ATHLETICS 2008

THE INTERNATIONAL TRACK AND FIELD ANNUAL

BY PETER MATTHEWS

ASSOCIATION OF TRACK & FIELD STATISTICIANS

SB

SPORTS BOOKS

Published by SportsBooks Ltd

SportsBooks Limited
PO Box 422
Cheltenham
GL50 2YN
United Kingdom
Tel: 01242 256755
Fax: 01242 254694
e-mail randall@sportsbooks.ltd.uk
Website www.sportsbooks.ltd.uk

This publication incorporates the ATFS Annual.

Photographs supplied by Mark Shearman, 22 Grovelands Road, Purley, Surrey, CR8 4LA.
Tel: 0208 660 0156 Fax: 0208 660 3437

British Library Cataloguing in Publication Data

Athletics: the international track and
field annual – 2008
1. Athletics. Track & Field events –
Serials
1. International athletics annual (London)
796.4'2'05

ISBN 9781899807 65 9

Cover design: Kath Grimshaw

Printed by Cromwell Press

CONTENTS

INTRODUCTION

IN COMPILING THIS essential handbook of our sport I have included all the usual features with just a few small innovations. I endeavour to pack in as much as possible and trust that the Annual provides all the key data for the last year and will be useful in the build-up to the Olympic Games in Beijing.

In addition to the deep world lists for 2007 I have included top world lists for 1957 and 1958, finding it fascinating in this nostalgic exercise to see the changes in standards to which we have become accustomed. Back in the late 1950s performance levels were rising fast and the setting of world records was thus far more common than nowadays as standards of living were developing from the War years and the ensuing years of austerity. Now the sport has become truly global, and it is always good to see that medals at major championships are distributed to a huge range of nations. Over the past two decades, however, the rate of change in performance levels has slowed considerably, or indeed stopped for some events. I find such trends fascinating and draw attention to my event-by-event summaries on pages 527-8.

While for most events 10th and 100th bests marks have been remarkably steady for the past 20 years and there was little change between 2006 and 2007, I found that, particularly for women, there was an increase in the number of athletes meeting base level standards. Of course, within this steady pattern there have been big demographic changes. For instance the collapse of distance running standards in the Western world has meant that far fewer Europeans make the lists than in previous years, but athletes from Africa etc. have more than replaced these. Also generally standards in the throws, and indeed the women's sprints, at the highest level are substantially lower than they were in the 1980s due both to the impact of drugs testing and to the change in economic priorities in Eastern Europe.

The increase in the number of athletes making the lists this year is an encouraging measure for the sport, but one still feels that there is a decline in public interest in all too many of the major powers in athletics. Realisation of this prompted the European AA to overhaul its competition structure.

One can commend governing bodies for taking initiatives to promote and improve the sport, but I, and so many other enthusiasts, am extremely concerned at the EAA plans. They have determined to hold European Championships biennially, noting that other Continental Championships are held more often than theirs, but seem to have failed to appreciate that, because of this, all eligible top athletes do not contest such events.

Every four years there has been a prime focus for Europeans – but the Championships will surely no longer be that when they are staged just weeks before the Olympic Games in 2012. Similarly the European Cup may also no longer attract the top athletes for, following their miserable decision a few years back to reduce the throws and jumps trials from six to four, thus spoiling the events for athletes and fans alike, the EAA are now proposing to seriously devalue the event by experiments such as "devil-take-the hindmost" in distance races and further reducing field event attempts. The EAA said that with a new 12-team format: "The emphasis will be on the country or the team as opposed to the individual athlete, and with the men and women's points counting towards one team effort we feel that the competitions will be exciting, energetic and unpredictable."

A once fine competition is in severe danger of being destroyed by this ludicrous 'change for change sake' mentality and seemingly a lack of understanding of what the current competition is about. The European Cup has always been a team event, with every performance by every athlete counting, and the joint scoring is likely to make the event much more predictable and reduce the competitivity.

I have endeavoured to keep this Annual as topical as possible – thus incorporating results right up to the beginning of April in the Biographies section, Records set in January-March 2008 and in the 2008 Indoor Rankings with results from the March 2008 World Indoor Championships and World Cross-Country Championships. Now for a great summer season!

Peter Matthews
2 April 2008

Information can be sent to me to 10 Madgeways Close, Great Amwell, Ware, Herts SG12 9RU, England. **Email**: p.jmatthews@tiscali.co.uk

Information or requests re sales, distribution, publication etc. to the publishers.

ABBREVIATIONS

The following abbreviations have been used for meetings with, in parentheses, the first year that they were held.

AAA (GBR) Amateur Athletic Association Championships (1880)
AAU (USA) Amateur Athletic Union Championships (1888) (now TAC)
Af-AsG Afro-Asian Games (2003)
AfCh African Championships (1979)
AfG African Games (1965)
Af-J African Junior Championships (1994)
AmCp America's Cup (World Cup Trial)
APM Adriaan Paulen Memorial, Hengelo
Aragón Gran Premio Internacional de Atletismo Gobierno de Aragón, Zaragoza (2004)
AsiC Asian Championships (1973)
AsiG Asian Games (1951)
Asi-J Asian Junior Championships (1990)
ASV Weltklasse in Köln, ASV club meeting (1934)
Athl Athletissima, Lausanne (1976)
Balk Balkan Games (1929), C – Championships
Barr (Cuba) Barrientos Memorial (1946)
BGP Budapest Grand Prix (1978)
Bisl Bislett Games, Oslo (1965) (Bergen 2004)
Bol Bolivar Games (1938)
BrGP British Grand Prix
CAC Central American and Caribbean Championships (1967)
CAG Central American and Caribbean Games (1926)
CalR California Relays (1942)
C.Asian Central Asian Championships
CAU Inter-counties, GBR (1934)
CISM International Military Championships (1946)
CG Commonwealth Games (1930)
Déca Décanation, Paris (C) (2005)
DNG DN Galan, Stockholm (1966)
Drake Drake Relays (1910)
EAsG East Asian Games (1993)
EC European Championships (1934)
ECCp European Clubs Cup (1975)
EChall European Challenge (10,000m 1997, Throws 2001)
ECp European Cup – track & field (1965), multi-events (1973)
EI European Indoor Championships (1970, Games 1966-9)
EICp European Indoor Cup (2003)
EJ European Junior Championships (1970)
EU23 European Under-23 Championships (1997) and European Under-23 Cup (1992-4)
FBK Fanny Blankers-Koen Games, Hengelo (formerly APM)
FlaR Florida Relays (1939)
FOT (USA) Final Olympic Trials (1920)
Franc Francophone Games (1989)
Gaz Gaz de France meeting, FRA (was BNP) (1968)
GGala Golden Gala, Roma (from 1980), Verona (1988), Pescara (1989), Bologna (1990)
GNR Great North Run – Newcastle to South Shields, GBR (1981)
GO Golden Oval, Dresden
GP Grand Prix
GPF IAAF Grand Prix Final (1985)
GS Golden Spike, Ostrava (1969)
Gugl Zipfer Gugl Grand Prix, Linz (1988)
GWG Goodwill Games (1986)
Herc Herculis, Monte Carlo, Monaco (1987)
IAAF International Amateur Athletic Federation
IAC IAC meeting (1968), formerly Coca-Cola
IAU International Association of Ultrarunners
IbAm Ibero-American Championships (1983)
ISTAF Internationales Stadionfest, Berlin (1921)
Jenner Bruce Jenner Classic, San Jose (1979)
Jerome Harry Jerome Track Classic (1984)
JUCO Junior Colleges Championships, USA
KansR Kansas Relays, Lawrence (1923)
Kuso Janusz Kusocinski Memorial (1954)
Kuts Vladimir Kuts Memorial
Macc Maccabiah Games, Israel (1932)
MAI Malmö AI Galan, Sweden (formerly Idag) (1958)
Mal Malinowski Memorial, Poland
Mast Masters pole vault, Grenoble (1987)
MedG Mediterranean Games (1951)
Mill Millrose Games, New York indoors (1908)
ModR Modesto Relays
MSR Mt. San Antonio College Relays (1959)
NA Night of Athletics, Heusden (2000) formerly Hechtel
NACAC North American, Central American & Caribbean Ch (2003)
NC National Championships
NC-w National Winter Championships
NCAA National Collegiate Athletic Association Championships, USA (1921)
NCAA-r NCAA Regional Championships (2003)
NCG Nelli Cooman Games, Stadskanaal, NED (1997)
NCp National Cup
NG National Games
Nik Nikaïa, Nice (1976)
NM Narodna Mladezhe, Sofia (1955)
N.Sch National Schools
Nurmi Paavo Nurmi Games (1957)
NYG New York Games (1989)
OD Olympischer Tag (Olympic Day)
Oda Mikio Oda Memorial Meeting, Hiroshima
OG Olympic Games (1896)
OT Olympic Trials
Owens Jesse Owens Memorial (1981)
PAm Pan American Games (1951)
PArab Pan Arab Championships (1977) (G-Games 1953)
PennR Pennsylvania Relays (1895)
PG Peugeot (Talbot) Games (1980), Royal Mail Parcels Games 1989-90, Parcelforce Games 1991
Prav (URS) Pravda Cup
PTS Pravda Televízia Slovnaft, Bratislava (1957) (now GPB)
Pre Steve Prefontaine Memorial (1976)
RdVin Route du Vin Half Marathon, Luxembourg
RomIC Romanian International Championships (1948)
RWC Race Walking Challenge Final (2007)
SACh South American Championships (1919)

SAsG	South Asian Games (1984)
SEAG	South East Asia Games (1959)
SEC	Southeast Conference Championships
SGP	IAAF Super Grand Prix
Slovn	Slovnaft, Bratislava (formerly PTS) (1990)
Spark	Sparkassen Cup, Stuttgart (indoor) (1987)
Spart	(URS) Spartakiad (1956)
Stra	Stramilano Half marathon, Milan
TexR	Texas Relays (1925)
USOF	US Olympic Festival
VD	Ivo Van Damme Memorial, Brussels (1977)
Veniz	Venizélia, Haniá, Crete (1936)
WAC	Western Athletic Conference Championships
WAF	World Athletics Finals, Monaco (2003)
WAfC	West African Championships
WAsG	West Asian Games (1997)
WCh	World Championships (1983)
WCp	World Cup – track & field (1977), marathon (1985) Walking – Lugano Trophy – men (1961), Eschborn Cup – women (1979)
WCT	World Championships Trial
WG	World Games, Helsinki (1961)
WI	World Indoor Championships (1987), World Indoor Games (1985)
WJ	World Junior Championships (1986)
WK	Weltklasse, Zürich (1962)
WMilG	World Military Games (or CISM)
WUG	World University Games (1923)
WY	World Youth Championships (1999)
Zat	Emil Zátopek Classic, Melbourne
Znam	Znamenskiy Brothers Memorial (1958)
-j, -y, -23	Junior, Youth or under-23

Dual and triangular matches are indicated by "v" (versus) followed by the name(s) of the opposition. Quadrangular and larger inter-nation matches are denoted by the number of nations and -N; viz 8-N designates an 8-nation meeting.

Events

CC	cross-country
Dec	decathlon
DT	discus
h	hurdles
Hep	heptathlon
HJ	high jump
HMar	half marathon
HT	hammer
JT	javelin
LJ	long jump
Mar	marathon
Pen	pentathlon
PV	pole vault
R	relay
SP	shot
St	steeplechase
TJ	triple jump
W	walk
Wt	weight

Miscellaneous abbreviations

+	Intermediate time in longer race
=	Tie (ex-aequo)
A	Made at an altitude of 1000m or higher
b	date of birth
D	Made in decathlon competition
dnf	did not finish
dnq	did not qualify
dns	did not start
exh	exhibition
h	heat
H	Made in heptathlon competition
hr	hour
i	indoors
kg	kilograms
km	kilometres
m	metres
M	mile
m/s	metres per second
mx	Made in mixed men's and women's race
nh	no height
O	Made in octathlon
P	Made in pentathlon
pb	personal best
Q	Made in qualifying round
qf	quarter final (or q in lists)
r	Race number in a series of races
sf	semi final (or s in lists)
w	wind assisted
WIR	world indoor record
WR	world record or best
y	yards
*	Converted time from yards to metres: For 200m: 220 yards less 0.11 second For 400m: 440 yards less 0.26 second For 110mh: 120yh plus 0.03 second

Countries

(IAAF membership reached 212 in 2006). IAAF and IOC abbreviations are now identical. Former IAAF abbreviations are shown in brackets in this list.

AFG	Afghanistan
AHO	Netherlands Antilles
AIA	Anguilla (ANG)
ALB	Albania
ALG	Algeria
AND	Andorra
ANG	Angola (ANO)
ANT	Antigua & Barbuda
ARG	Argentina
ARM	Armenia
ARU	Aruba
ASA	American Samoa (AMS)
AUS	Australia
AUT	Austria
AZE	Azerbaijan
BAH	Bahamas
BAN	Bangladash
BAR	Barbados
BDI	Burundi (BUR)
BEL	Belgium
BEN	Benin
BER	Bermuda
BHU	Bhutan
BIH	Bosnia Herzegovina (BSH)
BIZ	Belize
BLR	Belarus
BOL	Bolivia
BOT	Botswana
BRA	Brazil
BRN	Bahrain (BHR)
BRU	Brunei
BUL	Bulgaria
BUR	Burkina Faso (BKF)
CAF	Central African Republic
CAM	Cambodia
CAN	Canada
CAY	Cayman Islands
CGO	Congo
CHA	Chad
CHI	Chile

CHN	People's Republic of China
CIV	Côte d'Ivoire (Ivory Coast)
CMR	Cameroon
COD	Democratic Republic of Congo (ex ZAI Zaïre)
COK	Cook Islands (CKI)
COL	Colombia
COM	Comoros
CPV	Cape Verde Islands (CVD)
CRC	Costa Rica
CRO	Croatia
CUB	Cuba
CYP	Cyprus
CZE	Czech Republic
DEN	Denmark
DJI	Djibouti
DMA	Dominica (DMN)
DOM	Dominican Republic
ECU	Ecuador
EGY	Egypt
ENG	England
ERI	Eritrea
ESA	El Salvador
ESP	Spain
EST	Estonia
ETH	Ethiopia
FIJ	Fiji
FIN	Finland
FRA	France
FRG	Federal Republic of Germany (1948-90)
FSM	Micronesia
GAB	Gabon
GAM	The Gambia
GBR	United Kingdom of Great Britain & Northern Ireland
GBS	Guinea-Bissau
GDR	German Democratic Republic (1948-90)
GEO	Georgia
GEQ	Equatorial Guinea
GER	Germany (pre 1948 and from 1991)
GHA	Ghana
GIB	Gibraltar
GRE	Greece
GRN	Grenada
GUA	Guatemala
GUI	Guinea
GUM	Guam
GUY	Guyana
HAI	Haiti
HKG	Hong Kong, China
HON	Honduras
HUN	Hungary
INA	Indonesia
IND	India
IRI	Iran (IRN)
IRL	Ireland
IRQ	Iraq
ISL	Iceland
ISR	Israel
ISV	US Virgin Islands
ITA	Italy
IVB	British Virgin Islands (BVI)
JAM	Jamaica
JOR	Jordan
JPN	Japan
KAZ	Kazakhstan (KZK)
KEN	Kenya
KGZ	Kyrgyzstan
KIR	Kiribati
KOR	Korea
KSA	Saudi Arabia (from SAU)
KUW	Kuwait
LAO	Laos
LAT	Latvia
LBA	Libya
LBR	Liberia
LCA	St Lucia (STL)
LES	Lesotho
LIB	Lebanon
LIE	Liechtenstein
LTU	Lithuania (LIT)
LUX	Luxembourg
MAC	Macao
MAD	Madagascar
MAR	Morocco
MAS	Malaysia
MAW	Malawi
MDA	Moldova (MOL)
MDV	Maldives (MLD)
MEX	Mexico
MGL	Mongolia
MKD	Former Yugoslav Republic of Macedonia
MLI	Mali
MLT	Malta
MNE	Montenegro
MNT	Montserrat
MON	Monaco
MOZ	Mozambique
MRI	Mauritius
MSH	Marshall Islands
MTN	Mauritania
MYA	Myanmar (formerly BIR Burma)
NAM	Namibia
NCA	Nicaragua
NED	Netherlands (HOL)
NEP	Nepal
NFI	Norfolk Islands
NGR	Nigeria
NGU	Papua New Guinea (PNG)
NI	Northern Ireland
NIG	Niger
NMA	Northern Marianas Islands
NOR	Norway
NRU	Nauru (NAU)
NZL	New Zealand
OMA	Oman
PAK	Pakistan
PAN	Panama
PAR	Paraguay
PER	Peru
PHI	Philippines
PLE	Palestine (PAL)
PLW	Palau
PNG	Papua New Guinea
POL	Poland
POR	Portugal
PRK	North Korea (DPR Korea)
PUR	Puerto Rico
PYF	French Polynesia
QAT	Qatar
ROM	Romania (ROU from 2008)
RSA	South Africa
RUS	Russia
RWA	Rwanda
SAM	Samoa
SCG	Serbia & Montenegro (Crna Gora) (to 2006)
SCO	Scotland
SEN	Sénégal
SEY	Seychelles
SIN	Singapore
SKN	St Kitts & Nevis (STK)
SLE	Sierra Leone
SLO	Slovenia
SMR	San Marino
SOL	Solomon Islands
SOM	Somalia
SRB	Serbia
SRI	Sri Lanka
STP	São Tomé & Principé
SUD	Sudan
SUI	Switzerland
SUR	Surinam
SVK	Slovakia
SWE	Sweden
SWZ	Swaziland
SYR	Syria
TAN	Tanzania
TCH	Czechoslovakia (to 1991)
TGA	Tonga (TON)
THA	Thailand
TJK	Tadjikistan
TKM	Turkmenistan
TKS	Turks & Caicos Islands
TLS	East Timor
TOG	Togo
TPE	Taiwan (Chinese Taipei)
TRI	Trinidad & Tobago
TUN	Tunisia
TUR	Turkey
UAE	United Arab Emirates
UGA	Uganda
UKR	Ukraine
URS	Soviet Union (to 1991)
URU	Uruguay
USA	United States
UZB	Uzbekistan
VAN	Vanuatu
VEN	Venezuela
VIE	Vietnam
VIN	St Vincent & the Grenadines (STV)
WAL	Wales
YEM	Republic of Yemen
YUG	Yugoslavia (to 2002)
ZAM	Zambia
ZIM	Zimbabwe

ACKNOWLEDGEMENTS

WHILE IN THE end all the decisions as to the contents of this Annual are mine – I am enormously grateful to all those who help make this the supreme compilation of information on our sport.

A worldwide collection of experts, mostly members of the ATFS, work very hard on our key work of compiling the annual world lists. As they have been throughout the 24 years that I have produced the Annual, Jirí Havlín and Richard Hymans have been in the forefront of this work as has Milan Skocovsky for juniors, and I am indebted to them for their careful and expert attention to detail. Mirko Jalava has established an amazing depth of performance details for athletes and great topicality on his web site www.tilastopaja.net so that this is a wonderful reference source for us enthusiasts. Thanks also to such specialist contributors as Carlos Fernández for distance running, Dr. David E Martin, marathons, Raymund Herdt, walks, and Winfried Kramer for national records and widespread probing for results. Miguel Villaseñor read through the biographies and the lists with great care and came up with most useful corrections.

Throughout the year the area specialists contribute invaluable work: *Africa*: Yves Pinaud, *Asia*: Heinrich Hubbeling, *Central and South America*: Eduardo Biscayart and Luis Vinker.

The following specialists supplied information for their respective areas of interest and countries: *Records* György Csiki, *Ultrarunning* Andy Milroy, *Indoors* Ed Gordon, *Shot* Norbert Heinrich, *Multi events:* Hans van Kuijen.

Albania: Luigi Mengoni, *Australia*: Paul Jenes and David Tarbotton; *Austria*: Dr Karl Graf; *Belgium*: André de Hooghe and Alain Monet; *Bulgaria*: Alexander Vangelov; *China*: Mirko Jalava and Shen Xinsheng; *Cuba*: Basilio Fuentes and Alfredo Sánchez; *Czech Republic*: Milan Skocovsky, Jirí Havlín and Milan Urban; *Denmark*: Erik Laursen; *Estonia*: Erlend Teemägi and Enn Endjärv; *Finland*: Juhani Jalava, Mirko Jalava and Matti Hannus; *France*: Alain Bouillé and José Guilloto; *Germany*: Sven Kuus and Eberhard Vollmer; *Greece*: Thomas Konstas and Nikos Kriezis; *Hungary*: György Csiki; *Iceland*: Fridrik Oskarsson; *India*: R Murali Krishnan; *Ireland*: Pierce O'Callaghan and Liam Hennessy; *Israel*: David Eiger; *Italy*: Raul Leoni; *Japan*: Yoshimasa Noguchi, Akihiro Onishi and Ken Nakamura; *Latvia*: Andris Stagis; *Lithuania*: Stepas Misiunas; *Luxembourg*: Georges Klepper; *Montenegro*: Ivan Popovic, *Netherlands*: Wilmar Kortleever; *Norway*: Tore Johansen and Børre Lilloe; *Poland*: Zbigniew Jonik, Janusz Rozum and Tadeusz Wolejko; *Portugal:* Manuel Arons Carvalho; *Romania*: Alexandru Boriga; *Russia*: Sergey Tikhonov; *Serbia*: Ozren Karamata; *Slovakia*: Alfons Juck; *Slovenia*: Zdravko Peternelj; *South Africa:* Gert le Roux and Riël Haumann; *Spain*: José Luis Hernández, Carles Baronet and the AEEA team; *Sweden*: A.Lennart Julin, Owe Fröberg, Birger Fält and Peter Larsson; *Switzerland*: Alberto Bordoli and Antonin Hejda; *Syria and Arab world*: Fouad Habbash; *Trinidad:* Bernard Linley, *Turkey*: Nejat Kök, *Ukraine*: Yuriy Kostritsky; *UK*: Peter Matthews, Ian Hodge and Tony Miller; *USA*: Scott Davis, Garry Hill, Marty Post and *Track Newsletter*. Also various national federation lists and to those who post results or ranking lists to various web sites.

Also to Marco Buccellato, Mark Butler, Ottavio Castellini (IAAF), Justin Clouder, Carole Fuchs, José Maria García, Arild Gjerde, Grzegorz Gladzikowski, Stan Greenberg, Bob Hersh, Ove Karlsson, Alan Lindop, Rooney Magnusson, Bill Mallon, Gabriele Manfredini, Pino Mappa, David Martin, Phil Minshull, Walt Murphy, Galder Orobengoa, Jirí Ondracek, Lionel Peters, Bob Phillips, Ian Smith, Chris Turner and Rob Whittingham.

My apologies to anybody whose name I may have missed or who have corresponded with other key ATFS personnel, but all help, however small is deeply appreciated.

Keep the results flowing

During the year Mel Watman and I publish all marks that we know about to ATFS standards in *Athletics International*, of which there are 26 issues per year (by post or email). This serves as a base from which the lists in this book can be compiled, together with information from web sites and the major magazines that are published around the world, such as *Track & Field News* (USA) with its email results spin-off *Track Newsletter*, and *Leichtathletik* (Germany) and the newsletters with particular spheres of interest such as *Atletismo en España* by Francisco J Ascorbe and José Luis Hernández, and Luis Vinker's *South America Bulletin*.

Many of the national contributors to *Athletics International* are included in the list above. In order to ensure that the record of 2007 is as complete as possible I urge results contribution worldwide to AI, and then in turn our lists in *Athletics 2008* will be as comprehensive as we can make them.

Peter Matthews

THE ASSOCIATION OF TRACK & FIELD STATISTICIANS

The ATFS was founded in Brussels (at the European Championships) in 1950 and ever since has built upon the work of such key founding members as Roberto Quercetani, Don Potts and Fulvio Regli to produce authoritative ranking lists in the International Athletics Annual and elsewhere.

Current Executive Committee
President: Paul Jenes AUS
Vice-President: A.Lennart Julin SWE
Secretary General: Scott Davis USA
Treasurer: Rob Whittingham GBR
Past Presidents: Rooney Magnusson SWE, Dr Roberto Quercetani ITA
Committee: Jírí Havlín CZE, Nejat Kök TUR, Gert le Roux RSA, Bernard Linley TRI, Peter J Matthews GBR, Yves Pinaud FRA, Tatsumi Senda JPN, Luis R Vinker ARG

For details of ATFS Membership, which is open to keen statisticians, apply to the secretary: Scott Davis, 4432 Snowbird Circle, Cerritos, California 90703, USA; EMail: ssd@aol.com

Internet – Websites

IAAF	www.iaaf.org
IAU (Ultras)	www.iau.org.tw
Asian AA	www.asianathletics.org
CAC Confed.	www.athlecac.org
European AA	www.european-athletics.org
Oceania AA	www.oceania-athletics.com
S. American Fed.	www.consudatle.org
WMRA	www.wmra.info
World Masters	www.world-masters-athletics.org
Marathon Majors	www.worldmarathonmajors.com
Africa	www.africathle.com
Andorra	www.faa.ad
Argentina	www.cada-atletismo.org
Australia	www.athletics.org.au
Austria	www.oelv.at
Belgium	www.val.be
Bermuda	www.bermudatracknfield.com
Brazil	www.cbat.org.br
Bulgaria	www.bfla.org
magazine	www.athletics.netbg.com
Canada	www.athleticscanada.com
Chile	www.fedachi.cl
China	www.athletics.org.cn
Croatia	www.has.hr
Czech Republic	www.atletika.cz
Denmark	www.dansk-atletik.dk
England	www.englandathletics.org
Estonia	www.ekjl.ee
Finland	www.sul.fi
France	www.athle.org
Germany	www.leichtathletik.de
Great Britain	www.ukathletics.net
deep statistics	www.powerof10.info
Greece	www.segas.gr
also for results	www.athletix.org
Hong Kong	www.hkaaa.com
Hungary	www.masz.hu
Iceland	www.fri.is
India	www.indianathletics.org
Ireland	www.athleticsireland.ie
Israel	www.iaa.co.il
	http://members.tripod.com/~eiger
Italy	www.fidal.it
Jamaica	www.jaaaltd.com
Japan	www.rikuren.or.jp
Kenya	www.athleticskenya.org ?
Korea	www.kaf.go.kr
Latvia	www.lat-athletics.lv
Lithuania	www.laf.lt
Luxembourg	www.fla.lu
Macedonia	www.afm.org.mk
Moldova	www.fam.com.md/
Monaco	www.fma.mc
Montenegro	www.ascg.cg.yu
Netherlands	www.atletiek.nl
New Zealand	www.athletics.org.nz
Northern Ireland	www.niathletics.org
Norway	www.friidrett.no
Poland	www.pzla.pl
Portugal	www.fpatletismo.pt
Romania	www.fra.ro
Russia	www.rusathletics.com
	www.trackandfield.ru
Saudi Arabia	www.saaaf.com
Scotland	www.scottishathletics.org.uk
Serbia	www.asj.org.yu
Singapore	www.singaporeathletics.org.sg
Slovakia	www.saz.sk
Slovenia	www.atletska-zveza.si
South Africa	www.athletics.org.za
Spain	www.rfea.es
Sweden	www.friidrott.se
Switzerland	www.swiss-athletics.ch
Tunisia	www.tunisathle.africa-web.org
Turkey	www.taf.org.tr
Ukraine	www.uaf.org.ua
USA	www.usatf.org
Venezuela	www.feveatletismo.org.ve
Wales	www.welshathletics.org

Other recommended sites for statistics and results

AIMS	www.aims-association.org
ARRS	www.arrs.net
British historical	www.gbrathletics.net
Marathons	www.marathonguide.com
Masters Track & Field	www.mastersathletics.net
Men's shot put	www.menshotput.com
Mirko Jalava	www.tilastopaja.com
News (mainly US)	www.newsnow.co.uk/newsfeed/?name=Athletics
Runners World	www.runnersworld.com
Tracklion	sportslion.net/tracklion_e.html
Trackshark (USA)	www.trackshark.com
Track & Field News	www.trackandfieldnews.com
Walking (Sweden)	www.gangsport.com
World junior news	www.wjan.org
Olympic results etc	www.aafla.org (a.a. foundation of Los Angeles)

DIARY OF 2007

by Peter Matthews

A chronological survey of highlights in major events in the world of track and field athletics.
See Championships or National sections for more details of these events.

January

7 **Perth**, Australia. Steve Hooker and Paul Burgess both cleared 5.91 for 1-2 in the pole vault at the Drug Free Classic.

14 **Houston**, USA. Ryan Hall became the first American to break the hour for half marathon with 59:43.

21 **Seville**, Spain. A week after winning at Edinburgh, Kenenisa Bekele took his four-year win streak to 27 cross-country victories. Gelete Burka also had wins at both venues.

27 **Glasgow**, GBR. The five-way mini-international resulted in a tie for Britain and USA 50 from Germany 50, Sweden 46 and Commonwealth Select 43. Craig Pickering won the 60m in 6.55.

27 **Boston (Roxbury)**, USA. Tirunesh Dibaba improved the world indoor record for 5000m from the 14:32.93 that she had run on this track in 2005 to 14:27.42. Kilometre splits were 2:55.3 (Bridget Binning), 5:48.5 (Marina Muncan) with Ejegayehu Dibaba leading to near 3000m from where Dibaba led in 8:44.30 and 4000m in 11:40.98. Meseret Defar won the 3000m in 8:30.31 from Shalane Flanagan who set a North American record of 8:33.25. Dan Taylor scored an upset shot win with 21.57 from Christian Cantwell 21. 36 and Reese Hoffa 20.84. This meeting, with the Millrose Games, Tyson Invitational and US Championships, made up the USATF's Visa Championship Series.

28 **Gent**, Belgium. Tia Hellebaut is concentrating on the high jump these days but returned to the multi-events with 4877 points for pentathlon, fifth on the world all-time list. This included a Belgian indoor long jump record of 6.42.

28 **Moscow**, Russia. Ivan Ukhov high jumped 2.39, a mark which remained the year's best, at the "Moscow Winter" meeting.

28 **Osaka**, Japan. Yumiko Hara won the international women's marathon in a pb 2:23:48 from Mari Ozaki 2:24:39 and debutante Yuri Kano 2:24:43.

February

2 **New York**, USA. 100th Millrose Games. Gail Devers made an amazing comeback in only her second race since 2004 and the birth of a child in June 2005 to win the 60m hurdles in 7.86, easily a world age-40 best. 14,905 fans also saw Yelena Isinbayeva clear 4.82 in her first appearance in the USA and Bernard Lagat won his fifth Wanamaker Mile in 3:54.26 on the 148m track. Christian Cantwell beat Rees Hoffa 21.88 to 21.75 in the shot.

3 **Arnstadt**, Germany. Yaroslav Rybakov equalled his pb of 2.38 at the 31st High Jump with Music competition. Second was Andrey Silnov 2.36 and third Stefan Holm 2.34.

4 **Marugame**, Japan. Half marathon winners were Mekubo Mogusu 59:48 and Kayoko Fukushi 68:00.

4 **Stuttgart**, Germany. Sparkassen Cup. After just missing the world indoor record for 3000m in 2006, Meseret Defar took 4.14 off the mark with 8:23.72, but only beat Meselech Melkamu by 0.02. Olga Komyagina led at 1000m in 2:48.36 before the Ethiopians took over at 1800m and Defar passed 2000m in 5:38.95. In third place Jo Pavey set a Commonwealth record of 8:31.50. A series of other world-leading marks for the season included 6.49 for 60m by Olusoji Fasuba, 7.38 for 60m hurdles by Dayron Robles, who beat Liu Xiang 7.45, 5.88 pole vault by Björn Otto, 1:58.67 by Tetyana Petlyuk for 800m, and 7.85 in a heat by Susanna Kallur before 7.88 in the final of the 60mh.

9 **Fayetteville**, USA. Tyson Invitational. LaShawn Merritt ran the year's fastest indoor 400m of 45.54 and Allyson Felix ran a US 300m best of 36.33.

9 **Leipzig**, Germany. Merlene Ottey ran a world age-46 best of 7.30 for 60m indoors.

9 **Ra's Al Khaymah**, United Arab Emirates. Sammy Wanjiru of Kenya regained the world half marathon record with 58:53 through a scintillating display of front running. Behind him Patrick Makau ran 59:13 and Deriba Merga 59:44; they ran through 10k in 27:47.

9-11 **Russian Indoor Championships**, Volgograd. Anna Balakshina, Natalya Panteleyeva, Anna Yemashova and Olesya Chumakova combined for a world indoor record 8:18.54 for 4x800m, taking 0.17 off the 13 year-old mark.

10 **Donetsk**, Ukraine. Just as she had done in 2005 (with 4.87) and 2006 (4.91) Yelena Isinbayeva set a world indoor record with 4.93 at the Pole Vault Stars meeting. Her success, her 20th world record in all, came after two failures at 4.92. Kym Howe was second with a

Commonwealth record 4.72 and Paul Burgess won the men's event at 5.80 on count-back from Viktor Chistyakov and Oleksandr Korchmyd.

10-11 **UK Indoor Championships**, Sheffield. Nicola Sanders ran a world-leading 50.60 for 400m.

11 **Karlsruhe**, Germany. Liu Xiang needed an Asian record 7.42 to beat Dayron Robles 7.44 in the 60m hurdles. Marcus Brunson won the 60m in 6.46, the year's best time, and Christian Olsson had a strong triple jump victory with 17.44.

13 **Banská Bystrica**. Slovakia. World leading marks were set for men and women at the 14th edition of the high jump meeting held in a packed hall with 1200 spectators at the Europa Shopping Centre. Venelina Veneva's 2.02 equalled her personal best indoors (later lost through drugs disqualification) and Stefan Holm's win at 2.37 was his best for two years and his 100th competition at 2.30 or higher (62 outdoors, 38 indoors).

14 **Bydgoszcz**, Poland. Linus Thörnblad won the high jump with 2.34 on count-back from Yuriy Krymarenko and Yelena Isinbayeva the women's pole vault with 4.84.

17 **Balkan Indoor Championships**, Pireás, Greece. 19 year-old Tezdzhan Naimova ran a world-leading 7.13 for 60m.

17 **Birmingham**, GBR. Kenenisa Bekele took another of Haile Gebrselassie's marks as he ran a world best for 2000m of 4:49.99; splits were Wesley Cheruiyot 56.73, 1:55.50 and Hailu Dinku 2:25.82, 2:57.02 before Bekele injected a 57.83 400m through 1500m in 3:40.4 and 1600m 3:54.85 and a last 400m of 55.14 and 200m 26.31. Shadrack Korir was second in a Kenyan record 4:55.72. Bernard Lagat took the US 3000m record with 7:32.43, Nicola Sanders matched her 400m best of 50.60 and Irving Saladino set a South American record of 8.31 for long jump.

17-18 **German Indoor Championships**, Karlsruhe. Björn Otto cleared a world-leading 5.90 to win the pole vault from Danny Ecker 5.80.

20 **Stockholm**, Sweden. The 18th GE Globen Galen meeting, with a sell-out crowd of 10,500, included wins for all six Swedish European medallists of 2006 and three world indoor season leading marks: 7:30.51 for 3000m by Kenenisa Bekele, 4:03.73 for 1500m by Lidia Chojecka and 1:45.42 for 800m by Wilfred Bungei.

24 **Pireás**, Greece. Top mark was a 2.01 Spanish women's high jump record by Ruth Beitia.

24-25 **Swedish Indoor Championships**, Göteborg. A great high jump was won by Stefan Holm from Linus Thörnblad, as both men cleared 2.38.

24-25 **US Indoor Championships**, Boston (Roxbury). Christian Cantwell gained revenge for his 2006 loss by beating Reese Hoffa 21.72 to 21.21 in the shot to win the men's overall Visa Series title. Amber Campbell's 24.54 20lb weight throw was just 3cm short of Brittany Riley's recent world best. 39 year-old Jeff Hartwig won the pole vault with 5.80 and Tim Seaman won a tenth consecutive 5000m walk title to tie the record for any event. Other top marks included personal bests of 7.47 by Ron Bramlett in the 60m hurdles and 17.28 in the triple jump by Aarik Wilson.

25 **Yokohama**, Japan. Russia won the 25th women's international Ekiden in 2:14:48 from USA 2:16:04 and Japan 2:16:07.

March

2 **Melbourne**, Australia. First Grand Prix meeting in the IAAF World Athletics Tour 2007. Lisa Corrigan set an Oceania 1 mile record of 4:22.66.

2-4 **European Indoor Championships,** Birmingham, GBR. In all 570 athletes from 45 countries took part, nine athletes defended their titles from 2005 and six of the nine 2006 outdoor European champions to take part were successful. Top event for depth of marks was the women's pentathlon in which Carolina Klüft retained her title with 4944 points from Kelly Sotherton 4927 Commonwealth record and national records from Karin Ruckstuhl 4801, Austra Skujyte 4740 and Natalya Dobrynska 4739; 6th Jessica Ennis added 315 points to her best with 4716. Home fans were also thrilled by British 1-2s from Jason Gardener (6.51 for his fourth successive European Indoor gold) and Craig Pickering at 60m and Phillips Idowu (17.56) and Nathan Douglas at triple jump. Third titles were won by Kim Gevaert (60m 7.12 after world-leading Belgian record 7.10 in semi) and Roman Sebrle (heptathlon 6196), with Lidia Chojecka winning a unique 1500m/3000m double. Mikulás Konopka made a stunning improvement from 20.55 to 21.57 in the shot to take Slovakia's first European Indoor gold and there were championship bests from Idowu, Tia Hellebaut, high jump 2.05, and Belarus, women's 4x400m 3:27.83. *For leading results see Athletics 2007 p.607.*

9-10 **NCAA Indoor Championships**, Fayetteville, Arkansas. Brittany Riley added almost a metre to her world best for the 20lb weight with first 25.05 and then 25.56. Donald Thomas continued his meteoric progress to win the high jump with 2.33 and there were the world's fastest 200m times of the indoor season on a 200m track for Walter Dix 20.32 and Kerron Stewart (who also won the 60m in 7.15) 22.58. Team champions were Wisconsin (men) and Arizona State (women).

9-11 **Australian Championships,** Brisbane. Sally McLellan with 12.92 took 0.01 off the national record for 100m hurdles set twice by Pam Ryan back in 1972. American Brad Walker won the pole vault with 5.95, and this remained the top mark of 2007.

17 **Den Haag**, Netherlands. 33rd City-Pier-City race. Samuel Wanjiru took another 18 seconds off the world half marathon record that he set five weeks earlier with 58:35. He went through 10k in 27:27, 15k in 41:30 and 20k in a world record 55:31.

17-18 **European Winter Throwing Cup**, Yalta, Ukraine. Franka Dietzsch set a women's discus record for the event with 66.14. Team titles went to Russia (men) and Germany (women).

24 **World Cross-Country Championships**, Mombasa, Kenya. Zersenay Tadese took the men's title (just one race again this year) as he came from behind to overtake Kenenisa Bekele, who sensationally dropped out and thus lost his unbeaten CC record from 2001. Kenyans took places 2-5 to win the team title easily, adding those for both junior teams with 1-2-3-4 in the men's led by Asbel Kiprop and 1-2-3 in the women's led by Linet Masai. Ethiopia failed to complete a team in the men's race, but took the senior women's team title (Kenya 2nd) led by 2-3-4 finishers behind the champion, Kenyan-born Lornah Kiplagat of the Netherlands. 30,000 spectators packed a spectacular seaside setting, but the races were contested in temperatures reaching 38°C and humidity of 80%, terrible and ludicrous conditions for cross-country. *See Athletics 2007 p.608.*

April

1 **Berlin**, Germany. Patrick Makau Musyoki won the 27th Vattenfall Berlin Half Marathon from a record field of 18,531 runners with a new course record of 58:56, the fourth fastest ever time

1 **Brunssum**, Netherlands. Micah Kogo won the 10km in 27:07, just five seconds outside Haile Gebrselassie's world record on the roads.

4-7 **Austin**, USA. The 80th Clyde Littlefield Texas Relays, a massive meeting with high school and college and university events, was badly affected by wet and cold weather on the final day, as were other meetings at this time throughout the USA.

7 **European Cup 10,000m**, Ferrara, Italy. Elvan Abeylegesse won the women's race in 31:25.15 and André Pollmächer the men's in 28:17.17. Spain won both team contests.

13-15 49th **Mt SAC Relays**, Walnut, California, USA. Shalane Flanagan broke the North American 5000m record with 14:44.80.

14 **Wailuku**, Hawaii, USA. Top discus throwers extended their search for ideal wind conditions with two meetings in Hawaii. At the first Suzi Powell broke the US women's record with 67.67.

15 **Paris Marathon**, France. Despite warm (20°C) weather, fast times were run by the winners: Mubarak Shami 2:07:19 (Qatari record) and Wei Yanan 2:23:12.

15 Fortis **Rotterdam Marathon**, Netherlands. The weather was so sunny and hot (in excess of 27°C) that the organisers stopped the race after three and a half hours, advising participants to walk to the finish. However, the conditions did not prevent Joshua Chelanga clocking the admirable winning time of 2:08:21.

16 **Boston Marathon**, USA. The 2:14:13 run by Robert K. Cheruiyot was the slowest winning time for 30 years and seven minutes slower than he ran to win in 2006, as cold, rain and strong headwinds had their effect. Lidiya Grigoryeva was the women's winner in 2:29:18 (slowest since 1985).

22 Flora **London Marathon**, GBR. On a warm day (up to 20°C) Martin Lel, 1st in 2005 and 2nd in 2006, won in 2:07:41 in a sprint finish from Abderrahim Goumri 2:07:44 and Felix Limo 2:07:47. The women's winner was Zhou Chunxiu in 2:20:38, which was to remain the world's fastest time of 2007, from Gete Wami 2:21:45 and Constantina Tomescu 2:23:55. There were 35,694 finishers.

26-28 98th **Drake Relays**, Des Moines, USA. Highlights included a wind aided 13.00 110m hurdles by Anwar Moore, 5.81 pole vault by Jeff Hartwig, 21.72 shot by Christian Cantwell, a US collegiate women's hammer record of 72.51 by Brittany Riley and a world-leading mile time of 3:51.71 by Alan Webb.

26-28 113rd **Penn Relays**, Philadelphia, USA. The USA won 5-1 against Rest of the World teams, setting world year bests for national teams in the four standard relay events with 38.35, 2:59.18, 42.87 and 3:24.70 and also winning the women's 1600m medley in 3:38.89 while the opposition's only success came in the men's 4000m medley in 9:29.44. There were 39,166 spectators on the Friday (when lightning delayed events by two hours) and 46,363 on the Saturday.

28 **Dakar**, Sénégal. There was a crowd of about 50,000 at the Leopold Senghor Stadium for this IAAF GP meeting. In windy conditions Angelo Taylor won the 400m hurdles in 48.68 – his fastest time since 2004.

29 **Hamburg,** Germany. Rodgers Rop 2:07:32 led Kenyans to the first nine places in the marathon with two more men under 2:08.

29 **Stanford**, USA. 15 men, led by 20 year-old Galen Rupp's US collegiate record 27:33.38, broke 28 minutes for 10,000m at the Cardinal Invitational. A total of 26 men under 28:30 broke the previous world record of 22 and there were best ever marks for places 20-28. Jen Rhines won the women's 10,000m in 31:17.31 from Kim Smith's NZ record of 31:20.63.

May

1 **Baie Mahault**, Guadeloupe. Top mark came from LaShawn Merritt, 200m in 20.18.

1 **Sesto San Giovanni**, Italy. Rita Turova had her third consecutive win in the 50th edi-

tion of this race, recording a world-leading 20k time of 1:27:10 and heading three other women under 1:30.

3 **Salinas**, USA. Gerd Kanter used the usual helpful wind conditions at the Hartnell Discus meeting to throw 72.02, the top discus mark of 2007.

5 **Kingston**, Jamaica. Sprinters excelled, many in their first races of the outdoor season, with world-leading marks at the Jamaica International Invitational. Tyson Gay won the 200m in 19.97, Veronica Campbell returned for her first race since June 2006 for a narrow 100m win over Marshevet Hooker in 11.07; Kenia Sinclair ran 800m in 1:59.19 and Brigitte Foster-Hylton ran 100m hurdles in 12.71.

5 **Modesto Relays**, USA. Anwar Moore went to the top of the world list for 110m hurdles with 13.12.

5 **Osaka**, Japan. Jeremy Wariner clocked a world-leading 44.02 for 400m despite easing up before the finish at the IAAF Grand Prix meeting. Liu Xiang opened his season with 13.14 for 110m hurdles and Sally McLellan improved her Oceania record from 12.92 to 12.71.

5 **Xalapa**, Mexico. Jeff Hartwig pole vaulted 5.83 and Eder Sánchez set a Mexican record of 18:40.97 for 5000m walk.

5-6 **Desenzano del Garda, Italy.** Jessica Ennis added 101 points to her best in winning the heptathlon with 6388, including tying the British high jump record at 1.95. Decathlon winner Paul Terek was over 8000 for the first time since 2004 with 8134.

5-6 **IAU European 24 Hours Championship**, Madrid, Spain.

6 **Uberlandia**, Brazil. Keila Costa, who had set a triple jump pb of 14.43 in March, had three (wind-aided) jumps over 15m, topped by 15.10w/2.7.

9-12 **Caracas**, Venezuela. Triple jumpers, Osniel Tosca 17.52 and Yargelis Savigne 14.99, took full advantage of the 922m altitude venue of Caracas at the ALBA Games.

11 **Doha**, Qatar. Excellent early season world-leading outdoor marks were achieved by Wilfred Bungei (1:44.14 800m), Augustine Choge (3:31.73 1500m), Eliud Kipchoge (7:33.06 3000m), David Payne (13.12 110mh), Andreas Thorkildsen (86.39 JT), Allyson Felix (50.40 400m), Virginia Powell (12.66 100mH) and Blanka Vlasic (2.04 Croatian record HJ). Kamila Skolimowska set her 17th Polish hammer record with 76.83 in beating Tatyana Lysenko 75.73. Allyson Felix won the 400m in a pb 50.40 and also won the 100m in 11,27.

13 **Rio de Janeiro**, Brazil. Irving Saladino won the long jump.

16 **Fortaleza**, Brazil. Kim Kreiner threw the javelin 64.19 for a world-leading performance and North American record.

18-21 **Arab Championships**, Amman, Jordan.

19-20 **Halle**, Germany. Franka Dietzsch won the discus with the 2007 best mark of 68.06, and Christine Obergföll's javelin throw of 68.08 was the second longest of her career. Virgilijus Alekna extended his discus win streak to 27 with a 69.97 victory, while Betty Heidler won the women's hammer with 75.77 and had four throws beyond 75m.

20 **Belém**, Brazil. Jadel Gregório triple jumped 17.90 to add a centimetre to the 32 year-old South American record set by João Carlos de Oliveira. After 6.81 in Fortaleza Keila Costa improved again in the long jump, this time with a world leading 6.88.

20 **Carson, USA**. adidas Track Classic. Breaux Greer, 90.71 javelin, and Jenn Stuczynski, 4.84 pole vault, set North American records, and Meseret Defar broke the world best for 2 miles with 9:10.47 (4:35.4 + 4:35.1). Torri Edwards benefitted from a +2.0 wind to run a pb 100m of 10.90 just ahead of Veronica Campbell 10.91 and Lisa Barber pb 10.95 while the wind was over the limit at +2.5 in the men's race won by Tyson Gay in 9.79 from Derrick Atkins 9.86. In 200m action Wallace Spearmon won in 19.91 and LaShawn Merritt broke 20 sec for the first time with 19.98, and Allyson Felix won in 22.18. Other top marks came from Kenneth Ferguson, 48.15 pb in the 400m hurdles, Christian Cantwell 21.96 shot to beat Adam Nelson 21.47 and Reese Hoffa 21.36, and Michelle Perry 12.58 for 100m hurdles.

20 **European Race Walking Cup**, Leamington, GBR. Yohann Diniz was a surprise winner of the 20km as he took 1:22 off his two year-old best with a French record 1:18:58. Trond Nymark led the 50km by 34 sec at 40k but Vladimir Kanaykin produced a storming finish to pass him and win clearly in 3:40:57, just 17 sec outside his best. There was excellent standard in depth, not least in the women's race where Rita Turova 1:27:52 maintained her domination with her third win of the year and seventh in succession at 20km since 2005; she walked the final 5k in 20:58.

24-27 **Havana**, Cuba. The Barrientos Memorial meeting was combined this year with the Copa Cuba, the national championships. Yipsi Moreno won the hammer with 74.90 and Yargelis Savigne had a long jump/triple jump double with 6.66w and 14.54.

25-26 **NCAA Regional Championships** were held at Columbia MO (Mid-East), Des Moines (Mid-West), Eugene (West), Gainesville (East) as qualification meetings for the NCAA Nationals. At Gainesville Walter Dix won 100m and 200m in 10.05 and 19.69 (0.44 off his pb), and Natasha Hastings 200m and 400m in 22.61 and 50.23.

26 **Hengelo**, Netherlands. Fanny Blankers-Koen Games. A record ten men (previous best eight) broke 27:15 in the 10,000m won by Sileshi

Sihine in 26:48.73 from Eliud Kipchoge, 26:49.02 on his debut at the event, and Moses Mosop 26:49.55. Haile Gebrselassie was 5th in 26:52.81 in his first track race since 2004. The times for 8-11 and 15-18 were the quickest ever for those positions. World bests for the year were registered also by Paul Kipsiele Koech 8:01.05 in the steeplechase Gelete Burka 14:38.18 for 5000m, while Irving Saladino tied his year's longest jump of 8.53.

26-27 **Eugene**, USA. Maria Mutola won the 800m in 1:58.79, so that she has broken 2 min every year since 1991.

26-27 **European Champion Clubs Cup**, Albufeira, Portugal. Sports Club Luch of Moscow had a eleventh successive win in the women's event and ninth win in eleven years in the men's. Barbora Spotáková won the javelin with 65.19 and Australian Jana Rawlinson, competing for Panellinos of Greece, won both 400m and 400mh (51.94 and 55.52) in her first races since the birth of her son in December. Lyudmila Kolchanova recorded the best long jump of 2007 with a pb 7.21.

26-27 **Götzis,** Austria Carolina Klüft won the heptathlon for the fifth successive year but was closely challenged by Lyudmila Blonska as she won with 6681 points to 6626. Andrey Kravchenko won the decathlon with a European U23 record of 8617, a huge improvement on his previous best of 8013, from Roman Sebrle 8518 and Bryan Clay 8493. Clay looked set for a huge score after his best ever first day (4593) but managed only 36.14 in the discus, at which he has a best of 55.87.

26-27 **Sochi**, Russia. Subject to ratification Tatyana Lysenko set her fourth world hammer record with a first round 78.61 in hot weather (32ºC). There were also best marks for 2-3-4 from Gulfiya Khanafeyeva 77.36, Yelena Konevtseva 76.21) and Yekaterina Khoroshikh 74.87.

29 **Belgrade**, Serbia. 2nd Artur Takac Memorial meeting. Asafa Powell started his season as he had left off in 2006 with 9.97 (the 26th sub-10 second time of his career) in the 100m

June

1 **Dessau**, Germany. Vadim Vasilevskis beat Sergey Makarov 87.56 to 87.05 in the javelin.

2 **Kalamáta**, Greece. In his hometown Loúis Tsátoumas long jumped 8.66, the longest jump ever at sea level by a European, adding 30cm to the Greek record.

2 **La Coruña**, Spain. Francisco Fernández 1:18:50 and Rita Turova 1:28:44 had overwhelming victories in the fifth leg of the IAAF Race Walking Challenge 2007.

2 **Neerpelt**, Belgium. Eunice Jepkorir, with a previous best of 10:19.0, won the women's 3000m steeplechase in 9:25.84 followed by national records from Netsanet Achano ETH 9:28.03, Veerle Dejaeghere BEL 9:28.47 and the 16 year-old Norwegian Karoline Bjerkeli Grøvdal 9:33.19 (a world youth record).

2 **New York (Randall's Island)**, USA. Reebok GP. Tyson Gay won the 100m in 9.76 with the wind just over the limit at 2.2m/s from Derrick Atkins 9.83 and Jenn Stuczynski raised her recent American pole vault record of 4.84 to 4.88 (the classic 16 feet), for second equal on the world all-time list. Other top marks for the year came at 5000m from Tariku Bekele 13:04.05 and Tirunesh Dibaba 14:35.67 and in the sprint hurdles by Liu Xiang 12.92 (with Terrence Trammell second in a pb 12.95), and Virginia Powell 12.45. More super sprinting came from Wallace Spearmon who won the 200m in 19.82 from Usain Bolt 19.89, Veronica Campbell beat Torri Edwards 10.93 to 10.95 at 100m, in which Allyson Felix was third in a pb of 11.01 as well as winning the 400m in 50.53.

2-3 **Arles**, France. Tatyana Chernova, the 2006 World Junior champion, won the heptathlon with 6768 points. But for excess wind assistance at this notoriously windy venue this would have been a world junior record by 226 points.

3 **Glasgow**, GBR. Norwich Union Grand Prix. In miserably damp conditions, Goldie Sayers followed her British javelin record of 65.05 at Loughborough on 20 May with a 63.59 victory over Steffi Nerius 62.57 and Barbora Spotáková 62.26.

3 **Kuortane**. Finland. In their first clash of the year, Tero Pitkämäki beat Andreas Thorkildsen, 87.78 to 87.24 in the javelin.

6 **Turin**, Italy. Memorial Primo Nebiolo. Although beaten on countback by Kajsa Bergqvist, Antonietta Di Martino cleared 2.02 to break the Italian high jump record of 2.01 set in the year of her birth (1978) by Sara Simeoni.

6-9 **NCAA Championships**, Sacramento, USA. Walter Dix, clocked the swiftest legal 100m time of the season with a pb of 9.93, won the 200m in 20.32 and ran the second leg on their 38.60 winning 4x100m team to lead Florida State University (54) to a successful defence of the team title. LSU were second with 45 points in the men's competition with Auburn 34 3rd. Arizona State were the women's champions with from LSU 53 and Michigan 36. US Collegiate records were set by Michelle Sikes with 15:16.76 for 5000m and Anna Willard 9:38.08 for 3000m steeplechase, and other top women's marks came from Natasha Hastings, 50.15 for 400m, and Nicole Leach, 400m hurdles 54.32. *See USA section for winners.*

7-9 **South American Championships**, São Paulo, Brazil. Two continental records were set: Fábio Gomes da Silva, 5.77 pole vault, and Keila Costa, triple jump 14.57. Maurren Maggi (6.91) beat Costa (6.83) in the long jump. Brazilians won 29 of the 44 events, with Colombians next best with seven titles.

8-10 **Chinese World Championships Trials**, Suzhou. Li Zhenzhu, 3000m steeplechase 9:32.35, and Zheng Wenxiu, hammer 74.30, set Asian records.

9 **Haniá**, Greece. Loúis Tsátoumas was again in prime form as he won the long jump with 8.54.

9 **Zhukovskiy,** Russia. Znamenskiy Memorial. Gulnara Samitova-Galkina made a brilliant return to the event with a world leading steeplechase time of 9:14.37. Tatyana Lysenko won the hammer with 77.01 and Olga Komyagina took her break from pacemaking to win the 3000m in 8:43.95.

10 **Bydgoszcz**, Poland. European Athletics Festival. Five men threw over 80 in the hammer won with a Slovenian record 82.30 by Promoz Kozmus.

10 **Eugene**, USA. Prefontaine Classic. Daniel Kipchirchir Komen won the Bowerman Mile in 3:48.28 for a US all-comers record, well ahead of Bernard Lagat 3:50.56. Craig Mottram won the 2 miles in an Oceania record 8:03.50 (4:04.0 + 3:59.5) from Tariku Bekele 8:04.83 and Matt Tegenkamp 8:07.07 (North American record) and other world-leading times came from Melaine Walker 54.14 for 400m hurdles, Maria Mutola who won her 15th successive Prefontaine victory with 1:58.33 for 800m, and Gelete Burka 4:00.48 for 1500m. Michelle Perry beat Virginia Powell 12.51 to 12.58 at 100m hurdles.

15 **Oslo**, Norway. Bislett Games. Meseret Defar of Ethiopia smashed her world record for 5000m by almost 8 sec with 14:16.63 as Vivian Cheruiyot ran 14:22.51, also under the old record. Olga Komyagina set the pace through 2:50.74 and 5:42.60 before Defar led in 8:35.76 and 11:29.44, well ahead of schedule. Other highlights of this first Golden League meeting of the summer included 9.94 by Asafa Powell at 100m, 70.51 discus by Virgilijus Alekna, 50.26 by Sanya Richards at 400m, 4.85 pole vault by Yelena Isinbayeva and a fine javelin competition won by Tero Pitkämäki 88.78 from Breaux Greer 88.73 and Andreas Thorkildsen 87.79. Fast improving Eunice Jepkorir set a Kenyan steeplechase record of 9:19.44.

17 **Warsaw**, Poland. Kusocinski Memorial. Ivan Tikhon topped the world list for hammer with 82.58 while in the women's event Yipsi Moreno set a Cuban and CAC record of 76.36.

19 **Bangkok**, Thailand. Xie Limei set an Asian triple jump record of 14.73 at this Asian GP meeting.

19-20 **Kladno**, Czech Republic. Roman Sebrle won the decathlon with 8697, his highest total since winning the 2004 Olympic title. Dmitriy Karpov was second with 8553 points.

21-24 **USA Championships,** Indianapolis. Tyson Gay produced the fastest sprint double in history with 9.84 for 100m (equal pb) and 19.62 (second fastest ever) for 200m, winning both by big margins as second were Trindon Holliday 10.07 and Wallace Spearmon 19.89. Other world best performances for the year came in the 400m hurdles, 47.72 by James Carter and 53.28 by Tiffany Williams, US javelin record of 91.29 by Breaux Greer (winning his eighth successive title), and in the women's 400m which produced the biggest shock of the championships as Deedee Trotter 49.64, Natasha Hastings 49.84 and Mary Wineberg 50.24 all set pbs, leaving Sanya Richards (after an extravagant 50.02 semi) in fourth place 50.68 and off the 400m team for Osaka.

22-24 **Jamaican Championships**, Kingston. Usain Bolt broke Don Quarrie's 36 year-old Jamaican record, and his 19.75 was also a CAC record for 200m and Veronica Campbell had a superb 100m/200m double in 10.89 and 22.39, but Asafa Powell pulled up shortly after the finish of his 10.04 100m with a groin injury.

28-29 **European Cup Super League**, Munich, Germany. France and Germany finished on 116 points each with France winning the men's cup by dint of 6-4 on second places as each had four individual winners. Poland took third place. Russia took an eleventh consecutive women's victory by 20 points over France with Germany third. Christina Obergföll added 18cm to her European javelin record with 70.20 and there were world-leading marks also by Yuliya Pechonkina, 400mh 54.04 400mh (until Tiffany Williams ran 53.28 next day) and in both relays (Russia 42.78, Belarus 3:23.67). There were fourth wins in the event from four French athletes Mehdi Baala 1500m (he also has one at 800m), Ladji Doucouré 110mh, Bob Tahri 3000mSt and Muriel Hurtis-Houairi, 200m, and by the German Franka Dietzsch.

23-24 **European Cup**. Spain and Italy were men's winners and Great Britain and Italy women's winners in First League matches at Vaasa FIN and Milano ITA to win promotion to the Super League in 2008. Second League fixtures were staged at Odense DEN and Zenica BIH. Top marks included TJ 17.33 by Christian Olsson at Vaasa and an Italian record 2.03 high jump by Antonietta Di Martino, which gave her the greatest ever height differential, 34cm, by a woman high jumper, at Milano.

26-27 **Ostrava**, Czech Republic. Golden Spike IAAF Grand Prix. Haile Gebrselassie brought his tally of world records or world bests to 24 over a 13-year period by smashing Arturo Barrios' 1991 world records for 20,000m and one hour with 56:25.98 on the way to completing 21,285m. He went through 10,000m in 28:11.24. There was an Ethiopian 1-2-3 in the women's 5000m as Meseret Defar 14:30.18 was followed by pbs from Gelete Burka 14:31.20 and Meselech Melkamu 14:33.83 and Tatyana Lysenko produced the third longest women's hammer throw in history with 77.71.

28 **Strasbourg**, France. Mehdi Baala ran 3:31.05 for 1500m and Bob Tahri 5:17.19 for 2000m steeplechase.

29 **Moscow**, Russia. Yelena Soboleva ran the third best ever time for the women's mile with 4:15.63. The Cup meeting was held in a new stadium inside the Luzhniki Complex.

29-1 Jul **Japanese Championships**, Osaka. In his only competition prior to the World Championships, Koji Murofushi won his 13th successive hammer title with 79.24.

30-1 Jul **South American Junior Championships**, São Paulo, Brazil.

July

2 **Athens**, Greece. IAAF Grand Prix. Gulnara Samitova-Galkina clocked the fourth fastest ever steeplechase mark of 9:11.68 with Eunice Jepkorir second in 9:14.52, a Kenyan, African and Commonwealth record. The 30,000 spectators witnessed another world-leading mark as Tatyana Lebedeva made a spectacular start to her triple jump campaign with 15.08 in the third round and 15.14 in the fourth and Yuriy Borzakovskiy won a thrilling 800m in 1:44.38. Yelena Soboleva, in virtually a solo run once the pacemakers had gone, held off Maryam Jamal in the mile in a hand timed 3:58.3 to 3:59.0. In their first discus clash of the year Virgilijus Alekna beat Gerd Kanter 70.43 to 67.22.

4 **Salamanca**, Spain. Donald Thomas made a stunning European debut by high jumping 2.35.

4 **Zagreb**, Croatia. IAAF Grand Prix. Despite very wet conditions Tatyana Lysenko produced a great series of hammer throws topped by 76.74 and Irving Saladino long jumped 8.45.

4-5 62nd **Balkan Championships**, Sofia, Bulgaria.

6 **Saint-Denis**, France. Gaz de France meeting. Of the ten athletes who won IAAF Golden League jackpot scoring events in Oslo, only four remained in contention after this second leg: Sanya Richards (400m 49.52) and Yelena Isinbayeva (PV 4.91) who set world-leading marks and Michelle Perry (100mh 12.56) and Tero Pitkämäki (JT 89.70). Isinbayeva unsuccessfully attempted a world record 5.02. Alan Webb won a terrific 1500m race in 3:30.54, the fastest ever by a US-born athlete, from Mehdi Baala 3:31.01. Christian Olsson won the triple jump with 17.56 ahead of Nelson Évora's Portuguese record of 17.28 and there would have been very fast steeplechase times but for the bell being run a lap early, causing chaos.

6-8 **Pan-American Junior Championships**, São Paulo, Brazil.

7 **Bad Langensalza**, Germany. Karin Mey added 40 cm to her long jump best with a South African record 6.93 with Bianca Kappler 2nd at 6.90, and Chris Tomlinson set a British record with 8.29 when second to Gable Garenamotse 8.33w.

7-8 **European Cup of Combined Events**. Super League titles went to the British women at Szczecin, Poland and to the Belarussian men at Tallinn, Estonia, with the 1st League matches being held the other way round. Jessica Ennis led the first ever British success with a pb 6399 and Aleksandr Parkomenko was the individual decathlon winner with 8101. 2nd League events were held at Maribor, Slovenia.

8 **European Mountain Running Championships**, Cauterets, France. The Italian men achieved their 12th men's team win in 13 years).

10 **Lausanne**, Switzerland. Athletissima, IAAF Super Grand Prix. Tyson Gay's 19.78 200m was an astonishing run given the cold weather, leaving Usain Bolt 20.11 and Wallace Spearmon 20.42 well beaten. Liu Xiang also impressed with 13.01 for 110mh from Anwar Moore 13.12 and Torri Edwards beat Veronica Campbell 11.00 to 11.07 in the 100m. Brad Walker vaulted 5.91 before missing at the US record height of 6.04.

11-15 **IAAF World Youth Championships**, Ostrava, Czech Republic. World youth bests were set by Tatyana Kalmykova at 5000m walk 20:28.05 and the 15 year-old Wayne Davis with 13.18 for 110m over 91.4cm hurdles. Kalmykova and Bianca Perie (64.61 hammer) became the first athletes to retain World Youth titles. 1228 athletes took part, new championship records were set in 11 events and a record number of 41 countries won medals. The USA topped the medal table with 14 (7 gold, 4 silver and 3 bronze) from Kenya (6-4-1) and Russia (4-3-3).

12-15 **European Under-23 Championships**, Debrecen, Hungary. 904 athletes took part and there were ten new championship records, including 8492 decathlon by Andrey Kravchenko, 54.50 for 400mh by Angela Morosanu, and two featuring Simeon Williamson, 10.10 at 100m and 38.95 by Britain at 4x100m. Russia was easily the most successful nation with 15 gold, 9 silver and 11 bronze medals, from Britain 6-3-2, Germany 4-6-3 and Poland 4-2-3.

13 **Roma**, Italy. Golden Gala. Asafa Powell was back to his best as he finished close to a metre and a half clear of Derrick Atkins with 9.90 for 100m. Tero Pitkämäki was well beaten 88.36 to 86.09 by Andreas Thorkildsen in the javelin, but the other three Golden League jackpot contenders won again: Sanya Richards (400m 49.77), Yelena Isinbayeva (PV 4.90) and Michelle Perry (100mh world-leading 12.44). Pitkämäki's third round throw veered way over to the left and speared French long-jumper Salim Sdiri, who was badly hurt, but who recovered well over the ensuing months. There were 5000m wins from Sileshi Sihine 13:01.46 and Meriem Selsouli 14:36.52; and Blanka Vlasic high jumped 2.02 to win from Kajsa Bergqvist 2.00. Adil Kaouch won the 1500m in 3:30.77, but later lost that with a positive drugs test.

13-15 **NACAC U23 Championships**, San Salvador, El Salvador. Top mark was 20.19 for 200m by Jordan Vaden.

15 **Sheffield**, GBR. British Grand Prix. Kenenisa Bekele returned to top form with a brilliant 7:26.69 for 3000m on a depressingly chilly and wet evening. Allyson Felix virtually replicated her US championship 200m victory over Sanya Richards (22.34-22.43) with times of 22.35 and 22.44, followed by Veronica Campbell 22.60.

18 **Réthimno**, Greece. There was excellent weather with 30°C plus temperature in the 23rd annual Vardinoyannia meeting. Running his first serious 100m, Usain Bolt won in 10.03.

18-22 9th **All-Africa Games**, Alger, Algeria. Zersenay Tadese had a brilliant victory at 10,000m, finishing well clear of a talented field in a Games record 27:00.30. In the steeplechases, 19 year-old Willy Komen beat Ezekiel Kemboi 8:15.11 to 8:16.93 with 18 year-old Nahom Mesfin Tariku setting an Ethiopian junior record in third place, and new Kenyan star Ruth Bisibori ran barefoot to the women's title in 9:31.99.

19-22 **European Junior Championships**, Hengelo, Netherlands. There was a Norwegian 1-2 from Karoline Bjerkeli Grøvdal (9:44.34 for the first ever Norwegian EJ gold) and Kristine Eikrem Engeset and both broke the previous championship record. Bianca Perie followed her gold medals at the 2005 and 2007 World Youths and 2006 World Juniors with another here and the other 2006 World Junior champions to add a further gold were Artur Noga, who improved the championship record at 110m hurdles (99cm) to 13.42 and 13.36, and Kaire Leibak at women's triple jump. Daniejla Grgic (400m) was the one athlete to retain an EJ title won in 2005. Perhaps the top mark was Leonid Kivalov's 5.60 pole vault to match the championship record.

21 **Brasschaat**, Belgium. Alan Webb succeeded Steve Scott (3:47.69 in 1982) as North American 1 mile record holder by clocking 3:46.91, the world's quickest time for six years. He ran an even-paced race with quarter-miles in 56.2, 57.5, 56.9 and 56.3.

21 **Madrid**, Spain. IAAF GP meeting. Blanka Vlasic added a centimetre to her Croatian outdoor high jump record with 2.05 and wasn't too far away from making a world record 2.10, and Nelson Évora improved his Portuguese record from 17.28 to 17.51. Tatyana Lebedeva celebrated her 31st birthday with a brilliant long jump of 7.15 (her best for three years) and second was Naide Gomes with a Portuguese record 7.01.

21-22 **German Championships**, Erfurt. Franka Dietzsch her tenth discus title with 62.83 and top mark was 74.94 hammer from Berry Heidler.

22 **Lapinlahti**, Finland. Tero Pitkämäki missed his javelin pb by 30cm with 91.23.

22 **Tallinn**, Estonia. Vadim Vasilevskis set a Latvian javelin record of 90.73.

22-29 **Pan-American Games**, Rio de Janeiro, Brazil. Championship records were set in six men's and seven women's events, including top marks by Yargelis Savigne, TJ 14.80, and Yipsi Moreno, HT 75.20. Ana Guevara won the 400m in 50.34 to add to her 1999 and 2003 gold medals. Cuba headed the medal table with 12 gold, 8 silver and 10 bronze.

25 **Herculis, Monaco**. IAAF Super Grand Prix. 1:43.74 for 800m by Mbulaeni Mulaudzi and 8:29.52 for 3000m by Meriem Selsouli were world-leading marks and Christine Arron returned to top form with a 100m win in 11.06 over Carmelia Jeter and Me'Lisa Barber. Kenenisa Bekele won the 3000m in 7:29.32 with 20 year-old Moses Kipsiro second in a Ugandan record 7:32.03. Top field marks came from Blanka Vlasic 2.03 and Tatyana Lebedeva 15.10.

25 **Kaunas**, Lithuania. Virgilijus Alekna achieved his 36th successive discus victory but he needed 71.56, his longest throw of the year to beat Gerd Kanter 70.92.

25-29 **Asian Championships**, Amman, Jordan. Top mark came from Samuel Francis (Qatar, ex-Nigeria), as after a championships record 10.18 in his heat, he ran 9.99 for 100m. While the wind was legal for this race, performances were much affected by strong winds throughout the meeting. China topped the table (7-4-4), but 23 nations in all won medals. Susanthika Jayasinghe won a 100m/200m double in 11.19 and 22.99 to match the same feat in 2002 and 100m gold back in 1995.

28 **Heusden-Zolder**, Belgium. KBC Night of Athletics. The meeting was notable, as usual, for great depth in the middle and long distance events. Alan Webb took his best for 800m from 1:45.80 to 1:43.84 in beating Gary Reed 1:44.03. Three men broke 8:08 in the steeplechase, with Swedish and Bahraini records falling to Somalian-born Mustafa Mohamed 8:05.75 and Tareq Mubarak Taher (the former Kenyan Dennis Kipkirui Keter) 8:07.12. They were split by Morocco's Brahim Taleb (8:07.02). The women's steeplechase featured five inside 9:30, led by Hanane Ouhaddou's Moroccan record of 9:25.51 with six other national records in her wake.

28 **Zaragoza**, Spain. In very hot weather Kenenisa Bekele ran the year's top mark for 5000m in 2007 with 12:49.53, winning by 38 seconds. Another world-leading mark came from Maria Mutola, with 1:58.21 in the women's 800m.

28-29 **IAU 24 Hours World Challenge**, Drummondville, Canada. Ryoichi Sekiya retained his title with 263.562km and women's winner was Lyudmila Kalinina 236.848km. Team winners were, as in 2006, Japan (men) and Russia (women).

30 **Thessaloníki**, Greece. Blanka Vlasic

maintained her strong run of success with a Croatian record high jump 2.06.

31-3 Aug **Russian Championships**, Tula. Yekaterina Volkova and Tatyana Petrova went to second and third on the world all-time list for the 3000m steeplechase with 9:13.35 and 9:14.35. Another world leading-mark came from Olga Kotlyarova with 1:58.14 at 800m. Many other top women's marks included Yuliya Pechonkina 53.61 for 400mh, Svetlana Feofanova 4.75 pole vault and in a great long jump in which Lyudmila Kolchanova beat Irina Simagina 7.17 to 7.08.

August

2-5 **Chinese Championships**, Shijiazuang. Top marks included a 74.86 Asian hammer record by Zhang Wenxiu and world youth record 19.13 by Gong Lijiao in the women's shot.

3 **London Grand Prix**, London (CP), GBR. Reese Hoffa smashed his shot best with a final round 22.43 – the final throw of the competition after Christian Cantwell had taken the lead with 21.66. A magnificent triple jump contest was won by Aarik Wilson 17.58 from Leevan Sands 17.55w and Randy Lewis 17.43. Sanya Richards beat Allyson Felix 49.79 to 50.17 at 400m.

3-5 **Finnish Championships**, Lappeenranta. Tero Pitkämäki won his fourth successive Finnish javelin title with 89.43. Olli-Pekka Karjalainen won his tenth at the hammer and new Finn Frantz Kruger took his first title with 66.37 in the discus.

3-5 **French Championships**, Niort. Muriel Hurtis-Houairi won the 200m in 22.88, her first title since 2002.

4-5 **Spanish Championships**, San Sebastián. Spanish records were set by Francisco Javier Fernández. 10,000m 38:42.38, and Ruth Beitia, 2.02 high jump.

7 **Stockholm**, Sweden. The 41st DN Galan IAAF Super GP meeting was one of the greatest in its history. Jeremy Wariner ran the fastest 400m since 1999 with 43.50, Blanka Vlasic moved to third (indoors or out) on the world all-time list for high jump with 2.07 before unsuccessful attempts at a world record height of 2.10, and Kenenisa Bekele became the sixth fastest of all time at 3000m with 7:25.79. Allyson Felix scored an upset win, 49.70 to 49.72, over Sanya Richards at 400m, Belal Mansoor Ali set an Asian 1000m record of 2:15.23 and Paul K Koech went to the top of the 2007 steeplechase rankings with 7:59.42. The capacity crowd was treated to three Swedish wins: Stefan Holm raised his outdoor best for the season from 2.32 to 2.35, Carolina Klüft won the long jump and Susanna Kallur brought off a rare 100m hurdles victory over Michelle Perry. A US team of Ron Bramlett, Anwar Moore. David Payne and Aries Merritt improved the world best for 4x110m shuttle hurdle relay from 53.62 to 53.36.

9-12 **African Junior Championships**, Ouagadougou, Burkina Faso.

9-14 **World University Games**, Bangkok, Thailand. Yuliya Krevsun won the women's 800m by a huge margin in a world-leading time of 1:57.63, front-running through 400m in 56.17, and Games records were set by Halil Akkas, 8:20.83 for 3000m steeplechase, and by Jessica Augusto, 15:28.78 for 5000m.

10 **Leverkusen**, Germany. Christine Obergföll beat Steffi Nerius 67.04 to 65.72 in the javelin.

10-12 **Swedish Championships**, Eskilstuna. Anna Söderberg won her 15th successive discus title and Robert Kronberg his 11th at 110m hurdles. Ninth titles overall were won by Stefan Holm at high jump and Cecilia Nilsson at hammer, and Susanna Kallur took her seventh at 100m hurdles.

12 **Bochum-Wattenscheid**, Germany. Christina Obergföll retained her unbeaten record for the year as, with 65.42, she beat Steffi Nerius 64.68 and Barbora Spotáková 64.49.

25-2 Sep **World Championships,** Osaka, Japan. Tyson Gay and Allyson Felix, with three gold medals each, were the super-stars of a great championships in which the only major problem was excess heat throughout. But that helped terrific performances in many events although only Gay at 200m and Yekaterina Volkova at women's steeplechase set championship records. *See Championships section.*

September

4-15 **World Masters Championships**, Riccione, Misano and San Giovanni, Italy. Overall the most successful of 56 nations winning medals at this mammoth meeting were: Germany 108 gold, 106 silver and 101 bronze, Italy 89-75-55, USA 82-61-50, GBR 49-46-48, Australia 27-33-26 and Finland 25-20-24.

7 **Zürich**, Switzerland. Weltklasse, the first meeting in the re-constructed Letzigrund Stadium. Sanya Richards, with a world-leading 400m time of 49.36. and Yelena Isinbayeva, 4.80 PV, remained in the hunt for the Golden League jackpot, but Michelle Perry's dream of a share of the million dollars was dashed as she was third in 12.68 to Susanna Kallur 12.66 and Delloreen Ennis-London 12.68 in the 100m hurdles. Blanka Vlasic was again in top form with a 2.04 high jump. Xavier Carter bounced back from the knee injury that cost him a possible place in the team for Osaka by comfortably beating Usain Bolt 19.92 to 20.19 for 200m. The meeting was staged a little too soon after the World Champs for many top athletes.

8 **Paris (Charléty),** France. DécaNation. Result of the third edition of this 10-event international was: 1. FRA 104, 2. GER 102, 3. USA 100, 4. RUS 88, 5. UKR 63, 6. ESP 62, 7. ITA 59.

8 **IAU 100 Kilometres World Cup**, Win-

schoten, Netherlands. Shinichi Watanabe won the men's race in 6:23:21 and women's winner Norimi Sakurai clocked 7:00:27, taking 21 sec off the previous ARRS-recognised world best on a loop course by Ann Trason (USA) at the same venue in 1995, although Tomoe Abe of Japan recorded 6:33:11 on a point-to-point course in Yubetsu, Japan, in 2000.

8-9 **Finland v Sweden**, Göteborg. As in 2006 Finland's men just beat Sweden 203-199 but Sweden's women had a another clear win 219-189. Carolina Klüft once again demonstrated her amazing versatility by triple jumping 14.17w and 14.02, improving her pb from 13.87.

9 **Rieti**, Italy. Asafa Powell bounced back from his World Champs disappointment to run a world record 9.74 (reaction time 0.137, wind +1.7 m/s) in his 100m heat followed by 9.78/0.0 in the final. Janeth Jepkosgei maintained her brilliant form with 1:56.29 for 800m, Koji Murofushi produced his best hammer throw of the year 82.61 to beat Ivan Tikhon by 1cm, and Yargelis Savigne again beat Tatyana Lebedeva, 14.92 to 14.75 in the triple jump. Alfred Kirwa Yego ran his fastest 800m of the year, 1:44.50, but was well beaten by Belal Mansoor Ali 1:44.02 and Youssef Saad Kamel 1:44.11.

11 **Linz**, Austria. Gugl-Meeting. Dayron Robles clocked his season's best 110mh time of 13.05, into a 1.2m wind and in pouring rain, just 0.05 outside his pb.

14 **Brussels**, Belgium. 31st Van Damme Memorial. Meseret Defar took nearly 12 seconds off the world best for 2 miles that she had set earlier in the year with 8:58.58. En route she ran the quickest outdoor 3000m of the year, her 8:24.51 taking 0.15 sec off her Ethiopian record. Olga Komyagina, surely the best ever pace maker, led at 1000m in 2:48.29 before Defar took over. Defar's splits: 400m 67.4, 800m 2:14.7, 1200m 3:22.7, 1600m 4:31.5, 1M 4:33.07, 2000m 5:37.52 (sped up just after taking lead from Komyagina), 2400m 6:45.5, 2800m 7:52.8, 3200m 8:55.7. Yet again there was a superb 10,000m, ever the feature of this superb meeting, and Kenenisa Bekele ran the fastest time of the year, 26:46.18 from Moses Masai 26:49.20, Paul K Koech ran the fastest steeplechase of the year 7:58.80, and seven men led by Sileshi Sihine 12:50.16 broke 13 minutes for 5000m. Asafa Powell had almost 3m to spare when winning the 100m in 9.84 into a slight headwind and 18 year-old David Rudisha took 0.95 off his best to beat many of the world's best for 800m in 1:44.15. Sanya Richards reduced her 400m world best of the year to 49.29 in beating World medallists Nicola Sanders and Novlene Williams by over a second, and the other Golden League jackpot contender Yelena Isinbayeva also won again, but only on countback at 4.80 from Svetlana Feofanova.

15 **World Mountain Running Trophy**, Ovronnaz, Switzerland. Marco De Gaspari won a record fifth men's title (previously in 1997, 1999, 2001 and 2003), leading the Italian team to their 14th win in the 15 years that this competition has been determined as one men's race. The women's winner was Ana Pichrtová with the USA taking the team title.

16 **Berlin**, Germany. ISTAF. Sanya Richards, for the second successive year, and Yelena Isinbayeva shared the Golden League jackpot of $1 million. Richards produced another world-leading time of 49.27 to beat world champion Christine Ohuruogu by 1.13 secs and Isinbayeva cleared 4.82 before trying the world record height of 5.02. Blanka Vlasic completed five Golden League victories with a 2.00 high jump win. Susanna Kallur ran a pb 12.49 in a convincing 100m hurdles win over Michelle Perry 12.67 and 36 year-old Allen Johnson had his fourth ISTAF win in 13.33 for 110mh. *See Championships section for all Golden League event winners.*

19 **Warsaw**, Poland. Pedro's Cup. While he passed the chance of competing at the World Athletics Final, Jeremy Wariner maintained his brilliant form with a runaway 400m win in 44.43.

19-20 **Urumqi**, China. National Grand Prix Final. Xie Limei improved her Asian triple jump record of 14.73 to 14.90.

22-23 **World Athletics Finals**, Stuttgart, Germany. Top performance came in the final track event of the meeting when Dayron Robles matched Liu Xiang's world best time of the year for 110m hurdles with a CAC record 12.92. This was one of seven meeting records, the other top marks including Asafa Powell 9.83 for 100m and Sanya Richards 49.27 for 400m. Meseret Defar and Yelena Isinbayeva achieved record fourth successive WAF victories, winning for the third successive year were Paul Koech, Sanya Richards, Jamal and Michelle Perry, and Nadezhda Ostapchuk added to her 2004-05 victories. The one double winner was Edwin Soi – at 3000m and 5000m. Jaysuma Saidy Ndure made an amazing breakthrough to win the 200m in a Norwegian record 19.89, 0.36 under his previous best and Barbora Spotáková produced another Czech javelin record with 67.12.

16-17 **Talence**, France. Andrey Kravchenko, showing what might have been but for his false-starts disqualification in Osaka, finished well clear of Maurice Smith, Aleksey Drozdov and Roman Sebrle (2-4-1 at the Worlds) with a score of 8553, but Sebrle did enough to take the IAAF Combined Events Challenge for 2007 from Smith and Drozdov. The women's title went to Lyudmila Blonska who completed a fine season with a 6437 win.

23 **Shanghai**, China. Dayron Robles scored a convincing 110mh victory in 13.01 over Anwar Moore 13.20 and local favourite Liu Xiang 13.21.

After wins at 2.02 and 4.83, once again attempting world records were high jumper Blanka Vlasic and pole vaulter Yelena Isinbayeva, with the former getting close to 2.10 on one attempt. Wallace Spearmon produced a fantastic second half in the men's 100m to beat Tyson Gay by 0.06 in 9.96, a time that reduced his best from 10.11. Asafa Powell smashed a top field in 20.00 in just his second 200m race of the year. Kenenisa Bekele set a 1500m pb of 3:32.35 in second place to Daniel Komen's 3:31.75.

29 **Saransk**, Russia. IAAF Race Walking Challenge Final. Vladimir Kanaykin won the 20k on home ground in a world record 1:17:17 after 38:28 at halfway. Luke Adams finished well back with 1:21:01 in second place but won the Challenge series. Olga Kaniskina won the women's race in 1:26:47, the fastest time of the year, but the absent Rita Turova had already amassed enough points to take the series prize.

30 **Berlin Marathon**, Germany. Haile Gebrselassie took 29 seconds off Paul Tergat's world record with 2:04:26. He ran 5k splits of 14:44, 14:43, 14:50, 14:54 (20k 59:10), 14:55, 14:51, 14:43 and 14:30 and was on course for the record throughout, reaching halfway in 62:29. Two (Eshetu Wondimu and Rodgers Rop) of the original five pacemakers were able to stay with him to 30k in 1:28:56. Abel Kirui was second in a pb of 2:06:51. Gete Wami also defended her title, clocking 2:23:17, with second going to Irina Mikitenko, who ran 2:24:51, the best ever marathon debut by a German woman. There were 32,638 finishers.

30 **Great North Run, Newcastle to South Shields**, GBR. Paula Radcliffe ran well in her first race since the birth of baby Isla in December, but was well beaten by Kara Goucher, 66:57 to 67:53. Men's winner was Martin Lel in 60:10 from Samuel Wanjiru 60:18.

30 **Yokohama**, Japan. Sanya Richards continued her serene series of 400m wins with 50.27 in wet weather.

October

3 **Daegu**, Korea. Wallace Spearmon was again in top late season form, as he won both 100m (10.11) and 200m, in which his 19.88 was his sixth sub-20 sec time of 2007 (including one wind assisted). Aarik Wilson produced a brilliant series in the triple jump, topped by two jumps at 17.50.

7 LaSalle **Chicago Marathon**, USA. The 30th anniversary race will be remembered for record high temperatures (27º by the finish of the men's race and climbing later to 31°C) that slowed times considerably and for two fantastic finishes. Patrick Ivuti's winning margin was just five hundredths of a second as he and Jaouad Gharib ran 2:11:11 and in the women's race Adrian Pirtea was waving to the crowd and thought she had won in 2:33:52 not realising that Berhane Adere had been sprinting furiously far to her right on the men's side of the road and came through to win in 2:33:49. There were 35,867 starters but only 24,933 finishers as the organisers shut down the race at the halfway point with 3 hr and 50 min on the clock.

14 **IAAF World Road Running Championships**, Udine, Italy. Lornah Kiplagat took 24 sec off the world record for 20 kilometres with 62:57 en route to breaking Elana Meyer's world half marathon record by 19 seconds with 66:25 to win a $50,000 world record bonus as well as $30,000 first prize. She went through 5k in 15:38, 10k in 31:10 and 15k in 46:59 and second was Mary Keitany, who improved her best from 68:36 to 66:48. The perfect conditions were illustrated by the fact that most of the field set pbs – 17 of the first 20 and 39 of the 56 finishers. Similarly there were pbs from 18 of the first 20 and 61 of the 79 finishers in the men's race and here another defending champion won – in this case Zersenay Tadese in 58:59 from Patrick Makau Musyoki 59:02, Evans Cheruiyot 59:05 and Deriba Merga 59:16 with a record seven men breaking the 1 hour barrier. Kenya won both team titles.

15-18 4th **CISM World Military Games**, Hyderabad, India.

21 **Amsterdam**, Netherlands. Emmanuel Mutai, whose previous best was 2:13:06, headed some super-fast times with his 2:06:29 marathon win. Second was Richard Limo, whose 2:06:45 was the third fastest ever on debut at the distance. Eleven men under 2:10 was a new world record and there were best ever times for places 7 to 11.

21 **Scanzorosciate**, Italy. Monica Svensson improved the women's world best for 50km walk to 4:10:59.

29-2 Nov **Wuhan**, China. There were masses of great marks by juniors at the National City Games with a world junior record for the track 20,000m walk from Li Gaobo 1:20:11.72. Liu Nian ran the 3000m steeplechase in 9:26.25 for second on the women's junior all-time list, an astonishing result given her previous pb of 10:18.49, and 17 year-old Zhang Yingying won the 10,000m in 31:17.30, 1:12.93 off her pb.

30-1 Nov 2nd **Asian Indoor Games**, Macau. Top mark was 6.54 for 60m by Samuel Francis.

November

4 **New York,** USA. Held the day before the traditional race, the US Olympic Trial Marathon was run on a 5-loop course in Central Park. Ryan Hall completed a great year by winning in 2:09:02. The race was marred by the collapse (shortly after the 5 miles mark) and death of former US marathon champion Ryan Shay.

5 ING **New York City Marathon**, USA. Contesting her first marathon since winning the world title in August 2005, Paula Radcliffe beat Gete Wami in an epic race, 2:23:09 to 2:23;32,

with Wami, just five weeks after winning the Berlin marathon, taking the $500,000 prize as the female winner of the 2006-07 World Marathon Majors series. The top men ran conservatively for much of the race before Martin Lel and Abderrahim Goumri broke clear to finish in that order in 2:09:04 and 2:09:16. There was a world record 38,607 finishers.

21-24 11th **Pan-Arab Games**, Cairo, Egypt. The 18 year-old Sudanese Abubaker Kaki ran 1:43.90 for 800m, a 1.3 sec improvement on his pb and second on the world all-time list for juniors.

18 **Tokyo**, Japan. Mizuki Noguchi won the International Women's Marathon in 2:21:37 (halves of 71:18 and 70:19). Second was Selina Kosgei in 2:23:31.

23 **Chiba**, Japan. The annual international marathon relay was held this year for the first time as a mixed competition with alternating men's and women's legs. Japan 2:05:56 won clearly from Kenya 2:07:06.

December

2 **Fukuoka**, Japan. Samuel Wanjiru made a superb marathon debut by winning in a course record time of 2:06:39 from Deriba Merga (previous best 2:13:33) 2:06:50 and Atsushi Sato 2:07:13.

9 **European Cross-Country Championships**, Toro, Spain. Sergiy Lebid, who has competed in all 14 editions of this race, won for the seventh time and Stephanie Twell became the first woman to take the junior title twice. Marta Domínguez made her debut in the event to win the senior women's title and overall Britain was the most successful nation with four golds, two silver and two bronze from Spain (3-0-1) and France (2-1-1). Britain's 14 points from 1-2-4-6 in the junior women's race was the lowest ever.

7-12 24th **South East Asia Games**, Nakhon Ratchasima, Thailand. The host nation was the most successful with 17 gold, 9 silver and 9 bronze medals.

SUPERLATIVES

World Records

Most: Sergey Bubka USR/UKR set a total of 35 at pole vault: 17 outdoors from 5.85 (1984) to 6.14 (1994) and 18 indoors (9 ratified by IAAF) from 5.81 (1844) to 6.15 (1993).

Paavi Nurmi FIN set 22 official and 13 unofficial world records at distances from 1500m to 20,000m between 1921 and 1931.

The most world records by a woman at one event is 21 at pole vault (11 out, 10 in) by Yelena Isinbayeva RUS 2003-08.

Oldest: 41y 238d Yekaterina Podkopayeva RUS 4x800m indoor 8:18.71 Moskva 4 Feb 1994. **Youngest**: 14y 334d Wang Yan CHN 5000m walk 21:33.8 Jian 9 Mar 1986 (unratified). **Youngest male**: 17y 198d Thomas Ray PV 3.42m Ulverston 19 Sep 1879 (prior to IAAF jurisdiction, which began in 1913).

Most world records set in one day: 6 Jesse Owens USA at Ann Arbor 23 May 1935: 100y 9.4, LJ 8.13m, 220y straight (& 200m) 20.3, 220yh straight *(& 220y) 22.6.

Most official world records set in one field event competition: 3 Karl-Hans Riehm FRG 76.70, 77.56 & 78.50 hammer at Rehlingen 19 May 1975 (uniquely all six throws over previous WR of 76.66); 3 Mac Wilkins USA 69.80, 70.24 & 70.86 discus at San Jose 1 May 1976; 3 Alessandro Andrei ITA 22.72, 22.84 & 22.91 shot at Viareggio 12 Aug 1987; Indoors: 3 Tatyana Lebedeva RUS 15.16 (=), 15.25 & 15.36 triple jump at Budapest 6 Mar 2004.

Three men set four world records in one competition – the Olympic triple jump final at Ciudad de México on 17 Oct 1968; successively: 17.22 Giuseppe Genile ITA (who had set WR 17.10 in qualifying), 17.23 Viktor Saneyev URS, 17.27 Nelson Prudencio BRA, 17.39 Saneyev.

Olympic Games – see page 91

World Champions (excluding Olympics):

Oldest: Indoors: 44y 271d Yekaterina Podkopayeva RUS 1500m 197, Outdoors: 40y 268d Ellina Zvereva BLR DT 2001.

Youngest: 17y 248d Merlene Frazer JAM, but only ran heat of 4x100m 1991, 17y 333d or 18y 90d Tirunesh Dibaba ETH 5000m 2003; **Youngest man**: 18y 177d Ismael Kirui KEN 5000m 1993

Most gold medals: 10 Sergey Bubka URS/UKR (6 out, 4 in) PV 1983-97, 10 Maris Mutola MOZ (3 out, 7 in) 800m 1993-2006, 9 Michael Johnson USA (all outdoor) 200m, 400m, 4x400m 1991-9,

Most medals: 20 Merlene Ottey JAM (14 out, 6 in) 60m, 100m, 200m, 4x100m 1983-1997

Greatest High Jump height differntial: the greatest height cleared above an athlete's own head is 59cm by Frankin Jacobs USA 2.32m New York (indoors) 27 Jan 1978 and by Stefan Holm SWE 2.40m Madrid (indoors) 6 Mar 2005. The women's record is 34cm by Antonietta Di Martino ITA Milano 22 Jun 2007.

Longest winning sequence: 150 Iolanda Balas ROU at high jump 1956-67. Men's record: 122 Edwin Moses USA 400mh 1977-87.

Most finishers in a marathon: 38,607 New York City 4 Nov 2007.

ATHLETES OF 2007

By Peter Matthews

JUST AS ASAFA POWELL had been very nearly a universal choice for male world athlete of the year in 2006, so his conqueror at the Osaka World Championships, Tyson Gay, was the clear choice of most people for that accolade in 2007. Indeed Gay went further, for not only did he top the rankings at 100m, but also did so at 200m and added a third World gold with the sprint relay in Osaka.

Gay, born in Lexington, Kentucky, first came to prominence while at Barton County CC, for whom he won the 100m at the Junior College Nationals in 2002 and ran his fastest ever times of 10.01w for 3rd at 100m and 20.31w for 2nd at 200m at the age of 20 in 2003. He then went to the University of Arkansas, where he was coached by Lance Brauman, and had a terrific start at the NCAAs as he won the 100m in a pb 10.06 and was 4th at 200m in 20.39 after a pb 20.07 (6th fastest in the world that year) in his heat at 200m in 2004. He was 5th in the semis of the US Olympic Trials at 100m. A year later, after ducking under 20 seconds with 19.93 in the NCAA semis (3rd in the final in 20.16), he was 2nd in the US 200m to take his place at the World Championships, where he was the fourth man on the US clean sweep of 1-2-3-4, He also ran sub-20 times of 19.99 for 3rd in the London GP and 19.96 to win at the World Athletics Finals. That year he ran only four 100m races, with a best of 10.08, but he broke through at both sprints in 2006, to 9.84 and 19.68 for third equal and fourth equal on the world all-time lists and to rank as world 2nd at 100m and 1st at 200m. He was US champion at 100m and broke 10 seconds in each of his last six races while at 200m his four races sub-19.9 was just one short of Michael Johnson's record.

Gay went on from this great season in 2006 to even better things in 2007 and before his World Championships triumph ran the greatest ever sprint double (9.84 and 19.62) at the US Champs. His coach Brauman was in prison while Gay sped to glory on the track but kept in touch, and Gay was also aided by advice from former top sprinter Jon Drummond.

Tyson Gay in 2007

Won 11 of 12 individual finals and 4/4 relays

15 Apr	MSR	Walnut	4x100m	38.30
28 Apr	PennR	Philadelphia	4x100m	38.35
5 May		Kingston	200m	19.97/-0.5
20 May	adidas	Carson	100m	9.79w/2.5
	(1h2 10.18/0.4)			
2 Jun	GP	New York	100m	9.76w/2.1
22 Jun	NC	Indianapolis	100m	9.84/-0.5
	(1h2 9.98/1.9, 1s2 9.97/-1.1)			
24 Jun	NC	Indianapolis	200m	19.62/-0.3
	(1h4 20.66/-2.4, 1s2 20.15/-0.3)			
10 Jul	Athl	Lausanne	200m	19.78/0.0
15 Jul	BrGP	Sheffield	100m	10.13/-0.4
3 Aug	LGP	London (CP)	100m	10.02/-0.8
	(1h1 10.09/-0.6)			
26 Aug	WCh	Osaka	100m	9.85/-0.5
	(2h1 10.10/1.0, 1q2 10.06/-0.5, 1s2 10.00/0.1)			
30 Aug	WCh	Osaka	200m	19.76/-0.8
	(1h2 20.46/0.2, 1q3 20.08/0.9, 1s2 20.00/-0.4)			
1 Sep	WCh	Osaka	4x100m	37.78
7 Sep	WK	Zürich	4x100m	38.40
28 Sep	GP	Shangahi	100m	10.02/0.0 (2nd)
30 Sep	Super	Yokohama	100m	10.23/-1.4

WORLD RECORDS ARE increasingly rare commodities these days, and just four men set them outdoors in 2007: Asafa Powell with his 9.74 for 100m at Rieti, Samuel Wanjiru with half marathons in 58:53 and 58:33, Vladimir Kanaykin, 1:17:16 for 20km walk. and Haile Gebrselassie, first when he covered 21,285m in 1 hour at Ostrava (also breaking the 20,000m record in 56:26.0 en route) and then when he won the Berlin marathon in 2:04:26 (THE top single performance of 2007). Powell managed only 3rd in the World 100m, Wanjiru faded badly in the World Half marathon and although Kanaykin won both his 20km races (in the two fastest times of the year), he did not finish the 50km, his chosen event at the Worlds. Even the great Gebrselassie's record was not perfect, as he did not finish the London marathon and he was 5th at Hengelo in 26:52.81 in his first track 10,000m for three years, although he also had a fast New York half marathon win in 59:24.

Major contenders for top honours can certainly be claimed by those who were unbeaten in 2007 at their specialities. Not qualifying on the strictest criteria is Jeremy Wariner for he was left in his blocks at Sheffield, but other than that he won all his ten 400m finals, nearly all by wide margins. Rated by many as the greatest athlete of the present day, he is even closing on his mentor Michael Johnson's world record. Irving Saladino won all his nine long jump competitions, and Gay won all four at 200m (as did Walter Dix but he did not meet the best men). Kenenisa Bekele was second at 1500m in a marvellous pb of 3:32.35 in Shanghai, but won all his races at longer distances on the track: 4 at 3000m, 2 at 10,000m (including the World title). 1 each at 2000m (world indoor record), 2 miles and 5000m; the only blot on his record was his failure to finish in the World Cross-Country. Martin Lel won both his marathons (both top races).

Selections for World Top Ten

My selection of the top 10 athletes of 2007 together with the lists compiled by international experts polled by Track & Field News, by the IAAF and those of Athletics International readers:

	PJM	*TFN*	*IAAF*	*AI*
Tyson Gay USA	1	1	1	1
Jeremy Wariner USA	2	2	6	2
Kenenisa Bekele ETH	3	3	8	4
Haile Gebrselassie ETH	4	10	2/3	3
Irving Saladino PAN	5	4	4	7
Asafa Powell JAM	6	5	5	5
Reese Hoffa USA	7	8	11	10
Tero Pitkamaki FIN	8	9	9	9
Liu Xiang CHN	9	7	2/3	8
Zersenay Tadese ERI	10	-	10	-
Gerd Kanter EST	11	11	-	-
Bernard Lagat USA	–	6	7	6

Note Athletics International (AI) readers actually only voted for 1-2-3-4-5 and Track & Field News (TFN) does not consider road races, other than the marathon, or cross-country action.

100 Metres

IN 2006 THERE was keen anticipation over a clash between Asafa Powell and Justin Gatlin – but it never happened. There was similar anticipation in 2007 over a clash between Powell and Tyson Gay. Gay started in sensational form with wins in 9.79w at Carson and 9.76w at New York before his 9.84 win at the US Champs. Powell continued his sub-10 ways with 9.97 at Belgrade and 9.94 at Oslo, but the big men did not meet until the World Championships, and there Powell again tightened under pressure as Gay swept to a superb victory in 9.85 and Derrick Atkins stole second place. Powell was again in superb form after that, with a new world record of 9.74 in a heat at Rieti followed by 9.78 in the final in less favourable wind conditions, and big wins at Brussels in 9.84 and WAF 9.83 while Gay was beaten by Wallace Spearmon, 9.96 to 10.02 in Shanghai. Powell ran 8 of the 18 wind-legal sub 10.00 times to 4 by Gay, but ranks behind the American after that Osaka loss. He was 2-1 v Atkins, who ran three sub-10s and nine times (plus 9.86w and 9.83w behind Gay) inside his pre-season best of 10.08. The Nigerian Samuel Francis moved to Qatar and ran a sensational 9.99 to win the Asian title, but had little to back that up until his 10.10 CISM win in October. Trindon Holliday and Walter Dix were 2nd and 3rd in the US Champs, but turned down Osaka selection (for football and studies respectively). In reverse order these two men took NCAA 1-2, with Dix fourth fastest of the year with 9.93 in that race, but as both only had US seasons it is difficult to rank them with the rest of the world. Making a strong late-season surge was Jaysuma Saidy Ndure. The ex-Gambian was ineligible for the Worlds, but was second to Francis Obikwelu (false start in his Worlds heat) in Zürich, and to Powell in Brussels and WAF with a win in Berlin. 4-5-6 in the Worlds, well behind the top three, were African champion Olusoji Fasuba, Pan-Am champion Churandy Martina and Marlon Devonish. Win-loss records included Martina 3-2 v Michael Frater, WAF 3rd; Frater 2-2 v Devonish and 5-1 v Obikwelu; Obikwelu 4-4 v Devonish, 3-1 v Fasuba; Devonish 3-1 v Fasuba, 1-1 v Martina.

Most times at 10.05 or faster: Powell 11, Atkins 9+2w, Gay 7+2w, Dix 3+1w, Frater 2+1w, Holliday 1+2w. 18 'legal' times under 10.00 compared to 31 in 2006, 16 in 2005 and 33 in 2004.

1. Gay, 2. Powell, 3. Atkins, 4. Saidy Ndure, 5. Dix, 6. Holliday, 7. Spearmon, 8. Martina, 9. Frater, 10. Obikwelu

200 Metres

STANDARDS REMAINED HIGH at 200m with 7 men running 17 sub-20 second times compared to 6 running 16 in 2006. Tyson Gay ran sub-20 to win each of his four finals, headed by clear wins at US Champs (19.62 from Wallace Spearmon 19.89) and Worlds (19.76 from Usain Bolt 19.91 and Spearmon 20.05). Spearmon went 3-3 v Bolt, and had five (plus one windy) sub-20 times to four by the Jamaican. Xavier Carter did not finish in his US semi-final and raced sparingly but beat Bolt 2-0 while down 1-2 to Spearmon. Carter beat Spearmon 20.23 to 20.25 at Eugene, at Zürich it was 1. Carter 19.92, 2, Bolt 20.19, and at Brussels: 1. Spearmon 19.88, 2. Carter 20.04, 3, Bolt 20.14. The top four men are the same as in 2006, with Bolt swapping places with Carter. Behind these superstars Rodney Martin had a most consistent season including 3rd US Champs, 4th Worlds and 3rd WAF. As in the 100m Walter Dix, NCAA champion indoors and out, is hard to rank but won his four competitions in the USA and ran 19.69 at the NCAA-East meeting. Jaysuma Saidy Ndure improved from 20.25 to a startling 19.89 to win at the WAF, beating Spearmon and Martin, and LaShawn Merritt ran 19.98 at Carson behind Spearmon. Churandy Martina, Marvin Anderson and Chris Williams were 5-6-7 at the Worlds, but Martina only had three competitions while Anderson beat Williams 2-1. Johan Wissman was WAF 4th and beat Williams 2-0 and Anderson 1-0. Asafa Powell was eighth fastest with a fine win in Shanghai in 20.00, well ahead of Martin and Williams, but was not ranked as his only other races were 3rd in Eugene in 20.55 and a dnf in Yokohama.

Most times at 20.30 or better: Spearmon 14+1w, Bolt 12, Gay 7, Martin 6, Carter, Dix, Merritt, Anderson & Williams.

1. Gay, 2. Spearmon, 3. Bolt, 4. Carter, 5. Martin, 6. Dix, 7. Merritt, 8. Saidy Ndure, 9. Anderson, 10. Martina

400 Metres

JEREMY WARINER STUTTERED and was left in his blocks in bad weather at Sheffield, but otherwise won all ten competitions and was clearly number one for the fourth successive year. He improved his pb by 0.17 to 43.45 for third on the world all-time list, had six of the year's eight fastest times and his winning margin averaged an extraordinary 0.77. The closest anyone got was LaShawn Merritt, 0.18 behind at the London GP. Merritt moved to eighth on the world all-time list with his 43.96 (Wariner 43.50) at the Worlds and was 1st six times and 2nd five times in his 11 competitions. Angelo Taylor improved from a pb of 44.68 (2001) to 44.05 to beat Merritt by 0.01 at the US Champs (where Wariner was 4th at 200m) and completed a US 1-2-3 at the Worlds. These three men ran all the 19 fastest times of 2007. Chris Brown and Tyler Christopher were 1-2 at the Pan Ams and 4th and 6th respectively at the Worlds, with Christopher beating Worlds fifth placer Leslie Djhone 2-1 overall. Johan Wissman and Avard Moncur also made the World final but two men who were 4th in the semis, Gary Kikaya and John Steffensen (sub-45 in both heat and semi) had better records than Moncur. Kikaya beat Djhone 2-0 and Steffensen 4-0. Lionel Larry had a good US season (2nd NCAA, 3rd US Champs) but did not finish at the Pan Ams or in his Worlds heat. The 2006 top three (Wariner, Kikaya, Merritt) were the only men to remain in this year's top ten.

Most sub-45.00 times: Wariner & Merritt 11, Taylor 8, Brown & Christopher 5, Larry & Darrold Williamson 4, Kikaya, Steffensen & Wissman 3

1. Wariner, 2. Merritt, 3. Taylor, 4. Brown, 5. Christopher, 6. Wissman, 7. Kikaya, 8. Djhone, 9. Steffensen, 10. Larry

800 Metres

THIS WAS A poor year for 800m running with five men beating 1:44 (once each and the World race was unsatisfactory with 400m reached in 55.08 and 600m in 1:22.18. Credit, however goes to Gary Reed for making a race of it in the final lap and to Alfred Kirwa Yego for edging past him to win (in 1:47.09). But Kirwa Yego, who had run 1:44.54 in his semi in Osaka, was no better than third in any of his 11 other races and it is very difficult to determine who should rank top. Mbulaeni Mulaudzi ran the year's fastest of 1:43.74 in Monaco where Youssef Saad Kamel and Amine Laâlou also broke 1:44 closely followed by Reed, Khadevis Robinson and Dmitrijs Milkevics. The last two both went out in the semi-finals at the Worlds. Mulaudzi, who won 3 of his 10 and was 7th Worlds, was second to the Sudanese junior Abubaker Kaki at the African Games and to Kamel at the WAF (3. Belal Mansoor Ali, 4. Laâlou) and he was beaten 3-1 by Yuriy Borzakovskiy, who had four wins and three seconds prior to his World bronze but who was only 6th in Rieti and Brussels. Ali, 4th in his heat at the Worlds, won in Rieti and David Rudisha was an impressive winner in Brussels in 1:44.15 ahead of Mulaudzi, Kamel, Ali, Mohammed Al-Salhi, Borzakovskiy and Kamel. Rudisha, African junior champion, had the most impressive competitive record as he was unbeaten in ten races after 6th in Doha, but he did not contest the Worlds.

Alan Webb ran 1:43.84 to beat Reed 1:44.03 at Heusden, and was 2nd at Malmö to Rudisha, but had only one other 800m race. Win-loss records hardly help much: Mulaudzi was 2-2 v Kamel and v Abraham Chepkirwok (4th Worlds, 5th African G, 7th WAF), Reed was 1-1 v Borzakovskiy and Mulaudzi, Kamel 2-1 v Chepkirwok. Wilfred Bungei ran his season's best in his first outdoor race, 1:44.14 in Doha, and later won the Kenyan Trials and was 5th at the Worlds but did not have his usual depth of results and was 1-2 v Chepkirwok and 3-1 v Laâlou. Kaki went out in his heat at the Worlds, but won both the Arab Champs and the Pan Arab Games, making a 1.3 sec improvement on his pb to 1:43.90 at the latter. Overall there was little between the top men and although he lacked enough races against the others, Rudisha perhaps stands out most.

Most times sub-1:45: Reed 5, Kamel & Mulaudzi 4, Chepkirwok, Laâlou, Robinson & Ali 3.

1. Rudisha, 2. Borzakovskiy, 3. Reed, 4. Mulaudzi, 5. Kamel, 6. Ali, 7. Chepkirwok, 8. Bungei, 9. Laâlou, 10. Kirwa Yego

1500 Metres

BERNARD LAGAT RAN a fine tactical race to become a highly popular world champion, but this and the London GP were his only wins in seven 1500m or mile races. He ran his best times of 3:33.85 and 3:50.56 in the Eugene mile well behind Daniel Kipchirir Komen 3:48.2, and Komen also beat him in Berlin in Lagat's only post-Osaka 1500m. Komen fell in his semi at the Worlds but then won his last four races, including also Brussels, WAF and Shanghai. Mehdi Baala, disqualified in his Worlds semi for pushing, was WAF 2nd, had three wins in his six races including two 3:31s (so much faster than Lagat). For the first year since 1994 no man broke 3:30 for the 1500m and with all too many athletes having rather thin seasons the depth of times was way down as there were just 37 times sub 3:34 for 1500m or 3:51 for the mile compared to 73 in 2006. Alan Webb headed the list with his 3:30.54 Saint-Denis win and he also ran much the fastest mile as his 3:46.91 in Brasschaat broke Steve Scott's 25 year-old US record.

However, after six wins, Webb was 8th Worlds, 7th Zürich and 4th WAF, but still 3-1 v Lagat. Rashid Ramzi ran only twice, taking the World silver medal and coming 6th in Brussels, and Augustine Choge had only three races outdoors (plus two wins indoors, one over Komen), but those were wins in Doha and Glasgow and 2nd in Oslo, so that he was 2-0 v Shadrack Korir and Tarek Boukensa, respectively 3rd and 5th at the Worlds. The 2006 No. 1 Alex Kipchirchir was third in Rome in 3:31.58 behind Boukensa and Korir and 3rd in the Eugene mile but did not otherwise better 3:37. Adil Kaouch had crossed the line first in Rome in 3:30.77 and had 'won' his other race, the Oslo mile in 3:51.14 but he received a drugs ban so his marks were erased. Belal Mansour Ali was 11th at the Worlds and 6th WAF, but had good wins in Athens, Lausanne and Monaco, and was 2-2 against the Kenyans Korir, Asbel Kiprop (4th Worlds) and Suleiman Simotwo. 18 year-old Kiprop lacked fast times (best 3:35.24) but won the African Games title from Antar Zerguelaine and Boukensa.

Most times sub-3:34 or 3:51M: Komen 6, Boukensa & Korir 3.

1. Komen, 2. Lagat, 3. Baala, 4. Webb, 5. Choge, 6. Ramzi, 7. Boukensa, 8. Korir, 9. Ali, 10. Kiprop

3000 Metres/2 Miles

KENENISA BEKELE RAN the fastest time indoors, 7:30.51 at Stockholm, won a 2 miles in Hengelo, and then ran the three fastest 3000m times of the year: 7:25.79 at Stockholm, 7:26.69 at Sheffield and 7:29.32 at Monaco. Next quickest were Moses Kipsiro and Alistair Cragg, 2-3 at Monaco in 7:32.03 and 7:32.49 and Bernard Lagat a 7:32.43 win indoors at Birmingham with Markos Geneti, Augustine Choge and Paul Koech following, all under 7:34. Other fast races were at Doha in May, when Eliud Kipchoge (7:33.06), Jonas Cheruiyot and Joseph Ebuya broke 7:35, and at Rieti in September, when Thomas Longosiwa (7:32.79), Yusuf Biwott and Edwin Soi did so. Soi went on to a brilliant win in a slow race at the WAF from Ebuya, Mo Farah, Craig Mottram, Longosiwa, Kipchoge, Kipsiro, Cheruiyot and Biwott. Mottram set an Oceania 2 miles record with 8:03.50 (worth 7:30.4 on the Sparks formula) in Eugene from Tariku Bekele 8:04.83 and Matt Tegenkamp's North American best 8:07.07. Lagat won his only outdoor race, beating Soi, Kipsiro, Ebuya, Farah, T Bekele, Longosiwa, Tegenkamp and Cheruiyot in Zürich.

(indoors and out): 1. K Bekele, 2. Lagat, 3. Soi, 4. Mottram, 5. Kipsiro, 6. Ebuya, 7. Kipchoge, 8. Farah, 9. T Bekele, 10. Longosiwa

5000 Metres

KENENISA BEKELE RAN the year's fastest time – 12:49.53 at Zaragoza in July in his only 5000m race and finished 38 seconds ahead of the second man. But while in 2006 19 men had run 33 times under 13 minutes there was just one other sub-13 race in 2007 as seven men did so in Brussels, with Sileshi Sihine winning from Eliud Kipchoge, Moses Kipsiro, Joseph Ebuya, Thomas Longosiwa, Yusuf Biwott and Abraham Chebii. Tariku Bekele was 8th in 13:01.60, but he was the only man to run three times under 13:10, adding his win in New York and 2nd (to Craig Mottram) in Ostrava. Sihine also won the next fastest race with 13:01.46 in Rome from Kipchoge, Mushir Salim Jawher, Ahmed Baday and Leonard Komon, who all broke 13:05. Those two big wins are probably enough for Sihine to take top ranking even though he was only 6th in his third 5000m in a slow WAF race, won easily by Edwin Soi.

Bernard Lagat completed a World Champs double in a very slow race (his time 13:45.87), and he was followed home by Kipchoge, Kipsiro, Matt Tegenkamp, T Bekele and Mo Farah, but K Bekele and Sihine did not attempt to double up after the 10,000m. Lagat won his only other 5000m, the US Champs from Tegenkamp, but his time of 13:30.73 puts him 120th on the word list so he is very difficult to rate in merit terms. Kipchoge had five solid runs adding 3rd Kenyan Trials and 5th WAF to those three second places (above). Ebuya was 2-1 v Soi, as these men were 1-2 in Lille and 2-4 at the Kenyan Trials (won by Isaac Songok, who like Ebuya went out in his heat at the Worlds).

Micah Kogo was 2nd in New York, Lausanne and WAF with Moses Masai 3rd in the last.

1. Sihine, 2. Kipchoge, 3. Kipsiro, 4. K Bekele, 5. T Bekele, 6. Ebuya, 7. Soi, 8. Lagat, 9. Kogo, 10. Tegenkamp

10,000 Metres

KENENISA BEKELE WON the World title with a second 5000m in 13:22.5 for 27:05.90, a great time in the very hot weather of Osaka, and won at Brussels in the year's top time of 26:46.19. That took his career 10,000m record to nine wins in nine races from 2003. The top six ranked match their World Champs positions. Sileshi Sihine also won at Hengelo in 26:48.73, Martin Irungu Mathathi won at Kobe and was 2nd to Josephat Muchiri Ndambiri at the Kenyan Trials, and Zersenay Tadese won the African Games title from Tesfaye Tola (13th Worlds) and Gebre Gebremariam. The last was also 4th at Hengelo and 8th at Brussels. Running just one 10,000m race (26:49-26:53) were Moses Masai, 2nd at Brussels, and Eliud Kipchoge, Moses Mosop and Haile Gebrselassie, 2-3-5 at Hengelo. Also under 27 minutes, for 3rd in Brussels, was Micah Kogo (also 6th in the Kenyan Trials}. Three men ran 27:04 times at Neerpelt: Robert Sigei (7th Kenyan Trials, 5th Brussels), Josphat Kiprono (3rd Kenyan Trials, 8th Worlds) and Tola.

1. K Bekele, 2. Sihine, 3. Mathathi, 4. Tadese, 5. Muchiri, 6. Gebremariam, 7. Kipchoge, 8. Masai, 9. Mosop, 10. Gebrselassie

Half Marathon

THERE WERE AN unprecedented 25 sub-1 hour performances in 2007, and apart from Haile Gebrselassie's 59:24 on a New York course that was 30m downhill, these were all on certified courses. Samuel Wanjiru broke the world record with his 58:54 at Ra's Al Khaymah, when he was followed by Patrick Makau Musyoki 59:13, Deribe Merga 59:44 and Francis Kibiwott 60:08, and with 58:33 at The Hague (with a world 20km record 55:31 en route). Wanjiru was second to Martin Lel, 60:10 to 60:18 in the Great North Run, but faded to 51st in the World Championships at Udine. This race, held in perfect conditions, featured a record seven men under the hour. Zersenay Tadese (whose only other half marathon was a 61:26 win in Carceres) ran a most determined race to win in 58:59 from Musyoki 59:02, Evans Cheruiyot 59:05, Merga 59:16, Yonas Kifle 59:30, Diedonné Disi 59:32 and Marilson dos Santos 59:33. Musyoki ran four of the world's fastest times of 2007 – all under 59:20, as he also won in Berlin 58:56 from Kibiwott 59:26 and Cheruiyot 59:48, and Cheruiyot won in Rotterdam in 59:12 from Musyoki 59:19, Merga 59:25 and Patrick Ivuti 59:27 (Kibiwott 8th). Another man to run three sub-60s was Mekubo Mogusu in winning three Japanese races. Merga also took the African Games title and Disi won in New Delhi in 60:43. The slightly downhill Lisbon race was won by Robert Kipchumba (15th Worlds) in 60:34 with dos Santos 4th.

1.Tadese, 2. Musyoki, 3. Cheruiyot, 4. Wanjiru, 5. Merga, 6. Kifle, 7. Disi, 8. Kibiwott, 9. Mogusu, 10. Ivuti

Marathon

FOR THE THIRD successive year Haile Gebrselassie ran easily the fastest of the year and this time his 2:04:26 in Berlin was a world record. This was over two minutes quicker than the next men – four marathon debutants headed by Emmanuel Mutai 2:06:29. A strong case for top ranking can also be made for Martin Lel who won the top races in London (2:07:41) and New York (2:09:04). Kenyans dominated the event more than ever this year, and even though their top men were not in Osaka, a Kenyan also took the World title for the first time for 20 years as while it was far too hot and humid for marathon running Luke Kibet won in 2:15:59 by 1:19 from Mubarak Shami with Viktor Röthlin third. Their times can be put in context by their other marathons of 2007 (all wins): Kibet in Vienna 2:10:07, Shami in Paris 2:07:19, Röthlin in Zürich 2:08:20. Abderrahim Goumri did not finish in Osaka but was 2nd in both London and New York, and London had the top depth of talent as 3rd was Felix Limo, 4th Joauad Gharib and 5th Hendrick Ramaala (27th Worlds, 3rd New York).

Although Robert K Cheruiyot sealed the 2006-07 Marathon Majors title with his win in Boston, his 2:14:13 there with 2nd in Nairobi and 4th in Chicago in 2:16 times does not bring him into rankings contention. Joshua Chelanga had two good wins, Rotterdam and Seoul, both just outside 2:08, but quicker was Wilfred Kigen, 2nd in Hamburg 2:07:33 and 1st in Frankfurt 2:07:58. Amsterdam winner Mutai's previous marathon had been 7th in Rotterdam in 2:13:06 and the other new men at the top of the lists were: Samuel Wanjiru, who won Fukuoka on his debut in 2:06:39, Richard Limo, Amsterdam 2nd in 2:06:45, Deriba Merga, Fukuoka 2nd in 2:06:50 after 10th in Paris in 2:13:33. Abel Kirui was 2nd in Berlin in 2:06:51 after 3rd in Vienna in 2:10:41, and James Rotich coupled 3rd in Amsterdam 2:07:12 with 4th Hamburg. Another major race much affected by heat was Chicago won by Patrick Ivuti (5th Rotterdam) in a dramatic finish from Gharib, both 2:11:11; Felix Limo did not finish there.

1. Gebrselassie, 2. Lel, 3. Kibet, 4. Shami, 5. Röthlin, 6. Goumri, 7. Kirui, 8. Gharib, 9. Chelanga, 10. Ivuti

3000 Metres Steeplechase

AFTER FIVE YEARS at the top Saïf Saaeed Shaheen missed the entire season through injury, and Paul Koech stepped up to be a clear number one. Apart from the debacle in Paris where the race stopped a lap early and then the runners took off again (some missing a hurdle) Koech won all his seven races apart from a collapse in the Kenyan Trials and ran the four fastest times. Next quickest at 8:02.89 (2nd to Koech in Brussels) was Brimin Kipruto who led the Kenyan 1-2-3 at the World Champs from Ezekiel Kemboi and Richard Matelong. Kemboi beat the other two at the Kenyan Trials and was 3-1 v Matelong but did not run at the WAF, where Matelong and Kipruto were 2-3 behind Koech. Mustafa Mohamed broke the 31 year-old Swedish steeplechase record (set by Anders Gärderud) when he won at Heusden in 8:05.75 and he and the other top European Bob Tahri were 4th and 5th at the Worlds and 7th and 4th WAF. Halil Akkas was 6th at the Worlds and also won the World Universities title but his best of 8:18.43 was much slower than other contenders, with ten men beating 8:10. Of these Brahim Taleb (2nd Heusden 8:07.02 but no other times under 8:20) was disqualified at the Worlds, where Hamid Ezzine went out in the heats, but Reuben Kosgei was 4th in the Kenyan Trials and Tareq Mubarak Taher was Arab champion as well as 8th Worlds. Wesley Kiprotich had a solid season to 5th WAF and was 1-1 v Michael Kipyego and 19 year-old Willy Komen, who won the African Games title and was 3rd in Brussels.

Most times under 8:15: Koech 6, Kipruto 4, Tahri, Ezzine 3.

1. Koech, 2. Kipruto, 3. Kemboi, 4. Matelong, 5. Mohamed, 6. Tahri, 7. R Kosgei, 8. Taher, 9. W Komen, 10. Kiprotich

110 Metres Hurdles

AFTER BRONZE AND silver at previous championships Liu Xiang took gold in Osaka followed by Terrence Trammell, and both broke 13 seconds as they had done in New York three months earlier. The only other sub-13 time was run by Dayron Robles, to win the WAF title in 12.92 and match Liu at the top of the world list. Robles was 4th at the Worlds, a place behind David Payne, but was 2-2 v Liu and 4-2 v Trammell, ending with six successive wins post-Osaka and in all won 16 of his 20 races, while Liu won 7 of 9 and Trammell 3 of 8. After Liu and Robles, US athletes took the next seven spots on the world list and the eight places in these rankings. These men were pretty closely matched but Anwar Moore had the best overall record, with 1/2/1/4/2/4 in Golden League races and he was 7-4 v Payne, 5-2 v David Oliver, 7-2 v Allan Johnson and 9-5 v Ryan Wilson. Oliver beat Payne 6-5, including 3rd to 4th at the US Champs (5. Moore, 6. Aries Merritt, 7. Johnson) but Payne had quicker times and took the World bronze medal after flying in at the last minute as a late replacement for the injured Dominique Arnold (2nd US Champs). The amazing Johnson slips out of the top five for the first time since 1994 but still makes the top ten for the 14th time; he beat Wilson 7-2 and Merritt 3-2. Wilson was 4-3 v Oliver and 7-3 v Merritt. Shi Dongpeng was 5th at the Worlds, but just misses a ranking place as he lost 2-0 to Arnold, and just behind him are the top Europeans Ladji Doucouré, the 2005 number one, who was third in his semi at the Worlds, and Sergiy Demidyuk, 6th Worlds and 1st WUG. A record ten men broke 13.20.

Most times under 13.30: Robles 15, Payne 13, Moore & Oliver 11+1w, Liu & Trammell 10, Wilson 8, Shi 6, Merritt 5, Johnson & Doucouré 4, Arnold 2+1w.

1. Liu, 2. Robles, 3. Trammell, 4. Moore, 5. Payne, 6. Oliver, 7. Johnson, 8. Wilson, 9. Merritt, 10. Arnold

400 Metres Hurdles

KERRON CLEMENT WAS the world's fastest for the third successive year – winning the World title in 47.61 – but amazingly that was his only win in eleven competitions. However, his seven second places included running the same time, 48.35, as winner Marek Plawgo at the WAF, and overall he was 2-2 v Plawgo, who was the World bronze medallist, and 4-4 v James Carter, who had beaten him at the US Champs. Plawgo beat Carter (4th Worlds, 3rd WAF) 4-1, and while both these men were beaten by Félix Sánchez at the Worlds, their overall records were far superior. Nonetheless Sánchez made a terrific return to top form in Osaka and ranks ahead of Bershawn Jackson, who went out in the semis at the Worlds but who was 4th to Sánchez 7th at the WAF. Danny McFarlane, Periklís Iakovákis and Derrick Williams were 5-6-7 at the Worlds but I have slotted in Kenneth Ferguson (4th at the US Champs a place behind Williams, but 3-2 against him) and L J van Zyl, who ended badly, including exiting at the heats stage of the Worlds, but who had a good record earlier, including wins in Ostrava and Rome and at the African Games. Angelo Taylor concentrated on the flat 400m, but had four times under 48.8 and was WAF 5th. Williams, Michael Tinsley and Pan-Am champion Adam Kunkel just miss ranking.

Most times under 48.60: Carter 9, Clement 8, Iakovákis 4, Plawgo, Jackson, van Zyl & McFarlane 3.

1. Clement, 2. Plawgo, 3. Carter, 4. Sánchez, 5. Jackson, 6. McFarlane, 7. Iakovákis, 8. Taylor, 9. Ferguson, 10. van Zyl

High Jump

ONCE AGAIN MORE top marks were set in the intense indoor season than out – 22 (by 11 men) to 13 outdoors (by 9 men) at 2.33 or higher. Four men cleared 2.35 for the best outdoors: Donald Thomas (twice), Stefan Holm, Yaroslav Rybakov and Kyriakos Ioannou, but seven cleared at least that indoors, headed by Ivan Ukhov 2.39, Rybakov, Holm and Linus Thörnblad 2.38. The amazing story of Thomas continued so that less than two years after starting in the sport he was world champion and he also won the WAF title. He, Rybakov and Ioannou cleared 2.35 at the Worlds with medals decided on count-back and Holm was 4th at 2.33, but Holm was WAF 2nd (Rybakov 6th) and beat Thomas 3-2 and Rybakov 2-1 outdoors. Holm won the European Indoor title at 2.34 from Thörnblad 2.32 and won 6 of 7 indoors and 11 of 16 outdoors, while Thomas won 3/4 indoors and 7/14 outdoors.

I give Holm the top ranking including indoor form and Thomas just on outdoors. Holm was, however, outjumped indoors at Arnstadt when his 2.34 was behind Rybakov 2.38 and Andrey Silnov 2.36. Silnov, the 2006 number one, disappointed outdoors with a best of 2.30 and 11= at the Worlds. Ukhov had an outdoor best of only 2.20 after 2.39 and the Russian title indoors. Ioannou made a major advance from a 2006 best of 2.30 and beat Rybakov 2-1 but the latter had much better marks including indoors. Víctor Moya and Tomás Janku tied for fifth at the Worlds, but Janku beat Moya in their other three outdoor clashes (2-2 indoors), although Moya had much better marks. Andrey Tereshin failed to qualify for the World final and was 7th at the European Indoors but a good competitive record included 3-2 outdoors and 2-2 indoors v Janku. Thörnblad was 15th Worlds and 3rd WAF; outdoors he was 2-3 v Janku and 1-1 v Tereshin, but his position improves with indoor form. Elke Onnen was 7th at the Worlds but he was beaten 2-1 by Jesse Williams (dnq Worlds). Williams was 5-3 outdoors against Tora Harris, who beat him for the US indoor title, both men clearing 2.29.

Most competitions over 2.30m (outdoors/in): Holm 9/8, Thomas 7/3, Moya 5/4, Ioannou & Williams 5/0, Tereshin 4/3, Onnen 4/2, Rybakov 3/5, Thörnblad 2/7, Janku 2/6, Harris 2/2, Sokolovskiy 2/1, Manson 1/3, Silnov 1/2, Ukhov 0/6.

1. Thomas (2), 2. Holm (1), 3. Rybakov (4), 4. Ioannou (3), 5. Janku (6), 6. Tereshin (7), 7. Moya (8), 8. Thörnblad (5), 9. Williams (10), 10. Onnen (-). - Silnov (9). (Including indoors).

Pole Vault

BRAD WALKER TOPPED the world list for the second successive year and, with a 5.95 best, had four competitions at 5.90 or better to one each outdoors by Paul Burgess, Steve Hooker and Björn Otto. Walker won both World and WAF titles so was a clear number one even though he lost more often than he won. Indoors Otto was top at 5.90. Romain Mesnil took the World silver with 5.86, but his overall record was behind Danny Ecker (3rd Worlds, 4th WAF), Otto (5th, 2nd) and Hooker (9th, 3rd). Ecker was 4-1 (1-1 in) and Otto 4-2 v Hooker outdoors. Ecker was 8-4 v Otto outdoors, 2-3 indoors and they took gold and bronze respectively at the European Indoors, with Denys Yurchenko 2nd, all three at 5.71. Tim Lobinger was 5th European Indoors, 8th Worlds and 7th WAF and as ever a prolific competitor with 11 indoor & 26 outdoor competitions. Ecker (3rd), Otto (4th) and Lobinger (8th) had all cleared 5.81 at the Worlds, as did Igor Pavlov 4th, Yevgeniy Lukyanenko 6th and Alex Averbukh 7th. Averbukh otherwise had a best of 5.70 but the two Russians both had win-loss advantage over Lobinger. Turning 40 in September, Jeff Hartwig was over 5.80 twice both indoors and out, and won the US indoor title with second outdoors, but he did not qualify for the final at the Worlds in common with other top men including Burgess (best indoors, including a win at Donyetsk) and Giovanni Lanaro. Experience clearly counts in this event as all the men mentioned here were 26 or more in 2007 except for the 22 year-old Lukyanenko.

Most competitions over 5.80m (outdoors/in): Ecker 6/3, Hooker 6/2, Walker 6/1, Otto 4/4, Lobinger & Lanaro 3/-, Hartwig 2/2, Pavlov 2/1.

1. Walker, 2. Ecker, 3. Otto, 4. Hooker, 5. Mesnil, 6. Pavlov, 7. Lukyanenko, 8. Lobinger, 9. Averbukh, 10. Burgess. (Same including indoors).

Long Jump

IRVING SALADINO HAD a perfect season, winning his one indoor competition with a South American record 8.31 at Birmingham, and all eight outdoors. He had six of the world's top ten performances, starting with 8.53 at both Rio de Janeiro and Hengelo, and just once did he come under serious threat – when Andrew Howe set an Italian record of 8.47 in the final round of the Worlds, taking the lead by a centimetre from Saladino, but the Panamanian responded by adding 1cm to his South American record with 8.57. Howe won all four indoor contests to the European Indoors with 8.30, and won 7 of 9 outdoors, including at the WAF; his only other loss was to Nelson Évora in the European Cup 1B. Louís Tsátoumas, 2nd at the European Indoors, produced the year's top jump, 8.66 at Kalamáta followed a week later by 8.54 at Haniá, but had to end his season early after four wins and two third places outdoors. Although his bests of 8.31 and 8.37w were much less, US champion Dwight Phillips won 7 of 10 and was 3rd at the Worlds, where he was followed by Oleksiy Lukashevych, Khotso Mokoena and James Beckford. Of these men Lukashevych had worse marks than the others and was beaten 3-1 by Mokoena. Mokoena and Beckford were, however, beaten 2-0 by Brian Johnson, who was 2nd WAF although only 6th at the US Champs. Not qualifying for the World final were Chris Tomlinson 16th and Mohamed Al-Khuwalidi 18th, but the former had a solid set of performances including a British record of 8.29 and the latter won African and both Arab titles. Christian Relf set pbs of 8.08 to win the German title and 8.19 in qualifying at the Worlds (9th in the final) and he was 4th WAF, a place behind Mokoena, but did not have the depth of marks to make the top ten. Also just missing out were Miguel Pate and Trevell Quinley, who were 2nd and 3rd at the US Champs outdoors; Quinley beat Johnson to take the US indoor title.

Most competitions over 8.15m (outdoors/in): Saladino 9/1, Phillips 9, Howe 7/2, Beckford 6+1w, Tsátoumas 5+1w/2, Mokoena 4+3w/1, Johnson 4/1, Tomlinson 3, Al-Khuwalidi 2+2w

1. Saladino, 2. Howe, 3. Phillips, 4. Tsátoumas, 5. Mokoena, 6. Beckford, 7. Johnson, 8. Lukashevych (9), 9. Tomlinson (8), 10. Al-Khuwalidi. (Including indoors).

Triple Jump

IT WAS EXCEEDINGLY difficult to rank the top men in this event, particularly on outdoor form. The purest record was that of Christian Olsson who won his four major indoor competitions and outdoors was 2nd to Phillips Idowu 17.35 to 17.33 in Oslo, before he had three wins, European Cup 1A 17.33, Saint-Denis 17.56 and Rome 17.19. So he was 3-0 outdoors against Jadel Gregório, Nelson Évora and Aarik Wilson and 2-0 v Walter Davis. But injury then ended Olsson's season and the first three of these men jumped further. Gregório had the world's 1-3-4 marks with 17.90 at Belém, 17.70 at São Paulo and 17.59 for 2nd at the Worlds. There, however, he was beaten by Évora's 17.74, and he was below 17m in the four big meetings post-Osaka. Davis had been only 6th in Oslo and 10th in Saint-Denis but was 3rd at the Worlds and then won in Zürich, Brussels and WAF with 4th at Berlin. Against Gregório, Évora (3rd WAF) was 6-2 and Wilson (5th Worlds, 2nd WAF) 7-1, and Wilson was 6-4 v Évora. Davis was 4-3 v Évora and Wilson but, with a best of 17.35, had worse marks. Cuban champion Osniel Tosca was 2nd to Gregório at the Pan-Ams and 4th Worlds; he was 2-1 v Davis. The top marks indoors came from the British pair of Phillips Idowu and Nathan Douglas with 17.56 and 17.47 at the European Indoors, where Aleksandr Sergeyev was 3rd at 17.15 and Évora 5th at 16.97.

Douglas competed just three times outdoors before injury ended his season and Idowu also had injury niggles, so just five outdoor competitions, including 6th Worlds. Also restricted was Marian Oprea with just four competitions outdoors (three wins) and one indoors. Leevan Sands produced his best jump of 17.55w behind Wilson's 17.58 in London, and was 5-2 v Randy Lewis and 3-1 v Aleksandr Petrenko. In turn Lewis beat Petrenko 2-1 while Petrenko (10th Worlds) had win-loss advantage over men such as Danila Burkenya, Dmitrij Valukevic and Mykola Savolaynen. David Giralt was at his best indoors, but was also 7th at the Worlds.

Most competitions over 17.15 (outdoors/in): Wilson 10/1, Evora 7+1w/1, Tosca 6+1w/1, Gregório 5, Olsson 4/4, Davis 4, Valukevic 3, Lewis & Petrenko 2+1w, Idowu 2/1, Douglas 1/2, Giralt 1w/2.

1. Évora (2), 2. Olsson (1), 3. Wilson, 4. Gregório, 5. Davis, 6. Tosca, 7. Idowu, 8. Sands (10), 9. Lewis, 10. Petrenko, - Douglas (8), - Giralt (9). (Including indoors).

Shot

IN 2006 IT was close between Christian Cantwell and Reese Hoffa for top ranking, but in 2007 although they each had five of the top ten outdoor performances as well as the top indoor marks, Hoffa was a very clear number one. He won 3/6 indoors and 11/15 outdoors and was the one man over 22m – a pb 22.42 in London and 22.04 to win the World title. Although Cantwell had seven performances (two indoors) from 21.96 superior to the best of 21.61 by Adam Nelson, the latter was 2nd to Hoffa at both Worlds and WAF while Cantwell was 5th at WAF and in the US champs (he beat Hoffa to win the US Indoors). Andrey Mikhnevich was 3rd at both Worlds and WAF and was top European from Rutger Smith (4th Worlds, 6th WAF) and Tomasz Majewski (5th Worlds). Smith had a season's best of 21.19 behind Hoffa and Cantwell in London after starting his outdoor campaign with seven successive wins.

Joachim Olsen improved his Danish record to 21.61, but although he had 21.21 indoors, his next best outdoors was 20.82 and he had three no throws in the Worlds final. However, he was 3-0 outdoors (0-1 in) against Dan Taylor, who threw 21.00 or more twice indoors and five times outdoors. Taylor and German champion Peter Sack failed badly at the Worlds, but Taylor was 2-2 and Sack 6-3 outdoors against Ralf Bartels (7th Worlds and WAF). Mikulás Konopka left his past form behind with five throws of six over 21m in the European Indoor final, setting Slovakian records of 21.32 and 21.57 with his opening efforts, but outdoors exceeded 19m only twice – a best of 19.94 and 19.63 for 15th at the Worlds. Pavel Lyzhin was another to be much better indoors, 2nd at the European Indoors with 20.82 but an outdoor best of 20.02 and 20th Worlds. Consistent, however, was Miroslav Vodovnik who improved from 7th European Indoors to 6th Worlds.

Most competitions over 20.80 (outdoors/in): Hoffa 15/6, Cantwell 9/4, Smith 5, Taylor 4/3, Nelson 3, Olsen 2/2, Mikhnevich, Majewski & Sack 2.

1. Hoffa, 2. Nelson, 3. Cantwell, 4. Mikhnevich, 5. Smith, 6. Majewski (8), 7. Olsen (6), 8. Taylor (7), 9. Sack, 10. Bartels. (Including indoors).

Discus

GERD KANTER HAD challenged Virgilijus Alekna in the last couple of years but four more defeats in 2007 took him to 44 losses in their 45 clashes. However, while Alekna struggled at the end of the year after starting with 13 successive wins, Kanter came to the top with wins at both Worlds and WAF and in Tallinn. Alekna was also beaten by Robert Harting and Rutger Smith at the Worlds but was 2nd WAF. Alekna had 11 and Kanter 10 of the 22 marks over 68.40. The other man in that list was Frantz Kruger with 69.97 at the wind-friendly location of Helsingborg, but he was only 19th at the Worlds and just misses the rankings. Piotr Malachowski disappointed at the Worlds with 12th place, but otherwise had a most consistent season and beat Harting at the European Cup and was 3rd WAF. Gábor Máté had a 7-2 advantage over compatriot Zoltán Kövágó including 5th to 9th at the Worlds. Mario Pestano, 10th Worlds and 5th WAF, was beaten 3-0 by Máté but beat Kövágó 5-1. Ian Waltz beat Jared Rome 9-7 and these Americans produced good marks with favourable wind conditions but missed the World finals with 13th and 15th in qualifying, whereas the youngsters, African champion Omar El-Ghazaly and Asian champion Ehsan Hadadi, were 6th and 7th in the final. These two went 1-1 but Hadadi had a better set of marks; both were 3-0 v Kövágó, and 3-0 and 2-0 v Waltz.

Most competitions over 65m: Kanter 26, Alekna 17, Malachowski 11, Pestano 8, Rome 7, Waltz & Hadadi 6, Harting, Kruger, Máté & Smith 5; Kövágó 4.

1. Kanter, 2. Alekna, 3. Harting, 4. Smith, 5. Malachowski, 6. Máté, 7. Pestano, 8. Hadadi, 9. El-Ghazaly, 10. Kövágó

Hammer

IVAN TIKHON WON the World title for the third time and returned to top ranking. In all he won 10 of 13 with another big win at the WAF. Rankings at this event are straightforward and I have made just two adjustments to the World Champs top ten. Krisztián Pars, 2nd WAF, goes up a place from his 5th in Osaka; he was 4-1 v 4th placed Vadim Devyatovskiy and indeed he was 4-4 against Primoz Kozmus and Libor Charfreitag, the silver and bronze medallists. Also, although at his best for 9th in Osaka, Ola-Pekka Karjalainen had a thin season and Miloslav Konopka is up from his Worlds 10th. Neither of these two men threw over 80m, whereas Esref Apak, 11th at the Worlds, did so twice and Igor Vinichenko once, but their overall records were not enough for top ten places. Although 3rd at the WAF Koji Murofushi did not have the depth of marks to move higher than his Worlds place.

Most competitions over 80m/78.50m: Tikhon 9/11, Charfreitag 8/12, Pars 6/15, Kozmus 5/11, Devyatovskiy 3/8, Esser 3/6, Murofushi & Ziólkowski 2/4, Apak 2/3, Igor Vinichenko 1/3.

1. Tikhon, 2. Kozmus, 3. Charfreitag, 4. Pars, 5, Devyatovskiy, 6. Murofushi, 7. Ziólkowski , 8. Esser, 9. Konopka, 10. Karjalainen

Javelin

TERO PITKÄMÄKI AND Andreas Thorkildsen have had a thrilling series of competitions over the past three years, and this time the 2006 rankings are reversed and they revert to the 2005 order as the Finn beat the Norwegian 7-2. In all Pitkämäki won 14 of 16, Thorkildsen 6 of 14. Breaux Greer topped the world list with 91.29 to win the US title and was 3rd behind the big two at the Worlds and at three Golden League meetings after splitting them in Oslo. Vadims Vasilevskis was 4th at the Worlds and improved his best to 90.73 for third on the world list. There was quite a big gap in performances after the top four, but ranking fifth, despite only 10th at the Worlds, is Magnus Arvidsson, who had a splendidly consistent season culminating in WAF 3rd place and he beat Vasilevskis 3-1; he threw over his pre-season best of 81.75 in 15 of his 20 competitions. Sergey Makarov beat Aleksandr Ivanov 5-3 including at the Russian Champs, so just had the edge although he did not qualify for the World final in which Ivanov was 5th. The 20 year-old Robert Oosthuizen set a pb of 84.52 to take 6th place at the Worlds after earlier winning the African title and Guillermo Martínez won the Pan-American title before 9th at the Worlds. He had a 3-2 edge over Igor Janik (7th Worlds). Just missing a ranking spot are three Finns, Tero Järvenpää, Teemu Wirtkkala and Antti Ruuskanen.

Most competitions over 84m/82.50m: Pitkämäki 15/17, Thorkildsen 11/12, Arvidsson 9/13, Vasilevskis 8/10, Greer 7/8, Makarov 5/6, Ivanov 4/6, Martínez 3/8, Ruuskanen & Wirkkala 1/3.

1. Pitkämäki, 2. Thorkildsen, 3. Greer, 4. Vasilevskis, 5. Arvidsson, 6. Makarov, 7. Ivanov, 8. Oosthuizen, 9. Martínez, 10. Janik

Decathlon

ALREADY WELL ESTABLISHED as an all-time great, Roman Sebrle won the World title at his sixth attempt. He had the two top scores of the year: 8697 at Kladno and 8676 at Osaka. His 8067 for 4th at Talence was his 40th decathlon over 8000 points and he has 21 over 8500. It was, however, a case of what might have been but for Andrey Kravchenko's careless disqualification for two false starts in the 100m in Osaka, for the 21 year-old had impressed mightily with a 8617 to 8518 win over Sebrle in Götzis, a huge improvement from his 2006 best of 8013. Kravchenko did not finish at Kladno but had another big win with 8553 in moderate conditions in Talence. Maurice Smith was 8th at Götzis and won the Pan-Am title before adding 295 points to his CAC record with 8644 for the World silver and 2nd in Talence. Dmitriy Karpov was over 8500 points for 2nd Kladno and 3rd Worlds. Bryan Clay's scored 8493 for 3rd at Götzis, but he did not finish at the US and Worlds, which makes him difficult to rank. Aleksey Drozdov was 120 behind Clay when 4th at Götzis but went on to 4th Worlds, 3rd Talence and 1st CISM, and André Niklaus was 5th Götzis 8340 and 5th Worlds 8371. 6th (8357) to 9th (8243) at the Worlds all had other good marks: Aleksey Sysosyev was the Russian champion, Romain Barras 3rd Kladno 8298, Yordanis García (only 18 years old) 2nd Pan-Ams, and Arthur Abele 1st Ratingen 8269. Another man difficult to rank was Tom Pappas who did not finish at the Worlds but who won the US title with 8352.

1. Sebrle, 2. Kravchenko, 3. Smith, 4. Karpov, 5. Drozdov, 6. Niklaus, 7. Sysoyev, 8. Barras, 9. Clay, 10. Abele

20 Kilometres Walk

VLADIMIR KANAYKIN, WHO had not broken 1:21 before 2007, produced the fastest times in his two races: 1:17:36 to win the Russian title and 1:17:16 to win the IAAF Race Walking Challenge Final. Jefferson Pérez's best time was almost four minutes slower, 6th in Shenzhen in 1:21:14, but Pérez then won his three remaining races, Pan Am Cup, Pan Am Games and World Champs. The last was in 1:22:20, but of course with 32-34°C temperature in Osaka was worth far better in more temperate conditions. Francisco Javier Fernández had three wins, including at Shenzhen and La Coruña in the third and fourth fastest times of the year, before controversially sprinting past Hatem Ghoula at the finish to take the World silver medal. Ghoula had six 20k races, improving steadily from 18th at Shenzhen and won gold at the African Games. Valeriy Borchin (1st Russian went champs) and Ilya Markov (2nd Russian champs) were joint third fastest. Borchin went on to win European U23 gold, but was 9th in the European Cup, did not finish Worlds and dq in the Challenge final, while Markov was 12th at Shenzhen and 9th Worlds. Yohann Diniz won the European Cup, from Ivano Brugnetti and Igor Yerokhin, and also won the French title. A consistent series of performances enabled Luke Adams and Erik Tysse, 7th and 8th at the Worlds, to take the top two places in the IAAF Challenge from Fernández, Ghoula and Eder Sánchez (4th Worlds, 3rd Shenzhen). Sánchez also had a good win in Kraków from Tysse and Ghoula, with Adams 5th and Fernández dnf. Finishing 5th and 6th at the Worlds were Giorgio Rubino and Robert Heffernan, who had been 11th and 5th respectively in the European Cup. Li Gaobo was 2nd in Shenzhen and ended the year with a world junior record for 20,000m track, but was 13th at the Worlds.

1. Pérez, 2. Fernández, 3. Kanaykin, 4. Ghoula, 5. Sánchez, 6. Diniz, 7. Adams, 8. Li, 9. Heffernan, 10. Tysse

50 Kilometres Walk

ALEX SCHWAZER SET the one sub-3:40 time with 3:36:04 to win the Italian title in February, but the performance of the year was undoubtedly that of Nathan Deakes in winning the World title in 3:43:53, an extraordinary time in the heat and humidity of Osaka. He was followed home by Yohann Diniz, a fast finishing Schwazer and Denis Nizhegorodov all under 3:47, before Erik Tysse (who also had a win at Chula Vista) 3:51:52 and Mikel Odriozola 3:55:19. Nizhegorodov won the Russian title in 3:40:53, the year's second fastest time and the next five times on the world lists came in the European Cup, won by Vladimir Kanaykin (dnf Worlds) from Trond Nymark (8th), Oleg Kistin, Aleksey Voyevodin (dnf) and Yuriy Andronov with Jesús Ángel García sixth. Yu Chaohong won in Shenzhen from Sun Chao and García, but while Sun went on to 7th Worlds the other two were disqualified there.

1. Deakes, 2. Diniz, 3. Schwazer, 4. Nizhegorodov, 5. Kanaykin, 6. Nymark, 7. Tysse, 8. Kistkin, 9. Voyevodin, 10. Andronov

WOMEN ATHLETES OF 2007

JUST AS WITH the men, one athlete swept the polls in voting for the top honour – and that was Meseret Defar. In 2006 she had a series of epic races against her great rival Tirunesh Dibaba but they avoided each other in 2007, with Defar taking the World title at 5000m and Dibaba at 10,000m. But Defar also smashed the world record for 5000m, set an indoor world record for 3000m and took the 2 miles world best twice, first with 9:10.47 at Carson and then with 8:58.58 at Brussels. Now when I was at the van Damme meeting some commentators were dismissive of the 2 miles attempt as it was not a standard event. But meet organiser Wilfried Meert got it spot on, as so often, in setting up this race, for Defar's effort was a great one, noting that she set an Ethiopian record en route of 8:24.51. In all she won all her ten track races from 3000m to 5000m, although she did lose a road 10km – a minute behind Lornah Kiplagat

Meseret Defar in 2007

27 Jan	BIG	Boston (R)	3000m	8:30.31
3 Feb	Spark	Stuttgart	3000m	8:23.72 WR
25 Feb		San Juan	10kmRd	32:08 (2nd)
1Apr		Carlsbad	5kmRd	15:01
20 May	adidas	Carson	2M	9:10.47 WR
15 Jun	Bisl	Oslo	5000m	14:16.63
27 Jun	GS	Ostrava	5000m	14:30.18
17 Jul	AfG	Alger	5000m	15:02.72
1 Sep	WCh	Osaka (1h2 15:10.13)	5000m	14:57.91
14 Sep	VD	Brussels (3000m 8:24.51 NR)	2M	8:58.58 WR
16 Sep		London (HP)	5kmRd	15:08
23 Sep	WAF	Stuttgart	3000m	8:27.24
28 Sep		Shanghai	5000m	14:49.06

in San Juan, Puerto Rico.

Kiplagat, who beat Defar 31:05 to 32:08 in that 10km road race, was the only other athlete to set a world record at a standard event outdoors in 2007. She did so when she ran away with the World Half Marathon title in 66:25 at Udine in October (also going through 20km in a record 62:57). She thus completed a double, for she had also won the World Cross-country title at Mombasa in March. Otherwise she won her other CC race, won all three road 10km races and was 2nd in the road 15km at Nijmegen, but loses out with her one track race (6th 5000m at Hengelo) and one marathon (5th London).

As well as Defar, Tirunesh Dibaba (5000m) and Yelena Isinbayeva (PV) set world indoor records. She never really looking likely to challenge her outdoor WR of 5.01, although she tried several times, but Isinbayeva had a great year, as she won all her 18 competitions. Also trying many times for a world record (and getting close) was Blanca Vlasic at high jump. By the end of the year she was easily the world's best, winning in all 18 of her 19 outdoor competitions although she had won only three of nine indoors.

Although she raced sparingly Tirunesh Dibaba was unbeaten on the track – once each at 3000m and 10,000m and three times at 5000m, and Carolina Klüft won all three of her multi-event competitions – one indoor pentathlon and two outdoor heptathlons. Even more eye-catching was the running of Allyson Felix, who won three gold medals at the Worlds including the 200m by some five metres in 21.81. She was unbeaten at 200m (although only four meetings), and improved markedly at 100m (11.01) and 400m (49.70) showing at the longer distance that she was currently the only woman in the world able to challenge Sanya Richards at her best. The latter had that depressing 4th in the US 400m, but showed that she was back to her best with a series of major wins at the end of the year when she shared the IAAF Golden League jackpot with Isinbayeva.

100 Metres

JUST 0.02 SEPARATED Veronica Campbell from Lauryn Williams at the Worlds, but while Williams certainly peaked at the right time, she did not win a final until her last race of the year in Daegu. In contrast Campbell won 7/10 with four of the year's fastest times headed by 10.89 in Kingston. That was 0.01 quicker than run at Carson by Torri Edwards, who had 7 wins in 11 finals, beating Williams 11.02 to 11.16 at the US Champs. Third in that race in 11.17 was Carmelita Jeter, who made a remarkable improvement at the age of 27 from 11.48 in 2006 to the 11.02 with which she was third at the Worlds, 0.03 ahead of Edwards. Jeter and Williams were 7-7 in their clashes. Allyson Felix was 4th in the US Champs and 2nd WAF to Jeter, but was beaten 3-1 by Me'Lisa Barber, who was only 7th in her US Champs semi in 11.42 after a 10.95w heat. Barber beat Williams 4-1. The top Europeans were Kim Gevaert and Christine Arron, 5th and 6th at the Worlds and 3rd and 4th WAF respectively, with Arron 2-1 up on win-loss; an indication of how closely matched many of the world's top

Selections for World Top Ten

	PJM	*TFN*	*IAAF*	*AI*
Meseret Defar ETH	1	1	1	1
Allyson Felix USA	2	4	5	3
Yelena Isinbayeva RUS	3	2	4	5
Carolina Kluft SWE	4	5	2/3	4
Blanka Vlasic CRO	5	3	2/3	2
Tirunesh Dibaba ETH	6	6	–	8
Sanya Richards USA	7	8	8	7
Lornah Kiplagat NED	8	-	7	–
Janeth Jepkosgei KEN	9	10	6	6
Tatyana Lebedeva RUS	10	7	10	–
Valerie Vili NZL	11	-	11	–
Maryam Jamal BRN	12	12	9	9
Veronica Campbell JAM		9		10

Note *Athletics International* (AI) readers actually only voted for 1-2-3-4-5 and *Track & Field News* (TFN) does not consider road races other than the marathon.

women were is shown by both having win-loss advantage over Williams. Kerron Stewart, 2nd to Campbell in the Jamaican Champs, was 7th in the Worlds, but ran only once in Europe – third in Stockholm in 11.29 behind Lisa Barber 11.03 and Sanya Richards 11.05. Richards ran only one other 100m race, but that was 10.97 for fourth on the world lists when 2nd to Campbell's 10.90 in Shanghai, and well ahead of Jeter and Williams. Mikele Barber, who was 6th in the US Champs and won the Pan-Am title, beat the young Bulgarian Tezdzhan Naimova 2-1. The 2006 number one Sherone Simpson had a best of only 11.43 in 2007.

Most times under 11.00/11.15: Campbell 5/11, Edwards 2/13, L Barber 1+1w/4+2w, Richards 1/2, Jeter 8+1w, Stewart 5, L Williams 4+1w, Gevaert 4+1w, Mik. Barber 3+1w, Felix, Arron & Naimova 3

1. Campbell, 2. Edwards, 3. Jeter, 4. Williams, 5. Arron, 6. Barber, 7. Felix, 8. Gevaert, 9. Richards, 10. Stewart

200 Metres

ALLYSON FELIX RAN only four times at 200m, but was simply superb, winning all, and running 21.81, the worlds' fastest time since 1999, to win World gold. Veronica Campbell took the silver 0.53 behind with a further 0.29 to Susanthika Jayasinghe, who took the Asian title in her only other competition. Sanya Richards ran the 200m three times; she was only 0.09 behind Felix at both US Champs and in Sheffield but was below-par for 5th at the Worlds in 22.70. She was then a place behind Torri Edwards, but had four times faster than the best by Edwards, who had been 3rd at the US Champs. Kerron Stewart raced but once in Europe for 4th in London, but ran 22.41 in the NCAA-mideast race and 22.42 at the NCAAs with 22.51 for 2nd at the Jamaican Champs, all better than the top mark of WAF 4th placer Kim Gevaert, who had win-loss advantage on prolific racers LaShantea Moore and Debbie Ferguson McKenzie (5th and 2nd WAF). Muriel Hurtis-Houairi, who had mixed fortunes, running 22.38 in a heat of the French Champs and winning at the European Cup, won the WAF race but exiting in the quarter-finals at the Worlds; she was 3-3 v Ferguson and 1-3 v Moore. Rachelle Smith, US 5th placer, had a consistent season in the US and Europe and was 1-1 v Lauryn Williams (5th WAF). Difficult to rank as they competed only in the US collegiate season although well-placed on times are the NCAA 2-3, Simone Facey (best 22.49) and Ebonie Floyd, who was 4th on the world lists with 22.32 for NCAA-midwest victory.

Most times under 22.80: Felix & Moore 8, Stewart 7 (and 4 indoors), Campbell 6+1w, Edwards, Richards & Floyd 6, Smith 5, Jayasinghe & Facey 4, Gevaert, Hurtis, Ferguson, Bailey, Hastings & Mothersill 3

1. Felix, 2. Campbell, 3. Richards, 4. Edwards, 5. Jayasinghe, 6. Stewart, 7. Gevaert, 8. Moore, 9. Smith, 10. Hurtis-Houairi.

400 Metres

SANYA RICHARDS WAS only 4th in the US Champs but was clearly the world's number one with 10 wins in 12 races. She ran the five fastest times of the year, including world-leading times in Saint-Denis 49.52 and then in successive races at Zürich 49.36, Brussels 49.29, Berlin 49.27 and WAF 49.27. The World medallists, Novlene Williams (twice), Christine Ohuruogu and Nicola Sanders were 2nd 1.49, 1.05, 1.13 and 0.85 behind in those four races! In a terrific World final Ohuruogu and Sanders made it a British 1-2 with 49.61 and 49.65 in just passing Williams 49.66, all of them setting pbs in semis and final. Allyson Felix beat Richards 49.70 to 49.72 in Stockholm and showed with her wonderful relay leg in Osaka that she was the only 400m runner who could contest the status of world best with Richards, but with her programme of 100m and 200m running, ran 400m just five times, winning four, her one loss 50.17 to Richards 49.79 in London.

I have ranked the British pair ahead purely on depth of performances but Felix's 3-0 advantage of Williams was decisive. Ohuruogu had a remarkable return in August after serving a one-year ban through missing three random drugs tests and was 3-0 v Sanders, who made a delayed start to her outdoor campaign after her brilliant indoor running with two wins at 50.60 before her British record 50.02 to win the European Indoor title from Ilona Usovich 51.00. Ana Guevara won the Pan-Am title and was 4th at the Worlds, ending her campaign there. Deedee Trotter 49.64, Natasha Hastings 49.84 and Mary Wineberg 50.24 upset Richards at the US Champs, but Trotter suffered from the after-effects of a car accident with modest results in the top European races before 5th at the Worlds. Amy Mbacké Thiam had positive win-loss records against those three (4-0 v Trotter) and was 4th WAF; at the Worlds she jogged 54.31 in her heat in protest against her national federation. Natalya Antyukh won the Russian title and ran 49.93 in her semi before 7th in the final at the Worlds ahead of Usovich, who had run Belarus records in heat and semi, and Wineberg. Shericka Williams (6th WAF) and Hastings (NCAA champion indoors and out) went out in the semis at the Worlds.

Most times under 50.50: Richards 11, N Williams 7, Ohuruogu & Hastings 5, Sanders 4 (and 1 indoors), Felix, Guevara, Antyukh & Trotter 3.

1. Richards, 2. Ohuruogu, 3. Sanders, 4. Felix, 5. N Williams, 6. Guevara, 7. Thiam, 8. Trotter, 9. Hastings, 10. Wineberg

800 Metres

JANETH JEPKOSGEI WENT to the World

Championships with two wins in five races but in Osaka thrilled us with fast front-running victories in semi (1:56.17) and final (1:56.04) and went on to win her further five races, her 1:56.29 in Rieti giving her the year's three fastest times. Hasna Benhassi and Mayte Martínez took silver and bronze in Osaka with Olga Kotlyarova fourth. Benhassi was 1st twice and 2nd three times in her six competitions (only 8th in Athens), while Martínez went from her surprise pb of 1:57.62 in Osaka to 2nd behind Jepkosgei in Zürich, Berlin and WAF and 3rd in Rieti, where Svetlana Usovich was 2nd. Maria Mutola was hit by muscle failure in the finishing straight in Osaka but had previously won four of five races and was 2-1 v Benhassi. Kotlyarova beat Svetlana Cherkasova and Svetlana Klyuka to win the Russian title but was 6th in big races in Athens, Zürich and Rieti. Kenia Sinclair exited in the Worlds semis, but had important wins in Lausanne, Rome and Thessaloníki, and missing a world final spot by one place was Lucia Klocová, who won at the London GP, and these two rank ahead of the Worlds 5-6-7: Brigita Langerholc, Usovich and Klyuka. Usovich, 2-1 down to Klocová but 2-1 up on Langerholc, won the European Cup from Yuliya Krevsun, who won the World Universities title in 1:57.63, but who ten days after that at the Worlds was able to run just 2:02.45 in her heat. The European Indoor 1-2-3: Oksana Zbrozhek, Tetyana Petlyuk and Jolanda Ceplak, excelled indoors but fared less well outdoors. Zbrozhek did run two 1:58 times, but Ceplak failed a drugs test. Zuliya Calatayud, top ranked in 2005-06, had a best of 2:00.34.

Most times under 2:00 (outdoors/in): Jepkosgei 10, Martínez 7, Klocová, Mutola & Sinclair 6, Cherkasova, Kotlyarova & Elisa Cusma Piccione 5, Benhassi, Klyuka, Langerholc & Tamsyn Lewis 4, Zbrozhek 2/4, Petlyuk 1/4, Ceplak 1dq/5.

1. Jepkosgei, 2. Benhassi, 3. Martínez, 4. Mutola, 5. Kotlyarova, 6. Sinclair, 7. Klocová, 8. Usovich, 9. Langerholc, 10. Cherkasova

1500 Metres

YELENA SOBOLEVA RAN four of the six sub 4 minute times of 2007, including the two fastest – 3:57.30 en route to a 4:15.63 mile in Moscow and 3:58.3 in Athens with Maryam Jamal running the other two. However, after 2nd in Athens in 3:59.0 and only 13th in Saint-Denis (injured) when Soboleva won in 3:59.91, Jamal established a clear superiority with four successive wins: a 3:58.75 to 3:58.99 victory at the World Champs and then in Zürich, Brussels and WAF with Soboleva 2nd in each. The next group were closely matched. World Champs 3-7 were Iryna Lishchynska, Daniela Yordanova, Mariem Alaoui Selsouli, Viola Kibiwott and Yuliya Fomenko (née Chizhenko). Faster than any of those was Gelete Burka, winner at Eugene in 4:00.48 and 2nd in Saint-Denis in 4:00.68 and winner of Ethiopian and African titles. Lishchynska was 3rd in Oslo, Saint-Denis and at the Worlds, but fared less well later with 11 Zürich and 10th WAF; she was 2-2 v Olga Yegorova, who was only 6th at the Russian Champs but 1st to 4th in seven major races and 7th WAF; she beat Kibiwott 4-1 and Fomenko 5-2. Kibiwott beat Fomenko 4-2. Sarah Jamieson was 7th in her semi at the Worlds after 5th or 6th in four major European races and was 3rd at the WAF and Tatyana Tomashova had a 4th and three 6ths in top races. Yordanova had modest form apart from in Osaka and Selsouli had just one other 1500m (5th Athens). Just missing the rankings are Agnes Samaria (8th Worlds, 4th WAF with eight Namibian records in 2007) and Ibhissam Lakhoud (6th WAF); 2-2 in their clashes. Russian champion Natalya Panteleyeva was 9th at the Worlds and 10th was Lidia Chojecka, who won the European Indoor title from Panteleyeva and ran the fastest indoor time of 4:03.73.

Most times under 4:04 (or 4:23.6 mile): Jamal 8, Soboleva 6, Fomenko, Lishchynska & Yegorova 4, Jamieson 3

1. Jamal, 2. Soboleva, 3. Lishchynska, 4. Burka, 5, Yegorova, 6. Kibiwott, 7. Fomenko, 8. Jamieson, 9. Tomashova, 10. Yordanova.

3000 Metres/2 Miles

MESERET DEFAR RECORDED superb performances in her five races. Indoors she won at Boston in 8:30.31 and broke the world record with 8:23.72 at Stuttgart, and outdoors she set two world bests for 2 miles – 9:10.47 at Carson and 8:58.58 (3000m in 8:24.51 en route) in Brussels before winning the WAF race in 8:27.24. Vivien Cheruiyot had wins in Sheffield and Rieti before taking 2nd at the WAF in 8:28.66 ahead of Priscah Cherono 8:29.06 with Linet Masai well behind 4th. Cherono (née Jepleting) was also 2nd in Rieti and in the Brussels 2 miles. Meselech Melkamu was only 0.02 behind Defar's indoor world record but did not run a 3000m race outdoors. Jo Pavey was 3rd in Stuttgart in 8:31.50 (Lidia Chojecka 4th 8:38.21) but was below par for 6th in the European Indoors, won by Chojecka, and outdoors had second places at Sheffield and London. Five women broke 8:40 outdoors in both Monaco (1. Mariem Alaoui Selsouli 8:29.52, 2. Jennifer Rhines, 3. Kim Smith, 4. Shalane Flanagan, 5. Chojecka) and Rieti (3. Kara Goucher, 4. Smith, 5. Masai) and Flanagan ran a North American record 8:33.25 and Smith an Oceania record 8:38.14 behind Defar at Boston indoors.

Ranking (indoors and out): 1. Defar, 2. Cheruiyot, 3. Cherono, 4. Melkamu, 5. Alaoui Selsouli, 6. Smith, 7. Flanagan, 8. Chojecka, 9. Pavey, 10. Masai.

5000 Metres

ALTHOUGH THE 2005 and 2006 number one Tirunesh Dibaba won all her 5000m races in 2007 – a world record 14:27.42 indoors and in New York (14:35.67) and Saint-Denis outdoors, there can be no doubt that Meseret Defar deserved top ranking. She took 7.9 secs off her world record at the Bislett Games and went on to win four races – at Ostrava, African Games, Worlds and Shanghai. Vivian Cheruiyot ran the second fastest ever time of 14:22.51 in Oslo and was also 2nd to Defar at the Worlds with four wins, including at the WAF. Priscah Cherono and Sylvia Kibet were 3rd and 4th at the Worlds after 1-2 in the Kenyan Champs, with Kibet 2nd to Cherono's 3rd at the WAF. Meselech Melkamu was 2nd with Kibet 3rd at the African Games before 6th Worlds and 4th WAF and she was 3-0 against the 17 year-old Linet Masai (5th WAF). Gelete Burka won at Hengelo and was 2nd in 14:31.30 at Ostrava ahead of Melkamu, but was 10th at the Worlds, where Elvan Abeylegesse was 5th in her only major 5000m race. Jenn Rhines and Shalane Flanagan were 7th and 8th at the Worlds, with Flanagan earlier setting a North American record of 14:44.80 and winning the US title. Mariem Alaoui Selsouli was the year's sixth fastest outdoors with 14:36.52 to win in Rome from Kim Smith and was 6th in Oslo, a place ahead of Masai, and Florence Kiplagat was second in Hengelo and Saint-Denis.

Most times under 15 mins: Defar, Cheruiyot, Cherono 4, Melkamu 3.

1. Defar, 2. Cheruiyot, 3. T Dibaba, 4. Cherono, 5. Kibet, 6. Melkamu, 7. Burka, 8. Flanagan, 9. Smith, 10. Selsouli

10,000 Metres

CONDITIONS IN OSAKA were not conducive to fast times, but the race was dramatic with Tirunesh Dibaba overcoming a fall and stomach pains to take the gold from Elvan Abeylegesse with just these two under 32 minutes. Kara Goucher won a close tussle for the bronze from Jo Pavey (UK champion at 31:26.94) and Kim Smith. That was Dibaba's one 10,000m race of the year and Abeylegesse's other one was a decisive win in the European Cup. There was no other race that brought together the top women and the best depth of times came with six women under 31:40 in Kobe in April, a race won by Lucy Wangui in 31:32.52. and five young Chinese runners, headed by 17 year-old Zhang Yingying 31:17.30, under 31:40 at Wuhan in October. The year's fastest time was 31:00.27 by Mestawet Tufa and she also won the African Games title in 31:26.05, but failed to finish at the Worlds, and the year's second and third fastest came at Utrecht from Florence Kiplagat 31:06.30 (no other races) and Teyba Erkesso 31:13.67 (5th African Games). Another with just one race was Jenn Rhines who won at Stanford in 31:17.31 from Smith's NZ record 31:20.63. Only two women broke 31:45 three times – the Kenyans Wangui and Evelyne Kimwei all in Japanese races. Deena Kastor beat Goucher to win the US title and was 6th at the Worlds, a place ahead of Ejegayehu Dibaba, who ran 31:18.97 to win at Barakaldo, just ahead of Aheza Kiros (18th Worlds), with Philes Ongori 8th and Emily Chebet 9th. Amazingly Abeylegesse is the only one of the 2006 top ten to rank again this year (Dibaba was top in 2005).

1. T Dibaba, 2. Abeylegesse, 3. Goucher, 4. Pavey, 5. Smith, 6. Tufa, 7. Kastor, 8. E Dibaba, 9. Ongori, 10. Kiplagat

Half Marathon

THE WORLD LISTS are dominated by the World Championships race in Udine, in which Lornah Kiplagat broke the world record with 66:25. In all 17 women broke 70 minutes and there were pbs galore. Mary Keitany was a surprise 2nd in 66:48, but she had won her two previous races, in 68 minute times in France, and 3rd placed Pamela Chepchumba 68:06 had also won her two previous half marathons, Azpeitia and Philadelphia. Kayoko Fukushi was the year's third fastest, winning in Marugame in 68:00, and other fast winners were Mizuki Noguchi, 68:22 in Sapporo, 68:30 in Miyazaki and 68:54 in Sendai, and Benita Johnson, 68:28 in Berlin. Further World top placers (with other races) were 4. Bezenesh Bekele (3 Ra's Al Khaymah, 1 Lisbon), 5. Atsede Habtamu (2 New Delhi), 6. Evelyne Kimwei (8 Ra's, 3 Matsue, 3 Sapporo), 7. Chisato Osaki (1 Matsue, 5 Sapporo), 8. Luminita Talpos, 9. Alice Timbilil (2. Philadelphia, 3. New Delhi). Ra's winner was Berhane Adere and New Delhi winner Derebe Alemu. Mara Yamauchi was 2nd in both Matsue and Sapporo. Winners on slightly downhill courses were: Lisbon: Rita Jeptoo 67:08 and Great North Run: Kara Goucher 66:57 from Paula Radcliffe 67:53.

1. Kiplagat, 2. Keitany, 3. Chepchumba, 4. Noguchi, 5. Goucher, 6. Bekele, 7. Habtamu, 8. Yamauchi, 9. Kimwei, 10. Osaki

Marathon

THE WORLD'S GREATEST ever marathon runner, Paula Radcliffe, returned from the birth of her daughter to win in New York in 2:23:09. She was followed by Gete Wami, Jelena Prokopcuka, Lidiya Grigoryeva and Catherine Ndereba, but just one race was not quite enough to take top ranking with excellent form by the top two. Zhou Chunxiu ran the year's fastest time of 2:20:38 in London from Wami's 2:21:45 and Wami won the Marathon Majors title by adding a win in Berlin in 2:23:17 just five weeks before New York. Grigoryeva and Prokopcuka had earlier been 1-2 in Boston and Ndereba had won the World title in hot Osaka in 2:30:45 from

Zhou and Reiko Tosa, who had no other marathons. Mizuki Noguchi won the Tokyo marathon in 2:21:31 from Selina Kosgei 2:23:31. Wei Yanan (7th Worlds) ran the year's sixth fastest time to win in Seoul in 2:23:12 and Zhu Xiaolin was 4th in the Worlds after winning the Chinese title in 2:26:08. Constantina Tomescu (dnf New York) was 3rd in London in 2:23:55, Kosgei 4th in 2:24:13 and Lornah Kiplagat 5th 2:24:46. Three Japanese women beat 2:25 in the January Osaka race: Yumiko Hara (18th Worlds), Mari Ozaki (14th Worlds) and Yuri Kano (also winner in Sapporo).

1. Zhou, 2. Wami, 3. Radcliffe, 4. Noguchi, 5. Ndereba, 6. Kosgei, 7. Tosa, 8. Zhu, 9. Prokopcuka, 10. Grigoryeva

3000 Metres Steeplechase

YEKATERINA VOLKOVA AND Tatyana Petrova moved to second and third on the world all-time list with their 9:06.57 and 9:09.19 at the Worlds after the world record-holder Gulnara Galkina had run a swift opening kilometre in 3:00.35 before fading to 7th. Galkina had earlier made a fine return to the event with wins at the Znamenskiy Memorial in 9:14.37 and at Athens 9:11.68 while Volkova beat Petrova for the Russian title, 9:13.35 to 9:14.35. The only other sub 9:20 times were run by Eunice Jepkorir, 1st at Oslo in a Kenyan record 9:19.44 and 2nd in Athens in an African record 9:14.52, before she was 3rd at the Worlds in 9:20.09. Jepkorir went on to win the WAF title from Roisin McGettigan and Cristina Casandra with Volkova a tired fourth. 18 women under 9:30 compared to 10 in 2006, and 5 in 2005 and 2004. The consistent Casandra did so three times and was 6th at the Worlds, behind Ruth Bisibori 4th and Sophie Duarté 5th. Bisibori won the Kenyan title and then took African Games gold in 9:31.99 before world junior records of 9:25.25 in Osaka and 9:24.51 in Daegu. 8th to 11th at the Worlds were Rosa Morató, Arab champion Hanane Ouhaddou, McGettigan, and Veerle Dejaeghere, all of whom set national records sub 9:30 during the year. Another junior, Lou Nian of China, made an astonishing breakthrough to 9:26.25 in November from a previous best of 10:18.49. Petrova (4th) is the only one of the 2006 top ten to retain a top ten place.

Most times under 9:35: Jepkorir 6, Casandra & MacFarlane 5, Volkova & Bisibori 4, Duarte 3.

1. Volkova, 2. Petrova, 3. Jepkorir, 4. Galkina, 5. Bisibori, 6. Casandra, 7. Duarté, 8. Morató, 9. Ouhaddou, 10. McGettigan

100 Metres Hurdles

MICHELLE PERRY RANKS top for the third successive year with 12 wins in 18 races. She ran the year's fastest time of 12.44 in Rome and ran 12.46 in retaining her World title. It was close in Osaka as Perdita Felicien, Delloreen Ennis-London, Susanna Kallur and Virginia Powell followed within 0.1 of a second and 6th-8th LoLo Jones, Vonette Dixon and Angela Whyte completed the fastest ever times for places 5-8 with all running 12.66 or faster. Kallur had been beaten by Perry in their first four meetings, but had reversed that in Stockholm before unfortunate to be baulked by Perry in the World final. Post-Osaka, however, Kallur was on top with three wins over Perry: Zürich and Brussels (in both of which Ennis-London was 2nd and Perry 3rd) and Brussels, but Kallur was one of three women disqualified for false starts at the WAF, won by Perry from Josephine Onyia and Ennis-London. Ennis-London, who won Jamaican and Pan-American titles, was clearly world number three, beating Felicien 7-2 and also 2-1 v Powell, who beat Perry for the US title but who did not finish in Stockholm in her only European race. Jones, third in the US Champs, was a most prolific and consistent racer (25 times under 13.00) and was 4-3 v Canadian champion Whyte, who was 3rd at the Pan-Ams behind Ennis-London and Felicien, with Dixon 4th. Whyte beat Onyia, ineligible for the Worlds, 4-0, and Dixon 4-2. Sally McLellan took Pam Ryan's 35 year-old Oceania record with 12.92 in winning the Australian title and then improved to 12.71, with a series of good performances including 5th in her semi in Osaka. She did not meet Dawn Harper who had slightly better times, following 8th at the US Champs with ten wins on the 'B' circuit in Europe; her only opportunity to meet many of the best being in Stockholm and Linz, in both of which she came 4th.

Most times at 12.70 or faster: Perry 13, Kallur 9, Ennis-London & Powell 7, Jones & Whyte 5, Felicien 4+1w.

1. Perry, 2. Kallur, 3. Ennis-London, 4. Felicien, 5. Powell, 6. Jones, 7. Whyte, 8. Onyia, 9. Dixon, 10. Harper

400 Metres Hurdles

JANA RAWLINSON MADE a great return from the birth of her son in December 2006 to regain the World title and win 9 of 11 races, her only losses being to Yevgeniya Isakova at Saint-Denis and to Anna Jesien at the WAF. She ran three and Yuliya Pechonkina four of the 12 sub-54 sec times run during the year with the fastest being by Tiffany Williams 53.28 and Sheena Johnson 53.29 at the US Champs and then Rawlinson's 53.31 in Osaka. Pechonkina and Jesien were 2nd and 3rd in Osaka and Jesien ran 53.86 and 53.92 there. Isakova (6th Worlds, 4th WAF) was 3-2 v Williams (7th Worlds, 5th WAF) and ranking between these two is Melaine Walker, who just missed the World final (3rd semi) but was 3rd WAF and beat Williams 3-1. Johnson won the Pan-Am title but her second best was 54.55 for 5th in her Worlds semi. Nickiesha Wilson was 2nd at the NCAAs to Nicole Leach and 2nd at the Pan-Ams in a pb 54.94 before making a huge breakthrough at the Worlds with 53.94 in her semi and 54.10 for 4th in the final, but missed the other major races. Also making the World final were Huang Xiaoxiao (5th) and Tasha Danvers-Smith (8th). While Huang did not otherwise run outside China, Danvers-Smith had a decent record and was 3-1 v Johnson and Sandra Glover and 3-3 v Natalya Ivanova (4th semi Worlds), who was 6th with Danvers-Smith and Glover 7th and 8th at the WAF. Leach followed her unbeaten college season with 3rd US Champs (Glover 4th) and 3rd Pan-Ams but ran only 56.10 in her semi at the Worlds and did not run in Europe.

Most times under 54.0/55.0: Pechonkina 4/9, Rawlinson 3/11, Jesien 2/9, Williams 1/10, Johnson 1/5, Wilson 1/3, Isakova & Walker -/6, Ivanova -/5, Danvers-Smith, Glover, Huang, Leach, Angela Morosanu -/3.

1. Rawlinson, 2. Pechonkina, 3. Jesien, 4. Isakova, 5. Walker, 6. Williams, 7. Wilson, 8. Danvers-Smith, 9. Ivanova, 10. Huang

High Jump

BLANKA VLASIC HAD a stellar season outdoors, winning all but one of her 19 competitions, and upping her Croatian record four times from 2.04 to 2.07 with many attempts at a world record 2.10 and six performances in all at 2.04 or more. She was thus ahead of the 2.03 cleared by Antonietta Di Martino at Milan and then by Di Martino and Anna Chicherova to share the silver medals in Osaka behind Vlasic's 2.05. Indoors Tia Hellebaut cleared 2.05 to win the European Indoor title with Di Martino, Venelina Veneva and Ruth Beitia following 2-3-4 at 1.96 and Vlasic only 5th at 1.92; Vlasic won only 3 of 9 indoor competitions. Hellebaut had an earlier Belgian record at 2.00 but an outdoor best of 1.98 and was only 14th at the Worlds, where an unprecedented 16 women qualified at 1.94. After Vlasic, Yelena Slesarenko was the most prolific 2m jumper outdoors – 6 times to 3 by Di Martino and Kajsa Bergqvist, 2 by Chicherova and Yekaterina Savchenko – and was 3-2 outdoors against both Di Martino and Chicherova, who, however, outjumped her at both Worlds 2.03 to 2.00 and WAF 1.97 to 1.94 (for 2-3-4). Slesarenko was at her best with 2.02 to win in Oslo and at the European Cup and when 2nd in Zürich and Brussels with 2.01, while Chicherova was 9=, 4= and 6th in those Golden League events. Savchenko, 5th Worlds, was a clear choice for that ranking; outdoors she beat Chicherova 4-3 and was 4-0 against Beitia (6th Worlds) and 2-0 v Kajsa Bergqvist (7= Worlds). Bergqvist was 3-1 with 2 ties against Beitia (0-1 indoors). Also 7= at the Worlds were Vita Palamar, who returned to form this year and was 6th WAF, Emma Green (8th WAF), Marina Aitova (1st WUG) and Melanie Skotnik. Amy Acuff (12th Worlds and 5th WAF) was closely matched with this group.

Most competitions over 1.97m (indoors/out): Vlasic 18/5, Slesarenko 9/-, Chicherova & Savchenko 7/-, Beitia 6/2, Di Martino 4/3, Bergqvist 4/3, Veneva -/5, Hellebaut -/3.

1. Vlasic, 2. Di Martino, 3. Slesarenko, 4. Chicherova, 5. Savchenko, 6. Bergqvist, 7. Beitia (8), 8. Palamar (9), 9. Hellebaut (7), 10. Aitova (-). - Skotnik (10). (Including indoors).

Pole Vault

APART FROM NOT getting back to 5m form, Yelena Isinbayeva had a perfect season, winning all her 18 competitions – five indoors, including a world record 4.93, and 13 outdoors. She was over 4.80 16 times, but she had some company at such heights with Jenn Stuczynski and Svetlana Feofanova each recording two and Monika Pyrek one 4.80m plus performances. Stuczynski took the North American record to 4.84 and 4.88 but her season was curtailed by injury and she was restricted to 4.50 for 10th at the Worlds. Former world record holder Feofanova got steadily better and, although she and Monika Pyrek were beaten on countback by Katerina Badurová as all cleared 4.75 for 2-3-4 at the Worlds, these two had better records. Pyrek beat Feofanova 4-3 and Badurová 6-3 outdoors. Badurová made the greatest advance, from a previous best of 4.52 (2004) to Czech records of 4.65 indoors and 4.66, 4.70 and 4.75 outdoors.

Isinbayeva won at the WAF with 4.87 from Pyrek's pb of 4.82, Feofanova 4.82 and Tatyana Polnova 4.67. Then followed four women on 4.60 separated on count-back as 5. Yuliya Golubchikova, 6. Badurová, 7. Silke Spiegelburg, 8. Vanessa Boslak. Golubchikova improved from 4.60 in 2006 to 4.70 indoors before second to Feofanova 4.71 to 4.76 for silver at the European Indoors and 4.70 to 4.75 at the Russian Champs outdoors. Boslak was 5th, Golubchikova and Fabiana Murer 6=, Anna Rogowska 8th and Polnova 9th at the Worlds, but Golubchikova beat Polnova 8-6 outdoors (1-1 indoors) and was 4-4 v Boslak who was beaten 4-1 by Polnova, with Murer, the Pan-American champion, behind on win-loss those ranked 6-8th. Contesting tenth place in the rankings on outdoor form are Kym Howe (11th Worlds), Carolin Hingst, Spiegelburg and Gao Shuying. Rogowska excelled at the Worlds given that she had a pre-Osaka outdoor best of 4.40, but she was a force indoors with a best of 4.72 and was 3rd in the European Indoors.

Most competitions over 4.55m (outdoors/in): Pyrek 15/-, Isinbayeva 14/5, Feofanova 13/5, Badurová 12/3, Golubchikova 11/6, Polnova 11/1, Stuczynski 6/6, Hingst 6/1, Boslak 5/1, Murer 4/2, Howe 4/1 Spiegelburg 4/-, Gao 3/-, Rogowska 4/2, Pavla Rybová -/5.

1. Isinbayeva, 2. Feofanova, 3. Pyrek, 4. Badurová, 5. Golubchikova, 6. Stuczynski, 7. Polnova, 8. Boslak, 9. Murer (10), 10. Howe (-). - Rogowska (9). (Including indoors)

Long Jump

RUSSIANS TAKE THE first four rankings with the World 1-2-3 Tatyana Lebedeva, Lyudmila Kolchanova and Tatyana Kotova split by Irina Simagina. Lebedeva had four competitions at 7m plus (two wa), Kolchanova and Simagina two each, Naide Gomes one and Kotova one with wind aid. Lebedeva won 3 of 3 indoors and 8 of 9 outdoors, her one loss being 3rd behind Carolina Klüft and Oksana Udmurtova in Lausanne. Kolchanova showed modest form indoors with two thirds and a fifth and had only three outdoor competitions, but was over 7m in wins at Sochi and Russian Champs before 6.92 for World silver. Simagina and Kotova went 1-1 with the former having better marks; Kotova was 3-0 v Worlds 4th placer Gomes. Bianca Kappler and Maurren Maggi were 5-6 at the Worlds, but Maggi, South American and Pan-American champion, had three jumps at 6.90 or better to one by the German champion.

Keila Costa was a place behind Maggi in each of those three major events and 5th WAF, a place ahead of Kappler who was, however, 2-1 against her. Natalya Lebusova and Udmurtova were 3rd and 4th in the Russian Champs. Klüft had six wins and two second places outdoors and beat Udmurtova and Lebedeva in Lausanne but was beaten by Lebusova at Dubnica and had slightly weaker marks and lack of competition against ranking athletes. Her year's best was 6.85 in the Osaka heptathlon, but there she was outjumped by Lyudmila Blonska's 6.88. Gomes topped the indoor rankings with 6.89 to win the European Indoor title.

Most competitions over 6.70m (outdoors/in): Gomes 9+1w, Lebedeva 8, Maggi & Costa 7, Kotova 6+1w, Kappler & Lebusova 6, Simagina 5+1w, Kolchanova 5, Klüft 4+1w, Rybalko & Montaner 3, Udmurtova, Ikeda 2+1w, Upshaw 1+2w.

1. Lebedeva, 2. Kolchanova, 3. Simagina, 4. Kotova, 5. Gomes, 6. Maggi, 7. Kappler, 8. Lebusova, 9. Costa, 10. Klüft. (Including indoors)

Triple Jump

YARGELIS SAVIGNE PRODUCED one of the top performances of the 2007 World Championships with her CAC record 15.28 to hold off the challenge of favourites Tatyana Lebedeva 15.07 and Hrysopiyí Devetzí 15.04. These three were the only women over 15m during the year. Savigne had first done so with 15.09 at Alcalá and also won Cuban, Pan-American and WAF titles and in all won 12 (1 indoors) of 16 competitions. Lebedeva won five of eight and Devetzí two of six. There was a very close WAF: Savigne 14.78, Devetzí 14.75 and Lebedeva 14.72. Worlds 4-5 were Anna Pyatykh, who won the Russian title from Olesya Bufalova (10th Worlds), and Marija Sestak, who went 1-1. Worlds 6th placer Magdelin Martinez beat the 7th and WUG champion Olha Saladuha 4-1 and was 3-0 v Yamilé Aldama, who was 4th with Sestak 5th at the WAF but, although winning the African title, managed only 13.46 for 25th at the Worlds.

Chinese champion Xie Limei set Asian records at 14.73 and 14.90 and was unbeaten in Asian competition with 8th at the Worlds, a place ahead of Keila Costa, South American champion and 2nd at the Pan Ams (Mabel Gay 3rd) with 6th WAF and 2-2 v Aldama. Savigne topped the world indoor rankings with 14.80 followed by the European Indoor 1-2-3, Carlota Castrejana, Bufalova and Teresa Nzola, but those three did not jump as far outdoors.

Most competitions over 14.50m: Savigne 12+1i, Lebedeva 8, Devetzí 6, Pyatykh, Martinez & Sestak 4, Xie & Gay 3.

1. Savigne, 2. Lebedeva, 3. Devetzí, 4. Pyatykh, 5. Sestak, 6. Martinez, 7. Saladuha, 8. Xie, 9. Costa. 10. Aldama

Shot

VALERIE VILI AND Nadezhda Ostapchuk shared the top six marks of the year and had a terrific tussle at the Worlds, Vili winning 20.54 to 20.48 as both produced their bests of the year in the final round. Vili won 11 of of her 12 competitions, the exception being when Ostapchuk won at the WAF 20.45 to 20.40; she also beat Ostapchuk at Rovereto. Petra Lammert was the year's only other 20m putter with 20.04, and although 5th at the Worlds ranks ahead of the 3rd and 4th placers as she beat Nadine Kleinert 7-3 and Li Ling had a much inferior set of marks although she produced a pb of 19.38 in Osaka. Anna Omarova, with two marks over 19.60, was fifth best on performances and had six wins, including Russian Champs and a European Cup win over Lammert and Ostapchuk, and a second before slipping a little with 9th Worlds. Li Meiju and Gong Lijiao were 6th and 7th at the Worlds, with Li having a 3-2 advantage. Chiara Rosa, Yanina Pravalinskaya and Pan-Am champion Misleydis González finished 8th, 10th and 11th in Osaka and European Indoor champion Assunta Legnante (13th) and Anna Avdeyeva (14th) just missed rankings spots.

Most competitions over 19m: Lammert 15, Vili 9, Ostapchuk 8+1i, Kleinert 7+1i, Omarova 3.

1. Vili, 2. Ostapchuk, 3. Lammert, 4. Kleinert, 5. Li Ling, 6. Omarova, 7. Li Meiju, 8. Gong Lijiao, 9. Rosa, 10. Pravalinskaya

Discus

FRANKA DIETZSCH WON her third World title and with 15 wins in 19 competitions was very clearly world number one (previously in 1998-9 and 2006). Second and third on the world lists were the US Champs 1-2 Suzy Powell and Becky Breisch, but their top marks of 67.67 and 67.37 and a series of other long marks were helped by very favourable wind conditions, and neither made the World final (15th and 19th) with 6th and 4th respectively at WAF. Darya Pishchalnikova had five firsts, including the Russian title, and four seconds, including to Dietzsch at the European Cup and Worlds, in her nine competitions. Nicoleta Grasu completes a 1-2-3 unchanged from 2006 with 4th Worlds and 3rd WAF. World bronze medallist Yarelis Barrios also won Pan-Am and World University titles and was 1-1 v Vera Cechlová, who won 7/10 and was WAF 2nd but a non-qualifying 21st at the Worlds. Sun Taifeng was unbeaten at home and 5th at the Worlds, in her only meeting with non-Chinese competition, one place ahead of Olena Antonova. Yania Ferrales was 5-5 v Barrios, winning their early season clashes in Cuba before 2nd Pan-Ams and 11th Worlds. A place ahead of her at the Worlds was the veteran Iryna Yatchenko, who won her four home events and was 3rd in the European Cup. Just missing the top ten were the Worlds 7-8 Joanna Wisniewska and Nataliya Semenova, Elizna Naude, who did not compete at the Worlds after winning the African title, and Kateryna Karsak who beat Pishchalnikova to win the European U23 title but was 16th at the Worlds.

Most competitions over 63m: Dietzsch 14, Grasu 9, Pishchalnikova & Powell 6, Breisch 5, Ferrales 4, Barrios & Naude 3.

1. Dietzsch, 2. Pishchalnikova, 3. Grasu, 4. Barrios, 5. Cechlová, 6. Sun, 7. Ferrales, 8. Yatchenko, 9. Antonova, 10. Powell.

Hammer

THE EVENT'S RANKINGS are overshadowed by the pending enquiry into drugs abuse by top Russians Tatyana Lysenko and Yekaterina Khoroshikh. It seems that rather than introducing drugs into their system their coach may have induced them to take an oestrogen-reducing substance. Lysenko produced the top two throws of the year with a 'world record' 78.61 at Sochi and 77.71 at Ostrava; she had nine wins in 11 events before withdrawing from competition in July and would rank top if cleared. Khoroshikh was fifth on the world list with 76.63. Without Lysenko, in close competition for top ranking are the World 1-2 Betty Heidler and Yipsi Moreno, 2-2 in their clashes. Heidler did not compete at the WAF, won by Moreno. Kamila Skolimowska was next on the world list with her 17th Polish record of 76.83 but was beaten 2-0 by Zhang Wenxiu including when this pair were 3-4 at the Worlds. Yelena Konevtsova beat Olga Kuzenkova and Gulfiya Khanafeyeva to win the Russian title; they were 5th, 22nd and 10th respectively at the Worlds. Khanafeyeva was second on the world list with 77.36 and was 2-0 v Ivana Brkljacic, who improved her Croatian record to 74.62 and to 75.08 and excelled with 74.69 in qualifying at the Worlds, but managed only 68.16 for 11th in the final. She recovered, however, to take WAF 2nd place, with Clarisa Claretti (Worlds 7th) and Skolimowska 3rd and 4th. Manuèla Montebrun had four competitions over 73m and was 8th at the Worlds, where Eileen O'Keeffe excelled with 6th place. Oksana Menkova had throws of 73.94 to win the Belarus Cup and 73.03 for 3rd in the European Cup behind Lysenko and Heidler, but managed no valid throws in the World qualifying.

Most competitions over 72m: Heidler 13, Moreno 12, Montebrun 9, Skolimowska 8, Khanafeyeva, Konevtsova & Zhang 6, Menkova & Brittany Riley 3 – Lysenko 11, Khoroshikh 5

1. Heidler, 2. Moreno, 3. Zhang, 4. Skolimowska, 5. Konevtsova, 6. Khanafeyeva, 7. Brkljacic, 8. Montebrun, 9. O'Keeffe, 10. Claretti (1. Lysenko, 9. Khoroshikh if exonerated).

Javelin

CHRISTINA OBERGFÖLL WAS the clear favourite for the World title, unbeaten in nine competitions and topping the world list with a European record 70.20 at the European Cup. However, Barbora Spotáková took her Czech record to 66.40 and 67.07 to beat Obergföll (66.46) in Osaka with Steffi Nerius third and had another big win over the Germans at the WAF, so retains top ranking even though Obergföll had an overall 4-2 advantage. Nerius is a clear third; she was beaten by Obergföll in all their 11 contests until she was 2nd and Obergföll 3rd at the WAF. Osleidys Menéndez had only five competitions and although she beat Sonia Bisset at the Pan Ams decided that she was not in form to defend her World title. Bisset, who had beaten Menéndez in their two previous meetings, and Nikola Brejchová were 6th and 4th respectively at the Worlds and 5th and 6th WAF. Goldie Sayers broke the British record with 65.05 and then beat Nerius and Spotáková at Glasgow, the only athlete other than the top four to do so, but she was only 8th at Athens and 18th (non-qualifying) at the Worlds. Mariya Abakumova (7th Worlds) beat Sávva Líka (5th Worlds) 2-1 and Líka was 2-2 v Barbara Madejczk (9th Worlds). Just missing rankings were Linda Stahl (8th Worlds), Paula Tarvianen and African champion Justine Robbeson.

Most competitions over 62m: Nerius 15, Obergföll 14, Spotáková 12, Sayers, Bisset 3.

1. Spotáková, 2. Obergföll , 3. Nerius, 4. Bisset, 5. Brejchová, 6. Sayers, 7. Abakumova, 8. Líka, 9. Menéndez, 10. Madejczyk.

Heptathlon

CAROLINA KLÜFT TOOK her win streak at heptathlon to 19 from 2001 and is top for the sixth successive year. She scored 6681 at Götzis and took the World title with a European record 7032, a total exceeded only by the great Jackie Joyner-Kersee (six times). As Klüft competed only twice and the best three scores from selected events count, Lyudmila Blonska (6832 at the Worlds) was a clear winner of the IAAF Combined Events Challenge. She was second twice to Klüft and won at Kladno, UKR Champs and Talence. After her the Challenge order was Jessica Ennis (4th), Austra Skujyte (6th), Jennifer Oeser (7th), Lilli Schwarzkopf (5th), Kelly Sotherton (3rd) and Natalya Dobrynska (8th), but I have ranked them in their World Champs order (shown in brackets). Ennis was selected as Rising Star of the Year by the European AA and the 21 year-old improved her pb from 6287 (2006) to 6388 (1st Desenzano), 6399 (1st European Cup) and 6469 (Worlds). She was 170 points ahead of Sotherton at the European Cup but Sotherton scored 6510 at the Worlds. Pan-American champion Jessica Zelinka was 8th in the Challenge but did not compete at the Worlds. Rankings are pretty similar to 2006 with eight of the ten returning, the other two just missing out: Karin Ruckstuhl (4th 2006), who did not finish through injury at the Worlds after 6th in Götzis, and Karolina Tyminska. Just missing rankings places are Marie Collonvillé and Russian champion Anna Bogdanova, 9th and 10th at the Worlds (four points apart).

1. Klüft, 2. Blonska, 3. Sotherton, 4. Ennis, 5. Schwarzkopf, 6. Skujyte, 7. Oeser, 8. Chernova, 9. Dobrynska, 10. Zelinka

20 Kilometres Walk

RITA TUROVA DID not compete in Osaka or Saransk due to a hip injury but did enough to retain her top ranking with five major race wins and taking the IAAF World Race Walking Challenge. Olga Kaniskina started the year with third behind Alena Nartova and Tatyana Sibileva in the Russian winter champs and was beaten by Turova in their one clash, in the European Cup, but went on to be a brilliant winner of the World title and to record the year's fastest time of 1:26:47 in winning at the World Challenge final in her home town of Saransk. Second in that race was European Junior 10,000m champion Anna Kornikova, but that was her only 20k race. Tatyana Shemyakina was 5th in the Russian Champs and did not finish in Saransk but won the European U23 title and was 2nd at the Worlds. Second and third in the Challenge series were Kjersti Plätzer, with a win and four seconds before 4th at the Worlds, and Sabine Zimmer, 8th Worlds and 7th Saransk. Yelena Ginko was 3rd in the European Cup and in Kraków behind Turova and Elisa Rigaudo, but then was 16th Worlds and dnf Saransk, whereas Maria Vasco was 5th European Cup and 3rd Worlds and Tatyana Sibileva 6th and 9th in those races with 5th Saransk. Rigaudo was 4th European Cup but dnf Worlds. Further top Worlds placings came from Susana Feitor 5th, Claudia Stef 6th and Inês Henriques 7th; they were respectively 14th, 8th and 7th in the European Cup. Tatyana Korotkova and Lyudmila Arkhipova completed a Russian 1-2-3-4 in Saransk, but had been 11th and 8th in the Russian Champs, won by Irina Stankina.

Most times sub 1:31: Turova 5, Kaniskina 4, Arkhipova, Plätzer, Rigaudo, Sibileva 3.

1. Turova, 2. Kaniskina, 3. Shemyakina, 4. Plätzer, 5. Vasco, 6. Sibileva, 7. Zimmer, 8. Rigaudo, 9. Feitor, 10. Stef

• The winners of the Waterford Crystal **European Athlete of the Year** Awards for 2007 were Tero Ptikämäki and Blanka Vlasic. EAA Top 10:

Men: 1, Tero Pitkämäki, 2, Roman Sebrle, 3, Gerd Kanter, 4, Nelson Évora, 5, Ivan Tikhon, 6, Virgilijus Alekna, 7, Andrew Howe, 8, Yuriy Borzakovskiy, 9, Viktor Röthlin, 10, Francis Obikwelu.

Women: 1, Blanka Vlasic, 2, Carolina Klüft, 3, Yelena Isinbayeva, 4, Tatyana Lebedeva, 5, Franka Dietszch, 6, Susanna Kallur, 7, Barbora Spotáková, 8, Betty Heidler, 9, Kim Gevaert, 10, Naide Gomes.

EAA Rising Star Awards were presented to Andrew Howe (men) and Jessica Ennis (women).

Holm v Rybakov

A GREAT RIVALRY has developed in the high jump between Stefan Holm and Yaroslav Rybakov, who have both contested 14 of the 15 global or European championships 2001-2008. Holm, much the smaller of the two at 1.81m tall to Rybakov's 1.98m, has the advantage 9-5 in these clashes, but both have a terrific record of consistent top-quality performance when it matters most as the list shows:

	Championship	*Holm*	*Rybakov*
2001	World Indoor	2.32- 1	2.25- 7
	World	2.30- 4=	2.33- 2=
2002	European Indoor	2.30- 2	2.30- 3
	European	2.29- 2	2.31- 1
2003	World Indoor	2.35- 1	2.33- 2
	World	2.32- 2	2.25- 9
2004	World Indoor	2.35- 1	2.32- 2
	Olympics	2.36- 1	2.32- 6
2005	European Indoor	2.40- 1	2.38- 2
	World	2.29- 7	2.29- 2=
2006	World Indoor	2.30- 5	2.37- 1
	European	2.34- 3	2.30- 5
2007	European Indoor	2.34- 1	–
	World	2.33- 4	2.35- 2
2008	World Indoor	2.36- 1	2.34- 2

Up to Holm's 4th World title in 2008 his head-to-head career record against Rybakov in all competitions is 46-22 (plus 7 ties). All these are shown on Stefan's fantastic web site www.scholm.com.

CROSS-COUNTRY – NATIONAL CHAMPIONS 2007

	Men (longer distance)	**Women** (longer distance)
Algeria/Maghreb	Yahia Azaidj	Kenza Dahmani
Argentina	Juan Osvaldo Suárez	Sandra Amarillo
Australia (Sep)	Jeffrey Hunt	Anna Thompson
Austria	Günther Weidlinger	Andrea Mayr
Belgium	Rik Ceulemans	Natalie De Vos
Brazil	Gladson Barbosa	Ednalva da Silva
Bulgaria	Stanislav Lambev	Milka Mikhaylova
Canada (Dec)	Reid Coolsaet	Carmen Douma-Hussar
Chile	Roberto Echavarría	Erika Olivera
China	Yang Dinghong	Zhu Xiaolin
Croatia (Nov)	Zoran Zilic	Marija Schwarz
Cuba	Richard Pérez	Mariela González
Czech Republic	Milan Kocourek	Lenka Vsetecková
Denmark (Oct)	Steen Walter	Anna Holm Jørgensen
England	Frank Tickner	Liz Yelling
Estonia	Pavel Loskutov	Maria Sahharova
Ethiopia WC Trials	Tadesse Tola	Meselech Melkamu
Finland	Jussi Utriainen	Mari Järvenpää
France	Driss El Himer	Christelle Daunay
Germany	Stephan Hohl	Sabrina Mockenhaupt
Greece	Anastasásios Frágos	Kalliópi Astropetáki
Hungary	Balázs Ott	Simona Staicu
India	Sadasivam Raghunath	Pampa Chanda
Ireland	Gary Murray	Fionnuala Britton
Israel	Vodage Zvadye	Svetlana Bakhmand
Italy	Giuilano Battocletti	Renate Rungger
Kenya	Richard Matelong	Lornah Kiplagat NED
World Trials	Moses Mosop	Florence Kiplagat
Latvia	Mareks Floroseks	Daniele Fetcere
Lithuania	Vitalij Gorlukovic	Rasa Drazdauskaite
Luxembourg	Vincent Nothum	Pascale Schmoetten
Morocco	Anis Selmouni	Bouchra Chaabi
Netherlands	Michel Butter	Adrienne Herzog
New Zealand	Edwin Henshaw	Maria Akesson
Northern Ireland	Brian Campbell	Kelly Reid
Norway (Sep)	Henrik Sandstad	Kirsten Melkevik Otterbu
Poland	Marcin Chabowski	Justyna Bak
Portugal	Rui Pedro Silva	Jessica Augusto
Romania (Nov)	Marius Ionescu	Elena Timpau
Russia	Yevgeniy Rybakov	Olga Rossyeveva
Scotland	Mark Pollard	Freya Murray
Serbia	Sreten Ninkovic	Ana Subotic
Slovakia	Marcel Matanin	Ludmila Melicerová
Slovenia	Mitja Kosovelj	Jolanda Ceplak
South Africa (Sep)	Boy Soke	Dianahrose Phalula
Spain	Juan Carlos de la Ossa	Rosa Morató
Sweden	Mustafa Mohamed	Hanna Karlsson
Switzerland	Stéphane Joly	Anita Weyermann
Tunisia	Ridha Amri	Fatma Lanouar
Uganda	Boniface Kiprop	Dorcus Inzikuru
UK	Frank Tickner	Hayley Yelling
Ukraine (Mar)	Sergiy Zachepa	Kateryna Stetsenko
(Oct)	Igor Heletiy	Lyudmyla Kovalenko
USA Winter	Alan Culpepper	Deena Kastor
Wales	Jorge Thomas	Catherine Dugdale
Asian	Abdeullah Ahmad Hassan QAT	Maryam Jamal BRN
Balkan	Marius Ionescu ROM	Sonja Stolic SRB
European Clubs	Alberto García ESP	Rosa Morató ESP
Teams	adidas ESP	Maratona POR
Gulf	Abdulhaq Al-Qurashi BRN	
NACAC	Fazil Bizuneh USA	Malindi Elmore CAN
NCAA (Nov)	Josh McDougal (USA)	Sally Kipyego KEN
Nordic (Nov)	Jussi Utriainen FIN	Kirsten Melkevik Otterbu NOR
South American	Jorge Naranjo COL	Ednalva da Silva BRA
Southern Africa	Boy Soke RSA	Tabitha Tsatsa ZIM

	Men (short distance)	Women (short distance)
Austria	Martin Pröll	
Brazil	Hudson de Souza	Patricia Lobo
Bulgaria	Stanislav Lambev	Vanya Koleva
China	Dong Guojian	Zhoiu Chunxiu
Czech Republic	Zdenek Medlik	
Denmark	Jesper Faurschou	Anna Holm Jørgensen
Finland	Jukka Keskisalo	
France	Mohamed Belabbas	Marie-Noëlle Jacquet
Germany	Wolfram Müller	
Hungary	László Tóth	
India	Sunil Kumar	Jhuma Kathun
Israel	Gezachw Yossef	
Lithuania	Vitalij Gorlukovic	Gyte Norgiliene
Norway	Joachim Brøndbo	Kirsten Melkevik Otterbu
Russia	Aleksandr Krivchonkov	Yuliya Fomenko
Scotland	Alastair Hay	Morag Maclarty
Slovenia	Peter Kuznik	
Sweden	Erik Sjöqvist	Hanna Karlsson
Ukraine	Dmytro Baranovskiy	Yuliya Ruban
" (Oct)	Roman Pasichnyk	Yuliya Ruban
Gulf	Nasser Kareem Shamis QAT	
South American	Hudson de Souza BRA	Valeria Rodríguez ARG
Southern Africa	Mandla Maseko RSA	Chanelle Olivier RSA
World Military	Tareq Mubarak BRN	

Winners of EAA and IAAF Permit Cross-Country Races 2007

6 Jan	Belfast (IAAF)	Moses Kipsiro UGA	Etalemahu Kidane ETH
7 Jan	Amorebieta (EAA)	Micah Kogo KEN	Vivian Cheruiyot KEN
13 Jan	Edinburgh (IAAF)	Kenenisa Bekele ETH	Gelete Burka ETH
21 Jan	Sevilla (IAAF)	Kenenisa Bekele ETH	Gelete Burka ETH
28 Jan	Belgrade (EAA)	Kemal Koyuncu TUR	Sonja Stolic SER
13 Jan	Le Mans (FRA)	Edwin Soi KEN	Julie Coulard FRA
28 Jan	Hannut (EAA)	Simon Arusei KEN	Florence Kiplagat KEN
11 Feb	Diekirch (IAAF)	Khamis Zaman QAT	Veerle Dejaeghere BEL
25 Feb	Albufeira (IAAF)	Sergiy Lebid UKR	Dorcus Inzikuru UGA
4 Mar	San Vittore (IAAF)	Sergiy Lebid UKR	Maryam Jamal BRN
17 Nov	Oeiras (IAAF)	Imane Merga Jhida ETH	Mónica Rosa POR
18 Nov	Istanbul (EAA)	Halil Akkas TUR	Emebet Bacha ETH
18 Nov	Llodio (IAAF)	Joseph Ebuya KEN	Meselech Melkamu ETH
18 Nov	Roeselare (EAA)	Pieter Desmet BEL	Anuta Bobocel ROM
25 Nov	Leffinckroucke (EAA)	Imane Merga Jhida ETH	Linet Masai KEN
25 Nov	Soria (EAA)	Joseph Ebuya KEN	Meselech Melkamu ETH
2 Dec	Alcobendas (EAA)	Joseph Ebuya KEN	Eunice Jepkorir KEN
23 Dec	Brussels (IAAF)	Paul K. Koech KEN	Veerle Dejaeghere BEL

See ATHLETICS 2007 page 608 for results of the 2007 World Cross-Country Championships.

European Cross-Country Championships 2007

At Toro, Spain 8 December

Senior Men (10.7k)
1. Serhiy Lebid UKR 31:47
2. Mustafa Mohamed SWE 31:56
3. Rui Silva POR 31:58
4. Erik Sjöqvist SWE 32:00
5. José Manuel Martínez ESP 31:58
6. Jesús España ESP 32:05
7. Martin Fagan IRL 32:06
8. El Hassan Lahssini FRA 32:08
9. Ricardo Ribas POR 32:10
10. José Rios ESP 32:12
11. Andrew Baddeley GBR 32:14
12. Alberto García ESP 32:16
13. Pieter Desmet BEL 32:20
14. Carles Castillejo ESP 32:27
15. Mokhtar Benhari FRA 32:29

52 of 57 finished.

Teams: 1. ESP 33, 2. POR 64, 3. FRA 75, 4. GBR 81, 5. SWE 83, 6. BEL 92, 7. IRL 105, 8. ITA 139, 9. FIN 151

Under-23 Men (8.2k)
1. Kemal Koyuncu TUR 24:31
2. Yevgeniy Rybakov RUS 24:33
3. Andrew Vernon GBR 24:35
4. Andrea Lalli ITA 24:43
5. Stefano La Rosa ITA 24:44
6. Stepan Rahovtsov BLR 24:45
7. Artur Kozlowski POL 24:45
8. Lukasz Parszczynski POL 24:46

71 of 77 finished

Teams: 1. GBR 52, 2. POL 52, 3. RUS 65, 4, TUR 101, 5. FRA 105; 12 teams completed

Junior Men (6.7k)
1. Mourad Amdouni FRA 20:08
2. Florian Carvalho FRA 20:11
3. Dmytro Lashyn UKR 20:16
4. David Forrester GBR 20:21
5. Lee Carey GBR 20:22

86 of 89 finished.

Teams: 1. FRA 29, 2. GBR 48, 3. GER 57; 14 teams completed.

Senior Women (8.03k)
1. Marta Domínguez ESP 26:58
2. Julie Coulaud FRA 27:01
3. Rosa Morató ESP 27:04
4. Mariya Konovalova RUS 27:07
5. Anikó Kálovics HUN 27:10
6. Kate Reed GBR 27:11
7. Fionnuala Britton IRL 27:20
8. S. Bourgailh-Haddioui FRA 27:25
9. Hayley Yelling GBR 27:28
10. Liz Yelling GBR 27:31
11. Jessica Augusto POR 27:32
12. Iris Fuentes-Pila ESP 27:38

13. Nathalie De Vos BEL 27:40
14. Mónica Rosa POR 27:44
15. T. Holovchenko UKR 27:44
45 of 46 finished.
Teams: 1. ESP 33, 2. GBR 47, 3. POR 69, 4. FRA 77, 5. IRL 112, 6. ITA 140

Under-23 Women (6.7k)
1. Ancuta Bobocel ROM 22:35
2. Adriënne Herzog NED 22:37
3. K. Kowalska POL 22:44
4. Tatyana Shutova RUS 22:52
5. Felicity Milton GBR 23:02
6. Linda Byrne IRL 23:04
7. Marta Romo ESP 23:05
8. Katrina Wootton GBR 23:08
62 of 67 finished.
Teams: 1. GBR 47, 2. RUS 55, 3. POL 58, 4. BEL 82; 5, ESP 108; 11 teams completed

Junior Women (4.2k)
1. Stephanie Twell GBR 14:12
2. Danuta Urbanik POL 14:21
3. Charlotte Purdue GBR 14:22
4. Charlotte Roach GBR 14:27
5. Olga Skrypak UKR 14:28
6. Emily Pidgeon GBR 14:31
85 of 87 finished.
Teams: 1. GBR 14, 2. RUS 50, 3. UKR 57; 13 teams completed

2007 WORLD ROAD RACE REVIEW

By David E Martin

THE ACCOMPANYING LIST of winners of about 170 road races held in 2007 in 20 countries around the globe gives a sense of the world scene in this vibrant and topsy-turvy aspect of athletics. As with the marathon, Kenyan dominance on the road-racing podiums continues. In this present listing Kenyan men captured an amazing 109 out of 170 victories (64%!). Kenyan women also have been improving rapidly these past few years, shown here by their bringing home 73 out of 161 (45%) winners' medals. The most popular distance for these sub-marathon running contests has been 10km, but during the past several years the enthusiasm about attempting to complete a marathon has caused a corresponding increase in popularity of the half marathon.

At the front is the invited field of incredibly talented athletes from around the world, vying for sometimes enormous prize money payouts, while behind are the masses, delighted with the chance to compete in the same event as the champions. Because so many of these races are run from one city to the next, the odd race distance often causes difficulty in appreciating one's quality of effort, as the pace is not readily evident from the finish time.

Just as with the marathon, some of these races have become enormous spectacles, with a significant influence on the local economy, although they may remain relatively unknown elsewhere. Some events are meticulous in providing every entrant with an indication of their finish time, which then provides a useful data point for event management. For example, on 25 March in Chicago at the LaSalle Bank Shamrock Shuffle 8K, 11,007 men and 12,678 women finished, giving a total of 23,685 participants.

Other events simply indicate the total number of finishers without further breakdown, for example, the Vancouver Sun Run (10km) on 15 April – 42,683 participants. Still other events, such as the Peachtree Road Race 10km in Atlanta on July 4 and the Bay to Breakers 12K in San Francisco in May, only estimate their finish numbers. Another example is the J.P. Morgan Chase Corporate Challenge, a 3.5 mile run through the streets of Frankfurt, organized for members of corporate companies running on teams; on 13 June the event had 67,270 participants. And the Sydney, Australia newspapers reported that 64,713 entered the famous 14km Sun-Herald City-to-Surf run on 12 August.

When one considers the logistics of moving such a huge population such a long distance on foot, within a time limit, it is surprising that there aren't more deaths along the way. Running is a physiological stress, and many push themselves marginally too hard in the excitement of the event. And then there are the problems caused by inadequate hydration on warm days. Deaths do occur in such events, though they are few, estimated at one in around 65,000 participants and typically occurring among those with inadequate training or with pre-existing disease who likely would have met their demise earlier but for the healthy lifestyle brought on by chronic physical training, attention to sleep, nutrition, and hydration etc.

The world of distance running was thus shocked on 3 November in New York City when 28 year-old Ryan Shay, a superbly fit elite-level athlete competing in the USA's Olympic marathon team selection trials, collapsed and died of an apparent heart attack at just past the 8km point in the race. For several years he had been at the top of his game: national collegiate 10,000 m track champion in 2001, national road-racing champion at the marathon and half- marathon in 2003, national half-marathon and 20km road champion in 2004, national 15km road champion in 2005, and on and on. He was running in his eighth marathon, with a previous personal best of 2:14:09 at New York in 2004. It was known that his resting heart rate was very low, less than 30 beats per minute, compared to the more usual norm in the 40's for trained runners (sedentary resting heart rates are around 70 beats per minute). An enlarged left ventricle is a normal physiological adaptation to the stress of sustained submaximal work, and is considered desirable for optimal cardiac functioning.

Was Shay's heart diseased in some way that resulted in hypermyotrophic cardiomyopathy instead of the expected physiologic cardiac hypertrophy? Autopsy results have been inconclusive. None of the large and experienced assembled press corps for the event could recall an elite athlete death in any Olympic team trials selection race. It served as a sobering note to the 38,000+ assembled for the celebration of fitness and life that surrounds the New York City Marathon. It is the rarity of such events that keeps the lifestyle of endurance athletics so exciting.

Leading Road Races 2007

See also Major Championships and National Championships sections

Date	Race	Men	Women
1 Jan	Punta del Este 10km	Gustavo Comba ARG 28:50	Elisa Cobanea ARG 35:23
6 Jan	Miyazaki HMar	*Women only*	Mizuki Noguchi JPN 68:30
14 Jan	Egmond aan Zee HMar	Eshetu Wondimu ETH 60:14	Hilda Kibet KEN 73:25
14 Jan	Houston HMar USA Ch	Ryan Hall USA 59:43*	Elva Dryer USA 71:42
28 Jan	Austin HMar (dh)	Alene Emere Reta ETH 61:46	Kathy Butler GBR 71:12
28 Jan	Marrakech HMar	Mourad Maaroufi MAR 63:45	Meriem Wangari KEN 74:16
4 Feb	Coamo HMar	Evans Cheruiyot KEN 63:30	Getenesh Wami ETH 74:26
4 Feb	Eldoret HMar A	Benson Barus KEN 62:44	*Men only*
4 Feb	Granollers HMar	Stefano Baldini ITA 63:10	Marta Domínguez ESP 71:23
4 Feb	Málaga HMar	Silas Sang KEN 61:51	*Men only*
4 Feb	Marugame HMar	Mekubo Mogusu ETH 59:48*	Kayoko Fukushi JPN 68:00
9 Feb	Ra's Al Khaymah HMar	Samuel Wanjiru KEN 58:52 WR	Berhane Adere ETH 70:58
11 Feb	Himeji 10M	Terukazu Omori JPN 46:34	*Men only*
11 Feb	Karatsu 10M/10km	Cyrus Njui KEN 46:50	Pauline Wanguru KEN 32:16
11 Feb	Schoorl 10km NED Ch	Juwawo Wirimai ZIM 29:08	Hilda Kibet KEN 31:26
18 Feb	Ferrara HMar	Jackson Kirwa KEN 61:34	Helena Javornik SLO 70:57 WMR
18 Feb	Gava HMar	Nacho Casares ESP 62:47	Lidiya Vasilevskaya RUS 76:51
25 Feb	Kumamoto 30km	Willy Kangogo KEN 1:29:59	Mika Okunaga JPN 1:45:46
25 Feb	Ostia HMar	Benson Barus KEN 60:18	Souad Aït Salem ALG 70:29
25 Feb	San Juan 10km	Gilbert Okari KEN 28:08	Lornah Kiplagat KEN 31:05
10 Mar	Jacksonville 15km USA Ch	Mebrahtom Keflezighi USA 43:40	Deena Kastor USA 47:20
11 Mar	Alphen aan Rijn 20km	Eshetu Wondimu ETH 56:52*	Robe Guta ETH 67:46
11 Mar	Hastings HMar	Philemon Baaru KEN 63:22	Birhan Dagne ETH 76:02
11 Mar	Kyoto HMar	Samuel Nganga KEN 63:18	Ryoko Kizaki JPN 71:09
11 Mar	Paris HMar	Joseph Maregu KEN 60:22	Irene Kwambai KEN 70:26
11 Mar	Yamaguchi HMar	Kazuhiro Maeda JPN 62:10	Philes Ongori KEN 69:50
17 Mar	Den Haag HMar	Samuel Wanjiru KEN 58:35 WR	Hilda Kibet KEN 69:43
17 Mar	Virginia Beach 8km	Joseph Koskei KEN 22:27	Rehima Kedir ETH 25:46
18 Mar	Lisboa HMar	Robert Kipchumba KEN 60:34	Rita Jeptoo KEN 67:08
18 Mar	Matsue HMar	*Women only*	Chisato Osaki JPN 69:25
18 Mar	New York 8km USA Ch	Anthony Famiglietti USA 22:35	*Men only*
18 Mar	Virginia Beach HMar	Nicholas Kamakya KEN 63:08	Anca Fodor ROM 74:18
24 Mar	Mobile 10km	Samuel Ndereba KEN 28:01	Rehima Kedir ETH 32:02
24 Mar	Praha HMar	Patrick Ivuti KEN 61:00*	Liliya Shobukhova RUS 71:14
25 Mar	Málaga HMar	Wilson Chebet KEN 61:30	Tigist Tufa ETH 73:47
25 Mar	Venlo HMar	Elias Maindi KEN 61:53	Peninah Arusei KEN 70:49
25 Mar	Warszawa HMar	Michael Karonei KEN 63:25	Justyna Bak POL 72:14
25 Mar	Zapopan HMar (A)	Hillary Kimaiyo KEN 63:56	Madai Pérez MEX 72:51
31 Mar	Azpeitia HMar	Yared Asmerom ERI 60:28*	Pamela Chepchumba KEN 68:57*
31 Mar	Charleston 10km	Richard Kiplagat KEN 28:35	Rehima Kedir ETH 32:05
31 Mar	Richmond 10km	Teferi Bacha ETH 28:29	Magdalene Mukunzi KEN 32:24*
1 Apr	Barcelona 10km	Peter Kamais KEN 27:57	Eunice Jepkorir KEN 31:49
1 Apr	Berlin HMar	Patrick Musyoki KEN 58:56*	Benita Johnson AUS 68:28
1 Apr	Brunssum 10km	Micah Kogo KEN 27:07	Hilda Kibet KEN 32:24
1 Apr	Carlsbad 5km	Simon Ndirangu KEN 13:28	Meseret Defar ETH 15:01
1 Apr	Hilversum 10km	John Chipchumba KEN 32:34	Filomena Chepchirchir KEN 32:34

1 Apr	Milano HMar	Philemon Kipsang KEN 60:55	Aniko Kálovics HUN 68:58
1 Apr	Vitry-sur-Seine HMar	Enock Mitei KEN 61:01	Mary Keitany KEN 68:37
1 Apr	Washington 10M	Tadesse Tola ETH 46:01	Teyiba Erkesso ETH 51:44
7 Apr	Cape Town HMar	Willy Mwangi KEN 63:05	Helalia Johannes NAM 73:16
7 Apr	New Orleans 10km	George Misoi KEN 28:15	Teyiba Erkesso ETH 32:08
8 Apr	Paderborn 10km	Moses Kigen KEN 28:02	Peninah Arusei KEN 31:46
8 Apr	Paderborn HMar	Abel Kirui KEN 61:32	Beatrice Omwanza KEN 71:15
8 Apr	Tarsus HMar	Wilson Kiprotich KEN 62:05	Luminita Talpos ROM 72:29
9 Apr	Dongio 10km	Edwin Soi KEN 28:25	*Men only*
15 Apr	Caceres HMar	Zersenay Tadese ERI 61:26	*Men only*
15 Apr	Dublin 10km	Abraham Chebii KEN 28:47	Victoria Mitchell AUS 33:06
15 Apr	Vancouver 10km	Solomon Tsige ETH 29:22	Teyiba Erkesso ETH 32:05
29 Apr	Nice HMar	Isaac Kiplagat KEN 62:04	Anne Bererwe KEN 73:13
29 Apr	Würzburg 15km	Patrick Musyoki KEN 28:15	Peninah Arusei KEN 32:45
1 May	Marseille 10km	Edwin Soi KEN 28:01	Sylvia Kibet KEN 31:44
1 May	Puy-en-Velay 15km	Joseph Maregu KEN 44:16	Mary Keitany KEN 50:10
6 May	Berlin 25km	Patrick Musyoki KEN 1:14:22	Filomena Chepchirchir KEN 1:25:37
6 May	Edinburgh 10km	Hosea Macharinyang KEN 29:14	Jelena Prokopcuka LAT 32:53
6 May	Philadelphia 10M	Patrick Cheruiyot KEN 45:14*	Naomi Wangui KEN 53:43
6 May	Spokane 12km	John Korir KEN 34:18	Edna Kiplagat KEN 38:52
6 May	Toronto 10km (82m dh)	Stephen Koech KEN 27:47	Florence Jepkosgei KEN 31:42*
12 May	Göteborg HMar	Sylvester Kimeli KEN 64:03	K. Melkevik Otterbu NOR 72:38
13 May	Glasgow 10km	*Women only*	Vivian Cheruiyot KEN 32:08
13 May	Sendai HMar	Ombeche Mokamba KEN 62:29	Mizuki Noguchi JPN 68:54
19 May	New York City 10km	Dathan Ritzenhein USA 28:08*	*Men only*
20 May	Casablanca 10km	*Women only*	Zhor El Kamch MAR 31:56
20 May	Coban HMar	Duncan Kibet KEN 64:02	Neriah Asiba KEN 73:25
20 May	Manchester 10km	Micah Kogo KEN 27:21*	Jo Pavey GBR 31:47
20 May	Oviedo HMar	Akhoudaqui Mouhcine MAR 63:00	Malika Assahsah MAR 72:36
20 May	San Francisco 12km	John Korir KEN 34:43	Edna Kiplagat KEN 38:55
20 May	Santos 10km	Lawrence Kiprotich KEN 28:06	Ednalva da Silva BRA 33:12
20 May	Valencia HMar	Peter Korir KEN 62:24	Joan Aiyabei KEN 71:16
26 May	Ottawa 10km	Simon Bairu CAN 28:30	Catherine Ndereba KEN 33:02
27 May	Udine HMar ITA Ch	Salomon Rotich KEN 62:48	Nadia Ejjafini BRN 71:32
1 Jun	Clermont-Ferrand 10km	James Kibocha Theuri FRA 28:18	F. Klilech-Fauvel FRA 32:39
2 Jun	Albany 5km	*Women only*	Benita Johnson AUS 15:22
2 Jun	Groesbeek 10km	Jason Mbote KEN 27:52	Filomena Chepchirchir KEN 33:42
2 Jun	Neuss 10km/5km	Moses Kigen KEN 28:50	Ashu Kasim Rabu ETH 15:42
9 Jun	Green Bay 10km	John Korir KEN 28:09	Edna Kiplagat KEN 32:28
9 Jun	New York City 10km	*Women only*	Lornah Kiplagat NED 32:10
9 Jun	Zwolle HMar	Jason Mbote KEN 62:53	Filomena Chepchirchir KEN 74:06
10 Jun	Bern 5km	Women only	Aniko Kálovics HUN 16:16
10 Jun	Middletown 10km	Abdihakim Abdirahman USA 29:11	Yimenashu Taye ETH 33:21
10 Jun	Saltillo HMar	Duncan Kibet KEN 62:41	Elena Jiménez MEX 72:16
16 Jun	Languex 10km	Abdellah Falil MAR 27:56	Nadia Ejjafini BRN 32:39
16 Jun	Peoria 4M	John Korir KEN 17:54	Rehima Kedir ETH 20:27
17 Jun	Porto 15km	Peter Korir KEN 44:35	Tigist Tufa ETH 50:56
23 Jun	Ludwigshafen 10km	Jonathan Koilegei KEN 28:29	Caroline Chepkwony KEN 33:55
24 Jun	Heemskerk HMar	Charles Koech KEN 62:16	Soumiya el Abani MAR 75:37
30 Jun	Appingedam 10km	Abdellah Falil MAR 28:05	Genet Tetaneh ETH 33:26
1 Jul	Gold Coast HMar	Patrick Nyangelo TAN 63:00	Lisa Jane Weightman AUS 72:02
1 Jul	Durban HMar RSA Ch	Festus Langat KEN 62:11	Helalia Johannes NAM 71:15
1 Jul	London 10km	Stefano Baldini ITA 29:27	Hilda Kibet KEN 32:34
4 Jul	Atlanta 10km (dh)	Martin Irungu Mathathi KEN 28:01	Wude Ayelew ETH 31:44
4 Jul	Cedar Rapids 8km	Alene Emere Reta ETH 22:47	Magdalene Mukunzi KEN 26:11
8 Jul	Sapporo HMar	Mekubo Mogusu ETH 59:54	Mizuki Noguchi JPN 68:22
8 Jul	Utica 15km	Nicholas Kamakya KEN 43:51	Lidia Simon ROM 49:23
14 Jul	Kingsport 8km	Simon Ndirangu KEN 22:16	Ogla Kimaiyo KEN 25:52
15 Jul	London 10km	Ismael Kirui KEN 29:22	Hayley Yelling GBR 33:23
18 Jul	Voorthuizen 10km	Peter Kiprotich KEN 28:27	Peninah Arusei KEN 31:58
28 Jul	Moline 7M	Duncan Kibet KEN 32:15	Wude Ayelew ETH 36:57
29 Jul	Bogotá HMar (A)	Isaac Macharia KEN 63:38	Neriah Asiba KEN 76:07

29 Jul	Cardiff 10km	Francis Kibiwott KEN 28:36	Berhane Adere ETH 32:22
4 Aug	Cape Elizabeth 10km	Duncan Kibet KEN 27:52	Luminita Talpos ROM 32:21
5 Aug	New York City HMar	Haile Gebrselassie ETH 59:24	Hilda Kibet KEN 70:32
11 Aug	Stellenbosch 10km RSA Ch	Tshamano Setone RSA 28:47	Rene Kalmer RSA 32:28
12 Aug	Falmouth Heights 7M	Micah Kogo KEN 31:53	Catherine Ndereba KEN 36:31
12 Aug	Sydney 14km	Dickson Marwa TAN 41:10	Jessica Ruthe NZL 46:33
18 Aug	Amatrice 8.5km	Paul Kosgei KEN 24:11	Souad Aït Salem ALG 27:40
18 Aug	Parkersburg HMar	Alene Emere Reta ETH 62:39	Sharon Cherop KEN 72:26
19 Aug	San Diego HMar	Nelson Kiplagat KEN 64:25	Hiromi Ominami JPN 72:49
19 Aug	Sululta 20km ETH Ch (A)	Eshetu Gezahegn ETH 61:00	Bezunesh Bekele ETH 69:36
25 Aug	Flint 10M	Festus Langat KEN 47:11	Angelina Mutuka KEN 54:53
1 Sep	Lille HMar	Joseph Maregu KEN 59:45*	Mary Keitany KEN 68:43*
2 Sep	Bologna HMar	Daniel Kiprop Limo KEN 62:08	Vincenza Sicari ITA 71:36
2 Sep	Glasgow HMar	Isaac Macharia KEN 62:42	Peninah Arusei KEN 70:47
2 Sep	Tilburg 10M/10km	Wesley Langat KEN 46:11	Belaynesh Fikadu ETH 31:56
2 Sep	Virginia Beach HMar	Haron Toroitich KEN 62:20	Edna Kiplagat KEN 71:14
3 Sep	Park Forest 10M	Alene Emere Reta ETH 47:17	Leah Kiprono KEN 55:06
8 Sep	Praha 10km	Wilfred Taragon KEN 28:26	Irene Kwambai KEN 15:46
9 Sep	Bristol HMar	Tewodros Shiferaw ETH 63:01	Jane Muia KEN 70:26*
9 Sep	Hamburg 10km	Wilson Kipsang KEN 28:44	Anitha Kiptum KEN 32:11*
9 Sep	Pila HMar POL Ch	Michael Karonei KEN 63:25	Dorota Gruca POL 73:29
9 Sep	Rotterdam HMar	Evans Cheruiyot KEN 59:12	Berhane Adere ETH 71:11
9 Sep	Sheffield 10km	John Kibowen KEN 28:40	Benita Johnson AUS 32:55
16 Sep	Lisboa HMar	Emmanuel Mutai KEN 61:54	Bezunesh Bekele ETH 70:20
16 Sep	Philadelphia HMar	Julius Kibet KEN 62:02	P. Chepchumba KEN 68:45
16 Sep	Providence 5km	Simon Ndirangu KEN 13:46	Shalane Flanagan USA 15:26
23 Sep	Zaandam 10M	Zersenay Tadese ERI 45:52	Belaynesh Fikadu ETH 52:58
30 Sep	Milano 10km	David Chelule KEN 28:24	Nadia Ejjafini BRN 32:31
30 Sep	Remich HMar	Wilson Chebet KEN 60:13	Mary Ptikany KEN 70:13
30 Sep	South Shields HMar	Martin Lel KEN 60:10	Kara Goucher USA 66:57
30 Sep	Versailles 16.3k	Joseph Maregu KEN 46:38*	Mary Keitany KEN 68:43
7 Oct	Boston HMar	Thomas Nyariki KEN 62:20*	Edna Kiplagat KEN 73:36
7 Oct	Breda HMar	Jonathan Maiyo KEN 62:26	Emily Kimuria KEN 73:17
7 Oct	Utrecht 10km	Mark Tanui KEN 27:52	Lornah Kiplagat KEN 32:05
8 Oct	Boston 10km USA Ch	*Women only*	Deena Kastor USA 32:01
21 Oct	Madrid 10km	Kidane Tadesse ERI 28:51	Joan Aiyabei KEN 32:56
28 Oct	Morlaix 10km (dh)	Ruben Indidongo FRA 27:48	Esther Maina KEN 33:06
28 Oct	New Delhi HMar	Dieudonné Disi RWA 60:43	Derebe Alemu ETH 70:30
28 Oct	Portsmouth 10M	Luke Kibet KEN 47:31	Rose Cheruiyot KEN 53:44
4 Nov	Saint-Denis HMar	Ezekier Nizgimana TAN 62:29	Anne Bererwe KEN 72:58
11 Nov	Behobia HMar	José Manuel Martínez ESP 61:48	Sarah Kerubo KEN 69:26
11 Nov	Roanoke Island HMar	Samuel Kosgei KEN 62:34	Zemedkun Belaynesh ETH 73:55*
18 Nov	Boulogne-Billancourt HMar	Gideon Mitei KEN 62:37	Lydia Njeri KEN 73:27
18 Nov	Madrid 10km	Silas Kipruto KEN 28:00	Pamela Pertum KEN 32:30
18 Nov	Marseille 10km	Justus Kipchirchir KEN 28:39	Martha Komu KEN 33:18
18 Nov	Nijmegen 15km	Sileshi Sihine ETH 42:24	Bizunesh Bekele ETH 47:36
25 Nov	Kobe HMar	**Women only**	Julia Mombi KEN 69:45
2 Dec	Belo Horizonte 17.8km	Franck de Almeida BRA 53:13	Nancy Kipron KEN 62:41
2 Dec	Heerenberg 15km	Haile Gebrselassie ETH 42:36*	Derebe Alemu ETH 48:50
8 Dec	Nyeri HMar	Nathan Kosgei KEN 61:57*	S. Chemtai Kimaiyo KEN 73:55*
9 Dec	Kosa 10M	John Kariuki KEN 45:24	*Men only*
16 Dec	Sevilla HMar	Silas Sang KEN 60:34*	Hellen Cherono KEN 71:29
23 Dec	Okayama HMar	*Women only*	Evelyne Kimwei KEN 69:20
30 Dec	Houilles 10km	Micah Kogo KEN 27:56	Nadia Ejjafini BRN 32:10*
31 Dec	Bolzano 10km	Edwin Soi KEN 28:51	Sylvia Kibet KEN 16:02
31 Dec	Lisboa 10km	Moses Masai KEN 28:25	Jelena Prokopcuka LAT 33:16
31 Dec	Madrid 10km (55m dh)	Kiprono Menjo KEN 28:35	Vivian Cheruiyot KEN 31:50
31 Dec	São Paulo 15km	Robert Kipkoech Cheruiyot KEN 45:57	Alice Timbilil KEN 53:07
31 Dec	Trier 8km/5km	Moses Kipsiro UGA 22:30	Sabrina Mockenhaupt GER 16:01

*A = altitude > 1000 m, * = course record, WR = world record, WMR = world master's record*

2007 WORLD MARATHON REVIEW

By David E Martin

KENYAN MARATHON RUNNERS continue to impress the world with both their numbers and their performance quality, especially the men. Of the 1211 sub-2:20:00 performances by men that occurred in 2007, 559 of them (46%) belonged to Kenyans. Runner-up Ethiopia accounted for only 94 such efforts, with 85 for Japan. The accompanying list of marathon winners from around the world reveals these trends in top-level participation in a slightly different way – Kenyan men won 62% of the top races! Even their arch-rival Ethiopia has only 10 victories. On the women's side, Kenyan women are following in the footsteps of their male counterparts with a steady increase in victories – 28 on this accompanying list, compared to 45 last year. Following closely behind the Kenyan women to the victory stand are Ethiopia and Russia – with respectively 20 and 16 victories listed here.

Last year readers were introduced to a system for evaluating the strength of a nation's participation in the marathon. 100 points are awarded to the fastest performance by the 100 quickest marathon athletes worldwide, the 100th fastest athlete's performance is worth 1 point, and equal points are awarded to identical times in between. Sorting the 100 performances by nation, and then summing the totals, creates a list showing the relative strength of each marathoning nation. As seen in the table, from yet another perspective, the dominance of Kenya in 2007 over other countries is evident. Thus, it was not surprising that Kenya's influence would extend to the highest levels of competition – Catherine Ndereba and Luke Kibet were the gold medalists at the 2007 Osaka World Championships.

Nearly a quarter century has passed since the decision to include a women's marathon on the Olympic program. In that short span their increase in quality and depth of participation has been spectacular. An interesting statistical and physiological observation is evident when one examines the change in size of these athletes over time. Table Two compares the mean height and weight data for the top marathoners of 1984 and 2007 as reported in the respective ATFS Annuals. Notice that the men have not changed in dimensions significantly: they still average 1.70 cm in height and weigh c.60 kg. However, the women now average 9 cm less in height and 3 kg less in weight compared to 1984. Successful endurance running is all about increasing economy of motion and minimizing energy output with a quickening pace: the smaller the athlete, the less energy required to go the distance. It is thus also interesting that the present marathon world-record-holders do not "fit the mold." Thus, Paula Radcliffe is taller and heavier than the bulk of her challengers, while Haile Gebrselassie is smaller than the mean of his group.

Over the past few years, concern has been raised regarding just how large a marathon can become before failure occurs in provision of required logistical support. Excessive increases in number of participants can be managed using on-line computerized data entry systems that cease to function once a limit has been reached. Careful coordination of 'people power' - the mass of volunteers working at aid stations and traffic intersections – together with those under the purview of local governments is crucial. Presently the New York City Marathon is consistently the world's largest marathon race, with greater than 95% of its starters finishing, and finish totals averaging about 37,450. However, it was seen in 2007 that while careful race planning is the general rule, and that the mechanics of race preparation are well-organized, Mother Nature can wreak catastrophic havoc in mass participation events in ways that may cause a re-evaluation of estimates of appropriate size of such events. An unexpected early-spring heat wave In Europe during the second week of April raised temperatures to the low-to-mid-20s Celsius. Neither race personnel nor athletes could cope with the enormous increase in fluid intake needed to provide sweat for cooling. Rotterdam was most severely affected, and after 3½ hours stopped

Change in Mean Height & Weight of Top Marathoners Over 24 Years

	HEIGHT		*WEIGHT*
Men			
1984	170	1984	60
2007	172	2007	58
Gebrselassie	164		53
Women	cm.		kg.
1984	170	1984	51
2007	161	2007	48
Radcliffe	175		54

its race entirely. The heat was also oppressive in Paris with its field of >25,000. Even worse, during the fall (autumn) marathon season, the Midwestern USA was similarly struck with a heat wave early in October – races at Chicago and Minneapolis-St. Paul were most affected. In a fashion similar to Rotterdam, Chicago shut down its race after 3 hours and 50 minutes: 35,867 had started the event but there were only 24,933 recorded finishers. Perhaps the biggest factor in the inability to manage these events adequately was the enormous increase in fluid requirements. Runners can sweat one to two liters of water per hour, and if it is a hot day, it becomes impossible to provide sufficient water in cups and bottles at aid stations – plus water in bottles to splash on body parts.

At the front end of these races, performances seemed less affected, probably because the athletes were out on the course for a shorter period, and their enormous quantities of training raised their fluid volume for sweat production. Also, they have special drink bottles placed on tables to supplement the standard fluid fare. Not all races experienced unfortunate weather, however. However, at Berlin one week before the heat wave arrived, Haile Gebrselassie found conditions so perfect that he gathered together pacemakers Rodgers Rop and Eshetu Wondimu for a world record attempt, to better Paul Tergat's 2:04:55 set on this same course in 2003. Their 5 km splits through the first 30 km (1:28:56) ranged from 14:44 to 14:55, with a halfway split of 1:02:29. The weather was still overcast and cool (14-16°C), when Geb picked up the pace and soon found himself alone. His amazing second-half split of 1:01:57 allowed him to take 29 seconds off of Tergat's previous world mark and join Abebe Bikila and Belayneh Dinsamo as Ethiopia's third marathon world record-holder. The terrible heat of the upcoming Beijing Olympic marathon will preclude fast racing, but Geb's great desire is to join Bikila, Mamo Wolde, and Fatuma Roba as an Olympic marathon gold medalist representing Ethiopia. Stay tuned!

Relative Importance of Marathoning Nations Based on their 100 Fastest Athlete Best Performances

	MEN		*WOMEN*		*TOTAL*	
NAT	*No.*	*Pts*	*No.*	*Pts*	*No.*	*Points*
KEN	65	3156	16	871	81	4027
JPN	5	196	17	865	22	1061
ETH	8	431	10	515	18	946
CHN	2	129	9	601	11	730
RUS	1	55	11	495	12	550
PRK	–	–	6	314	6	314
MAR	3	229	–	–	3	229
GBR	1	6	4	217	5	223
GER	–	–	4	210	4	210
NED	1	66	1	90	2	156
ROM	–	–	2	134	2	134
ITA	2	14	3	115	5	129
QAT	2	129	–	–	2	129
KOR	1	75	1	40	2	115
HUN	–	–	2	92	2	92
UKR	1	88	–	–	1	88
ALG	–	–	1	87	1	87
ERI	1	86	–	–	1	86
RSA	2	83	–	–	2	83
LAT	–	–	1	82	1	82

WINNERS OF 2007 MARATHONS

4 Jan	Tiberias	Musir Salem Jawher BRN	2:13:14	Nili Avramski ISR	2:39:26
12 Jan	Dubai	William Todoo Rotich KEN	2:09:53	Magarsa Askale Tafa ETH	2:27:19
14 Jan	Houston	Katera Feyissa Tusse ETH	2:11:39	Dire Tune Arissi ETH	2:26:52
14 Jan	Lahore	Edrees Kamal Eisa QAT	2:15:26	Merima Denboba ETH	2:32:54
14 Jan	Tempe	Terife Yae ETH	2:14:13	Zekiros Adanech ETH	2:31:43
21 Jan	Mumbai	John Ekiru Kelai KEN	2:12:27	Yang Fengxia CHN	2:36:16
28 Jan	Marrakech	Samuel Chumba KEN	2:11:43	Alina Gherasim ROM	2:39:52
28 Jan	Miami	Teshome Gelana ETH	2:17:51	Ramilya Burangulova RUS	2:40:25
28 Jan	Osaka	*Women only*		Yumiko Hara JPN	2:23:48
4 Feb	Beppu	Atsushi Fujita JPN	2:10:23	*Men only*	
10 Feb	Port Elizabeth NC	George Mofokeng RSA	2:13:50	Poppy Mlambo RSA	2:39:19
11 Feb	Sevilla	Sylvester Kipyego Chebee KEN	2:15:16	Faustina Maria Ramos ESP	2:45:34
18 Feb	Austin (dh)	Jynocel Basweti KEN	2:14:02	Zebenaye Moges ETH	2:39:46
18 Feb	Nobeoka	Shinji Tateishi JPN	2:15:48	*Men only*	
18 Feb	Tokyo	Daniel Njenga KEN	2:09:45	Hitomi Niiya JPN	2:31:02
18 Feb	Valencia	Samson Loywapet KEN	2:12:04	Zinash Alemu ETH	2:39:08

25 Feb	Busseto	Joshua Kipchumba Rop KEN	2:16:30	Ilaria Bianchi ITA	2:37:07
4 Mar	Barcelona	Johnstone Chebii KEN	2:12:04	Kristijna Loonen NED	2:42:03
4 Mar	Hong Kong	Stephen Loruo Kamar KEN	2:17:03	Rose Kerubo Nyangacha KEN	2:38:19
4 Mar	Los Angeles	Fred Mogaka Tumbo KEN	2:17:14	Ramilya Burangulova RUS	2:37:54
4 Mar	Moshi (A)	Andreas Sylvin TAN	2:18:47	Banuelia Briyton TAN	2:42:10
4 Mar	Otsu	Samson Ramadhani TAN	2:10:43	*Men only*	
4 Mar	Torreón	Pablo Olmedo MEX	2:11:34	Maria Elena Valencia MEX	2:31:16
11 Mar	Nagoya	*Women only*		Yasuko Hashimoto JPN	2:28:49
18 Mar	Kuala Lumpur	Cyprian Kiogara KEN	2:17:38	Winfridah Nyasikera KEN	2:48:09
18 Mar	Roma	Elias Kemboi Chelimo KEN	2:09:36	Souad Aït Salem ALG	2:25:08
18 Mar	Seoul	Lee Bong-ju KOR	2:08:04	Wei Yanan CHN	2:23:12
25 Mar	Treviso (dh)	Benjamin Pseret KEN	2:10:18	Shitaye Gemechu ETH	2:28:03
31 Mar	Xiamen NC	Li Zhuhong CHN	2:13:17	Zhu Xiaolin CHN	2:26:08
1 Apr	Jeonju	Kil Kyong-sun KOR	2:15:57	Chang Jin-sook KOR	2:32:14
1 Apr	Thessaloniki	David Kimutai Kosgei KEN	2:13:49	Elizabeth Chemweno KEN	2:36:05
1 Apr	Zürich	Viktor Röthlin SUI	2:08:20	Nina Podnebesnova RUS	2:37:00
9 Apr	Pyongyang	Pak Song-chol PRK	2:12:41	Jong Yong-ok PRK	2:26:02
9 Apr	Utrecht	Mariko Kiplagat KEN	2:11:16	Joanna Gront POL	2:47:11
15 Apr	Debno	Pawel Ochal POL	2:15:31	Natalya Kulesh BLR	2:40:46
15 Apr	Linz	Oleksandr Kuzin UKR	2:07:33	Eva Maria Gradwohl AUT	2:37:36
15 Apr	Nagano	Nephat Kinyanjui KEN	2:13:32	Alevtina Ivanova RUS	2:27:49
15 Apr	Paris	Mubarak Hassan Shami QAT	2:07:19	Magarsa Askale Tafa ETH	2:25:07
15 Apr	Rotterdam	Joshua Chelanga KEN	2:08:21	Hiromi Ominami JPN	2:26:37
15 Apr	Torino	Philemon Kirwa Tarbei KEN	2:10:24	Aniko Kálovics HUN	2:29:24
16 Apr	Boston (dh)	Robert K. Cheruiyot KEN	2:14:13	Lidiya Grigoryeva RUS	2:29:18
21 Apr	Beograd	John Katio Maluni KEN	2:11:53	Olivera Jevtic SRB	2:35:46
22 Apr	Bonn	David Kiplagat Kuino KEN	2:14:05	Christiane Dobmeier GER	2:47:07
22 Apr	Enschede	Thomson Cherogony KEN	2:11:35	Ingrid Prigge NED	2:42:31
22 Apr	London	Martin Lel KEN	2:07:41	Zhou Chunxiu CHN	2:20:38
22 Apr	Madrid	Jonathan Kipkosgei Kibet KEN	2:12:42	Pauline Chepkorir KEN	2:48:46
22 Apr	Padova	Paul Kipkemei Kogo KEN	2:10:39	Vincenza Sicari ITA	2:30:35
28 Apr	Nashville	Simon Wangai KEN	2:13:52	Olena Shurhno UKR	2:37:52
29 Apr	Brescia	Philemon Boit KEN	2:13:05	Muliye Lemma Gurma ETH	2:45:36
29 Apr	Hamburg	Rodgers Rop KEN	2:07:32	Ayelech Worku ETH	2:29:14
29 Apr	Wien	Luke Kibet KEN	2:10:07	Luminita Talpos ROM	2:32:21
6 May	Düsseldorf	Bellor Yator KEN	2:09:48	Luminita Zaituc GER	2:29:37
6 May	Génève	Tesfaye Eticha ETH	2:18:37	Elfenesh Menaku ETH	2:43:58
6 May	Hannover	Daniel Muruki Mbogo KEN	2:14:46	Monica Njeru KEN	2:46:19
6 May	Johannesburg (A)	Portipher Dombojena ZIM	2:16:14	Simona Staicu HUN	2:38:34
6 May	Kraków	Matthew Kosgei KEN	2:18:16	Kateryna Stesenko UKR	2:39:08
6 May	Mainz	Andriy Naumov UKR	2:14:04	Ilona Pfeiffer GER	2:46:13
6 May	Trieste	Ottaviano Andriani ITA	2:10:57	Anne Kosgei KEN	2:33:14
6 May	Vancouver	Thomas Omwenga KEN	2:25:23	Claudia Camargo ARG	2:35:50
6 May	Vitoria NC	Oscar Martínez ESP	2:14:55	Maria Teresa Pulido ESP	2:36:17
6 May	Zhengzhou	Elijah Chemwolo Mutai KEN	2:13:20	Bai Xue CHN	2:33:51
7 May	Belfast	John Mutai Kipyator KEN	2:16:24	Marashet Jimma ETH	2:41:38
13 May	Essen	Jonathan Keiyo KEN	2:13:31	Mary Ptikany KEN	2:30:05
13 May	Praha	Helder Ornelas POR	2:11:49	Nailya Yulamanova RUS	2:33:10
13 May	Salzburg	Michael Rotich KEN	2:18:41	Eva Maria Gradwohl AUT	2:46:32
13 May	Vise Maastricht	Eric Gerome BEL	2:17:48	Inge van Bergen BEL	2:47:33
20 May	Luxembourg	Alex Malinga UGA	2:17:17	Ruth Kutol Kipkoech KEN	2:41:26
20 May	Riga	Johnstone K. Changwony KEN	2:18:30	Lyudmila Rodina LAT	2:50:07
27 May	Mombasa	Peter Kemboi KEN	2:09:21	Juliet Jepchirchir KEN	2:52:49
27 May	Ottawa	David Cheruiyot KEN	2:10:35	Lioudmila Kortchaguina CAN	2:31:57
3 Jun	San Diego (dh)	Daniel Kipkoech Yego KEN	2:09:04	Hellen Jemaiyo Kimutai KEN	2:32:40
3 Jun	São Paulo	Reuben C. Mutumwo KEN	2:16:05	Jacqueline Jerotich Chebor KEN	2:40:12
9 Jun	Mont Saint-Michel	Mark Saina KEN	2:15:21	Elizabeth Chemweno KEN	2:39:20
9 Jun	Stockholm	Philip Bandawe ZIM	2:20:56	Kirsten Melkevik Otterbu NOR	2:37:03
10 Jun	Addis Ababa (A)	Tsegaye Tadesse ETH	2:15:53	Tigist Abedi ETH	2:43:48
10 Jun	Caen	Jonathan Kipkoskei Kibet KEN	2:15:36	Alina Gherasim ROM	2:42:22

16 Jun	Cheboksary NC	Aleksey Sokolov RUS	2:15:52	Deana Usanova RUS	2:45:27
16 Jun	Duluth	Wesley Ngetich Kimutai KEN	2:15:55	Mary Akor USA	2:35:40
17 Jun	Dalian	Zhang Wenliang CHN	2:19:01	Jiang Yuanyuan CHN	2:41:01
24 Jun	Rio de Janeiro	Elson Alex Gracioli BRA	2:18:31	Marily dos Santos BRA	2:42:18
24 Jun	San Luis Potosi (A)	Edilberto Mendez MEX	2:18:14	Adriana Sánchez MEX	2:37:37
1 Jul	Gold Coast	Toyokazu Nishimura JPN	2:20:07	Ayumi Hayashi JPN	2:33:22
4 Aug	Omsk	Sergey Lukin RUS	2:18:39	Iraida Pudorkina RUS	2:39:00
26 Aug	Ciudad de México (A)	Hilary Kipchirchir KEN	2:16:06	Anne Kibor Jelagat KEN	2:38:26
9 Sep	Sapporo	Julius Gitahi KEN	2:17:26	Yuri Kano JPN	2:30:43
16 Sep	Cape Town	Mluleki Nobanda RSA	2:14:46	Samukeliso Moyo ZIM	2:41:30
16 Sep	Groningen	Mohamed Ikoko Msandeki KEN	2:14:22	Rimma Pushkina RUS	2:45:52
16 Sep	Karlsruhe	Ben Kimutai Kimwole KEN	2:14:37	Irene Cherop KEN	2:39:04
23 Sep	Odense	Daniel Kiprugut KEN	2:15:54	Irina Songerlainen RUS	2:42:17
23 Sep	Sydney	Julius Maritim KEN	2:14:37	Naoko Tsuchiya JPN	2:43:09
23 Sep	Warszawa	Pawel Ochal POL	2:12:21	Valentyna Poltavska UKR	2:40:18
30 Sep	Berlin	Haile Gebrselassie ETH	2:04:26	Getenesh Wami ETH	2:23:17
30 Sep	Toronto	John Ekiru Kelai KEN	2:09:30	Asha Gigi ETH	2:33:16
30 Sep	Zaragoza	Peter Korir KEN	2:12:31	Elena Moreno ESP	2:37:21
6 Oct	St. Paul	Mykola Antonenko UKR	2:13:54	Svetlana Ponomarenko RUS	2:34:09
7 Oct	Chicago	Patrick Ivuti KEN	2:11:11	Berhane Adere ETH	2:33:49
7 Oct	Köln	Daniel Kiprugut Too KEN	2:11:05	Sabrina Mockenhaupt GER	2:29:33
7 Oct	Kosice	William Biama KEN	2:09:53	Natalya Kulesh BLR	2:34:50
13 Oct	Baltimore	John Thuo Itati KEN	2:16:24	Gladys Asiba KEN	2:36:27
13 Oct	Hartford	Mohammed Awol ETH	2:17:15	Tetyana Belovol UKR	2:42:19
14 Oct	Bruxelles	Jonathan Kiptoo Yego KEN	2:12:16	Rael Jepyator Kimaiyo KEN	2:41:20
14 Oct	Eindhoven	Philip Singoei KEN	2:07:57	Lydia Kurgat KEN	2:39:27
14 Oct	Essen	Stefan Koch GER	2:17:17	Romy Spitzmueller GER	2:41:49
14 Oct	Graz	Michael Rotich KEN	2:14:20	Peris Poywo KEN	2:55:03
14 Oct	Poznan	Paul Tangus KEN	2:16:24	Ewa Brych Pajak POL	2:39:59
21 Oct	Amsterdam	John Emmanuel Mutai KEN	2:06:29	Magdalene Chemjor KEN	2:28:16
21 Oct	Beijing	Nephat Kinyanjui KEN	2:08:09	Chen Rong CHN	2:27:05
21 Oct	Carpi (dh)	Noah Kiplagat Serem KEN	2:11:18	Aniko Kálovics HUN	2:28:17
21 Oct	Detroit	Christopher Kiprotich KEN	2:15:15	Anzhelika Averkova UKR	2:34:50
21 Oct	Dresden	Leonid Shvetsov RUS	2:16:19	Krystyna Kuta POL	2:41:54
21 Oct	Gyeongju	Edwin Komen KEN	2:09:44	Youn Sun-sook KOR	2:35:53
21 Oct	Lausanne	William Kwambai KEN	2:12:18	Zhanna Malkova RUS	2:47:11
21 Oct	Porto	Edwin Kimutai KEN	2:15:12	Marisa Barros POR	2:31:31
21 Oct	Reims	David Kemboi Kiyeng KEN	2:09:08	Martha Komu KEN	2:32:48
28 Oct	Chunchon	Victor Mangusho KEN	2:14:01	Choi Kyung-hee KOR	2:35:25
28 Oct	Frankfurt	Wilfred Kigen KEN	2:07:58	Melanie Kraus GER	2:28:56
28 Oct	Guadalajara (A)	Cornelius Lel KEN	2:15:32	Viola Bor KEN	2:38:20
28 Oct	Istanbul	David Cheruiyot KEN	2:11:00	Atsede Bayisa Tesema ETH	2:29:08
28 Oct	Ljubljana	Oleksandr Sitkovskyy UKR	2:12:49	Tetyana Filonyuk UKR	2:34:58
28 Oct	Nairobi (A)	John Njoroge Thuita KEN	2:15:50	Rose Cheshire Jepkosgei KEN	2:44:14
28 Oct	Venezia	Jonathan Kosgei KEN	2:12:27	Linah Cheruiyot KEN	2:27:02
29 Oct	Dublin	Aleksey Sokolov RUS	2:09:07	Alina Ivanova RUS	2:29:20
3 Nov	New York	Ryan Hall USA	2:09:02	*USA Men's Olympic Trial*	
4 Nov	Athína	Benjamin Kiprotich Korir KEN	2:14:40	Svetlana Ponomarenko RUS	2:33:19
4 Nov	Buenos Aires	Juan Carlos Cardona COL	2:16:07	Sirlene Souza de Pinho BRA	2:39:08
4 Nov	New York	Martin Lel KEN	2:09:04	Paula Radcliffe GBR	2:23:09
4 Nov	Seoul	Joshua Chelanga KEN	2:08:14	Lee Eun-jung KOR	2:29:32
4 Nov	Soweto	Teboho Sello LES	2:18:51	Mamorallo Tjoka LES	2:47:57
11 Nov	Hangzhou	Eric Kiptoon KEN	2:18:00	Xie Sainan CHN	2:33:08
11 Nov	Ravenna	Julius Kirwa Choge KEN	2:14:05	Francesca Marin ITA	2:51:53
18 Nov	Bangkok	John Chirchir Tubei KEN	2:18:27	Fridah Chepkite Lodepa KEN	2:51:42
18 Nov	Beirut	Tamrat Elanso ETH	2:19:46	Adaneche Beyene Jemilu ETH	2:41:24
18 Nov	Tokyo	*Women only*		Mizuki Noguchi JPN	2:21:37
25 Nov	Firenze	Paul Kipkemboi Ngeny KEN	2:12:50	Vincenza Sicari ITA	2:33:14
25 Nov	San Sebastián	Abdelhadi El Mouaziz MAR	2:12:45	Kristijna Loonen NED	2:47:12
25 Nov	Shanghai	Samuel Tum KEN	2:13:01	Lidia Simon ROM	2:29:28

26 Nov	La Rochelle	Johnstone Chebii KEN	2:14:17	Flora Kandie KEN	2:37:13
1 Dec	Memphis	Genna Tufa ETH	2:17:38	Atalech Ketema ETH	2:43:44
2 Dec	Fukuoka	Samuel Wanjiru KEN	2:06:39	*Men only*	
2 Dec	Las Vegas	Christopher Cheboiboch KEN	2:16:49	Sylvia Skvortsova RUS	2:29:01
2 Dec	Macau	Ri Kum-song PRK	2:17:40	Pyo Un-suk PRK	2:38:27
2 Dec	Mazatlán	Robert Onyancha KEN	2:19:50	Lucy Njeri KEN	2:37:07
2 Dec	Milano	Evans Cheruiyot KEN	2:09:16	Pamela Chepchumba KEN	2:25:36
2 Dec	Sacramento	Laban Moiben KEN	2:14:31	Wioletta Kryza POL	2:39:20
2 Dec	Singapore	Elijah Mbogo KEN	2:14:23	Alem Ashebir ETH	2:37:08
9 Dec	Dallas	James Koskei KEN	2:15:09	Emily Samoei KEN	2:35:25
9 Dec	Hofu	Kazuya Nakamori JPN	2:15:40	*Men only*	
9 Dec	Reggio Emilia	Benazzouz Slimani MAR	2:17:28	Stefania Benedetti ITA	2:35:28
10 Dec	Honolulu	Ambesse Tolossa ETH	2:17:26	Alevtina Biktimirova RUS	2:33:07
16 Dec	Monterrey	Christopher Toroitich KEN	2:13:33	Karina Pérez MEX	2:33:48
16 Dec	Taipei	Hillary Bett KEN	2:17:09	Tabitha Tsatsa ZIM	2:33:01

A = altitude over 1000m, (dh) *= downslope > 1 m/km. See also World and Pan-American Championships*

Review of Ultrarunning 2007

by Andy Milroy

THE PROMISE OF greater African involvement in standard ultras did not materialise in 2007 – instead the Japanese continued their advance, and Russians continued to provide the main opposition. Japan won three of the four national team titles contested in World ultra events, and were second in the other. Their strength in distance running is based in part on their long tradition within the sport, but it is also due to their systematic development programmes and support for distance running which is lacking in much of the rest of the world. There are well over 10,000 Japanese ultrarunners, numerous ultra events and several 100km races with over a thousand entrants.

Japan clearly led the way at 100km with five performances in the top seven men's performances, and four of the top five women's. Thirty year-old Shinichi Watanabe ran the fastest time of the year in winning the World 100km at Winschoten, eclipsing his previous top ranked mark set on the potentially aided Lake Saroma course earlier. His fellow countryman, Kenji Nakanishi, was his closest opposition in both races. The European Championship was incorporated in the World 100km, and three Russians. Oleg Kharitonov, Igor Tyazhkorob and Aleksey Izmaylov, took the medals by finishing 3-4-5. Japan beat Russia for the team title by just under ten minutes, but both were well clear of all other opposition. France took European silver medals.

The picture was similar in the women's event, in which Norimi Sakurai was the dominant force. She too had run the fastest time prior to the World 100km at Yubetsu, Lake Saroma, but her 7:00:27 at Winschoten was the fastest ever performance by a woman on a loop course. Laurence Klein (Fricotteaux) of France managed to split her from her teammate Hiroko Sho, who had run the second fastest time of the year at Yubetsu. The first Russian was 4th-placed Marina Myshlyanova, but the Russian 100km women seem to focus their efforts on the Comrades, and for a number of years we have not seen their true strength in the World 100km. Japan made it a team double as they had three women under eight hours (two under 7:30). The French, led by Fricotteaux, the European champion, took second place and the European team title from Germany.

Watanabe and Sakurai were clearly the top 100km runners, and with the European and World events being held simultaneously, there was little opportunity for runners to shine elsewhere. Grigoriy Murzin, the former world champion, was one of the few and his 6:39:22 at Bezana in Spain made him the fourth best performer of the year.

At 24 Hours Ryoichi Sekiya dominated, winning the World 24 Hour with 263km, then later in the year in Taiwan pulling out to 275km, some 18km better than the next performer. With Masayuki Otaki coming third in the World 24, there was a strong Japanese presence in the other championship event. The sole African presence was Mohamed Magroun, the former Tunisian who now competes for France, who took second place. Russians dominated the European 24 Hour track championships in Madrid as 39 year-old Anatoliy Kruglikov covered 257km and Vladimir Bychkov 251km for second. Spaniard José Luis Posado took the bronze on home territory with 247km.

Last year a Japanese took the women's world 24 hour title, but this year the Russians came back in force. Lyudmila Kalinina won with 236.848km from France's Brigitte Bec, with another Russian Galina Yeremina third; and in the European track championships in Madrid, Kalinina again emerged as winner with 233.307 km. Second in that race was Italian Monica Casiraghi (217km) and third Rosario Muñoz who ran 210km on home soil. Last year's world champion, Sumie Inagaki JPN ran 232km in Taipei and a new runner to be reckoned with, Michaela Dimitriadu CZE, ran 232km at Kladno. Japan took the World men's team title from France and Germany, and Russia took the women's team title from Japan and France.

There was a renaissance of the 48 Hour event with four men over 400km, the leading performer being once again a Japanese, Masayuki Otaki, with 426.448km on the track at Surgères in France. There were new world bests on the road from Germany's Wolfgang Schwerk 420.00km, and indoors 426.178km by Ireland's Tony Mangan. Kenji Okiyama of Japan was the fourth runner over 400km, indoors behind Mangan. The top women's 48 Hour event was on the track at Surgères where Russians Galina Yeremina and Irina Koval took the top two slots with 367.336km and 355.876 from Michaela Dimitriadu 353.161km.

The 6 Day event recovered sharply in 2007 with five races held world wide. Wolfgang Schwerk of Germany dominated with the top two marks of the year, running 1010.080km on the track at Erkrath in Germany and 936km in Athens. Only Yiannis Kouros has run further in modern times. Cornelia Bullig (740,000) and Martina Hausmann (715.430) of Germany were the top two women with AUS/GBR Catherine Cunningham running 712.939 in New York. Second at Athens behind Schwerk was Katsuhiro Tanaka JPN 784km, and Hiroko Okiyama set a Japanese women's record of 696km when third in Athens behind Bullig and Hausmann with Lin Mong-Chi TPE fourth with 613km. Such Asian success is a probable indication for the future; remember that Sumie Inagaki JPN ran a world track best for 48 Hours last year.

The longest event of the year on a certifed course was the 3100 miler in New York, won by Pekka Aalto of Finland in 43 days 4:26:32; he ran under 14 days for the first 1000 miles, the best performance at that distance in 2007.

History and tradition also has a great attraction for ultrarunners with two classic point-to-point events. There was a new record for the down course at the 90km Comrades Marathon from Pietermaritzburg to Durban as Russian Leonid Shvetsov ran 5:20:49 well clear of Grigoriy Murzin RUS 5:30:20, and the first South African, Mncedisi Mkhize 5:32:58. With runners from Lesotho and Zimbabwe and with five South Africans in the top ten, the Comrades shows what a potential impact Africans could make on the 100km. Female Russian strength in depth was shown as the Nurgaliyeva twins once again dominated the women's Comrades race – Olesya winning in 6:10:11 from Yelena 6:10:40 – and with Madina Biktagirova, Marina Myshlyanova and Alena Vinitskaya 3rd, 5th and 6th (4th was South African Farwa Mentoor), but regrettably this was not on show at the World 100km.

The 146km Spartathlon from Athens to Sparta was won for the second year running by American Scott Jurek, some twenty minutes slower than in 2006, 23:12:14, followed by the Pole Piotr Kurylo in 24:29:41 and Valmir Nunes of Brazil 25:37:40. The first woman was the Japanese Akiko Sakamoto 31:09:24 from Brigitte Bec FRA (second in the World 24 Hours) 31:56:03 and Kimie Noto of Japan 32:11:05.

Another ultra permutation available is the stage race, with a specific distance to be covered each day. The 17-stage 1205km Deutschlandlauf across Germany was won by yet another Japanese, Hiroko Okiyama, in an elapsed time of 124:40:33 from Trond Sjavik 132:44:15 and the Swiss Jörg Knupfer third 139:29:11. The first woman was Susanne Mahlstedt in 166:22:40. The Trans-Gaule 18 day/1050km stage race across France was won by the Swiss Martin Wagen in an elapsed time of 103:19:42, from Jochen Hoschele (GER) 109:41:09 with Chen Ching-Hu of Taipei third in 113:45:16. The first woman was Elke Streicher of Germany in 123:37:44.

The virtual absence of African runners from standard ultras like the 100km gives some indication of what the world distance running scene would be like without the Kenyans, Ethiopians and other African nations. Runners from Russia, Japan, Korea and Taipei are filling the void. However the performance of the French national ultra squad shows what can be achieved by consistent, long-term federation national support for Ultrarunning. The Comrades offered some $180,000 US in total prize money in 2007, set to rise to 1.4 million Rand ($210,000) in 2008. If that level of prize money was available in 100km events, then it is likely that African runners would be tempted to move up to the event and potentially could change the present world ultra scene drastically.

IAAF WORLD CHAMPIONSHIPS 2007

Aug 25 – Sep 2, Osaka, Japan

STARS OF A splendid World Championships were the American athletes who each won three gold medals – Tyson Gay and Allyson Felix. There were no world records and only two championship records – from Gay at 200m and Yekaterina Volkova in the women's steeplechase – but world leading marks for 2007 were set in six men's and eight women's events and in many events the best ever qualifying marks or bests ever by place were recorded.

The clash between Gay and Asafa Powell at 100m was much touted as the most eagerly awaited one, but Gay blew away his Jamaican rival who once again tightened under pressure, and went on to win the 200m clearly before running very fast in the sprint relay even if there were bad baton changes at either end. The running of Felix is such an aesthetic delight. Her win at 200m was no surprise but she left a huge margin between herself and rivals such as Veronica Campbell and Sanya Richards. Then the timetabling of the relays on separate days made it easier for her to run both – first contributing a sharp second leg to the US 4 x 100m and then one of the greatest ever 400m legs for the 4 x 400m. Her 48.0 in taking the US team from fourth to first has been bettered only once in World Champs history by Jarmila Kratochvílová's 47.75 in 1983, but that was a different era. Jeremy Wariner was another top star, both for his 43.46 victory at 400m and for his amazing 43.10 final relay leg when out on his own to anchor the US relay team. Then there was Franka Dietzsch winning a third discus title on a record ninth appearance and Bernard Lagat's double at 1500m and 5000m.

The Championships were much affected by the very hot weather in Osaka. That helped most events but the distance runners suffered from the heat and high humidity. The walks and marathons started at 7-8 am, but even for these the lowest temperature was 25°C for the start of the 50k walk and in each it rose to 30°C plus. So the performances of many of the athletes, such as Nathan Deakes in the 50km walk, were truly remarkable. The Ethiopians Kenenisa Bekele and Tirunesh Dibaba showed special tenacity in retaining their 10,000m titles.

Sadly the Japanese team performed modestly and all too many of their athletes were way below par. The largest crowd (apart perhaps from the final day) of 35,000 came to watch that men's hammer, but generally attendances were disappointing, reflecting the lack of interest in the sport in Japan and their lack of potential medallists. Fortunately Reiko Tosa came through with a gutsy marathon bronze on the final day to prevent no medals for the host nation – although they had won the team gold in the men's marathon World Cup right at the start, this not counting in the medal table.

Medals and Points (8 for 1st to 1 for 8th)

66 nations placed athletes in top eight, 46 won medals, 22 won gold.

	Nation	G	S	B	Medals	Pts
1.	USA	14	4	8	26	249
2.	RUS	4	9	3	16	191
3.	KEN	5	3	5	13	123
4.	JAM	1	6	3	10	98
5.	GER	2	2	3	7	84
6.	GBR	1	1	3	5	61
7.	CHN	1	1	1	3	51
8.	ETH	3	1	-	4	44
9=	CUB	1	1	13		43
9=	POL	-	-	3	3	43
11.	BLR	1	1	1	3	39
12.	FRA	-	2	-	2	38
13.	ESP	-	1	2	3	34
14.	CZE	2	1	-	3	33
15=	ITA	-	2	1	3	30
15=	UKR	-	1	1	2	30
17.	SWE	1	-	-	1	29
18.	BAH	1	2	-	3	28
19.	JPN	-	-	1	1	25
20=	BRA	-	1	-	1	20
20=	SLO	-	1	-	1	20
22.	POR	1	-	-	1	19
23=	AUS	2	-	-	2	18
23=	CAN	-	2	-	2	18
23=	NOR	-	1	-	1	18
26.	BRN	1	1	-	2	16
27.	ROM	-	-	-	-	15
28=	GRE	-	-	1	1	14
28=	MAR	-	1	-	1	14
28=	TUR	-	1	-	1	14
31.	NZL	1	-	-	1	12

32= MEX, NED (1B), UGA (1B) 11; 35= BEL (1B), ERI 10; 37= DOM (1S), EST (1G), FIN (1G) 9; 41= CRO (1G), ECU (1G), HUN, KAZ (1B), LTU, AHO, PAN (1G) 8; 48= ALG, QAT (1S), SUI (1B) 7; 51= CYP, IRL, NGR, SRI, SVK, TUN 6; 57= BUL, LAT 5; 59. EGY 59; 60= IRI, IRN, KSA, SEN 2; 64= CAY, NAM, TRI 1.

Overall the final placings table for nations looked remarkably similar to that of 2005. Then the USA won 14 gold, 8 silver and 3 bronze with 248 points and here their tally was 14, 4, 8 and 249. Russia slipped a little from 7 gold and 218.5 points to 4 and 191 but were still clearly second while Kenya moved up to third with 123 points and five gold medals from 82 and 1 in 2005. All the top ten nations of 2005 were in the top 12 this time, being joined by Britain, up from 14th to 6th, and Poland, up from 12th to 9=. Britain's score, headed by the remarkable 1-2 in the women's 400m, was despite only two (6th places) by men in individual events.

There were clean sweeps of the medals in three events: men's 400m from the USA, steeplechase from Kenya and women's long jump from Russia. Preliminary figures indicate that about 1980 athletes, and 200 IAAF federations took part.

Men

100 Metres (h, qf 25th, sf, F 26th -0.5)

AFTER NOBUHARU ASAHARA (10.14) had been fastest in round 1, Powell easing up after 60m, ran 10.01 from Atkins 10.02, and Gay won his race in 10.06 in the quarter-finals. Atkins won the first semi in 10.04 from Powell, who had been 2m clear before switching off the power, 10.08, and Gay, recovering from a slight stumble out of the blocks, ran 10.00 in the second. The final was held in 30°C heat on a lightning fast track, and but for a 0.5m headwind the world record might have been threatened. Powell (lane 4) got the better start and was well clear at halfway but Gay (lane 5) was never flustered and, when he drew level Powell "just panicked and tightened up". Gay went on to win in 9.85 and Powell admitted: "When I saw I wasn't in gold medal contention I gave up; I just stopped running." He was passed by his second cousin Atkins, who took second with a Bahamian record 9.91. Francis Obikwelu was disqualified for false starting in the first round, and only one American made the semi-finals as Mark Jelks was injured and J-Mee Samuels was only 5th in his qf in 10.29. For the first time eight different nations were represented in the final with Martina the first finalist at any event from Netherlands Antilles.

1. Tyson Gay USA	9.85
2. Derrick Atkins BAH	9.91
3. Asafa Powell JAM	9.96
4. Olusoji Fasuba NGR	10.07
5. Churandy Martina AHO	10.08
6. Marlon Devonish GBR	10.14
7. Matic Osovnikar SLO	10.23
8. Marc Burns TRI	10.29

Gay (0.143 reaction time) 10m splits of 1.90, 1.04, 0.92, 0.87, 0.86, 0.85 (6.44 at 60m), 0.84 (= 11.83mps/26.46mph), 0.85, 0.86, 0.86; Atkins (0.137) 1.90, 1.03, 0.94, 0.88, 0.87, 0.85 (6.47), 0.86, 0.85, 0.86, 0.87; Powell (0.145) 1.87, 1.04, 0.92, 0.88, 0.86, 0.85 (6.42), 0.86, 0.87, 0.88, 0.93.

200 Metres (h, qf 28th, sf 29th, F 30th -0.8)

GAY RAN THE sixth sub-19.80 run of his career to equal Michael Johnson's record tally and complete a superb 9.85/19.76 combination to emulate Maurice Greene's 1999 double of 9.80 & 19.90 and to break Johnson's 1995 championship record of 19.79. Goúsis reduced his pb from 20.43 to 20.11 for the fastest ever first round time in World Champs from Bolt 20.12, and in the second round Gay went even quicker at 20.08 ahead of Anderson's pb 20.13 with Bolt also winning in 20.13. The two semis were won by Bolt 20.03, just ahead of Spearmon, and Gay 20.00 from another pb 20.06 by Anderson. In the final, Bolt (15) held a narrow lead over Gay (14) but by halfway Gay led 10.13 to 10.15 and pulled away in the straight. Spearmon, who stumbled out of his blocks, was down at 100m in 10.32 but ran the fastest last 50 (4.97) to Gay's 5.01 and Bolt's 5.06 to take bronze 0.01 ahead of Martin's pb.

1. Tyson Gay USA	19.76*
2. Usain Bolt JAM	19.91
3. Wallace Spearmon USA	20.05
4. Rodney Martin USA	20.06
5. Churandy Martina AHO	20.28
6. Marvin Anderson JAM	20.28
7. Chris Williams JAM	20.57
8. Anástasios Goúsis GRE	20.75

400 Metres (h 28th, sf 29th, F 31st)

AFTER THEY HAD won their semi-finals in 44.34, 44.31 and 44.45 respectively, Wariner retained his title in 43.45, the fastest in the world since Michael Johnson's world record in 1999m and Merritt and Taylor gave the US a clean sweep. 100m splits showed Wariner 10.75, 20.92, 31.58 with his last 100m in 11.87; Merritt 10.77, 20.88, 31.68 and 12.28; Taylor 10.88, 20.90, 31.88 and 12.44. Along the finishing straight Wariner's strength and relaxation paid huge dividends as he finished over 4m clear of Merritt, who became the ninth member of the all-American sub-44 club. There was great depth as Brown (32.1 at 300) in fourth place broke the Bahamian record (as he had done in 2005) and in the semis there were national records by Djhone (44.46) and Wissman (44.56) while Christopher ran 44.47. Brown's 44.50 was the fastest ever first round, heading six men under 45 secs, and Bastian Swillims ran the fastest ever non-qualifying time (45.44) in a World Champs first round. Nery Brenes improved his Costa Rican record from 46.00 to 45.01.

1. Jeremy Wariner USA	43.45
2. LaShawn Merritt USA	43.96
3. Angelo Taylor USA	44.32

4. Christopher Brown BAH	44.45
5. Leslie Djhone FRA	44.59
6. Tyler Christopher CAN	44.71
7. Johan Wissman SWE	44.72
8. Avard Moncur BAH	45.40

800 Metres (h 30th, sf 31st, F 2nd)

KAMEL WAS QUICKEST in the heats at 1:45.25 with 18 men at 1:46.00 or better and Samwel Mwera's 1:46.24 was the fastest ever non-qualifying time in a W.Champs first round. Thanks to a 50.33 first lap by Khadevis Robinson (4th in 1:45.45), 1:44.54 was recorded by Kirwa in the first semi, and Reed and Borzakovskiy won the others in 1:44.92 and 1:45.12, with Mulaudzi and Chepkirwok also running sub-1:45 times. Defending champion Rashid Ramzi was eliminated at this stage. Reed led from 200 in 25.60 in the final, but slowed the pace so much that the first lap took a funereal 55.08. He was joined in the front at 600 in 1:22.18 by the junior Chepkirwok, who launched his bid but didn't have the speed or strength to maintain it, and Reed led for most of the finishing straight.

Although further forward than normal, Borzakovskiy left it too late to catch him but the small rather-hunched Kirwa Yego (20, the youngest ever 800 champion), who entered the straight in third place, managed to edge past in the last stride with less than half a second separating first from last! He covered the final 200m in 24.6 as against 24.9 for Reed and 24.8 for Borzakovskiy. 1:47.09 was by far the slowest ever time to take this title (1:45.08 by Wilson Kipketer in 1995 was the previous worst) and the slowest for a global title since Tom Courtney's 1:47.75 at the 1956 Olympics.

1. Alfred Kirwa Yego KEN	1:47.09
2. Gary Reed CAN	1:47.10
3. Yuriy Borzakovskiy RUS	1:47.39
4. Abraham Chepkirwok UGA	1:47.41
5. Wilfred Bungei KEN	1:47.42
6. Amine Laâlou MAR	1:47.45
7. Mbulaeni Mulaudzi RSA	1:47.52
8. Mohammed Al Salhi KSA	1:47.58

1500 Metres (h 25th, sf 27th, F 29th)

LAGAT RAN A perfect tactical race to take his first global title. Mehdi Baala was fastest in the first round at 3:38.65 but was disqualified for pushing in his semi, where another favourite Daniel Kipchirchir Komen fell. Webb was an early leader in the final with 58.63 at 400m but after 700m Kiprop took over, passing 800 in 1:58.08, the bell in 2:41.51 and 1200 in 2:55.21, closely followed by Webb, Korir, Lagat and defending champion Ramzi. Kiprop continued to lead around the final bend but, with Webb fading and Ramzi hemmed in at a crucial moment, Lagat's kick proved the deadliest as he sped through the last 100 in 12.65 (Ramzi 12.95, Kibet 13.10), 200 in 25.9 and 400 in 53.0. Ramzi extricated himself in time to chase home a frustrated second, and Korir – who had only just scraped into the final after 7th in his semi – overhauled Kiprop (who set a pb) for the bronze. This was the closest ever World Champs 1500m as the first eight finished within a second. Canadian Kevin Sullivan (9th semi) made an event record eighth appearance.

1. Bernard Lagat USA	3:34.77
2. Rashid Ramzi BRN	3:35.00
3. Shadrack Korir KEN	3:35.04
4. Asbel Kiprop KEN	3:35.24
5. Tarek Boukensa ALG	3:35.26
6. Antar Zerguelaine ALG	3:35.29
7. Arturo Casado ESP	3:35.62
8. Alan Webb USA	3:35.69
9. Andrew Baddeley GBR	3:35.95
10. Nicholas Willis NZL	3:36.13
11. Belal Mansoor Ali BRN	3:36.44
12. Sergio Gallardo ESP	3:37.03
13. Juan Carlos Higuero ESP	3:38.43
14. Youssef Baba MAR	3:38.78

5000 Metres (h 30th, F 2nd)

LAGAT PRODUCED A last 200 in 25.9 and final 400 of 52.3, kilometre of 2:23.4 and 1600m of 4:00.3 for just the third 1500/5000m double in global championships, emulating Paavo Nurmi in 1924 and Hicham El Guerrouj in 2004 at the Olympics. The first kilometre took 3:00.35, slower than in the women's race, and that was followed by 2:46.72, 2:49.92 and 2:45.47 to 4000m, when the race began to burst into life. Farah moved ahead approaching 4400m (62.75 lap) and was ahead at the bell in 12:53.08 (27.87 for that 200). The 2003 champion Kipchoge sprinted ahead at 4800m, that full lap having taken just 54.35, but Lagat (5th with 200 to go) had more fire power in the finishing straight and took the race by 0.13 in by far the slowest winning time in World Champs history. Surprisingly, Kenyans Isaac Songok and Joseph Ebuya failed to progress from a slow first heat won in 13:46.42; ten qualified from the second, won by Kipchoge in 13:33.37.

1. Bernard Lagat USA	13:45.87
2. Eliud Kipchoge KEN	13:46.00
3. Moses Kipsiro UGA	13:46.75
4. Matt Tegenkamp USA	13:46.78
5. Tariku Bekele ETH	13:47.33
6. Mohammed Farah GBR	13:47.54
7. Jesus España ESP	13:50.55
8. Abraham Feleke ETH	13:51.01
9. Felix Kibore QAT	13:51.18
10. Ali Abdalla ERI	13:52.69
11. Adam Goucher USA	13:53.17
12. Hicham Bellani MAR	13:55.44
13. Craig Mottram AUS	13:56.24
14. Juan Luis Barrios MEX	13:59.86
15. Benjamin Limo KEN	14:01.25

10,000 Metres 27th)

BEKELE AND SIHINE were 1-2 as in 2005 with Matathi and Tadese moving up two places apiece. It looked as if Bekele might lose a 10,000m for the first time when Sihine opened up an 8m lead along the final back straight ... but only for a few seconds. Bekele caught the luckless Sihine (his runner-up in three previous Olympic or World Champs races) and sprinted past 130m from the finish for his third world 10,000m title. Tadese made it a remarkably quick race in 32°C as, despite periodic attempts by Gebremariam to slow it down, the Eritrean ran kilometres of 2:44.15, 2:43.17, 2:45.61, 2:44.89 and 2:45.16 to reach halfway in 13:42.98 with ten men still in close formation. Kilometres of 2:45.85 and 2:43.91 by Tadese reduced his immediate pursuers to six and after an eighth of 2:41.84 it was down to four men. Mathathi struck with three laps to go as the gallant Tadese dropped away from medal contention, and the penultimate kilometre was covered in 2:40.99. Mathathi led at the bell in 26:09.99, just ahead of Sihine with Bekele a few metres back. Both Ethiopians quickly took over and Bekele ran his last 200 in 27.48, last lap in 55.51 (to 59.0 by Sihine, 62.2 by Mathathi) and final 1km in 2:30.33. He ran the first half in 13:43.4, the second in 13:22.5 for a time that his agent Jos Hermens claimed was "maybe world record pace in normal weather". There were no Europeans in the field of 22, a far cry from the inaugural championship in 1983 when Europeans filled seven of the first eight places.

1. Kenenisa Bekele ETH	27:05.90
2. Sileshi Sihine ETH	27:09.03
3. Martin Mathathi KEN	27:12.17
4. Zersenay Tadese ERI	27:21.37
5. Josphat M Ndambiri KEN	27:31.41
6. Gebre Gebremariam ETH	27:44.58
7. Abdi Abdirahman USA	27:56.62
8. J. Kiprono Menjo KEN	28:25.67
9. Dathan Ritzenhein USA	28:28.59
10. Boniface Kiprop UGA	28:30.99
11. Galen Rupp USA	28:41.71
12. Kensuke Takezawa JPN	28:51.69
13. Tadesse Tola ETH	28:51.75
14. Alejandro Suárez MEX	28:52.19
15. Wilson Busienei UGA	29:24.72

Marathon (25th)

MOST OF THE world's best were not here, but Kibet overcame horrendous weather conditions far better than anyone else to triumph by over 400m in the slowest time to win a global championship since the high altitude Mexico City Olympics of 1968, but he had the largest winning margin in World Champs history. Temperature was 28°C with 81% humidity at the 7 am start and rose to 33°C by the finish. 57 of the 84 starters finished. Halfway was reached in 68:29 with a lead group of about 30 runners and Kibet made his move approaching 30k, with only the Kenyan-born Shami for company. Kiplagat and Shami fought for second for a while, but the latter eventually finished eighth in a state of collapse. Meanwhile a strong finish enabled Röthlin to snatch third place. Japan, with their scorers 5-6-7, successfully defended the World Marathon Cup. First marathon medals in global champs for SUI and QAT, highest ever placing for ERI.

1. Luke Kibet KEN	2:15:59
2. Mubarak Hassan Shami QAT	2:17:18
3. Viktor Röthlin SUI	2:17:25
4. Yared Asmerom ERI	2:17:41
5. Tsuyoshi Ogata JPN	2:17:42
6. Satoshi Osaki JPN	2:18:06
7. Toshinari Suwa JPN	2:18:35
8. William Kiplagat KEN	2:19:21
9. Janne Holmén FIN	2:19:36
10. José M. Martínez ESP	2:20:25
11. Dan Robinson GBR	2:20:30
12. Alex Malinga UGA	2:20:36
13. Tomoyuki Sato JPN	2:20:53
14. Gashaw Asfaw ETH	2:20:58
15. Park Ju-young KOR	2:21:49

World Cup: 1. JPN 6:54:23, 2. KOR 7:12:08, 3. KEN 7:12:33, 4. USA 7:15:00, 5. ETH 7:19:08, 6. TAN 7:23:20, 7. ISR 7:23:22, 8. POR 7:24:48, 9. CHN 7:31:02.

3000 Metres Steeple (h 26th, F 28th)

THE KENYAN TRIO swept the medals (as in 1997) and did so with ease as the winner Kipruto celebrated with his arms aloft in delight for half of the finishing straight. Kemboi took his third successive silver medal with Matelong the bronze, so that Kenya has now won 7 of the 11 World titles and 19 of the 33 medals from 1983. Taher was fastest in qualifying at 8:19.99 and the final started very slowly with Mohamed leading at 1000m in 2:52.63 but quickened with a second kilometre of 2:44.80. At the bell it was Mohamed from Kemboi, Kipruto and Taher in 7:11.10. Taher led briefly on the last lap but along the back straight Kemboi went ahead followed by Kipruto.

1. Brimin Kipruto KEN	8:13.82
2. Ezekiel Kemboi KEN	8:16.94
3. Richard Matelong KEN	8:17.59
4. Mustafa Mohamed SWE	8:19.82
5. Bouabdellah Tahri FRA	8:20.27
6. Halil Akkas TUR	8:22.51
7. Eliseo Martín ESP	8:22.91
8. Tareq Mubarak Taher BRN	8:22.95
9. Abdelkader Hachlaf MAR	8:24.18
10. Roba Gary ETH	8:25.93
11. Abubaker Ali Kamal KSA	8:26.90
12. Nahom Mesfin Tariku ETH	8:28.86
dq. José Luis Blanco ESP	–
dq. Brahim Taleb MAR	–
dnf. Ali Ahmed Al-Amri KSA	–

110mh (h 29th, sf 30th, F 31st +1.7)

AFTER BRONZE IN 2003 and silver in 2005, Liu added World gold to Olympic. He ran a fine race from lane 9, marred only by hitting the ninth hurdle hard. As in Athens 2004 Trammell was second and Payne, only called up to replace the injured Dominique Arnold at the last minute, took bronze. Payne, who had arrived the night before, ran 13.27 in the fastest heat won by Shi in 13.22, and ran the quickest time (13.19) in the semis, in which Robles 13.21 and Trammell 13.32 were the other winners and defending champion Doucouré (3rd in 13.36) was eliminated. Demidyuk and Quiñónez set national records and all times for 2-8 were the fastest in World Champs history.

1. Liu Xiang CHN	12.95
2. Terrence Trammell USA	12.99
3. David Payne USA	13.02
4. Dayron Robles CUB	13.15
5. Shi Dongpeng CHN	13.19
6. Sergiy Demidyuk UKR	13.22
7. Jackson Quiñónez ESP	13.33
8. Maurice Wignall JAM	13.39

400mh (h 25th, sf 26th, F 28th)

CLEMENT STUTTERED BEFORE several of the hurdles – but was still much too good for the opposition and he won in 47.61, the world's fastest time of 2007. Sánchez surprised with a season's best 48.70 for the fastest time of the first round and won the second semi with 48.35, although that was not as fast as Plawgo's 48.18 in the previous race in which 48.44 by Kenji Narisako in 5th was the fastest non-qualifying time in World Champs history. Sánchez, in his fastest since winning Olympic gold in 2004, and Plawgo were surprising medallists behind Clement. McFarlane ran a world M35 record of 48.32 in 5th. Defending champion Bershawn Jackson was eliminated in the semis; he was heading for a win when he rammed the last hurdle and staggered home third in 48.95. L.J. van Zyl and Dai Tamesue, didn't make it through their heats.

1. Kerron Clement USA	47.61
2. Felix Sánchez DOM	48.01
3. Marek Plawgo POL	48.12
4. James Carter USA	48.40
5. Danny McFarlane JAM	48.59
6. Periklís Iakovákis GRE	49.25
7. Derrick Williams USA	52.97
dnf. Adam Kunkel CAN	–

High Jump (Q 2.29 27th, F 29th)

A RECORD 15 men over 2.29 in qualifying made it best ever marks for places 13-15. Thomas, in just his second year in athletics, took gold with a first-time clearance at 2.35 with Rybakov and Ioannou, who set national records at 2.33 and 2.35 and became the first Cypriot to win a medal at any event, clearing on their second attempts. Holm and Rybakov, who collected his third World Champs silver medal, had clean sheets all the way to 2.33. Dragutin Topic (31= 2.19) made a record seventh World Champs HJ appearance.

1. Donald Thomas BAH	2.35
2. Yaroslav Rybakov RUS	2.35
3. Kyriakos Ioannou CYP	2.35
4. Stefan Holm SWE	2.33
5= Victor Moya CUB	2.30
5= Tomás Janku CZE	2.30
7. Eike Onnen GER	2.26
8. Jaroslav Bába CZE	2.26
9. Kabelo Kgosiemang BOT	2.26
10. Tom Parsons GBR	2.26
11= Andrey Silnov RUS	2.21
11= Michal Bieniek POL	2.21
13. Jesse de Lima BRA	2.21
14. Martyn Bernard GBR	2.21
15. Linus Thörnblad SWE	2.16

Pole Vault (Q 5.85m 30th, F 1st)

FIVE MEN WERE still jumping at 5.91, but no one succeeded and Walker, first time, and Mesnil second time, were the only men to clear 5.86. Ecker took bronze with a clear card to 5.81. This was the highest quality contest for depth as there were the best ever marks for places 7 to 11 and eight men cleared 5.81 with one other (Hooker) passing that height in an unsuccessful gamble. Lobinger made his sixth final in a PV record seventh Worlds appearance. Ten men jumped 5.70 to qualify, augmented by Averbukh and da Silva 5.65.

1. Brad Walker USA	5.86
2. Romain Mesnil FRA	5.86
3. Danny Ecker GER	5.81
4. Igor Pavlov RUS	5.81
5. Björn Otto GER	5.81
6. Yevgeniy Lukyanenko RUS	5.81
7. Alex Averbukh ISR	5.81
8. Tim Lobinger GER	5.81
9. Steve Hooker AUS	5.76
10. Fábio da Silva BRA	5.76
11. Maksym Mazuryk UKR	5.76
12. Denys Yurchenko UKR	5.66

Long Jump (Q 8.15m 29th, F 30th)

THERE WAS A superb finish to this competition. Seeking his third straight title, Phillips opened with 8.30, and that was matched in the second round by Saladino, who became the outright leader with his third effort of 8.46. Mokoena, who had led the qualifying with 8.28, moved into third with 8.19, only to be displaced by Howe's penultimate leap of 8.20. In the final round. Lukashevych briefly took third with 8.25, but then Howe touched down at the Italian record distance of 8.47 for the lead. His celebrations were as wild as those of his mother, who had urged him on very loudly, but there were still two jumps to go. Phillips made only 8.22 as, disgracefully, a victory ceremony was staged over those last two jumps. After having to wait for the anthem it was down to Saladino – and he broke the sand at 8.57 for a South American record and gold.

1. Irving Saladino PAN	8.57/0.0
2. Andrew Howe ITA	8.47/-0.2
3. Dwight Phillips USA	8.30/0.4
4. Oleksiy Lukashevych UKR	8.25/0.2
5. Khotso Mokoena RSA	8.19/-0.1
6. James Beckford JAM	8.17/0.1
7. Ndiss Kaba Badji SEN	8.01/0.1
8. Ahmed Bin Marzouq KSA	7.98/0.0
9. Christian Reif GER	7.95/-0.4
10. Miguel Pate USA	7.94/-0.6
11. Hussein Al-Sabee KSA	7.84/0.4
nj. Trevell Quinley USA	–

Triple Jump (Q 17.10m 26th, F 27th)

ÉVORA LED THE qualifying round with 17.22 and registered 17.41 with just the second jump of the final, to which the only close response was a 17.33 opener by defending champion Davis. Early in the second round Idowu moved into third with 17.07, only to be overtaken by Wilson's 17.21. Then Tosca jumped 17.32 in the third round, while Évora set a formidable target for everyone with a Portuguese record of 17.74. Gregório's third jump was a monster foul of something in excess of 17.80 but it wasn't until the fifth round that he was able to move from sixth to second with 17.59 (with 12cm to spare on the board). Wilson's final round 17.31 left him 3cm short of a medal. Évora (23), who was born in the Ivory Coast, became the first man to win a World gold medal for Portugal.

1. Nelson Évora POR	17.74/1.4
2. Jadel Gregório BRA	17.59/0.3
3. Walter Davis USA	17.33/1.0
4. Osniel Tosca CUB	17.32/1.1
5. Aarik Wilson USA	17.31/0.6
6. Phillips Idowu GBR	17.09/-0.9
7. David Giralt CUB	16.91/0.7
8. Alexander Martinez SUI	16.85/1.3
9. Kim Deok-hyeon KOR	16.71/1.1
10. Aleksandr Petrenko RUS	16.66/0.8
11. Zhong Minwei CHN	16.66/1.5
12. Dimitrios Tsiámis GRE	16.59/-1.1

Shot (Q 20.20m & F 25th)

HOFFA TOOK THE lead in the first round with 21.81 and improved to 22.04 in the third as four of his valid throws were good enough for victory. As so often, title holder Nelson raised his game with his opening (and only valid) throws of 21.47 and 21.61 gaining him the sixth silver medal (also Olympics 2000 and 2004, Worlds of 2001 and 2003 and World Indoors 2001), and to become the first four-time World medallist. Behind the two American spinners, 2003 world champion Mikhnevich – whose uses the glide technique – took bronze. Another strong medal contender, Olsen, fouled out in the final. Ten men went over 20m in qualifying, headed by Smith 21.04, and Anton Lyuboslavskiy's 19.91 was the best non-qualifier ever.

1. Reese Hoffa USA	22.04
2. Adam Nelson USA	21.61
3. Andrey Mikhnevich BLR	21.27
4. Rutger Smith NED	21.13
5. Tomasz Majewski POL	20.87
6. Miroslav Vodovnik SLO	20.67
7. Ralf Bartels GER	20.45
8. Yuriy Belov BLR	20.34
9. Dylan Armstrong CAN	20.23
10. Pavel Sofin RUS	19.62
nt. Joachim Olsen DEN	–
nt. Dorian Scott JAM	–

Discus (Q 64.50m 26th, F 28th)

PRIOR TO OSAKA KANTER had lost 44 of 45 clashes with Alekna – but won here. There were anxious moments as he was only 12th with 58.81 after two rounds of the qualifying contest before unleashing a 67.45 throw to top the pb of 66.60 by Smith and 66.54 by Alekna. In the final Kanter took a first round lead with 64.89, was overtaken in the second round by Harting 65.59 and Smith 65.98, and then produced what turned out to be the winner of 68.94 with his third throw, backing that up with a final 68.84. Alekna, who had won his previous 37 competitions from August 2005, was unable to meet the challenge as he had been held back by an injury to his right calf. In the battle for silver Smith, who became the first man to win World Champs medals in both shot (silver 2005) and discus, threw 66.42 in round 3 but Harting topped that with 66.68 in round 5. Eight of the 12 finalists threw further in qualifying.

1. Gerd Kanter EST	68.94
2. Robert Harting GER	66.68
3. Rutger Smith NED	66.42
4. Virgilijus Alekna LTU	65.24
5. Gábor Máté HUN	64.71
6. Omar El Ghazaly EGY	64.58
7. Ehsan Hadadi IRI	64.53
8. Aleksander Tammert EST	64.33
9. Zoltán Kövágó HUN	63.04
10. Mario Pestano ESP	62.70
11. Rashid Al-Dosari QAT	62.60
12. Piotr Malachowski POL	60.77

Hammer (Q 77.00m 26th, F 27th)

THE HOPES OF Japan rested with Murofushi and (in only his second competition of the year) he threw creditably, improving steadily to a final 80.46, but that was good only for sixth. Charfreitag led the qualifiers with 80.61 and was third at 80.93 at halfway in the final behind Kozmus 82.12 and Devyatovskiy 80.95. Tikhon hooked his first two efforts far to the left, out of the sector, but just qualified for the top eight with 79.35. Devyatovskiy improved to 81.22 in round 4 while in round 5 Tikhon progressed to 80.77 for 4th and Charfreitag to 81.60 just ahead of Devyatovskiy's 81.57.

In the final round, after Pars took over 4th with 80.93 Tikhon delivered his thunderbolt ... a world leading mark of 83.63. Victory was not yet assured and all credit to Kozmus, who recovered sufficiently from seeing the gold medal slip from his grasp by extending his best to 82.29. For the first time ever, seven men exceeded 80m (previous best six at 1987 Worlds) and there were the best ever marks for each place 4-12. That was all the more remarkable as there was a long delay to the proceedings when in the first round an errant delivery from Konopka left a hole in the cage netting, requiring some desperate running repairs to be made. Tikhon (31) became the first to win three world hammer titles, breaking the record he shared with his coach Sergey Litvinov (1983 & 1987) and Andrey Abduvaliyev (1993 & 1995), and he is the first field eventer ever to move from 8th to 1st in the final three rounds of a World Champs. Al-Zankawi became the first Kuwaiti world finalist.

1. Ivan Tikhon BLR	83.63
2. Primoz Kozmus SLO	82.29
3. Libor Charfreitag SVK	81.60
4. Vadim Devyatovskiy BLR	81.57
5. Krisztian Pars HUN	80.93
6. Koji Murofushi JPN	80.46
7. Szymon Ziólkowski POL	80.09
8. Markus Esser GER	79.66
9. Olli-Pekka Karjalainen FIN	78.35
10. Miloslav Konopka SVK	78.09
11. Esref Apak TUR	76.59
12. Mohamed Al-Zankawi KUW	76.04

Javelin (Q 82.00m 31st, F 2nd)

PITKÄMÄKI EXPERIENCED A shaky qualification in tenth place with only 80.62, well behind Vasilevskis 87.37 and Greer 86.78, as the two previous winners Makarov (18th 78.22) and Värnik (24th 75.96) were the principal casualties. After Ivanov 85.18 and Oosthuizen 84.52 had led the first round of the final, in the second round consecutively Pitkämäki reached 89.16, Vasilevskis 85.19 and Thorkildsen 88.61. The Finn kept up the pressure with 87.72 in the fourth round and Greer replaced Vasilevskis in third place with a fifth round 86.21. Thorkildsen had to settle for silver, as in 2005, when his last attempt fell short at 87.33 and so Pitkämäki was able to relax for his final effort in the knowledge that he was the new champion. The result was a mighty throw of 90.33.

1. Tero Pitkämäki FIN	90.33
2. Andreas Thorkildsen NOR	88.61
3. Breaux Greer USA	86.21
4. Vadim Vasilevskis LAT	85.19
5. Aleksandr Ivanov RUS	85.18
6. Robert Oosthuizen RSA	84.52
7. Igor Janik POL	83.38
8. Tero Järvenpää FIN	82.10
9. Guillermo Martínez CUB	82.03
10. Magnus Arvidsson SWE	81.98
11. Eriks Rags LAT	80.01
12. Teemu Wirkkala FIN	78.01

Decathlon (31st–1st)

THERE WAS A major shock at the start as one of the main medal contenders, Andrey Kravchenko went out, having made two false starts in the 100m. Defending champion Bryan Clay, having started well with 10.44 for 100m, dropped out with an injury in the high jump, and at the end of day one Smith led with 4525 from Karpov 4439, Sebrle 4434, Drozdov 4353 and Tom Pappas 4342. Smith excelled with pbs at 100m 10.62 and 400m 47.48 and near-pbs at LJ 7.50 and SP 17.32 and increased his lead with 110mh 13.91 and DT 52.36 to 6431 to 6259 by Karpov and 6210 by Sebrle. Another pb for Smithc ame with 4.80 PV but an arm injury held him back to just 53.61 in the javelin, whereas Sebrle came up with a pb 71.18 to take the lead with 7966 to 7922 Smith and 7904 Karpov. There was little chance of Sebrle relinquishing that advantage in the 1500m and finally at 32 he won the only major honour to have eluded him.

The magnificent Smith provided the closest finish ever at World Champs as he added 295 points to his CAC record with 8644 to rank second to Daley Thompson on the Commonwealth all-time list. Karpov added another bronze to those he gained at the 2003 Worlds and 2004 Olympics with 8586. There were personal bests by Drozdov, Niklaus, Sysoyev and García (18, the youngest ever Worlds decathlon competitor), who set a Cuban record and ranks second on the world junior all-time list.

1. Román Sebrle CZE	8676
2. Maurice Smith JAM	8644
3. Dmitriy Karpov KAZ	8586
4. Aleksey Drozdov RUS	8475
5. André Niklaus GER	8371
6. Aleksey Sysoyev RUS	8357
7. Romain Barras FRA	8262
8. Yordanis García CUB	8257
9. Arthur Abele GER	8243
10. Paul Terek USA	8120
11. Hans Van Alphen BEL	8034
12. Attila Zsivóczky HUN	8017
13. Jake Arnold USA	8004
14. Aleksandr Parkhomenko BLR	7984
15. François Gourmet BEL	7974

4 x 100 Metres Relay (h 31st, F 1st)

IN THE HEATS Asafa Powell had stormed past Leroy Dixon for 38.02 (Jamaican record) to 38.10 USA, and had Jamaica not been so diabolically poor at passing the baton the same might have happened in the final. As it was, Powell took over far behind in fifth place and the US team – although with dreadful second and third exchanges but fast runs by Spearmon and Gay – won in 37.78 for the seventh US win in 11 World Champs. Powell ran a fantastic last leg, reportedly timed at 8.84 for a flying 100m, to take his team into second place with another national record. He overtook Japan (Asian record), Brazil and, on the line, Britain for whom Devonish won a record fourth World Champs relay medal. There were the fastest ever times for 4th and 5th places.

1. USA	37.78	Patton, Spearmon, Gay, Dixon
2. JAM	37.89	Anderson, Bolt, Carter, Powell
3. GBR	37.90	Malcolm, Pickering, Devonish, Lewis-Francis
4. BRA	37.99	de Lima, Ribeiro, de Moraes, Viana
5. JPN	38.03	Tsukahara, Suetsugu, Takahira, Asahara
6. GER	38.62	Ostwald, Unger, Kosenkow, Reus
dnf. NGR	–	Metu, Isaac, Oriala, Fasuba
dnf. POL	–	Bielczyk, Chyla, Jedrusinski, Kuc

4 x 400 Metres Relay (h 1st, F 2nd)

LaSHAWN MERRITT GAVE the USA a lead of some 6m, and Angelo Taylor, Darrold Williamson and Wariner (43.10 on his own!) came up with the third quickest ever time and the team won by some 30m. Wariner's time was the second fastest ever relay split to Michael Johnson's 42.9 at the 1993 Worlds. Bahamas (fastest in the heats with 3:00.37) were best of the rest and their first man, Avard Moncur, won a fourth successive medal at the event. The American success meant they had won all four relays, a feat they achieved at the 1984 Olympics but unique to the World Champs. The distinction of running the fastest non-USA split fell to Britain's anchorman Martyn Rooney (44.17 heat, 44.29 final).

1. USA	2:55.56	Merritt 44.4, Taylor 43.7, Williamson 44.32, Wariner 43.10
2. BAH	2:59.18	Moncur 45.2, Mathieu 45.0, A Williams 44.54, Brown 44.41
3. POL	3:00.05	Plawgo 45.5, Dabrowski 44.6, Marciniszyn 44.81, Kozlowski 45.15
4. JAM	3:00.76	Blackwood 45.4, Chambers 44.3, Green 44.50, Ayre 46.54
5. RUS	3:01.62	Dyldin 46.2, Frolov 44.9, Svechkar 45.31, Alekseyev 45.20
6. GBR	3:02.94	Steele 46.3, Tobin 45.4, Buck 47.0, Rooney 44.29
7. DOM	3:03.56	Sánchez 46.4, Tapia 45.3, Santa 46.54, Peguero 45.32
8. GER	3:07.40	Schultz 45.7, Kirch 45.8, Gaba 49.33 (fell), Swillims 46.51

20 Kilometres Walk (26th)

PÉREZ WON HIS third successive world title. The 33 year-old respected the conditions (32-34°C) and allowed Ivano Brugnetti to open up a 17 sec lead by halfway (42:14 to 42:31). Pérez passed the Italian (who was later disqualified) at 13k and shared the lead with Ghoula at 15k (62:31) with Fernández 2 sec behind. Pérez opened up a 20 sec lead over Ghoula (making his eighth World Champs appearance) by the finish. Ghoula appeared to be a safe second ... until Fernández unleashed a stupefying finish which carried him past the unsuspecting Tunisian in the final stride or two. The Spaniard (with no previous warnings) was disqualified for this charge but was later reinstated following an appeal, while Ghoula was happy enough to win Africa's first ever walking medal and the first ever World Champs medal for Tunisia in any event. Pérez covered his 5k segments in 21:41, 20:50, 20:00 and 19:49. 32 of 42 men finished.

1. Jefferson Pérez ECU	1:22:20
2. Francisco J. Fernández ESP	1:22:40
3. Hatem Ghoula TUN	1:22:40
4. Eder Sánchez MEX	1:23:36
5. Giorgio Rubino ITA	1:23:39
6. Robert Heffernan IRL	1:23:42
7. Luke Adams AUS	1:23:52
8. Erik Tysse NOR	1:24:10
9. Ilya Markov RUS	1:24:35
10. Alex Schwazer ITA	1:24:39
11. Koichi Morioka JPN	1:24:46
12. Rolando Saquipay ECU	1:25:03
13. Li Gaobo CHN-J	1:25:30
14. Matej Tóth SVK	1:25:57
15. Park Chil-sung KOR	1:26:08

50 Kilometres Walk (1st)

DESPITE THE GRUELLING weather conditions Deakes recorded the fine time of 3:43:53, finishing in an emotional state 29 sec ahead of Diniz. Santiago Pérez of Spain took an early lead until caught by Yu Chaohong, who speedily built up a 42 sec lead over Pérez at 10k (45:54) while defending champion Sergey Kirdyapkin led the main group, including Deakes, in a very pedestrian 47:23. Yu's lead stretched to 1:41 by 15k but at 20k (1:31:30) it was down to 18 sec over Vladimir Kanaykin, Yamazaki and Deakes. Yu was soon caught and Kanaykin, Deakes and Yamazaki reached halfway in 1:53:35, followed by Diniz 1:53:49, a fading Yu 1:55:04, Nizhegorodov and Schwazer 1:55:49. Yu was disqualified shortly afterwards and Deakes made his bid for glory between 30 and 35k with only Diniz (who led briefly) able to stay in touch. By 40k, though, Deakes was 39 sec clear. Schwazer closed considerably with a final 10k in 43:12 (4:08 last kilometre) as against 44:48 by Deakes and 44:38 by Diniz. Deakes' 10k splits were 47:23, 44:25, 43:51, 43:26 and 44:48. Yamazaki, fading fast, was unfortunately misdirected into the stadium a lap short, and crossed the finish apparently in fifth place in 3:48:12 before the error was realised.

Just 31 of the 52 starters finished, non-finishers included Kanaykin and Kirdyapkin.

1.	Nathan Deakes AUS	3:43:53
2.	Yohann Diniz FRA	3:44:22
3.	Alex Schwazer ITA	3:44:38
4.	Denis Nizhegorodov RUS	3:46:57
5.	Erik Tysse NOR	3:51:52
6.	Mikel Odriozola ESP	3:55:19
7.	Sun Chao CHN	3:55:43
8.	Trond Nymark NOR	3:57:22
9.	Horacio Nava MEX	3:58:17
10.	Jarkko Kinnunen FIN	3:58:22
11.	Antti Kempas FIN	3:59:34
12.	Donatas Skarnulis LTU	3:59:48
13.	Eddy Riva FRA	4:00:44
14.	David Boulanger FRA	4:01:30
15.	António Pereira POR	4:02:09

Women

100 Metres (h, qf 26th; sf, F 27th -0.2)

ALTHOUGH THERE WAS the slowest winning time in World Champs history, just 0.002 separated Campbell and Williams – 11.006 to 11.008 – and the first five were just 0.04 apart. Williams got her customary fast start and led at 50m in 6.06; it took a long time to finalise the verdict from the photo-finish. Jeter 11.07 and Gevaert 11.09 were fastest in the first round, and Campbell in the second round with 11.08. The semis were won by Edwards 11.02 and Campbell 10.99. Merlene Ottey (3h1 11.64) became at 47y 108d, the oldest ever World Champs competitor and Irina Khabarova ran 11.38 for fifth in her quarter final at the age of 41.

1.	Veronica Campbell JAM	11.01
2.	Lauryn Williams USA	11.01
3.	Carmelita Jeter USA	11.02
4.	Torri Edwards USA	11.05
5.	Kim Gevaert BEL	11.05
6.	Christine Arron FRA	11.08
7.	Kerron Stewart JAM	11.12
8.	Oludamola Osayomi NGR	11.26

200 Metres (h, qf 29th, sf 30th, F 31st +1.7)

FELIX RAN THE fastest time of 22.50 in the first round with Jayasinghe running 22.55 in both first and second round, in which Richards was quickest at 22.31. Felix sauntered through the first semi in 22.21 ahead of Campbell 22.44 and Richards won the second in 22.50. Campbell ran the first 100m of the final in 11.10 closely followed by Felix 11.15, before Felix closed in awe-inspiring fashion with 50ms in 5.13 and 5.53 to 5.33 and 5.91 by Campbell so that her 5m winning margin was the widest in a global 200m championship since Fanny Blankers-Koen's 6m advantage at the 1948 Olympics and her 21.81 was the world's fastest time since Inger Miller won the 1999 world title. Jayasinghe (11.45 at 100m) took the bronze.

1.	Allyson Felix USA	21.81
2.	Veronica Campbell JAM	22.34
3.	Susanthika Jayasinghe SRI	22.63
4.	Torri Edwards USA	22.65
5.	Sanya Richards USA	22.70
6.	Aleen Bailey JAM	22.72
7.	LaShauntea Moore USA	22.97
8.	Cydonie Mothersill CAY	23.08

400 Metres (h 26th, sf 27th, F 29th)

ARGUABLY THE TWO best women 400m runners – Sanya Richards and Allyson Felix – were not in this event, but there was the closest ever 1-2-3 at the event at World Champs. Novlene Williams, who had run the fastest times in first-round 50.21 and semis 49.66, blasted away through 200m in 23.37 to lead at 300m in 35.73 ahead of Antyukh 35.9, Ohuruogu (23.78 at 200m) 36.12 and Sanders (24.08) 36.17. The Britons proved strongest in the last 100m and produced a dip finish while Williams stayed upright. Both Ohuorogu 50.16 and Sanders 49.77 had run pbs in the semis and improved those in this epic final for the first ever British 1-2 in women's World Champs history and first British medals at women's 400m. 49.66 is the fastest qualifying time and 50.37 by Shericka Williams (4s2) was the fastest non-qualifying time in World Champs history.

1.	Christine Ohuruogu GBR	49.61
2.	Nicola Sanders GBR	49.65
3.	Novlene Williams JAM	49.66
4.	Ana Guevara MEX	50.16
5.	Deedee Trotter USA	50.17
6.	Natalya Antyukh RUS	50.33
7.	Ilona Usovich BLR	50.54
8.	Mary Wineberg USA	50.96

800 Metres (h 25th, sf 26th, F 28th)

JEPKOSGEI WAS FASTEST at 1:58.95 in the first round and won her semi in a Kenyan record 1:56.17 with a brilliant front-running display (splits of 26.91, 56.54 and 1:26.25). Behind her Benhassi ran 1:56.84 and Mutola 1:56.98, and Svetlana Usovich won the other semi in a pb 1:58.11. Lucia Klocová's 1:58.62 was the fastest ever World Champs non-qualifying time and defending champion Calatayud trailed in last. Jepkosgei looked unbeatable and she adopted the same tactics in the final, racing through in 26.58 (already 5m clear), 56.16 and 1:26.19, at which point Mutola 1:26.7 and Benhassi 1:26.79 were closest. Benhassi narrowed the gap but Jepkosgei pulled away magnificently in the finishing straight as Mutola, running in her ninth Worlds and seeking a fourth title, collapsed on the infield with a muscle injury with 80m to go. Jepkosgei finished 7m clear in another national record of 1:56.04, the world's fastest time for four years. Martínez, who had been last just behind Benhassi at the bell, sped home in the finishing straight to claim bronze and a pb.

1. Janeth Jepkosgei KEN	1:56.04
2. Hasna Benhassi MAR	1:56.99
3. Mayte Martínez ESP	1:57.62
4. Olga Kotlyarova RUS	1:58.22
5. Brigita Langerholc SLO	1:58.52
6. Svetlana Usovich BLR	1:58.92
7. Svetlana Klyuka RUS	2:00.90
dnf. Maria Mutola MOZ	–

1500 Metres (h 29th, sf 31st, F 2nd)

SOBOLEVA ENSURED A fast pace in the final, leading through 65.82 at 400, 2:09.57 at 800, 2:57.37 at the bell and 3:12.66 at 1200, but Jamal tracked her all the way, and edged past along the back straight. With 200m to go Jamal held a 2m lead over Soboleva with Selsouli a further 10m back in an isolated third place. Covering the last lap in 61.2, Jamal held on to win in a swift 3:58.75 and become the first woman to win a World Champs medal for Bahrain. Soboleva finished a stride behind while an exhausted Selsouli was picked off in the final straight by the very fast finishing Lishchynska and Yordanova. Bouchra Chaabi ran 4:11.51 for the fastest ever non-qualifying time in a first round of World Champs and after Jamal had won the first semi in 4:14.86 the second, won by Lishchynska in 4:03.84, was much quicker.

1. Maryam Yusuf Jamal BRN	3:58.75
2. Yelena Soboleva RUS	3:58.99
3. Iryna Lishchynska UKR	4:00.69
4. Daniela Yordanova BUL	4:00.82
5. Mariem Alaoui Selsouli MAR	4:01.52
6. Viola Kibiwott KEN	4:02.10
7. Yuliya Fomenko RUS	4:02.46
8. Agnes Samaria NAM	4:07.61
9. Nataliya Panteleyeva RUS	4:07.82
10. Lidia Chojecka POL	4:08.64
11. Nataliya Tobias UKR	4:10.56
12. Iris Fuentes-Pila ESP	4:14.00

5000 Metres (h 29th, F 1st)

AFTER UNREMARKABLE HEATS, with Abeylegesse fastest at 15:06.26, the final began slowly. Cheruiyot led at 3000m in 9:11.99, but it was not until the last two laps that the tempo changed dramatically. Defar took off at the bell and found a final lap of 58.58 (28.18 last 200) more than sufficient to hold off Cheruiyot, who was followed home by her colleagues Jepleting and Kibet. Defar's kilometre splits were 3:00.4, 3:04.7, 3:06.9, 3:01.1 and 2:45.4.

1. Meseret Defar ETH	14:57.91
2. Vivian Cheruiyot KEN	14:58.50
3. Priscah Cherono KEN	14:59.21
4. Sylvia Kibet KEN	14:59.26
5. Elvan Abeylegesse TUR	15:00.88
6. Meselech Melkamu ETH	15:01.42
7. Jennifer Rhines USA	15:03.09
8. Shalane Flanagan USA	15:03.86
9. Jo Pavey GBR	15:04.77
10. Gelete Burka ETH	15:07.46
11. Mariya Konovalova RUS	15:09.71
12. Silvia Weissteiner ITA	15:11.81
13. Olga Kravtsova BLR	15:11.82
14. Kayoko Fukushi JPN	15:19.40
15. Jessica Augusto POR	15:24.93

10,000 Metres (25th)

TIRUNESH DIBABA RETAINED her title but it was tough. There were 22 starters and the pace was slow (De Vos led at 5000m in 16:29.24) but Dibaba fell back suffering from stomach pains just before 5k and a lap later fell with Mestawet Tufa and Benita Johnson at the back of the field. However, she managed to rejoin the pack and responded when Abeylegesse dashed ahead and ran the eighth kilometre in 3:07.62 and the ninth in 3:02.45. Abeylegesse led by a stride at the bell (30:55.27) but immediately Dibaba launched a prolonged kick, clocking 60.14 (29.38 + 30.73) for the last lap and 2:47.18 for the final kilometre to leave her opponent 25m behind. She covered the first half in 16:31.4, the second in 15:24.0. In a battle for the bronze Goucher ran the race of her life to overtake Pavey with 200m to go with Smith fifth.

1. Tirunesh Dibaba ETH	31:55.41
2. Elvan Abeylegesse TUR	31:59.40
3. Kara Goucher USA	32:02.05
4. Jo Pavey GBR	32:03.81
5. Kimberley Smith NZL	32:06.89
6. Deena Kastor USA	32:24.58
7. Ejegayehu Dibaba ETH	32:30.44
8. Philes Ongori KEN	32:30.74
9. Emily Chebet KEN	32:31.21
10. Kayoko Fukushi JPN	32:32.85
11. Nathalie De Vos BEL	32:38.60
12. Inga Abitova RUS	32:40.39
13. Katie McGregor USA	32:44.76
14. Megumi Kinukawa JPN	32:45.19
15. Akane Wakita JPN	32:48.68

Marathon (2nd)

AS THE TEMPERATURE rose to 32°C (although in the stadium 37° was recorded), it was no surprise that Ndereba's time was eight minutes slower than when she finished second in 2005 and it was the slowest Worlds winning time. The halfway point was reached in 76:33 by close to 30 runners. Eight were in the lead group at 35k before the fastest 5k stretch of the race (17:25) left Zhou, Zhu and Ndereba level at 40k, with a grimacing Tosa 2 sec behind and Jeptoo another 9 sec back. Zhu fell away, enabling the gritty Tosa, the 2001 silver medallist, to win Japan's only medal of these championships. Meanwhile, Ndereba timed her run to perfection and drew away from Zhou to win by nearly 50m and reclaim the title she won in 2003. Zhou became China's first ever marathon medallist at World or Olympics. 57 of 67 finished.

1. Catherine Ndereba KEN	2:30:37
2. Zhou Chunxiu CHN	2:30:45

3. Reiko Tosa JPN 2:30:55
4. Zhu Xiaolin CHN 2:31:21
5. Lidia Simon ROM 2:31:26
6. Kiyoko Shimahara JPN 2:31:40
7. Rita Jeptoo KEN 2:32:03
8. Edith Masai KEN 2:32:22
9. Mara Yamauchi GBR 2:32:55
10. Lyubov Morgunova RUS 2:33:41
11. Zhang Shujing CHN 2:33:46
12. Gulnara Vygovskaya RUS 2:33:57
13. Nina Rillstone NZL 2:33:58
14. Mari Ozaki JPN 2:35:04
15. Madaí Pérez MEX 2:35:17

World Cup: 1. KEN 7:35:02, 2. CHN 7:35:52, 3. JPN 7:37.39, 4. RUS 7:50:34, 5. ITA 8:12:41, 6. USA 8:13:24, 7. ETH 8:58:46

3000 Metres Steeple (h 25th, F 27th)

GALKINA (NÉE SAMITOVA) led through a swift opening kilometre of 3:00.35 just ahead of Jepkorir, but slowed a lap later and eventually finished a distant seventh. Volkova took over and held an 8m lead over Petrova and Jepkosgei at 2000m (6:05.46). At the bell (7:51.15) she was 12m clear of Petrova and went on to win in a championship record 9:06.57, a time second only to Galkina's 2004 world record of 9:01.59. Petrova completed a Russian 1-2 in the fourth quickest ever time, while Jepkorir took the bronze ahead of Kenyan team-mate Bisibori who set a world junior record following an African junior record of 9:31.20 in her heat. This was easily the greatest women's steeplechase race with best ever marks for 2nd to 11th places and a record six under 9:30. Fastest in the heats was Casandra with 9:29.39 and Hatti Dean (GBR) become the fastest ever non-qualifier with 9:43.23, but Alesya Turova, in her first race of the year, did not finish.

1. Yekaterina Volkova RUS 9:06.57*
2. Tatyana Petrova RUS 9:09.19
3. Eunice Jepkorir KEN 9:20.09
4. Ruth Bisibori KEN-J 9:25.25
5. Sophie Duarté FRA 9:27.51
6. Cristina Casandra ROM 9:29.63
7. Gulnara Galkina RUS 9:30.24
8. Rosa Morató ESP 9:36.84
9. Hanane Ouhaddou MAR 9:37.87
10. Roisin McGettigan IRL 9:39.80
11. Veerle Dejaeghere BEL 9:40.10
12. Fionnuala Britton IRL 9:48.09
13. Sara Moreira POR 10:00.40
14. Mardrea Hyman JAM 10:16.24

dnf. Wioletta Janowska POL –

100mh (h 27th, sf 28th, F 29th -0.1)

KALLUR (12.66) WAS fastest in the heats and Perry (12.55) in the semis, in which all the other women ran between 12.61 and 12.67. Perry retained her title in a very close race as her dip gained her the verdict from Felicien, the 2003 champion who ran her quickest time since 2004, and Ennis-London, who ran a pb at the age of at 32. Tantalisingly out of the medals, a further 0.01 back, was Kallur in a pb 12.51. She led, just, to the 8th hurdle but was impeded on the last hurdle as Perry's knee and arm were well into her lane. Places 5-8 in the final were fastest ever in any race and the 0.2 separating 1st from 8th made it the closest ever World Champs finish. Priscilla Lopes (CAN) ran 12.94 for the fastest ever non-qualifying time in a first round of World Champs.

1. Michelle Perry USA 12.46
2. Perdita Felicien CAN 12.49
3. Delloreen Ennis-London JAM 12.50
4. Susanna Kallur SWE 12.51
5. Virginia Powell USA 12.55
6. LoLo Jones USA 12.62
7. Vonette Dixon JAM 12.64
8. Angela Whyte CAN 12.66

400mh (h 27th, sf 28th, F 30th)

AFTER WILLIAMS WAS fastest in round one with 54.24, the 2003 and 2005 champions Rawlinson (53.57) and Pechonkina (53.82), with Jesien (Polish record 53.86) were semi-final winners. That was also the final order. Williams, in lane 9, was ahead for the first half but faded to seventh when Rawlinson and Pechonkina fought it out along the finishing straight and Jesien finished strongly. Perchonkina's silver was her seventh World Champs medal (4 400mh, 3 4x400m). Wilson, who had lowered her pb to 53.97 in the semis, was fourth. Tetyana Tereshchuk's 54.38 semi is the fastest ever non-qualifying time in World Champs.

1. Jana Rawlinson AUS 53.31
2. Yuliya Pechonkina RUS 53.50
3. Anna Jesien POL 53.92
4. Nickiesha Wilson JAM 54.10
5. Huang Xiaoxiao CHN 54.15
6. Yevgeniya Isakova RUS 54.50
7. Tiffany Williams USA 54.63
8. Natasha Danvers-Smith GBR 54.94

High Jump (Q 1.94 31st, F 2nd)

16 women cleared the requisite 1.94 in qualifying compared to the previous record of 11 female jumpers over 1.94 in any competitiion (Rome 2003). That made for a lengthy final but, after European champion Hellebaut and defending champion Bergqvist went early, a record five women cleared 2m or higher and three jumped at least 2.03. At that height Vlasic went over first time for the lead, while Di Martino – equalling her Italian record and world differential best of 34cm – and Chicherova, with a new outdoor pb, made it at the second attempt. Out went Olympic champion Slesarenko (close at 2.03) and Savchenko, whose 2.00 clearance had tied her best. Vlasic (the cleared 2.05 at the third attempt before unsuccessfully attempting a world record 2.10.

1. Blanka Vlasic CRO		2.05
2= Anna Chicherova RUS		2.03
2= Antonietta Di Martino ITA		2.03
4. Yelena Slesarenko RUS		2.00
5. Yekaterina Savchenko RUS		2.00
6. Ruth Beitia ESP		1.97
7= Marina Aitova KAZ		1.94
7= Kajsa Bergqvist SWE		1.94
7= Emma Green SWE		1.94
7= Vita Palamar UKR		1.94
7= Melanie Skotnik FRA		1.94
12. Amy Acuff USA		1.94
13. Miruna Mataoanu ROM		1.90
14. Tia Hellebaut BEL		1.90
15= Barbora Laláková CZE		1.90
15= Lavern Spencer LCA		1.90

Pole Vault (Q 4.55m 26th, F 28th)

ISINBAYEVA NEED JUST four jumps to retain her title 4.55 in qualifying and 4.65 and two at 4.80 in the final. She then had three failures at a world record 5.02. Silver went to Badurová, who equalled her Czech record of 4.70 at the third try and then made 4.75 first time. Feofanova and Pyrek (equal pb) cleared 4.75 at the second try with bronze to the Russian on countback. Boslak tied her French record of 4.70 in fifth. The heights from third to ninth were the best ever for those placings and nine women over 4.60 compares with the previous record of five. In qualifying 12 women over 4.55, 15 over 4.50 and 25 over 4.35 are records for any meeting (previous bests 6, 9 and 15). The 4.50s by Agirre (equalling her Spanish record), Gao and Schwartz were the highest ever non-qualifying marks. Stuczynski, equal no 2 of all-time at 4.88 but competing with an ankle injury, pulled out after two failures at 4.65.

1. Yelena Isinbayeva RUS	4.80
2. Katerina Badurová CZE	4.75
3. Svetlana Feofanova RUS	4.75
4. Monika Pyrek POL	4.75
5. Vanessa Boslak FRA	4.70
6= Yuliya Golubchikova RUS	4.65
6= Fabiana Murer BRA	4.65
8. Anna Rogowska POL	4.60
9. Tatyana Polnova RUS	4.60
10. Jennifer Stuczynski USA	4.50
11. Kym Howe AUS	4.50
nh. Silke Spiegelburg GER	–

Long Jump (Q 6.75m 27th, F 28th)

THIS WAS RUSSIA'S first medal sweep in a World Champs women's event. After Kappler 6.81 and then Gomes 6.87 led the way in the first round, Lebedeva leapt into a lead she was never to forfeit with 7.03 (7.08 from take-off), matching that in round three and with a fifth jump of 6.98 that was also further than anyone else. Gomes, who led the qualifiers with Kolchanova at 6.96, was still in second place going into the final round but was passed by both three-time silver medallist Kotova 6.90 and then Kolchanova 6.92. Maggi, who had registered 6.95 (7.07 from take-off) in qualifying, could manage only 6.80 for sixth in the final, while defending champion Madison was never a factor and 2003 champion Barber was 16th with 6.51 in qualifying.

1. Tatyana Lebedeva RUS	7.03/0.3
2. Lyudmila Kolchanova RUS	6.92/-0.3
3. Tatyana Kotova RUS	6.90/0.5
4. Nadia Gomes POR	6.87/0.7
5. Bianca Kappler GER	6.81/-0.7
6. Maurren Maggi BRA	6.80/1.2
7. Keila Costa BRA	6.69/0.0
8. Brittney Reese USA	6.60/-1.5
9. Anju Bobby George IND	6.53/0.9
10. Tianna Madison USA	6.47/0.9
11. Viktoriya Rybalko UKR	6.45/0.0
12. Jana Veldáková SVK	6.21/-1.8

Triple Jump (Q 14.40m 29th, F 31st)

DEVETZÍ PRODUCED THE best ever qualifying mark in a World Champs with 15.09 (Savigne was next best at 14.67) and started the final with 15.04, to which Lebedeva responded with 14.75. Then Savigne added 19cm to her pb with 15.28 for sixth on the world all time list. Devetzi fouled her next four attempts and finished with 14.75, but Lebedeva never gave up and her final two jumps were 15.07 for the silver medal and 15.01. The Cuban winner had one other big jump – measured at only 14.73 but 15.02 from take-off to landing. Carlota Castrejana's 14.16 is the longest ever non-qualifying jump at World Champs, and other non-qualifiers included the London-based pair of defending champion Smith (13.47) and Aldama (13.46), both of whom had been injured this year.

1. Yargelis Savigne CUB	15.28/0.9
2. Tatyana Lebedeva RUS	15.07/0.8
3. Hrysopiyí Devetzí GRE	15.04/-0.2
4. Anna Pyatykh RUS	14.88/0.3
5. Marija Sestak SLO	14.72/0.2
6. Magdelín Martínez ITA	14.71/1.3
7. Olga Saladuha UKR	14.60/0.7
8. Xie Limei CHN	14.50/0.9
9. Keila Costa BRA	14.40/1.1
10. Olesya Bufalova RUS	14.39/0.7
11. Olga Rypakova KAZ	14.32/1.4
12. Dana Veldáková SVK	14.09/-0.1

Shot (Q 18.35m & F 26th)

WORLD-LEADER AND defending champion Ostapchuk only just qualified for the final in last place with 18.23, but then opened with 20.04, to which Vili, who had led the qualifying with 19.45, responded with 19.89. Vili improved to 19.95 in the fifth round in which Kleinert consolidated her third place from 19.45 in round two to 19.77 to take her third medal in her sixth World final. With the penultimate throw of the event Vili launched the shot, 20.54, adding 34cm to her Commonwealth and Oceania records, and with the last Ostapchuk came very close with 20.48. Vili became the youngest ever world shot champion at 22.

1. Valerie Vili NZL	20.54
2. Nadezhda Ostapchuk BLR	20.48
3. Nadine Kleinert GER	19.77
4. Li Ling CHN	19.38
5. Petra Lammert GER	19.33
6. Li Meiju CHN	18.83
7. Gong Lijiao CHN	18.66
8. Chiara Rosa ITA	18.39
9. Anna Omarova RUS	18.20
10. Yanina Pravalinskaya BLR	18.17
11. Misleydis González CUB	18.14
12. Yumileidi Cumbá CUB	17.93

Discus (Q 62.50m 27th, F 29th)

THE 39 YEAR-OLD DIETZSCH had the longest throw (65.17) in a qualifying round in which the 2nd, 3rd and 4th longest throwers of the year (Powell, Breisch and Cechlová) were eliminated but in which seven women produced longer throws than they did in the final. Dietzsch became champion for a third time and, competing in her ninth World Champs, the second oldest ever world gold medallist, producing the winning distance of 66.61 with just the third throw of the contest and throwing 66.48 in the second round. Barrios held second from a pb of 63.90 in the first round until Pishchalnikova recorded 65.14 in the third round and a pb of 65.78 in the fifth. The 2003 champion Yatchenko, aged 41, reached the final for a record seventh time.

1. Franka Dietzsch GER	66.61
2. Darya Pishchalnikova RUS	65.78
3. Yarelis Barrios CUB	63.90
4. Nicoleta Grasu ROM	63.40
5. Sun Taifeng CHN	63.22
6. Olena Antonova UKR	62.41
7. Joanna Wisniewska POL	61.35
8. Natalya Semenova UKR	61.17
9. Ma Xuejun CHN	59.37
10. Iryna Yatchenko BLR	58.67
11. Yania Ferrales CUB	58.20
12. Melina Robert-Michon FRA	57.81

Hammer (Q 71.00m 28th, F 30th)

SEVEN WOMEN EXCEEDED 70m in qualifying, headed by 74.69, the longest ever throw outside of a final, from Brkljacic. 68.15 by Martina Denisová (SVK) was the best ever non-qualifying mark in World Champs (note 68.21 in 04 OG) and there were best ever marks for 15 (=), 16, 18-22, but defending champion Kuzenkova was 22nd with 66.56. In the final nine over 70m bettered the previous world record of eight and the previous best at the World Champs of four. Brkljacic managed only 68.16 as Moreno 72.84 and Skolimowska 73.75 took first round leads, and Heidler took over with 74.76 in the second. Moreno threatened that lead with 74.33 in the fourth round, and after being demoted to third by Zhang Wenxiu 74.39 in the next, had a final throw of 74.74, just 2cm short of denying Heidler gold.

1. Betty Heidler GER	74.76
2. Yipsi Moreno CUB	74.74
3. Zhang Wenxiu CHN	74.39
4. Kamila Skolimowska POL	73.75
5. Yelena Konevtsova RUS	72.45
6. Eileen O'Keeffe IRL	70.93
7. Clarissa Claretti ITA	70.74
8. Manuela Montebrun FRA	70.36
9. Arasay Thondike CUB	70.20
10. Gulfiya Khanafeyeva RUS	69.08
11. Ivana Brkljacic CRO	68.16
12. Yunaika Crawford CUB	67.56

Javelin (Q 61.00m 29th, F 31st)

TWO CZECHS LED the qualifiers: Brejchová 64.20 and Spotáková 63.77, with world-leader Obergföll only ninth best with 60.77. Taina Kolkkala's 59.52 was the longest ever non-qualifying throw at a World Champs. Spotáková opened the final with a Czech record of 66.40 and improved to 67.07 in the third. Obergföll started with 64.01 and 65.26 before a final round 66.46. Brejchová threw 63.73 for third place in the third round, only to lose out in the fourth to 64.42 by Nerius, who moved to the bronze medal spot from 8th at 59.96; it was a third medal and record sixth final for her.

1. Barbora Spotáková CZE	67.07
2. Christina Obergföll GER	66.46
3. Steffi Nerius GER	64.42
4. Nikola Brejchová CZE	63.73
5. Sávva Líka GRE	63.13
6. Sonia Bisset CUB	61.74
7. Mariya Abakumova RUS	61.43
8. Linda Stahl GER	61.03
9. Barbara Madejczyk POL	58.37
10. Olga Ivankova UKR	57.87
11. Felicia Moldovan ROM	55.71
12. Paula Tarvainen FIN	53.50

Heptathlon (25-26th)

KLÜFT GAVE A wonderful display to became the first heptathlete to win three world titles. She equalled her 100mh pb of 13.15 and added 1cm to her high jump best with 1.95. Then in the long jump she produced two of her best ever efforts with 6.85 and 6.84 on her way to the European record score of 7032. In second place Blonska scored 6832 for a Ukrainian record and an improvement of nearly 400 points over her pre-2007 best, while despite another abysmal showing in the javelin Sotherton took the bronze with 6510, her second highest score. Ennis set pbs of 12.97 for 100mh and 23.15 for 200m and maintained her exciting progress with her highest score of 6469 in fourth place. Skujyté soared from 23rd place to fourth with a heptathlon world best shot put of 17.03 and after 52.63 in the javelin was lying third but lost three places with the 800m. There were 36 competitors in all.

1.	Carolina Klüft SWE	7032
2.	Lyudmila Blonska UKR	6832
3.	Kelly Sotherton GBR	6510
4.	Jessica Ennis GBR	6469
5.	Lilli Schwarzkopf GER	6439
6.	Austra Skujyté LTU	6380
7.	Jennifer Oeser GER	6378
8.	Nataliya Dobrynska UKR	6327
9.	Marie Collonvillé FRA	6244
10.	Anna Bogdanova RUS	6243
11.	Ida Marcussen NOR	6226
12.	Kylie Wheeler AUS	6184
13.	Sonja Kesselschläger GER	6149
14.	Jolanda Keizer NED	6102
15.	Karolina Tyminska POL	6092

4 x 100 Metres Relay (h & F 1st)

THE HEATS WERE won by Belgium (NR 42.85) and USA 42.24 (from Jamaica 42.70), and the Americans took gold in a world leading 41.98 but it was close as on the final leg Campbell (10.06) sped to within 0.03 of Edwards (10.21). This was the ninth women's 4x100 medal for Jamaica and seventh for the USA at 11 Worlds. The British squad was in third place at the last change but Gevaert, who had withdrawn from the 200m semis to be fresh for this race, ran down Maduaka to snatch bronze in a national record time with a 10.17 leg and earn Belgium's first relay medal at Worlds or Olympics.

1. USA	41.98	L Williams, Felix, Mik. Barber, Edwards
2. JAM	42.01	Brooks, Stewart, Facey, Campbell
3. BEL	42.75	Borlée, Mariën, Ouédraogo, Gevaert
4. GBR	42.87	Turner, Douglas, Freeman, Maduaka
5. RUS	42.97	Grigoryeva, Rusakova, Gushchina, Polyakova
6. BLR	43.37	Shulyak, Safronnikova, Nevmerzhitskaya, Dragun
7. GER	43.51	Wakan, Tschirch, Kedzierski, Sailer
8. POL	43.57	Jeschke, Korczynska, Jedrusinska, Klocek

4 x 400 Metres Relay (h 1st, F 2nd)

THE USA AND Russia were closely matched as they won the heats in 3:23.37 and 3:23.49, but in the final it was very different. Shericka Williams gave Jamaica a slight first leg lead over Britian but then Felix ran a fabulous leg of 48.0 to take the USA from fourth place into a lead they would never lose. Richards brought the USA home safely in the world's quickest time since 1993, and a splendid 48.93 by Novlene Williams assured Jamaica of second place in a time of 3:19.73 for a Commonwealth and CAC record, with Sanders, making up at least six metres on the Russian Antyukh, snatching third place in a national record with a 48.76 leg, the fastest ever UK split.

1. USA	3:18.55	Trotter 51.2, Felix 48.0, Wineberg 50.24, Richards 49.07
2. JAM	3:19.73	S Williams 50.5, Lloyd 50.1, Prendergast 50.18, N Williams 48.93
3. GBR	3:20.04	Ohuruogu 50.6, Okoro 50.9, McConnell 49.79, Sanders 48.76
4. RUS	3:20.25	Litvinova 51.1, Nazarova 50.0, Veshkurova 49.79, Antyukh 49.40
5. BLR	3:21.88	Yushchenko 51.4, Khlyustova 50.7, I Usovich 49.97, S Usovich 49.78
6. POL	3:26.49	Radecka 51.8, Prokopek 50.6, Setowska-Dyrk 52.58, Jesien 51.44
7. CUB	3:27.05	Martínez 52.2, Pernía 51.8, Calatayud 52.20, Terrero 50.85
8. MEX	3:29.14	Rodríguez 53.7, Medina 51.6, Vela 53.20, Guevara 50.66

20 Kilometres Walk (31st)

KANISKINA LED THE whole way in debilitatingly hot and humid conditions with some rain. She was 20 sec clear of her training companion Shemyakina after 5k (22:21), was 44 sec up at halfway in 44:33 (22:12) and 56 sec ahead at 15k in 1:06:46 (22:13). She lost ground during the closing kilometres (23:23 final 5k) but still finished 33 sec in front of her Russian team-mate. Vasco walked the fastest second half (45:53 + 44:54) to finish only 5 sec behind Shemyakina after being 36 sec behind at halfway. Defending champion Ivanova, who had not raced this year, dropped out in the first few minutes before the walkers had even left the stadium – when fourth of the Russians who were spaced out ahead of the field. 33 of 42 finished.

1.	Olga Kaniskina RUS	1:30:09
2.	Tatyana Shemyakina RUS	1:30:42
3.	María Vasco ESP	1:30:47
4.	Kjersti Plätzer NOR	1:31:24
5.	Susana Feitor POR	1:32:01
6.	Claudia Stef ROM	1:32:47
7.	Inês Henriques POR	1:33:06
8.	Sabine Zimmer GER	1:33:23
9.	Tatyana Sibileva RUS	1:33:29
10.	Mayumi Kawasaki JPN	1:33:35
11.	Vera Santos POR	1:34:28
12.	María José Poves ESP	1:35:06
13.	Beatriz Pascual ESP	1:35:13
14.	Melanie Seeger GER	1:35:30
15.	Song Hongjuan CHN	1:35:44

• **Contesting record 8th final at one event**: Maria Mutola (800m).

• **Competing at record 9th Championships**: Men: Tim Berrett (19th 50kmW); Women: Franka Dietzsch (1st DT), Jackie Edwards (dnq 27th LJ), Laverne Eve (dnq 20th JT), Susana Feitor (5th 20kmW), Maria Mutola (dnf 800m).

2007 CHAMPIONSHIPS

IAAF World Half Marathon Championships

At Udine, Italy 14 October

Men

1. Zersenay Tadese ERI 58:59
2. Patrick Makau KEN 59:02
3. Evans Cheruiyot KEN 59:05
4. Deriba Merga ETH 59:16
5. Yones Kifle ERI 59:30
6. Dieudonné Disi RWA 59:32
7. Marilson dos Santos BRA 59:33
8. Dickson Marwa Mkami TAN 60:24
9. Atsushi Sato JPN 60:25
10. Cuthbert Nyasango ZIM 60:26
11. Fabiano Joseph TAN 60:27
12. Raji Assefa ETH 60:31
13. Michael Tesfay ERI 60:39
14, Saadoun Al-Dawoodi QAT 60:39
15. Robert Kipchumba KEN 60:47
16. Samson Kiflemariam ERI 60:52
17. Nicholas Kiprono UGA 60:57
18. Tariku Jifar ETH 61:28
19. Ezekiel Ngimba TAN 61:28
20. Pierre Joncheray FRA 61:36.

79 of 82 finished

Teams: 1. KEN 2:58:54, 2. ERI 2:59:08, 3. ETH 3:01:15, 4. TAN 3:02:19, 5. QAT 3:04:03, 6. RWA 3:04:14, 7. JPN 3:04:53, 8. UGA 3:05:09, 9. BRA 3:05:14, 10. RSA 3:08:32, 11. ITA 3:08:39, 12. AUT 3:10:59, 13. ESP 3:11:04, 14. RUS 3:11:15; 17 nations scored.

Women

1. Lornah Kiplagat NED 66:25 WR
2. Mary Keitany KEN 66:48
3. Pamela Chepchumba KEN 68:06
4. Bezunesh Bekele ETH 68:07
5. Atsede Habtamu ETH 68:29
6. Evelyne Kimwei KEN 68:39
7. Chisato Ozaki JPN 68:56
8. Luminita Talpos ROM 69:01
9. Alice Timbilil KEN 69:09
10. Alina Gherasim ROM 69:14
11. Atsede Baysa ETH 69:15
12. Akane Taira JPN 69:17
13. Yoshimi Ozaki JPN 69:26
14. Irina Timofeyeva RUS 69:29
15. Alina Ivanova RUS 69:32
16. Deena Kastor USA 69:38
17. Olga Glok RUS 69:58
18. Lidia Simon ROM 70:08
19. Genet Getaneh ETH 70:30
20. Krisztina Papp HUN 70:53

56 of 62 finished

Teams: 1. KEN 3:23:33, 2. ETH 3:25:51, 3. JPN 3:27:39, 4. ROM 3:28:23, 5. RUS 3:28:59, 6. USA 3:36:26, 7. ITA 3:35:05, 8. COL 3:53:14, 8 nations scored

5th IAAF World Youth Championships

At Ostrava, Czech Republic 11-15 July

In all 1228 athletes took part, new championship records were set in 11 events and a record number of 41 countries won medals.

100m	1. Dexter Lee JAM 10.51
(-0.4)	2. Nickel Ashmeade JAM 10.54
	3. Kenneth Gilstrap USA 10.65
200m	1. Ramone McKenzie JAM 20.67
(-0.2)	2. Ramil Guliyev AZE 20.72
	3. Nickel Ashmeade JAM 20.76
400m	1. Chris Clarke GBR 46.74
	2. Kirani James GRN 46.96
	3. Vladimir Krasnov RUS 47.03
800m	1. Geoffrey Kibet KEN 1:49.99
	2. Ali Al-Deraan KSA 1:50.10
	3. Amine El Manaoui MAR 1:50.12
1500m	1. Fredrick Musyoki KEN 3:44.27
	2. Josphat Mitunga KEN 3:44.68
	3. Dawit Wolde ETH 3:45.03
3000m	1. Daniel Salel KEN 7:57.18
	2. Lucas Rotich KEN 7:59.67
	3. Hicham El Amrani MAR 8:00.98
2000mSt	1. Legese Lamiso ETH 5:30.81
	2. Silas Kosgei Kiptum KEN 5:32.88
	3. Abdellah Dacha MAR 5:34.49
110mh	1. Wayne Davis USA 13.18*
(0.2)	2. William Wynne USA 13.44
(91.4cm)	3. Denis Semenov KAZ 13.82
400mh	1. William Wynne USA 49.01*
(84cm)	2. Reginald Wyatt USA 50.33
	3. Amaurys Valle CUB 50.37
HJ	1. Wang Chen CHN 2.22
	2. Sergey Mudrov RUS 2.22
	3. Josh Hall AUS 2.20
PV	1. Nico Wieler GER 5.26*
	2= Manuel Concepción ESP 4.85
	2= Shiota Doi JPN 4.85
LJ	1. Yasimichi Konishi JPN 7.52w/2.2
	2. Daisuke Yoshiyama JPN 7.32/1.1
	3. Christian Taylor USA 7.29/0.8
TJ	1. Christian Taylor USA 15.98/0.6
	2. Aleksey Federov RUS 15.59/0.2
	3. Gennadiy Chudinov RUS 15.54/0.2
SP 5kg	1, David Storl GER 21.40
	2. Marin Premeru CRO 20.42
	3. Dmytro Savytskyy UKR 20.15
DT 1.5kg	1. Mykyta Nesterenko UKR 68.54
	2. Marin Premeru CRO 64.20
	3. Andrius Gudzius LTU 61.59
HT 5kg	1. Andriy Martynyuk UKR 76.09
	2. Daniel Szabó HUN 75.30
	3. Richard Olbrich GER 75.18
JT 700g	1. Tuomas Laaksonen FIN 79.71
	2. Hamish Peacock AUS 76.31
	3. Edgars Rütins LAT 74.65
Octathlon	1. Shane Brathwaite BAR 6261
	2. Jaroslav Hedvicák CZE 6212

	3. Adam Bevis AUS 6212
10kmW	1. Stanislav Emelyanov RUS 41:49.91*
	2. Pedro Daniel Gómez MEX 43:11.87
	3. Vito Di Bari ITA 43:36.13
MedleyR	1. USA (Sweeney, Gilstrap, Wynne, Fortsun) 1:51.34
	2. JPN 1:51.42 3. JAM 1:52.18
Women	
100m (0.9)	1. Asha Philip GBR 11.46
	2. Rosângela Santos BRA 11.46
	3. Ashlee Nelson GBR 11.58
200m (-1.9)	1. Bárbara Leoncio BRA 23.50
	2. Chalonda Goodman USA 23.54
	3. Nivea Smith BAH 23.69
400m	1. Yuliya Baraley UKR 53.57
	2. Latoya McDermott JAM 54.12
	3. Alexandra Stuková SVK 54.46
800m	1. Elena Mirela Lavric ROM 2:04.29
	2. Alison Leonard GBR 2:05.36
	3. Juana Ivis Méndez CUB 2:05.42
1500m	1. Sammary Cherotich KEN 4:15.47
	2. Jordan Hasay USA 4:17.24
	3. Sheila Chepkirui Kiprotich KEN 4:19.26
3000m	1, Mercy Cherono KEN 8:53.94*
	2. Mahlet Melese ETH 8:56.98
	3. Sule Utura ETH 9:06.48
2000mSt	1. Caroline Chepkurui KEN 6:22.30*
	2. Christine Kambua KEN 6:22.49
	3. Karoline Bjerkeli Grøvdal NOR 6:25.30
100mh (-1.3) (76.2cm)	1. Julian Purvis USA 13.41
	2. Shermaine Williams JAM 13.48
	3. Anne Zagre BEL 13.58
400mh	1. Dalilah Muhammad USA 57.25
	2. Andreea Ionescu ROM 57.33
	3. Ryann Krais USA 57.50
HJ	1. Natalya Mamlina RUS 1.89
	2. Misha-Gaye DaCosta JAM 1.84
	3= Aleksandrina Klimentinova BUL 1.81
	3= Elena Vallortigara ITA 1.81
PV	1. Vicky Parnov AUS 4.35*
	2. Ekateríni Stefanídi GRE 4.25
	3. Petra Olsen SWE 4.05
LJ	1, Darya Klishina RUS 6.47*/1.3
	2. Ivana Spanovic SRB 6.41/0.5
	3. Mariya Shumilova RUS 6.29/1.0
TJ	1. Dailenis Alcántara CUB 13.63/1.0
	2. Yosleidis Rivalta CUB 13.32/0.3
	3. Maja Bratkic SLO 12.96/-1.3
SP	1. Aliona Hryshko BLR 15.91
	2. Samira Burkhardt GER 15.36
	3. Sophie Kleeberg GER 14.94
DT	1. Julia Fischer GER 51.39
	2. Sandra Perkovic CRO 51.25
	3. Jin Yuanyuan CHN 51.20
HT	1. Bianca Perie ROM 64.61*
	2. Adriána Papadopoúlou-Fatála GRE 56.32
	3. Barbara Spiler SLO 55.97
JT	1. Tazmin Brits RSA 51.71
	2. Carita Hinkka FIN 51.61
	3. Sini Kiiski FIN 50.75
Hep	1. Katerina Cachová CZE 5641
	2. Carolin Schäfer GER 5544
	3. Elisa-Sophie Döbel GER 5494
5000mW	1, Tatyana Kalmykova RUS 20:28.05*
	2. Irina Yumanova RUS 21:21.14
	3. Panayióta Tsinopoúlou GRE 22:49.15
Medley R	1. USA (Goodman, A Purvis, Krais, E Alexander) 2:05.74
	2. JAM 2:06.77 3. CAN 2:09.08

** = Championships or Games record throughout the championships section*

Medal & Points Table Leaders

Nat	G	S	B	Pts
USA	7	4	3	145
RUS	4	3	3	99
KEN	6	4	1	91
GER	3	2	3	88
AUS	1	1	2	82
JAM	2	5	2	70
JPN	1	3	-	60
UKR	3	-	1	53
GBR	2	1	1	53
ROM	2	1	-	44
ETH	1	1	2	42

41 nations won medals

IAAF World Race Walking Challenge

2007 events were: Naucalpan MEX 10-11 Mar, Shenzhen CHN 24-25 Mar, Rio Maior POR 14 Apr, Sesto San Giovanni ITA 1 May, La Coruña ESP 2 Jun, Karków POL 23 Jun, final at Saransk, RUS 29 Sep. Walkers needed to compete at four or more of the eight events to qualify and final positions were based on the best positions from any three races, with 10 points for a win, nine for 2nd, eight for 3rd, and so on, down to 10th. Prize money was awarded to the first eight – from $30,000 for 1st to $5000 for 8th.

Men: 1. Luke Adams AUS 36, 2. Erik Tysse NOR 33, 3. Francisco Javier Fernández ESP 32, 4. Eder Sánchez MEX 28, 5. Hatem Ghoula TUN 28, 6. Ivano Brugnetti ITA 10, 7= Jared Tallent AUS, João Vieira POR 6. Only competed in two races: Nathan Deakes AUS 22, Jefferson Pérez ECU 19, Vladimir Kanaykin RUS 18.

Women: 1. Rita Turova BLR 40, 2. Kjersti Plätzer NOR 37, 3. Sabine Zimmer GER 27, 4. Elisa Rigaudo ITA 20, 5. Yelena Ginko BLR 17, 6. Claudia Stef ROM 16, 7. Jane Saville AUS 13, 8. Susana Feitor POR 12. Only competed in 2/3 races: Olga Kaniskina RUS 28, Jiang Jing CHN 15, Song Hongjuan CHN, Bai Yanmin CHN 13.

23rd WMRA World Mountain Running Trophy 2006

At Ovronnaz, Switzerland 15 September

Men (12.15km, 939 height difference): 1. Marco De Gasperi ITA 51:50, 2. Tesfaye Yohannes ERI 52:20, 3. Ermias Tesfazghi ERI 53:03, 4. Joseph Symonds SCO 53:03, 5. Adam Grice ENG 53:11. **Team:** 1. ITA 30, 2. ERI 30, 3. SUI 61, 4. FRA 98, 5. ENG 102; **Women** (8.1km, 626 HD): 1. Anna Pichrtová CZE 39:12, 2. Andrea Mayr AUT 39:53, 3. Laura Haefili USA 41:20, 4. Elisa Desco ITA 41:26, 5, Maria Rodríguez COL 41:38. **Team:** 1. USA 23, 2. CZE 24, 3. ITA 29, 4. ENG 50, 5. FRA 57; **Junior Men** (8.1km, 626m HD): Geoffrey Kusuro UGA 34:27, **Team:** ERI 9; **Junior Women** (4.05km, 313m HD): Lara Tamsett AUS 20:48, **Team:** AUS 4.

IAAF World Combined Events Challenge

The IAAF World Combined Events Challenge is based on the sum of the best scores achieved in any three of the 13 designated competitions during the year. The men's decathlon winner, for the fourth time, was Roman Sebrle and the women's heptathlon winner Lyudmila Blonska. Having won for the previous four years, Carolina Klüft only contested two heptathlons. Andrey Kravchenko did complete three decathlons – and the combined score from these at 25,662 would have given him the series, but unfortunately his European U23 Championships win (8492) did not count. As well as Talence he also won at Götzis (8617).

Men Decathlon

1	Roman Sebrle CZE	25,261	8518 Götzis	8676 Worlds	8067 Talence
2	Maurice Smith JAM	25,220	8278 Pan Ams	8644 Worlds	8298 Talence
3	Aleksey Drozdov RUS	24,972	8373 Götzis	8475 Worlds	8124 Talence
4	Romain Barras FRA	24,473	8064 Götzis	8147 Arles	8262 Worlds
5	Paul Terek USA	24,318	8134 Desenzano	8064 US Champs	8120 Worlds
6	Hans Van Alphen BEL	24,011	7930 Eur Cup-1	8047 WUG	8034 Worlds
7	Jacob Minah GER	23,856	7759 Götzis	7998 Ratingen	8099 WUG
8	Norman Müller GER	23,843	8255 Götzis	8244 Ratingen	7344 Worlds
9	François Gourmet BEL	23,807	7925 Arles	7908 Eur Cup-1	7974 Worlds
10	Ryan Harlan USA	23,471	7901 NACAC	7883 US Ch	7687 Pan Ams

Women Heptathlon

1	Lyudmila Blonska UKR	19,895	6626 Götzis	6832 Worlds	6437 Talence
2	Jessica Ennis GBR	19,256	6388 Desenzano	6399 Eur Cup	6469 Worlds
3	Austra Skujyte LTU	18,994	6277 Götzis	6337 Eur Cup-2	6380 Worlds
4	Jennifer Oeser GER	18,994	6366 Götzis	6250 Ratingen	6378 Worlds
5	Lilli Schwarzkopf GER	18,984	6202 Götzis	6343 Ratingen	6439 Worlds
6	Kelly Sotherton GBR	18,949	6210 Götzis	6229 Eur Cup	6510 Worlds
7	Nataliya Dobrynska UKR	18,699	6134 Arles	6327 Worlds	6238 Talence
8	Jessica Zelinka CAN	18,697	6343 Götzis	6218 Arles	6136 Pan Ams
9	Kylie Wheeler AUS	18,440	6158 Arles	6098 Ratingen	6184 Worlds
10	Karolina Tyminska POL	18,300	6164 Götzis	6044 Eur Cup	6092 Worlds

Prize Money: 1st $30,000, 2nd $20,000, 3rd $15,000, 4th $10,000, 5th $8000, 6th $7000, 7th $6000, 8th $5000

World University Games

At Bangkok, Thailand 9-14 August

100m (-0.9) 1. Simeon Williamson GBR 10.22
2. Zhang Peimeng CHN 10.30
3. Neville Wright CAN 10.37

200m (0.2) 1. Amr Ibrahim Seoud EGY 20.74
2. Leigh Julius RSA 20.96
3. Tomoya Kamiyama JPN 20.97

400m 1. Sean Wroe AUS 45.49
2. Piotr Klimczak POL 46.06
3. Dmitriy Buryak RUS 46.22

800m 1. Ehsan Mohajershojaei IRI 1:46.04
2. Fabiano Peçanha BRA 1:46.11
3. Livio Sciandra ITA 1:46.19

1500m 1. Samir Khadar ALG 3:39.62
2. Alvaro Rodríguez ESP 3:39.78
3. Fabiano Peçanha BRA 3:40.98

5000m 1. Halil Akkas TUR 14:08.47
2. Yuki Matsuoka JPN 14:09.33
3. Simon Ayeko UGA 14:10.13

10,000m 1. Mohamed Fadil MAR 30:19.41
2. Simon Ayeko UGA 30:22.58
3. Stephen Mokoka RSA 30:31.78

HMar 1. Mohamed Fadil MAR 65:49
2. Najim El Gady MAR 66:04
3. Takashi Toyoda JPN 66:30

3000mSt 1. Halil Akkas TUR 8:20.83*
2. Barnabas Kirui KEN 8:22.07
3. Ion Luchianov MDA 8:23.83

110mh (-0.2) 1. Sergiy Demydyuk UKR 13.33
2. Ji Wei CHN 13.57
3. Anselmo da Silva BRA 13.58

400mh 1. Petrus Koekemoer RSA 49.06
2. Kurt Couto MOZ 49.12
3. Javier Culson PUR 49.35

HJ 1. Aleksandr Shustov RUS 2.31
2. Kyriacos Ioannou CYP 2.26
3. Oleksandr Nartov UKR 2.26

PV 1. Alexander Straub GER 5.60
2. Leonid Kivalov RUS 5.60
3. Dmitriy Starodubtsev RUS 5.50

LJ 1. Robert Crowther AUS 8.02/0.6
2. Chao Chih-Chien TPE 7.95/0.8
3. Roman Novotny CZE 7.88/0.9

TJ 1. Kim Deok-hyeon KOR 17.02/0.7
2. Viktor Kuznyetsov UKR 16.94/0.0
3. Wu Bo CHN 16.64/-0.7

SP 1. Maksim Sidorov RUS 20.01
2. Maris Urtans LAT 19.38
3. Chang Ming-Huang TPE 19.36

DT 1. Gerhard Mayer AUT 61.55
2. Omar El-Ghazaly EGY 60.89
3. Mart Israel EST 60.32

HT 1. Aleksandr Vashchilo BLR 76.94
2. Aleksandr Kozuklo BLR 74.52
3. Igor Vinichenko RUS 73.94

JT 1 Vadims Vasilevskis LAT 83.92
2. Igor Janik POL 82.28
3. Ainars Kovals LAT 82.23

Dec 1. Jacob Minah GER 8099
2. Hans Van Alphen BEL 8047
3. Carlos Eduardo Chinin BRA 7920

20kmW 1. Chu Yafei CHN 1:24:37

2. Park Chil-sung KOR 1:24:42
3. Koichiro Morioka JPN 1:25:10

4x100m 1. THA (Autas, Sondee, Suwannaramgsri, Suwonprateep) 39.15
2. RSA (Dreyer, Julius, Kotze, Prinsloo) 39.20
3. CHN (Wang X, Zhang P, Du B, Yin H) 39.30

4x400m 1. POL (Banka, Klimczak, Kedzia, Dabrowski) 3:02.05
2. AUS (Grant, Ormrod, Milburn, Wroe) 3:02.76
3. RUS (Aleksandrov, Kruglyakov, Antimanis, Buryak) 3:05.04

Women

100m (-0.8) 1. Johanna Manninen FIN 11.46
2. Olena Chebanu UKR 11.56
3. Audra Dagelyte LTU 11.65

200m (1.3) 1. Iryna Shtangyeyeva UKR 22.95
2. Kadi-Ann Thomas GBR 23.28
3. Hanna Mariën BEL 23.48

400m 1. Olga Tereshkova KAZ 51.62
2. Danijela Grgic CRO 51.88
3. Ksenia Zadorina RUS 51.89

800m 1. Yuliya Krevsun UKR 1:57.63
2. Yekaterina Kostetskaya RUS 1:59.52
3. Charlotte Best GBR 2:01.50

1500m 1. Olesya Chumakova RUS 4:09.32
2. Tetyana Holovchenko UKR 4:10.46
3. Sylwia Ejdys POL 4:11.51

5000m 1. Jessica Augusto POR 15:28.78*
2. Tetyana Holovchenko UKR 15:40.56
3. Elizaveta Grechishnikova RUS 15:50.58

10,000m 1. Ksenia Agafonova RUS 32:20.94
2. Ryoko Kizaki JPN 32:55.11
3. Jo Bun-hui PRK 33:20.55

HMar 1. Kim Kum-ok PRK 72:31
2. Lei Terada JPN 72:37
3. Jong Yong-ok PRK 73:56

3000mSt 1. Dobrinka Shalamanova BUL 9:45.04
2. Valentina Horpynych UKR 9:45.55
3. Türkan Erismis TUR 9:46.12

100mh (-0.3) 1. Yevgeniya Volodzko BLR 13.03
2. Nevin Yanit TUR 13.07
3. Yevgeniya Snigur UKR 13.08

400mh 1. Tatyana Azarova KAZ 55.52
2. Anastasiya Rabchenyuk UKR 55.98
3. Jonna Tilgner GER 56.27

HJ 1. Marina Aitova KAZ 1.92
2= Ariane Friedrich GER 1.90
3= Anna Ustinova KAZ 1.90

PV 1. Aleksandra Kiryashova RUS 4.40
2. Kristina Gadschiew GER 4.40
3. Nicola Büchler SUI 4.35

LJ 1. Olga Rypakova KAZ 6.85/-0.7
2. Yelena Sokolova RUS 6.61/0.4
3. Stilianí Pilátou GRE 6.52/-0.3

TJ 1. Olga Saladuha UKR 14.79/0.4
2. Dana Veldáková SVK 14.41/0.1
3. Yarianna Martínez CUB 14.25/0.9

SP 1. Irina Tarasova RUS 17.46
2. Yuliya Leontyuk BLR 17.20
3. Magdalena Sobieszek POL 16.88

DT 1. Yarelys Barrios CUB 61.36
2. Dani Samuels AUS 60.47
3. Dragana Tomasevic SRB 56.82

HT 1. Darya Pchelnik BLR 68.74
2. Eileen O'Keeffe IRL 68.46
3. Lenka Ledvinová CZE 66.41

JT 1. Buoban Pamang THA 61.40
2. Monica Stoian ROM 61.19
3. Urszula Jasinska POL 60.63

Hep 1. Viktorija Zemaityte LTU 5971
2. Sara Aerts BEL 5904
3. Hanna Melnychenko UKR 5852

20kmW 1. Jiang Qiuyan CHN 1:35:22
2. Lidia Mongelli ITA 1:37:23
3. Snezhana Yurchenko BLR 1:37:26

4x100m 1. FIN (Hannula, Keskitalo, Ranta, Manninen) 43.48
2. THA (Jaksunin, Klomdee, Thavoncharoen, Saenrat) 43.92
3. UKR (Chebanu, Tonkovyd, Shtangyeyeva, Shepetyuk) 43.99

4x400m 1. UKR (Pygyda, Yefremova, Zavorodnya, Shcherbak) 3:29.59
2. RUS (Shulikova, Voynova, Kochetova, Zadorina) 3:30.49
3. GBR (Massey, Finucane, Thomas, Harding) 3:33.70

Medals and Placing Table Leaders

Nat	*G*	*S*	*B*	*Pts*
RUS	6	4	6	200
UKR	5	6	4	149
JPN	-	3	3	85
BLR	3	2	6	73
CHN	2	2	2	69
GER	2	2	1	56
KAZ	4	1	-	55
RSA	1	2	1	54
POL	1	2	3	50
AUS	2	2	-	48
GBR	1	-	1	47
ITA	-	1	1	42
THA	2	1	-	37
BRA	-	1	3	34
TUR	2	1	1	32
MAR	2	1	-	30
PRK	1	-	2	30
LAT	1	1	1	29
LTU	1	-	1	28
FIN	2	-	-	25
CAN	-	-	1	25

Athletes from 46 nations won medals.

9th All-Africa Games

At Alger, Algeria 18-22 July

100m (0.6) 1. Olusoji Fasuba NGR 10.18
2. Eric Nkansah GHA 10.35
3. Uchenna Emedolu NGR 10.37

200m (-0.7) 1. Leigh Julius RSA 20.81
2. Seth Amoo GHA 20.88
3. Obinna Metu NGR 20.94

400m 1. California Molefe BOT 45.59
2. Young Talkmore Nyongani ZIM 45.76
3. Mathieu Gnaligo BEN 45.89

800m 1. Abubaker Kaki SUD 1:45.22
2. Mbulaeni Mulaudzi RSA 1:45.54
3. Justus Koech KEN 1:45.80

1500m 1. Asbel Kiprop KEN 3:38.97
2. Anter Zerguelaine ALG 3:39.04
3. Tarek Boukensa ALG 3:39.18

5000m 1. Moses Kipsiro UGA 13:12.51
2. Kiprono Menjo KEN 13:12.64
3. Tariku Bekele ETH 13:13.43

10,000m 1. Zersenay Tadese ERI 27:00.30*
2. Tadesse Tola ETH 27:28.08
3. Gebregziabher Gebremariam ETH 27:41.24

HMar 1. Deriba Merga ETH 62:24*
2. Martin Sulle TAN 63:01
3. Yonas Kifle ERI 63:19

3000mSt 1. Willy Komen KEN 8:15.11
2. Ezekiel Kemboi KEN 8:16.93
3. Nahom Mesfin Tariku ETH 8:17.21

110mh: (0.0) 1. Selim Nurudeen NGR 13.59*
2. Berlioz Randriahihaja MAD 13.72
3. Shaun Bownes RSA 13.

400mh 1. L.J. van Zyl RSA 48.74
2. Pieter de Villiers RSA 48.91
3. Alwyn Myburgh RSA 48.91

HJ 1. Kabelo Kgosiemang BOT 2.27*
2. Abderahmane Hammad ALG 2.24
3= Obiora Arinze NGR 2,20
3= Mohammed Benhadja ALG 2.20

PV 1. Abderrahman Tamedda TUN 5.10
2. Karim Sène SEN 5.10
3. Hamdo Dhouibi TUN 4.90

LJ 1. Gable Garenamotse BOT 8.08/0.7
2. Arnaud Casquette MRI 8.03/1.4
3. Khotso Mokoena RSA 7.99/0.6

TJ 1. Ndiss Kaba Badji SEN 16.80/0.0
2. Hugo Mamba CMR 16.61/0.0
3. Andrew Owusu GHA 16.32/1.0

SP 1. Yasser Fathi Ibrahim EGY 19.20
2. Roelie Potgieter RSA 19.02
3. Mohammed Meddeb TUN 17.94

DT 1. Omar El-Ghazaly EGY 62.28
2. Yasser Fathi Ibrahim EGY 61.58
3. Hannes Hopley RSA 57.79

HT 1. Chris Harmse RSA 76.73*
2. Mohsen Anani EGY 72.00
3. Saber Souid TUN 70.01

JT 1. Robert Oosthuizen RSA 78.05
2. Hardus Pienaar RSA 76.70
3. Mohamed Ali Kbabou TUN 71.77

Dec 1. Hamdi Dhouibi TUN 7838
2. Boualem Lamri ALG 7473
3. Larbi Bouraada ALG 7349

20kmW 1. Hatem Ghoula TUN 1:22:33
2. David Kimutai KEN 1:24:16
3. Mohamed Ameur ALG 1:25:12

4x100m 1. NGR (Isaac, Metu, Oriala, Fasuba) 38.91
2. RSA 39.11 3. ZIM 39.16

4x400m 1. BOT (Kamberuka, Makwala, Ngwigwa, Kelautswe) 3:03.16
2. NGR 3:03.99 3. ZIM 3:04.84

Women

100m (0.6) 1. Damola Osayomi NGR 11.20
2. Nombulelo Mkenku RSA11.27
3. Vida Anim GHA 11.33

200m (-0.8) 1. Damola Osayomi NGR 23.21
2. Vida Anim GHA 23.29
3. Amandine Allou Affoué CIV 23.44

400m 1. Amantie Montsho BOT 51.13
2. Joy Eze NGR 51.20
3. Shade Abugan NGR 51.44

800m 1. Leonora Piuza MOZ 2:02.83
2. Agnes Samaria NAM 2:03.17
3. Nahida Touhami ALG 2:03.79

1500m 1. Gelete Burka ETH 4:06.89*
2. Veronica Nyaruai Wanjiru KEN 4:09.11
3. Agnes Samaria NAM 4:09.18

5000m 1. Meseret Defar ETH 15:02.72*
2. Meselech Melkamu ETH 15:03.86
3. Sylvia Kibet KEN 15:06.39

10,000m 1. Mestawet Tufa ETH 31:26.05
2. Edith Masai KEN 31:31.18
3. Irene Kwambai KEN 31:36.67

HMar 1. Souad Aït Salem ALG 73:35
2. Atseda Bayisa ETH 73:54
3. Kenza Dahmani ALG 74:10

3000mSt 1. Ruth Bisibori KEN 9:31.99*
2. Mekdes Bekele ETH 9:49.95
3. Netsanet Achano ETH 9:51.63

100mh (1.3) 1. Toyin Augustus NGR 13.23
2. Jessica Ohanaja NGR 13.27
3. Fatmata Fofanah GUI 13.51

400mh 1. Muna Jabir Ahmed SUD 54.93
2. Aïssata Soulama BUR 55.49
3. Joke Odumosu NGR 55.80

HJ 1. Doreen Amata NGR1.89
2. Anika Smit RSA 1.89
3. Marcoleen Pretorius RSA 1.83

PV 1. Leila Ben-Youssef TUN 3.85
2. Ahmed Eman Nesrim EGY 3.60
3. Eva Thornton RSA 3.60

LJ 1. Janice Josephs RSA 6.79/0.1
2. Blessing Okagbare NGR 6.46/1.8
3. Yah Koïta MLI 6.35w/2.2

TJ 1. Yamilé Aldama SUD 14.46/0.5
2. Chinoye Ohadugha NGR 14.21/-0.3
3. Iworima Otonye NGR 13.83/0.9

SP 1. Vivian Chukwuemeka NGR 17.60
2. Simoné du Toit RSA 16.77
3. Veronica Abrahmse RSA 15.75

DT 1. Elizna Naude RSA 58.40
2. Monia Kari TUN 55.15
3. Vivian Chukwuemeka NGR 52.52

HT 1. Marwa Hussein EGY 65.70
2. Florence Ezeh TIG 59.55
3. Vivian Chukwuemeka NGR 58.15
drugs dq (2) Susan Adeoye Olufunke NGR 64.04

JT 1. Justine Robbeson RSA 58.09
2. Lindy Leveau-Agricole SEY 56.49
3. Sunette Viljoen RSA 54.46

Hep 1. Margaret Simpson GHA 6278
2. Patience Okoro NGR 5161
3. Béatrice Kamboule BUR 4994

20kmW 1, Cheima Trabelsi TUN 1:49:13
2. Mercy Njoroge KW}EN 1:49:18
3. Ararissa Abissa Asnakch ETH 1:49:29

4x100m 1. GHA (Salifu, Dankwah, Addy, Anim) 43.84
2. NGR 43.85; 3. CIV 44.48

4x400m 1. NGR 3:29.74
2. RSA 3:33.62 3. SUD 3:34.84

17th Asian Championships

At Amman, Jordan 25-29 July

100m 1. Samuel Francis QAT 9.99*

(0.9) 2. Masahide Ueno JPN 10.26
3. Ibrahim Al-Waleed QAT 10.30

200m 1. Kenji Fujimitsu JPN 20.85
(0.8) 2. Ibrahim Al-Waleed QAT 20.98
3. Khalil Al-Hanahneh JOR 21.03

400m 1. Prasanna Amarasekara SRI 46.71
2. Reza Bouazar IRI 46.90
3. Mohammad Akefian IRI 46.93

800m 1, Mohammed Al-Salhi KSA 1:51.73
2. Sadjad Moradi IRI 1:52.22
3. Ali Abubaker Kamal QAT 1: 52.22

1500m 1. Mohammed Othman Shaween KSA 3:46.85
2. Sadjad Moradi IRI 3:47.01
3. Ali Abubaker Kamal QAT 3:47.22

5000m 1. Felix K. Kibore QAT 14:07.12
2. Abdullah Ahmad Hassan QAT 14:08.66
3. Ishaq Issa Abdeen BRN 14:18.47

10,000m 1. Abdullah Ahmad Hassan QAT 29:45.95
2. Ali Saadoun Al-Dawoodi QAT 29:58.33
3. Hassan Mahbood Ali BRN 30:05.12

3000mSt 1. Ali Ahmad Ali-Amri KSA 8:40.25
2. Kamal Ali Thamer QAT 8:40.49
3. Moustafa Shebto QAT 8:47.99

110mh 1. Tasuku Tanonaka JPN 13.51
(5.3) 2. Mohammed Al-Thawadi QAT 13.55
3. Wu Youjia CHN 13.68

400mh 1. Yevgeniy Meleshenko KAZ 50.01
2. Yosuke Tsushima JPN 50.14
3. Joseph Abraham IND 50.28

HJ 1. Lee Hup Wei MAS 2.24
2. Jean-Claude Rabbath LIB 2.21
3. Satoru Kubota JPN 2.21

PV 1. Mohammad Mohsen Rabbani IRI 5.35
2. Kim Do-kyun KOR 5.25
3. Takafumi Suzuki JPN 5.10

LJ 1. Mohammed Al-Khuwalidi KSA 8.16w/3.7
2. Saleh Al-Haddad KUW 8.05w/5.2
3. Li Runrun CHN 7.84w/2.3

TJ 1. Renjith Maheswary IND 17.19w/2.5
2. Kim Duk-hyun KOR 17.00/1.8
3. Bibu Mathew IND 16.64w/5.2

SP 1. Navpreet Singh IND 19.70
2. Chang Ming-Huang TPE 19.66
3. Khalid Al-Suwaidi QAT 19.51

DT 1. Ehsan Hadadi IRI 65.38*
2. Rasheed Al-Dosari QAT 63.49
3. Abbas Samimi IRI 61.29

HT 1. Ali Mohamed Al-Zankawi KUW 75.71
2. Dilshod Nazarov TJK 75.70
3. Hiroaki Doi JPN 70.74

JT 1. Chen Qi CHN 78.07
2. Park Jae-myong KOR 75.77
3. Jung Sang-jin KOR 70.95

Dec 1. Ahmed Hassan Moussa QAT 7678
2. Hadi Sepehrzad IRI 7667w
3. Pavel Andreyev UZB 7484

20kmW 1. Cui Zhide CHN 1:30:21.30
2. Shin Il-yong KOR 1:31:33.4
3. Rustam Kuvatov KAZ 1:32:37.5

4x100m 1. THA (Pooltong, Sondee, Suwannarangsri, Suwonprateep) 39.34
2. QAT 39.64; 3. CHN 39.71

4x400m 1. KSA (Younas, Shaween, Al-Sabani, Al-Salhi) 3:05.96
2. SRI 3:07.29 3. IND 3:07.94

Women

100m 1. Susanthika Jayasinghe SRI 11.19
(3.1) 2. Vu Thi Huong VIE 11.33
3. Zou Yiting CHN 11.54

200m 1. Susanthika Jayasinghe SRI 22.99
(1.9) 2. Sujani Bhuddika SRI 23.28
3. Vu Thi Huong VIE 23.30

400m 1. Chitra Soman IND 53.03
2. Asami Tanno JPN 53.20
3. Menaka Wickramesinghe SRI 54.11

800m 1. Truong Thanh Hang VIE 2:04.77
2. Sinimole Paulose IND 2:06.15
3. Ayako Jinnouchi JPN 2:08.75

1500m 1. Sinimol Paulose IND 4:25.67
2. Sara Bakheet Youssef BRN 4:26.21
3. Truong Thanh Hang VIE 4:26.77

5000m 1. Karima Saleh Jassem BRN 16:40.87
2. Preeja Sreedharan IND 16:56.16
3. Kim Mi-gyong PRK 18:21.32

10,000m 1. Karima Saleh Jassem BRN 34:26.39
2. Preeja Sreedharan IND 36:04.54
3. Kim Mi-gyong PRK 38:29.90

3000mSt 1. Zhao Yanni CHN 10:48.18*
2. Bara'h Marouane JOR 12:03.04
3. Leila Mojavery IRI 12;12.40

100mh 1. Mami Ishino JPN 13.26
(1.9) 2. He Liyuan CHN 13.31
3. Lee Yeon-kyong KOR 13.50

400mh 1. Satomi Kubokura JPN 56.74
2. Ruan Zhuofen CHN 57.63
3. Galina Pedan KGZ 59.13

HJ 1. Tatyana Effimenko KGZ 1.94*
2. Yekaterina Yevseyeva KAZ 1.91
3. Anna Ustinova KAZ 1.91

PV 1. Rosalinda Samsu MAS 4.20
2. Rachel Yang Bing Jie SIN 3.50

LJ 1. Olga Rypakova KAZ 6.66w/2.4
2. Anju Bobby George IND 6.65/1.3
3. Jung Soon-ok KOR 6.60w/2.9

TJ 1. Olga Rypakova KAZ 14.69*/1.6
2. Sha Li CHN 14.03w/2.3
3. Irina Litvinenko KAZ 13.80w/5.2

SP 1. Liu Xiangrong CHN 17.65
2. Lee Mi-young KOR 16.58
3. Lin Chia-Ying TPE 16.46

DT 1. Xu Shaoyang CHN 61.30
2. Li Yanfeng CHN 61.13
3. Krishna Poonia IND 55.38

HT 1. Liao Xiaoyan CHN 60.58
2. Kang Na-ru KOR 57.38
3, Huang Chih-Feng TPE 55.37

JT 1. Buoban Phamang THA 58.35*
2. Kim Kyong-ae KOR 53.01
3. Nadeeka Lakmali SRI 52.59

Hep 1. Irina Naumenko KAZ 5617
2. Javur J. Shobha IND 5356
3. Sushmita Singha Roy IND 5154

20kmW 1. Jiang Qiuyan CHN 1:36:15.9
2. Bai Yanmin CHN 1:38:09.6
3. Svetlana Tolstaya KAZ 1:41:53.0

4x100m 1. THA 44.31 2. JPN 45.06
3. TPE 46.48

4x400m 1. IND 3:33.39
2. JPN 3:33.82 3. KAZ 3:50.81

Placing & Medal Table

Nat	*G*	*S*	*B*	*Pts*
IND	5	5	5	183
JPN	4	5	4	149
QAT	4	7	5	135
CHN	7	5	4	133
IRI	2	4	3	101
KOR	-	7	3	92
KAZ	4	1	5	86
SRI	3	2	2	66
KSA	5	-	-	62
BRN	2	1	2	48
TPE	-	1	3	48
THA	3	-	-	43
MAS	2	-	-	37
VIE	1	1	2	37

22 nations won medals, 27 scored points

6th European Under-23 Championships

At Debrecen, Hungary 12-15 July

100m (0.2)
1. Simeon Williamson GBR 10.10*
2. Craig Pickering GBR 10.14
3. Martial Mbandjock FRA 10.27

200m (-1.9)
1. Visa Hongisto FIN 20.84
2. Vojtech Sulc CZE 20.91
3. Rikki Fifton GBR 21.02

400m
1. Denis Alekseyev RUS 45.69
2. Zeljko Vincek CRO 45.69
3. Kacper Kozlowski POL 45.86

800m
1. Marcin Lewandowski POL 1:49.94
2. Oleksandr Osmolovych UKR 1:50.21
3. Abdesslam Merabet FRA 1:50.31

1500m
1. Álvaro Rodríguez ESP 3:44.00
2. Yohan Durand FRA 3:44.38
3. Barnabás Bene HUN 3:44.47

5000m
1. Noureddine Smail FRA 13:53.15
2. Andrey Safronov RUS 13:54.04
3. Kemal Koyuncu TUR 13:54.32

10,000m
1. Anatoliy Rybakov RUS 29:09.89
2. Michel Butter NED 29:12.95
3. Daniele Meucci ITA 29:18.26.

3000mSt
1. Mah. Mekhissi-Benabbad FRA 8:33.91
2. Ildar Minshin RUS 8:34.27
3. Balázs Ott HUN 8:35.04

110mh (-0.4)
1. Kostadínos Douvalídis GRE 13.49
2. Adrien Deghelt BEL 13.59
3. Emanuele Abate ITA 13.66

400mh
1. David Greene GBR 49.58
2. Fadil Belaabouss FRA 49.58
3. Milan Kotur CRO 50.14

HJ
1. Linus Thörnblad SWE 2.24
2. Benjamin Lauckner GER 2.21
3. Jussi Viita FIN 2.21

PV
1. Pavel Prokopenko RUS 5.75
2. Jesper Fritz SWE 5.70
3. Denys Fedas UKR 5.65

LJ
1. Michal Rosiak POL 7.94/0.8
2. Petteri Lax FIN 7.89/0.2
3. Roman Novotny CZE 7.87/0.4

TJ
1. Gary White GBR 16.33/-0.2
2. Adrian Swiderski POL 16.29/-0.6
3. Yuriy Zharavlyev RUS 16.22/-0.3

SP
1. Jakub Giza POL 19.87
2. Luka Rujevic SRB 19.55
3. Aleksandr Grekov RUS 19.13

DT
1. Martin Wierig GER 61.10
2. Jan Marcell CZE 58.48
3. Apostolos Parellis CYP 58.16

HT
1. Yuriy Shayunov BLR 74.92
2. Kristóf Németh HUN 72.56
3. Marcel Lomnicky SVK 72.17

JT
1. Alexander Vieweg GER 79.56
2. Karlis Alainis LAT 76.83
3. Oleksandr Pyatnytsya UKR 76.28

Dec
1. Andrey Kravchenko BLR 8492*
2. Pascal Behrenbruch GER 8239
3. Arkadiy Vasilyev RUS 8179

20kmW
1. Valeriy Borchin RUS 1:20:43
2. Andrey Krivov RUS 1:21:51
3. Sergey Bakulin RUS 1:23:33

4x100m
1. GBR (Scott, Pickering, Fifton, Ellington 38.95*
2. POR (Gonçalves, Abrantes, Martins, Nascimento) 39.37
3. FIN (Hämäläinen, Hongisto, Jokinen, Astrand) 39.53

4x400m
1. RUS (Maksim Dyldin, Alekseyev, Artyom Sergeyenkov, Anton Kokorin) 3:02.13*
2. POL (Klimczyk, Baranowski, Dabrowski, Kozlowski) 3:04.76
3. GER (Plass, Schwalm, Bos, Grothkopp) 3:05.25

Women

100m (-2.0)
1. Verena Sailer GER 11.66
2. Montell Douglas GBR 11.66
3. Myriam Soumare FRA 11.68

200m (-1.1)
1. Yuliya Chermoshanskaya RUS 23.19
2. Nelly Banco FRA 23.36
3. Marta Jeschke POL 23.42

400m
1. Lyudmila Litvinova RUS 51.25
2. Olga Shulikova RUS 51.57
3. Kseniya Zadorina RUS 51.78

800m
1. Mariya Shapayeva RUS 2:00.86*
2. Élodie Guégan FRA 2:01.26
3. Vanja Perisic CRO 2:01.34

1500m
1. Abby Westley GBR 4:15.48
2. Lizi Brathwaite GBR 4:16.45
3. Tatyana Beltyukova RUS 4:16.49

5000m
1. Laura Kenney GBR 16:22.28
2. Olga Minina BLR 16:27.31
3. Marta Romo ESP 16:29.56

10,000m
1. Olga Minina BLR 33:06.37
2. Irina Sergeyeva RUS 33:08.69
3. Alina Alekseyeva RUS 33:09.63

3000mSt
1. Katarzyna Kowalska POL 9:39.40*
2. Ancuta Bobocel ROM 9:41.84
3. Sara Moreira POR 9:42.47

100mh (-0.3)
1. Nevin Yanit TUR 12.90
2. Christina Vukicevic NOR 13.08
3. Jessica Ennis GBR 13.09

400mh
1. Angela Morosanu ROM 54.50*
2. Irina Obedina RUS 55.19
3. Zuzana Hejnová CZE 55.93

HJ
1. Svetlana Shkolina RUS 1.92
2. Asonia Steryiou GRE 1.92
3. Ebba Jungmark SWE 1.89

PV
1. Aleksandra Kiryashova RUS 4.50
2. Anna Schultze GER 4.35
3. Anna Battke GER 4.35

LJ 1. Anna Nazarova RUS 6.81/0.0
2. Denisa Scerbová CZE 6.80w/2.1
3. Yelena Sokolova RUS 6.71/0.0
TJ 1. Liliya Kulyk UKR 14.39/0.4
2. Yekaterina Kayukova RUS 14.11
3. Anastasiya Taranova RUS 13.99w
SP 1. Irina Tarasova RUS 18.26
2. Denise Hinrichs GER 17.56
3. Anna Avdeyeva RUS 17.47
DT 1. Kateryna Karsak UKR 64.40*
2. Darya Pishchalnikova RUS 64.15
3. Veronika Watzek AUT 57.15
HT 1. Mariya Smolyachkova BLR 69.34
2. Lenka Ledvinová CZE 67.63
3. Nataliya Zolotuhina UKR 67.00
JT 1. Linda Stahl GER 62.17*
2. Annike Suthe GER 57.86
3. Madara Palameika LAT 57.07
Hep 1. Viktorija Zemaityte LTU 6219
2. Jolanda Keizer NED 6219
3. Julia Mächtig GER 6151
20kmW 1. Tatyana Shemyakina RUS 1:28:48*
2. Svetlana Solovyova RUS 1:33:58
3. Olga Mikhaylova RUS 1:34:41
4x100m 1. RUS (Yuna Mekhti-Zade, Kseniya Vdovkina, Natalya Murinovich, Chermoshanskaya) 43.67
2. GER (Elbe, Sailer, Peters, Möllinger) 43.75
3. POL (Siemieniako, Klocek, Jeschke, Brzezinska) 43.78
4x400m 1. RUS (Shulikova. Zadorina, Yelena Novikova, Litvinova) 3:26.58*
2. FRA (Lacorbelle, Behi, Michanol, Sigère) 3:30.56
3. UKR (Plotitsnya, Karandyuk, Irhina, Pescheva) 3:33.90

Placing & Medal Table

Nat	*G*	*S*	*B*	*Pts*
1. RUS	15	9	11	334
2. GER	4	6	3	140
3. GBR	6	3	2	132
4. POL	4	2	3	131
5. FRA	2	5	3	106
6. UKR	2	1	4	78
7. BLR	4	1	0	65
8. CZE	0	4	2	62
9. ROM	1	1	0	47
10. ITA	0	0	2	46
11. NED	0	2	0	45
12. ESP	1	0	1	39
13. FIN	1	1	2	37
14. HUN	0	1	2	37
15. GRE	1	1	0	34
16. SWE	1	1	1	28

34 nations won medals

European Junior (U20) Championships

At Hengelo, Netherlands 19-22 July

100m (0.2) 1. Julian Reus GER 10.38
2. Yannick Lesourd FRA 10.53
3. Giuseppe Aita ITA 10.57
200m (-1.0) 1. Alex Nelson GBR 20.83
2. Julian Reus GER 20.87
3. Luke Fagan GBR 21.08
400m 1. Yannick Fonsat FRA 46.34
2. Marcin Klaczanski POL 46.46
3. Eric Krüger GER 46.49
800m 1. Robin Schembera GER 1:47.98
2. James Brewer GBR 1:48.08
3. Adam Kszczot POL 1:48.10
1500m 1. Mario Scapini ITA 4:01.31
2. Victor Corrales ESP 4:01.44
3. Merihun Crespi ITA 4:01.83
5000m 1. Mourad Amdouni FRA 14:08.27
2. Mohamed Elbendir ESP 14:14.79
3. Dmytro Lashyn UKR 14:15.26
10,000m 1. Dmytro Lashyn UKR 29:51.58
2. Matti Markowski GER 30:10.75
3. Roman Pozdyaykin RUS 30:13.70
3000mSt 1. Jakub Holusa CZE 8:50.30
2. Alexandru Ghinea ROM 8:50.42
3. Carlos Alonso ESP 8:50.95
110mh (1.5) (99cm) 1. Artur Noga POL 13.36*
2. Vladimir Zhukov RUS 13.46
3. Gianni Frankis GBR 13.47
400mh 1. Silvio Schirrmeister GER 50.60
2. Vyacheslav Sakayev RUS 50.72
3. Toby Ulm GBR 50.99
HJ 1. Oleksandr Nartov UKR 2.23
2= Andriy Protsenko UKR 2.21
2= Raul Spank GER 2.21
PV 1. Leonid Kivalov RUS 5.60*
2. Yevgeniy Ageyev RUS 5.50
3. Lukasz Michalski POL 5.45
LJ 1. Olivier Huet FRA 7.78/1.8
2. Ivan Slepov RUS 7.61/1.9
3. Marcos Caldeira POR 7.58/2.0
TJ 1. Lyukman Adams RUS 16.50/0.0
2. Ilya Yefremov RUS 16.49/-0.7
3. Dmitriy Platnitskiy BLR 16.49/0.9
SP 6kg 1. Aleksandr Bulanov RUS 19.95
2. António Silva POR 19.66
3. Nikola Kisanic CRO 19.63
DT 1.75kg 1. Nikolay Sedyuk RUS 62.72*
2. Ivan Hryshyn UKR 62.28
3. Joni Mattila FIN 58.05
HT 6kg 1. Arno Laitinen FIN 71.94
2. Adrian Pop ROM 70.80
3. Aleksey Tsitsorin BLR 70.23
JT 1. Matthias De Zordo GER 78.59
2. Roman Avramenko UKR 75.24
3. Thomas Smet BEL 72.56
Dec Jnr 1. Matthias Prey GER 7908
2. Rok Derzanic SLO 7560
3. Rico Freimuth GER 7524
10,000mW 1. Sergey Morozov RUS 40:02.88
2. Matteo Giupponi ITA 40:54.88
3. Lluis Torla 41:06.32
4x100m 1. GER (Christ, Reus, Hering, Brandt) 39.81
2. GBR (Sobodu, Nelson, Fagan, Yearwood) 39.83
3. FRA (Figaro, Lesourd, Mignot, Nubret) 40.21
4x400m 1. GBR (Levine, Davis, Persent, McGrath) 3:08.21
2. GER (Nabow, Krüger, Schneider, Schembera) 3:08.64
3. FRA (Naprix, Françcois, Rolland, Fonsat) 3:09;10

Women

100m (0.7)
1. Ezinne Okparaebo NOR 11.45
2. Inna Eftimova BUL 11.52
3. Katerina Cechová CZE 11.58

200m (-0.2)
1. Hayley Jones GBR 23.37
2. Yelizaveta Bryzhina UKR 23.66
3. Inna Eftimova BUL 23.78

400m
1. Danijela Grgic CRO 52.45
2. Kseniya Ustalova RUS 52.92
3. Olga Fomina RUS 53.68

800m
1. Mirela Lavric ROM 2:02.84
2. Emma Jackson GBR 2:03.23
3. Machteld Mulder NED 2:03.72

1500m
1. Cristina Vasiloiu ROM 4:15.30
2. Stephanie Twell GBR 4:16.03
3. Daniela Donisa ROM 4:18.19

3000m
1. Cristina Vasiloiu ROM 9:13.51
2. Natalya Popkova RUS 9:14.17
3. Daniela Donisa ROM 9:14.54

5000m
1. Natalya Popkova RUS 16:08.95
2. Ingunn Opsal NOR 16:14.59
3. Emily Pidgeon GBR 16:31.30

3000mSt
1. Karoline Bjerkeli Grøvdal NOR 9:44.34*
2. Kristine Eikrem Engeset NOR 9:47.35
3. Polina Jelizarova LAT 10:03.91

100mh (0.8)
1. Aleksandra Fedoriva RUS 13.12
2. Laetitia Denis FRA 13.35
3. Marina Andryukhina RUS 13.50

400mh
1. Fabienne Kohlmann GER 56.42
2. Perri Shakes-Drayton GBR 56.46
3. Anastasiya Ott RUS 57.27

HJ
1. Erika Wiklund SWE 1.82
2. Liene Karsuma LAT 1.82
3. Mirela Demireva BUL 1.82

PV
1. Minna Nikkanen FIN 4.35
2. Tina Michel GER 4.25
3. Anna Katharina Schmid SUI 4.25

LJ
1. Manuela Galtier FRA 6.44/-0.2
2. Eloyse Leseur FRA 6.34/0.4
3. Yuliya Pidluzhnaya RUS 6.28/0.0

TJ
1. Kaire Leibak EST 14.02w/2.7
2. Hanna Knyazheva UKR 13.85/0.0
3. Cristina Bujin ROM 13.57/1.3

SP
1. Melissa Boekelman NED 16.51
2. Alena Kopets BLR 16.10
3. Isabell von Loga GER 15.74

DT
1. Vera Karmishina RUS 55.16
2. Sandra Perkovic CRO 55.42
3. Tamara Apostolico ITA 52.21

HT
1. Bianca Perie ROM 64.35
2. Katerina Safránková CZE 62.95
3. Natalya Shayunova BLR 62.73

JT
1. Vira Rebryk UKR 58.48
2. Sinta Ozolina LAT 57.01
3. Urszula Kuncewicz POL 54.83

Hep
1. Aiga Grabuste LAT 5920
2. Eliska Klucinová CZE 5709
3. Nikol Ogrodníková CZE 5607

10kmW
1. Anisya Kornikova 43:27.20
2. Yelena Shumkina RUS 46:24.74
3. Alena Kostromitina RUS 46:41.56

4x100m
1. GBR (Shand-Whittingham, Nelson, H Jones, Philip) 44.52
2. UKR (Titimets, Pogrebnyak, Yaroshchuk, Bryzhina) 44.77
3. POL (Ksaizek, Popowicz, Ceglarek, Wedler) 45.32

4x400m
1. RUS (Fomina, Ott, Vrkhovskaya, Ustalova) 3:33.95
2. GBR (Beesley, Jones, Duck, Shakes-Drayton) 3:37.29
3. GER (Ullmann, Cremer, Schmidt, Kohlmann) 3:37.32

Placing Table of Leading Nations

NAT	*G*	*S*	*B*	*Pts*
RUS	10	8	6	230
GER	7	5	4	213
FRA	4	3	2	146
GBR	4	6	4	141
UKR	3	6	1	102
ROM	4	2	3	96
POL	1	1	4	88
ITA	1	1	3	55
LAT	1	2	1	42
ESP	0	2	2	42
BLR	0	1	3	42
CZE	1	2	2	41
FIN	2	0	1	39
NOR	2	2	0	35
CRO	1	1	1	33
BUL	0	1	2	29

European Cup

Super League at München, Germany 23-24 June

Men: 1. FRA 116, 2. GER 116, 3. POL 110, 4. GBR 101, 5. RUS 93, 6. GRE 70, 7. UKR 58.5, 8. BEL 53.5

100m (0.2)
1. Craig Pickering GBR 10.15
2. Martial Mbandjock FRA 10.29
3. Christian Blum GER 10.37

200m (1.0)
1. Marlon Devonish GBR 20.33
2. David Alerte FRA 20.34
3. Anastásios Goúsis GRE 20.43

400m
1. Leslie Djhone FRA 45.54
2. Tim Benjamin GBR 45.67
3. Bastian Swillims GER 45.95

800m
1. Pawel Czapiewski POL 1:49.00
2. Michael Rimmer GBR 1:49.06
3. Robin Schembera GER 1:49.06

1500m
1. Mehdi Baala FRA 3:47.36
2. Andrew Baddeley GBR 3:48.08
3. Franek Haschke GER 3:48.54

3000m
1. Bouabdellah Tahri FRA 7:51.32
2. Sergey Ivanov RUS 8:02.47
3. Bartosz Nowicki POL 8:02.47

5000m
1. Monder Rizki BEL 14:15.46
2. Arne Gabius GER 14:16.09
3. Aleksandr Orlov RUS 14:16.57

3000mSt
1. Filmon Ghirmai GER 8:38.78
2. Mah. Mekhissi-Benabbad FRA 8:39.34
3. Andrew Lemoncello GBR 8:39.94

110mh (0.4)
1. Ladji Doucouré FRA 13.35
2. Andy Turner GBR 13.48
3. Thomas Blaschek GER 13.51

400mh
1. Periklís Iakovákis GRE 48.35
2. Marek Plawgo POL 48.90
3. Naman Keïta FRA 48.90

HJ
1. Eike Onnen GER 2.30
2. Andrey Tereshin RUS 2.30
3. Aleksander Walerianczyk POL 2.24

PV 1. Tim Lobinger GER 5.70
2. Romain Mesnil FRA 5.65
3. Roman Yurchenko UKR 5.60
LJ 1. Louis Tsátoumas GRE 8.16/-0.9
2. Marcin Starzak POL 7.82/-1.0
3. Nils Winter GER 7.70/1.4
TJ 1. Alksandr Petrenko RUS 17.29/1.6
2. Phillips Idowu GBR 17.21/0.7
3. Mykola Savolaynen UKR 17.09/0.2
SP 1. Peter Sack GER 20.28
2. Carl Myerscough GBR 19.96
3. Tomasz Majewski POL 19.93
DT 1. Piotr Malachowski POL 66.09
2. Robert Harting GER 63.90
3. Aleksandr Borichevskiy RUS 60.79
HT 1. Szymon Ziólkowski POL 77.99
2. Marjus Esser GER 74.68
3. Aléxandros Papadimitríou GRE 73.83
JT 1. Aleksandr Ivanov RUS 82.57
2. Vitolio Tipotio FRA 79.69
3. Igor Janik POL 78.70
4x100m 1. GBR (Edgar, Pickering, Devonish, Lewis-Francis) 38.30
2. FRA (Nthépé, Alerte, De Lépine, Mbandjock) 38.40
3. GER (Blum, Helmke, Kosenkow, Reus) 38.56
4x400m 1. POL (Kozlowski, Marciniszyn, Rysiukiewicz, Dabrowski) 3:01.70
2. GER (Schultz, Gaba, Bos, Swillims) 3:01.77
3. GBR (Steele, Strachan, Rooney, Caines) 3:01.92

Women: 1. RUS 127, 2. FRA 107, 3. GER 94.5, 4. POL 89, 5. UKR 81. 6. BLR 80, 7. GRE 75, 8. ESP 64.5.

100m (1.1) 1. Yevgeniya Polyakova RUS 11.20
2. Verena Sailer GER 11.35
3. Natalya Safronnikova BLR 11.36
200m (-2.0) 1. Muriel Hurtis-Houairi FRA 22.83
2. Natalya Rusakova RUS 22.92
3. Iryna Shtanhyeyeva UKR 23.12
400m 1. Faní Halkiá GRE 51.85
2. Zhanna Kashcheyeva RUS 51.87
3. YulyanaYushchenko BLR 52.09
800m 1. Svetlana Usovich BLR 2:00.71
2. Yuliya Krevsun UKR 2:01.12
3. Oksana Zbrozhek RUS 2:01.14
1500m 1. Sylwia Ejdys POL 4:17.05
2. Yuliya Fomenko RUS 4:17.12
3. Maria Martins FRA 4:17.23
3000m 1. Gulnara Galkina RUS 8:47.92
2. Lidia Chojecka POL 8:54.72
3. Dolores Checa ESP 8:58.35
5000m 1. Olga Kravtsova BLR 15:20.35
2. Sabrina Mockenhaupt GER 15:23.96
3. Kalliópi Astropekáki GRE 15:46.22
3000mSt 1. Katarzyna Kowalska POL 9:45.35
2. Sophie Duarté FRA 9:50.02
3. Iríni Kokkinaríou GRE 9:53.83
100mh (0.9) 1. Yevgeniya Snigur UKR 12.92
2. Adrianna Lamalle FRA 12.94
3. Aleksandra Antonova RUS 12.97
400mh 1. Yuliya Pechonkina RUS 54.04
2. Anna Jesien POL 54.88
3. Ulrike Urbansky GER 55.74
HJ 1. Yelena Slesarenko RUS 2.02
2. Ruth Beitia ESP 1.98
3. Mélanie Skotnik FRA 1.95
PV 1. Monika Pyrek POL 4.65
2. Nataliya Kushch UKR 4.38
3. Vanessa Boslak FRA 4.38
LJ 1. Eunice Barber FRA 6.73/0.9
2. Tatyana Kotova RUS 6.73/0.3
3. Concepción Montaner ESP 6.72/-0.2
TJ 1. Teresa N'Zola Meso Ba FRA 14.69/2.0
2. Hrisopiyí Devetzí GRE 14.58/-2.8
3. Viktoriya Gurova RUS 14.46/-1.2
SP 1. Anna Omarova RUS 19.69
2. Petra Lammert GER 19.47
3. Nadezhda Ostapchuk BLR 18.52
DT 1. Franka Dietzsch GER 63.60
2. Darya Pishchalnikova RUS 63.27
3. Irina Yatchenko BLR 62.54
HT 1. Tatyana Lysenko RUS 75.86
2. Betty Heidler GER 73.55
3. Oksana Menkova BLR 73.03
JT 1. Christina Obergföll GER 70.20*
2. Oksana Gromova RUS 60.15
3. Barbara Madejczyk POL 59.36
4x100m 1. RUS (Gushchina, Rusakova, Khabarova, Polyakova) 42.78
2. FRA (Louami, Hurtis-Houairi, Banco, Arron) 43.09
3. GER (Wakan, Schielke, Tschirch, Sailer) 43.33
4x400m 1. BLR (Yushchenko, Khlyustova, S Usovich, I Usovich) 3:23.67
2. POL (Radecka, Bejnar, Wójcik, Prokopek) 3:26.36
3. FRA (Anacharsis, Lacordelle, Michanol, Désert) 3:28.62

First League Group A at Vaasa, Finland 23-24 June

Men: 1. ESP 111, 2. SWE 107, 3. NED 101.5, 4. CZE 93.5, 5. FIN 88.5, 6. SUI 81, 7. IRL 76, 8. SVK 59.5. **Winners: 100m**: Guus Hoogmoed NED 10.15, **200m**: Paul Hession IRL 20.61, **400m**: Johan Wissman SWE 45.77, **800m**: Antonio Manuel Reina ESP 1:47.58, **1500m**: Arturo Casado ESP 3:56.38, **3000m**: Sergio Gallardo ESP 8:03.37, **5000m**: Jesús España ESP 14:20.8, **3000mSt**: Mustafa Mohamed SWE 8:26.03, **110mh**: Gregory Sedoc NED 13.77, **400mh**: Jussi Heikkilä FIN 50.60, **HJ**: Stefan Holm SWE 2.30, **PV**: Jesper Fritz SWE 5.45, **LJ**: Tommi Evilá FIN 7.90, **TJ**: Christian Olsson SWE 17.33, **SP/DT**: Rutger Smith NED 20.44/64.51, **HT**: Miloslav Konopka SVK 78.35, **JT**: Tero Pitkämäki FIN 85.56, **4x100m**: SUI 39.31, **4x400m**: ESP 3:06.30.

Women: 1. GBR 131, 2. SWE 110, 3. CZE 102, 4. FIN 98, 5. NED 78, 6. IRL 76, 7. NOR 73, 8. SVK 505. **Winners: 100m**: Johanna Manninen FIN 11.27, **200m**: Joice Maduaka 23.31, **400m**: Lee McConnell GBR 52.27, **800m**: Lucia Klocová SVK 2:01.62, **1500m**: Abby Westley GBR 4:21.12, **3000m**: Mari Järvenpää FIN 9:30.75, **5000m**: Jo Pavey GBR 15:43.86, **3000mSt**: Hatti Dean GBR 9:42.66, **100mh**: Susanna Kallur SWE 12.92, **400mh**: Natasha Danvers-Smith GBR 55.86, **HJ**: Kajsa Bergqvist SWE 1.92, **PV**: Katerina Badurová CZE 4.45, **LJ**: Carolina Klüft SWE 6.75, **TJ**: Martina Darmovzalová CZE 13.96, **SP**: Helena Engman SWE 17.60, **DT**: Vera Cechlová CZE 61.65,

HT: Eileen O'Keeffe IRL 69.44, **JT**: Goldie Sayers GBR 60.41, **4x100m/4x400m**: GBR 43.24/3:29.51.

First League Group B at Milano, Italy 23-24

Men: 1. ITA 135, 2. SLO 105, 3. POR 102, 4. ROM 98, 5. HUN 89, 6. BLR 85, 7. BUL 57, 8. SRB 46. **Winners: 100m/200m**: Francis Obikwelu POR 10.12/20.85, **400m**: Andea Barberi ITA 46.02, **800m**: Ioan Zaizan ROM 1:49.57, **1500m**: Christian Obrist ITA 3:43.41, **3000m**: Stefano La Rosa ITA 8:06.40, **5000m**: Marius Ionescu ROM 14:08.46, **3000mSt**: Bostjan Buc SLO 8:47.48, **110mh**: Damjan Zlatnar SLO 13.76, **400mh**: Gianni Carabelli ITA 50.73, **HJ**: Andrea Bettinelli ITA 2.30, **PV**: Spas Bukhalov BUL 5.50, **LJ/TJ**: Nelson Évora POR 8.10/17.35w, **SP**: Yuriy Belov BLR 20.47, **DT**: Gábor Máté HUN 65.96, **HT**: Ivan Tikhon BLR 79.40, **JT**: Csongor Olteán HUN 75.45, **4x100m/ 4x400m**: ITA 39.09/ 3:05.11.

Women: 1, ITA 139, 2, ROM 123, 3, POR 95.5, 4, BUL 84, 5, HUN 82, 6, SLO 72.5, 7, SRB 61.5, 8, CYP 58.5. **Winners: 100m/ 200m**: Lalova BUL 11.26/23.00, **400m**: Ionela Tîrlea ROM 51.98, **800m**: Liliana Barbulescu-Popescu ROM 2:01.92, **1500m**: Cristina Vasiloiu ROM 4:09.06, **3000m/5000m**: Silvia Weissteiner ITA 8:59.30/15:30.96, **3000mSt**: Cristina Casandra ROM 9:38.86, **100mh**: Edit Vári HUN 13.06, **400mh**: Benedetta Ceccarelli ITA 56.50, **HJ**: Antonietta Di Martino ITA 2.03, **PV**: Krisztina Molnár HUN 4.35, **LJ**: Naide Gomes POR 6.80, **TJ**: Magdalin Martínez ITA 14.57, **SP**: Chiara Rosa ITA 19.15, **DT**: Nicoleta Grasu ROM 61.75, **HT**: Clarissa Claretti ITA 68.68, **JT**: Zahra Bani ITA 60.20, **4x100m**: ITA 43.98, **4x400m**: ROM 3:30.22.

Second League Group A at Odense, Denmark 23-24 June

Men: 1. AUT 120.5, 2. NOR 118, 3. LAT 111, 4. EST 109.5, 5. DEN 104, 6. LTU 72, 7. ISL 50, 8. AND 30, **Women:** 1. BEL 124, 2. LTU 117, 3. LAT 109, 4. AUT 102, 5. EST 101, 6. DEN 83.5, 7. ISL 61.5, 8. AND 20.

Second League Group B at Zenica. Bosnia 23-24 June

Men: 1. TUR 232, 2. CRO 226, 3. CYP 209, 4. ISR 208, 5. MDA 196.5, 6. BIH 158.5, 7. LUX 151, 8. AZE 142.5, 9. GEO 124.5, 10. MNE 115, 11. ARM 106, 12. AASSE (Athletic Association of the Small States of Europe) 72, 13. ALB 66, 14. MKD 57, **Women:** 1. TUR 254, 2. CRO 246, 3. SUI 243, 4. MDA 217, 5. ISR 180, 6. BIH 155.5, 7. LUX 149, 8, MNE 118, 9. AZE 110.5, 10. ARM 98, 11. GEO 90.5, 12. ALB 78, 13. AASSE 55, 14. MKD 46.5.

European Cup Combined Events

At Tallinn, Estonia 7-8 July

Super League Men: 1. BLR 23,749, 2. FRA 23,246, 3. NED 23,022, 4. RUS 22,765, 5. EST 22,734, 6. ESP 22,464, 7. ITA 22,088, 8. HUN 21,696. **Ind:** 1. Aleksandr Parkhomenko BLR 8101, 2. Nikolay Shubenok BLR 8020, 3. Julien Choffart FRA 7916, 4. Mattias Cerlati FRA 7912, 5. Eugène Martineau NED 7877.

First League Women: 1. NED 17,353, 2. SUI 16,835, 3. ITA 16,697, 4. EST 16,588, 5. BLR 16,525, 6. CZE 16,457, 7. ESP 15,845, 8. LAT 14,383. **Ind:** 1. Karin Ruckstuhl NED 6080, 2. Yvonne Wisse NED 5974, 3. Simone Oberer SUI 5936.

At Szczecin, Poland 7-8 July

First League Men: 1. BEL 23,712, 2. POL 22,520, 3. FIN 22,145, 4. UKR 22,096, 5. SWE 21,913, 6. GBR 21,467, 7. LAT 20,149, 8. GRE 17,078. **Ind:** 1. Hans Van Alphen BEL 7930, 2. François Gourmet BEL 7908, 3. Frédéric Xhonneux BEL 7874.

Super League Women: 1. GBR 18,329, 2. RUS 17,289, 3. UKR 17,243, 4. POL 17,093, 5. GRE 16,725, 6. FRA 16,559, 7. FIN 16,431, 8. SWE 15,148. **Ind:** 1. Jessica Ennis GBR 6399, 2. Kelly Sotherton GBR 6229, 3. Hanna Melnychenko UKR 6143, 4. Karolina Tyminska POL 6044, 5. Aryiró Stratáki GRE 5917.

Second League. At Maribor, Slovenia 7-8 July

Men: 1. NOR 22,280, 2. CZE 21,945, 3. SUI 21,363, 4. AUT 19,977, 5. LTU 19,756, 6. TUR 17,747, 7. SLO 17,507, 8. CRO 15,835, **Ind:** Hans Olav Uldal NOR 7963.

Women: 1. HUN 16,056, 2. LTU 14,984, 3. SLO 14,566, 4. AUT 14,487. **Ind:** Austra Skujyte LTU 6337.

European Winter Throws Cup

At Yalta, Ukraine 17-18 March

Men: 1. RUS 4287, 2. BLR 4256, 3. UKR 4081; **SP**: 1. Yuriy Bilonog UKR 19.95, 2. Pavel Lyzhin BLR 19.86; 3. Manuel Martínez ESP 19.10; **DT**: 1. Gerd Kanter EST 65.43. 2. Piotr Malachowski POL 65.06. 3. Ercüment Olgundeniz TUR 64.34; **HT**: 1. Primoz Kozmus SLO 77.99, 2. Ivan Tikhon BLR 77.79, 3. Esref Apak TUR 76.68; **JT**: 1. Igor Sukhomlinov RUS 83.34, 2. Magnus Arvidsson SWE 76.27, 3. Ainars Kovals LAT 74.64. **Women:** 1. GER 4406, 2. ITA 4132, 3. BLR 4032; **SP**: 1. Petra Lammert GER 18.67, 2. Assunte Legnante ITA 18.31, 3. Yuliya Leontyuk BLR 17.92; **DT**: 1. Franka Dietzsch GER 66.14*, 2. Mélina Robert-Michon FRA 63.48, 3. Olena Antonova UKR 60.30; **HT**: 1. Manuèla Montebrun FRA 72.65, 2. Tatyana Lysenko RUS 72.05. 3. Ester Balassini ITA 68.70; **JT**: 1. Steffi Nerius GER 63.14, 2. Goldie Sayers GBR 60.02, 3. Zahra Bani ITA 58.95.

European Cup 10,000m

At Ferrara, Italy 7 April

Men: 1. Andreas Pollmächer GER 28:17.17, 2. Günther Weidlinger AUT 28:19.11, 3. Carlos Castillejo ESP 28:32.7; **Team:** 1. ESP 1:26:55.09, 2. ITA 1:27:44.24, 3. POR 1:27:48.78. **Women:** 1. Elvan Abeylegesse TUR 31:25.15, 2. Tetyana Holovchenko UKR 31:59.98, 3. Nathalie De Vos BEL 32:07.62; **Team:** 1. ESP 1:39:02.23, 2. ITA 1:39:40.51.

European Cup of Race Walking

At Leamington, GBR 20 May

Men 20km: 1. Yohann Diniz FRA 1:18:58, 2. Ivano Brugnetti ITA 1:19:36, 3. Igor Yerokhin RUS 1:20:09, 4. Ivan Trotskiy BLR 1:20:13, 5. Robert Heffernan IRL 1:20:15, 6. André Höhne GER 1:20:32, 7. João Vieira POR 1:20:42, 8. Sergey Chernov BLR 1:21:02, 9. Valeriy Borchin RUS 1:21:13, 10. Giorgio Rubino ITA 1:21:17. 53 of 61 finished. **Team:** 1. BLR 29, 2. ITA 32, 3. ESP 39, 4. RUS 46, 5. POR 54, 6. FRA 62.

Men 50km: 1. Vladimir Kanaykin RUS 3:40:57, 2. Trond Nymark NOR 3:41:31, 3. Oleg Kistkin RUS 3:41:51, 4. Aleksey Voyevodin RUS 3:41:52, 5. Yuriy Andronov RUS 3:42:55, 6. Jesús Ángel García ESP 3:46:08, 7. Santiago Pérez ESP 3:46:56. 8. Marco De Luca ITA 3:47:04, 9. Rafal Fedaczynsky POL 3:48:07, 10. Francisco José Pinardo ESP 3:50:53. 36 of 47 finished. **Team:** 1. RUS 8, 2. ESP 23, 3. FRA 43, 4. POR 52. 5. ITA 60, 6. LAT 79
U20 Men 10km: 1. Sergey Morozov RUS 40:25, 2, Miguel Ángel López ESP 40:49, 3. Dmitriy Shorin RUS 41:38. **Team:** 1. RUS 4, 2. ESP 6, 3. FRA 25, 4. BLR 26
Women 20 km: 1. Rita Turova BLR 1:27:52, 2. Olga Kaniskina RUS 1:28:13, 3. Yelena Ginko BLR 1:28:29, 4. Elisa Rigaudo ITA 1:29:15, 5. Maria Vasco ESP 1:29:17, 6. Tatyana Sibileva RUS 1:30:11, 7. Inês Henriques POR 1:30:24, 8. Claudia Stef ROM 1:30:34, 9. Beatriz Pascual ESP 1:30:37, 10. Alena Nartova RUS 1:30:44. 53 of 57 finished. **Team:** 1. BLR 16, 2. RUS 18, 3. ESP 25, 4. POR 39, 5. ITA 45, 6. ROM 59.
U20 Women 10km: 1. Anisya Kornikova RUS 43:17, 2. Yelena Shumkina RUS 44:29, 3. Irina Yumanova RUS 45:45. **Team:** 1. RUS 3, 2. ROM 9, 3. UKR 20, 4. ITA 21

15th Pan-American Games

At Rio de Janeiro, Brazil 22-29 July

Men

100m (1.0) 1. Churandy Martina AHO 10.15
2. Darvis Patton USA 10.17
3. Brendan Christian ANT 10.26

200m 1. Brendan Christian ANT 20.37
2. Marvin Anderson JAM 20.38
3. Rubin Williams USA 20.57

400m 1. Chris Brown BAH 44.85
2. Tyler Christopher CAN 45.05
3. Chris Lloyd DMA 45.40

800m 1. Yeimar López CUB 1:44.58*
2. Kléberson Davide BRA 1:45.47
3. Fabiano Peçanha BRA 1:45.54

1500m 1. Hudson de Souza BRA 3:36.32*
2. Juan Luis Barrios MEX 3:37.71
3. Byron Piedra ECU 3:37.88

5000m 1. Ed Moran USA 13:25.60*
2. Juan Luis Barrios MEX 13:29.87
3. Marílson dos Santos BRA 13:30.68

10,000m 1. David Galván MEX 28:08.74*
2. Marílson dos Santos 28:09.30
3. Alejandro Suárez MEX 28:09.95

Mar 1. Franck de Almeida BRA 2:14:03
2. Amado García GUA 2:14:27
3. Procopio Franco MEX 2:15:18

3000mSt 1. Josh McAdams USA 8:30.49
2. Michael Spence USA 8:32.11
3. José Alberto Sánchez CUB 8:36.07

110mh (0.4) 1. Dayron Robles CUB 13.25
2. David Payne USA 13.43
3. Yoel Hernández CUB 13.50

400mh 1. Adam Kunkel CAN 48.24
2. Bayano Kamani PAN 48.70
3. LaRon Bennett USA 49.07

HJ 1. Víctor Moya CUB 2.32
2. Donald Thomas BAH 2.30
3. James Grayman ANT 2.24

PV 1. Fábio Gomes da Silva BRA 5.40
2. Giovanni Lanaro MEX 5.30
3. Germán Chiaraviglio ARG 5.20

LJ 1. Irving Saladino PAN 8.28/-0.5
2. Wilfredo Martínez CUB 7.92/0.1
3. Bashir Ramzy USA 7.90/0.6

TJ 1. Jadel Gregório BRA 17.27/0.5
2. Osniel Tosca CUB 16.92/0.1
3. Yoandris Betanzos CUB 16.90/0.7

SP 1. Dylan Armstrong CAN 20.10
2. Dorian Scott JAM 20.06
3. Carlos Véliz CUB 19.75

DT 1. Michael Robertson USA 59.24
2. Adam Kuehl USA 57.50
3. Dariusz Slowik CAN 57.37

HT 1. James Steacy CAN 73.77
2. Kibwe Johnson USA 73.23
3. Juan Ignacio Cerra ARG 72.12

JT 1. Guillermo Martínez CUB 77.66
2. Mike Hazle USA 75.33
3. Alexon Maximiano BRA 75.04

Dec 1. Maurice Smith JAM 8278*
2. Yordanis García CUB 8113
3. Carlos Eduardo Chinin BRA 7977

20kmW 1. Jefferson Pérez ECU 1:22:08
2. Rolando Saquipay ECU 1:23:28
3. Gustavo Restrepo COL 1:24:51

50kmW 1. Xavier Moreno ECU 3:52:07
2. Horacio Nava MEX 3:52:35
3. Omar Zepeda MEX 3:56:04

4x100m 1. BRA (V de Lima, Ribeiro, Morães, Viana) 38.81
2. CAN (Adu-Bobie, Henry, Connaughton, Barnett) 38.87
3. USA (Samuels, Edwards, Williams, Patton) 38.88

4x400m 1. BAH (A Williams, Moncur, Matheau, Brown) 3:01.94
2. USA (Nixon, Torrance, Bennett, Neville) 3:02.44
3. DOM (Santa, Peguero, Tapia, Sánchez) 3:02.48

Women

100m (0.8) 1. Mikele Barber USA 11.02*
2. Mechelle Lewis USA 11.24
3. Chandra Sturrup BAH 11.29

200m (-0.6) 1. Roxana Díaz CUB 22.90
2. Sheri-Ann Brooks JAM 22.92
3. Sherry Fletcher GRN 22.96

400m 1. Ana Guevara MEX 50.34
2. Christine Amertil BAH 50.99
3. Indira Terrero CUB 51.09

800m 1. Diane Cummins CAN 1:59.75
2. Rosibel García COL 2:00.02
3. Zulia Calatayud CUB 2:00.34

1500m 1. Juliana dos Santos BRA 4:13.36
2. Mary Jayne Harrelson USA 4:15.24
3. Rosibel García COL 4:15.78

5000m 1. Megan Metcalfe CAN 15:35.78
2. Cack Ferrell USA 15:42.01
3. Nora Rocha MEX 15:43.80

10,000m 1. Sara Slattery USA 32:54.41*
2. Dulce María Rodríguez MEX 32:56.75
3. Lucélia Peres BRA 33:19.48

Mar 1. Mariela González CUB 2:43:11
2. Márcia Narloch BRA 2:45:10

3. Sirlene de Pinho BRA 2:47:36

3000mSt 1. Sabine Heitling BRA 9:51.13*
2. Talis Apud MEX 9:55.43
3. Zenaide Vieira BRA 9:55.71

100mh (0.0) 1. Delloreen Ennis-London JAM 12.65*
2. Perdita Felicien CAN 12.65*
3. Angela Whyte CAN 12.72

400mh 1. Sheena Johnson USA 54.64
2. Nikiesha Wilson JAM 54.94
3. Nicole Leach USA 54.97

HJ 1. Romary Rifka MEX 1.95
2. Nicole Forrester CAN 1.95
3. Lavern Spencer LCA 1.87

PV 1. Fabiana Murer BRA 4.60*
2. April Steiner USA 4.40
3. Yarisley Silva CUB 4.30

LJ 1. Maurren Maggi BRA 6.84/0.0
2. Keila Costa BRA 6.73/-0.2
3. Yargelis Savigne CUB 6.66/0.0

TJ 1. Yargelis Savigne CUB 14.80*/0.5
2. Keila Costa BRA 14.38/-0.3
3. Mabel Gay CUB 14.26/0.0

SP 1. Misleidis González CUB18.83
2. Yumileidi Cumbá CUB 18.28
3. Cleopatra Borel-Brown TRI 18.22

DT 1. Yarelis Barrios CUB 61.72
2. Yania Ferrales CUB 61.71
3. Elisângela Adriano BRA 60.27

HT 1. Yipsi Moreno CUB 75.20*
2. Arasay Thondike CUB 69.70
3. Jennifer Dahlgren ARG 68.37

JT 1. Osleidis Menéndez CUB 62.34
2. Sonia Bisset CUB 60.68
3. Lavern Eve BAH 58.10

Hep 1. Jessica Zelinka CAN 6136
2. Gretchen Quintana CUB 6000
3. Lucimara Silva BRA 5873

20kmW 1. Cristina López ESA 1:38:59
2. Miriam Ramón ECU 1:40:03
3. Esther Sánchez MEX 1:41:47

4x100m 1. JAM (Brooks, Rowe, Bailey, Dowdie) 43.58
2. USA (Woods, Lewis, Weatherspoon, Barber) 43.62
3. CUB (Benavides, Díaz, Lazo, Tejeda) 43.80

4x400m 1. CUB (Martínez, Pernía, Calatayud, Terrero) 3:27.51
2. MEX (Rugerio, Medina, Rodríguez, Guevara) 3:27.75
3. USA (Dunn, Perkins, L Wilson, Leach) 3:27.84

Medal Table of Leading Nations

Nat	*G*	*S*	*B*
CUB	12	8	10
BRA	9	5	9
USA	6	12	6
CAN	6	4	2
MEX	3	7	5
JAM	3	4	
BAH	2	2	2
ECU	2	2	1
PAN	1	1	-
ANT	1	-	2

20 nations won medals

South American Championships

45th edition, At São Paulo, Brazil 7-9 June

Men

100m (-0.7) 1. Vicente de Lima BRA 10.36
2. Franklin Nazareno ECU 10.37
3. Álvaro Gómez COL 10.66

200m (0.4) 1. Sandro Rodrigues Viana BRA 20.54
2. Heber Viera URU 20.59
3. Daniel Grueso COL 20.66

400m 1. Andrés Silva URU 45.89
2. Rodrigo Bargas BRA 46.15
3. Fernando de Almeida BRA 46.38

800m 1. Kléberson Davide BRA 1:49.61
2. Gustavo Aguirre ARG 1:49.98
3. André de Santana BRA 1:50.10

1500m 1. Byron Piedra ECU 3:42.53
2. Leandro de Oliveira BRA 3:43.26
3. Eduardo Villanueva VEN 3:43.40

5000m 1. Javier Guarín COL 13:51.19*
2. Javier Carriqueo ARG 13:55.37
3. William Naranjo COL 13:56.99

10,000m 1. Sérgio da Silva BRA 29:57.80
2. Ubiratan dos Santos BRA 30:12.36
3. Didimo Sánchez VEN 31:15.30

3000mSt 1. Sergio Lobos CHI 8:37.83
2. Gládson Barbosa BRA 8:43.69
3. José Gregorio Peña VEN 8:54.43

110mh (-0.8) 1. Anselmo da Silva BRA 13.56
2. Éder Antônio de Souza BRA 13.58
3. Francisco Castro CHI 14.31

400mh 1. Raphael Fernandes BRA 49.81
2. Maurício Teixeira BRA 50.39
3. José Céspedes VEN 50.62

PV 1. Fábio Gomes da Silva BRA 5.77*
2. Germán Chiaraviglio ARG 5.40
3= Javier Benítez ARG 5.20
3= João Gabriel Sousa BRA 5.20

HJ 1. Jessé de Lima BRA 2.24
2. Fábio Baptista BRA 2.21
3. Gilmar Mayo COL 2.21

LJ 1. Rogério Bispo BRA 7.94/1.4
2. Hugo Chila ECU 7.81/0.8
3. Rodrigo de Araújo BRA 7.77/1.2

TJ 1. Jefferson Sabino BRA 16.68/-0.3
2. Hugo Chila ECU 16.37/0.1
3. Leonardo dos Santos BRA 15.89/-1.1

SP 1. Germán Lauro ARG 19.65
2. Marco Antonio Verni CHI 19.22
3. Yojer Medina VEN 18.44

DT 1. Germán Lauro ARG 57.12
2. Ronald Julião BRA 56.53
3. Julián Angulo COL 54.68

HT 1. Juan Ignacio Cerra ARG 72.96
2. Patricio Palma CHI 66.56
3. Wágner Domingos BRA 65.15

JT 1. Pablo Pietrobelli ARG 76.52
2. Víctor Fatecha PAR 75.95
3. Júlio César de Oliveira BRA 74.56

Dec 1. Gonzalo Barroilhet CHI 7504
2. Danilo Mendes Xavier BRA 7288
3. Sinval de Oliveira BRA 7243

4x100m 1. BRA (V. de Lima, N. André, B. de Morães, Rodrigues Viana) 38.77

	2. COL (Hechevarría, G. Mosquera, Gómez, Grueso) 39.80
	3. ARG (Garaventa, Jiménez, Wilken, Altamirano) 39.91
4x400m	1. BRA (R. Fernandes, E. Vasconcelos, R. Bargas, F. de Almeida) 3:04.36
	2. VEN (Céspedes, Silvera, Rivas, Rodríguez) 3:05.88
	3. PAN (Gibson, Edmund, Rodríguez, Edwards) 3:09.67
20kmW	1. James Rendón COL 1:24:25.4
	2. Rolando Saquipay ECU 1:25:55.2
	3. Juan Manuel Cano ARG 1:28:28.5
Women	
100m	1. Lucimar de Moura BRA 11.20
(0.2)	2. Felipa Palacios COL 11.43
	3. Thaíssa Barbosa Presti BRA 11.63
200m	1. Lucimar de Moura BRA 23.00
(-0.5)	2. Felipa Palacios COL 23.10
	3. Thaíssa Barbosa Presti BRA 23.58
400m	1. Josiane Tito BRA 52.67
	2. Sheila Ferreira BRA 53.19
	3. Lucy Jaramillo ECU 53.44
800m	1. Marian Burnett GUY 2:03.57
	2. Muriel Coneo COL 2:08.99
	3. Marcela Britos URU 2:10.30
1500m	1. Rosibel García COL 4:20.36
	2. Marian Burnett GUY 4:20.69
	3. Zenaide Vieira BRA 4:22.08
5000m	1. Ednalva da Silva BRA 16:09.96
	2. Lucélia Peres BRA 16:16.07
	3. Bertha Sánchez COL 16:21.17
10,000m	1. Lucélia Peres BRA 34:11.95
	2. Inés Melchor PER 34:13.23
	3. Bertha Sánchez (COL) 34:23.89
3000mSt	1. Zenaide Vieira BRA 10:07.93*
	2. Ángela Figueroa COL 10:13.88
	3. Michelle Costa BRA 10:24.35
100mh	1. Brigitte Merlano COL 13.27
(0.0)	2. Gilvaneide Parrela BRA 13.40
	3. Lucimara da Silva BRA 13.48
400mh	1. Lucimar Teodoro BRA 57.36
	2. Luciana França BRA 58.38
	3. Lucy Jaramillo ECU 58.81
HJ	1. Caterine Ibargüen COL 1.84
	2. Solange Witteveen ARG 1.81
	3. Marielys Rojas VEN 1.78
PV	1. Fabiana Murer BRA 4.50*
	2. Alejandra García ARG 4.20
	3. Joana Costa BRA 4.20
LJ	1. Maurren Maggi BRA 6.91/1.0
	2. Keila Costa BRA 6.83/0.2
	3. Caterine Ibargüen COL 6.18/0.9
TJ	1. Keila Costa BRA 14.57/0.2*
	2. Fernanda Delfino BRA 13.63/0.7
	3. Jennifer Arveláez VEN 13.52/1.0
SP	1. Elisângela Adriano BRA 17.41
	2. Luz Dary Castro COL 16.35
	3. Natalia Ducó CHI 16.20
DT	1. Elisângela Adriano BRA 59.85
	2. Luz Dary Castro COL 52.23
	3. Renata de Figueirêdo BRA 51.69
HT	1. Eli Johana Moreno COL 61.93
	2. Katiuscia de Jesus BRA 61.57
	3. Johana Ramírez COL 61.10
JT	1. Alessandra Resende BRA 57.75
	2. Zuleima Araméndiz COL 57.55
	3. Leryn Franco PAR 53.80
Hep	1. Lucimara da Silva BRA 5803*
	2. Elizete da Silva BRA 5727
	3. Daniela Crespo ARG 4856
4x100m	1. BRA (Barbosa Presti, Alves dos Santos, de Moura, Ignácio) 43.54
	2. COL (Palacios, Merlano, Brock, Hinestroza) 44.68
	3. CHI (Pavez, Díaz, Mackenna, Riderelli) 45.34
4x400m	1. BRA (Teodoro, Almirão, Ferreira, Tito) 3:33.34
	2. COL (Palacios, García, Brock, Idrobo) 3:43.52
	3. CHI (Riderelli, Pavez, Díaz, Mackenna) 3:55.13

Medal Table of Leading Nations

NAT	*G*	*S*	*B*
BRA	28	17	16
COL	7	10	9
ARG	4	5	4
CHI	2	2	4
ECU	1	5	2
URU	1	1	1
GUY	1	1	-
VEN	-	1	7
PAR	-	1	1
PER	-	1	-
PAN	-	-	1

African Junior Championships

At Ouagadougou, Burkina Faso 9-13 August

Men: 100m/200m: Gabriel Mvumvure ZIM 10.51/21.03, **400m**: Julius Kirwa KEN 46.56, **800m**: David Rudisha KEN 1:46.51, **1500m**: Cornelius Ndiwa KEN 3:46.47, **5000m/10,000m**: Mathew Kisorio KEN 14:13.25/29:34.96, **3000mSt**: Abel Mutai KEN 8:29.76, **110mh**-J: Louw Smit RSA 13.98, **400mh**: John Kituu KEN 52.02, **HJ**: Karim Samir Lotfy EGY 2.17, **PV**: Karim El Mafhoum MAR 4.60, **LJ**: Keenan Watson RSA 7.79w, **TJ**: Sief Islam Temancini ALG 15.58, 6k **SP**: J.P.Hoffmann RSA 19.03, 1.75k **DT**: Victor Hogan RSA 56.35, 6k **HT**: Moustafa Mohamed Hisham EGY 66.36, **JT**: Mohamed Ali Kbabou TUN 71.47, **Dec**: Mehdi Mouaci ALG 6604, **4x100m**: RSA 40.61, **4x400m**: KEN 3:09.90, **10,000mW**: Maher ben Hilma 53:09.98. **Women: 100m/200m**: Nombulelo Mkenku RSA 11.65/23.96, **400m**: Pamela Jelimo JEN 54.93, **800m**: Lydia Wafula KEN 2:06.05, **1500m/3000m**: Emebet Etea Bedada ETH 4:17.39/9:07.53, **5000m**: Mary Wachera KEN 15:50.55, **3000mSt**: Mueni Mutua KEN 10:02.46, **100mh**: Félicité Traore BKF 14.26, **400mh**: Fayza Omer SUS 58.59, **HJ**: Marcoleen Pretorius RSA 1.75, **LJ/TJ**: Yamina Hjaji MAR 5.97/12.33, **SP**: Mohamed Atteya Walaa EGY 12.95, **DT**: Mariam Traore MLI 36.50, **HT**: Abdel Zackaria Noura EGY 42.84, **JT**: Gerlize de Klerk RSA 49.18, **Hep**: Katia Amokrane 4316, **4x100m**: RSA 46.60, **4x400m**: KEN 3:49.52, **10,000mW**: Bekashe Aynalem ETH 52:53.79.

15th Arab Championships

At Amman, Jordan 18-21 May

Men: 100m: Yahya Ibrahim Hassan KSA 10.42, **200m**: Abdullah Ibrahim Al-Waleed QAT 20.94w, **400m**: Ismail Daif MAR 46.30, **800m**: Abubaker Kaki SUD 1:45.9*, **1500m**: Mohamed Moustaoui MAR 3:36.90*, **5000m/10,000m**: Mohamed Amyn MAR 13:53.58/28:26.2*, **HMar**: Mustapha Ahmed Shebto QAT 62:21, **3000mSt**: Tarek Mubarak Taher BRN 8:31.08, **110mh**: Mohamed Aissa Al-Thawadi QAT 13.94, **400mh**: Idris Abdelaziz Al-Housaoui KSA 51.14, **HJ**: Jean-Claude Rabbath LIB 2.23*, **PV**: Ali Makki Al-Sabagha KUW 5.10, **LJ**: Mohamed Salim Al-Khuwalidi KSA 7.95*, **TJ**: Tareq Bougtaïb MAR 16.39, **SP** Ahmed Hassan Gholoum KUW 19.18, **DT**: Omar El Ghazali EGY 63.66*, **HT**: Ali Mohamed Al-Zankawi KUW 76.90*, **JT**: Mohamed Ali Kbabou TUN 71.54, **Dec**: Mohamed Jassem Al-Qaree KSA 7366, **4x100m/4x400m**: KSA 39.53*/3:07.76, **20kmW:** Hassanine Sbai TUN 1:26:13. **Women: 100m/200m**: Rakia Al-Gasara BRN 11.35*/22.7w, **400m/Hep**: Mona Jabir Ahmed SUD 53.11*/4815, **800m**: Saida El Mehdi MAR 2:06.8, **1500m**: Siham Hilali MAR 4:18.71, **5000m/3000mSt**: Hanane Ouhaddou MAR 15:49.19*/9:53.28*, **10,000m**: Nadia Ejjafini BRN 33:25.31*, **HMar**: Karima Jassem BRN 74:33*, **100mh**: Lamia El Habz MAR 14.0, **400mh**: Hanane Skhiyi MAR 57.01, **HJ**: Karima Ben Othman TUN 1.70, **PV**: Nisrine Dinar MAR 4.00*, **LJ/TJ**: Yamile Aldama SUD 6.34/14.35*, **SP**: Wafa El Baghdadi EGY 14.70, **DT**: Monia Kari TUN 50.32, **HT**: Marwa Ahmed Hussein EGY 60.63, **JT**: Hanaa Ramadhan Omar EGY 48.56, **4x100m/4x400m**: MAR 47.03/3:43.46, **10,000mW**: Chaïma Trabelsi TUN 50:06.0.

11th Pan Arab Games

At Cairo, Egypt 4-8 November

Men: 100m/200m: Amr Ibrahim Seoud EGY 10.38/20.69, **400m**: Nagmeldin El Abubakr SUD 46.16, **800m/1500m**: Abubaker Kaki SUD 1:43.90/3:47.92, **5000m/3000mSt**: Abdelkadr Hachlaf MAR 13:39.75/ 8:39.84, **10,000m**: Mahboud Hassan BRN 29:29.48, **HMar**: Brahim Beloua MAR 62:30, **110mh**: Othmane Hadj Lazib ALG 14.03, **400mh**: Abderahmane Hamadi ALG 50.77, **HJ**: Salem Al-Enazy KUW 2.20, **PV**: Karim Mafhoum MAR 5.00, **LJ**: Mohamed Al-Khuwalidi KSA 8.19, **TJ**: Tareq Bougtaïb MAR 16.46, **SP**: Khaled Habash Al-Suwaidi QAT 19.56, **DT**: Sultan Al-Dawoodi KSA 58.63, **HT**: Mohsen Anani EGY 74.22, **JT**: Mohamed Ali Kbabou TUN 71.41, **Dec**: Ahmed Hassan Moussa QAT 7383, **4x100m/4x400m**: KSA 39.99/3:04.74, **20,000mW**: Hassanine Sbai TUN 1:36:00.2*. **Women: 100m/200m**: Greta Taslakian LIB 12.07/23.56. **400m**: Nawal El Jack SUD 54.15, **800m**: Amina Bakheet SUD 2:07.95, **1500m**: Seltana Aït-Hammou MAR 4:23.54, **5000m**: Safa Issaoui TUN 19:13.96, **10,000m**: Nadia Ejjafini BRN 32:29.53, **HMar**: Karima Jassem BRN 75:15, **100mh**: Lamia El Habz MAR 14.21, **400mh/Hep**: Mona Jabir Ahmed SUD 56.07/4594, **HJ**: Karima Ben Othman TUN 1.77, **PV**: Leila Ben Youssef TUN 3.80, **LJ**: Fatima Zahra Dkouk MAR 6.16, **TJ**: Fadoua Al-Boza SYR 12.61, **SP**: Wafa El Baghdadi EGY 15.29, **DT**: Monia Kari TUN 52.79, **HT**: Marwa Ahmed Hussein EGY 62.83*, **JT**: Hanaa Ramadhan Omar EGY 48.28, **4x100m**: MAR 47.52, **4x400m**: SUD 3:38.56, **10,000mW**: Chaïma Trabelsi TUN 53:52.0.

Leaders in medal table: MAR 10G-9S-4B, SUD 8-7-3, TUN 7-1-4, EGY 6-8-9, KSA 4-8-4, BRN 3-1-6, QAT 2-6-3, ALG 2-1-7. *17 nations won medals.*

Asian Race Walking Championships

At Nomi, Japan 25 March

Men 20km: Takayuki Tanii JPN 1:21:09; **Women 20km:** Mayumi Kawasaki JPN 1:28:56.

April 15, Kobe, Japan

Men 50km: Zhao Chengliang CHN 3:44:26.

2nd Asian Indoor Championships

At Macau 30 October - 1 November

Men: 60m: Samuel Francis QAT 6.54*, **400m**: Wang Liangyu CHN 46.08*, **800m**: Mohamed Al-Azimi KUW 1:49.62*, **1500m**: Chatholi Hamza IND 3:50.22*, **3000m**: Charles Bett Koech QAT 8:04.69*, **60mh:** Wu Youxia CHN 7.82, **HJ**: Rashid Al-Mannai QAT-J 2.24*, **PV**: Liu Feiliang CHN 5.30*, **LJ**: Hussein Al-Sabee KSA 7.93*, **TJ**: Roman Valiyev KAZ 16.57*, **SP**: Sultan Al-Hebshi KSA 18.99*, **Hep**: P.J.Vinod IND 5561*, **4x400m**: KSA 3:11.29*. **Women: 60m:** Nongnuch Sanrat THA 7.28*, **400m**: Tang Xiaoyin CHN 53.56, **800m**: Liu Qing CHN 2:06.13, **1500m**: Sinimol Paulose IND 4:22.56, **3000m**: Chen Xiaofang CHN 9:23.11*, **60mh:** Nataliya Ivoninskaya KAZ 8.33*, **HJ**: Noengruthai Chaipetch THA 1.91*, **PV**: Desy Margawati INA 3.75, **LJ**: Chen Yaling CHN 6.45, **TJ**: Irina Litvinenko KAZ 13.56, **SP**: Li Fengfeng CHN 16.33, **Pen:** Irina Naumenko KAZ 4179, **4x400m**: KAZ 3:37.59*.

62nd Balkan Championships

At Sofia, Bulgaria 4-5 July

Men: 100m/200m: Florin Suciu ROM 10.43/21.06, **400m**: Dmiítrios Grávalos GRE 46.85, **800m**: Ioan Zaizan ROM 1:48.67, **1500m**: Cristian Vorovenci ROM 3:49.38, **3000m**: Cosmin Suteu ROM 8:20.65, **5000m**: Marius Ionescu ROM 14:46.48, **3000mSt**: Osman Bas TUR 9:05.67, **110mh**: Ioánnis Lazarídis GRE 14.15, **400mh**: Sotírios Iakovákis GRE 50.15, **HJ**: Dragutin Topic SRB 2.21, **PV**: Spas Bukhalov BUL 5.50, **LJ**: Nikolay Atanasov BUL 8.16, **TJ**: Alin Anghel ROM 16.45, **SP**: Hamza Alic BIH 19.98, **DT**: Sergiu Ursu ROM 62.14, **HT**: Fatih Eryildirim TUR 72.92, **JT**: Levente Bartha ROM 74.21, **4x100m/4x400m**: GRE 39.90/3:09.07; **Women: 100m/200m**: Tezdzhan Naimova BUL 11.07/22.70, **400m**: Dímitra Dóva GRE 53.20, **800m**: Eléni Filándra GRE 2:04.51, **1500m**: Daniela Yordanova BUL 4:16.67, **3000m/5000m**: Alemitu Bekele TUR 8:55.51/16:47.08, **3000mSt**: Iríni Kokkinaríou GRE 9:52.78, **100mh**: Carmen Ghilase ROM 13.43, **400mh**: Hristína Hantzí-Neag GRE 55.94, **HJ**: Persefóni Hatzinákou GRE 1.92, **PV**: Slavica Semenjuk SRB 4.20, **LJ**: Alina Militaru ROM 6.66, **TJ**: Mariya Dimitrova BUL 13.87, **SP**: Anca Heltne ROM 16.47, **DT**: Dragana Tomasevic SRB 56.74, **HT**: Mihaela Melinte ROM 67.85, **JT**: Rumyana Karapetrova BUL 57.62,

4x100m: BUL 43.91, **4x400m**: GRE 3:37.11. Drugs dq: **400m/800m** Teodora Kolarova BUL 52.50/2:02.18, **4x400m** BUL 3:35.73 inc. Kolarova.

Walks: *At Galati, Romania 14 April.* **Men 20km:** Recep Çelik TUR 1:23:10. **Women 20km:** Alina Olaru ROM 1:33:14.

Mar: *At Istanbul 28 October.* **Men:** Iaroslav Muschinski MDA 2:11:58. **Women:** Bahar Dogan TUR 2:37:31.

East African Championships

At Kampala, Uganda 30-31 May

Men: 100m: Gelcha Wotere ETH 10.72, **200m/400m**: Nagmeldin El-Abubakr SUD 21.12/45.90, **800m**: Abubaker Kaki SUD 1:45.80, **1500m**: Sore Abduissa ETH 3:39.01, **5000m**: Amanuel Woldeselassie ETH 13:39.6, **10,000m**: Kwang Samweli TAN 28:42.19, **3000mSt**: Simon Ayeko UGA 8:42.6, **110mh/400mh**: Julius Bungei KEN 14.79/50.2, **HJ**: Mohammed Younis SUD 2.00, **PV**: Karim El Mafhoum MAR 4.60, **LJ/TJ**: Geoffrey Okello UGA 6.72/14.37, **SP**: Charles Anywar UGA 12.61, **DT**: Daniel Rubangakene UGA 38.95, **JT**: Sammy Keskeny KEN 68.34, **4x100m/4x400m**: KEN 40.7/3:07.78. **Women: 100m**: Joyce Sakari KEN 12.22, **200m/400m/100mh/400mh**: Muna Jabir Ahmed SUD 23.89/51.61/14.31/55.8, **800m**: Catherine Webombesa UGA 2:08.21, **1500m**: Aite Tusa ETH 4:16.94, **5000m**: Fortuna Zegerghis ERI 16:20.48, **LJ**: Evelyne Amucu 5.50, **SP**: Annet Kabasindi 10.96, **DT/JT**: Cecilia Kiplagat 41.64/52.25, **4x100m/4x400m**: KEN 47.31/3:34.44.

NACAC (North American, Central American & Caribbean) Under-23 Championships)

At San Salvador, El Salvador 13-15 July

Men: 100m: Richard Thompson TRI 10.33, **200m**: Jordan Vaden USA 20.17*, **400m**: Calvin Smith USA 45.52, **800m**: Golden Coachman USA 1:49.01, **1500m**: Pablo Solares MEX 3:45.29*, **5000m**: Ben Bruce USA 14:27.90, **10,000m**: Julio César Pérez MEX 29:38.31*, **3000mSt**: Mike Spence USA 8:39.51*, **110mh**: Dexter Faulk USA 13.35*, **400mh**: LaRon Bennett USA 48.76*, **HJ**: Adam Shunk USA 2.23, **PV**: José Francisco Montano MEX 5.15, **LJ**: Carlos Jorge DOM 7.89, **TJ**: Marc Kellman USA 16.50, **SP**: Rhuben Williams USA 18.43, **DT**: Nick Petrucci USA 56.17, **HT**: Jacob Freeman USA 70.32*, **JT**: Justin St. Clair USA 73.16*, **Dec**: Darvin Colon HON 6330, **4x100m**: USA (D Omole, Vaden, M Mitchell, R Edwards) 38.99*, **4x400m**: USA (McCoy, Smith, Mitchell, Neville) 3:02.78, **20kmW**: Walter Sandoval ESA 1:28:29*; **Women: 100m**: Mechelle Lewis USA 11.37, **200m**: Virgil Hodge SKN 22.73w, **400m**: Debbie Dunn USA 52.68, **800m/1500m**: Mary Jayne Harrelson USA 2:05.10/4:30.09, **5000m**: Whitney McDonald 16:42.12, **3000mSt**: Kristen Anderson USA 10:21.82*, **100mh**: Candice Davis USA 13.12, **400mh**: Latosha Wallace USA 56.54, **HJ**: Lavern Spencer LCA 1.89, **PV**: Becky Holliday USA 4.15, **LJ**: Shameka Marshall 6.34, **TJ**: Ayanna Alexander TRI 13.29w, **SP**: Cleopatra Borel-Brown TRI 17.53*, **DT**: Stephanie Trafton USA 59.27*, **HT**: Jessica Cosby USA 65.15, **JT**: Ana Erika Gutiérrez MEX 51.52, **Hep**: Maria Carrillo ESA 5022, **4x100m**: JAM (Palmer, Whyte, McLaughlin, Dowdie) 43.73, **4x400m**: USA (Wallace, Woods, Wilson, Dunn) 3:29.15, **10kmW**: Cristina López ESA 44:16.21*.

At Santo Domingo, Dominican Republic: **Dec**: Ryan Harlan USA 7901.

Pan-American Race Walking Cup

At Camboriú, Brazil 21-22 April

Men: 20kmW: 1. Jefferson Pérez ECU 1:25:08, 2. Gustavo Restrepo COL 1:25:09, 3. Luis Fernando López COL 1:25:26; **50kmW**: 1. Álvaro García MEX 4:04:52, 2. Fredy Hernández COL 4:05:16, 3. Fausto Quinde ECU 4:10:08. **Women 20kmW**: 1. Cristina López ESA 1:39:21, 2 Miriam Ramón ECU 1:39:42; 3. Yadira Guamán ECU 1:41:08.

14th Pan-American Junior Championships

At São Paulo, Brazil 6-8 July

Men: 100m: Keston Bledman TRI 10.32, **200m**: Arthur Wims USA 20.80, **400m**: Bryshon Nellum USA 45.40, **800m**: Andrew Heaney CAN 1:48.52, **1500m**: Matthew Centrowitz USA 3:56.63, **5000m**: Diego Borrego MEX 14:33.16, **10,000m**: Kenny Klotz USA 31:04.57, **3000mSt**: Marvin Blanco VEN 9:04.38, **110mh-J/400mh**: Johnny Dutch USA 13.46*/50.82, **HJ**: Jamal Wilson BAH 2.11, **PV**: Scott Roth USA 5.30, **LJ**: Jorge McFarlane PER 7.59, **TJ**: Héctor Fuentes CUB 16.61, 6k **SP**: Nicholas Robinson USA 18.60, 1.75k **DT**: Luke Bryant USA 59.45*, 6k **HT**: Walter Henning USA 69.89, **JT**: Víctor Fatecha PAR 75.43*, **Dec**-J: Diego de Araújo BRA 7100, **4x100m**: USA 39.43, **4x400m**: TRI 3:05.70, **10kmW**: Mauricio Arteaga ECU 43:30.64. **Women: 100m**: Lynne Layne USA 11.24*, **200m**: Bianca Knight USA 23.17, **400m**: Bobby-Gaye Wilkins JAM 51.72*, **800m**: Latavia Thomas USA 2:06.59, **1500m**: Jessica Pixler USA 4:21.09, **3000m**: Nicole Blood USA 9:22.35, **5000m**: Marie-Louise Aselin CAN 17:40.28, **3000mSt**: Danielle Woods CAN 10:13.98, **100mh**: Kristi Castlin USA 13.02*, **400mh**: Queen Harrison USA 56.25*, **HJ**: Lesyani Mayor CUB 1.85, **PV**: Alicia Rue USA 4.20*, **LJ**: Jamesha Youngblood USA 6.40, **TJ**: Ke'Nyia Richardson USA 13.55, **SP**: Natalia Ducó CHI 16.40, **DT**: Emily Pendleton USA 49.09, **HT**: Marynna de Jesús Dias BRA 60.26, **JT**: Jucilene de Lima BRA 49.42, **Hep**: Brian Theisen CAN 5413, **4x100m/4x400m**: USA 43.71/3:29.67, **10kmW**: Ingrid Hernández COL 48:48.24*. **Medal Table Leaders:** USA 24-16-8, CAN 4-5-4, BRA 3-2-6, TRI 2-5-3, CUB 2-3-8, JAM 2-5-5.

37th South American Junior Championships

At São Paulo, Brazil 30 June - 1 July

Men: 100m: Alonso Edwards PAN 10.28*, **200m**: Dax Danns GUY 21.27, **400m/400mh**: Juan Pablo Maturana COL 47.25/52.43, **800m**: Lutimar Paes BRA 1:50.94, **1500m/3000mSt**: Marvin Blanco VEN 3:54.71/9:16.75, **5000m**: Robson Pereira de Lima BRA 15:01.05, **10,000m**: Jefferson Peña COL 31:06.05#, **110mh-J/LJ**: Jorge McFarlane PER 13.76/7.52,

400mh: Víctor Solarte VEN 51.30, **HJ**: Diego Ferrín ECU 2.08, **PV**: Rodrigo Tenorio CHI 4.80, **TJ**: Alafans Delfino BRA 15.53, 6k **SP**: Yosner Ortiz VEN 17.88, 1.75k **DT**: Luis Schneider BRA 52.44, 6k **HT**: Rhaony Caldas BRA 61.21, **JT**: Víctor Fatecha PAR 73.07, **Dec**: J: Diego de Araújo BRA 7100#, **4x100m**: COL 40.48, **4x400m**: BRA 3:08.68, **10,000mW**: Mauricio Arteaga ECU 43:30.64#. **Women: 100m**: Rosângela Santos BRA 11.56, **200m**: Bárbara Leôncio BRA 23.69, **400m**: María Alejandra Idrobo COL 54.24, **800m**: Madelene Rondón VEN 2:09.43, **1500m**: Evangelina Thomas ARG 4:45.30, **3000m**: Viviana Acosta ECU 10:18.35, **5000m**: Claudia Ramírez URU 18:18.32, **3000mSt**: Rocío Huillca PER 11:11.57, **100mh/TJ**: Giselle de Albuquerque BRA 13.96/12.95, **400mh**: Keila Escobar COL 59.26, **HJ**: Tamara Maass CHI 1.75, **PV**: Keisa Monterola VEN 4.15, **LJ**: Vanessa Spínola 5.79, **SP**: Natalia Ducó CHI 16.67, **DT**: Fernanda Borges BRA 44.44, **HT**: Marynna de Jesús Dias BRA 57.14, **JT**: Jucilene de Lima 47.53, **Hep**: Giovanna Cavaleti BRA 4957#, **4x100m/4x400m**: BRA 44.42/3:43.44, **10,000mW**: Ingrid Hernández COL 48:48.24#. **Medal Table Leaders:** BRA 17G-17S-16B, COL 7-11-8, VEN 6-6-6, CHI 3-5-3, PER 3-2-6, ECU 3-3-6, ARG 0-5-7. # held at Pan-American Juniors.

24th South East Asia Games

At Nakhon Ratchasima, Thailand 7-12 December

Men: 100m/200m: Suryo Agung Wibowo INA 10.25*/20.76, **400m**: Julius Felicisimo Nierras PHI 46.56, **800m/1500m**: Nguyen Dinh Cuong VIE 1:51:16/3:45.31*, **5000m/10,000m**: Boonthung Srisung THA 14:18.03/30:51.66, **Mar:** Yahuza INA 2:23:46, **110mh**: Rayzamshah Wan Sofian MAS 13.91*, **400mh**: Apisit Kuttiyawan THA 50.38, **3000mSt**: Rene Herrera PHI 8:54.21, **HJ**: Lee Hup Wei MAS 2.19, **PV**: Sompong Saombankuay THA 5.10*, **LJ**: Henry Dagmil PHI 7.87*, **TJ**: Theerayut Philakong THA 16.44*, **SP**: Chatchawal Polyemg THA 17.43*, **DT**: Wansawang Sawasdee THA 54.13, **HT**: Arniel Ferrera PHI 60.98*, **JT**: Sanya Buathong THA 68.65, **Dec**: Vu Van Huyen VIE 7457*, **4x100m**: THA 38.95*, **4x400m**: MAS 3:07.95, **20kmW**: Teoh Boon Lim MAS 1:30:37. **Women: 100m/200m**: Vu Thi Huong VIE 11.47/23.47, **400m**: Saowalee Kaewchuy THA 54.75, **800m/1500m**: Truong Thanh Hang VIE 2:02.39*/4:11.60*, **5000m/10,000m**: Triyaningsih INA 15: 54.32*/34:07.35, **Mar:** Sunisa Sailomyen THA 2:43:33, **100mh**: Dedeh Erawati INA 13.51, **400mh**: Wassana Winatho THA 57.21, **HJ**: Bui Thi Nung VIE 1.88, **PV**: Roslinda Samsu MAS 4.00, **LJ**: Marestella Torres PHI 6.31, **TJ**: Thitima Muangjan THA 13.85*, **SP**: Zhang Guirong SIN 17.21, **DT**: Dwi Ratanawati INA 50.05, **HT**: Siti Shahidah Abdullah MAS 52.93, **JT**: Buoban Phamang THA 55.97*, **Hep**: Wassana Winatho THA 5889*, **4x100m/4x400m**: THA 44.00*/3:38.26, **20kmW**: Yuan Yu Fang MAS 1:41:47.

West African Championships

At Cotonou, Bénin 29 June - 1 July

Men: 100m: Mouhamadiu Lamine Niang SEN 10.71, **200m**: Narcisse Tevoedjre BEN 22.58, **400m**: Bawa Fuseini GHA 48.66, **800m**: Abdoulaye Wagne SEN 1:48.70, **1500m**: Assand Diallo SEN 3:52.24, **5000m/10,000m**: Romaric Yoro BEN 15:02.61/32:09.75, **3000mSt**: Tchendo Malabou TOG 9:34.38, **110mh**: Samuel Okon NGR 14.09, **400mh**: Barnabé Bationo BEN 51.59, **HJ**: Olivier Sanou BUR 2.10, **LJ**: Stanley Gagbeke NGR 7.60, **TJ**: Relwende Kaboré BUR 15.91, **SP**: Moussa Diarra NLI 14.65, **DT/JT**: Kenechukwu Ezeofor NGR 51.35/65.16, **4x100m**: SEN 40.16. **Women: 100m**: Emem Eden NGR 11.80, **200m**: Jopy Eze NGR 24.38, **400m**: Sekinat Adesanya NGR 53.04, **800m**: Seynabou Paye SEN 2:11.61, **1500m/5000m**: Bentille Allassane 4:38.30/17:41.34, **100mh**: Béatrice Kamboulé BUR 13.80, **400mh**: Mary Onfeweng NGR 60.98, **HJ**: Doreen Amata NGR 1.83, **LJ**: Chinazom Amadi NGR 6.06, **TJ**: Otonye Iworima NGR 13.72, **SP**: Nakani Coulibaly MLI 12.08, **DT**: Adeoye Funde NGR 40.36, **JT**: Ihuefo Sorochukwu NGR 46.00, **4x100m**: NGR 45.01.

IAU 100km World Cup

At Einschoten, Netherlands 8 September

Men: 1. Shinichi Watanabe JPN 6:23:21, 2. Kenji Nakanishi JPN 6:30:21, 3. Oleg Kharitonov RUS 6:30:22, 4. Igor Tyazhkorob RUS 6:42:30, 5. Aleksey Izmaylov RUS 6:45:10; **Team:** 1. JPN 19:48.14, 2. RUS 19:58:02, 3. USA 20:43:33. **Women:** 1. Norimi Sakurai JPN 7:00:27, 2. Laurence Fricotteaux FRA 7:26:44 rec, 3. Hiroko Sho JPN 7:27:12, 4. Marina Myshlyanova RUS 7:39:18, 5. Monica Carlin ITA 7:40:36, **Team:** 1 JPN 22:25:11, 2. FRA 23:12:23, 3. GER 23:52:44.

Also included European Championships

IAU World 24 Hours Championships

At Drummondville, Canada 28-29 July

Men: 1. Ryoichi Sekiya JPN 263.562k, 2. Mohamed Magroun FRA 257.018, 3. Masayuki Otaki JPN 253.814, 4. Phil McCarthy USA 248.613, 5. Fabien Hoblea FRA 248.505; **Team:** 1. JPN 761.841, 2. FRA 742.206, 3. GER 673.092. **Women:** 1. Lyudmila Kalinina RUS 236.848, 2. Brigtte Bec FRA 233.137, 3. Galina Yeremina RUS 230.288, 4. Yasuke Kanchira JPN 221.383, 5. Monique Muhlen LUX 217.776; **Team:** 1. RUS 671.329, 2. JPN 641.208, 3. FRA 614.488.

IAU European 24 Hours Championships

At Madrid, Spain 5-6 May

Men: 1, Anatoliy Kruglikov RUS 257.358k, 2. Vladimir Bychkov RUS 251.631, 3. José Luis Poasdo ESP 247.937. **Women:** 1. Lyudmila Kalinina RUS 233.307, 2. Monika Casiraghi ITA 217.989, 3. Rosario Muñoz ESP 210.721.

European Mountain Racing Championships

At Cauterets, France 8 July

Men (12.8km, 1570m height difference): 1. Ahmet Arslan TUR 68:39, 2. Marco De Gasperi ITA 68:50, 3. Marco Gaiardo ITA 69:09; **Team:** 1. ITA 15, 2. FRA 31, 3. GER 36; **Junior Men** (8.5km. 1010m hd): Mehmet Akkoyun TUR 48:27; **Team:** TUR 6. **Women** (8.5km

IAAF Golden League

There were six meetings in the Golden League in 2007. The jackpot of $1 million, shared by athletes who won at all six meetings, was shared by Sanya Richards (for the second successive year) and Yelena Isinbayeva.

Winners of Golden League events 2007:

Event	*Oslo 15/6*	*St-Denis 6/7*	*Rome 13/7*	*Zürich 7/9*	*Brussels 14/9*	*Berlin 16/9*
Men						
100m	A Powell	D Atkins	A Powell	F Obikwelu	A Powell	J Saidy Ndure
1500m	B Kipruto	A Webb	A Kaouch	M Baala	D K Komen	D K Komen
110mh	A Moore	D Robles	A Moore	D Robles	D Robles	A Johnson
TJ	P Idowu	C Olsson	C Olsson	W Davis	W Davis	A Wilson
JT	T Pitkämäki	T Pitkämäki	A Thorkildsen	A Thorkildsen	T Pitkämäki	T Pitkämäki
Women						
100m	S Durst	T Edwards	T Edwards	C Arron	V Campbell	C Jeter
400m	S Richards	S Richards	S Richards	S Richards	S Richards	S Richards
100mh	M Perry	M Perry	M Perry	S Kallur	S Kallur	S Kallur
HJ	Y Slesarenko	B Vlasic	B Vlasic	B Vlasic	B Vlasic	B Vlasic
PV	Y Isinbayeva	Y Isinbayeva	Y Isinbayeva	Y Isinbayeva	Y Isinbayeva	Y Isinbayeva

2008 Dates; June 1 - Berlin; June 6 - Oslo; July 11 - Rome; July 18 - Paris; Aug 29 - Zürich; Sep 5 - Brussels.

The disciplines designated as Jackpot events 2008 are (men) **100m, 400m, 1500m, 400mh, LJ, JT**; (women) **200m, 800m, 100mh, HJ**. As in 2007 athletes would have to win at all six meetings for a share of the $1 million prize. Should no athlete manage six wins, then anyone with five victories would share $500,000.

1010m hd): 1. Anita Håkenstad Evertsen NOR 51:45, 2. Anna Pichrtová CZE 52:34, 3. Kirsten Melkevik Otterbu NOR 52:56; **Team:** 1. SUI 17, 2. CZE 22. 3. ITA 29; **Junior Women** (4km. 450m hd): Lucija Krkoc SLO 23:343, **Team:** GBR 8.

World Marathon Majors 2006-07

Men: 1. Robert K. Cheruiyot KEN 80, 2. Martin Lel KEN 65, 3. Haile Gebrselassie ETH 50, 4. Felix Limo KEN 35, 5. Abderrahim Goumri MAR 30, 6=, Marilson dos Santos BRA, Patrick Ivuti KEN, Luke Kibet KEN, Stephen Kiogora KEN & Daniel Njenga KEN 25.

Women: 1. Gete Wami ETH 80, 2. Jelena Prokopcuka LAT 65, 3. Berhane Adere ETH 55, 4. Chunxiu Zhou CHN 40, 5. Catherine Ndereba KEN 36, 6. Rita Jeptoo KEN 35, 7. Lidiya Grigoryeva RUS 31, 8. Deena Kastor USA 26, 9. Paula Radcliffe GBR 25, 10=, Salina Kosgei KEN & Reiko Tosa JPN 20.

World Athletics Final 2007

Stuttgart on 9-10 September.

Prize Money for each event: 1st $30,000, 2nd $20,000, 3rd $12,000, 4th $7000, 5th $5000, 6th $4000, 7th $3000, 8th $2000. Also at 1500m, 5000m, 3000mSt: 9th to 12th each $1000. No valid performance – half the money for last position.

Results with scores (and positions in brackets) from the Grand Prix season, and leading scorers who did not compete in Stuttgart.

Maximum 5 GP scores (20 for 1st) to count.

Men

100 Metres (a): (-0.3)

1. Asafa Powell JAM 9.83*	96 (1)
2. Jaysuma Saidy Ndure NOR 10.06	73 (4)
3. Michael Frater JAM 10.11	62 (6)
4. Francis Obikwelu POR 10.17	72 (5)
5. Marlon Devonish GBR 10.18	74 (3)
6. Churandy Martina AHO 10.23	60 (7)
7. Matic Osovnikar SLO 10.35	29 (19=)
dq Olusoji Fasuba NGR DQ	52 (9)

Other GP leaders prior to WAF:
Derrick Atkins BAH 82, Shawn Crawford USA 54, Nesta Carter JAM 48, Tyson Gay USA 46

200 Metres (b): (1.3)

1. Jaysuma Saidy Ndure NOR 19.89	57 (5)
2. Wallace Spearmon USA 20.18	80 (1)
3. Rodney Martin USA 20.27	62 (4)
4. Johan Wissman SWE 20.30	51 (6=)
5. Chris Williams JAM 20.39	51 (6=)
6. J.J. Johnson USA 20.48	64 (3)
7. Brian Dzingai ZIM 20.56	36 (10)
8. Paul Hession IRL 20.58	44 (9)

Other GP leaders prior to WAF:
Usain Bolt JAM 74, Xavier Carter USA 47, Shawn Crawford USA 34

400 Metres (a)

1. LaShawn Merritt USA 44.58	86 (1)
2. Tyler Christopher CAN 44.87	56 (6)
3. Angelo Taylor USA 44.92	55 (7)
4. Gary Kikaya COD 45.58	64 (3)
5. John Steffensen AUS 46.16	62 (4)
6. Martyn Rooney GBR 46.25	-
7. Alleyne Francique GRN 46.27	35 (13=)
8. Sanjay Ayre JAM 46.32	58 (5)

Other GP leaders prior to WAF:
Jeremy Wariner USA 80, Darrold Williamson USA 54, Tim Benjamin GBR 40

800 Metres (a)

1. Youssef Saad Kamel BRN 1:45.61	62 (2)
2. Mbulaeni Mulaudzi RSA 1:45.67	76 (1)
3. Belal Mansour Ali BRN 1:45.93	52 (5)
4. Amine Laâlou MAR 1:46.18	48 (7=)
5. Mohammed Al-Salhi KSA 1:46.99	56 (4)
6. Manuel Olmedo ESP 1:47.06	37 (10=)

7. Abraham Chepkirwok UGA 1:47.29 60 (3)
8. Dmitrijs Milkevics LAT 1:47.35 24 (18=)
Other GP leaders prior to WAF:
Yuriy Borzakovskiy RUS 50, David Rudisha KEN 48, Khadevis Robinson USA 45

1500 Metres (b)
1. Daniel Kipchirchir Komen KEN 3:37.96 76 (1)
2. Mehdi Baala FRA 3:38.35 36 (10=)
3. Suleiman Simotwo KEN 3:38.36 56 (6=)
4. Alan Webb USA 3:38.84 36 (10=)
5. Kevin Sullivan CAN 3:38.91 36 (10=)
6. Belal Mansour Ali BRN 3:38.93 59 (4=)
7. Andrew Baddeley GBR 3:39.14 56 (6=)
8. Nicholas Kemboi KEN 3:39.20 33 (15=)
9. Mohamed Moustaoui MAR 3:42.49 42 (8)
10. Shadrack Korir KEN 3:47.05 60 (3)
Other GP leaders prior to WAF:
Tarek Boukensa ALG 61, Bernard Lagat USA 59, Adil Kaouch MAR 40, Augustine Choge KEN 36

3000 Metres (a)
1. Edwin Soi KEN 7:48.81 38 (5)
2. Joseph Ebuya KEN 7:49.70 48 (3)
3. Mo Farah GBR 7:49.89 28 (10)
4. Craig Mottram AUS 7:49.89 34 (6)
5. Thomas Longosiwa KEN 7:50.62 30 (7=)
6. Eliud Kipchoge KEN 7:50.93 20 (12=)
7. Moses Kipsiro UGA 7:51.22 50 (1=)
8. Jonas Cheruiyot KEN 7:51.26 41 (4)
9. Yusuf Biwott KEN 7:51.28 15 (18=)
10. Bisluke Kiplagat KEN 8:07.01 17 (14)
Other GP leaders prior to WAF:
Kenenisa Bekele ETH 50, Alistair Cragg IRL 30, Boniface Songok KEN 29

5000 Metres (b)
1. Edwin Soi KEN 13:38.16 31 (3)
2. Micah Kogo KEN 13:39.91 25 (4)
3. Moses Masai KEN 13:39.96 -
4. Joseph Ebuya KEN 13:40.43 23 (5)
5. Eliud Kipchoge KEN 13:40.49 40 (2)
6. Sileshi Sihine ETH 13:41.04 50 (1)
7. Mo Farah GBR 13:41.61 -
8. Thomas Longosiwa KEN 13:42.39 10 (19=)
9. Craig Mottram AUS 13:42.81 20 (7)
10. Shadrack Kosgei KEN 13:50.61 19 (8)
11. Markos Geneti ETH 13:50.98 -
Other GP leaders prior to WAF:
Tariku Bekele ETH 22, Ahmed Baday NAR 18

3000m Steeplechase (b)
1. Paul Kipsiele Koech KEN 8:00.67 76 (1)
2. Richard Matelong KEN 8:07.66 26 (7=)
3. Brimin Kipruto KEN 8:11.05 43 (2)
4. Bouabdellah Tahri FRA 8:14.38 32 (3)
5. Wesley Kiprotich KEN 8:14.88 22 (13=)
6. Julius Nyamu KEN 8:17.91 30 (4)
7. Mustafa Mohamed SWE 8:20.33 26 (7=)
8. Steve Slattery USA 8:20.94 29 (5)
9. Collins Kosgei KEN 8:24.27 26 (7=)
10. Günther Weidlinger AUT 8:32.15 22 (13=)
11. Hamid Ezzine MAR 8:45.22 27 (6)
Other GP leaders prior to WAF:
Reuben Kosgei KEN, Michael Kipyego KEN 24

110 Metres Hurdles (a): (0.0)
1. Dayron Robles CUB 12.92* 86 (2)
2. David Payne USA 13.08 70 (5=)
3. Terrence Trammell USA 13.15 64 (7=)
4. Anwar Moore USA 13.18 88 (1)
5. Ladji Doucouré FRA 13.27 42 (11)
6. Allen Johnson USA 13.36 70 (5=)
7. Serhiy Demydyuk UKR 13.37 34 (14=)
dq. Ryan Wilson USA 78 (3)
Other GP leaders prior to WAF:
Aries Merritt USA 72, Liu Xiang CHN 72, David Oliver USA 60

400 Metres Hurdles (b)
1. Marek Plawgo POL 48.35 52 (5)
2. Kerron Clement USA 48.35 62 (4)
3. James Carter USA 48.36 80 (1)
4. Bershawn Jackson USA 48.58 28 (12=)
5. Angelo Taylor USA 49.27 66 (3)
6. Kenneth Ferguson USA 49.45 45 (7)
7. Félix Sánchez DOM 49.61 35 (8)
8. L.J. van Zyl RSA 49.62 68 (2)
Other GP leaders prior to WAF:
Alwyn Myburgh RSA 49, Derrick Williams USA 34

High Jump (b)
1. Donald Thomas BAH 2.32 34 (6)
2. Stefan Holm SWE 2.30 68 (1)
3. Linus Thörnblad SWE 2.27 29.5 (7)
4. Germaine Mason GBR 2.27 46 (3=)
5. Tora Harris USA 2.27 37 (5)
6. Yaroslav Rybakov RUS 2.27 -
7. Tomáš Janku CZE 2.24 46 (3=)
8. Jesse Williams USA 2.24 59 (2)
Other GP leaders prior to WAF:
Kyriakos Ioannou CYP 23

Pole Vault (a)
1. Brad Walker USA 5.91 66 (1)
2. Björn Otto GER 5.86 36.7 (7)
3. Steve Hooker AUS 5.81 60 (2)
4. Danny Ecker GER 5.81 58 (3)
5. Denys Yurchenko UKR 5.70 13.5 (19)
6. Jeff Hartwig USA 5.70 40 (6)
7. Tim Lobinger GER 5.60 42 (5)
8. Igor Pavlov RUS 5.60 44 (4)
Other GP leaders prior to WAF:
Daichi Sawano JPN 36.5, Alex Averbukh ISR 34.5

Long Jump (b)
1. Andrew Howe ITA 8.35/0.7 36 (6=)
2. Brian Johnson USA 8.16/0.0 60 (1=)
3. Khotso Mokoena RSA 8.12/0.1 50 (4)
4. Christian Reif GER 8.01/1.0 -
5. Chris Tomlinson GBR 7.93/0.2 55 (3)
6. Oleksiy Lukashevych UKR 7.78/-0.2 26 (13=)
7. John Moffitt USA 7.72/0.0 36 (6=)
8. Miguel Pate USA 7.71/0.2 47 (5)
Other GP leaders prior to WAF:
Irving Saladino PAN 60, Gable Garenamotse BOT, Issam Nima ALG 35

Triple Jump (a)
1. Walter Davis USA 17.35/0.7 60 (5)
2. Aarik Wilson USA 17.34/0.6 86 (1)
3. Nelson Évora POR 17.30/0.2 72 (2)
4. Randy Lewis GRN 17.21/0.6 54 (7)
5. Leevan Sands BAH 17.07/0.8 62 (4)
6. Jadel Gregório BRA 16.95/0.0 60 (3)
7. Dmitrij Valukevic SVK 16.63/0.8 33 (10)
8. Aleksandr Petrenko RUS 16.44/0.1 34 (9)
Other GP leaders prior to WAF:
Christian Olsson SWE 56, Osniel Tosca CUB 42

Shot (a)

1. Reese Hoffa USA 20.98	60 (1)
2. Adam Nelson USA 20.95	14 (13)
3. Andrey Mikhnevich BLR 20.88	38 (3)
4. Dan Taylor USA 20.74	33 (5)
5. Christian Cantwell USA 20.25	44 (2)
6. Rutger Smith NED 20.01	34 (4)
7. Ralf Bartels GER 19.49	28 (7)
8. Garrett Johnson USA 19.26	32 (6)

Other GP leaders prior to WAF:
Tomasz Majewski POL 26

Discus (a)

1. Gerd Kanter EST 66.54	35 (3)
2. Virgilijus Alekna LTU 65.94	60 (1)
3. Piotr Malachowski POL 65.35	41 (2)
4. Robert Harting GER 65.25	-
5. Mario Pestano ESP 63.25	32 (5)
6. Jarred Rome USA 62.05	23 (6)
7. Zoltán Kővágó HUN 61.58	21 (7)
8. Ian Waltz USA 61.14	34 (4)

Other GP leaders prior to WAF:
Ehsan Hadadi IRI 20, Frantz Kruger FIN 19

Hammer (b)

1. Ivan Tikhon BLR 82.05	26 (1)
2. Krisztián Pars HUN 78.42	20 (3=)
3. Koji Murofushi JPN 77.95	10 (8)
4. Miloslav Konopka SVK 77.95	11 (7)
5. Vadim Devyatovskiy BLR 77.81	14 (5)
6. Primoz Kozmus SLO 76.78	22 (2)
7. Libor Charfreitag SVK 75.89	20 (3=)
8. Szymon Ziólkowski POL 74.54	12 (6)

Javelin (b)

1. Tero Pitkämäki FIN 88.19	80 (1=)
2. Andreas Thorkildsen NOR 85.06	80 (1=)
3. Magnus Arvidsson SWE 83.37	56 (4)
4. Teemu Wirkkala FIN 80.20	48 (5)
5. Eriks Rags LAT 77.40	46 (6)
6. Aleksandr Ivanov RUS 76.09	36 (9=)
7. Stefan Wenk GER 75.87	-
8. Peter Esenwein GER 72.91	26 (13=)

Other GP leaders prior to WAF:
Breaux Greer USA 58. Guillermo Martínez CUB 42, Robert Oosthuizen RSA 40

Women

100 Metres (b): (-0.6)

1. Carmelita Jeter USA 11.10	74 (4)
2. Allyson Felix USA 11.15	54 (8)
3. Christine Arron FRA 11.20	78 (3)
4. Kim Gevaert BEL 11.29	50 (9=)
5. Lauryn Williams USA 11.31	60 (6)
6. Sheri-Ann Brooks JAM 11.33	64 (5)
7. Ivet Lalova BUL 11.59	-
8. Joice Maduaka GBR 11.61	-

Other GP leaders prior to WAF:
Torri Edwards USA 90, Me'Lisa Barber USA 80, Veronica Campbell JAM 58, Stephanie Durst USA 5-

200 Metres (a) (0.5)

1. Muriel Hurtis-Houairi FRA 22.73	32 (8)
2. Debbie Ferguson McKenzie BAH 22.74	45 (4)
3. Lashauntea Moore USA 22.78	50 (2)
4. Kim Gevaert BEL 22.84	54 (1)
5. Lauryn Williams USA 22.94	48 (3)
6. Joice Maduaka GBR 23.36	15 (15)
7. Stephanie Durst USA 23.50	26 (11)

Other GP leaders prior to WAF:
Rachelle Smith USA 42, Torri Edwards USA 36, Cydonie Mothersill CAY 34, Sheri-Ann Brooks JAM 31

400 Metres (b)

1. Sanya Richards USA 49.27	100 (1)
2. Novlene Williams JAM 50.12	80 (2)
3. Christine Ohuruogu GBR 50.20	28 (13=)
4. Ami Mbacké Thiam SEN 50.33	78 (3)
5. Nicola Sanders GBR 50.44	60 (5=)
6. Shericka Williams JAM 50.64	60 (5=)
7. Mary Wineberg USA 50.73	54 (7)
8. Ilona Usovich BLR 51.38	38 (9)

Other GP leaders prior to WAF:
Allyson Felix USA 66, Deedee Trotter USA 44

800 Metres (b)

1. Janeth Jepkosgei KEN 1:57.87	72 (1)
2. Mayte Martínez ESP 1:58.14	65 (2)
3. Marilyn Okoro GBR 1:58.76	39 (10)
4. Lucia Klocová SVK 1:58.94	58 (4)
5. Brigita Langerholc SLO 1:59.56	40 (8=)
6. Svetlana Cherkasova RUS 1:59.63	41 (7)
7. Elisa Cusma Piccione ITA 1:59.67	43 (6)
8. Jemma Simpson GBR 2:00.78	44 (5)

Other GP leaders prior to WAF:
Kenia Sinclair JAM 60, Maria Mutola MOZ 40, Hazel Clark USA 38

1500 Metres (a)

1. Maryam Jamal BRN 4:01.23	100 (1)
2. Yelena Soboleva RUS 4:05.35	62 (3)
3. Sarah Jamieson AUS 4:05.43	46 (7)
4. Agnes Samaria NAM 4:05.44	36 (9)
5. Viola Kibiwott KEN 4:06.00	48 (4=)
6. Ibhissam Lakhoud MAR 4:06.01	42 (8)
7. Olga Yegorova RUS 4:07.67	64 (2)
8. Yuliya Fomenko RUS 4:08.14	53 (6)
9. Carmen Douma-Hussar CAN 4:08.33	27 (11)
10. Iryna Lishchynska UKR 4:13.82	58 (4=)
11. Siham Hilali MAR 4:16.51	26 (12=)

Other GP leaders prior to WAF:
Malindi Elmore CAN 31

3000 Metres (b)

1. Meseret Defar ETH 8:27.24	20 (5=)
2. Vivian Cheruiyot KEN 8:28.66	20 (5=)
3. Priscah Cherono KEN 8:29.06	24 (1=)
4. Linet Masai KEN 8:42.54	10 (18=)
5. Sylvia Kibet KEN 8:46.10	22 (4)
6. Jessica Augusto POR 8:56.65	24 (1=)
7. Helen Clitheroe GBR 9:02.41	18 (11=)
8. Hattie Dean GBR 9:16.93	-
9. Bizunesh Urgesa ETH 9:18.52	15 (13)
10. Mahlet Melese ETH 9:25.74	-
11. Donna MacFarlane AUS 9:34.37	-

Other GP leaders prior to WAF:
Jo Pavey GBR 24, Mariem Alaoui Selsouli MAR, Lauren Fleshman USA, Kim Smith NZL 20

5000 Metres (a)

1. Vivian Cheruiyot KEN 14:56.94	36 (3=)
2. Sylvia Kibet KEN 14:57.37	-
3. Priscah Cherono KEN 14:58.97	33 (7)
4. Linet Masai KEN 15:02.74	36 (3=)
5. Meselech Melkamu ETH 15:06.20	37 (2)
6. Kseniya Agafonova RUS 15:56.35	-

Other GP leaders prior to WAF:
Kim Smith NZL 44, Meseret Defar ETH 33, Jen Rhines USA 34, Tirunesh Dibaba ETH 30, Lauren Fleshman USA 29

3000m Steeplechase (a)
1. Eunice Jepkorir KEN 9:35.03 34 (3)
2. Roísín McGettigan IRL 9:35.86 17 (8=)
3. Cristina Casandra ROM 9:36.38 31 (4)
4. Yekaterina Volkova RUS 9:40.21 10 (13=)
5. Korine Hinds JAM 9:40.50 47 (1)
6. Helen Clitheroe GBR 9:41.59 15 (10)
7. Donna MacFarlane AUS 9:41.77 42 (2)
8. Hatti Dean GBR 9:41.86 12 (12)
9. Mardrea Hyman JAM 9:51.03 17 (8=)
10. Lisa Galaviz USA 9:51.73 19 (6=)
Other GP leaders prior to WAF:
Mekdes Bekele ETH 24, Wioletta Janowska POL 19

100 Metres Hurdles (b): (-0.3)
1. Michelle Perry USA 12.68 96 (1=)
2. Josephine Onyia ESP 12.70 60 (5)
3. Delloreen Ennis-London JAM 12.72 72 (4)
4. Perdita Felicien CAN 12.83 45 (8)
5. Vonette Dixon JAM 12.90 27 (15)
dq. Susanna Kallur SWE 96 (1=)
dq. Sally McLellan AUS 52 (6)
dq. Lolo Jones USA 74 (3)
Other GP leaders prior to WAF:
Adrianna Lamalle FRA 46, . Danielle Carruthers USA 43, Virginia Powell USA, Angela Whyte CAN 42

400 Metres Hurdles (a)
1. Anna Jesien POL 54.17 56 (3)
2. Jana Rawlinson AUS 54.19 76 (1)
3. Melaine Walker JAM 54.31 72 (2)
4. Yevgeniya Isakova RUS 54.99 40 (6)
5. Tiffany Williams USA 55.01 39 (7)
6. Natalya Ivanova RUS 55.60 51 (5)
7. Tasha Danvers-Smith GBR 55.76 31 (8=)
8. Sandra Glover USA 55.82 52 (4)
Other GP leaders prior to WAF:
Markita James USA 31

High Jump (a)
1. Blanka Vlašic CRO 2.00 100 (1)
2. Antonietta Di Martino ITA 1.97 45 (9)
3. Anna Chicherova RUS 1.97 51 (6=)
4. Yelena Slesarenko RUS 1.94 83 (2)
5. Amy Acuff USA 1.94 46 (8)
6. Vita Palamar UKR 1.94 51 (6=)
7. Ruth Beitia ESP 1.94 66 (3=)
8. Emma Green SWE 1.85 39 (11)
Other GP leaders prior to WAF:
Kajsa Bergqvist SWE 66, Tia Hellebaut BEL 58, Yekaterina Savchenko RUS 41

Pole Vault (a)
1. Yelena Isinbayeva RUS 4.87 100 (1)
2. Monika Pyrek POL 4.82 78 (3)
3. Svetlana Feofanova RUS 4.82 81 (2)
4. Tatyana Polnova RUS 4.67 53 (6)
5. Yuliya Golubchikova RUS 4.60 69 (4)
6. Katerina Badurová CZE 4.60 66 (5)
7. Silke Spiegelburg GER 4.60 51 (7)
8. Vanessa Boslak FRA 4.60 23 (13)
Other GP leaders prior to WAF:
Jenn Stuczynski USA 35, Kym Howe AUS 33.5

Long Jump (a)
1. Tatyana Lebedeva RUS 6.78/0.6 36 (4=)
2. Grace Upshaw USA 6.64/0.5 35 (6)
3. Oksana Udmurtova RUS 6.52/0.9 31 (7)
4. Kumiko Ikeda JPN 6.48/-0.3 56 (1)
5. Keila Costa BRA 6.46/0.4 30 (8)
6. Bianca Kappler GER 6.42/-0.4 10 (19=)
7. Malgorzata Trybanska POL 6.36/-0.3 36 (4=)
8. Rose Richmond USA 6.32/0.1 40 (2=)
Other GP leaders prior to WAF:
Carolina Klüft SWE 40, Brianna Glenn USA 28

Triple Jump (b)
1. Yargelis Savigne CUB 14.78/0.4 42 (2=)
2. Hrisopiyí Devetzí GRE 14.75/0.4 -
3. Tatyana Lebedeva RUS 14.72/0.6 64 (1)
4. Yamilé Aldama SUD 14.41/0.3 28 (5)
5. Marija Sestak SLO 14.31/0.4 42 (2=)
6. Keila Costa BRA 14.13/0.5 26 (7)
7. Carlota Castrejana ESP 13.91/0.1 31 (4)
8. Dana Veldáková SVK 13.81/0.0 27 (6)
Other GP leaders prior to WAF:
Xie Limei CHN 18

Shot (b)
1. Nadezhda Ostapchuk BLR 20.45 16 (2)
2. Valerie Vili NZL 20.40 12 (5=)
3. Nadine Kleinert GER 19.36 14 (4)
4. Petra Lammert GER 19.12 8 (11=)
5. Cleopatra Borel-Brown TRI 18.66 15 (3)
6. Chiara Rosa ITA 17.82 -
7. Kristin Heaston USA 17.26 12 (5=)
Other GP leaders prior to WAF:
Li Ling CHN 18, Jill Camarena USA 12, Yumileidi Cumbá CUB, Lee Mi-young KOR 10

Discus (b)
1. Franka Dietzsch GER 62.58 22 (1=)
2. Vera Cechlová CZE 62.04 21 (3)
3. Nicoleta Grasu ROM 61.75 15 (7)
4. Becky Breisch USA 60.26 17 (4)
5. Beatrice Faumuina NZL 58.68 22 (1=)
6. Suzy Powell USA 57.85 16 (5=)
7. Anna Söderberg SWE 57.54 11 (9)
8. Elisângela Adriano BRA 54.10 -
Other GP leaders prior to WAF:
Dani Samuels AUS 16

Hammer (a)
1. Yipsi Moreno CUB 73.76 27 (5)
2. Ivana Brkljacic CRO 73.22 35 (3)
3. Clarissa Claretti ITA 70.34 8 (9=)
4. Kamila Skolimowska POL 70.20 39 (1)
5. Arasay Thondike CUB 69.51 8 (9=)
6. Kathrin Klaas GER 69.00 11 (8)
7. Ester Balassini ITA 63.90 18 (6)
Other GP leaders prior to WAF:
Tatyana Lysenko RUS 36, Betty Heidler GER 29, Yekaterina Khoroshikh RUS 17, Zhang Wenxiu CHN 8

Javelin (a)
1. Barbora Špotáková CZE 67.12 50 (1=)
2. Steffi Nerius GER 64.90 43 (3)
3. Christina Obergföll GER 62.47 50 (1=)
4. Barbara Madejczyk POL 60.03 21 (8)
5. Sonia Bisset CUB 59.23 32 (4)
6. Nikola Brejchová CZE 58.27 29 (5)
7. Mercedes Chilla ESP 58.25 25 (6)
8. Linda Stahl GER 55.62 -
Other GP leaders prior to WAF:
Kim Kreiner USA 24, Zahra Bani ITA 19

IAAF World Athletics Tour – Major Meetings 2007/2008

THE IAAF introduced a new concept with the World Athletics Tour in 2006. Under this brand there were 23 of these higher quality meetings in 2007 (24 in 2006 and 24 again in 2008). At least one meeting from each Continental area is included in the Tour. Tour points from these meetings and also from designated Continental Permit meetings determine qualification for the World Athletics Final. held in Stuttgart in 2006-08.

The World Athletics Tour meetings are designated: GL – Golden League, SGP – Super Grand Prix, GP – Grand Prix, EAP European Premium Meeting,. Also: ASI Grand Prix, EAA European Permit, NAC NACAC Area Premit Meeting.

2007 date		*Meeting*	*2008 date*	
2 Mar	GP	Telstra Melbourne Track Classic, AUS	21 Feb	GP
28 Apr	GP	Grand Prix, Dakar, SEN	17 May	GP
28 Apr		Conseil General, Fort-de-France, Martinique	3 May	NAC
1 May	NAC	Grand Prix de Guadeloupe, Baie Mahault	1 May	NAC
5 May	NAC	Jamaica International, Kingston, JAM	3 May	NAC
5 May	GP	Osaka, JPN	10 May	GP
11 May	SGP	Doha, QAT	9 May	SGP
12 May	NAC	Félix Sánchez Invitational, Santo Domingo DOM	10 May	NAC
19 May	EAP	Gran Premio Andalucia, Seville (2007), Jérez (2008), ESP	24 Jun	EAP
19 May	NAC	Ponce Grand Prix, PUR	17 May	NAC
19 May	NAC	Adidas Track Classic, Carson, USA	20 May	NAC
		Manaus, Brazil	22 May	NAC
20 May	GP	Grande Premio Brasil de Atletismo, Belém BRA	25 May	GP
26 May	GP	Thales FBK Games, Hengelo, NED	24 May	GP
29 May		Memorial Artur Takac, Beograd, SRB	29 May	EAA
1 Jun	EAA	Anhalt 2007/2008, Dessau, GER	30 May	EAA
2 Jun	EAA	Papaflessia, Kalamáta, GRE	4 Jun	EAA
2 Jun	GP	Reebok Grand Prix, New York, USA	31May	GP
3 Jun	EAA	Norwich Union Grand Prix, Glasgow, GBR	8 Jun	EAA
6 Jun		Askina 2008, Kassel, GER	6 Jun	EAA
8 Jun	EAP	Memorial Primo Nebiolo, Turin, ITA	6 Jun	EAP
8 Jun	EAP	Lille Métropole, Villeneuve d'Ascq, FRA	27 Jun	EAP
9 Jun	EAA	Venizelia, Haniá, GRE	7 Jun	EAA
9 Jun	NAC	Harry Jerome Track Classic, Burnaby, CAN	21 Jun	
9 Jun	EAA	Znamenskiy Memorial, Zhukovskiy, RUS	15 Jun	EAP
10 Jun	EAP	European Athletics Festival, Bydgoszcz, POL	1 Jul	EAP
10 Jun	GP	Prefontaine Classic, Eugene, Oregon, USA	8 Jun	GP
13 Jun	EAA	Riga Cup, LAT	11 Jun	EAA
13 Jun	EAP	Josef Odlozil Memorial, Prague, CZE	16 Jun	EAP
		Moscow Open, RUS	11 Jun	EAA
15 Jun	GL	Exxon Mobil Bislett Games, Oslo, NOR	6 Jun	GL
17 Jun	EAP	Janusz Kusocinski Memorial, Warsaw, POL	15 Jun	EAP
19 Jun	ASI	Asian Grand Prix, Bangkok, THA	23 Jun	ASI
		Asian Grand Prix, Korat THA	26 Jun	ASI
27 Jun	GP	Golden Spike, Ostrava, CZE	12 Jun	GP
27 Jun		Sollentuna GP, SWE	27 Jun	EAA
28 Jun	EAP	Luzern Spitzen Leichtathletik, SUI	16 Jul	EAP
28 Jun	EAA	Velenje, SLO	26 Jun	EAA
30 Jun	EAA	Cezmi Or Memorial, Istanbul, TUR	28 Jun	EAA
30 Jun	EAA	Cork City Sports, IRL	12 Jul	EAA
2 Jul	GP	Tsiklitiria, Athens, GRE	16 or 18 Jun	GP
4 Jul	GP	Grand Prix Zagreb, CRO	9 Sep	GP
4 Jul	EAA	Gran Premio Diputación de Salamanca, ESP	2 Jul	EAA
6 Jul	GL	Gaz de France Paris Saint-Denis, FRA	18 Jul	GL
8 Jul	EAA	Citta de Padova, ITA	31 Aug	EAA
10 Jul	SGP	Athletissima, Lausanne, SUI	2 Sep	SGP
13 Jul	GL	Golden Gala, Rome, ITA	11 Jul	GL
14 Jul		EWE Athletics, Cuxhaven, GER	12 Jul	EAA
15 Jul	GP	British Grand Prix, Sheffield (2007), Gateshead (2008), GBR	31 Aug	GP
18 Jul	EAP	Vardinoyiannia, Réthimno, GRE	14 Jul	EAP
21 Jul	GP	Atletismo Madrid 2012, ESP	5 Jul	GP
22 Jul	EAP	Tallinn, EST	3 Jun	EAP
25 Jul	EAA	Kaunas 2007/2008, LTU	8 Jun	EAA
–		Reunion Ciudad de Barcelona	19 Jul	EAA

28 Jul	SGP	Herculis Zepter, Monaco, MON	29 Jul	SGP
28 Jul	EAP	KBC Night of Athletics, Heusden-Zolder, BEL	20 Jul	EAP
28 Jul	EAP	Gobierno de Aragón, Zaragoza, ESP	31 May	EAA
30 Jul	EAP	Thessaloniki, GRE	9 Jul	EAP
3 Aug	SGP	Norwich Union London Grand Prix, (CP), GBR	25-26 Jul	SGP
7 Aug	SGP	DN Galan, Stockholm, SWE	22 Jul	SGP
–		Karelia Games, Lappeenranta, FIN	3 Aug	EAA
7 Sep	GL	Weltklasse, Zürich, SUI	29 Aug	GL
9 Sep	GP	Rieti, ITA	7 Sep	GP
11 Sep	EAP	Gugl Meeting, Linz, AUT	16 Jul	EAP
12 Sep	EAP	Palio Citta della Quercia, Rovereto, ITA	10 Sep	EAP
14 Sep	GL	Memorial Van Damme, Brussels, BEL	5 Sep	GL
16 Sep	GL	ISTAF, Berlin, GER	1 Jun	GL
18 Sep	EAA	Athletic Bridge, Dubnica nad Váhom, SVK	7 Sep	EAA
28 Sep	IAAF	Shanghai, CHN		

INDOORS

IAAF and EAAA – respective indoor permit meetings

2007 date	*Meeting*		*2008 date*	
7 Jan	EAA	Christmas Starts. Yekaterinburg, RUS	7 Jan	–
28 Jan	IAAF	Russian Winter, Moscow, RUS	27 Jan	IAAF
2 Feb	IAAF	Millrose, New York USA	1 Feb	IAAF
3 Feb	EAA	Gubernator Cup, Samara, RUS	2 Feb	EAA
3-4 Feb	EAA	Reva Hotels Cup, Tallinn, EST (combined events)	15-16 Feb	EAA
4 Feb	IAAF	Sparkassen Cup, GER	2 Feb	IAAF
4 Feb	IAAF	KBC Indoor, Gent, BEL	24 Feb	IAAF
6 Feb	EAA	Internationales, Düsseldorf, GER	8 Feb	EAA
7 Feb	EAA	Eduard Grigoryan Memorial, Moscow, RUS	16 Feb	EAA
10 Feb	EAA	Zepter Pole Vault Stars, Donestk, UKR	16 Feb	EAA
10 Feb	IAAF	Reunión Internacional Ciudad de Valencia, ESP	9 Feb	IAAF
11 Feb	IAAF	BW-Bank Meeting, Karlsuhe, GER	10 Feb	IAAF
14 Feb	IAAF	Athína 2008, Pireás, GRE	13 Feb	IAAF
14 Feb	EAA	Pedro's Cup, Bydgoszcz, POL	20 Feb	EAA
17 Feb	IAAF	Birmingham Indoor Grand Prix, GBR	16 Feb	IAAF
20 Feb	IAAF	GE Galan, Stockholm, SWE	21 Feb	IAAF

IAAF WORLD COMBINED EVENTS CHALLENGE 2007 & 2008

5/6 May	Multistra, Desenzano del Garda, ITA	10-11 May
26/27 May	Hypo-Mehrkampf Meeting, Götzis, AUT	31 May-1 Jun
2/3 Jun	Arles, FRA	7-8 Jun
16/17 Jun	Ruhrgas Mehrkampf Meeting, Ratingen, GER	21-22 Jun
22/23 Sep	Decastar Meeting, Talence, FRA	13-14 Sep

IAAF WORLD RACE WALKING CHALLENGE 2007 & 2008

10/11 Mar	Naucalpan (2007), Chihuahua (2008) MEX	8-9 Mar
24/25 Mar	Shenzhen (2007), Beijing (2008), CHN	18-19 Apr
14 Apr	Rio Maior, POR	5 Apr
1 May	Sesto San Giovanni, ITA	1 May
2 Jun	La Coruña, ESP	7 Jun
23 Jun	Krakow, POL	24 May
29 Sep	Race Walking Challenge Final. Saransk, RUS (2007)	20-21 Sep

AFRICA – CAA Grand Prix 2008 (with 2007 dates of these meeings first)

Nairobi KEN 12/12 May, Brazzaville CGO 20/20 May, Rabat MAR 17/14 Jun

2007: Réduit MRI 9 Apr, 31 Mar, Yaoundé CMR 14 Apr, Bamako MLI 20 Apr, Pretoria RSA 20 Apr, Abuja NGR 5 May, Khartoum SUD ? May, Alger ALG 21 Jun, Tunis TUN 30 Jun

Asian Grand Prix 2007

Also New Delhi IND 23 Jun, Pune IND 27 Jun

Other EAA Permit Meetings 2007

Lapinlahti 22 Jul, Banská Bystrica 16 Sep.

OCEANIA Permit Meeings 2008

Canberra AUS 27 Jan, Sydney AUS 16 Feb, Auckland NZL 19 Feb

SOUTH AMERICA Grand Prix Sudamericano 2008(with 2007 dates of these meeings first)

Uberlândia BRA 6/1 May, Rio de Janeiro BRA 13/18 May, Fortaleza BRA 16/21 May

2007: Rosario ARG 8 Mar, Mar del Plata ARG 10-11 Mar, Buenos Aires ARG 14-15 Mar, San Carlos URU 12 Apr, Asunción PAR 21 Apr, Valparaiso CHI 22 Apr, San Fernando CHI 25 Apr, Medellín COL 28 Apr, Santiago CHI 28 Apr, Caracas VEN 24-25 May, La Paz BOL 1 Jun, Cochabamba BOL 3 Jun, Bogotá COL 30 Jun

OLYMPICS 2008

THE FIRST OLYMPIC GAMES of the modern era were staged in Athens, Greece from the 6th to 15th April 1896. Those in Beijing 2008, the Games of the XXIX Olympiad, will be the 26th to be staged, including the intercalated Games of 1906.

Just 59 athletes from ten nations contested the athletics events in 1896. In 2000 there was a record participation for a summer Games, at all sports, with 10,651 competitors from 200 nations. 1995 competitors (1079 men and 916 women) from 196 nations contested the athletics events at the 2004 Games.

Olympic Games Records (after 2004)

Men		
100m	9.84	Donovan Bailey CAN 1996
200m	19.32	Michael Johnson USA 1996
400m	43.49	Michael Johnson USA 1996
800m	1:42.58	Vebjørn Rodal NOR 1996
1500m	3:32.07	Noah Ngeny KEN 2000
5000m	13:05.59	Saïd Aouita MAR 1984
10000m	27:05.10	Kenenisa Bekele ETH 2004
Mar	2:09:21	Carlos Lopes POR 1984
3000mSt	8:05.51	Julius Kariuki KEN 1988
110mh	12.91	Liu Xiang CHN 2004
400mh	46.78	Kevin Young USA 1992
HJ	2.39	Charles Austin USA 1996
PV	5.95	Tim Mack USA 2005
LJ	8.90A	Bob Beamon USA 1968
TJ	18.17w	Mike Conley USA 1992
	18.09	Kenny Harrison USA 1996
SP	22.47	Ulf Timmermann GDR 1988
DT	69.89	Virgilijus Alekna LTU 2004
HT	84.80	Sergey Litvinov URS 1988
JT	90.17	Jan Zelezny CZE 2000
old	94.58	Miklós Németh HUN 1976
Dec	8893	Román Sebrle CZE
4x100mR	37.40	USA 1992
4x400mR	2:55.74	USA 1992
20kmW	1:18:59	Robert Korzeniowski POL 2000
50kmW	3:38:29	Vyacheslav Ivanenko URS 1988
Women		
100m	10.62	Florence Griffith-Joyner USA 1988
	10.54w	Florence Griffith-Joyner USA 1988
200m	21.34	Florence Griffith-Joyner USA 1988
400m	48.25	Marie-José Pérec FRA 1996
800m	1:53.43	Nadezhda Olizarenko URS 1980
1500m	3:53.96	Paula Ivan ROM 1988
3000m	8:26.53	Tatyana Samolenko URS 1988
5000m	14:40.79	Gabriela Szabo ROM 2000
10000m	30:17.49	Derartu Tulu ETH 2000
Mar	2:23:14	Naoko Takahashi JPN 2000
100mh	12.37	Joanna Hayes USA 2004
400mh	52.82	Deon Hemmings JAM 1996
	52.82	Faní Halkiá GRE 2004
HJ	2.06	Yelena Slesarenko RUS
PV	4.91	Yelena Isinbayeva RUS
LJ	7.40	Jackie Joyner-Kersee USA 1988
TJ	15.33	Inessa Kravets UKR 1996
SP	22.41	Ilona Slupianek GDR 1980
DT	72.30	Martina Hellmann GDR 1988
HT	75.02	Olga Kuzenkova RUS 2004
JT	68.91	Trine Hattestad NOR 2000
old	74.68	Petra Felke GDR 1988
Hep	7291	Jackie Joyner-Kersee USA 1988
4x100mR	41.60	GDR 1980
4x400mR	3:15.17	USSR 1988
20kmW	1:29:05	Wang Liping CHN 2000

A at high altitude, Mexico City 2240m

Most gold medals - all events

Men

10 Raymond Ewry USA StHJ and StLJ 1900-04-06-08, StTJ 1900-04

9 Paavo Nurmi FIN 1500m 1924, 5000m 1924, 10000m 1920-28, 3000mSt 1924, CC 1920-24, CC team 1920-24

9 Carl Lewis USA 100m, 200m, LJ & 4x100mR 1984; 100m, LJ 1988; LJ, 4x100mR 1992; LJ 1996

5 Martin Sheridan USA DT 1904-06-08, SP 1906, DT Greek style 1908

5 Ville Ritola FIN 10000m, 3000mSt, CC team & 3000m team 1924, 5000m 1928

5 Michael Johnson USA 200m 1996, 400m 1996-2000, 4x400m 1992-2000

4 thirteen men

Women

4 Fanny Blankers-Koen NED 100m, 200m, 80mh & 4x100mR 1948

4 Betty Cuthbert AUS 100m, 200m, 4x100mR 1956, 400m 1964

4 Bärbel Eckert/Wöckel GDR 200m & 4x100mR 1976-80

4 Evelyn Ashford USA 100m 1984, 4x100mR 1984-88-92

Most medals - all events

G gold, S silver, B bronze

Men

12 Paavo Nurmi FIN 9G as above; 3S 5000m 1920-28, 3000mSt 1928

10 Raymond Ewry USA 10G as above

10 Carl Lewis USA 9G as above; 1S 200m 1988

9 Martin Sheridan USA 5G as above; 3S StHJ, StLJ & Stone 1906; 1B StLJ 1908

8 Ville Ritola FIN 5G as above; 3S 5000m & CC 1924, 10000m 1928

7 Eric Lemming SWE 4G JT 1906-08-12 freestyle 1908, 3B SP, Pen, Tug of War 1906

Women

8 Merlene Ottey JAM 3S 100m, 200m 1996; 4x100mR 2000; 5B 4x100mR 1980, 1996; 100m 1984, 200m 1984-92

7 Shirley Strickland/de la Hunty AUS 3G 80mh 1952-56, 4x100mR 1956; 1S 4x100mR 1948; 3B 100m 1948-52, 80mh 1948 (later evidence showed that she should also have been awarded the 1948 200m bronze)

7 Irena Kirszenstein/Szewinska POL 3G 200m 1968, 400m 1976, 4x100mR 1964; 2S 200m & LJ 1964, 2B 100m 1968, 200m 1972

Most gold medals at one Games: Men: 5 Paavo Nurmi FIN 1924; Women: 4 Fanny Blankers-Koen NED *as above*

Most medals at one Games: Men: 6 – 4 gold, 2 silver – Ville Ritola FIN 1924; Women: 5 – 3 gold, 2 bronze – Marion Jones 2000

Most Games contested: 6 Lia Manoliu ROM 1952-72 at women's discus, Tessa Sanderson GBR 1976-96 at women's javelin

Most finals or first eight at the same event: 5 Vladimir Golubnichiy URS 20kmW 1960-76: 1-3-1-2-7

Oldests – Men

Winner	42y 23d	Pat McDonald USA 56lb Wt 1920
Medallist	48y 115d	Tebbs Lloyd Johnson GBR 3rd 50kmW 1948
Competitor	52y 199d	Percy Wyer CAN Mar 1936

Oldests – Women

Winner	39y 315d	Ellina Zvereva BLR DT 2000
Medallist	40y 143d	Merlene Ottey JAM 4x100mR 2000
Competitor	48y 234d	Lourdes Klitzkie GUM 63rd Mar 1988

Youngests – Men

Winner	17y 263d	Bob Mathias USA Dec 1948
Medallist	17y 169d	Frank Castleman USA 2nd 200mh 1904
	17y 206d	Pál Simon HUN 3rd Medley relay 1908
		born 1891, but exact date unknown, 17-206 is oldest possible
Ind. medal	17y 263d	Bob Mathias as above

Youngests – Women

Winner	15y 123d	Barbara Pearl Jones USA 4x100mR 1952
Ind.winner	16y 123d	Ulrike Meyfarth FRG HJ 1972
Medallist	15y 123d	Barbara Pearl Jones as above
Ind. medal	16y 115d	Dorothy Odam GBR 2nd HJ 1936

y – years, d – days

Medal table of leading nations 1896-2004 including 1906 Games

	Men			*Women*			*Total*
Nation	**Gold**	**Silver**	**Bronze**	**Gold**	**Silver**	**Bronze**	**Medals**
USA	273	207	166	45	27	22	740
USSR/CIS	37	37	42	34	29	35	214
United Kingdom	44	63	43	8	20	17	195
Germany *	13	27	38	18	16	19	131
GDR	14	19	14	25	28	24	121
Finland	48	33	30	1	2	-	114
Sweden	19	25	41	2	-	4	91
Australia	6	11	13	12	10	13	65
France	8	20	19	6	1	5	59
Italy	15	8	21	3	7	3	57
Kenya	16	20	14	-	3	1	54
Canada	12	10	17	2	5	7	53
Poland	14	8	5	8	8	8	51
Hungary	7	14	16	3	1	2	43
Jamaica	4	12	7	3	9	8	43
Russia	2	4	7	10	13	6	42
Greece	4	7	14	3	6	1	35
Romania	-	1	1	10	13	9	34
Cuba	5	8	6	4	3	6	32
Ethiopia	10	3	8	4	2	4	31
Czechoslovakia	8	7	3	3	2	2	25
South Africa	5	6	6	1	4	1	23
Japan	5	5	6	1	2	1	20
New Zealand	7	1	7	1	-	2	18
Norway	5	2	7	1	2	1	18
Bulgaria	1	-	1	4	7	5	18
Morocco	5	3	5	1	1	1	16
Netherlands	-	-	5	6	2	1	14
Brazil	3	3	7	-	-	-	13
China	1	-	1	4	3	4	13
Belarus	-	2	2	3	1	4	12
Spain	2	4	4	-	-	1	11
Nigeria	-	2	3	1	2	3	11
Mexico	3	4	2	-	1	-	10
Belgium	2	6	2	-	-	-	10
Ukraine	1	1	3	1	1	3	10

In all 82 nations have won medals at track and field events

* Germany 1896-1952 and from 1992, Federal Republic of Germany 1956-88. Medals won by the combined German teams of 1956, 1960 and 1964 have been allocated to FRG or GDR according to the athlete's origin. Note that tug of war events, held from 1900 to 1920 have been excluded.

Olympic Games Athens 2004 – Medallists

100 Metres (+0.6)
1. Justin Gatlin USA 9.85
2. Francis Obikwelu POR 9.86
3. Maurice Greene USA 9.87

200 Metres (+1.2)
1. Shawn Crawford USA 19.79
2. Bernard Williams USA 20.01
3. Justin Gatlin USA 20.03

400 Metres
1. Jeremy Wariner USA 44.00
2. Otis Harris USA 44.16
3. Derrick Brew USA 44.42

800 Metres
1. Yuriy Borzakovskiy RUS 1:44.45
2. Mbulaeni Mulaudzi RSA 1:44.61
3. Wilson Kipketer DEN 1:44.65

1500 Metres
1. Hicham El Guerrouj MAR 3:34.18
2. Bernard Lagat KEN 3:34.30
3. Rui Silva POR 3:34.68

5000 Metres
1. Hicham El Guerrouj MAR 13:14.39
2. Kenenisa Bekele ETH 13:14.59
3. Eliud Kipchoge KEN 13:15.10

10,000 Metres
1. Kenenisa Bekele ETH 27:05.10*
2. Sileshi Sihine ETH 27:09.39
3. Zersenay Tadesse ERI 27:22.57

Marathon
1. Stefano Baldini ITA 2:10:55
2. Meb Keflezighi USA 2:11:29
3. Vanderlei de Lima BRA 2:12:11

3000 Metres Steeplechase
1. Ezekiel Kemboi KEN 8:05.81
2. Brimin Kipruto KEN-J 8:06.11
3. Paul K Koech KEN 8:06.64

110 Metres Hurdles (+0.3)
1. Liu Xiang CHN 12.91* WR
2. Terrence Trammell USA 13.18
3. Anier García CUB 13.20

400 Metres Hurdles
1. Félix Sánchez DOM 47.63
2. Danny McFarlane JAM 48.11
3. Naman Keïta FRA 48.26

High Jump
1. Stefan Holm SWE 2.36
2. Matt Hemingway USA 2.34
3. Jaroslav Bába CZE 2.34

Pole Vault
1. Tim Mack USA 5.95*
2. Toby Stevenson USA 5.90
3. Giuseppe Gibilisco ITA 5.85

Long Jump
1. Dwight Phillips USA 8.59/1.0
2, John Moffitt USA 8.47/0.9
3. Joan Lino Martínez ESP 8.32/1.3

Triple Jump
1. Christian Olsson SWE 17.79/1.4
2. Marian Oprea ROM 17.55/0.7
3. Danila Burkenya RUS 17.48/0.4

Shot
1. Yuriy Belonog UKR 21.16
2. Adam Nelson USA 21.16
3. Joachim Olsen DEN 21.07

Discus
1. Virgilijus Alekna LTU 69.89*
2. Zoltán Kövágó HUN 67.04
3. Aleksander Tammert EST 66.66

Hammer
1. Koji Murofushi JPN 82.91
2. Ivan Tikhon BLR 79.81
3. Esfref Apak TUR 79.51

Javelin
1. Andreas Thorkildsen NOR 86.50
2. Vadims Vasilevskis LAT 84.95
3. Sergey Makarov RUS 84.84

Decathlon
1. Román Sebrle CZE 8893*
2. Bryan Clay USA 8820
3. Dmitriy Karpov KAZ 8725

4 x 100 Metres Relay
1. GBR 38.07
2. USA 38.08
3. NGR 38.23

4 x 400 Metres Relay
1. USA 2:55.91
2. AUS 3:00.60
3. NGR 3:00.90

20 Kilometres Walk
1. Ivano Brugnetti ITA 1:19:40
2. Francisco Javier Fernández ESP 1:19:45
3. Nathan Deakes AUS 1:20:02

50 Kilometres Walk
1. Robert Korzeniowski POL 3:38:46
2. Denis Nizhegorodov RUS 3:42:50
3. Aleksey Voyevodin RUS 3:43:34

Women

100 Metres (-0.1)
1. Yuliya Nesterenko BLR 10.93
2. Lauryn Williams USA 10.96
3. Veronica Campbell JAM 10.97

200 Metres (+0.8)
1. Veronica Campbell JAM 22.05
2. Allyson Felix USA-J 22.18
3. Debbie Ferguson BAH 22.30

400 Metres
1. Tonique Williams-Darling BAH 49.41
2. Ana Guevara MEX 49.56
3. Natalya Antyukh RUS 49.89

800 Metres
1. Kelly Holmes GBR 1:56.38
2. Hasna Benhassi MAR 1:56.43
3. Jolanda Ceplak SLO 1:56.43

1500 Metres
1. Kelly Holmes GBR 3:57.90
2. Tatyana Tomashova RUS 3:58.12
3. Maria Cioncan ROM 3:58.39

5000 Metres
1. Meseret Defar ETH 14:45.65
2. Isabella Ochichi KEN 14:48.19
3. Tirunesh Dibaba ETH-J 14:51.83

10,000 Metres
1. Xing Huina CHN 30:24.36
2. Ejegayehu Dibaba ETH 30:24.98
3. Derartu Tulu ETH 30:26.42

Marathon
1. Mizuki Noguchi JPN 2:26:20
2. Catherine Ndereba KEN 2:26:32

3. Deena Kastor USA 2:27:20

100 Metres Hurdles (+1.5)

1. Joanna Hayes USA 12,37*
2. Olena Krasovska UKR 12.45
3. Melissa Morrison USA 12.56

400 Metres Hurdles

1. Faní Halkiá GRE 52.82*
2. Ionela Tîrlea-Manolache ROM 53.38
3. Tatyana Tereshchuk UKR 53.44

High Jump

1. Yelena Slesarenko RUS 2.06*
2. Hestrie Cloete RSA 2.02
3. Viktoriya Styopina UKR 2.02

Pole Vault

1. Yelena Isinbayeva RUS 4.91*
2. Svetlana Feofanova RUS 4.75
3. Anna Rogowska POL 4.70

Long Jump

1. Tatyana Lebedeva RUS 7.07/1.3
2. Irina Simagina RUS 7.05/0.8
3. Tatyana Kotova RUS 7.05/1.8

Triple Jump

1. Françoise Mbango CMR 15.30/0.6
2. Hrysopiyí Devetzí GRE 15.25/-0.1
3. Tatyana Lebedeva RUS 15.14/0.7

Shot

1. Yumeileidi Cumbá CUB 19.59
2. Nadine Kleinert GER 19.55
3. Svetlana Krivelyova RUS 19.49

Discus

1. Natalya Sadova RUS 67.02
2. Anastasia Kelesídou GRE 66.68
3. Irina Yatchenko BLR 66.17

Hammer

1. Olga Kuzenkova RUS 75.02*
2. Yipsi Moreno CUB 73.36
3. Yunaika Crawford CUB 73.16

Javelin

1. Osleidys Menéndez CUB 71.53*
2. Steffi Nerius GER 65.82
3. Mirela Manjani GRE 64.29

Heptathlon

1. Carolina Klüft SWE 6952
2. Austra Skujytė LTU 6435
3. Kelly Sotherton GBR 6424

4 x 100 Metres Relay

1. JAM 41.73
2. RUS 42.27
3. FRA 42.54

4 x 400 Metres Relay

1. USA 3:19.01
2. RUS 3:20.16
3. JAM 3:22.00

20 Kilometres Walk

1. Athanasia Tsoumeléka GRE 1:29:12
2. Olimpiada Ivanova RUS 1:29:16
3. Jane Saville AUS 1:29:25

* Olympic record

OLYMPIC QUALIFICATION STANDARDS & DATES 2008

Dates are given in final columns for days in August for each round (Q - qualifying)

Event	Men A	Men B	Women A	Women B	Men's Comp	Women's Comp
100m	10.21	10.28	11.32	11.42	h/q 15, s/F 16	h/q 16, s/F 17
200m	20.59	20.75	23.00	23.20	h/q 18, S 19, F 20	h/q 19, s 20, F 21
400m	45.55	45.95	51.55	52.35	h 18, s 19, F 21	h 16, s 17, F 19
800m	1:46.00	1:47.00	2:00.00	2:01.30	h 20, s21, F 23	h 15, s 16, F 18
1500m	3:36.60	3:39.00	4:07.00	4:08.00	h 15, s 17, F 19	h 19, s 21, F 23
5000m	13:21.50	13:28.00	15:09.00	15:24.00	h 20, F 23	h 19, F 22
10,000m	27:50.00	28:10.00	31:45.00	32:20.00	17	15
Marathon	2:15:00	2:18:00	2:37:00	2:42.00	24	17
3000m S/C	8:24.60	8:32.00	9:46.00	9:55.00	h 16, F 18	h 15, F 17
110/100mH	13.55	13.72	12.96	13.11	h 18,q 19, s 20, F 21	h 17, s 18, F 19
400mH	49.20	49.50	55.60	56.50	h 15, s 16, F 18	h 17, s 18, F 20
HJ	2.30	2.27	1.95	1.91	Q 17, F 19	Q 21, F 23
PV	5.70	5.55	4.45	4.30	Q 20, F 22	Q 16, F 18
LJ	8.20	8.05	6.72	6.60	Q 16, F 18	Q19, F 22
TJ	17.10	16.80	14.20	14.00	Q18, F 21	Q 15, F 17
SP	20.30	19.80	18.35	17.20	Q & F 15	Q & F 16
DT	64.50	62.50	61.00	59.00	Q 16m F 19	Q 15, F 18
HT	78.50	74.00	69.50	67.00	Q 15, F 17	Q 18, F 20
JT	81.80	77.80	60.50	56.00	Q 21, F 23	Q 19, F 21
Dec/Hep	8000	7700	6000	5800	21/22	15/16
20kmW	1:23:00	1:24:30	1:33:30	1:38:00	16	21
50kmW	4:00:00	4:07:00			22	
4x100mR					h 21, F 22	h 21, F 22
4x400mR					h 22, F 23	h 22, F 23

Relays: There will be a maximum of 16 qualified teams in each event, based on the aggregate of the two fastest times achieved by national teams at IAAF recognised international events from 1 Jan 2007 to 16 July 2008.

The first 20 runners in the men's and women's marathons in the 2007 World Championships in Osaka will be considered as having met 'A' qualification standard.

A country may enter a maximum of 3 qualified athletes in each individual event if all entered athletes meet the A qualification standard, or 1 athlete per event if they have met the B standard only. Countries without any qualified athletes may enter their best male athlete and their best female athlete for one event each, with the exception of the combined events, 10,000m and steeplechase. Athletes must reach cont. page 118

WORLD LISTS 1957 & 1958

! = world record

TOP LISTS 1957

100 YARDS

9.3!	David Sime USA	1	Raleigh	18 May
9.3!	Bobby Morrow USA	1	Austin	14 Jun
9.3!	Ira Murchison USA	2	Austin	14 Jun
9.4	Ollan Cassell USA	1	Clarksville	11 May
9.4	Hayes Jones USA	1	Charleston	24 May
9.4	Willie White USA	1	Modesto	25 May
9.4	Paul Williams USA	1	Sheppard AFB	13 Jun
9.3w	three men			

10th best 9.5, 57 to 9.6

100 METRES

10.2	Leamon King USA	1	Oslo	16 Jul
10.2	Manfred Germar FRG	1	Köln	31 Jul
10.2	José T da Conçeicão BRA	1	São Paulo	24 Nov
10.3	nine men, 100th best 10.6			

200 METRES (* 220y less 0.1 sec.)

20.8	Manfred Germar GER	1	Hannover	15 Sep
20.9*	Bobby Morrow USA	1	Austin	15 Jun
21.0	five men			

Half turn

20.4	Manfred Germar GER	1	Köln	31 Jul
20.6	Ed Collymore USA	2	Köln	31 Jul
20.9	Leonid Bartenyev URS	1	Kiev	23 Jun

10th best inc. half turn 21.0, 100th 21.5

220 YARDS (Straight Track)

20.4	Michael Agostini TRI	1	Fresno	25 Apr
20.4	David Sime USA	1	Raleigh	18 May
20.6	Ray Norton USA	1	San Jose	4 May
20.6A	Ken Christensen USA	1	Salt Lake City	4 May
20.6	Bobby Morrow USA	1	Compton	31 May
	20.0w	1	Abilene	23 Mar
20.1w	Bill Woodhouse USA	2	Abilene	23 Mar

400 METRES (* 440y less 0.3 sec.)

46.0+	Thomas Courtney USA	1	Oslo	16 Jul
46.2*	Mike Larrabee USA	1	Port Elizabeth	30 Mar
46.3	Charles Jenkins USA	1	Borås	5 Aug
46.4*	Bob McMurray USA	1	San Diego	8 Jun
46.5	four men; 10th best 46.7, 100th 47.9			

800 METRES (* 880y less 0.7 sec.)

1:45.8	Thomas Courtney USA	1	Oslo	9 Aug
1:46.0	Roger Moens BEL	1	Oslo	31 Jul
1:46.5*	Don Bowden USA	1	Austin	15 Jun
1:46.6	Derek Johnson GBR	2	Oslo	9 Aug
1:46.9	Arnie Sowell USA	1	Bordeaux	29 Jun
1:47.1*	Ron Delany IRL	2	Austin	15 Jun

10th best 1:47.5, 100th 1:50.8

1000 METRES

2:19.3	Thomas Courtney USA	1	Göteborg	4 Jul
2:19.4	Stefan Lewandowski POL	1	Feuerbach	16 Jul
2:19.6	Stanislav Jungwirth TCH	1	Bratislava	1 Sep

1500 METRES

3:38.1!	Stanislav Jungwirth TCH	1	Stará Boleslav	12 Jul
3:40.2!	Olavi Salsola FIN	1	Turku	11 Jul
3:40.2!	Olavi Salonen FIN	2	Turku	11 Jul
3:40.3	Olavi Vuorisalo FIN	3	Turku	11 Jul
3:40.8	Dan Waern SWE	4	Turku	11 Jul
3:41.1	Jonas Pipyne URS	1	Moskva	4 Aug

10th best 3:42.0, 100th 3:50.6

1 MILE

3:57.2!	Derek Ibbotson GBR	1	London (WC)	19 Jul
3:58.5	Dan Waern SWE	1	Malmö	4 Sep
3:58.7	Don Bowden USA	1	Stockton	1 Jun
3:58.8	Ron Delany IRL	2	London (WC)	19 Jul
3:58.9	Mervyn Lincoln AUS	1	Melbourne	23 Mar
3:58.9	Roger Moens BEL	2	Malmö	4 Sep

10th best 4:00.2, 100th 4:11.4

3000 METRES

7:58.2	Zdzislaw Krzyszkowiak POL	1	Warszawa	9 Jun
7:59.0	Kazimierz Zimny POL	2	Warszawa	9 Jun
7:59.6	István Rozsavölgyi HUN	1	Budapest	27 Oct

10th best 8:07.6, 50th 8:16.6

5000 METRES

13:35.0!	Vladimir Kuts URS	1	Roma	13 Oct
13:51.8	Miklós Szabó HUN	1	Moskva	4 Aug
13:52.0	Friedrich Janke GDR	2	Moskva	4 Aug
13:54.2	Allan Lawrence AUS	3	Moskva	4 Aug
13:54.4	Pyotr Bolotnikov URS	4	Moskva	4 Aug
13:55.8	Zdzislaw Krzyszkowiak POL	1	Köln	31 Jul

10th best 13:58.6, 100th 14:25.6

3 Miles

13:20.8	Derek Ibbotson GBR	1	London (WC)	13 Jul
13:25.9	Albert Thomas AUS	1	Melbourne	8 Dec
13:27,2	Murray Halberg NZL	1	Auckland	28 Dec

10,000 METRES

29:06.4	George Knight GBR	1	Warszawa	7 Sep
29:09.8	Pyotr Bolotnikov URS	1	Moskva	29 Aug
29:10.0	Vladimir Kuts URS	2	Moskva	29 Aug
29:16.4	Allan Lawrence AUS	2	Moskva	30 Jul
29:19.4	Nikolay Pudov URS	3	Moskva	29 Aug
29:19.6	Yuriy Zakharov URS	4	Moskva	29 Aug

10th best 29:24.8, 100th 30:53.4

6 Miles

28:10.4	Allan Lawrence AUS	1	Auckland	21 Dec

MARATHON

2:19:50	Sergey Popov URS	1	Moskva	1 Sep
2:20:05	John J Kelley USA	1	Boston	20 Apr
2:21:24	Franjo Mihalic YUG	1	Moskva	4 Aug
2:21:39	Ivan Filin URS	2	Moskva	1 Sep
2:21:40	Kurao Hiroshima JPN	1	Fukuoka	1 Dec
2:22:00	Albert Ivanov URS	3	Moskva	1 Sep

10th best 2:22:34, 100th c. 2:35:30

3000m STEEPLECHASE

8:40.4	Semyon Rzhishchin URS	1	Moskva	31 Aug
8:44.4	Ernst Larsen NOR	1	Oslo	16 Jul
8:45.8	Ludvik Vesely TCH	2	Oslo	16 Jul
8:45.8	Gyula Varga HUN	1	Budapest	13 Oct
8:47.8	Bohumir Zhanal TCH	1	Brno	13 Oct
8:48.0	Sergey Ponomaryev URS	1	Gorkiy	24 Jul

10th best 8:49.0, 100th 9:13.4

110m HURDLES (y = 120y h)

13.4y!	Milton Campbell USA	1	Compton	31 May
13.4y!	Elias Gilbert USA	2	Compton	31 May
13.5y	Lee Calhoun USA	3	Compton	31 May
13.6	Willie Stevens USA	1	Gävle	26 Jul
13.7	Martin Lauer FRG	2	Köln	31 Jul
13.7y	Hayes Jones USA	1	Dayton	21 Jun
13.7yw	Charles Pratt USA	1	Fort Hood	15 Jun

10th best 14.0, 100th 14.6

200m HURDLES (* 220y less 0.1 sec.)

22.7*!	Elias Gilbert USA	1	San Diego	8 Jun
22.8*	Lee Calhoun USA	2	San Diego	8 Jun
22.9+	Martin Lauer FRG 1/2 t	1	Köln	2 Oct
23.0A*	Gerhardus Potgieter RSA	1	Nylstroom	2 Mar

220y HURDLES (Straight Track)

22.2!	Ancel Robinson USA	1	Austin	15 Jun
22.5	Rod Perry USA	1s1	Austin	14 Jun
22.5	Elias Gilbert USA	2	Austin	15 Jun

400m HURDLES (* 440y less 0.3 sec.)

50.2+	Josh Culbreath USA	1	Oslo	9 Aug
50.4*	Gerhardus Potgieter RSA	1	Queenstown	20 Apr
50.5	Aubrey Lewis USA	1	Köln	31 Jul
50.6*	Glenn Davis USA	1	Dayton	21 Jun
51.1	Igor Ilin URS	1	Moskva	14 Jul
51.1	Tom Farrell GBR	1	London (WC)	23 Aug

10th best 51.6, 100th 53.7

HIGH JUMP

2.16!x	Yuriy Styepanov URS	1	Leningrad	13 Jul
2.15x	Vladimir Sitkin URS	1	Odessa	29 Sep
2.14x	Igor Kashkarov RUS	1	Moskva	8 Aug
2.115	Floyd Smith USA	1	Chicago	23 Jun
2.105	Donald Stewart USA	1	Austin	11 May
2.095	Charles Dumas USA	1	Compton	31 May
2.09	Charles Porter AUS	1	Brisbane	9 Feb

x made with built-up shoe, which was banned in 1958
10th best 2.06, 100th 1.98

POLE VAULT

4.82	Robert Gutowski USA	1	Austin	15 Jun
4.72i	Robert Richards USA	1=	New York	9 Feb
	4.64	1	El Monte	26 Jul
4.64	Don Bragg USA	1	Villanova	25 May
4.63	Ronald Morris USA	1	Palo Alto	13 Apr
4.59	Joe Rose USA	1	Tempe	12 Apr
4.57	Jim Brewer USA	1	Phoenix	17 May

10th best 4.50, 100th 4.20

LONG JUMP

8.10	Gregory Bell USA	1	Austin	14 Jun
7.80	Henryk Grabowski POL	1	Chorzów	5 Oct
7.78	Ernest Shelby USA	1	Compton	31 May
7.77	Igor Ter-Ovanesyan URS	1	Kiev	23 Aug
7.76	Carroll Hamilton USA	1	Madison	20 Apr
7.74	Jorma Valkama FIN	1	Vaasa	6 Sep

10th best 7.68, 100th 7.33

TRIPLE JUMP

16.29	Oleg Ryakhovskiy URS	1	Moskva	2 Sep
16.04	Konstantin Tsigankov URS	1	Moskva	6 Jul
16.00	Vitold Kreer URS	1	Kharkov	17 Sep
16.00	Dmitriy Yefremov URS	1	Odessa	3 Oct
15.98	Leonid Shcherbakov URS	2	Moskva	2 Sep
15.95	Arsentiy Tyerkel URS	1	Moskva	2 Jun
15.95	Vilhjálmur Einarsson ISL	1	Athína	6 Oct

10th best 15.90, 100th 14.95

SHOT

18.94	William Nieder USA	1	Lawrence	20 Apr
18.55	Parry O'Brien USA	1	Bucuresti	15 Sep
18.30	Dave Owen USA	1	Austin	15 Jun
18.05	Jirí Skobla TCH	1	Athína	14 Aug
17.97i	Ken Bantum USA	2	New York	16 Feb
17.89	Don Vick USA	1	Los Angeles	14 Jun
17.62	Dave Davis USA	2	Los Angeles	14 Jun

10th best 17.41, 100th 15.95

DISCUS

58.28	Jack Ellis USA	1	New Britain	24 Aug
56.80	Rink Babka USA	1	Aalborg	11 Aug
56.49	Al Oerter USA	1	Austin	15 Jun
55.85	Parry O'Brien USA	1	Vancouver	4 May
55.05	József Szécsényi HUN	1	Praha	13 Sep
55.01	Otto Grigalka URS	1	London (WC)	24 Aug

10th best 54.60, 100th 49.64

HAMMER

66.70	Mikhail Krivonosov URS	1	Athína	29 Jun
65.91	Harold Connolly USA	1	Dayton	21 Jun
64.93	Albert Hall USA	1	New York	8 Jun
64.73	Zvonko Bezjak YUG	1	Zagreb	11 Jun
64.56	Michael Ellis GBR	1	Hannover	15 Sep
64.36	Fyodor Tkachev URS	1	Uzhgorod	7 Apr

10th best 63.25, 100th 56.14

JAVELIN

84.00	Egil Danielsen NOR	1	Hamar	6 Oct
83.73	Vladimir Kuznyetsov URS	1	Genoa	19 Oct
83.37	Jan Kopyto POL	1	Warszawa	13 Oct
83.34	Viktor Tsibulenko URS	1	Kiev	16 Sep
82.98	Janusz Sidlo POL	1	Warszawa	9 Jun
81.47	Franklin Held USA	1	Modesto	25 May

10th best 78.94, 100th 69.36

DECATHLON (1952 tables)

7379	Vasiliy Kuznetsov URS	1	Moskva	1 Sep
	(7269 on current tables)			
7294	Yuriy Kutyenko URS	1	Moskva	3 Aug
7193	Walter Meier GDR	2	Moskva	3 Aug
7164	Charles Pratt USA	1	Kingsburg	29 Jun
7151	Walter Tschudi SUI	1	Bruxelles	28 Jul
6981	David Edstrom (USA)	2	Kingsburg	29 Jun

10th best 6735, 50th 5925

20 KILOMETRES WALK

1:27:28.6	Leonid Spirin URS	1	Moskva	7 Jul
1:28:38.4	Valentin Guk URS	1	Kiev	13 Apr
1:29:08.0	Anatoliy Vedyakov URS	1	Leningrad	21 May
1:29:28.6	Mikhail Lavrov RUS	1	Kursk	29 Jun
1:29:38.0	Antanas Mikenas URS	2	Moskva	7 Jul
1:30:22.0	Grigoriy Panichkin URS	3	Moskva	7 Jul

50 KILOMETRES WALK

4:10:08.2	Sergey Lobastov URS	1	Podebrady	6 Oct
4:12:18.2	Ladislav Moc TCH	2	Podebrady	6 Oct
4:14:33.2	Mikhail Lavrov URS	1	Moskva	2 Sep
4:15:13.8	Josef Dolezal TCH	4	Podebrady	6 Oct
4:17:58.8t	Milan Skront CZE	1	Opava	15 Sep
4:19:05.0	Anatoliy Vedyakov URS	3	Moskva	2 Sep

4x100m: 39.9y! Texas Univ. USA 1 Lawrence 20 Apr
39.9y! Abilene Christian Coll USA 1 Fresno 11 May

4x400m: 3:07.3 FR Germany 1 Hannover 15 Sep
3:08.0 GBR 2 Hannover 15 Sep

WOMEN

100 YARDS

10.5	Marlene Mathews AUS	1	Sydney	12 Jan
	10.1w	1	Sydney	2 Feb
10.6	Betty Cuthbert AUS	1	Sydney	7 Dec
	10.4w	2	Sydney	2 Feb
10.5w	Erica Willis AUS	3	Sydney	2 Feb

100 METRES

11.5	Vyera Krepkina URS	1	Moskva	29 Aug
11.6	Nina Dyekonskaya URS	1	Moskva	25 May
11.6	Tamara Buyanova URS	1	Moskva	27 Jun
11.6	Galina Popova URS	1	Moskva	27 Jun
11.6	Maria Itkina URS	1	Moskva	6 Jul
11.6	Hannie Bloemhof NED	1	Bucuresti	14 Sep
	11.5w	1	Den Haag	11 Aug
11.5w	Wendy Hayes AUS	1	Melbourne	9 Mar

10th best 11.7, 50th 12.0

200 METRES (* 220y less 0.1 sec.)

23.8*	Betty Cuthbert AUS	1	Sydney	9 Feb
23.8*	Marlene Mathews AUS	1	Sydney	14 Dec
23.8	Maria Itkina URS	1	Minsk	- Jul
23.9	Gisela Köhler GDR	1	Moskva	3 Aug
24.0*	Nancy Boyle AUS	2	Melbourne	14 Feb
24.0	Haether Young GBR	1	Warszawa	9 Jun
24.0	Albina Kobranova URS	1	London (WC)	24 Aug
24.0	Claud. Masdammer GUY	1	Georgetown	1 Sep
23,6w	Hannie Bloemhof NED	1	Den Haag	11 Aug
23.8w	Ria van Kuik NED	2	Den Haag	11 Aug

10th best 24.1, 50th 24.8

400 METRES

53.6!	Maria Itkina URS	1	Moskva	6 Jul
54.4	Albina Khomutova URS	1	Moskva	1 Aug
54.7	Ursula Donath GDR	2	Moskva	1 Aug
54.9	Poplina Lazareva	1	Moskva	14 Jul
55.3	Yekaterina Parlyuk URS	1	Moskva	29 Aug
55.3	Tatyana Avramova URS	1	Bucuresti	14 Sep

10th best 55.6, 50th 57.4

800 METRES

2:05.6	Yeliz. Yermolayeva URS	1	Moskva	2 Sep
2:05.8	Nina Otkalenko URS	1	Leningrad	15 Jul
2:06.8	Diane Leather GBR	1	London (WC)	23 Aug
2:07.6	Ursula Donath GDR	1	Leipzig	17 Jun

2:07.6	Dzidra Levitska URS	3	Moskva	2 Sep
2:07.9	Florica Otel ROM	1	Aue	30 Jun

10th best 2:08.7, 50th 2:13.2

1500 METRES

4:29.7+	Diane Leather GBR	1	London (WC)	19 Jul
4:32.2+	Maureen Smith GBR	2	London (WC)	19 Jul

1 MILE

4:50.6	Diane Leather GBR	1	London (WC)	19 Jul
4:51.6	Maureen Smith GBR	2	London (WC)	19 Jul

80 METRES HURDLES

10.8	Nelli Yeliseyeva URS	1	Moskva	1 Aug
10.8	Gisela Köhler GDR	2	Moskva	1 Aug
10.8	Galina Bystrova URS	1	Moskva	17 Aug
10.9	Erika Fisch FRG	1	Hamburg	20 Jul
10.9	Edeltraud Eiberle FRG	1P	Oberhausen	28 Jul
10.9	Kreszentia Kopp FRG	1	Schwandorf	4 Aug
10.9	Mariya Golubnichaya URS	1	Moskva	15 Aug
10.8w	Wendy Hayes AUS	1	Melbourne	14 Feb

10th best 11.0, 50th 11.4

HIGH JUMP

1.77!x	Cheng Feng-jung CHN	1	Bejing	17 Nov
1.76!	Iolanda Balas ROM	1	Bucuresti	13 Oct
1.75	Taisia Chenchik URS	1	Bucuresti	17 Sep
1.70	Mariya Pisaryeva URS	1	Kharkov	15 Sep
1.70	Lyudmila Mochilina URS	1	Kharkov	17 Sep
1.68	Mary Donaghy NZL	1	Dunedin	2 Mar

10th best 1.67, 50th 1.60

x made with built-up shoe, which was banned in 1958

LONG JUMP

6.28	Nina Kazmina URS	1	Moskva	17 Aug
6.27	Elzbieta Krzesinska POL	1	Chorzów	6 Oct
6.23	Beverley Weigel NZL	1	Auckland	9 Feb
6.17	Galina Bystrova URS	1	Odessa	16 Oct
6.15	Annel. Seonbuchner FRG	1	Lindau	8 Sep
6.11	Vilve Maremäe URS	1	Leningrad	11 Jul

10th best 6.03, 50th 5.83

SHOT

16.50	Tamara Tyshkevich URS	1	Kharkov	7 Sep
16.29	Valerie Sloper NZL	1	Christchurch	7 Dec
16.26	Galina Zybina URS	1	Moskva	3 Aug
16.17	Zinaida Doynikova URS	1	Moskva	8 Aug
16.13	Mariya Kuznetsova URS	1	Bel. Tserkev	8 Aug
15.89	Tamara Press URS	4	Moskva	29 Aug

10th best 15.01, 50th 13.67

DISCUS

55.19	Nina Ponomaryeva URS	1	Moskva	20 Jul
53.16	Tamara Press URS	1	Moskva	8 Aug
52.57	Stepanka Mertová TCH	1	Brno	13 Oct
52.04	Irina Beglyakova URS	2	Moskva	3 Aug
51.51	Anton. Zolotukhina URS	1	Odessa	14 Oct
51.30	Doris Müller FRG	1	Oldenburg	7 Sep

10th best 50.59, 50th 45.93

JAVELIN

54.81	Galina Zybina URS	1	Moskva	30 Aug
53.80	Dana Zátopková TCH	1	Praha	19 Oct
53.77	Almut Brömmel FRG	1	Kiel	15 Sep
53.36	Inese Jaunzeme URS	1	Riga	30 Jun
53.28	Urszula Figwer POL	1	Kraków	30 Jun
52.69	Eleonora Bogun URS	1	Stalinabad	27 Oct

10th best 50.88, 50th 46.15

PENTATHLON (1954 tables)

4846!	Galina Bystrova URS	1	Odessa	16 Oct
4527	Lidiya Shmakova URS	2	Gorkiy	24 Jul
4517	Aleksandra Chudina URS	2	Moskva	2 Sep
4508	Edeltraud Eiberle FRG	1	Oberhausen	28 Jul
4445	Sofia Burdelenko URS	1	Kharkov	30 Jun
4441	Vilve Maremäe URS	1	Leningrad	15 Jul

4x100m: 45.6	USSR	1	London (WC)	23 Aug
45.9	Great Britain	2	London (WC)	23 Aug

TOP LISTS 1958

100 YARDS

9.3!	Ray Norton USA	1	San Jose	12 Apr
9.4	Eugene White USA	1	Tallahassee	29 Mar
9.4	John Moon USA	1	Montgomery	19 Apr
9.4	David Sime USA	1	Durham	29 Apr
9.4	Dee Givens USA	1	Stillwater	3 May
9.4	Ira Murchison USA	1	Kalamazoo	10 May
9.4	Hayes Jones USA	1	Normal	24 May
9.4	Bobby Morrow USA	1	Modesto	31 May
9.4	Keith Gardner JAM	1	Cardiff	19 Jul

9.3w four men. 10th best 9.5, 88 to 9.6

100 METRES

10.2	Heinz Futterer FRG	1s	Hannover	20 Jul
10.2	Armin Hary FRG	2s	Hannover	20 Jul
10.2	Manfred Germar FRG	1	Hannover	20 Jul
10.2	Ira Murchison USA	1	Moskva	27 Jul
10.2	Ed Collymore USA	2	Moskva	27 Jul
10.2	Michael Agostini TRI	1	Köln	29 Aug

10th best 10.3, 100th 10.5

200 METRES (* 220y less 0.1 sec.)

20.6*	Ed Collymore USA	1	Berkeley	14 Junl
20.6	Manfred Germar GER	1	Wuppertal	1 Oct
20.7*	Orlando Hazley USA	1	Stillwater	8 May
20.7*	Les Carney USA	1	Berkeley	13 Jun

20.8 Four men. 10th best 21.0, 100th 21.5

Half turn

20.6	Michael Agostini TRI	1	Köln	29 Aug

220 YARDS (Straight Track)

20.3	Ed Collymore USA	1	Compton	6 Jun
20.4	Ira Murchison USA	1	Kalamazoo	10 May
20.4	Keith Gardner JAM	1	Columbia	17 May
20.4	Dee Givens USA	2	Columbia	17 May
20.0w	Bill Woodhouse USA	1	Abilene	19 Apr
20.0w	Ira Davis USA	1	West Chester	9 May
20.0w	Ray Norton USA	1	Sanger	7 Jun

400 METRES (* 440y less 0.3 sec.)

45.4*!	Glenn Davis USA	1	Berkeley	14 Jun
45.5*	Eddie Southern USA	1	Bakersfield	21 Jun
45.8*	Charles Jenkins USA	2	Bakersfield	21 Jun
46.0	Malcolm Spence RSA	1	Hagfors	18 Aug
46.1*	George Kerr JAM	2	Lafayette	24 May

46.3 Five men; 10th best 46.3, 100th 47.6

800 METRES (* 880y less 0.7 sec.)

1:46.6*	Herb Elliott AUS	1	London (WC)	4 Aug
1:46.7	Zbigniew Makomaski POL	1	Warszawa	2 Aug
1:46.8	Thomas Courtney USA	2	Warszawa	2 Aug
1:46.8	Paul Schmidt FRG	1	Bremen	26 Aug
1:46.9	Tadeusz Kazmierski POL	3	Warszawa	2 Aug
1:47.0	Herbert Missalla FRG	2	Bremen	26 Aug
1:47.0	Brian Hewson GBR	1	Colombes	13 Sep
1:47.0	Mike Rawson GBR	2	Colombes	13 Sep

10th best 1:47.6, 100th 1:50.5

1000 METRES

2:18.1!	Dan Waern SWE	1	Turku	19 Sep
2:18.8	Zbigniew Orywal POL	2	Turku	19 Sep
2:19.2	Brian Hewson GBR	1	London (WC)	30 Aug

1500 METRES

3:36.0!	Herb Elliott AUS	1	Göteborg	28 Aug
3:38.8	Murray Halberg NZL	2	Oslo	5 Sep
3:39.0	Stanislav Jungwirth TCH	2	Göteborg	28 Aug
3:39.8	Arne Hamarsland NOR	3	Oslo	5 Sepl
3:40.0	István Rozsavölgyi HUN	4	Göteborg	28 Aug
3:40.8	Olavi Vuorisalo FIN	1	Stockholm	22 Aug

10th best 3:41.1, 100th 3:49.4

1 MILE

3:54.5!	Herb Elliott AUS	1	Dublin	6 Aug
3:55.9	Mervyn Lincoln AUS	2	Dublin	6 Aug

3:57.5 Ron Delany IRL 3 Dublin 6 Aug
3:57.5 Murray Halberg NZL 4 Dublin 6 Aug
5:58.6 Albert Thomas AUS 5 Dublin 6 Aug
3:58.9 Brian Hewson GBR 2 London (WC) 3 Sep
10th best 4:00.5, 100th 4:10.6

3000 METRES

7:58.0 Jerzy Chromik POL 1 Warszawa 15 Jun
7:59.0 Siegfried Herrmann GDR2 Warszawa 15 Jun
8:00.7 Zdzislaw Krzyszkowiak POL 3 Warszawa 9 Jun

2 MILES

8:32.0! Albert Thomas AUS 1 Dublin 7 Aug
8:33.0 Murray Halberg NZL 1 London (WC) 3 Sep
8:33.4 Jerzy Chromik POL 2 London (WC) 3 Sep

5000 METRES

13:51.6 Gordon Pirie GBR 1 Göteborg 28 Aug
13:52.2 Kazimierz Zimny POL 1 Warszawa 1 Aug
13:52.2 Miroslav Jurek CZE 2 Göteborg 28 Aug
13:53.2 Zdzislaw Krzyszkowiak POL 1 Erfurt 25 Sep
13:53.8 Peter Clark GBR 1 Colombes 13 Sep
13:54.6 Marian Jochman POL 2 Warszawa 1 Aug
10th best 13:59.4, 100th 14:24.6

3 Miles

13:10.8! Albert Thomas AUS 1 Dublin 9 Jul
13:15.0 Murray Halberg NZL 1 Cardiff 22 Jul
13:22.4 Stanley Eldon GBR 1 London (WC) 12 Jul

10,000 METRES

28:56.0 Zdzislaw Krzyszkowiak POL 1 Stockholm19 Aug
28:58.6 Yevgeniy Zhukov RUS 2 Stockholm 19 Aug
29:02.2 Nikolay Pudov URS 3 Stockholm 19 Aug
29:02.8 Stanley Eldon GBR 4 Stockholm 19 Aug
29:03.2 Stanislav Ozog POL 5 Stockholm 19 Aug
29:03.8 John Merriman GBR 6 Stockholm 19 Aug
10th best 29:06.4, 100th 30:35.4

MARATHON

2:15:17! Sergey Popov URS 1 Stockholm 24 Aug
2:19:56 Li Tun-Yung CHN 1 Tsinan 21 Dec
2:20:07 Nikolay Rumyantsev RUS 1 Tbilisi 2 Nov
2:20:51 Ivan Filin URS 2 Stockholm 24 Aug
2:21:01 John J Kelley USA 1 Yonkers 18 May
2:21:15 Fred Norris GBR 3 Stockholm 24 Aug
10th best 2:21:51

3000m STEEPLECHASE

8:32.0! Jerzy Chromik POL 1 Warszawa 2 Aug
8:33.6 Zdzislaw Krzyszkowiak POL 2 Warszawa 2 Aug
8:35.6 Semyon Rzhishchin URS 1 Tallinn 21 Jul
8:37.4 Hans Huneke FRG 1 Kassel 3 Aug
8:37.6 Hermann Buhl FRG 2 Kassel 3 Aug
8:40.6 Sergey Ponomaryev URS 2 Tallinn 21 Jul
10th best 8:42.4, 100th 9:09.6

110m HURDLES (y = 120y h)

13.6 Hayes Jones USA 1 Budapest 6 Aug
13.6 Ancel Robinson USA 2 Budapest 6 Aug
13.6y Elias Gilbert USA 1 San Diego 7 Jun
13.7 Martin Lauer FRG 2 Köln 9 Jul
13.8 Anatoliy Mikhailov URS 1 Nalchik 11 May
13.8 Keith Gardner JAM Göteborg 28 Aug
13.8 Stanko Lorger YUG 1 Celje 6 Sep
13.8y Francis Washington USA 1 Baltimore 10 May
10th best 13.9, 100th 14.5

200m HURDLES (* 220y less 0.1 sec.)

22.6*! Charles Tidwell 1 Berkeley 14 Jun
22.8* Francis Washington USA 2 Berkeley 14 Jun
22.9 Elias Gilbert USA 1 Zürich 17 Jul

220y HURDLES (Straight Track)

22.1! Elias Gilbert USA 1 Raleigh 17 May
22.3 Francis Washington USA 2 Raleigh 17 May

400m HURDLES (* 440y less 0.3 sec.)

49.2! Glenn Davis USA 1 Budapest 6 Aug
49.4*! Gerhardus Potgieter RSA 1 Cardiff 22 Jul
50.3* Josh Culbreath USA 2 Bakersfield 22 Jun
50.3* David Lean AUS 2 Cardiff 22 Jul
50.7* Willie Atterberry USA 3 Bakersfield 22 Jun
50.9 Helmut Janz FRG 2 Köln 9 Jul
10th best 51.2, 100th 53.5

HIGH JUMP

2.12 Charles Dumas USA 1 Los Angeles 26 Apr
2.12 Yuriy Styepanov URS 1 Moskva 28 Jul
2.12 Richard Dahl SWE 1 Stockholm 24 Aug
2.10 Stig Pettersson SWE 1 Borås 8 Aug
2.10 Jirí Lansky TCH 2 Stockholm 24 Aug
2.10 Igor Kashkarov RUS 1 Moskva 27 Aug
2.10 John Thomas USA 1 Odawara 14 Sep
10th best 2.09, 100th 1.99

POLE VAULT

4.68 Robert Gutowski USA 1 Compton 6 Jun
4.65 Ron Morris USA 1 Athína 10 Aug
4.64i Don Bragg USA 1 Philadelphia 24 Jan
4.56 1 Athens GA 26 Mar
4.60 Georgios Roubanis GRE1 München 12 Jul
4.57i Jerry Welbourn USA 2 Philadelphia 24 Jan
4.57 Eeles Landström FIN 1 Helsinki 16 Jul
4.56 four men; 10th best 4.53, 100th 4.27

LONG JUMP

8.00 Gregory Bell USA 1 Kalamazoo 10 May
7.94 Ernest Shelby USA 1 Moskva 27 Jul
7.84 Mike Herman USA 1 New York 19 Apr
7,83 Henk Visser NED 1 Den Haag 15 Jun
7.82 Ira Davis USA 1 Philadelphia 24 May
7.81 Henryk Grabowski POL 1 Bydgoszcz 19 Jul
7.81 Igor Ter-Ovanesyan URS 1 Stockholm 20 Aug
10th best 7.69, 100th 7.36

TRIPLE JUMP

16.59! Oleg Ryakhovskiy URS 1 Moskva 28 Jul
16.43 Józef Schmidt POL 1 Stockholm 23 Aug
16.43 Vitold Kreer URS 1 Tbilisi 2 Nov
16.25 Adhemar F da Silva 1 Rio de Janeiro9 Nov
16.19 Konstantin Tsigankov URS 1 Moskva 7 Aug
16,12 Leonid Shcherbakov URS 1 Kiev 2 Aug
10th best 15.92, 100th 15.07

SHOT

19.23 Parry O'Brien USA 1 Modesto 31 May
18.60 Dallas Long USA 2 Compton 6 Jun
18.30 Dave Davis USA 3 Compton 6 Jun
18.36 William Nieder USA 1 San Jose 3 May
17.96 Arthur Rowe GBR 1 Colombes 13 Sep
17.93 Vartan Ovsepyan URS 1 Tbilisi 28 Oct
10th best 17.41, 100th 15.95

DISCUS

57,42 Rink Babka USA 1 Budapest 6 Aug
57.35 Al Oerter USA 1 Austin 28 Mar
56.94 Otto Grigalka URS 1 Kharkov 26 Sep
56.78 Edmund Piatkowski POL 1 Prague 20 Jun
56.60 József Szécsényi HUN 1 Szeged 10 Aug
56.60 Vladimir Trusenyev URS Q Tbilisi 29 Oct
10th best 55.94, 100th 49.82

HAMMER

68.68! Harold Connolly USA 1 Bakersfield 20 Jun
67.23 Albert Hall USA 1 Fort Lee 13 Jun
66.80 Mikhail Krivonosov URS 1 Nalchik 11 May
66.66 Fyodor Tkachev URS 1 Uzhgorod 29 Nov
66.34 Vasiliy Rudenkov URS 1 Zagreb 29 Jun
66.13 Anatoliy Samotsvetov URS 1 Augsburg 21 Sep
10th best 64.59, 100th 57.21

JAVELIN

84.90 Vladimir Kuznyetsov URS 1 Nalchik 12 Oct
82.49 Egil Danielsen NOR 1 Oslo 26 Aug
81.97 Janusz Sidlo POL 1 Warszawa 1 Aug
81.63 Knut Fredriksson SWE 1 Gävle 26 Jul
81.06 Michel Macquet FRA 1 Thonon-I-B 10 Aug

80.72 Giovanni Lievore ITA 1 Roma 12 Oct
10th best 78.94, 100th 69.36

DECATHLON (1952 tables)

8302! Rafer Johnson USA 1 Moskva 28 Jul
8042 Vasiliy Kuznetsov URS 1 Tbilisi 1 Nov
(RJ 7789, VK 7658 on current tables)
7989 Yuriy Kutyenko URS 1 Lvov 29 Aug
7736 David Edstrom (USA) 2 Kingsburg 25 Jun
7625 Yang Chun-Kuang TPE 2 Palmyra 5 Jul
7559 Uno Palu URS 2 Tbilisi 1 Nov
10th best 7137, 50th 6221

20 KILOMETRES WALK

1:27:05.0t Vladimir Golubnichiy URS 1 Simferopol 23 Sep
1:27:38.6t Grigoriy Panichkin URS 1 Stalinabad 9 May
1:28:56,6t Valentin Guk URS 2 Nalchik 21 Apr
1:29:11.8 Leonid Spirin URS 1 Tallinn 21 Jul
1:29;55.0 Grigoriy Klimov URS 2 Moskva 6 Jul
1:30:21.4 Anatoliy Vedyakov URS 3 Moskva 6 Jul

50 KILOMETRES WALK

4:10:13.0 Aleksandr Linde URS 1 Riga 10 Sep
4:10:37.8 Mikhail Lavrov URS 1 Tbilisi 2 Nov
4:10:39.0 Mikhail Korchunov URS 2 Tbilisi 2 Nov
4:16:08.0 Aleksandr Seryy URS 3 Tbilisi 2 Nov
4:16:08.6 Sergey Lobastov URS 1 Moskva 23 Aug
4:17:15.4 Yevg. Maskinskov URS 1 Stockholm22 Aug

4x100m: 39.5! Germany 1 Köln 29 Aug
39.7y! Abilene Christian Coll USA 1 Fresno 11 May
4x400m: 3:05.8 USA 1 Warszawa 2 Aug
3:08.1y South Africa 1 Cardiff 26 Jul

WOMEN

100 YARDS

10.3! Marlene Willard AUS 1 Sydney 1 Mar
10.4 Betty Cuthbert AUS 1 Sydney 20 Mar
10.4 Wendy Hayes AUS 3 Sydney 20 Mar
10.3w Barbara Jones USA 1 New York 19 Jul
10.3w Nancy Boyle AUS 1 Lumsden 13 Jan

100 METRES

11.3! Vyera Krepkina URS 1 Kiev 13 Sep
11.5 Inge Fuhrmann FRG 1 Hannover 19 Jun
11.5 Maria Itkina URS 1 Minsk 11 Sep
11.5 Guseppina Leone ITA 1 Roma 12 Sep
11.6 six women, 10th best 11.6, 50th 11.9

200 METRES (* 220y less 0.1 sec.)

23.3*! Marlene Willard AUS 1 Sydney 22 Mar
23.4* Betty Cuthbert AUS 1 Sydney 8 Mar
23.7 Christa Stubnick GDR 1 Jena 19 Jul
23.7 Maria Itkina URS 1 Moskva 8 Aug
23.8* Kay Johnson AUS 3 Sydney 22 Mar
23.8* Heather Young GBR 3 Cardiff 24 Jul
10th best 23.9, 50th 24.7
Half turn: 23.7A* Anne Shaw RSA 1 Bloemf'tein5 May

400 METRES

53.6! Maria Itkina URS 1 Warszawa 14 Jun
54.4 Betty Cuthbert AUS 1 Göteborg 24 Augr
54.6 Yekaterina Parlyuk URS 1 Nalchik 11 May
55.2 Zinaida Kotova URS 1 Tbilisi 28 Oct
55.3*! Molly Hiscox GBR 1 London (WC) 2 Aug
55.4 Nina Otkalenko URS 1 Krasnodar 12 Jul
10th best 55.6, 50th 57.0, * 440y less 0.3 sec.

800 METRES

2:05.8 Nina Otkalenko URS 1 Kiev 30 Jul
2:06.3 Yeliz. Yermolayeva URS 1 Tallinn 21 Jul
2:06.3 Lyudmila Lisenko URS 1 Tbilisi 31 Oct
2:06.4 Zoya Yelkhova URS 2 Tbilisi 31 Oct
2:06.6 Vyera Mukhanova URS 2 Tallinn 21 Jul
2:06.6 Diane Leather GBR 2 Stockholm 24 Aug
2:06.6 Dzidra Levitska URS 3 Stockholm 24 Aug
10th best 2:08.2, 50th 2:12.5

1500 METRES

4:32.8 Aranka Kazi HUN 1 Budapest 23 Oct

80 METRES HURDLES

10.6! Galina Bystrova URS 1 Krasnodar 8 Sep
10.8 Norma Thrower AUS 1 Sydney 23 Mar
10.6w 1 Sydney 22 Mar
10.8 Margaret Stuart NZL 1 Hastings 7 Apr
10.8 Avis Brain NZL 2 Hastings 7 Apr
10.8 Kreszentia Kopp FRG 1 Nürnberg 2 Jul
10.8 Gisela Birkemeyer GDR 1 Potsdam 6 Jul
10.8 Rimma Kosheleva URS 2 Krasnodar 8 Sep
10.8 Zinaida Burenkova URS 3 Krasnodar 8 Sep
10.8 Nina Vinogradova URS 1 Nalchik 12 Oct
10th best 10.9, 50th 11.2

HIGH JUMP

1.83! Iolanda Balas ROM 1 Bucuresti 19 Oct
1.765 Taisia Chenchik URS 1 Chelyabinsk 14 Jun
1.75 Cheng Feng-jung CHN 1 -- --
1.725 Micheline Mason AUS 1 Sydney 15 Sep
1.705 Mary Donaghy NZL 2 Cardiff 22 Jul
1.70i Lyudmila Nabatova URS 1 Orenburg 18 Jan
1.70 Mariya Pisaryeva URS Budapest 24 May
1.70 Luiza Slobozhanina URS 1 Minsk 13 Aug
10th best 1.67, 50th 1.60
x made with built-up shoe, which was banned in 1958

LONG JUMP

6.28 Lyudmila Radchenko URS 1 Kiev 7 Sep
6.21 Erika Fisch FRG 1 Köln 29 Aug
6.18 Margaret Matthews USA 1 Budapest 6 Aug
6.16 Willye White USA 1 Warszawa 2 Aug
6.16 Nina Protchenko URS 1 Moskva 28 Aug
6.14 Liesel Jacobi FRG 1 Stockholm 22 Aug
6.16w Beverley Weigel NZL 1 London (WC) 2 Aug
10th best 6.10, 50th 5.87

SHOT

16.66 Galina Zybina URS 1 Tbilisi 29 Oct
16.54 Tamara Press URS 1 Tallinn 20 Jul
16.54 Earlene Brown USA 1 Moskva 20 Jul
16.47 Valerie Sloper NZL 1 Christchurch25 Oct
16.35 Zinaida Doynikova URS 2 Tbilisi 29 Oct
15.95 Lyudmila Zhdanova URS 4 Tbilisi 29 Oct
10th best 15.77, 50th 13.94

DISCUS

54.38 Tamara Press URS 1 Nalchik 20 Apr
54.36 Nina Ponomaryeva URS 2 Nalchik 20 Apr
53.89 Kriemhild Hausmann FRG 1 Nijmwegen 27 Jul
52.73 Yevg. Kuznyetsova URS 1 Nalchik 2 May
52.53 Lamara Tugushi URS 2 Tbilisi 31 Oct
52.46 Stepanka Mertová TCH 1 Bratislava 29 Jun
10th best 51.75, 50th 46.72

JAVELIN

57.49! Birute Zalogaitite URS 1 Tbilisi 30 Oct
57.40! Anna Pazera AUS 1 Cardiff 24 Jul
56,67 Dana Zátopková TCH 1 Bucuresti 13 Sep
54.98 Galina Zybina URS 1 Brno 5 Jul
54.66 Jutta Neumann FRG 1 Berlin 22 Jun
54.10 Almut Brömmel FRG 2 Berlin 22 Jun
10th best 53.13, 50th 47.07

PENTATHLON (1954 tables)

4872! Galina Bystrova URS 1 Tbilisi 2 Nov
4648 Edeltraud Eiberle FRG 1 Ludwigsburg31 Aug
4627 Nina Vinogradova URS 2 Stockholm 21 Aug
4623 Lidiya Shmakova URS 2 Krasnodar 18 May
4593 Galina Grinvald URS 1 Minsk 14 Aug
4494 Barendina Hobers NED 4 Stockholm 21 Aug

4x100m: 44.8 USA 1 Moskva 27 Julg
44.8 FR Germany 1 Kassel 3 Aug

OBITUARY 2007

See ATHLETICS 2007 for obituaries of the following who died in early 2007: Herman Brix, Adrian Callan, Olgierd Cieply, Maria Cioncan, Ali de Vries, Helmut Ebert, Berwyn Jones, Emil Kiszka, Ken Lorraway, Karl Engebret Lunaas, Yelena Romanova, Adolfas Varanauskaite, Willye White, Yang Chaung-kwang.

Arne ANDERSSON (Sweden) (b. 30 Jun 1942 Stockholm) on 7 October. A hammer thrower, he competed in 13 internationals for Sweden and had a best of 63.44 (1970).

Richard ASHENHEIM (Jamaica) (b. 20 Aug 1927 St. Andrews) on 14 December in Bermuda. He was a sprinter while at Jamaica College and while studying law at Wadham College, Oxford. Pbs: 100y 10.2/10.1w, 220y 23.3 in 1949. He practised as an attorney at law for over 50 years after admittance to the Jamaican Bar in 1950, and, following in his family tradition, he was director of *The Gleaner* newspaper (founded in 1834 by his great great grandfather) for 43 years. An ATFS member from 1957, he was the top statistician for Jamaica and the region. He was an ever-present as a journalist at major events from the 1948 Olympic Games and played a major part in organising the 1966 Commonwealth Games in Kingston while he was president of the Jamaican AA.

Richard Francis **'Dick' AULT** (USA) (b. 10 Dec 1925) on 16 July in Jefferson City. He finished fourth at 400m hurdles in the 1948 Olympics. In 1949 he was 2nd in 51.9 to Charles Moore's 51.1 at the AAU but ran the next six fastest times in the world that year with a pb of 51.4 and a 440yh world record of 52.2 at Oslo on 31 August. Other pbs: 440y 48.2 & 120yH 15.2 (both 1949).

Sixten BORG (Sweden) (b. 26 Jun 1923 Almundsryd) on 27 March. He founded one of the world's great meetings, the DN Galan in Stockholm in 1967, linking the Stockholm clubs with the newspaper *Dagens Nyheter*.

Hallgeir BRENDEN (Norway) (b. 10 Dec 1929 Trysil) on 21 September in Lillehammer. Norwegian 3000m steeplechase champion in 1953 and 1954, he took part in 13 internationals 1950-4. Pbs: 400mH 57.4 (1954), 800m 1:55.8 (1954), 1500m 3:53.8 (1954), 1M 4:16.2 (1950), 3000m 8:35.8 (1952), 5000m 15:12.2 (1951) and 3000mSC 8:54.6 (1954). He was best known, however, as a cross-country skier, winning Olympic gold medals at 18k in 1952 and 15k in 1956 and silver at 4x10k relay in 1952 and 1960.

Roscoe Lee BROWNE (USA) (b. 2 May 1925 Woodbury, New Jersey) on 11 April in Los Angeles. He was 6th in the US Olympic Trials 1500m in 1948 and AAU indoor 1000 yards champion in 1950 and 1951. A member of the New York Pioneer Club, he ran his pb of 1:49.3 for 800m in 1951 when 2nd to Mal Whitfield in the US Champs and was ranked no 2 in the world by *Track & Field News*. Blessed with a distinctively rich voice and dignified bearing, Browne went on to make his mark in Hollywood films, including roles in Alfred Hitchcock's "Topaz" (1969) and William Wyler's "The Liberation of L.B. Jones" (1970), and he was the narrator in "Babe" (1995). He also worked extensively on TV, winning an Emmy Award for an episode of "The Cosby Show" in 1986.

Robert Alfred **'Bob' CLARK** (GBR) (b. 15 May 1935) in November in Peterborough. He was 11th in the European 20km walk in 1962. Pbs: 2MW 13:27.0 (1964), 7MW 51:28.0 (1960), 20kmW 1:32:30 (1961), 50kmW 4:50:14 (1962), 1 Hr 13,053m (1960).

Theodore **'Ted' CORBITT** (USA) (b. 31 Jan 1920 South Carolina) on 12 December in Houston. He made a huge inspirational contribution to distance running as an athlete and official. He graduated from the University of Cincinnati with a masters' degree in physical education and, adapting Emil Zátopek's training methods, ran his first marathon at age 31 and the following year (1952) was 44th in the Olympics. He won the US marathon title in 1954 and had a pb of 2:26:44 (1958). He ran a total of 199 marathons and ultra races and set American records at 50 miles, 100 miles and 24 hours. He became in 1958 the first President of the Road Runners Club of America, and while President of the New York Road Runners Club campaigned for a masters category (40+) for runners. His 1964 book, "Measuring Road Running Courses", provided the benchmark for certified road race courses.

Bertha CROWTHER (née Piggott) (GBR) (b. 9 Dec 1921) on 8 August in London. She won the silver medal at the 1950 European Championships at pentathlon with 3048 points (3409 on 1954 tables) and was 5th at high jump. At the 1948 Olympic Games she was 6th at high jump and at the 1950 Empire Games equalled her (1948) best of 1.60m in taking the high jump silver medal, also 5th at javelin, 9th at long jump and heats of the 80m hurdles. She was the winner of the first WAAA Pentathlon in 1949 with 327p (3901 on the 1954 tables for a British record) and again in 1950 with 2949 pts and also WAAA 80mh champion in 1946. pb LJ 5.50 (1950).

Richard DAHL (Sweden) (b. 5 Aug 1933 Landskrona) on 8 August. Generally overshadowed by compatriot Stig Pettersson, he caused the big surprise at the 1958 Europeans as he won the high jump gold medal with 2.12 (joint top mark in the world that year) from a previous pb of 2.08. He represented Sweden on 13 further occasions and at Swedish championships was 2nd in 1957 and 1958, 3rd in 1960.

Annual progression: 1948- 1.45, 1949- 1.60, 1950- 1.65, 1951- 1.81, 1952- 1.84, 1953- 1.88, 1954- 1.90, 1955- 1.95, 1956- 2.00, 1957- 2.04, 1958- 2.12, 1959- 2.08, 1960- 2.00, 1961- 2.03, 1962- 1.85, 1963- 1.85, 1964-1.80.

Harold **'Hal' DAVIS** (USA) (b. 5 Jan 1921 Salinas, California) on 12 August in California. The 'California Comet' would surely have been the favourite for Olympic sprint titles, but his chances were dashed by World War II. He came to the fore while at Salinas Junior College in 1940 and in 1941 he equalled Jesse Owens' world 100m record of 10.2 despite an 0.9m/sec headwind at Compton. In 1942, by then a student at the University of California, he tied the world 100 yards record of 9.4 at Fresno but although the mark was accepted by the NCAA it was not ratified by the IAAF as he was using starting blocks of an unapproved type. He was AAU champion at 100m in 1940, 1942-3 and at 200m each year 1940-3 and won the NCAA sprint double at 100y and 220y in 1942-3. He was unbeaten at the furlong 1940-3 and lost just one important race at 100, to Barney Ewell in the 1941 AAU 100m. Ever a poor starter, but a brilliant finisher, on that occasion he was some 3m down at half way only to finish at such speed that he finished just a few centimetres down as both he and Ewell were given 10.3. That was his only defeat in four years at the top 1940-3 in which time he never lost a race in the furlong.

Annual progression at 100y, 100m and 220y (straightaway): 1938 - 9.7, 21.0; 1939 - 9.7, 21.0; 1940 - 9.5, 10.3, 20.4 (200m); 1941 - 9.5. 10.2, 20.5 (20.2w); 1942 - 9.4, 10.5, 20.4 (21.2 on turn); 1943 - 9.5, 10.3, 20.9 (20.2w 200m).

Antonio DE GAETANO (Italy) (b. 18 May 1934 Ancona) on 21 August in Roseto, Teramo. He was 12th at 50km walk at the 1960 Olympics and had 12 internationals for Italy 1958-67. pb 50kmW 4:25:42 (1960). His son Giusppe was also an Italian international.

Jack DIANETTI (USA) (b. 22 Jul 1928) on 21 December in Englewood, Florida. He was the world's fastest junior at 880y (1:50.8 for 2nd at the NCAAs) and mile (4:12.0) in 1947, times which ranked him 7= and 10= among the seniors that year. In 1948 he was 2nd in the NCAA for Michigan State University and 5th in the US Olympic Trials at 800m. He was a schoolteacher in East Rochester for 33 years.

Satimkul DZHUMANAZAROV (Kyrgyzstan) (b. 17 Sep 1951 Kok-Tyub) on 2 April. He was the 1980 Olympic marathon bronze medallist (representing the USSR) in 2:11:35. He was also 11th in the 1978 Europeans and 5th in the 1981 World Champs in 2:12:31. Pbs: 5000m 13:53.4, 10,000m 28:14.0 (1978), Mar 2:11:16 (1980).

Moshe GENUTH (Israel) on 21 June in Jerusalem, aged 55. An ATFS member since 1989 and Israel's best known athletics historian, his main work "The History of Athletics in the Modern Era" published in 1995, was the first book of its kind written in Hebrew, covering all major historic events, worldwide, from the beginning of the 19th century until 1992. He had just finished work on a new edition of that book amidst physical hardships due to his illness.

Lilita GERIKA-ZAGERE (Latvia) (b. 28 Oct 1941) on 7 April. She ran the first leg on the Latvian team that set a world record of 3:43.2 for 4x400m in 1969. In all she won 15 Latvian titles and set 10 Latvian records. Pbs: 100m 11.7 (1966), 200m 24.1 (1966), 400m 53.5 (1965).

Alastair K. **'Scotchy' GORDON** (Australia) (b.30 Oct 1928) on 25 April in Adelaide. He was 4th at 100y and 220y and a gold medallist in the 4x110y relay at the 1950 British Empire Games. Pbs 100y 9.8 (1953), 100m 10.5 (1952, equalled AUS record), 220y 21.8 (1953). He later became a successful coach at St Peter's College, his pupils including Tania van Heer, who won two gold medals (both relays) and a bronze (100m) at the 1998 Commonwealth Games.

Bob GRANT (Australia) (b. 26 Apr 1934) on 25 June. Australian javelin champion 1955-7 with a best of 65.76 in the qualifying round of the 1956 Melbourne Olympics, just missing the final.

Jim GRANT (Jamaica) (b. 8 Jan 1947) on 23 July in Iowa City, USA. He represented Jamaica at the Commonwealth Games in 1966 (heats) and 1970 (semi). After studying at Eastern Michigan University, Ypsilanti, he coached in Jamaica for 11 years during which time he guided Bert Cameron, world 400m champion in 1983, at St Jago HS and then for 23 years of the women`s team at Iowa University, with 12 years as head coach. Pbs: 440y 46.8, 440yh 51.2 (JAM record) (both 1970).

Jan Erik **GULBRANDSEN** (Norway) (b. 29 May 1938) on 4 September. A member of SK Vidar Oslo, he set seven Norwegian records at 400mh from 52.7 in 1958 to 51.5 (twice) in 1964 and one at decathlon with 6296 points (1952 tables, 6551 on 1985 tables) in 1959. He was a semi-finalist at the 1960 Olympics and went out in the heats at the 1958 and 1962 Europeans at 400mh. He was Norwegian champion at 110mh 1960-2, 400mh 1957-64, Pentathlon and Decathlon 1959 and a regular on the national team 1958-67.

Oiva HALMETOJA (Finland) (b. 31 Mar 1920 Maaninka) on 21 February at Varkaus. A dive bomber lookout in the War against Russia in 1939-44 on 204 flights, he injured his rib cage, which ended his shot putting career (pb 14.07). There was no problem with the hammer, however, and he placed 19th in the 1952 Olympic Games and 14th in the 1954 Europeans. He threw his pb of 57.17 against Hungary in Helsinki in 1955 and won four Finnish titles (1952-5). He later became an eminent figure in the Finnish Athletics Federation (SUL), and was deputy President in the 1970s.

Terry HARRISON (Australia) (b. 7 Dec 1945) on 20 October in Sydney. He was Australian 10,000m champion in 1972 in 30:19.2 and had a marathon pb of 2:20:23 (1972). His son Nick ran in the 2004 Olympic marathon.

John HART (GBR) (b. 7 Apr 1928 Balfron) on 10 June. He represented Britain in the 120y hurdles in 1946 and 1949 and Scotland in the 1950 Empire Games. Second to Don Finlay in the 1949 AAA Champs, he was Scottish champion 1946-50; pb 15.0 in 1949. A Scottish rugby international in 1951, he served as hon. secretary of the International Rugby Football Board from 1971 to 1986.

Peter HEIDENSTROM (New Zealand) (b. 20 June 1929) in June. Long crippled by arthritis, he was a world renowned authority on athletics, an ATFS member for over 55 years, who put his extensive records and encyclopaedic knowledge into the most comprehensive book on New Zealand athletics ever written: *Athletes of the Century* (1992) containing detailed information covering 100 years of men and women's track, field and long distance events. Ill health prevented him from attending the 2007 New Zealand Champs, the first he had missed in over 50 years. He invented a wind graph with which he could calculate to the hundredth of a second the effect of head or tail winds on the human body. His enormous contribution to athletics included being the NZ correspondent for *Track & Field News* for over 50 years and to this annual and *Athletics International*.

Walter HESKETH (GBR) (b. 30 Oct 1930) on 15 June in Manchester. He set a UK record for 6 miles in the Britain v France match at the White City in 1951 when he trounced Gordon Pirie in 29:13.8, shattering Pirie's record of 29:32.0. In contrast to Pirie (who regained the record the next year) he raced very little on the track but made his mark at cross country, winning the prestigious English 'National' in 1952 and placing fourth in the International Championship in 1951 & 1952.

Horst IHLENFELD (Germany/GDR) (b. 24 Nov 1926 Berlin) on 8 June in Berlin. GDR long jump champion 1953-5 and UIE Student Games bronze medallist 1953. He set GDR records with 7.36 & 7.39 (1953) and 7.51 (1955). HJ pb 1.86 (1958)

Trenton James **JACKSON** (USA) (b. 28 Feb 1942) on 25 March in Rochester, NY. He ran 9.4w for 100y while in high school in 1961 and in 1964 he was 3rd NCAA 100m for University of Illinois and an Olympic 100m semi-finalist. Pbs: 100y 9.4, 100m 10.1 and 220y 20.8 (all 1964), 440y 48.5i (1965). He was also a star basketball player and later played pro football for the Philadelphia Eagles and the Washington Redskins in the NFL. He was a basketball coach at Franklin High School, Rochester for 26 years, retiring in 2001.

Inez JACQUEMART (Belgium) (b. 8 Aug 1962) on 22 April in a diving accident. She was four times Belgian champion at 100km and was 9th in the European 100km in 2002. She had a narrow escape in the December 2004 tsunami disaster in Thailand, just making refuge on the fourth floor of her hotel. pb 100k 8:31:58 (2004).

Charles "**Deacon**" **JONES** (USA) (b. 31 Aug 1934 St.Paul. Minnesota) on 7 September in Hillside. Illinois. He started steeplechasing in 1956 and 9th in the Olympics that years with 7th in 1960; he was silver medallist at the 1959 Pan American Games and US champion in 1957-8 and 1961. He set a US high school mile record with 4:17.6 in 1954 and was NCAA champion for the University of Iowa at cross-country 1955 and 2 miles in 1957. Pbs: 1M 4:06.5i (1961), 2M 8:57.6 (1957), 3000mSC 8:42.4 (1961).

Tom JONES (USA) (b. 1944) on 21 March in Gainesville. He was NCAA champion at 200m and 4x100m in 1966 for UCLA and was successively a head coach at North Carolina State 1978-84, Texas-El Paso 1984-8, Arizona State 1988-92 and of the highly successful women's team at the University of Florida 1992-2007. Pbs: 100y 9.5 (1966), 220y 20.8 (1965), 21.02 and 20.68w (1966).

Moira JOUBERT (South Africa) (b. 17 Sep 1951 Bloemfontein) on 28 November in Pretoria. She was South African champion at 100m hurdles in 1972 and 1973 and set eight national records from 14.8 in 1969 to 13.4 in 1973, the last was also an African record. She was a well-known painter.

Veikko KARVONEN (Finland) (b. 5 Jan

1926 Sakkola) on 1 August in Turku. One of the world's top marathoners throughout the 1950s, he won 15 of the 35 marathons that he ran during his career, winning the 1954 European gold medal after bronze in 1950 (6th 1958) and taking Olympic bronze in 1956 with 5th in 1952. He had major wins at Enschede 1951, Boston 1954, Fukuoka and Athens 1955, and was Finnish champion in 1951 and 1954. His best time was 2:18:56.6 for 3rd in the Finish Champs in 1956. Pbs: 5000m 14:51.4, 10000m 30:52.0, 25,000m 1:19:38.6 (all 1956).

Annual progression at Marathon: 1949- 2:45:07, 1950- 2:32:45 (11), 1951- 2:28:08 (1), 1952- 2:25:19 (8), 1953- 2:25:47 (4), 1954- 2:24:52 (3), 1955- 2:21:22 (1), 1956- 2:18:56.6 (3), 1957- 2:23:54, 1958- 2:22:46. 1959- 2:24:37.

Vladimir KAZANTSEV (Russia) (b. 4 May 1923 Alekseyev Khvalnsk) on 22 November in Moscow. He set world records prior to the first official ratification for the 3000m steeplechase with 8:49.8 (9.8 secs better than the previous best) in 1951 and 8:48.6 in 1952. He was, however, well beaten by the American Horace Ashenfelter who set a new mark of 8:45.4 (8:45.68) to win the 1952 Olympic title in Helsinki as Kazantsev took silver with 8:51.6. He won World Student (UIE) titles at 5000m in 1949 and 1951 and was Russian champion at 5000m 1948, 1950-1, 10,000m in 1951, and 3000m steeple in 1950-3. Pbs: 3000m 8:18.4 (1951), 5000m 14:08.8 (1952), 10,000m 30:21.8 (1951).

Henri KLEIN (France) (b. 23 Sep 1919 Mulhouse) on 18 May. He was French 1500m champion in 1948, going out in the heats of the Olympic Games. He had 8 internationals 1947-51. Pbs: 800m 1:54.0 (1948), 1000m 2:26.5 (1948), 1500m 3:52.8 (1948), 3000m 8:42.0 (1950).

Andrey KURENNOY (Russia) (b. 12 May 1972) in December. He improved at triple jump from 16.92 in 1994 to take the World University Games gold in 1995 in Fukuoka, Japan with 17.30 and made a further advance to 17.44 to win the Russian title in 1997. Also 4th WUG 1997 and European Cup 2001.

Maria KWASNIEWSKA-MALESZEWSKA (Poland) (b. 15 Aug 1913 Lodz) on 17 October in Warsaw. She won the bronze medal in the javelin at the 1936 Berlin Olympics and was also 4th (and 6th at pentathlon) at the 1934 World Games and 6th at the 1946 European Championships. She set five Polish records from 39.81 in 1934 to 44.03 in 1936, the last remaining the national record until 1952, and was Polish champion in 1931, 1934-6, 1939 and 1946. She worked on behalf of the IAAF and the Polish Olympic Committee and in many different bodies related to sport.

Stefan LEWANDOWSKI (Poland) (b. 30 May 1930 Gdansk) on 2 December. He competed at the Olympic Games in 1952 (heat 800m) and 1960 (heats 800m and 1500m) and the 1958 Europeans (heat 1500m) and represented Poland in 22 internationals 1953-60. He was Polish champion at 800m in 1959 and 1500m in 1955. From 1953 he set three Polish records for 800m and five for 1500m to bests of 1:46.5 and 3:41.0 in what was very much his best year 1959, when he was respectively 2nd and 5th on the world lists at those events with 3rd at 1000m in 2:19.0 and 5th at 1M in 4:00.6. He also set six records at 1000m to 2:19.4 in 1957 and one at 2000m – 5:07.2 (1959). pb 400m 48.4 (1956), 1M 4:00.6 (1957).

Annual progression at 800m, 1500m: 1951- 1:56.1, 1952- 1:52,8, 3:53.8; 1953- 1:53.2, 3:49.2; 1954- 1:51.7, 3:50.8; 1955- 1:50.5, 3:43.4; 1956- 1:48.5, 3:45.4; 1957- 1:49.5, 3:42.3; 1958- 1:49.7, 3:41.1; 1959- 1:46.5, 3:41.0; 1960- 1:49.2, 3:44.3; 1961- 1:51.8, 3:52.4.

Vincenzo LOMBARDO (Italy) (b. 21 Jan 1932 Santo Stefano di Camastra, Messina) on 3 December in Milano. He competed at the Olympics in 1952 (ht 400m) and 1956 (qf 200m 4th 4x100m) and in 14 internationals 19652-60.1952-60. Italian champion at 400m 1952, 1954-5, he set an Italian record for 200m at 21.1 in 1955 and 1957 and had pbs: 100m 10.7 (1955), 400m 47.2 (1960). He rose to become a general of the "Guardia di Finanza", Customs Service, being very active against criminal gangs, and was also chairman of the FIDAL Regional Committee in Lombardia. He had two daughters who became internationals: Patrizia (100mh 13.10 '87 ITA record) and Rosanna (400m 53.54 '84).

Stephen Hunter **McCOOKE** (GBR) (b. 4 Sep 1918) on 16 March in Broughshane. He placed 12th in the 1948 Olympic 10,000m, and had pbs: 3 miles 14:30.6, 6M 30:27.6 (both 1948).

Bernard **Darcy McGONAGLE** (New Zealand) (b. 4 Jan 1938) on 27 April in Whangerei. NZ champion at pole vault 1966 and 1971-2 and 1974 and 7th at the 1962 Commonwealth Games. pb 4.35 (1966). He became a leading PV coach and official.

Herbert Henry **McKENLEY** (Jamaica) (b. 10 Jul 1922 Clarendon) on 26 November in Kingston. He was a versatile sprinter with the unique distinction for a male athlete of making Olympic finals at 100m, 200m and 400m. He was at his best at the one-lap with world 440y records of 46.3 in 1947 and 46.0 in 1948 (and unratified 46.2 in 1946 and 1947), but he tended to go off too fast as shown by the fact that he reached 220y in these races in estimated times of 21.0, 21.2, (20.9 and 20.8). He improved the 400m record to 45.9 (46.00 auto) at Milwaukee (AAU Champs) on 2 Jul 1948. He won Olympic silver medals at 400m in 1948 and 1952, being surprisingly beaten on each occasion by Jamaican compatriots, Arthur Wint and George

Rhoden. In the 1952 Games McKenley ran a 44.6 relay leg, the fastest ever at the time, for Jamaica's gold medal winning team. He was 4th at 200m in 1948 and 2nd at 100m in 1952. He also won the AAU 440y in 1945, 1947 and 1948, and the NCAA 440y for the University of Illinois in 1946 and 1947. 'Hustling Herb' was for many years the head coach for the Jamaican Olympic team. Other bests: 100y 9.6 (1946) and 9.4w (1947), 100m 10.2 (1951), 200m 20.8 (1950), 220y straight 20.6 (1946) and 20.2w (1947), 300m 32.4 (1948), 500y 55.8i (1949).

At his funeral the Jamaican Prime Minister Bruce Golding announced that a statue would be erected by the government at the entrance of the National Stadium in honour of one the country's greatest athletes.

Annual progression at 100y, 100m, 200m (and 220y straight), 400m: 1941- (8=) 10.0y, 21.6*; 1942- 9.8u, 10.9, 21.2 (4); 1943- 21.4ySt (10), 47.7 (3=); 1944- 21.6ySt (6=), 48.0* (6); 1945- 9.9y, 48.4 (8=), 47.1?; 1946- 9.6 (3=), 10.5 (6=), 20.9e* (2). 20.6ySt (1), 45.9* (1); 1947- 9.4w, 10.4 (4=)/20.2w, 20.7A/20.3*w (2=), 20.2w, 20.7ySt (2=), 45.9A* (1); 1948- 21.2 (9), 45.7* (1); 1949- 9.7, 10.3 (1=), 20.9* (1), 20.9ySt, 46.2 (1=); 1950- 10.5/10.4w (7=), 20.8/20.6w (2), 46.0 (2); 1951- 10.4 (5=), 21.1 (4=), 46.1* (2); 1952- 10.4 (3=), 20.8* (2=), 45.9 (1=); 1953- 21.2* (9=), 47.1* (9=).

Raymond MARCILLAC (France) (b. 11 Apr 1917 Levallois-Perret) on 13 April in Paris. He had 5 internationals 1937-9 and was French 400m champion in 1939 and 1944. Pb 400m 48.4 (1944). He became a journalist, film producer and TV presenter, creating RTF's sports service in 1958 and becoming director of news in 1963.

Sir Arthur Gregory George **MARSHALL** (GBR) (b. 4 Dec 1903 Cambridge) on 16 March near Linton, aged 103. A Cambridge "Blue" at 440y, he went to the Paris Olympic Games in 1924 as a reserve for the 4x400m relay but did not run. He went on to make a huge impact in the world of aviation. An engineering graduate, he obtained his pilot's licence (which he held for 60 years!) in 1928 and became a master flying instructor in 1931. His methods were adopted by the RAF with Marshall flying schools training more than 20,000 pilots and instructors during the Second World War. He was also a test pilot and was chairman of the motor and aerospace engineering firm Marshall of Cambridge (founded by his father), one of the largest privately owned companies in Britain, from 1942 until his retirement in 1989, aged 86. It was Marshall Aerospace which designed Concorde's distinctive nose. He was knighted in 1974.

Mizan MEHARI (Australia) (b. 28 Dec 1980) committed suicide on 10 May in Mount Ainslie, Canberra. He was 12th for Australia in the 2000 Olympic 5000m. He ran a world age-15 best of 13:33.76 for 5000m in 1996 in which year he ran for Ethiopia in the 1500m at the 1996 World Juniors in Sydney. He remained in Australia with three other Ethiopians and gained Australian citizenship in 1999. He won the Australian cross-country title in 1997 and 1998 and was coached by Dick Telford at the Australian Institute of Sport. Other pbs: 1500m 3:42.36 (1997), 3000m 7:53.40 (1998), 5000m 13:20.85 (1998).

Mary MITCHELL (later LOGAN) (New Zealand) died in Dargaville in late March at the age of 94. She was the first prominent NZ women's javelin thrower, taking the national record from 28.90 in 1936 to 38.30 in 1941, winning national titles each year 1939-41 and placing 4th in the 1938 Empire Games with 35.96. She also set an NZ long jump record with 4.82 in 1935 and was the second best at high jump with a best of 1.36 in 1941.

Andrew John **NORMAN** (b. 21 Sep 1943 Suffolk) in Birmingham on 24 September on his return from the World Athletics Final in Stuttgart where he acted as IAAF Advertising Commissioner. Having an 880y best of 1:55.7 in 1962, he joined the Metropolitan Police that year and speedily became secretary of their athletics club and earned rapid promotion to sergeant. He organised open meetings for the Southern Counties AAA and became their coaching secretary. His hard-working, no-nonsense approach led to his having a huge influence on the sport – directing the IAC meeting at Crystal Palace, helping many top athletes with their racing programmes and becoming promotions officer of the British Athletics Federation after leaving the Met Police in 1984. This was a period of major change in athletics as it moved into the professional age pushed on by leaders such as Norman. He also served one term as EAA Council Member 1991-4. Often involved in controversial issues during this era (a most successful one for British athletics) he was dismissed from his BAF job in 1994 after a coroner's inquiry into the death of respected athletics journalist Cliff Temple had concluded that unfair allegations made by Norman against Temple were a contributing factor in the latter's suicide. Norman went on to be involved in organising meetings in South Africa and Baltic countries and currently was helping events in Hungary (where he had played a major role in directing the 1998 European Championships in Budapest) and Slovakia and, as an agent, managing several top current athletes. His second wife was javelin world record holder Fatima Whitbread.

Birgit NYHED (Sweden) (b. 30 Sep 1911 Lund, née Lundström) on 4 May. At discus she was 6th in the 1936 Olympics and 4th in the 1938 Europeans, setting four national records from 1936 to 44.38 in 1938. She was Swedish champion at javelin and sling ball 1934, discus 1935, 1937-41 and 1944; shot 1941.

Parry O'BRIEN (USA) (b. 28 Jan 1932 Santa Monica, Califonia) on 21 April while competing in a masters' swim meet in Santa Clarita, California. In a long career as a shot putter, he was Olympic champion in 1952 and 1956, won the silver medal in 1960, and was fourth in 1964. He was Pan-American champion in 1955 and 1959 and won AAU titles indoors nine times (1953-61) and outdoors eight times (1951-5, 1958-60). He was also the Sullivan Award winner in 1959. The complete master of his event, and pioneer of the step-back O'Brien technique, he set the record win streak by a male athlete with 116 consecutive victories between July 1952 and June 1956. He set 15 world records with ten performances ratified by the IAAF, from 18.00 in 1953 to 19.30 in 1959. His 18.42 in 1954 was the first ever 60ft put. Although he was surpassed by younger throwers, O'Brien continued to improve and recorded a best of 19.69 in 1966. While at the University of Southern California he was NCAA champion in 1952 and 1953. He also won the AAU discus title in 1955 and had a best at that event of 60.00m in 1965. He also ran 100m in 10.8 in 1951.

He had a successful career in commercial banking, real estate and civil engineering and, returning to throwing, set world age group records in the 1980s.

Annual progression at SP/DT (position in world rankings): 1949- 14.62, 1950- 16.42 (11), 38.51; 1951- 17.00 (3), 47.40; 1952- 17.48 (2), 51.93 (10); 1953- 18.04 (1), 53.45 (4); 1954- 18.54 (1), 56.12 (2); 1955- 18.12i/18.10 (1), 53.90 (9); 1956- 19.25 (1), 56.46 (4); 1957- 18.55 (2), 55.85 (4); 1958- 19.23 (1), 56.06 (9); 1959- 19.30 (2), 56.43 (6); 1960- 19.33 (3), 54.61 (36); 1961- 19.24i/18.97 (3), 57.31 (9); 1962- 18.88i/18.70 (8), 58.88 (9); 1963- 19.11i/19.10 (5), 56.52 (20=); 1964- 19.45 (4), 56.06 (42); 1965- 18.20 (34), 60.00 (10); 1966- 19.69 (4), 57.51 (32=); 1967- 19.01i (17), 53.40; 1968- 18.12i (59).

Alfred Adolph **OERTER** (USA) (b. 19 Sep 1936 Astoria, New York) on 1 October in Fort Myers, Florida. He achieved the then unique feat of winning four successive Olympic titles, with the discus at each Games from 1956 to 1968. On each occasion he beat the reigning world record holder (four different men), throwing pbs and Olympic records in 1956 (56.36), 1960 (59.18), 1964 (61.00) and 1968 (64.78). The 1964 win in Tokyo came despite having torn cartilages in his lower rib cage just six days earlier and having had to have won a neck harness for most of the year due to a cervical disc injury. He also won the Pan-American title in 1959, the AAU six times between 1959 and 1966, and the NCAA for the University of Kansas in 1957 and 1958. He set four world records from 61.10m in 1962 to 62.94 in 1964. The former was the first officially accepted mark over 200ft, although Oerter himself had thrown over that mark with 61.73m at Fayetteville, Arkansas on 5 Apr 1958, but this was disallowed due to a 2.5% downhill slope.

After winning his fourth Olympic gold medal with a personal best in 1968, he retired to concentrate on his career as a systems analyst and computer engineer. He had won each of his Olympic titles when others were favoured ahead of him and, especially in 1964, against considerable adversity, for then he had neck and rib injuries. After a decade out of competition, however, he made an awe-inspiring comeback and improved his best to 69.46 at the age of 43 in 1980. He placed fourth that year in the US Olympic Trials, but by then the US Government had determined to boycott the Games in Moscow. If that competition had been 'for real' who can say but that his tremendous competitive spirit might not once again have returned him to the Olympic arena. Even in 1985, at the age of 49, he had a season's best of 64.40, 31 years after he had set a US high school discus record. In recent years he had been an award-winning abstract painter.

Annual progression at DT (position in world rankings): 1955- 52.27 (17), 1956- 56.36 (5), 1957- 56.49 (3), 1958- 57.35 (2); 1959- 58.12 (3); 1960- 59.18 (2); 1961- 58.05 (5),1962- 62.45 (1), 1963- 62.62 (1); 1964- 62.94 (2), 1966- 63.22 (3),1967- 62.03 (9) 1968- 64.78 (2), 1969- 61.88 (13), 1976- 53.40; 1977- 62.50 (32=), 1978- 62.62 (37), 1979- 67.46 (7), 1980- 69.46 (2), 1981- 68.76 (3), 1982- 66.12 (22), 1983- 67.90 (11), 1984- 63.92 (48), 1985- 64.40 (37). pb SP 17.37i (1958).

Esko OLKKONEN (Finland) (b. 18 Feb 1948 Oulainen) on 14 April at Oulu. Finnish 110m hurdles champion in 1970 with a pb of 14.3 (1971), he went into coaching after a career-ending knee injury and worked for SUL in various posts for almost 30 years. Highly regarded as a technical expert of hurdling, his coaching duties were sadly ended in 2001 when it was found he had been supplying doping substances to one of his young athletes.

Dr. Austin **Robin**ette **PINNINGTON** (GBR) (b. 13 Jun 1929) in April. He ran at the European Championships (heats 100m, 4th 4x100m) and also ran against France in 1950. While studying medicine at Oxford University, he equalled the English Native record of 9.8 when running for Oxford and Cambridge against Cornell and Princeton in 1950. Other pbs: 9.7dh (1950), 200m 22.0 (1953), 21.7yw (1952), 220yhSt 24.7 (1952).

Wilhelm PORRASSALMI (Finland) (b. 18 Dec 1930 Kälviä) on 21 December at Kokkola. He missed European long jump gold in Bern in 1954 by frustrating millimetres after a controversial foul to finish 5th. He won against France in Helsinki in 1956 with a Finnish record 7.62, which was broken later the same year by

Jorma Valkama, whom he never beat in Finnish championships (two silvers, two bronzes). Porrassalmi was injured in the Melbourne 1956 Olympic qualifying round and finished 9th at the 1958 Europeans.

Rupert Aldworth **POWELL** (GBR) (b. 18 Sep 1916) on 30 March. A graduate of Oxford University, he competed for Britain against France at long jump in 1938 and in two post-War internationals at high hurdles in 1946-7. Pbs: 120yh 15.2 (1946), 220yh 25.0 (1939), LJ 7.25 (1938).

Lavize PUCE-ALDZERE (Latvia) (b. 15 May 1911) on 9 July. She was 5th in the 1938 European Championships javelin with 40.20 (the first Latvian over 40m). In all she won 40 Latvian titles at shot, discus and javelin and set 23 Latvian records at shot and javelin. Pbs: SP 13.11 (1948), JT 47.78 (1952).

Sven RAPP (Sweden) (b. 13 Feb 1920 Stockholm) on 28 May. He made his only appearance for Sweden when 4th in the European 10,000m in 1946. Pbs: 3000m 8:37.6 (1946), 5000m 14:36.6 (1947), 10000m 30.29.6 (1948), 20,000m 1:05.41 (1949), 1 hour 18434m (1949).

Robert **'Bob' REID** (GBR) (b. 1 Feb 1920 Ayrshire) in July. After winning the Scottish Youths Cross-country title in 1937 and 1938, he became the youngest ever senior champion in 1939. That year he made his debut in the International CC Champs and he ran in that event each year 1946-52, with a best of 12th in 1948. His family moved to Birmingham in 1939 and, previously with Doon Harriers, he joined Birchfield Harriers. He was 2nd in the English National CC in 1946 and won a further Scottish CC title in 1950.

Edward ROMANOWSKI (Poland) (b. 30 Jul 1944 Warsaw) on 11 November in Warsaw. He ran the third leg on the Polish 4x100m team that set a European record 39.2 in 1965 and he also ran at 4x100m in the finals of the 1966 Europeans and 1968 Olympics, making the heats and semis respectively at 200m at those meetings. Polish champion at 200m in 1968, pbs 100m 10.3 (1964), 200m 20.80 (1968).

Wilbur ROSS (USA) (b. 1927) in Hollywood, Florida on 10 August at the age of 80. He won the AAU pentathlon in 1949 and 1950, was 2nd at decathlon in 1944 and was twice placed at 400m hurdles. pb 440yh 54.2 (1947). He became recognised throughout the world as one of the premier hurdles coaches in history and author of *The Hurdler's Bible*. He was an athlete at Baldwin Wallace College and coached at the University of Maryland Eastern Shore and at Winston Salem State University and mentored such luminaries as Greg Foster, Roger Kingdom and Renaldo Nehemiah.

Lucas Kipkemboi **SANG (Kenya)** (b. 12 Feb 1963) was a victim of the violence in Kenya as he was reportedly either hacked or stoned to death and his body burnt near Chepkoilel on 31 December. A member of the Kalenjin tribe and respected business man in Eldoret, in 1988 he ran a hand-timed 45.3A in Nairobi and was a quarter-finalist in a pb 45.72 at 400m (& 8th at 4x400m with a 45.08 leg) at the Olympics. He ran on the African team that was 3rd in the World Cup 4x400m in 1989, and that year set an 800m pb of 1:46.21. He later acted as pacemaker at many meetings.

François SCHEWETTA (France) (b. 23 Sep 1919, Ile de Bréhat, Brittany) on 8 October. He won an Olympic silver medal at 4x400m in 1948 and was 4th at 4x400m at the 1950 Europeans, with 14 internationals 1948-50. Pbs: 400m 48.3 (1948), 800m 1:53.6 (1949).

Ryan SHAY (USA) (b. 4 May 1979 Ypsilanti, Mich) of suspected cardiac arrest during the early stages of the US Olympic marathon trial in Central Park, New York on 3 November. He was NCAA 10,000m champion in 2001 and won US titles at the marathon (2003), half marathon (2003 & 2004), 20k (2004) and 15k (2005). Pbs: 3000m 7:58.73i (2002), 5000m 13:35.08 (2002), 10,000m 28:26.91 (2000), Mar 2:14:29 (2003). In July he married Alicia Craig (25), the NCAA 10,000m champion in 2003 and 2004 with a best time of 32:19.97.

Michel SIMÉON (France) (b. 21 Sep 1927 Enghein-les-Bains) on 13 July. He was French long jump champion in 1948 and had 4 internationals 1948-50. pb 7.17 (1948).

Richard Swift **'Dick' STEANE** (GBR) (b. 26 Sep 1939) on 3 June. His best sprint times were 10.59 when 4th at 100m in the 1963 World University Games (where he won a gold medal in the 4x400m) and 20.66 for 200m at high altitude Mexico City in the 1968 Olympics where he reached the semi-finals. His best sea level 200m time was 20.9 in 1967. Other pbs: 100y 9.9 (1962), 9.7w (1960), 100m 10.59 (1963), 10.5 (1962); 300y 30.7 (1966), 400m 48.6 (1964).

Magdalena Catherine '**Dalene**' **SWANEPOEL** (South Africa) (b. 7 Nov 1930 Hopetown) on 2 June in Pretoria. At the Commonwealth Games she won the javelin and was third in the shot in 1954 and in 1958 was second in the javelin, leading until the 4th round with 48.73 when Australia's Polish-born Anna Pazera produced a totally unexpected world record of 57.41, and fourth in the shot. She won eight national javelin titles between 1949 and 1963 and was five times shot champion between 1953 and 1958. She set 11 South African records at shot from 12.10 in 1953 to 13.53 in 1958 and 9 at javelin from 40.82 in 1953 to 49.29 in 1960.

Robert TAYLOR (USA) (b. 14 Sep 1948 Tyler, Texas) on 13 November in Missouri City. In the celebrated incident at the 1972 Olympic Games in Munich, he was the only member of the US 100m runners to make it in time to compete in the quarter finals. Without any warm-up he came second in his race in an auto-timed pb of 10.16 and went on to the silver medal in 10.24, a metre behind Valeriy Borzov; later he ran the second leg on the gold medal-winning 4x100m US team. He had ranked 10th in the world in 1969 when he set his 100y pb of 9.2 and 1972 was his only other top-10 year – he ran 9.0w for 100y in April, won the AAU title and was third in US Olympic Trials in his hand-timed best of 10.0 (9.9w in his quarter-final). pb 220y 20.8 (1970). He was a student at Texas Southern University and later coached there.

Henry David **'H.D.' THOREAU** Jr. (USA) (b. 13 Apr 1923 Denver) on 29 December in Palo Alto. He attended the 1932 Olympics aged 9 and was a lifetime track and field fan and statistician. A graduate of Stanford University, he first worked for the Pacific Coast Athletic Commission and then for the NCAA, for whom he edited their college sports guides. He was general manager of the 1960 Winter Olympics at Squaw Valley and a track and field announcer for CBS. He became a successful businessman in real estate and investment banking. He was the co-commissioner for athletics at the 1984 Olympics in Los Angeles.

George Peter **Michael VARAH** (GBR) (b. 19 Oct 1944 Blackburn) on 4 April of pneumonia. He ran the second leg in 1:48.9 for the British team that broke the world record for 4x880y with 7:14.6 at Crystal Palace, London on 22 June 1966 (disallowed because a false time was called out to John Boulter). He ran in four internationals for GB in 1966-7 and was 4th in his heat at the 1966 Commonwealth Games. A member of Hercules Wimbledon AC and Loughborough University, he ran his pb of 1:48.2 for 880y when 4th in the 1967 AAAs. The son of Chad Varah, the founder of the Samaritans and co-founder of the *Eagle* comic, he taught at Rugby School for five years before joining the probation service. He was Chief Probation Officer for Surrey from 1988 to 2004, and was Deputy Lieutenant of Surrey and had been nominated as High Sheriff of Surrey for 2008/09.

Antti VISKARI (Finland) (b. 1 May 1928 Joutseno) on 4 June in Imatra. He won the Boston Marathon in 1956 in a very fast 2:14:14, although the course was later found to be 1183 yards short. Two months earlier he had won a most unusual Finnish trial race, circling the 160m unbanked cinder indoor track at Otaniemi, near Helsinki, for a distance of 20,000m twice the same afternoon in times of 1:03:54.8 and 1:12:47.4! On 21 Oct 1956 in Lappeenranta he broke Emil Zátopek's 30,000m track world record with 1:35:03.6 (this remained the Finnish record for 16 years). An army sergeant and later frontier guard on the Russian border, he was 53rd in the 1960 Olympic marathon, having finished 3rd in Tunis earlier in the year in his pb 2:21:27. He was 2nd once and 3rd three times at Finnish Championships. Pbs: 5000m 14:36.8 (1955), 10,000m 30:09.0 (1956), 25,000m 1:18:24.4 (1956, Finnish record).

Göran WAXBERG (Sweden) (b. 23 May 1919 Kolbäck) on 17 January. Bronze medallist at decathlon at the 1946 European Championships and Swedish champion at decathlon 1942-5 and pentathlon 1943-5. He topped the world list in 1943 with 7008 points (1934 tables, 6594 on 1985 tables) and set a Swedish record for pentathlon (which lasted for 27 years) with 3574 points (1944, 3651 on 1985 tables). Pb LJ: 7.30w (1943).

Alice **Eileen WEARNE** (Australia) (b. 30 Jan 1912) on 6 July at Kingswood, New South Wales. She was Australia's oldest Olympian (4th in her 100m heat in 1932). She was third at 220y and took gold in the medley relay at the 1938 British Empire Games and was Australian 100y champion in 1932 and 1936 (running 11.2 on each occasion) and 2nd in 1935. She was also 2nd at 220y in 1935 and 1936 and 3rd in 1937. AUS records: 100y 11.0 (1937), 100m 12.3 (1932); pb 220y 25.0 (1938).

Max WEBER (Germany/GDR) (b. 24 Jan 1922 Nebra) on 29 August in Leipzig-Wiederitzsch. At 50km walk he was European bronze medallist and 13th at the 1960 Olympics. He was GDR champion at 10,000m 1953 & 1958, 20km 1955 & 1958, 25km 1954, 50km 1955-8 & 1960. In all he set 18 GDR walks records. with pbs: 10,000m 44:47.2 (1955), 20km 1:32:34.6 (1956), 30,000m 2:26:15.8 (1956), 50km 4:17:28.2 (1958). 1Hr 13115m (1955), 2Hr 23835m (1959).

John WINTER (Australia) (b. 3 Dec 1924 Perth) on 5 December. He improved from 38= in the world in 1946 with 1.94 to 8= in 1947 with a national record of 2.00 and jumped his all-time best of 2.01 in 1948 for 7= on the year list behind six Americans. However, he cleared 2.03 in an exhibition in Adelaide in late May prior to leaving for the Olympic Games and in London, with his more fancied American rivals well below form on the heavy cinder run-up, his eastern cut-off leap of 1.98 was sufficient for a clear victory. Shortly afterwards he won for the British Empire team against the USA again at 1.98, and that was also his winning height in the 1950 British Empire Games. He was Australian champion in 1947, 1948 and 1950 and AAA champion in 1948.

John Youie **WOODRUFF** (USA) (b. 5 July 1915 Connellsville, Pennsylvania) on 30 October at his home in Fountain Hills, Arizona. The last survivor of the 12 American men who won gold medals at the 1936 Olympics, his nine-foot stride carried him to victory in the 800m in Berlin and immediately after that he ran on the US team that set a world record of 7:35.8 for 4x880y against the British Empire at the White City, London at the age of 21 while still a freshman at the University of Pittsburgh. For them he won the IC4A 440y/880y double and the NCAA 880y each year 1937-9. He won the AAU 800m in 1937 and that year was deprived of a world record when he won the '800m' in 1:47.8 at the Pan-American Exposition Games held at the Dallas Cotton Bowl, but the distance on this five lap to a mile clay track was then found to be about 5ft/1.52m short. He ran his fastest time for 880y of 1:47.7 on a five-lap track at Dartmouth University track at Hanover, NH in March 1940. That was far superior to the world record (Sydney Wooderson's 1:49.2) but it was run indoors so ineligible. The time (1:47.0 at 800m en route) was close to Rudolf Harbig's 1:46.6 for 800m and indeed nobody was to run as fast after that until 1955. A supreme talent, he was unbeaten at 800m/880y from 2nd to Charles Beetham at the 1936 AAU to his retirement in 1940, after he had run a US 800m record of 1:48.6 at Compton – what a race it could have been between him and Harbig! The first great black American middle distance runner (his grandparents were slaves in the Virginia tobacco fields), he became an officer in the US Army, serving in WW II and Korea, and retiring in 1957 as a lieutenant colonel. Other pbs: 400m 46.8 (1936), 440y 47.0 (1937), 1M 4:12.8 (1939). He was later well known as an official at New York and New Jersey meetings.

Annual progression at 800m (position on world list): 1936- 1:49.9 (2), 1937-1:48.0 (0.2 added to 798.42m time)/1:49.6* (1), 1938- 1:50.6* (4=), 1939-1:50.5* (4), 1940- 1:47.0+i/1:48.6 (1).

Gyula ZSIVÓTZKY (Hungary) (b. 25 Feb 1937 Budapest) on 29 September in Budapest. He was a highly consistent hammer thrower throughout the 1960s and voted as the best Hungarian athlete of the 20th century. His brilliant championships record was: Olympics: 1960 2nd, 1964 2nd, 1968 1st, 1972 5th; Europeans: 1958 3rd, 1962 1st, 1966 2nd, 1969 4th, 1971 11th; World Student Games: 1957 3rd, 1959 1st, 1961 1st, 1963 2nd, 1965 1st. He was Hungarian champion each year from 1958 to 1970 and AAA champion in 1965 and 1966. He set 17 Hungarian records 1958-68, including seven European records from 68.22 in 1960, and was the first European over 70m with 70.42 in 1962 and two world records, 73.74 in 1965 and 73.76 in 1968.

Annual progression at HT (position in world rankings): 1953- 46.52, 1954- 51.16, 1955- 53.07, 1956- 59.69 (29), 1957- 62.38 (15), 1958- 64.10 (13); 1959- 65.72 (5); 1960- 69.53 (2); 1961- 65.41 (11),1962- 70.42 (2), 1963- 69.06 (2); 1964- 69.09 (4), 1965- 73.75 (1) 1966- 71.94 (1), 1967- 68.96 (6), 1968- 73.76 (1), 1969- 72.58 (5), 1970- 70.96 (8); 1971- 73.06 (9), 1972- 72.04 (17), 1973- 64.20.

His son **Attila Zsivoczky** (note slight change of spelling) (b. 29 Apr 1977) was 3rd in the 2005 Worlds and 2nd in the 2006 Europeans at decathlon, with his best score a Hungarian record 8554 in 2000.

Died in 2006

Anton BOLINDER (Sweden) (b. 3 Jun 1915 Los) on 7 December. He won the European high jump title in 1946 with his best ever jump of 1.99 – and on his debut for the Swedish team! He then competed in 3 internationals 1947-8. He was Swedish champion in 1946 and 1948 and was 2nd in 1934 and 1944.

Jean VERNIER (France) (b. 21 Jul 1923 Grand Charmont) on 8 July. He set French records of 5:18.6 (1947) and 5:17.4 (1950) for 2000m and 8:19.6 (1949) for 3000m in 1969 and had 20 internationals 1947-52. At 1500m he was French champion in 1947 and 8th in the 1950 Europeans (also heats 1948 & 1952 Olympics). Other pbs: 800m 1:54.1 (1948), 1000m 2:26.7 (1948), 1500m 3:48.6 (1949), 1M 4:10.0 (1949), 5000m 14:45.2 (1947).

Died in 2008

Hermann BLAZEJEZAK (Germany) (b. 3 Jun 1912 Hildesheim) on 13 January in Mönchengladbach. He was the last survivor of Germany's team at the 1936 Olympics, where he was the second fastest 400m heat winner in his best ever time of 47.9 and won his quarter-final in 48.2 but trailed home last (49.2) in his semi. Two years later he ran the first leg for Germany's winning 4x400m team at the European Champs. Other pbs: 100m 10.8 (1937), 200m 22.0 (1937).

Gary CADOGAN (GBR) (b. 8 Oct 1966 London) of cancer on 19 January. A member of Shaftesbury Barnet Harriers, six years after his 400m best of 46.37 he made his debut with 52.2 at 400m hurdles in May 1993. He then progressed rapidly so that within a month he won the CAU title in 50.05 and the UK in 49.80. He also won the AAA title and ran 49.25 in the heats of the World Champs (before 7th semi-final). He topped the British rankings in 1994 with his pb of 49.07 and that year he was 4th at the Commonwealth Games, 8th at the Europeans and 6th at the World Cup. He received a two-year drugs ban on 28 Nov 1998, but a UK Athletics panel later cleared him and Doug Walker, finding that it could not be proven beyond reasonable doubt that the nandrolene present in their samples was derived from a prohibited substance. He did not compete again.

Maryvonne DUPUREUR (France) (b. 24 May 1937 Saint-Brieuc, née Samson) on 7 January in Paris. At 800m she won the silver medal behind Ann Packer at the 1964 Olympic Games in Tokyo. In this race she improved the French record from 2:03.9 that she had run twice earlier in the year to 2:01.9. In all she set seven French records from 2:08.1 in 1963 and also set French records of 56.0 for 400m in 1963 (with a pb of 55.0 in 1964) and 4:33.23 and 4:27.9 for 1500m in 1969. She ran in the heats in 1960 and was 8th in 1968 at the Olympics and in all had 24 internationals (14 wins) 1960-9. She was French champion at 400m 1959, 1963-4; 800m 1960, 1963-4, 1967-9; and 1500m 1969.

Annual progression at 800m (position on world list): 1959- 2:15.5, 1960- 2:10.7, 1961- 2:11.2, 1963- 2:07.5 (15), 1964- 2:01.9 (3), 1967- 2:05.0 (13), 1968- 2:04.0 (14), 1969- 2:04.9 (14).

Stephen Arusei **KIPKORIR** (Kenya) (b. 24 Oct 1970 Moi's Bridge) was killed in a car crash between Nakuru and Eldoret in February. After 3:38.78 for 1500m in 1995, he burst to the fore in 1996, when he was 14th at the World CC (7th finisher for the winning Kenyan team) and at 1500m won the Kenyan title before running 3:31.82 at Lausanne and going on to the Olympic bronze. He had a big win at Monaco in 3:32.17 in his next race, but never ran as fast again with bests of 3:34.54 in 1997 and 3:34.47 in 1999. Other bests: 1M 3:57.4e (1995), 2000m 4:54.80 (1995), 3000m 7:38.44 (1996), 2M 8:25.37 (1995), 5000m 13:26.49 (1996). He served as a soldier in the Kenyan army.

Ernest **Eddie KIRKUP** (GBR) (b. 12 Jul 1929) on 5 January. He set his marathon pb of 2:22:27.8 in winning the AAA title in 1957 and was 4th at the 1958 Commonwealth Games.

Wesley NGETICH (Kenya) (b. 15 Dec 1977) became a victim of the unrest in Kenya when he was shot and killed by a poisoned arrow in Trans Mara on 21 January. He set his marathon pb when 2nd in Houston in 2:12:10 in 2006 and won the Grandma's Marathon in Duluth in 2005 and 2007.

Bjørn Andreas **PAULSON** (Norway) (b. 21 Jun 1923 Bergen) on 14 January in Skien. He took the Olympic silver medal at high jump in 1948 with 1.95, just 1cm below the pb that he set to win the Norwegian title that year. Annual bests in his brief career: 1947- 1.87, 1948- 1.96, 1949- 1.95, 1950- 1.85.

Bozidar RADULOVIC (Serbia) (b. 28 Feb 1924 Belgrade) on 3 January in Belgrade. He set a Yugoslav record for 400mh with 54.4 (1953), was national champion in 1951, 1953, 1955 and 1957 and competed in 11 internationals.

Glenda REISER (Canada) (b. 16 Jun 1955) on 6 January in Ottawa after a long illness. She set world age bests for 1500m at 16 – 4:15.7 and at 17 – a Canadian record of 4:06.71 in her heat at the 1972 Olympic Games before 7th in her semi-final. Still a junior, she won Commonwealth gold in 4:07.78 in 1974. She was Canadian champion at 800m in 1972 and at 1500m in 1972 and 1973. Other pbs (all in 1973): 800m 2:03.17, 1000m 2:41.4, 1M 4:35.13, all these bests being Canadian junior records. She gave up running for her medical career, becoming a doctor.

Ralph TATE (USA) (b. 10 Jan 1921) on 9 January in Sand Springs, Oklahoma. He was the world's fastest 120y hurdler in both 1943 and (after war service) in 1946 with 14.0. He was also a fine long jumper, world no 2 in 1943 with 7.60 and 3rd in the 1942 NCAAs for Oklahoma State (where he later became a successful track coach), and was the USA's leading triple jumper in 1946 with 14.61 to win the AAU title.

Donald Rae **WITTMAN** (Canada) (b. 9 Oct 1936 Herbert, Sasketchewan) on 19 January in Winnipeg. He broadcast for CBS Sports for over 40 years and was their "voice of athletics". He was even better known in Canada for his work on ice hockey and Canadian football.

DRUGS BANS

THE IAAF HAS a longstanding history in the fight against doping and continues to take a lead in the world of sport, conducting far more tests than any other international federation including at all major IAAF competitions since 1977. The IAAF budgeted $2.8 million for its drugs testing programme in 2007 and for the calendar year 1 January to 31 December 2007 conducted 3277 doping control tests (1426 in-competition tests and 1759 out-of-competition plus 92 pre-competition). This IAAF testing forms part of a world-wide programme where approximately 20,000 samples were collected in the sport of track and field in 2007.

The largest ever anti-doping programme at an athletics event was implemented at the IAAF World Championships in Osaka, and no positive tests were recorded during the championships or in the pre-competition testing at the athletes' village – the first championships with such an outcome since the first edition in 1983. In all 1132 samples were collected from a total of 976 individuals. Also 82 athletes were tested during their team training camps in

Japan as part of the ongoing IAAF out-of-competition testing programme, and that produced one positive result. 534 tests were conducted pre-competition including 429 blood screens for profiling purposes for indication of possible EPO abuse. During the championships a total of 598 tests were conducted. Of these, 179 were urine tests for detection of EPO, a further 103 were blood samples for detection of blood transfusions, while the remaining 316 were standard urine tests.

Drugs bans in 2007

Suspension: Life - life ban, y = years, m = months, W = warning and disqualification, P = pending hearing

Leading athletes

Men	*Name*	*Date*
Kenta Bell USA	24 Jun	W
Jeff Chakouian USA	5 Sep	1y
Silvao Chesani ITA	26 Aug	W
Giuseppe Gibilisco ITA		2y
Konstadínos Filippídis GRE	16 Jun	2y
Omar Jimila MAR	15 Apr	3y
Adil Kaouch MAR	13 Jul	2y
Héni Kechi FRA	19 Jun	3m
Naman Keïta FRA	20 Aug	2y
Mikko Kyrrö FIN	5 Aug	W
Florent Lacasse FRA	18 May	2y
Jesse Lipscombe CAN	14 May	6m
Jaysima Saidy Ndure NOR	28 Jun	W
Eric Thompson USA	21 Jun	1y
Jaanus Uudmäe EST	23 Jun	W
Khalid Zoubaa FRA	27 Jan	3y
Women		
Susan Olufunke Adeoye NGR	5 Jul	W
Süreyya Ayhan Kop TUR	Sep	Life
Mihaela Botezan ROM	28 Apr	2y
Jolanda Ceplak SLO	18 Jun	2y
Susan Chepkemei KEN	10 Sep	1y
Hind Dehiba FRA	23 Jan	2y
Lyubov Denisova RUS	20 Mar	2y
Adriana Fernández ESP	Sep	6m
Alena Ivanova BLR	14 Jan	2y
Marian Jones USA	(from 8 Oct)	2y
Lisa Kehler GBR	7 Jul	W
Yekaterina Khoroshikh RUS	9 May	P
Teodora Kolarova BUL	26 Jun	2y
Yekaterina Koneva RUS	14 Feb	2y
Olesya Kravchenko RUS	7 Feb	2y
Tatyana Lysenko RUS	9 May	P
Vanya Stambolova BUL	24 Jan	2y
Binnaz Uslu TUR	13 Mar	2y
Venelina Veneva BUL	24 Jan	2y

4 years: Ling Peng CHN-J (19 Sep);
3 years: El Mokhtar Ajjaji MAR (18 Mar), Saïd Bel Harizi FRA (29 Jun)
2 years: Gaetano De Cillis ITA (1 Apr), Brumo Miguel Fortes Andre POR (11 Feb), Jasmine Joseph IND (12 Feb), Ahmadreza Khanfari IRI (8 May), Gajendra Kumar IND (11 Feb), Kavian Mosazadeh IRI (24 May), Jamie Payne TRI (17 Mar), Pablo López Sánchez-Rey (6-13 May), Yuriy Sechnev RUS (6 Oct), Marco Francesco Segato ITA (25 Feb), Seyed Shahrokh IRI (20 Oct), Vadim Shmagaylo RUS (21 Apr), Abdeljabbar Sihammane MAR (7 Jan), Aleksandr Slepov (9 Jun), Tomas Turkis LTU (15 Sep), Wang Yaqi CHN (22 Aug), Christin Zoladkiewicz GER (7 Sep)
6 months: Dawid Nikodem POL (27 Jan), Mikolaj Lewanski POL (30 Jun);
5 months: Samuel Bonaudo FRA;
3 months: Franck Gauthier FRA (9 Apr);
2 months: Stefano Savi ITA (31 Jul)
Public warning: Jonathan Bacabas BEL (23 Jun). Luzia Souza Pinto BRA (1 Apr)
? Gajendra Singh IND (Feb), Jasmin Joseph IND (Feb)

Add to 2006 List

Men		
Ridouane Es-Saadi BEL	15 Jan	Life
Justin Gatlin USA	22 Apr	4y
Dorian Scott JAM	29 Jul	W
Fernando Silva POR	4 Dec	2y
Women		
Ibifuro Tobin-West NGR	10 Feb	2y

2 years: Mehdi Asadi IRN (21 Jul), Mukesh Beniwal IND (10 Jul), Rajendra Bhandari NEP (25-26 Aug), Arzu Berk TUR (12 Nov), Dong Dingrui CHN (11 May), Michal Fiala CZE (27 Aug), Sapour Ghanbari IRI (21 Jul), Iglandini González COL (31 Aug), Mohammad Goudarzi IRN (22 Jun), Matsusalem de Lima BRA (22 Oct), Seyed Shahrokh Madhdavi IRI (20 Oct), Mohsen Moghadam IRI (22 Jun), Farid Soltani Mohammadi IRI (21 Jul), Marcelo Moreira BRA (24 Sep), Charles Nyakundi KEN (2 Apr), Jamie Payne TRI (17 Mar), Rosalba Ravi Pinto ITA (25 Mar), Mojtaba Poustchi Khorasani IRN (20 Jul), Anil Senova TUR (24 Jun), Reza Shirian IRN (21 Jul), Sebastian Varga ROM (9 Sep)
6 months: Julien Balsen FRA (9 Dec), José Manuel Oliveira da Silva POR (28 Jan);
3 months: Thierry Blocodon FRA (17 Dec)
Public warning: Ofense Mogawane RSA (22 Jun), Giuseppe Mucerino ITA (11 Mar)
LaTasha Jenkins, who tested positive test for nandolene in July 2006, was cleared at a USADA arbitration hearing because of procedural mistakes in the testing, but this is being contested by WADA.

Add to athletes failing drugs test in 2005

Men		
Nils Engevik NOR	17 Jul	2y
Anil Kumar IND	1 Sep	2y

A re-evaluation of the career of Sin Kim Dan

By Bob Phillips

MYSTERIOUS. The same description has been used by both Robert Parienté and Roberto Quercetani in their comprehensive histories of athletics regarding the exploits of an athlete known to them as Sin Kim Dan but now referred to, presumably in the light of heightened linguistic awareness, as Shin Gheum Dan. She ran 51.2 for 400m and 1:58.0 for 800m during September and October of 1964 in her home town of Pyongyang, in North Korea, and neither performance was ever ratified. The official world records then stood at 51.9 and 2:01.2.

Yet the 51.9 which had received IAAF approval had been set by the same lady two years before, and she had also run 51.4 and 1:59.1 (the first sub-two-minutes ever achieved) at an international meeting in 1963. So what was the mystery? In essence, it was a mere matter of bureaucracy because North Korea had withdrawn from the IAAF and the 1963 performances were achieved at the "Games of the New Emerging Forces" (GANEFO) in Jakarta, Indonesia, which were, in any case, not recognised by the IAAF. If more accessible proof of her ability was needed, then Sin Kim Dan provided it by her appearances at the annual Znamenskiy brothers memorial meeting in Moscow between 1960 and 1967, winning convincingly at 400 and 800m on four occasions.

Her eight record-breaking or record-equalling performances included three at 400 and 800m before she ran her officially-accepted 51.9 which were not submitted for ratification. The "records" were as follows in chronological order, with the current official world record (WR) in brackets:

22 Oct 1960, Pyongyang, 400m 53.0 (WR 53.4)
1 May 1961, Pyongyang, 800m 2:01.2 (WR 2:04.3)
30 Jun 1962, Moscow, 400m 53.0 (WR 53.4)
23 Oct 1962, Pyongyang, 400m 51.9 (WR 53.4)
12 Nov 1963, Djakarta, 800m 1:59.1 (WR 2:01.2)
13 Nov 1963, Djakarta, 400m 51.4 (WR 51.9)
5 Sep 1964, Pyongyang, 800m 1:58.0 (WR 2:01.2)
21 Oct 1964, Pyongyang, 400m 51.2 (WR 51.9)

In both 1960 and 1964 she was deprived of an opportunity to take part in the Olympic Games, when she would undoubtedly have challenged strongly for medals. Roberto Quercetani draws attention to another aspect of Sin Kim Dan's eligibility in referring to the fact that "some Western correspondents who had seen her in previous years in Moscow and/or Djakarta expressed doubts as to her femininity". Such scepticism seems to have been countered in the fullness of time by the knowledge that she subsequently married and had two children. Additionally, the Spanish statisticians' group, AEEA, in its 2003 publication of biographies of 500 leading women athletes, states that a medical examination of Sin Kim Dan by Japanese doctors pronounced her "100 per cent woman" [Yet even the AEEA referred to her as *"esta misterioso norcoreana"*!]

This eligibility test took place in Tokyo in 1964 when she arrived with her North Korean team-mates for the Olympics, but the entire contingent returned home after three days because the suspension of six of their number, including herself, for taking part in the banned GANEFO meeting was not lifted. During her stay in Tokyo, Sin Kim Dan had a brief meeting with her father, who lived in Seoul, and whom she had not seen for 14 years because of the partition of North and South Korea.

The 800m in Tokyo was won, astonishingly, in only her seventh attempt at the distance by Britain's Ann Packer, who had already taken the silver medal at 400m, and her time of 2:01.2 equalled the official world record. In his book, *Olympic Diary Tokyo 1964*, published the following year, Neil Allen, who had reported the Games for *The Times* newspaper, pointed out: "Because she is scrupulously fair, Ann would be the first to admit that she won in the absence of Sin Kim Dan", and he then said of the surprise gold-medallist, "But I do not think for a moment that she is a shadow champion. We will never know how good she could have been since this is her last year in the sport. My opinion, taking into account her lack of experi-

Note: the name "Sin Kim Dan" has been used throughout this article because that is how she was known when she was competing.

ence at 800m and the burden of the 400 before, is that she could certainly beat 1:59.0".

When I spoke with Neil Allen recently about the Tokyo Games he recalled that he had been the one to tell Ann Packer in Tokyo that Sin Kim Dan had gone home, and Packer – typically generous in nature – expressed heartfelt pity for the plight of the woman who might well have beaten her.

The belief that Packer could beat 1:59 says as much about the absent Korean as it does of the British winner. While Western experts might have found it difficult to accept that a rugged peasant woman from a secretive country with no tradition in the event could run so much faster than Miss Packer, pretty as a picture and engaged to be married to Britain's valiant team captain, Robbie Brightwell, the fact is that such times as the North Korean had achieved, and that Neil Allen thought Packer could have achieved, were to be proved perfectly feasible for women in the not too distant future. In 1974 the imperious Irena Szewinska was to run 400m in 49.9. Three years earlier another splendid runner of whom there were no doubts, the supremely elegant Hildegard Falck, had covered 800m in 1:58.5.

It was Neil Allen, too, who recorded a first-hand account of what it was like to run against Sin Kim Dan. In his highly informative and entertaining *On the Track* column for the monthly magazine *World Sports* in January 1964 he related in detail a conversation with the European 800m champion from Holland, Gerda Kraan, who had also taken part in the Znamenskiy 800 the previous year.

The headline to the column was "A SUPERWOMAN ... but she can be beaten", and Kraan recalled: "When Dan burst away with a first 200m in 27 seconds, and then runs the opening 400m in 57.2 seconds, I felt I had no chance. I went past the bell in about 61 seconds. Imagine it! About four seconds behind the world record-holder! I kept running, just running. And with about 200m to go suddenly I heard this noise. Ooosh! Ooosh! At first I did not realise what it was. Then I saw that Dan was suddenly tired. She was breathing in gasps. At last I knew that she was human. She could be beaten. I woke up too late, but I only lost by 1.3 seconds. Next time it could be different". Unfortunately for both, there was to be no next time. Kraan reached her peak when she won her European title in 1962 in 2:02.8 and was 7th in the 1964 Olympic final.

Sin Kim Dan had been born on 3 July 1938 and was one of nine children in the family. She apparently started running at the age of 14 but by 1958 her best times for 400 and 800m were still not at all exceptional – 66.0 and 2:28.2, though achieved without any training. Russian and Korean coaches are said to have recognised her potential at a youth festival in Pyongyang, and their judgement was amply and promptly rewarded. During the winter of 1958-9 she was persuaded to train as much as three hours a day on a track covered with sawdust, totalling 199 kilometres (124 miles) in February alone, which indicates that she was running some six kilometres (four miles) a day. One of her sessions was 12 x 200m in 34-35 seconds, and while this was probably more than Ann Packer did it was still hardly of Zátopek proportions.

Of above average build – 1.73m tall and weighing 62kg – she contested her first serious races in April 1959: 200m in 26.8, 400m in 59.9, 800m in 2:17.1. Her training continued at an intense but modified level, amounting to 120 kilometres in April and 110 kilometres in May, and an article originally published in Moscow and then translated for the March 1962 issue of the magazine, *World Athletics*, edited by Mel Watman, mentions that she ran 400m in 55.9 in Moscow during 1959, which was presumably at the Znamenskiy meeting. This was startling enough progress, already putting her in the top 30 in the world for the year in an underdeveloped and non-Olympic event, but there was much more to come.

Remarkable breakthrough

In August she ran 100m in 12.4, and in September 200m in 24.8, ranking 58th equal in the world for the year and 2nd in Asia to Chiang Yu-ming, of China (24.4). In October in Peking she ran 800m in 2:09.7 and 400m in 54.4 on successive days. This was a remarkable breakthrough. The 800m time was to rank 33rd equal in the world for the year, and as 20 of those ahead of her were from the Soviet Union there were only actually eight countries with faster performers: the others being Great Britain, Hungary, Holland (Gerda Kraan), Germany, Romania, Poland and France. Just three women in the world were faster at 400m that year, led by a new world record 53.4 for Maria Itkina, of the USSR, from Australia's Betty Cuthbert and Britain's Molly Hiscox. Altogether, Sin Kim Dan had 30 races during the year, including 10 at 400m (one of which was a 54.6 in China in November) and eight at 800m.

The training was maintained at a very high level into 1960, and one day's work in April of that year is recorded as being as follows: 15 minutes running (presumably to warm up); general exercises, 2 x 30m, "runs with acceleration" (two on the straight, two round a bend), 12 starts of 30-40m, 8 x 200m (29, 26, 28, 26.5, 27, 27, 27, 26.5) with 12 minutes rest between each, and two sets of 15 squat jumps with dumbbells. She raced regularly, three times at 100m, four at 200m and six each at 400 and 800m by the end of July, with electrifying results: 53.8 for 400m in April and 2:06.9 for 800m in June.

Then she went to the Znamenskiy meeting in Moscow and ran Lyudmila Shevtsova, of the USSR, desperately close in a world-record 800m, 2:04.3 to 2:04.5. Both runners were inside the previous record of 2:05.0 set by the magnificent Nina Otkalenko, also of the USSR, five years before. Sin Kim Dan's training in the 10 days leading up to the Moscow 800m had included on one day 2 x 200m in 24.4 and 24.8, with a 12-minute break in between, and on another day 10 x 200m in 31-32sec, with a 200m jog between each, and one wonders how many women in the world, even in the Soviet Union, were putting in as much quality work as this.

Very few athletes in history had progressed from obscurity to the highest level in as short time as had Sin Kim Dan, and this was to be the only defeat of her career. Two months later Shevtsova won the Olympic title in precisely the same time, with Australia's Brenda Jones 2nd in 2:04.4. North Korea was not affiliated to the International Olympic Committee and so could not take part in the Games. Further 400m times by Sin Kim Dan of 53.5 and 53.0 (her first world record, albeit unofficial) followed in Pyongyang in October. A photograph of Sin Kim Dan in the Moscow 800m gives no reason to doubt her gender, though it has to be said that other photos taken during her career are less flattering. Of course, she is by no means the only woman athlete to whom such a judgement could apply.

Her 2:01.2 for 800m in Pyongyang in May of 1961 was far faster then Shevtsova but justifies the historians' claims of "mysteriousness" because no details are known of it and it was not ratified, though less than a year later its feasibility was affirmed as the time was equalled by Dixie Willis, of Australia, and this performance was officially recognised. At the Znamenskiy meeting in July Sin Kim Dan beat Gerda Kraan by a street at 400m on the first day, 53.5 to 55.7, with the official world record-holder, Maria Itkina, notably absent, though she had run 53.8 a week or so before, and then won at 800m from Kraan the next day. Sin Kim Dan's time was 2:04.6, and Kraan's a national record 2:06.4, with the world record-holder, Shevtsova, a distant 4th in 2:08.0.

Returning for the Znamenskiy meeting in 1962, Sin Kim Dan produced another marvellous double – the greatest yet of its type in history – winning the 400m in 53.0 to equal her own unofficial world record and the 800m the next day in 2:01.4, just two-tenths slower than Willis's world record. Both races were solitary ventures, with 2nd places going to Barbara Mayer, of East Germany, in 55.5 and Lyudmila Lysenko (previously Shevtsova) in 2:06.3. Sin Kim Dan's first lap in the 800 was 58.4, which was not much slower than she had run against Kraan the previous year. In October her Pyongyang 400m time of 51.9 (2nd place in the race, 58.1!) was officially ratified now that North Korea was affiliated to the IAAF. It was 1.5sec faster than Itkina's previous official record.

The 1963 season was presumably undertaken, at least at the start, in the belief that Sin Kim Dan would get her chance to prove herself against all-comers at the following year's Olympics, for which the 400m for women was to be introduced at long last, and there would, of course, also be an 800m. She began in April with a 2:06.3 for 800m, and her annual demonstration at the Znamenskiy meeting entailed the customary wins at both 400 and 800m. She ran the first 200 of the 400 in 23.9, which must have caused some consternation for that Dutch girl of fond memory, Tilly van der Zwaard, who had placed 3rd to Maria Itkina and Britain's Joy Grieveson in the previous year's European Championships. Sin Kim Dan won in 52.5 – a time which only she had ever beaten – with van der Zwaard a remote 2nd in 55.0. The 800m race was the one described so graphically by Gerda Kraan to Neil Allen, with the Korean weakening for once to a modest (for her) time of 2:04.6 ahead of Kraan's 2:05.9.

Outlawed by the IAAF

Confirmatory times of 53.4 and 2:05.0 for Sin Kim Dan followed in October, and then came that ill-fated GANEFO meeting. The problem was that it was taking place in Indonesia, which had been outlawed by the IAAF for refusing permission to Israeli athletes to take part in the previous year's Asian Games. The countries involved at GANEFO included Albania, Algeria, China, Indonesia, Iraq, Morocco, Tunisia and the United Arab Republic, among others, but the whole affair was really of very little sporting significance, other than Sin Kim Dan's succession of victories. On 11 November she won her heat of the 800m in 2:10.1 and then took the 200m final in 23.5 to equal the Asian record, with 2nd place recording 25.8! On 12 November she won the 800m in 1:59.1, passing the bell in under 57sec with a lead of 70m, and eventually winning by 110m (2nd place for Liu Cheng-ping, of China, in 2:18.4)! On 13 November she won her 400m heat in 54.9 and the final in 51.4 (2nd place, Chiang Yu-ming, of China, 57.7).

Sin Kim Dan started the 1964 season with 53.6 for 400m in April and 53.2 for 400 and 2:03.5 for 800 in May. Then in September came her sensational 1:58.0 for 800m, again achieved in obscure circumstances, plus a 52.8 for 400m. As a defiant gesture, she ran 400 and 800m again within a couple of days or so of the Olympic finals and produced times of

51.2 (the fastest ever) and 1:59.0 (the 2nd fastest ever) which presumably made a point which satisfied the country's political leaders if not her. No performances were recorded for her in 1965, but she returned the next year at the second GANEFO meeting, winning the 400 in 53.1 (4th fastest in the world for the year) and the 800 in 2:03.7 (equal 6th fastest). In 1967 she was back in Moscow for further Znamenskiy successes in 53.3 (7th in the world) and 2:04.6 (16th in the world).

It was a grand final flourish. The best of the Soviet women seemed to be avoiding her yet again at 400m on the first day as she won by the usual huge margin, with Tamara Byelitskaya 2nd in 55.5. In the next day's 800m Sin Kim Dan led by 15m after half a lap in 27.5sec and by 50m at the bell in 57.0sec before slowing to 2:04.6 at the finish – still comfortably ahead of the 2:06.5 for Katlin Prodan, of the USSR.

Neil Allen provided an early and fitting epitaph to her career in the article which he wrote for *World Sports* at the beginning of 1964.

"The sudden rise to power, the powerful legs that are nearer to those of Vladimir Kuts than a young woman, and the barriers of geography and language have made Sin Kim Dan seem an inexplicable, unbeatable freak", he suggested. "In fact, she is just another exciting example of the progress of track and field's standards, and I am convinced she can be beaten by someone with the same application and determination".

World All-Time Best Performances – Women's 400m As at the end of 1967

51.2	Sin Kim Dan (North Korea)	(1)	Pyongyang	21.10.64
51.4	Sin Kim Dan	(1)	Jakarta	13.11.63
51.9	Sin Kim Dan	(1)	Pyongyang	23.10.62
52.0	Betty Cuthbert (Australia)	(1)	Tokyo (OG)	17.10.64
52.1*	Judy Pollock (Australia)	(1)	Perth, W. Aus	27. 2.65
52.2	Ann Packer (GB)	(2)	Tokyo (OG)	17.10.64
52.4	Charlette Cooke (USA)	(1)	Mexico City	16.10.67
52.5	Sin Kim Dan	(1)	Moscow	2. 7.63
52.5	Cooke	(1)	Santa Barbara, Cal	2. 7.67
52.6*	Pollock	(1)	Melbourne	8. 1.66
52.6*	Pollock	(1)h	Kingston, Jam (CG)	6. 8.66
52.6+	Pollock	(1)	Melbourne	19. 2.67
52.6	Kathy Hammond (USA)	(2)	Santa Barbara, Cal	2. 7.67

* 440 yards time less 0.3sec, + made during 440 yards race.

World All-Time Best Performances – Women's 800m As at the end of 1967

1:58.0	Sin Kim Dan (North Korea)	(1)	Pyongyang	5. 9.64
1:59.0	Sin Kim Dan	(1)	Pyongyang	23.10.64
1:59.1	Sin Kim Dan	(1)	Jakarta	12.11.63
2:01.0	Judy Pollock (Australia)	(1)	Helsinki	28. 6.67
2:01.1	Ann Packer (GB)	(1)	Tokyo (OG)	20.10.64
2:01.1+	Pollock	(1)	Stockholm	5. 7.67
2:01.2	Sin Kim Dan	(1)	Pyongyang	1. 5.61
2:01.2+	Dixie Willis (Australia)	(1)	Perth, W. Aus	3. 3.62
2:01.4+	Marise Chamberlain (NZ)	(2)	Perth, W. Aus	3. 3.62
2:01.4	Sin Kim Dan	(1)	Moscow	1. 7.62

+ made during 880 yards race.

Sin Kim Dan is the only athlete from North Korea to have set a world record in athletics. Indeed, very few athletes from this most closed of societies have registered on a world scene. Their only athlete to have won a global title has been Yong song-ok, who won the World women's marathon title in 1999 in a national record 2:26:59. Ham Bong-sil improved that record to 2:25:31 when 5th in the 2003 World marathon and the only other top six placing in a global championships was 6th by Mun Gyung-ae in the women's marathon at the 1992 Olympic Games.

IAAF Rule Changes 2007

By Robert Hersch

THE IAAF CONGRESS, at its meeting in Osaka prior to last year's World Championships, approved several changes in the rules of competition that will be of interest to statisticians and fans.

Records and Statistics:

Chip times will now be acceptable for records in road events, both running and race walking. (Rule 260.22(a))

Records in events timed by fully automatic timing will not be accepted without evidence of the zero control test. (Rule 260.22(c)). This test has been required by the rules for some time (Rule 165.19) and the new rule should not be a problem assuming the officials know that they must keep the test and provide it to the relevant Federation so that it can be sent with the record application.

As of January 1, 2009, records in events of 400m and less will require the use of starting blocks linked to IAAF-approved automatic false start detection apparatus. (Rule 260.22(f)).

Alternative formats were authorized in the vertical jumps in competition other than major international championships and Games. (Rule 181.6) Thus the competition could involve allowing athletes to a total number of attempts, rather than limiting them to three per height. The IAAF Council later decided that clearances on fourth or subsequent attempts at a given height can count as qualifying heights for championships, but should not count as records. Statisticians will have to determine whether such clearances should be included on main lists without notation.

Running events

The indoor 300m race will now be run entirely in lanes. (Rule 214.6). This was the practice in a number of major indoor 300m in recent years, notwithstanding the fact that it was contrary to the rules.

There was a major revision in the rules relating to the draw for lanes after the first round in events that begin in lanes. Under the new rule, there will three draws. Assuming an 8-lane track, the first four runners in the ranking order will draw for the four preferred lanes; then the next two will draw for lanes 7 and 8, and then the last two will draw for lanes 1 and 2, which are generally considered the least desirable.

Two rule changes should help eliminate some of the controversies that have surrounded starting (such as the incidents at the last two editions of the World Athletics Final). There will now be a Start Referee assigned to the starts to facilitate the processing of protests involving starts. (Rule 125.2) And the rules now deal specifically with what happens when an athlete causes the start to be aborted, *e.g.*, by raising a hand. If the referee determines that this was done without a valid reason, the athlete can be yellow-carded for improper conduct, but it will not be considered a false start. (Rule 162.5)

Some minor revisions were made to the chart that documents the recommended procedures regarding the numbers of heats and the qualifying procedures in running events. In a few situations, the chart now calls for three semifinals instead of two. (Rule 166.2)

Field events

Jump-offs will now begin at the height after the last one cleared by the tied athletes, rather than the lowest height at which any of the tied athletes lost the right to compete. This could make a difference where an athlete passes a number of heights before finally failing. (Rule 181.8(c)(i))

A new rule permits the referee to allow a field event athlete to advance to the final three rounds in an event, pending the resolution of a protest regarding a jump or throw that was initially ruled a foul, but that would have qualified the athlete for the final three rounds if the Jury of Appeal determines that the foul call was erroneous. This is analogous to the current rule that protects the rights of runners who have protested a false start disqualification. (Rule 146.4(b))

General

The Congress confirmed the rule that had been passed by Council earlier in the year dealing with the use of technical devices such as prostheses. As was well reported, research was undertaken to determine how that rule should be applied to the specific prostheses used by

Oscar Pistorius of South Africa, whose success has generated international publicity.

In certain invitational meetings (not those that are part of the World Athletics Tour), mixed competition will now be permitted in field events and in races of 5000m or longer. (Rule 147)

Other amendments, as usual, dealt with technical matters such as the specifications of the hammer handle, the dimensions of spikes, the placement of cones on indoor tracks, the markers used by field event athletes, the inclination of runways, the maximum depth of the water in the steeplechase, and the marking of the finish line to facilitate the alignment of photo finish cameras.

Officials and others wishing to read the actual text of the current rules can purchase the rule book from the IAAF, or can download the rules from the IAAF's web site. It is noteworthy that the new edition of the rule book bears the date of a single year, 2008, rather than the usual two years. Because of the recent amendments to the World Anti-Doping Code, which will require changes in the IAAF's antidoping rules effective January 1, 2009, the IAAF will publish a book dated 2009 near the end of this year.

AIMS Silver Jubilee

By AIMS Secretary, Hugh Jones

AIMS (the Association of International Marathons and Distance Races) became 25 years old during 2007. It came into being at a time when marathon running was experiencing its first boom, with up to 15,000 people taking part in the biggest events. But perhaps more significantly it seemed as if every city in the world suddenly wanted a marathon, and many organisers responded to the demand. In doing so they soon came to appreciate the advantages of co-operating at an international level

The official foundation of AIMS was enacted at the Establishing Congress held in the Park Lane Hotel, London on 6 May, attended by 28 Marathon race directors. At this stage it was called "The Association of International Marathons", and was the outgrowth of a series of meetings that had been held over the previous eighteen months in Honolulu, New York and Boston, mainly directed towards the establishment of a "World Circuit" of Marathons. The Circuit idea eventually fell by the wayside but other reasons remained for Marathon directors to continue to meet, not least in order to formalise an administrative system for the measurement of marathons to ensure they were of the correct length. All members of the Association were to meet strict measurement criteria to prove that they were indeed of Marathon length.

Boston Marathon race director Will Cloney became the first President of AIMS, with Chris Brasher of the London Marathon as Vice-President. Allan Steinfeld became Chair of the AIMS Standards Committee and worked tirelessly to help race directors learn the technical requirements to produce a good race. "Exchanging information, knowledge and expertise" was one of the objectives enshrined in the Articles of Association adopted on foundation. The others were the overriding aim "to foster and promote road running throughout the World", and a professed desire "to work with IAAF on all matters relating to international Marathons."

A monthly Newsletter was produced from June 1982 to keep members up to date with AIMS business and record the results of member races. An AIMS Yearbook was published from 1985 allowing direct communication with the runners who participated in AIMS races. This opened the way for AIMS to establish a platform from which member races, through their joint efforts, could directly promote themselves to the running community. The yearbook was one plank of this platform, but member races had already realised that sending their entry forms for distribution to runners at fellow members' events was an effective way to attract foreign runners. Foreign participation was particularly valued not just for the international gloss it provided, but also for the impact it had on the local economy. The New York Marathon, the prototype of a big city event and a founder member of AIMS had already generated a significant "niche" tourist industry around its race.

Chris Brasher, whose term lasted from 1983-1987, expressed two of AIMS purposes, technical improvement and foreign promotion, in one phrase: "travel with confidence, race with enjoyment". At the 4th World Congress of AIMS in Manila, at which Chris Brasher handed over to Bob Dalgleish of the Glasgow Marathon, the Association expanded to embrace road races of distances other than the Marathon. The Berlin 25km and the Gothenburg Half Marathon were two of the first non-Marathon events to join.

Bob Dalgleish's Presidency of AIMS was cut short by his untimely death in October 1990 and Hiroaki Chosa, of the Fukuoka Marathon, was appointed as interim President. By this time AIMS had grown to include 87 members.

Through the efforts of Allan Steinfeld as Technical Chairman, backed up by the General Secretary Andy Galloway, great progress had been made in developing a cadre of measurers around the world. The system of measurement developed by AIMS was officially adopted by IAAF in 1988, and enshrined in their rule book.

This convergence between AIMS and IAAF was a welcome development, but it had not been typical of relations in the 1980s. The first decade of AIMS' existence was partly propelled by a feeling that IAAF had not ventured sufficiently far out of the stadium to address the problems and potential of road running. AIMS believed that some IAAF member federations saw road running largely as a mass tax base that could be exploited to support the activities of a track and field elite. The relationship between the two bodies was at times abrasive.

Well placed

Hiroaki Chosa's assumption of the Presidency presented an opportunity to bring AIMS closer to the world governing body. As a member of the IAAF Cross Country and Road Running Committee, he was well placed to bridge the gulf that separated the two organisations. He received his mandate from the 7th World Congress of AIMS, held in Bangkok in November 1991.

Following this a significant transformation of the AIMS Yearbook took place. Since 1988 it had been published twice yearly, but the "yearbook" had been between 44 and 64 pages in A5 format and between the colours covers, entirely in black and white. The new magazine, titled *Distance Running* was in A4 format with more pages and much greater colour content.

Through the good offices of the new President the September 1992 – March 1993 edition of Distance Running became a joint publication of AIMS and IAAF, which it has remained ever since. Several Japanese sponsors were recruited and membership grew to exceed 100.

In co-operation with two of its main partners AIMS developed specific Awards. With ASICS, from 1992, a "Golden Shoe" was awarded annually to the most outstanding male and female runners of the year – and this award was made to a succession of the sports' household names. With Citizen, AIMS teamed up to recognise "World Fastest Times", at a time when IAAF was reticent about calling road performances "world records".

AIMS has often acted as a channel for the diffusion of ideas and innovation within the worldwide running community. One of the most important such innovations was when the ChampionChip company introduced new technology to time races. A transponder worn on the foot was activated to record time as it passed through a magnetic field generated at the timing point. Despite, or perhaps because of, the initial difficulties with the system problems were quickly rectified and ChampionChip became the timing system of choice.

Organisers could now subcontract this race function to professional timing companies and save vast amount of manpower, allowing a less cluttered finish line and consequently better exposure for race sponsors. Individual runners could be recorded as they passed over the start line as well as the finish line, allowing them to know exactly how long it took them to cover the race distance. The need to cross the start line as soon as possible after the gun was fired was reduced (although race positions still depend upon "gun time") and safety in such starts was enhanced. Timing points along the course could be used to identify those runners who had short-cut the course.

With such advantages for race organisers it was not surprising that the chip timing system spread so rapidly among the AIMS membership and ChampionChip, in becoming a sponsor of AIMS, developed a direct channel to their core market.

Also in Berlin at around the same time, the Berlin Marathon race director Horst Milde proposed the establishment of an AIMS Marathon Museum of Running. It took much longer than the chip timing system did to come to fruition, but after approval at the 9th World Congress of AIMS in Macau in 1994 the concept was pursued consistently over the years in partnership with the Berlin Sports Museum. After major reconstruction of the Berlin Olympic Stadium the AIMS Marathon Museum of Running has finally found a permanent home.

The 10th World Congress of AIMS, held in Barcelona in 1996, brought significant changes of personnel and redefined some of AIMS key functions. Andy Galloway, who had been the General Secretary since foundation, resigned his post, which was taken up by Hugh Jones. Hiroaki Chosa continued as AIMS President with several new Board members who subsequently played important roles in meeting the challenge posed by an increase in membership that by the turn of the Millennium had become something close to an influx.

Paco Borao, as Membership Director, oversaw this increase. Gordon Rogers, as Technical Director, dedicated great effort to generating a comprehensive database of course measurements, Accurate measurement has had always been a central tenet of AIMS membership, and this brought the organisation into an ever closer relationship with IAAF. At least partly as a result, in 2004 IAAF finally agreed that, subject to meeting certain criteria, road races should be able to claim official IAAF world records.

Distance Running grew to match the new size and reach of the Association. First in 2000, and then in 2004, it added new editions so that by 2005 each issue of the now quarterly publication had more pages than the old yearbook. Assisted by the advent of widespread digital photography it became produced in full colour on all pages. It also portrayed a more accurate representation of the sport of running than either AIMS or IAAF formally admitted. In belated recognition of this AIMS, at their 17th World Congress in 2007, undertook another change of name to the Association of International Marathons and Distance Races.

Alongside Distance Running the AIMS website has grown into a valuable source of information for runners and race organisers alike, and holds the potential to become an essential means of managing the Association.

Approaching the 25th anniversary of its foundation, AIMS had reason to look back at the past. In January and February 2003 the first two Presidents of the Association, Will Cloney and Chris Brasher, passed away. Sue Richardson, who had been deeply involved with AIMS from the days of Chris Brasher's presidency, died in September 2005. Even when she left employment at the London Marathon and took a position with IAAF, she still attended AIMS meetings and provided a valuable link between the two organisations. Her death left a gap in the ability of IAAF to deal with road running matters which was only filled in 2007, with the appointment of Sean Wallace Jones to the new position of IAAF Road Race Co-ordinator.

But there were also more optimistic developments. In 2006 AIMS launched a Children's series, by assisting selected member events develop children's races as part of their programme. Also in 2006 AIMS cooperated with ChampionChip to introduce an award to recognise innovation in the organisation of road races. In 2007 the inaugural AIMS Marathon Symposium was arranged to take place in the town of Marathon.

Since foundation AIMS has burgeoned to almost ten times the size that it was in 1982, counting 235 members in 85 countries and territories throughout the world. Membership fees are the largest single contributor to the AIMS budget and the Association consequently remains a member-centred organisation, existing to provide a platform from which members can better develop and promote their events, especially on an international stage. To mark the 25th anniversary of AIMS a Silver Jubilee brochure has been produced in which the story of the Association has been recorded. This can be viewed and downloaded through the AIMS website at www.aimsworldrunning.org.

Miscellaneous Marathon Facts

Most times under various limits:

Men

sub-2:06s: 3 Haile Gebrselassie, Khalid Khannouchi
sub-2:07s: 6 Gebrselassie, 4 Felix Limo, 3 Khannouchi, Sammy Korir, Evans Rutto, Paul Tergat
sub-2:08s: 8 Khannouchi, 6 Gebrselassie, Josephat Kiprono, F Limo
sub-2:09s: 11 Korir, 9 Khannouchi, 8 Abdelkader El Mouaziz
sub-2:10s: 13 Stefano Baldini, El Mouaziz, 12 Korir
sub-2:11s: 17 El Mouaziz, 15 Korir, 14 Baldini

Women

sub-2:20s: 4 Paula Radcliffe, 3 Catherine Ndereba
sub-2:21s: 5 Radcliffe
sub-2:22s: 5 Radcliffe, Ndereba
sub-2:23s: 6 Catherine Ndereba, 5 Radcliffe
sub-2:24s: 9 Ndereba, 7 Radcliffe, 6 Constantina Tomescu, Zhou Chunxiu
sub-2:25s: 10 Ndereba

Continued from page 94... Olympic Qualifying Conditions.

the qualification standards from 1 Jan 2007 (1 Sep 2006 for marathon, combined events and walks) until 23 July 2008 for individual events or until 16 July 2008 for relay events in order to be eligible to participate.

Performances achieved in mixed events between male and female participants, held completely in the stadium, will not be accepted, nor will wind-assisted performances or hand timed marks in 100m, 200m, 400m, 110mh and 400mh. Indoor performances will be accepted.

For the marathon and 50k walk, senior athletes only (aged 20 and over on 31 Dec 2008) will be accepted and Junior athletes (18 or 19 on 31 Dec 2008) may compete in any other event. Youth athletes (16 or 17 on 31 Dec 2008) may compete in any event except the throws, decathlon, 10,000m, marathon and walks. Athletes younger than 16 on 31 Dec 2008 cannot be entered in any event.

ATHLETICS BOOKS 2007/08

Reviewed by Peter Matthews

National Athletics Records for all countries in the world (2007 edition. A5 204pp. By Winfried Kramer, Fouad Habash, Heinrich Hubbeling & Yves Pinaud. This ATFS publication sets out the national records of 230 countries and territories. In general, the records listed are those supplied by National Federations but in some cases statistically reliable marks that were not recognised for bureaucratic reasons are included. The oldest record shown is Sylvio Cator's Haitian long jump record of 7.93, a world record in 1928. From Winfried Kramer, Kohlrodweg 12, 66539 Neunkirchen-Kohlhof, Germany; price 25 euro or US$35; payment in advance by cash or international money order.

All Time 1000 Performances by Giuseppe Mappa. The fourth edition of this massive work (first three editions 1987, 1998 and 2001 with Roberto Quercetani) is now published on CD rather than in printed form. It covers all men's Olympic events plus 1 mile, 3000m and half marathon and in additions to details of top marks includes an alphabetical index of athletes. Price is 30 euros inc. postage from the author at 6 Piazza della Costituzione, 50129 Firenze, Italy. Email g.mappa@winalltime.it

Leichtathletik im 19, Jahrhundert Band II, by Hubert Hamacher. 747pp. €25, including postage, from: Hans Waynberg (see DGLD address below). This is the second volume of a substantial series about world athletics in the late nineteenth century. The first spanned the years 1891-1900. This covers 1881-90, and provides a text in German that is a condensed international history of the sport from its classical origins to the period under analysis. This is followed by an event-by-event round-up of significant results, championships and a fifty-deep listing for each year.

The 1948 Olympics – How London Rescued the Games. By Bob Phillips. This is a terrific book – a highly readable account of how London was awarded the 1948 Games and succeeded in staging a vital sports extravaganza despite the severe period of austerity that Britain was undergoing in the aftermath of World War II. The author, well known to athletics enthusiasts, describes each of the events for each of the sports in most authoritative fashion, with full results of all finals and a host of anecdotes illustrating what the Games felt like as well as paying tribute to the contestants. Price £16.99. Published by SportsBooks Ltd, 1 Evelyn Court, Malvern Road, Cheltenham, GL50 2JR, UK. E-mail: randall@sportsbooks.ltd.uk

The 1908 Olympics - The First London Games by Keith Baker. PB format 178pp. Published to commemorate the centenary of the first London Olympics this is an intriguing glimpse of the Olympic scene of a century ago. Baker reminds us that the 1908 Games had been awarded by the IOC to Rome but the damage and devastation caused by the Mount Vesuvius eruption in 1906 led to the Italians withdrawing for financial reasons. There was plenty of controversy and drama. Stories include the luckless marathoner Dorando Pietri and the largely overlooked winner, Johnny Hayes together with the often bitter squabbles between the British and American teams, which came to the boil in the US-boycotted 400m. £7.99 post free (UK) + £3 postage for rest of Europe or £5 for rest of world; SportsBooks (as above).

Weltrekorde und Weltrekordler – 100m, 200m Women. A4 184pp. Manfred Holzhausen continues his series of splendidly detailed surveys (in German) of world records and world record holders. There are details of all WR races with profiles (and illustrations) of record breakers for the women's 100m and 200m; also tables of annual world bests and results of sprints at major championships. 15 euros (including postage) from Manfred Holzhausen, Dresdener Str. 4, 41516 Grevenbroich, Germany. (m.holzhausen@planet- interkom.de).

The Men's Javelin Throw – History and Statistics by Tony Isaacs. A5 76pp. **Part 2** (the first concentrated on world records, annual top tens and area champions) gives full results for the javelin at all Olympic Games and World Championships (including Juniors, Youths and Masters). **Part 3** covers Inter-continental Games and Championships such as Universiade, World Military Championships, Commonwealth, Francophone and Mediterranean Games. Each booklet £5 or 10 euros (banknotes) from Tony Isaacs, 43 St George's Road, Felixstowe, Sussex IP11 9PN, England. E-mail: tony.isaac2@tinyworld.co.uk.

Statistics Handbook – European Athletics Indoor Championships (2007). A5 536pp. Edited for the European AA by Mirko Jalava with national indoor records by György Csiki. Complete results of all European Indoor Championships from 1970 with index of all competitors and comprehensive statistical analysis by athlete/nation etc. Also 50-deep indoor all-time lists.

The European Under 23 Athletics Statistical Handbook (2007 edition). A5 212pp. European U23 Champs results. all-time lists (20-25 performances, 80-100 performers), national best performances and progressions of European bests. 20 euro (inc. postage) in cash to Roberto Camano, Via Barzilai, 11 20146 Milano, Italy or by bank transfer to bank account: Banco di Brescia - Agenzia 21 Milano. Account number: 17505. IBAN: IT95M0350001622000000017505, SWIFT CODE: BCABIT21.

Combined Events Annual 2007 by Hans van Kuijen. A5, 216pp. The 15th edition of this attractively produced annual includes top 200 men's decathlon and women's heptathlon lists for 2007 and all scores over 7500 and 5600 respectively with deep all-time world lists. Also results of major events, profiles and complete career details for 100 of the world's top multi-eventers, records etc. In Europe: 25 euro or £20 sterling cash (add £10 for cheques). Payments to bank account 52.31.27.898 of ABN-AMRO, Helmond, BIC code ABNANL2A. Outside Europe: US $45 cash or $65 cheques– from Hans van Kuijen, de Bergen 66, 5706 RZ Helmond, Netherlands. Email: hvankuijen@wxs.nl. Back numbers for 2001, 2002, 2005, 2006: 15 Euro each.

Statistic Handbook – Götzis Mehrkampfmeeting by Hans van Kuijen. A5 108pp. Contains history, highlights and all results from 1975 to 2007 from this top multi-events meeting with many stats including index of all participants. 17.50 euro (inc. postage and packing), details above.

Statistic Handbook – European Cup Combined Events by Hans van Kuijen. A5 208pp. Contains history, highlights and all results from 1973 to 2007 with overview of competing countries, and many stats including index of all participants. 25 euro (inc. postage and packing), details above.

World All-Time Lists. A4 272pp. Luis Leite has updated to 15 Dec 2007 his world lists – 500 deep for all men's and women's Olympic events with top 50 performances. He also shows the best performances using his scoring tables. Each book (men and women) 20 euro within Europe, 25 euro elsewhere or the pair for 35 euro (40 outside Europe) from Luis at Av. Alm. Gago Coutinho 154, 1700-033 Lisboa, Portugal.

TAFWA All-Time Indoor List 2008. A5 220pp. Ed Gordon's excellent annual compilation of world all-time indoor lists of performers (over 200 deep) and performances (c. 150 deep) for all events, men and women was updated to include the 2007 season. New editions appear in December each year – in book form and on CD. Contact ed@gordon007.net.

400 Metres Men – Outdoor automatic timing. By Carlos Baronet. Very deep all-time lists of more than 100 countries, including top 1000 USA, all European sub-47.00 and rankings averages. 25 euros or USD 35 (payment in advance by cash or international money order) from the author at Carrer Roca, 3; 08519 Folgueroles (Barcelona), or by e-mail: trackinsun@telefonica.net

The Book of Cross Country in Europe. A5 168pp. By Ignacio Mansilla. Coincident with the 2007 event in December this book (in Spanish and English) gives the history of the European Cross Country Championships. There are complete results of all events (from 1993) and index of all competitors. Also 1-2-3 for all International and World Champs with section of fine colour photographs.

Ignacio Mansilla has also written the 396-page **Historia del Campo a través en España**, published by the RFEA. The text is in Spanish, but there are 160 pages of detailed results of Spanish championship results with provincial champions, all Spanish results from international races and details of all the major Spanish CC races. The two books are on sale for 20 euros (plus postage 10.20 euros in Europe) from RFEA, Avda, Valladolid 81 - 1 °- 28.008 Madrid, Spain.

Prove Multiple di Atletica Leggera in Italia dalle origini al 1968 (Multi Events in Italy before 1968) by Gabriele Manfredini. 380pp. Anyone with a particular interest in Italian all-round athletes of 40 years or more ago will appreciate the huge amount of research which went into this lovingly produced large format book. It's in Italian but the names, figures and photos need no translation. Statistics include complete results of all Olympic decathlons 1912-68. Available from the author at Via Puccini 23, 56022 Castelfranco di Sotto (Pisa), Italy; 20 euro in cash.

Jack White "The Gateshead Clipper" 1837-1910, by Warren Roe. 76pp. An illustrated booklet on the life of Jack White, the famous pedestrian. £4 to UK addresses, 10 Euros banknote to Europe or 10 dollars banknote to USA from Warren Roe, 36 Ravenscourt Grove, Hornchurch, Essex RM12 6HS. E-mail: warrenroe1@yahoo.com

Stan Greenberg's Olympic Almanack 2008. 300pp. Published by SportsBooks Ltd, PO Box 422, Cheltenham GL50 2YN, UK; price £14.99. www.sportsbooksltd.uk. This is the seventh of the author's well researched books on Olympic history. It contains just about every fact that any Olympic enthusiast could possibly want to know, with athletics of course taking pride of place.

Running The Race, Eric Liddell – Olympic Champion and Missionary by John W. Keddie. Large paperback 256pp. £8.95 from by Evangelical Press, Faverdale North, Darlington, DL3 0PH, England. www.evangelicalpress.org. John Keddie is the ideal man to write this story for as he says in his introduction "Uniquely among all biographers of Eric Liddell, I believe, I approach this as an evangelical Christian who has participated in athletics and rugby at a high level, as well as being keenly involved in sporting history". Quite so, and this is a fascinating story both of Liddell's athletics (Olympic 400m gold in 1924) and rugby (playing seven times for Scotland as a wing) career and of his Christian work and faith to his premature death in a Japanese internment camp in China in 1945. The author researched Liddell's athletics career from first being inspired by Liddell as a teenager and full details are included here.

Collecting Books on Athletics and the Olympic Games: a Bibliography and History by Richard Bond. Contents include a detailed study of statistical works and the most significant Olympic books published in the English language. A limited edition of 100 copies, each numbered and signed by the author, will be available for £35 plus postage. Contact the author at 12 Lytham Close, Ashton-under-Lyne, OL6 9ER, UK or e-mail richard.bond@jlservices.co.uk

Atletismo Argentino – Ranking Permanate. A5 243pp. By Luis Vinker, Edgardo Fontana, Rubén Aguilera and Salvador Fontana. Argentina all-time lists to 31 Dec 2006 (50 performers, 10 performances, top 10 juniors). Plus profiles of top stars over the years. Published by Centro Regional de Desarrolo, Raúl Tacca 707, Planta Alta, S3000JRO Santa Fe, Argentina.

Bulgarian Athletics 1926-2006 by Aleksandar Vangelov. 240x158m 384pp. This fine book includes lists of Bulgarian champions 1926-54, then top 3s in the championships and annual lists 10-15 deep for all events each year 1955-2006. Cost 25 euros, including postage if sent by registered letter to the author at "Ilinden" Bl.1 Ap.44, 1309 Sofia, Bulgaria.

Cuba Y FL Mundo 1924-2004 by Lázaro Betancourt and Basilio Fuentes. Gives a comparison of Cuban results event by event for these 80 years. Contact basilio@inder.cu.

Seniorska Prvenstva Jugoslavije by Ljubisa Gajic. A5 194pp. Comprehensive results of all Yugoslav national championships 1920-2005 with summaries of achievements and a statistical profile of the top Yugoslav Athlete of the 20th Century for each event. Price 25 euros or $30 US, cash only, from Ljubisa Gajic, Vukasina Stefanovica 9, 35000 Jagodina, Serbia.

ANNUALS

European Athletics Yearbook 2006-07. A5 520pp. From the European Athletic Association, Avenue Louis-Ruchonnet 18, CH-1003 Lausanne, Switzerland (25 euro in Europe, 30 euro elsewhere), or see www.European-athletics.org. The book includes 100-deep European lists for 2006 (and U23, junior, indoor and 50-deep all-time lists) compiled by Mirko Jalava plus a wealth of other useful information.

L'Athlétisme Africain/African Athletics 2007. A5, 152p. By Yves Pinaud. 26th edition of this splendid book has 100 deep men's and women's lists for Africa for 2006, with all-time lists, national championships and major meetings results. 20 euro, £15 or US $30 from Polymédias, 103 rue de Paris, 46 rue des Bordeaux, 94220 Charenton-le-pont, France. (also available booklist with very extensive list of athletics books and magazines for sale).

Asian Athletics 2006 rankings. A5 96 pages. Heinrich Hubbeling does a magnificent annual job of compiling Asian statistics. Top 30s for 2006 for athletes from Asian nations, with continuation lists for countries other than China and Japan, indicating new national records, and full lists of Asian records. Euro 15/US $20 in cash or by International Money Order from the author, Haydnstrasse 8, 48691 Vreden, Germany. Copies also available for 1998, 2004 and 2005 at Euro 10/US $13 each.

Athletics Australia Handbook of Records and Results 2006. A5 324p. Comprehensive records, results and lists for 2006 with all-time lists (c. 40 deep per event) compiled by Paul Jenes. Contact Athletics Australia (athletics@athletics.org.au).

British Athletics 2007. The NUTS Annual, edited by Rob Whittingham, Peter Matthews, Tony Miller and Justin Clouder. Deep UK ranking lists for all age groups in 2006, top 12 merit rankings, all-time lists, results etc. £16 UK, £18 rest of Europe, £20 outside Europe; from Umbra Athletics Ltd, Unit 1, Bredbury Business Park, Bredbury Park Way, Stockport, SK6 2SN, England. All orders by credit card to www.umbraathletics.com worldwide post-free for £16.

Athlérama 2006. A5, 608pp. The French Annual, edited by Jean Gilbert and Patricia Doilin with a strong team of compilers, is again a superb reference book. Packed with information on French athletics – deep year lists, indexes, athlete profiles, results and all-time lists for all age groups. Extras include French top ten lists for 1956 and top marks for 1906. Also many colour photos. 25 euros from the FFA, 33 avenue Pierre de Coubertin, 75640 Paris CEDEX 13, France.

DAF i Tal 2006. A5 260 pages. The Danish athletics annual, edited by Erik Laursen, provides most comprehensive lists of records for all age groups with 2006 and all-time lists. Contact the Dansk Athletic Federation, Idrattens Hus, 2605 Brondby, Denmark or erik.laursen@privat.dk

DLV Leichtathletik Jahrbuch 2007. A5 366pp. The official yearbook of the German Federation. Directory and review, with articles on top athletes, detailed results of 2007 meetings, records and top tens, also many illustrations in colour. Euro 19.50 plus postage, from Deutsche Leichtathletik Marketing GmbH, Postfach 10 04 63, 64219 Darmstadt, Germany. See www.leichtathketik.de

DLV Leichtathletik Bestenliste 2007. A5 384pp. The DLV's ranking lists for 2007 for all events compiled by Eberhard Vollmer, generally 50-deep for seniors and Jugend-A, 30-deep for other age groups. Also German records. Euro 15 as above,

Eesti Kergejõustiku Aastaraamat 2007. 270pp. An attractively produced annual with comprehensive Estonian ranking lists indoors and out for 2006, with results and records. From the Estonian Athletic Federation, Regati pst. 1, 11911 Tallinn, Estonia.

Yleisurheilu 2007. A5 672pp. The splendid Finnish Yearbook, published by Suomen Urheiluliitto (Finnish Athletics) and compiled by Juhani and Mirko Jalava, contains not only every conceivable statistic for Finnish athletics in 2007 but also world indoor, outdoor and junior lists for the year as at November. 17 euros plus postage and packaging. Orders by e-mail to juhani@tilastopaja.fi

Israeli Athletics 2007/8 Annual. 240 x 170mm, 54pp. By David Eiger. Records, championship results, 2007 top 20s and all-time lists, with profiles of leading Israeli athletes. 7 euro or US $10 from David Eiger, 10 Ezra Hozsofer Str, Herzliya 46 371, Israel.

Latvijas Vieglatletikas Gadagramata 2008. A5 351 pp. Comprehensive coverage of Latvian athletics for 2007, including records, all-time lists, results and biographies, compiled by Andris Stagis. From the Latvian Athletic Association, Augsiela 1, Riga LV-1009, Latvia.

Scottish Athletics Yearbook 2007. A5 296p. Edited by Arnold Black for the SATS. Comprehensive review of Scottish athletics in 2006 with articles, deep Scottish lists for all age groups, event reviews and championship results, all-time lists and records and a 4-page section of colour photographs. £6 (£7.50 inc. postage in the UK, £9 elsewhere), sterling cheques only, payable to S.A.T.S. From Arnold Black, 19 Millbrae Crescent, Langside, Glasgow G42 9UW, UK.

South African Athletics Annual 2007. A5 208 pages. Edited by Riël Hauman. The 55th edition of this Annual includes 2006 and all-time lists, records and results. Also included is a South African Athletics Hall of Fame that lists all the nation's medallists at major games and championships. From SA Athletics Annual, PO Box 688, BelaBela 0480, South Africa at 70 SA Rand per copy (surface mail) and 100 SA Rand (by airmail)…or the equivalent in US Dollars, euros or Sterling. No cheques.

Anuario Athlético Español Ranking 2006/2007. At 936 pages this is surely the largest national annual ever. It has everything about Spanish athletics with immense depth of results and annual lists for 2007 as well as records, all-time lists, details of all Spanish champions, lists of Spanish international matches, biographies of current stars and details of Spanish participation at major events. Also colour photographs. 20 euros plus postage (10.20 in Europe) from the Federación Española de Atletismo (RFEA), Avda. Valladolid 81 - 1º - 28.008 Madrid SPAIN. Email: publicaciones@rfea.es.

Swiss Athletics 2006. A5 366pp. The 33rd edition of this Annual provides the usual comprehensive compilation of Swiss records, results, year and all-time top ten lists (by ATFS members Antonin Hejda and Alberto Bordoli). There are also statistical profiles of 22 top Swiss athletes. From the SLV, Industriering 43/Postfach 45, 3250 Lyss.

2007 USA Track & Field Media Guide & FAST Annual (general editors: Jill Geer & Scott Davis). A5 726pp. The first 292 pages is the USATF Media Guide with detailed profiles on top athletes and lists of all US champions from 1985 and there follows the 29th edition of the FAST Annual with 50-deep US lists for 2006 and all-time, with 12-deep junior and college all-time lists. The massive final index section includes annual progressions and championships details for top American athletes. $24 ($32 airmail) from Scott Davis, 4432 Snowbird Circle, Cerritos, CA 90703, USA.

Statistical bulletins

The **Asociación Española de Estadósticos de Atletismo** (AEEA) have celebrated their 20th birthday this year with a special publication, fully maintaining their flow of magnificent statistical publications. This book gives the full history of the association with details of all members and their meetings through the years with plenty of colour photographs. Listed are the 79 publications (with a total of 16,013 pages!) that they have produced together with several more in conjunction with the Spanish Federation (another 4499 pages). This book includes an index of these publications by author. Then there are 100-deep junior indoor lists for Spain followed by indoor lists for youths 30-50 deep per event and other articles. See their web site at www.rfea.es/estadis/aeea/entrada.htm. Membership (four bulletins per year) is 55 euros (61 euros outside Europe) from AEEA secretary Ignacio Mansilla, E-mail: imc987@terra.es

The **DGLD – German** statistical group, the Deutschen Gesellschaft für Leichtathletik-Dokumentation produces annual national ranking lists (**Deutsche Bestenliste**) for Germany and impressive bulletins of up to 268 pages, packed with historical articles and statistical compilations. Each issue (three per year) includes statistical profiles of athletes born in 70 years ago, 75, 80, 85, 90 etc. Membership, with free Deutsche Bestenliste – euro 55 per year. Contact Hans Waynberg, Grefrather Weg 100, 41464 Neuss/Rh, Germany. Website: www.leichtathletik-dgld.de

No. 47 included three top names aged 70 in 2007 – Klaus Grogorenz and the walkers Dieter Lindner and Gerhard Sperling. The series giving full details of progressive German indoor bests continued with the men's walks events, and there was an extensive section giving progressive records 1898-2006 followed by year lists for 1948 and 1949 for Saxony (a continuing series). There were also interviews with Manfred Matuschewski and Helga Hoffmann.

No. 48 detailed progressive German men's indoor high jump bests, a complete survey of German performances in the European Junior Championships 1964-2005, and progressive German seniors records (M30 to M80) for various events.

No. 49 included progressive German indoor records for men's pole vault, results of 85 years of German women's javelin championships 1922-2006, progressive GDR indoor records for all events and outdoors for non-standard events and more progressive German seniors records.

The DGLD is also publishing a series of books dealing with the history of 100 years of athletics in Germany, event-by-event – **100 Jahre Leichtathletik in Deutschland**. The latest to be published are (obtainable from Hans Waynberg. above):

Marathonlauf Teil III - Frauen by Dr Karl Lennartz (price euro 30).

Band 10 – 400m-Hürdenlauf (also with 200mh) by Harry Themel (price euro 15).

Editions covering men's Marathon, HJ, SP, 110mh, 800m, 1500m, 5000m and women's Walks are still available (DT, men's walks sold out).

TRACK STATS. The NUTS quarterly bulletin, edited by Bob Phillips, includes a wealth of fascinating statistics and articles. A5, 68-80 pages. Annual subscription (4 issues) is £17 (UK), £21 (rest of Europe) or £26 (elsewhere); contact Liz Sissons, 9 Fairoak Lane, Chessington, Surrey KT9 2NS, UK.

For instance the **November 2007 issue** included interviews with Alastair McCorquodale and Jack Emery by David Thurlow; the British athletics scene in 1937; the forgotten English Championships of the 1920s by Richard Bond; and a review by Peter Lovesey of a new book on "Deerfoot" (Louis Bennett).

In 2008 there will be a special edition of Track Stats to commemorate the 50th Anniversary of the founding of the NUTS. This will include a detailed statistical survey of British athletics 1958-2007 with many feature articles.

Track Stats Historical Series: the NUTS event booklets (series editor Peter Matthews) – giving great historical coverage of British athletics. Progressive UK records (senior and U20), indoors and out, age bests, very deep UK performer and performance all-time lists, best performances for each decade and yearly bests from 1827, results of all British and English internationals, all British performances at major international championships, national and area champions, and biographies of leading athletes. Price for each booklet inc. postage: £5 in UK, $8 or 8 euro in cash in sterling or Money Orders from outside Britain from Dave Terry, 34 Windmill Hill, Ruislip, Middlesex HA4 8PX, UK.
(Email mdterry@dial.pipex.com). The most recent is: **No. 12 Pole Vault** (men and women) by Ian Tempest. A5, 73pp The first record mark (3.15m) dates back to 1849 and the author documents the event's evolution to the end of 2007. Of particular fascination is the period in the 1880s when the leading performers, drawn from the English Lake District, were pole climbers. UK all-time performers are listed to 4.42m for men and 3.13m for women, with performances to 5.30 and 3.90 respectively.

IAAF Handbooks

Contact the IAAF for their extensive list of publications and videos for sale at 17 rue Princesse Florestine, BP 359, MC 98007, Monaco. Prices (by Visa, Master Card or eurocard) include postage by airmail. Email to: headquarters@iaaf.org. Payment by credit card (Visa, Mastercard or eurocard only), quoting name on card, number of card, expiry date, name and address and signature.

IAAF Statistics Handbook, Osaka 2007. A5 654pp. Another superb work by Mark Butler, this book includes comprehensive statistics, including full results for all IAAF World Championships 1983-2005 plus medallists from major championships, world record progressions, national records, all-time lists and biographical profiles. $20.

Also available are the statistics handbooks published in 2006 for World Indoors, World Juniors and World Cup and there will be a **World Indoor Championships – Valencia 2008 Statistics** handbook.

IAAF Directory and Calendar 2008. A5, 278 pages. Essential reference with contact details for officials, organisations and national federations, plus calendar and lists of records and champions. $16.

Progression of IAAF World Records (2007 edition). A5 546pp. This is the 6th edition of this great work initiated by the late Ekkehard zur Megede and maintained to the 2003 edition by Richard Hymans. It has now been updated in house by the IAAF technical manager Imre Matrahazi, and contains additions to June 2007. Comprehensive details are given for performances dating back as far as 1827 as the marks are fleshed out with such additional information as intermediate times, field event series and the complete result.

This edition includes world records for road events, officially recognised by the IAAF from 1 January 2003. There is an index of all the record breakers with dates of birth and height and weight where available. The new method of production had unfortunately meant that corrections and additions from research by statisticians into old records have not been included. Price $32.

Polymédias, 103 rue de Paris, 94220 Charenton le Pont, France, has a very extensive catalogue of sports books and magazines **la mémoire du sport** including rare historical items available at www.polymedias.fr.

Umbra Athletics have invaluable books for the statistician. List from Unit 1, Bredbury Business Park, Bredbury Park Way, Stockport, SK6 2SN, England (email: julie@umbra.co.uk). These include books that Rob Whittingham (Treasurer) holds for the ATFS. Includes: IAAF Statistics Handbooks, some ATFS Annuals. Also: National Athletics records – various editions 1975-98, Race Walking World Statistics (many in the 1980s), British Athletics Annuals 1990-2008, and other national publications. ATFS Track & Field Performances Through The Years Volumes 2, 3 and 4 (£20 each).

Scottie. By Norman Harris. Last Side Publishing Ltd. A format paperback 172pp. Norman Harris makes a belated return to athletics writing (previous books include **The Legend of Lovelock** and **The Lonely Breed**) with the story of Neville Scott, the New Zealander who was seventh in the 1956 Olympic 1500 metres final. From that high point his life descended into alcoholism and self-destruction. This is the story of his reconstruction. NZ and Australian readers should contact www.scottiethebook.com. The rest of the world can buy it for £10 from www.sportsbooks.ltd.uk

ATFS annuals. SportsBooks has some copies of past ATFS annuals. They are from 1992, 1995, 1995, 1997, 1998, 1999, 2000, 2001, 2002, 2003, 2004, 2005, 2006, 2007. Contact SportsBooks 1 Evelyn Court, Malvern Road, Cheltenham, GL50 2JR, UK or www.sportsbooks.ltd.uk

Amendments to ATHLETICS 2007

p.11 **Diary:** Millrose Games on 3 Feb
p.19 Helsinki GP on 26 Jul
p.34 100m rankings – next is Campbell not Williams
p.49 **European Cross-Country**. Men: Fernando Silva was disqualified from his 2nd place. Move 3-15 up a place and add 15. José Manuel Martínez ESP 28:32. Men's team amend: 2. ESP 44, 3. POR 49
p.55 8 Oct marathon at Köln
p.74 **World Junior Champs 2006** : 3000mSt: dq (2) Taher (over-age) the rest up a place.
p.81 **Central American & Caribbean Games 2006**: SP: Damien Scott dq. so: 1. Paumier, 2. do Proenza. 3. Yojer Medina COL 17.94
p.85 South American Ch 400mh: 2. Montenegro 50.16
p.86 Balkan Champs in Bosnia & Herzegovina; European Cup 10,000m: women – Abeylegesse 30:21.67
p.88 World Athletics Final held at Stuttgart (not Monaco). Men 100m (+0.9); LJ: 5 Pate 8.26/0.2
p.93 3rd line from foot: Bamaka MLI
p.95 World Champs. Ellina Zvereva was oldest ever world champion at 40y 268d as she was elevated from 2nd to 1st in 2001 discus on disqualification of Natalya Sadova.
p.97 **Obituary**: Brouwer b. 29 Oct 1930
p.98 Frenn 7th 1975 Pan-Ams.
p.100 Kepp-Ojastu (Estonia). Lipp b. 21 Jun 1922 Verner Ljunggren – brother John silver at 1950 EC
p.101 Maffei won 1938 EC with pb 7.607
p.102 Mart Paama
p.103 Rogers also won AAU HJ 1936. pb 1.587 (1936)
p.105 Tóth. 10th at 1971 EC (not 27 in 1972).
p.107 Kiszka 100m 10.5 not 10.50
p.108 Willye B. WHITE (USA) (b. 1 Jan 1939 Money, Mississippi) on 6 February 2007 in Evanston, Illinois. First US athlete to compete at five OG… OG from 1960 to 1972. 60y 6.8i (1968).
p.119 **Farewell**: Jan Zelezny won three Olympic and three World titles (not four European!)
p.128 Jenner WR 8634 on current tables; pbs 1500m 4:12.61, JT 69.48 (1972); O'Brien JT 66.90 (1996)
p.181 Irish Champs W DT: Katewicz POL
p.203 Lornah Kiplagat b.1.5.74
p.233 TRI 200m champion 2006: Armstrong 20.65
p.235 UKR HJ champion 2006: Myhalchenko 1.95
Corrections to **Records** shown in current section.
p.338 Women's Hammer all-time: 31/10) to 75.18, adjust other totals
p.595 First IAAF women's hammer record 23 Feb 94
p.607 **European Indoor Champs 2007**: W HJ: dq (3) Veneva, so move up from there, 3. Beitia etc.
p.608 **World Cross-Country 2007**: Senior Men: add 7. Tadesse Tola ETH and move rest down a place. Adjust team scores: 1. KEN 29, 2. MAR 152, 3. UGA 191, 4. ERI 209, 5. QAT 244, 6. TAN 315, 7. RWA 360, 8. GBR 383, 9. AUS 416, 10. POR 526

2006 World Lists

General note - due to a fault in publishing, accented capital letters in my files have been missed out – accents on Évora, Épinal, Århus etc.
100m: 10.32 Becerra 14.11.85; 10.24w Phiri ZAM not GBR, 10.31w Witherspoon 5.6.85
200m: 20.73 Breland 16.4.84; wa: add 20.75 Amr Ibrahim Seoud EGY 10.6.86 25 Aug
400m: 45.35 Wroe at Canberra
800m: 1:45.27 Belal Mansoor Ali (& 1500m 3:34.30, 1M 3:56.18), 1:47.41 Arturo Casado, 1:47.62 Neunhäuserer, add: 1:47.7A Alex Sang KEN .83 30 Jun
1500m: add: 3:40.3A Jonathan Komen KEN 4.2.82 15 Jun; Jnr: 3:41.35 El Kaam MAR, 3:42.1A Josephat Kithii KEN-Y .90 6 NC Nairobi 29 Jun, 3:42.2A Lalang
2000m: 5:01.8+ Kenenisa Bekele ETH 13.6.82 & 5:02.1+ Augustine Choge KEN-J 21.1.87 25 Aug, 5:02.8+ Yusuf Biwott KEN 12.11.86 11 Jul
3000m: Jnr: 7:57.78 Fekadu 13.3.88
2M: 8:26.96 Patrick Kimeli 22.4.89 (& 3000mSt 8:37.4A)
5000m: 13:07.47 Moses Kigen 10.1.83 (& 10km 28:24, HMar 61:17), 13:17.57 Chepkok 5.7.88 (& 10000m 28:23.46), 13:18.24 Muge .83, 13:22.15 Jawher BRN, add 13:36.7A F.Lebo KEN 30 Jun, 13:41.4 Moussati 15.12.79; Jnrs: add 13:42.7A Simon Gichuki KEN .87 4 NC-J Nairobi 22 Jul, 13:43.0 Gitawo 3.1.88
15km/HMar: 43:42/62:23 James Rotich 22.12.78
10M: 45:15+ Cheruiyot .82
20km: add 56:41 Kipchumba 2 WCh Debrecen 8 Oct
HMar: add 61:45 Peter Kiprotich KEN 27.2.79 1 Glasgow 3 Sep (178/55, 61:49- 03), 61:56 Chebii 3 San Jose 8 Oct (from 61:57), 62:16 Kirui 4.4.78 (& 10k 28:35), 62:35 Abdelkébir Lamaâchi MAR 30 Apr
Mar: 2:10:09 Makori 15 Oct, 2:10:17A Hosea Rotich 2.10.79
100km: 6:59:40 Crowther 17.5.73
3000mSt: 8:15.21 Ngetich b. 20.1.81 (& 2000mSt 5:31.14), 8:37.4 Patrick Lagat Kimeli 22.4.89; Jnrs: 8:42.8A Hezekyas Siasy ETH 5.12.88 1 Addis Ababa 16 Apr (8:43.4)
110mh: 13.73 Castelo Branco is family name b. 6.11.79, 13.81A Brown 29.11.84, 13.84/13.66w Cotto 8.8.84, 13.86 Traoré 26.4.85, 13.82w Thornton 3.1.85 (& 400mh 49.62)
200 Metres Hurdles (heading missing on p.401)
400mh: 50.16 Montenegro 6.10.81
HJ: Rybakov at WI: 2.22, 2.26, 2.30, 2.33 all /1; 2.36i Tereshin 2.30/1, Thörnblad at WI 2.18, 2.22, 2.26, 2.30 all /1; 2.30 Zhang Shufeng 24.11.84, 2.21 Darvin Edwards
PV: 5.81 Mesnil 13.6.77, 5.62i Jeremy Scott 21.5.81, 5.50Ai Ryland & Johnson, 5.45i Gripich 21.9.86. Exhibition: 5.50 Piantella at Pordenone
LJ: 8.08i/8.05 Évora, 7.86 Reeves 20.9.81, 7.81w Tennell 11.9.87, Jnrs: Crowther 7.88 1.2; 7.82 Janmanee at NC, 7.75 Su Xiongfeng 21.3.87 (not Y), delete 7.74 Jin Zutao (b. 1983)
TJ: 17.23 Évora, 16.25/16.55w Rhoulac 13.12.83, doubtful 16.62 Dagen 30.9.78; Jnrs: delete 16.07 Jin Zutao
SP: Hoffa 21.65i at Mill, 19.41 Caulfield Q; best out: Dorian Scott # 20.34dq, so best 20.33 1 NC Kingston 24 Jun
DT: 66.31 Pestano 2 but 1 NC
HT: Devyatovskiy 81.95 & Vorontsov 80.51 6 Jul; 78.62 Krivitskiy add NC, 71.99 Delli Carri at Benevento
JT: 77.27 Kozlov 20.4.85. 76.96 Alexon Maximiano Porto Alegre 16 Sep (from 74.76) (170/72, 75.84- 05), add 76.82A Tommie du Toit RSA 17.8.82 1 Potchefstroom 1 Dec (72.16A- 05); 100th 76.01
Jnr Dec: 7348 Itani JT 55.38
4x100m: 38.94 GER (Kosenkow); add hand timed: 40.2A KEN (Armed Forces) 29 Jun
10000mW: delete 39:51.02 Trofimov
20kmW: 1:19:27 Burayev 23.8.82
100km: Scanzoresciate (also women 50km - see p.122)

Women

100m: hand/Junior: add 11.3 Sergien Kouanga CMR-J 4.8.89 1 Yaoundé 29 Jul
200m: 23.39 Huang Huijiang 22.4.90 (& Juniors)
400m: 50.78 Danijela Grgic , 52.18 Chen Jingwen 8.2.90
800m: Jepkosgei (twice), 2:02.24 Green 10.8.82

1500m: 4:14.69 He Pan 1.5.88 (not -Y), 4:15.43 Jepkosgei
3000m: 15/11 under 8:40, numbering wrong from there
5000m: 15:33.53 Grechshnikova 12.12.83, 15:39.46 Song Xiaoxue 13.2.87 (not -Y, also in 10000m 33:29.60, HMar 71:27)
5000m/10000m: Lornah Kiplagat b.1.5.74!
10km: (23/16) to 31:34, 32:43 Bor 26.12.79
15km: 47:10+ Tomescu 8 Oct
HMar: 71:30 Chepchirchir 1.12.81, 72:47 Emmah Kariuki 4.1.81
Mar: 2:27:57 Magarsa Askale Tafa 27.9.84
3000mSt: 10:10.11 Achamo 14.12.87 (so add to Juniors) 1 Bilbao 1 Jul, 10:19.16 Chepkoech .84; numbering 1 out from (60), 100th 10:06.34
60mh: (16/9/) to 7.88 (delete JAM for Golding-Clarke 2nd mark at 7.87) and adjust counts
100mh: 13.14/13.10w Ohanaja 6.12.85
400mh: 57.79 Onyemuwa 28 Jul (from 57.93)
HJ: Vlasic at WI 1.84, 1.91, 1.96 all /1; add 1.86i Olena Holosha UKR 26.1.82 22 Feb; Best out: 1.90 Styopina 7=, Mendia 5=, Kuptsova 4=
PV: Rogowska at WI: 4.40/1, 4.55/1; 4.45 Zhang Yingning 2.1.90 (world U18 record), 4.32I & 4.20i at Épinal, 4.24 twice on 13 May; move numbering from 60 to 100 down one place, 192 listed
LJ: delete 6.49 Tobin-West¶ (2-year drugs dq)
SP: 19.64i Kleinert on 12 Mar, Lammert at Ueckermünde, (29/7) to 19.39, 17.92 Gong 24.1.89
DT: Pishchalnikova 64.24 ECp-S, add 55.06 Monia Kari TUN 14.4.71 1 May; Jnrs: 53.18 Jin Yuanyuan 24.1.90
HT: 71.67 Klaas 6.2.84, 65.53 Anita Wlodarczyk 1 Wolstyn 1 Oct (from 63.28). 100th best 63.86. add 62.58 Mariya Bespalova RUS 21.5.86 23 Apr
JT: Scherwin 64.08, & 62.44 & 60.41 marks at Århus
Hep: 6021w Zemaityte, 5930 Émilie Boulleret
4x100m: Jnrs 44.18 JAM - Calvert, Sutherland, Leroy, ?
4x400m: 3:39.6A KEN (Prisons) 1 Jul (see at 3:39.79)
3000mW: 12:23.58 Plätzer 1
5000mW: 20:42.01 Kaniskina 10 Jun
10kmW: 45:03+ Bai Yanmin (& 20km 1:30:41), 45:04 Chai Xue 21.10.88 (& 20km 1:32:07) and 3 (not in 20k), best track: 44:44.5 Milusauskaite
20kmW: 1:36:01 Li Li 18.6.87 (& 50000mW 22:07.31), 1:39:18 Zhou Tongjie CHN-Y 8.4.91

World Indoor Lists 2007

Men: 60m: delete 6.60 Farmer; **PV**: 5.70 Mesnil 13.6.77, 5.65 Gripich 21.9.86
Women: 300m: 36.99 drugs dq Stabolova ¶; **60mh:** Feb 2 New York Mill - at New York (MSG) not (A); **HJ**: 2.02 drugs dq Veneva ¶ - best pre positive test 1.96 1 Hustopece 20 Jan; 1.93 Hartmann 8q, 1.92 Yekaterina Yevseyeva KAZ-J 22.6.88 3 Mar; **PV**: 4.27 Tavares POR; **SP**: 19.29 Kleinert

Amendments to Previous World Lists

1956: TJ: 16.26w +4.0 Einarsson - 15.83 1 Karlstad 6 Oct
1964: 220y Straight: 20.9 not 20.1 Bruce Airheart
1986: SP: 19.86i John Smith 1 Charleston 21 Feb (from 19.72i)
1994: The men's 20,000m and women's 10,000m walks, held on 7 April were track events, and the winning performances were both world records. It was erroneously assumed at the time that these two events were held on the road (as were the 10 Apr 1994 men's 50km and women's 20km) and the times published as such in ATHLETICS 1995.
20,000mW track: 1. Bo Lingtang 1:18:03.3 WR, 2. Tan Mingjun 1:18:45.2, 3. Chen Shaoguo 1:19:15.7, 4. Li Mingcai 1:20:01.1, 5. Zhou Yongsheng 1:20:06.0, 6. Tian Niantang 1:20:59.1, 7. Jiao Baozhong 1:21:24.9, 8. Hao Huanquan 23.12.74 1:21:25.8, 9. Gao Yunbin 1:21:26.9, 10. Wang Lifeng .3.74 1:21:37.0, 11. Liu Haiming J-11.5.76 1:21:59.6 (from 1:24:55.8), 12. Yang Jun 1:22:16.2, 13. Mao Xinyuan 2.7.71 1:22:35.0 (from 1:24:57.0), 14. Shen Weihui 25.5.73 1:23:04.0, 15. Wang Shangjun 1:23:18.0, 16. Wang Yinghang J-15.2.77 1:23:18.2, 17. Cui Qiangnian 1:23:34.7. 18. Xi Shaohui 1:23:51.7, 19. Yang Yongjian 28.4.73 1:24:15.0, 20. Zang Jianbo 1:24:33.0. 100th best 1:24:18
50kmW (10 Apr): 10. Fu Youliang 4:02:03, 11. Zang Jungbo 4:02:46, 12. Liu Yunfeng 4:03:27, 13. Wang Aiguo 4:03:59, 14. Wang Shangjun 4:05:10, 15. Li Zhiqiang 4:06:56, 16. Hu Zhenrong 4:07:20, 17. Yu Guohui 4:08:42, 18. Xi Shaohui 4:08:57. 100th best 4:05:48.
Women 10,000mW track: (notes times of first 9 correctly shown in index) 1. Gao Hongmiao 41:37.9 WR, 2. Gu Yan 42:19.2, 3. Liu Hongyu 42:48.5, 4. Li Chunxiu 43:00.3, 5. Kong Yan 43:02.3, 6. Zhang Qinghua 43:25.2, 7. Li Jingxue 43:40.3, 8. Feng Haixia 44:00.0, 9. Wei Linkun 44:25.0, 10. Tong Lijun 44:52.0, 11. Tang Yinghua 10.2.73 45:25.8, 12. Li Hong 45:30.0, 13. Wang Jinli 45:46.6, 14. Wang Liping J-8.7.76 45:54.3, 15. Yuan Yufang 45:58.1, 16. Song Lijuan 46:05.4 (best track time), 18. Pan Hailian J-4.11.77 46:17.1, 19. Niu Hongyan 46:25.8.
20kmW: add date of 10 Apr and NC to seven entries for Beijing in April, Note Feng Haixia b. 23.2.75, Sun Chunfang 1.3.77, add 1:38:12 Pan Hainlian 4.11.77 8
1997: SP 19.57i Andrey Mikhenevich at Minsk 9 Jan
2002: LJ: 8.03 Jin Zutao 4.12.83 (not 9.1.87, so not world age-15 best)
2003: 3000m 7:45.59, 5000m 13:19.29, 10km 27:48 Moses Kigen 10.1.83; Women: HJ: 1.88 Olena Motok UKR 16.1.82 2 Berdichev 8 Sep (different athlete from Kholosha 1.90)
2004: 10km 27:54, HMar 61:38 Moses Kigen 10.1.83; W 200m: 22.05 0.8 Campbell.
2005: 3000m: 7:53.12 Kimeli 22.4.89, 5000m 13:25.55, HMar 61:39 Moses Kigen 10.1.83; PV: 5.50 Randall Flach 25.12.82; SP: 19.48 Conrad Woolsey (178/124) 1 Columbia 1 Aug (from 19.41).

2004 NCAA Champs: Tyson Gay has been stripped of his NCAA 100m title (10.06), which goes to Michael Frater JAM (10.06) as a result of the annulment of the University of Arkansas' team victories in 2004 and 2005.
2005 World Youth Champs: 2000mSt: Tareq Mubarak Taher BRN stripped of gold after being found to be over-age. So revised to: 1. Abel Kiprop KEN, 2. Bisluke Kiplagat KEN, 3. Abdelghani Aït Bahmad MAR 5:26.52.
2005 Asian Champs: DT: dq (3) Anil Kumar, so 3rd Abbas Samimi IRI 59.08
2006 World Cross-Country: Junior team: 5. QAT 83, 6. BRN 101 (after Taher (19th) dq.

The IAAF Council determined that **Marion Jones** should lose all her results from 1 Sep 2000. All-time lists in this Annual have been accordingly adjusted. This has huge repercussions on major event results as Jones loses: OG: '00- 1/3R (1, 3 LJ, 1 4x400), '04- (5 LJ); WCh: '01- 2/dq1R (1); WCp: '02- 1/2R; GP 100m 2000, 2002; overall GP 2002. And those relay race results are also annulled. She also loses her title of IAF Athlete of the Year for 2000. Thus, for instance, Debbie Ferguson becomes World champion for 200m 2001 and Grand Prix champion at 100m 2002.

With thanks to Gerald Borman, José Maria García, Norbert Heinrich, Heinrich Hubbeling, Richard Hymans, Mirko Jalava, Galder Orobengoa, Ireneusz Pawlik, Yves Pinaud. Miguel Villaseñor

HALL OF FAME 2008

EACH YEAR WE add five new athletes to our Hall of Fame – a mix of past and current stars, taking special consideration of athletes who have just retired. Any current stars can only be included if they have already had at least ten years in international competition.

Of those who died during 2007, Parry O'Brien and All Oerter were already included in our Hall of Fame, but we have included one great man who sadly passed away during the past year – Herb McKenley.

Inclusion of the following five athletes brings the total so far recognised to 61. Nominations for additions are welcomed by the Editor.

Bob HAYES (USA) (b. 20 Dec 1942 Jacksonville, Florida, d. 18 Sep 2002 Jacksonville).

The Olympic 100m champion of 1964 in a world record equalling time of 10.0 (10.06 automatic timing), Robert Lee Hayes won with awesome power by a clear two metres margin. He won a second gold medal when he anchored the US sprint relay team to a world record. He had run the first automatically timed sub-10 second time with 9.91 in the semi-final, but the wind, at 5.3m/s, was well over the permitted limit. In April 1963 at Walnut, California he ran the first ever sub-10 second 100 metres on hand timing with 9.9, but that too was aided by wind assistance of 5m/s.

His first world record had been an unratified 9.3 for 100 yards in 1961, and after 9.2 in 1962 he became the first to run 9.1 with a world record at St Louis on 21 Jun 1963 to take the AAU title. He was also the first to break 6 seconds for 60 yards indoors when he won the AAU title on 22 Feb 1964 in 5.9 (5.99 automatic timing) after tying the record of 6.0 six times in the preceding five weeks, and in 1963 he unofficially equalled the world 220y turn record of 20.5. He won the AAU 100y or 100m title each year 1962-4 and while at Florida A & M won the NCAA 200m in 1964.

Having played football at Florida A & M he turned professional for the Dallas Cowboys as a wide receiver and was twice chosen All-Pro. He had a sensational rookie season with 46 pass receptions for 1003 yards and an average of 21.8 yards per carry and played with Dallas for ten years and then one year with the San Francisco 49ers. When the Cowboys won the Super Bowl in 1971, Hayes became the first and only athlete ever to win an Olympic gold medal and a Super Bowl ring. He ran into trouble with the law and served a two-year jail sentence for drugs possession and dealing.

Stefka KOSTADINOVA BUL (b. 25 Mar 1965 Plovdiv. Later Petrova).

Kostadinova, 1.80m tall, still holds the world record for the high jump at 2.09 set when she won the World title in Rome in 1987, following earlier records at 2.07 and 2.08m in 1986. She won the World Cup in 1985, the European Cup in 1985 and 1987 and the European title in 1986, adding the Olympic silver medal in 1988. She was 6th in the 1991 World Championships, but returned to consistent 2 metre-plus jumping in 1992, although she disappointed with only 1.94 for 4th in the Olympics. She was back at the top with the World title in 1995 and the Olympic title at her third attempt in 1996.

Indoors she set three world bests in 1987-8 (2.04m to 2.06m), was European Indoor champion in 1985, 1987, 1988 and 1994 and won a record five World Indoor titles in 1985, 1987, 1989, 1993 and 1997. She retired at the end of that year after two operations on her left foot, having jumped two metres or higher in 130 competitions indoors or out from her first at the age of 19 in 1984, far ahead of any rival, with 21 of the 26 all-time performances at 2.05m or more to that time.

She married her coach Nikolai Petrov on 6 Nov 1989. In 1999 she became a vice-president of the Bulgarian Federation and in 2000 was elected Deputy Minister of the newly established Bulgarian Agency for Youth & Sport. She now chairs the Bulgarian Olympic Committee.

Herb McKENLEY JAM. See Obituary.

Iván PEDROSO CUB (b. 17 Dec 1972 Ciudad Habana).

From the retirement of Carl Lewis and Mike Powell, Iván Lázaro Pedroso Soler, who won an extraordinary nine world titles, was clearly the world's top long jumper for several years. He won World Indoor gold at each of the five championships from 1993 to 2001, thus emulating Stefka Kostadinova's record number of wins at any event, and outdoors, after not registering a jump in the 1993 final, won in 1995, 1997, 1999 and 2001. He was at his peak when he was clearly the world top long jumper in 1995 – he had a narrow foul at 9.03m at the Pan-American Games and jumped 8.96 at Sestriere. This was shown to have a wind of just 1.2 m/s, but allegations were made of interference by an official standing in front of the gauge and the mark was not recognised. He was unbeaten in 26 LJ competitions 1995 to January 1996, but hamstring surgery meant that he was not fully fit at the Olympics and he was 12th (after 4th in 1992). He was back at the top in 1997, and won 84/99 competitions from 1997 to 2001. Time after time he showed the priceless ability to respond to competition and to produce his best jump in the last round, as he did in Sydney 2000 when he responded to Jai Taurima's 8.49m with 8.55m.

He set three Cuban and Central American records to 8.71m in 1995. TJ best 16.05 (1991).

Other championships: World Juniors: 4th 1990; World Cup: 1st 1992 and 1998, 2nd 2002; World University Games: 1st 1997; Pan-American Games: 3rd 1991, 1st 1995, 1999 and 2003, 4th 2007; CAC Games: 1st 1998, 2nd 2006. He won the IAAF Grand Prix in 1995, 1997 and 1999 and the Goodwill Games 1998 and 2001. Keeping going, he was 7th at the Olympics in 2004, but did not qualify for the final at the 2005 Worlds. 2007 was his 17th successive year long jumping 8.15 or more.

Derartu TULU ETH (b. 21 Mar 1972 Bejoki, Arusi province). Tulu was a double Olympic champion, three times world cross-country champion and set Ethiopian records from 1500m to the half marathon, including three African records at 10,000m. In 1992 she became the first black African woman to win an Olympic gold medal when she set an African record 31:06.02 to win the 10,000m in Barcelona. She waited for the runner-up, Elana Meyer of South Africa, at the finish line, before the two of them went on a lap of honour, symbolizing hope for the new Africa with South Africa's return to international sport.

Tulu, a most elegant runner, had been World Junior champion at 10,000m in 1990, 2nd in the World Cross-country in 1991 and African champion at both 3000m and 10,000m in 1990 and 1992, when she went through the year undefeated on the track, adding also World Cup success at both those events. She missed most of 1993 season through injury and did not return to top form until 1995, when she won the World Cross-country title and was second in the World 10,000m. She was 4th in the World Cross and the Olympic 10,000m in 1996 before regaining her World CC title in 1997.

She married decathlete Zewde Deboba in 1988 and gave birth to a daughter Tsion in 1998. She returned to road racing in 1999 and showed that she was back at the top in 2000 with the world CC title and Olympic 10,000m, when she smashed the African record with a brilliant 30:17.49, compared to her previous best of 30:56.4. In 2001 she won the World title and at the Goodwill Games over 10,000m.

She made her marathon debut with fifth place in Boston in 1997 in a time of 2:30:28. Feeling her way at this distance she was 6th London (2:26:09) and 3rd Tokyo (2:26:38) in 2000 before beating a top-class field in London 2001 in 2:23:57. Later in the year she won in Tokyo in 2:25:08. In 2004 she was third in the Olympic 10,000m, and in 2005 fourth in the World marathon in a personal best 2:23:30 and the winner of the Great North Run in 67:33.

Other best times: 1500m 4:12.08 (1992), 3000m 8:46.32 (2000), 5000m 14:44.22 (2003), Half marathon 67:03 (2001).

Previous Hall of Fame inductees

Men: Bob Beamon USA, Abebe Bikila ETH, Valeriy Brumel RUS, Sergey Bubka UKR, Ron Clarke AUS, Sebastian Coe GBR, Jonathan Edwards GBR, Hicham El-Guerrouj MAR, Herb Elliott AUS, Haile Gebrselassie ETH, Vladimir Golubnichiy RUS, Gunder Hägg SWE, Rudolf Harbig GER, Colin Jackson GBR, Bruce Jenner USA, Michael Johnson USA, Rafer Johnson USA, Kip Keino KEN, Wilson Kipketer DEN, Robert Korzeniowski POL, Carl Lewis USA, Bob Mathias USA, Noureddine Morceli ALG, Edwin Moses USA, Paavo Nurmi FIN, Dan O'Brien USA, Parry O'Brien USA, Al Oerter USA, Jesse Owens USA, Viktor Saneyev RUS, Yuriy Sedykh RUS, Peter Snell NZL, Daley Thompson GBR, Lasse Viren FIN, Cornelius Warmerdam USA, Emil Zátopek CZE, Jan Zelezny CZE.

Women: Iolanda Balas ROM, Fanny Blankers-Koen NED, Nadezhda Chizhova RUS, Gail Devers USA, Heike Drechsler GER, Ruth Fuchs GDR, Florence Griffith-Joyner USA, Jackie Joyner-Kersee USA, Tatyana Kazankina RUS, Marita Koch GDR, Ingrid Kristiansen NOR, Faina Melnik RUS, Maria Mutola MOZ, Ramona Neubert GDR, Merlene Ottey JAM/SLO, Paula Radcliffe GBR, Gabriela Szabo ROM, Irena Szewinska POL, Grete Waitz NOR.

Women's 2m High Jumping

As mentioned on the previous page Stefka Kostadinova dominated women's high jumping in her era. Now Blanka Vlasic is challenging her world record. This table shows the number of competitions by the top women at 2.00m or better and at 2.05m or better to March 2008.

Name	*2.00+*	*2.05+*	*Years*
Stefka Kostadinova	130	21	1984-97
Kajsa Bergqvist	52	4	2000-07
Blanka Vlasic	45	5	2003-08
Heike Henkel	45	2	1989-93
Inga Babakova	43	1	1991-2003
Yelena Slesarenko	26	1	2004-08
Hestrie Cloete	24	2	1999-2004
Alina Astafei	20	-	1988-96
Anna Chicherova	16		2002-07
Tamara Bykova	15	1	1983-9
Venelina Veneva	15+1dq	-	1998-2007

Also 5 or more: Silvia Costa & Marina Kuptsova 9, Yelena Yelesina & Vita Palamar 8, Louise Ritter & Tatyana Motkova 7, Tia Hellebaut 6 (1), Monica Iagar 6, Lyudmila Andonova 5 (1), Ulrike Meyfarth & Chaunte Howard 5

Al Oerter, who died in October last year, on his way to his first Olympic gold in Melbourne in 1956. (Photograph courtesy of Track & Field News)

Deratu Tulu tracks Elana Meyer on her way to victory in the Barcelona Olympic 10,000m

Meseret Defar, the female athlete of the year, beats Vivian Cheruiyot in the Osaka World Championships 5000m

Allyson Felix, World 200m champion.

Reese Hoffa

Bernard Lagat wins the World Championships 1500m. Later he was to add the 5000m title.

(Top) Gerd Kanter the World discus champion.
(Below) World high jump champion Blanka Vlasic.

(Top) Valerie Vili, World shot champion.
(Below) Lornah Kiplagat – after her 2007 World Half Marathon victory in a world record time.

NATIONAL CHAMPIONS 2007 and BIOGRAPHIES OF LEADING ATHLETES

By Peter Matthews

THIS SECTION incorporates biographical profiles of 784 of the world's top athletes, 414 men and 370 women, listed by nation. Also listed are national champions at standard events in 2007 for the leading countries prominent in athletics (for which I have such details).

The athletes profiled have, as usual, changed quite considerably from the previous year, not only that all entries have been updated, but also that many newcomers have been included to replace those who have retired or faded a little from the spotlight. The choice of who to include is always invidious, but I have concentrated on those who are currently in the world's top 10-15 per event, those who have the best championship records and some up-and-coming athletes who I consider may make notable impact during the coming year.

Since this section was introduced in the 1985 Annual, biographies have been given for a total of 3627 different athletes (2083 men and 1524 women).

The ever continuing high turnover in our sport is reflected in the fact that there are even more newcomers to this section than usual (144 in all, 75 men, 69 women), as well as 12 athletes (6 men, 6 women) reinstated from previous Annuals. The athlete to have had the longest continuous stretch herein is Franka Dietzsch 19 years and two athletes have been included 17 times: Yoelbis Quesada and Maria Mutola.

No doubt some of those dropped from this compilation will also again make their presence felt; the keen reader can look up their credentials in previous Annuals, and, of course, basic details may be in the athletes' index at the end of this book.

Athletes included in these biographies are identified in the index at the end of this Annual by * for those profiled in this section and by ^ for those who were included in previous Annuals.

The biographical information includes:

a) Name; date and place of birth; height (in metres); weight (in kilograms).
b) Previous name(s) for married women; club or university; occupation.
c) Major championships record – all placings in such events as the Olympic Games, World Championships, European Championships, Commonwealth Games, World Cup and European Cup Super League; leading placings in finals of the World Indoor Championships, European or World Junior Championships, European Under-23 Championships and other Continental Championships; and first three to six in European Indoors or World University Games.
IAAF Grand Prix first three at each event or overall.
World Athletics Final (WAF) winners
d) National (outdoor) titles won or successes in other major events.
e) Records set: world, continental and national; indoor world records/bests (WIR/WIB).
f) Progression of best marks over the years at each athlete's main event(s).
g) Personal best performances at other events.
h) Other comments.

See Introduction to this Annual for lists of abbreviations used for events and championships.

Note that for comparison purposes decathlons and heptathlons made before the introduction of the current tables have been rescored using the 1984 IAAF Tables, except those marked *, for which event breakdowns were unavailable. Women's pentathlons (p) have not been rescored.

Information given is as known at 1 April 2008 (to include performances at the World Indoor Championships and the World Cross-country Championships as well as some other early indoor and outdoor events of 2008).

I am most grateful to various ATFS members who have helped check these details. Additional information or corrections would be welcomed for next year's Annual.

Peter Matthews

ALBANIA

Governing body: Federata Shqiptare e Atletikes, Rruga Dervish Hima n 31, Tirana.

National Championships first held in 1945 (women 1946). **2001 Champions**: **Men**: 100m/LJ: Admir Bregu 10.93/7.35, 200m: Gjergj Shtepani 22.29, 400m: Eusebio Halili 50.07, 800m/1500m: Neritan Hasanaj 1:59.01/3:59.48, 5000m: Gene Lugja 16:02.89, 10,000m: Florian Balaj 34:16.49, 3000mSt: Bledar Mesi 9:40.13, 110mh: Elton Bitinka 14.20, 400mh: Marjan Potani 58.39, HJ/PV: *not held*, TJ: Gledi Gojashi 14.03, SP: Manfred Koleci 14.51, DT: Adriatik Hoxha 34.99, HT: Ardit Merdanaj 61.25, JT: Vladimir Sokoli 61.10. **Women**: 100m: Arta Sadria 12.50, 200m/400m: Klodiana Shala 25.64/57.99, 800m/1500m/3000m: Luiza Gega 2:13.47/4:34.61/10:18.21, 5000m: Nurie Shala 18:55.04, 10,000m: Myrvete Pervetica 42:42.12, 100mh: Anila Meta 14.50, 400mh: Denisa Thengjilli 65.41, HJ: Laura Derhemi 1.70, PV/SP: *not held*; LJ/TJ: Rigerta Selenica 5.62/12.82, DT: Atfiete Tola 19.03, HT: Emiliana Ciko 50.81, JT: Gerta Batushaj 36.72.

ALGERIA

Governing body: Fédération Algerienne d'Athlétisme, BP n°61, Dely-Ibrahim, Alger. Founded 1963.

Tarek BOUKENSA b. 19 Nov 1981 Annaba 1.78m 62kg.
At 1500m: OG: '04- sf; WCh: '03- sf, '05- 8, '07- 5; WJ: '00- 8; AfG: '07- 3; AfCh: '02- 5, '06- 3. World 4k CC: '04- 12.
Progress at 1500m: 2000- 3:41.08, 2001- 3:36.22, 2002- 3:35.08, 2003- 3:34.57, 2004- 3:32.35, 2005- 3:34.68/3:32.7+u, 2006- 3:31.58, 2007- 3:30.92. pbs: 800m 1:46.10 '06, 1000m 2:16.13 '06, 1M 3:49.95 '06, 2000m 4:57.20 '07, 3000m 7:43.23 '05.

Issam NIMA b. 8 Apr 1979 1.86m 74kg.
At LJ: WCh: '05- 11, '07- dnq 17; WI: '06- 8; AfG: '07- 4; AfCh: '02- 4, '06- 3; WUG: '05- 2. Pan-Arab champion 2004.
Six Algerian long jump records 2005-7.
Progress at LJ: 1998- 7.27, 1999- 7.60, 2000- 7.38, 2001- 7.45, 2002- 7.78/7.93w, 2004- 7.97/7.99w, 2005- 8.13, 2006- 8.17/8.37w, 2007- 8.26. pbs: 100m 10.56 '06, TJ 16.03 '05.

ARGENTINA

Governing body: Confederación Argentina de Atletismo, 21 de Noviembre No. 207. 3260 Concepción del Uruguay, Entre Ríos. Founded 1954 (original governing body founded 1919).

National Championships first held in 1920 (men), 1939 (women). **2007 Champions: Men**: 100m: Agustín Muniagorri 10.79, 200m: Mariano Jiménez 21.66, 400m: Esteban Brandán 48.3, 800m/1500m: Leonardo Price 1:56.11/3:54.91, 5000m: Javier Carriqueo 14:19.05, 10.000m: Santiago Figueroa 30:24.97, HMar: Ulises Sanguinetti 67:57, Mar: Oscar Cortínez 2:19:40, 3000St: Mariano Mastromarino 9:15.94, 110mh: Mariano Romero 15.00, 400mh: José Ignacio Pignataro 52.55, HJ: Santiago Guerci 2.09, PV: Germán Chiaraviglio 5.20, LJ: Julián Cherit 6.99, TJ: Martín Falico 15.30w, SP/DT: Germán Lauro 18.08/56.26, HT: Juan Ignacio Cerra 66.91, JT: Pablo Pietrobelli 72.54, Dec: Gerardo Canale 6950, 20000mW: Juan Manuel Cano 1:24:13.0. **Women**: 100m: Vanesa Wohlgemuth 12.02, 200m: Jacqueline Rombaldoni 25.06, 400m: Juliana Menéndez 57.1, 800m: Julieta Fraguio 2:20.57, 1500m/3000mSt: Rosa Godoy 4:31.55/10:29.60, 5000m: Valeria Rodríguez 16:59.49, 10,000m: María Gómez 34:53.49, Mar: Estela Martínez 2:48:54, 100mh: Soledad Donzino 14.33, 400mh: Verónica Pronzati 62.29, HJ: Delfina Blaquier 1.70, PV: Alejandra García 4.00, LJ: Andrea Morales 5.88, TJ: Silvia Sastre 12.55w, SP/DT: Rocío Comba 15.22/51.70, HT: Karina Moya 53.95, JT: Romina Maggi 48.19, Hep: Daniela Crespo 4670.

AUSTRALIA

Governing body: Athletics Australia, Suite 22, Fawkner Towers, 431 St.Kilda Rd, Melbourne, Victoria 3004. Founded 1897.

National Championships first held in 1893 (men) (Australasian until 1927), 1930 (women). **2007 Champions**: **Men**: 100m/200m: Joshua Ross 10.08/20.51, 400m: Sean Wroe 45.80, 800m: Nick Bromley 1:48.42, 1500m: Mark Fountain 3:42.31, 3000m: Mark Tucker 8:00.11, 5000m: Craig Mottram 13:32.67, 10,000m: Collis Birmingham 28:39.91, Mar: Damon Harris 2:27:58, 3000mSt: Peter Nowill 8:34.95, 110mh: Justin Merlino 13.55, 400mh: Brendan Cole 50.78, HJ: Liam Zamel-Paez 2.21, PV: Steve Hooker 5.50, LJ: Tim Parravicini 8.01, TJ: Alwyn Jones 16.80w, SP: Justin Anlezark 18.55, DT: Benn Harradine 60.89, HT: Pavlo Milinevskyy 66.57, JT: Jarrod Bannister 83.70, Dec: Erik Surjan 7706, 20kW: Luke Adams 1:25:10, 50kW:.Jarrod Tallent 3:44:45. **Women**: 100m/100mh: Sally McLellan 11.23/12.91, 200m: Melanie Kleeberg 23.46, 400m/800m: Tamsyn Lewis 51.71/2:00.71, 1500m: Lisa Corrigan 4:15.25, 3000m: Eloise Wellings 9:35.88, 5000m: Benita Johnson 15:36.45, 10,000m: Melinda Vernon 34:28.85, Mar: Eliza Mayger 2:46:34, 3000mSt: Donna MacFarlane 9:34.21, 400mh: Lauren Boden 58.40 HJ: Ellen Pettitt 1.83, PV: Kym Howe 4.55, LJ: Bronwyn Thompson 6.63, TJ: Jeanette Bowles 13.08, SP/DT: Dani Samuels 16.17/60.40 (Ana Po'uhila TGA 16.17), HT: Karyne Di Marco 61.53, JT: Kim Mickle 57.24, Hep: Kylie Wheeler 6044, 10kW: Megan Szirom 47:31, 20kW: Claire Woods 1:41:56.

Luke ADAMS b. 22 Oct 1976 Myumi, Tanzania 1.89m 70kg. Bankstown. Studied industrial design.
At 20kW: OG: '04- 16; WCh: '03- 5, '05- 10, '07- 7.; CG: '02- 2, '06- 2; WCp: '04- 14, '06- 18. At

10,000mW: WJ: '94- 24. Won AUS 20kW 2003, 30kW 1998.
Progress at 20kW: 1995- 1:30:21, 1996- 1:25:27, 1999- 1:23:52, 2000- 1:24:18, 2001- 1:26:31, 2002- 1:23:56, 2003- 1:19:35, 2004- 1:21:24, 2005- 1:19:19, 2006- 1:20:49, 2007- 1:20:30, 2008- 1:20:32. pbs: 3000mW 11:48.4 '95. 5000mW 18:59.43 '07, 10,000mW 40:04.88 '05, 30kW 2:17:33 '02; 50kW 3:53:19 '07.

Paul BURGESS b. 14 Aug 1979 Perth 1.84m 83kg. Stirling Swans.
At PV: OG: '00- dnq 16=, '04- 11=; WCh: '07- dnq 21=; CG: '98- 2, '02- 2; WJ: '96- 1, '98- 3=; WCp: '98- 7, '02- 5=. Won WAF 2006, AUS 2000, 2002, 2005-06.
Oceania indoor pole vault record 5.80 in 2006.
Progress at PV: 1994- 3.90, 1995- 5.25, 1996- 5.35, 1997- 5.51, 1998- 5.60, 1999- 5.50, 2000- 5.60, 2001- 5.71, 2002- 5.75, 2003- 5.70, 2004- 5.77, 2005- 6.00, 2006- 5.92, 2007- 5.91.
Former gymnast.

Nathan DEAKES b. 17 Aug 1977 Geelong 1.83m 66kg. Bellarine.
At 20kW(/50kW): OG: '00- 8/6, '04- 3/dq; WCh: '99- 7, '01- 4/dq, '07- 1; CG: '98- 3, '02- 1/1, '06- 1/1; WCp: '04- 3, '06- 5. At 10,000mW: WJ: '96- 3. Won GWG 20000mW 2001, AUS 20kW 2000-02, 2004-06; 50kW 1999 (t), 2005-06.
Walk records: World 50km 2006, Commonwealth & Oceania 20km 2001 & 2005, 20,000m track (1:19:48.1) 2001; 30km 2006, 50km 2003, 5000m 2006.
Progress at 20kW, 50kW: 1996- 1:26:27, 1997- 1:23:58, 1998- 1:23:25, 1999- 1:20:15, 3:52:53; 2000- 1:21:03, 3:47:29; 2001- 1:18:14, 3:43:43; 2002- 1:21:07, 3:52:40; 2003- 3:39:43, 2004- 1:19:11, 2005- 1:17:33, 3:47.51; 2006- 1:19:07, 3:35:47; 2007- 1:19:34, 3:43:53. pbs: 3000mW 11:17.0 '98, 5000mW 18:45.19 '06, 10,000m 38:44.87 '02, 30kW 2:05:06 '06, 35kW 2:29:11e '06.
Unable to compete at 2005 Worlds due to a hamstring injury, returned for second Commonwealth Games double in 2006 before world record and title at 50km..

Steve HOOKER b. 16 Jul 1982 Melbourne 1.87m 82kg. Box Hill.
At PV: OG: '04- 28=; WCh: '05- dnq 17=, '07- 9; CG: '06- 1; WJ: '00- 4; WI: '08- 3; WCp: '06- 1. AUS champion 2008.
Progress at PV: 1999- 5.00, 2000- 5.20, 2001- 5.30, 2002- 5.25, 2003- 5.45, 2004- 5.65, 2005- 5.87, 2006- 5.96, 2007- 5.91. pbs: 100m 10.6, 10.68w '05, 200m 21.1 '05, LJ 7.10 '05.
Played Australian Rules football before taking up pole vaulting. His father Bill was 6th CG 800m 1974, had pbs: 800m 1:45.36 '73, 400mh pb 50.6 '69, and his mother Erica (née Nixon) was 6th LJ, 4th Pen 1974 and 2nd LJ 1978 (in pb 6.58) at CG.

Scott MARTIN b. 12 Oct 1982 Wodonga, Victoria 1.90m 130kg. Ringwood.
At SP/(DT): WCh: '07- dnq 14; CG: '06- 3/1; WJ: '00- 11/dnq 15; WI: '08- 7; WCp: '06- 4/5; WY: '98- 6. Won AUS SP 2006, DT 2004-06.
Australian shot record 2008
Progress at SP, DT: 1999- 16.43, 2000- 17.60, 51.70; 2001- 18.41, 54.90; 2002- 18.29, 58.22; 2003- 18.81, 62.19; 2004- 19.53, 63.78; 2005- 20.10, 63.78; 2006- 20.38, 64.00; 2007- 20.52, 61.65; 2008- 21.27.

Craig MOTTRAM b. 18 Jun 1980 Frankston, Victoria 1.88m 71kg. Deakin. Degree from Deakin University
At 5000m (1500m): OG: '00- h, '04- 8; WCh: '01- (sf), '05- 3, '07- 13; CG: '02- 6, '06- 2 (9). At 3000m: WI: '01-04-08: 8/10/5; WCp: '02- 1, '06- 1. World CC: '99- 17J, 4k: '01-02-04-06: 8/5/9/11; 12k: '04-05: 13/22. Won AUS 1500m 2002, 3000m 2008, 5000m 2002, 2004-08; 10,000m 2001.
Oceania records 1M 2005, 2000m 2006, 3000m (3) 2002-06, 5000m (4) 2002-04, 2M 2005; indoor 3000m (7:34.50) 2008
Progress at 5000m: 1999- 13:40.48, 2000- 13:26.20, 2001- 13:23.94, 2002- 13:12.04, 2003- 13:17.81, 2004- 12:55.76, 2005- 12:56.13, 2006- 12:58.19, 2007- 13:04.97. pbs: 800m 1:52.90, 1500m: 3:33.97 '06, 3:32.7e '05; 1M 3:48.98 '05, 2000m 4:50.76 '06, 3000m 7:32.19 '06, 2M 8:11.27 '05, 10,000m 27:50.55 '03.
Former AUS junior triathlon champion. British parents, his father Brian played football for Wimbledon.

John STEFFENSEN b. 30 Aug 1982 Perth 1.80m 71kg. University of Western Australia.
At 400m: OG: '04- 2R; WCh: '03- hR, '05- 8, '07- sf; CG: '06- 1/1R. Australian champion 2006.
Progress at 400m: 2002- 47.14, 2003- 46.07, 2004- 45.63, 2005- 45.31, 2006- 44.73, 2007- 44.82. pbs: 200m 20.79/20.76w '07, LJ 7.18/7.28w '02.
Was a state champion boxer.

Women

Kym HOWE b. 12 Jun 1980 Perth 1.77m 63kg. Married name Nadin. Curtin. Child care worker.
At PV: OG: '04- dnq 16; WCh: '07- 11; CG: '02- 2, '06- 1; WJ: '98- 11; WCp: '06- nh. Won AUS 1999, 2004-05, 2007.
Three Commonwealth & Oceania pole vault records 2006-07, OCE indoor record 2007.
Progress at PV: 1997- 3.60, 1998- 3.90, 1999- 4.16, 2000- 4.20, 2001- 4.30, 2002- 4.45, 2003- 4.30, 2004- 4.40, 2005- 4.40, 2006- 4.62, 2007- 4.72i/4.65.
Member of Western Australian junior gymnastics team 1993-6.

Sarah JAMIESON b. 24 Mar 1975 Perth 1.76m 56kg. Essendon.
At 1500m: OG: '00/04- h; WCh: '07- sf; CG: '02- 5, '06- 2 (5 5000m); WJ: '94- h (h 800m); WUG: '99- 4; WCp: '02- 8, '06- 3. Won AUS 1999, 2002, 2005-06. World 4k CC: '04- 15, '05- 13.
Oceania 1500m record 2006.
Progress at 1500m: 1992- 4:26.02, 1993- 4:21.56, 1994- 4:19.9, 1995- 4:16.30, 1996- 4:15.00, 1997-

4:20.89, 1998- 4:20.41, 1999- 4:12.89, 2000- 4:06.09, 2001- 4:19.72, 2002- 4:08.54, 2003- 4:16.89, 2004- 4:04.73, 2005- 4:06.80, 2006- 4:00.93, 2007- 4:03.71. pbs: 800m 2:02.81 '99, 1000m 2:42.35 '00, 1M 4:23.40 '07, 3000m 8:48.41 '07, 5000m 15:02.90 '06.

Benita JOHNSON b. 6 May 1979 Mackay, QLD 1.67m 49kg. née Willis. University of Queenland.
At 3000m: WI: '01- 6, '03- 7. At 5000m (1500m): OG: '00- h; WCh: '01- 12; CG: '02- 6 (h); WJ: '98- (7); WUG: '99- (5); WCp: '02- 4. At 10,000m: OG: '04- 24; WCh: '03- 8, '05- 19, '07- 17; CG: '06- 4. World HMar: '03- 3; CC: 4km: '01-02-03-06: 6/4/5/4; 8km: '04-05-06-08: 1/7/4/11. Won AUS 5000m 2003, 2005-07; 10,000m 2004, 2006.
Oceania records: 3000m (2) 2001-03, 5000m (3) 2001-02, 2000m & 10,000m 2003, Mar 2006.
Progress at 5000m, 10,000m, Mar: 1997- 16:11.57, 1998- 16:31.2, 2000- 15:21.37, 2001- 15:04.18, 2002- 14:47.60, 2003- 14:54.52, 30:37.68; 2004- 15:16.61, 31:49.9, 2:38:03; 2005- 15:21.02, 31:55.15, 2:26:32; 2006- 15:13.46, 31:14.80, 2:22:36; 2007- 15:36.45, 32:55.94, 2:29:47. pbs: 800m 2:05.41 '00, 1500m 4:07.05 '00, 1M 4:32.61 '06, 2000m 5:37.71 '03, 3000m 8:38.06 '03, HMar 67:55 '04, 25km 1:23:25 '06, 30km 1:40:12 '06.
Became Australia's first World CC champion in 2004 and later won Great North Run half marathon. Under-18 international at hockey. Married Cameron Johnson 2 Feb 2002. Younger sister Caitlin has 400m pb 52.75 '06 (1R CG '06).

Tamsyn LEWIS b. 20 Jul 1978 Melbourne 1.73m 60kg. Sandringham AC.
At 800m/4x400mR: OG: '00- sf, '04- h; WCh: '99-01-03-07: h/sf/sf/h; CG: '98- 6/1R, '02- 5/1R, 06- 1R (sf 400m); WI: '99- 2R, 08- 1; WCp: '98/02- 8. At 400m: WJ: '94-6, '96- sf/3R. Won AUS 400m 2005, 2007-08, 800m 1998-2003, 2007-08.
Progress at 800m: 1997- 2:07.49, 1998- 2:01.71, 1999- 2:00.95, 2000- 1:59.21, 2001- 2:00.86, 2002- 1:59.73, 2003- 1:59.35, 2004- 2:00.96, 2005- 2:11.37, 2006- 2:05.10, 2007- 1:59.37, 2008- 1:59.59. pbs: 200m 24.16 '00, 24.1 '06; 400m 51.44 '08.
Father Greg Lewis had 100m pb 10.1 '72, 1R CG 1974; mother Carolyn Wright won seven AUS high jump titles.

Donna MacFARLANE b. 18 Jun 1977 Melbourne 1.76m 57kg. née Tyberek. Sandy Bay. Radio producer.
At 3000mSt: WCh: '07- h; CG: '06- 3. AUS champion 2007-08.
Progress at 3000mSt: 2000- 10:31.10. 2005- 9:51.60, 2006- 9:25.05, 2007- 9:26.63, 2008- 9:29.93. pbs: 800m 2:06.39 '06, 1000m 2:45.68 '08, 1500m 4:10.37mx '07, 4:15.83 '06, 1M 4:33.52 '07, 3000m 8:50.65 '06, 5000m 15:46.43 '07.
Australian junior 1500m champion 1997, retired to start a family; made dramatic return 2005/06.

Sally McLELLAN b. 19 Sep 1986 Sydney 1.66m 60kg. Griffith University.
At (100m)/100mh: WCh: '07- sf/sf; CG: '06- 7/dq/3R; WJ: 3/4; WY: '03- 1; WCp: '06-8/4. AUS champion 100m & 100mh 2005-07.
Two Oceania 100mh records 2007.
Progress at 100mh: 2003- 14.01, 2004- 13.30, 2005- 13.01, 2006- 12.95, 2007- 12.71, 2008- 12.81. pbs: 60m 7.39 '07, 100m 11.14 '07, 200m 23.36 '06, 200mh 27.54 '06, 400mh 62.98 '07.

Victoria MITCHELL b. 25 Apr 1982 Melbourne 1.64m 48kg. Eureka AC. Was at Ballarat University and Butler University, USA.
At 3000mSt: WCh: '07- h; CG: '06- 4; WUG: '05- 2; WCp: '06- 4. Won AUS 2003, NCAA 2005.
Progress at 3000mSt: 2001- 10:29.5, 2002- 10:09.53, 2003- 10:17.55, 2004- 10:13.31, 2005- 9:47.54, 2006- 9:30.84, 2007- 9:45.20. pbs: 1500m 4:18.01 '06, 1M 4:38.05 '06, 3000m 8:58.42 '06, 5000m 15:36.15 '06.

Jana RAWLINSON b. 9 Nov 1982 Sydney 1.81m 68kg. née Pittman. Multelink Hills and Panellínios GRE.
At 400mh(/400m): OG: '00- h; '04- 5; WCh: '03- 1, '07- 1; CG: '02- 1/1R, '06- 1/1R; WJ: '00- 1/1; WY: '99- 1/7; WCp: '02- 3. AUS champion 2001-03.
Equalled official world junior record 400mh 2000. Oceania 300m best 2003.
Progress at 400mh: 1998- 59.75, 1999- 56.23, 2000- 55.20A/55.63, 2001- 55.93, 2002- 54.14, 2003- 53.22, 2004- 53.43, 2005- 53.44, 2006- 53.82, 2007- 53.31. pbs: 100m 11.77 '03, 200m 23.52 '03, 300m 36.34 '03, 400m 50.43 '03, 800m 2:04.03 '05, 100mh 13.92 '00.
Won the 400m/400mh double at the 2000 World Juniors, the first woman to achieve this feat at an IAAF/IOC event. Named the IAAF Rising Star for 2000. Set world age 19 400mh record in 2002. World champ at Yth, Jnr, Snr. Had arthroscopic knee surgery just a couple of weeks before OG 2004. Married British 400m hurdler Chris Rawlinson (1 CG 2002) on 31 Mar 2006; their son Cornelius born on 14 Dec 2006.

Bronwyn THOMPSON b. 29 Jan 1978 Rockhampton, Queensland 1.77m 68kg. Southern Suburbs. Paediatric physiotherapist.
At LJ: OG: '00- dnq 16, '04- 4; WCh: '03- 7, '07- dnq 21; CG: '02- 6, '06- 1; WCp: '06- 4. Australian champion 2002-03, 2006-08.
Oceania long jump records 2001 & 2002, Commonwealth record 2002.
Progress at LJ: 1992- 5.42, 1993- 5.60, 1994- 6.04/6.14w, 1995- 6.10; 1996- 6.10/6.15w, 1997- 5.95, 2000- 6.56/6.64w, 2001- 6.88, 2002- 7.00, 2003- 6.73/6.75w, 2004- 6.96, 2005- 6.59/6.73w, 2006- 6.97, 2007- 6.72. pbs: 100m 11.77 '03, 200m 24.19 '03.
Serious knee injury after 2004 Olympics. Three jumps over 6.90 at 2006 CG, despite jumping from behind the board (7.15 from jump to take-off on best jump). Married Jason Chipperfield on 31 Mar 2006.

Kylie WHEELER b. 17 Jan 1980 Perth 1.80m

64kg. University of Western Australia.
At Hep: WCh: '05- 15, '07- 12; CG: '02- 2, '06- 2; WUG: '03- 1. At 400mh: WJ: '98- sf. Won AUS Hep 2003-08.
Progress at Hep: 1996- 4700, 1997- 4586, 1998- 4859, 1999- 5059, 2000- 5583, 2001- 5702, 2002- 5962, 2003- 6031, 2004- 6296, 2005- 6231, 2006- 6298, 2007- 6184. pbs: 100m 12.09 '07, 11.81w '05, 11.6w '02; 200m 23.99 '05, 400m 54.49 '99, 800m 2:09.98 '05, 100mh 13.63 '06, 13.58w '07; 400mh 58.11 '00, HJ 1.86 '05, LJ 6.57 '03, 6.66w '04; SP 13.33 '07, JT 41.10 '07.

AUSTRIA

Governing body: Österreichischer Leichtathletik Verband, 1040 Vienna, Prinz Eugenstrasse 12. Founded 1902.

National Championships first held in 1911 (men), 1918 (women). **2007 Champions**: **Men**: 100m: Roland Kwitt 10.57, 200m/400m: Clemens Zeller 21.11/46.20, 800m: Andreas Rapatz 1:54.08, 1500m: Daniel Spitzl 3:46.48, 5000m/10,000m/3000mSt: Günther Weidlinger 14:08.21/29:07.66/9:09.15, HMar: Martin Pröll 65:31, Mar: Markus Hohenwarter 2:24:41, 110mh: Elmar Lichtenegger 13.72, 400mh: Gotthard Schöpf 52.84, HJ: Martin Kalss 2.02, PV: David Kreuzhuber 4.70, LJ: Michael Mülschl 7.52, TJ: Alexander Leprich 15.16, SP: Martin Gratzer 17.73, DT: Gerhard Mayer 59.81, HT: Benjamin Siart 64.59, JT: Klaus Ambrosch 70.25, Dec: Markus Walser 6870, 20kW: Alexander Maier 1:49:59. 50kW: Johann Siegele 5:09:26. **Women**: 100m/200m: Nora Ivanova-Edletzberger 11.87/23.51, 400m/800m/400mh: Sabine Kreiner 55.20/2:09.69/59.08, 1500m: Sylvia Aschenberger 4:41.41, 1500m/10,000m/3000mSt: Andrea Mayr 4:25.66/34:05.34/10:30.30, 5000m: Susanne Pumper 17:35.47, HMar/Mar: Eva-Maria Gradwohl 74:33/2:46:31, 100mh: Victoria Schreibeis 13.42, HJ: Monika Gollner 1.71, PV: Doris Auer 3.90, LJ: Junel Anderson 6.15, TJ: Michaela Egger 12.64, SP/DT: Veronika Watzek 14.98/58.77, HT: Julia Siart 51.09, JT: Elisabeth Pauer 50.13, Hep: Marion Obermayr 4983, 10kW/20kW: Vera Toporek 52:45/1:51:49.

Günther WEIDLINGER b. 5 Apr 1978 Braunau 1.69m 54kg. SU IGLA Harmonie Linz. Soldier.
At 3000mSt: OG: '00- 8; WCh: '99- 9, '03- h, '05- 12, '07- h; EC: '98- h, '02- 12, '06- 7; WJ: '96- 4; EU23: '99- 1; EJ: '95- 8, '97- 1. At 3000m: WI: '03/06- 10; EI: '05- 4, '07- 7. At 5000m: OG: '04- h. Eur CC: '97-8-02-04-05: 2J/4/10/4/5. Won World Univs CC 2000. Won AUT 1500m 1999-2000, 5000m 2004-05, 2007; 10,000m 2003-05, 2007; 3000mSt 1998-9, 2006-07; CC 2001-02, 2006-07.
Austrian records: 1500m 2000, 3000mSt (3) 1999, 2M & 5000m 2005, HMar 2007.
Progress at 3000mSt: 1995- 9:02.15, 1996 8:38.97, 1997- 8:31.43, 1998- 8:23.13, 1999- 8:10.83, 2000- 8:11.51, 2001- 8:23.62, 2002- 8:23.91, 2003- 8:17.90, 2005- 8:12.26, 2006- 8:20.91, 2007- 8:15.35. pbs: 800m 1:51.82 '00, 1500m 3:34.69 '00, 1M 3:59.40 '00, 3000m 7:44.19i '03, 7:48.46 '04; 2M 8:21.88 '05, 5000m 13:13.44 '05, 10,000m 28:19.11 '07, Road: 10km 28:15 '07, 20km 58:38 '07, HMar 61:42 '07.

BAHAMAS

Governing body: Bahamas Association of Athletics Associations, P.O.Box SS 5517, Nassau. Founded 1952.

National Champions 2007: **Men**: 100m: Derrick Atkins 10.13, 200m: Michael Mathieu 20.82, 400m: Chris Brown 44.88, 800m: Kenneth Wallace-Whitfield 1:52.34, 110mh: Shamar Sands 13.86, 400mh: Nathan Arnett 51.94, HJ: Donald Thomas 2.30, PV, LJ: Osbourne Moxey 7.91, TJ: Leevan Sands 16.53. **Women**: 100m: Chandra Sturrup 11.39, 200m: Debbie Ferguson McKenzie 23.23, 400m: Shakeitha Henfield 55.53, 100mh: Tiavanni Thompson 13.60, LJ: Jackie Edwards 6.63, SP: Aymara Albury 15.56, JT: Laverne Eve 59.70.

Derrick ATKINS b. 5 Jan 1984 Jamaica 1.85m 84kg. Degeree in education from Dickinson State University, USA.
At 100m/4x100mR: WCh: '05- h, '07- 2; PAm: '03- h; CAG: '06- 2/2R. Won NACAC 2006, BAH 2005-07.
Five Bahamas 100m records 2006-07.
Progress at 100m: 2001- 10.75, 2002- 10.66/10.60w, 2003- 10.30, 2004- 10.36, 2005- 10.21, 2006- 10.08/10.03w, 2007- 9.91/9.83w. pbs: 55m 6.25i '04, 200m 20.50/20.48w '07.
Moved to Bahamas at age 2. Second cousin of Asafa Powell.

Christopher BROWN b. 15 Oct 1978 1.78m 68kg. Was at Norfolk State University.
At 400m/4x400mR: OG: '00- qf/4R, '04- sf; WCh: '01-03-05-07- h&2R/sf&3R/4&2R/4&2R; CG: '02- 7/3R, '06- 4; PAm: '07- 1/1R; CAG: '98- 3R, '99- 1R, '03- 2/1R; WI: '06- 3, '08- 3; BAH champion 2002, 2004, 2007. At 800m: CG: '98- h.
Bahamas records 400m 2007, 800m 1998.
Progress at 400m: 1997- 47.46, 1998- 46.44, 1999- 45.96, 2000- 45.08, 2001- 45.45, 2002- 45.11, 2003- 44.94A/45.16, 2004- 45.09, 2005- 44.48, 2006- 44.80, 2007- 44.45. pbs: 200m 21.05 '03, 20.56w '06; 800m 1:49.54 '98.
Had fastest split (43.42 anchor leg) in 2005 World 4x400m.

Leevan SANDS b. 16 Aug 1981 Nassau 1.90m 75kg. Was at Auburn University, USA.
At TJ (LJ): OG: '04- dnq 27; WCh: '03- 3, '05- 4 (dnq), '07- dnq 21; CG: '02- 3; WJ: '98- dnq, '00- 5 (dnq 19); PAm: '99- 6, '07- 6; won CAC LJ 2005, TJ 2003, CAm-J 1998, 2000; NCAA LJ 2003 & TJ 2004, BAH LJ 2003.
Bahamas triple jump record 2002.
Progress at TJ: 1998- 15.70, 1999- 16.00/16.02w, 2000- 16.22, 2001- 16.39, 2002- 17.50, 2003- 17.40, 2004- 17.41, 2005- 17.30/17.39w, 2006- 16.99i/17.10idq, 2007- 17.23/17.55w. pbs: 20m

22.09 '07, LJ 8.13 '05, 8.28w '03.
6-month suspension after testing positive for a banned stimulant, methamphetamine, Feb 2006.

Donald THOMAS b. 1 Jul 1984 1.90m 75kg Lindenwood University, USA.
At HJ: WCh: '07- 1; CG: '06- 4; PAm: '07- 2; CAG: '06- 4=. Won WAF, NCAA indoors & BAH 2007.
Progress at HJ: 2006- 2.24, 2007- 2.35.
A basketball player, he made a sensational start by clearing 2.22 indoors in January 2006 with no high jump training since he had jumped at school five years earlier. 19 months later he was world champion.

Women

Christine AMERTIL b. 18 Aug 1979 Nassau 1.68m 53kg. Studied accountancy at Southeastern Louisiana University, USA.
At 400m: OG: '00- h, '04- 7; WCh: '03- sf, '05- sf (h 200m), '07- sf; CG: '02- 8, '06- 4; WI: '03- 2, '06- 3; WCp: '06- 1R. At 4x100mR: CAC: '03- 1R. Won BAH 400m 2004-05.
Progress at 400m: 1999- 52.99, 2000- 52.00, 2001- 52.70, 2002- 50.82, 2003- 51.11i/51.25, 2004- 50.17, 2005- 50.09, 2006- 50.34i/50.51, 2007- 50.99. pbs: 60m 7.50i '03, 100m 11.49 '05, 200m 22.58 '05.

Tonique DARLING b. 17 Jan 1976 Nassau 1.68m 59kg. née Williams. Was at University of Georgia, then South Carolina.
At 400m: OG: '00- h, '04- 1; WCh: '97- qf, '99- h, '03- 5, '05- 1; CG: '06- 2; PAm: '99- h; CAC: '99- 2, '05- 1; WI: '04- 3; WCp: '06- 1R. At 200m: CAC: '03- 3.
Three BAH 400m records 2004, CAC indoor 400m record 50.87 '04.
Progress at 400m: 1994- 53.72, 1995- 52.40, 1996- 52.42, 1997- 52.15, 1998- 51.99, 1999- 52.01, 2000- 52.35, 2003- 50.24, 2004- 49.07, 2005- 49.30, 2006- 50.11. pbs: 55m 6.99i '97, 60m 7.49i '97, 100m 11.72 '97, 200m 22.77 '04, 300m 35.6+ '04.
Married sprinter Dennis Darling (pb 400m 45.82 '97) on 11 April 2003. Won $500,000 as share of Golden League jackpot 2004.

Debbie FERGUSON McKENZIE b. 16 Jan 1976 Nassau 1.70m 57kg. Graduate of University of Georgia, USA.
At 100m/4x100mR (/200m): OG: '96- sf/res (2)R, '00- 8/5/1R, '04- 7/3/4R; WCh: '95- 4R (h), '97- sf, '99- sf/5/1R, '01- 5/1, '03- sf/qf, '07- sf/sf; CG: 94- (sf), '02- 1/1/1R; WJ: '92- qf/sf, '94- 5/4; PAm: '99- (1); WCp: '02- (1)/1R, '06- 1R. Won GP 100m 2002 (2nd 200m 2001), CAC 100m 1997, 200m 1995, NCAA 100m & 200m 1998, PAm-J 100m & 200m 1995, CAC-J 100m 1994, GWG 200m 2001.
Bahamas 200m record 1999.
Progress at 100m, 200m: 1991- 11.75, 24.26; 1992- 11.79, 23.97w; 1993- 23.82/23.32w, 1994- 11.48/11.1, 23.32/23.1; 1995- 11.19/10.9w, 22.86/22.7; 1996- 11.26/11.07Aw, 22.92; 1997- 11.20, 1998- 10.97/10.94w, 22.53; 1999- 10.98/10.91w, 22.19; 2000- 10.96, 22.37; 2001- 11.04, 22.39; 2002- 10.91, 22.20; 2003- 10.97, 22.50A/22.65; 2004- 11.04, 22.30; 2006- 11.14/11.06w, 22.56/22.4; 2007- 11.12, 22.49. pbs: 55m 6.71i '99, 60m 7.20i '04, 400m 54.68 '92.
Won three gold medals at 2002 CG, winning both 100m and 200m in Games records. Married Andrew McKenzie on 23 Dec 2005.

BAHRAIN

Governing body: Bahrain Athletics Association, PO Box 29269, Manama. Founded 1974.

Belal Mansoor ALI b. JohnYego (KEN) 17 Oct 1983 or 17 Oct 1988 (accepted by IAAF) Kenya 1.70m 61kg.
At (800m)/1500m: WCh: '05- 7/5, '07- h/11; WJ: '06- 7/3; WY: '05- 1. World CC: '05- 10J.
Asian 1000m record 2007. World youth bests for 800m and 1500m (with 1988 birthdate).
Progress at 800m, 1500m: 2004- 1:46.8A, 2005- 1:44.34, 3:33.86; 2006- 1:45.27, 3:34.30; 2007- 1:44.02, 3:31.49. pbs: 1000m 2:15.23 '07, 1M 3:56.17 '07.

Youssef Saad KAMEL formerly Gregory Konchellah (KEN) b. 29 Mar 1983 Kenya 1.84m 70kg.
At 800m: OG: '04- h; WCh: '05/07- sf; WI: '08- 3; AsiG: '06- 1; WCp: '06- 1. Won WAF 2004, 2007; Pan Arab 2004-05, Asian indoor 2008.
Asian and three BRN 800m records 2004, Asian indoor record (1:45.26) 2008.
Progress at 800m, 1500m: 2003- 1:45.88, 2004- 1:43.11, 2005- 1:43.96, 2006- 1:43.61, 3:34.45; 2007- 1:43.87, 3:34.59. pbs: 600m 1:16.01 '03, 1000m 2:19.71 '03.
Son of Billy Konchellah (world 800m champion 1987 and 1991), he changed nationality to Bahrain in 2003.

Rashid Mohamed **RAMZI** b. 17 Jul 1980 Safi, Morocco 1.72m 65kg. né Khoula. Army corporal.
At (800m)/1500m: OG: '04- sf; WCh: '05- 1/1, '07- h/2; WI: '04- (2), '08- 5; AsiG: '02- 1, '06- 3; AsiC: '02- 2, '03- 1; Af-J: '99- 2.
Four Asian 1500m records 2004-06, Asian indoor 80m 1004Bahrain 1M 2005.
Progress at 800m, 1500m: 1998- 1:51.49, 1999- 3:43.2, 2000- 3:42.9, 2001- 3:40.1, 2002- 1:46.5, 3:44.85; 2003- 1:47.56, 3:39.30; 2004- 1:46.15i, 3:30.25; 2005- 1:44.24, 3:30.00; 2006- 1:44.05, 3:29.14; 2007- 1:45.64, 3:35.00. pbs: 1000m 2:16.5+ '06, 1M 3:51.33 '05.
In 2005 he became the first man to win a global 800m/1500m double since Peter Snell OG 1964. He won the 1500m silver medal for Morocco at the 1999 African Junior Championships, but he seemed unable to break into top flight athletics and was unemployed when a friend of his rec-

ommended he relocate to Bahrain. He moved at the end of 2001 and gained Bahraini citizenship on joining the armed forces. Coached by Khalid Boulami, he is compiling an excellent championships record and after surprisingly winning the 2004 World Indoor silver he made an amazing breakthrough at 1500m, taking his pb from 3:39.30 to Asian records of 3:31.87 and 3:30.25.

Tareq Mubarak TAHER b. Dennis Kipkurui Keter (KEN) 24 Mar 1984 Kenya 1.78m 68kg.
At 3000mSt: WCh: 05- 15, '07- 8; AsiG: '06- 1; won Arab Ch 2007. At 3000m: WCp: '06- 8. Disqualified as over-age WJ: '06- (2); WY 2000mSt '05- (1); World CC: '05-06: (9J/19J). Bahrain 3000mSt record 2007.
Progress at 3000mSt: 2005- 8:16.26, 2006- 8:11.36, 2007- 8:07.12. pbs: 1500m 3:44.3A '04, 3000m 7:48.82 '02, 50000m 13:30.52 '03, 2000mSt 5:23.95 '05.
Entered by Bahrain as born 1 Dec 1989 in major events 2005-06 – all invalidated by IAAF in 2007.

Women

Maryam Yusuf **JAMAL** b. 16 Sep 1984 Alkesa,Arsi Province, Ethiopia 1.55m 44kg. Stade Lausanne, Switzerland.
At (800m)/1500m: WCh: '05- 5, '07- 1; WI: '06- 3, '08- 4; AsiG: '06- 1/1; WCp: '06- 1. Won WAF 2005-07, Swiss CC 2003, P.Arab 800m, 1500m & 5000m 2005, Arab 4k CC 2006, Asian CC 2007.
Records: Two Asian 1M 2007, Bahrain 800m, 1500m (3), 3000m (3), 5000m 2005-06. Asian indoor 1500m 2006 & 2008.
Progress at 1500m, 5000m: 2003- 4:18.12, 2004- 4:07.78, 15:19.45mx; 2005- 3:56.79, 14:51.68; 2006- 3:56.18, 2007- 3:58.75, 15:20.28; 2008- 3:59.79i. pbs: 800m 1:59.04 '06, 1M 4:17.75 '07, 2000m 5:41.9 '05, 3000m 8:28.87 '05, HMar 71:43 '04.
Formerly Ethiopian Zenebech Kotu Tola, based in Switzerland, ran series of fast times after converting to Jamal of Bahrain in 2005. Married to Mnashu Taye (now Tareq Yaqoob BRN).

BELARUS

Governing body: Belarus Athletic Federation, Kalinovskogo Street 111, Minsk 220119. Founded 1991.

National Champions 2007: **Men**: 100m: Dmitriy Holub 10.91, 200m: Maksim Piskunov 21.94, 400m: Dmitriy Paluyan 48.14, 800m: Sergey Peshko 1:51.95, 1500m: Andrey Korotko 3:51.87, 5000m: Gennadiy Verkhovodkin 14:19.28, 10,000m: Igor Teteryukov 30:17.20, 3000mSt: Sergey Berdnik 9:01.72, 110mh: Maksim Lynsha 13.85, 400mh: Andrey Kozlovskiy 51.92, HJ: Sergey Kobyak 2.15, PV: Stanislav Tsivonchik 4.60, LJ: Aleksey Tsapik 7.35, TJ: Dmitriy Dziatsuk 15.95, SP: Andrey Mikhnevich 20.65, DT: Aleksandr Malashevich 60.47, HT: Pavel Krivitskiy 76.18, JT: Vadim Yevtukhovich 67.62, Dec: Dmitriy Kisel 7355, 20km: Nikolay Seredovich 1:22:12. **Women**: 100m/200m: Natalya Safronnikova 11.72/23.67, 400m: Irina Khlyustova 52.42, 800m/1500m: Svetlana Kovgan 2:03.80/4:23.83, 5000m/10,000m: Olga Kravtsova 15:27.17/31:58.52, 3000mSt: Natalya Grigoryeva 10:35.90, 100mh: Yevgeniya Volodzko 13.46;, 400mh: Christina Vedernikova 58.57, HJ: Alena Ivanova 1.86, PV: Yuliya Taratynova 3.80, LJ: Veronika Shutkova 6.47, TJ: Natalya Safronova 13.44, SP: Nadezhda Ostapchuk 19.54, DT: Ellina Zvereva 60.20, HT: Darya Pchelnik 69.74, JT: Natalya Shimchuk 50.55, Hep: Tatyana Alisevich 5911, 20kW: Snezhana Yurchenko 1:33:05.

Vadim DEVYATOVSKIY b. 20 Mar 1977 Novopolotsk 1.94m 120kg. Brest.
At HT: OG: '04- 4; WCh: '03- 7, '05- 2, '07- 4; EC: '06- 3; WJ: '94- 5, '96- 2; EU23: '99- 4; WUG: '05- 1. BLR champion 2000, 2006.
Progress at HT: 1994- 67.20, 1995- 68.82?/64.60, 1996- 74.18, 1997- 69.64, 1998- 75.00, 1999- 76.77, 2000- 81.36, 2003- 79.90, 2004- 82.91, 2005- 84.90, 2006- 82.95, 2007- 82.94.
Two year drugs ban from positive test on 18 Sep 2000.

Andrey KRAVCHENKO b. 4 Jan 1986 Petrikov, Gomel region 1.87m 84kg.
At Dec: WCh: '07- dq 100; WJ: '04- 1; EJ: 05- 1. At Oct: WY: '03- 2. At Hep: WI: '08- 2; EI: '07- 3. World youth record for octathlon (6415) 2003.
Progress at Dec: 2005- 7833, 2006- 8013, 2007- 8617. pbs: 60m 7.03i '08, 100m 10.86 '07, 400m 47.17 '07, 1000m 2:39.92i '05, 1500m 4:24.44 '06, 60mh 8.04i '07, 110mh 13.93 '07, HJ 2.19i '05, 2.16 '04; PV 5.30i '08, 5.15 '07; LJ 7.90 '07, SP 14.00 '07, DT 44.08 '07, JT 64.35 '07, Hep 6234i '08.
Added 604 points to his pb to win with a European U23 record at Götzis 2007.

Pavel LYZHIN b. 24 Mar 1981 1.89m 110kg. Army.
At SP(/DT): OG: '04= dnq 17;' WCh: '03-05-07: dnq 14/nt/20; EC: '06- 10; WJ: '00- 4/7; EU23: '01- 8, '03- 1; EJ: '99- 4/2; EI: '02- 6, '07- 2; WUG: '03- 2, '05- 5. BLR champion 2001, 2004.
Progress at SP: 1999- 17.98, 2000- 19.12, 2001- 20.12, 2002- 20.15, 2003- 20.86, 2004- 20.92, 2005- 20.38, 2006- 20.85, 2007- 20.82i/20.02. pb DT 61.72 '07.

Andrey MIKHNEVICH b. 12 Jul 1976 Bobruysk 2.01m 135kg.
At SP: OG: '00- 9, '04- 5; WCh: '01- dq 10, '03- 1, '05- 6, '07- 3; EC: '98- dnq 17, '06- 2; WUG: '97- 6, '03- 1; WI: '99-04-06-08: 8/6/2/4; EI: '07- 5. BLR champion 2000, 2005-07.
Progress at SP: 1992- 13.06, 1993- 15.02, 1994- 16.74, 1995- 17.36, 1996- 19.24, 1997- 19.57i/19.27, 1998- 20.07i/19.90, 1999- 20.52i/20.30, 2000- 20.48i/20.12, 2001- 20.92, 2003- 21.69, 2004- 21.23,

2005- 21.08, 2006- 21.60, 2007- 21.27.
Two year drugs ban from positive test on 4 Aug 2001, when he lost 10th at the World Champs. Threw 21.66 four days after return from ban in August 2003, world title 2 weeks later. Married Natalya Khoroneko on 17 Mar 2007.

Ivan TIKHON b. 24 Jul 1976 Slonim 1.86m 110kg.
At HT: OG: '00- 4, '04- 2; WCh: 97- nt (12), '01- dnq 22, '03- 1, '05- 1, '07- 1; EC: '98- dnq 30, '02- 9, '06- 1; EU23: 97- 1; EJ: '95- 9; WUG: '03- 1; WCp: '06- 2. Won WAF 2005, 2007; BLR 2001-05.
Two Belarus hammer records 2005.
Progress at HT: 1994- 62.66, 1995- 66.84, 1996- 75.32, 1997- 77.46, 1998- 78.03, 1999- 70.37, 2000- 79.85, 2001- 78.73, 2002- 79.04, 2003- 84.32, 2004- 84.46, 2005- 86.73, 2006- 81.12, 2007- 83.63.
Missed Yuriy Sedykh's 19 year-old world record by just 1cm at Brest on 3 Jul 2005.

Women

Natalya KHORONEKO b. 25 May 1982 Nevinnomysk, Russia 1.80m 85kg.
At SP: OG: '04- 5; WCh: '05- 8; EC: '06- 1; WJ: '00- 3; WY: '99- 2; EJ: '01- 1; EU23: '03- 1; WI: '04- 9, '06- 1; WUG: '05- 1; WCp: '06- 4. Won WAF 2006, BLR 2001, 2004-06.
Progress at SP: 1999- 16.12, 2000- 16.58, 2001- 17.25, 2002- 17.20, 2003- 18.05, 2004- 20.04, 2005- 19.78, 2006- 20.17.
Married Andrey Mikhnevich on 17 Mar 2007, their son Ilya was born on 11 Aug 2007.

Yuliya NESTERENKO b. 15 Jun 1979 Brest 1.73m 61kg. née Bartsevich.
At 100m/4x100mR: OG: '04- 1; WCh: '03- 7R, '05- 8/3R: EC: '02- sf, '06- 6. At 60m: WI: '04-3. Won BLR 100m 2002.
Three Belarus 100m records 2004.
Progress at 100m: 2000- 11.87, 2001- 11.53/11.32w/11.1, 2002- 11.29, 2003- 11.45, 2004- 10.92, 2005- 11.08, 2006- 11.28. pbs: 60m 7.10i '04, 200m 22.91 '04.
Her four best times at 100m (all sub 11.00) were run in the four rounds of the 2004 Olympics. Married to 400m runner Dmitriy Nesterenko (47.19 '02).

Nadezhda OSTAPCHUK b. 12 Oct 1980 1.80m 90kg. Luch Moskva, RUS.
At SP: OG: '04- 4; WCh: '99- dnq 17, '01- 7, '03- 2, '05- 1, '07- 2; EC: '02- 5, '06- 2; WJ: '98- 1; EJ: '99- 1; EU23: '01- 1; WI: '01-03-04-06-08: 2/2/7/6/2, EI: '00- 6, '05- 1; Won WAF 2004, 2007; 2nd GP 2001. Won WAF 2005, BLR 1999-2000, 2007.
Three Belarus shot records 2005.
Progress at SP: 1997- 14.23, 1998- 18.23, 1999- 18.73, 2000- 19.13i/18.83, 2001- 19.73, 2002- 19.40, 2003- 20.56i/20.12, 2004- 20.36, 2005- 21.09, 2006- 20.86i/20.56, 2007- 20.48.

Yanina PRAVALINSKAYA b. 26 Dec 1976 Grodno 1.86m 87kg. née Korolchik.
At SP: OG: '00- 1; WCh: '97- dnq 18; '99- 4, '01- 1, '07- 10; EC: '98- 3; EU23: '97- 3 (3 DT); EJ: '95- 2; WI: '01- 9, '03- 7. BLR champion 2000, (2003).
BLR shot record 2000 and 2001.
Progress at SP: 1994- 16.00, 1995- 17.07, 1996- 17.48, 1997- 18.67, 1998- 19.23, 1999- 19.58, 2000- 20.56, 2001- 20.61, 2003- 19.39, 2007- 19.24. pb DT 59.90 '97.
Two year drugs ban for positive test at Dortmund 15 Jun 2003.

Marina SMOLYACHKOVA b. 10 Feb 1985 Minsk 1.77m 78kg.
At HT: OG: '04- dnq 25; EC: '06- 4; WJ: '02- 10, '04- 1; WY: '01- 3; E23: '05- 6, '07- 1; EJ: '03- 2; WCp: '06- 5.
BLR hammer record 2004.
Progress at HT: 1999- 51.32, 2000- 57.70, 2001- 60.34, 2002- 60.47, 2003- 67.08, 2004- 70.39, 2005- 69.86, 2006- 72.75, 2007- 71.74.

Alesya TUROVA b. 6 Dec 1979 Dubrovno 1.80m 64kg.
At 1500m: WCh: '01- 7, '03- sf, '05- h; EC: '02- 7; WJ: '98- h; EU23: '99- 5, '01- 1; EJ: '97- 11; WI: '01-03-04: 6/7/7; EI: '02- 3, '05- 5; ECp: '01- 4. At 3000mSt: WCh: '07- h; EC: '06- 1; WCp: '06- 1; Won WAF 2006, BLR 2006.
Two world 3000m steeple records 2002; BLR records: 2000m & 3000m (3), 5000m 2000-01.
Progress at 1500m, 3000mSt: 1997- 4:24.64, 1998- 4:21.53, 1999- 4:12.8, 2000- 4:05.99, 2001- 4:07.25, 2002- 3:59.89, 9:16.51; 2003- 4:03.32, 9:20.28; 2004- 4:04.42i, 2005- 4:02.21, 2006- 4:06.46i, 9:20.16. pbs: 800m 2:02.11i '03, 2:04.52 '99; 1M 4:33.88i '02, 2000m 5:42.55 '01, 3000m 8:32.89 '01, 5000m 15:23.84 '00.
Sister Rita (b. 28 Dec 1980) – see below – they won a unique double at 2006 Europeans.

Margarita **'Rita' TUROVA** b. 28 Dec 1980 Vitebsk 1.74m 55kg.
At 20kW: OG: '04- 4; WCh: '05- 2; EC: '06- 1; WCp: '06- 1; ECp: '07- 1. At 5000mW: WJ: '98- 5; EJ: '97-12, '99- 3.
World indoor best 5000m walk 2005, two BLR 20km walk records 2005-06.
Progress at 20kW: 2001- 1:29:31, 2004- 1:29:06, 2005- 1:27:05, 2006- 1:26:11, 2007- 1:27:10. pbs: 5000mW 20:32.77i '05, 21:48.11 '99; 10kW 42:05 '05. Won IAAF Race Walking Challenge 2005.

Ilona USOVICH b. 14 Nov 1982 Cherven 1.67m 55kg.
At 400m/4x400mR: WCh: '05- sf, '07- 7; EC: '06- 5/2R; EJ: '03- h; WI: '04-06-08: 2R/3R/2R; EI: '05- 4, '07- 2/1R; ECp: '07- 1R.
Three Belarus 400m records 2006-07.
Progress at 400m: 2003- 53.62, 2004- 52.31, 2005- 50.96, 2006- 50.69, 2007- 50.31. pbs: 800m 2:02.94i/2:03.12 '07.
Younger sister of Svetlana.

Svetlana USOVICH b. 14 Oct 1980 1.65m 52kg.
At 400m/4x400mR: OG: '04- sf; WCh: '03- sf; EC: '02- 7, '06- 2R; WI: '03- 6, '04/08- 2R; EI: '02- 1R, '05- 2, '07- 1R. At 800m: WCh: '05- sf, '07- 6; ECp: '07- 1/1R.

Belarus 400m record 2004.
Progress at 400m, 800m: 1999- 54.69, 2000- 53.68, 2001- 52.47, 2002- 51.64, 2003- 51.39, 2:05.55; 2004- 50.79, 2005- 50.55i/51.87, 1:58.17; 2006- 2:01.76i, 2007- 52.10, 1:58.11.

Irina YATCHENKO b. 31 Oct 1965 Gomel 1.86m 105kg. Grodno. Sports instructor.
At DT: OG: '92- 7, '96- 12, '00- 3, '04- 3; WCh: '91- 7, '95- 9, '97- 5, '99- 9, '01- 9, '03- 1, '07-10; EC: '90- 5, '98- 8, '06- 10; ECp: '95-96-07: 3/3/3. 2nd GP 1992. BLR champion 1997, 2003-04.
Progress at DT: 1982- 50.72, 1983- 57.04, 1984- 59.54, 1985- 60.56, 1986- 57.58, 1987- 63.00, 1988- 67.44, 1989- 62.38, 1990- 68.60, 1991- 64.92, 1992- 68.94, 1993- 58.74, 1995- 66.14, 1996- 65.80, 1997- 68.32, 1998- 64.00, 1999- 66.18, 2000- 66.51, 2001- 66.65, 2002- 64.23, 2003- 67.32, 2004- 69.14, 2005- 60.25, 2006- 61.90, 2007- 64.87.
Oldest ever world champion at 37y 298d in 2003. Married to hammer thrower Igor Astapkovich.

BELGIUM

Governing bodies: Ligue Royale Belge d'Athlétisme, Stade Roi Baudouin, avenue du Marathon 199B, 1020 Bruxelles (KBAB/LRBA). Vlaamse Atletiekliga (VAL); Ligue Belge Francophone d'Athlétisme (LBFA). Original governing body founded 1889.
National Championships first held in 1889 (women 1921). **2007 Champions**: **Men**: 100m: Kristof Beyens 10.54, 200m: Anthony Ferro 20.79, 400m: Kevin Borlée 46.38, 800m: Matthias Rosseeuw 1:53.00, 1500m: Kim Ruell 3:52.89, 5000m/10,000m: Guy Fays 14:30.13/29:39.73, HMar: Rik Ceulemans 66:58, Mar: Eric Gerome 2:17:54, 3000mSt: Pieter Desmet 8:30.78, 110mh: Adrien Deghelt 13.71, 400mh: Vincent Vanryckeghem 50.25, HJ: Timothy Hubert 2.12, PV: Kevin Rans 5.45, LJ: Gert Messiaen 7.36, TJ: Corentin Debailleul 15.29, SP/DT: Wim Blondeel 18.85/50.81, HT: Walter De Wyngaert 65.92, JT: Tom Goyvaerts 75.20, Dec: Frédéric Xhonneux 7798, 20000mW: Frank Buytaert 1:53:16. **Women**: 100m/200m: Kim Gevaert 11.22/22.77, 400m: Elke Bogemans 54.42, 800m: Lieselot Matthys 2:09.35, 1500m/3000mSt: Veerle Dejaeghere 4:20.12/9:57.97, 5000m: Sigrid Vanden Bempt 16:26.54, 10,000m: Anja Smolders 35:49.98, HMar: Louise Deldicque 83:55, Mar: Veerle D;Haese 2:54:34 100mh: Eline Berings 13.33, 400mh: Doukje Vermyl 60.79, HJ: Sabrina De Leeuw 1.82, PV: Karen Pollefeyt 3.90, LJ: Tia Hellebaut 6.41, TJ: Jolien Van Brempt 12.48, SP: Catherine Timmermans 16.01, DT: Veerle Blondeel 47.71, HT: Patricia Blondeel 52.27, JT: Melissa Dupre 50.02, Hep: Isabel Poelmans 5060, 10,000mW: Myriam Nicolas 64:37.

Women

Kim GEVAERT b. 5 Aug 1978 Leuven 1.70m 60kg. Vilvoorde AC.
At 100m/(200m): OG: '00- dnq 15, '04- sf/6; WCh: '99- qf/qf, '01- qf/sf, '03- sf/sf, '05- sf/7, '07- 5/sf/3R; EC: '98- h/sf, '02- 2/2, '06- 1/1; WJ: '96- sf/7; EU23: '99- 3/5; EJ: '95- (6), '97- 5; WUG: '99- 4/1, '01- 2; WCp: '02- (7), '06- 4/2. At 60m: WI: '04-06-08: 2/3/4; EI: '00-02-05-07: 6/1/1/1. Won BEL 100m 1996, 1998-2007; 200m 1995-2001, 2004-07.
Belgian records: 100m (11) 1998-2006, 200m (8) 1999-2006, 400m 2005.
Progress at 100m, 200m: 1994- 12.02, 1995- 11.63, 23.92; 1996- 11.68/11.60w, 23.59; 1997- 11.52, 23.84/23.58w; 1998- 11.40, 23.10; 1999- 11.17, 23.03; 2000- 11.34, 23.09; 2001- 11.26, 22.94; 2002- 11.15, 22.53; 2003- 11.21, 22.64; 2004- 11.14, 22.48; 2005- 11.12, 22.68; 2006- 11.04, 22.20; 2007- 11.05/11.04w, 22.62. pbs: 60m 7.10i '07, 400m 51.45 '05, TJ 11.67 '03.
'La Gazelle de Kampenhout', who was an award-winning classical pianist, set ten Belgian records in 2002 and 2004. She became Belgium's first ever European women's champion indoors in 2002 and outdoors in 2006. Member of EAA Athletes Commission 2002-06.

Tia HELLEBAUT b. 16 Feb 1978 Antwerpen 1.82m 62kg. Atletica '84. Chemistry graduate.
At HJ: OG: '04- 12; WCh: '05- 6, '07- 14; EC: '06- 1; WI: '06- 6; EI: '07- 1; WCp: '06- 2. At Hep: WCh: '01- 14, '03- dnf; EJ: '97- 11; EU23: '99- 7. At Pen: WI: '04- 5, '08- 1. Won BEL HJ 2000, 2002-03, 2005; LJ 2006-07, Hep 1999-2000, 2002.
Belgian records: HJ (8) 2004-06, Hep 2006, Indoor HJ (7) 2006-07, Indoor LJ 2006 & 2007, Pen 2004 & 2007.
Progress at HJ, Hep: 1992- 1.56, 1993- 1.70, 1994- 1.73, 4731; 1995- 1.76, 5167; 1996- 1.78, 5104; 1997- 1.75+, 5197; 1998- 1.81, 5381; 1999- 1.87i/1.82, 5629; 2000- 1.89, 5646; 2001- 1.89i/1.87, 5859; 2002- 1.85, 5584; 2003- 1.91, 6019; 2004- 1.95, 5954; 2005- 1.93, 2006- 2.03, 6201; 2007- 2.05i/1.98. pbs: 200m 24.65 '06, 800m 2:14.75 '06, 50mh 7.34i '04, 60mh 8.34i '07, 100mh 13.91 '05, LJ 6.42i/6.41 '07, TJ 12.54i '01, SP 13.85i '08, 13.10 '99; JT 44.37 '01, Pen 4877i '07.
Belgian records at 2.01 and 2.03 to win EC gold 2006 and indoor records at 2.01, 2.03, 2.05 to win EI 2007.

BOTSWANA

Governing body: Botswana Athletics Association, PO Box 2399, Gaborone. Founded 1972.

Gable GARENAMOTSE b. 28 Feb 1977 1.83m 75kg. Was at University of Wales in Cardiff.
At LJ (TJ): OG: '04- dnq 25; WCh: '99-03-07- dnq 41/27/20; CG: '98- (6), '02- 2, '06- 2; WI: '08- 4; AfG: '99- (6), '03- 5, '07- 1; AfCh: '00-02-06: 8/8/4 (4 TJ '00); WUG: '01- 3.
Botswana records LJ 1997-2006, TJ 1998-9.
Progress at LJ: 1996- 7.41, 1997- 7.67, 1998- 7.53A,

1999- 7.63A, 2000- 7.65A, 2001- 7.99/8.26w, 2002- 8.01i/7.91, 2003- 8.14, 2004- 7.98, 2005- 8.07, 2006- 8.27, 2007- 8.18/8.34w. pbs: 60m 6.93i '03, TJ 16.05 '98.

First athlete from Botswana to win a Commonwealth Games medal.

BRAZIL

Governing body: Confederação Brasileira de Atletismo (CBAt), Avenida Rio Purus No. 103 – Conj. Vieiralves, Bairro N.Sra das Graças, Manaus, AM 69053-050. Founded 1914 (Confederação 1977).

2007 National Champions: Men: 100m/200m: Sandro Viana 10.28/20.68, 400m: Sanderlei Parrela 46.02, 800m: Kléberson Davide 1:47.51, 1500m: Hudson de Souza 3:43.01, 5000m/10,000m: Marílson dos Santos 13:43.41/29:08.21, 3000mSt: Gladson Barbosa 8:47.61, 110mh: Anselmo da Silva 13.65, 400mh: Raphael Fernandes 49.29, HJ: Jessé de Lima 2.27, PV: Fábio Gomes da Silva 5.50, LJ: Rogério Bispo 7.97, TJ: Jadel Gregório 17.70, SP: Gustavo de Mendonça 17.86. DT: Ronald Julião 55.69, HT: Wágner Domingos 66.12, JT: Júlio César de Oliveira 74.00, Dec: Carlos Chinin 7854, Dec: Ivan da Silva 7538, 20kmW: José Alessandro Baggio 1:30:36, 50kmW: Mario José dos Santos 4:06:29. **Women:** 100m: Luciana dos Santos 11.49, 200m: Thaíssa Presti 23.33, 400m: Maria Laura Almirão 52.16, 800m: Josiano Tito 2:02.68, 1500m: Juliana de Azevedo 4:15.08, 5000m/10,000m: Ednalva da Silva 16:01.70/33:11.73, 3000mSt: Zenaide Vieira 9:58.10, 100mh: Fabiana Morae 13.64, 400mh: Lucimar Teodoro 56.54, HJ: Eliana da Silva 1.82, PV: Fabiana Murer 4.50, LJ/TJ: Keila Costa 6.76/13.91, SP/DT: Elisângela Adriano 17.16/56.97, HT: Josiane Soares 61.51, JT: Alessandra Resende 55.17, Hep: Lucimara da Silva 5822, 20000mW: Cisiane Lopes 1:39:32.5.

Jadel GREGÓRIO b. 16 Sep 1980 Jandaia do Sul, Paraná 2.02m 102kg. BM&F Atletismo.

At TJ: OG: '04- 5 (dnq 32 LJ); WCh: '03- 5, '05- 6, '07- 2; PAm: '03- 2, '07- 1; SACh: '01- 1, 03- 1; WI: '03-04-06: 6/2/2; WUG: '01- 3; WCp: '02- 5, '06- 2. Won Ib-Am 2002; BRA TJ 2001-05, 2007; LJ 2002, 2004.

South American triple jump record 2007, indoors (3) 2002-06.

Progress at TJ: 1999- 16.07, 2000- 16.48, 2001- 17.13, 2002- 17.35i/17.08, 2003- 17.11/17.37w, 2004- 17.72, 2005- 17.73, 2006- 17.56i/17.54, 2007- 17.90. pbs: HJ 2.10 '99, LJ 8.22 '04, 8.26w '07.

In 2007 he broke the 32 year-old South American record set by João Carlos da Oliveira.

Marílson Gomes **dos SANTOS** b. 6 Aug 1977 Brasília, DF 1.74m 58kg. BM&F Atletismo.

At Mar: WCh: '05- 10. At 5000m(/10,000m): PAm: '03- 3/2, '07- (2); SAm: '03- 1; WJ: '96- dnq; WCp: '06- 5. At HMar: WCh: '07- 7; WUG: '97- 1, '99- 1. Won IbAm 5000m 2006, BRA 5000m 2003, 2007; 10,000m 2003-04, 2006-07; SAm CC 2008.

South American records 5000m 2006, 10,000m, 15km, 20km & HMar 2007, two BRA 10,000m records 2006-07.

Progress at 5000m, 10,000m, Mar: 1995- 14:29.7, 30:19.05; 1996- 14:18.3, 29:52.5; 1997- 14:08.1, 29:30.41; 1998- 14:20.08, 29:12.05; 1999- 14:05.35, 28:54.9; 2000- 13:52.19, 28:39.87; 2001- 14:03.47, 29:02.89; 2002- 14:00.68, 28:34.59; 2003- 13:48.52, 28:22.58; 2004- 13:48.07, 28:21.38, 2:08:48; 2005- 13:40.8, 29:05.42, 2:13:40; 2006- 13:19.43, 27:48.49, 2:09:58; 2007- 13:22.11, 27:28.12, 2:08:37. Road pbs: 15km 42:15 '07, 20km 56:32 '07, HMar 59:33 '07. Won New York City Marathon 2006.

Fábio GOMES da SILVA b. 4 Aug 1983 Campinas, São Paulo 1.78m 74kg. BM&F Atletismo.

At PV: WCh: '07- 10; WJ: '02- 12; PAm: '07- 1; SACh: '05- 06-07: 1/3/1. Won Ib-Am 2004; and SACh-j 2002; BRA 2005-07.

South American pole vault record 2007.

Progress at PV: 1999- 4.75, 2000- 5.01, 2001- 5.16, 2002- 5.17, 2003- 5.25, 2004- 5.55, 2005- 5.50, 2006- 5.65, 2007- 5.77.

Women

Keila da Silva **COSTA** b. 6 Feb 1983 Recife 1.70m 62kg. BM&F Atletismo.

At LJ/TJ: OG: '04- dnq 31/-; WCh: '07- 7/9; PAm: 07- 2/2; SACh: '01- -/1, '03- 1/1, '05- 2/2, '07- 2/1; WJ: '00- -/11, '02- dnq 18/3; WI: '08- 7/-. Won IbAm LJ 2006, SAm-J TJ 2000, BRA LJ & TJ 2003-05, 2007.

South American TJ record 2007, indoor record (14.11) 2006, S.Am junior records TJ 2001, LJ 2002.

Progress at LJ, TJ: 1998- 11.74/11.91w, 1999- 5.83, 12.62; 2000- 6.05A/5.88, 13.23/13.65w, 2001- 6.20/6.24w, 14.00/14.15w; 2002- 6.46, 13.78/13.80w; 2003- 6.52, 13.68/13.69w; 2004- 6.61, 13.80/13.82w; 2005- 6.63, 13.95; 2006- 6.59, 14.17; 2007- 6.88, 14.57/15.10w.

Maurren Higa **MAGGI** b. 25 Jun 1976 São Carlos, São Paulo 1.78m 66kg. BM&F Atletismo.

At LJ (/100mh): OG: '00- dnq 25; WCh: '99- 8/qf, '01- 7/h, '07- 6; PAm: '99- 1/2, '07- 1 (4 TJ); SACh: '97- 2/1, '99- 1/1, '01- 1/1, '07- 1; WUG: '99- 3, '01- 1/2/2R; WI: '03- 3. Won GP 2002, GWG 2001, IbAm 2000, 2002; SA-J 100mh 1994, BRA 100mh 1997-2000, LJ 1999-2002, 2006; TJ 2002.

South American (BRA) records: LJ 1 (3) 1999, 100mh 4 (6) 1999-2001, TJ 2002-03 (3); S.Am indoor LJ (4) 2003-08.

Progress at 100mh, LJ, TJ: 1994- 14.13, 5.86; 1995- 14.46/14.3w, 5.75/6.02w; 1996- 13.99, 6.47; 1997- 13.67/13.53w, 6.54; 1998- 13.60, 6.42; 1999- 12.86, 7.26A/6.79/6.81w, 2000- 6.93, 2001- 12.71, 6.94/6.98w, 13.60; 2002- 7.02/7.17w, 14.32; 2003-

7.06, 14.53; 2006- 6.84/6.86Aw, 14.02; 2007- 6.95, 14.44; 2008- 6.89i. pbs: 60mh 8.12i '00.

Father intended to name her Maureen (after first wife of Ringo Starr), but name was misspelled on both certificate. Formerly a gymnast, made huge breakthrough in 1999 with her 7.26 LJ at the high altitude of Bogotá from a previous best of 6.79. Two year ban for positive drugs test 14 Jun 2003, later reversed by CBAT but not by IAAF. Daughter Sophia (with former F1 driver Antonio Pizzonia) was born in December 2004.

Fabiana de Almeida **MURER** b. 16 Mar 1981 Campinas, São Paulo 1.72m 64kg. BM&F Atletismo. Degree in physiotherapy.

At PV: WCh: '05- dnq 15. '07- 6=; WJ: '98- dnq 14=, '00- 10; PAm: '99- 9, '07- 1; WI: '08- 3=; SACh: '99-01-05-06-07: 3/6/2/1/1; WCp: '06- 2. Ibero-American champion 2006, SAm-J 1998-2000, BRA 2005-07.

Eight South American pole vault records 2006 & 10 indoors 2006-08, 12 BRA records 2004-06.

Progress at PV: 1998- 3.66, 1999- 3.81, 2000- 3.90, 2001- 3.91, 2002- 3.70, 2003- 4.06, 2004- 4.25, 2005- 4.40, 2006- 4.66, 2007- 4.66i/4.65, 2008- 4.70i.

BRITISH VIRGIN ISALNDS

Tahesia HARRIGAN b. 15 Feb 1982 BVI 1.57m 50kg. Was at University of Minnesota, then Alabama, USA.

At 100m(/200m): WCh: '05- qf, '07- qf/qf; CG: '02- sf, '06- 5; PAm: '07- 4; CAG: '06- 1. At 60m: '08- 3.

IVB records 100m, 200m, 400m, LJ, TJ.

Progress at 100m: 1997- 11.84, 1999- 11.96, 2000- 11.93, 2002- 11.37, 2005- 11.29, 2006- 11.13/11.02w, 2007- 11.17. pbs: 55m 6.75i '06, 60m 7.09i '08, 200m 22.98 '07, 400m 55.60 '07, LJ 6.17i '06, 6.06 '05; TJ 11.93i '06.

Went to high school in Tallahassee, Florida. Son, Khamauri, born 2004.

BULGARIA

Governing body: Bulgarian Athletics Federation, 75 bl. Vassil Levski, Sofia 1000. F'd 1924.

National Championships first held in 1926 (men), 1938 (women). **2007 Champions**: **Men**: 100m: Desulav Gunev 10.2, 200m: Kiril Kirilov 21.07, 400m: Marin Minchev 49.4, 800m/1500m: Sava Todorov 1:52.09/3:51.01, 5000m/10,000m: Dimcho Mitsov 15:02.96/31:10.77, HMar: Aleksandar Panovski 69:41, Mar/3000mSt: Stanislav Lambev 2:27:03/9:12.0, 110mh: Milen Valkanov 15.09, 400mh: Lazar Katuchev 54.22, HJ: Kalin Zlatanov 2.05, PV Spas Bukhalov 5.70, LJ: Nikolay Atanasov 7.84, TJ: Zhivko Petkov 15.97, SP: Georgi Ivanov 18.63, DT: Mikhail Selenski 52.17, HT: Rosen Zhelev 58.40, JT: Kolyo Neshev 74.32, Dec: Borislav Borisov 5146, 20kW: 20kW: Tenyo Georgiev 1:51:27. **Women**: 100m: Monika Ivanova 11.88, 200m: Tezdzhan Naimova 22.43, 400m/800m/400mh: Teodora Kolarova 52.32/2:04.37/56.48, 1500m: Daniela Yordanova 4:09.9, 5000m: Dobrinka Shalamanova 16:23.10, 10,000m/HMar: Milka Mikhaylova 35:41.46/ 77:18, Mar: Dobrinka Shalamanova 2:48:22, 3000mSt: Rumyana Panovska 10:59.77, 100mh: Magdalena Mladenova 14.45, HJ: Mirela Demireva 1.83, PV: Vera Chavdarova 4.00, LJ: Antoniya Yordanova 6.40, TJ: Mariya Dimitrova 13.89w, SP: Yana Georgieva 13.47, DT: Tsvetanka Khristova 53.67, HT: Siyana Kirilova 49.20, JT: Khristina Georgieva 46.62, Hep: Anita Petrova 4252, 20kW: Iliana Nyagolova 1:52:58

Women

Ivet LALOVA b. 18 May 1984 Sofia 1.68m 56kg. Levski Sofia, Panellínios GRE.

At 100m/200m: OG: '04- 4/5; WCh: '07- qf/-; WJ: '02- sf/-; WY: '01- h/sf; EJ: '03: 1/1; EI: '05- -/1. Won BUL 100m 2004-05, 200m 2004.

Bulgarian 100m record 2004.

Progress at 100m, 200m: 1998- 13.0, 27.2; 1999- 12.71, 2000- 12.14, 25.24; 2001- 11.72, 24.03; 2002- 11.59, 24.4; 2003- 11.14, 22.87; 2004- 10.77, 22.51/22.36w; 2005- 11.03, 22.76; 2007- 11.26/11.15w, 23.00. pb 60m 7.21i '04.

Broke her leg in a collision with another athlete on 14 Jun 2005. Her 10.77 for 100m is the best mark of the 21st century. Her father Miroslav Lalov had 100m best of 10.4 and was BUL 200m champion in 1966, her mother Liliya (née Petrunova) was a heptathlete.

Tezdzhan NAIMOVA b. 1 May 1987 Parvomay 1.63m 54kg. Lokomotiv 2004 Plovdiv.

At 100m/200m: WCh: '07- sf/sf; WJ: '06- 1/1; EJ: '05: 4/7. At 60m: EI: '07- 5. Won Balkan 100m & 200m 2007, BUL 100m 2006, 200m 2007.

Progress at 100m, 200m: 2003- 11.14, 22.87; 2004- 11.85/11.78w, 24.33; 2005- 11.61, 23.82; 2006- 11.23/11.11w, 22.99; 2007- 11.04, 22.43. pb 60m 7.13i '07.

Daniela YORDANOVA b. 8 Mar 1976 Slivnitsa 1.65m 52kg. CMA Varna.

At 1500m/(5000m): OG: '00- (10), '04- 5; WCh: '01- sf/h, '03- 7, '05- h, '07- 4; EC: '02- 5, '06- 3; WI: '04- 4, '08- 5; EI: '02- 5; WCp: '06- 4. At 3000m: EI: '00- 5. Won Balkan 1500m & 3000m 2007, BUL 1500m 1999, 2007; 5000m 1998, 10,000m 2006.

Bulgarian records 2000m 2004, 3000m (3) 2000-01, 5000m (3) 2000, 10,000m 2006.

Progress at 1500m, 5000m: 1994- 4:48.94, 19:10.48; 1995- 4:39.59, 17:42.73; 1996- 4:43.26i, 17:50.77; 1997- 17:13.25, 1998- 4:08.83, 16:16.46; 1999- 4:11.93, 16:07.28; 2000- 4:03.83, 14:56.95; 2001- 4:01.68, 2002- 4:00.65, 2003- 4:01.83, 2004- 3:59.10, 2005- 4:11.64, 2006- 3:59.37, 2007- 4:00.82. pbs: 800m 2:03.02 '01, 1000m 2:42.02i '06, 2000m 5:35.83 '04, 3000m 8:30.59 '01, 10,000m 32:40.23 '06.

CANADA

Governing body: Athletics Canada, Suite 300-2197 Riverside Drive, Ottawa, Ontario K1H 7X3. Formed as Canadian AAU in 1884.

National Championships first held in 1884 (men), 1925 (women). **2007 champions: Men**: 100m: Nicolas Macrozonaris 10.35, 200m: Brian Barnett 20.52, 400m: Tyler Christopher 45.10, 800m: Gary Reed 1:44.93, 1500m: Ryan McKenzie 3:45.97, 5000m: Reid Coolsaet 13:34.55, 10,000m: Eric Gillis 29:23.36, Mar: Matthew McInnis 2:18:06, 3000mSt: Matthew Kerr 8:47.90, 110mh: Charles Allen 13.58w, 400mh: Adam Kunkel 50.52, HJ: Michael Mason 2.27, PV: Jason Wurster 5.36; LJ: Frederic Miyoupo 7.50, TJ: Sean Jestadt 15.53, SP: Dylan Armstrong 19.86; DT: Jason Tunks 62.32, HT: James Steacy 74.80; JT: Scott Russell 76.87, Dec: Massimo Bertocchi 7704, 20000mW: Tim Berrett 1:34:17. **Women**: 100m: Toyin Olupona 11.60, 200m/400m: Esther Akinsulie 23.56/52.81, 800m: Diane Cummins 2:02.49, 1500m: Hilary Stellingwerff 4:12.66, 5000m: Megan Metcalfe 15:45.14, 10,000m: Beth Wightman 33:30.52, Mar: Lioudmila Kortchaguina 2:31:56, 3000mSt: Danelle Woods 10:17.24, 100mh: Perdita Felicien 12.50w, 400mh: Sarah Wells 59.06, HJ: Nicole Forrester 1.92, PV: Kelsie Hendry 4.31, LJ/TJ: Tabia Charles 6.52/13.60w, SP/DT: Lieja Tunks 17.43/54.91. HT: Sultana Frizell 63.87, JT: Krista Woodward 54.89, Hep: Susan Coltman 5495, 20000mW: Rachel Lavallée 1:44:27.

Dylan ARMSTRONG b. 15 Jan 1981 Kamloop, British Columbia 1.93m 114kg. Kamloops TC. Was at University of Texas.
At SP: WCh: '07- 9; PAm: '07- 1. At HT: WCh: '01- dnq 31; WJ: '00- 2 (dnq DT); PAm-J: '99- 1. Won Canadian HT 2001-02, SP 2005-07.
Five Canadian 400mh records 2006-07.
Progress at SP: 1999- 16.16, 2000- 16.30, 2001- 18.07, 2004- 19.55, 2005- 19.83, 2006- 20.62, 2007- 20.72. pbs: DT 54.60 '00, HT 71.51 '03, Wt 22.78i '03.

Tyler CHRISTOPHER b. 3 Oct 1983 Chilliwack, British Columbia 1.88m 84kg. Edmonton International.
At 400m: WCh: '03- hR, '05- 3, '07- 6; PAm: '07- 2; WI: '08- 1. Canadian champion 2004, 2006-07. At 200m: WJ: '02- sf.
Canadian records 300m 2004, 400m (3) 2005.
Progress at 400m: 2002- 46.53, 2003- 45.61, 2004- 45.25, 2005- 44.44, 2006- 44.98, 2007- 44.47. pbs: 60m 6.69i '07, 200m 20.49 '05, 300m 31.77 '04.
Former long and triple jumper.

Adam KUNKEL b. 24 Feb 1981 Walkerton, Ontario 1.80m 80kg. Legacy Athletics.
At 400mh: WCh: '03- h, '07- dnf; PAm: '03- 7, '07- 1. Canadian champion 2003-07.
Five Canadian 400mh records 2006-07.
Progress at 400mh: 1999- 52.00, 2000- 53.41, 2001- 49.87, 2002- 50.22, 2003- 49.49, 2004- 49.87, 2005- 49.90, 2006- 48.77, 2007- 48.24. pbs: 60m 6.86i '06, 100m 10.55 '00, 200m 21.10 '03, 400m 46.44 '06, 110mh 14.33 '98.

Gary REED b. 25 Oct 1981 Corpus Christie, Texas, USA 1.75m 66kg. Kamloops.
At 800m: OG: '04- sf; WCh: '01- hR; '03- h, '05- 8, '07- 2; CG: '06- ht; WCp: '06- 4; Canadian champion 2003-05, 2007.
Five Canadian 800m records 2005-06.
Progress at 800m: 2002- 1:48.08, 2003- 1:45.34, 2004- 1:44.92, 2005- 1:44.33, 2006- 1:43.93, 2007- 1:44.03. pbs: 300m 34.10 '01, 400m 46.45 '06, 600m 1:14.72 '03, 1000m 2:18.68 '07.
Began as long/triple jumper, then a decathlete (4th PAm Jnrs 1999).

Jason TUNKS b. 7 May 1975 London, Ontario 2.00m 125kg. London Western. Was at Southern Methodist University, USA.
At DT (SP): OG: '96- dnq 33, '00- 6, '04- dnq 15; WCh: '97- 9, '99- dnq 20, '01- 9, '03- 11, '05- 8; WJ: '94- 8 (10); CG: '98-02-06: 3/2/2; PAm: '99- 3 (5), '03- 1; WCp: '02- 5, '06- 9. Won NCAA 1997; Canadian SP 1997, DT 1995, 1997-2005, 2007.
Commonwealth & 2 CAN discus records 1998.
Progress at DT: 1992- 48.38, 1993- 51.52, 1994- 58.76, 1995- 58.66, 1996- 63.86, 1997- 65.20, 1998- 67.88, 1999- 65.54, 2000- 66.28, 2001- 67.70, 2002- 66.50, 2003- 65.84/66.55dh, 2004- 66.15, 2005- 66.59, 2006- 66.50, 2007- 62.87. pb SP 19.06 '97.
Was married to Teri Steer (USA, pb SP 19.21 '01). Now married to **Lieja Koeman** (NED, b. 10 Mar 1976, pb 18.82 '03, 3 EI 02, 11 OG 04 & WCh 05}.

Women

Diane CUMMINS b. 19 Jan 1974 Durban, South Africa 1.65m 50kg. Pacific Sport.
At 800m/4x400m (1500m): OG: '04- sf; WCh: '01- 5, '03- 6, '05/07- sf; CG: '98- sf/3R, '02- 2 (9), '06- 5; PAm: '99- 5, '07- 1; won CAN 800m 1998, 2000-07.
Canadian records: 800m 2001, 1000m 2002.
Progress at 800m: 1997- 2:08.65, 1998- 2:03.45, 1999- 2:02.14, 2000- 2:01.95, 2001- 1:58.39, 2002- 1:58.79, 2003- 1:58.89, 2004- 1:59.22, 2005- 2:00.10, 2006- 1:59.31, 2007- 1:59.75. pbs: 400m 53.89 '01, 1000m 2:34.14 '02, 1500m 4:05.02 '01, 1M 4:42.42i '02. Came to Canada from South Africa in November 1994.

Carmen DOUMA-HUSSAR b. 12 Mar 1977 Cambridge, Ontario 1.72m 57kg. née Douma. Graduate of Villanova University, USA.
At 1500m: OG: '04- 9; WCh: '05- 9, '07- h; CG: '06- 5; WI: '04- 2; WCp: '06- 6. Won NCAA 1998 (and indoor mile 1998, 2000), Canadian 2003, 2005-06.
Progress at 1500m: 1995- 4:28.42, 1996- 4:26.59, 1998- 4:16.04, 1999- 4:19.69, 2000- 4:16.09, 2001- 4:40.84M, 2002- 4:14.60, 2003- 4:08.09, 2004- 4:02.31, 2005- 4:02.29, 2006- 4:03.82, 2007- 4:05.91. pbs: 800m 2:02.43 '04, 1000m 2:36:26 '05, 1M

4:26.76 '07, 3000m 8:53.83 '05.
Married Christopher Hussar December 2001.

Dana ELLIS b. 7 Dec 1979 Kitchener, Ontario 1.62m 57kg. KWTF. Was at University of Waterloo.
At PV: OG: '04- 6=; WCh: '05- 6=; CG: '02- 6, '06- 4=; PAm: '03- 6, '07- nh. Canadian champion 2004-05
Six Canadian pole vault records 2004-07.
Progress at PV: 1998- 3.35, 1999- 3.65, 2000- 4.02A, 2001- 4.10, 2002- 4.20A, 2003- 4.30, 2004- 4.47, 2005- 4.51, 2006- 4.45, 2007- 4.52.
She was a member of the Canadian gymnastics team for seven years and took up vaulting after injuries. Married to US pole vaulter Ross Buller (pb 5.81 '01, US champion 2006).

Perdita FELICIEN b. 29 Aug 1980 Oshawa, Ontario 1.65m 63kg. Phoenix TC. Studied kinesiology at University of Illinois, USA.
At 100mh: OG: '00- h, '04- dnf; WCh: '01- sf, '03- 1, '05- sf, '07- 2; PAm: '03- 2, '07- 2. At 60mh: WI: '04- 1. Won FrancG 2001, CAN 2000, 2002-07, NCAA 2002-03.
Canadian 100mh records 2003 & 2004.
Progress at 100mh: 1998- 13.69/13.47w, 1999- 13.69, 2000- 12.91, 2001- 12.73, 2002- 12.83/12.77w, 2003- 12.53, 2004- 12.46/12.45w, 2005- 12.58, 2006- 12.58, 2007- 12.49. pbs: 60m 7.37i '02, 100m 11.62 '01, 200m 24.21 '02, 50mh 6.80i '04, 60mh 7.75i '04.
Improved her best from 12.68 to 12.53 to win World 100mh in 2003 and from 7.90 to 7.75 to win World Indoor 60mh in 2004. Fell in 2004 Olympic final.

Angela WHYTE b. 22 May 1980 Edmonton 1.70m 57kg. Graduate of University of Idaho, USA.
At 100mh: OG: '04- 6; WCh: '01- h, '03/05- sf, '07- 8; CG: '02- 5, '06- 2; PAm: '03- 5, '07- 3. Canadian champion 2001.
Progress at 100mh: 1998-, 1999- 13.97/13.43Aw, 2000- 13.37A/13.58, 2001- 13.09/12.82w, 2002- 13.03/13.00w, 2003- 12.78, 2004- 12.69, 2005- 12.88, 2006- 12.69, 2007- 12.63/12.55w. pbs: 60m 7.36i '08, 100m 11.63 '03, 11.37w '04; 200m 23.60 '07, 800m 2:19.91 '03, 55mh 7.48iA '03, 60mh 7.92i '08, 400mh 58.74 '01, HJ 1.68 '03, LJ 6.21i '08, 6.15 '07; SP 11.98 '03, JT 37.79 '03, Hep 5745 '03.

Jessica ZELINKA b. 3 Sep 1981 London, Ontario 1.73m 62kg. Calgary AB.
At Hep: WCh: '05- 11; CG: '06- 4; PAm: '07- 1; WJ: '00- 5 (h 100mh). Won CAN Hep 2001, 2004-06. Three Canadian heptathlon records 2006-07.
Progress at Hep: 1996- 4700, 1997- 4586, 1998- 4859, 1999- 5059, 2000- 5583, 2001- 5702, 2002- 5962, 2003- 6031, 2004- 6296, 2005- 6137, 2006- 6314, 2007- 6343. pbs: 50m 6.56i '02, 60m 7.53i '04, 100m 12.10A '06, 200m 24.03 '06, 23.90w '04; 800m 2:10.75 '06, 60mh 8.19i '06, 100mh 13.08 '06, HJ 1.79 '07, LJ 6.19/6.23w '06, SP 14.97 '07, JT 43.67 '07, Pen 4386i '07.

CAYMAN ISLANDS

Governing Body: Cayman Islands Amateur Athletic Association, PO Box 527, George Town, Grand Cayman. Founded 1980.

Women

Cydonie MOTHERSILL b. 19 Mar 1978 Kingston, Jamaica 1.70m 54kg. Was at Clemson University, USA.
At 200m(/100m): OG: '96- (h), '00- qf/qf, '04- sf; WCh: '97- (h), '01- 3, '03- sf, '05- 8, '07- 8; WJ: '96- sf/6; CG: '02- 5, '06- 4; PAm: '99- 5, '03- 2; PAm-J: '97- 3/3; WI: '03- 4; WCp: '06- 7/1R; won CAC 2001, 2003, 2005.
Cayman Islands records 100m 1994-2006, 200m 1994-05, 400m 1998-9.
Progress at 200m: 1994- 24.31, 1995- 23.83, 1996- 23.65, 1997- 23.80, 1998- 23.48, 1999- 22.81, 2000- 22.66, 2001- 22.54, 2002- 22.76, 2003- 22.45/22.41w, 2004- 22.40, 2005- 22.39/22.26w, 2006- 22.57/22.56w, 2007- 22.52. pbs: 60m 7.36i '03, 100m 11.08/11.02w '06, 300m 35.82 '00, 400m 53.13 '99.
Married to Ato Modibo TRI (400m 44.87 '01).

CHILE

Governing body: Federación Atlética de Chile, Calle Santo Toribio No 660, Ñuñoa, Santiago de Chile. Founded 1914.
National Champions 2007: **Men**: 100m/200m: Cristian Reyes 10.64/21.02, 400m: Roberto Cortés 48.90, 800m: Andy Muñoz 1:53.56, 1500m: Enzo Yáñez 3:53.85, 5000m/10,000m/Mar: Roberto Echeverría 14:33.47/29:43.93/2:16:05, 3000mSt: Aquiles Zúñiga 10:07.65, 110mh: Francisco Castro 14.21, 400mh: Gustavo Gutiérrez 52.66, HJ: Ángelo Orellana 1.95, PV: José Francisco Nava 4.70, LJ: Daniel Pineda 7.05, TJ: Jacobo Fariña 13.68, SP: Marco Antonio Verni 16.96, DT: Maximiliano Alonso 51.34, HT: Patricio Palma 65.89, JT: Ignacio Guerra 70.01, 20kW/20000mW: Yerko Araya 1:28:34/1:29:17, 50kW: Cristian Bascuñan 4:07:09. **Women**: 100m: Daniela Pavez 12.01, 200m: María Carolina Díaz 25.08, 400m/800m: Gladys Tapia 57.41/2:13.00, 1500m: Ingrid Galloso 4:39.15, 5000m/10,000m: Clara Morales 17:19.4/36:20.28, Mar: Susana Rebolledo 2:48:34 3000mSt: *none,* 100mh: Francisca Guzmán 13.78, 400mh: Karen Sauterel 63.98, HJ/PV: *none,* LJ/TJ: Macarena Reyes 5.64/12.01, SP: Marcela Barrientos 12.42, DT: Ximena Araneda 43.69, HT: Odette Palma 56.37, JT: *none,* 20000mW: Josette Sepúlveda 1:51:49, 20kW: Vanesa Contreras 1:51:48.

CHINA

Governing body: Athletic Association of the People's Republic of China, 2 Tiyuguan Road, Beijing 100763.
National Championships first held in 1910 (men), 1959 (women). **2007 Champions**: **Men**:

100m: Zhang Peimeng 10.34, 200m: Liu Haitao 21.21, 400m: Liu Xiaosheng 46.41, 800m: Li Xiangyu 1:52.24, 1500m: Xu Song 3:43.14, 5000m: Dong Guojian 14:07.61, 10,000m: Feng Zhandong 29:53.01, Mar:, 3000mSt: Lin Xiangqian 8:41.51, 110mh: Shi Dongpeng 13.31, 400mh: Qu Yongjian 49.87, HJ: Huang Haiqiang 2.24, PV: Yang Yansheng 5.60, LJ: Gao Hongwei 8.03, TJ: Gu Junjie 16.94, SP: Yan Yongguang 19.04, DT: Wu Tao 61.49, HT: Zhao Yihai 70.63, JT: Qin Qiang 76.94, Dec: Zhu Hengjun 7408, 20kW: Wang Hao 1:23:19, 50kW: Xing Shucai 3:54:53. **Women**: 100m: Jiang Lan 11.72, 200m Qin Wangping 23.57, 400m: Tang Xiaoyin 52.90, 800m/1500m: Liu Qing 2:02.29/4:16.56, 5000m: Zhang Yingying 15:36.23, 10,000m: Bai Xue 33:33.49, Mar:, 3000mSt: Zhu Yanmei 9:53.12, 100mh: Zhang Rong 13.49, 400mh: Huang Xiaoxiao 55.31, HJ: Zhao Wei 1.84, PV: Wu Sha 4.30, LJ: Chen Yaling 6.59, TJ: Xie Limei 14.42, SP: Gong Lijiao 19.13, DT: Sun Taifeng 62.92, HT: Zhang Wenxiu 74.86, JT: Chang Chunfeng 58.43, Hep: Cao Lan 5452, 20kW: Jiang Qiuyan 1:32:47.

HAN Yucheng b. 16 Dec 1978 1.82m 60kg. Liaoning.
At 20kW (50kW): OG: '04- 40 (dnf); WCh: '05- (dnf), '07- 29; WCp: '04- 4, '06- 3; AsiG: '06- 1; AsiC: '03- 1. Won CHN 20kW 2004, 50kW 2004-05. Asian 50km records 2004 & 2005.
Progress at 20kW, 50kW: 2003- 1:20:00, 3:54:45; 2004- 1:19:30, 3:39:10; 2005- 1:18:31, 3:36:20; 2006- 1:18:35, 2007- 1:19:15, 4:03:53. pbs: 10,000mW 39:39.12 '06, 30kW 2:12:39 '05.

LI Gaobo b. 23 Jul 1989 1.76m 55kg. Jiangsu province.
At 20kW: WCh: '07- 13. Won CHN NG 2005.
World youth 20km walk record 2005, junior 20,000m track record (1:20:11.72) 2007.
Progress at 20kW: 2004- 1:22:41, 2005- 1:18:07, 2006- 1:18:17, 2007- 1:19:03. pbs: 5000mW 20:54.76 '05. 10,000mW 40:51.75 '07.

LIU Xiang b. 13 Jul 1983 Shanghai 1.89m 82kg.
At 110mh: OG: '04- 1; WCh: '01- sf, '03- 3, '05- 2, '07- 1; WJ: '00- 4; WUG: '01- 1; AsiG: '02- 1, '06- 1; AsiC: '02- 1, '05- 1; WCp: '02- dnf, '06- 2. Won WAF 2006, CHN 2002, 2004-06; CHN NG 2005, E.Asian 2001, 2005. At 60mh: WI: '03-04-08: 3/2/1.
World 110mh records 2004 & 2006, five Asian & CHN records 2002-06; World junior records 110mh 2002, indoors 50mh (6.53 and 6.52) & 60mh (7.61 and 7.55). Seven Asian indoor 60mh records 2002-07.
Progress at 110mh: 1999- 14.19, 2000- 13.75, 2001- 13.32, 2002- 13.12, 2003- 13.17, 2004- 12.91, 2005- 13.05, 2006- 12.88, 2007- 12.92. pbs: 200m 21.27 '02. 50mh 6.52i '02, 60mh 7.42i '07, HJ 2.04 '98.
With his brilliant Olympic 110mh win in 2004 he tied the world record of 12.91 and become the first Chinese man to win a global athletics gold medal. Took world record to 12.88 at Lausanne 2006. Set world age records 16 (13.94)-17-18 in 2000-02.

SHI Dongpeng b. 6 Jan 1984 1.91m 75kg. Hebei.
At 110mh: OG: '04- h; WCh: '03-05-07: 6/sf/5; WJ: '02- 2; AsiG: '02- 4, '06- 2; AsiC: '03- 1, '05- 2; Won Asi-J 2001, CHN 2003, 2007.
World U18 110mh record 2001.
Progress at 110mh: 2000- 14.10, 2001- 13.43, 2002- 13.50, 2003- 13.40, 2004- 13.50, 2005- 13.29, 2006- 13.28, 2007- 13.19. pbs: 100m 10.95 '06, 50mh 6.75i '04, 60mh 7.63i '06.

XING Shucai b. 4 Aug 1984 1.72m 60kg. Yunnan.
At 50kW: WCh: '05- dnf; WCp: '04- 14. Chinese champion 2007.
Progress at 20kW, 50kW: 2003- 1:22:58, 4:24:46; 2004- 1:21:53, 3:40:22; 2005- 1:18:27, 3:37:58; 2006- 1:24:38, 3:45:52; 2007- 3:54:19. pb 10,000mW 40:55.42 '04.

YU Chaohong b. 12 Dec 1976 1.75m 63kg. Yunnan.
At 20kW: WCh: '03- 15, '05- dq; WCp: '99- 16; AsiG: '02- 2. At 50kW: OG: '04- 4; WCh: '07- dq; WCp: '04- 2, '06- 11. Won E.Asian 20kW 2005, CHN 20kW 2002-03, 2005; 50kW 2003, NG 50kW 2005. Asian 50km walk record 2005.
Progress at 20kW, 50kW: 1995- 1:25:33, 1997- 4:00:47, 1999- 1:23:09, 2000- 1:23:35, 3:58:44; 2001- 1:21:04, 3:47:04, 2002- 1:21:45, 3:58:57; 2003- 1:18:56, 3:44:11; 2004- 1:21:04, 3:42:28; 2005- 1:18:30, 3:36:06; 2006- 1:21:34, 3:43:58; 2007- 3:49:27. pbs: 30kW 2:10:58 '04, 35kW 2:33:04 '04.

ZHAO Chengliang b. 1 Jun 1984 1.70m 62kg. Yunnan.
At 50kW: WCh: '05- 5, '07- dq; AsiC: '07- 1; WCp: '04- 19, '06- 8.
Progress at 20kW, 50kW: 2003- 1:26:55, 2004- 1:23:03, 3:43:09; 2005- 1:20:20, 3:36:13; 2006- 1:21:23, 3:47:32; 2007- 3:44:26. pbs: 30kW 2:12:32 '05, 35kW 2:34:33 '05.

Women

GAO Shuying b. 28 Oct 1979 1.80m 66kg. Shanghai.
At PV: OG: '00- 10, '04- dnq 24=; WCh: '01- 5, '03- 9, '05- 5. '07- dnq 14; WJ: '98- 8; AsiG: '02- 1, '06- 1; AsiC: '02/03/05- 1/4/1; WUG: '01- 1; WCp: '02- 4, '06- 3. Won CHN 2000-02, 2004, 2006; E.Asian & CHN NG 2001.
Nine Asian pole vault records 2000-07.
Progress at PV: 1996- 3.30, 1997- 3.70, 1998- 3.90, 1999- 4.10, 2000- 4.35, 2001- 4.52, 2002- 4.45i/4.43, 2003- 4.40, 2004- 4.45, 2005- 4.53, 2006- 4.50, 2007- 4.64.

GONG Lijiao b. 24 Jan 1989 1.75m 80kg. Hebei.
At SP: WCh: '07- 7. Chinese champion 2007, Asian indoor 2008.
Progress at SP: 2005- 15.41i, 2006- 17.92, 2007- 19.13. pb JT 53.94 '07.

HE Dan b. 22 Jul 1984 1.60m 46kg. Army.
At 20kW: WCp: '06- 4; AsiG: '06- 3.
Progress at 20kW: 2003- 1:35:49, 2004- 1:34:18, 2005- 1:28:35, 2006- 1:28:20. pbs: 10kW 44:50R '06.

HUANG Xiaoxiao b. 3 Mar 1983 1.81m 62kg. Shandong.
At 400mh: OG: '04- sf; WCh: '05- 5, '07- 5; AsiG: '06- 1; AsiC: '03- 1, '05- 1; WUG: '03- 2; WCp: '06- 6. Won E.Asian 2005, CHN 400mh 2003, 2007; CHN NG 400m 2003, 2005; 400mh 2005.
Progress at 400mh: 2001- 55.15, 2002- 56.96, 2003- 55.10, 2004- 54.83, 2005- 54.18, 2006- 54.69, 2007- 54.00. pbs: 200m 24.28 '00, 400m 51.93 '03.

JIANG Jing b. 23 Oct 1985 1.72m 50kg. Jiangsu.
At 20kW: OG: '04- 32; WCh: '05- dq, '07- dnf; WCp: '04- 2. Chinese champion 2004-05.
Progress at 20kW: 2003- 1:29:42, 2004- 1:27:34, 2005- 1:27:19, 2006- 1:28:55, 2007- 1:29:45. pb 10kW 44:07 '04.

LI Ling b. 7 Feb 1985 1.79m 85kg. Liaoning.
At SP: WCh: '07- 4; AsiG: '06- 1; AsiC: '05- 3; WCp: '06- 5. Chinese champion 2006.
Progress at SP: 2002- 15.45, 2003- 16.55, 2004- 17.34, 2005- 18.68, 2006- 19.05, 2007- 19.38.

LI Meiju b. 3 Oct 1979 1.79m 85kg. Hebei.
At SP: OG: '04- 9; WCh: '03- 11, '05- 7, '07- 6; WJ: '00- 2; AsiG: '02- 1, '06- 2, AsiC: '03- 1, '05- 1; WI: '03-04-08: dnq 10/5/3; WUG: '05- 2. Won CHN 2002, 2004-05; NG 2001, 2005; Af-AsG 2003.
Progress at SP: 1998- 15.89, 1999- 16.62, 2000- 17.48, 2001- 18.92, 2002- 18.95, 2003- 18.96, 2004- 18.89, 2005- 19.05, 2006- 18.54, 2007- 19.09, 2008- 19.09i.

LIU Hong b. 12 May 1987 1.64m 55kg. Guangdong.
At 20kW: WCh: '07- 19; WCp: '06- 6; AsiG: '06- 1. At 10,000mW: WJ: '06- 1.
Progress at 20kW: 2004- 1:35:04, 2005- 1:29:39, 2006- 1:28:26, 2007- 1:29:41. pbs: 3000mW 12:18.18 '05, 5000mW 21:30.03 '06, 10kW 44:50R, 45:12.84t '06.

MA Xuejun b. 26 Mar 1985 1.77m 83kg. Hebei.
At DT: WCh: '07- 9; AsiG: '06- 2; WJ: '02- 1, '04- 1; WY: '01- 1. Won Asi-J 2004, CHN 2006.
Progress at DT: 1999- 52.79, 2001- 58.65, 2002- 58.85, 2003- 60.20, 2004- 57.85, 2005- 61.87, 2006- 65.00, 2007- 62.57.

SONG Aimin b. 15 Mar 1978 1.77m 83kg. Hebei.
At DT: OG: '04- dnq 25; WCh: '03- 7, '05- 10, '07- dnq 14; AsiG: '02- 2, '06- 1; AsiC: '05- 1; WUG: '05- 2; WCp: '06- 3. Won Asi-J 1997, E.Asian 2005, CHN 2001-03.
Progress at DT: 1997- 55.84, 1998- 56.64, 1999- 60.50, 2000- 60.39, 2001- 62.34, 2002- 62.28, 2003- 65.33, 2004- 64.90, 2005- 65.23, 2006- 63.52, 2007- 62.64.

SONG Hongjuan b. 4 Jul 1984 1.66m 50kg. Jilin.
At 20kW: OG: '04- 14; WCh: '03- dq, '05- 9, '07- 15; WCp: '04- 6; Chinese champion 2003-04.
World junior records 20,000m walk (1:29:23.4) and 20km road 2003.
Progress at 20kW: 2000- 1:43:04, 2001- 1:40:38, 2003- 1:27:16, 2004- 1:26:46, 2005- 1:28:26, 2006- 1:34:12, 2007- 1:28:25. pb 10kW 43:44 '04.

SUN Taifeng b. 26 Aug 1982 1.87m 90kg. Tianjin.
At DT: WCh: '07- 5. Won CHN 2007.
Progress at DT: 1999- 44.00, 2000- 52.49, 2001- 55.40, 2002- 53.66, 2003- 54.98, 2004- 58.09, 2005- 61.08, 2006- 62.98, 2007- 64.98.

XIE Limei b. 27 Jun 1986 1.68m 50kg. Fujian.
At TJ: WCh: '07- 8; WJ: '04- 2; AsiG: '06- 1; WI: '08- 8. Won CHN 2006-07. Asian TJ record 2007.
Progress at TJ: 2002- 13.51, 2003- 13.89, 2004- 14.08, 2005- 14.38, 2006- 14.54, 2007- 14.90. pb LJ 6.41 '06.

XING Huina b. 25 Feb 1984 Weifang, Shandong province 1.66m 50kg.
At (5000m)/10,000m: OG: '04- 9/1; WCh: '03- 7, '05- 5/4; AsiG: '02- 4/3. Won CHN 1500m 2003-04, 5000m 2004-05, CHN NG 5000m & 10,000m 2005. World junior 10,000m record 2003.
Progress at 5000m, 10,000m: 2000- 16:11.09, 2001- 14:56.15, 36:38.91; 2002- 15:42.99, 31:42.58; 2003- 15:00.02, 30:31.55; 2004- 14:56.01, 30:24.36; 2005- 14:43.64, 30:27.18; 2006- 15:26.84, 32:04.32; 2007- 15:36.94. pbs: 1500m 4:03.98dq '05, 4:09.01 '03, 3000m 8:53.5 '05.

ZHANG Wenxiu b. 22 Mar 1986 Dalian 1.81m 102kg. Army.
At HT: OG: '04- 7; WCh: '01- 11, '03- dnq 14, '05- 5, '07- 3; WJ: '02- dnq 20; AsiG: '06- 1; AsiC: '05- 1; WCp: '06- 4. Won Asi-J 2002, CHN 2004, 2006-07; NG 2003.
Six Asian hammer records 2001-07, world youth record 2003, two world junior record 2004-05.
Progress at HT: 2000- 60.30, 2001- 66.30, 2002- 67.13, 2003- 70.60, 2004- 72.42, 2005- 73.24, 2006- 74.15, 2007- 74.86.
World age bests at 15-16-18.

ZHOU Chunxiu b. 15 Nov 1978 Jiangsu province 1.63m 44kg. Henan.
At Mar: OG: '04- 33; WCh: '05- 5, '07- 2; AsiG: '06- 1; Chinese champion 2003-05. World HMar: '04- 12.
Progress at 10,000m, Mar: 2000- 33:14.63, 2003- 32:13.96, 2:23:41; 2004- 33:03.04, 2:23:28; 2005- 31:09.03, 2:21:11; 2006- 32:42.46, 2:19:51; 2007- 32:44.13, 2:20:38. pbs: 1500m 4:16.59 '98, 3000m 9:34.68 '00, 5000m 15:22.46 '03, HMar 69:58 '07.
Six wins in 14 marathons to 2007. Four sub 2:30 runs in 2005 (first woman to do so in one year), won Seoul in pb 2:23:24 and improved by 2:13 for 2nd in Beijing. Won Seoul 2006, London 2007.

ZHU Xiaolin b. 20 Feb 1984 1.66m 50kg. Liaoning.
At Mar: WCh: '07- 4. Won Chinese 1500m 2006, Mar & CC 2007.
Progress at Mar: 2002- 2:23:57, 2004- 2:41:04, 2005- 2:32:27, 2006- 2:28:27, 2007- 2:26:08. pbs: 800m 2:18.51 '06, 1500m 4:12.73 '05, 3000m 9:04.64i '02, 5000m 15:22.35 '05, 10,000m 32:27.38 '07, HMar 73:24 '07.
Won Dalian Marathon 2002, 2005-06.

COLOMBIA

Governing body: Federación Colombiana de Atletismo, Calle 28 No. 25-18, Apartado Aéreo 6024, Santafé de Bogotá. Founded 1937.
National Champions 2007: Men: 100m: Harlin Hechavarría 10.43, 200m: Daniel Grueso 20.66, 400m: Yeimer Mosquera 47.30, 800m/1500m: Freddy Espinoza 1:50.08/3:49.37, 5000m/10,000m: Javier Guarín 14:15.04/30:05.93, Mar: Juan Carlos Cardona 2:26:20, 3000mSt: Wilder Álvarez 9:19.50, 110mh: Jeison Rivas 14.32, 400mh: Juan Pablo Maturana 51.35, HJ: Gilmar Mayo 2.16, PV: Víctor Medina 4.80, LJ: Lewis Asprilla 7.64w, TJ: John Murillo 15.93, SP: Jiovanny García 17.55, DT: Julián Angulo 52.81, HT: Jacobo de León 58.10, JT: Noraldo Palacios 74.34, Dec: Andrés Mantilla 6827, 20kW: Gustavo Restrepo 1:23:45, 20000mW: Luis F.López 1:24:22.7. **Women:** 100m/200m: Felipa Palacios 11.58w/23.42, 400: Alejandra Idrobo 54.53, 800m/1500m: Rosibel García 2:05.60/ 4:27.71, 5000m: Bertha Sánchez 17:02.266, 10,000m: Lina Arias 34:48.57, HMar: , Mar: Ruby Milena Riativa 2:49:34, 100mh: Brigitte Merlano 13.18w, 400mh: Keila Escobar 59.42, HJ/LJ/TJ: Caterine Ibargüen 1.82/6.22/12.66, PV: Milena Agudelo 3.90, SP/DT: Luz Dary Castro 16.06/50.19, HT: Johana Moreno 61.73, JT: Zuleima Araméndiz 55.72, Hep: Alejandra Gómez 4109, 20,000mW/ 20kW: Sandra Zapata 1:42:09.0t/1:42:30.

DEMOCRATIC REPUBLIC OF CONGO

Governing Body: Fédération d'Athlétisme du Congo, BP 1527 Kinshasa 1. Founded 1949.

Gary KIKAYA b. 4 Feb 1978 Lubumbashi 1.84m 75kg. Studied sociology at University of Tennessee.
At 400m: OG: '04- sf; WCh: '03/05/07- sf; AfCh: '06- 1; WI: '04- 3; WCp: '06- 2; Won NCAA 2002, indoor 2003.
African 400m record 2006. COD records 200m & 400m 2001-06.
Progress at 400m: 2000- 46.51A, 2001- 45.58A, 2002- 44.53, 2003- 44.99, 2004- 44.80, 2005- 44.81, 2006- 44.10, 2007- 44.60A/44.77. pbs: 55m 6.20i '05, 200m 20.40 '06, 300m 31.95 '05.
2004 World Indoor bronze was the first ever global medal for his country. COD recortds in three successive 400m races in 2006, 44.46, 44.43 and 44.10 (2nd WAF). Lived in South Africa for a decade as his father was Congo's ambassador there.

CROATIA

Governing body: Hrvatski Atletski Savez, Tg Sportova 11, 10000 Zagreb. Founded 1912.
National Champions 2007: **Men**: 100m: Goran Pelic 10.59, 200m: Zeljko Vincek 21.08, 400m: Ivan Rimac 48.28, 800m: Dalibor Pavic 1:55.09, 1500m: Mahmoud Al-Mufleh 4:00.93, 3000m/5000m/10,000m/HMar: Slavko Petrovic 8:53.62/15:38.88/31:49.95/66:27, Mar: Hrvoje Kovac 2:49:47, 3000mSt: Zoran Zilic 9:32.55, 110mh: Nenad Varda 15.15, 400mh: Milan Kotur 50.94, HJ/Dec: Aleksandar Puklavec 2.05/6585, PV: Nenad Pavlicek 4.70, LJ: Ivan Pucelj 7.60, TJ: Milan Ljubotina 15.35, SP: Nenad Mulabegovic 19.99, DT: Martin Maric 55.87, HT: Andras Haklits 72.75, JT: Goran Vukovic 70.47, 5kW: Zelimir Haubrih 26:41. **Women**: 100m: Maja Golub 11.54, 200m/400m: Danijela Grgic 24.01/53.06, 800m: Anita Banovic 2:04.68, 1500m/3000m: Marina Milkovic 4:54.15/10:24.92, 5000m: Ljiljana Culirk 17:06.70, 10,000m/Mar: Lidija Rajcic 37:40.67/2:59:25, HMar: Antonija Orlic 83:50, 100mh: Andrea Ivancevic 13.85, 400mh: Nikolina Horvat 59.66, HJ: Ana Simic 1.65, PV: Ivona Jerkovic 3.80, LJ: Petra Karanikic 6.08, TJ: Marija Babic 12.1612.16, SP: Mateja Greguric 14.49, DT: Vera Begic 56.13, HT: Ivana Brkljacic 72.63, JT: Ivana Vukovic 53.18, Hep: Ivana Loncarek 4585.

Women

Ivana BRKLJACIC b. 25 Jan 1983 Vinningen-Schweningen, Germany 1.70m 65kg. Mladost Zagreb.
At HT: OG: '00- 11, '04- dnq 13; WCh: '01- 8, '03/05- dnq 36/15, '07- 11; EC: '02/06- dnq 17/21; WJ: '98- dnq 15, '00- 1, '02- 1; WY: '99- 3; EU23: '03- 8; EJ: '99- 5, '01- 1. CRO champion 1999, 2001-02, 2004, 2006-07.
12 Croatian hammer records 1998-2007.
Progress at HT: 1998- 56.84, 1999- 58.51, 2000- 68.18, 2001- 66.49, 2002- 66.54, 2003- 68.03, 2004- 69.38, 2005- 71.00, 2006- 71.34, 2007- 75.08. pbs: SP 12.90 '04, DT 42.84 '04.

Blanka VLASIC b. 8 Nov 1983 Split 1.92m 75kg. ASK PK Split.
At HJ: OG: '00- dnq 17, '04- 11; WCh: '01- 6, '03- 7, '05- dnq 19=, '07- 1; EC: '02- 5=, '06- 4; WJ: '00- 1, '02- 1; WY: '99- 8; EU23: '03- 1; EJ: '01- 7; WI: '03-04-06-08: 4/3/2/1; EI: '07- 4. Won WAF 2007, MedG 2001, CRO 2001-02, 2005.
Nine Croatian high jump records 2003-07.
Progress at HJ: 1998- 1.68, 1999- 1.80, 2000- 1.93, 2001- 1.95, 2002- 1.96, 2003- 2.01, 2004- 2.03, 2005- 1.95, 2006- 2.05i/2.03, 2007- 2.07.
Won 5/6 Golden League HJs 2007 and in that year she had 24 attempts at the WR of 2.10. Her father Josko set the Croatian decathlon record with 7659 (1983) and named his daughter after Casablanca, where he won Mediterranean Games title.

Janeth Jepkosgei on her way to winning the World 800m championship.

Maryam Jamal beats Yelena Soboleva to win the World 1500m

(To) Donald Thomas World high jump champion.
(Below) Dayron Robles (left) wins the World Athletics Final 110m hurdles.

Yargelis Savigne, World triple jump champion.

Edwin Soi who won both 3000m and 5000m at the World Athletics Final.

World pole vault champion Brad Walker.

Andrew Howe, pipped at the last for the World long jump title, was given the European AAA Rising Star Award.

Barbora Spotáková, World javelin champion.

CUBA

Governing body: Federación Cubana de Atletismo, Calle 13 y C Vedado 601, Zona Postal 4, La Habana 10400. Founded 1922.

National Champions 2007: Men: 100m: Michel Herrera 10.30w, 200m: David Lescay 21.17, 400m: William Collazo 46.71, 800m: Yeimar López 1:49.6, 1500m: Maury Surel Castillo 3:41.87, 5000m: Liván Luque 14:27.24, 10,000m: Richard Pérez 30:04.17, 3000mSt: José A. Sánchez 9:01.87, 110mh: Dayron Robles 13.17, 400mh: Yacnier Luis 50.05, HJ: Víctor Moya 2.31, PV: Lázaro Borges 5.20, LJ: Héctor Fuentes 7.99w, TJ: Osniel Tosca 17.26, SP: Carlos Véliz 19.62, DT: Yunier Lastre 56.90, HT: Noleisis Bicet 70.01, JT: Guillermo Martínez 79.21, Dec: Yordanis García 8013, 20kW: Yubraile Hernández 1:35:56. **Women**: 100m: Virgen Benavies 11.42w, 200m: Roxana Díaz 23.32, 400m: Indira Terrero 51.00, 800m; Juana Méndez 2:05.48, 1500m: Yadira Bataille 4:23.20, 5000m: Dailín Belmonte 16:40.25, 10,000m: Mariela González 34:41.45, 100mh: Yenima Arencibia 13.37, 400mh: Daimí Pernía 58.50, HJ: Lesyaní Mayor 1.75, PV: Yarisley Silva 4.00, LJ/TJ: Yargelis Savigne 6.66w/14.54, SP: Misleydis González 18.37, DT: Yania Ferrales 58.04, HT: Yipsi Moreno 74.90, JT: Maria de la C. Álvarez 60.95, Hep: Dailenis Mensoney 5317, 20kW: Leislis Rodríguez 1:44:25.

Yoandri BETANZOS b. 15 Feb 1982 Ciego de Ávila 1.79m 71kg
At TJ: OG: '04- 4; WCh: '03- 2, '05- 2, '07- dnq 20; WJ: '00- 2; WY: '99- 2; PAm: '03- 1; CAG: '06- 1; WUG: '01- 5; WI: '04- 3, '06- 3; Won WAF 2005-06, CAC 2005, PAm-J 2001, Cuban 2002-06.
Progress at TJ: 1998- 14.96, 1999- 15.94/16.07w, 2000- 16.82, 2001- 16.84/16.86w, 2002- 17.29, 2003- 17.28, 2004- 17.53, 2005- 17.46, 2006- 17.63/17.67w, 2007- 17.12i/16.96/17.21w. pb HJ 2.10.

Yordani GARCÍA b. 21 Nov 1988 San Luis, Pinar del Río 1.93m 88kg.
At Dec: WCh: '07- 8; PAm: '07- 2; WJ: '06- 2; Cuban champion 2006-07. At Oct: WY: '05- 1.
Cuban & CAC junior decathlon record 2007. World youth octathlon record (6482) 2005.
Progress at Dec: 2005- 6765, 2006- 7879h, 2007- 8257. pbs: 100m 10.67 '07, 400m 49.25 '07, 1500m 4:46.53 '06, 110mh 14.01 '07, 14.0 '06; HJ 2.09 '07, PV 4.80'07, LJ 7.15 '07, SP 15.39 '07, DT 45.93 '07, JT 68.74 '07.

David GIRALT b. 26 Aug 1984 Santiago de Cuba 1.82m 72kg.
At TJ: OG: '04- dnq 17; WCh: '03-05-07: 4/8/7; WJ: '02- 1, WY: '01- 2; WI: '08- 2. Won PAm-J 2003 (2 LJ), Ib-Am 2004.
Progress at TJ: 2000- 15.23, 2001- 16.33, 2002- 16.84, 2003- 17.31, 2004- 17.12, 2005- 17.14, 2006- 16.97/17.06w, 2007- 17.39i/17.10/17.18w, 2008- 17.50. pb LJ 7.70 '02.
Father (also David) had LJ pbs 8.22/8.32w and was third in the World Cup in 1979.

Yoel HERNÁNDEZ b. 12 Dec 1977 Manacas, Villa Clara 1.84m 77kg.
At 110mh: OG: '00/04- sf; WCh: '99-01-03-07: 6/4/7/sf; WJ: '94- sf, '96- 1; PAm: '99- 2, '07- 3; Won Cuban 2002, IbAm 2004. At 60mh: WI: '01-04-06-08: 5/7/8/8.
Progress at 110mh: 1994- 14.20, 1995- 13.81, 1996- 13.81/13.72w, 1997- 13.70, 1998- 13.45, 1999- 13.24, 2000- 13.24/13.20w, 2001- 13.30, 2002- 13.30, 2003- 13.49, 2004- 13.29/13.28w, 2005- 13.39/13.32w, 2006- 13.39, 2007- 13.23. pbs: 100m 10.62 '07, 200m 21.10 '02, 50mh 6.42i '00, 60mh 7.40i '00.

Guillermo MARTÍNEZ b. 28 Jun 1981 Camagüey 1.90m 101kg.
At JT: OG: '04- dnq 17; WCh: '05- 10, '07- 9; PAm: '07- 1; CAG: '07- 1. Cuban champion 2004-07.
Cuban & CAC javelin record 2006.
Progress at JT: 1999- 64.66, 2000- 70.82, 2001- 73.50, 2002- 75.90, 2003- 75.35, 2004- 81.45, 2005- 84.06, 2006- 87.17, 2007- 85.93.

Víctor Rafael **MOYA** b. 24 Oct 1982 Santiago de Cuba 1.96m 80kg.
At HJ: WCh: '05- 2=, '07- 5=; WI: '06- 4, '08- 5; PAm: '07- 1; CAG: '06- 1. Won WAF & CAC 2005, Cuban 2006-07.
Progress at HJ: 1999- 2.00, 2000- 2.05, 2001- 2.10, 2002- 2.21, 2003- 2.18, 2004- 2.25, 2005- 2.35, 2006- 2.31, 2007- 2.33.
Set pbs at 2.32 and 2.35 to win 2005 WAF title.

Yoelbi Luis **QUESADA** b. 4 Aug 1973 Trinidad, Sancti Spíritus 1.81m 71kg. Adidas.
At TJ: OG: '92- 6, '96- 3, '00- 4, '04- 8; WCh: '91- 7, '93- 12, '95- 4, '97- 1, '99- 10, '03- 9; WI: '93-5-9-03: 5/2/4/3; WJ: '90- 2, '92- 1; WUG: '97- 1, '99- 1; WCp: '94- 1, '98- 3; PAm: '91-5-9-03: 1/1/1/3; CAG: '93- 1, '98- 1. Won CAC-J 1990, PAmJ 1991, IbAm 1992, Cuban 1991-5, 1997-8, 2002. 2nd GP 1996.
Cuban triple jump record 1997.
Progress at TJ: 1989- 16.11, 1990- 16.68, 1991- 17.13, 1992- 17.23, 1993- 17.68, 1994- 17.61, 1995- 17.67/17.97w, 1996- 17.75, 1997- 17.85, 1998- 17.43i/17.27, 1999- 17.40, 2000- 17.37, 2001- 16.55, 2002- 17.42, 2003- 17.27i/16.97, 2004- 17.13, 2005- 17.03. 2006- 17.02/17.38w, 2007- 17.07. pb LJ 7.88 '94.
World age bests for each age 15-19 in 1989-93.

Dayron ROBLES b. 19 Nov 1986 Guantánamo 1.92m 80kg.
At 110mh: WCh: '05- sf, '07- 4; WJ: '04- 2, WY: '03- 6; CAG: '06- 1; PAm: '07- 1; WCp: '06- 3; won PAm-J 2005, WAF 2007, Cuban 2006-07. At 60mh: WI: '06- 2.
Three Cuban & CAC 110mh records 2006-07, CAC junior record 2005. Two CAC 60mh indoor records 2008.

Progress at 110mh: 2002- 15.01, 2003- 14.30, 2004- 13.75, 2005- 13.46/13.2/13.41w, 2006- 13.00, 2007- 12.92. pbs: 100m 10.70 '06, 200m 21.85 '06, 50mh 6.39i '08, 60mh 7.33i '08.

Osniel TOSCA b. 30 Jun 1984 Santa Clara 1.78m 60kg.
At TJ: WCh: '07- 4; WJ: '02- 7; WY: '01- 3; PAm: '07- 2; WI: '08- 6. NACAC champion 2006, Cuban 2007.
Progress at TJ: 2000- 15.14, 2001- 16.05, 2002- 16.45, 2003- 16.61, 2004- 17.17, 2005- 17.08, 2006- 17.01, 2007- 17.52. pb LJ 7.00 '03.

Women

Yarelis BARRIOS b. 12 Jul 1983 Pinar del Rio 1.72m 89kg.
At DT: WCh: '07- 3; WJ: '02- 7; PAm: '07- 1; CAG: '06- 2; WUG: '07- 1. Won CAC 2005.
Progress at DT: 1999- 44.45, 2000- 50.22, 2001- 48.92, 2002- 54.10, 2003- 58.37, 2004- 59.51, 2005- 60.61, 2006- 61.01, 2007- 63.90.

Zulia Inés **CALATAYUD** b. 9 Nov 1979 Playa, La Habana 1.69m 59kg. Graduated in PE from University of Havana.
At 800m: OG: '00- 6, '04- 8; WCh: '99- h, '01- sf, '05- 1, '07- sf; PAm: '99- 2; CAG: '06- 1; WCp: '02- 4, '06- 1; Won WAF 2005-06, Ib-Am 2004. At 400m: WJ: '98- sf. Won Cuban 400m 1999, 800m 1999-2001.
Progress at 800m: 1995- 2:18.9, 1996- 2:13.80, 1997- 2:12.7, 1999- 2:00.67, 2000- 1:58.66, 2001- 1:58.60, 2002- 1:56.09, 2004- 1:59.21, 2005- 1:57.92, 2006- 1:56.91, 2007- 2:00.34. pbs: 200m 24.33/24.2 '98, 400m 50.87 '01, 1000m 2:34.31 '02, 1500m 4:21.73 '06. Missed 2003 season with shin injuries.

Yunaika CRAWFORD b. 2 Nov 1982 Marianao, La Habana 1.65m 75kg.
At HT: OG: '04- 3; WCh: '03/05- dnq 20/26, '07- 12; WJ: '00- 3; WY: '99- 2; PAm: '03- 2; CAG: '06- 2; Won PAm-J 2001, CAC 2001, Cuban 2005.
Progress at HT: 1995- 38.86, 1997- 48.98, 1998- 58.92, 1999- 62.71, 2000- 65.88, 2001- 65.67, 2002- 70.62, 2003- 70.69, 2004- 73.16, 2005- 69.30, 2006- 71.92, 2007- 68.82.

Yumileidi CUMBÁ b. 11 Feb 1975 Guantánamo 1.83m 100kg. PE student.
At SP: OG: '96- dnq 13, '00- 6, '04- 1; WCh: '99- 6, '01- 8, '03- dnq 13, '05- 6, '07- 12; PAm: '95- 3, '99- 2, '03- 1; CAG: '93- 2, '98- 1, '06- 1; WJ: '92- 4, '94- 2; WI: '99-01-03-04-06: 6/5/6/2/5; WUG: '99- 1, '01- 1; WCp: '98-02-06: 4/2/3. Won CAC 2005, Cuban 1994-5, 1998, 2000-06; IbAm 2002, 2004. CAC junior shot record 1994.
Progress at SP: 1990- 14.53, 1991- 15.84, 1992- 17.44, 1993- 17.70, 1994- 18.78, 1995- 19.11, 1996- 18.57, 1998- 19.20, 1999- 19.29, 2000- 19.48, 2001- 19.10i/19.00, 2002- 19.39, 2003- 19.31, 2004- 19.97, 2005- 19.06, 2006- 19.66, 2007- 18.81. pb DT 42.84 '93.

Yania FERRALES b. 28 Jul 1977 Morón, Ciego de Avila 1.80m 86kg.
At DT: OG: '04- nt; WCh: '05- dnq 14, '07- 11; PAm: '03- 3, '07- 2; CAG: '06- 1; WJ: '96- dnq 18; WCp: '06- 7. CAC champion 2001, 2003; Ibero-American 2004, Cuban 2000-01, 2004-07, CAC-J 1996.
Progress at DT: 1995- 45.64, 1996- 51.94, 1997- 53.82, 1998- 56.40, 1999- 56.94, 2000- 57.40, 2001- 56.90, 2002- 59.04, 2003- 61.34, 2004- 62.88, 2005- 64.52, 2006- 66.00, 2007- 64.97, 2008- 65.02.

Mabel GAY b. 5 May 1983 Santiago de Cuba 1.86m 71kg.
At TJ: WCh: '03- 5, '05- dnq 18; WJ: '02- 1; WY: '99- 1; PAm: '03- 1, '07- 3; CAG: '06- 1; WI: '04- 9; Won CAC-J 2002, IbAm 2002, Cuban 2003-04, 2006. CAC junior TJ record 2002.
Progress at TJ: 1997- 13.00, 1998- 13.48, 1999- 13.82, 2000- 14.02, 2001- 14.05, 2002- 14.29, 2003- 14.52, 2004- 14.57i/14.20, 2005- 14.21/14.44w, 2006- 14.27, 2007- 14.66.
World age 17 record in 1999.

Misleydis GONZÁLEZ b. 19 Jun 1978 Bayamo, Granma 1.79m 75kg.
At SP: OG: '04- 7; WCh: '05- 10, '07- 11; PAm: '03- 4, '07- 1; CAG: '06- 2; WI: '04- 6. '08- 4; WUG: '05- 3; won CAC 2001, 2003; Cuban 2007.
Progress at SP: 1994- 12.41, 1995- 14.48, 1996- 15.80, 1997- 15.87, 1998- 15.76, 1999- 16.19, 2000- 17.55, 2001- 17.54, 2002- 17.79, 2003- 18.11, 2004- 18.73, 2005- 18.92, 2006- 19.10, 2007- 18.97.

Osleidys MENÉNDEZ b. 14 Nov 1979 Martí, Matanzas 1.78m 80kg.
At JT: OG: '00- 3, '04- 1; WCh: '97- 7, '99- 4, '01- 1, '03- 5, '05- 1; WJ: '96- 1, '98- 1; WUG: '01- 1; PAm: '99- 1, '03- 3, '07- 1; CAG: '98- 2, '06- 2; WCp: '02- 1. Won GWG 2001, ÍbAm 2004, PAm-J 1995, 1997; Cuban 1997, 1999-2002-05; CAC 1997, GP 2002 (3rd 2000), WAF 2004-05.
World javelin records 2001 & 2005. Eight CAC bests and one world (66.45 '99) new javelin 1999-2001.
Progress at JT: 1994- 53.98, 1995- 54.30, 1996- 62.54, 1997- 66.92, 1998- 68.17, 1999- 67.59; new 1999- 66.49, 2000- 67.83, 2001- 71.54, 2002- 67.40, 2003- 63.96, 2004- 71.53, 2005- 71.70, 2006- 65.02, 2007- 62.34.
On 1 July 2001 she became the first Cuban woman to set a world record in athletics. World age 19 best in 1999.

Yipsi MORENO b. 19 Nov 1980 Camagüey 1.68m 70kg.
At HT: OG: '00- 4, '04- 2; WCh: '99- 18, '01- 1, '03- 1, '05- 2, '07- 2; WJ: '98- 4; PAm: '99- 2, '03- 1; CAG: '06- 1; WUG: '01- 2; WCp: '02- 2, '06- 3. Won WAF 2003, 2005, 2007, PAm-J 1997, IbAm 2004, Cuban 2000-04, 2007.
World junior hammer record 1999, 21 CAC records 1999-2007.
Progress at HT: 1996- 53.94, 1997- 61.96, 1998-

61.00, 1999- 66.34, 2000- 69.36, 2001- 70.65, 2002- 71.47, 2003- 75.14, 2004- 75.18, 2005- 74.95, 2006- 74.69, 2007- 76.36, 2008- 75.00.

Yargelis SAVIGNE b. 13 Nov 1984 Niceto Pérez, Guantánamo 1.65m 53kg.
At (LJ)/TJ: WCh: '05- 4/2, '07- 1; WJ: '02- (dnq); PAm: '03- (3), '07- 3/1; WI: '06- 6/5, '08- 1. Won WAF TJ 2007, CAC LJ & TJ 2005, Cuban LJ 2006-07, TJ 2007.
Records: three Cuban TJ 2005-07, CAC indoor 2008.
Progress at LJ, TJ: 1998- 12.13, 1999- 5.60, 12.65; 2000- 5.92, 12.70; 2001- 6.24, 13.03; 2002- 6.46, 2003- 6.63, 2004- 6.60A/6.52, 2005- 6.77/6.88w, 14.82; 2006- 6.67/6.81w, 14.91; 2007- 6.79i/6.66/ 6.81w, 15.28; 2008- 6.77i, 15.05i.

Anay TEJEDA b. 3 Apr 1983 Marianao, La Habana 1.65m 59kg
At 100mh: OG: '04- h; WCh: '05/07- sf; WJ: '00- 7, '02- 1; WY: '99- 3; PAm: '03- 8, '07- 5; CAG: '06- 1. Cuban champion 2002-05. At 60mh: WI: '08- 3.
Progress at 100mh: 1998- 14.00, 1999- 13.56, 2000- 13.38, 2001- 13.20/13.07w, 2002- 12.89/12.6/12.81w, 2003- 12.99, 2004- 12.74, 2005- 12.95, 2006- 12.72, 2007- 12.80. pbs: 60m 7.43i '08, 100m 11.81, 11.36w '06; 200m 24.2 '02, 50mh 6.91i '05, 60mh 7.90i '08.

Arasay THONDIKE b. 28 May 1986 Pinar del Río 1.68m 71kg.
At HT: WCh: '07- 9; PAm: '07- 2; WY: '03- 7. Won PAm-J 2005. CAC junior hammer record 2005.
Progress at HT: 2000- 41.35, 2002- 55.76, 2003- 59.62, 2004- 63.71, 2005- 68.74, 2006- 69.26, 2007- 71.14, 2008- 70.78.

CYPRUS

Governing body: Amateur Athletic Association of Cyprus, PO Box 25356, 1309 Nicosia. Founded 1983. **National Champions**: **Men**: 100m/200m: Ioannis Georgallis 10.51w/21.41w, 400m: Marios Mardas 49.03, 800m: Neofytos Lemonaris 1:56.84, 1500m/5000m/10,000m: Alexandros Kalogerogiannis 4:02.36/14:59.86/31:30.5, Mar: Michael Keenan 2:35:42, 3000mSt: Panayiotis Kyprianou 9:28.60, 110mh: Stefanos Ioannou 13.86, 400mh: Constantinos Constantinou 52.81, HJ: Yiannis Constantinou 2.14, PV/LJ: Andreas Efstathiou 4.90/7.21, TJ: Stelios Kapsalis 15.81, SP: Georgios Aresti 17.96, DT: Apostolos Parellis 57.60, HT: Petros Sofianos 63.91, JT: Ioannis Stylianou 67.29, Dec: Savvas Savva 6066. **Women**: 100m: Melina Menelaou 12.18w, 200m: Eleni Artymata 23.18, 400m: Alissa Kallinicou 54.59, 800m: Stella Christoforou 2:15.41, 1500m/5000m: Marilena Sofocleous 4:40.13/18:08.75, Mar: Deborah Webb GBR 3:03:00, 3000mSt: Evgenia Korkokiou 11:17.25, 100mh: Polyxeni Herodotou 14.19, 400mh: Ramona Papaioannou 63.60, HJ: Effrosíni Drósou GRE 1.78, PV: Anna Fitidou 4.10, LJ: Irini Charalambous 5.95, TJ: Thomaida Polydorou 12.98w, SP: Olympia Menelaou 15.89, DT: Zacharoula Georgiadou 50.13, HT: Paraskevi Theodorou 64.46, JT: Alexandra Tsisiou 54.20, Hep: Andri Papaconstantinou 4026.

Kyriakos IOANNOU b. 26 Jul 1984 Limassol 1.93m 66kg. GS Olympia Limassol. Student of PE at University of Athens.
At HJ: OG: '04- dnq 18=; WCh: '05- 10, '07- 3; CG: '06- 3; WJ: '02- dnq; WY: '01- dnq; EJ: '03- 6=; EU23: '05- 4; WI: '08- 3=; WUG: '07- 2. Won Med G 2005, Greek 2005, 2007, CYP 2004-05.
Nine Cyprus high jump records 2004-07.
Progress at HJ: 2001- 2.00, 2002- 2.15, 2003- 2.17, 2004- 2.28, 2005- 2.27, 2006- 2.30i/2.23, 2007- 2.35. First athlete from Cyprus to win a medal at Olympics or World Championships.

CZECH REPUBLIC

Governing body: Cesky atleticky svaz, Diskarská 100, 169 00 Praha 6 -Strahov, PO Box 40. AAU of Bohemia founded in 1897.
National Championships first held in 1907 (Bohemia), 1919 (Czechoslovakia), 1993 CZE.
2007 Champions: **Men**: 100m: Rostislav Sulc 10.72, 200m: Jirí Vojtík 21.01, 400m: Rudolf Götz 46.94, 800m: Richard Svoboda 1:53.89, 1500m: Václav Janousek 3:47.89, 5000m: Jan Polásek 15:01.65, 10,000m/Mar: Pavel Faschingbauer 30:18.52/2:18:55, HMar: Róbert Stefko 70:15, 3000mSt: Petr Mikulenka 8:55.94, 110mh: Petr Svoboda 13.80, 400mh: Jindrich Simánek 50.49, HJ: Tomás Janku 2.30, PV: Michal Balner 5.50, LJ: Roman Novotny 7.98, TJ: Petr Hnízdil 16.16, SP: Petr Stehlík 19.18, DT: Libor Malina 58.97, HT: Lukás Melich 72.01, JT: Miroslav Guzdek 75.09, Dec: Pavel Baar 7047, 20kW/50kW: Milos Holusa 1:32:04/4:15:40. **Women**: 100m: Pavlina Vostatkova 11.94, 200m: Stepánka Klapacová 23.76, 400m: Jitka Bartonicková 53.70, 800m: Alena Rücklová 2:08.92, 1500m: Marcela Lustigová 4:25.15, 5000m/10,000m: Petra Kamínková 16:18.23/35:51.37, HMar: Ivana Sekyrová 79:48, Mar: Veronika Brychcínová 2:40:50, 3000mSt: Katerina Pechácková 10:37.91, 100mh/Hep: Michaela Hejnová 13.97/5618, 400mh: Zuzana Bergrová 57.83, HJ: Romana Dubnova 1.93, PV: Katerina Badurová 4.60, LJ: Denisa Scerbová 6.56, TJ: Martina Darmovzalová 13.84w, SP: Jana Kárniková 15.54, DT: Vera Cechlová 61.19, HT: Lenka Ledvinová 62.08, JT: Barbora Spotáková 58.17, 20kW: Barbora Dibelková 1:43:14.

Jaroslav BÁBA b. 2 Sep 1984 Karviná 1.96m 82kg. SSK Vítkovice.
At HJ: OG: '04- 3; WCh: '03- 11, '05- 5=, '07- 8; WJ: '02- 8; WY: '01- 10=; EU23: '05- 1; EJ: '03- 1; WI: '03-04-08: 9/3=/9; EI: '05- 4. Won CZE 2003, 2005. Czech high jump record 2005.
Progress at HJ: 1997- 1.72i, 1998- 1.81i/1.75, 1999- 1.93i/1.92, 2000- 1.95, 2001- 2.16i/2.15, 2002- 2.27/2.28et, 2003- 2.32i/2.30, 2004- 2.34,

2005- 2.37i/2.36, 2006- 2.28i, 2007- 2.29, 2008- 2.30i. pb TJ 15.43 '03.

Tomás DVORÁK b. 11 May 1972 Gottwaldov (now Zlín) 1.86m 88kg. Dukla Praha. Soldier.
At Dec: OG: '96- 3 (h 110mh), '00- 6, '04- dnf; WCh: '93- 10, '95- 5, '97- 1, '99- 1, '01- 1, '03- 4, '05- 8; EC: '94- 7, '98- 5,'02- dnf, '06- 12; ECp: '94- 3, '95- 1, '99- 1; WJ: '90-17; EJ: '91- 2; won GWG 2001. At Hep: WI: '95-7-9-03: 2/dnf/4/5; EI: '94-6-8-00-02: 4/2/4/1/2. Won Czech 110mh 1994-2001, Dec 1991.
World decathlon record 1999, three Czech 1996-9. European indoor heptathlon record 2000.
Progress at Dec: 1989- 6999, 1990- 7251w/7138, 1991- 7748, 1992- 7392, 1993- 8054, 1994- 8313, 1995- 8347, 1996- 8664, 1997- 8837, 1998- 8592, 1999- 8994, 2000- 8900, 2001- 8902, 2002- 8226, 2003- 8242, 2004- 8211, 2005- 8105, 2006- 7997, 2007- 8020. pbs: 60m 6.90i '97, 100m 10.54 '99, 200m 21.39 '98, 400m 47.56 '97, 1000m 2:34.60i '98, 1500m 4:27.63 '03, 50mh 6.59i '96, 60mh 7.76i '00, 110mh 13.61/13.6 '97, HJ 2.09 '00, PV 5.00 '97, LJ 8.07 '01, SP 16.88 '00, DT 50.28 '00, JT 72.32 '99, Hep 6424i '00.
Set four pbs en route to Olympic bronze in 1996 and six pbs when he won World gold in 1997. In 1999 he won all his four decathlons and added 103 points to Dan O'Briens' world record, missing 9000 by just six points and setting five pbs. After 2nd 1996-8, won at Götzis 1999 and 2000 and Talence 2000 before injury held him back to sixth in Sydney. Won the IAAF Combined Events Challenge in 1999 and 2001. Has 35 decathlons over 8000 points 1993-2007 (14 over 8500). Married Gabriela Vánová (pb LJ 6.28/6.30w '93, daughter of his ex-coach).

Tomás JANKU b. 27 Dec 1974 Jablonec nad Nisou 1.91m 75kg. Dukla Praha.
At HJ: OG: '96- 14, '04- dnq 30; WCh: '97/03- dnq 28/16=, '07- 5=; EC: '98- 12, '02- 5, '06- 2; WI: '99- 6=, '03- 6; EI: '98-02-07: 3/6/4; WJ: '92- 7; EJ: '93- 3; WUG: '97- 4; WCp: '06- 1; ECp: '93-8-9: 8/3/3. Won CZE 1992-4, 1996, 1998-2000, 2002, 2005-07.
Progress at HJ: 1988- 1.63, 1989- 1.77, 1990- 1.86, 1991- 2.05, 1992- 2.21, 1993- 2.20, 1994- 2.21, 1995- 2.22i/2.20, 1996- 2.29, 1997- 2.29, 1998- 2.31i/2.28, 1999- 2.32, 2000- 2.25, 2001- 2.16, 2002- 2.30, 2003- 2.30, 2004- 2.33, 2005- 2.27i/2.24, 2006- 2.34, 2007- 2.34i/2.30. pb TJ 15.56 '96.
Brother of Jan Janku (b. 10 Aug 1971) pb 2.30 '96, 2.29 '97. They set a world record for synchronised high jumping, clearing 2.18m in May 1997. Coached by his father Jan (pb 2.11 '71).

Roman SEBRLE b. 26 Nov 1974 Lanskroun 1.86m 88kg. Dukla Praha. Soldier.
At Dec: OG: '00- 2, '04- 1; WCh: '97- 9, '99- dnf, '01- 10, '03- 2, '05- 2, '07- 1; EC: '98- 6, '02- 1, '06- 1; WUG: '97- 1; ECp: '97-8-9: 1/2/2. At Hep: WI: '99- 01-03-04-06-08: 3/1/3/1/3/dnf; EI: '00-02-05-07: 2/1/1/1. At 110mh: ECp: '99- 6. At LJ: ECp: '05- 7. Won Czech Dec 1996, LJ 1998.
World decathlon record 2001, European indoor heptathlon record 2004.
Progress at Dec: 1991- 5187, 1992- 6541, 1993- 7066, 1994- 7153, 1995- 7642, 1996- 8210, 1997- 8380, 1998- 8589, 1999- 8527, 2000- 8757, 2001- 9026, 2002- 8800, 2003- 8807, 2004- 8893, 2005- 8534, 2006- 8526, 2007- 8697. pbs: 60m 6.87i '02, 100m 10.64 '01, 200m 21.74 '04, 400m 47.66 '07, 1000m 2:37.86i '01, 1500m 4:21.98 '01, 60mh 7.84i '02, 110mh 13.79 '99, 13.68w '01; HJ 2.15 '00, PV 5.20 '03, LJ 8.11 '01, SP 16.47 '07, DT 49.37 '03, JT 71.18 '07, Hep 6438i '04.
Married Eva Kasalová (b. 4 Dec 1976, pb 800m 2:02.79 '98), on 14 Oct 2000. At Götzis in 2001 he became the first decathlete to exceed 9000 points with the current scoring tables, setting five pbs. Won again at Götzis 2002-05 and at Talence in 2004-05, and he won IAAF Combined Challenge in 2004-05 and 2007. Has 21 decathlons over 8500 and 40 over 8000 (66 in all).

Svatoslav TON b. 20 Oct 1978 Brno 1.92m 75kg. Dukla Praha.
At HJ: OG: '04- 8; WCh: '05/07- dnq 21/19=; EC: '02- 6, '06- 6=; WJ: '96- 2=; EU23: '01- 7; EJ: '95- dnq, '97- 10; EI: '05- 7; ECp: '05- 3. Czech champion 2004.
Progress at HJ: 1992- 1.64, 1993- 1.86, 1994- 2.08i/2.05, 1995- 2.16, 1996- 2.24i/2.21, 1997- 2.27i/2.25, 1998- 2.20, 1999- 2.20, 2000- 2.25, 2001- 2.26, 2002- 2.30i/2.28, 2004- 2.33, 2005- 2.33i/2.30, 2006- 2.33i/2.32, 2007- 2.30. pb LJ 7.74 '97.

Women

Katerina BADUROVÁ b. 18 Dec 1982 Ostrava 1.67m 50kg. Dukla Praha.
At PV: OG: '04- 12; WCh: '07- 2; EC: '02/06- dnq 28/16; WY: '99- 5=. Czech champion 2001, 2004, 2007.
Four Czech pole vault records 2007.
Progress at PV: 1996- 2.55, 1997- 3.50, 1998- 3.70i/3.50, 1999- 4.20, 2000- 4.30, 2001- 4.30, 2002- 4.30i/4.22, 2003- 4.00, 2004- 4.52, 2005- 4.20, 2006- 4.42, 2007- 4.75.

Nikola BREJCHOVÁ b. 25 Jun 1974 Gottwaldov (now Zlín) 1.78m 75kg. née Tomecková. PSK Olymp Praha. Sports instructor.
At JT: OG: '96- dnq 25, '00- 8, '04- 4; WCh: '93- dnq 22, '95-97-99 dnq 17/26/21, '01- 4, '07- 4; EC: '98- dnq 13, '02- dnq 14; WJ: '92- 11; EJ: '91- 2, '93- 5; WUG: '01- 2; ECp: '98-9-01: 2/5/2; E23Cp: '94- 5. Czech champion 1993-2002.
11 Czech new javelin records 1999-2004.
Progress at JT: 1987- 32.22, 1988- 39.80, 1989- 42.24, 1990- 49.22, 1991- 55.80, 1992- 59.78, 1993- 57.48, 1994- 56.68, 1995- 63.80, 1996- 64.50, 1997- 62.96, 1998- 64.18; new: 1999- 60.92A, 2000- 64.19, 2001- 65.71, 2002- 61.43, 2004- 65.91, 2006- 65.26, 2007- 64.29.
Married in 2002, daughter Valerie born 13 Dec 2005.

Véra CECHLOVÁ b. 19 Nov 1978 Litomerice 1.78m 78kg. née Pospísilová. PSK Olymp Praha.
At (SP/)DT: OG: '04- 4; WCh: '01- 6, '03- 5, '05- 3, '07- dnq 21; EC: '02- 4, '06- 7; EU23: '99- 3; EJ: '97- 12/8; ECp: '01- 7/4; Won WAF 2003-04, 2nd GP 2002. Won CZE SP 2001-02, DT 2003-07.
Progress at DT: 1992- 28.24, 1993- 34.28, 1994- 39.48, 1995- 40.24, 1996- 45.72, 1997- 50.00, 1998- 54.67, 1999- 58.17, 2000- 58.28, 2001- 63.20, 2002- 64.10, 2003- 67.71, 2004- 66.42, 2005- 66.81, 2006- 65.44, 2007- 66.18. pb SP 16.92 '01.
Married wrestler Jakub Cechl on 17 Oct 2003.

Pavla RYBOVÁ b. 20 May 1978 Chomutov 1.70m 68kg. née Hamácková. Dukla Praha.
At PV: OG: '00- dnq 22=, '04- 11; WCh: '99- 6=, '01- 8, '05- 3, '07- dnq 19=; EC: '98- 12=, '06- 10; EJ: '97- 5; EU23: '99- 7=; WUG: '99- 1; WI: '99-01-08: 7/1/7; EI: '00-02-05-07: 1/6/6/4; ECp: '99- 3, '01- 3. Czech champion 1999, 2003, 2005-06.
Czech pole vault record 2003.
Progress at PV: 1993- 2.40i, 1994- 3.20, 1995- 3.21i/3.28i exh, 1997- 3.95, 1998- 4.15, 1999- 4.40, 2000- 4.45, 2001- 4.56i/4.47, 2002- 4.56i/4.30A, 2003- 4.60, 2004- 4.45, 2005- 4.55i/4.51, 2006- 4.50, 2007- 4.64i/4.50/4.51exh, 2008- 4.53i.
Married Jirí Ryba (b. 15 Jun 1976, Dec: 6 WCh '01, 3 EJ '95, pb 8339 '00) on 16 Sep 2006.

Barbora SPOTÁKOVÁ b. 30 Jun 1981 Jablonec nad Nisou 1.82m 80kg. Dukla Praha.
At JT: OG: '04- dnq 23; WCh: '05- dnq 13, '07- 1; EC: '02- dnq 17, '06- 2; EU23: '03- 6; WUG: '03- 4, '05- 1; won WAF 2006-07, Czech 2003, 2005-07. At Hep: WJ: '00- 4.
Six Czech javelin records 2006-07.
Progress at JT: 1996- 31.32, 1997- 37.28, 1998- 44.56, new: 1999- 41.69, 2000- 54.15, 2001- 51.97, 2002- 56.76, 2003- 56.65, 2004- 60.95, 2005- 65.74, 2006- 66.21, 2007- 67.12. pbs: 200m 25.11w '00, 800m 2:18.29 '00, 60mh 8.68i '07, 100mh 13.99 '00, 400mh 62.68 '98, HJ 1.78 '00, LJ 5.60 '00, SP 14.53 '07, DT 36.80 '02, Dec 6749 '04, Hep 5873 '00.

DENMARK

Governing body: Dansk Athletik Forbund, Idraettens Hus, Brøndby Stadion 20, DK-2605 Brøndby. Founded 1907.
National Championships first held in 1894. **2007 Champions**: **Men**: 100m/200m/LJ: Morten Jensen 10.89/21.12/7.71, 400m: Nicklas Hyde 46.99, 800m: Jacob Carstensen 1:52.49, 1500m: Alladin Bouhania 3:54.60, 5000m/10,000m/HMar: Jesper Faurschou 14:35.18/29:50.19/65:39, Mar: Søren Palshøj 2:22:01, 3000mSt: Stephan A. Jensen 9:27.80, 110mh: Yon Yde Bentsen 14.41, 400mh: Andreas Bube 52.41, HJ: Jens Møller Boeriis 2.06, PV: Martin Stensvig 4.35, TJ: Anders Møller 16.33, SP/DT: Joachim B. Olsen 20.66/54.88, HT: Simon Colin 64.60, JT: Lars Møller 70.86, Dec: Niels Uth 6275, 5000mW/10,000mW/20kmW: Jacob Sorensen 23:04.51/46:41.6/1:37:24, 50kmW: Andreas Nielsen 5:07:56. **Women**: 100m/400mh: Sara Petersen 12.07/58.93, 200m: Julie Scherer 24.61, 400m: Helene Scherer 56.24, 800m: Rikke Rønholt 2:07.10, 1500m: Ida Fallesen 4:51.18, 5000m/10,000m/HMar: Maria S.Møller 17:26.56/35:12.68/77:10, Mar: Lene Duus 2:57:14, 100mh/HJ: Anne Møller 14.26/1.70, PV: Anita Tørring 3.75, LJ: Lotte Thiesen 5.72, TJ: Lisbeth Bertelsen 12.75, SP: Mette O. Rosentjørn 13.34, DT: Marianne Simonsen 41.26, HT: Vanessa Mortensen 56.44, JT: Jane Lindved 48.09, Hep: Tine Bach Ejlersen 4809, 3000mW/5000mW/10kmW: Josefine Klausen 18:30.93/30:10.7/63:54.

Joachim B **OLSEN** b. 31 May 1977 Aalborg 1.84m 142kg. Studied history at the University of Idaho, USA. Århus 1900.
At SP: OG: '00- dnq 17, '04- 3; WCh: '99- dnq 22, 01- 10, '03- dns, '05- 7, '07- nt; EC: '02- 2, '06- 3; EU23: '99- 2; WI: '03-04-06: 8/3/3; EI: '02-05-07: 2/1/3. At DT: WJ: '96- dnq 23. Won WAF 2004, NCAA 2000, DEN SP 1997-2003, 2007; DT 1999-03, 2007.
Six Danish shot records 2000-07 (and 14 indoor 1999-2004).
Progress at SP: 1994- 13.27, 1995- 14.54, 1996- 14.89, 1997- 17.11, 1998- 18.40, 1999- 19.75, 2000- 20.88, 2001- 20.43, 2002- 21.57, 2003- 20.85, 2004- 21.63i/21.46, 2005- 21.32, 2006- 21.35i/21.33, 2007- 21.61. pb DT 60.67 '02.

Women

Christina SCHERWIN b. 11 Jul 1976 Viborg 1.76m 67kg. IF Sparta.
At JT: OG: '04- dnq 29; WCh: '05- 4; EC: '02- dnq 18, '06- 5; WJ: '94- 5; WUG: '03- 2; won Danish JT 2000, 2002-03, 2005-06; SP 2002-3, 2005-06.
Danish records: javelin (8) 2000-06, shot (5) 2003-06.
Progress at JT: 1991- 44.04, 1992- 45.46, 1993- 53.48, 1994- 55.70, 1995- 43.48, 1996- 50.78, 1997- 52.10, 1998- 53.63, new: 1999- 53.61, 2000- 59.00, 2002- 55.99, 2003- 56.80, 2004- 59.36, 2005- 63.43, 2006- 64.83, 2007- 59.94. pb SP 15.24 '06.

DOMINICAN REPUBLIC

Governing body: Federación Dominicana de Asociaciones de Atletismo. Avenida J.F. Kennedy, esquina Ortega y Gasset. Centro Olímpico "Juan Pablo Duarte". Santo Domingo. Founded 1953.

Félix SÁNCHEZ b. 30 Aug 1977 New York, USA 1.78m 73kg. Was at University of Southern California.
At 400mh: OG: '00- sf, '04- 1; WCh: '99- ht, '01- 1, '03- 1, '05- dnf, '07- 2; PAm: '99- 4, '03- 1/3R, '07- 4/3R; CAG: '02- 1R; WCp: '02- 1R. Won NCAA 2000, GWG 2001, GP 2002 (3rd overall), WAF 2003.
Three CAC 400mh records 2001-03. DOM records: 400mh (11) 1997-2003, 400m (3) 2001-02.

Progress at 400m, 400mh: 1995- 51.33, 1996- 51.19, 1997- 46.36, 50.01; 1998- 51.30, 1999- 48.60, 2000- 48.33, 2001- 44.90, 47.38; 2002- 45.14, 47.35; 2003- 45.22A/45.33, 47.25; 2004- 46.28, 47.63; 2005- 46.32, 48.24; 2006- 49.10, 2007- 48.01. pbs: 100m 10.45 '05, 200m 20.87 '01, 800m 1:49.36 '04.
Born in New York and raised in California, he first competed for the Dominican Republic, where his parents were born, in 1999 after placing 6th in US 400mh. He took a share of the Golden League jackpot in 2002 and won 43 successive 400mh races (including 7 heats) from loss to Dai Tamesue on 2 Jul 2001 until he pulled up in Brussels on 3 Sep 2004.

ECUADOR

Governing body: Federación Ecuatoriana de Atletismo, Casilla 01-01-736, Cuenca. F'd 1925.

Jefferson PÉREZ b. 1 Jul 1974 Cuenca 1.74m 59kg. Graduate of business management from University of Azuay.
At 20kW: OG: '92- dnf, '96- 1, '00- 4, '04- 4 (12 50kW); WCh: '95- 32, '97- 14, '99- 2, '01- 8, '03- 1, '05- 1, '07- 1; WCp: '97-02-04-06: 1/1/1/2; PAm: '95-99-03-07: 1/3/1/1; SAmCh: '93- 1, '05- 1. Won IbAm 2002, SAm Cup 1994-5, 1997-8, 2006; PAm Cup 2003, 2007. At 10kW: WJ: '90- 3, '92- 1; won SAm-J 1989-93, PAm-J 1993. At 50km: WCp: '99- dnf.
World best 20km walk 2003, South American record 1997 & 2003, 9 Ecuador records 20kW 1992-2003, 50kW 2003 & 2004.
Progress at 20kW, 50kW: 1992- 1:25:50.5, 1993- 1:24:03, 1994- 1:23:27, 1995- 1:22:53, 1996- 1:20:07/1:20:55.4t, 1997- 1:18:24, 1998- 1:19:19, 1999- 1:20:46, 2000- 1:20:18, 2001- 1:22:20, 2002- 1:19:08, 2003- 1:17:21, 3:56:04; 2004- 1:18:42, 3:53:04; 2005- 1:18:35, 2006- 1:19:08, 2007- 1:21:14. pbs: 5000mW 19:49.54i '90, 10,000mW 39:50.73 '93, 10kW 38:24 '02, 35kW 2:38:04 '04.
In 1996 he became the youngest ever Olympic walking champion and Ecuador's first medallist at any sport. He then walked 459km from Quito, along the Pan-American Freeway at an altitude of 2500 to 4800m, to his home-town of Cuenca, as a religious promise. The Ecuador postal authorities issued a stamp with his picture, and the National Central Bank, in 1996, a special coin for the tenth anniversary of his win. Tied record with third World Cup win in 2004. Set world age 16 best for 10,000m walk with 40:08.23 in 1990.

EGYPT

Governing body: Egyptian Amateur Athletic Federation, Sport Federation Building, El Estad El Bahary, Nasr City – Cairo. Founded 1910.

Omar Ahmed **EL-GHAZALY** b. 9 Feb 1984 Cairo 2.00m 130kg. Student
At DT: OG: '04- dnq 33; WCh: '07- 6; AfG: '03- 1, '07- 1; AfCh: '00-02-06: 7/3/1; WJ: '00- dnq 17, '02- 10; WY: '01- 3; Af-J '01-2, '03-1; WUG: '05- 2, '07- 2; WCp: '06- 4. Arab champion 2000, 2003-05, 2007.
Five Egyptian discus records 2006-07. World junior record (65.88) with 1.75kg discus in 2003.
Progress at DT: 2000- 55.35, 2001- 51.42, 2002- 52.53, 2003- 59.77, 2004- 61.46, 2005- 64.36, 2006- 65.33, 2007- 66.58.

ERITREA

Governing body: Eritream National Athletics Federation, PO Box 1117, Asmara. F'd 1992.

Yonas KIFLE b. 24 Mar 1977 1.68m 55kg.
At 10,000m: OG: '00- h, '04- 16; WCh: '05- 11; At 5000m: WCh: '99/01- h, AfCh: '02- 6. World CC: 2002-04-05-06-08: 8/9/15/7/20; 20k: '06- 10; HMar: '02-04-05-07: 4/11/3/5.
Eritrean records: 5000m (2) 2001-02, 10,000m 2004, HMar 2002, Mar 2007.
Progress at 10,000m: 2000- 28:07.15, 2004- 27:40.92, 2005- 27:35.72. pbs: 3000m 7:53.02 '02, 5000m 13:17.72 '02, Road: 15km 42:07 '07, 20km 56:30 '07, HMar 59:30 '07, Mar 2:07:34 '07.

Zersenay TADESE b. 8 Feb 1982 Adi Bana 1.60m 56kg. C.A. Adidas. Madrid, Spain.
At (5000m)/10,000m: OG: '04- 7/3; WCh: '03- (8), '05- 14/6, '07- 4; AfG: '02- 6, '07- 1. World CC: 2002-03-04-05-06-07-08: 30/9/6/2/4/1/3; 20k: '06- 1; HMar: '02-03-07: 21/7/1.
Eritrean records 3000m (2), 2M, 5000m (4), 10,000m (5) HMar (2) 2003-07.
Progress at 5000m, 10,000m: 2002- 13:48.79, 28:47.29; 2003- 13:05.57, 28:42.79; 2004- 13:13.74, 27:22.57; 2005- 13:12.23, 27:04.70; 2006- 12:59.27, 26:37.25; 2007- 27:00.30. pbs: 3000m 7:39.93 '05, 2M 8:19.34 '07, Road: 15km 41:27 '05, 10M 45:52 '07. 20km 56:01 '06, HMar 58:59 '07.
Won Eritrea's first medal at Olympics in 2004 and World CC in 2005 and first gold in the World 20k in 2006. Ran 59:05 for the fastest ever half marathon to win the Great North Run (slightly downhill overall) in 2005. Won a national road cycling title in 2001 before taking up athletics. His younger brother **Kidane** was 16th in 2005 World Junior CC.

ESTONIA

Governing body: Eesti Kergejôustikuliit, Pirita tee 12, Tallinn 10127. Founded 1920.
National Championships first held in 1917. **2007 Champions**: **Men**: 100m: Henri Sool 10.71, 200m/400m: Taavi Liiv 21.59/47.41, 800m: Sergo Treufeld 1:50.62, 1500m: Nikolai Vedehin 3:47.38, 5000m: Tiidrek Nurme 15:27.02, 10,000m: Taivo Püi 31:06.65, HMar: Pavel Loskutov 66:22, Mar: Aleksei Saveljev 2:29:33, 3000mSt: Aleksei Saveljev 9:09.95, 110mh: Rene Oruman 14.10, 400mh: Aarne Nirk 51.86, HJ: Marko Aleksejev 2.13, PV: Eigo Siimu 4.80, LJ: Gerri Pärson 7.67, TJ: Jaanus Uudmäe 16.22, SP: Taavi Peetre 19.64, DT: Gerd Kanter 67.82, HT: Margus Hunt 62.94, JT: Risto Mätas 75.97, Dec: Aigar Kukk 7307,

20kW/50kW: Margus Luik 1:30:36/4:30:18. **Women**: 100m: Ksenija Balta 11.76, 200m: Ebe Reier 24.30, 400m/400mh: Maris Mägi 54.47/59.58, 800m: Jekaterina Duman 2:09.84, 1500m: Liina Tsernov 4:33.68, 5000m/3000mSt: Jekaterina Patjuk 17:04.44/10:37.54, HMar: Sigrid Valdre 79:03, Mar: Kaja Vals 3:07:25, 100mh: Mirjam Liimask 13.57, HJ: Anna Iljustsenko 1.85, PV: Lembi Vaher 3.85, LJ: Sirkka-Liisa Kivine 6.30, TJ: Kaire Leibak 13.52, SP: Anu Teesaar 15.56. DT: Eha Rünne 52.83, HT: Maris Röngelep 57.21, JT: Jana Trakmann 50.06, Hep: Kaie Kand 5876, 10kW/20kW: Jekaterina Jutkina 54:52/1:56:22.

Gerd KANTER b. 6 May 1979 Tallinn 1.96m 126kg. Kalev, Tallinn. Business management graduate.
At DT: OG: '04- dnq 19; WCh: '03- dnq 25, '05- 2, '07- 1; EC: '02- 12, '06- 2; EU23: '01- 5; WUG:'05- 1. Won WAF 2007, Estonian 2004-07.
Five Estonian discus records 2004-06.
Progress at DT: 1998- 47.37, 1999- 49.65, 2000- 57.68, 2001- 60.47, 2002- 66.31, 2003- 67.13, 2004- 68.50, 2005- 70.10, 2006- 73.38, 2007- 72.02. pb SP 17.31i '04, 16.11 '00.
Threw over 70m in four rounds at Helsingborg on 4 Sep 2006; a feat matched only by Virgilijs Alekna.

Aleksander TAMMERT b. 2 Feb 1973 Tartu 1.96m 126kg. Audentes, Tallinn. Was at Southern Methodist University, USA.
At DT: OG: '96- dnq 25, '00- 9, '04- 3; WCh: '95- dnq 23, '97- 12, '99- 10, '01- dnq 16, '03- 7, '05- 4. '07- 8; EC: '98- dnq 20, '02- 5, '06- 3; WUG: '97- 5, '99- 4, '01- 1. Won EST SP 1998, 2002, DT 1993-5, 1997-2003, 2005.
Nine Estonian discus records 1998-2006.
Progress at DT: 1990- 42.06, 1991- 48.24, 1992- 51.12, 1993- 54.54, 1994- 55.50, 1995- 60.24, 1996- 64.80, 1997- 64.78, 1998- 65.35, 1999- 66.95, 2000- 67.41, 2001- 67.10, 2002- 67.75, 2003- 66.63, 2004- 68.48, 2005- 67.93, 2006- 70.82, 2007- 64.41. pbs: SP 18.41 '01, HT 52.09 '99.
Father (also Aleksander) won 1966 European Junior shot, pbs: SP 19.41 '76, DT 54.98 '77.

Andrus VÄRNIK b. 27 Sep 1977 Anstla 1.82m 100kg. Löunalövi, Vöru.
At JT: OG: '00- dnq 15, '04- 6; WCh: '03- 2, '05- 1; EC: '02- dnq 21. EST champion 1999-2000, 2003-06. Two Estonian javelin records 2002-03.
Progress at JT: 1994- 65.22, 1995- 62.28, 1996- 68.36, 1997- 72.20, 1998- 69.96, 1999- 77.19, 2000- 82.16, 2001- 80.83, 2002- 85.47, 2003- 87.83, 2004- 87.58, 2005- 87.19, 2006- 84.85. 2007- 75.96. pb SP: 14.20 '03.
Became Estonia's first world champion in 2005.

ETHIOPIA

Governing body: Ethiopian Athletic Federation, Addis Ababa Stadium, PO Box 3241, Addis Ababa. Founded 1961.

2007 Champions: **Men**: 100m: Watere Gelelcha 10.3, 400m: Zemenu Kassa 46.7, 800m: Eshetu Zewde 1:50.9, 1500m: Derese Mekonnen 3:38.7, 5000m: Ali Abdosh 14:04.3, 10,000m: Tadessa Tola 28:48.4, 3000mSt: Roba Gari 8:31.5, 110mh: Ubang Abaya 14.2, 400mh: Feleke Degela 51.2, HJ: Ygula Ubang 1.95, LJ: Galwat Galkot 7.19, SP: Sisay Mekonnen 13.00, JT: Anteneh Tameru 61.81, 20kW: Cherenet Mikore 1:33:56. **Women**: 400m: Abebe Megersa 56.0, 800m: Mestawot Tadesse 2:05.0, 1500m: Gelete Burka 4:10.9, 3000m: Mahlet Melese 9:30.8, 5000m: Werkitu Ayanu 15:51.3, 10,000m: Mestawot Tufa 33:26.8, 3000mSt: Netsanet Achamo 10:12.0, 100mh/400mh: Terhas Haileselassie 15.7/61.7, HJ: Haregewoin Mengistu 1.49, LJ/TJ: Emebet Tilahun 5.55/11.75, SP: Roman Abera 11.48, DT: Mitiku Tilahun 37.09, 20kW: Asnakech Ararsa 1:44:30.

Kenenisa BEKELE b. 13 Jun 1982 near Bekoji, Arsi Province 1.60m 54kg.
At 5000m(/10,000m): OG: '04- 2/1; WCh: '03- 3/1, '05- (1), '07- (1); WJ: '00- 2; AfG: '03- 1; AfCh: '06- 1. At 3000m: WY: '99- 2; WI: '06- 1; WCp: '06- 2. World CC: '99- 9J, 4k: '01- 1J/2 4k, '02-03-04-05-06: all 1/1, '08- 1. Won WAF 3000m 2003, 5000m 2006.
World records: 5000m 2004, 10,000m 2004 & 2005, indoor 5000m (12:49.60) 2004, 2000m 2007, 2M 2008; World junior record 3000m 2001.
Progress at 5000m, 10,000m: 2000- 13:20.57, 2001- 13:13.33, 2002- 13:26.58, 2003- 12:52.26, 26:49.57; 2004- 12:37.35, 26:20.31; 2005- 12:40.18, 26:17.53; 2006- 12:48.09, 2007- 12:49.53, 26:46.19. pbs: 1500m 3:32.35 '07, 1M 3:56.2+ '07, 2000m 4:49.99i/4:58.98 '07, 3000m 7:25.79 '07, 2M 8:04.35i '08, 8:13.51 '07; Rd 15km 42:42 '01.
Has won a record 20 (12 individual, 8 team) world CC gold medals from his record winning margin of 33 seconds for the World Juniors in 2001, a day after coming second in senior 4km. He is the only man to win both World senior CC races in the same year, and did so five times. He was unbeaten in 27 CC races from Dec 2001 to March 2007 when he did not finish in the World Cross. Has won all his nine 10,000m track races including three major gold medal, from a brilliant debut win over Haile Gebrselassie at Hengelo in June 2003. He ran 3000m in 7:30.77 on his indoor debut in 2004 to win in Stuttgart and has run three world indoor records/bests at Birmingham, with outdoor world records at 5000m and 10,000m, in all cases beating Gebrselassie's mark.
His fiancée Alem Techale (b. 13.12.87, the 2003 World Youth 1500m champion) died of a heart attack on 4 Jan 2005.

Tariku BEKELE b. 21 Jan 1987 near Bekoji 1.65m 52kg.
At 5000m: WCh: '05- 7, '07- 5; WJ: '04- 3, '06- 1; AfG: '07- 3. At 3000m: WY: '03- 2; WI: '06- 6, '08-

1; won WAF 3000m 2006. World CC: '05- 6J, '06- 3J. World junior indoor 2M best 2006.
Progress at 5000m: 2004- 13:11.97, 2005- 12:59.03, 2006- 12:53.81, 2007- 13:01.60. pbs: 2000m 5:00.1 '06, 3000m 7:29.11 '06, 2M 8:04.83 '07.
Younger brother of Kenenisa Bekele.

Dejene BERHANU b. 12 Dec 1980 Addis Alem 1.82m 64kg.
At 5000m: WCh: '05- 8. At 10,000m: OG: '04- 5; AfCh: '00- 2, '02- 5; AfG: '03- 3. At Mar: '07- 31. World CC: '03- 20, '05- 6; 4k: '04- 11, '05- 7. Won ETH CC 2001, 4k CC 2005; E.Afr 4k 2004.
Ethiopian half marathon record 2004.
Progress at 5000m, 10,000m, Mar: 2000- 13:36.58, 28:41.11; 2002- 13:26.74, 28:46.21; 2003- 13:14.05, 27:14.61; 2004- 12:54.15, 28:21.38A '04; 2005- 12:56.24, 27:12.22, 2:11:48; 2006- 2:08:46. pbs: 1500m 3:44.65 '00, HMar 59:37 '04.
Brilliant winner of Great North Run in 2004 in 59:37 and 2nd in 2005.

Abreham CHERKOS Feleke b. 23 Sep 1989 1.58m 52kg.
At 5000m: WCh: '07- 8; WJ: '06- 2; AfG: '07- 4. At 3000m: WY: '05- 1; WI: '08- 3.
World youth 3000m, 2M & 5000m records 2006, world junior indoor 3000m best (7:38.03) 2008.
Progress at 5000m: 2006- 12:54.19, 2007- 13:05.83. pbs: 1500m 3:42.91 '05, 2000m 5:02.4 '06, 3000m 7:32.37 '06, 2M 8:16.07 '06.

Abebe DINKESA Negera b. 6 Mar 1984 Dendhi, near Ambo 1.69m 55kg.
At 10,000m: WCh: '05- 7; AfCh: '04- 2, '06- 3. World HMar: '04- 10, CC: '02- 9J, '05- 4. Won ETH CC 2005-06.
Progress at 5000m, 10,000m: 2002- 13:40.33, 2004- 13:23.85, 27:23.60; 2005- 12:55.58, 26:30.74; 2006- 13:13.40, 28:05.07. pbs: 3000m 7:32.9+ '05, 2M 8:28.22i '06; Road: 15km 43:28 '05, HMar 61:53 '05.
Ran 10,000m pbs at Hengelo with 27:23.60 in 2004 and 26:30.74 in 2005. Won Great Ethiopian Run 2004.

Gebre-egziabher GEBREMARIAM b. 10 Sep 1984 Tsenkanet, Tigray region 1.78m 56kg.
At 10,000m (5000m): OG: '04- (4); WCh: '03- (6), '05- 15, '07- 6; WJ: '02- 1 (3); AfG: '03- 2, '07- 3. World CC: '02-03-04-05-06-08: 1J/3/2&2/9(4k)/13/17._Won ETH CC 2003, 5000m & 10,000m 2005. E.Afr 2004.
Progress at 5000m, 10,000m: 2001- 14:13.74A, 31:04.61A; 2002- 13:12.14, 27:25.61; 2003- 12:58.08, 28:03.03; 2004- 12:55.59, 26:53.73; 2005- 12:52.80, 27:11.57; 2006- 13:30.95, 27:03.95; 2007- 13:10.29, 26:52.33. pbs: 3000m 7:39.48 '05, 2M 9:34.82i '06, Mar 2:12:01 '04, 3000mSt 8:57.7A '02.
Married Worknesh Kidane on 4 Feb 2006.

Haile GEBRSELASSIE b. 18 Apr 1973 Arssi 1.64m 53kg.
At 10,000m (5000m): OG: '96- 1, '00- 1, '04- 5; WCh: '93- 1 (2), '95- 1, '97- 1, '99- 1, '01- 3, '03- 2; WJ: '92- 1 (1); AfG: '93- 3 (2). At 3000m: WI: '97- 1, '99- 1 (1 1500m), '03- 1. Won GP 3000m 1995, 1998. World CC: '91-2-3-4-5-6: 8J/2J/7/3/4/5; HMar: '01- 1; Rd Rly team: '94- 2.
World records 5000m (4) 1994-8, 10,000m (3) 1995-8, 20000m & 1Hr 2007; 10km road (27:02) 2002, 15km & 10M road 2005, 20km, HMar & 25km 2006, Marathon 2007; Indoors 2000m 1998, 3000m (7:30.72 '96, 7:26.15 '98), 5000m (13:10.98 '96, 12:59.04 '97, 12:50.38 '99); World best 2M 1995 (8:07.46) & 1997, indoors 8:04.69 (2003). ETH records 1993-9: 1500m (3), 1M (1), 3000m (6), 5000m (6), 10,000m (3), marathon (3) 2002-06.
Progress at 5000m, 10,000m, marathon: 1992- 13:36.06, 28:03.99; 1993- 13:03.17, 27:30.17; 1994- 12:56.96, 27:15.00; 1995- 12:44.39, 26:43.53; 1996- 12:52.70, 27:07.34; 1997- 12:41.86, 26:31.32; 1998- 12:39.36, 26:22.75; 1999- 12:49.64, 27:57.27; 2000- 12:57.95, 27:18.20; 2001- 27:54.41, 2002- 28:16.50, 2:06:35; 2003- 12:54.36, 26:29.22; 2004- 12:55.51, 26:41.58; 2005- 2:06:20, 2006- 2:05:56, 2007- 26:52.81, 2:04:26. pbs: 800m 1:49.35i '97, 1000m 2:20.3+i '98, 1500m 3:31.76i '98, 3:33.73 '99; 1M 3:52.39 '99, 2000m 4:52.86i '98, 4:56.1 '97; 3000m 7:25.09 '98, 2M 8:01.08 '97, 10M 45:23.80 '07, 20000m 56:25.98 '07, 1Hr 21285m '07; Road: 15km 41:22 '05, 10M 44:24 '05, 20km 55:48 '06, HMar 58:55 '06, 25km 1:11:37 '06.
A beautifully smooth runner, perhaps the greatest ever. After finishing a place behind Ismael Kirui at two successive World Junior CC championships, he outkicked his rival for a brilliant double at the 1992 World Juniors. He set the first of his 25 world records in Hengelo in 1994 at 5000m and in 1995 he took 8.7 secs off the 10,000m WR and regained the 5000m record by taking 10.91 secs off Kiptanui's mark. Between these feats he won the World 10,000m, with 25.1 for the last 200m!. He ran the second 5000m in c.13:11.6 to win the 1996 Olympic 10,000m and in 1997 took 6.76 secs off the world 10,000m record in Oslo. In 1998 he regained both the 5000m and 10,000m world records. From 1992 to 2004 he had 13 wins in 19 races at 10,000m, 26/28 at 3000m/2M, and 28/36 at 5000 including 16 successive 1996 to 2000. He has 9/9 wins at half marathon 2001-08. After missing the 2002 summer season through injury he set a world 10km road record of 27:02 at Doha, Qatar in December for a reward of $1 million.
He had run c.2:48 for the marathon at the age of 15, but made his senior debut at the distance at London 2002, when he was third in 2:06:35 and won at Amsterdam in 2:06:20 in 2005. In 2006 he was 9th in London, then won the Berlin and Fukuoka marathons, but dnf London 2007. He smashed the world record with 2:04:26 to win the Berlin Marathon in 2007.
Based during the summer in the Netherlands. His brother Tekeye had marathon pb 2:11:45 '94 and was 13th in 1991 World Cup.

Markos GENETI b. 30 May 1984 Walega 1.75m 55kg.
At 5000m: WJ: '02- 2; AfG: '03- 4. At 3000m: WY: '01- 1; WI: '04- 3. At 1500m: WCh: '05- sf. World CC: '07- 14.
Progress at 5000m: 2001- 13:50.14, 2002- 13:28.83, 2003- 13:11.87, 2004- 13:17.57, 2005- 13:00.25, 2006- 13:13.98, 2007- 13:07.65. pbs: 1500m 3:33.83 '05, 3000m 7:32.69i '07, 7:38.11 '05; 2M 8:08.39i '04, 8:19.61 '06.

Ibrahim JEYLAN Gashu b. 12 Jun 1989 1.58m 52kg. Muger Cement.
At 10,000m: WJ: '06- 1. At 3000m: WY: '05- 1. World CC: '06- 5J, '08- 1J.
Two world youth 10,000m records 2006.
Progress at 5000m, 10,000m: 2006- 13:09.38, 27:02.81; 2007- 13:17.99, 27:50.53. pbs: 3000m 8:04.21 '05.

Deresse MEKONNEN Tsigu b. 20 Oct 1987 1.75m 60kg.
At 1500m: WCh: '07- h; WI: '08- 1; AfG: '07- 5.
Progress at 1500m: 2007- 3:36.41, 2008- 3:35.51i.

Deriba MERGA Ejigu b. 26 Oct 1980 1.60m 54kg.
World 20km Rd: '06- 6, HMar: '07- 4.
Two world youth 10,000m records 2006
Progress at 10,000m, Mar: 2007- 27:02.62, 2:06:50. pbs: Road: 15km 41:34 '07, 20km 56:13 '07, HMar 59:16 '07, 30km 1:30:05 '07.
Marathon career: 2006- dnf Boston, 2007- 10th Paris 2:13:33, 2nd Fukuoka.

Sileshi SIHINE b. 29 Jan 1983 Sheno 1.71m 55kg.
At (5000m)/10,000m: OG: '04- 2; WCh: '03- 3, '05- 2/2, '07- 2; WJ: '02- 2; AfG: '03- 1. World CC: '02-03-04-06-07-08: 6J/7/3/2 & 12 4k/16/15. World HMar: '05- 4. Won WAF 5000m 2004-05, Ethiopian 5000m 2003, 10,000m 2003-04, Af-AsG 10,000m 2003.
Progress at 5000m, 10,000m: 2002- 13:21.81, 27:26.12; 2003- 13:06.53, 26:58.76; 2004- 12:47.04, 26:39.69; 2005- 13:13.04, 26:57.27; 2006- 13:06.72i. 2007- 12:50.16, 26:48.73. pbs: 2000m 5:01.2i+ '04, 5:02.2 '05; 3000m 7:29.92 '05, 2M 8:27.03i '06; Road: 15km 41:38 '04, HMar 61:14 '05.
Six major silver medals.

Women

Berhane ADERE b. 21 Jul 1973 Shewa District 1.70m 48kg.
At 10,000m (5000m): OG: '96- 18, '00- 12; WCh: '95- h, '97- 4, '99- 7, '01- 2, '03- 1 (10), '05- 2; AfCh: '93- 1 (5 3000m). At 5000m: AfCh: '98- 1, '02- 1; WCp: '98- 3. At 3000m: WI: '03- 1, '04- 2; WCp: '02- 1; 3rd GP 2002. World CC: '96-7-00: 10/14/14; HMar: '01-02-03: 3/1/2. Won Rd Rly team '96, ETH 3000m & 10,000m 1993.
Records: African 5000m and 10,000m 2003, World indoor 3000m (8:29.15) 2002, 5000m 2004, African indoor 5000m 2003; Ethiopian 2000m 2003, 3000m 1997 and 2001, marathon 2006 (2).
Progress at 5000m, 10,000m, Mar: 1992- 34:13.3, 1993- 32:48.52, 1995- 15:44.46, 32:02.94; 1996- 14:59.17, 32:21.09; 1997- 15:08.22, 31:48.95; 1998- 15:22.34, 32:06.42; 1999- 14:54.88, 31:32.51; 2000- 14:52.61, 30:51.30; 2001- 14:51.67, 31:32.70, 2:41:50; 2002- 14:33.65, 2003- 14:29.32, 30:04.18; 2004- 14:36.92; 2005- 14:31.09, 30:25.41; 2006- 14:49.03, 2:20:42; 2007- 2:33:49. pbs: 1500m 4:05.54i, 4:06.46 '02; 2000m 5:35.62 '03; 3000m 8:25.62 '01; road: 15km 47:48 '05, 10M 53:16 '98, HMar 67:32 '03.
Fourth London marathon (2:21:56) and first in Great North Run 2006 and Chicago Marathon 2006-07. Married to Lemme Erpassa (five team medals at World CC 1988-97), son Aleme born in 1994.

Gelete BURKA Bati b. 15 Feb 1986 Kofele 1.65m 45kg.
At 1500m: WCh: '05- 8; WI: '08- 3; AfG: '07- 1. At 5000m: WCh: '07- 10. World CC: '03-05-06-07-08: 3J/1J/1 4k/4/6. Won ETH 1500m 2004-05, 2007; 5000m 2005, 4k CC 2006.
African indoor 1500m record 2008, junior 2005.
Progress at 1500m, 5000m: 2003- 4:10.82, 16:23.8A, 2004- 4:06.10, 2005- 3:59.60, 14:51.47; 2006- 4:02.68, 14:40.92; 2007- 4:00.48, 14:31.20; 2008- 3:59.75i. pbs: 800m 2:07.05 '03, 1M 4:30.81 '03, 2000m 5:37.82 '06, 3000m 8:25.92 '06.
Married Taddele Gebrmehden in 2007.

Meseret DEFAR b. 19 Nov 1983 Addis Ababa 1.55m 42kg.
At 5000m: OG: '04- 1; WCh: '03- h, '05- 2; WJ: '00- 2, '02- 1; AfG: '03- 1; AfCh: '00- 2, '06- 1; WCp: '06- 1. At 3000m: WJ: '02- 1; WY: '99- 2; WI: '03-04-06-08: 3/1/1/1. Won WAF 3000m 2004-07, 5000m 2005. World CC: '02- 13J.
Records: World 5000m 2006 & 2007, indoor 3000m 2007, 2M (3) 2007-08, African 5000m 2005, Ethiopian 3000m (2) 2006-07. World 5k road best 14:46 Carlsbad 2006.
Progress at 3000m, 5000m: 1999- 9:02.08, 2000- 8:59.90, 15:08.36; 2001- 8:52.47, 15:08.65; 2002- 8:40.28, 15:26.45; 2003- 8:38.31, 14:40.34; 2004- 8:33.44i/8:36.46, 14:44.81; 2005- 8:30.05i/8:33.57, 14:28.98; 2006- 8:24.66, 14:24.53; 2007- 8:23.72i/8:24.51, 14:16.63. pbs: 1500m 4:06.12 '06, 1M: 4:28.5ei '06, 4:33.07+ '07; 2000m 5:34.74i/5:38.0 '06, 2M 8:58.58 '07, 10kmRd 32:08 '07.
Married to Teodros Hailu. IAAF woman athlete of the year 2007.

Ejegayehu DIBABA b. 25 Jun 1982 Chefe, Arsi region 1.60m 46kg.
At (5000m/)10,000m: OG: '04- 2; WCh: '03- 9, '05- 3/3, '07- 7; AfG: '03- 1; AfCh: '06- dnf; won Af-AsG 2003. At 5000m: AfCh: '02- 3. World CC 4k: '03-04: 9/10/14; 8k: '04-06: 2/14.
Progress at 5000m, 10,000m: 2001- 15:32.31, 32:24.20; 2002- 15:56.02, 2003- 14:41.67, 31:01.07; 2004- 14:32.74, 30:24.98; 2005- 14:37.34, 30:18.39; 2006- 14:33.52, 2007- 14:45.22, 31:18.97. pbs: 2000m 5:46.0+ '06, 3000m 8:29.55 '06.
Older sister of Tirunesh Dibaba.

Tirunesh DIBABA b. 1 Jun 1985 Chefe, Arsi region 1.60m 47kg.
At 5000m(/10,000m): OG: '04- 3; WCh: '03- 1, '05- 1/1, '07- (1); WJ: '02- 2; AfG: '03- 4; AfCh: '06- 2. At 3000m: WCp: '06- 1. World CC: '01-02-03-05-06-07-08: 5J/2J/1J/1/1/2/1; 4k: '04-05: 2/1. Won WAF 5000m 2006, ETH 4k CC & 5000m 2003. 8k CC 2005.
World indoor 5000m records 2005 (14:32.93) & 2007, World junior 5000m records 2003-04, indoor best 8:33.56 '04, world road 5k best 14:51 '05.
Progress at 5000m: 2002- 14:49.90, 2003- 14:39.94, 2004- 14:30.88, 2005- 14:32.42, 30:15.67; 2006- 14:30.40, 2007- 14:27.42i/14:35.67, 31:55.41. pbs: 2000m 5:42.7 '05, 3000m 8:29.55 '06.
In 2003 she became, at 18 years 90 days, the youngest ever world champion at an individual event and in 2005 the first woman to win the 5000m/10,000m double (with last laps of 58.19 and 58.4) at a global event after earlier in the year winning both World CC titles. Sister of Ejagayou Dibaba; their younger sister **Genzebe** won the 2008 World Junior CC.

Meselech MELKAMU b. 19 Apr 1985 Debre Markos 1.58m 47kg.
At 5000m: WCh: '05- 4, '07- 6; AfG: '07- 2; AfCh: '06- 6; WJ: '04- 1. At 3000m: WI: '08- 2. World CC: '03-04-05-06-07-08: 4J/1J/4 & 6/3 & 3/3/9. Won ETH 5000m 2004, 4k CC 2005, CC 2006-07.
Progress at 5000m: 2003- 15:27.93, 2004- 15:00.02, 2005- 14:38.97, 2006- 14:37.44, 2007- 14:33.83. pbs: 1500m 4:07.52 '07, 1M 4:33.94 '03, 2000m 5:39.2i+ '07, 5:46.3+ '07; 3000m 8:23.74i '07, 8:34.73 '05, 10km Rd 31:41 '06.

Mestawet TUFA b. 14 Sep 1983 Bekoji 1.57m 45kg.
At 10,000m: WCh: '07- dnf; AfG: '07- 1; At 3000m: WJ: '00- 5; WY: '01- 2. World CC: '01-06-08: 10J/7/2.
Progress at 5000m, 10,000m: 2002- 15:48.50, 2004- 15:02.43, 2005- 15:39.50, 2006- 14:59.05, 2007- 14:51.72, 31:00.27. pbs: 2000m 5:49.2+ '06, 3000m 8:47.41 '06, Road: 15km 49:00 '05, HMar 73:39A '03.

Getenesh WAMI b. 11 Dec 1974 Debre Birhan 1.54m 45kg.
At 10,000m (5000m): OG: '96- 3, '00- 2 (3); WCh: '95- 18, '97- dnf, '99- 1, '01- 3; WJ: '92- 2; AfG: '95- 3, '99- 1; AfCh: '92- 4. Won GP 3000m 1998, 2nd 5000m 1996. World CC: '91-2: 5J/9J, '95-6-7-8-9-00-01-05: 5/1/3/3/1/2/2 &1 4k/8; Rd Rly team: '96/8- 1/1.
African records 5000m 2000, 10,000m 1999. ETH 3000m (3) 1997-8, 5000m (5) 1996-2000, Mar 2002.
Progress at 5000m, 10,000m, Mar: 1992- 32:34.68, 1994- 36:15.0A, 1995- 15:28.65, 32:17.41; 1996- 14:46.45, 31:06.65; 1997- 14:54.05, 32:05.73; 1998- 14:36.08, 34:23.4A; 1999- 15:25.5, 30:24.56; 2000- 14:30.88, 30:22.48; 2001- 14:31.69, 31:49.98; 2002- 2:22:20, 2004- 2:32:07, 2005- 14:58.58, 2:27:40; 2006- 2:21:34, 2007- 2:21:45. pbs: 1500m 4:01.47 '98, 2000m 5:39.9 '01, 3000m 8:27.62 '01, 10M Rd 51:30 '05, HMar 69:58+ '07.
Has won 19 individual and team medals at World CC. After missing the 2002 track season, she became the second fastest ever marathon debutante when winning at Amsterdam. Won Berlin Marathon 2006-07, 2nd London & New York 2007. Married Geteneh Tessema November 1999, daughter Eva born August 2003.

FINLAND

Governing body: Suomen Urheiluliitto, Radiokatu 20, SF-00240 Helsinki. Founded 1906.
National Championships first held in 1907 (men), 1913 (women). **2007 Champions**: **Men**: 100m: Nghi Tran 10.60, 200m: Visa Hongisto 20.98, 400m: Juhani Mikkola 47.77, 800m: Mikko Lahtio 1:48.85, 1500m: Jonas Hamm 3:49.80, 5000m/10,000m/HMar: Jussi Utriainen 14:08.65/29:43.14/65:59, Mar: Marko Vaittinen 2:28:12, 3000mSt: Joonas Harjamäki 8:53.11, 110mh: Antti Korkealaakso 13.89, 400mh: Jussi Heikkilä 50.53, HJ: Oskari Frösén 2.27, PV: Matti Mononen 5.45, LJ: Petteri Lax 7.97w, TJ: Johan Meriluoto 16.18, SP: Robert Häggblom 20.07, DT: Frantz Kruger 66.37, HT: Olli-Pekka Karjalainen 76.57, JT: Tero Pitkämäki 89.43, Dec: Jaakko Ojaniemi 7613, 20kW: Antti Kempas 1:27:32, 50kW: Heikki Lahtinen 5:35:17. **Women**: 100m: Johanna Manninen 11.40, 200m: Sari Keskitalo 23.71, 400m: Kirsi Mykkänen 53.87, 800m/1500m: Mari Järvenpää 2:04.70/4:24.70, 5000m: Elina Lindgren 16:54.57, 10,000m: Annemari Sandell-Hyvärinen 35:23.78, HMar/Mar: Hanna Jantunen 77:06/2:47:24, 3000mSt: Sandra Eriksson 10:24.73, 100mh: Johanna Halkoaho 13.35, 400mh: Ilona Ranta 57.21, HJ: Hanna Mikkonen 1.86, PV: Minna Nikkanen 4.25, LJ: Elina Sorsa 6.17, TJ: Natalia Kilpeläinen-Bäck 13.87, SP: Suvi Helin 15.32, DT: Anita Hietalahti 55.46, HT: Merja Korpela 68.65, JT: Paula Tarvainen 61.03, Hep: Salla Rinne 5894, 10kW: Karoliina Kaasalainen 50:29, 20kW: Tiina Muininen 1:51:22.

Tommi EVILÄ b. 6 Apr 1980 Tampere 1.94m 83kg. Tampereen Pyrintö. Student at Technical University of Tampere.
At LJ: WCh: '05- 3; WJ: '98- 10; EU23: '01- 5; EI: '05- 4. Finnish champion 2001, 2003-06.
Two Finnish long jump records 2005.
Progress at LJ: 1995- 6.42, 1996- 6.85, 1997- 7.48, 1998- 7.48/7.51w, 1999- 7.45/7.49w, 2000- 7.69/7.80w, 2001- 8.04/8.11w, 2002- 7.76/7.88w, 2003- 7.96, 2004- 8.15, 2005- 8.19/8.27w, 2006- 8.02, 2007- 7.98/8.41w. pbs: 60m 6.97i '01, 100m 10.89 '01, TJ 15.55i/15.53 '03.

Tero JÄRVENPÄÄ b. 2 Oct 1984 Tampere 1.88m 95kg. Tampereen Pyrintö,
At JT: WCh: '07- 8; EC: '06- dnq 17; WY: '01- 3; EU23: '05- 5; EJ: '03- 2; WUG: '05- 2.
Progress at JT: 2001- 66.53, 2002- 70.85, 2003- 80.43, 2004- 80.13, 2005- 84.05, 2006- 84.95, 2007- 84.35.

Olli-Pekka KARJALAINEN b. 7 Mar 1980 Töysä 1.94m 115kg. Töysän Veto. Political science student at University of Helsinki.
At HT: OG: '00/04- dnq 34/15; WCh: '99- 11, '01- 10, '03- dnq 14, '05- 5, '07- 9; EC: '02- 8, '06- 2; WJ: '98- 1; EJ: '97- 3, '99- 1; EU23: '01- 2; ECp: '02- 1, '06- 3. Won WAF 2004, Finnish 1998-2007.
World junior hammer record 1999, three Finnish 2002-04.
Progress at HT: 1995- 48.26, 1996- 58.80, 1997- 69.84, 1998- 75.08, 1999- 78.33, 2000- 80.55, 2001- 80.54, 2002- 81.70, 2003- 80.20, 2004- 83.30, 2005- 79.81, 2006- 80.84, 2007- 78.35.

Frantz KRUGER b. 22 May 1975 Kempton Park, RSA 2.03m 125kg. Former medical student at Free State University, Bloemfontein.
At DT: OG: '00- 3, '04- 5; WCh: '99- dnq 17, '01- 8, '03- 6, '05- 6, '07- dnq 19; CG: '98- 2, '02- 1; WJ: '94- 1; AfG: '99- 1; AfCh: '98- 1, '04- 1; WUG: '97- 6, '99- 1; WCp: '98- 3. Won GWG 2001, RSA 1996, 1999-2005; Finnish 2007, Af-J SP & DT 1994.
Discus records: three African and Commonwealth 2000-02, Finnish 2007.
Progress at DT: 1993- 58.28, 1994- 58.52, 1995- 60.06, 1996- 60.66, 1997- 61.64, 1998- 65.73, 1999- 67.38, 2000- 69.75A, 2001- 69.96, 2002- 70.32, 2003- 66.70, 2004- 66.59, 2005- 67.30, 2006- 65.10, 2007- 69.97.
Set RSA U13 record for 200m individual medley swimming. Married **Heli Koivula** FIN (b. 27 Jun 1975; 2 EC TJ 2002, pb 14.39 '03, 14.83w '02) on 28 June 2003. He gained Finnish citizenship on 14 Jun 2007.

Tero PITKÄMÄKI b. 19 Dec 1982 Ilmajoki 1.95m 92kg. Nurmon Urheilijat. Electrical engineering student.
At JT: OG: '04- 8; WCh: '05- 4, '07- 1; EC: '06- 2; EU23: '03- 3; EJ: '01- 6; ECp: '06- 1. Won WAF 2005, 2007; Finnish 2004-07.
Progress at JT: 1999- 66.83, 2000- 73.75, 2001- 74.89, 2002- 77.24, 2003- 80.45, 2004- 84.64, 2005- 91.53, 2006- 91.11, 2007- 91.23.

Women

Mikaela INGBERG b. 29 Jul 1974 Vaasa 1.74m 75kg. Vasa Idrottssällskap.
At JT: OG: '96- 7, '00- 9, '04- dnq 13; WCh: '95- 3, '97- 4, '99- 9, '01- 6, '03- 4, '05- 9; EC: '94- dnq 16, '98- 3, '02- 3, '06- 10; EJ: '91- 15, '93- 1; WCp: '98- 3, '02- 3; 2nd GP 2002. Finnish champion 1994, 1999-2000, 2002, 2004-05.
Finnish javelin record 2000.
Progress at JT: 1987- 33.70, 1988- 41.78, 1989- 43.92, 1990- 51.96, 1991- 52.30, 1992- 54.00, 1993- 58.26, 1994- 58.70, 1995- 65.16, 1996- 65.66, 1997- 67.32, 1998- 66.43; new 1999- 61.50, 2000- 64.03, 2001- 63.13, 2002- 63.50, 2003- 63.55, 2004- 62.53, 2005- 61.06, 2006- 60.16, 2007- 60.70. pbs: HJ 1.57 '88, SP 12.67 '99, DT 39.56 '95.

Paula TARVAINEN b. 17 Feb 1973 Pori 1.67m 68kg. née Huhtaniemi. Noormarkun Nopsa.
At JT: OG: '04- dnq 28; WCh: '01-03: dnq 13/20; '05- 6, '07- 12; EC: '02- 10, '06- 11. Finnish champion 2001, 2003, 2006-07.
Finnish javelin record 2003.
Progress at JT: 1990- 33.84, 1991- 48.34, 1992- 52.50, 1993- 57.34, 1994- 51.64, 1995- 56.68, 1996- 55.24, 1997- 56.08, 1998- 58.10; new 1999- 58.44, 2000- 61.01, 2001- 63.05, 2002- 62.35, 2003- 64.90, 2004- 62.63, 2005- 62.64, 2006- 63.56, 2007- 63.58.

FRANCE

Governing body: Fédération Française d'Athlétisme, 33 avenue Pierre de Coubertin, 75640 Paris cedex 13. Founded 1920.
National Championships first held in 1888 (men), 1918 (women). **2007 Champions: Men**: 100m: Lueyi Dovy 10.41, 200m: David Alerte 20.33, 400m: Leslie Djhone 45.19, 800m: Driss Yousfi 1:50.60, 1500m: Abdelkader Bakhtache 3:40.51, 5000m: Malik Bahloul 13:51.28, 10,000m: El Hassan Lahssini 27:59.93, HMar: Brahim Lahlafi 64:34, Mar: David Antoine 2:20:36, 3000mSt: Mohamed-Khaled Belabbas 8:33.48, 110mh: Ladji Doucouré 13.43, 400mh: Fadil Bellaabouss 49.29, HJ: Mickaël Hanany 2.24, PV: Jérôme Clavier 5.70, LJ: Kafetien Gomis 7.91, TJ: Julien Kapek 17.10, SP: Yves Niaré 20.08, DT: Bertrand Vili 61.05, HT: Frédéric Pouzy 70.80, JT: Vitolio Tipotio 75.78, Dec: Rudy Bourguignon 7703, 20kW: Yohann Diniz 1:23:16, 50kW: Sébastien Biche 3:58:16. **Women**: 100m: Carima Louami 11.54, 200m: Muriel Hurtis-Houairi 22.88, 400m: Solen Désert 51.42, 800m: Élodie Guégan 2:02.74, 1500m: Maria Martins 4:14.30, 5000m: Samira Mezeghrane 16:34.51, HMar: Fatiha Klilech-Fauvel 73:12, Mar: Béatrice Ceveno 2:45:01, 3000mSt: Sophie Duarté 9:39.01, 100mh: Adrienna Lamalle 12.94, 400mh: Aurore Kassambara 56.23, HJ: Mélanie Skotnik 1.95, PV: Vanessa Boslak 4.60, LJ: Eunice Barber 6.66; TJ: Teresa N'Zola 14.14w, SP: Laurence Manfrédi 17.50, DT: Mélina Robert-Michon 61.40, HT: Manuèla Montebrun 71.36, JT: Nadia Vigliano 56.84, Hep; Antoinette Nana Djimou Ida 5982, 20kW: Many Loriou 1:45:17.

Mehdi BAALA b. 17 Aug 1978 Strasbourg 1.83m 65kg. Lille Métropole Athlétisme.
At 1500m (800m): OG: '00- 4, '04- h; WCh: '01- 12, '03- 2, '05- sf (6), '07- dq sf; EC: '02- 1, '06- 1; WJ: '96- h; EU23: '99- 3; EJ: '97- 7; EI: '00- 3; WCp: '02-3; ECp: '00-01-02-04-07: 1 (1)/2/1/1/1. Won FRA 800m 2001, 1500m 2002, 2005.
French records 800m 2002, 1000m (2) 2002-03, 1500m (2) 2003, 2000m 2005.
Progress at 800m, 1500m: 1994- 1:56.5, 4:08.1; 1995- 1:53.76, 3:48.74; 1996- 1:49.62, 3:43.50; 1997- 1:50.08, 3:45.34; 1998- 1:49.57, 3:41.86; 1999- 1:46.41, 3:34.83; 2000- 1:46.24, 3:32.05; 2001- 1:46.94, 3:31.97; 2002- 1:43.15, 3:32.03;

2003- 1:44.17, 3:28.98; 2004- 1:45.52, 3:31.25; 2005- 1:44.74, 3:30.80; 2006- 1:44.04, 3:32.01; 2007- 3:31.01. pbs: 1000m 2:13.96 '03, 2000m 4:53.12 '05, 3000m 8:08.06i '98, 8:23.69 '98.

Married Hanane Sabri (ht WC 1500m '01, FRA champion 2001) in September 2000. His elder brother Samir won 2002 French marathon.

Romain BARRAS b. 1 Aug 1980 Calais 1.94m 86kg. SO Calais.

At Dec: OG: '04- 13; WCh: '05- 7, '07- 7; EC: '06- 8; EU23: '01- 4; WUG: '01- 5, 03- 1; ECp: '03-04-06: 1/6/1; French, MedG & Franc G champion 2005. At Hep: EI: '07- 6.

Progress at Dec: 1998- 6505, 1999- 7147, 2000- 7609, 2001- 7876, 2002- 7835, 2003- 8196, 2004- 8067, 2005- 8185, 2006- 8416w/8138, 2007- 8298. pbs: 60m 7.21i '07, 100m 11.02 '03, 10.94w '06; 400m 48.21 '06, 1000m 2:39.89i '06, 1500m 4:21.79 '06, 50mh 7.09i '04, 6.8i '03; 60mh 8.14i '01, 110mh 14.13 '06, HJ 2.01 '03, PV 5.05 '07, LJ 7.35 '05, SP 15.51i '07, 15.35 '04; DT 47.21 '04, JT 65.84 '05, Hep 5895i '06.

Jérome CLAVIER b. 3 May 1983 Chambray-lès-Tours 1.85m 73kg. Athletic Trois Tours.

At PV: WCh: '07- dnq 20; WJ: '02- 6; EU23: '03- dnq, '05- 3; WI: '08- 4; EI: '07- 6; ECp: '05- 7; French champion 2007.

Progress at PV: 1998- 3.90, 1999- 4.40, 2000- 4.80, 2001- 5.10, 2002- 5.40, 2003- 5.56i/5.50, 2004- 5.65i/5.60, 2005- 5.63, 2006- 5.65i/5.561, 2007- 5.70, 2008- 5.80i. pb Dec 6307 '01.

Yohann DINIZ b. 1 Jan 1978 Epernay 1.85m 66kg. EFS Reims Athlétisme.

At 20kW: ECp: '07- 1; At 50kW: WCh: '05- dq, '07- 2; EC: '06- 1; ECp: '05- 4. Won French 20kW 2007, 50kW 2005.

French records 5000mW 2006 & 2007, 50kW 2006, 20kW 2005 & 2007.

Progress at 20kW, 50kW: 2001- 1:35:05.0t, 2002- 1:30:40, 2003- 1:26:54.99t, 2004- 1:24:25, 3:52:11.0t; 2005- 1:20:20, 3:45:17; 2006- 1:23:19, 3:41:39; 2007- 1:18:58, 3:44:22. pbs: 5000mW 18:35.54 '07, 10kW 39:35+ '07, 1HrW 14,914m '05.

Leslie DJHONE b. 18 Mar 1981 Abidjan, CIV 1.87m 76kg. Lagardère Paris Racing.

At 400m/4x400m: OG: '04- 7; WCh: '03- 5/1R, '05- h, '07- 5; EC: '02- 3R, '06- 3/1R; EU23: '03- 1; ECp: '04-06-07: 3/1R/1. At LJ/4x100m: WJ: '98- dnq, '00- 2R; EU23: '01- 4/4R, '03- 2R; EJ: '99- 1/1R. At 200m: ECp: '03- 5. Won FRA 200m 2004, 400m 2006-07.

French 400m records 2004 & 2007.

Progress at 400m: 2001- 47.01, 2002- 45.63, 2003- 44.83, 2004- 44.64, 2005- 45.56, 2006- 44.91, 2007- 44.46. pbs: 100m 10.52 '03, 200m 20.51i '03, 20.67 '04; 300m 32.18 '03, LJ: 7.92 '99, 8.06w '01.

Began as a long jumper, winning the European Junior title in 1999, before turning to 400m.

Ladji DOUCOURÉ b. 28 Mar 1983 Juvisy-sur-Orge 1.83m 75kg. Viry Evry Nord Sud Essonne.

At 110mh/4x100mR: OG: '04- 8; WCh: '03- sf, '05- 1, '07- sf; EC: '06- sf; WJ: '00- 3/2R; EU23: '03- 1; ECp: '01-03-05-06-07: 7/1/1&3R/1/1; French champion 2004-05, 2007. At 100mh: WY: '99- 1. At 60mh: WI: '03- 4; EI: '05- 1. At Dec: EJ: '01- 1/2R.

Four French 110mh records 2004-05. European indoor 50mh record 2005.

Progress at 110mh: 2000- 13.75, 2001- 13.58, 2002- 13.87/13.73w, 2003- 13.23, 2004- 13.06, 2005- 12.97, 2006- 13.21, 2007- 13.27. pbs: 60m 6.78i '00, 100m 10.48 '01, 200m 20.75 '01, 400m 46.82 '01, 50mh 6.36i '05, 55mh 7.14i '04, 60mh 7.42i '05, PV 4.45 '01, LJ 7.82i '01, 7.57/7.73w '01, SP 12.97 '03, Dec 7794 '01.

Improved from 7.64 to 7.61 and 7.58 (for surprise 4th place) at 60mh at 2003 World Indoors. Set two French records (13.18 and 13.06) at 2004 Olympics before smashing into a hurdle in final and two more French records (13.02 and 12.97) before winning World title in 2005. Father came from Mali, mother from Sénegal.

Romain MESNIL b. 13 Jun 1977 Le Plessis Bouchard 1.88m 82kg. AC Paris Joinville. IT Engineer.

At PV: OG: '00/04- dnq 31/18; WCh: '99- nh, '01- 5, '03- dnq, '07- 2; EC: '02- dnq, '06- 2=; EU23: '99-1; WJ: '96- dnq 13=; WI: '99-01-03-04: 6=/3/7/7; WCp: '06- 4; ECp: '00-03-04-06-07: 5/1/1/1/2. French champion 2000-03.

Progress at PV: 1993- 4.30, 1994- 4.65, 1995- 5.15, 1996- 5.30, 1997- 5.40, 1998- 5.80, 1999- 5.93, 2000- 5.75, 2001- 5.86i/5.85, 2002- 5.75, 2003- 5.95, 2004- 5.80, 2005- 5.75, 2006- 5.81, 2007- 5.86. pb Dec 5724 '98.

Former gymnast. Married to Karine Bénézech (PV 3.75i '99).

Salim SDIRI b. 26 Oct 1978 Ajaccio, Corsica 1.85m 80kg, USM Montargis.

At LJ: OG: '04- 12; WCh: '03- dnq 13, '05- 5; EC: '02- 7, '06- 10; WI: '03- 7; EI: '07- 3; WCp: '06- 5; ECp: '02-04-05-06-07: 3/2/2/2/5; won Med G 2005, French 2003-06.

Progress at LJ: 1999- 7.43, 2000- 7.95, 2001- 7.83, 2002- 8.23, 2003- 8.29w, 2004- 8.24, 2005- 8.25, 2006- 8.27i/8.22, 2007- 8.13i/8.01. pbs: 100m 10.87 '04, 10.6w '01; TJ 16.10 '00.

Seriously injured when speered by a javelin at Rome Golden Gala 2007.

Bouabdellah 'Bob' TAHRI b. 20 Dec 1978 Metz 1.91m 68kg. Athlétisme Metz Métropole.

At 3000mSt: OG: '00- h, '04- 7; WCh: '99- 12, '01- 5, '03- 4, '05- 8, '07- 5; EC: '98- 10, '02- 4, '06- 3; WJ: '96- 7; WCp: '06- 3; ECp: '00-01-02-04: 1/1/1/1. At 5000m: EJ: '97- 1; ECp: '05- 2. At 3000m: EI: '07- 2; ECp: '07- 1; At 1500m: ECp: '03- 4. World CC: '97-04: 22J/15 4k; Eur CC: '05- 4. Won FRA 1500m 2004, 2006; 3000mSt 1998.

European record 3000mSt 2003, best 2000mSt 2002.

Progress at 3000mSt: 1996- 8:44.65, 1998- 8:19.75,

1999- 8:12.24, 2000- 8:16.14, 2001- 8:09.23, 2002- 8:10.83, 2003- 8:06.91, 2004- 8:14.26, 2005- 8:09.58, 2006- 8:09.53, 2007- 8:09.06. pbs: 800m 1:48.96 '01, 1000m 2:20.34 '05, 1500m 3:34.85 '02, 1M 3:52.95 '02. 2000m 4:57.58 '02, 3000m 7:38.41i '07, 7:42.49 '05; 5000m 13:12.29 '07, 10km Rd 28:52 '06, HMar 66:12 '03, 2000mSt 5:15.96 '02.

Women

Christine ARRON b. 13 Sep 1973 Abymes, Guadeloupe 1.77m 64kg. Neuilly Plaisance Sports.

At 100m/(200m)/4x100m: OG: '00- sf/4R, '04- sf/sf/3R; WCh: '97- 4/3R, '99- 6/2R, '03- 5/1R, '05- 3/3/4R, '07- 6; EC: '98- 1/1R, ECp: '97-8-9-00-03-04-05-07: 2R/2&3R/1&1R/2&1R/1&1R/1&1R (1 200m '97)/1&1/2R; WJ: '92- sf. At 60m: WI: '04- 7, '06- 4. Won French 100m 2000, 2003-04; 200m 1997, 2004-05. MedG 200m 1997.

European and four French 100m records 1998.

Progress at 100m, 200m: 1988- 12.04, 1989- 11.64/11.6, 25.43; 1990- 12.41/12.3/12.0w, 1991- 11.97, 24.4; 1992- 11.51, 23.75; 1993- 11.93/11.92w, 1994- 24.18, 1995- 23.92, 1996- 23.26, 1997- 11.03, 22.62/22.57w, 1998- 10.73, 22.95i; 1999- 10.97, 22.26; 2000- 10.99/10.89w, 2001- 11.15, 23.42/23.14w; 2003- 11.01/10.95w, 22.92; 2004- 10.95, 22.60; 2005- 10.93/10.82w, 22.31; 2006- 11.33/11.25w, 22.80i; 2007- 11.04, 22.88. pbs: 50m 6.05+ '99, 60m 7.00+ '99, 7.06i '06; 400m 53.76 '95.

Superstar of the 1998 European Championships: followed a majestic 100m victory in a European record 10.73 with an awesome final sprint relay leg to take France to gold. First set French age records at 14 in 1988 (for 80m and 150m). Breakthrough in 1997, setting a French indoor 200m record (23.13), stepping in for Marie-José Pérec to win European Cup 200m and placing 4th in World 100m. Son Ethan born 28 Jun 2002. Won five of six Golden League 100m races in 2005.

Eunice BARBER b. 17 Nov 1974 Freetown, Sierra Leone 1.75m 68kg. EFS Reims.

At Hep (LJ): OG: '92- 26 (h 100mh), '96- 5 (dnq), '00- dnf, '04- (dnq); WCh: '93- dnf, '95- 4, '97- dnf, '99- 1 (qf 100mh), '01- dnf, '03- 2 (1), '05- 2 (3), '07- (dnq 16); EC: '06- dnf; WJ: '92- 14; ECp: '99- 1. At Pen: WI: '97- 6. At LJ: AfG: '95- 1; ECp: '99-01-03-06-07: 1/2/1/2/1; won WAF 2003, FRA HJ 2006, LJ 1998-9, 2007; Hep 1996.

French records: LJ 1999 & 2003, heptathlon record 1999 & 2005. African heptathlon record 1996 and indoor pentathlon 1997. SLE records 100m, 200m, 100mh, HJ, LJ, SP, JT, Hep 1992-8.

Progress at LJ, Hep: 1990- 5.47, 1991- 5.66, 1992- 6.02, 5048; 1993- 5.94, 5308; 1994- 5.93, 5378; 1995- 6.57/6.70Aw, 6340; 1996- 6.59/6.66w, 6416; 1997- 6.70, 1998- 6.86i/6.75/6.90w, 1999- 7.01, 6861; 2000- 6.85, 6842; 2001- 6.97, 6736; 2003- 7.05, 6755; 2004- 6.61i/6.37, 2005- 6.80, 6889; 2006- 6.61, 2007- 6.73. pbs: 60m 7.36i '00, 100m 11.52 '06, 200m 23.53 '99, 800m 2:10.55 '01, 60mh 8.11i '00, 100mh 12.78 '01, 12.62w '05; 200mh 27.47 '99, HJ 1.93 '99, SP 14.12 '07, JT 53.10 '05, Pen 4558i '97.

French citizen in February 1999; previously represented Sierra Leone, but living in Reims from 1992. After concentrating on the long jump and taking the French record to 7.01, she returned in 1999 to the heptathlon with wins at 6461 (Arles) and 6505 (European Cup) before adding 356 points to her pb in Seville to take the world title; a win at Talence (6514) secured the IAAF Combined Events Challenge. Won at Götzis with world's best score of 2000, but then held back by injuries; returned for Olympics but unable to continue beyond long jump in heptathlon. In 2001 she won again at Götzis, and started the World Championships heptathlon in great form with a clear lead after two events, but then made the terrible of error of having three no throws in the shot and withdrew. Back at her best in 2005 after injury in 2004.

Vanessa BOSLAK b. 11 Jun 1982 Lesquin 1.70m 57kg. Lille Métropole Athlétisme. Physiotherapy student.

At PV: OG: '04- 6=, WCh: '05- 8, '07- 5; EC: '02- 11=, '06- dnq 17=; WJ: '98- 6; '00- 3=; EU23: '03- 2; EJ: '01- 3; WI: '04- 5=, '06- 5; EI: '07- 6=; ECp: '01-02-04-06-07: 5/3/5/2/3; won Med G 2005, French 2001, 2003-05, 2007.

13 French pole vault records 2002-07.

Progress at PV: 1995- 3.25, 1996- 3.76, 1997- 3.90, 1998- 4.10, 1999- 4.15i/4.11, 2000- 4.32, 2001- 4.33i/4.30, 2002- 4.46, 2003- 4.50, 2004- 4.51, 2005- 4.60, 2006- 4.70, 2007- 4.70. pb JT 44.27 '99. Broke her ankle at Saint-Denis in July 2006.

Marie COLLONVILLÉ b. 23 Nov 1973 Amiens 1.63m 55kg. Amiens UC

At Hep: OG: '04- 7; WCh: '97-99-01-05-07: 12/9/11/6/9; EC: '94- 19, '98- 8, '06- dnf; WUG: '97- 3 (3 HJ); ECp: '96-7-8-00: 6/4/1/5. At Pen: WI: '97- 8, '03- 3; EI: '98- 5, '05- 6. Won MedG Hep 2005, FRA HJ 1997, Hep 1995, 1999, 2002.

Inaugural world decathlon record 2004.

Progress at Hep: 1991- 4882, 1992- 5233, 1993- 5638, 1994- 5995, 1995- 5833, 1996- 6143, 1997- 6350, 1998- 6218, 1999- 6188, 2000- 6119, 2001- 5887, 2002- 6083, 2003- 6007, 2004- 6279, 2005- 6248, 2006- 6170, 2007- 6244. pbs: 60m 8.09i '04, 100m 12.44 '05, 200m 24.71 '97, 24.68w '04; 400m 56.15 '04, 800m 2:10.90 '99, 1500m 5:06.09 '04, 50mh 7.33i '04, 60mh 8.48i '05, 100mh 13.52 '00, 13.2w '98; 400mh 59.56 '95, HJ 1.94 '97, PV 3.64i '05, 3.60 '02; LJ 6.67 '07, SP 12.87i '03, 12.73 '06; DT 35.28 '04, JT 50.74 '97, Pen 4644i '03, Dec 8150 '04. Accomplished pianist.

Sophie DUARTÉ b. 31 Jul 1981 Rodez 1.70m 54kg. AC Paris Joinville.

At 3000mSt: WCh: '07- 5; EU23: '03- 9; ECp: '07- 2. French champion 2007.

Two French 3000mSt records 2007.

Progress at 3000mSt: 2003- 10:17.76, 2004- 10:29.13,

2005- 10:07.73, 2006- 10:14.36, 2007- 9:27.51. pb 800m 2:14.26 '04, 1500m: 4:18.91 '07, 3000m 9:26.43 '07, 5000m 17:29.37 '01.

Muriel HURTIS-HOUAIRI b. 25 Mar 1979 Bondy 1.80m 68kg. AC Bobigny Athlétisme.
At (100m)/200m/4x100m: OG: '00- sf/4R, '04- qf/3R; WCh: '99- sf/2R, '01- 2R, '03- 3/1R, '07- qf; EC: '02- 1/1R, '06- sf; WJ: '98- 1/2R; EJ: '97- 2/4R; EU23: '99- 2/1R; WI: '01- 5, '03- 1; EI: '00- 1, '02- 1; WCp: '02- 2/3R; ECp: '00-02-03-04-07: 1&1R/1&1R/3&1R/1&1R/1&2R (1 100m '02). At 60m: WI: '04- 5. Won WAF 200m 2003, 2007; French 200m 2000, 2002, 2007.
Progress at 100m, 200m: 1995- 11.95, 23.91/23.76w; 1996- 11.89/11.8, 23.92; 1997- 11.80, 23.79; 1998- 11.43, 22.76/22.72w, 1999- 11.33/11.3, 22.31; 2000- 11.36/11.28w, 22.70; 2001- 11.51, 23.06i/23.35/ 23.14w; 2002- 10.96, 22.43/22.35w, 2003- 11.08/10.97w, 22.41; 2004- 11.21, 22.76; 2006- 11.66, 23.26/23.22w; 2007- 11.31, 22.38. pbs: 50m 6.14i '03, 60m 7.09i '03, 400m 54.44 '98, LJ 6.04i '97, 5.86 '95.
Married to rap-singer K-mel. Son Leyhan born 21 March 2005.

Manuèla MONTEBRUN b. 13 Nov 1979 Laval 1.75m 85kg. Stade Laval. Student.
At HT: OG: '00/04- dnq 24/15; WCh: '99-01-03-05-07: 12/5/3/4/8; EC: '98- dnq 26, '02- 3; WJ: '98- 5; EU23: '99- 4, '01- 1; WUG: '99- 3, '01- 1; ECp: '00-01-02-03-04-05-07: 3/4/2/1/5/2/4. French champion 2000-05, 2007.
Ten French hammer records 1999-2005.
Progress at HT: 1996- 47.34, 1997- 52.58, 1998- 62.79, 1999- 68.11, 2000- 71.18, 2001- 70.28, 2002- 72.54, 2003- 74.50/75.20dh, 2004- 72.73, 2005- 74.66, 2006- 72.13, 2007- 73.71. pb SP 13.99 '99.

Teresa N'ZOLA MESO Ba b. 30 Nov 1983 Luanda, Angola 1.68m 53kg. Lyon OU.
At TJ: WCh: '07- dnq 17; ECh: '06- 9; EU23: '05- 8; EI: '07- 3; ECp: '06- 7, '07- 1. French champion 2007.
TJ records: Angola 2002, French 2007.
Progress at TJ: 1998- 11.38, 1999- 12.11, 2000- 12.69, 2001- 13.11, 2002- 13.49, 2003- 13.82i/13.33, 2004- 13.60, 2005- 14.03, 2006- 14.07/14.17w, 2007- 14.69. pbs: 50m 7.07i '02, 100m 12.33 '07, 200m 25.79 '07, 400mh 66.12 '07, LJ 6.32 '07.
Naturalised as French in 2003. Married name Ba.

Mélanie SKOTNIK b. 8 Nov 1982 Hersbrück, Germany 1.82m 59kg. Alsace Nord Athlétisme.
At HJ: WCh: '05- dnq 15=, 07- 7=; WJ: '00- 5; WY: '99- 5; EU23: '03- 5; EI: '07- 5=; ECp: '05-06-07- 3/6/3. German champion 2003, French 2005 & 2007.
French high jump record 2007.
Progress at HJ: 1995- 1.61, 1996- 1.65, 1997- 1.72, 1998- 1.72, 1999- 1.85, 2000- 1.86, 2001- 1.86, 2002- 1.88, 2003- 1.97i/1.91, 2004- 1.93i/1.90, 2005- 1.95, 2006- 1.93i/1.92, 2007- 1.97i/1.96.
French mother. Switched nationality from Germany to France with effect from 6 Mar 2005.

GERMANY

Governing body: Deutscher Leichtathletik Verband (DLV), Alsfelder Str. 27, 64289 Darmstadt. Founded 1898.
National Championships first held in 1891. **2007 Champions**: **Men**: 100m: Alexander Kosenkow 10.35, 200m: Daniel Schnelting 20.88, 400m: Bastian Swillims 46.21, 800m: Moritz Höft 1:48.30, 1500m: Carsten Schlangen 3:41.59, 5000m: Arne Gabius 14:03.97, 10,000m: Jan Fitschen 29:17.30, HMar: Stefan Koch 63:35, Mar: Philipp Büttner 2:20:17, 3000mSt: Filmon Ghirmai 8:39.35, 110mh: Thomas Blaschek 13.59, 400mh: Thomas Goller 50.97, HJ: Benjamin Lauckner 2.26, PV: Danny Ecker 5.70, LJ: Christian Reif 8.08, TJ: Andreas Pohle 16.65, SP: Peter Sack 20.66, DT: Robert Harting 63.79, HT: Markus Esser 78.48, JT: Stephan Steding 80.44, Dec: Lars Albert 7679, 10,000mW/20kW: André Höhne 40:08.71/ 1:24:40, 50kW: Maik Berger 3:54:24. **Women**: 100m: Verena Sailer 11.39, 200m: Cathleen Tschirch 23.07, 400m: Claudia Hoffmann 52.30, 800m: Monika Gradzki 2:04.97, 1500m: Antje Möldner 4:16.12, 5000m/10,000m: Sabrina Mockenhaupt 15:23.71/31:56.09, HMar: Irina Mikitenko 70:03, Mar: Iona Pfeiffer 2:46:13, 3000mSt: Julia Hiller 10:11.47, 100mh: Carolin Nytra 13.24, 400mh: Ulrike Urbansky 55.21, HJ: Ariane Friedrich 1.93, PV: Silke Spiegelburg 4.50, LJ: Bianca Kappler 6.67, TJ: Katja Demut 13.91, SP: Petra Lammert 19.30, DT: Franka Dietzsch 62.83, HT: Betty Heidler 74.94, JT: Christina Obergföll 66.59, Hep: Julia Mächtig 5887, 5000mW: Ulrike Sischka 23:22.00, 20kW: Sabine Zimmer 1:32:14.

Arthur ABELE b. 30 Jul 1986 Muttlangan 1.84m 80kg. SSV Ulm.
At Dec: WCh: '07- 9; WJ: '04- 7; EJ: '05- 2; ECp: '04- 4.
Progress at Dec: 2006- 8012, 2007- 8269. pbs: 60m 7.11i '06, 100m 10.84 '07, 200m 22/.04 '06, 400m 48.25 '06, 1000m 2:44.65i '06, 1500m 4:18.00 '07, 60mh 8.00i '06, 110mh 13.91 '07, 400mh 51.71 '04, HJ 2.04 '07. PV 4.70 '07, LJ 7.47 '06, SP 13.71 '07, DT 41.28 '07, JT 67.31 '06, Hep 5488i '06.

Ralf BARTELS b. 21 Feb 1978 Malchin 1.86m 128kg. SC Neubrandenburg. Soldier.
At SP: OG: '04- 8; WCh: '01- dnq 17, '03- 5, '05- 3, '07- 7; EC: '02- 3, '06- 1; WJ: '96- 1; EU23: '99- 6; EJ: '95- 4, '97- 1; WCp: '02- 3; ECp: '01-02-03-04-05-06: 4/4/5/3/1/3. German champion 2002-06.
Progress at SP: 1995- 17.63, 1996- 18.71, 1997- 18.35, 1998- 18.50, 1999- 18.95, 2000- 19.34, 2001- 20.30, 2002- 20.85, 2003- 20.67, 2004- 20.88, 2005- 21.36, 2006- 21.43i/21.13, 2007- 20.75.

Pascal BEHRENBRUCH b. 19 Jan 1985 Offenbach 1.96m 96kg. LG Eintracht Frankfurt.
At Dec: EC: '06- 5; EJ: '03- 10; EU23: '07- 2.
Progress at Dec: 2005-7842, 2006- 8209, 2007- 8239. pbs: 60m 7.17i '06, 100m 10.90 '06, 400m

48.48 '06, 1000m 2:53.39i '06, 1500m 4:24.16 '06, 60mh 8.28i '06, 110mh 14.10 '07, HJ 2.00 '05, PV 4.60 '05, LJ 7.12 '06, 7.32w '07, SP 16.15 '06, DT 49.91 '07, JT 69.55 '07, Hep 5604i '06.

Thomas BLASCHEK b. 5 Apr 1981 Gera 1.89m 83kg. LAZ Leipzig.
At 110mh: WCh: '05/07- sf; EC: '06- 2; WJ: '00- 2; EJ: '99- 3; EU23: '03- sf; ECp: '05-06-07: 2/5/3. At 60mh: WI: '06- 6, '08- 5; EI: '05- 5. Won German 110mh 2005-07, 60mh indoors 2005-07.
Progress at 110m: 1999- 13.93, 2000- 13.78, 2001- 13.81, 2002- 13.84, 2003- 13.66, 2004- 13.62, 2005- 13.31, 2006- 13.33/13.27w, 2007- 13.33. pb 60mh 7.57i '06.

Lars BÖRGELING b. 16 Apr 1979 Neuss 1.89m 86kg. TSV Bayer 04 Leverkusen. Student.
At PV: OG: '04- 6; WCh: '03- dnq 13, '05- dnq; EC: '02- 2, '06- nh; WJ: '96- 8=, '98- 2; EU23: '99- 2, '01- 1; EJ: '97- 1; EI: '02- 3; WCp: '02- 3; ECp: '03- 3, '04- 3=. German champion 2002, 2006.
Progress at PV: 1993- 3.83, 1994- 4.30, 1995- 4.60, 1996- 5.20, 1997- 5.50, 1998- 5.62, 1999- 5.80, 2000- 5.75ex/5.70, 2001- 5.80, 2002- 5.85, 2003- 5.80, 2004- 5.80, 2005- 5.77, 2006- 5.80, 2007- 5.75i/5.71. pbs: Dec 6478 '99.

Danny ECKER b. 21 Jul 1977 Leverkusen 1.92m 80kg. TSV Bayer 04 Leverkusen.
At PV: OG: '00- 8, '04- 5; WCh: '99- 4=, '01- 11, '05- nh, '07- 3; EC: '98- 4; WI: '99- 3; EI: '98- 3, '07- 1; WJ: '96- 3; ECp: '98- 4. GER champion 2004, 2007.
Progress at PV: 1990- 2.90, 1991- 3.30, 1992- 3.80, 1993- 4.40, 1994- 4.70, 1995- 5.12, 1996- 5.61, 1997- 5.72i/5.71, 1998- 5.93, 1999- 5.90, 2000- 5.90, 2001- 6.00i/5.85, 2002- 5.82i/5.70, 2004- 5.75, 2005- 5.75, 2006- 5.86, 2007- 5.87 pbs: HJ 2.00 '99, LJ 6.83 '99.
Son of Heide Rosendahl, 1972 Olympic LJ champion (and 2nd Pen) (WR 6.84 '70), and US basketball player John Ecker.

Peter ESENWEIN b. 7 Dec 1967 Göppingen 1.88m 100kg. LAZ Salamander Kornwestheim-Ludwigsburg. Building company manager.
At JT: OG: '04- dnq 20; WCh: '07- dnq 13; EC: '06- 6; ECp: '04- 2.
Progress at JT: 1984- 57.42, 1985- 65.96, new: 1986- 67.48, 1987- 70.48, 1988- 73.88, 1990- 78.06, 1991- 82.42, 19920 76.86, 1993- 78.26, 1994- 76.58, 1995- 78.00, 1996- 78.88, 1997- 85.70, 1998- 84.17, 2000- 84.79, 2001- 81.74, 2002- 82.97, 2003- 83.03, 2004- 87.20, 2005- 87.20, 2006- 85.30, 2007- 82.78.
At bobsleigh was 2nd in 4-man at 1989 World Juniors and was brakeman for Christoph Langen in 2001-02.

Markus ESSER b. 3 Feb 1980 Leverkusen 1.80m 99kg. TSV Bayer 04 Leverkusen. Soldier.
At HT: OG: '00- dnq 35; WCh: '05- 4, '07- 8; EC: '06- 4; WJ: '98- 12; EJ: '99- 3; EU23: '01- 7; ECp: '04-05-06-07: 2/3/4/2. German champion 2006-07.
Progress at HT: 1997- 64.78, 1998- 73.10, 1999- 70.29, 2000- 76.66, 2001- 75.69, 2002- 76.94, 2003- 78.13, 2004- 79.01, 2005- 80.00, 2006- 81.10, 2007- 80.68.

Robert HARTING b. 18 Oct 1984 Cottbus 2.01m 115kg. SCC Berlin.
At DT: WCh: '07- 2; ECh: '06- dnq 13; ECp: '07- 2; WJ: '02- dnq 13; EU23: '05- 1. German champion 2007.
Progress at DT: 2002- 54.25, 2003- 59.54, 2004- 64.05, 2005- 66.02, 2006- 65.22, 2007- 66.93. pb SP 18.63 '07.

André HÖHNE b. 10 Mar 1978 Berlin 1.85m 72kg. SCC Berlin. Soldier.
At 20kW: OG: '04- 8 (dnf 50km); WCh: '01- dnf, '03- 13, '05- 4, '07- dnf; EC: '98- 23, '02- 11, '06- 11; EU23: '99- 12; WCp: '04- 15, '06- 16; ECp: '07- 6. At 10,000mW: EJ: '97- 2. Won German 10kW 2002, 2006-07; 20kW 2005-07, 50kW 2006.
Progress at 20kW: 1996- 1:36:12, 1997- 1:31:00, 1998- 1:25:04, 1999- 1:24:22, 2000- 1:22:05, 2001- 1:22:49, 2002- 1:21:38, 2003- 1:20:44, 2004- 1:21:27, 2005- 1:20:00, 2006- 1:21:52, 2007- 1:20:32. pbs: 3000mW 11:31.76i '05, 5000mW 19:12.33i '06, 19:51.0 '04; 10,000mW 39:24.9 '04, 35kW 2:38:58 '04, 50kW 3:49:00 '04.

Karsten KOBS b. 16 Sep 1971 Dortmund 1.96m 125kg. Teutonia Lanstrop.
At HT: OG: '96/00- dnq 18/31, '04- 8; WCh: '93-95-03: dnq 16/16/17, '97- 9, '99- 1; EC: '94- 10, '98- 3, '02- dnq 14, '06- 8; WJ: '90- 4; EJ: '89- 10; WCp: '02- 3; ECp: '93-5-6-9-00-01-02-03: 7/3/1/3/3/5/5/1; E23Cp: '92- 2. German champion 1996, 1999-2005. 3rd GP 2000.
Progress at HT: 1988- 59.80, 1989- 65.02, 1990- 70.02, 1991- 71.82, 1992- 74.36, 1993- 75.94, 1994- 76.30, 1995- 76.80, 1996- 78.92, 1997- 79.08, 1998- 81.21, 1999- 82.78, 2000- 80.21, 2001- 79.15, 2002- 81.49, 2003- 80.63, 2004- 79.11, 2005- 79.46, 2006- 80.82, 2007- 77.92. pb SP 15.53 '98.
Improved every year of his career until he reached the world number one ranking in 1999. His father, Reiner, had HT pb of 58.90 (1974).

Tim LOBINGER b. 3 Sep 1972 Rheinbach 1.93m 86kg. LG Stadtwerke München.
At PV: OG: '96- 7, '00- 13, '04- 11=; WCh: '93- dnq, '95- 11, '97- 4, '99- 6, '03- 5, '05- 5=, '07- 8; EC: '94- dnq 21=, '98- 2, '02- 3, '06- 2=; WI: '97-03-04-06-08: 5/1/5/3/5; EI: '96-98-02-05-07: 6/1/1/3/5; WJ: '90- dnq; EJ: '91- 3; WCp: '98- 2; ECp: '93-4-5-6-7-00-02-07: 5/3/nh/2/3/2/1/1; E23Cp: '92- 1, '94- 4. Won WAF 2003, GP 2000, 3rd 1997, 2002; German champion 1993-4, 1997-2000, 2003, 2005.
Four German pole vault records 1996-9.
Progress at PV: 1986- 3.46, 1987- 3.90, 1988- 4.60, 1989- 4.85, 1990- 5.32, 1991- 5.35, 1992- 5.50, 1993- 5.55, 1994- 5.60, 1995- 5.70, 1996- 5.91, 1997- 6.00, 1998- 5.92, 1999- 6.00, 2000- 5.95i/5.85, 2001- 5.80,

2002- 5.90, 2003- 5.91, 2004- 5.80, 2005- 5.93, 2006- 5.90, 2007- 5.83, 2008- 5.81i. pbs: 110mh 14.78 '99, HJ 1.97 '99, DT 42.76 '99, Dec 7346 '99.
Set (then) world decathlon PV best of 5.75 in 7346 decathlon at Leverkusen 1999. His ex-wife **Petra** (b. 24 Jan 1967 Siegen-Weidenau, née Laux) set four German indoor TJ records from 14.15 '96 to 14.36 '97 (5 WI), outdoor pb 14.31/14.35w '97; German champion 1992, 1996-7, 10 WCh 1997.

Michael MÖLLENBECK b. 12 Dec 1969 Wesel 2.00m 130kg. TV Wattenscheid. Businessman.
At DT: OG: '96- dnq, '00- 10, '04- dnq 20; WCh: '95- dnq 16, '99- 6, '01- 3, '03- 5, '05- 3; EC: '02- 3. '06- 5; WJ: '88- 9; EJ: '87- 6; WCp: '02- 4; ECp: '02-03-04-05: 1/2/1/2. Won GER 2002, 2004-05.
Progress at DT: 1988- 53.00, 1989- 59.26, 1990- 60.16, 1991- 58.86, 1992- 62.12, 1993- 62.82, 1994- 58.26, 1995- 65.78, 1996- 67.44, 1997- 66.66, 1998- 67.18, 1999- 67.00, 2000- 65.49, 2001- 67.61, 2002- 67.64, 2003- 67.42, 2004- 66.36, 2005- 66.56, 2006- 65.52, 2007- 65.29. pb SP 16.78 '95.
Threw pb in first round of 2001 World DT final. Married discus thrower Anja Gündler (1 EJ 91, 5 WCh 93, pb 64.63 '98) in 1996.

André NIKLAUS b. 30 Aug 1981 Berlin 1.90m 84kg. LG Nike Berlin.
At Dec: WCh: '03- 8, '05- 4, '07- 5; WJ: '00- 3; EU23: '01-03- 1/1; EJ: '99- 4; ECp: '04- 4. At Hep: WI: '06- 1.
Progress at Dec: 1996- 7368, 1997- 7835, 1998- 7979, 1999- 8363, 2000- 7847, 2001- 8206, 2002- dnf, 2003- 8060, 2004- 7929, 2005- 8316, 2006- 8239, 2007- 8371. pbs: 60m 7.06i '06, 100m 10.91 '03, 400m 48.55 '00, 1000m 2:40.38i '06, 1500m 4:19.09 '04, 60mh 8.04i '08, 110mh 14.28 '06, HJ 2.07i '06, 2.06 '07; PV 5.40i '03, 5.30 '05; LJ 7.64i '06, 7.49 '07; SP 14.60 '06, DT 46.13 '05, JT 63.28 '07, Hep 6192i '06.

Eike ONNEN b. 3 Aug 1982 Hannover 1.94m 83kg. LG Hannover.
At HJ: WCh: '07- 7; EU23: '03- 5; ECp: '06- 7=, '07- 1.
Progress at HJ: 1997- 1.74, 1998- 1.95, 1999- 2.06, 2000- 2.10, 2001- 2.12, 2002- 2.15, 2003- 2.23, 2004- 2.22i, 2005- 2.26, 2006- 2.28, 2007- 2.34. pbs: PV 4.12 '00, LJ 6.74 '00.

Björn OTTO b. 16 Oct 1977 Frechen 1.88m 84kg. LAZ Bayer Uerdingen/Dormagen.
At PV: WCh: '07- 5; WI: '04- 11=; EI: '00-05-07: 6/4/3; WUG: '99-01-03-05: 8/7/3=/1.
Progress at PV: 1991- 3.20, 1992- 3.20, 1993- 4.10, 1994- 4.71, 1995- 5.00, 1996- 5.30i/5.20, 1997- 5.40, 1998- 5.52sq/5.40, 1999- 5.55/5.60ex, 2000- 5.65/5.71ex, 2001-5.51/5.63ex, 2002-5.63sq/5.60, 2003- 5.72i/5.70, 2004- 5.82i/5.70, 2005- 5.80, 2006- 5.85, 2007- 5.90.

Peter SACK b. 27 Jul 1979 Schkeudotz 1.92m 135kg. LAZ Leipzig.
At SP: OG: '04- dnq 28; WCh: '07- dnq; WJ: '98- 4; EU23: '01- 9; EJ: '97- 3; WI: '08- 8; ECp: '07- 1. German champion 2007.
Progress at SP: 1995- 13.41, 1996- 14.88, 1997- 17,36, 1998- 18.23, 1999- 18.51i/18.13, 2000- 17.20, 2001- 18.55, 2002- 18.80, 2003- 19.96i/19.87, 2004- 20.32, 2005- 19.78i/19.68, 2006- 20.83, 2007- 21.00. 2008- 20.88i. pb DT 48.83 '99.
His brother René Sack (b. 14 Jul 1976) had pb 19.84 '02.

Fabian SCHULZE b. 16 Apr 1979 Filderstadt 1.92m 79kg. LAZ Salamander Kornwestheim-Ludwigsburg.
At PV: WY: '01- 6; EU23: '05- 2; EJ: '03- 3; EI: '05- 5.
Progress at PV: 1998- 2.92, 1999- 3.72, 2000- 4.41, 2001- 4.90, 2002- 5.11, 2003- 5.45, 2004- 5.70, 2005- 5.70, 2006- 5.81, 2007- 5.83i/5.41.

Women

Kirsten BOLM b. 4 Mar 1975 Frechen 1.81m 70kg. MTG Mannheim. Was at Brigham Young University, USA, now studying psychology at Heidelberg.
At 100mh: OG: '04- sf; WCh: '99- qf, '01- h, '05- 4; EC: '02- h, '06- 2=; WJ: '92- 5, '94- 1 (5 LJ); WUG: '99- 5/3R; WCp: '02- 7; ECp: '99-01-02-04-05-06: 6/3/2/7/2/2; Won German 2000-02, 2004-06. At 60mh: WI: '06- 5; EI: '02-05-07: 3/3/3.
Progress at 100mh: 1991- 13.49, 1992- 13.42, 1993- 13.52, 1994- 13.26, 1995- 13.60, 1996- 13.57, 1998- 13.75, 1999- 13.04/12.86Aw, 2000- 12.92, 2001- 12.98. 2002- 12.84, 2004- 12.80/12.66w, 2005- 12.59. 2006- 12.65, 2007- 13.15. pbs: 60m 7.41i '02, 100m 11.68A '00, 200m 24.05i '02, 24.12A '00; 50mh 7.12i '01, 60mh 7.89i '02, HJ 1.81 '00, LJ 6.55 '94.

Franka DIETZSCH b. 22 Jan 1968 Wolgast 1.83m 95kg. SC Neubrandenburg. Bank employee.
At DT: OG: '92- 12, '96- 4, '00- 6, '04- dnq 27; WCh: '91-93-95-97-99-01-03-05-07: dnq 13/8/7/dnq/1/4/dnq 14/1/1; EC: '94- 9, '98- 1, '06- 2; WJ: '86- 2; WUG: '89- 4; WCp: '98- 1, '06- 1; ECp: '97-9-01-02-03-04-05-06-07: 2/3/1/3/4/2/1/1/1; Won GP 2000, 2nd 1998; WAF 2006-07. GER champion 1997-2001, 2003-07.
Progress at DT: 1981- 27.70, 1982- 43.80, 1983- 50.04, 1984- 51.16, 1985- 56.94, 1986- 64.34, 1987- 66.34, 1988- 65.56, 1989- 68.26, 1990- 67.42, 1991- 61.22, 1992- 64.64, 1993- 62.06, 1994- 62.76, 1995- 62.26, 1996- 66.66, 1997- 67.66, 1998- 68.91, 1999- 69.51, 2000- 68.06, 2001- 65.87A, 2002- 64.12, 2003- 66.00, 2004- 66.12, 2005- 66.56, 2006- 68.51, 2007- 68.06. pb SP 15.02 '85.

Ariane FRIEDRICH b. 10 Jan 1984 Nordhausen/Harz 1.78m 60kg. Eintracht Frankfurt.
At HJ: EU23: '05- 3; EJ: '03- 1; WI: '08- 8=; ECp: 04-05-07: 3/7/4; WUG: '05- 3.
Progress at PV: 1998- 1.62, 1999- 1.68, 2000- 1.73, 2001- 1.81, 2002- 1.86, 2003- 1.88, 2004- 1.92, 2005- 1.90, 2006- 1.91, 2007- 1.94, 2008- 2.02i.

Betty HEIDLER b. 14 Oct 1983 Berlin 1.74m 80kg. LG Eintracht Frankfurt. Student.
At HT: OG: '04- 4; WCh: '03- 11, '05- dnq 29, '07- 1; EC: '06- 5; EU23: '03- 4; WJ: '00/02- dnq 19/17; EJ: '01- 9, ECp: '04-06-07: 3/nt/2. Won WAF 2006, German 2005-07.
Six German hammer records 2004-06.
Progress at HT: 1999- 42.07, 2000- 56.02, 2001- 60.54, 2002- 63.38, 2003- 70.42, 2004- 72.73, 2005- 72.19, 2006- 76.55, 2007- 75.77.
Surgery on her left knee at the end of 2007.

Carolin HINGST b. 18 Sep 1980 Donauwörth 1.70m 60kg. USC Mainz.
At PV: OG: '04- dnq 22=; WCh: '01- 10, '03- dnq 15=, '05- 10, '07- dnq 17=; EC: '02- dnq 13=; EU23: '01- 3; WI: '04- dnq 9; EI: '05- 4; ECp: 04-05-07: nh/2/5=. German champion 2004.
Progress at PV: 1999- 3.60, 2000- 4.01, 2001- 4.50, 2002- 4.50, 2003- 4.51, 2004- 4.66, 2005- 4.65i/4.50, 2006- 4.52, 2007- 4.70i/4.61, 2008- 4.65i. pbs: 100mh 14.54 '98, HJ 1.75 '98, LJ 5.81 '98.

Bianca KAPPLER b. 8 Aug 1977 Hamburg 1.80m 62kg. LC asics Rehlingen.
At LJ: OG: '04- 9; WCh: '03/05- dnq 14/19, '07- 5; EC: '02- dnq 15; WI: '04- dnq 14; EI: '05- bronze; ECp: '02-03-04-07: 3/7/5/8. German champion 2003, 2005, 2007.
Progress at LJ: 1992- 5.42, 1993- 5.66, 1994- 5.72, 1995- 5.89, 1996- 5.98, 1997- 6.14, 1998- 6.16, 1999- 6.40, 2000- 6.55, 2001- 6.50, 2002- 6.65, 2003- 6.69, 2004- 6.71, 2005- 6.66/6.69w, 2007- 6.90. pbs: 60m 7.53i '05, 100m 11.88 '07, 200m 24.36 '02, 800m 2:22.30 '99, 100mh 14.49 '99, HJ 1.77 '99, SP 10.95 '97, JT 36.92 old '97, Hep 5520 '99.
Awarded an extra bronze medal at 2005 European Indoors after what was possibly her best jump (next 6.53) was wrongly registered as 6.96 and video evidence showed that it was in the range of the third placer's 6.59. Gave birth to a daughter on 20 May 2006.

Sonja KESSELSCHLÄGER b. 20 Jan 1978 Finsterwalde 1.77m 66kg. SC Neubrandenburg.
At Hep: OG: '04- 6; WCh: '03- 8, '05- 10, '07- 13; EC: '02- 9; WJ: '96- 7; EJ: '97- 3; EU23: '99- 3; WUG: '01- 3; ECp: '01-02- 3/3; German champion 2005. At Pen: WI: '03- 4, '06- 4; EI: '00-02-05: 6/5/5.
Progress at Hep: 1994- 5005, 1995- 5236, 1996- 5620, 1997- 5753, 1998- 5763, 2000- 6039, 2001- 6064, 2002- 6205, 2003- 6175, 2004- 6287, 2005- 6221, 2006- 6101, 2007- 6184. pbs: 200m 24.52 '02, 400m 55.94i '05, 800m 2:11.95 '04, 60mh 8.35i '04, 100mh 13.34 '03, HJ 1.85 '00, LJ 6.42 '04, SP 14.94i '08, 14.53 '04; JT 46.06 '96, Pen 4587i '05.

Nadine KLEINERT b. 20 Oct 1975 Magdeburg 1.90m 90kg. SC Magdeburg.
At SP: OG: '00- 8, '04- 2; WCh: '97- 7, '99- 2, '01- 2, '03- 7, '05- 5, '07- 3; EC: '98- 6, '02- 6, '06- 6; WJ: '92- 12, '94- 6; EU23: '94- 3Cp, '97- 1; EJ: '93- 2; WI: '99-01-04-06: 5/4/3/2; EI: '96-98-00: 5/5/2; ECp: '99-01-04-05: 2/1/3/2. Won GP 1999. German champion 1998, 2000-01, 2005.
Progress at SP: 1990- 13.85, 1991- 15.08, 1992- 16.32, 1993- 17.07, 1994- 17.44, 1995- 17.13, 1996- 18.37, 1997- 18.91, 1998- 19.22, 1999- 19.61, 2000- 19.81, 2001- 19.86, 2002- 19.24, 2003- 19.33i/19.14, 2004- 19.55, 2005- 20.06, 2006- 19.64i/19.15, 2007- 19.77. pb DT 50.99 '01.

Petra LAMMERT b. 3 Mar 1984 Freudenstadt 1.82m 85kg. SC Neubrandenberg.
At SP: WCh: '05- dnq 15, '07- 5; EC: '06- 3; EJ: '03- 3; EU23: '05- 1; WI: '06- 4; EI: '05- 4; ECp: '06- 1, '07- 2. German champion 2006-07.
Progress at SP: 2001- 13.55, 2002- 15.18, 2003- 16.23, 2004- 18.01i/17.16, 2005- 19.81, 2006- 19.64, 2007- 20.04.

Irina MIKITENKO b. 23 Aug 1972 Bakanas, Kazakhstan 1.58m 49kg. née Volynskaya. TV Wattenscheid 01.
At 5000m: OG: '96- h, '00- 5, '04- 7; WCh: '99- 4, '01- 5, '03- h; ECp: '99-00-03-06: 2/2/4/5. At 10,000m: EC: '98- 8, '06- 9; WCp: '98- 5. 3rd GP 3000m 1999. World 4k CC: '00- 19. Won Central Asian 1500m 1995; German 10,000m 1998, 2006; 5000m 1999-2000, 2006.
German records 3000m 2000, 5000m (3) 1999.
Progress at 5000m, 10,000m: 1995- 15:47.85, 1996- 15:49.59, 1997- 15:48.29, 1998- 15:18.86, 32:10.61; 1999- 14:42.03, 31:38.68; 2000- 14:43.59; 2001- 14:53.00, 31:29.55; 2003- 14:56.64, 31:38.48; 2004- 14:55.43, 32:04.86; 2006- 15:28.00, 31:44.82; 2007- 32:42.95. pbs: 800m 2:09.97 '98, 1500m 4:06.08 '01, 2000m 5:40.6 '01, 3000m 8:30.39 '00, HMar 68:51 '08, Mar 2:24:51 '07.
Made fine marathon debut with 2nd Berlin 2007. German parents; changed nationality from Kazakhstan to Germany in March 1998. Her husband Alexander had 5000m pb of 13:39.95 (1994); son Alexander, and daughter Vanessa (born in July 2005). Her father-in-law Leonid Mikitenko won the 1966 European bronze medal at 10,000m with pbs of 13.36.4 for 5000m and 28:12.4 at 10,000m.

Sabrina MOCKENHAUPT b. 6 Dec 1980 Siegen 1.56m 46kg. Kölner Verein für Marathon.
At 10,000m (5000m): OG: '04- 15; WCh: '03- dnf, '05- 17; EC: '02- 10, '06- 8 (6); EU23: '01- 4; ECp: '05- 1. At 5000m: EJ: '99- 4 (8 3000m); WCp: '02- 7, '06- 6; ECp: '02-04-05-07: 4/3/4/2; World Military champion 2002. At 3000m: WI: '04- 7; EI: '02-05-07: 8/3/4; ECp: '01-03-06: 6/3/4. Eur CC: '00-03-05: 17/15/2. Won GER 5000m 2001-05, 2007; 10,000m 2003-05, 2007; CC 2005, SC CC 2007.
Progression at 10,000m: 2000- 33:12.97mx, 2001- 32:38.1, 2002- 32:08.52, 2003- 32:11.95, 2004- 31:23.35, 2005- 31:21.28, 2006- 31:40.28, 2007- 31:56.09. pbs: 1500m 4:14.83 '07, 2000m 5:44.98i '05, 3000m 8:44.65 '03, 5000m 15:03.47 '04, HMar 70:35 '06, Mar 2:29:33 '07.

Steffi NERIUS b. 1 Jul 1972 Bergen/Rügen 1.78m 72kg. TSV Bayer 04 Leverkusen. PE teacher.
At JT: OG: '96- 9, '00- 4, '04- 2; WCh: '93- 9, '95- 11, '99- dnq 16, '01- 5, '03- 3, '05- 3, '07- 3; EC: '98- 6, '02- 2, '06- 1; EJ: '91- 3; WUG: '97- 5; WCp: '92- 6, '02- 4, '06- 1; ECp: '95-01-02-03-04-05: 1/2/3/1/2/1. 2nd GP 1996. German champion 2001, 2003-06.
Progress at JT: 1985- 30.12, 1987- 45.16, 1988- 48.00, 1989- 56.88, 1990- 56.14, 1991- 60.02, 1992- 59.46, 1993- 63.88, 1995- 68.42, 1996- 69.42, 1997- 64.58, 1998- 67.33; new: 1999- 61.56. 2000- 65.76, 2001- 63.72, 2002- 64.55, 2003- 64.42, 2004- 65.82, 2005- 66.52, 2006- 65.82, 2007- 65.78.
Was a GDR youth volleyball champion. Threw personal best in last round of 2004 Olympics to move from 4th to 2nd.

Christina OBERGFÖLL b. 22 Aug 1981 Lahr (Baden) 1.75m 78kg. LG Offenburg. Student.
At JT: OG: '04-dnq 15; WCh: '05- 2, '07- 2; EC: '06- 4; EU23: '01- 9, '03- 8; WJ: '00- 8; ECp: '07- 1. German champion 2007.
European javelin records 2005 & 2007.
Progress at JT: 1997- 49.20, 1998- 48.52, new: 1999- 50.57, 2000- 54.50, 2001- 56.83, 2002- 60.61, 2003- 57.40, 2004- 63.34, 2005- 70.03, 2006- 66.91, 2007- 70.20.
Made a wondrous breakthrough at the 2005 World Champs to take her pb from 64.59 to a European record 70.03 and the silver medal.

Jennifer OESER b. 29 Nov 1983 Brunsbüttel 1.76m 64kg. TSV Bayer 04 Leverkusen. Policewoman.
At Hep: WCh: '07- 7; EC: '06- 4; WJ: '02- 8; EU23: '03- 1. German champion 2006.
Progress at Hep: 2000- 5167, 2001- 5531, 2002- 5595, 2003- 5901, 2004- 5936, 2005- 5637, 2006- 6376, 2007- 6378. pbs 200m 24.32 '07, 800m 2:13.85 '07, 60mh 8.81i '06, 100mh 13.51 '07, HJ 1.86 '06, LJ 6.28 '06, SP 14.21 '07, JT 48.52 '06, Pen 4307i '06.

Anastasija **'Nastja' REIBERGER** b. 19 Sep 1977 Omsk, Russia 1.70m 59kg.née Ryshich/Ryjikh. ABC Ludwigshafen.
At PV: WCh: '99- nh; EC: '98- 4=, '06- 9; WI: '99- 1, '04- 8; EU23: '99- 2.
Pole vault records: four World junior and five European junior 1996, three German 1999.
Progress at PV: 1992- 2.90, 1993- 3.50, 1994- 3.71, 1995- 3.80, 1996- 4.15, 1997- 4.10, 1998- 4.32/4.42ex, 1999- 4.50i/4.44, 2000- 4.31, 2001- 4.30i/4.11, 2002- 4.40, 2003- 4.32, 2004- 4.50i/4.40, 2005- 4.35, 2006- 4.63, 2007- 4.52.
Her family left Omsk in Siberia in 1992 to live in Ulm. Her mother Yekaterina Ryzhikh (née Yefimova b. 20 Jan 1959) had HJ pb 1.91i '85 and 1.89 '81; her father, Vladimir, is a pole vault coach. Her sister Elisaveta 'Lisa' has pb 4.35 '06, 1 WY 03,1 WJ 04.

Lilli SCHWARZKOPF b. 28 Aug 1983 Novo Pokrovka, Kyrgyzhstan 1.74m 63kg. LC Paderborn. Student.
At Hep: WCh: '05- 13, '07- 5; EC: '06- 3; WJ: '02- 5; EU23: '05- 2. German champion 2004.
Progress at Hep: 2001- 5079, 2002- 5597, 2003- 5735, 2004- 6161, 2005- 6146, 2006- 6420, 2007- 6439. pbs 200m 24.78 '06, 800m 2:09.63 '06, 60mh 8.54i '07, 100mh 13.50 '07, HJ 1.83 '07, LJ 6.35i/6.34 '07, SP 14.83i '08, 14.26 '06; JT 54.44 '07, Pen 4641i '08.

Melanie SEEGER b. 8 Jan 1977 Brandenburg/ Havel 1.66m 49kg. SC Potsdam.
At 20kW: OG: '04- 5; WCh: '99- 33, '01- 7, '03- 8, '05- 11, '07- 14; EC: '98- dnf, '02- 14, '06- 10; EU23: '97- 8, '99- 3; WCp: '04- 9; ECp: '03- 9. At 5000mW: WJ: '96- 4; EJ: '93- 10, '95- 4. Won German 5000mW 2001-05, 20kW 2001, 2005.
Four German records 20km walk 2001-04.
Progress at 20kW: 1999- 1:34:17, 2000- 1:32:10, 2001- 1:30:41, 2002- 1:31:08, 2003- 1:29:44, 2004- 1:28:17, 2005- 1:30:21, 2006- 1:29:15, 2007- 1:29:32. pbs: 3000mW 11:50.48i '04, 12:49.62 '02, 5000mW 20:18.87i '04, 20:56.19 '03; 10kW 43:12 '02.

Silke SPIEGELBURG b. 17 Mar 1986 Georgsmarienhütte 1.73m 62kg. TSV Bayer 04 Leverkusen.
At PV: OG: '04- dnq 13; WCh: '07- nh; EC: '06- 6; WJ: '02- 8; WY: '01- 1; EU23: '07- 4; EJ: '03- 1, '05- 1; WI: '06- 8; EI: '07- 5. German champion 2005-07. World junior pole vault record 2005.
Progress at PV: 1998- 2.75, 1999- 3.30, 2000- 3.75, 2001- 4.00, 2002- 4.20, 2003- 4.20i/4.15, 2004- 4.40, 2005- 4.48i/4.42, 2006- 4.56, 2007- 4.60.
Her brother **Richard** (b. 12 Aug 1977) has PV pb 5.85 '01; 6= WCh 01, 1 WUG 99. Older brothers: Henrik pb 4.80, Christian (b. 15 Apr 1976) 5.51 '98.

Claudia TONN b. 18 Apr 1981 Viernheim 1.82m 70kg. LC Paderborn. Physiotherapy student.
At Hep: OG: '04- 12; EU23: '03- 4. At Pen: EI: '05- 9.
Progress at Hep: 1999- 5163, 2000- 5206, 2001- 5476, 2002- 5628, 2003- 5842, 2004- 6169, 2005- 6054, 2006- 6373, 2007- 6108, pbs: 200m 24.43 '06, 800m 2:07.87 '07, 60mh 8.56i '05, 100mh 13.84 '06, HJ 1.83 '04, LJ 6.75 '06, SP 13.10 '06, JT 41.81 '05, Pen 4566i '08.

GHANA

Governing body: Ghana Athletics Association, National Sports Council, PO Box 1272, Accra. Founded 1944.

Ignisious GAISAH b. 20 Jun 1983 1.86m 70kg. Formerly known as Anthony Essuman. Lives in the Netherlands.
At LJ: OG: '04- 6; WCh: '03- 4, '05- 2; CG: '06- 1; AfG: '04- 1, '06- 1; WI: '06- 1; WCp: '06- 4. Won WAF 2004.
Nine Ghana long jump records 2003-06, African junior record 2002, indoor record 2006.

Progress at LJ: 1998- 7.35, 1999- 7.42, 2000- 7.40, 2002- 8.12, 2003- 8.30, 2004- 8.32, 2005- 8.34, 2006- 8.43/8.51w, 2007- 8.08.

Women

Margaret Esi **SIMPSON** b. 31 Dec 1981 Kumase 1.62m 53kg.
At Hep: OG: '04- 9; WCh: '01- 13, '03- dnf, '05- 3, '07- dnf; CG: '02- 3; WJ: '00- dnf; AfG: '03- 1, '07- 1; AfCh: '00- 5, '02- 1, '04- 1. Won Af-J 1999.
African heptathlon record 2005, Ghana records at HJ, JT and eight heptathlon 1999-2004.
Progress at Hep: 1999- 5366, 2000- 5543, 2001- 5836, 2002- 6105w/6004, 2003- 6152, 2004- 6306, 2005- 6423, 2007- 6278. pbs: 200m 24.54 '04, 800m 2:17.02 '05, 100mh 13.41 '05, HJ 1.85 '05, LJ 6.32 '05, SP 13.33 '05, JT 56.36 '05, Dec 7014 '07. Child born July 2006.

GREECE

Governing body: Hellenic Amateur Athletic Association (SEGAS), 137 Siggroú Avenue, 171 21 Nea Smirni, Athens. Founded 1897.
National Championships first held in 1896 (men), 1930 (women). **2007 Champions**: **Men**: 100m: Efthímios Steryioúlis 10.29, 200m: Anastásios Goúsis 20.85, 400m: Dimítrios Grávalos 46.39, 800m/1500m: Konstadínos Nakópoulos 1:51.90/3:46.62, 5000m: Anastásios Frággos 14:23.37, 10,000m: Konstadínos Poúlios 30:00.13, Mar: Yeóryios Karavídas 2:23:51, 3000mSt: Panayiótis Kókoros 8:51.36, 110mh: Konstadínos Douvalídis 13.59, 400mh: Periklís Iakovákis 49.13, HJ: Kyriacos Ioannou CYP 2.27, PV: Mários Evaggélou 5.30, LJ: Loúis Tsátoumas 8.37, TJ: Dimítrios Tsiámis 16.97, SP: Andréas Anastasópoulos 19.22, DT: Spirídon Arabatzís 59.72, HT: Aléxandros Papadimitríou 75.55, JT: Yeóryios Íltsios 78.94, Dec: Konstadínos Karamousalís 7273, 20kW: Theódoros Koupídis 1:32:06, 50kW: Konstadínos Stefanópoulos 4:14:22. **Women**: 100m: María Karastamáti 11.39, 200m: Eleni Artymata CYP 23.68, 400m: Faní Halkiá 52.06, 800m: Eléni Filándra 2:04.10, 1500m/5000m: Kalliópi Astropekáki 4:19.93/ 16:45.53, 10,000m: Ekaterini Asimakopoúlou 34:27.14, Mar: Magdaliní Gazéa 2:41:31, 3000mSt: Iríni Kokkinaríou 9:42.97, 100mh: Flóra Redoúmi 13.01, 400mh: Hristína Hantzí-Neag 56.40, HJ: Persefóni Hatzinákou 1.84, PV: Afrodíti Skafída 4.31, LJ/TJ: Hrisopiyí Devetzí 6.56/15.01w, SP: Iríni Hrisovaládou Terzóglou 16.30, DT: Dorothéa Kalpakídou 53.66, HT: Alexándra Papayeoryíou 68.88, JT: Sávva Líka 58.40, Hep: Aléna-Mária Pádi 5779w, 20kW: Athiná Papayiánni 1:39:38.

Periklís IAKOVÁKIS b. 24 Mar 1979 Pátra 1.85m 76kg. Olympiakós SF Piraeus. Student of Economics at University of Athens. Air Force officer.
At 400mh/4x400mR: OG: '00- h, '04- sf; WCh: '99- h, '01- sf, '03- 3, '05- sf, '07- 6; EC: '98- hR, '02- 5, '06- 1; WJ: '98- 1; EJ: '97- 2/2R; EU23: '99- 3, '01- 2; WUG: '01- 4; ECp: '99-00-03-07: 6/4/2&2R/1. Won WAF 2006, Med.Games 2001, Greek 1998-2007. At 400m: WJ: '96- h; ECp: '97- 8.
Six Greek 400mh records 2002-06.
Progress at 400mh: 1997- 51.6, 1998- 49.82, 1999- 49.53, 2000- 49.35, 2001- 48.87, 2002- 48.66, 2003- 48.17, 2004- 48.47, 2005- 48.24, 2006- 47.82, 2007- 48.35. pbs: 100m 11.1 '96, 200m 21.62 '97, 400m 46.35 '02. 110mh 15.09 '02. LJ 6.58 '95.
Older brother Thomás (b. 1976), pbs 100m 10.89 '03, 200m 21.39 '99, 400m 47.96 '98; younger brother Sotírios (b. 1982), pbs 400m 46.45 '07, 400mh 49.9 '05.

Louis TSÁTOUMAS b. 12 Feb 1982 Messíni 1.87m 76kg. Olympiakós SF Piraeus.
At LJ: OG: '04- dnq 22; WCh: '03- 12; EC: '06- 8; WJ: '00- dnq 21; WY: '99- 4; EU23: '03- 1; EJ: '01- 1; WI: '06- 4; EI: '07- 2; WCp: '06- nj; ECp: '03- 1, '07- 1; Greek champion 2003-07.
Greek long jump record 2007.
Progress at LJ: 1996- 6.56, 1997- 7.07, 1998- 7.41/7.43w, 1999- 7.64, 2000- 7.52, 2001- 7.93/7.98w, 2002- 8.17, 2003- 8.34, 2004- 8.19/8.37w, 2005- 8.15i/8.14, 2006- 8.30, 2007- 8.66. pb 200m 22.3 '98. 8.66 is best ever by European at sea-level.

Women

Hrisopiyí DEVETZÍ b. 2 Jan 1976 Alexand—roúpoli 1.70m 60kg. Olympiakós SF Piraeus. Physiotherapist. Air Force officer.
At TJ (/LJ): OG: '04- 2; WCh: '03- 8, '05- 5, 07- 3; EC: '02- 7, '06- 2/10; WI: '04- 3, '08- 2; WCp: 06- 2/3; ECp: '03-04-05-07: 4/2/2/2(6). Won WAF TJ 2005, Greek LJ 2006-07, TJ 2002-07, Balkan LJ 2000.
Greek triple jump record 2004.
Progress at LJ, TJ: 1990- 5.35, 1991- 5.32, 1992- 5,67, 11.76; 1993- 5.70, 12.48; 1994- 5.81, 12.52; 1995- 5.70, 12.52/12.83w; 1996- 5.78, 12.72i/12.69/12.77w; 1997- 5.07, 12.70i/12.59; 1998- 5.64, 13.44; 1999- 6.21, 13.61/13.66w; 2000- 6.19, 13.48; 2001- 5.94, 14.00/14.12w; 2002- 6.15, 14.15; 2003- 6.36, 14.84i/14.34; 2004- 6.24, 15.32; 2005- 6.56, 14.89; 2006- 6.83, 15.05; 2007- 6.69, 15.09; 2008- 15.00i. pbs: HJ 1.64 '96, JT 32.26 '92.
From previous TJ best of 14.15, jumped 14.48i and 14.84i in 2003 but only 13.93 at World Indoors. She won national championship medals in gymnastics as a child.

Faní HALKIÁ b. 2 Feb 1979 Lárisa 1.75m 64kg. Olympiakós SF Piraeus. Air Force officer.
At 400mh/4x400mR: OG: '04- 1; WCh: '03- hR, '07- sf; EC: '06- 2; WJ: '98- h; EJ: '97- h; ECp: '04- 1/3R. At 400m: WI: '04- 6; WCp: '06- 5; ECp: '07- 1. Won Greek 400m 2007, 400mh 1998, 2004, Balkan 400mh 1997.
Greek records 400mh (7) 2003-04, 400m 2004.
Progress at 400mh: 1995- 62.37, 1996- 61.40,

1997- 59.17, 1998- 59.99, 1999- 61.99, 2002- 58.80, 2003- 56.40, 2004- 52.77, 2006- 53.71, 2007- 55.66. pbs: 100m 12.47/12.2 '03, 200m 23.30 '07, 400m 50.56 '04, 100mh 14.45 '03, HJ 1.55 '94.
Having been a promising junior, she had many injuries and gave up athletics for two years after a poor year in 1999. In this time she worked mainly as a journalist. Coached by Yeóryios Panayiotópoulos, she made rapid progress to her triumphant year in 2004 when she set Greek 400mh records at 56.03, 54.88, 54.16 and 53.99 (all her pre-OG races), then 53.85 and 52.77 at the Olympic Games before winning the gold medal with 52.82. Missed almost all 2005 season with a foot injury.

Vojsavva **'Sávva' LÍKA** b. 27 Jun 1970 Korçé, Albania 1.68m 70kg. Panellínos YS Athens.
At JT: OG: '04- 9; WCh: '05- dnq 22, '07- 5; EC: '06- dnq 17; WCp: '06- 6; ECp: '07- 6. Greek champion 2003-04, 2006-07.
Progress at JT: 1988- 52.20 (old JT), 1999- 52.15, 2000- 57.61, 2001- 58.53, 2002- 56.27, 2003- 60.07, 2004- 62.89, 2005- 57.88, 2006- 60.28, 2007- 63.13. pb SP 13.06 '04.
As Albanian set national junior record in 1998. Travelled on foot all the way from the Greek-Albanian border to Athens! Practically out of action from 1989 until her relocation in Athens in 1997, during that period she worked mainly as a PE teacher in Albania.

GRENADA

Governing body: Grenada Athletic Assocation, PO Box 419, St George's. Founded 1924.

Randy LEWIS b. 14 Oct 1980 1.88m 74kg. Marketing graduate of Wichita State University, USA
At TJ: OG: '04- dnq 28; WCh: '05- dnq 24; CG: '02- 8 LJ, '06- 6; PAm: '07- 7.
Grenada TJ record from 1998.
Progress at TJ: 1997- 15.66w, 1998- 15.66A, 1999- 15.75, 2000- 16.15i/15.78, 2002- 16.29i/16.06, 2003- 16.80, 2004- 17.34, 2005- 16.88, 2006- 17.31, 2007- 17.43, 2008- 17.27i. pb LJ 7.07 '02.

HUNGARY

Governing body: Magyar Atlétikai Szövetség, 1146 Budapest, Istvánmezei út 1-3. Founded 1897.
National Championships first held in 1896 (men), 1932 (women). **2007 Champions**. **Men**: 100m: Roland Németh 10.48, 200m: Péter Miklós 21.23, 400m: Róbert Mucsi 47.59, 800m: Támas Kazi 1:49.64, 1500m: Balázs Csillag 3:47.76, 5000m: Tibor Végh 14:31.80, 10,000m: Albert Minczér 29:59.58, HMar/3000mSt: Balázs Ott 67:21/8:50.45, Mar: Tamás Tóth 2:24:40, 110mh: Balázs Baji 14.48, 400mh: Balázs Molnár 52.03, HJ: Árpád Lehoczky 2.10, PV: Zoltán Szörényi 5.30, LJ: Dániel Ecseki 7.62, TJ: Péter Ungvári 15.02, SP: Lajos Kürthy 19.12, DT: Gábor Máté 64.80, HT: Krisztián Pars 79.82, JT: Csongor Olteán 72.39, Dec: Attila Szabó 7545, 20kW: Gyula Dudás 1:27:45, 50kW: Zoltán Czukor 4:09:31. **Women**: 100m: Zsófia Rózsa 11.92, 200m/400m: Barbara Petráhn 23.93/52.68, 800m: Krisztina Kácser 2:10.25, 1500m/5000m: Zsófia Erdélyi 4:25.91/16:46.94, 10,000m: Simona Staicu 34:08.49, HMar: Krisztina Papp 71:49, Mar: Judit Földing-Nagy 2:47:10, 3000mSt: Eszter Erdélyi 10:32.45, 100mh: Edit Vári 13.38, 400mh: Réka Skoumal 59.92, HJ: Dóra Györffy 1.87, PV: Krisztina Molnár 4.20, LJ: Katalin Deák 6.10, TJ: Rita Babos 13.06, SP: Anita Márton 14.38, DT: Katalin Császár 49.83, HT: Vanda Nickl 64.39, JT: Xénia Frajka 55.08, Hep: Zita Óvári 5559; 10,000mW: Katalin Varró 50:49.05, 20kW: Edina Füsti 1:40:08.

Zoltán KÖVAGÓ b. 10 Apr 1979 Szolnok 2.04m 127kg. Budapesti Honvéd SE. Army lieutenant.
At DT: OG: '00- dnq, '04- 2; WCh: '01-03: dnq 20/19, '05- 10, '07- 9; EC: '02- 7; WJ: '96- 4, '98- 1; EJ: '97- 3; EU23: '99- 6, '01- 1. HUN champion 2001, 2004-05.
Progress at DT: 1995- 49.78, 1996- 59.70, 1997- 62.16, 1998- 60.27, 1999- 63.23, 2000- 66.76, 2001- 66.93, 2002- 65.98, 2003- 66.03, 2004- 68.93, 2005- 66.00, 2006- 69.95, 2007- 66.42. pb SP 15.93 '01.

Gábor MÁTÉ b. 9 Feb 1979 Békéscsaba 1.99m 104kg. Csabai Atléták SE. Was at Auburn University, USA.
At DT: OG: '00- dnq 23, '04- 11; WCh: '03- dnq, '05- dnq 26, '07- 5; EC: '06- 11; WJ: '98- 3; EU23: '99- 4, '01- 3; WUG: '05- 3. HUN champion 2006-07, NCAA 1999-2000.
Progress at DT: 1995- 43.42, 1996- 48.50, 1997- 55.30, 1998- 59.01, 1999- 61.74, 2000- 66.54/66.91dh, 2001- 63.41, 2002- 65.33, 2003- 65.05/66.99dh, 2004- 65.35, 2005- 65.42, 2006- 63.38, 2007- 66.45. pbs: SP 18.77i/18.72 '03, HT 65.68 '03, Wt 19.78 '03

Krisztián PARS b. 18 Feb 1982 Körmend 1.88m 104kg. Dobó SE.
At HT: OG: '04- 5; WCh: '05- 7, '07- 5; EC: '06- 6; WY: '99- 1; EJ: '01- 1; EU23: '03- 1. HUN champion 2005-07.
World junior records with 6kg hammer: 80.64 & 81.34 in 2001.
Progress at HT: 1998- 54.00, 1999- 61.92, 2000- 66.80, 2001- 73.09, 2002- 74.18, 2003- 78.81, 2004- 80.90, 2005- 80.03, 2006- 82.45, 2007- 81.40. pbs: SP 15.60 '05, DT 53.80 '06.

Attila ZSIVOCZKY b. 29 Apr 1977 Budapest 1.93m 82kg. Debreceni SC. Was at Kansas State University, USA.
At Dec: OG: '00- 8, '04- 6; WCh: '99- 10, '01- 4, '03- dnf, '05- 3, '07- 12; EC: '98- 16, '06- 2; WJ: '96- 1; EU23: '97- 4, '99- 1; ECp: '98-9-01-06: 5/5/2/2. At Hep: EI: '00-02-05: 4/5/5.
Hungarian decathlon record 2000.
Progress at Dec: 1995- 7242, 1996- 7582, 1997-

7804, 1998- 8103, 1999- 8379, 2000- 8554, 2001- 8371, 2002- 8175, 2003- 7923, 2004- 8287, 2005- 8480, 2006- 8390, 2007- 8017. pbs: 60m 7.11i '00, 100m 10.90 '05, 10.64w '00; 400m 47.93 '00, 1000m 2:34.79i '98, 1500m 4:20.94 '99, 60mh 8.14i '06, 110mh 14.54 '06, 14.52w '05; HJ 2.23i '98, 2.22 '94; PV 4.91i '02, 4.90 '01; LJ 7.31 '99, SP 15.96 '05, DT 49.58 '05, JT 66.79 '06, Hep 6033i '00.

Son of Gyula Zsivótzky (OG: 60- 2, 64- 2, 68- 1, 72- 5; EC: 58- 3, 62- 1, 66- 2, 69- 4) who set two world hammer records – 73.74 '65 and 73.76 '68.

Women

Anikó KÁLOVICS b. 13 May 1977 Szombathely 1.75m 60kg. Zalaszám ZAC.

At 10,000m: OG: '00- h, '04- 20; WCh: '03- 20; EC: '98- 12, '02- 14; EU23: '97- 4; EJ: '95- 6. At 5000m: WCh: '05- h; WJ: '96- 11 (h 3000m). World 20k: '06- 11. Eur CC: '01-02-03-04-05-06-07: 15/4/3/8/5/4/5. Won HUN 5000m 1998, 2000, 2002-03, 10,000m 1997-8, 2004, HMar 2003-04, CC 1998, 2004.

HUN records HMar 2002 & 2007, 10,000m 2003.

Progress at 10,000m: 1993- 40:56.30, 1994- 35:21.46, 1995- 35:49.59, 1996- 35:29.07, 1997- 33:06.56, 1998- 32:53.32; 2000- 32:16.4, 2001- 32:48.76, 2002- 32:22.61, 2003- 31:40.31, 2004- 31:56.36. pbs: 800m 2:18.89 '96, 1500m 4:29.01 '97, 3000m 9:08.24 '04, 5000m 15:10.21 '04, Road: 15km 49:24 '04, 10M: 52:28 '05, 20km 66:20 '06, HMar 68:58 '07, Mar 2:26:44dh '06.

Won at Carpi on marathon debut 2006 and in Turin and Carpi 2007.

ICELAND

Governing body: Frjálsíthróttasamband Islands, Engjavegur 6, IS-104 Reykjavik. F'd 1947.

National Championships first held in 1927. **2007 Champions: Men**: 100m/200m/400m: Sveinn Elias Eliasson 10.66w/21.55/49.37, 800m/1500m: Björn Margeirsson 1:56.94/4:04.08, 5000m: Kári Steinn Karlsson 14:45.16, 110mh/400mh: Einar Dadi Lárusson 14.73w/55.71, HJ: Örn Davidsson 1.88, PV: Gauti Ásbjörnsson 4.10, LJ: Halldór Lárusson 7.31w, TJ: Eølafur Gudmundsson 13.70, SP/DT: Ódinn Björn Thorsteinsson 18.10/50.71, HT: Bergur Ingi Pétursson 64.85, JT: Sigurdur Karlsson 59.59. **Women:** 100m/200m/400m/400mh: Silja Úlfarsdóttir 11.88w/24.80/57.82/60.72, 800m: Stefanía Valdimarsdóttir 2:18.35, 3000m: Frída Rún Thórardóttir 10:25.34, 100mh: Kriston Birna Ólafsdóttor 14.26w, HJ: Dagrún Inga Thorsteinsdóttir 1.67, PV: Hulda Thorsteinsdóttir 3.40, LJ: Hafdís Sigurdjardóttir 5.90w, TJ: Agústa Tryggvadóttir 11.60w, SP/DT: Ásdís Hjálmsdóttir 13.03/42.66, HT: Kristbjörg Helga Ingvarssdóttir 47.66, JT: Vigdís Gudjónsdóttir 43.22.

INDIA

Governing body: Athletics Federation of India, Room No.1148, Gate No 28, East Block, Jawaharlal Nehru Stadium, Lodi Complex, New Delhi 110003. Founded 1946.

National Championships first held as Indian Games in 1924. **2007 Champions: Men**: 100m: Sameer Mon 10.53, 200m: Arunjith 20.92, 400m: Bibin Mathew 47.55, 800m: Sajeesh Joseph 1:47.42, 1500m: Chatholi Hamza 3:39.9, 5000m: Sunil Kumar 14:00.80; 10,000m: Surendra Singh 29:04.7, 3000mSt: Om Prakash 8:48.06, 110mh: Pandi Muthu Swami 14.10, 400mh: Kuldev Singh 50.70, HJ: Benedict Starli 2.19, PV: K. P. Bimin 4.80, LJ: Shiv Shankar Yadav 7.73, TJ: Amarjeet Singh 16.53, SP: Satyendra Kumar 18.05, DT: Harpreet Singh 52.24, HT: Harinder Singh 62.28, JT: Anil Singh 72.84, Dec: Jora Singh 6960, 20kW: Babubhai Panocha 1:23:40. **Women**: 100m: N.Sharda 11.83, 200m/400m: Satti Geetha 24.09/54.71, 800m/1500m: Sinimol Paulose 2:02.02/4:15.5, 5000m/10,000m: Preeja Sreedharan 15:45.96/33:25.0, 3000mSt: Sudha Singh 10:18.76, 100mh: Poonam Bojanna 14.08, 400mh: V.Leelavathi 60.3, HJ: Sahana Kumari 1.82, PV: V.S.Surekha 3.75, LJ: Resmi Bose 6.06, TJ: Kulwinder Kaur 12.84, SP: Manpreet Kaur 13.62, DT: Krishna Poona 52.34, HT: Ritu Rani 55.94, JT: Mukesh Kumari 45.96, Hep: J. J. Shobha 5508, 20000mW: Y.Bala Devi 1:47:08.04.

Anju Bobby GEORGE b. 19 Apr 1977 Cheeranchira, Kerala 1.77m 70kg. née Markose. Customs & Excise officer.

At LJ: OG: '04- 6; WCh: '03- 3, '05- 5, '07- 9; CG: '02- 3, '06- 6, AsiG: '02- 1 (4 TJ), '06- 2; AsiC: '05- 1, '07- 2; WI: '03- 7; won Af-AsG 2003, S.Asian 2006.

Indian records LJ (6) 1999–2004, TJ 2001 & 2002.

Progress at LJ: 1996- 6.13, 1997- 6.20, 1998- 6.12, 1999- 6.37, 2000- 6.59, 2001- 6.74, 2002- 6.74, 2003- 6.70, 2004- 6.83, 2005- 6.75, 2006- 6.54, 2007- 6.65. pb TJ 13.67 '02.

Married triple jumper Bobby George in 2001.

IRAN

Governing body: Amateur Athletic Federation of Islamic Republic of Iran, PO Box 15875-6891, Shahid Keshvari Sports Complex, Razaneh Junibi St Mirdamad Ave, Tehran. Founded 1936.

Ehsan HADADI b. 21 Jan 1985 1.98m 115kg.

At DT: WCh: '07- 7; WJ: '04- 1; AsiG: '06- 1; AsiC: '03- 8, '05- 1, '07- 1; AsiJ: '04- 1; WCp: '06- 2. W.Asian champion 2005.

Four Asian discus records 2005-07.

Progress at DT: 2002- 53.66, 2003- 54.40, 2004- 54.96, 2005- 65.25, 2006- 63.79, 2007- 67.95.

IRELAND

Governing Body: The Athletic Association of Ireland (AAI), Unit 19, Nortwood Court, Northwood Business Campus, Santry, Dublin 9. Founded in 1999. Original Irish AAA founded in 1885.

National Championships first held in 1873. **2007**

Champions: **Men**: 100m/200m: Paul Hession 10.45/20.30, 400m: David Gillick 46.34, 800m/1500m: David Campbell 1:49.45/3:45.21, 5000: Martin Fagan 13:56.13, 10,000m: Gary Thornton 29:57.06, HMar: Tergia Sergio 69:05, Mar: Michael O'Connor 2:25:48, 3000mSt: Mark Kirwan 9:06.84, 110mh: Ian McDonald 14.62, 400mh: Jonathan Miller 52.39, HJ: Mark Crowley GBR 2.08, PV: Anthony McCreery 4.90, LJ: Stephen Fleming 7.24, TJ: Denis Finnegan 14.18, SP/DT: Eoin Leen 15.36/50.54, HT: Patrick McGrath 66.96, JT: Mindaugas Kurcenkovas 55.90, Dec: Philip Kearney 5606, 10,000mW: Robert Heffernan 39:11.78, 20kW: Colin Griffin 1:25:40, 30kW: Jamie Costin 2:19:40. **Women**: 100m: Emily Maher 11.83, 200m/400m: Joanne Cuddihy 23.63/51.86, 800m: Orla Drumm 2:06.15, 1500m: Mary Cullen 4:17.20, 5000m: Maria McCambridge 16:01.84, HMar: Gladys Daniel 85:57, Mar: Pauline Curley 2:42:30, 3000mSt: Roisin McGettigan 9:56.17, 100mh: Derval O'Rourke 13.45, 400mh: Michelle Carey 57.23, HJ: Deidre Ryan 1.80, PV: Zoë Brown GBR 3.95, LJ: Kelly Proper 6.17, TJ: Mary McLoone 11.57, SP: Eva Massey GBR 15.45, DT/HT: Eileen O'Keeffe 44.75/73.21, JT: Anita White 44.97, Hep: Geraldine Finegan 4166, 5000mW: Ann Loughnane 24:36.30, 20kW: Catriona McMahon 1:57:27.

Alistair CRAGG b. 13 Jun 1980 Johannesburg, South Africa 1.83m 59kg. Clonliffe H. Studied marketing at University of Arkansas.
At 5000m: OG: '04- 12; WCh: '07- h; EC: '06- dnf; At 3000m: WI: '06- 4; EI: '05- 1, '07- 6. World 4k CC: '04- 16. Won Irish 1500m 2004, NCAA 5000m 2003, 10,000m 2004 (indoor 3000m 2003-04, 5000m 2002-04).
Progress at 5000m,10,000m: 1998- 14:27.82, 1999- 14:25.04, 2000- 13:49.25, 2002- 13:22.07, 29:33.77; 2003- 13:25.59, 28:20.29; 2004- 13:12.74, 28:46.64; 2006- 13:08.97, 2007- 13:07.10, 27:39.55. pbs 1500m 3:36.18 '07, 1M 3:55.04i '06, 4:03.70 '02; 3000m 7:32.49 '07, 2M 8:23.75 '06.
Ran for South Africa at 1998 & 1999 World Junior CC, but held Irish passport through two Irish grandparents.

Women

Roisin McGETTIGAN b. 23 Aug 1980 Wicklow 1.70m 55kg. Sll Chulainn. Was at Providence College, USA.
At 3000mSt: WCh: '05- h, '07- 10; EC: '06- h; EU23: '03- 10; WUG: '05- 6; Won Irish 800m 2006, 1500m 2003, 3000mSt 2007.
Eight Irish 3000m steeplechase records 2001-07.
Progress at 3000mSt: 2001- 10:24.35, 2002- 10:08.24, 2003- 9:50.12, 2004- 9:45.60, 2005- 9:46.12, 2006- 9:32.04, 2007- 9:28.29. pbs: 800m 2:04.9 '03, 1500m 4:10.34 '03, 1M 4:32.35i '05, 4:35.55 '04; 3000m 9:03.11i/9:10.87 '06, 5000m 16:00.64 '07.

Eileen O'KEEFFE b. 31 May 1981 Kilkenny 1.70m 80kg. Kilkenny City Harriers. Nurse.
At HT: OG: '04- h; WCh: '05- dnq 24, '07- 6; EC: '02/06- dnq 15/17; WJ: '00- dnq 26; EU23: '03- dnq; WUG: '03-05-07: 4/6/2; Won AAA 2006, Irish DT 2002, 2004-05, 2007, HT 2001-07.
17 Irish hammer records 2002-07.
Progress at 100mh: 1998- 38.03, 1999- 47.97, 2000- 53.54, 2001- 57.08, 2002- 61.10, 2003- 63.25, 2004- 64.66, 2005- 69.36, 2006- 69.32, 2007- 73.21. pb DT 46.64 '00.

Derval O'ROURKE b. 28 May 1981 Cork 1.68m 57kg. Leevale. Graduate of University College Dublin; sports administrator for Dublin City University.
At 100mh: OG: '04- h; WCh: '05/07- sf; EC: '06- 2=; WJ: '00- sf; EU23: '01- 7, '03- 4; EJ: '99- sf; WUG: '05- 3; Irish champion 2001-02, 2004-07. At 60mh: WI: '06- 1.
Five Irish 100mh records 2003-06.
Progress at 100mh: 1998- 14.29/13.88w, 1999- 13.82, 2000- 13.49, 2001- 13.57, 2002- 13.38, 2003- 12.96, 2004- 13.39, 2005- 13.00/12.95w, 2006- 12.72, 2007- 12.88. pbs: 60m 7.59i '05, 100m 11.54 '05, 11.43w '07; 50mh 6.80i '06, 60mh 7.84i '06.
Set six Irish records at 60mh from 8.02 to 7.84 to win World Indoor title in 2006.

ISRAEL

Governing body: Israeli Athletic Association, PO Box 24190, Tel Aviv 61241. Founded as Federation for Amateur Sport in Palestine 1931.
National Championships first held in 1935.
2007 Champions: 100m: Alex Trembach 10.80, 200m/110mh: Michael Illin 21.56/13.96, 400m: Yuriy Shapsai 48.05, 800m/1500m: Gezachw Yossef 1:53.79/3:50.52, 5000m: Brihon Voba 14:44.18, 10,000m: Ayele Setegne 30:37.52, HMar/Mar: Asaf Bimro 66:39/2:17:35, 3000mSt: Itai Maggidi 9:10.45 400mh: Yuriy Pelles 52.82, HJ: Niki Palli 2.25, PV: Alex Averbukh 5.70, LJ: Yinon Israeli 7.64, TJ: Vladimir Borisenko 15.41, SP: Shai Shelev 16.23, DT: Felix Gromadskiy 49.19, HT: Issar Yazbin 62.34, JT: Vadim Bavikin 67.83, Dec: Ruslan Khamad 6629. **Women**: 100m/200m: Rita Pogorleov 11.84/24.63, 400m/400mh: Liat Anav 57.24/61.89, 800m/1500m/3000mSt: Irina Weingarten 2:16.02/4:42.51/11:23.43, 5000m/10,000m/HMar/Mar: Nili Abramski 16:59.70/36:29.72/75:41/ 2:39:25 (57 national titles), 100mh: Irina Lenskiy 13.30, HJ: Ma'ayan Foreman 1.80, PV: Olga Dogadko 4.03, LJ: Rotem Battat 6.03, TJ: Niva Ziv 12.65, SP/DT: Sivan Jean 16.03/51.00, HT: Yevgeniya Zabolotniy 42.11, JT: Dorit Naor 3994, Hep: Yulia Pushkaryov 4138.

Alex AVERBUKH b. 1 Oct 1974 Irkutsk. Siberia 1.78m 76kg. Maccabi Tel-Aviv.
At PV: OG: '00- 10=, '04- 8; WCh: '99- 3, '01- 2, '03- dnq, '07- 7; EC: '02- 1, '06- 1; WI: '01- 4, '06-

4=; EI: '00- 1; EJ: '93- dnq; WUG: '01- 1; WCp: '06- 5=; 2nd GP 2002. EI Hep: '98- 6. Won ISR PV 2000-02, 2004-07; RUS Dec 1997.
Six ISR pole vault records 1999-2003 (from 5.80).
Progress at PV, Dec: 1991- 4.95, 1993- 5.30, 1994- 5.20, 1995- 5.50, 7598w; 1996- 5.40, 7716; 1997- 5.60, 8084; 1998- 5.70, 7658; 1999- 5.81, 2000- 5.85, 2001- 5.91, 2002- 5.85, 2003- 5.93, 2004- 5.85, 2005- 5.65, 2006- 5.81i/5.80, 2007- 5.81. pbs: 60m 6.89i '98, 6.6i '97; 100m 10.64 '00, 400m 48.74 '98, 1500m 4:33.79 '97, 60mh 8.36i '98, 8.2i '97; 110mh 14.14 '97, HJ 2.06 '95, LJ 7.53i/7.50 '97, SP 15.12 '98, DT 41.51 '00, JT 53.26 '97, Hep 6144i '98.
His father Valeriy had a decathlon best of 7557 points and his brother Yevgeniy (died 1996 in a car crash) an 800m best of 1:48.18. Emigrated from Russia to Israel, and became a citizen on 3 August 1999, just in time to compete at World Championships. In 1999 he became Israel's first World medallist and at Munich 2002 he became Israel's first European outdoor champion.

ITALY

Governing Body: Federazione Italiana di Atletica Leggera (FIDAL), Via Flaminia Nuova 830, 00191 Roma. Constituted 1926. First governing body formed 1896.
National Championships first held in 1897 (one event)/1906 (men), 1927 (women). **2007 champions**: **Men**: 100m: Koura Kaba Fantoni 10.57, 200m/LJ: Andrew Howe 20.53/8.40w, 400m: Andrea Barberi 45.79, 800m: Livio Sciandra 1:51.18, 1500m: Christian Obrist 3:50.37, 5000m/10,000m: Daniele Meucci 14:07.01/29:33.71, HMar: Giuliano Battocletti 63:14, Mar: Migidio Bourifa 2:10:30, 3000mSt: Yuri Floriani 8:43.84, 110mh: Emanuele Abate 14.00, 400mh: Claudio Citterio 51.12, HJ: Filippo Campiolo 2.26, PV: Mateo Rubbiani 5.20, TJ: Fabrizio Donato 16.97, SP: Paolo Capponi 18.99, DT: Hannes Kirchler 60.24, HT: Nicola Vizzoni 77.98, JT: Daniele Crivellaro 72.30, Dec: Paulo Mottadelli 7517, 10,000mW/20kW/50kW: Alex Schwazer 40:39. 21/1:25:16/3:36:04. **Women**: 100m/200m: Anita Pistone 11.78/23.76, 400m: Daniela Reina 52.31, 800m: Elisa Cusma 2:02.59, 1500m: Silvia Wessteiner 4:15.27, 5000m: Claudia Pinna 16:39.34, 10,000m: Gloria Marconi 33:26.95, HMar: Anna Incerti 71:56, Mar: Ivana Iozzia 2:35:26, 3000mSt: Elena Romagnolo 9:51.93, 100mh: Micol Cattaneo 13.52, 400mh: Benedetta Ceccarelli 56.59, HJ: Antonietta Di Martino 1.91, PV: Anna Giordano Bruno 4.30, LJ: Tania Vicenzino 6.50, TJ: Magdelin Martinez 14.22, SP: Chiara Rosa 19.13, DT: Cristiana Checchi 57.93, HT: Clarissa Claretti 67.95, JT: Claudia Coslovich 59.88, Hep: Elisa Trevisan 5690, 5000mW: Elisa Rigaudo 21:45.46, 20kW: Gisella Orsini 1:38:41.

Stefano BALDINI b. 25 May 1971 Castelnovo di Sotto, Reggio Emilia 1.76m 60kg. Works for Corradini Excelsior Rubiera.
At Mar: OG: '00- dnf, '04- 1; WCh: '01- 3, '03- 3, '05- dnf; EC: '98- 1, '06- 1. At 10,000m (5000m): OG: '96- 18 (sf); WCh: '95- 18, '97- 9; EC: '94- 20, '02- 4; WJ: '90- (6); EJ: '89- (9); ECp: '95- 1. World HMar: '96- 1, '97- 9. Eur CC: '99- 10. Won ITA 10,000m 1993-6, 2001-02; HMar 1995, 1998, 2001, 2004, 2006.
Italian records: half marathon 1997 & 2000, marathon 1997, 2002 & 2006.
Progress at 10,000m, Mar: 1990- 29:48.5, 1992- 28:50.16, 1993- 28:25.98, 1994- 27:57.86, 1995- 27:50.17, 2:11:01sh; 1996- 27:43.98; 1997- 28:07.81, 2:07:57; 1998- 27:55.92, 2:09:33; 2000- 2:09:45, 2001- 28:21.38, 2:08:51; 2002- 27:50.98, 2:07:29; 2003- 2:07:56, 2004- 2:08:37, 2005- 2:09:25, 2006- 2:07:22, 2007- 2:11:58. pbs: 1500m 3:45.7 '91, 3000m 7:43.14 '96, 5000m 13:23.43 '96, HMar 60:50w '00, 60:56 '97.
Four wins in 22 marathons: Rome and EC 1998, Madrid 2001, OG 2004; 2nd London 1997 & 2003, 3rd New York 1997, pb when 5th London 2006. On 9 Oct 1999 married **Virna De Angeli** (b. 27 Feb 1976) (2 WJ 400mh 1994, Italian record 400m 51.31 '97), but they are now separated. Older brother Marco (b. 14 May 1968) had marathon best of 2:16:32 sh '95.

Ivano BRUGNETTI b. 1 Sep 1976 Milano 1.76m 61kg. Fiamme Gialle Ostia.
At 20kW: OG: '04- 1; WCh: '05- dnf, '07- dq; EC: '06- 17; WCp: '04- 6, '06- 15; ECp: '07- 2. At 50kW: OG: '00- dnf; WCh: '99- 1; WCp: '99- 26. At 10,000mW: EJ: '95- 14. Won ITA 10,000mW 1999, 2006; 20kW 2003-04.
Progress at 20kW, 50kW: 1995- 1:30:33, 1997- 1:26:51, 4:06:43; 1998- 1:25:12, 4:02:15; 1999- 1:25:44, 3:47:54; 2000- 1:21:21, 2001- 1:24:38, 4:08:35; 2002- 1:26:08, 2003- 1:22:01, 2004- 1:19:40, 2005- 1:22:50, 2006- 1:21:47, 2007- 1:19:36. pbs: 5000mW 18:08.86i '07, 10,000mW 37:58.6 '05 (world best), 30kW: 2:10:06 '99, 35kW 2:33:43 '99.
He finished second at the 1999 World Championships, but two years later the winner German Skurygin (Rus) received a two-year ban from a positive drugs test in Seville, and Brugnetti was awarded the gold.

Fabrizio DONATO b. 14 Aug 1976 Latina 1.89m 82kg. Fiamme Galle Ostia.
At TJ: OG: '00/04- dnq 25/21; WCh: '03/07- dnq 13/32; EC: '02- 4, '06- dnq 16; EJ: '95- 5; WI: '01- 6, '08- 4; EI: '02- 4; ECp: '00-02-03-04-06: 2/2/1/6/1. Won MedG 2001, Italian 2000, 2004, 2006-07.
Italian triple jump record 2000.
Progress at TJ: 1992- 12.88, 1993- 14.36, 1994- 15.27, 1995- 15.81, 1996- 16.35, 1997- 16.40A, 1998- 16.73, 1999- 16.66i/16.53w, 2000- 17.60, 2001- 17.05, 2002- 17.17, 2003- 17.16, 2004- 16.90, 2005- 16.65/16.68w, 2006- 17.33i/17.24, 2007- 16.97/17.06w, 2008- 17.27i. pb LJ 8.02i '07, 8.00 '06.
He married Patrizia Spuri (400m pb 51.74 '98, 8 EC 98) on 27 Sep 2003.

Andrew HOWE b. 12 May 1985 Los Angeles, USA 1.84m 73kg. Aeronautica Militare.

At (200m)/LJ: OG: '04- (h); WCh: '05- (qf), '07- 2; EC: '06- 1; WJ: '02- 5 4x100mR, '04- 1/1; WY: '01- 3; WI: '06- 3; EI: '07- 1; WCp: '06- 2; ECp: '06- 1. Won WAF LJ 2007, Italian 200m & LJ 2007. Italian LJ record 2007. European Junior 200m record 2004.
Progress at 200m, LJ: 1998- 5.88, 1999- 6.51, 2000- 7.52, 2001- 20.99/20.91w, 7.61; 2002- 21.15/21.0, 7.38; 2003- 21.03, 7.63i/7.47; 2004- 20.28, 8.11; 2005- 20.52, 8.02; 2006- 8.41, 2007- 20.53, 8.47. pbs: 100m 10.27 '06, 10.24w '04; 150m 15.3 '04, 300m 33.7 '04, 400m 46.03 '06, 110mh 14.65 '02, HJ 2.06 '00, TJ 16.27 '02.
Left the USA with his mother Renée Felton (100mh 13.72 '81) at age five in 1990 – she married an Italian, Ugo Besozzi. Andrew set many Italian age group records. From a previous best of 7.61 he set Italian junior LJ records with 7.93, 8.01, 8.04 and 8.07 in 2004. improving to 8.11 to win World Junior gold. He followed this with a pb 20.86 in his heat, then a national junior record 20.72 in his semi and an amazing European junior record 20.28 to win the 200m.

Alex SCHWAZER b. 26 Dec 1984 Vipiteno (Bolzano) 1.85m 73kg. Carabinieri Bologna.
At 50kW (20kW): WCh: '05- 3, '07- 3 (10); EC: '06- dnf; EU23: '05- (dnf); ECp: '05- 6. Won ITA 10,000m & 20kW 2007, 50kW 2005, 2007-08.
Italian 50km walk records 2005 and 2007.
Progress at 50kW: 2004- 4:00:51, 2005- 3:41:54, 2007- 3:36:04. pbs: 10,000mW 40:39.21 '05, 20kW 1:21:38 '06, 30kW: 2:12:20 '04, 35kW 2:36:40 '05.
Rapid improvement in 2005 with 3:56:59 in January, 3:49:42 in May and 3:41:54 to win the World bronze medal at the age of 20 in August.

Women

Ester BALASSINI b. 20 Oct 1977 Bologna 1.73m 74kg. Fiamme Gialle.
At HT: OG: '00- dnq, '04- dnq 26; WCh: '01/05- dnq; EC: '98- dnq 20, '02- 6, '06- dnq 19; EU23: '97- 10, '99- 5; ECp: '98-9-00-01-02-03-05: 4/7/6/5/4/4/4; Won MedG 2005, ITA 1998-2001, 2005.
17 Italian hammer records 1998-2005.
Progress at HT: 1996- 46.64, 1997- 56.04, 1998- 61.73, 1999- 64.44, 2000- 66.17, 2001- 68.50, 2002- 68.54, 2003- 70.43, 2004- 71.28, 2005- 73.59, 2006- 72.11, 2007- 71.96. pb DT 38.52.
Formerly a rollerskate dancer. Married to Cristiano Andrei (DT 64.49 '03).

Zahra BANI b. 31 Dec 1979 Mogadishu, Somalia 1.73m 73kg. Fiamme Azzurre Roma.
At JT: WCh: '05- 5, '0- dnq 14; EC: '06- 9; WJ: '98- dnq 26; EU23: '99- 6; WUG: '05- 6, ECp: '05- 3. Italian champion 2005-06.
Progress at JT: 1995- 39.12, 1996- 43.66, 1997- 47.92, 1998- 51.35, 1999- 53.78, new: 2000- 54.26, 2001- 54.98, 2002- 55.34, 2003- 56.50, 2004- 59.10, 2005- 62.75, 2006- 62.44, 2007- 62.09.
Born in Somalia to old colonial family from Livorno/Tuscany. The family went to Italy/ Turin in 1989, due to the Somali civil war.

Clarissa CLARETTI b. 7 Oct 1980 Fermo, Macerata 1.70m 70kg. Aeronautica Militare.
At HT: OG: '04- dnq 28; WCh: '03- dnq 28, '05- 9, '07- 7; EC: '02- 8; EU23: '01- dnq; EJ: '99- dnq; WUG: '05- 4. ITA champion 2002-03, 2006-07.
Progress at HT: 1997- 39.36, 1998- 48.96, 1999- 55.83, 2000- 60.83, 2001- 63.54, 2002- 68.23, 2003- 67.43, 2004- 69.40, 2005- 70.59, 2006- 71.98, 2007- 71.43. She is also a football referee.

Antonietta DI MARTINO b. 1 Jun 1978 Cava de' Tirreni, Salerno 1.69m 58kg. Fiamme Gialle Ostia.
At HJ: WCh: '01- 12, '07- 2=; EC: '06- 10; WI: '06- 5; EI: '07- 2; ECp: '01-02-05: 3=/7=/5. Italian champion 2000-01, 2006-07.
Three Italian high jump records 2007.
Progress at HJ: 1993- 1.63, 1994- 1.71, 1995- 1.69, 1996- 1.66, 1997- 1.78, 1998- 1.73, 1999- 1.63, 2000- 1.88, 2001- 1.98, 2002- 1.91, 2003- 1.96i/1.90, 2004- 1.86, 2005- 1.90, 2006- 1.96i/1.94, 2007- 2.03. pbs: 200m 25.93 '00, 800m 2:24.21 '01, 60mh 8.94i '01, 100hm 14.11 '01, LJ 5.60 '01, SP 11.74 '01, JT 46.64 '01, Pen 3980i '01, Hep 5687w/5542 '01.
Has the record for the greatest ever height differential, 34cm, by a woman high jumper.

Assunta LEGNANTE 14 May 1978 Napoli 1.87m 118kg. AS Camelot. Studied political science at Macerata University.
At SP: WCh: '03- 8, '05- 12, '07- dnq 13; EC: '02- 8, '06- 5; WJ: '96- dnq 13; EJ: '95- 11, '97- 3; EU23: '99- 3; WI: '03- 8, '04- dnq 12; EI: '00- dnq 16, '02- 2, '05- 6, '07- 1; ECp: 01-02-03-05: 3/5/4/3; WUG: '05- 4. Won MedG 2001, ITA 2002-04.
Three Italian shot records 2004-06.
Progress at SP: 1993- 12.33, 1994- 14.33i/13.89, 1995- 15.23, 1996- 15.87, 1997- 16.56i/16.52, 1998- 16.12i/15.95, 1999- 16.61, 2000- 17.84, 2001- 17.79, 2002- 19.20i/18.23, 2003- 18.43, 2004- 18.92, 2005- 18.80, 2006- 19.04, 2007- 19.01i/18.85. pbs: DT 42.74, JT 50.93 '03.

Magdelin MARTINEZ b. 10 Feb 1976 Camagüey, Cuba 1.78m 63kg. Assindustria Padova.
At TJ: OG: '04- 7; WCh: '01- 4, '03- 3, '05- 8, '07- 6; EC: '02- 6, '06- dnq 14; WJ: '94- 9; PAm: '99- 3; WI: '03- 5, '04- 5; EI: '05- 2; ECp: '02-03-05: 3/2/3. Italian champion 2002, 2007.
Five Italian triple jump records 2002-04.
Progress at TJ: 1992- 12.82, 1993- 13.07, 1994- 13.60, 1995- 13.74, 1996- 14.13/14.17w, 1997- 13.78/14.96w, 1998- 14.26, 1999- 14.14/14.18w, 2000- 14.40, 2001- 14.59, 2002- 14.73, 2003- 14.90, 2004- 15.03/15.24Aw, 2005- 14.69, 2006- 14.25, 2007- 14.71. pb LJ 6.67/6.74w '04.
Changed nationality from Cuba to Italy in 2001 after marrying an Italian, Giuseppe Picotti, in 1999.

Elisa RIGAUDO b. 17 Jun 1980 Cuneo 1.68m 56kg. Fiamme Galle Ostia.
At 20kW: OG: '04- 6; WCh: '03- 10, '05- 7, '07- dnf; EC: '06- 3; EU23: '03- 1; WCp: '02-04-06: 16/5/10; ECp: '07- 4. At 5000mW: WJ: '98- 7; EJ: '99-6. Won MedG 20kW 2005, Italian 5000mW 2004, 2007; 20kW 2004-05.
Progress at 20kW: 1999- 1:42:40. 2000- 1:32:50, 2001- 1:29:54, 2002- 1:30:42, 2003- 1:30:34, 2004- 1:27:49, 2005- 1:29:26, 2006- 1:28:37, 2007- 1:29:15. pbs: 3000mW 11:57.00i '04, 12:28.92 '02; 5000mW 20:56.29 '02, 10kW 43:06.4t '04.

Chiara ROSA b. 28 Jan 1983 Camposampiero, Padova 1.78m 112kg. Fiamme Azzurre Roma. Language student at Padua University.
At SP: WCh: '05- dnq 18, '07- 8; EC: '06- 8; WJ: '00- 12, '02- 4; EJ: '01- 7; EU23: '03- 4, '05- 3; WI: '08- 5; WUG: '05- 5. Italian champion 2005-07. Italian shot record 2007.
Progress at SP: 1999- 15.14, 2000- 15.44, 2001- 15.62, 2002- 16.96, 2003- 17.06, 2004- 17.76, 2005- 18.71, 2006- 18.42, 2007- 19.15. pb DT 45.33 '06

JAMAICA

Governing body: Jamaica Amateur Athletic Association, PO Box 272, Kingston 5. Founded 1932. **2007 Champions**: **Men**: 100m: Asafa Powell 10.04, 200m: Usain Bolt 19.75, 400m: Sanjay Ayre 45.07, 800m: Auldwin Sappleton 1:47.11, 1500m: Shawn Pitter 3:54.27, 5000m/10,000m: Wainard Talbert 14:58.98/31:47.41, 110mh: Maurice Wignall 13.67, 400mh: Danny McFarlane 48.52, HJ: David Edwards-Brennan 1.95, LJ: James Beckford 7.86, TJ: Kenneth Sylvester 16.06, SP: Dorian Scott 19.79, DT: Maurice Smith 55.49, JT: Anundrea Clarke 61.27. **Women**: 100m/200m: Veronica Campbell 10.89/22.39, 400m: Novlene Williams 50.06, 800m/1500m: Kenia Sinclair 1:59.11/4:19.93, 3000mSt: Korene Hinds 9:56.04, 100mh: Delloreen Ennis-London 12.62, 400mh: Melaine Walker 54.98, HJ: Peaches Roach 1.81, LJ: Chlesea Hammond 6.87w, TJ: Trecia Smith 14.35, SP: Zara Northover 16.08, DT: Nadia ;lexander 43.96, HT: Natalie Grant 59.43, JT: Kateema Rettie 54.95.

Marvin ANDERSON b. 12 May 1982 Trelawny 1.75m 69kg. Was at University of Southern California.
At 200m/4x100mR: WCh: '07- 6/2R; PAm: '07- 2; WJ: '00- 6; won CAC-J 100 '00.
Progress at 200m: 2000- 20.84, 2001- 21.01, 2002- 21.39, 2003- 21.20, 2004- 20.84, 2005- 20.75/20.36w, 2006- 20.65; 2007- 20.06. pbs: 100m 10.15/10.03w '07, 400m 49.07 '07.

James BECKFORD b. 9 Jan 1975 St Mary 1.83m 73kg. Was a PE student at Blinn JC, USA.
At LJ (TJ): OG: '96- 2, '00- dnq 14, '04- 4; WCh: '95- 2 (6/4R), '97- 4, '01- 7, '03- 2, '05- 9, '07- 6; CG: '02- nj; WI: '97-9-04-08: 5/5/2/6; CAG: '98- 1. 2nd GP LJ 1997, 1999 (3rd 1995). Won JAM LJ 1995-8, 2000, 2002, 2004-05, 2007; TJ 1995.
Commonwealth records: LJ 1995 & 1997, TJ 1995, Jamaican records: LJ (5), TJ (4) 1994-7.
Progress at LJ, TJ: 1993- 7.53, 15.70; 1994- 8.13/8.29w, 17.29; 1995- 8.45/8.68w, 17.92; 1996- 8.52, 16.43i; 1997- 8.62, 1998- 8.60/8.61w, 16.09; 1999- 8.50, 2000- 8.42, 2001- 8.41, 2002- 8.21/8.25w, 2003- 8.28, 2004- 8.31, 2005- 8.28/8.36w, 2006- 8.25, 2007- 8.37. pbs: 60m 6.79i '04, 100m 10.78 '05.
An outstanding long/triple jumper, now concentrating on the long jump. After positive test for ephedrine on 25 June 1997 was re-admitted to competition with the IAAF new warning procedure and thus competed at the World Champs.

Usain BOLT b. 21 Aug 1986 Trelawny 1.96m 86kg. Student.
At 200m/4x100mR: OG: '04- h; WCh: '05- 8, '07- 2/2R; WJ: 02- 1/2R/2R; WY: '01- sf, '03- 1; WCp: '06- 2; won PAm-J 2003, CAC 2005, JAM 2005, 2007.
CAC 200m record 2007, WJR 200m 2003 & 2004, World U18 200m record 2003.
Progress at 200m, 400m: 2001- 21.81, 48.28; 2002- 20.58, 47.12; 2003- 20.13, 45.35; 2004- 19.93, 2005- 19.99, 2006- 19.88, 2007- 19.75, 45.28. pb 100m 10.03 '07.
In 2002, after running 20.61 to win the CAC U17 200m title, he became the youngest ever male world junior champion at 15y 332d and set a world age best with 20.58, with further age records for 16 and 17 in 2003-04. Won IAAF 'Rising Star' award for men in 2002 and again in 2003.

Omar O. **BROWN** b. 21 Jun 1982 Trelawny 1.77m 70kg. University of Arkansas, USA.
At 200m/4x100mR: WCh: '05- h; CG: '06- 1; WJ: '00- 4; WY: '99- 2/1R (3 100m).
Progress at 200m: 1998- 21.47, 1999- 21.09, 2000- 20.89, 2003- 21.02i, 2004- 20.66/20.36w, 2005- 20.43, 2006- 20.33, 2007- 20.72. pbs: 60m 6.72i '04, 100m 10.27/10.20w '00, 300m 33.20i '06, 400m 46.00 '05.
Married Olympic and World champion Veronica Campbell on 3 Nov 2007.

Ricardo CHAMBERS b. 21 Jun 1982 Trelawny 1.77m 73kg. Florida State University, USA.
At 400m/4x400mR: WCh: '07- sf; CAG: '06- 5/1R. Won JAM & NACAC 2006, NCAA 2007.
Progress at 400m: 2003- 46.42, 2004- 46.02, 2005- 44.87, 2006- 44.71, 2007- 44.62. pbs: 100m 10.73 '04, 200m 21.08 '05, 800m 1:53.34i '07.

Michael FRATER b. 6 Oct 1982 Manchester 1.70m 67kg. Political science graduate of Texas Christian University.
At 100m/4x100mR: OG: '04- sf; WCh: '03- sf, '05- 2; CG: '02- sf, '06- sf/1R; PAm: '03- 1; WJ: '00- 5. Won NCAA 100m 2004, JAM 100m 2006.
Progress at 100m: 1999- 10.73/10.47w, 2000- 10.46, 2001- 10.26, 2002- 10.21/10.05w, 2003-

10.13, 2004- 10.06, 2005- 10.03, 2006- 10.06, 2007- 10.03/9.95w. pbs: 60m 6.64i '02, 200m 20.63, 20.45w '02; 400m 49.13 '07.
Older brother Lindel was former Jamaican champion, pb 100m 10.07 '00, 9.9w '98.

Jermaine GONZALES b. 26 Nov 1984 St. Catherine 1.90m 72kg.
At 400m/4x400mR: OG: '04- hR; CG: '06- 3/3R; WJ: '02- 3/2R; WY: 01- 3.
Progress at 400m: 2001- 47.51, 2002- 45.80, 2003- 46.15i/46.81, 2004- 45.41, 2005- 46.51, 2006- 44.85, 2007- 45.78.

Danny McFARLANE b. 14 Feb 1972 St Mary 1.85m 81kg. Was at University of Oklahoma, USA.
At 400m/4x400mR: OG: '00- 8/3R; WCh: '93- 7R, '95- sf/2R, '97- 3R, '99- sf/3R, '01- 3R, '07- 5; CG: '02- dnf R; WI: '01- 3/3R, '03- 2R; PAm: '99- 1R. Won CAC 1997, 2001. At 400mh: OG: '04- 2; WCh: '03- 4/2R, '05- sf. Won JAM 400mh 2003-04, 2006-07.
Progress at 400m, 400mh: 1993- 45.82, 1994- 45.74, 1995- 44.90, 1996- 46.18i/46.23, 1997- 45.47, 1998- 45.61, 1999- 45.37, 2000- 45.26, 2001- 45.20A/45.59, 2002- 45.66, 2003- 45.72, 48.30; 2004- 46.86, 48.00, 2005- 48.53, 2006- 48.47, 2007- 48.32. pb 200m 21.17 '95.

Asafa POWELL b. 23 Nov 1982 St Catherine 1.90m 88kg. Sports medicine student at Kingston University of Technology.
At 100m/4x100mR: OG: '04- 5 (dns 200); WCh: '03- dq, '07- 3/2R; CG: '02- sf/2R, '06- 1/1R; PAm-J: '01- 2R. Won JAM 100m 2003-05, 2007; 200m 2006; WAF 100m 2004, 2006-07; 200m 2004.
Four world 100m records, five CAC & Commonwealth 2005-07, ssven JAM 2004-7.
Progress at 100m, 200m: 2001- 10.50, 2002- 10.12, 20.48; 2003- 10.02/9.9, 2004- 9.87, 20.06; 2005- 9.77, 2006- 9.77, 19.90; 2007- 9.74, 20.00. pbs: 60m 6.56i '04, 400m 47.17 '07.
Disqualified for false start in World quarters 2003 after fastest time (10.05) in heats. In 2004 he tied the record of nine sub-10 second times in a season and in 2005 he took the world record for 100m at Athens, tying that at Gateshead and Zürich in 2006, when he ran a record 12 sub-10 times and was world athlete of the year. Took record to 9.74 in Rieti 2007. His elder brother Donovan Powell (b. 31 Oct 1971) won the 1996 US indoor 60m and was 6th WI 60m 1999 (pbs 60m 6.51i '96, 100m 10.07/9.7 '95).

Dorian SCOTT b. 1 Feb 1982 Springfield, USA 1.85m 136kg. Was at Florida State University.
At SP: WCh: '05- dnq 27, '07- nt; CG: '06- 2; PAm: '03- 10, '07- 2; WI: '08- 6; WCp: '06- 5. CAC champion 2005, JAM 2003-07.
CAC shot record 2008, 4 indoors 2006-08, 15 JAM records 2004-08.
Progress at SP: 2001- 17.53, 2002- 17.54, 2003- 19.43, 2004- 19.46, 2005- 20.21, 2006- 20.52i/20.33, 2007- 20.60, 2008- 21.45. pb DT 52.61 '05.
Lost 2006 CAC Games shot gold after positive test for a stimulant.

Maurice SMITH b. 28 Sep 1980 St Catherine 1.90m 90kg. Graduated in adult education from Auburn University, USA.
At Dec: OG: '04- 14; WCh: '05- dnf, '07- 2; CG: '06- 2; PAm: '07- 1; CAC champion 2001, NACAC 2005. Won NCAA indoor Hep 2005, JAM SP 2001, DT 2001, 2005, 2007; JT 2000..
Three CAC decathlon records 2006-07, four Jamaican 2005-07.
Progress at Dec: 1999- 6996, 2000- 7090, 2001- 7755, 2003- 7925w/7854, 2004- 8024, 2005- 8232, 2006- 8349, 2007- 8644. pbs: 60m 6.94i '05, 100m 10.62 '07, 400m 47.48 '07, 1000m 2:39.32i '05, 1500m 4:29.95 '06, 60mh 7.88i '05, 110mh 13.76 '06, HJ 2.03A '01, PV 4.80 '07, LJ 7.51 '06, SP 17.41 '07, DT 55.49 '07, JT 62.07 '02, Hep 6035i '05 (CAC record)

Dwight THOMAS b. 23 Sep 1980 Kingston 1.85m 82kg. adidas.
At 100m/4x100mR: OG: '04- sf; WCh: '03- sf, '05- 5; CG: '02- 4=/2R; PAm: '99- 3R; WJ: '98- 3/1R. At 200m: OG: '00- qf/4R. At 60m: WI: '03- sf. At 60mh: WI: '04- 8. Won CAC-J 110mh 1998, PAm-J 100m & 200m 1999, Jamaican 100m & 200m 2002.
Progress at 100m: 1998- 10.38, 1999- 10.37, 2000- 10.12, 2001- 10.19, 2002- 10.15, 2003- 10.19, 2004- 10.12, 2005- 10.00, 2006- 10.11, 2007- 10.15/10.07w. pbs: 55m 6.27i '01, 60m 6.61i '03, 200m 20.32 '07, 60mh 7.59i '04, 110mh 13.34 '04.

Kemel THOMPSON b. 25 Sep 1974 Kingston 1.80m 75kg. Took masters degree in sports science at Loughborough University, UK, was at South Florida University, USA.
At 400mh: OG: '00- h, '04- sf; WCh: '99- sf, '03- 5, '05- sf; CG: '98- 6, '06- 3; WCp: '06- 4; Jamaican champion 1999-2000, 2002, 2005.
Progress at 400mh: 1996- 50.52, 1997- 49.71, 1998- 49.39, 1999- 48.82, 2000- 48.56, 2002- 48.57, 2003- 48.05, 2004- 48.06, 2005- 48.09, 2006- 48.57, 2007- 49.28. pbs: 400m 46.97 '99, 300mh 35.22 '02.
Lived in USA from age 13; in Britain from 2001.

Maurice WIGNALL b. 17 Apr 1976 St Andrew 1.86m 75kg. Was at George Mason University, USA. Graphic designer.
At 110mh (LJ): OG: '04- 4; WCh: '97- (nj), '01- h, '05- 7, '07- 8; CG: '02- 3, '06- 1; PAm: '99- 7 (6); WUG: '01- 5. At 60mh: WI: '04- 3, '06- 4=. Won JAM 110mh 1997, 1999, 2001-05, 2007; LJ 1999.
Four Jamaican records 110mh 2002-04.
Progress at 110mh: 1993- 14.56, 1994- 14.59/14.2, 1995- 13.93, 1996- 13.98, 1997- 13.75, 1999- 13.66, 2000- 13.71, 2001- 13.70, 2002- 13.49, 2003- 13.28, 2004- 13.17, 2005- 13.20, 2006- 13.26, 2007- 13.29. pbs: 60mh 7.48i '04, LJ 8.09 '97.
Former long jumper (won NCAA indoor 1999).

Christopher WILLIAMS b. 15 Mar 1972 Manchester 1.78m 68kg. Went to Riverside CC, USA.
At 200m/4x400mR (100m): OG: '00- sf/3R (qf, 4 4x100m), '04- sf; WCh: '99- sf, '01- 2/3R, '03- qf, '05- sf, '07- 7; CG: '02- dq h/2R, '06- 3/1R; PAm: '99- 7 (3 4x100m), '03- 2; WI: '01- 4; WCp: '02- 2R. Won CAC 1999, JAM 100m 2001, 200m 1999-2001, 2004.
Progress at 200m: 1996- 20.69, 1997- 20.95, 1999- 20.48/20.40w, 2000- 20.02, 2001- 20.11, 2002- 20.84, 2003- 20.54, 2004- 20.34, 2005- 20.19, 2006- 20.19, 2007- 20.17. pbs: 60m 6.61i '01, 100m 10.05 '00, 10.03w '07; 400m 46.30 '96.

Women

Aleen BAILEY b. 25 Nov 1980 St Mary 1.70m 64g. Student at University of South Carolina.
At 100m/(200m)/4x100mR: OG: '04- 5/4/1R; WCh: '01- (h), '03- 6, '05- sf/2R, '07- (6); WJ: '96- 2R, '98- 3R; PAmJ: '99- 1/1, '07- (5)/1R; WCp: '06- 1R. Won NCAA 100m & 200m (and indoor 200m) 2003, Jamaican 100m & 200m 2001, 2003.
Progresion at 100m, 200m: 1995- 12.10, 1996- 11.67, 23.99; 1997- 11.60/11.55w, 23.65; 1998- 11.37, 23.96/23.16w, 1999- 11.41, 23.37; 2000- 11.47/11.38w, 23.45/22.86w; 2001- 11.14, 22.59; 2002- 11.33, 22.54; 2003- 11.07, 22.59; 2004- 11.04, 22.33; 2005- 11.07, 23.00/22.75w; 2006- 11.27, 23.70; 2007- 11.17, 22.60. pbs: 60m 7.23i '03, 400m 54.43 '07.

Sheri-Ann BROOKS b. 11 Feb 1983 Manchester 1.70m 64kg. Zion TC. Florida International University.
At (100m)/200m/4x100mR: WCh: '05- h, '07- (sf)/2R; CG: '06- 1/5/1R; PAm: '07- 2/1R. Won NCAA 200m 2005.
Progress at 100m, 200m: 2003- 11.85, 2004- 11.52, 24.11/23.98w; 2005- 11.24/11.23w, 22.80/22.74w; 2006- 11.19, 22.81; 2007- 11.05, 22.78. pbs: 55m 6.75i '05, 60m 7.29i '05, 400m 53.95 '06.

Veronica CAMPBELL-BROWN b. 15 May 1982 Trelawny 1.63m 61kg. Was at University of Arkansas, USA.
At 100m/(200m)/4x100mR: OG: '00- 2R, '04- 3/1/1R; WCh: '05- 2/4/2R, '07- 1/2/2R; CG: '02- 2/2R, '06- (2); WJ: '98- qf, '00- 1/2R (1); WY: '99- 1/1R. Won WAF 100m 2004-05, 200m 2004, CAC-J 100m 2000, JAM 100m 2002, 2004-05, 2007; 200m 2004-05, 2007.
CAC junior 100m record 2000.
Progress at 100m, 200m: 1999- 11.49, 23.73; 2000- 11.12/11.1, 22.87; 2001- 11.13/22.92; 2002- 11.00, 22.39; 2004- 10.91, 22.05; 2005- 10.85, 22.35/22.29w; 2006- 10.99, 22.51; 2007- 10.89, 22.34. pbs: 60m 7.04i '06, 400m 52.24i '05.
In 2000 became the first woman to become World Junior champion at both 100m and 200m. Unbeaten at 200m in 28 finals (42 races in all) from 11 March 2000 to 22 July 2005 (lost to Alyson Felix). Married Omar Brown (1 CG 200m 2006) on 3 Nov 2007.

Vonette DIXON b. 26 Nov 1975 Hanover 1.70m 62kg. Graduate of Auburn University, USA.
At 100mh: WCh: '01- 8, '03- 9, '05- sf, '07- 7; CG: '02- 2.
Progress at 100mh: 1994- 15.13/15.0, 1995- 14.29, 1996- 13.52/13.30w, 1997- 13.26, 1998- 13.52, 1999- 13.40, 2000- 12.90, 2001- 12.83, 2002- 12.83/12.82w, 2003- 12.72, 2004- 12.76, 2005- 12.67, 2006- 12.82/12.80w, 2007- 12.64. pbs: 55m 6.79i '00, 60m 7.33i '00, 100m 11.47/11.40w '00, 200m 23.57/23.48w '00, 50mh 6.85i '02, 55mh 7.55i '00, 60mh 7.92i '02.

Delloreen ENNIS-LONDON b. 5 Mar 1975 St Catherine 1.78m 67kg. née Ennis. Business management graduate of Abilene Christian University, USA.
At 100mh: OG: '00- 4, '04- sf; WCh: '99- 7, '05- 2, '07- 3; CG: '06- 3; WJ: '92- sf; PAm: '07- 1. 3rd GP 2000. JAM champion 1999-2001, 2004, 2005 (tie), 2007; CAC 2003. CAC 100mh record 2000.
Progress at 100mh: 1992- 13.81, 1994- 13.96, 1996- 13.53/13.30w, 1997- 13.60/13.51w, 1998- 13.27/13.1w, 1999- 12.71/12.60w, 2000- 12.52, 2001- 12.57, 2003- 12.70, 2004- 12.51, 2005- 12.57, 2006- 12.74, 2007- 12.50. pbs: 60m 7.39i '99, 100m 11.50 '99, 11.30w '04; 55mh 7.56i '99, 60mh 7.92i '04, 400mh 62.75 '98.
Coached by her husband Lincoln London.

Brigitte FOSTER-HYLTON b. 7 Nov 1974 St Elizabeth 1.70m 62kg. Was at Southwest Texas State University, USA.
At 100mh: OG: '00- 8, '04- sf; WCh: '01- sf, '03- 2, '05- 3; CG: '98- 5/2R, '02- dns, '06- 1; PAm: '03- 1; WCp: '02- 2, '06- 1; 2nd GP 2002. JAM champion 2002-03, 2005 (tie), 2006. At 60mh: WI: '03- 6. Three CAC 100mh records 2002-03.
Progress at 100mh: 1993- 14.22, 1996- 13.34, 1998- 13.19/13.13w/12.9w, 1999- 13.35, 2000- 12.70, 2001- 12.70, 2002- 12.49, 2003- 12.45, 2004- 12.56, 2005- 12.55, 2006- 12.49, 2007- 12.71. pbs: 60m 7.32i '04; 100m 11.17 '03, 200m 23.51/23.35w '98, 400m 53.81 '07, 60mh 7.96i '03, 400mh 64.62 '93.

Lacena GOLDING-CLARKE b. 20 Mar 1975 Clarendon 1.68m 57kg. Was at Auburn University, USA.
At 100mh/4x100mR: OG: '04- 5; WCh: '03- 8, '07- sf; CG: '02- 1, '06- 4; PAm: '03- 3/3R. At LJ: OG: '96- dnq; WCh: '95- dnq 20, '97- dnq 18; CG: '98- 4; WJ: '92- 6, '94- 8; CAG: '98- 1; CAC: '99- 1; PAm-J '93- 1. At 60mh: WI: '01-03-04-06-08: 8/4/6/6/4; Won JAM LJ 1994, 1996-9.
Progress at 100mh: 1994- 13.98, 1995- 13.22/13.19w/13.0w, 1997- 13.05/13.04w, 1998- 13.00, 1999- 13.11, 2000- 12.93, 2001- 12.97, 2002- 12.74/12.70w, 2003- 12.72, 2004- 12.69, 2005- 12.68/12.67w, 2006- 12.87/12.84w, 2007- 12.85. pbs: 55m 6.89i '97, 100m 11.69/11.64w '97, 200m 23.99 '98, 50mh 6.83i '00, 55mh 7.37Ai '98, 60mh 7.83i '06, HJ 1.71i '94, 1.70 '95; LJ 6.87 '98, TJ 12.03 '98, JT 41.02 '95, Hep 5750 '98.
Married to 400m runner **Davian Clarke** (b. 30

Apr 1976) pb 44.83 '04, five World, three WI, two CG, one Olympic 4x400 medals.

Korene HINDS b. 18 Jan 1976 St. Catherine 1.63m 54kg. Post-graduate degree in education from Kansas State University, USA.
At 3000mSt: WCh: '05- 4, '07- h; WCp: '06- 6. JAM champion 2007.
Five CAC 3000m steeplechase records 2002-05.
Progress at 3000mSt: 2002- 9:58.9, 2003- 10:00.44, 2004- 9:50.64, 2005- 9:30.12, 2006- 9:41.01, 2007- 9:28.86. pbs: 600m 1:29.43 '98, 800m 2:03.62 '07, 1500m 4:17.00 '02, 1M 4:40.78i '01, 3000m 9:08.55i '03, 9:10.10 '00.
Ran in 1991 World CC as a 15 year-old. First ran the steeplechase in 2002. Lives in Albuquerque.

Sherone SIMPSON b. 12 Aug 1984 Manchester, Jamaica 1.73m 58kg. Kingston University of Technology.
At 100m/(200m)/4x100mR: OG: '04- 6/1R; WCh: '05- 6/2R; CG: '06- (1)/1R; WJ: '02- 1R; PAm-J: '03- 2; WCp: '06- 1/1R. Won WAF 100m 2006, JAM 100m & 200m 2006.
Progress at 100m, 200m: 2000- 12.54, 2001- 12.17, 25.01; 2002- 11.60, 24.21; 2003- 11.37/11.1, 23.60; 2004- 11.01, 22.70; 2005- 10.97, 22.54; 2006- 10.82, 22.00; 2007- 11.43, 22.76. pbs: 400m 51.25 '08, 100mh 14.10 '02.

Kenia SINCLAIR b. 14 July 1980 St Catherine 1.67m 54kg. Was at Seton Hall University, USA.
At 800m: WCh: '05/07- sf; CG: '06- 2; WI: '06- 2. Won JAM 800m 2005-07, 1500m 2006-07.
Five Jamaican 800m records 2005-06.
Progress at 800m: 2002- 2:05.26i/2:07.39, 2003- 2:03.21, 2005- 1:58.88, 2006- 1:57.88, 2007- 1:58.61. pbs: 1000m 2:37.37 '05, 1500m 4:05.56 '07, 1M 4:32.33i '05, 3000m 9:52.71i '02.
Based in Gainesville, Florida.

Trecia-Kaye SMITH b. 5 Nov 1975 Westmoreland 1.85m 77kg. Graduated in physiotherapy from University of Pittsburgh, USA.
At TJ: OG: '04- 4; WCh: '97- dnq 31, '01- 8, '05- 1, '07- dnq 24; CG: '02- 3, '06- 1; WI: '04- 4, '06- 4; WCp: '02- 4, '06- 4. At LJ: WJ: '94- 11. Won NCAA LJ 1997, 1999; TJ 1998; JAM TJ 2001-02, 2004-05, 2007.
Commonwealth triple jump record 2004. Six Jamaican records 1997-2004.
Progress at TJ: 1996- 13.55/13.58w, 1997- 14.22, 1998- 14.05i/13.98, 1999-14.02i/13.91/13.95w, 2000- 13.76/13.92w, 2001- 14.12A/14.88w, 2002- 14.32, 2003- 13.96i/13.55/13.89w, 2004- 15.16, 2005- 15.11, 2006- 15.05, 2007- 14.35. pbs: 200m 24.39 '97, 60mh 8.10i '98, 100mh 14.48 '97, 14.36w '99; HJ 1.81 '97, LJ 6.74 '01, 6.84w '97; SP 14.74 '98, DT 44.20 '98, JT 44.52 '98, Pen 4080i '99, Hep 5931 '97.
Set national TJ records of 14.57 in qualifying and 14.70 and 14.71 in final at 2004 World Indoors and outdoors improved from 14.34 to 15.16.

Kerron STEWART b. 16 Apr 1984 St. Catherine 1.75m 61kg. Adult education student at Auburn University, USA.
At 100m/(200m)/4x100mR: WCh: '07- 7/2R; WJ: '02- 4/1R; WY: '01- 2/2R. Won NCAA 200m 2007, indoor 60m & 200m 2007.
Progress at 100m, 200m: 2000- 11.89, 24.09w; 2001- 11.70, 23.90; 2002- 11.46, 24.21; 2003- 11.34, 23.50; 2004- 11.40, 23.63i/23.66; 2005- 11.63, 23.77i/24.22/23.46w; 2006- 11.03, 22.65; 2007- 11.03, 22.41. pbs: 55m 6.71i '06, 60m 7.14i '07, 400m 52.08 '08.

Melaine WALKER b. 1 Jan 1983 1.65m 53kg. Social work graduate of University of Texas, USA.
At 400mh/4x400mR: WCh: '07- sf; CG: '02- 4; WJ: '00- 3/2R, '02- 2 (5 100mh); CAG: '06- 3/2R; Jamaican champion 2006-07. At 200m: WJ: '98- 5/3 4x100R; WY: '99-2.
Progress at 400mh: 1999- 58.99, 2000- 56.96, 2001- 55.62, 2002- 55.84, 2003- 57.24, 2004- 56.62, 2005- 55.09, 2006- 54.87, 2007- 54.14. pbs: 60m 7.40i '05, 100m 11.63 '99, 200m 23.51 '99, 400m 51.61 '08, 60mh 8.05i '06, 100mh 12.75 '06.

Novlene WILLIAMS b. 26 Apr 1982 St Ann 1.70m 57kg. Studied recreation at University of Florida, USA.
At 400m/4x400mR: OG: '04- sf/3R; WCh: '05- 2R, '07- 3/2R; CG: '06- 3; PAm: '03- 6/2R; WI: '06- 5; WCp: '06- 3/1R. Won JAM 400m 2006-07.
Progress at 400m: 1999- 55.62, 2000- 53.90, 2001- 54.99, 2002- 52.05, 2003- 51.93, 2004- 50.59, 2005- 51.09, 2006- 49.53, 2007- 49.66. pbs: 200m 23.39 '07, 500m 1:11.83i '03.
Younger sister Clora Williams (b. 26.11.83) has 400m pb 51.06 '06, won NCAA 2006.

Shericka WILLIAMS b. 17 Sep 1985 1.70m 64kg. Kingston University of Technology.
At 400m/4x400mR: WCh: '05- sf/2R, '07- sf/2R; CG: '06- 5; WCp: '06- 1R; won JAM 400m 2005.
Progress at 400m: 2003- 55.44, 2004- 53.52, 2005- 50.97, 2006- 50.24, 2007- 50.37. pbs: 100m 11.34 '07, 200m 22.55 '06.

Nickiesha WILSON b. 28 Jul 1986 Kingston 1.73m 64kg. Student at Louisiana State University, USA.
At 400mh: WCh: '07- 4; PAm: '07- 2; PAm-J: '05-1.
Progress at 400mh: 2005- 57.38, 2006- 56.77, 2007- 53.97. pbs: 200m 24.51i '06, 400m 53.77i '07, 60mh 8.01i '07, 100mh 12.93 '07.

JAPAN

Governing body: Nippon Rikujo-Kyogi Renmei, 1-1-1 Jinnan, Shibuya-Ku, Tokyo 150-8050. Founded 1911.

National Championships first held in 1914 (men), 1925 (women). **2007 Champions**: **Men**: 100m: Naoki Tsukahara 10.34, 200m: Shingo Suetsugu 20.20, 400m: Yuzo Kanemaru 45.64, 800m: Masato Yokota 1:49.51, 1500m: Fumikazu Kobayashi , 5000m/10,000m: Takayuki Matsumiya

13:52.64/28:56.27, Mar: Mitsuru Kubota 2:12:50, 3000mSt: Yoshitaka Iwamizu 8:32.75, 110mh: Masato Naito 13.55, 400mh: Dai Tamesue 48.87, HJ: Naoyuki Daigo 2.21, PV: Daichi Sawano 5.65, LJ: Daisuke Arakawa 7.90, TJ: Takanori Sugibayashi 16.90, SP: Satoshi Hatase 18.47, DT: Shigeo Hatakeyama 56.50, HT: Koji Murofushi 79.24, JT: Yukifumi Murakami 79.85, Dec: Hiromasa Tanaka 7550, 20kW: Koichiro Morioka 1:23:58, 50kW: Yuki Yamazaki 3:47:40. **Women**: 100m: Momoko Takahashi 11.61, 200m: Sakie Nobuoka 23.79, 400m: Asami Tanno 52.48, 800m: Ayako Jinouchi 2:05.11, 1500m: Mika Yoshikawa 4:16.80, 5000m/10,000m: Kayoko Fukushi 15:27.41/32:13.58, Mar: Yasuko Hashimoto 2:28:49, 3000mSt: Minori Hayakari 9:46.59, 100mh: Mami Ishino 13.31, 400mh: Satomi Kubokura 56.09, HJ: Miyuki Aoyama 1.90, PV: Takayo Kondo 4.30, LJ: Kumiko Ikeda 6.59, TJ: Fumiyo Yoshida 13.16, SP: Yoko Toyonaga 15.67, DT: Yuka Murofushi 53.81, HT: Masumi Aya 63.43, JT: Yuki Ebihara 57.19, Hep: Yuki Nakata 5544, 20kW: Masumi Fuchise 1:29:36.

Koji MUROFUSHI b. 8 Oct 1974 Shizuoka 1.87m 100kg. Graduate of Chukyo University. Mizuno.
At HT: OG: '00- 9, '04- 1; WCh: '95- dnq, '97- 10, '99- dnq 14, '01- 2, '03- 3, '07- 6; WJ: '92- 8; AsiG: '94- 2, '98- 1, '02- 1; AsiC: '93-5-8-02: 2/2,/2/1; WCp: '02- 2 (9 DT), '06- 1. Won GWG 2001, GP 2002 (2nd 2000), WAF 2006. Won E.Asian 1997, 2001; Japanese 1995-2007.
18 Japanese hammer records 1998-2003, Asian records 2001 & 2003.
Progress at HT: 1991- 61.76, 1992- 66.30, 1993- 68.00, 1994- 69.54, 1995- 72.32, 1996- 73.82, 1997- 75.72, 1998- 78.57, 1999- 79.17, 2000- 81.08, 2001- 83.47, 2002- 83.33, 2003- 84.86, 2004- 83.15, 2005- 76.47, 8006- 82.01, 2007- 82.62. pb DT 44.64 '96.
His father Shigenobu Murofushi won a record five Asian Games gold medals 1970-86 and held the Japanese hammer record with 75.96 (Los Angeles 1984) until Koji broke it for the first time on 26 Apr 1998. His mother was the 1968 European Junior javelin champion, Serafina Moritz (Romania).
His sister **Yuka** (b. 11 Feb 77) holds Japanese records: DT 58.62 '07 and HT 67.77 '04; 6th WJ DT 1996.

Kenji NARISAKO b. 25 Jul 1984 1.85m 74kg. Student at University of Tsukuba.
At 400mh: WCh: '05/07- sf; WJ: '02- h; WY: '01- 3; AsiG: '06- 1; WUG: '05- 1. JPN champion 2006.
Progress at 400mh: 2001- 51.33, 2002- 51.49, 2003- 50.53, 2004- 48.54, 2005- 48.09, 2006- 47.93, 2007- 48.44. pbs: 400m 46.02 '05, 110mh 14.77/14.62w '02.

Atsushi SATO b. 8 May 1978 1.70m 55kg.
At Mar: WCh: '03- 10. World HMar: '02- 8, '07- 9. At 10,000m: AsiG: '02- 6.
Japanese half marathon record 2007.
Progress at Mar: 2000- 2:09:50, 2001- 2:14:41, 2003- 2:08:50, 2004- 2:08:36, 2005- 2:19:44, 2007- 2:07:13. pbs: 3000m 8:00.83 '04, 5000m 13:33.62 '04, 10,000m 27:56.86 '04, HMar 60:25 '07.
Married (2007) **Miho Sugimori** (b. 14 Apr 1978) 800m 2:00.45 '05 (JPN record), 100m 2:41.08 '02 (Asian record), 1500m 4:09.30 '05.

Daichi SAWANO b. 16 Sep 1980 1.82m 70kg. Nishi Sports. Was at Nihon University.
At PV: OG: '04- 13=; WCh: '03- dns, '05- 8, '07- dnq; AsiG: '06- 1; AsiC: '02- 1, '05- 1; WCp: '02- nh, '06- 2. Won Asian indoor 2008, JPN champion 1999-2000, 2003-04, 2006.
Three Japanese pole vault records 2003-05.
Progress at PV: 1994- 3.80, 1995- 4.30, 19960 4.80, 1997- 5.25, 1998- 5.40, 1999- 5.50, 2000- 5.45, 2001- 5.52, 2002- 5.51, 2003- 5.75, 2004- 5.80, 2005- 5.83, 2006- 5.75, 2007- 5.75.

Shingo SUETSUGU b. 2 Jun 1980 Kumamoto pref. 1.78m 68kg. Mizuno. Studied at Tokai University.
At 200m/4x100mR (100m): OG: '00- sf, '04- (qf)/4R; WCh: '01- sf, '03- 3, '05- sf, '07- qf; AsiG: '02- 1/2R. '06- 1/2R; AsiC: '05- (2); WCp: '06- 3. Won E.Asian 2001, JPN 100m 2003-04; 200m 2001, 2003, 2006-07.
Asian 200m record 2003.
Progress at 100m, 200m: 1996- 10.63, 21.62; 1997- 10.52, 21.37; 1998- 10.37, 21.08; 1999- 10.46, 21.36; 2000- 10.19, 20.26; 2001- 10.31, 20.30; 2002- 10.05, 20.37; 2003- 10.03, 20.03; 2004- 10.10, 2005- 10.15, 20.55; 2006- 10.26/10.12w, 20.25; 2007- 10.23, 20.20. pb 400m 45.99 '02.

Dai TAMESUE b. 3 May 1978 Hiroshima 1.70m 67kg. Graduate of Hosei University.
At 400mh: OG: '00- h, '04- sf; WCh: '01- 3, '03- sf, '05- 3, '07- h; AsiG: '02- 3. Japanese champion 2001-05, 2007. At 400m: WJ: '96- 4/2R.
Two Japanese records 2001.
Progress at 400mh: 1996- 49.09, 1998- 49.19, 1999- 49.12, 2000- 48.47, 2001- 47.89, 2002- 48.69, 2003- 48.94, 2004- 48.46, 2005- 48.10, 2007- 48.73. pbs: 200m 20.97 '06, 400m 45.94 '96.
One of the shortest ever top-class 400m hurdlers. Has set national records at each age group.

Women

Kayoko FUKUSHI b. 25 Mar 1982 Itayanagi, Aiomori pref. 1.61m 45kg. Wacoal.
At 5000m/(10,000m): OG: '04- (26); WCh: '03- h/11, '05- 12/11, '07- 14/10; WJ: '00- 4; AsiG: '02- 2/2. '06- (1); WCp: '06- 3 (5 3000m). World 20km: '06- 6; CC: '02- 15, '06- 6. Won JPN 5000m 2002, 2004-07; 10,000m 2002-07.
World 15km record & Asian 20km & HMar records 2006, Japanese records: 3000m 2002, 5000m (4) 2002-05.
Progress at 5000m, 10,000m: 1998- 16:56.35, 1999- 16:38.69, 35:37.54; 2000- 15:29.70, 2001- 15:10.23, 31:42.05; 2002- 14:55.19, 30:51.81; 2003- 15:09.02, 31:10.57; 2004- 14:57.73, 31:05.68; 2005-

14:53.22, 31:03.75; 2006- 15:03.17, 30:57.90; 2007- 15:05.73, 32:13.58. pbs: 3000m 8:44.40 '02, 15km 46:55 '06, 20km 63:41 '06, HMar 67:26 '06.
Set Japanese junior records at 3000m, 5000m and 10,000m in 2001.

Yumiko HARA b. 9 Jan 1982 Ashikaga, Tochigi pref. 1.63m 43kg. Kyocera.
At Mar: WCh: '05- 6, '07- 18.
Progress at 10,000m, Mar: 1999- 33:13.99, 2000- 34:02.90, 2001- 31:48.50, 2002- 32:31.59, 2003- 31:51.80, 2004- 32:15.86, 2005- 31:24.33, 2:24:19; 2007- 2:23:48. pbs: 5000m 15:38.81 '04, HMar 69:28 '02.
Won at Nagoya in 2005 on marathon debut and at Osaka in 2007.

Kumiko IKEDA b. 10 Jan 1981 Sakata, Yamagata pref. 1.66m 54kg. Suzuki Motor. Fukushima University.
At LJ: WCh: '01- 11, '03/05/07- dnq 22/15/25; WJ: '00- 3 (sf 100mh); AsiG: '02- 7, '06- 1; AsiC: '02- 5; WUG: '01- 3. Won Japanese 100mh 2001, 2004-05; LJ 2003, 2005-07; E.Asian LJ 2005.
Japanese long jump record 2006.
Progress at LJ: 1992- 5,18, 1993- 5.97, 1994- 6.04, 1995- 6.19, 1996- 5.85, 1997- 6.07, 1998- 6.14, 1999- 6.10, 2000- 6.43, 2001- 6.78, 2002- 6.41, 2003- 6.64, 2004- 6.65, 2005- 6.69, 2006- 6.86, 2007- 6.73. pbs: 60mh 8.37i '04, 100mh 13.04/12.90w '06.

Mizuki NOGUCHI b. 3 Jul 1978 Kanagawa 1.50m 41kg. Globary.
At 10,000m: WCh: '01- 13. At Mar: OG: '04- 1; WCh: '03- 2. World HMar: '99-00-01-02: 2/4/4/9. Won Asian CC 1999, E.Asian HMar 2001, JPN Mar 2003.
Asian marathon record 2005. World road records 25km 1:22:12 & 30km 1:38:48 in 2005 Berlin Marathon.
Progress at 10,000m, Mar: 1999- 33:09.98, 2000- 32:05.23, 2001- 31:51.13, 2002- 31:50.18, 2:25:35; 2003- 31:59.28, 2:21:18; 2004- 31:21.03, 2:26:20, 2005- 31:44.29, 2:19:12; 2006- 31:50.13, 2007- 2:21:37. pbs: 3000m 9:24.51 '98, 5000m 15:34.36 '99, Rd: 15km 48:11 '01, HMar 67:43 '06, 30km 1:39:09 '04.
Formerly excelling at half marathon, she won the Nagoya marathon on debut in 2002 and again at Osaka in January 2003, at the Olympics in 2004, in Berlin 2005 and Tokyo 2007.

Mari OZAKI b. 16 Jul 1975 Hirakata, Osaka pref. 1.62m 48kg. Noritz.
At 10,000m: WCh: '01- 19, '05- 15. At Mar: WCh: '07- 14. Won JPN 5000m 2003.
Progress at 10,000m, Mar: 1999- 31:58.05, 2000- 32:03.00, 2001- 31:50.56, 2002- 32:44.9, 2003- 31:46.57, 2:23:30, 2004- 31:47.47, 2005- 31:34.15, 2:23:59; 2006- 31:45.48, 2007- 2:24:39. pbs: 3000m 8:59.4 '00, 5000m 15:12.76 '03, HMar 69:33 '02.
Ran 2:23:30 for fifth on debut at Osaka 2003 (fifth fastest ever debut) and was second at Osaka in 2005 and 2007.

Yoko SHIBUI b. 14 Mar 1979 Kuroiso, Tochigi pref. 1.65m 46kg. Mitsui-Sumitomo.
At Mar: WCh: '01- 4. At 10,000m: WCh: '03- 14. Japanese records 10,000m 2002, Marathon 2004.
Progress at 10,000m, Mar: 1997- 33:53.20, 1999- 32:43.02, 2000- 31:48.89, 2001- 31:48.73, 2:23:11; 2002- 30:48.89, 2:21:22; 2003- 31:42.01, 2004- 32:17.72, 2:19:41; 2005- 32:34.11, 2:27:40; 2006- 32:39.42, 2:23:58; 2007- 31:48.87, 2:34:15. pbs: 3000m 9:11.37 '96, 5000m 15:18.92 '02, 15km 49:07 '02, HMar 69:20+ '02.
Ran the fastest ever debut marathon by a woman with 2:23:11 to win at Osaka in January 2001. Her breakthrough came with a 31:59 ekiden road relay leg in January 2000 and she had shown brilliant form with 10km legs of 31:09 and 31:11 in November 2000. She was third in the 2002 Chicago Marathon and returned from injuries to win the Berlin Marathon in 2004 in 2:19:41. 2nd Nagoya 2006.

Reiko TOSA b. 11 Jun 1976 Matsumaya, Ehime pref. 1.67m 45kg. Mitsui Sumitomo. Graduate of Matsuyama University.
At Mar: OG: '04- 5; WCh: '01- 2, '07- 3. Japanese champion 2004. At HMar: WCh: '99- 5.
Progress at Mar: 1998- 2:54:57, 2000- 2:24:36, 2001- 2:26:06, 2002- 2:22:46, 2004- 2:23:57, 2006- 2:24:11, 2007- 2:30:55. pbs: 3000m 9:43.00 '98, 5000m 15:37.08 '00, 10,000m 32:07.66 '05, HMar 69:36 '99.
Won Nagoya Marathon 2004 and Tokyo 2006, 2nd Nagoya (2:24:36) and Tokyo (2:24:47) 2000; 3rd Boston 2006, 4th London 2002.

KAZAKHSTAN

Governing body: Athletic Federation of the Republic of Kazakhstan, Abai Street 48, 480072 Almaty. Founded 1959.
2007 National Champions: Men: 100m: Grigoriy Volodin 10.73, 200m: Rinat Galiyev 21.75, 400m: Sergey Zankov 47.58, 800m/1500m: Mikhail Kolganov 1:52.05/3:56.28, 5000m/3000mSt: Artyom Kosinov 14:51.89/9:05.78, 10,000m: Takhir Mamashayev 31:40.89, 110mh: Nazar Mukhamedzhan 14.25, 400mh: Yevgeniy Meleshenko 51.71, HJ: Sergey Zasimovich 2.24, PV: Aleksandr Akhmedov 5.10, LJ: Konstantin Safronov 7.45, TJ: Yevgeniy Ektov 16.26, SP: Sergey Rubtsov 17.44, DT: Yevgeniy Buchatskiy 53.56, HT: ? 51.05, JT: Yegor Stepanov 60.64, Dec: Pavel Dubitskiy 7194, 20,000mW: Rustam Kuvatov 1:29:03.4. **Women**: 100m/100mh: Anastasiya Vinogradova 11.78/13.31, 200m: Tatyana Azarova 23.63, 400m: Olga Tereshkova 53.39, 800m: Viktoriya Yalovtseva 2:08.09, 1500m: Svetlana Lukasheva 4:29.34, 5000m/10,000m: Irina Smolnikova 17:28.61/ 36:13.06, 3000m St: Marina Podkorytova/89 10:59.52, 400mh: Tatyana Azarova 56.72, HJ: Anna Ustinova 1.92, PV: Yelena Klimova 3.70, LJ/TJ: Olga Rypakova 6.57w/14.05, SP: Iolanta Ulyeva 15.98, DT: Valeriya Sychkova 44.34, HT: Tatyana Bem

50.63, Hep: Irina Naumenko 6069, 20000mW: Svetlana Tolstaya 1:40:39.9.

Dmitriy KARPOV b. 23 Jul 1981 Karaganda 1.98m 98kg.
At Dec: OG: '04- 3; WCh: '03- 3, '05- dnf, '07- 3; WJ: '00- 4; AsiG: '02- 2, '06- 1; won E.Asian 2001. At Hep: WI: '04- 4, '08- 3. At 110mh: AsiC: '02- 5. Won KAZ 200m 2003, Dec 1999.
Two Asian decathlon records 2004, indoor heptathlon 2004 & 2007.
Progress at Dec: 1999- 7105, 2000- 7620, 2001- 7567, 2002- 7995, 2003- 8374, 2004- 8725, 2006- 8438, 2007- 8586. pbs: 60m 7.04i '04, 100m 10.69 '06, 10.50w '04; 200m 21.65 '03, 400m 46.81 '04, 1000m 2:42.34i '04, 1500m 4:32.34 '06, 60mh 7.87i '04, 110mh 13.93 '02, HJ 2.12 '03, PV 5.20i '08, 5.00 '07; LJ 8.05 '02, SP 16.47 '06, DT 52.80 '04, JT 60.31 '06, Hep 6229i '08.
Set national record of 8253 to win at Desenzano in 2003 from previous best of 7995. Then three pbs en route to World bronze and another KAZ record with 8374. In 2004 he was third at Götzis with 8512 and set three pbs in his 8725 for Olympic bronze. Did not compete in 2005 apart from two false starts in World Champs decathlon 100m, but won at Ratingen and Talence after 2nd Götzis in 2006 to win the IAAF Combined Events Challenge.

Women

Marina AITOVA b. 13 Sep 1982 1.80m 60kg. née Korzhova.
At HJ: OG: '04- dnq 31=; WCh: '03- dnq 22=, '07- 7=; AsiG: '02- 2, '06- 1; AsiC: '00- 2, '02- 3; WJ: '00- 9=; WY: '99- 4; WI: '08- 5; WUG: '07- 1; WCp: '06- 3. Won Asi-J 2001, Af-AsG & C.Asian G 2003, Asian indoor 2006, KAZ 2002-04.
Progress at HJ: 1999- 1.86, 2000- 1.90, 2001- 1.86i/1.85, 2002- 1.94, 2003- 1.89, 2004- 1.91i/1.89, 2005- 1.75, 2006- 1.95, 2007- 1.96, 2008- 1.96i. pb LJ 6.00 '01.

Olga RYPAKOVA b. 30 Nov 1984 Kamenogorsk 1.78m 53kg. née Alekseyeva.
At TJ/(LJ): WCh: '07- 11; WJ: '00- (dnq 23); AsiG: '06- (3); AsiC: '07- 1/1; WUG: '07- (1); WCp: '06- (8). At Hep: WJ: '02- 2; WY: '01- 4; AsiG: ''06- 2; won C.Asian 2003. At Pen: WI: '06- 7. Won KAZ LJ 2005, 2008; TJ 2008, Hep 2006.
Asian indoor TJ record 2008.
Progress at LJ, TJ: 2000- 6.23, 2001- 6.00, 2002- 6.26, 2003- 6.34i/6.14, 2004- 6.53i, 2005- 6.60, 2006- 6.63, 2007- 6.85, 14.69; 2008- 14.58i. pbs: 200m 24.83 '02, 800m 2:20.12 '02, 60mh 8.67i '06, 100mh 14.02 '06, HJ 1.92 '06, SP 13.04 '06, JT 41.60 '03, Hep 6122 '06.

KENYA

Governing body: Kenya Amateur Athletic Association, PO Box 46722, 00100 Nairobi. Founded 1951.
2007 National Champions: **Men**: 100m: Tom Musinde 10.49, 200m/400m: Ezra Sambu 21.68/45.73, 800m: Justus Koech 1:45.7, 1500m: Asbel Kiprop 3:43.0, 5000m: Thomas Longosiwa 13:49.6, 10,000m: Joseph Birech 28:09.4, 3000mSt: Ezekiel Kemboi 8:26.2, 400mh: Julius Bungei 50.42, HJ: Silas Katonen 2.15, PV: Wesley Cheruiyot 4.10, LJ/TJ: Paul Koech 7.63/15.95, SP: Gideon Mengich 15.60, DT: Joshua Pondo 48.80, HT: Morris Omoro 52.00, JT: Sammy Keskeny 69.40, 20kW: David Kimutai 1:23:06. **Women**: 100m/200m: Joyce Zakary 11.92/23.60, 400m: Elizabeth Muthoka 53.04, 800m: Charity Wandia 2:04.1, 1500m: Florence Kiplagat 4:09.0, 5000m: Sylvia Kibet 16:05.67, 10,000m: Edith Masai 33:25.2, 3000mSt: Ruth Bosiberi 9:50.1, 100mh/LJ: Florence Wasike 14.67/5.67, 400mh: Callen Nyakawa 58.24, HJ/TJ: Janeth Chepchumba 1.70/12.37, PV: Veronica Chebet 2.40, SP: Priscila Isiao 12.95, DT/JT: Cecilia Kiplagat 42.23/51.71, HT: Rebecca Kerubo 40.84, 20kW: Mary Njoki 1:46:32.

Yusuf Kibet **BIWOTT** b. 12 Nov 1986 1.75m 64kg.
World 4k CC: 06- 20.
Progress at 5000m: 2006- 13:08.13, 2007- 12:58.49. pbs: 1500m 3:34.04 '06, 2000m 4:59.48i '07, 5:01.1+ '06; 3000m 7:33.39 '07.

Wilfred Kipkemboi **BUNGEI** b. 24 Jul 1980 Kabirisang, near Kapsabet 1.72m 60kg. Nandi (Kalenjin).
At 800m: OG: '04- 5; WCh: '01- 2, '05- 4, '07- 5; WJ: '98- 2; WI: '03- 3, '06- 1. Won WAF 2003, 2005. World record 4x800m 2006.
Progress at 800m: 1998- 1:47.21, 1999- 1:45.14, 2000- 1:44.23, 2001- 1:42.96, 2002- 1:42.34, 2003- 1:42.52, 2004- 1:43.06, 2005- 1:43.70, 2006- 1:43.31, 2007- 1:44.14. pbs: 400m 46.99 '06, 600m 1:14.94 '99, 1000m 2:18.60 '02.

Solomon BUSENDICH b. 10 Jan 1984 1.65m 58kg.
At 5000m/10,000m: WJ: '02- 4/3, Af-J: '01- 2/1. World CC: '03- 3J.
Progress at Mar: 2004- 3:38.66, 2005- 3:33.43, 2006- 2:08:52. pbs: 3000m 7:45.07 '03, 5000m 13:12.83 '03, 10,000: 28:05.99 '03, Road: 15km 42:26 '07, HMar 60:13 '07.
Won in Amsterdam in his first completed marathon in 2006.

Abrahim CHEBII Kosgei b. 23 Dec 1979 Kaptabuk, near Kapsowar 1.72m 63kg. Keiyo.
At 5000m: OG: '04- dnf; WCh: '03- 5; Won GP 3000m 2002. World 4k CC: '00-04-05: 5/19/2.
Progress at 5000m, 10,000m: 1999- 13:30.41, 2000- 13:01.9, 2001- 13:12.53, 27:04.20; 2002- 12:58.98, 2003- 12:52.99, 2004- 13:08.01, 2005- 13:22.53, 2006- 13:04.54, 2007- 12:59.63. pbs: 1500m 3:38.5A '04, 1M 3:55.31 '00, 2000m 5:00.5e '06, 3000m 7:33.42 '07, 2M 8:13.28 '08.
Won 2002 GP 3000m final with 50.68 last lap and outsprinted Gebrselassie in Paris and both Geb and Bekele in Rome in 2003 5000m races.

Joshua CHELANGA b. 7 Apr 1973 1.68m 56kg.

At Mar: WCh: '07- 1.
Progress at Mar: 2001- 2:10:29, 2002- 2:12:40, 2004- 2:07:05, 2005- 2:09:10, 2006- 2:18:08, 2007- 2:08:14. pbs: 5000m 13:16.76 '00, 10,000m 27:36.62 '97, HMar 61:01 '02, 3000mSt 8:25.4A '04.
Won Rotterdam and Seoul marathons 2007.

Evans Kiprop CHERUIYOT b. 10 May 1982.
World HMar: '07- 3.
pbs: 5000m 13:38.59 '05. Road: 10km 27:35 '07, 15km 41:34 '07, 20km 56:13 '07, HMar 59:05 '07, Mar 2:09:15 '07.
Won at Milan on marathon debut 2007.

Robert Kipkoech CHERUIYOT b. 26 Sep 1978 Kapsabet 1.86m. Nandi.
Progress at Mar: 2002- 2:08:59, 2003- 2:10:11, 2004- 2:12:14, 2005- 2:11:01, 2006- 2:07:14, 2007- 2:14:13. pbs: 10km 27:57 '04, HMar 59:21 '05.
Great record in Lisbon half marathon: 3-3-2-2-2 in 2003-07, three sub 1 hour. Major marathon wins: Milan 2002, Boston 2003, 2006 and 2007, Chicago 2006.

Augustine Kiprono **CHOGE** b. 21 Jan 1987 Kipsigat, Nandi 1.62m 53kg.
At 5000m: CG: '06- 1; WJ: '04- 1. At 3000m: WY: '03- 1. At 1500m: WCh: '05- h. World CC: '0305-06-08: 4/1J/7 (4k)/12. Won E.African Youth 800m/1500m/3000m 2003, Junior 1500m 2004.
World youth 5000m record 2004, world junior 3000m record 2005.
Progress at 1500m, 5000m: 2003- 3:37.48, 13:20.08; 2004- 3:36.64, 12:57.01; 2005- 3:33.99, 12:53.66; 2006- 3:32.48, 12:56.41; 2007- 3:31.73. pbs: 800m 1:48.4 '04, 1M 3:51.62 '07, 2000m 4:56.30i '07, 3000m 7:28.78 '05, 10,000m 29:06.5A '02.
At 17 in 2004 he become youngest to break 13 minutes for 5000m.

Joseph EBUYA b. 20 Jun 1987 Nyandarua district 1.76m 60kg. South Rift. Turkana.
At 5000m: WCh: '07- h; CG: '06- 4; WJ: '06- 3 (2 10,000m). World CC: '06- 4J, '08- 4.
World junior indoor 2M best 2006.
Progress at 5000m: 2005- 13:03.79, 2006- 12:58.03, 2007- 12:51.00. pbs: 3000m 7:34.66 '07, 2M 8:18.33 '07, 10,000m 28:53.46 '06, 10kmRd 28:49 '06.

Patrick Mutuku **IVUTI** b. 30 Jun 1978 Machakos 1.65m 52kg.
At 10,000m: OG: '00- 4. World CC: '96-7-9-00-01-03: 9J/6J/2/4/7/2.
Progress at 5000m, 10,000m, Mar: 1999- 28:48.0A, 2000- 13:02.68, 27:09.79; 2001- 13:24.48, 28:53.7A; 2002- 13:21.91, 27:05.88; 2004- 28:24.6A, 2005- 2:07:46, 2006- 2:14:23, 2007- 28:13.8A, 2:11:11. pbs: 3000m 7:38.69 '02, HMar 59:31 '00.
Fifth in Chicago marathon on debut in 2005, won in 2007.

Charles KAMATHI b. 18 May 1978 Mathari, Nyeri 1.65m 51kg. Police corporal.
At 10,000m: OG: '04- 13; WCh: '01- 1, '03- 7, '05- 12; AfCh: '04- 1. World CC: '00-01-02-04-05: 7/3/5/5/10; HMar: '02- 9. Won KEN 5000m 2004, 10,000m 2001.
Progress at 5000m, 10,000m: 1999- 13:05.29, 26:51.49; 2000- 13:23.24; 2001- 13:05.16, 27:22.58; 2002- 13:02.51, 28:20.98A; 2003- 13:15.33, 27:29.12; 2004- 13:11.41, 26:59.93; 2005- 13:11.98, 27:28.35; 2006- 13:22.48, 2007- 27:36.12. pbs: 1500m 3:41.6? '99, 3000m 7:41.89 '03, road: 10M 46:01 '03, HMar 60:22 '02, Mar 2:11:25 '07.
Made a sensational debut in European competition when he won at 10,000m in 26:51.49 in Brussels in September 1999. He had won in India in July at 3000m 7:56.56 and 5000m 13:45.91 in his only previous races outside Kenya, where he had been 2nd at 5000m and 10,000m in the Kenyan Police Championships (c. 14:01 and 28:57) and had a 5000m best of c.13:43.

John KARIUKI b. 10 Nov 1986 1.71m 55kg.
Progress at 5000m, 10,000m: 2001- 13:49.38, 2002- 13:37.25, 2003- 13:27.18, 28:02.72, 2004- 13:26.94, 27:46.47; 2005- 13:12.12, 27:28.69; 2006- 13:14.49, 27:14.84; 2007- 13:18.39, 27:30.50. pbs: 1500m 3:42.59 '03, 3000m 7:51.21 '02.
World age-15 best for 3000m 2002.

Ezekiel KEMBOI Cheboi b. 25 May 1982 Matira, near Kapsowar, Marakwet District 1.75m 62kg.
At 3000mSt: OG: '04- 1; WCh: '03- 2, '05- 2, 07- 2; CG: '02- 2, '06- 1; AfG: '03- 1, '07- 2; AfCh: '02- 4, '06- dq; Af-J: '01- 1. Kenyan champion 2003, 2006-07.
Progress at 3000mSt: 2001- 8:23.66, 2002- 8:06.65, 2003- 8:02.49, 2004- 8:02.98, 2005- 8:09.04, 2006- 8:09.29, 2007- 8:05.50. pbs: 1500m 3:40.8A '04, 3000m 7:56.8A '05.

Luke KIBET b. 12 Apr 1983 Kaplelach, Uasin Gushu district. Prison guard.
At Mar: WCh: '07- 1.
Progress at Mar: 2004- 2:11:13, 2005- 2:08:52, 2006- 2:10:00, 2007- 2:10:07. pbs: 3000m 8:02.45 '05, 5000m 14:08.13A '04, 10,000m 28:15.0A '07, HMar 60:00 '04, 3000mSt 8:25.4A '04.
Marathon wins: Taipei 2006, Vienna 2007.

Mike Kipruto **KIGEN** b. 15 Jan 1986 Keiyo district 1.70m 54kg.
At 5000m/(10,000m): AfCh: '06- 2/2; WCp: '06- 2. World CC: '06- 5. Won Kenyan 5000m 2006.
Progress at 5000m: 2005- 13:22.48, 2006- 12:58.58. pbs: 3000m 7:35.87 '06, 2M 8:20.09 '05, 10,000m 28:03.70 '06.

Alex KIPCHIRCHIR Rono b. 26 Nov 1984 Sergoit, Uasin Gishu 1.88m 63kg.
At 800m: WJ: '02- 1; CG: '06- 1; AfCh: '06- 1. At 1500m: WCh: '05- 7; AfCh: '06- 1; WCp: '06- 1; won WAF 2006
World junior 1 mile record 2003.
Progress at 1500m: 2002- 3:32.95, 2003- 3:31.42, 2004- 3:30.46, 2005- 3:30.82, 2006- 3:31.36, 2007- 3:31.58. pbs: 800m 1:45.0A '06, 1:45.54 '05; 1000m 2:16.94 '05, 1M 3:50.25 '03.
World age 18 1500m best 2003.

Eliud KIPCHOGE b. 5 Nov 1984 Kapsisiywa, Nandi 1.67m 52kg.
At 5000m: OG: '04- 3; WCh: '03- 1, '05- 4, '07- 2. At 3000m: WI: '06- 3. World CC: '02-03-04-05: 5J/1J/4/5. Won WAF 5000m 2003, 3000m 2004, Kenyan CC 2005.
World junior 5000m record 2003. World road best 4M 17:10 '05.
Progress at 1500m, 5000m, 10,000m: 2002- 13:13.03, 2003- 3:36.17, 12:52.61; 2004- 3:33.20, 12:46.53; 2005- 3:33.80, 12:50.22; 2006- 3:36.25i, 12:54.94; 2007- 3:39.98, 12:50.38, 26:49.02. pbs: 1M 3:50.40 '04, 2000m 4:59.?+ '04, 3000m 7:27.72 '04, 2M 8:07.68 '05. 10km Rd 26:55dh '06, 27:34 '05.
Kenyan Junior CC champion 2002-03, followed World Junior CC win by winning the World 5000m title, becoming at 18 years 298 days the second youngest world champion. Age 19 bests for 3000m & 5000m 2004. Ran 26:49.02 in 10,000m debut at Hengelo in 2007.

Robert KIPCHUMBA b. 24 Feb 1984 Kaptul, Marakwet District 1.73m 53kg. Soldier.
At 10,000m: WJ: '00- 1. World 20k: '06- 2, HMar: '07- 15; CC: '00- 1J.
World youth 10,000m record 2001.
Progress at 10,000m: 2000- 27:43.14, 2001- 27:25.55, 2002- 29:57.7A, 2003- 29:39.2A, 2004- 27:55.74, 2006- 29:07.0A. pbs: 3000m 7:44.36 '06, 5000m 13:19.76 '01, Road: 20km 56:41 '06, HMar 59:28 '06.
Won 2000 WJ 10,000m title at 16 years 235 days. Married Rose Cherotich in 2000.

Sammy KIPKETER b. 29 Sep 1981 Keiyo 1.66m 52kg.
At 5000m: WCh: '01- 6; CG: '02- 1. At 10,000m: AfG: '03- 6. 3rd GP 3000m 2000. World CC: '99- 6J, '03- 14; 4k: '00-01-02: 2/4/4. Won KEN 4k CC 2002.
Official world junior record 3000m 1999. World road bests 5km 13:00 2000 & 2001, 10km 27:18 '01, 27:11 '02.
Progress at 5000m, 10,000m: 1999- 12:58.10, 2000- 12:54.07, 2001- 12:59.34, 2002- 12:56.99, 26:49.38; 2003- 12:52.33, 27:13.42; 2004- 13:25e+, 27:03.61; 2005- 13:01.55, 26:52.60; 2006- 13:29.3A, 2007- 27:14.04. pbs: 1500m 3:40.0A '01, 2000m 5:00.0e '99, 3000m 7:33.62 '01, HMar 61:25 '06.
World age-17 bests at 3000m and 5000m 1999.

Asbel KIPROP b. 30 Jun 1989 Uasin Gishu, Eldoret. North Rift
At 1500m: WCh: '07- 4; AfG: '07- 1. World CC: '07- 1J.
pbs: 1500m: 3:35.24 '07, 3000m 7:42.32 '07.
Father David Kebenei was a 1500m runner.

Wesley KIPROTICH b. 31 Jul 1979 Kericho 1.79m 64kg.
At 3000mSt: CG: '06- 2.
Progress at 3000mSt: 2004- 8:05.68, 2005- 8:09.43, 2006- 8:15.32, 2007- 8:14.88. pbs: 1500m 3:43.37 '05, 3000m 7:57.00 '00, 5000m 14:05.64 '05, 2000mSt 5:16.46 '05.

Wilson KIPROTICH Kebenei b. 20 Jul 1980.
At World 20k: '06- 3, HMar: '04- 8.
pbs: Road: 10km 27:37 '04, 20km 57:15 '06, HMar 59:27 '05.

Brimin KIPRUTO b. 31 Jul 1985 Korkitony, Marakwet District 1.76m 54kg.
At 3000mSt: OG: '04- 2; WCh: '05- 3, '07- 1; Af-J: '03- 2. At 1500m: WJ: '04- 3. At 2000St: WY: '01- 2. World 4k CC: '06- 18.
Progress at 3000mSt: 2002- 8:33.0A, 2003- 8:34.5A, 2004- 8:05.52, 2005- 8:04.22, 2006- 8:08.32, 2007- 8:02.89. pbs: 1500m 3:35.23 '06, 2000m 4:58.76i '07, 3000m 7:43.20i '07, 7:47.33 '06.
First name is actually Firmin, but he has stayed with the clerical error of Brimin written when he applied for a birth certificate in 2001.

Bernard KIPYEGO Kiprop b. 16 Jul 1986 Keiyo district 1.60m 50kg.
At 10,000m: Af-J: '03- 7. World CC: '05- 2J, '07- 3.
Progress at 10,000m: 2003- 29:29.09, 2004- 28:18.94, 2005- 27:04.45, 2006- 27:19.45, 2007- 26:59.51. pbs: 3000m 7:54.91 '05, 5000m 13:09.96 '05, Road: 15km 43:15 '07, 10M 46:21 '07.

Michael KIPYEGO b. 2 Oct 1983 Marakwet 1.62m 58kg.
At 3000mSt: WCh: '03- h; WJ: '02- 1. At 3000m: WY: '99- 8; Af-J: '01- 2. World CC: '02-03-07: 12J/4 4k/6.
Progress at 3000mSt: 2001- 8:41.26, 2002- 8:22.90, 2003- 8:13.02, 2004- 8:23.14, 2005- 8:10.66, 2006- 8:14.99, 2007- 8:11.62. pbs: 1500m 3:39.93 '05, 3000m 7:53.18 '05.

Abel KIRUI b. 4 Jun 1982.
Progress at Mar: 2006- 2:15:22, 2007- 2:06:51. pbs: 1500m 3:46.10 '05, 3000m 7:55.90 '06, 5000m 13:52.71 '05, 10,000m 28:30.15 '05; Road: 10km 28:08 '07, 15km 42:22 '07, HMar 60:11 '07.
2nd Berlin Marathon 2007.

Paul Kiprop **KIRUI** b. 5 Feb 1980.
World HMar: '02- 10, '04- 1.
Progress at Mar: 2004- 2:14:04, 2005- 2:11:28, 2006- 2:06:44, 2007- 2:07:12. pbs: 10km 28:37 '03, HMar 60:18 '06.
Had four wins in five half marathons 2003-04. 2nd Milan marathon 2005.

Alfred KIRWA YEGO b. 28 Nov 1986 1.75m 56kg.
At 800m: WCh: '05- h, '07- 1; WJ: '04- 2; AfCh: '06- 3.
Progress at 800m: 2004- 1:47.39, 2005- 1:44.45, 2006- 1:43.89, 2007- 1:44.50. pbs: 1500m 3:37.95 '04.

Paul Kipsiele **KOECH** b. 10 Nov 1981 Cheplanget, Buret District 1.68m 57kg.
At 3000mSt: OG: '04- 3; WCh: '05- 7; AfG: '03- 2; AfCh: '06- 1; WCp: '06- 2; won WAF 2005-07. At 3000m: WI: 08- 2.
Progress at 3000mSt: 2001- 8:15.92, 2002- 8:05.44,

2003- 7:57.42, 2004- 7:59.65, 2005- 7:56.37, 2006- 7:59.94, 2007- 7:58.80. pbs: 1500m 3:37.92 '07, 3000m 7:33.46i '07, 7:33.93 '05; 2M 8:06.48i (2008), 5000m 13:11.26 '05.

Micah KOGO b. 3 Jun 1986 1.70m 60kg.
Progress at 5000m, 10,000m: 2004- 14:02.99, 2005- 13:16.31, 2006- 13:00.07, 26:35.63; 2007- 13:10.68, 26:58.42. pbs: 2000m 5:03.05 '06, 3000m 7:38.67 '07, 2M 8:20.88 '05
Won Van Damme 10,000m in Brussels in 2006 for 6th world all-time.

Ismael Kipngetich **KOMBICH** b. 6 Dec 1985 1.83m 73kg.
At 800m: AfG: 07- dnf; AfCh: '06- 7. At 1500m: CG: '06- ht.
Progress at 800m: 2004- 1:51.57A, 2005- 1:46.83/1:46.8A, 2006- 1:44.24, 2007- 1:45.15. pbs: 400m 47.87 '07, 1500m 3:40.68 '06.

Daniel Kipchirchir **KOMEN** b. 27 Nov 1984 1.75m 60kg.
At 1500m: WCh: '05- h, '07- sf; WI: '06- 2, '08- 2; won WAF 2007. At 5000m: Af-J: '03- 2.
Progress at 1500m: 2004- 3:34.66, 2005- 3:29.72, 2006- 3:29.02, 2007- 3:31/75. pbs: 800m 1:47.3A '05, 1000m 2:16.9+ '06, 1M 3:48.28 '07, 3000m 7:31.98 '05, 5000m 13:16.26 '04.

Willy KOMEN b. 22 Dec 1987 1.68m 55kg.
At 3000mSt: WJ: '06- 1; AfG: '07- 1; Af-J: '05- 1.
Progress at 3000mSt: 2004- 8:33.0A, 2005- 8:35.82, 2006- 8:14.00, 2007- 8:11.18. pbs: 1500m 3:40.0A '07, 3000m 7:50.34i '07, 5000m 14:01.42 '07.

Leonard Patrick **KOMON** b. 10 Jan 1988 1.63m 52kg.
World CC: '06-07-08: 2J/4J/2.
Progress at 5000m: 2006- 13:04.12, 2007- 13:04.79. pbs: 3000m 7:37.69 '06, 2M 8:22.56 '07.

John Cheruiyot **KORIR** b. 13 Dec 1981 Kiramwok, Bomet district 1.72m 57kg. Army private.
At 10,000m: OG: '00- 5, '04- 6; WCh: '01- 8, '03- 5; CG: '02- 4; AfCh: '02- 2, '06- 4. World CC: '00-01-03-04-05: 3J/28/6/11/9; HMar: '03- 4, '04- 4. Won Kenyan 10,000m 2000, 2003; CC 2001, 2003.
Progress at 5000m,10,000m: 1999- 13:24.22, 27:38.86; 2000- 13:09.58, 27:24.75; 2001- 13:19.58, 27:49.34A; 2002- c.13:24+, 26:52.87; 2003- 13:17.7, 27:17.24; 2004- 13:20.31, 27:05.14; 2005- 27:30.46; 2006- 13:29.18, 28:10.83; 2007- 27:26.31. pbs: 3000m 7:43.35 '00, HMar 61:02 '03.
Ran fastest ever 10,000m at high altitude, 27:48.42, to win 2000 Kenyan title.

Sammy KORIR b. 12 Dec 1971 Nandi 1.60m 61kg. FILA Milan.
At HMar: WCh: '99- 11.
Progress at Mar: 1996- 2:12:33, 1997- 2:08:02, 1998- 2:08:13, 1999- 2:08:27, 2001- 2:08:14, 2002- 2:08:10, 2003- 2:04:56, 2004- 2:06:49, 2005- 2:10:53, 2006- 2:06:38, 2007- 2:08:01, 20008- 2:07:32. pb HMar 60:15 '98.
Has won 9 of his 19 marathons: Florence and Cancun 1996, Amsterdam 1997 and 1998, Turin 1999; Beppu and San Diego 2002, Rotterdam 2006, Seoul 2008. Second, just one second behind Paul Tergat's world record at Berlin 2003 and 2nd London 2004. 3rd Rotterdam 1997, Tokyo 2006, Dubai 2008. Has a record 11 times sub 2:09.

Shadrack KORIR b. 14 Dec 1978 Nandi district 1.70m 54kg.
At 1500m: WCh: '07- 3; AfCh: '06- 7. At 3000m: WI: '06- 5. Won Kenyan 1500m 2006.
Progress at 1500m, 5000m: 1999- 3:42.34, 2001- 3:35.16, 2002- 3:36.32, 13:14.02; 2003- 3:37.92, 13:16.92; 2005- 3:41.8A, 13:09.92; 2006- 3:31.96, 2007- 3:31.18. pbs: 1M 3:52.78 '07, 2000m 4:55.72i '07, 4:56.62 '01; 3000m 7:37.35i '07, 7:37.50 '06; 2M 8:14.84i '06, 8:19.53 '05.
Younger brother of Laban Rotich (1 CG, AfCh & WCp 1998, pbs 1500m 3:29.91 '98, 1M 3:47.65 '97).

Paul KOSGEI Malakwen b. 22 Apr 1978 Marakwet 1.75m 57kg.
At 3000mSt: WCh: '99- 7. At 10,000m: WCh: '01- 7; CG: '02- 2; AfCh: '02- 1. At 5000m: WCp: '02- 2. World CC: '97- 3J, 4k: '98-9-00: 3/2/3; 12k: '01- 5; HMar: '02- 1; Rd Rly team: '98- 1. Won KEN 10,000m 2002, 4km CC 1999.
World junior record 3000m steeplechase 1997, Kenyan HMar record 2006.
Progress at 5000m, 10,000m, 3000mSt: 1997- 8:07.69, 1998- 8:07.86, 1999- 8:07.13, 2000- 13:05.44, 27:38.22, 8:29.57; 2001- 13:06.29, 27:51.87A; 2002- 13:20.92, 27:44.14A; 2003- 27:21.56. pbs: 1500m: 3:42.7A '00, 2000m 5:03.1+ '00, 3000m 7:39.15 '00, HMar 59:07 '06, Mar 2:09:31 '07, 2000mSt 5:19.78 '98.
Won his heat at 1999 World Champs in 8:10.34, the fastest ever time in a preliminary round, but stopped steeplechasing in 2000 due to a knee injury. Ran world road best 10km 27:03 in 2000, and won the World Half marathon title in his first major race at the distance followed by the fastest ever 10,000m at high altitude, 27:44.14 to win the Kenyan title, and Great North Run half marathon win in 59:58 in 2002.

Reuben KOSGEI b. 2 Aug 1979 Kapsabet 1.70m 55kg.
At 3000mSt: OG: '00- 1; WCh: '01- 1, '03- dnf; CG: '06- 3; WJ: '98- 1; Af-J: '97- 1. Kenyan champion 2000.
Progress at 3000mSt: 1998- 8:23.76, 1999- 8:12.33, 2000- 8:03.92, 2001- 7:57.29, 2002- 8:05.87, 2003- 8:09.65, 2005- 8:12.57, 2006- 8:08.79, 2007- 8:07.12. pbs: 1500m 3:37.24 '00, 3000m 7:41.86i '00, 10,000m 29:09.6A '02.
After his World Championship win in 2001, he improved his best ever time to 8:03.22 at Zürich and to 7:57.29, fourth fastest of all-time at the event, at Brussels, behind Brahim Boulami. Had two years of Achilles problems before good return in 2005-06.

Martin LEL b. 29 Oct 1978 Kapsabet 1.71m 54kg.
World HMar: '03- 1.
Progress at Mar: 2002- 2:10:02, 2003- 2:10:30, 2004- 2:13:38, 2005- 2:07:26, 2006- 2:06:41, 2007- 2:07:41. pbs: 10km 28:13 '07, 15km 42:41 '07, 10M 45:40 '07, HMar 59:30 '06.
Exclusively a road runner. Marathons: dnf Prague and 2nd in Venice 2002, 3rd Boston 2003-04, 1st New York 2003 and 2007 and London 2005 and 2007 (2nd 2006).

Benjamin LIMO b. 23 Aug 1974 Chepkongony, Keiyo 1.78m 65kg. Army engineer.
At 5000m: WCh: '99- 2, '05- 1, '07- 15; CG: '02- 2, '06- 3; AfG: '03- 7; AfCh: '02- 2. Won GP 3000m 1999. World 4k CC: '98-9-01-03-06: 4/1/3/3/4; Rd Rly team: '98- 1. Won KEN 5000m 2002, 2005.
Progress at 5000m: 1998- 13:07.38, 1999- 12:55.86, 2000- 12:55.82, 2001- 12:59.53, 2002- 12:57.24, 2003- 12:54.99, 2004- 13:31.25, 2005- 12:55.26, 2006- 12:58.29, 2007- 13:16.66. pbs: 1500m 3:37.59 '99, 2000m 4:59.2e '99, 3000m 7:28.67 '99, 2M 8:10.59 '06, 10,000m 27:42.43 '04.
Only began running seriously in November 1997. Has great finishing speed. Uncle of Sally Barsosio (1997 World 10,000m champion).

Felix LIMO b. 22 Aug 1980 Nandi 1.74m 58kg.
World best for 15km road with 41:29 at Nijmegen 2001.
Progress at 10,000m, Mar: 1998- 28:48A, 1999- 28:23.30, 2000- 27:04.54, 2001- 27:26.86; 2003- 2:06:42, 2004- 2:06:14, 2005- 2:07:02, 2006- 2:06:39, 2007- 2:07:47. pbs: 3000m 7:40.67 '01, 5000m 13:16.42 '01, HMar 61:12 '06.
Made second fastest ever marathon debut when 2nd at Amsterdam in 2003. Won at Rotterdam (2:06:14) and Berlin (2:06:44) in 2004, Chicago 2005 and London 2006. 3rd Rotterdam 2005, London 2007.

Richard Kipkemei **LIMO** b. 18 Nov 1980 Cheptigit 1.67m 53kg. Kalenjin.
At 5000m: OG: '00- 10; WCh: '01- 1, '03- 7; CG: '98- 3; AfG: '99- 6. At 3000mSt: AfCh: '98- 2. World CC: '98-9-02-03-04: 2J/2J/4/4/32. Won KEN 5000m 2001, CC 2002.
World junior records 3000m 1998, 2M 1999.
Progress at 5000m, 10,000m: 1998- 13:21.59, 1999- 12:58.15, 2000- 12:58.70, 2001- 12:56.72, 27:25.27; 2002- 12:57.52, 26:50.20; 2003- 13:01.13, 26:56.63; 2004- 12:59.37, 27:09.61; 2005- 13:09.52, 28:16.7A. pbs: 1500m 3:43.3A '02, 2000m 5:00.6 '99, 3000m 7:32.23 '01, 2M 8:13.47 '99, 3000mSt 8:20.67 '98.
2nd Amsterdam in 2:06:45 on marathon debut 2007.

Thomas Pkemei **LONGOSIWA** b. 14 Jan 1982 1.75m 57kg. North Rift.
At 5000m: AfG: '07- 6. World CC: '06- 13J (but dq after birthdate found to be 1982). Won Kenyan 5000m 2007.
Progress at 5000m: 2006- 13:35.3A, 2007- 12:51.95. pbs: 3000m 7:32.79 '07, 10,000m 28:11.3A '06.

Benjamin MAIYO b. 6 Oct 1978 Trans Nzoia 1.75m 58kg.
At 10,000m: WCh: '99- 7; AfG: '99- 5; AfCh: '02- 3.
Progress at 5000m, 10,000m, Mar: 1998- 13:18.98, 27:34.38; 1999- 13:02.38, 28:01.8A; 2000- 13:02.28, 28:28.7A; 2001- 13:05.43, 27:07.55; 2002- 13:02.95, 28:06.0A; 2003- 13:14.75, 29:07.7A; 2004- 27:30.30, 2:13:07; 2005- 2:07:09, 2006- 2:08:21. pbs: 1500m 3:42.30 '99, 2000m 5:01.9+ '00; 3000m 7:32.36 '00, HMar 61:59 '02, Mar 2:13:17 '04.
2nd Los Angeles and Chicago marathons 2005, 2nd Boston 2006.

Patrick MAKAU Musyoki b. 2 Mar 1985. Machakos Province. Birchfield H, GBR.
World HMar: '07- 2.
pbs: 3000m 7:54.50 '07, 5000m 13:42.84 '06. Road: 10km 27:27 '07, 15km 41:34 '07, 20km 55:53 '07, HMar 58:56 '07.

Moses MASAI b. 1 Jun 1986 1.72m 57kg.
At 10,000m: WJ: '04- 10. World CC: '04-05-08: 16J/7J/5. Won Afr-j 5000 & 10,000m 2005, Kenyan CC 2006.
World junior marathon record 2005.
Progress at 10,000m: 2004- 27:07.29, 2005- 28:08.6A, 2006- 27:03.20, 2007- 26:49.20. pbs: 1500m 3:43.1A '05, 3000m 7:47.29 '07, 5000m 13:08.81 '07, Mar 2:10:13 '05.
Marathon wins (while a junior) at Hannover 2004 and Essen 2005. His sister **Linet Masai** won the World Junior CC in 2007.

Richard Kipkemboi **MATELONG** b. 14 Oct 1983 Lenape, Narok District 1.79m 65g. Police.
At 3000mSt: WCh: '07- 3; AfCh: '04- 2. Won Kenyan CC 2007.
Progress at 3000mSt: 2004- 8:05.96, 2005- 8:10.97, 2006- 8:07.50, 2007- 8:06.66. pbs: 1500m 3:41.79 '05, 3000m 7:48.71 '05, 5000m 13:30.4A '06, 10,000m 28:18.4A '07.

Martin Irungu MATHATHI b. 25 Dec 1985 Nyahururu 1.67m 49kg. Suzuki, Japan.
At 10,000m: WCh: '05- 5, '07- 3. World CC: '06- 3.
Progress at 5000m, 10,000m: 2003- 14:09.3A, 27:43.16; 2004- 13:03.84, 27:22.46; 2005- 13:05.99, 27:08.42; 2006- 13:05.55, 27:10.51; 2007- 13:22.13, 27:09.90. pbs: 1500m 3:38.57 '06, 10M Rd 44:51 '04 (world junior best).
Posted a brilliant series of times in road races in Japan at the end of 2004.

Josphat Kiprono MENJO b. 20 Aug 1979 1.83m 62kg.
At 5000m: AfG: '07- 2; AfCh: '06- 5. At 10,000m: WCh: '07- 8.
Progress at 5000m, 10,000m: 2004- 13:48.7A, 2005- 13:14.38, 2006- 13:09.24, 27:29.45; 2007- 13:06.69, 27:04.61. pbs: 3000m 7:44.47 '05, 2M 8:18.96 '07, HMar 64:09 '04.

Moses MOSOP b. 17 Jul 1985 Kamasia, Marakwet 1.72m 57kg.

At 10,000m: OG: '04- 7; WCh: '05- 3. World CC: '02-03-05-07: 10J/7J/18/2. Won KEN 10,000m 2006.
Progress at 5000m, 10,000m: 2002- 29:38.6A, 2003- 13:11.75, 27:13.66; 2004- 13:09.68, 27:30.66; 2005- 13:06.83, 27:08.96; 2006- 12:54.46, 27:17.00; 2007- 13:07.89, 26:49.55. pbs: 3000m 7:36.88 '06.

Leonard MUCHERU b. 13 Jun 1978 Nyandarua 1.82m 66kg.
At 5000m: AsiG: '06- 2. At 3000m: WI: '03- 7. World 4km CC: '00- 4.
Bahrain 5000m & Marathon records 2007.
Progress at 5000m: 2000- 13:21.14, 2001- 13:14.94, 2002- 13:21.68, 2003- 13:01.76, 2004- 13:00.40, 2005- 12:59.79, 2006- 13:22.15, 2007- 13:02.89. pbs: 1500m 3:33.79 '01, 1M 3:49.75 '01, 3000m 7:35.35 '01, Mar 2:11:10 '07, 3000mSt 8:47.34 '00.
Mucheru took up Bahrain citizenship in 2003 and changed his name to Mushir Salim Jawher. He was eligible to compete for Bahrain from 16 March 2006, but on 4 Jan 2007 he ran in Israel, a country not recognised by Bahrain, winning at Tiberias on his marathon debut. The Bahrain Athletic Union in conjunction with government authorities decided to strike Jawher's name off the sport union records and to strip him of his nationality but he was reinstated after apologising. However, he regained Kenyan citizenship on 31 Oct 2007.

Emmanuel MUTAI b. 1 Apr 1978.
Progress at Mar: 2007- 2:06:29. pbs: 10,000m 28:21.14 '06, Road: 10km 27:51 '06, HMar 60:49 '06.
Made marathon debut with 7th in Rotterdam in 2:13:06 in 2007, then won in Amsterdam.

Josphat Muchiri NDAMBIRI b. 12 Feb 1985 1.72m 52kg. Komori, Japan.
At 10,000m: WCh: '07- 5.
Progress at 5000m, 10,000m: 2001- 13:54.65, 29:06.30; 2002- 13:36.77, 28:45.05; 2003- 13:36.14, 28:02.09; 2004- 13:27.53, 27:46.10; 2005- 13:05.33, 27:19.19; 2006- 13:09.39, 27:04.79; 2007- 13:18.49, 27:28.38. pbs: 1500m 3:38.72 '04, 3000m 7:42.98 '06, HMar 62:10 '05.

Gideon NGATUNY b. 10 Oct 1986 Kilgoris 1.73m 55kg. Nissin Foods Corporation, Japan.
At World CC: '07- 4, '08- 7.
Progress at 5000m, 10,000m: 2006- 13:15.9, 27:28.42; 2007- 13:12.62, 27:11.36. pbs: 3000m 7:56.48 '06.

Daniel NJENGA b. 7 May 1976 1.76m 61kg.
World Junior record when winning Japanese 3000m steeplechase title in 1994.
Progress at 3000mSt, Mar: 1993- 8:41.46, 1994- 8:19.21, 1995- 8:27.03, 2:20:28; 1996- 8:28.67, 1997- 8:30.50, 1998- 8:32.14, 1999- 2:11:49, 2001- 2:20:58, 2002- 2:06:16, 2003- 2:07:41, 2004- 2:07:44, 2005- 2:07:14, 2006- 2:07:40, 2007- 2:09:45. pbs: 1500m 3:43.43 '94, 5000m 13:36.55 '96, 10,000m 27:51.83 '02, HMar 60:39 '96.
Based in Japan. Huge breakthough when 2nd at Chicago 2002 in his seventh marathon, and was third in 2003 & 2005 and second 2004 & 2006. Won Tokyo 2004 and 2007.

Rodgers ROP b. 16 Feb 1976 Nandi 1.72m 52kg.
Progress at Mar: 2001- 2:09:51, 2002- 2:08:07, 2003- 2:11:11, 2004- 2:13:57, 2005- 2:10:31, 2006- 2:07:34, 2007- 2:07:32. Road pbs: 10km 28:01 '01, 10M 45:56 '01, HMar 59:49 '04, 25k 1:13:44 '01 (world best).
Marathons: After third in New York 2001, achieved a unique double in 2002 by being first to win Boston (2:09:02) and New York (2:08:07) in the same year. 2nd New York 2003 and pb for 6th London 2006. Won Hamburg 2007.

David RUDISHA b. 17 Dec 1988 1.82m 70kg.
At 800m: WJ: '06- 1/4R; Af-J: '07- 1.
Progress at 800m: 2006- 1:46.3A, 2007- 1:44.15.
His father Daniel won 4x400m silver medal at 1968 Olympics with 440y pb 45.5A '67.

Evans RUTTO b. 8 Apr 1978 Marakwet 1.68m 56kg.
World CC: 1999- 5; HMar: '01- 6.
Progress at 5000m, 10,000m, Mar: 1999- 13:24.84, 28:06.60; 2000- 13:02.71, 27:21.32; 2001- 13:28.25, 2003- 2:05:50, 2004- 2:06:16. 2005- 2:07:28, 2006- 2:09:35. pbs: 2000m 5:02.3+ '99; 3000m 7:36.38 '00; Road: 10km 28:19 '02, 15km 43:15 '01; 10M 46:26 '01, HMar 60:30 '01.
Ran fastest ever debut marathon when he won at Chicago 2003 and won again at London (2:06:19) and Chicago (2:06:16) 2004. His father Kilimo Yano was a 29 min 10,000m runner.

Suleiman SIMOTWO b. 21 Apr 1980 Kaptama, Mount Elgon district 1.82m 70kg. PE instructor in Kenyan Police.
At 1500m: WI: '08- 7. Won Kenyan 800m 2005.
Progress at 1500m: 2002- 3:42.2A, 2003- 3:36.98, 2004- 3:34.48, 2005- 3:31.85, 2006- 3:31.67, 2007- 3:31.89. pbs: 800m 1:45.5A '05, 1000m 2:18.13i '08, 2:19.31 '04; 1M 3:50.82 '05, 2000m 4:59.06 '03, 3000m 7:48.38 '03.

Edwin SOI b. 3 Mar 1986 1.68m 53kg.
At 3000m: WI: '08- 4; won WAF 3000m & 5000m 2007 (2nd both 2006). World 4k CC: '06-07: 8/9.
Progress at 5000m, 10,000m: 2002- 29:06.5A, 2004- 13:22.57, 2005- 13:10.78, 2006- 12:52.40, 27:14.83; 2007- 13:10.21. pbs: 1500m 3:44.76 '05, 2000m 5:01.9 '06, 3000m 7:31.84 '06, 2M 8:16.98 '07.

Isaac Kiprono **SONGOK** b. 25 Apr 1984 Kaptel, near Kapsabet, Nandi region 1.76m 54kg.
At 1500m: OG: '04- 12; WCh: '03- 9; WJ: '02- 7; WY: '01- 1; At 5000m: WCh: '05- 10, '07- h. World 4k CC: '04-05-06: 7/3/2. Won KEN 1500m 2003, 4k CC 2005.
World U18 records 1M (3:54.56) & 2000m (4:56.86, also U20 record) 2001.
Progress at 1500m, 5000m: 2001- 3:35.55, 13:37.3A; 2002- 3:34.20, 2003- 3:31.54, 2004- 3:30.99, 2005- 3:31.72, 12:52.29; 2006- 3:31.85, 12:48.66; 2007-

13:15.70. pbs: 800m 1:50.5A '03, 1M 3:54.56 '01, 2000m 4:56.86 '01, 3000m 7:28.72 '06.
National primary school champion at 5000m in 1999 and 2000.

Paul TERGAT b. 17 Jun 1969 Kabarnet, Barango 1.82m 62kg. Air Force sergeant (SPTE). Tugen.
At 10,000m: OG: '96- 2, '00- 2; WCh: '95- 3, '97- 2, '99- 2. At Mar: OG: '04- 10. World HMar: '92-4-9-00: 5/11/1/1. World CC: '93-4-5-6-7-8-9-00: 10/4/1/1/1/1/1/3. Won Kenyan CC 1992, 1995-6.
World records: 10,000m 1997, marathon 2003. World road best 15km 1994 (42:13), half marathon 59:17 '98 and 59:06 '00 (40m dh at Lisbon). 58:51 at Milano 1996 was on a course 49m short. Two Kenyan marathon record 2002-03.
Progress at 5000m, 10,000m, Mar: 1991- 29:46.8A, 1992- 13:48.64, 1993- 13:20.16, 27:18.43; 1994- 13:15.07, 27:23.89; 1995- 13:07.49, 27:14.08; 1996- 12:54.72, 26:54.41; 1997- 12:49.87, 26:27.85; 1998- 12:58.74, 26:44.44; 1999- 12:55.37, 27:10.08; 2000- 12:55.18, 27:03.87; 2001- 2:08:15, 2002- 2:05:48, 2003- 2:04:55, 2004- 2:14:45, 2005- 2:09:30, 2006- 2:10:10, 2007- 2:08:06. pbs: 1500m 3:42.3 '96, 1M 3:58.4 '96, 2000m 4:57.4 '96, 3000m 7:28.70 '96, HMar 59:06 '00, 58:51sh '96.
A former basketball player, he made a major impact when he won the Kenyan CC in 1992. Won a record five successive World CC titles. Won the Stramilano half marathon each year 1994-9 and unbeaten at that distance 1995-2000. On the track he won four silver medals and a bronze behind Haile Gebrselassie in global 10,000m races. He was 2nd in his first three marathons: London (2:08:15), Chicago (2:08:56) 2001 and London (2:05:48) 2002 and then 4th at Chicago (2:06:18) 2002 and London 2003 before his world record 2:04:55 at Berlin 2003. He won the New York Marathon in 2005 (3rd 2006).

Samuel WANJIRU Kamau b. 10 Nov 1986 Nyahururu 1.64m 52kg. Toyota Yushu Company.
At 10,000m: Japanese champion 2005.
Three world half marathon records 2005 (59:16) & 2007 (58:53 & 58:33), 20km 2007; junior 10,000m 2005.
Progress at 10,000m: 2002- 28:36.08, 2003- 28:20.06, 2004- 28:00.14, 2005- 26:41.75, 2007- 27:20.99. pbs: 1500m 3:49.28 '03, 5000m 13:09.5+ '05, 15km 41:40 '07, 10M 45:10 '05, 20km 55:31 '07, HMar 58:33 '07, Mar 2:06:39 '07.
Left Kenya in 2002 to go to school in Japan and that year ran world age 15 record for 10,000m. Won at Fukuoka on marathon debut 2007.

Women

Ruth BISIBORI Nyanga b. 2 Jan 1988 Dachuba, Kisii district 1.70m 50kg. Police.
At 3000mSt: WCh: '07- 4; AfG: '07- 1.
Two world junior (four African junior) 3000mSt records 2007.
Progress at 3000mSt: 2005- 10:12.0A, 2007- 9:24.51. pbs: 3000m 8:54.42 '07, 5000m 15:26.65 '07, 10,000m 34+ '04.

Pamela CHEPCHUMBA b. 8 Mar 1979 Kapsait, West Pokot 1.55m 44kg.
World CC: '93-4-5-01-02-03-07: 2J/7J/10J/5/9/6dq/6; HMar '00-02-07: 5/5/3.
Progress at Mar: 2001- 2:43:56, 2005- 2:41:02, 2006- 2:29:48, 2007- 2:25:36. pbs: 1500m 4:23.97 '08, 3000m 8:42.24 '01, 5000m 14:56.75 '01, 10,000m 34:05.2A '01; Road: 31:19 '07, 15km 47:46 '07, 20km 64:40 '07, HMar 68:06 '07, 3000mSt 10:19.16 '06.
Two-year ban after positive test for EPO at the 2003 World Cross. Won Milan Marathon 2007. Married to Boaz Kimaiyo (Mar 2:08:46 '02), two daughters

Salome CHEPCHUMBA b. 29 Sep 1982 1.74m 57kg. North Rift.
At 3000mSt: WCh: '05- 5. World 4k CC: '01- 34. Won Kenyan 2000mSt 2003, 3000mSt 2004.
Kenyan 3000m steeplechase record 2004.
Progress at 3000mSt: 2004- 9:29.81, 2005- 9:31.44, 2006- 9:26.07, 2007- 9:52.00. pbs: 1500m 4:21.95 '04, 3000m 8:51.5A '00, 5000m 16:03.72 '06, 2000mSt 6:21.93 '05.

Priscah CHERONO b. 27 Jun 1980 1.60m 47kg. née Jepleting.
At 5000m: WCh: '05- 7, '07- 3; WJ: '96- 8, '98- 7; AfCh: '04- 2. Kenyan champion 2004. World CC J/4k: '97-8-02-03-04-06: 2J/11J/18/11/4/2, '08- 7.
Progress at 5000m: 1996- 15:39.1A, 1998- 16:07.12, 1999- 16:24.4A, 2001- 16:42.4A, 2002- 15:41.13A, 2003- 15:35.7A, 2004- 14:54.24, 2005- 14:44.00, 2006- 14:35.30, 2007- 14:42.00. pbs: 800m 2:07.8A '99, 1500m 4:16.76 '06, 3000m 8:29.06 '07, 2M 9:14.09 '07 (Kenyan best), 10km Rd 31:53 '02.

Vivian CHERUIYOT b. 11 Sep 1983 Keiyo 1.53m 39kg. Panellinos, Greece.
At 5000m: OG: '00- 14; WCh: '07- 2; WJ: '02- 3; AfG '99- 3. At 3000m: WY: '99- 3. World CC: '98-9-00-01-02-04-06: 5J/2J/1J/4J/3J/8 4k/8 4k/8.
Kenyan 5000m record 2007.
Progress at 5000m: 1999- 15:42.79A, 2000- 15:11.11, 2001- 15:59.4A, 2002- 15:49.7A, 2003- 15:44.8A, 2004- 15:13.26, 2006- 14:47.43, 2007- 14:22.51. pbs: 1500m 4:06.65 '07, 2000m 5:48.3+ '06, 3000m 8:28.66 '07, 10km Rd 32:25 '06.

Eunice JEPKORIR b. 17 Feb 1982 Eldama Ravine 1.64m 48kg.
At 3000mSt: WCh: '07- 3; won WAF 2007. At 20km: WCh: '06- 14. World CC: '04- 7.
African, Commonwealth and two Kenyan 3000mSt records 2007.
Progress at 3000mSt: 2005- 10:19.0A, 2006- 10:39.18, 2007- 9:14.52. pbs: 5000m 15:09.05 '04, 10,000m 32:58.0A '03, 2000mSt 6:25.2A '03, Road: 10km 31:38 '04, 20km 66:47 '06, Mar 2:45:22 '05.

Janeth JEPKOSGEI b. 13 Dec 1983 Kabirirsang, near Kapsabet 1.67m 47kg. North Rift.
At 800m: WCh: '07- 1; CG: '06- 1; AfCh: '06- 1;

WJ: '02- 1; WY: '99- h; WCp: '06- 2; won WAF 2007. Five Kenyan 800m records 2005-07.
Progress at 800m: 1999- 2:11.0A, 2001- 2:06.21, 2002- 2:00.80, 2003- 2:03.05, 2004- 2:00.52, 2005- 1:57.82, 2006- 1:56.66, 2007- 1:56.04. pbs: 600m 1:25.08+ '07, 1000m 2:37.98 '02, 1500m 4:11.91 '04.
Brilliant front-running victory at 2007 Worlds.

Rita Sitienei **JEPTOO** b. 15 Feb 1981 Eldoret.
At Mar: WCh: '05- 7, '07- 7; World 20k: '06- 3; HMar: '04- 14.
African record 20km road 2006.
Progress at Mar: 2004- 2:28:11, 2005- 2:24:22, 2006- 2:23:38, 2007- 2:32:03. pbs: 3000m 9:38.13 '98, 5000m 15:56.90 '02, 10,000m 33:23.04A '05; Road: 10km 31:50 '07, 20km 63:47 '06, HMar 67:08 '07. Won marathons at Stockholm and Milan 2004, Boston 2006.

Mary Jepkosgei **KEITANY** b. 18 Jan 1982 Kisok, Kabarnet 1.68m 53kg.
World HMar: '07- 2.
pbs: 1500m 4:24.33 '99, 10,000m 32:18.07 '07; Road: 10km 31:10 '07, 15km 47:01 '07, 20km: 63:18 '07, HMar 66:48 '07, Mar 2:29:45 '05.

Sylvia KIBET Kibiwott b. 18 Mar 1984 Kapchorwa, Keiyo district 1.57m 44kg. Kenya Police.
At 5000m: WCh: '07- 4; AfG: '07- 3; AfCh: '06- 3. At 3000m: WI: '08- 4, won Afr-Y 1998. At 1500m: WY: '99- 2.
Progress at 5000m: 2006- 15:02.54, 2007- 14:57.37. pbs: 1500m 4:11.50 '06, 3000m 8:40.09 '06, 2M 9:16.62 '07, 10,000m 31:39.34 '06, HMar 71:37 '06.
Did not compete in 2001-02. Married Erastus Limo in 2003, daughter Britney Jepkosgei bon in 2004. Older sister **Hilda Kibet** NED (b. 27 Mar 1981, HMar 69:43 '07, Mar 2:32:10 '07, 5 World CC 2008), and cousin of Lornah Kiplagat.

Viola KIBIWOTT b. 22 Dec 1983. 1.57m 45kg.
At 1500m: WCh: '07- 6; CG: '06- 7; WJ: '02- 1. World CC: '00-01-02: 3J/1J/1J.
Progress at 1500m: 2004- 4:06.64, 2006- 4:08.74, 2007- 4:02.10. pbs: 800m 2:04.99 '07, 3000m 8:40.14 '03, 2M 9:18.26 '07, 5000m 15:32.87 '03.

Evelyne Kemunto **KIMWEI** b. 25 Aug 1987 1.46m 40kg. Panasonic, Japan.
At HMar: WCh: '07- 6. World CC: '04- 16J.
Progress at 10,000m: 2005- 31:42.51, 2006- 31:16.50, 2007- 31:36.20. pbs: 3000m 9:06.84 '07, 5000m 15:14.05 '05, HMar 68:39 '07.

Gladys KIPKEMBOI b. 15 Oct 1986 1.56m 45kg.
At 3000mSt: WJ: '04- 1.
African junior 3000m steeplechase record 2004.
Progress at 3000mSt: 2004- 9:47.26, 2006- 9:32.68, 2007- 9:46.46. pb 3000m 9:08.22 '06.

Florence Jebet **KIPLAGAT** b. 27 Feb 2007 1.55m 42kg.
At 5000m: WJ: '06- 2. World CC: '07- 5. Won Kenyan 1500m 2007.
Progress at 5000m, 10,000m: 2006- 15:32.34, 2007- 14:40.74, 31:06.20. pb 1500m 4:09.0A '07.

Jeruto KIPTUM b. 29 Sep 1982 Metkei, Keiyo district 1.66m 50kg.
At 3000mSt: WCh: '05- 3; CG: '06- 6; AfCh: '06- 1; WCp: '06- 2. At 800m: WJ: '99- 7. At 1500m: AfCh: '04- 3. World 4k CC: '01- 34. Kenyan champion 2000mSt 2003, 3000mSt 2005-06.
Five Kenyan 3000m steeplechase records 2005-06.
Progress at 3000mSt: 2005- 9:26.95, 2006- 9:23.35. pbs: 800m 2:06.1A '99, 1500m 4:08.6A '00, 3000m 9:01.90 '99, 5000m 15:32.23 '06.

Salina KOSGEI b. 16 Nov 1976 Simotwo, Keiyo district 1.62m 58kg. Kenya Prisons Service.
At 10,000m: WCh: '03- 19; CG: '02- 1. At 800m: CG: '94- 5. Won Kenyan 10,000m 2003.
Progress at 5000m, 10,000m, Mar: 1998- 15:50.43, 2002- 15:20.17, 31:27.83; 2003- 15:01.79, 32:09.15; 2004- 32:49.0A, 2:24:32; 2005- 2:25:30, 2006- 16:01.4A, 2:23:22; 2007- 2:23:31. pbs: 800m 2:03.38 '94, 1500m 4:19.9 '98, 3000m 9:34.35 '02, HMar 67:52 '06.
Won four successive Kenyan Schools titles at heptathlon, as well as at 200m, 800m and on both winning relay teams in her final year. Won Paris marathon on debut 2004, Prague 2005, Singapore 2006; ran pb for 2nd Berlin 2006 and Tokyo 2007. Married (1995) Barnabas Kinyor (3rd Commonwealth 400mh 1994), children born 1996 and 2001.

Edith Chewanjel **MASAI** b. 4 Apr 1967 Chepkoya, Mt Elgon 1.68m 55kg. Police sergeant.
At 5000m: OG: '04- dnf; WCh: '01- 7, '03- 3; CG: '02- 2; AfG: '03- 6. At 10,000m: WCh: '05- 5; AfG: '07- 2; AfCh: '06- 1. AT Mar: WCh: '07- 8. World 20km: '06- 5; 4km CC: '01-02-03-04: 3/1/1/1. Won WAF 3000m 2003, KEN 1500m 2004, 5000m 2001-03, 2006; 10,000m 2006-07, 4km CC 2002.
African 3000m record 2002, Kenyan 5000m 2005 & 2006, 10,000m 2005. World W35 3000m 2002, 5000m 2006, 10,000m 2005, W40 10,000m record 2007.
Progress at 5000m, 10,000m: 2001- 14:45.86, 2002- 14:48.14, 2003- 14:45.35, 2004- 14:42.64, 2005- 14:37.20, 30:30.26; 2006- 14:33.84, 31:27.96; 2007- 31:31.18. pbs: 1500m 4:18.6A '04, 2000m 5:38.2 '06, 3000m 8:23.23 '02; Road: 15km 48:37 '01, 10M 52:45 '02, 20km 63:52 '06, HMar 67:16 '06, Mar 2:27:06 '05.
Son Griffin born 1990. Ran successfully in primary school, but only started running seriously after she separated from her husband in 1999. Won third successive World 4k CC title in 2004. Ran 31:27 for road 10km in 2001 but did not make track debut at 10,000m until 2005, when she also won at Hamburg on her marathon debut.

Linet Chepkwemoi **MASAI** b. 5 Dec 1989 Mount Elgon 1.70m 55kg.

World CC: '07- 1J, '08- 3.
pbs: 3000m 8:38.97 '07, 5000m 14:55.50 '07.
Younger sister of Moses Masai.

Catherine NDEREBA b. 21 Jul 1972 Gatunganga, Nyeri district 1.60m 45kg.
At Mar: OG: 04- 2; WCh: '03- 1, '05- 2, '07- 1. At HMar: WCh: '99- 3. Won Kenyan 10,000m 2005. World marathon record in Chicago 2001.
Progress at Mar: 1999- 2:27:34, 2000- 2:21:33, 2001- 2:18:47, 2002- 2:19:26, 2003- 2:19:55, 2004- 2:24:27, 2005- 2:22:01, 2006- 2:25:05, 2007- 2:29:08. pbs: 1500m 4:22.1A '01, 3000m 9:25.10 '99, 5000m 15:27.84 '00, 10,000m 32:17.58 '00; Road 5km 15:07 '98, 10km 31:02 '01, 15km 48:06 '01, 10M 52:25 '98, HMar 67:54 '01.
Married to Anthony Maina. Has had great success on the US road running circuit, where she was top ranked in 1996 and 1998, having had a baby, Jane, in 1997. Sixth in Boston on her debut, 8 wins in 16 marathons: Boston and Chicago in both 2000 and 2001 before 2003 Worlds, and Boston 2004-05, Osaka 2006. 2nd in New York 1999 and 2003 (2:23:03), in Boston (2:21:12) and Chicago 2002 and London 2003. Record 10 sub-2:26 marathons. Her sister **Anastasha** (b. 27 Sep 1974) won marathons in 2002 at Turin in 2:29:27 and Venice in 2:29:03, making them the fastest marathoning sisters. Her brother **Samuel** ran 10km road best of 28:01 in 2007.

Isabella Bosibori **OCHICHI** b. 28 Oct 1979 Keroka, Kisii 1.62m 48kg. Police corporal.
At 5000m: OG: '04- 2; WCh: '03- 6, '05- 8; CG: '06- 1; AfG: '03- 3; AfCh: '06- 4 (2 10,000m). World CC: 4k: '02-03-04-05-06: 3/4/5/3/10; 8k: '05- 5; HMar: '01- 8. Won Kenyan CC 2003.
Progress at 5000m: 1997- 16:24.46, 2000- 16:54.1A, 2001- 16:34.0A, 2002- 15:01.42, 2003- 14:47.70, 2004- 14:46.42, 2005- 14:38.21, 2006- 14:46.99. pbs: 800m 2:07.4A '05, 1500m 4:14.5A '05, 2000m 5:39.47 '04, 3000m 8:31.32 '04, 10,000m 31:29.43 '06; Road: 10km 30:27 '05, 15km 47:54 '01, 10M 51:08 '05, HMar 68:38 '01.
Married to marathoner David Maina. European base in Brest, France.

Margaret OKAYO b. 30 May 1976 Masaba, Kisii district 1.50m 39kg. Sergeant in police service.
At Mar: OG: '04- dnf. At HMar: WCh: '99- 13.
Progress at Mar: 1999- 2:26:00, 2000- 2:26:36, 2001- 2:24:21, 2002- 2:20:43, 2003- 2:22:31, 2004- 2:22:35, 2005- 2:25:22, 2006- 2:29:16. pbs: 5000m 15:30.0A '01, Road: 10km 32:32 '99, 15km 49:09 '99, HMar 67:23 '03.
7 wins in 16 marathons. Made a brilliant debut with 2:26:00 for 2nd at Chicago 1999, and won at San Diego 2000 and 2001, New York 2001 and 2003 (3rd 2000, 4th 2004, 6th 2002), Boston and Milan 2002, London 2004 (4th 2005).

Lucy WANGUI Kabuu b. 24 Mar 1984 Uasin Gishu 1.55m 41kg. Suzuki, Japan.
At (5000m)/10,000m: OG: '04- 9; CG: '06- 3/1. World 4k CC: '05- 5.
Progress at 10,000m: 2002- 32:54.70, 2003- 31:06.20, 2004- 31:05.90, 2005- 31:22.37, 2006- 31:29.66. 2007- 31:32.52. pbs: 1500m 4:09.60 '02, 3000m 8:55.56 '07, 5000m 14:56.09 '06, HMar 69:47 '04.

KOREA

Governing body: Korea Athletics Federation, 10 Chamshil Dong, Songpa-Gu, Seoul. Founded 1945. **National Champions 2007**: **Men:** 100m: Limhee-nam 10.62, 200m: Park Se-jung 21.48, 400m: Cho Sung-kwon 47.02, 800m:Lee Jae-hoon 1:51.74, 1500m: Lee Du-haeng 3:48.00, 5000m: Cho Keun-hyung 14:18.50, 10,000m: Lee Du-haeng 29:49.48, Mar: Kil Kyong-sun 2:15:57, 3000mSt: Ahn Hyun-woo 9:17.07, 110mh: Lee Jung-joon 13.94, 400mh: Yoo Kyung-min 52.13, HJ: Kim Jong-pyo 2.15, PV: Kim Do-kyun 5.20, LJ: Suh Suk-kyun 7.76, TJ: Kim Duk-hyung 16.57, SP: Hwang In-sung 18.10, DT: Choi Jong-bum 55.46, HT: Lee Yeon-Chul 70.42, JT: Park Jae-myong 78.27, Dec: Kim Kun-woo 7289, 20kW: Shin Il-yong 1:24:00. **Women**: 100m/200m: Oh Hyung-mi 11.83/25.18, 400m: Lee Yun-kyong 55.74, 800m: Huh Yeon-jung 2:08.90, 1500m: Nam Son-ha 4:28.52, 5000m: Kim Seung-eun 16:35.36, 10,000m: Choi Kyung-hee 35:22.09, Mar: Chang Jin-sook 2:32:14, 3000mSt: Kwon Keun-young 10:41.43, 100mh: Lee Yeon-kyong 13.45, 400mh: Chung Sul-mi 60.17, HJ: Chung Mi-jung 1.75, PV: Chung So-hee 3.20, LJ: Jung Soon-ok 6.66, TJ: Jung Hye-kyung 13.49, SP: Lee Mi-young 17.21, DT: Kim Min-young 50.21, HT: Kang Na-ru 58.84, JT: Kim Kyong-ae 56.29, Hep: Chung Su-hye 5013.

KUWAIT

Governing body: Kuwait Association of Athletic Federation, PO Box 5499, 13055 Safat, Kuwait. Founded 1957.

Mohammed AL-AZIMI b. 16 Jun 1982 1.76m 70kg.
At 800m: OG: '00- h 4x400mR, '04- h; WCh: '05/07- sf; AsiG: '06- 2; Asi-J: '01- 3.
Kuwait records 800m (6) & 1500m 2003-06.
Progress at 800m: 1999- 1:49.53, 2000- 1:50.99, 2001- 1:49.55, 2003- 1:47.44, 2004- 1:45.25, 2005- 1:46.67, 2006- 1:44.13, 2007- 1:44.55. pbs: 1500m 3:42.75 '06.

LATVIA

Governing body: Latvian Athletic Association, 1 Augsiela Str, Riga LV-1009. Founded 1921.
National Championships first held in 1920 (men), 1922 (women). **2007 Champions**: **Men**: 100m/200m: Elvijs Misans 10.63/21.10, 400m: Aleksandrs Makarovs 49.82, 800m: Normunds Silins 1:52.49, 1500m/3000m: Valerijs Zolnerovics 3:48.00/8:21.12, 5000m/10,000m: Sandis Bralitis 14:44.79/30:41.6, HMar: Dmitrijs Slesarenoks 74:29, Mar: Modris Liepins 2:46:21,

3000mSt: Konstantins Savcuks 9:16.49, 110mh: Karlis Daube 14.50, 400mh: Valdis Iljanovs 52.74, HJ: Normunds Pupols 2.10, PV: Egons Lacis 4.50, LJ: Andrejs Maskancevs 7.69, TJ: Maksims Tkacovs 15.72, SP: Maris Urtans 20.11, DT: Oskars Silcenoks 53.98, HT: Igors Sokolovs 76.22, JT: Ainars Kovals 82.02, Dec: Edgars Erins 7961, 20kW/50kW: Ingus Janevics 1:25:30/3:53:57. **Women**: 100m: Zanda Grava 12.22, 200m/400m: Marina Surnina 24.84/54.98, 800m: Tereza Vimba 2:14.24, 1500m/3000m: Irina Poluskina 4:16.88/9:45.16, 5000m Ilona Marhele 17:14.52, 10,000m: Anita Cuhnova 38:33.9, HMar: Jelena Prokopcuka 79:39, Mar: Anita Liepina 3:10:19, 3000mSt: Polina Jelizarova 10:14.8, 100mh: Aiga Grabuste 14.13, 400mh: Ieva Zunda 57.10, HJ: Natalja Cakova 1.85, PV: Maira Bluma 2.80, LJ: Ilva Janite 5.63, TJ: Sabine Skrodere 13.07, SP: Diana Ozolina 12.75, DT: Laura Igaune 47.98, HT: Vaira Kumermane (Godmane) 56.72, JT: Sinta Ozolina 56.16, Hep: Jesenija Volzankina 5799, 10kW/20kW: Jolanta Dukure 48:43/1:32:29.

Ainars KOVALS b. 21 Nov 1981 Riga 1.92m 100kg. LU/LSK.
At JT: WCh: '05- 7, '07- dnq 14; EC: '06- 5; EU23: '01- 4, '03- 6; WUG: '05- 1, '07- 3. Latvian champion 2005, 2007.
Progress at JT: 1997- 57.56, 1998- 63.09, 1999- 70.55, 2000- 72.68, 2001- 76.58, 2002- 75.05, 2003- 80.75, 2004- 82.13, 2005- 82.22, 2006- 85.95, 2007- 82.23. pb SP 14.84i '06, 14.58 '04.

Dmitrijs MILKEVICS b. 6 Dec 1981 Riga 1.81m 72kg. Studied business administration at University of Nebraska, USA.
At 800m: OG: '04- sf; WCh: '05- h, '07- sf; EC: '06- 4; WI: '06- 4, '08- 4. Won NCAA 800m 2005, Latvian 400m 2001-02, 2006.
Latvian 800m record 2006.
Progress at 800m: 2003- 1:49.4, 2004- 1:45.60, 2005- 1:44.74, 2006- 1:43.67, 2007- 1:44.37. pbs 100m 10.7 '00, 200m 21.87 '02, 21.7 '03; 400m 46.44 '03, 600m 1:15.60i '05, 1000m 2:22.82i '05.

Stanislav(s) OLIJAR(S) b. 22 Mar 1979 Chelyabinsk, Russia 1.90m 80kg. ASK.
At 110mh: OG: '00- sf, '04- 5; WCh: '97-99-03-05-07: qf/sf/h/sf/sf; EC: '98- sf, '02- 2, '06- 1; WJ: '96- h (dnq LJ), '98- 1; EJ: '97- 2; EU23: '99- 2; WCp: '02- 3, '06- 4. At 60mh: WI: '01-03-04-06-08: 8/6/4/4=/3=; EI: '00-02-05: 1/3/dq. Won LAT 100m 1999, 110mh 2002.
Five Latvian 110mh records 2000-03.
Progress at 110mh: 1996- 14.52, 1997- 13.62, 1998- 13.49, 1999- 13.28, 2000- 13.25, 2001- 13.29, 2002- 13.15A/13.22, 2003- 13.08, 2004- 13.20, 2005- 13.11, 2006- 13.15, 2007- 13.38. pbs: 60m 6.70i '98, 6.6i '01; 100m 10.42A/10.33w '02, 200m 20.91A '03, 20.95 '02; 400m 46.66 '00, 50mh 6.46i '03, 60mh 7.49i '02, LJ 7.94i '00, 7.57A '97.
His mother (and coach) Ludmila Olijar (b. 5 Feb 1958) set the Latvian record holder for 100mh 12.90 (1989).

Eriks RAGS b. 1 Jun 1975 Ventspils 1.83m 93kg. Ventspils.
At JT: OG: '00- dnq 26, '04- 7; WCh: '97- dnq 22, '99- 10, '01- 8, '03- dnq 17, '05- 6, '07- 11; EC: '98- dnq 21, '02- 4, '06- 9; WJ: '94- dnq 28; EU23: '97- 4; WUG: '99- 1, '01- 1. 2nd GP 2001. Latvian champion 1997, 1999-2003, 2006.
Five Latvian javelin records 1999-2001.
Progress at JT: 1991- 63.50, 1992- 60.90, 1993- 65.22, 1994- 68.42, 1995- 75.32, 1996- 76.92, 1997- 79.04, 1998- 80.50, 1999- 83.78, 2000- 83.61, 2001- 86.47, 2002- 86.44, 2003- 86.32A, 2004- 85.83, 2005- 82.35, 2006- 85.99, 2007- 83.35.

Vadims VASILEVSKIS b. 5 Jan 1982 Riga 1.87m 82kg. ASK.
At JT: OG: '04- 2; WCh: '05- dnq 16, '07- 4; EC: '02- dnq 16, '06- 4; WJ: '00- 8; EU23: '03- 7; EJ: '01- 7; WUG: '07- 1.
Three Latvian javelin records 2006-07.
Progress at JT: 1998- 59.17, 1999- 63.82, 2000- 73.07, 2001- 73.25, 2002- 81.92, 2003- 77.81, 2004- 84.95, 2005- 81.30, 2006- 90.43, 2007- 90.73.
Set personal bests in qualifying (84.43) and final at 2004 Olympics.

Women

Jelena PROKOPCUKA b. 21 Sep 1976 Riga 1.68m 51kg. née Chelnova. Arkadija/ASK.
At (5000m)/10,000m: OG: '96- (h), '00- 9/19, '04- 7; WCh: '97- (h), '03- 10, '05- 12; EC: '98- (16), '02- 5, '06- 6; EU23: '97- 5/6. At 3000m (/10,000m): WJ: '94: h/13; EJ: '95- 5/4; EI: '98- 4, '00- 4. World HMar: '01- 5, '02- 3. Won LAT 1500m 1994, 1997-8, 2003, 3000m 1992-3, 1998-9, 2002, 2006; 5000m 1995-7, 2002, 2005; 10,000m 2003-04, HMar 1995, 1999, 2003, 2007; CC 2001-02.
Latvian records 3000m (3) 2000-06, 5000m (4) 1997-2000, 10,000m (5) 2000-06, 1 Hour 2003, HMar 2001 & 2005, Mar (3) 2002-05.
Progress at 5000m, 10,000m, Mar: 1994- 35:22.44, 1995- 16:20.7, 34:21.84; 1996- 15:59.00, 33:59.9; 1997- 15:40.68, 33:41.51; 1998- 15:30.76, 33:29.04; 1999- 16:09.22, 2000- 14:47.71, 31:27.86; 2001- 15:14.73, 32:02.96; 2002- 15:08.28, 31:17.72, 2:29:36; 2003- 15:02.04, 31:06.14, 2:24:01; 2004- 31:04.10, 2:26:51; 2005- 15:03.10, 31:04.55, 2:22:56; 2006- 15:17+, 30:38.78, 2:23:48; 2007- 15:33.93, 32:43.2, 2:26:13. pbs: 400m 60.46 '98, 800m 2:05.82 '00, 1500m 4:12.36 '00, 3000m 8:42.86 '06, 15km 48:47 '01, 1 Hour 17,776m '03, HMar 68:11 '05.
45 Latvian titles including indoors. Married to Aleksandrs Prokopchuks (LAT marathon record 2:15:56 '95). Marathons: 7th London & 3rd Chicago 2003, 4th Boston & 5th New York 2004, won Osaka 2005, New York 2005-06 (3rd 2007), 2nd Boston 2006 & 2007.

LITHUANIA

Governing body: Athletic Federation of

Lithuania, Statybininku 12/10, Vilnius LT 03201. Founded 1921.

National Championships first held in 1921 (women 1922). **2007 Champions: Men:** 100m/200m: Zilvinas Adomavicius 10.82/21.75, 400m: Linas Bruzas 47.95, 800m: Egidijus Svegzda 1:53.36, 1500m: Vitalij Kozlov 3:52.35, 5000m/3000mSt: Tomas Matijosius 14:41.56/ 9:19.86, 10,000m: Dainius Saucikovas 31:57.66, HMar/Mar: Aurimas Skinulis 71:28/2:35:15, 110mh: Evaldas Pranckus 15.01, 400mh: Arturas Kulnis 51.19, HJ: Rimantas Melinis 2.10, PV: Eimantas Spitrys 3.80, LJ: Vytautas Seliukas 7.25, TJ: Mantas Dilys 15.99, SP: Paulius Luozys 17.35, DT: Aleksas Abromavicius 54.86, HT: Zydrunas Vasiliauskas 56.43, JT: Tomas Intas 73.25, Dec: Tadas Volkavicius 7335, 20kW/50kW: Tadas Suskevicius 1:25:42/3:57:48/ **Women**: 100m: Audra Dagelyte 11.50, 200m: Edita Lingyte 24.21, 400m: Jurate Kudirkaite 54.23, 800m: Jekaterina Sakovic 2:04.46, 1500m: Rasa Drazdauskaite 4:21.83, 5000m: Vaida Zusinaite 17:04.13, 10,000m: Remalda Kergyte 35:21.04, HMar: Gyte Norgiliene 84:07, Mar: Modesta Kaminskiene 3:06:52, 3000mSt: Gintare Kubiliute 11:31.95, 100m: Sonata Tamosaityte 14.23, 400mh: Natalija Piliusina 61.00, HJ: Karina Vnukova 1.85, PV: Vitalija Dejeva 3.30, LJ/SP: Austra Skujyte 6.15/16.71, TJ: Ieva Staponkute 12.71, DT: Zinaida Sendriute 55.25, HT: Vaida Keleciute 52.65, JT: Indre Jakubaityte 60.46, Hep: Agne Jakubauskaite 4595, 10kW: Brigita Virbalyte 45:50, 20kW: Neringa Aidietyte 1:35:33.

Virgilijus ALEKNA b. 13 Feb 1972 Terpeikiai, Kupiskis 2.00m 130kg. Graduate of Lithianian Academy of Physical Culture and (from 1995) guard of the Lithuanian president.

At DT: OG: '96- 5, '00- 1, '04- 1; WCh: '95- dnq 19, '97- 2, '99- 4, '01- 2, '03- 1, '05- 1, '07- 4; EC: '98- 3, '02- 2, '06- 1; WCp: '98- 1, '06- 1. Won WAF 2003, 2005-06; GP 2001 (2nd 1999). LTU champion 1998, 2000-05.

Four Lithuanian discus records 2000.

Progress at DT: 1990- 52.84, 1991- 57.16, 1992- 60.86, 1993- 62.84, 1994- 64.20, 1995- 62.78, 1996- 67.82, 1997- 67.70, 1998- 69.66A, 1999- 68.25, 2000- 73.88, 2001- 70.99, 2002- 66.90, 2003- 69.69, 2004- 70.97, 2005- 70.67, 2006- 71.08, 2007- 71.56. pb SP: 19.99 '97.

His 72.35 and 73.88 at the 2000 LTU Championships were the second and third longest ever discus throws. His 70.17 to win the 2005 World title (coming from 2nd at 68.10 with the last throw) was the first ever 70m throw at a global championships. He has 17 competitions and 26 throws over 70m. 37 successive wins from August 2005 to 4th at Worlds August 2007. Married on 4 Mar 2000 Kristina Sablovskyte (pb LJ 6.14 '96, TJ 12.90 '97, sister of Remigija Nazaroviene).

Women

Austra SKUJYTE b. 12 Aug 1979 Birzai 1.88m 80kg. Graduated in kinesiology from Kansas State University, USA.

At Hep: OG: '00- 12, '04- 2; WCh: '01- 6, '03- 10, '05- 4, '07- 6; EC: '02- 4; WJ: '98- 6; EU23: '99- 6, '01- 3. At Pen: WI: '04- 3, '08- 5; EI: '07- 4. Won NCAA 2001-02; LTU 100mh 2000, 2005; HJ 2005, LJ 2005, 2007; SP 2001-02, 2004-05. 2007; Hep 1997. World decathlon record 2005.

Progress at Hep: 1997- 4930, 1998- 5606, 1999- 5724, 2000- 6104, 2001- 6150w, 2002- 6275, 2003- 6213, 2004- 6435, 2005- 6386, 2007- 6380. pbs: 100m 12.49 '05, 200m 24.82 '04, 24.79w '07; 400m 57.19 '05, 800m 2:15.92 '04, 1500m 5:15.86 '05, 60mh 8.69i '04, 100mh 14.02/13.83w '04; HJ 1.89i/1.86 '06; PV 3.20 '06, LJ 6.39i '05, 6.32 '04, 6.40w '01; SP 17.05 '06, DT 51.30 '02, JT 52.63 '07, Pen 4740i '07, Dec 8358 '05.

Set three pbs in 2004 Olympics, including two seconds off 800m best to secure silver.

LUXEMBOURG

Governing body: Fédération Luxembourgeoise d'Athlétisme, BP 503, L-2015 Luxembourg. Founded 1928.

2007 National Champions: **Men**: 100m/200m: Yoann Bebon 10.90/21.73, 400m: Jacques Frisch 49.09, 800m: Mikel Schumacher 1:53.11, 1500m: François Kauffman 3:59.77, 5000m: Pascal Groben 14:54.15, 10,000m/HMar: Vincent Nothum 31:21.84/67:29, Mar: Patrick Lenertz 2:37:57, 110mh: Claude Godart 14.09, HJ: Jeff Reuter 1.90, PV: Mike Gira 4.60, LJ: Patrick Hansen 6.95, TJ: Benjamin Kraemer 14.16, SP: David Hengen 14.13, DT: Marcel Weber 40.06, HT: Steve Tonizzo 52.04, JT: Tun Wagner 54.80. **Women**: 100m/200m/LJ: Chantal Hayen 12.30/25.48/6.42, 400m/100mh: Martine Bomb 57.22/14.41, 800m/1500m: Véronique Hansen 2:14.85/4:42.33, 3000m/HMar: Anna Logelin 10:19.18/-, 10,000m: Liz May 35:45.21, Mar: Pascale Schmoetten 2:55:41, 3000mSt: Anne Flies 13:50.97, HJ: Liz Kuffer 1.65, PV: Stephanie Vieillevoye 3.40, TJ: Natahlaie Gieres 11.03, SP: Kim Schartz 13.20, DT/HT: Vanessa Bignoli 40.60/35.21, JT: Nadia Bellagamba 32.40.

MEXICO

Governing body: Federación Mexicana de Atletismo, Anillo Periférico y Av. del Conscripto, 11200 México D.F. Founded 1933.

2007 National Champions: Men: 100m: Dan Morales 10.61, 200m: Juan Pedro Toledo 20.92, 400m/400mh: Héctor Rodríguez 47.52/52.32, 800m: Martell Munguía 1:51.53, 1500m: Isaías Haro 3:52.13, 5000m: José David Galván 14:16.98, Mar: Pablo Olmedo 2:11:34, 3000mSt: Josafath González 9:01.54, 110mh: Alejandro Hernández 14.90, HJ: Jorge Rouco 2.15, PV: Cristian Sánchez 5.05, LJ/TJ: Luis Alberto Rivera 7.50/15.42, SP:

Mario Ramos 16.82, DT: Jesús Sánchez 53.21, HT: Santiago Loera 60.92, JT: Luis Enrique Guzmán 71.32, Dec: Alberto Zárate 6560, 20kW: Claudio Vargas 1:24:10. **Women:** 100m/200m: Zudikey Rodríguez 11.82/23.74, 400m: Gabriela Medina 52.09, Cristina Guevara 2:06.88, 1500m: Yamilé Alaluf 4:33.92, 5000m: Marisol Romero 16:51.57, Mar: María Elena Valencia 2:31:16, 3000mSt: Talis Apud 10:51.65, 100mh: Violeta Ávila 13.88, 400mh: Elisa Barrón 60.42, HJ: Romary Rifka 1.92, PV: Cecilia Villar 3.80, LJ: Claudett Martínez 6.12, TJ: Aidé Villarreal 12.65, SP: Tamara Lechuga 15.17, DT: Irais Estrada 47.52, HT: Jéssica Ponce de León 62.35, JT: Ana Gutiérrez 53.73, Hep: Mariana Abuela 4949, 20kW: María Esther Sánchez 1:39:21.

Éder SÁNCHEZ b. 21 May 1986 Toluca 1.76m 67kg.
At 20kW: WCh: '05- 8, '07- 4; CAG: '06- 2; won MEX 2006. At 10,000mW: WJ: '02- 4; WCp: '04- 2J. CAC junior record 20kW 2005.
Progress at 20kW: 2005- 1:19:02, 2006- 1:23:24A, 2007- 1:20:08. pbs: 5000mW 18:40.97A '07, 10,000mW 40:46.29 '04, 10km Rd: 39:42 '07.

Women

Ana Gabriela **GUEVARA** b. 4 Mar 77 Nogales, Sonora 1.73m 61kg.
At 400m/4x400m (800m): OG: '00- 5, '04- 2; WCh: '99- sf, '01- 3, '03- 1, '05- 3, '07- 4; WI: '99- 4; WJ: '96- sf; PAm: '99- 1, '03- 1, '07- 1; CAG: '98- 2 (2), '02- 1/1R; WUG: '97- (6); WCp: '02- 1. Won WAF 2003-04, GP 2002 (2nd overall), GWG 2001, IbAm 1998.
Four CAC 400m records 2002-03, MEX records 400m (9) 1998-2003, 800m (2) 1998. World best 300m 2003.
Progress at 400m, 800m: 1996- 54.75A, 2:09.80; 1997- 52.46A, 2:02.90; 1998- 50.65, 2:01.12; 1999- 50.70, 2:03.69, 2000- 49.70A/49.96, 2:02.88; 2001- 49.97; 2002- 49.16, 2003- 48.89, 2004- 49.53, 2005- 49.81, 2006- 50.43, 2007- 50.16. pbs: 200m: 23.78A '98, 300m 35.30A '03, 35.7+ '04, 35.92 '01.
She became the first Mexican woman to win a medal at any IAAF World Championship in track when 3rd in Edmonton 400m. Unbeaten in 24 successive 400m finals from then to loss to Tonique Williams-Darling in Rome on 2 July 2004, including 12 in 2002, when she shared the Golden League jackpot, and 8 in 2003. Played semi-professional basketball to December 1995.

Madaí PÉREZ b. 2 Feb 1980 Tlaxcala 1.57m 45kg.
At Mar: WCh: '05- 11. At 10,000m: PAm: '03- 5. At 5000m: CAG: '06- 3. World HMar: '05- 6. Won CAC-J 5000m 1998, PAm-J 5000m 1999, NACAC HMar 1999, 2001; MEX 10,000m 2003.
CAC marathon record 2006, CAC junior record 5000m & 10,000m 1999.
Progress at Mar: 2003- 2:31:24, 2004- 2:27:08, 2005- 2:26:50, 2006- 2:22:59. 2007- 2:30:16. pbs: 1500m 4:24.19 '03, 3000m 9:17.63 '05, 5000m 15:57.86A '06, 10,000m 32:22.09 '06, HMar 70:15+ '06.
4th Chicago Marathon 2006, 3rd Boston 2007. Married Odilón Cuahutle (Mar 2:17:15 '03) in 2001, daughter Kenjiro born 2002.

MOROCCO

Governing Body: Fédération Royale Marocaine d'Athlétisme, Complex Sportif Prince Moulay Abdellah, PO Box 1778 R/P, Rabat. F'd 1957.
2007 National Champions: Men: 100m: Aziz Ouhadi 10.47, 200m: Khalid Zougari Idrissi 20.82, 400m: Ali Nagmeldin SUD 45.62, 800m: Aboubakar Kaki SUD 1:45.49, 1500m: Zakaria Mazouzi 3:43.99, 5000m: Anis Salmouni 13:49.34, 3000mSt: Jilali Ismaili 8:38.57, 110mh: Zakaria Benslimmane 15.15, 400mh: El Houcine Ayade 51.47, HJ: Otmane Dyane 2.05, PV: Karim EL Mafhoum 5.00, LJ: Yahya Berrabeh 7.89, TJ: Younès Moudrik 16.12, SP/DT: Nabil Kiram 16.06/56,16, HT: Driss Barid 59.17, JT: Mohamed Driouchi 60.93. **Women**: 100m/200m: Fadoua Adili 11.92/24.68, 400m: Nawal El Jak SUD 52.84, 800m: Malika Akkaoui 2:05.20, 1500m: Halima Hachlaf 4:30.9, 5000m: Maria Laghrissi 16:40.08, 3000mSt: Ibtissam Guermouen 11:10.99, 110mh: Houria Mouhandis 14.24, 400mh: Mona Jabir SUD 55.15, HJ: Meryem Ouahbi 1.55, PV: Nisrine Dinar 3.80, LJ: Fatima Zahra Dkouk ?, LJ: Jamaa Chnaik 12.79, SP/DT: Rachida Lakhal 12.67.42.84, HT: Mouna Dani 56.30, JT: Nezha Marzak 43.49.

Hicham BELLANI b. 15 Sep 1979 1.80m 64kg. BEPA.
At 5000m: OG: '04- 9; WCh: '05- h. '07- 12; WUG: '03- 3; MAR 2002. At 3000m: WI: '04- 9. World 4k CC: '06- 14.
Progress at 5000m: 2001- 13:54.74, 2003- 13:15.03, 2004- 13:05.72, 2005- 12:59.67, 2006- 12:55.52, 2007- 13:30.35. pbs: 1500m 3:33.71 '07, 2000m 4:59.9 '07, 3000m 7:33.71 '06, HMar 61:44 '03.

Mouhcine CHÉHIBI b. 28 Jan 1978 1.82m 70kg. Efs Reims, France.
At 800m: OG: '00- sf, '04- 4; WCh: '99/03- h, '05/07- sf; AfCh: '00- 3; WUG: '01- 6.
Progress at 800m: 1999- 1:46.15, 2000- 1:46.2, 2001- 1:46.54, 2002- 1:47.15, 2003- 1:45.73, 2004- 1:44.62. 2005- 1:44.46, 2006- 1:44.16, 2007- 1:45.52. pbs: 600m 1:18.86 '00, 1000m 2:20.43i '05, 2:21.43 '03; 1500m 3:45.84 '04.
Disqualified for pushing at 2003 Worlds. Married to Hasna Benhassi (2 OG 800m 2004).

Jaouad GHARIB b. 22 May 1972 Khenifra province 1.76m 60kg.
At Mar: OG: '04- 11; WCh: '03- 1, '05- 1. At 10,000m: WCh: '01- 11; AfCh: '02- 8. At 3000m: WI: '03- 11. World HMar: '01- 9, '02- 2; CC: '02- 10. Won MedG 10,000m 2001.
Progress at 5000m, 10,000m, Mar: 2001- 13:19.69, 27:29.51; 2002- 13:20.59, 28:02.09i/28:57.12; 2003-

2:08:31, 2004- 2:07:02 (2:07:12?), 2005- 2:07:49, 2006- 2:07:19, 2007- 2:07:54. pbs: 3000m 7:39.22 '01, 2M 8:29.23i '02, 15km 43:08 '01, HMar 59:56 '04.
Began running at 22, made sudden emergence into top class in 2001. Sixth in 2:09:15 at Rotterdam 2003 on marathon debut and won world title in next marathon; London: 3rd 2004, 2nd 2005, 8th 2006, 4th 2007. 3rd Fukuoka marathon 2006, 2nd Chicago 2007.

Abderrahim GOUMRI b. 21 May 1976 Safi 1.67m 60kg.
At 5000m: OG: '04- 13; WCh: '03- 10. At 10,000m: WCh: '01- 16, '05- 8; AfCh: '02- 4. At 3000m: WI: '03- 9. At Mar: WCh: '07- dnf. World CC: '95-02-03-04-06-07: 25J/7/15/14/11/21; 4k: '03- 10, '05- 18; HMar: '03- 12.
Progress at 5000m, 10,000m: Mar, 1999- 13:20.70, 2001- 13:03.60, 27:26.01; 2002- 13:00.76, 27:52.62i/28:45.92; 2003- 13:05.81, 2004- 12:59.04, 2005- 12:50.25, 27:02.62; 2006- 12:57.89; 2007- 2:07:44. pbs: 1500m 3:39.80 '98, 1M 4:02.46 '99, 2000m 5:02.2 '06, 3000m 7:32.36 '01, HMar 61:19 '01.
Second London (debut) and New York Marathons 2007.

Abdelkader HACHLAF b. 3 July 1979 1.82m 68kg.
At 1500m: WCh: '01- 8; AfCh: '02- 3; WI: '03- 3, '04- dq 4. At 3000mSt: WCh: '03- 13, '07- 9; AfCh: '06- 2; won P.Arab G 5000m & 3000mSt 2007, Mar 1500m 2000. World 4k CC: '03- 16.
Progress at 1500m, 3000mSt: 2000- 3:39.28, 2001- 3:33.59, 2002- 3:33.66, 8:20.64; 2003- 3:35.03, 8:15.33; 2004- 3:37.61i, 2006- 3:38.96, 8:08.78; 2007- 8:17.03. pbs: 800m 1:46.9 '04, 1M 3:52.20 '02, 2000m 4:57.97 '01, 2000mSt 5:23.02 '07.
Two-year drugs ban 2004-06 after disqualification at 2004 World Indoors,

Abdelaati IGUIDER b. 25 Mar 1987 Errachidia 1.68m 50kg.
At 1500m: WCh: '07- h; WJ: '04- 1, '06- 2.
Progress at 1500m: 2004- 3:35.53, 2005- 3:35.63, 2006- 3:32.68, 2007- 3:32.75. pbs: 800m 1:47.14 '07, 1000m 2:19.14 '07, 1M 3:59.79 '07, 3000m 7:41.95 '07.

Amine LAÂLOU b. 13 May 1982 Salé 1.78m 57kg.
At 800m: OG: '04- sf; WCh: '03-05-07: h/sf/6; WJ: '00- sf; WY: '99-h; WI: '04- 4; AfCh: '02- h; AfJ: '01- 2; MAR champion 2003.
Moroccan 800m record 2006.
Progress at 800m: 2000- 1:51.55, 2001- 1:49.94, 2002- 1:46.5, 2003- 1:45.20, 2004- 1:43.68, 2005- 1:44.22, 2006- 1:43.25, 2007- 1:43.94. pb 400m 47.21 '04, 47.0 '03.

Mohamed MOUSTAOUI b. 2 Apr 1985 Khouribga 1.74m 60kg.
At 1500m: WCh: '07- sf; AfCh: '06- 5; WJ: '04- 4; AfJ: '03- 2; Arab champion 2007. World CC: '04- 14J, '05- 14 4k.
Progress at 1500m: 2003- 3:42.9, 2004- 3:37.44, 2005- 3:36.20, 2006- 3:32.51, 2007- 3:32.67. pbs: 800m 1:47.42 '05, 1M 3:53.03 '06, 2000m 5:00.98i '07, 3000m 7:46.82i '07, 7:49.57 '05; 2M 8:26.49i '05, 5000m 13:22.61 '05.

Women

Mariem ALAOUI SELSOULI b. 8 Apr 1984 Marrakech 1.65m 49kg.
At 1500m: WCh: '07- 5; WJ: '02- 5. At 3000m: WJ: '02- 2; WY: '01- 5; WI: '06- 6, '08- 3; Af-J: '03- 1. At 5000m: AfC: '06- 5; WUG: '05- 5. World CC: '03- 13J, '06- 15 4k, '07- 17. Won W.Students CC 2004. Moroccan 800m record 2006.
Progress at 1500m, 5000m: 2002- 4:13.9, 2003- 4:18.37, 2004- 4:19.59, 2005- 4:08.30, 16:07.99; 2006- 4:07.13, 15:04.46; 2007- 4:01.52, 14:36.52. pbs: 800m 2:13.81 '05, 3000m 8:29.52 '07.

Hasna BENHASSI b. 1 Jun 1978 Marrakech 1.66m 55kg. Panellínios, Greece.
At 800m: OG: '00- 8, '04- 2 (12 1500m); WCh: '97- sf, '05- 2, '07- 2; AfCh: '98- 2, '00- 1; WJ: '96- sf; WI: '99- 5, '06- 3; won WAF 2004, MedG 1997, Moroccan 1996. At 1500m: WI: '01- 1, '03- 8; AfCh: '02- 3.
MAR records 800m (4), 1000m, 1500m (2) 1998-2004.
Progress at 800m, 1500m: 1995- 2:11.0, 1996- 2:04.6, 4:31.4; 1997- 2:00.48, 4:27.1; 1998- 1:58.47, 4:05.15; 1999- 1:57.45, 4:05.29; 2000- 1:58.47, 4:14.28; 2001- 1:59.86i, 4:04.48i; 2002- 4:05.28, 2003- 2:01.08, 4:02.54; 2004- 1:56.43, 4:04.42; 2005- 1:58.41, 2006- 1:58.24, 4:20.86; 2007- 1:56.84. pbs: 400m 54.04 '00, 1000m 2:33.15 '99, 1M 4:32.99 '98.
Married to Mouhcine Chéhibi, daughter Farah born on 7 Dec 2001.

MOZAMBIQUE

Governing body: Federaçao Moçambicana de Atletismo,Parque dos Continuardores, CP 1094, Maputo. Founded 1978.

Maria de Lurdes **MUTOLA** b. 27 Oct 1972 Maputo 1.62m 61kg.
At 800m (1500m): OG: '88- h, '92- 5 (9), '96- 3, '00- 1, '04- 4; WCh: '91- 4, '93- 1, '95 dq sf, '97- 3, '99- 2, '01- 1, '03- 1, '05- 4, '07- dnf; WI: '93-5-7-9-01-03-04-06-08: 1/1/1/2/1/1/1/1/3; CG: '98- 1, '02- 1, '06- 3; AfCh: '88-90-3-8-02: 2/1/1/1/1 (1 1500m 90); AfG: '91- 1, '95- 1, '99- 1; WCp: '92- 1/3R, '94- 1, '98- 1, '02- 1. Won WAF 2003, GWG 1994, 2001; GP 1993, 1995 (won overall), 1999 (2nd overall), 2001; 2nd 1997.
Records: World 1000m 1995, two WIR 1000m (2:32.08 '96 and 2:30.94 '99). African: 800m (8) 1991-4, 1000m (4) 1993-5; Commonwealth 800m 1997. African junior 800m (3) and 1500m 1991. MOZ 200m to 3000m.
Progress at 800m, 1500m: 1988- 2:04.36, 1989- 2:05.7, 4:31.5; 1990- 2:13.54, 4:25.27; 1991- 1:57.63,

4:12.72; 1992- 1:57.49, 4:02.60; 1993- 1:55.43, 4:04.97; 1994- 1:55.19, 4:13.93; 1995- 1:55.72, 4:01.6mx; 1996- 1:57.07, 4:01.63; 1997- 1:55.29, 4:09.1mx; 1998- 1:56.11, 1999- 1:56.04, 2000- 1:56.15, 4:02.39; 2001- 1:56.85, 2002- 1:56.16, 4:01.50; 2003- 1:55.55, 2004- 1:56.51, 4:07.57; 2005- 1:58.49i/1:58.96, 2006- 1:56.77, 2007- 1:56.98. pbs: 200m 23.86 '94, 300m 37.16mx '94, 400m 51.37 '94, 600m 1:22.87 '02, 1000m 2:29.34 '95, 1M 4:36.09 '91, 2000m 6:03.84 '92, 3000m 9:27.37 '91, 5000m 18:15.1 '90; Rd 1M 4:32.4 '95.

A star soccer player at school in Maputo, she was enabled to attend school in Eugene, Oregon, USA by a grant from the Olympic Solidarity Committee. 50 successive wins in 800m finals 1992-6 (apart from disqualification for stepping out of her lane in her World semi-final) ending with Olympic bronze in 1996, and 39 successive wins at 800m including 12 heats in 2002-04. Became Mozambique's first ever CG champion in 1998 and in 2002 the first athlete ever to win four individual World Cup titles. She was the sole winner of the Golden League jackpot of £1 million in 2003, and now has a record seven World indoor titles with two outdoors in a record nine appearances at each. Her 1:56.36 for 800m in 1998 was disallowed as a world indoor record as she ran inside the lane. 12 successive wins at Zürich 1993-2004. She has run 193 sub-2 minute 800m times from 1991 to March 2008.

NAMIBIA

Governing body: Namibia AAU, PO Box 195, Swakopmund. Founded 1990.

Agnes SAMARIA b. 11 Aug 1972 Otjiwarongo 1.66m 56kg.

At 800m/(1500m): OG: '04- sf; WCh: '01- h, '03/05- sf; '07- sf/8; CG: '02- 3; AfCh: '02- 2, '06- 6; AfG: '07- 2/3.

Namibian records 400m, 800m, 1000m, 1500m, 1M from 2000.

Progress at 800m, 1500m: 2000- 2:03.99, 2001- 2:00.81A, 4:14.40; 2002- 1:59.15, 4:13.22; 2003- 2:01.51, 2004- 1:59.16, 4:14.61; 2005- 1:59.91, 2006- 2:07.65, 2007- 1:59.76, 4:05.44. pbs: 400m 53.83A '01, 1000m 2:34.19 '02, 1M 4:25.01 '07.

NETHERLANDS

Governing body: Koninklijke Nederlandse Atletiek Unie (KNAU), Postbus 60100, NL-6800 JC Arnhem. Founded 1901.

National Championships first held in 1910 (men), 1921 (women). **2007 Champions: Men**: 100m/200m: Guus Hoogmoed 10.26/20.48, 400m: Youssef el Rhalfioui 46.67, 800m: Arnoud Okken 1:50.30; 1500m: Bram Rouwen 4:08.08, 5000m: Michel Butter 13:55.56, 10,000m: Marco Gielen 29:14.88, HMar: Koen Raymaekers 62:30, Mar: Luc Krotwaar 2:15:28, 3000mSt: Simon Vroemen 8:35.40, 110mh: Gregory Sedoc 13.67, 400mh: Eelco Veldhuijzen 50.77, HJ: Martijn Nuijens 2.21, PV: Rens Blom 5.42, LJ: Joost van Bennekom 7.28, TJ: David van Hetten 14.91, SP/DT: Rutger Smith 20.38/63.63, HT: Ronald Gram 63.18, JT: Elliott Thijssen 69.42, Dec: Pelle Rietveld 7484, 20kW: Jacques van Bremen 1:37:34, 50kW: Victor Mennen 4:49:55. **Women**: 100m/200m: Pascal van Assendelft 11.79/23.86, 400m: Annemarie Schulte 53.49, 800m: Machteld Mulder 2:10.72, 1500m: Marije te Raa 4:42.90, 5000m: Selma Borst 16:40.62, 10,000m: Daphne Panhuysen 34:11.92, HMar: Merel de Knegt 74:21, Mar: Madja Wijenberg 2:37:25, 3000mSt: Andrea Deelstra 10:21.56, 100m: Femke van der Meij 13.42, 400mh: Tamara Ruben 57.92, HJ: Karin Ruckstuhl 1.82, PV: Rianna Galiart 4.01, LJ: Yvonne Wisse 6.10, TJ: Brenda Baar 12.72, SP: Denise Kemkers 17.00, DT: Monique Jansen 54.10, HT: Maaike Schetters 58.50, JT: Bregje Crolla 54.53, Hep: Jolanda Kiezer 6092.

Rens BLOM b. 1 Mar 1977 Munstergeleen 1.78m 75kg. AV Unitas & TSV Bayer 04 Leverkusen, GER.

At PV: OG: '00- dnq 15, '04- 9=; WCh: '01- nh, '03- dnq 14, '05- 1; EU23: '97- 10, '99- 5=; WI: '03- 3, '04- nh; EI: '00- 3; WUG: '97- 4; ECp: '04- 6. Dutch champion 2001-05, 2007.

Three Dutch pole vault records 1997-2004.

Progress at PV: 1990- 3.41, 1991- 3.90, 1992- 4.05, 1993- 4.70, 1994- 5.10i, 1995- 5.00, 1996- 5.40, 1997- 5.62, 1998- 5.60i/5.55, 1999- 5.70i/5.50, 2000- 5.75, 2001- 5.70, 2002- 5.65, 2003- 5.75, 2004- 5.81, 2005- 5.80, 2006- 5.50, 2007- 5.60.

In 2005 he became the first Dutch athlete to won gold at the World Championships, after which he was appointed a Knight in the Order of Orange-Nassau. Series of injury problems have held him back since then. Father Wim set pbs in 1967 of 100m 10.5, 200m 21.4/21.1w.

Kamiel MAASE b. 20 Oct 1971 Nijmegen 1.90m 70kg. Graduate of Universities of Texas and Leiden. Leiden.

At 10,000m (5000m): OG: '04- 14; WCh: '97- 11, '99- 8, '01- 10, '03- 8; EC: '98- 8, '02- 9 (5); WUG: '97- 1; ECp: '04- (5). At Mar: OG: '00- 13; EC: '06- 9. World HMar: '99- 13. Eur CC '96-00-01-02: 20/7/2/11. Won NED 5000m 1995-7, 1999-2001, 2003-04; HMar 2004, Mar 2003 & 2005-06, CC 1997-9, 2002-06.

Dutch records: 10,000m (3) 1997-2002, 5000m 2000 & 2002, Marathon 2003 & 2007.

Progress at 10,000m, Mar: 1995- 28:52.99, 1996- 28:01.4, 1997- 27:35.72, 1998- 27:51.42, 1999- 27:34.02, 2:10:08; 2000- 27:56.94, 2:16:24; 2001- 28:02.37, 2002- 27:26.29, 2003- 27:45.46, 2:08:31; 2004- 27:51.99, 2005- 2:12:51, 2006- 2:10:45, 2007- 28:31.02, 2:08:21. pbs: 1500m 3:42.84 '01, 1M 4:04.7 '96, 3000m 7:45.44 '99, 5000m 13:13.06 '02, Road: 15km 43:33 '07, 10M 46:44 '07, HMar 62:08 '00, 30km 1:30:20 '03.

Rutger SMITH b. 9 Jul 1981 Groningen 1.97m 129kg. Groningen Atletiek.

At SP (/DT): OG: '04- dnq 14/16; WCh: '03- dnq 25/15, '05- 2, '07- 4/3; EC: '02- 8. '06- 4/7; WJ: '00- 1/3; EU23: '03- 3/1; EJ: '99- 1/1; WI: '03- dnq 10, '08- 5; EI: '05- 2; ECp: '04- 2/2. Won NED SP 2000, 2002-07; DT 2002-07.
Three Dutch shot records 2005-06.
Progress at SP, DT: 1998- 15.23, 51.18; 1999- 18.27, 53.81; 2000- 19.48, 58.74; 2001- 18.92i/18.21, 59.96; 2002- 20.52, 64.69; 2003- 20.52, 62.70; 2004- 20.94, 63.79; 2005- 21.41, 65.51; 2006- 21.62, 64.60; 2007- 21.19, 67.63; 2008- 20.89i.
First athlete to win World Championships medals in shot and discus.

Bram SOM b. 20 Feb 1980 Terborg 1.78m 67kg. Atletico '73 (Gendringen). Sergeant in Dutch army.
At 800m: OG: '00- h, '04- sf; WCh: '01/03- sf, '07- h; EC: '02- 6, '06- 1; WJ: '98- 5; EJ: '99- 3; EU23: '01- 5; WI: '03- 5; WCp: '06- 2. Dutch champion 2000-01, 2003-04, 2006.
Progress at 800m: 1995- 2:01.27, 1996- 1:53.31, 1997- 1:49.55, 1998- 1:47.99, 1999- 1:46.58, 2000- 1:44.01, 2001- 1:43.98, 2002- 1:45.86, 2003- 1:44.22, 2004- 1:44.37, 2006- 1:43.45, 2007- 1:45.61. pbs: 100m 10.97, 200m 21.56 '01, 400m 46.87 '01, 600m 1:15.37 '04, 1000m 2:17.81i '03, 2:20.18 '99; 1500m 3:48.86 '01.
Achilles operations at end of 2005 and 2007 seasons.

Women

Lornah KIPLAGAT b. 1 May 1974 Kabeimit, Kenya 1.66m 49kg. AV Hylas (Alkmaar). Married to Pieter Langerhorst NED.
At 10,000m: OG: '04- 5; WCh: '03- 4; EC: '06- 5. World 20k: '06- 1; HMar: '05- 2, '07- 1; CC: '04-06-07: 6/5 (4k) & 2/1; Eur CC: '05- 1. Won Dutch 10,000m 2006, Mar 2005.
World road bests 10 miles 2002 & 2006, 20km (3) and HMar (3) 2003-07, European record 15km 2007, Dutch records 10,000m & Marathon 2003.
Progress at 10,000m, Mar: 1997- 2:33:50, 1998- 2:34:03, 1999- 2:25:29, 2000- 2:22:36, 2001- 2:27:56, 2002- 2:23:55, 2003- 30:12.53, 2:22:22; 2004- 30:31.92, 2:28:21; 2005- 2:28:10, 2006- 30:37.26, 2:32:31; 2007- 2:24:46. pbs: 3000m 8:52.82 '00, 5000m 14:51.95mx '02, 14:56.43 '03; Road: 5M 25:09 '97 (former world best), 10km 30:32 '02, 15km 46:59 '07, 10M 50:50 '06, 20km 62:57 '07, HMar 66:25 '07.
Four wins in 16 marathons: Los Angeles 1997 and 1998, Amsterdam 1999, Osaka 2002. Capped a series of fine road runs with second in Chicago marathon 2000. 4th Boston 2001, 4th Osaka and 3rd New York 2003, 5th London 2007. Switched from Kenyan to Dutch (citizen from 23 July 2003).

Karin RUCKSTUHL b. 2 Nov 1980 Baden, Switzerland 1.81m 65kg. AAC (Amsterdam). PhD student in geophysics.
At Hep: OG: '04- 16; WCh: '05- 8, '07- dnf; EC: '02- 14, '06- 2; EU23: '01- 13. At Pen: WI: '04- 4, '06- 2; EI: '05- 4, '07- 3. Won NED 100mh 2006, HJ 2004, 2006-07; LJ 2001, 2003-04, 2006; TJ 1999, 2001.
Dutch heptathlon records 2005 & 2006.
Progress at Hep: 1998- 4836, 1999- 5329, 2000- 5269, 2001- 5735, 2002- 5858, 2003- 6017, 2004- 6206, 2005- 6318, 2006- 6423, 2007- 6260. pbs: 100m 11.88w '06, 200m 24.22/24.02w '06; 400m 55.28i '07, 800m 2:11.97 '06, 50mh 7.33i '06, 60mh 8.30i '07, 100mh 13.17 '06, 200mh 27.57 '04, HJ 1.88i '07, 1.85 '04; LJ 6.64 '07, TJ 12.90i/12.77 '00, SP 14.34 '04, JT 43.61 '05, Pen 4801i '07.

NETHERLANDS ANTILLES

Churandy MARTINA b. 3 Jul 1984 Willemstad, Curaçao 1.80m 68kg. Nike. Studied civil engineering at University of Texas at El Paso, USA.
At 100m/(200m): OG: '04- qf; WCh: '03- h, '05- qf, '07- 5/5; WJ: '00- h/h, '02- qf; WY: '99- sf; PAm: '03- sf, '07- 1; CAG: '06- 1/1R.
AHO records: 100m 2004-06, 200m 2003-07, 400m 2007.
Progress at 100m, 200m: 2000- 10.73, 21.73; 2001- 10.64A, 21.55; 2002- 10.30, 20.81; 2003- 10.29, 20.71; 2004- 10.13, 20.75; 2005- 10.13/9.93Aw, 20.32/20.31w; 2006- 10.04A/10.06/9.76Aw/9.99w, 20.27A; 2007- 10.06, 20.20. pbs: 60m 6.72i '06, 400m 46.13A '07.

NEW ZEALAND

Governing body: Athletics New Zealand, PO Box 741, Wellington.
National Championships first held in 1887 (men), 1926 (women). **2007 Champions: Men**: 100m: James Dolphin & Chris Donaldson 10.56, 200m: James Dolphin 21.31, 400m: Cory Innes 46.97, 800m: Tim Hawkes 1:50.84, 1500m: Richard Olsen 3:52.41, 5000m: Rees Buck 14:26.02, 10,000m: Scott Winton 29:38.90, HMar: Nicholas Browne 71:45, Mar: Stafford Thompson 2:27:11, 3000mSt: Neville Smith 9:21.64, 110mh: James Mortimer 14.07, 400mh: Kieran Cocks 56.56, HJ: Grant Knaggs 2.10, PV: Jeremy McColl 4.60, LJ: Brent Newdick 7.15, TJ: Charles Nicolson 14.35, SP/DT: Patrick Hillier 15.97/48.11, HT: Philip Jensen 62.20, JT: Stuart Farquhar 76.85, 3000mW: Glen Burrell 12:36.15, 20kW: Tony Sargisson 1:32:03, 50kW: David Sim 5:15:20. **Women**: 100m/200m/400m: Monique Williams 11.78/23.95/56.19, 800m/1500m: Kellie Palmer 2:08.66/4:32.70, 5000m: Belinda Wimmer 17:10.30, HMar: Annabelle Latz 83:42, Mar: Melanie Burke 2:42:16, 3000mSt: Maria Åkesson 11:06.74, 100mh: Andrea Miller 13.70, 400mh: Gemma Radford 67.07, HJ: Sarah Cowley 1.76, PV: Melina Hamilton 4.10, LJ: Jessica Penney 5.82, TJ: Marissa Pritchard 12.37, SP: Valerie Vili 18.84, DT: Beatrice Faumuina 60.71, HT: Debbie McCaw 52.99, JT: Keshia Grant 43.15, Hep: Jennifer James 4202, 3000mW/20kW: Michelle Lei 15:28.82/1:56:04.

Nick WILLIS b. 25 Apr 1983 Lower Hutt 1.83m 68kg. Economics graduate of University of Michigan, USA.
At 1500m: OG: '04- sf, WCh: '05- sf, '07- 10; CG: '06-1; WJ: '02- 4; WI: '08- dq; WCp: '06- 3. NZ champion 2006, NCAA indoor 2005.
NZ 1500m records 2005 & 2006.
Progress at 1500m: 2001- 3:43.54, 2002- 3:42.69, 2003- 3:36.58, 2004- 3:32.64, 2005- 3:32.38, 2006- 3:32.17, 2007- 3:35.85. pbs: 800m 1:45.54 '04, 1M 3:52.75 '06, 3000m 7:44.90i '04, 7:45.97 '05; 5000m 13:27.54 '05.
His brother Steve (b. 25 Apr 1975) had pbs: 1500m 3:40.29 '99, 1M 3:59.04 '00.

Women

Beatrice FAUMUINA b. 23 Oct 1974 Auckland 1.85m 115kg. Auckland City.
At DT (SP): OG: '96- dnq 23, '00- 12, '04- 7; WCh: '95- dnq 28, '97- 1, '99- 5, '03- 13, '05- 4, '07- dnq 25; CG: '94- 2 (9), '98- 1 (4), '02- 1, '06- 4; WJ: '92- 5; WCp: '98- 4, '02- 1. 3rd GP 2000. Won NZ DT 1993-2000, 2002-07; SP 1994, 1997-9.
Eleven NZ discus records 1993-7.
Progress at DT: 1990- 45.06, 1991- 46.04, 1992- 53.02, 1993- 55.20, 1994- 57.94, 1995- 60.28, 1996- 64.04, 1997- 68.52, 1998- 67.58, 1999- 64.62, 2000- 65.41A, 2001- 61.54, 2002- 65.05, 2003- 65.53 irreg/65.35, 2004- 66.08, 2005- 65.09, 2006- 63.30, 2007- 62.20. pbs: SP 16.96 '98, HT 44.24 '95.
First major success was winning 1992 Pacific Schools Games DT. 37 successive wins at discus 1997-8. Parents came from Western Samoa.

Kimberley SMITH b. 19 Nov 1981 Papakura 1.66m 49kg. Was at Providence College.
At 5000m: OG: '04- h; WUG: '05- 1; WCp: '06- 4. At 10,000m: WCh: '05- 15, '07- 5. At 3000m: WI: '08- 6. World CC: '05- 12. Won NCAA 5000m and indoor 3000m & 5000m 2004; NZ 5000m 2002, 2006; CC 2002.
Oceania records: 3000m 2007, indoor 1M 2008, 3000m 2007, 5000m 2005. NZ records 5000m (3) 2005-07, 10,000m 2005 & 2007.
Progress at 5000m, 10,000m: 2002- 16:30.10, 2003- 15:47.92, 2004- 15:09.72, 33:45.81; 2005- 14:50.46i/15:05.68, 31:21.00, 2006- 14:56.58, 2007- 14:49.41, 31:20.63. pbs: 1500m 4:11.25 '04, 1M 4:24.14i '04, 3000m 8:35.31 '07.

Valerie VILI b. 6 Oct 1984 Rotorua 1.93m 123kg. née Adams. Auckland City.
At SP: OG: '04- 8; WCh: '03- 5, '05- 3, '07- 1; CG: '02- 2, '06- 1; WJ: '02- 1; WY: '99- 10, '01- 1; WI: '04- 10, '08- 1; WCp: '02- 6, '06- 1. Won NZL SP 2001-07, DT 2004, HT 2003.
Five Oceania & Commonwealth shot records 2005-07, 18 NZ 2002-07, OCE indoor 2004 & 2008.
Progress at SP: 1999- 14.83, 2000- 15.72, 2001- 17.08, 2002- 18.40, 2003- 18.93, 2004- 19.29, 2005- 19.87, 2006- 20.20, 2007- 20.54, 2008- 20.19i. pbs: DT 58.12 '04, HT 58.75 '02.
Matched her age with metres at the shot from 14 to 18 and missed that at 19 by only two months. Her father came from England and her mother from Tonga. She married New Caledonia thrower Bertrand Vili (SP 17.81 '02, DT 61.05 '07 4 ECp '07 for France) in November 2004.

NIGERIA

Governing body: The Athletic Federation of Nigeria, P.O.Box 211, Marina, Lagos. F'd 1944.
2007 National Champions: **Men**: 100m:Olusoji Fasuba 10.32, 400m: Weigopwa 46.43. LJ: Stanley 7.85w. **Women** 100m: Kemasuode 11.42, 400m: Ekpukpon 51.86, 100mh: Toyin Augustus 13.62, 400H: Onyemuwa 57.27, HJ: Amata 1.85, LJ/TJ: Okagbare 6.50/14.13, SP: Chukwuemeka 18.14, HT: Adeoye 61.04.

Uchenna EMEDOLU b. 17 Sep 1976 Adazi-Ani, Aniocha 1.83m 79kg. Benfica, Portugal.
At 100m/(200m): OG: '00- (qf), '04- sf/3R; WCh: '01- sf/sf, '03- 6/8, '05- sf/qf; CG: '02- 2/qf; AfG: '03- 2/1, '07- 3/1R; AfCh: '02- 2, '06- 2/1/1R; WCp: '02- 1/3R, '06- 4. Won NGR 200m 2001-03, 2005.
Progress at 100m, 200m: 1999- 21.08, 2000- 10.54/10.2, 20.69, 2001- 10.11/10.06w, 20.34; 2002- 10.06/10.00w, 20.31; 2003- 9.97, 20.38; 2004- 10.05/9.99w, 20.39; 2005- 10.13, 20.55/20.22w; 2006- 10.14/10.10w, 20.51; 2007- 10.23, 20.66/20.0h. pb 60m 6.66i '02.

Olusoji Adetokunbo **FASUBA** b. 9 Jul 1984 Sapele, Delta State 1.76m 76kg.
At 100m/(200m)/4x100m: OG: '04- 3R; WCh: '03- 4R, '05- sf/qf, '07- 4; CG: '06- 2; AfG: '07- 1/1R; AfCh: '04- 1, '06- 1/1R. Won Af-AsG 2003. At 60m: WI: '06- 5, '08- 1. Won NGR 100m 2006-07. African 100m record 2006.
Progress at 100m: 2002- 10.52/10.1, 2003- 10.15, 2004- 10.09, 2005- 10.09A/10.08w/9.8A, 2006- 9.85, 2007- 10.07. pbs: 60m 6.49i '07, 200m 20.52 '04.
At Doha in 2006 he improved from 10.09 to 9.93 (heats and 9.85 (final); next best is 10.07. Father is a Yoruban, mother is Evelyn Quarrie from Jamaica, first cousin of Don Quarrie.

NORWAY

Governing body: Norges Fri-Idrettsforbund, Serviceboks 1, Ullevaal Stadium, 0840 Oslo. Founded 1896.
National Championships first held in 1897 (men), 1947 (women). **2007**: **Men**: 100m/200m: Jaysuma Saidy Ndure 10.14/20.75, 400m: Quincy Douglas 47.89, 800m: Stian Flo 1:53.67, 1500m: Morten Kolstø Velde 3:51.36, 5000m: Bård Kvalheim 14:27.86, 10,000m: Urige Arado Buta 30:02.26, HMar: Urige Buta ETH 65:29, Mar: Trond Idland 2:21:25, 3000mSt: Bjørnar Ustad Kristensen 8:42.31, 110mh: Elvind Stavang 14.76 , 400mh: Andreas Totsås 51.64, HJ: Brede Raa Ellingsen 2.10, PV: Benjamin Jensen 4.70, LJ: Lars Ytterhaug 7.28, TJ: Lars Eric Sæther 15.35,

SP/DT: Gaute Myklebust 17.11/55.99, HT: Steffen Nerdal 63.22, JT: Ronny Nilsen 73.01, Dec: Benjamin Jensen 7191, 5000mW/10,000mW/20kW: Erik Tysse 18:32.46/40:13.12/1:22:03. **Women**: 100m: Ezinne Okparaebo 11.70, 200m: Elisabeth Slettum 23.85, 400m: Irene Høvik Helgesen 54.60, 800m: Ingvill Måkestad 2:06.59, 1500m: Kristine Eikrem Engeset 4:15.35, 5000m: Ingunn Opsal 16:07.04, 10,000m: Kirsten Melkevik Otterbu 36:11.53, HMar: Chrsitina Bus Holth 80:23, Mar: Marit Årthun 2:59:58, 3000mSt: Silje Fjørtoft 10:08.11, 100mh: Christina Vukicevic 13.34, 400mh: Rachel Nordtømme 60.29, HJ: Anne Gerd Eieland 1.84, PV: Cathrine Larsåsen 4.15, LJ: Margrethe Renstrøm 6.33, TJ: Margrethe Renstrøm 12.84, SP: Charlotte Lund Abrahamsen 14.25, DT: Grete Etholm Snyder 52.91, HT: Mona Holm 65.14, JT: Ina Cathrin Kartum 50.33, Hep: Silje Pettersen 3914, 3000mW: Kjersti Tysse Plätzer 12:34.69, 5000mW/10kW: Hanne Liland 26:22.2/55:02.

Trond NYMARK b. 28 Dec 1976 Bergen 1.80m 64kg. TIF Viking, Bergen.
At 50kW: OG: '04- 13; WCh: '99/01- dnf, '03- 8, '05- 4, '07- 8; EC: '02- 5, '06- 4; WCp: '06- 2; ECp: '07- 2. At 20kW: EC: '98- 19; EU23: '97- 14. Won NOR 10,000m W 1997-8, 20kW 1997, 2000, 2004; 50kW 1998-9, 2004-05.
NOR record 30km walk 2000, 50km walk 2005 & 2006.
Progress at 50kW: 1998- 3:57:52, 1999- 3:54:36, 2000- 3:53:10, 2002- 3:49:27, 2003- 3:46:14, 2004- 3:44:55, 2005- 3:44:04, 2006- 3:41:30, 2007- 3:41:31. pbs: 3000mW 11:47.0 '00, 5000mW 19:53.44i '02, 20:07.11 '00; 10,000mW: 42:17.2 '02, 20kW 1:22:52.4t '04, 30kW 2:12:56 '00, 35kW 2:35:51 '06.

Jaysuma SAIDY NDURE b. 1 Jan 1984 Bakau, The Gambia 1.92m 72kg. IL I BUL.
At (100m)/200m: OG: '04- qf/qf; WCh: '03- h, '05- sf; CG: '02- qf, '06- sf; WJ: '02- h; AfG: '03- h/sf; AfCh: '04- 3/6. Won WAF 20m 2007, Norwegian 100m & 200m 2007.
Records: Gambian 100m & 200m 2005-06, Norwegian 100m (3) and 200m 2007.
Progress at 100m, 200m: 2002- 10.73/10.59w, 21.20; 2003- 10.52/10.51w, 21.18; 2004- 10.26, 20.69; 2005- 10.31/10.18w, 20.51/20.14w, 2006- 10.27, 20.47; 2007- 10.06, 19.89. pb 60m 6.55i '08.
Having lived in Oslo from 2001, became a Norwegian citizen in November 2006.

Andreas THORKILDSEN b. 1 Apr 1982 Kristiansand 1.88m 90kg. Kristiansands IF.
At JT: OG: '04- 1; WCh: '01- dnq 26, '03- 11, '05- 2, '07- 2; EC: '02- dnq 15, '06- 1; WJ: '00- 2; EU23: '03- 5; EJ: '99- 7, '01- 2; EY: '97- 1. Won WAF 2006, Norwegian 2001-06.
World junior javelin record 2001, seven Norwegian records 2005-06.
Progress at JT: 1996- 53.82, 1998- 61.57, 1999- 72.11, 2000- 77.48, 2001- 83.87, 2002- 83.43, 2003- 85.72, 2004- 86.50, 2005- 89.60, 2006- 91.59, 2007- 89.51.
His mother Bente Amundsen was a Norwegian champion at 100mh (pb 14.6), father Tomm was a junior international with bests of 100m 10.9 and javelin 71.64. Partner is Christina Vukicevic (NJR for 2nd WJ 100mh in 13.34 in 2006).

Erik TYSSE b. b. 4 Dec 1980 Bergen 1.84m 59kg. IL Norna-Salhus.
At 20kW/(50kW): WCh: '03- 19, '05- 13, '07- 8/5; EC: '02- 17, '06- 7; WCp: '06: 9; ECp: '05-07- 8/11. At 10,000mW: WJ: '98- 26; EJ: '99-16. Won NOR 5000mW 2000-02, 2004-07, 10,000mW 2000-04, 2006-07, 20kW 2001-03, 2005-07; 50kW 2006.
Norwegian walks records: 3000m 2007, 5000m (2) 2005-07, 10,000m 2006, 20km (3) 2005-06.
Progress at 20kW/50kW: 1998- 1:33:47, 1999- 1:30:49, 2000- 1:26:28.3t, 2001- 1:25:41, 2002- 1:22:29, 2003- 1:22:43, 2004- 1:22:15, 2005- 1:21:11, 2006- 1:19:38, 3:54:37; 2007- 1:20:31, 3:51:52. pbs: 3000mW 11:06.8 '07, 5000mW 18:32.46 '07, 10,000mW 39:20.2 '06.
Brother of Kjersti Plätzer.

Women

Kjersti TYSSE PLÄTZER b. 18 Jan 1972 Bergen 1.74m 54kg. née Tysse. IL Norna-Salhus, Bergen.
At 20kW: OG: '00- 2, '04- 12; WCh: '99- 9, '01/03- dq, '07- 4; EC: '94- 16, '98- 9, '02- dq, '06- 4; WCp: '02- 5; ECp: '00- 3, '03- 6. At 5000mW: WJ: '86- 5. Won NOR 3000mW 2002, 2004-05, 2007; 5000mW 1985-7, 1992, 1994-6, 1998-2002, 2006; 10kW 1994-5, 1998, 2000-02, 2006; 20kW 1998-9, 2004, 2006.
World bests 1M walk 2001, 1500m walk 2002, 3km road (11:41) 2003, 5km road 2006. NOR walks records: 3000m (3), 5000m (4), 10km (6), 10,000m, 20km (4) 1996-2002.
Progress at 10kW, 20kW: 1986- 48:01, 1987- 45:45, 1994- 46:10, 1995- 45:12, 1996- 44:40, 1:39:36; 1998- 42:44, 1:32:55; 1999- 41:54, 1:28:35; 2000- 43:21.1t, 1:27:53; 2001- 42:23, 1:29:55, 2002- 41:16, 1:28:55; 2003- 43:59, 1:28:49; 2004- 42:52, 1:30:49; 2006- 42:48, 1:28:23; 2007- 42:51, 1:27:41. pbs: 1500mW 5:47.03 '02, 1MW 6:16.45 '01, 3000mW 11:59.3i '04, 12:01.91 '02; 5000mW 20:37.83 '01, 19:46R '06; 15kW 1:05:12 '00; running: 3000m 10:43.19 '01, 5000m 17:57.55 '01.
She has a record 3 gold medals in all NOR walks championships. Married to Stephan Plätzer GER (b. 12 Sep 66), pbs 800m 1:46.53 '89, 1500m 3:40.26 '89. Daughter Kiara Lea born 13 Oct 1997, son Sebastian born 5 Jun 2005.
Her brother is Erik Tysse (qv).

Susanne WIGENE b. 12 Feb 1978 Haugesund 1.68m 50kg. IK Tjalve.
At 5000m (/10,000m): WCh: 05- 13; EC: '06- 7/2; EU23: '99- 8; At 3000m: EJ: '97- 5. Won NOR 1500m 1999, 5000m 1998, 2004-05; 3000mSt 2000; Nordic CC 2004.
Four Norwegian 3000mSt records 2000-04.

Progress at 5000m, 10,000m: 1998- 15:57.44, 1999- 15:41.57, 2000- 16:20.72, 32:58.68; 2002- 16:04.24, 2003- 15:42.02, 2004- 15:12.27, 2005- 14:48.53, 2006- 14:52.68, 30:32.36; 2007- 15:24.25. pbs: 800m 2:13.39 '96, 1500m 4:13.01 '05, 1M 4:51.29 '99, 3000m 8:40.23 '05, 3000mSt 9:45.21 '04, Road: 20km 68:16 '04, HMar 75:01 '03.

PANAMA

Governing body: Federación Pananeña de Atletismo, Apartado 0815-00067, Panama 4. Founded 1945.

Bayano KAMANI b. 17 Apr 1980 Houston, USA 1.88m 79kg. Was at Baylor University.
At 400mh: OG '04- 5; WCh: '03- h, '05- 7, '07- sf; PAm: '07- 2; SACh: '03- 1; CAG: '06- 1; WUG: '99- 2; NCAA champion 1999, 2001.
South American 400mh record 2005, indoor 400m (46.26) 2005; Six Panama records 2004-05.
Progress at 400mh: 1996- 51.71, 1997- 50.82, 1998- 49.86, 1999- 48.68, 2000- 48.43, 2001- 48.99, 2002- 50.05, 2003- 49.82, 2004- 48.23, 2005- 47.84, 2006- 48.84, 2007- 48.70. pb 400m 46.20i '01, 46.32 '01; 55mh 7.56i '97, 60mh 8.09i '98.
Lives in Los Angeles. Opted for his father's Panamanian nationality in 2003; his mother came from Barbados.

Irving SALADINO b. 23 Jan 1983 Ciudad de Colón 1.83m 70kg
At LJ: OG: '04- dnq 36; WCh: '05- 6, '07- 1; WJ: '02- dnq; PAm: '07- 1; CAG: '06- 1; SACh: '03- 3; WI: '06- 2; WCp: '06- 1; won WAF & IbAm 2006, SAm U23 2004.
South American LJ records 2006, indoors (7) 2006-08, Panama records 2002-06.
Progress at LJ: 2001- 7.11, 2002- 7.51A/7.39, 2003- 7.46, 2004- 8.12A/7.74, 2005- 8.29/8.51w, 2006- 8.56/8.65w, 2007- 8.57, 2008- 8.42i. pbs: 100m 10.4 '04, TJ 14.47 '04.
Set South American indoor record in qualifying and four more in final of WI 2006 for the first medal ever for Panama at World Championships. Clear world number one in 2006, winning 15/16 outdoors and in 2007 when he won all nine competitions.

POLAND

Governing body: Polski Zwiazek Lekkiej Atletyki (PZLA), ul. Kopernika 30, 00-336 Warszawa. Founded 1919.

National Championships first held in 1920 (men), 1922 (women). **2007 Champions**: **Men**: 100m/200m: Marcin Jedrusinski 10.37/20.84, 400m: Daniel Dabrowski 45.33, 800m: Pawel Czapiewski 1:48.97, 1500m: Bartosz Nowicki 3:42.05, 5000m: Henryk Szost 13:58.89, 10,000m: Michal Kaczmarek 28:37.44, HMar: Arkadiusz Sowa 63:42, Mar: Pawel Ochal 2:15:31, 3000mSt: Tomasz Szymkowiak 8:27.97, 110mh: Tomasz Scigaczewski 13.74, 400mh: Marek Plawgo 48.90, HJ: Aleksander Walerianczyk 2.28, PV: Przemyslaw Czerwinski 5.70, LJ: Marcin Starzak 8.02, TJ: Pawel Kruhlik 16.13, SP: Tomasz Majewski 20.07, DT: Piotr Malachowski 63.16, HT: Szymon Ziólkowski 76.80, JT: Igor Janik 79.13, Dec Marcin Drózdz 7497, 20kW: Rafal Augustyn 1:23:38, 50kW: Grzegorz Sudol 3:55:22. **Women**: 100m: Daria Korczynska 11.53, 200m: Monika Bejnar 23.31, 400m: Zuzanna Radecka-Pakaszewska 52.14, 800m: Ewelina Setowska-Dryk 2:03.62, 1500m: Sylwia Ejdys 4:15.56, 5000m: Wioletta Janowska 15:59.59, 10,000m: Lidia Chojecka 32:55.10, HMar: Dorota Gruca 73:29, Mar: Arleta Meloch 2:41:45, 3000mSt: Katarzyna Kowalska 9:47.11, 100mh: Joanna Kocielnik 13.25, 400mh: Weronika Zielinska 59.52, HJ: Kamila Stepaniuk 1.86, PV: Monika Pyrek 4.60, LJ: Malgorzata Trybanska 6.80, TJ: Joanna Skibinska 14.04, SP: Krystyna Zabawska 17.57, DT: Wioletta Potepa 60.14, HT: Kamila Skolimowska 71.90, JT: Urszula Jasinska 59.20, Hep: Karolina Tyminska 6200, 20kW: Katarzyna Kwoka 1:37:56.

Igor JANIK b. 18 Jan 1983 2.00m 112kg. AZS AWFIS Gdansk.
At JT: WCh: '07- 7; WJ: '02- 1; EU23: '03- 2, '05- 1; EJ: '01- 6; WUG: '03-05-07: 1/2/5; ECp: '05-06-07: 5/3/3. Polish champion 2007.
Progress at JT: 2001- 72.08, 2002- 78.90, 2003- 82.54, 2004- 74.49, 2005- 77.25, 2006- 82.86, 2007- 83.38.

Tomasz MAJEWSKI b. 30 Aug 1981 Nasielsk 2.04m 135kg. AZS-AWF Warszawa. Studying politics at Cardinal Wyszynski University.
At SP: OG: '04- dnq 18; WCh: '05- 9, '07- 5; EC: '06- 8; EU23: '03- 4; WI: '04-06-08: 4/7/3; EI: '05- dnq 10; WUG: '03- 5, '05- 1; ECp: '03-04-05-06-07: 4/4/4/6/3. Polish champion 2002-05, 2007.
Progress at SP: 1998- 12.91, 1999- 15.77, 2000- 17.77, 2001- 18.34, 2002- 19.33, 2003- 20.09, 2004- 20.83i/20.52, 2005- 20.64, 2006- 20.66, 2007- 20.87, 2008- 20.93i. pb DT 51.79 '07.

Piotr MALACHOWSKI b. 7 Jun 1983 Zuromin 1.94m 125kg. Slask Wroclaw.
At DT: WCh: '07- 12; EC: '06- 6; WJ: '02- 6; EU23: '03- 9, '05- 2; EJ: '01- 5; ECp: '06- 1, '07- 1. Polish champion 2007.
Polish discus records 2006 & 2007.
Progress at DT: 2001- 54.19, 2002- 56.84, 2003- 57.83, 2004- 62.04, 2005- 64.74, 2006- 66.21, 2007- 66.61.

Marek PLAWGO b. 25 Feb 1981 Ruda Slaska 1.83m 72kg. Warszawianka. Studying at University of Economics.
At 400mh: OG: '04- 6; WCh: '01- sf, '07- 3/3R; EC: '06- 2; WJ: '00- 1/3R; EU23: '03- 1/1R; EJ: '99- 4; WCp: '06- 3; ECp: '01- 2, '05- 2/2R, '07- 2. Won WAF 2007, POL 2001, 2003, 2005-07. At 400m/4x400m: EC: '02- 4; EI: '02- 1/1R; ECp: '02- 3.
Three Polish 400mh records 2001-07, 600m 2005.

Progress at 400mh: 1999- 51.97, 2000- 49.23, 2001- 48.16, 2002- 48.25, 2003- 48.45, 2004- 48.16, 2005- 48.99, 2006- 48.57, 2007- 48.12. pbs: 100m 10.60 '01, 200m 20.61 '02, 300m 32.77 '02, 400m 45.35 '02, 600m 1:16.03 '05.
Ran Polish indoor records 45.49 and 45.39 at 2002 European Indoors.

Grzegorz SUDOL b. 28 Aug 1978 Nowa Deba 1.76m 63kg. AZS-AWF Kraków. PE student.
At 50kmW: OG: '04- 7; WCh: '03/05- dq, '07- 21; EC: '02- 10, '06- 10. At 20kmW: ECp: '05- 9. At 10,000mW: WJ: '96- 7, EJ: '97- 10. Won POL 50km 2002, 2007-08.
Progress at 50kmW: 2002- 3:50:37, 2003- 3:55:40, 2004- 3:49:09, 2006- 3:50:24, 2007- 3:55:22, 2008- 3:45:47. pbs: 3000mW 11:25.93i/11:29.20 '05, 5000mW 18:55.01i/19:10.53 '05, 10kmW 39:01 '05, 20kmW 1:21:03 '05.

Szymon ZIÓLKOWSKI b. 1 Jul 1976 Poznan 1.92m 120kg. AZS Poznan. Student.
At HT: OG: '96- 10, '00- 1, '04- dnq 13; WCh: '95- dnq 22, '99- dnq 23, '01- 1, '05- 3, '07- 7; EC: '98- 5, '02- dnq 15, '06- 5; WJ: '94- 1; EJ: '93- 7, '95- 1; EU23: '97- 2; ECp: '95-6-9-01-04-05-06-07: 6/2/2/1/1/1/1/1. Polish champion 1996-7, 1999-2002, 2004-07.
Six Polish hammer records 2000-01.
Progress at HT: 1991- 55.96, 1992- 63.84, 1993- 67.34, 1994- 72.48, 1995- 75.42, 1996- 79.52, 1997- 79.14, 1998- 79.58, 1999- 79.01, 2000- 81.42, 2001- 83.38, 2002- 79.78, 2003- 76.97, 2004- 79.41, 2005- 79.35, 2006- 82.31, 2007- 80.70. pbs: SP 15.25 '95, DT 49.58 '00.
His sister Michalina (b. 1983) was second in the 2000 Polish U18 Championships, pb 58.33 '04. Married javelin thrower (50.90 '98 (old), 50.64 '99) Joanna Domagala in December 2000.

Women

Lidia CHOJECKA b. 25 Jan 1977 Siedlce 1.66m 46kg. Pogon Siedlce. Teacher.
At 1500m (/3000m): OG: '00- 5, '04- 6; WCh: '99- 9, '01- 5, '07- 10; EC: '98- 6, '02- 9, '06- 5; WJ: '94- 7, '96- 5; EJ: '95- 1; EU23: '97- 2, '99- 1; WUG: '97- 3; WI: '97-9-04-06: 3/3/8/(3); EI: '98- 2, '00- (2), '05- (1), '07- 1/1; WCp: '06- 5/2; ECp: '99-02-04-07: (2)/2&3/(2)/(2). At 5000m: ECp: '06- 4. Eur CC: '02- 13. Won POL 800m 1996, 1500m 1999-2000, 2002; 10,000m 2007.
POL records: 1500m 2000, 3000m (4) 1999-2002, 5000m 2002.
Progress at 1500m: 1993- 4:40.84, 1994- 4:18.70, 1995- 4:15.27, 1996- 4:11.36, 1997- 4:05.74, 1998- 4:03.32, 1999- 4:01.36, 2000- 3:59.22, 2001- 4:03.51, 2002- 4:04.84, 2003- 4:03.58i/4:08.73, 2004- 3:59.27, 2005-4:04.84i,2006-4:01.43,2007-4:03.73i/4:05.10. pbs: 800m 1:59.97 '99, 1000m 2:36.97i '03, 2:40.49 '98; 1M 4:24.44i '00, 4:25.18 '98; 2000m 5:48.15 '02, 3000m 8:31.69 '02, 5000m 15:04.88 '02, 10,000m 32:55.10 '07.
Former married name Okninska (12 May 2001).

Wioletta FRANKIEWICZ b. 9 Jun 1977 Piotrków Trybunalski 1.77m 54kg. Former married name Janowska. AZS-AWF Kraków.
At 3000mSt (1500m): OG: '04- (sf); WCh: '05- 14 (h), '07- dnf (h); EC: '06- 3; WCp: '06- 3. At 5000m: ECp: '05- 2. Won Polish 1500m 2005, 5000m 2002, 2004, 2007; 3000mSt 2006.
Polish 3000mSt record 2006, world best 2000mSt 2006.
Progress at 1500m, 3000mSt: 1995- 4:41.98, 1996- 4:24.27, 1997- 4:21.49, 1998- 4:37.47, 1999- 4:21.73, 10:18.10; 2002- 4:07.84, 2003- 4:10.31, 2004- 4:03.09, 2005- 4:03.68, 9:25.09; 2006- 4:08.31, 9:17.15; 2007- 4:09.51, 9:28.97. pbs: 800m 2:06.67i '04, 2:06.86 '03; 1000m 2:36.97 '04, 2000m 5:43.62i '06, 3000m 8:44.42 '05, 5000m 15:08.38 '05, 10,000m 32:16.27 '04, 2000mSt 6:03.38 '06.

Anna JESIEN b. 10 Dec 1978 Sokolow Podlaski 1.68m 57kg. née Olichwierczuk. AZS-AWF Warszawa. Economist.
At 400mh: OG: '00/04- h; WCh: '01- sf, '03- h, '05- 4; EC: '02- 3, '06- 6; WCp: '06- 3; ECp: '99-02-05-06-07: 7/2&3R/2&2R/5/2. Won WAF 2007, Polish 400m 2006, 400mh 1999-2000, 2002-03, 2005.
Three Polish 400mh records 2005-07.
Progress at 400mh: 1995- 66.84, 1996- 61.34, 1997- 58.97, 1998- 58.21, 1999- 56.43, 2000- 55.75, 2001- 55.61, 2002- 55.11, 2003- 55.38, 2004- 55.85, 2005- 53.96, 2006- 54.48, 2007- 53.86. pbs: 100m 12.14 '01, 200m 24.19 '00, 300m 38.33 '02, 400m 51.74 '07, 100mh 14.1 '05, 14.49 '99, 14.23w '01.
Coached by her husband (married on 8 Oct 2001) Pawel Jesien (400mh pb 51.08 '00).

Barbara MADEJCZYK b. 30 Sep 1976 Ustka 1.80m 81kg. Jantar Ustka. PE teacher.
At JT: OG: '04- 12; WCh: '05- dnq 16, '07- 9; EC: '06- 7; EJ: '95- dnq 15; WUG: '03- 1; WCp: '04- 4; ECp: '04-05-06-07: 6/2/1/3. Polish champion 2003-06.
Three Polish records 2005-06.
Progress at JT: 1990- 33.26, 1991- 45.78, 1992- 45.50, 1993- 46.48, 1994- 48.22, 1995- 50.98, 1996- 52.82, 1997- 54.76, 1998- 56.89, new: 1999- 53.22, 2000- 55.10, 2001- 59.54, 2002- 59.19, 2003- 59.89, 2004- 61.36, 2005- 63.03, 2006- 64.08, 2007- 61.66. pbs: SP 14.42 '01.

Wioletta POTEPA b. 13 Dec 1980 Ciechanów 1.89m 95kg. AZS-AWF Warszawa.
At DT: OG: '04- dnq 16; WCh: '05/07- dnq 19/17; EC: '06- 5; WJ: '98- dnq 17 (6 SP); EJ: '97- 9, '99-1 (5 SP); EU23: '01- 5; WUG: '03- 4, '05- 1; WCp: '06- 4. Polish champion 2004, 2006-07.
Progress at DT: 1996- 40.24, 1997- 47.14, 1998- 53.32, 1999- 56.47, 2000- 58.14, 2002- 59.58, 2003- 60.80, 2004- 62.90, 2005- 63.67, 2006- 66.01, 2007- 61.62. pb SP 16.44 '99.

Monika PYREK b. 11 Aug 1980 Gdynia 1.70m 54kg. MKL Szczecin. Law graduate of University of Gdansk.

At PV: OG: '00- 7, '04- 4; WCh: '01- 3, '03- 4=, '05- 2, '07- 4; EC: '98- 7, '02- dnq 13=, '06- 2; WJ: '98- 2=; EU23: '01- 1; EJ: '97- 10, '99- 4; WI: '03-04-06-08: 3/5=/4/3=; EI: '02- 3, '05- 3; WCp: '06- 5; ECp: '02-04-06-07: 4/2/1/1. Polish champion 1999-2002, 2004-07 and indoors 1998-2006. 41 Polish pole vault records 1996-2004 (and 28 indoors 1996-2006), European record 2001.
Progress at PV: 1995- 2.30, 1996- 3.60, 1997- 3.83, 1998- 4.15, 1999- 4.21i/4.16, 2000- 4.40, 2001- 4.61, 2002- 4.62, 2003- 4.60, 2004- 4.72, 2005- 4.70, 2006- 4.76i/4.75, 2007- 4.82, 2008- 4.70i. pb HJ 1.72 '03.

Anna ROGOWSKA b. 21 May 1981 Gdynia 1.71m 55kg. SKLA Sopot. PE student.
At PV: OG: '04- 3; WCh: '03- 7, '05- 6=, '07- 8; EC: '02- 7=; EU23: '03- 3; WI: '03-04-08: 6=/7/6; WI: '06- 2; EI: '05- 2, '07- 3; ECp: '05- 1.
Nine Polish pole vault records 2004-05.
Progress at PV: 1997- 2.60, 1998- 2.90, 1999- 3.40, 2000- 3.60, 2001- 3.90, 2002- 4.40, 2003- 4.47i/4.45, 2004- 4.71, 2005- 4.83, 2006- 4.80i/4.70, 2007- 4.72i/4.60, 2008- 4.62i.
Coached by fiancé Jacek Torlinski (PV 4.85 '97).

Kamila SKOLIMOWSKA b. 4 Nov 1982 Warszawa 1.80m 105kg. Skra Warszawa. Graduate of Warsaw University.
At HT: OG: '00- 1, '04- 5; WCh: '99- 21, '01- 4, '03- 8, '05- 7, '07- 4; EC: '98- 7, '02- 2, '06- 3; WJ: '98- dnq, '00- dnq 20; WY: '99- 1; EU23: '03- 1; EJ: '97- 1; WUG: '05- 1; WCp: '02- 5, '06- 1; ECp: '99-02-04-05-06-07: 4/6/4/1/2/6; Won GPF & GWG 2001. Polish champion 1996-7, 1999-2007. Five World junior hammer records 1999-2001, 17 Polish hammer records 1996-2007.
Progress at HT: 1996- 47.66, 1997- 63.48, 1998- 62.72, 1999- 66.62, 2000- 71.16, 2001- 71.71, 2002- 72.60, 2003- 71.38, 2004- 72.57, 2005- 74.27, 2006- 75.29, 2007- 76.83.
Youngest ever Polish champion and record holder (at 13y 229d), won European Junior title at 14y 264d and became the youngest Olympic champion in Sydney 2000 at 17y 331d. Set world age bests at each age 14-19 and was the first junior over 70m. Father, Robert, was junior world champion at weightlifting in 1976 and 7th at super-heavyweight at the 1980
Olympics (his weight 155kg). Mother, Teresa Wenta, had DT pb 40.32 '77 as a junior.

Karolina TYMINSKA b. 4 Oct 1984 Swiebodzin 1.78m 61kg. AZS-AWFis Gdansk.
At Hep: WCh: '07- 15; EC: '06- dnf; EU23: '05- dnf (LJ dnq 17); ECp: '04-06-07: 7/3/4. Polish champion 2006-07. At Pen: WI: '08- 6; EI: '05- 8, '07- 7.
Progress at Hep: 2002- 5147, 2004- 5787, 2005- 6026, 2006- 6402, 2007- 6200. pbs: 100m 12.15 '05, 200m 23.44 '06, 800m 2:05.53 '06, 60mh 8.50i '08, 100mh 13.81/13.80w '06, HJ 1.74 '06, LJ 6.59 '06, SP 14.69i '08, 14.68 '07; JT 40.70 '06, Pen 4769i '08.

PORTUGAL

Governing body: Federação Portuguesa de Atletismo, Largo da Lagoa, 1799-538 Linda-a-Velha. Founded in 1921.

National Championships first held in 1910 (men), 1937 (women). **2007 Champions**: **Men**: 100m: Arnaldo Abrantes 10.33 200m: Francis Obikwelu 20.46, 400m: Paulo Ferreira 47.93, 800m: Tiago Rodrigues 1:50.61, 1500m: Adelino Monteiro 4:00.17, 5000m: José Rocha 14:15.66, 10,000m: António Silva 29:38.2. Mar: Vasco Azevedo 2:19:35, 3000mSt: Mário Teixeira 8:37.02, 110mh: Luis Sá 13.99, 400mh: Edivaldo Monteiro 49.57, HJ: Paulo Gonçalves 2.13, PV: Edi Maia 4.85, LJ/TJ: Nelson Évora 8.00/17.26, SP: Marco Fortes 18.51, DT: Jorge Grave 55.06, HT: Vítor Costa 70.55, JT: Elias Leal 63.47, Dec: Tiago Marlo 7090, 20000mW: João Vieira 1:27:04.97, 50kW: Jorge Costa 4:03:00. **Women**: 100m: Sónia Tavares 11.81, 200m: Andreia Felisberto 25.14, 400m/400mh: Patricia Lopes 53.89/59.57, 800m: Sandra Teixeira 2:01.57, 1500m: Jessica Augusto 4:16.25, 5000m: Cláudia Pereira 17:43.60, 10,000m: Dulce Félix 34:24.57, Mar: Fatima Silva 2:47:49, 3000mSt: Sara Moreira 9:45.84, 100mh: Mónica Lopes 13.93, HJ: Marisa Anselmo 1.75, PV: Sandra Tavares 4.14, LJ: Naide Gomes 6.73, TJ: Marta Godinho 13.69w, SP/JT: Sílvia Cruz 15.36/59.74, DT: Teresa Machado 54.84, HT: Vânia Silva 65.21, Hep: : Carina Gomes 4865w, 10,000mW/20kW: Susana Feitor 44:13.87/1:31:35.

Nelson ÉVORA b. 20 Apr 1984 Côte d'Ivoire 1.81m 64kg Benfica.
At (LJ/)TJ: OG: '04- dnq 40; WCh: '05- dnq 14, '07- 1; EC: '06- 6/4; WJ: '02- dnq 18/6; EJ: '03- 1/1; WI: '06- 6, '08- 3; EI: '07- 5; Won POR LJ 2006-07, TJ 2003-04, 2006- 07.
Six Portuguese triple jump records 2006-07.
Progress at TJ: 1999- 14.35, 2000- 14.93i, 2001- 16.15, 2002- 15.87, 2003- 16.43, 2004- 16.85i/16.04, 2005- 16.89, 2006- 17.23, 2007- 17.74. pbs: HJ 2.07i '05, 1.98 '99; LJ 8.10 '07.
Originally from Cape Verde Islands (from where his parents went to live in Côte d'Ivoire, relocating to Portugal when he was five), switching to Portugal in 2002. Became Portugal's first male world champion in 2007.

Francis Obiorah **OBIKWELU** b. 22 Nov 1978 Onitsha, Nigeria 1.95m 74kg. Sporting Club de Portugal.
At (100m/)200m: OG: '96- sf, '00- sf, '04- 2/5; WCh: '97- 2R (sf), '99- 3/3R, '03- h, '05- (4), '07- h/sf; EC: '02- 1/2, '06- 1/1; WI: '97- 3, '99- 4; WJ: '96- 1/1; AfG: '99- 2/1/1R; WCp: '02- 3/1, '06- 2/4. 3rd GP 200m 1999, 2001. At 400m: WJ: '94- sf; Af-J: '94- 2. At 60m: WI: '04- 6. Won NGR 100m 1999, 200m 1997, 1999; POR 100m 2004-06, 200m 2002-03, 2007.
European 100m record 2004; Two Nigerian

200m records 1999; POR records: 100m (5), 200m (6) 2002-04.
Progress at 100m, 200m: 1994- 21.16, 1995- 10.31, 21.22; 1996- 10.12, 20.24; 1997- 10.10, 20.53/20.27Aw; 1998- 10.01, 20.17; 1999- 10.01A/10.13/10.11w, 19.84; 2000- 9.97, 20.01; 2001- 9.98, 20.33; 2002- 10.01, 20.18; 2003- 10.11, 20.41; 2004- 9.86, 20.12; 2005- 10.04, 20.48; 2006- 9.99/9.84w, 20.01, 2007- 10.06/9.99w, 20.38. pbs: 50m 5.79i '04, 60m 6.54i '05, 400m 46.29 '98.
An Ibo, and thus in an ethnic minority group in Nigeria, he emigrated to Portugal in 1994 and became a citizen on 26 October 2001.

Rui SILVA b. 3 Aug 1977 Vila Chã de Ourique 1.75m 65kg. Sporting Club de Portugal.
At 1500m: OG: '00- h, '04- 3; WCh: '99- sf (fell), '01- 7, '03- 5, '05- 3; EC: '98- 2, '02- 3; WJ: '96- 6; EJ: '95- 8; EU23: '99- 1; WI: '99- 5, '01- 1; EI: '98- 1, '02- 1; WCp: '98- 2. At 3000m: WI: '04- 2; EI: '00- 2. Eur CC: '07- 3. Won POR 800m 2002-05, 1500m 1999, 2001; CC sh 2000-02.
Portuguese records 1997-2002: 800m, 1000m (2), 1500m (6), 1M (2), 2000m.
Progress at 1500m: 1994- 3:50.9, 1995- 3:44.8, 1996- 3:40.09, 1997- 3:44.6, 1998- 3:34.00, 1999- 3:30.88, 2000- 3:32.60, 2001- 3:30.36, 2002- 3:30.07, 2003- 3:32.97, 2004- 3:30.90, 2005- 3:32.91, 2006- 3:34.00, 2007- 3:35.92. pbs: 800m 1:44.91 '02, 1000m 2:16.30 '99, 1M 3:49.50 '02, 2000m 4:54.66 '99, 3000m 7:39.44i '00, 7:46.41 '04; 5000m 13:19.20 '04, 10km Rd 28:07 '05, HMar 70:04 '07.

João VIEIRA b. 20 Feb 1976 Portimão 1.74m 58kg. Clube de Natação de Rio Maior.
At 20kW: OG: '04- 10; WCh: '99/01- dq, '03- 17, '05- dnf, '07- 25; EC: '98- 20, '02- 12; '06- 3; WCp: '06- 8; ECp: '03- 4, '07- 7. At 10,000mW: WJ: '94- 11; Won POR 20kW 1996, 1999-2007, 50kW 2005, 2008.
Portuguese records: 5000mW 2000, 20kW (3) 2002-06, 50kW 2004.
Progress at 20kW: 1995- 1:33:51, 1996- 1:23:49, 1997- 1:20:59, 1998- 1:22:50, 1999- 1:22:46, 2000- 1:22:53, 2001- 1:22:52, 2002- 1:20:44, 2003- 1:20:30, 2004- 1:20:48, 2005- 1:21:56, 2006- 1:20:09, 2007- 1:20:42. pbs: 5000m 18:33.16 '00, 10,000mW 40:36.6 '98, 30kW 2:09:49 '04, 50kW 3:52:00 '04.
Twin brother Sergio set POR 20km walk record at 1:20:58 in 1997.

Women

Susana FEITOR b. 28 Jan 1975 Alcobertas 1.60m 52kg. Clube de Natação de Rio Maior.
At 20kW: OG: '00- 14, '04- 20; WCh: '99- 4, '01- dq, '03- 9, '05- 3, '07- 5; EC: '02- dnf, '06- 14; WCp: '99- 9, '02- 14; ECp: '03- 5, '05- 2. At 10kW: OG: '92- dq, '96- 13; WCh: '91- 13, '93- 11, '95- 17, '97- h; EC: '94- 8, '98- 3; EU23: '97- 3; WUG: '95- 4, '97- 4, '01- 2; WCp: '93- 8, '95- 15; ECp: '96- 3. At 5000mW: WJ: '90- 1, '92- dq, 94- 2; EJ: '89- 6, '91- 2, '93- 1. Won POR 10kW 1992, 1994-2000, 2002-04, 2007; 20kW 1998-9, 2001-04, 2007-08.
POR walks records 1989-2001: 3000m (10), 5000m (9), 10km (9), 20km (3), 20,000m track (1:29:36.4 WR '01). World junior 5000m best (21:01.8) '93.
Progress at 10kW, 20kW: 1991- 45:37, 1992- 45:24, 1993- 43:44, 1994- 43:30, 1995- 44:05, 1996- 43:37, 1997- 44:26, 1998- 42:55, 1:31:03, 1999- 44:36, 1:30:13; 2000: 43:55, 1:28:19; 2001- 42:39, 1:27:55; 2002- 44:24, 1:31:12; 2003- 44:07.80t, 1:29:08; 2004- 44:31.21t, 1:29:13; 2005- 44:25+, 1:28:44; 2006- 44:57, 1:31:43; 2007- 44:13.87, 1:31:15. Track pbs: 3000mW 12:08.30 '01, 5000mW 20:40.24 '01, 10,000mW 44:07.80 '03.
Had a hugely successful junior career to her world silver medal in front of her home crowd in 1994, four years after she had won this title.

Naide GOMES b. 20 Nov 1979 São Tome e Principe 1.81m 70kg. Sporting Club de Portugal.
At LJ/(Hep): OG: '04- (13); WCh: '05- dnq 17/7, '07- 4; EC: '02- 10/18, '06- 2; AfrG: '99- (5); WUG: '05- 2; WI: '06- 3, '08- 1; EI: '05-07: 1/1; WCp: '06- 2. At Pen: WI: '03- 5, '04- 1; EI: '02- 2. At 100mh: OG: '00- h. Won POR Hep 2001, 100mh 2004-05, HJ 2002, LJ 2002, 2004, 2006-07.
Portuguese records LJ (7) 2002-07 Heptathlon (2) 2002-05, indoor HJ & Pen 2004, LJ 2005-06.
Progress at LJ, Hep: 1996- 5.60, 1997- 5.63, 4578; 1998- 5.80, 1999- 5.81, 4964; 2000- 6.15, 5671; 2001- 6.36, 5606w; 2002- 6.57, 6160; 2003- 6.53, 6120; 2004- 6.51, 6151; 2005- 6.72, 6230; 2006- 6.82/6.84w, 2007- 7.01, 2008- 7.00i. pbs: 60m 7.84i '04, 200m 24.87 '05, 400m 57.91i '05, 800m 2:16.31 '05, 60mh 8.39i '05, 100mh 13.50 '05, HJ 1.88i '04, 1.86 '02; TJ 11.73 '99, SP 15.08i/14.71 '04, JT 42.86 '00, Pen 4759i '04.
Changed nationality from São Tome e Principe (for whom she set 30 national records – at 100mh, HJ, LJ, TJ. SP, JT & Hep) to Portugal in 2001. Set pbs at HJ (Portuguese record) and SP en route to WI gold in 2004. Full name is Enezenaide do Rosario da Vera Cruz Gomes.

QATAR

Governing body: Qatar Association of Athletics Federation, PO Box 8139, Doha. Founded 1963.

Samuel FRANCIS b. 27 Mar 1987 Nigeria 1.90m 80kg
At 100m: WCh: '07- h; AsiC: '07-1. Won Asian indoor 60m 2007.
Asian 100m record 2007.
Progression at 100m: 2006- 10.44, 2007- 9.99. pbs: 60m 6.54i '07, 200m 20.91 '07.
Ex-Nigeria, eligible for Qatar from 13 Jul 2007.

Abdullah Ahmad HASSAN b. 4 Apr 1981 Keiyo, Kenya 1.70m 54kg. Formerly Albert CHEPKURUI KEN.
At 10,000m: WCh: '03- 4, '07- dnf; AsiG: '06- 4; AsiC: '03- 1, '07- 1 (2 5000m). World CC: '99-02-05-06-07-08: 5J/6/3/14/12/8; 4k: '01-04-05: 6/4/8; HMar: '04- 3. Won Asian CC 2007.
Asian records 5000m (2) (13:04.65 '03, 2004), 10,000m (2) 2003.

Progress at 5000m, 10,000m: 1998- 13:49.48, 1999- 13:25.18, 2000- 12:59.90, 2001- 13:18.71, 28:06.86; 2002- 13:12.22, 26:50.67; 2003- 12:56.27, 26:38.76; 2004- 13:02.03, 26:59.54; 2005- 13:27.61, 2006- 28:05.47, 2007- 27:33.87. pbs: 1500m 3:42.42 '00, 3000m 7:43.01 '99, HMar 62:36 '04.
Three Asian records in month after transferring from Kenya to Qatar on 9 Aug 2003. He had been 4th in Kenyan 10,000m Trials on 26 July 2003! Tendon injury curtailed his 2005 season.

James KWALIA Chepkurui b. 12 Jun 1984 Kenya 1.76m 68kg.
At 5000m: WCh: '05- 13; AsiG: '06- 1; AsiC: '05- 1. At 3000m: WY: '01- 3, WI: '08- 9.
World junior 1 mile record 2003.
Progress at 5000m: 2001- 13:44.3, 2002- 13:14.34, 2003- 12:54.58, 2004- 13:02.24, 2005- 13:21.36, 2006- 13:29.53. pbs: 1500m 3:37.02 '06, 1M 3:50.39 '03, 2000m 4:59.11 '03, 3000m 7:28.28 '04.
Kenyan who received Qatar passport on 5 Aug 2004 and IAAF agreement to his transfer of allegiance from 28 Oct 2004.

Saïf Saeed SHAHEEN b. 15 Oct 1982 Keiyo, Kenya 1.77m 64kg. Formerly Stephen Cherono.
At 3000mSt: WCh: '03- 1, '05- 1; CG: '02- 1; AfCh: '02- 3; WCp: '06- 1 (1 5000m) won KEN 2002, WAF 2003-04, 3rd GP 2001. At 2000mSt: WY: '99- 1. At 1500m/5000m: AsiC: '03- 2/2. At 3000m: WI: '06- 2. World CC: 4k: '04-05-06: 5/4/9; 12k: '05- 8.
World record 3000m steeplechase 2004, world junior record 2001; Asian records: 3000m 2004, 5000m 2006, 3000mSt (4) 2003-04, indoor 3000m (7:39.77) 2006.
Progress at 5000m, 3000mSt: 1997- 8:43.0A, 1999- 8:19.12, 2000- 8:16.27, 2001- 7:58.66, 2002- 13:11.55, 7:58.10, 2003- 12:48.81, 7:57.38; 2004- 13:14.65, 7:53.63; 2005- 7:55.51, 2006- 12:51.98, 7:56.32. pbs: 1500m 3:33.51 '06, 2000m 5:03.06 '01, 3000m 7:34.67 '04, 2M 8:18.80 '99, 2000mSt 5:14.53 '05 (Asian best).
World age 17-18-19 records for 3000mSt 2000-02. 28 succcessive steeplechase wins (inc. 2 heats) from 16 Aug 2002 to 2006. Controversially transferred allegiance from Kenya to Qatar and set first Asian record (3000mSt 8:02.48) nine days after citizenship granted (9 Aug 2003) and also won the first global gold medal for Qatar. Brother of **Abraham Cherono** (b. 21 Jul 1980): 3 CG 02, 5 WCh 03, pb 8:10.33 '03, & **Christopher Kosgei** (b. 14 Aug 1974): WCh: 95- 2, 99- 1; pb 8:05.43 '99.

Mubarak Hassan SHAMI b. 2 Dec 1980 Baringo, Kenya 1.74m 63kg. Formerly Richard Yatich KEN.
At Mar: WCh: '07- 2; AsiG: '06- 1. World 20k: '06- 8, HMar: '05- 2, CC: '07- 8. Won Gulf & W.Asian HMar 2005.
Qatar records half marathon 2005, marathon 2007; Asian road 15km best 2006.
Progress at Mar: 2005- 2:09:22, 2006- 2:11:11, 2007- 2:07:19, 2008- 2:08:23. pbs: 10km 28:17 '03, 15km 42:51 '06, 20km 57:33 '06, HMar 60:47 '07.
Won Prague Marathon 2006, Paris 2007, Lake Biwa 2008.

ROMANIA

Governing body: Federatia Romana de Atletism, 2 Primo Nebiolo Str, 011349 Bucuresti. Founded 1912.
National Championships first held in 1914 (men), 1925 (women). **2007 Champions**: **Men**: 100m/200m: Florin Suciu 10.24/20.88, 400m: Ioan Vieru 46.35, 800m/1500m: Ioan Zaizan 1:49.13/3:44.90, 5000m/3000mSt: Mircea Bogdan 14:14.89/8:29.10, 10,000m: Marius Ionescu 29:40.06, 20kmRd:, Mar: Petrea Hristea 2:24:27. 110mh: Alexandru Mihailescu 14.26, 400mh: Gilberto Vîdeanu 51.87, HJ: Bogdan Popa 2.14, PV: Tiberiu Agoston 4.60, LJ: Claudiu Bujin 7.70, TJ: Marian Oprea 17.19, SP: Gheorghe Guset 19.62, DT: Sergiu Ursu 60.49, HT: Cosmin Sorescu 73.13, JT: Levente Bartha 72.87, Dec: Bogdan Bârcâlaiâ 6714, 10,000mW: Alin Ciobotaru 43:24.30, 20kW:, 50kW: Silviu Casandra 4:18:03. **Women**: 100m/200m/400mh: Ionela Tirlea 11.56/22.93/56.10, 400m: Angela Morosanu 52.70, 800m: Corina Dumbravean 2:00.21, 1500m: Liliana Popescu 4:10.41, 5000m/10,000m: Adriana Pîrtea 16:05.65/34:39.23, 20kmRd:, Mar: Alina Gherasim 2:42:31, 3000mSt: Cristina Casandra 9:32.47, 100mh: Carmen Ghilase 13.32, HJ: Ana Maria Mataoanu 1.92, PV: Monika Gombar 3.70, LJ: Alina Militaru 6.51, TJ: Adelina Gavrila 14.20, SP: Anca Heltne 17.07, DT: Ileana Brindusoiu 54.10, HT: Mihaela Melinte 68.07, JT: Monica Stoian 57.90, Hep: Diana Dumitrescu 5331, 10kW/20kW: Claudia Stef 43:27/1:31:44.

Gheorghe GUSET b. 28 May 1968 Zalau 1.85m 142kg. CSM Armatura Zalau.
At SP: OG: '00/04- dnq 30/15; WCh: '99-01-03-05: dnq 18/14/17/13; EC: '98- 10, '02- 7, '06- dnq 19; ECp: '94- dq 3; WI: '01-03-06: 9/dq/5; EI: '00- 4, '05- 5. Balkan champion 1999-2002, 2004-05; ROM 1990, 1992-3, 1998-2007.
5 Romanian shot records 1990-9 (indoors 2005).
Progress at SP: 1984- 12.60i/12.48, 1985- 15.17, 1986- 16.51, 1987- 17.66, 1988- 18.66, 1989- 18.57i, 1990- 19.71, 1991- 20.33, 1992- 19.63, 1993- 19.81, 1994- 19.56i/19.97dq, 1998- 20.27, 1999- 20.84, 2000- 20.76i/20.66, 2001- 20.68i/20.39, 2002- 20.40, 2003- 20.48, 2004- 20.54, 2005- 20.93i/20.75, 2006- 21.04i/20.77, 2007- 19.91i/19.62.
Four-year drugs ban 1994-8.

Marian OPREA b. 6 Jun 1982 Pitesti 1.90m 77kg. Rapid Bucuresti & Dinamo Bucuresti. Sports teacher.
At TJ: OG: '04- 2; WCh: '01- dnq 13, '03- dnq 17, '05- 3; EC: '02- dnq 14, '06- 3; WJ: '00- 1, WY: '99- 4; EU23: '03- 2; EJ: '99- 3, '01- 1; WI: '03-04-06: 8/5/4; EI: '02- 2; WUG: '01- 2; WCp: '06- 3. ROM champion 2001, 2003-07; Balkan 2001-03.
Romanian TJ records 2003 and 2005.

Progress at TJ: 1997- 14.37, 1998- 14.78, 1999- 15.98, 2000- 16.49, 2001- 17.11/17.13w, 2002- 17.29i/17.11/17.39w, 2003- 17.63, 2004- 17.55, 2005- 17.81, 2006- 17.74i/17.56, 2007- 17.32. pb LJ 7.73 '05.
Silver medal in 2004 was best ever Olympic placing by a Romanian male.

Women

Cristina CASANDRA b. 1 Feb 1977 Zalău 1.68m 50kg. née Iloc. CSM Suceava. Sports teacher.
At 3000mSt: WCh: '05- 7, '07- 6; EC: '06- 10; ECp: '02-03-05-06: 2/2/1/6. At 5000m: WJ: '96- 3. Won ROM 3000mSt 2000-07; Balkan 2002-03.
Two world 3000m steeplechase bests 2000, seven ROM records 2000-07.
Progress at 3000mSt: 2000- 9:40.20, 2001- 9:45.12, 2002- 9:33.16, 2003- 9:40.49, 2004- 9:31.96, 2005- 9:35.95, 2006- 9:38.82, 2007- 9:28.53. pbs: 1500m 4:20.46 '96, 2000m 5:56.82 '00, 3000m 9:02.94 '01, 2M 9:52.25i '07. 5000m 15:22.64 '99, 2000mSt 6:16.58 '05 (ROM rec).
Married to her coach Silviu Casandra (b. 27 Oct 1975) 20kW pb 1.21.35 '00.

Adelina GAVRILA b. 26 Nov 1978 Brăila 1.74m 55kg. Rapid Bucuresti & Farul Constanta. Sports teacher.
At TJ: OG: '04- 15; WCh: '99- 11, '01- dnq 15, '03- 9, '07- dnq 15; EC: '98- 11, '06- 7; WJ: '96- 3; EJ: '97- 1; EU23: '99- 3; WUG: '99- 3; WI: '01-03-04: 8/8/7; EI: '05- 5, '07- 5; ECp: '03- 3, '06- 3. Won Balkan 1999, 2001, ROM 2000, 2003-04, 2006-07.
Progress at TJ: 1995- 13.69: 1996- 13.50, 1997- 13.62, 1998- 14.53, 1999- 14.71, 2000- 14.44, 2001- 14.18, 2002- 14.29i/14.13w, 2003- 14.76i/14.75, 2004- 14.71, 2005- 14.58i/14.23, 2006- 14.41, 2007- 14.29i/14.20/14.21w. pb LJ 6.24 '01.

Nicoleta GRASU b. 11 Sep 1971 Secuieni 1.76m 88kg. née Gradinaru. Administration officer. Dinamo Bucuresti & Enka TUR.
At DT: OG: '92- dnq 13, '96- 7, '00- dnq 19, '04- 6; WCh: '93- 7, '95- dnq 18, '97- 10, '99- 3, '01- 2, '05- 5, '07- 4; EC: '94- 4, '98- 3, '06- 3; WJ: '90- 6; WUG: '97- 3, '99- 1; WCp: '98- 2; ECp: '97-9-00-01-02-05-06: 4/2/1/3/2/4/3; E23Cp: '92- 1. Won Balkan 1992, 1997-9; ROM 1992-3, 1995-7, 1999-2002, 2004-06. 3rd GP 1996.
Progress at DT: 1985- 36.02, 1986- 43.56, 1987- 50.82, 1988- 51.06, 1989- 52.54, 1990- 56.02, 1991- 59.90, 1992- 65.66, 1993- 65.16, 1994- 64.40, 1995- 64.62, 1996- 65.26, 1997- 64.68, 1998- 67.80, 1999- 68.80, 2000- 68.70, 2001- 68.31, 2002- 64.90, 2004- 64.92, 2005- 64.89, 2006- 65.21, 2007- 65.60. pb SP 15.00i '92, 14.56 '91.
Married her coach Costel Grasu (b. 5 Jul 1967) DT pb 67.08 '92; 4 OG 1992.

Felicia MOLDOVAN b. 29 Sep 1967 Mîgura Ilvei 1.69m 70kg. née Tilea. Steaua Bucuresti. Teacher.
At JT: OG: '96- 10, '00- dnq 15, '04- 11; WCh: '93- 8, '95- 2, '97- 5, '99- 11, '01/05- dnq 16/23, '07- 11; EC: '90- dq (9), '94- 3, '98- 10, '02- 9, '06- dnq 16; WUG: '95- 1; ECp: '93-4-7-02-05-06: 1/3/2/2/5/2. Won ROM 1990, 1994, 1996-8, 2004-06.
Romanian JT record 1996, new spec (2) 1999-2000.
Progress at JT: 1981- 36.62, 1982- 44.00, 1983- 48.40, 1984- 46.80, 1985- 47.74, 1986- 51.42, 1987- 51.44, 1988- 47.42, 1989- 59.54, 1990- 64.02, 1993- 65.62, 1994- 66.40, 1995- 65.22, 1996- 69.26, 1997- 65.76, 1998- 65.10, 1999- 65.27; new: 1999- 60.97, 2000- 63.12, 2001- 62.27, 2002- 63.89, 2004- 63.01, 2005- 61.65, 2006- 62.14, 2007- 61.90.
Two-year drugs ban after positive test for steroids when 9th at 1990 Europeans. Married rowing coach Doru Moldovan in June 1997.

Claudia STEF b. 25 Feb 1978 Craiova 1.60m 48kg. née Iovan. CSM Universitatea Craiova & Dinamo Bucuresti. Sports teacher.
At 20kW: WCh: '99- 11, '03- 5, '05- 8, '07- 6; EC: '02- 5, '06- 5; WCp: '99-02-04-06: 6/6/12/11; ECp: '05- 4, '07- 8; EU23: '99- 1. At 10kW: EC: 98- 12; ECp: '98- 3; WUG: '99- 1. At 5000mW: WJ: '96- 3; EJ: '97- 1. Won ROM 10kW 1998, 2007; 20kW 2007.
World indoor best 3000mW 1999.
Progress at 10kW, 20kW: 1996- 44:52, 1997- 43:52, 1998- 43:11, 1999- 42:37, 1:29:39; 2000- 44:35dq/44:52, 1:29:39; 2002- 42:35, 1:29:57; 2003- 44:12, 1:29:09; 2004- 44:08, 1:27:41; 2005- 44:43, 1:29:54; 2006- 42:53, 1:29:27; 2007- 1:30:34. pbs: 3000mW 12:24.47 '97, 11:40.33i '99; 5000mW 20:30.8 '98.
Won IAAF Race Walking Challenge 2006. Two year drugs ban from 20 May 2000.

Ionela TÎRLEA-MANOLACHE b. 9 Feb 1976 Horezu 1.69m 54kg. Dinamo Bucuresti & CSM Calarasi. Sports teacher. Married Daniel Manolache on 20 Mar 2004.
At 400mh/4x400mR (200m): OG: '96- 7, '00- 6, '04- 2; WCh: '95- 7, '01- 6, '03- 4, '07- sf (h 200m, sf 400m); EC: '94- 7, '98- 1/4, '02- 1; WJ: '94- 1/3R; EJ: '93- 1, '95- 1; WUG: '95- 2; WCp: '98- 4, '02- 4; ECp: '93- (7), '94- 7 (8), '97- 8, '99- 3R (4, 1-400, 4-100), '01- 2 (2), '02 (5), '03- 1 (2), '05- (2); WI: '97- 4, '99- (1); E23Cp: '94- 1 (2). At 400m: WUG: '99- 1; WJ: '92- 3/1R; WI: '97- 4, '04- 4/3R; EI: '94- 4, '96- 4, '98- 2; E23Cp: '92- 2 (4). Won ROM 100m 1998, 2001, 2007; 200m 1998-9, 2002, 2007; 400m 1996, 1999; 400mh 1994-6, 2007; Balkan 200m 2002.
Romanian records: 100m (2) 1998-9, 200m (3) 1998-9, 400m (2) 1998-9, 400mh (6) 1996-9. European Junior 400mh record 1995.
Progress at 200m, 400m, 400mh: 1991- 24.51, 1992- 23.84, 52.13; 1993- 23.49, 56.30H; 1994- 23.60, 56.25H; 1995- 23.54, 55.26H; 1996- 54.40, 1997- 23.07, 52.06i, 55.04; 1998- 22.65/22.5A, 50.32, 53.37; 1999- 22.35, 49.88, 53.25; 2000- 51.84, 54.35; 2001- 22.77, 52.64i, 54.65; 2002- 23.04, 54.61; 2003- 22.78, 52.19, 53.87; 2004- 23.13, 50.48,

53.32; 2005- 23.26, 52.09; 2007- 22.93, 51.59, 55.41. pbs: 60m 7.24i '99, 100m 11.30 '99, 300m 36.20A '03.

Constantina TOMESCU b. 23 Jan 1970 Turburea 1.65m 48kg. née Dita. CSM Drobeta Turnu Severin. Sports teacher.
At 10,000m: EC: '02- 7, '06- 11. At Mar: OG: '04- 20; WCh: '99- 19, '01- 10, '03- dnf, '05- 3; EC: '98- 17; World CC: '98- 16; 20km: '06- 2; HMar: '99-03-04-05: 12/5/3/1; Eur CC: '99- 2. Won ROM 10,000m 1998, HMar 2002 CC 1998; Balkan 5000m 2002, 10,000m 1997-8.
Records: World 30km road 2006, European 20km road 2006. Romanian: half marathon 2006, marathon (2) 2005.
Progress at Mar: 1997- 2:35:32, 1998- 2:34:35, 1999- 2:36:28, 2000- 2:37:57, 2001- 2:26:39, 2002- 2:23:54, 2003- 2:23:35, 2004- 2:23:45, 2005- 2:21:30, 2006- 2:24:25, 2007- 2:23:55. pbs: 5000m 15:28.91 '00, 10,000m 31:49.47 '06, Road: 15km 47:10 '06, 20km 63:23 '06, HMar 68:07 '05, 30km 1:38:30 '06.
Led World marathon by almost 2 mins at 20k in 2001 and by 32sec at 5k in 2003. Stayed in lead to win Chicago 2004 (2nd 2003 and 2005); 2nd London 2005 (3rd 2004, 2007). Married to her coach Valeriu Tomescu, son Raphael born 1995.

RUSSIA

Governing body: All-Russia Athletic Federation, Luzhnetskaya Nab. 8, Moscow 119992. Founded 1911.

National Championships first held 1908, USSR women from 1922. **2007 Champions**: **Men**: 100m/200m: Ivan Teplykh 10.36/20.81, 400m: Maksim Dyldin 45.64, 800m: Yutriy Borzavovskiy 1:45.45, 1500m: Vyacheslav Shabunin 3:40.89, 5000m: Aleksandr Orlov 13:42.10, 10,000m: Aleksey Aleksandrov 28:40.26, HMar: Sammy Tum 62:40, Mar: Aleksey Sokolov 2:15:52, 3000mSt: Roman Usov 8:33.35, 110mh: Igor Peremota 13.60, 400mh: Aleksandr Derevyagin 49.35, HJ: Yaroslav Rybakov 2.30, PV: Igor Pavlov 5.70, LJ: Ruslan Gataullin 7.90, TJ: Aleksandr Petrenko 17.06, SP: Anton Lyuboslavskiy 20.77, DT: Bogdan Pishchalnikov 64.95, HT: Aleksey Zagornyi 77.90, JT: Sergey Makarov 86.56, Dec: Aleksey Sysoyev 8267, 20kW: Vladimir Kanaykin 1:17:36, 50kW: Denis Nizhegorodov 3:40:53. **Women**: 100m: Yevgeniya Polyakova 11.09, 200m: Natalya Rusakova 22.71, 400m: Natalya Antyukh 50.10, 800m: Olga Kotlyarova 1:58.14, 1500m: Natalya Pantelyeva 4:05.19, 5000m/3000mSt: Yekaterina Volkova 15:00.02/9:13.35, 10,000m: Inga Abitova 31:26.08, HMar: Rashida Khayrutdinova 70:38, Mar: Deana Usanova 2:45:27, 100mh: Tatyana Pavliy 12.90, 400mh: Yuliya Pechonkina 53.61, HJ: Anna Chicherova 2.01, PV: Svetlana Feofanova 4.75, LJ: Lyudmila Kolchanova 7.17 , TJ: Anna Pyatykh 14.60, SP: Anna Omarova 19.34, DT: Darya Pishchalnikova 63.90, HT: Yelena Konevstova 73.95, JT: Lada Chernova 63.35, Hep: Anna Bogdanova 5883, 20kW: Irina Stankina 1:29:56.
Note: Clubs abbreviations: Dyn – Dynamo, TU – Trade Union sports society, VS – Army, YR – Yunest Rossii.

Yuriy ANDRONOV b. 6 Nov 1971 1.80m 68kg.
At 50kW: OG: '04- 9; EC: '06- 3; WCp: '04- 3; ECp: '01-05-07: 12/3/5.
Progress at 50kW: 1991- 4:06:49, 1993- 3:59:28, 1994- 3:52:30, 1995- 3:57:54, 1996- 3:47:04, 1997- 3:54:52, 1999- 3:50:34, 2001- 3:52:57, 2002- 3:42:06, 2003- 3:48:26, 2004- 3:46:49, 2005- 3:42:34, 2006- 3:42:38, 2007- 3:42:55. pbs: 5000mW 19:09.7i '02, 20kW: 1:22:42.0t '02, 30kW 2:07:23 '04, 35kW 2:28:01 '03.

Sergey BAKULIN b. 13 Nov 1986 Morovia reg. 1.75m 62kg. Mordovia VS.
At 20kW: EC: '06- 5; WCp: '06- 6.
Progress at 20kW: 2006- 1:19:54, 2007- 1:19:14, 2008- 1:18:18. pb 10kW: 39:03 '06.

Valeriy BORCHIN b. 3 Jul 1986 Mordoviya 1.78m 63kg. Saransk VS.
At 20kW: WCh: '07- dnf; EC: '06- 2; EU23: '07- 1; ECp: '07- 9; Russian champion 2006.
Progress at 20kW: 2006- 1:20:00, 2007- 1:18:56, 2008- 1:17:55. pb 10kW: 39:45 '06.
Served one year drugs ban 2005-06.

Yuriy BORZAKOVSKIY b. 12 Apr 1981 Kratovo, Moskva reg. 1.82m 72kg. Moskva Dyn.
At 800m/4x400mR: OG: '00- 6, '04- 1; WCh: '03- 2, '05- 2, '07- 3; EC: '02- 2R; EJ: '99- 1; WI: '01- 1, '06- 3; EI: '00- 1; ECp: '99- 1, '02- 1; 2nd GP 2001. At 400m: EC: '02- sf; EU23: '01- 1; At 1500m: ECp: '03- 3. Won Russian 800m 2004, 1500m 2005, 2007.
Records: Two world junior indoor 800m 2000, European Junior 800m (2) & 1000m 2000; four Russian 800m 2001.
Progress at 800m: 1997- 1:52.8i/1:53.69, 1998- 1:47.71, 1999- 1:46.13, 2000- 1:44.33, 2001- 1:42.47, 2002- 1:44.20, 2003- 1:43.68, 2004- 1:43.92, 2005- 1:44.18, 2006- 1:43.42, 2007- 1:44:38. pbs: 200m 22.56 '99, 400m 45.84 '00, 1000m 2:17.40 '00, 1500m 3:40.28 '05, 3000m 8:32 '99.
He won at the World Youth Games in 1998, and at 18 had a startling victory in sprinting to victory in the European Cup 800m. In 2000 he set a hugely impressive Russian senior and world junior record 1:44.38 in Dortmund. He did not compete at the 2001 Worlds or 2002 Europeans at 800m, although he ran a 44.75 last leg in the European 4x400m. He typically leaves himself a tremendous amount to do on the second lap of his 800m races but Olympic success in 2004 came from a remarkably even-paced race.

Viktor BURAYEV b. 23 Aug 1982 Zarechnyi, Penza Reg. 1.76m 58kg. Saransk VS.
At 20kW: OG: '04- 22; WCh: '01- 3, '03- dq, '05- dnf; EC: '02- 4, '06- 4; WCp: '04- 7, '06- 7; ECp: '01- 1. At 10kW: WJ: '00- 3. Won RUS 20kW 2002-03. World junior walks records 10,000m 2000, 20km 2001.

Progress at 20kW: 1999- 1:28:18, 2001- 1:18:06, 2002- 1:20:36, 2003- 1:20:56, 2004- 1:20:14, 2005- 1:18:48, 2006- 1:19:27, 2007- 1:19:57, 2008- 1:19:27. pbs: 5000mW 19:12.0 '02, 10,000mW 38:46.4 '00. Youngest ever men's walk medallist at 18 years 264 days at the 2001 Worlds, when he was the only junior to win a medal that year.

Danil BURKENYA b. 20 Jul 1978 Ashkhabad, Turkmenistan 1.98m 82kg. Moskva VS.
At TJ: OG: '04- 3; WCh: '05/07- dnq 19/23; EC: '06- 6; WI: '04- 7, '08- 8; EJ: '97- 9; WCp: '06- 5; ECp: '04-05-06: 2/2/nj. At LJ: OG: '00- dnq 26; WCh: '01/03- dnq 19/30; EC: '02- 5; EJ: '97- 5; EI: '98- 4; ECp: '01-02: 1/4. Won RUS LJ 2000-02, TJ 2004, 2006.
Progress at LJ, TJ: 1994- 6.18, 13.73; 1995- 6.77, 15.28; 1996- 7.08, 14.87; 1997- 7.81, 16.29; 1998- 7.68, 16.36/16.40w; 1999- 8.07i/8.00, 16.30i; 2000- 8.12, 16.14; 2001- 8.31, 2002- 8.19/8.35w '02, 2003- 8.23, 16.58i; 2004- 7.84, 17.68; 2005- 17.10, 2006- 17.42, 2007- 17.48. pb 100m 10.98 '97.

Aleksey DROZDOV b. 3 Dec 1983 Klintsy, Bryansk Reg. 1.84m 80kg. Bryansk VS.
At Dec: WCh: '05- 10, '07- 4; EC: '06- 3; EU23: '03- 8, '05- 1; Russian champion 2005. At Hep: WI: '06- 5; EI: '05- 6.
Progress at Dec: 2002- 7037, 2003- 7536, 2004- 7805, 2005- 8196, 2006- 8350, 2007- 8475. pbs: 60m 6.7i '05, 6.94i '06; 100m 11.04 '07, 400m 50.27 '06, 1000m 2:43.17i '05, 1500m 4:32.93 '06, 60mh 8.0i '05, 8.19i '06; 110mh 14.74 '06, HJ 2.12 '07, PV 5.00 '06, LJ 7.58i '06, 7.35 '03; SP 16.98i/16.61 '06, DT 51.76 '06, JT 68.97 '07, Hep 6225i '06.

Pavel GERASIMOV b. 29 May 1979 Aleksin, Tula reg. 1.90m 83kg. Moskva VS.
At PV: OG: '00- dnq 26=, '04- 13=; WCh: '03- dnq 17, '05- 3; EC: '02- 12; WJ: '98- 1; EJ: '97- 2; WI: '01- 5, EI: '02- 6. Russian champion 2000.
Progress at PV: 1995- 4.40, 1996- 5.10i/5.00, 1997- 5.30, 1998- 5.55, 1999- 5.65/5.70ex, 2000- 5.90, 2001- 5.81i/5.50, 2002- 5.80i/5.60, 2003- 5.67, 2004- 5.77i/5.75, 2005- 5.70, 2006- 5.50i, 2007- 5.65i/5.60, 2008- 5.75i.

Aleksandr IVANOV b. 25 May 1982 Leningrad 1.94m 100kg. Luch Moskva.
At JT: OG: '04- 5; WCh: '01- 10, '03- 12, '05- 5, '07- 5; EC: '02- 6, '06- 8; EU23: '03- 1; EJ: '01- 1; WJ: '00- 6; WY: '99- 3; WCp: '06- 3; ECp: '04-05-07: 1/2/1. Won RUS 2002, 2004, World Military 2003.
Progress at JT: 1998- 67.97, 1999- 71.76, 2000- 77.11, 2001- 83.55, 2002- 87.62, 2003- 88.90, 2004- 87.73, 2005- 84.24, 2006- 84.22, 2007- 86.71.
Mother Valentina (née Tikhonova) had JT best of 59.10 in 1980.

Vladimir KANAYKIN b. 21 Mar 1985 Mordoviya 1.70m 60kg. Saransk VS.
At 50kW: WCh: '05- dq. '07- dnf; EC: '06- 9; ECp: '07- 1; Won RWC 30kW 2007, RUS 20km 2007, 50km 2005-06. At 10,000mW: WJ: '02- 1, '04- 2; WY: '01- 1.
World record 20km walk 2007, three world bests 30km & 35km walk 2004-06 (each to win Russian winter 35k).
Progress at 20kW. 50kW: 2003- 1:21:23, 2004- 1:22:00, 3:40:40; 2005- 1:21:11, 3:40:40; 2006- 1:21:20, 3:45:57; 2007- 1:17:16, 3:40:57. pbs: 5000mW 20:20.26 '03, 10,000mW: 40:58.48 '04, 10kW: 38:16 '04, 30kW 2:01:13 '06, 35kW 2:21:31 '06.
Disqualified when well clear of field in 2004 at World Cup junior 10km.

Sergey KIRDYAPKIN b. 16 Jan 1980 Insar, Mordoviya Rep. 1.78m 67kg. Saransk VS.
At 50kW: WCh: '05- 1, '07- dnf; ECp: '05- 2.
Progress at 50kW: 2001- 4:08:16, 2002- 3:52:19, 2004- 3:43:20, 2005- 3:38:08, 2006- 4:23:27; pbs: 20kW 1:23:07 '05, 30kW 2:05:06 '03, 35kW 2:25:57 '05.

Yevgeniy LUKYANENKO b. 23 Jan 1985 Slavyansk-na-Kubani 1.90m 80kg. Krasnodar VS.
At PV: WCh: '07- 6; WI: '08- 1; ECp: '07- nh.
Progress at PV: 2002- 4.90, 2003- 5.10, 2004- 5.30i/5.00, 2005- 5.40, 2006- 5.60, 2007- 5.81, 2008- 5.90i.

Sergey MAKAROV b. 19 Mar 1973 Lyubertsy 1.92m 100kg. Moskva Dyn.
At JT: OG: '96- 6, '00- 3, '04- 3; WCh: '97- 5, '99- 9, '01- 7, '03- 1, '05- 3, '07- dnq 18; EC: '98- 4, '02- 2; WCp: '98- 2, '02- 1; ECp: '96-7-8-9-00-01-02-03-06: 2/4/2/2/2/2/1/1/2; E23Cp: '94- 2. Won GWG 1998, WAF 2003, RUS 1996-7, 2000-01, 2003, 2005-07.
Six Russian records 1996-2002.
Progress at JT: 1991- 73.48, 1992- 76.08, 1993- 75.78, 1994- 82.54, 1995- 84.42, 1996- 88.86, 1997- 88.54, 1998- 86.96, 1999- 89.93, 2000- 89.92, 2001- 88.42, 2002- 92.61, 2003- 90.11, 2004- 86.19, 2005- 90.33, 2006- 88.49, 2007- 87.46.
Married to Oksana Ovchinnikova (b. 21 Jul 1971, Russian 'old' javelin record 68.72 '96. 2 WJ 1990). His father Aleksandr Makarov (b. 11 Feb 1951) was 2nd in the 1980 Olympic JT with a pb 89.64 (old javelin).

Ilya MARKOV b. 19 Jun 1972 Asbest, Sverdlovsk reg. 1.74m 65kg. Yekaterinburg VS. Soldier.
At 20kW: OG: '96- 2, '00- 15; WCh: '95- 4, '97- dq, '99- 1, '01- 2, '03- 8, '05- dq, '07- 9; EC: '94- 18, '98- 1; WUG: '97- 1; WCp: '95-3-9: 30/3/7; ECp: '03- 5, '05- 1. Won RUS 1995, GWG 1998. At 10kW: WJ: '90- 1; EJ: '91- 1.
Progress at 20kW: 1991- 1:33:46, 1992- 1:23:27, 1993- 1:20:19, 1994- 1:24:07, 1995- 1:18:53, 1996- 1:18:48, 1997- 1:18:30, 1998- 1:19:46, 1999- 1:18:50, 2000- 1:20:53, 2001- 1:19:36, 2003- 1:20:05, 2004- 1:19:25, 2005- 1:18:17, 2006- 1:18:18, 2007- 1:18:56, 2008- 1:19:18. pbs: 3000mW 11:08.2i '92, 5000mW 18:36.71i '99, 18:46.96 '01; 10,000mW 39:15.6 '98.

Denis NIZHEGORODOV b. 26 Jul 1980 Saransk 1.80m 61kg. Saransk VS.

At 50kW: OG: '04- 2; WCh: '03- 5, '07- 4; EC: '06- dq; Russian champion 2003-04, 2007. At 20kW: EU23: '01- 5; WUG: '01- 4; ECp: '00- 17, '01- 7. World best (no drugs test) 50km walk 2004.
Progress at 20kW, 50kW: 2000- 1:21:47, 2001- 1:18:20; 2003- 1:23:23, 3:38:23; 2004- 3:35:29, 2005- dnf, 2006- 1:22:45, 3:38:02; 2007- 3:40:53. pbs: 30kW 2:05:08 '06, 35kW 2:24:50 '06.

Igor PAVLOV b. 18 Jul 1979 Moskva 1.87m 83kg. Moskva VS.
At PV: OG: '04- 4; WCh: '05- 4, '07- 4; WI: '04- 1; EI: '05- 1; WUG: '03- 2. Russian champion 2005-07.
Progress at PV: 1998- 5.10, 1999- 5.30i, 2000- 5.55/5.70sq, 2001- 5.60i, 2002- 5.40, 2003- 5.65/5.75ex, 2004- 5.80, 2005- 5.90i/5.80, 2006- 5.60, 2007- 5.81, 2008- 5.81i.

Aleksandr PETRENKO 8 Feb 1983 Kaliningrad 1.89m 81kg. Luch Moskva.
At TJ: WCh: '07- 10; EC: '06- 11; WJ: '02- 4; EU23: '05- 2; WUG: '05- 5; EI: '05- 3, '07- 6; ECp: '07- 1; Russian champion indoors and out 2007.
Progress at TJ: 1999- 15.00, 2000- 15.09i, 2001- 16.20, 2002- 16.26. 2003- 16.46i/16.38, 2004- 16.79,2005-17.03,2006-17.09,2007-17.29/17.41w. pb LJ 7.63 '03.

Aleksandr POGORELOV b. 10 Jan 1980 Zheleznogorsk, Kursk region 2.01m 97kg. Bryansk Dyn.
At Dec: OG: '04- 11; WCh: '03- dnf, '05- 5; EC: '02- 8, '06- 4; EJ: '99- dnf; ECp: '02-03-06: 5/2/3. At Hep: WI: '03-04-06-08: 6/6/6/dnf; EI: '05- 2, '07- 2.
Progress at Dec: 1997- 5750, 1998- 6356, 1999- 6895, 2001- 7354, 2002- 8163, 2003- 8072, 2004- 8084, 2005- 8429, 2006- 8245. pbs: 60m 6.90i '06, 6.7i '04; 100m 10.86 '05, 400m 50.16 '05, 1000m 2:52.16i '07, 1500m 4:47.00 '04, 60mh 7.93i '06, 7.9i '04; 110mh 14.14 '05, HJ 2.15 '02, PV 5.10 '05, LJ 7.80i '08, 7.74 '02; SP 16.12i/16.07 '05, DT 48.44 '05, JT 61.38 '06, Hep 6229i '06.

Yaroslav RYBAKOV b. 22 Nov 1980 Mogilyev, Belarus 1.98m 82kg. Moskva VS.
At HJ: OG: '04- 6; WCh: '01- 2=, '03- 9, '05- 2=, '07- 2; EC: '02- 1, '06- 5; WJ: '98- 5; EJ: '99- 3; WI: '01-03-04-06-08: 7/2/2/1/2; EI: '02- 3, '05- 2; WCp: '02- 1; ECp: '01-02-03: 1/2/1; Won WAF 2003, 2nd GP 2002. Won Russian 2002-04, 2007.
Progress at HJ: 1997- 2.10i/2.09, 1998- 2.20, 1999- 2.19i/2.18, 2000- 2.28, 2001- 2.33, 2002- 2.31, 2003- 2.34,2004-2.32,2005-2.38i/2.33,2006-2.37i/2.33, 2007- 2.38i/2.35, 2008- 2.38i. pbs: LJ 7.44i '98, Hep 5570i '98.

Aleksandr SERGEYEV 29 Jul 1983 Kimry, Tver region 1.91m 81kg. Moskva TU.
At TJ: WJ: '02- 3; EC: '06- 10; EU23: '03- 5, '05- 1; WI: '04- dnq 13; EI: '02-05-07: 6/dnq 9/3; WUG: '05- 1.
Progress at TJ: 2000- 15.51i/15.46w, 2001- 16.38, 2002- 16.89i/16.62 2003- 16.80, 2004- 17.23i/17.11, 2005- 17.11, 2006- 17.07, 2007- 17.15i/16.83. pb LJ 7.50 '03, 7.58w '05.

Andrey SILNOV b. 9 Sep 1984 Shakhty, Rostov Reg. 1.98m 83kg. Russian Army.
At HJ: WCh: '07 11=; EC: '06- 1; E23: '05- 9; WCp: '06- 2; ECp: '06- 1. Russian champion 2006.
Progress at HJ: 2002- 2.10, 2003- 2.10, 2004- 2.15, 2005- 2.28, 2006- 2.37, 2007- 2.36i/2.30, 2008- 2.37i.

Pavel SOFYIN b. 4 Sep 1981 Lyubertsky, Moskva region 2.00m 120kg. Moskva TU.
At SP: OG: '04- dnq; WCh: '03- dnq, '07- 10; EC: '06- 5; WJ: '00- 7; EU23: '03- 2; EJ: '99- 6; WI: '06- 4; EI: '05- 8; WCp: '06- 3; ECp: '05-06-07: 6/1/5. Russian champion 2006.
Progress at SP: 1999- 17.12, 2000- 18.42, 2001- 18.44, 2002- 19.63, 2003- 20.33, 2004- 19.89, 2005- 20.05, 2006- 20.68i/20.59, 2007- 20.38.

Aleksey SYSOYEV b. 8 Mar 1985 Kamyshin, Volgograd region 1.94m 96kg. Volgograd Dyn.
At Dec: WCh: '05- dnf, '07- 6; EC: '06- 10; WJ: '04- 2; EU23: '05- 2; EJ: '03- 2; Russian champion 2006-07.
Progress at Dec: 2005- 8090, 2006- 8108, 2007- 8357. pbs: 60m 6.88i '06, 100m 10.80 '07, 10.72w '05; 400m 48.42 '07, 1000m 2:41.90i '06, 1500m 4:28.96 '03, 60mh 8.25i '06, 110mh 14.59 '07, HJ 2.18i '07, 2.16 '05, PV 4.90 '07, LJ 7.15 '07, SP 16.59i '08, 16.16 '07; DT 53.49 '05, JT 59.60 '05, Hep 6119i '08.

Andrey TERESHIN b. 15 Dec 1982 Kineshma, Ivanovo Reg. 1.95m 77kg. Moskva VS.
At HJ: WCh: '05/07- dnq 23=/24; EU23: '03- 2; WI: '06- 2; EI: '05- 8, '07- 7; WUG: '03- 6=; ECp: '07- 2.
Progress at HJ: 2000- 2.15, 2001- 2.18, 2002- 2.24, 2003- 2.24, 2004- 2.28i/2.26, 2005- 2.32, 2006- 2.36i/2.31, 2007- 2.35i/2.34, 2008- 2.36i.

Ivan UKHOV b. 29 Mar 1986 Chelyabinsk 1.92m 83kg. Sverdlovsk TU.
At HJ: WJ: '04- dnq 13; EC: '06- 12=; EJ: '05- 1; WUG: '05- 4.
Progress at HJ: 2004- 2.15, 2005- 2.30, 2006- 2.37i/2.33, 2007- 2.39i/2.20, 2008- 2.36i.
Former discus thrower.

Vyacheslav VORONIN b. 5 Apr 1974 Vladikavkaz 1.91m 78kg. Moskva Dyn.
At HJ: OG: '00- 10, '04- 9; WCh: '99- 1, '01- 2=, '05- 8; EJ: '93- 2; WI: '99- 2, '01- 9; EI: '98- 2, '00- 1; ECp: '99- 2, '04- 5=. Won GP 2000, RUS champion 1999, 2005.
Russian high jump record 2000.
Progress at HJ: 1990- 1.85, 1991- 2.07, 1992- 2.15, 1993- 2.18, 1995- 2.18, 1996- 2.29, 1997- 2.26/2.30sq, 1998- 2.32i/2.28, 1999- 2.37, 2000- 2.40, 2001- 2.37, 2002- 2.26i, 2003- 2.24i/2.21, 2004- 2.32, 2005- 2.33, 2006- 2.28, 2007- 2.32i/2.30.

Aleksey VOYEVODIN b. 9 Aug 1970 Marat, Penza Reg. 1.78m 65kg. Saransk VS.
At 50kW: OG: '04- 3; WCh: '95- 15, '97- 10, '01- dnf, '03- 4, '05- 2, '07- dnf; EC: '02- 2; WCp: '95-02-04: 10/1/1; ECp: '98-01-03-05-07: 4/6/2/1/4.

Won RUS 50kW 2001-02.
Progress at 50kW: 1993- 4:04:44, 1994- 3:52:36, 1995- 3:48:55, 1996- 3:45:37, 1997- 3:41:33, 1998- 3:46:31, 1999- 3:51:43, 2000- 3:50:27, 2001- 3:44:32, 2002- 3:40:16, 2003- 3:38:01, 2004- 3:42:44, 2005- 3:41:03, 2007- 3:41:52. pbs: 5000mW 19:19.0 '02, 10,000mW 39:22.0i '01, 20kW 1:19:31 '98, 30kW 2:05:18 '04, 35kW 2:26:25 '04.
His wife **Yuliya Voyevodina** (b. 7.10.71) has 20kW pb 1:27:53 '04, 13 OG 04, 10 WCh 05.

Women

Mariya ABAKUMOVA b. 15 Jan 1986 Stavropol 1.79m 80kg. Krasnodar VS.
At PV: WCh: '07- 7; WJ: '04- dnq 25; WY: '03- 4; EU23: '07- 6; EJ: '05- 1; ECp: '05- 7.
Progress at JT: 2002- 51.81, 2003- 51.41, 2004- 58.26, 2005- 59.53, 2006- 60.12, 2007- 64.28.

Inga ABITOVA b. 6 Mar 1982 Novokuibyshevsk 1.53m 47kg. Novokuibyshevsk Dyn
At 10,000m: WCh: '07- 12; EC: '06- 1. Eur CC: '01- 4J, '05- 7. Won RUS 10,000m 2007.
Progress at 10,000m, Mar: 2004- 2:43:48, 2005- 32:25.83, 2:38:20; 2006- 30:31.42, 2:33:55; 2007- 31:26.08, 2:34:25. pbs: 1500m 4:20.10 '00, 3000m 9:02.88 '06, 5000m 15:15.05 '06, HMar 71:06 '05.
Son Yegorka born 2003. Won Belgrade Marathon 2004.

Natalya ANTYUKH b. 26 Jun 1981 Leningrad 1.82m 73kg. Moskva VS.
At 400m/4x400mR: OG: '04- 3/2R; WCh: '05- sf/1R, '07- 6; EC: '02- 2R; WI: '03-04-06: 1R/GR/1R; EI: '02- 1, '07- 2R; WCp: '02- 3R; ECp: '01- 3/1R, '05- 1/1R, '06- 1R. At 200m: ECp: '04- 2. Won Russian 400m 2007.
Progress at 400m: 2000- 54.79, 2001- 51.19, 2002- 51.17i/51.24, 2003- 51.73i/52.28, 2004- 49.85, 2005- 50.67, 2006- 50.37i/50.47, 2007- 49.93. pbs: 200m 22.75 '04, 300m 36.0+ '04, 400mh 58.30 '00.

Anna BOGDANOVA b. 21 Oct 1984 Sankt-Peterburg 1.78m 66kg. St. Peterburg.
At Hep: WCh: '07- 10; Russian champion 2007. At Pen: WI: '08- 3.
Progress at Hep: 2004- 5250, 2006- 5785, 2007- 6289. pbs: 200m 25.00 '07, 800m 2:10.98 '07, 60mh 8.32i '08, 100mh 13.65 '07, HJ 1.86 '07, LJ 6.51i '08, 6.46 '04, 6.59w '07; SP 14.56i '08, 13.43 '07; JT 39.91 '07, Hep 4762i '08.
Her faher Andrey Bogdanov won a silver medal at 4x200m freestyle swimming at the 1996 Olympics.

Galina BOGOMOLOVA b. 15 Oct 1977 Beloretsk, Bashkorstan 1.59m 43kg. Beloretsk VS.
At 10,000m (5000m): OG: '00- h, '04- 22; WCh: '03- 6, '05- 8; EC: '06- 4; WJ: '96- 12 (h 3000m); EU23: '97- 7/7. At 3000m: WI: '03- 6; ECp: '00- 2. At Mar: WCh: '07- dnf. World HMar: '03- 17, '05- 4. Eur CC: '02- 2, '03- 10. Won RUS 10,000m 2000, 2003, 2005-06.
Russian 10,000m record (30:46.48) 2003.
Progress at 5000m, 10,000m, Mar: 1996- 16:29.56, 1997- 15:53.45, 33:34.44; 1998- 16:18.06, 33:56.04; 1999- 15:52.72, 2000- 15:08.61, 31:29.66; 2002- 15:39.14, 2003- 15:13.08, 30:26.20; 2004- 14:59.72, 32:15.31; 2005- 30:33.75, 2:31:54; 2006- 15:17+, 30:35.90, 2:20:47; 2008- 2:22:53. pbs: 1500m 4:10.00 '04, 3000m 8:42.03 '05, Road: 15km 49:56 '05, HMar 70:15 '06.
Won Rome marathon 2008, 5th London and 2nd Chicago 2006.

Olesya BUFALOVA b. 6 Oct 1982 Makhoshevskaya, Adygeya 1.65m 56kg. Maikop TU.
At TJ: WCh: '07- 10; EC: '06- 5; WI: 08- 7; EI: '07- 2. At 400mh: WY: '99- 5.
Progress at TJ: 2001- 13.09, 2005- 13.67, 2006- 14.50, 2007- 14.50i/14.49, 2008- 14.54i. pbs: 100mh 14.07 '99, 400mh 59.96 '99.

Svetlana CHERKASOVA b. 20 May 1978 Belogorsk, Khabarovsk region 1.72m 57kg. née Belosurova. Luch Moskva.
At 800m: OG: '04- sf; WCh: '01- sf, '05- 7, '07- h; EC: '02- sf, '06- 8; EI: '02- 5; WCp: '02- 5. Russian champion 2001.
Progress at 800m: 1998- 2:07.75, 1999- 2:00.91, 2000- 1:59.23, 2001- 1:57.59, 2002- 1:58.84, 2003- 1:59.28, 2004- 1:57.50, 2005- 1:56.93, 2006- 1:57.23, 2007- 1:58.37. pbs: 400m 52.76 '05, 600m 1:26.84i '02, 1000m 2:34.08 '01, 1500m 4:05.55 '03, 2000m 5:40.49 '07.
Husband Aleksey Cherkasov has 2.15 HJ best.

Tatyana CHERNOVA b. 29 Jan 1988 Krasnodar 1.89m 63kg. Krasnodar VS.
At Hep: WCh: '07- dnf; WJ: '06- 1; WY: '05- 1. At Pen: WI: '08- 7.
Progress at Hep: 2006- 6227, 2007- 6768w. pbs: 200m 23.50 '07, 800m 2:10.10i '08, 2:15.05 '07; 60mh 8.38i '08, 100mh 13.47, 13.07w '07, 400mh 56.14 '07, HJ 1.87 '07, LJ 6.61 '07, SP 13.57 '07, JT 54.49 '06, Pen 4717i '08.
Her mother Lyudmila (née Zenina) won an Olympic gold medal (ran in the heats) for 4x400m at the 1980 Olympics, pbs: 200m 22.9 '82, 400m 50.91 '83.

Anna CHICHEROVA b. 22 Jul 1982 Yerevan, Armenia 1.80m 57kg. Moskva VS.
At HJ: OG: '04- 6; WCh: '03- 6, '05- 4, '07- 2=; EC: '06- 7=; WJ: '00- 4; WY: '99- 1; EJ: '01- 2; WUG: '05- 1; WI: '04- 2; EI: '05- 1, '07- 5=; ECp: '06- 3. Russian champion 2004, 2007.
Progress at HJ: 1998- 1.80, 1999- 1.89, 2000- 1.90, 2001- 1.92, 2002- 2.00i/1.89, 2003- 2.04i/2.00, 2004- 2.04i/1.98, 2005- 2.01i/1.99, 2006- 1.96i/1.95, 2007- 2.03.
Moved with family to Russia at the beginning of the 1990s.

Svetlana FEOFANOVA b. 16 Jul 1980 Moskva 1.64m 53kg. Moskva TU.
At PV: OG: '00- dnq, '04- 2; WCh: '01- 2, '03- 1, '07- 3; EC: '02- 1, '06- 4; WI: '01-03-04-06-08: 2/1/3/3/5; EI: '02- 1, '07- 1; WCp: '02- 2; ECp: '00-02-06: 1/1/nh; 2nd GP 2001. Russian champion 2001, 2006.

World pole vault record 2004, 9 European records 2001-04, 11 Russian 2000-04, 9 world indoor 2002-04 (4.71-4.85), 13 European indoor 2001-04.
Progress at PV: 1998- 3.90, 1999- 4.10, 2000- 4.50, 2001- 4.75, 2002- 4.78, 2003- 4.80i/4.75, 2004- 4.88, 2005- 4.70i, 2006- 4.70, 2007- 4.82, 2008- 4.71i.
Was a top gymnast, winning Russian titles at youth, junior and U23 level at asymmetric bars and floor exercises. Set five indoor world records in a month in 2002. Missed 2005 outdoor season due to a herniated disc.

Yuliya FOMENKO b. 30 Aug 1979 Arkhangelsk 1.66m 54kg. née Chizhenko. Moskva reg. VS.
At 1500m: WCh: 05- dq, '07- 7; EC: '06- 2; WI: '06- 1, '08- 2; ECp: '05- 1, '07- 2. At 3000m: WCp: '06- 7. Won Russian 800m 2006, 1500m 2005.
European indoor 1000m record 2006.
Progress at 800m, 1500m: 2001- 2:06.80, 2002- 2:05.32, 4:16.79; 2003- 2:03.08, 4:07.21; 2004- 2:05.43, 4:04.58; 2005- 2:01.08, 3:58.68; 2006- 1:57.07, 3:55.68; 2007- 2:01.04, 4:00.7; 2008- 3:59.41i. pbs: 400m 53.81 '06, 1000m 2:32.16i/2:33.49 '06, 1M 4:24.79 '07, 2000m 5:50.95i '03, 3000m 8:53.80i '05, 8:59.67 '06; 5000m 16:27.19 '01.
Finished 2nd in World 1500m in 2005, but then disqualified for baulking Miryam Jamal. Married Pavel Fomenko (HJ 2.32i/2.31 '02, 3 EI '05) in 2006.

Olesya FORSHEVA b. 8 Jul 1979 Nizhniy Tagil, Sverdlovsk 1.71m 60kg. née Krasnomovets. Moskva reg. Dyn.
At 400m/4x400mR: OG: '04- 2R; WCh: '05- 1R; WI: '04- 2/1R, '06- 1/1R.
World indoor 4x400m record 2004.
Progress at 400m: 2001- 53.31, 2003- 53.77, 2004- 50.19, 2005- 50.77, 2006- 50.04i. pbs: 200m 23.09 '05, 300m 36.62i '04, 500m 1:08.84i '04.
Breakthrough in 2004 indoor season to win EI Cup and take silver and gold at World Indoors. Married to **Dmitriy Forshev** (b. 30 May 1976) – 400m 45.62 '03, Russian champion 2005.

Gulnara GALKINA b. 9 Jul 1978 Naberezhnye Chelny, Tatarstan 1.74m 56kg. née Samitova. Naberezhnye Chelny Dyn.
At 3000mSt: WCh: '07- 7; ECp: '03- 1. At 1500m: WI: '04- 3. At 3000m: ECp: '04- 1, '07- 1. At 5000m: OG: '04- 6; WCh: '03- 7. Won RUS 1500m 2004, 5000m 2003-04, 3000mSt 2003, indoor 1500m & 3000m 2004.
Two world records and four Russian records 3000m steeplechase 2003-04.
Progress at 5000m, 3000mSt: 2003- 14:54.38, 9:08.33; 2004- 14:53.70, 9:01.59; 2006- 9:53.83, 2007- 9:11.68. pbs: 800m 2:01.40 '07, 1000m 2:35.91i '04, 1500m 4:01.29 '04, 1M 4:20.23 '07, 2000m 5:31.03 '07, 3000m 8:41.72i '04, 8:47.92 '07.
Great breakthrough in 2003, starting with world indoor 3000mSt best of 9:29.54. Married Anton Galkin (400m 44.83 '04) in 2004. Missed 2005 and raced only twice in 2006.

Yuliya GOLUBCHIKOVA b. 27 Mar 1983 Moskva 1.75m 57kg. Moskva City Sport Society.
At PV: WCh: '07- 6=; WJ: '02- 2; EI: '07- 2; ECp: '07- 7.
Progress at PV: 1997- 2.80, 1998- 3.60, 1999- 3.70i/3.60, 2000- 3.60i, 2002- 4.35, 2003- 4.30, 2004- 4.30, 2005- 4.40, 2006- 4.60, 2007- 4.71i/4.70, 2008- 4.75i.

Lidiya GRIGORYEVA b. 21 Jan 1974 Smychka, Chuvashiya 1.64m 58kg. Novocheboksarsk TU.
At 10,000m: OG: '00- 9, '04- 8; EC: '06- 3; WCh: '03- 16. World HMar: '00-03-05: 11/4/7. Won Russian 10,000m 2004, CC 1998.
Progress at 10,000m, Mar: 1997- 34:32.08, 1998- 2:41:04; 1999- 32:49.64, 2:35:38; 2000- 31:21.27, 2:32:40; 2001- 32:36.6, 2003- 30:57.83, 2004- 31:01.15, 2:34:39; 2005- 31:20.58, 2:27:01; 2006- 30:32.72, 2:25:10; 2007- 32:03.02, 2:28:37. pbs: 1M 4:36.82 '04, 3000m 8:45.73 '04, 5000m 15:17.21 '04, 15:17+ '06; HMar 69:32 '03.
Won Paris marathon 2005, Los Angeles 2006 (when she collected $155,000 plus a Honda Accord car) and Boston 2007.

Viktoriya GUROVA b. 22 May 1982 Sochi 1.78m 63kg. Krasnodar TU.
At TJ: OG: '04- dnq 21; WCh: '05- 10; EU23: '03- 1; EJ: '01- 3; WUG: '03- 2; EI: '05- 1; ECp: '06- 2, '07- 3.
Progress at TJ: 1998- 12.56, 1999- 13.02, 2000- 13.44, 2001- 13.75/13.92w, 2002- 14.22, 2003- 14.37, 2004- 14.65, 2005- 14.74i/14.38, 2006- 14.60, 2007- 14.46. pb LJ 6.72 '07.

Yuliya GUSHCHINA b. 4 Mar 1983 Novocherkask 1.75m 63kg. Moskva reg. VS.
At 200m(/100m)/4x100mR: WCh: '05- 6, '07- 5R; EC: '06- 2/5/1R; EU23: '03- 3; WCp: '06- 3/5/1R; ECp: '05- 1R, '06- (1)/1R, '07- 1R, At 4x400mR: WI: '06- GR, '08- 1R; ECp: '05/07- 1R. Won Russian 200m 2005.
World indoor records 4x200m 2005, 4x400m 2006.
Progress at 200m: 2002- 23.92/23.88w, 2003- 23.58, 2004- 23.06, 2005- 22.53, 2006- 22.69/22.52w, 2007- 22.75. pbs: 60m 7.24i '07, 7.2i '03; 100m 11.13 '06, 400m 51.26i '06, 51.94 '03.

Yevgeniya ISAKOVA b. 27 Nov 1978 Leningrad 1.75m 67kg. St Petersburg VS.
At 400mh: WCh: '07- 6; EC: '06- 1; ECp: '06- 2; Russian champion 2006.
Progress at 400mh: 1997- 60.46, 2001- 56.55, 2003- 57.98, 2003- 56.25, 2004- 55.62, 2005- 54.39, 2006- 53.93, 2007- 54.11. pbs: 400m 52.14 '05, 800m 2:04.61 '00.

Yelena ISINBAYEVA b. 3 Jun 1982 Volgograd 1.74m 66kg. Volgograd VS. PE student.
At PV: OG: '00- dnq, '04- 1; WCh: '03- 3, '05- 1, '07- 1; EC: '02- 2, '06- 1; WJ: '98- 9, '00- 1, WY: '99- 1; EU23: '03- 1; EJ: '99- 5, '01- 1; WI: '01-03-04-06-08: 7/2/1/1/; EI: '05- 1; WCp: '06- 1. Won WAF 2004-07, Russian 2002.

11 outdoor world pole vault records 2003-05, 10 indoor 2004-08 (inc. 3 absolute WR), world junior indoor records 2000 and 2001.
Progress at PV: 1997- 3.30, 1998- 4.00, 1999- 4.20, 2000- 4.45i/4.40, 2001- 4.47i/4.46, 2002- 4.60/4.65ex, 2003- 4.82, 2004- 4.92, 2005- 5.01, 2006- 4.91, 2007- 4.93i/4.91, 2008- 4.95i.
Former gymnast. Set world age bests at 17-18-19 in 2000-02. World titles as Youth, junior and senior. World indoor records in all four competitions 2005 and a further five outdoors in 2005. These included the first 5m vault by a woman (at the London GP) followed by 5.01 to win the World title by 41 cm. Shared Golden League jackpot in 2007.

Olimpiada IVANOVA b. 26 Aug 1970 Munsyuty, Chuvashiya 1.68m 54kg. Moskva VS.
At 20kW: OG: '04- 2; WCh: '03- dnf, '05- 1, '07- dnf; EC: '02- 1; WCp: '02- 2, '06- 2; ECp: '00- 1; RUS champion 2004. At 10kW: WCh: '97- drugs dq (2); WCp: '93- 12, '97- 2; won GWG 1994. At 5000mW: EJ: '85- 9.
World best 20km walk 2001, world record 2005.
Progress at 10kW, 20kW: 1987- 45:15, 1992- 45:18, 1993- 42:24, 1994- 42:30.31t, 1995- 41:30, 1996- 41:46, 1:30:58; 1997- 41:24, 1999- 43:31, 1:28:21; 2000- 42:43, 1:26:08; 2001- 42:34, 1:24:50; 2002- 43:26, 1:26:42; 2004- 43:46, 1:26:54; 2005- 42:54, 1:25:41; 2006- 43:39, 1:27:26. pbs: 3000mW 12:02.2 '95, 2MW 12:54.98i '96, 5000mW 20:50.6i '97, 20:56.10 '94, 20:51R '97.
Lost her 1997 World silver medal when she tested positive for Stanozolol, receiving a two-year ban. World best 20km walk time when she won Russian winter championship in March 2001 and official record to win 2005 World title.

Olga KANISKINA b. 19 Jan 1985 Napolnaya Tavla, Mordoviya 1.60m 43kg. Saransk VS. Mathematics student at Uversity of Mordovia.
At 20kW: WCh: '07- 1; EC: '06- 2; WCp: '06- 5; EU23: '05- 2; ECp: '07- 2; won RWC 2007.
Progress at 20kW: 2005- 1:29:25, 2006- 1:26:02, 2007- 1:26:47, 2008- 1:25:11. pbs: 3000mW 12:23.5 '05, 5000mW 20:38.2 '05, 10kW 43:12R '06.

Gulfiya KHANAFEYEVA b. 4 Jun 1982 1.70m 84kg. Moskva TU.
At HT: WCh: '07- 10; EC: '06- 2; EU23: '03- 3; EJ: '01- 10; WUG: '03- 2; ECp: '05- 3. Russian champion 2006. World hammer record 2006.
Progress at HT: 1998- 51.10, 1999- 53.80, 2000- 57.20, 2001- 61.10, 2002- 62.19/64.50dq, 2003- 68.92, 2004- 72.71, 2005- 70.76, 2006- 77.26, 2007- 77.36. She had a 3-month ban in 2002 after testing positive for a stimulant.

Yekaterina KHOROSHIKH b. 21 Jan 1983 Shakhty, Rostov Reg. 1.65m 75kg. Rostov VS.
At HT: WCh: '05- dnq; EC: '06- dnq 22; WJ: '02- 11; EU23: '05- 1.
Progress at HT: 2001- 48.78, 2002- 61.73, 2003- 64.42, 2004- 68.44, 2005- 73.08, 74.31 irreg; 2006- 76.63, 2007- 74.87.
Suspended and awaiting drug test enquiry after positive test on 9 May 2007.

Irina KHUDOROSHKINA b. 13 Oct 1968 Tonarskiy Karaganda reg, Kazakhstan. 1.82m 100kg. Moskva Dyn.
At SP: OG: '96- 3, '04- dq (1); EC: '06- 7; EI: '96- 2, '07- 2; ECp: '06- 2. Russian champion 1994, 1996, 1997 (disq), 2006.
Progress at SP: 1986- 15.01i/14.34, 1987- 16.82, 1988- 17.52, 1989- 18.53, 1990- 19.16, 1991- 18.53, 1992- 18.61i/18.21, 1993- 18.89, 1994- 19.81, 1995- 19.54, 1996- 20.32, 1997- 18.54/18.95dq, 2000- 18.56, 2001- 18.67, 2002- 18.92, 2003- 19.31i/18.81, 2004- 18.38i (18.75i/17.70dq), 2006- 18.84, 2007- 19.01i/18.87.
Two-year drugs ban June 1997 and again from 10 Feb 2004.

Anisya KIRDYAPKINA b. 23 Oct 1989 1.65m 51kg. née Kornikova. Mordovia TU.
At 10,000mW: EJ: '07- 1; ECp: '07- 1J.
Progress at 20kW: 2007- 1:28:00, 2008- 1:25:30. pbs: 5000mW 21:06.3 '06, 10,000mW 43:27.30 '06, 42:59R '07.

Svetlana KLYUKA b. 27 Dec 1978 Belogorsk, Khabarovsk reg. 1.70m 62kg. Moskva VS.
At 800m: WCh: '03- sf, '07- 7; EC: '06- 2; WUG: '05- 1; ECp: '05- 3, '06- 1.
Progress at 800m: 2002- 2:00.97, 2003- 1:58.47, 2004- 1:59.55, 2005- 1:57.35, 2006- 1:57.21, 2007- 1:58.63. pbs: 400m 52.14 '06, 1000m 2:39.42i '06, 2:40.60 '07.

Lyudmila KOLCHANOVA b. 1 Oct 1979 Sharya, Kostroma. 1.75m 60kg. Kostroma TU.
At LJ: WCh: '07- 2; EC: '06- 1; WUG: '05- 1; EI: '05- 5; WCp: '06- 1. Russian champion 2007.
Progress at LJ: 2000- 6.20, 2001- 6.12i/6.07, 2002- 6.32, 2003- 6.09i/6.07, 2004- 6.54, 2005- 6.79, 2006- 7.11, 2007- 7.21. pbs: HJ 1.82 ?, TJ 13.88 '04.
Having been a high jumper, she played basketball before returning to athletics in 2000.

Olga KOMYAGINA b. 10 Feb 1974 Toksovo 1.68m 57kg. St-Peterburg VS.
At 1500m: ECh: '98- 11; WI: 99- 4; EI: '02- 6; ECp: '98- 1. At 3000m: WI: 08- 5. World 4k CC: '06- 16
Progress at 1500m: 1997- 4:13.81, 1998- 4:04.99, 1999- 4:05.44, 2000- 4:02.32, 2001- 4:03.98, 2002- 4:05.71, 2003- 4:04.77, 2005- 4:12.85, 2006- 4:04.33i, 2007- 4:04.5. pbs: 800m 2:00.64 '99, 1000m 2:36.76i '06, 1M 4:23.49i '08, 4:25.71 '99; 2000m 5:39.06 '01, 3000m 8:35.67i '06, 8:42.58 '99.
Surely the best ever pacemaker, providing just what is asked for in so many GP races and record attempts from 1999 to date. Married to Innokenty Zharov (400m 45.88 '93), daughter Katya born in 2004.

Yelena KONEVTSOVA b. 11 Mar 1981 Klin 1.83m 77kg. née Tauryanina. Moskva Dyn.
At HT: OG: '04- dnq 16; WCh: '03- dnq 24, '07- 5; EC: '02- dnq 23. Russian champion 2007.

Progress at HT: 1997- 48.44, 1998- 55.19, 1999- 53.75, 2000- 60.41, 2001- 63.85, 2002- 67.35, 2003- 69.59, 2004- 73.68, 2005- 67.51, 2006- 75.07, 2007- 76.21.

Olga KOTLYAROVA b. 12 Apr 1976 Sverdlovsk 1.80m 66kg. Accountancy graduate. Yekaterinburg TU.
At 800m/4x400mR: WCh: '07- 4; EC: '06- 1; WI: '06- 5; WCp: '06- 3/3R. At 400m: OG: '96- qf/5R, '00- 8/3R; WCh: '97- sf, '99- 8/1R; EC: '98- 3/2R; WJ: '94- 4R; EJ: '95- 1/2R; EU23: '97- 2R; WI: '97- 1R, '99- 1R, '01- 2/1R, '04- 1R; EI: '96- 2; WUG: '97- 2/1R; WCp: '98- 3R; ECp: '96-7-9-04: 4&3R/3&1R/2&1R/1. Won Russian 400m 1998, 800m 2007.
World indoor 4x400m record 1997, 1999, 2004.
Progress at 400m, 800m: 1994- 53.67, 1995- 52.03/51.8, 1996- 51.17, 1997- 50.63, 1998- 50.38, 1999- 50.32, 2000- 49.95, 2:05.17, 2001- 50.42i/50.81A, 2003- 52.86, 2004- 49.77, 1:57.96; 2005- 52.00, 1:57.55; 2006- 50.99, 1:57.24; 2007- 52.14, 1:58.14. pbs: 50m 6.2i '98, 200m 23.35A '98, 300m 36.91+ '99, 500m 1:07.68i '03, 600m 1:23.44i '04 (world best).
Gave birth to daughter Tatyana in 2002.

Tatyana KOTOVA b. 11 Dec 1976 Kokand, Uzbekistan 1.82m 60kg. Moskva TU.
At LJ: OG: '00- 4, '04- 3; WCh: '99- dnq 13, '01- 2, '03- 2, '05- 2, '07- 3; EC: '02- 1; WI: '99-01-03-04-06: 1/2/1/2/1; EU23: '97- 1; WCp: '02- 1; ECp: '02-06-07: 1/1/2; 2nd GP 2002. Won WAF 2005, Russian 1999-2001, 2005.
Progress at LJ: 1994- 6.32, 1995- 6.32, 1996- 6.65, 1997- 6.76, 1998- 6.82/6.97w, 1999- 6.99/7.01w, 2000- 7.04 (7.05iu), 2001- 7.12, 2002- 7.42, 2003- 6.94, 2004- 7.05, 2005- 6.96/7.20w, 2006- 7.12, 2007- 6.90/7.10w. pbs: HJ 1.75 '95, TJ 13.69i/13.64 '98.
Born in Uzbekistan, she moved to Taboshari (Tajikistan) and now lives in Central Siberia. Her father came from Cherkassy in the Ukraine. Shared Golden League jackpot 2000. Achieved the world's best long jump for eight years in 2002. Married her coach Vladimir Kudyavtsev in 2007.

Olga KUZENKOVA b. 4 Oct 1970 Smolensk 1.76m 75kg. Moskva Dyn. Army Officer, has a diploma in physical education.
At HT: OG: '00- 2, '04- 1; WCh: '99- 2, '01- 2, '03- 2, '05- 1, '07- dnq 22; EC: '98- 2, '02- 1; WUG: '97- 2; ECp: '97-8-9-00-02-03-04: 1/1/2/1/1/3/2; 3rd GP 2001. RUS champion 1992-4, 1997-2004; CIS 1992, WAF 2004.
Eleven world hammer records 1992-8 (six officially ratified), inc. unratified 69.46 '96 and 73.80 '98 due to no drugs testing procedures; 66.84 in 1994 was the first record for the event accepted by the IAAF. 14 Russian records 1992-2000.
Progress at HT: 1990- 59.50, 1991- 61.52, 1992- 65.40, 1993- 64.64, 1994- 66.84, 1995- 68.16, 1996- 69.46, 1997- 73.10, 1998- 73.80, 1999- 74.30, 2000- 75.68, 2001- 73.62, 2002- 73.07, 2003- 74.98, 2004- 75.02, 2005- 75.10, 2007- 72.36.
Became the first 70m hammer thrower in 1997. After five championship silver medals at last won gold at the 2002 Europeans. Child born in 2006. World W35 record 2007.

Tatyana LEBEDEVA b. 21 Jul 1976 Sterlitamsk, Bashkortostan 1.71m 61kg. Volgograd VS.
At TJ (/LJ): OG: '00- 2, '04- 3/1; WCh: '99- 4, '01- 1, '03- 1, '05- dns, '07- 1/2; EC: '98- 5, '06- 1; WJ: '94- 3/10; EJ: '95- 2/6; WI: '01- 2, '04- 1/1, '06- 1; EI: '00- 1; WUG: '01- 1; WCp: '98- 2, '06- 1; ECp: '00-01: 1/1. GP: 3rd 1999, 2nd 2001. Won WAF LJ 2006-07, TJ 2003, 2006; GWG TJ 2001, Russian TJ 1998-2001, LJ 2004.
Three Russian triple jump records 2000-04.
Progress at LJ, TJ: 1991- 12.91, 1992- 13.03, 1993- 6.17, 13.13i/12.94; 1994- 6.65, 13.69; 1995- 13.88, 1996- 13.62, 1997- 13.89i/13.56, 1998- 14.45/14.58w, 1999- 14.89, 2000- 15.32, 2001- 6.71i, 15.25; 2003- 6.82, 15.18; 2004- 7.33, 15.36i/15.34; 2005- 6.70, 15.11; 2006- 6.97/7.09w, 15.23; 2007- 7.15, 15.14.
Won 2001 World gold by massive margin of 65cm. Married to Nikolay Medveyev (400mh), daughter Anastasiya born in August 2002. Set three world indoor records (15.16, 15.25, 15.36) at WI 2004, and next day completed unique double with LJ gold. Sole winner of the Golden League Jackpot for 6/6 wins at TJ in 2005.

Tatyana LYSENKO b. 9 Oct 1983 Bataisk, Rostov region 1.86m 81kg. Bataisk VS.
At HT: OG: '04- dnq 19; EC: '06- 1; WCh: '05- 3; EU23: '03- 5; WUG: '03- 5; WCp: '06- 2; ECp: '06- 1. Russian champion 2005.
Four world hammer records, seven Russian records 2005-07.
Progress at HT: 2000- 49.08, 2001- 55.73, 2002- 61.85, 2003- 67.19, 2004- 71.54, 2005- 77.06, 2006- 77.80, 2007- 78.61.
Suspended and awaiting drug test enquiry after positive test on 9 May 2007.

Natalya NAZAROVA b. 26 May 1979 Moskva 1.68m 57kg. Luch Moskva.
At 400m/4x400mR: OG: '00- sf/3resR, '04- 8/2R; WCh: '99- 6/1R, '03- 4/2R, '07- 4R; EC: '02- 2R; WJ: '98- 1/2R; WI: '99-03-04-06-08: 1R,/1&1R/1&1R/4&1R/2&1R; EI: '00- 2; EJ: '97- 7; WUG: '05- 1; WCp: '02- 3R; ECp: '99- 1R. Russian champion 1999-2000, 2003-04.
World indoor 4x400m world records 1999 & 2004.
Progress at 400m: 1995- 55.79, 1996- 54.59, 1997- 52.94, 1998- 51.50, 1999- 50.48, 2000- 50.10, 2002- 51.15, 2003- 49.78, 2004- 49.65, 2005- 51.31, 2006- 49.98i/51.09, 2007- 50.52. pbs: 100m 11.57 '99, 200m 23.01/22.9 '99, 300m 36.3+ '03, 500m 1:07.36i '04 (world best), 600m 1:26.35i '00.
Plays violin and piano.

Yelena OLEYNIKOVA b. 9 Dec 1976 Zernograd, Rostov-na-Donu reg. 1.78m 57kg. Luch Moskva.

At TJ: WCh: '01- dnq 14, '03- 14; EC: '02- 3; EI: '02- 3, '05- 7; WUG: '01- 3; WCp: '02- 6.
Progress at TJ: 1995- 12.79, 1996- 13.22, 1997- 13.38, 1998- 13.58, 1999- 13.85, 2000- 14.25, 2001- 14.59, 2002- 14.83, 2003- 14.56/14.70w, 2004- 14.57/14.63w, 2005- 14.33i/14.29, 2006- 14.63, 2007- 13.88i.

Anna OMAROVA b. 3 Oct 1981 Pyatigorsk 1.80m 108kg. née Tolokina. Moskva VS. Economics student.
At SP: WCh: '07- 9; WJ: 00- 5; WI: '08- 8; EI: '07- 6; ECp: '07-1. Russian champion 2007.
Progress at SP: 1997- 12.98, 1998- 15.88i/14.18, 1999- 13.45, 2000- 16.12, 2001- 17.13, 2003- 17.28, 2004- 17.12, 2005- 17.04i/16.70, 2006- 18.40, 2007- 19.69. pb DT 51.62 '07.
Daughter Aminat born in 2002.

Natalya PANTELYEVA b. 18 Aug 1983 Dzerzhinsk 1.70m 56kg. Moskva Dyn.
At 1500m: WCh: '07- 9; EU23: '05- 5; EI: '05- 2. At 800m: WJ: '02- 7.
World indoor 4x800m record 2007.
Progress at 1500m: 2003- 4:16.19, 2004- 4:13.57, 2005- 4:13.84, 2006- 4:00.81, 2007- 4:03.2. pbs: 800m 1:59.21 '06, 1000m 2:36.71 '06, 1M 4:27.18 '07, 2000m 5:36.52 '07.

Yuliya PECHONKINA b. 21 Apr 1978 Krasnoyarsk 1.80m 66kg. née Nosova. Moskva reg. VS.
At 400mh/4x400mR: OG: '00- sf, '04- 8; WCh: '01- 2/3R, '03- 3/2R, '05- 1/1R, '07- 2; EC: '98- h; WJ: '96- h; EJ: '97- 6; WCp: '02- 1/3R, '06- 1/3R; ECp: '01- 1/2R, '02- 1, '07- 1. RUS champion 1999, 2001, 2003-05. At 400m: WI: '01- 1R, '03- 1R; EI: '02- 5, '05- 1R.
World record 400m hurdles 2003, indoor 4x200m 2005.
Progress at 400mh: 1993- 63.47, 1994- 60.86, 1995- 60.30, 1996- 57.04, 1997- 57.53, 1998- 56.13, 1999- 53.98, 2000- 54.31, 2001- 53.84, 2002- 53.10, 2003- 52.34, 2004- 53.31, 2005- 52.90, 2006- 53.14, 2007- 53.50. pbs: 200m 23.26i '05, 300m 37.09i '05, 400m 51.00i '03, 500m 1:09.69i '03.
Married **Yevgeniy Pechonkin** (b. 9 Oct 1973, 110mh: 1 WJ 92, 2 EJ 91, pb 13.38 '96) on 15 Aug 2001; now separated. She married again in 2005.

Irina PETROVA b. 25 May 1985 Mordovia reg. 1.74m 50kg. Russian Army.
At 20kW: WCp: '06- 3; EU23: '05- 1. At 10kW: WJ: '04- 1; EJ: '03- 1; ECp: 03- 1J.
Progress at 20kW: 2005- 1:30:18, 2006- 1:26:14. pbs: 3000mW 12:02.4 '06, 5000mW 20:36.2 '05, 10kW 43:12R '06.

Lyudmila PETROVA b. 7 Oct 1968 Karakly, Chuvashiya 1.60m 44kg. née Yakimova. Novocheboksary TU.
At 10,000m: OG: '96- 14; WCh: '01- 6. At Mar: OG: '04- 8; EC: '98- 9. World HMar: '97-9-02: 7/18/13. Won RUS 10,000m 1996.
World W35 & Russian marathon record 2006.
Progress at 10,000m, Mar: 1995- 33:41.40, 1996- 31:58.84, 1997- 32:14.39, 2:39:26; 1998- 2:30:26, 1999- 2:29:13, 2000- 31:52.75, 2:25:45; 2001- 32:04.94, 2:26:18; 2002- 2:22:33, 2003- 31:36.76, 2:23:14; 2004- 2:26:02, 2005- 2:26:29, 2006- 2:21:29. pbs: 3000m 8:59.15i/9:00.2 '96, 5000m 15:20.44 '96, Rd 15km 48:31 '98, HMar 69:26 '00.
Two wins in 19 marathons: Moscow 1998, New York 2000. 3rd 2002 and 2nd 2004 and 2006 at London. Did not run 1987-94, when her two daughters were born. Husband killed in a car crash in 2005.

Tatyana PETROVA b. 8 Apr 1983 Cheboksary 1.60m 53kg. Moskva VS.
At 3000mSt: WCh: '07- 2; EC: '06- 2; WCp: '06- 6. At 5000m/10,000m: EU23: '05- 2/1. Eur CC: '01- 19J, '02- 4J.
World best indoor 3000mSt 9:07.00 '06.
Progress at 10,000m, 3000mSt: 2003- 10:05.70, 2004- 32:37.88, 2005- 32:17.49, 2006- 9:22.82, 2007- 9:09.19. pbs: 1500m 4:23.95i '02, 3000m 8:44.13 '06, 5000m 15:46.58 '03, 10km Rd 32:10 '07, Mar 2:31:03 '06.

Darya PISHCHALNIKOVA b. 19 Jul 1985 Astrakhan 1.90m 103kg. Saransk VS
At DT: WCh: '07- 2; EC: '06- 1; WJ: '02- 8, '04- 2; WY: '01- 2; E23: '05- 2; EJ: '03- 3; EY: '01- 1; WCp: '06- 4; ECp: '06- 2, '07- 2. Won Russian 2007.
Progress at DT: 2000- 50.48, 2001- 55.26, 2002- 56.24, 2003- 54.80, 2004- 58.26, 2005- 60.62, 2006- 65.55, 2007- 65.78. pb SP 14.02i '02.
Older brother **Bogdan Pishchalnikov** (26.8.82) has DT pb 64.95 '07 (3 EU23 03. 7 WCp 06). Their father Vitaliy had DT pb 67.76 '84 and mother Tatyana DT pb 61.62 '84.

Tatyana POLNOVA b. 20 Apr 1979 Slavyansk-na-Kubani 1.73m 64kg. née Zaykova. Krasnodar TU.
At PV: WCh: '05- 4, '07- 9; EC: '06- 3; WJ: '98- 10; WUG: '03- 1; EI: '05- 5; ECp: '03-04: 2/3. Won WAF 2003.
Progress at PV: 1995- 3.00, 1996- 3.75, 1997- 3.85, 1998- 4.10i/3.90, 2000- 4.20, 2001- 4.20, 2002- 4.60, 2003- 4.70, 2004- 4.78, 2005- 4.60i/4.52, 2006- 4.65, 2007- 4.72.
Former gymnast, coached by her husband Sergey Polnov. She competed for Turkey 1998-2000 (eeting NRs at 4.20) as Tuna Köstem, but reverted to Russia.

Svetlana POSPELOVA b. 24 Dec 1979 Leningrad 1.68m 65kg. St Petersburg Dyn.
At 400m/4x400mR: OG: '00- dq h; WCh: '03- 8/res (2)R, '05- 4/1R; EC: '06- 7/1R; WJ: '98- h/2R; EU23: '99- 1R; EI: '00- 1/1R, '05- 1/1R; WCp: '06- 3R; ECp: '00- 1, '03- 1/1R, '06- 1. Won Russian 200m 2000, 400m 2005-06.
Progress at 400m: 1996- 56.50, 1997- 55.17, 1998- 53.80, 1999- 52.58, 2000- 50.47, 2003- 50.70, 2004- 51.69. 2005- 49.80, 2006- 49.99, 2007- 51.13. pbs: 60m 7.20i '05, 100m 11.32 '05, 200m 22.39 '05, 300m 35.8+ '05.
Two-years drugs ban from positive test after

elimination in Olympic 400m heat 2000.

Anna PYATYKH b. 4 Apr 1981 Moskva 1.76m 64kg. Moskva VS.
At TJ: OG: '04- 8; WCh: '03- 4, '05- 3, '07- 5; EC: '02- 8, '06- 3; WJ: '00- 2; EJ: '99- 3; WI: '03- 4, '06- 2; ECp: '02-03-04-05: 1/1/1/1. Russian champion 2004, 2006.
Progress at TJ: 1998- 12.98, 1999- 13.59, 2000- 14.19, 2001- 14.21/14.22w, 2002- 14.67, 2003- 14.79, 2004- 14.85, 2005- 14.88, 2006- 15.02/15.17w, 2007- 14.88. pb LJ 6.72 '07.

Olga RYABINKINA b. 24 Sep 1976 Bryansk 1.90m 87kg. St. Peterburg Dyn. Teacher.
At SP: OG: '00- 10, '04- dnq 13; WCh: '03- dnq 16, '05- 2; EC: '06- 4; EJ: '95- 3 (4 DT); WI: '06- 3; EI: '05- 3, '07- 3; WCp: '06- 2; ECp: '04- 1, '05- 1. Russian champion 2005.
Progress at SP: 1993- 15.61, 1994- 16.52, 1995- 17.40, 1996- 17.75, 1997- 17.98, 1998- 17.51, 1999- 17.99, 2000- 19.32, 2001- 17.85, 2002- 19.36, 2003- 19.36i/19.07, 2004- 19.12, 2005- 19.65, 2006- 19.54, 2007- 18.58i. pb DT 61.66 '98.

Yekaterina SAVCHENKO b. 3 Jun 1977 Omsk 1.80m 60kg. née Aleksandrova. Omsk TU.
At HJ: WCh: '01- dnq, '07- 5; EC: '06- 7=; WI: '06- 4, '08- 7; EI: '05- 6; WJ: '94- 7=; EJ: '95- 7; WUG: '99- 5. Russian champion 2001, 2006.
Progress at HJ: 1994- 1.88, 1995- 1.90, 1996- 1.94, 1997- 1.93, 1998- 1.96i/1.90, 1999- 1.92, 2000- 1.90, 2001- 1.96, 2003- 1.97, 2004- 1.98i, 2005- 1.97, 2006- 1.98i/1.95, 2007- 2.00, 2008- 2.00i.

Tatyana SHEMYAKINA b. 3 Sep 1987 Makarovka, Mordoviya 1.61m 51kg. Saransk VS.
At 20kW: WCh: '07- 2; EU23: '07- 1. At 10,000mW: WJ: '06- 2.
Progress at 20kW: 2007- 1:28:48. 2008- 1:25:46. pbs: 10,000mW 44:26.5 '06, 10kmW 43:57 '07.

Tatyana SIBILYEVA b. 17 May 1980 Chelyabinsk 1.59m 42kg. Chelyabinsk VS.
At 20kW: WCh: '07- 9; EU23: '01- 4; WUG: '03- 1, '05- 3; ECp: '07- 7. At 10,000mW: WJ: '06- 2.
Progress at 20kW: 1998- 1:29:53, 2000- 1:30:51, 2001- 1:27:33, 2002- 1:32:17, 2003- 1:27:54, 2004- 1:29:12, 2005- 1:31:18, 2006- 1:28:58, 2007- 1:28:51, 2008- 1:26:16. pbs: 10kW 44:05 '07, 45:09.3t '06.

Irina SIMAGINA b. 25 May 1982 Ryazan 1.71m 60kg. Luch Moskva.
At LJ: OG: '04- 2; WJ: '00- 6; WY: '99- 5; EU23: '03- 2; WUG: '03- 1; WI: '08- 3; EI: '02- 4; ECp: '04- 1, '05- 1. Won WAF 2004.
Progress at LJ: 1999- 6.32i/6.12, 2000- 6.38, 2001- 6.41i/6.11, 2002- 6.74i/6.58, 2003- 6.83, 2004- 7.27, 2005- 7.04, 2007- 7.11, 2008- 6.96i.

Yelena SLESARENKO b. 28 Feb 1982 Volgograd 1.78m 57kg. née Sivushenko. Volgograd VS.
At HJ: OG: '04- 1; WCh: '07- 4; EC: '06- 5; EU23: '03- 2; EJ: '01- 4; WUG: '03- 3; WI: '04-06-08: 1/1/2; EI: '02- 5=; WCp: '06- 1; ECp: '04- 1, '07- 1. Won WAF 2004, Russian 2005.
Progress at HJ: 1999- 1.82, 2000- 1.88, 2001- 1.94i/1.88, 2002- 1.97, 2003- 1.98i/1.96, 2004- 2.06, 2005- 2.00, 2006- 2.02i/2.00, 2007- 2.02, 2008- 2.02i.
Tied Russian indoor record to win gold at 2004 World Indoors and set a Russian record of 2.06 to win Olympic gold.

Yelena SOBOLEVA b. 3 Oct 1982 Bryansk 1.76m 66kg. Lokomotiv Moskva.
At 1500m: WCh: '05- 4, '07- 2; EC: '06- 4; EU23: '03- 6; WI: '06- 2, '08- 1. Won Russian 1500m 2006. Three WIR 1500m 2006-08.
Progress at 800m, 1500m: 2002- 2:04.43, 2003- 2:01.65, 4:12.02; 2004- 4:11.98, 2005- 2:00.59, 4:01.14; 2006- 1:57.28, 3:56.43; 2007- 1:59.49, 3:57.30; 2008- 1:58.49i, 3:57.71i. pbs: 1000m 2:32.40i '06, 2:36.50 '05; 1M 4:15.63 '07, 2000m 5:36.43 '07, 3000m 8:55.89 '05.

Tatyana TOMASHOVA b. 1 Jul 1975 Perm 1.64m 50kg. Perm VS.
At 1500m: OG: '04- 2; WCh: '03- 1, '05- 1; EC: '02- 3, '06- 1; WCp: '02- 2, '06- 2; ECp: '02- 3. At 5000m: OG: '00- 13; WCh: '01- 10; ECp: '00- 1. Won GP 3000m 2001 (2nd 2002), RUS 1500m 2001-03, 5000m 2000.
Russian 5000m record 2000.
Progress at 1500m, 5000m: 1996- 4:17.97, 15:48.13; 1997- 4:16.39, 1998- 4:13.50, 1999- 4:08.5?, 15:26.67; 2000- 4:04.80, 14:53.00; 2001- 4:03.31, 14:39.22; 2002- 4:01.28, 14:47.85; 2003- 3:58.52, 2004- 3:58.12, 2005- 3:59.05, 2006- 3:56.91, 2007- 4:02.8. pbs: 800m 2:04.0 '99, 1000m 2:34.91 '05, 1M 4:24.84 '07, 2000m 5:43.3 '01, 3000m 8:25.56 '01, road 10km 32:48 '99.

Oksana UDMURTOVA b. 1 Feb 1982 Grakovo, Udmurtiya 1.72m 56kg. Volgograd VS.
At LJ: WCh: '05- 6; EC: '06- 3; WI: '06- 7; Russian champion 2006. At TJ: EI: '07- 4.
Progress at LJ, TJ: 2000- 6.29, 2001- 6.41, 2003- 6.78, 2004- 6.60, 2005- 6.86, 2006- 7.02, 2007- 6.92, 14.41i/14.35; 2008- 14.94i.

Tatyana VESHKUROVA b. 23 Sep 1981 Perm 1.80m 70kg. Yekaterinburg TU.
At 400m/4x400mR: WCh: '07- sf; EC: '06- 2/1R; WI: res 1R; EI: '07- 5; WCp: '06- 4/3R; ECp: '06- 1R.
Progress at 400m: 2003- 54.30, 2004- 53.51, 2005- 53.33, 2006- 49.99, 2007- 50.22. pbs: 60m 7.66i '04, 100m 11.88 '05, 200m 23.58i/23.63 '06, 300m 37.51i '07, 600m 1:10.78i '07.

Yekaterina VOLKOVA b. 16 Feb 1978 Zhelznogorsk, Kursk region 1.69m 55kg. Kursk VS.
At 3000mSt: WCh: '05- 2, '07- 1; ECp: '02- 7. Won Russian 5000m 2007, 300mSt 2000-01, 2005.
Russian 3000m steeplechase record 2001.
Progress at 3000mSt: 1999- 10:04.46, 2000- 9:52.40, 2001- 9:41.54, 2002- 10:37.78, 2003- 9:32.31, 2005- 9:20.49, 2007- 9:06.57. pbs: 1000m 2:39.57i '06, 1500m 4:09.03 '05, 1M 4:29.60 '05, 3000m 8:45.09i '06, 8:54.64 '05, 5000m 15:00.02 '07, 2000mSt 6:27.69 '00.
Married to Artem Mastrov (800m 1:46.04 '00).

Olga YEGOROVA b. 28 Mar 1972 Novocheboksarsk, Chuvashiya 1.60m 48kg. Cheboksary Dyn. Economist.
At 1500m: OG: '04- 11; WCh: '05- 2; WJ: '90- 9; EJ: '91- 3. At 3000m: WI: '97/9/01- 6/6/1; EI: '98- 8, '00- 6; ECp: '98-9-03: 1/3/1. At 5000m: OG: '00- 8; WCh: '99- h, '01- 1, '03- h; EC: '98- 11, '02- 4; WCp: '02- 1; ECp: '02- 1; won RUS 1999, GWG 2001.
European 5000m record 2001, 2 Russian records 2000-01.
Progress at 1500m, 3000m, 5000m: 1989- 4:14.76, 1990- 4:18.26, 1991- 4:17.09, 1996- 16:00.07, 1997- 4:12.73i, 15:42.47, 1998- 15:32.74, 1999- 4:07.38, 8:33.02, 15:22.80; 2000- 4:04.75, 8:49.18i/8:53.76, 14:42.91; 2001- 4:02.76, 8:23.26, 14:29.32; 2002- 4:04.11, 8:46.24i, 14:48.29; 2003- 4:01.00, 8:38.00, 14:55.19; 2004- 4:01.15, 2005- 3:59.47, 2006- 4:01.31, 2007- 4:01.2. pbs: 800m 2:06.01 '03, 1M 4:20.10 '07, 2000m 5:39.30i '00, 5:39.9 '01; 2000mSt 6:28.2 '96.
Daughter Yevgeniya born June 1994.

Yelena ZADOROZHNAYA b. 3 Dec 1977 Ust-Kut, Irkutsk reg. 1.57m 42kg. Irkutsk VS.
At 5000m (1500m): OG: '04- 4; WCh: '01- 6, '03- 4 (8); EC: '02- 3; ECp: '01- 1, '03- 1. At 3000m: WI: '01- 3, '04- 6; EI: '02- 3; WCp: '02- 3; ECp: '02- 2, '05- 3. At 1500m: EU23: '99- 2; ECp: '00- 2; won GP 2002. At 3000mSt: WCh: '05- 6.
Russian 5000m record 2001.
Progress at 1500m, 5000m, 3000mSt: 1998- 4:12.70, 1999- 4:09.03, 2000- 4:03.32, 2001- 4:02.16, 14:40.47; 2002- 3:59.94, 15:15.22; 2003- 4:00.12, 14:51.61; 2004- 4:01.38, 14:55.31; 2005- 4:03.65, 15:15.85, 9:32.41. pbs: 800m 2:01.74 '98, 1000m 2:37.71i '04, 1M 4:24.11i '01, 2000m 5:41.61i '02, 5:43.38 '03; 3000m 8:25.40 '01.

Olga ZAYTSEVA b. 29 Jul 1975 Leningrad 1.76m 67kg. St Peterburg YR.
At 400m/4x400mR: EC: '06- 3/1R; EU23: '05- 1/1R. At 200m: ECp: '06- 1/1R. Won Russian 200m 2006.
Progress at 400m: 2004- 51.09, 2005- 50.06, 2006- 49.49. pbs: 200m 22.67 '06, 600m 1:06.76i '06.

Oksana ZBROZHEK b. 12 Jan 1978 1.67m 49kg. Moskva TU
At 800m: WJ: '96- sf; EI: '07- 1; ECp: '07- 3.
Progress at 800m: 1996- 2:05.52, 1997- 2:07.7, 1998- 2:04.99, 1999- 2:05.96, 2001- 2:00.46, 2002- 2:01.79, 2003- 2:01.92, 2004- 1:58.06, 2005- 2:00.56, 2006- 2:02.13, 2007- 1:58.80. pbs: 400m 53.49 '07, 1000m 2:32.21i '07, 1500m 4:08.16 '05, 1M 4:33.73 '05. Expecting a baby in 2008.

Olesya ZYKINA b. 7 Oct 1980 Kaluga 1.70m 62kg. Tula Dyn.
At 400m/4x400m: OG: '00- res (3)R, '04- 2R; WCh: '01- 6/3R, '03- 6/2R, '05- 6/res(1)R; EC: '02- 1/2R; WJ: '98- 2R (8 100m); EJ: '99- 1/1R; WI: '01-03-04-08: 3&1R/1R/GR/1&R; EI: '07- 3/2R; WCp: '02- 3/3R; ECp: '00- 1R. Russian champion 2001-02.
Progress at 400m: 1999- 51.31, 2000- 50.36, 2001- 50.15, 2002- 50.44, 2003- 50.39, 2004- 50.44, 2005- 50.73, 2006- 51.86, 2007- 51.04. pbs: 60m 7.47i '04, 100m 11.84 '98, 200m 22.55 '05, 22.3 '99; 300m 36.6+ '03, 36.69i '04, 36.70 '01.

SAINT KITTS & NEVIS

Governing body: Saint Kitts Amateur Athletic Association, PO Box 932, Basseterre, St Kitts. Founded 1961.

Kim COLLINS b. 5 Apr 1976 St Kitts 1.75m 64kg. Studied sociology at Texas Christian University, USA.
At 100m (/200m): OG: '96- qf, 00- 7/sf, '04- 6; WCh: '97- h, 99- h/h, '01- 6/3=, '03- 1, '05- 3, '07- sf; CG: '02- 1; PAm: '07- 5; CAC: '99- 2, '01- 1/1, '03- 1; WCp: '02- 2/2R. At 60m: WI: '03- 2, '08- 2=. Won NCAA indoor 60m & 200m 2001.
SKN records: 100m from 1996, 200m from 1998, 400m 2000.
Progress at 100m, 200m: 1995- 10.63, 21.85; 1996- 10.27, 21.06; 1998- 10.18/10.16w, 20.88/20.78w; 1999- 10.21, 20.43, 2000- 10.13A/10.15/10.02w, 20.31A/20.18w; 2001- 10.04A/10.00?/9.99w, 20.20/20.08w; 2002- 9.98, 20.49; 2003- 9.99/9.92w, 20.40w; 2004- 10.00, 20.98; 2005- 10.00, 2006- 10.33, 21.53; 2007- 10.14. pbs: 60m 6.53i '00, 400m 46.93 '00.
The first athlete from his country to make Olympic and World finals and in 2003 the first to win a World Indoor medal and a World title. There is a 'Kim Collins Highway' in St Kitts.

SAUDI ARABIA

Governing body: Saudi Arabian Athletics Federation, PO Box 5802, Riyadh 11432. Founded 1963.

Mohamed Salim **AL-KHUWALIDI** b. 19 Jun 1981 Al Dharan 1.88m 82kg. Works for Saudi Aramco.
At LJ: WCh: '07- dnq 18; AsiG: '02- 9; AsiC: '03- 9, '07- 1; WI: '08- 3; WCp: '06- 3; Asian indoor champion 2004 & 2008, Gulf 2002, Arab Ch & P.Arab G 2007.
Asian long jump record 2006, two KSA records 2005-06.
Progress at LJ: 1998- 7.32, 1999- 7.55, 2002- 7.91/8.18w, 2003- 8.02, 2004- 8.12, 2005- 8.44, 2006- 8.48, 2007- 8.25, 2008- 8.24i. pb 200m 21.09 '03.

Mohammed AL-SALHI b. 11 May 1986 1.83m 72kg.
At 800m: OG: '04- h; WCh: '05- sf, '07- 8; WY: '03- 1; AsiG: '06- 6/1R; AsiC: '05- 4, '07- 1; Gulf champion 2005. At 400m: AsiG: '02- sf; Asi-J '04- 1. Five KSA 800m records 2003-05, World U18 record 2003.
Progress at 800m: 2003- 1:46.48, 2004- 1:48.42, 2005- 1:44.80, 2006- 1:43.99, 2007- 1:44.88. pbs: 400m 45.75 '03, 1000m 2:24.50 '03.

SENEGAL

Governing body: Fédération Sénégalaise d'Athlétisme, BP 1737, Stade Iba Mar DIOP, Dakar. Founded 1960.

Women

Amy Mbacké THIAM b. 10 Nov 1976 Kaolack 1.83m 70kg. Racing Club de France.
At 400m: OG: '00- sf, '04- h; WCh: '99- sf, '01- 1, '03- 3, '05- 8, '07- h; AfG: '99- 3; AfCh: '98- 4, '06- 1. French champion 1998-2000, 2005-06; SEN champion 1996, 1998-9, 2004.
Eight SEN 400m records 1999-2001.
Progress at 400m: 1996- 54.40, 1997- 53.25, 1998- 51.60, 1999- 50.77, 2000- 50.88, 2001- 49.86, 2002- 50.96, 2003- 49.95, 2004- 50.82, 2005- 50.69, 2006- 50.54, 2007- 50.15. pbs: 100m 11.84 '98, 200m 23.10 '05, 23.0A '99; 300m 36.0+ '03, 36.37 '00.
In 2001 she became the first athlete to win a world title for Senegal in any sport.

SERBIA

Governing body: Athletic Federation of Serbia, Strahinjica Bana 73a, 11000 Beograd. Founded in 1921 (as Yugoslav Athletic Federation).
National Championships (Yugoslav) first held in 1920 (men) and 1923 (women). **2007 Champions**: **Men**: 100m/200m: Marko Jankovic 10.67/21.57, 400m: Robert Muci 48.09, 800m: Predrag Randjelovic 1:53.37, 1500m: Miloš Vuckovic 3:52.17, 3000m: Velimir Bojovic 8:28.09, 5000m: Saša Stolic 15:02.6, Mar: Nikola Stamenic 2:34:05, 3000mSt: Darko Živanovic 9:09.68, 110mh: Miroslav Novakovic 14.25, 400mH: Damir Andjelov 55.73, HJ: Dragutin Topic 2.22, PV: Igor Šarcevic 4.00, LJ: Milan Milenkovic 7.25, TJ: Kosta Randjic 15.25, SP/DT: Luka Rujevic 19.64/55.63, HT: Laslo Eperješi 60.83, JT: Kristijan Kovac 65.80, Dec: *not held*, 10,000mW/20km: Predrag Filipovic 41:53.8/1:28:33. **Women**: 100m: Tanja Mitic 11.54, 200m: Nataša Lacaracki 24.70, 400m: Marija Petrovic 58.30, 800m: Marija Papic 2:09.51, 1500m: Snežana Kostic 4:34.32, 3000m/5000m: Ana Subotic 9:44.86/16:49.51, Mar: Olivera Jevtic 2:35:46, 3000mSt: Milana Gavrilov 11:13.2, 100mh: Jelena Jotanovic 14.00, 400mH: Ivana Avdalovic 63.06, HJ: Andrijana Nešic 1.60, PV: Slavica Semenjuk 4.15, LJ: Mirjana Djuric 5.50, TJ: Biljana Topic 13.90, SP: Dijana Šefcic 15.18, DT: Dragana Tomaševic 61.52, HT: Dunja Etinski 44.72, JT: Tatjana Jelaca 48.04, Hep/walks: *not held*.

Women

Olivera JEVTIC b. 24 Jul 1977 Titovo Uzice 1.74m 52kg. AC Mladost, Uzice.
At 10,000m (/5000m): OG: '00- 11/dnf; WCh: '97- h/h, '99- 10, '01- 12/h; EC: '98- 4/4, '02- 6/dnf; EU23: '97- 1, '99- 1/3; WJ: '94- (3000m 10), 96- -/2 (3000m 5); EJ: '95- 2 (3000m 3). At Mar: OG: '04- 6; WCh: '03- 8; EC: '06- 2. World HMar: '98-99-01-02: 4/21/7/6; CC: '95-00-01-04: 17J/15/9/12; Eur CC: '96-7-8-9-00-01-03-05-06: 13/3/3/3/3/4/6/4/3. Won YUG 1500m & 5000m 1996, HMar 1998-9, 2002; Mar 2007; CC 1994-7, 1999; Balkan 5000m 1998, CC 2002.
YUG/SRB records: 5000m (7) 1995-2000, 10,000m (2) 1998-2000, HMar (3) 1998-2002, Mar 2003.
Progress at 5000m, 10,000m, Mar: 1995- 16:03.34, 33:48.61; 1996- 15:40.59, 32:38.0; 1997- 15:34.65, 32:43.42; 1998- 15:16.61, 31:34.26; 1999- 15:19.08, 31:57.67; 2000- 15:11.25, 31:29.65; 2001- 15:26.84, 31:33.08; 2002- 15:40.24, 31:47.82, 2:26:44dq; 2003- 2:25:23, 2004- 15:33.37, 2:27:34; 2005- 2:31:43, 2006- 15:45.99, 2:29:38; 2007- 2:35:46. pbs: 800m 2:12.41 '93, 1500m 4:16.16 '98, 3000m 8:59.21 '98, Rd: 10km 31:31 '01, 15km 49:06 '01, HMar 69.18 '02.
Has women's record five European CC medals.
At Marathon: Third in New York on debut 2002, but disqualified (public warning) for positive test for ephedrine. Won Rotterdam 2003, Belgrade 2007, 3rd Boston 2004.

SLOVAKIA

Governing body: Slovak Athletic Federation, Junácka 6, 832 80 Bratislava. Founded 1939.
National Championships first held in 1939. **2007 Champions: Men**: 100m/200m: Matús Mentel 10.84/21.75, 400m/800m: Peter Znava 47.02/1:50.94, 1500m: Jaroslav Szabo 3:56.27, 5000m: Miroslav Vanko 14:52.60, 10,000m: Imrich Magyar 30:57.81, HMar: Marcel Matanin 70:03, Mar: Imrich Pastor 2:21:59, 3000mSt: Pavol Michalcik 9:35.21, 110mh: Matús Janecek 14.12, 400mh: Peter Hort 52.62, HJ: Peter Horák 2.18, PV: Tomás Ondrejko 4.80, LJ: Marián Hruska 7.51, TJ: Dmitrij Valukevic 16.97, SP: Daniel Vanek 19.39, DT: Jozef Páricka 42.41, HT: Libor Charfreitag 80.24, JT: Marián Bokor 75.49, Dec: Ondrej Hort 6697, 20kW: Matej Tóth 1:29:28, 50kW: Milos Batovsky 3:54:10. **Women**: 100m: Barbora Simková 12.22, 200m: Alexandra Stuková 24.27, 400m: Lucia Klocová 53.99, 800m/1500m: Petra Mráziková 2:15.48/4:36.09, 5000m: Katarina Beresová 17:20.49, 10,000m/HMar: Dana Janecková 36:53.24/83:56, Mar: Anna Balosaková 3:12:59, 3000mSt: Kristina Guttmanová 11:33.54, 100mh: Miriam Bobková 13.44, 400mh: Miriam Hrdlicková 59.38, HJ: Iveta Srnková 1.80, PV: Slavomíra Slúková 3.85, LJ: Jana Veldáková 6.19, TJ: Dana Veldáková 14,14, SP: Martina Zatková 13.24, DT: Ivona Tomanová 47.73, HT: Nikola Lomnická 56.69, JT: Jana Katrenciková 42.65, Hep: Silvia Koblisková 4141, 5000mW: Mária Gáliková 22:10.72, 20kW: Zuzana Maliková 1:32:19.

Libor CHARFREITAG b. 11 Sep 1977 Trnava 1.91m 117kg. Studied at Southern Methodist University, USA. ASK Slavia Trnava.
At HT: OG: '00- dnq 30, '04- 7; WCh: '99-01-03: dnq 32/18/13, '05- 9, '07- 3; EC: '02- 7, '06- dnq 14; WJ: '96- dnq 13. NCAA champion 1998, 2000; SVK 1998-9, 2002-07.

12 SVK hammer records 1996-2003, six European indoor bests 35lb weight 2003-05.
Progress at HT: 1993- 49.42, 1994- 54.32, 1995- 56.90, 1996- 66.82, 1997- 66.44, 1998- 72.30, 1999- 75.18, 2000- 77.22, 2001- 77.65, 2002- 79.20, 2003- 81.81, 2004- 79.84, 2005- 80.85, 2006- 78.04, 2007- 81.60. pbs: SP 17.27i/16.69 '00, DT 51.88 '00; 35lb Wt 25.68i '05.
Won first Slovak World Champs medal since 1997.

Mikulás KONOPKA b. 23 Jan 1979 Rimavska Sobota 1.93m 110kg. Dukla Banská Bystrica.
At SP: OG: '00- dnq 24, '04- 10; WCh: '01- dnq 22, '05- 11, '07- dnq 15; EC: '98- dnq, '06- dnq 12; EU23: '99- 1, '01- 1; WJ: '96- 5, '98- 1; EJ: '97- 2; EI: '02- (3)dq, '05- 6, '07- 1. SVK champion 2000, 2005-06.
Three Slovakian shot records 2001.
Progress at SP: 1995- 15.42, 1996- 17.35, 1997- 18.60, 1998- 19.68, 1999- 19.71, 2000- 19.94, 2001- 20.66, 2002- 20.87idq/19.61i, 2004- 20.34, 2005- 20.61, 2006- 20.30i/20.11, 2007- 21.57i/19.94. pb DT 51.42 '99.
2-years drugs disqualification after third place EI 2002. Stunning breakthrough at 2007 EI with all puts over 21m from previous indoor best 20.55. His twin brother **Miloslav** set SVK hammer record 78.58 '01, improving pb to 81.33 '04, WCh: '03- 9, '07- 10; EU23: '01- 03.

Miloslav KONOPKA b. 23 Jan 1979 Rimavska Sobota 1.89m 102kg. VSK Univerzita Brno.
At HT: OG: '00/04- dnq 32/14; WCh: '01-03-05-07: dnq 28/9/dnq 20/10; EC: '02- 10, '06- dnq 13; WJ: '98- 5; EU23: '01- 3; EJ: '97- nt. SVK champion 2001-02.
Slovakian hammer record 2001.
Progress at HT: 1996- 63.84, 1997- 65.52, 1998- 71.27, 1999- 71.96, 2000- 76.12, 2001- 78.58, 2002- 79.98, 2003- 78.44, 2004- 81.33, 2005- 76.74, 2006- 78.25, 2007- 79.83.
Twin brother of shot putter Mikulás.

Dmitrij VALUKEVIC b. 31 May 1981 Vitrysland, Belarus 1.86m 78kg. Spartak Dubnica.
At TJ: OG: '04- dnq 30; WCh: '03- dnq 16, '05- 10, '07- dnq 13; EC: '06- dnq 15; EU23: '03- 1; WI: '04- 4, '08- 5. BLR champion 2002, SVK 2005-07.
Six SVK triple jump records 2005-07.
Progress at TJ: 1998- 15.52, 2000- 16.39, 2001- 16.62, 2002- 16.68i/16.53, 2003- 17.57, 2004- 17.31i/16.78, 2005- 17.19, 2006- 17.19i/17.06/ 17.34w, 2007- 17.35, 2008- 17.14i. pb LJ 7.86 '05.
Dmitriy Valyukevich of Belarus until gaining Slovak nationality in January 2005, having trained with Aleksandr Beskrovniy in Slovakia for the previous three years. Improved from 16.81 to 16.83 in qualifying and then 17.16, 17.51 and 17.57 in the final of the European U23s in 2003. His father Gennadiy had best of 17.53 in 1986, won the 1979 EI title (2nd 1982 and 1983) and set world indoor bests that year at 17.19 and 17.29. His mother Irina had a long jump best of 7.17 '87 and was WUG champion in 1985.

Women

Lucia KLOCOVÁ b. 20 Nov 1983 1.70m 57kg. AK ZTS Marrin.
At 800m: OG: '04- sf; WCh: '03/05/07- sf; EC: '06- sf; WJ: '00- 3, '02- 2; EU23: '03- 2, '05- 5; EJ: '01- 1. Won SVK 400m 2007, 800m 2004, 2006.
Progress at 800m: 1998- 2:11.63, 2000- 2:04.00, 2001- 2:03.06, 2002- 2:01.59, 2003- 2:00.60, 2004- 2:00.79, 2005- 2:00.64, 2006- 2:00.28, 2007- 1:58.62. pbs: 400m 52.98 '07, 1000m 2:39.74i '03.

SLOVENIA

Governing body: Atletska Zveza Slovenije, Vodnikova cesta 155, 1000 Ljubljana. Current organisation founded 1948.

2007 National Champions: **Men**: 100m/200m: Matic Osovnikar 10.28/20.71, 400m: Sebastjan Jagarinec 46.93, 800m: Borut Veber 1:55.33, 1500m: Peter Kastelic 3:58.06, 3000m: Mitja Krevs 8:43.19, 5000m: Robert Kotnik 16:07.11, 10,000m/HMar: Roman Kejzar 30:23.09/67:24, Mar: Bostjan Hrovat 2:33:12, 3000mSt: Bostjan Buc 8:49.57, 110mh: Damjan Zlatnar 13.90, 400mh: Marko Prezelj 54.81, HJ: Rozle Prezelj 2.20, PV: Andrej Poljanec 5.40, LJ: Bostjan Fridrih 7.56, TJ: Andrej Batagelj 16.15w, SP: Miroslav Vodovnik 20.40, DT: Tadej Hribar 53.48, HT: *not held*, JT: Matija Kranjc 72.44. **Women**: 100m: Merlene Ottey 11.69, 200m: Sabina Veit 23.47w, 400m: Brigita Langerholc 53.22, 800m/1500m: Sonja Roman 2:06.11/4:17.67, 3000m/5000m: Petra Sink 10:09.05/17:52.38, HMar/Mar: Helena Javornik 77:46/2:35:45, 3000mSt: Daneja Grandovec 11:16.25, 100mh: Radmila Vukmirovic 13.75, 400mh: Ana Kopcavar 62.50, HJ: Marusa Novak 1.74, PV: Ivana Abramic 3.50, LJ: Nina Kolaric 6.42w, TJ: Marija Sestak 14.12, SP: Spela Hus 13.32, DT: Tamara Stojkovic 43.02, HT: Ana Susec 63.89, JT: Martina Ratej 53.71, Hep: Maja Petan 5068.

Primoz KOZMUS b. 30 Sep 1979 Novo Mesto 1.88m 106kg. FIT Brezice.
At HT: OG: '00- dnq 38, '04- 6; WCh: '03- 5, '07- 2; EC: '02- dnq 25, '06- 7; EU23: '99- 12, '01- 14; WJ: '98- dnq. SLO champion 1999-2004, 2006.
Nine SLO hammer records 2000-07.
Progress at HT: 1995- 45.82, 1996- 54.10, 1997- 61.08, 1998- 66.28, 1999- 70.11, 2000- 76.84, 2001- 71.17, 2002- 75.87, 2003- 81.21, 2004- 79.34, 2006- 80.38, 2007- 82.30.
Older sister Simona set Slovenian women's hammer record (58.60 '01).

Miroslav VODOVNIK b. 11 Sep 1977 Maribor 1.97m 130kg. AD Almont Slovenska Bistrica.
At SP: OG: '04- 11; WCh: '03/05- dnq 23/20, '07- 6; WJ: '96- dnq SP & DT; WI: '04- dnq 12; EI: '07- 7. SLO champion 2000-07.
Five SLO shot records 2004-06.
Progress at SP: 1993- 13.30, 1994- 14.8-0, 1995- 16.84, 1996- 17.01, 1997- 17.25, 1998- 17.55, 1999-

18.72, 2000- 17.64, 2001- 18.04, 2002- 18.23, 2003- 20.46, 2004- 20.56, 2005- 20.30, 2006- 20.76, 2007- 20.67, 2008- 20.68i. pb DT 53.61 '04.

Women

Brigita LANGERHOLC b. 23 Jul 1976 Kranj 1.70m 56kg. Triglav, Kranj. Was at University of Southern California, USA. Marketing and finance manager.

At 800m: OG: '00- 4; WCh: '99/03- sf, '01/05- h, '07- 5; EC: '02- sf, '06- 5; EI: '07- 6; WUG: '99- 2, '01- 1; won NCAA 2001. At 400m: EJ: '93- 7, '95- 5; EU23: '97- 5; ECp: '98- 8. Won SLO 400m 1996-8, 2000-02, 2006-07; 800m 1996, 1998-9, 2005.

SLO records: 400m (4) 2000, 800m (4) 1999-2000.

Progress at 800m: 1991- 2:12.69, 1992- 2:23.52, 1993- 2:17.81, 1994- 2:17.54, 1995- 2:11.36, 1996- 2:06.57, 1998- 2:04.16, 1999- 1:59.87, 2000- 1:58.51, 2001- 1:59.86, 2002- 1:58.97, 2003- 2:00.47, 2004- 2:00.77, 2005- 2:01.41, 2006- 1:59.30, 2007- 1:58.41. pbs: 100m 12.01 '00, 200m 24.32 '00, 400m 52.02 '00, 600m 1:25.84 '07, 1000m 2:37.47 '06.

Marija SESTAK b. 17 Apr 1979 Kragujevac, Serbia 1.78m 56kg. née Martinovic. AD MASS Ljubljana.

At TJ: OG: '00- dnq 22; WCh: '97- dnq 33, '07- 5; WJ: '96- dnq 20, '98- 3; EU23: '99- 8, '01- 2; EJ: '97- 2; WI: '08- 3; EI: '02- 6. Won YUG/SRB LJ 1996, 2000-01, TJ 1996-9, 2001, 2003; SLO LJ 2006, TJ 2007, Balkan Indoor TJ 2002.

Six YUG triple jump records 1997-2000, three SLO records 2006-07.

Progress at TJ: 1992- 11.80, 1993- 11.93, 1994- 12.10, 1995- 12.63, 1996- 13.09/13.33w, 1997- 13.62, 1998- 13.47, 1999 13.24, 2000- 14.06, 2001- 14.00, 2002- 14.26i/13.81, 2003- 13.20, 2006- 14.53, 2007- 14.92, 2008- 15.08i. pb LJ 6.59i, 6.58 '07.

Switch from Serbia to Slovenia (recognised from 13 July 2006), having not competed in 2004-05. Married to Matija Sestak (b. 30 Dec 1972, SLO recs 300m 32.34 '04, 400m 45.43 '99).

SOUTH AFRICA

Governing body: Athletics South Africa, PO Box 2712, Houghton 2041. Original body founded 1894.

National Championships first held in 1894 (men), 1929 (women). **2007 Champions**: **Men**: 100m/200m: Sherwin Vries 10.54/20.79, 400m: Jan van der Merwe 46.31, 800m: Mbulaeni Mulaudzi 1:46.09, 1500m: Juan van Deventer 3:46.85, 5000m: Boy Soke 13:48.11, 10,000m: Coolboy Ngamole 28:57, HMar: Hendrick Ramaala 62:42, Mar: George Mofokeng 2:13:50, 3000mSt: Ruben Ramolefi 8:28.93, 110mh: Ruan de Vries 14.45, 400mh: Alwyn Myburgh 48.97, HJ: Ramsay Carelse 2.20, PV: Riaan Botha 4.80, LJ: Khotso Mokoena 8.16, TJ: Tumelo Thagane 16.27w, SP: Roelie Potgieter 18.63, DT: Johannes van Wyk 59.12, HT: Chris Harmse 74.35, JT: Robert Oosthuizen 81.24, Dec: Terry Wepener 6668, 20kW: Thami Hlatswayo 1:33:22, 50kW: Thabiso Thagane 5:10:31. **Women**: 100m/200m: Geraldine Pillay 11.59/23.45, 400m: Estie Wittstock 53.85, 800m: Lebogang Phalula 2:06.15, 1500m/5000m: Rene Kalmer 4:14.75/15:35.00, 10,000m/Mar: Poppy Mlambo 35:20.67/2:39:19, HMar: Zintle Xiniwe 76:53, 3000mSt: Tebogo Masehla 10:07.12, 100mh/LJ: Janice Josephs 13.83/6.62, 400mh: Amanda Kotze 58.46, HJ: Anika Smit 1.85, PV: Sylma Jordaan 3.50, TJ: Arlien Muller 12.36, SP: Simoné du Toit 16.87, DT: Elizna Naude 61.00, HT: Karin le Roux 47.90, JT: Justine Robbeson 57.54, Hep: Janice Josephs 5101 (only 6 ev.), 20kW: Nicolene Cronje 1:41:28, 50kW: Trudi Carstens 5:42:30.

Khotso MOKOENA b. 6 Mar 1985 Heidelberg, Gauteng 1.90m 73kg. Peak Performance AC, Johannesburg.

At LJ/(TJ): OG: '04- (dnq 29); WCh: '05- 7, '07- 5; CG: '06- 4/2; WJ: '02- 12, '04- 2/1; AfG: '03- (2), '07- 3; AfCh: '06- 2/2; WI: '06- 5, '08- 1. At HJ: WY: '01- 5. Won RSA LJ 2005-07, TJ 2004-06.

RSA records LJ (2) 2005-06, TJ (2) 2004-05, African junior TJ record 2004.

Progress at LJ, TJ: 2001- 7.17A, 2002- 7.82A, 16.03A; 2003- 7.84A/7.83, 16.28; 2004- 8.09, 16.96A/16.77; 2005- 8.37A/8.22, 17.25; 2006- 8.39/8.45w, 16.95; 2007- 8.34A/8.28/8.32w, 16.75; 2008- 8.25. pbs: HJ 2.10 '01.

Mbulaeni MULAUDZI b. 8 Sep 1980 Muduluni Village, Limpopo Province 1.71m 62kg. University of Johannesburg AC.

At 800m: OG: '04- 2; WCh: '01-03-05-07: 6/3/sf/7; CG: '02- 1; AfG: '03- 2, '07- 2; AfCh: '00-02-06: 2/3/6; WI: '04-06-08: 1/2/2; WCp: '06- 3; Won WAF 2006, AfrJ 1999, RSA 2001-03, 2005-08.

RSA 1000m record 2007.

Progress at 800m: 1998- 1:50.33A, 1999- 1:48.33A; 2000- 1:45.55, 2001- 1:44.01, 2002- 1:43.81, 2003- 1:42.89, 2004- 1:44.56, 2005- 1:44.08, 2006- 1:43.09, 2007- 1:43.74. pbs: 400m 46.3 '07, 600m 1:17.25i '05, 1000m 2:15.86 '07, 1500m 3:39.70 '02.

Alwyn MYBURGH b. 13 Oct 1980 Vanderbijlpark 1.88m 71kg. Rainbow AC, Vaal Triangle.

At 400mh: OG: '00- sf, '04- 7; WCh: '01/03- sf, '07- h; CG: '06- 2; AfG: '07- 3; AfCh: '06- 2; WUG: '01- 1; AfJ: '99- 1. RSA champion 2007.

Progress at 400mh: 1998- 52.48A, 1999- 50.15A; 2000- 49.07A/49.11, 2001- 48.09, 2002- 48.39A/49.80, 2003- 48.61, 2004- 48.21, 2005- 48.75, 2006- 48.23, 2007- 48.64. pbs: 100m 10.66A '99, 200m 21.11A '01, 20.9A '06; 400m 46.28A '04.

His father Hugo Myburgh had a 400mh best of 50.04 in 1974 and mother Hybré de Lange set South African records of 13.2 and 13.48 for 100mh, 26.36 for 200mh and 57.6 for 400mh in 1974.

John **Robert OOSTHUIZEN** b. 23 Jan 1987 1.88m 101kg. Maties AC, Stellenbosch

At JT: WCh: '07- 6; CG: '06- 5; AfG: '07- 1; WJ: '06- 1; WY: '03- 2; RSA champion 2007-08.

Afrian junior javelin record 2006.
Progress at JT: 2005- 75.94, 2006- 83.07, 2007- 84.52, 2008- 86.80.
His father and coach Johan had JT best of 80.92 (1990).

Hendrick RAMAALA b. 2 Feb 1972 GaMalepo, Pietersburg 1.72m 58kg. Mr Price AC. Law graduate of Witwatersrand University.
At 10,000m: OG: '96- h; WCh: '95- 17, '97- 14, '99- 11; AfG: '99- 7. At Mar: OG: '00- 12, '04- dnf; WCh: '03- 9, '05- dnf, '07- 27. World HMar: '97-8-9-01-02: 4/2/2/4/15. Won SA 5000m 1995, 1999; 10,000m 1995, 1999-2001, 2008; HMar 1997, 2005, 2007; CC 1998.
RSA records 10,000m (3) 1997-9, HMar 1997, 2000.
Progress at 10,000m, Mar: 1995- 27:54.59, 1996- 27:57.8, 1997- 27:36.30, 1998- 27:30.57, 1999- 27:29.94, 2000- 27:46.38, 2:09:43; 2001- 27:38.36, 2:11:18; 2002- 28:02.37, 2:10:06; 2003- 27:43.07, 2:08:58; 2004- 28:35.56, 2:09:28; 2005- 29:20.13, 2:08:32; 2006- 2:06:55, 2007- 2:07:56. pbs: 1500m 3:52.14 '03, 3000m 8:06.03A '04, 5000m 13:24.43 '98, HMar 59:20 '00 & RSA rec 60:07 '97.
Won Great North Run half marathon 1997, 2003 & 2006. Did not finish on his marathon debut at Chicago 1999, won Mumbai and New York 2004, 2nd New York 2005 (3rd 2007), 3rd London 2005-6 (5th 2007). Partner of French distance runner Rodica Moroianu.

Louis J. van ZYL b. 20 Jul 1985 1.86m 75kg. Tuks AC, Pretoria.
At 400mh: WCh: '05- 6, '07- h; CG: '06- 1/2R; AfG: '07- 1; AfCh: '06- 1; WJ: '02- 1, '04- 4/2R; WY: '01- 3; WCp: '06- 2; RSA champion 2003, 2005-06, 2008.
Progress at 400mh: 2001- 51.14A, 2002- 48.89, 2003- 49.22, 2004- 49.06, 2005- 48.11, 2006- 48.05, 2007- 48.24. pbs: 100m 10.62 '07, 10.3Aw '03, 10.5A '01; 200m 21.20A/21.19w '05, 21.0A '03; 400m 46.28A '05, 45.9A '07; 300mh 35.76 '04.
Ran world U18 record of 48.89 to win World Junior title in 2002 after world age record at 15 in 2001. Commonwealth Games record to win 400mh gold and ran brilliant final leg in 4x400m to take RSA from fifth to second in 2006.

Women

Elizna NAUDE b. 14 Sep 1978 Vereeniging 1.80m 105kg. Tuks AC, Pretoria. Teacher
At DT: OG: '04- dnq 20; WCh: '05- dnq 13; CG: '02- 6, '06- 1; AfG: '99- 3, '03- 1, '07- 1; AfCh: '02-04-06: 3/1/1; WUG: '01-03- 5/5; WCp: '98- 7, '06- 8. Won RSA DT 1998, 2000-2007, African junior 1997.
Three African discus records 2004-07, four RSA 2002-07.
Progress at DT: 1994- 43.32, 1995- 45.46, 1996- 46.64, 1997- 49.60, 1998- 52.51A, 1999- 55.92A, 2000- 58.51, 2001- 58.30, 2002- 60.99, 2003- 57.44, 2004- 61.79A, 2005- 63.17A, 2006- 61.55, 2007- 64.87.

Justine ROBBESON b. 15 May 1985 Benoni 1.67m 65kg. University of North West, Potchefstroom.
At JT: AfG: '03- 2, '07- 1; AfCh: '06- 1; WY: '01- 2; WUG: '05- 3; WCp: '06- 3. At Hep: WJ: '04- 1. Won RSA 100mh 2005, JT 2007, Hep 2003.
Two African javelin records 2006, African junior heptathlon record 2004.
Progress at JT: 1999- 43.30A, 2000- 45.51A, 2001- 51.93, 2002- 54.17A, 2003- 51.42, 2004- 55.82A, 2005- 59.46A, 2006- 62.80, 2007- 62.51A. pbs: 200m 24.83 '03, 100mh 13.56 '04, HJ 1.78 '03, LJ 6.26A '02, 6.14 '04, 6.24w '05; SP 13.15 '07, DT 36.92 '03, Hep 5868 '04.
Forced by back injury sustained high jumping to give up heptathlon and concentrate on javelin.

SPAIN

Governing body: Real Federación Española de Atletismo, Avda. Valladolid, 81 – 1°, 28008 Madrid, Spain. Founded 1918.

National Championships first held in 1917 (men), 1931 (women). **2007 Champions**: **Men**: 100m: Ángel David Rodríguez 10.41, 200m: Alberto Dorrego 21.66, 400m: Mark Ujakpor 47.19, 800m: Manuel Olmedo 1:49.31, 1500m: Juan Carlos Higuero 3:40.41, 5000m: Jesús España 13:30.24, 10,000m: Ayad Lamdassem 27:56.60, HMar: Ricardo Serrano 64:21, Mar: Óscar Martín 2:14:55, 3000mSt: Antonio Jiménez 8:21.88, 110mh: Jackson Quiñónez 13.44, 400mh: José M. Romera 50.63, HJ: Javier Bermejo 2.20, PV: Javier Gazol 5.15, LJ: Joan Lino Martínez 7.81, TJ: Andrés Capellán 16.31, SP: German Millán 18.54, DT: Mario Pestano 66.12, HT: Moisés Campeny 70.45, JT: Gustavo Dacal 73.13, Dec: David Gómez 7470, 10,000mW/20kW: Francisco Javier Fernández 38:07.75/1:19:52, 50kW: Jesús Ángel García 3:52:22. **Women**: 100m/200m: Belén Recio 11.71/23.94, 400m: Begoña Garrido 54.71, 800m: Mayte Martínez 2:06.18, 1500m: Iris Fuentes-Pila 4:23.06, 5000m: Marta Romo 15:50.25, 10,000m/HMar: Yesenia Centeno 32:54.29/73:25, Mar: Teresa Pulido 2:36:17, 3000mSt: Rosa Morató 9:51.63, 100mh: Josephine Onyia 12.89, 400mh: Laia Forcadell 58.34, HJ: Ruth Beitía 2.02, PV: Naroa Agirre 4.30, LJ: Concepción Montaner 6.48, TJ: Carlota Castrejana 14.25, SP/DT: Irache Quintanal 16.44/54.09, HT: Berta Castells 64.44, JT: Mercedes Chilla 59.02, Hep: Ana Capdevila 5532, 10,000mW: Teresa Linares 47:39.24, 20kW: María José Poves 1:33:14.

Arturo CASADO b. 26 Jan 1983 Madrid 1.87m 71kg. Adidas.
At 1500m: WCh: '05- 5, '07- 7; EC: '06- 4; WJ: '02- 6, EU23: '03- 7, '05- 1; EJ: '01- 3; WI: '08- 4; EI: '05- 4, '07- 3; Won Med G 2005, Spanish 2005.
Progress at 1500m: 2000- 3:57.76, 2001- 3:46.15, 2002- 3:43.66, 2003- 2:41.52, 2004- 3:38.04, 2005-

3:35.64, 2006- 3:35.45, 2007- 3:34.09. pbs: 800m 1:46.98 '07, 1000m 2:20.50 '06, 1M 3:52.38 '07, 3000m 7:55.77i '06, 5000m 14:21.0 '03, 10kmRd 29:18 '05.

Jesús ESPAÑA b. 21 Aug 1978 Madrid 1.73m 56kg. C.A. Valdemoro.
At 1500m: EJ '97- 9. At 3000m: WI: '03- 4; WCp: '06- 6; ECp: '05- 1; EI: '02- 3=, '07- 3. At 5000m: WCh: '05- h, '07- 7; EC: '02- 11, '06- 1; ECp: '03- 2. Eur CC: '07- 6. Won Spanish 5000m 2003, 2005-07; indoor 3000m 2003 & 2007.
Progress at 5000m: 1998- 14:33.34, 1999- 14:22.1, 2000- 14:28.24, 2002- 13:22.66, 2003- 13:29.24, 2004- 13:18.31, 2005- 13:15.44, 2006- 13:16.74, 2007- 13:30.24. pbs: 800m 1:51.18 '00, 1500m 3:36.53 '02, 2000m 5:05.34 '02, 3000m 7:38.26 '06, 10,000m 29:03.20 '00, 10km Rd 28:33 '01.

Francisco Javier FERNÁNDEZ b. 6 Mar 1977 Guadix, Granada 1.75m 65kg. Agrupaejido.
At 20kW: OG: '00- 7, '04- 2; WCh: '99- 15, '01- dnf, '03- 2, '05- 2, '07- 2; EC: '98- 3, '02- 1, '06- 1; WCp: '97-99-06: 47/12/1; EU23: '97- 2; ECp: '98-00-01-03: 1/3/4/1; won Med G 2005, Spanish 20kW 1998-2004, 2007; 10,000mW 2007. At 10kW: WJ: '96- 1; EJ: '95- 2.
World 20km walk best 2002. Spanish walks records 1999-2007: 5000m (3), 10,000m (2), 10km (3), 20km (2).
Progress at 20kW: 1997- 1:21:59, 1998- 1:20:31, 1999- 1:21:55, 2000- 1:18:56, 2001- 1:19:47, 2002- 1:17:22, 2003- 1:18:00, 2004- 1:19:19, 2005- 1:17:52, 2006- 1:18:31, 2007- 1:18:50. pbs: 3000mW 12:27.27 '02, 5000mW 18:27.34/18:24.13i '07; 10,000mW 38:07.65 '07, 10kmRd 37:52 '02 (all Spanish records).
Won IAAF Race Walking Challenge 2005-06. Coached by Robert Korzeniowski from 2005.

Jesús Ángel GARCÍA b. 17 Oct 1969 Madrid 1.72m 64kg. Canal de Isabel II.
At 50kW: OG: '92- 10, '96- dnf, '00- 12, '04- 5; WCh: '93-5-7-9-01-03-05-07: 1/5/2/dnf/2/6/dq/dq; EC: '94- 4, '98- dq, '02- 3, '06- 2; WCp: '93-5-7-9-02-04-06: 2/2/1/4/dq/6/6; ECp: '96-8-00-01-07: 1/2/1/1/6. At 20kW: WUG: '91- 5; ECp: '05- 14. Won Spanish 50kW 1997, 2000, 2007.
Progress at 50kW: 1991- 4:05:10, 1992- 3:48:24, 1993- 3:41:41, 1994- 3:41:28, 1995- 3:41:54, 1996- 3:46:59, 1997- 3:39.54, 1998- 3:43:17, 1999- 3:40:40, 2000- 3:42:51, 2001- 3:43:07, 2002- 3:44:33, 2003- 3:43:56, 2004- 3:44:42, 2005- 3:48:19, 2006- 3:42:48, 2007- 3:46:08. pbs: 5000mW 19:33.3 '01, 10,000mW 40:32.85 '04, road: 10kW 40:25 '99, 20kW 1:23:09 '05, 30kW 2:08:47 '01, 35km 2:31:06 '94.
In 1997 he married Carmen Acedo, who won a rhythmic gymnastics world title in 1993.

Juan Carlos HIGUERO b. 3 Aug 1978 Aranda de Duero (Burgos) 1.80m 60kg. Promoaranda.
At 1500m (5000m): OG: '00- 8, '04- sf; WCh: '03- 11, '05- 6, '07- 13; EC: '02- 5, '06- 3 (3); EU23: '99- h; EJ: '97- (3). WI: '01-03-04-08: 9/8/h/3; EI: '00-02-05-07: 6/2/2/1; ECp: '03-05-06: 1/1/2. Eur CC: '96-97: 3J/4J. Won Spanish 1500m 2000, 2002-03, 2006-07.
Progress at 1500m: 1997- 3:50.90, 1998- 3:41.24, 1999- 3:39.57, 2000- 3:36.63, 2001- 3:32.30, 2002- 3:33.72, 2003- 3:31.61, 2004- 3:32.95, 2005- 3:33.72, 2006- 3:31.57, 2007- 3:32.18. pbs: 800m 1:45.87 '07, 1000m 2:18.23 '06, 1M 3:52.49 '02, 2000m 5:04.26 '05, 3000m 7:48.46i '05, 7:53.41 '07; 5000m 13:32.69 '07, 10kmRd 28:37 '03, 3000mSt 9:51.34 '95.

Antonio David **JIMÉNEZ** b. 18 Feb 1977 Sevilla 1.78m 63kg. Reebok RC
At 3000mSt: OG: '04- 14; WCh: '01- 6, '05- 6, '07- h, EC: '02- 1,'06- 5; EU23: '99- 3; ECp: '01-03-05-06: 2/4/1/1; Won MedG 2001. At 3000m: WI: '04- 4; EI: '02- 2. World 4k CC: '02- 7. Eur CC: '00- 17, '01- 3. Won Spanish 4k CC 2002, 3000mSt 2001-02, 2004-07.
Two Spanish records 2000mSt 2001-05.
Progress at 3000mSt: 1995- 9:24.74, 1996- 9:17.93, 1997- 9:19.3, 1998- 8:54.90, 1999- 8:37:29, 2000- 8:20:34, 2001- 8:11.52, 2002- 8:17.77, 2003- 8:15.82, 2004- 8:14.30, 2005- 8:14.05, 2006- 8:11.55, 2007- 8:21.33. pbs: 1500m 3:43.23 '02, 2000m 5:04.91 '02, 3000m 7:46.49i '02, 7:50.30 '00; 2000mSt 5:18.65 '05.

José Manuel 'Chema' **MARTÍNEZ** b. 22 Oct 1971 Madrid 1.76m 63kg. Nike Runnig.
At 10,000m: OG: '04- 9; WCh: '99- 19, '01- 12, EC: '02- 1, '06- 2; WUG: '99- 1. At Mar: WCh: '03- 16, '05- 30, '07- 10; EC: '06- dnf. Eur CC: '00-02-06-07: 9/15/15/5. Won Spanish 10,000m 2004-05, CC 2002.
Progress at 10,000m, Mar: 1993- 29:22.72, 1994- 29:19.42, 1995- 29:15.8, 1996- 28:51.97, 1997- 28:11.67, 1998- 28:16.39, 1999- 27:51.82, 2000- 27:53.9, 2001- 27:54.81, 2002- 27:41.76, 2:09:55; 2003- 27:30.56, 2:08:09; 2004- 27:41.49, 2:13:14; 2005- 27:42.90, 2:11:56; 2006- 28:12.06, 2:11:06; 2007- 2:10:12. pbs: 1500m 3:48.49 '97, 2000m 5:06.33 '04, 3000m 7:39.64 '04, 5000m 13:11.13 '06, HMar 63:17 '04.
Third in Rotterdam on marathon debut 2002 and again in 2003. Won the European 10,000m with a 56.6 last lap. Wife Nuria Moreno was an international hockey player.

Manuel MARTÍNEZ b. 7 Dec 1974 León 1.85m 132kg. D.Manuel Martínez.
At SP: OG: '96- dnq 15, '00- 6, '04- 4; WCh: '93- 11, '95- dnq 21, '97- dnq 13, '01- 4, '03/05/07- dnq 15/16/nt; EC: '94- dnq 14, '98- 7, '02- 5, '06- 9; WI: '95-7-9-01-03-04-06: 4/5/4/3/1/5/6; EI: '94-96-98-00-02-05: 4/7/6/2/1/3; WJ: '92- 2; EJ: '93- 1; WUG: '01- 1; WCp: '02- 6; ECp: '93-5-6-7-8-01-03-05-06: 7/4/4/3/3/1/1/2/2; E23Cp: '94- 1. Won Spanish 1993-8, 2000-06 (also indoors 1993-2007); IbAm 1998, 2000, 2004; MedG 2001. 16 Spanish shot records 1993-2002.
Progress at SP: 1991- 15.57, 1992- 18.14, 1993- 19.53, 1994- 20.16, 1995- 19.97i/19.69, 1996- 20.12, 1997- 20.37i/20.27, 1998- 20.50i/20.08; 1999-

20.79i/20.04, 2000- 20.55, 2001- 21.35, 2002- 21.47, 2003- 21.24i/21.08, 2004- 21.15, 2005- 20.51i/20.43, 2006- 20.58, 2007- 19.48. pb DT 48.04 '98.

Juan Manuel MOLINA b. 15 Mar 1979 Cieza, Murcia 1.73m 67kg. UCAM-Athleo Cieza Golf.
At 20kW: OG: '04- 5; WCh: '05- 3, '07- 16; EC: '02- 3, '06- dq; EU23: '99- 4, '01- 1; WUG: '01- 2, '05- 1; WCp: '02-04-06: 8/8/12; ECp: '01- 10, '05- 2. At 10kW: WJ: '98- 4; EJ: '97- 6. Won Spanish 20kW 2005.
Spanish record 20,000m walk 1:22:31.8 '01.
Progress at 20kW: 1999- 1:23:39, 2000- 1:22:43, 2001- 1:21:51, 2002- 1:20:18, 2003- 1:21:57, 2004- 1:20:29, 2005- 1:19:44, 2006- 1:21:09, 2007- 1:20:44. pbs: 3000mW 12:31.20 '02, 5000mW 18:54.03 '07, 10,000mW 39:30.36 '04, 10kW 38:46 '05, 30kW 2:11:05 '00, 50kW 3:55:12 '06.

Mikel ODRIOZOLA b. 25 May 1973 San Sebastián 1.80m 62kg. Real Sociedad FIACT.
At 20kW: WCh: '99- 18. At 50kW: OG: '00- 24; WCh: '01- 15, '03- 14, '05- dq, '07- 6; EC: '98- 4, '02- dq, '06- 5; WCp: '06- 4. Won Spanish 50kW 2001-03, 2005-06.
Spanish record 30km walk 2003.
Progress at 50kW: 1996- 4:11:45, 1997- 3:57:15, 1998- 3:47:24, 1999- 3:51:01, 2000- 3:45:57, 2001- 3:45:22, 2002- 3:47:55, 2003- 3:42:03, 2005- 3:41:47, 2006- 3:44:59, 2007- 3:55:19. pbs: 5000mW 19:28.9 '00, 10,000mW 41:27.13 '07, 10kW 40:30 '05, 20kW 1:22:29 '00, 30kW 2:05:28 '03.

Mario PESTANO b. 8 Apr 1978 Santa Cruz de Tenerife 1.95m 120kg. Tenerife Cajacanarias.
At DT: OG: '04- dnq 12; WCh: '99/01- dnq 30/22, '03- 8, '05- 11, '07- 10; EC: '02- 4, '06- 4; EU23: '99- 3; EJ: '97- 11; WCp: '02- 3; ECp: '01-03-05-06: 2/5/1/3. Won WAF 2004, IbAm 2004, MedG 2005, Spanish 2001-07.
Six Spanish discus records 2001-07.
Progress at DT: 1995- 49.36, 1996- 50.56, 1997- 53.68, 1998- 54.96, 1999- 61.73, 2000- 61.63, 2001- 67.92, 2002- 67.46, 2003- 64.99, 2004- 68.00, 2005- 66.57, 2006- 66.31, 2007- 68.26. pb SP 18.75i '00, 18.64 '02.

Jackson QUIÑÓNEZ b. 12 Jun 1980 Esmeraldas, Ecuador 1.90m 91kg. FC Barcelona.
At 110m: OG: '04- qf; WCh: '03- sf, '05- h, '07- 7; PAm: '99- h, '03- 6; SACh: '01- 4, '03- 2; Won Spanish 2006-07. At 60mh: WI: '08- 7; EI: '07- 3.
Records at 110mh: Ecuador 1998-2004, four Spanish 2006-07.
Progress at 110mh: 1997- 14.93/14.86w, 1998- 14.28/13.9, 1999- 14.26, 2000- 14.06, 2001- 13.64A/13.89/13.82w, 2002- 13.64, 2003- 13.59, 2004- 13.44, 2005- 13.45, 2006- 13.34, 2007- 13.33. pbs: 100m 10.52A '00, 200m 21.41A '00, 60mh 7.52i '08, HJ 2.20 '01.
Switched from Ecuador (from whom he played at basketball) to Spain with IAAF approval 28 Oct 2006.

Antonio Manuel REINA b. 13 Jun 1981 Osuna, Sevilla 1.86m 71kg. Nike Running.
At 800m: OG: '04- sf; WCh: '01- h/7R, '03- sf/5R, '05- sf, '07- h; EC: '02- sf; WJ: '00- 3; EU23: '01- 1; WI: '03- 4; EI: '02- 3, '05- 2; WCp: '02- 1; ECp: '03- 1, '05- 1; Won Med G 2005, Spanish 400m 2005, 800m 2001-05.
Two Spanish 800m records 2002
Progress at 800m: 1998- 1:54.44, 1999- 1:51.75, 2000- 1:47.33, 2001- 1:46.00, 2002- 1:43.83, 2003- 1:44.37, 2004- 1:43.89, 2005- 1:44.18, 2007- 1:45.32. pbs: 200m 21.83 '05, 400m 45.98 '05, 1000m 2:20.50 '01, 1500m 3:59.6 '00.
Improved in 2002 from a best of 1:45.25 (3rd in European Indoors) to a Spanish outdoor record 1:44.11 at San Sebastián and then 1:43.83 in a thrilling World Cup victory in Madrid.

Julio REY b. 13 Jan 1972 Toledo 1.66m 51kg. Adidas.
At Mar: OG: '04- 58; WCh: '01- 37, '03- 2, '05- 8, '07- dnf; EC: '02- 3, '06- 3. At 10,000m: WCh: '97- 8; EC: '98- dnf. World HMar: '02- 11. World CC: '97- 9; Eur CC: '95-7-8: 20/7/9. Won Spanish 10,000m 1997, HMar 2004, CC 1997-8.
Spanish marathon record 2006.
Progress at 10,000m, Mar: 1995- 28:18.6, 1996- 28:00.79, 1997- 27:55.19, 1998- 27:47.33, 2:08:33; 1999- 2:07:37dq, 2001- 2:07:46, 2002- 27:51.59, 2:11:14; 2003- 2:07:27, 2004- 2:24:54, 2005- 2:07:38, 2006- 2:06:52, 2007- 2:11:36. pbs: 3000m 7:54.40 '97, 5000m 13:22.13 '98, HMar 62:10 '02.
Two year-drugs ban after 3rd Rotterdam marathon 1999. Won Hamburg marathon 2001, 2003 & 2005-06; 2nd Fukuoka 2005. His brother Fernando (b. 16 Apr 1980) has 10,000m pb 28:14.90 '04.

Women

Naroa AGIRRE b. 15 May 1979 San Sebastián 1.77m 64kg. At. San Sebastián
At PV: OG: '04- 6=; WCh: '03- dnq 13=, '05- 9, '07- dnq 13; EC: '02- 10; WI: '06- 6, '08- 9; ECp: '04-06: 7/4. Won IbAm 2004.
Nine Spanish PV records 2002-07.
Progress at PV: 1995- 2.90, 1996- 3.30, 1997- 3.50, 1998- 3.50, 1999- 4.00, 2000- 4.10, 2001- 4.05, 2002- 4.40, 2003- 4.45, 2004- 4.47, 2005- 4.45, 2006- 4.50, 2007- 4.56i/4.50. pbs: 100m 12.71 '97, 200m 25.86 '00, 60mh 9.38i '01, HJ 1.61i '98, LJ 6.35 '07, TJ 12.58 '01, Pen 3574i '98.
Actress on Basque TV. Coached by her husband, Jon Karla Lizeaga (PV 5.31 '95).

Ruth BEITIA b.1 Apr 1979 Santander 1.92m 71kg. Valencia Terra i Mar. Student of physical therapy at University of Santander.
At HJ: OG: '04- dnq 16=; WCh: '03- 11=, '05- dnq 19=, '07- 6; EC: '02- 11, '06- 9; WJ: '96- dnq, '98- 8, EU23: '01- 1; EJ: '97- 9; WI: '01-03-06-08: 7/5=/3/4; EI: '05- 2, '07- 3; WCp: '02- 6=; ECp: '03-04-06-07: 2/6/2/2; Won Med G 2005, Spanish 2003, 2006-07.

Nine Spanish HJ records 1998-2007.
Progress at HJ: 1989- 1.29, 1990- 1.39, 1991- 1.50, 1992- 1.55, 1993- 1.66, 1994- 1.74, 1995- 1.80, 1996- 1.85, 1997- 1.86, 1998- 1.89, 1999- 1.83, 2000- 1.86i/1.85, 2001- 1.94i/1.91, 2002- 1.94, 2003- 2.00, 2004- 2.00i/1.96, 2005- 1.99i/1.97, 2006- 1.98i/1.97; 2007- 2.02, 2008- 1.99i. pbs: 200m 25.26 '02, 100mh 14.95 '97, 14.93w '00; LJ 6.04 '03, TJ 10.93 '99.
Her sister Inmaculada (b. 8 Sep 1975) has TJ pb 13.43 '00.

Carlota CASTREJANA b. 25 Apr 1973 Logroño 1.88m 70kg. La Rioja Atletismo.
At TJ: OG: '00/04- dnq 18/18; WCh: '03- dnq 22, '05- 11, '07- dnq 13; EC: '02- 11, '06- 11; WI: '03- 6; EI: '98-00-02-05-07: 8/9/8/3/1 (10 LJ '02); WCp: '02- 3; ECp: '03-04-06-07: 5/4/5/5. Won IbAm 2000. At HJ: WI: '95- dnq. Won Spanish HJ 1996, TJ 2000-06.
Spanish TJ records 2002 & 2005 (seven indoors 2003-07), HJ 1989.
Progress at TJ: 1998- 13.61i/13.58/13.63w, 1999- 14.05A/14.05i, 2000- 14.10, 2001- 13.99, 2002- 14.51, 2003- 14.32i/14.17, 2004- 14.37, 2005- 14.60, 2006- 14.27; 2007- 14.64i/14.47. pbs: HJ 1.89i '95, 1.89 '96; LJ 6.47 '98, 6.73w '06.
Was a member of the Spanish Olympic basketball team (came 5th) in 1992.

Mercedes CHILLA b.19 Jan 1980 Jerez de la Frontera 1.70m 60kg. Puma Chapín Jerez.
At JT: OG: '04- dnq 22; WCh: '05/07- dnq 15/27; EC: '06- 3; WJ: '98- dnq 23; EU23: '01- 2; EJ: '99- 10; WUG: '01- 6, '03- 3; ECp: '03-04-06-07: 6/5/3/4; Won Spanish 2003-07.
Three Spanish JT records 2000-06.
Progress at JT: 1996- 39.16, 1997- 50.08, 1998- 53.45, 1999- 55.32; new: 1999- 54.41, 2000- 57.91, 2001- 57.78, 2002- 57.78, 2003- 59.22, 2004- 62.32, 2005- 60.22, 2006- 63.20, 2007- 62.19. pbs: SP 13.27i '06, 12.90 '00; DT 34.69 '04.

Marta DOMÍNGUEZ b. 3 Nov 1975 Palencia 1.63m 52kg. Nike Running.
At 5000m: OG: '00- h; WCh: '99- 9, '01- 2, '03- 2, '05- 14; EC: '98- 3, '02- 1, '06- 1 (7 10,000m); EU23: '97- 3 (1500m 5); WCp: '02- 2; ECp: '06- 2. At 3000m: WI: '95-7-01-03-04: 6/5/4/2/4; EI: '96-8-00-02-07: 3/3/3/1/2; ECp: '96- 3. At 1500m: OG: '96- h; WCh: '95- sf; WJ: '94- 2; EJ: '93- 1. World 4k CC: '00- 14; Eur CC: '07- 1. Won Spanish 1500m 1996, 5000m 1998-2003, 10,000m 2006.
Spanish records 3000m 2000, 10,000m 2006.
Progress at 3000m, 5000m, 10,000m: 1990- 10:15.0, 1991- 9:47.03, 1993- 9:35.16, 1994- 9:24.10, 1995- 9:01.79i, 1996- 8:53.34i/9:06.27, 1997- 8:52.74i/9:01.96, 15:41.91; 1998- 8:44.10, 14:59.49; 1999- 8:46.14, 15:16.93; 2000- 8:28.80, 15:26.00; 2001- 8:36.33, 14:58.12; 2002- 8:47.93, 15:10.67; 2003- 8:41.14i/8:50.6+, 14:48.33; 2004- 8:51.05i, 2005- 9:05.56, 14:54.98; 2006- 8:43.45, 14:56.18, 30:51.69; 2007- 8:44.40i. pbs: 800m 2:06.1 '95, 1000m 2:50.1 '91, 1500m 4:06.08 '00, 2000m 5:46.64i '03, HMar 71:23 '07.

Maria Teresa **'Mayte' MARTÍNEZ** b. 17 May 1976 Valladolid 1.68m 56kg. Adidas.
At 800m: OG: '00/04- sf; WCh: '01- 7, '05- 5, '07- 3, EC: '02- 2, '06- 7, WJ: '94- h; EJ: '95- 6; WI: '03- 3, '08- 4; EI: '02- 4, '05- 2; WCp: '02- 2; ECp: '03- 3, '06- 3. At 1500m: EI: '07- 5. Won Spanish 800m 2000-02, 2004-07.
Spanish 1000m record 2007.
Progress at 800m: 1991- 2:14.48, 1992- 2:13.09, 1993- 2:07.99, 1994- 2:05.68, 1995- 2:05.00, 1996- 2:08.81i, 1997- 2:06.84, 1998- 2:05.49i, 2000- 1:59.60, 2001- 1:59.76, 2002- 1:58.29, 2003- 1:59.53i/1:59.62, 2004- 1:58.58, 2005- 1:59.40, 2006- 1:59.60, 2007- 1:57.62. pbs: 400m 53.67 '03, 1000m 2:33.06 '07, 1500m 4:05.05 '05.
Married her coach Juan Carlos Granado on 20 Sep 2003.

Concepción MONTANER b.14 Jan 1981 L'Eliana, Valencia 1.70m 56kg. C.A.L'Elianna Llanera.
At LJ: OG: '00- dnq, WCh: '03- 12, '05- 11, '07- dnq 15; EC: '02- 4, '06- dnq 13; WJ: '98- h 4x100m, '00- 1, EU23: '01- 2; EJ: '99- 2; WI: '03-04-06-08: 9/7/4/5; EI: '07- 2; WCp: '02- 3; ECp: '03-04-06-07: 2/8/8/3. Spanish champion 2003-05.
Progress at LJ: 1996- 5.62/5.75w, 1997- 5.43/5.51w, 1998- 5.95/5.96w, 1999- 6.47, 2000- 6.64/6.79w, 2001- 6.61i/6.57/6.67w, 2002- 6.89, 2003- 6.78i/6.69/6.70w, 2004- 6.65i/6.59, 2005- 6.92, 2006- 6.76i/6.72, 2007- 6.84. pbs: 50m 6.46+i '01, 60m 7.47i '01, 100m 11.71 '01, 200m 24.65 '07, TJ 11.98 '97.

Rosa Maria MORATÓ b. 19 Jun 1979 Navarcles, Barcelona 1.58m 46kg. Valencia Terra I Mar.
At 3000mSt: WCh: '05- h, '07- 8, EC: '06- h; ECp: '03-04-06: 4/3/2. At 5000m/10,000m: ECp: '07- 5/4. Eur CC: '98-05-06-07: 10J/9/12/3. Won Spanish 3000mSt 2003-07, CC 2008.
Spanish records 2000mSt 2004, 3000mSt (6) 2003-07.
Progress at 3000mSt: 1998- 10:57.6, 2003- 10:01.70, 2004- 9:51.08, 2005- 9:54.20, 2006- 9:42.51, 2007- 9:26.23. pbs: 800m 2:09.87 '03, 1000m 2:48.80 '00, 1500m 4:16.75 '03, 1M 4:51.3 '02, 3000m 8:58.79 '06, 5000m 15:59.05 '07, 10,000m 32:23.61 '07, 2000mSt 6:28.22 '04.

Josephine ONYIA b. 15 Jul 1986 Sululere, Nigeria 1.66m 60kg. Valencia Terra i Mar.
At 100mh: WY: '03- 4; Af-J: '03- 2. Spanish champion 2007.
Progress at 100mh: 2003- 13.76, 2004- 13.48/13.30w, 2005- 13.36/13.26w, 2006- 12.78/12.70w, 2007- 12.67. pbs: 60m 7.35i '08, 100m 11.37/11.23w '07, 200m 24.20 '04, 23.62w '07; 50mh 6.78+i '06, 60mh 7.84i '08.
Became a Spanish citizen on 10 May 2007.

María VASCO b. 26 Dec 1975 Barcelona 1.56m 45kg. A.E. Blanc i Blau.
At 20kW: OG: '00- 3, '04- 7; WCh: '99- 10, '01- 5,

'03- dnf, '05- 4, '07- 3; EC: '02- dnf, '06- 15; WCp: '99-02-04: 23/8/3; ECp: '01-03-07: 7/3/5. At 10kW: OG: '96- 28; WCh: '95- 26; EC: '98- 5; EU23: '97- 2; WCp '95- 26, '97- 22. At 5000mW: WJ: '90- 15, '92- 6, '94- 4; EJ: '93- 4. Won Spanish 10kW 1996 10,000mW (t) 1997-9, 2001-05; 20kW 1998, 2001-04.
Spanish records 5000m (3) 1997-2007, 10,000m track (4) 1996-2001, 10km 1998, 20km (6) 1998-2004.
Progress at 10kW, 20kW: 1993- 47:11, 1994- 47:05, 1995- 44:53, 1996- 44:51.60t, 1997- 43:54, 1998- 43:02, 1:34:11; 1999- 43:35, 1:32:38; 2000- 43:33.92t, 1:30:20; 2001- 43:02.04t, 1:30:09; 2002- 43:51, 1:28:47; 2003- 44:22, 1:28:10; 2004- 44:07+, 1:27:36; 2005- 43:59, 1:28:51; 2006- 44:43, 1:32:50; 2007- 45:28+, 1:29:17. pbs: 3000mW 12:20.44 '04, 5000mW 20:57.11 '07.

SRI LANKA

Governing body: Athletic Association of Sri Lanka, n°33 Torrington Avenue, Colombo 7. Founded 1922.
National Champions 2007: **Men:** 100m: D.P.A.B. G.Silva 10.78, 200m: S.M.Weerasooriya 21.55, 400m: Deepal Mudunegedara 47.97, 800m: T.P.K. Mendis 1:52.31, 1500m: Chamara Wijesinghe 3:53.11, 5000m/10,000m: Mahalingama Ajanthan 14:43.59/30:31.83, 3000mSt: Sunil Ranjith 9:09.78, 110mh: Nuwan Tharanga 14.56, 400mh: Yasariri Ajith 51.72, HJ: Nalin Priyantha Rathnasiri 2.11, PV: Ruwan Pradeep Perera 4.50, LJ: Ravindran Ratheesan 7.15, TJ: Chamara Nuwan Gammage 15.9, SP: W.U.L.O.R.Perera 15.87, DT: Talavou F.Alaileema 49.95, JT: Harshana Gunathilake 71.24, Dec: Mohammad Sameer 6086, 20kW: B. N.M.Nayanananda 1:39:33. **Women**: 100m: Jani Chaturangani De Silva 11.91, 200m: D.D.P. Priadharshani 24.81, 400m: Chandrika Subashini 54.41, 800m: K.L.L.Gunawardana 2:10.21, 1500m: Shanika Samanmali 4:28.95, 5000m: Dalugoda Inoka 17:38.37, 10,000m: Lakmini Bogahawatta 37:28.82, 100mh: Lakshika Maduwanthi 14.9, , HJ: Priyangika Madumanthi 1.80, PV: Anne Piyumali 2.50, LJ: N.C.D. Priyadharshani 5.98, TJ: Ruwani Rubasinghe 12.76, SP: Nadeeka Muthunayaka 13.54, DT: Padma Nandan Wijesundara 44.17, JT: Nadeeka Lakmali 53.95, 20kW: Gallage Geetha Nandani 1:51:16.

Women

Susanthika JAYASINGHE b. 17 Dec 1975 Al Gama 1.70m 62kg. Married Dhammika Nandakumara 1994.
At 200m (/100m): OG: '96- (qf); '00- sf/3; WCh: '95- h/qf, '97- 2, '99- (qf), '01- h, '03- qf, '07- 3/qf; CG: '02- 4/dq h; WI: '01- 4; AsiG: '94- 2, '02- /1, '06- 3/2; AsiC: '95- 1/2, '02- 1/1, '07- 1/1; WCp: '02- 2/4; Won Asi-J 200m 1994, S.Asian 100m/200m 1995.
Two Asian 200m records 1997, SRI records: 100m (4) 1995-2000, 200m (6) 1993-2000. Asian indoor records 50m 2001, 60m 1999, 200m 2001.
Progress at 100m, 200m: 1992- 12.36, 25.67; 1993- 12.17, 24.56; 1994- 11.49, 23.16; 1995- 11.30, 22.95; 1996- 11.18, 23.18; 1997- 11.25+/11.38, 22.33; 1998- 11.27, 23.28; 1999- 11.17, 22.74; 2000- 11.04, 22.28; 2001- 11.37, 22.63; 2002- 11.08, 22.82; 2003- 11.20, 23.16; 2004- 23.24, 2006- 11.33, 22.99; 2007- 11.13, 22.55. pbs: 50m 6.31i '01, 60m 7.09i '99.
Suspended after random doping test in April 1998, but cleared by Sri Lankan AAA; she claimed she was the victim of a conspiracy (she also also been cleared after a positive test in 1995). In 2000 she became the first Sri Lankan woman to win an Olympic medal.

SUDAN

Governing body: Sudan Athletic Associatio, PO Box 13274, 11 111 Khartoum. Founded 1959.
Abubaker KAKI Khamis b. 21 Jun 1989 Elmuglad 1.71m 60kg.
At 800m: WCh: '07- h; WJ: '06- 6; WI: '08- 1; AfG: '07- 1. At 1500m: WY: '05- 3, Won Pan Arab G 800m & 1500m 2007.
World indoor junior best 1000m 2008.
Progress at 800m: 2005- 1:48.43, 2006- 1:45.78, 2007- 1:43.90, 2008- 1:44.81i. pbs: 1000m 2:15.77i '08, 1500m 3:45.06 '05, 10km Rd 30:18 '07.

Women

Yamilé ALDAMA b. 14 Aug 1972 La Habana 1.73m 62kg. married name Dodds. Shaftesbury Barnet Harriers, GBR.
At TJ: OG: '00- 4, '04- 5; WCh: '97- dnq 13, '99- 2, '05- 4, '07- dnq 25; PAm: '99- 1; AfG: '07- 1; AfC: '04- 1, '06- 1; CAG: '98- 1; WI: '97-9-04-06-08: 6/7/2/3/5; WCp: '98- 3, '06- 3. Won IbAm 1996, 1998; Cuban 1997-2000, AAA 2003; Arab HJ, 2005, LJ & TJ 2005, 2007.
Nine CAC triple jump records 1999-2003 (if still eligible), CAC indoor (14.65 and 14.88) 2003, three African and Sudan records 2004. SUD records HJ (1.85) 2004, LJ 2005 & 2007.
Progress at TJ: 1994- 13.92, 1995- 13.84, 1996- 14.43, 1997- 14.46, 1998- 14.55, 1999- 14.77, 2000- 14.47, 2001- 13.85i, 2002- 14.40/14.54w, 2003- 15.29, 2004- 15.28, 2005- 14.82, 2006- 14.86i/14.78, 2007- 14.58, 2008- 14.47i. pbs: 100mh 14.97/14.8 '92, HJ 1.88 '92, LJ 6.34 '07, Hep 5246 '93.
Aldama, who last competed for Cuba in 2000, began to compete for Sudan in 2004. She had moved to London with Scottish husband Andrew Dodds in 2001, in which year her son Amil was born, and hoped to be eligible for Britain but a three-year waiting period meant that she was unable to gain a passport in sufficient time to compete at the 2003 Worlds (or 2004 Olympics).

SWEDEN

Governing body: Svenska Friidrottsförbundet, Box 11, 171 18 Solna. Founded 1895.

National Championships first held in 1896 (men), 1927 (women). **2007 Champions**: **Men**: 100m: Johan Engberg 10.80, 200m: Johan Wissman 20.73, 400m: Thomas Nikitin 46.14, 800m: Mattias Claesson 1:48.64, 1500m: Rizak Dirshe 3:52.75, 5000m: Mustafa Mohamed 14:09.99, 10,000m: Erik Sjöqvist 29:16.93, HMar: Henrik Ahnström 66:19, Mar: Kent Claesson 2:28:20, 3000mSt: Per Jacobsen 8:44.73, 110mh: Robert Kronberg 13.83, 400mh: Niklas Larsson 52.16, HJ: Stefan Holm 2.31, PV: Gustaf Hultgren 5.25, LJ: Michel Tornéus 7.85, TJ: Anton Andersson 17.10, SP: Nick Fertitta USA 17.39, DT: Niklas Arrhenius 56.44, HT: Mattias Jons 70.34, JT: Magnus Arvidsson 80.43, Dec: Daniel Almgren 7552, 10,000mW/20kW/50kW: Fredrik Svensson 44:29.9/1:34:15/4:06:03. **Women**: 100m: Lena Berntsson 11.83, 200m: Lena Aruhn 24.43, 400m: Beatrice Dahlgren 54.30, 800m: Johanna Hallberg 2:11.66, 1500m: Kajsa Haglund 4:21.45, 5000m: Hanna Karlsson 16:36.20, 10,000m: Lilian Magnusson 34:32.21, HMar/Mar: Anna Rahm 73:31/2:39:02, 300mSt: Christin Johansson 10:12.18, 100mh: Susanna Kallur 12.90, 400mh: Erica Mårtensson 57.71, HJ: Emma Green 1.92, PV: Hanna-Mia Persson 4.20, LJ: Erica Jarder 6.02, TJ: Maria Augutis 12.94, SP: Helena Engman 17.54, DT: Anna Söderberg 58.95, HT: Cecilia Nilsson 68.31, JT: Annika Petersson 57.31, Hep: Nadja Casadei 5444, 5000mW/10,000mW: Ellinor Hogrell 26:28.3/55:33.1, 20kW: Siw Ibanez 1:51:29.

Magnus ARVIDSSON b. 20 Feb 1983 1.91m 100kg. KA 2 IF.
At JT: WCh: '07- 10; EC: '06- 10; WJ: '02- dnq 22; EU23: '03- dnq, 05- 3; Swedish champion 2006-07.
Progress at JT: 2000- 50.99, 2001- 63.84; 2002- 69.60, 2003- 70.08, 2004- 73.98, 2005- 77.83, 2006- 81.75, 2007- 85.75. pb SP 13.19 '05.

Stefan HOLM b. 25 May 1976 Forshaga 1.81m 70kg. Kils AIK.
At HJ: OG: '00- 4, '04- 1; WCh: '99- 10=, '01- 4=, '03- 2, '05- 7, '07- 4; EC: '98- 7, '02- 2, '06- 3; WJ: '94- 7=; EJ: '93- 11, '95- 6; WI: '97-9-01-03-04-06-08: 8=/6=/1/1/1/5/1; EI: '98-00-02-05-07: 12/4/2/1/1; WUG: '99- 4; ECp: '00-04: 1/1. Won GP 2002, WAF 2004, GWG 2001, Swedish 1998-2003, 2005-07.
Progress at HJ: 1987- 1.40, 1988- 1.51, 1989- 1.61, 1990- 1.83, 1991- 1.94, 1992- 2.09i/2.06, 1993- 2.14, 1994- 2.18, 1995- 2.21, 1996- 2.26, 1997- 2.30i/2.22, 1998- 2.33, 1999- 2.32, 2000- 2.34, 2001- 2.34i/2.33, 2002- 2.35, 2003- 2.36i/2.34, 2004- 2.37i/2.36, 2005- 2.40i/2.36, 2006- 2.34, 2007- 2.38i/2.35, 2008- 2.37i. pbs: 60m 7.33i '03, 100m 11.42 '99, 110mh 16.23 '99, LJ 7.18 '99; TJ 12.35i '91.
One of the smallest top high jumpers, he equalled the world best of 59cm cleared above own head with his 2.40 to win the 2005 European Indoor title. Is 83-47 v Staffan Strand 1989-2007 per his superb web site www.scholm.com. Won 8/8 indoors in both 2003 and 2004, also unbeaten in 14 outdoor events 2004. 122 competitions (71 outdoors, 48 indoors) over 2.30 from 1997 to 2008.

Alhaji JENG b. 13 Dec 1981 Banjul, The Gambia 1.85m 77kg. Örgryte IS.
At PV: WCh: '07- dnq 15=; EC: '06- dnq; WJ: '00- 8; EU23: '01- 6; WI: '06- 2, '08- 7. Swedish champion 2006.
Progress at PV: 1996- 3.90i/3.60, 1997- 4.27, 1998- 4.80, 1999- 5.30, 2000- 5.40, 2001- 5.49, 2002- 5.41, 2003- 5.56i/5.40, 2004- 5.61, 2005- 5.75sq/5.71i/5.65, 2006- 5.80, 2007- 5.70, 2008- 5.71i. pbs: 60mh 8.53i '03, 110mh 15.43 '01, HJ 2.00i '03, 1.94 '97; LJ 7.07i '03, Hep 5668i '03.
Family moved to Sweden when he was three weeks old. Gambia record in 1999, Swedish nationality from 2000.

Mustafa MOHAMED b. 1 Mar 1979 Mogadishu, Somalia 1.72m 54kg. Hälle IF.
At 3000St: OG: '04- 13; WCh: '03- h, '05- 10, '07- 4; EC: '06- 4; ECp: '04- 4; WJ: '98- 8. At 10,000m: EU23: '99-5, '01- 8; EJ: '97- 2. Eur CC: '97- 98-06-07; 3J/6J/3/2. Won SWE 5000m 2005, 2007; 3000mSt 2002-03, 2006.
Swedish 3000mSt record 2007.
Progress at 3000mSt: 1996- 9:37.38, 1998- 8:42.55, 1999- 8:40.84, 2002- 8:32.07, 2003- 8:23.35, 2004- 8:18.05, 2005- 8:15.51, 2006- 8:14.67, 2007- 8:05.75. pbs: 1500m 3:44.17 '07, 1M 4:00.02 '05, 3000m 7:59.40 '06, 5000m 13:32.08 '07, 10,000m 28:49.14 '02, HMar 63:35 '02.
Moved to Sweden at the age of 11. At Heusden in 2007 he broke the 31 year-old Swedish steeplechase record set by Anders Gärderud at the Montreal Olympics.

Christian OLSSON b. 25 Jan 1980 Göteborg 1.92m 74kg. Örgryte IS.
At TJ (/HJ): OG: '00- dnq 17, '04- 1; WCh: '01- 2, '03- 1; EC: '02- 1, '06- 1; EU23: '01- 1; EJ: '99- 2/1; WI: '03- 1, '04- 1; EI: '02- 1; WCp: '02- 3; ECp: '00-04: 4/1. Won WAF 2003, GP 2002, Swedish LJ 2006, TJ 2000-01, 2003.
Six Swedish triple jump records 2001-04. WIR 2004.
Progress at TJ: 1995- 12.20w, 1996- 12.44, 1998- 14.48, 1999- 16.30/16.59w, 2000- 16.97, 2001- 17.49, 2002- 17.80i/17.64, 2003- 17.77/17.92w, 2004- 17.83i/17.79, 2006- 17.67, 2007- 17.56. pbs: 100m 10.9 '06, 110mh 16.21 '98, HJ 2.28i '02, 2.28 '03; PV 4.04 '99, LJ 7.71 '02, 7.84w '03.
Considered himself a high jumper, but took his TJ best from 14.48 to 16.27w in his first competition of 1999 and had a superb season at his new event in 2001 when he was the only man to defeat Jonathan Edwards (and did so twice). He challenged Edwards again in 2002, losing 4-5, and was easily the world number one in 2003, when unbeaten outdoors. First jumped 17m on 14 June 2001, and from then has been under that just twice in 94 meetings to July 2007. Shared

Golden League jackpot 2004. Missed 2005 season and 2007 Worlds through injury and has had four operations.

Linus THÖRNBLAD b. 6 Mar 1985 Lund 1.80m 76kg. IFK Lund.
At HJ: OG: '04- dnq 24; WCh: '07- 15; EC: '06- 4; WJ: '02- dnq, '04- 4; WY: '01- dnq; EU23: '05- 10; EJ: '03- 3; WI: '06- 3; EI: '07- 2.
Progress at HJ: 2000- 1.90i, 2001- 2.06, 2002- 2.19, 2003- 2.30, 2004- 2.27, 2005- 2.31i/2.26, 2006- 2.34, 2007- 2.38i/2.31, 2008- 2.35i.

Johan WISSMAN b. 2 Dec 1982 Helsingborg 1.80m 75kg. IFK Helsingborg.
At 200m: OG: '04- qf; WCh: '03/05- sf; EC: '02- qf, '06- 2; WJ: '00- h; E23: '03- 3; WI: '04- 2; ECp: '04- 2. At 400m: WCh: '07- 7; EJ: '01- 2; WI: '08- 2; EI: '07- 4. Won Swedish 100m 2004, 200m 2001, 2003-04, 2006-07; 400m 2002, 2005.
Swedish records 200m (5) 2002-07, 400m (5) 2007. Euopean indoor best 300m (32.61) 2001.
Progress at 200m, 400m: 1999- 21.78, 48.03; 2000- 21.23, 47.30; 2001- 20.81, 46.40; 2002- 20.51, 46.17; 2003- 20.43, 45.80; 2004- 20.50, 45.57; 2005- 20.46/20.26w, 46.23; 2006- 20.38, 47.26i; 2007- 20.30, 44.56. pbs: 60m 6.84i '04, 100m 10.44 '02, 10.34w '03; 300m 32.40 '03, 3000mSt 11:12.75 '98. LJ 6.81 '00.

Women

Emma GREEN b. 8 Dec 1984 Bergsjön 1.80m 62kg. Örgryte IS.
At HJ: WCh: '05- 3, '07- 7=; EC: '06- 11; WJ: '02- 9; EU23: '05- 2; EJ: '03- 3; EI: '05- 8. At 200m: ECp: '06- 5. Won Swedish HJ 2005, 2007 (indoors 2004-07), LJ 2005.
Progress at HJ: 1998- 1.66i, 1999- 1.71, 2000- 1.75i/1.73, 2001- 1.82, 2002- 1.82, 2003- 1.86, 2004- 1.90, 2005- 1.97, 2006- 1.96i/1.92, 2007- 1.95, 2008- 1.98i. pbs: 60m 7.42i '06, 100m 11.58 '06, 200m 23.02 '06, LJ 6.41 '05, TJ 13.69i '06, 13.39 '07.
Her uncle Göte Green ran 47.9 for 400m.

Susanna KALLUR b. 16 Feb 1981 Huntington, New York, USA 1.70m 61kg. Falu IK. Was at University of Illinois, USA,
At 100mh: OG: '04- sf; WCh: '01/03/05- sf, '07- 4; WJ: '98- 3, '00- 1/3R; EC: '02- 7, '06- 1; EU23: '01- 1, '03- 1; EJ: '99- 5; WCp: '06- 2; ECp: '06- 1. At 60mh: WI: '03-04-06: 7/5/3; EI: '05- 1, '07- 1 (7 60m). Won Swedish 100m 2005, 100mh 1998, 2000, 2002-05, 2007.
World indoor 60mh record 2008.
Progress at 100mh: 1997- 14.11, 1998- 13.48, 1999- 13.41, 2000- 13.02, 2001- 12.74, 2002- 12.94, 2003- 12.88, 2004- 12.67, 2005- 12.65, 2006- 12.52, 2007- 12.49. pbs: 50m 6.56i '00, 60m 7.24i '07, 100m 11.30 '06, 200m 23.32 '05, 50mh 6.67i '08, 60mh 7.68i '08, HJ 1.72 '98, PV 3.00i '98, LJ 6.11 '01, TJ 11.67i '97, 11.22 '98; SP 10.80i '02, Pen 3917i '02, Hep 5282 '98.
Twin sister (a few minutes younger) **Jenny** has pbs: 60mh 7.92i '05 (2 EI 05, 8 WI 06); 100mh 12.85 '04 (2 EU23 01, 6 WCh 05, 7 EC 06). Their father Anders played for the New York Islanders at ice hockey, winning Stanley Cup four times.

Carolina KLÜFT b. 2 Feb 1983 Borås 1.78m 65kg. IFK Växjö.
At Hep (LJ): OG: '04- 1 (11); WCh: '03- 1, '05- 1, '07- 1; EC: '02- 1, '06- 1 (6); WJ: '00- 1, '02- 1; EJ: '01- 1; ECp: '06- 1. At Pen: WI: '03- 1; EI: '02-05-07: 3/1/1. At LJ: EU23: '03- 1, '05- 1; WI: '04- 3. Won SWE 100m 2003-04, 200m 2005, HJ 2004, LJ 2001-02, 2006; Hep 2001.
Two world junior heptathlon records 2002, European record 2007, seven Swedish records 2002-03.
Progress at LJ, Hep: 1998- 5.75, 1999- 6.13, 5162; 2000- 6.23, 6056; 2001- 6.26/6.33w, 6022; 2002- 6.48/6.59w, 6542; 2003- 6.86, 7001; 2004- 6.97, 6952; 2005- 6.87/6.92w, 6887; 2006- 6.67, 6740; 2007- 6.85, 7032. pbs: 60m 7.40i '05, 100m 11.48 '04, 200m 22.98 '03, 400m 52.98i '08, 53.17 '02; 800m 2:08.89 '05, 60mh 8.19i '03, 100mh 13.15 '05, HJ 1.95 '07, PV 3.16 '01, TJ 14.02/14.17w '07, SP 15.05 '06, DT 33.96 '00, JT 50.96 '06, Pen 4948i '05.
Thirteen gold medals and two bronze in 16 major championship competitions and has 19 successive heptathlon wins 2001-07 and three successive indoor pentathlon wins 2003-07. Won IAAF 'Rising Star' award for women in 2002, when she was the world's top heptathlete while still a junior. Added 398 points to her Swedish indoor record when she won 2003 World Indoor title with 4933, setting pbs at first four events. Set five pbs en route to winning World title (for third on world all-time list) in 2003. Her winning margin at the Athens Olympics was the widest ever, 517 points. Set Swedish LJ record at 6.92 twice at World indoors 2004. Won at Götzis each year 2003-07 and won the IAAF Combined Events Challenge each year 2003-06. Her mother Ingalill had long jump pb 6.09/6.20w (1979). Married (2007) to Patrik Kristiansson (b. 3 Jun 1977, PV 5.85 '02 SWE record, 3 WCh '03 4 EC '02, 2 EI '02).

Anna SÖDERBERG b. 11 Jun 1973 Knista, Örebro prov. 1.77m 85kg. Ullevi FK. Was at Northern Arizona University, USA.
At DT: OG: '00/04- dnq 24/35; WCh: '97- 11, '99- dnq 18, '03- 8, '05- 11, '07- dnq 18; EC: '98/02- dnq 15/15, '06- 11; WJ: '92- dnq. Won SWE DT 1993-2007, HT 1996-7.
Ten Swedish discus records 1994-9.
Progress at DT: 1986- 28.62, 1987- 35.50, 1988- 41.52, 1989- 46.44, 1990- 45.06, 1991- 48.80, 1992- 52.88, 1993- 52.24, 1994- 58.74, 1995- 56.84, 1996- 59.96, 1997- 61.30, 1998- 64.00, 1999- 64.54, 2000- 62.91, 2001- 59.18, 2002- 59.33, 2003- 61.61, 2004- 60.50, 2005- 61.26. 2006- 64.00, 2007- 62.98. pbs: HJ 1.67 '94, SP 16.30 '99, HT 59.45 '99.

SWITZERLAND

Governing body: Schweizerischer Leichtathletikverband (SLV), Haus des Sports, Postfach 606, 3000 Bern 22. Formed 1905 as Athletischer Ausschuss des Schweizerischen Fussball-Verbandes.

National Championships first held in 1906 (men), 1934 (women). **2007 Champions**: **Men**: 100m: Marco Cribari 10.35, 200m: Marc Schneeberger 20.47, 400m: Thomas Zaugg 47.17, 800m: Ueli Albert 1:48.72, 1500m: Mirco Zwahlen 3:52.25, 5000m: Daniel Vögeli 14:41.45, 10,000m: Ivan Pongeli 31:49.70, HMar: David Valtério 69:17, Mar: Bruno Invernizzi 2:28:54, 3000mSt: Markus Hagmann 9.01.16, 110mh: Andreas Kundert 13.59, 400mh: Christian Grossenbacher 51.34, HJ: David Zumbach 2.06, PV: Olivier Frey 5.20, LJ: Julien Fivaz 7.46, TJ: Alexander Martínez 16.60w, SP: Roger Strasser 15.98, DT: Daniel Schaerer 52.76, HT: Florian Lambercier 54.33, JT: Felix Loretz 74.11, Dec: David Gervasi 7659, 10,000mW/20kW/50kW: Bruno Grandjean 46:16.10/1:40:07/4:32:25. **Women**: 100m/200m: Fabienne Weyermann 11.64/24.19, 400m: Elle Sprunger 54.38, 800m: Marjolein Terwiel 2:08.33, 1500m: Valérie Lehmann 4:23.43, 5000m: Mirja Jenni 16:26.12, 10,000m/HMar: Deborah Büttel 35:49.45/76:43, Mar: Patrizia Morceli-Bieri 2:49:50, 3000mSt: Nicole Gmeiner 11:04.98, 100mh/JT: Linda Züblin 13.63/49.29, 400mh: Martina Naef 56.83, HJ: Beatrice Lundmark 1.80, PV: Anna Katharina Schmid 4.30, LJ: Simone Oberer 6.21, TJ: Barbara Leuthard 12.77, SP: Claudia Egli 14.13, DT: Karin Hagmann 50.52, HT: Rebecca Bähni 55.69, Hep: Sylvie Dufour 6112, 10,000mW: Marie Polli 48:02, 20kW: Laura Polli 1:40:02.

Alexander MARTÍNEZ b. 23 Aug 1977 Nueva Gerona, Isla de la Juventud 1.84m 82kg. LC Zürich.

At TJ: WCh: '07- 8; EC: '06- 9; 3rd GP 2002. Swiss champion 2006-07.

Six Swiss triple jump records 2006-07 (from 16.34)

Progress at TJ: 1995- 15.53, 1996- 15.88, 1998- 16.67, 1999- 16.50, 2000- 16.80, 2001- 17.06, 2002- 17.32, 2003- 17.06, 2004- 17.09, 2005- 17.51, 2006- 17.13, 2007- 17.13. pb LJ 7.60 '05.

Lives in Zürich, married a Swiss wife Marion (with whom he has won international salsa dancing competitions, but now separated) and gained Swiss citizenship on 22 Feb 2006.

Viktor RÖTHLIN b. 14 Oct 1974 1.72m 60kg. TV Alpnach.

At Mar: OG: '00- 36, '04- dnf; WCh: '07- 3; EC: 02- 16, '06- 2. At 10,000m: EC: '98- 19. At 5000m: EJ: '93- 6. Won Swiss 5000m 1997, 2001, 2004, CC 1998, 2004.

Three Swiss marathon records 2004-08.

Progress at Mar: 1999- 2:13:36, 2000- 2:12:53, 2001- 2:10:54, 2002- 2:16:16, 2003- 2:11:05, 2004- 2:09:56, 2005- 2:11:00, 2006- 2:11:50, 2007- 2:08:20, 2008- 2:07:23. pbs: 1500m 3:49.59 '95, 3000m 8:00.43 '98, 5000m 13:40.28 '99, 10,000m 28:22.53 '00, HMar 62:16 '06.

Won Zürich Marathon 2004, 2007; Tokyo 2008.

TANZANIA

Governing body: Tanzania Amateur Athletic Association, PO Box 2172, Dar es Salaam. Founded 1954.

Fabiano JOSEPH Naasi b. 24 Dec 1985 Babati, Mbulu district 1.58m 48kg. Iraqw.

At 10,000m (/5000m): OG: '04- 10/h; WCh: '03- 13, '05- (15); CG: '06- 3/5; WJ: '04- (6). World HMar: '03-04-05-07: 2/2/1/11; CC: '03-04: 19/7. Won AAA 10,000m 2003.

Progress at 10,000m: 2002- 29:04.7, 2003- 27:32.63, 2004- 28:01.94, 2005- 28:33.44, 2006- 27:51.99. pbs: 3000m 7:54.12 '04, 5000m 13:12.76 '06; Road: 15km 42:35 '07, 20km 57:21 '07, HMar 60:14 '07, Mar 2:13:24 '06.

TRINIDAD & TOBAGO

Governing body: National Amateur Athletic Association of Trinidad & Tobago, PO Box 605, Port of Spain, Trinidad. Fd. 1945, reformed 1971.

National Champions 2007: **Men**: 100m: Darrel Brown 9.88w, 200m: Emmanuel Callender 20.77, 400m: Renny Quow 45.74, 800m: Jamaal James 1:47.85, 1500m: Gavyn Nero 3:57.36, 5000m: Denzil Ramirez 14:54.16, 110mh: Mikel Thomas 14.14, 400mh: Keston Toney 53.41, HJ: Kevin Huggins 2.03, LJ: LeJuan Simon 7.74, TJ: Christopher Hercules 15.90, SP: Wade Franklyn 13.47, DT: Kellon Marshall 46.79, JT: Kerren Brown 57.82. **Women**: 100m: Sasha Springer 11.31, 200m: Nandelle Cameron 23.47, 400m: Britney St. Louis 54.09, 800m: Melissa De Leon 2:06.67, 1500m: Dawnell Collymore 5:00.23, 3000m: Shermin Lasaldo 11:12.37, 100mh: Afesha Dunbar 16.58w, 400mh: Janeil Bellille 57.70, HJ: Deandra Daniel 1.70, LJ: Rhonda Watkins 6.26, TJ: Ayanna Alexander 13.31w, SP: Cleopatra Borel-Brown 18.29, DT: Annie Alexander 52.71, JT: Kwema Philander 36.11, Hep: Natoya Baird 4743.

Darrel BROWN b. 11 Oct 1984 Arima 1.79m 85kg. Silver Bullet/Nike. Was at Southern Union CC, Alabama, USA.

At 100m/4x100mR: OG: '04- 7R; WCh: '01- 2R, '03- 2, '05- sf/2R; CG: '06- qf; WJ: '00- 4; 02- 1/3R; WY: '01- 1; PAm: '03- 2R. Won CAC 100m 2005, CAC-J 100m 2000, 2002; 200m 2000; TRI 100m 2001, 2007.

World junior 100m record 2003.

Progress at 100m, 200m: 1998- 10.79, 22.41; 1999- 10.67, 21.20; 2000- 10.34, 21.14/20.76w; 2001- 10.24, 20.41; 2002- 10.09, 20.97; 2003- 10.01, 2004- 10.11A, 2005- 9.99, 20.61; 2006- 10.11, 2007- 10.02/9.88w, 20.51. pbs: 55m 6.15i '03, 60m 6.59i '04.

Set world age records for 100m at 15, 16, 17 and

18, the last a WJR 10.01 in the quarter-finals before his silver medal in the final in 2003; the youngest 100m medallist in World Championship history. At 16 years 305 days for the 4x100m bronze in 2001 he is the youngest ever World medallist. Elder brother Darron has 100m pb 10.49 '04.

Marc BURNS b. 7 Jan 1983 1.83m 91kg. Rebirth/adidas. Was at Auburn University, Alabama.
At 100m/4x100mR: OG: '04- h; WCh: '01- 2R, '03- h, '05- 7/2R, '07- 8; CG: '06- 3; WJ: '00- 3; 02- 2/3R; PAm: '03- 2R; WCp: '06- 3. Won WAF 2005, PAm-J 2001, TRI 2002, 2005.
Progress at 100m: 1998- 10.51, 2000- 10.40, 2001- 10.28, 2002- 10.18, 2003- 10.28/10.24w, 2004- 10.12/9.99w, 2005- 9.96, 2006- 10.02, 2007- 10.15/10.06w. pbs: 60m 6.61i '04, 200m 20.57 '05.

Richard THOMPSON b. 7 Jun 1985 1.88m 80kg. Student at Louisiana State University.
At 100m: WCh: '07- qf; PAm: '07- h. Won NCAA 60m indoor 2008.
Progress at 100m: 2004- 10.55, 2005- 10.66/10.61w, 2006- 10.27/10.26w, 2007- 10.09/9.95w. pbs: 60m 6.51i '08, 200m 20.90 '07.

TUNISIA

Governing body: Fédération Tunisienne d'Athlétisme, B.P. 264, Cité Mahrajane 1082, Tunis. Founded 1957.

Hatem GHOULA b. 7 Jun 1973 Paris, France 1.80m 67kg. Zitouna Sports.
At 20kW: OG: '96- 33, '00- 36, '04- 11; WCh: '93-95-7-9-01-03-05-07: 32/30/9/16/10/14/5/3; AfG: '95-03-07: dq/1/1; AfCh: 96-98-00-02: 1/1/1/1; WCp: '99-02-06: 15/9/4. Won Francophone Games 1997, 2001, Arab Ch 1995, 1999, 2004.
World best 5000m walk 1997, African records at 10,000mW 1998, 20000mW track (1:22.51.84) 1994, 20kW 1997, 50kW 2002 & 2007.
Progression at 20kW: 1991- 1:46:47.6t, 1992- 1:39:03.0t, 1993- 1:33.24, 1994- 1:22:51.84t, 1995- 1:20:37, 1996- 1:21:45, 1997- 1:19:02, 1998- 1:23:19, 1999- 1:19:46, 2000- 1:25:38, 2001- 1:21:41, 2002- 1:23:49, 3:59:56; 2003- 1:21:12, 2004- 1:20:38, 2005- 1:20:19, 2006- 1:19:36, 2007- 1:20:40, 3:58:44. pbs: 3000mW 11:34.3 '99, 5000mW 18:05.49 '07, 10,000mW 38:24.31 '98.
Moved back from France to Southern Tunisia at the age of 15.

TURKEY

Governing body: Türkiye Atletizm Federasyonu, 19 mayis Spor Kompleksi, Ulus-Ankara. Founded 1922.

National Champions 2007: **Men**: 100m/200m: Ismail Arslan 10.61/21.57w, 400m: Firat Akten 48.90, 800m: Serhat Polat 1:52.51, 1500m: Kemal Koyuncu 3:49.49, 5000m: Murat Ertas 14:20.53, 10,000m: Mehmet Caglayan 31:12.15, Mar: Abdil Ceylan 2:16:12, 3000mSt: Osman Bas 9:25.70, 110mh: Caglar Kahramanoglu 14.72, 400mh: Tuncay Örs 51.31, HJ: Serdar Demirci 2.10, PV: Ibrahim Aydin 4.40, LJ: Koray Imrak 7.34, TJ: Hasim Yilmaz 15.56, SP: Hüseyin Atici 17.59, DT: Özkan Kaya 49.66, HT: Fatih Eryildirim 75.49, JT: Hulki Zümbül 60.03, Dec: Hikmet Tugsuz 6313. **Women**:100m/200m: Burcu Sentürk 11.58/23.94w, 400m: Özge Gürler 53.57, 800m: Yeliz Kurt 2:06.96, 1500m: Dudu Karakaya 4:36.07, Mar: Bahar Dogan 2:37:28, 3000mSt: Gülcan Mingir 11:25.60, 100mh: Ceren Nalbantoglu 14.52, 400mh: Nagihan Karadere 57.45, HJ: Candeger Oguz 1.86, PV: Songül Kiliç 3.50, LJ/TJ: Mukadder Ulusoy 6.09/13.76w, SP: Zeynep Uzun 14.21, DT: Ahu Sulak 52.27, HT: Zübeyde Yildiz 61.36, JT: Suzan Balkesen 42.07, Hep: Serpil Koçak 5043.

Halil AKKAS b. 1 Jul 1983 Kütahya 1.75m 60kg. Fenerbahce.
At 3000mSt (5000m): WCh: 05- h, '07- 6; EC: '06- (4); WJ: '02- 6; EU23: '03- 5, '05- 2; WUG: '05- 1, '07- 1 (1). At 1500m: WI: '06- 4; At 3000m: EI: '07- 4. European CC: '02- 3J, '05- 17.
TUR records 2000m 2007, 3000mSt (5) 2003-07.
Progress at 3000mSt: 2002- 8:50.17, 2003- 8:33.68, 2004- 8:40.90, 2005- 8:22.00, 2006- 9:08.75, 2007- 8:18.43. pbs: 1500m 3:39.48 '07, 2000m 5:01.29 '07, 3000m 7:45.74i '07, 7:54.60 '05; 5000m 13:28.39i '06, 13:46.53 '06.

Esref APAK b. 3 Jan 1982 Kalecik 1.86m 100kg. ENKA.
At HT: OG: '04- 3; WCh: '05- dnq 18, '07- 11; EC: '06- dnq 19; WJ: '00- 1; EU23: '03- 2; EJ: '01- 3; WUG: '05- 2; won Med G 2005, Turkish 2001-03.
20 Turkish hammer records 2000-05.
Progress at HT: 1999- 57.93, 2000- 69.97, 2001- 72.82, 2002- 73.24, 2003- 77.57, 2004- 81.27, 2005- 81.45, 2006- 79.80, 2007- 80.31.

Women

Elvan ABEYLEGESSE b. 11 Sep 1982 Addis Ababa, Ethiopia 1.59m 40kg. Enka.
At (1500m)/5000m: OG: '04- 8/12; WCh: '03- 5, '07- 5 (2 10,000m); EC: '02- 7, '06- 3 (dnf 10,000m); WJ: '00- 6/6; WY: '99- (5 3000m); EU23: '03- 1; EJ: '99- 2, '01- 1/1. At 10,000m: ECp: '06-07: 1/1. Won WAF 5000m 2003-04. World CC: '99- 9J; Eur CC: '00-01-02-03: 3J/1J/3/2.
World 5000m record 2004. Turkish records 2000m 2003, 3000m 2002, 10,000m 2006.
Progress at 1500m, 5000m, 10,000m: 1999- 4:24.1, 16:06.40; 2000- 4:18.7, 16:33.77; 2001- 4:11.31, 15:21.12, 33:29.20; 2002- 4:11.00, 15:00.49; 2003- 4:07.25, 14:53.56; 2004- 3:58.28, 14:24.68; 2005- 15:08.59; 2006- 4:11.61, 14:59.29, 30:21.67; 2007- 15:00.88, 31:25.15. pbs: 800m 2:07.10 '04, 2000m 5:33.83 '03, 3000m 8:31.94 '02.
Known as Hewan Abeye ETH, then as Elvan

Can on move to Turkey. In 2004 she became the first Turkish athlete to set a world record.

UGANDA

Governing body: Uganda Athletics Federation, PO Box 22726, Kampala. Founded 1925.

Abraham CHEPKIRWOK b. 18 Nov 1988 1.76m 62kg.
At 800m: WCh: '07- 4; WJ: '06- 3; AfG: '07- 5.
Progress at 800m: 2005- 1:50.1A, 2006- 1:45.0A, 2007- 1:44.78. pb 1000m 2:20.75 '07.

Boniface KIPROP b. 12 Oct 1985 Kapchorwa District 1.67m 53kg. Kalenjin.
At (5000m)/10,000m): OG: '04- 4; WCh: '03- (h), '05- 11/4, '07- 10; CG: '06- 1; WJ: '04- 5/1; AfG: '03- 6/4, '07- 6; Af-J: '01- 1/2, '03- 1/1; World CC: '00-02-03-04-05-06-08: 27J/3J/2J/2J/7/22/16.
World junior 10,000m record 2004. Ugandan records 3000m (4) 2002-06, 5000m (7) 2003-06, 10,000m (3) 2003-05.
Progress at 5000m, 10,000m: 2001- 14:06.93, 28:45.76; 2002-13:55.5, 2003- 13:16.21, 27:15.88; 2004- 13:05.47, 27:04.00; 2005- 12:58.43, 26:39.77; 2006- 12:57.11, 26:41.95; 2007- 13:07.46, 28:05.66. pb 3000m 7:40.58 '06.
World age 17 and 18 10,000m records 2003-04. Previously known as Boniface Toroitich Tirop. Brother Martin Toroitich (11 WJ CC 2002).

Moses KIPSIRO b. 2 Sep 1986 Chesimat 1.74m 59kg.
At 5000m(/10,000m): WCh: '05- h, '07- 3; CG: '06- 7; AfG: '07- 1; Af Ch: 3/1. World CC: '03-05-08: 18J/21J/13.
UGA records: 3000m (3) 2005-07, 5000m 2007.
Progress at 5000m: 2005- 13:13.81, 2006- 13:01.88, 2007- 12:50.72. pbs: 1500m 3:42.57 '05, 2000m 5:03.99+ '06, 3000m 7:32.03 '07, 10,000m 28:03.46 '07.

Women

Dorcus INZIKURU b. 2 Feb 1982 Veurra, Arua district 1.58m 49kg. Camelot, Italy.
At 3000mSt: WCh: '05- 1; CG: '06- 1. At 5000m: OG: '04- h; WCh: '03- h; WJ: '00- 1; CG: '02- 4; AfG: '99- 6, '03- 2; AfCh: '02- 2; won WAF 2005. At 3000m: WY: '99- 8. World CC: '00- 10J, '05- 18 4k.
Five African 3000mSt records 2003-05, three Commonwealth 2004-05; Ugandan 1M 2003, 3000m (3) 1999-2003, 5000m (4) 1999-2004, 3000mSt (6) 2003-05. Africa & Commonwealth 2000mSt record 2005.
Progress at 5000m, 3000mSt: 1998- 17:10.9, 1999- 16:05.5, 2000- 16:12.0, 2002- 15:18.01, 2003- 15:54.81, 9:39.51; 2004- 15:05.30, 9:29.30; 2005- 15:42.22, 9:15.04; 2006- 15:47.59, 9:19.51. pbs: 800m 2:03.00 '03, 1500m 4:14.90 '03, 1M 4:36.05 '03, 3000m 8:46.29 '03, HMar 74:01 '06, 2000mSt 6:04.46 '05 (world best).
Uganda's first World and Commonwealth champion. Her father Jackson Luluwa was a distance runner. Married to Martin Boscop Acidri, Italian doctor; daughter Emmanuella born 29 Ded 2007.

UKRAINE

Governing body: Ukrainian Athletic Federation, P.O. Box 607, Kiev 01019. Founded 1991.
National Champions 2007: **Men**: 100m/200m: Dmytro Hlushchenko 10.39/20.90, 400m: Oleksiy Rachkovskyy 47.09, 800m/1500m: Ivan Heshko 1:47.41/3:41.19, 5000m: Vasyl Matviychuk 14:08.28, 10,000m: Sergiy Lebid 28:24.56, Mar: Yuriy Hychun 2:18:56, 3000mSt: Vadym Slobodenyuk 8:38.43, 110mh: Sergiy Demydyuk 13.76, 400mh: Stanislav Melnykov 51.39, HJ: Viktor Shapoval 2.24, PV: Denys Yurchenko 5.65, LJ: Oleksiy Lukashevych 8.02, TJ: Mykola Savolaynen 17.02, SP: Yuriy Bilonog 20.20, DT: Stanislav Nesterovskyy 61.82, HT: Yevgen Vynogradov 76.51, JT: Oleg Statsenko 76.06, Dec: Mykola Shulha 7583, 20kW: Andriy Kovenko 1:22:52, 50kW:. **Women**: 100m/200m: Iryna Shtangyeyeva 11.50/23.28, 400m: Oksana Shcherbak 51.93, 800m: Yuliya Krevsun 1:59.60, 1500m: Iryna Lishchynska 4:11.73, 5000m: Tetyana Holovchenko 15:26.88, 10,000m: Nataliya Berkut 32:09.28, Mar: Tetyana Bulyshchenko 2:43:03, 3000mSt: Nataliya Tobias 9:49.42, 100mh: Yevgeniya Snigur 13.00, 400mh: Anastasiya Rabchenyuk 55.48, HJ: Vita Palamar 1.95, PV: Nataliya Kushch 4.35, LJ: Viktoriya Rybalko 6.76, TJ: Olga Saladuha 14.41, SP: Tetyana Nasonova 16.25, DT: Kateryna Karsak 64.02, HT: Nataliya Zolotuhina 69.24, JT: Tetyana Lyahovych 58.09, Hep: Lyudmyla Blonska 6733, 20kW: Vera Zozulya 1:30:02.

Yuriy BILONOG b. 9 Mar 1974 Belopol'ye 2.00m 135kg. Odessa Dyn & Sporting Clube de Portugal. Sports instructor.
At SP: OG: '00- 5, '04- 1; WCh: '97- 4, '99- 5, '01- 6, '03- 3 (dnq DT), '05- 4; EC: '98- 3, '02- 1, '06- 6; WI: '95-7-9-01-03-04: 5/1/3/8/3/8; WJ: '92- 1; WUG: '95- 1, '97- 1, '01- 2; WCp: '02- 5; ECp: '96-02-06: 3/1/5. 2nd GP 1998, 2002; 2nd overall 2000. Won UKR SP 1999, 2001, 2003, 2005-07; DT 2001, 2003, 2006.
UKR shot records 2000 & 2003.
Progress at SP: 1990- 15.60, 1991- 17.91, 1992- 19.02, 1993- 18.39, 1994- 18.72, 1995- 20.05, 1996- 21.20i/20.05, 1997- 21.02i/20.75, 1998- 20.92, 1999- 20.89i/20.65, 2000- 21.64, 2001- 20.98, 2002- 21.37, 2003- 21.81, 2004- 21.16, 2005- 20.93, 2006- 20.84, 2007- 20.20. pb DT 65.53 '03.
Mother-in-law Valentina Korsak: DT 63.92 '84.

Sergiy DEMIDYUK b. 5 Jun 1982 1.95m 80kg.
At 110mh: OG: '04- h; WCh: '05- 5, '07- 6; EC: '06- 8; EU23: '03- sf; WUG: '05- 3, '07- 1; ECp: '06- 4. UKR champion 2003-07. At 60mh: EI: '07- 5. Four UKR 110m hurdles records 2004-07.
Progress at 110mh: 2001- 14.19, 2002- 14.08/13.6, 2003- 13.92, 2004- 13.37, 2005- 13.38, 2006- 13.46, 2007- 13.22. pbs: 100m 10.70 '06, 60mh 7.53i '07.

Ivan HESHKO b. 19 Aug 1979 Klivodin, Kitsman region 1.80m 70kg. Kistman Dynamo.
At 1500m (/800m): OG: '00- h, '04- 5/sf; WCh: '03- 3, '05- 4, '07- h; EC: '02- h, '06- 2; WJ: '98- 11/h; EU23: '99- 4, '01- 2; WI: '03-04-06: 5/2/1; EI: '05- 1; WUG: '05- 1; WCp: '06- 2; ECp: '02- 5/8, '06- 2/1. Won WAF 1500m 2004-05, UKR 800m 2003, 2005, 2007; 1500m 2000-04, 2007.
UKR records: 1500m & 1M 2004, 2000m 2000.
Progress at 1500m: 1996- 3:54.94, 1997- 3:46.21, 1998- 3:43.56, 1999-3:42.33, 2000- 3:38.48, 2001- 3:37.10, 2002- 3:37.07, 2003- 3:32.01, 2004- 3:30.33, 2005- 3:31.91, 2006- 3:31.08, 2007- 3:35.03. pb 800m 1:45.41 '03, 1000m 2:19.04 '01, 1M 3:50.04 '04, 2000m 5:03.91 '00, 3000m 7:52.33 '01.

Yuriy KRYMARENKO b. 11 Aug 1983 Berdychiv 1.87m 65kg.
At HJ: WCh: '05- 1, '07- dnq 21=; EU23: '05- 3; WUG: '05- 6=. UKR champion 2005.
Progress at HJ: 2000- 2.05, 2001- 2.15, 2002- 2.15, 2003- 2.22, 2004- 2.23, 2005- 2.33, 2006- 2.31i/2.20, 2007- 2.34i/2.27.

Sergiy LEBID b. 15 Jul 1975 Pridneprovsk 1.80m 65kg. Donetsk ZS. Based in Italy.
At 5000m (10,000m): OG: '00- 7, 04- h; WCh: '99/01/05- h; EC: '98- 15, '02- 3, '06 (5); WUG: '99- 1, '01- 1, '03- 1; EU23: '97- 7 (2). At 3000m: EI: '98- 5; WCp: '02- 7. World CC: '00-01-05: 8/2/14; 4k: '01- 10; Eur CC: '95-7-8-9-00-01-02-03-04-05-06-07: 11/3/1/7/2/1/1/1/1/1/11/1. Won UKR 1500m 1998, 2005; 5000m 1995-6, 1999-2001, 2003-04; 10,000m 2003, 2007.
UKR records 3000m (3) 1998-2002, 5000m (4) 1999-2002, HMar (2) 2001-03.
Progress at 5000m: 1993- 14:23.54, 1994- 14:11.27, 1995- 13:52.39, 1996- 13:39.31, 1997- 13:50.51, 1998- 13:30.23, 1999- 13:18.18, 2000- 13:27.53, 2001- 13:14.51, 2002- 13:10.78, 2003- 13:15.15, 2004- 13:13.03, 2005- 13:12.35, 2006- 13:36.92. pbs: 1500m 3:38.44 '05, 3000m 7:35.06 '02, 2M 8:21.57i '01, 10,000m 28:09.71 '06, 10km Rd 27:58 '07, HMar 61:49 '03.
Has run in all 15 European CC Championships with a record 7wins. Married Olena Gorodnichova (1500m 4:05.78 '99) on 23 April 2003.

Oleksiy LUKASHEVICH b. 11 Jan 1977 Dnepropetrovsk 1.75m 72kg. Dnepropetrovsk Dyn.
At LJ: OG: '00- 4, '04- dnq; WCh: '97/99/03: dnq 16/22/17, '01- 6, '07- 4; EC: '98- dnq 20, '02- 1, '06- 3; WJ: '96- 1; EU23: '97- 3; EI: '98-00-02: 1/4/4; WUG: '99- 1; WCp: '02- 7; ECp: '06- 4. 3rd GP 2001. UKR champion 1996, 2000, 2006-07.
Progress at LJ: 1994- 7.68, 1995- 7.57, 1996- 7.91/8.10w, 1997- 7.95/8.09w, 1998- 8.06i/8.03, 1999- 8.16/8.17w, 2000- 8.27, 2001- 8.20, 2002- 8.26, 2003- 8.19, 2004- 7.97i/7.92, 2005- 8.01i/7.95, 2006- 8.17, 2007- 8.25.

Maksym MAZURYK b. 2 Apr 1983 Donetsk 1.90m 85kg.
At PV: WCh: '07- 11; EC: '06- 8; WJ: '02- 1; EU23: '03- 3, '05- 6.
Progress at PV: 1999- 4.49i, 2000- 4.90, 2001- 5.00, 2002- 5.55, 2003- 5.50i/5.45, 2004- 5.75, 2005- 5.65, 2006- 5.70, 2007- 5.76, 2008- 5.81i.

Andriy SOKOLOVSKYY b. 16 Jul 1978 Moskva, Russia 1.96m 80kg. Vinnista Dyn. Sports instructor.
At HJ: OG: '00- dnq 16=, '04- 5; WCh: '99/01- dnq 27=/21=, '03- 8, '05- 13; EC: '06- dnq 19=; WI: '99-01-03-04-06: 6=/2/8/7/6; EU23: '99- 2; EI: '02- 4; ECp: '02- 4. UKR champion 2000-01, 2003-04, 2006.
Progress at HJ: 1997- 2.10, 1998- 2.22, 1999- 2.32, 2000- 2.28, 2001- 2.35i/2.34, 2002- 2.36, 2003- 2.33, 2004- 2.35, 2005- 2.38, 2006- 2.36i/2.28, 2007- 2.35i/2.30.

Denys YURCHENKO b. 27 Jan 1978 Donetsk 1.74m 74kg. Donetsk Dyn.
At PV: OG: '00- dnq, '04- 9=; WCh: '03- 6=, '05- dnq 17=, '07- 12; EC: '02- 6=, '06- dnq; EJ: '97- nh; WI: '03- 3, '06- nh; EI: '05- 2, '07- 2; ECp: '02- 2=. Won UKR 2000, 2002-03, 2006-07.
Progress at PV: 1997- 5.20, 1998- 5.50, 1999- 5.59, 2000- 5.72, 2001- 5.70i/5.65/5.71ex, 2002- 5.75, 2003- 5.81, 2004- 5.75i/5.70/5.75ex, 2005- 5.85i/5.75, 2006- 5.70, 2007- 5.72.

Women

Olena ANTONOVA b. 16 Jun 1972 Nikopol 1.82m 95kg. Dnepropetrovsk U.
At DT: OG: '96/00- dnq 29/13, '04- 5; WCh: '97- dnq 13, '99- 7, '01- dnq 16, '03- 4, '05- 8, '07- 6; EC: '98- 11; EJ: '91- 3; WUG: '97- 4; ECp: '97-8-00-05-06: 3/3/6/2/6. UKR champion 1995-2005.
Progress at DT: 1989- 55.84, 1990- 57.30, 1991- 57.12, 1992- 61.94, 1993- 58.34, 1994- 59.80, 1995- 61.54, 1996- 63.60, 1997- 61.62, 1998- 65.44, 1999- 64.32, 2000- 66.67, 2001- 64.20, 2002- 63.40, 2003- 65.90, 2004- 67.30, 2005- 65.89, 2006- 62.83, 2007- 62.41. pb HT 56.28 '95.

Lyudmyla BLONSKA b. 9 Nov 1977 1.75m 62kg. née Shevchuk.
At Hep: WCh: '07- 2; EC: '02- 13, '06- 5; WUG: '05- 1; UKR champion 2007. At Pen: WI: '06- 1, '08- 8. Two UKR heptathlon records 2007.
Progress at Hep: 1997- 4809, 1998- 5590, 1999- 5765, 2000- 5592, 2002- 6039, 2003- 6316/6425 dq, 2005- 6378, 2006- 6448, 2007- 6832. pbs: 200m 23.80 '07, 800m 2:12.18 '07, 60mh 8.26i '08, 100mh 13.13 '07, HJ 1.92 '07, LJ 6.88 '07, SP 14.77 '07, JT 51.53 '07, Pen 4685i '06.
Two-year drugs ban from 8 June 2003. Set HJ and LJ pbs en route to World silver in 2007. Won at Talence and the IAAF Combined Events Challenge 2007. Coached by husband Sergiy.

Nataliya DOBRYNSKA b. 29 May 1982 Khmelnitsky 1.82m 77kg. Vinnitsa K.
At Hep: OG: '04- 8; WCh: '05- 9, '07- 8; EC: '06- 6; EU23: '03- 5; EJ: '01- 10. At Pen: WI: '04- 2, '08- 4; EI: '05- 3, '07- 5.

Progress at Hep: 1999- 5226, 2000- 5322, 2001- 5742, 2002- 5936, 2003- 5877, 2004- 6387, 2005- 6299, 2006- 6356, 2007- 6327. pbs: 100m 11.60/11.2 '95, 200m 24.84 '05, 24.61w '04; 800m 2:15.38 '04, 60mh 8.39i '06, 100mh 13.66 '06, HJ 1.86 '06, LJ 6.56 '06, SP 17.18i '08, 16.31 '07; JT 47.24 '04, Pen 4758i '08.
Four pbs en route to UKR pentathlon record 4727 and WI silver medal 2004.

Iryna LISHCHYNSKA b. 15 Jan 1976 Makeevka 1.65m 53kg. née Nedelenko. Donetsk U.
At 800m: WCh: '99- h; EC: '98- h; WUG: '97- 1; EU23: '97- 1; ECp: '97- 2, '98- 2. At 1500m: OG: '04- h; WCh: '03- sf, '07- 3; EC: '02- 10, '06- 8; WJ: '94- 6; WI: '03- 5; ECp: '02- 5. Won UKR 800m 1999, 1500m 2001-02, 2004, 2007.
Progress at 800m, 1500m: 1993- 2:07.04, 1994- 2:02.6, 1996- 2:05.03, 1997- 2:00.16, 1998- 1:59.15, 1999- 2:00.01, 2001- 2:03.36, 4:05.38; 2002- 2:00.45, 4:03.78; 2003- 2:01.22, 4:02.60; 2004- 2:01.99, 4:03.74; 2005- 2:07.43i, 4:14.71i; 2006- 1:59.97, 4:00.04; 2007- 4:00.69. pbs: 400m 53.88 '98, 1M 4:28.31 '02, 3000m 9:04.24i '03, 5000m 16:57.15 '07.

Viktoriya PALAMAR b. 12 Oct 1977 1.87m 66kg. Kyiv ZS.
At HJ: OG: '00- 7; WCh: '01- 5, '03- 5, '05- 5, '07- 7=; WJ: '96- 6=; WI: '01-03-08: 5=/4/3; EI: '00- 5; WUG: '01- 1; ECp: '05- 2. UKR champion 2001, 2007.
Progress at HJ: 1992-, 1993- 1.83, 1994- 1.91, 1995- 1.88, 1996- 1.89, 1997- 1.88, 1998- 1.89, 1999- 1.93, 2000- 1.98, 2001- 1.99, 2002- 1.95, 2003- 2.01, 2004- 2.00i/1.94, 2005- 1.95, 2007- 2.00, 2008- 2.01i.

Tetyana PETLYUK b. 22 Feb 1982 Kiev 1.74m 60kg. Student at Sports University of Kiev.
At 800m: OG: '04- sf; WCh: '05/07- sf; EC: '06- 4; WJ: '00- 6; WY: '99- 2; EU23: '03- 7; EJ: '01- 3; WI: '08- 2; EI: '07- 2; ECp: '04- 7, '06- dnf; UKR champion 2004, 2006.
Progress at 800m: 1999- 2:06.97, 2000- 2:04.74, 2001- 2:03.07, 2002- 2:02.41, 2003- 2:02.45, 2004- 1:59.48, 2005- 2:01.78, 2006- 1:57.34, 2007- 1:58.67i/1:59.85, 2008- 1:59.58i. pbs: 400m 53.26 '04, 1000m 2:34.76i '07.

Olga SALADUHA b. 4 Jun 1983 Donetsk 1.75m 55kg.
At TJ: WCh: '07- 7; EC: '06- 4; WJ: '02- 5; EC: '06- 4; EU23: '05- 4; EJ: '01- 9; WI: '08- 6; WUG: '05- 2, '07- 1; WCp: '06- 6; ECp: '06- 1, '07- 4. UKR champion 2007.
Progress at TJ: 1999- 12.86, 2000- 13.26, 2001- 13.48, 2002- 13.66i/13.63, 2003- 13.26i/13.03, 2004- 13.22, 2005- 14.04, 2006- 14.41/14.50w, 2007- 14.79. pb LJ 6.37 '06.

Irina SEKACHOVA b. 21 Jul 1976 Vasil'kov 1.65m 72kg. Vasil'kov Dyn.
At HT: OG: '00- dnq 16, '04- 8; WCh: '03- dnq 23, '05- 6; EC: '98- dnq, 02- dnq 14, '06- 8; ECp: '00-02-04-06-07: 7/3/1/3/8. UKR champion 1996, 2000-06.
Eight Ukraine hammer records 1998-2006.
Progress at HT: 1995- 53.64, 1996- 55.42, 1997- 56.46, 1998- 62.83, 1999- 65.93, 2000- 69.53, 2001- 67.00, 2002- 68.70, 2003- 72.96, 2004- 74.16, 2005- 70.30, 2006- 74.31, 2007- 71.83.

Tetyana TERESHCHUK-Antipova. b. 11 Oct 1969 Lugansk 1.85m 63kg. Kyiv Dyn.
At 400mh: OG: '96- sf, '00- 5, '04- 3; WCh: '95- 5, '97- 4, '99- 7, '03- 5, '05- 7, '07- sf; EC: '94- 6, '98- 2, '06- 3; WUG: '97- 1; WCp: '06- 4; ECp: '94-5-6-8-00-06: 2/3/4/1/1/3. Won GWG 2001, 3rd/2nd GP 1997/2000. UKR champion 1994, 1996, 1999, 2001.
Seven UKR 400mh records 1997-04.
Progress at 400mh: 1989- 57.58, 1990- 57.98, 1991- 57.19, 1993- 58.20/57.9, 1994- 54.96, 1995- 54.88, 1996- 54.68, 1997- 53.64, 1998- 53.40, 1999- 53.46, 2000- 53.98, 2001- 53.89A/54.01, 2002- 54.28A, 2003- 54.26, 2004- 53.37, 2005- 55.09, 2006- 54.12, 2007- 54.38. pbs: 200m 24.03 '97, 100mh 12.8 '95, 13.12A '98, 13.14 '97.
Set UKR 400mh records in four successive races in 12 days in 1997: World semi and final, then Zürich and Monaco. Missed 2001 Worlds & 2002 Europeans through injury. Fifth UKR record in Olympic semi 2004.

Antonina YEFREMOVA b. 19 Jul 1981 1.76m 61kg. Donetsk Dyn. Business student at Donetsk Academy.
At 400m: OG: '04- sf; WCh: '03- sf, '05- h; EC: '02- 6; WJ: '00- sf; EU23: '01- 1 (2 4x100mR); WI: '09- 4; WCp: '02- 5R; ECp: '02-04-05: 1/2&2R/2&3R; WUG: '05- 3R. UKR champion 2002-05.
Progress at 400m- 1999- 54.85, 2000- 51.95, 2001- 52.29, 2002- 50.70, 2003- 51.36, 2004- 50.74, 2005- 51.40, 2007- 52.09, 2008- 51.53i. pb 200m 23.4 '03.

UNITED KINGDOM

Governing body: UK Athletics, Athletics House, Central Boulevard, Blythe Valley Park, Solihull. West Midlands B90 8AJ. Founded 1999 (replacing British Athletics, founded 1991, which succeeded BAAB, founded 1932). The Amateur Athletic Association was founded in 1880 and the Women's Amateur Athletic Association in 1922.

National Championships (first were English Championships 1866-79, then AAA 1880-2006, WAAA from 1922). **2007 UK Champions**: **Men**: 100m/200m: Marlon Devonish 10.31/20.79, 400m: Andrew Steele 45.70, 800m: Michael Rimmer 1:47.06, 1500m: Andrew Baddeley 3:43.25, 5000m: Mohamed Farah 13:40.19, 10,000m: Peter Nicholls 28:40.05, HMar: Philip Wicks 64:43, Mar: Dan Robinson 2:14:14, 3000mSt: Andrew Lemoncello 8:42.57, 110mh: Andrew Turner 13.54, 400mh: Dale Garland 49.79, HJ: Martyn Bernard 2.24, PV: Steve Lewis 5.61, LJ: Chris Tomlinson 7.99, TJ: Tosin Oke 16.59, SP: Carl Myerscough 19.39, DT: Emeka Udechuku 60.83, HT: Andy Frost

71.02, JT: Nick Nieland 73.95, Dec: Ben Hazell 7508, 5000mW: Dominic King 20:57.90. **Women**: 100m/200m: Jeanette Kwakye 11.59/23.66, 400m: Nicola Sanders 51.33, 800m: Jemma Simpson 2:00.91, 1500m: Katrina Wootton 4:09.57, 5000m/10,000m: Joanne Pavey 15:17.77/31:26.94, HMar: Liz Yelling 70:46, Mar: Mara Yamauchi 2:25:41, 3000mSt: Helen Clitheroe 9:47.49, 100mh/HT: Jessica Ennis 13.25/1.87, 400mh: Natasha Danvers-Smith 55.43, PV: Kate Dennison 4.20, LJ: Kelly Sotherton 6.53, TJ: Nadia Williams 13.58, SP: Eva Massey 16.63, DT: Philippa Roles 57.83, HT: Zoe Derham 64.99, JT: Goldie Sayers 63.02, Hep: Phyllis Agbo 5471, 5000mW: Johanna Jackson 22:03.65. **National Road Walk Champions**: Men: 20kW: Andrew Penn 1:35:24. 50kW: Scott Davis 4:35:39; Women 10kW/20kW: Johanna Jackson 47:49/1:38:34.

Andrew BADDELEY b. 20 June 1982 Upton, Wirral 1.86m 70k. Harrow, Graduated in aerospace engineering at Cambridge University.
At 1500m: WCh: '07- 9; EC: '06- 6; CG: '06- 12; WUG: '05- 2; ECp: '06- 6, '07- 2. Won AAA/UK 2006-07.
Progress at 1500m: 1998- 4:01.5, 1999- 3:52.79, 2000- 3:46.36, 2001- 3:52.15, 2002- 3:45.96, 2003- 3:45.87, 2004- 3:39.11, 2005- 3:36.43, 2006- 3:36.52, 2007- 3:34.74. pbs: 800m 1:46.32 '07, 1000m 2:16.99 '07, 1M 3:51.95 '07, 3000m 7:45.10i '08, 7:54.74 '07; 5000m 14:12.15 '05.

Dwain CHAMBERS b. 5 Apr 1978 London 1.80m 83kg. Belgrave H.
At 100m/4x100mR: OG: '00- 4; WCh: '97- resR, '99- 3/2R, '01- 4 (qf 200m), '03- dq (4/2R); EC: '98- 2/res 1R, '02- dq (1/1R). '06- 7/1R; CG: '98- sf/1R, '02- 8; WJ: '96- 5; EJ: '95 & '97- 1/1R; WCp: '98- 3/1R, '02- dq (5), '06- 2R; ECp: '99-00-02-06: 1/1R/dq (1&1R)/2. Won AAA 2000-1, 2003; GWG 2001. At 60m: WI: '08- 2=.
World junior 100m record 1997, European 100m record 2002.
Progression at 100m: 1994- 10.75/10.56w, 1995- 10.41, 1996- 10.42, 1997- 10.06, 1998- 10.03rA/10.10, 1999- 9.97, 2000- 10.08, 2001- 9.99/9.97w?, 2002- 9.87 dq, 2003- 10.03/10.0 dq, 2006- 10.07. pbs: 50m 5.57+ '99, 60m 6.41+ '99, 6.54i '08; 200m 20.31 '01, 20.27dq '02.
Positive test for tetrahydrogestrinome (THG) 1 Aug 2003 which resulted in a two-year ban. He also admitted to drug taking in 2002 and as a result all his results from 1 Jan 2002 were annulled, including his European title and record for 100m. Older sister Christine Chambers (b. 4 Mar 1969) was 8th at 100m at 1987 European Juniors. pbs: 60m 7.46i '92, 100m 11.84 '87, 11.68w '92.

Marlon DEVONISH b. 1 Jun 1976 Coventry 1.83m 76kg. Coventry Godiva.
At 200m/4x100mR (100m): OG: '00- hR, '04- 1R; WCh: '97- (qf), '99- sf/2R, '01- 8, '03- dq R(2), '05- sf/3R (sf), 07- (6)/3R; EC: '98- res 1R (5), '02- 3/dq (1)R; CG: '98- 1R (8), '02- 2/1R, '06- sf (8); WJ: '94- res 1R; EJ: '95- 1/1R; EU23: '97- 1R (3); WI: '03- 1; WCp: '98- 1R, '02- 3, '06- 2R; ECp: '97-9-00-01-02-03-05-06: 3R/1R/1R/2&2R/1&dq(1)R/3R/1R/3R/1&1R. Won AAA 100m 2006, 200m 1997, 2001-02, 2006; UK 100m & 200m 2007.
Progress at 100m, 200m: 1992, 11.1, 1993- 10.84/10.66w, 21.94/21.8w; 1994- 10.57/10.52w, 21.25/21.20w; 1995- 10.55/10.44w, 20.94/20.88w; 1996- 10.41, 20.86; 1997- 10.22/10.13w, 20.65/20.61w; 1998- 10.13, 20.92; 1999- 10.17, 20.25; 2000- 10.27, 20.59; 2001- 10.30/10.29w, 20.29; 2002- 10.32/10.30w, 20.19/20.18w; 2003- 10.56, 20.50; 2004- 10.32/10.28w, 20.70; 2005- 10.13, 20.41/20.34w; 2006- 10.16, 20.53/20.49w; 2007- 10.06, 20.33. pbs: 60m 6.71i '00, 400m 46.83 '00.

Nathan DOUGLAS b. 4 Dec 1982 Oxford 1.83m 72kg. Oxford City. Sports science graduate of Loughborough University.
At TJ: OG: '04- dnq 13; WCh: '05- dnq 15; EC: '06- 2; WI: '06- 7; EI: '05- 4, '07- 2; ECp: '05- 5, '06- 4. Won AAA 2004-05.
Progress at TJ: 1999- 14.31, 2000- 15.18, 2001- 15.50, 2002- 15.69/16.13w, 2003- 16.30, 2004- 16.95, 2005- 17.64, 2006- 17.42, 2007- 17.47i/17.18. pbs: 60m 6.9i '02, 100m 10.74w '03, 10.7/10.6w '02; LJ 7.40 '02.

Mohamed FARAH b. 23 March 1983 Mogadishu, Somalia 1.75m 65kg. Newham & Essex Beagles.
At 5000m: WCh: '07- 6; EC: '06- 2; CG: '06- 9; WJ: '00- 10; WY: '99- 6; EJ: '01- 1; EU23: '03 & '05- 2. At 3000m: WI: '08- 6; EI: '05- 6, '07- 5; ECp: '05-06: 2/2. World CC: '07- 11; Eur CC: '99-00-01-04-05-06: 5J/7J/2J/15/21/1. Won UK 5000m 2007.
Progress at 5000m: 2000- 14:05.72, 2001- 13:56.31, 2002- 14:00.5, 2003- 13:38.41, 2004- c.14:25, 2005- 13:30.53, 2006- 13:09.40, 2007- 13:07.00. pbs: 800m 1:48.69 '03, 1500m 3:38.02 '06, 1M 3:56.49 '05, 2000m 5:06.34 '06, 3000m 7:38.15 '06, 2M 8:20.47 '07, 2000mSt 5:55.72 '00; road: 10km 28:37 '06, 10M 48:59 '05.
Joined his father in England in 1993.

Phillips IDOWU b. 30 Dec 1978 Hackney, London 1.92m 89kg. Belgrave H.
At TJ: OG: '00- 6, '04- nj; WCh: '01- 9, '07- 6; EC: '02- 5, '06- 5; CG: '02- 2, '06- 1; EU23: '99-5; EJ: '97- 4; WI: '08- 1; EI: '07- 1; ECp: '04- 3, '07- 2. Won AAA 2000, 2002, 2006.
Progress at TJ: 1995- 13.90, 1996- 15.12/15.53w, 1997- 15.86/16.34w, 1998- 16.35, 1999- 16.41, 2000- 17.12, 2001- 17.33/17.38w, 2002- 17.68, 2004- 17.47, 2005- 17.30i/16.96; 2006- 17.50, 2007- 17.56i/17.35, 2008- 17.75i. pbs: 60m 6.81i '04, 100m 10.60 '06, LJ 7.83 '00.

Mark LEWIS-FRANCIS b. 4 Sep 1982 Birmingham 1.83m 85kg. Birchfield H.
At 100m/4x100mR: OG: '04- sf/1R; WCh: '01- sf, '03- sf, '05- qf/3R, '07- sf/3R; EC: '06- 5/1R;

CG: '02- 7, '06- sf; WJ: '00- 1/1R; WY: '99- 1; EJ: '99- 2, '01- 1/1R; WCp: '06- 2R; ECp: '01-03-04-05-07: 1&2R/1/dq&1R/2&1R/1R. At 60m: WI: '01- 3, '03- 4; EI: '02- 2, '05- dq 2. Won AAA 100m 2002.
World junior record 60m indoors 2001.
Progress at 100m: 1996- 11.37/11.31w, 1997- 10.93, 1998- 10.49/10.36w, 1999- 10.31/10.26w, 2000- 10.10, 2001- 10.12/9.97w?, 2002- 10.04/9.97w, 2003- 10.07, 2004- 10.12, 2005- 10.13/10.10w, 2006- 10.16/10.13w, 2007- 10.17. pbs: 50m 5.73i '02, 60m 6.51i '01, 200m 20.94 '02, 20.78w '05.

Craig PICKERING b. 16 October 1986 Sussex 1.81m 82kg. Marshall Milton Keynes.
At 100m/4x100mR: WCh: '07- sf/3R; WY: '03- 3; EU23: '07- 2; EJ: '05- 1; ECp: '07- 1/1R. At 60m: EI: '07- 2.
Progress at 100m: 2001- 11.12/11.00w, 2002- 10.70, 2003- 10.53, 2004- 10.41, 2005- 10.22, 2006- 10.34, 2007- 10.14. pbs: 60m 6.55i '07, 200m 21.34 '04, 21.17w '07.

Greg RUTHERFORD b. 17 Nov 1986 Milton Keynes 1.88m 84kg. Marshall Milton Keynes.
At LJ: WCh: '07- dnq 21; EC: '06- 2; CG: '06- 8; EJ: '05- 1; ECp: '06- 9. Won AAA 2005-06.
Progress at LJ: 1999- 5.04, 2001- 6.16, 2003- 7.04, 2004- 7.28, 2005- 8.14, 2006- 8.26, 2007- 7.96. pbs: 60m 6.80i '05, 100m 10.38 '05.
His great-grandfather Jock Rutherford played 11 internationals for England at football 1904-08.

Chris TOMLINSON b. 15 Sep 1981 Middlesbrough 1.97m 81kg. Newham & Essex Beagles.
At LJ: OG: '04- 5; WCh: '03- 9, '05/07- dnq 14/16; EC: '02- 6, '06- 9; CG: '02- 6, '06- 6; WJ: '00- 12; WI: '04- 6, '08- 2; EI: '07- 5; WCp: '02- 6; ECp: '01-02-03-04: 2/1/5/1; AAA champion 2004.
British long jump records 2002 and 2007.
Progress at LJ: 1996- 5.91/6.09w, 1997- 6.82w/6.44, 1998- 7.23i, 1999- 7.44i/7.40, 2000- 7.62, 2001- 7.75, 2002- 8.27, 2003- 8.16, 2004- 8.25/8.28w, 2005- 7.95i/7.82/7.83w, 2006- 8.09, 2007- 8.29, 2008- 8.18i. pbs: 100m 10.69 '02, 10.61w/10.6 '01; 200m 21.73 '02, TJ 15.35 '01.
Jumped 8.27 at Tallahassee in April 2002, from a previous best of 7.87 (and 8.19w), to break the 34-year-old British record set by Lynn Davies.

Women

Natasha DANVERS-SMITH b. 19 Sep 1977 London 1.75m 61kg. Shaftesbury Barnet. Was at University of Southern California, USA. Married her coach Darrel Smith Jnr on 1 November 2003.
At 400mh/4x400mR: OG: '00- 8; WCh: '99/01- h, '03- sf, '07- 8; CG: '02- 7, '06- 2; EC: '98: h/3R res, '02- 7, '06- 7; CG: '98- 5; EU23: '99- 1; ECp: '00-01-02-03: 3R/8/3/2; WUG: '99- 5/3R, '01- 1/2R; AAA 1998, 2002, 2006; UK 2007; NCAA 2000. At 100mh: WJ: '96- 6; EJ: '95- 2; ECp: '03- 7.
Progression at 400mh: 1993- 66.9, 1997- 56.84, 1998- 55.69, 1999- 55.75, 2000- 54.95, 2001- 54.94, 2002- 55.68, 2003- 54.02, 2005- 57.47, 2006- 54.82, 2007- 54.08. pbs: 200m 24.99 '00, 300m 37.80 '00, 400m 53.26 '98, 800m 2:06.25 '08, 60mh 8.32i '96, 100mh 12.96 '03, 12.8w '99; HJ 1.82 '98.
Son Jaden born in December 2004.

Jessica ENNIS b. 28 Jan 1986 Sheffield 1.64m 57kg. Sheffield. Studying psychology at University of Sheffield.
At Hep: WCh: '07- 4; EC: '06- 8; CG: '06- 3; WJ: '04- 8; WY: '03- 5; EJ: '05- 1; WUG: '05- 3; ECp: '06- 4, '07- 1. At Pen: EI: '07- 6. At 100mh: EU23: '07- 3. Won UK 100mh & HJ 2007.
UK high jump record 2007.
Progress at Hep: 2001- 4801, 2002- 5194, 2003- 5116, 2004- 5542, 2005- 5910, 2006- 6287, 2007- 6469. pbs: 60m 7.47i '07, 100m 12.0 '05, 200m 23.15 '07, 800m 2:10.91 '07, 60mh 8.18i '07, 100mh 12.97 '07, HJ 1.95 '07, LJ 6.40/6.54w '07, SP 13.28i/12.89 '07, JT 38.07 '07, Hep 4716i '07.
Set four pbs in adding 359 points to best score for third at 2006 Commonwealth Games.

Jeanette KWAKYE b. 20 Mar 1983 1.62m 52kg. Woodford Green with Essex Ladies. Studied politics at Loughborough University.
At 100m/4x400m: WCh: '07- qf; WJ: '02- sf/3R; EU23: '03- 7. At 60m: WI: '08- 2; EI: '07- 4.
Progress at 100m: 1997- 12.11, 1998- 12.11/11.93w/11.8w, 2000- 12.10, 2001- 12.03/11.88w, 2002- 11.70, 2003- 11.54, 2004- 11.57/11.44w, 2005- 11.58, 2006- 11.44, 2007- 11.26/11.24w. pbs: 60m 7.08i '08, 200m 23.11 '07.

Rebecca LYNE b. 4 Jul 1982 Sheffield 1.73m 52kg. Hallamshire Harriers.
At 800m: CG: '02- h; EC: '06- 3; EU23: '03- 1; WUG: '05- 9; WJ: '00- h; EJ: '01- 4; WCp: '06- 4; ECp: '06- 8. Won AAA 2006.
Progress at 800m: 1997- 2:15.52, 1998- 2:14.63, 1999- 2:07.29, 2000- 2:05.27, 2001- 2:05.05, 2002- 2:02.45, 2003- 2:01.76, 2004- 2:01.26, 2005- 2:01.98, 2006- 1:58.20, 2007- 2:00.86. pbs: 400m 54.9 '05, 55.38 '01; 1000m 2:48.84i '03, 1500m 4:06.85 '06.

Christine OHURUOGU b. 17 May 1984 Forest Gate, London 1.75m 70kg. Newham & Essex Beagles. Studied linguistics at University College, London.
At 400m: OG: '04- sf/4R; WCh: '05- sf/3R, '07- 1/3R; CG: '06- 1; EU23: '05- 2/2R; EJ: '03- 3; Won AAA 400m 2004.
Progress at 400m: 2001- 55.29, 2003- 54.21, 2004- 50.50, 2005- 50.73, 2006- 50.28, 2007- 49.61. pbs: 60m 7.39i '06, 100m 11.90i '06, 200m 23.40 '04.
Played for England U17 and U19 at netball. Withdrawn from GB European Champs team in 2006 after missing three drugs tests, receiving a one-year ban.

Joanne PAVEY b. 20 Sep 1973 Honiton 1.62m 51kg. née Davis. Bristol.
At 5000m (10,000m): OG: '00- 12, '04- 5 (h

1500m); WCh: '05- 15, '07- 9 (4); EC: '02- 5, '06- 4; CG: '02- 5, '06- 2; WCp: '02- 3; ECp: '02-03: 2/2, '07- (4). At 3000m: WI: '04- 5; EI: '07- 6. At 1500m: WCh: '97- sf, '03- 10. Eur CC: '04-3, '06-8. Won UK 1500m 1997, AAA 5000m 2001, 2006; UK 5000m & 10,000m 2007.
2 Commonwealth indoor 3000m records 2004-07.
Progress at 1500m, 3000m, 5000m, 10,000m: 1988- 4:27.9, 1989- 4:30.91, 1990- 4:26.7, 1993-9:56.1, 1994-4:23.36, 1995- 4:28.46, 1996- 4:21.14, 9:37.6; 1997- 4:07.28, 9:05.87; 1998- 8:58.2, 2000-8:36.70, 14:58.27; 2001- 8:36.58, 15:00.56; 2002-4:11.16, 8:31.27, 14:48.66; 2003- 4:01.79, 8:37.89, 15:09.04; 2004- 4:12.50, 8:34.55i/8:40.22, 14:49.11; 2005- 4:16.3i, 8:33.79, 14:40.71; 2006- 4:05.91, 8:38.80, 14:39.96; 2007- 8:31.50i/8:44.13, 15:04.77, 31:26.94. pbs: 800m 2:09.68 '90, 1M 4:30.77 '97, 2000m 5:41.2i '07, 5:41.6 '05; 2M 9:32.00i '07, Road: 10M 52:46 '06, HMar 70:40 '08.
Set a British under-15 record at 1500m with 4:27.9 in 1988 and won four national titles at U15/U17 level, but did not compete much in the early 1990s, also missing two years through injury 1998-2000. Married to middle-distance runner Gavin Pavey.

Paula RADCLIFFE b. 17 Dec 1973 Northwich 1.73m 54kg. Bedford & County. Degree in European languages from Loughborough University.
At 10,000m (Mar): OG: '00- 4, '04- dnf (dnf); WCh: '99- 2, '01- 4, '05- 9 (1); EC: '98- 5, '02- 1; At 5000m: OG: '96- 5; WCh: '95- 5, '97- 4; CG: '02- 1; ECp: '98-9-01-04: 1/1/2/1 (2 1500m '98); 3rd GP 1997. At 3000m: WCh: '93- 7; WJ: '92- 4; EJ: '91-4; ECp: '97- 3. World HMar: '00-01-03: 1/1/1; CC: '91- 15J, '92- 1J, '93-5-6-7-8-9-00-01-02: 18/18/19/2/2/3/5 (4 4k)/1 (2 4k)/1. Eur CC: '98- 1, '03- 1. Won AAA 5000m 1996, 2000; Mar 2002-03; UK 5000m 1997, CC 1994-5.
Records: World marathon 2002 & 2003; half marathon 2003; Commonwealth & UK 1998-2004: 3000m (3), 5000m (4), 10,000m (5); UK 5000m (6) 1996-2004. European 10,000m 2002, HMar 2000 & 2001, Marathon 2002.
Progress at 1500m, 3000m, 5000m, 10,000m, Mar: 1988- 4:41.0, 1989- 4:34.9, 1990- 4:31.3, 9:41.4; 1991- 4:23.68, 9:23.29; 1992- 4:16.82, 8:51.78, 16:16.77i; 1993- 4:11.6, 8:40.40; 1994- 4:23.84, 1995- 4:06.84, 8:40.82, 14:49.27; 1996- 4:08.42, 8:37.07, 14:46.76; 1997- 4:06.93, 8:35.28, 14:45.51; 1998- 4:05.81, 8:38.84, 14:51.27, 30:48.58; 1999-4:06.71, 8:27.40, 14:43.54, 30:27.13; 2000- 4:11.45, 8:28.85, 14:44.36, 30:26.97; 2001- 4:05.37, 8:26.97, 14:32.44, 30:55.80; 2002- 8:22.20, 14:31.42, 30:01.09, 2:17:18; 2003- 2:15:25, 2004- 8:39.08+, 14:29.11, 30:17.15, 2:23:10; 2005- 4:13.13, 8:50.18, 15:16.29+, 30:42.75, 2:17:42; 2007- 2:23:09. pbs: 400m 58.9 '92, 800m 2:05.22 '95, 1000m 2:47.17 '93, 1M 4:24.94 '96, 2000m 5:37.1 '02, 2M 9:17.4e '04; Road: 15km 46:41 '03, 10M 50:01 '03, HMar 65:40 '03, 30km 1:36:36 '03, 20M 1:43:33 '03.
Has 7 wins in 8 marathons inc London 2002-03, 2005, Chicago 2003, New York 2004, 2007. In 2002 she won at London in 2:18:56, the fastest women's debut by over four minutes and beating the women's only world record by over three minutes, then improved the world record by 1:29 with 2:17:18 in Chicago. In 2003 she ran a world 10km road best of 30:21 in San Juan and a world record 2:15:25 at the London Marathon. After illness and injury, returned with the fastest ever half marathon, 65:40 to win the Great North Run. Improved women's only world best to win London marathon 2005 with fourth sub-2:20 time, 2:17:42 and won World gold. Had made fastest ever track debut for 10,000m, 30:48.58 when 2nd in 1998 European Challenge. Set European half marathon record to win Great North Run in 2000 and won the World Half marathon by 33 secs. Won 5th Avenue Mile 1996 & 1997. Married Gary Lough (1500m 3:34.76 '95) on 15 April 2000. Gave birth to daughter Isla on 17 Jan 2007. Her great aunt Charlotte Radcliffe won an Olympic swimming silver medal at 4x100m freestyle relay in 1920.

Nicola SANDERS b. 23 Jun 1982 High Wycombe 1.71m 59kg. Windsor, Slough, Eton & Hounslow.
At 400m: WCh: '07- 2/3R; EC: '06- 6/4R; EI: '07-1/3R. Won AAA 2006, UK 2007. At 400mh/4x400mR: WCh: '05- sf/3R; CG: '05- 4; WUG: '05- 6/4R; WJ: '00- 5; WY: '99- 4; EJ: '99- 3; Won Comm Yth G 2000, AAA 2005.
Progress at 400m, 400mh: 1998- 56.30, 1999-55.66, 58.96; 2000- 56.48, 59.68; 2001- 56.97i/57.07, 61.1; 2002- 56.54, 58.72; 2003- 58.99H, 2004-53.77, 2005- 51.95, 55.61; 2006- 50.68, 55.32; 2007-49.65. pbs: 100m 12.15/11.89w '98, 200m 23.31i+/24.08+ '07, 300m 36.0i+/36.17+ '07, 100mh 15.0 '02, Hep 4285 '99.

Goldie SAYERS b. 16 Jul 1982 Newmarket 1.71m 70kg. Belgrave H.
At OG: '04- dnq 20; WCh: '05- 12, '07- dnq 18; EC: '06- 12; CG: '02- 6, '06- 5; WJ: '00- 6; WY: '99- 5; EJ: '01- 2; EU23: '03- 11; WUG: '03- 5, '05-4; ECp: '03-04-06: 7/7/7. AAA champion 2003-06, UK 2007.
Progress at JT: 1996- 41.56, 1997- 45.10, 1998-51.92, new: 1999- 51.06, 2000- 54.48, 2001- 55.40, 2002- 58.20, 2003- 56.29, 2004- 60.85, 2005- 61.45, 2006- 60.41, 2007- 65.05, 2008- 63.65.

Kelly SOTHERTON b. 13 November 1976 Newport, Isle of Wight 1.80m 66kg. Birchfield H.
At Hep (LJ): OG: '04- 3; WCh: '05- 5 (8), '07- 3; EC: '06- 7 (dnq 15); CG: '02- 7, '06- 1; EU23: '97-10; ECp: 04- (2), '07- 2. At Pen: WI: '08- 2; EI: '05- 2, '07- 2. Won AAA LJ 2005-06, UK 2007.
Commonwealth indoor pentathlon records 2005 & 2007.
Progress at Hep: 1994- 4823, 1995- 4961, 1996-4930, 1997- 5585, 1998- 4599 dnf, 2000- 5428, 2001- 5410, 2002- 5794, 2003- 6059, 2004- 6424, 2005- 6547, 2006- 6396, 2007- 6510. pbs: 60m

7.70i '02, 100m 11.85, 11.80w '97, 11.8 '02; 200m 23.40 '07, 400m 52.47i '08, 54.17 '97; 800m 2:07.94 '05, 60mh 8.17i '08, 100mh 13.21 '07, 400mh 58.30 '02, HJ 1.88i/1.87 '07, LJ 6.68 '04, TJ 11.88/11.95w '02, SP 14.57i '07, 14.27 '06; JT 40.81 '04, Pen 4927i '07.

Mara YAMAUCHI b. 13 Aug 1973 Oxford 1.62m 52kg. née Myers. Harrow. Graduate of Oxford University.
At Mar: WCh: '05- 18, 07- 9; won AAA 2006, UK 2007. At 10,000m: EC: '06- 13; CG: '06- 3. Won ENG CC 1998.
Progress at Mar: 2004- 2:39:16, 2005- 2:27:38, 2006- 2:25:13, 2007- 2:25:41, 2008- 2:25:10. pbs: 1500m 4:25.56 '98, 3000m 9:16?+ '06; 5000m 15:28.58 '06, 10,000m 31:49.40 '06; Road: 10km 31:40+ '07, 15km 48:08+ '07, 10M 54:13 '07, 20km 65:12+ '07, 30km 1:41:52+ '06, HMar 68:45 '07.
Lived in Kenya until she was 8. Made her international debut for Britain at the 1997 European CC, but dropped out of athletics for a few years while she worked as a diplomat in Japan for the Foreign & Commonwealth Office. She married Shigetoshi Yamauchi while in Japan, and returned to racing in England with great success in 2003. Won Osaka Marathon 2008.

USA

Governing body: USA Track and Field, One RCA Dome, Suite #140, Indianapolis, IN 46225. Founded 1979 as The Athletics Congress, when it replaced the AAU (founded 1888) as the governing body.
National Championships first held in 1876 (men), 1923 (women). **2007 Champions**: **Men**: 100m/200m: Tyson Gay 9.84/19.62, 400m: Angelo Taylor 44.05, 800m: Khadevis Robinson 1:44.37, 1500m: Alan Webb 3:34.82, 5000m: Bernard Lagat 13:30.73, 10,000m: Abdi Abdirahman 28:13.51, HMar/Mar: Ryan Hall 59:43/2:09:02, 3000mSt: Josh McAdams 8:24.46, 110mh: Terrence Trammell 13.08, 400mh: James Carter 47.72, HJ: Jim Dilling 2.27, PV: Brad Walker 5.70, LJ: Dwight Phillips 8.36w, TJ: Aarik Wilson 17.06, SP: Reese Hoffa 21.47, DT: Michael Robertson 64.04, HT: A.G. Kruger 78.10, JT: Breaux Greer 91.29, Dec: Tom Pappas 8352, 20000mW/50kmW: Kevin Eastler 1:26:43.28/4:05:44. **Women**: 100m: Torri Edwards 11.02, 200m: Allyson Felix 22.34, 400m: Deedee Trotter 49.64, 800m: Alysia Johnson 1:59.47, 1500m: Treniere Clement 4:07.04, 5000m: Shalane Flanagan 14:51.75, 10,000m/Mar: Deena Kastor 31:57.00/2:35:09, HMar: Elva Dryer 71:42, 3000mSt: Jenny Barringer 9:34.64, 100mh: Virginia Powell 12.63, 400mh: Tiffany Williams 53.28, HJ: Amy Acuff 1.89, PV: Jenn Stuczynski 4.45, LJ: Grace Upshaw 6.74w, TJ: Shani Marks 14.08, SP: Kristin Heaston 18.74, DT: Suzy Powell 60.63, HT: Brittany Riley 72.41, JT: Dana Pounds 59.65, Hep: Hyleas Fountain 6090, 20000mW: Teresa Vaill 1:37:28.70.

NCAA Championships first held in 1921 (men), 1982 (women). **2007 Champions**: **Men**: 100m/200m: Walter Dix 9.93/20.32, 400m: Ricardo Chambers JAM 44.66, 800m: Andrew Ellerton CAN 1:47.48, 1500m: Lopez Lomong SUD 3:37.07, 5000m: Chris Solinsky 13:35.12, 10,000m: Shadrack Songok KEN 28:55.83, 3000mSt: Barnabas Kirui KEN 8:20.36, 110mh: Tyron Akins 13.42, 400mh: Isa Phillips JAM 48.51, HJ: Scott Sellers 2.32, PV: Tommy Skipper 5.50, LJ: DaShalle Andrews 7.68, TJ: Ray Taylor 16.37w, SP: Noah Bryant 20.04, DT: Niklas Arrhenius SWE 62.84, HT: Jake Dunkleberger 71.87, JT: Justin Ryncavage 73.58, Dec: Jake Arnold 8215. **Women**: 100m: Sherry Fletcher GRN 11.20, 200m: Kerron Stewart JAM 22.42, 400m: Natasha Hastings 50.15, 800m: Alysia Johnson 1:59.29, 1500m: Brie Felnagle 4:09.93, 5000m: Michelle Sikes 15:16.76, 10,000m: Sally Kipyego KEN 32:55.71, 3000mSt: Anna Willard 9:38.08, 100mh: Tiffany Ofili 12.80, 400mh: Nicole Leach 54.32, HJ: Destinee Hooker 1.92, PV: April Kubishta 4.25, LJ: Rhomda Watkins TRI 6.96w, TJ: Yvette Lewis 13.73, SP: Jessica Pressley 18.00, DT: Keleche Anyanwu 57.58, HT: Jennifer Dahlgren ARG 70.72, JT: Lindsey Blaine 55.56, Hep: Jacquelyn Johnson 5984.

Dominique ARNOLD b. 14 Sep 1973 Compton, California 1.85m 88kg. Nike. Studied fine arts at Washington State University.
At 110mh: WCh: '05- 4; PAm: '99- 4. 3rd GP 2001. Won USA 2006, NCAA 1996. At 60mh: WI: '06- 3. US & N.American 110mh record 2006.
Progress at 110mh: 1992- 14.55, 1993- 14.17, 1995- 14.00, 1996- 13.46/13.32w, 1998- 13.54/13.5/ 13.48w, 1999- 13.21/13.2, 2000- 13.11, 2001- 13.14, 2002- 13.70A, 2003- 13.35, 2004- 13.31, 2005- 13.01, 2006- 12.90, 2007- 13.17. pbs: 200m 21.0 '99, 50mh 6.68i '98, 55mh 7.15i '98, 60mh 7.51i '00.
Withdrew from 2007 Worlds team due to injury.

Kenwood '**Kenta' BELL** b. 16 Mar 1977 Kilgore, Texas 1.83m 77kg. Studied criminology at Northwestern State University, Louisiana.
At TJ: OG: '04- 9; WCh: '03- 6, '05- 7, '07- dnq 30; WI: '01- 9; WUG: '01- 1 (6 LJ); US champion 2003.
Progress at 110mh: 1998- 15.85i/16.02w, 1999- 16.52/16.67w, 2000- 17.22, 2001- 17.22, 2002- 17.63, 2003- 17.59, 2004- 17.58/17.76Aw, 2005- 17.11, 2006- 17.29/17.58w, 2007- 17.26. pb LJ 8.05 '00.
Dq (public warning) at US Champs 2007.

Ron BRAMLETT b. 22 Oct 1979 Frankfurt, Germany 1.81m 68kg. Advertising graduate from University of Alabama, formerly Middle Tennessee State.
At 110mh: WUG: '01- 4; won NCAA 2001-02.
Progress at 110mh: 1998- 14.01/13.93w, 1999- 13.72, 2000- 13.47, 2001- 13.43/13.39w, 2002- 13.35, 2003- 13.27, 2004- 13.26, 2005- 13.31, 2006- 13.39, 2007- 13.28. pbs: 60m 6.74i '06, 100m 10.45 '03, 200m 21.24 '02, 50mh 6.50i '05, 55mh 7.03i '02, 60mh 7.47i '07.

Christian CANTWELL b. 30 Sep 1980 Jefferson City, Missouri 1.98m 145kg. Studied hotel and restaurant management at University of Missouri.
At SP: WCh: '05- 5; WI: '04- 1, '08- 1; won WAF 2003, US 2005. At DT: PAm-J: '99- 2.
Progress at SP: 1999- 15.85, 2000- 19.67, 2001- 19.71, 2002- 21.45, 2003- 21.62, 2004- 22.54, 2005- 21.67, 2006- 22.45, 2007- 21.96, 2008- 22.18i. pbs: DT 59.32 '01, HT 57.18 '01, Wt 22.04i '03.
After three competitions over 22m in 2004, was 4th in the US Olympic Trials. Married Teri Steer (b. 3 Oct 1975, SP pb 19.21 '01, 3 WI 1999) on 29 Oct 2005.

James CARTER b. 7 May 1978 Baltimore 1.86m 77kg. Nike. Was at Hampton College.
At 400mh: OG: 00- 4, '04- 4; WCh: '01- sf, '05- 2, '07- 4; WCp: '02- 1/2R; 3rd GP 2002. US champion 2002, 2004, 2007.
Progress at 400mh: 1998- 50.17, 1999- 49.45, 2000- 48.04, 2001- 48.44, 2002- 47.57, 2003- 48.88, 2004- 47.68, 2005- 47.43, 2006- 48.16, 2007- 47.72. pbs: 60m 6.74i '07, 200m 21.03i/21.20 '04, 400m 46.21 '01, 55mh 7.44i '99, 60mh 8.15i '99, LJ 7.25 '99, TJ 15.61i '99.

Xavier CARTER b. 8 Dec 1985 Palm Bay, Florida 1.91m 89kg. Nike. Student at Louisiana State University.
Won NCAA 100m & 400m 2006.
Progress at 200m, 400m: 1999- 22.20, 49.71; 2001- 46.95, 2002- 21.02, 46.90; 2003- 20.69, 45.88; 2004- 20.69i/20.72/20.5, 45.44/45.3; 2005- 20.02, 45.65; 2006- 19.63, 44.53; 2007- 19.92, 45.26. pbs: 60m 6.74i '05, 100m 10.09, 10.08w '06.
Played for LSU as wide receiver at American football. Youngest ever to break 50 secs for 400m (49.71 at age 13) with world age record also for 200m.

Bryan CLAY b. 3 Jan 1980 Austin, Texas 1.80m 83kg. Nike. Was at Azusa Pacific University.
At Dec: OG: '04- 2; WCh: '01/03/07- dnf, '05- 1; PAm-J: '99- 1. US champion 2004-05. At Hep: WI: '04-06-08: 2/2/1.
Progress at Dec: 1999- 7312, 2000- 7373, 2001- 8169, 2002- 8230, 2003- 8482, 2004- 8820, 2005- 8732. 2006- 8677, 2007- 8493. pbs: 60m 6.65i '04, 100m 10.36 '05, 400m 47.78 '05, 1000m 2:49.41i '04, 1500m 4:38.93 '01, 60mh 7.74i '08, 110mh 13.74 '06, HJ 2.10i '06, 2.09 '07; PV 5.10 '04, LJ 7.96/8.06w '04, SP 16.25 '05, DT 55.87 '05, JT 72.00 '05, Hep 6371i '08.
Moved from Texas to Hawaii at age five. Brilliant breakthrough with four pbs in 2004 World Indoor heptathlon. Set decathlon discus WR with 55.87 during 2005 US Champs. Set pbs at SP, 400m and JT when winning World gold in 2005. Won Götzis 2006.

Kerron CLEMENT b. 31 Oct 1985 Port of Spain, Trinidad 1.88m 84kg. Nike. Student at University of Florida.
At 400mh/4x400mR: WCh: '05- 4, '07- 1/res 1R; WJ: '04- 1/1R; WCp: '06- 1. US champion 2005-06, NCAA 2004-05.
World junior 4x400m record 2004, world indoor records: 400m 2005, 4x400m 2006.
Progress at 400m, 400mh: 2002- 49.77H, 2003- 50.13H, 2004- 45.90, 48.51; 2005- 44.57i, 47.24; 2006- 44.71, 47.39; 2007- 44.48, 47.61. pbs: 100m 10.23 '07, 200m 20.40i '05, 20.49 '07; 300m 31.94i '06, 55mh 7.28i '05, 60mh 7.80i '04, 110mh 13.78 '04.
Born in Trinidad, moved to Texas in 1998, US citizenship confirmed in 2005. Ran world-leading 47.24, the world's fastest time since 1998, to win 2005 US 400mh title.

Shawn CRAWFORD b. 14 Jan 1978 Van Wyck, SC 1.81m 86kg. Nike. Was at Clemson University.
At 200m/4x100mR (100m): OG: '04- 1/2R (4); WCh: '01- 3=, '05- (sf); WI: '01- 1; Won US 2001, 2004; GWG & GP 2001, NCAA 2000. At 60m: WI: '04- 2.
Progress at 100m, 200m: 1996- 10.62, 21.57; 1997- 10.51w, 20.83; 1998- 10.34/10.15w, 20.44A/20.12w; 1999- 10.41, 20.39; 2000- 10.16, 20.09; 2001- 10.09, 20.17; 2002- 9.94, 19.85A/20.29; 2003- 10.07, 20.02; 2004- 9.88/9.86w, 19.79; 2005- 9.99/9.98w, 20.12; 2006- 10.01, 2007-10.13/9.96w, 20.21. pb 60m 6.47i '04.
US indoor record 20.26 to win NCAA indoor 200m 2000. Disqualified in 2003 WI semis. Calls himself 'The Cheetah Man' after racing against a zebra and a cheetah on Fox TV in 2003, made his TV acting debut in October 2004.

Walter DAVIS b. 2 Jul 1979 LaFayette, Louisiana 1.88m 83kg. Nike. Studied sociology at Louisiana State University.
At TJ/(LJ): OG: '00- 11, '04- 11/dnq 23; WCh: '01- 5, '03- dnq 15/7, '05- 1/dnq 19, '07- 3/dnq; WI: '03- 2, '06- 1; WCp: '02- 2, '06- 1. Won WAF 2007, US 2002, 2005-06; NCAA 2001-02 (& LJ 2002).
Progress at LJ, TJ: 1997- 7.24, 15.67; 1998- 15.29w, 1999- 7.88i/7.70, 16.38/16.47w; 2000- 8.16, 17.07/17.08w, 2001- 8.14i/8.13/8.19w, 17.22; 2002- 8.15i/8.12/8.15w, 17.59; 2003- 8.24, 17.55; 2004- 8.25, 17.63; 2005- 7.98, 17.62i/17.57; 2006- 8.36, 17.73i/17.71; 2007- 8.24, 17.35. pbs: 60m 6.78i '01, 100m 10.44w '05, 200m 20.98 '96, 20.87w '95, 20.6w '94.
All-state basketball player in high school.

Walter DIX b. 31 Jan 1986 Coral Springs, Florida 1.75m 80kg. Nike. Student at Florida State University.
Won NCAA 100m 2005, 2007; 200m 2006-07.
World junior 200m indoor best (20.37) 2005.
Progress at 100m, 200m: 2002- 10.72/10.67w, 2003- 10.41/10.29w, 21.04/20.94w; 2004- 10.28, 20.62/20.54w; 2005- 10.06/9.96w, 20.18; 2006- 10.12, 20.25; 2007- 9.93, 19.69. pbs: 55m 6.19i '07, 60m 6.59i '06, LJ 7.39 '04.

Kenneth FERGUSON b. 22 Mar 1984 Detroit 1.86m 73kg. Was at University of South Carolina.
At (110mh)/400mh/4x400mR: WJ: '02- 5/2/1R; PAm-J '03- 1/1/1R.
Progress at 400mh: 2001- 52.99, 2002- 49.38, 2003- 48.79, 2004- 49.50, 2005- 48.51, 2006- 48.80, 2007- 48.15. pbs: 400m 45.91 '07, 55mh 7.16i '03 (WJR), 60mh 7.66i '04, 110mh 13.53 '03.

Tyson GAY b. 9 Sep 1982 Lexington 1.83m 73kg. Marketing student at University of Arkansas.
At 100m/(200m)/4x100mR: WCh: '05- 3, '07- 1/1/1R; WCp: '06- 1/1R. Won WAF 200m 2005-06, US 100m & 100m 2007.
Progress at 100m, 200m: 2000- 10.56, 21.27; 2001- 10.28, 21.23; 2002- 10.27/10.08w, 20.88/20.21w; 2003- 10.01w, 21.15/20.31w; 2004- 10.06/10.10w, 20.07; 2005- 10.08, 19.93; 2006- 9.84, 19.68; 2007- 9.84/9.76w, 19.62. pbs: 60m 6.55i '05, 400m 47.08i '07.
Ran four 200m races in under 19.85 in 2006 and now the all-time best for 100m/200m combined. Greatest ever sprint double (9.84 and 19.62) at 2007 US Champs.

John GODINA b. 31 May 1972 Fort Sill, Oklahoma 1.93m 129kg. adidas. Studied biology at UCLA.
At SP/(DT): OG: '96- 2/dnq 14, '00- 3/dnq 17, '04- 9; WCh: '95- 1/10, '97- 1/5, '99- 7/dnq 16, '01- 1/dnq 21, '03- 8, '05- dnq 17; WI: '97-9-01-03: 3/2/1/2; WCp: '98- 1/4. Won GP SP 1996 (3rd 2000), 3rd DT 1997. Won US SP 1998-9, 2001, 2003; DT 1997-8, NCAA SP 1995, DT 1994-5, PAm-J SP & DT 1991; GWG SP 1998.
Progress at SP, DT: 1990- 53.58, 1991- 17.75, 58.60; 1992- 19.68, 61.52; 1993- 20.03, 60.48; 1994- 20.03, 62.24; 1995- 22.00, 64.92; 1996- 21.25, 64.58; 1997- 21.75, 67.40; 1998- 21.78, 69.91; 1999- 22.02, 69.05; 2000- 21.51, 68.32; 2001- 21.95, 67.66; 2002- 21.91, 64.71; 2003- 21.23i/21.08, 64.03/66.38dh; 2004- 21.71, 2005- 22.20, 2006- 20.50i, 2007- 20.60.
Four world shot gold medals. Undefeated in 24 shot competitions July 1997 to February 1999. 4th in the US trials shot in 1997, but gained World place with a 'wild card' for a defending champion; came second but took gold after the disqualification of Aleksandr Bagach. He achieved the best ever one day SP-DT double with 21.58 and 69.91 at Salinas in 1998. He stepped into the US Olympic shot team after the withdrawal of CJ Hunter in 2000 and took bronze.

Breaux GREER b. 19 Oct 1976 Houston 1.88m 102kg. adidas. Was at Northeast Louisiana University.
At JT: OG: '00- 12, '04- 12; WCh: '01- 4, '03- dnq 14, '07- 3; PAm: '03- 3. Won WAF 2004, US 2000-07.
Four North American javelin records 2004-07.
Progress at JT: 1995- 70.92, 1996- 79.98, 1997- 78.12, 1998- 79.68, 2000- 82.63, 2001- 87.00, 2002- 81.78, 2003- 82.10, 2004- 87.68, 2005- 87.65, 2006- 85.45, 2007- 91.29.
Set five pbs in 2001, including those to win US title (85.23) and in first round of World final.

Ryan HALL b. 14 Oct 1982 Big Bear Lake, California 1.80m 64kg. Graduate of Stanford University.
At 5000m: WCh: '05- h. World 4k CC: '06- 19; 20k: '06- 11. Won HMar & Mar 2007, CC 2006; NCAA 5000m 2005.
US records: 20km 2006, HMar 2007.
Progress at 5000m, Mar: 2004- 13:45.00, 2005- 13:16.03, 2006- 13:28.89, 2007- 2:08:24. pbs: 800m 1:51.07 '01, 1500m 3:42.70 '01, 1M 4:05.50 '05, 3000m 7:53.8+ '06, 2M 8:26.26 '06, 10,000m 28:07.93 '07, Road: 15km 42:21 '07, 10M 45:33 '07, 20km 57:06e '07, HMar 59:43 '07.
Made marathon debut in 2007: 7th London 2:08:24, 1st US Trial 2:09:02. Married to **Sara Bei-Hall** (b. 15 Apr 1983) pbs: 1500m 4:08.99 '07, 5000m 15:20.88 '06, 12 WI 3000m '06.

Trey HARDEE b. 7 Feb 1984 Birmingham, Alabama 1.96m 95kg. Mississippi State University.
At Dec: won NCAA 2005.
Progress at Dec: 2003- 7544, 2004- 8041, 2005- 7881, 2006- 8465. pbs: 60m 6.71i '06, 100m 10.58 '04, 10.28w '06; 200m 20.98 '06, 400m 47.51 '06, 1000m 2:48.16i '05, 1500m 4:42.23 '06, 60mh 7.76i '06, 110mh 13.98, 13.83w '06; HJ 2.04i/2.01 '05, PV 5.30Ai/5.20 '06, LJ 7.85i '07, 7.37, 7.70w '06, SP 14.78 '06, DT 48.33 '05, JT 60.00 '06, Hep 6208Ai '06.

Jeff HARTWIG b. 25 Sep 1967 St Louis 1.90m 82kg. Nike. Was at Arkansas State University.
At PV: OG: '96- 11=; WCh: '99/07- dnq 14=/15=; WI: '99- 2, '06- nh; WCp: '98- 3, '02- 2. Won GWG 1998, US 1998-9, 2002-03; GP 2002 (2nd 1999).
Four US pole vault records 1998-2000. World M35 record indoors and out 2004, M40 indoors 2008.
Progress at PV: 1983- 3.35, 1984- 3.81, 1985- 4.42, 1986- 4.57, 1987- 4.90, 1988- 5.10, 1989- 5.34, 1990- 5.40i/5.35, 1991- 5.35, 1992- 5.60i/5.50, 1993- 5.35, 1994- 5.63, 1995- 5.72, 1996- 5.80, 1997- 5.85, 1998- 6.01, 1999- 6.02, 2000- 6.03, 2001- 5.90, 2002- 6.02i/5.90, 2003- 5.80i/5.70, 2004- 5.88i/5.81, 2005- 5.76i/5.68, 2006- 5.85i/5.71, 2007- 5.85i/5.83A, 2008- 5.65i.
The first 6m-vaulter from the USA, Hartwig is also a snake rancher, with a herd of pythons and boa constrictors. Clearly headed world rankings in 2000, but failed to clear his opening height in the qualifying round of the US Trials, when he had problems with his eyes.

Reese HOFFA b. 8 Oct 1977 Evans, Georgia 1.82m 133kg. New York AC. Was at University of Georgia.
At SP: OG: '04- dnq 22; WCh: '03- dnq, '07- 1; PAm: '03- 1; WI: '04-06-08: 2/1/2; WUG: '01- 9; WCp: '06- 2; won WAF 2006-07, USA 2007.

Progress at SP: 1998- 19.08, 1999- 19.35, 2000- 19.79, 2001- 20.22, 2002- 20.47, 2003- 20.95, 2004- 21.67, 2005- 21.74i/21.29, 2006- 22.11i/21.96, 2007- 22.43. pbs: DT 58.46 '99, HT 60.05 '02.
Added 37cm to his best to win World Indoor gold 2006.

Trindon HOLLIDAY b. 27 Apr 1986 Baton Rouge 1.65m 72kg. Student at Louisiana State University. 2nd NCAA & US 100m 2007; NCAA 60m indoor 2008.
Progress at 100m: 2002- 10.59, 2003- 10.51w, 2005- 10.47/10.43w, 2007- 10.02. pbs: 60m 6.54i '08, 200m 21.33 '02.
Plays as a wide receiver for the LSU Tigers at American Football.

Bershawn JACKSON b. 8 May 1983 Miami 1.73m 69kg. Nike. Studied accountancy at St Augustine's University, Raleigh.
At 400mh: WCh: '03- h (dq), '05- 1, '07- sf/res 1R; WJ: '02- 3/1R. Won WAF 2004-05, US 2003, US indoor 400m 2005.
Progress at 400mh: 2000- 52.17, 2001- 50.86, 2002- 50.00, 2003- 48.23, 2004- 47.86, 2005- 47.30, 2006- 47.48, 2007- 48.13. pbs: 200m 21.03/20.46w '04, 400m 45.06 '07, 600m 1:18.65i '06.

Allen JOHNSON b. 1 Mar 1971 Washington DC 1.78m 70kg. Nike. Was at University of North Carolina.
At 110mh: OG: '96- 1, '00- 4, '04- h (fell); WCh: '95- 1, '97- res (1) 4x400mR, '99- sf, '01- 1, '03- 1, '05- 3; WCp: '94-8-02-06: 2/2R/2/1; 2nd GP 1995 & 2001. Won WAF 2003-04, GWG 2001, US 1996-7, 2000-03, 2005. At 60mh: WI: '95-03-04-08: 1/1/1/2. US & N.American 110mh record 1996 and indoor 60mh 2004.
Progress at 110mh: 1990- 14.4, 1991- 14.11, 1992- 13.63, 1993- 13.47/13.34w, 1994- 13.25/13.23Aw, 1995- 12.98, 1996- 12.92, 1997- 12.93, 1998- 12.98, 1999- 13.01, 2000- 12.97, 2001- 13.04, 2002- 13.04, 2003- 12.97, 2004- 13.05, 2005- 12.99, 2006- 12.96, 2007- 13.23. pbs: 60m 6.62i '98, 100m 10.41/10.10w '99, 200m 20.26 '97, 400m 48.27 '96, 50mh 6.40i '05, 55mh 7.03i '94, 60mh 7.36i '04, 400mh 52.00 '91, HJ 2.11 '89, LJ 8.14i/7.91w '93, 7.85 '91; TJ 14.83 '89.
Ranked in world top ten for 14 years from 1994 and has won seven global high hurdles titles. In 1996 he missed the world record by just 0.01 at the US Trials, Had to withdraw from the 1999 World semis through injury. In 2004 he won his third World Indoor 60mh title in 7.36 to tie the US record and improve his pb of 7.38 '95. World M35 records in 2006 of 13.01 and 12.96 (to win at World Cup). He has a record eleven 'legal' sub-13 time for 110mh.

Brian JOHNSON b. 25 Mar 1980 Houma, LA 1.96m 91kg. Nike. Studied political science at Southern University.
At LJ: WCh: '05- dnq 13; WI: '06- 7; WCp: '06- 6. Won US 2006, US indoor 2005, NCAA 2003.
Progress at LJ: 1999- 7.48/7.67w, 2000- 7.65/8.04w, 2001- 8.01/8.06w, 2002- 8.07A/8.33w, 2003- 8.28i/8.05, 2004- 8.06/8.15w, 2005- 8.33, 2006- 8.33, 2007- 8.31. pbs: 55m 6.28i '03, 60m 6.72i '03, 100m 10.24 '02, 10.18w '05; 200m 20.65 '03.
Former basketball player.

Meb(rahtom) **KEFLEZIGHI** b. 5 May 1975 Asmara, Eritrea 1.70m 58kg. Nike. Was at UCLA.
At Mar: OG: '04- 2; At 10,000m: OG: '00- 12; WCh: '01- 23, '03- 16, '05- dnf; PAm: '99- 5. At 5000m: WCp: '02- 4. World CC: '01-02-03: 13/14/11. Won US 10,000m 2000, 2002, 2004; CC 2001-02; NCAA 5000m, 10,000m, indoor 5000m & CC 1997.
US records: 10,000m 2001, 20km road 58:57 '03.
Progress at 10,000m, Mar: 1995- 30:41.24, 1996- 29:55.75, 1997- 28:26.55, 1998- 28:16.79, 1999- 28:29.27, 2000- 27:53.63, 2001- 27:13.98, 2002- 27:20.15, 2:12:35; 2003- 27:57.59, 2:10:03; 2004- 27:24.10, 2:09:53; 2005- 28:10.57, 2:09:56; 2006- 28:18.74, 2:09:56; 2007- 27:41.26, 2:15:09. pbs: 1500m 3:42.29 '98, 1M 4:02.24i/4:02.86 '98, 3000m 7:48.81 '03, 2M 8:27.2 '01, 5000m 13:11.77 '00, Road: 15km 42:48 '02, HMar 61:28 '06.
Emigrated from war-torn Eritrea at age of 10, first to Italy and then to San Diego, USA in 1987. US citizen on 2 July 1998. 2nd New York Marathon 2004 (3rd 2005), 3rd Boston 2006.

Khalid KHANNOUCHI b. 22 Dec 1971 Meknès, Morocco 1.65m 57kg. New Balance.
At Mar: WCh: '01- dnf. At 5000m: WUG: '93- 1. World best for the marathon 1999 and 2002. World best road 20km 1998 (57:37). Moroccan records HMar and Mar 1997, US marathon records 2000 and 2002.
Progress at Mar: 1997- 2:07:10, 1998- 2:07:19, 1999- 2:05:42, 2000- 2:07:01, 2002- 2:05:38, 2004- 2:08:44, 2006- 2:07:04, 2007- 2:12:34. pbs: 3000m 8:01.89i '96, 5000m 13:41.6 '95, 10,000m 29:00.8 sh '89; Rd: 5km 13:24 '97, 10km 27:47 '98, 15km 42:57 '98, HMar 60:27 '97.
Five marathon wins: Chicago 1997 (fastest ever debut, just 20 seconds off the world record), 1999 (world record 2:05:42, 2000 and 2002 (2:05:56); London 2002 (world record 2:05:38. Also Chicago: 2nd 1998 and 5th 2004; London 3rd 2000, 4th 2006. Won 1993 WUG 5000m in Buffalo, New York, USA. Feeling that he was not appreciated in Morocco, he returned to Buffalo and eventually settled in Brooklyn, becoming a US citizen in 2000. He is coached and managed by his wife Sandra Natal, who ran for the Dominican Republic in the 1991 World marathon.

Bernard LAGAT b. 12 Dec 1974 Kapsabet, Kenya 1.75m 61kg. Studied business management at Washington State University, USA.
At 1500m: OG: '00- 3, '04- 2; WCh: '01- 2, '05- sf, '07- 1 (1 5000m); WI: '03- 2; AfCh: '02- 1; WUG: '99- 1; WCp: '02- 1; 2nd GP 1999-2000-02. At

3000m: WI: '01- 6, '04- 1. Won WAF 3000m 2005, KEN 1500m 2002, US 1500m 2006, 5000m 2006-07, NCAA 5000m 1999 (and indoor 1M/3000m). Records: Commonwealth and KEN 1500m 2001, N.American 1500m 2005, indoor 3000m 2007.
Progress at 1500m, 5000m: 1996- 3:37.7A, 1997- 3:41.19, 13:50.33; 1998- 3:34.48, 13:42.73; 1999- 3:30.56, 13:36.12; 2000- 3:28.51, 13:23.46; 2001- 3:26.34, 13:30.54; 2002- 3:27.91, 13:19.14; 2003- 3:30.55, 2004- 3:27.40, 2005- 3:29.30, 12:59.29; 2006- 3:29.68, 12:59.22; 2007- 3:33.85, 13:30.73. pbs: 800m 1:46.00 '03, 1000m 2:16.25 '07, 1M 3:47.28 '01, 2000m 4:55.49 '99, 3000m 7:32.43i '07, 7:33.51 '00.
Gave up his final year of scholastic eligibility (as under NCAA rules no payments can be received) at his university in order to compete (for money) in the 1999 GP Final, in which he was 2nd. He was 2nd to Hicham El Guerrouj six times in 2001, including his 3:26.34 at Brussels for 2nd on the world all-time list, and six times in 2002. Withdrew from 2003 Worlds after testing positive for EPO, but this was later repudiated. Lives in Tucson, Arizona and revealed in 2005 that he had gained US citizenship. In 2006 he became the first man ever to win 1500m/5000m double at US Champs and in 2007 the first to do this double at the World Champs.
From a large family, one sister **Mary Chep-kemboi** competed at the 1982 Commonwealth Games and won an African title at 3000m, and another **Evelyne Jerotich Langat** has a 71:35 half marathon pb. Of his brothers **William Cheseret** has a marathon pb of 2:12:09 '04 and **Robert Cheseret** won the NCAA 5000m in 2004 and 10,000m in 2005, pbs 5000m 13:13.23 and 10,000m 28:20.11 in 2005.

Lionel LARRY b. 14 Sep 1986 1.75m 68kg. Student at University of Southern California.
At 400m: WCh: '07- h; PAm: '07- dnf. At 200m: WY: '03- sf.
Progress at 400m: 2004- 47.28, 2005- 45.78, 2006- 45.38, 2007- 44.67. pbs: 100m 10.52/10.37w/10.0w '04; 200m 20.73 '04.

Daniel LINCOLN b. 22 Oct 1980 Ruston, Louisiana 1.90m 72kg. Nike. Graduate of University of Arkansas, now at medical school.
At 3000mSt: OG: '04- 11; WCh: '03- h, '05- 13. Won US 3000mSt 2004-06; NCAA 3000mSt 2001-03, 10,000m 2003.
US & N.American 3000m steeple record 2006.
Progress at 3000mSt: 2000- 8:44.43, 2001- 8:26.91, 2002- 8:22.34, 2003- 8:24.10, 2004- 8:15.02, 2005- 8:12.65, 2006- 8:08.82, 2007- 8:28.32. pbs: 1500m 3:40.05 '04, 1M 3:57.68 '04, 3000m 7:40.0e '05, 2M 8:13.70 '06, 5000m 13:32.27 '04, 10,000m 28:20.20 '03. Won unique NCAA 10,000m/3000mSt double in 2003.

Tim MACK b. 15 Sep 1972 Cleveland 1.88m 78kg. Nike. Graduate of University of Tennessee.
At PV: OG: '04- 1; WCh: '01- 9, '03- 6=. Won WAF 2004, GWG 2001, US 2004.
Progress at PV: 1993- 5.31, 1994- 5.52, 1995- 5.60, 1996- 5.65, 1998- 5.70, 1999- 5.70i/5.43, 2000- 5.81, 2001- 5.81, 2002- 5.85i/5.84, 2003- 5.76, 2004- 6.01, 2005- 5.85, 2006- 5.75, 2007- 5.86.
Became the world's 11th 6m vaulter with 6.01 at the World Athletics Finals after pbs of 5.90 to win US title and 5.95 to win Olympic title in 2004. Shoulder surgery in October 2006,

Andra MANSON b. 30 Apr 1984 Brenham, Texas 1.96m 75kg. Was at University of Texas.
At HJ: WJ: '02- 1; WI: '08- 3=; won NCAA 2004.
Progress at HJ: 2001- 2.13, 2002- 2.31, 2003- 2.22, 2004- 2.32, 2005- 2.26i/2.23, 2006- 2.28i/2.26, 2007- 2.33i/2.30, 2008- 2.30i. pb 100m 10.81 '07.
Won 2002 World Junior title with US junior record 2.31.

Rodney MARTIN b. 22 Dec 1982 Las Vegas 1.80m 73kg. Nike. Criminal justice graduate of University of Southern California.
At 200m/4x100mR: WCh: '07- 4/res 1R. At 100m: WUG: '01- 1/1R.
Progress at 200m: 2000- 21.30, 2001- 21.35w, 2002- 20.81w, 2003- 20.89/20.57w, 2004- 20.84, 2005- 20.34, 2006- 20.14, 2007- 20.06. pbs: 100m 10.24 '06. pbs: 55m 6.35i '04, 60m 6.75i '05.

Aries MERRITT b. 24 Jul 1985 Marietta, Georgia 1.88m 75kg. Sports management student at University of Tennessee.
At 110mh: WJ: '04- 1; won NCAA 60mh indoors & 110mh 2006.
Progress at 110mh: 2004- 13.47, 2005- 13.38/13.34w, 2006- 13.12, 2007- 13.09. pbs: 55m 6.43i '05, 60m 6.97i '05, 200m 21.31 '05, 55mh 7.10i '06, 60mh 7.51i '06, 7.5i '04; 400mh 51.94 '04.

LaShawn MERRITT b. 27 Jun 1986 Portsmouth, Virginia 1.88m 82kg. Nike. Studying sports management at Old Dominion University.
At 400m/4x400mR: WCh: '05- res(1)R, '07- 2/1R; WJ: '04- 1/1R (1 at 4x100); WI: '06- 1R; WCp: '06- 1/1R; won WAF 2007.
World junior records 4x100m and 4x400m 2004, World indoor 400m junior best (44.93) 2005.
Progress at 200m, 400m: 2002- 21.46, 2003- 21.33, 47.9?; 2004- 20.72/20.69w, 45.25; 2005- 20.38, 44.66; 2006- 20.10, 44.14; 2007- 19.98, 43.96. pbs: 55m 6.33i '04, 60m 6.68i '06, 100m 10.47/10.38w '04, 300m 31.31 '06.
World age-18 400m record with 44.66 in 2005 and world low-altitude 300m best 2006. Spent a year at East Carolina University before signing for Nike and returning home to Portsmouth.

Derek MILES b. 28 Sep 1972 Sacramento 1.91m 82kg. Bell Athletics. History graduate of University of South Dakota. Academic advisor at Arkansas State University.
At PV: OG: '04- 7; WCh: '03- 6=, WI: '03- 5, '08- 8.
Progress at PV: 1997- 5.50, 1998- 5.35, 1999- 5.40Ai/5.35, 2000- 5.65, 2001- 5.82, 2002- 5.82i/5.74, 2003- 5.81, 2004- 5.81, 2005- 5.85i/5.81,

2006- 5.65i/5.50, 2007- 5.75, 2008- 5.80Ai.

John MOFFITT b. 21 Dec 1980 Winnsboro, Louisiana 1.85m 75kg. Louisiana State University.
At LJ: OG: '04- 2; NCAA champion 2004.
Progress at LJ: 2001- 7.68/7.92w, 2002- 7.83/7.95w, 2003- 8.08i/8.02, 2004- 8.47, 2005- 8.16i/7.96, 2006- 8.23i/8.11, 2007- 8.19. pbs: TJ 16.79i/16.69w '04, 16.53 '03.

Anwar MOORE b. 5 Mar 1979 1.82m 75kg. Was at St. Augustine's University.
Progress at 110mh: 2000- 13.9/14.33w, 2001- 14.18, 2002- 13.66, 2003- 13.44, 2004- 13.35, 2005- 13.23/13.20w, 2006- 13.39, 2007- 13.12/13.00w. pbs: 55m 6.25i '03, 60m 6.72i '03, 100m 10.42 '05, 200m 21.63 '04, 21.19w '02; 55mh 7.17i '03, 60mh 7.52i '06.

Adam NELSON b. 7 Jul 1975 Atlanta 1.83m 115kg. Graduate of Dartmouth University. Training as a financial consultant.
At SP: OG: '00- 2, '04- 2; WCh: '01- 2, '03- 2, '05- 1, '07- 2; WI: '01- 2; WJ: '94- 1; WUG: '99- 2; WCp: '02- 1. GP 2002 (2nd 2000 and 3rd overall). Won WAF 2005, PAm-J 1993, GWG 2001, NCAA 1997, US 2000, 2002, 2004, 2006.
Progress at SP: 1993- 16.56, 1994- 18.34, 1995- 18.27, 1996- 19.14, 1997- 19.62, 1998- 20.61, 1999- 20.64, 2000- 22.12, 2001- 21.53, 2002- 22.51, 2003- 21.29, 2004- 21.68, 2005- 21.92, 2006- 22.04, 2007- 21.61, 2008- 22.40i. pb DT 56.18 '96.
Had a great season in 2000, when he improved his best from 20.64 to 21.70 and then the world's longest throw for four years, 22.12 (to take the US title) in July. Further improvement as world number one in 2002. Small for a shot putter, but very fast and dynamic in the circle. Played American Football at high school and college.

David OLIVER b. 24 Apr 1982 Orlando 1.88m 93kg. Studied marketing at Howard University.
At 110mh: WCh: '07- sf.
Progress at 110mh: 2001- 14.04, 2002- 13.92/13.88w, 2003- 13.60, 2004- 13.55, 2005- 13.29/13.23w, 2006- 13.20, 2007- 13.14. pbs: 60m 6.88i '04, 55mh 7.04i '07, 60mh 7.55i '08.
Mother, Brenda Chambers, had 400mh pb 58.54 '80.

Tom PAPPAS b. 6 Sep 1976 Azalea, Oregon 1.96m 95kg. Nike. Was at University of Tennessee.
At Dec: OG: '00- 5, '04- dnf; WCh: '99- dnf, '03- 1, '07- dnf. Won PAm-J 1995, NCAA 1999, US 2000, 2002-03, 2006-07. At Hep: WI: '03- 1.
Progress at Dec: 1995- 7198, 1996- 7499, 1997- 7677, 1999- 8463, 2000- 8467, 2001- 8323, 2002- 8583, 2003- 8784, 2004- 8732, 2006- 8319, 2007- 8352. pbs: 60m 6.89i '03, 100m 10.65 '03, 10.63w '04; 400m 47.58 '03, 1000m 2:49.32i '04, 1500m 4:35.14 '95, 55mh 7.27i '03, 60mh 7.80i '03, 110mh 13.90 '04, HJ 2.21 '00, PV 5.20 '02, LJ 7.96 '03, SP 16.66i '08, 16.53 '06; DT 52.18 '03, JT 66.56 '00, Hep 6361i '03.
Won Talence decathlon 2002 and IAAF Combined Events Challenge 2003. Four pbs in World Indoor heptathlon win 2003. Grandfather was a professional wrestler, father (Nick) set a world motor speed record. Younger brother Billy (b. 22 Feb 1979) has decathlon best of 7745 '03. Tom married Kim Shiemenz (heptathlon 6209A '03) in 2004.

Miguel PATE b. 13 Jun 1979 St Francisville, Louisiana 1.88m 84kg. Nike. Studying criminal justice at University of Alabama.
At LJ: WCh: '01- 4, '05- dnq 16, '07- 10; WI: '03- 3; WUG: '01- 1. Won US 2001, 2005; NCAA 2000-01.
Progress at LJ: 1997- 7.28, 1998- 7.68/7.73w, 1999- 7.63, 2000- 8.26, 2001- 8.20/8.48w, 2002- 8.59i/8.45, 2003- 8.46A/8.27, 2004- 7.96A, 2005- 8.45, 2006- 8.27, 2007- 8.24. pbs: 55m 6.39i '01, 100m 10.50 '02, 200m 21.41 '01, HJ 2.18i '00, 2.13 '97; TJ 16.52i '02, 16.48 '01.

Darvis PATTON b. 4 Dec 1977 Dallas 1.83m 75kg. adidas. Was at Texas Christian University.
At 200m/4x100m: OG: '04- res 2R; WCh: '03- 2/1R, '07- 1R; PAm: '07- 2 100m/3R. Won US 200m 2003.
Progress at 100m, 200m: 1998- 10.3, 20.49w; 2000- 10.22w/10.09w, 20.29; 2001- 10.16/10.14w, 20.31; 2002- 10.14, 20.12; 2003- 10.00/9.97w, 20.03, 2004- 10.12/9.89w, 20.17/20.07w; 2005- 10.27; 2006- 10.19, 20.50; 2007- 10.11, 20.49. pbs: 60m 6.58i '03, LJ 8.12 '01, TJ 16.17i '98.
Versatile performer came into his own at 200m in 2002, when he was 2nd in the US Champs indoors and out. Turned to athletics after dislocating his hip playing American football as a teenager.

David PAYNE b. 24 Jul 1982 Cincinnati 1.85m 81kg. Was at University of Cincinnati.
At 110mh: WCh: '07- 3; PAm: '07- 1.
Progress at 110mh: 2002- 13.92, 2003- 13.53, 2004- 13.48/13.42w, 2005- 13.33, 2006- 13.31, 2007- 13.02. pbs: 100m 10.56 '07, 200m 21.15 '07, 60mh 7.51i '07, 400mh 51.16 '04.

Dwight PHILLIPS b. 1 Oct 1977 Decatur, Georgia 1.81m 82kg. Nike. Was at University of Kentucky, then Arizona State University.
At LJ: OG: '00- 8, '04- 1; WCh: '01- 8, '03- 1, '05- 1, '07- 3; WI: '03- 1; PAm: '99- 7. Won WAF 2003, 2005; US 2003-04, 2007.
Progress at LJ: 1996- 7.14, 1997- 7.26, 1999- 8.18, 2000- 8.21/8.30w, 2001- 8.13/8.23w, 2002- 8.38, 2003- 8.44, 2004- 8.60, 2005- 8.60, 2006- 8.32 2007- 8.31/8.37w. pbs: 50m 5.70i '05, 60m 6.47i '05, 100m 10.14 '05, 10.06w '07, 200m 20.68 '02, 400m 46.80 '97, TJ 16.41 '99.
World number one 2003-05, winning 34 of 42 competitions in those three years.

Khadevis ROBINSON b. 19 Jul 1976 Dallas 1.83m 74kg. Nike. Degree in social work from Texas Christian University.
At 800m: OG: '04- h; WCh: '99/01- h, '03/05/07-

sf; WI: '99/03/06- sf (gold 4x400m 1999); WCp: '06- 6. Won US 800m 1999, 2005-07, indoors 1999, 2006; NCAA 1998.
US record 4x800m 2006.
Progress at 800m: 1994- 1:53+, 1995- 1:48.61, 1996- 1:47.85, 1997- 1:47.46, 1998- 1:45.72, 1999- 1:45.23, 2000- 1:45.40, 2001- 1:45.15, 2002- 1:44.41, 2003- 1:45.03, 2004- 1:44.89, 2005- 1:44.62, 2006- 1:43.68, 2007- 1:44.27. pbs: 400m 46.55 '98, 600m 1:15.23 '05.

Andrew ROCK b. 23 Jan 1982 Marshfield, Wisconsin 1.88m 75kg. adidas. Studied finance at Wisconsin La Crosse University.
At 400m/4x400m: WCh: '05- 2/1R; OG: '04- res (1)R. US champion 2006.
Progress at 400m: 2001- 46.52, 2002- 46.08, 2003- 45.29, 2004- 44.66, 2005- 44.35, 2006- 44.45, 2007- 45.12. pbs: 200m 20.84 '03, 300m 32.4 '05, 600m 1:18.53i '04.
Won Olympic relay gold in 2004, having run third leg in the heat. Improved pb from 44.66 to 44.35 in taking 2005 World silver. Married Missy Buttry (won NCAA 5000m 2003-05, pb 15:37.48 '03) on 6 Oct 2007.

Mike RODGERS b. 24 Apr 1985 Brenham, Texas 1.96m 75kg. Studied kinesiology at Oklahoma Baptist University.
At 60m: WI: '08- 4, US indoor champion 2008/
Progress at 100m: 2004- 10.55/10.31w, 2005- 10.30/10.25w, 2006- 10.29/10.18w, 2007- 10.10, 10.07w. pbs: 60m 6.54i '08, 200m 20.88 '05.

Jarred ROME b. 21 Dec 1976 Seattle 1.94m 140kg. Studied business education at Boise State University.
At DT: OG: '04- dnq 13; WCh: '05- 7, '07- dnq 15; WUG: '01- 8. US champion 2004.
Progress at DT: 1996- 53.14, 1997- 59.46, 1998- 59.78, 1999- 56.86, 2000- 64.00, 2001- 65.53, 2002- 65.92, 2003- 62.24, 2004- 67.51, 2005- 67.39, 2006- 67.25, 2007- 68.37. pb SP 20.40 '06.
Was a quarterback in high school.

Leonard SCOTT b. 19 Jan 1980 Zachary, Louisiana 1.81m 84kg. Nike. Studied sociology at the University of Tennessee.
At 100m: WCh: '05- 6. At 60m: WI: '06- 1.
Progress at 100m: 1997- 10.56, 1998- 10.34, 1999- 10.29/9.83w, 2000- 10.26A/10.18w, 2001- 10.05, 2002- 10.13, 2004- 10.01, 2005- 9.94, 2006- 9.91, 2007- 10.09. pbs: 50m 5.58i '05, 55m 6.07i '99, 60m 6.46i '05, 200m 20.34 '01, 20.08w '99.
He missed the 2003 season while with the Pittsburgh Steelers Football team, although he did not play a game in the NFL. Slimmed down from 89kg to 80kg in a year and a half on his return to track.

Wallace SPEARMON b. 24 Dec 1984 Chicago 1.88m 78kg. Student at University of Arkansas.
At 200m/4x100mR: WCh: '05- 2, '07- 3/1R; WCp: '06- 1/1R. US champion 2006, NCAA 2004-05. At 4x400m: WI: '06- 1R. WIR 4x400m 2006. Two US indoor 200m records 2005.
Progress at 100m, 200m: 2003- 21.05, 2004- 10.38, 20.25/20.12w; 2005- 10.35/10.21w, 19.89; 2006- 10.11, 19.65; 2007- 9.96, 19.82. pbs: 60m 6.70i '08, 300m 31.88i '06 (world indoor best), 400m 45.22.
His father (also Wallace, b. 3 Sep 1962) had pbs: of 100m 10.19 '87, 10.05w '86, 10.0w '81; 200m 20.27/20.20w '87. 1 WUG 200/4x100m, 3 PAm 200m 1987.

Toby STEVENSON b. 19 Nov 1976 Odessa, Texas 1.86m 82kg. ZMA. Economics graduate of Stanford University.
At PV: OG: '04- 2; PAm: '03- 1, won NCAA 1998.
Progress at PV: 1994- 4.87, 1995- 5.18, 1996- ?, 1997- 5.40i/5.37, 1998- 5.55, 1999- 5.55, 2000- 5.73A, 2001- 5.40, 2002- 5.74, 2003- 5.75, 2004- 6.00, 2005- 5.90, 2006- 5.82, 2007- 5.70.
Wears a protective helmet while vaulting. Withdrew injured after warm-up at 2005 Worlds.

Angelo TAYLOR b. 29 Dec 1978 Albany, Georgia 1.88m 84kg. Nike. Was at Georgia Tech University. Electrician.
At 400mh/4x400mR: OG: '00- 1/dq (res 1)R, '04- sf; WCh: '99- h/1R, '01- sf/1R, '07- (3 400m)/1R; WJ: '96- 3; won GP 2000 (and overall), PAm-J 1997, NCAA 1998, US 400mh 1999-2001, 400m 2007, indoor 400m 1999.
Progress at 400m, 400mh: 1995- -, 52.76, 1996- 46.7, 50.18; 1997- 46.19i/46.81, 48.72; 1998- 45.14, 47.90; 1999- 45.50i, 48.15; 2000- 44.89, 47.50; 2001- 44.68, 47.95; 2002- 44.85, 48.87; 2003- 46.32, 48.94; 2004- 45.85, 48.03; 2006- 45.24, 49.44; 2007- 44.05, 48.45. pbs: 200m 20.60 '07, 300m 32.67 '02, TJ 14.76 '96.
Brilliant year in 1998, with fastest ever time by a 19 year-old and losing just twice (to Bryan Bronson) at 400mh. Went out in his heat (misjudging the finish) when favourite for 1999 World 400mh, but made amends with relay gold, and, after winning Olympic gold in 2000, stumbled off the last hurdle in 2001 World 400mh semi.

Dan TAYLOR b. 12 May 1982 Cleveland 1.98m 145kg. Construction management graduate of Ohio State University.
At SP: WCh: '07- dnq 34; PAm: '03- 4. Won NCAA indoor 2003-04.
Progress at SP: 2001- 18.31, 2002- 20.01i/19.15, 2003- 21.33i/20.44, 2004- 20.62, 2005- 20.75, 2006- 21.59, 2007- 21.57i/21.18. pbs: DT 59.00 '03, HT 69.35 '04, Wt 24.01i '04.
Achieved unique NCAA SP/Wt double 2004.

Matt TEGENKAMP b. 19 Jan 1982 Lee's Summit, Missouri 1.83m 57kg. Studied human ecology at University of Wisconsin.
At 5000m: WCh: '07- 4; WCp: '06- 3. World CC: '01- 5J. North American 2M record 2007.
Progress at 5000m: 2001- 13:49.64, 2002- 13:44.77, 2004- 13:30.90, 2005- 13:25.36, 2006- 13:04.90, 2007- 13:07.41. pbs: 1500m 3:34.25 '07, 1M 3:56.38

'06, 2000m 5:01.3 '06, 3000m 7:35.68 '07, 2M 8:07.07 '07, 10,000m 29:59.35 '02.

Terrrence TRAMMELL b. 23 Nov 1978 Atlanta 1.88m 84kg. Mizuno. Studied retail management at University of South Carolina.
At 110mh/4x100m: OG: '00- 2, '04- 2; WCh: '01- sf, '03- 2, '05- 5, '07- 2; WUG: '99- 1/1R; Won US 2004, 2007; NCAA 1999-2000. At 60mh: WI: '01- 1, '06- 1 (60m 3).
Progress at 110mh: 1997- 13.87, 1998- 13.32, 1999- 13.28, 2000- 13.16, 2001- 13.23, 2002- 13.17, 2003- 13.17, 2004- 13.09, 2005- 13.02, 2006- 13.02, 2007- 12.95. pbs: 55m 6.12i '99, 60m 6.45Ai '00, 6.46i '03; 100m 10.04 '00, 200m 20.74 '98, 20.45w '99; 55mh 6.94i '99, 60mh 7.42i '03.
Twice world indoor champion at 60mh and joint fifth fastest of all-time at flat 60m indoors. After 13.02 for 110mh in 2005 and 2006 broke 13 seconds for first time at New York in 2007. Injured in heats of World Indoor 60m 2003.

Brad WALKER b. 21 Jun 1981 Aberdeen, South Dakota 1.88m 86kg. Nike. Graduated in business administration from University of Washington
At PV: WCh: '05- 2, '07- 1; WI: '06- 1, '08- 2; Won WAF 2005, 2007; US 2005, 2007; indoors 2005-06, NCAA indoor 2003-04.
Progress at PV: 1999- 4.80, 2000- 5.12, 2001- 5.48i/5.36, 2002- 5.64, 2003- 5.80i/5.65, 2004- 5.82, 2005- 5.96, 2006- 6.00, 2007- 5.95, 2008- 5.85i.

Ian WALTZ b. 15 Apr 1977 Ashland, Oregon 1.86m 122kg. Studied kinesiology at Washington State University.
At DT: OG: '04- dnq 21; WCh: '05- 5, '07- dnq 13; WJ: '96- 5 (6 SP); WCp: '06- 3. US champion 2005-06.
Progress at DT: 1996- 57.78, 1997- 59.85, 1998- 64.44, 1999- 58.50, 2000- 60.54, 2001- 60.30, 2002- 63.84, 2003- 62.55, 2004- 66.14, 2005- 66.95, 2006- 68.91, 2007- 67.98. pb SP 20.10 '02.
Good American footballer (defensive end) in high school.

Jeremy WARINER b. 31 Jan 1984 Irving, Texas 1.88m 67kg. Student of outdoor recreation at Baylor University.
WIR 4x400m 2006.
At 400m/4x400mR: OG: '04- 1/1R; WCh: '05- 1/1R, '07- 1/1R; PAm-J: '03- 2/1R. US Champion 2004-05, NCAA 2004, WAF 2006.
Progress at 200m, 400m: 2001- 21.33/21.23w, 46.68; 2002- 21.17/20.8/20.41w, 45.57; 2003- 20.78, 45.13; 2004- 20.59, 44.00; 2005- 20.52w, 43.93; 2006- 20.19, 43.62; 2007- 20.35, 43.45. pbs: 100m 10.52w '02, 300m 31.58+ '07.
His 43.93 to win 2005 World title was world's fastest 400m time for five years, his 43.62 to win Rome GP in 2006 the fastest for seven years and his 43.45 to win the 2007 World title took him to third on the world all-time list. He shared the Golden League jackpot and won all eleven 400m races in 2006 with three sub-44 times (a record seven sub-44.25s and 10 sub 44.50s) until he dropped out in Shanghai. Won all 10 races in 2007 after from failure to start in Sheffield.

Alan WEBB b. 13 Jan 1983 Ann Arbor, Michigan 1.76m 64kg. Nike. Was at University of Michigan.
At 1500m: OG: '04- h; WCh: '05- 9, '07- 8. Won US 1500m 2004-05, 2007.
US records 1M 2007, 2M 2005.
Progress at 1500m/1M: 1999- 4:06.94M, 2000- 3:47.4/4:03.33M, 2001- 3:38.26/3:53.43M, 2002- 3:41.46, 2003- 3:42.87/3:58.84M, 2004- 3:32.73/3:50.73M, 2005- 3:32.52/3:48.92M, 2006- 4:00.87M, 2007- 3:30.54/3:46.91M. pbs: 800m 1:43.84 '07, 1000m 2:20.32 '05, 3000m 7:39.28 '05, 2M 8:11.48 '05, 5000m 13:10.86 '05, 10,000m 27:34.72 '06.
Broke Jim Ryun's high school record for sophomores in 1999 and in 2001 became the first high schooler to break 4 minutes indoors and outdoors broke Ryun's 36 year-old high school record with 3:53.43.

Ryan WHITING b. 24 Nov 1986 Pennsylvania 1.90m 116kg. Civil engineering student at Arizona State University.
At SP: Won NCAA indoor 2008.
Progress at SP: 2006- 19.75, 2007- 20.35, 2008- 21.73i. pb DT 61.11 '08.

Derrick WILLIAMS b. 25 Mar 1982 1.81m 73kg. Reebok. Was at North Texas University.
At 400mh: WCh: '07- 7.
Progress at 400mh: 2001- 51.23, 2003- 50.14, 2004- 51.72, 2005- 50.89, 2006- 48.68, 2007- 48.26. pbs: 55mh 7.29i '05, 60mh 7.85i '05, 110mh 13.96/13.59w '03.

Jesse WILLIAMS b. 27 Dec 1983 Modesto 1.84m 75kg. Nike. Graduate of University of Southern California, formerly at North Carolina State.
At HJ: WCh: '05/07- dnq 15/26; WJ: '02- 4=; WI: '08- 6=; Won NCAA indoors and out 2005-06.
Progress at HJ: 2001- 2.16, 2002- 2.21, 2003- 2.24, 2004- 2.24, 2005- 2.30, 2006- 2.32, 2007- 2.33, 2008- 2.32i. pb LJ 7.53 '06.
Also a wrestler in high school.

Darold WILLIAMSON b. 19 Feb 1983 San Antonio, Texas 1.88m 77kg. Student of communications at Baylor University.
At 400m/4x400mR: OG: '04- 1R; WCh: '05- 7/1R, '07- 1R; WJ: '02- 1/1R; WCp: '06- 1R. Won NCAA 2005. WIR 4x400m 2006.
Progress at 400m: 2000- 46.94, 2001- 46.12, 2002- 45.23, 2003- 44.95, 2004- 44.51, 2005- 44.27, 2006- 44.88, 2007- 44.68. pbs: 200m 20.91 '01, 300m 32.42 '06, 32.1+ '07.

Aarik WILSON b. 25 Oct 1982 Falon, Nevada 1.91m 88kg. Was at Indiana University.
At TJ: WCh: '07- 5; PAm: '03- 5; WI: '08- 7. Won US indoors and out 2007, NCAA indoor LJ & TJ 2005.
Progress at TJ: 2000- 15.28A, 2001- 15.57, 2002-

16.68, 2003- 16.99i/16.69, 2004- 16.96A/16.91/16.97Aw, 2005- 16.94, 2006- 17.32, 2007- 17.58. pb LJ 8.17i '05, 8.07/8.11w '07.

Ryan WILSON b. 19 Dec 1980 1.88m 79kg. Graduate (art) of University of Southern California.
At 110mh: won NCAA 2003.
Progress at 110mh: 2000- 14.00/13.79w, 2001- 13.69, 2002- 13.55, 2003- 13.35, 2004- 13.65/13.58w, 2005- 13.99, 2006- 13.22, 2007- 13.02. pbs: 50mh 6.78i '02, 55mh 7.25i '06, 60mh 7.83i '04, 400mh 49.33 '03.

Women

Amy ACUFF b. 14 Jul 1975 Port Arthur, Texas 1.88m 66kg. Asics. Graduate of UCLA (biology) and Academy of Oriental Medicine, Austin. Part-time model.
At HJ: OG: '96- dnq 24=, '00- dnq 31, '04- 4; WCh: '95-97-99-01-03-05-07: 8=/dnq 14/9/10=/9=/8/12; WI: '01-03-08: 4/10/6; WJ: '92- 9, '94-3=; WUG: '97- 1; WCp: '06- 3=. 3rd GP 2001. Won PAm-J 1993, NCAA 1995-6, US 1995, 1997, 2001, 2003, 2005, 2007.
Progress at HJ: 1988- 1.73, 1990- 1.83, 1991- 1.89, 1992- 1.90, 1993- 1.93, 1994- 1.89, 1995- 1.98, 1996- 1.94, 1997- 2.00, 1998- 1.94, 1999- 1.95, 2000- 1.91, 2001- 1.98, 2002- 1.95, 2003- 2.01, 2004- 2.00, 2005- 1.93, 2006- 1.96, 2007- 1.95.
Married **Tye Harvey** (b. 25 Sep 1974, PV: 2 WI 03, 5.93i '01, 5.80 '00) in October 2004.

Jenny ADAMS b. 8 Jul 1978 Tomball, Texas 1.65m 55kg. Nike. Corporate communications graduate of University of Houston.
At 100mh: WCh: '01- 5 (nj LJ), '03- 6. Won US LJ 2001, NCAA LJ 2000.
Progress at 100mh: 1995- 14.45w, 1996- 13.98/13.93w, 1997- 13.47, 1998- 13.25/13.22w, 1999- 12.98/12.86w, 2000- 12.86, 2001- 12.63/12.61w, 2002- 12.80/12.71w, 2003- 12.67, 2004- 12.66, 2005- 12.89/12.88w, 2006- 12.66, 2007- 12.82/12.75w. pbs: 60m 7.47i '00, 100m 11.58 '00, 200m 23.51 '03, 60mh 7.95i '03, LJ 6.68i/6.75w '01, 6.64 '00.

Me'Lisa BARBER b. 4 Oct 1980 Livingston, New Jersey 1.60m 52kg. Nike. Was at University of South Carolina.
At 100m/4x100mR: WCh: '05- 5/1R. At 400m/4x400mR: WCh: '03- 1R; PAm: '03- 5/1R; WUG: '01- 3R. At 60m: WI: '06- 1. Won US 100m 2005.
Progress at 100m, 200m, 400m: 1997- 11.86/11.78w, 24.20; 1998- 11.57, 23.93/23.63w, 57.21i; 1999- 11.40, 23.57/23.16w; 2000- 11.59, 23.23; 2001- 11.46/11.44w, 23.43/23.06w, 52.18; 2002- 11.35, 23.01, 50.87; 2003- 23.51, 52.04; 2004- 51.95, 2005- 11.04/10.87w, 22.37; 2006- 11.03, 22.92; 2007- 10.95. pbs: 60m 7.01i '06, 300m 37.54 '03.
Twin sister of Mikele.

Mikele BARBER b. 4 Oct 1980 Livingston, New Jersey 1.57m 50kg. Nike. Was at University of South Carolina.
At 100m/4x100mR: WCh: '07- 1R; PAm: '07- 1/2R. At 400m/4x400mR: WJ: '98- 8/3R; WUG: '99-2/1R, '01- 3/3R; won NCAA 2000.
Progress at 100m, 200m, 400m: 1996- 24.2w, 55.3; 1997- 24.07/23.92w. 54.03; 1998- 23.94/23.2w, 52.56; 1999- 11.67, 23.05/22.99w, 51.03; 2000- 22.98/22.84w, 50.98; 2001- 23.21/22.71w, 50.63; 2003- 23.06i/23.46, 51.92i/52.43; 2006- 11.27, 23.42; 2007- 11.02, 22.73. pbs: 60m 7.27i '06, 300m 37.99i '00

Becky BREISCH b. 10 Oct 1982 Edwardsburg, Michigan 1.80m 104kg. Nike. Was at University of Nebraska.
At DT: WCh: '05-07- dnq 18/19; Won NCAA SP 2003, DT 2004, NACAC DT 2004.
Progress at DT: 1999- 46.16, 2000- 47.83, 2001- 48.23, 2002- 55.67, 2003- 58.69, 2004- 63.12, 2005- 63.53, 2006- 62.75, 2007- 67.37. pbs: SP 18.46 '06, 20lbWt 19.87i '04.

Danielle CARRUTHERS b. 22 Dec 1979 Paducah, Kentucky 1.73m 62kg. Nike. Was at University of Indiana.
At 100mh: WUG: '01- 8. At 60mh: WI: '06- 4. Won US indoor 60mh 2005-06.
Progress at 100mh: 1998- 13.88/13.77w, 2000- 13.33, 2001- 12.96/12.79w, 2002- 12.68, 2003- 12.79, 2004- 12.56, 2005- 12.72/12.63w, 2006- 12.74, 2007- 12.89. pbs: 55m 6.79i '00, 60m 7.26i '02, 100m 11.43/11.42w '01, 200m 23.24 '01, 50mh 6.85i '02, 55mh 7.55i '00, 60mh 7.88i '06.

Damu CHERRY b. 29 Nov 1977 Tampa 1.63m 59kg. Nike. Was at University of Florida.
At 60mh: WI: '06- 7.
Progress at 100mh: 1999- 13.32, 2000- 13.26/13.24w, 2001- 12.85, 2002- 12.98, 2003- 12.68dq, 2006- 12.44, 2007- 12.74. pbs: 55m 6.88i '03, 60m 7.54i '03, 100m 11.53 '07, 200m 23.94 '01, 60mh 7.85i '08, 7.84idq '03.
Two year drugs ban – positive test 18 Feb 2003.

Hazel CLARK b. 3 Oct 1977 Livingston, NJ 1.78m 55kg. Nike. Was at University of Florida.
At 800m: OG: '00- 7, '04- h; WCh: '01- sf, '05- 8, '07- sf; PAm: '03- 7; WCp: '06- 6. US champion 2005-06, NCAA 1998.
Progress at 800m: 1994- 2:10.24, 1995- 2:05.50, 1996- 2:05.08i/2:06.66, 1997- 2:01.42, 1998- 2:00.23, 1999- 2:01.77i/2:02.01, 2000- 1:58.75, 2001- 1:59.95, 2002- 2:05.24, 2003- 2:01.71, 2004- 1:59.32, 2005- 1:57.99, 2006- 1:59.10, 2007- 1:59.43. pbs: 400m 53.69 '98, 1000m 2:36.47 '01, 1500m 4:16.04 '00, 1M 4:40.82 '00.
Sister of **Joetta** (b. 1 Aug 1962) who competed at four Olympics 1988-2000 (7th 1992) and five World Champs (7th 1997) and ranked in US top ten at 800m for 22 successive years 1979-2000; pb 1:57.84 (1998). Their brother (and coach) J J Clark married Jearl Miles-Clark and their father is the celebrated school principal, Joe Clark, portrayed in the movie *Lean On Me*.

Candice DAVIS b. 26 Oct 1985 Ann Arbor,

Michigan 1.70m 62kg. Was at University of Southern California.
At 60mh: WI: '08- 2.
Progress at 100mh: 2001- 13.76, 2002- 13.69/13.51w, 2003- 13.66, 2004- 13.93/13.80w, 2005- 13.21/13.13w, 2006- 13.07A/13.10/13.05w, 2007- 12.90/12.88w. pbs: 60m 7.65i '07, 100m 11.54 '07, 60mh 7.90i '08.

Lashinda DEMUS b. 10 Mar 1983 Palmdale, California 1.70m 62kg. Nike. Student at University of South Carolina.
At 400mh/4x400mR: OG: '04- sf; WCh: '05- 2; WJ: '02- 1/1R; WCp: '06- 2/2R. Won WAF 2005-06, PAm-J 1999, US 2005-06, NCAA 2002.
Two world junior records 400mh 2002.
Progress at 400mh: 1998- 64.61, 1999- 57.04, 2001- 55.76, 2002- 54.70, 2003- 55.65, 2004- 53.43, 2005- 53.27, 2006- 53.02. pbs: 50m 6.64i '01, 60m 7.73i '01, 100m 11.5 '01, 200m 24.0 '01, 23.50w '05; 400m 51.24 '02, 500y 1:05.8i '01, 800m 2:08.91i '06, 2:09.16 '04; 55mh 7.65i '04, 60mh 8.11i '04, 100mh 13.08 '04, 12.93w '05.
Twin sons Duane and Donte born 5 Jun 2007. Her mother, Yolanda Rich, had a 400m best of 52.19 in 1980.

Nichole DENBY b. 10 Oct 1982 Los Angeles 1.63m 52kg. Nike. Was at University of Texas.
At 100mh: WCh: '07- sf; Won NCAA 2004.
Progress at 100mh: 1998- 14.20, 1999- 13.53/13.36w, 2000- 13.20, 2001- 13.41/13.39w, 2002- 13.17, 2003- 12.98, 2004- 12.62, 2005- 12.79/12.66w, 2006- 12.84/12.77w, 2007- 12.80/12.72w. pbs: 60m 7.43i '04, 100m 11.67 '00, 50mh 6.90i+ '05, 60mh 7.93i '07, LJ 5.91i '04.

Stacy DRAGILA b. 25 Mar 1971 Auburn, California 1.72m 62kg. née Mikaelson. Nike. Graduate of Idaho State University.
At PV: OG: '00- 1, '04- dnq 18=; WCh: '99- 1, '01- 1, '03- 4=, '05- dnq 16; WI: '97-9-01-03-04: 1/8/4/dnq/2. Won GWG 2001, GP 2001, US 1996-7, 1999-2001, 2003-05.
7 world pole vault records 1999-2001 & world outdoor best 2004, 10 WIR 1997-2003. 18 US records 1996-2004 (and 24 indoors 1995-2004).
Progress at PV: 1995- 3.70, 1996- 4.20, 1997- 4.45, 1998- 4.48i/4.42A, 1999- 4.60, 2000- 4.70b/4.63, 2001- 4.81, 2002- 4.72, 2003- 4.78i/4.62, 2004- 4.83, 2005- 4.60, 2007- 4.50. pbs: 55mh 8.30i '03, 100mh 13.88A '98, HJ 1.70 '97, LJ 5.89/6.07w '02; SP 10.80 '02, JT 44.28A '98, Hep 5488A '98.
Won first women's world vault titles both indoors 1997 and outdoors 1999 (both in world records) and inaugural Olympic title. Surgery on right Achilles in June 2006.

Stephanie DURST b. 11 Apr 1982 1.68m 58kg. Nike. Sociology graduate of Louisiana State University.
Progress at 100m, 200m:1998- 24.22, 2000- 24.10, 2001- 11.60/11.42w, 23.33/23.05w; 2002- 11.39, 22.48/22.46w; 2003- 22.86, 2004- 11.54, 22.66/22.60w, 2005- 11.24, 22.64; 2006- 11.13, 22.51; 2007- 11.09, 22.51. pb 60m 7.25i '06.

Torri EDWARDS b. 31 Jan 1977 Fontana, Cal. 1.63m 52kg. Nike/HSI. Studied sociology at University of Southern California.
At 100m/(200m)/4x100mR: OG: '00- qf/sf/3R; WCh: '01- dq1 resR, '03- 1/2/2R, '07- 4/4/1R; PAm: '99- 2R; WUG: '99- 5/1R; WCp: '06- 2. At 60m: WI: '03- 3, '04- 4. Won US 100m 2007.
Progress at 100m, 200m: 1994- 24.52, 1995- 11.84w, 23.94/23.60w; 1996- 11.48, 23.60/23.1; 1997- 11.55A/11.35w, 23.43; 1998- 11.11/11.05w, 22.88/22.87w; 1999- 11.10/11.05w, 22.89/22.84w; 2000- 11.06/10.92w, 22.65; 2001- 11.11/11.09w, 2002- 11.11, 2003- 10.93, 22.28; 2004- 11.00dq, 22.38dq, 2006- 11.06/10.86w, 22.50; 2007- 10.90, 22.51. pbs: 50m 6.31i '02, 60m 7.10i '06.
She finished 2nd at 100m and 3rd at 200m at the 2003 Worlds, positions that were elevated to gold and silver through the disqualification of Kelli White for drugs abuse. Received drugs ban from 24 Apr 2004, but reinstated early in November 2005 as nikethamide downgraded to public warning and one year's ineligibility.

Allyson FELIX b. 18 Nov 1985 Los Angeles 1.68m 57kg. adidas. Graduated in elementary education from University of Southern California.
At 200m: OG: '04- 2; WCh: '03- qf, '05- 1, '07- 1/1R/1R; WJ: '02- 5; PAm: '03- 3. At 100m: WY: '01- 1 (1 Medley R). Won WAF 200m 2005-06, US 200m 2004-05, 2007.
World junior record 200m 2004 after unratified (no doping test) at age 17 in 2003.
Progress at 100m, 200m, 400m: 2000- 12.19/11.99w, 23.90; 2001- 11.53, 23.31/23.27w; 2002- 11.40, 22.83/22.69w, 55.01; 2003- 11.29/11.12w, 22.11A/22.51, 52.26; 2004- 11.16, 22.18, 51.83A; 2005- 11.05, 22.13, 51.12; 2006- 11.04, 22.11; 2007- 11.01, 21.81, 49.70. pbs: 50m 6.43i '02, 60m 7.32i '04, 300m 36.33i '07.
First teenager to won a World sprint title. Unbeaten in ten 200m competitions 2005 and in five 2007. Starred at 2007 Worlds wth three gold medals, record 0.53 winning margin at 200m and both relays, with 48.0 400m leg. Older brother Wes Felix won World Junior bronze at 200m and gold in WJR at 4x100m in 2002, pbs: 100m 10.23 '05, 200m 20.43 '04.

Shalane FLANAGAN b. 8 Jul 1981 Boulder 1.65m 50kg. Nike. Was at University of North Carolina.
At 5000m: OG: '04- h; WCh: '05- h, '07- 8. World 4k CC: '05- 20. Won US 5000m 2005, CC 2008, 4km CC 2004-05, indoor 3000m 2007, NCAA CC 2002-03, indoor 3000m 2003. North American records: 5000m and indoor 3000m 2007
Progress at 5000m: 2001- 16:29.68, 2003- 15:20.54, 2004- 15:05.08, 2005- 15:10.96, 2007- 14:44.80. pbs: 800m 2:09.28 '02, 1500m 4:05.86 '07, 1M 4:37.41i '01, 3000m 8:33.25i/8:35.34 '07.
Brilliant return in 2007 after missing 2006 with a

foot injury. Mother, Cheryl Bridges, set marathon world best with 2:49:40 in 1971 and was 4th in 1969 International CC.

Hyleas FOUNTAIN b. 14 Jan 1981 Columbus, Georgia 1.70m 60kg. Nike. University of Georgia.
At Hep: WCh: '05- 12, '07- dnf; US champion 2005. At Pen: WI: '06- 8. Won NCAA Hep 2003, LJ 2004; US Junior HJ 2000, Hep 2007.
Progress at Hep: 2001- 4905, 2002- 5673w, 2003- 5999, 2004- 6035, 2005- 6502, 2006- 6148, 2007- 6090. pbs: 200m 23.53 '03, 800m 2:16.79 '06, 55mh 7.61i '05, 60mh 8.15i '04, 100mh 13.09 '05, HJ 1.88 '05, LJ 6.67 '05, TJ 13.40 '04, SP 12.76i '06, 12.69 '07; JT 46.90 '05, Pen 4417i '05.

Sandra GLOVER b. 30 Dec 1968 Palestine, Texas 1.73m 59kg. née Cummings. Nike. Teacher, graduate of University of Houston.
At 400mh: OG: '00- sf; WCh: '99- 5, '01- 8, '03- 2, '05- 3; WCp: '02- 2; Won WAF 2003-04, US 1999-2002. 3rd GP 1999, 2001.
Progress at 400mh: 1988- 61.08, 1989- 59.99, 1990- 57.68, 1991- 56.97, 1992- 55.77, 1993- 56.76, 1994- 56.66, 1995- 57.39, 1996- 56.31mx/56.92, 1997- 55.63, 1998- 55.11, 1999- 53.65, 2000- 53.33, 2001- 54.30, 2002- 54.40, 2003- 53.34, 2004- 53.40, 2005- 53.32, 2006- 54.15, 2007- 54.59. pbs: 200m 23.73 '00, 100mh 13.79/13.62w '91.
Made huge improvement in 1999 at the age of 30. Coached by her husband, Don Glover.

Kara GOUCHER b. 9 Jul 1978 Queens, New York 1.70m 59kg. née Grgas-Wheeler. Nike. Studied psychology at Colorado State University.
At 10,000m: WCh: '07- 3. At 3000m: WCp: '06- 3. World 4k CC: '06- 21. At 3000m: WCp: '06- 5. Won NCAA 3000m, 5000m & CC 2000.
Progress at 5000m, 10,000m: 1999- 16:57.31, 2000- 15:28.78, 2001- 15:31.77, 2003- 15:42.97, 33:44.86; 2004- 16:30.35, 2005- 15:17.55, 2006- 15:08.13, 31:17.12; 2007- 14:55.02, 32:02.05. pbs: 800m 2:08.60 '07, 1500m 4:05.14 '06, 1M 4:46.45i '06, 3000m 8:34.99 '07, 2M 9:41.32 '07, HMar 66:57 '07.
After surprise World 10,000m bronze, made brilliant half marathon debut to win Great North Run 2007 with American best.
Married (2001) **Adam Goucher** (18 Feb 1975) (pbs: 1500m 3:36.64 '01, 1M 3:54.17 '99, 2000m 4:58.92 '99, 3000m 7:34.96 '01, 2M 8:12.73 '06, 5000m 13:10.00 '06, 10,000m 27:59.41 '06).

Dawn HARPER b. 13 May 1984 1.68m 57kg. Nike. Was at UCLA.
At 100mh: won PAm-J 2003.
Progress at 100mh: 2002- 13.63, 2003- 13.33/13.21w, 2004- 13.16/12.91w, 2005- 12.91, 2006- 12.80A/12.86, 2007- 12.67. pbs: 60m 7.70i '05, 100m 11.66 '07, 200m 23.97 '06, 60mh 7.98i '06.

Natasha HASTINGS b. 23 Jul 1986 Brooklyn, NY 1.73m 63kg. Reebok. Student of exercise science at Unversty of South Carolina.
At 400m/4x400m: WCh: '07- sf/res 1R; WJ: '04- 1/1R; WY: '03- 1. Won NCAA indoors and out 2007. World junior 500m best 2005.
Progress at 400m: 2000- 54.21, 2001- 55.06, 2002- 53.42, 2003- 52.09, 2004- 52.04, 2005- 51.34, 2006- 51.45, 2007- 49.84. pbs: 55m 7.08i '02, 100m 11.61 '04, 200m 22.61 '07, 300m 35.9+ '07, 500m 1:10.05i '05.
Father from Jamaica, mother Joanne Gardner was British (ran 11.89 to win WAAA U15 100m at 14 in 1977).

Joanna HAYES b. 23 Dec 1976 Williamsport, Pa. 1.65m 58kg. Sociology graduate of UCLA.
At 100mh: OG: '04- 1; WCh: '05- dq (fell); PAmJ: '95- 1; won WAF 2004. At 400mh: WCh: '99- h, '03- sf; PAm: '99- 5, '03- 1; WUG: '99- 2; won NCAA 1999. At 60mh: WI: '04- 4.
Progress at 100mh, 400mh: 1994- 14.02/13.80w, 59.12; 1995- 13.38/13.06w, 59.02; 1996- 13.15, 58.32; 1997- 13.04, 56.38; 1998- 12.93, 57.09; 1999- 12.89, 54.57; 2000- 12.67, 54.97; 2003- 12.83/12.65w, 54.66; 2004- 12.37, 55.74; 2005- 12.47, 2006- 12.76, 2007- 13.28/12.78w. pbs: 100m 11.41 '04, 60mh 7.83i '04.
Missed Olympics in 2000 (4th at 400mh and 5th at 100mh in US Trials) and did not compete in 2001-02 while working at the Jackie Joyner-Kersee Youth Center in East St. Louis. Then returned to LA.

Monique HENDERSON b. 18 Feb 1983 San Diego 1.70m 54kg. Reebok. Student at UCLA.
At 400m/4x400m: OG: '04- 1R; WCh: '05- 7; WJ: '02- 1/1R; PAm: '07- 6; WCp: '06- 2R. NCAA champion 2005.
Progress at 400m: 1996- 54.79, 1997- 53.83, 1998- 52.93, 1999- 51.96, 2000- 50.74, 2001- 51.34, 2002- 51.10, 2003- 51.96, 2004- 50.53, 2005- 49.96, 2006- 50.14, 2007- 50.82. pbs: 60m 7.50i '03, 100m 11.34 '05, 200m 22.71 '04, 300m 35.8 '05.

Monique HENNAGAN b. 26 May 1976 Columbia, SC 1.73m 57kg. Nike. Degree in psychology from University of North Carolina.
At 400m/4x400mR: OG: '00- qf/1R, '04- 4/1R; WCh: '01- sf, '05- hR, '07- res 1R; WI: '99- 3R, '01- 5/4R, '03- 5/3R; WJ: '92- sf/4R, '94- 2/1R; PAm-J: '93- 2/2R; WCp: '02- 2R. Won US 400m 2004-05, NCAA 800m 1996.
Progress at 400m: 1992- 53.58, 1993- 52.30, 1994- 52.19, 1995- 52.32, 1996- 51.44, 1997- 52.00, 1998- 51.11, 1999- 51.05, 2000- 50.82, 2001- 50.98, 2002- 51.04, 2003- 51.46, 2004- 49.56, 2005- 50.24, 2006- 51.46, 2007- 51.19. pbs: 60m 7.42i '04, 100m 11.26 '05, 200m 22.87 '05, 300m 36.52 '01, 800m 2:02.5 '96.

Chaunte HOWARD b. 12 Jan 1984 Templeton, California 1.75m 59kg. Was at Georgia Tech University.
At HJ: OG: '04- dnq 26=; WCh: '05- 2; PAm-J: '03- 3; Won US 2006, NCAA 2004, indoors 2004-05
Progress at HJ: 2000- 1.75, 2001- 1.84, 2002- 1.87,

2003- 1.89, 2004- 1.98A, 2005- 2.00, 2006- 2.01, 2008- 1.95. pbs: 100m 11.83 '05, 100mh 13.78 '04, LJ 6.26 '02, TJ 12.93 '04, 12.98w '05.
Marriued to Mario Lowe (b. 20 Apr 1980, TJ pb 16.15 '02), daughter Jasmine born 30 Jul 2007.

Carmelita JETER b. 24 Nov 1979 Los Angeles 1.63m 53kg. Was at California State University, Dominguez Hills.
At 100m/4x100mR: WCh: '07- 3/res 1R; won WAF 2007.
Progress at 100m: 2000- 11.69, 2002- 11.46w, 2003- 11.61/11.43w, 2004- 11.56, 2006- 11.48, 2007- 11.02. pbs: 60m 7.16i '07, 200m 22.82 '07.
Younger brother Eugene plays NBA basketball for the Miami Heat.

Sheena JOHNSON b. 1 Oct 1982 Camden, New Jersey 1.65m 58kg. Nike. Student at UCLA.
At 400mh: OG: '04- 4; WCh: '07- sf; WJ: '98- h. Won US 2004, NCAA 2003-04.
Progress at 400mh: 1998- 58.61, 1999- 59.12, 2000- 56.82, 2001- 56.02, 2002- 55.71, 2003- 54.24, 2004- 52.95, 2005- 54.72, 2006- 53.90, 2007- 53.29. pbs: 60m 7.40i '07, 100m 11.68 '06, 200m 23.42 '07, 400m 52.85 '06, 60mh 8.04 '07, 100mh 12.75 '04, LJ 6.10/6.16w '00, TJ 12.67 '00.

Lori '**Lolo**' **JONES** b. 5 Aug 1982 Des Moines 1.68m 60kg. Nike. Spanish & economic graduate of Louisiana State University.
At 100mh: Ch: '07- 6; Won NACAC 2004. At 60mh: WI: '08- 1; won NCAA indoor 2003, US indoor 2007-08.
Progress at 100mh: 2000- 14.04, 2001- 13.31/13.17w/12.7w, 2002- 12.84, 2003- 12.90, 2004- 12.77, 2005- 12.76, 2006- 12.56, 2007- 12.57. pbs: 55m 6.87i '03, 60m 7.27i '03, 100m 11.24 '06, 200m 23.76 '04, 23.50w '03; 55mh 7.57i '03, 60mh 7.77i '08, 400mh 59.95 '00.

Deena KASTOR b. 14 Feb 1973 Waltham, Mass. née Drossin. 1.63m 48kg.Asics. Graduate of University of Arkansas.
At 10,000m: OG: '00- h; WCh: '99- 11, '01- 11, '03- 12, '07- 6; WUG: '97- 1. At Mar: OG: '04- 3. World CC: '99-00-01-02-03: 10/12/12/2/2; HMar: '07- 16; Won US 10,000m 2000-01, 2003-04, 2007; HMar 2004, CC 1997, 1999-2003, 2007.
N.American records: 10,000m 2002, 15km road & Mar 2003, 10M, 20k, HMar, Mar 2006.
Progress at 5000m, 10,000m, Mar: 1992- 16:21.47, 1993- 15:52.80i/16:07.73, 1994- 16:39.62, 34:10.89; 1996- 16:29.17, 34:13.75; 1997- 15:43.63, 32:47.44; 1998- 15:07.83, 1999- 14:56.84, 32:00.72; 2000- 14:51.62, 31:51.05; 2001- 15:08.02, 32:05.14, 2:26:58; 2002- 15:13.93, 30:50.32, 2:26:53; 2003- 15:08.14, 31:17.86. 2:21:16; 2004- 15:29.30, 31:09.65, 2:27:20; 2005- 15:52.0, 31:45.08, 2:21:25; 2006- 2:19:36, 2007- 14:52.21, 31:57.00, 2:35:09. pbs: 1500m 4:07.82 '00, 2000m 5:42.76 '01, 3000m 8:42.59 '00, 2M 9:35.89 '02; Road: 5km 14:54 '02, 15km 47:15 '03, 10M 51:31 '06, 20km 64:07 '06, HMar 67:34 '06, 25km 1:21:57 '05, 30km 1:38:29 '05.
Seventh in New York on marathon debut 2001. 3rd London Marathon 2003, won Chicago 2005 and London 2006. Married her massage therapist Andrew Kastor on 14 September 2003.

Muna LEE b. 30 Oct 1981 Little Rock, Arkansas 1.72m 50kg. Studied fashion and design at Louisiana State University.
At 100m/4x100mR: WCh: '05- 7/1R. At 200m: OG: '04- 7=. Won NCAA indoor 60m 2003-04, 200m 2002-03.
Progress at 100m, 200m: 1998- 24.72, 1999- 11.66, 24.08; 2000- 11.36, 23.83; 2001- 11.17/11.13w, 23.04i/23.12/22.53w; 2002- 11.19, 22.66/22.33w; 2003- 11.04/10.97w, 22.49i/22.74; 2004- 11.12/11.00w, 22.36/22.22w; 2005- 11.09/10.99w, 22.46; 2006- 11.13, 22.77; 2007- 11.10, 22.90. pbs: 55m 6.73i '03, 60m 7.11i '05.

Tianna MADISON b. 30 Aug 1985 Elyria, Ohio 1.68m 60kg. Student at University of Tennessee.
At LJ: WCh: '05- 1, '07- 10; WI: '06- 2; PAm-J: '03- 4, NCAA champion indoors and out 2005.
Progress at LJ: 2000- 5.73, 2001- 6.07, 2002- 6.20, 2003- 6.28, 2004- 6.60, 2005- 6.89/6.92w, 2006- 6.80i/6.60, 2007- 6.60/6.61w. pbs: 55m 6.75i '05, 60m 7.27i '05, 100m 11.41 '05, 11.35w '04; 200m 23.56i '05, 23.66 '04.
Set pbs in qualifying and final of 2005 Worlds.

LaShauntea MOORE b. 31 Jul 1983 Akron, Ohio 1.70m 56kg. adidas. Was at University of Arkansas. Training to be a nurse.
At 200m: OG: '04- sf, WCh: '07- 7; WY: '99- 1/1 MedR; won NCAA 2004.
Progress at 200m: 1998- 23.86w, 1999- 23.26, 2001- 23.59/23.40w, 2002- 23.13/22.89w, 2003- 23.09/22.81w, 2004- 22.63/22.37w, 2005- 22.93, 2006- 22.89/22.64w, 2007- 22.46. pbs: 60m 7.36i '03, 100m 11.26 '04, 11.10w '07; 400m 54.92 '07.

Michelle PERRY b. 1 May 1979 Granada Hills, California 1.73m 64kg. Studied sociology at UCLA.
At 100mh: WCh: '05- 1, '07- 1; PAm: '03- 4; won WAF 2005-07, US 2005. At Hep: OG: '04- 14.
Progress at 100mh: 1995- 14.36, 1996- 14.37/13.19w, 1997- 13.87/13.82w, 1998- 13.41, 1999- 13.26/13.08w/12.9w, 2000- 13.15/13.03w, 2001- 13.18, 2003- 12.80, 2004- 12.74, 2005- 12.43, 2006- 12.43, 2007- 12.44. pbs: 100m 11.34 '07, 200m 22.91 '04, 400m 54.80 '03, 800m 2:12.81 '04, 60mh 7.84i '06, 400mh 56.23 '01, HJ 1.70 '04, LJ 6.14 '01, 6.23w '05; SP 12.07 '03, JT 40.73 '04, Hep 6126 '04.

Suzy POWELL b. 3 Sep 1976 Modesto 1.78m 73kg. Asics. Was at UCLA.
At DT: OG: '96- dnq 33, '00- dnq 15; WCh: '97-01-07: dnq 21/18/15, '03- 9; WJ: '92- 10, '94- 3; PAm: '03- 4; US champion 1996, 2007; PAm-J 1995. US discus record 2007.
Progress at DT: 1990- 46.31, 1991- 49.66, 1992- 51.72, 1993- 55.06, 1994- 57.40, 1995- 58.06, 1996- 60.58, 1997- 65.22, 1998- 65.05, 1999- 60.89, 2000-

65.30, 2001- 64.50, 2002- 69.44dh/65.48, 2003- 65.38, 2004- 63.58, 2005- 62.35, 2006- 63.14, 2007- 67.67. pb JT 54.62 '97.

69.44 at La Jolla in 2002 was acclaimed as US discus record but throwing area later found to be downhill. Married Tim Roos in November 2004.

Virginia POWELL b. 7 Sep 1983 Seattle 1.78m 63kg. Student at University of Southern California.

At 100mh: WCh: '05- sf, '07- 5; WY: '99- 8/2R; WCp: '06- 3. Won US 100mh 2006-07, NCAA 100mh & indoor 60mh 2005-06.

Progress at 100mh: 2000- 14.07, 2001- 13.39, 2002- 13.62, 2003- 13.07, 2004- 13.07, 2005- 12.61, 2006- 12.48, 2007- 12.45. pbs: 60m 7.21i '06, 100m 11.10/10.93Aw '06, 200m 23.29 '06, 60mh 7.84i '06.

Brittney REESE b. 9 Sep 1986 1.73m 64kg. Student at University of Mississippi.

At LJ: WCh: '07- 8; 2nd US & NCAA 2007.

Progress at LJ: 2004- 6.31, 2007- 6.83, 2008- 6.87i. pbs: 60m 7.29i '05, HJ 1.88i '08, 1.83 '07; TJ 13.02i '08.

Played basketball at Gulf Coast Community College in 2005-06 and no athletics.

Sanya RICHARDS b. 26 Feb 1985 Kingston, Jamaica 1.73m 61kg. Nike. University of Texas.

At (200m)/400m/4x400m: OG: '04- 6/1R; WCh: '03- sf/1R, '05- 2, '07- (5)/1R; WJ: '02- 3/2; WCp: '06- 1/1. Won WAF 2005-07, US 2003, 2005-06; NCAA 2003.

US & N.American 400m record 2006, world junior indoor bests 200m, 400m (2) 2004.

Progress at 200m, 400m: 1999- 23.84, 2000- 23.57, 54.34; 2001- 23.09, 53.49; 2002- 23.01, 50.69; 2003- 22.80i/22.86, 50.58; 2004- 22.49i/22.73, 49.89; 2005- 22.53, 48.92; 2006- 22.17, 48.70; 2007- 22.31, 49.27. pbs: 60m 7.21i '04, 100m 10.97 '07, 300m 35.6 '05, LJ 6.08 '01.

Left Jamaica at the age of 12 and gained US citizenship on 20 May 2002. Her 48.92 at Zürich in 2005 and then 48.70 at the World Cup in 2006 (to beat 22 year-old US record) were the world's fastest 400m times since 1996. Unbeaten in 13 finals outdoors at 400m in 2006 and after WAF win scored 200m/400m double at World Cup. Shared Golden League jackpot 2006 and 2007.

Brittany RILEY b. 26 Aug 1986 Flossmoor, Illinois 1.73m 89kg. Student at University of Southern Illinois.

At HT: WCh: '07- dnq 38; PAm: '07- 5; US champion 2007.

Three world indoor 20lb weight records 2007.

Progress at HT: 2005- 59.72, 2006- 66.30, 2007- 72.51. pbs: SP 15.15i/14.22 '07, DT 51.85 '07, 20lbWt 25.56i '07.

Jillian SCHWARTZ b. 19 Sep 1979 Evanston 1.73m 63kg. Nike. Was at Duke University.

At PV: OG: '04- dnq 17; WCh: '03- dnq 18=, '05- 11, '07- dnq 15; WI: '04- 4.

Progress at PV: 1999- 3.56, 2000- 4.10, 2001- 4.20, 2002- 4.50, 2003- 4.45, 2004- 4.60, 2005- 4.55, 2006- 4.61i/4.50, 2007- 4.50, 2008- 4.63i.

Rachelle SMITH b. 30 Jun 1981 Norfolk, Virginia 1.60m 52kg. née Boone. Nike. Was at Indiana University.

At 200m: WCh: '05- 2; US champion 2006.

Progress at 100m, 200m: 1999- 3.56, 2000- 11.49/11.39w, 23.37; 2001- 11.22/11.32w, 23.29/22.94w; 2002- 11.53, 22.99i/23.35; 2003- 11.22, 22.87; 2004- 11.37/11.26w, 22.69; 2005- 11.17/11.02w, 22.22; 2006- 11.20/11.04w, 22.31; 2007- 11.13, 22.31. pbs: 60m 7.21i '03, 400m 54.19 '05.

Shauna SMITH b. 10 Sep 1983 Sheridan, Wyoming 1.78m 64kg. University of Wyoming.

At 400mh: WCh: '05- sf; Won NCAA 2005.

Progress at 400mh: 2001- 59.70, 2002- 58.89, 2003- 57.09, 2004- 54.42, 2005- 54.21, 2006- 54.76, 2007- 55.94. pbs: 60m 7.54iA '05, 200m 23.53A '04, 400m 51.79i '04, 53.04A '02; 55mh 7.84iA '04, 60mh 8.33iA '04, 100mh 13.29 '04.

Shalonda SOLOMON b. 19 Dec 1985 Inglewood, California 1.69m 56kg. Student at University of South Carolina.

At (100m)/200m/4x100m: WJ: '04- 1/1R; PAm-J: '03- 1/1. Won NCAA 200m 2006, NCAAC 100m & 200m 2006.

Progress at 100m, 200m: 2001- 11.57/11.37w, 23.65/23.22w; 2002- 11.51/11.46w, 23.31; 2003- 11.35/11.25w, 22.93; 2004- 11.41/11.32w, 22.82; 2005- 11.29, 22.74/22.72w; 2006- 11.09/11.07w, 22.36/22.30w; 2007- 11.33, 22.77. pbs: 55m 6.73i '06, 60m 7.21i '06, 300m 36.93i '07, 400m 53.47 '08.

Jennifer STUCZYNSKI b. 6 Feb 1982 Freedonia, New York 1.80m 64kg. adidas. Graduate of Roberts Wesleyan University, now studying child psychology.

At PV: WCh: '06- 10; WI: '08- 2;WCp: '06- nh; US champion 2006-07, indoors 2005, 2007.

Two North American pole vault records 2007.

Progress at PV: 2002- 2.75, 2004- 3.49, 2005- 4.57i/4.26, 2006- 4.68i/4.66, 2007- 4.88. pbs: 55mh 8.07i '05, JT 46.82 '05.

All-time top scorer at basketball at her university, then very rapid progress at vaulting.

Aretha THURMOND b. 14 Aug 1976 Seattle 1.81m 98kg. née Hill. Was at University of Washington.

At DT: OG: '96/04- dnq 34/19; WCh: '99/03/05: dnq 24/20/21; PAm: '99- 1, '03- 1; WUG: '97- 6; WCp: '06- 2. US champion 2003-04, 2006.

Progress at DT: 1992- 43.38, 1993- 47.48, 1994- 50.52, 1995- 54.84, 1996- 60.50, 1997- 59.92, 1998- 65.62dh/63.68, 1999- 62.15, 2000- 62.91, 2001- 61.64, 2002- 65.21, 2003- 65.10/66.23dh, 2004- 65.86, 2005- 64.56, 2006- 64.41. pb SP 15.91i/15.67 '98.

Withdrew due to a collapsed lung from 1999 WUG and Worlds after 2nd in US 200m. Married Reedus Thurmond (DT pb 62.06 '00) in May

2005, their son Theo born 4 Jun 2007 (she competed at US Champs 16 days later).

De'Hashia **'Deedee' TROTTER** b. 8 Dec 1982 Twentynine Palms, California 1.78m 60kg. adidas. Degree in criminal justice from University of Tennessee.
At 400m/4x400mR: OG: '04- 5/1R; WCh: '03- sf/res (1)R, '05- 5, '07- 5/1R; PAm: '03- 1R; WCp: '06- 2R. Won US 2007, NCAA 2004.
Progress at 400m: 1998- 58.61, 1999- 59.12, 2000- 56.82, 2001- 56.02, 2002- 53.66, 2003- 50.66, 2004- 50.00, 2005- 49.88, 2006- 49.80, 2007- 49.64. pbs: 55m 6.93i '04, 60m 7.46i '05, 100m 11.65 '02, 200m 23.04 '06, 300m 35.8+ '07, LJ 6.00 '02.

Grace UPSHAW b. 25 Sep 1975 Berkeley 1.78m 65kg. Graduated in American studies from University of California, Berkeley.
At LJ: OG: '04- 10; WCh: '03- 8, '05- 7, '07- dnq 19. US champion 2003, 2005, 2007; indoors 2002.
Progress at LJ: 1994- 5.80, 1995- 5.79, 1996- 5.98/6.19w, 1997- 6.24, 2000- 6.47A/6.38, 2001- 6.62/6.70w, 2002- 6.60/6.75w, 2003- 6.73/6.99w, 2004- 6.84/6.88w, 2005- 6.73/6.87w, 2006- 6.75/6.79w, 2007- 6.72/6.74w. pbs: 60m 7.63i '04, 100m 11.81 '02, 200m 24.16 '02.
After graduating she did not compete in 1998-9, returning in 2000. Daughter of Monte Upshaw, who set a US high school long jump record of 7.72 in 1954 (second best in the world that year).

Angela WILLIAMS b. 30 Jan 1980 Bellflower, California 1.56m 52kg. Nike/HSI. Graduate of University of Southern California.
At 100m/4x100mR: WCh: '01- sf/res (dq1)R, '03- 2R; WJ: '98- 2/1R; PAm: '99- 2/2R, '03- 2/1R; WUG: '99- 1/1R; PAm-J: '95- 2, '97- 1/1R; Won NCAA 1999-2002. At 60m: WI: '01-03-08: 2/2/1.
Progress at 100m: 1990- 12.85, 1992- 12.10, 1993- 11.79, 1994- 11.78, 1995- 11.24, 1996- 11.73/11.4w, 1997- 11.14/10.98w, 1998- 11.11/11.10w, 1999- 11.04/10.96w, 2000- 11.12/11.1/11.01w, 2001- 11.18/11.01w, 2002- 11.06, 2003- 11.15/11.08w, 2004- 11.15, 2005- 11.29/11.25w, 2006- 11.48, 2007- 11.06. pbs: 50m 6.17i '01, 55m 6.73i '03, 60m 7.05i '08, 200m 23.02 '98, 22.78w '00; 400m 53.40 '95, 800m 2:16.78 '92, LJ 6.00/6.06w '98.
Became just the third woman ever to win four NCAA titles at one event.

Lauryn WILLIAMS b. 11 Sep 1983 Pittsburgh 1.57m 57kg. Nike. Finance graduate of University of Miami.
At 100m/4x100mR: OG: '04- 2; WCh: '03- res (1)R, '05- 1/1R, '07- 2/1R; WJ: '02- 1/2R; PAm: '03- 1/1R. Won NCAA 2004. At 60m: WI: '06- 1.
Progress at 100m, 200m: 1999- 12.00/11.6, 24.2; 2000- 11.70, 24.31; 2001- 11.65/11.60w, 23.85; 2002- 11.33, 23.64/23.63w; 2003- 11.12, 23.25; 2004- 10.96/10.94w, 22.46; 2005- 10.88, 22.27; 2006- 11.09, 22.87; 2007- 11.01, 22.70. pbs: 55m 6.70i '04, 60m 7.01i '06.

Tiffany WILLIAMS b. 5 Feb 1983 Miami 1.59m 57kg. née Ross. Graduated in retail management from University of Southern Carolina.
At 400mh: WCh: '07- 7; WJ: '02- 4/1R. Won US 2007.
Progress at 400mh: 2000- 58.50, 2001- 57.91, 2002- 55.22, 2003- 55.89, 2005- 54.56, 2006- 53.79, 2007- 53.28. pbs: 200m 24.35i '06, 400m 52.43i '05, 52.45 '06; 55mh 7.63i '03, 60mh 8.29i '05, 100mh 12.99 '05.
Married to Steven Williams, they have a daughter, Samya, botn in 2004..

Mary WINEBERG b. 3 Jan 1980 Brooklyn, New York 1.78m 61kg. née Danner. Education graduate of University of Cincinnati.
At 400m/4x400m: WCh: '07- 8/1R; WI: '03- 3R, '06- 2R.
Progress at 400m: 1998- 57.6, 2000- 53.88, 2002- 52.62, 2004- 51.54A/51.88, 2005- 52.99, 2006- 51.27, 2007- 50.24. pbs: 60m 7.81i '07, 100m 11.97 '07, 200m 23.82i/23.94 '06, 300m 36.3+ '07.

Shareese WOODS b. 20 Feb 1985 Fort Lee, Virginia 1.64m 57kg. Was at UNC Charlotte.
At 400m/4x400m: WI: '08- 3/3R. At 200m/4x100m: PAm: '07- 7/2R.
Progress at 200m, 400m: 2004- 54.91, 2005- 23.42/23.39w, 52.47; 2006- 22.95/22.70w, 52.93; 2007- 22.74, 52.80; 2008- 51.41i. pbs: 55m 6.85i '07, 60m 7.43i '07, 100m 11.37/11.26w '06.

VENEZUELA

Governing body: Federación Venezolana de Atletismo, Apartado Postal 29059, Caracas. Founded 1948.

National Champions 2007(National Games): **Men**: 100m: Ronald Amaya 10.41, 200m: José Eduardo Acevedo 20.88, 400m: Luis Luna 47.26, 800m/1500m: Edwar Villanueva 1:47.16/3:43.54, 5000m: Didimo Sánchez 14:28.18, 10,000m: Lervis Arias 30:32.12, HMar: Danny Corniele 68:36, 3000mSt: Marvin Blanco 8:42.82, 110mh: Jonathan Davis 14.23, 400mh: Víctor Solarte 50.84, HJ: Daniel Rodríguez 2.13, PV: César González 5.00, LJ: Esteban Copland 7.93, TJ: Johnny Rodríguez 15.92, SP: Yojer Medina 17.29, DT: Héctor Hurtado 55.68, HT: Aldo Bello 65.38, JT: Manuel Fuenmayor 71.21, Dec: Juan Carlos Jaramillo 7149, 20kW: Mario Romero 1:39:31. **Women**: 100m: Fiorela Molina 11.82, 200m: Prisciliana Chourio 24.47, 400m: Eliana Pacheco 52.77, 800m: Madelene Rondón 2:07.01, 1500m: Valentina Medina 4:34.77, 5000m/10,000m: Zuleima Amaya 17:00.38/34:33.42, HMar: Isabel Montilla 76:07, 3000mSt: Yeisy Álvarez 10:52.92, 100mh: Sandrine Legenort 14.15, 400mh: Magdalena Mendoza 59.34, HJ: Marielis Rojas 1.83, PV: Keisa Monterola 4.15, LJ/TJ: Yennifer Arveláez 6.05/13.76, SP: Ahymara Espinoza 14.23, DT: María Cubillán 50.17, HT: Rosa Rodríguez 63.61, JT: María de los Ángeles González 50.12, Hep: Thaimara Rivas 5266, 20kW: Milángela Rosales 1:45:50.

INTRODUCTION TO WORLD LISTS AND INDEX

Records

World, World U20 and U18, Olympic, Continental and Area records are listed for standard events. In running events up to and including 400 metres, only fully automatic times are shown. Marks listed are those which are considered statistically acceptable by the ATFS, and thus may differ from official records. These are followed by road bests and bests by masters/veterans.

World All-time and Year Lists

These lists are presented in the following format: Mark, Wind reading (where appropriate), Name, Nationality (abbreviated), Date of birth, Position in competition, Meeting name (if significant), Venue, Date of performance.

In standard events the best 30 or so performances are listed followed by the best marks for other athletes. Position, meet and venue details have been omitted for reasons of space beyond 100th in year lists.

In the all-time lists performances which have been world records (or world bests, thus including some unratified marks) are shown with WR against them .

Juniors (U20) are shown with-J after date of birth, and Youths (U18) with -Y.

Indexes

These contain the names of all athletes ranked with full details in the world year lists for standard events (and others such as half marathon). The format of the index is as follows:

Family name, First name, Nationality, Birthdate, Height (cm) and Weight (kg), 2007 best mark, Lifetime best (with year) as at the end of 2006.

* indicates an athlete who is profiled in the Biographies section, and ^ one who has been profiled in previous editions.

General Notes

Altitude aid

Marks set at an altitude of 1000m or higher have been suffixed by the letter "A" in events where altitude may be of significance.

Although there are no separate world records for altitude assisted events, it is understood by experts that in all events up to 400m in length (with the possible exclusion of the 110m hurdles), and in the horizontal jumps, altitude gives a material benefit to performances. For events beyond 800m, however, the thinner air of high altitude has a detrimental effect.

Supplementary lists are included in relevant events for athletes with seasonal bests at altitude who have low altitude marks qualifying for the main list.

Some leading venues over 1000m

Addis Ababa ETH	2365m
Air Force Academy USA	2194
Albuquerque USA	1555
Antananarivo MAD	1350
Bloemfontein RSA	1392
Bogotá COL	2644
Boulder USA	1655
Bozeman USA	1467
Calgary CAN	1045
Cali COL	1046
Ciudad de Guatemala GUA	1402
Ciudad de México MEX	2247
Cochabamba BOL	2558
Colorado Springs USA	1823
Cuenca ECU	2561
Denver USA	1609
El Paso USA	1187
Flagstaff USA	2107
Fort Collins USA	1521
Germiston RSA	1661
Guadalajara MEX	1567
Harare ZIM	1473
Johannesburg RSA	1748
Krugersdorp RSA	1740
La Paz BOL	3630
Logan USA	1372
Medellín COL	1541
Monachil ESP	2320
Nairobi KEN	1675
Pietersburg RSA	1230
Pocatello USA	1361
Potchefstroom RSA	1351
Pretoria RSA	1400
Provo USA	1380
Reno USA	1369
Roodepoort RSA	1720
Rustenburg RSA	1157
Salt Lake City USA	1321
Secunda RSA	1628
Sestriere ITA	2050
Soría ESP	1056
South Lake Tahoe USA	1909
Tunja COL	2810
Windhoek NAM	1725
Xalapa MEX	1420

Some others over 500m

Almaty KZK	847
Ankara TUR	902
Bern SUI	555
Blacksburg USA	634
Boise USA	818
Canberra AUS	581
La Chaux de Fonds SUI	997
Caracas VEN	922
Edmonton CAN	652
Jablonec CZE	598
Las Vegas USA	619
Lubbock USA	988
Madrid ESP	640

Magglingen SUI	751
Malles ITA	980
Moscow, Idaho USA	787
München GER	520
Nampa, Idaho USA	760
Salamanca ESP	806
Santiago de Chile CHI	520
(Apoquindo)	950
São Paulo BRA	725
Sofia BUL	564
Spokane USA	576
Taiyuan CHN	780
Trípoli GRE	655
Tucson USA	728
Uberlandia BRA	852

350m-500m

Annecy FRA	448
Banská Bystrica SVK	362
Fayetteville USA	407
Genève SUI	385
Götzis AUS	448
Johnson City USA	499
Lausanne SUI	375
Rieti ITA	402
Sindelfingen GER	440
Stuttgart GER	415
Tashkent UZB	477
Zürich SUI	410

Automatic timing

In the main lists for sprints and hurdles, only times recorded by fully automatic timing devices are included.

Hand timing

In the sprints and hurdles supplementary lists are included for races which are hand timed. Any athlete with a hand timed best 0.01 seconds or more better than his or her automatically timed best has been included, but hand timed lists have been terminated close to the differential levels considered by the IAAF to be equivalent to automatic times, i.e. 0.24 sec. for 100m, 200m, 100mh, 110mh, and 0.14 sec. for 400m and 400mh. It should be noted that this effectively recognises bad hand timekeeping, for there should be no material difference between hand and auto times, but what happens is that badly trained timekeepers anticipate the finish, having reacted to the flash at the start.

In events beyond 400m, auto times are integrated with hand timed marks, the latter identifiable by times being shown to tenths. All-time lists also include some auto times in tenths of a second, identified with the symbol ′.

Indoor marks

Indoor marks are included in the main lists for field events and straightway track events, but not for other track events. This is because track sizes vary in circumference (200m is the international standard) and banking, while outdoor tracks are standardised at 400m. Outdoor marks for athletes whose seasonal bests were set indoors are shown in a supplemental list.

Mixed races

For record purposes athletes may not, except in road races, compete in mixed sex races. Statistically there would not appear to be any particular logic in this, and women's marks set in such races are shown in our lists – annotated with mx. In such cases the athlete's best mark in single sex competition is appended.

Field event series

Field event series are given (where known) for marks in the top 30 performances lists.

Tracks and Courses

As well as climatic conditions, the type and composition of tracks and runways will affect standards of performance, as will the variations in road race courses.

Wind assistance

Anemometer readings have been shown where available in the lists for sprints and horizontal jumps in metres per second to one decimal place. If the figure was given to two decimal places, it has been rounded to the next tenth upwards, e.g. a wind reading of +2.01m/s, beyond the IAAF legal limit of 2.0, is rounded to +2.1; or -1.22m/s is rounded up to -1.2.

For multi-events a wind-assisted mark in one in which an event is aided by a wind over 4.0m/s and the average of the three wind-measured events is > 2m/s.

Drugs bans

The IAAF Council may decertify an athlete's records, titles and results if he or she is found to have used a banned substance before those performances. Performances at or after such a positive finding are shown in footnotes. Such athletes are shown with ¶ after their name in year lists, and in all-time lists if at any stage of their career they have served a drugs suspension of a year or more (thus not including athletes receiving public warnings or 3 month bans for stimulants etc., which for that year only are indicated with a #). This should not be taken as implying that the athlete was using drugs at that time. Nor have those athletes who have subsequently unofficially admitted to using banned substances been indicated; the ¶ is used only for those who have been caught.

Venues

From time to time place names are changed. Our policy is to use names in force at the time that the performance was set. Thus Leningrad prior to 1991, Sankt-Peterburg from its re-naming.

Amendments

Keen observers may spot errors in the lists. They are invited to send corrections as well as news and results for 2008.

Peter Matthews, 10 Madgeways Close, Great Amwell, Ware, Herts SG12 9RU, England

WORLD & CONTINENTAL RECORDS

As at end of 2007. **Key**: W = World, Afr = Africa, Asi = Asia, CAC = Central America & Caribbean, Eur = Europe, NAm = North America, Oce = Oceania, SAm = South America, Com = Commonwealth, W20 = World Junior (U20), W18 = World Youth (U18, not officially ratified by IAAF).
Successive columns show: World or Continent, performance, name, nationality, venue, date.
A altitude over 1000m, + timing by photo-electric-cell, # awaiting ratification, § not officially ratified

100 METRES

W,CAC,Com	9.74	Asafa POWELL	JAM	Rieti	9 Sep 2007
NAm	9.79	Maurice GREENE	USA	Athína	16 Jun 1999
Afr	9.85	Olusoji FASUBA	NGR	Doha	12 May 2006
Eur	9.86	Francis OBIKWELU	POR	Athína	22 Aug 2004
Oce	9.93	Patrick JOHNSON	AUS	Mito	5 May 2003
Asi	9.99	Samuel FRANCIS	QAT	Amman	26 Jul 2007
SAm	10.00A	Róbson da SILVA	BRA	Ciudad de México	22 Jul 1988
W20	10.01	Darrel BROWN	TRI	Saint-Denis	24 Aug 2003
W18	10.23	Rynell PARSON	USA	Indianapolis	21 Jun 2007
	10.23 ?	Tamunoski ATORUDIBO	NGR	Enugu	23 Mar 2002

200 METRES

W, NAm	19.32	Michael JOHNSON	USA	Atlanta	1 Aug 1996
Afr, Com	19.68	Frank FREDERICKS	NAM	Atlanta	1 Aug 1996
Eur	19.72A	Pietro MENNEA	ITA	Ciudad de México	12 Sep 1979
CAC	19.75	Usain BOLT	JAM	Kingston	24 Jun 2007
SAm	19.89	Claudinei da SILVA	BRA	München	11 Sep 1999
Oce	20.06A	Peter NORMAN	AUS	Ciudad de México	16 Oct 1968
Asi	20.03	Shingo SUETSUGU	JPN	Yokohama	7 Jun 2003
W20	19.93	Usain BOLT	JAM	Hamilton, BER	11 Apr 2004
W18	20.13	Usain BOLT	JAM	Bridgetown	20 Jul 2003

400 METRES

W, NAm	43.18	Michael JOHNSON	USA	Sevilla	26 Aug 1999
Afr	44.10	Gary KIKAYA	COD	Stuttgart	9 Sep 2006
CAC	44.14	Roberto HERNÁNDEZ	CUB	Sevilla	30 May 1990
Com	44.17	Innocent EGBUNIKE	NGR	Zürich	19 Aug 1987
SAm	44.29	Sanderlei PARRELA	BRA	Sevilla	26 Aug 1999
Eur	44.33	Thomas SCHÖNLEBE	GER	Roma	3 Sep 1987
Oce	44.38	Darren CLARK	AUS	Seoul	26 Sep 1988
Asi	44.56	Mohamed AL-MALKY	OMN	Budapest	12 Aug 1988
W20	43.87	Steve LEWIS	USA	Seoul	28 Sep 1988
W18	45.14	Obea MOORE	USA	Santiago de Chile	2 Sep 1995

800 METRES

W, Eur	1:41.11	Wilson KIPKETER	DEN	Köln	24 Aug 1997
Com	1:41.73	Sebastian COE	GBR	Firenze	10 Jun 1981
SAm	1:41.77	Joaquim CRUZ	BRA	Koln	26 Aug 1984
Afr	1:42.28	Sammy KOSKEI	KEN	Koln	26 Aug 1984
NAm	1:42.60	Johnny GRAY	USA	Koblenz	28 Aug 1985
CAC	1:42.85	Norberto TELLEZ	CUB	Atlanta	31 Jul 1996
Asi	1:43.11	Youssef Saad KAMEL	BRN	Zürich	6 Aug 2004
Oce	1:44.3 m	Peter SNELL	NZL	Christchurch	3 Feb 1962
W20	1:43.64	Japheth KIMUTAI	KEN	Zürich	13 Aug 1997
W18	1:46.25	Benson ESHO	KEN	Pergine Valsugana	23 Jul 2004

1000 METRES

W, Afr, Com	2:11.96	Noah NGENY	KEN	Rieti	5 Sep 1999
Eur	2:12.18	Sebastian COE	GBR	Oslo	11 Jul 1981
NAm	2:13.9	Rick WOHLHUTER	USA	Oslo	30 Jul 1974
SAm	2:14.09	Joaquim CRUZ	BRA	Nice	20 Aug 1984
Oce	2:16.57	John WALKER	NZL	Oslo	1 Jul 1980
CAC	2:17.0	Byron DYCE	JAM	København	15 Aug 1973
Asi	2:15.23	Belal Mansoor ALI	BRN	Stockholm	7 Aug 2007
W20	2:15.00	Benjamim KIPKURUI	KEN	Nice	17 Jul 1999
W18	2:17.59	Japheth KIMUTAI	KEN	København	23 Aug 1995

1500 METRES

W, Afr	3:26.00	Hicham EL GUERROUJ	MAR	Roma	14 Jul 1998
Com	3:26.34	Bernard LAGAT	KEN	Bruxelles	24 Aug 2001
Eur	3:28.95	Fermin CACHO	ESP	Zürich	13 Aug 1997

NAm	3:29.30	Bernard LAGAT	USA	Rieti	28 Aug 2005
Asi	3:29.14	Rashid RAMZI	BRN	Roma	14 Jul 2006
Oce	3:31.96	Simon DOYLE	AUS	Stockholm	3 Jul 1991
SAm	3:33.25	Hudson Santos de SOUZA	BRA	Rieti	28 Aug 2005
CAC	3:36.60	Stephen AGAR (later CAN)	DMN	Abbotsford	2 Jun 1996
W20	3:30.24	Cornelius CHIRCHIR	KEN	Monaco	19 Jul 2002
W18	3:33.72	Nicholas KEMBOI	KEN	Zürich	18 Aug 2006

1 MILE

W, Afr	3:43.13	Hicham El GUERROUJ	MAR	Roma	7 Jul 1999
Com	3:43.40	Noah NGENY	KEN	Roma	7 Jul 1999
Eur	3:46.32	Steve CRAM	GBR	Oslo	27 Jul 1985
NAm	3:46.91	Alan WEBB	USA	Brasschaat	21 Jul 2007
Asi	3:47.97	Daham Najim BASHIR	QAT	Oslo	29 Jul 2005
Oce	3:48.98	Craig MOTTRAM	AUS	Oslo	29 Jul 2005
SAm	3:51.05	Hudson de SOUZA	BRA	Oslo	29 Jul 2005
CAC	3:57.34	Byron DYCE	JAM	Stockholm	1 Jul 1974
W20	3:50.25	Alex KIPCHIRCHIR	KEN	Rieti	7 Sep 2003
W18	3:54.56	Isaac SONGOK	KEN	Linz	20 Aug 2001

2000 METRES

W, Afr	4:44.79	Hicham EL GUERROUJ	MAR	Berlin	7 Sep 1999
Com	4:48.74	John KIBOWEN	KEN	Hechtel	1 Aug 1998
Oce	4:50.76	Craig MOTTRAM	AUS	Melbourne	9 Mar 2006
Eur	4:51.39	Steve CRAM	GBR	Budapest	4 Aug 1985
NAm	4:52.44	Jim SPIVEY	USA	Lausanne	15 Sep 1987
Asi	4:55.57	Mohammed SULEIMAN	QAT	Roma	8 Jun 1995
W18, W20	4:56.86	Isaac SONGOK	KEN	Berlin	31 Aug 2001
SAm	5:03.34	Hudson Santos de SOUZA	BRA	Manaus	6 Apr 2002
CAC	5:03.4	Arturo BARRIOS	MEX	Nice	10 Jul 1989

3000 METRES

W, Afr, Com	7:20.67	Daniel KOMEN	KEN	Rieti	1 Sep 1996
Eur	7:26.62	Mohammed MOURHIT	BEL	Monaco	18 Aug 2000
Asi	7:30.76	Jamal Bilal SALEM	QAT	Doha	13 May 2005
NAm	7:30.84	Bob KENNEDY	USA	Monaco	8 Aug 1998
Oce	7:32.19	Craig MOTTRAM	AUS	Athína	17 Sep 2006
CAC	7:35.71	Arturo BARRIOS	MEX	Nice	10 Jul 1989
SAm	7:39.70	Hudson Santos de SOUZA	BRA	Lausanne	2 Jul 2002
W20	7:28.78	Augustine CHOGE	KEN	Doha	13 May 2005
W18	7:32.37	Abreham FELEKE	ETH	Lausanne	11 Jul 2006

5000 METRES

W, Afr	12:37.35	Kenenisa BEKELE	ETH	Hengelo	31 May 2004
Com	12:39.74	Daniel KOMEN	KEN	Bruxelles	22 Aug 1997
Eur	12:49.71	Mohammed MOURHIT	BEL	Bruxelles	25 Aug 2000
Asi	12:51.98	Saif Saaeed SHAHEEN	QAT	Roma	14 Jul 2006
Oce	12:55.76	Craig MOTTRAM	AUS	London	30 Jul 2004
NAm	12:58.21	Bob KENNEDY	USA	Zürich	14 Aug 1996
CAC	13:07.79	Arturo BARRIOS	MEX	London (CP)	14 Jul 1989
SAm	13:19.43	Marilson DOS SANTOS	BRA	Kassel	8 Jun 2006
W20	12:52.61	Eliud KIPCHOGE	KEN	Oslo	27 Jun 2003
W18	12:54.19	Abreham FELEKE	ETH	Roma	14 Jul 2006

10,000 METRES

W, Afr	26:17.53	Kenenisa BEKELE	ETH	Bruxelles	26 Aug 2005
Com	26:27.85	Paul TERGAT	KEN	Bruxelles	22 Aug 1997
Asi	26:38.76	Abdullah Ahmad HASSAN	QAT	Bruxelles	5 Sep 2003
Eur	26:52.30	Mohammed MOURHIT	BEL	Bruxelles	3 Sep 1999
CAC	27:08.23	Arturo BARRIOS	MEX	Berlin	18 Aug 1989
NAm	27:13.98	Mebrahtom KEFLEZIGHI	USA	Stanford	4 May 2001
SAm	27:28.12	Marilson DOS SANTOS	BRA	Neerpelt	2 Jun 2007
Oce	27:31.92	Shaun CREIGHTON	AUS	Melbourne	25 Nov 1996
W20	26:41.75	Samuel WANJIRU	KEN	Bruxelles	26 Aug 2005
W18	27:02.81	Ibrahim JAYLAN Gashu	ETH	Bruxelles	25 Aug 2006

HALF MARATHON

W, Afr, Com	58:33	Samuel WANJIRU	KEN	Den Haag	17 Mar 2007
SAm	59:33	Marilson DOS SANTOS	BRA	Udine	14 Oct 2007
NAm	59:43	Ryan HALL	USA	Houston	14 Jan 2007

Eur	59:52	Fabian RONCERO	ESP	Berlin	1 Apr 2001
Oce	60:02	Darren WILSON	AUS	Tokyo	19 Jan 1997
Asi	60:25	Atsushi SATO	JPN	Udine	14 Oct 2007
CAC	60:14	Armando QUINTANILLA	MEX	Tokyo	21 Jan 1996
W20	59:16	Samuel WANJIRU	KEN	Rotterdam	11 Sep 2005
W18	60:38	Faustin BAHA Sulle	TAN	Lille	4 Sep 1999

MARATHON

W. Afr	2:04:26	Haile GEBRSELASSIE	ETH	Berlin	30 Sep 2007
Com	2:04:55	Paul TERGAT	KEN	Berlin	28 Sep 2003
NAm	2:05:38	Khalid KHANNOUCHI (ex MAR)	USA	London	14 Apr 2002
SAm	2:06:05	Ronaldo da COSTA	BRA	Berlin	20 Sep 1998
Asi	2:06:16	Toshinari TAKAOKA	JPN	Chicago	13 Oct 2002
Eur	2:06:36	António PINTO	POR	London	16 Apr 2000
	2:06:36	Benoît ZWIERZCHIEWSKI	FRA	Paris	6 Apr 2003
CAC	2:07:19	Andrés ESPINOSA	MEX	Boston	18 Apr 1994
Oce	2:07:51	Rob DE CASTELLA	AUS	Boston	21 Apr 1986
W20	2:10:13	Moses MASAI	KEN	Essen	17 Apr 2005
W18	2:11:43	LI He	CHN	Beijing	14 Oct 2001

Boston course has an overall net drop of 139m (0.33%), and in 1994 there was a strong following wind.

3000 METRES STEEPLECHASE

W,Asi	7:53.63	Saïf Saaeed SHAHEEN	QAT	Bruxelles	3 Sep 2004
Afr	7:55.28	Brahim BOULAMI	MAR	Bruxelles	24 Aug 2001
Com	7:55.72	Bernard BARMASAI	KEN	Köln	24 Aug 1997
Eur	8:04.95	Simon VROEMEN	NED	Bruxelles	26 Aug 2005
NAm	8:08.82	Daniel LINCOLN	USA	Roma	14 Jul 2006
Oce	8:14.05	Peter RENNER	NZL	Koblenz	29 Aug 1984
SAm	8:14.41	Wander MOURA	BRA	Mar del Plata	22 Mar 1995
CAC	8:25.69	Salvador MIRANDA	MEX	Barakaldo	9 Jul 2000
W20	7:58.66	Stephen CHERONO (now Shaheen)	KEN	Bruxelles	24 Aug 2001
W18	8:18.51	Ronald KIPCHUMBA	KEN	Bruxelles	3 Sep 2004

110 METRES HURDLES

W, Asi	12.88	LIU Xiang	CHN	Lausanne	11 Jul 2006
NAm	12.90	Dominique ARNOLD	USA	Lausanne	11 Jul 2006
Eur, Com	12.91	Colin JACKSON	GBR/Wal	Stuttgart	20 Aug 1993
CAC	12.92	Dayron ROBLES	CUB	Stuttgart	23 Sep 2007
Afr	13.26	Shaun BOWNES	RSA	Heusden	14 Jul 2001
Oce	13.29	Kyle VANDER-KUYP	AUS	Göteborg	11 Aug 1995
SAm	13.29	Redelen DOS SANTOS	BRA	Lisboa	13 Jun 2004
	13.29	Paulo César VILLAR	COL	Cartagena	26 Jul 2006
W20	13.12	LIU Xiang (with 3'6" hurdles)	CHN	Lausanne	2 Jul 2002
W18	13.43	SHI Dongpeng	CHN	Shanghai	6 May 2001
W18 (91cm)	13.18	Wayne DAVIS	USA	Ostrava	12 Jul 2007

400 METRES HURDLES

W, NAm	46.78	Kevin YOUNG	USA	Barcelona	6 Aug 1992
Afr, Com	47.10	Samuel MATETE	ZAM	Zürich	7 Aug 1991
CAC	47.25	Felix SÁNCHEZ	DOM	Saint-Denis	29 Aug 2003
Eur	47.37	Stéphane DIAGANA	FRA	Lausanne	5 Jul 1995
Asi	47.53	Hadi Sou'an AL-SOMAILY	KSA	Sydney	27 Sep 2000
SAm	47.84	Bayano KAMANI	PAN	Helsinki	7 Aug 2005
Oce	48.28	Rohan ROBINSON	AUS	Atlanta	31 Jul 1996
W20	48.02	Danny HARRIS	USA	Los Angeles	17 Jun 1984
W18 (84mc)	49.01	William WYNNE	USA	Ostrava	15 Jul 2007

HIGH JUMP

W, CAC	2.45	Javier SOTOMAYOR	CUB	Salamanca	27 Jul 1993
Eur	2.42	Patrik SJÖBERG	SWE	Stockholm	30 Jun 1987
	2.42 i§	Carlo THRÄNHARDT	FRG	Berlin	26 Feb 1988
NAm	2.40 i§	Hollis CONWAY	USA	Sevilla	10 Mar 1991
		Charles AUSTIN	USA	Zürich	7 Aug 1991
Asi	2.39	ZHU Jianhua	CHN	Eberstadt	10 Jun 1984
Com	2.38i	Steve SMITH	GBR/Eng	Wuppertal	4 Feb 1994
	2.38	Troy KEMP	BAH	Nice	12 Jul 1995
Afr, Com	2.38	Jacques FREITAG	RSA	Oudtshoorn	5 Mar 2005
Oce	2.36	Tim FORSYTH	AUS	Melbourne	2 Mar 1997
SAm	2.33	Gilmar MAYO	COL	Pereira	17 Oct 1994
W20	2.37	Dragutin TOPIC	YUG	Plovdiv	12 Aug 1990
		Steve SMITH	GBR	Seoul	20 Sep 1992

W18	2.33	Javier SOTOMAYOR	CUB	La Habana	19 May 1984

POLE VAULT

W, Eur	6.15 i§	Sergey BUBKA	UKR	Donetsk	21 Feb 1993
	6.14 A	Sergey BUBKA	UKR	Sestriere	31 Jul 1994
Oce, Com	6.05	Dmitriy MARKOV	AUS	Edmonton	9 Aug 2001
Afr	6.03	Okkert BRITS	RSA	Köln	18 Aug 1995
NAm	6.03	Jeff HARTWIG	USA	Jonesboro	14 Jun 2000
Asi	5.92i	Igor POTAPOVICH	KAZ	Stockholm	19 Feb 1998
	5.90	Grigoriy YEGOROV	KAZ	Stuttgart 19 Aug 1993 & London (CP)	10 Sep 1993
	5.90	Igor POTAPOVICH	KAZ	Nice	10 Jul 1996
CAC	5.82	Giovanni LANARO	MEX	Walnut	15 Apr 2007
SAm	5.77	Fabio Gomes DA SILVA	BRA	São Paulo	7 Jun 2007
W20	5.80	Maksim TARASOV	RUS	Bryansk	14 Jul 1989
W18	5.51	Germán CHIARAVIGLIO	ARG	Pôrto Alegre	1 May 2004

LONG JUMP

W, NAm	8.95	Mike POWELL	USA	Tokyo	30 Aug 1991
Eur	8.86 A	Robert EMMIYAN	ARM	Tsakhkadzor	22 May 1987
CAC	8.71	Iván PEDROSO	CUB	Salamanca	18 Jul 1995
Com	8.62	James BECKFORD	JAM	Orlando	5 Apr 1997
SAm	8.57	Irving SALADINO	PAN	Osaka	30 Aug 2007
Oce	8.49	Jai TAURIMA	AUS	Sydney	28 Sep 2000
Asi	8.48	Mohamed Salim AL-KHUWALIDI	KSA	Sotteville	2 Jul 2006
Afr	8.46	Cheikh TOURÉ	SEN	Bad Langensalza	15 Jun 1997
W20	8.34	Randy WILLIAMS	USA	München	8 Sep 1972
W18	8.25	Luis Alberto BUENO	CUB	La Habana	28 Sep 1986

TRIPLE JUMP

W, Eur, Com	18.29	Jonathan EDWARDS	GBR/Eng	Göteborg	7 Aug 1995
NAm	18.09	Kenny HARRISON	USA	Atlanta	27 Jul 1996
CAC	17.92	James BECKFORD	JAM	Odessa, Texas	20 May 1995
SAm	17.90	Jadel GREGÓRIO	BRA	Belém	20 May 2007
Oce	17.46	Ken LORRAWAY	AUS	London (CP)	7 Aug 1982
Asi	17.37	Tareq BOUGTAÏB	MAR	Khémisset	14 Jul 2007
Afr	17.37	Ndabezinhle MDHLONGWA	ZIM	Lafayette	28 Mar 1998
W20	17.50	Volker MAI	GDR	Erfurt	23 Jun 1985
W18	16.89	GU Junjie	CHN	Dalian	25 Aug 2000

SHOT

W, NAm	23.12	Randy BARNES	USA	Westwood	20 May 1990
Eur	23.06	Ulf TIMMERMANN	GER	Hania	22 May 1988
Afr, Com	21.97	Janus ROBBERTS	RSA	Eugene	2 Jun 2001
SAm	21.14	Marco Antonio VERNI	CHI	Santiago de Chile	29 Jul 2004
Oce	20.96	Justin ANLEZARK	AUS	Brisbane	5 Apr 2003
CAC	20.78	Alexis PAUMIER	CUB	La Habana	29 Jul 2000
Asi	20.61	Sultan Mubarak AL-HEBSHI	KSA	Donetsk	5 Jul 2007
W20	21.05 i§	Terry ALBRITTON	USA	New York	22 Feb 1974
	20.65 §	Mike CARTER	USA	Boston	4 Jul 1979
	20.39	Janus ROBBERTS	RSA	Germiston	7 Mar 1998
W18	18.73	Karsten STOLZ	GER	Essen	2 Sep 1981
W20 6kg	21.96	Edis ELKASEVIC	CRO	Zagreb	20 Jun 2002
W18 5kg	22.72	Marin PREMERU	CRO	Varazdin	13 Oct 2007

DISCUS

W, Eur	74.08	Jürgen SCHULT	GDR	Neubrandenburg	6 Jun 1986
NAm	72.34 ¶	Ben PLUCKNETT	USA	Stockholm	7 Jul 1981
	71.32 §	Ben PLUCKNETT	USA	Eugene	4 Jun 1983
CAC	71.06	Luis DELIS	CUB	La Habana	21 May 1983
Afr, Com	70.32	Frantz KRUGER	RSA	Salon-de-Provence	26 May 2002
Asi	67.95	Ehsan HADADI	IRI	Minsk (Staiki)	9 Jun 2007
SAm	66.32	Jorge BALLIENGO	ARG	Rosario	15 Apr 2006
Oce	65.62 §	Werner REITERER	AUS	Melbourne	15 Dec 1987
	65.06	Wayne MARTIN	AUS	Newcastle	3 Jan 1979
W20	65.62 §	Werner REITERER	AUS	Melbourne	15 Dec 1987
	63.64	Werner HARTMANN	FRG	Strasbourg	25 Jun 1978
W18	58.62	Michal HODUN	POL	Santiago de C hile	21 Oct 2000
W20 1.75kg	67.32	Margus HUNT	EST	Beijing	16 Aug 2006
W18 1.5kg	72.31	Mykyta NESTERNKO	UKR	Beograd	26 Jul 2007

¶ Disallowed by the IAAF following retrospective disqualification for drug abuse, but ratified by the AAU/TAC

HAMMER

W, Eur	86.74	Yuriy SEDYKH	UKR/RUS	Stuttgart	30 Aug 1986
Asi	84.86	Koji MUROFUSHI	JPN	Praha	29 Jun 2003
NAm	82.52	Lance DEAL	USA	Milano	7 Sep 1996
Afr, Com	80.63	Chris HARMSE	RSA	Durban	15 Apr 2005
Oce	79.29	Stuart RENDELL	AUS	Varazdin	6 Jun 2002
CAC	77.78	Alberto SANCHEZ	CUB	La Habana	15 May 1998
SAm	76.42	Juan CERRA	ARG	Trieste	25 Jul 2001
W20	78.33	Olli-Pekka KARJALAINEN	FIN	Seinäjoki	5 Aug 1999
W18	73.66	Vladislav PISKUNOV	UKR	Live	11 Jun 1994
W20 6kg	82.62	Yevgeniy AYDAMIROV	RUS	Tula	22 Jul 2006
W18 5kg	83.28	József HORVÁTH	HUN	Szombathely	10 May 2001

JAVELIN

W, Eur	98.48	Jan ZELEZNY	CZE	Jena	25 May 1996
Com	91.46	Steve BACKLEY	GBR/Eng	Auckland (NS)	25 Jan 1992
NAm	91.29	Breaux GREER	USA	Indianapolis	21 Jun 2007
Afr	88.75	Marius CORBETT	RSA	Kuala Lumpur	21 Sep 1998
Oce	88.20	Gavin LOVEGROVE	NZL	Oslo	5 Jul 1996
Asi	87.60	Kazuhiro MIZOGUCHI	JPN	San José	27 May 1989
CAC	87.17	Guillermo MARTÍNEZ	CUB	Saint-Denis	8 Jul 2006
SAm	84.70	Edgar BAUMANN	PAR	San Marcos	17 Oct 1999
W20	83.87	Andreas THORKILDSEN	NOR	Fana	7 Jun 2001
W18	79.96	Aki PARVIAINEN	FIN	Pyhäselkä	12 Sep 1991

DECATHLON

W,Eur	9026	Roman SEBRLE	CZE	Götzis	27 May 2001
NAm	8891	Dan O'BRIEN	USA	Talence	5 Sep 1992
Com	8847	Daley THOMPSON	GBR/Eng	Los Angeles	9 Aug 1984
Asi	8725	Dmitriy KARPOV	KAZ	Athína	24 Aug 2004
CAC	8644	Maurice SMITH	JAM	Osaka	1 Sep 2007
Oce	8490	Jagan HAMES	AUS	Kuala Lumpur	18 Sep 1998
SAm	8291 m	Tito STEINER	ARG	Provo	23 Jun 1983
	8266	Pedro da SILVA	BRA	Walnut	24 Apr 1987
Afr	8023	Hamdi DHOUIBI	TUN	Helsinki	10 Aug 2005
W20	8397	Torsten VOSS (with 3'6" hurdles)	GDR	Erfurt	7 Jul 1982
W18	8104h	Valter KÜLVET	EST	Viimsi	23 Aug 1981
	7829	Valter KÜLVET	EST	Stockholm	13 Sep 1981

4 X 100 METRES RELAY

W, NAm	37.40	USA (Marsh, Burrell, Mitchell, C.Lewis)	Barcelona	8 Aug 1992
	37.40	USA (Drummond, Cason, Mitchell, Burrell)	Stuttgart	21 Aug 1993
Com	37.69	CAN (Esmie, Gilbert, Surin, Bailey)	Atlanta	3 Aug 1996
Eur	37.73	GBR (Gardener, Campbell, Devonish, Chambers)	Sevilla	29 Aug 1999
CAC	37.89	JAM (Anderson, Boit, Carter, Powell)	Osaka	1 Sep 2007
SAm	37.90	BRA (V Lima, Ribeiro, A da Silva, Cl da Silva)	Sydney	30 Sep 2000
Afr	37.94	NGR (O Ezinwa, Adeniken, Obikwelu, D Ezinwa)	Athína	9 Aug 1997
Asi	38.03	JPN (Tsukahara, Suetsugu, Takahira, Asahara)	Osaka	1 Sep 2007
Oce	38.17	AUS (Henderson, Jackson, Brimacombe, Marsh)	Göteborg	12 Aug 1995
W20	38.66	USA (Kimmons, Omole, Williams, Merritt)	Grosseto	18 Jul 2004
W18	40.03	JAM (W Smith, M Frater, Spence, O Brown)	Bydgoszcz	18 Jul 1999

4 X 400 METRES RELAY

W, NAm	2:54.20	USA (Young, Pettigrew, Washington, Johnson)	Uniondale, NY	22 Jul 1998
Eur	2:56.60	GBR (Thomas, Baulch, Richardson, Black)	Atlanta	3 Aug 1996
CAC, Com	2:56.75	JAM (McDonald, Haughton, McFarlane, Clarke)	Athína	10 Aug 1997
SAm	2:58.56	BRA (C da Silva, A J dosSantos, de Araújo, Parrela)	Winnipeg	30 Jul 1999
Afr	2:58.68	NGR (Chukwu, Monye, Nada, Udo-Obong)	Sydney	30 Sep 2000
Oce	2:59.70	AUS (Frayne, Clark, Minihan, Mitchell)	Los Angeles	11 Aug 1984
Asi	3:00.76	JPN (Karube, K Ito, Osakada, Omori)	Atlanta	3 Aug 1996
W20	3:01.09	USA (Johnson, Merritt, Craig, Clement)	Grosseto	18 Jul 2004
W18	3:12.05	POL (Zrada, Kedzia, Grzegorczyk, Kowalski)	Kaunas	5 Aug 2001

20 KILOMETRES WALK

W, Eur	1:17:16	Vladimir KANAYKIN	RUS	Saransk	29 Sep 2007
SAm	1:17:21	Jefferson PÉREZ	ECU	Saint-Denis	23 Aug 2003
CAC	1:17:25.6 t	Bernardo SEGURA	MEX	Fana	7 May 1994
Oce, Com	1:17:33	Nathan DEAKES	AUS	Cixi	23 Apr 2005
Asi	1:17:41	ZHU Hongyu	CHN	Cixi	23 Apr 2005
Afr	1:19:02	Hatem GHOULA	TUN	Eisenhüttenstadt	10 May 1997

NAm	1:21:03	Arturo HUERTA	CAN	Etobicoke	7 Jul 2000
W20	1:18:06 §	Viktor BURAYEV	RUS	Adler	4 Mar 2001
W18	1:18:07	LI Gaobo	CHN	Cixi	23 Apr 2005

20,000 METRES TRACK WALK

W, CAC	1:17:25.6	Bernardo SEGURA	MEX	Fana	7 May 1994
Eur	1:18:35.2	Stefan JOHANSSON	SWE	Fana	15 May 1992
Oce, Com	1:19:48.1	Nathan DEAKES	AUS	Brisbane	4 Sep 2001
Asi	1:20:24.4	LI Mingcai	CHN	Jinan	15 Mar 1992
SAm	1:20:55.4	Jefferson PÉREZ	ECU	Fana	4 May 1996
NAm	1:22:27.0	Tim BERRETT	CAN	Edmonds, WA	9 Jun 1996
Afr	1:22:51.84	Hatem GHOULA	TUN	Leutkirch	8 Sep 1994
W20	1:20:11.72	LI Gaobo	CHN	Wuhan	2 Nov 2007
W18	1:24:28.3	ZHU Hongjun	CHN	Xian	15 Sep 1999

50 KILOMETRES WALK

W,Oce, Com	3:35:47	Nathan DEAKES	AUS	Geelong	2 Dec 2006
Eur	3:36:03	Robert KORZENIOWSKI	POL	Saint-Denis	27 Aug 2003
	3:35:29 #	Denis NIZHEGORODOV (no doping test)	RUS	Cheboksary	13 Jun 2004
Asi	3:36:06	YU Chaohong	CHN	Nanjing	22 Oct 2005
CAC	3:41:20	Raúl GONZÁLEZ	MEX	Praha-Podebrady	11 Jun 1978
NAm	3:47:48	Marcel JOBIN	CAN	Québec	20 Jun 1981
SAm	3:52:07	Xavier MORENO	ECU	Rio de Janeiro	28 Jul 2007
Afr	3:58:44	Hatem GHOULA	TUN	Santa Eularia des Riu	4 Mar 2007
W20	3:41:10	ZHAO Jianguo	CHN	Wajima	16 Apr 2006
W18	3:45:46	YU Guoping	CHN	Guangzhou	23 Nov 2001

50,000 METRES TRACK WALK

W, Eur	3:40:57.9	Thierry TOUTAIN	FRA	Héricourt	29 Sep 1996
CAC	3:41:38.4	Raúl GONZÁLEZ	MEX	Fana	25 May 1979
Oce, Com	3:43:50.0	Simon BAKER	AUS	Melbourne	9 Sep 1990
Asi	3:48:13.7	ZHAO Yongshen	CHN	Fana	7 May 1994
NAm	3:56:13.0	Tim BERRETT	CAN	Saskatoon	21 Jul 1991
SAm	4:14:28.5	Jorge LOREFICE	ARG	Buenos Aires	9 May 1993
	4:14:28.5	Benjamin LOREFICE	ARG	Buenos Aires	9 May 1993
Afr	4:21:44.5	Abdelwahab FERGUÈNE	ALG	Toulouse	25 Mar 1984

World Records at other men's track & field events recognised by the IAAF

20,000m	56:25.98+	Haile GEBRSELASSIE	ETH	Ostrava	27 Jun 2007
1 Hour	21,285 m	Haile GEBRSELASSIE	ETH	Ostrava	27 Jun 2007
25km	1:13:55.8+	Toshihiko SEKO	JPN	Christchurch	22 Mar 1981
30km	1:29:18.8	Toshihiko SEKO	JPN	Christchurch	22 Mar 1981
4 x 200m	1:18.68	Santa Monica Track Club	USA	Walnut	17 Apr 1994
		(Michael Marsh, Leroy Burrell, Floyd Heard, Carl Lewis)			
4 x 800m	7:02.43	Kenya Team	KEN	Bruxelles	25 Aug 2006
		(Joseph Mutua, William Yiampoy, Ismael Kombich, Wilfred Bungei)			
4 x l500m	14:38.8 m	F.R.Germany Teal	GER	Köln	17 Aug 1977
		(Thomas Wessinghage, Harald Hudak, Michael Lederer, Karl Fleschen)			

Track Walking

2 Hours	29,572m+	Maurizio DAMILANO	ITA	Cuneo	3 Oct 1992
30km	2:01:44.1	Maurizio DAMILANO	ITA	Cuneo	3 Oct 1992

WOMEN

100 METRES

W, NAm	10.49	Florence GRIFFITH JOYNER	USA	Indianapolis	16 Jul 1988
Eur	10.73	Christine ARRON	FRA	Budapest	19 Aug 1998
CAC, Com	10.74	Merlene OTTEY	JAM	Milano	7 Sep 1996
Asi	10.79	LI Xuemei	CHN	Shanghai	18 Oct 1997
Afr	10.90	Glory ALOZIE	NGR	La Laguna	5 Jun 1999
	10.84 §	Chioma AJUNWA	NGR	Lagos	11 Apr 1992
Oce	11.12A	Melinda GAINSFORD/TAYLOR	AUS	Sestriere	31 Jul 1994
SAm	11.17A	Lucimar de MOURA	BRA	Bogotá (sf)	25 Jun 1999
	11.17A	Lucimar de MOURA	BRA	Bogotá	25 Jun 1999
W20	10.88	Marlies OELSNER/GÖHR	GDR	Dresden	1 Jul 1977
W18	11.13	Chandra CHEESEBOROUGH	USA	Eugene	21 Jun 1976

200 METRES

W, NAm	21.34	Florence GRIFFITH JOYNER	USA	Seoul	29 Sep 1988
CAC, Com	21.64	Merlene OTTEY	JAM	Bruxelles	13 Sep 1991
Eur	21.71	Marita KOCH	GDR	Chemnitz	10 Jun 1979
	21.71 §	Marita KOCH	GDR	Potsdam	21 Jul 1984

	21.71	Heike DRECHSLER	GDR	Jena	29 Jun 1986
	21.71 §	Heike DRECHSLER	GDR	Stuttgart	29 Aug 1986
Asi	22.01	LI Xuemei	CHN	Shanghai	22 Oct 1997
Afr	22.06 A§	Evette DE KLERK	RSA	Pietersburg	8 Apr 1989
	22.07	Mary ONYALI	NGR	Zürich	14 Aug 1996
Oce	22.23	Melinda GAINSFORD-TAYLOR	AUS	Stuttgart	13 Jul 1997
SAm	22.60A	Lucimar de MOURA	BRA	Bogotá	26 Jun 1999
W20	22.18	Allyson FELIX	USA	Athína	25 Aug 2004
	22.11A §	Allyson FELIX (no doping control)	USA	Ciudad de México	3 May 2003
W18	22.58	Marion JONES	USA	New Orleans	28 Jun 1992

400 METRES

W, Eur	47.60	Marita KOCH	GDR	Canberra	6 Oct 1985
Oce, Com	48.63	Cathy FREEMAN	AUS	Atlanta	29 Jul 1996
NAm	48.70	Sanya RICHARDS	USA	Athína	16 Sep 2006
Afr	49.10	Falilat OGUNKOYA	NGR	Atlanta	29 Jul 1996
CAC	48.89 #	Ana GUEVARA	MEX	Saint-Denis	27 Aug 2003
SAm	49.64	Ximena RESTREPO	COL	Barcelona	5 Aug 1992
Asi	49.81	MA Yuqin	CHN	Beijing	11 Sep 1993
W20	49.42	Grit BREUER	GER	Tokyo	27 Aug 1991
W18	50.01	LI Jing	CHN	Shanghai	18 Oct 1997

800 METRES

W, Eur	1:53.28	Jarmila KRATOCHVÍLOVÁ	CZE	München	26 Jul 1983
CAC	1:54.44	Ana Fidelia QUIROT	CUB	Barcelona	9 Sep 1989
Afr	1:55.19	Maria Lurdes MUTOLA	MOZ	Zürich	17 Aug 1994
Com	1:55.29	Maria Lurdes MUTOLA	MOZ	Köln	24 Aug 1997
Asi	1:55.54	LIU Dong	CHN	Beijing	9 Sep 1993
NAm	1:56.40	Jearl MILES CLARK	USA	Zürich	11 Aug 1999
SAm	1:56.68	Letitia VRIESDE	SUR	Göteborg	13 Aug 1995
Oce	1:58.25	Toni HODGKINSON	NZL	Atlanta	27 Jul 1996
W20, W18	1:57.18	WANG Yuan	CHN	Beijing	8 Sep 1993

1000 METRES

W, Eur	2:28.98	Svetlana MASTERKOVA	RUS	Bruxelles	23 Aug 1996
Afr	2:29.34	Maria Lurdes MUTOLA	MOZ	Bruxelles	25 Aug 1995
Com	2:29.66	Maria Lurdes MUTOLA	MOZ	Bruxelles	23 Aug 1996
NAm	2:31.80	Regina JACOBS	USA	Brunswick	3 Jul 1999
SAm	2:32.25	Letitia VRIESDE	SUR	Berlin	10 Sep 1991
CAC	2:33.21	Ana Fidelia QUIROT	CUB	Jerez de la Frontera	13 Sep 1989
Asi	2:33.6 §	Svetlana ULMASOVA	UZB	Podolsk	5 Aug 1979
Oce	2:38.54	Alison WRIGHT	NZL	Berlin	17 Aug 1979
W20	2:35.4a	Irina NIKITINA	RUS	Podolsk	5 Aug 1979
	2:35.4	Katrin WÜHN	GDR	Potsdam	12 Jul 1984
W18	2:38.58	Jo WHITE	GBR	London (CP)	9 Sep 1977

1500 METRES

W, Asi	3:50.46	QU Yunxia	CHN	Beijing	11 Sep 1993
Eur	3:52.47	Tatyana KAZANKINA	RUS	Zürich	13 Aug 1980
Afr	3:55.30	Hassiba BOULMERKA	ALG	Barcelona	8 Aug 1992
NAm	3:57.12	Mary DECKER/SLANEY	USA	Stockholm	26 Jul 1983
Com	3:57.41	Jackline MARANGA	KEN	Monaco	8 Aug 1998
Oce	4:00.93	Sarah JAMIESON	AUS	Stockholm	25 Jul 2006
CAC	4:01.84	Yvonne GRAHAM	JAM	Monaco	25 Jul 1995
SAm	4:05.67	Letitia VRIESDE	SUR	Tokyo	31 Aug 1991
W20	3:51.34	LANG Yinglai	CHN	Shanghai	18 Oct 1997
W18	3:54.52	ZHANG Ling	CHN	Shanghai	18 Oct 1997

1 MILE

W, Eur	4:12.56	Svetlana MASTERKOVA	RUS	Zürich	14 Aug 1996
NAm	4:16.71	Mary SLANEY	USA	Zürich	21 Aug 1985
Com	4:17.57	Zola BUDD	GBR/Eng	Zürich	21 Aug 1985
Asi	4:17.75	Maryam Yusuf JAMAL	BRN	Bruxelles	14 Sep 2007
Afr	4:20.79	Hassiba BOULMERKA	ALG	Oslo	6 Jul 1991
Oce	4:22.66	Lisa CORRIGAN	AUS	Melbourne	2 Mar 2007
CAC	4:24.64	Yvonne GRAHAM	JAM	Zürich	17 Aug 1994
SAm	4:30.05	Soraya TELLES	BRA	Praha	9 Jun 1988
W20	4:17.57	Zola BUDD	GBR	Zürich	21 Aug 1985
W18	4:30.81	Gelete BURKA	ETH	Heusden	2 Aug 2003

2000 METRES

W, Eur	5:25.36	Sonia O'SULLIVAN	IRL	Edinburgh	8 Jul 1994
Com	5:26.93	Yvonne MURRAY	GBR/Sco	Edinburgh	8 Jul 1994
Asi	5:29.43+§	WANG Junxia	CHN	Beijing	12 Sep 1993
NAm	5:32.7	Mary SLANEY	USA	Eugene	3 Aug 1984
Afr	5:35.62	Berhane ADERE	ETH	Ostrava	12 Jun 2003
Oce	5:37.71	Benita JOHNSON	AUS	Ostrava	12 Jun 2003
W20	5:33.15	Zola BUDD	GBR	London (CP)	13 Jul 1984
W18	5:46.5+	Sally BARSOSIO	KEN	Zürich	16 Aug 1995

3000 METRES

W, Asi	8:06.11	WANG Junxia	CHN	Beijing	13 Sep 1993
Eur	8:21.42	Gabriela SZABO	ROM	Monaco	19 Jul 2002
Com	8:22.20	Paula RADCLIFFE	Eng	Monaco	19 Jul 2002
Afr	8:23.23	Edith MASAI	KEN	Monaco	19 Jul 2002
NAm	8:25.83	Mary SLANEY	USA	Roma	7 Sep 1985
Oce	8:35.31	Kim SMITH	NZL	Monaco	25 Jul 2007
CAC	8:37.07	Yvonne GRAHAM	JAM	Zürich	16 Aug 1995
SAm	9:02.37	Delirde BERNARDI	BRA	Linz	4 Jul 1994
W20	8:28.83	Zola BUDD	GBR	Roma	7 Sep 1985
W18	8:36.45	MA Ningning	CHN	Jinan	6 Jun 1993

5000 METRES

W, Afr	14:16.63	Meseret DEFAR	ETH	Oslo	15 Jun 2007
Eur	14:24.68	Elvan ABEYLEGESSE	TUR	Bergen (Fana)	11 Jun 2004
Asi	14:28.09	JIANG Bo	CHN	Shanghai	23 Oct 1997
Com	14:29.11	Paula RADCLIFFE	Eng	Bydgoszcz	20 Jun 2004
NAm	14:44.80	Shalane FLANAGAN	USA	Walnut	13 Apr 2007
Oce	14:47.60	Benita JOHNSON	AUS	Berlin (P)	6 Sep 2002
CAC	15:04.32	Adriana FERNÁNDEZ	MEX	Gresham	17 May 2003
SAm	15:22.01	Carmen de OLIVEIRA	BRA	Hechtel	31 Jul 1993
W20	14:30.88	Tirunesh DIBABA	ETH	Bergen (Fana)	11 Jun 2004
W18	14:45.71	SONG Liqing	CHN	Shanghai	21 Oct 1997

10,000 METRES

W, Asi	29:31.78	WANG Junxia	CHN	Beijing	8 Sep 1993
Eur, Com	30:01.09	Paula RADCLIFFE	GBR/Eng	München	6 Aug 2002
Afr	30:04.18	Berhane ADERE	ETH	Saint-Denis	23 Aug 2003
Oce	30:37.68	Benita JOHNSON	AUS	Saint-Denis	23 Aug 2003
NAm	30:50.32	Deena DROSSIN	USA	Stanford	3 May 2002
CAC	31:10.12	Adriana FERNANDEZ	MEX	Brunswick	1 Jul 2000
SAm	31:47.76	Carmen de OLIVEIRA	BRA	Stuttgart	21 Aug 1993
W20	30:31.55	XING Huina	CHN	Saint-Denis	23 Aug 2003
W18	31:11.26	SONG Liqing	CHN	Shanghai	19 Oct 1997

HALF MARATHON

W, Eur	66:25	Lornah KIPLAGAT	NED	Udine	14 Oct 2007
Afr, Com	66:44	Elana MEYER	RSA	Tokyo	15 Jan 1999
Asi	67:26	Kayoko FUKUSHI	JPN	Marugame	5 Feb 2006
Oce	67:48	Kerryn McCANN	AUS	Tokyo	10 Jan 2000
NAm	68:34	Joan BENOIT	USA	Philadelphia	16 Sep 1984
CAC	68:34 dh?	Olga APPELL	MEX	Tokyo	24 Jan 1993
	69:28	Adrian FERNÁNDEZ	MEX	Kyoto	9 Mar 2003
SAm	71:15	Silvana PEREIRA	BRA	Florianópolis	13 Jul 1991
W20	68:41	Evelyne KIMWEI	KEN	Kobe	19 Nov 2006
W18	72:59	SUN Lamei	CHN	Beijing	21 Oct 2007

MARATHON

W, Eur, Com	2:15:25	Paula RADCLIFFE	GBR/Eng	London	13 Apr 2003
Afr	2:18:47	Catherine NDEREBA	KEN	Chicago	7 Oct 2001
Asi	2:19:12	Mizuki NOGUCHI	JPN	Berlin	25 Sep 2005
NAm	2:19:36	Deena KASTOR	USA	London	23 Apr 2006
Oce	2:22:36	Benita JOHNSON	AUS	Chicago	22 Oct 2006
CAC	2:22:59	Madai PÉREZ	MEX	Chicago	22 Oct 2006
SAm	2:27:41	Carmen de OLIVEIRA	BRA	Boston (dh 139m & w)a	18 Apr 1994
W20	2:23:37	LIU Min	CHN	Beijing	14 Oct 2001

3000 METRES STEEPLECHASE

W, Eur	9:01.59	Gulnara SAMITOVA	RUS	Iráklio	4 Jul 2004

Afr,Com	9:14.52	Eunice JEPKORIR	KEN	Athína	2 Jul 2007
Oce	9:24.29	Melissa ROLLISON	AUS	Melbourne	22 Mar 2006
Asi	9:26.25	LIU Nian	CHN	Wuhan	2 Nov 2007
CAC	9:27.21	Mardrea HYMAN	JAM	Monaco	9 Sep 2005
NAm	9:28.75	Lisa GALAVIZ	USA	Heusden	28 Jul 2007
SAm	9:46.52	Zenaide VIEIRA	BRA	Neerpelt	2 Jun 2007
W20	9:24.51	Ruth BISIBORI	KEN	Daegu	3 Oct 2007
W18	9:33.19	Karoline Bjerkeli GRØVDAL	NOR	Neerpelt	2 Jun 2007

100 METRES HURDLES

W, Eur	12.21	Yordanka DONKOVA	BUL	Stara Zagora	20 Aug 1988
NAm	12.33	Gail DEVERS	USA	Sacramento	23 Jul 2000
Asi	12.44	Olga SHISHIGINA	KAZ	Luzern	27 Jun 1995
Afr, Com	12.44	Glory ALOZIE	NGR	Sevilla	28 Aug 1999
CAC	12.45	Brigitte FOSTER	JAM	Eugene	24 May 2003
SAm	12.71	Maurren MAGGI	BRA	Manaus	19 May 2001
Oce	12.71	Sally McLELLAN	AUS	Osaka	5 May 2007
W20	12.84	Aliuska LÓPEZ	CUB	Zagreb	16 Jul 1987
W18	12.95	Candy YOUNG	USA	Walnut	16 Jun 1979

400 METRES HURDLES

Eur, W	52.34	Yuliya PECHONKINA	RUS	Tula	8 Aug 2003
NAm	52.61	Kim BATTEN	USA	Göteborg	11 Aug 1995
Com	52.74	Sally GUNNELL	GBR/Eng	Stuttgart	19 Aug 1993
CAC	52.82	Deon HEMMINGS	JAM	Atlanta	31 Jul 1996
Afr	52.90	Nezha BIDOUANE	MAR	Sevilla	25 Aug 1999
Oce	53.17	Debbie FLINTOFF-KING	AUS	Seoul	28 Sep 1988
Asi	53.96	HAN Qing	CHN	Beijing	9 Sep 1993
	53.96	SONG Yinglan	CHN	Guangzhou	22 Nov 2001
SAm	55.94	Lucimar TEODORO	BRA	São Paulo	6 Jun 2004
W20	54.40	WANG Xing	CHN	Nanjing	21 Oct 2005
W18	55.15	HUANG Xiaoxiao	CHN	Guangzhou	22 Nov 2001

HIGH JUMP

W, Eur	2.09	Stefka KOSTADINOVA	BUL	Roma	30 Aug 1987
Afr, Com	2.06	Hestrie CLOETE	RSA	Saint-Denis	31 Aug 2003
CAC	2.04	Silvia COSTA	CUB	Barcelona	9 Sep 1989
NAm	2.03	Louise RITTER	USA	Austin	8 Jul 1988
		Louise RITTER	USA	Seoul	30 Sep 1988
Oce	1 98	Vanessa WARD	AUS	Perth	12 Feb 1989
	1.98	Alison INVERARITY	AUS	Ingolstadt	17 Jul 1994
Asi	1.98i #	Svetlana ZALEVSKAYA	KAZ	Samara	2 Mar 1996
	1.97	JIN Ling	CHN	Hamamatsu	7 May 1989
	1.97 #	Svetlana ZALEVSKAYA	KAZ	Pierre-Benité	14 Jun 1996
	1.97	Svetlana ZALEVSKAYA	KAZ	Lausanne	5 Jul 2000
	1.97	Tatyana EFIMENKO	KGZ	Roma	11 Jul 2003
SAm	1.96	Solange WITTEVEEN	ARG	Oristano	8 Sep 1997
W20	2.01	Olga TURCHAK	KAZ	Moskva	7 Jul 1986
	2.01	Heike BALCK	GDR	Chemnitz	18 Jun 1989
W18	1.96A	Charmaine GALE	RSA	Bloemfontein	4 Apr 1981
	1.96	Olga TURCHAK	UKR	Donetsk	7 Sep 1984

POLE VAULT

W, Eur	5.01	Yelena ISINBAYEVA	RUS	Helsinki	12 Aug 2005
NAm	4.88	Jennifer STUCZYNSKI	USA	New York	2 Jun 2007
Oce, Com	4.72 i	Kym HOWE	AUS	Donetsk	10 Feb 2007
	4.65	Kym HOWE	AUS	Saulheim	30 Jun 2007
SAm	4.66	Fabiana de MURER	BRA	Monaco	20 Aug 2006
	4.66	Fabiana de MURER	BRA	Bruxelles	25 Aug 2006
	4.66 i	Fabiana de MURER	BRA	Paris (Bercy)	23 Feb 2007
Asi	4.64	GAO Shuying	CHN	New York	2 Jun 2007
Afr	4.42	Elmarie GERRYTS	RSA	Wesel	12 Jun 2000
CAC	4.30	Yarisley SLVA	CUB	Rio de Janeiro	23 Jul 2007
W20	4.48i	Silke SPIEGELBURG	GER	Münster	25 Aug 2005
	4.46	Yelena ISINBAYEVA	RUS	Berlin	31 Aug 2001
W18	4.46i	ZHANG Yingning	CHN	Shanghai	15 Mar 2007
	4.40	ZHANG Yingning	CHN	Osaka	5 May 2007
	4.40	Valeriya VOLIK	RUS	Kazan	8 Jul 2006
	4.40	Vicky PARNOV	AUS	Saulheim	30 Jun 2007

LONG JUMP

W, Eur	7.52	Galina CHISTYAKOVA	RUS	Sankt-Peterburg	11 Jun 1988
NAm	7.49	Jackie JOYNER-KERSEE	USA	New York	22 May 1994
	7.49A #	Jackie JOYNER-KERSEE	USA	Sestriere	31 Jul 1994
SAm	7.26A	Maurren MAGGI	BRA	Bogotá	26 Jun 1999
CAC,Com	7.16A	Elva GOULBOURNE	JAM	Ciudad de México	22 May 2004
Afr	7.12	Chioma AJUNWA	NGR	Atlanta	1 Aug 1996
Asi	7.01	YAO Weili	CHN	Jinan	5 Jun 1993
Oce	7.00	Bronwyn THOMPSON	AUS	Melbourne	7 Mar 2002
W20	7.14	Heike DAUTE/Drechsler	GDR	Bratislava	4 Jun 1983
W18	6.91	Heike DAUTE/Drechsler	GDR	Jena	9 Aug 1981

TRIPLE JUMP

W, Eur	15.50	Inessa KRAVETS	UKR	Göteborg	10 Aug 1995
Afr,Com	15.30	Françoise MBANGO ETONE	CMR	Athína (Round 2	23 Aug 2004
	15.30	Françoise MBANGO ETONE	CMR	Athína (Round 6)	23 Aug 2004
CAC	15.29	Yamilé ALDAMA	CUB	Roma	11 Jul 2003
Asi	14.90	XIE Limei	CHN	Urumqi	20 Sep 2007
SAm	14.57	Keila da Silva COSTA	BRA	São Paulo	9 Jun 2007
NAm	14.45	Tiombé HURD	USA	Sacramento	11 Jul 2004
Oce	14.04	Nicole MLADENIS	AUS	Perth	7 Dec 2003
W20	14.62	Tereza MARINOVA	BUL	Sydney	25 Aug 1996
W18	14.57	HUANG Qiuyan	CHN	Shanghai	19 Oct 1997

SHOT

W, Eur	22.63	Natalya LISOVSKAYA	RUS	Moskva	7 Jun 1987
Asi	21.76	LI Meisu	CHN	Shijiazhuang	23 Apr 1988
CAC	20.96	Belsy LAZA	CUB	Ciudad de México	2 May 1992
Oce, Com	20.54	Valerie VILI	NZL	Osaka	26 Aug 2007
NAm	20.18	Ramona PAGEL	USA	San Diego	25 Jun 1988
SAm	19.30	Elisângela ADRIANO	BRA	Tunja	14 Jul 2001
Afr	18.35	Vivian CHUKWUEMEKA	NGR	Ijebu Ode	17 Apr 2006
	18.43 §	Vivian CHUKWUEMEKA	NGR	Walnut	19 Apr 2003
W20	20.54	Astrid KUMBERNUSS	GDR	Orimattila	1 Jul 1989
W18	19.08	Ilke WYLUDDA	GDR	Chemnitz	9 Aug 1986

DISCUS

W, Eur	76.80	Gabriele REINSCH	GDR	Neubrandenburg	9 Jul 1988
Asi	71.68	XIAO Yanling	CHN	Beijing	14 Mar 1992
CAC	70.88	Hilda RAMOS	CUB	La Habana	8 May 1992
Oce, Com	68.72	Daniela COSTIAN	AUS	Auckland	22 Jan 1994
NAm	67.67	Suzy POWELL	USA	Wailuku	14 Apr 2007
Afr	64.87	Elizna NAUDE	RSA	Stellenbosch	2 Mar 2007
SAm	61.96	Elisângela ADRIANO	BRA	São Leopoldo	21 May 1998
W20	74.40	Ilke WYLUDDA	GDR	Berlin	13 Sep 1988
W18	65.86	Ilke WYLUDDA	GDR	Neubrandenburg	1 Aug 1986

HAMMER

W, Eur	77.80	Tatyana LYSENKO	RUS	Tallinn	15 Aug 2006
	78.61 §	Tatyana LYSENKO	RUS	Sochi	26 May 2007
CAC	76.36	Yipsi MORENO	CUB	Warszawa	17 Jun 2007
Asi	74.86	ZHANG Wenxiu	CHN	Shijiazhuang	3 Aug 2007
NAm	73.87	Erin GILREATH	USA	Carson	25 Jun 2005
SAm	72.94	Jennifer DAHLGREN	ARG	Athens, GA	13 Apr 2007
Oce, Com	71.45	Candice SCOTT	TRI	Marietta	15 May 2005
Afr	68.48	Marwa Ahmed HUSSEIN	EGY	Cairo	18 Feb 2005
W20	73.24	ZHANG Wenxiu	CHN	Changsha	24 Jun 2005
W18	70.60	ZHANG Wenxiu	CHN	Nanning	5 Apr 2003

JAVELIN

W, CAC	71.70	Osleidys MENÉNDEZ	CUB	Helsinki	14 Aug 2005
Eur	70.20	Christina OBERGFÖLL	GER	München	23 Jun 2007
Oce, Com	66.80	Louise CURREY	AUS	Gold Coast	5 Aug 2000
NAm	64.19	Kim KREINER	USA	Fortaleza	16 May 2007
Asi	63.92	WEI Jianhua	CHN	Beijing	18 Aug 2000
Afr	62.80	Justine ROBBESON	RSA	Kuortane	24 Jun 2006
SAm	62.62A	Sabina MOYA	COL	Ciudad de Guatemala	12 May 2002
W20, W18	62.93	XUE Juan	CHN	Changsha	27 Oct 2003

HEPTATHLON

W, NAm	7291	Jackie JOYNER-KERSEE	USA	Seoul	24 Sep 1988
Eur	7032	Carolina KLÜFT	RUS	Osaka	26 Aug 2007
Asi	6942	Ghada SHOUAA	SYR	Götzis	26 May 1996
Com	6831	Denise LEWIS	GBR/Eng	Talence	30 Jul 2000
Oce	6695	Jane FLEMMING	AUS	Auckland	28 Jan 1990
CAC	6527	Diane GUTHRIE-GRESHAM	JAM	Knoxville	3 Jun 1995
Afr	6423	Margaret SIMPSON	GHA	Götzis	29 May 2005
SAm	6017	Conceição GEREMIAS	BRA	Caracas	25 Aug 1983
W20	6542	Carolina KLÜFT	SWE	München	10 Aug 2002
W18	6185	SHEN Shengfei	CHN	Shanghai	18 Oct 1997

DECATHLON

W, Eur	8358	Austra SKUJYTE	LTU	Columbia, MO	15 Apr 2005
Asi	7798	Irina NAUMENKO	KAZ	Talence	26 Sep 2004
NAm	7064	Breanna EVELAND	USA	Columbia, MO	14 Apr 2006
Afr, Com	6915	Margaret SIMPSON	GHA	Réduit	19 Apr 2007
SAm	6570	Andrea BORDALEJO	ARG	Rosario	28 Nov 2004

4 X 100 METRES RELAY

W, Eur	41.37	GDR (Gladisch, Rieger, Auerswald, Göhr)	Canberra	6 Oct 1985
NAm	41.47	USA (Gaines, Jones, Miller, Devers)	Athína	9 Aug 1997
CAC, Com	41.73	JAM (Lawrence, Simpson, Bailey, Campbell)	Athína	27 Aug 2004
Asi	42.23	Sichuan CHN (Xiao Lin, Li Yali, Liu Xiaomei, Li Xuemei)	Shanghai	23 Oct 1997
Afr	42.39	NGR (Utondu, Idehen, Opara-Thompson, Onyali)	Barcelona	7 Aug 1992
SAm	42.97A	BRA (Moura, de Jesús, dos Santos, Neto)	Bogotá	10 Jul 2004
Oce	42.99A	AUS (Massey, Broadrick, Lambert, Gainsford-Taylor)	Pietersburg	18 Mar 2000
W20	43.29	USA (Knight, Tarmoh, Olear, Mayo)	Eugene	8 Aug 2006
W18	44.05	GDR (Koppetsch, Oelsner, Sinzel, Brehmer)	Athína	24 Aug 1975

4 X 400 METRES RELAY

W, Eur	3:15.17	URS (Ledovskaya, Nazarova, Pinigina, Bryzgina)	Seoul	1 Oct 1988
NAm	3:15.51	USA (D.Howard, Dixon, Brisco, Griffith Joyner)	Seoul	1 Oct 1988
CAC, Com	3:19.73	JAM (S Williams, Lloyd, Prendergast, N Williams)	Osaka	2 Sep 2007
Afr	3:21.04	NGR (Bisi Afolabi, Yusuf, Opara, Ogunkoya)	Atlanta	3 Aug 1996
Oce	3:23.81	AUS (Peris, Lewis, Gainsford-Taylor, Freeman)	Sydney	30 Sep 2000
Asi	3:24.28	CHN / Hebei (An, Bai, Cao, Ma)	Beijing	13 Sep 1993
SAm	3:26.82	BRA (Almirão, Coutinho, Tito, Teodoro)	Helsinki	13 Aug 2005
W20	3:27.60	USA (Anderson, Kidd, Smith, Hastings)	Grosseto	18 Jul 2004
W18	3:36.98	GBR (Ravenscroft, E McMeekin, Kennedy, Pettett)	Duisburg	26 Aug 1973

10 KILOMETRES WALK

W, Eur	41:04	Yelena NIKOLAYEVA	RUS	Sochi	20 Apr 1996
Asi	41:16	WANG Yan	CHN	Eisenhüttenstadt	8 May 1999
Oce, Com	41:30	Kerry SAXBY-JUNNA	AUS	Canberra	27 Aug 1988
CAC	42:42	Graciela MENDOZA	MEX	Naumburg	25 May 1997
NAm	44:17	Michelle ROHL	USA	Göteborg	7 Aug 1995
SAm	45:03	Geovanna IRUSTA	BOL	Podebrady	19 Apr 1997
Afr	45:06A	Susan VERMEULEN	RSA	Bloemfontein	17 Apr 1999
W20	41:55	Irina STANKINA	RUS	Adler	11 Feb 1995
W18	43:28	Aleksandra KUDRYASHOVA	RUS	Adler	19 Feb 2006

10,000 METRES TRACK WALK

W, Eur	41:56.23	Nadyezhda RYASHKINA	RUS	Seattle	24 Jul 1990
Oce, Com	41:57.22	Kerry SAXBY-JUNNA	AUS	Seattle	24 Jul 1990
Asi	42:30.13	GAO Hongmiao	CHN	Nanjing	24 Oct 1995
NAm	44:30.1 m	Alison BAKER	CAN	Fana	15 May 1992
	44:06 no kerb	Michelle ROHL	USA	Kenosha	2 Jun 1996
CAC	44:16.21	Cristina LÓPEZ	ESA	San Salvador	13 Jul 2007
SAm	45:59.95	Geovanna IRUSTA	BOL	Rio de Janeiro	20 May 2000
Afr	47:32.54A	Nicolene CRONJE	RSA	Pretoria	19 Mar 2005
W20	42:49.7 §	GAO Hongmiao	CHN	Jinan	15 Mar 1992
	43:11.34	Vera SOKOLOVA	RUS	Kaunas	21 Jul 2005
W18	42:56.09	GAO Hongmiao	CHN	Tangshan	27 Sep 1991

20,000 METRES TRACK WALK

W, Eur	1:26:52.3	Olimpiada IVANOVA	RUS	Brisbane	6 Sep 2001
Oce,Com	1:33:40.2	Kerry SAXBY-JUNNA	AUS	Brisbane	6 Sep 2001
CAC	1:34:56.7	Maria del Rosario SÁNCHEZ	MEX	Xalapa	16 Jul 2000

NAm	1:33:28.2	Teresa VAILL	USA	Carson	25 Jun 2005
SAm	1:35:33.4	Alessandra PICAGEVICZ	BRA	Itajai	15 May 2004
Asi	1:36:18.2	LI Yuxin	CHN	Qufu	27 Sep 1999
Afr	1:36:43.43A	Nicolene CRONJE	RSA	Germiston	20 Mar 2004
W20	1:29:32.4 #	SONG Hongjuan	CHN	Changsha	24 Oct 2003
W18	1:37:33.9	GAO Kelian	CHN	Xian	18 Sep 1999

20 KILOMETRES WALK

W, Eur	1:24:50 §	Olimpiada IVANOVA	RUS	Adler	4 Mar 2001
	1:25:41	Olimpiada IVANOVA	RUS	Helsinki	7 Aug 2005
Asi	1:26:22	WANG Yan	CHN	Guangzhou	19 Nov 2001
Oce, Com	1:27:44	Jane SAVILLE	AUS	Naumburg	2 May 2004
CAC	1:30:03	Graciela MENDOZA	MEX	Mézidon-Canon	2 May 1999
SAm	1:31:25	Miriam RAMÓN	ECU	Lima	7 May 2005
NAm	1:31:51	Michelle ROHL	USA	Kenosha	13 May 2000
Afr	1:36:18	Susan VERMEULEN	RSA	Mézidon-Canon	2 May 1999
W20	1:27:16	SONG Hongjuan	CHN	Yangzhou	14 Apr 2003
W18	1:30:52	JIANG Kun	CHN	Dandong	13 Apr 2001

World Records at other track & field events recognised by the IAAF

1 Hour	18,340 m	Tegla LOROUPE	KEN	Borgholzhausen	7 Aug 1998
20km	1:05:26.6	Tegla LOROUPE	KEN	Borgholzhausen	3 Sep 2000
25km	1:27:05.84	Tegla LOROUPE	KEN	Mengerskirchen	21 Sep 2002
30km	1:45:50.0	Tegla LOROUPE	KEN	Warstein	6 Jun 2003
4x200m	1:27.46	USA (Jenkins, Colanda, N Perry, M Jones)		Philadelphia	29 Apr 2000
4x800m	7:50.17	USSR (Olizarenko, Gurina, Borisova, Podyalovskaya)		Moskva	5 Aug 1984

WORLD BESTS AT NON-STANDARD EVENTS

50m	5.53+	Bruny Surin	CAN	Sevilla (in 100m)	22 Aug 1999
	5.53+	Ben Johnson ¶	CAN	Rome (in 100m)	30 Aug 1987
	drugs dq 5.52	Ben Johnson		Seoul (in 100m)	24 Sep 1988
60m	6.38+	Bruny Surin	CAN	Sevilla (in 100m)	22 Aug 1999
	6.38+	Ben Johnson ¶	CAN	Roma (in 100m)	30 Aug 1987
drugs dq	6.37+	Ben Johnson	CAN	Seoul (in 100m)	24 Sep 1988
150m	14.8	Pietro Mennea	ITA	Cassino	22 May 1983
	14.93+	John Regis	GBR	Stuttgart (in 200m)	20 Aug 1993
300m	30.85A	Michael Johnson	USA	Pretoria	24 Mar 2000
	31.31	LaShawn Merritt	USA	Eugene	8 Aug 2006
500m	1:00.08	Donato Sabia	ITA	Busto Arsizio	26 May 1984
600m	1:12.81	Johnny Gray	USA	Santa Monica	24 May 1986
2 miles	7:58.61	Daniel Komen	KEN	Hechtel	19 Jul 1997
2000m Steeple	5:14.43	Julius Kariuki	KEN	Rovereto	21 Aug 1990
200mh	22.55	Laurent Ottoz	ITA	Milano	31 May 1995
(hand time)	22.5	Martin Lauer	FRG	Zürich	7 Jul 1959
220yh straight	21.9	Don Styron	USA	Baton Rouge	2 Apr 1960
300mh	34.48	Chris Rawlinson	GBR	Sheffield	30 Jun 2002
35lb weight	25.41	Lance Deal	USA	Azusa	20 Feb 1993
Pentathlon	4282 points	Bill Toomey	USA	London (CP)	16 Aug 1969
(1985 tables)		(7.58, 66.18, 21.3, 44.52, 4:20.3)			
Double decathlon	14185 points	Kip Janvrin	USA	Turku	7/8 Sep 2002

11.42, 6.79, 200mh 25.31, 13.63, 5k 18:23.97, 2:02.46, 1.87, 400m 50642, HT 34.27, 3kSt 11:22.96
15.23, DT 40.91, 200m 22.56, 4.93, 10:13.16, 400mh 54.40, 58.31, 4:45.76, TJ 13.18, 10k 42:37.71

3000m track walk	10:47.11	Giovanni De Benedictis	ITA	San Giovanni Valdarno	19 May 1990
5000m track walk	18:05.49	Hatem Ghoula	TUN	Tunis	1 May 1997
10,000m track walk	37:58.6	Ivano Brugnetti	ITA	Sesto San Giovanni	23 Jul 2005
10 km road walk	37:11	Roman Rasskazov	RUS	Saransk	28 May 2000
30 km road walk	2:01:13+	Vladimir Kanaykin	RUS	Adler	19 Feb 2006
35 km road walk	2:21:31	Vladimir Kanaykin	RUS	Adler	19 Feb 2006
100 km road walk	8:38:07	Viktor Ginko	BLR	Scanzorosciate	27 Oct 2002

Women

50m	5.93+	Marion Jones	USA	Sevilla (in 100m)	22 Aug 1999
60m	6.85+	Marion Jones	USA	Sevilla (in 100m)	22 Aug 1999
150m	16.10+	Florence Griffith-Joyner	USA	Seoul (in 200m)	29 Sep 1988
300m	34.1+	Marita Koch	GDR	Canberra (in 400m)	6 Oct 1985
500m	1:05.9	Tatána Kocembová	CZE	Ostrava	2 Aug 1984
600m	1:22.63	Ana Fidelia Quirot	CUB	Guadalajara, ESP	25 Jul 1997
2 miles	8:58.58	Meseret Defar	ETH	Bruxelles	14 Sep 2007
2000m Steeple	6:03.38	Wioletta Janowska	POL	Gdansk	15 Jul 2006
200mh	25.6	Patricia Girard	FRA	Nantes	23 Aug 2001
	25.82	Patricia Girard	FRA	Nantes	22 Sep 1999
300mh	39.00	Jana Pittman	AUS	Meilen	11 Jul 2004

	38.6	Mame Tacko Diouf	SEN	Dakar	21 Feb 1999
Double heptathlon	10798 pts	Milla Kelo	FIN	Turku	7/8 Sep 2002
	100mh 14.89, HJ 1.51, 500m 5:03.74, 400mh 62.18, SP 12.73, 200m 25.16, 100m 12.59				
	LJ 5.73w, 400m 56.10, JT 32.69, 800m 2:23.94, 200mh 28.72, DT 47.86, 3000m 11:48.68				
3000m track walk	11:48.24	Ileana Salvador	ITA	Padova	29 Aug 1993
5000m track walk	20:02.60	Gillian O'Sullivan	IRL	Dublin	13 Jul 2002
50 km road walk	4:10:59	Monika Svensson	SWE	Scanzorosciate	21 Oct 2007
100km road walk	10:04:50	Jolanta Dukure	LAT	Scanzorosciate	21 Oct 2007

LONG DISTANCE WORLD BESTS – MEN TRACK

	hr:min:sec	*Name*	*Nat*	*Venue*	*Date*
15,000m	0:42:18.7+	Haile Gebrselassie	ETH	Ostrava	27 Jun 2007
10 miles	0:45:23.8+	Haile Gebrselassie	ETH	Ostrava	27 Jun 2007
15 miles	1:11:43.1	Bill Rodgers	USA	Saratoga, Cal.	21 Feb 1979
20 miles	1:39:14.4	Jack Foster	NZL	Hamilton, NZ	15 Aug 1971
30 miles	2:42:00+	Jeff Norman	GBR	Timperley, Cheshire	7 Jun 1980
50 km	2:48:06	Jeff Norman	GBR	Timperley, Cheshire	7 Jun 1980
40 miles	3:48:35	Don Ritchie	GBR	London (Hendon)	16 Oct 1982
50 miles	4:51:49	Don Ritchie	GBR	London (Hendon)	12 Mar 1983
100 km	6:10:20	Don Ritchie	GBR	London (CP)	28 Oct 1978
150 km	10:34:30	Denis Zhalybin	RUS	London (CP)	20 Oct 2002
100 miles	11:28:03	Oleg Kharitonov	RUS	London (CP)	20 Oct 2002
200 km	15:10:27+	Yiannis Kouros	AUS	Adelaide	4-5 Oct 1997
200 miles	27:48:35	Yiannis Kouros	GRE	Montauban	15-16 Mar 1985
500 km	60:23.00+ ??	Yiannis Kouros	GRE	Colac, Aus	26-29 Nov 1984
500 miles	105:42:09+	Yiannis Kouros	GRE	Colac, Aus	26-30 Nov 1984
1000 km	136:17:00	Yiannis Kouros	GRE	Colac, Aus	26-31 Nov 1984
1500 km	10d 17:28:26	Petrus Silkinas	LTU	Nanango, Qld	11-21 Mar 1998
1000 mile	11d 13:54:58+	Petrus Silkinas	LTU	Nanango, Qld	11-22 Mar 1998
2 hrs	37.994 km	Jim Alder	GBR	Walton-on-Thames	17 Oct 1964
12 hrs	162.400 km +	Yiannis Kouros	GRE	Montauban	15 Mar 1985
24 hrs	303.506 km #	Yiannis Kouros	AUS	Adelaide	4-5 Oct 1997
48 hrs	473.797 km	Yiannis Kouros	AUS	Surgères	3-5 May 1996
6 days	1036.8 km	Yiannis Kouros	GRE	Colac, Aus	20-26 Nov 2005

LONG DISTANCE ROAD RECORDS & BESTS – MEN

Where superior to track bests (over 10km) and run on properly measured road courses. (I) IAAF recognition.

10 km (I)	0:27:02	Haile Gebrselassie	ETH	Doha	11 Dec 2002
15 km (I)	0:41:22+ §	Haile Gebrselassie	ETH	Tilburg	4 Sep 2005
	0:41:29	Felix Limo	KEN	Nijmegen	11 Nov 2001
10 miles	0:44:24 §	Haile Gebrselassie	ETH	Tilburg	4 Sep 2005
	0:44:45	Paul Koech	KEN	Amsterdam-Zaandam	21 Sep 1997
20 km (I)	0:55:31+	Samuel Wanjiru	KEN	Den Haag	17 Mar 2007
25 km (I)	1:12:45	Paul Kosgei	KEN	Berlin	9 May 2004
	1:11:37 §	Haile Gebrselassie	ETH	Alphen aan den Rijn	12 Mar 2006
30 km (I)	1:28:00	Takayuki Matsumiya	JPN	Kumamoto	27 Feb 2005
20 miles	1:35:22+	Steve Jones	GBR	Chicago	10 Oct 1985
30 miles	2:37:31+	Thompson Magawana	RSA	Claremont-Kirstenbosch	12 Apr 1988
50km	2:43:38+	Thompson Magawana	RSA	Claremont-Kirstenbosch	12 Apr 1988
40 miles	3:45:39	Andy Jones	CAN	Houston	23 Feb 1991
50 miles	4:50:21	Bruce Fordyce	RSA	London-Brighton	25 Sep 1983
100 km (I)	6:13:33	Takahiro Sunada	JPN	Yubetsu	21 Jun 1998
1000 miles	10d:10:30:35	Yiannis Kouros	GRE	New York	21-30 May 1988
Ekiden (6) (I)	1:57:06 #	Kenya	KEN	Chiba	23 Nov 2005
5 stages	1:55:59	Ethiopia	ETH	Chiba	24 Nov 2003
	10k Dejene Birhanu, 5k Hailu Mekonnen, 10k Gebr. Gebremariam, 5k Markos Geneti, 12.195k Sileshi Sihine				
12 hrs	162.543 km	Yiannis Kouros	GRE	Queen's, New York	7 Nov 1984

LONG DISTANCE WORLD BESTS – WOMEN TRACK

15 km	0:49:44.0+	Silvana Cruciata	ITA	Roma	4 May 1981
10 miles	0:54:21.8	Lorraine Moller	NZL	Auckland	9 Jan 1993
20 miles	1:59:09 !	Chantal Langlacé	FRA	Amiens	3 Sep 1983
30 miles	3:12:25+	Carolyn Hunter-Rowe	GBR	Barry, Wales	3 Mar 1996
50 km	3:18:52+	Carolyn Hunter-Rowe	GBR	Barry, Wales	3 Mar 1996
40 miles	4:26:43	Carolyn Hunter-Rowe	GBR	Barry, Wales	7 Mar 1993
50 miles	5:48:12.0+	Norimi Sakurai	JPN	San Giovanni Lupatoto	27 Sep 2003
100 km	7:14:05.8	Norimi Sakurai	JPN	San Giovanni Lupatoto	27 Sep 2003
150 km	13:45:54	Hilary Walker	GBR	Blackpool	5-6 Nov 1988
100 miles	14:25:45+	Edit Bérces	HUN	San Giovanni Lupatoto	22 Sep 2002

200 km	18:31:43+	Edit Bérces	HUN	San Giovanni Lupatoto	22 Sep 2002
200 miles	39:09:03	Hilary Walker	GBR	Blackpool	5-7 Nov 1988
500 km	77:53:46	Eleanor Adams	GBR	Colac, Aus.	13-16 Nov 1989
500 miles	130:59:58+	Sandra Barwick	NZL	Campbelltown, AUS	18-23 Nov 1990
1000 km	8d 00:27:06+	Eleanor Robinson	GBR	Nanango, Qld	11-19 Mar 1998
1500 km	12d 06:52:12+	Eleanor Robinson	GBR	Nanango, Qld	11-23 Mar 1998
1000 miles	13d 02:16:49	Eleanor Robinson	GBR	Nanango, Qld	11-24 Mar 1998
2 hrs	32.652 km	Chantal Langlacé	FRA	Amiens	3 Sep 1983
12 hrs	147.600 km	Ann Trason	USA	Hayward, Cal	3-4 Aug 1991
24 hrs	250.106 km	Edit Bérces	HUN	San Giovanni Lupatoto	22 Sep 2002
48 hrs	377.892 km	Sue Ellen Trapp	USA	Surgères	2-4 May 1997
6 days	883.631 km	Sandra Barwick	NZL	Campbelltown, AUS	18-24 Nov 1990

! Timed on one running watch only, # lap recorded by computer

LONG DISTANCE ROAD RECORDS & BESTS – WOMEN

	hr:min:sec	*Name*	*Nat*	*Venue*	*Date*
10 km (l)	0:30:21	Paula Radcliffe	GBR	San Juan	23 Feb 2003
15 km (l)	0:46:55+	Kayoko Fukushi	JPN	Marugame	5 Feb 2006
	0:46:41+ dh	Paula Radcliffe	GBR	Newcastle	21 Sep 2003
10 miles	0:50:50	Lornah Kiplagat	KEN	Zaandam	17 Sep 2006
	0:50:01+ dh	Paula Radcliffe	GBR	Newcastle	21 Sep 2003
20 km (l)	1:02:57+	Lornah Kiplagat	NED	Udine	14 Oct 2007
	1:02:21+ dh	Paula Radcliffe	GBR	Newcastle	21 Sep 2003
Half mar (l) qv +	1:05:40 dh	Paula Radcliffe	GBR	South Shields	21 Sep 2003
25 km (l)	1:21:31+	Constantina Tomescu	ROM	Chicago	22 Oct 2006
	1:20:36e+ dh	Paula Radcliffe	GBR	London	13 Apr 2003
30 km (l)	1:38:30+	Constantina Tomescu	ROM	Chicago	22 Oct 2006
	1:36:36+ dh	Paula Radcliffe	GBR	London	13 Apr 2003
20 miles	1:43:33+	Paula Radcliffe	GBR	London	13 Apr 2003
30 miles	3:01:16+	Frith van der Merwe	RSA	Claremont-Kirstenbosch	25 Mar 1989
50 km	3:08:39	Frith van der Merwe	RSA	Claremont-Kirstenbosch	25 Mar 1989
40 miles	4:26:13+	Ann Trason	USA	Houston	23 Feb 1991
50 miles	5:40:18	Ann Trason	USA	Houston	23 Feb 1991
100 km (l)	6:33:11	Tomoe Abe	JPN	Yubetsu	25 Jun 2000
100 miles	13:47:41	Ann Trason	USA	Queen's, New York	4 May 1991
200 km	19:00:31	Eleanor Adams	GBR	Milton Keynes (indoor)	3-4 Feb 1990
1000 km	7d 01:11:00+	Sandra Barwick	NZL	New York	16-23 Sep 1991
1000 miles	12d 14:38:40	Sandra Barwick	NZL	New York	16-29 Sep 1991
Ekiden (6 stages)	2:11:22	(l)	ETH	Chiba	24 Nov 2003
	Berhane Adere, Tirunesh Dibaba, Eyerusalem Kuma, Ejegayou Dibaba, Meseret Defar, Werknesh Kidane				
12 hours	144.840 km	Ann Trason	USA	Queen's, New York	4 May 1991
24 hours	243.657 km	Sigrid Lomsky	GER	Basel	1-2 May 1993

100 KILOMETRES CONTINENTAL RECORDS

W, Asi	6:13:33	Takahiro SUNADA	JPN	Yubetsu	21 Jun 1998
Eur	6:16:41	Jean-Paul PRAET	BEL	Torhout	24 Jun 1989
SAm	6:18:09	Valmir NUNES	BRA	Winschoten	16 Sep 1995
Afr	6:25:07	Bruce FORDYCE	RSA	Stellenbosch	4 Feb 1989
Oce	6:29:23	Tim SLOAN	AUS	Ross-Richmond	23 Apr 1995
NAm	6:30:11	Tom JOHNSON	USA	Winschoten	16 Sep 1995
WOMEN					
W, Asi	6:33:11	Tomoe ABE	JPN	Yubetsu	25 Jun 2000
NAm	7:00:48	Ann TRASON	USA	Winschoten	16 Sep 1995
Eur	7:10:32	Tatyana ZHYRKOVA	RUS	Winschoten	11 Sep 2004
SAm	7:20:22	Maria VENANCIO	BRA	Cubatão	8 Aug 1998
Afr	7:31:47	Helena JOUBERT	RSA	Winschoten	16 Sep 1995
Oce	7:40:58	Linda MEADOWS	AUS	North Otago	18 Nov 1995

WORLD INDOOR RECORDS

Men to March 2008

50 metres	5.56A	Donovan Bailey	CAN	Reno	9 Feb 1996
60 metres	6.39	Maurice Greene	USA	Madrid	3 Feb 1998
	6.39	Maurice Greene	USA	Atlanta	3 Mar 2001
200 metres	19.92	Frank Fredericks	NAM	Liévin	18 Feb 1996
400 metres	44.57	Kerron Clement	USA	Fayetteville	12 Mar 2005
800 metres	1:42.67	Wilson Kipketer	KEN	Paris (Bercy)	9 Mar 1997
1000 metres	2:14.96	Wilson Kipketer	KEN	Birmingham	20 Feb 2000
1500 metres	3:31.18	Hicham El Guerrouj	MAR	Stuttgart	2 Feb 1997
1 mile	3:48.45	Hicham El Guerrouj	MAR	Gent	12 Feb 1997

2000 metres #	4:52.86	Haile Gebrselassie	ETH	Birmingham	16 Feb 1998
3000 metres	7:24.90	Daniel Komen	KEN	Budapest	6 Feb 1998
2 miles #	8:04.69	Haile Gebrselassie	ETH	Birmingham	21 Feb 2003
5000 metres	12:49.60	Kenenisa Bekele	ETH	Birmingham	20 Feb 2004
10000 metres #	27:50.29	Mark Bett	KEN	Gent	10 Feb 2002
50 m hurdles	6.25	Mark McKoy	CAN	Kobe	5 Mar 1986
60 m hurdles	7.30	Colin Jackson	GBR	Sindelfingen	6 Mar 1994
High jump	2.43	Javier Sotomayor	CUB	Budapest	4 Mar 1989
Pole vault	6.15	Sergey Bubka	UKR	Donetsk	21 Feb 1993
Long jump	8.79	Carl Lewis	USA	New York	27 Jan 1984
Triple jump	17.83	Aliecer Urrutia	CUB	Sindelfingen	1 Mar 1997
	17.83	Christian Olsson	SWE	Budapest	7 Mar 2004
Shot	22.66	Randy Barnes	USA	Los Angeles	20 Jan 1989
Javelin #	85.78	Matti Närhi	FIN	Kajaani	3 Mar 1996
35 lb weight #	25.86	Lance Deal	USA	Atlanta	4 Mar 1995
3000m walk #	10:31.42	Andreas Erm	GER	Halle	4 Feb 2001
5000m walk	18:07.08	Mikhail Shchennikov	RUS	Moskva	14 Feb 1995
10000m walk	38:31.4	Werner Heyer	GDR	Berlin	12 Jan 1980
4 x 200m	1:22.11	United Kingdom		Glasgow	3 Mar 1991
		(Linford Christie, Darren Braithwaite, Ade Mafe, John Regis)			
4 x 400m	3:01.96	USA (not ratified – no EPO analysis)		Fayetteville	11 Feb 2006
		(Kerron Clement, Wallace Spearmon, Darold Williamson, Jeremy Wariner)			
4 x 800m	7:13.94	USA/Global Athletics & Marketing		Boston (Roxbury)	6 Feb 2000
		(Joey Woody, Karl Paranya, Rich Kenah, David Krummenacker)			
Heptathlon	6476 points	Dan O'Brien	USA	Toronto	13/14 Mar 1993
	(6.67 60m, 7.84 LJ, 16.02 SP, 2.13 HJ, 7.85 60mh, 5.20 PV, 2:57.96 1000m)				

Women

50 metres	5.96+	Irina Privalova	RUS	Madrid	9 Feb 1995
60 metres	6.92	Irina Privalova	RUS	Madrid 11 Feb 1993 &	19 Feb 1995
200 metres	21.87	Merlene Ottey	JAM	Liévin	13 Feb 1993
400 metres	49.59	Jarmila Kratochvílová	CZE	Milano	7 Mar 1982
800 metres	1:55.82	Jolanda Ceplak	SLO	Wien	3 Mar 2002
1000 metres	2:30.94	Maria Lurdes Mutola	MOZ	Stockholm	25 Feb 1999
1500 metres	3:58.28	Yelena Soboleva	RUS	Moskva	18 Feb 2006
1 mile	4:17.14	Doina Melinte	ROM	East Rutherford	9 Feb 1990
2000 metres #	5:30.53	Gabriela Szabo	ROM	Sindelfingen	8 Mar 1998
3000 metres	8:23.72	Meseret Defar	ETH	Stuttgart	3 Feb 2007
2 miles #	9:23.38	Regina Jacobs	USA	Boston (Roxbury)	27 Jan 2002
5000 metres	14:27.42	Tirunesh Dibaba	ETH	Boston (Roxbury)	27 Jan 2007
50 m hurdles	6.58	Cornelia Oschkenat	GDR	Berlin	20 Feb 1988
60 m hurdles	7.69	Lyudmila Narozhilenko	RUS	Chelyabinsk	4 Feb 1990
High jump	2.08	Kajsa Bergqvist	SWE	Arnstadt	4 Feb 2006
Pole vault	4.93	Yelena Isinbayeva	RUS	Donetsk	10 Feb 2007
Long jump	7.37	Heike Drechsler	GDR	Wien	13 Feb 1988
Triple jump	15.36	Tatyana Lebedeva	RUS	Budapest	5 Mar 2004
Shot	22.50	Helena Fibingerová	CZE	Jablonec	19 Feb 1977
Javelin #	61.29	Taina Uppa/Kolkkala	FIN	Mustasaari	28 Feb 1999
20 lb weight #	24.23	Erin Gilreath	USA	Bloomington	18 Feb 2005
3000m walk	11:35.34 #	Gillian O'Sullivan	IRL	Belfast	15 Feb 2003
	11:40.33	Claudia Iovan/Stef	ROM	Bucuresti	30 Jan 1999
5000m walk #	20:37.77	Margarita Turova	BLR	Minsk	13 Feb 2005
10000m walk	43:54.63	Yelena Ginko	BLR	Mogilyov	
4 x 200m	1:32.41	Russia		Glasgow	29 Jan 2005
		(Yekaterina Kondratyeva, Irina Khabarova, Yuliya Pechonkina, Yuliya Gushchina)			
4 x 400m	3:23.37	Russia		Glasgow	28 Jan 2006
		(Yuliya Gushchina, Olga Kotlyarova, Olga Zaytseva, Olesya Krasnomovets)			
4 x 800m	8:14.53	Sverdlovskaya Region	RUS	Moskva	10 Feb 2008
		(Yevgeniya Zinurova, Olga Kotlyarova, Mariya Savinova, Natalya Ignatova))			
Pentathlon	4991 points	Irina Belova	RUS	Berlin	14/15 Feb 1992
		(8.22 60mh, 1.93 HJ, 13.25 SP, 6.67 LJ, 2:10.26 800m)			

events not officially recognised by the IAAF

¶ The IAAF stripped Johnson of his records in January 1990, after he had admitted long-term steroid use.

WORLD VETERANS/MASTERS RECORDS

MEN – aged 35 or more

100 metres	9.97A	Linford Christie (2.4.60)	GBR	Johannesburg	23 Sep 1995
200 metres	20.11	Linford Christie (2.4.60)	GBR	Villeneuve d'Ascq	25 Jun 1995
400 metres	45.76	Ibrahima Wade (6.9.68)	FRA	Saint-Denis	23 Jul 2004
800 metres	1:43.36	Johnny Gray (19.6.60)	USA	Zürich	16 Aug 1995

1000 metres	2:18.8+	William Tanui (22.2.64)	KEN	Rome	7 Jul 1999
1500 metres	3:32.45	William Tanui (22.2.64)	KEN	Athína	16 Jun 1999
1 mile	3:52.04	Marcus O'Sullivan (22.12.61)	IRL	Berlin	26 Aug 1997
2000 metres	4:58.3+ e	William Tanui (22.2.64	KEN	Monaco	4 Aug 1999
	4:57.31i	William Tanui		Sindelfingen	28 Feb 1999
3000 metres	7:37.23	John Kibowen (21.4.69)	KEN	Doha	14 May 2004
5000 metres	13:01.32	John Kibowen (21.4.69)	KEN	Roma	2 Jul 2004
10000 metres	27:17.48	Carlos Lopes (18.2.47)	POR	Stockholm	2 Jul 1984
20000 metres	57:44.4+	Gaston Roelants (5.2.37)	BEL	Bruxelles	20 Sep 1972
1 Hour	20,784m	Gaston Roelants (5.2.37)	BEL	Bruxelles	20 Sep 1972
Half Marathon	59:10 dh	Paul Tergat (17.6.69)	KEN	Lisboa	13 Mar 2005
	61:00	Brahim Lahlafi (5.4.68)	FRA	Paris	11 Mar 2007
Marathon	2:07:12	Carlos Lopes (18.2.47)	POR	Rotterdam	20 Apr 1985
3000m steeple	8:04.95	Simon Vroemen (11.5.69)	NED	Bruxelles	26 Aug 2005
110m hurdles	12.96	Allen Johnson (1.3.71)	USA	Athína	17 Sep 2006
400m hurdles	48.32	Danny McFarlane (24.2.72)	JAM	Osaka	26 Aug 2007
High jump	2.30i	Charles Austin (19.12.67)	USA	Boston	2 Mar 2003
	2.27	Charles Austin (19.12.67)	USA	Austin	5 Apr 2003
	2.27	Dragutin Topic (12.3.71)	SRB	Sofia	7 Jul 2007
Pole vault	5.88i	Jeff Hartwig (25.9.67)	USA	Jonesboro	22 Feb 2004
	5.83A	Jeff Hartwig	USA	Xalapa	5 May 2007
Long jump	8.50	Larry Myricks (10.3.56)	USA	New York	15 Jun 1991
	8.50	Carl Lewis (1.7.61)	USA	Atlanta	29 Jul 1996
Triple jump	17.92	Jonathan Edwards (10.5.66)	GBR	Edmonton	6 Aug 2001
Shot	22.67	Kevin Toth ¶ (29.12.67)	USA	Lawrence	19 Apr 2003
Discus	71.56	Virgilijus Alekna (13.2.72)	LTU	Kaunas	25 Jul 2007
Hammer	83.62	Igor Astapkovich (4.1.63)	BLR	Minsk (Staiki)	20 Jun 1998
Javelin	92.80	Jan Zelezny (16.6.66)	CZE	Edmonton	12 Aug 2001
Decathlon	8241	Kip Janvrin (8.7.65)	USA	Eugene	22 Jun 2001
		(10.98, 7.01, 14.21, 1.89, 48.41, 14.72, 45.59, 5.20, 60.41, 4:14.96)			
20 km walk	1:18:44	Vladimir Andreyev (7.9.66)	RUS	Cheboksary	12 Jun 2004
20000m t walk	1:20:55.4+	Maurizio Damilano (6.4.57)	ITA	Cuneo	3 Oct 1992
50 km walk	3:36:03	Robert Korzeniowski (30.7.68)	POL	Saint-Denis	27 Aug 2003
50000m t walk	3:49:29.7	Alain Lemercier (11.1.57)	FRA	Franconville	3 Apr 1994

MEN – aged 40 or more

100 metres	10.29	Troy Douglas (30.11.62)	NED	Leiden	7 Jun 2003
200 metres	20.64	Troy Douglas (30.11.62)	NED	Utrecht	9 Aug 2003
400 metres	47.82	Enrico Saraceni (19.5.64)	ITA	Århus	25 Jul 2004
	47.5u	Lee Evans (25.2.47)	USA		Apr 1989
800 metres	1:50.34	Jim Sorensen (10.5.67)	USA	Bloomington	30 Jun 2007
	1:48.81i	Johnny Gray (19.6.60)	USA	Atlanta	3 Mar 2001
1000 metres	2:26.71i	Eamonn Coghlan (21.11.52)	IRL	Gainesville	21 Jan 1994
1500 metres	3:44.06	Jim Sorensen (10.5.67)	USA	Los Angeles	4 Jun 2007
1 mile	4:02.53	David Moorcroft (10.4.53)	GBR	Belfast	19 Jun 1993
	3:58.15i	Eamonn Coghlan (21.11.52)	IRL	Boston	20 Feb 1994
3000 metres	8:03.69	Tony Bernardo (9.12.66)	AND	Palafrugell	26 May 2007
5000 metres	13:43.15	Mohamed Ezzher (26.4.60)	FRA	Sotteville	3 Jul 2000
10000 metres	28:30.88	Martti Vainio (30.12.50)	FIN	Hengelo	25 Jun 1991
1 Hour	19.710k	Steve Moneghetti (26.9.62)	AUS	Geelong	17 Dec 2005
Marathon	2:08:46	Andrés Espinosa (4.2.63)	MEX	Berlin	28 Sep 2003
3000m steeple	8:38.40	Angelo Carosi (20.1.64)	ITA	Firenze	11 Jul 2004
110m hurdles	13.97	David Ashford (24.1.63)	USA	Indianapolis	3 Jul 2004
	13.79 ?	Roger Kingdom (26.8.62)	USA	Slippery Rock	23 Jun 2004
400m hurdles	52.62	Antônio Dias Ferreira (2.3.60)	BRA	Rio de Janeiro	23 Jul 2000
High jump	2.15	Glen Conley (9.1.57)	USA	Albany	2 Aug 1997
Pole vault	5.50A ?	Larry Jessee (31.3.52)	USA	El Paso	24 Aug 1996
Long jump	7.68A	Aaron Sampson (20.9.61)	USA	Cedar City, UT	21 Jun 2002
	7.57	Hans Schicker (3.10.47)	FRG	Kitzingen	16 Jul 1989
Triple jump	16.58	Ray Kimble (19.4.53)	USA	Edinburgh	2 Jul 1993
Shot	21.41	Brian Oldfield (1.6.45)	USA	Innsbruck	22 Aug 1985
Discus	69.46	Al Oerter (19.9.36)	USA	Wichita	31 May 1980
Hammer	82.23	Igor Astapkovich (4.1.63)	BLR	Minsk	10 Jul 2004
Javelin	85.92	Jan Zelezny (16.6.66)	CZE	Göteborg	9 Aug 2006
Pentathlon	3510 pts	Werner Schallau (8.9.38)	FRG	Gelsenkirchen	24 Sep 1978
		6.74, 59.20, 23.0, 43.76, 5:05.7			
Decathlon	7525 pts	Kip Janvrin (8.7.65)	USA	San Sebastián	24 Aug 2005
		11.56, 6.78, 14.01, 1.80, 49.46, 15.40, 42.70, 4.70, 58.43, 4:25.87			
20 km walk	1:21:36	Willi Sawall (7.11.41)	AUS	Melbourne	4 Jul 1982
20000m t walk	1:24:58.8	Marcel Jobin (3.1.42)	CAN	Sept Isles	12 May 1984
50 km walk	3:49:06	José Marín (21.1.50)	ESP	Badalona	22 Mar 1992
50000m t walk	3:51:54.5	José Marín (21.1.50)	ESP	Manresa	7 Apr 1990

4x100m	42.20	SpeedWest TC (Frank Strong, Cornell Stephenson, Kettrell Berry, Willie Gault)	USA	Irvine	2 May 2004
4x400m	3:20.83	S Allah, K Morning, E Gonera, R Blackwell	USA	Philadelphia	27 Apr 2001

WOMEN – aged 35 or more

100 metres	10.74	Merlene Ottey (10.5.60)	JAM	Milano	7 Sep 1996
200 metres	21.93	Merlene Ottey (10.5.60)	JAM	Bruxelles	25 Aug 1995
400 metres	50.27	Jearl Miles Clark (4.9.66)	USA	Madrid	20 Sep 2002
800 metres	1:56.53	Lyubov Gurina (6.8.57)	RUS	Hechtel	30 Jul 1994
1000 metres	2:31.5	Maricica Puica (29.7.50)	ROM	Poiana Brasov	1 Jun 1986
1500 metres	3:57.73	Maricica Puica (29.7.50)	ROM	Bruxelles	30 Aug 1985
1 mile	4:17.33	Maricica Puica (29.7.50)	ROM	Zürich	21 Aug 1985
2000 metres	5:28.69	Maricica Puica (29.7.50)	ROM	London	11 Jul 1986
3000 metres	8:23.23	Edith Masai (4.4.67)	KEN	Monaco	19 Jul 2002
5000 metres	14:33.84	Edith Masai (4.4.67)	KEN	Oslo	2 Jun 2006
10000 metres	30:30.26	Edith Masai (4.4.67)	KEN	Helsinki	6 Aug 2005
Half Marathon	67:16	Edith Masai (4.4.67)	KEN	Berlin	2 Apr 2006
Marathon	2:21:29	Lyudmila Petrova (7.10.68)	RUS	London	23 Apr 2006
3000m steeple	9:50.29	Natalya Cherepanova (9.3.67)	RUS	Tula	10 Aug 2003
100m hurdles	12.40	Gail Devers (19.11.66)	USA	Lausanne	2 Jul 2002
400m hurdles	52.94	Marina Styepanova (1.5.50)	RUS	Tashkent	17 Sep 1986
High jump	2.01	Inga Babakova (27.6.67)	UKR	Oslo	27 Jun 2003
Pole vault	4.50	Stacy Dragila (25.3.71)	USA	Eugene	27 May 2007
Long jump	6.99	Heike Drechsler (16.12.64)	GER	Sydney	29 Sep 2000
Triple jump	14.42	Inessa Kravets (5.10.66)	UKR	Waszawa	15 Jun 2003
	14.44i	Inessa Kravets (5.10.66)	UKR	Moskva	30 Jan 2003
Shot	21.46	Larisa Peleshenko (29.2.64)	RUS	Moskva	26 Aug 2000
	21.47i	Helena Fibingerová (13.7.49)	CZE	Jablonec	9 Feb 1985
Discus	69.60	Faina Melnik (9.7.45)	RUS	Donetsk	9 Sep 1980
Hammer	72.36	Olga Kuzenkova (4.10.70)	RUS	Tula	2 Aug 2007
Javelin	66.00	Tatyana Shikolenko (10.5.68)	RUS	Tula	10 Aug 2003
Heptathlon	6533 pts	Jane Frederick (7.4.52) 13.60, 1.82, 15.50, 24.73; 6.29, 49.70, 2:14.88	USA	Talence	27 Sep 1987
5000m walk	20:12.41	Elisabetta Perrone (9.7.68)	ITA	Rieti	2 Aug 2003
10km walk	42:42+	Tamara Kovalenko (5.6.64)	RUS	Moskva	19 May 2000
10000m t walk	43:26.5	Elisabetta Perrone (9.7.68)	ITA	Saluzzo	4 Aug 2004
20km walk	1:25:59	Tamara Kovalenko (5.6.64)	RUS	Moskva	19 May 2000
20000m t walk	1:27:49.3	Yelena Nikolayeva (1.2.66)	RUS	Brisbane	6 Sep 2001
4x100m	48.63	Desmier, Sulter, Andreas, Apavou	FRA	Eugene	8 Jun 1989
4x400m	3:50.80	Mitchell, Mathews, Beadnall, Gabriel	GBR	Gateshead	8 Aug 1999

WOMEN – aged 40 or more

100 metres	10.99	Merlene Ottey (10.5.60)	JAM	Thessaloniki	30 Aug 2000
200 metres	22.72	Merlene Ottey (10.5.60)	SLO	Athína	23 Aug 2004
400 metres	53.05A	María Figueirêdo (11.11.63)	BRA	Bogotá	10 Jul 2004
	53.14	María Figueirêdo (11.11.63)	BRA	San Carlos, VEN	19 Jun 2004
800 metres	1:59.25	Yekaterina Podkopayeva (11.6.52)	RUS	Luxembourg	30 Jun 1994
1000 metres	2:36.16	Yekaterina Podkopayeva (11.6.52)	RUS	Nancy	14 Sep 1994
	2:36.08i	Yekaterina Podkopayeva (11.6.52	RUS	Liévin	13 Feb 1993
1500 metres	3:59.78	Yekaterina Podkopayeva (11.6.52)	RUS	Nice	18 Jul 1994
1 mile	4:23.78	Yekaterina Podkopayeva (11.6.52)	RUS	Roma	9 Jun 1993
3000 metres	9:11.2	Joyce Smith (26.10.37)	GBR	London	30 Apr 1978
	9:02.83i	Lyubov Kremlyova (21.12.61)	RUS	Moskva	22 Jan 2002
5000 metres	15:20.59	Elena Fidatov (24.7.60)	ROM	Bucuresti	7 Aug 2000
10000 metres	31:31.18	Edith Masai (4.4.67)	KEN	Alger	21 Jul 2007
Half Marathon	70:32	Helena Javornik (26.3.66)	SLO	Klagenfurt	19 Aug 2007
Marathon	2:26:51	Priscilla Welch (22.11.44)	GBR	London	10 May 1987
3000m steeple	10:38.98	Soraya Telles (15.9.58)	BRA	Rio de Janeiro	5 Jun 1999
100 m hurdles	13.55	Clova Court (10.2.60)	GBR	Bedford	19 Aug 2000
400 m hurdles	58.35	Barbara Gähling (20.3.65)	GER	Erfurt	21 Jul 2007
	58.3 h	Gowry Retchakan (21.6.60)	GBR	Hoo	3 Sep 2000
High jump	1.76	Debbie Brill (10.3.53) W45 record	CAN	Gateshead	6 Aug 1999
	1.76A	Patricia Porter (27.8.62)	USA	Albuquerque	6 Jun 2004
Pole vault	3.60	Larissa Lowe (19.8.63)	NED	Kingston	24 Apr 2004
	3.60i	Carla Forcellini (7.11.59)	ITA	Sindelfingen	12 Mar 2004
	3.60i	Larissa Lowe (19.8.63)	NED	Sindelfingen	12 Mar 2004
Long jump	6.41	Vera Olenchenko (21.3.59)	RUS	Rostov-na-Donu	26 Jun 2000
Triple jump	12.77i	Katalin Deák (4.3.68)	HUN	Budapest	8 Mar 2008
	12.49	Dana Urnánková (8.4.62)	CZE	Turnov	19 May 2002
Shot	19.05	Antonina Ivanova (25.12.32)	RUS	Oryol	28 Aug 1973
	19.16i	Antonina Ivanova	RUS	Moskva	24 Feb 1974
Discus	67.10	Ellina Zvereva (16.11.60)	BLR	Edmonton	11 Aug 2001

Hammer	59.29	Oneithea Lewis (11.6.60)	USA	Princeton	10 May 2003
Javelin	61.96	Laverne Eve (16.6.65)	BAH	Monaco	9 Sep 2005
Heptathlon	4359 pts	Conceição Geremias (23.7.56)	BRA	São Caetano do Sul	7 Sep 1997
		15.61, 1.57, 12.14, 28.26, 5.49, 32.08, 2:56.10			
5000m walk	22:49.06	Suzanne Griesbach (22.4.45)	FRA	Annecy	9 Aug 1987
10km walk	45:09+	Kerry Saxby-Junna (2.6.61)	AUS	Edmonton	9 Aug 2001
20km walk	1:33:04	Graciela Mendoza (23.3.63)	MEX	Lima	7 May 2005
20000m t walk	1:33:28.15t	Teresa Vaill (20.11.62)	USA	Carson	25 Jun 2005
4x100m	48.22	Cadinot, Barilly, Valouvin, Lapierre	FRA	Le Touquet	24 Jun 2006
4x400m	3:57.28	Loizou, Kay, Smithe, Cearns	AUS	Brisbane	14 Jul 2001

WORLD AND CONTINENTAL RECORDS SET IN 2007

OUTDOORS - MEN

Not ratified

100	W18	10.23	Rynell PARSON	USA	Indianapolis	21 Jun 07
	Asi	9.99	Samuel A. FRANCIS	QAT	Amman	26 Jul 07
	W,CAC,Com	9.74	Asafa POWELL	JAM	Rieti	9 Sep 07
200	CAC	19.75	Usain BOLT	JAM	Kingston	24 Jun 07
800	W40	1:50.34	Jim SORENSEN	USA	Bloomington	30 Jun 07
1000	Asi	2:15.23	Belal Mansoor ALI	BRN	Stockholm	7 Aug 07
1500	W40	3:44.06	Jim SORENSEN	USA	Eagle Rock	3 Jun 07
1M	NAm	3:46.91	Alan WEBB	USA	Brasschaat	21 Jul 07
3000	W40	8:03.69	Toni BERNADO	AND	Palafrugell	26 May 07
2M	Oce	8:03.50	Craig MOTTRAM	AUS	Eugene	10 Jun 07
	NAm	8:07.07	Matthew TEGENKAMP	USA	Eugene	10 Jun 07
10000	SAm	27:28.12	Marilson DOS SANTOS	BRA	Neerpelt	2 Jun 07
10k	SAm	27:48+	Marilson DOS SANTOS	BRA	Udine	14 Oct 07
15000	W	42:18.7	Haile GEBRSELASSIE	ETH	Ostrava	27 Jun 07
15k	SAm	42:15+	Marilson DOS SANTOS	BRA	Udine	14 Oct 07
	Asi	42:36+	Atsushi SATO	JPN	Udine	14 Oct 07
10M (track)	W	45:23.8	Haile GEBRSELASSIE	ETH	Ostrava	27 Jun 07
20000	W	56:26.0	Haile GEBRSELASSIE	ETH	Ostrava	27 Jun 07
20k	W,Com	55:31+	Samuel WANJIRU	KEN	Den Haag	17 Mar 07
1Hr (track)	W	21.285k	Haile GEBRSELASSIE	ETH	Ostrava	27 Jun 07
HMar	NAm	59:43	Ryan HALL	USA	Houston	14 Jan 07
	W,Afr,Com	58:53 #	Samuel WANJIRU	KEN	R'as Al Khaymah	9 Feb 07
	W35	61:00	Brahim LAHLAFI	FRA	Paris	11 Mar 07
	W,Afr,Com	58:33	Samuel WANJIRU	KEN	Den Haag	17 Mar 07
	SAm	59:33	Marilson DOS SANTOS	BRA	Udine	14 Oct 07
	Asi	60:25	Atsushi SATO	JPN	Udine	14 Oct 07
30k	Afr	1:28:56+	Haile GEBRSELASSIE	ETH	Berlin	30 Sep 07
	Afr	1:28:56+	Eshetu WONDIMU	ETH	Berlin	30 Sep 07
	Afr,Com	1:28:56+	Rodgers ROP	KEN	Berlin	30 Sep 07
Mar	W,Afr	2:04:26	Haile GEBRSELASSIE	ETH	Berlin	30 Sep 07
110H/91	W18	13.18	Wayne DAVIS	USA	Ostrava	12 Jul 07
110H	CAC	12.92	Dayron ROBLES	CUB	Stuttgart	23 Sep 07
400H/84	W18	49.01	William WYNNE	USA	Ostrava	15 Jul 07
400H	W35	48.83	Danny McFARLANE	JAM	Carson	20 May 07
	W35	48.52	Danny McFARLANE	JAM	Kingston	23 Jun 07
	W35	48.32	Danny McFARLANE	JAM	Osaka	26 Aug 07
HJ	W35=	2.27	Dragutin TOPIC	SRB	Sofia	7 Jul 07
PV	CAC	5.73	Giovanni LANARO	MEX	Walnut	15 Apr 07
	CAC	5.82	Giovanni LANARO	MEX	Walnut	15 Apr 07
	W35=	5.81	Jeff HARTWIG	USA	Des Moines	28 Apr 07
	W35	5.83A	Jeff HARTWIG	USA	Xalapa	5 May 07
	SAm	5.77	Fabio Gomes DA SILVA	BRA	São Paulo	7 Jun 07
LJ	SAm	8.57	Irving SALADINO	PAN	Osaka	30 Aug 07
TJ	SAm	17.90	Jadel GREGÓRIO	BRA	Belém	20 May 07
	Afr	17.37	Tareq BOUGTAïB	MAR	Khémisset	14 Jul 07
SP/5kg	W18	22.79	Marin PREMERU	CRO	Varazdin	13 Oct 07
SP	Asi	20.61	Sultan Mubarak AL-HEBSHI	KSA	Donetsk	5 Jul 07
DT/1.5kg	W18	71.95	Mykyta NESTERENKO	UKR	Yalta	19 May 07
	W18	72.31	Mykyta NESTERENKO	UKR	Beograd	26 Jul 07
DT	W18	60.60	Mykyta NESTERENKO	UKR	Kiev	19 Apr 07
	W18	62.79	Mykyta NESTERENKO	UKR	Kiev	22 May 07
	Asi	66.83	Ehsan HADADI	IRI	Tehran	24 May 07
	Asi	67.88	Ehsan HADADI	IRI	Tehran	24 May 07
	Asi	67.95	Ehsan HADADI	IRI	Minsk (Staiki)	9 Jun 07
	W35	71.56	Virgilijus ALEKNA	LTU	Kaunas	25 Jul 07
JT	NAm	90.71	Breaux GREER	USA	Carson	20 May 07
	NAm	91.29	Breaux GREER	USA	Indianapolis	21 Jun 07

Dec	CAC	8644	Maurice SMITH	JAM	Osaka	1 Sep 07
		(10.62/0.7, 7.50/0.0, 17.32, 1.97, 47.48, 13.91/-0.2, 52.36, 4.80, 53.61, 4:33.52)				
4x100	Asi	38.21	Tsukahara, Suetsugu, Takahira, Asahara	JPN	Osaka	31 Aug 07
	Asi	38.03	Tsukahara, Suetsugu, Takahira, Asahara	JPN	Osaka	1 Sep 07
	CAC	37.89	Anderson, Bolt, Carter, Powell	JAM	Osaka	1 Sep 07
4x110H	W	53.36	Bramlett, Moore, Payne, Merritt	USA	Stockholm	7 Aug 07
10kW	Asi	39:21.51t	SHIN Il-Yong	KOR	Andong	22 May 07
20000W	W20	1:20:11.72	LI Gaobo	CHN	Wuhan	2 Nov 07
20kW	W,Eur	1:17:16	Vladimir KANAYKIN	RUS	Saransk	29 Sep 07
50kW	Afr	3:58:44	Hatem GHOULA	TUN	Santa Eularia des Riu	4 Mar 07
	SAm	3:52:07	Xavier MORENO	ECU	Rio de Janeiro	28 Jul 07

OUTDOORS - WOMEN

1M	Oce	4:22.66	Lisa CORRIGAN	AUS	Melbourne	2 Mar 07
	Asi	4:22.34	Maryam Yusuf JAMAL	BRN	Genéve	9 Jun 07
	Asi	4:17.75	Maryam Yusuf JAMAL	BRN	Bruxelles	14 Sep 07
3000	Oce	8:35.31	Kim SMITH	NZL	Monaco	25 Jul 07
2M	W	9:10.47	Meseret DEFAR	ETH	Carson	20 May 07
	Oce	9:43.53	Georgie CLARKE	AUS	Carson	20 May 07
	W	8:58.58	Meseret DEFAR	ETH	Bruxelles	14 Sep 07
5000	NAm	14:44.80	Shalane FLANAGAN	USA	Walnut	13 Apr 07
	W,Afr	14:16.63	Meseret DEFAR	ETH	Oslo	15 Jun 07
10000	W40	31:31.18	Edith MASAI	KEN	Alger	21 Jul 07
15k	Eur	46:59+	Lornah KIPLAGAT	NED	Udine	14 Oct 07
20k	W,Eur	62:57+	Lornah KIPLAGAT	NED	Udine	14 Oct 07
	Com	63:18+	Mary KEITANY	KEN	Udine	14 Oct 07
HMar	W40	70:57	Helena JAVORNIK	SLO	Ferrara	18 Feb 07
	W40	70:32	Helena JAVORNIK	SLO	Klagenfurt	19 Aug 07
	NAm	66:57 dh	Kara GOUCHER	USA	South Shields	30 Sep 07
	W,Eur	66:25	Lornah KIPLAGAT	NED	Udine	14 Oct 07
	W18	72:59	SUN Lamei	CHN	Beijing	21 Oct 07
2000SC	NAm	6:25.98	Kelly STRONG	USA	Seattle	16 Mar 07
	NAm	6:20.66	Carrie VICKERS	USA	Nashville	5 May 07
3000SC	SAm	9:52.09	Zenaide VIEIRA	BRA	Belém	20 May 07
	SAm	9:46.52	Zenaide VIEIRA	BRA	Neerpelt	2 Jun 07
	W18	9:33.19	Karoline Bjerkeli GRØVDAL	NOR	Neerpelt	2 Jun 07
	Asi	9:32.35	LI Zhenzhu	CHN	Suzhou	10 Jun 07
	Afr,Com	9:14.52	Eunice JEPKORIR	KEN	Athína	2 Jul 07
	NAm	9:28.75	Lisa GALAVIZ	USA	Heusden	28 Jul 07
	W20	9:25.25	Ruth BISIBORI	KEN	Osaka	27 Aug 07
	W20	9:24.51	Ruth BISIBORI	KEN	Daegu	3 Oct 07
	Asi	9:26.25	LIU Nian	CHN	Wuhan	2 Nov 07
100H	Oce	12.92	Sally McLELLAN	AUS	Brisbane	11 Mar 07
	Oce	12.71	Sally McLELLAN	AUS	Osaka	5 May 07
400H	W40	58.35	Barbara GÄHLING	GER	Erfurt	21 Jul 07
PV	Asi	4.55	GAO Shuying	CHN	Walnut	13 Apr 07
	W35	4.30A	Stacy DRAGILA	USA	Provo	27 Apr 07
	W18=	4.40	ZHANG Yingning	CHN	Osaka	5 May 07
	NAm	4.84	Jennifer STUCZYNSKI	USA	Carson	20 May 07
	W35	4.50	Stacy DRAGILA	USA	Eugene	27 May 07
	NAm	4.88	Jennifer STUCZYNSKI	USA	New York	2 Jun 07
	Asi	4.64	GAO Shuying	CHN	New York	2 Jun 07
	Oce,Com	4.65	Kym HOWE	AUS	Saulheim	30 Jun 07
	W18=	4.40	Vicky PARNOV	AUS	Saulheim	30 Jun 07
	CAC	4.30	Yarisley SILVA	CUB	Rio de Janeiro	23 Jul 07
TJ	SAm	14.57	Keila da SILVA COSTA	BRA	Sao Paulo	9 Jun 07
	Asi	14.73	XIE Limei	CHN	Bangkok	19 Jun 07
	Asi	14.90	XIE Limei	CHN	Urumqi	20 Sep 07
SP	W18	19.13	GONG Lijao	CHN	Shijiazhuang	4 Aug 07
	Oce,Com	20.54	VILI Valerie	NZL	Osaka	26 Aug 07
DT	Afr	64.87	Elizna NAUDE	RSA	Stellenbosch	2 Mar 07
	NAm	67.67	Suzy POWELL-ROOS	USA	Wailuku	14 Apr 07
HT	CAC	75.64	Yipsi MORENO	CUB	Kingston	3 Mar 07
	SAm	72.17	Jennifer DAHLGREN	ARG	Athens	13 Apr 07
	SAm	72.94	Jennifer DAHLGREN	ARG	Athens	13 Apr 07
	W,Eur	78.61 #	Tatyana LYSENKO	RUS	Sochi	26 May 07
	Asi	74.30	ZHANG Wenxiu	CHN	Suzhou	8 Jun 07
	CAC	76.36	Yipsi MORENO	CUB	Warszawa	17 Jun 07
	W35	72.36	Olga KUZENKOVA	RUS	Tula	2 Aug 07
	Asi	74.86	ZHANG Wenxiu	CHN	Shijiazhuang	3 Aug 07
JT	NAm	64.19	Kim KREINER	USA	Fortaleza	16 May 07

	Eur	70.20	Christina OBERGFÖLL	GER	München	23 Jun 07
Hep	Eur	7032	Carolina KLÜFT	SWE	Osaka	26 Aug 07
			(13.15/0.1, 1.95, 14.81, 23.38/0.3, 6.85/1.0, 47.98, 2:12.56)			
Dec	Afr,Com	6915h	Margaret SIMPSON	GHA	Réduit	19 Apr 07
			(12.3, 5.73, 12.42, 1.72, 62.2, 14.0, 32.17, 2.50, 47.67, 5:41.7)			
4x400	CAC,Com	3:19.73	S.Williams, Lloyd, Prendergast, N.Williams			
				JAM	Osaka	2 Sep 07
5000W	W18,W20	20:28.05	Tatyana KALMYKOVA	RUS	Ostrava	12 Jul 07
10000W	CAC	44:16.21	Cristina LÓPEZ	ESA	San Salvador	13 Jul 07
50kW	W	4:10:59	Monica SVENSSON	SWE	Scanzorosciate	21 Oct 07
100kW	W	10:04:50	Jolanta DUKURE	LAT	Scanzorosciate	21 Oct 07

See ATHLETICS 2007 for Indoor Records set in January - March 2007

Additions: Men

1500	W20	3:36.28	Bilal Mansoor ALI	BRN	Stockholm	20 Feb 07
35 lb Wt	Oce	21.17	Simon WARDHAUGH	AUS	Nampa	1 Dec 07

Women

PV	Asi	4.46	ZHANG Yingning	CHN	Shanghai	15 Mar 07
4x400	Asi	3:37.59	Khadjimuratova, Azarova, Gavryushenko, Tereshkova			
				KAZ	Macau	1 Nov 07

WORLD AND CONTINENTAL RECORDS SET IN JAN–MAR 2008

INDOORS - MEN

60	SAm	6.58 (twice)	Vicente DE LIMA	BRA	Paris (B)	22 Feb 08
400	W40	48.95	Enrico SARACENI	ITA	Aubière	22 Mar 08
500	Afr	1:00.82	Gakologelwang MASHETO	BOT	New York (A)	8 Feb 08
800	Asi	1:45.26	Yusuf Saad KAMEL	BRN	Valencia	9 Mar 08
1000	W20	2:15.77	Abubaker KAKI	SUD	Stockholm	21 Feb 08
	Asi	2:17.06	Bilal Mansoor ALI	BRN	Gent	24 Feb 08
Mile	CAC	3:59.36	Pablo SOLARES	MEX	Houston	12 Jan 08
	CAC	3:58.60 o/s	David FREEMAN	PUR	Lexington	2 Feb 08
	CAC	3:58.50	Pablo SOLARES	MEX	Fayetteville	15 Feb 08
3000	Oce	7:34.50	Craig MOTTRAM	AUS	Boston (R)	26 Jan 08
	W20	7:38.03	Abraham CHERKOS FELEKE	ETH	Stuttgart	2 Feb 08
2M	W,Afr	8:04.35	Kenenisa BEKELE	ETH	Birmingham	16 Feb 08
	Com	8:06.48	Paul KOECH	KEN	Birmingham	16 Feb 08
60H	CAC	7.36	Dayron ROBLES	CUB	Stuttgart	2 Feb 08
	CAC	7.33	Dayron ROBLES	CUB	Düsseldorf	8 Feb 08
HJ	W35=	2.30	Dragutin TOPIC	SRB	Novi Sad	7 Feb 08
PV	W40	5.36A	Pat MANSON	USA	Reno	4 Jan 08
	W40	5.40A, 5.50A	Jeff HARTWIG	USA	Reno	4 Jan 08
	W40	5.51	Jeff HARTWIG	USA	Vermillion	19 Jan 08
	W40	5.60	Jeff HARTWIG	USA	Dormagen	25 Jan 08
	W40	5.65	Jeff HARTWIG	USA	Cottbus	30 Jan 08
	W40	5.70	Jeff HARTWIG	USA	Stuttgart	2 Feb 08
	SAm	5.61	Fabio Gomes DA SILVA	BRA	Donetsk	16 Feb 08
	SAm	5.61	Fabio Gomes DA SILVA	BRA	Stockholm	21 Feb 08
	W20	5.68	Raphael HOLZDEPPE	GER	Halle	1 Mar 08
LJ	SAm	8.42	Irving SALADINO	PAN	Athína (P)	13 Feb 08
	Asi	8.24	Mohamed AL-KHUWALIDI	KSA	Doha	16 Feb 08
TJ	Com	17.75	Phillips IDOWU	GBR	Valencia	9 Mar 08
SP	Oce	20.83	Scott MARTIN	AUS	Valencia	7 Mar 08
	CAC	20.62	Dorian SCOTT	JAM	Valencia	7 Mar 08
Wt	W20	21.41	Walter HENNING	USA	State College	25 Jan 08
	Oce	21.21	Simon WARDHAUGH	AUS	Nampa	2 Feb 08
	Oce	21.35	Simon WARDHAUGH	AUS	Nampa	9 Feb 08
	W20	21.47	Walter HENNING	USA	Boston	24 Feb 08
	W20	21.48, 21.66	Walter HENNING	USA	Chapel Hill	28 Feb 08
	W20	21.93, 22.02	Walter HENNING	USA	Fayetteville	15 Mar 08
	Oce	21.61, 21.83, 21.93	Simon WARDHAUGH	AUS	Fayetteville	15 Mar 08
Hep	Asi	6229	Dmitriy KARPOV	KAZ	Tallinn	16 Feb 08
		(7.07, 7.21, 16.23, 2.07 / 7.99, 5.15, 2:43.69)				
	SAm	5765 (with 55m)	Gonzalo BARROILHET	CHI	Chapel Hill	29 Feb 08
		(6.79/55, 6.99, 13.75, 1.94 / 7.49/55H, 5.27, 2:54.30)				
	SAm	5951	Gonzalo BARROILHET	CHI	Fayetteville	15 Mar 08
		(7.19, 7.42, 13.74, 2.02 / 7.98, 5.05, 2:49.30)				
4x800	Eur	7:15.77	Moskovskaya Region	RUS	Moskva	10 Feb 08
			(Trubetskoy, Bukreyev, Bogdanov, Borzakovskiy)			
Distance Medley W		9:25.97	Texas University	USA	Fayetteville	16 Feb 08
			(Miller, Fortson, Hernandez, Manzano)			

INDOORS - WOMEN

200	W20	22.48, 22.40	Bianca KNIGHT	USA	Fayetteville	14 Mar 08
1500	W,Eur	3:58.05	Yelena SOBOLEVA	RUS	Moskva	10 Feb 08
	W,Eur	3:57.71	Yelena SOBOLEVA	RUS	Valencia	9 Mar 08
	Afr	3:59.75	Gelete BURKA	ETH	Valencia	9 Mar 08
	Asi	3:59.79	Maryam Yusuf JAMAL	BRN	Valencia	9 Mar 08
Mile	Oce	4:24.14	Kimberley SMITH	NZL	Boston	8 Feb 08
2M	W,Afr	9:10.50	Meseret DEFAR	ETH	Boston (R)	26 Jan 08
	Oce,Com	9:13.94	Kimberley SMITH	NZL	Boston (R)	26 Jan 08
5000	W35	15:59.56	Yuliya VINOKUROVA	RUS	Moskva	8 Feb 08
60H	W,Eur	7.68	Susanna KALLUR	SWE	Karlsruhe	10 Feb 08
PV	W,Eur	4.95	Yelena ISINBAYEVA	RUS	Donetsk	16 Feb 08
	SAm	4.70	Fabiana de MURER	BRA	Valencia	8 Mar 08
LJ	SAm	6.86, 6.87	Maurren Higa MAGGI	BRA	Stuttgart	2 Feb 08
	W40	6.21	Katalin DEÁK	HUN	Budapest (Sy)	8 Mar 08
	SAm	6.89	Maurren Higa MAGGI	BRA	Valencia	9 Mar 08
TJ	CAC	14.89, 15.05	Yargelis SAVIGNE	CUB	Valencia	8 Mar 08
	Asi	14.48, 14.58	Olga RYPAKOVA	KAZ	Valencia	8 Mar 08
	W35	14.47	Yamilé ALDAMA	SUD	Valencia	8 Mar 08
	W40	12.69, 12.77	Katalin DEÁK	HUN	Budapest (Sy)	8 Mar 08
SP	Oce,Com	19.72	Valerie VILI	NZL	Valencia	8 Mar 08
	Oce,Com	20.19	Valerie VILI	NZL	Valencia	9 Mar 08
4x400	Asi	3:37.46	India	IND	Doha	16 Feb 08
			(Mandeep Kaur, Manjeet Kaur, Jose, Soman)			
4x800	W,Eur	8:14.53	Sverdlovskaya Region	RUS	Moskva	10 Feb 08
			(Zinurova, Kotlyarova, Savinova, Ignatova)			
10000W	W	43:54.63	Yelena GINKO	BLR	Mogilyov	22 Feb 08

OUTDOORS - MEN

30k	Afr	1:28:01+	Haile GEBRSELASSIE	ETH	Dubai	18 Jan 08
SP	Oce	21.26	Scott MARTIN	AUS	Melbourne	21 Feb 08
	CAC	21.45	Dorian SCOTT	JAM	Tallahassee	28 Mar 08
DT (1.5kg)	W18	72.97	Mykita NESTERENKO	UKR	Antalya	30 Mar 08
		74.32	Mykita NESTERENKO	UKR	Antalya	30 Mar 08
JT	Oce	89.02	Jarrod BANNISTER	AUS	Brisbane	29 Feb 08
10kW	W20	39:13	Edikt KHAYBULLIN	RUS	Adler	24 Feb 08

OUTDOORS - WOMEN

Mar	W20	2:22:38	ZHANG Yingying	CHN	Xiamen	5 Jan 08
PV	CAC	4.30, 4.40, 4.50	Yarisley SILVA	CUB	La Habana	8 Feb 08
JT	Afr	63.49A	Justine ROBBESON	RSA	Potchefstroom	16 Feb 08
20kW	W,Eur	1:25:11	Olga KANISKINA	RUS	Adler	23 Feb 08
	W20	1:25:30	Anisya KIRDYAPKINA	RUS	Adler	23 Feb 08

SPLIT TIMES IN WORLD RECORDS

Men			400m	800m	1200m	1600m	2000m	2400m	2800m	
800m	1:41.11	Kipketer 1997	49.3	1:41.11						(200m 23.8, 600m 1:14.6)
1000m	2:11.96	Ngeny 1999	49.66	1:44.62						(200m 24.12, 600m 1:17.14)
1500m	3:26.00	El Guerrouj 1998	54.3	1:50.7	2:46.4					(1000m 2:18.8)
1M	3:43.13	El Guerrouj 1999	55.2	1:51.2	2:47.0					(1000m 2:19.2)
2000m	4:44.79	El Guerrouj 1999	57.1	1:55.4	2:52.4	3:49.60				
3000m	7:20.67	Komen 1996	57.6	1:57.0	2:54.9	3:53.6	4:53.4	5:51.3	6:51.2	(1500m 3:38.6)
2M	7:58.61	Komen 1997	58.6	2:00.4		3:58.4	4:58.2	5:56.7	6:57.5	(1M 3:59.2)
5000m	12:37.35	Bekele 2004	kms: 2:33.24, 5:05.47, 7:37.34, 10:07.93, last 400m 57.9							
10,000m	26:17.53	Bekele 2005	kms: 2:40.6, 5:16.4, 7:53.3, 10:30.4, 13:09.4, 15:44.66, 18:23.98, 21:04.63, 23:45.09, 26:17.53, last 400m 57.1							
3kmSt	7:53.63	Shaheen 2004	1000m 2:36.13, 2000m 5:18.09							

Women			400m	800m	1200m	1600m	2000m	
800m	1:53.28	Kratochvílová 1983	56.1	1:53.28				(600m 1:25.0)
1000m	2:28.98	Masterkova 1996	58.3	1:59.8				(200m 28.4, 600m 1:29.1)
1500m	3:50.46	Qu Yunxia 1993	57.2	2:00.8	3:05.2			
1M	4:12.56	Masterkova 1996	62.0	2:06.7	3:12.2			(1000m 2:39.5, 1500m 3:56.77)
2000m	5:25.36	O'Sullivan 1994	64.9	2:07.8	3:14.8	4:23.5	5:25.36	

			1km	2km	3km	4km	5km	6km	7km	8km	9km
3000m	8:06.11	Wang J 1993	2:42.0	5:29.7	(last 400m 62.7)						
2M	8:58.58	Defar 2008	2:48.4	5:37.5	8:24.51	(1M 4:33.07, last 400m 62.6)					
5000m	14:16.63	Defar 2008	2:51.0	5:42.9	8:35.8	11:29.5	14:16.63				
10000m	29:31.78	Wang J 1993	2:54.7	5:56.6	8:59.2	12:02.8	15:05.7	18:10.1	21:14.4	23:59.9	26:44.8
3kmSt	9:01.59	Samitova 2004	1000m 2:58.9, 2000m 5:59.4								

Marriages

Fayyaz Ahmed GBR	Julie Crane GBR	20 May 07
Cristiano Andrei ITA	Ester Balassini ITA	
Tim Benjamin GBR	Natalie Lewis GBR	28 Sep 07
Veronica Campbell JAM	Omar Brown JAM	3 Nov 07
Pavel Fomenko RUS	Yuliya Chizhenko RUS	2006
William Frullani ITA	Hanna Melnychenko UKR	Jun 07
Graham Hood CAN	Malindi Elmore CAN	May 07
Stepan Janácek CZE	Grazyna Prokopek POL	Oct 07
Andrey Mikhnevich BLR	Natalya Khoroneko BLR	17 Mar 07
Andrew Rock USA	Missy Buttry USA	6 Oct 07
Denni Rypakov KAZ	Olga Alekseyeva KAZ	
Atsushi Sato JPN	Miho Sugimori JPN	
Ryan Shay USA	Alicia Craig USA	7 Jul 07
Obadele Thompson BAR	Marion Jones USA	24 Feb 07

Retired – Women

Sonia Bisset CUB, Yvonne Buschbaum GER, Damayanthi Darsha SRI, Karin Ertl GER, Suzy Favor-Hamilton, USA, Ludmila Formanová CZE, Laura Gerraughty USA, Ana Guevara MEX ?, Susanne Keil GER, Karin Mayr-Krifka AUT, Gillian O'Sullivan IRL, Daimí Pernía CUB, Natalya Sazanovich BLR, Sabine Schulte GER, Anita Weyermann SUI

Further recent women's name changes

Original	*Married name*
Julia Bennett GBR	Machin
Ileana Brandusoiu ROM	Sorescu
Makalesi Buikiobo FIJ	Batimala
Samira Chellah FRA	Mezeghrane
Dawn Cleary USA	Cromer
Mary Danner USA	Wineberg
Martina Darmovzalová CZE	Sestáková
Oksana Golodkova UKR	Shcherbak
Yuliya Gurtovenko UKR	Krevsun
Elena Iagar ROM	Antoci
Svetlana Ivanova RUS	Saykova
LaVerne Jones ISV	Ferrette
Tatyana Khmeleva RUS	Aryasova
Anna Kornikova RUS	Kirdyapkina
Marina Korzova KAZ	Aitova
Kristal Kostiew USA	Yush
Olesya Krasnomovets RUS	Forsheva
Jurgita Krinickaite LTU	Meskauskiene
Yevgeniya Likhuta BLR	Volodko
Marina Malashitskaya BLR	Parkhomenko
Marija Martinovic SLO	Sestak
Kara Nwidobie GBR	Sharpe
Mariya Pantyukhova RUS	Konovalova
Oksana Potapova RUS	Zhukovskaya
Anastasija 'Nastja' Ryshich GER	Reiberger
Gulnara Samitova RUS	Galkina
Natalya Shipitsyna RUS	Ignatova
Charlene Snelgrove GBR	Thomas
Elisabete Tavares POR	Ribeiro-Ansel (in FRA)
Snezana Vukmirovic SLO	Rodic
Shakeema Walker USA	Welsch
Galina Yegorova RUS	Saykina
Yulyana Zhalneryuk BLR	Yushchenko

Transfer of Nationality/Allegiance

Name	*From*	*To*	*IAAF Noted*
Men			
Jon Brown	GBR	CAN	22.1.08
Viktor Chistiakov	AUS	RUS	12.2.07
Tumatai Dauphin	PYF	FRA	18.7.07
Dominique DeGrammont	HAI	USA	4.3.07
Fabian Florant	DOM	NED	16.2.08* (24.6.08)
Samuel Francis	NGR	QAT	13.7.07
Ali Hakimi	TUN	SUI	2007
Tommy/Tamas Kafri	ISR	HUN	5.6.07
Hassan Khallouki	MAR	FRA	2.3.06
Felix Kibor(e)	KEN	QAT	13.7.07
Charles Koech	KEN	QAT	13.7.07
Frantz Kruger	RSA	FIN	14.6.07* (20.8.07)
Brahim Lahlafi	FRA	MAR	15.3.07
Ayad Lamdassem	MAR	ESP	25.5.07
Lopez Lomong	SUD	USA	6.7.07
Luis Méliz	CUB	ESP	28.12.07* (27.12.08)
Yazaldes Nascimento	STP	POR	12.6.07
Jérôme Romain	FRA	DMA	10.1.08
Jaysuma Saidy Ndure	GAM	NOR	–.12.06* (Dec 09)
Rodrigue Sialo Ngboda	CAF	FRA	15.3.07
Allen Simms	PUR	USA	9.2.08* (30.7.08)
Women			
Ruky Abdulai	GHA	CAN	Feb 08
Kim Barret-Losada	JAM	PUR	2006
Kia Davis	USA	LBR	2008
Fabienne Féraez	FRA	BEN	
Hilda Kibet	KEN	NED	13.10.07
Lucia Kimani	KEN	BIH	6.6.07
Josephine Onyia	NGR	ESP	20.4.07* (20.4.08)
Sara Salmon	GBR	AUS	12.3.07
Colleen Scott	JAM	USA	26.4.07
Svetlana Sudak/Torun	BLR	TUR	8.6.07
Saskia Triesscheijn	GER	NED	13.3.07

* not eligible to compete in international championships for new nation until later date.

Change of name and nationality

Men	
Tommy Kafri ISR	Tamás Mezei HUN
Ronald Kipchumba KEN	Saleh Besheer Madjed BRN
Dominic Kiprono Koech KEN	Khamis Sultan Dawood BRN
Stephen Lorua Kamar KEN	Nasar Sakar Saaed BRN
Bellor Minigwo Yator KEN	Yasser Belal Mansour QAT
Women	
Monica Jepkoech KEN	Mona Salem Jaber BRN

Retired – Men

André Bucher SUI, Davian Clarke JAM, Tim Goebel GER, Julian Golding GBR, Maurice Greene USA, Conny Karlsson FIN, Patrik Kristiansson SWE, Kipkirui Misoi KEN, Iván Pedroso CUB, Djabir Saïd Guerni ALG, Brandon Simpson JAM/BRN, Andriy Skvaruk UKR, Savanté Stringfellow USA, Patric Suter SUI, Andriy Skvaruk UKR, Yeoryios Theodoridis GRE.

WORLD MEN'S ALL-TIME LISTS

100 METRES

Mark	Wind	Name		Nat	Born	Pos	Meet	Venue	Date
9.74 WR	1.7	Asafa	Powell	JAM	23.11.82	1h2	GP	Rieti	9 Sep 07
9.77 WR	1.6		Powell			1	SGP	Athína	14 Jun 05
9.77 WR	1.5		Powell			1	BrGP	Gateshead	11 Jun 06
9.77 WR	1.0		Powell			1rA	WK	Zürich	18 Aug 06
9.78	0.0		Powell			1	GP	Rieti	9 Sep 07
9.79 WR	0.1	Maurice	Greene	USA	23.7.74	1rA	GP II	Athína	16 Jun 99
9.80	0.2		Greene			1	WCh	Sevilla	22 Aug 99
9.82	-0.2		Greene			1	WCh	Edmonton	5 Aug 01
9.83	-0.3		Powell			1	WAF	Stuttgart	22 Sep 07
9.84 WR	0.7	Donovan	Bailey	CAN	16.12.67	1	OG	Atlanta	27 Jul 96
9.84	0.2	Bruny	Surin	CAN	12.7.67	2	WCh	Sevilla	22 Aug 99
9.84	1.8		Powell			1		Kingston	7 May 05
9.84	1.0	Tyson	Gay	USA	9.9.82	2rA	WK	Zürich	18 Aug 06
9.84	-0.5		Gay			1	NC	Indianapolis	22 Jun 07
9.84	-0.3		Powell			1	VD	Bruxelles	14 Sep 07
9.85 WR	1.2	Leroy	Burrell	USA	21.2.67	1rA	Athl	Lausanne	6 Jul 94
9.85	0.8		Greene			1	GGala	Roma	7 Jul 99
9.85	0.6	Justin	Gatlin ¶	USA	10.2.82	1	OG	Athína	22 Aug 04
9.85	0.6		Powell			1	GS	Ostrava	9 Jun 05
9.85	1.7	Olusoji	Fasuba	NGR	9.7.84	2	SGP	Doha	12 May 06
9.85	0.1		Powell			1	Gaz	Saint-Denis	8 Jul 06
9.85	0.5		Powell			1	GGala	Roma	14 Jul 06
9.85	-0.5		Gay			1	WCh	Osaka	26 Aug 07
9.86 WR	1.2	Carl	Lewis	USA	1.7.61	1	WCh	Tokyo	25 Aug 91
9.86	-0.4	Frank	Fredericks (10)	NAM	2.10.67	1rA	Athl	Lausanne	3 Jul 96
9.86	0.2		Greene			1	WCh	Athína	3 Aug 97
9.86	1.8	Ato	Boldon	TRI	30.12.73	1rA	MSR	Walnut	19 Apr 98
9.86	-0.4		Boldon			1		Athína	17 Jun 98
9.86	0.1		Boldon			2rA	GP II	Athína	16 Jun 99
9.86	0.4		Boldon			1rA	Athl	Lausanne	2 Jul 99
9.86	-0.2		Greene			1	ISTAF	Berlin	1 Sep 00
9.86	0.6	Francis	Obikwelu	POR	22.11.78	2	OG	Athína	22 Aug 04
9.86	0.2		Powell			1rA	DNG	Stockholm	25 Jul 06
9.86	-0.5		Powell			1	ISTAF	Berlin	3 Sep 06
		(34 performances by 12 athletes)							
9.87	0.3	Linford	Christie ¶	GBR	2.4.60	1	WCh	Stuttgart	15 Aug 93
9.87A	-0.2	Obadele	Thompson	BAR	30.3.76	1	WCp	Johannesburg	11 Sep 98
9.88	1.8	Shawn	Crawford	USA	14.1.78	1	Pre	Eugene	19 Jun 04
9.91	1.2	Dennis	Mitchell ¶	USA	20.2.66	3	WCh	Tokyo	25 Aug 91
9.91	0.9	Leonard	Scott	USA	19.1.80	2	WAF	Stuttgart	9 Sep 06
9.91	-0.5	Derrick	Atkins	BAH	5.1.84	2	WCh	Osaka	26 Aug 07
9.92	0.3	Andre	Cason	USA	20.1.69	2	WCh	Stuttgart	15 Aug 93
9.92	0.8	Jon	Drummond	USA	9.9.68	1h3	NC	Indianapolis	12 Jun 97
		(20)							
9.92	0.2	Tim	Montgomery ¶	USA	28.1.75	2	NC	Indianapolis	13 Jun 97
9.92A	-0.2	Seun	Ogunkoya	NGR	28.12.77	2	WCp	Johannesburg	11 Sep 98
9.92	1.0	Tim	Harden	USA	27.1.74	1		Luzern	5 Jul 99
9.93AWR	1.4	Calvin	Smith	USA	8.1.61	1	USOF	USAF Academy	3 Jul 83
9.93	-0.6	Michael	Marsh	USA	4.8.67	1	MSR	Walnut	18 Apr 92
9.93	1.8	Patrick	Johnson	AUS	26.9.72	1		Mito	5 May 03
9.93	0.0	Walter	Dix	USA	31.1.86	1	NCAA	Sacramento	8 Jun 07
9.94	0.2	Davidson	Ezinwa ¶	NGR	22.11.71	1	Gugl	Linz	4 Jul 94
9.94	-0.2	Bernard	Williams	USA	19.1.78	2	WCh	Edmonton	5 Aug 01
9.95AWR	0.3	Jim	Hines	USA	10.9.46	1	OG	Ciudad de México	14 Oct 68
		(30)							
9.95A	1.9	Olapade	Adeniken	NGR	19.8.69	1A		El Paso	16 Apr 94
9.95	0.8	Vincent	Henderson	USA	20.10.72	1		Leverkusen	9 Aug 98
9.95	1.8	Joshua 'J.J.'	Johnson	USA	10.5.76	1r6	MSR	Walnut	21 Apr 02
9.95	0.6	Deji	Aliu	NGR	22.11.75	1	Afr G	Abuja	12 Oct 03
9.95	1.8	John	Capel	USA	27.10.78	3	Pre	Eugene	19 Jun 04
9.96	0.1	Mel	Lattany	USA	10.8.59	1r1		Athens, Ga.	5 May 84
9.96	1.2	Ray	Stewart	JAM	18.3.65	6	WCh	Tokyo	25 Aug 91
9.96	0.8	Kareem	Streete-Thompson	CAY/USA	30.3.73	2h3	NC	Indianapolis	12 Jun 97
9.96	1.0	Marc	Burns	TRI	7.1.83	1	NC	Port of Spain	25 Jun 05
9.96	0.0	Wallace	Spearmon	USA	24.12.84	1	Golden	Shanghai	28 Sep 07
		(40)							

Mark	Wind	Name		Nat	Born	Pos	Meet	Venue	Date
9.97	0.2	Dwain	Chambers ¶	GBR	5.4.78	3	WCh	Sevilla	22 Aug 99
9.97	0.6	Uchenna	Emedolu	NGR	17.9.76	2	Afr G	Abuja	12 Oct 03
9.98A	0.6	Silvio	Leonard	CUB	20.9.55	1	WPT	Guadalajara	11 Aug 77
9.98	0.3	Daniel	Effiong ¶	NGR	17.6.72	2s1	WCh	Stuttgart	15 Aug 93
9.98	1.4	Percy	Spencer	JAM	24.2.75	1	NC	Kingston	20 Jun 97
9.98	1.6	Leonard	Myles-Mills	GHA	9.5.73	1	NCAA	Boise	5 Jun 99
9.98	0.4	Jason	Gardener	GBR	18.9.75	3rA	Athl	Lausanne	2 Jul 99
9.98	0.4	Coby	Miller	USA	19.10.76	1s1	NCAA	Durham	2 Jun 00
9.98	0.2	Kim	Collins	SKN	5.4.76	1	CG	Manchester	27 Jul 02
		(49)	100th man 10.05, 200th 10.11, 300th 10.15, 400th 10.19						

9.99 seven men: Brian Lewis, MGrimes ¶, A A Zakari ¶, Darrel Brown, R Pognon, M Brunson, S Francis

Faulty wind gauge – possibly wind assisted

Mark	Wind	Name		Nat	Born	Pos	Meet	Venue	Date
9.97		Mark	Lewis-Francis	GBR	4.9.82	1q3	WCh	Edmonton	4 Aug 01

Doubtful wind reading

Mark	Wind	Name		Nat	Born	Pos	Meet	Venue	Date
9.91	-2.3	Davidson	Ezinwa ¶	NGR	22.11.71	1		Azusa	11 Apr 92

Low altitude marks for athletes with lifetime bests at high altitude

9.94 0.1 Ogunkoya 1 AfCh Dakar 19 Aug 98 — 9.97 1.6 C Smith 1 WK Zürich 24 Aug 83

9.96 0.6 O Thompson 2 DNG Stockholm 30 Jul 99 — 9.97 1.2 Adeniken 1 TexR Austin 4 Apr 92

Wind-assisted – 17 performances to 9.84, performers listed to 9.94

Mark	Wind	Name		Nat	Born	Pos	Meet	Venue	Date
9.69A	5+	Obadele	Thompson	BAR	30.3.76	1		El Paso	13 Apr 96
9.76A	6.1	Churandy	Martina	AHO	3.7.84	1		El Paso	13 May 06
9.76	2.2	Tyson	Gay	USA	9.9.82	1	GP	New York	2 Jun 07
9.78	5.2	Carl	Lewis	USA	1.7.61	1	OT	Indianapolis	16 Jul 88
9.78	3.7	Maurice	Greene	USA	23.7.74	1	GP II	Stanford	31 May 04
9.79	5.3	Andre	Cason	USA	20.1.69	1h4	NC	Eugene	16 Jun 93
9.79	4.5		Cason			1s1	NC	Eugene	16 Jun 93
9.79	2.9		Greene			1	Pre	Eugene	31 May 98
9.79	2.5		Gay			1	adidas	Carson	20 May 07
9.80	4.3		Lewis			1q2	WCh	Tokyo	24 Aug 91
9.83	7.1	Leonard	Scott	USA	19.1.80	1r1	Sea Ray	Knoxville	9 Apr 99
9.83	2.2	Derrick	Atkins	BAH	5.1.84	2	GP	New York	2 Jun 07
9.84	3.3		Greene			1h2	NC	New Orleans	19 Jun 98
9.84	3.5		Greene			1	Pre	Eugene	30 May 99
9.84	3.4	Justin	Gatlin	USA	10.2.82	1	Pre	Eugene	4 Jun 05
9.84	3.4		Powell			2	Pre	Eugene	4 Jun 05
9.84	5.4	Francis	Obikwelu	POR	22.11.78	1		Zaragoza	3 Jun 06
9.85	4.8	Dennis	Mitchell ¶	USA	20.2.66	2	NC	Eugene	17 Jun 93
9.85A	3.0	Frank	Fredericks	NAM	2.10.67	1		Nairobi	18 May 02
9.86	2.6	Shawn	Crawford	USA	14.1.78	1	GP	Doha	14 May 04
9.87	11.2	William	Snoddy	USA	6.12.57	1		Dallas	1 Apr 78
9.87	4.9	Calvin	Smith	USA	8.1.61	1s2	OT	Indianapolis	16 Jul 88
9.87	2.4	Michael	Marsh	USA	4.8.67	1rA	MSR	Walnut	20 Apr 97
9.88	2.3	James	Sanford	USA	27.12.57	1		Los Angeles (Ww)	3 May 80
9.88	5.2	Albert	Robinson	USA	28.11.64	4	OT	Indianapolis	16 Jul 88
9.88	4.9	Tim	Harden	USA	27.1.74	1	NC	New Orleans	20 Jun 98
9.88	4.5	Coby	Miller	USA	19.10.76	1		Auburn	1 Apr 00
9.88	3.6	Patrick	Johnson	AUS	26.9.72	1		Perth	8 Feb 03
9.88	3.0	Darrel	Brown	TRI	11.10.84	1	NC	Port of Spain	23 Jun 07
9.89	4.2	Ray	Stewart	JAM	18.3.65	1s1	PAm	Indianapolis	9 Aug 87
9.90	5.2	Joe	DeLoach	USA	5.6.67	5	OT	Indianapolis	16 Jul 88
9.90	7.1	Kenny	Brokenburr	USA	29.10.68	2r1	Sea Ray	Knoxville	9 Apr 99
9.91	5.3	Bob	Hayes	USA	20.12.42	1s1	OG	Tokyo	15 Oct 64
9.91	4.2	Mark	Witherspoon	USA	3.9.63	2s1	PAm	Indianapolis	9 Aug 87
9.91	3.7	Nicolas	Macrozonaris	CAN	22.8.80	1	NC	Edmonton	22 Jun 02
9.91	3.7	Steve	Mullings ¶	JAM	29.11.82	1	Aragón	Zaragoza	28 Jul 07
9.92A	4.4	Chidi	Imo ¶	NGR	27.8.63	1s1	AfG	Nairobi	8 Aug 87
9.92A	2.8	Olapade	Adeniken	NGR	19.8.69	1rA		Sestriere	29 Jul 95
9.92	2.8	Kim	Collins	SKN	5.4.76	1rA	Tex R	Austin	5 Apr 03
9.92	3.7	Joshua 'J.J.'	Johnson	USA	10.5.76	2	Aragón	Zaragoza	28 Jul 07
9.92	3.7	Clement	Campbell	JAM	19.2.75	3	Aragón	Zaragoza	28 Jul 07
9.93	7.5	Pablo	Montes	CUB	23.11.47	1s1	CAC	Panama City	1 Mar 70
9.93	5.3	Erick	Wilson	USA	10.1.82	1	JUCO	Levelland	10 May 03
9.94	2.7	Vitaliy	Savin	KZK	23.1.66	1	CIS Ch	Moskva	22 Jun 92
9.94	2.5	Daniel	Effiong ¶	NGR	17.6.72	2	TexR	Austin	9 Apr 94
9.94	7.0	Ousmane	Diarra	MLI	30.9.66	1		La Laguna	13 Jul 96
9.94	5.2	Osmond	Ezinwa	NGR	22.11.71	1		Pula	4 Sep 96
9.94	3.9	Vincent	Henderson	USA	20.10.72	1s1	WUG	Catania	29 Aug 97
9.94	2.8	Bryan	Howard	USA	7.10.76	2r7	MSR	Walnut	16 Apr 00

Rolling start 9.89w 3.7 Patrick Jarrett ¶ JAM 2.10.77 1 Pre Eugene 27 May 01

Mark	Wind	Name		Nat	Born	Pos	Meet	Venue	Date
Hand timing									
9.7	1.9	Donovan	Powell ¶	JAM	31.10.71	1rA		Houston	19 May 95
9.7	1.9	Carl	Lewis	USA	1.7.61	2rA		Houston	19 May 95
9.7	1.9	Olapade	Adeniken	NGR	19.8.69	3rA		Houston	19 May 95
9.7w	3.8	Osvaldo	Lara	CUB	13.7.55	1		Santiago de Cuba	24 Feb 82
9.7w	6.6	Rod	Mapstone	AUS	19.11.69	1r1		Perth	21 Dec 96
9.7w	8.1	Sayon	Cooper	LBR	24.4.74	1		Abilene	28 Mar 98
Disqualified for drug abuse									
9.77	1.7	Justin	Gatlin ¶	USA	10.2.82	1	SGP	Doha	12 May 06
9.78 WR	2.0	Tim	Montgomery ¶	USA	28.1.75	1	GPF	Paris (C)	14 Sep 02
9.79	1.1	Ben	Johnson ¶	CAN	30.12.61	-	OG	Seoul	24 Sep 88
9.83	1.0		Johnson			(1)	WCh	Roma	30 Aug 87
9.84	2.0		Montgomery			1	Bisl	Oslo	13 Jul 01
9.85	-0.2		Montgomery			2	WCh	Edmonton	5 Aug 01
9.86	1.1		Gatlin			1h1	SGP	Doha	12 May 06
9.87	2.0	Dwain	Chambers ¶	GBR	5.4.78	2	GPF	Paris (C)	14 Sep 02
9.7w ht	3.5		Johnson	CAN	30.12.61	1		Perth	24 Jan 87

200 METRES

Mark	Wind	Name		Nat	Born	Pos	Meet	Venue	Date
19.32 WR	0.4	Michael	Johnson	USA	13.9.67	1	OG	Atlanta	1 Aug 96
19.62	-0.3	Tyson	Gay	USA	9.9.82	1	NC	Indianapolis	24 Jun 07
19.63	0.4	Xavier	Carter	USA	8.12.85	1	Athl	Lausanne	11 Jul 06
19.65	0.0	Wallace	Spearmon	USA	24.12.84	1		Daegu	28 Sep 06
19.66 WR	1.7		Johnson			1	NC	Atlanta	23 Jun 96
19.68	0.4	Frank	Fredericks	NAM	2.10.67	2	OG	Atlanta	1 Aug 96
19.68	-0.1		Gay			1	WAF	Stuttgart	10 Sep 06
19.69	0.9	Walter	Dix	USA	31.1.86	1	NCAA-r	Gainesville	26 May 07
19.70	0.4		Gay			2	Athl	Lausanne	11 Jul 06
19.71A	1.8		Johnson			1rA		Pietersburg	18 Mar 00
19.72A WR	1.8	Pietro	Mennea	ITA	28.6.52	1	WUG	Ciudad de México	12 Sep 79
19.73	-0.2	Michael	Marsh	USA	4.8.67	1s1	OG	Barcelona	5 Aug 92
19.75	1.5	Carl	Lewis	USA	1.7.61	1	TAC	Indianapolis	19 Jun 83
19.75	1.7	Joe	DeLoach (10)	USA	5.6.67	1	OG	Seoul	28 Sep 88
19.75	0.2	Usain	Bolt	JAM	21.8.86	1	NC	Kingston	24 Jun 07
19.76	-0.8		Gay			1	WCh	Osaka	30 Aug 07
19.77	0.6		Johnson			1	DNG	Stockholm	8 Jul 96
19.77	0.7	Ato	Boldon	TRI	30.12.73	1rA		Stuttgart	13 Jul 97
19.78	0.0		Gay			1	Athl	Lausanne	10 Jul 07
19.79	1.7		Lewis			2	OG	Seoul	28 Sep 88
19.79	1.0		Johnson			1	OT	New Orleans	28 Jun 92
19.79	0.5		Johnson			1	WCh	Göteborg	11 Aug 95
19.79	1.2	Shawn	Crawford	USA	14.1.78	1	OG	Athína	26 Aug 04
19.79	0.2		Gay			1	VD	Bruxelles	25 Aug 06
19.80	-0.9		Lewis			1	OG	Los Angeles	8 Aug 84
19.80	0.4		Boldon			3	OG	Atlanta	1 Aug 96
19.81	0.3		Fredericks			1	GPF	Fukuoka	13 Sep 97
19.82A	2.0		Lewis			1		Sestriere	11 Aug 88
19.82	1.1		Fredericks			1	Bisl	Oslo	5 Jul 96
19.82	1.6		Boldon			1rA	DNG	Stockholm	7 Jul 97
19.82	1.3		Spearmon			1	GP	New York	2 Jun 07
		(31/13)							
19.83A WR	0.9	Tommie	Smith	USA	6.6.44	1	OG	Ciudad de México	16 Oct 68
19.84	1.7	Francis	Obikwelu	NGR	22.11.78	1s2	WCh	Sevilla	25 Aug 99
19.85	-0.3	John	Capel	USA	27.10.78	1	NC	Sacramento	23 Jul 00
19.85	-0.5	Konstadínos	Kedéris ¶	GRE	11.7.73	1	EC	München	9 Aug 02
19.86A	1.0	Don	Quarrie	JAM	25.2.51	1	PAm	Cali	3 Aug 71
19.86	1.6	Maurice	Greene	USA	23.7.74	2rA	DNG	Stockholm	7 Jul 97
19.87	0.8	Lorenzo	Daniel	USA	23.3.66	1	NCAA	Eugene	3 Jun 88
		(20)							
19.87A	1.8	John	Regis	GBR	13.10.66	1		Sestriere	31 Jul 94
19.87	1.2	Jeff	Williams	USA	31.12.65	1		Fresno	13 Apr 96
19.88	-0.3	Floyd	Heard	USA	24.3.66	2	NC	Sacramento	23 Jul 00
19.88	0.1	Joshua 'J.J'	Johnson	USA	10.5.76	1	VD	Bruxelles	24 Aug 01
19.89	-0.8	Claudinei	da Silva	BRA	19.11.70	1	GPF	München	11 Sep 99
19.89	1.3	Jaysuma	Saidy Ndure (GAM)	NOR	1.1.84	1	WAF	Stuttgart	23 Sep 07
19.90	1.3	Asafa	Powell	JAM	23.11.82	1	NC	Kingston	25 Jun 06
19.92A	1.9	John	Carlos	USA	5.6.45	1	FOT	Echo Summit	12 Sep 68
		above mark made with illegal brush spikes							
19.96	-0.9	Kirk	Baptiste	USA	20.6.63	2	OG	Los Angeles	8 Aug 84

Mark	Wind	Name		Nat	Born	Pos	Meet	Venue	Date
19.96	0.4	Robson (30)	da Silva	BRA	4.9.64	1	VD	Bruxelles	25 Aug 89
19.96	-0.3	Coby	Miller	USA	19.10.76	3	NC	Sacramento	23 Jul 00
19.97	-0.9	Obadele	Thompson	BAR	30.3.76	1	Super	Yokohama	9 Sep 00
19.98	1.7	Marcin	Urbas	POL	17.9.76	2s2	WCh	Sevilla	25 Aug 99
19.98	0.3	Jordan	Vaden	USA	15.9.78	2	NC	Indianapolis	25 Jun 06
19.98	1.4	LaShawn	Merritt	USA	27.6.86	2	adidas	Carson	20 May 07
19.99	0.6	Calvin	Smith	USA	8.1.61	1	WK	Zürich	24 Aug 83
20.00	0.0	Valeriy	Borzov	UKR	20.10.49	1	OG	München	4 Sep 72
20.00	0.0	Justin	Gatlin ¶	USA	10.2.82	1		Monterrey	11 Jun 05
20.01	-1.0	Michael	Bates	USA	19.12.69	3rA	WK	Zürich	19 Aug 92
20.01	0.1	Bernard (40)	Williams	USA	19.1.78	2	VD	Bruxelles	24 Aug 01
20.02	1.7	Christopher	Williams	JAM	15.3.72	1r5	MSR	Walnut	16 Apr 00
20.03	1.6	Clancy	Edwards	USA	9.8.55	1		Los Angeles (Ww)	29 Apr 78
20.03	1.5	Larry	Myricks ¶	USA	10.3.56	2	TAC	Indianapolis	19 Jun 83
20.03	1.2	Jon	Drummond	USA	9.9.68	1	VD	Bruxelles	22 Aug 97
20.03	0.6	Shingo	Suetsugu	JPN	2.6.80	1	NC	Yokohama	7 Jun 03
20.03	0.6	Darvis	Patton	USA	4.12.77	1s1	WCh	Saint-Denis	28 Aug 03
20.04	1.7	Kenny	Brokenburr	USA	29.10.68	2r5	MSR	Walnut	16 Apr 00
20.05	1.0	Roy	Martin	USA	25.12.66	3	OT	Indianapolis	20 Jul 88
20.05	1.0	Albert	Robinson	USA	28.11.64	4	OT	Indianapolis	20 Jul 88
20.05	-0.1	Ramon	Clay	USA	29.6.75	1	Athl	Lausanne	4 Jul 01
		(50)	100th man 20.19, 200th man 20.32, 300th man 20.41						
Wind-assisted 3 performances to 19.81, performers listed to 20.00									
19.61	>4.0	Leroy	Burrell	USA	21.2.67	1	SWC	College Station	19 May 90
19.70	2.7		Johnson			1s1	NC	Atlanta	22 Jun 96
19.79A	4.0		Marsh			1		Sestriere	21 Jul 92
19.83	9.2	Bobby	Cruse	USA	20.3.78	1r2	Sea Ray	Knoxville	9 Apr 99
19.86	4.6	Roy	Martin	USA	25.12.66	1	SWC	Houston	18 May 86
19.86	4.0	Justin	Gatlin ¶	USA	10.2.82	1h2	NCAA	Eugene	30 May 01
19.90	3.8	Steve	Mullings ¶	JAM	29.11.82	1		Fort Worth	17 Apr 04
19.91		James	Jett	USA	28.12.70	1		Morgantown	18 Apr 92
19.93	2.4	Sebastián	Keitel	CHI	14.2.73	1		São Leopoldo	26 Apr 98
19.94	4.0	James	Sanford	USA	27.12.57	1s1	NCAA	Austin	7 Jun 80
19.94	3.7	Chris	Nelloms	USA	14.8.71	1	Big 10	Minneapolis	23 May 92
19.94	2.3	Kevin	Little	USA	3.4.68	1s3	NC	Sacramento	17 Jun 95
19.95	3.4	Mike	Roberson	USA	25.3.56	1h3	NCAA	Austin	5 Jun 80
19.96	2.2	Rohsaan	Griffin	USA	21.2.74	1s1	NC	Eugene	26 Jun 99
19.98	2.1	Aaron	Armstrong	TRI	14.10.77	1	NC	Port of Spain	26 Jun 05
19.99	2.7	Ramon	Clay	USA	29.6.75	2s1	NC	Atlanta	22 Jun 96
20.00A	3.4	Olapade	Adeniken	NGR	19.8.69	1	WAC	USAF Academy	23 May 92
Low altitude marks for athletes with lifetime bests at high altitude									
19.94	0.3	Regis 2 WCh Stuttgart 20 Aug 93			19.96 0.0		Mennea 1	Barletta	17 Aug 80
Suspended under IAAF rules									
19.86	1.5	Justin	Gatlin ¶	USA	10.2.82	1	SEC	Starkville	12 May 02
Hand timing			*" during 220 yards race, * 220 yards less 0.1 seconds*						
19.7A		James	Sanford	USA	27.12.57	1		El Paso	19 Apr 80
19.7A	0.2	Robson C.	da Silva	BRA	4.9.64	1	AmCp	Bogotá	13 Aug 89
19.8"	WR1.3	Don	Quarrie	JAM	25.2.51	1	Pre	Eugene	7 Jun 75
19.8*	WR1.3	Steve	Williams	USA	13.11.53	2	Pre	Eugene	7 Jun 75
19.8	1.6	James	Mallard	USA	29.11.57	1	SEC	Tuscaloosa	13 May 79
19.8*w	9.0	Carl	Lawson	JAM	27.10.47	1		Moscow, ID	19 May 73
19.8*w	3.4	James	Gilkes	GUY	21.9.52	1	NCAA	Austin	8 Jun 74
19.8w	4.4	Desmond	Ross	USA	30.12.61	1	Big8	Manhattan	11 May 85

300 METRES

In 300m races only, not including intermediate times in 400m races

Mark	Name		Nat	Born	Pos	Meet	Venue	Date
30.85A	Michael	Johnson	USA	13.9.67	1		Pretoria	24 Mar 00
31.31	LaShawn	Merritt	USA	27.6.86	1		Eugene	8 Aug 06
31.48	Danny	Everett	USA	1.11.66	1		Jerez de la Frontera	3 Sep 90
31.48	Roberto	Hernández	CUB	6.3.67	2		Jerez de la Frontera	3 Sep 90
31.56		Johnson			1		Salamanca	22 Jul 94
31.56	Doug	Walker ¶	GBR	28.7.73	1		Gateshead	19 Jul 98
31.61	Anthuan	Maybank	USA	30.12.69	1		Durham	13 Jul 96
31.67	John	Regis	GBR	13.10.66	1	Vaux	Gateshead	17 Jul 92
31.70	Kirk	Baptiste	USA	20.6.63	1	Nike	London (CP)	18 Aug 84
31.73	Thomas	Jefferson	USA	8.6.62	1	DCG	London (CP)	22 Aug 87
31.74	Gabriel	Tiacoh (10)	CIV	10.9.63	1		La Coruña	6 Aug 86
31.77	Tyler	Christopher	CAN	3.10.83	1		Sainte-Anne	20 May 04
31.82	Steve	Lewis	USA	16.5.69	2	Vaux	Gateshead	17 Jul 92

400 METRES

Mark Wind	Name		Nat	Born	Pos	Meet	Venue	Date
43.18 WR	Michael	Johnson	USA	13.9.67	1	WCh	Sevilla	26 Aug 99
43.29 WR	Butch	Reynolds ¶	USA	8.6.64	1	WK	Zürich	17 Aug 88
43.39		Johnson			1	WCh	Göteborg	9 Aug 95
43.44		Johnson			1	NC	Atlanta	19 Jun 96
43.45	Jeremy	Wariner	USA	31.1.84	1	WCh	Osaka	31 Aug 07
43.49		Johnson			1	OG	Atlanta	29 Jul 96
43.50	Quincy	Watts	USA	19.6.70	1	OG	Barcelona	5 Aug 92
43.50		Wariner			1	DNG	Stockholm	7 Aug 07
43.62		Wariner			1rA	GGala	Roma	14 Jul 06
43.65		Johnson			1	WCh	Stuttgart	17 Aug 93
43.66		Johnson			1	NC	Sacramento	16 Jun 95
43.66		Johnson			1rA	Athl	Lausanne	3 Jul 96
43.68		Johnson			1	WK	Zürich	12 Aug 98
43.68		Johnson			1	NC	Sacramento	16 Jul 00
43.71		Watts			1s2	OG	Barcelona	3 Aug 92
43.74		Johnson			1	NC	Eugene	19 Jun 93
43.75		Johnson			1		Waco	19 Apr 97
43.76		Johnson			1	GWG	Uniondale, NY	22 Jul 98
43.81	Danny	Everett	USA	1.11.66	1	OT	New Orleans	26 Jun 92
43.83		Watts			1	WK	Zürich	19 Aug 92
43.84		Johnson			1	OG	Sydney	25 Sep 00
43.86A WR	Lee	Evans	USA	25.2.47	1	OG	Ciudad de México	18 Oct 68
43.86		Johnson			1	Bisl	Oslo	21 Jul 95
43.87	Steve	Lewis	USA	16.5.69	1	OG	Seoul	28 Sep 88
43.88		Johnson			1	WK	Zürich	16 Aug 95
43.90		Johnson			1		Madrid	6 Sep 94
43.91		Reynolds			2	NC	Atlanta	19 Jun 96
43.91		Wariner			1	Gaz	Saint-Denis	8 Jul 06
43.92		Johnson			1	Athl	Lausanne	2 Jul 99
43.92		Johnson			1	Pre	Eugene	24 Jun 00
	(30/7)							
43.96	LaShawn	Merritt	USA	27.6.86	2	WCh	Osaka	31 Aug 07
43.97A	Larry	James	USA	6.11.47	2	OG	Ciudad de México	18 Oct 68
44.05	Angelo	Taylor	USA	29.12.78	1	NC	Indianapolis	23 Jun 07
	(10)							
44.09	Alvin	Harrison ¶	USA	20.1.74	3	NC	Atlanta	19 Jun 96
44.09	Jerome	Young ¶	USA	14.8.76	1	NC	New Orleans	21 Jun 98
44.10	Gary	Kikaya	COD	4.2.78	2	WAF	Stuttgart	9 Sep 06
44.13	Derek	Mills	USA	9.7.72	1	Pre	Eugene	4 Jun 95
44.14	Roberto	Hernández	CUB	6.3.67	2		Sevilla	30 May 90
44.15	Anthuan	Maybank	USA	30.12.69	1rB	Athl	Lausanne	3 Jul 96
44.17	Innocent	Egbunike	NGR	30.11.61	1rA	WK	Zürich	19 Aug 87
44.16	Otis	Harris	USA	30.6.82	2	OG	Athína	23 Aug 04
44.18	Samson	Kitur	KEN	25.2.66	2s2	OG	Barcelona	3 Aug 92
44.20A	Charles	Gitonga	KEN	5.10.71	1	NC	Nairobi	29 Jun 96
	(20)							
44.21	Ian	Morris	TRI	30.11.61	3s2	OG	Barcelona	3 Aug 92
44.21	Antonio	Pettigrew	USA	3.11.67	1		Nassau	26 May 99
44.26	Alberto	Juantorena	CUB	3.12.50	1	OG	Montreal	29 Jul 76
44.27	Alonzo	Babers	USA	31.10.61	1	OG	Los Angeles	8 Aug 84
44.27	Darold	Williamson	USA	19.2.83	1s1	NCAA	Sacramento	10 Jun 05
44.28	Andrew	Valmon	USA	1.1.65	4	NC	Eugene	19 Jun 93
44.28	Tyree	Washington	USA	28.8.76	1		Eagle Rock	12 May 01
44.29	Derrick	Brew	USA	28.12.77	1	SEC	Athens, Ga	16 May 99
44.29	Sanderlei	Parrela	BRA	7.10.74	2	WCh	Sevilla	26 Aug 99
44.30	Gabriel	Tiacoh	CIV	10.9.63	1	NCAA	Indianapolis	7 Jun 86
	(30)							
44.30	Lamont	Smith	USA	11.12.72	4	NC	Atlanta	19 Jun 96
44.31	Alejandro	Cárdenas	MEX	4.10.74	3	WCh	Sevilla	26 Aug 99
44.33	Thomas	Schönlebe	GDR	6.8.65	1	WCh	Roma	3 Sep 87
44.34	Darnell	Hall	USA	26.9.71	1	Athl	Lausanne	5 Jul 95
44.35	Andrew	Rock	USA	23.1.82	2	WCh	Helsinki	12 Aug 05
44.36	Iwan	Thomas	GBR	5.1.74	1	NC	Birmingham	13 Jul 97
44.37	Roger	Black	GBR	31.3.66	2rA	Athl	Lausanne	3 Jul 96
44.37	Davis	Kamoga	UGA	17.7.68	2	WCh	Athína	5 Aug 97
44.37	Mark	Richardson	GBR	26.7.72	1	Bisl	Oslo	9 Jul 98
44.38	Darren	Clark	AUS	6.9.65	3s1	OG	Seoul	26 Sep 88
	(40)							

Mark	Wind	Name		Nat	Born	Pos	Meet	Venue	Date
44.40		Fred	Newhouse	USA	8.11.48	2	OG	Montreal	29 Jul 76
44.41A		Ron	Freeman	USA	12.6.47	3	OG	Ciudad de México	18 Oct 68
44.43A		Ezra	Sambu	KEN	4.9.78	1	WCT	Nairobi	26 Jul 03
44.44		Tyler	Christopher	CAN	3.10.83	3	WCh	Helsinki	12 Aug 05
44.45A		Ronnie	Ray	USA	2.1.54	1	PAm	Ciudad de México	18 Oct 75
44.45		Darrell	Robinson	USA	23.12.63	2	Pepsi	Los Angeles (Ww)	17 May 86
44.45		Avard	Moncur	BAH	2.11.78	1		Madrid	7 Jul 01
44.45		Leonard	Byrd	USA	17.3.75	1	GP	Belém	5 May 02
44.45		Chris	Brown	BAH	15.10.78	4	WCh	Osaka	31 Aug 07
44.46		Leslie	Djhone	FRA	18.3.81	2s3	WCh	Osaka	29 Aug 07
		(50)	100th man 44.69, 200th 44.99, 300th 45.24						
Hand timing									
44.1		Wayne	Collett	USA	20.10.49	1	OT	Eugene	9 Jul 72
44.2*		John	Smith	USA	5.8.50	1	AAU	Eugene	26 Jun 71
44.2		Fred	Newhouse	USA	8.11.48	1s1	OT	Eugene	7 Jul 72

600 METRES

Mark	Wind	Name		Nat	Born	Pos	Meet	Venue	Date
1:12.81		Johnny	Gray	USA	19.6.60	1		Santa Monica	24 May 86
1:13.2 + ?		John	Kipkurgat	KEN	16.3.44	1		Pointe-à-Pierre	23 Mar 74
1:13.49		Joseph	Mutua	KEN	10.12.78	1		Liège (NX)	27 Aug 02
1:13.80		Earl	Jones	USA	17.7.64	2		Santa Monica	24 May 86

800 METRES

Mark	Wind	Name		Nat	Born	Pos	Meet	Venue	Date
1:41.11	WR	Wilson	Kipketer	DEN	12.12.70	1	ASV	Köln	24 Aug 97
1:41.24	WR		Kipketer			1rA	WK	Zürich	13 Aug 97
1:41.73!	WR	Sebastian	Coe	GBR	29.9.56	1		Firenze	10 Jun 81
1:41.73			Kipketer			1rA	DNG	Stockholm	7 Jul 97
1:41.77		Joaquim	Cruz	BRA	12.3.63	1	ASV	Köln	26 Aug 84
1:41.83			Kipketer			1	GP II	Rieti	1 Sep 96
1:42.17			Kipketer			1	TOTO	Tokyo	16 Sep 96
1:42.20			Kipketer			1	VD	Bruxelles	22 Aug 97
1:42.27			Kipketer			1	VD	Bruxelles	3 Sep 99
1:42.28		Sammy	Koskei	KEN	14.5.61	2	ASV	Köln	26 Aug 84
1:42.32			Kipketer			1	GP II	Rieti	8 Sep 02
1:42.33	WR		Coe			1	Bisl	Oslo	5 Jul 79
1:42.34			Cruz			1r1	WK	Zürich	22 Aug 84
1:42.34		Wilfred	Bungei	KEN	24.7.80	2	GP II	Rieti	8 Sep 02
1:42.41			Cruz			1	VD	Bruxelles	24 Aug 84
1:42.47		Yuriy	Borzakovskiy	RUS	12.4.81	1	VD	Bruxelles	24 Aug 01
1:42.49			Cruz			1		Koblenz	28 Aug 85
1:42.51			Kipketer			1	Nik	Nice	10 Jul 96
1:42.52			Bungei			1	VD	Bruxelles	5 Sep 03
1:42.54			Cruz			1	ASV	Köln	25 Aug 85
1:42.55		André	Bucher	SUI	19.10.76	1rA	WK	Zürich	17 Aug 01
1:42.57			Kipketer			1	Herc	Monaco	4 Aug 99
1:42.58		Vebjørn	Rodal	NOR	16.9.72	1	OG	Atlanta	31 Jul 96
1:42.59			Kipketer			1	Herc	Monaco	10 Aug 96
1:42.60		Johnny	Gray	USA	19.6.60	2r1		Koblenz	28 Aug 85
1:42.61			Kipketer			1rA	WK	Zürich	14 Aug 96
1:42.61			Kipketer			1rA	Athl	Lausanne	2 Jul 97
1:42.62		Patrick	Ndururi	KEN	12.1.69	2rA	WK	Zürich	13 Aug 97
1:42.65			Gray			1	WK	Zürich	17 Aug 88
1:42.69		Hezekiél	Sepeng ¶	RSA	30.6.74	2	VD	Bruxelles	3 Sep 99
1:42.69		Japheth	Kimutai	KEN	20.12.78	3	VD	Bruxelles	3 Sep 99
		(31/12)							
1:42.79		Fred	Onyancha	KEN	25.12.69	3	OG	Atlanta	31 Jul 96
1:42.81		Jean-Patrick	Nduwimana	BDI	9.5.78	2rA	WK	Zürich	17 Aug 01
1:42.85		Norberto	Téllez	CUB	22.1.72	4	OG	Atlanta	31 Jul 96
1:42.88		Steve	Cram	GBR	14.10.60	1rA	WK	Zürich	21 Aug 85
1:42.89		Mbulaeni	Mulaudzi	RSA	8.9.80	2	VD	Bruxelles	5 Sep 03
1:42.91		William	Yiampoy	KEN	17.5.74	3	GP II	Rieti	8 Sep 02
1:42.97		Peter	Elliott	GBR	9.10.62	1		Sevilla	30 May 90
1:42.98		Patrick	Konchellah	KEN	20.4.68	2	ASV	Köln	24 Aug 97
		(20)							
1:43.03		Kennedy/Kenneth	Kimwetich	KEN	1.1.73	2		Stuttgart	19 Jul 98
1:43.06		Billy	Konchellah	KEN	20.10.62	1	WCh	Roma	1 Sep 87
1:43.08		José Luiz	Barbosa	BRA	27.5.61	1		Rieti	6 Sep 91
1:43.09		Djabir	Saïd Guerni	ALG	29.3.77	5	VD	Bruxelles	3 Sep 99
1:43.11		Youssef Saad	Kamel	BRN	29.3.83	1rB	WK	Zürich	6 Aug 04

Mark Wind	Name		Nat	Born	Pos	Meet	Venue	Date
1:43.15	Mehdi	Baala	FRA	17.8.78	5	GP II	Rieti	8 Sep 02
1:43.16	Paul	Ereng	KEN	22.8.67	1	WK	Zürich	16 Aug 89
1:43.17	Benson	Koech	KEN	10.11.74	1		Rieti	28 Aug 94
1:43.20	Mark	Everett	USA	2.9.68	1rA	Gugl	Linz	9 Jul 97
1:43.22	Pawel	Czapiewski	POL	30.3.78	5rA	WK	Zürich	17 Aug 01
	(30)							
1:43.25	Amine	Laâlou	MAR	13.5.82	1	GGala	Roma	14 Jul 06
1:43.26	Sammy	Langat (Kibet)	KEN	24.1.70	1rB	WK	Zürich	14 Aug 96
1:43.30	William	Tanui	KEN	22.2.64	2		Rieti	6 Sep 91
1:43.31	Nixon	Kiprotich	KEN	4.12.62	1		Rieti	6 Sep 92
1:43.33	Robert	Chirchir	KEN	26.11.72	3		Stuttgart	19 Jul 98
1:43.33	William	Chirchir	KEN	6.2.79	6	VD	Bruxelles	3 Sep 99
1:43.33	Joseph Mwengi	Mutua	KEN	10.12.78	1rA	WK	Zürich	16 Aug 02
1:43.35	David	Mack	USA	30.5.61	3r1		Koblenz	28 Aug 85
1:43.38	David (Singoei)	Kiptoo	KEN	26.6.65	2	Herc	Monaco	10 Aug 96
1:43.38	Rich	Kenah	USA	4.8.70	3rA	WK	Zürich	13 Aug 97
	(40)							
1:43.38	Arthémon	Hatungimana	BDI	21.1.74	3	VD	Bruxelles	24 Aug 01
1:43.44 WR	Alberto	Juantorena	CUB	3.12.50	1	WUG	Sofiya	21 Aug 77
1:43.45	Bram	Som	NED	20.2.80	2rA	WK	Zürich	18 Aug 06
1:43.50	Mahjoub	Haïda	MAR	1.7.70	2	GGala	Roma	14 Jul 98
1:43.5* WR	Rick	Wohlhuter	USA	23.12.48	1		Eugene	8 Jun 74
1:43.54	William	Wuyke	VEN	21.5.58	2		Rieti	7 Sep 86
1:43.55	Philip	Kibitok	KEN	23.3.71	3	GP II	Rieti	1 Sep 96
1:43.56	Rob	Druppers	NED	29.4.62	4	ASV	Köln	25 Aug 85
1:43.57	Mike	Boit	KEN	6.1.49	1	ISTAF	Berlin	20 Aug 76
1:43.57	Joseph	Tengelei	KEN	8.12.72	3rB	WK	Zürich	16 Aug 95
	(50)	100th man 1:44.10, 200th man 1:44.91, 300th man 1:45.35						
Indoors		! *photo-electric cell time*						
1:42.67		Kipketer			1	WI	Paris (B)	9 Mar 97

1000 METRES

Mark Wind	Name		Nat	Born	Pos	Meet	Venue	Date
2:11.96 WR	Noah	Ngeny	KEN	2.11.78	1	GP II	Rieti	5 Sep 99
2:12.18 WR	Sebastian	Coe	GBR	29.9.56	1	OsloG	Oslo	11 Jul 81
2:12.66		Ngeny			1	Nik	Nice	17 Jul 99
2:12.88	Steve	Cram	GBR	14.10.60	1		Gateshead	9 Aug 85
2:13.40 WR		Coe			1	Bisl	Oslo	1 Jul 80
2:13.56	Kennedy/Kenneth	Kimwetich	KEN	1.1.73	2	Nik	Nice	17 Jul 99
2:13.73	Noureddine	Morceli	ALG	28.2.70	1	BNP	Villeneuve d'Ascq	2 Jul 93
2:13.9 WR	Rick	Wohlhuter	USA	23.12.48	1	King	Oslo	30 Jul 74
2:13.96	Mehdi	Baala	FRA	17.8.78	1		Strasbourg	26 Jun 03
2:14.09	Joaquim	Cruz	BRA	12.3.63	1	Nik	Nice	20 Aug 84
2:14.28	Japheth	Kimutai	KEN	20.12.78	1	DNG	Stockholm	1 Aug 00
2:14.41	William	Yiampoy (10)	KEN	17.5.74	2	GP II	Rieti	5 Sep 99
2:14.43	Laban	Rotich	KEN	20.1.69	1	Nik	Nice	16 Jul 97
2:14.50	Abdi	Bile	SOM	28.12.62	1		Jerez de la Frontera	13 Sep 89

1500 METRES

Mark Wind	Name		Nat	Born	Pos	Meet	Venue	Date
3:26.00 WR	Hicham	El Guerrouj	MAR	14.9.74	1	GGala	Roma	14 Jul 98
3:26.12		El Guerrouj			1	VD	Bruxelles	24 Aug 01
3:26.34	Bernard	Lagat	KEN/USA	12.12.74	2	VD	Bruxelles	24 Aug 01
3:26.45		El Guerrouj			1 rA	WK	Zürich	12 Aug 98
3:26.89		El Guerrouj			1	WK	Zürich	16 Aug 02
3:26.96		El Guerrouj			1	GP II	Rieti	8 Sep 02
3:27.21		El Guerrouj			1	WK	Zürich	11 Aug 00
3:27.34		El Guerrouj			1	Herc	Monaco	19 Jul 02
3:27.37 WR	Noureddine	Morceli	ALG	28.2.70	1	Nik	Nice	12 Jul 95
3:27.40		Lagat			1rA	WK	Zürich	6 Aug 04
3.27.52		Morceli			1	Herc	Monaco	25 Jul 95
3:27.64		El Guerrouj			2rA	WK	Zürich	6 Aug 04
3:27.65		El Guerrouj			1	WCh	Sevilla	24 Aug 99
3:27.91		Lagat			2	Herc	Monaco	19 Jul 02
3:28.12	Noah	Ngeny	KEN	2.11.78	2	WK	Zürich	11 Aug 00
3:28.21+		El Guerrouj			1	in 1M	Roma	7 Jul 99
3.28.37		Morceli			1	GPF	Monaco	9 Sep 95
3:28.37		El Guerrouj			1	Herc	Monaco	8 Aug 98
3:28.38		El Guerrouj			1	GP	Saint-Denis	6 Jul 01
3:28.40		El Guerrouj			1	VD	Bruxelles	5 Sep 03
3:28.51		Lagat			3	WK	Zürich	11 Aug 00

Mark Wind	Name		Nat	Born	Pos	Meet	Venue	Date
3:28.57		El Guerrouj			1rA	WK	Zürich	11 Aug 99
3:28.6+		Ngeny			2	in 1M	Roma	7 Jul 99
3:28.73		Ngeny			2	WCh	Sevilla	24 Aug 99
3:28.84		Ngeny			1	GP	Paris (C)	21 Jul 99
3:28.86 WR		Morceli			1		Rieti	6 Sep 92
3:28.91		El Guerrouj			1rA	WK	Zürich	13 Aug 97
3:28.92		El Guerrouj			1	VD	Bruxelles	22 Aug 97
3:28.93		Ngeny			1	GPF	München	11 Sep 99
3:28.95	Fermín	Cacho	ESP	16.2.69	2rA	WK	Zürich	13 Aug 97
3:28.98	Mehdi	Baala	FRA	17.8.78	2	VD	Bruxelles	5 Sep 03
	(31/6)							
3:29.02	Daniel Kipchirchir	Komen	KEN	27.11.84	1	GGala	Roma	14 Jul 06
3:29.14	Rashid	Ramzi	BRN	17.7.80	2	GGala	Roma	14 Jul 06
3:29.18	Vénuste	Niyongabo	BUR	9.12.73	2	VD	Bruxelles	22 Aug 97
3:29.29	William	Chirchir	KEN	6.2.79	3	VD	Bruxelles	24 Aug 01
	(10)							
3:29.46 WR	Saïd	Aouita	MAR	2.11.59	1	ISTAF	Berlin	23 Aug 85
3:29.46	Daniel	Komen	KEN	17.5.76	1	Herc	Monaco	16 Aug 97
3:29.51	Ali	Saïdi-Sief ¶	ALG	15.3.78	1	Athl	Lausanne	4 Jul 01
3:29.67 WR	Steve	Cram	GBR	14.10.60	1	Nik	Nice	16 Jul 85
3:29.77	Sydney	Maree	USA	9.9.56	1	ASV	Köln	25 Aug 85
3:29.77	Sebastian	Coe	GBR	29.9.56	1		Rieti	7 Sep 86
3:29.91	Laban	Rotich	KEN	20.1.69	2rA	WK	Zürich	12 Aug 98
3:30.04	Timothy	Kiptanui	KEN	5.1.80	2	GP	Saint-Denis	23 Jul 04
3:30.07	Rui	Silva	POR	3.8.77	3	Herc	Monaco	19 Jul 02
3:30.18	John	Kibowen	KEN	21.4.69	3rA	WK	Zürich	12 Aug 98
	(20)							
3:30.24	Cornelius	Chirchir	KEN	5.6.83	4	Herc	Monaco	19 Jul 02
3:30.33	Ivan	Heshko	UKR	19.8.79	2	VD	Bruxelles	3 Sep 04
3:30.46	Alex	Kipchirchir	KEN	26.11.84	3	VD	Bruxelles	3 Sep 04
3:30.54	Alan	Webb	USA	13.1.83	1	Gaz	Saint-Denis	6 Jul 07
3:30.55	Abdi	Bile	SOM	28.12.62	1		Rieti	3 Sep 89
3:30.57	Reyes	Estévez	ESP	2.8.76	3	WCh	Sevilla	24 Aug 99
3:30.58	William	Tanui	KEN	22.2.64	3	Herc	Monaco	16 Aug 97
3:30.67	Benjamin	Kipkurui	KEN	28.12.80	2	Herc	Monaco	20 Jul 01
3:30.72	Paul	Korir	KEN	15.7.77	3	VD	Bruxelles	5 Sep 03
3:30.77 WR	Steve	Ovett	GBR	9.10.55	1		Rieti	4 Sep 83
	(30)							
3:30.83	Fouad	Chouki ¶	FRA	15.10.78	3	WK	Zürich	15 Aug 03
3:30.92	José Luis	González	ESP	8.12.57	3	Nik	Nice	16 Jul 85
3:30.92	Tarek	Boukensa	ALG	19.11.81	1	GGala	Roma	13 Jul 07
3:30.94	Isaac	Viciosa	ESP	26.12.69	5	Herc	Monaco	8 Aug 98
3:30.99	Robert	Rono	KEN	11.10.74	3	VD	Bruxelles	30 Aug 02
3:30.99	Isaac	Songok	KEN	25.4.84	3rA	WK	Zürich	6 Aug 04
3:31.01	Jim	Spivey	USA	7.3.60	1	R-W	Koblenz	28 Aug 88
3:31.04	Daham Najim	Bashir (David Nyaga)	QAT	8.11.78	2	SGP	Doha	13 May 05
3:31.10	Adil	Kaouch	MAR	1.1.79	3	GGala	Roma	14 Jul 06
3:31.13	José Manuel	Abascal	ESP	17.3.58	1		Barcelona	16 Aug 86
	(40)							
3:31.13	Mulugueta	Wondimu	ETH	28.2.85	2rA	NA	Heusden	31 Jul 04
3:31.17	Robert K.	Andersen	DEN	12.12.72	5rA	WK	Zürich	13 Aug 97
3:31.18	Shadrack	Korir	KEN	14.12.78	2	GGala	Roma	13 Jul 07
3:31.21	José Antonio	Redolat	ESP	17.2.76	1	DNG	Stockholm	17 Jul 01
3:31.28	Enock	Koech	KEN	4.4.81	3rA	WK	Zürich	17 Aug 01
3:31.40	William	Kemei	KEN	22.2.69	2	Nik	Nice	12 Jul 95
3:31.45	Driss	Maazouzi	FRA	15.10.69	6	Herc	Monaco	19 Jul 02
3:31.48	Azzedine	Sediki	MAR	21.5.70	3rA	ASV	Köln	18 Aug 95
3:31.48	Andrés	Díaz	ESP	12.7.69	2	Herc	Monaco	18 Aug 00
3:31.49	Belal Mansoor	Ali	BRN	17.10.83	1	GP	Athína	2 Jul 07
	(50)	100th man 3:33.10, 200th 3:34.69, 300th 3:35.78, 400th 3:36.53						
Drugs disqualification								
3:30.77	Adil	Kaouch ¶	MAR	1.1.79	1	GGala	Roma	13 Jul 07

1 MILE

3:43.13 WR	Hicham	El Guerrouj	MAR	14.9.74	1	GGala	Roma	7 Jul 99
3:43.40	Noah	Ngeny	KEN	2.11.78	2	GGala	Roma	7 Jul 99
3:44.39 WR	Noureddine	Morceli	ALG	28.2.70	1		Rieti	5 Sep 93
3:44.60		El Guerrouj			1	Nik	Nice	16 Jul 98
3:44.90		El Guerrouj			1	Bisl	Oslo	4 Jul 97
3:44.95		El Guerrouj			1	GGala	Roma	29 Jun 01
3:45.19		Morceli			1	WK	Zürich	16 Aug 95

MEN All-time

Mark Wind	Name		Nat	Born	Pos	Meet	Venue	Date
3:45.64		El Guerrouj			1	ISTAF	Berlin	26 Aug 97
3:45.96		El Guerrouj			1	BrGP	London (CP)	5 Aug 00
3:46.24		El Guerrouj			1	Bisl	Oslo	28 Jul 00
3:46.32 WR	Steve	Cram	GBR	14.10.60	1	Bisl	Oslo	27 Jul 85
3:46.38	Daniel	Komen	KEN	17.5.76	2	ISTAF	Berlin	26 Aug 97
3:46.70	Vénuste	Niyongabo	BUR	9.12.73	3	ISTAF	Berlin	26 Aug 97
3:46.76	Saïd	Aouita	MAR	2.11.59	1	WG	Helsinki	2 Jul 87
3:46.78		Morceli			1	ISTAF	Berlin	27 Aug 93
3:46.91	Alan	Webb	USA	13.1.83	1		Brasschaat	21 Jul 07
3:46.92		Aouita			1	WK	Zürich	21 Aug 85
3:47.10		El Guerrouj			1	BrGP	London (CP)	7 Aug 99
3:47.28	Bernard	Lagat	KEN/USA	12.12.74	2	GGala	Roma	29 Jun 01
3:47.30		Morceli			1	VD	Bruxelles	3 Sep 93
3:47.33 WR	Sebastian	Coe	GBR	29.9.56	1	VD	Bruxelles	28 Aug 81
	(21/10)							
3:47.65	Laban	Rotich	KEN	20.1.69	2	Bisl	Oslo	4 Jul 97
3:47.69	Steve	Scott	USA	5.5.56	1	OsloG	Oslo	7 Jul 82
3:47.79	José Luis	González	ESP	8.12.57	2	Bisl	Oslo	27 Jul 85
3:47.88	John	Kibowen	KEN	21.4.69	3	Bisl	Oslo	4 Jul 97
3:47.94	William	Chirchir	KEN	6.2.79	2	Bisl	Oslo	28 Jul 00
3:47.97	Daham Najim	Bashir (David Nyaga)	QAT	8.11.78	1	Bisl	Oslo	29 Jul 05
3:48.17	Paul	Korir	KEN	15.7.77	1	GP	London (CP)	8 Aug 03
3:48.23	Ali	Saïdi-Sief ¶	ALG	15.3.78	1	Bisl	Oslo	13 Jul 01
3:48.28	Daniel Kipchirchir	Komen	KEN	27.11.84	1	Pre	Eugene	10 Jun 07
3:48.38	Andrés	Díaz	ESP	12.7.69	3	GGala	Roma	29 Jun 01
	(20)							
3:48.40 WR	Steve	Ovett	GBR	9.10.55	1	R-W	Koblenz	26 Aug 81
3:48.80	William	Kemei	KEN	22.2.69	1	ISTAF	Berlin	21 Aug 92
3:48.83	Sydney	Maree	USA	9.9.56	1		Rieti	9 Sep 81
3:48.98	Craig	Mottram	AUS	18.6.80	5	Bisl	Oslo	29 Jul 05
3:49.08	John	Walker	NZL	12.1.52	2	OsloG	Oslo	7 Jul 82
3:49.20	Peter	Elliott	GBR	9.10.62	2	Bisl	Oslo	2 Jul 88
3:49.22	Jens-Peter	Herold	GDR	2.6.65	3	Bisl	Oslo	2 Jul 88
3:49.31	Joe	Falcon	USA	23.6.66	1	Bisl	Oslo	14 Jul 90
3:49.34	David	Moorcroft	GBR	10.4.53	3	Bisl	Oslo	26 Jun 82
3:49.34	Benjamin	Kipkurui	KEN	28.12.80	3	VD	Bruxelles	25 Aug 00
	(30)							
3:49.40	Abdi	Bile	SOM	28.12.62	4	Bisl	Oslo	2 Jul 88
3:49.45	Mike	Boit	KEN	6.1.49	2	VD	Bruxelles	28 Aug 81
3:49.50	Rui	Silva	POR	3.8.77	3	GGala	Roma	12 Jul 02
3:49.56	Fermín	Cacho	ESP	16.2.69	2	Bisl	Oslo	5 Jul 96
3:49.60	José Antonio	Redolat	ESP	17.2.76	4	GGala	Roma	29 Jun 01
3:49.75	Leonard	Mucheru	KEN	13.6.78	5	GGala	Roma	29 Jun 01
3:49.77	Ray	Flynn	IRL	22.1.57	3	OsloG	Oslo	7 Jul 82
3:49.77	Wilfred	Kirochi	KEN	12.12.69	2	Bisl	Oslo	6 Jul 91
3:49.80	Jim	Spivey	USA	7.3.60	3	Bisl	Oslo	5 Jul 86
3:49.83	Vyacheslav	Shabunin	RUS	27.9.69	6	GGala	Roma	29 Jun 01
	(40)							
3:49.91	Simon	Doyle	AUS	9.11.66	4	Bisl	Oslo	6 Jul 91
3:49.95	Tarek	Boukensa	ALG	19.11.81	6	Bisl	Oslo	29 Jul 05
3:49.98	Thomas	Wessinghage	FRG	22.2.52	3	ISTAF	Berlin	17 Aug 83
	(43)	50th man 3:50.38, 100th man 3:52.02, 200th man 3:54.39, 300th 3:55.80						
Indoors: 3:49.78	Eamonn	Coghlan	IRL	24.11.52	1		East Rutherford	27 Feb 83

2000 METRES

Mark	Name		Nat	Born	Pos	Meet	Venue	Date
4:44.79 WR	Hicham	El Guerrouj	MAR	14.9.74	1	ISTAF	Berlin	7 Sep 99
4:46.88	Ali	Saïdi-Sief ¶	ALG	15.3.78	1		Strasbourg	19 Jun 01
4:47.88 WR	Noureddine	Morceli	ALG	28.2.70	1		Paris	3 Jul 95
4:48.36		El Guerrouj			1		Gateshead	19 Jul 98
4:48.69	Vénuste	Niyongabo	BUR	9.12.73	1	Nik	Nice	12 Jul 95
4:48.74	John	Kibowen	KEN	21.4.69	1		Hechtel	1 Aug 98
4:49.00		Niyongabo			1		Rieti	3 Sep 97
4:49.55		Morceli			1	Nik	Nice	10 Jul 96
4:50.08	Noah	Ngeny	KEN	2.11.78	1	DNG	Stockholm	30 Jul 99
4:50.76	Craig	Mottram	AUS	18.6.80	1		Melbourne (OP)	9 Mar 06
4:50.81 WR	Saïd	Aouita	MAR	2.11.59	1	BNP	Paris	16 Jul 87
4:51.17		El Guerrouj			1	ISTAF	Berlin	31 Aug 01
4:51.30	Daniel	Komen	KEN	17.5.76	1		Milano	5 Jun 98
4:51.39 WR	Steve	Cram (10)	GBR	14.10.60	1	BGP	Budapest	4 Aug 85
4:49.99ind	Kenenisa	Bekele	ETH	13.6.82	1		Birmingham	17 Feb 07

Mark Wind		Name	Nat	Born	Pos	Meet	Venue	Date

3000 METRES

Mark Wind		Name	Nat	Born	Pos	Meet	Venue	Date
7:20.67 WR	Daniel	Komen	KEN	17.5.76	1		Rieti	1 Sep 96
7:23.09	Hicham	El Guerrouj	MAR	14.9.74	1	VD	Bruxelles	3 Sep 99
7:25.02	Ali	Saïdi-Sief ¶	ALG	15.3.78	1	Herc	Monaco	18 Aug 00
7:25.09	Haile	Gebrselassie	ETH	18.4.73	1	VD	Bruxelles	28 Aug 98
7:25.11 WR	Noureddine	Morceli	ALG	28.2.70	1	Herc	Monaco	2 Aug 94
7:25.16		Komen			1	Herc	Monaco	10 Aug 96
7:25.54		Gebrselassie			1	Herc	Monaco	8 Aug 98
7:25.79	Kenenisa	Bekele	ETH	13.6.82	1	DNG	Stockholm	7 Aug 07
7:25.87		Komen			1	VD	Bruxelles	23 Aug 96
7:26.02		Gebrselassie			1	VD	Bruxelles	22 Aug 97
7:26.03		Gebrselassie			1	GP II	Helsinki	10 Jun 99
7:26.5 e		Komen			1	in 2M	Sydney	28 Feb 98
7:26.62	Mohammed	Mourhit ¶	BEL	10.10.70	2	Herc	Monaco	18 Aug 00
7:26.69		K Bekele			1	BrGP	Sheffield	15 Jul 07
7:27.18	Moses	Kiptanui	KEN	1.10.70	1	Herc	Monaco	25 Jul 95
7:27.3+		Komen			1	in 2M	Hechtel	19 Jul 97
7:27.42		Gebrselassie			1	Bisl	Oslo	9 Jul 98
7:27.50		Morceli			1	VD	Bruxelles	25 Aug 95
7:27.59	Luke	Kipkosgei	KEN	27.11.75	2	Herc	Monaco	8 Aug 98
7:27.67		Saïdi-Sief			1	Gaz	Saint-Denis	23 Jun 00
7:27.72	Eliud	Kipchoge (10)	KEN	5.11.84	1	VD	Bruxelles	3 Sep 04
7:27.75	Tom	Nyariki	KEN	27.9.71	2	Herc	Monaco	10 Aug 96
7:28.04		Kiptanui			1	ASV	Köln	18 Aug 95
7:28.28		Kipkosgei			2	Bisl	Oslo	9 Jul 98
7:28.28	James	Kwalia	KEN	12.6.84	2	VD	Bruxelles	3 Sep 04
7:28.41	Paul	Bitok	KEN	26.6.70	3	Herc	Monaco	10 Aug 96
7:28.45	Assefa	Mezegebu	ETH	19.6.78	3	Herc	Monaco	8 Aug 98
7:28.56		Kipchoge			1	SGP	Doha	13 May 05
7:28.67	Benjamin	Limo	KEN	23.8.74	1	Herc	Monaco	4 Aug 99
7:28.70	Paul	Tergat	KEN	17.6.69	4	Herc	Monaco	10 Aug 96
	(30/16)							
7:28.72	Isaac K.	Songok	KEN	25.4.84	1	GP	Rieti	27 Aug 06
7:28.78	Augustine	Choge	KEN	21.1.87	2	SGP	Doha	13 May 05
7:28.93	Salah	Hissou	MAR	16.1.72	2	Herc	Monaco	4 Aug 99
7:28.94	Brahim	Lahlafi	MAR	15.4.68	3	Herc	Monaco	4 Aug 99
	(20)							
7:29.09	John	Kibowen	KEN	21.4.69	3	Bisl	Oslo	9 Jul 98
7:29.11	Tariku	Bekele	ETH	21.1.87	2	GP	Rieti	27 Aug 06
7:29.34	Isaac	Viciosa	ESP	26.12.69	4	Bisl	Oslo	9 Jul 98
7:29.45 WR	Saïd	Aouita	MAR	2.11.59	1	ASV	Köln	20 Aug 89
7:29.92	Sileshi	Sihine	ETH	29.9.83	1	GP	Rieti	28 Aug 05
7:30.09	Ismaïl	Sghyr	MAR/FRA	16.3.72	2	Herc	Monaco	25 Jul 95
7:30.36	Mark	Carroll	IRL	15.1.72	5	Herc	Monaco	4 Aug 99
7:30.50	Dieter	Baumann ¶	GER	9.2.65	6	Herc	Monaco	8 Aug 98
7:30.53	El Hassan	Lahssini	MAR	1.1.74	6	Herc	Monaco	10 Aug 96
7:30.53	Hailu	Mekonnen	ETH	4.4.80	1	VD	Bruxelles	24 Aug 01
	(30)							
7:30.62	Boniface	Songok	KEN	25.12.80	3	VD	Bruxelles	3 Sep 04
7:30.76	Jamal Bilal	Salem	QAT	12.9.78	4	SGP	Doha	13 May 05
7:30.78	Mustapha	Essaïd	FRA	20.1.70	7	Herc	Monaco	8 Aug 98
7:30.84	Bob	Kennedy	USA	18.8.70	8	Herc	Monaco	8 Aug 98
7:30.99	Khalid	Boulami	MAR	7.8.69	1	Nik	Nice	16 Jul 97
7:31.13	Julius	Gitahi	KEN	29.4.78	6	Bisl	Oslo	9 Jul 98
7:31.14	William	Kalya	KEN	4.8.74	3	Herc	Monaco	16 Aug 97
7:31.59	Manuel	Pancorbo	ESP	7.7.66	7	Bisl	Oslo	9 Jul 98
7:31.84	Edwin	Soi	KEN	3.3.86	1	Athl	Lausanne	11 Jul 06
7:31.98	Daniel	Kipchirchir Komen	KEN	27.11.84	3	FBK	Hengelo	29 May 05
	(40)							
7:32.03	Moses	Kipsiro	UGA	2.9.86	2	Herc	Monaco	25 Jul 07
7:32.1 WR	Henry	Rono	KEN	12.2.52	1	Bisl	Oslo	27 Jun 78
7:32.19	Craig	Mottram	AUS	18.6.80	1	WCp	Athína	17 Sep 06
7:32.23	Richard	Limo	KEN	18.11.80	5	VD	Bruxelles	24 Aug 01
7:32.32	Enrique	Molina	ESP	25.2.68	5	Bisl	Oslo	4 Jul 97
7:32.36	Million	Wolde	ETH	17.3.79	3	Gaz	Saint-Denis	23 Jun 00
7:32.36	Benjamin	Maiyo	KEN	6.10.78	2	GPII	Athína	28 Jun 00
7:32.36	Abderrahim	Goumri	MAR	21.5.76	6	VD	Bruxelles	24 Aug 01
7:32.37	Abreham	Cherkos Feleke	ETH	23.9.89	2	Athl	Lausanne	11 Jul 06
7:32.38	Abiyote	Abate	ETH	20.11.80	7	VD	Bruxelles	24 Aug 01
	(50)	100th man 7:36.40, 200th man 7:41.00, 300th 7:43.35, 400th 7:45.57						

Mark	Wind	Name		Nat	Born	Pos	Meet	Venue	Date
Indoors									
7:24.90			Komen			1		Budapest	6 Feb 98
7:26.15			Gebrselassie			1		Karlsruhe	25 Jan 98
7:26.80			Gebrselassie			1		Karlsruhe	24 Jan 99
7:28.29			Gebrselassie			1		Karlsruhe	28 Feb 03

2 MILES

Mark	Wind	Name		Nat	Born	Pos	Meet	Venue	Date
7:58.61	WR	Daniel	Komen	KEN	17.5.76	1		Hechtel	19 Jul 97
7:58.91			Komen			1		Sydney	28 Feb 98
8:01.08	WR	Haile	Gebrselassie	ETH	18.4.73	1	APM	Hengelo	31 May 97
8:01.72			Gebrselassie			1	BrGP	London (CP)	7 Aug 99
8:01.86			Gebrselassie			1	APM	Hengelo	30 May 99
8:03.50		Craig	Mottram	AUS	18.6.80	1	Pre	Eugene	10 Jun 07
8:04.83		Tariku	Bekele	ETH	21.1.87	2	Pre	Eugene	10 Jun 07
8:07.07		Matt	Tegenkamp	USA	19.1.82	3	Pre	Eugene	10 Jun 07
Indoors									
8:04.69			Gebrselassie			1	GP	Birmingham	21 Feb 03
8:05.12i		Kenenisa	Bekele	ETH	13.6.82	1	GP	Birmingham	18 Feb 06
8:06.61		Hicham	El Guerrouj	MAR	14.9.74	1		Liévin	23 Feb 03

5000 METRES

Mark	Wind	Name		Nat	Born	Pos	Meet	Venue	Date
12:37.35	WR	Kenenisa	Bekele	ETH	13.6.82	1	FBK	Hengelo	31 May 04
12:39.36	WR	Haile	Gebrselassie	ETH	18.4.73	1	GP II	Helsinki	13 Jun 98
12:39.74	WR	Daniel	Komen	KEN	17.5.76	1	VD	Bruxelles	22 Aug 97
12:40.18			K Bekele			1	Gaz	Saint-Denis	1 Jul 05
12:41.86	WR		Gebrselassie			1	WK	Zürich	13 Aug 97
12:44.39	WR		Gebrselassie			1	WK	Zürich	16 Aug 95
12:44.90			Komen			2	WK	Zürich	13 Aug 97
12:45.09			Komen			1	WK	Zürich	14 Aug 96
12:46.53		Eliud	Kipchoge	KEN	5.11.84	1	GGala	Roma	2 Jul 04
12:47.04		Sileshi	Sihine	ETH	29.9.83	2	GGala	Roma	2 Jul 04
12:48.09			K Bekele			1	VD	Bruxelles	25 Aug 06
12:48.25			K Bekele			1	WK	Zürich	18 Aug 06
12:48.66		Isaac K.	Songok	KEN	25.4.84	2	WK	Zürich	18 Aug 06
12:48.81		Stephen	Cherono	KEN	15.10.82	1	GS	Ostrava	12 Jun 03
		(now Saïf Saaeed Shaheen QAT)							
12:48.98			Komen			1	GGala	Roma	5 Jun 97
12:49.28		Brahim	Lahlafi	MAR	15.4.68	1	VD	Bruxelles	25 Aug 00
12:49.53			K Bekele			1	Aragón	Zaragoza	28 Jul 07
12:49.64			Gebrselassie			1	WK	Zürich	11 Aug 99
12:49.71		Mohammed	Mourhit ¶	BEL	10.10.70	2	VD	Bruxelles	25 Aug 00
12:49.87		Paul	Tergat (10)	KEN	17.6.69	3	WK	Zürich	13 Aug 97
12:50.16			Sihine			1	VD	Bruxelles	14 Sep 07
12:50.22			Kipchoge			1	VD	Bruxelles	26 Aug 05
12:50.24		Hicham	El Guerrouj	MAR	14.9.74	2	GS	Ostrava	12 Jun 03
12:50.25		Abderrahim	Goumri	MAR	21.5.76	2	VD	Bruxelles	26 Aug 05
12:50.38			Kipchoge			2	VD	Bruxelles	14 Sep 07
12:50.72		Moses	Kipsiro	UGA	2.9.86	3	VD	Bruxelles	14 Sep 07
12:50.80		Salah	Hissou	MAR	16.1.72	1	GGala	Roma	5 Jun 96
12:50.86		Ali	Saïdi-Sief ¶	ALG	15.3.78	1	GGala	Roma	30 Jun 00
12:51.00		Joseph	Ebuya	KEN	20.6.87	4	VD	Bruxelles	14 Sep 07
12:51.32			K Bekele			1	Gaz	Saint-Denis	8 Jul 06
		(30/16)							
12:51.95		Thomas	Longosiwa	KEN	14.1.82	5	VD	Bruxelles	14 Sep 07
12:52.33		Sammy	Kipketer	KEN	29.9.81	2	Bisl	Oslo	27 Jun 03
12:52.40		Edwin	Soi	KEN	3.3.86	2	Gaz	Saint-Denis	8 Jul 06
12:52.80		Gebre-egziabher	Gebremariam	ETH	10.9.84	3	GGala	Roma	8 Jul 05
		(20)							
12:52.99		Abraham	Chebii	KEN	23.12.79	4	Bisl	Oslo	27 Jun 03
12:53.41		Khalid	Boulami	MAR	7.8.69	4	WK	Zürich	13 Aug 97
12:53.66		Augustine	Choge	KEN	21.1.87	4	GGala	Roma	8 Jul 05
12:53.72		Philip	Mosima	KEN	2.1.77	2	GGala	Roma	5 Jun 96
12:53.81		Tariku	Bekele	ETH	21.1.87	4	GGala	Roma	14 Jul 06
12:53.84		Assefa	Mezegebu	ETH	19.6.78	1	VD	Bruxelles	28 Aug 98
12:54.07		John	Kibowen	KEN	21.4.69	4	WCh	Saint-Denis	31 Aug 03
12:54.15		Dejene	Berhanu	ETH	12.12.80	3	GGala	Roma	2 Jul 04
12:54.19		Abreham	Cherkos Feleke	ETH	23.9.89	5	GGala	Roma	14 Jul 06
12:54.46		Moses	Mosop	KEN	17.7.85	3	Gaz	Saint-Denis	8 Jul 06
		(30)							
12:54.58		James	Kwalia	KEN	12.6.84	5	Bisl	Oslo	27 Jun 03

Mark Wind		Name	Nat	Born	Pos	Meet	Venue	Date
12:54.70	Dieter	Baumann ¶	GER	9.2.65	5	WK	Zürich	13 Aug 97
12:54.85	Moses	Kiptanui	KEN	1.10.70	3	GGala	Roma	5 Jun 96
12:54.99	Benjamin	Limo	KEN	23.8.74	3	Gaz	Saint-Denis	4 Jul 03
12:55.52	Hicham	Bellani	MAR	15.9.79	7	GGala	Roma	14 Jul 06
12:55.58	Abebe	Dinkesa	ETH	6.3.84	2	Gaz	Saint-Denis	1 Jul 05
12:55.63	Mark	Bett	KEN	22.12.76	2	Bisl	Oslo	28 Jul 00
12:55.76	Craig	Mottram	AUS	18.6.80	2	GP	London (CP)	30 Jul 04
12:55.85	Boniface	Songok	KEN	25.12.80	4	VD	Bruxelles	26 Aug 05
12:55.94	Tom	Nyariki	KEN	27.9.71	1	DNG	Stockholm	7 Jul 97
	(40)							
12:56.27	Albert	Chepkurui	KEN	4.4.81	6	Bisl	Oslo	27 Jun 03
	(Abdullah Ahmad Hassan QAT from August 2003)							
12:56.29	Paul	Koech	KEN	25.6.69	6	WK	Zürich	13 Aug 97
12:56.50	Luke	Kipkosgei	KEN	27.11.75	5	Bisl	Oslo	28 Jul 00
12:56.72	Richard	Limo	KEN	18.11.80	1	WK	Zürich	17 Aug 01
12:57.05	Mulugueta	Wondimu	ETH	28.2.85	2	ISTAF	Berlin	12 Sep 04
12:57.11	Boniface	Kiprop	UGA	12.10.85	1	DNG	Stockholm	25 Jul 06
12:57.23	Worku	Bikila	ETH	6.5.68	3	GGala	Roma	8 Jun 95
12:57.79	David	Chelule	KEN	7.7.77	5	GGala	Roma	7 Jul 99
12:58.21	Bob	Kennedy	USA	18.8.70	5	WK	Zürich	14 Aug 96
12:58.39WR	Saïd	Aouita	MAR	2.11.59	1	GGala	Roma	22 Jul 87
	(50)	100th man 13:05.05, 200th 13:12.34, 300th 13:17.44, 400th 13:20.12, 500th 13:22.68						
Indoors								
12:49.60		Bekele			1		Birmingham	20 Feb 04
12:50.38		Gebrselassie			1		Birmingham	14 Feb 99

10,000 METRES

Mark Wind		Name	Nat	Born	Pos	Meet	Venue	Date
26:17.53WR	Kenenisa	Bekele	ETH	13.6.82	1	VD	Bruxelles	26 Aug 05
26:20.31WR		K Bekele			1	GS	Ostrava	8 Jun 04
26:22.75WR	Haile	Gebrselassie	ETH	18.4.73	1	APM	Hengelo	1 Jun 98
26:27.85WR	Paul	Tergat	KEN	17.6.69	1	VD	Bruxelles	22 Aug 97
26:28.72		K Bekele			1	FBK	Hengelo	29 May 05
26:29.22		Gebrselassie			1	VD	Bruxelles	5 Sep 03
26:30.03	Nicholas	Kemboi	KEN/QAT	25.11.83	2	VD	Bruxelles	5 Sep 03
26:30.74	Abebe	Dinkesa	ETH	6.3.84	2	FBK	Hengelo	29 May 05
26:31.32WR		Gebrselassie			1	Bisl	Oslo	4 Jul 97
26:35.63	Micah	Kogo	KEN	3.6.86	1	VD	Bruxelles	25 Aug 06
26:36.26	Paul	Koech	KEN	25.6.69	2	VD	Bruxelles	22 Aug 97
26:37.25	Zersenay	Tadese	ERI	8.2.82	2	VD	Bruxelles	25 Aug 06
26:38.08WR	Salah	Hissou	MAR	16.1.72	1	VD	Bruxelles	23 Aug 96
26:38.76	Abdullah Ahmad	Hassan (10)	QAT	4.4.81	3	VD	Bruxelles	5 Sep 03
	(Formerly Albert Chepkurui KEN)							
26:39.69	Sileshi	Sihine	ETH	29.9.83	1	FBK	Hengelo	31 May 04
26:39.77	Boniface	Kiprop	UGA	12.10.85	2	VD	Bruxelles	26 Aug 05
26:41.58		Gebrselassie			2	FBK	Hengelo	31 May 04
26:41.75	Samuel	Wanjiru	KEN	10.11.86	3	VD	Bruxelles	26 Aug 05
26:41.95		Kiprop			3	VD	Bruxelles	25 Aug 06
26:43.53WR		Gebrselassie			1	APM	Hengelo	5 Jun 95
26:46.19		K Bekele			1	VD	Bruxelles	14 Sep 07
26:46.44		Tergat			1	VD	Bruxelles	28 Aug 98
26:47.89		Koech			2	VD	Bruxelles	28 Aug 98
26:48.73		Sihine			1	FBK	Hengelo	26 May 07
26:49.02	Eliud	Kipchoge	KEN	5.11.84	2	FBK	Hengelo	26 May 07
26:49.20	Moses	Masai	KEN	1.6.86	2	VD	Bruxelles	14 Sep 07
26:49.38	Sammy	Kipketer	KEN	29.9.81	1	VD	Bruxelles	30 Aug 02
26:49.55	Moses	Mosop	KEN	17.7.85	3	FBK	Hengelo	26 May 07
26:49.57		Bekele			1	WCh	Saint-Denis	24 Aug 03
26:49.90	Assefa	Mezegebu	ETH	19.6.78	2	VD	Bruxelles	30 Aug 02
	(30/18)							
26:50.20	Richard	Limo	KEN	18.11.80	3	VD	Bruxelles	30 Aug 02
26:51.49	Charles	Kamathi (20)	KEN	18.5.78	1	VD	Bruxelles	3 Sep 99
26:52.23WR	William	Sigei	KEN	11.10.69	1	Bisl	Oslo	22 Jul 94
26:52.30	Mohammed	Mourhit ¶	BEL	10.10.70	2	VD	Bruxelles	3 Sep 99
26:52.33	Gebre-egziabher	Gebremariam	ETH	10.9.84	4	FBK	Hengelo	26 May 07
26:52.87	John Cheruiyot	Korir	KEN	13.12.81	5	VD	Bruxelles	30 Aug 02
26:52.93	Mark	Bett	KEN	22.12.76	6	VD	Bruxelles	26 Aug 05
26:58.38WR	Yobes	Ondieki	KEN	21.2.61	1	Bisl	Oslo	10 Jul 93
26:59.51	Bernard	Kipyego	KEN	16.7.86	4	VD	Bruxelles	14 Sep 07
27:02.62	Abderrahim	Goumri	MAR	21.5.76	3	FBK	Hengelo	29 May 05
27:02.62	Deriba	Merga	ETH	26.10.80	6	FBK	Hengelo	26 May 07

Mark	Wind	Name		Nat	Born	Pos	Meet	Venue	Date
27:02.81		Ibrahim	Jeylan	ETH	12.6.89	4	VD	Bruxelles	25 Aug 06
		(30)							
27:04.18		Robert Kipngetich	Sigei	KEN	3.1.82	1		Neerpelt	2 Jun 07
27:04.20		Abraham	Chebii	KEN	23.12.79	1		Stanford	4 May 01
27:04.54		Felix	Limo	KEN	22.8.80	2	VD	Bruxelles	25 Aug 00
27:04.61		Josphat Kiprono	Menjo	KEN	20.8.79	2		Neerpelt	2 Jun 07
27:04.79		Josphat	Muchiri Ndambiri	KEN	12.2.85	1rA		Oita	30 Sep 06
27:04.89		Tadesse	Tola	ETH	31.10.87	3		Neerpelt	2 Jun 07
27:04.92		Mohamed Ali	Abdosh	ETH	28.8.87	7	FBK	Hengelo	26 May 07
27:05.88		Patrick	Ivuti	KEN	30.6.78	6	VD	Bruxelles	30 Aug 02
27:06.17		John	Yuda	TAN	9.6.79	7	VD	Bruxelles	30 Aug 02
27:06.44		Worku	Bikila	ETH	6.5.68	1	VD	Bruxelles	25 Aug 95
		(40)							
27:06.45		Habte	Jifar	ETH	29.1.76	1	APM	Hengelo	30 May 99
27:06.47		Habtamu	Fikadu	ETH	13.3.88	8	FBK	Hengelo	26 May 07
27:06.59		Ismael	Kirui	KEN	20.2.75	2	VD	Bruxelles	25 Aug 95
27:07.55		Benjamin	Maiyo	KEN	6.10.78	2		Stanford	4 May 01
27:07.91	WR	Richard	Chelimo	KEN	21.4.72	1	DNG	Stockholm	5 Jul 93
27:08.23	WR	Arturo	Barrios	MEX	12.12.63	1	ISTAF	Berlin	18 Aug 89
27:08.42		Martin Irungu	Mathathi	KEN	25.12.85	1		Kobe	24 Apr 05
27:10.34		Josphat	Machuka	KEN	12.12.73	4	VD	Bruxelles	25 Aug 95
27:11.17		Julius	Gitahi	KEN	29.4.78	1		Kobe	26 Apr 98
27:11.36		Gideon	Ngatuny	KEN	10.10.86	2		Kobe	22 Apr 07
		(50)	100th man 27:25.48, 200th 27:39.76, 300th 27:47.33, 400th 27:54.33						

20,000 METRES & 1 HOUR

Mark	Distance	Name		Nat	Born	Pos	Meet	Venue	Date
56:25.98+	21 285m	Haile	Gebrselassie	ETH	18.4.73	1		Ostrava	27 Jun 07
56:55.6+	21 101	Arturo	Barrios	MEX	12.12.63	1		La Flèche	30 Mar 91
57:24.19+	20 944	Jos	Hermens	NED	8.1.50	1		Papendal	1 May 76
57:18.4+	20 943	Dionísio	Castro	POR	22.11.63	1		La Flèche	31 Mar 90

HALF MARATHON

Included are the slightly downhill courses: Newcastle to South Shields 30.5m, Tokyo 33m. Lisboa (Spring) 69m

Mark	Wind	Name		Nat	Born	Pos	Meet	Venue	Date
58:33		Samuel	Wanjiru	KEN	10.11.86	1		Den Haag	17 Mar 07
58:53			Wanjiru			1		Ra's Al Khaymah	9 Feb 07
58:55		Haile	Gebrselassie	ETH	18.4.73	1		Tempe	15 Jan 06
58:56		Patrick	Makau	KEN	2.3.85	1		Berlin	1 Apr 07
58:59		Zersenay	Tadese	ERI	8.2.82	1	WCh	Udine	14 Oct 07
59:02			Makau			2	WCh	Udine	14 Oct 07
59:05	dh		Tadese			1	GNR	South Shields	18 Sep 05
59:05		Evans	Cheruiyot	KEN	5.10.82	3	WCh	Udine	14 Oct 07
59:06	dh	Paul	Tergat	KEN	17.6.69	1		Lisboa	26 Mar 00
59:07		Paul	Kosgei	KEN	22.4.78	1		Berlin	2 Apr 06
59:10	dh		Tergat			1		Lisboa	13 Mar 05
59:12			E Cheruiyot			1		Rotterdam	9 Sep 07
59:13			Makau			2		Ra's Al Khaymah	9 Feb 07
59:16			Wanjiru			1		Rotterdam	11 Sep 05
59:16			Tadesse			1		Rotterdam	10 Sep 06
59:16		Deriba	Merga	ETH	26.10.80	4	WCh	Udine	14 Oct 07
59:17			Tergat			1		Milano	4 Apr 98
59:19			Makau			2		Rotterdam	9 Sep 07
59:20	dh	Hendrick	Ramaala	RSA	2.2.72	2		Lisboa	26 Mar 00
59:21	dh	Robert Kipkoech	Cheruiyot (10)	KEN	26.9.78	2		Lisboa	13 Mar 05
59:22			Tergat			1	Stra	Milano	17 Apr 99
59:24	dh		Gebrselassie			1		New York (dh 30m)	5 Aug 07
59:25			Merga			3		Rotterdam	9 Sep 07
59:26		Francis	Kibiwott	KEN	15.9.78	2		Berlin	1 Apr 07
59:27	dh	Wilson	Kiprotich Kebenei	KEN	20.7.80	3		Lisboa	13 Mar 05
59:27		Patrick	Ivuti	KEN	30.6.78	4		Rotterdam	9 Sep 07
59:28		Robert	Kipchumba	KEN	24.2.84	2		Rotterdam	10 Sep 06
59:29			E Cheruiyot			2		Berlin	2 Apr 06
59:30	dh	Martin	Lel	KEN	29.10.78	1		Lisboa	26 Mar 06
59:30		Yonas	Kifle	ERI	24.3.77	5	WCh	Udine	14 Oct 07
		(30/16)							
59:32		Dieudonné	Disi	RWA	24.4.78	6	WCh	Udine	14 Oct 07
59:33		Marilson	dos Santos	BRA	6.8.77	7	WCh	Udine	14 Oct 07
59:35	dh	Robert	Cheruiyot	KEN	20.12.74	2		Lisboa	26 Mar 06
59:37	dh	Dejene	Berhanu	ETH	12.12.80	1	GNR	South Shields	26 Sep 04
		(20)							

Mark	Wind	Name		Nat	Born	Pos	Meet	Venue	Date
59:38	dh	Faustin	Baha	TAN	30.5.82	4		Lisboa	26 Mar 00
59:43	dh	António	Pinto	POR	22.3.66	1		Lisboa	15 Mar 98
59:43		Ryan	Hall	USA	14.10.82	1	NC	Houston	14 Jan 07
59:45		Joseph	Maregu	KEN	.77	1		Lille	1 Sep 07
59:47		Moses	Tanui	KEN	20.8.65	1		Milano	3 Apr 93
59:48		Mekubo	Mogusu	KEN	25.12.86	1		Marugame	4 Feb 07
59:49	dh	Rodgers	Rop	KEN	16.2.76	1		Lisboa	28 Mar 04
59:51	dh	William	Kiplagat	KEN	21.6.72	5		Lisboa	26 Mar 00
59:51	w	Tesfaye	Tola	ETH	19.10.74	1		Malmö	12 Jun 00
59:52		Fabián	Roncero	ESP	19.10.70	1		Berlin	1 Apr 01
		(30)							
59:53		Philip	Rugut	KEN	18.5.77	2	NC	Udine	29 Sep 02
59:56		Shem	Kororia	KEN	25.9.72	1	WCh	Kosice	4 Oct 97
59:56	dh	Jaouad	Gharib	MAR	22.5.72	4		Lisboa	28 Mar 04
60:00		Kenneth	Cheruiyot	KEN	2.8.74	3	WCh	Kosice	4 Oct 97
60:00	dh	Luke	Kibet	KEN	19.6.73	6		Lisboa	28 Mar 04
60:01		Paul	Koech	KEN	25.6.69	1	WCh	Uster	27 Sep 98
60:01	dh	Japhet	Kosgei	KEN	20.12.68	1		Lisboa	21 Mar 99
60:02		Benson	Masya	KEN	14.5.70	1	GNR	South Shields	18 Sep 94
60:02		Darren	Wilson	AUS	9.8.68	1		Tokyo	19 Jan 97
60:02		John	Yuda	TAN	9.6.79	2	GNR	South Shields	6 Oct 02
		(40)							
60:04		Joseph	Kimani	KEN	21.9.72	2		Lisboa	15 Mar 98
60:04		Tesfaye	Jifar	ETH	23.4.76	2	WCh	Bristol	7 Oct 01
60:05		Jackson	Koech	KEN	26.12.78	2	GNR	South Shields	21 Sep 03
60:06		Steve	Moneghetti	AUS	26.9.62	1		Tokyo	24 Jan 93
60:08		Eshetu	Wondimu	ETH	26.1.82	4		Berlin	1 Apr 07
60:09	Sh?	Paul	Evans	GBR	13.4.61	1		Marrakesh	15 Jan 95
60:10		Jonathan	Maiyo	KEN	.88	5		Rotterdam	9 Sep 07
60:11		Matthews	Temane	RSA	14.12.60	1	NC	East London	25 Jul 87
60:11		Zithulele	Sinqe	RSA	9.6.63	2	NC	East London	25 Jul 87
60:11		Todd	Williams	USA	7.3.69	2		Tokyo	24 Jan 93
60:11		Abel	Kirui	KEN	4.6.82	6		Rotterdam	9 Sep 07
		(51)	100th man 60:43, 200th 61:03, 300th 61:20, 400th 61:32, 500th 61:41						
Short course									
58:51		Paul	Tergat	KEN	17.6.69	1	Stra	Milano 49m sh	30 Mar 96
59:24		Sammy	Lelei	KEN	14.8.64	1		Lisboa 97m	13 Mar 93
59:46		Josephat	Kiprono	KEN	12.12.73	2	Stra	Milano 49m	30 Mar 96

MARATHON

In second column: L = loop course or start and finish within 30%, P = point-to-point or start and finish more than 30% apart, D = point-to-point and downhill over 1/1000

Mark		Name		Nat	Born	Pos	Meet	Venue	Date
2:04:26	L	Haile	Gebrselassie	ETH	18.4.73	1		Berlin	30 Sep 07
2:04:55	L WR	Paul	Tergat	KEN	17.6.69	1		Berlin	28 Sep 03
2:04:56	L	Sammy	Korir	KEN	12.12.71	2		Berlin	28 Sep 03
2:05:38	L WR	Khalid	Khannouchi	MAR/USA	22.12.71	1		London	14 Apr 02
2:05:42	L WR		Khannouchi			1		Chicago	24 Oct 99
2:05:48	L		Tergat			2		London	14 Apr 02
2:05:50	L	Evans	Rutto	KEN	8.4.78	1		Chicago	12 Oct 03
2:05:56	L		Khannouchi			1		Chicago	13 Oct 02
2:05:56	L		Gebrselassie			1		Berlin	24 Sep 06
2:06:05	L WR	Ronaldo da	Costa	BRA	7.6.70	1		Berlin	20 Sep 98
2:06:14	L	Felix	Limo	KEN	22.8.80	1		Rotterdam	4 Apr 04
2:06:15	L	Titus	Munji	KEN	20.12.79	3		Berlin	28 Sep 03
2:06:16	L	Moses	Tanui	KEN	20.8.65	2		Chicago	24 Oct 99
2:06:16	L	Daniel	Njenga (10)	KEN	7.5.76	2		Chicago	13 Oct 02
2:06:16	L	Toshinari	Takaoka	JPN	24.9.70	3		Chicago	13 Oct 02
2:06:16	L		Rutto			1		Chicago	10 Oct 04
2:06:18	L		Tergat			4		Chicago	13 Oct 02
2:06:18	L		Rutto			1		London	18 Apr 04
2:06:20	L		Gebrselassie			1		Amsterdam	16 Oct 05
2:06:23	L	Robert	Cheboror	KEN	9.9.78	1		Amsterdam	17 Oct 04
2:06:29	L	Emmanuel	Mutai	KEN	1.4.78	1		Amsterdam	21 Oct 07
2:06:33	L	Gert	Thys	RSA	12.11.71	1		Tokyo	14 Feb 99
2:06:33	L	Michael	Rotich	KEN	26.10.82	1		Paris	6 Apr 03
2:06:35	L		Gebrselassie			3		London	14 Apr 02
2:06:36	L	António	Pinto	POR	22.3.66	1		London	16 Apr 00
2:06:36	L	Benoit	Zwierzchlewski	FRA	19.8.76	2		Paris	6 Apr 03
2:06:38	L		S Korir			1		Rotterdam	9 Apr 06

Mark	Wind	Name		Nat	Born	Pos	Meet	Venue	Date
2:06:39	L	William	Kipsang	KEN	.77	1		Amsterdam	19 Oct 03
2:06:39	L		F Limo			1		London	23 Apr 06
2:06:39	L	Samuel	Wanjiru	KEN	10.11.86	1		Fukuoka	2 Dec 07
2:06:41	L	Martin	Lel	KEN	29.10.78	2		London	23 Apr 06
		(31/20)							
2:06:44	L	Josephat	Kiprono	KEN	12.12.73	1		Berlin	26 Sep 99
2:06:44	L	Paul	Kirui	KEN	5.2.80	2		Rotterdam	9 Apr 06
2:06:45	L	Richard	Limo	KEN	18.11.80	2		Amsterdam	21 Oct 07
2:06:46	L	Abdelkader	El Mouaziz	MAR	1.1.69	5		Chicago	13 Oct 02
2:06:47	L	Fred	Kiprop	KEN	3.6.74	1		Amsterdam	17 Oct 99
2:06:47	L	Raymond	Kipkoech	KEN	19.4.78	1		Berlin	29 Sep 02
2:06:47	L	Wilson	Onsare	KEN	15.6.76	3		Paris	6 Apr 03
2:06:48	L	Driss	El Himer	FRA	4.4.74	4		Paris	6 Apr 03
2:06:49	L	Tesfaye	Jifar	ETH	23.4.76	2		Amsterdam	17 Oct 99
2:06:49	L	Simon	Biwott	KEN	3.3.70	2		Berlin	29 Sep 02
		(30)							
2:06:49	L	Joseph	Riri	KEN	21.10.73	2		Berlin	26 Sep 04
2:06:50	L WR	Belayneh	Dinsamo	ETH	28.6.65	1		Rotterdam	17 Apr 88
2:06:50	L	William	Kiplagat	KEN	21.6.72	3		Amsterdam	17 Oct 99
2:06:50	L	Deriba	Merga	ETH	26.10.80	2		Fukuoka	2 Dec 07
2:06:51	L	Atsushi	Fujita	JPN	6.11.76	1		Fukuoka	3 Dec 00
2:06:51	L	Abel	Kirui	KEN	4.6.82	2		Berlin	30 Sep 07
2:06:52	L	Vincent	Kipsos	KEN	22.6.76	3		Berlin	29 Sep 02
2:06:52	L	Charles E	Kibiwott	KEN	8.8.74	3		Rotterdam	9 Apr 06
2:06:52	L	Julio	Rey ¶	ESP	13.1.72	1		Hamburg	23 Apr 06
2:06:54	L	Ondoro	Osoro	KEN	3.12.67	1		Chicago	11 Oct 98
		(40)							
2:06:55	L	Hendrick	Ramaala	RSA	2.2.72	3		London	23 Apr 06
2:06:57	L	Takayuki	Inubishi	JPN	11.8.72	2		Berlin	26 Sep 99
2:06:57	L	Tesfaye	Tola	ETH	19.10.74	4		Amsterdam	17 Oct 99
2:07:02	L	Sammy	Lelei	KEN	14.8.64	1		Berlin	24 Sep 95
2:07:02	L	Jaouad	Gharib	MAR	22.5.72	3	(2:07:12?)	London	18 Apr 04
2:07:05	L	Joshua	Chelanga	KEN	7.4.73	3		Berlin	26 Sep 04
2:07:06	L	Ian	Syster	RSA	20.1.76	5		London	14 Apr 02
2:07:07	L	Ahmed	Salah	DJI	31.12.56	2		Rotterdam	17 Apr 88
2:07:07	L	Paul	Koech	KEN	25.6.69	2		Chicago	12 Oct 03
2:07:09	L	Japheth	Kosgei	KEN	28.12.68	1		Rotterdam	18 Apr 99
2:07:09	L	Benjamin	Maiyo	KEN	6.10.78	2		Chicago	9 Oct 05
		(51)	100th man 2:07:55, 200th 2:08:48, 300th 2:09:26, 400th 2:10:04, 500th 2:10:29						

2000 METRES STEEPLECHASE

Mark	Wind	Name		Nat	Born	Pos	Meet	Venue	Date
5:14.43		Julius	Kariuki	KEN	12.6.61	1		Rovereto	21 Aug 90
5:14.53		Saïf Saeed	Shaheen	QAT	15.10.82	1	SGP	Doha	13 May 05
5:15.96		Bouabdallah	Tahri	FRA	20.12.78	1		Tomblaine	19 Jun 02
5:16.22		Phillip	Barkutwo	KEN	6.10.66	2		Rovereto	21 Aug 90
5:16.46		Wesley	Kiprotich	KEN	31.7.79	2	SGP	Doha	13 May 05
5:16.85		Eliud	Barngetuny	KEN	20.5.73	1		Parma	13 Jun 95
5:18.28		Richard	Kosgei	KEN	29.12.70	2		Parma	13 Jun 95
5:18.36		Alessandro	Lambruschini	ITA	7.1.65	1		Verona	12 Sep 89
5:18.38		Azzedine	Brahmi	ALG	13.9.66	1		Verona	17 Jun 92
5:18.51		John	Langat	KEN	27.11.74	1		Rovereto	29 Aug 01
5:18.60		Stanley	Kibiwott	KEN	8.8.69	2		Rovereto	29 Aug 01

3000 METRES STEEPLECHASE

Mark	Wind	Name		Nat	Born	Pos	Meet	Venue	Date
7:53.63	WR	Saïf Saaeed	Shaheen	QAT	15.10.82	1	VD	Bruxelles	3 Sep 04
		(Formerly Stephen	Cherono KEN)						
7:55.28	WR	Brahim	Boulami ¶	MAR	20.4.72	1	VD	Bruxelles	24 Aug 01
7:55.51			Shaheen			1	VD	Bruxelles	26 Aug 05
7:55.72	WR	Bernard	Barmasai	KEN	6.5.74	1	ASV	Köln	24 Aug 97
7:56.16		Moses	Kiptanui	KEN	1.10.70	2	ASV	Köln	24 Aug 97
7:56.32			Shaheen			1	SGP	Athína	3 Jul 06
7:56.34			Shaheen			1	GGala	Roma	8 Jul 05
7:56.37		Paul Kipsiele	Koech	KEN	10.11.81	2	GGala	Roma	8 Jul 05
7:56.94			Shaheen			1	WAF	Monaco	19 Sep 04
7:56.54			Shaheen			1	WK	Zürich	18 Aug 06
7:57.28			Shaheen			1	SGP	Athína	14 Jun 05
7:57.29		Reuben	Kosgei	KEN	2.8.79	2	VD	Bruxelles	24 Aug 01
7:57.38			Shaheen			1	WAF	Monaco	14 Sep 03
7:57.42			P K Koech			2	WAF	Monaco	14 Sep 03
7:58.09			Boulami			1	Herc	Monaco	19 Jul 02

Mark	Wind	Name		Nat	Born	Pos	Meet	Venue	Date
7:58.10			Cherono			2	Herc	Monaco	19 Jul 02
7:58.50			Boulami			1	WK	Zürich	17 Aug 01
7:58.66			S Cherono			3	VD	Bruxelles	24 Aug 01
7:58.80			P K Koech			1	VD	Bruxelles	14 Sep 07
7:58.98			Barmasai			1	Herc	Monaco	4 Aug 99
7:59.08	WR	Wilson	Boit Kipketer	KEN	6.10.73	1	WK	Zürich	13 Aug 97
7:59.18	WR		Kiptanui			1	WK	Zürich	16 Aug 95
7:59.42			P K Koech			1	DNG	Stockholm	7 Aug 07
7.59.52			Kiptanui			1	VD	Bruxelles	25 Aug 95
7:59.65			P K Koech			1	GGala	Roma	2 Jul 04
7:59.94			P K Koech			1	GGala	Roma	14 Jul 06
8:00.06			Shaheen			1	VD	Bruxelles	5 Sep 03
8:00.35			Barmasai			2	WK	Zürich	13 Aug 97
8:00.29			P K Koech			1	DNG	Stockholm	25 Jul 06
8:00.42			P K Koech			2	VD	Bruxelles	5 Sep 03
		(30/7)							
8:01.69		Kipkirui	Misoi	KEN	23.12.78	4	VD	Bruxelles	24 Aug 01
8:02.49		Ezekiel	Kemboi	KEN	25.5.82	2	WK	Zürich	15 Aug 03
8:02.89		Brimin	Kipruto	KEN	31.7.85	2	VD	Bruxelles	14 Sep 07
		(10)							
8:03.41		Patrick	Sang	KEN	11.4.64	3	ASV	Köln	24 Aug 97
8:03.57		Ali	Ezzine	MAR	3.9.78	1	Gaz	Saint-Denis	23 Jun 00
8:03.74		Raymond	Yator	KEN	7.4.81	3	Herc	Monaco	18 Aug 00
8:03.89		John	Kosgei	KEN	13.7.73	3	Herc	Monaco	16 Aug 97
8:04.95		Simon	Vroemen	NED	11.5.69	2	VD	Bruxelles	26 Aug 05
8:05.01		Eliud	Barngetuny	KEN	20.5.73	1	Herc	Monaco	25 Jul 95
8:05.35	WR	Peter	Koech	KEN	18.2.58	1	DNG	Stockholm	3 Jul 89
8:05.37		Philip	Barkutwo	KEN	6.10.66	2		Rieti	6 Sep 92
8:05.4	WR	Henry	Rono	KEN	12.2.52	1		Seattle	13 May 78
8:05.43		Christopher	Kosgei	KEN	14.8.74	2	WK	Zürich	11 Aug 99
		(20)							
8:05.51		Julius	Kariuki	KEN	12.6.61	1	OG	Seoul	30 Sep 88
8:05.68		Wesley	Kiprotich	KEN	1.8.79	4	VD	Bruxelles	3 Sep 04
8:05.75		Mustafa	Mohamed	SWE	1.3.79	1	NA	Heusden-Zolder	28 Jul 07
8:05.96		Richard	Matelong	KEN	14.10.83	6	VD	Bruxelles	3 Sep 04
8:05.99		Joseph	Keter	KEN	13.6.69	1	Herc	Monaco	10 Aug 96
8:06.77		Gideon	Chirchir	KEN	24.2.66	2	WK	Zürich	16 Aug 95
8:06.88		Richard	Kosgei	KEN	29.12.70	2	GPF	Monaco	9 Sep 95
8:06.91		Bouabdellah	Tahri	FRA	20.12.78	3	Gaz	Saint-Denis	4 Jul 03
8:07.02		Brahim	Taleb	MAR	16.2.85	2	NA	Heusden-Zolder	28 Jul 07
8:07.12		Tareq Mubarak	Taher	BRN	24.3.84	3	NA	Heusden-Zolder	28 Jul 07
		(30)							
8:07.13		Paul	Kosgei	KEN	22.4.78	2	GP II	Saint-Denis	3 Jul 99
8:07.18		Obaid Moussa	Amer ¶	QAT	18.4.85	4	OG	Athína	24 Aug 04
8:07.44		Luis Miguel	Martín	ESP	11.1.72	2	VD	Bruxelles	30 Aug 02
8:07.59		Julius	Nyamu	KEN	1.12.77	5	VD	Bruxelles	24 Aug 01
8:07.62		Joseph	Mahmoud	FRA	13.12.55	1	VD	Bruxelles	24 Aug 84
8:07.96		Mark	Rowland	GBR	7.3.63	3	OG	Seoul	30 Sep 88
8:08.02	WR	Anders	Gärderud	SWE	28.8.46	1	OG	Montreal	28 Jul 76
8:08.12		Matthew	Birir	KEN	5.7.72	3	GGala	Roma	8 Jun 95
8:08.14		Sa'ad Shaddad	Al-Asmari	KSA	24.9.68	4	DNG	Stockholm	16 Jul 02
8:08.57		Francesco	Panetta	ITA	10.1.63	1	WCh	Roma	5 Sep 87
		(40)							
8:08.78		Alessandro	Lambruschini	ITA	7.1.65	3	WCh	Stuttgart	21 Aug 93
8:08.78		Abdelkader	Hachlaf	MAR	3.7.78	4	GGala	Roma	14 Jul 06
8:08.82		Dan	Lincoln	USA	22.10.80	5	GGala	Roma	14 Jul 06
8:09.02		Abdelaziz	Sahere	MAR	18.9.67	5	GGala	Roma	8 Jun 95
8:09.03		Elarbi	Khattabi	MAR	16.5.67	3	GGala	Roma	7 Jul 99
8:09.09		Eliseo	Martín	ESP	5.11.73	3	WCh	Saint-Denis	26 Aug 03
8:09.09		David	Chemweno	KEN	18.12.81	2	NA	Heusden-Zolder	23 Jul 05
8:09.11		Bronislaw	Malinowski	POL	4.6.51	2	OG	Montreal	28 Jul 76
8:09.17		Henry	Marsh	USA	15.3.54	1	R-W	Koblenz	28 Aug 85
8:09.18		Boguslaw	Maminski	POL	18.12.55	2	VD	Bruxelles	24 Aug 84
		(50)	100th man 8:14.02, 200th 8:19.88, 300th 8:23.26						
Drugs disqualification: 7:53.17			Brahim Boulami ¶	MAR	20.4.72	1	WK	Zürich	16 Aug 02

110 METRES HURDLES

Mark	Wind	Name		Nat	Born	Pos	Meet	Venue	Date
12.88	WR 1.1		Liu Xiang	CHN	13.7.83	1rA	Athl	Lausanne	11 Jul 06
12.90	1.1	Dominique	Arnold	USA	14.9.73	2rA	Athl	Lausanne	11 Jul 06
12.91	WR 0.5	Colin	Jackson	GBR	18.2.67	1	WCh	Stuttgart	20 Aug 93

Mark	Wind	Name		Nat	Born	Pos	Meet	Venue	Date
12.91	WR 0.3		Liu Xiang			1	OG	Athína	27 Aug 04
12.92	WR -0.1	Roger	Kingdom	USA	26.8.62	1	WK	Zürich	16 Aug 89
12.92	0.9	Allen	Johnson	USA	1.3.71	1	NC	Atlanta	23 Jun 96
12.92	0.2		Johnson			1	VD	Bruxelles	23 Aug 96
12.92	1.5		Liu Xiang			1	GP	New York	2 Jun 07
12.92	0.0	Dayron	Robles	CUB	19.11.86	1	WAF	Stuttgart	23 Sep 07
12.93	WR -0.2	Renaldo	Nehemiah	USA	24.3.59	1	WK	Zürich	19 Aug 81
12.93	0.0		Johnson			1	WCh	Athína	7 Aug 97
12.93	-0.6		Liu Xiang			1	WAF	Stuttgart	9 Sep 06
12.94	1.6	Jack	Pierce	USA	23.9.62	1s2	NC	Atlanta	22 Jun 96
12.95	0.6		Johnson			1	OG	Atlanta	29 Jul 96
12.95	1.5	Terrence	Trammell	USA	23.11.78	2	GP	New York	2 Jun 07
12.95	1.7		Liu Xiang			1	WCh	Osaka	31 Aug 07
12.96	0.4		Johnson			1	WCp	Athína	17 Sep 06
12.97A	2.0		Kingdom			1		Sestriere	11 Aug 88
12.97A	-1.6		Jackson			1A		Sestriere	28 Jul 93
12.97	-0.5		Johnson			1		Stuttgart	13 Jul 97
12.97	1.5		Johnson			1	NC	Sacramento	23 Jul 00
12.97	0.0		Johnson			1	Gaz	Saint-Denis	4 Jul 03
12.97	1.0	Ladji	Doucouré (10)	FRA	28.3.83	1	NC	Angers	15 Jul 05
12.98	1.5		Kingdom			1	OG	Seoul	26 Sep 88
12.98	0.2		Jackson			1	TOTO	Tokyo	15 Sep 94
12.98	0.2		Johnson			1	ASV	Köln	18 Aug 95
12.98	-0.3		Johnson			1rA	WK	Zürich	12 Aug 98
12.98	0.6	Mark	Crear	USA	2.10.68	1		Zagreb	5 Jul 99
12.99	1.2		Jackson			1	VD	Bruxelles	3 Sep 93
12.99	-0.3		Jackson			1		Madrid	6 Sep 94
12.99	0.2		Johnson			1	NC	Carson	24 Jun 05
12.99	1.7		Trammell			2	WCh	Osaka	31 Aug 07
		(32/11)							
13.00	0.5	Anthony	Jarrett	GBR	13.8.68	2	WCh	Stuttgart	20 Aug 93
13.00	0.6	Anier	García	CUB	9.3.76	1	OG	Sydney	25 Sep 00
13.01	0.3	Larry	Wade ¶	USA	22.11.74	1rA	Athl	Lausanne	2 Jul 99
13.02	1.5	Ryan	Wilson	USA	19.12.80	3	GP	New York	2 Jun 07
13.02	1.7	David	Payne	USA	24.7.82	3	WCh	Osaka	31 Aug 07
13.03	-0.2	Greg	Foster	USA	4.8.58	2	WK	Zürich	19 Aug 81
13.03	1.0	Reggie	Torian	USA	22.4.75	1	NC	New Orleans	21 Jun 98
13.05	1.4	Tony	Dees ¶	USA	6.8.63	1		Vigo	23 Jul 91
13.05	-0.8	Florian	Schwarthoff	GER	7.5.68	1	NC	Bremen	2 Jul 95
		(20)							
13.08	1.2	Mark	McKoy	CAN	10.12.61	1	BNP	Villeneuve d'Ascq	2 Jul 93
13.08	0.0	Stanislav	Olijar	LAT	22.3.79	2	Athl	Lausanne	1 Jul 03
13.09	0.1	Aries	Merritt	USA	24.7.85	1	DNG	Stockholm	7 Aug 07
13.12	1.5	Falk	Balzer ¶	GER	14.12.73	2	EC	Budapest	22 Aug 98
13.12	1.0	Duane	Ross	USA	5.12.72	3	WCh	Sevilla	25 Aug 99
13.12	1.9	Anwar	Moore	USA	5.3.79	1	ModR	Modesto	5 May 07
13.13	1.6	Igor	Kovác	SVK	12.5.69	1	DNG	Stockholm	7 Jul 97
13.15	0.3	Robin	Korving	NED	29.7.74	5rA	Athl	Lausanne	2 Jul 99
13.14	-0.5	David	Oliver	USA	24.4.82	2	SGP	Doha	11 May 07
13.17	-0.4	Sam	Turner	USA	17.6.57	2	Pepsi	Los Angeles (Ww)	15 May 83
		(30)							
13.17	0.0	Tonie	Campbell	USA	14.6.60	3	WK	Zürich	17 Aug 88
13.17	0.5	Courtney	Hawkins	USA	11.7.67	1		Ingolstadt	26 Jul 98
13.17	0.4	Mike	Fenner	GER	24.4.71	1		Leverkusen	9 Aug 98
13.17	-0.1	Maurice	Wignall	JAM	17.4.76	1s1	OG	Athína	26 Aug 04
13.18	0.5	Emilio	Valle	CUB	21.4.67	3s1	OG	Atlanta	29 Jul 96
13.19	1.9	Steve	Brown	USA/TRI	6.1.69	1h4	NC	Atlanta	21 Jun 96
13.19	1.7		Shi Dongpeng	CHN	6.1.84	5	WCh	Osaka	31 Aug 07
13.20	2.0	Stéphane	Caristan	FRA	31.5.64	1	EC	Stuttgart	30 Aug 86
13.20	1.8	Aleksandr	Markin ¶	RUS	8.9.62	1	Znam	Leningrad	11 Jun 88
13.20	1.7	Larry	Harrington	USA	24.11.70	2s1	NC	Atlanta	22 Jun 96
		(40)							
13.21	WR 0.6	Alejandro	Casañas	CUB	29.1.54	1	WUG	Sofiya	21 Aug 77
13.21	1.8	Vladimir	Shishkin	RUS	12.1.64	2	Znam	Leningrad	11 Jun 88
13.21	0.9	Eugene	Swift	USA	14.9.64	3	NC	Atlanta	23 Jun 96
13.22	-0.2	Terry	Reese	USA	20.6.67	2	ASV	Köln	24 Aug 97
13.22	1.5	Dawane	Wallace	USA	30.12.76	4	NC	Sacramento	23 Jul 00
13.22	-0.1	Joel	Brown	USA	31.1.80	2	Bisl	Oslo	29 Jul 05
13.22	1.7	Sergiy	Demydyuk	UKR	5.6.82	6	WCh	Osaka	31 Aug 07

Mark	Wind	Name		Nat	Born	Pos	Meet	Venue	Date
13.23	-0.1	Charles	Allen	CAN	29.3.77	4s1	OG	Athína	26 Aug 04
13.23	0.1	Arend	Watkins	USA	23.5.79	1	SGP	Ath na	14 Jun 05
13.23	0.4	Yoel	Hernández	CUB	12.12.77	4r2	GP	Athína	2 Jul 07
13.23	1.6	Eric	Mitchum	USA	2.8.84	1	Aragón	Zaragoza	28 Jul 07
		(51)	100th man 13.34, 200th 13.47, 300th 13.57, 400th 13.63						
Rolling start but accepted by race officials									
13.10A	2.0	Falk	Balzer ¶	GER	14.12.73	1	WCp	Johannesburg	13 Sep 98
Doubtful timing									
13.06	1.3	Mike	Fenner	GER	24.4.71	1		Scheessel	4 Jun 95
13.08	1.3	Eric	Kaiser ¶	GER	7.3.71	2		Scheessel	4 Jun 95
Wind-assisted marks			*Performances to 12.98, performers to 13.22*						
12.87	2.6	Roger	Kingdom	USA	26.8.62	1	WCp	Barcelona	10 Sep 89
12.91	3.5	Renaldo	Nehemiah	USA	24.3.59	1	NCAA	Champaign	1 Jun 79
12.94A	2.8		Jackson			1rA		Sestriere	31 Jul 94
12.95	2.6		Jackson			2	WCp	Barcelona	10 Sep 89
13.00	2.6	Anwar	Moore	USA	5.3.79	1	DrakeR	Des Moines	28 Apr 07
13.06	2.1	Mark	McKoy	CAN	10.12.61	1	Gugl	Linz	13 Aug 92
13.14	2.9	Igor	Kazanov	LAT	24.9.63	1r1	Znam	Leningrad	8 Jun 86
13.15	2.1	Courtney	Hawkins	USA	11.7.67	1		Salamanca	10 Jul 98
13.18	4.7	Robert	Reading	USA	9.6.67	1		Azusa	23 Apr 94
13.20	2.4	Arthur	Blake	USA	19.8.66	2	IAC	Edinburgh	6 Jul 90
13.20	3.1	Yoel	Hernández	CUB	12.12.77	2		Camagüey	10 Mar 00
13.20	2.1	Anwar	Moore	USA	5.3.79	1	DNG	Stockholm	26 Jul 05
13.21A	2.5	Eric	Cannon	USA	2.3.67	2	NCAA	Provo	3 Jun 89
Hand timing									
12.8	1.0	Renaldo	Nehemiah	USA	24.3.59	1		Kingston	11 May 79
13.0 WR	1.8	Guy	Drut	FRA	6.12.50	1	ISTAF	Berlin	22 Aug 75
13.0	1.0	Greg	Foster	USA	4.8.58	2		Kingston	11 May 79
13.0	0.8	Mark	McKoy	CAN	10.12.61	1	Nik	Nice	16 Jul 85
13.0		Stéphane	Caristan	FRA	25.1.64	1		Creteil	3 May 86
13.0		Vladimir	Shishkin	RUS	12.1.64	1		Stayki	7 May 88
13.0* WR	2.0	Rod	Milburn	USA	18.5.50	1s1	AAU	Eugene	25 Jun 71
13.0	0.4	Tomasz	Scigaczewski	POL	18.11.78	1	NC	Wroclaw	28 Jun 98
Wind-assisted									
12.8	2.4	Colin	Jackson	GBR	18.2.67	1		Sydney	10 Jan 90
12.9	4.1	Mark	Crear	USA	2.10.68	1rA	S&W	Modesto	8 May 93
13.0		Alejandro	Casañas	CUB	29.1.54	1	Barr	La Habana	22 May 77
13.0		Tonie	Campbell	USA	14.6.60	1		Los Angeles	16 Jul 86
13.0		Keith	Talley	USA	28.1.64	1		Tuscaloosa	26 Mar 88
13.0	4.1		Li Tong	CHN	6.5.67	2rA	S&W	Modesto	8 May 93

400 METRES HURDLES

Mark	Name		Nat	Born	Pos	Meet	Venue	Date
46.78 WR	Kevin	Young	USA	16.9.66	1	OG	Barcelona	6 Aug 92
47.02 WR	Edwin	Moses	USA	31.8.55	1		Koblenz	31 Aug 83
47.03	Bryan	Bronson	USA	9.9.72	1	NC	New Orleans	21 Jun 98
47.10	Samuel	Matete	ZAM	27.7.68	1rA	WK	Zürich	7 Aug 91
47.13 WR		Moses			1		Milano	3 Jul 80
47.14		Moses			1	Athl	Lausanne	14 Jul 81
47.17		Moses			1	ISTAF	Berlin	8 Aug 80
47.18		Young			1	WCh	Stuttgart	19 Aug 93
47.19	Andre	Phillips	USA	5.9.59	1	OG	Seoul	25 Sep 88
47.23	Amadou	Dia Bâ	SEN	22.9.58	2	OG	Seoul	25 Sep 88
47.24	Kerron	Clement	USA	31.10.85	1	NC	Carson	26 Jun 05
47.25	Félix	Sánchez	DOM	30.8.77	1	WCh	Saint-Denis	29 Aug 03
47.27		Moses			1	ISTAF	Berlin	21 Aug 81
47.30	Bershawn	Jackson	USA	8.5.83	1	WCh	Helsinki	9 Aug 05
47.32		Moses			1		Koblenz	29 Aug 84
47.35		Sánchez			1rA	WK	Zürich	16 Aug 02
47.37		Moses			1	WCp	Roma	4 Sep 81
47.37		Moses			1	WK	Zürich	24 Aug 83
47.37		Moses			1	OT	Indianapolis	17 Jul 88
47.37		Young			1	Athl	Lausanne	7 Jul 93
47.37	Stéphane	Diagana (10)	FRA	23.7.69	1	Athl	Lausanne	5 Jul 95
47.38		Moses			1	Athl	Lausanne	2 Sep 86
47.38	Danny	Harris ¶	USA	7.9.65	1	Athl	Lausanne	10 Jul 91
47.38		Sánchez			1rA	WK	Zürich	17 Aug 01
47.39		Clement			1	NC	Indianapolis	24 Jun 06
47.40		Young			1	WK	Zürich	19 Aug 92
47.42		Young			1	ASV	Köln	16 Aug 92

Mark Wind	Name		Nat	Born	Pos	Meet	Venue	Date
47.43		Moses			1	ASV	Köln	28 Aug 83
47.43	James	Carter	USA	7.5.78	2	WCh	Helsinki	9 Aug 05
47.45 WR		Moses			1	AAU	Los Angeles (Ww)	11 Jun 77
	(30/12)							
47.48	Harald	Schmid	FRG	29.9.57	1	EC	Athína	8 Sep 82
47.50	Angelo	Taylor	USA	29.12.78	1	OG	Sydney	27 Sep 00
47.53	Hadi Soua'an	Al-Somaily	KSA	21.8.76	2	OG	Sydney	27 Sep 00
47.54	Derrick	Adkins	USA	2.7.70	2	Athl	Lausanne	5 Jul 95
47.54	Fabrizio	Mori	ITA	28.6.69	2	WCh	Edmonton	10 Aug 01
47.60	Winthrop	Graham	JAM	17.11.65	1	WK	Zürich	4 Aug 93
47.67	Bennie	Brazell	USA	2.6.82	2	NCAA	Sacramento	11 Jun 05
47.75	David	Patrick	USA	12.6.60	4	OT	Indianapolis	17 Jul 88
	(20)							
47.81	Llewellyn	Herbert	RSA	21.7.77	3	OG	Sydney	27 Sep 00
47.82 WR	John	Akii-Bua	UGA	3.12.49	1	OG	München	2 Sep 72
47.82	Kriss	Akabusi	GBR	28.11.58	3	OG	Barcelona	6 Aug 92
47.82	Periklis	Iakovákis	GRE	24.3.79	2	GP	Osaka	6 May 06
47.84	Bayano	Kamani	PAN	17.4.80	2s1	WCh	Helsinki	7 Aug 05
47.89	Dai	Tamesue	JPN	3.5.78	3	WCh	Edmonton	10 Aug 01
47.91	Calvin	Davis	USA	2.4.72	1s2	OG	Atlanta	31 Jul 96
47.92	Aleksandr	Vasilyev	BLR	26.7.61	2	ECp	Moskva	17 Aug 85
47.93	Kenji	Narisako	JPN	25.7.84	3	GP	Osaka	6 May 06
47.94	Eric	Thomas	USA	1.12.73	1	GGala	Roma	30 Jun 00
	(30)							
47.97	Maurice	Mitchell	USA	14.5.71	2rA	WK	Zürich	14 Aug 96
47.97	Joey	Woody	USA	22.5.73	3	NC	New Orleans	21 Jun 98
47.98	Sven	Nylander	SWE	1.1.62	4	OG	Atlanta	1 Aug 96
48.00	Danny	McFarlane	JAM	14.2.72	1s2	OG	Athína	24 Aug 04
48.02A	Ockert	Cilliers	RSA	21.4.81	1		Pretoria	20 Feb 04
48.02	Michael	Tinsley	USA	21.4.84	1s2	NC	Indianapolis	22 Jun 07
48.04	Eronilde	de Araújo	BRA	31.12.70	2	Nik	Nice	12 Jul 95
48.05	Ken	Harnden	ZIM	31.3.73	1	GP	Paris	29 Jul 98
48.05	Kemel	Thompson	JAM	25.9.74	1	GP	London (CP)	8 Aug 03
48.05	LjJ. 'Louis'	van Zyl	RSA	20.7.85	1	CG	Melbourne	23 Mar 06
	(40)							
48.06	Oleg	Tverdokhleb	UKR	3.11.69	1	EC	Helsinki	10 Aug 94
48.06	Ruslan	Mashchenko	RUS	11.11.71	1	GP II	Helsinki	13 Jun 98
48.09	Alwyn	Myburgh	RSA	13.10.80	1	WUG	Beijing	31 Aug 01
48.12A WR	David	Hemery	GBR	18.7.44	1	OG	Ciudad de México	15 Oct 68
48.12	Marek	Plawgo	POL	25.2.81	3	WCh	Osaka	28 Aug 07
48.13	Dinsdale	Morgan	JAM	19.11.72	2	GGala	Roma	14 Jul 98
48.13	Marcel	Schelbert	SUI	26.2.76	3	WCh	Sevilla	27 Aug 99
48.14	Chris	Rawlinson	GBR	19.5.72	1rB	WK	Zürich	11 Aug 99
48.15	Kenneth	Ferguson	USA	22.3.84	1	adidas	Carson	20 May 07
48.16	Tony	Rambo	USA	30.5.60	3s1	OT	Los Angeles	17 Jun 84
48.16	Rickey	Harris ¶	USA	29.9.81	1	NCAA	Baton Rouge	31 May 02
	(51)	100th man 48.58, 200th man 49.10, 300th man 49.38						
Drugs Disqualification	47.15	Bronson			1	GWG	Uniondale, NY	19 Jul 98

HIGH JUMP

2.45 WR	Javier	Sotomayor	CUB	13.10.67	1		Salamanca	27 Jul 93
2.44 WR		Sotomayor			1	CAC	San Juan	29 Jul 89
2.43 WR		Sotomayor			1		Salamanca	8 Sep 88
2.43i		Sotomayor			1	WI	Budapest	4 Mar 89
2.42 WR	Patrik	Sjöberg	SWE	5.1.65	1	DNG	Stockholm	30 Jun 87
2.42i WR	Carlo	Thränhardt	FRG	5.7.57	1		Berlin	26 Feb 88
2.42		Sotomayor			1		Sevilla	5 Jun 94
2.41 WR	Igor	Paklin	KGZ	15.6.63	1	WUG	Kobe	4 Sep 85
2.41i		Sjöberg			1		Pireás	1 Feb 87
2.41i		Sotomayor			1	WI	Toronto	14 Mar 93
2.41		Sotomayor			1	NC	La Habana	25 Jun 94
2.41		Sotomayor			1	TSB	London (CP)	15 Jul 94
2.40 WR	Rudolf	Povarnitsyn	UKR	13.6.62	1		Donetsk	11 Aug 85
2.40i		Thränhardt			1		Simmerath	16 Jan 87
2.40i		Sjöberg			1		Berlin	27 Feb 87
2.40		Sotomayor			1	NC	La Habana	12 Mar 89
2.40		Sjöberg			1	ECp-B	Bruxelles	5 Aug 89
2.40		Sotomayor			1	AmCp	Bogota	13 Aug 89
2.40	Sorin	Matei	ROM	6.7.63	1	PTS	Bratislava	20 Jun 90
2.40i	Hollis	Conway	USA	8.1.67	1	WI	Sevilla	10 Mar 91

Mark	Wind	Name		Nat	Born	Pos	Meet	Venue	Date
2.40			Sotomayor			1		Saint Denis	19 Jul 91
2.40		Charles	Austin	USA	19.12.67	1	WK	Zürich	7 Aug 91
2.40			Sotomayor			1	Barr	La Habana	22 May 93
2.40			Sotomayor			1	TSB	London (CP)	23 Jul 93
2.40			Sotomayor			1	WCh	Stuttgart	22 Aug 93
2.40i			Sotomayor			1		Wuppertal	4 Feb 94
2.40i			Sotomayor			1	TSB	Birmingham	26 Feb 94
2.40			Sotomayor			1		Eberstadt	10 Jul 94
2.40			Sotomayor			1	Nik	Nice	18 Jul 94
2.40			Sotomayor			1	GWG	Sankt-Peterburg	29 Jul 94
2.40			Sotomayor			1	WCp	London (CP)	11 Sep 94
2.40			Sotomayor			1	PAm	Mar del Plata	25 Mar 95
2.40		Vyacheslav	Voronin	RUS	5.4.74	1	BrGP	London (CP)	5 Aug 00
2.40i		Stefan	Holm	SWE	25.5.76	1	EI	Madrid	6 Mar 05
		(34/10)							
2.39	WR		Zhu Jianhua	CHN	29.5.63	1		Eberstadt	10 Jun 84
2.39i		Dietmar	Mögenburg	FRG	15.8.61	1		Köln	24 Feb 85
2.39i		Ralf	Sonn	GER	17.1.67	1		Berlin	1 Mar 91
2.39i		Ivan	Ukhov	RUS	29.3.86	1		Moskva	28 Jan 07
2.38i		Gennadiy	Avdeyenko	UKR	4.11.63	2	WI	Indianapolis	7 Mar 87
2.38		Sergey	Malchenko	RUS	2.11.63	1		Banská Bystrica	4 Sep 88
2.38		Dragutin	Topic ¶	YUG	12.3.71	1		Beograd	1 Aug 93
2.38i		Steve	Smith	GBR	29.3.73	2		Wuppertal	4 Feb 94
2.38i		Wolf-Hendrik	Beyer	GER	14.2.72	1		Weinheim	18 Mar 94
2.38		Troy	Kemp	BAH	18.6.66	1	Nik	Nice	12 Jul 95
		(20)							
2.38		Artur	Partyka	POL	25.7.69	1		Eberstadt	18 Aug 96
2.38i		Matt	Hemingway	USA	24.10.72	1	NC	Atlanta	4 Mar 00
2.38i		Yaroslav	Rybakov	RUS	22.11.80	1		Stockholm	15 Feb 05
2.38		Jacques	Freitag	RSA	11.6.82	1		Oudtshoorn	5 Mar 05
2.38		Andriy	Sokolovskyy	UKR	16.7.78	1	GGala	Roma	8 Jul 05
2.38i		Linus	Thörnblad	SWE	6.3.85	2	NC	Göteborg	25 Feb 07
2.37		Valeriy	Sereda	RUS	30.6.59	1		Rieti	2 Sep 84
2.37		Tom	McCants	USA	27.11.62	1	Owens	Columbus	8 May 88
2.37		Jerome	Carter	USA	25.3.63	2	Owens	Columbus	8 May 88
2.37		Sergey	Dymchenko	UKR	23.8.67	1		Kiyev	16 Sep 90
		(30)							
2.37i		Dalton	Grant	GBR	8.4.66	1	EI	Paris	13 Mar 94
2.37i		Jaroslav	Bába	CZE	2.9.84	2		Arnstadt	5 Feb 05
2.37		Andrey	Silnov	RUS	9.9.84	1	Herc	Monaco	20 Aug 06
2.36	WR	Gerd	Wessig	GDR	16.7.59	1	OG	Moskva	1 Aug 80
2.36		Sergey	Zasimovich	KZK	6.9.62	1		Tashkent	5 May 84
2.36		Eddy	Annys	BEL	15.12.58	1		Ghent	26 May 85
2.36i		Jim	Howard	USA	11.9.59	1		Albuquerque	25 Jan 86
2.36i		Jan	Zvara	CZE	12.2.63	1	vGDR	Jablonec	14 Feb 87
2.36i		Gerd	Nagel	FRG	22.10.57	1		Sulingen	17 Mar 89
2.36		Nick	Saunders	BER	14.9.63	1	CG	Auckland	1 Feb 90
		(40)							
2.36		Doug	Nordquist	USA	20.12.58	2	TAC	Norwalk	15 Jun 90
2.36		Georgi	Dakov	BUL	21.10.67	2	VD	Bruxelles	10 Aug 90
2.36		Lábros	Papakóstas	GRE	20.10.69	1	NC	Athína	21 Jun 92
2.36i		Steinar	Hoen	NOR	8.2.71	1		Balingen	12 Feb 94
2.36		Tim	Forsyth	AUS	17.8.73	1	NC	Melbourne	2 Mar 97
2.36		Sergey	Klyugin	RUS	24.3.74	1	WK	Zürich	12 Aug 98
2.36		Konstantin	Matusevich	ISR	25.2.71	1		Perth	5 Feb 00
2.36		Martin	Buss	GER	7.4.76	1	WCh	Edmonton	8 Aug 01
2.36		Aleksander	Walerianczyk	POL	1.9.82	1	EU23	Bydgoszcz	20 Jul 03
2.36		Michal	Bieniek	POL	17.5.84	1		Biala Podlaska	28 May 05
2.36i		Andrey	Tereshin	RUS	15.12.82	1	NC	Moskva	17 Feb 06
		(51)	100th man 2.33, 200th 2.30, 300th 2.28, 400th 2.27						

Best outdoor marks for athletes with indoor bests

2.39	Conway	1	USOF	Norman	30 Jul 89
2.38	Avdeyenko	2=	WCh	Roma	6 Sep 87
2.37	Thranhardt	2		Rieti	2 Sep 84
2.37	Smith	1	WJ	Seoul	20 Sep 92
2.36	Mögenburg	3		Eberstadt	10 Jun 84
2.36	Howard	1		Rehlingen	8 Jun 87
2.36	Zvara	1		Praha	23 Aug 87
2.36	Grant	4	WCh	Tokyo	1 Sep 91
2.36	Hoen	1		Oslo	1 Jul 97
2.36	Holm	1		Eberstadt	18 Jul 04
2.36	Bába	2=	GGala	Roma	8 Jul 05

Ancillary jumps – en route to final marks

2.40 Sotomayor 8 Sep 88 | 2.40 Sotomayor 29 Jul 89 | 2.40 Sotomayor 5 Jun 94

POLE VAULT

Mark	Wind	Name		Nat	Born	Pos	Meet	Venue	Date
6.15i		Sergey	Bubka	UKR	4.12.63	1		Donetsk	21 Feb 93
6.14i			Bubka			1		Liévin	13 Feb 93
6.14A	WR		Bubka			1		Sestriere	31 Jul 94
6.13i			Bubka			1		Berlin	21 Feb 92
6.13	WR		Bubka			1	TOTO	Tokyo	19 Sep 92
6.12i			Bubka			1	Mast	Grenoble	23 Mar 91
6.12	WR		Bubka			1		Padova	30 Aug 92
6.11i			Bubka			1		Donetsk	19 Mar 91
6.11	WR		Bubka			1		Dijon	13 Jun 92
6.10i			Bubka			1		San Sebastián	15 Mar 91
6.10	WR		Bubka			1	MAI	Malmö	5 Aug 91
6.09	WR		Bubka			1		Formia	8 Jul 91
6.08i			Bubka			1	NC	Volgograd	9 Feb 91
6.08	WR		Bubka			1	Znam	Moskva	9 Jun 91
6.07	WR		Bubka			1	Super	Shizuoka	6 May 91
6.06	WR		Bubka			1	Nik	Nice	10 Jul 88
6.05	WR		Bubka			1	PTS	Bratislava	9 Jun 88
6.05i			Bubka			1		Donetsk	17 Mar 90
6.05i			Bubka			1		Berlin	5 Mar 93
6.05			Bubka			1	GPF	London (CP)	10 Sep 93
6.05i			Bubka			1	Mast	Grenoble	6 Feb 94
6.05			Bubka			1	ISTAF	Berlin	30 Aug 94
6.05			Bubka			1	GPF	Fukuoka	13 Sep 97
6.05		Maksim	Tarasov	RUS	2.12.70	1	GP II	Athína	16 Jun 99
6.05		Dmitriy	Markov (ex BLR)	AUS	14.3.75	1	WCh	Edmonton	9 Aug 01
6.03	WR		Bubka			1	Ros	Praha	23 Jun 87
6.03i			Bubka			1		Osaka	11 Feb 89
6.03		Okkert	Brits	RSA	22.8.73	1	ASV	Köln	18 Aug 95
6.03		Jeff	Hartwig	USA	25.9.67	1		Jonesboro	14 Jun 00
6.02i		Rodion	Gataullin	RUS	23.11.65	1	NC	Gomel	4 Feb 89
6.02			Bubka			1	GP	Atlanta	18 May 96
6.02			Hartwig			1	NC	Eugene	27 Jun 99
6.02			Tarasov			1	WCh	Sevilla	26 Aug 99
6.02i			Hartwig			1	IHS	Sindelfingen	10 Mar 02
		(34/6)							
6.01		Igor	Trandenkov	RUS	17.8.66	1	NC	Sankt Peterburg	4 Jul 96
6.01		Tim	Mack	USA	15.9.72	1	WAF	Monaco	18 Sep 04
6.00		Tim	Lobinger	GER	3.9.72	1	ASV	Köln	24 Aug 97
6.00i		Jean	Galfione	FRA	9.6.71	1	WI	Maebashi	6 Mar 99
		(10)							
6.00i		Danny	Ecker	GER	21.7.77	1		Dortmund	11 Feb 01
6.00		Toby	Stevenson	USA	19.11.76	1eA	CalR	Modesto	8 May 04
6.00		Paul	Burgess	AUS	14.8.79	1		Perth	25 Feb 05
6.00		Brad	Walker	USA	21.6.81	1		Jockgrim	19 Jul 06

Most competitions at 6 metres or more: S Bubka 44, Hartwig 8, Gataullin & Tarasov 7, Brits 3, Markov & Lobinger 2

Mark	Wind	Name		Nat	Born	Pos	Meet	Venue	Date
5.98		Lawrence	Johnson	USA	7.5.74	1		Knoxville	25 May 96
5.97		Scott	Huffman	USA	30.11.64	1	NC	Knoxville	18 Jun 94
5.96		Joe	Dial	USA	26.10.62	1		Norman	18 Jun 87
5.96		Steve	Hooker	AUS	16.7.82	1	ISTAF	Berlin	3 Sep 06
5.95		Andrei	Tivontchik	GER	13.7.70	1	ASV	Köln	16 Aug 96
5.95		Michael	Stolle	GER	17.12.74	1	Herc	Monaco	18 Aug 00
		(20)							
5.95		Romain	Mesnil	FRA	13.6.77	1		Castres	6 Aug 03
5.94i		Philippe	Collet	FRA	13.12.63	1	Mast	Grenoble	10 Mar 90
5.93i		Billy	Olson	USA	19.7.58	1		East Rutherford	8 Feb 86
5.93i		Tye	Harvey	USA	25.9.74	2	NC	Atlanta	3 Mar 01
5.93		Aleksandr	Averbukh	ISR	1.10.74	1	GP	Madrid (C)	19 Jul 03
5.92		István	Bagyula	HUN	2.1.69	1	Gugl	Linz	5 Jul 91
5.92		Igor	Potapovich	KZK	6.9.67	2		Dijon	13 Jun 92
5.92		Dean	Starkey	USA	27.3.67	1	Banes	São Paulo	21 May 94
5.91	WR	Thierry	Vigneron	FRA	9.3.60	2	GGala	Roma	31 Aug 84
5.91i		Viktor	Ryzhenkov	UZB	25.8.66	2		San Sebastián	15 Mar 91
		(30)							
5.91A		Riaan	Botha	RSA	8.11.70	1		Pretoria	2 Apr 97
5.90		Pierre	Quinon	FRA	20.2.62	2	Nik	Nice	16 Jul 85
5.90i		Ferenc	Salbert	FRA	5.8.60	1	Mast	Grenoble	14 Mar 87
5.90		Miroslaw	Chmara	POL	9.5.64	1	BNP	Villeneuve d'Ascq	27 Jun 88
5.90i		Grigoriy	Yegorov	KZK	12.1.67	1		Yokohama	11 Mar 90

Mark	Wind	Name		Nat	Born	Pos	Meet	Venue	Date
5.90		Denis	Petushinskiy ¶	RUS	29.1.67	1	Znam	Moskva	13 Jun 93
5.90i		Pyotr	Bochkaryov	RUS	3.11.67	1	EI	Paris	12 Mar 94
5.90		Jacob	Davis	USA	29.4.78	1	Tex R	Austin	4 Apr 98
5.90		Viktor	Chistyakov	RUS/AUS	9.2.75	1		Salamanca	15 Jul 99
5.90		Pavel	Gerasimov	RUS	29.5.79	1		Rüdlingen	12 Aug 00
		(40)							
5.90		Nick	Hysong	USA	9.12.71	1	OG	Sydney	29 Sep 00
5.90		Giuseppe	Gibilisco	ITA	5.1.79	1	WCh	Saint-Denis	28 Aug 03
5.90i		Igor	Pavlov	RUS	18.7.79	1	EI	Madrid	5 Mar 05
5.90i		Björn	Otto	GER	16.10.77	1	NC	Leipzig	17 Feb 07
5.89		Kory	Tarpenning ¶	USA	27.2.62	1	OT	Indianapolis	21 Jul 88
5.87		Earl	Bell	USA	25.8.55	1		Jonesboro	14 May 88
5.87		Oscar	Janson	SWE	22.7.75	1		Somero	29 Jun 03
5.86		Vasiliy	Bubka	UKR	26.11.60	1		Chelyabinsk	16 Jul 88
5.86		Bill	Payne	USA	21.12.67	1	SWC	Houston	19 May 91
5.86		Valeri	Bukrejev	EST	15.6.64	1		Somero	3 Jul 94
5.86A		Pavel	Burlachenko	RUS	7.4.76	1		Pretoria	23 Mar 01
		(51)	100th man 5.80, 200th 5.70, 300th 5.61, 400th 5.56						

Best outdoor marks for athletes with lifetime bests indoors

6.00	Gataullin	Tokyo	16 Sep 89	5.90	Yegorov	2	WCh	Stuttgart	19 Aug 93
5.98	Galfione	Amiens	23 Jul 99	5.86	Bochkaryov	5	OG	Atlanta	2 Aug 96
5.93	Ecker	Ingolstadt	26 Jul 98	5.86	Otto	2	WAF	Stuttgart	23 Sep 07

Ancillary jump: 6.05i Bubka 13 Feb 93

Outdoors on built-up runway

Mark	Wind	Name		Nat	Born	Pos	Meet	Venue	Date
5.90		Pyotr	Bochkaryov	RUS	3.11.67	1		Karlskrona	28 Jun 96

Exhibition or Market Square competitions

Mark	Wind	Name		Nat	Born	Pos	Meet	Venue	Date
6.00		Jean	Galfione	FRA	9.6.71	1		Besançon	23 May 97
5.95		Viktor	Chistiakov	RUS/AUS	9.2.75	1		Chiari	8 Sep 99
5.86		Gennadiy	Sukharev	BLR	3.2.65	1		Bisceglie	23 Jul 91
5.86i		Larry	Jessee	USA	31.3.52	1		Newcastle	16 Oct 85

LONG JUMP

Mark	Wind	Name		Nat	Born	Pos	Meet	Venue	Date
8.95 WR	0.3	Mike	Powell	USA	10.11.63	1	WCh	Tokyo	30 Aug 91
8.90A WR	2.0	Bob	Beamon	USA	29.8.46	1	OG	Ciudad de México	18 Oct 68
8.87	-0.2	Carl	Lewis	USA	1.7.61	*	WCh	Tokyo	30 Aug 91
8.86A	1.9	Robert	Emmiyan	ARM	16.2.65	1		Tsakhkadzor	22 May 87
8.79	1.9		Lewis			1	TAC	Indianapolis	19 Jun 83
8.79i	-		Lewis			1		New York	27 Jan 84
8.76	1.0		Lewis			1	USOF	Indianapolis	24 Jul 82
8.76	0.8		Lewis			1	OT	Indianapolis	18 Jul 88
8.75	1.7		Lewis			1	PAm	Indianapolis	16 Aug 87
8.74	1.4	Larry	Myricks ¶	USA	10.3.56	2	OT	Indianapolis	18 Jul 88
8.74A	2.0	Erick	Walder	USA	5.11.71	1		El Paso	2 Apr 94
8.72	-0.2		Lewis			1	OG	Seoul	26 Sep 88
8.71	-0.4		Lewis			1	Pepsi	Los Angeles (Ww)	13 May 84
8.71	0.1		Lewis			1	OT	Los Angeles	19 Jun 84
8.71	1.9	Iván	Pedroso	CUB	17.12.72	1		Salamanca	18 Jul 95
8.70	0.8		Myricks			1	TAC	Houston	17 Jun 89
8.70	0.7		Powell			1		Salamanca	27 Jul 93
8.70	1.6		Pedroso			1	WCh	Göteborg	12 Aug 95
8.68	1.0		Lewis			Q	OG	Barcelona	5 Aug 92
8.68	1.6		Pedroso			1		Lisboa	17 Jun 95
8.67	0.4		Lewis			1	WCh	Roma	5 Sep 87
8.67	-0.7		Lewis			1	OG	Barcelona	6 Aug 92
8.66	0.8		Lewis			*	MSR	Walnut	26 Apr 87
8.66	1.0		Myricks			1		Tokyo	23 Sep 87
8.66	0.9		Powell			1	BNP	Villeneuve d'Ascq	29 Jun 90
8.66A	1.4		Lewis			*		Sestriere	31 Jul 94
8.66	0.3		Pedroso			1		Linz	22 Aug 95
8.66	1.6	Loúis	Tsátoumas	GRE	12.2.82	1		Kalamáta	2 Jun 07
8.65	0.2		Lewis			1	VD	Bruxelles	24 Aug 84
8.65	0.7		Lewis			1	TAC	San José	26 Jun 87
8.65	1.5		Pedroso			1	OD	Jena	3 Jun 00
		(31/8)							
8.63	0.5	Kareem	Streete-Thompson	CAY/USA	30.3.73	1	GP II	Linz	4 Jul 94
8.62	0.7	James	Beckford	JAM	9.1.75	1		Orlando	5 Apr 97
		(10)							
8.60	0.5	Dwight	Phillips	USA	1.10.77	1	GP	Linz	2 Aug 04
8.59i		Miguel	Pate	USA	13.6.79	1	NC	New York	1 Mar 02
8.56i	-	Yago	Lamela	ESP	24.7.77	2	WI	Maebashi	7 Mar 99

Mark	Wind	Name		Nat	Born	Pos	Meet	Venue	Date
8.57	0.0	Irving	Saladino	PAN	23.1.83	1	WCh	Osaka	30 Aug 07
8.54	0.9	Lutz	Dombrowski	GDR	25.6.59	1	OG	Moskva	28 Jul 80
8.53	1.2	Jaime	Jefferson	CUB	17.1.62	1	Barr	La Habana	12 May 90
8.52	0.7	Savanté	Stringfellow	USA	6.11.78	1	NC	Stanford	21 Jun 02
8.51	1.7	Roland	McGhee	USA	15.10.71	2		São Paulo	14 May 95
8.50	0.2	Llewellyn	Starks	USA	10.2.67	2		Rhede	7 Jul 91
8.49	2.0	Melvin	Lister	USA	29.8.77	1	SEC	Baton Rouge	13 May 00
		(20)							
8.49	0.6	Jai	Taurima	AUS	26.6.72	2	OG	Sydney	28 Sep 00
8.48	0.8	Joe	Greene	USA	17.2.67	3		São Paulo	14 May 95
8.48	0.6	Mohamed Salim	Al-Khuwalidi	KSA	19.6.81	1		Sotteville	2 Jul 06
8.47	1.9	Kevin	Dilworth	USA	14.2.74	1		Abilene	9 May 96
8.47	0.9	John	Moffitt	USA	12.12.80	2	OG	Athína	26 Aug 04
8.47	-0.2	Andrew	Howe	ITA	12.5.85	2	WCh	Osaka	30 Aug 07
8.46	1.2	Leonid	Voloshin	RUS	30.3.66	1	NC	Tallinn	5 Jul 88
8.46	1.6	Mike	Conley	USA	5.10.62	2		Springfield	4 May 96
8.46	1.8	Cheikh Tidiane	Touré	SEN	25.1.70	1		Bad Langensalza	15 Jun 97
8.45	2.0	Nenad	Stekic	YUG	7.3.51	1	PO	Montreal	25 Jul 75
		(30)							
8.44	1.7	Eric	Metcalf	USA	23.1.68	1	TAC	Tampa	17 Jun 88
8.43	0.8	Jason	Grimes	USA	10.9.59	•	TAC	Indianapolis	16 Jun 85
8.43	1.8	Giovanni	Evangelisti	ITA	11.9.61	1		San Giovanni Valdarno	16 May 87
8.43i	-	Stanislav	Tarasenko	RUS	23.7.66	1		Moskva	26 Jan 94
8.43	0.1	Luis Felipe	Méliz	CUB	11.8.79	2	OD	Jena	3 Jun 00
8.43	-0.2	Ignisious	Gaisah	GHA	20.6.83	2	GGala	Roma	14 Jul 06
8.41	1.5	Craig	Hepburn	BAH	10.12.69	1	NC	Nassau	17 Jun 93
8.41i	-	Kirill	Sosunov	RUS	1.11.75	2	WI	Paris (B)	8 Mar 97
8.40	1.4	Douglas	de Souza	BRA	6.8.72	1		São Paulo	15 Feb 95
8.40	0.4	Robert	Howard	USA	26.11.75	1	SEC	Auburn	17 May 97
		(40)							
8.40	2.0	Gregor	Cankar	SLO	25.1.75	1		Celje	18 May 97
8.40	0.0		Lao Jianfeng	CHN	24.5.75	1	NC	Zhaoqing	28 May 97
8.39	0.8	Dion	Bentley	USA	26.8.71	2	NCAA	New Orleans	3 Jun 93
8.39	1.7	Khotso	Mokoena	RSA	6.3.85	1		Lapinlahti	16 Jul 06
8.39	-0.4	Ahmad Fayez	Marzouk	KSA	6.9.79	1		Lemgo	13 Aug 06
8.38	0.4	Konstantin	Semykin	RUS	26.5.60	1	Drz	Moskva	17 Aug 84
8.38	1.1		Huang Geng	CHN	10.7.70	1	NC	Taiyuan	18 May 95
8.38i	–	Vitaliy	Shkurlatov	RUS	25.5.79	1		Samara	30 Jan 00
8.37A	0.4	Leroy	Burrell	USA	21.2.67	2	NCAA	Provo	2 Jun 89
8.37	1.5	Bogdan	Tudor	ROM	1.2.70	2		Bad Cannstatt	9 Jul 95
8.37i		Joan Lino	Martínez	ESP	17.1.78	1	EI	Madrid	6 Mar 05
		(51)	100th man 8.29, 200th 8.21, 300th 8.14						
Irregular conditions: 8.39	1.2	Joan	Lino Martínez	CUB	17.1.78	1		La Habana	5 Feb 99
Wind-assisted marks performances to 8.68, performers to 8.40									
8.99A	4.4	Mike	Powell	USA	10.11.63	1		Sestriere	21 Jul 92
8.96A	1.2+	Iván	Pedroso	CUB	17.12.72	1		Sestriere	29 Jul 95
8.95A	3.9		Powell			1		Sestriere	31 Jul 94
8.91	2.9	Carl	Lewis	USA	1.7.61	2	WCh	Tokyo	30 Aug 91
8.90	3.7		Powell			1	S&W	Modesto	16 May 92
8.79	3.0		Pedroso			1	Barr	La Habana	21 May 92
8.77	3.9		Lewis			1	Pepsi	Los Angeles (Ww)	18 May 85
8.77	3.4		Lewis			1	MSR	Walnut	26 Apr 87
8.73	4.6		Lewis			Q	TAC	Sacramento	19 Jun 81
8.73	3.2		Lewis			Q	TAC	Indianapolis	17 Jun 83
8.73A	2.6		Powell			1		Sestriere	31 Jul 91
8.73	4.8		Pedroso			1		Madrid	20 Jun 95
8.72	2.2		Lewis			1	NYG	New York	24 May 92
8.72A	3.9		Lewis			2		Sestriere	31 Jul 94
8.70	2.5		Pedroso			1		Padova	16 Jul 95
8.68	4.1		Powell			1	NC	Knoxville	18 Jun 94
8.68	4.9	James	Beckford	JAM	9.1.75	1	JUCO	Odessa, Tx	19 May 95
8.66A	4.0	Joe	Greene	USA	17.2.67	2		Sestriere	21 Jul 92
8.65	3.3	Irving	Saladino	PAN	23.1.83	1	SGP	Athína	3 Jul 06
8.64	3.5	Kareem	Streete-Thompson	CAY/USA	30.3.73	2	NC	Knoxville	18 Jun 94
8.63	3.9	Mike	Conley	USA	5.10.62	2	TAC	Eugene	20 Jun 86
8.57	5.2	Jason	Grimes	USA	10.9.59	1	vFRG,AFR	Durham	27 Jun 82
8.53	4.9	Kevin	Dilworth	USA	14.2.74	1		Fort-de-France	27 Apr 02
8.51	3.7	Ignisious	Gaisah	GHA	20.6.83	1	AfCh	Bambous/MRI	9 Aug 06
8.49	2.6	Ralph	Boston	USA	9.5.39	1	FOT	Los Angeles	12 Sep 64
8.49	4.5	Stanislav	Tarasenko	RUS	23.7.66	2		Madrid	20 Jun 95

Mark	Wind	Name		Nat	Born	Pos	Meet	Venue	Date
8.48	2.8	Kirill	Sosunov	RUS	1.11.75	1		Oristano	18 Sep 95
8.48	3.4	Peter	Burge	AUS	3.7.74	1		Gold Coast (RB)	10 Sep 00
8.46	3.4	Randy	Williams	USA	23.8.53	1		Eugene	18 May 73
8.46		Vernon	George	USA	6.10.64	1		Houston	21 May 89
8.44		Keith	Talley	USA	28.1.64	Q		Odessa, Tx	16 May 85
8.42		Anthony	Bailous	USA	6.4.65	Q		Odessa, Tx	16 May 85
8.42A	4.5	Milan	Gombala	CZE	29.1.68	3		Sestriere	21 Jul 92
8.41	4.3	Shamil	Abbyasov	KGZ	16.4.57	2	vUSA	Indianapolis	3 Jul 82
8.41	3.3	Andre	Ester	USA	27.4.65	1	TexR	Austin	4 Apr 87
8.41A	3.2	Nelson	Ferreira Jr	BRA	1.1.73	1	IbAm	Medellín	10 May 96
8.41	2.6	Hussein	Al-Sabee	KSA	14.11.79	1		Carson	22 May 04
8.41	3.8	Tommy	Evilä	FIN	6.4.80	1	v SWE	Göteborg	8 Sep 07
8.40	4.3	Henry	Hines	USA	12.2.49	1	CalR	Modesto	27 May 72
8.40	2.1	Anthuan	Maybank	USA	30.12.69	1	DrakeR	Des Moines	24 Apr 93
8.40	3.4	Konstadínos	Koukodímos	GRE	14.9.69	1	ECp I	Valencia	11 Jun 94
Exhibition: 8.46		Yuriy	Naumkin	RUS	4.11.68	1		Iglesias	6 Sep 96

Best outdoors

8.56 1.3 Lamela 1 Torino 24 Jun 99   8.38 1.1 Sosunov 1 ECp Sankt-Peterburg 27 Jun 98

8.46A 0.0 Pate 1 Cd. de México 3 May 03 and 8.45 1.5 2 NC Stanford 21 Jun 02, 8.48w 5.6 1 Fort Worth 21 Apr 01

Ancillary marks – other marks during series (to 8.66/8.68)

Mark	Wind	Name	Date	Mark	Wind	Name	Date	Mark	Wind	Name	Date
8.84	1.7	Lewis	30 Aug 91	8.89Aw	2.4	Pedroso	29 Jul 95	8.75Aw	3.4	Powell	21 Jul 92
8.71	0.6	Lewis	19 Jun 83	8.84Aw	3.8	Powell	21 Jul 92	8.73w	2.4	Lewis	18 May 85
8.68	0.3	Lewis	18 Jul 88	8.83w	2.3	Lewis	30 Aug 91	8.73w		Powell	16 May 92
8.68	0.0	Lewis	30 Aug 91	8.80Aw	4.0	Powell	21 Jul 92	8.71Aw		Powell	31 Jul 91
8.67	-0.2	Lewis	5 Sep 87	8.78Aw		Powell	21 Jul 92	8.68w	3.7	Lewis	16 Aug 87
8.66		Lewis	26 Apr 87	8.75w	2.1	Lewis	16 Aug 87	8.68w	4.1	Lewis	16 Aug 87

TRIPLE JUMP

Mark	Wind	Name		Nat	Born	Pos	Meet	Venue	Date
18.29 WR	1.3	Jonathan	Edwards	GBR	10.5.66	1	WCh	Göteborg	7 Aug 95
18.09	-0.4	Kenny	Harrison	USA	13.2.65	1	OG	Atlanta	27 Jul 96
18.01	0.4		Edwards			1	Bisl	Oslo	9 Jul 98
18.00	1.3		Edwards			1	McD	London (CP)	27 Aug 95
17.99	0.5		Edwards			1	EC	Budapest	23 Aug 98
17.98 WR	1.8		Edwards			1		Salamanca	18 Jul 95
17.97 WR	1.5	Willie	Banks	USA	11.3.56	1	TAC	Indianapolis	16 Jun 85
17.93	1.6		Harrison			1	DNG	Stockholm	2 Jul 90
17.92	1.6	Khristo	Markov	BUL	27.1.65	1	WCh	Roma	31 Aug 87
17.92	1.9	James	Beckford	JAM	9.1.75	1	JUCO	Odessa, Tex	20 May 95
17.92	0.7		Edwards			1	WCh	Edmonton	6 Aug 01
17.90	1.0	Vladimir	Inozemtsev	UKR	25.5.64	1	PTS	Bratislava	20 Jun 90
17.90	0.4	Jadel	Gregório	BRA	16.9.80	1	GP	Belém	20 May 07
17.89A WR	0.0	João Carlos	de Oliveira	BRA	28.5.54	1	PAm	Ciudad de México	15 Oct 75
17.88	0.9		Edwards			2	OG	Atlanta	27 Jul 96
17.87	1.7	Mike	Conley	USA	5.10.62	1	TAC	San José	27 Jun 87
17.86	1.3	Charles	Simpkins (10)	USA	19.10.63	1	WUG	Kobe	2 Sep 85
17.86	0.3		Conley			1	WCh	Stuttgart	16 Aug 93
17.86	0.7		Edwards			1	CG	Manchester	28 Jul 02
17.85	0.9	Yoelbi	Quesada	CUB	4.8.73	1	WCh	Athína	8 Aug 97
17.84	0.7		Conley			1		Bad Cannstatt	4 Jul 93
17.83i	-	Aliecer	Urrutia	CUB	22.9.74	1		Sindelfingen	1 Mar 97
17.83i		Christian	Olsson	SWE	25.1.80	1	WI	Budapest	7 Mar 04
17.82	1.6		Edwards			1	WG	Helsinki	25 Jun 96
17.81	2.0		Markov			1	Nar	Sofia	31 May 87
17.81	1.0	Marian	Oprea	ROM	6.6.82	1	Athl	Lausanne	5 Jul 05
17.80	0.6		Markov			1	BGP	Budapest	11 Aug 86
17.80i			Olsson			1		Göteborg	5 Mar 02
17.79	-0.8		Harrison			1	OD	Berlin	4 Jul 90
17.79	-0.7		Edwards			1	WK	Zürich	14 Aug 96
17.79	1.4		Olsson			1	OG	Athína	22 Aug 04
		(31/14)							
17.78	1.0	Nikolay	Musiyenko	UKR	16.12.59	1	Znam	Leningrad	7 Jun 86
17.78	0.6	Lázaro	Betancourt ¶	CUB	18.3.63	1	Barr	La Habana	15 Jun 86
17.78	0.8	Melvin	Lister	USA	29.8.77	1	NC/OT	Sacramento	17 Jul 04
17.77	1.0	Aleksandr	Kovalenko	RUS	8.5.63	1	NC	Bryansk	18 Jul 87
17.77i	-	Leonid	Voloshin	RUS	30.3.66	1		Grenoble	6 Feb 94
17.75	0.3	Oleg	Protsenko	RUS	11.8.63	1	Znam	Moskva	10 Jun 90
		(20)							
17.74	1.4	Nelson	Évora	POR	20.4.84	1	WCh	Osaka	27 Aug 07
17.73i		Walter	Davis	USA	2.7.79	1	WI	Moskva	12 Mar 06
17.72i		Brian	Wellman	BER	8.9.67	1	WI	Barcelona	12 Mar 95

Mark	Wind	Name		Nat	Born	Pos	Meet	Venue	Date
17.69	1.5	Igor	Lapshin	BLR	8.8.63	1		Stayki	31 Jul 88
17.68	1.2	Phillips	Idowu	GBR	30.12.78	2	CG	Manchester	28 Jul 02
17.66	1.7	Ralf	Jaros	GER	13.12.65	1	ECp	Frankfurt-am-Main	30 Jun 91
17.68	0.4	Danil	Burkenya	RUS	20.7.78	1	NC	Tula	31 Jul 04
17.65	1.0	Aleksandr	Yakovlev	UKR	8.9.57	1	Znam	Moskva	6 Jun 87
17.65	0.8	Denis	Kapustin	RUS	5.10.70	2	Bisl	Oslo	9 Jul 98
17.64	1.4	Nathan	Douglas	GBR	4.12.82	1	NC	Manchester (SC)	10 Jul 05
		(30)							
17.63	0.9	Kenta	Bell	USA	16.3.77	1c2	MSR	Walnut	21 Apr 02
17.63	1.0	Yoandri	Betanzos	CUB	15.2.82	1		La Habana	4 Feb 06
17.62i		Yoel	García	CUB	25.11.73	2		Sindelfingen	1 Mar 97
17.60	0.6	Vladimir	Plekhanov	RUS	11.4.58	2	NC	Leningrad	4 Aug 85
17.60	1.9	Fabrizio	Donato	ITA	14.8.76	1		Milano	7 Jun 00
17.59i	-	Pierre	Camara	FRA	10.9.65	1	WI	Toronto	13 Mar 93
17.59	0.3	Vasiliy	Sokov	RUS	7.4.68	1	NC	Moskva	19 Jun 93
17.59	0.8	Charles	Friedek	GER	26.8.71	1		Hamburg	23 Jul 97
17.58	1.5	Oleg	Sakirkin	KZK	23.1.66	2	NC	Gorkiy	23 Jul 89
17.58	1.6	Aarik	Wilson	USA	25.10.82	1	LGP	London (CP)	3 Aug 07
		(40)							
17.57A	0.0	Keith	Connor	GBR	16.9.57	1	NCAA	Provo	5 Jun 82
17.57	0.2	Dmitriy	Valyukevich/Valukevic	BLR/SVK	31.5.81	1	EU23	Bydgoszcz	19 Jul 03
17.56	1.9	Maris	Bruziks	LAT	25.8.62	1		Riga	3 Sep 88
17.55	0.3	Vasiliy	Grishchenkov	RUS	23.1.58	1	Spart	Moskva	19 Jun 83
17.55	0.9	Serge	Hélan	FRA	24.2.64	2	EC	Helsinki	13 Aug 94
17.55	0.8	Dimítrios	Tsiámis	GRE	12.1.82	1	ECp-1B	Thessaloníki	18 Jun 06
17.53	1.0	Aleksandr	Beskrovniy	RUS	5.4.60	2	Spart	Moskva	19 Jun 83
17.53	1.6	Zdzislaw	Hoffmann	POL	27.8.59	1		Madrid	4 Jun 85
17.53	1.0	Gennadiy	Valyukevich	BLR	1.6.58	1		Erfurt	1 Jun 86
17.53	1.6	Al	Joyner	USA	19.1.60	Q	TAC	San José	26 Jun 87
17.53	0.9	Milán	Mikulás	CZE	1.4.63	1	NC	Praha	17 Jul 88
17.53	1.9	Oleg	Denishchik	BLR	10.11.69	2	NC	Kiyev	12 Jul 91
17.53	0.5	Aleksandr	Glavatskiy	BLR	2.5.70	2	WK	Zürich	12 Aug 98
		(53)	100th man 17.31, 200th 17.09, 300th 16.95						

Wind-assisted marks – performances to 17.81, performers to 17.55

Mark	Wind	Name		Nat	Born	Pos	Meet	Venue	Date
18.43	2.4	Jonathan	Edwards	GBR	10.5.66	1	ECp	Villeneuve d'Ascq	25 Jun 95
18.20	5.2	Willie	Banks	USA	11.3.56	1	OT	Indianapolis	16 Jul 88
18.17	2.1	Mike	Conley	USA	5.10.62	1	OG	Barcelona	3 Aug 92
18.08	2.5		Edwards			1	BUPA	Sheffield	23 Jul 95
18.03	2.9		Edwards			1	GhG	Gateshead	2 Jul 95
18.01	3.7		Harrison			1	NC	Atlanta	15 Jun 96
17.97	7.5	Yoelbi	Quesada	CUB	4.8.73	1		Madrid	20 Jun 95
17.93	5.2	Charles	Simpkins	USA	19.10.63	2	OT	Indianapolis	16 Jul 88
17.92	3.4	Christian	Olsson	SWE	25.1.80	1	GP	Gateshead	13 Jul 03
17.91	3.2		Simpkins			1	TAC	Eugene	21 Jun 86
17.86	3.9		Simpkins			1	OT	New Orleans	21 Jun 92
17.86	5.7	Denis	Kapustin	RUS	5.10.70	1		Sevilla	5 Jun 94
17.84	2.3		Conley			2	TAC	Eugene	21 Jun 86
17.82	3.6		Banks			1	Jen	San José	31 May 86
17.81	4.6	Keith	Connor	GBR	16.9.57	1	CG	Brisbane	9 Oct 82
17.76A	2.2	Kenta	Bell	USA	16.3.77	1		El Paso	10 Apr 04
17.75		Gennadiy	Valyukevich	BLR	1.6.58	1		Uzhgorod	27 Apr 86
17.75	7.1	Brian	Wellman	BER	8.9.67	2		Madrid	20 Jun 95
17.73	4.1	Vasiliy	Sokov	RUS	7.4.68	1		Riga	3 Jun 89
17.67	5.4	Yoandri	Betanzos	CUB	15.2.82	1		Bilbao	1 Jul 06
17.63	4.3	Robert	Cannon	USA	9.7.58	3	OT	Indianapolis	16 Jul 88
17.59	2.1	Jerome	Romain	DMN	12.6.71	3	WCh	Göteborg	7 Aug 95
17.58	5.2	Al	Joyner	USA	19.1.60	5	OT	Indianapolis	16 Jul 88
17.56	3.7	Ron	Livers	USA	20.7.55	1	AAU	Walnut	17 Jun 79
17.55	3.6	Zdzislaw	Hoffmann	POL	27.8.59	1	Kuso	Warszawa	9 Jun 84
17.55	2.5	Leevan	Sands	BAH	16.8.81	2	LGP	London (CP)	3 Aug 07

Best outdoor marks for athletes with indoor bests

Mark	Wind	Name	Pos	Meet	Venue	Date
17.79	1.4	Olsson	1	OG	Athína	22 Aug 04
17.75	1.0	Voloshin	2	WCh	Tokyo	26 Aug 91
17.71	-0.7	Davis	1	NC	Indianapolis	25 Jun 06
17.70	1.7	Urrutia	1	GP II	Sevilla	6 Jun 96
17.62A	0.1	Wellman	1		El Paso	15 Apr 95

Ancillary marks – other marks during series (to 17.78/17.84w)

Mark	Wind	Name	Date
17.99	0.1	Harrison	27 Jul 96
18.39w	3.7	Edwards	25 Jun 95
18.06w	4.9	Banks	16 Jul 88
17.90w	2.5	Edwards	25 Jun 95
17.84w	2.1	Edwards	23 Aug 98

A mark made at an altitude of 1000m or higher, i – indoors, Q – in qualifying competition, WR – world record

SHOT

Mark	Wind	Name		Nat	Born	Pos	Meet	Venue	Date
23.12	WR	Randy	Barnes ¶	USA	16.6.66	1		Los Angeles (Ww)	20 May 90
23.10			Barnes			1	Jen	San José	26 May 90
23.06	WR	Ulf	Timmermann	GDR	1.11.62	1	Veniz	Haniá	22 May 88
22.91	WR	Alessandro	Andrei	ITA	3.1.59	1		Viareggio	12 Aug 87
22.86		Brian	Oldfield	USA	1.6.45	1	ITA	El Paso	10 May 75
22.75		Werner	Günthör	SUI	1.6.61	1		Bern	23 Aug 88
22.67		Kevin	Toth ¶	USA	29.12.67	1	Kans R	Lawrence	19 Apr 03
22.66i			Barnes			1	Sunkist	Los Angeles	20 Jan 89
22.64	WR	Udo	Beyer	GDR	9.8.55	1		Berlin	20 Aug 86
22.62	WR		Timmermann			1		Berlin	22 Sep 85
22.61			Timmermann			1		Potsdam	8 Sep 88
22.60			Timmermann			1	vURS	Tallinn	21 Jun 86
22.56			Timmermann			1		Berlin	13 Sep 88
22.55i			Timmermann			1	NC	Senftenberg	11 Feb 89
22.54		Christian	Cantwell	USA	30.9.80	1	GP II	Gresham	5 Jun 04
22.52		John	Brenner	USA	4.1.61	1	MSR	Walnut	26 Apr 87
22.51			Timmermann			1		Erfurt	1 Jun 86
22.51		Adam	Nelson (10)	USA	7.7.75	1		Gresham	18 May 02
22.47			Timmermann			1		Dresden	17 Aug 86
22.47			Günthör			1	WG	Helsinki	2 Jul 87
22.47			Timmermann			1	OG	Seoul	23 Sep 88
22.45			Oldfield			1	ITA	El Paso	22 May 76
22.45			Cantwell			1	GP	Gateshead	11 Jun 06
22.43			Günthör			1	v3-N	Lüdenscheid	18 Jun 87
22.43		Reese	Hoffa	USA	8.10.77	1	LGP	London (CP)	3 Aug 07
22.42			Barnes			1	WK	Zürich	17 Aug 88
22.40			Barnes			1		Rüdlingen	13 Jul 96
22.39			Barnes			2	OG	Seoul	23 Sep 88
22.36 @			Timmermann			1		Athína	16 May 88
22.35			Cantwell			1		Carson	22 May 04
		(30/11)	@ competitive meeting but unsanctioned by GDR federation						
22.24		Sergey	Smirnov	RUS	17.9.60	2	vGDR	Tallinn	21 Jun 86
22.20		John	Godina	USA	31.5.72	1		Carson	22 May 05
22.10		Sergey	Gavryushin	RUS	27.6.59	1		Tbilisi	31 Aug 86
22.09		Sergey	Kasnauskas	BLR	20.4.61	1		Stayki	23 Aug 84
22.09i		Mika	Halvari	FIN	13.2.70	1		Tampere	7 Feb 00
22.02i		George	Woods	USA	11.2.43	1	LAT	Inglewood	8 Feb 74
22.02		Dave	Laut	USA	21.12.56	1		Koblenz	25 Aug 82
22.00	WR	Aleksandr	Baryshnikov	RUS	11.11.48	1	vFRA	Colombes	10 Jul 76
21.98		Gregg	Tafralis ¶	USA	9.4.58	1		Los Gatos	13 Jun 92
		(20)							
21.97		Janus	Robberts	RSA	10.3.79	1	NCAA	Eugene	2 Jun 01
21.96		Mikhail	Kostin	RUS	10.5.59	1		Vitebsk	20 Jul 86
21.93		Remigius	Machura ¶	CZE	3.7.60	1		Praha	23 Aug 87
21.92		Carl	Myerscough ¶	GBR	21.10.79	1	NCAA	Sacramento	13 Jun 03
21.87		C.J.	Hunter ¶	USA	14.12.68	2	NC	Sacramento	15 Jul 00
21.85	WR	Terry	Albritton	USA	14.1.55	1		Honolulu	21 Feb 76
21.83i		Aleksandr	Bagach ¶	UKR	21.11.66	1		Brovary	21 Feb 99
21.82	WR	Al	Feuerbach	USA	14.1.48	1		San José	5 May 73
21.82		Andy	Bloom	USA	11.8.73	1	GPF	Doha	5 Oct 00
21.81		Yuriy	Belonog	UKR	9.3.74	1	NC	Kiev	3 Jul 03
		(30)							
21.78	WR	Randy	Matson	USA	5.3.45	1		College Station	22 Apr 67
21.77i		Mike	Stulce ¶	USA	21.7.69	1	v GBR	Birmingham	13 Feb 93
21.77		Dragan	Peric	YUG	8.5.64	1		Bar	25 Apr 98
21.76		Mike	Carter	USA	29.10.60	2	NCAA	Eugene	2 Jun 84
21.74		Janis	Bojars	LAT	12.5.56	1		Riga	14 Jul 84
21.73		Augie	Wolf ¶	USA	3.9.61	1		Leverkusen	12 Apr 84
21.69		Reijo	Ståhlberg	FIN	21.9.52	1	WCR	Fresno	5 May 79
21.69		Andrey	Mikhnevich ¶	BLR	12.7.76	1	WCh	Saint-Denis	23 Aug 03
21.68		Geoff	Capes	GBR	23.8.49	1	4-N	Cwmbrân	18 May 80
21.68		Edward	Sarul	POL	16.11.58	1		Sopot	31 Jul 83
		(40)							
21.67		Hartmut	Briesenick	GDR	17.3.49	1		Potsdam	1 Sep 73
21.63i		Joachim	Olsen	DEN	31.5.77	1		Tallinn	25 Feb 04
21.62		Rutger	Smith	NED	9.7.81	1		Leiden	10 Jun 06
21.61		Kevin	Akins	USA	27.1.60	1	S&W	Modesto	14 May 83
21.60		Jim	Doehring ¶	USA	27.1.62	2		Los Gatos	13 Jun 92

Mark Wind	Name		Nat	Born	Pos	Meet	Venue	Date
21.59	Dan	Taylor	USA	12.5.82	2	Reebok	New York (RI)	3 Jun 06
21.58	Vladimir	Kiselyov	UKR	1.1.57	3	Drz	Moskva	17 Aug 84
21.57i	Mikulás	Konopka ¶	SVK	23.1.79	1	EI	Birmingham	2 Mar 07
21.53	Yevgeniy	Mironov ¶	RUS	1.11.49	1	NC	Kiyev	24 Jun 76
21.51	Ralf	Reichenbach	FRG	31.7.50	1	ISTAF	Berlin	8 Aug 80

(50) 100th man 21.01, 200th 20.55, 300th 20.13

Not recognised by GDR authorities

22.11	Rolf	Oesterreich	GDR	24.8.49	1		Zschopau	12 Sep 76

Drugs disqualification

22.84		Barnes			1		Malmö	7 Aug 90
21.82	Mike	Stulce ¶	USA	21.7.69	1		Brenham	9 May 90

Best outdoor marks for athletes with lifetime bests indoors

21.70	Stulce ¶	1	OG	Barcelona	31 Jul 92	21.57	Olsen	2	NCAA	Baton Rouge	1 Jun 02
21.63	Woods	2	CalR	Modesto	22 May 76	21.50	Halvari	1		Hämeenkyrö	9 Jul 95

Ancillary marks – other marks during series (to 22.42)

22.84 WR	Andrei	12 Aug 87	22.72 WR	Andrei	12 Aug 87	22.55	Barnes	20 May 90
22.76	Barnes	20 May 90	22.70	Günthör	23 Aug 88	22.49	Nelson	18 May 02
22.74	Andrei	12 Aug 87	22.58	Beyer	20 Aug 86	22.45	Timmermann	22 May 88
						22.44	Barnes	20 May 90

DISCUS

Mark Wind	Name		Nat	Born	Pos	Meet	Venue	Date
74.08 WR	Jürgen	Schult	GDR	11.5.60	1		Neubrandenburg	6 Jun 86
73.88	Virgilijus	Alekna	LTU	13.2.72	1	NC	Kaunas	3 Aug 00
73.38	Gerd	Kanter	EST	6.5.79	1		Helsingborg	4 Sep 06
72.02		Kanter			1eA		Salinas	3 May 07
71.86 WR	Yuriy	Dumchev	RUS	5.8.58	1		Moskva	29 May 83
71.70	Róbert	Fazekas ¶	HUN	18.8.75	1		Szombathely	14 Jul 02
71.56		Alekna			1		Kaunas	25 Jul 07
71.50	Lars	Riedel	GER	28.6.67	1		Wiesbaden	3 May 97
71.32	Ben	Plucknett ¶	USA	13.4.54	1	Pre	Eugene	4 Jun 83
71.26	John	Powell	USA	25.6.47	1	TAC	San José	9 Jun 84
71.26	Rickard	Bruch	SWE	2.7.46	1		Malmö	15 Nov 84
71.26	Imrich	Bugár (10)	CZE	14.4.55	1	Jen	San José	25 May 85
71.25		Fazekas			1	WCp	Madrid (C)	21 Sep 02
71.18	Art	Burns	USA	19.7.54	1		San José	19 Jul 83
71.16 WR	Wolfgang	Schmidt	GDR	16.1.54	1		Berlin	9 Aug 78
71.14		Plucknett			1		Berkeley	12 Jun 83
71.14	Anthony	Washington	USA	16.1.66	1eA		Salinas	22 May 96
71.12		Alekna			1	WK	Zürich	11 Aug 00
71.08		Alekna			1		Réthimno	21 Jul 06
71.06	Luis Mariano	Delís ¶	CUB	12.12.57	1	Barr	La Habana	21 May 83
71.06		Riedel			1	WK	Zürich	14 Aug 96
71.00		Bruch			1		Malmö	14 Oct 84
70.99		Alekna			1		Stellenbosch	30 Mar 01
70.98	Mac	Wilkins	USA	15.11.50	1	WG	Helsinki	9 Jul 80
70.98		Burns			1	Pre	Eugene	21 Jul 84
70.97		Alekna			1		Réthimno	23 Jun 04
70.93		Kanter			1		Helsingborg	28 Jun 07
70.92		Schmidt	FRG		1		Norden	9 Sep 89
70.92		Kanter			2		Kaunas	25 Jul 07
70.86 WR		Wilkins			1		San José	1 May 76

(30/15)

Mark Wind	Name		Nat	Born	Pos	Meet	Venue	Date
70.82	Aleksander	Tammert	EST	2.2.73	1		Denton	15 Apr 06
70.54	Dmitriy	Shevchenko ¶	RUS	13.5.68	1		Krasnodar	7 May 02
70.38 WRU	Jay	Silvester	USA	27.8.37	1		Lancaster	16 May 71
70.32	Frantz	Kruger	RSA/FIN	22.5.75	1		Salon-de-Provence	26 May 02
70.06	Romas	Ubartas ¶	LIT	26.5.60	1		Smalininkay	8 May 88

(20)

Mark Wind	Name		Nat	Born	Pos	Meet	Venue	Date
70.00	Juan	Martínez ¶	CUB	17.5.58	2	Barr	La Habana	21 May 83
69.95	Zoltán	Kövágó	HUN	10.4.79	1		Salon-de-Provence	25 May 06
69.91	John	Godina	USA	31.5.72	1		Salinas	19 May 98
69.70	Géjza	Valent	CZE	3.10.53	2		Nitra	26 Aug 84
69.62	Knut	Hjeltnes ¶	NOR	8.12.51	2	Jen	San José	25 May 85
69.62	Timo	Tompuri	FIN	9.6.69	1		Helsingborg	8 Jul 01
69.46	Al	Oerter	USA	19.9.36	1	TFA	Wichita	31 May 80
69.44	Georgiy	Kolnootchenko	BLR	7.5.59	1	vUSA	Indianapolis	3 Jul 82
69.40	Art	Swarts ¶	USA	14.2.45	1		Scotch Plains	8 Dec 79
69.36	Mike	Buncic	USA	25.7.62	1		Fresno	6 Apr 91

(30)

Mark Wind	Name		Nat	Born	Pos	Meet	Venue	Date
69.28	Vladimir	Dubrovshchik	BLR	7.1.72	1	NC	Stayki	3 Jun 00

Mark	Wind	Name		Nat	Born	Pos	Meet	Venue	Date
69.26		Ken	Stadel	USA	19.2.52	2	AAU	Walnut	16 Jun 79
68.94		Adam	Setliff	USA	15.12.69	1		Atascadero	25 Jul 01
68.91		Ian	Waltz	USA	15.4.77	1		Salinas	24 May 06
68.90		Jean-Claude	Retel	FRA	11.2.68	1		Salon-de-Provence	17 Jul 02
68.88		Vladimir	Zinchenko	UKR	25.7.59	1		Dnepropetrovsk	16 Jul 88
68.64		Dmitriy	Kovtsun ¶	UKR	29.9.55	1		Riga	6 Jul 84
68.58		Attila	Horváth	HUN	28.7.67	1		Budapest	24 Jun 94
68.52		Igor	Duginyets	UKR	20.5.56	1	NC	Kiyev	21 Aug 82
68.50		Armin	Lemme	GDR	28.10.55	1	vUSA	Karl-Marx-Stadt	10 Jul 82
		(40)							
68.48	WR	John	van Reenen	RSA	26.3.47	1		Stellenbosch	14 Mar 75
68.44		Vaclovas	Kidykas	LIT	17.10.61	1		Sochi	1 Jun 88
68.37		Jarred	Rome	USA	21.12.76	1		Wailuku	16 Apr 07
68.30		Stefan	Fernholm	SWE	2.7.59	1		Västerås	15 Jul 87
68.26		Mario	Pestano	ESP	8.4.78	2	GP	Athína	2 Jul 07
68.12		Markku	Tuokko ¶	FIN	24.6.51	1	WCR	Fresno	5 May 79
68.12		Iosif	Nagy	ROM	20.11.46	2		Zaragoza	22 May 83
68.12		Erik	de Bruin ¶	NED	25.5.63	1		Sneek	1 Apr 91
68.08		Hein-Direck	Neu ¶	FRG	13.2.44	1		Bremerhaven	27 May 77
68.00		Svein Inge	Valvik	NOR	20.9.56	1		Juarez	31 May 82
		(50)	100th man 66.62, 200th 64.94, 300th 63.54						

Subsequent to or at drugs disqualification ! recognised as US record

Mark	Wind	Name		Nat	Born	Pos	Meet	Venue	Date
72.34!		Ben	Plucknett ¶	USA	13.4.54	(1)	DNG	Stockholm	7 Jul 81
71.20			Plucknett			(1)	CalR	Modesto	16 May 81
70.93			Fazekas			(1)	OG	Athína	23 Aug 04
70.84		Kamy	Keshmiri ¶	USA	23.1.69	(1)		Salinas	27 May 92

Sloping ground

Mark	Wind	Name		Nat	Born	Pos	Meet	Venue	Date
72.08		John	Powell	USA	25.6.47	1		Klagshamn	11 Sep 87
69.80		Stefan	Fernholm	SWE	2.7.59	1		Klagshamn	13 Aug 87
69.44		Adam	Setliff	USA	15.12.69	1		La Jolla	21 Jul 01
68.46		Andy	Bloom	USA	11.8.73	2cA		La Jolla	25 Mar 00

Ancillary marks – other marks during series (to 70.90)

72.35 Alekna 3 Aug 00 72.30 Kanter 4 Sep 06 71.08 Plucknett 4 Jun 83

HAMMER

Mark	Wind	Name		Nat	Born	Pos	Meet	Venue	Date
86.74	WR	Yuriy	Sedykh	RUS	11.6.55	1	EC	Stuttgart	30 Aug 86
86.73		Ivan	Tikhon	BLR	24.7.76	1	NC	Brest	3 Jul 05
86.66	WR		Sedykh			1	vGDR	Tallinn	22 Jun 86
86.34	WR		Sedykh			1		Cork	3 Jul 84
86.04		Sergey	Litvinov	RUS	23.1.58	1	OD	Dresden	3 Jul 86
85.74			Litvinov			2	EC	Stuttgart	30 Aug 86
85.68			Sedykh			1	BGP	Budapest	11 Aug 86
85.60			Sedykh			1	PTG	London (CP)	13 Jul 84
85.60			Sedykh			1	Drz	Moskva	17 Aug 84
85.20			Litvinov			2		Cork	3 Jul 84
85.14			Litvinov			1	PTG	London	11 Jul 86
85.14			Sedykh			1	Kuts	Moskva	4 Sep 88
85.02			Sedykh			1	BGP	Budapest	20 Aug 84
84.92			Sedykh			2	OD	Dresden	3 Jul 86
84.90		Vadim	Devyatovskiy ¶	BLR	20.3.77	1		Staiki	21 Jul 05
84.88			Litvinov			1	GP-GG	Roma	10 Sep 86
84.86		Koji	Murofushi	JPN	8.10.74	1	Odlozil	Praha	29 Jun 03
84.80			Litvinov			1	OG	Seoul	26 Sep 88
84.72			Sedykh			1	GWG	Moskva	9 Jul 86
84.64			Litvinov			2	GWG	Moskva	9 Jul 86
84.62		Igor	Astapkovich	BLR	4.1.63	1	Expo	Sevilla	6 Jun 92
84.60			Sedykh			1	8-N	Tokyo	14 Sep 84
84.58			Sedykh			1	Znam	Leningrad	8 Jun 86
84.48		Igor	Nikulin	RUS	14.8.60	1	Athl	Lausanne	12 Jul 90
84.46			Sedykh			1		Vladivostok	14 Sep 88
84.46			Tikhon			1		Minsk	7 May 04
84.40		Jüri	Tamm	EST	5.2.57	1		Banská Bystrica	9 Sep 84
84.36			Litvinov			2	vGDR	Tallinn	22 Jun 86
84.32			Tikhon			1		Staiki	8 Aug 03
84.26			Sedykh			1	Nik	Nice	15 Jul 86
84.26			Astapkovich			1		Reims	3 Jul 91
		(31/8)							
84.19		Adrián	Annus ¶	HUN	28.6.73	1		Szombathely	10 Aug 03
83.68		Tibor	Gécsek ¶	HUN	22.9.64	1		Zalaegerszeg	19 Sep 98
		(10)							

Mark Wind		Name	Nat	Born	Pos	Meet	Venue	Date
83.46	Andrey	Abduvaliyev	TJK/ UZB	30.6.66	1		Adler	26 May 90
83.43	Aleksey	Zagornyy	RUS	31.5.78	1		Adler	10 Feb 02
83.40 @	Ralf	Haber	GDR	18.8.62	1		Athína	16 May 88
	82.54				1		Potsdam	9 Sep 88
83.38	Szymon	Ziółkowski	POL	1.7.76	1	WCh	Edmonton	5 Aug 01
83.30	Olli-Pekka	Karjalainen	FIN	7.3.80	1		Lahti	14 Jul 04
83.04	Heinz	Weis	GER	14.7.63	1	NC	Frankfurt	29 Jun 97
83.00	Balázs	Kiss	HUN	21.3.72	1	GP II	Saint-Denis	4 Jun 98
82.78	Karsten	Kobs	GER	16.9.71	1		Dortmund	26 Jun 99
82.64	Günther	Rodehau	GDR	6.7.59	1		Dresden	3 Aug 85
82.62	Sergey	Kirmasov ¶	RUS	25.3.70	1		Bryansk	30 May 98
	(20)	@ competitive meeting but unsanctioned by GDR federation						
82.62	Andrey	Skvaruk	UKR	9.3.67	1		Koncha-Zaspa	27 Apr 02
82.54	Vasiliy	Sidorenko	RUS	1.5.61	1		Krasnodar	13 May 92
82.52	Lance	Deal	USA	21.8.61	1	GPF	Milano	7 Sep 96
82.45	Krisztián	Pars	HUN	18.2.82	1		Celje	13 Sep 06
82.40	Plamen	Minev	BUL	28.4.65	1	NM	Plovdiv	1 Jun 91
82.38	Gilles	Dupray	FRA	2.1.70	1		Chelles	21 Jun 00
82.30	Primoz	Kozmus	SLO	30.9.79	1		Bydgoszcz	10 Jun 07
82.28	Ilya	Konovalov	RUS	4.3.71	1	NC	Tula	10 Aug 03
82.24	Benjaminas	Viluckis	LIT	20.3.61	1		Klaipeda	24 Aug 86
82.24	Vyacheslav	Korovin	RUS	8.9.62	1		Chelyabinsk	20 Jun 87
	(30)							
82.23	Vladislav	Piskunov ¶	UKR	7.6.78	2		Koncha-Zaspa	27 Apr 02
82.22	Holger	Klose	GER	5.12.72	1		Dortmund	2 May 98
82.16	Vitaliy	Alisevich	BLR	15.6.67	1		Parnu	13 Jul 88
82.08	Ivan	Tanev	BUL	1.5.57	1	NC	Sofia	3 Sep 88
82.00	Sergey	Alay	BLR	11.6.65	1		Stayki	12 May 92
81.88	Jud	Logan ¶	USA	19.7.59	1		State College	22 Apr 88
81.81	Libor	Charfreitag	SVK	11.9.77	3	Odlozil	Praha	29 Jun 03
81.79	Christophe	Épalle	FRA	23.1.69	1		Clermont-Ferrand	30 Jun 00
81.78	Christoph	Sahner	FRG	23.9.63	1		Wemmetsweiler	11 Sep 88
81.70	Aleksandr	Seleznyov	RUS	25.1.63	2		Sochi	22 May 93
	(40)							
81.66	Aleksandr	Krykun	UKR	1.3.68	1		Kiev	29 May 04
81.64	Enrico	Sgrulletti	ITA	24.4.65	1		Ostia	9 Mar 97
81.56	Sergey	Gavrilov	RUS	22.5.70	1	Army	Rostov	16 Jun 96
81.56	Zsolt	Németh	HUN	9.11.71	1		Veszprém	14 Aug 99
81.52	Juha	Tiainen	FIN	5.12.55	1		Tampere	11 Jun 84
81.49	Valeriy	Svyatokho	BLR	20.7.81	1	NCp	Brest	27 May 06
81.45	Esref	Apak	TUR	3.1.82	1	Cezmi	Istanbul	4 Jun 05
81.44	Yuriy	Tarasyuk	BLR	11.4.57	1		Minsk	10 Aug 84
81.35	Wojciech	Kondratowicz	POL	18.4.80	1		Bydgoszcz	13 Jul 03
81.33	Miloslav	Konopka	SVK	23.1.79	1		Banská Bystrica	29 May 04
	(50)	100th man 79.56, 200th 77.00, 300th 75.03						

Ancillary marks – other marks during series (to 84.85)

86.68	Sedykh	30 Aug 86	85.82	Sedykh	22 Jun 86	85.42	Litvinov	3 Jul 86	85.20	Sedykh	3 Jul 84
86.62	Sedykh	30 Aug 86	85.52	Sedykh	13 Jul 84	85.28	Sedykh	30 Aug 86	85.04	Sedykh	13 Jul 84
86.00	Sedykh	3 Jul 84	85.46	Sedykh	30 Aug 86	85.26	Sedykh	11 Aug 86	84.98	Sedykh	4 Sep 88
86.00	Sedykh	22 Jun 86	85.42	Sedykh	11 Aug 86	85.24	Sedykh	11 Aug 86	84.92	Litvinov	3 Jul 86

JAVELIN

Mark Wind		Name	Nat	Born	Pos	Meet	Venue	Date
98.48 WR	Jan	Zelezny	CZE	16.6.66	1		Jena	25 May 96
95.66 WR		Zelezny			1	McD	Sheffield	29 Aug 93
95.54A WR		Zelezny			1		Pietersburg	6 Apr 93
94.64		Zelezny			1	GS	Ostrava	31 May 96
94.02		Zelezny			1		Stellenbosch	26 Mar 97
93.09	Aki	Parviainen	FIN	26.10.74	1		Kuortane	26 Jun 99
92.80		Zelezny			1	WCh	Edmonton	12 Aug 01
92.61	Sergey	Makarov	RUS	19.3.73	1		Sheffield	30 Jun 02
92.60	Raymond	Hecht	GER	11.11.68	1	Bisl	Oslo	21 Jul 95
92.42		Zelezny			1	GS	Ostrava	28 May 97
92.41		Parviainen			1	ECp-1A	Vaasa	24 Jun 01
92.28		Zelezny			1	GPF	Monaco	9 Sep 95
92.28		Hecht			1	WK	Zürich	14 Aug 96
92.12		Zelezny			1	McD	London (CP)	27 Aug 95
92.12		Zelezny			1	TOTO	Tokyo	15 Sep 95
91.82		Zelezny			1	McD	Sheffield	4 Sep 94
91.69	Kostadínos	Gatsioúdis	GRE	17.12.73	1		Kuortane	24 Jun 00
91.68		Zelezny			1	GP	Gateshead	1 Jul 94

Mark	Wind	Name		Nat	Born	Pos	Meet	Venue	Date
91.59		Andreas	Thorkildsen	NOR	1.4.82	1	Bisl	Oslo	2 Jun 06
91.53		Tero	Pitkämäki	FIN	19.12.82	1		Kuortane	26 Jun 05
91.50			Zelezny			1	Kuso	Lublin	4 Jun 94
91.50A			Zelezny			1		Pretoria	8 Apr 96
91.50			Hecht			1		Gengenbach	1 Sep 96
91.46	WR	Steve	Backley	GBR	12.2.69	1		Auckland	25 Jan 92
91.40			Zelezny			1	BNP	Villeneuve d'Ascq	2 Jul 93
91.34			Zelezny			1		Cape Town	8 Apr 97
91.33			Pitkämäki			1	WAF	Monaco	10 Sep 05
91.31			Parviainen			2	WCh	Edmonton	12 Aug 01
91.30			Zelezny			1	ISTAF	Berlin	1 Sep 95
91.29		Breaux	Greer	USA	19.10.76	1	NC	Indianapolis	21 Jun 07
		(30/9) 68 performances over 90m (most: Zelezny 35, Parviainen 8, Hecht & Pitkämäki 6, Makarov 5)							
90.73		Vadims	Vasilevskis (10)	LAT	5.1.82	1		Tallinn	22 Jul 07
90.60		Seppo	Räty	FIN	27.4.62	1		Nurmijärvi	20 Jul 92
90.44		Boris	Henry	GER	14.12.73	1	Gugl	Linz	9 Jul 97
89.16A		Tom	Petranoff	USA	8.4.58	1		Potchefstroom	1 Mar 91
89.10	WR	Patrik	Bodén	SWE	30.6.67	1		Austin	24 Mar 90
88.90		Aleksandr	Ivanov	RUS	25.5.82	1	Znam	Tula	7 Jun 03
88.75		Marius	Corbett	RSA	26.9.75	1	CG	Kuala Lumpur	21 Sep 98
88.70		Peter	Blank	GER	10.4.62	1	NC	Stuttgart	30 Jun 01
88.24		Matti	Närhi	FIN	17.8.75	1		Soini	27 Jul 97
88.22		Juha	Laukkanen	FIN	6.1.69	1		Kuortane	20 Jun 92
88.20		Gavin	Lovegrove	NZL	21.10.67	1	Bisl	Oslo	5 Jul 96
		(20)							
88.00		Vladimir	Ovchinnikov	RUS	2.8.70	1		Tolyatti	14 May 95
87.83		Andrus	Värnik	EST	27.9.77	1		Valga	19 Aug 03
87.82		Harri	Hakkarainen	FIN	16.10.69	1		Kuortane	24 Jun 95
87.60		Kazuhiro	Mizoguchi	JPN	18.3.62	1	Jen	San José	27 May 89
87.40		Vladimir	Sasimovich	BLR	14.9.68	2		Kuortane	24 Jun 95
87.34		Andrey	Moruyev	RUS	6.5.70	1	ECp	Birmingham	25 Jun 94
87.20		Viktor	Zaytsev	UZB	6.6.66	1	OT	Moskva	23 Jun 92
87.20		Peter	Esenwein	GER	7.12.67	1		Rehlingen	31 May 04
87.17		Dariusz	Trafas	POL	16.5.72	1		Gold Coast (RB)	17 Sep 00
87.17		Guillermo	Martínez	CUB	28.6.81	2	GP	Saint-Denis	8 Jul 06
		(30)							
87.12		Tom	Pukstys	USA	28.5.68	2	OD	Jena	25 May 97
87.12		Emeterio	González	CUB	11.4.73	1	OD	Jena	3 Jun 00
86.98		Yuriy	Rybin	RUS	5.3.63	1		Nitra	26 Aug 95
86.94		Mick	Hill	GBR	22.10.64	1	NC	London (CP)	13 Jun 93
86.80		Einar	Vihljálmsson	ISL	1.6.60	1		Reykjavik	29 Aug 92
86.74		Pål Arne	Fagernes	NOR	8.6.74	q	OG	Sydney	22 Sep 00
86.67		Andrew	Currey	AUS	7.2.71	1		Wollongong	22 Jul 01
86.64		Klaus	Tafelmeier	FRG	12.4.58	1	NC	Gelsenkirchen	12 Jul 87
86.63		Harri	Haatainen	FIN	5.1.78	2	GP II	Gateshead	19 Aug 01
86.50		Tapio	Korjus	FIN	10.2.61	1		Lahti	25 Aug 88
		(40)							
86.47		Eriks	Rags	LAT	1.6.75	2	BrGP	London	22 Jul 01
85.96		Kimmo	Kinnunen	FIN	31.3.68	3	NC	Seinäjoki	8 Aug 99
85.95		Ainars	Kovals	LAT	21.11.81	Q	EC	Göteborg	7 Aug 06
85.75		Magnus	Arvidsson	SWE	20.2.83	1	GP	Osaka	5 May 07
85.74		Dmitriy	Polyunin ¶	UZB	6.4.69	2	OT	Moskva	23 Jun 92
85.74A		Miroslav	Guzdek	CZE	3.8.75	1		Germiston	5 Apr 02
85.70		Andrey	Shevchuk	RUS	8.3.70	2	Slovn	Bratislava	1 Jun 93
85.67		Mark	Roberson	GBR	13.3.67	2		Gateshead	19 Jul 98
85.60		William	Hamlyn-Harris	AUS	14.1.78	1		Canberra	31 Jan 04
85.42		Andreas	Linden	GER	20.2.65	2		Mülheim-Kärlich	17 Sep 95
		(50)	100th man 83.38, 200th 80.46, 300th 78.98					new javelin introduced in 1986	

Ancillary marks – other marks during series (to 91.40)

95.34	Zelezny	29 Aug 93	92.26	Zelezny	26 Mar 97	91.44	Zelezny	25 May 96
92.88	Zelezny	25 May 96	91.88	Zelezny	27 Aug 95	91.44	Zelezny	26 Mar 97
92.30	Zelezny	26 Mar 97	91.48	Zelezny	15 Sep 95			

Javelins with roughened tails, now banned by the IAAF

Mark	Wind	Name		Nat	Born	Pos	Meet	Venue	Date
96.96	WR	Seppo	Räty	FIN	27.4.62	1		Punkalaidun	2 Jun 91
94.74	Irreg		Zelezny			1	Bisl	Oslo	4 Jul 92
91.98	WR		Räty			1	Super	Shizuoka	6 May 91
90.82		Kimmo	Kinnunen	FIN	31.3.68	1	WCh	Tokyo	26 Aug 91
87.00		Peter	Borglund	SWE	29.1.64	1	vFIN	Stockholm	13 Aug 91
85.52		Dag	Wennlund	SWE	9.10.63	1	NC	Helsingborg	27 Jul 91

Downhill: 87.88 Antti Ruuskanen FIN 21.2.84 1 Savonlinna 16 Sep 07

DECATHLON

Mark Wind	Name			Nat	Born	Pos	Meet	Venue		Date
9026 WR	Roman	Sebrle		CZE	26.11.74	1		Götzis		27 May 01
	10.64/0.0	8.11/1.9	15.33	2.12	47.79	13.92/-0.2	47.92	4.80	70.16	4:21.98
8994 WR	Tomás	Dvorák		CZE	11.5.72	1	ECp	Praha		4 Jul 99
	10.54/-0.1	7.90/1.1	16.78	2.04	48.08	13.73/0.0	48.33	4.90	72.32	4:37.20
8902		Dvorák				1	WCh	Edmonton		7 Aug 01
	10.62/1.5	8.07/0.9	16.57	2.00	47.74	13.80/-0.4	45.51	5.00	68.53	4:35.13
8900		Dvorák				1		Götzis		4 Jun 00
	10.54/1.3	8.03/0.0	16.68	2.09	48.36	13.89/-1.0	47.89	4.85	67.21	4:42.33
8893		Sebrle				1	OG	Athína		24 Aug 04
	10.85/1.5	7.84/0.3	16.36	2.12	48.36	14.05/1.5	48.72	5.00	70.52	4:40.01
8891 WR	Dan	O'Brien		USA	18.7.66	1		Talence		5 Sep 92
	10.43w/2.1	8.08/1.8	16.69	2.07	48.51	13.98/-0.5	48.56	5.00	62.58	4:42.10
8847 WR	Daley	Thompson		GBR	30.7.58	1	OG	Los Angeles		9 Aug 84
	10.44/-1.0	8.01/0.4	15.72	2.03	46.97	14.33/-1.1	46.56	5.00	65.24	4:35.00
8844w		O'Brien				1	TAC	New York		13 Jun 91
	10.23	7.96	16.06	2.08	47.70	13.95W/4.2	48.08	5.10	57.40	4:45.54
8842		Sebrle				1		Götzis		30 May 04
	10.92/0.5	7.86w/3.3	16.22	2.09	48.59	14.15/0.3	47.44	5.00	71.10	4:34.09
8837		Dvorák				1	WCh	Athína		6 Aug 97
	10.60/0.8	7.64/-0.7	16.32	2.00	47.56	13.61/0.8	45.16	5.00	70.34	4:35.40
8832 WR	Jürgen	Hingsen		FRG	25.1.58	1	OT	Mannheim		9 Jun 84
	10.70w/2.9	7.76/	16.42	2.07	48.05	14.07/0.2	49.36	4.90	59.86	4:19.75
8825 WR		Hingsen				1		Bernhausen		5 Jun 83
	10.92/0.0	7.74	15.94	2.15	47.89	14.10	46.80	4.70	67.26	4:19.74
8824		O'Brien				1	OG	Atlanta		1 Aug 96
	10.50/0.7	7.57/1.4	15.66	2.07	46.82	13.87/0.3	48.78	5.00	66.90	4:45.89
8820	Bryan	Clay		USA	3.1.80	2	OG	Athína		24 Aug 04
	10.44w/2.2	7.96/0.2	15.23	2.06	49.19	14.13/1.5	50.11	4.90	69.71	4:41.65
8817		O'Brien				1	WCh	Stuttgart		20 Aug 93
	10.57/0.9	7.99/0.4	15.41	2.03	47.46	14.08/0.0	47.92	5.20	62.56	4:40.08
8815	Erki	Nool		EST	25.6.70	2	WCh	Edmonton		7 Aug 01
	10.60/1.5	7.63/2.0	14.90	2.03	46.23	14.40/0.0	43.40	5.40	67.01	4:29.58
8812		O'Brien				1	WCh	Tokyo		30 Aug 91
	10.41/-1.6	7.90/0.8	16.24	1.91	46.53	13.94/-1.2	47.20	5.20	60.66	4:37.50
8811		Thompson				1	EC	Stuttgart		28 Aug 86
	10.26/2.0	7.72/1.0	15.73	2.00	47.02	14.04/-0.3	43.38	5.10	62.78	4:26.16
8807		Sebrle				1		Götzis		1 Jun 03
	10.78/-0.2	7.86/1.2	15.41	2.12	47.83	13.96/0.0	43.42	4.90	69.22	4:28.63
8800		Sebrle				1		Götzis		2 Jun 02
	10.95/0.5	7.79/1.8	15.50	2.12	48.35	13.89/1.6	48.02	5.00	68.97	4:38.16
8800		Sebrle				1	EC	München		8 Aug 02
	10.83/1.3	7.92/0.8	15.41	2.12	48.48	14.04/0.0	46.88	5.10	68.51	4:42.94
8792	Uwe	Freimuth		GDR	10.9.61	1	OD	Potsdam		21 Jul 84
	11.06/	7.79/	16.30	2.03	48.43	14.66/	46.58	5.15	72.42	4:25.19
8784	Tom	Pappas		USA	6.9.76	1	NC	Stanford		22 Jun 03
	10.78/0.2	7.96/1.4	16.28	2.17	48.22	14.13/1.7	45.84	5.20	60.77	4:48.12
8774 WR		Thompson				1	EC	Athína		8 Sep 82
	10.51/0.3	7.80/0.8	15.44	2.03	47.11	14.39/0.9	45.48	5.00	63.56	4:23.71
8762	Siegfried	Wentz		FRG	7.3.60	2		Bernhausen		5 Jun 83
	10.89	7.49/	15.35	2.09	47.38	14.00	46.90	4.80	70.68	4:24.90
8757		Sebrle				2		Götzis		4 Jun 00
	10.64/1.3	7.88/1.6	15.19	2.15	49.05	13.99/-1.0	47.21	4.75	67.23	4:35.06
8755		O'Brien				1	GWG	Uniondale, NY		20 Jul 98
	10.71/-2.3	7.78w/2.2	15.67	2.11	48.04	13.67/0.4	48.87	5.20	66.31	5:08.77
8750		Pappas				1	WCh	Saint-Denis		27 Aug 03
	10.80/-0.5	7.62/1.1	16.11	2.09	47.58	13.99/0.0	46.94	5.10	65.90	4:44.31
8744		Dvorák				1	WCh	Sevilla		25 Aug 99
	10.60/0.1	7.98/0.1	16.49	2.00	48.42	13.75/0.7	46.26	4.60	70.11	4:39.87
8742		Nool				3		Götzis		4 Jun 00
	10.69/1.3	7.78/1.8	14.14	1.97	47.18	14.37/-0.1	44.16	5.55	69.10	4:35.59
	(30/10)									
8735	Eduard	Hämäläinen		FIN/BLR	21.1.69	1		Götzis		29 May 94
	10.50w/2.1	7.26/1.0	16.05	2.11	47.63	13.82/-3.0	49.70	4.90	60.32	4:35.09
8727	Dave	Johnson		USA	7.4.63	1		Azusa		24 Apr 92
	10.96/0.4	7.52w/4.5	14.61	2.04	48.19	14.17/0.3	49.88	5.28	66.96	4:29.38
8725	Dmitriy	Karpov		KAZ	23.7.81	3	OG	Athína		24 Aug 04
	10.50w/2.2	7.81/-0.9	15.93	2.09	46.81	13.97/1.5	51.65	4.60	55.54	4:38.11
8709	Aleksandr	Apaychev		UKR	6.5.61	1	vGDR	Neubrandenburg		3 Jun 84
	10.96/	7.57/	16.00	1.97	48.72	13.93/	48.00	4.90	72.24	4:26.51

Mark Wind	Name			Nat	Born	Pos	Meet	Venue		Date
8706	Frank	Busemann		GER	26.2.75	2	OG	Atlanta		1 Aug 96
	10.60/0.7	8.07/0.8	13.60	2.04	48.34	13.47/0.3	45.04	4.80	66.86	4:31.41
8698	Grigoriy	Degtyaryov		RUS	16.8.58	1	NC	Kiyev		22 Jun 84
	10.87/0.7	7.42/0.1	16.03	2.10	49.75	14.53/0.3	51.20	4.90	67.08	4:23.09
8694	Chris	Huffins		USA	15.4.70	1	NC	New Orleans		20 Jun 98
	10.31w/3.5	7.76w/2.5	15.43	2.18	49.02	14.02/1.0	53.22	4.60	61.59	4:59.43
8680	Torsten	Voss		GDR	24.3.63	1	WCh	Roma		4 Sep 87
	10.69/-0.3	7.88/1.2	14.98	2.10	47.96	14.13/0.1	43.96	5.10	58.02	4:25.93
8667 WR	Guido	Kratschmer		FRG	10.1.53	1		Bernhausen		14 Jun 80
	10.58w/2.4	7.80/	15.47	2.00	48.04	13.92/	45.52	4.60	66.50	4:24.15
8644	Steve	Fritz		USA	1.11.67	4	OG	Atlanta		1 Aug 96
	10.90/0.8	7.77/0.9	15.31	2.04	50.13	13.97/0.3	49.84	5.10	65.70	4:38.26
	(20)									
8644	Maurice	Smith		JAM	28.9.80	2	WCh	Osaka		1 Sep 07
	10.62/0.7	7.50/0.0	17.32	1.97	47.48	13.91/-0.2	52.36	4.80	53.61	4:33.52
8634 WR	Bruce	Jenner		USA	28.10.49	1	OG	Montreal		30 Jul 76
	10.94/0.0	7.22/0.0	15.35	2.03	47.51	14.84/0.0	50.04	4.80	68.52	4:12.61
8627	Robert	Zmelík		CZE	18.4.69	1		Götzis		31 May 92
	10.62w/2.1	8.02/0.2	13.93	2.05	48.73	13.84/1.2	44.44	4.90	61.26	4:24.83
8626	Michael	Smith		CAN	16.9.67	1		Götzis		26 May 96
	11.23/-0.6	7.72/0.6	16.94	1.97	48.69	14.77/-2.4	52.90	4.90	71.22	4:41.95
8617	Andrey	Kravchenko		BLR	4.1.86	1		Götzis		27 May 07
	10.86/0.2	7.90/0.9	13.89	2.15	47.46	14.05/-0.1	39.63	5.00	64.35	4:29.10
8603	Dean	Macey		GBR	12.12.77	3	WCh	Edmonton		7 Aug 01
	10.72/-0.7	7.59/0.4	15.41	2.15	46.21	14.34/0.0	46.96	4.70	54.61	4:29.05
8583w	Jón Arnar	Magnússon		ISL	28.7.69	1	ECp-2	Reykjavik		5 Jul 98
	10.68/2.0	7.63/2.0	15.57	2.07	47.78	14.33W/5.2	44.53	5.00	64.16	4:41.60
	8573					3		Götzis		31 May 98
	10.74/0.5	7.60/-0.2	16.03	2.03	47.66	14.24/0.7	47.82	5.10	59.77	4:46.43
8574	Christian	Plaziat		FRA	28.10.63	1	EC	Split		29 Aug 90
	10.72/-0.6	7.77/1.1	14.19	2.10	47.10	13.98/0.7	44.36	5.00	54.72	4:27.83
8574	Aleksandr	Yurkov		UKR	21.7.75	4		Götzis		4 Jun 00
	10.69/0.9	7.93/1.8	15.26	2.03	49.74	14.56/-0.9	47.85	5.15	58.92	4:32.49
8571	Lev	Lobodin		RUS	1.4.69	3	EC	Budapest		20 Aug 98
	10.66w/2.2	7.42/0.2	15.67	2.03	48.65	13.97/0.9	46.55	5.20	56.55	4:30.27
	(30)									
8566	Sebastian	Chmara		POL	21.11.71	1		Alhama de Murcia		17 May 98
	10.97w/2.9	7.56/1.2	16.03	2.10	48.27	14.32/1.8	44.39	5.20	57.25	4:29.66
8554	Attila	Zsivoczky		HUN	29.4.77	5		Götzis		4 Jun 00
	10.64w/2.1	7.24/-1.0	15.72	2.18	48.13	14.87/-0.9	45.64	4.65	63.57	4:23.13
8548	Paul	Meier		GER	27.7.71	3	WCh	Stuttgart		20 Aug 93
	10.57/0.9	7.57/1.1	15.45	2.15	47.73	14.63/0.0	45.72	4.60	61.22	4:32.05
8547	Igor	Sobolevskiy		UKR	4.5.62	2	NC	Kiyev		22 Jun 84
	10.64/0.7	7.71/0.2	15.93	2.01	48.24	14.82/0.3	50.54	4.40	67.40	4:32.84
8534	Siegfried	Stark		GDR	12.6.55	1		Halle		4 May 80
	11.10w	7.64	15.81	2.03	49.53	14.86w	47.20	5.00	68.70	4:27.7
8534w/8478	Antonio	Peñalver		ESP	1.12.68	1		Alhama de Murcia		24 May 92
	10.76w/3.9	7.42W/6.2 (7.19w/4.0)	16.50	2.12	49.50	14.32/0.8	47.38	5.00	59.32	4:39.94
8526	Francisco Javier	Benet		ESP	25.3.68	2		Alhama de Murcia		17 May 98
	10.72w/2.9	7.45/-1.2	14.57	1.92	48.10	13.83/1.8	46.12	5.00	65.37	4:26.81
8526	Kristjan	Rahnu		EST	29.8.79	1		Arles		5 Jun 05
	10.52w/2.2	7.58/1.6	15.51	1.99	48.60	14.04w/3.1	50.81	4.95	60.71	4:52.18
8524	Sébastien	Levicq		FRA	25.6.71	4	WCh	Sevilla		25 Aug 99
	11.05/0.2	7.52/-0.4	14.22	2.00	50.13	14.48/0.6	44.65	5.50	69.01	4:26.81
8519	Yuriy	Kutsenko		RUS	5.3.52	3	NC	Kiyev		22 Jun 84
	11.07/0.5	7.54/-0.1	15.11	2.13	49.07	14.94/0.3	50.38	4.60	61.70	4:12.68
	(40)									
8506	Valter	Külvet		EST	19.2.64	1		Stayki		3 Jul 88
	11.05/-1.4	7.35/0.4	15.78	2.00	48.08	14.55/-0.8	52.04	4.60	61.72	4:15.93
8500	Christian	Schenk		GER	9.2.65	4	WCh	Stuttgart		20 Aug 93
	11.22/-0.9	7.63/0.0	15.72	2.15	48.78	15.29/0.0	46.94	4.80	65.32	4:24.44
8491	Aleksandr	Nevskiy		UKR	21.2.58	2		Götzis		20 May 84
	10.97/-1.6	7.24/1.2	15.04	2.08	48.44	14.67/1.0	46.06	4.70	69.56	4:19.62
8490	Jagan	Hames		AUS	31.10.75	1	CG	Kuala Lumpur		18 Sep 98
	10.77/0.0	7.64/0.8	14.73	2.19	49.67	14.07/0.4	46.40	5.00	64.67	5:02.68
8485	Konstantin	Akhapkin		RUS	19.1.56	1	NC	Moskva		2 Aug 82
	11.10/0.2	7.72/0.2	15.25	2.02	49.14	14.38/1.8	45.68	4.90	62.42	4:19.60
8485	Stefan	Schmid		GER	6.5.70	1	OT	Ratingen		23 Jul 00
	10.82/0.0	7.59/-0.6	14.14	2.01	48.99	14.20/-1.6	44.24	5.06	67.63	4:31.76

MEN All-time

Mark	Wind	Name		Nat	Born	Pos	Meet	Venue	Date
8475		Aleksey	Drozdov	RUS	3.12.83	4	WCh	Osaka	1 Sep 07
		10.97/0.2 7.25/-0.3 16.49 2.12 50.00 14.76/1.4 48.62 5.00 63.51 4:36.93							
8466 WR		Nikolay	Avilov	UKR	6.8.48	1	OG	München	8 Sep 72
		11.00/ 7.68/ 14.36 2.12 48.45 14.31/ 46.98 4.55 61.66 4:22.82							
8465		Trey	Hardee	USA	7.2.84	1	TexR	Austin	6 Apr 06
		10.35w/2.5 7.70w/3.0 14.45 1.99 49.11 13.83w/3.1 48.24 5.20 60.00 5:06.73							
8462w		Kip	Janvrin	USA	8.7.65	1	vGER	Edwardsville	18 Jul 96
		10.61W/4.1 7.34w/3.1 14.64 1.96 48.20 14.48W/5.7 45.84 5.00 61.82 4:20.12							
		(50) 100th man 8288, 200th 8122, 300th 8002							

4 x 100 METRES RELAY

Mark	Nat	Team	Pos	Meet	Venue	Date
37.40 WR	USA	Marsh, Burrell, Mitchell, C Lewis	1	OG	Barcelona	8 Aug 92
37.40 WR	USA	Drummond, Cason, D Mitchell, L Burrell	1s1	WCh	Stuttgart	21 Aug 93
37.48	USA	Drummond, Cason, D Mitchell, L Burrell	1	WCh	Stuttgart	22 Aug 93
37.50 WR	USA	Cason, Burrell, Mitchell, C Lewis	1	WCh	Tokyo	1 Sep 91
37.59	USA	Drummond, Montgomery, B Lewis, Greene	1	WCh	Sevilla	29 Aug 99
37.59	USA	Conwright, Spearmon, Gay, Smoots	1	WCp	Athína	16 Sep 06
37.61	USA	Drummond, Williams, B Lewis, Greene	1	OG	Sydney	30 Sep 00
37.65	USA	Drummond, Williams, C Johnson, Greene	1	ISTAF	Berlin	1 Sep 00
37.67 WR	USA	Marsh, Burrell, Mitchell, C Lewis	1	WK	Zürich	7 Aug 91
37.69	CAN	Esmie 10.47, Gilbert 9.02, Surin 9.25, Bailey 8.95	1	OG	Atlanta	3 Aug 96
37.73	GBR	Gardener, Campbell, Devonish, Chambers	2	WCh	Sevilla	29 Aug 99
37.75	USA	Cason, Burrell, Mitchell, Marsh	1h2	WCh	Tokyo	31 Aug 91
37.77	GBR	Jackson, Jarrett, Regis, Christie	2	WCh	Stuttgart	22 Aug 93
37.77	USA A	Drummond, B Williams, Patton, Greene	1	ISTAF	Berlin (P)	10 Aug 03
37.78	USA	Patton 10.28, Spearmon 9.22, Gay 9.05, Dixon 9.23	1	WCh	Osaka	1 Sep 07
37.79 WR	FRA	Morinière, Sangouma, Trouabal, Marie-Rose	1	EC	Split	1 Sep 90
37.79 WR	Santa Monica TC/USA	Marsh, Burrell, Heard, C Lewis	1	Herc	Monaco	3 Aug 91
37.79	USA – Santa Monica TC	Marsh, Burrell, Heard, C Lewis	1	MSR	Walnut	17 Apr 94
37.82	USA	Drummond, Williams, B.Lewis, Greene	1s1	OG	Sydney	29 Sep 00
37.83 WR	USA	Graddy, R Brown, C Smith, C Lewis	1	OG	Los Angeles	11 Aug 84
37.83	CAN	Esmie, Gilbert, Surin, Mahorn	3	WCh	Stuttgart	22 Aug 93
37.86 WR	USA	E King, Gault, C Smith, C Lewis	1	WCh	Helsinki	10 Aug 83
37.86	CAN	Esmie, Gilbert, Surin, Bailey	1	WCh	Athína	10 Aug 97
37.87	FRA	Morinière, Sangouma, Trouabal, Marie-Rose	2	WCh	Tokyo	1 Sep 91
37.88	USA	(HSI) Drummond, B Williams, C.Johnson, Greene	1	TexR	Austin	7 Apr 01
37.89	Santa Monica TC (USA)	Marsh, Burrell, Heard, C Lewis	1	TexR	Austin	9 Apr 94
37.89	JAM	Anderson 10.60, Bolt 9.05, N Carter 9.40, Powell 8.84	2	WCh	Osaka	1 Sep 07
37.90	USA	McRae, L McNeill, Glance, C Lewis	1	WCh	Roma	6 Sep 87
37.90	USA	Drummond, Harden, Mitchell, Greene	1	GWG	Uniondale, NY.	22 Jul 98
37.90	BRA	de Lima, Ribeiro, A da Silva, Cl da Silva	2	OG	Sydney	30 Sep 00
37.90	GBR	Malcolm, Pickering 9.06, Devonish, Lewis-Francis	3	WCh	Osaka	1 Sep 07
		(31 by 6 nations) Further bests by nations:				
37.94	NGR	O Ezinwa, Adeniken, Obikwelu, D Ezinwa	1s2	WCh	Athína	9 Aug 97
38.00	CUB	Simón, Lamela, Isasi, Aguilera	3	OG	Barcelona	8 Aug 92
38.02	URS	Yevgenyev, Bryzgin, Muravyov, Krylov	2	WCh	Roma	6 Sep 87
38.03	JPN	Tsukahara, Suetsugu 9.08, Takahira, Asahara	5	WCh	Osaka	1 Sep 07
		(10)				
38.10	TRI	Pierre, Burns, Harper, Brown	2	WCh	Helsinki	13 Aug 05
38.12	GHA	Duah, Nkansah, Zakari, Tuffour	1s1	WCh	Athína	9 Aug 97
38.17	AUS	Henderson, Jackson, Brimacombe, Marsh	1s2	WCh	Göteborg	12 Aug 95
38.29	GDR	Schröder, Kübeck, Prenzler, Emmelmann	2	vUSA	Karl-Marx-Stadt	9 Jul 82
38.33	POL	Zwolinski, Licznerski, Dunecki, Woronin	2	OG	Moskva	1 Aug 80
38.37	ITA	Tilli, Simionato, Pavoni, Mennea	2	WCh	Helsinki	10 Aug 83
38.45	AHO	Goeloe, Raffaela, Duzant, Martina	6	WCh	Helsinki	13 Aug 05
38.46	URS/RUS	Zharov, Krylov, Fatun, Goremykin	4	EC	Split	1 Sep 90
38.47	RSA	Nagel, du Plessis, Newton, Quinn	1	WCh	Edmonton	12 Aug 01
38.53	UKR	Rurak, Osovich, Kramarenko, Dologodin	1	ECp	Madrid	1 Jun 96
		(20, with RUS and UKR for USSR)				
38.54	FRG	Heer, Haas, Klein, Schweisfurth	1	R-W	Koblenz	28 Aug 88
38.60	ESP	Feo, José, Mayoral, Berlanga	3s1	WCh	Athína	9 Aug 97
38.60	CIV	Meité, Douhou, Sonan, N'Dri	3s1	WCh	Edmonton	12 Aug 01
38.61	GRE	Séggos, Alexópoulos, Panayiotópoulos, Hoídis	2	ECp	Paris (C)	19 Jun 99
38.63	SWE	Karlsson, Mårtensson, Hedner, Strenius	3s2	OG	Atlanta	2 Aug 96
38.63	NED	Beck, T Douglas, van Balkom, C Douglas	5s1	WCh	Saint-Denis	30 Aug 03
38.67	HUN	Karaffa, Nagy, Tatár, Kovács	1	BGP	Budapest	11 Aug 86
38.80	THA	Natenee, Sophanich, Janthana, Suwonprateep	1	AsiC	Jakarta	31 Aug 00
38.81	CHN	Li Xiaoping, Lin Wei, Huang Danwei, Chen Wenzhong	2h3	WCh	Göteborg	12 Aug 95
38.81	ISR	Jaar, Jablonka, Kafri, Porkhomovskiy	3h2	WCh	Sevilla	28 Aug 99
38.82	TCH/CZE	Matousek, Demec, Kynos, Bohman	4	OG	München	10 Sep 72

Mark	Wind	Name	Nat	Born	Pos	Meet	Venue	Date
Multi-nation team								
37.82		Drummond/USA, Jarrett/GBR, Regis/GBR, Mitchell/USA			2	MSR	Walnut	17 Apr 94
Drugs dsqualification								
37.91		NGR Asonze ¶, Obikwelu, Effiong, Aliu			(3)	WCh	Sevilla	29 Aug 99

4 x 200 METRES RELAY

Mark	Wind	Name	Nat	Born	Pos	Meet	Venue	Date
1:18.68	WR	USA – Santa Monica Track Cluc						
		Marsh 20.0, Burrell 19.6, Heard 19.7, C Lewis 19.4			1	MSR	Walnut	17 Apr 94
1:19.10		World All-Stars			2	MSR	Walnut	17 Apr 94
		Drummond USA 20.4, Mitchell USA 19.3, Bridgewater USA 20.3, Regis GBR 19.1						
1:19.11	WR	Santa Monica TC/USA M.Marsh, L Burrell, Heard, C Lewis			1	Penn	Philadelphia	25 Apr 92
1:19.16		USA Red Team Crawford, Clay, Patton, Gatlin			1	PennR	Philadelphia	26 Apr 03
1:19.38	WR	Santa Monica TC/USA Everett, Burrell, Heard, C Lewis			1	R-W	Koblenz	23 Aug 89
1:19.39		USA Blue Drummond, Crawford, B Williams, Greene			1	PennR	Philadelphia	28 Apr 01
1:19.45		Santa Monica TC/USA DeLoach, Burrell, C.Lewis, Heard			1	Penn	Philadelphia	27 Apr 91
1:19.47		Nike Int./USA Brokenburr, A Harrison, Greene, M Johnson			1	Penn	Philadelphia	24 Apr 99
Best non-US nations								
1:20.79		Central Arizona DC/Jamaica			1		Walnut	24 Apr 88
		Bucknor, Campbell, O'Connor, Davis)						
1:21.10		ITA Tilli, Simionato, Bongiorno, Mennea			1		Cagliari	29 Sep 83
1:21.22		POL Tulin, Balcerzak, Pilarczyk, Urbas			2		Gdansk	14 Jul 01
1:21.29		GBR Adam, Mafe, Christie, Regis			1		Birmingham	23 Jun 89

4 x 400 METRES RELAY

Mark	Wind	Name	Nat	Born	Pos	Meet	Venue	Date
2:54.20	WR	USA Young 44.3, Pettigrew 43.2, Washington 43.5, M Johnson 43.2			1	GWG	Uniondale, NY	22 Jul 98
2:54.29	WR	USA Valmon 44.43, Watts 43.59, Reynolds 43.36, Johnson 42.91			1	WCh	Stuttgart	22 Aug 93
2:55.56		USA Merritt 44.4, Taylor 43.7, Williamson 44.32, Wariner 43.10			1	WCh	Osaka	2 Sep 07
2:55.74	WR	USA Valmon 44.6, Watts 43.00, M.Johnson 44.73, S Lewis 43.41			1	OG	Barcelona	8 Aug 92
2:55.91		USA O Harris 44.5, Brew 43.6, Wariner 43.98, Williamson 43.83			1	OG	Athína	28 Aug 04
2:55.99		USA L Smith 44.62, A Harrison 43.84, Mills 43.66, Maybank 43.87			1	OG	Atlanta	3 Aug 96
2:56.16A	WR	USA Matthews 45.0, Freeman 43.2, James 43.9, Evans 44.1			1	OG	Ciu. México	20 Oct 68
2:56.16	WR	USA Everett 43.79, S Lewis 43.69, Robinzine 44.74, Reynolds 43.94			1	OG	Seoul	1 Oct 88
2:56.35		USA A Harrison 44.36, Pettigrew 44.17, C Harrison 43.53, Johnson 44.29			1	OG	Sydney	30 Sep 00
2:56.45		USA J Davis 45.2, Pettigrew 43.9, Taylor 43.92, M Johnson 43.49			1	WCh	Sevilla	29 Aug 99
2:56.47		USA Young 44.6, Pettigrew 43.1, Jones 44.80, Washington 44.80			1	WCh	Athína	10 Aug 97
2:56.60		GBR I Thomas 44.92, Baulch 44.19, Richardson 43.62, Black 43.87			2	OG	Atlanta	3 Aug 96
2:56.60		USA Red Taylor 45.0, Pettigrew 44.2, Washington 43.7, Johnson 43.7			1	PennR	Philadelphia	29 Apr 00
2:56.65		GBR Thomas 44.8, Black 44.2, Baulch 44.08, Richardson 43.57			2	WCh	Athína	10 Aug 97
2:56.75		JAM McDonald 44.5, Haughton 44.4, McFarlane 44.37, Clarke 43.51			3	WCh	Athína	10 Aug 97
2:56.91		USA Rock 44.7, Brew 44.3, Williamson 44.40, Wariner 43.49			1	WCh	Helsinki	14 Aug 05
2:57.29		USA Everett 45.1, Haley 44.0, McKay 44.20, Reynolds 44.00			1	WCh	Roma	6 Sep 87
2:57.32		USA Ramsey 44.9, Mills 44.6, Reynolds 43.74, Johnson 44.11			1	WCh	Göteborg	13 Aug 95
2:57.32		BAH McKinney 44.9, Moncur 44.6, A.Williams 44.43, Brown 43.42			2	WCh	Helsinki	14 Aug 05
2:57.53		GBR Black 44.7, Redmond 44.0, Regis 44.22, Akabusi 44.59			1	WCh	Tokyo	1 Sep 91
2:57.54		USA Byrd 45.9, Pettigrew 43.9, Brew 44.03, Taylor 43.71			1	WCh	Edmonton	12 Aug 01
2:57.57		USA Valmon 44.9, Watts 43.4, D.Everett 44.31, Pettigrew 44.93			2	WCh	Tokyo	1 Sep 91
2:57.87		USA L Smith 44.59, Rouser 44.33, Mills 44.32, Maybank 44.63			1s2	OG	Atlanta	2 Aug 96
2:57.91		USA Nix 45.59, Armstead 43.97, Babers 43.75, McKay 44.60			1	OG	Los Angeles	11 Aug 84
2:57.97		JAM McDonald , Haughton , McFarlane, D Clarke			1	PAm	Winnipeg	30 Jul 99
2:58.00		POL Rysiukiewicz 45.6, Czubak 44.2, Haczek 44.0, Mackowiak 44.2			2	GWG	Uniondale, NY	22 Jul 98
2:58.07		JAM Ayre 44.9, Simpson 44.9, Spence 44.48, Clarke 43.81			3	WCh	Helsinki	14 Aug 05
2:58.19		BAH Moncur 45.1, C Brown 44.5, McIntosh 44.42, Munnings 44.13			2	WCh	Edmonton	12 Aug 01
2:58.22		GBR Sanders 45.85, Akabusi 44.48, Regis 43.93, Black 43.96			1	EC	Split	1 Sep 90
2:58.23		USA Ramsey 44.6, Mills 44.0, Lyles 44.41, Hall 45.22			1h1	WCh	Göteborg	12 Aug 95
		(30/5) Further bests by nations:						
2:58.56		BRA Parrela, da Silva, dos Santos, de Araújo			2	PAm	Winnipeg	30 Jul 99
2:58.68		NGR Chukwu 45.18, Monye 44.49, Bada 44.70, Udo-Obong 44.31			2	OG	Sydney	30 Sep 00
2:58.96		FRA Djhone 45.4, Keita 44.7, Diagana 44.69, Raquil 44.15			2	WCh	Saint-Denis	31 Aug 03
2:59.13		CUB Martínez 45.6, Herrera 44.38, Tellez 44.81, Hernández 44.34			1h2	OG	Barcelona	7 Aug 92
2:59.63		KEN D Kitur 45.4, S Kitur 45.13, Kipkemboi 44.76, Kemboi 44.34			3h2	OG	Barcelona	7 Aug 92
		(10)						
2:59.70		AUS Frayne 45.38, Clark 43.86, Minihan 45.07, Mitchell 45.39			4	OG	Los Angeles	11 Aug 84
2:59.86		GDR Möller 45.8, Schersing 44.8, Carlowitz 45.3, Schönlebe 44.1			1	vURS	Erfurt	23 Jun 85
2:59.95		YUG Jovkovic, Djurovic, Macev, Brankovic 44.3			2h3	WCh	Tokyo	31 Aug 91
2:59.96		FRG Dobeleit 45.7, Henrich 44.3, Itt 45.12, Schmid 44.93			4	WCh	Roma	6 Sep 87
3:00.16		URS Lovachov, Lomtyev, Kurochkin, Markin 43.9			1	Drz	Moskva	18 Aug 84
3:00.20		RSA			4	WCh	Sevilla	29 Aug 99
		van Oudtshoorn 46.5, Mokganyetsi 44.5, A Botha 45.43, Malherbe 43.78						
3:00.44		RUS Kliger 45.71, Kosov 45.14, Vdovin 44.66, Golovastov 44.93			5	WCh	Stuttgart	22 Aug 93

Mark Wind		Name	Nat	Born	Pos	Meet	Venue	Date
3:00.64	SEN	Diarra 46.53, Dia 44.94, Ndiaye 44.70, Faye 44.47			4	OG	Atlanta	3 Aug 96
3:00.76	JPN	Karube 45.88, Ito 44.86, Osakada 45.08, Omori 44.94			5	OG	Atlanta	3 Aug 96
3:00.79	ZIM	Chiwira 46.2, Mukomana 44.6, Ngidhi 45.79, Harnden 44.20			2h3	WCh	Athína	9 Aug 97
3:01.05	TRI	Delice, A Daniel, De Silva, Morris			1h1	OG	Barcelona	7 Aug 92
	(20 inc. RUS/URS)							
3:01.12	FIN	Lönnqvist 46.7, Salin 45.1, Karttunen 44.8, Kukkoaho 44.5			6	OG	München	10 Sep 72
3:01.37	ITA	Bongiorni 46.2, Zuliani 45.0, Petrella 45.3, Ribaud 44.9			4	EC	Stuttgart	31 Aug 86
3:01.42	ESP	I Rodríguez 46.0, Canal 44.1, Andrés 45.88, Reina 45.48			4h1	WCh	Edmonton	11 Aug 01
3:01.60	BAR	Louis 46.67, Peltier 44.97, Edwards 45.04, Forde 44.92			6	OG	Los Angeles	11 Aug 84
3:01.61	BUL	Georgiev 45.9, Stankulov 46.0, Raykov 45.07, Ivanov 44.66			2h1	WCh	Stuttgart	21 Aug 93
3:02.02	DOM	Peguero, Santa, Vidal, Sánchez			3	PAm	Santo Domingo	9 Aug 03
3:02.09	UGA	Govile 46.72, Kyeswa 44.60, Rwamu 46.40, Okot 44.37			7	OG	Los Angeles	11 Aug 84
3:02.11	MAR	Kasbane, Dahane, Belcaid, Lahlou 44.5			1h2	WCh	Tokyo	31 Aug 91
3:02.21	GRE	Régas 46.8, Doúpis 45.4, Grávalos 45.41, P Iakovákis 44.57			4	ECp-S	München	24 Jun 07
3:02.24	BOT	Molefe, Kilego, Moseki, Kubisa			1	AfG	Abuja	15 Oct 03

4 x 800 METRES RELAY

7:02.43	KEN	Mutua 1:46.73, Yiampoy 1:44.38, Kombich 1:45.92, Bungei 1:45.40	1 VD	Bruxelles	25 Aug 06
7:02.82	USA	J Harris 1:47.05, Robinson 1:44.03, Burley 1:46.05, Krummenacker 1:45.69	2 VD	Bruxelles	25 Aug 06
7:03.89 WR	GBR	Elliott 1:49.14, Cook 1:46.20, Cram 1:44.54, Coe 1:44.01	1	London (CP)	30 Aug 82
7:04.70	RSA	van Oudtshoorn 1:46.9, Sepeng 1:45.2, Kotze 1:48.3, J Botha 1:44.3	1	Stuttgart	6 Jun 99
7:06.66	QAT	Sultan 1:45.81, Al-Badri 1:46.71, Suleiman 1:45.89, Ali Kamal 1:48.25	4 VD	Bruxelles	25 Aug 06

4 x 1500 METRES RELAY

14:38.8 WR	FRG	Wessinghage 3:38.8, Hudak 3:40.2, Lederer 3:42.6, Fleschen 3:37.3	1	Köln	16 Aug 77
14:40.4 WR	NZL	Polhill 3:42.9, Walker 3:40.4, Dixon 3:41.2, Quax 3:35.9	1	Oslo	22 Aug 73
14:45.63	URS	Kalutskiy, Yakovlev, Legeda, Lotarev	1	Leningrad	4 Aug 85
14:46.16	Larios, ESP	Jiménez 3:40.9, Pancorbo 3:41.2, A García 3:43.9, Viciosa 3:40.2	1	Madrid	5 Sep 97
14:46.3	USA	Aldridge, Clifford, Harbour, Duits	1	Bourges	23 Jun 79
14:48.2	FRA	Begouin, Lequement, Philippe 3:42.2, Dien 3:37.2	2	Bourges	23 Jun 79

4 x 1 MILE RELAY

15:49.08	IRL	Coghlan 4:00.2, O'Sullivan 3:55.3, O'Mara 3:56.6, Flynn 3:56.98	1	Dublin	17 Aug 85
15:59.57	NZL	Rodhers 3:57.2, VBowden 4:02.5, Gilchrist 4:02.8, Walker 3:57.07	1	Auckland	2 Mar 83

3000 METRES TRACK WALK

10:47.11	Giovanni	De Benedictis	ITA	8.1.68	1		S.Giovanni Valdarno	19 May 90
10:56.22	Andrew	Jachno	AUS	13.4.62	1		Melbourne	7 Feb 91
10:56.34+	Roman	Mrázek	SVK	21.1.62	1k	PTS	Bratislava	14 Jun 89
11:00.2+	Jozef	Pribilinec	SVK	6.7.60	1k		Banská Bystrica	30 Aug 85
11:00.56	David	Smith	AUS	24.7.55	1		Perth	24 Jan 87
11:03.01	Vladimir	Andreyev	RUS	7.9.66	2		Formia	13 Jul 97
Indoors								
10:31.42	Andreas	Erm	GER	12.3.76	1		Halle	4 Feb 01
10:54.61	Carlo	Mattioli	ITA	23.10.54	1		Milano	6 Feb 80
10:56.88	Reima	Salonen	FIN	19.11.55	1		Turku	5 Feb 84
11:00.86+	Frants	Kostyukevich	BLR	4.4.63	1k	EI	Genova	28 Feb 92

5000 METRES TRACK WALK

18:05.49	Hatem	Ghoula	TUN	7.6.73	1		Tunis	1 May 97
18:17.22	Robert	Korzeniowski	POL	30.7.68	1		Reims	3 Jul 92
18:27.34	Francisco Javier	Fernández	ESP	6.3.77	1		Villeneuve d'Ascq	8 Jun 07
18:28.80	Roman	Mrázek	SVK	21.1.62	1	PTS	Bratislava	14 Jun 89
18:30.43	Maurizio	Damilano	ITA	6.4.57	1		Caserta	11 Jun 92
ndoors								
18:07.08	Mikhail	Shchennikov	RUS	24.12.67	1		Moskva	14 Feb 95
18:08.86	Ivano	Brugnetti	ITA	1.9.76	1	NC	Ancona	17 Feb 07
18:11.41	Ronald	Weigel	GDR	8.8.59	1mx		Wien	13 Feb 88
18:15.25	Grigoriy	Kornev	RUS	14.3.61	1		Moskva	7 Feb 92
18:16.54 ?	Frants	Kostyukevich	BLR	4.4.63	2	NC	Gomel	4 Feb 89
18:19.97	Giovanni	De Benedictis	ITA	8.1.68	1	EI	Genova	28 Feb 92
18:22.25	Andreas	Erm	GER	12.3.76	1	NC	Dortmund	25 Feb 01
18:23.18	Rishat	Shafikov	RUS	23.1.70	1		Samara	1 Mar 97
18:24.13	Francisco Javier	Fernández	ESP	6.3.77	1		Belfast	17 Feb 07
18:27.15	Alessandro	Gandellini	ITA	30.4.73	1	NC	Genova	12 Feb 00
18:27.80	Jozef	Pribilinec	SVK	6.7.60	2	WI	Indianapolis	7 Mar 87
18:27.95	Stefan	Johansson	SWE	11.4.67	3	EI	Genova	28 Feb 92
18:30.91	Aleksandr	Yargunkin	RUS	6.1.81	1		Yekaterinburg	7 Jan 07
18:31.63	Vladimir	Andreyev	RUS	7.9.66	2		Moskva	7 Feb 92

10,000 METRES TRACK WALK

Mark	Wind	Name		Nat	Born	Pos	Meet	Venue	Date
37:58.6		Ivano	Brugnetti	ITA	1.9.76	1		Sesto San Gioavnni	23 Jul 05
38:02.60		Jozef	Pribilinec	SVK	6.7.60	1		Banská Bystrica	30 Aug 85
38:06.6		David	Smith	AUS	24.7.55	1		Sydney	25 Sep 86
38:07.65		Francisco Javier	Fernández	ESP	6.3.77	1	NC	San Sebastián	5 Aug 07
38:12.13		Ronald	Weigel	GDR	8.8.59	1		Potsdam	10 May 86
38:18.0+		Valdas	Kazlauskas	LTU	23.2.58	1		Moskva	18 Sep 83
38:24 0+		Bernardo	Segura	MEX	11.2.70	1	SGP	Fana	7 May 94
38:24.31		Hatem	Ghoula	TUN	7.6.73	1		Tunis	30 May 98
38:26.4		Daniel	García	MEX	28.10.71	1		Sdr Omme	17 May 97
38:26.53		Robert	Korzeniowski	POL	30.7.68	1		Riga	31 May 02
38:37.6+		Jefferson	Pérez	ECU	1.7.74	1	in 20k	Fana	9 May 98
38:38.0		Walter	Arena	ITA	30.5.64	1		Catania	13 Apr 90
38:40.18		Giovanni	De Benedictis	ITA	8.1.68	1	NC	Cesenatico	1 Jul 95
38:41.17		Andrey	Yurin	UKR	20.1.84	1		Kiev	22 Jun 05
Indoors									
38:31.4		Werner	Heyer	GDR	14.11.56	1		Berlin	12 Jan 80

20 KILOMETRES WALK

Mark	Wind	Name		Nat	Born	Pos	Meet	Venue	Date
1:17:16		Vladimir	Kanaykin	RUS	21.3.85	1	RWC	Saransk	29 Sep 07
1:17:21	WR	Jefferson	Pérez	ECU	1.7.74	1	WCh	Saint-Denis	23 Aug 03
1:17:22	WR	Francisco Javier	Fernández	ESP	6.3.77	1		Turku	28 Apr 02
1:17:23		Vladimir	Stankin	RUS	2.1.74	1	NC-w	Adler	8 Feb 04
1:17:25.6t		Bernardo	Segura	MEX	11.2.70	1	SGP	Fana	7 May 94
1:17:33		Nathan	Deakes	AUS	17.8.77	1		Cixi	23 Apr 05
1:17:36			Kanaykin			1	NC	Cheboksary	17 Jun 07
1:17:41			Zhu Hongjun	CHN	18.8.83	2		Cixi	23 Apr 05
1:17:46		Julio	Martínez	GUA	27.9.73	1		Eisenhüttenstadt	8 May 99
1:17:46		Roman	Rasskazov	RUS	28.4.79	1	NC	Moskva	19 May 00
1:17:52			Fernández			1		La Coruña	4 Jun 05
1:17:53			Cui Zhide (10)	CHN	11.1.83	3		Cixi	23 Apr 05
1:17:56		Alejandro	López	MEX	9.2.75	2		Eisenhüttenstadt	8 May 99
1:18:00			Fernández			2	WCh	Saint-Denis	23 Aug 03
1:18:03.3t	WR		Bo Lingtang	CHN	12.8.70	1	NC	Beijing	7 Apr 94
1:18:05		Dmitriy	Yesipchuk	RUS	17.11.74	1	NC-w	Adler	4 Mar 01
1:18:06		Viktor	Burayev	RUS	23.8.82	2	NC-w	Adler	4 Mar 01
1:18:06		Vladimir	Parvatkin	RUS	10.10.84	1	NC-w	Adler	12 Mar 05
1:18:07			Rasskazov			1	NC-w	Adler	20 Feb 00
1:18:07			Rasskazov			3	WCh	Saint-Denis	23 Aug 03
1:18:07			Li Gaobo	CHN	23.7.89	4		Cixi	23 Apr 05
1:18:12		Artur	Meleshkevich	BLR	11.4.75	1		Brest	10 Mar 01
1:18:13	WR	Pavol	Blazek	SVK	9.7.58	1		Hildesheim	16 Sep 90
1:18:14		Mikhail	Khmelnitskiy	BLR	24.7.69	1	NC	Soligorsk	13 May 00
1:18:14			Deakes			1		Dublin	16 Jun 01
1:18:14		Noé	Hernández (20)	MEX	15.3.78	4	WCh	Saint-Denis	23 Aug 03
1:18:16		Vladimir	Andreyev	RUS	7.9.66	2	NC	Moskva	19 May 00
1:18:17			Parvatkin			2	NC-w	Adler	8 Feb 04
1:18:17		Ilya	Markov	RUS	19.6.72	2	NC-w	Adler	12 Mar 05
1:18:17			Li Gaobo			1		Yangzhou	22 Apr 06
		(30/22)							
1:18:18		Yevgeniy	Misyulya	BLR	13.3.64	1		Eisenhüttenstadt	11 May 96
1:18:20	WR	Andrey	Perlov	RUS	12.12.61	1	NC	Moskva	26 May 90
1:18:20		Denis	Nizhegorodov	RUS	26.7.80	3	NC-w	Adler	4 Mar 01
1:18:22		Robert	Korzeniowski	POL	30.7.68	1		Hildesheim	9 Jul 00
1:18:23		Andrey	Makarov	BLR	2.1.71	2	NC	Soligorsk	13 May 00
1:18:27		Daniel	García	MEX	28.10.71	2	WCp	Podebrady	19 Apr 97
1:18:27			Xing Shucai	CHN	4.8.84	5		Cixi	23 Apr 05
1:18:30			Yu Chaohong	CHN	12.12.76	6		Cixi	23 Apr 05
		(30)							
1:18:31			Han Yucheng	CHN	16.12.78	7		Cixi	23 Apr 05
1:18:32			Li Zewen	CHN	5.12.73	4	WCp	Podebrady	19 Apr 97
1:18:33			Liu Yunfeng	CHN	3.8.79	8		Cixi	23 Apr 05
1:18:35.2t		Stefan	Johansson	SWE	11.4.67	1	SGP	Fana	15 May 92
1:18:36		Mikhail	Shchennikov	RUS	24.12.67	1	NC	Sochi	20 Apr 96
1:18:37		Aleksandr	Pershin	RUS	4.9.68	2	NC	Moskva	26 May 90
1:18:37		Ruslan	Shafikov	RUS	27.6.75	1	NC-w23	Adler	11 Feb 95
1:18:39			Lu Ronghua	CHN	21.2.83	9		Cixi	23 Apr 05
1:18:40.0t	WR	Ernesto	Canto	MEX	18.10.59	1	SGP	Fana	5 May 84
1:18:41		Igor	Kollár	SVK	26.6.65	3		Eisenhüttenstadt	11 May 96
		(40)							

Mark Wind	Name		Nat	Born	Pos	Meet	Venue	Date
1:18:42	Andreas	Erm	GER	12.3.76	2	ECp	Eisenhüttenstadt	17 Jun 00
1:18:44		Chu Yafei	CHN	5.9.88	5		Yangzhou	22 Apr 06
1:18:45	Stepan	Yudin	RUS	3.4.80	4	NC-w	Adler	12 Mar 05
1:18:45		Dong Jimin	CHN	10.10.85	6		Yangzhou	22 Apr 06
1:18:45.2t		Tan Mingjun	CHN	17.7.70	2	NC	Beijing	7 Apr 94
1:18:48	Rishat	Shafikov	RUS	23.1.70	2		Cheboksary	30 Aug 98
1:18:51	Frants	Kostyukevich	BLR	4.4.63	3	NC	Moskva	26 May 90
1:18:54	Maurizio	Damilano	ITA	6.4.57	1	7N	La Coruña	6 Jun 92
1:18:56	Grigoriy	Kornev	RUS	14.3.61	4	NC	Moskva	26 May 90
1:18:56	Valeriy	Borchin	RUS	3.7.86	1	NC-w	Adler	17 Feb 07
	(50)	100th man 1:19:51, 200th 1:21:01, 300th 1:21:55						
Probable short course								
1:18:33	Mikhail	Shchennikov	RUS	24.12.67	1	4-N	Livorno	10 Jul 93
1:18:49WR?	Daniel	Bautista	MEX	4.8.52	1	LT	Eschborn	29 Sep 79

30 KILOMETRES WALK

2:01:13+	Vladimir	Kanaykin	RUS	21.3.85	1	in 35k	Adler	19 Feb 06
2:01:44.1t	Maurizio	Damilano	ITA	6.4.57	1		Cuneo	3 Oct 92
2:01:47+		Kanaykin			1	in 35k	Adler	13 Mar 05
2:02:27+		Kanaykin			1	in 35k	Adler	8 Feb 04
2:02:41	Andrey	Perlov	RUS	12.12.61	1	NC-w	Sochi	19 Feb 89
2:02:45	Yevgeniy	Misyulya	BLR	13.3.64	1		Mogilyov	28 Apr 91
2:03:06	Daniel	Bautista	MEX	4.8.52	1		Cherkassy	27 Apr 80
2:03:50+	Vladimir	Parvatkin	RUS	10.10.84	2	in 35k	Adler	19 Feb 06
2:03:56.5t	Thierry	Toutain	FRA	14.2.62	1		Héricourt	24 Mar 91
2:04:00	Aleksandr	Potashov	BLR	12.3.62	1		Adler	14 Feb 93
2:04:24	Valeriy	Spitsyn	RUS	5.12.65	1	NC-w	Sochi	22 Feb 92
2:04:30	Vitaliy	Matsko (10)	RUS	8.6.60	2	NC-w	Sochi	19 Feb 89
2:04:49+	Semyon	Lovkin	RUS	14.7.77	1=	in 35k	Adler	1 Mar 03
2:04:49+	Stepan	Yudin	RUS	3.4.80	1=	in 35k	Adler	1 Mar 03
2:04:50+	Sergey	Kirdyapkin	RUS	16.1.80	2	in 35k	Adler	13 Mar 05
2:04:55.5t	Guillaume	Leblanc	CAN	14.4.62	1		Sept-Iles	16 Jun 90

35 KILOMETRES WALK

2:21:31	Vladimir	Kanaykin	RUS	21.3.85	1	NC-w	Adler	19 Feb 06
2:23:17		Kanaykin			1	NC-w	Adler	8 Feb 04
2:23:17		Kanaykin			1	NC-w	Adler	13 Mar 05
2:24:25	Semyon	Lovkin	RUS	14.7.77	1	NC-w	Adler	1 Mar 03
2:24:50	Denis	Nizhegorodov	RUS	26.7.80	2	NC-w	Adler	19 Feb 06
2:25:38	Stepan	Yudin	RUS	3.4.80	2	NC-w	Adler	1 Mar 03
2:25:57	Sergey	Kirdyapkin	RUS	16.1.80	2	NC-w	Adler	13 Mar 05
2:25:58	German	Skurygin ¶	RUS	15.9.63	1	NC-w	Adler	20 Feb 98
2:26:25	Aleksey	Voyevodin	RUS	9.8.70	2	NC-w	Adler	8 Feb 04
2:26:46	Oleg	Ishutkin	RUS	22.7.75	1	NC-w	Adler	9 Feb 97
2:26:51	Yuriy	Andronov	RUS	6.11.71	3	NC-w	Adler	19 Feb 06
2:27:02	Yevgeniy	Shmalyuk (10)	RUS	14.1.76	1	NC-w	Adler	20 Feb 00
2:27:07	Dmitriy	Dolnikov	RUS	19.11.72	2	NC-w	Adler	20 Feb 98
2:27:21	Pavel	Nikolayev	RUS	18.12.77	3	NC-w	Adler	20 Feb 98
2:27:29	Nikolay	Matyukhin	RUS	13.12.68	2	NC-w	Adler	9 Feb 97

50 KILOMETRES WALK

3:35:29	Denis	Nizhegorodov	RUS	26.7.80	1	NC	Cheboksary	13 Jun 04
3:35:47	Nathan	Deakes	AUS	17.8.77	1	NC	Geelong	2 Dec 06
3:36:03 WR	Robert	Korzeniowski	POL	30.7.68	1	WCh	Saint-Denis	27 Aug 03
3:36:04	Alex	Schwazer	ITA	26.12.84	1	NC	Rosignano Solvay	11 Feb 07
3:36:06		Yu Chaohong	CHN	12.12.76	1	NG	Nanjing	22 Oct 05
3:36:13		Zhao Chengliang	CHN	1.6.84	2	NG	Nanjing	22 Oct 05
3:36:20		Han Yucheng	CHN	16.12.78	1	NC	Nanning	27 Feb 05
3:36:39 WR		Korzeniowski			1	EC	München	8 Aug 02
3:36:42	German	Skurygin ¶	RUS	15.9.63	2	WCh	Saint-Denis	27 Aug 03
3:37:26 WR	Valeriy	Spitsyn	RUS	5.12.65	1	NC	Moskva	21 May 00
3:37:41 WR	Andrey	Perlov (10)	RUS	12.12.61	1	NC	Leningrad	5 Aug 89
3:37:46	Andreas	Erm	GER	12.3.76	3	WCh	Saint-Denis	27 Aug 03
3:37:58		Xing Shucai	CHN	4.8.84	2	NC	Nanning	27 Feb 05
3:38:01	Aleksey	Voyevodin	RUS	9.8.70	4	WCh	Saint-Denis	27 Aug 03
3:38:02		Nizhegorodov			1	WCp	La Coruña	14 May 06
3:38:08	Sergey	Kirdyapkin	RUS	16.1.80	1	WCh	Helsinki	12 Aug 05
3:38:17 WR	Ronald	Weigel	GDR	8.8.59	1	IM	Potsdam	25 May 86
3:38:23		Nizhegorodov			5	WCh	Saint-Denis	27 Aug 03
3:38:29	Vyacheslav	Ivanenko	RUS	3.3.61	1	OG	Seoul	30 Sep 88

Mark	Wind	Name		Nat	Born	Pos	Meet	Venue	Date
3:38:31	WR		Weigel			1		Berlin	20 Jul 84
3:38:43		Valentí	Massana	ESP	5.7.70	1	NC	Orense	20 Mar 94
3:38:46			Korzeniowski			1	OG	Athína	27 Aug 04
3:38:56			Weigel			2	OG	Seoul	30 Sep 88
3:38:56			Zhao Chengliang			3	NC	Nanning	27 Feb 05
3:39:10			Han Yucheng			1	NC-w	Guangzhou	22 Mar 04
3:39:17			Dong Jimin	CHN	10.10.85	4	NC	Nanning	27 Feb 05
3:39:21		Vladimir	Potemin	RUS	15.1.80	2	NC	Moskva	21 May 00
3:39:22		Sergey	Korepanov	KAZ	9.5.64	1	WCp	Mézidon-Canon	2 May 99
3:39:34		Valentin	Kononen	FIN	7.3.69	1		Dudince	25 Mar 00
3:39:34			Potemin			2	NC	Cheboksary	13 Jun 04
		(30/21)							
3:39:45		Hartwig	Gauder	GDR	10.11.54	3	OG	Seoul	30 Sep 88
3:39:54		Jesús Angel	García	ESP	17.10.69	1	WCp	Podebrady	20 Apr 97
3:40:02		Aleksandr	Potashov	BLR	12.3.62	1	NC	Moskva	27 May 90
3:40:07		Andrey	Plotnikov	RUS	12.8.67	2	NC	Moskva	27 May 90
3:40:08		Tomasz	Lipiec ¶	POL	10.5.71	2	WCp	Mézidon-Canon	2 May 99
3:40:12		Oleg	Ishutkin	RUS	22.7.75	2	WCp	Podebrady	20 Apr 97
3:40:13		Nikolay	Matyukhin	RUS	13.12.68	3	WCp	Mézidon-Canon	2 May 99
3:40:23			Gadasu Alatan	CHN	27.1.84	3	NG	Nanjing	22 Oct 05
3:40:40		Vladimir	Kanaykin	RUS	21.3.85	1	NC	Saransk	12 Jun 05
		(30)							
3:40:46	WR	José	Marin	ESP	21.1.50	1	NC	Valencia	13 Mar 83
3:40:57.9t		Thierry	Toutain	FRA	14.2.62	1		Héricourt	29 Sep 96
3:41:10			Zhao Jianguo	CHN	19.1.88	1	AsiC	Wajima	16 Apr 06
3:41:20	WR	Raúl	González	MEX	29.2.52	1		Podebrady	11 Jun 78
3:41:20			Zhao Yongsheng	CHN	16.4.70	1	WCp	Beijing	30 Apr 95
3:41:28.2t		René	Piller	FRA	23.4.65	1	SGP	Fana	7 May 94
3:41:30			Ni Liang	CHN	26.7.86	4	NG	Nanjing	22 Oct 05
3:41:30		Trond	Nymark	NOR	28.12.76	2	WCp	La Coruña	14 May 06
3:41:39		Yohann	Diniz	FRA	1.1.78	1	EC	Göteborg	10 Aug 06
3:41:47		Mikel	Odriozola	ESP	25.5.73	1	NC	El Prat de Llobregat	27 Feb 05
		(40)							
3:41:51		Venyamin	Nikolayev	RUS	7.10.58	2	NC	Leningrad	3 Aug 85
3:41.51		Oleg	Kistkin	RUS	13.5.83	3	ECp	Leamington	20 May 07
3:41:56		Yevgeniy	Shmalyuk	RUS	14.1.76	6	WCp	Mézidon-Canon	2 May 99
3:42:00		Stanislav	Vezhel	BLR	11.10.58	3	NC	Moskva	27 May 90
3:42:03		Carlos	Mercenario	MEX	3.5.67	1	WCp	San José	2 Jun 91
3:42:04		Yevgeniy	Yevsyukov	RUS	2.1.50	3	NC	Leningrad	3 Aug 85
3:42:06		Yuriy	Andronov	RUS	6.11.71	2	NC	Cheboksary	26 May 02
3:42:20		Pavel	Szikora	SVK	26.3.52	1		Dudince	4 Apr 87
3:42:20		Viktor	Ginko	BLR	7.12.65	2		Palma de Mallorca	5 Mar 95
3:42:36		Reima	Salonen	FIN	19.11.55	1	NC	Vantaa	24 May 86
		(50)	100th man 3:46:44, 200th 3:51:36						

100 KILOMETRES WALK

Mark	Wind	Name		Nat	Born	Pos	Meet	Venue	Date
8:38.07		Viktor	Ginko	BLR	7.12.65	1		Scanzorosciate	27 Oct 02
8:43:30			Ginko			1		Scanzorosciate	29 Oct 00
8:44:28			Ginko			1		Scanzorosciate	19 Oct 03
8:48:28		Modris	Liepins	LAT	30.8.66	1		Scanzorosciate	28 Oct 01
8:54:35		Aleksey	Rodionov	RUS	5.3.57	1		Scanzorosciate	15 Nov 98
8:55:12		Pascal	Kieffer	FRA	6.5.61	1		Besançon	18 Oct 92
8:55:40		Vitaliy	Popovich	UKR	22.10.62	1		Scanzorosciate	31 Oct 99
8:58:12		Gérard	Lelièvre	FRA	13.11.49	1		Laval	7 Oct 84
8:58:47		Zóltan	Czukor	HUN	18.12.62	2		Scanzorosciate	27 Oct 02

Some notes on all-time lists at end of 2007

Dominance: Yelena Isinbayeva has best 19 PV performances, Bubka has best 17 (plus the first 8 of the 9 6.05 marks)
Most changes: Women's Hammer: five new marks in both all-time top ten performances and top performers.
No changes in top 50s – men's 800m, women's 1500m (top change 131st Selsouli 4:10.52), women's discus.
Men 800m: The top mark of 1:43.74 does not make the top 227 performances at 1:43.7 or better.
Men PV: The only change in top 50 – 5.90i Björn Otto as 31=.
Men LJ: 8.13 Jesse Owens 1935 ranks 313= performer; this is easily the top mark of the pre-War era at any event
Men Shot: Mikulás Konopka is the only newcomer to top 100; HT: Primoz Kozmus at 27th only change to top 80.
Women 200m: Allyson Felix 21.81 (12=) only change to top 50.
Women 800m: Jepkosgei 1:56.04 (26th) only change to top 50, then 95= Martínez 1:57.62.
Unusually for recent years – first change in 10,000m was 31:00.27 Tufa for 42nd.
Women Shot: Valerie Vili at 41= only change in top 50.
Women Discus: Only changes in the world top 100 came in the wind-favourable conditions in Hawaii by Suzy Powell and Becky Breisch at 51st and 56th respecively, and from Darya Pishchalnikova, up a few places to 92nd.

WOMEN'S ALL-TIME WORLD LISTS

100 METRES

Mark	Wind	Name		Nat	Born	Pos	Meet	Venue	Date
10.49WR	0.0	Florence	Griffith-Joyner	USA	21.12.59	1q1	OT	Indianapolis	16 Jul 88
		@ Probably strongly wind-assisted, but recognised as a US and world record							
10.61	1.2		Griffith-Joyner			1	OT	Indianapolis	17 Jul 88
10.62	1.0		Griffith-Joyner			1q3	OG	Seoul	24 Sep 88
10.65A	1.1	Marion	Jones ¶	USA	12.10.75	1	WCp	Johannesburg	12 Sep 98
10.70	1.6		Griffith-Joyner			1s1	OT	Indianapolis	17 Jul 88
10.70	-0.1		Jones			1	WCh	Sevilla	22 Aug 99
10.71	0.1		Jones			1		Chengdu	12 May 98
10.71	2.0		Jones			1s2	NC	New Orleans	19 Jun 98
10.72	2.0		Jones			1	NC	New Orleans	20 Jun 98
10.72	0.0		Jones			1	Herc	Monaco	8 Aug 98
10.72	0.0		Jones			1	Athl	Lausanne	25 Aug 98
10.73	2.0	Christine	Arron	FRA	13.9.73	1	EC	Budapest	19 Aug 98
10.74	1.3	Merlene	Ottey	JAM	10.5.60	1	GPF	Milano	7 Sep 96
10.75	0.6		Jones			1	GGala	Roma	14 Jul 98
10.76WR	1.7	Evelyn	Ashford	USA	15.4.57	1	WK	Zürich	22 Aug 84
10.76	0.9		Jones			1	VD	Bruxelles	22 Aug 97
10.76	0.3		Jones			1q4	WCh	Sevilla	21 Aug 99
10.77	0.9	Irina	Privalova	RUS	22.11.68	1rA	Athl	Lausanne	6 Jul 94
10.77	-0.9		Jones			1rA	WK	Zürich	12 Aug 98
10.77	0.7	Ivet	Lalova	BUL	18.5.84	1	ECp-1A	Plovdiv	19 Jun 04
10.78A	1.0	Dawn	Sowell	USA	27.3.66	1	NCAA	Provo	3 Jun 89
10.78	1.7		Ottey			1	Expo	Sevilla	30 May 90
10.78	0.4		Ottey			1	GPF	Paris	3 Sep 94
10.78	1.1		Jones			1	BrGP	London (CP)	5 Aug 00
10.79AWR	0.6		Ashford			1	USOF	USAF Academy	3 Jul 83
10.79	1.7		Ottey			1		Vigo	23 Jul 91
10.79	0.0		Li Xuemei	CHN	5.1.77	1	NG	Shanghai	18 Oct 97
10.79	-0.6		Jones			1	GP	Osaka	9 May 98
10.79	-0.1	Inger	Miller	USA	12.6.72	2	WCh	Sevilla	22 Aug 99
10.80		four performances: 1 by Ottey, 3 by Jones							
		(30 performances by 10 athletes)							
10.81WR	1.7	Marlies	Göhr'	GDR	21.3.58	1	OD	Berlin	8 Jun 83
10.82	-1.0	Gail	Devers	USA	19.11.66	1	OG	Barcelona	1 Aug 92
10.82	0.4	Gwen	Torrence	USA	12.6.65	2	GPF	Paris	3 Sep 94
10.82	-0.3	Zhanna	Pintusevich-Block	UKR	6.7.72	1	WCh	Edmonton	6 Aug 01
10.82	-0.7	Sherone	Simpson	JAM	12.8.84	1	NC	Kingston	24 Jun 06
10.83	1.7	Marita	Koch	GDR	18.2.57	2	OD	Berlin	8 Jun 83
10.83@	0.0	Sheila	Echols	USA	2.10.64	1q2	OT	Indianapolis	16 Jul 88
10.83	-1.0	Juliet	Cuthbert	JAM	9.4.64	2	OG	Barcelona	1 Aug 92
10.83	0.1	Ekateríni	Thánou ¶	GRE	1.2.75	2s1	WCh	Sevilla	22 Aug 99
10.84	1.3	Chioma	Ajunwa ¶	NGR	25.12.70	1		Lagos	11 Apr 92
		(20)							
10.84	1.9	Chandra	Sturrup	BAH	12.9.71	1	Athl	Lausanne	5 Jul 05
10.85	2.0	Anelia	Nuneva	BUL	30.6.62	1h1	NC	Sofiya	2 Sep 88
10.85	0.4	Veronica	Campbell	JAM	15.5.82	1	WK	Zürich	19 Aug 05
10.86	0.6	Silke	Gladisch/Möller	GDR	20.6.64	1	NC	Potsdam	20 Aug 87
10.86@	0.0	Diane	Williams	USA	14.12.60	2q1	OT	Indianapolis	16 Jul 88
		10.94A	0.6			2	USOF	USAF Academy	3 Jul 83
10.86	1.2	Chryste	Gaines	USA	14.9.70	1	WAF	Monaco	14 Sep 03
10.88	0.4	Lauryn	Williams	USA	11.9.83	2	WK	Zürich	19 Aug 05
10.89	1.8	Katrin	Krabbe ¶	GDR	22.11.69	1		Berlin	20 Jul 88
10.89	0.0		Liu Xiaomei	CHN	11.1.72	2	NG	Shanghai	18 Oct 97
10.90	1.4	Glory	Alozie	NGR/ESP	30.12.77	1		La Laguna	5 Jun 99
		(30)							
10.90	2.0	Torri	Edwards	USA	31.1.77	1	adidas	Carson	20 May 07
10.91	0.2	Heike	Drechsler'	GDR	16.12.64	2	GWG	Moskva	6 Jul 86
10.91	1.1	Savatheda	Fynes	BAH	17.10.74	2	Athl	Lausanne	2 Jul 99
10.91	1.5	Debbie	Ferguson	BAH	16.1.76	1	CG	Manchester	27 Jul 02
10.92	0.0	Alice	Brown	USA	20.9.60	2q2	OT	Indianapolis	16 Jul 88
10.92	1.1	D'Andre	Hill	USA	19.4.73	3	NC	Atlanta	15 Jun 96
10.92	0.1	Yuliya	Nesterenko	BLR	15.6.79	1s1	OG	Athína	21 Aug 04
10.93	1.8	Ewa	Kasprzyk	POL	7.9.57	1	NC	Grudziadz	27 Jun 86
10.93	1.0	Tayna	Lawrence	JAM	17.9.75	3	VD	Bruxelles	30 Aug 02
10.94	1.0	Carlette	Guidry	USA	4.9.68	1	TAC	New York	14 Jun 91
		(40)							

Mark	Wind	Name		Nat	Born	Pos	Meet	Venue	Date
10.95	1.0	Bärbel	Wöckel'	GDR	21.3.55	2	NC	Dresden	1 Jul 82
10.95	2.0	Me'Lisa	Barber	USA	4.10.80	2	adidas	Carson	20 May 07
10.96	1.2	Marie-José	Pérec	FRA	9.5.68	1	NC	Dijon	27 Jul 91
10.96	2.0	Galina	Malchugina	RUS	17.12.62	2	CIS Ch	Moskva	22 Jun 92
10.96	1.0	Eldece	Clarke-Lewis	BAH	13.2.65	1	Conseil	Fort-de-France	29 Apr 00
10.96	0.4	Muriel	Hurtis	FRA	25.3.79	1	ECp-S	Annecy	22 Jun 02
10.97	0.0	Angella	Issajenko' ¶	CAN	28.9.58	3	ASV	Köln	16 Aug 87
10.97	0.2	Mary	Onyali	NGR	3.2.68	1q2	WCh	Stuttgart	15 Aug 93
10.97	0.1	Pauline	Davis-Thompson	BAH	9.7.66	3	NC	Nassau	21 Jul 00
10.97	0.1	LaTasha	Colander	USA	23.8.76	1	NC/OT	Sacramento	10 Jul 04
10.97	-0.7	Sanya	Richards	USA	26.2.85	2	Golden	Shanghai	28 Sep 07
		(51)	100th women 11.07, 200th 11.17, 300th 11.24						
Probably semi-automatic timing									
10.87	1.9	Lyudmila	Kondratyeva	RUS	11.4.58	1		Leningrad	3 Jun 80
Low altitude best: 10.91	1.6		Sowell			1	TAC	Houston	16 Jun 89
Wind-assisted to 10.78 performances and 10.95 performers									
10.54	3.0		Griffith-Joyner			1	OG	Seoul	25 Sep 88
10.60	3.2		Griffith-Joyner			1h1	OT	Indianapolis	16 Jul 88
10.68	2.2		Jones			1	DNG	Stockholm	1 Aug 00
10.70	2.6		Griffith-Joyner			1s2	OG	Seoul	25 Sep 88
10.75	4.1		Jones			1h3	NC	New Orleans	19 Jun 98
10.77	2.3	Gail	Devers	USA	19.11.66	1	Jen	San José	28 May 94
10.77	2.1		Jones			1	Pre	Eugene	31 May 98
10.77	2.3	Ekateríni	Thánou ¶	GRE	1.2.75	1		Rethymno	28 May 99
10.78	3.1		Ashford			1		Modesto	12 May 84
10.78	5.0	Gwen	Torrence	USA	12.6.65	1q3	OT	Indianapolis	16 Jul 88
10.78	2.3		Ottey			1s2	WCh	Tokyo	27 Aug 91
10.79	3.3	Marlies	Göhr'	GDR	21.3.58	1	NC	Cottbus	16 Jul 80
10.80	2.9	Pam	Marshall	USA	16.8.60	1	TAC	Eugene	20 Jun 86
10.80	2.8	Heike	Drechsler'	GDR	16.12.64	1	Bisl	Oslo	5 Jul 86
10.82	2.2	Silke	Gladisch/Möller	GDR	20.6.64	1s1	WCh	Roma	30 Aug 87
10.84	2.9	Alice	Brown	USA	20.9.60	2	TAC	Eugene	20 Jun 86
10.86	2.2	Torri	Edwards ¶	USA	31.1.77	1		Réthimno	21 Jul 06
10.87	3.0	Me'Lisa	Barber	USA	4.10.80	1s1	NC	Carson	25 Jun 05
10.89	3.1	Kerstin	Behrendt	GDR	2.9.67	2		Berlin	13 Sep 88
10.91	4.6	Carlette	Guidry	USA	4.9.68	1s1	NCAA	Eugene	31 May 91
10.92	3.3	Bärbel	Wöckel'	GDR	21.3.55	2	NC	Cottbus	16 Jul 80
10.92	3.4	Angella	Taylor' ¶	CAN	28.9.58	1s2	CG	Brisbane	4 Oct 82
10.93	3.8	Sonia	Lannaman	GBR	24.3.56	1	ECp/sf	Dublin	17 Jul 77
10.93	3.3	Ingrid	Auerswald'	GDR	2.9.57	3	NC	Cottbus	16 Jul 80
10.93	4.2	Holli	Hyche	USA	6.9.71	2h2	NC	Eugene	16 Jun 93
10.93A	3.1	Virginia	Powell	USA	7.9.83	1h1	NCAA-r	Provo	26 May 06
10.94	3.9	Jackie	Washington	USA	17.7.62	1		Houston	18 May 86
10.94A	3.0	Evette	de Klerk'	RSA	21.8.65	1h	NC	Germiston	20 Apr 90
Hand timing									
10.6	0.1	Zhanna	Pintusevich	UKR	6.7.72	1		Kiev	12 Jun 97
10.7		Merlene	Ottey	JAM	10.5.60	1h	NC	Kingston	15 Jul 88
10.7	1.1	Juliet	Cuthbert	JAM	9.4.64	1	NC	Kingston	4 Jul 92
10.7		Mary	Onyali	NGR	3.2.68	1	NC	Lagos	22 Jun 96
10.7	-0.2	Svetlana	Goncharenko	RUS	28.5.71	1		Rostov-na-Donu	30 May 98
10.7w	2.6	Savatheda	Fynes	BAH	17.10.74	1	NC	Nassau	22 Jun 95
Drugs disqualification									
10.75	-0.4		Jones			1	OG	Sydney	23 Sep 00
10.78	0.1		Jones			1	ISTAF	Berlin	1 Sep 00
10.85	0.9	Kelli	White ¶	USA	1.4.77	1	WCh	Saint-Denis	24 Aug 03
10.79w	2.3	Kelli	White ¶	USA	1.4.77	1		Carson/Los Angeles	1 Jun 03

200 METRES

21.34WR	1.3	Florence	Griffith-Joyner	USA	21.12.59	1	OG	Seoul	29 Sep 88
21.56WR	1.7		Griffith-Joyner			1s1	OG	Seoul	29 Sep 88
21.62A	-0.6	Marion	Jones ¶	USA	12.10.75	1	WCp	Johannesburg	11 Sep 98
21.64	0.8	Merlene	Ottey	JAM	10.5.60	1	VD	Bruxelles	13 Sep 91
21.66	-1.0		Ottey			1	WK	Zürich	15 Aug 90
21.71WR	0.7	Marita	Koch	GDR	18.2.57	1	v Can	Karl-Marx-Stadt	10 Jun 79
21.71WR	0.3		Koch			1	OD	Potsdam	21 Jul 84
21.71WR	1.2	Heike	Drechsler'	GDR	16.12.64	1	NC	Jena	29 Jun 86
21.71WR	-0.8		Drechsler			1	EC	Stuttgart	29 Aug 86
21.72	1.3	Grace	Jackson	JAM	14.6.61	2	OG	Seoul	29 Sep 88
21.72	-0.1	Gwen	Torrence	USA	12.6.65	1s2	OG	Barcelona	5 Aug 92
21.74	0.4	Marlies	Göhr'	GDR	21.3.58	1	NC	Erfurt	3 Jun 84

Mark	Wind		Name	Nat	Born	Pos	Meet	Venue	Date
21.74	1.2	Silke	Gladisch'	GDR	20.6.64	1	WCh	Roma	3 Sep 87
21.75	-0.1	Juliet	Cuthbert (10)	JAM	9.4.64	2s2	OG	Barcelona	5 Aug 92
21.76	0.3		Koch			1	NC	Dresden	3 Jul 82
21.76	0.7		Griffith-Joyner			1q1	OG	Seoul	28 Sep 88
21.76	-0.8		Jones			1	WK	Zürich	13 Aug 97
21.77	-0.1		Griffith-Joyner			1q2	OT	Indianapolis	22 Jul 88
21.77	1.0		Ottey			1	Herc	Monaco	7 Aug 93
21.77	-0.3		Torrence			1	ASV	Köln	18 Aug 95
21.77	0.6	Inger	Miller	USA	12.6.72	1	WCh	Sevilla	27 Aug 99
21.78	-1.3		Koch			1	NC	Leipzig	11 Aug 85
21.79	1.7		Gladisch			1	NC	Potsdam	22 Aug 87
21.80	-1.1		Ottey			1	Nik	Nice	10 Jul 90
21.80	0.4		Jones			1	GWG	Uniondale, NY	20 Jul 98
21.81	-0.1	Valerie	Brisco	USA	6.7.60	1	OG	Los Angeles	9 Aug 84
21.81	0.4		Ottey			1	ASV	Köln	19 Aug 90
21.81	-0.6		Torrence			1	OG	Barcelona	6 Aug 92
21.81	0.0		Torrence			1	Herc	Monaco	25 Jul 95
21.81	1.6		Jones			1	Pre	Eugene	30 May 99
21.81	1.7	Allyson	Felix	USA	18.11.85	1	WCh	Osaka	31 Aug 07
		(31/13)							
21.83	-0.2	Evelyn	Ashford	USA	15.4.57	1	WCp	Montreal	24 Aug 79
21.85	0.3	Bärbel	Wöckel'	GDR	21.3.55	2	OD	Potsdam	21 Jul 84
21.87	0.0	Irina	Privalova	RUS	22.11.68	2	Herc	Monaco	25 Jul 95
21.93	1.3	Pam	Marshall	USA	16.8.60	2	OT	Indianapolis	23 Jul 88
21.95	0.3	Katrin	Krabbe ¶	GDR	22.11.69	1	EC	Split	30 Aug 90
21.97	1.9	Jarmila	Kratochvílová	CZE	26.1.51	1	PTS	Bratislava	6 Jun 81
21.99	0.9	Chandra	Cheeseborough	USA	10.1.59	2	TAC	Indianapolis	19 Jun 83
		(20)							
21.99	1.1	Marie-José	Pérec	FRA	9.5.68	1	BNP	Villeneuve d'Ascq	2 Jul 93
22.00	1.3	Sherone	Simpson	JAM	12.8.84	1	NC	Kingston	25 Jun 06
22.01	-0.5	Anelia	Nuneva'	BUL	30.6.62	1	NC	Sofiya	16 Aug 87
22.01	0.0		Li Xuemei	CHN	5.1.77	1	NG	Shanghai	22 Oct 97
22.04A	0.7	Dawn	Sowell	USA	27.3.66	1	NCAA	Provo	2 Jun 89
22.05	0.8	Veronica	Campbell	JAM	15.5.82	1	OG	Athína	25 Aug 04
22.06A	0.7	Evette	de Klerk'	RSA	21.8.65	1		Pietersburg	8 Apr 89
22.07	-0.1	Mary	Onyali	NGR	3.2.68	1	WK	Zürich	14 Aug 96
22.10	-0.1	Kathy	Cook'	GBR	3.5.60	4	OG	Los Angeles	9 Aug 84
22.13	1.2	Ewa	Kasprzyk	POL	7.9.57	2	GWG	Moskva	8 Jul 86
		(30)							
22.14	-0.6	Carlette	Guidry	USA	4.9.68	1	NC	Atlanta	23 Jun 96
22.17A	-2.3	Zhanna	Pintusevich	UKR	6.7.72	1		Monachil	9 Jul 97
		22.24	-0.3			2	VD	Bruxelles	30 Aug 02
22.17	0.6	Sanya	Richards	USA	26.2.85	2	WAF	Stuttgart	9 Sep 06
22.18	-0.6	Dannette	Young-Stone	USA	6.10.64	2	NC	Atlanta	23 Jun 96
22.18	0.9	Galina	Malchugina	RUS	17.12.62	1s2	NC	Sankt Peterburg	4 Jul 96
22.18	0.5	Merlene	Frazer	JAM	27.12.73	1s2	WCh	Sevilla	25 Aug 99
22.19	1.5	Natalya	Bochina	RUS	4.1.62	2	OG	Moskva	30 Jul 80
22.19	0.0	Debbie	Ferguson	BAH	16.1.76	1	GP II	Saint-Denis	3 Jul 99
22.20	2.0	Kim	Gevaert	BEL	5.8.78	1	NC	Bruxelles	9 Jul 06
22.21 WR	1.9	Irena	Szewinska'	POL	24.5.46	1		Potsdam	13 Jun 74
		(40)							
22.22	-0.9	Falilat	Ogunkoya	NGR	12.5.68	1	AfCh	Dakar	22 Aug 98
22.22	0.6	Beverly	McDonald	JAM	15.2.70	2	WCh	Sevilla	27 Aug 99
22.22	0.3	Rachelle	Smith (Boone)	USA	30.6.81	2	NC	Carson	26 Jun 05
22.23	0.8	Melinda	Gainsford-Taylor	AUS	1.10.71	1		Stuttgart	13 Jul 97
22.23A	1.8	Carol	Rodríguez	PUR	16.12.85	1h1	NCAA-r	Provo	26 May 06
22.24	0.3	Gesine	Walther	GDR	6.10.62	2	NC	Dresden	3 Jul 82
22.24	0.1	Maya	Azarashvili	GEO	6.4.64	1		Kiyev	16 Aug 88
22.25A	0.8	Angella	Taylor'	CAN	28.9.58	1		Colorado Springs	20 Jul 82
22.25	1.3	Cathy	Freeman	AUS	16.2.73	1	CG	Victoria	26 Aug 94
22.25	1.8	Andrea	Philipp	GER	29.7.71	2s1	WCh	Sevilla	25 Aug 99
		(50)	100th woman 22.43, 200th 22.69, 300th 22.84						
Wind-assisted			*Performers listed to 22.22*						
21.82	3.1	Irina	Privalova	RUS	22.11.68	1	Athl	Lausanne	6 Jul 94
22.16	3.1	Dannette	Young-Stone	USA	6.10.64	2	Athl	Lausanne	6 Jul 94
22.16	3.2	Nanceen	Perry	USA	19.4.77	1		Austin	6 May 00
22.18A	2.8	Melinda	Gainsford-Taylor	AUS	1.10.71	1		Pietersburg	18 Mar 00
22.19A	3.1	Angella	Taylor'	CAN	28.9.58	1		Colorado Springs	21 Jul 82
22.22	2.7	LaTasha	Jenkins	USA	19.12.77	1s1	NCAA	Boise	4 Jun 99
22.22	4.0	Muna	Lee	USA	30.10.81	1	NCAA-r	Baton Rouge	29 May 04

Mark	Wind	Name		Nat	Born	Pos	Meet	Venue	Date
Hand timing									
21.9	-0.1	Svetlana	Goncharenko	RUS	28.5.71	1		Rostov-na-Donu	31 May 98
22.0	-0.6	Marina	Molokova	RUS	24.8.62	1	Ros	Praha	23 Jun 87
21.6w	2.5	Pam	Marshall	USA	16.8.60	1	TAC	San José	26 Jun 87
Drugs disqualification									
22.05	-0.3	Kelli	White ¶	USA	1.4.77	1	WCh	Saint-Denis	28 Aug 03
22.18i		Michelle	Collins ¶	USA	12.2.71	1	WI	Birmingham	15 Mar 03

300 METRES

Times in 300m races only

Mark		Name		Nat	Born	Pos	Meet	Venue	Date
35.30A		Ana Gabriela	Guevara	MEX	4.3.77	1		Ciudad de México	3 May 03
35.46		Kathy	Cook'	GBR	3.5.60	1	Nike	London (CP)	18 Aug 84
35.46		Chandra	Cheeseborough	USA	10.1.59	2	Nike	London (CP)	18 Aug 84
Drugs dq: 35.68		Marion	Jones ¶	USA	12.10.75	1	MSR	Walnut	22 Apr 01
Indoors									
35.45		Irina	Privalova	RUS	22.11.68	1		Moskva	17 Jan 93
35.48	#	Svetlana	Goncharenko	RUS	28.5.71	1		Tampere	4 Feb 98

400 METRES

Mark		Name		Nat	Born	Pos	Meet	Venue	Date
47.60	WR	Marita	Koch	GDR	18.2.57	1	WCp	Canberra	6 Oct 85
47.99	WR	Jarmila	Kratochvílová	CZE	26.1.51	1	WCh	Helsinki	10 Aug 83
48.16	WR		Koch			1	EC	Athína	8 Sep 82
48.16			Koch			1	Drz	Praha	16 Aug 84
48.22			Koch			1	EC	Stuttgart	28 Aug 86
48.25		Marie-José	Pérec	FRA	9.5.68	1	OG	Atlanta	29 Jul 96
48.26			Koch			1	GO	Dresden	27 Jul 84
48.27		Olga	Vladykina'	UKR	30.6.63	2	WCp	Canberra	6 Oct 85
48.45			Kratochvílová			1	NC	Praha	23 Jul 83
48.59		Tatána	Kocembová'	CZE	2.5.62	2	WCh	Helsinki	10 Aug 83
48.60	WR		Koch			1	ECp	Torino	4 Aug 79
48.60			Vladykina			1	ECp	Moskva	17 Aug 85
48.61			Kratochvílová			1	WCp	Roma	6 Sep 81
48.63		Cathy	Freeman	AUS	16.2.73	2	OG	Atlanta	29 Jul 96
48.65			Bryzgina'			1	OG	Seoul	26 Sep 88
48.70		Sanya	Richards	USA	26.2.85	1	WCp	Athína	16 Sep 06
48.73			Kocembová			2	Drz	Praha	16 Aug 84
48.77			Koch			1	v USA	Karl-Marx-Stadt	9 Jul 82
48.82			Kratochvílová			1	Ros	Praha	23 Jun 83
48.83		Valerie	Brisco	USA	6.7.60	1	OG	Los Angeles	6 Aug 84
48.83			Pérec			1	OG	Barcelona	5 Aug 92
48.85			Kratochvílová			2	EC	Athína	8 Sep 82
48.86			Kratochvílová			1	WK	Zürich	18 Aug 82
48.86			Koch			1	NC	Erfurt	2 Jun 84
48.87			Koch			1	VD	Bruxelles	27 Aug 82
48.88			Koch			1	OG	Moskva	28 Jul 80
48.89	WR		Koch			1		Potsdam	29 Jul 79
48.89			Koch			1		Berlin	15 Jul 84
48.89		Ana Gabriela	Guevara	MEX	4.3.77	1	WCh	Saint-Denis	27 Aug 03
48.92			Richards			1	WK	Zürich	19 Aug 05
		(30/9)							
49.05		Chandra	Cheeseborough	USA	10.1.59	2	OG	Los Angeles	6 Aug 84
			(10)						
49.07		Tonique	Williams-Darling	BAH	17.1.76	1	ISTAF	Berlin	12 Sep 04
49.10		Falilat	Ogunkoya	NGR	12.5.68	3	OG	Atlanta	29 Jul 96
49.11		Olga	Nazarova ¶	RUS	1.6.65	1s1	OG	Seoul	25 Sep 88
49.19		Mariya	Pinigina'	UKR	9.2.58	3	WCh	Helsinki	10 Aug 83
49.24		Sabine	Busch	GDR	21.11.62	2	NC	Erfurt	2 Jun 84
49.28	WR	Irena	Szewinska'	POL	24.5.46	1	OG	Montreal	29 Jul 76
49.28		Pauline	Davis	BAH	9.7.66	4	OG	Atlanta	29 Jul 96
49.29		Charity	Opara ¶	NGR	20.5.72	1	GGala	Roma	14 Jul 98
49.30		Petra	Müller'	GDR	18.7.65	1		Jena	3 Jun 88
49.30		Lorraine	Fenton'	JAM	8.9.73	2	Herc	Monaco	19 Jul 02
		(20)							
49.40		Jearl	Miles-Clark	USA	4.9.66	1	NC	Indianapolis	14 Jun 97
49.42		Grit	Breuer ¶	GER	16.2.72	2	WCh	Tokyo	27 Aug 91
49.43		Kathy	Cook'	GBR	3.5.60	3	OG	Los Angeles	6 Aug 84
49.43A		Fatima	Yusuf	NGR	2.5.71	1	AfG	Harare	15 Sep 95
49.47		Aelita	Yurchenko	UKR	1.1.65	2	Kuts	Moskva	4 Sep 88
49.49		Olga	Zaytseva	RUS	10.11.84	1	NCp	Tula	16 Jul 06
49.53		Vanya	Stambolova ¶	BUL	28.11.83	1	GP	Rieti	27 Aug 06

Mark Wind	Name		Nat	Born	Pos	Meet	Venue	Date
49.53	Novlene	Williams	JAM	26.4.82	1		Shanghai	23 Sep 06
49.56	Bärbel	Wöckel'	GDR	21.3.55	1		Erfurt	30 May 82
49.56	Monique	Hennagan	USA	26.5.76	1	NC/OT	Sacramento	17 Jul 04
	(30)							
49.57	Grace	Jackson	JAM	14.6.61	1	Nik	Nice	10 Jul 88
49.58	Dagmar	Rübsam'	GDR	3.6.62	3	NC	Erfurt	2 Jun 84
49.59	Marion	Jones	USA	12.10.75	1r6	MSR	Walnut	16 Apr 00
49.59	Katharine	Merry	GBR	21.9.74	1	GP	Athína	11 Jun 01
49.61	Ana Fidelia	Quirot	CUB	23.3.63	1	PAm	La Habana	5 Aug 91
49.61	Christine	Ohuruogu	GBR	17.5.84	1	WCh	Osaka	29 Aug 07
49.64	Gwen	Torrence	USA	12.6.65	2	Nik	Nice	15 Jul 92
49.64	Ximena	Restrepo	COL	10.3.69	3	OG	Barcelona	5 Aug 92
49.64	Deedee	Trotter	USA	8.12.82	1	NC	Indianapolis	23 Jun 07
49.65	Natalya	Nazarova	RUS	26.5.79	1	NC	Tula	31 Jul 04
	(40)							
49.65	Nicola	Sanders	GBR	23.6.82	2	WCh	Osaka	29 Aug 07
49.66	Christina	Lathan'	GDR	28.2.58	3	OG	Moskva	28 Jul 80
49.66	Lillie	Leatherwood	USA	6.7.64	1	TAC	New York	15 Jun 91
49.67	Sandra	Myers	ESP	9.1.61	1	Bisl	Oslo	6 Jul 91
49.70	Allyson	Felix	USA	18.11.85	1	DNG	Stockholm	7 Aug 07
49.74	Anja	Rücker	GER	20.12.72	2	WCh	Sevilla	26 Aug 99
49.75	Gaby	Bussmann	FRG	8.10.59	4	WCh	Helsinki	10 Aug 83
49.77	Olga	Kotlyarova	RUS	12.4.76	3	GGala	Roma	2 Jul 04
49.79	Sandie	Richards	JAM	6.11.68	2	WCh	Athína	4 Aug 97
49.79	Donna	Fraser	GBR	7.11.72	4	OG	Sydney	25 Sep 00
	(50)	100th woman 50.34, 200th 50.98, 300th 51.30						
Low altitude best: 49.77		Yusuf			6	OG	Atlanta	29 Jul 96
Hand timing								
48.9	Olga	Nazarova ¶	RUS	1.6.65	1	NP	Vladivostok	13 Sep 88
49.2A	Ana Fidelia	Quirot	CUB	23.3.63	1	AmCp	Bogotá	13 Aug 89

600 METRES

Mark	Name		Nat	Born	Pos	Meet	Venue	Date
1:22.63	Ana Fidelia	Quirot	CUB	23.3.63	1		Guadalajara, ESP	25 Jul 97
1:22.87	Maria Lurdes	Mutola	MOZ	27.10.72	1		Liège (NX)	27 Aug 02
1:23.5	Doina	Melinte	ROM	27.12.56	1		Poiana Brasov	27 Jul 86
1:23.78	Natalya	Khrushchelyova	RUS	30.5.73	2		Liège (NX)	2 Sep 03

800 METRES

Mark	Name		Nat	Born	Pos	Meet	Venue	Date
1:53.28 WR	Jarmila	Kratochvílová	CZE	26.1.51	1		München	26 Jul 83
1:53.43 WR	Nadezhda	Olizarenko'	UKR	28.11.53	1	OG	Moskva	27 Jul 80
1:54.44	Ana Fidelia	Quirot	CUB	23.3.63	1	WCp	Barcelona	9 Sep 89
1:54.68		Kratochvílová			1	WCh	Helsinki	9 Aug 83
1:54.81	Olga	Mineyeva	RUS	1.9.52	2	OG	Moskva	27 Jul 80
1:54.82		Quirot			1	ASV	Köln	24 Aug 97
1:54.85 WR		Olizarenko			1	Prav	Moskva	12 Jun 80
1:54.94 WR	Tatyana	Kazankina ¶	RUS	17.12.51	1	OG	Montreal	26 Jul 76
1:55.04		Kratochvílová			1	OsloG	Oslo	23 Aug 83
1:55.05	Doina	Melinte	ROM	27.12.56	1	NC	Bucuresti	1 Aug 82
1:55.1 '		Mineyeva			1	Znam	Moskva	6 Jul 80
1:55.19	Maria Lurdes	Mutola	MOZ	27.10.72	1	WK	Zürich	17 Aug 94
1:55.19	Jolanda	Ceplak ¶	SLO	12.9.76	1rA	NA	Heusden	20 Jul 02
1:55.26	Sigrun	Wodars/Grau	GDR	7.11.65	1	WCh	Roma	31 Aug 87
1:55.29		Mutola			2	ASV	Köln	24 Aug 97
1:55.32	Christine	Wachtel (10)	GDR	6.1.65	2	WCh	Roma	31 Aug 87
1:55.41		Mineyeva			1	EC	Athína	8 Sep 82
1:55.42	Nikolina	Shtereva	BUL	25.1.55	2	OG	Montreal	26 Jul 76
1:55.43		Mutola			1	WCh	Stuttgart	17 Aug 93
1:55.46	Tatyana	Providokhina	RUS	26.3.53	3	OG	Moskva	27 Jul 80
1:55.5		Mineyeva			1	Kuts	Podolsk	21 Aug 82
1:55.54	Ellen	van Langen	NED	9.2.66	1	OG	Barcelona	3 Aug 92
1:55.54		Liu Dong	CHN	24.12.73	1	NG	Beijing	9 Sep 93
1:55.55		Mutola			1	GP	Madrid (C)	19 Jul 03
1:55.56	Lyubov	Gurina	RUS	6.8.57	3	WCh	Roma	31 Aug 87
1:55.60	Elfi	Zinn	GDR	24.8.53	3	OG	Montreal	26 Jul 76
1:55.62		Mutola			1A	WK	Zürich	4 Aug 93
1:55.68	Ella	Kovacs	ROM	11.12.64	1	RomIC	Bucuresti	2 Jun 85
1:55.69	Irina	Podyalovskaya	RUS	19.10.59	1	Izv	Kiyev	22 Jun 84
1:55.70		Wodars			2	WCp	Barcelona	9 Sep 89
	(30/18)							
1:55.74	Anita	Weiss'	GDR	16.7.55	4	OG	Montreal	26 Jul 76

Mark	Wind	Name		Nat	Born	Pos	Meet	Venue	Date
1:55.87		Svetlana	Masterkova	RUS	17.1.68	1	Kuts	Moskva	18 Jun 99
		(20)							
1:55.96		Lyudmila	Veselkova	RUS	25.10.50	2	EC	Athína	8 Sep 82
1:55.96		Yekaterina	Podkopayeva'	RUS	11.6.52	1		Leningrad	27 Jul 83
1:55.99		Liliya	Nurutdinova ¶	RUS	15.12.63	2	OG	Barcelona	3 Aug 92
1:56.0	WR	Valentina	Gerasimova	KAZ	15.5.48	1	NC	Kiyev	12 Jun 76
1:56.0		Inna	Yevseyeva	UKR	14.8.64	1		Kiyev	25 Jun 88
1:56.04		Janeth	Jepkosgei	KEN	13.12.83	1	WCh	Osaka	28 Aug 07
1:56.07		Tatyana	Andrianova	RUS	10.12.79	1	NC	Tula	11 Jul 05
1:56.09		Zulia	Calatayud	CUB	9.11.79	1	Herc	Monaco	19 Jul 02
1:56.1		Ravilya	Agletdinova'	BLR	10.2.60	2	Kuts	Podolsk	21 Aug 82
1:56.2 '		Totka	Petrova ¶	BUL	17.12.56	1		Paris	6 Jul 79
		(30)							
1:56.2		Tatyana	Mishkel	UKR	10.6.52	3	Kuts	Podolsk	21 Aug 82
1:56.21		Martina	Kämpfert'	GDR	11.11.59	4	OG	Moskva	27 Jul 80
1:56.21		Zamira	Zaytseva	UZB	16.2.53	2		Leningrad	27 Jul 83
1:56.21		Kelly	Holmes	GBR	19.4.70	2	GPF	Monaco	9 Sep 95
1:56.24			Qu Yunxia	CHN	25.12.72	2	NG	Beijing	9 Sep 93
1:56.40		Jearl	Miles-Clark	USA	4.9.66	3	WK	Zürich	11 Aug 99
1:56.42		Paula	Ivan	ROM	20.7.63	1	Balk	Ankara	16 Jul 88
1:56.43		Hasna	Benhassi	MAR	1.6.78	2	OG	Athína	23 Aug 04
1:56.44		Svetlana	Styrkina	RUS	1.1.49	5	OG	Montreal	26 Jul 76
1:56.51		Slobodanka	Colovic	YUG	10.1.65	1		Beograd	17 Jun 87
		(40)							
1:56.53		Patricia	Djaté	FRA	3.1.71	3	GPF	Monaco	9 Sep 95
1:56.56		Ludmila	Formanová	CZE	2.1.74	4	WK	Zürich	11 Aug 99
1:56.57		Zoya	Rigel	RUS	15.10.52	3	EC	Praha	31 Aug 78
1:56.59		Natalya	Khrushchelyova	RUS	30.5.73	2	NC	Tula	31 Jul 04
1:56.60		Natalya	Tsyganova	RUS	7.2.71	1	NC	Tula	25 Jul 00
1:56.6		Tamara	Sorokina'	RUS	15.8.50	5	Kuts	Podolsk	21 Aug 82
1:56.61		Yelena	Afanasyeva	RUS	1.3.67	3	WK	Zürich	13 Aug 97
1:56.62		Tina	Paulino	MOZ	7.7.73	2	NYG	New York	22 May 93
1:56.64		Nadezhda	Loboyko	KAZ	30.6.61	1	NC	Kiyev	7 Jul 90
1:56.64		Stephanie	Graf	AUT	26.4.73	2	OG	Sydney	25 Sep 00
		(50)	100th woman 1:57.70, 200th 1:58.88, 300th 1:59.60						
Indoors: 1:55.85		Stephanie	Graf	AUT	26.4.73	2	EI	Wien	3 Mar 02

1000 METRES

Mark	Wind	Name		Nat	Born	Pos	Meet	Venue	Date
2:28.98	WR	Svetlana	Masterkova	RUS	17.1.68	1	VD	Bruxelles	23 Aug 96
2:29.34	WR	Maria Lurdes	Mutola	MOZ	27.10.72	1	VD	Bruxelles	25 Aug 95
2:30.6	WR	Tatyana	Providokhina	RUS	26.3.53	1		Podolsk	20 Aug 78
2:30.67	WR	Christine	Wachtel	GDR	6.1.65	1	ISTAF	Berlin	17 Aug 90
2:30.85		Martina	Kämpfert'	GDR	11.11.59	1		Berlin	9 Jul 80
2:31.50		Natalya	Artyomova ¶	RUS	5.1.63	1	ISTAF	Berlin	10 Sep 91
2:31.5		Maricica	Puica	ROM	29.7.50	1		Poiana Brasov	1 Jun 86
2:31.51		Sandra	Gasser ¶	SUI	27.7.62	1		Jerez de la Frontera	13 Sep 89
2:31.6 '		Beate	Liebich	GDR	21.2.58	2		Berlin	9 Jul 80
2:31.65		Olga	Dvirna	RUS	11.2.53	1		Athína	1 Sep 82

1500 METRES

Mark	Wind	Name		Nat	Born	Pos	Meet	Venue	Date
3:50.46	WR		Qu Yunxia	CHN	25.12.72	1	NG	Beijing	11 Sep 93
3:50.98			Jiang Bo	CHN	13.3.77	1	NG	Shanghai	18 Oct 97
3:51.34			Lang Yinglai	CHN	22.8.79	2	NG	Shanghai	18 Oct 97
3:51.92			Wang Junxia	CHN	9.1.73	2	NG	Beijing	11 Sep 93
3:52.47	WR	Tatyana	Kazankina ¶	RUS	17.12.51	1	WK	Zürich	13 Aug 80
3:53.91			Yin Lili ¶	CHN	11.11.79	3	NG	Shanghai	18 Oct 97
3:53.96		Paula	Ivan'	ROM	20.7.63	1	OG	Seoul	1 Oct 88
3:53.97			Lan Lixin	CHN	14.2.79	4	NG	Shanghai	18 Oct 97
3:54.23		Olga	Dvirna	RUS	11.2.53	1	NC	Kiyev	27 Jul 82
3:54.52			Zhang Ling (10)	CHN	13.4.80	5	NG	Shanghai	18 Oct 97
3:55.0 '	WR		Kazankina ¶			1	Znam	Moskva	6 Jul 80
3:55.01			Lan Lixin			1h2	NG	Shanghai	17 Oct 97
3:55.07			Dong Yanmei	CHN	16.2.77	6	NG	Shanghai	18 Oct 97
3:55.30		Hassiba	Boulmerka	ALG	10.7.68	1	OG	Barcelona	8 Aug 92
3:55.33		Süreyya	Ayhan ¶	TUR	6.9.78	1	VD	Bruxelles	5 Sep 03
3:55.38			Qu Yunxia			2h2	NG	Shanghai	17 Oct 97
3:55.47			Zhang Ling			3h2	NG	Shanghai	17 Oct 97
3:55.60			Ayhan			1	WK	Zürich	15 Aug 03
3:55.68		Yuliya	Chizhenko	RUS	30.8.79	1	Gaz	Saint-Denis	8 Jul 06
3:55.82			Dong Yanmei			4h2	NG	Shanghai	17 Oct 97

Mark Wind	Name		Nat	Born	Pos	Meet	Venue	Date
3:56.0 WR		Kazankina ¶			1		Podolsk	28 Jun 76
3:56.14	Zamira	Zaytseva	UZB	16.2.53	2	NC	Kiyev	27 Jul 82
3:56.18	Maryam	Jamal	BRN	16.9.84	1	GP	Rieti	27 Aug 06
3:56.22		Ivan			1	WK	Zürich	17 Aug 88
3:56.31		Liu Dong	CHN	24.12.73	5h2	NG	Shanghai	17 Oct 97
3:56.43	Yelena	Soboleva	RUS	3.10.82	2	Gaz	Saint-Denis	8 Jul 06
3:56.50	Tatyana	Pozdnyakova	RUS	4.3.56	3	NC	Kiyev	27 Jul 82
3:56.56		Kazankina ¶			1	OG	Moskva	1 Aug 80
3:56.63	Nadezhda	Ralldugina (20)	UKR	15.11.57	1	Drz	Praha	18 Aug 84
3:56.65	Yekaterina	Podkopayeva'	RUS	11.6.52	1		Rieti	2 Sep 84
	(30/21)							
3:56.7 '	Lyubov	Smolka	UKR	29.11.52	2	Znam	Moskva	6 Jul 80
3:56.7	Doina	Melinte	ROM	27.12.56	1		Bucuresti	12 Jul 86
3:56.77+	Svetlana	Masterkova	RUS	17.1.68	1	WK	Zürich	14 Aug 96
3:56.8 '	Nadezhda	Olizarenko'	UKR	28.11.53	3	Znam	Moskva	6 Jul 80
3:56.91	Lyudmila	Rogachova	RUS	30.10.66	2	OG	Barcelona	8 Aug 92
3:56.91	Tatyana	Tomashova	RUS	1.7.75	1	EC	Göteborg	13 Aug 06
3:56.97	Gabriela	Szabo	ROM	14.11.75	1	Herc	Monaco	8 Aug 98
3:57.03		Liu Jing	CHN	3.2.71	6h2	NG	Shanghai	17 Oct 97
3:57.05	Svetlana	Guskova	MDA	19.8.59	4	NC	Kiyev	27 Jul 82
	(30)							
3:57.12	Mary	Decker/Slaney	USA	4.8.58	1	vNord	Stockholm	26 Jul 83
3:57.22	Maricica	Puica	ROM	29.7.50	1		Bucuresti	1 Jul 84
3:57.40	Suzy	Favor Hamilton	USA	8.8.68	1	Bisl	Oslo	28 Jul 00
3:57.4 '	Totka	Petrova ¶	BUL	17.12.56	1	Balk	Athína	11 Aug 79
3:57.41	Jackline	Maranga	KEN	16.12.77	3	Herc	Monaco	8 Aug 98
3:57.46		Zhang Linli	CHN	6.3.73	3	NG	Beijing	11 Sep 93
3:57.71	Christiane	Wartenberg'	GDR	27.10.56	2	OG	Moskva	1 Aug 80
3:57.71	Carla	Sacramento	POR	10.12.71	4	Herc	Monaco	8 Aug 98
3:57.72	Galina	Zakharova	RUS	7.9.56	1	NP	Baku	14 Sep 84
3:57.73	Natalya	Yevdokimova	RUS	17.3.78	2	GP	Rieti	28 Aug 05
	(40)							
3:57.90	Kelly	Holmes	GBR	19.4.70	1	OG	Athína	28 Aug 04
3:57.92	Tatyana	Dorovskikh ¶	UKR	12.8.61	4	OG	Barcelona	8 Aug 92
3:58.12	Naomi	Mugo	KEN	2.1.77	5	Herc	Monaco	8 Aug 98
3:58.20	Anita	Weyermann	SUI	8.12.77	6	Herc	Monaco	8 Aug 98
3:58.2 '	Natalia	Marasescu' ¶	ROM	3.10.52	1	NC	Bucuresti	13 Jul 79
3:58.28	Elvan	Abeylegesse	TUR	11.9.82	1	ECCp-A	Moskva	30 May 04
3:58.29	Violeta	Szekely' ¶	ROM	26.3.65	1	Herc	Monaco	18 Aug 00
3:58.37	Tatyana	Providokhina	RUS	26.3.53	1	Kuts	Podolsk	22 Aug 82
3:58.38	Kutre	Dulecha	ETH	22.8.78	7	Herc	Monaco	8 Aug 98
3:58.39	Maria	Cioncan	ROM	19.6.77	3	OG	Athína	28 Aug 04
	(50)	100th woman 4:00.35, 200th 4:03.75, 300th 4:05.70						

1 MILE

Mark Wind	Name		Nat	Born	Pos	Meet	Venue	Date
4:12.56 WR	Svetlana	Masterkova	RUS	17.1.68	1	WK	Zürich	14 Aug 96
4:15.61 WR	Paula	Ivan'	ROM	20.7.63	1	Nik	Nice	10 Jul 89
4:15.63	Yelena	Soboleva	RUS	3.10.82	1		Moskva	29 Jun 07
4:15.8	Natalya	Artyomova ¶	RUS	5.1.63	1		Leningrad	5 Aug 84
4:16.71 WR	Mary	Slaney (Decker)	USA	4.8.58	1	WK	Zürich	21 Aug 85
4:17.25	Sonia	O'Sullivan	IRL	28.11.69	1	Bisl	Oslo	22 Jul 94
4:17.33	Maricica	Puica	ROM	29.7.50	2	WK	Zürich	21 Aug 85
4:17.57	Zola	Budd'	GBR	26.5.66	3	WK	Zürich	21 Aug 85
4:17.75	Maryam	Jamal	BRN	16.9.84	1	VD	Bruxelles	14 Sep 07
4:18.13	Doina	Melinte	ROM	27.12.56	1	Bisl	Oslo	14 Jul 90
	4:17.14i				1		East Rutherford	9 Feb 90

2000 METRES

Mark Wind	Name		Nat	Born	Pos	Meet	Venue	Date
5:25.36 WR	Sonia	O'Sullivan	IRL	28.11.69	1	TSB	Edinburgh	8 Jul 94
5:26.93	Yvonne	Murray	GBR	4.10.64	2	TSB	Edinburgh	8 Jul 94
5:28.69 WR	Maricica	Puica	ROM	29.7.50	1	PTG	London (CP)	11 Jul 86
5:28.72 WR	Tatyana	Kazankina ¶	RUS	17.12.51	1		Moskva	4 Aug 84
5:29.43+		Wang Junxia	CHN	9.1.73	1h2	NG	Beijing	12 Sep 93
5:29.64	Tatyana	Pozdnyakova	UKR	4.3.56	2		Moskva	4 Aug 84
5:30.19	Zola	Budd'	GBR	26.5.66	3	PTG	London (CP)	11 Jul 86
5:30.92	Galina	Zakharova	RUS	7.9.56	3		Moskva	4 Aug 84
Indoors: 5:30.53	Gabriela	Szabo	ROM	14.11.75	1		Sindelfingen	8 Mar 98

3000 METRES

Mark Wind	Name		Nat	Born	Pos	Meet	Venue	Date
8:06.11 WR		Wang Junxia	CHN	9.1.73	1	NG	Beijing	13 Sep 93

Mark	Wind	Name		Nat	Born	Pos	Meet	Venue	Date
8:12.18			Qu Yunxia	CHN	25.12.72	2	NG	Beijing	13 Sep 93
8:12.19	WR		Wang Junxia			1h2	NG	Beijing	12 Sep 93
8:12.27			Qu Yunxia			2h2	NG	Beijing	12 Sep 93
8:16.50			Zhang Linli	CHN	6.3.73	3	NG	Beijing	13 Sep 93
8:19.78			Ma Liyan	CHN	6.9.68	3h2	NG	Beijing	12 Sep 93
8:21.26			Ma Liyan			4	NG	Beijing	13 Sep 93
8:21.42		Gabriela	Szabo	ROM	14.11.75	1	Herc	Monaco	19 Jul 02
8:21.64		Sonia	O'Sullivan	IRL	28.11.69	1	TSB	London (CP)	15 Jul 94
8:21.84			Zhang Lirong	CHN	3.3.73	5	NG	Beijing	13 Sep 93
8:22.06	WR		Zhang Linli			1h1	NG	Beijing	12 Sep 93
8:22.20		Paula	Radcliffe	GBR	17.12.73	2	Herc	Monaco	19 Jul 02
8:22.44			Zhang Lirong			2h1	NG	Beijing	12 Sep 93
8:22.62	WR	Tatyana	Kazankina ¶	RUS	17.12.51	1		Leningrad	26 Aug 84
8:23.23		Edith	Masai (10)	KEN	4.4.67	3	Herc	Monaco	19 Jul 02
8:23.26		Olga	Yegorova	RUS	28.3.72	1	WK	Zürich	17 Aug 01
8:23.75			Yegorova			1	GP	Saint-Denis	6 Jul 01
8:23.96			Yegorova			1	GGala	Roma	29 Jun 01
8:24.19			Szabo			2	WK	Zürich	17 Aug 01
8:24.31			Szabo			1	GP	Paris	29 Jul 98
8:24.51+		Meseret	Defar	ETH	19.11.83	1	in 2M	Bruxelles	14 Sep 07
8:24.66			Defar			1	DNG	Stockholm	25 Jul 06
8:25.03			Szabo			1	WK	Zürich	11 Aug 99
8:25.40		Yelena	Zadorozhnaya	RUS	3.12.77	2	GGala	Roma	29 Jun 01
8:25.56		Tatyana	Tomashova	RUS	1.7.75	3	GGala	Roma	29 Jun 01
8:25.59			Szabo			1	GP	Paris (C)	21 Jul 99
8:25.62		Berhane	Adere	ETH	21.7.73	3	WK	Zürich	17 Aug 01
8:25.82			Szabo			1	VD	Bruxelles	3 Sep 99
8:25.83		Mary	Slaney	USA	4.8.58	1	GGALA	Roma	7 Sep 85
8:25.92		Gelete	Burka	ETH	15.2.86	2	DNG	Stockholm	25 Jul 06
		(30/17)							
8:26.48		Zahra	Ouaziz	MAR	20.12.69	2	WK	Zürich	11 Aug 99
8:26.53		Tatyana	Samolenko' ¶	UKR	12.8.61	1	OG	Seoul	25 Sep 88
8:26.78	WR	Svetlana	Ulmasova	UZB	4.2.53	1	NC	Kiyev	25 Jul 82
		(20)							
8:27.12	WR	Lyudmila	Bragina	RUS	24.7.43	1	v USA	College Park	7 Aug 76
8:27.15		Paula	Ivan'	ROM	20.7.63	2	OG	Seoul	25 Sep 88
8:27.62		Gete	Wami	ETH	11.12.74	4	WK	Zürich	17 Aug 01
8:27.83		Maricica	Puica	ROM	29.7.50	2	GGALA	Roma	7 Sep 85
8:28.66		Vivian	Cheruiyot	KEN	11.9.83	2	WAF	Stuttgart	23 Sep 07
8:28.80		Marta	Domínguez	ESP	3.11.75	3	WK	Zürich	11 Aug 00
8:28.83		Zola	Budd'	GBR	26.5.66	3	GGALA	Roma	7 Sep 85
8:28.87		Maryam	Jamal	BRN	16.9.84	1	Bisl	Oslo	29 Jul 05
8:29.02		Yvonne	Murray	GBR	4.10.64	3	OG	Seoul	25 Sep 88
8:29.06		Priscah	Cherono	KEN	27.6.80	3	WAF	Stuttgart	23 Sep 07
		(30)							
8:29.14		Lydia	Cheromei	KEN	11.5.77	5	WK	Zürich	11 Aug 00
8:29.36		Svetlana	Guskova	MDA	19.8.59	2	NC	Kiyev	25 Jul 82
8:29.52		Mariem Alaoui	Selsouli	MAR	8.4.84	1	Herc	Monaco	25 Jul 07
8:29.55		Tirunesh	Dibaba	ETH	1.6.85	1	LGP	London (CP)	28 Jul 06
8:30.18		Mariya	Pantyukhova	RUS	14.8.74	4	WK	Zürich	11 Aug 99
8:30.22		Carla	Sacramento	POR	10.12.71	2	Herc	Monaco	4 Aug 99
8:30.39		Irina	Mikitenko	GER	23.8.72	6	WK	Zürich	11 Aug 00
8:30.45		Yelena	Romanova	RUS	20.3.63	4	OG	Seoul	25 Sep 88
8:30.59		Daniela	Yordanova	BUL	8.3.76	5	GP	Saint-Denis	6 Jul 01
8:30.66		Fernanda	Ribeiro	POR	23.6.69	3	Herc	Monaco	4 Aug 99
		(40)							
8:30.95		Tegla	Loroupe	KEN	9.5.73	2	Herc	Monaco	18 Aug 00
8:31.27		Joanne	Pavey	GBR	20.9.73	4	VD	Bruxelles	30 Aug 02
8:31.32		Isabella	Ochichi	KEN	28.10.79	1	Gaz	Saint-Denis	23 Jul 04
8:31.67		Natalya	Artyomova ¶	RUS	5.1.63	5	OG	Seoul	25 Sep 88
8:31.69		Lidia	Chojecka	POL	25.1.77	5	VD	Bruxelles	30 Aug 02
8:31.75		Grete	Waitz'	NOR	1.10.53	1	OsloG	Oslo	17 Jul 79
8:31.94		Elvan	Abeylegesse	TUR	11.9.82	6	VD	Bruxelles	30 Aug 02
8:32.00		Elana	Meyer'	RSA	10.10.66	1		Durban	29 Apr 91
8:32.0		Tatyana	Pozdnyakova	UKR	4.3.56	1		Ryazan	11 Aug 84
8:32.17		Angela	Chalmers	CAN	6.9.63	1	CG	Victoria	23 Aug 94
		(50)	100th woman 8:38.13, 200th 8:45.07, 300th 8:49.91						

Indoors

Mark		Name		Nat	Born	Pos	Meet	Venue	Date
8:23.72		Meseret	Defar	ETH	19.11.83	1	Spark	Stuttgart	3 Feb 07
8:23.74		Meselech	Melkamu	ETH	19.4.85	2	Spark	Stuttgart	3 Feb 07

Mark	Wind	Name		Nat	Born	Pos	Meet	Venue	Date
8:27.86		Liliya	Shobukhova	RUS	13.11.77	1	NC	Moskva	17 Feb 06
8:29.00		Olesya	Syreva	RUS	25.11.83	2	NC	Moskva	17 Feb 06

5000 METRES

Mark	Wind	Name		Nat	Born	Pos	Meet	Venue	Date
14:16.63	WR	Meseret	Defar	ETH	19.11.83	1	Bisl	Oslo	15 Jun 07
14:22.51		Vivian	Cheruiyot	KEN	11.9.83	2	Bisl	Oslo	15 Jun 07
14:24.53	WR		Defar			1		New York (RI)	3 Jun 06
14:24.68	WR	Elvan	Abeylegesse	TUR	11.9.82	1	Bisl	Bergen (Fana)	11 Jun 04
14:28.09	WR		Jiang Bo	CHN	13.3.77	1	NG	Shanghai	23 Oct 97
14:28.98			Defar			1	VD	Bruxelles	26 Aug 05
14:29.11		Paula	Radcliffe	GBR	17.12.73	1	ECpS	Bydgoszcz	20 Jun 04
14:29.32		Olga	Yegorova	RUS	28.3.72	1	ISTAF	Berlin	31 Aug 01
14:29.32		Berhane	Adere	ETH	21.7.73	1	Bisl	Oslo	27 Jun 03
14:29.82			Dong Yanmei	CHN	16.2.77	2	NG	Shanghai	23 Oct 97
14:30.18			Defar			1	GS	Ostrava	27 Jun 07
14:30.40		Tirunesh	Dibaba	ETH	1.6.85	1	Bisl	Oslo	2 Jun 06
14:30.63			T Dibaba			1	VD	Bruxelles	25 Aug 06
14:30.88		Gete	Wami (10)	ETH	11.12.74	1	NA	Heusden	5 Aug 00
14:30.88			T Dibaba			2	Bisl	Bergen (Fana)	11 Jun 04
14:31.09			Adere			2	VD	Bruxelles	26 Aug 05
14:31.20		Gelete	Burka	ETH	15.2.86	2	GS	Ostrava	27 Jun 07
14:31.27	WR		Dong Yanmei			1h1	NG	Shanghai	21 Oct 97
14:31.30			Jiang Bo			2h1	NG	Shanghai	21 Oct 97
14:31.42			Radcliffe			1	CG	Manchester	28 Jul 02
14:31.48		Gabriela	Szabo	ROM	14.11.75	1	ISTAF	Berlin	1 Sep 98
14:31.69			Wami			2	ISTAF	Berlin	31 Aug 01
14:32.08		Zahra	Ouaziz	MAR	20.12.69	2	ISTAF	Berlin	1 Sep 98
14:32.33			Liu Shixiang ¶	CHN	13.1.71	3h1	NG	Shanghai	21 Oct 97
14:32.42			T Dibaba		5	1		New York (RI)	11 Jun 05
14:32.44			Radcliffe			3	ISTAF	Berlin	31 Aug 01
14:32.57			T Dibaba			1	GGala	Roma	8 Jul 05
14:32.74		Ejagayehu	Dibaba	ETH	25.6.82	3	Bisl	Bergen (Fana)	11 Jun 04
14:32.79			Adere			2	GGala	Roma	8 Jul 05
14:32.90			Defar			3	GGala	Roma	8 Jul 05
		(30/15)							
14:33.04		Werknesh	Kidane	ETH	21.11.81	2	Bisl	Oslo	27 Jun 03
14:33.83		Meselech	Melkamu	ETH	19.4.85	3	GS	Ostrava	27 Jun 07
14:33.84		Edith	Masai	KEN	4.4.67	3	Bisl	Oslo	2 Jun 06
14:35.18		Sentayehu	Ejigu	ETH	21.6.85	4	Bisl	Bergen (Fana)	11 Jun 04
14:35.30		Priscah	Jepleting/Cherono	KEN	27.6.80	4	Bisl	Oslo	2 Jun 06
		(20)							
14:36.45	WR	Fernanda	Ribeiro	POR	23.6.69	1		Hechtel	22 Jul 95
14:36.52		Mariem Alaoui	Selsouli	MAR	8.4.84	1	G Gala	Roma	13 Jul 07
14:37.33	WR	Ingrid	Kristiansen'	NOR	21.3.56	1		Stockholm	5 Aug 86
14:38.21		Isabella	Ochichi	KEN	28.10.79	4	VD	Bruxelles	26 Aug 05
14:39.22		Tatyana	Tomashova	RUS	1.7.75	4	ISTAF	Berlin	31 Aug 01
14:39.83		Leah	Malot	KEN	7.6.72	1	ISTAF	Berlin	1 Sep 00
14:39.96			Yin Lili ¶	CHN	11.11.79	4	NG	Shanghai	23 Oct 97
14:39.96		Jo	Pavey	GBR	20.9.73	3	VD	Bruxelles	25 Aug 06
14:40.41			Sun Yingjie ¶	CHN	3.10.77	1	AsiG	Busan	12 Oct 02
14:40.47		Yelena	Zadorozhnaya	RUS	3.12.77	1	ECp-S	Bremen	24 Jun 01
		(30)							
14:40.74		Florence	Kiplagat	KEN	27.2.87	2	FBK	Hengelo	26 May 07
14:41.02		Sonia	O'Sullivan	IRL	28.11.69	2	OG	Sydney	25 Sep 00
14:41.23		Ayelech	Worku	ETH	12.6.79	1	BrGP	London (CP)	5 Aug 00
14:42.03		Irina	Mikitenko	GER	23.8.72	3	ISTAF	Berlin	7 Sep 99
14:42.53		Zhor	El Kamch	MAR	15.3.73	5	GGala	Roma	11 Jul 03
14:43.64			Xing Huina	CHN	25.2.84	5	WCh	Helsinki	13 Aug 05
14:43.87		Zakia	Mrisho	TAN	19.2.84	6	WCh	Helsinki	13 Aug 05
14:43.90		Margaret	Maury	FRA	15.5.74	2	VD	Bruxelles	3 Sep 04
14:44.05		Elana	Meyer	RSA	10.10.66	2		Hechtel	22 Jul 95
14:44.22		Derartu	Tulu	ETH	21.3.72	1	VD	Bruxelles	5 Sep 03
		(40)							
14:44.50		Roberta	Brunet	ITA	20.5.65	2	ASV	Köln	16 Aug 96
14:44.80		Shalane	Flanagan	USA	7.8.81	1	MSR	Walnut	13 Apr 07
14:44.95		Julia	Vaquero	ESP	18.9.70	3	Bisl	Oslo	5 Jul 96
14:45.33			Lan Lixin	CHN	14.2.79	2h2	NG	Shanghai	21 Oct 97
14:45.35		Regina	Jacobs ¶	USA	28.8.63	1	NC	Sacramento	21 Jul 00
14:45.71			Song Liqing ¶	CHN	20.1.80	3h2	NG	Shanghai	21 Oct 97
14:45.95		Tegla	Loroupe	KEN	9.5.73	3	BrGP	London (CP)	5 Aug 00

Mark Wind		Name	Nat	Born	Pos	Meet	Venue	Date
14:45.98	Pauline	Korikwiang	KEN	1.3.88	7	Bisl	Oslo	2 Jun 06
14:46.41	Rose	Cheruiyot	KEN	21.7.76	3	ASV	Köln	16 Aug 96
14:46.71	Sally	Barsosio	KEN	21.3.78	3	VD	Bruxelles	22 Aug 97
	(50)	100th woman 14:58.60, 200th 15:10.52, 300th 15:18.92, 400th 15:24.53						
Indoors: 14:27.42	Tirunesh	Dibaba	ETH	1.6.85	1	BIG	Boston (R)	27 Jan 07

10,000 METRES

Mark Wind		Name	Nat	Born	Pos	Meet	Venue	Date
29:31.78 WR		Wang Junxia	CHN	9.1.73	1	NG	Beijing	8 Sep 93
30:01.09	Paula	Radcliffe	GBR	17.12.73	1	EC	München	6 Aug 02
30:04.18	Berhane	Adere	ETH	21.7.73	1	WCh	Saint-Denis	23 Aug 03
30:07.15	Werknesh	Kidane	ETH	21.11.81	2	WCh	Saint-Denis	23 Aug 03
30:07.20		Sun Yingjie ¶	CHN	3.10.77	3	WCh	Saint-Denis	23 Aug 03
30:12.53	Lornah	Kiplagat (KEN)	NED	1.5.74	4	WCh	Saint-Denis	23 Aug 03
30:13.37		Zhong Huandi	CHN	28.6.67	2	NG	Beijing	8 Sep 93
30:13.74 WR	Ingrid	Kristiansen'	NOR	21.3.56	1	Bisl	Oslo	5 Jul 86
30:15.67	Tirunesh	Dibaba	ETH	1.6.85	1		Sollentuna	28 Jun 05
30:17.15		Radcliffe			1	GP	Gateshead	27 Jun 04
30:17.49	Derartu	Tulu (10)	ETH	21.3.72	1	OG	Sydney	30 Sep 00
30:18.39	Ejegayehu	Dibaba	ETH	25.6.82	2		Sollentuna	28 Jun 05
30:19.39		Kidane			1	GP II	Stanford	29 May 05
30:21.67	Elvan	Abeylegesse	TUR	11.9.82	1	ECp	Antalya	15 Apr 06
30:22.48	Gete	Wami	ETH	11.12.74	2	OG	Sydney	30 Sep 00
30:22.88	Fernanda	Ribeiro	POR	23.6.69	3	OG	Sydney	30 Sep 00
30:23.07	Alla	Zhilyayeva	RUS	5.2.69	5	WCh	Saint-Denis	23 Aug 03
30:23.25		Kristiansen			1	EC	Stuttgart	30 Aug 86
30:24.02		T Dibaba			1	WCh	Helsinki	6 Aug 05
30:24.36		Xing Huina	CHN	25.2.84	1	OG	Athína	27 Aug 04
30:24.56		Wami			1	WCh	Sevilla	26 Aug 99
30:24.98		E Dibaba			2	OG	Athína	27 Aug 04
30:25.41		Adere			2	WCh	Helsinki	6 Aug 05
30:26.00		E Dibaba			3	WCh	Helsinki	6 Aug 05
30:26.20	Galina	Bogomolova	RUS	15.10.77	6	WCh	Saint-Denis	23 Aug 03
30:26.42		Tulu			3	OG	Athína	27 Aug 04
30:26.97		Radcliffe			4	OG	Sydney	30 Sep 00
30:27.13		Radcliffe			2	WCh	Sevilla	26 Aug 99
30:27.18		Xing Huina			4	WCh	Helsinki	6 Aug 05
30:28.26		Sun Yingjie			1	AsiG	Busan	8 Oct 02
	(30/17)							
30:30.26	Edith	Masai	KEN	4.4.67	5	WCh	Helsinki	6 Aug 05
30:31.42	Inga	Abitova	RUS	6.3.82	1	EC	Göteborg	7 Aug 06
30:32.03	Tegla	Loroupe	KEN	9.5.73	3	WCh	Sevilla	26 Aug 99
	(20)							
30:32.36	Susanne	Wigene	NOR	12.2.78	2	EC	Göteborg	7 Aug 06
30:32.72	Lidiya	Grigoryeva	RUS	21.1.74	3	EC	Göteborg	7 Aug 06
30:37.68	Benita	Johnson	AUS	6.5.79	8	WCh	Saint-Denis	23 Aug 03
30:38.09		Dong Yanmei	CHN	16.2.77	1	NG	Shanghai	19 Oct 97
30:38.78	Jelena	Prokopcuka	LAT	21.9.76	6	EC	Göteborg	7 Aug 06
30:39.41		Lan Lixin	CHN	14.2.79	2	NG	Shanghai	19 Oct 97
30:39.98		Yin Lili ¶	CHN	11.11.79	3	NG	Shanghai	19 Oct 97
30:47.22		Dong Zhaoxia	CHN	13.11.74	4	NG	Shanghai	19 Oct 97
30:47.59	Sonia	O'Sullivan	IRL	28.11.69	2	EC	München	6 Aug 02
30:47.72		Wang Dongmei	CHN	3.12.72	5	NG	Shanghai	19 Oct 97
	(30)							
30:48.89	Yoko	Shibui	JPN	14.3.79	1		Stanford	3 May 02
30:50.32	Deena	Drossin/Kastor	USA	14.2.73	2		Stanford	3 May 02
30:51.69	Marta	Domínguez	ESP	3.11.75	7	EC	Göteborg	7 Aug 06
30:51.81	Kayoko	Fukushi	JPN	25.3.82	2	AsiG	Busan	8 Oct 02
30:52.51	Elana	Meyer	RSA	10.10.66	1	WCp	London (CP)	10 Sep 94
30:55.67	Irene	Kwambai	KEN	25.10.78	2		Utrecht	17 Jun 05
30:55.83		Liu Shixiang ¶	CHN	13.1.71	6	NG	Shanghai	19 Oct 97
30:57.07	Liz	McColgan	GBR	24.5.64	1	APM	Hengelo	25 Jun 91
30:57.21	Olga	Bondarenko'	RUS	2.6.60	2	EC	Stuttgart	30 Aug 86
30:57.70	Leah	Malot	KEN	7.6.72	2	NA	Heusden-Zolder	5 Aug 00
	(40)							
30:59.92	Merima	Hashim	ETH	.81	3	NA	Heusden-Zolder	5 Aug 00
31:00.27	Mestawet	Tufa	ETH	14.9.83	1		Valkenswaard	26 Jun 07
31:03.60	Marleen	Renders	BEL	24.12.68	4	NA	Heusden-Zolder	5 Aug 00
31:03.62	Kathrin	Ullrich'	GER	14.8.67	1	ECp	Frankfurt-am-Main	30 Jun 91
31:04.00	Lyudmila	Biktasheva	RUS	25.7.74	3	EC	München	6 Aug 02

Mark	Wind	Name		Nat	Born	Pos	Meet	Venue	Date
31:04.34		Jane	Wanjiku	KEN	14.6.79	1		Kobe	25 Apr 04
31:04.49		Derebe	Alemu	ETH	5.6.83	1		Uden	3 Jul 04
31:05.57		Maura	Viceconte	ITA	3.10.67	5	NA	Heusden-Zolder	5 Aug 00
31:05.90		Lucy	Wangui	KEN	24.3.84	9	OG	Athína	27 Aug 04
31:06.20		Florence	Kiplagat	KEN	27.2.87	1	NED Ch	Utrecht	17 May 07
		(50)	100th woman 31:23.92, 200th 31:45.82, 300th 32:00.05, 400th 32:14.50						

HALF MARATHON

Slightly downhill courses included: Newcastle-South Shields 30.5m, Tokyo 33m (to 1998), Lisboa (Spring) 69m

Mark	Wind	Name		Nat	Born	Pos	Meet	Venue	Date
65:40	dh	Paula	Radcliffe	GBR	17.12.73	1	GNR	South Shields	21 Sep 03
65:44	dh	Susan	Chepkemei	KEN	25.6.75	1		Lisboa	1 Apr 01
66:25		Lornah	Kiplagat	NED	1.5.74	1	WCh	Udine	14 Oct 07
66:34	dh		Kiplagat			2		Lisboa	1 Apr 01
66:40*		Ingrid	Kristiansen	NOR	21.3.56	1	NC	Sandnes	5 Apr 87
66:43	dh	Masako	Chiba	JPN	18.7.76	1		Tokyo	19 Jan 97
66:44		Elana	Meyer	RSA	10.10.66	1		Tokyo	15 Jan 99
66:47			Radcliffe			1	WCh	Bristol	7 Oct 01
66:48		Mary	Keitany	KEN	18.1.82	2	WCh	Udine	14 Oct 07
66:49		Esther	Wanjiru	KEN	27.3.77	2		Tokyo	15 Jan 99
66:56			L Kiplagat			1	City-Pier	Den Haag	25 Mar 00
66:57	dh	Kara	Goucher	USA	9.7.78	1		South Shields	30 Sep 07
67:03	dh	Derartu	Tulu (10)	ETH	21.3.72	3		Lisboa	1 Apr 01
67:07	dh		Radcliffe			1	GNR	South Shields	22 Oct 00
67:08	dh	Rita	Jeptoo	KEN	15.2.81	1		Lisboa	18 Mar 07
67:11	dh	Liz	McColgan	GBR	24.5.64	1		Tokyo	26 Jan 92
67:12	dh	Tegla	Loroupe	KEN	9.5.73	1		Lisboa	10 Mar 96
67:16		Edith	Masai	KEN	4.4.67	1		Berlin	2 Apr 06
67:19	dh	Sonia	O'Sullivan	IRL	28.11.69	1	GNR	South Shields	6 Oct 02
67:22			Meyer			1		Tokyo	24 Jan 93
67:23		Margaret	Okayo	KEN	30.5.76	1		Udine	28 Sep 03
67:24	dh		Loroupe			1		Lisboa	26 Mar 00
67:26		Kayoko	Fukushi	JPN	25.3.82	1		Marugame	5 Feb 06
67:29			Meyer			1		Kyoto	8 Mar 98
67:32			Loroupe			1		Den Haag	28 Mar 98
67:32	dh	Berhane	Adere	ETH	21.7.73	2	GNR	South Shields	21 Sep 03
67:33			Meyer			1		Tokyo	10 Jan 00
67:33	dh		Tulu			1	GNR	South Shields	18 Sep 05
67:34		Deena	Kastor	USA	14.2.73	2		Berlin	2 Apr 06
67:35			Radcliffe			1	WCh	Vilamoura	4 Oct 03
		(30/19)	* uncertain course measurement						
67:43		Mizuki	Noguchi (20)	JPN	3.7.78	2		Marugame	5 Feb 06
67:48		Kerryn	McCann	AUS	2.5.67	3		Tokyo	10 Jan 00
67:50	dh	Catherina	McKiernan	IRL	30.11.69	1		Lisboa	15 Mar 98
67:52	dh	Salina	Kosgei	KEN	16.11.76	1		Lisboa (dh 69m)	26 Mar 06
67:54		Catherine	Ndereba	KEN	21.7.72	1		Den Haag	24 Mar 01
67:55	dh	Benita	Johnson	AUS	6.5.79	1	GNR	South Shields	26 Sep 04
67:56	dh	Susie	Power	AUS	26.3.75	2	GNR	South Shields	6 Oct 02
67:58		Uta	Pippig ¶	GER	7.9.65	1		Kyoto	19 Mar 95
67:59	w	Restituta	Joseph	TAN	30.7.71	1		Malmö	12 Jun 00
68:06		Pamela	Chepchumba ¶	KEN	8.3.79	3	WCh	Udine	14 Oct 07
68:07+		Constantina	Tomescu	ROM	23.1.70	1	in Mar	Chicago	22 Oct 06
		(30)							
68:07		Bezunesh	Bekele	ETH	18.9.83	4	WCh	Udine	14 Oct 07
68:09	dh	Cristina	Pomacu	ROM	15.9.73	2		Lisboa	15 Mar 98
68:09	dh	Werknesh	Kidane	ETH	21.11.81	2	GNR	South Shields	18 Sep 05
68:11	dh	Joyce	Chepchumba	KEN	6.11.70	1		Lisboa	28 Mar 04
68:11	dh	Jelena	Prokopcuka	LAT	21.9.76	3	GNR	South Shields	18 Sep 05
68:18	dh	Izumi	Maki	JPN	10.12.68	2		Tokyo	21 Jan 96
68:18	dh	Yoshiko	Ichikawa	JPN	18.4.76	3		Tokyo	19 Jan 97
68:21	dh	Albertina	Dias	POR	26.4.65	3		Lisboa	10 Mar 96
68:23	dh	Fernanda	Ribeiro	POR	23.6.69	3		Lisboa	26 Mar 00
68:29		Atsede	Habtamu	ETH	26.10.87	5	WCh	Udine	14 Oct 07
		(40)							
68:30	dh	Maria	Guida	ITA	23.1.66	4		Lisboa	10 Mar 96
68:32		Mikie	Takanaka	JPN	6.10.80	2		Miyazaki	6 Jan 02
68:33	dh	Lisa	Ondieki	AUS	12.5.60	2		Tokyo	26 Jan 92
68:34		Joan	Benoit	USA	16.5.57	1		Philadelphia	16 Sep 84
68:34	dh	Olga	Appell	MEX	2.8.63	2		Tokyo	24 Jan 93
68:34		Asmae	Leghzaoui ¶	MAR	30.8.76	1		Marrakech	31 Jan 99
68:34		Lidia	Simon	ROM	4.9.73	4		Tokyo	10 Jan 00

Mark	Wind	Name		Nat	Born	Pos	Meet	Venue	Date
68:35		Takako	Kotorida	JPN	2.4.77	2		Yamaguchi	9 Mar 03
68:38		Colleen	de Reuck	RSA	13.4.64	1	NC	Durban	23 Jul 89
68:38		Isabella	Ochichi	KEN	79	2		Nice	22 Apr 01
		(50)	100th woman 69:23, 200th 70:01, 300th 70:37, 400th 71:05						

MARATHON

Note Boston times included, but course is downhill overall (139m) and sometimes, as in 1994, strongly wind-aided
In second column: first character: L = loop course or start and finish within 30%, P = point-to-point or start and finish more than 30% apart, D + point-to-point and downhil over 1/1000
Second character: M mixed marathon (men and women), W women only race or separated start by time

Mark	Wind	Name		Nat	Born	Pos	Meet	Venue	Date
2:15:25	LM	Paula	Radcliffe	GBR	17.12.73	1		London	13 Apr 03
2:17:18	LM		Radcliffe			1		Chicago	13 Oct 02
2:17:42	LW		Radcliffe			1		London	17 Apr 05
2:18:47	LM	Catherine	Ndereba	KEN	21.7.72	1		Chicago	7 Oct 01
2:18:56	LW		Radcliffe			1		London	14 Apr 02
2:19:12	LM	Mizuki	Noguchi	JPN	3.7.78	1		Berlin	25 Sep 05
2:19:26	LM		Ndereba			2		Chicago	13 Oct 02
2:19:36	LW	Deena	Kastor	USA	14.2.73	1		London	23 Apr 06
2:19:39	LM		Sun Yingjie ¶	CHN	3.10.77	1		Beijing	19 Oct 03
2:19:41	LM	Yoko	Shibui	JPN	14.3.79	1		Berlin	26 Sep 04
2:19:46	LM	Naoko	Takahashi	JPN	6.5.72	1		Berlin	30 Sep 01
2:19:51	L		Zhou Chunxiu	CHN	15.11.78	1		Seoul	12 Mar 06
2:19:55	LM		Ndereba			2		London	13 Apr 03
2:20:38	LW		Zhou Chunxiu			1		London	22 Apr 07
2:20:42	L	Berhane	Adere	ETH	21.7.73	1		Chicago	22 Oct 06
2:20:43	LM	Tegla	Loroupe (10)	KEN	9.5.73	1		Berlin	26 Sep 99
2:20:43	DM	Margaret	Okayo	KEN	30.5.76	1		Boston	15 Apr 02
2:20:47	LM		Loroupe			1		Rotterdam	19 Apr 98
2:20:47	L	Galina	Bogomolova	RUS	15.10.77	2		Chicago	22 Oct 06
2:20:57	LW		Radcliffe			1	WCh	Helsinki	14 Aug 05
2:21:01	LM		Sun Yingjie ¶			1	NG	Beijing	16 Oct 05
2:21:06	LM	Ingrid	Kristiansen	NOR	21.3.56	1		London	21 Apr 85
2:21:11	LM		Zhou Chunxiu			2	NG	Beijing	16 Oct 05
2:21:12	DM		Ndereba			2		Boston	15 Apr 02
2:21:16	LM		Drossin/Kastor			3		London	13 Apr 03
2:21:18	LW		Noguchi			1		Osaka	26 Jan 03
2:21:21	LM	Joan	Benoit'	USA	16.5.57	1		Chicago	20 Oct 85
2:21:21	LM		Sun Yingjie			2		Beijing	20 Oct 02
2:21:22	LM		Shibui			3		Chicago	13 Oct 02
2:21:25	LM		Kastor			1		Chicago	9 Oct 05
2:21:29	LW	Lyudmila	Petrova	RUS	7.10.68	2		London	23 Apr 06
2:21:30	LM	Constantina	Dita/Tomescu	ROM	23.1.70	2		Chicago	9 Oct 05
2:21:31	LM	Svetlana	Zakharova	RUS	15.9.70	4		Chicago	13 Oct 02
		(33/17)							
2:21:34	L	Getenesh	Wami	ETH	11.12.74	1		Berlin	25 Sep 06
2:21:45	DM	Uta	Pippig ¶	GER	7.9.65	1		Boston	18 Apr 94
2:21:45	LW	Masako	Chiba	JPN	18.7.76	2		Osaka	26 Jan 03
		(20)							
2:21:46	LW	Susan	Chepkemei	KEN	25.6.75	3		London	23 Apr 06
2:21:51	LW	Naoko	Sakamoto	JPN	14.11.80	3		Osaka	26 Jan 03
2:22:12	LW	Eri	Yamaguchi	JPN	14.1.73	1		Tokyo	21 Nov 99
2:22:22	LW	Lornah	Kiplagat	KEN	1.5.74	4		Osaka	26 Jan 03
2:22:23	LM	Catherina	McKiernan	IRL	30.11.69	1		Amsterdam	1 Nov 98
2:22:36	L	Benita	Johnson	AUS	6.5.79	3		Chicago	22 Oct 06
2:22:46	LW	Reiko	Tosa	JPN	11.6.76	4		London	14 Apr 02
2:22:54	LW	Lidia	Simon	ROM	4.9.73	1		Osaka	30 Jan 00
2:22:56	LW	Harumi	Hiroyama	JPN	2.9.68	2		Osaka	30 Jan 00
2:22:56	LW	Jelena	Prokopcuka	LAT	21.9.76	1		Osaka	30 Jan 05
		(30)							
2:22:59	L	Madai	Pérez	MEX	2.2.80	4		Chicago	22 Oct 06
2:23:05	LM	Marleen	Renders	BEL	24.12.68	1		Paris	7 Apr 02
2:23:12	L		Wei Yanan ¶	CHN	6.12.81	1		Seoul	18 Mar 07
2:23:17	LM		Zhang Shujing	CHN	13.9.78	3		Beijing	20 Oct 02
2:23:21	DM	Fatuma	Roba	ETH	18.12.73	1		Boston	20 Apr 98
2:23:22	LW	Joyce	Chepchumba	KEN	6.11.70	1		London	18 Apr 99
2:23:22	L	Salina	Kosgei	KEN	16.11.76	2		Berlin	25 Sep 06
2:23:26	LM	Hiromi	Ominami	JPN	15.11.75	2		Berlin	26 Sep 04
2:23:29	LM	Rosa	Mota	POR	29.6.58	3		Chicago	20 Oct 85
2:23:30	LW	Mari	Ozaki	JPN	16.7.75	5		Osaka	26 Jan 03
		(40)							

Mark	Wind	Name		Nat	Born	Pos	Meet	Venue	Date
2:23:30	LW	Derartu	Tulu	ETH	21.3.72	4	WCh	Helsinki	14 Aug 05
2:23:31	LW	Esther	Wanjiru	KEN	27.3.77	3		Osaka	30 Jan 00
2:23:33	DM	Valentina	Yegorova	RUS	16.2.64	2		Boston	18 Apr 94
2:23:37	LM		Liu Min	CHN	29.11.83	1		Beijing	14 Oct 01
2:23:38	DW	Rita	Jeptoo	KEN	15.2.81	1		Boston	17 Apr 06
2:23:43	DM	Olga	Markova	RUS	6.8.68	1		Boston	20 Apr 92
2:23:43	LM	Takami	Ominami	JPN	15.11.75	1		Rotterdam	21 Apr 02
2:23:47	LM	Maura	Viceconte	ITA	3.10.67	1		Wien	21 May 00
2:23:48	LW	Yumiko	Hara	JPN	9.1.82	1		Osaka	28 Jan 07
2:23:51	LW	Lisa	Martin/Ondieki	AUS	12.5.60	1		Osaka	31 Jan 88
		(50)	100th woman 2:25:46, 200th 2:27:34, 300th 2:28:54, 400th 2:29:56, 500th 2:31:08						
Drugs dq: 2:20:23	LM		Wei Yanan ¶	CHN	6.12.81	1		Beijing	20 Oct 02

2000 METRES STEEPLECHASE

Mark	Name		Nat	Born	Pos	Meet	Venue	Date
6:03.38	Wioletta	Janowska	POL	9.6.77	1		Gdansk	15 Jul 06
6:04.46	Dorcus	Inzikuru	UGA	2.2.82	1	GP II	Milano	1 Jun 05
6:11.63	Livia	Tóth	HUN	7.1.80	2		Gdansk	15 Jul 06
6:11.84	Marina	Pluzhnikova	RUS	25.2.63	1	GWG	Sankt-Peterburg	25 Jul 94
6:14.52	Svetlana	Rogova	RUS	4.8.67	1	Znam	Moskva	11 Jun 92

3000 METRES STEEPLECHASE

Mark	Name		Nat	Born	Pos	Meet	Venue	Date
9:01.59 WR	Gulnara	Samitova/Galkina	RUS	9.7.78	1		Iráklio	4 Jul 04
9:06.57	Yekaterina	Volkova	RUS	16.2.78	1	WCh	Osaka	27 Aug 07
9:08.33 WR		Samitova			1	NC	Tula	10 Aug 03
9:09.19	Tatyana	Petrova	RUS	8.4.83	2	WCh	Osaka	27 Aug 07
9:09.84		Samitova			1		Réthimno	23 Jun 04
9:11.68		Galkina			1	GP	Athína	2 Jul 07
9:13.35		Volkova			1	NC	Tula	31 Jul 07
9:14.35		Petrova			1	NC	Tula	31 Jul 07
9:14.37		Galkina			1	Znam	Zhukovskiy	9 Jun 07
9:14.52	Eunice	Jepkorir	KEN	17.2.82	2	GP	Athína	2 Jul 07
9:15.04	Dorcus	Inzikuru	UGA	2.2.82	1	SGP	Athína	14 Jun 05
9:16.46		Inzikuru			1	GP	Rieti	28 Aug 05
9:16.51 WR	Alesya	Turova	BLR	6.12.79	1		Gdansk	27 Jul 02
9:17.15	Wioletta	Frakiewicz/Janowska	POL	9.6.77	1	SGP	Athína	3 Jul 06
9:18.24		Inzikuru			1	WCh	Helsinki	8 Aug 05
9:19.44		Jepkorir			1	Bisl	Oslo	15 Jun 07
9:19.51		Inzikuru			1	CG	Melbourne	22 Mar 06
9:20.09		Jepkorir			3	WCh	Osaka	27 Aug 07
9:20.16		Turova			1	Herc	Monaco	20 Aug 06
9:20.28		Turova			1	GS	Ostrava	12 Jun 03
9:20.33		Inzikuru			1	Odlozil	Praha	27 Jun 05
9:20.49		Volkova			2	WCh	Helsinki	8 Aug 05
9:21.40		Samitova			1	GP	Rieti	5 Sep 04
9:21.72 WR		Turova			1	GS	Ostrava	12 Jun 02
9:21.80		Inzikuru			1	WAF	Monaco	9 Sep 05
9:21.94	Lyubov	Ivanova ¶	RUS	2.3.81	2	SGP	Athína	3 Jul 06
9:22.29 WR	Justyna	Bak	POL	1.8.74	1		Milano	5 Jun 02
9:22.48		Janowska			1	GP	Rieti	27 Aug 06
9:22.82		Petrova			1	v3N	Birmingham	19 Aug 06
9:22.96		Petrova			3	SGP	Athína	3 Jul 06
9:23.35	Jeruto	Kiptum	KEN	12.12.81	2	GP	Rieti	27 Aug 06
	(31/10)							
9:24.29	Melissa	Rollison	AUS	13.4.83	2	CG	Melbourne	22 Mar 06
9:24.51	Ruth	Bisibori	KEN	2.1.88	1		Daegu	3 Oct 07
9:25.05	Donna	MacFarlane	AUS	18.6.77	3	CG	Melbourne	22 Mar 06
9:25.51	Hanane	Ouhaddou	MAR	.82	1	NA	Heusden-Zolder	28 Jul 07
9:26.07	Salome	Chepchumba	KEN	29.9.82	3	GP	Rieti	27 Aug 06
9:26.23	Rosa María	Morató	ESP	19.6.79	2	NA	Heusden-Zolder	28 Jul 07
9:26.25		Liu Nian	CHN	26.4.88	1		Wuhan	2 Nov 07
9:26.55	Yelena	Sidorchenkova	RUS	30.5.80	3	NC	Tula	31 Jul 07
9:27.21	Mardrea	Hyman	JAM	22.12.72	3	WAF	Monaco	9 Sep 05
9:27.51	Sophie	Duarté	FRA	31.7.81	5	WCh	Osaka	27 Aug 07
	(20)							
9:28.03	Netsanet	Achano	ETH	14.12.87	2		Neerpelt	2 Jun 07
9:28.29	Roisin	McGettigan	IRL	23.8.80	3	NA	Heusden-Zolder	28 Jul 07
9:28.47	Veerle	Dejaeghere	BEL	1.8.73	3		Neerpelt	2 Jun 07
9:28.53	Cristina	Casandra	ROM	1.2.77	1	Vard	Réthimno	18 Jul 07
9:28.75	Lisa	Galaviz	USA	30.11.79	4	NA	Heusden-Zolder	28 Jul 07
9:28.86	Korine	Hinds	JAM	18.1.76	3	Bisl	Oslo	15 Jun 07

Mark	Wind	Name		Nat	Born	Pos	Meet	Venue	Date
9:29.32		Brianna	Shook	USA	6.1.81	1	NA	Heusden-Zolder	31 Jul 04
9:30.20		Livia	Tóth	HUN	7.1.80	4	WAF	Monaco	9 Sep 05
9:30.35		Bouchra	Chaabi	MAR	22.9.80	3		Iráklio	4 Jul 04
9:30.84		Victoria	Mitchell	AUS	25.4.82	4	SGP	Athína	3 Jul 06
		(30)							
9:31.43		Julie	Coulaud	FRA	7.8.82	4	GP	Athína	2 Jul 07
9:32.05		Mekdes	Bekele	ETH	20.1.87	5	Bisl	Oslo	15 Jun 07
9:32.35			Li Zhenzhu	CHN	13.12.85	1	WCT	Suzhou	10 Jun 07
9:32.36			Zhu Yanmei	CHN	16.10.86	2	WCT	Suzhou	10 Jun 07
9:32.41		Yelena	Zadorozhnaya	RUS	3.12.77	5	WAF	Monaco	9 Sep 05
9:32.54		Kate	McIlroy	NZL	26.8.81	5	NA	Heusden-Zolder	22 Jul 06
9:32.68		Gladys	Kipkemboi	KEN	15.10.86	6	NA	Heusden-Zolder	22 Jul 06
9:33.12		Élodie	Olivarès	FRA	22.5.76	2	NA	Heusden	20 Jul 02
9:33.19		Karoline Bjerkeli	Grøvdal	NOR	14.6.90	4		Neerpelt	2 Jun 07
9:33.95		Jenny	Barringer	USA	23.8.86	1		Paris	8 Sep 07
		(40)							
9:34.28		Kristine Eikrem	Engeset	NOR	15.11.88	6	Bisl	Oslo	15 Jun 07
9:34.72		Anna	Willard	USA	31.3.84	2	NC	Indianapolis	23 Jun 07
9:35.28		Sigrid	Vanden Bempt	BEL	10.2.81	3	NA	Heusden	31 Jul 04
9:35.51		Natalya	Izmodenova	RUS	1.1.81	5	SGP	Athína	14 Jun 05
9:37.88		Ancuta	Bobocel	ROM	3.10.87	2	Vard	Réthimno	18 Jul 07
9:38.31		Melanie	Schulz	GER	27.8.79	1	NC	Wattenscheid	6 Jul 02
9:38.31		Fatiha Bahi	Azzouhoum	ALG	8.3.83	6	SGP	Athína	14 Jun 05
9:38.48		Svetlana	Ivanova	RUS	18.8.83	2	GS	Ostrava	30 May 06
9:38.55		Christin	Johansson	SWE	26.1.78	7	NA	Heusden-Zolder	28 Jul 07
9:38.56		Hatti	Dean	GBR	2.2.82	3	BrGP	Sheffield	15 Jul 07
		(50)	100th woman 9:51.16						

100 METRES HURDLES

Mark	Wind	Name		Nat	Born	Pos	Meet	Venue	Date
12.21 WR	0.7	Yordanka	Donkova	BUL	28.9.61	1		Stara Zagora	20 Aug 88
12.24	0.9		Donkova			1h		Stara Zagora	28 Aug 88
12.25 WR	1.4	Ginka	Zagorcheva	BUL	12.4.58	1	v TCH,GRE	Drama	8 Aug 87
12.26 WR	1.5		Donkova			1	Balk	Ljubljana	7 Sep 86
12.26	1.7	Lyudmila	Narozhilenko ¶	RUS	21.4.64	1rB		Sevilla	6 Jun 92
		(now Ludmila Engquist SWE)							
12.27	-1.2		Donkova			1		Stara Zagora	28 Aug 88
12.28	1.8		Narozhilenko			1	NC	Kiyev	11 Jul 91
12.28	0.9		Narozhilenko			1rA		Sevilla	6 Jun 92
12.29 WR	-0.4		Donkova			1	ASV	Köln	17 Aug 86
12.32	1.6		Narozhilenko			1		Saint-Denis	4 Jun 92
12.33	1.4		Donkova			1		Fürth	14 Jun 87
12.33	-0.3	Gail	Devers	USA	19.11.66	1	NC	Sacramento	23 Jul 00
12.34	-0.5		Zagorcheva			1	WCh	Roma	4 Sep 87
12.35 WR	0.1		Donkova			1h2	ASV	Köln	17 Aug 86
12.36 WR	1.9	Grazyna	Rabsztyn	POL	20.9.52	1	Kuso	Warszawa	13 Jun 80
12.36 WR	-0.6		Donkova			1	NC	Sofiya	13 Aug 86
12.36	1.1		Donkova			1		Schwechat	15 Jun 88
12.37	1.4		Donkova			1	ISTAF	Berlin	15 Aug 86
12.37	0.7		Devers			1	WCh	Sevilla	28 Aug 99
12.37	1.5	Joanna	Hayes	USA	23.12.76	1	OG	Athína	24 Aug 04
12.38	0.0		Donkova			1	BGP	Budapest	11 Aug 86
12.38	-0.7		Donkova			1	EC	Stuttgart	29 Aug 86
12.38	0.2		Donkova			1	OG	Seoul	30 Sep 88
12.39	1.5	Vera	Komisova'	RUS	11.6.53	1	GGala	Roma	5 Aug 80
12.39	1.5		Zagorcheva			2	Balk	Ljubljana	7 Sep 86
12.39	1.8	Natalya	Grigoryeva ¶	UKR	3.12.62	2	NC	Kiyev	11 Jul 91
12.39	-0.7		Devers			1	WK	Zürich	11 Aug 00
12.40	0.4		Donkova			1	GWG	Moskva	8 Jul 86
12.40	1.2		Devers			1rA	Athl	Lausanne	2 Jul 02
		(29/8) – 7 performances at 12.42							
12.42	1.8	Bettine	Jahn	GDR	3.8.58	1	OD	Berlin	8 Jun 83
12.42	2.0	Anjanette	Kirkland (10)	USA	24.2.74	1	WCh	Edmonton	11 Aug 01
12.43	-0.9	Lucyna	Kalek (Langer)	POL	9.1.56	1		Hannover	19 Aug 84
12.43	-0.3	Michelle	Perry	USA	1.5.79	1s1	NC	Carson	26 Jun 05
12.44	-0.5	Gloria	Uibel (-Siebert)	GDR	13.1.64	2	WCh	Roma	4 Sep 87
12.44	-0.8	Olga	Shishigina ¶	KAZ	23.12.68	1		Luzern	27 Jun 95
12.44	0.4	Glory	Alozie	NGR/ESP	30.12.77	1	Herc	Monaco	8 Aug 98
12.44	0.6	Damu	Cherry ¶	USA	29.11.77	2rA	Athl	Lausanne	11 Jul 06
12.45	1.3	Cornelia	Oschkenat'	GDR	29.10.61	1		Neubrandenburg	11 Jun 87
12.45	1.4	Brigitte	Foster-Hylton	JAM	7.11.74	1	Pre	Eugene	24 May 03

Mark	Wind	Name		Nat	Born	Pos	Meet	Venue	Date
12.45	1.5	Yelena	Krasovskaya	UKR	17.8.76	2	OG	Athína	24 Aug 04
12.45	1.4	Virginia	Powell	USA	7.9.83	1	GP	New York	2 Jun 07
		(20)							
12.46	0.7	Perdita	Felicien	CAN	29.8.80	1	Pre	Eugene	19 Jun 04
12.47	1.1	Marina	Azyabina	RUS	15.6.63	1s2	NC	Moskva	19 Jun 93
12.49	0.9	Susanna	Kallur	SWE	16.2.81	1	ISTAF	Berlin	16 Sep 07
12.50	0.0	Vera	Akimova'	RUS	5.6.59	1		Sochi	19 May 84
12.50	-0.1	Delloreen	Ennis-London	JAM	5.3.75	3	WCh	Osaka	29 Aug 07
12.51	1.4	Miesha	McKelvy	USA	26.7.76	2	Pre	Eugene	24 May 03
12.52	-0.4	Michelle	Freeman	JAM	5.5.69	1s1	WCh	Athína	10 Aug 97
12.53	0.2	Tatyana	Reshetnikova	RUS	14.10.66	1rA	GP II	Linz	4 Jul 94
12.53	-0.4	Svetla	Dimitrova ¶	BUL	27.1.70	1	Herc	Stara Zagora	16 Jul 94
12.53	1.0	Melissa	Morrison	USA	9.7.71	1	DNG	Stockholm	5 Aug 98
		(30)							
12.54	0.4	Kerstin	Knabe	GDR	7.7.59	3	EC	Athína	9 Sep 82
12.54	0.9	Sabine	Paetz/John'	GDR	16.10.57	1		Berlin	15 Jul 84
12.56	1.2	Johanna	Klier'	GDR	13.9.52	1		Cottbus	17 Jul 80
12.56	1.2	Monique	Ewanje-Epée	FRA	11.7.67	1	BNP	Villeneuve d'Ascq	29 Jun 90
12.56	0.7	Danielle	Carruthers	USA	22.12.79	2	Pre	Eugene	19 Jun 04
12.56	-0.2	Lolo	Jones	USA	5.8.82	1	NA	Heusden-Zolder	22 Jul 06
12.59 WR	-0.6	Anneliese	Ehrhardt	GDR	18.6.50	1	OG	München	8 Sep 72
12.59	0.0	Natalya	Shekhodanova ¶	RUS	29.12.71	1	NC	Sankt Peterburg	3 Jul 96
12.59	1.0	Patricia	Girard ¶	FRA	8.4.68	2s2	OG	Atlanta	31 Jul 96
12.59	0.2	Brigita	Bukovec	SLO	21.5.70	2	OG	Atlanta	31 Jul 96
		(40)							
12.59	0.4	Kirsten	Bolm	GER	4.3.75	1	LGP	London (CP)	22 Jul 05
12.60	1.7	Mariya	Koroteyeva	RUS	10.11.81	4s1	OG	Athína	23 Aug 04
12.60	0.4	Priscilla	Lopes	CAN	26.8.82	2	NCAA	Sacramento	9 Jun 06
12.61	0.3	Svetlana	Gusarova	KAZ	29.5.59	2	NC	Leningrad	3 Aug 85
12.61	0.2	Jackie	Joyner-Kersee	USA	3.3.62	1	Jenn	San José	28 May 88
12.61	1.4	Katie	Anderson	CAN	9.1.68	1		Villeneuve d'Ascq	13 Jun 99
12.62	1.2	Mihaela	Pogacian'	ROM	27.1.58	2	BNP	Villeneuve d'Ascq	29 Jun 90
12.62	1.1	Yuliya	Graudyn	RUS	13.11.70	1A	ISTAF	Berlin	30 Aug 94
12.62	1.7	Nichole	Denby	USA	10.10.82	1	NCAA	Austin	11 Jun 04
12.63	1.8	Zofia	Bielczyk	POL	22.9.58	1h1	Kuso	Warszawa	18 Jun 79
12.63	1.4	Heike	Terpe/Theele	GDR	4.10.64	2	NC	Jena	27 Jun 86
12.63	0.0	Angie	Vaughn	USA	4.11.76	1	GP	Edwardsville	25 Jul 98
12.63	2.0	Jenny	Adams	USA	8.7.78	5	WCh	Edmonton	11 Aug 01
12.63	1.4	Angela	Whyte	CAN	22.5.80	4	adidas	Carson	20 May 07
		(54)	100th woman 12.74, 200th 12.91, 300th 13.05, 400th 13.14						

Wind assisted performances to 12.39, performers to 12.62

Mark	Wind	Name		Nat	Born	Pos	Meet	Venue	Date
12.28	2.7	Cornelia	Oschkenat'	GDR	29.10.61	1		Berlin	25 Aug 87
12.29	3.5		Donkova			1	Athl	Lausanne	24 Jun 88
12.29	2.7	Gail	Devers	USA	19.11.66	1	Pre	Eugene	26 May 02
12.35	2.4	Bettine	Jahn	GDR	3.8.58	1	WCh	Helsinki	13 Aug 83
12.37	2.7	Gloria	Uibel/Siebert'	GDR	13.1.64	2		Berlin	25 Aug 87
12.39	2.8		Rabsztyn			1	4-N	Bremen	24 Jun 79
12.40	2.1	Michelle	Freeman	JAM	5.5.69	1	GPF	Fukuoka	13 Sep 97
12.41	2.2	Olga	Shishigina ¶	KAZ	23.12.68	1rA	Athl	Lausanne	5 Jul 95
12.42	2.4	Kerstin	Knabe	GDR	7.7.59	2	WCh	Helsinki	13 Aug 83
12.44	2.6	Melissa	Morrison	USA	9.7.71	1		Carson	22 May 04
12.45	2.1	Perdita	Felicien	CAN	29.8.80	1	NC	Victoria	10 Jul 04
12.50	2.7	Svetla	Dimitrova ¶	BUL	27.1.70	1		Saint-Denis	10 Jun 94
12.51	3.2	Johanna	Klier'	GDR	13.9.52	1	NC	Cottbus	17 Jul 80
12.51	3.6	Sabine	Paetz/John'	GDR	16.10.57	1		Dresden	27 Jul 84
12.51A	3.3	Yuliya	Graudyn	RUS	13.11.70	1		Sestriere	31 Jul 94
12.53	2.2	Mihaela	Pogacian	ROM	27.1.58	1	IAC	Edinburgh	6 Jul 90
12.55	4.3	Angela	Whyte	CAN	22.5.80	2	NC	Windsor	14 Jul 07
12.61	4.0	Jenny	Adams	USA	8.7.78	1h1	NC	Eugene	23 Jun 01
12.62	2.9	Eunice	Barber	FRA	17.11.74	1H		Arles	4 Jun 05

Probably hand timed Officially 12.36, but subsequent investigations showed this unlikely to have been auto-timed

Mark	Wind	Name		Nat	Born	Pos	Meet	Venue	Date
12.4	0.7	Svetla	Dimitrova ¶	BUL	27.1.70	1		Stara Zagora	9 Jul 97

Hand timed

Mark	Wind	Name		Nat	Born	Pos	Meet	Venue	Date
12.3 WR	1.5	Anneliese	Ehrhardt	GDR	18.6.50	1	NC	Dresden	22 Jul 73
12.3		Marina	Azyabina	RUS	15.6.63	1		Yekaterinburg	30 May 93
12.0w	2.1	Yordanka	Donkova	BUL	28.9.61	1		Sofiya	3 Aug 86
12.1w	2.1	Ginka	Zagorcheva	BUL	12.4.58	2		Sofiya	3 Aug 86

400 METRES HURDLES

Mark	Name		Nat	Born	Pos	Meet	Venue	Date
52.34 WR	Yuliya	Nosova-Pechonkina'	RUS	21.4.78	1	NC	Tula	8 Aug 03

Mark Wind	Name		Nat	Born	Pos	Meet	Venue	Date
52.61 WR	Kim	Batten	USA	29.3.69	1	WCh	Göteborg	11 Aug 95
52.62	Tonja	Buford-Bailey	USA	13.12.70	2	WCh	Göteborg	11 Aug 95
52.74 WR	Sally	Gunnell	GBR	29.7.66	1	WCh	Stuttgart	19 Aug 93
52.74		Batten			1	Herc	Monaco	8 Aug 98
52.77	Faní	Halkiá	GRE	2.2.79	1s2	OG	Athína	22 Aug 04
52.79	Sandra	Farmer-Patrick	USA	18.8.62	2	WCh	Stuttgart	19 Aug 93
52.82	Deon	Hemmings	JAM	9.10.68	1	OG	Atlanta	31 Jul 96
52.82		Halkiá			1	OG	Athína	25 Aug 04
52.84		Batten			1	WK	Zürich	12 Aug 98
52.89	Daimí	Pernía	CUB	27.12.76	1	WCh	Sevilla	25 Aug 99
52.90		Buford			1	WK	Zürich	16 Aug 95
52.90	Nezha	Bidouane	MAR	18.9.69	2	WCh	Sevilla	25 Aug 99
52.90		Pechonkina			1	WCh	Helsinki	13 Aug 05
52.94 WR	Marina	Styepanova' (10)	RUS	1.5.50	1s	Spart	Tashkent	17 Sep 86
52.95	Sheena	Johnson	USA	1.10.82	1	NC/OT	Sacramento	11 Jul 04
52.96A		Bidouane			1	WCp	Johannesburg	11 Sep 98
52.97		Batten			1	NC	Indianapolis	14 Jun 97
52.97		Bidouane			1	WCh	Athína	8 Aug 97
52.98		Hemmings			1rA	WK	Zürich	13 Aug 97
52.99		Hemmings			1s1	OG	Atlanta	29 Jul 96
53.01		Pechonkina			1	NC	Tula	11 Jul 05
53.02	Irina	Privalova	RUS	22.11.68	1	OG	Sydney	27 Sep 00
53.02	Lashinda	Demus	USA	10.3.83	1	SGP	Athína	3 Jul 06
53.03A		Hemmings			2	WCp	Johannesburg	11 Sep 98
53.05		Bidouane			1	GGala	Roma	7 Jul 99
53.05		Pechonkina			1		Tula	13 Jun 05
53.06		Batten			1	Herc	Monaco	16 Aug 97
53.06		Batten			1	Gaz	Paris	29 Jul 98
53.07		Demus			1	NC	Indianapolis	25 Jun 06
	(30/13)							
53.11	Tatyana	Ledovskaya	BLR	21.5.66	1	WCh	Tokyo	29 Aug 91
53.17	Debbie	Flintoff-King	AUS	20.4.60	1	OG	Seoul	28 Sep 88
53.21	Marie-José	Pérec	FRA	9.5.68	2	WK	Zürich	16 Aug 95
53.22	Jana	Pittman/Rawlinson	AUS	9.11.82	1	WCh	Saint-Denis	28 Aug 03
53.24	Sabine	Busch	GDR	21.11.62	1	NC	Potsdam	21 Aug 87
53.25	Ionela	Tîrlea-Manolache	ROM	9.2.76	2	GGala	Roma	7 Jul 99
53.28	Tiffany	Williams	USA	5.2.83	1	NC	Indianapolis	24 Jun 07
	(20)							
53.32	Sandra	Glover	USA	30.12.68	3	WCh	Helsinki	13 Aug 05
53.36	Andrea	Blackett	BAR	24.1.76	4	WCh	Sevilla	25 Aug 99
53.36	Brenda	Taylor	USA	9.2.79	2	NC/OT	Sacramento	11 Jul 04
53.37	Tetyana	Tereshchuk	UKR	11.10.69	3s2	OG	Athína	22 Aug 04
53.47	Janeene	Vickers	USA	3.10.68	3	WCh	Tokyo	29 Aug 91
53.48	Margarita	Ponomaryova'	RUS	19.6.63	3	WCh	Stuttgart	19 Aug 93
53.58	Cornelia	Ullrich'	GDR	26.4.63	2	NC	Potsdam	21 Aug 87
53.63	Ellen	Fiedler'	GDR	26.11.58	3	OG	Seoul	28 Sep 88
53.65A	Myrtle	Bothma'	RSA	18.2.64	mx		Pretoria	12 Mar 90
	53.74A				1		Johannesburg	18 Apr 86
53.72	Yekaterina	Bikert	RUS	13.5.80	2	NC	Tula	30 Jul 04
	(30)							
53.86	Anna	Jesien	POL	10.12.78	1s3	WCh	Osaka	28 Aug 07
53.88	Debbie-Ann	Parris	JAM	24.3.73	3s1	WCh	Edmonton	6 Aug 01
53.93	Yevgeniya	Isakova	RUS	27.11.78	1	EC	Göteborg	9 Aug 06
53.96		Han Qing ¶	CHN	4.3.70	1	NG	Beijing	9 Sep 93
53.96		Song Yinglan	CHN	14.9.75	1	NG	Guangzhou	22 Nov 01
53.97	Nickiesha	Wilson	JAM	28.7.86	2s3	WCh	Osaka	28 Aug 07
54.00		Huang Xiaoxiao	CHN	3.3.83	2s2	WCh	Osaka	28 Aug 07
54.02 WR	Anna	Ambraziené'	LTU	14.4.55	1	Znam	Moskva	11 Jun 83
54.02A	Judit	Szekeres ¶	HUN	18.11.66	1		Roodepoort	23 Jan 98
54.02	Natasha	Danvers	GBR	19.9.77	2	GGala	Roma	11 Jul 03
	(40)							
54.03	Heike	Meissner	GER	29.1.70	5	OG	Atlanta	31 Jul 96
54.04	Gudrun	Abt	FRG	3.8.62	6	OG	Seoul	28 Sep 88
54.05A	Surita	Febbraio ¶	RSA	27.12.73	1		Pretoria	4 Apr 03
54.11	Anna	Knoroz	RUS	30.7.70	3	Nik	Nice	18 Jul 94
54.14	Yekaterina	Fesenko/Grun	RUS	10.8.58	1	WCh	Helsinki	10 Aug 83
54.14	Melaine	Walker	JAM	1.1.83	1	Pre	Eugene	10 Jun 07
54.15	Ann-Louise	Skoglund	SWE	28.6.62	4	EC	Stuttgart	30 Aug 86
54.15	Michelle	Johnson	USA	12.4.74	5	WK	Zürich	11 Aug 99

Mark Wind	Name		Nat	Born	Pos	Meet	Venue	Date
54.16	Raasin	McIntosh	USA	29.4.82	5	NC/OT	Sacramento	11 Jul 04
54.17	Tonya	Williams	USA	5.10.74	3	Athl	Lausanne	3 Jul 96
	(50)	100th woman 54.82, 200th 55.67, 300th 56.18, 400th 56.54						
Drugs disqualification: 53.38		Jiang Limei ¶	CHN	.3.70	(1)	NG	Shanghai	22 Oct 97

HIGH JUMP

Mark Wind	Name		Nat	Born	Pos	Meet	Venue	Date
2.09 WR	Stefka	Kostadinova	BUL	25.3.65	1	WCh	Roma	30 Aug 87
2.08 WR		Kostadinova			1	NM	Sofiya	31 May 86
2.08i	Kajsa	Bergqvist	SWE	12.10.76	1		Arnstadt	4 Feb 06
2.07 WR	Lyudmila	Andonova ¶	BUL	6.5.60	1	OD	Berlin	20 Jul 84
2.07 WR		Kostadinova			1		Sofiya	25 May 86
2.07		Kostadinova			1		Cagliari	16 Sep 87
2.07		Kostadinova			1	NC	Sofiya	3 Sep 88
2.07i	Heike	Henkel'	GER	5.5.64	1	NC	Karlsruhe	8 Feb 92
2.07	Blanka	Vlasic	CRO	8.11.83	1	DNG	Stockholm	7 Aug 07
2.06		Kostadinova			1	ECp	Moskva	18 Aug 85
2.06		Kostadinova			1		Fürth	15 Jun 86
2.06		Kostadinova			1		Cagliari	14 Sep 86
2.06		Kostadinova			1		Wörrstadt	6 Jun 87
2.06		Kostadinova			1		Rieti	8 Sep 87
2.06i		Kostadinova			1		Pireás	20 Feb 88
2.06		Bergqvist			1		Eberstadt	26 Jul 03
2.06	Hestrie	Cloete	RSA	26.8.78	1	WCh	Saint-Denis	31 Aug 03
2.06	Yelena	Slesarenko	RUS	28.2.82	1	OG	Athína	28 Aug 04
2.06		Vlasic			1		Thessaloníki	30 Jul 07
2.05 WR	Tamara	Bykova	RUS	21.12.58	1	Izv	Kiyev	22 Jun 84
2.05		Kostadinova			1		Wörrstadt	14 Jun 86
2.05		Kostadinova			1		Rieti	7 Sep 86
2.05i		Kostadinova			1	WI	Indianapolis	8 Mar 87
2.05		Kostadinova			1	Bisl	Oslo	4 Jul 87
2.05		Kostadinova			1		Padova	13 Sep 87
2.05		Kostadinova			1	BGP	Budapest	12 Aug 88
2.05		Henkel			1	WCh	Tokyo	31 Aug 91
2.05i		Kostadinova			1	NC	Sofiya	1 Feb 92
2.05		Kostadinova			1		San Marino	4 Jul 92
2.05		Kostadinova			1	Toto	Fukuoka	18 Sep 93
2.05	Inga	Babakova	UKR	27.6.67	1		Tokyo	15 Sep 95
2.05		Kostadinova			1	OG	Atlanta	3 Aug 96
2.05		Bergqvist			1		Poznan	18 Aug 02
2.05		Cloete			1	ISTAF	Berlin (P)	10 Aug 03
2.05i		Vlasic			1		Banská Bystrica	14 Feb 06
2.05		Bergqvist			1	LGP	London (CP)	28 Jul 06
2.05i	Tia	Hellebaut	BEL	16.2.78	1	EI	Birmingham	3 Mar 07
2.05		Vlasic			1	GP	Madrid	21 Jul 07
2.05		Vlasic			1	WCh	Osaka	2 Sep 07
	(39/10)							
2.04	Silvia	Costa	CUB	4.5.64	1	WCp	Barcelona	9 Sep 89
2.04i	Alina	Astafei	GER	7.6.69	1		Berlin	3 Mar 95
2.04	Venelina	Veneva ¶	BUL	13.6.74	1		Kalamáta	2 Jun 01
2.04i	Anna	Chicherova	RUS	22.7.82	1		Yekaterinburg	7 Jan 03
2.03 WR	Ulrike	Meyfarth	FRG	4.5.56	1	ECp	London (CP)	21 Aug 83
2.03	Louise	Ritter	USA	18.2.58	1		Austin	8 Jul 88
2.03	Tatyana	Motkova	RUS	23.11.68	2		Bratislava	30 May 95
2.03	Níki	Bakoyiánni	GRE	9.6.68	2	OG	Atlanta	3 Aug 96
2.03i	Monica	Iagar/Dinescu	ROM	2.4.73	1		Bucuresti	23 Jan 99
2.03i	Marina	Kuptsova	RUS	22.12.81	1	EI	Wien	2 Mar 02
	(20)							
2.03	Antonietta	Di Martino	ITA	1.6.78	1	ECp-1B	Milano	24 Jun 07
2.02i	Susanne	Beyer'	GDR	24.6.61	2	WI	Indianapolis	8 Mar 87
2.02	Yelena	Yelesina	RUS	4.4.70	1	GWG	Seattle	23 Jul 90
2.02	Viktoriya	Styopina	UKR	21.2.76	3	OG	Athína	28 Aug 04
2.02	Ruth	Beitia	ESP	1.4.79	1	NC	San Sebastián	4 Aug 07
2.01 WR	Sara	Simeoni	ITA	19.4.53	1	v Pol	Brescia	4 Aug 78
2.01	Olga	Turchak	UKR	5.3.67	2	GWG	Moskva	7 Jul 86
2.01	Desiré	du Plessis	RSA	20.5.65	1		Johannesburg	16 Sep 86
2.01i	Gabriele	Günz	GDR	8.9.61	2		Stuttgart	31 Jan 88
2.01	Heike	Balck	GDR	19.8.70	1	vSU-j	Karl-Marx-Stadt	18 Jun 89
	(30)							
2.01i	Ioamnet	Quintero	CUB	8.9.72	1		Berlin	5 Mar 93

Mark	Wind	Name		Nat	Born	Pos	Meet	Venue	Date
2.01		Hanne	Haugland	NOR	14.12.67	1	WK	Zürich	13 Aug 97
2.01i		Tisha	Waller	USA	1.12.70	1	NC	Atlanta	28 Feb 98
2.01		Yelena	Gulyayeva	RUS	14.8.67	2		Kalamata	23 May 98
2.01		Vita	Palamar	UKR	12.10.77	2=	WK	Zürich	15 Aug 03
2.01		Amy	Acuff	USA	14.7.75	4	WK	Zürich	15 Aug 03
2.01		Irina	Mikhalchenko	UKR	20.1.72	1		Eberstadt	18 Jul 04
2.01		Chaunte	Howard	USA	12.1.84	1	NC	Indianapolis	24 Jun 06
2.00	WR	Rosemarie	Ackermann'	GDR	4.4.52	1	ISTAF	Berlin	26 Aug 77
2.00i		Coleen	Sommer'	USA	6.6.60	1		Ottawa	14 Feb 82
		(40)							
2.00		Charmaine	Gale/Weavers	RSA	27.2.64	1		Pretoria	25 Mar 85
2.00i		Emilia	Dragieva'	BUL	11.1.65	3	WI	Indianapolis	8 Mar 87
2.00		Lyudmila	Avdyeyenko'	UKR	14.12.63	1	NC	Bryansk	17 Jul 87
2.00		Svetlana	Isaeva/Leseva	BUL	18.3.67	2	v TCH,GRE	Drama	8 Aug 87
2.00i		Larisa	Kositsyna	RUS	14.12.63	2	NC	Volgograd	11 Feb 88
2.00		Jan	Wohlschlag'	USA	14.7.58	1	Bisl	Oslo	1 Jul 89
2.00		Yolanda	Henry	USA	2.12.64	1	Expo	Sevilla	30 May 90
2.00		Biljana	Petrovic ¶	YUG	28.2.61	1		St. Denis	22 Jun 90
2.00		Tatyana	Shevchik ¶	BLR	11.6.69	1		Gomel	14 May 93
2.00i		Britta	Bilac'	SLO	4.12.68	1		Frankfurt	9 Feb 94
		(50)							
2.00i		Yuliya	Lyakhova	RUS	8.7.77	1		Wuppertal	5 Feb 99
2.00		Zuzana	Hlavonová	CZE	16.4.73	1	Odlozil	Praha	5 Jun 00
2.00		Dóra	Györffy	HUN	23.2.78	1	NC	Nyíregyháza	26 Jul 01
2.00		Viktoriya	Seryogina	RUS	22.5.73	1	Univ Ch	Bryansk	11 Jun 02
2.00i		Svetlana	Lapina	RUS	12.4.78	3=	NC	Moskva	26 Feb 03
2.00		Daniela	Rath	GER	6.5.77	1	ECp-S	Firenze	22 Jun 03
2.00		Yekaterina	Savchenko'	RUS	3.6.77	1		Dudelange	1 Jul 07
		(57)	100th woman 1.97, 200th 1.94, 300th 1.92						

Best outdoor marks

2.03	Hellebaut	1	EC	Göteborg	11 Aug 06	2.00	Quintero	1	Herc	Monaco	7 Aug 93
2.03	Chicherova	2=	WCh	Osaka	2 Sep 07	2.00	Kositsyna	1		Chelyabinsk	16 Jul 88
2.02	Iagar/Dinescu	1		Budapest	6 Jun 98	2.00	Bilac	1	EC	Helsinki	14 Aug 94
2.02	Kuptsova	1	FBK	Hengelo	1 Jun 03	2.00	Waller	1	MSR	Walnut	18 Apr 99
2.01	Astafei	2		Wörrstadt	27 May 95	2.00	Chicherova	1		Moskva	15 Jul 03

Ancillary jumps – 2.06 Kostadinova 30 Aug 87 2.05i Henkel 8 Feb 92 2.05i Bergqvist 4 Feb 06

POLE VAULT

Mark	Wind	Name		Nat	Born	Pos	Meet	Venue	Date
5.01	WR	Yelena	Isinbayeva	RUS	3.6.82	1	WCh	Helsinki	12 Aug 05
5.00	WR		Isinbayeva			1	LGP	London (CP)	22 Jul 05
4.95	WR		Isinbayeva			1	GP	Madrid	16 Jul 05
4.93	WR		Isinbayeva			1	Athl	Lausanne	5 Jul 05
4.93			Isinbayeva			1	VD	Bruxelles	26 Aug 05
4.93i			Isinbayeva			1		Donetsk	10 Feb 07
4.92	WR		Isinbayeva			1	VD	Bruxelles	3 Sep 04
4.91	WR		Isinbayeva (this jump on 25 Aug)			1	OG	Athína	25 Aug 04
4.91i			Isinbayeva			1		Donetsk	12 Feb 06
4.91			Isinbayeva			1	LGP	London (CP)	28 Jul 06
4.91			Isinbayeva			1	Gaz	Saint-Denis	6 Jul 07
4.90	WR		Isinbayeva			1	GP	London (CP)	30 Jul 04
4.90i			Isinbayeva			1	EI	Madrid	6 Mar 05
4.90			Isinbayeva			1	Athl	Lausanne	11 Jul 06
4.89	WR		Isinbayeva			1		Birmingham	25 Jul 04
4.89i			Isinbayeva			1		Liévin	26 Feb 05
4.88	WR	Svetlana	Feofanova	RUS	16.7.80	1		Iráklio	4 Jul 04
4.88i			Isinbayeva			1	GP	Birmingham	18 Feb 05
4.88		Jennifer	Stuczynski	USA	6.2.82	1	GP	New York	2 Jun 07
4.87	WR		Isinbayeva			1	GP	Gateshead	27 Jun 04
4.87i			Isinbayeva			1		Donetsk	12 Feb 05
4.87			Isinbayeva			1	WAF	Stuttgart	22 Sep 07
4.86i	WR		Isinbayeva			1	WI	Budapest	6 Mar 04
4.85i	WR		Feofanova			1		Athína (P)	20 Feb 04
4.85			Isinbayeva			1	Bisl	Oslo	15 Jun 07
4.84i			Isinbayeva			1		Bydgoszcz	14 Feb 07
4.84			Stuczynski			1	adidas	Carson	20 May 07
4.83i	WR		Isinbayeva			1		Donetsk	15 Feb 04
4.83		Stacy	Dragila	USA	25.3.71	1	GS	Ostrava	8 Jun 04
4.83			Isinbayeva			1	WAF	Monaco	19 Sep 04
4.83		Anna	Rogowska	POL	21.5.81	2	VD	Bruxelles	26 Aug 05

Mark Wind	Name		Nat	Born	Pos	Meet	Venue	Date
4.83		Isinbayeva			1	Golden	Shanghai	28 Sep 07
	(33/5)	6 performances at 4.80: Feofanova 3, Isinbayeva 2, Rogowska 1						
4.82	Monika	Pyrek	POL	11.8.80	2	WAF	Stuttgart	22 Sep 07
4.78	Tatyana	Polnova	RUS	20.4.79	2	WAF	Monaco	19 Sep 04
4.77	Annika	Becker	GER	12.11.81	1	NC	Wattenscheid	7 Jul 02
4.75	Katerina	Badurová	CZE	18.12.82	2	WCh	Osaka	28 Aug 07
4.72i	Kym	Howe	AUS	12.6.80	2		Donetsk	10 Feb 07
	(10)							
4.71i	Yuliya	Golubchikova	RUS	27.3.83	2	EI	Birmingham	4 Mar 07
4.70i	Carolin	Hingst	GER	18.9.80	1		Ludwigshafen	14 Jan 07
4.70	Yvonne	Buschbaum	GER	14.7.80	1	NC	Ulm	29 Jun 03
4.70	Vanessa	Boslak	FRA	11.6.82	2	ECp-S	Málaga	28 Jun 06
4.67i	Kellie	Suttle	USA	9.5.73	1		Jonesboro	16 Jun 04
4.66i	Christine	Adams	GER	28.2.74	1	IHS	Sindelfingen	10 Mar 02
4.66	Carolin	Hingst	GER	18.9.80	1		Karlsruhe	21 Jul 04
4.66	Fabiana	Murer	BRA	16.3.81	1	Herc	Monaco	20 Aug 06
4.65	Mary	Sauer/Vincent	USA	31.10.75	2		Madrid (C)	3 Jul 02
4.65	Anastasiya	Ivanova/Shvedova	RUS	3.5.79	1	Odlozil	Praha	13 Jun 07
4.64i	Pavla	Hamácková/Rybová	CZE	20.5.78	4		Bydgoszcz	14 Feb 07
	(20)							
4.64		Gao Shuying	CHN	28.10.79	2	GP	New York	2 Jun 07
4.63	Nastja	Ryshich	GER	19.9.77	1		Nürnberg	29 Jul 06
4.62	Kym	Howe	AUS	12.6.80	1	CG	Melbourne	25 Mar 06
4.61i	Jillian	Schwartz	USA	19.9.79	1		Jonesboro	13 Jun 06
4.60 WR	Emma	George	AUS	1.11.74	1		Sydney	20 Feb 99
4.60Ai	Mel	Mueller	USA	16.11.72	1		Flagstaff	9 Feb 02
4.60	Yelena	Belyakova	RUS	7.4.76	1	NC	Tula	10 Aug 03
4.60A	Andrea	DuToit	USA	28.2.78	1		Albuquerque	1 May 04
4.60	Thórey Edda	Elisdóttír	ISL	30.6.77	2	SGP	Madrid	17 Jul 04
4.60	Tracy	O'Hara	USA	20.7.80	1	GP II	Stanford	30 May 05
4.60	Chelsea	Johnson	USA	20.12.83	1	Pac-10	Eugene	14 May 06
	(30)							
4.60Ai	April	Steiner	USA	22.4.80	2		Reno	19 Jan 07
4.60Ai	Lacy	Janson	USA	20.2.83	1		Albuquerque	16 Feb 07
4.60	Silke	Spiegelburg	GER	17.3.86	7	WAF	Stuttgart	22 Sep 07
4.58	Tatiana	Grigorieva	AUS	8.10.75	2		Daegu	28 Sep 06
4.57	Anzhela	Balakhonova	UKR	18.12.72	1	NC	Yalta	4 Jul 04
4.57	Julia	Hütter	GER	26.7.83	1=		Leverkusen	10 Aug 07
4.56i	Nicole	Rieger/Humbert	GER	5.2.72	1		Stockholm	25 Feb 99
4.56i	Naroa	Agirre	ESP	15.5.79	1	NC	Sevilla	17 Feb 07
4.56	Anna	Battke	GER	3.1.85	1		Weissach im Tal	8 Jul 07
4.55	Krisztina	Molnár	HUN	8.4.76	1		Beckum	20 Aug 06
	(40)							
4.55	Alana	Boyd	AUS	10.5.84	1		Perth	7 Jan 07
4.54	Nicole	McEwen	USA	1.4.80	3	GP	New York	2 Jun 07
4.53i	Amy	Linnen	USA	15.7.82	1	NCAA	Fayetteville	8 Mar 02
4.53	Joanna	Piwowarska	POL	4.11.83	2	SGP	Doha	12 May 06
4.53i	Becky	Holliday	USA	12.3.80	1		Jonesboro	14 Feb 07
4.52i	Andree	Pickens	USA	17.6.80	1		Jonesboro	23 May 07
4.52	Dana	Ellis-Buller	CAN	7.12.79	1		Chula Vista	18 Aug 07
4.51	Daniela	Bártová	CZE	6.5.74	1	Slovn	Bratislava	9 Jun 98
4.51i	Zsuzsanna	Szabó	HUN	6.5.73	1		Budapest	4 Feb 99
4.51	Kirsten	Belin	SWE	2.5.81	1		Göteborg	27 Aug 02
4.51i	Natalya	Kushch	UKR	5.3.83	6		Donetsk	12 Feb 06
	(51)	100th woman 4.37, 200th 4.25						

Outdoor bests

4.70	Golubchikova	1	NCp	Tula	8 Jul 07
4.66	Hingst	1		Karlsruhe	21 Jul 04
4.65	Howe	1		Saulheim	30 Jun 07
4.60	Suttle	1	ModR	Modesto	12 May 01
4.60	Hamácková	1	ECp-1B	Velenje	21 Jun 03
4.60	Mueller	1		Atascadero	9 Jul 03
4.60	Schwartz	1		Phoenix	14 May 04
4.58	Janson	1		Winston-Salem	20 Apr 06
4.51	Humbert	1		Salamanca	13 Jul 01

Ancillary jumps: 4.96 WR Isinbayeva 22 Jul 05 4.85 Isinbayeva 24 Aug 04

Street competition, raised runway, slightly uphill

4.62	Melissa	Mueller	USA	16.11.72	1	Clovis	4 Aug 01

LONG JUMP

Mark	Wind	Name		Nat	Born	Pos	Meet	Venue	Date
7.52 WR	1.4	Galina	Chistyakova	RUS	26.7.62	1	Znam	Leningrad	11 Jun 88
7.49	1.3	Jackie	Joyner-Kersee	USA	3.3.62	1	NYG	New York	22 May 94
7.49A	1.7		Joyner-Kersee			1		Sestriere	31 Jul 94
7.48	1.2	Heike	Drechsler	GER	16.12.64	1	v ITA	Neubrandenburg	9 Jul 88
7.48	0.4		Drechsler			1	Athl	Lausanne	8 Jul 92

Mark	Wind		Name	Nat	Born	Pos	Meet	Venue	Date
7.45 WR	0.9		Drechsler'			1	v URS	Tallinn	21 Jun 86
7.45 WR	1.1		Drechsler			1	OD	Dresden	3 Jul 86
7.45 WR	0.6		Joyner-Kersee			1	PAm	Indianapolis	13 Aug 87
7.45	1.6		Chistyakova			1	BGP	Budapest	12 Aug 88
7.44 WR	2.0		Drechsler			1		Berlin	22 Sep 85
7.43 WR	1.4	Anisoara	Cusmir/Stanciu	ROM	28.6.62	1	RomIC	Bucuresti	4 Jun 83
7.42	2.0	Tatyana	Kotova	RUS	11.12.76	1	ECp-S	Annecy	23 Jun 02
7.40	1.8		Daute' (Drechsler)			1		Dresden	26 Jul 84
7.40	0.7		Drechsler			1	NC	Potsdam	21 Aug 87
7.40	0.9		Joyner-Kersee			1	OG	Seoul	29 Sep 88
7.39	0.3		Drechsler			1	WK	Zürich	21 Aug 85
7.39	0.5	Yelena	Byelevskaya'	BLR	11.10.63	1	NC	Bryansk	18 Jul 87
7.39			Joyner-Kersee			1		San Diego	25 Jun 88
7.37i	-		Drechsler			1	v2N	Wien	13 Feb 88
7.37A	1.8		Drechsler			1		Sestriere	31 Jul 91
7.37		Inessa	Kravets ¶	UKR	5.10.66	1		Kiyev	13 Jun 92
7.36	0.4		Joyner			1	WCh	Roma	4 Sep 87
7.36	1.8		Byelevskaya			2	Znam	Leningrad	11 Jun 88
7.36	1.8		Drechsler			1		Jena	28 May 92
7.35	1.9		Chistyakova			1	GPB	Bratislava	20 Jun 90
7.34	1.6		Daute'			1		Dresden	19 May 84
7.34	1.4		Chistyakova			2	v GDR	Tallinn	21 Jun 86
7.34			Byelevskaya			1		Sukhumi	17 May 87
7.34	0.7		Drechsler			1	v URS	Karl-Marx-Stadt	20 Jun 87
7.33	0.4		Drechsler			1	v URS	Erfurt	22 Jun 85
7.33	2.0		Drechsler			1		Dresden	2 Aug 85
7.33	-0.3		Drechsler			1	Herc	Monaco	11 Aug 92
7.33	0.4	Tatyana	Lebedeva	RUS	21.7.76	1	NC	Tula	31 Jul 04
		(33/8)							
7.31	1.5	Yelena	Kokonova'	UKR	4.8.63	1	NP	Alma-Ata	12 Sep 85
7.31	1.9	Marion	Jones ¶	USA	12.10.75	1	Pre	Eugene	31 May 98
		(10)							
7.27	-0.4	Irina	Simagina	RUS	25.5.82	2	NC	Tula	31 Jul 04
7.26A	1.8	Maurren	Maggi ¶	BRA	25.6.76	1	SACh	Bogotá	26 Jun 99
7.24	1.0	Larisa	Berezhnaya	UKR	28.2.61	1		Granada	25 May 91
7.21	1.6	Helga	Radtke	GDR	16.5.62	2		Dresden	26 Jul 84
7.21	1.9	Lyudmila	Kolchanova	RUS	1.10.79	1		Sochi	27 May 07
7.20 WR	-0.5	Valy	Ionescu	ROM	31.8.60	1	NC	Bucuresti	1 Aug 82
7.20	2.0	Irena	Ozhenko'	LTU	13.11.62	1		Budapest	12 Sep 86
7.20	0.8	Yelena	Sinchukova'	RUS	23.1.61	1	BGP	Budapest	20 Jun 91
7.20	0.7	Irina	Mushayilova	RUS	6.1.67	1	NC	Sankt-Peterburg	14 Jul 94
7.17	1.8	Irina	Valyukevich	BLR	19.11.59	2	NC	Bryansk	18 Jul 87
		(20)							
7.16		Iolanda	Chen	RUS	26.7.61	1		Moskva	30 Jul 88
7.16A	-0.1	Elva	Goulbourne	JAM	21.1.80	1		Ciudad de México	22 May 04
7.14	1.8	Niole	Medvedyeva ¶	LTU	20.10.60	1		Riga	4 Jun 88
7.14	1.2	Mirela	Dulgheru	ROM	5.10.66	1	Balk G	Sofiya	5 Jul 92
7.12	1.6	Sabine	Paetz/John'	GDR	16.10.57	2		Dresden	19 May 84
7.12	0.9	Chioma	Ajunwa ¶	NGR	25.12.70	1	OG	Atlanta	2 Aug 96
7.11	0.8	Fiona	May	ITA	12.12.69	2	EC	Budapest	22 Aug 98
7.09 WR	0.0	Vilma	Bardauskiene	LTU	15.6.53	Q	EC	Praha	29 Aug 78
7.09	1.5	Ljudmila	Ninova	AUT	25.6.60	1	GP II	Sevilla	5 Jun 94
7.08	0.5	Marieta	Ilcu ¶	ROM	16.10.62	1	RumIC	Pitesti	25 Jun 89
		(30)							
7.07	0.0	Svetlana	Zorina	RUS	2.2.60	1		Krasnodar	15 Aug 87
7.06	0.4	Tatyana	Kolpakova	KGZ	18.10.59	1	OG	Moskva	31 Jul 80
7.06	-0.1	Niurka	Montalvo	CUB/ESP	4.6.68	1	WCh	Sevilla	23 Aug 99
7.06		Tatyana	Ter-Mesrobyan	RUS	12.5.68	1		Sankt Peterburg	22 May 02
7.05	0.6	Lyudmila	Galkina	RUS	20.1.72	1	WCh	Athína	9 Aug 97
7.05	-0.4	Eunice	Barber	FRA	17.11.74	1	WAF	Monaco	14 Sep 03
7.04	0.5	Brigitte	Künzel/Wujak	GDR	6.3.55	2	OG	Moskva	31 Jul 80
7.04	0.9	Tatyana	Proskuryakova'	RUS	13.1.56	1		Kiyev	25 Aug 83
7.04	2.0	Yelena	Yatsuk	UKR	16.3.61	1	Znam	Moskva	8 Jun 85
7.04	0.3	Carol	Lewis	USA	8.8.63	5	WK	Zürich	21 Aug 85
		(40)							
7.03	0.6	Níki	Xánthou	GRE	11.10.73	1		Bellinzona	18 Aug 97
7.03i	-	Dawn	Burrell	USA	1.11.73	1	WI	Lisboa	10 Mar 01
7.02	1.5	Oksana	Udmurtova	RUS	1.2.82	2	SGP	Doha	12 May 06
7.01	-0.4	Tatyana	Skachko	UKR	18.8.54	3	OG	Moskva	31 Jul 80
7.01	-0.3	Eva	Murková	SVK	29.5.62	1	PTS	Bratislava	26 May 84

Mark	Wind	Name		Nat	Born	Pos	Meet	Venue	Date
7.01	-1.0	Marina	Kibakina'	RUS	2.8.60	1		Krasnoyarsk	10 Aug 85
7.01	1.4		Yao Weili	CHN	6.5.68	1	NC	Jinan	5 Jun 93
7.01	1.1	Shana	Williams	USA	7.4.72	Q	NC	Atlanta	21 Jun 96
7.01	2.0	Naide	Gomes	POR	10.11.79	2	GP	Madrid	21 Jul 07
7.00	2.0	Jodi	Anderson	USA	10.11.57	1	OT	Eugene	28 Jun 80
7.00		Margarita	Butkiene	LTU	19.8.49	1		Vilnius	25 May 83
7.00	-0.2	Birgit	Grosshennig	GDR	21.2.65	2		Berlin	9 Jun 84
7.00	0.6	Silvia	Khristova'	BUL	22.8.65	1		Sofiya	3 Aug 86
7.00		Susen	Tiedtke ¶	GER	23.1.69	2		Seoul	18 Aug 91
7.00	1.8	Bronwyn	Thompson	AUS	29.1.78	1	GP II	Melbourne	7 Mar 02
		(55)	100th woman 6.88, 200th 6.78, 300th 6.71						
Drugs dq: 7.03	0.1		Xiong Qiying ¶	CHN	14.10.67	Q	NG	Shanghai	21 Oct 97

Wind assisted *Performances to 7.35, performers to 7.02*

Mark	Wind	Name		Nat	Born	Pos	Meet	Venue	Date
7.63A	2.1	Heike	Drechsler	GER	16.12.64			Sestriere	21 Jul 92
7.45	2.6		Joyner-Kersee			1	OT	Indianapolis	23 Jul 88
7.39	2.6		Drechsler			1		Padova	15 Sep 91
7.39	2.9		Drechsler			1	Expo	Sevilla	6 Jun 92
7.39A	3.3		Drechsler			2		Sestriere	31 Jul 94
7.36	2.2		Chistyakova			1	Znam	Volgograd	11 Jun 89
7.35	3.4		Drechsler			1	NC	Jena	29 Jun 86
7.23A	4.3	Fiona	May	ITA	12.12.69	1		Sestriere	29 Jul 95
7.19A	3.7	Susen	Tiedtke ¶	GER	23.1.69	1		Sestriere	28 Jul 93
7.17	3.6	Eva	Murková	SVK	29.5.62	1		Nitra	26 Aug 84
7.14A	4.5	Marieke	Veltman	USA	18.9.71	2		Sestriere	29 Jul 95
7.12A	5.8	Níki	Xánthou	GRE	11.10.73	3		Sestriere	29 Jul 95
7.12A	4.3	Nicole	Boegman	AUS	5.3.67	4		Sestriere	29 Jul 95
7.09	2.9	Renata	Nielsen	DEN	18.5.66	2		Sevilla	5 Jun 94
7.08	2.2	Lyudmila	Galkina	RUS	20.1.72	1		Thessaloniki	23 Jun 99
7.07A	5.6	Valentina	Uccheddu	ITA	26.10.66	5		Sestriere	29 Jul 95
7.07A	2.7	Sharon	Couch	USA	13.9.67	1		El Paso	12 Apr 97
7.07A	w	Erica	Johansson	SWE	5.2.74	1		Vygieskraal	15 Jan 00
7.06	3.4		Ma Miaolan	CHN	18.1.70	1	NG	Beijing	10 Sep 93

Best at low altitude:
7.06 0.8 Maggi ¶ 1 Milano 3 Jun 03 | 7.12w 3.4 May 1 NC Bologna 25 May 96
7.17w 2.6 1 São Paulo 13 Apr 02

Ancillary marks – other marks during series (to 7.34/7.36w)
7.45 1.0 Chistyakova 11 Jun 88 | 7.47Aw 3.1 Drechsler 21 Jul 92 | 7.38w 2.2 Chistyakova 11 Jun 88
7.37 Drechsler 9 Jul 88 | 7.39Aw 3.1 Drechsler 21 Jul 92 | 7.36w Joyner-Kersee 31 Jul 94

TRIPLE JUMP

Mark	Wind	Name		Nat	Born	Pos	Meet	Venue	Date
15.50 WR	0.9	Inessa	Kravets ¶	UKR	5.10.66	1	WCh	Göteborg	10 Aug 95
15.36i		Tatyana	Lebedeva	RUS	21.7.76	1	WI	Budapest	6 Mar 04
15.34	-0.5		Lebedeva			1		Iráklio	4 Jul 04
15.33	-0.1		Kravets			1	OG	Atlanta	31 Jul 96
15.33	1.2		Lebedeva			1	Athl	Lausanne	6 Jul 04
15.32	0.5		Lebedeva			1	Super	Yokohama	9 Sep 00
15.32	0.9	Hrisopiyi	Devetzí	GRE	2.1.76	Q	OG	Athína	21 Aug 04
15.30	0.6	Françoise	Mbango-Etone	CMR	14.4.76	1	OG	Athína	23 Aug 04
15.29	0.3	Yamilé	Aldama	CUB/SUD	14.8.72	1	GGala	Roma	11 Jul 03
15.28	0.3		Aldama			1	GP	Linz	2 Aug 04
15.28	0.9	Yargelis	Savigne	CUB	13.11.84	1	WCh	Osaka	31 Aug 07
15.27	1.3		Aldama			1	GP	London (CP)	8 Aug 03
15.25	-0.8		Lebedeva			1	WCh	Edmonton	10 Aug 01
15.25	-0.1		Devetzí			2	OG	Athína	23 Aug 04
15.23	0.8		Lebedeva			1		Réthimno	23 Jun 04
15.23	0.6		Lebedeva			1	SGP	Athína	3 Jul 06
15.21	1.2		Aldama			2		Réthimno	23 Jun 04
15.20	0.0	Sarka	Kaspárková	CZE	20.5.71	1	WCh	Athína	4 Aug 97
15.20	-0.3	Tereza	Marinova	BUL	5.9.77	1	OG	Sydney	24 Sep 00
15.19	0.5		Lebedeva			1	Athl	Lausanne	11 Jul 06
15.18	0.3	Iva	Prandzheva ¶	BUL	15.2.72	2	WCh	Göteborg	10 Aug 95
15.18	-0.2		Lebedeva			1	WCh	Saint-Denis	26 Aug 03
15.16	0.1	Rodica	Mateescu ¶ (10)	ROM	13.3.71	2	WCh	Athína	4 Aug 97
15.16i	-	Ashia	Hansen	GBR	5.12.71	1	EI	Valencia	28 Feb 98
15.16	0.7	Trecia	Smith	JAM	5.11.75	2	GP	Linz	2 Aug 04
15.15	1.7		Hansen			1	GPF	Fukuoka	13 Sep 97
15.15	1.4		Lebedeva			1	EC	Göteborg	9 Aug 06
15.14	-0.1		Mateescu			1	RomIC	Bucuresti	14 Jun 97
15.14	0.3		Lebedeva			1	VD	Bruxelles	5 Sep 03

Mark	Wind	Name		Nat	Born	Pos	Meet	Venue	Date
15.14	0.7		Lebedeva			3	OG	Athína	23 Aug 04
15.14	0.9		Lebedeva			1	GP	Athína	2 Jul 07
		(31/12)							
15.09 WR	0.5	Anna	Biryukova	RUS	27.9.67	1	WCh	Stuttgart	21 Aug 93
15.09	-0.5	Inna	Lasovskaya	RUS	17.12.69	1	ECCp-A	Valencia	31 May 97
15.07	-0.6	Paraskeví	Tsiamíta	GRE	10.3.72	Q	WCh	Sevilla	22 Aug 99
15.03i		Iolanda	Chen	RUS	26.7.61	1	WI	Barcelona	11 Mar 95
15.03	1.9	Magdelin	Martinez	ITA	10.2.76	1		Roma	26 Jun 04
15.02	0.9	Anna	Pyatykh	RUS	4.4.81	3	EC	Göteborg	8 Sep 06
15.00	1.2	Kène	Ndoye	SEN	20.11.78	2		Iráklio	4 Jul 04
14.98	1.8	Sofiya	Bozhanova ¶	BUL	4.10.67	1		Stara Zagora	16 Jul 94
		(20)							
14.98	0.2	Baya	Rahouli	ALG	27.7.79	1	MedG	Almeria	1 Jul 05
14.96	0.7	Yelena	Govorova	UKR	18.9.73	4	OG	Sydney	24 Sep 00
14.94i	–	Cristina	Nicolau	ROM	9.8.77	1	NC	Bucuresti	5 Feb 00
14.92	1.3	Marija	Sestak	SLO	17.4.79	1		Ljubljana	3 Jun 07
14.90	1.0		Xie Limei	CHN	27.6.86	1		Urumqi	20 Sep 07
14.83i	-	Yelena	Lebedenko	RUS	16.1.71	1		Samara	1 Feb 01
14.83	0.5	Yelena	Oleynikova	RUS	9.12.76	1	Odlozil	Praha	17 Jun 02
14.79	1.7	Irina	Mushayilova	RUS	6.1.67	1	DNG	Stockholm	5 Jul 93
14.79	0.4	Olga	Saladuha	UKR	4.6.83	1	WUG	Bangkok	13 Aug 07
14.76	0.9	Galina	Chistyakova/Cistjaková	RUS/SVK	26.7.62	1		Luzern	27 Jun 95
		(30)							
14.76	1.1	Gundega	Sproge	LAT	12.12.72	3		Sheffield	29 Jun 97
14.76i		Adelina	Gavrila	ROM	26.11.78	1	NC	Bucuresti	22 Feb 03
14.74i		Viktoriya	Gurova	RUS	22.5.82	1	EI	Madrid	6 Mar 05
14.72	1.8		Huang Qiuyan	CHN	25.1.80	1	NG	Guangzhou	22 Nov 01
14.70i		Oksana	Rogova	RUS	7.10.78	1		Volgograd	6 Feb 02
14.69	1.2	Anja	Valant	SLO	8.9.77	3		Kalamáta	4 Jun 00
14.69	1.2	Simona	La Mantia	ITA	14.4.83	1		Palermo	22 May 05
14.69	2.0	Teresa	N'zola Meso	FRA	30.11.83	1	ECp-S	München	23 Jun 07
14.69	1.6	Olga	Rypakova	KAZ	30.11.84	1	AsiC	Amman	28 Jul 07
14.67	1.2	Ólga	Vasdéki	GRE	26.9.73	1	Veniz	Haniá	28 Jul 99
		(40)							
14.66	1.9		Ren Ruiping	CHN	1.2.76	1	Oda	Hiroshima	29 Apr 97
14.65	0.3	Fiona	May	ITA	12.12.69	1	ECp	Sankt-Peterburg	27 Jun 98
14.65	2.0	Natalya	Safronova	BLR	11.4.74	1	NCp	Stayki	3 Jun 00
14.65i		Nadezhda	Bazhenova	RUS	22.9.78	1		Pireás	20 Feb 02
14.61	2.0	Yusmay	Bicet	CUB	8.12.83	1		La Habana	4 Mar 04
14.60	0.7	Niurka	Montalvo	CUB/ESP	4.6.68	1	NC	La Habana	24 Jun 94
14.60	0.4	Carlota	Castrejana	ESP	25.4.73	2	MedG	Almeria	1 Jul 05
14.58	0.3	Yelena	Donkina	RUS	15.3.73	2	NC	Tula	10 Jul 97
14.57		Irina	Vasilyeva	RUS	9.4.79	2		Moskva	23 Jun 01
14.57	0.2	Keila	Costa	BRA	6.2.83	1	SAmC	São Paulo	9 Jun 07
		(50)	100th woman 14.25, 200th 14.01, 300th 13.80						
Wind assisted			*Performances to 15.14, performers to 14.55*						
15.24A	4.2	Magdelin	Martinez	ITA	10.2.76	1		Sestriere	1 Aug 04
15.17	2.4	Anna	Pyatykh	RUS	4.4.81	2	SGP	Athína	3 Jul 06
15.10	2.7	Keila	Costa	BRA	6.2.83	1		Uberlandia	6 May 07
14.99	6.8	Yelena	Govorova	UKR	18.9.73	1	WUG	Palma de Mallorca	11 Jul 99
14.88	3.8	Trecia	Smith	JAM	5.11.75	1	Kans R	Lawrence	21 Apr 01
14.84	4.1	Galina	Chistyakova	RUS	26.7.62	1		Innsbruck	28 Jun 95
14.83	8.3		Ren Ruiping	CHN	1.2.76	1	NC	Taiyuan	21 May 95
14.83	2.2	Heli	Koivula	FIN	27.6.75	2	EC	München	10 Aug 02
14.75	4.2	Jelena	Blazevica	LAT	11.5.70	1	v2N	Kaunas	23 Aug 97
14.71	2.5	Simona	La Mantia	ITA	14.4.83	1		Roma	25 Jun 04
14.67	3.0	Yusmay	Bicet	CUB	8.12.83	2		Zaragoza	8 Jun 04
14.66	3.2	Sheila	Hudson	USA	30.6.67	1	NC	Sacramento	17 Jun 95

Best outdoor mark for athlete with all-time best indoors

14.97WR	0.9	Chen	1	NC	Moskva	18 Jun 93	14.65	0.4	Gurova	2	NC	Tula	1 Aug 04
14.75	1.1	Gavrila	3	GP II	Rieti	7 Sep 03	14.60		Bazhenova	1		Moskva	23 Jun 01
14.70	1.3	Nicolau	1	EU23	Göteborg	1 Aug 99	14.59	1.1	Rogova	*	EU23	Göteborg	1 Aug 99
									14.65w 2.6	2	EU23	Göteborg	1 Aug 99

Ancillary marks – other marks during series (to 15.16)

15.30	0.5	Mbango	23 Aug 04	15.28	-0.3	Ledebeva	4 Jul 04	15.25i		Ledebeva	6 Mar 04
15.21	-0.2	Mbango	23 Aug 04	15.19	1.0	Lebedeva	3 Jul 06	15.17	0.4	Aldama	2 Aug 04
15.17	-0.1	Mbango	23 Aug 04	15.16	1.7	Lebedeva	9 Sep 00	15.16	-0.2	Ledebeva	26 Aug 03
15.16i		Ledebeva	6 Mar 04								

SHOT

22.63 WR		Natalya	Lisovskaya	RUS	16.7.62	1	Znam	Moskva	7 Jun 87
22.55			Lisovskaya			1	NC	Tallinn	5 Jul 88

Mark Wind	Name		Nat	Born	Pos	Meet	Venue	Date
22.53 WR		Lisovskaya			1		Sochi	27 May 84
22.53		Lisovskaya			1		Kiyev	14 Aug 88
22.50i	Helena	Fibingerová	CZE	13.7.49	1		Jablonec	19 Feb 77
22.45 WR	Ilona	Slupianek' ¶	GDR	24.9.56	1		Potsdam	11 May 80
22.41		Slupianek			1	OG	Moskva	24 Jul 80
22.40		Slupianek			1		Berlin	3 Jun 83
22.38		Slupianek			1		Karl-Marx-Stadt	25 May 80
22.36 WR		Slupianek			1		Celje	2 May 80
22.34		Slupianek			1		Berlin	7 May 80
22.34		Slupianek			1	NC	Cottbus	18 Jul 80
22.32 WR		Fibingerová			1		Nitra	20 Aug 77
22.24		Lisovskaya			1	OG	Seoul	1 Oct 88
22.22		Slupianek			1		Potsdam	13 Jul 80
22.19	Claudia	Losch	FRG	10.1.60	1		Hainfeld	23 Aug 87
22.14i		Lisovskaya			1	NC	Penza	7 Feb 87
22.13		Slupianek			1		Split	29 Apr 80
22.06		Slupianek			1		Berlin	15 Aug 78
22.06		Lisovskaya			1		Moskva	6 Aug 88
22.05		Slupianek			1	OD	Berlin	28 May 80
22.05		Slupianek			1		Potsdam	31 May 80
22.04		Slupianek			1		Potsdam	4 Jul 79
22.04		Slupianek			1		Potsdam	29 Jul 79
21.99 WR		Fibingerová			1		Opava	26 Sep 76
21.98		Slupianek			1		Berlin	17 Jul 79
21.96		Fibingerová			1	GS	Ostrava	8 Jun 77
21.96		Lisovskaya			1	Drz	Praha	16 Aug 84
21.96		Lisovskaya			1		Vilnius	28 Aug 88
21.95		Lisovskaya			1	IAC	Edinburgh	29 Jul 88
	(30/4)							
21.89 WR	Ivanka	Khristova	BUL	19.11.41	1		Belmeken	4 Jul 76
21.86	Marianne	Adam	GDR	19.9.51	1	v URS	Leipzig	23 Jun 79
21.76		Li Meisu	CHN	17.4.59	1		Shijiazhuang	23 Apr 88
21.73	Natalya	Akhrimenko	RUS	12.5.55	1		Leselidze	21 May 88
21.69	Viktoriya	Pavlysh ¶	UKR	15.1.69	1	EC	Budapest	20 Aug 98
21.66		Sui Xinmei ¶	CHN	29.1.65	1		Beijing	9 Jun 90
	(10)							
21.61	Verzhinia	Veselinova	BUL	18.11.57	1		Sofiya	21 Aug 82
21.60i	Valentina	Fedyushina	UKR	18.2.65	1		Simferopol	28 Dec 91
21.58	Margitta	Droese/Pufe	GDR	10.9.52	1		Erfurt	28 May 78
21.57 @	Ines	Müller'	GDR	2.1.59	1		Athína	16 May 88
	21.45				1		Schwerin	4 Jun 86
21.53	Nunu	Abashidze ¶	UKR	27.3.55	2	Izv	Kiyev	20 Jun 84
21.52		Huang Zhihong	CHN	7.5.65	1	NC	Beijing	27 Jun 90
21.46	Larisa	Peleshenko ¶	RUS	29.2.64	1	Kuts	Moskva	26 Aug 00
21.45 WR	Nadezhda	Chizhova	RUS	29.9.45	1		Varna	29 Sep 73
21.43	Eva	Wilms	FRG	28.7.52	2	HB	München	17 Jun 77
21.42	Svetlana	Krachevskaya'	RUS	23.11.44	2	OG	Moskva	24 Jul 80
	(20)	*@ competitive meeting, but unsanctioned by GDR federation*						
21.31 @	Heike	Hartwig'	GDR	30.12.62	2		Athína	16 May 88
	21.27				1		Haniá	22 May 88
21.27	Liane	Schmuhl	GDR	29.6.61	1		Cottbus	26 Jun 82
21.22	Astrid	Kumbernuss	GER	5.2.70	1	WCh	Göteborg	5 Aug 95
21.21	Kathrin	Neimke	GDR	18.7.66	2	WCh	Roma	5 Sep 87
21.19	Helma	Knorscheidt	GDR	31.12.56	1		Berlin	24 May 84
21.15i	Irina	Korzhanenko ¶	RUS	16.5.74	1	NC	Moskva	18 Feb 99
21.10	Heidi	Krieger	GDR	20.7.65	1	EC	Stuttgart	26 Aug 86
21.09	Nadezhda	Ostapchuk	BLR	12.10.80	1		Staiki	21 Jul 05
21.06	Svetlana	Krivelyova	RUS	13.6.69	1	OG	Barcelona	7 Aug 92
21.05	Zdenka	Silhavá' ¶	CZE	15.6.54	2	NC	Praha	23 Jul 83
	(30)							
21.01	Ivanka	Petrova-Stoycheva	BUL	3.2.51	1	NC	Sofiya	28 Jul 79
21.00	Mihaela	Loghin	ROM	1.6.52	1		Formia	30 Jun 84
21.00	Cordula	Schulze	GDR	11.9.59	4	OD	Potsdam	21 Jul 84
20.96	Belsy	Laza	CUB	5.6.67	1		Ciudad de México	2 May 92
20.95	Elena	Stoyanova ¶	BUL	23.1.52	2	Balk	Sofiya	14 Jun 80
20.91	Svetla	Mitkova	BUL	17.6.64	1		Sofiya	24 May 87
20.80	Sona	Vasícková	CZE	14.3.62	1		Praha	2 Jun 88
20.72	Grit	Haupt/Hammer	GDR	4.6.66	3		Neubrandenburg	11 Jun 87
20.61	María Elena	Sarría	CUB	14.9.54	1		La Habana	22 Jul 82

Mark Wind		Name	Nat	Born	Pos	Meet	Venue	Date
20.61	Yanina	Korolchik ¶	BLR	26.12.76	1	WCh	Edmonton	5 Aug 01
	(40)							
20.60	Marina	Antonyuk	RUS	12.5.62	1		Chelyabinsk	10 Aug 86
20.54		Zhang Liuhong	CHN	16.1.69	1	NC	Beijing	5 Jun 94
20.54	Valerie	Vili	NZL	6.10.84	1	WCh	Osaka	26 Aug 07
20.53	Iris	Plotzitzka	FRG	7.1.66	1	ASV	Köln	21 Aug 88
20.50i	Christa	Wiese	GDR	25.12.67	2	NC	Senftenberg	12 Feb 89
20.47	Nina	Isayeva	RUS	6.7.50	1		Bryansk	28 Aug 82
20.47		Cong Yuzhen	CHN	22.1.63	2	IntC	Tianjin	3 Sep 88
20.44	Tatyana	Orlova	BLR	19.7.55	1		Staiki	28 May 83
20.40		Zhou Tianhua ¶	CHN	10.4.66	1		Beijing	5 Sep 91
20.34	Stephanie	Storp	FRG	28.11.68	1		Wolfsburg	1 Jul 90
	(50)	100th woman 19.58, 200th 18.70						

Best outdoor marks

21.08 Fedyushina 1 Leselidze 15 May 88 | 20.82 Korzhanenko ¶ 1 Rostov na Donu 30 May 98
21.06 drugs dq (1) OG Athína 18 Aug 04

Ancillary marks – other marks during series (to 22.09)

22.60	Lisovskaya (WR)	7 Jun 87	22.20	Slupianek	13 Jul 80	22.12	Slupianek	13 Jul 80
22.40	Lisovskaya	14 Aug 88	22.19	Lisovskaya	5 Jul 88	22.11	Slupianek	7 May 80
22.34	Slupianek	11 May 80	22.14	Slupianek	25 May 80	22.10	Slupianek	25 May 80
22.33	Slupianek	2 May 80	22.14	Slupianek	13 Jul 80	22.09	Slupianek	7 May 80

DISCUS

76.80 WR	Gabriele	Reinsch	GDR	23.9.63	1	v ITA	Neubrandenburg	9 Jul 88
74.56 WR	Zdenka	Silhavá' ¶	CZE	15.6.54	1		Nitra	26 Aug 84
74.56	Ilke	Wyludda	GDR	28.3.69	1	NC	Neubrandenburg	23 Jul 89
74.44		Reinsch			1		Berlin	13 Sep 88
74.40		Wyludda			2		Berlin	13 Sep 88
74.08	Diana	Gansky'	GDR	14.12.63	1	v URS	Karl-Marx-Stadt	20 Jun 87
73.90		Gansky			1	ECp	Praha	27 Jun 87
73.84	Daniela	Costian ¶	ROM	30.4.65	1		Bucuresti	30 Apr 88
73.78		Costian			1		Bucuresti	24 Apr 88
73.42		Reinsch			1		Karl-Marx-Stadt	12 Jun 88
73.36 WR	Irina	Meszynski	GDR	24.3.62	1	Drz	Praha	17 Aug 84
73.32		Gansky			1		Neubrandenburg	11 Jun 87
73.28	Galina	Savinkova'	RUS	15.7.53	1	NC	Donetsk	8 Sep 84
73.26 WR		Savinkova			1		Leselidze	21 May 83
73.26		Sachse/Gansky			1		Neubrandenburg	6 Jun 86
73.24		Gansky			1		Leipzig	29 May 87
73.22	Tsvetanka	Khristova ¶	BUL	14.3.62	1		Kazanlak	19 Apr 87
73.10	Gisela	Beyer	GDR	16.7.60	1	OD	Berlin	20 Jul 84
73.04		Gansky			1		Potsdam	6 Jun 87
73.04		Wyludda			1	ECp	Gateshead	5 Aug 89
72.96		Savinkova			1	v GDR	Erfurt	23 Jun 85
72.94		Gansky			2	v ITA	Neubrandenburg	9 Jul 88
72.92	Martina	Opitz/Hellmann	GDR	12.12.60	1	NC	Potsdam	20 Aug 87
72.90		Costian			1		Bucuresti	14 May 88
72.78		Hellmann			2		Neubrandenburg	11 Jun 87
72.78		Reinsch			1	OD	Berlin	29 Jun 88
72.72		Wyludda			1		Neubrandenburg	23 Jun 89
72.70		Wyludda			1	NC-j	Karl-Marx-Stadt	15 Jul 88
72.54		Gansky			1	NC	Rostock	25 Jun 88
72.52		Hellmann			1		Frohburg	15 Jun 86
72.52		Khristova			1	BGP	Budapest	11 Aug 86
	(31/10)							
72.14	Galina	Murashova	LTU	22.12.55	2	Drz	Praha	17 Aug 84
71.80 WR	Maria	Vergova/Petkova	BUL	3.11.50	1	NC	Sofiya	13 Jul 80
71.68		Xiao Yanling ¶	CHN	27.3.68	1		Beijing	14 Mar 92
71.58	Ellina	Zvereva' ¶	BLR	16.11.60	1	Znam	Leningrad	12 Jun 88
71.50 WR	Evelin	Schlaak/Jahl	GDR	28.3.56	1		Potsdam	10 May 80
71.30	Larisa	Korotkevich	RUS	3.1.67	1	RusCp	Sochi	29 May 92
71.22	Ria	Stalman	NED	11.12.51	1		Walnut	15 Jul 84
70.88	Hilda Elia	Ramos ¶	CUB	1.9.64	1		La Habana	8 May 92
70.80	Larisa	Mikhalchenko	UKR	16.5.63	1		Kharkov	18 Jun 88
70.68	Maritza	Martén	CUB	16.8.63	1	Ib Am	Sevilla	18 Jul 92
	(20)							
70.50 WR	Faina	Melnik	RUS	9.6.45	1	Znam	Sochi	24 Apr 76
70.34 @	Silvia	Madetzky	GDR	24.6.62	3		Athína	16 May 88
	69.34				1		Halle	26 Jun 87
70.02	Natalya	Sadova ¶	RUS	15.6.72	1		Thessaloniki	23 Jun 99
69.86	Valentina	Kharchenko	RUS	.49	1		Feodosiya	16 May 81

WOMEN All-time

Mark	Wind	Name		Nat	Born	Pos	Meet	Venue	Date
69.72		Svetla	Mitkova	BUL	17.6.64	2	NC	Sofiya	15 Aug 87
69.68		Mette	Bergmann	NOR	9.11.62	1		Florø	27 May 95
69.51		Franka	Dietzsch	GER	22.1.68	1		Wiesbaden	8 May 99
69.50		Florenta	Craciunescu'	ROM	7.5.55	1	Balk	Stara Zagora	2 Aug 85
69.14		Irina	Yatchenko	BLR	31.10.65	1		Staiki	31 Jul 04
69.08		Carmen	Romero	CUB	6.10.50	1	NC	La Habana	17 Apr 76
		(30)							
69.08		Mariana	Ionescu/Lengyel	ROM	14.4.53	1		Constanta	19 Apr 86
68.92		Sabine	Engel	GDR	21.4.54	1	v URS,POL	Karl-Marx-Stadt	25 Jun 77
68.80		Nicoleta	Grasu	ROM	11.9.71	1		Poiana Brasov	7 Aug 99
68.64		Margitta	Pufe'	GDR	10.9.52	1	ISTAF	Berlin	17 Aug 79
68.62			Yu Hourun	CHN	9.7.64	1		Beijing	6 May 88
68.62			Hou Xuemei	CHN	27.2.62	1	IntC	Tianjin	4 Sep 88
68.60		Nadezhda	Kugayevskikh	RUS	19.4.60	1		Oryol	30 Aug 83
68.58		Lyubov	Zverkova	RUS	14.6.55	1	Izv	Kiyev	22 Jun 84
68.52		Beatrice	Faumuiná	NZL	23.10.74	1	Bisl	Oslo	4 Jul 97
68.38		Olga	Burova'	RUS	17.9.63	2	RusCp	Sochi	29 May 92
		(40)							
68.18		Tatyana	Lesovaya	KAZ	24.4.56	1		Alma-Ata	23 Sep 82
68.18		Irina	Khval	RUS	17.5.62	1		Moskva	8 Jul 88
68.18		Barbara	Hechevarría	CUB	6.8.66	2		La Habana	17 Feb 89
67.96		Argentina	Menis	ROM	19.7.48	1	RomIC	Bucuresti	15 May 76
67.90		Petra	Sziegaud	GDR	17.10.58	1		Berlin	19 May 82
67.82		Tatyana	Belova	RUS	12.2.62	1		Irkutsk	10 Aug 87
67.80		Stefenia	Simova ¶	BUL	5.6.63	1		Stara Zagora	27 Jun 92
67.72		Ekateríni	Vóggoli	GRE	30.10.70	1	NC	Athína	10 Jun 04
67.71		Vera	Pospísilová/Cechlová	CZE	19.11.78	1		Réthimno	6 Jul 03
67.70		Anastasía	Kelesídou	GRE	28.11.72	2		Réthimno	29 May 99
		(50)	100th woman 65.40, 200th 63.18						

Unofficial meeting

Mark	Wind	Name		Nat	Born	Pos	Meet	Venue	Date
78.14		Martina	Hellmann	GDR	12.12.60	1		Berlin	6 Sep 88
75.36		Ilke	Wyludda	GDR	28.3.69	2		Berlin	6 Sep 88

Downhill: 69.44 Suzy Powell USA 3.9.76 1 La Jolla 27 Apr 02

Ancillary marks – other marks during series (to 72.92)

73.32	Reinsch	13 Sep 88	73.28	Gansky	27 Jun 87	73.10	Reinsch	9 Jul 88
73.28	Gansky	11 Jun 87	73.16	Wyludda	13 Sep 88	73.06	Gansky	27 Jun 87
						72.92	Hellmann	20 Aug 87

HAMMER

Mark	Wind	Name		Nat	Born	Pos	Meet	Venue	Date
78.61		Tatyana	Lysenko	RUS	9.10.83	1		Sochi	26 May 07
77.80	WR		Lysenko			1		Tallinn	15 Aug 06
77.71			Lysenko			1	GS	Ostrava	27 Jun 07
77.41	WR		Lysenko			1	Znam	Zhukovskiy	24 Jun 06
77.36		Gulfiya	Khanafeyeva	RUS	4.6.82	2		Sochi	26 May 07
77.30			Lysenko			1		Adler	22 Apr 07
77.26	WR		Khanafeyeva			1	NC	Tula	12 Jun 06
77.06	WR		Lysenko			1	Kuts	Moskva	15 Jul 05
77.01			Lysenko			1	Znam	Zhukovskiy	9 Jun 07
76.94			Khanafeyeva			1		Moskva	31 May 06
76.93			Khanafeyeva			1	RUSCp	Tula	15 Jul 06
76.86		Oksana	Menkova	BLR	28.3.82	1	Klim	Minsk	23 Jun 06
76.83		Kamila	Skolimowska	POL	4.11.82	1	SGP	Doha	11 May 07
76.74			Lysenko			1		Zagreb	4 Jul 07
76.67			Lysenko			1	EC	Göteborg	8 Aug 06
76.66		Olga	Tsander	BLR	18.5.76	1		Staiki	21 Jul 05
76.63		Yekaterina	Khoroshikh	RUS	21.1.83	2	Znam	Moskva	24 Jun 06
76.55		Betty	Heidler	GER	14.10.83	1		Leverkusen	28 Jul 06
76.54			Lysenko			1	GP	Zagreb	31 Aug 06
76.50			Lysenko			1	ECp-S	Málaga	29 Jun 06
76.36		Yipsi	Moreno	CUB	19.11.80	1	Kuso	Waszawa	17 Jun 07
76.34			Lysenko			2	NC	Tula	12 Jun 06
76.24			Lysenko			1		Birmingham	20 Aug 06
76.21		Yelena	Konevtsova	RUS	11.3.81	3		Sochi	26 May 07
76.11			Heidler			2	GP	Zagreb	31 Aug 06
76.09			Heidler			1		Thum	15 Aug 06
76.07	WR	Mihaela	Melinte ¶	ROM	27.3.75	1		Rüdlingen	29 Aug 99
75.97	WR		Melinte			1		Clermont-Ferrand	13 May 99
75.95			Lysenko			1		Moskva	29 Jun 05
75.95			Lysenko			1	NC	Tula	13 Jul 05
		(30/10)							
75.68		Olga	Kuzenkova	RUS	4.10.70	1	NCp	Tula	4 Jun 00

Mark	Wind	Name		Nat	Born	Pos	Meet	Venue	Date
75.08		Ivana	Brkljacic	CRO	25.1.83	2	Kuso	Waszawa	17 Jun 07
74.86			Zhang Wenxiu	CHN	22.3.86	1	NC	Shijiazhuang	3 Aug 07
74.66		Manuèla	Montebrun	FRA	13.11.79	1	GP II	Zagreb	11 Jul 05
74.31		Iryna	Sekachova	UKR	21.7.76	1	NC	Kiev	22 Jul 06
73.87		Erin	Gilreath	USA	11.10.80	1	NC	Carson	25 Jun 05
73.84		Martina	Danisová ¶	SVK	21.3.83	1	NC	Trnava	1 Jul 06
73.59		Ester	Balassini	ITA	20.10.77	1	NC	Bressanone	25 Jun 05
73.45		Kathrin	Klaas	GER	8.2.84	2eA		Halle	19 May 07
73.21		Eileen	O'Keeffe	IRL	31.5.81	1	NC	Dublin	21 Jul 07
		(20)							
73.16		Yunaika	Crawford	CUB	2.11.82	3	OG	Athína	25 Aug 04
72.94		Jennifer	Dahlgren	ARG	27.8.84	1		Athens	13 Apr 07
72.75		Marina	Smolyachkova	BLR	10.2.85	2		Minsk (Staiki)	22 Jul 06
72.74		Susanne	Keil	GER	18.5.78	1		Nikiti	15 Jul 05
72.51			Liu Yinghui	CHN	29.6.79	2	WUG	Izmir	16 Aug 05
72.51		Brittany	Riley	USA	26.8.86	1	DrakeR	Des Moines	28 Apr 07
72.36			Gu Yuan	CHN	9.5.82	2		Padova	3 Jul 04
72.09		Tatyana	Konstantinova	RUS	18.11.70	2	Znam	Moskva	4 Jun 99
72.01		Anna	Norgren-Mahon	USA	19.12.74	1		Walnut	27 Jul 02
71.98		Clarissa	Claretti	ITA	7.10.80	2	NC-w	Ascoli Piceno	5 Mar 06
		(30)							
71.78		Yelena	Priyma	RUS	2.12.83	5		Sochi	26 May 07
71.45		Candice	Scott	TRI	17.9.80	1		Marietta	15 May 05
71.38		Amélie	Perrin	FRA	30.3.80	1		Sotteville	2 Jul 06
71.29		Darya	Pchelnik	BLR	20.12.81	1		Minsk (Staiki)	28 Jul 07
71.14		Arasay	Thondike	CUB	28.5.86	5	Kuso	Warszawa	17 Jun 07
71.11		Stéphanie	Falzon	FRA	7.1.83	1		Sasolburg	23 Jan 07
71.12		Bronwyn	Eagles	AUS	23.8.80	1		Adelaide	6 Feb 03
70.79		Katalin	Divós ¶	HUN	11.5.74	2	GP	Doha	18 May 01
70.78		Jessica	Cosby	USA	31.5.82	1	NC	Indianapolis	23 Jun 06
70.73		Andrea	Bunjes	GER	5.2.76	Q	OG	Athína	23 Aug 04
		(40)							
70.72		Brooke	Krueger/Billett	AUS	9.7.80	1	NC	Sydney	5 Feb 06
70.67			Zhao Wei	CHN	27.1.79	1		Nanning	5 Apr 03
70.62		Dawn	Ellerbe	USA	3.4.74	1	Penn R	Philadelphia	28 Apr 01
70.62		Yelena	Matoshko	BLR	23.6.82	2		Minsk (Staiki)	28 Jul 07
70.33		Alexándra	Papayeoryíou	GRE	17.12.80	1	Balk	Zenica	3 Sep 06
70.33		Amber	Campbell	USA	5.6.81	1		Provo	2 Jun 07
70.03		Loree	Smith	USA	6.11.82	1		Fort Collins	13 May 05
69.92		Lyudmila	Gubkina	BLR	13.8.73	1		Staiki	19 Aug 00
69.91		Nadezhda	Pavlyukovskaya	BLR	6.6.85	3	Klim	Minsk (Staiki)	9 Jun 07
69.80		Svetlana	Sudak	BLR/TUR	20.3.71	4		Staiki	21 Jul 05
		(50)	100th woman 67.52, 200th 63.08						
Downhill: 75.20		Manuéla	Montebrun	FRA	13.11.79	1		Vineuil	18 May 03

Ancillary marks – other marks during series to 76.24

77.32	Lysenko	27 Jun 07	76.80	Lysenko	22 Apr 07	76.28	Khanafeyeva	26 May 07
77.06	Lysenko	24 Jun 06	76.71	Lysenko	15 Aug 06	76.24	Lysenko	4 Jul 07
77.05	Lysenko	26 May 07	76.39	Lysenko	15 Aug 06			

Drugs disqualification: 70.34 Melissa Price ¶ USA 5.9.79 1 NC Stanford 19 Jun 03

JAVELIN

Mark	Wind	Name		Nat	Born	Pos	Meet	Venue	Date
71.70	WR	Osleidys	Menéndez	CUB	14.11.79	1	WCh	Helsinki	14 Aug 05
71.54	WR		Menéndez			1		Réthimno	1 Jul 01
71.53			Menéndez			1	OG	Athína	27 Aug 04
70.20		Christina	Obergföll	GER	22.8.81	1	ECp-S	München	23 Jun 07
70.03			Obergföll			2	WCh	Helsinki	14 Aug 05
69.82			Menéndez			1	WUG	Beijing	29 Aug 01
69.53			Menéndez			1	WCh	Edmonton	7 Aug 01
69.48	WR	Trine	Hattestad	NOR	18.4.66	1	Bisl	Oslo	28 Jul 00
68.91			Hattestad			1	OG	Sydney	30 Sep 00
68.47			Menéndez			1	GP	Helsinki	25 Jul 05
68.40			Menéndez			1		Tartu	19 Jun 01
68.32			Hattestad			1	ISTAF	Berlin	1 Sep 00
68.23			Menéndez			1		La Habana	5 Mar 04
68.22	WR		Hattestad			1	GGala	Roma	30 Jun 00
68.19	WRu		Hattestad			1		Fana	28 Jul 99
68.08			Obergföll			1		Halle	19 May 07
67.99			Menéndez			1		Iráklio	4 Jul 04
67.92			Hattestad			1	DNG	Stockholm	1 Aug 00
67.88			Obergföll			1	GP	Athína	2 Jul 07

Mark	Wind	Name		Nat	Born	Pos	Meet	Venue	Date
67.87			Menéndez			1	SGP	Madrid	17 Jul 04
67.83			Menéndez			2	ISTAF	Berlin	1 Sep 00
67.76			Hattestad			1	VD	Bruxelles	25 Aug 00
67.67		Sonia	Bisset	CUB	1.4.71	1		Salamanca	6 Jul 05
67.51	WR	Miréla	Manjani/Tzelíli	GRE	21.12.76	2	OG	Sydney	30 Sep 00
67.47			Manjani			1	EC	München	8 Aug 02
67.40			Menéndez			1	Athl	Lausanne	2 Jul 02
67.34			Menéndez			Q	OG	Sydney	29 Sep 00
67.24			Menéndez			1	WAF	Monaco	9 Sep 05
67.20		Tatyana	Shikolenko	RUS	10.5.68	1	Herc	Monaco	18 Aug 00
67.14			Menéndez			1	NC	La Habana	10 Mar 02
67.12		Barbora	Spotáková	CZE	30.6.81	1	WAF	Stuttgart	22 Sep 07
		(31/7)							
66.91		Tanja	Damaske	GER	16.11.71	1	NC	Erfurt	4 Jul 99
66.80		Louise	Currey	AUS	24.1.69	1		Gold Coast (RB)	5 Aug 00
66.52		Steffi	Nerius	GER	1.7.72	Q	WCh	Helsinki	12 Aug 05
		(10)							
65.91		Nikola	Brejchová'	CZE	25.6.74	1	GP	Linz	2 Aug 04
65.30		Claudia	Coslovich	ITA	26.4.72	1		Ljubljana	10 Jun 00
65.29		Xiomara	Rivero	CUB	22.11.68	1		Santiago de Cuba	17 Mar 01
65.17		Karen	Forkel	GER	24.3.70	2	NC	Erfurt	4 Jul 99
65.08		Ana Mirela	Termure ¶	ROM	13.1.75	1	NC	Bucuresti	10 Jun 01
65.05		Goldie	Sayers	GBR	16.7.82	1		Loughborough	20 May 07
64.90		Paula	Huhtaniemi/Tarvainen	FIN	17.2.73	1	NC	Helsinki	10 Aug 03
64.89		Yekaterina	Ivakina	RUS	4.12.64	4	Bisl	Oslo	28 Jul 00
64.87		Kelly	Morgan	GBR	17.6.80	1	NC	Birmingham	14 Jul 02
64.83		Christina	Scherwin	DEN	11.7.76	3	WAF	Stuttgart	9 Sep 06
		(20)							
64.62		Joanna	Stone	AUS	4.10.72	2		Gold Coast (RB)	5 Aug 00
64.62		Nikolett	Szabó	HUN	3.3.80	1		Pátra	22 Jul 01
64.61		Oksana	Makarova	RUS	21.7.71	2	ECp	Paris (C)	19 Jun 99
64.49		Valeriya	Zabruskova	RUS	29.7.75	1	Znam	Tula	7 Jun 03
64.46		Dörthe	Friedrich	GER	21.6.73	1	NC	Wattenscheid	7 Jul 02
64.28		Mariya	Abakumova	RUS	15.1.86	2	ECCp	Albufeira	26 May 07
64.19		Kim	Kreiner	USA	26.7.77	1		Fortaleza	16 May 07
64.08		Barbara	Madejczyk	POL	30.9.76	1	ECp-S	Málaga	28 Jun 06
64.06		Taina	Uppa/Kolkkala	FIN	24.10.76	1		Pihtipudas	23 Jul 00
64.03		Mikaela	Ingberg	FIN	29.7.74	6	ISTAF	Berlin	1 Sep 00
		(30)							
63.92			Wei Jianhua	CHN	23.3.79	1		Beijing	18 Aug 00
63.89		Felicia	Tilea-Moldovan ¶	ROM	29.9.67	2	WK	Zürich	16 Aug 02
63.73		Laverne	Eve	BAH	16.6.65	1		Nashville	22 Apr 00
63.69			Li Lei	CHN	4.5.74	1	OT	Jinzhou	8 Jun 00
63.65		Indre	Jakubaitité	LTU	24.1.76	1		Kaunas	14 Sep 07
63.35		Lada	Chernova	RUS	1.1.70	1	NC	Tula	31 Jul 07
63.32		Khristina	Georgieva	BUL	3.1.72	3	GP	Athína	28 Jun 00
63.32		Nora Aída	Bicet	CUB	29.10.77	2		Tallinn	21 Jul 04
63.20		Mercedes	Chilla	ESP	19.1.80	2	Herc	Monaco	20 Aug 06
63.14		Aggelikí	Tsiolakoúdi	GRE	10.5.76	5	EC	München	8 Aug 02
		(40)	50th woman 62.53, 100th 59.81						
63.13		Sávva	Líka	GRE	27.6.70	5	WCh	Osaka	31 Aug 07
63.07		Tetyana	Lyahovych	UKR	20.5.79	Q	OG	Athína	25 Aug 04
62.93			Xue Juan	CHN	10.2.86	1	NG	Changsha	27 Oct 03
62.89		Voisávva	Líka	GRE	27.6.70	1	NC	Athína	11 Jun 04

Ancillary marks – other marks during series (to 66.70)

69.42	Menéndez	7 Aug 01	67.72	Obergföll	19 May 07	67.51	Tzelíli	30 Sep 00
68.60	Menéndez	27 Aug 04	67.61	Hattestad	28 Jul 99			

Specification changed from 1 May 1999. See ATHLETICS 2000 for Old specification all-time list. Top six:

Mark	Wind	Name		Nat	Born	Pos	Meet	Venue	Date
80.00	WR	Petra	Felke	GDR	30.7.59	1		Potsdam	9 Sep 88
77.44	WR	Fatima	Whitbread	GBR	3.3.61	Q	EC	Stuttgart	28 Aug 86
74.76	WR	Tiina	Lillak	FIN	15.4.61	1		Tampere	13 Jun 83
74.20	WR	Sofía	Sakorafa	GRE	29.4.57	1	NC	Haniá	26 Sep 82
73.58		Tessa	Sanderson	GBR	14.3.56	1		Edinburgh	26 Jun 83
72.70		Anna	Veroúli ¶	GRE	13.11.56	1		Haniá	20 May 84

HEPTATHLON

Mark	Wind	Name		Nat	Born	Pos	Meet	Venue	Date
7291	WR	Jackie	Joyner-Kersee	USA	3.3.62	1	OG	Seoul	24 Sep 88
		12.69/0.5	1.86	15.80	22.56/1.6	7.27/0.7		45.66	2:08.51
7215	WR		Joyner-Kersee			1	OT	Indianapolis	16 Jul 88
		12.71/-0.9	1.93	15.65	22.30/ 0.0	7.00/-1.3		50.08	2:20.70

Mark Wind	Name		Nat	Born	Pos	Meet	Venue	Date
7158 WR		Joyner-Kersee			1	USOF	Houston	2 Aug 86
	13.18/-0.5	1.88	15.20	22.85/1.2	7.03w/2.9	50.12	2:09.69	
7148 WR		Joyner-Kersee			1	GWG	Moskva	7 Jul 86
	12.85/0.2	1.88	14.76	23.00/0.3	7.01/-0.5	49.86	2:10.02	
7128		Joyner-Kersee			1	WCh	Roma	1 Sep 87
	12.91/0.2	1.90	16.00	22.95/1.2	7.14/0.9	45.68	2:16.29	
7044		Joyner-Kersee			1	OG	Barcelona	2 Aug 92
	12.85/-0.9	1.91	14.13	23.12/0.7	7.10/1.3	44.98	2:11.78	
7032	Carolina	Klüft	SWE	2.2.83	1	WCh	Osaka	26 Aug 07
	13.15/0.1	1.95	14.81	23.38/0.3	6.85/1.0	47.98	2:12.56	
7007	Larisa	Nikitina ¶	RUS	29.4.65	1	NC	Bryansk	11 Jun 89
	13.40/1.4	1.89	16.45	23.97/1.1	6.73w/4.0	53.94	2:15.31	
7001		Klüft			1	WCh	Saint-Denis	24 Aug 03
	13.18/-0.4	1.94	14.19	22.98/1.1	6.68/1.0	49.90	2:12.12	
6985	Sabine	Braun	GER	19.6.65	1		Götzis	31 May 92
	13.11/-0.4	1.93	14.84	23.65/2.0	6.63w/2.9	51.62	2:12.67	
6979		Joyner-Kersee			1	TAC	San José	24 Jun 87
	12.90/2.0	1.85	15.17	23.02/0.4	7.25/2.3	40.24	2:13.07	
6952		Klüft			1	OG	Athína	21 Aug 04
	13.21/0.2	1.91	14.77	23.27/-0.1	6.78/0.4	48.89	2:14.15	
6946 WR	Sabine	Paetz'	GDR	16.10.57	1	NC	Potsdam	6 May 84
	12.64/0.3	1.80	15.37	23.37/0.7	6.86/-0.2	44.62	2:08.93	
6942	Ghada	Shouaa	SYR	10.9.72	1		Götzis	26 May 96
	13.78/0.3	1.87	15.64	23.78/0.6	6.77/0.6	54.74	2:13.61	
6935 WR	Ramona	Neubert	GDR	26.7.58	1	v URS	Moskva	19 Jun 83
	13.42/1.7	1.82	15.25	23.49/0.5	6.79/0.7	49.94	2:07.51	
6910		Joyner			1	MSR	Walnut	25 Apr 86
	12.9/0.0	1.86	14.75	23.24w/2.8	6.85/2.1	48.30	2:14.11	
6897		John'			2	wOG	Seoul	24 Sep 88
	12.85/0.5	1.80	16.23	23.65/1.6	6.71/ 0.0	42.56	2:06.14	
6889	Eunice	Barber	FRA	17.11.74	1		Arles	5 Jun 05
	12.62w/2.9	1.91	12.61	24.12/1.2	6.78w/3.4	53.07	2:14.66	
6887		Klüft			1	WCh	Helsinki	7 Aug 05
	13.19/-0.4	1.82	15.02	23.70/-2.5	6.87/0.2	47.20	2:08.89	
6878		Joyner-Kersee			1	TAC	New York	13 Jun 91
	12.77	1.89	15.62	23.42	6.97/0.4	43.28	2:22.12	
6875		Nikitina			1	ECp-A	Helmond	16 Jul 89
	13.55/-2.1	1.84	15.99	24.29/-2.1	6.75/-2.5	56.78	2:18.67	
6861		Barber			1	WCh	Sevilla	22 Aug 99
	12.89/-0.5	1.93	12.37	23.57/0.5	6.86/-0.3	49.88	2:15.65	
6859	Natalya	Shubenkova	RUS	25.9.57	1	NC	Kiyev	21 Jun 84
	12.93/1.0	1.83	13.66	23.57/-0.3	6.73/0.4	46.26	2:04.60	
6858	Anke	Vater/Behmer (10)	GDR	5.6.61	3	OG	Seoul	24 Sep 88
	13.20/0.5	1.83	14.20	23.10/1.6	6.68/0.1	44.54	2:04.20	
6847		Nikitina			1	WUG	Duisburg	29 Aug 89
	13.47	1.81	16.12	24.12	6.66	59.28	2:22.07	
6845 WR		Neubert			1	v URS	Halle	20 Jun 82
	13.58/1.8	1.83	15.10	23.14/1.4	6.84w/2.3	42.54	2:06.16	
6845	Irina	Belova ¶	RUS	27.3.68	2	OG	Barcelona	2 Aug 92
	13.25/-0.1	1.88	13.77	23.34/0.2	6.82/0.0	41.90	2:05.08	
6842		Barber			1		Götzis	4 Jun 00
	12.97/0.2	1.88	12.23	23.84/0.5	6.85/-0.1	51.91	2:11.55	
6841		Joyner			1		Götzis	25 May 86
	13.09/-1.3	1.87	14.34	23.63/-0.8	6.76/-0.3	48.88	2:14.58	
6837		Joyner-Kersee			1	WCh	Stuttgart	17 Aug 93
	12.89/0.1	1.81	14.38	23.19/0.0	7.04/1.4	43.76	2:14.49	
6831	Denise	Lewis	GBR	27.8.72	1		Talence	30 Jul 00
	13.13/1.0	1.84	15.07	24.01w/3.6	6.69/-0.4	49.42	2:12.20	
6832	Lyudmila	Blonska ¶	UKR	9.11.77	2	WCh	Osaka	26 Aug 07
	13.25/0.1	1.92	14.44	24.09/0.3	6.88/1.0	47.77	2:16.68	
	(32/13)							
6803	Jane	Frederick	USA	7.4.52	1		Talence	16 Sep 84
	13.27/1.2	1.87	15.49	24.15/1.6	6.43/0.2	51.74	2:13.55	
6768w	Tatyana	Chernova	RUS	29.1.88	1		Arles	3 Jun 07
	13.04w/6.1	1.82	13.57	23.59w/5.2	6.61/1.2	53.43	2:15.05	
6765	Yelena	Prokhorova	RUS	16.4.78	1	NC	Tula	23 Jul 00
	13.54/-2.8	1.82	14.30	23.37/-0.2	6.72/1.0	43.40	2:04.27	
6750		Ma Miaolan	CHN	18.1.70	1	NG	Beijing	12 Sep 93
	13.28/1.5	1.89	14.98	23.86/	6.64/	45.82	2:15.33	

Mark Wind	Name		Nat	Born	Pos	Meet	Venue		Date
6741	Heike	Drechsler	GER	16.12.64	1		Talence		11 Sep 94
	13.34/-0.3	1.84	13.58	22.84/-1.1	6.95/1.0		40.64	2:11.53	
6703	Tatyana	Blokhina	RUS	12.3.70	1		Talence		11 Sep 93
	13.69/-0.6	1.91	14.94	23.95/-0.4	5.99/-0.3		52.16	2:09.65	
6702	Chantal	Beaugeant ¶	FRA	16.2.61	2		Götzis		19 Jun 88
	13.10/1.6	1.78	13.74	23.96w/3.5	6.45/0.2		50.96	2:07.09	
	(20)								
6695	Jane	Flemming	AUS	14.4.65	1	CG	Auckland		28 Jan 90
	13.21/1.4	1.82	13.76	23.62w/2.4	6.57/1.6		49.28	2:12.53	
6660	Ines	Schulz	GDR	10.7.65	3		Götzis		19 Jun 88
	13.56/0.4	1.84	13.95	23.93w/2.8	6.70/0.7		42.82	2:06.31	
6658	Svetla	Dimitrova ¶	BUL	27.1.70	2		Götzis		31 May 92
	13.41/-0.7	1.75	14.72	23.06w/2.4	6.64/1.9		43.84	2:09.60	
6646	Natalya	Grachova	UKR	21.2.52	1	NC	Moskva		2 Aug 82
	13.80	1.80	16.18	23.86	6.65w/3.5		39.42	2:06.59	
6635	Sibylle	Thiele	GDR	6.3.65	2	GWG	Moskva		7 Jul 86
	13.14/0.6	1.76	16.00	24.18	6.62/1.0		45.74	2:15.30	
6635	Svetlana	Buraga	BLR	4.9.65	3	WCh	Stuttgart		17 Aug 93
	12.95/0.1	1.84	14.55	23.69/0.0	6.58/-0.2		41.04	2:13.65	
6633	Natalya	Roshchupkina	RUS	13.1.78	2	NC	Tula		23 Jul 00
	14.05/-2.8	1.88	14.28	23.47/-0.2	6.45/0.4		44.34	2:07.93	
6623	Judy	Simpson'	GBR	14.11.60	3	EC	Stuttgart		30 Aug 86
	13.05/0.8	1.92	14.73	25.09/0.0	6.56w/2.5		40.92	2:11.70	
6619	Liliana	Nastase	ROM	1.8.62	4	OG	Barcelona		2 Aug 92
	12.86/-0.9	1.82	14.34	23.70/0.2	6.49/-0.3		41.30	2:11.22	
6616	Malgorzata	Nowak'	POL	9.2.59	1	WUG	Kobe		31 Aug 85
	13.27w/4.0	1.95	15.35	24.20/0.0	6.37w/3.9		43.36	2:20.39	
	(30)								
6604	Remigija	Nazaroviene'	LTU	2.6.67	2	URSCh	Bryansk		11 Jun 89
	13.26/1.4	1.86	14.27	24.12/0.7	6.58/0.9		40.94	2:09.98	
6604	Irina	Tyukhay	RUS	14.1.67	3		Götzis		28 May 95
	13.20/-0.7	1.84	14.97	24.33/1.7	6.71/0.5		43.84	2:17.64	
6598	Svetlana	Moskalets	RUS	22.1.69	1	NC	Vladimir		17 Jun 94
	13.20/0.8	1.82	13.78	23.56/0.1	6.74/0.8		42.48	2:14.54	
6591	Svetlana	Sokolova	RUS	9.1.81	1	NC	Tula		23 Jun 04
	13.56/1.1	1.82	15.09	24.02/0.6	6.26/0.3		45.07	2:07.23	
6577	DeDee	Nathan	USA	20.4.68	1		Götzis		30 May 99
	13.28/-0.1	1.76	14.74	24.23/0.2	6.59/1.6		50.08	2:16.92	
6573	Rita	Ináncsi	HUN	6.1.71	3		Götzis		29 May 94
	13.66/2.0	1.84	13.94	24.20w/2.5	6.78/1.4		46.28	2:16.02	
6572	Heike	Tischler	GDR	4.2.64	2	EC	Split		31 Aug 90
	14.08/-0.9	1.82	13.73	24.29/0.9	6.22/-0.7		53.24	2:05.50	
6563	Natalya	Sazanovich	BLR	15.8.73	2	OG	Atlanta		28 Jul 96
	13.56/-1.6	1.80	14.52	23.72/-0.3	6.70/1.1		46.00	2:17.92	
6552	Nadezhda	Vinogradova'	RUS	1.5.58	2	NC	Kiyev		21 Jun 84
	13.92/1.0	1.80	15.19	23.84/0.2	6.67/0.1		38.60	2:06.80	
6551	Yelena	Martsenyuk	RUS	21.2.61	2		Staiki		2 Jul 88
	13.54/-0.4	1.82	15.32	24.25/0.3	6.25/0.7		47.56	2:12.72	
	(40)								
6547	Kelly	Sotherton	GBR	13.11.76	2		Götzis		29 May 05
	13.27/1.1	1.85	13.84	23.77/1.7	6.67/-0.6		37.21	2:10.29	
6546	Mona	Steigauf	GER	17.1.70	1	WUG	Catania		27 Aug 97
	13.13/1.6	1.85	12.83	24.14/1.7	6.56/1.3		43.86	2:11.15	
6542	Urszula	Wlodarczyk	POL	22.12.65	4	WCh	Athína		4 Aug 97
	13.55/0.3	1.81	14.16	24.48/0.1	6.63/0.6		44.18	2:09.59	
6541	Mila	Kolyadina	RUS	31.12.60	4	v GDR	Moskva		19 Jun 83
	14.05	1.82	16.28	24.81	6.48/0.8		48.26	2:15.26	
6539	Tatyana	Shpak	UKR	17.11.60	3		Staiki		2 Jul 88
	13.57/-0.4	1.76	15.30	23.61/0.5	6.52/-0.6		39.28	2:07.25	
6536	Yekaterina	Smirnova	RUS	22.10.56	3	v GDR	Moskva		19 Jun 83
	13.41	1.82	14.82	24.84	6.56/1.1		45.66	2:13.38	
6531	Peggy	Beer	GDR	15.9.69	3	EC	Split		31 Aug 90
	13.27/-0.2	1.82	13.46	23.99/0.4	6.38/0.9		42.10	2:05.79	
6527	Diane	Guthrie-Gresham	JAM	24.10.71	1	NCAA	Knoxville		3 Jun 95
	13.86w/2.5	1.86	13.80	24.91/-1.3	6.92w/2.5		49.04	2:20.82	
6523	Sabine	Everts	FRG	4.3.61	1	v URS	Mannheim		10 Jun 82
	13.45	1.89	12.39	23.73	6.75		36.02	2:07.73	
6502	Hyleas	Fountain	USA	14.1.81	3		Götzis		29 May 05
	13.09/1.1	1.88	12.13	23.87/1.7	6.67/-0.9		46.90	2:22.81	
	(50)	100th woman 6350, 200th 6151, 300th 6019							

DECATHLON

Mark Wind	Name		Nat	Born	Pos	Meet	Venue	Date
8358 WR	Austra	Skujyte	LTU	12.8.79	1		Columbia, MO	15 Apr 05
	12.49/1.6 46.19 3.10 48.78 57.19 14.22w/2.4 6.12/1.6 16.42 1.78							5:15.86
8150 WR	Marie	Collonvillé	FRA	23.11.73	1		Talence	26 Sep 04
	12.48/0.4 34.69 3.50 47.19 56.15 13.96/0.4 6.18/1.0 11.90 1.80							5:06.09
7885	Mona	Steigauf	GER	17.1.70	1		Ahlen	21 Sep 97
	12.15/1.2 5.93 12.49 1.73 55.34 13.75/0.2 34.68 3.10 42.24							5:07.95
7798	Irina	Naumenko	KAZ	13.2.80	2		Talence	26 Sep 04
	12.58/0.4 34.63 3.30 37.57 55.91 14.42/0.4 5.98/1.0 12.51 1.77							4:59.03
7742	Anna	Snetkova	RUS	25.2.79	1		Krasnodar	20 Sep 03
	12.66 36.90 3.70 37.50 58.88 14.19 5.98 13.48 1.69							5:17.67

IAAF approved order: 100m, DT, PV, JT, 400m / 100mh, LJ, SP, HJ, 1500m, 1997/2000 events used men's order

4 x 100 METRES RELAY

Mark	Nat	Name	Pos	Meet	Venue	Date
41.37 WR	GDR	Gladisch, Rieger, Auerswald, Göhr	1	WCp	Canberra	6 Oct 85
41.47	USA	Gaines, Jones, Miller, Devers	1	WCh	Athína	9 Aug 97
41.49	RUS	Bogoslovskaya, Malchugina, Voronova, Privalova	1	WCh	Stuttgart	22 Aug 93
41.49	USA	Finn, Torrence, Vereen, Devers	2	WCh	Stuttgart	22 Aug 93
41.52	USA	Gaines, Jones, Miller, Devers	1h1	WCh	Athína	8 Aug 97
41.53 WR	GDR	Gladisch, Koch, Auerswald, Göhr	1		Berlin	31 Jul 83
41.55	USA	Brown, Williams, Griffith, Marshall	1	ISTAF	Berlin	21 Aug 87
41.58	USA	Brown, Williams, Griffith, Marshall	1	WCh	Roma	6 Sep 87
41.60 WR	GDR	Müller, Wöckel, Auerswald, Göhr	1	OG	Moskva	1 Aug 80
41.61A	USA	Brown, Williams, Cheeseborough, Ashford	1	USOF	USAF Academy	3 Jul 83
41.63	USA	Brown, Williams, Cheeseborough, Ashford	1	v GDR	Los Angeles	25 Jun 83
41.65	USA	Brown, Bolden, Cheeseborough, Ashford	1	OG	Los Angeles	11 Aug 84
41.65	GDR	Gladisch, Koch, Auerswald, Göhr	1	ECp	Moskva	17 Aug 85
41.68	GDR	Möller, Krabbe, Behrendt, Günther	1	EC	Split	1 Sep 90
41.69	GDR	Gladisch, Koch, Auerswald, Göhr	1	OD	Potsdam	21 Jul 84
41.73	GDR	Möller, Behrendt, Lange, Göhr	1		Berlin	13 Sep 88
41.73	JAM	Lawrence, Simpson, Bailey, Campbell	1	OG	Athína	27 Aug 04
41.76	GDR	Gladisch, Koch, Auerswald, Göhr	1	WCh	Helsinki	10 Aug 83
41.78	FRA	Girard, Hurtis, Félix, Arron	1	WCh	Saint-Denis	30 Aug 03
41.78	USA	Daigle, Lee, Barber, L.Williams	1	WCh	Helsinki	13 Aug 05
		(20 performances by 5 nations) from here just best by nation				
41.92	BAH	Fynes, Sturrup, Davis-Thompson, Ferguson	1	WCh	Sevilla	29 Aug 99
42.08mx	BUL	Pavlova, Nuneva, Georgieva, Ivanova	mx		Sofiya	8 Aug 84
	42.29	Pencheva, Nuneva, Georgieva, Donkova	1		Sofiya	26 Jun 88
42.23	CHN	(Sichuan) Xiao Lin, Li Yali, Liu Xiaomei, Li Xuemei	1	NG	Shanghai	23 Oct 97
42.39	NGR	Utondu, Idehen, Opara-Thompson, Onyali	2h2	OG	Barcelona	7 Aug 92
42.43	GBR	Hunte, Smallwood, Goddard, Lannaman (10)	3	OG	Moskva	1 Aug 80
42.56	BLR	Nesterenko, Sologub, Nevmerzhitskaya, Dragun	3	WCh	Helsinki	13 Aug 05
42.59	FRG	Possekel, Helten, Richter, Kroniger	2	OG	Montreal	31 Jul 76
42.71	POL	Tomczak, Pakula, Pisiewicz, Kasprzyk	3	ECp	Moskva	17 Aug 85
42.75	BEL	Borlée, Marien, Ouédraogo, Gevaert	3	WCh	Osaka	1 Sep 07
42.77	CAN	Bailey, Payne, Taylor, Gareau	2	OG	Los Angeles	11 Aug 84
42.89	CUB	Ferrer, López, Duporty, Allen	6	WCh	Stuttgart	22 Aug 93
42.96	UKR	Tkalich, Kravchenko, Pastushenko, Maydanova	1		Kiev	6 Jul 03
42.97A	BRA	K Santos, de Moura, Neto, L dos Santos	1	SAm-r	Bogotá	10 Jul 04
42.98	CZE/TCH	Sokolová, Soborová, Kocembová, Kratochvilová	1	WK	Zürich	18 Aug 82
42.99A	AUS	Massey, Broadrick, Lambert, Gainsford-Taylor	1		Pietersburg	18 Mar 00
	(20)					
43.03A	COL	M.Murillo, Palacios, Obregón, D Murillo	2	SAm-r	Bogotá	10 Jul 04
43.07	GRE	Tsóni, Kóffa, Vasarmídou, Thánou	2	MedG	Bari	18 Jun 97
43.19	GHA	Akoto, Twum, Anim, Nsiah	5s1	OG	Sydney	29 Sep 00
43.25A	RSA	Hartman, Moropane, Holtshausen, Seyerling	2		Pietersburg	18 Mar 00
43.35	KAZ	Aleksandrova, Kvast, Miljauskiene, Sevalnikova	2	SPART	Taskent	16 Sep 86
43.37	FIN	Pirtimaa, Hanhijoki, Hernesniemi, Salmela	7	WCh	Stuttgart	22 Aug 93
43.44A	NED	van den Berg, Sterk, Hennipman, Bakker	4	OG	Ciudad de México	20 Oct 68
43.44	ITA	Pistone, Graglia, Grillo, Levorato	1		Barletta	26 Jul 00
43.61	MAD	Rahanitraniriana, Ratsimbazafy, Rakotozafy, Rakotondrabé	4h4	OG	Sydney	29 Sep 00
43.61	SWE	Rienas, Klüft, J.Kallur, S.Kallur (30)	1	v FIN	Göteborg	27 Aug 05

Best at low altitude

Mark	Nat	Name	Pos	Meet	Venue	Date
42.99	BRA	da Costa, de Moura, Ignâcio, L.dos Santos	5	WCh	Helsinki	13 Aug 05
43.03	COL	M.Murillo, Palacios, Obregón, N.González	3h2	WCh	Helsinki	12 Aug 05
43.18	AUS	Wilson, Wells, Robertson, Boyle	5	OG	Montreal	31 Jul 76
43.48	NED	Cooman, Tromp, Olyslager, Vader	5s1	OG	Seoul	1 Oct 88

One or more athlete susbsequently drugs dq

Mark	Nat	Name	Pos	Meet	Venue	Date
41.67	USA	A Williams, Jones ¶, L Williams, Colander	(1)	3-N	München	8 Aug 04
41.67	USA	A Williams, Jones ¶, L Williams, Colander	(1h1)	OG	Athína	26 Aug 04
41.71	USA	White ¶, Gaines, Miller, Jones ¶	(1)	WCh	Edmonton	11 Aug 01

4 x 200 METRES RELAY

Mark	Wind	Nat	Name	Pos	Meet	Venue	Date
1:27.46	WR	USA Blue	Jenkins, Colander-Richardson, Perry, M Jones	1	Penn	Philadelphia	29 Apr 00
1:28.15	WR	GDR	Göhr, R.Müller, Wöckel, Koch	1		Jena	9 Aug 80
1:29.24		Nike International USA	Roberts, Miller, Green, M Jones	1	Penn	Philadelphia	25 Apr 98

4 x 400 METRES RELAY

Mark	Wind	Nat	Name	Pos	Meet	Venue	Date
3:15.17	WR	URS		1	OG	Seoul	1 Oct 88
			Ledovskaya 50.12, O.Nazarova 47.82, Pinigina 49.43, Bryzgina 47.80				
3:15.51		USA		2	OG	Seoul	1 Oct 88
			D.Howard 49.82, Dixon 49.17, Brisco 48.44, Griffith-Joyner 48.08				
3:15.92	WR	GDR	G.Walther 49.8, Busch 48.9, Rübsam 49.4, Koch 47.8	1	NC	Erfurt	3 Jun 84
3:16.71		USA	Torrence 49.0, Malone 49.4, Kaiser-Brown 49.48, Miles 48.78	1	WCh	Stuttgart	22 Aug 93
3:16.87		GDR	Emmelmann 50.9, Busch 48.8, Müller 48.9, Koch 48.21	1	EC	Stuttgart	31 Aug 86
3:18.29		USA		1	OG	Los Angeles	11 Aug 84
			Leatherwood 50.50, S.Howard 48.83, Brisco-Hooks 49.23, Cheeseborough 49.73				
3:18.29		GDR	Neubauer 50.58, Emmelmann 49.89, Busch 48.81, Müller 48.99	3	OG	Seoul	1 Oct 88
3:18.38		RUS		2	WCh	Stuttgart	22 Aug 93
			Ruzina 50.8, Alekseyeva 49.3, Ponomaryova 49.78, Privalova 48.47				
3:18.43		URS		1	WCh	Tokyo	1 Sep 91
			Ledovskaya 51.7, Dzhigalova 49.2, Nazarova 48.87, Bryzgina 48.67				
3:18.55		USA	Trotter 51.2, Felix 48.0, Wineberg 50.24, Richards 49.07	1	WCh	Osaka	2 Sep 07
3:18.58		URS	I.Nazarova, Olizarenko, Pinigina, Vladykina	1	ECp	Moskva	18 Aug 85
3:18.63		GDR	Neubauer 51.4, Emmelmann 49.1, Müller 48.64, Busch 49.48	1	WCh	Roma	6 Sep 87
3:19.01		USA	Trotter 49.8, Henderson 49.7, Richards 49.81, Hennagan 49.73	1	OG	Athína	28 Aug 04
3:19.04	WR	GDR	Siemon' 51.0, Busch 50.0, Rübsam 50.2, Koch 47.9	1	EC	Athína	11 Sep 82
3:19.12		URS	Baskakova, I.Nazarova, Pinigina, Vladykina	1	Drz	Praha	18 Aug 84
3:19.23	WR	GDR	Maletzki 50.05, Rohde 49.00, Streidt 49.51, Brehmer 49.79	1	OG	Montreal	31 Jul 76
3:19.49		GDR	Emmelmann, Busch, Neubauer, Koch 47.9	1	WCp	Canberra	4 Oct 85
3:19.50		URS	Yurchenko 51.2, O.Nazarova 50.2, Pinigina 49.09, Bryzgina 49.03	2	WCh	Roma	6 Sep 87
3:19.60		USA	Leatherwood, S.Howard, Brisco-Hooks, Cheeseborough	1		Walnut	25 Jul 84
3:19.62		GDR	Kotte, Brehmer, Köhn, Koch 48.3	1	ECp	Torino	5 Aug 79
			(20/4 with USSR and Russia counted separately)				
3:19.73		JAM	S Williams 50.5, Lloyd 50.1, Prendergast 50.18, NWilliams 48.93	2	WCh	Osaka	2 Sep 07
3:20.04		GBR	Ohuruogu 50.6, Okoro 50.9, McConnell 49.79, Sanders 48.76	3	WCh	Osaka	2 Sep 07
3:20.32		CZE/TCH		2	WCh	Helsinki	14 Aug 83
			Kocembová 48.93, Matejkovicová 52.13, Moravcíková 51.51, Kratochvílová 47.75				
3:21.04		NGR	Afolabi 51.13, Yusuf 49.72, Opara 51.29, Ogunkoya 48.90	2	OG	Atlanta	3 Aug 96
3:21.21		CAN	Crooks 50.30, Richardson 50.22, Killingbeck ¶ 50.62, Payne 50.07	2	OG	Los Angeles	11 Aug 84
3:21.88		BLR	Yushchenko 51.4, Khlyustova 50.7, I Usovich 49.97, S Usovich 49.78	5	WCh	Osaka	2 Sep 07
		(10)					
3:21.94		UKR	Dzhigalova, Olizarenko, Pinigina, Vladykina	1	URSCh	Kiyev	17 Jul 86
3:22.34		FRA	Landre 51.3, Dorsile 51.1, Elien 50.54, Pérec 49.36	1	EC	Helsinki	14 Aug 94
3:22.49		FRG	Thimm 50.81, Arendt 49.95, Thomas 51.50, Abt 50.23	4	OG	Seoul	1 Oct 88
3:23.81		AUS	Peris-K 51.71, Lewis 51.69, Gainsford-T 51.06, Freeman 49.35	5	OG	Sydney	30 Sep 00
3:24.23		CUB	Bonne 51.91, Duporty 50.92, Morales 51.31, Quirot 50.09	2h2	OG	Atlanta	2 Aug 96
3:24.28		CHN	(Hebei) An X, Bai X, Cao C, Ma Y	1	NG	Beijing	13 Sep 93
3:24.49		POL	Guzowska 52.2, Bejnar 50.2, Prokopek 50.47, Jesien 51.59	4	WCh	Helsinki	14 Aug 05
3:25.68		ROM	Ruicu 52.69, Rîpanu 51.09, Barbu 52.64, Tîrlea 49.26	2	ECp	Paris (C)	20 Jun 99
3:25.7a		FIN	Eklund 53.6, Pursiainen 50.6, Wilmi 51.6, Salin 49.9	2	EC	Roma	8 Sep 74
3:25.81		BUL	Ilieva, Stamenova, Penkova, Damyanova	1	v Hun,Pol	Sofiya	24 Jul 83
		(20)					
3:26.33		GRE	Kaidantzi 53.2, Goudenoúdi 51.6, Boudá 51.76, Halkiá 49.75	3	ECpS	Bydgoszcz	20 Jun 04
3:26.69		ITA	Perpoli 51.81, Spuri 51.62, Carbone 52.61, De Angeli 50.65	5	ECp	Paris (C)	20 Jun 99
3:26.82		BRA	Almirão 52.3, Coutinho 52.1, Tito 51.56, Teodoro 50.82	2h2	WCh	Helsinki	13 Aug 05
3:26.89		IND	R Kaur 53.1, Beenamol 51.4, Soman 52.51, M Kaur 49.85	3h2	OG	Athína	27 Aug 04
3:27.08		CMR	Nguimgo 51.7, Kaboud 52.1, Atangana 51.98, Béwouda 51.35	7	WCh	Saint-Denis	31 Aug 03
3:27.54		LTU	Navickaite, Valiuliene, Mendzoryte, Ambraziene	3	SPART	Moskva	22 Jun 83
3:27.14		MEX	Rodríguez 53.3, Medina 51.2, Vela 52.94, Guevara 49.70	4h2	WCh	Osaka	1 Sep 07
3:27.57		ESP	Merino 52.2, Lacambra 52.0, Myers 50.85, Ferrer 52.56	7	WCh	Tokyo	1 Sep 91
3:27.86		HUN	Orosz, Forgács, Tóth, Pál	5	OG	Moskva	1 Aug 80
3:28.02		SEN	Diop 51.27, M T Diouf 51.70, A Diouf 52.53, Thiam 51.52	4h3	OG	Sydney	29 Sep 00

5000 METRES WALK (TRACK)

Mark	Wind	Name	Nat	Born	Pos	Meet	Venue	Date
20:02.60	WR	Gillian O'Sullivan	IRL	21.8.76	1	NC	Dublin (S)	13 Jul 02
20:03.0	WR	Kerry Saxby-Junna	AUS	2.6.61	1		Sydney	11 Feb 96
20:07.52	WR	Beate Anders/Gummelt	GDR	4.2.68	1	vURS	Rostock	23 Jun 90
20:11.45		Sabine Zimmer	GER	6.2.81	1	NC	Wattenscheid	2 Jul 05
20:12.41		Elisabetta Perrone	ITA	9.7.68	1	NC	Rieti	2 Aug 03
20:18.87		Melanie Seeger	GER	8.1.77	1	NC	Braunschweig	10 Jul 04
20:21.69		Annarita Sidoti	ITA	25.7.69	1	NC	Cesenatico	1 Jul 95

Mark Wind	Name		Nat	Born	Pos	Meet	Venue	Date

10 KILOMETRES WALK

Mark Wind	Name		Nat	Born	Pos	Meet	Venue	Date
41:04 WR	Yelena	Nikolayeva	RUS	1.2.66	1	NC	Sochi	20 Apr 96
41:16		Wang Yan	CHN	3.5.71	1		Eisenhüttenstadt	8 May 99
41:16	Kjersti	Plätzer (Tysse)	NOR	18.1.72	1	NC	Os	11 May 02
41:17	Irina	Stankina	RUS	25.3.77	1	NC-w	Adler	9 Feb 97
41:24	Olimpiada	Ivanova ¶	RUS	26.8.70	2	NC-w	Adler	9 Feb 97
41:29 WR	Larisa	Ramazanova	RUS	23.9.71	1	NC	Izhevsk	4 Jun 95
41:30 WR	Kerry	Saxby-Junna	AUS	2.6.61	1	NC	Canberra	27 Aug 88
41:30		O Ivanova			2	NC	Izhevsk	4 Jun 95
41:31	Yelena	Gruzinova	RUS	24.12.67	2	NC	Sochi	20 Apr 96
41:37.9t		Gao Hongmiao	CHN	17.3.74	1	NC	Beijing	7 Apr 94
41:38	Rossella	Giordano (10)	ITA	1.12.72	1		Naumburg	25 May 97
41:41		Nikolayeva			2		Naumburg	25 May 97
41:45		Liu Hongyu	CHN	11.1.75	2		Eisenhüttenstadt	8 May 99
41:46	Annarita	Sidoti	ITA	25.7.69	1		Livorno	12 Jun 94
41:46		O Ivanova			1	NC/w	Adler	11 Feb 96
41:47		Saxby-Junna			1		Eisenhüttenstadt	11 May 96
41:48		Li Chunxiu	CHN	13.8.69	1	NG	Beijing	8 Sep 93
41:49		Ramazanova			3	NC	Sochi	20 Apr 96
41:49		Nikolayeva			1	OG	Atlanta	29 Jul 96
41:50	Yelena (20/14)	Arshintseva	RUS	5.4.71	1	NC-w	Adler	11 Feb 95
41:51	Beate	Anders/Gummelt	GER	4.2.68	2		Eisenhüttenstadt	11 May 96
41:56	Yelena	Sayko	RUS	24.12.67	2	NC/w	Adler	11 Feb 96
41:56.23t	Nadezhda	Ryashkina	RUS	22.1.67	1	GWG	Seattle	24 Jul 90
42:01	Tamara	Kovalenko	RUS	5.6.64	3	NC-w	Adler	11 Feb 95
42:01	Olga	Panfyorova	RUS	21.8.77	1	NC-23	Izhevsk	16 May 98
42:05+	Margarita (20)	Turova	BLR	28.12.80	1+	in 20k	Adler	12 Mar 05
42:06	Valentina	Tsybulskaya	BLR	19.2.68	4		Eisenhüttenstadt	8 May 99
42:07	Ileana	Salvador	ITA	16.1.62	1		Sesto San Giovanni	1 May 92
42:09	Elisabetta	Perrone	ITA	9.7.68	4		Eisenhüttenstadt	11 May 96
42:11	Nina	Alyushenko	RUS	29.5.68	3	NC	Izhevsk	4 Jun 95
42:13	Natalya	Misyulya	BLR	16.4.66	5		Eisenhüttenstadt	8 May 99
42:13.7t	Madelein	Svensson	SWE	20.7.69	2	SGP	Fana	15 May 92
42:15		Gu Yan	CHN	17.3.74	3	WCp	Podebrady	19 Apr 97
42:15	Erica	Alfridi	ITA	22.2.68	5		Naumburg	25 May 97
42:15	Jane	Saville	AUS	5.11.74	6		Eisenhüttenstadt	8 May 99
42:16	Alina (30)	Ivanova	RUS	16.3.69	1		Novopolotsk	27 May 89
42:16	Norica	Cîmpean	ROM	22.3.72	1		Calella	9 May 99
42:17	Katarzyna	Radtke	POL	31.8.69	5		Eisenhüttenstadt	11 May 96
42:19+	Iraida	Pudovkina	RUS	2.11.80	2	in 20k	Adler	12 Mar 05
42:20	Sari	Essayah	FIN	21.2.67	4	WCh	Göteborg	7 Aug 95
42:29	Olga	Kardopoltseva	BLR	11.9.66	4		Eisenhüttenstadt	10 May 97
42:31	Vera	Nacharkina'	RUS	17.2.66	1	NC	Izhevsk	16 May 98
42:32	Maya	Sazonova	KAZ	28.5.68	4	Rus Ch	Sochi	20 Apr 96
42:34	Mária	Rosza/Urbaník	HUN	12.2.67	7	WCh	Göteborg	7 Aug 95
42:35	Claudia	Iovan/Stef ¶	ROM	25.2.78	2	NC	Alba Iulia	15 Sep 02
42:37	Olga (40)	Lukyanchuk	UKR	7.12.76	1		Mukachevo	21 Oct 00

50th woman 42:46.7, 100th 43:30, 200th 44:27, 300th 45:03

Probable short course: Livorno 10 Jul 93: 1. Ileana Salvador ITA 16.1.62 41:30, 2. Elisabeta Perrone 9.7.68 41:56

Best track times

Mark	Name		Nat	Born	Pos	Meet	Venue	Date
41:57.22	Kerry	Saxby-Junna	AUS	2.6.61	2	GWG	Seattle	24 Jul 90
42:11.5	Beate	Anders/Gummelt	GER	4.2.68	1	SGP	Fana	15 May 92
42:19.2		Gu Yan	CHN	17.3.74	2	NC	Beijing	7 Apr 94
42:23.7	Ileana	Salvador		16.1.62	2	SGP	Fana	8 May 93
42:30.13		Gao Hongmiao	CHN	17.3.74	1		Nanjing	24 Oct 95
42:30.31	Olimpiada	Ivanova ¶	RUS	26.8.70	1	GWG	Sankt-Peterburg	26 Jul 94
42:37.0	Sari	Essayah	FIN	21.2.67	3	SGP	Fana	8 May 93

20 KILOMETRES WALK

Mark Wind	Name		Nat	Born	Pos	Meet	Venue	Date
1:24:50	Olimpiada	Ivanova ¶	RUS	26.8.70	1	NC-w	Adler	4 Mar 01
1:25:18	Tatyana	Gudkova	RUS	23.1.78	1	NC	Moskva	19 May 00
1:25:20	Olga	Polyakova	RUS	23.9.80	2	NC	Moskva	19 May 00
1:25:29	Irina	Stankina	RUS	25.3.77	3	NC	Moskva	19 May 00
1:25:41 WR		O Ivanova			1	WCh	Helsinki	7 Aug 05
1:25:59	Tamara	Kovalenko	RUS	5.6.64	4	NC	Moskva	19 May 00
1:26:02	Olga	Kaniskina	RUS	19.1.85	1	NC-w	Adler	19 Feb 06
1:26:08		Ivanova			5	NC	Moskva	19 May 00

Mark	Wind	Name		Nat	Born	Pos	Meet	Venue	Date
1:26:11		Margarita	Turova	BLR	28.12.80	1	NC	Nesvizh	15 Apr 06
1:26:14		Irina	Petrova	RUS	26.5.85	2	NC-w	Adler	19 Feb 06
1:26:22	WR		Wang Yan	CHN	3.5.71	1	NG	Guangzhou	19 Nov 01
1:26:22	WR	Yelena	Nikolayeva (10)	RUS	1.2.66	1	ECp	Cheboksary	18 May 03
1:26:23			Wang Liping	CHN	8.7.76	2	NG	Guangzhou	19 Nov 01
1:26:27			Turova			1	WCp	La Coruña	13 May 06
1:26:28		Iraida	Pudovkina	RUS	2.11.80	1	NC-w	Adler	12 Mar 05
1:26:35			Liu Hongyu	CHN	11.1.75	3	NG	Guangzhou	19 Nov 01
1:26:42			O Ivanova			1	EC	München	7 Aug 02
1:26:46			Song Hongjuan	CHN	4.7.84	1	NC	Guangzhou	20 Mar 04
1:26:47			Kaniskina			1	RWC	Saransk	29 Sep 07
1:26:48			Ivanova			1	ECp	Eisenhüttenstadt	17 Jun 00
1:26:48			Ivanova			1	ECp	Dudince	19 May 01
1:26:50		Natalya	Fedoskina	RUS	25.6.80	2	ECp	Dudince	19 May 01
1:26:52			Nikolayeva			1	WCh	Saint-Denis	24 Aug 03
1:26:52.3	t		Ivanova			1	GWG	Brisbane	6 Sep 01
1:26:54			Ivanova			1	NC	Cheboksary	12 Jun 04
1:26:57		Lyudmila	Yefimkina	RUS	22.8.81	3	NC-w	Adler	19 Feb 06
1:27:02			Nikolayeva			1	NC	Cheboksary	25 May 02
1:27:05			Turova			2	WCh	Helsinki	7 Aug 05
1:27:08			Turova			1	EC	Göteborg	9 Aug 06
1:27:09		Elisabetta	Perrone	ITA	9.7.68	3	ECp	Dudince	19 May 01
		(30/17)							
1:27:14		Antonina	Petrova	RUS	25.1.77	1	NC-w	Adler	1 Mar 03
1:27:19			Jiang Jing	CHN	23.10.85	1	NC	Nanning	25 Feb 05
1:27:22		Gillian	O'Sullivan (20)	IRL	21.8.76	1		Sesto San Giovanni	1 May 03
1:27:23		Larisa	Yemelyanova (Safronova)	RUS	6.1.80	2	NC-w	Adler	1 Mar 03
1:27:29		Erica	Alfridi	ITA	22.2.68	4	ECp	Dudince	19 May 01
1:27:30	WB	Nadezhda	Ryashkina	RUS	22.1.67	1	NC-w	Adler	7 Feb 99
1:27:30		Tatyana	Kozlova	RUS	2.9.83	2	NC-w	Adler	12 Mar 05
1:27:33		Tatyana	Sibilyeva	RUS	17.5.80	2	NC-w	Adler	4 Mar 01
1:27:35		Tatyana	Korotkova	RUS	24.4.80	2	NC	Cheboksary	12 Jun 04
1:27:36		María	Vasco	ESP	26.12.75	3	WCp	Naumburg	2 May 04
1:27:37			Bai Yanmin	CHN	29.6.87	1	NG	Nanjing	20 Oct 05
1:27:41		Claudia	Iovan/Stef ¶	ROM	25.2.78	1		La Coruña	5 Jun 04
1:27:41		Kjersti	Tysse/Plätzer	NOR	18.1.72	2		Sesto San Giovanni	1 May 07
		(30)							
1:27:44		Jane	Saville	AUS	5.11.74	4	WCp	Naumburg	2 May 04
1:27:46		Norica	Cîmpean	ROM	22.3.72	1		Békéscsaba	28 Mar 99
1:27:49		Elisa	Rigaudo	ITA	17.6.80	5	WCp	Naumburg	2 May 04
1:27:53		Yuliya	Voyevodina	RUS	17.10.71	7	WCp	Naumburg	2 May 04
1:27:54			Song Lijuan	CHN	9.2.75	2		Beijing	1 May 95
1:27:55		Susana	Feitor	POR	28.1.75	1		Rio Maior	7 Apr 01
1:27:56		Sabine	Zimmer	GER	6.2.81	1		Hildesheim	5 Jun 04
1:27:58			Yang Yawei	CHN	16.10.83	2		Cixi	23 Apr 05
1:28:00		Anisya	Kornikova	RUS	23.10.89	2	RWC	Saransk	29 Sep 07
1:28:01			Jiang Qiuyan	CHN	5.7.83	3		Cixi	23 Apr 05
		(40)							
1:28:07			Tang Yinghua	CHN	18.5.73	4		Cixi	23 Apr 05
1:28:10		Valentina	Tsybulskaya	BLR	19.2.68	3	WCh	Saint-Denis	24 Aug 03
1:28:11		Yelena	Ginko	BLR	30.7.76	5	RUS-w	Adler	12 Mar 05
1:28:13		Marina	Smyslova	RUS	25.2.66	3	NC	Cheboksary	12 Jun 04
1:28:17		Melanie	Seeger	GER	8.1.77	9	WCp	Naumburg	2 May 04
1:28:18			Kong Yan	CHN	6.7.73	3		Beijing	1 May 95
1:28:19		Vira	Zozulya	UKR	31.8.70	1	NC-w	Yevpatoriya	23 Feb 03
1:28:20			He Dan	CHN	22.7.84	1		Yangzhou	22 Apr 06
1:28:22			Shi Na	CHN	17.2.81	5		Cixi	23 Apr 05
1:28:23			Song Xiaoling	CHN	21.12.87	2		Yangzhou	22 Apr 06
		(50)	100th best woman 1:30:22, 200th 1:32:49						

50 KILOMETRES WALK

Mark	Name		Nat	Born	Pos	Venue	Date
4:10:59	Monica	Svensson	SWE	26.12.78	1	Scanzorosciate	21 Oct 07
4:12:16	Yelena	Ginko	BLR	30.7.76	1	Scanzorosciate	17 Oct 04
4:16:27	Jolanta	Dukure	LAT	20.9.79	1	Paralepa	9 Sep 06
4:28:13	Evaggelía	Xinoú	GRE	22.11.81	2	Scanzorosciate	17 Oct 04
4:28:53	Neringa	Aidietité	LTU	5.6.83	1	Ivano-Frankivsk	1 Oct 06
4:29:56	Natalia	Bruniko	ITA	23.2.73	2	Scanzorosciate	27 Oct 02
4:33:45	Lyudmila	Yegorova	UKR	4.10.74	3	Scanzorosciate	17 Oct 04
4:36:45	Yelena	Krivokhizha	UKR	10.3.79	3	Scanzorosciate	28 Oct 01
4:37:40	Martina	Gabrielli	ITA	15.2.86	2	Scanzorosciate	15 Oct 06

JUNIOR MEN'S ALL-TIME LISTS

100 METRES

Mark	Wind	Name		Nat	Born	Pos	Meet	Venue	Date
10.01	0.0	Darrel	Brown	TRI	11.10.84	1q3	WCh	Saint-Denis	24 Aug 03
10.05		Davidson	Ezinwa	NGR	22.11.71	1		Bauchi	4 Jan 90
10.06	2.0	Dwain	Chambers	GBR	5.4.78	1	EJ	Ljubljana	25 Jul 97
10.06	1.5	Walter	Dix	USA	31.1.86	1h1	NCAA-r	New York	27 May 05
10.07	2.0	Stanley	Floyd	USA	23.6.61	1		Austin	24 May 80
10.07	1.1	DaBryan	Blanton	USA	3.7.84	1h2	NCAA-r	Lincoln, NE	30 May 03
10.07	0.2	Tamunosiki	Atorudibo	NGR	21.3.85	1s2	NC	Abuja	9 Jul 04
10.08	0.0	Andre	Cason	USA	13.1.69	1	NC-j	Tallahassee	24 Jun 88
10.08	0.0	Justin	Gatlin	USA	10.2.82	1	NCAA	Eugene	2 Jun 01
10.08A	1.9	Obadele	Thompson	BAR	30.3.76	3		El Paso	16 Apr 94
10.08	0.7	J-Mee	Samuels	USA	20.5.87	1		Greensboro	24 Jul 05
10.09A	1.8	Mel	Lattany	USA	10.8.59	2r2	USOF	USAF Academy	30 Jul 78
Wind assisted to 10.07									
9.83	7.1	Leonard	Scott	USA	19.1.80	1		Knoxville	9 Apr 99
9.96	4.5	Walter	Dix	USA	31.1.86	1rA	TexR	Austin	9 Apr 05
9.97	??	Mark	Lewis-Francis	GBR	4.9.82	1q3	WCh	Edmonton	4 Aug 01
10.05	2.1	J-Mee	Samuels	USA	20.5.87	1s2		Greensboro	23 Jul 05
10.05	3.0	Keston	Bledman	TRI	8.3.88	3	NC	Port of Spain	23 Jun 07
10.07	2.9	Lee	McRae	USA	23.1.66	2h5	NCAA	Austin	30 May 85

200 METRES

Mark	Wind	Name		Nat	Born	Pos	Meet	Venue	Date
19.93	1.4	Usain	Bolt	JAM	21.8.86	1		Hamilton, BER	11 Apr 04
20.07	1.5	Lorenzo	Daniel	USA	23.3.66	1	SEC	Starkville	18 May 85
20.13	1.7	Roy	Martin	USA	25.12.66	1		Austin	11 May 85
20.16A	-0.2	Riaan	Dempers	RSA	4.3.77	1	NC-j	Germiston	7 Apr 95
20.18	1.0	Walter	Dix	USA	31.1.86	1s2	NCAA	Sacramento	9 Jun 05
20.22	1.7	Dwayne	Evans	USA	13.10.58	2	OT	Eugene	22 Jun 76
20.23	0.5	Michael	Timpson	USA	6.6.67	1		State College	16 May 86
20.24	0.2	Joe	DeLoach	USA	5.6.67	3		Los Angeles	8 Jun 85
20.24	0.2	Francis	Obikwelu	NGR	22.11.78	2rB		Granada	29 May 96
20.28	0.1	Andrew	Howe	ITA	12.5.85	1	WJ	Grosseto	16 Jul 04
20.29 four men: Clinton Davis USA 1983, Christian Malcolm GBR 1998, Justin Gatlin USA & Yusuke Omae JPN 2001									
Wind assisted									
19.86	4.0	Justin	Gatlin	USA	10.2.82	1h2	NCAA	Eugene	30 May 01
20.01	2.5	Derald	Harris	USA	5.4.58	1		San José	9 Apr 77
20.08	9.2	Leonard	Scott	USA	19.1.80	2r2		Knoxville	9 Apr 99
20.10	4.6	Stanley	Kerr	USA	19.6.67	2r2	SWC	Houston	18 May 86
Hand timing: 19.9		Davidson	Ezinwa	NGR	22.11.71	1		Bauchi	18 Mar 89

400 METRES

Mark	Name		Nat	Born	Pos	Meet	Venue	Date
43.87	Steve	Lewis	USA	16.5.69	1	OG	Seoul	28 Sep 88
44.66	Hamdam Odha	Al-Bishi	KSA	5.5.81	1	WJ	Santiago de Chile	20 Oct 00
44.66	LaShawn	Merritt	USA	27.6.86	1		Kingston	7 May 05
44.69	Darrell	Robinson	USA	23.12.63	2	USOF	Indianapolis	24 Jul 82
44.73A	James	Rolle	USA	2.2.64	1	USOF	USAF Academy	2 Jul 83
44.75	Darren	Clark	AUS	6.9.65	4	OG	Los Angeles	8 Aug 84
44.75	Deon	Minor	USA	22.1.73	1s1	NCAA	Austin	5 Jun 92
44.93	Nagmeldin	El Abubakr	SUD	22.2.86	1	Is.Sol	Makkah	14 Apr 05
45.01	Thomas	Schönlebe	GDR	6.8.65	1		Berlin	15 Jul 84
45.01	Jerome	Young	USA	14.8.76	1	NC-j	Walnut	24 Jun 95
45.04A	Wayne	Collett	USA	20.10.49	1q2	OT	Echo Summit	13 Sep 68
45.04	Brandon	Couts	USA	17.2.79	1	DrakeR	Des Moines	25 Apr 98
44.9+A	Steve	Williams	USA	13.11.53	1	WAC	El Paso	13 May 72

800 METRES

Mark	Name		Nat	Born	Pos	Meet	Venue	Date
1:43.64	Japheth	Kimutai	KEN	20.12.78	3rB	WK	Zürich	13 Aug 97
1:43.90	Abubaker	Kaki	SUD	21.6.89	1	PArabG	Cairo	22 Nov 07
1:44.15	David	Rudisha	KEN	17.12.88	1	VD	Bruxelles	14 Sep 07
1:44.27	Majid Saeed	Sultan	QAT	3.11.86	1	AsiC	Inchon	4 Sep 05
1:44.3*	Jim	Ryun	USA	29.4.47	1	USTFF	Terre Haute	10 Jun 66
1:44.3	Joaquim	Cruz	BRA	12.3.63	1		Rio de Janeiro	27 Jun 81
1:44.33	Yuriy	Borzakovskiy	RUS	12.4.81	2s2	OG	Sydney	25 Sep 00
1:44.39	Mohammed	Al-Salhi	KSA	11.5.86	1		Lapinlahti	3 Jul 05
1:44.45	Alfred	Kirwa Yego	KEN	28.11.86	3rA	Bisl	Oslo	29 Jul 05
1:44.46	Nicholas	Wachira	KEN	19.11.82	5	GP II	Rieti	2 Sep 01
1:44.56	Benjamin	Kipkurui	KEN	28.12.80	2		Rehlingen	24 May 99
1:44.69	William	Chirchir	KEN	6.2.79	6	Herc	Monaco	8 Aug 98

1000 METRES

Mark	Wind	Name		Nat	Born	Pos	Meet	Venue	Date
2:15.00		Benjamin	Kipkurui	KEN	28.12.80	5	Nik	Nice	17 Jul 99
2:16.84		Ali	Hakimi	TUN	24.4.76	1		Lindau	28 Jul 95
2:16.86		Japheth	Kimutai	KEN	20.12.78	1	VD	Bruxelles	22 Aug 97
2:17.10		Julius	Achon	UGA	12.12.76	1		Rhede	30 Jul 95

1500 METRES

Mark	Wind	Name		Nat	Born	Pos	Meet	Venue	Date
3:30.24		Cornelius	Chirchir	KEN	5.6.83	4	Herc	Monaco	19 Jul 02
3:31.13		Mulugueta	Wondimu	ETH	28.2.85	2rA	NA	Heusden	31 Jul 04
3:31.42		Alex	Kipchirchir	KEN	26.11.84	5	VD	Bruxelles	5 Sep 03
3:31.54		Isaac	Songok	KEN	25.4.84	1	NA	Heusden	2 Aug 03
3:32.48		Augustine	Choge	KEN	21.1.87	1	ISTAF	Berlin	3 Sep 06
3:32.68		Abdelaati	Iguider	MAR	25.3.87	5	VD	Bruxelles	25 Aug 06
3:32.91		Noah	Ngeny	KEN	2.11.78	9	Herc	Monaco	16 Aug 97
3:33.16		Benjamin	Kipkurui	KEN	28.12.80	1rB	WK	Zürich	11 Aug 99
3:33.24		William	Chirchir	KEN	6.2.79	8rA	WK	Zürich	12 Aug 98
3:33.72		Nicholas	Kemboi	KEN	18.12.89	1-23	WK	Zürich	18 Aug 06
3:34.03		Bernard	Kiptum	KEN	8.10.86	8	ISTAF	Berlin	4 Sep 05
3:34.17		Michael	Too	KEN	3.8.83	4	GP	Doha	15 May 02

1 MILE

Mark	Wind	Name		Nat	Born	Pos	Meet	Venue	Date
3:50.25		Alex	Kipchirchir	KEN	26.11.84	2	GP II	Rieti	7 Sep 03
3:50.39		James	Kwalia	KEN	12.6.84	1	FBK	Hengelo	1 Jun 03
3:50.41		Noah	Ngeny	KEN	2.11.78	2	Nik	Nice	16 Jul 97
3:50.69		Cornelius	Chirchir	KEN	5.6.83	5	GGala	Roma	12 Jul 02
3:51.3		Jim	Ryun	USA	29.4.47	1		Berkeley	17 Jul 66

2000 METRES

Mark	Wind	Name		Nat	Born	Pos	Meet	Venue	Date
4:56.86		Isaac	Songok	KEN	25.4.84	6	ISTAF	Berlin	31 Aug 01
4:59.11		James	Kwalia	KEN	12.6.84	5		Naimette	2 Sep 03
4:59.14		Ali	Saïdi-Sief	ALG	15.3.78	9	Gaz	Villeneuve d'Ascq	29 Jun 97
4:59.02 i		Remi	Limo Ndiwa	KEN	3.2.88	4	GP	Birmingham	17 Feb 07

3000 METRES

Mark	Wind	Name		Nat	Born	Pos	Meet	Venue	Date
7:28.78		Augustine	Choge	KEN	21.1.87	2	SGP	Doha	13 May 05
7:29.11		Tariku	Bekele	ETH	21.1.87	2	GP	Rieti	27 Aug 06
7:30.67		Kenenisa	Bekele	ETH	13.6.82	2	VD	Bruxelles	24 Aug 01
7:30.91		Eliud	Kipchoge	KEN	5.11.84	2	VD	Bruxelles	5 Sep 03
7:32.37		Abreham Cherkos	Feleke	ETH	23.9.89	2	Athl	Lausanne	11 Jul 06
7:33.00		Hailu	Mekonnen	ETH	4.4.80	2		Stuttgart	6 Jun 99
7:34.32		Richard	Limo	KEN	18.11.80	4	VD	Bruxelles	3 Sep 99
7:34.58		Sammy	Kipketer	KEN	29.9.81	5	VD	Bruxelles	3 Sep 99
7:35.52		Philip	Mosima	KEN	2.1.77	1	GP	London (CP)	12 Jul 96
7:35.53		James	Kwalia	KEN	12.6.84	5	VD	Bruxelles	5 Sep 03
7:36.78		Joseph	Ebuya	KEN	20.6.87	4	BrGP	Gateshead	11 Jun 06

5000 METRES

Mark	Wind	Name		Nat	Born	Pos	Meet	Venue	Date
12:52.61		Eliud	Kipchoge	KEN	5.11.84	3	Bisl	Oslo	27 Jun 03
12:53.66		Augustine	Choge	KEN	21.1.87	4	GGala	Roma	8 Jul 05
12:53.72		Philip	Mosima	KEN	2.1.77	2	GGala	Roma	5 Jun 96
12:53.81		Tariku	Bekele	ETH	21.1.87	4	GGala	Roma	14 Jul 06
12:54.07		Sammy	Kipketer	KEN	29.9.81	2	GGala	Roma	30 Jun 00
12:54.19		Abreham	Cherkos Feleke	ETH	23.9.89	5	GGala	Roma	14 Jul 06
12:54.58		James	Kwalia	KEN	12.6.84	5	Bisl	Oslo	27 Jun 03
12:56.15		Daniel	Komen	KEN	17.5.76	2	GG	Roma	8 Jun 95
12:57.05		Mulugueta	Wondimu	ETH	28.2.85	2	ISTAF	Berlin	12 Sep 04
12:58.03		Joseph	Ebuya	KEN	20.6.87	6	Gaz	Saint-Denis	8 Jul 06
12:58.08		Gebre-egziabher	Gebremariam	ETH	10.9.84	6	WCh	Saint-Denis	31 Aug 03

10,000 METRES

Mark	Wind	Name		Nat	Born	Pos	Meet	Venue	Date
26:41.75		Samuel	Wanjiru	KEN	10.11.86	3	VD	Bruxelles	26 Aug 05
27:02.81		Ibrahim	Jeylan	ETH	12.6.89	4	VD	Bruxelles	25 Aug 06
27:04.00		Boniface	Kiprop	UGA	12.10.85	5	VD	Bruxelles	3 Sep 04
27:04.45		Bernard Kipyego	Kiprop	KEN	16.7.86	4	FBK	Hengelo	29 May 05
27:06.47		Habtanu	Fikadu	ETH	13.3.88	8	FBK	Hengelo	26 May 07
27:07.29		Moses	Masai	KEN	1.6.86	7	VD	Bruxelles	3 Sep 04
27:11.18		Richard	Chelimo	KEN	21.4.72	1	APM	Hengelo	25 Jun 91
27:12.42		Sammy	Alex	KEN	1.6.89	1		Tokamchi	29 Sep 07
27:13.66		Moses	Mosop	KEN	17.7.85	7	VD	Bruxelles	5 Sep 03
27:17.82		Addis	Abebe	ETH	5.9.70	2	WG	Helsinki	29 Jun 89

Mark	Wind	Name		Nat	Born	Pos	Meet	Venue	Date

3000 METRES STEEPLECHASE

7:58.66		Stephen	Cherono	KEN	15.10.82	3	VD	Bruxelles	24 Aug 01
8:03.74		Raymond	Yator	KEN	7.4.81	3	Herc	Monaco	18 Aug 00
8:05.52		Brimin	Kipruto	KEN	31.7.85	1	FBK	Hengelo	31 May 04
8:07.18		Moussa	Omar Obaid	QAT	18.4.85	4	OG	Athína	24 Aug 04
8:07.69		Paul	Kosgei	KEN	22.4.78	5	DNG	Stockholm	7 Jul 97
8:09.37		Abel	Cheruiyot/Yugut	KEN	26.12.84	2	NA	Heusden	2 Aug 03
8:12.91		Thomas	Kiplitan	KEN	15.6.83	7	GP	Doha	15 May 02
8:14.00		Williy	Komen	KEN	22.12.87	1	WJ	Beijing	19 Aug 06
8:16.69		Ronald	Kipchumba Rutto	KEN	8.10.87	4	FBK	Hengelo	29 May 05
8:16.76		Kipkirui	Misoi	KEN	23.10.78	2		Dortmund	8 Jun 97
8:17.21		Nahom	Mesfin Tariku	ETH	3.6.89	3	AfG	Alger	18 Jul 07
8:18.11		Bisluke	Kiplagat	KEN	8.8.88	3	WJ	Beijing	19 Aug 06

110 METRES HURDLES (106cm)

13.12	1.6		Liu Xiang	CHN	13.7.83	1rB	Athl	Lausanne	2 Jul 02
13.23	0.0	Renaldo	Nehemiah	USA	24.3.59	1r2	WK	Zürich	16 Aug 78
13.40	-1.0		Shi Dongpeng	CHN	6.1.84	1	NC	Shanghai	14 Sep 03
13.44	-0.8	Colin	Jackson	GBR	18.2.67	1	WJ	Athína	19 Jul 86
13.46	1.8	Jon	Ridgeon	GBR	14.2.67	1	EJ	Cottbus	23 Aug 85
13.46	-1.6	Dayron	Robles	CUB	19.11.86	1	PAm-J	Windsor	29 Jul 05
13.47	1.9	Holger	Pohland	GDR	5.4.63	2	vUSA	Karl-Marx-Stadt	10 Jul 82
13.47	1.2	Aries	Merritt	USA	24.7.85	4	NCAA	Austin	12 Jun 04
13.49	0.6	Stanislav	Olijar	LAT	22.3.79	1		Valmiera	11 Jul 98
13.50	0.7	Jason	Richardson	USA	4.4.86	3	NCAA	Sacramento	10 Jun 05
Wind assisted									
13.41	2.6	Dayron	Robles	CUB	19.11.86	2	CAC	Nassau	10 Jul 05
13.42	4.5	Colin	Jackson	GBR	18.2.67	2	CG	Edinburgh	27 Jul 86
13.42	2.6	Antwon	Hicks	USA	12.3.83	1	WJ	Kingston	21 Jul 02
13.47	2.1	Frank	Busemann	GER	26.2.75	1	WJ	Lisboa	22 Jul 94

99 cm Hurdles

13.23	1.5	Artur	Noga	POL	2.5.88	1	WJ	Beijing	20 Aug 06
13.25*		Arthur	Blake	USA	19.8.66	1		Winter Park	11 May 84
13.30		Chris	Nelloms	USA	14.8.71	1		Dayton	26 May 90
Wind assisted				*120 yards time plus 0.03					
13.15	2.7	Brendan	Ames	USA	6.10.88	1	NC-j	Indianapolis	21 Jun 07
13.18		Arthur	Blake	USA	19.8.66	1	GWest	Sacramento	9 Jun 84
13.26	2.8	Ted	Ginn	USA	12.4.85	1h1		Columbus	5 Jun 04
13.28		Thomas	Wilcher	USA	11.4.64	1			82
Hand timed:	12.9y	Renaldo	Nehemiah	USA	24.3.59	1		Jamaica, NY	30 May 77

400 METRES HURDLES

48.02		Danny	Harris	USA	7.9.65	2s1	OT	Los Angeles	17 Jun 84
48.51		Kerron	Clement	USA	31.10.85	1	WJ	Grosseto	16 Jul 04
48.62		Brandon	Johnson	USA	6.3.85	2	WJ	Grosseto	16 Jul 04
48.68		Bayano	Kamani	USA	17.4.80	1	NCAA	Boise	4 Jun 99
48.72		Angelo	Taylor	USA	29.12.78	2	NCAA	Bloomington	6 Jun 97
48.74		Vladimir	Budko	BLR	4.2.65	2	DRZ	Moskva	18 Aug 84
48.76A		Llewellyn	Herbert	RSA	21.7.77	1		Pretoria	7 Apr 96
48.79		Kenneth	Ferguson	USA	22.3.84	1	SEC	Knoxville	18 May 03
48.89		Louis	van Zyl	RSA	20.7.85	1	WJ	Kingston	19 Jul 02
48.94		Ibrahim	Al-Hamaidi	KSA	28.8.85	3	WJ	Grosseto	16 Jul 04
49.07		Mubarak	Al-Nubi	QAT	30.12.77	1	WJ	Sydney	23 Aug 96
49.09		Dai	Tamesue	JPN	3.5.78	1		Hiroshima	14 Oct 96

HIGH JUMP

2.37		Dragutin	Topic	YUG	12.3.71	1	WJ	Plovdiv	12 Aug 90
2.37		Steve	Smith	GBR	29.3.73	1	WJ	Seoul	20 Sep 92
2.36		Javier	Sotomayor	CUB	13.10.67	1		Santiago de Cuba	23 Feb 86
2.35i		Vladimir	Yashchenko	UKR	12.1.59	1	EI	Milano	12 Mar 78
		2.34				1	Prv	Tbilisi	16 Jun 78
2.35		Dietmar	Mögenburg	FRG	15.8.61	1		Rehlingen	26 May 80
2.34		Tim	Forsyth	AUS	17.8.73	1	Bisl	Oslo	4 Jul 92
2.33			Zhu Jianhua	CHN	29.5.63	1	AsiG	New Delhi	1 Dec 82
2.33		Patrik	Sjöberg	SWE	5.1.65	1	OsloG	Oslo	9 Jul 83
2.32i		Jaroslav	Bába	CZE	2.9.84	3		Arnstadt	8 Feb 03
2.32			Huang Haiqiang	CHN	8.2.88	1	WJ	Beijing	17 Aug 06

POLE VAULT

5.80		Maksim	Tarasov	RUS	2.12.70	1	vGDR-j	Bryansk	14 Jul 89
5.75		Konstadínos	Filippídis	GRE	26.11.86	2	WUG	Izmir	18 Aug 05

Mark	Wind	Name		Nat	Born	Pos	Meet	Venue	Date
5.71		Lawrence	Johnson	USA	7.5.74	1		Knoxville	12 Jun 93
5.71		Germán	Chiaraviglio	ARG	16.4.87	1	WJ	Beijing	19 Aug 06
5.70		Viktor	Chistyakov	RUS	9.2.75	1		Leppävirta	7 Jun 94
5.70		Artyom	Kuptsov	RUS	22.4.84	1	Znam	Tula	7 Jun 03
5.67i		Leonid	Kivalov	RUS	1.4.88	1	NC-j	Penza	1 Feb 07
5.65		Rodion	Gataullin	UZB	23.11.65	2	NC	Donetsk	8 Sep 84
5.65		István	Bagyula	HUN	2.1.69	1	WJ	Sudbury	28 Jul 88
5.65i		Jacob	Davis	USA	29.4.78	1	Big 12	Lincoln	21 Feb 97
		5.62				2		Austin	5 Apr 97
5.62		Gérald	Baudouin	FRA	15.11.72	1	NC-j	Dreux	7 Jul 91
5.62		Lars	Börgeling	GER	16.4.79	1		Mannheim	13 Jun 98

LONG JUMP

Mark	Wind	Name		Nat	Born	Pos	Meet	Venue	Date
8.34	0.0	Randy	Williams	USA	23.8.53	Q	OG	München	8 Sep 72
8.28	0.8	Luis Alberto	Bueno	CUB	22.5.69	1		La Habana	16 Jul 88
8.24	0.2	Eric	Metcalf	USA	23.1.68	1	NCAA	Indianapolis	6 Jun 86
8.24	1.8	Vladimir	Ochkan	UKR	13.1.68	1	vGDR-j	Leningrad	21 Jun 87
8.22		Larry	Doubley	USA	15.3.58	1	NCAA	Champaign	3 Jun 77
8.22		Iván	Pedroso	CUB	17.12.72	1		Santiago de Cuba	3 May 91
8.22i		Viktor	Kuznetsov	UKR	14.7.86	1		Brovary	22 Jan 05
8.21A	2.0	Vance	Johnson	USA	13.3.63	1	NCAA	Provo	4 Jun 82
8.20	1.5	James	Stallworth	USA	29.4.71	Q	WJ	Plovdiv	9 Aug 90
8.18		LaMonte	King	USA	18.12.59	2	CalR	Modesto	20 May 78
8.18		Petr	Lampart	CZE	31.3.83	1		Brno	15 Sep 02
Wind assisted									
8.40	3.2	Kareem	Streete-Thompson	CAY	30.3.73	1		Houston	5 May 91
8.35	2.2	Carl	Lewis	USA	1.7.61	1	NCAA	Austin	6 Jun 80
8.29	2.3	James	Beckford	JAM	9.1.75	1		Tempe	2 Apr 94
8.23	4.4	Peller	Phillips	USA	23.6.70	1		Sacramento	11 Jun 88
8.21	2.8	Masaki	Morinaga	JPN	27.3.72	1		Hamamatsu	7 Sep 91

TRIPLE JUMP

Mark	Wind	Name		Nat	Born	Pos	Meet	Venue	Date
17.50	0.4	Volker	Mai	GDR	3.5.66	1	vURS	Erfurt	23 Jun 85
17.42	1.3	Khristo	Markov	BUL	27.1.65	1	Nar	Sofiya	19 May 84
17.40A	0.4	Pedro	Pérez	CUB	23.2.52	1	PAm	Cali	5 Aug 71
17.31	-0.2	David	Giralt Jr.	CUB	26.8.84	Q	WCh	Saint-Denis	23 Aug 03
17.29	1.3	James	Beckford	JAM	9.1.75	1		Tempe	2 Apr 94
17.27		Aliecer	Urrutia	CUB	22.9.74	1		Artemisa	23 Apr 93
17.23	0.2	Yoelbi	Quesada	CUB	4.8.73	1	NC	La Habana	13 May 92
17.23	0.0		Gu Junjie	CHN	5.5.85	1		Hefei	26 Sep 04
17.11	1.4	Marian	Oprea	ROM	6.6.82	2	WUG	Beijing	31 Aug 01
17.03	0.6	Osiris	Mora	CUB	3.10.73	2	WJ	Seoul	19 Sep 92
17.13w	4.1	Marian	Oprea	ROM	6.6.82	1	ECp-1B	Budapest	24 Jun 01
17.13w	4.6	Kenneth	Hall	USA	17.4.86	1		Eugene	29 Jul 04

SHOT

Mark	Wind	Name		Nat	Born	Pos	Meet	Venue	Date
21.05i		Terry	Albritton	USA	14.1.55	1	AAU	New York	22 Feb 74
		20.38				2	MSR	Walnut	27 Apr 74
20.65		Mike	Carter	USA	29.10.60	1	vSU-j	Boston	4 Jul 79
20.39		Janus	Robberts	RSA	10.3.79	1	NC	Germiston	7 Mar 98
20.20		Randy	Matson	USA	5.3.45	2	OG	Tokyo	17 Oct 64
20.20		Udo	Beyer	GDR	9.8.55	2	NC	Leipzig	6 Jul 74
20.13		Jeff	Chakouian	USA	20.4.82	2		Atlanta	18 May 01
19.99		Karl	Salb	USA	19.5.49	4	OT	Echo Summit	10 Sep 68
19.95		Edis	Elkasevic	CRO	18.2.83	1		Velenje	15 Jun 02
19.74		Andreas	Horn	GDR	31.1.62	2	vSU-j	Cottbus	24 Jun 81
19.71		Vladimir	Kiselyov -1	UKR	1.1.57	1		Yalta	15 May 76
19.69		Mikulás	Konopka	SVK	23.1.79	2	NC	Nitra	11 Jul 98
6 kg Shot		(* 6.25kg shot)							
21.96		Edis	Elkasevic	CRO	18.2.83	1	NC-j	Zagreb	29 Jun 02
21.47			Elkasevic			1	WJ	Kingston	16 Jul 02
21.25			Gao Yong	CHN	12.10.89	1		Jinzhou	1 Sep 06
21.24		Georgi	Ivanov	BUL	13.3.85	1	NC-j	Sofia	12 Jun 04
21.11		Magnus	Lohse	SWE	28.7.84	1		Lerum	19 Jun 03
21.11			Wang Like	CHN	2.4.89	1	SDG	Yantai	15 Oct 06
21.03*		Udo	Beyer	GDR	9.8.55	1		Frankfurt an der Oder	13 Jul 93
21.03		Carl	Myerscough	GBR	21.10.79	1		Street	13 May 98

DISCUS

Mark	Wind	Name		Nat	Born	Pos	Meet	Venue	Date
65.62		Werner	Reiterer	AUS	27.1.68	1		Melbourne	15 Dec 87
63.64		Werner	Hartmann	FRG	20.4.59	1	vFRA	Strasbourg	25 Jun 78

Mark	Wind	Name		Nat	Born	Pos	Meet	Venue	Date
63.26		Sergey	Pachin	UKR	24.5.68	2		Moskva	25 Jul 87
63.22		Brian	Milne	USA	7.1.73	1		State College	28 Mar 92
62.79		Mykyta	Nesterenko	UKR	15.4.91	1		Kyiv	22 May 07
62.52		John	Nichols	USA	23.8.69	1		Baton Rouge	23 Apr 88
62.36		Nuermaimaiti	Tulake	CHN	8.3.82	2	NG	Guangzhou	21 Nov 01
62.16		Zoltán	Kővágó	HUN	10.4.79	1		Budapest	9 May 97
62.04		Kenth	Gardenkrans	SWE	2.10.55	2		Helsingborg	11 Aug 74
62.04			Wu Tao	CHN	3.10.83	1	NGP	Shanghai	18 May 02
1.75kg Discus									
67.32		Margus	Hunt	EST	14.7.87	1	WJ	Beijing	16 Aug 06
65.88		Omar	El-Ghazaly	EGY	9.2.84	1		Cairo	7 Nov 03
65.55		Mihai	Grasu	ROM	21.4.87	1	NC	Bucuresti	23 Jul 06
64.51			Wu Tao	CHN	3.10.83	1	WJ	Kingston	18 Jul 02
64.50		Michael	Möllenbeck	GER	12.12.69	1		Rhede	18 Jun 88
64.35		Emeka	Udechuku	GBR	10.7.79	1		Basildon	21 Jun 98

HAMMER

Mark	Wind	Name		Nat	Born	Pos	Meet	Venue	Date
78.33		Olli-Pekka	Karjalainen	FIN	7.3.80	1	NC	Seinäjoki	5 Aug 99
78.14		Roland	Steuk	GDR	5.3.59	1	NC	Leipzig	30 Jun 78
78.00		Sergey	Dorozhon	UKR	17.2.64	1		Moskva	7 Aug 83
76.54		Valeriy	Gubkin	BLR	3.9.67	2		Minsk	27 Jun 86
76.42		Ruslan	Dikiy	TJK	18.1.72	1		Togliatti	7 Sep 91
75.52		Sergey	Kirmasov	RUS	25.3.70	1		Kharkov	4 Jun 89
75.42		Szymon	Ziolkowski	POL	1.7.76	1	EJ	Nyíregyhazá	30 Jul 95
75.24		Christoph	Sahner	FRG	23.9.63	1	vPOL-j	Göttingen	26 Jun 82
75.22		Yaroslav	Chmyr	UKR	29.11.66	1		Kiyev	9 Sep 85
75.20		Igor	Nikulin	RUS	14.8.60	2		Leselidze	1 Jun 79
6kg Hammer (* 6.25kg hammer)									
82.62		Yevgeniy	Aydamirov	RUS	11.5.87	1	NC-j	Tula	22 Jul 06
81.34		Krisztián	Pars	HUN	18.2.82	1		Szombathely	2 Sep 01
81.04		Werner	Smit	RSA	14.9.84	1		Bellville	29 Mar 03
80.51		Andrey	Azarenkov	RUS	26.9.85	1		Adler	7 Feb 04
80.34*		David	Chaussinand	FRA	19.4.73	1		Clermont-Ferrand	24 Oct 92
80.30		Fréderic	Kuhn	FRA	10.7.68	1		Saint-Etienne	11 Oct 87
80.12		Anatoliy	Pozdnyakov	RUS	1.2.87	2	NC-j	Tula	22 Jul 06

JAVELIN

Mark	Wind	Name		Nat	Born	Pos	Meet	Venue	Date
83.87		Andreas	Thorkildsen	NOR	1.4.82	1		Fana	7 Jun 01
83.55		Aleksandr	Ivanov	RUS	25.5.82	2	NC	Tula	14 Jul 01
83.07		Robert	Oosthuizen	RSA	23.1.87	1	WJ	Beijing	19 Aug 06
82.52		Harri	Haatainen	FIN	5.1.78	4		Leppävirta	25 May 96
81.80		Sergey	Voynov	UZB	26.2.77	1		Tashkent	6 Jun 96
80.94		Aki	Parviainen	FIN	26.10.74	4	NC	Jyväskylä	5 Jul 92
80.57		Teemu	Wirkkala	FIN	14.1.84	1		Espoo	14 Sep 03
80.43		Tero	Järvenpää	FIN	2.10.84	3	NC	Helsinki	11 Aug 03
80.30		Konstadínos	Gatsioúdis	GRE	17.12.73	1	NC	Athína	20 Jun 92
80.26		Vladimir	Ovchinnikov	RUS	2.8.70	Q	OG	Seoul	24 Sep 88
80.03		Lohan	Rautenbach	RSA	6.2.86	1	NC	Durban	16 Apr o5

DECATHLON

Mark	Name		Nat	Born	Pos	Meet	Venue	Date
8397	Torsten	Voss	GDR	24.3.63	1	NC	Erfurt	7 Jul 82
	10.76 7.66 14.41 2.09 48.37 14.37 41.76 4.80 62.90 4:34.04							
8257	Yordani	Garcia	CUB	21.11.88	8	WCh	Osaka	1 Sep 07
	10.73/0.7 7.15/0.2 14.94 2.09 49.25 14.08/-0.2 42.91 4.70 68.74 4:55.42							
8114	Michael	Kohnle	FRG	3.5.70	1	EJ	Varazdin	26 Aug 89
	10.95 7.09/0.1 15.27 2.02 49.91 14.40 45.82 4.90 60.82 4:49.43							
8104	Valter	Külvet	EST	19.2.64	1		Viimsi	23 Aug 81
	10.7 7.26 13.86 2.09 48.5 14.8 47.92 4.50 60.34 4:37.8							
8082	Daley	Thompson	GBR	30.7.58	1	ECp/s	Sittard	31 Jul 77
	10.70/0.8 7.54/0.7 13.84 2.01 47.31 15.26/2.0 41.70 4.70 54.48 4:30.4							
8041		Qi Haifeng	CHN	7.8.83	1	AsiG	Busan	10 Oct 02
	11.09/0.2 7.22/0.0 13.05 2.06 49.09 14.54/0.0 43.16 4.80 61.04 4:35.17							
8036	Christian	Schenk	GDR	9.2.65	5		Potsdam	21 Jul 84
	11.54 7.18 14.26 2.16 49.23 15.06 44.74 4.20 65.98 4:24.11							
7938	Frank	Busemann	GER	26.2.75	1		Zeven	2 Oct 94
	10.68/1.6 7.37/1.1 13.08 2.03 50.41 14.34/-1.1 39.84 4.40 63.00 4:37.31)							
7913	Raul	Duany	CUB	4.1.75	2		La Habana	26 May 94
	11.50 7.13 13.99 2.10 49.70 14.77 37.76 4.50 65.58 4:24.03							
7906	Mikhail	Romanyuk	UKR	6.2.62	1	EJ	Utrecht	21 Aug 81
	11.26/1.8 7.11w/3.7 13.50 1.98 49.98 14.72w/4.0 42.94 4.90 59.74 4:30.63							

Mark	Wind	Name		Nat	Born	Pos	Meet	Venue	Date

IAAF Junior specifiaction with 99cm 110mh, 6kg shot, 1.75kg Discus

Mark			Nat	Born	Pos	Meet	Venue	Date
8131	Arkadiy	Vasilyev	RUS	19.1.87	1		Sochi	27 May 06
	11.28/-0.8 7.70/2.0 14.59 2.00 49.17 14.67/0.6 46.30 4.70 56.96 4:32.10							
8126	Andrey	Kravchenko	BLR	4.1.86	1	WJ	Grosseto	15 Jul 04
	11.09/-0.5 7.46-0.2 14.51 2.16 48.98 14.55*/0.4 43.41 4.50 52.84 4:28.46							
8047	Aleksey	Sysoyev	RUS	8.3.85	2	WJ	Grosseto	15 Jul 04
	10.86/-0.2 6.84/0.9 16.94 1.95 49.72 15.25*/0.3 53.80 4.30 57.44 4:34.84							

10,000 METRES WALK

Mark			Nat	Born	Pos	Meet	Venue	Date
38:46.4	Viktor	Burayev	RUS	23.8.82	1	NC-j	Moskva	20 May 00
38:54.75	Ralf	Kowalsky	GDR	22.3.62	1		Cottbus	24 Jun 81
39:28.45	Andrey	Ruzavin	RUS	28.9.86	1	EJ	Kaunas	23 Jul 05
39:44.71	Giovanni	De Benedictis	ITA	8.1.68	1	EJ	Birmingham	7 Aug 87
39:49.22		Pei Chuang	CHN	5.12.81	2	NSG	Chengdu	8 Sep 00
39:50.32		Cui Jin	CHN	1.12.87	2		Jinzhou	30 Aug 06
39:50.73	Jefferson	Pérez	ECU	1.7.74	1	PAmJ	Winnipeg	15 Jul 93
39:55.52	Ilya	Markov	RUS	19.6.72	1	WJ	Plovdiv	10 Aug 90
39:56.49	Alberto	Cruz	MEX	6.6.72	2	WJ	Plovdiv	10 Aug 90
39:59.58	Sergey	Tyulenyev	RUS	14.3.71	1		Kharkov	4 Jun 90

20 KILOMETRES WALK

Mark			Nat	Born	Pos	Meet	Venue	Date
1:18:06	Viktor	Burayev	RUS	23.2.82	2	NC-w	Adler	4 Mar 01
1:18:07		Li Gaobo	CHN	23.7.89	4		Cixi	23 Apr 05
1:18:44		Chu Yafei	CHN	5.9.88	5		Yangzhou	22 Apr 06
1:18:57		Bai Xuejin	CHN	6.6.87	7		Yangzhou	22 Apr 06
1:19:02	Éder	Sánchez	MEX	21.5.86	11		Cixi	23 Apr 05
1:19:14		Xu Xingde	CHN	12.6.84	3	NC	Yangzhou	12 Apr 03
1:19:34		Li Jianbo	CHN	14.11.86	16		Cixi	23 Apr 05
1:19:38		Yu Guohui	CHN	13.4.77	2	NC	Zhuhai	10 Mar 96
1:20:15		Sun Chao	CHN	8.1.87	10		Yangzhou	22 Apr 06
1:20:28		Liu Wenjun	CHN	8.1.87	22		Cixi	23 Apr 05

4 x 100 METRES RELAY

Mark	Nat	Team	Pos	Meet	Venue	Date
38.66	USA	Kimmons, Omole, I Williams, L Merritt	1	WJ	Grosseto	18 Jun 04
39.05	GBR	Edgar, Grant, Benjamin, Lewis-Francis	1	WJ	Santiago de Chile	22 Oct 00
39.05	JAM	Barnes, Rose, Jervis, Blake	1	WJ	Beijing	20 Aug 06
39.17	TRI	Simpson, Burns, Holder, Brown	3	WJ	Kingston	21 Jul 02
39.25	FRG	Dobeleit, Klameth, Evers, Lübke	1	EJ	Schwechat	28 Aug 83
39.30	JPN	Matsumaga, Noda, Takahira, Aikawa	1	AsiC-j	Bangkok	28 Oct 02
39.33	FRA	Pognon, Calligny, Doucoure, Djhone	2	WJ	Santiago de Chile	22 Oct 00
39.51	CIV	Y.Sonan, Ahmed Douhou, A.Byo, Ibrahim Meité	1	Afr-J	Bouaké	22 Jul 95

4 x 400 METRES RELAY

Mark	Nat	Team	Pos	Meet	Venue	Date
3:01.09	USA	B Johnson, L Merritt, Craig, Clement	1	WJ	Grosseto	18 Jul 04
3:03.80	GBR	Grindley, Patrick, Winrow, Richardson	2	WJ	Plovdiv	12 Aug 90
3:04.06	JAM	S Clarke, Bolt, Myers, Gonzales	2	WJ	Kingston	21 Jul 02
3:04.22	CUB	Cadogan, Mordoche, González, Hernández	2	WJ	Athína	20 Jul 86
3:04.50	RSA	le Roux, Gebhardt, Julius, van Zyl	2	WJ	Grosseto	18 Jul 04
3:04.58	GDR	Preusche, Löper, Trylus, Carlowitz	1	EJ	Utrecht	23 Aug 81
3:04.74	AUS	McFarlane, Batman, Thom, Vincent	1	WJ	Annecy	2 Aug 98
3:05.33	JPN	Ota, Noda, Suzuki, Sasaki	3	WJ	Grosseto	18 Jul 04

JUNIOR WOMEN'S ALL-TIME LISTS

100 Metres

Mark	Wind			Nat	Born	Pos	Meet	Venue	Date
10.88	2.0	Marlies	Oelsner	GDR	21.3.58	1	NC	Dresden	1 Jul 77
10.89	1.8	Katrin	Krabbe	GDR	22.11.69	1rB		Berlin	20 Jul 88
11.03	1.7	Silke	Gladisch	GDR	20.6.64	3	OD	Berlin	8 Jun 83
11.04	1.4	Angela	Williams	USA	30.1.80	1	NCAA	Boise	5 Jun 99
11.08	2.0	Brenda	Morehead	USA	5.10.57	1	OT	Eugene	21 Jun 76
11.11	0.2	Shakedia	Jones	USA	15.3.79	1		Los Angeles (Ww)	2 May 98
11.11	1.1	Joan Uduak	Ekah	NGR	16.12.80	5	Athl	Lausanne	2 Jul 99
11.12	2.0	Veronica	Campbell	JAM	15.5.82	1	WJ	Santiago de Chile	18 Oct 00
11.12	1.2	Alexandria	Anderson	USA	28.1.87	1	NC-j	Indianapolis	22 Jun 06
11.13	2.0	Chandra	Cheeseborough	USA	10.1.59	2	OT	Eugene	21 Jun 76
11.13	-1.0	Grit	Breuer	GDR	16.2.72	1		Jena	6 Jun 90
11.13	1.5	Ashley	Owens	USA	19.11.85	1	WJ	Grosseto	14 Jul 04

Uncertain timing: 10.99 1.9 Natalya Bochina RUS 4.1.62 2 Leningrad 3 Jun 80

Wind assisted to 11.11

Mark	Wind			Nat	Born	Pos	Meet	Venue	Date
10.96	3.7	Angela	Williams	USA	30.1.80	1		Las Vegas	3 Apr 99

Mark	Wind	Name		Nat	Born	Pos	Meet	Venue	Date
10.97	3.3	Gesine	Walther	GDR	6.10.62	4	NC	Cottbus	16 Jul 80
11.02	2.1	Nikole	Mitchell	JAM	5.6.74	1	Mutual	Kingston	1 May 93
11.04	5.6	Kelly-Ann	Baptiste	TRI	14.10.86	1rB	TexR	Austin	9 Apr 05
11.06	2.2	Brenda	Morehead	USA	5.10.57	1s	OT	Eugene	21 Jun 76
11.09		Angela	Williams	TRI	15.5.65	1		Nashville	14 Apr 84

200 METRES

Mark	Wind	Name		Nat	Born	Pos	Meet	Venue	Date
22.11A	-0.5	Allyson	Felix	USA	18.11.85	1		Ciudad de México	3 May 03
		22.18	0.8			2	OG	Athína	25 Aug 04
22.19	1.5	Natalya	Bochina	RUS	4.1.62	2	OG	Moskva	30 Jul 80
22.37	1.3	Sabine	Rieger	GDR	6.11.63	2	vURS	Cottbus	26 Jun 82
22.42	0.4	Gesine	Walther	GDR	6.10.62	1		Potsdam	29 Aug 81
22.45	0.5	Grit	Breuer	GER	16.2.72	2	ASV	Köln	8 Sep 91
22.51	2.0	Katrin	Krabbe	GDR	22.11.69	3		Berlin	13 Sep 88
22.52	1.2	Mary	Onyali	NGR	3.2.68	6	WCh	Roma	3 Sep 87
22.58	0.8	Marion	Jones	USA	12.10.75	4	TAC	New Orleans	28 Jun 92
22.70		Marita	Koch	GDR	18.2.57	1		Halle	16 May 76
22.70A	1.9	Kathy	Smallwood	GBR	3.5.60	2	WUG	Ciudad de México	12 Sep 79
22.71	-0.6	Simone	Facey	JAM	7.5.85	1		Kingston	27 Mar 04
Indoors:	22.49i	Sanya	Richards	USA	26.2.85	2rA	NCAA	Fayetteville	12 Mar 04
Wind assisted to 22.66									
22.34	2.3	Katrin	Krabbe	GDR	22.11.69	1	WJ	Sudbury	30 Jul 88
22.49	2.3	Brenda	Morehead	USA	5.10.57	1	OT	Eugene	24 Jun 76
22.53	2.5	Valerie	Brisco	USA	6.7.60	2	AAU	Walnut	17 Jun 79
22.64	2.3	Chandra	Cheeseborough	USA	16.1.59	2	OT	Eugene	24 Jun 76
22.65	3.5	Shakedia	Jones	USA	15.3.79	1	NC-j	Edwardsville IL	27 Jun 98
22.66	5.0	Lauren	Hewitt	AUS	25.11.78	3	NC	Melbourne	2 Mar 97

400 METRES

Mark	Name		Nat	Born	Pos	Meet	Venue	Date
49.42	Grit	Breuer	GER	16.2.72	2	WCh	Tokyo	27 Aug 91
49.77	Christina	Brehmer	GDR	28.2.58	1		Dresden	9 May 76
49.89	Sanya	Richards	USA	26.2.85	2	NC/OT	Sacramento	17 Jul 04
50.01		Li Jing	CHN	14.2.80	1	NG	Shanghai	18 Oct 97
50.19	Marita	Koch	GDR	18.2.57	3	OD	Berlin	10 Jul 76
50.59	Fatima	Yusuf	NGR	2.5.71	1	HGP	Budapest	5 Aug 90
	50.5 hand				1	NC	Lagos	25 Aug 90
50.74	Monique	Henderson	USA	18.2.83	1		Norwalk	3 Jun 00
50.78	Danijela	Grgic	CRO	28.9.88	1	WJ	Beijing	17 Aug 06
50.86	Charity	Opara	NGR	20.5.72	2		Bologna	7 Sep 91
50.87	Denean	Howard	USA	5.10.64	1	TAC	Knoxville	20 Jun 82
50.87	Magdalena	Nedelcu	ROM	12.5.74	1	NC-j	Bucuresti	31 Jul 92

800 METRES

Mark	Name		Nat	Born	Pos	Meet	Venue	Date
1:57.18		Wang Yuan	CHN	8.4.76	2h2	NG	Beijing	8 Sep 93
1:57.45	Hildegard	Ullrich	GDR	20.12.59	5	EC	Praha	31 Aug 78
1:57.62		Lang Yinglai	CHN	22.8.79	1	NG	Shanghai	22 Oct 97
1:57.63	Maria	Mutola	MOZ	27.10.72	4	WCh	Tokyo	26 Aug 91
1:57.77		Lu Yi	CHN	10.4.74	4	NG	Beijing	9 Sep 93
1:57.86	Katrin	Wühn	GDR	19.11.65	1		Celje	5 May 84
1:58.16		Lin Nuo	CHN	18.1.80	3	NG	Shanghai	22 Oct 97
1:58.18	Marion	Hübner	GDR	29.9.62	2		Erfurt	2 Aug 81
1:58.24	Christine	Wachtel	GDR	6.1.65	3		Potsdam	25 May 84
1:58.37	Gabriela	Sedláková	SVK	2.3.68	4	ISTAF	Berlin	21 Aug 87
1:59.01		Liu Qifang	CHN	.2.79	4h3	NG	Shanghai	21 Oct 97

1500 METRES

Mark	Name		Nat	Born	Pos	Meet	Venue	Date
3:51.34		Lang Yinglai	CHN	22.8.79	2	NG	Shanghai	18 Oct 97
3:53.91		Yin Lili	CHN	11.11.79	3	NG	Shanghai	18 Oct 97
3:53.97		Lan Lixin	CHN	14.2.79	4	NG	Shanghai	18 Oct 97
3:54.52		Zhang Ling	CHN	13.4.80	5	NG	Shanghai	18 Oct 97
3:59.60	Gelete	Burka	ETH	15.2.86	5	GP	Rieti	28 Aug 05
3:59.81		Wang Yuan	CHN	8.4.76	7	NG	Beijing	11 Sep 93
3:59.96	Zola	Budd	GBR	26.5.66	3	VD	Bruxelles	30 Aug 85
4:00.05		Lu Yi	CHN	10.4.74	8	NG	Beijing	11 Sep 93
4:01.71		Li Ying	CHN	24.6.75	4h2	NG	Beijing	10 Sep 93
4:03.45	Anita	Weyermann	SUI	8.12.77	1	Athl	Lausanne	3 Jul 96
4:03.5	Svetlana	Guskova	MDA	19.8.59	3	Kuts	Podolsk	13 Aug 78
1 MILE: 4:17.57	Zola	Budd	GBR	26.5.66	3	WK	Zürich	21 Aug 85
2000 METRES: 5:33.15	Zola	Budd	GBR	26.5.66	1		London	13 Jul 84

3000 METRES

Mark	Wind	Name		Nat	Born	Pos	Meet	Venue	Date
8:28.83		Zola	Budd	GBR	26.5.66	3	GG	Roma	7 Sep 85
8:35.89		Sally	Barsosio	KEN	21.3.78	2	Herc	Monaco	16 Aug 97
8:36.45			Ma Ningning	CHN	1.6.76	4	NC	Jinan	6 Jun 93
8:38.97		Linet	Masai	KEN	5.12.89	5	GP	Rieti	9 Sep 07
8:39.90		Gelete	Burka	ETH	15.2.86	3	SGP	Doha	13 May 05
8:40.08		Gabriela	Szabo	ROM	14.11.75	3	EC	Helsinki	10 Aug 94
8:40.28		Meseret	Defar	ETH	19.11.83	10	VD	Bruxelles	30 Aug 02
8:41.86		Tirunesh	Dibaba	ETH	2.6.85	11	VD	Bruxelles	30 Aug 02
8:42.38		Pauline	Korikwiang	KEN	1.3.88	3	GS	Ostrava	30 May 06
8:42.39			Li Ying	CHN	24.6.75	8	NG	Beijing	13 Sep 93

5000 METRES

Mark	Wind	Name		Nat	Born	Pos	Meet	Venue	Date
14:30.88		Tirunesh	Dibaba	ETH	2.6.85	2	Bisl	Bergen (Fana)	11 Jun 04
14:35.18		Sentayehu	Ejigu	ETH	21.6.85	4	Bisl	Bergen (Fana)	11 Jun 04
14:39.96			Yin Lili	CHN	11.11.79	4	NG	Shanghai	23 Oct 97
14:45.33			Lan Lixin	CHN	14.2.79	2h2	NG	Shanghai	21 Oct 97
14:45.71			Song Liqing	CHN	20.1.80	3h2	NG	Shanghai	21 Oct 97
14:45.90			Jiang Bo	CHN	13.3.77	1		Nanjing	24 Oct 95
14:45.98		Pauline	Korikwiang	KEN	1.3.88	7	Bisl	Oslo	2 Jun 06
14:46.71		Sally	Barsosio	KEN	21.3.78	3	VD	Bruxelles	22 Aug 97
14:47.40		Worknesh	Kidane	ETH	21.11.81	7	OG	Sydney	25 Sep 00
14:48.07		Zola	Budd	GBR	26.5.66	1	McV	London (CP)	26 Aug 85
14:50.51		Workitu	Ayanu	ETH	19.4.87	2		New York (RI)	3 Jun 06

10,000 METRES

Mark	Wind	Name		Nat	Born	Pos	Meet	Venue	Date
30:31.55			Xing Huina	CHN	25.2.84	7	WCh	Saint-Denis	23 Aug 03
30:39.41			Lan Lixin	CHN	14.2.79	2	NG	Shanghai	19 Oct 97
30:39.98			Yin Lili	CHN	11.11.79	3	NG	Shanghai	19 Oct 97
30:59.92		Merima	Hashim	ETH	.81	3	NA	Heusden	5 Aug 00
31:06.20		Lucy	Wangui	KEN	24.3.84	1rA		Okayama	27 Sep 03
31:11.26			Song Liqing	CHN	20.1.80	7	NG	Shanghai	19 Oct 97
31:15.38		Sally	Barsosio	KEN	21.3.78	3	WCh	Stuttgart	21 Aug 93
31:16.50		Evelyne	Kimwei	KEN	25.8.87	1		Kobe	21 Oct 06
31:17.30			Zhang Yingying	CHN	4.1.90	1		Wuhan	2 Nov 07
31:21.25			Xie Fang	CHN	26.12.89	2		Wuhan	2 Nov 07
31:23.07			Chen Huirong	CHN	1.6.88	3		Wuhan	2 Nov 07

MARATHON

Mark	Wind	Name		Nat	Born	Pos	Meet	Venue	Date
2:23:37			Liu Min	CHN	29.11.83	1		Beijing	14 Oct 01
2:23:57			Zhu Xiaolin	CHN	20.4.84	4		Beijing	20 Oct 02
2:25:48			Jin Li	CHN	29.5.83	6		Beijing	14 Oct 01
2:26:34			Wei Yanan	CHN	6.12.81	1		Beijing	15 Oct 00
2:27:05			Chen Rong	CHN	18.5.88	1		Beijing	21 Oct 07
2:27:20			Zhang Yingying	CHN	4.1.90	2		Beijing	21 Oct 07
2:27:30			Ai Dongmei	CHN	15.10.79	3	NG	Beijing	4 Oct 97
2:27:37			Lu Cui	CHN	26.3.85	10		Beijing	20 Oct 02

3000 METRES STEEPLECHASE

Mark	Wind	Name		Nat	Born	Pos	Meet	Venue	Date
9:24.51		Ruth	Bisibori	KEN	2.1.88	1		Daegu	3 Oct 07
9:26.25			Liu Nian	CHN	26.4.88	1		Wuhan	2 Nov 07
9:30.70		Melissa	Rollison	AUS	13.4.83	1	GWG	Brisbane	4 Sep 01
9:33.19		Karoline Bjerkeli	Grøvdal	NOR	14.6.90	4		Neerpelt	2 Jun 07
9:34.28		Kristine Eikrem	Engeset	NOR	15.11.88	6	Bisl	Oslo	15 Jun 07
9:40.95		Caroline	Chepkurui	KEN	12.3.90	1	WJ	Beijing	17 Aug 06
9:46.19		Ancuta	Bobocel	ROM	3.10.87	2	WJ	Beijing	17 Aug 06
9:46.67		Mekdes	Bekele	ETH	20.1.87	1h1	WJ	Beijing	15 Aug 06
9:47.26		Gladys Jerotich	Kipkemboi	KEN	15.10.86	1	WJ	Grosseto	15 Jul 04
9:48.33			Jin Yuan	CHN	11.2.88	2		Eagle Rock	3 Jun 07

100 METRES HURDLES

Mark	Wind	Name		Nat	Born	Pos	Meet	Venue	Date
12.84	1.5	Aliuska	López	CUB	29.8.69	2	WUG	Zagreb	16 Jul 87
12.88	1.5	Yelena	Ovcharova	UKR	17.6.76	2	ECp	Villeneuve d'Ascq	25 Jun 95
12.89	1.3	Anay	Tejeda	CUB	3.4.83	1		Padova	1 Sep 02
12.91	1.8	Kristina	Castlin	USA	7.7.88	1	NCAA-r	Gainesville	26 May 07
12.92	0.0		Sun Hongwei	CHN	24.11.79	6	NG	Shanghai	18 Oct 97
12.95	1.5	Candy	Young	USA	21.5.62	2	AAU	Walnut	16 Jun 79
12.95A	1.5	Cinnamon	Sheffield	USA	8.3.70	2	NCAA	Provo	3 Jun 89
12.98	1.8	Queen	Harrison	USA	10.9.88	5	NCAA	Sacramento	8 Jun 07
13.00	0.7	Gloria	Kovarik	GDR	13.1.64	3h2	NC	Karl-Marx-Stadt	16 Jun 83

Mark	Wind	Name		Nat	Born	Pos	Meet	Venue	Date
13.00	2.0	Lyudmila	Khristosenko	UKR	14.10.66	1	NC-j	Krasnodar	16 Jul 85
13.01	0.4	Sally	McLellan	AUS	19.9.86	1		Brisbane	27 Nov 05
Wind assisted to 12.99									
12.81	3.4	Anay	Tejeda	CUB	3.4.83	1	WJ	Kingston	21 Jul 02
12.82	2.1	Kristina	Castlin	USA	7.7.88	1		College Park	21 Apr 07
12.90	3.0	Adrianna	Lamalle	FRA	27.9.82	1		Fort-de-France	28 Apr 01

400 METRES HURDLES

54.40			Wang Xing	CHN	30.11.86	2	NG	Nanjing	21 Oct 05
54.70		Lashinda	Demus	USA	10.3.83	1	WJ	Kingston	19 Jul 02
54.93			Li Rui	CHN	22.11.79	1	NG	Shanghai	22 Oct 97
55.11		Kaliese	Spencer	JAM	6.4.87	1	WJ	Beijing	17 Aug 06
55.15			Huang Xiaoxiao	CHN	3.3.83	2	NG	Guangzhou	22 Nov 01
55.20		Lesley	Maxie	USA	4.1.67	2	TAC	San Jose	9 Jun 84
55.20A		Jana	Pittman	AUS	9.11.82	1		Pietersburg	18 Mar 00
55.22		Tiffany	Ross	USA	5.2.83	2	NCAA	Baton Rouge	31 May 02
55.26		Ionela	Tîrlea	ROM	9.2.76	1	Nik	Nice	12 Jul 95
55.35		Nicole	Leach	USA	18.7.87	1s2	NCAA	Sacramento	9 Jun 06
55.43			Li Shuju	CHN	20.7.81	1h2	NG	Shanghai	21 Oct 97
Drugs disqualification: 54.54			Peng Yinghua ¶	CHN	21.2.79	(2)	NG	Shanghai	22 Oct 97

HIGH JUMP

2.01		Olga	Turchak	KZK	5.3.67	2	GWG	Moskva	7 Jul 86
2.01		Heike	Balck	GDR	19.8.70	1	vURS-j	Karl-Marx-Stadt	18 Jun 89
2.00		Stefka	Kostadinova	BUL	25.3.65	1		Sofiya	25 Aug 84
2.00		Alina	Astafei	ROM	7.6.69	1	WJ	Sudbury	29 Jul 88
1.98		Silvia	Costa	CUB	4.5.64	2	WUG	Edmonton	11 Jul 83
1.98		Yelena	Yelesina	RUS	5.4.70	1	Druzh	Nyiregyháza	13 Aug 88
1.97		Svetlana	Isaeva	BUL	18.3.67	2		Sofiya	25 May 86
1.96A		Charmaine	Gale	RSA	27.2.64	1	NC-j	Bloemfontein	4 Apr 81
1.96i		Desislava	Aleksandrova	BUL	27.10.75	2	EI	Paris	12 Mar 94
1.96		Marina	Kuptsova	RUS	22.12.81	1	NC	Tula	26 Jul 00
1.96		Blanka	Vlasic	CRO	8.11.83	1	WJ	Kingston	20 Jul 02

POLE VAULT

4.48i		Silke	Spiegelburg	GER	17.3.86	2		Münster	25 Aug 05
		4.42				3		Beckum	21 Aug 05
4.47i		Yelena	Isinbayeva	RUS	3.6.82	1		Budapest	10 Feb 01
		4.46				2	ISTAF	Berlin	31 Aug 01
4.46i			Zhang Yingning	CHN	6.1.90	1		Shanghai	15 Mar 07
		4.45				1		Changsha	29 Oct 06
4.45i			Zhao Yingying	CHN	15.2.86	3		Madrid	24 Feb 05
		4.40				1		Nanjing	1 May 04
4.42		Yvonne	Buschbaum	GER	14.7.80	1		Rheinau-Freistett	27 Jun 99
4.41		Floé	Kühnert	GER	6.3.84	1		Mannheim	15 Jun 02
4.40		Valeriya	Volik	RUS	15.11.89	1	NC-23	Kazan	8 Jul 06
4.40		Vicky	Parnov	AUS	24.10.90	2		Saulheim	30 Jun 07
4.40			Zhou Yang	CHN	16.5.88	1		Wuhan	2 Nov 07
4.37i		Ekateríni	Stefanídi	GRE	4.2.90	1		Athína (P)	20 Feb 05
4.35		Yuliya	Golubchikova	RUS	27.3.83	2	Mos Ch	Moskva	28 Jun 02
4.35		Elizaveta 'Lisa'	Ryshich	GER	27.9.88	1j		Mannheim	7 Jul 06
4.35		Minna	Nikkanen	FIN	9.4.88	1	EJ	Hengelo	21 Jul 07
Exhibition: 4.45		Yvonne	Buschbaum	GER	14.7.80	1		Zeiskam	17 Jul 99

LONG JUMP

7.14	1.1	Heike	Daute	GDR	16.12.64	1	PTS	Bratislava	4 Jun 83
7.00	-0.2	Birgit	Grosshennig	GDR	21.2.65	2		Berlin	9 Jun 84
6.94	-0.5	Magdalena	Khristova	BUL	25.2.77	2		Kalamáta	22 Jun 96
6.91	0.0	Anisoara	Cusmir	ROM	28.6.62	1		Bucuresti	23 May 81
6.90	1.4	Beverly	Kinch	GBR	14.1.64	*	WCh	Helsinki	14 Aug 83
6.88	0.6	Natalya	Shevchenko	RUS	28.12.66	2		Sochi	26 May 84
6.84		Larisa	Baluta	UKR	13.8.65	2		Krasnodar	6 Aug 83
6.82	1.8	Fiona	May	GBR	12.12.69	*	WJ	Sudbury	30 Jul 88
6.81	1.6	Carol	Lewis	USA	8.8.63	1	TAC	Knoxville	20 Jun 82
6.81	1.4	Yelena	Davydova	KZK	16.11.67	1	NC-j	Krasnodar	17 Jul 85
6.80	0.2		Peng Fengmei	CHN	2.7.79	2	NGP	Chengdu	18 Apr 98
Wind assisted									
7.27	2.2	Heike	Daute	GDR	16.12.64	1	WCh	Helsinki	14 Aug 83
6.93	4.6	Beverly	Kinch	GBR	14.1.64	5	WCh	Helsinki	14 Aug 83
6.88	2.1	Fiona	May	GBR	12.12.69	1	WJ	Sudbury	30 Jul 88
6.84	2.8	Anu	Kaljurand	EST	16.4.69	2		Riga	4 Jun 88

TRIPLE JUMP

Mark	Wind	Name		Nat	Born	Pos	Meet	Venue	Date
14.62	1.0	Teresa	Marinova	BUL	5.9.77	1	WC	Sydney	25 Aug 96
14.57	0.2		Huang Qiuyan	CHN	25.1.80	1	NG	Shanghai	19 Oct 97
14.52	0.6	Anastasiya	Ilyina	RUS	16.1.82	q	WJ	Santiago de Chile	20 Oct 00
14.46	1.0		Peng Fengmei	CHN	2.7.79	1		Chengdu	18 Apr 98
14.43	0.6	Kaire	Leibak	EST-J	21.5.88	1	WJ	Beijing	17 Aug 06
14.38	-0.7		Xie Limei	CHN	27.6.86	1	AsiC	Inchon	1 Sep 05
14.37i	-		Ren Ruiping	CHN	1.2.76	3	WI	Barcelona	11 Mar 95
		14.36	0.0			1	NC	Beijing	1 Jun 94
14.32	-0.1	Yelena	Lysak ¶	RUS	19.10.75	1		Voronezh	18 Jun 94
14.29	1.2	Mabel	Gay	CUB	5.5.83	1		La Habana	5 Apr 02
14.23			Li Jiahui	CHN	8.8.79	1	Asi-J	Bangkok	6 Nov 97
14.22	1.2	Yusmay	Bicet	CUB	8.12.83	2		La Habana	23 Feb 02
14.21	1.8	Dailenis	Alcántara	CUB	10.8.91	1		La Habana	1 Mar 07
Wind assisted									
14.83A	8.3		Ren Ruiping	CHN	1.2.76	1	NC	Taiyuan	21 May 95
14.43	2.7	Yelena	Lysak ¶	RUS	19.10.75	1	WJ	Lisboa	21 Jul 94

SHOT

Mark	Wind	Name		Nat	Born	Pos	Meet	Venue	Date
20.54		Astrid	Kumbernuss	GDR	5.2.70	1	vFIN-j	Orimattila	1 Jul 89
20.51i		Heidi	Krieger	GDR	20.7.65	2		Budapest	8 Feb 84
		20.24				5		Split	30 Apr 84
20.23		Ilke	Wyludda	GDR	28.3.69	1	NC-j	Karl-Marx-Stadt	16 Jul 88
20.12		Ilona	Schoknecht	GDR	24.9.56	2	NC	Erfurt	23 Aug 75
20.02			Cheng Xiaoyan	CHN	30.11.75	3	NC	Beijing	5 Jun 94
19.90		Stephanie	Storp	FRG	28.11.68	1		Hamburg	16 Aug 87
19.63			Wang Yawen	CHN	23.8.73	1		Shijiazhuang	25 Apr 92
19.57		Grit	Haupt	GDR	4.6.66	1		Gera	7 Jul 84
19.48		Ines	Wittich	GDR	14.11.69	5		Leipzig	29 Jul 87
19.42		Simone	Michel	GDR	18.12.60	3	vSU	Leipzig	23 Jun 79
19.23			Zhang Zhiying	CHN	19.7.73	1	NC-j	Hangzhou	8 May 92

DISCUS

Mark	Wind	Name		Nat	Born	Pos	Meet	Venue	Date
74.40		Ilke	Wyludda	GDR	28.3.69	2		Berlin	13 Sep 88
		75.36 unofficial meeting				2		Berlin	6 Sep 88
67.38		Irina	Meszynski	GDR	24.3.62	1		Berlin	14 Aug 81
67.00		Jana	Günther	GDR	7.1.68	6	NC	Potsdam	20 Aug 87
66.80		Svetla	Mitkova	BUL	17.6.64	1		Sofiya	2 Aug 83
66.60		Astrid	Kumbernuss	GDR	5.2.70	1		Berlin	20 Jul 88
66.34		Franka	Dietzsch	GDR	22.1.68	2		Saint-Denis	11 Jun 87
66.30		Jana	Lauren	GDR	28.6.70	1	vURS-j	Karl-Marx-Stadt	18 Jun 89
66.08			Cao Qi	CHN	15.1.74	1	NG	Beijing	12 Sep 93
65.96		Grit	Haupt	GDR	4.6.66	3		Leipzig	13 Jul 84
65.22		Daniela	Costian	ROM	30.4.65	3		Nitra	26 Aug 84

HAMMER

Mark	Wind	Name		Nat	Born	Pos	Meet	Venue	Date
73.24			Zhang Wenxiu	CHN	22.3.86	1	NC	Changsha	24 Jun 05
71.71		Kamila	Skolimowska	POL	4.11.82	1	GPF	Melbourne	9 Sep 01
70.39		Mariya	Smolyachkova	BLR	10.2.85	1		Staiki	26 Jun 04
69.73		Natalya	Zolotukhina	UKR	4.1.85	1		Kiev	24 Jul 04
68.74		Arasay	Thondike	CUB	28.5.86	2	Barr	La Habana	2 May 05
68.50		Martina	Danisová	SVK	21.3.83	1		Kladno	16 Jun 01
68.49		Anna	Bulgakova	RUS	17.1.88	6		Sochi	26 May 07
68.40		Bianca	Achilles	GER	17.4.81	1		Dortmund	25 Sep 99
68.18		Ivana	Brkljacic	CRO	25.1.83	1		Pula	28 Apr 00
67.38		Bianca	Perie	ROM	1.6.90	1	WJ	Beijing	16 Aug 06

JAVELIN

Mark	Wind	Name		Nat	Born	Pos	Meet	Venue	Date
62.93			Xue Juan	CHN	10.2.86	1	NG	Changsha	27 Oct 03
61.99			Wang Yaning	CHN	4.1.80	1	NC	Huizhou	14 Oct 99
61.79		Nikolett	Szabó	HUN	3.3.80	1		Schwechat	23 May 99
61.61			Chang Chunfeng	CHN	4.5.88	1	NC-j	Chengdu	4 Jun 07
61.49			Liang Lili	CHN	16.11.83	1	NC	Benxi	1 Jun 02
61.38		Annika	Suthe	GER	15.10.85	1-j		Halle	23 May 04
60.45		Sandra	Schaffarzik	GER	22.6.87	1	WJ	Beijing	19 Aug 06
Pre 1999 specification									
71.88		Antoaneta	Todorova	BUL	8.6.63	1	ECp	Zagreb	15 Aug 81
71.82		Ivonne	Leal	CUB	27.2.66	1	WUG	Kobe	30 Aug 85
70.12		Karen	Forkel	GDR	24.9.70	1	EJ	Varazdin	26 Aug 89
68.94		Trine	Solberg	NOR	18.4.66	1	vURS	Oslo	16 Jul 85

Mark	Wind	Name		Nat	Born	Pos	Meet	Venue	Date
68.38		Antje	Kempe	GDR	23.6.63	Q	EC	Athína	8 Sep 82
68.17		Osleidys	Menéndez	CUB	14.11.79	1	WJ	Annecy	29 Jul 98
67.32		Regina	Kempter	GDR	4.4.67	2	NC	Jena	27 Jun 86

HEPTATHLON

Mark		Name		Nat	Born	Pos	Meet	Venue	Date
6768w		Tatyana	Chernova	RUS	29.1.88	1		Arles	3 Jun 07
		13.04w/6.1	1.82	13.57	23.59w/5.2	6.61/1.2		53.43	2:15.05
	6227					1	WJ	Beijing	19 Aug 06
		13.70/1.6	1.80	12.18	24.05/0.3	6.35/-0.4		50.51	2:25.49
6542		Carolina	Klüft	SWE	2.2.83	1	EC	München	10 Aug 02
		13.33/-0.3	1.89	13.16	23.71/-0.3	6.36/1.1		47.61	2:17.99
6465		Sibylle	Thiele	GDR	6.3.65	1	EJ	Schwechat	28 Aug 83
		13.49	1.90	14.63	24.07	6.65		36.22	2:18.36
6436		Sabine	Braun	FRG	19.6.65	1	vBUL	Mannheim	9 Jun 84
		13.68	1.78	13.09	23.88	6.03		52.14	2:09.41
6428		Svetla	Dimitrova ¶	BUL	27.1.70	1	NC	Sofiya	18 Jun 89
		13.49/-0/7	1.77	13.98	23.59/-0.2	6.49/0.7		40.10	2:11.10
6403		Emilia	Dimitrova	BUL	13.11.67	6	GWG	Moskva	7 Jul 86
		13.73	1.76	13.46	23.17	6.29		43.30	2:09.85
6276		Larisa	Nikitina	RUS	29.4.65	8	URS Ch	Kiyev	21 Jun 84
		13.87/1.6	1.86	14.04	25.26/-0.7	6.31/0.1		48.62	2:22.76
6218		Jana	Sobotka	GDR	3.10.65	6	OD	Potsdam	21 Jul 84
		14.40	1.74	13.28	24.19	6.27		43.64	2:06.83
6198		Anke	Schmidt	GDR	5.2.68	7		Götzis	24 May 87
		13.80/0.9	1.72	13.32	23.82/0.3	6.63/2.0		35.78	2:12.44
6194		Camelia	Cornateanu	ROM	23.1.67	2	NC	Pitesti	8 Aug 86
		14.35	1.86	14.70	24.97	6.15		38.94	2:11.93
Drugs disqualification: 6534		Svetla	Dimitrova	BUL	27.1.70	H	ECp	Helmond	16 Jul 89
		13.30/1.0	1.84	14.35	23.33/-2.2	6.47/-1.4		39.20	2:13.56

10 KILOMETRES WALK

Mark	Name		Nat	Born	Pos	Meet	Venue	Date
41:55	Irina	Stankina	RUS	25.3.77	1	NCw-j	Adler	11 Feb 95
41:57		Gao Hongmiao	CHN	17.3.74	2	NG	Beijing	8 Sep 93
42:44		Long Yuwen	CHN	1.8.75	3	NC	Shenzen	18 Feb 93
42:45		Li Yuxin	CHN	4.12.74	4		Shenzhen	18 Feb 93
42:47		Liu Hongyu	CHN	1.12.75	5	NC	Shenzen	18 Feb 93
42:50		Gu Yan	CHN	17.3.74	4	NG	Beijing	8 Sep 93
42:53.9t		Tan Lihong	CHN	13.2.73	6	NC	Jinan	15 Mar 92
42:59	Anisya	Kornikova	RUS	23.10.89	1	NC-j/w	Adler	17 Feb 07
43:07		Song Lijuan	CHN	1.2.76	6	NG	Beijing	8 Sep 93
43:10.4		Zhang Qinghua	CHN	6.3.73	8	NC	Jinan	15 Mar 92

20 KILOMETRES WALK

Mark	Name		Nat	Born	Pos	Meet	Venue	Date
1:27:16		Song Hongjuan	CHN	4.7.84	1	NC	Yangzhou	14 Apr 03
1:27:34		Jiang Jing	CHN	23.10.85	2	WCp	Naumburg	2 May 04
1:27:35	Natalya	Fedoskina	RUS	25.6.80	2	WCp	Mézidon-Canon	2 May 99
1:27:37		Bai Yanmin	CHN	29.6.87	1	NG	Nanjing	20 Oct 05
1:28:00	Anisya	Kornikova	RUS	23.10.89	2	RWC	Saransk	29 Sep 07
1:28:23		Song Xiaoling	CHN	21.12.87	2		Yangzhou	22 Apr 06
1:28:26		Liu Hong	CHN	12.5.87	3		Yangzhou	22 Apr 06

4 X 100 METRES RELAY

Mark	Nat	Team	Pos	Meet	Venue	Date
43.29	USA (Blue)	Knight, Tarmoh, Olear, Mayo	1		Eugene	8 Aug 06
43.40	JAM	Simpson, Stewart, McLaughlin, Facey	1	WJ	Kingston	20 Jul 02
43.44A	NGR	Utondu, Iheagwam, Onyali, Ogunkoya	1	AfrG	Nairobi	9 Aug 87
43.48	GDR	Breuer, Krabbe, Dietz, Henke	1	WJ	Sudbury	31 Jul 88
	Unsanctioned race 43.33	Breuer, Krabbe, Dietz, Henke	1		Berlin	20 Jul 88
43.68	FRA	Vouaux, Jacques-Sebastien, Kamga, Banco	3	WJ	Grosseto	18 Jul 04
43.87	URS	Lapshina, Doronina, Bulatova, Kovalyova	1	vGDR-j	Leningrad	20 Jun 87
43.98	BRA	Silva, Leoncio, Krasucki, Santos	2	PAm-J	São Paulo	7 Jul 07
44.04	CUB	Riquelme, Allen, López, Valdivia	2	WJ	Sudbury	31 Jul 88

4 X 400 METRES RELAY

Mark	Nat	Team	Pos	Meet	Venue	Date
3:27.60	USA	Anderson, Kidd, Smith, Hastings	1	WJ	Grosseto	18 Jul 04
3:28.39	GDR	Derr, Fabert, Wöhlk, Breuer	1	WJ	Sudbury	31 Jul 88
3:29.66	JAM	Stewart, Morgan, Walker, Hall	1	PennR	Philadelphia	28 Apr 01
3:30.03	RUS	Talko, Shapayeva, Soldatova, Kostetskaya	2	WJ	Grosseto	18 Jul 04
3:30.38	AUS	Scamps, R Poetschka, Hanigan, Andrews	1	WJ	Plovdiv	12 Aug 90
3:30.46	GBR	Wall, Spencer, James,. Miller	2	WJ	Kingston	21 Jul 02
3:30.72	BUL	Kireva, Angelova, Rashova, Dimitrova	3	v2N	Sofiya	24 Jul 83
3:30.84	NGR	Abugan, Odumosu, Eze, Adesanya	2	WJ	Beijing	20 Aug 06

MEN'S WORLD LISTS 2007

60 METRES INDOORS

Mark	Name		Nat	Born	Pos	Meet	Venue	Date
6.46	Marcus	Brunson	USA	24.4.78	1		Karlsruhe	11 Feb
6.49	Olusoji	Fasuba	NGR	9.7.84	1	Spark	Stuttgart	3 Feb
6.51		Brunson			2	Spark	Stuttgart	3 Feb
6.51	Jason	Gardener	GBR	17.9.75	1	EI	Birmingham	4 Mar
6.52	Jacoby	Ford	USA	27.7.87	1		Clemson	24 Feb
6.53		Fasuba			1h2	Spark	Stuttgart	3 Feb
6.53		Ford			1h1		Clemson	23 Feb
6.54		Brunson			1h3	Spark	Stuttgart	3 Feb
6.54	Preston	Perry	USA	13.9.83	1		Houston	10 Feb
6.54		Fasuba			1		Paris	23 Feb
6.54	Samuel	Francis (NGR)	QAT	27.3.87	1	AsiG	Macau	30 Oct
6.55	Craig	Pickering	GBR	16.10.86	1		Glasgow	27 Jan
6.55	Shawn	Crawford	USA	14.1.78	1	BIG	Boston (R)	27 Jan
6.55	Demi	Omole	USA	29.7.85	1r2		Notre Dame	3 Feb
6.55		Pickering			2h2	Spark	Stuttgart	3 Feb
6.55	Ronald	Pognon	FRA	16.11.82	1		Aubière	9 Feb
6.55		Francis			1s1	AsiG	Macau	30 Oct
	(17/10)							
6.56	DaBryan	Blanton	USA	3.7.84	1	NC	Boston (R)	25 Feb
6.56	Travis	Padgett	USA	13.12.86	1	NCAA	Fayetteville	10 Mar
6.56	Yahya Saed	Al-Kahes	KSA	19.2.86	2	AsiG	Macau	30 Oct
6.57	Brendan	Christian	ANT	11.12.83	2		Houston	10 Feb
6.59	Christian	Blum	GER	10.3.87	1	NC	Leipzig	17 Feb
6.59		Wen Yongyi	CHN	3.01.87	1r1	NGP	Beijing	20 Mar
6.60	Trell	Kimmons	USA	13.7.85	1		Fayetteville	20 Jan
6.60	Mark	Jelks	USA	10.4.84	3	BIG	Boston (R)	27 Jan
6.60	Mikhail	Yegorychev	RUS	21.7.77	1		Moskva	28 Jan
6.60	Fredi	Mayola	CUB	1.11.77	3h2	Spark	Stuttgart	3 Feb
	(20)							
6.60A	John	Woods	USA	19.6.82	1		Golden	16 Feb
6.60	Ronnie	Pines	USA	27.8.83	1		Norman	17 Feb
6.60	Simeon	Williamson	GBR	16.1.86	3	GP	Birmingham	17 Feb
6.60	Morné	Nagel	RSA	23.2.78	1		Chemnitz	23 Feb
6.60	Clement	Campbell	JAM	19.12.75	2		Chemnitz	23 Feb
6.60		Du Bing	CHN	8.4.85	1r2	NGP	Beijing	20 Mar
6.61	Gregory	Bolden	USA	30.6.84	1r2		New York	3 Feb
6.61	Jarkko	Ruostekivi	FIN	5.4.85	3		Aubière	9 Feb
6.61	Kael	Becerra	CHI	4.11.85	1		Valencia	10 Feb
6.61	Francis	Obikwelu	POR	22.11.78	2h2	GP	Birmingham	17 Feb
	(30)							
6.61	Paul	Hession	IRL	27.1.83	2h1	ECh	Birmingham	3 Mar
6.61	Walter	Dix	USA	31.1.86	1h1	NCAA	Fayetteville	9 Mar
6.62	Simone	Collio	ITA	27.12.79	2h1		Wien	30 Jan
6.62	Nicolas	Macrozonaris	CAN	22.8.80	1		Saskatoon	4 Feb
6.62	Ronny	Ostwald	GER	7.4.74	2	NC	Leipzig	17 Feb
6.62	Massimiliano	Donati	ITA	16.6.79	1	NC	Ancona	18 Feb
6.62	Ivory	Williams	USA	2.5.85	1h2	NC	Boston (R)	4 Feb
6.62	Kyle	Farmer	USA	15.4.83	3	NC	Boston (R)	25 Feb
6.62	Fabio	Cerutti	ITA	26.9.85	2s2	EI	Birmingham	3 Mar
6.63	Anson	Henry	CAN	9.3.79	1		Samara	3 Feb
	(40)							
6.63	Ryan	Scott	GBR	20.2.87	3s1	EI	Birmingham	3 Mar
6.63	Matic	Osovnikar	SLO	19.1.80	4	EI	Birmingham	4 Mar
6.63	Ibrahim	Kabia	USA	28.7.86	5	NCAA	Fayetteville	10 Mar
6.63		Zhang Peimeng	CHN	13.3.87	2r2	NGP	Beijing	20 Mar
6.64	Johnie	Drake	USA	28.3.83	1		Ann Arbor	20 Jan
6.64	Lerone	Clarke	JAM	12.6.81	2	Mill	New York	2 Feb
6.64	Julian	Reus	GER-J	29.4.88	1	NC-j	Sindelfingen	11 Feb
6.64	Lukasz	Chyla	POL	31.3.81	1	NC	Spala	17 Feb
6.64	Chinedu	Oriala	NGR	17.12.81	3		Paris	23 Feb
6.64	Jeremy	Hall	USA-J	27.1.88	1	SEC	Lexington	25 Feb
	(50)							
6.64	Ricardo	Shaw	USA	19.6.77	2s1	NC	Boston (R)	25 Feb
6.64	Richard	Thompson	TRI	7.6.85	2	SEC	Lexington	25 Feb
6.64	Rubin	Williams	USA	9.7.83	3h1	NCAA	Fayetteville	9 Mar

Outdoors: Times during 100m: 26 Aug Osaka: 6.42 Asafa Powell, 6.44 Tyson Gay, 6.47 Derrick Atkins, 6.60 Marlon Devonish

100 METRES

Mark	Wind	Name		Nat	Born	Pos	Meet	Venue	Date
9.74	1.7	Asafa	Powell	JAM	23.11.82	1h2	GP	Rieti	9 Sep
9.78	0.0		Powell			1	GP	Rieti	9 Sep
9.83	-0.3		Powell			1	WAF	Stuttgart	22 Sep
9.84	-0.5	Tyson	Gay	USA	9.9.82	1	NC	Indianapolis	22 Jun
9.84	-0.3		Powell			1	VD	Bruxelles	14 Sep
9.85	-0.5		Gay			1	WCh	Osaka	26 Aug
9.90	0.5		Powell			1	GGala	Roma	13 Jul
9.91	-0.5	Derrick	Atkins	BAH	5.1.84	2	WCh	Osaka	26 Aug
9.93	0.0	Walter	Dix	USA	31.1.86	1	NCAA	Sacramento	8 Jun
9.94	0.9		Powell			1rA	Bisl	Oslo	15 Jun
9.95	0.3		Atkins			1	GP	Athína	2 Jul
9.96	-0.5		Powell			3	WCh	Osaka	26 Aug
9.96	0.0	Wallace	Spearmon	USA	24.12.84	1	Golden	Shanghai	28 Sep
9.97	0.5		Powell			1	Takac	Beograd	29 May
9.97	-1.1		Gay			1s2	NC	Indianapolis	22 Jun
9.98	2.0		Atkins			1		Berkeley	28 Apr
9.98	1.9		Gay			1h2	NC	Indianapolis	21 Jun
9.99	0.9	Samuel	Francis (NGR)	QAT	27.3.87	1	AsiC	Amman	26 Jul
10.00	-0.1		Atkins			1	Gaz	Saint-Denis	6 Jul
10.00	0.1		Gay			1s2	WCh	Osaka	26 Aug
10.01	1.3	Joshua 'J.J.'	Johnson	USA	10.5.76	1h1	Aragón	Zaragoza	28 Jul
10.01	1.8	Mickey	Grimes	USA	10.10.76	1h2	Aragón	Zaragoza	28 Jul
10.01	0.8		Powell			1q1	WC	Osaka	25 Aug
10.02	1.3	Darrel	Brown	TRI	11.10.84	1		Kingston	5 May
10.02	1.8	Trindon	Holliday (10)	USA	27.4.86	1s1	NCAA	Sacramento	6 Jun
10.02	0.5		Atkins			2	GGala	Roma	13 Jul
10.02	1.8	Clement	Campbell	JAM	19.2.75	2h2	Aragón	Zaragoza	28 Jul
10.02	-0.8		Gay			1	LGP	London	3 Aug
10.02	0.8		Atkins			2q1	WCh	Osaka	25 Aug
10.02	0.0		Gay			2	Golden	Shanghai	28 Sep
		(30/11)							
10.03	0.7	Usain	Bolt	JAM	21.8.86	1rA	Vard	Réthimno	18 Jul
10.03	0.0	Michael	Frater	JAM	6.10.82	2	GP	Rieti	9 Sep
10.04	1.9	Mark	Jelks	USA	10.4.84	1h4	NC	Indianapolis	21 Jun
10.05	1.3	Steve	Mullings	JAM	29.11.82	2h1	Aragón	Zaragoza	28 Jul
10.06	0.9	Francis	Obikwelu	POR	22.11.78	2rA	Bisl	Oslo	15 Jun
10.06	1.3	Marlon	Devonish	GBR	1.6.76	1rB	Athl	Lausanne	10 Jul
10.06	0.1	Churandy	Martina	AHO	3.7.84	1s1	PAm	Rio de Janeiro	23 Jul
10.06	-0.3	Jaysuma	Saidy Ndure (GAM)	NOR	1.1.84	2	WAF	Stuttgart	22 Sep
10.07	1.9	Leroy	Dixon	USA	20.6.83	2h4	NC	Indianapolis	21 Jun
		(20)							
10.07	-0.5	Olusoji	Fasuba	NGR	9.7.84	4	WCh	Osaka	26 Aug
10.08	1.9	Joshua	Ross	AUS	9.2.81	1	NC	Brisbane	10 Mar
10.09	0.0	Travis	Padgett	USA	13.12.86	3	NCAA	Sacramento	8 Jun
10.09	1.9	Monzavous Rae	Edwards	USA	7.5.81	2h2	NC	Indianapolis	21 Jun
10.09	-1.1	Leonard	Scott	USA	19.1.80	2s2	NC	Indianapolis	22 Jun
10.09	1.9	Richard	Thompson	TRI	7.6.85	1s1	NC	Port of Spain	23 Jun
10.10	1.9	Michael	Rodgers	USA	24.4.85	3h2	NC	Indianapolis	21 Jun
10.10	1.9	Demi	Omole	USA	29.7.85	3h4	NC	Indianapolis	21 Jun
10.10	0.2	Simeon	Williamson	GBR	16.1.86	1	EU23	Debrecen	13 Jul
10.11	1.2	Yohan	Blake	JAM-J	26.12.89	1	Carifta	Providenciales	7 Apr
		(30)							
10.11	1.1	Darvis	Patton	USA	4.12.77	2h1	adidas	Carson	20 May
10.11	1.0	Nesta	Carter	JAM	10.10.85	3	NC	Kingston	23 Jun
10.12	1.8	DaBryan	Blanton	USA	3.7.84	1		Salamanca	4 Jul
10.13	1.3	Ivory	Williams	USA	2.5.85	1rA	ModR	Modesto	5 May
10.13	1.9	Shawn	Crawford	USA	14.1.78	4h4	NC	Indianapolis	21 Jun
10.13	1.3	Tyrone	Edgar	GBR	29.3.82	2rB	Athl	Lausanne	10 Jul
10.13	0.8	Matic	Osovnikar	SLO	19.1.80	3q1	WCh	Osaka	25 Aug
10.14A	0.0	Vicente Lenilson	de Lima	BRA	4.6.77	1		La Paz	1 Jun
10.14	1.9	Preston	Perry	USA	13.9.83	4h2	NC	Indianapolis	21 Jun
10.14	1.9	Keston	Bledman	TRI-J	8.3.88	2s1	NC	Port of Spain	23 Jun
		(40)							
10.14	0.2	Craig	Pickering	GBR	16.10.86	2	EU23	Debrecen	13 Jul
10.14	1.0	Nobuharu	Asahara	JPN	21.6.72	1h1	WCh	Osaka	25 Aug
10.14	1.7	Kim	Collins	SKN	5.4.76	3h2	GP	Rieti	9 Sep
10.14	0.0	Simone	Collio	ITA	27.12.79	4	GP	Rieti	9 Sep
10.15	1.3	Marvin	Anderson	JAM	12.5.82	2rA	ModR	Modesto	5 May

Mark	Wind	Name		Nat	Born	Pos	Meet	Venue	Date
10.15	1.3	Lerone	Clarke	JAM	2.10.81	3=		Kingston	5 May
10.15	1.9	Guus	Hoogmoed	NED	27.9.81	1	ECp-1A	Vaasa	23 Jun
10.15	0.2	Dwight	Thomas	JAM	23.9.80	1	NA	Heusden-Zolder	28 Jul
10.15	1.7	Marc	Burns	TRI	7.1.83	4h2	GP	Rieti	9 Sep
10.15	0.6	Naoki	Tsukahara	JPN	10.5.85	1		Tokyo	16 Sep
		(50)							
10.16A	1.9	John	Woods	USA	19.6.82	1		Fort Collins	21 Apr
10.16	2.0	Jeff	Laynes	USA	3.10.70	2		Berkeley	28 Apr
10.16A	0.0	José Carlos	Moreira	BRA	28.9.83	1	Iriarte	Cochabamba	3 Jun
10.16	1.6	Martial	Mbandjock	FRA	14.10.85	1s2	EU23	Debrecen	12 Jul
10.16	1.0	Brendan	Christian	ANT	11.12.83	1h2	WCh	Osaka	25 Aug
10.16	0.0	Rikki	Fifton	GBR	17.6.85	4	Golden	Shanghai	28 Sep
10.17	0.9	Adam	Miller	AUS	22.6.84	1s2	NC	Brisbane	10 Mar
10.17	1.8	Mike	LeBlanc	CAN	25.2.87	2s1	NCAA	Sacramento	6 Jun
10.17	1.3	Patrick	Johnson	AUS	26.9.72	4h1	Aragón	Zaragoza	28 Jul
10.17	-0.6	Mark	Lewis-Francis	GBR	4.9.82	2q3	WCh	Osaka	25 Aug
		(60)							
10.18	1.7	Chris	Williams	JAM	15.3.72	2	GP	Dakar	28 Apr
10.18	0.9	Kendall	Stevens	USA	26.1.83	2h3	NC	Indianapolis	21 Jun
10.18	1.9	Paul	Hession	IRL	27.1.83	2	ECp-1A	Vaasa	23 Jun
10.18	1.6	Henry (Jenris)	Vizcaíno	CUB	16.5.80	2h1	PAm	Rio de Janeiro	23 Jul
10.18	1.8	Ángel David	Rodríguez	ESP	25.4.80	5h2	Aragón	Zaragoza	28 Jul
10.19	1.8	Orlando	Reid	JAM	3.7.82	3s1	NCAA	Sacramento	6 Jun
10.19	0.9	Ricardo	Williams	JAM	29.9.76	3	Odlozil	Praha	13 Jun
10.19	1.9	Garry	Jones	USA	24.7.84	5h2	NC	Indianapolis	21 Jun
10.20	1.1	Dwight	Phillips	USA	1.10.77	2h3	adidas	Carson	20 May
10.20	1.9	Carlos	Moore	USA	8.5.84	6h2	NC	Indianapolis	21 Jun
		(70)							
10.20	-0.6	Anson	Henry	CAN	9.3.79	3q3	WCh	Osaka	25 Aug
10.21	1.5	Gregory	Bolden	USA	30.6.84	1		Lake Buena Vista	24 Mar
10.21	1.8	Chris	Johnson	USA	28.4.82	1		Monroe	28 Apr
10.21	-1.3	Terrence	Trammell	USA	23.11.78	2		Baie Mahault	1 May
10.21	0.5	Michael Ray	Garvin	USA	29.9.86	1h1	NCAA-r	Gainesville	25 May
10.21	0.9	Jordan	Vaden	USA	15.9.78	4h3	NC	Indianapolis	21 Jun
10.22A	1.1	Franklin	Nazareno	ECU	24.4.87	1		Cuenca	10 Mar
10.22	1.7	Deji	Aliu	NGR	22.11.75	3	GP	Dakar	28 Apr
10.22	1.9	Kelly	Willie	USA	7.9.82	5h4	NC	Indianapolis	21 Jun
10.22	-0.5	J-Mee	Samuels	USA	20.5.87	5	NC	Indianapolis	22 Jun
		(80)							
10.22	-0.2	Bernard	Williams	USA	19.1.78	2		Liège (NX)	25 Jul
10.23	2.0	Kerron	Clement	USA	31.10.85	1		Coral Gables	14 Apr
10.23	1.1	Jacoby	Ford	USA	27.7.87	1h2		College Park	20 Apr
10.23	0.0	Uchenna	Emedolu	NGR	17.9.76	2		Abuja	5 May
10.23	0.4	Shingo	Suetsugu	JPN	2.6.80	1	GP	Osaka	5 May
10.23	1.9	Kyle	Farmer	USA	15.4.83	6h4	NC	Indianapolis	21 Jun
10.23	1.2	Rynell	Parson	USA-Y	11.7.90	1	NC-j	Indianapolis	21 Jun
10.23	0.0	Uche	Isaac	NGR	10.4.81	3		Malles	4 Aug
10.24	0.9	Anthony	Alozie	NGR	18.8.86	2s2	AUS Ch	Brisbane	10 Mar
10.24	0.5	Bennie	Robinson	USA	6.7.82	1		Azusa	13 Apr
		(90)							
10.24A	1.4	Brian	Barnett	CAN	10.2.87	1		Calgary	17 Jun
10.24	1.5	Kaaron	Conwright	USA	8.8.76	4h1	NC	Indianapolis	21 Jun
10.24	1.9	Mardy	Scales	USA	10.9.81	7h4	NC	Indianapolis	21 Jun
10.24	1.2	Scott	Wims	USA-J	30.5.88	2	NC-j	Indianapolis	21 Jun
10.24	0.0	Florin	Suciu	ROM	18.5.83	1	NC	Bucuresti	27 Jul
10.24	0.6	Shigeyuki	Kojima	JPN	25.9.79	2		Kakogawa	4 Aug
10.25	1.5	Christiaan	Krone	RSA	30.8.84	1		Durban	30 Mar
10.25	1.0	Carl	Barrett	JAM	21.4.75	1rB		Kingston	5 May
10.25	1.4	Leigh	Julius	RSA	25.3.85	3	GP	Rio de Janeiro	13 May
10.25	1.1	Daniel	Bailey	ANT	9.9.86	3h3	adidas	Carson	20 May
		(100)							
10.25	1.2	Jacques	Riparelli	ITA	27.3.83	2		Génève	9 Jun
10.25	1.6	Jeff	Demps	USA-Y	8.1.90	1s3	AAA JO	Knoxville	1 Aug
10.25	-0.1	Suryo Agung	Wibowo	INA	8.10.83	1	SEAG	Nakhon Ratchasima	7 Dec

10.26	1.6	Jason	Heard	USA	11.7.83	31 Mar
10.26	1.3	Andre	Ammons	USA	12.11.78	5 May
10.26	1.9	Dwayne	Grant	GBR	17.7.82	5 May
10.26A	1.0	Emanuel	Parris	CAN	7.10.82	19 May
10.26	1.1	Marcus	Brunson	USA	24.4.78	20 May
10.26	1.1	Christian	Blum	GER	10.3.87	26 May
10.26	1.8	Michael	Coleman	USA	26.1.87	6 Jun
10.26	1.2	Mark	Findlay	GBR	20.3.78	9 Jun
10.26	1.1	Caimin	Douglas	NED	11.5.77	23 Jun
10.26	1.5	Guillaume	Guffroy	FRA	18.9.85	30 Jun
10.26	0.7	Tom	Musinde	KEN	22.4.79	18 Jul
10.26	0.9	Masahide	Ueno	JPN	10.9.83	26 Jul
10.26	1.1	Leevan	Yearwood	GBR-J	10.2.88	26 Aug
10.26	0.9	Brian	Dzingai	ZIM	29.4.81	9 Sep

Mark	Wind	Name		Nat	Born	Date
10.27A	1.0	Sherwin	Vries	RSA	22.3.80	2 Feb
10.27	1.8	Rubin	Williams	USA	9.7.83	6 Jun
10.27	0.6	Marquis	Davis	USA	14.8.80	8 Jun
10.27	-0.1	David	Alerte	FRA	18.9.84	6 Jul
10.27	-0.1	Rosario	La Mastra	ITA	2.1.84	25 Aug
10.27	0.0		Zhang Peimeng	CHN	13.3.87	28 Sep
10.28	1.8	Ambrose	Ezenwa	AUS	10.4.77	7 Jan
10.28	0.0	Jacey	Harper	TRI	20.5.80	7 Apr
10.28	1.3	Brian	Witherspoon	USA	5.6.85	20 Apr
10.28	1.7	Yahya Ibrahim	Hassan	KSA	6.2.86	26 Apr
10.28	2.0	Josh	Norman	USA	26.7.80	5 May
10.28	1.3	Ainsley	Waugh	JAM	17.9.81	20 May
10.28	1.2	Xavier	Carter	USA	8.12.85	26 May
10.28	0.5	Jason	Gardener	GBR	18.9.75	29 May
10.28	1.5	Luca	Verdecchio	ITA	24.5.78	9 Jun
10.28	0.4	Sandro	Viana	BRA	26.3.77	21 Jun
10.28	0.0	Alonso	Edwards	PAN-J	8.12.89	30 Jun
10.28	1.8	Matt	Shirvington	AUS	25.10.78	4 Jul
10.28	1.2	Ryan	Scott	GBR	20.2.87	12 Jul
10.28	0.4		Wen Yongyi	CHN	3.1.87	21 Jul
10.28	0.0	Julian	Reus	GER-J	29.4.88	3 Aug
10.29	0.4	Brent	Gray	USA	16.9.86	17 Mar
10.29		Marcus	Duncan	TRI	4.12.86	10 May
10.29	1.8	Richard	Adu-Bobie	CAN	12.1.85	6 Jun
10.29	1.0	Efthímios	Steryioúlis	GRE	9.2.85	15 Jun
10.29	1.1	Emmanuel	Callander	TRI	10.5.84	22 Jun
10.29	1.7	Shannon	King	CAN	3.5.86	30 Jun
10.29	0.5	Fabio	Cerutti	ITA	26.9.85	12 Jul
10.29	0.0	Nicolas	Macrozonaris	CAN	22.8.80	27 Jul
10.29	1.2	Eric Pacôme	Ndri	CIV	24.3.78	12 Aug
10.30	-1.7	Jeremy	Hall	USA-J	27.1.88	24 Mar
10.30	1.7	Abdullah Ibrahim	Al Waleed	QAT	7.5.84	26 Apr
10.30A	1.0	Neville	Wright	CAN	21.12.80	19 May
10.30	1.3	Justyn	Warner	CAN	28.6.87	26 May
10.30	0.9	Dariusz	Kuc	POL	24.4.86	13 Jun
10.31	0.6	Courtney	Thomas	USA	4.3.87	21 Apr
10.31	1.0	Andrew	Hinds	BAR	25.4.84	5 May
10.31	1.6	Arnaldo	Abrantes	POR	27.11.86	12 May
10.31	1.2	Basilio	de Morães	BRA	11.5.82	16 May
10.31	0.4	Trell	Kimmons	USA	13.7.85	20 May
10.31	0.4	Eric	Nkansah	GHA	12.12.74	24 May

Mark	Wind	Name		Nat	Born	Date
10.31	1.2	Rodney	Martin	USA	22.12.82	26 May
10.31	1.5	Manuel	Reynaert	FRA	5.6.85	30 Jun
10.31	1.7	Delwayne	Delaney	SKN	4.8.82	13 Jul
10.32A	1.0	Snyman	Prinsloo	RSA	22.5.84	2 Feb
10.32		Yoan	Frias	CUB	4.7.86	22 Feb
10.32	0.4	Evander	Wells	USA	7.12.87	12 May
10.32	1.5	Jerome	Avery	USA	18.4.78	12 May
10.32	0.0	Jeremy	Rankin	USA-Y	23.9.90	19 May
10.32	-0.1	Tyree	Gailes	USA	24.2.83	27 May
10.32A	0.0	Kael	Becerra	CHI	4.11.85	1 Jun
10.32	-0.2	Chris	Berrian	USA	17.4.83	3 Jun
10.32	2.0	Andrey	Yepishin	RUS	10.6.81	9 Jun
10.32	0.0	Chinedu	Oriala	NGR	17.12.81	20 Jun
10.32	0.2	Igor	Gostev	RUS	24.10.85	29 Jun
10.32	1.3	Cláudio Roberto	Sousa	BRA	14.10.79	18 Aug
10.32	-0.1	Christian	Malcolm	GBR	3.6.789	23 Aug
10.33A	1.7	Ryan	Campbell	USA	29.3.86	31 Mar
10.33	-0.9	Brian	Mariano	AHO	22.1.85	27 May
10.33	-0.7	Ahmad	Rashad	USA	12.12.87	28 May
10.33	0.9	Aimé Issa	Nthépé	FRA	26.6.73	5 Jun
10.33	1.2	Leon	Baptiste	GBR	23.5.85	9 Jun
10.33	1.0	Anastásios	Goúsis	GRE	7.7.79	15 Jun
10.33	0.9	Dexter	Lee	JAM-Y	18.1.91	23 Jun
10.33	1.3	James	Dasaolu	GBR	5.9.87	23 Jun
10.33	0.3	Dmitriy	Hlushchenko	UKR	17.2.81	25 Jul
10.33	-1.0	Obinna	Metu	NGR-J	12.7.88	23 Aug
10.33	0.8		Liu Yuan-Kai	TPE	2.12.81	15 Sep
10.33	-0.1	Wachara	Sondee	THA	9.4.83	7 Dec
10.34	0.0	Cédric Mongha	Nabe	SUI	16.6.83	12 May
10.34	-0.9	Jamaal	Charles	USA	27.12.86	12 May
10.34	1.0	D.J.	Smith	USA	26.8.85	12 May
10.34	1.7	Orion	Nicely	JAM	28.2.84	25 May
10.34A	0.0	Rafael	Ribeiro	BRA	23.6.86	1 Jun
10.34	0.2		Lu Bin	CHN	19.5.87	8 Jun
10.34	1.0	Jarkko	Ruostekivi	FIN	5.4.85	20 Jun
10.34	0.2	Shane	Crawford	USA-J	4.6.88	6 Jul
10.34	0.0	Jan	Zumer	SLO	9.6.82	10 Jul
10.34	0.9	Roland	Németh	HUN	19.9.74	21 Jul
10.34	2.0	Daniel	Adolia	FRA	12.9.82	3 Aug
10.34	0.0	Tim	Abeyie	GBR	7.11.82	11 Aug
10.34	0.2	Ronny	Ostwald	GER	7.4.74	12 Aug

(199)

Wind assisted

Mark	Wind	Name		Nat	Born	Pos	Meet	Venue	Date
9.76	2.2	Tyson	Gay	USA	9.9.82	1	GP	New York	2 Jun
9.79	2.5		Gay			1	adidas	Carson	20 May
9.83	2.2	Derrick	Atkins	BAH	5.1.84	2	GP	New York	2 Jun
9.86	2.5		Atkins			2	adidas	Carson	20 May
9.88	3.0	Darrel	Brown	TRI	11.10.84	1	NC	Port of Spain	23 Jun
9.91	3.7	Steve	Mullings	JAM	29.11.82	1	Aragón	Zaragoza	28 Jul
9.92	3.7	Joshua 'J.J.'	Johnson	USA	10.5.76	2	Aragón	Zaragoza	28 Jul
9.92	3.7	Clement	Campbell	JAM	19.2.75	3	Aragón	Zaragoza	28 Jul
9.95	3.0	Richard	Thompson	TRI	7.6.85	2	NC	Port of Spain	23 Jun
9.95	3.7	Michael	Frater	JAM	6.10.82	4	Aragón	Zaragoza	28 Jul
9.96	2.2	Shawn	Crawford	USA	14.1.78	3	GP	New York	2 Jun
9.99	3.7	Mickey	Grimes	USA	10.10.76	5	Aragón	Zaragoza	28 Jul
9.99	3.7	Francis	Obikwelu	POR	22.11.78	6	Aragón	Zaragoza	28 Jul
10.01	2.8	Brendan	Christian	ANT	11.12.83	1r2	KansR	Lawrence	21 Apr
10.02	3.9	DaBryan	Blanton	USA	3.7.84	1		Fort Worth	21 Apr
10.02	2.2	Mark	Jelks	USA	10.4.84	1r1	KansR	Lawrence	21 Apr
10.03	2.1	Brian	Dzingai	ZIM	29.4.81	1		Clermont, FL	19 May
10.03	2.8	Chris	Williams	JAM	15.3.72	1		Port of Spain	26 May
10.03	2.8	Marvin	Anderson	JAM	12.5.82	2		Port of Spain	26 May
10.05	3.8	Travis	Padgett	USA	13.12.86	1		Clemson	7 Apr
10.05	3.0	Keston	Bledman	TRI-J	8.3.88	3	NC	Port of Spain	23 Jun
10.06	2.5	Dwight	Phillips	USA	1.10.77	4	adidas	Carson	20 May
10.06	3.0	Marc	Burns	TRI	7.1.83	4	NC	Port of Spain	23 Jun
10.07		Michael	Rodgers	USA	24.4.85	1		Plainview	21 Apr
10.07	2.5	Dwight	Thomas	JAM	23.9.80	5	adidas	Carson	20 May
10.10	2.4	Michael Ray	Garvin	USA	29.9.86	2h3	NCAA	Sacramento	6 Jun
10.11	8.0	Amr Ibrahim	Seoud	EGY	10.6.86	1		El Maadi	6 Apr
10.11A	4.4	Nicolas	Macrozonaris	CAN	22.8.80	1h2		Provo	1 Jun
10.11	4.0	Ivory	Williams	USA	2.5.85	3h5	NC	Indianapolis	21 Jun
10.12	2.5	Garry	Jones	USA	24.7.84	7	adidas	Carson	20 May
10.12A	4.4	Anson	Henry	CAN	9.3.79	2h2		Provo	1 Jun
10.12	6.5	Tomoyuki	Arai	JPN	14.6.81	1h1	Nambu	Sapporo	15 Jul

Mark	Wind	Name		Nat	Born	Pos	Meet	Venue	Date
10.12	3.7	Patrick	Johnson	AUS	26.9.72	8	Aragón	Zaragoza	28 Jul
10.13	2.6	J-Mee	Samuels	USA	20.5.87	2		Fayetteville	21 Apr
10.13	4.4	Ricardo	Williams	JAM	29.9.76	3		Fort Worth	21 Apr
10.14	2.7	Ernest	Wiggins	USA	18.6.82	1h4		Clermont	19 May
10.14	6.5	Shigeyuki	Kojima	JPN	25.9.79	2h1	Nambu	Sapporo	15 Jul
10.15	2.6	Anthony	Alozie	NGR	18.8.86	2		Perth	7 Jan
10.15	3.0	Jacey	Harper	TRI	20.5.80	5	NC	Port of Spain	23 Jun
10.16	2.4	Mike	LeBlanc	CAN	25.2.87	3h3	NCAA	Sacramento	6 Jun
10.16	4.2	Masahide	Ueno	JPN	10.9.83	1s2	AsiC	Amman	26 Jul
10.17	2.6	Orlando	Reid	JAM	3.7.82	2h2	NCAA	Sacramento	6 Jun
10.17	2.9	Miklós	Szebeny	HUN	13.3.87	1		Budapest	16 Jun
10.18	2.2	Michael	Mitchell	USA	16.5.81	1		Cerritos	24 Mar
10.18	2.3	Jason	Heard	USA	11.7.83	1rB	MSR	Walnut	15 Apr
10.18	3.0	Emmanuel	Callander	TRI	10.5.84	6	NC	Port of Spain	23 Jun
10.18	3.9	Julien	Dunkley	JAM	20.12.75	1		New York	14 Jul
10.19	3.9	Tyree	Gailes	USA	24.2.83	4		Fort Worth	21 Apr
10.20	3.0	Ahmad	Rashad	USA	12.12.87	1	Pac-10	Stanford	13 May
10.20	2.1	Marquis	Davis	USA	14.8.80	3		Clermont, FL	19 May
10.20	2.4	Gregory	Bolden	USA	30.6.84	5h3	NCAA	Sacramento	6 Jun
10.20	2.9	Richard	Adu-Bobie	CAN	12.1.85	1h4		Ottawa	1 Jul
10.21	3.9	Brant	Gilbert	USA	8.10.81	5		Fort Worth	21 Apr
10.21	2.1	Kamil	Masztak	POL	16.7.84	1		Bydgoszcz	10 Jun
10.22	2.6	Steven	Tucker	AUS	3.12.82	3		Perth	7 Jan
10.22	3.7	Christian	Malcolm	GBR	3.6.79	1		Clermont	21 Apr
10.22	3.0	Jan	Zumer	SLO	9.6.82	3		Donnas	15 Jul
10.23	2.1	Przemyslaw	Rogowski	POL	9.2.80	2		Bydgoszcz	10 Jun
10.23	3.9	Lee	Prowell	GUY	11.1.75	2		New York	14 Jul
10.23	8.5	Masanori	Kumagai	JPN	20.10.86	1		Rifu	15 Jul

10.24	2.6	Yahya Ibrahim Hassan		KSA	6.2.86	18 Apr
10.24	2.6	Brent	Gray	USA	16.9.86	6 Jun
10.24	2.3	Mark	Findlay	GBR	20.3.78	30 Jun
10.24	5.7	Lukasz	Chyla	POL	31.3.81	15 Sep
10.25	2.9	Ashhad	Agyapong	USA	23.9.85	4 May
10.25	2.3	Alonso	Edwards	PAN-J	8.12.89	9 May
10.25	2.2	Trell	Kimmons	USA	13.7.85	2 Jun
10.25	2.9	Gergely	Németh	HUN	8.7.81	16 Jun
10.25	2.2	Guillaume	Guffroy	FRA	18.9.85	30 Jun
10.26	2.6	Ambrose	Ezenwa	AUS	10.4.77	7 Jan
10.26	2.3	Maurice	Mitchell	USA-J	22.12.89	21 Apr
10.26	2.9	Jason	Moore	USA	3.3.86	4 May
10.26	4.2	Marcus	Duncan	TRI	4.12.86	19 May
10.26	2.4	Tyrell	Cuffy	CAY-J	6.9.88	25 May
10.26	2.2	Delwayne	Delaney	SKN	4.8.82	6 Jun
10.26	2.2	Rubin	Williams	USA	9.7.83	6 Jun
10.26	2.9	Pierre	Browne	CAN	14.1.80	1 Jul
10.26	4.2	Siriroj	Darasuriyong	THA	8.10.84	26 Jul
10.27	6.5	Hirofumi	Nakagawa	JPN	3.1.80	15 Jul
10.27	4.2	Abduallah Ibrahim Al-Waleed		QAT	7.5.84	26 Jul
10.27		Mikhail	Yegorychev	RUS	21.7.77	9 Aug
10.28A	3.1	D.J. (Dejuan)	Smith	USA	26.8.85	6 Apr
10.28	2.6	Daniel	Batman	AUS	20.3.81	7 Jan
10.28	3.0	Hank	Palmer	CAN	16.3.85	14 Apr
10.28	2.6	Shomari	Wilson	USA	6.6.76	21 Apr
10.28	2.6	Marcus	Pugh	USA	30.4.86	21 Apr
10.28	4.2	Denison	Collins	CAN	24.10.83	12 May
10.28	2.1	Leon	Covington	USA	9.12.86	19 May
10.28	2.3	Chris	Johnson	CAN-J	.88	2 Jun
10.28	2.4	Desislav	Gunev	BUL	21.1.86	9 Jun
10.29		Jonathan	Davis	BAH-J	20.3.88	14 Apr
10.29	3.7	Leon	Baptiste	GBR	23.5.85	21 Apr
10.29	2.6	Ravyn	Hayward	USA	23.9.85	21 Apr
10.29	4.3	Eric	Nkansah	GHA	12.12.74	12 May
10.29	4.3	Aimé-Issa	Nthépé	FRA	26.6.73	12 May
10.29	2.2	Justyn	Warner	CAN	28.6.87	6 Jun
10.29	3.0	Niconnor	Alexander	TRI	4.2.77	23 Jun
10.29		Aziz	Ouhadi	MAR	24.7.84	14 Jul
10.29	2.1		Lim Hee-nam	KOR	29.5.84	15 Jul
10.30	3.1	Manuel	Reynaert	FRA	5.6.85	6 May
10.30	4.3	Lee-Roy	Newton	RSA	19.12.78	12 May
10.30	2.1	Michael	Herrera	CUB	5.6.85	26 May
10.30	3.0	Melvin	Nero	TRI	13.11.80	23 Jun
10.30	6.5	Hitoshi	Saito	JPN	9.10.86	15 Jul
10.30	5.7	Marcin	Nowak	POL	2.8.77	15 Sep
10.31	2.5	Heber	Viera	URU	29.4.79	11 Mar
10.31	2.9	Aulton	Kohn	USA	15.1.85	31 Mar
10.31		Markie	Faust	USA	25.8.87	14 Apr
10.31		DeRico	Tilley	USA	10.2.77	14 Apr
10.31	5.4	Jamaal	Charles	USA	27.12.86	21 Apr
10.31	5.0	Ryan	Moseley	GBR	8.10.82	27 May
10.31	2.4	Jahvid	Best	USA-J	30.1.89	2 Jun
10.31	4.2	Umanga Surendra Sanjeewa		SRI	21.5.81	26 Jul
10.32		Philip	Redrick	USA		15 Mar
10.32	3.1	Garrion	Martin	USA		18 Mar
10.32	4.2	Teddy	Poole	USA	.86	19 May
10.32	3.0	D'Angelo	Cherry	USA-Y	1.8.90	2 Jun
10.32	2.1	Shinji	Takahira	JPN	18.7.84	15 Jul
10.32	3.6	Shintaro	Kimura	JPN	30.6.87	8 Sep
10.33	2.8	Ihsan	McPherson	USA	25.1.84	21 Apr
10.33		Trenton E.	Guy	USA-J	6.10.89	2 May
10.33	4.3	Jorge Célio	Sena	BRA	31.1.85	6 May
10.33	5.0	Gavin	Eastman	GBR	28.6.80	27 May
10.33	2.5	Andrew	Turner	GBR	19.9.80	2 Jun
10.33	2.2	Shane	Crawford	USA-J	4.6.88	21 Jun
10.34w		12 men				

Best at low altitude 10.18 1.4 de Lima 1 Rio de Janeiro 13 May

10.29 1.4 J Woods 13 May 10.30 1.0 Vries 25 Aug 10.31 0.7 Moreira 14 Apr 10.29w? Parris 1 Jul

Doubtful timing

10.02	-0.4		Grimes			1		Atlanta	2 Jun
10.10	0.1	Julien	Dunkley	JAM	20.12.75	1		Durham	12 May
10.16	-1.5	Ernest	Wiggins	USA	18.6.82	1		Orlando	3 Mar
10.21	0.1	Wachara	Sondee	THA	9.4.83	1s1	SEAG	Bangkok	5 Oct
10.23	0.1	Dennis	Boone	USA	26.9.86	2		Durham	12 May
10.23	-0.4	Andre	Sturdivant	USA	5.7.81	2		Atlanta	2 Jun

10.26	0.1	Chris	Davis	USA	1.3.86	12 May
10.27	+0.1	Taweesak	Poonthong	THA	7.7.87	5 Oct
10.28	1.9	Ruslan	Abbasov	AZE	24.6.86	21 Jul
10.31*	0.1	Thomas	Hunter	USA	14.12.83	12 May
10.34	+0.1	John H.	Muray	INA	6.6.78	5 Oct

Doubtful times and/or wind readings

Ouagadougou 24 Apr: (-2.7?) 1. Béranger Bosse CAF 9.3.85, 2. Marius Loua CIV 27.7.82 10.27

Mark	Wind	Name		Nat	Born	Pos	Meet	Venue	Date
Hand timed									
9.8	1.7	Henry (Jenris)	Vizcaíno	CUB	16.5.80	1h1		La Habana	14 Jun
9.9	0.1	Luis Alexander	Reyes	CUB	22.10.77	1h2		La Habana	14 Jun
10.0A		Morné	Nagel	RSA	23.2.78	1		Pretoria	16 Jan
10.0		Adeyote	Durotoye	NGR	9.5.86	1		Bauchi	25 Feb
10.0A		Tom	Musinde	KEN	22.4.79	1		Nairobi	29 Sep
10.0A		Fanuek	Kenosi	BOT-J	3.5.88	1		Gaborone	3 Nov

10.1		Carl	Barrett	JAM	21.4.75	14 Apr	10.1A		Fabrice	Coiffic	MRI	25.8.84	15 Aug
10.1		Keston	Bledman	TRI-J	8.3.88	14 Apr	10.1	0.9	Daniel	Burgess	AUS	18.3.85	8 Dec

JUNIORS

See main list for top 5 juniors. 10 performances by 5 men to 10.25. Additional marks and further juniors:

Blake	10.18	1.5	1h1	Carifta	Providenciales	7 Apr	10.21	-0.9	1		Kingston	31 Mar
	10.19	-0.3	2s3	NC	Kingston	23 Jun						
Bledman	10.18	1.7	1		Port of Spain	26 May	10.19	1.5	1h4	PAm	Rio de Janeiro	23 Jul

Mark	Wind	Name		Nat	Born	Pos	Meet	Venue	Date
10.26	1.1	Leevan	Yearwood	GBR	10.2.88	1		London (He)	26 Aug
10.28	0.0	Alonso	Edwards	PAN	8.12.89	1	SAmC-j	São Paulo	30 Jun
10.28	0.0	Julian	Reus	GER	29.4.88	1	NC-j	Ulm	3 Aug
10.30	-1.7	Jeremy	Hall	USA	27.1.88	1		Tucson	24 Mar
10.32	0.0	Jeremy	Rankin (10)	USA-Y	23.9.90	1		Lakewood	19 May
10.33	0.9	Dexter	Lee	JAM-Y	18.1.91	1	NC-j	Kingston	23 Jun
10.33	-1.0	Obinna	Metu	NGR	12.7.88	2r2		Osaka	23 Aug
10.34	0.2	Shane	Crawford	USA	4.6.88	3	PAm-J	São Paulo	6 Jul
10.36	0.9	Aaron	Rouget-Serret	AUS	21.1.88	3h2	NC	Brisbane	10 Mar
10.36	1.8	Jonathan	Williams	USA	8.4.88	1		Fresno	31 Mar
10.36	1.2	Jahvid	Best	USA	30.1.89	1h2		Sacramento	28 Apr
10.36	1.4	Masashi	Eriguchi	JPN	17.12.88	1		Hong Kong	8 Jul
10.39	0.7	Dax	Danns	GUY	27.3.88	2h1	Big 12	Lincoln	12 May
10.39	1.9	Charles	Saseun	USA		1		Norwalk	25 May
10.39	0.9	Nickel	Ashmeade (20)	JAM-Y	4.7.90	2	NC-y	Kingston	23 Jun
10.39	-0.9	Tyrell	Cuffy	CAY	6.9.88	1		Carolina	30 Jun

Wind assisted See main list for top junior (10.05w Bledman). Additional men to 10.34w

Mark	Wind	Name		Nat	Born	Pos	Meet	Venue	Date
10.25	2.3	Alonso	Edwards	PAN	8.12.89	1	ALBA	Caracas	9 May
10.26	2.3	Maurice	Mitchell	USA	22.12.89	1rC	KansR	Lawrence	21 Apr
10.26	2.4	Tyrell	Cuffy	CAY	6.9.88	1s1	NAIA	Fresno	25 May
10.28	2.3	Chris	Johnson	CAN	.88	6		Cork	2 Jun
10.29		Jonathan	Davis	BAH	20.3.88	1		Mobil	14 Apr
10.31	2.4	Jahvid	Best	USA	30.1.89	1		Sacramento	2 Jun
10.32	3.0	DeAngelo	Cherry	USA-Y	1.8.90	1h1		Orlando	2 Jun
10.33		Trenton	Guy	USA	6.10.89	1		Huntersville	2 May
10.33	2.2	Shane	Crawford	USA	4.6.88	1h1	NC-j	Indianapolis	21 Jun
10.34	4.2	Shogo	Arao	JPN	16.8.88	1		Oita	13 May
10.34		Antoine	Adams	SKN	31.8.88	1		Dallas	22 May

200 METRES

Mark	Wind	Name		Nat	Born	Pos	Meet	Venue	Date
19.62	-0.3	Tyson	Gay	USA	9.9.82	1	NC	Indianapolis	24 Jun
19.69	0.9	Walter	Dix	USA	31.1.86	1	NCAA-r	Gainesville	26 May
19.75	0.2	Usain	Bolt	JAM	21.8.86	1	NC	Kingston	24 Jun
19.76	-0.8		Gay			1	WCh	Osaka	30 Aug
19.78	0.0		Gay			1	Athl	Lausanne	10 Jul
19.82	1.3	Wallace	Spearmon	USA	24.12.84	1	GP	New York	2 Jun
19.88	0.7		Spearmon			1	VD	Bruxelles	14 Sep
19.88	0.1		Spearmon			1	Color	Daegu	3 Oct
19.89	1.3		Bolt			2	GP	New York	2 Jun
19.89	-0.3		Spearmon			2	NC	Indianapolis	24 Jun
19.89	1.3	Jaysuma	Saidy Ndure (GAM)	NOR	1.1.84	1	WAF	Stuttgart	23 Sep
19.91	1.4		Spearmon			1	adidas	Carson	20 May
19.91	-0.8		Bolt			2	WCh	Osaka	30 Aug
19.92	0.2	Xavier	Carter	USA	8.12.85	1	WK	Zürich	7 Sep
19.96	1.0		Bolt			1	Hampton	Port of Spain	27 May
19.97	-0.5		Gay			1		Kingston	5 May
19.98	1.4	LaShawn	Merritt	USA	27.6.86	2	adidas	Carson	20 May
20.00	-0.4		Gay			1s2	WC	Osaka	29 Aug
20.00	-0.3	Asafa	Powell	JAM	23.11.82	1	Golden	Shanghai	28 Sep
20.02	-0.3		Merritt			1	Olympic	Thessaloníki	30 Jul
20.03	-0.4		Bolt			1s1	WCh	Osaka	29 Aug
20.04	0.7		Carter			2	VD	Bruxelles	14 Sep
20.05	-0.4		Spearmon			2s1	WCh	Osaka	29 Aug
20.05	-0.8		Spearmon			3	WCh	Osaka	30 Aug
20.06	-0.1		Bolt			1	LGP	London (CP)	3 Aug

Mark	Wind	Name		Nat	Born	Pos	Meet	Venue	Date
20.06	-0.4	Marvin	Anderson	JAM	12.5.82	2s2	WCh	Osaka	29 Aug
20.06	-0.8	Rodney	Martin	USA	22.12.82	4	WCh	Osaka	30 Aug
20.08	1.2		Spearmon			1	BrGP	Sheffield	15 Jul
20.08	1.2		Bolt			2	BrGP	Sheffield	15 Jul
20.08	0.9		Gay			1q3	WC	Osaka	28 Aug
		(30/10)							
20.11	0.0	Anastásios	Goúsis	GRE	7.7.79	1h4	WCh	Osaka	28 Aug
20.17	1.3	Chris	Williams	JAM	15.3.72	3	GP	New York	2 Jun
20.17	1.8	Jordan	Vaden	USA	15.9.78	1	NACAC	El Salvador	15 Jul
20.20	1.2	Shingo	Suetsugu	JPN	2.6.80	1	NC	Osaka	30 Jun
20.20	-0.4	Churandy	Martina	AHO	3.7.84	4s1	WCh	Osaka	29 Aug
20.21	1.4	Shawn	Crawford	USA	14.1.78	3	adidas	Carson	20 May
20.23	0.0	Brendan	Christian	ANT	11.12.83	3h4	WCh	Osaka	28 Aug
20.28	0.3	Brian	Dzingai	ZIM	29.4.81	2q1	WCh	Osaka	28 Aug
20.29	0.2	Clement	Campbell	JAM	19.2.75	3	NC	Kingston	24 Jun
20.30	0.1	Paul	Hession	IRL	27.1.83	1	NC	Dublin	21 Jul
		(20)							
20.30	1.3	Johan	Wissman	SWE	2.11.82	4	WAF	Stuttgart	23 Sep
20.31	2.0	Michael	Herrera	CUB	5.6.85	1	ALBA	Caracas	11 May
20.31	0.2	Brian	Barnett	CAN	10.2.87	1h3	WCh	Osaka	28 Aug
20.31	0.0	Marcin	Jedrusinski	POL	28.9.81	4h4	WCh	Osaka	28 Aug
20.32A	-1.0	Morné	Nagel	RSA	23.2.78	1		Pretoria	9 Mar
20.32	0.6	Reggie	Witherspoon	USA	31.5.85	1h1	Big 12	Lincoln	12 May
20.32	0.6	Dwight	Thomas	JAM	23.9.80	1		Bydgoszcz	10 Jun
20.32	-0.3	Joshua 'J.J.'	Johnson	USA	10.5.76	1	DNG	Stockholm	7 Aug
20.33	0.9	Michael	Mitchell	USA	16.5.81	1rA	MSR	Walnut	15 Apr
20.33	1.0	Marlon	Devonish	GBR	1.6.76	1	ECp-S	München	24 Jun
		(30)							
20.33	1.4	David	Alerte	FRA	18.9.84	1	NC	Niort	5 Aug
20.35	0.6	Ricardo	Williams	JAM	29.9.76	1	GP	Belém	20 May
20.35	-0.3	Jeremy	Wariner	USA	31.1.84	4	NC	Indianapolis	24 Jun
20.37	1.8	Till	Helmke	GER	6.5.84	1		Wetzlar	28 Jul
20.38	1.3	Charles	Clark	USA	10.8.87	1s2	NCAA	Sacramento	7 Jun
20.38	0.9	Francis	Obikwelu	POR	22.11.78	3q3	WCh	Osaka	28 Aug
20.40	-0.3	Rubin	Williams	USA	9.7.83	5	NC	Indianapolis	24 Jun
20.43	1.6	Greg	Nixon	USA	12.9.81	1		Tucson	31 Mar
20.43	1.7	Evander	Wells	USA	7.12.87	1		Atlanta	31 Mar
20.43	1.6	Bryshon	Nellum	USA-J	1.5.89	1		Sacramento	2 Jun
		(40)							
20.43A	0.0	Sandro	Viana	BRA	26.3.77	1	Iriarte	Cochabamba	3 Jun
20.44	-0.1	Kristof	Beyens	BEL	13.7.83	2h6	WCh	Osaka	28 Aug
20.47A	0.0	Franklin	Nazareno	ECU	24.4.87	2	Iriarte	Cochabamba	3 Jun
20.47	0.7	Marc	Schneeberger	SUI	5.7.81	1	NC	Lausanne	29 Jul
20.47	0.3	Bernard	Williams	USA	19.1.78	1		Uden	4 Aug
20.48	0.0	Tobias	Unger	GER	10.7.79	1		Regensburg	9 Jun
20.48	-0.5	Guus	Hoogmoed	NED	27.9.81	1	NC	Amsterdam	1 Jul
20.48	0.2	Patrick	Johnson	AUS	26.9.72	3h3	WCh	Osaka	28 Aug
20.48	0.0	Arnaldo	Abrantes	POR	27.11.86	5h4	WCh	Osaka	28 Aug
20.49	1.3	Kerron	Clement	USA	31.10.85	1		Coral Gables	14 Apr
		(50)							
20.49	1.3	Darvis	Patton	USA	4.12.77	5	GP	New York	2 Jun
20.49	-0.9	Chris	Berrian	USA	17.4.83	1		Eagle Rock	3 Jun
20.50	0.1	Derrick	Atkins	BAH	5.1.84	1		Leverkusen	10 Aug
20.51	1.0	Darrel	Brown	TRI	11.10.84	2		Port of Spain	27 May
20.51	0.5	Orlando	Reid	JAM	3.7.82	2s1	NCAA	Sacramento	7 Jun
20.51	0.5	Brent	Gray	USA	16.9.86	3s1	NCAA	Sacramento	7 Jun
20.51	-0.2	Christiaan	Krone	RSA	30.8.84	1	Kuso	Warszawa	17 Jun
20.51	1.4	Eddy	De Lepine	FRA	30.3.84	2	NC	Niort	5 Aug
20.51	0.2	Matic	Osovnikar	SLO	19.1.80	4h2	WCh	Osaka	28 Aug
20.52	0.6	Courtney	Thomas	USA	4.3.87	2h1	Big 12	Lincoln	12 May
		(60)							
20.52	1.2	Shinji	Takahira	JPN	18.7.84	2	NC	Osaka	30 Jun
20.53	0.2	Joshua	Ross	AUS	9.2.81	1		Lignano	15 Jul
20.53	-2.1	Andrew	Howe	ITA	12.5.85	1	NC	Padova	28 Jul
20.54	0.9	Paulvince	Obuon	KEN	18.11.83	1		Lincoln	5 May
20.54	-0.1	Marco	Cribari	SUI	7.7.85	1		Génève	9 Jun
20.54	0.2	Steve	Mullings	JAM	29.11.82	5	NC	Kingston	24 Jun
20.56	1.1	Ahmad	Rashad	USA	12.12.87	1	Pac-10	Stanford	13 May
20.56	0.6	Vicente Lenilson	de Lima	BRA	4.6.77	2	GP	Belém	20 May
20.56	1.0	Chris	Lloyd	DMA	10.10.80	3		Port of Spain	27 May

Mark	Wind	Name		Nat	Born	Pos	Meet	Venue	Date
20.56	0.2	Visa	Hongisto	FIN	9.4.87	5h2	WCh	Osaka	28 Aug
		(70)							
20.56	0.5	Alessandro	Cavallaro	ITA	22.2.80	1s2	CISM	Hyderabad	17 Oct
20.57	0.9	Willie	Perry	USA	16.5.87	3	NCAA-r	Gainesville	26 May
20.58	0.7	Ramone	McKenzie	JAM-Y	15.11.90	1	Carifta	Providenciales	9 Apr
20.58	1.5	Edino	Steele	JAM	6.1.87	1		Cerritos	25 Apr
20.58	0.9	Michael Ray	Garvin	USA	29.9.86	1h1	NCAA-r	Gainesville	25 May
20.59	0.4	Heber	Viera	URU	29.4.79	2	SACh	São Paulo	9 Jun
20.59	0.2	Sebastian	Ernst	GER	11.10.84	2rA	DLV	Bochum-Wattenscheid	12 Aug
20.60A	1.0	Sherwin	Vries	RSA	22.3.80	1		Pretoria	9 Mar
20.60	1.7	Angelo	Taylor	USA	29.12.78	2		Atlanta	31 Mar
20.60	0.4	Naoki	Tsukahara	JPN	10.5.85	1h1	NC	Osaka	29 Jun
		(80)							
20.61	1.3	Scott	Wims	USA-J	30.5.88	5s2	NCAA	Sacramento	7 Jun
20.62	1.0	Yohan	Blake	JAM-J	26.12.89	1		Kingston	31 Mar
20.62	2.0	Alonso	Edwards	PAN-J	8.12.89	2	ALBA	Caracas	10 May
20.62	0.1	Daniel	Schnelting	GER	9.3.86	1rB	DLV	Bochum-Wattenscheid	12 Aug
20.63A	1.4	Paul	Smith	USA	29.5.84	1		Provo	28 Apr
20.63	1.0	Alexander	Kosenkow	GER	14.3.77	6	ECp-S	München	24 Jun
20.63	-0.6	Obinna	Metu	NGR-J	12.7.88	1h3	AfG	Alger	21 Jul
20.64	-1.5	Jody	Johnson	USA	13.11.85	1		Sacramento	24 Mar
20.64	-0.4	Gary	Kikaya	COD	4.2.78	2		Greensboro	21 Apr
20.64	-0.2	Jeremy	Dodson	USA	30.8.87	1h2	Big 12	Lincoln	12 May
		(90)							
20.64	1.3	Nate	Probasco	USA	10.7.83	6s2	NCAA	Sacramento	6 Jun
20.64	0.0	Hitoshi	Saito	JPN	9.10.86	2h3	NC	Osaka	29 Jun
20.64	1.0	Amr Ibrahim	Seoud	EGY	10.6.86	1h2	PArabG	Cairo	23 Nov
20.65	0.0	Brian	Witherspoon	USA	5.6.85	1		Atlanta	12 May
20.65	0.4	Leigh	Julius	RSA	25.3.85	1		Brazzaville	27 May
20.65	1.6	Jahvid	Best	USA-J	30.1.89	2		Sacramento	2 Jun
20.65	0.2	James	Dolphin	NZL	17.6.83	6h2	WCh	Osaka	28 Aug
20.66A	1.2	Daniel	Grueso	COL	30.7.85	1	NC	Medellín	5 May
20.66	0.2	Uchenna	Emedolu	NGR	17.9.76	4	SGP	Doha	11 May
20.66	-0.2	Jacobi	Mitchell	BAH	4.1.86	2h2	Big 12	Lincoln	12 May
		(100)							
20.66	0.4	Marcus	Pugh	USA	30.4.86	2	Big 12	Lincoln	13 May

Mark	Wind	Name		Nat	Born	Date
20.67	0.1	David	Dickens	USA	19.3.85	11 May
20.67	0.6	Basílio	de Moraes	BRA	11.5.82	20 May
20.67	0.7	Tim	Abeyie	GBR	7.11.82	4 Jul
20.68	1.3	Ashhad	Agyapong	USA	23.9.85	12 May
20.68	1.0	Mickey	Grimes	USA	10.10.76	27 May
20.69	1.8	Marek	Niit	EST	9.8.87	5 Jun
20.69	1.2	Tomoya	Kamiyama	JPN-J	21.2.88	30 Jun
20.70	0.0	Domenik	Peterson	USA	12.12.84	14 Apr
20.70	0.6	Ainsley	Waugh	JAM	17.9.81	20 May
20.71	0.0	Mark	Jelks	USA	10.4.84	28 Apr
20.71	-0.6	Phil	DeRosier	USA	11.4.84	26 May
20.71	0.0	Chris	Lambert	GBR	6.4.81	16 Jun
20.72	0.9	Arman	Dixon	USA	25.6.86	26 May
20.72	0.5	Roman	Smirnov	RUS	2.9.84	27 May
20.72	1.3	Jared	Connaughton	CAN	20.7.85	7 Jun
20.72	0.2	Omar	Brown	JAM	21.6.82	24 Jun
20.72	-0.2	Ramil	Guliyev	AZE-Y	29.5.90	15 Jul
20.72	1.2	Seth	Amoo	GHA	20.3.83	21 Jul
20.73	0.0	Kelvin	Love	USA	18.5.86	17 Mar
20.73	1.2	Kenji	Fujimitsu	JPN	1.5.86	30 Jun
20.74	-1.5	Joe	Turner	USA	.87	24 Mar
20.74	0.7	Trey	Harts	USA	17.10.87	12 May
20.74	0.0	Zhang Peimeng		CHN	13.3.87	19 Sep
20.75A	-0.5	Kagisho	Kumbane	RSA-J	21.11.88	5 May
20.75	-1.0	Kyle	Farmer	USA	15.4.83	2 Jun
20.75A	1.2	Josué	Mena	ESP	22.8.83	14 Jul
20.75	-0.9	Gavin	Smellie	CAN	26.6.86	15 Jul
20.75	0.1	Marquis	Davis	USA	14.8.80	30 Jul
20.76A	1.0	Hank	Palmer	CAN	16.3.85	19 May
20.76	-0.2	Nickel	Ashmeade	JAM-Y	4.7.90	15 Jul
20.76	0.8	Surya	Agung Wibowo	INA	8.10.83	11 Dec
20.77	-0.6	Marvin	Bien-Aimé	HAI	20.10.83	26 May
20.77A	0.0	Nilson	André	BRA	30.1.86	3 Jun
20.77	1.3	Maurice	Mitchell	USA-J	22.12.89	10 Jun
20.77	1.3	Emmanuel	Callander	TRI	10.5.84	24 Jun
20.78	-0.3	Mitsuru	Hasegawa	JPN	12.6.84	5 May
20.78	0.7	Ryan	Campbell	USA	29.3.86	12 May
20.79	-0.4	John	Steffensen	AUS	30.8.82	2 Mar
20.79	1.7	Ravyn	Hayward	USA	23.9.85	21 Apr
20.79		Lavarius	Giles	USA		22 Apr
20.79	1.2	Marco	Torrieri	ITA	14.5.78	20 May
20.79	1.9	Anthony	Ferro	BEL	12.12.80	5 Aug
20.80A	-1.0	Snyman	Prinsloo	RSA	22.5.84	9 Mar
20.80	-1.5	Joel	Stallworth	USA	18.1.83	24 Mar
20.80	2.0	Kyle	Stevenson	USA-J	18.7.88	31 Mar
20.80	0.1	Aulton	Kohn	USA	15.1.85	6 May
20.80	-0.6	Marquis	Horn	USA		26 May
20.80	0.1	Ingo	Schultz	GER	26.7.75	1 Jul
20.80	2.0	Lee	Prowell	GUY	11.1.75	13 Jul
20.80	1.7	Claudio Roberto	Souza	BRA	14.10.79	14 Jul
20.80	0.1	Michael	Mathieu	BAH	24.6.84	25 Jul
20.80	0.1	Rikki	Fifton	GBR	17.6.85	25 Aug
20.81	0.9	Daniel	Batman	AUS	20.3.81	17 Feb
20.81	2.0	Abidemi	Omole	USA	29.7.85	31 Mar
20.81	0.1	Jacey	Harper	TRI	20.5.80	7 Apr
20.81	0.0	Derrick	Brew	USA	28.12.77	12 May
20.81	0.4	Ivan	Teplykh	RUS	2.8.85	2 Aug
20.81	2.0	Khalil	Al Hanahneh	JOR	11.5.80	24 Nov
20.82	1.1	Lewis	Banda	ZIM	16.8.82	31 Mar
20.82	-0.2	Mike	Myer	USA	17.7.87	12 May
20.82	0.6	Leon	Baptiste	GBR	23.5.85	28 Jun
20.82	0.2	Idriss Khalid	Zougari Idrissi	MAR-J	24.1.88	30 Jun
20.82	-0.8	Tyler	Christopher	CAN	3.10.83	30 Sep
20.83	0.0	Carlos	Moore	USA	8.5.84	7 Apr
20.83	0.5	Ricki	Bratton	USA		21 Apr
20.83	0.6	Jamaal	Charles	USA	27.12.86	12 May
20.83	0.2	Yusuke	Ishitsuka	JPN	19.6.67	13 May
20.83	-1.0	Jamial	Rolle	BAH	16.4.80	2 Jun
20.83	1.5	Jirí	Vojtík	CZE	2.7.81	1 Jul
20.83	-0.9	Tyrell	Cuffy	CAY-J	6.9.88	8 Jul
20.83	1.8	Obra	Hogans	USA	29.6.82	14 Jul
20.83	1.8	Delwayne	Delaney	SKN	4.8.82	15 Jul
20.83	-1.0	Alex	Nelson	GBR-J	21.3.88	21 Jul
20.84	0.0	Ato	Modibo	TRI	19.6.79	7 Apr
20.84	0.9	Travis	Padgett	USA	13.12.86	26 May
20.84	-0.3	Kelly	Willie	USA	7.9.82	24 Jun
20.84	0.0	Zhao Jiahuan		CHN	9.5.85	19 Sep
20.84	0.5	Liu Yuan-Kai		TPE	2.12.81	24 Oct

Mark	Wind	Name		Nat	Born	Pos	Meet	Venue	Date
20.84	0.8	Sittichai	Suwonprateep	THA	17.11.80				11 Dec
20.85A		Juan Pedro	Toledo	MEX	17.6.78				1 Apr
20.85	-0.4	Daniel	Caines	GBR	15.5.79				21 Apr
20.85	1.7	Michael	Rhue	USA	8.9.86				25 May
20.85	0.0	Christian	Blum	GER	10.3.87				9 Jun
20.85	2.0	Jan	Zumer	SLO	9.6.82				28 Jul
20.85	0.1	Kamil	Masztak	POL	16.7.84				12 Aug
20.85	2.0	Joel	Brown	USA	31.1.80				9 Sep

(187)

Wind assisted

19.87	2.2		Spearmon			1		Fayetteville	21 Apr
20.30	3.1	Joshua 'J.J'	Johnson	USA	10.5.76	1		Salamanca	4 Jul
20.37	3.0	Edino	Steele	JAM	6.1.87	1h1		Cerritos	24 Apr
20.39	2.6	Leigh	Julius	RSA	25.3.85	1		Durban	31 Mar
20.48	2.1	Derrick	Atkins	BAH	5.1.84	1		Berkeley	28 Apr
20.48	4.5	Teddy	Poole	USA	.86	1	JUCO	Coffeyville	19 May
20.51	4.7	Joshua	Ross	AUS	9.2.81	1	NC	Brisbane	11 Mar
20.56	3.1	Marquis	Davis	USA	14.8.80	5		Salamanca	4 Jul
20.62	2.5	Ainsley	Waugh	JAM	17.9.81	5	Bisl	Oslo	15 Jun
20.63	2.2	J-Mee	Samuels	USA	20.5.87	1		Fayetteville	21 Apr
20.64	3.8	Shingo	Takada	JPN	26.9.85	1		Nara	20 May
20.65	2.1	Obra	Hogans	USA	29.6.82	1h3		New York	13 Jul

20.67	2.2	Travis	Padgett	USA	13.12.86	25 May
20.68	2.6	Ambrose	Ezenwa	AUS	10.4.77	20 Jan
20.68	2.6	Jan	van der Merwe	RSA	16.3.84	31 Mar
20.71	3.5	Andrew	Turner	GBR	19.9.80	2 Jun
20.73	2.2	Aulton	Kohn	USA	15.1.85	25 May
20.75	4.5	Dwight	Mullings	JAM	10.12.86	19 May
20.75	4.5	Marcus	Duncan	TRI	4.12.86	19 May
20.76	3.0	John	Steffensen	AUS	30.8.82	10 Feb
20.77		Gil	Roberts	USA-J	15.3.89	4 May
20.78	3.2	Adam	Miller	AUS	22.6.84	25 Feb
20.79	4.2	Sergio	Mullins	RSA	12.5.80	31 Mar
20.81	2.1	Tremaine	Smith	USA	16.4.86	28 Apr
20.82	4.4	Lukas	Hulett	USA-J	18.4.88	5 May
20.82	3.9	Masahiro	Naiki	JPN	17.7.84	20 May
20.83	2.2	Jared	Lewis	CAN	14.1.86	21 Apr
20.84	2.5	Caimin	Douglas	NED	11.5.77	15 Jun
20.85		Rabah	Yousif	SUD	11.12.86	28 May

Doubtful timing 20.50 0.4 Marcin Nowak POL 2.8.77 1 Kielce 21 Jul

Ouagadougou 24 Apr: 1. Marius Loua CIV 27.7.72 20.73, 2. Béranger Bossé CAF 9.3.85 20.75

Hand timed

20.0	0.0	Uchenna	Emedolu	NGR	17.9.76	1	Abuja	5 May
20.2		Xavier	Brown	JAM	21.2.83	1	Arima	30 Jun
20.3	0.0	Stefano	Anceschi	ITA	18.6.84	2	Abuja	5 May
20.4	1.9	Joseph	Batangdon	CMR	29.7.78	1	Giessen	21 Apr
20.4	0.8	Jorge	Valcárcel	CUB-J	16.4.88	1	Santiago de Cuba	30 Jun
20.4	0.8	David	Lescay	CUB-J	19.2.89	2	Santiago de Cuba	30 Jun

20.5	0.0	Obinna	Metu	NGR-J	12.7.88	5 May
20.5	0.4	Marek	Niit	EST	9.8.87	29 May
20.5	0.4	Oleg	Zhuravlev	UZB	17.5.82	3 Jun
20.5		Ramil	Guliyev	AZE-Y	29.5.90	3 Jun
20.5		Ruslan	Abbasov	AZE	24.6.86	3 Jun

Indoors

20.67i	Chris	Dykes	USA	15.8.87	9 Mar
20.70i	Idrissa	M'Barke	FRA	30.3.83	18 Feb
20.77i	Milton	Campbell	USA	15.5.76	10 Feb

Best at low altitude

20.47	0.2	Viana	3h2	WCh	Osaka	28 Aug
20.59	-1.0	Nagel	1		Stellenbosch	2 Mar
20.66	0.4	Grueso	3	SACh	São Paulo	9 Jun
20.73	0.4	Nazareno				9 Jun
20.79	-2.4	Vries				17 Mar
20.83	1.7	André				14 Jul

JUNIORS

See main list for top 7 juniors. 13 performances by 8 men to 20.67. Additional marks and further juniors:

Nellum	20.58	1.0	1		Norwalk	19 May	20.45w 3.5 1h2 Sacramento 1 Jun
McKenzie	20.63	1.2	1	NC-j	Kingston	24 Jun	
Wims	20.66	0.6	1		Des Moines	26 May	20.67 0.6 3h1 Big 12 Lincoln, NE 12 May
Metu	20.66	0.0	2s2	AfG	Alger	21 Jul	

20.69	1.2	Tomoya	Kamiyama	JPN	21.2.88	4	NC	Osaka	30 Jun
20.72	-0.2	Ramil	Guliyev	AZE-Y	29.5.90	2	WY	Ostrava	15 Jul
20.75A	-0.5	Kagisho	Kumbane (10)	RSA	21.11.88	1		Gaborone	5 May
20.76	-0.2	Nickel	Ashmeade	JAM-Y	4.7.90	3	WY	Ostrava	15 Jul
20.77	1.3	Maurice	Mitchell	USA	22.12.89	1		Independence	10 Jun
20.80	2.0	Kyle	Stevenson	USA	18.7.88	1B		Atlanta	31 Mar
20.82	0.2	Idriss Khalid	Zougari Idrissi	MAR	24.1.88	1		Meknès	30 Jun
20.83	-0.9	Tyrell	Cuffy	CAY	6.9.88	2	PAm-J	São Paulo	8 Jul
20.83	-1.0	Alex	Nelson	GBR	21.3.88	1	EJ	Hengelo	21 Jul
20.86	1.5	Darryl	Jenkins	USA	10.9.89	1	Jnr Oly	Walnut	28 Jul
20.86	-0.7	Luke	Fagan	GBR	31.7.88	3	NC	Manchester	29 Jul
20.87A	-0.7	Mychal	Dungey	USA	13.10.88	1		Albuquerque	2 Jun
20.87	-1.0	Julian	Reus (20)	GER	29.4.88	2	EJ	Hengelo	21 Jul
20.87	0.1	Chris	Clarke	GBR-Y	25.1.90	2		Leverkusen	10 Aug

Wind assisted One performance (Nellum, above) to 20.67. Additional men to 20.85

20.77		Gil	Roberts	USA	15.3.89	1h2	Moore	4 May
20.82	4.4	Lukas	Hulett	USA	18.4.88	1B	Lincoln	5 May

Hand timed

20.5	0.0	Obinna	Metu	NGR	12.7.88	3	Abuja	5 May
20.5		Ramil	Guliyev	AZE	29.5.90	1	Baku	3 Jun

Mark	Name		Nat	Born	Pos	Meet	Venue	Date

300 METRES

Mark	Name		Nat	Born	Pos	Meet	Venue	Date
32.35	Greg	Nixon	USA	12.9.81	1		Villeneuve d'Ascq	8 Jun
32.50	Fernada	Blakely	USA	28.9.81	1		Eugene	27 May
32.53	Milton	Campbell	USA	15.5.76	2		Eugene	27 May

Mark	Name		Nat	Born	Date
32.70	Chris	Berrian	USA	17.4.83	27 May
32.71	Yuzo	Kanemaru	JPN	18.9.87	22 Apr
32.71	Daniel	Batman	AUS	20.3.81	15 Dec
32.74	Marc	Schneeberger	SUI	5.7.81	12 May
32.75	Guus	Hoogmoed	NED	27.9.81	20 May
32.90	Leslie	Djhone	FRA	18.3.81	8 Jun
32.91	Chris	Lloyd	DMA	10.10.80	8 Jun

Indoors: 32.23# LaShawn Merritt USA 27.6.86 1 Notre Dame 2 Feb

During 400m races: 24 Jun Indianapolis USA Ch: 31.8 LaShawn Merritt, 31.9 Angelo Taylor, 32.1 Darold Williamson, 32.3 Lionel Larry, 32.4 Bershawn Jackson; 7 Aug Stockholm: 31.8 Wariner
31 Aug WCh Osaka: 31.58 Jeremy Wariner. 31.68 LaShawn Merritt, 31.88 Angelo Taylor, 32.1 Chris Brown

400 METRES

Mark	Name		Nat	Born	Pos	Meet	Venue	Date
43.45	Jeremy	Wariner	USA	31.1.84	1	WCh	Osaka	31 Aug
43.50		Wariner			1	DNG	Stockholm	7 Aug
43.96	LaShawn	Merritt	USA	27.6.86	2	WCh	Osaka	31 Aug
44.02		Wariner			1	GP	Osaka	5 May
44.02		Wariner			1	Golden	Shanghai	28 Sep
44.05	Angelo	Taylor	USA	29.12.78	1	NC	Indianapolis	23 Jun
44.05		Wariner			1	LGP	London	3 Aug
44.05		Wariner			1	ISTAF	Berlin	16 Sep
44.06		Merritt			2	NC	Indianapolis	23 Jun
44.23		Merritt			2	LGP	London	3 Aug
44.31		Merritt			1s3	WCh	Osaka	29 Aug
44.32		Taylor			3	WCh	Osaka	31 Aug
44.34		Wariner			1s2	WCh	Osaka	29 Aug
44.35		Taylor			1		Atlanta	12 May
44.38		Merritt			1	Herc	Monaco	25 Jul
44.43		Wariner			1	FBK	Hengelo	26 May
44.43		Wariner			1	Pedro's	Warszawa	19 Sep
44.44		Merritt			1s2	NC	Indianapolis	22 Jun
44.44		Merritt			1rA	GGala	Roma	13 Jul
44.45		Taylor			1s1	WCh	Osaka	29 Aug
44.45	Chris	Brown	BAH	15.10.78	4	WCh	Osaka	31 Aug
44.46	Leslie	Djhone	FRA	18.3.81	2s3	WCh	Osaka	29 Aug
44.47	Tyler	Christopher	CAN	3.10.83	3s3	WCh	Osaka	29 Aug
44.48	Kerron	Clement	USA	31.10.85	2	DNG	Stockholm	7 Aug
44.50		Brown			1h1	WCh	Osaka	28 Aug
44.52		Brown			2s2	WCh	Osaka	29 Aug
44.55		Taylor			2rA	GGala	Roma	13 Jul
44.56	Johan	Wissman	SWE	2.11.82	2s1	WCh	Osaka	29 Aug
44.58		Merritt			1	WAF	Stuttgart	22 Sep
44.59		Djhone			5	WCh	Osaka	31 Aug
	(30/8)							
44.60A	Gary	Kikaya	COD	4.2.78	1		Xalapa	5 May
44.62	Ricardo	Chambers	JAM	7.10.84	2		Atlanta	12 May
	(10)							
44.67	Lionel	Larry	USA	14.9.86	2s2	NC	Indianapolis	22 Jun
44.68	Darold	Williamson	USA	19.2.83	2	GP	Osaka	5 May
44.82	John	Steffensen	AUS	30.8.82	2h1	WCh	Osaka	28 Aug
44.86	Avard	Moncur	BAH	2.11.78	3s1	WCh	Osaka	29 Aug
44.92	Arizmendi	Peguero	DOM	7.8.80	3h1	WCh	Osaka	28 Aug
44.95	Alleyne	Francique	GRN	7.6.76	1h3	WCh	Osaka	28 Aug
44.98	Sanjay	Ayre	JAM	19.6.80	4	DNG	Stockholm	7 Aug
45.01	Nery	Brenes	CRC	25.9.85	1h6	WCh	Osaka	28 Aug
45.02	Derrick	Brew	USA	28.12.77	3s2	NC	Indianapolis	22 Jun
45.05	Michael	Blackwood	JAM	29.8.76	3	Herc	Monaco	25 Jul
	(20)							
45.06	Bershawn	Jackson	USA	8.5.83	3s1	NC	Indianapolis	22 Jun
45.12	Andrew	Rock	USA	23.1.82	5	DNG	Stockholm	7 Aug
45.12	Ato	Modibo	TRI	19.6.79	3s2	WCh	Osaka	29 Aug
45.19	Jamaal	Torrance	USA	20.7.83	4s1	NC	Indianapolis	22 Jun
45.22	Michael	Mathieu	BAH	24.6.83	1rA		Osaka	23 Aug
45.23	David	Gillick	IRL	9.7.83	1		Génève	9 Jun
45.24	Fernada	Blakely	USA	28.9.81	3		Atlanta	12 May
45.24	David	Neville	USA	1.6.84	2s2	NC	Indianapolis	22 Jun
45.25	Nagmeldin	El Abubakr	SUD	22.2.86	1s3	AfG	Alger	19 Jul

Mark	Name		Nat	Born	Pos	Meet	Venue	Date
45.25	Sean	Wroe	AUS	18.3.85	5s1	WCh	Osaka	29 Aug
	(30)							
45.26	Xavier	Carter	USA	8.12.85	2		Glasgow	3 Jun
45.26	Andrae	Williams	BAH	11.7.83	3	NC	Nassau	23 Jun
45.28	Usain	Bolt	JAM	21.8.86	3		Kingston	5 May
45.28	Tim	Benjamin	GBR	2.5.82	5	GP	London (CP)	3 Aug
45.29	William	Collazo	CUB	31.8.86	3h6	WCh	Osaka	28 Aug
45.31	Greg	Nixon	USA	12.9.81	1rB	adidas	Carson	20 May
45.31	Andrew	Steele	GBR	19.9.84	2		Génève	9 Jun
45.33	LeJerald	Betters	USA-J	6.2.88	1	Big 12	Lincoln	13 May
45.33	Daniel	Dabrowski	POL	23.9.83	1	NC	Poznan	1 Jul
45.35	Renny	Quow	TRI	25.8.87	2h4	PAm	Rio de Janeiro	23 Jul
	(40)							
45.36	California	Molefe	BOT	2.5.80	4h6	WCh	Osaka	28 Aug
45.37	Hakeem	Mohammed	USA	.85	1	NCAA-2	Charlotte	26 May
45.38	Bryshon	Nellum	USA-J	1.5.89	1	NC-j	Indianapolis	23 Jun
45.40	Chris	Lloyd	DMA	10.10.80	1	KansR	Lawrence	21 Apr
45.40	Joel	Stallworth	USA	18.1.83	2	NCAA-2	Charlotte	26 May
45.40	Erison	Hurtault	USA	29.12.84	3	NCAA	Sacramento	9 Jun
45.40	Young Talkmore	Nyongani	ZIM	2.9.83	4h4	WCh	Osaka	28 Aug
45.41	Lesiba	Masheto	BOT	1.11.84	1		Tucson	17 Mar
45.42	Chris	Troode	AUS	10.2.83	2		Canberra	27 Jan
45.44	Bastian	Swillims	GER	9.12.82	4h1	WCh	Osaka	28 Aug
	(50)							
45.47	Martyn	Rooney	GBR	3.4.87	4h2	WCh	Osaka	28 Aug
45.47	Lewis	Banda	ZIM	16.8.82	5h2	WCh	Osaka	28 Aug
45.48	Milton	Campbell	USA	15.5.76	4		Atlanta	12 May
45.52	Calvin	Smith	USA	10.12.87	1	NACAC	San Salvador	15 Jul
45.54	Brice	Panel	FRA	13.6.83	2		La Chaux de Fonds	12 Aug
45.56	Reggie	Witherspoon	USA	31.5.85	1h2	Big 12	Lincoln	12 May
45.57	Michael	Bingham	USA	13.4.86	5	NCAA	Sacramento	9 Jun
45.62	Quentin	Iglehart-Summers	USA	15.6.87	1	NCAA-r	Des Moines	26 May
45.62	Saul	Weigopwa	NGR	14.6.84	1		Brazzaville	27 May
45.63	Vladislav	Frolov	RUS	24.7.80	1h		Tula	18 Jun
	(60)							
45.64	Yuzo	Kanemaru	JPN	18.9.87	1	NC	Osaka	1 Jul
45.64	Rickey	Harris	USA	29.9.81	1rB	GP	Madrid	21 Jul
45.64	Maksim	Dyldin	RUS	15.5.87	1	NC	Tula	2 Aug
45.66	Obra	Hogans	USA	29.6.82	2		Baie Mahault	1 May
45.67	Ingo	Schultz	GER	26.7.75	1		Erfurt	8 Jul
45.68	Nathaniel	McKinney	BAH	19.1.82	2		Atlanta	2 Jun
45.69	Denis	Alekseyev	RUS	26.12.87	1	EU23	Debrecen	13 Jul
45.69	Zeljko	Vincek	CRO	16.6.86	2	EU23	Debrecen	13 Jul
45.70	Godday	James	NGR	9.1.84	3s3	AfG	Alger	19 Jul
45.71	Leford	Green	JAM	14.11.86	4	NC	Kingston	24 Jun
	(70)							
45.72	Rabah	Yousif	SUD	11.12.86	1	BIG	Bedford	10 Jun
45.73A	Ezra	Sambu	KEN	4.9.78	1	NC	Nairobi	16 Jun
45.74	Andrea	Barberi	ITA	15.1.79	5h7	WCh	Osaka	28 Aug
45.77	Edino	Steele	JAM	6.1.87	1		San Mateo	19 May
45.77A	Rodrigo	Bargas	BRA	4.2.86	1	Iriarte	Cochabamba	3 Jun
45.77	Siraj	Williams	LBR	5.3.84	8	NCAA	Sacramento	9 Jun
45.77	Marcin	Marciniszyn	POL	7.9.82	2	NC	Poznan	1 Jul
45.77A	George	Kwoba	KEN	9.11.74	1	WCT	Nairobi	28 Jul
45.78	Otis	Harris	USA	30.6.82	3	Sánchez	Santo Domingo	12 May
45.78	Jermaine	Gonzales	JAM	26.11.84	3rB	adidas	Carson	20 May
	(80)							
45.79		Liu Xiaosheng	CHN-J	5.1.88	1	WCT	Suzhou	9 Jun
45.80	Lancford	Spence	JAM	15.12.82	1		Lauderdale Lakes	7 Apr
45.80	Aaron	Buzard	USA	11.10.84	2	Big 10	State College, Pa	13 May
45.80	Kacper	Kozlowski	POL	7.12.86	2	Kuso	Warszawa	17 Jun
45.82	Elvis	Lewis	USA	30.4.87	1		Storrs	6 May
45.83	Corenelius	Duncan	USA	9.5.86	1		Houston	12 May
45.83	Clemens	Zeller	AUT	2.7.84	1		Villach	16 Jun
45.84	Kamghe	Gaba	GER	13.1.84	2		Kassel	6 Jun
45.85	Bryan	Steele	JAM	23.3.84	1rB	Sánchez	Santo Domingo	12 May
45.86	Artem	Sergeyenkov	RUS	10.6.86	2		Sochi	26 May
	(90)							
45.87	Alex	Harcourt	USA	.85	2	Pac-10	Stanford	13 May
45.88	Michael	Mitchell	USA	16.5.81	1		Walnut	10 Mar

Mark	Name		Nat	Born	Pos	Meet	Venue	Date
45.89	James	Groce	USA-J	12.5.88	2		State College, Pa	13 May
45.89	Andrés	Silva	URU	27.3.86	1	SAmC	São Paulo	8 Jun
45.89	Mathieu	Gnaligo	BEN	13.12.86	3	AfG	Alger	20 Jul
45.90	Mathieu	Lahaye	FRA	25.12.83	3	NC	Niort	4 Aug
45.90	Robert	Tobin	GBR	20.12.83	1r2		Osaka	23 Aug
45.91	Kenneth	Ferguson	USA	22.3.84	4		Baie Mahault	1 May
45.91	Yuki	Yamaguchi	JPN	22.2.84	5	GP	Osaka	5 May
45.91	David	Dickens	USA	19.3.85	3	SEC	Tuscaloosa	13 May
	(100)							

45.92	Félix	Martinez	PUR	4.2.85	19 May
45.92	Allodin	Fothergill	JAM	2.7.87	24 Jun
45.93	Anton	Kokorin	RUS	5.4.87	13 Jul
45.94	Rafal	Wieruszewski	POL	24.2.81	28 Aug
45.95		Wang Langyu	CHN	9.8.84	19 Jun
45.96	Jamel	Ashley	USA	17.4.79	21 Jun
45.97A	Sanderlei	Claro Parrela	BRA	7.10.74	3 Jun
45.99	Domenik	Peterson	USA	12.12.84	14 Apr
45.99	Daniel	Caines	GBR	15.5.79	12 May
45.99	Carlos	Santa	DOM	7.1.78	28 Aug
46.00	Dirk	Homewood	USA	21.1.82	20 May
46.00A	Anderson	Jorge dos Santos	BRA	23.4.72	3 Jun
46.00A	Thomas	Musembi	KEN	26.4.77	16 Jun
46.01	Lukas	Hulett	USA-J	18.4.88	12 May
46.02	Bruce	Davis	USA		26 May
46.03	Kurt	Mulcahy	AUS-J	12.5.89	20 Jan
46.03	Michael	Mason	JAM	26.4.87	15 Jul
46.03	Eric	Milazar	MRI	1.6.75	18 Jul
46.03	Andrey	Rudnitskiy	RUS	12.10.79	2 Aug
46.04	Zwede	Hewitt	TRI-J	10.6.89	7 Jul
46.04	Paul	McKee	IRL	15.11.77	12 Aug
46.05	Osmar	Cisneros	CUB-J	19.11.89	16 Mar
46.05	Leonard	Byrd	USA	17.3.75	14 Apr
46.05	Michael	Tinsley	USA	21.4.84	21 Apr
46.05A	David	Kirui	KEN	15.12.74	16 Jun
46.05	Mitch	Potter	USA	16.9.80	21 Jun
46.05	Yoshihiro	Horigome	JPN	2.1.81	30 Jun
46.06	Andretti	Bain	BAH	1.12.85	21 Apr
46.06A	Salesio	Njiru	KEN	9.4.70	28 Jul
46.06	Piotr	Klimczak	POL	18.1.80	11 Aug
46.08	Johnny	Jacob	USA	6.1.82	26 May
46.08	Bolaji	Lawal	NGR	26.6.76	19 Jul
46.09	Mark	Ormrod	AUS	1.12.82	13 Jan
46.09	Justin	Oliver	USA	7.11.87	14 Apr
46.09	Yoel	Tapia	DOM	11.9.84	15 Jul
46.10	Ioan	Vieru	ROM	4.1.79	10 Jun
46.11	Witold	Banka	POL	18.1.80	23 Aug
46.12	Elias	Koech	KEN	4.6.85	12 May
46.12	Matthias	Bos	GER	17.1.85	6 Jun
46.12	Dwight	Mullings	JAM	10.12.86	24 Jun
46.13A	Churandy	Martina	AHO	3.7.84	31 Mar
46.13	Richard	Buck	GBR	14.11.86	28 Jul
46.13	Ben	Offereins	AUS	12.3.86	15 Dec
46.14	Thomas	Nikitin	SWE	15.11.82	11 Aug
46.15	Herbert	Nichols	USA	20.12.83	5 May
46.15	Drew	Morano	USA	28.3.85	11 May
46.15	Luis	Luna	VEN	27.12.83	25 May
46.15	Yusuke	Ishitsuka	JPN	19.6.87	1 Jul
46.16	Gil	Roberts	USA-J	15.3.89	16 Jun
46.18	Marcus	Dillon	TRI	8.11.87	8 Jun
46.20	Terrence	Reid	USA	19.1.86	13 May
46.20	Zacharia	Kamberuka	BOT	28.12.87	26 May
46.20	Fernando	de Almeida	BRA	3.8.85	23 Jun
46.21A	Nathan	Vadeboncoeur	CAN	6.11.84	19 May
46.21	Fernando	Augustin	MRI	25.4.80	19 Jul
46.22	Marvin	Stevenson	USA	26.9.84	21 Apr
46.22	Niko	Verekauta	FIJ	16.2.87	5 Aug
46.22	Dmitriy	Buryak	RUS	5.6.87	11 Aug
46.22	Dimítrios	Régas	GRE	17.9.86	28 Aug
46.23	Dylan	Grant	AUS-J	14.3.88	2 Mar
46.23	Manteo	Mitchell	USA		31 Mar
46.23	Sean	Wright	USA	22.11.78	13 May
46.23A	Nelton	Ndebele	ZIM	6.6.85	27 May
46.23	Idrissa	M'Barke	FRA	30.3.83	5 Aug
46.24	Donald	Sanford	USA	2.8.87	21 Apr
46.24	Frankie	Wright	USA		25 May
46.24	Karjuan	Williams	USA	5.7.87	26 May
46.24	Naman	Keïta ¶	FRA	9.4.78	17 Jun
46.24	Terrill	McCombs	USA-J	12.3.88	23 Jun
46.24	Keston	Nelson	CAN	2.4.81	14 Jul
46.25	Alfred	Robinson	USA	13.2.86	12 May
46.26	Claudio	Licciardello	ITA	11.1.86	26 May
46.26	Stefano	Braciola	ITA	5.12.75	23 Jun
46.26	Wojciech	Chybinski	POL	26.2.84	1 Jul
46.26	Tyree	Washington	USA	28.8.76	30 Jul
46.27	Ade	Alleyne-Forte	TRI-J	11.10.88	7 Jul
46.28	Riker	Hylton	JAM-J	13.12.88	31 Mar
46.28	Antonio	McKay	USA-J		14 Apr
46.28	Richard	Strachan	GBR	18.11.86	13 May
46.28	Jamil	James	TRI	16.9.86	26 May
46.28	Ramon	Miller	BAH	17.2.87	24 Jun
46.28		Wang Xiaoxu	CHN	24.3.84	20 Jul
46.29	Bernard	Middleton	USA	21.12.85	13 May
46.29	Kelly	Willie	USA	7.9.82	20 May
46.29	Jimmie	Gordon	USA	2.9.84	8 Jun
46.29	Richard	Maunier (186)	FRA	8.12.77	9 Jun

Best at low altitude

44.77 Kikaya 2 FBK Hengelo 26 May

46.02 Sanderlei Claro Parrela 22 Jun | 46.03 Rodrigo Bargas 22 Jun | 46.26 Anderson Jorge dos Santos 22 Jun

Indoors

46.11 Reginald Dardar USA 31.10.85 25 Feb

Hand timing

45.2	Nagmeldin	El Abubakr	SUD	22.2.86	1	NC	Khartoum	10 Sep
45.7A	Nelton	Ndebele	ZIM	6.6.85	1		Harare	30 Jun

45.9A	L.J.	van Zyl	RSA	20.7.85	9 Mar
45.9A	Thomas	Musembi	KEN	26.4.77	3 Jun
45.9A	Gabriel	Chikomo	ZIM	29.3.76	30 Jun
46.1	Joel	Milburn	AUS	17.3.86	1 Dec

Doubtful timing

Durham 12 May: 1. Randy Curry USA 4.11.83 45.20, 2. Keith McMillan USA 3.6.80 45.75, 3. Bedawi Gomez TRI 46.08
La Habana 21 Jun: 1. Osmar Cisneros CUB-J 19.11.89 44.8, 2. Sergio Hierrezuelo CUB 15.3.82 45.6

JUNIORS

See main list for top 4 juniors. 10 performances by 5 men to 45.89. Additional marks and further juniors:

Nellum	45.40	1	PAm-J	São Paulo	7 Jul
	45.54	1		Sacramento	2 Jun
Betters	45.62	1h4	Big 12	Lincoln	12 May
	45.77	2	NCAA-r	Des Moines	26 May
	45.66	6	NCAA	Sacramento	9 Jun
Liu X	45.87	1		Guangzhou	20 Jul

Hand timed: 46.2 David Rudisha KEN 17.12.68 1 Nairobi 13 Jun

46.01	Lukas	Hulett	USA	18.4.88	2h2	Big12	Lincoln	12 May
46.03	Kurt	Mulcahy	AUS	12.5.89	2		Brisbane	20 Jan
46.04	Zwede	Hewitt	TRI	10.6.89	2	PAm-J	São Paulo	7 Jul
46.05	Osmar	Cisneros	CUB	19.11.89	1		Camagüey	16 Mar
46.16	Gil	Roberts	USA	15.3.89	1		Greensboro	16 Jun

MEN 2007

Mark	Name		Nat	Born	Pos	Meet	Venue	Date
46.23	Dylan	Grant (10)	AUS	14.3.88	4	GP	Melbourne	2 Mar
46.24	Terrill	McCombs	USA	12.3.88	2	NC	Indianapolis	23 Jun
46.27	Ade	Alleyne-Forte	TRI	11.10.88	3	PAm-J	São Paulo	7 Jul
46.28	Riker	Hylton	JAM	13.12.88	1		Kingston	31 Mar
46.28	Antonio	McKay	USA		1		Atlanta	14 Apr
46.31	Nigel	Levine	GBR	30.4.89	2	BIG	Bedford	10 Jun
46.31	Willie	de Beer	RSA	14.3.88	3s3	WUG	Bangkok	9 Aug
46.32A	Julius	Kirwa	KEN	3.5.89	2	EAf Ch	Kampala	31 May
46.34	Mitsuhiro	Abiko	JPN	25.10.88	3		Tokyo	19 May
46.34	Yannick	Fonsat	FRA	16.6.88	1	EJ	Hengelo	21 Jul
46.38	Kevin	Borlee (20)	BEL	22.2.88	2	NC	Bruxelles	5 Aug

600 METRES

Mark	Name		Nat	Born	Pos	Meet	Venue	Date
1:16.11	Peter	Znava	SVK	6.10.82	1		Pliezhausen	13 May
1:16.23	Joseph	Mutua	KEN	10.12.78	1		Bottrop	24 May

800 METRES

#: Belal Mansoor Ali – date of birth accepted by IAAF as 17.10.88

Mark	Name		Nat	Born	Pos	Meet	Venue	Date
1:43.74	Mbulaeni	Mulaudzi	RSA	8.9.80	1	Herc	Monaco	25 Jul
1:43.84	Alan	Webb	USA	13.1.83	1	NA	Heusden-Zolder	28 Jul
1:43.87	Youssef Saad	Kamel	BRN	29.3.83	2	Herc	Monaco	25 Jul
1:43.90	Abubaker	Kaki	SUD-J	21.6.89	1	PArabG	Cairo	22 Nov
1:43.94	Amine	Laâlou	MAR	13.5.82	3	Herc	Monaco	25 Jul
1:44.02	Belal Mansoor	Ali #	BRN	17.10.83	1	GP	Rieti	9 Sep
1:44.03	Gary	Reed	CAN	25.10.81	2	NA	Heusden-Zolder	28 Jul
1:44.11		Kamel			2	GP	Rieti	9 Sep
1:44.14	Wilfred	Bungei	KEN	24.7.80	1	SGP	Doha	11 May
1:44.15	David	Rudisha	KEN-J	17.12.88	1	VD	Bruxelles	14 Sep
1:44.17		Reed			4	Herc	Monaco	25 Jul
1:44.27	Khadevis	Robinson (10)	USA	19.7.76	5	Herc	Monaco	25 Jul
1:44.37		Robinson			1	NC	Indianapolis	24 Jun
1:44.37	Dmitrijs	Milkevics	LAT	6.12.81	6	Herc	Monaco	25 Jul
1:44.38	Yuriy	Borzakovskiy	RUS	12.4.81	1	GP	Athína	2 Jul
1:44.40		Mulaudzi			2	VD	Bruxelles	14 Sep
1:44.43		Kamel			3	VD	Bruxelles	14 Sep
1:44.49		Kamel			1rA	GP	Madrid	21 Jul
1:44.50	Alfred	Kirwa Yego	KEN	28.11.86	3	GP	Rieti	9 Sep
1:44.54	Nick	Symmonds	USA	30.12.83	1	Pre	Eugene	10 Jun
1:44.54	Nabil	Madi	ALG	9.6.81	3	NA	Heusden-Zolder	28 Jul
1:44.54		Kirwa Yego			1s1	WC	Osaka	31 Aug
1:44.55	Mohamed	Al-Azimi	KUW	16.6.82	2	GP	Athína	2 Jul
1:44.56		Al-Azimi			1	Bisl	Oslo	15 Jun
1:44.58	Yeimar	López	CUB	20.8.82	1	PAm	Rio de Janeiro	28 Jul
1:44.60	Fabiano	Peçanha	BRA	5.6.82	1h3	WUG	Bangkok	11 Aug
1:44.66		Reed			3	GP	Athína	2 Jul
1:44.69	Jonathan	Johnson	USA	5.3.82	4	NA	Heusden-Zolder	28 Jul
1:44.71		Borzakovskiy			2	Pre	Eugene	10 Jun
1:44.71		Mulaudzi			2s1	WCh	Osaka	31 Aug
	(30/19)							
1:44.78	Abraham	Chepkirwok (20)	UGA-J	18.11.88	5	GP	Athína	2 Jul
1:44.86	Justus	Koech	KEN	19.3.80	6	GP	Athína	2 Jul
1:44.88	Mohammed	Al-Salhi	KSA	11.5.86	1		Alger	21 Jun
1:44.94	Dmitriy	Bogdanov	RUS	11.4.79	5	GP	Rieti	9 Sep
1:45.1A	Richard	Kiplagat	KEN	3.7.87	2		Nairobi	29 Sep
1:45.13	Manuel	Olmedo	ESP	17.5.83	7	GP	Rieti	9 Sep
1:45.15	Isaac	Kombich	KEN	16.10.85	7	GP	Athína	2 Jul
1:45.17	Michael	Rimmer	GBR	3.2.86	1	DNG	Stockholm	7 Aug
1:45.32	Mouhcine	Chéhibi	MAR	28.1.78	9	GP	Athína	2 Jul
1:45.32	Antonio Manuel	Reina	ESP	13.6.81	5	GP	Madrid	21 Jul
1:45.34	Gilbert	Kipchoge	KEN	4.5.83	2	Nebiolo	Torino	8 Jun
	(30)							
1:45.47	Kléberson	Davide	BRA	20.7.85	2	PAm	Rio de Janeiro	28 Jul
1:45.52	Marcin	Lewandowski	POL	13.6.87	3	FBK	Hengelo	26 May
1:45.54	Edwin	Letting	KEN	15.5.84	1		Huelva	13 Sep
1:45.55	Alex	Kipchirchir	KEN	26.11.84	5	SGP	Doha	11 May
1:45.61	Bram	Som	NED	20.2.80	4	FBK	Hengelo	26 May
1:45.64	Rashid	Ramzi	BRN	17.7.80	2h3	WCh	Osaka	30 Aug
1:45.69	Duane	Solomon	USA	28.12.84	3	NC	Indianapolis	24 Jun
1:45.7A	Leonard	Kibet	KEN-J	16.12.88	1s2	NC	Nairobi	14 Jun
1:45.79	Joseph Lopez	Lomong	SUD/USA	1.1.85	5	NC	Indianapolis	24 Jun

Mark	Name		Nat	Born	Pos	Meet	Venue	Date
1:45.84	Achraf	Tadili	CAN	8.7.80	2	NC	Windsor	15 Jul
	(40)							
1:45.87	Juan Carlos	Higuero	ESP	3.8.78	7	GP	Madrid	21 Jul
1:45.88	Arnoud	Okken	NED	20.4.82	6	NA	Heusden-Zolder	28 Jul
1:45.89	René	Herms	GER	17.7.82	1		Leverkusen	10 Aug
1:45.90	Ehsan	Mohajershojaei	IRI	21.3.83	2h3	WUG	Bangkok	11 Aug
1:45.90	Yassine	Bensghir	MAR	3.1.83	4h5	WCh	Osaka	30 Aug
1:45.91	Pawel	Czapiewski	POL	30.3.78	5	GS	Ostrava	27 Jun
1:45.92	Jebreh	Harris	USA	22.9.78	1rB	NA	Heusden-Zolder	28 Jul
1:45.93	Livio	Sciandra	ITA	23.9.80	3		Lignano	15 Jul
1:46.05	Dave	Campbell	IRL	28.1.82	5		Lignano	15 Jul
1:46.07	Robin	Schembera	GER-J	1.10.88	2		Leverkusen	10 Aug
	(50)							
1:46.11	Floyd	Thompson	USA	22.11.79	6	NC	Indianapolis	24 Jun
1:46.12	Abdoulaye	Wagne	SEN	30.1.81	4	AfG	Alger	20 Jul
1:46.20	Brandon	Shaw	USA	11.9.81	6		Lignano	15 Jul
1:46.22	Elliot	Blount	USA	25.6.79	7		Lignano	15 Jul
1:46.24	Abdesslam	Kennouche	ALG	7.10.80	2rB	NA	Heusden-Zolder	28 Jul
1:46.24	Samwel	Mwera	TAN	3.6.85	5h6	WCh	Osaka	30 Aug
1:46.25	Tarek	Boukensa	ALG	19.11.81	2		Alger	21 Jun
1:46.26	Nahashon	Ruto	KEN	23.9.77	3		Salamanca	4 Jul
1:46.27	Daniel	Kandie	KEN	.77	8	NA	Heusden-Zolder	28 Jul
1:46.32	Andrew	Baddeley	GBR	20.6.82	1		Watford	30 Jun
	(60)							
1:46.33	Eduardo	Villanueva	VEN	29.12.84	6h4	WCh	Osaka	30 Aug
1:46.35	Jeff	Riseley	AUS	11.11.86	5	DNG	Stockholm	7 Aug
1:46.40	Sadjad	Moradi	IRI	30.3.83	1		Tehran	24 May
1:46.43	Mattias	Claesson	SWE	26.7.86	6h3	WCh	Osaka	30 Aug
1:46.45	Jozef	Repcík	SVK	3.8.86	6	GS	Ostrava	27 Jun
1:46.46	Thomas	Chamney	IRL	16.4.84	8		Lignano	15 Jul
1:46.48	Eugenio	Barrios	ESP	3.11.76	7	DNG	Stockholm	7 Aug
1:46.50	Sherridan	Kirk	TRI	11.2.81	1		Fortaleza	16 May
1:46.5A	Gezahegn	Alemu	ETH	.85	1		Addis Ababa	1 Jun
1:46.5A	Jimmy	Adar	UGA	1.11.87	2		Kampala	3 Jun
	(70)							
1:46.62	Trent	Riter	USA	15.6.82	3s2	NC	Indianapolis	22 Jun
1:46.65	Christian	Obrist	ITA	20.11.80	1		Olbia	21 Jul
1:46.66	Andrew	Ellerton	CAN	18.11.83	3		Padova	8 Jul
1:46.66	Sergio	Gallardo	ESP	22.3.79	4rB	GP	Madrid	21 Jul
1:46.67		Li Xiangyu	CHN	21.10.85	1		Eugene	9 Jun
1:46.67	Tetlo	Emmen	USA	24.1.84	4rB	NA	Heusden-Zolder	28 Jul
1:46.67	Julien	Barré	FRA	21.2.84	5rB	NA	Heusden-Zolder	28 Jul
1:46.69	James	McIlroy	GBR	30.12.76	2		Manchester	9 Jun
1:46.7	Saïd	Doulal	MAR	17.12.79	1		Casablanca	24 Jun
1:46.71	Ryan	Brown	USA	17.9.84	1		Uden	4 Aug
	(80)							
1:46.73	Kevin	Elliott	USA	7.11.78	5s2	NC	Indianapolis	22 Jun
1:46.75	David	Krummenacker	USA	24.5.75	2		Brasschaat	21 Jul
1:46.75	Gareth	Balch	GBR	18.5.83	3		Breda	18 Aug
1:46.77	Thomas	Matthys	BEL	4.9.85	9	NA	Heusden-Zolder	28 Jul
1:46.79	Golden	Coachman	USA	24.7.84	4s1	NC	Indianapolis	22 Jun
1:46.8A	George	Koech	KEN-J	.88	1		Kakamega	21 Apr
1:46.8A	Francis	Kakonzi	KEN	.77	5	NC	Nairobi	16 Jun
1:46.81	Bartosz	Nowicki	POL	26.2.84	4		Bydgoszcz	10 Jun
1:46.82	Najim	Mansour	ALG-J	8.6.88	3rB	GGala	Roma	13 Jul
1:46.84	Aldwyn	Sappleton	JAM	21.12.81	2h3	PAm	Rio de Janeiro	27 Jul
	(90)							
1:46.86	Ramil	Aritkulov	RUS	1.3.78	3		Moskva	29 Jun
1:46.86	Ådne Svahn	Dæhlin	NOR	26.6.82	6rB	NA	Heusden-Zolder	28 Jul
1:46.88	Martin	Conrad	GER	8.1.86	4		Breda	18 Aug
1:46.89	René	Bauschinger	GER	12.6.85	4		Leverkusen	10 Aug
1:46.90	Richard	Hill	GBR	12.2.86	3h3	WUG	Bangkok	11 Aug
1:46.92	Dustin	Emrani	USA	6.1.85	1		Indianapolis	27 Jun
1:46.92	Geoffrey	Rono	KEN	21.4.87	2		Rovereto	12 Sep
1:46.94	David	Freeman	PUR	28.4.82	1	DrakeR	Des Moines	28 Apr
1:46.98	Arturo	Casado	ESP	26.1.83	5rB	GP	Madrid	21 Jul
1:46.99	Samson	Ngoepe	RSA	28.1.85	2	NC	Durban	17 Mar
	(100)							
1:46.99	Ioan	Zaizan	ROM	21.7.83	6	WUG	Bangkok	14 Aug

Note: A made at an altitude of 1000m or more, h made in a heat, q quarter-final, s semi-final, -J Juniors, -Y Youths

Mark	Name		Nat	Born	Date
1:47.00	Jamaal	James	TRI-J	4.9.88	13 May
1:47.0	Joseph	Mutua	KEN	10.12.78	14 Jun
1:47.04	Andrea	Longo	ITA	26.6.75	8 Jun
1:47.04	Michael	Coltherd	GBR	28.12.82	30 Jun
1:47.05	Isaac	Sang	KEN	24.8.78	4 Aug
1:47.06	Lachlan	Renshaw	AUS	4.2.87	15 Apr
1:47.06	Andy	González	CUB	17.10.87	28 Jul
1:47.07	Yuriy	Koldin	RUS	1.11.83	1 Aug
1:47.08	Matthew	Scherer	USA	21.11.83	12 May
1:47.08	Maurizio	Bobbato	ITA	17.2.79	8 Jun
1:47.08	Neville	Miller	USA	22.12.82	21 Jun
1:47.08	Ivan	Nesterov	RUS	10.2.85	29 Jun
1:47.09	Miguel	Quesada	ESP	18.9.79	4 Jul
1.47.1A	Geoffrey	Kibet	KEN-Y	5.6.90	13 Jun
1:47.11	Reuben	Twijukye	UGA	25.12.86	13 May
1:47.13	Glody	Dube	BOT	2.7.78	28 Apr
1:47.14A	Florent	Lacasse ¶	FRA	21.1.81	2 Feb
1:47.14	Abdelaati	Iguider	MAR	25.3.87	4 Aug
1:47.15	Steffen	Co	GER	22.3.77	7 Jul
1:47.16	Masato	Yokota	JPN	19.11.87	30 Aug
1:47.19	Saïd	Ahmed	USA	10.12.82	2 Jun
1:47.19	Matthias	Rosseeuw	BEL	22.5.85	28 Jul
1:47.23	Gustavo	Aguirre	ARG	8.4.77	28 Jul
1:47.26	Timothy	Kiptanui	KEN	5.1.80	25 Jul
1:47.26	James	Brewer	GBR-J	18.6.88	10 Aug
1:47.28	Jackson	Langat	KEN	15.12.80	28 Apr
1:47.28	Kevin	Hicks	USA	7.11.84	22 Jun
1:47.28	Nick	Bromley	AUS	23.3.84	27 Jun
1:47.28	Linus	Ndiwa	KEN		14 Jul
1:47.29	Ismail Ahmed	Ismail	SUD	10.9.84	20 Apr
1:47.30	Driss	Yousfi	FRA	23.7.83	18 Aug
1:47.33	Samson	Serem	KEN	.85	9 Jun
1:47.34	Andrew	Osagie	GBR-J	19.2.88	20 May
1.47.4	William Filip	(Rabih Khoudi)	SUD-J	18.10.88	10 Sep
1:47.41	Ivan	Heshko	UKR	19.8.79	7 Jul
1:47.42	Sajeesh	Joseph	IND	14.1.87	26 Oct
1:47.43	Cosmas	Rono Kipkorir	KEN	12.12.84	2 Mar
1:47.43	Samuel	Burley	USA	13.2.81	15 Apr
1:47.43	Assane	Diallo	SEN	10.2.75	24 Jun
1:47.43	Rui	Silva	POR	3.8.77	21 Jul
1:47.44	Abdesslam	Merabet	FRA	30.7.87	12 Jul
1:47.45	Martell	Munguia	MEX	6.6.82	12 May
1:47.47	Jeff	Lastennet	FRA	26.8.87	21 Jul
1:47.48	José Manuel	Cortés	ESP	10.6.83	13 Sep
1:47.5A	Silah	Kimutai	KEN		18 May
1:47.5	Samir	Khadar	ALG	10.6.86	19 May
1:47.53	Onalenna	Baloyi (Oabona)	BOT	6.5.84	14 Jul
1:47.53	Mahamoud	Farah	DJI-J	4.9.88	19 Jul
1:47.54	Hiroshi	Sasano	JPN	23.9.78	28 Jul
1:47.54	Ramesan	Rajeev	IND	2.3.85	26 Oct
1:47.55	Paul	Harris	USA	30.3.86	12 May
1:47.56	Prince	Mumba	ZAM	28.8.84	7 Jul

Mark	Name		Nat	Born	Date
1:47.56	Andrey	Osipov	RUS	6.3.83	1 Aug
1:47.58	Grzegorz	Krzosek	POL	10.1.76	6 Jun
1:47.59	Miroslaw	Formela	POL	31.10.78	17 Jun
1:47.64	Dmitrijs	Jurkevics	LAT	7.1.87	13 Jun
1:47.69	Ali Abubaker	Kamal	QAT	8.11.83	28 Apr
1:47.69	Pablo	Solares	MEX	22.12.84	12 May
1:47.70	Elias	Koech	KEN	4.6.85	9 Jun
1:47.71	Marcus	Mayes	USA	10.3.85	26 May
1:47.71	David	McCarthy	IRL	16.7.83	7 Jul
1:47.71	Brice	Etes	FRA	11.4.84	25 Jul
1:47.71	Georg	Eberhardt	GER-J	10.10.88	28 Jul
1:47.72	Aunese	Curreen	SAM	23.12.81	30 Aug
1:47.74	Hugo	de Haan	NED	6.11.84	18 Aug
1:47.75	Philemon	Kimutai	KEN	12.8.83	9 Jun
1:47.76	Steve	Sherer	USA	5.5.81	3 Jun
1:47.77	Moritz	Hoeft	GER	3.12.80	6 Jun
1:47.77	Graeme	Oudney	GBR	11.4.85	9 Jun
1:47.78	Mouhcine	El Amine	MAR	8.1.82	30 Jun
1:47.78	Vitalij	Kozlov	LTU	5.3.87	12 Jul
1:47.79	Werner	Botha	AUS	17.12.85	2 Mar
1:47.79	Dominic	Tanui	KEN	2.2.83	28 Apr
1:47.79	Leonardo	Price	ARG	21.2.79	14 Jul
1:47.79	John	Litei	KEN	2.6.83	2 Jul
1:47.79	Gareth	Hyett	NZL	13.2.80	15 Jul
1:47.81A	Robert	Lathouwers	NED	8.7.83	3 Feb
1:47.81	Takeshi	Kuchino	JPN	7.4.86	15 Jul
1:47.81	Mikko	Lahtio	FIN	21.9.84	12 Aug
1:47.83	Jimmy	Lomba	FRA	30.6.78	21 Jul
1:47.86	Maury Surel	Castillo	CUB	19.10.84	17 Mar
1:47.86	Darren	St.Clair	GBR	6.4.85	23 May
1:47.87	Jason	Stewart	NZL	21.11.81	10 Aug
1:47.88	Badr	Rassioui	MAR	.86	12 May
1:47.88	Oleksandr	Osmolovych	UKR	8.10.85	7 Jul
1:47.89	Zach	Glavash	USA	14.6.84	25 May
1:47.89	Mohamed	Moro	ITA/MAR	5.3.84	21 Jul
1:47.90	Alex	McClary	USA	31.10.85	21 Apr
1:47.90	Nils	Schumann	GER	20.5.78	17 Jun
1:47.90	Diego	Ruíz	ESP	5.2.82	29 Jun
1:47.91	Joeri	Jansen	BEL	28.5.79	26 May
1:47.91	Tiago	Rodrígues	POR	19.6.85	12 Jul
1:47.92	André	Olivier	RSA-J	29.12.89	31 Mar
1:47.92	Moritz	Waldmann	GER	23.7.85	10 Aug
1:47.92	Andrew	Maloney	CAN	7.12.82	11 Aug
1:47.92	Nico	Herrera	VEN	31.7.83	21 Dec
1:47.93	Elphas	Sang	KEN		24 Mar
1:47.95	Mohd Othman	Shahween	KSA	15.2.86	16 Oct
1:47.96	Russell	Brown	USA	6.3.85	8 Jul
1:47.96	Hikaru	Miyazaki	JPN	31.7.86	20 Oct
1:47.98	Yarrick	Kincaid (202)	USA		26 May
Indoors					
1:47.80	Shaun	Smith	JAM	19.4.83	2 Mar
1:47.90	Alex	McClary	USA	31.10.85	2 Mar

JUNIORS

See main list for top 7 juniors. 11 performances by 3 men to 1:45.35. Additional marks and further juniors:

Chepkirwok	1:44.84	3s1	WCh	Osaka	31 Aug	1:45.14	3	SGP	Doha	11 May
	1:44.95	3	Bisl	Oslo	15 Jun	1:45.35	1	APM	Hengelo	26 May
Kaki	1:45.2	1		Khartoum	10 Sep	1:45.22	1	AfG	Alger	20 Jul
Rudisha	1:45.10	1	MAI	Malmö	2 Jul					

If junior: note Belal Mansoor Ali 1:44.74 1 GS Ostrava 27 Jun, 1:44.89 4 VD Bruxelles 14 Sep

Mark	Name		Nat	Born	Pos	Meet	Venue	Date
1:47.00	Jamaal	James	TRI	4.9.88	1	SEC	Tuscaloosa	13 May
1.47.1A	Geoffrey	Kibet	KEN-Y	5.6.90	1		Nairobi	13 Jun
1:47.26	James	Brewer (10)	GBR	18.6.88	6		Leverkusen	10 Aug
1:47.34	Andrew	Osagie	GBR	19.2.88	3		Loughborough	20 May
1.47.4	William	Filip (Rabih Khoudi)	SUD	18.10.88	2		Khartoum	10 Sep
1:47.53	Mahamoud	Farah	DJI	4.9.88	5s2	AfG	Alger	19 Jul
1:47.71	Georg	Eberhardt	GER	10.10.88	8B	NA	Heusden-Zolder	28 Jul
1:47.92	André	Olivier	RSA	29.12.89	1		Port Elizabeth	31 Mar
1:48.04	Sebastian	Keiner	GER	22.8.89	2r1		Dessau	1 Jun
1:48.04	Hamid	Oualich	FRA	26.4.88	6		Noisy-le-Grand	12 Jun
1:48.10	Adam	Kszczot	POL	2.9.89	3	EJ	Hengelo	22 Jul
1:48.19	Ali Saad	Al-Daraan	KSA-Y	17.4.90	7	SGP	Doha	11 May
1:48.24A	Abdissa	Sore (20)	ETH	.89	4	E.Af Ch	Kampala	31 May

1000 METRES

2:15.23	Belal Mansoor	Ali	BRN	17.10.83	1	DNG	Stockholm	7 Aug

Mark	Name		Nat	Born	Pos	Meet	Venue	Date
2:15.86	Mbulaeni	Mulaudzi	RSA	8.9.80	2	DNG	Stockholm	7 Aug
2:16.25	Bernard	Lagat	USA	12.12.74	3	DNG	Stockholm	7 Aug
2:16.27	Yassine	Bensghir	MAR	3.1.83	4	DNG	Stockholm	7 Aug
2:16.99	Andrew	Baddeley	GBR	20.6.82	5	DNG	Stockholm	7 Aug
2:17.73	Mehdi	Baala	FRA	17.8.78	1		Tomblaine	18 Sep
2:18.12	Edwin	Letting	KEN	15.5.84	6	DNG	Stockholm	7 Aug

2:18.68	Gary	Reed	CAN	25.10.81	7 Aug
2:18.79	Abdesslam	Kennouche	ALG	7.10.80	12 May
2:18.92	Rizak	Dirshe	SWE	5.1.72	7 Aug
2:19.14	Abdelaati	Iguider	MAR	25.3.87	7 Aug
2:19.33	Edward	Mutai	KEN	28.8.84	15 Jul
Indoors					
2:18.75	Arnoud	Okken	NED	20.4.82	11 Feb
2:19.47	Tarek	Boukensa	ALG	19.11.81	11 Feb

Best Junior: 2:20.75i Abraham Chepkirwok UGA 18.11.88 5 Karlsruhe 11 Feb

1500 METRES

Mark	Name		Nat	Born	Pos	Meet	Venue	Date
3:30.54	Alan	Webb	USA	13.1.83	1	Gaz	Saint-Denis	6 Jul
3:30.92	Tarek	Boukensa	ALG	19.11.81	1	GGala	Roma	13 Jul
3:31.01	Mehdi	Baala	FRA	17.8.78	2	Gaz	Saint-Denis	6 Jul
3:31.05		Baala			1		Strasbourg	28 Jun
3:31.18	Shadrack	Korir	KEN	14.12.78	2	GGala	Roma	13 Jul
3:31.49	Belal Mansoor	Ali	BRN	17.10.83	1	GP	Athína	2 Jul
3:31.58	Alex	Kipchirchir	KEN	26.11.84	3	GGala	Roma	13 Jul
3:31.73	Augustine	Choge	KEN	21.1.87	1	SGP	Doha	11 May
3:31.75	Daniel Kipchirchir	Komen	KEN	27.11.84	1	Golden	Shanghai	28 Sep
3:31.89	Suleiman	Simotwo	KEN	21.4.80	4	GGala	Roma	13 Jul
3:31.98		Simotwo			2	SGP	Doha	11 May
3:32.13	Youssef	Baba (10)	MAR	7.8.79	3	SGP	Doha	11 May
3:32.18	Juan Carlos	Higuero	ESP	3.8.78	5	GGala	Roma	13 Jul
3:32.28		Ali			1	Herc	Monaco	25 Jul
3:32.35		Boukensa			4	SGP	Doha	11 May
3:32.35	Kenenisa	Bekele	ETH	13.6.82	2	Golden	Shanghai	28 Sep
3:32.44		Komen			2	GP	Athína	2 Jul
3:32.55		Komen			6	GGala	Roma	13 Jul
3:32.67	Mohammed	Moustaoui	MAR	2.4.85	2	Herc	Monaco	25 Jul
3:32.67		Komen			1	VD	Bruxelles	14 Sep
3:32.75	Abdelaati	Iguider	MAR	25.3.87	7	GGala	Roma	13 Jul
3:32.76		Korir			5	SGP	Doha	11 May
3:32.77		Boukensa			3	Gaz	Saint-Denis	6 Jul
3:32.81+		Komen			1	Pre	Eugene	10 Jun
3:32.81		Korir			4	Gaz	Saint-Denis	6 Jul
3:32.83		Baba			3	GP	Athína	2 Jul
3:33.04	Yassine	Bensghir	MAR	3.1.83	3	Herc	Monaco	25 Jul
3:33.16		Korir			4	GP	Athína	2 Jul
3:33.43	Sergio	Gallardo	ESP	22.3.79	8	GGala	Roma	13 Jul
3:33.52		Komen			6	SGP	Doha	11 May
	(30/16)							
3:33.71	Hicham	Bellani	MAR	15.9.79	6	GP	Athína	2 Jul
3:33.85+	Bernard	Lagat	USA	12.12.74	2	Pre	Eugene	10 Jun
3:34.04	Bernard	Kiptum	KEN	8.10.86	7	GP	Athína	2 Jul
3:34.09	Arturo	Casado	ESP	26.1.83	9	GGala	Roma	13 Jul
	(20)							
3:34.16	Kevin	Sullivan	CAN	20.3.74	5	Gaz	Saint-Denis	6 Jul
3:34.25	Matt	Tegenkamp	USA	19.1.82	8	GP	Athína	2 Jul
3:34.32	Anter	Zerguelaine	ALG	4.1.85	9	GP	Athína	2 Jul
3:34.33	Reyes	Estévez	ESP	2.8.76	1	DLV	Bochum-Wattenscheid	12 Aug
3:34.52	Mounir	Yemmouni	FRA	12.10.83	5	Herc	Monaco	25 Jul
3:34.59	Youssef Saad	Kamel	BRN	29.3.83	3	Golden	Shanghai	28 Sep
3:34.62	Kamel	Boulahfane	ALG	1.7.76	10	GP	Athína	2 Jul
3:34.74	Andrew	Baddeley	GBR	20.6.82	1	BrGP	Sheffield	15 Jul
3:35.00	Rashid	Ramzi	BRN	17.7.80	2	WCh	Osaka	29 Aug
3:35.03	Ivan	Heshko	UKR	19.8.79	10	GGala	Roma	13 Jul
	(30)							
3:35.09	Yusuf	Biwott	KEN	12.11.86	2	DLV	Bochum-Wattenscheid	12 Aug
3:35.10	Remi	Limo Ndiwa	KEN-J	3.2.88	6	Herc	Monaco	25 Jul
3:35.24	Asbel	Kiprop	KEN-J	30.6.89	4	WCh	Osaka	29 Aug
3:35.29	Leonel	Manzano	USA	12.9.84	2	NC	Indianapolis	24 Jun
3:35.32	Christian	Obrist	ITA	20.11.80	3	GP	Rieti	9 Sep
3:35.72	Jonathan	Rankin	USA	9.2.82	5	GP	Rieti	9 Sep
3:35.72	Geoffrey	Rono	KEN	21.4.87	4	VD	Bruxelles	14 Sep
3:35.8+	Adil	Kaouch ¶	MAR	1.1.79	2	Bisl	Oslo	15 Jun
3:35.85	Nick	Willis	NZL	25.4.83	1	adidas	Carson	20 May

MEN 2007

Mark	Name		Nat	Born	Pos	Meet	Venue	Date
3:35.92	Rui	Silva	POR	3.8.77	2	BrGP	Sheffield	15 Jul
	(40)							
3:36.04	Badr	Rassioui	MAR	.86	3	NA	Heusden-Zolder	28 Jul
3:36.04	Mekonnen	Gebremedhin	ETH-J	11.10.88	4	NA	Heusden-Zolder	28 Jul
3:36.13	Bouabdellah	Tahri	FRA	20.12.78	2	Athl	Lausanne	10 Jul
3:36.13	Nicholas	Kemboi	KEN-J	18.12.89	2	LGP	London (CP)	3 Aug
3:36.18	Alistair	Cragg	IRL	13.6.80	2	adidas	Carson	20 May
3:36.22	Diego	Ruiz	ESP	5.2.82	1		Huelva	13 Sep
3:36.27	Brimin	Kipruto	KEN	31.7.85	1	Bisl	Oslo	15 Jun
3:36.32	Hudson	de Souza	BRA	25.2.77	1	PAm	Rio de Janeiro	25 Jul
3:36.40	Álvaro	Fernández	ESP	7.4.81	2	Bisl	Oslo	15 Jun
3:36.41	Deresse	Mekonnen	ETH	20.10.87	1		Herrera	19 May
	(50)							
3:36.49	Rob	Myers	USA	5.8.80	3	adidas	Carson	20 May
3:36.54	Carsten	Schlangen	GER	31.12.80	3	DLV	Bochum-Wattenscheid	12 Aug
3:36.82	William	Chirchir	KEN	6.2.79	13	GP	Athína	2 Jul
3:36.86	Samson	Serem	KEN	.85	2		Strasbourg	28 Jun
3:36.95	Chris	Lukezic	USA	24.4.84	4	NC	Indianapolis	24 Jun
3:37.04	Álvaro	Rodríguez	ESP	25.5.87	3	Bisl	Oslo	15 Jun
3:37.04	Paul	Melly	KEN	4.1.81	3		Strasbourg	28 Jun
3:37.07	Joseph Lopez	Lomong	SUD/USA	1.1.85	1	NCAA	Sacramento	9 Jun
3:37.13	Adam	Goucher	USA	18.2.75	5	adidas	Carson	20 May
3:37.23	Elkanah	Angwenyi	KEN	5.2.83	9	VD	Bruxelles	14 Sep
	(60)							
3:37.25	Samir	Khadar	ALG	10.6.86	1		Alger	21 Jun
3:37.27	Chris	Solinsky	USA	5.12.84	1		Oordegem	7 Jul
3:37.29	Paul	Korir	KEN	15.7.77	1		Cuxhaven	14 Jul
3:37.41	Cornelius	Ndiwa	KEN-J	.88	2		Huelva	13 Sep
3:37.42	Mark	Fountain	AUS	10.3.82	5	LGP	London (CP)	3 Aug
3:37.47	Hassan	Mourhit	BEL	2.1.82	7	NA	Heusden-Zolder	28 Jul
3:37.56	Russell	Brown	USA	3.3.85	3	NCAA	Sacramento	9 Jun
3:37.58	Juan	van Deventer	RSA	26.3.83	1		Rehlingen	28 May
3:37.59	Abdelghani	Hamamraoui	ALG	.83	4		Strasbourg	28 Jun
3:37.61	Timothy	Kiptanui	KEN	5.1.80	8	NA	Heusden-Zolder	28 Jul
	(70)							
3:37.67	Johan	Cronje	RSA	13.4.82	9	SGP	Doha	11 May
3:37.71	Ali	Maataoui	MAR	15.12.80	2		Herrera	19 May
3:37.71	Juan Luis	Barrios	MEX	24.6.83	2	PAm	Rio de Janeiro	25 Jul
3:37.75	Haron	Keitany	KEN	.84	10	NA	Heusden-Zolder	28 Jul
3:37.79	Daham Najim	Bashir	QAT	8.11.79	2rA	GP	Madrid	21 Jul
3:37.85	Wolfram	Müller	GER	8.7.81	5	DLV	Bochum-Wattenscheid	12 Aug
3:37.88	Byron	Piedra	ECU	9.8.82	3	PAm	Rio de Janeiro	25 Jul
3:37.92	Paul Kipsiele	Koech	KEN	25.11.81	5		Glasgow	3 Jun
3:37.96	Vincent	Rono	KEN		4	NCAA	Sacramento	9 Jun
3:38.1A	Vickson	Polonet	KEN	2.7.85	8h3	NC	Nairobi	14 Jun
	(80)							
3:38.11	Abdesslam	Kennouche	ALG	7.10.80	2		Rehlingen	28 May
3:38.15	Khoudir	Aggoune	ALG	5.1.81	5		Strasbourg	28 Jun
3:38.16	Guillaume	Eraud	FRA	1.7.81	4	Bisl	Oslo	15 Jun
3:38.17	Gustavo	Platas	ESP	19.2.81	4		Huelva	13 Sep
3:38.18	Mohamed Othman	Shahween	KSA	15.2.86	2		Alger	21 Jun
3:38.19	Ate	van der Burgt	NED	17.3.78	11rA	NA	Heusden-Zolder	28 Jul
3:38.20	Jeremy	Roff	AUS	22.11.83	3	GP	Melbourne	2 Mar
3:38.2+	Craig	Mottram	AUS	18.6.80	9	in 1M	Oslo	15 Jun
3:38.24	Abdelkader	Bakhtache	FRA	30.1.82	6		Strasbourg	28 Jun
3:38.33	Neil	Speaight	GBR	9.9.78	7	BrGP	Sheffield	15 Jul
	(90)							
3:38.40	Philemon	Kimutai	KEN	12.8.83	3	Kuso	Warszawa	17 Jun
3:38.42	Ali Abubaker	Kamal	QAT	8.11.83	3		Bilbao	23 Jun
3:38.46	Nick	McCormick	GBR	11.9.81	6	Bisl	Oslo	15 Jun
3:38.48	Youcef	Abdi	AUS	7.12.77	5	GP	Melbourne	2 Mar
3:38.49	Manuel	Damião	POR	4.7.78	2		Alcalá de Henares	7 Jul
3:38.50	Stephen	Davies	GBR	16.2.84	8	BrGP	Sheffield	15 Jul
3:38.56	Jeff	Riseley	AUS	11.11.86	9	BrGP	Sheffield	15 Jul
3:38.62	Javier	Carriqueo	ARG	29.5.79	4	PAm	Rio de Janeiro	25 Jul
3:38.63	Gareth	Hyett	NZL	13.2.80	6	GP	Melbourne	2 Mar
3:38.66	Adrian	Blincoe	NZL	4.11.79	11	BrGP	Sheffield	15 Jul
	(100)							

3:38.68	Ryan	McKenzie	CAN	13.10.78	7 Jul
3:38.7A	Gideon	Gathumba	KEN	9.3.80	29 Sep
3:38.74	Moses	Barmasai	KEN	1.6.86	28 Jul
3:38.76	Bikila	Demma	ETH-J	18.7.89	2 Jul

Mark	Name		Nat	Born	Date
3:38.77	Zakaria	Maazouzi	MAR	15.6.85	9 Jun
3:38.80	Sadjad	Moradi	IRI	30.3.83	1 Jul
3:38.90	David	Freeman	PUR	28.4.82	19 May
3:38.90	Christoph	Lohse	GER	26.11.83	12 Aug
3:39.00	Saïd	Ahmed	USA	10.12.82	20 May
3:39.01A	Abdissa	Sore	ETH-J	.89	31 May
3:39.01	Vyacheslav	Shabunin	RUS	27.9.69	17 Jun
3:39.03	Pedro Antonio	Esteso	ESP	13.10.76	9 Sep
3:39.08	Edward	Mutai	KEN	28.8.84	3 Jun
3:39.08	Felipe	Carnicer	ESP	25.3.83	23 Jun
3:39.09	Mitchell	Kealey	AUS	28.1.84	22 Jul
3:39.10	Collis	Birmingham	AUS	27.12.84	15 Jul
3:39.14	Brad	Woods	AUS	25.4.86	28 Jul
3:39.19	Bartosz	Nowicki	POL	26.2.84	13 Sep
3:39.2	Lachlan	Chisholm	AUS	4.5.80	1 Aug
3:39.22	Franek	Haschke	GER	28.3.80	6 Jun
3:39.30	Rizak	Dirshe	SWE	5.1.72	28 Jul
3:39.31	Hailu	Mekonnen	ETH	4.4.80	14 Jul
3:39.34	Solomon	Barngetuny	KEN		2 Jul
3:39.35		Gu Ming	CHN	16.3.83	20 May
3:39.36	José Antonio	Redolat	ESP	17.2.76	2 Jun
3:39.4A	Dejene	Edeba	ETH		6 May
3:39.44	John	Jefferson	USA	30.12.82	28 Jul
3:39.48	Halil	Akkas	TUR	1.7.83	29 Apr
3:39.50	Hassan	Khallouki	FRA	4.2.79	28 May
3:39.58	Fabiano	Peçanha	BRA	5.6.82	25 Jul
3:39.59	Gabe	Jennings	USA	25.1.79	22 Jun
3:39.62	Eugenio	Barrios	ESP	3.11.76	2 Jul
3:39.62	Ian	Dobson	USA	6.2.82	21 Jul
3:39.67	Mulugeta	Wondimu	ETH	28.2.85	23 May
3:39.72	Bernard	Kirui	KEN	12.12.85	15 Jun
3:39.80	Kurt	Benninger	CAN	1.1.85	9 Jun
3:39.81	Philip	Lagat	KEN	16.2.83	21 Apr
3:39.81	Andy	McClary	USA	31.10.85	24 Jun
3:39.81	Jesús	España	ESP	21.8.78	21 Jul
3:39.85	Jermaine	Mays	GBR	23.12.82	9 Jun
3:39.87	Barnabás	Bene	HUN	27.8.86	23 May
3:39.9	Chatholi	Hamza	IND	1.11.81	23 Oct
3:39.91	Tom	Brooks	USA	10.1.78	2 Jul
3:39.93	Max	Smith	NZL	20.10.84	9 Jun
3:39.96	Garrett	Heath	USA	3.11.85	14 Jul
3:39.98+	Eliud	Kipchoge	KEN	5.11.84	10 Jun
3:40.0A	Willy	Komen Rutto	KEN	22.12.87	29 Sep
3:40.02	Abdelaziz Naji	El Idrissi	ITA/MAR	8.12.86	11 Jul
3:40.06	Will	Leer	USA		22 Jun
3:40.07	Joseph	Boit	KEN	.78	30 May
3:40.10	Michael	Coltherd	GBR	28.12.82	9 Jun
3:40.10	Francisco	España	ESP	27.10.84	23 Jun
3:40.11	David	Krummenacker	USA	24.5.75	20 May
3:40.15	Paul	Hoffman	AUS	17.6.82	2 Mar
3:40.17	Ben	True	USA		7 Jun
3:40.22	Pablo	Solares	MEX	22.12.84	7 Jun
3:40.31	Mahiedine	Mekhissi Benabbad	FRA	15.3.85	28 Jun

Mark	Name		Nat	Born	Date
3:40.37	Nabil	Madi	ALG	9.6.81	26 May
3:40.37	Christian	Neunhauserer	ITA	21.6.78	30 Jun
3:40.37	Sean	Graham	USA	6.3.80	21 Jul
3:40.38	Reid	Coolsaet	CAN	29.7.79	21 Jul
3:40.43	Peter	Biwott Kipkorir	KEN	22.8.76	6 Jun
3:40.45	Bernard	Chepkok	KEN	17.1.84	23 May
3:40.51	Boaz	Cheboiywo Kipsang	KEN	2.8.78	21 Apr
3:40.52	Mykola	Labovskyy	UKR	4.5.83	28 Jul
3:40.53	Jonas	Stifel	GER	5.9.80	1 Jun
3:40.58	Mohamed	Kallouche	MAR	7.6.85	7 Jul
3:40.60	Thomas	Lancashire	GBR	2.7.85	3 Aug
3:40.68	Wesley	Cheruiyot	KEN-J	10.12.88	27 May
3:40.75	Thorben	Grothaus	GER	3.2.84	12 Aug
3:40.76	Benjamin	Kiplagat	UGA-J	4.3.89	1 Jun
3:40.76	Fumikazu	Kobayashi	JPN	21.3.78	14 Jun
3:40.76	Mohamed-Khaled	Belabbas	FRA	4.7.81	11 Aug
3:40.78	Stephen	Pifer	USA	7.12.84	26 May
3:40.78	Chris	Warburton	GBR	23.8.83	28 May
3:40.80	David	Torrence	USA	26.11.85	22 Jun
3:40.82	Mbulaeni	Mulaudzi	RSA	8.9.80	16 Sep
3:40.85	Jonathon	Riley	USA	29.12.78	15 Jul
3:40.86	Benson	Esho	KEN	2.2.87	26 May
3:40.95	Jeff	See	USA	6.6.86	22 Jun
3:40.96	Liam	Reale	IRL	16.3.83	28 Jul
3:40.97	Leandro	de Oliveira	BRA	2.2.82	30 May
3:40.99	Issak	Zemikael	ERI-J	12.3.89	22 Jul
3:41.0A	Adunga	Assefa	ETH		6 May
3:41.03	Tom	Van Rooy	BEL	30.1.82	21 Jul
3:41.03	Elijah	Boit Kiprono	KEN	4.7.86	28 Jul
3:41.05	Steve	Sherer	USA	5.5.81	27 May
3:41.07	Kazuya	Watanabe	JPN	7.7.87	14 Jun
3:41.12	Ross	Toole	GBR	8.10.86	30 Jun
3:41.12	Ricardo Filipe	Giehl	GER	5.6.85	12 Aug
3:41.13	Jordan	McNamara	USA		9 Jun
3:41.17	Peter	van der Westhuizen	RSA	21.12.84	26 May
3:41.2A	Amos	Korir	KEN	.80	21 Apr
3:41.22	Mark	Carroll	IRL	15.1.72	9 Jun
3:41.25	Dawit	Wolde	ETH-Y	19.5.91	13 Sep
3:41.27	Eduard	Villanueva	VEN	29.12.84	6 Jul
3:41.28	Patrick	Tarpy	USA		9 Jun
3:41.28	Abdelkader	Hachlaf	MAR	3.7.79	13 Jun
3:41.30	Hatem	Hamdi	TUN	2.9.86	21 Jun
3:41.34	Samwel	Mwera Chegere	TAN	3.6.85	14 Sep

(200)

Indoors

Mark	Name		Nat	Born	Date
3:39.05	Isaac K.	Songok	KEN	25.4.84	20 Feb
3:39.78	Laban	Rotich	KEN	20.1.69	3 Feb
3:40.13	Juan Carlos	Esteso	ESP	13.10.76	24 Feb
3:40.80	Gilbert	Kipchoge	KEN	4.5.83	6 Feb
3:41.03	James	Nolan	IRL	27.1.77	3 Feb
3:41.06	Driss	Maazouzi	FRA	15.10.69	3 Feb
3:41.21	Joeri	Jansen	BEL	28.5.79	24 Feb

Drugs disqualification: 3:30.77dq Adil Kaouch ¶ MAR 1.1.79 1 GGala Roma 13 Jul

JUNIORS

See main list for top 5 juniors. 16 performances by 4 men to 3:35.8. Additional marks and further juniors:

Kiprop	3:35.5A	1	WCT	Nairobi	28 Jul	3:35.81	12	GP	Athína	2 Jul
Limo Ndiwa	3:35.91	2	NA	Heusden-Zolder	28 Jul	3:37.24i	4		Pireás	24 Feb
Mekonnen	3:36.45	1		Barakaldo	14 Jul					
Kemboi	3:36.49	4		Shanghai	28 Sep	3:36.90	4	BrGP	Sheffield	15 Jul

If junior: note Belal Mansoor Ali – two in main list plus 3:35.24 7 SGP Doha 11 May, 3:35.41 1 Athl Lausanne 10 Jul

Mark	Name		Nat	Born	Pos	Meet	Venue	Date
3:38.76	Bikila	Demma	ETH-J	18.7.89	3		Malmö	2 Jul
3:39.01A	Abdissa	Sore	ETH-J	.89	1	E.AfCh	Kampala	31 May
3:40.68	Wesley	Cheruiyot	KEN-J	10.12.88	1		Brazzaville	27 May
3:40.76	Benjamin	Kiplagat	UGA-J	4.3.89	7		Dessau	1 Jun
3:40.99	Issak	Zemikael (10)	ERI-J	12.3.89	10	AfG	Alger	22 Jul
3:41.25	Dawit	Wolde	ETH-Y	19.5.91	13		Huelva	13 Sep
3:41.5A	Josphat Mitunga	Kithii	KEN	28.12.90	3		Kakamega	21 Apr
3:41.65	Emmanuel	Bor	KEN	14.4.88	4	WUG	Bangkok	12 Aug
3:41.7A	Abel Kiprop	Mutai	KEN	2.10.88	1h4		Kakamega	21 Apr
3:42.0A	Bernard Muinde	Matheka	KEN	18.7.88	6s2	NC	Nairobi	14 Jun
3:42.40	A.J.	Acosta	USA	13.4.88	2r2		Eugene	20 Apr
3:42.4	Adil	Beryami	MAR-Y	23.1.90	1		Casablanca	24 Jun
3:42.79	Otmane	Belharbazi	FRA	3.11.88	10r1		Ninove	11 Aug
3:42.84	Mourad	Amdouni	FRA	21.1.88	11r1		Ninove	11 Aug
3:43.09	Kamil	Zielinski (20)	POL	17.1.89	3		Wroclaw	22 Jun

1 MILE

Mark	Name		Nat	Born	Pos	Meet	Venue	Date
3:46.91	Alan	Webb	USA	13.1.83	1		Brasschaat	21 Jul
3:48.28	Daniel Kipchirchir	Komen	KEN	27.11.84	1	Pre	Eugene	10 Jun
3:50.56	Bernard	Lagat	USA	12.12.74	2	Pre	Eugene	10 Jun
3:51.14	Adil	Kaouch ¶	MAR	1.1.79	1	Bisl	Oslo	15 Jun
3:51.62	Augustine	Choge	KEN	21.1.87	2	Bisl	Oslo	15 Jun
3:51.95	Andrew	Baddeley	GBR	20.6.82	3	Bisl	Oslo	15 Jun
3:52.10	Alex	Kipchirchir	KEN	26.11.84	3	Pre	Eugene	10 Jun
3:52.35	Belal Mansoor	Ali	BRN	17.10.83	5	Bisl	Oslo	15 Jun
3:52.38	Arturo	Casado	ESP	26.1.83	6	Bisl	Oslo	15 Jun
3:52.78	Shadrack	Korir	KEN	14.12.78	4	Pre	Eugene	10 Jun
3:52.85	Sergio	Gallardo	ESP	22.3.79	7	Bisl	Oslo	15 Jun
3:53.08	Suleiman	Simotwo	KEN	21.4.80	8	Bisl	Oslo	15 Jun
3:54.24	Jonathan	Rankin	USA	9.2.82	1		Manchester (Str)	11 Aug
3:54.54	Craig	Mottram	AUS	18.6.80	3	GP	New York	2 Jun
3:55.09	Nick	Willis	NZL	25.4.83	4	GP	New York	2 Jun
3:56.17	Isaac	Songok	KEN	25.4.84	11	Bisl	Oslo	15 Jun
3:56.21	Kevin	Sullivan	CAN	20.3.74	5	Pre	Eugene	10 Jun

Mark	Name		Nat	Born	Date
3:56.37	Tarek	Boukensa	ALG	19.11.81	15 Jun
3:56.46	Max	Smith	NZL	20.10.84	21 Jul
3:56.6	Adam	Goucher	USA	18.2.75	10 Jun
3:57.02	Chris	Lukezic	USA	24.4.84	2 Jun
3:57.07	Jonathon	Riley	USA	29.12.78	11 Aug
3:57.19	Eliud	Kipchoge	KEN	5.11.84	10 Jun
3:57.20	Robert	Curtis	USA	28.11.84	14 May
3:57.26	Jason	Jabaut	USA	13.3.82	2 Jun
3:57.46	Josh	McDougall	USA	1.6.85	31 Mar
3:57.46	Gareth	Hyett	NZL	13.2.80	21 Jul
3:57.82	Moumin	Geele	SOM	6.4.86	11 Aug
3:57.84	Seth	Summerside	USA	14.2.84	21 Jul
3:57.95	Lachlan	Chisholm	AUS	4.5.80	11 Aug
3:58.01	Robert	Myers	USA	5.8.80	10 Jun
3:58.03	Thomas	Lancashire	GBR	2.7.85	25 Aug
3:58.12	Nicholas	Kemboi	KEN-J	18.12.89	10 Jun
3:58.18	Juan Luis	Barrios	MEX	24.6.83	15 Apr
3:58.32	Bernard	Kiptum Kiptanui	KEN	8.10.86	11 Aug
3:58.4	Sean	Graham	USA	6.3.80	10 Jun
3:58.44	Chris	Warburton	GBR	23.8.83	11 Aug
3:58.45	Mitchell	Kealey	AUS	28.1.84	8 Jul
3:58.46	Saïd	Ahmed	USA	10.12.82	10 Jun
3:58.54	Joseph Lopez	Lomong	SUD/USA	1.1.85	14 Apr
3:58.62	David	Torrence	USA	26.11.85	28 Apr
3:58.70	Jeff	See	USA	6.6.86	3 Jun
3:58.74	Dame	Tasama Faisa	ETH	12.10.87	21 Jul
3:58.8	Sean	O'Brien	USA	4.8.80	10 Jun
3:58.86	Mark	Fountain	AUS	10.3.82	6 Jul
3:58.89	Brad	Woods	AUS	25.4.86	8 Jul

9 more men under 4 minutes

Indoors

Mark	Name		Nat	Born	Pos	Meet	Venue	Date
3:55.58	Mark	Fountain	AUS	10.3.82	1	Tysn	Fayetteville	9 Feb
3:56.2+	Kenenisa	Bekele	ETH	13.6.82	1	GP	Birmingham	17 Feb

Mark	Name		Nat	Born	Date
3:56.72#	Nick	Symmonds	USA	30.12.83	13 Jan
3:57.76	Berhanu	Alemu	ETH	16.7.82	3 Feb
3:58.64	Eliud	Njubi	KEN	27.7.79	20 Jan
3:58.78#	Leonel	Manzano	USA	12.9.84	24 Feb
3:58.85	James	Nolan	IRL	27.1.77	27 Jan
3:58.88	Gareth	Turnbull	IRL	14.5.79	3 Feb

7 more men under 4 minutes

Best Junior: 3:58.12 Nicholas Kemboi KEN 18.12.89 8 Pre Eugene 10 Jun

2000 METRES

Mark	Name		Nat	Born	Pos	Meet	Venue	Date
4:56.56	Mehdi	Baala	FRA	17.8.78	1		Villeneuve d'Ascq	9 Jun
4:57.20	Tarek	Boukensa	ALG	19.11.81	2		Villeneuve d'Ascq	9 Jun
4:58.98+	Kenenisa	Bekele	ETH	13.6.82	1	in 3k	Monaco	25 Jul
4:59.88+		K Bekele			1	in 3k	Stockholm	7 Aug
4:59.9+	Hicham	Bellani	MAR	15.9.79	2	in 3k	Monaco	25 Jul

Mark	Name		Nat	Born	Date
5:00.74	Remi	Limo Ndiwa	KEN-J	3.2.88	9 Jun
5:00.82	Bernard	Kiplagat	KEN-J	10.8.88	9 Jun
5:01.29	Halil	Akkas	TUR	1.7.83	3 Jun
5:01.4+	Alistair	Cragg	IRL	13.6.80	25 Jul
5:02.18+	Sahle	Warga	ETH	.81	9 Sep
5:02.5+	Yusuf	Biwott	KEN	12.11.86	9 Sep
5:02.7+	Edwin	Soi	KEN	3.3.86	9 Sep
5:02.9+	Thomas	Longosiwa	KEN	14.1.82	9 Sep
5:03.2+	Mark	Kiptoo	KEN	21.6.76	9 Sep

Monaco 25 Jul: 3-4-5- 5:00.3, 5:00.7, 5:01.1, possibly Kipsiro, Baday, Jawher

Indoors

Mark	Name		Nat	Born	Pos	Meet	Venue	Date
4:49.99	Kenenisa	Bekele	ETH	13.6.82	1	GP	Birmingham	17 Feb
4:55.72	Shadrack	Korir	KEN	14.12.78	2	GP	Birmingham	17 Feb
4:56.30	Augustine	Choge	KEN	21.1.87	1		Aubière	9 Feb
4:58.76	Brimin	Kipruto	KEN	31.7.85	3	GP	Birmingham	17 Feb
4:59.02	Remi	Limo Ndiwa	KEN-J	3.2.88	4	GP	Birmingham	17 Feb
4:59.48	Yusuf	Biwott	KEN	12.11.86	2		Aubière	9 Feb
5:00.98	Mohammed	Moustaoui	MAR	2.4.85	2		Aubière	9 Feb

3000 METRES

Mark	Name		Nat	Born	Pos	Meet	Venue	Date
7:25.79	Kenenisa	Bekele	ETH	13.6.82	1	DNG	Stockholm	7 Aug
7:26.69		K Bekele			1	BrGP	Sheffield	15 Jul
7:29.32		K Bekele			1	Herc	Monaco	25 Jul
7:32.03	Moses	Kipsiro	UGA	2.9.86	2	Herc	Monaco	25 Jul
7:32.49	Alistair	Cragg	IRL	13.6.80	3	Herc	Monaco	25 Jul
7:32.79	Thomas	Longosiwa	KEN	14.1.82	1	GP	Rieti	9 Sep
7:33.06	Eliud	Kipchoge	KEN	5.11.84	1	SGP	Doha	11 May

Mark	Name		Nat	Born	Pos	Meet	Venue	Date
7:33.39	Yusuf	Biwott	KEN	12.11.86	2	GP	Rieti	9 Sep
7:34.07	Edwin	Soi	KEN	3.3.86	3	GP	Rieti	9 Sep
7:34.37	Jonas	Cheruiyot	KEN	11.1.84	2	SGP	Doha	11 May
7:34.66	Joseph	Ebuya	KEN	20.6.87	3	SGP	Doha	11 May
7:34.94	Ahmed Ibrahim	Baday (10)	MAR	12.1.79	4	Herc	Monaco	25 Jul
7:35.00	Craig	Mottram	AUS	18.6.80	2	BrGP	Sheffield	15 Jul
7:35.44		J Cheruiyot			2	DNG	Stockholm	7 Aug
7:35.64		Longosiwa			3	DNG	Stockholm	7 Aug
7:35.68	Matt	Tegenkamp	USA	19.1.82	4	DNG	Stockholm	7 Aug
7:35.88	Boniface	Songok	KEN	25.12.80	4	SGP	Doha	11 May
7:35.99	Mushir Salem	Jawher	BRN	13.6.78	5	Herc	Monaco	25 Jul
7:36.34	Tefere Maregu	Zewdie	ETH	23.10.82	5	SGP	Doha	11 May
7:36.70	Ali	Maataoui	MAR	11.12.80	5	DNG	Stockholm	7 Aug
	(20/16)							
7:36.74	Abraham	Chebii	KEN	23.12.79	4	GP	Rieti	9 Sep
7:36.90	Chris	Solinsky	USA	5.12.84	3	BrGP	Sheffield	15 Jul
7:37.69	Bernard	Kiplagat	KEN-J	10.8.88	6	SGP	Doha	11 May
7:37.77	Khalid	El Amri	MAR	20.3.77	7	SGP	Doha	11 May
	(20)							
7:37.93	Hicham	Bellani	MAR	15.9.79	7	Herc	Monaco	25 Jul
7:38.10	Isaac	Songok	KEN	25.4.84	8	SGP	Doha	11 May
7:38.62	Remi	Limo Ndiwa	KEN-J	3.2.88	6	DNG	Stockholm	7 Aug
7:38.67	Micah	Kogo	KEN	3.6.86	7	DNG	Stockholm	7 Aug
7:38.77	Bernard	Lagat	USA	12.12.74	1	WK	Zürich	7 Sep
7:38.83	Mark	Kiptoo	KEN	21.6.76	5	GP	Rieti	9 Sep
7:39.02	Robert Kipngetich	Sigei	KEN	3.1.82	8	DNG	Stockholm	7 Aug
7:39.03	Dathan	Ritzenhein	USA	30.12.82	4	BrGP	Sheffield	15 Jul
7:39.07	Leonard Patrick	Komon	KEN-J	10.1.88	8	Herc	Monaco	25 Jul
7:40.88	Edwin	Kipkorir	KEN-J	3.9.89	5	BrGP	Sheffield	15 Jul
	(30)							
7:41.27	Anthony	Famiglietti	USA	8.11.78	1	adidas	Carson	20 May
7:41.51	Shadrack	Kosgei	KEN	24.11.84	6	GP	Rieti	9 Sep
7:41.86	Mohamed	Farah	GBR	23.3.83	5	WK	Zürich	7 Sep
7:41.95	Abdelaati	Iguider	MAR	25.3.87	1		Herrera	19 May
7:42.32	Asbel	Kiprop	KEN-J	30.6.89	1	Nebiolo	Torino	8 Jun
7:42.35	Tariku	Bekele	ETH	21.1.87	6	WK	Zürich	7 Sep
7:42.63	Bikila	Demma Daba	ETH-J	18.7.89	2		Herrera	19 May
7:42.64	James	Kosgei	KEN	.84	1		Liège (NX)	25 Jul
7:42.86	Juan Luis	Barrios	MEX	24.6.83	2	adidas	Carson	20 May
7:42.88+	Mark	Bett	KEN	22.12.76	1	GGala	Roma	13 Jul
	(40)							
7:42.94	Dickson	Marwa Mkami	TAN	6.3.82	2	Nebiolo	Torino	8 Jun
7:43.29	Jesús	España	ESP	21.8.78	3		Herrera	19 May
7:43.30	Josphat	Boit	KEN	26.11.83	3	adidas	Carson	20 May
7:43.67	Sahle	Warga	ETH	.81	2		Liège (NX)	25 Jul
7:43.70	Tadesse	Tola	ETH	31.10.87	5		Herrera	19 May
7:43.82	Seth	Summerside	USA	14.2.84	4	adidas	Carson	20 May
7:44.30	Felix	Kibore	QAT-J	18.2.88	10	SGP	Doha	11 May
7:44.39	Lishan	Yegezu	ETH	6.10.85	3		Liège (NX)	25 Jul
7:44.62	Bisluke	Kiplagat	KEN-J	8.8.88	4	Nebiolo	Torino	8 Jun
7:44.?+	Sileshi	Sihine	ETH	29.9.83	2	in 5k	Bruxelles	14 Sep
	(50)							
7:45.43	Edward	Mutai	KEN	28.8.84	5	Vard	Réthimno	18 Jul
7:45.51	Adil	Kaouch ¶	MAR	1.1.79	1		Castellón	9 Jun
7:45.76	Boaz	Cheboiywo	KEN	2.8.78	5	adidas	Carson	20 May
7:45.83	Moses	Mosop	KEN	17.7.85	6	Gaz	Saint-Denis	6 Jul
7:45.84	Bolota	Asmerom	USA	12.10.78	1		Oordegem	7 Jul
7:46.01	Collis	Birmingham	AUS	27.12.84	3		Sydney	17 Feb
7:46.16	Rob	Koborsi	USA	4.10.83	6	adidas	Carson	20 May
7:46.26	Francisco Javier	Alves	ESP	3.9.80	8	GP	Rieti	9 Sep
7:46.38	Moustafa	Shebto	QAT	4.7.86	2		Oordegem	7 Jul
7:46.65	John	Thuo	KEN	27.11.85	6	Nebiolo	Torino	8 Jun
	(60)							
7:46.70	Sultan Khamis	Zaman	QAT	23.7.85	4		Liège (NX)	25 Jul
7:46.74	Jan	Fitschen	GER	2.5.77	1	DLV	Bochum-Wattenscheid	12 Aug
7:46.93	Hosea	Macharinyang	KEN	12.6.86	7	Nebiolo	Torino	8 Jun
7:46.94	Monder	Rizki	BEL	16.8.79	3		Oordegem	7 Jul
7:47.29	Moses	Masai	KEN	1.6.86	4	Kuso	Warszawa	17 Jun
7:47.37	David	Siele	KEN-J	.88	2	GP	Dakar	28 Apr
7:47.68	Abdullah Ahmad	Hassan	QAT	4.4.81	6	Vard	Réthimno	18 Jul

Mark	Name		Nat	Born	Pos	Meet	Venue	Date
7:47.69	Abdi	Abdirahman	USA	1.1.77	7	adidas	Carson	20 May
7:47.69	Sean	Graham	USA	6.3.80	1		Gent	15 Jul

Mark	Name		Nat	Born	Date
7:48.03	Ian	Dobson	USA	6.2.82	15 Jul
7:48.06	Stephen	Kiprotich	UGA-J	18.4.89	25 Jul
7:48.12	Isaac	Tanui Kiprotich	KEN	19.12.86	21 Jul
7:48.29	David	Chemweno	KEN	18.12.81	17 Jun
7:48.35	Sammy	Kipketer	KEN	29.9.81	28 Apr
7:48.60	Solomon	Tsige	ETH	23.1.85	25 Jul
7:48.9+	John	Kibowen	KEN	21.4.69	3 Aug
7:49.06	Essa Ismail	Rashed	QAT	14.12.86	15 Jul
7:49.20	Simon	Bairu	CAN	8.8.83	15 Jul
7:49.30	Wilfred	Taragon	KEN	9.6.85	5 Jun
7:49.33	Hillary	Kiprono	KEN	.85	8 Jun
7:49.99	Benjamin	Kiplagat	KEN-J	4.3.89	28 Apr
7:50.04	Ben	Limo	KEN	23.8.74	4 Jul
7:50.06	Eric	Chirchir	KEN	20.11.83	8 Jun
7:50.34	Ed	Moran	USA	27.5.81	7 Aug

Mark	Name		Nat	Born	Date
7:50.78	Mohamed-Khaled	Belabbas	FRA	4.7.81	5 Jun
7:50.97	Kiprono	Menjo	KEN	20.8.79	20 Jun
7:51.29	Bernard Muinde	Matheka	KEN-J	18.7.88	25 Jul
7:51.32	Bouabdellah	Tahri	FRA	20.12.78	382 Jun
7:51.61	Kamal Ali	Thamer	QAT-J	12.11.88	15 Jul
7:52.24	Jamel	Chatbi	MAR	30.4.84	21 Jul
7:52.44	Arne	Gabius	GER	22.3.81	28 May
7:52.52	Adrian	Blincoe	NZL	4.11.79	13 Jun
7:52.71	Geoffrey	Kipngeno Siele	KEN	10.4.84	12 Aug
7:52.97	Ronald	Kipchumba Rutto	KEN	8.10.87	17 Jun
7:53.00	Tim	Nelson	USA	27.2.84	15 Jul
7:53.15	Steve	Slattery	USA	14.8.80	20 May
7:53.2+	Kensuke	Takezawa	JPN	11.10.86	3 Aug
7:53.41	Juan Carlos	Higuero	ESP	3.8.78	19 May
7:53.65	Filmon	Ghirmai	GER	25.1.79	12 Aug
7:53.97	Jason	Woolhouse	NZL	9.9.80	17 Feb

Indoors

Mark	Name		Nat	Born	Pos	Meet	Venue	Date
7:32.43	Bernard	Lagat	USA	12.12.74	1	GP	Birmingham	17 Feb
7:32.69	Markos	Geneti	ETH	30.5.84	2	GP	Birmingham	17 Feb
7:33.09	Augustine	Choge	KEN	21.1.87	3	GP	Birmingham	17 Feb
7:33.46	Paul K.	Koech	KEN	10.11.81	4	GP	Birmingham	17 Feb
7:37.35	Shadrack	Korir	KEN	14.12.78	1	Spark	Stuttgart	3 Feb
7:37.47	Daniel Kipchirchir	Komen	KEN	27.11.84	2		Stuttgart	9 Feb
7:38.41	Bouabdallah	Tahri	FRA	20.12.78	3		Stuttgart	9 Feb
7:40.17	Kevin	Sullivan	CAN	20.3.74	1	Tyson	Fayetteville	9 Feb
7:43.20	Brimin	Kipruto	KEN	31.7.85	1		Valencia	10 Feb
7:45.74	Halil	Akkas	TUR	1.7.83	3		Stockholm	20 Feb
7:45.96	Mohamed Ali	Abdosh	ETH	28.8.87	3	BIG	Boston (R)	27 Jan
7:46.61	Alberto	García	ESP	22.2.71	4		Valencia	10 Feb
7:46.82	Mohammed	Moustaoui	MAR	2.4.85	1		Gent	4 Feb

Mark	Name		Nat	Born	Date
7:48.71	José Antonio	Redolat	ESP	17.2.76	3 Feb
7:48.79	Günther	Weidlinger	AUT	5.4.78	20 Feb
7:48.88	Cosimo	Calandro	ITA	11.3.82	3 Feb
7:49.10	Isaac	Sang	KEN	24.8.78	6 Feb
7:49.17	Khoudir	Aggoune	ALG	5.1.81	4 Feb
7:49.27	Erik	Sjöqvist	SWE	4.12.72	20 Feb
7:49.48	Juan Carlos	Higuero	ESP	3.8.78	4 Feb
7:49.73	Jonathon	Riley	USA	29.12.78	24 Feb

Mark	Name		Nat	Born	Date
7:49.74	Joseph Lopez	Lomong	SUD/USA	1.1.85	10 Mar
7:50.15	Arne	Gabius	GER	22.3.81	3 Feb
7:50.34	Willy	Komen Rutto	KEN	22.12.87	4 Feb
7:52.07	Mark	Carroll	IRL	15.1.72	9 Feb
7:52.59	Henrik	Skoog	SWE	17.4.79	3 Feb
7:52.70	Vyacheslav	Shabunin	RUS	27.9.69	3 Feb
7:53.08#	Colby	Wissel	USA	25.4.85	3 Mar
7:53.30	Sergey	Ivanov	RUS	3.3.79	2 Mar

JUNIORS

See main list for top 9 juniors. 12 performances by 8 men to 7:45.0. Additional marks and further juniors:

Limo Ndiwa	7:39.08	1	Vard	Réthimno	18 Jul					
Komon	7:40.76	3	Vard	Réthimno	18 Jul	7:43.96	6		Herrera	19 May
	7:42.99	7	GP	Rieti	9 Sep					

Mark	Name		Nat	Born	Pos	Meet	Venue	Date
7:48.06	Stephen	Kiprotich (10)	UGA	18.4.89	6		Liège (NX)	25 Jul
7:49.99	Benjamin	Kiplagat	KEN	4.3.89	6	GP	Dakar	28 Apr
7:51.29	Bernard Muinde	Matheka	KEN	18.7.88	8		Liège (NX)	25 Jul
7:51.61	Kamal Ali	Thamer	QAT	12.11.88	4		Gent	15 Jul
7:54.08	Geoffrey	Kusuro	UGA	12.2.89	4	DLV	Bochum-Wattenscheid	12 Aug
7:56.29	Ismail Adam	Khamis	BRN	12.2.89	9		Liège (NX)	25 Jul
7:57.18	Daniel Lemashon	Salel	KEN-Y	11.12.90	1	WY	Ostrava	14 Jul
7:58.19	John	Sombol	KEN	6.4.88	6		Stavanger	13 Jun
7:59.67	Lucas Kimeli	Rotich	KEN-Y	16.4.90	2	WY	Ostrava	14 Jul
8:00.39	Mathew	Kisorio	JEN	16.5.89	1		Avezzano	16 Sep
8:00.98	Hicham	El Amrani (20)	MAR-Y	30.1.91	3	WY	Ostrava	14 Jul
Best European: 8:10.07		Mourad Amdouni	FRA	21.1.88	3		Marseille	15 Jun

2 MILES

Mark	Name		Nat	Born	Pos	Meet	Venue	Date
8:03.50	Craig	Mottram	AUS	18.6.80	1	Pre	Eugene	10 Jun
8:04.83	Tariku	Bekele	ETH	21.1.87	2	Pre	Eugene	10 Jun
8:07.07	Matt	Tegenkamp	USA	19.1.82	3	Pre	Eugene	10 Jun
8:11.16		Mottram			1	LGP	London (CP)	3 Aug
8:11.74	Dathan	Ritzenhein	USA	30.12.82	4	Pre	Eugene	10 Jun
8:13.51	Kenenisa	Bekele	ETH	13.6.82	1	FBK	Hengelo	26 May
8:15.90	Benjamin	Limo	KEN	23.8.74	5	Pre	Eugene	10 Jun
8:16.77	Jonas	Cheruiyot	KEN	11.1.84	6	Pre	Eugene	10 Jun
8:16.98	Edwin	Soi	KEN	3.3.86	2	FBK	Hengelo	26 May
8:18.33	Joseph	Ebuya	KEN	20.6.87	4	FBK	Hengelo	26 May
8:18.70	Remi	Limo Ndiwa	KEN-J	3.2.88	5	FBK	Hengelo	26 May
8:18.96	Josphat Kiprono	Menjo	KEN	20.8.79	6	FBK	Hengelo	26 May
8:19.33	Ali	Maataoui	MAR	11.12.80	7	FBK	Hengelo	26 May

Mark	Name		Nat	Born	Pos	Meet	Venue	Date
8:19.34	Zersenay	Tadese	ERI	8.2.82	7	Pre	Eugene	10 Jun
8:20.47	Mohamed	Farah	GBR	23.3.83	2	LGP	London (CP)	3 Aug
8:20.83	Shadrack	Kosgei	KEN	24.11.84	8	FBK	Hengelo	26 May
8:21.34	John	Kibowen	KEN	21.4.69	3	LGP	London (CP)	3 Aug
8:22.56	Leonard Patrick	Komon	KEN-J	10.1.88	9	FBK	Hengelo	26 May

8:23.81	Juan Luis	Barrios	MEX	24.6.83	10 Jun
8:23.97	Alan	Webb	USA	13.1.83	10 Jun
8:24.58	Abraham	Chebii	KEN	23.12.79	10 Jun
8:24.69	Kensuke	Takezawa	JPN	11.10.86	3 Aug
8:24.98	Ian	Dobson	USA	6.2.82	3 Aug
8:26.46	Adam	Goucher	USA	18.2.75	10 Jun
8:27.64	Sean	Graham	USA	6.3.80	10 Jun
8:28.46	Edwin	Kipkorir	KEN-J	3.9.89	26 May

Indoors

8:23.94	Shadrack	Korir	KEN	14.12.78	28 Jan
8:24.10	Isaac	Sang	KEN	24.8.78	28 Jan
8:24.18	Boniface	Songok	KEN	25.12.80	28 Jan
8:24.44	Mark	Bett	KEN	22.12.76	28 Jan

5000 METRES

Mark	Name		Nat	Born	Pos	Meet	Venue	Date
12:49.53	Kenenisa	Bekele	ETH	13.6.82	1	Aragón	Zaragoza	28 Jul
12:50.16	Sileshi	Sihine	ETH	29.9.83	1	VD	Bruxelles	14 Sep
12:50.38	Eliud	Kipchoge	KEN	5.11.84	2	VD	Bruxelles	14 Sep
12:50.72	Moses	Kipsiro	UGA	2.9.86	3	VD	Bruxelles	14 Sep
12:51.00	Joseph	Ebuya	KEN	20.6.87	4	VD	Bruxelles	14 Sep
12:51.95	Thomas	Longosiwa	KEN	14.1.82	5	VD	Bruxelles	14 Sep
12:58.49	Yusuf	Biwott	KEN	12.11.86	6	VD	Bruxelles	14 Sep
12:59.63	Abraham	Chebii	KEN	23.12.79	7	VD	Bruxelles	14 Sep
13:01.46		Sihine			1	GGala	Roma	13 Jul
13:01.60	Tariku	Bekele	ETH	21.1.87	8	VD	Bruxelles	14 Sep
13:02.10		Kipchoge			2	Ggala	Roma	13 Jul
13:02.89	Mushir Salem	Jawher (10)	BRN	13.6.78	3	GGala	Roma	13 Jul
13:03.82	Ahmed Ibrahim	Baday	MAR	12.1.79	4	GGala	Roma	13 Jul
13:04.05		T Bekele			1	GP	New York	2 Jun
13:04.79	Leonard Patrick	Komon	KEN-J	10.1.88	5	GGala	Roma	13 Jul
13:04.97	Craig	Mottram	AUS	18.6.80	1	GS	Ostrava	27 Jun
13:05.42		T Bekele			2	GS	Ostrava	27 Jun
13:05.83	Abreham	Cherkos Feleke	ETH-J	23.9.89	3	GS	Ostrava	27 Jun
13:06.51	Sahle	Warga	ETH	.81	9	VD	Bruxelles	14 Sep
13:06.52	Bekana	Daba	ETH-J	29.7.88	1		Brasschaat	21 Jul
13:06.69	Josphat Kiprono	Menjo	KEN	20.8.79	1		Gavá	30 Jun
13:06.71	Robert Kipngetich	Sigei	KEN	3.1.82	6	GGala	Roma	13 Jul
13:07.00	Mohamed	Farah	GBR	23.3.83	10	VD	Bruxelles	14 Sep
13:07.10	Alistair	Cragg (20)	IRL	13.6.80	2		Brasschaat	21 Jul
13:07.30	Jonas	Cheruiyot	KEN	11.1.84	7	GGala	Roma	13 Jul
13:07.41	Matt	Tegenkamp	USA	19.1.82	11	VD	Bruxelles	14 Sep
13:07.46	Boniface	Kiprop	UGA	12.10.85	8	GGala	Roma	13 Jul
13:07.65	Markos	Geneti	ETH	30.5.84	3		Brasschaat	21 Jul
13:07.89	Moses	Mosop	KEN	17.7.85	4	GS	Ostrava	27 Jun
13:08.81	Moses	Masai	KEN	1.6.86	1	Takac	Beograd	29 May
	(30/26)							
13:09.85	Hosea	Macharinyang	KEN	12.6.86	2	Takac	Beograd	29 May
13:10.21	Edwin	Soi	KEN	3.3.86	1	Athl	Lausanne	10 Jul
13:10.29	Gebre-egziabher	Gebremariam	ETH	10.9.84	6	GS	Ostrava	27 Jun
13:10.68	Micah	Kogo	KEN	3.6.86	2	Athl	Lausanne	10 Jul
	(30)							
13:11.32	Tefere Maregu	Zewdie	ETH	23.10.82	9	GS	Ostrava	27 Jun
13:11.37	Juan Luis	Barrios	MEX	24.6.83	1	MSR	Walnut	13 Apr
13:11.85	Shadrack	Kosgei	KEN	24.11.84	10	GS	Ostrava	27 Jun
13:11.93	Anthony	Famiglietti	USA	8.11.78	2	MSR	Walnut	13 Apr
13:12.18	David	Galván	MEX	6.4.76	3	MSR	Walnut	13 Apr
13:12.24	Chris	Solinsky	USA	5.12.84	4	NA	Heusden-Zolder	28 Jul
13:12.29	Bouabdellah	Tahri	FRA	20.12.78	4		Villeneuve d'Ascq	8 Jun
13:12.60	Mark	Kiptoo	KEN	21.6.76	3	Takac	Beograd	29 May
13:12.62	Gideon	Ngatuny	KEN	10.10.86	1		Yokohama	24 Jun
13:13.08	Mohamed Ali	Abdosh	ETH	25.8.87	12	GS	Ostrava	27 Jun
	(40)							
13:13.18	Sammy	Alex	KEN-J	1.6.89	1		Nobeoka	26 May
13:13.20	Takayuki	Matsumiya	JPN	21.2.80	5	NA	Heusden-Zolder	28 Jul
13:13.40	Bernard	Kipyego	KEN	16.7.86	2		Nobeoka	26 May
13:13.95	Silas	Kipruto	KEN	.84	6	NA	Heusden-Zolder	28 Jul
13:14.85	Jan	Fitschen	GER	2.5.77	7	NA	Heusden-Zolder	28 Jul
13:15.16	Bolota	Asmerom	USA	12.10.78	8	NA	Heusden-Zolder	28 Jul
13:15.70	Isaac K.	Songok	KEN	25.4.84	13	GS	Ostrava	27 Jun
13:15.79	Khoudir	Aggoune	ALG	5.1.81	9	NA	Heusden-Zolder	28 Jul
13:15.87	Mourad	Maaroufit	MAR	.82	4		Brasschaat	21 Jul

Mark	Name		Nat	Born	Pos	Meet	Venue	Date
13:15.91	Wilfred (50)	Taragon	KEN	9.6.85	3		Rovereto	12 Sep
13:16.06	Dathan	Ritzenhein	USA	30.12.82	5		Brasschaat	21 Jul
13:16.13	Khalid	El Amri	MAR	20.3.77	14	GS	Ostrava	27 Jun
13:16.66	Benjamin	Limo	KEN	23.8.74	9	GGala	Roma	13 Jul
13:16.74	Boniface	Songok	KEN	25.12.80	15	GS	Ostrava	27 Jun
13:16.87	Girma	Assefa	ETH	20.2.86	3		Nobeoka	26 May
13:17.28	Adrian	Blincoe	NZL	4.11.79	16	GS	Ostrava	27 Jun
13:17.45	Mark	Bett	KEN	22.12.76	1	MAI	Malm	2 Jul
13:17.99	Ibrahim	Jeylan	ETH-J	12.6.89	11	GGala	Roma	13 Jul
13:17.99	Lishan	Yegezu	ETH	6.10.85	10	NA	Heusden-Zolder	28 Jul
13:18.25	Samuel (60)	Wanjiru	KEN	10.11.86	4		Nobeoka	26 May
13:18.32	Yu	Mitsuya	JPN	18.12.84	5		Nobeoka	26 May
13:18.39	John	Kariuki	KEN	10.11.86	6		Nobeoka	26 May
13:18.49	Josphat Muchiri	Ndambiri	KEN	12.2.85	1		Shizuoka	30 Apr
13:18.82	Tadesse	Tola	ETH	31.10.87	6		Villeneuve d'Ascq	8 Jun
13:18.87	Ian	Dobson	USA	6.2.82	1rB	NA	Heusden-Zolder	28 Jul
13:19.00	Kensuke	Takezawa	JPN	11.10.86	11	NA	Heusden-Zolder	28 Jul
13:19.27	Kevin	Sullivan	CAN	20.3.74	4	MSR	Walnut	13 Apr
13:19.27	Adam Ismail	Khamis	BRN-J	12.2.89	1		Pergine Valsugana	7 Jul
13:19.31	Jamal Bilal	Salem	QAT	12.9.78	7		Villeneuve d'Ascq	8 Jun
13:19.68	Ryan (70)	Kirkpatrick	USA	10.9.78	5	MSR	Walnut	13 Apr
13:19.92	Jonathon	Riley	USA	29.12.78	2rB	NA	Heusden-Zolder	28 Jul
13:20.35	Ed	Moran	USA	27.5.81	6	MSR	Walnut	13 Apr
13:20.43	Josh	McDougal	USA	1.6.85	7	MSR	Walnut	13 Apr
13:20.72	Boaz	Cheboiywo	KEN	2.8.78	12	NA	Heusden-Zolder	28 Jul
13:20.89	Felix	Kibore	KEN/QAT-J	18.2.88	1		Ninove	11 Aug
13:21.05	Dejene	Gebremeskel	ETH-J	24.11.89	6		Brasschaat	21 Jul
13:21.13	Moses	Kigen	KEN	10.1.83	1		Kassel	6 Jun
13:21.39	Abdelaziz Naji	El Idrissi	ITA/MAR	8.12.86	2		Ninove	11 Aug
13:21.49	Yuichiro	Ueno	JPN	29.7.85	3rB	NA	Heusden-Zolder	28 Jul
13:21.53	Reid (80)	Coolsaet	CAN	29.7.79	4rB	NA	Heusden-Zolder	28 Jul
13:21.74	Geoffrey	Kipngeno Siele	KEN	10.4.84	2		Kassel	6 Jun
13:22.11	Marílson	dos Santos	BRA	6.8.77	3		Kassel	6 Jun
13:22.13	Martin Irungu	Mathathi	KEN	25.12.85	2		Gifu	22 Sep
13:22.39	Paul	Morrison	CAN	25.9.80	5rB	NA	Heusden-Zolder	28 Jul
13:22.50	Bado	Worku	ETH-J	22.7.88	3		Alger	21 Jun
13:22.67	Benjamin	Kiplagat	UGA-J	4.3.89	4		Kassel	6 Jun
13:23.50	Sean	Graham	USA	6.3.80	6rB	NA	Heusden-Zolder	28 Jul
13:23.65	Ali	Abdallah Afringi	ERI	2.11.82	7	AfG	Alger	22 Jul
13:24.26	Charles	Koech	QAT	29.12.83	3		Ninove	11 Aug
13:24.88	Hillary (90)	Chenonge	KEN	30.5.85	7		Nobeoka	26 May
13:24.94	Daniel	Gitau (or Gitawo)	KEN	1.10.87	1		Yokohama	30 Apr
13:25.18	Dickson	Marwa Mkami	TAN	6.3.82	4		Lugano	15 Jun
13:25.34	Dereje	Tadesse	ETH	24.1.87	6	Takac	Beograd	29 May
13:25.37	Erik	Sjöqvist	SWE	4.12.72	7rB	NA	Heusden-Zolder	28 Jul
13:25.53	Josh	Rohatinsky	USA	7.3.82	8	MSR	Walnut	13 Apr
13:25.91	Simon	Bairu	CAN	8.8.83	8rB	NA	Heusden-Zolder	28 Jul
13:26.30	Bernard	Kiplagat	KEN-J	10.8.88	7	Takac	Beograd	29 May
13:26.60	Isaac	Kimurine	KEN	.86	1		Marano	14 Sep
13:27.40	Stephen	Kiprotich	UGA-J	18.4.89	9rB	NA	Heusden-Zolder	28 Jul
13:27.48	Arne (100)	Gabius	GER	22.3.81	5		Kassel	6 Jun

13:27.63	Nicholas	Makau	KEN-Y	15.10.90	26 May
13:27.63	Edwin	Kipkorir	KEN-J	3.9.89	28 Jul
13:27.94	Davis	Kabiru	KEN	1.5.83	26 May
13:28.43	Mathew	Kisorio	KEN-J	16.5.89	14 Sep
13:28.75	Francisco Javier	Alves	ESP	3.9.80	12 Sep
13:28.84	Katsuhiro	Maeda	JPN	19.4.81	26 May
13:29.02+	Joseph	Kosgei	KEN	25.8.74	26 May
13:29.05	Ali Saadoun	Al-Dawoodi	QAT	29.6.84	11 Aug
13:29.30	Alejandro	Suárez	MEX	30.11.80	13 Apr
13:29.41	Cyrus Gichobi	Njui	KEN	11.2.86	26 May
13:29.56	Kidane	Tadesse	ERI	.87	14 Jul
13:30.07	Seth	Summerside	USA	14.2.84	13 Apr
13:30.12	Brent	Vaughn	USA	4.9.84	29 Apr
13:30.24	Jesús	España	ESP	21.8.78	5 Aug
13:30.29	Samuel Ndungu	Wanjiku	KEN-J	4.4.88	30 Apr
13:30.35	Hicham	Bellani	MAR	15.9.79	28 Jul
13:30.49	Galen	Rupp	USA	8.5.86	20 Apr
13:30.68	Matt	Gabrielson	USA	28.7.78	21 Jul
13:30.73	Barnard	Lagat	USA	12.12.74	22 Jun
13:31.11	Ayad	Lamdassem	ESP	11.10.81	30 Jun
13:31.27	Cuthbert	Nyasango	ZIM	17.9.82	14 Jul
13:31.50	Adam	Goucher	USA	18.2.75	22 Jun
13:31.61	Bernard	Chepkok	KEN	17.1.84	29 May
13:31.78	Tesfaye	Assefa	ETH	20.12.83	26 May
13:32.08	Mustafa	Mohamed	SWE	1.3.79	6 Jun
13:32.14	Ali	Maataoui	MAR	15.12.80	10 Jul
13:32.43	Sergio	Sánchez	ESP	1.10.82	5 Aug
13:32.46	Sultan Khamis	Zaman	QAT	23.7.85	28 Jul
13:32.49	Kamiel	Maase	NED	20.10.71	21 Jul
13:32.69	Juan Carlos	Higuero	ESP	3.8.78	30 Jun

Mark	Name		Nat	Born	Date
13:32.80	Hassan	Mahboub Ali	BRN	31.12.81	7 Jul
13:33.10	Alan	Culpepper	USA	15.9.72	13 Apr
13:33.20	Mark	Carroll	IRL	15.1.72	26 May
13:33.24	Brian	Olinger	USA	2.6.83	21 Jul
13:33.27	Dame	Tasama Faisa	ETH	12.10.87	28 Jul
13:33.44	Kyle	King	USA	28.7.81	26 May
13:33.52	Imame	Marga Jidha	ETH-J	15.10.88	2 Jul
13:33.55	Tom	Compernolle	BEL	13.11.75	28 Jul
13:33.68	Abdihakem	Abdirahman	USA	2.12.78	29 Apr
13:33.77	José Antonio	Redolat	ESP	17.2.76	30 Jun
13:33.81	Christopher	Thompson	GBR	17.4.81	6 Jun
13:33.94	Julius	Nyamu	KEN	1.12.77	16 May
13:34.17	Willy	Kimutai Kangogo	KEN	12.2.84	26 May
13:34.22	Collis	Birmingham	AUS	27.12.84	9 Feb
13:34.41	Mike	Kigen	KEN	15.1.86	29 Jun
13:34.42	Michael	Aish	NZL	24.7.76	20 Apr
13:34.44	Terukazu	Omori	JPN	3.9.79	20 Apr
13:34.54	Salim	Saiti	KEN	28.12.85	8 Jun
13:34.86	Aleksandr	Orlov	RUS	23.2.81	29 Jun
13:34.92	Abraham	Rotich	KEN	14.2.79	14 Jul
13:34.99	Paul	Melly	KEN	4.1.81	23 Jun
13:35.12	Mutai	Kiprono	KEN	23.12.87	4 May
13:35.26	Philipp	Bandi	SUI	28.9.77	28 Jul
13:35.38	Amanuel	Woldeselassie	ERI	15.10.78	22 Jul
13:35.44	Patrick	Kimeli	KEN-J	22.4.89	6 Jun
13:35.48	Solomon	Tsige Asfav	ETH	23.1.85	28 Jul
13:35.56	Ryan	McKenzie	CAN	13.10.78	29 Apr
13:35.86	Andrew	Carlson	USA	27.4.82	28 Jul
13:36.03	Steve	Slattery	USA	14.8.80	29 Apr
13:36.03	Eric	Gillis	CAN	8.3.80	21 Jul
13:36.13	Atsushi	Sato	JPN	8.5.78	17 Jun
13:36.18	Satoshi	Irifune	JPN	14.12.75	26 May
13:36.29A	Haurun	Njoroge	KEN-J	11.6.88	20 Oct
13:36.36	Abdellah	Falil	MAR	76	23 Jun
13:36.5A	Charles	Kamathi	KEN	18.5.78	26 May
13:36.51	Yuki	Matsuoka	JPN	14.1.86	10 Jun
13:36.76	Jefferson	Siekei	KEN	12.3.83	23 Sep
13:36.91	Thomas	Morgan	USA	10.5.81	26 May
13:37.47	Ricardo	Serrano	ESP	29.10.80	5 Aug
13:37.63	Essa Ismail	Rashed	QAT	14.12.86	28 Jul
13:37.69	Yuta	Takahashi	JPN	13.4.87	10 Jun
13:37.71	Aaron	Aguayo	USA	27.7.84	29 Apr
13:38.06	Merzak Ould	Bouchiba	ALG	27.4.75	8 Jun
13:38.19	Dieudonne	Gahungu	BDI	16.4.86	28 Jul
13:38.28	Anderson	Smith	USA	16.3.82	26 May
13:38.33	Eduard	Bordukov	RUS	30.6.79	9 Jun
13:38.35	Daniel	Browne	USA	24.6.75	26 May
13:38.39	Manuel Ángel	Penas	ESP	9.11.77	5 Aug
13:38.48	Pavel	Naumov	RUS	27.12.79	9 Jun
13:38.51	Stephem	Haas	USA	18.4.83	29 Apr
13:38.6	Bitan ?	Kariuki	KEN-Y	21.8.90	6 Oct
13:38.92	Abera	Ertiban	ETH-J	13.3.88	8 Jun
13:39.07	Jason	Woolhouse	NZL	9.9.80	29 Apr
13:39.13	Amanuel	Mesel Tikue	ERI-Y	29.12.90	22 Jul
13:39.14	Martin	Waweru	KEN-J	6.2.88	26 May
13:39.41	Pierre	Joncheray	FRA	9.9.82	8 Jun
13:39.45	Kazuya	Watanabe	JPN	7.7.87	19 May
13:39.5A	Richard	Matelong	KEN	14.10.83	14 Jun
13:39.51	Wilson	Busienei	UGA	18.8.81	2 Jul
13:39.52	Andrey	Safronov	RUS	16.12.85	9 Jun
13:39.57	Gunther	Weidlinger	AUT	5.4.78	29 May
13:39.59	Lewis	Korir	KEN		1 Jul
13:39.61	Filmon	Ghirmai	GER	25.1.79	23 May
13:39.75	Abdelkader	Hachlaf	MAR	3.7.79	24 Nov
13:39.83	Moorosi	Soke	RSA	11.2.83	22 Jul
13:39.88	Bobby	Curtis	USA	28.11.84	8 Jun
13:40.01	Micah	Chelagat Njeru	KEN-J	5.8.88	7 Apr
13:40.02	Sergey	Yemelyanov	RUS	24.11.78	9 Jun
13:40.05	Demissie	Tsege	ETH-J	13.3.88	8 Jun
	(200)				

Indoors

Mark	Name		Nat	Born	Date
13:39.88i	Peter	Kosgei	KEN	3.2.83	9 Mar

JUNIORS

See main list for top 12 juniors. 13 performances by 9 men to 13:22.50. Additional marks and further juniors:

Komon	13:08.87	12	VD	Bruxelles	14 Sep	13:20.93	1	Lugano	15 Jun
Cherkos	13:14.90	4	AfG	Alger	22 Jul				
Alex	13:20.19	2		Yokohama	15 Apr				

13:27.63	Nicholas	Makau	KEN-Y	15.10.90	8		Nobeoka	26 May
13:27.63	Edwin	Kipkorir	KEN	3.9.89	2	Aragón	Zaragoza	28 Jul
13:28.43	Mathew	Kisorio	KEN	16.5.89	2		Marano	14 Sep
13:30.29	Samuel Ndungu	Wanjiku	KEN	4.4.88	3		Yokohama	30 Apr
13:33.52	Imame	Marga Jidha	ETH	15.10.88	3	MAI	Malmö	2 Jul
13:35.44	Patrick	Kimeli	KEN	22.4.89	8		Kassel	6 Jun
13:36.29A	Haurun	Njoroge	KEN	11.6.88	2		Naka	20 Oct
13:38.6	Bitan ?	Kariuki (20)	KEN-Y	21.8.90	1		Kure	6 Oct
Top European: 13:56.03	Morhad	Amdouni	FRA	21.6.88	5		Carquefou	22 Jun

10,000 METRES

Mark	Name		Nat	Born	Pos	Meet	Venue	Date
26:46.19	Kenenisa	Bekele	ETH	13.6.82	1	VD	Bruxelles	14 Sep
26:48.73	Sileshi	Sihine	ETH	29.9.83	1	FBK	Hengelo	26 May
26:49.02	Eliud	Kipchoge	KEN	5.11.84	2	FBK	Hengelo	26 May
26:49.20	Moses	Masai	KEN	1.6.86	2	VD	Bruxelles	14 Sep
26:49.55	Moses	Mosop	KEN	17.7.85	3	FBK	Hengelo	26 May
26:52.33	Gebre-egziabher	Gebremariam	ETH	10.9.84	4	FBK	Hengelo	26 May
26:52.81	Haile	Gebrselassie	ETH	18.4.73	5	FBK	Hengelo	26 May
26:58.42	Micah	Kogo	KEN	3.6.86	3	VD	Bruxelles	14 Sep
26:59.51	Bernard	Kipyego	KEN	16.7.86	4	VD	Bruxelles	14 Sep
27:00.30	Zersenay	Tadese (10)	ERI	8.2.82	1	AfG	Alger	19 Jul
27:02.62	Deriba	Merga	ETH	26.10.80	6	FBK	Hengelo	26 May
27:04.18	Robert Kipngetich	Sigei	KEN	3.1.82	1		Neerpelt	2 Jun
27:04.61	Josphat Kiprono	Menjo	KEN	20.8.79	2		Neerpelt	2 Jun
27:04.89	Tadesse	Tola	ETH	31.10.87	3		Neerpelt	2 Jun
27:04.92	Mohamed Ali	Abdosh	ETH	28.8.87	7	FBK	Hengelo	26 May
27:05.90		K Bekele			1	WC	Osaka	27 Aug
27:06.47	Habtamu	Fikadu	ETH-J	13.3.88	8	FBK	Hengelo	26 May
27:09.03		Sihine			2	WC	Osaka	27 Aug
27:09.90	Martin Irungu	Mathathi	KEN	25.12.85	1		Kobe	22 Apr
27:11.36	Gideon	Ngatuny	KEN	10.10.86	2		Kobe	22 Apr

Mark	Name		Nat	Born	Pos	Meet	Venue	Date
27:11.93	Eshetu	Wondimu	ETH	26.1.82	9	FBK	Hengelo	26 May
27:12.17		Mathathi			3	WC	Osaka	27 Aug
27:12.42	Sammy	Alex (20)	KEN-J	1.6.89	1		Tokamchi	29 Sep
27:14.02		Ngatuny			1		Kumagaya	19 May
27:14.04	Sammy	Kipketer	KEN	29.9.81	10	FBK	Hengelo	26 May
27:15.68	Raji	Assefa	ETH	18.2.86	11	FBK	Hengelo	26 May
27:16.48		Sigei			5	VD	Bruxelles	14 Sep
27:17.43		Alex			1		Shibetsu	17 Jun
27:20.99	Samuel	Wanjiru	KEN	10.11.86	2		Shibetsu	17 Jun
27:21.37		Tadese			4	WC	Osaka	27 Aug
27:22.28	Dieudonné	Disi	RWA	24.4.78	6	VD	Bruxelles	14 Sep
	(31/24)							
27:26.31	John Cheruiyot	Korir	KEN	13.12.81	7	VD	Bruxelles	14 Sep
27:28.12	Marílson	dos Santos	BRA	6.8.77	4		Neerpelt	2 Jun
27:28.38	Josphat Muchiri	Ndambiri	KEN	12.2.85	3		Kobe	22 Apr
27:28.82	Abera	Ertiban	ETH-J	13.3.88	5		Neerpelt	2 Jun
27:29.43	Geoffrey	Kipngeno	KEN	10.4.84	6		Neerpelt	2 Jun
27:30.50	John	Kariuki	KEN	10.11.86	4		Kobe	22 Apr
	(30)							
27:30.67	Abiyote	Guta	ETH	1.1.85	7		Neerpelt	2 Jun
27:30.94	Khalid	El Amri	MAR	20.3.77	12	FBK	Hengelo	26 May
27:31.46	Abdi	Abdirahman	USA	1.1.77	13	FBK	Hengelo	26 May
27:33.02	Wilfred	Taragon	KEN	9.6.85	14	FBK	Hengelo	26 May
27:33.48	Galen	Rupp	USA	8.5.86	1		Stanford	29 Apr
27:33.87	Abdullah Ahmad	Hassan	QAT	4.4.81	15	FBK	Hengelo	26 May
27:33.96	David	Galván	MEX	6.4.76	2		Stanford	29 Apr
27:35.85	Patrick	Kimeli	KEN-J	22.4.89	8		Neerpelt	2 Jun
27:36.12	Charles	Kamathi	KEN	18.5.78	2		Kumagaya	19 May
27:38.56	Simon	Ndirangu	KEN	1.11.85	3		Stanford	29 Apr
	(40)							
27:38.58	Dickson	Marwa Mkami	TAN	6.3.82	16	FBK	Hengelo	26 May
27:39.55	Alistair	Cragg	IRL	13.6.80	4		Stanford	29 Apr
27:41.26	Mebrahtom	Keflezighi	USA	5.5.75	10	VD	Bruxelles	14 Sep
27:42.91	Jorge	Torres	USA	22.8.80	5		Stanford	29 Apr
27:43.13	Ed	Moran	USA	27.5.81	6		Stanford	29 Apr
27:43.64	James	Carney	USA	24.5.78	7		Stanford	29 Apr
27:43.67	Girma	Assefa	ETH	20.2.86	1		Fukuroi	14 Oct
27:43.92	Alejandro	Suárez	MEX	30.11.80	8		Stanford	29 Apr
27:44.73	Daniel	Gitau	KEN	1.10.87	1		Yokohama	20 Oct
27:45.59	Kensuke	Takezawa	JPN	11.10.86	9		Stanford	29 Apr
	(50)							
27:45.63	Mbuthi Davis	Kabiru	KEN	1.5.83	2		Fukuroi	14 Oct
27:46.37	Michael	Aish	NZL	24.7.76	10		Stanford	29 Apr
27:47.57	Josphat	Boit	KEN	26.11.83	11		Stanford	29 Apr
27:48.03	Samuel Ndungu	Wanjiku	KEN-J	4.4.88	3		Fukuroi	14 Oct
27:48.40	Micah	Njeru	KEN-J	5.8.88	4		Fukuroi	14 Oct
27:50.05	Alan	Culpepper	USA	15.9.72	12		Stanford	29 Apr
27:50.53	Ibrahim	Jeylan	ETH-J	12.6.89	17	FBK	Hengelo	26 May
27:50.71	Simon	Bairu	CAN	8.8.83	13		Stanford	29 Apr
27:51.34	Harry	Sugut	KEN	4.5.85	18	FBK	Hengelo	26 May
27:51.39	Jacob	Wanjuki	KEN	16.1.86	6		Fukuroi	14 Oct
	(60)							
27:51.51	Dereje Raya	Tadesse	ETH	24.1.87	9		Neerpelt	2 Jun
27:51.65	Yuki	Sato	JPN	26.11.86	7		Fukuroi	14 Oct
27:51.90	Terukazu	Omori	JPN	3.9.79	3		Fukuroi	2 Jun
27:51.92	Hillary	Chenonge	KEN	30.5.85	2rB		Kobe	21 Apr
27:52.35	Willy	Kangogo Kimutai	KEN	12.2.84	2		Kitakyushu	12 May
27:52.78	Bekele	Gebretsadik	ETH	27.9.86	3rB		Kobe	21 Apr
27:52.79	Mekubo	Mogusu	KEN	25.12.86	1		Tokyo	8 Jun
27:53.78	Takeshi	Makabe	JPN	3.2.82	1		Yokohama	2 Dec
27:55.17	Katsuhiro	Maeda	JPN	19.4.81	2		Yokohama	2 Dec
27:55.56	André	Pollmächer	GER	22.3.83	10		Neerpelt	2 Jun
	(70)							
27:55.86	Josh	Rohatinsky	USA	7.3.82	14		Stanford	29 Apr
27:56.60	Ayad	Lamdassem	ESP	11.10.81	1	NC	Avilés	28 Jul
27:56.63	Cyrus	Njui	KEN	11.2.86	4rB		Kobe	21 Apr
27:56.92	Reid	Coolsaet	CAN	29.7.79	15		Stanford	29 Apr
27:57.34	Cuthbert	Nyasango	ZIM	17.9.82	2	Esp Ch	Avilés	28 Jul
27:58.41	Hosea	Macharinyang	KEN	12.6.85	1		Bilbao	23 Jun
27:59.32	Tesfaye	Assefa	ETH	20.12.83	8		Fukuroi	14 Oct

Mark	Name		Nat	Born	Pos	Meet	Venue	Date
27:59.69	Musabeker	Marda	MAR	4.2.82	1	FRA Ch	Marseille	15 Jun
27:59.93	El Hassan	Lahssini	FRA	1.1.75	2	1 NC	Marseille	15 Jun
28:00.22	Satoru	Kitamura	JPN	4.2.86	6		Fukuroi	2 Jun
	(80)							
28:02.51	Seth	Summerside	USA	14.2.84	16		Stanford	29 Apr
28:03.44	Ryan	Shay	USA	4.5.79	17		Stanford	29 Apr
28:03.83	Kenji	Noguchi	JPN	23.2.75	18		Stanford	29 Apr
28:04.40	Kenta	Murozuka	JPN	12.2.86	3		Yokohama	2 Dec
28:04.46	Tim	Nelson	USA	27.2.84	19		Stanford	29 Apr
28:04.74	Ali Saadoun	Al-Dawoodi	QAT	29.6.84	1		Liège (NX)	28 Jun
28:04.86	Edward	Muge	KEN	26.6.83	5	AfG	Alger	19 Jul
28:05.30	Daniel Muchunu	Mwangi	KEN	1.1.84	4		Kumagaya	19 May
28:05.66	Boniface	Kiprop	UGA	12.10.85	6	AfG	Alger	19 Jul
28:06.26	Nicodemus	Naimadu	KEN	24.4.84	1		Stanford	31 Mar
	(90)							
28:06.43	Richard	Kiplagat	KEN	5.1.81	20		Stanford	29 Apr
28:07.57	Takashi	Horiguchi	JPN	26.9.79	4		Yokohama	2 Dec
28:07.65	Stephen	Samoei	KEN	20.6.82	2		Stanford	31 Mar
28:07.93	Ryan	Hall	USA	14.10.82	3		Stanford	31 Mar
28:08.67		Ren Longyun	CHN	12.10.87	1		Wuhan	1 Nov
28:09.4A	Joseph Kiptoo	Birech	KEN	4.1.84	1	NC	Nairobi	16 Jun
28:10.14	Juan Carlos	Romero	MEX	15.12.77	21		Stanford	29 Apr
28:10.57	Augustine Gatimu	Ndirangu	KEN	.84	9		Fukuroi	14 Oct
28:10.68	Daisuke	Shimizu	JPN	2.8.82	5		Yokohama	2 Dec
28:10.73	Dan	Browne	USA	24.6.75	22		Stanford	29 Apr
	(100)							

28:11.38	Joseph	Gitawo	KEN-J	3.1.88	11 Jul
28:11.6A	Sammy	Kitwara	KEN		16 Jun
28:11.67	Nicholas	Makau	KEN-Y	15.10.90	28 Nov
28:11.8A	Barnabas	Kosgei Kiplagat	KEN	20.8.86	16 Jun
28:12.5A	John	Mutai	KEN	22.4.76	16 Jun
28:12.92	Nasser Jamal	Nasser	QAT-J	19.11.88	28 Jun
28:13.12	Atsushi	Sato	JPN	8.5.78	21 Sep
28:13.8A	Patrick	Ivuti	KEN	30.6.78	16 Jun
28:14.36	Haurun	Njoroge	KEN-J	11.6.88	14 Oct
28:15.0A	Luke	Kibet	KEN	12.4.83	16 Jun
28:15.18	Takashi	Ota	JPN	27.4.76	28 Nov
28:15.22	Jason	Hartmann	USA	21.3.81	31 Mar
28:15.52	Naoki	Okamoto	JPN	26.5.84	2 Dec
28:15.77	Takayuki	Matsumiya	JPN	21.2.80	11 Jul
28:16.47	Shadrack	Songok	KEN	25.4.84	13 Apr
28:16.12	Seigo	Ikegami	JPN	2.6.80	2 Dec
28:16.58	Moustafa	Shebto	QAT	4.7.86	28 Jun
28:16.98	Jefferson	Siekei	KEN	12.3.83	29 Sep
28:16.98	Takeshi	Takahashi	JPN	2.4.83	2 Dec
28:17.77	Thomas	Kipkosgei	KEN	.78	23 Jun
28:17.87	Juan Carlos	de la Ossa	ESP	25.11.76	28 Jul
28:18.30	Martin	Fagan	IRL	26.6.83	29 Apr
28:18.4A	Richard	Matelong	KEN	14.10.83	26 May
28:18.64	Yoshitaka	Iwamizu	JPN	20.6.79	14 Oct
28:19.10	Matthew	Cheboi Kiptoo	KEN	.82	28 Jul
28:19.11	Günther	Weidlinger	AUT	5.4.78	7 Apr
28:19.31	Martin	Mukule	KEN-J	14.12.89	9 Dec
28:19.80	Peter	Kariuki	KEN	31.12.85	14 Oct
28:20.36	Atsushi	Ikawa	JPN	13.12.83	28 Nov
28:20.36	Kosaku	Hoshina	JPN	31.8.84	9 Dec
28:20.94	Noriaki	Takahashi	JPN	26.7.82	2 Dec
28:21.03	Tomohiro	Seto	JPN	19.10.76	2 Dec
28:21.29	Kevin	Chelimo	KEN	14.2.83	31 Mar
28:21.31	Masato	Kihara	JPN	13.7.86	22 Apr
28:21.68	Samuel Tsegay	Tesfamarian	ERI-J	24.10.88	19 Jul
28:22.37	Pablo	Olmedo	MEX	8.5.75	13 Apr
28:22.45	Tomoo	Tsubota	JPN	16.6.77	28 Nov
28:22.62	Mark	Kiptoo	KEN	21.6.76	18 Oct
28:22.93	Paul	Kuira	KEN-Y	25.1.91	29 Apr
28:23.75	Yoshihiro	Yamamoto	JPN	20.4.83	14 Oct
28:23.89	Yuki	Iwai	JPN	30.12.82	14 Oct
28:23.99	Yoichiro	Akiyama	JPN	25.12.79	14 Oct
28:24.38	James Kibocha	Theuri	FRA	30.10.78	15 Jun
28:24.48	Japhet	Ngojoy	KEN	31.12.87	31 Mar
28:24.56	Sergiy	Lebid	UKR	15.7.75	7 Jul
28:24.56	Yusei	Nakao	JPN	28.2.84	2 Dec
28:24.66	Kenta	Oshima	JPN	29.6.79	20 Oct
28:25.02	Hideaki	Date	JPN	11.4.85	22 Apr
28:25.02	Koji	Watanabe	JPN	20.2.78	11 Jul
28:25.05	Fekadu	Lemma	ETH	.82	2 Jun
28:25.08	Takahiro	Mori	JPN	22.5.87	20 Oct
28:25.45	Yuki	Matsuoka	JPN	14.1.86	11 Jul
28:25.47	Hiroshi	Yamada	JPN	2.11.82	28 Nov
28:25.69	Fasil	Bizuneh	USA	5.5.78	13 Apr
28:26.2	Mohammed	Amyn	MAR	25.5.76	18 May
28:26.26	Julius	Kiptoo	KEN	4.9.77	23 Jun
28:26.49	Tomoaki	Bungo	JPN	28.1.86	20 Oct
28:26.6	Hassan Mahboub (Silas Kirui)		BRN	31.12.81	18 May
28:26.61	Hiroyuki	Ono	JPN	3.10.86	19 May
28:26.72	Satoshi	Irifune	JPN	14.12.75	3 Jun
28:27.35	Yoshinori	Oda	JPN	5.12.80	22 Apr
28:27.4	Ahmed Ibrahim	Baday	MAR	12.1.79	18 May
28:27.53	Joseph	Mwaniki	KEN-J	29.11.88	17 Jun
28:27.53	Martin	Waweru	KEN-J	6.2.88	20 Oct
28:27.65	Josh	McDougal	USA	1.6.85	29 Apr
28:28.01	Steve	Sundell	USA	7.5.82	13 Apr
28:28.04	Andrew	Lemoncello	GBR	12.10.82	31 Mar
28:28.10	Ed	Torres	USA	22.8.80	29 Apr
28:28.56	Shinji	Kanagawa	JPN	17.1.82	11 Jul
28:28.59	Dathan	Ritzenhein	USA	30.12.82	27 Aug
28:28.78	Kazuo	Ietani	JPN	25.8.77	11 Jul
28:28.92	Clodoaldo	da Silva	BRA	19.8.76	27 Jul
28:29.16	Sean	Quigley	USA	8.2.85	31 Mar
28:29.59	Kuflom	Sium	ERI	.87	28 Jul
28:30.03	Rob	Koborsi	USA	4.10.83	29 Apr
28:30.4A	Julius	Nyamu	KEN	1.12.77	25 May
28:30.53	Matt	Downin	USA	10.2.77	31 Mar
28:30.77	Ombeche	Mokamba	KEN	7.4.82	21 Apr
28:30.93	Viatliy	Shafar	UKR	27.1.82	7 Jul
28:31.02	Kamiel	Maase	NED	20.10.71	2 Jun
28:31,3A	Thomas	Nyariki	KEN	27.9.71	17 May
28:32.70	Carles	Castillejo	ESP	18.8.78	7 Apr
28:32.82	Yoshikazu	Kawazoe	JPN	26.9.87	12 May
28:32.9A	Stephen	Kiprotich	UGA-J	18.4.89	8 Jul
28:33.34	Tomoyuki	Sato	JPN	31.1.81	12 May
28:33.84	Julius	Gitahi	KEN	29.4.78	15 Apr
28:33.84	Rui Pedro	Silva	POR	6.5.81	2 Jun
28:34.0	Naoto	Morimoto	JPN	14.5.83	24 Nov
28:34.00	Kazuki	Ikenaga	JPN	17.2.84	28 Nov
28:34.98	Vasyl	Matviychuk	UKR	13.1.82	7 Apr
28:35.28	Tomoya	Shirayanagi	JPN	7.7.81	2 Dec
28:35.71	Hidekazu	Sato	JPN	7.6.86	2 Dec
28:35.95	John	Moore	USA	24.4.84	29 Apr
28:36.12	Ryan	Kirkpatrick	USA	10.9.78	29 Apr
28:36.31	Masayuki	Obata	JPN	5.4.80	22 Apr
28:36.31	Tomoya	Adachi	JPN	18.12.85	12 May
28:36.40	Yu	Mitsuya	JPN	18.12.84	1 Dec
28:37.0A	Wilson	Kipsang	KEN	26.6.77	25 May
28:37.05	Killian	Lonergan	IRL	6.7.74	2 Jun
28:37.14	John	Kanyi (200)	KEN	6.9.80	2 Jun

JUNIORS

See main list for top 7 juniors. 14 performances by 9 men to 28:14.0. Additional marks and further juniors:

Fikadu 27:40.64 9 VD Bruxelles 14 Sep 28:06.00 7 AfG Alger 19 Jul
Njeru 27:51.62 2 Fukuroi 2 Jun 27:51.81 1r2 Kobe 12 Apr

Mark	Name		Nat	Born	Pos	Meet	Venue	Date
28:11.38	Joseph	Gitawo	KEN-J	3.1.88	7		Fukagawa	11 Jul
28:11.67	Nicholas	Makau	KEN-Y	15.10.90	2		Hachioji	28 Nov
28:12.92	Nasser Jamal	Nasser (10)	QAT	19.11.88	2		Liège (NX)	28 Jun
28:14.36	Haurun	Njoroge	KEN	11.6.88	10		Fukuroi	14 Oct
28:19.31	Martin	Mukule	KEN	14.12.89	1		Yokohama	9 Dec
28:21.68	Samuel	Tsegay Tesfamarian	ERI	24.10.88	8	AfG	Alger	19 Jul
28:22.93	Paul	Kuira	KEN-Y	25.1.91	2	Oda	Hiroshima	29 Apr
28:27.53	Joseph	Mwaniki	KEN	29.11.88	5		Shibetsu	17 Jun
28:27.53	Martin	Waweru	KEN	6.2.88	5		Yokohama	20 Oct
28:32.9A	Stephen	Kiprotich	UGA	18.4.89	1		Kampala	8 Jul
28:38.58	Abraham	Niyonkuru	BDI	26.12.89	9	AfG	Alger	19 Jul
28:42.76	Adam Ismail	Khamis Issa	BRN	12.2.89	3	CISM	Hyderabad	18 Oct
28:48.08	Takuya	Nakayama (20)	JPN	29.9.89	18		Yokohama	20 Oct
Top European: 29:14.49	Mohamed	Elbendir	ESP	28.9.88	13	NC	Avilès	28 Jul

20,000M 1 HOUR

Mark	Name		Nat	Born	Pos	Meet	Venue	Date
56:25.98+ 21 285m	Haile	Gebrselassie	ETH	18.4.73	1	GS	Ostrava	27 Jun
	and 42:18.70 at 15,000m							
59:06.75+ 20 271	Daniel Kiprop	Limo	KEN	10.12.83	2	GS	Ostrava	27 Jun

10 KILOMETRES ROAD

Mark	Name		Nat	Born	Pos	Meet	Venue	Date
27:07	Micah	Kogo	KEN	3.6.86	1		Brunssum	1 Apr
27:21		Kogo			1		Manchester	20 May
27:24	Zersenay	Tadese	ERI	8.2.82	2		Manchester	20 May
27:27+	Samuel	Wanjiru	KEN	10.11.86	1	in HMar	Den Haag	17 Mar
27:27+	Patrick	Makau	KEN	2.3.85	1=	in HMar	Berlin	1 Apr
27:27+	Francis	Kibiwott	KEN	15.9.78	1=	in HMar	Berlin	1 Apr
27:27+	Evans	Cheruiyot	KEN	5.10.82	1=	in HMar	Berlin	1 Apr
27:27+	Eshetu	Wondimu	ETH	26.1.82	1=	in HMar	Berlin	1 Apr
Other where superior to track bests								
27:30+	Moses	Kigen	KEN	10.1.83	5=	in HMar	Berlin	1 Apr
27:30+	Wilfred	Taragon	KEN	9.6.85	5=	in HMar	Berlin	1 Apr
27:35+		Makau			1=	in HMar	Udine	14 Oct
27:35+		E Cheruiyot			1=	in HMar	Udine	14 Oct
27:35+		Merga			1=	in HMar	Udine	14 Oct
27:43+	Mekubo	Mogusu	KEN	25.12.86	1	in HMar	Sapporo	8 Jul
27:49+	Yonas	Kifle	ERI	24.3.77	7	in HMar	Udine	14 Oct
27:51	Wilson	Kipsang	KEN	.80	1		Hem	26 Aug
27:52	Jason	Mbote	KEN	5.1.77	1		Groesbeek	2 Jun
27:52	Mark	Tanui	KEN	.77	1		Utrecht	7 Oct
27:52	Duncan	Kibet	KEN	25.4.78	1		Cape Elizabeth	4 Aug
27:54	Allan	Masai Ndiwa	KEN	.84	2		Utrecht	7 Oct
27:56	Charles	Koech	KEN	27.7.83	2		Groesbeek	2 Jun
27:56	Abdellah	Falil	MAR	.76	1		Languex	16 Jun
27:56	John	Yuda	TAN	9.6.79	3		Cape Elizabeth	4 Aug
27:57	Peter	Kamais	KEN	7.11.76	1		Barcelona	1 Apr
27:58	Ben	Kimwole	KEN	.78	3		Groesbeek	2 Jun
27:58	Sergiy	Lebid	UKR	15.7.75	2		Houilles	30 Dec
27:59	Eshetu	Gezhagne	ETH	20.9.82		in HMar	Berlin	1 Apr
27:59	Ali Mabrouk	El Zaidi	LBA	13.1.74	4		Groesbeek	2 Jun
28:00	Silas	Kipruto	KEN	.84	1		Madrid	18 Nov
28:01	Samuel	Ndereba	KEN	2.2.77	1		Mobile	24 Mar
28:01	Edwin	Soi	KEN	3.3.86	1		Marseille	1 May
28:02	Nicholas	Manza	KEN	2.3.85	2		Mobile	24 Mar
28:02	Paul	Kosgei	KEN	22.4.78	3		Houilles	30 Dec
28:03	Mark	Kiptoo	KEN	21.6.76	3		Marseille	1 May
28:04	Adil	Annani	MAR	30.6.80	3		Utrecht	7 Oct
28:05	Stanley	Kipkosgei Salil	KEN	2.4.86	2		Paderborn	7 Apr
28:05+	Robert	Kipchumba	KEN	24.2.84	11	in HMar	Udine	14 Oct
28:05+	Nicholas	Kiprono	UGA	7.11.87	12	in HMar	Udine	14 Oct
28:05+	Fabiano	Joseph	TAN	24.12.85	14	in HMar	Udine	14 Oct
28:05+	Samson	Kiflemariam	ERI	23.1.84	15	in HMar	Udine	14 Oct
28:05+	Atsushi	Sato	JPN	8.5.78	17	in HMar	Udine	14 Oct
28:06	Lawrence	Kiprotich	KEN	20.8.86	1		Santos	20 May
28:07	Mohammed	Farah	GBR	23.3.83	3		Manchester	20 May
28:07+	Jonathan	Maiyo	KEN-J	.88	5	in HMar	Rotterdam	9 Sep

Mark	Name		Nat	Born	Pos	Meet	Venue	Date
28:08+	Patrick	Ivuti	KEN	30.6.78	6=	in HMar	Rotterdam	9 Sep
28:08+	Abel	Kirui	KEN	4.6.82	6=	in HMar	Rotterdam	9 Sep
28:08	Gilbert	Okari	KEN	2.7.78	1		San Juan	25 Feb
28:08	Dathan	Ritzenhein	USA	30.12.82	1		New York	19 May
28:08	Nourredine	Athamna	ALG	25.5.84	4		Utrecht	7 Oct
28:09	Cosmas	Koech	KEN	9.10.85	2		San Juan	25 Feb
28:09+	Francis	Kiprop	KEN	4.6.82	3	in HMar	Den Haag	17 Mar
28:09+	Solomon	Busendich	KEN	10.1.84	3	in HMar	Den Haag	17 Mar
28:09	José Manuel	Martínez	ESP	22.10.71	4		Manchester	20 May
28:09	John	Korir	KEN	15.12.75	1		Green Bay	9 Jun
28:10	Nicholas	Makau	KEN-Y	15.10.90	2		Lahore	14 Jan
28:10+	Stephen	Chelimo	KEN	9.8.85		in HMar	Den Haag	17 Mar
28:10	Stanley	Muiruri Nganga	KEN	30.6.86	5		Groesbeek	2 Jun

Mark	Name		Nat	Born	Date
28:11+	Charles Munyeki Kiama		KEN	2.11.86	17 Mar
28:11+	William	Kipsang	KEN	26.6.77	17 Mar
28:13	Martin	Lel	KEN	28.10.78	25 Feb
28:14	William	Chebor	KEN	.81	4 Aug
28:15	George	Kirwa Misoi	KEN	.84	7 Apr
28:17	Linus	Maiyo	KEN	26.2.83	7 Apr
28:17+	Michael	Tesfay	ERI	23.9.76	14 Oct
28:18	Geoffrey	Kusuro	UGA-J	12.2.89	1 May
28:18	James Kibocha Theuri		FRA	30.10.78	1 Jun
28:19	Johnstone	Chepkwony	KEN	5.5.84	7 Apr
28:19	Mathew	Koech	KEN	1.1.83	29 Apr
28:20	Thomas	Nyariki	KEN	27.9.71	9 Jun
28:20+	Philemon	Baaru Gitia	KEN	20.5.81	9 Sep
28:20	Joseph	Kiptoo	KEN		7 Oct
28:22	Mohamed	Fadil	MAR	15.11.81	7 Oct
28:23	Mohammed	Amyn	MAR	25.3.76	4 Aug
28:23	Wilson	Busienei	UGA	18.8.81	14 Oct
28:24	Charles	Korir	KEN-J	.88	26 Aug
28:24	David	Chelule	KEN	7.7.77	30 Sep
28:24+	Tariku	Jifar	ETH	18.7.84	14 Oct
28:25+	Luke	Kipkosgei	KEN	27.11.75	17 Mar
28:25+	Sammy	Kipruto	KEN	22.11.78	17 Mar
28:25	Benoît	Zwierzchiewski	FRA	19.8.76	25 Mar
28:25	Charles	Ngolepus	KEN	.84?, .68	7 Apr
28:25	Craig	Mottram	AUS	18.6.80	19 May
28:25	Mohamed	Hadji	MAR	.79	7 Oct
28:25+	Mohamed Abdu Bakhet		QAT	25.12.87	14 Oct
28:26+	Wilson	Chebet	KEN	.85	30 Sep
28:26+	John	Kales	KEN	.84	30 Sep
28:26+	Francis	Bowen	KEN	12.10.73	30 Sep
28:26+	Jacob	Yator	KEN	5.8.82	30 Sep
28:26+	Ezekiel	Ngimba	TAN	17.8.85	14 Oct
28:26	Joel	Kimurer Kemboi	KEN	.88	11 Nov
28:27	Peter	Kiprotich	KEN	.79	18 Jul
28:27	Justus	Kiprono	KEN	28.2.87	8 Sep
28:27+	Josphat	Kamzee	KEN	.84	30 Sep
28:27+	Isaac	Kiprop	KEN	10.9.86	14 Oct
28:28	Charles	Kibet	KEN-J		9 Sep
28:28+	Ahmad Juma	Jaber	QAT	29.12.83	14 Oct
28:29	Tefera	Bacha	ETH	.85	31 Mar
28:29	Jonathan	Koilegei	KEN	.79	23 Jun
28:30	William	Kiplagat	KEN	21.6.72	18 Jul
28:30	Phillimon	Serem	KEN	.78	11 Nov
28:31+	James	Yatich	BRN	22.10.84	11 Mar
28:31+	Rodgers	Rop	KEN	16.2.76	11 Mar
28:31	Tefera	Demesse	ETH	15.12.82	19 May
28:31	Ruggero	Pertile	ITA	8.8.74	30 Sep
28:32+	Paul	Kimaiyo	KEN	4.3.80	11 Mar
28:32	Elijah	Sang	KEN	.83	30 Jun
28:33	Abraham	Chebii	KEN	23.12.79	9 Apr
28:33	Said	Azouzi	MAR	.79	23 Jun
28:33	Salim	Saiti	KEN	.86	24 Jun
28:33	Tsegay	Kebede	ETH	.87	30 Jun
28:33	Charles	Munyeki	KEN	2.11.86	4 Aug
28:34	Fred	Mogaka Tumbo	KEN	18.6.78	31 Mar
28:34	Joseph	Kipkemboi Koskei	KEN	29.11.80	31 Mar
28:34	Chala	Lemi	ETH	26.2.87	26 May
28:35	Elijah	Keitany	KEN	.83	23 Jun
28:36	Abera	Eritiban	ETH-J	13.3.88	14 Jan
28:36+	Yared	Asmeron	ERI	3.2.79	31 Mar
28:36+	Elijah	Mbogo	KEN-J	.88	30 Sep
28:37+	Philemon Kipsang Kipchumba		KEN	.77	1 Apr
28:37+	Jackson	Kirwa Kiprono	KEN	.86	1 Apr
28:37+	Alphonce	Yatich Kibor	KEN	21.12.83	1 Apr
28:37	Mark	Tucker	AUS	15.8.79	22 Jul
28:37	Driss	El Himer	FRA	4.4.74	30 Dec
28:25 dh	Boaz	Cheboiywo	KEN	2.8.78	4 Jul

82m downhill: May 6, Toronto: 1. Stephen Koech KEN 27:47, 2. Isaac Arusei KEN 27:49, 3. Philip Koech KEN 27:50

15 KILOMETRES ROAD

And see splts at 15km in 10M lists on next page

Mark	Name		Nat	Born	Pos	Meet	Venue	Date
41:29+	Samuel	Wanjiru	KEN	10.11.86	1	in HMar	Ra's Al Khaymah	9 Feb
41:30+		Wanjiru			1	in HMar	Den Haag	17 Mar
41:34+	Zersenay	Tadese	ERI	8.2.82	1	in HMar	Udine	14 Oct
41:34+	Deriba	Merga	ETH	26.10.80	2	in HMar	Udine	14 Oct
41:34+	Patrick	Makau	KEN	2.3.85	3	in HMar	Udine	14 Oct
41:34+	Evans	Cheruiyot	KEN	5.10.82	4	in HMar	Udine	14 Oct
41:46+		Makau			1=	in HMar	Berlin	1 Apr
41:46+	Francis	Kibiwott	KEN	15.9.78	1=	in HMar	Berlin	1 Apr
41:46+		E Cheruiyot			1=	in HMar	Berlin	1 Apr
41:46+	Eshetu	Wondimu	ETH	26.1.82	1=	in HMar	Berlin	1 Apr
42:06+	Mekubo	Mogusu	KEN	25.12.86	1	in HMar	Sapporo	8 Jul
42:07+	Dieudonné	Disi	RWA	24.4.78	5	in HMar	Udine	14 Oct
42:13+		Makau			1=	in HMar	Rotterdam	9 Sep
42:13+		Merga			1=	in HMar	Rotterdam	9 Sep
42:13+	Patrick	Ivuti (10)	KEN	30.6.78	1=	in HMar	Rotterdam	9 Sep
42:14+		E Cheruiyot			4	in HMar	Rotterdam	9 Sep
42:15+		Mogusu			1	in HMar	Marugame	4 Feb
42:15+	Yonas	Kifle	ERI	24.3.77	6	in HMar	Udine	14 Oct
42:15+	Marílson	dos Santos	BRA	6.8.77	7	in HMar	Udine	14 Oct
42:22+	Jonathan	Maiyo	KEN-J	.88	5=	in HMar	Rotterdam	9 Sep
42:22+	Abel	Kirui	KEN	4.6.82	5=	in HMar	Rotterdam	9 Sep
42:24	Sileshi	Sihine	ETH	29.9.83	1		Nijmegen	18 Nov

Mark	Name		Nat	Born	Pos	Meet	Venue	Date
42:25+	Fabiano	Joseph	TAN	24.12.85	7	in HMar	Rotterdam	9 Sep
42:26+	Solomon	Busendich	KEN	10.1.84	2	in HMar	Den Haag	17 Mar
42:29+	Francis	Kiprop	KEN	4.6.82	3	in HMar	Den Haag	17 Mar
	(25/18)							
42:34+	William	Kipsang	KEN	26.6.77	4	in HMar	Den Haag	17 Mar
42:35+	Dickson	Marwa Mkawi (20)	TAN	9.3.82	8	in HMar	Udine	14 Oct
42:35+	Cuthbert	Nyasango	ZIM	17.9.82	10	in HMar	Udine	14 Oct
42:35+	Raji	Assefa	ETH	18.2.86	11	in HMar	Udine	14 Oct
42:36+	Atsushi	Sato	JPN	8.5.78	12	in HMar	Udine	14 Oct
42:36	Haile	Gebreselassie	ETH	18.4.73	1		s'Heerenberg	2 Dec
42:39+	Robert	Kipchumba	KEN	24.2.84	14	in HMar	Udine	14 Oct
42:40+	Ali Saadoun	Al-Dawoodi	QAT	29.6.84	15	in HMar	Udine	14 Oct
42:41+	William	Chebor	KEN	.81	1	in HMar	Azpeitia	31 Mar
42:42	Ali Mabrouk	El Zaidi	LBA	13.1.74	2		s'Heerenberg	2 Dec
42:43+	Charles Munyeki	Kiama	KEN	2.11.86		in HMar	Den Haag	17 Mar
42:48+	Stephen	Chelimo	KEN	9.8.85		in HMar	Den Haag	17 Mar
	(30)							
42:50+	Nicholas	Kiprono	UGA	7.11.87	16	in HMar	Udine	14 Oct
42:50+	Samson	Kiflemariam	ERI	23.1.84	17	in HMar	Udine	14 Oct
42:55+	Michael	Tesfay	ERI	23.9.76	18	in HMar	Udine	14 Oct
42:57+	Abdullah Ahmad	Hassan	QAT	4.4.81	19	in HMar	Udine	14 Oct
43:03+	Benson	Barus	KEN	4.7.80	1	in HMar	Ostia	25 Feb
43:03+	Philemon	Kipsang Kipchumba	KEN	.77	1=	in HMar	Milano	1 Apr
43:03+	Jackson	Kirwa Kiprono	KEN	.86	1=	in HMar	Milano	1 Apr
43:03+	Paul	Kimaiyo	KEN	4.3.80	1=	in HMar	Milano	1 Apr
43:04+	Jonathan	Kipkorir	KEN		2=	in HMar	Ostia	25 Feb
43:04+	Stanley	Kipleting Biwott	KEN	.86	2=	in HMar	Ostia	25 Feb
	(40)							
43:08+	Girma	Assefa	ETH	20.6.86	2	in HMar	Sapporo	8 Jul
43:18+	Luke	Kipkosgei	KEN	27.11.75		in HMar	Den Haag	17 Mar
43:18+	Philemon	Baaru Gitia	KEN	20.5.81		in HMar	Rotterdam	9 Sep
43:20+	Sammy	Kipruto	KEN	22.11.78		in HMar	Den Haag	17 Mar
43:22+	Charles	Koech	KEN	27.7.83		in HMar	Den Haag	17 Mar
43:22	Shimelis	Girma	ETH	12.6.87	1		Istanbul	28 Oct
43:24+	Ben	Kimwole	KEN	.78		in HMar	Den Haag	17 Mar
43:26	Stanley	Kipkosgei	KEN	2.4.86	1		Kerzers	17 Mar
43:26	Moses Mwengi	Macharia	KEN	.73	2		Istanbul	28 Oct
43:27+	Tariku	Jifar	ETH	18.7.84	20	in HMar	Udine	14 Oct
	(50)							
43:27+	Ezekiel	Ngimba	TAN	17.8.85	21	in HMar	Udine	14 Oct
43:27+	Mohamed Abdu	Bakhet	QAT	25.12.87	22	in HMar	Udine	14 Oct
43:27	Joel	Melly	KEN	.84	3		Istanbul	28 Oct

43:30+	Wilson	Busienei	UGA	18.8.81	14 Oct
43:31+	Paul	Kirui	KEN	5.2.80	9 Sep
43:39+	Ombeche	Mokamba	KEN	7.4.82	13 May
43:40	Mebrahtom	Keflezighi	USA	5.5.75	10 Mar
43:42	Bernard	Kiprop	KEN	16.7.86	18 Nov
43:44+	Ahmad Juma	Jaber	QAT	29.12.83	14 Oct
43:47	Mark	Tanui	KEN	.77	6 May
43:50+	Masato	Kihara	JPN	13.7.86	20 Oct

10 MILES ROAD

15km splits in 2nd column

Mark	15km	Name		Nat	Born	Pos	Meet	Venue	Date
45:24		John	Kariuki	KEN	10.11.86	1r1		Kosa	9Dec
45:33+	42:21	Ryan	Hall	USA	14.10.82	1	in HMar	Houston	14Jan
45:40+	42:41dh	Martin	Lel	KEN	29.10.78	1=	in HMar	Newcastle	30Sep
45:40+	42:41dh	Samuel	Wanjiru	KEN	10.11.86	1=	in HMar	Newcastle	30Sep
45:45		Girma	Assefa	ETH	20.2.86	2r1		Kosa	9Dec
45:52	42:58	Zersenay	Tadese	ERI	8.2.82	1		Zaandam	23Sep
46:01		Tadesse	Tola	ETH	31.10.87	1		Washington	1Apr
46:03		Micah	Njeru	KEN-J	5.8.88	3r1		Kosa	9Dec
46:04		John	Yuda	TAN	9.6.79	2		Washington	1Apr
46:11		John	Korir	KEN	15.12.75	3		Washington	1Apr
		(10)							
46:11	43:05	Wesley	Langat	KEN	13.8.86	1		Tilburg	2Sep
46:12		Nicholas	Manza	KEN	2.3.85	4		Washington	1Apr
46:21	43:16	Bernard	Kiprop	KEN	16.7.86	2		Zaandam	23Sep
46:27	43:17	Wilson	Kipsang	KEN	.80	2		Tilburg	2Sep
46:28		Hideaki	Date	JPN	11.4.85	1		Kosa	9Dec
46:32		Kenji	Noguchi	JPN	23.2.75	2		Kosa	9Dec
46:34		Terukazu	Omori	JPN	3.9.79	1		Himeji	11Feb
46:34		Takeshi	Takahashi	JPN	2.4.83	3		Kosa	9Dec
46:35		Masato	Imai	JPN	2.4.84	4		Kosa	9Dec
46:35		Yuki	Sato	JPN	26.11.86	5		Kosa	9Dec
46:38+		Macdonald	Ondara	KEN	8.12.84	1	in HMar	San Jose	14Oct

Mark		Name		Nat	Born	Pos	Meet	Venue	Date
46:39	43:23	Charles	Koech	KEN/QAT	29.12.83	3		Tilburg	2Sep
46:44	43:33	Kamiel	Maase	NED	20.10.71	4		Tilburg	2Sep
46:44		Kazuhiro	Maeda	JPN	19.4.81	6		Kosa	9Dec
46:46		Samuel	Ndereba	KEN	2.2.77	5		Washington	1Apr
46:50		Cyrus	Njui	KEN	11.2.86	1		Karatsu	11Feb
46:50	43:32	Joseph Kiptoo	Birech	KEN	4.1.84	5		Tilburg	2Sep
46:50	43:51	James	Rotich	KEN	22.12.78	3		Zaandam	23Sep

46:53	Samuel	Rongo (43:35)	KEN	.72	2 Sep
46:53	Tomoyuki	Sato	JPN	31.1.81	9 Dec
46:54	Takaki	Koda	JPN	27.3.84	9 Dec
46:55	Tomoya	Adachi	JPN	18.12.85	9 Dec
46:56	Tsukasa	Morita	JPN	24.1.83	9 Dec
46:57	Julius	Muriuki (43:45)	KEN	.85	2 Sep
46:57	Willy	Kangogo Kimutai	KEN	12.2.84	9 Dec
46:57	Kazuharu	Takai	JPN	10.5.84	9 Dec
46:58	Keita	Akiba	JPN	27.11.79	11 Feb
46:58	Joseph	Mwaniki	KEN-J	29.11.88	9 Dec
46:58	Ken-ichiro	Setoguchi	JPN	12.12.80	9 Dec
46:58	Makoto	Tobimatsu	JPN	18.8.80	9 Dec
46:59	Kemsuke	Takezawa	JPN	11.10.86	11 Feb
46:59	John	Kanyi	KEN	6.9.80	9 Dec

Point-to-point, 48m dh and wind assisted: 6 May, Philadelphia: 1. Patrick Cheruiyot KEN 12.6.67 45:14. 2. Benson Cheruiyot KEN .83 45:19.

20 KILOMETRES ROAD

See times in Half Marathon lists – plus

56:52	Eshetu	Wondimu	ETH	26.1.82	1		Alphen aan den Rijn	11 Mar
57:01		Mogusu			1		Tachikawa	20 Oct
57:21+	Fabiano	Joseph	TAN	24.12.85	9	in HMar	Udine	14 Oct
57:37	James	Yatich	BRN	22.10.84	3		Alphen aan den Rijn	11 Mar
57:39+	Robert	Kipchumba	KEN	24.2.84	15	in HMar	Udine	14 Oct
58:02+	William Chebon	Chebor	KEN	22.12.82		in HMar	Den Haag	17 Mar
58:03	Rodgers	Rop	KEN	16.2.76	4		Alphen aan den Rijn	11 Mar
58:07	Musau	Mwanzia	KEN	.83	1		Paris	14 Oct
58:08	Paul	Kimaiyo	KEN	4.3.80	5		Alphen aan den Rijn	11 Mar
58:08	Jonathan	Maiyo	KEN-J	.88	2		Paris	14 Oct
58:09	Philemon	Terer	KEN	.85	3		Paris	14 Oct
58:10	Sammy	Kibet	KEN	.82	4		Paris	14 Oct
58:12	Jacob	Kitur	KEN	.80	5		Paris	14 Oct
58:27	John	Kales	KEN	.84	6		Paris	14 Oct
58:35+	Philemon	Baaru Gitia	KEN	20.5.81		in HMar	Den Haag	17 Mar
58:40	Masato	Kihara	JPN	13.7.86	2		Tachikawa	20 Oct

Distance? 10 Nov, Kabarnet (A) all KEN: 1. Moses Kigen 56:14, 2. Stephen Kemboi 56:16, 3. Agnello Rutto 56:41; 4. Yator Minigwo 5hamer 57:11, 6. Jacob Chamer 57:11, 8. Wilson Kipsang 57:24.

HALF MARATHON

20km times in 2nd column

58:33	55:31	Samuel	Wanjiru	KEN	10.11.86	1		Den Haag	17 Mar
58:53	55:50		Wanjiru			1		Ra's Al Khaymah	9 Feb
58:56	55:53	Patrick	Makau	KEN	2.3.85	1		Berlin	1 Apr
58:59	56:13	Zersenay	Tadese	ERI	8.2.82	1	WCh	Udine	14 Oct
59:02	56:13		Makau			2	WCh	Udine	14 Oct
59:05	56:13	Evans	Cheruiyot	KEN	5.10.82	3	WCh	Udine	14 Oct
59:12	56:20		E Cheruiyot			1		Rotterdam	9 Sep
59:13			Makau			2		Ra's Al Khaymah	9 Feb
59:16	56:13	Deriba	Merga	ETH	26.10.80	4	WCh	Udine	14 Oct
59:19	56:20		Makau			2		Rotterdam	9 Sep
59:24dh		Haile	Gebrselassie	ETH	18.4.73	1		New York (dh 30m)	5 Aug
59:25	56:20		Merga			3		Rotterdam	9 Sep
59:26		Francis	Kibiwott	KEN	15.9.78	2		Berlin	1 Apr
59:27	56:20	Patrick	Ivuti	KEN	30.6.78	4		Rotterdam	9 Sep
59:30	56:30	Yonas	Kifle	ERI	24.3.77	5	WCh	Udine	14 Oct
59:32	56:31	Dieudonné	Disi (10)	RWA	24.4.78	6	WCh	Udine	14 Oct
59:33	56:32	Marílson	dos Santos	BRA	6.8.77	7	WCh	Udine	14 Oct
59:43	57:06e	Ryan	Hall	USA	14.10.82	1	NC	Houston	14 Jan
59:44			Merga			3		Ra's Al Khaymah	9 Feb
59:45		Joseph	Maregu	KEN	.77	1		Lille	1 Sep
59:48	56:42	Mekubo	Mogusu	KEN	25.12.86	1		Marugame	4 Feb
59:48			Cheruiyot			3		Berlin	1 Apr
59:54	56:50		Mogusu			1		Sapporo	8 Jul
59:58			Mogusu			1		Ichinoseki	23 Sep
60:08			Kibiwott			4		Ra's Al Khaymah	9 Feb
60:08		Eshetu	Wondimu	ETH	26.1.82	4		Berlin	1 Apr
60:10		Jonathan	Maiyo	KEN-J	.88	5		Rotterdam	9 Sep
60:10dh	57:10	Martin	Lel	KEN	29.10.78	1	GNR	South Shields (dh 30.5m)	30Sep
60:11		Abel	Kirui	KEN	4.6.82	6		Rotterdam	9 Sep
60:13	56:58	Solomon (30/19)	Busendich	KEN	10.1.84	2		Den Haag	17 Mar

Mark		Name		Nat	Born	Pos	Meet	Venue	Date
60:13		Wilson	Chebet (20)	KEN	12.7.85	1	RdVin	Remich	30 Sep
60:14		Fabiano	Joseph	TAN	24.12.85	7		Rotterdam	9 Sep
60:17	56:58	Francis	Kiprop	KEN	4.6.82	3		Den Haag	17 Mar
60:18	57:04	Benson	Barus	KEN	4.7.80	1		Ostia	25 Feb
60:24	57:21	Dickson	Marwa Mkami	TAN	9.3.82	8	WCh	Udine	14 Oct
60:25	57:07	William	Kipsang	KEN	26.6.77	4		Den Haag	17 Mar
60:25	57:24	Atsushi	Sato	JPN	8.5.78	9	WCh	Udine	14 Oct
60:26	57:21	Cuthbert	Nyasango	ZIM	17.9.82	10	WCh	Udine	14 Oct
60:28		Yared	Asmeron	ERI	3.2.79	1		Azpeitia	31 Mar
60:29dh		Abdi	Abdirahman	USA	1.1.77	2		New York	5 Aug
60:31	57:25	Raji	Assefa	ETH	18.2.86	12	WCh	Udine	14 Oct
		(30)							
60:34dh		Robert	Kipchumba	KEN	24.2.84	1		Lisboa (69m dh)	18 Mar
60:34		Silas	Sang	KEN	21.8.78	1		Los Palacios	16 Dec
60:35		Shadrack	Kiplagat	KEN	9.12.77	2		Paris	11 Mar
60:38		Robert K.	Cheruiyot	KEN	26.9.78	5		Ra's Al Khaymah	9 Feb
60:39		John	Yuda	TAN	9.6.79	6		Ra's Al Khaymah	9 Feb
60:39		Moses Kipkosgei	Kigen	KEN	10.1.83	5		Berlin	1 Apr
60:39	57:39	Michael	Tesfay	ERI	23.9.76	13	WCh	Udine	14 Oct
60:39	57:31	Ali Saadoun	Al-Dawoodi	QAT	29.6.84	14	WCh	Udine	14 Oct
60:42		Wilfred	Taragon	KEN	25.2.85	6		Berlin	1 Apr
60:43		Abdellah	Falil	MAR	.76	4		Paris	11 Mar
		(40)							
60:43dh		Jaouad	Gharib	MAR	22.5.72	3		Lisboa	18 Mar
60:47		Mubarak Hassan	Shami	QAT	2.12.80	5		Paris	11 Mar
60:47		John	Kales	KEN	.84	2	RdVin	Remich	30 Sep
60:48		James	Yatich	KEN	22.10.84	1		Muscat	2 Feb
60:48		Isaac	Macharia	KEN	25.11.80	2		New Delhi	28 Oct
60:51dh		Emmanuel	Mutai	KEN	1.4.78	5		Lisboa	18 Mar
60:51		William Chebon	Chebor	KEN	22.12.82	2		Azpeitia	31 Mar
60:52		Jackson	Kirwa Kiprono	KEN	.86	2		Lille	1 Sep
60:52	57:39	Samson	Kiflemariam	ERI	23.1.84	16	WCh	Udine	14 Oct
60:55		Philemon	Kisang Kipchumba	KEN	.77	1		Milano	1 Apr
		(50)							
60:57		Matthew	Koech	KEN	1.1.83	8		Ra's Al Khaymah	9 Feb
60:57	57:46	Nicholas	Kiprono	UGA	7.11.87	17	WCh	Udine	14 Oct
60:59	57:36	Jonathan Kosgei	Kipkorir	KEN	.82	2		Ostia	25 Feb
61:00		Brahim	Lahlafi	FRA	15.4.68	6		Paris	11 Mar
61:01		Enock	Mitei	KEN	26.11.80	1		Ivry-Vitry	1 Apr
61:03	57:46	Stephen	Chelimo	KEN	9.8.85	5		Den Haag	17 Mar
61:03dh		James	Kipsang Kwambai	KEN	.76	3		New York	5 Aug
61:04	57:41	Charles Munyeki	Kiama	KEN	2.11.86	6		Den Haag	17 Mar
61:04dh		Festus	Langat	KEN	.85	6		Lisboa	18 Mar
61:07		Paul	Kirui	KEN	5.2.80	10		Rotterdam	9 Sep
		(60)							
61:10		Jacob	Yator	KEN	5.8.82	1		Barcelona	11 Feb
61:11		Macdonald	Ondara	KEN	8.12.84	1		San Jose	14 Oct
61:13		Francis	Bowen	KEN	12.10.73	4	RdVin	Remich	30 Sep
61:16		Sammy	Kibet	KEN	.82	2		Reims	21 Oct
61:18	57:56	Luke	Kipkosgei	KEN	27.11.75	7		Den Haag	17 Mar
61:20	57:55	Stanley	Kipleting Biwott	KEN	.86	3		Ostia	25 Feb
61:26dh		Paul	Kosgei	KEN	22.4.78	7		Lisboa	18 Mar
61:27	58:08	Charles	Koech	QAT	29.12.83	9		Den Haag	17 Mar
61:27		Philemon	Kirwa Tarbei	KEN	20.10.78	3		Lille	1 Sep
61:28	58:27	Tariku	Jifar	ETH	18.7.84	18	WCh	Udine	14 Oct
		(70)							
61:28	58:27	Ezekiel	Ngimba	TAN	17.8.85	19	WCh	Udine	14 Oct
61:31	58:25	Girma	Assefa	ETH	20.6.86	2		Sapporo	8 Jul
61:32		Hillary	Kipchumba	KEN		3		San Jose	14 Oct
61:33	58:12	Sammy	Kipruto	KEN	22.11.78	10		Den Haag	17 Mar
61:36		James Kibocha	Theuri	FRA	30.10.78	4		Lille	1 Sep
61:36	58:31	Pierre	Joncheray	FRA	9.9.82	20	WCh	Udine	14 Oct
61:36		Tesfaye	Sandiku	ETH	.83	4		Reims	21 Oct
61:37		Tadesse	Tola	ETH	31.10.87	11		Ra's Al Khaymah	9 Feb
61:37		Musau	Mwanzia	KEN	.83	5		Lille	1 Sep
61:38	58:33	Mohamed Abdu	Bakhet	QAT	25.12.87	21	WCh	Udine	14 Oct
		(80)							
61:38	58:31	Kidane	Gemechu	ETH	23.6.85	22	WCh	Udine	14 Oct
61:39		Albert	Matebor	KEN	20.12.80	6		Lille	1 Sep
61:39		Allan	Masai Ndiwa	KEN		1		Dordrecht	14 Oct
61:40		Andrew	Chopa	TAN		3		Ivry-Vitry	1 Apr

Mark		Name		Nat	Born	Pos	Meet	Venue	Date
61:40		Elijah	Mbogo	KEN-J	.88	5		Reims	21 Oct
61:42		Tadesse	Feyisa	ETH	.81	12		Ra's Al Khaymah	9 Feb
61:42	58:38	Günther	Weidlinger	AUT	5.4.78	23	WCh	Udine	14 Oct
61:46	58:31	Abdullah Ahmad	Hassan	QAT	4.4.81	24	WCh	Udine	14 Oct
61:47		Denis Musembi	Ndiso	KEN	31.12.83	8		Lille	1 Sep
61:48		Musabeker (90)	Marda	MAR	4.2.82	9		Lille	1 Sep
61:48		William	Todoo Rotich	KEN	.80	2		Porto	23 Sep
61:49		Paul	Kimaiyo	KEN	4.3.80	3	Str	Milano	1 Apr
61:50		Josphat	Kamzee	KEN	.84	5	RdVin	Remich	30 Sep
61:50		Ernest	Kebenei	KEN	.83	2		Dordrecht	14 Oct
61:51		Philemon	Terer	KEN	.85	6		Reims	21 Oct
61:52		Philemon	Baaru Gitia	KEN	20.5.81	12		Rotterdam	9 Sep
61:52		Joseph	Mwaniki	KEN-J	29.11.88	1		Hakodate	30 Sep
61:53		Elias	Maindi	KEN	.80	1		Venio	25 Mar
61:53		Mark	Tanui	KEN	.77	3		Dordrecht	14 Oct
61:54		Stephen (100)	Kibiwott	KEN	.80	3		Praha	24 Mar

61:55	Martin Hhaway	Sulle	TAN	28.12.82	9 Feb
61:58	Samwel	Kwaangu (58:48)	TAN	30.11.85	14 Oct
61:59	Isaac	Kiplagat	KEN		23 Sep
61:59	Yuko	Matsumiya	JPN	21.2.80	30 Sep
61:59	Sylvain	Rukundo (58:56)	RWA-J	20.12.88	14 Oct
62:00	Abel	Maina	KEN		1 Sep
62:02	Mariko	Kipchumba Kiplagat	KEN	.75	1 Apr
62:02	Julius	Kibet Koskei	KEN	6.4.82	16 Sep
62:03	Kamiel	Maase	NED	20.10.71	11 Feb
62:03	Patrick	Mbuvi	KEN		28 Oct
62:04	Thomas	Nyariki	KEN	27.9.71	16 Sep
62:04	Wilson	Kiprotich Kebenei	KEN	20.7.80	28 Oct
62:05	John	Kiprotich	KEN-J	.89	23 Sep
62:05	Wilson	Busienei (58:52)	UGA	18.8.81	14 Oct
62:07	James	Kibet (58:52)	UGA	5.6.86	14 Oct
62:08	Emmanuel	Biwott	KEN		25 Mar
62:08	Daniel	Limo Kiprop	KEN	10.12.83	2 Sep
62:08	Ahmad Juma	Jaber (58:59)	QAT	29.12.83	14 Oct
62:08	Kazuhiro	Maeda	JPN	19.4.81	14 Oct
62:09	Tewodros	Shiferaw	ETH	21.9.80	25 Mar
62:09	Ricardo	Serrano	ESP	29.10.80	14 Oct
62:10	Daniel	Rono	KEN	13.7.78	11 Mar
62:10	Stefano	Baldini	ITA	25.5.71	1 Apr
62:10	Mustafa	Riyadh	BRN	5.8.75	15 Apr
62:11	Takayuki	Matsumiya	JPN	21.2.80	4 Feb
62:11	Matthew	Cheboi Kiptoo	KEN	.82	2 Sep
62:11	David	Kemboi Kiyeng	KEN	.83	23 Sep
62:14	Terukazu	Omori	JPN	3.9.79	11 Mar
62:14	Naoto	Yoneda	JPN	6.1.81	11 Mar
62:15	Toru	Okada	JPN	22.4.78	11 Mar
62:15	Brahim	Beloua	MAR	.72	15 Apr
62:15	Wilberforce	Talel Kapkeny	KEN	10.1.80	16 Sep
62:15	Mohamed	Fadil	MAR	15.11.84	14 Oct
62:16	Kazuyoshi	Shimozato	JPN	9.4.81	11 Mar
62:16	John	Kibowen	KEN	21.4.69	23 Sep
62:17	Bekele	Gebretsadik	ETH	27.9.86	11 Mar
62:17	Ruggero	Pertile	ITA	8.8.74	14 Oct
62:18	Kazuo	Ietani	JPN	25.8.77	11 Mar
62:19	Yoshinori	Oda	JPN	5.12.80	11 Mar
62:19	Cyrus	Njui	KEN	11.2.86	11 Mar
62:19	David	Kilel	KEN	21.5.84	16 Dec
62:20	Fasil	Bizuneh	USA	5.5.78	14 Jan
62:20	Kenji	Noguchi	JPN	23.2.75	11 Mar
62:20	Haron	Toroitich	KEN	.78	2 Sep
62:20	Urige	Buta	ETH	28.11.82	30 Sep
62:21	Youssef Othman	Qader	QAT	5.4.85	2 Feb
62:21	Masahiro	Fujita	JPN	14.5.77	11 Mar
62:21	Moustafa	Shebto	QAT	4.7.86	21 May
62:21	Samuel	Ndereba	KEN	.78	7 Oct
62:22	Mebrathom	Keflezighi	USA	5.5.75	14 Jan
62:22	John Cheruiyot	Korir	KEN	13.12.81	24 Mar
62:23	Mohamed	Ikoki Msandeki	TAN	31.12.85	2 Feb
62:23	Ken-ichi	Shiraishi	JPN	6.4.82	11 Mar
62:23	Kensuke	Takahashi	JPN	30.5.78	11 Mar
62:23	David	Kipsang	KEN	.74	30 Sep
62:24	James	Kosgei Cheptuiyon	KEN	.84	18 Feb
62:24	Satoshi	Osaki	JPN	4.6.76	11 Mar
62:24	John	Kanyi	KEN	6.9.80	11 Mar
62:24	Peter	Korir	KEN	.70	20 May
62:24	Lusapho	April	RSA	24.5.82	14 Oct
62:24	Vincent	Krop	KEN	1.1.83	21 Oct
62:24	Nahashon	Rugut Kipngetich	KEN	.84	28 Oct
62:26	Fernando	Rey	ESP	16.4.80	14 Oct
62:27	Chiharu	Takada	JPN	9.7.81	11 Mar
62:27	Elijah	Nyabuti	KEN	10.10.79	1 Apr
62:27	Isaac	Tanui Kiprotich	KEN	19.12.86	9 Apr
62:27	Yusuf	Songoka	KEN	5.2.79	2 Sep
62:29	Arata	Fujiwara	JPN	12.9.81	4 Feb
62:29	Takeshi	Kumamoto	JPN	6.1.84	11 Mar
62:29	Hiromichi	Ueki	JPN	11.11.84	11 Mar
62:29	Ombeche	Mokamba	KEN	7.4.82	13 May
62:29+	Peter	Kiprotich	KEN	.79	30 Sep
62:29+	Rodgers	Rop	KEN	16.2.76	30 Sep
62:29+	Wilson	Kipkemboi Kigen	KEN	15.9.80	30 Sep
62:29	Philip	Rugut	KEN	18.5.77	28 Oct
62:29	Ezechiel	Nizigimana	TAN-Y	30.3.90	4 Nov
62:29	Khalid	El Boumlili	MAR	10.4.78	18 Nov
62:30	Takeshi	Maekawa	JPN	18.12.85	4 Feb
62:30	Yoshiro	Tanigawa	JPN	20.10.79	11 Mar
62:30	Koen	Raymaekers	NED	31.1.80	17 Mar
62:30	Mutai	Kiprono	KEN	23.12.87	8 Jul
62:30+	Andrew	Limo	KEN	15.3.84	30 Sep
62:31	Takuya	Fukatsu	JPN	10.11.87	4 Feb
62:31	Leonard	Kipyego Kipkoech	KEN		11 Feb
62:31dh	Philip	Manyim	KEN	24.3.78	18 Mar
62:31	Alex	Kirui	KEN		20 May
62:31	James	Melly	KEN		3 Jun
62:31	Adil	Ennani	MAR	30.6.80	14 Oct
62:31	Henry	Kiplagat	KEN	.82	28 Oct
62:32	Stephen	Njenga Wainaina	KEN	20.12.84	4 Feb
62:32	Ali Mabrouk	El Zaidi	LBA	13.1.74	23 Nov
62:32	Justus	Kiprono	KEN	28.2.87	2 Sep
62:33	Tetsuo	Nishimura	JPN	27.10.78	8 Jul
62:33	Joseph	Lomala Kimosop	KEN	.82	2 Sep
62:33	Kazuki	Ikenaga	JPN	17.2.84	30 Sep
62:33	Jacob	Wanjuki	KEN	16.1.86	23 Nov
62:33	Abdelkebir	Lamachi	MAR	12.6.80	16 Dec
62:34	Luc	Krotwaar	NED	25.1.68	17 Mar
62:34	Kazuyuki	Maeda	JPN	10.2.80	30 Sep
62:34	Mohamed	Hadji	MAR	.79	14 Oct
62:34	Samuel (201)	Kosgei	UGA	18.6.84	11 Nov

61:46dh Alene Emere ETH 25.6.82 1 Austin (114m dh) 28 Jan

Questionable distance: 22 Sep Ngereny: 1. William Muturi Karanja KEN 60:57, 2. Peter Kioi KEN 62:17

JUNIORS

See main list for top 3 juniors. Further men:

61:59	58:56	Sylvain	Rukundo	RWA-J	20.12.88	26	WCh	Udine	14 Oct
62:05		John	Kiprotich	KEN-J	.89	1		Torino	23 Sep

MEN 2007

Mark	Name		Nat	Born	Pos	Meet	Venue	Date
62:29	Ezechiel	Nizigimana	TAN-Y	30.3.90	1		Saint-Denis	4 Nov
62:36	Patrick	Kimeli	KEN-J	22.4.89	11	RdVin	Remich	30 Sep
62:39	Nathan	Chebet	UGA-J	.88	3		Saint-Denis	4 Nov
63:09	Kiyonori	Takahara	JPN	16.3.88	2		Ageo	18 Nov
63:40		Jeon Eun-hoi	KOR	15.5.88	29		Marugame	4 Feb

25 KILOMETRES ROAD

Mark	Name		Nat	Born	Pos	Meet	Venue	Date
1:14:05+	Haile	Gebrselassie	ETH	18.4.73	1	in Mar	Berlin	30 Sep
1:14:05+	Eshetu	Wondimu	ETH	26.1.82	1=	in Mar	Berlin	30 Sep
1:14:05+	Rodgers	Rop	KEN	16.2.76	1=	in Mar	Berlin	30 Sep
1:14:05+	Andrew	Limo	KEN	15.3.84	1=	in Mar	Berlin	30 Sep
1:14:22	Patrick	Makau	KEN	2.3.85	1		Berlin	6 May
1:14:25	Julius	Kibet	KEN	6.4.82	1		Grand Rapids	12 May
1:14:38+	Philip	Singoei	KEN	31.12.75	1	in Mar	Eindhoven	14 Oct
1:14:46+	Mubarak Hassan	Shami	QAT	2.12.80	1	in Mar	Paris	15 Apr
1:14:49	Brian	Sell	USA	11.4.78	2		Grand Rapids	12 May

30 KILOMETRES ROAD

Mark	Name		Nat	Born	Pos	Meet	Venue	Date
1:28:56+	Haile	Gebrselassie	ETH	18.4.73	1=	in Mar	Berlin	30 Sep
1:28:56+	Eshetu	Wondimu	ETH	26.1.82	1=	in Mar	Berlin	30 Sep
1:28:56+	Rodgers	Rop	KEN	16.2.76	1=	in Mar	Berlin	30 Sep
1:29:42+	Samuel	Muturi	KEN	2.5.86	1=	in Mar	Hamburg	29 Apr
1:29:59	Willy	Kangogo Kimutai	KEN	12.2.84	1		Kumamoto	25 Feb
1:30:01+	James	Rotich	KEN	22.12.78		in Mar	Hamburg	29 Apr
1:30:01+	Abel	Kirui	KEN	4.6.82	4=	in Mar	Berlin	30 Sep
1:30:01+	Philip	Manyim	KEN	24.3.78	4=	in Mar	Berlin	30 Sep
1:30:01+	Philip	Serem	KEN	3.10.78	4=	in Mar	Berlin	30 Sep
1:30:02+	Josphat Kiprotich	Kenei	KEN	.78		in Mar	Hamburg	29 Apr
1:30:02+	Wilfred	Kigen	KEN	23.2.75		in Mar	Hamburg	29 Apr
1:30:03+	Matthew	Sigei	KEN	30.4.83		in Mar	Hamburg	29 Apr

1:30:05+ in Paris Mar: Mubarak Hassan Shami; in Berlin Mar: Salim Kipsang, Mesfin Adimasu
1:30:05+ in Fukuoka Mar: Deriba Merga, Samuel Wanjiru, Atsushi Sato, Isaac Macharia, Fabiano Joseph
1:30:06+ in Fukuoka Mar: Kensuke Takahashi, Shigeru Aburaya; 1:30:14+ in Hamburg Mar: Joseph Ngeny
25 Feb Kumamoto (all JPN): 2. Kazuhiro Maeda 19.4.81 1:30:07, 3. Ken-ichi Shiraishi 6.4.82 1:30:08, 4. Naoto Yoneda 6.1.81 1:30:10, 5, Takayuki Ota 29.11.82 1:30:14, 6. Koichi Sakai 11.3.86 1:30:15

MARATHON

L = loop course, P = point-to-point, D = downhill over 1/1000

Mark		Name		Nat	Born	Pos	Meet	Venue	Date
2:04:26	L	Haile	Gebrselassie	ETH	18.4.73	1		Berlin	30 Sep
2:06:29	L	Emmanuel	Mutai	KEN	1.4.78	1		Amsterdam	21 Oct
2:06:39	L	Samuel	Wanjiru	KEN	10.11.86	1		Fukuoka	2 Dec
2:06:45	L	Richard	Limo	KEN	18.11.80	2		Amsterdam	21 Oct
2:06:50	L	Deriba	Merga	ETH	26.10.80	2		Fukuoka	2 Dec
2:06:51	L	Abel	Kirui	KEN	4.6.82	2		Berlin	30 Sep
2:07:12	L	James	Rotich	KEN	22.12.78	3		Amsterdam	21 Oct
2:07:12	L	Paul	Kirui	KEN	5.2.80	4		Amsterdam	21 Oct
2:07:13	L	Atsushi	Sato	JPN	8.5.78	3		Fukuoka	2 Dec
2:07:19	L	Mubarak Hassan	Shami (10)	QAT	2.12.80	1		Paris	15 Apr
2:07:29	L	Salim	Kipsang	KEN	22.12.79	3		Berlin	30 Sep
2:07:32	L	Rodgers	Rop	KEN	16.2.76	1		Hamburg	29 Apr
2:07:33	L	Oleksandr	Kuzin	UKR	21.10.74	1		Linz	15 Apr
2:07:33	L	Wilfred	Kigen	KEN	23.2.75	2		Hamburg	29 Apr
2:07:34	L	Yonas	Kifle	ERI	24.3.77	5		Amsterdam	21 Oct
2:07:41	L	Martin	Lel	KEN	29.10.78	1		London	22 Apr
2:07:42	L	Josphat Kiprotich	Kenei	KEN	.78	3		Hamburg	29 Apr
2:07:44	L	Abderrahim	Goumri	MAR	21.5.76	2		London	22 Apr
2:07:47	L	Felix	Limo	KEN	22.8.80	3		London	22 Apr
2:07:51	L	Jason	Mbote (20)	KEN	5.1.77	6		Amsterdam	21 Oct
2:07:53	L	Shadrack	Kiplagat	KEN	9.12.77	7		Amsterdam	21 Oct
2:07:54	L	Jaouad	Gharib	MAR	22.5.72	4		London	22 Apr
2:07:56	L	Hendrick	Ramaala	RSA	2.2.72	5		London	22 Apr
2:07:57	L	Philip	Singoei	KEN	31.12.75	1		Eindhoven	14 Oct
2:07:58	L		Kigen			1		Frankfurt	28 Oct
2:08:01	L	Philip	Manyim	KEN	24.3.78	4		Berlin	30 Sep
2:08:04	L		Lee Bong-ju	KOR	11.10.70	1		Seoul	18 Mar
2:08:06	L	Paul	Tergat	KEN	17.6.69	6		London	22 Apr
2:08:09	L	Nephat	Kinyanjui	KEN	30.6.77	1		Beijing	21 Oct
2:08:11	L	Hosea	Kiprop Rotich	KEN	2.8.79	2		Frankfurt	28 Oct
2:08:14	L	Joshua	Chelanga	KEN	7.4.73	1		Seoul	4 Nov
		(31/30)							

Mark		Name		Nat	Born	Pos	Meet	Venue	Date
2:08:15	L		Ren Longyun	CHN	12.10.87	2		Beijing	21 Oct
2:08:16	L	Tsegaye	Kebede	ETH	.87	8		Amsterdam	21 Oct
2:08:20	L	Viktor	Röthlin	SUI	14.10.74	1		Zürich	1 Apr
2:08:20	L	Abderrahim	Bouramdane	MAR	1.1.78	2		Seoul	4 Nov
2:08:21	L	Kamiel	Maase	NED	20.10.71	9		Amsterdam	21 Oct
2:08:24	L	Ryan	Hall	USA	14.10.82	7		London	22 Apr
2:08:37	L	Marílson Gomes	dos Santos	BRA	6.8.77	8		London	22 Apr
2:08:38	L	Laban	Kipkemboi	KEN	30.12.77	3		Seoul	18 Mar
2:08:38	L	Sammy	Kurgat	KEN	.75	3		Frankfurt	28 Oct
2:08:45	L	Edwin	Komen	KEN	.80	4		Seoul	18 Mar
		(40)							
2:08:49	L	Peter	Kiprotich	KEN	.79	4		Frankfurt	28 Oct
2:08:56	L		Han Gang	CHN	10.11.78	3		Beijing	21 Oct
2:09:01	L	Yirefu	Berhanu	ETH	1.1.86	3		Seoul	4 Nov
2:09:04	D	Daniel	Yego	KEN	28.8.79	1		San Diego (dh 76m)	3 Jun
2:09:04	L	Benson	Barus	KEN	4.7.80	4		Seoul	4 Nov
2:09:07	L	Aleksey	Sokolov	RUS	14.11.79	1		Dublin	29 Oct
2:09:08	L	David	Kemboi Kiyeng	KEN	.83	1		Reims	21 Oct
2:09:16	L	Evans	Cheruiyot	KEN	5.10.82	1		Milano	2 Dec
2:09:20	L	John	Birgen	KEN	8.5.74	2		Milano	2 Dec
2:09:21	L	Peter	Kemboi	KEN	.78	1		Mombasa	27 May
		(50)							
2:09:30	L	John	Kelai	KEN	29.12.76	1		Toronto	30 Sep
2:09:31	L	Paul	Kosgei	KEN	22.4.78	10		Amsterdam	21 Oct
2:09:33	L	Albert	Matebor	KEN	20.12.80	5		Frankfurt	28 Oct
2:09:36	L	Elias	Kemboi	KEN	10.3.84	1		Roma	18 Mar
2:09:36	L	Daniel	Rono	KEN	13.7.78	2		Toronto	30 Sep
2:09:39	L	Matthew	Sigei	KEN	30.4.83	5		Hamburg	29 Apr
2:09:40	L	Yuko	Matsumiya	JPN	21.2.80	4		Fukuoka	2 Dec
2:09:42	L	Nicholas	Chelimo	KEN		5		Seoul	4 Nov
2:09:45	L	Daniel	Njenga	KEN	7.5.76	1		Tokyo	18 Feb
2:09:45	L	Charles	Kibiwott	KEN	8.8.74	2		Gyeongju	21 Oct
		(60)							
2:09:46	L	David	Kemboi	KEN	.75	2		Reims	21 Oct
2:09:46	L	Simon	Njoroge	KEN		6		Frankfurt	28 Oct
2:09:48	L	Bellor	Yator	KEN	.84	1		Düsseldorf	6 May
2:09:49	L	Mesfin	Adimasu	ETH	5.3.85	5		Berlin	30 Sep
2:09:49	L	Francis	Kiprop	KEN	4.6.82	11		Amsterdam	21 Oct
2:09:53	L	William	Todoo Rotich	KEN	.80	1		Dubai	12 Jan
2:09:53	L	Gashaw	Melesse	ETH	26.9.78	2		Paris	15 Apr
2:09:53	L	William	Biama	KEN	.85	1		Kosice	7 Oct
2:09:56	L	Paul	Biwott	KEN	18.4.78	2		Eindhoven	14 Oct
2:09:56	L	Wilson	Kipkemboi Kigen	KEN	15.9.80	3		Gyeongju	21 Oct
		(70)							
2:09:59	L	David Mandago	Kipkorir	KEN	15.12.74	4		Beijing	21 Oct
2:10:04	L	Takayuki	Matsumiya	JPN	21.2.80	2		Rotterdam	15 Apr
2:10:07	L	Luke	Kibet	KEN	12.4.83	1		Wien	29 Apr
2:10:12	L	José Manuel	Martínez	ESP	22.10.71	2		Roma	18 Mar
2:10:13	L	Kennedy	Mburu Mugo	KEN		2		Mombasa	27 May
2:10:13	L	Elijah	Sang	KEN	.83	7		Frankfurt	28 Oct
2:10:15	L	Abraham	Chelanga	KEN	.84	3		Reims	21 Oct
2:10:18	D	Benjamin	Pseret	KEN	.80	1		Treviso (dh 96m)	25 Mar
2:10:19	D	David	Maiyo	KEN	5.11.76	2		Treviso	25 Mar
2:10:20	L	Kasine	Adilo	ETH		3		Toronto	30 Sep
		(80)							
2:10:23	L	Atsushi	Fujita	JPN	6.11.76	1		Oita	4 Feb
2:10:24	L	Philemon Kirwa	Tarbei	KEN	20.10.78	1		Torino	15 Apr
2:10:25	L	Jonathan Kosgei	Kipkorir	KEN	.82	3		Roma	18 Mar
2:10:25	L	Joseph	Ngeny	KEN	20.7.77	6		Hamburg	29 Apr
2:10:27	D	Phillip Kiplagat	Biwott	KEN	.77	3		Treviso	25 Mar
2:10:27	D	Asnake	Fekadu	KEN	.82	4		Treviso	25 Mar
2:10:27	L	James	Mwangi Macharia	KEN	23.6.84	2		Wien	29 Apr
2:10:28	L	Jackson	Koech	KEN	26.12.78	7		Hamburg	29 Apr
2:10:30	L	Migidio	Bourifa	ITA	31.1.69	4		Roma	18 Mar
2:10:30	L	Shigeru	Aburaya	JPN	8.2.77	5		Fukuoka	2 Dec
		(90)							
2:10:31	L	Lee	Troop	AUS	22.3.73	6		Berlin	30 Sep
2:10:34	L	Joseph	Wambua Mutiso	KEN		2		Dubai	12 Jan
2:10:36	L	David	Cheruiyot	KEN	5.5.81	1		Ottawa	27 May
2:10:37	L	Tomas	Abyu	GBR	5.5.78	2		Dublin	29 Oct

Mark		Name		Nat	Born	Pos	Meet	Venue	Date
2:10:39	D	Paul Kipkemei	Kogo	KEN	.83	1		Padova (dh 73m)	22 Apr
2:10:39	L	Norman	Dlomo	RSA	18.4.75	3		Milano	2 Dec
2:10:40	L	Musa	Kanda	KEN	.73	3		Dubai	12 Jan
2:10:40	D	Alberico	Di Cecco	ITA	19.4.74	2		Padova	22 Apr
2:10:41	L	Francis	Bowen	KEN	12.10.73	8		Frankfurt	28 Oct
2:10:43	L	Samson (100)	Ramadhani	TAN	25.12.82	1	L.Biwa	Otsu	4 Mar

Mark		Name		Nat	Born	Date
2:10:45	L	Tesfaye	Tola	ETH	19.10.74	18 Mar
2:10:47	L	William	Kiplagat	KEN	21.6.72	4 Mar
2:10:47	L	Francis	Kipketer	KEN	17.4.76	15 Apr
2:10:47	L	Luka	Chelimo	KEN		21 Oct
2:10:49	L	Vincent	Kiplagat	KEN	10.8.84	27 May
2:10:51	L	Dmytro	Baranovskyy	UKR	28.7.79	18 Mar
2:10:51	L	Yusuf	Songoka	KEN	5.2.79	15 Apr
2:10:53	L	Simon	Wangai	KEN	12.11.78	30 Sep
2:10:57	L	Ottaviano	Andriani	ITA	4.1.74	6 May
2:10:58	L	Alphonce	Yatich Kibor	KEN	21.12.83	12 Jan
2:10:58	D	Christopher	Cheboiboch	KEN	3.3.77	3 Jun
2:11:00		David Emmanuel	Cheruiyot	KEN	.70	28 Oct
2:11:01	L	Japhet	Kosgei	KEN	1.9.68	28 Oct
2:11:02	L	Grigoriy	Andreyev	RUS	7.1.76	28 Oct
2:11:04	L	William	Kipsang	KEN	26.6.77	15 Apr
2:11:04	D	Mark	Yatich	KEN	4.12.76	28 Oct
2:11:05	L	Hillary	Bett	KEN	.80	15 Apr
2:11:05	L	Stanley	Nganga	KEN	30.6.86	6 May
2:11:05	L	Daniel	Kiprugut Too	KEN	25.4.78	7 Oct
2:11:05	D	Tariku	Jifar	ETH	18.7.84	28 Oct
2:11:07	L	Dathan	Ritzenhein	USA	30.12.82	3 Nov
2:11:08	L	Sammy	Chumba	KEN	9.8.78	14 Oct
2:11:08	L	Yirdawe	Dejene	ETH		29 Oct
2:11:10	L	Daniele	Caimmi	ITA	17.12.72	15 Apr
2:11:10	D	Mushir Salem	Jawher	BRN	13.6.78	28 Oct
2:11:11	L	Patrick	Ivuti	KEN	30.6.78	7 Oct
2:11:11	L	Thomson	Cherogony	KEN	12.11.78	21 Oct
2:11:13	L	Sammy	Kipruto	KEN	22.11.78	29 Apr
2:11:14	L	Samson	Barmao	KEN	17.4.82	15 Apr
2:11:14	L	Hillary	Kipchirchir	KEN	30.4.81	27 May
2:11:14	D	Raymond	Kipkoech	KEN	19.4.78	28 Oct
2:11:15	L	Ambesse	Tolossa	ETH	28.8.77	4 Mar
2:11:15	L	Dmitriy	Semyonov	RUS	4.7.75	28 Oct
2:11:16	L	Mariko	Kiplagat	KEN	.75	9 Apr
2:11:18	L	Ahmed	Ezzobayry	FRA	6.6.78	15 Apr
2:11:18	D	Noah	Serem	KEN	.76	21 Oct
2:11:22	D	Tomoyuki	Sato	JPN	31.1.81	18 Feb
2:11:25	L	Charles	Kamathi	KEN	18.5.78	2 Dec
2:11:27	L	Samuel	Muturi Mugo	KEN	2.5.86	7 Oct
2:11:28	L	Joseph	Ngurane	KEN	.75	6 May
2:11:33	L	Benjamin	Itok	KEN	.72	7 Oct
2:11:34	L	Pablo	Olmedo	MEX	8.5.75	4 Mar
2:11:36	L	Julio	Rey	ESP	13.1.72	15 Apr
2:11:39	L	Katera	Feyissa	ETH	.83	14 Jan
2:11:40	L	Khalid	El Boumlili	MAR	10.4.78	12 Jan
2:11:40	L	Simon	Munyutu	FRA	27.12.77	21 Oct
2:11:40	L	Brian	Sell	USA	11.4.79	3 Nov
2:11:47	L	Andrew	Limo	KEN	15.3.84	15 Apr
2;11:47	L	Mulugeta	Wondimu	ETH	28.2.85	14 Oct
2:11:49	L	Héledr	Ornelas	POR	6.5.74	14 Oct
2:11:52	L	Kensuke	Takahashi	JPN	30.5.78	2 Dec
2:11:53	L	Jon	Maluni	KEN	29.12.80	21 Apr
2:11:55	L	Francisco	Bautista	MEX	17.9.72	4 Mar
2:11:58	L	Stefano	Baldini	ITA	25.5.71	4 Nov
2:11:59	L	Anersissa	Ketema	ETH	17.4.84	29 Apr
2:11:59	D	Iaroslav	Musinschi	MDA	8.8.76	28 Oct
2:12:00	L	Haron	Toroitich	KEN	.78	29 Apr
2:12:00	D	Sylvester	Chebii	KEN	.82	3 Jun
2:12:00	L	Arkadiusz	Sowa	POL	2.3.79	30 Sep
2:12:01	L	Simon	Bor	KEN	13.2.69	7 Oct
2:12:01	L	John	Kirui	KEN	.78	14 Oct
2:12:02	L	Youssef	Galmin	MAR	19.4.78	28 Jan
2:12:04	L	Samson	Loywapet	KEN	24.12.72	18 Feb
2:12:04	L	Johnstone	Chebii	KEN		4 Mar
2:12:05	L	Tekele	Tefera	ETH		18 Feb
2:12:05	L	Hosea	Kiptanui	KEN	.78	6 May
2:12:06	L	Isaac	Macharia	KEN	25.11.80	15 Apr
2:12:07	L	Vitaliy	Shafar	UKR	27.1.82	14 Oct
2:12:08	L	Edward	Kiprop	KEN	.87	27 May
2:12:08	L	Joseph	Kahugu	KEN	7.6.71	30 Sep
2:12:09	L	David	Kirui Kiptoo	KEN	29.12.77	18 Feb
2:12:10	D	Joseph	Chirlee	KEN	.81	3 Jun
2:12:15	L	Vincent	Kipsos	KEN	22.6.76	28 Oct
2:12:16	L	Jonathan	Kiptoo Yego	KEN	.76	14 Oct
2:12:18	L	William	Kwambai	KEN	3.11.76	21 Oct
2:12:19	L	Ben	Kipruto	KEN	22.2.82	18 Feb
2:12:19	L	Jonathan	Keiyo	KEN		14 Oct
2:12:20	L	Pawel	Ochal	POL	17.7.81	23 Sep
2:12:21	L	Tomohiro	Seto	JPN	19.10.76	30 Sep
2:12:22	L	Yuriy	Abramov	RUS	9.12.76	28 Oct
2:12:24	L	José Telles	de Souza	BRA	22.4.71	2 Dec
2:12:25	L	Benjamin	Kiptoo	KEN	.79	21 Oct
2:12:25	L	James	Kwambai	KEN	.76	4 Nov
2:12:28	L	Yusuke	Kataoka	JPN	19.8.79	21 Oct
2:12:31	L	Peter	Korir	KEN	.70	30 Sep
2:12:31	D	Josephat	Kipkemboi Yego	KEN	1.4.74	28 Oct
2:12:34	L	Khalid	Khannouchi	USA	22.12.71	3 Nov
2:12:36	L	Laban	Kagika	KEN	17.7.78	4 Mar
2:12:39	L	Samson	Kosgei	KEN	.74	18 Mar
2:12:41	L		Park Song-chol	PRK		8 Apr
2:12:42	L	Jonathan	Kibet	KEN	.68	22 Apr
2:12:42	D	Mohamed	Msenduki Ikoki	TAN	3.12.85	28 Oct
2:12:44	L	Kazushi	Hara	JPN	16.11.80	4 Feb
2:12:44	L	Satoshi	Irifune	JPN	14.12.75	18 Feb
2:12:45	L	Jacob	Chesire	KEN	.82	7 Oct
2:12:45	L	Abdelhadi	El Mouaziz	MAR	.77	25 Nov
2:12:46	L	Rachid	Kisri	MAR	1.3.75	4 Feb
2:12:46	L	Ignacio	Cáceres	ESP	18.6.76	30 Sep
2:12:49	L	David	Ramard	FRA	3.2.78	28 Oct
2:12:49	L	Oleksandr	Sitkovskyy (200)	UKR	9.6.78	28 Oct
Best on non-downhill courses						
2:11:57	L	Daniel	Yego	KEN	28.8.79	2 Dec
Drugs disqualification						
2:10:44	L	Omar	Jimila ¶	MAR	29.4.78	15 Apr

JUNIORS

Mark		Name	Nat	Born	Pos	Venue	Date
2:18:45	L	Hu Kaijun	CHN	15.3.89	21	Beijing	21 Oct

100 KILOMETRES

Mark	Name		Nat	Born	Pos	Meet	Venue	Date
6:23:21	Shin-ichi	Watanabe	JPN	16.11.76	1	WCp	Winschoten	8 Sep
6:29:57		Watanabe			1		Yubetsu	24 Jun
6:30:21	Kenji	Nakanishi	JPN	4.6.80	2	WCp	Winschoten	8 Sep
6:30:22	Oleg	Kharitonov	RUS	13.4.68	3	WCp	Winschoten	8 Sep
6:38:02		Nakanishi			2		Yubetsu	24 Jun
6:39:22	Grigoriy	Murzin	RUS	23.1.70	1		Santa Cruz de Bezana	29 Sep
6:40:24	Toshikazu	Goda	JPN	20.5.79	3		Yubetsu	24 Jun
6:42:30	Igor	Tyazhkorob	RUS	4.12.67	4	WCp	Winschoten	8 Sep
6:45:10	Aleksey	Izmaylov	RUS	17.12.70	5	WCp	Winschoten	8 Sep
6:46:50	Martin (10/8)	Lukes	NZL	27.5.71	6	WCp	Winschoten	8 Sep
6:47:10	Pascal	Fétizon	FRA	30.8.62	7	WCp	Winschoten	8 Sep

Mark	Name		Nat	Born	Pos	Meet	Venue	Date
6:48:21	Takenori	Kaga (10)	JPN	26.9.68	4		Yubetsu	24 Jun
6:49:02	Giorgio	Calcaterra	ITA	11.2.72	1		Firenze	27 May
6:49:08	Aleksey	Izmaylov	RUS	17.12.70	1	NC	Puschino	21 Apr
6:49:31	Howard	Nippert	USA	15.7.65	8	WCp	Winschoten	8 Sep

6:51:36	Marco	Boffo	ITA	21.1.75	8 Sep
6:52:31	János	Zabari	HUN	23.2.68	8 Sep
6:52:52	Gregory	Crowther	USA	17.5.73	8 Sep
6:53:02	Bernard	Bretaud	FRA	17.8.67	19 May
6:54:32	Mitsuru	Shinohara	JPN	29.4.67	8 Sep
6:55:21	Regis	Lacombe	FRA	21.8.67	19 May
6:55:56	Vasily	Spiridonov	RUS	12.10.72	21 Apr
6:56:05	Jean-Marc	Bordus	FRA	11.11.60	19 May
6:56:15	Michael	Sommer	GER	2.3.64	24 Mar
6:56:23	Anatoli	Kruglikov	RUS	9.10.57	21 Apr
6:58:11	Toru	Sakuta	JPN	.4.66	24 Jun
6:58:30	Christophe	Bachelier	FRA	21.8.66	8 Sep
6:58:34	Yuriy	Slastenikov	RUS	.64	2 Sep
6:58:53	Takehiro	Matsushita	JPN	26.11.78	8 Sep
6:59:03	Jörg	Hooss (28)	GER	12.9.64	24 Mar
Indoors					
6:53:39	Aleksandr	Vishnyagov	RUS	9.8.76	28 Jan
6:59:41	Igor	Tyazhkorob	RUS	4.12.67	28 Jan

24 HOURS

Mark	Name		Nat	Born	Pos	Meet	Venue	Date
275.684km	Ryoichi	Sekiya	JPN	27.12.56	1		Soochow	25 Nov
263.562		Sekiya			1	WCh	Drummondville	29 Jul
257.358 t	Anatoliy	Kruglikov	RUS	9.10.57	1	EC	Madrid	6 May
257.18	Mohamed	Magroun	FRA	15.7.59	2	WCh	Drummondville	29 Jul
253.814	Masayuki	Otaki	JPN	5.6.65	3	WCh	Drummondville	29 Jul
253.765	Claude	Hardel	FRA	20.1.59	1	NC	Montigny-en-Gohelle	8 Apr
251.631 t	Vladimir	Bychkov	RUS	13.5.67	2	EC	Madrid	6 May
251.602 t	Aleksey	Arefiev	RUS	24.3.72	1		Moscow	6 May
250.612	Yiannis	Kouros	AUS	13.2.56	1		Wörschach	22 Jul
249.771	Patrice	Bruneteau	FRA	4.8.64	2	NC	Montigny-en-Gohelle	8 Apr
248.613	Philip	McCarthy (10)	USA	.68	4	WCh	Drummondville	29 Jul
248.505	Fabien	Hoblea	FRA	5.3.65	5	WCh	Drummondville	29 Jul

247.937 t	José Luis	Posado	ESP	7.8.54	6 May
244.465	Makoto	Suzuki	JPN	.67	29 Jul
242.239	Ralf	Steisslinger	GER	7.12.65	13 May
240.711	Didier	David	FRA	27.6.53	28 Apr

Indoor

254.700	Kenji	Okiyama	JPN	5.6.65	1		Brno	17 Mar

246.580	Henrik	Olsson	SWE	8.8.75	9 Dec
241.210	Reima	Hartikainen	SWE	24.3.63	2 Dec

2000 METRES STEEPLECHASE

Mark	Name		Nat	Born	Pos	Meet	Venue	Date
5:17.19	Bouabdellah	Tahri	FRA	20.12.78	1		Strasbourg	28 Jun
5:19.96	Roba	Gari	ETH	12.4.82	1		Herrera	19 May
5:23.02	Abdelkader	Hachlaf	MAR	3.7.79	2		Herrera	19 May
5:23.68	Elijah	Chelimo	KEN	.87	3		Herrera	19 May
5:25.64	David	Chemweno	KEN	18.12.81	4		Herrera	19 May
5:26.60	Youcef	Abdi	AUS	7.12.77	2		Strasbourg	28 Jun

5:28.97	Bisluke	Kiplagat	KEN-J	8.8.88	19 May
5:29.20	José Luis	Blanco	ESP	3.6.75	19 May
5:29.37	Eliseo	Martín	ESP	5.11.73	19 May
5:30.81	Legese	Lamiso	ETH-Y	13.1.90	13 Jul
5:31.40	Saïd	Tbibi	MAR	17.1.85	28 Jun
5:32.0	Andrey	Farnosov	RUS	9.7.80	21 Jul

List does not include intermediate times in 3000m steeplechase races

JUNIORS

Mark	Name		Nat	Born	Pos	Meet	Venue	Date
5:28.97	Bisluke	Kiplagat	KEN	8.8.88	5		Herrera	19 May
5:30.81	Legese	Lamiso	ETH-Y	13.1.90	1	WY	Ostrava	13 Jul
5:32.88	Silas	Kosgei Kiptum	KEN	25.5.90	2	WY	Ostrava	13 Jul
5:34.49	Abdellah	Dacha	MAR	26.1.92	3	WY	Ostrava	13 Jul
5:36.39	Abdelghani	Aït Bahmad	MAR	28.7.89	2		Bottrop	24 May
5:37.30	Jonathan	Muia Ndiku	KEN	18.9.91	4	WY	Ostrava	13 Jul

3000 METRES STEEPLECHASE

Mark	Name		Nat	Born	Pos	Meet	Venue	Date
7:58.80	Paul K.	Koech	KEN	10.11.81	1	VD	Bruxelles	14 Sep
7:59.42		Koech			1	DNG	Stockholm	7 Aug
8:00.67		Koech			1	WAF	Stuttgart	23 Sep
8:01.05		Koech			1	FBK	Hengelo	26 May
8:02.89	Brimin	Kipruto	KEN	31.7.85	2	VD	Bruxelles	14 Sep
8:05.50	Ezekiel	Kemboi	KEN	25.5.82	1	GP	Athína	2 Jul
8:05.75	Mustafa	Mohamed	SWE	1.3.79	1	NA	Heusden-Zolder	28 Jul
8:06.66	Richard	Matelong	KEN	14.10.83	2	GP	Athína	2 Jul
8:06.98		Kipruto			3	GP	Athína	2 Jul
8:07.02	Brahim	Taleb	MAR	16.2.85	2	NA	Heusden-Zolder	28 Jul
8:07.12	Reuben	Kosgei	KEN	2.8.79	4	GP	Athína	2 Jul
8:07.12	Tareq Mubarak	Taher	BRN	24.3.84	3	NA	Heusden-Zolder	28 Jul
8:07.66		Matelong			2	WAF	Stuttgart	23 Sep
8:07.83		Mohamed			2	DNG	Stockholm	7 Aug
8:08.08		Koech			1	Pre	Eugene	10 Jun
8:09.06	Bouabdellah	Tahri	FRA	20.12.78	1		Longeville-lès-Metz	15 Jul
8:09.72	Hamid	Ezzine (10)	MAR	5.10.83	5	GP	Athína	2 Jul

Mark	Name		Nat	Born	Pos	Meet	Venue	Date
8:10.01		Koech			1	GS	Ostrava	27 Jun
8:10.98		Ezzine			4	NA	Heusden-Zolder	28 Jul
8:11.05		Kipruto			3	WAF	Stuttgart	23 Sep
8:11.18	Willy	Komen	KEN	22.12.87	3	VD	Bruxelles	14 Sep
8:11.24		Taher			3	DNG	Stockholm	7 Aug
8:11.50		Ezzine			4	DNG	Stockholm	7 Aug
8:11.62	Michael	Kipyego	KEN	2.10.83	5	DNG	Stockholm	7 Aug
8:11.77		Tahri			4	VD	Bruxelles	14 Sep
8:11.94		R Kosgei			2	GS	Ostrava	27 Jun
8:12.46		Komen			3	GS	Ostrava	27 Jun
8:13.66	James	Kosgei	KEN	.84	5	NA	Heusden-Zolder	28 Jul
8:13.82		Kipruto			1	WCh	Osaka	28 Aug
8:14.22	Mahiedine	Mehkhissi Benabbad	FRA	15.3.85	6	NA	Heusden-Zolder	28 Jul
	(30/14)							
8:14.32	Collins	Kosgei	KEN	4.8.86	1	Odlozil	Praha	13 Jun
8:14.88	Wesley	Kiprotich	KEN	1.8.79	5	WAF	Stuttgart	23 Sep
8:15.02	Pieter	Desmet	BEL	7.6.83	7	NA	Heusden-Zolder	28 Jul
8:15.05	Roba	Gari	ETH	12.4.82	1		Brazzaville	27 May
8:15.35	Günther	Weidlinger	AUT	5.4.78	5	GS	Ostrava	27 Jun
8:15.66	Julius	Nyamu	KEN	1.12.77	6	GP	Athína	2 Jul
	(20)							
8:15.69	Steve	Slattery	USA	14.8.80	4	VD	Bruxelles	14 Sep
8:16.28	Elijah	Chelimo	KEN	.87	1		Neerpelt	2 Jun
8:16.55	Vincent	Zouaoui Dandrieux	FRA	12.10.80	8	NA	Heusden-Zolder	28 Jul
8:16.75	Bjørnar Ustad	Kristensen	NOR	26.1.82	9	NA	Heusden-Zolder	28 Jul
8:17.03	Abdelkader	Hachlaf	MAR	3.7.79	3	FBK	Hengelo	26 May
8:17.21	Nahom	Mesfin Tariku	ETH-J	3.6.89	3	AfG	Alger	18 Jul
8:17.71	Abdellatif	Chemlal	MAR	11.1.82	7	DNG	Stockholm	7 Aug
8:17.90	Caleb	Ngetich	KEN	20.1.81	4	Odlozil	Praha	13 Jun
8:18.34	Youcef	Abdi	AUS	7.12.77	10	NA	Heusden-Zolder	28 Jul
8:18.43	Halil	Akkas	TUR	1.7.83	1		Izmir	22 May
	(30)							
8:19.29	Brian	Olinger	USA	2.6.83	11	NA	Heusden-Zolder	28 Jul
8:20.18	Ruben	Ramolefi	RSA	17.7.78	1		Stellenbosch	2 Mar
8:20.34	Aaron	Aguayo	USA	27.7.84	12	NA	Heusden-Zolder	28 Jul
8:20.36	Barnabas	Kirui	KEN	12.12.85	1	NCAA	Sacramento	8 Jun
8:20.43	Bisluke	Kiplagat	KEN-J	8.8.88	5	FBK	Hengelo	26 May
8:20.57	David	Chemweno	KEN	18.12.81	6	FBK	Hengelo	26 May
8:20.86	Krijn	Van Koolwijk	BEL	30.8.81	13	NA	Heusden-Zolder	28 Jul
8:21.20	Ali Abubaker	Kamal	QAT	8.11.83	5h1	WCh	Osaka	26 Aug
8:21.33	Antonio David	Jiménez	ESP	18.2.77	14	NA	Heusden-Zolder	28 Jul
8:21.36	Josh	McAdams	USA	26.3.80	2	Pre	Eugene	10 Jun
	(40)							
8:21.73	Benjamin	Kiplagat	UGA-J	4.3.89	1		Velenje	28 Jun
8:22.23	Filmon	Ghirmai	GER	25.1.79	6	Odlozil	Praha	13 Jun
8:22.47	José Luis	Blanco	ESP	3.6.75	2	NC	San Sebastián	4 Aug
8:22.57	Henry	Talam	KEN	12.2.81	1		Málaga	2 Jun
8:22.91	Eliseo	Martín	ESP	5.11.73	7	WCh	Osaka	28 Aug
8:23.12	Mircea-Florin	Bogdan	ROM	6.5.82	1		Stanford	29 Apr
8:23.21	Rubén	Palomeque	ESP	14.8.80	3	NC	San Sebastián	4 Aug
8:23.31	Yoshitaka	Iwamizu	JPN	20.6.79	4	Pre	Eugene	10 Jun
8:23.38	Elijah	Kibwalei	KEN	.84	3		Cottbus	20 Jun
8:23.40	César	Pérez	ESP	7.4.75	4	NC	San Sebastián	4 Aug
	(50)							
8:23.56	Rabia	Makhloufi	ALG	.86	10	GP	Athína	2 Jul
8:23.61	Ali Ahmed	Al-Amri	KSA	28.12.87	4h3	WCh	Osaka	26 Aug
8:23.74	Andrew	Lemoncello	GBR	12.10.82	3		Longeville-lès-Metz	15 Jul
8:23.83	Ion	Luchianov	MDA	31.1.81	3	WUG	Bangkok	13 Aug
8:24.54	Martin	Dent	AUS	8.2.79	2		Sydney	17 Feb
8:25.11	Moustafa	Shebto	QAT	4.7.86	4		Longeville-lès-Metz	15 Jul
8:25.15	Vadym	Slobodenyuk	UKR	17.3.81	4		Bydgoszcz	10 Jun
8:25.42	Abdelhakim	Zilali	FRA	20.6.83	5		Longeville-lès-Metz	15 Jul
8:25.71	Nicodemus	Naimadu	KEN	24.4.84	5	Pre	Eugene	10 Jun
8:25.71	Kamal Ali	Thamer	QAT-J	12.11.88	1		Leverkusen	10 Aug
	(60)							
8:26.42	Bostjan	Buc	SLO	13.4.80	7h3	WCh	Osaka	26 Aug
8:26.52	Tomasz	Szymkowiak	POL	5.7.83	1		Warszawa	19 Sep
8:26.94	Peter	Nowill	AUS	15.6.79	2		Stanford	29 Apr
8:26.96	Angelo	Iannelli	ITA	27.7.76	6		Cottbus	20 Jun
8:27.34	Tom	Brooks	USA	10.1.78	3	NC	Indianapolis	24 Jun

Mark	Name		Nat	Born	Pos	Meet	Venue	Date
8:27.64	Anthony	Famiglietti	USA	8.11.78	4	NC	Indianapolis	24 Jun
8:27.73	Collins	Ngeno	KEN	14.4.83	5	GP	Madrid	21 Jul
8:28.32	Dan	Lincoln	USA	20.10.80	5	NC	Indianapolis	24 Jun
8:28.82	Irba	Lakhal	FRA	12.2.75	6		Longeville-lès-Metz	15 Jul
8:28.89	Luis Miguel	Martín	ESP	11.1.72	13	GP	Athína	2 Jul
	(70)							
8:29.12	Kim	Hogarth	NZL	18.12.75	4		Stanford	29 Apr
8:29.13	Jamel	Chatbi	MAR	30.4.84	1		Uden	4 Aug
8:29.76	Abel	Mutai	KEN-J	2.10.88	1	Afr-J	Ouagadougou	9 Aug
8:29.99	Yakob	Garso	ETH-J	.88	2	Afr-J	Ouagadougou	9 Aug
8:30.00	Víctor	García	ESP	13.3.85	6	NC	San Sebastián	4 Aug
8:30.0A	Patrick	Nthiwa	KEN	30.6.83	4	NC	Nairobi	16 Jun
8:30.05	Mohamed-Khaled	Belabbas	FRA	4.7.81	10	Odlozil	Praha	13 Jun
8:30.09	Radoslaw	Poplawski	POL	16.1.83	2	NC	Poznan	1 Jul
8:30.41	Jermaine	Mays	GBR	23.12.82	11	Odlozil	Praha	13 Jun
8:30.51	Itai	Maggidi	ISR	9.1.81	16	NA	Heusden-Zolder	28 Jul
	(80)							
8:30.81	Mateusz	Demczyszak	POL	18.1.86	3	NC	Poznan	1 Jul
8:31.0A	David	Langat	KEN	.80	5	NC	Nairobi	16 Jun
8:31.18	Andrey	Farnosov	RUS	9.7.80	1	Znam	Zhukosvkiy	9 Jun
8:31.26	Max	King	USA	24.2.80	1		Eugene	26 May
8:31.28	Michal	Kaczmarek	POL	19.9.77	5		Bydgoszcz	10 Jun
8:31.31	Hubert	Pokrop	POL	2.11.85	4	NC	Poznan	1 Jul
8:31.40	Frank	Tickner	GBR	12.10.83	13	Odlozil	Praha	13 Jun
8:31.54	Rafal	Snochowski	POL	31.10.83	2		Warszawa	19 Sep
8:31.65	Mike	Spence	USA	20.5.78	6	NC	Indianapolis	24 Jun
8:31.72	Henrik	Skoog	SWE	17.4.79	13	DNG	Stockholm	7 Aug
	(90)							
8:32.03	Solomon	Kandie	KEN	28.8.78	2		Stanford	31 Mar
8:32.10	Ronald	Kipchumba Rutto	KEN	8.10.87	2		Rehlingen	28 May
8:32.2A	Henry	Kipkorir	KEN		1		Kakamega	21 Apr
8:32.29	Daham Najim	Bashir	QAT	8.11.79	9	FBK	Hengelo	26 May
8:32.45	Matteo	Villani	ITA	28.8.82	2h2	WUG	Bangkok	11 Aug
8:32.49	Martin	Pröll	AUT	21.3.81	15	Odlozil	Praha	13 Jun
8:32.55	Marcin	Chabowski	POL	28.5.86	10	GS	Ostrava	27 Jun
8:32.74	Benjamin	Bruce	USA	10.9.82	9	Pre	Eugene	10 Jun
8:32.79	Steffen	Uliczka	GER	17.7.84	7		Cottbus	20 Jun
8:32.94	Hillary	Kiprono	KEN	.85	3		Velenje	28 Jun
	(100)							

8:33.28	Yuri	Floriani	ITA	25.12.81	28 Jun
8:33.33	Bill	Nelson	USA	11.9.84	8 Jun
8:33.35	Roman	Usov	RUS	4.6.78	31 Jul
8:33.60	Simon	Ayeko	UGA	10.5.87	11 Aug
8:33.66	Abdelghani	Aït Bahmad	MAR-J	28.7.89	15 Jul
8:34.11	Ildar	Minshin	RUS	5.2.85	31 Jul
8:34.17	Pyotr	Ivanenko	RUS	11.1.86	19 Jun
8:34.24	Mário	Teixeira	POR	20.9.74	30 Jun
8:34.28	Augustus	Maiyo	KEN	10.5.83	11 Aug
8:34.31	Haron	Lagat	KEN	15.8.83	8 Jun
8:34.34	Lukasz	Parszczynski	POL	4.5.85	10 Jun
8:34.42	Corey	Nowitzke	USA	26.4.84	8 Jun
8:34.59	Patrick	Terer	KEN-J	.89	9 Aug
8:34.64	Abdelgafour	El Asri	MAR	20.6.79	14 Jul
8:34.66	Per	Jacobsen	SWE	30.12.77	26 Jul
8:34.70	Øystein	Sylta	NOR	3.3.78	2 Jun
8:34.77	Francisco Javier	Lara	ESP	24.6.76	4 Aug
8:34.78	David	Cheromei	KEN	.85	13 Apr
8:34.78	Jan	Förster	GER	25.2.82	8 Jun
8:34.84	Emmanuel	Mkhabela	RSA	19.7.79	9 Feb
8:34.92	Glen	Comish	GBR	27.10.79	30 Jun
8:34.96	Saïd	Tbibi	MAR	17.1.85	16 Jun
8:35.04	Balázs	Ott	HUN	23.9.85	15 Jul
8:35.15	Andrey	Olshanskiy	RUS	24.1.78	27 Jun
8:35.16	Anderson	Smith	USA	16.3.82	29 Apr
8:35.25	Koen	Wilssens	BEL	15.3.81	28 May
8:35.37	Kevin	Davis	USA	4.2.84	24 Jun
8:35.40	Simon	Vroemen	NED	11.5.69	1 Jul
8:35.4A	Evans	Taiget	KEN		21 Apr
8:35.42	Isaac	Tanui Kiprotich	KEN	19.12.86	6 Jul
8:35.55	Mariusz	Gizynski	POL	26.6.81	28 May
8:35.71	Kyle	Alcorn	USA	18.3.85	8 Jun
8:36.02	Frédéric	Denis	FRA	3.3.75	26 May
8:36.07	José Alberto	Sánchez	CUB	2.9.86	28 Jul
8:36.11	Yoann	Kowal	FRA	28.5.87	13 Jul
8:36.15	Gládson	Barbosa	BRA	16.8.79	13 May
8:36.23	Valerijs	Zolnerovics	LAT	19.4.85	13 Jul
8:36.6	Abraham	Cherono	KEN	21.7.80	5 May
8:36.64	Jamal Bilal	Salem	QAT	12.9.78	20 May
8:36.98	Alberto	Paulo	POR	3.10.85	13 Jul
8:37.0	Hicham	Sadok	MAR	18.5.84	24 Jun
8:37.3A	Abraham	Chirchir	KEN		14 Jun
8:37.30	Luke	Gunn	GBR	22.3.85	8 Jun
8:37.8A	Ezekiel	Melly	KEN		15 Jun
8:37.83	Sergio	Lobos	CHI	1.12.82	8 Jun
8:38.02	David	Olson	USA		8 Jun
8:38.05	Celso	Ficagna	BRA	5.8.75	2 Jun
8:38.57	Jilali	Smaïli	MAR	8.7.79	30 Jun
8:38.70	Luke	Watson	USA	20.8.80	20 Apr
8:38.92	Robert	Watson	CAN	83	20 Apr
8:39.20	Tom	Chorny	USA	23.11.76	22 Jun
8:39.3A	Joseph	Ngetich	KEN	86	15 Jun
8:39.44	Ahmed	Hamzaoui	MAR	23.3.80	19 May
8:39.90	Imed	Zaidi	TUN	20.12.78	30 Jun
8:39.94	Peter	Kosgei	KEN	3.2.83	26 May
8:40.0A	Daniel	Kamau (156)	KEN		14 Jun

One hurdle missing: 6 Jul, Saint-Denis: 1. Tahri 8:08.47, 2. P K Koech 8:12.73, 3. Kipruto 8:12.88, 4. Matelong 8:12.98

JUNIORS

See main list for top 6 juniors. 10 performances by 4 men to 8:27.0. Additional marks and further juniors:

Mesfin	8:17.52	2		Neerpelt	2 Jun	8:26.68	7	GS	Ostrava	27 Jun
	8:20.57	1		Huelva	13 Sep					
Bis. Kiplagat	8:24.50	3		Neerpelt	2 Jun	8:26.59	8	Odlozil	Praha	13 Jun

MEN 2007

Mark	Name		Nat	Born	Pos	Meet	Venue	Date
Ben. Kiplagat	8:25.55	4	Cottbus	20 Jun				
8:33.66	Abdelghani	Aït Bahmad	MAR	28.7.89	7		Longeville-lès-Metz	15 Jul
8:34.59	Patrick	Terer	KEN	.89	3	Afr-J	Ouagadougou	9 Aug
8:42.82	Marvin	Blanco	VEN	16.6.88	1		Barinas	20 Dec
8:43.4A	Lemese	Lamiso (10)	ETH-Y	13.1.90	3	NC	Addis Ababa	6 May
8:44.34	Atsuro	Kikuchi	JPN	10.3.88	1		Tokyo	9 Jun
8:46.8A	Patrick	Langat	KEN	22.4.89	1		Nairobi	3 Jun
8:47.48	Mousa Youssef	Idriss	SUD	17.6.88	5	CISM	Hyderabad	18 Oct
8:49.23		Xu Shengming	CHN	3.1.88	2		Wuhan	2 Nov
8:50.30	Jakub	Holuša	CZE	20.2.88	1	EJ	Hengelo	20 Jul
8:50.4	Ben	Siwa	UGA	27.5.89	2	E.Af Ch	Kampala	31 May
8:50.42	Alexandru	Ghinea	ROM	6.3.89	2	EJ	Hengelo	20 Jul
8:50.95	Carlos	Alonso	ESP	15.9.89	3	EJ	Hengelo	20 Jul
8:50.99	Olivier	Lavoie	CAN	.88	2		Newfoundland	3 Aug
8:51.1	Osmany	Calzado (20)	CUB	27.6.88	2		Santa Clara	16 Jun

60 METRES HURDLES INDOORS

Mark	Name		Nat	Born	Pos	Meet	Venue	Date
7.38	Dayron	Robles	CUB	19.11.86	1	Spark	Stuttgart	3 Feb
7.42		Liu Xiang	CHN	13.7.83	1		Karlsruhe	11 Feb
7.44		Robles			2		Karlsruhe	11 Feb
7.45		Liu Xiang			2	Spark	Stuttgart	3 Feb
7.47	Ron	Bramlett	USA	22.10.79	1	NC	Boston (R)	25 Feb
7.48		Robles			1		Stockholm	20 Feb
7.49		Robles			1		Göteborg	31 Jan
7.51		Robles			1		Paris	23 Feb
7.51		Bramlett			1h1	NC	Boston (R)	24 Feb
7.51	David	Payne	USA	24.7.82	2	NC	Boston (R)	25 Feb
7.52		Bramlett			1	GP	Birmingham	17 Feb
7.52		Robles			2	GP	Birmingham	17 Feb
7.52	Anwar	Moore	USA	5.3.79	1s1	NC	Boston (R)	25 Feb
7.53		Robles			1h1	Spark	Stuttgart	3 Feb
7.53		Liu Xiang			1rA		Düsseldorf	6 Feb
7.53		Bramlett			3		Karlsruhe	11 Feb
7.53	Sergiy	Demydyuk	UKR	5.6.82	4		Karlsruhe	11 Feb
7.54		Bramlett			2s1	NC	Boston (R)	25 Feb
7.55	Andy	Turner (19/6)	GBR	19.9.80	1	NC	Sheffield	11 Feb
7.56	David	Oliver	USA	24.4.82	1h3	NC	Boston (R)	24 Feb
7.58	Yevgeniy	Borisov	RUS	7.3.84	1		Moskva	28 Jan
7.58	Jackson	Quiñónez	ESP	12.6.80	1	NC	Sevilla	18 Feb
7.58	Dexter (10)	Faulk	USA	14.4.84	4	NC	Boston (R)	25 Feb
7.59	Robert	Kronberg	SWE	15.8.76	1	NC	Göteborg	25 Feb
7.60	Joel	Brown	USA	31.1.80	2	BIG	Boston (R)	27 Jan
7.60	Thomas	Blaschek	GER	5.4.81	1		Chemnitz	23 Feb
7.61	Aries	Merritt	USA	24.7.85	1r2	Mill	New York	2 Feb
7.61	Stanislav	Olijar	LAT	22.3.79	1	NC	Riga	16 Feb
7.61	Mike	Wray	USA	24.3.87	1h1	NCAA	Fayetteville	9 Mar
7.62	Marcel	van der Westen	NED	1.8.76	1s2	EI	Birmingham	2 Mar
7.63	Paulo	Villar	COL	28.7.78	2		Paris	23 Feb
7.63	Gregory	Sedoc	NED	16.10.81	1	EI	Birmingham	2 Mar
7.64	(20)	Shi Dongpeng	CHN	6.1.84	4	Spark	Stuttgart	3 Feb
7.64	Allan	Scott	GBR	27.12.82	3s1	EI	Birmingham	2 Mar
7.64	Jeff	Porter	USA	27.11.85	1	NCAA	Fayetteville	9 Mar
7.66	Petr	Svoboda	CZE	10.10.84	2		Praha	3 Feb
7.66	Maksim	Lynsha	BLR	6.4.85	1	Univ Ch	Minsk	15 Feb
7.66	Antwon	Hicks	USA	12.3.83	3s2	NC	Boston (R)	25 Feb
7.67	John	Yarbrough	USA	16.8.85	1	SEC	Lexington	25 Feb
7.67	Dominic	Berger	USA	19.5.86	1h2	NCAA	Fayetteville	9 Mar
7.68	Cédric	Lavanne	FRA	13.11.80	1		Mondeville	27 Jan
7.68	Felipe	Vivancos	ESP	16.6.80	2		Valencia	10 Feb
7.68	Tyrone (30)	Akins	USA	6.1.86	2	SEC	Lexington	25 Feb
7.68		Wu Youjia	CHN	6.5.83	1r2	NGP	Shanghai	16 Mar
7.69	Igor	Peremota	RUS	14.1.81	2		Yekaterinburg	7 Jan
7.70	Elmar	Lichtenegger	AUT	25.4.74	2h2	EI	Birmingham	2 Mar
7.70	Alleyne	Lett	GRN	7.1.83	1h3	NCAA	Fayetteville	9 Mar
7.71	Willi	Mathiszik	GER	17.6.84	2h1	Spark	Leipzig	9 Feb
7.71	Aubrey	Herring	USA	19.9.78	3h1	NC	Boston (R)	24 Feb

Mark	Wind	Name		Nat	Born	Pos	Meet	Venue	Date
7.72		Maurice	Wignall	JAM	17.4.76	6		Karlsruhe	11 Feb
7.72		Samuel	Coco-Viloin	FRA	19.10.87	1	NC23	Paris	25 Feb
7.73		Adrien	Deghelt	BEL	10.5.85	1		Wien	30 Jan
7.73		Kevin	Craddock	USA	25.6.87	1r1	Tyson	Fayetteville	9 Feb
		(40)							
7.73		Brandon	Hon	USA	7.7.79	1		Akron	16 Feb
7.73		Marlon	Odom	USA	4.12.82	5	NCAA	Fayetteville	9 Mar
7.74		Alexander	John	GER	3.5.86	1r2		Chemnitz	20 Jan
7.74		Damjan	Zlatnar	SLO	16.12.77	2		Wien	30 Jan
7.74		Shamar	Sands	BAH	30.4.85	2r1	Tyson	Fayetteville	9 Feb
7.74		Bano	Traoré	FRA	25.4.85	1s2	NC	Aubière	18 Feb
7.74		Andreas	Kundert	SUI	1.10.84	1	NC	St. Gallen	18 Feb
7.74		Dimitri	Bascou	FRA	20.7.87	2	NC23	Paris	25 Feb
7.74		Thomas	Hilliard	USA	16.7.84	3h1	NCAA	Fayetteville	9 Mar
7.75			Ji Wei	CHN	5.2.84	2r2	NGP	Beijing	21 Mar
		(50)							
Best Junior: 7.78		Erik	Balnuweit	GER	21.9.88	1h1		Chemnitz	23 Feb

110 METRES HURDLES

Mark	Wind	Name		Nat	Born	Pos	Meet	Venue	Date
12.92	1.5		Liu Xiang	CHN	13.7.83	1	GP	New York	2 Jun
12.92	0.0	Dayron	Robles	CUB	19.11.86	1	WAF	Stuttgart	23 Sep
12.95	1.5	Terrence	Trammell	USA	23.11.78	2	GP	New York	2 Jun
12.95	1.7		Liu Xiang			1	WCh	Osaka	31 Aug
12.99	1.7		Trammell			2	WCh	Osaka	31 Aug
13.01	0.0		Liu Xiang			1	Athl	Lausanne	10 Jul
13.01	-0.4		Robles			1	Golden	Shanghai	28 Sep
13.02	1.5	Ryan	Wilson	USA	19.12.80	3	GP	New York	2 Jun
13.02	1.7	David	Payne	USA	24.7.82	3	WCh	Osaka	31 Aug
13.05	-1.2		Robles			1	Gugl	Linz	11 Sep
13.07	0.0		Robles			1		Dubnica	16 Sep
13.08	0.5		Trammell			1	NC	Indianapolis	24 Jun
13.08	0.0		Payne			2	WAF	Stuttgart	23 Sep
13.09	0.1	Aries	Merritt	USA	24.7.85	1	DNG	Stockholm	7 Aug
13.10	0.1		Wilson			2	DNG	Stockholm	7 Aug
13.11	0.4		Robles			1r2	GP	Athína	2 Jul
13.12	1.9	Anwar	Moore	USA	5.3.79	1	ModR	Modesto	5 May
13.12	-0.5		Payne			1	SGP	Doha	11 May
13.12	0.0		Moore			2	Athl	Lausanne	10 Jul
13.13	0.5		Robles			1	Gaz	Saint-Denis	6 Jul
13.13	0.5		Moore			2	Gaz	Saint-Denis	6 Jul
13.14	0.8		Liu Xiang			1	GP	Osaka	5 May
13.14	-0.5	David	Oliver	USA	24.4.82	2	SGP	Doha	11 May
13.14	0.4		Oliver			2r2	GP	Athína	2 Jul
13.15	-0.5		Trammell			3	SGP	Doha	11 May
13.15	1.5		Payne			4	Reebok	New York	2 Jun
13.15	0.5		Liu Xiang			3	Gaz	Saint-Denis	6 Jul
13.15	1.7		Robles			4	WC	Osaka	31 Aug
13.15	-0.2		Robles			1	WK	Zürich	7 Sep
13.15	0.0		Trammell			3	WAF	Stuttgart	23 Sep
		(30/8)							
13.17	0.5	Dominique	Arnold	USA	14.9.73	2	NC	Indianapolis	24 Jun
13.19	1.7	(10)	Shi Dongpeng	CHN	6.1.84	5	WCh	Osaka	31 Aug
13.22	1.7	Sergiy	Demidyuk	UKR	5.6.82	6	WCh	Osaka	31 Aug
13.23	0.4	Yoel	Hernández	CUB	12.12.77	4r2	GP	Athína	2 Jul
13.23	1.6	Eric	Mitchum	USA	2.8.84	1	Aragón	Zaragoza	28 Jul
13.23	-0.2	Allen	Johnson	USA	1.3.71	3	WK	Zürich	7 Sep
13.27	0.5	Ladji	Doucouré	FRA	28.3.83	6	Gaz	Saint-Denis	6 Jul
13.27	0.6	Andrew	Turner	GBR	19.9.80	3h5	WCh	Osaka	29 Aug
13.28	1.6	Ron	Bramlett	USA	22.10.79	2	Aragón	Zaragoza	28 Jul
13.29	-0.4	Maurice	Wignall	JAM	17.4.76	3s1	WCh	Osaka	30 Aug
13.31	1.6	Joel	Brown	USA	31.1.80	3	Aragón	Zaragoza	28 Jul
13.33	1.8	Thomas	Blaschek	GER	5.4.81	1		Dessau	1 Jun
		(20)							
13.33	-0.4	Jackson	Quiñónez	ESP	12.6.80	4s1	WCh	Osaka	30 Aug
13.34	0.1	Linnie	Yarbrough	USA	9.9.82	1		Tampa	9 Mar
13.34	1.0	Dexter	Faulk	USA	14.4.84	2		Tomblaine	18 Sep
13.36	0.8	Antwon	Hicks	USA	12.3.83	1		Chambéry	15 Jul
13.36	1.6	Robby	Hughes	USA	10.10.78	5	Aragón	Zaragoza	28 Jul
13.37	0.8	Gregory	Sedoc	NED	16.10.81	2	FBK	Hengelo	26 May

Mark	Wind	Name		Nat	Born	Pos	Meet	Venue	Date
13.38	1.9	Larry	Wade	USA	22.11.74	3	ModR	Modesto	5 May
13.38	-0.2	Stanislav	Olijar	LAT	22.3.79	1h3	WCh	Osaka	29 Aug
13.39A	2.0	Shaun	Bownes	RSA	24.10.70	1		Potchefstroom	19 May
13.40	0.0		Ji Wei	CHN	5.2.84	1	NGP	Urumqi	20 Sep
		(30)							
13.42	-1.7	Richard	Phillips	JAM	26.1.83	1		Atlanta	2 Jun
13.42	-1.0	Tyrone	Akins	USA	6.1.86	1	NCAA	Sacrameto	8 Jun
13.43	1.7	Masato	Naito	JPN	31.7.80	1		Kumagaya	19 May
13.45	0.7	John	Yarbrough	USA	16.8.85	1h3	NCAA	Sacramento	6 Jun
13.47	2.0	Igor	Peremota	RUS	14.1.81	1		Sochi	26 May
13.47	-1.7	Shamar	Sands	BAH	30.4.85	2		Atlanta	2 Jun
13.48	1.3	Kevin	Craddock	USA	25.6.87	1	Pac-10	Stanford	13 May
13.49	-0.4	Konstadínos	Douvalídis	GRE	10.3.87	1	EU23	Debrecen	14 Jul
13.51	0.5	Aubrey	Herring	USA	19.9.78	1	Takac	Beograd	29 May
13.51	0.4	Robert	Kronberg	SWE	15.8.76	3h1	WCh	Osaka	29 Aug
		(40)							
13.52	1.9	Marlon	Odom	USA	4.12.82	1h1	NCAA	Sacramento	6 Jun
13.52	1.2	Alleyne	Lett	GRN	7.1.83	1s2	NCAA	Sacramento	6 Jun
13.52	0.0	Anselmo Gomes	da Silva	BRA	22.3.81	1		Salamanca	4 Jul
13.54	0.2		Xing Yanan	CHN	17.6.83	2	WCT	Suzhou	9 Jun
13.54	1.7	Bano	Traoré	FRA	25.4.85	1s1	NC	Niort	5 Aug
13.55	1.5	Justin	Merlino	AUS	10.12.86	1	NC	Brisbane	11 Mar
13.55	0.7	Jared	MacLeod	CAN	3.4.80	4		Luzern	28 Jun
13.55	2.0	Yuji	Ohashi	JPN	5.9.83	2	Nambu	Sapporo	15 Jul
13.55	1.0	Joseph-Berlioz	Randriamihaja	MAD	30.11.75	2s2	FRA Ch	Niort	5 Aug
13.56	0.8	Damjan	Zlatnar	SLO	16.12.77	1		Novo Mesto	19 Jun
		(50)							
13.56	1.6	Felipe	Vivancos	ESP	16.6.80	7	Aragón	Zaragoza	28 Jul
13.56	0.9	Yevgeniy	Borisov	RUS	7.3.84	2s1	WUG	Bangkok	9 Aug
13.57	1.8	Jeff	Porter	USA	27.11.85	2s1	NCAA	Sacramento	6 Jun
13.57	0.7	Adrien	Deghelt	BEL	10.5.85	1		Oordegem	7 Jul
13.58	1.7	Kenji	Yahata	JPN	4.11.80	2		Kumagaya	19 May
13.58	-0.8	Éder Antônio	de Souza	BRA	15.10.86	2	SAmC	São Paulo	7 Jun
13.59	0.8	Tasuku	Tanonaka	JPN	23.9.78	3	GP	Osaka	5 May
13.59	1.8	Kai	Kelley	USA	8.11.86	3s1	NCAA	Sacramento	6 Jun
13.59	0.4	Alexander	John	GER	3.5.86	1		Mannheim	22 Jun
13.59	0.0	Selim	Nurudeen	NGR	1.2.83	1	AfG	Alger	19 Jul
		(60)							
13.59	1.3	Andreas	Kundert	SUI	1.10.84	1	NC	Lausanne	29 Jul
13.60	1.7	Dániel	Kiss	HUN	12.2.82	1		Debrecen	19 May
13.60	-1.7	Chris	Thomas	USA	9.2.81	3		Atlanta	2 Jun
13.60	1.2	Jonathan	McDowell	USA	28.10.84	4s2	NCAA	Sacramento	6 Jun
13.60	0.7	Mohammed	Al-Thawadi	QAT	18.11.81	2	CISM	Hyderabad	17 Oct
13.61	1.8	Thomas	Hilliard	USA	16.7.84	4s1	NCAA	Sacramento	6 Jan
13.61	1.5	Willi	Mathiszik	GER	17.6.84	2h2		Kassel	6 Jun
13.61	0.1	Ryan	Brathwaite	BAH-J	6.6.88	3h1	PAm	Rio de Janeiro	27 Jul
13.61	0.1	Bashir	Ramzy	USA	4.5.79	4h1	PAm	Rio de Janeiro	27 Jul
13.62	-0.2	Emanuele	Abate	ITA	8.7.85	4	WUG	Bangkok	10 Aug
		(70)							
13.63	0.0	Matheus	Inocêncio	BRA	17.5.81	1		São Paulo	7 Mar
13.63	1.3	Karl	Jennings	CAN	14.5.79	2		Berkeley	28 Apr
13.63	0.8	Marcel	van der Westen	NED	1.8.76	4	FBK	Hengelo	26 May
13.63	0.7	Charles	Derrickson	USA	17.7.87	2h3	NCAA	Sacramento	6 Jun
13.63	-0.1	Jens	Werrmann	GER	29.6.85	1	NC-23	Hannover	26 Aug
13.63	0.6	Dudley	Dorival	HAI	1.9.75	4h5	WCh	Osaka	29 Aug
13.64	1.7	Thiago	Castelo Branco	BRA	6.11.79	1h2		São Paulo	14 Apr
13.64	1.8	Petr	Svoboda	CZE	10.10.84	1		Ried/Innkreis	28 Jul
13.65	0.1		Wu Youjia	CHN	6.5.83	1h1	AsiC	Amman	28 Jul
13.65	0.0	Jacoby	DuBose	USA	11.12.82	3	DLV	Bochum-Wattenscheid	12 Aug
		(80)							
13.66	0.2	Charles	Allen	CAN	29.3.77	4		Kassel	6 Jun
13.66	1.2	Julius	Jiles-Tindall	USA	14.2.86	5s2	NCAA	Sacramento	6 Jun
13.66	-0.2	Maksim	Lynsha	BLR	6.4.85	7	WUG	Bangkok	10 Aug
13.67		Decosma	Wright	JAM	1.9.82	1		Columbia	31 Mar
13.67	1.1	Jermaine	Cooper	USA	31.8.80	1r3		Atlanta	11 May
13.67A	2.0	Hennie	Kotze	RSA	4.2.84	2		Potchefstroom	19 May
13.67	-0.6		Huang Hao	CHN	7.10.87	2h2	NC	Shijiazhuang	4 Aug
13.68	0.5	Dominic	Berger	USA	19.5.86	1h1		College Park	20 Apr
13.68	1.1	William	Sharman	GBR	12.9.84	3rB	Bisl	Oslo	15 Jun
13.68	0.7	Josh	Walker	USA	6.5.82	2		Albertville	12 Jul
		(90)							

Mark	Wind	Name		Nat	Born	Pos	Meet	Venue	Date
13.68	-0.2		Yin Jing	CHN-J	23.5.88	4	NC	Shijiazhuang	5 Aug
13.68	-0.5	Elmar	Lichtenegger	AUT	25.5.74	1		Kapfenberg	11 Aug
13.69	2.0	Yoichi	Iwafune	JPN	12.6.85	3	Nambu	Sapporo	15 Jul
13.70	1.0	Justin	Lindsey	USA	25.8.79	1h2		New York	13 Jul
13.71	1.5	James	Mortimer	NZL	1.3.83	2	Aus Ch	Brisbane	11 Mar
13.71	0.5	Logan	Taylor	USA	3.4.86	1		Los Angeles	28 Apr
13.71	1.8	Eric	Keddo	JAM	1.7.84	2		Clermont, FL	19 May
13.71	-1.9	Richard	Alleyne	GBR	7.5.83	1		Nivelles	30 Jun
13.71	0.7	Fred	Townsend	USA	19.2.82	2		Oordegem	7 Jul
13.72	1.5	Greg (100)	Eyears	AUS	21.8.81	3	NC	Brisbane	11 Mar
13.72	0.6	Héctor	Cotto	PUR	8.8.84	2		Greensboro	21 Apr
13.72	1.5	Enrique	Llanos	PUR	7.5.80	1h1		Lynchburg	4 May
13.73	1.4	Ricardo	Melbourne	JAM	26.2.82	1h3		Fairfax	31 Mar

13.73	0.5	Allan	Scott	GBR	27.12.82	29 May
13.73	2.0	Samuel	Coco-Viloin	FRA	19.10.87	5 Jun
13.73	0.0	Rodrigo	Pereira	BRA	2.4.85	23 Jun
13.73	0.0	Tomasz	Scigaczewski	POL	18.11.78	1 Jul
13.74	-1.6	Brandon	Hon	USA	7.7.79	24 Mar
13.74	0.1	Anier	García	CUB	9.3.76	26 May
13.74	1.2	Thomas	Mack	USA	28.8.85	6 Jun
13.74	0.4	Mariusz	Kubaszewski	POL	11.7.82	24 Jun
13.74	-0.4	Stanislav	Sajdok	CZE	22.7.83	27 Jun
13.75	1.1	Jan	Cech	CZE	17.6.81	24 May
13.75	-1.7	Corey	Taylor	USA	2.5.81	2 Jun
13.76	0.6	Keith	Hopkins	USA	14.4.86	26 May
13.76	2.0	Dimitri	Bascou	FRA	20.7.87	5 Jun
13.76	-0.2	Aymen	Ben Ahmed	TUN	1.3.86	30 Jun
13.77	-1.0	Dermillo	Wise	USA	7.11.83	26 May
13.77	0.1	Sergey	Chepiga	RUS	5.6.82	18 Jun
13.77	-0.7	Ivo	Burkhardt	GER	7.12.77	14 Jul
13.78		Ron	Andrews	USA	12.10.79	28 Apr
13.78	1.4	Sheldon	Leith	JAM	17.9.83	4 May
13.78	1.5	Terry	Ross	USA	8.2.85	26 May
13.78	0.0	Paul	Dittmer	GER	1.1.87	22 Jun
13.78	0.5	Ricky	Pinkney	USA	21.12.84	13 May
13.79A	0.2	Ruan	de Vries	RSA	1.2.86	26 Jan
13.79	0.6	Márcio	de Souza	BRA	24.1.75	14 Apr
13.79	1.6	Cédric	Lavanne	FRA	13.11.80	2 Jun
13.79	0.1	Helge	Schwarzer	GER	26.11.85	14 Jul
13.80	1.3	Timothy	Bogdanof	USA	9.11.79	28 Apr
13.80	-0.6	Juan	Walker	USA	19.8.85	13 May
13.80	0.0	Hideki	Nomoto	JPN	13.3.84	29 Jun
13.81	0.3	Andrew	Brunson	USA	4.4.86	28 Apr
13.81	1.5	Darius	Reed	USA-J	1.2.88	26 May
13.81	0.1	Martin	Hoffmann	GER	7.4.84	16 Jun
13.81	1.3	David	Ilariani	GEO	20.1.81	30 Jun
13.81	0.5	Samuel	Okon	NGR	6.6.86	18 Jul
13.81	1.2	Andrea	Alterio	ITA	11.6.73	12 Aug
13.82	1.7	Yakov	Petrov	RUS	16.5.83	9 Jun
13.83	-0.1	Maurice	Smith	JAM	28.9.80	27 May
13.83	0.8	Aléxandros	Theofánov	GRE	25.2.81	2 Jul
13.83	0.7	Artur	Kohutek	POL	1.5.71	17 Oct
13.84		Ignacio	Morales	CUB	28.1.87	26 Jan
13.84	-1.4	Andrea	Giaconi	ITA	11.4.74	25 Apr
13.84	2.0	Satoru	Tanigawa	JPN	5.7.72	15 Jul
13.85	1.7		Park Tae-kyong	KOR	30.7.80	19 May
13.85	0.0	Michael	Illin	ISR	8.10.84	10 Jun
13.85	0.8	Stephanos	Ioannou	CYP	12.6.82	2 Jul
13.85	-1.1		Lee Jung-joon	KOR	26.3.84	3 Oct
13.86	1.0	Dominique	DeGrammont	HAI	13.3.79	10 Mar
13.86	1.7	Damien	Broothaers	BEL	13.3.83	12 May
13.86	0.0	David	Hughes	GBR	31.5.84	20 May
13.87	0.6	Ryan	Fontenot	USA	4.5.86	26 May
13.87	1.0	Kota	Kumamoto	JPN	5.11.83	29 Jun
13.87	-0.2	Sven	Pieters	BEL	5.6.76	4 Aug
13.87	0.0		Yan Xu	CHN	20.5.87	31 Oct
13.88	-0.2	Yasunori	Yoshioka	JPN	19.5.75	15 Apr
13.88	1.5	Ioánnis	Lazarídis	GRE	7.1.84	2 Jun
13.88	0.6	Rene	Oruman	EST	7.1.84	1 Jul
13.88	-1.7	Othman	Hadj Lazib	ALG	15.5.83	8 Jul
13.88	-0.4	Julien	Fenes	FRA	17.7.84	20 Jul
13.89A	0.2	Frikkie	van Zyl	RSA	30.7.81	26 Jan
13.89	1.4	Fawaz	Al Shammari	KUW	3.4.77	30 Jun
13.89	1.2	Antti	Korkealaakso	FIN	14.2.84	11 Jul
13.89	0.7	Alexandru	Mihailescu	ROM	16.8.82	18 Oct
13.90	0.5	DeLon	Isom	USA-J	1.5.88	12 May
13.90	0.0	Erik	Balnuweit	GER-J	21.9.88	9 Jun
13.90	1.4	Pavel	Filyev	RUS	5.3.85	31 Jul
13.90		Rouhollah	Ashgari	IRI	8.1.82	21 Aug
13.90	0.0		Li Haolun	CHN-J	15.6.88	1 Nov
13.91	1.2	Joey	Scott	USA	12.5.78	31 Mar
13.91	0.2	Javier	Culson	PUR	25.7.84	31 Mar
13.91	0.5	Arthur	Abele	GER	30.7.86	10 Jun
13.91	-0.3	Ryazamshah	Wan Sofian	MAS-J	11.1.88	10 Dec
13.92	0.0	William	Vese	USA	17.8.86	24 Mar
13.92	0.4		Chen Ming	CHN	8.3.84	19 May
13.92	0.1	Yutaro	Furukawa	JPN	3.6.85	19 May
13.93	-0.6	Andrey	Kravchenko	BLR	4.1.86	17 May
13.93	-0.5	Pete	Smith	JAM		26 May
13.93	0.3	Lukas	Erdmann	GER	16.5.83	9 Jun
13.93	0.5	Elton	Bitincka	ALB	26.5.85	7 Jul
13.93	-0.6	Masayuki	Ida	JPN	11.8.87	22 Jul
13.93	-1.6	Falk	Balzer	GER	14.12.73	18 Aug
13.94	0.0	Bryan	Clay	USA	3.1.80	12 May
13.94	1.9	Robert	Williams	USA	10.8.87	6 Jun
13.94	0.4	Stephen	Jones	BAR	25.7.78	27 Jul
13.94	0.3	Nick	Gayle	GBR	4.1.85	11 Aug
13.95	1.8	Lewis	Edmonson	USA	26.2.79	21 Apr
13.95	-1.0	Derek	Johnson	USA	5.11.85	26 May
13.95	0.2	Andre	English	USA	10.12.84	9 Jun
13.95	0.4	Dominic	Girdler	GBR	6.3.82	10 Jun
13.95	1.3	Claude	Godart	LUX	20.10.80	16 Jun
13.95	1.7	Fábio	dos Santos	BRA	11.10.83	23 Jun
13.95	0.5	Andrés	Amador	PUR	6.11.84	30 Jun
13.95	0.3	Gianni	Frankis	GBR-J	16.4.88	11 Aug
13.95	-0.3	Suphan (195)	Wongsriphuck	THA	31.5.77	10 Dec

Faulty timing: 5 Oct, Bangkok: (-0.1) 1. Narongdech Janjai THA 20.5.81 13.82, 2. Mohd Faiz Mohamad MAS 14.1.83 13.93

Wind assisted

13.00	2.6	Anwar	Moore	USA	5.3.79	1	DrakeR	Des Moines	28 Apr
13.43	2.6	John	Yarbrough	USA	16.8.85	1rB	DrakeR	Des Moines	28 Apr
13.45	2.6	Aubrey	Herring	USA	19.9.78	4	DrakeR	Des Moines	28 Apr
13.50	2.5	Marlon	Odom	USA	4.12.82	1		Fort Worth	21 Apr
13.51	5.3	Tasuku	Tanonaka	JPN	23.9.78	1	AsiC	Amman	29 Jul
13.52	4.3	Felipe	Vivancos	ESP	16.6.80	4h1	Aragón	Zaragoza	28 Jul
13.54	2.7	Dominic	Berger	USA	19.5.86	1		College Park	21 Apr
13.55	5.3	Mohammed	Al-Thawadi	QAT	18.11.81	2	AsiC	Amman	29 Jul
13.56	2.6	Josh	Walker	USA	6.5.82	7	DrakeR	Des Moines	28 Apr
13.58	2.7	Charles	Allen	CAN	29.3.77	1	NC	Windsor, ON	14 Jul
13.59	2.1	Keith	Hopkins	USA	14.4.86	1		West Lafayette	21 Apr
13.61	2.6	Dudley	Dorival	HAI	1.9.75	2		New York	14 Jul

MEN 2007

Mark	Wind	Name		Nat	Born	Pos	Meet	Venue	Date
13.63	2.7	Andrew	Brunson	USA	4.4.86	2		College Park	21 Apr
13.68	2.5	Eric	Keddo	JAM	1.7.84	1		Clermont	9 Jun
13.70	2.5	Juan	Walker	USA	19.8.85	2		Clermont	9 Jun
13.71	3.5	Tomasz	Scigaczewski	POL	18.11.78	2		Bydgoszcz	10 Jun
13.71	2.6	Stanislav	Sajdok	CZE	22.7.83	1		Budapest	7 Jul

13.73 3.0 Sheldon Leith JAM 17.9.83 21 Apr
13.77 2.7 Terry Ross USA 8.2.85 6 Jun
13.77 2.2 Aléxandros Theofánov GRE 25.2.81 11 Jul
13.80 2.3 Park Tae-kyong KOR 30.7.80 22 Apr
13.81 3.0 Damien Broothaerts BEL 13.3.83 6 May
13.81 3.4 Lee Jung-joon KOR 26.3.84 23 May
13.81 2.9 Artur Kohutek POL 1.5.71 15 Sep
13.82 2.3 Yakov Petrov RUS 16.5.83 5 Jun
13.83 2.5 Chris Pinnock JAM 26.3.79 21 Apr
13.83 3.3 Julien Fenes FRA 17.7.84 30 Jun
13.83 2.2 Ioánnis Lazarídis GRE 7.1.84 11 Jul
13.85 3.7 Justin Gaymon USA 13.12.86 27 Apr
13.87 2.9 Azim Smith USA 31 Mar
13.88 2.7 Javier Garcia-Tunon USA 21 Apr
13.88 5.3 Ali Hussein Al Zaki KSA 11.5.85 29 Jul
13.90 5.3 Tyrell Ross USA 9.1.87 5 May
13.90 2.3 Stephen Jones BAR 25.7.78 5 Jun
13.91 3.2 Daniel Cook USA 6.6.85 17 Mar
13.94 2.6 Stevy Telliam FRA 5.5.77 30 Jun
13.95 2.3 Naoya Hisada JPN 29.8.80 21 Oct

Best at low altitude

13.62 1.9 Bownes 1h2 Chambéry 15 Jul
13.91 -0.9 Kotze 9 Aug
13.95 0.8 de Vries 15 Jun

Doubtful timing

13.33 1.6 Linnie Yarbrough USA 9.9.82 1 Orlando 3 Mar
13.59 Mohammed Al-Thawadi QAT 18.11.81 1 Kielce 21 Jul

12 May, Durham (all USA): (0.1) 1. Carrington Queen 21.9.87 13.60, 2. Kevin Watson 16.9.82 13.65, 3, Gabriel Rolston .85 13.74

Hand timed

13.4 0.5 Ignacio Morales CUB 28.1.87 1h1 La Habana 8 Jun
13.4 Yevgeniy Borisov RUS 7.3.84 1 Zhukovskiy 21 Jul
13.6 Anier García CUB 9.3.76 16 Mar
13.6 David Arzola CUB-J 24.2.89 16 Mar
13.7A Ruan de Vries RSA 1.2.86 16 Jan
13.3w 2.3 Ignacio Morales CUB 28.1.87 1 La Habana 8 Jun
13.5 w? Márcio de Souza BRA 24.1.75 22 Jul
13.6 w? Thiago Castelo Branco BRA 6.11.79 22 Jul

JUNIORS

See main list for top 2 juniors. 6 performances by 2 men to 13.78. Additional marks and further juniors:

Brathwaite 13.62 -0.2 4h3 WCh Osaka 29 Aug; 13.77 0.1 1h1 NC Bridgetown 24 Jun
13.70 0.4 4 PAm Rio de Janeiro 28 Jul
Yin Jing 13.78 -0.8 1h3 WUG Bangkok 9 Aug

Mark	Wind	Name		Nat	Born	Pos	Meet	Venue	Date
13.81	1.5	Darius	Reed	USA	1.2.88	3	NCAA-r	Eugene	26 May
13.90	0.5	DeLon	Isom	USA	1.5.88	2h2	SEC	Tuscaloosa	12 May
13.90	0.0	Erik	Balnuweit	GER	21.9.88	2A		Regensburg	9 Jun
13.90	0.0		Li Haolun	CHN	15.6.88	1		Wuhan	1 Nov
13.91	-0.3	Ryazamshah	Wan Sofian	MAS	11.1.88	1	SEAG	Nakhon Ratchasima	10 Dec
13.95	0.3	Gianni	Frankis	GBR	16.4.88	2h1	LEAP	Loughborough	11 Aug
13.99	-1.0	Omo	Osaghae	USA	18.5.88	4	Big 12	Lincoln	13 May
13.99	0.5	Marcus	Pope (10)	USA	1.2.89	4		Carolina	30 Jun
14.01	-0.2	Yordani	García	CUB	21.11.88	1D	PAm	Rio de Janeiro	24 Jul
14.02	1.6	Jin	Nakamura	JPN	13.5.89	1		Saga	6 Aug
14.03	1.4	João	Almeida	POR	5.4.88	2	NC	Lisboa	28 Jul
14.06		Ivan	Byzin	RUS	10.9.88	1		Sankt-Peterburg	7 Jun
14.07	0.3	Yume	Moses	JPN	1.2.88	3h4	NC	Osaka	29 Jun
14.08	-0.3	Callum	Priestley	GBR	13.2.89	5	NC	Manchester	28 Jul
14.08	0.0	Artur	Noga	POL	2.5.88	1r1		Sosnowiec	8 Sep

Wind assisted

14.03 3.3 Yume Moses JPM 1.2.88 1 Katsuura 3 Nov

Hand timed: 13.6 David Arzola CUB-J 24.2.89 2h2 Camagüey 16 Mar

99 cm Hurdles

Mark	Wind	Name		Nat	Born	Pos	Meet	Venue	Date
13.36	1.5	Artur	Noga	POL	2.5.88	1	EJ	Hengelo	22 Jul
		13.42 0.8 1s2 EJ Hengelo 22 Jul			13.43	0.7 1	NC-j	Biala Podlaska	28 Jun
13.42	0.2	Ryan	Brathwaite	BAR	6.6.88	1	Carifta	Providenciales	9 Apr
13.46	0.9	Johnny	Dutch	USA	20.1.89	1	PAm-J	São Paulo	6 Jul
13.46	1.5	Vladimir	Zhukov	RUS	28.2.88	2	EJ	Hengelo	22 Jul
13.46	-0.8	Robert	Griffin	USA-Y	12.2.90	1		Knoxville	2 Aug
13.47	0.8	Gianni	Frankis	GBR	16.4.88	2s2	EJ	Hengelo	22 Jul
		13.47 1.5 3 EJ Hengelo 22 Jul			10 performances by 7 men to 13.47				
13.47	0.1	Mohammed	Koné	FRA	22.10.88	1		Narbonne	28 Jul
13.49	0.2	Keiron	Stewart	JAM	21.11.89	2		Providenciales	9 Apr
13.51	0.9	Jorge Armando	McFarlane	PER	20.2.88	2	PAm-J	São Paulo	6 Jul
13.54	-0.2	Erik	Balnuweit	GER	21.9.88	1h1		Erfurt	8 Jul
13.60	2.0	Terry	Prentice	USA	7.1.89	1		Folsom	10 Jun
13.61	1.3		Lu Guoliang	CHN	23.1.88	1		Cangzhou	14 Jun
13.61	1.5	Abdelrahman	Idris Taher	EGY	14.2.89	1r1		Mannheim	23 Jun
13.61	1.9	João	Almeida	POR	5.4.88	2s1	EJ	Hengelo	22 Jul
13.62	0.8	Callum	Priestley	GBR	13.2.89	3s2	EJ	Hengelo	22 Jul
13.64	0.8	Brendan	Ames	USA	6.10.88	1		Littleton	14 Apr

Mark	Wind	Name		Nat	Born	Pos	Meet	Venue	Date
13.65	-0.7	Wayne	Davis	USA-Y	22.8.91	1		Greensboro	16 Jun
13.65	0.7	Warren	Weir	JAM	31.10.89	2	NC	Kingston	24 Jun

Wind assisted

Mark	Wind	Name		Nat	Born	Pos	Meet	Venue	Date
13.15	2.7	Brendan	Ames	USA	6.10.88	1	NC-j	Indianapolis	21 Jun
		13.32 3.0 1h2 NC-j Indianapolis 21 Jun							
13.36	2.7	Johnny	Dutch	USA	20.1.89	2	NC-j	Indianapolis	21 Jun
		13.37 3.5 1h3 NC-j Indianapolis 21 Jun				13.39	3.2 1	Greensboro	19 May
13.42	2.7	Bryce	Brown	USA	17.9.88	3	NC-j	Indianapolis	21 Jun
13.50	2.2	Terry	Prentice	USA	7.1.89	1	Jnr Oly	Walnut	29 Jul
13.52		Oscar	Spurlock	USA	1.8.89	1		Dallas	31 Mar
13.53	3.2	Charlton	Rolle	USA	18.5.89	2		Greensboro	19 May
13.58	2.1		Li Haolun	CHN	15.6.88	1		Hong Kong	8 Jul

Hand timing

Mark	Wind	Name		Nat	Born	Pos	Meet	Venue	Date
13.2		Johnny	Dutch	USA	20.1.89	1		Clayton	2 May
13.4	0.5	Yoisel	Pumariega	CUB	4.2.88	1h		La Habana	8 Jun
		13.1w 2.3				1		La Habana	8 Jun
13.4	1.1	David	Arzola	CUB	24.2.89	1		Santiago de Cuba	27 Jun
		13.2w 2.3				2		La Habana	8 Jun

200 METRES HURDLES

Mark	Wind	Name		Nat	Born	Pos	Meet	Venue	Date
23.09		Naoki	Ihara	JPN	22.4.82	1r2		Katsuura	7 Oct

400 METRES HURDLES

Mark	Name		Nat	Born	Pos	Meet	Venue	Date
47.61	Kerron	Clement	USA	31.10.85	1	WCh	Osaka	28 Aug
47.72	James	Carter	USA	7.5.78	1	NC	Indianapolis	23 Jun
47.80		Clement			2	NC	Indianapolis	23 Jun
48.01	Fólix	Sánchez	DOM	30.8.77	2	WCh	Osaka	28 Aug
48.02	Michael	Tinsley	USA	21.4.84	1s2	NC	Indianapolis	22 Jun
48.08		Clement			2s2	NC	Indianapolis	22 Jun
48.12	Marek	Plawgo	POL	25.2.81	3	WCh	Osaka	28 Aug
48.13	Bershawn	Jackson	USA	8.5.83	1	GP	Osaka	5 May
48.15	Kenneth	Ferguson	USA	22.3.84	1	adidas	Carson	20 May
48.15		Jackson			1	GP	Athína	2 Jul
48.16		Ferguson			2	GP	Athína	2 Jul
48.18		Plawgo			1s1	WCh	Osaka	26 Aug
48.22		Carter			2	GP	Osaka	5 May
48.24	L.J. (Louis)	van Zyl	RSA	20.7.85	1	GGala	Roma	13 Jul
48.24	Adam	Kunkel	CAN	24.2.81	1	PAm	Rio de Janeiro	27 Jul
48.25		Carter			3	GP	Athína	2 Jul
48.26	Derrick	Williams (10)	USA	25.3.82	3	NC	Indianapolis	23 Jun
48.26		Clement			2	GGala	Roma	13 Jul
48.30		Carter			1	Athl	Lausanne	10 Jul
48.30		Carter			2s1	WCh	Osaka	26 Aug
48.31		Clement			2	Athl	Lausanne	10 Jul
48.31		Carter			3	GGala	Roma	13 Jul
48.32		van Zyl			4	GP	Athína	2 Jul
48.32	Danny	McFarlane	JAM	14.2.72	3s1	WCh	Osaka	26 Aug
48.35	Periklís	Iakovákis	GRE	24.3.79	1	ECp-S	München	23 Jun
48.35		Sánchez			1s2	WCh	Osaka	26 Aug
48.35		Plawgo			1	WAF	Stuttgart	22 Sep
48.35		Clement			2	WAF	Stuttgart	22 Sep
48.36		Carter			3	WAF	Stuttgart	22 Sep
48.37		Carter			1		New York	2 Jun
	(30/12)							
48.44	Kenji	Narisako	JPN	25.7.84	5s1	WCh	Osaka	26 Aug
48.45	Angelo	Taylor	USA	29.12.78	1	Herc	Monaco	25 Jul
48.51	Isa	Phillips	JAM	22.4.84	1	NCAA	Sacramento	9 Jun
48.64	Alwyn	Myburgh	RSA	13.10.80	5	GP	Athína	2 Jul
48.70	Bayano	Kamani	PAN	17.4.80	2	PAm	Rio de Janeiro	27 Jul
48.73	Dai	Tamesue	JPN	3.5.78	3	GP	Osaka	5 May
48.76	LaRon	Bennett	USA	25.11.82	1	NACAC	San Salvador	14 Jul
48.88	Jonathan	Williams	BIZ	29.8.83	2	NACAC	San Salvador	14 Jul
	(20)							
48.89	Pieter	de Villiers	RSA	13.7.82	1		Chambéry	15 Jul
48.90	Naman	Keïta ¶	FRA	9.4.78	3	ECp-S	München	23 Jun
48.98	Rickey	Harris	USA	29.9.81	2		Lignano	15 Jul
49.02	Brandon	Johnson	USA	6.3.85	2	NCAA	Sacramento	9 Jun
49.04	Pieter	Koekemoer	RSA	12.1.82	2		Durban	31 Mar
49.07	Javier	Culson	PUR	25.7.84	4		Kingston	5 May

Mark	Name		Nat	Born	Pos	Meet	Venue	Date
49.11	Gianni	Carabelli	ITA	30.5.79	2r2	Vard	Réthimno	18 Jul
49.11	Aleksandr	Derevyagin	RUS	24.3.79	4s2	WCh	Osaka	26 Aug
49.12	Kurt	Couto	MOZ	14.5.85	2	WUG	Bangkok	13 Aug
49.13	Ibrahima	Maïga	MLI	14.3.79	3	GP	Dakar	28 Apr
	(30)							
49.16	Minás	Alozídis	GRE	7.7.84	8	GP	Athína	2 Jul
49.17	Fadil	Bellaabous	FRA	15.6.86	6s1	WCh	Osaka	26 Aug
49.21	Damian	Prince	USA	23.10.86	1	NCAA-2	Charlotte	26 May
49.22A	Ockert	Cilliers	RSA	21.4.81	1		Pretoria	9 Mar
49.24	Markino	Buckley	JAM	16.4.86	3	NC	Kingston	23 Jun
49.25	Justin	Gaymon	USA	13.12.86	1	SEC	Tuscaloosa	13 May
49.27	Reuben	McCoy	USA	16.3.86	4s1	NC	Indianapolis	22 Jun
49.28	Kemel	Thompson	JAM	25.9.74	4		Tarare	14 Jul
49.29	Raphael	Fernandes	BRA	8.11.84	1	NC	São Paulo	24 Jun
49.30	Mahau	Sugimachi	BRA	13.11.84	2	NC	São Paulo	24 Jun
	(40)							
49.30	Dean	Griffiths	JAM	27.1.80	5	PAm	Rio de Janeiro	27 Jul
49.31	Edivaldo	Monteiro	POR	28.4.76	5s2	WCh	Osaka	26 Aug
49.34	Adrian	Findlay	JAM	1.10.82	1rB		Atlanta	2 Jun
49.34	Julius	Bungei	KEN	16.6.84	4	AfG	Alger	21 Jul
49.47		Meng Yan	CHN	30.9.80	1		Bangkok	19 Jun
49.48	Bryan	Steele	JAM	23.3.84	4	NACAC	San Salvador	14 Jul
49.51	Joseph	Abraham	IND	11.9.81	7s1	WCh	Osaka	26 Aug
49.53	Masahira	Yoshikata	JPN	23.8.82	3	NC	Osaka	30 Jun
49.56	Robert	Griffin	USA-Y	12.2.90	1	AAU JO	Knoxville	1 Aug
49.56	Yevgeniy	Meleshenko	KAZ	19.1.81	8s1	WCh	Osaka	26 Aug
	(50)							
49.57	Osmar	Cisneros	CUB-J	19.11.89	1	ALBA	Caracas	11 May
49.58	Eric	Dudley	USA	18.4.80	4h2	NC	Indianapolis	21 Jun
49.58	David	Greene	GBR	11.4.86	1	EU23	Debrecen	14 Jul
49.61	LaBronze	Garrett	USA	9.11.76	1		Fortaleza	16 May
49.63	Thomas	Hilliard	USA	16.7.84	1h1	SEC	Tuscaloosa	11 May
49.65	Sébastien	Maillard	FRA	2.5.81	1		La Chaux de Fonds	12 Aug
49.70	William	Wynne	USA-Y	30.1.90	1	NC-j	Indianapolis	23 Jun
49.71	Gregory	Little	JAM	20.2.83	2		Fortaleza	16 May
49.72	Brendan	Cole	AUS	29.5.81	1		Neerpelt	2 Jun
49.74	Ian	Weakley	JAM	24.2.74	2B	Odlozil	Praha	13 Jun
	(60)							
49.74	Vladimir	Antmanis	RUS	12.3.84	1h2	NC	Tula	31 Jul
49.75	Brian	Derby	USA	18.2.81	1		Holmdel	9 Jun
49.76	Heni	Kéchi	FRA	31.8.80	1		Génève	8 Jun
49.78	Bryan	Scott	USA	1.3.85	1		Tucson	24 Mar
49.78	Takayuki	Koike	JPN	12.10.84	2		Gifu	22 Sep
49.79	Ben	Clark	USA	25.11.80	5s2	NC	Indianapolis	22 Jun
49.79	Yosuke	Tsushima	JPN	24.12.81	4	NC	Osaka	30 Jun
49.79	Dale	Garland	GBR	13.10.80	1	NC	Manchester	28 Jul
49.82	Yacnier	Luis	CUB	24.1.82	1h2	NC/Barr	La Habana	27 May
49.83	Naohiro	Kawakita	JPN	10.7.80	5	NC	Osaka	30 Jun
	(70)							
49.87		Ou Yongjian	CHN	1.7.84	1	NC	Shijiazhuang	5 Aug
49.89	Naoki	Ihara	JPN	22.4.82	6	NC	Osaka	30 Jun
49.90	Andrew	Peresta	USA	12.10.85	7s2	NC	Indianapolis	22 Jun
49.90	Sergio	Hierrezuelo	CUB	15.3.82	5h2	PAm	Rio de Janeiro	25 Jul
49.92	Joe	Greene	USA	20.11.87	4	NCAA	Sacramento	9 Jun
49.92	Joey	Woody	USA	22.5.73	2h1	NC	Indianapolis	21 Jun
49.92	Yoshihiro	Chiba	JPN	29.4.79	2h2	NC	Osaka	29 Jun
49.93	Orentheus	Hutcherson	USA	18.11.76	4h4	NC	Indianapolis	21 Jun
49.97		Zhu Zhi	CHN	25.8.82	1	NGP	Urumqi	20 Sep
49.99	Yasmani	Copello	CUB	15.4.87	2	ALBA	Caracas	11 May
	(80)							
50.07	Johnny	Dutch	USA-J	20.1.89	2	NC-j	Indianapolis	23 Jun
50.07	Yasuhiro	Fueki	JPN	20.12.85	1r2		Tokyo	16 Sep
50.08	Maurício	Teixeira	BRA	22.3.82	3	NC	São Paulo	24 Jun
50.10	Sotirios	Iakovákis	GRE	20.9.82	3	NC	Athína	16 Jun
50.10	Reggie	Wyatt	USA-Y	17.9.90	2		Greensboro	16 Jun
50.13	Fred	Sharpe	USA	21.8.78	3		Atlanta	31 Mar
50.13	Laurent	Ottoz	ITA	10.4.70	1		Rieti	20 May
50.14	Michal	Uhlík	CZE	9.3.80	1		Kladno	2 Jun
50.14	Andrés	Silva	URU	27.3.86	2		Alcalá de Henares	7 Jul
50.14	Milan	Kotur	CRO	15.4.86	3	EU23	Debrecen	14 Jul
	(90)							

Mark	Name		Nat	Born	Pos	Meet	Venue	Date
50.17	Steven	Green	GBR	15.1.83	2	NC	Manchester	28 Jul
50.18	Luis	Montenegro	CHI	6.10.81	3	ALBA	Caracas	11 May
50.18	Sean	Bergstedt	USA	4.5.85	2	NCAA-2	Charlotte	26 May
50.19	Eelco	Veldhuyzen	NED	19.7.84	2		Génève	8 Jun
50.21	Tomohisa	Inose	JPN	17.9.87	3h3	NC	Osaka	29 Jun
50.25	Thiago	Sales	BRA	12.8.86	4	NC	São Paulo	24 Jun
50.25	Vincent	Vanryckeghem	BEL	18.1.87	1	NC	Bruxelles	5 Aug
50.25	Idriss Abdulaziz	Al-Housaoui	KSA	5.1.84	1	CISM	Hyderabad	16 Oct
50.26	O'Neil	Wright	LBR	3.5.80	2	BEL Ch	Bruxelles	5 Aug
50.28	Jussi (100)	Heikkilä	FIN	21.3.83	5	NCAA-r	Gainesville	26 May
50.28	Ben	Carne	GBR	11.6.86	3		Génève	8 Jun

Mark	Name		Nat	Born	Date
50.29	Adrian	Walker	USA	1.10.83	13 May
50.32		Yu Zipei	CHN-J	1.2.88	20 Sep
50.37	Thomas	Goller	GER	28.10.77	9 Jun
50.37	Thiago	Bueno	BRA	21.2.83	24 Jun
50.37	Wouter	le Roux	RSA	17.1.86	15 Jul
50.38	Apisit	Kuttiyawan	THA	29.1.81	7 Dec
50.40	Stepán	Tesarik	CZE	6.7.78	13 Jun
50.40	Koji	Yasuhara	JPN	6.12.86	29 Jun
50.42	El Hadji Seth	Mbow	SEN	2.4.85	11 Aug
50.43	Sean	Williams	USA	7.6.83	24 Mar
50.44	Kevin	Hutton	USA		21 Apr
50.44	Ricardo	Lima	POR	2.1.85	13 Jul
50.47	Hideki	Yano	JPN	13.12.85	29 Jun
50.47	Go	Tanabe	JPN	21.3.86	29 Jun
50.49	Antonio	Vieillesse	MRI	24.1.86	27 May
50.49	Thomas	Kortbeek	NED	2.4.81	10 Jun
50.49	Jindrich	Simánek	CZE	27.5.79	1 Jul
50.50A	Johann	Hanekom	RSA	3.12.86	9 Mar
50.51	José Manuel	Céspedes	VEN	20.10.86	18 May
50.53	Quentin	Seigel	GER-J	7.4.88	4 Aug
50.55	Diego	Venâncio	BRA	10.5.85	20 May
50.56	Hamza	Deyaf	USA	4.12.85	6 Jun
50.59	Javonie	Small	USA	.82	14 Apr
50.59	Nicola	Cascella	ITA	2.7.85	30 Sep
50.60	Silvio	Schirrmeister	GER-J	7.12.88	21 Jul
50.63	Nick	Robinson	USA	14.1.86	13 May
50.63	James	Fredrickson	USA	27.6.86	13 May
50.63	Benjamin	Chevrol	FRA	13.3.86	8 Jun
50.63	José Maria	Romera	ESP	2.9.80	5 Aug
50.64	Kai	Kelley	USA	8.11.86	13 May
50.65	Pláton	Gavélas	GRE	21.5.80	12 May
50.66	Susumu	Saito	JPN	5.5.84	29 Jun
50.66		Li Guangjin	CHN	28.11.85	23 Jul
50.67	Jansen	Hyde	USA	10.4.87	28 Apr
50.70	Yuki	Iwataki	JPN	29.11.86	29 Jun
50.70	Tuncay	Ors	TUR	19.2.86	4 Jul
50.70	Aleksey	Mishanin	RUS	30.5.81	31 Jul
50.70	Hiroaki	Masuoka	JPN	18.2.86	16 Sep
50.70	Kuldev	Singh	IND	4.4.81	26 Oct
50.72	Vyacheslav	Sakayev	RUS-J	12.1.88	21 Jul
50.73	Vincent	Kerssies	NED	11.7.80	9 Jun
50.74	Taketoshi	Nomura	JPN	4.7.83	10 Jun
50.75	Reggie	Rucker	USA	7.10.83	12 May
50.75		Zhang Chong	CHN	24.2.87	5 Aug
50.77	Abderahmane	Hamadi	ALG	24.3.84	24 Nov
50.79	Elon	Simms	USA	4.2.87	13 May
50.79	Roman	Matveyev	RUS	7.11.82	4 Jul
50.80	Mickaël	François	FRA-J	12.3.88	6 Jul
50.81	Shogo	Shimizu	JPN	1.10.87	13 May
50.81	Michael	Bultheel	BEL	30.6.86	14 May
50.81	Ari-Pekka	Lattu	FIN	22.6.78	25 Jul
50.82	John	Cassleman	USA	16.8.84	13 May
50.83	Andretti	Bain	BAH	1.12.85	26 May
50.83	Justin	Boyd	USA	25.8.85	26 May
50.84A	Llewellyn	Herbert	RSA	21.7.77	2 Feb
50.84	Víctor José	Solarte	VEN	6.1.86	21 Dec
50.85	Ondrej	Danek	CZE	26.11.81	2 Jun
50.85	(159) Hafedh	Mohd Hussein	SUD	12.5.87	20 Jul

Best at low altitude

49.36	Cilliers	4	WUG	Bangkok	13 Aug	
50.81	Hanekom	3r3		Tarare	14 Jul	

Hand timed: 50.0 (49.97?) Abdoulaye Issa Chérif SEN 22.10.84 2 Ouagadougou 24 Apr

JUNIORS

See main list for top 5 juniors. 10 performances by 5 men to 50.25. Additional marks and further juniors:

Griffin	50.07	1h6	Knoxville	30 Jul				
Cisneros	49.97	1	La Habana	2 Mar	50.23	1	La Habana	23 Feb
Wynne	50.01	1h2 NC-j	Indianapolis	22 Jun	50.09	1r4	Greensboro	16 Jun

Mark	Name		Nat	Born	Pos	Meet	Venue	Date
50.32		Yu Zipei	CHN	1.2.88	3	NGP	Urumqi	20 Sep
50.53	Quentin	Seigel	GER	7.4.88	1	NC-j	Ulm	4 Aug
50.60	Silvio	Schirrmeister	GER	7.12.88	1	EJ	Hengelo	21 Jul
50.72	Vyacheslav	Sakayev	RUS	12.1.88	2	EJ	Hengelo	21 Jul
50.80	Mickaël	François (10)	FRA	12.3.88	2		Saint-Denis	6 Jul
50.92	Jason	Perez	USA	3.4.88	3	NC-j	Indianapolis	23 Jun
50.99	Ross	Harlan	USA	18.4.88	1	NAIA	Fresno	26 May
50.99	Toby	Ulm	GBR	19.5.89	3	EJ	Hengelo	21 Jul
51.05	Juan Pablo	Maturana	COL	5.2.88	4	SACh	São Paulo	9 Jun
51.11	Nathan	Arnette	BAH-Y	15.12.90	1	Carifta	Providenciales	8 Apt
51.21	Tim	Grier	USA	18.1.88	3	Big 12	Lincoln	13 May
51.24	Tomoharu	Kino	JPN	4.8.89	1		Yuwa	6 Oct
51.33	Ryo	Watanabe	JPN	8.5.89	2		Saga	4 Aug
51.37	Kenya	Nagahisa	JPN	20.10.89	1		Osaka	23 Jun
51.38	Lee	Moore (20)	USA	20.12.88	1		Knoxville	1 Aug

HIGH JUMP

2.39i Ivan Ukhov RUS 29.3.86 1 Moskva 28 Jan
2.15/1 2.20/1 2.24/1 2.28/1 2.31/1 2.33/1 2.35/x 2.37/1 2.39/1 2.41/xxx
2.34i 1 Chelyabinsk 15 Feb 2.15/1 2.24/1 2.30/1 2.34/1 2.37/xxx

2.38i Yaroslav Rybakov RUS 22.11.80 1 Arnstadt 3 Feb
2.20/1 2.25/1 2.28/1 2.31/1 2.34/2 2.36/1 2.38/2 2.41/xxx
2.35i 2 Moskva 28 Jan 2.20/1 2.24/1 2.28/1 2.31/1 2.33/1 2.35/1 2.37/x 2.39/xx

MEN 2007

Mark Name Nat Born Pos Meet Venue Date

2.35 2 WCh Osaka 29 Aug 2.21/1 2.26/1 2.30/1 2.33/1 2.35/2 2.37/xxx 2.36/xxx
2.34 1= Kuso Warszawa 17 Jun 2.10/1 2.15/1 2.20/1 2.25/1 2.28/2 2.30/1 2.32/2 2.34/2 /
2.33i 2 Banská Bystrica 13 Feb 2.20/1 2.27/1 2.30/1 2.30/2 2.37/x 2.39/xx
2.33i 1 Birmingham 17 Feb 2.20/1 2.24/1 2.27/1 2.30/2 2.33/1 2.36/xxx
2.38i Stefan Holm SWE 25.5.76 1 NC Göteborg 25 Feb
2.18/1 2.22/1 2.26/1 2.30/1 2.32/x 2.34/1 2.36/1 2.38/1 2.40/xx
2.37i 1 Banská Bystrica 13 Feb 2.20/1 2.24/1 2.27/1 2.30/1 2.33/2 2.35/1 2.37/1 2.39/xx
25 Feb and 13 Feb – both also 2.41/x,
2.35 1 DNG Stockholm 7 Aug 2.20/1 2.24/1 2.27/1 2.30/2 2.33/2 2.35/2 2.37/xxx
2.34i 3 Arnstadt 3 Feb 2.20/1 2.25/2 2.28/1 2.31/1 2.34/2 2.38/xxx
2.34i 1 EI Birmingham 4 Mar 2.20/1 2.25/1 2.29/1 2.32/3 2.34/2 2.41/xxx
2.33i 1 Stockholm 20 Feb 2.20/1 2.24/1 2.27/1 2.30/1 2.33/1 2.41/xxx
2.33 4 WCh Osaka 29 Aug 2.21/1 2.26/1 2.30/1 2.33/1 2.35/xxx
2.38i Linus Thörnblad SWE 6.3.85 2 NC Göteborg 25 Feb
2.18/1 2.22/1 2.26/1 2.30/3 2.32/1 2.34/x 2.36/1 2.38/1 2.40/xxx
2.34i 1 Bydgodzcz 14 Feb 2.20/1 2.24/1 2.28/1 2.30/3 2.32/1 2.34/1 2.37/xxx
2.36i Andrey Silnov RUS 9.9.84 2 Arnstadt 3 Feb
2.20/1 2.25/1 2.28/2 2.31/1 2.34/3 2.36/2 2.38/xxx
2.35i Andriy Sokolovskyy UKR 16.7.78 1 Wuppertal 26 Jan
2.14/1 2.22/1 2.28/2 2.30/1 2.35/1 2.37/xx
2.35i Andrey Tereshin RUS 15.12.82 3 Moskva 28 Jan
2.15/1 2.20/2 2.24/1 2.28/3 2.31/x 2.33/2 2.35/3 2.37/xxx
2.34 1= Kuso Warszawa 17 Jun 2.15/1 2.20/1 2.25/1 2.28/1 2.30/1 2.32/3 2.34/2 2.36/xxx
2.33i 1 Hustopece 20 Jan 2.10/1 2.15/1 2.20/1 2.24/2 2.27/1 2.30/3 2.33/3
2.35 Donald Thomas BAH 1.7.84 1 Salamanca 4 Jul
2.14/2 2.19/1 2.23/1 2.25/2 2.31/1 2.35/3
2.35 1 WCh Osaka 29 Aug 2.21/2 2.26/2 2.30/1 2.33/3 2.35/1 2.37/xxx
2.34 1 Auburn 21 Apr 2.13/1 2.22/2 2.26/2 2.30/2 2.34/2 2.39/xxx
2.33i 1 NCAA Fayetteville 10 Mar 2.14/1 2.19/1 2.22/1 2.25/1 2.28/1 2.33/1 2.37/xxx
2.35 Kyricaos Ioannou CYP 26.7.84 3 WCh Osaka 29 Aug
2.16/1 2.21/1 2.26/1 2.30/2 2.33/2 2.35/2 2.37/xxx
2.34i Tomás Jankú CZE27.12.74 1 Brno 6 Feb
2.10/1 2.20/1 2.26/2 2.30/1 2.34/3 2.37/xxx
2.33i 1 Praha 15 Feb 2.10/1 2.19/1 2.25/3 2.31/2 2.33/1 2.35/xx
2.34i Yuriy Krymarenko UKR 11.8.83 2 Bydgoszcz 14 Feb
2.15/1 2.20/1 2.24/1 2.28/3 2.30/1 2.32/1 2.34/3 2.36/xxx
2.34 Eike Onnen GER 3.8.82 1 Garbsen 20 May
2.19/1 2.25/1 2.31/2 2.34/1 2.37/x 2.39/xx
2.33i Andra Manson USA 30.4.84 1 Fayetteville 10 Feb
2.18/1 2.24/2 2.27/1 2.30/2 2.33/1 2.36/xxx
2.33 Jesse Williams USA 27.12.83 1 Los Angeles 24 Mar
2.33 Scott Sellers USA 16.8.86 1 Big 12 Lincoln 13 May
2.05/1 2.10/1 2.15/1 2.20/1 2.24/1 2.27/2 2.30/2 2.33/3
2.33 Víctor Moya CUB 24.10.82 1 Alcalá de Henares 7 Jul
(35/16) 2.20/1 2.27/1 2.31/2 2.33/2
2.32i Vyacheslav Voronin RUS 5.4.74 1 Yekaterinburg 18 Feb
2.32 Dmytro Demyanyuk UKR 30.6.83 1 Kyiv 3 Aug
2.31i Tora Harris USA 21.9.78 5 Moskva 28 Jan
2.31 Aleksandr Shustov RUS 13.8.84 1 WUG Bangkok 11 Aug
(20)
2.30i Svatoslav Ton CZE 20.10.78 3 Ostrava 23 Jan
2.30i Jim Dilling USA 23.4.85 1 Madison 27 Jan
2.30i Michal Bieniek POL 17.5.84 2 Brno 6 Feb
2.30i Andrea Bettinelli ITA 6.10.78 2 Iagar Bucuresti 9 Feb
2.30i Peter Horák SVK 7.12.83 4 Banská Bystrica 13 Feb
2.30i Oleksandr Nartov UKR-J 21.5.88 1 v3N Mogilev 24 Feb
2.30i Martyn Bernard GBR 15.12.84 Q EI Birmingham 3 Mar
2.30i Aleksander Walerianczyk POL 1.9.82 Q EI Birmingham 3 Mar
2.30 Gerardo Martínez MEX 9.3.79 1 MSR Walnut 15 Apr
2.30 Naoyuki Daigo JPN 18.1.81 1 GP Osaka 5 May
(30)
2.30 Huang Haiqiang CHN-J 8.2.88 1 WCT Suzhou 10 Jun
2.30 Germaine Mason GBR 20.1.83 3 Pre Eugene 10 Jun
2.30 Aleksey Dmitrik RUS 12.4.84 2 Biberach 16 Jun
2.30 Sergey Zasimovich KAZ 11.3.86 1 Bangkok 19 Jun
2.30 Pavel Fomenko RUS 29.6.76 4 GP Athína 2 Jul
2.29 Jaroslav Bába CZE 2.9.84 Q WCh Osaka 27 Aug
2.29 Jessé Farias de Lima BRA 17.2.81 Q WCh Osaka 27 Aug
2.29 Kabelo Mmono Kgosimang BOT 7.1.86 Q WCh Osaka 27 Aug
2.29 Tom Parsons GBR 5.5.84 Q WCh Osaka 27 Aug

Mark	Name		Nat	Born	Pos	Meet	Venue	Date
2.28i	Viktor	Shapoval	UKR	17.10.79	2		Trinec	25 Jan
	(40)							
2.28i	Keith	Moffatt	USA	20.6.84	2		Gainesville	27 Jan
2.28i	Artyom	Zaytsev	BLR	7.12.84	1	NC	Mogilev	8 Feb
2.28i	Grzegorz	Sposób	POL	12.2.76	3	Iagar	Bucuresti	9 Feb
2.28i	Ivan	Ilyichev	RUS	14.10.86	1	NC-23	Volgograd	15 Feb
2.28	Will	Littleton	USA	14.10.83	1		Austin	24 Mar
2.28	Abderahmane	Hammad	ALG	27.5.77	1		Alger	2 Jul
2.28	Oskari	Frösén	FIN	24.1.76	1		Donnas	15 Jul
2.28	Samson	Oni	GBR	25.6.81	1		London (CP)	25 Aug
2.27i	Robert	Wolski	POL	8.12.82	1		Dresden	24 Jan
2.27i	Filippo	Campioli	ITA	21.2.82	1	v FIN	Tampere	4 Feb
	(50)							
2.27i	Michael	Mason	CAN	30.9.86	1		Seattle	10 Feb
2.27i	Nicola	Ciotti	ITA	5.10.76	2	NC	Ancona	18 Feb
2.27i	Stefan	Vasilache	ROM	9.5.79	1	BalkC	Pireás	21 Feb
2.27i	Mark	Boswell	CAN	28.7.77	4		Novi Sad	22 Feb
2.27i	Niki	Palli	ISR	28.5.87	Q	EI	Birmingham	3 Mar
2.27	Dusty	Jonas	USA	19.4.86	1		Lincoln NE	29 Apr
2.27	Rozle	Prezelj	SLO	26.9.79	1		Maribor	3 Jul
2.27	James	Grayman	ANT	11.10.85	1		Pergine Valsugana	7 Jul
2.27	Lisvany	Pérez	CUB	24.1.82	2		Alcalá de Henares	7 Jul
2.27	Dragutin	Topic	SRB	12.3.71	1		Sofia	7 Jul
	(60)							
2.27	James	Nieto	USA	2.11.76	1		Lignano	15 Jul
2.27	Javier	Bermejo	ESP	23.12.78	3	Aragón	Zaragoza	28 Jul
2.27	Osku	Torro	FIN	21.8.79	2	NC	Lappeenranta	5 Aug
2.26i	Mikhail	Tsvetkov	RUS	4.5.80	2		Moskva	13 Jan
2.26i	Adam	Shunk	USA	29.8.79	1		Greencastle	10 Feb
2.26	Trevor	Barry	BAH	14.6.83	1		Auburn	7 Apr
2.26	Benjamin	Lauckner	GER	3.4.87	1	NC	Erfurt	22 Jul
2.25Ai	Matt	Hemingway	USA	24.10.72	1		Air Force Academy	27 Jan
2.25i	Stijn	Stroobants	BEL	15.4.84	5	Iagar	Bucuresti	9 Feb
2.25i	Bohdan	Bondarenko	UKR-J	30.8.89	2		Kyiv	28 Feb
	(70)							
2.25	Eugene	Hutchinson	USA	29.9.83	1		Eugene	17 Mar
2.25A	Onnanye	Ramohube	BOT	2.3.79	1		Gaborone	5 May
2.25	Mickaël	Hanany	FRA	25.3.83	6	Kuso	Warszawa	17 Jun
2.24i	Martijn	Nuyens	NED	18.11.83	1		Otrokovice	27 Jan
2.24i	Jean-Claude	Rabbath	LIB	12.7.77	4		Weinheim	7 Feb
2.24i	Sergey	Klyugin	RUS	24.3.74	7=		Novi Sad	22 Feb
2.24i	Vadim	Kolesnikov	RUS	24.5.85	1		Bryansk	22 Feb
2.24i	Mickaël	Diaz	FRA	28.10.86	1	NC-23	Paris	25 Feb
2.24	Kane	Brigg	AUS-J	14.1.88	1		Gold Coast	1 Jun
2.24	Andrei	Mîtîcov	MDA	15.11.86	1	NC	Chisinau	2 Jun
	(80)							
2.24	Heikki	Taneli	FIN	12.6.80	2		Joensuu	7 Jun
2.24	Adam	Scarr	GBR	7.5.85	1	BIG	Bedford	10 Jun
2.24	Dimítrios	Hondrokoúkis	GRE-J	26.1.88	1	NC-23	Thessaloniki	30 Jun
2.24		Lee Hup-Wei	MAS	5.5.87	1	AsiC	Amman	25 Jul
2.24	Raul	Spank	GER-J	13.7.88	1	NC-j	Ulm	5 Aug
2.24i	Rashid	Al-Mannai	QAT-J	18.7.88	1	AsiG	Macau	1 Nov
2.23i	Giulio	Ciotti	ITA	5.10.76	6		Brno	6 Feb
2.23i	Marko	Aleksejev	EST	14.2.79	1	NC	Tallinn	11 Feb
2.23i	Robert	Mitchell	GBR	14.9.80	2	NC	Sheffield	11 Feb
2.23i	Vitaliy	Samoylenko	UKR	22.5.84	3	NC	Sumy	12 Feb
	(90)							
2.23	Ramsey	Carelse	RSA	30.10.85	1		Bellville	24 Feb
2.23	Marcus	Harris	USA	5.5.83	1		Houston	24 Mar
2.23		Tsao Chih-Hao	TPE	21.9.81	1		Yilan	31 Mar
2.23	Randal	Carter	USA-J	7.4.89	1		Omaha	18 May
2.23	Rafael	Gonçalves	POR	12.5.77	1		Leiria	1 Jun
2.23	Matthew	Carter	USA	21.11.85	1		Eagle Rock	3 Jun
2.23	Kyle	Lancaster	USA	15.8.83	4	NCAA	Sacramento	8 Jun
2.23	Konstadinos	Baniótis	GRE	6.11.86	2	NC	Athína	16 Jun
2.23	Matthias	Haverney	GER	21.7.85	2	NC	Erfurt	22 Jul
2.23	Mark	Taylor	AUS	29.5.80	1		Sydney	15 Dec

(100)

2.22i	Zoltán	Vaská	HUN	17.4.84	10 Feb
2.22i	Kyley	Johnson	USA	8.8.78	3 Mar
2.22i	Ryan	Fritz	USA	4.5.87	10 Mar
2.22	Jason	House	USA-J	15.5.88	10 Mar
2.22	Ed	Wright	USA	3.3.86	26 May
2.22	Mohamed	Benhadja	ALG	24.11.81	3 Jun

Mark	Name		Nat	Born	Date	Mark	Name		Nat	Born	Date
2.22	Grégory	Gabella	FRA	22.6.80	8 Jun	2.20i	Andriy	Karmelyuk	UKR	9.2.79	25 Jan
2.22	Boubacar	Sere	BUR	15.3.84	27 Jun	2.20	Yunier	Carrillo	CUB	1.10.81	25 Jan
2.22	Mustapha	Raifak	FRA	9.9.75	5 Jul	2.20i	Sergey	Kabyak	BLR	7.3.87	27 Jan
2.22		Wang Chen	CHN-Y	27.2.90	14 Jul	2.20i	Sergey	Goleshev	BLR	30.6.84	27 Jan
2.22	Sergey	Mudrov	RUS-Y	8.9.90	14 Jul	2.20i	Aleksandr	Veryutin	BLR	18.11.79	8 Feb
2.22	Hari Shankar	Roy	IND	4.4.86	20 Sep	2.20i	Raividas	Stanis	LTU	3.2.87	9 Feb
2.22	Sylwester	Bednarek	POL-J	28.4.89	21 Sep	2.20i	Mihail	Tomarás	GRE	7.6.72	10 Feb
2.22	Fábio	Baptista	BRA	19.10.84	21 Oct	2.20i	Fedor	Getov	RUS	14.3.84	11 Feb
2.21i	Martin	Lloyd	GBR	18.6.80	28 Jan	2.20i	Kyryilo	Shchavinskyy	UKR	23.7.82	12 Feb
2.21i	Joel	Spolén	SWE	27.11.83	31 Jan	2.20i	Andrey	Chubsa	BLR	29.11.82	15 Feb
2.21i	Ilya	Krivetskiy	RUS	24.8.86	15 Feb	2.20i	László	Boros	HUN	3.2.82	18 Feb
2.21i	Tone	Belt	USA	10.2.87	18 Feb	2.20i	Michael	Isler	SUI	11.5.84	18 Feb
2.21	Liam	Zamel-Paez	AUS-J	4.8.88	9 Mar	2.20i	Branko	Djuricic	SRB	5.1.81	22 Feb
2.21	Cedric	Norman	USA	5.10.81	10 Mar	2.20i	Derek	Watkins	CAN	5.4.81	24 Feb
2.21	D'Ornoir	Flax	USA	9.11.84	18 Mar	2.20i		Wang Hao	CHN	2.2.85	21 Mar
2.21	Jerome	Miller	USA	14.8.86	31 Mar	2.20	David	Pendergrass	USA	25.5.83	30 Mar
2.21	Grant	Lindsey	USA-J	11.11.88	20 Apr	2.20	Jonathan	Golden	USA	5.3.86	31 Mar
2.21	Daniel	Olson	USA	27.9.82	21 Apr	2.20	Hikaru	Tsuchiya	JPN	1.2.86	2 Apr
2.21	Mark	Davis	USA	26.10.87	21 Apr	2.20	Julio	Luciano	DOM	10.10.77	13 Apr
2.21	Joe	Kindred	USA	15.9.87	21 Apr	2.20		Qu Zhaobing	CHN-Y	11.6.91	28 Apr
2.21	Matt	Turner	USA	21.7.86	28 Apr	2.20	Hervé	Paris	FRA	21.3.83	6 May
2.21		Zhang Shufeng	CHN	24.11.84	5 May	2.20	Bayo	Adio	NGR	24.9.85	12 May
2.21	Gilmar	Mayo	COL	30.9.69	8 Jun	2.20	Kirill	Shymanskyy	UKR	23.10.85	18 May
2.21	Stéphane	Toinon	FRA	16.10.83	8 Jun	2.20	Matthias	Franta	GER	4.12.84	19 May
2.21	Darwin	Edwards	LCA	11.9.86	10 Jun	2.20	Jamal Fakhri	Al Qasim	KSA	3.12.83	21 May
2.21	Nerijus	Buzas	LTU	1.5.84	13 Jun	2.20	Fabrice	Saint-Jean	FRA	21.11.80	25 May
2.21	Jamal	Wilson	BAH-J	1.9.88	24 Jun	2.20A	David	Hoffman	USA	22.4.75	2 Jun
2.21	Dalibor	Hon	CZE	2.8.78	30 Jun	2.20	Nikólaos	Giósis	GRE	22.9.80	6 Jun
2.21	Sandro	Finesi	ITA	5.4.80	7 Jul	2.20	Ivan	Diggs	USA	28.11.85	8 Jun
2.21	Jussi	Viita	FIN	26.9.85	15 Jul	2.20	Alessandro	Talotti	ITA	7.10.80	8 Jun
2.21	Radu	Tucan	MDA	13.5.86	15 Jul	2.20		Zhao Kuansong	CHN	11.2.86	10 Jun
2.21	Michal	Kabelka	SVK	4.2.85	15 Jul	2.20	Hamza	Labadi	ALG	4.3.85	11 Jun
2.21	Andriy	Protsenko	UKR-J	20.5.88	21 Jul	2.20	Roman	Guliy	UKR	7.4.79	12 Jun
2.21	Silvano	Chesani	ITA-J	17.7.88	21 Jul	2.20	Andretty	Lisboa	BRA	26.12.82	13 Jun
2.21	Satoru	Kubota	JPN	29.10.82	25 Jul	2.20	Normunds	Pupols	LAT	10.5.84	23 Jun
2.21	Hashim Issa	Al Oqabi	KSA	31.1.87	25 Jul	2.20		Li Bing	CHN	1.2.79	8 Jul
2.21	Bryan	Hall	GBR	17.11.81	25 Aug	2.20	Josh	Hall	AUS-Y	3.4.90	14 Jul
2.21	Robbie	Grabarz	GBR	3.10.87	25 Aug	2.20	Obiora	Arinze	NGR	15.12.85	22 Jul
2.21		Kim Jong-pyo	KOR	28.3.84	11 Oct	2.20		Ceng Hui	CHN		24 Jul
2.21i		Kim Young-min	KOR	11.2.83	1 Nov	2.20	Wilbert	Pennings	NED	12.2.75	1 Aug
2.20i	Jan Peter	Larsen	NED	18.3.79	7 Jan	2.20	Mathias	Cianci	FRA	25.10.82	12 Aug
2.20i	Stefan	Häfner	GER	30.1.84	13 Jan	2.20	Alan	McKie	GBR-J	14.10.88	2 Sep
2.20i	Stanislav	Malyarenko	RUS	19.5.85	20 Jan	2.20	Davide	Marcandelli	ITA	9.11.87	30 Sep
2.20i	Kwaku	Boateng	CAN	30.6.74	20 Jan	2.20	Albert	Bravo	VEN	29.8.87	24 Oct
2.20i	Lubos	Benko	SVK	27.2.74	20 Jan	2.20	Salem Sayar	Al Anezi	KUW	4.9.83	24 Nov
2.20i	Andrea	Lemmi	ITA	12.5.84	20 Jan		(197)				

Best outdoors

2.35	Holm	1	DNG	Stockholm	7 Aug	2.27	Horák	3=	GS	Ostrava	27 Jun
2.35	Rybakov	2	WCh	Osaka	29 Aug	2.27	N Ciotti	6	GP	Athína	2 Jul
2.34	Tereshin	1=	Kuso	Warszawa	17 Jun	2.27	M Mason	1	NC	Windsor	14 Jul
2.31	Thörnblad	1	Golden	Shanghai	28 Sep	2.27	Krymarenko	2	Aragón	Zaragoza	28 Jul
2.30	Dilling	1	DrakeR	Des Moines	28 Apr	2.26	Shunk	3	DrakeR	Des Moines	28 Apr
2.30	Manson	2	Big 12	Lincoln	13 May	2.26	Nartov	1		Yalta	12 Jun
2.30	Ton	1		Praha	19 May	2.26	Shapoval	4	WUG	Bangkok	11 Aug
2.30	Voronin	2	Takac	Beograd	29 May	2.25	Palli	1		Tel Aviv	18 Feb
2.30	T Harris	1	Pre	Eugene	10 Jun	2.25	Moffatt	1		Atlanta	12 May
2.30	Walerianczyk	3	Kuso	Warszawa	17 Jun	2.25	Tsvetkov	1	Isr Ch	Tel Aviv	4 Jul
2.30	Bieniek	4	Kuso	Warszawa	17 Jun	2.24	Sposób	2	GP	Osaka	5 May
2.30	Bettinelli	1	ECp-1B	Milano	23 Jun	2.24	Ilyichev	2		Sochi	27 May
2.30	Jankú	1	NC	Trinec	30 Jun	2.24	Vasilache	1	Rom IC	Bucuresti	10 Jun
2.30	Silnov	1		Eberstadt	8 Sep	2.23	Hemingway	2	DrakeR	Des Moines	26 Apr
2.30	Sokolovskyy	2		Thessaloníki	30 Jul	2.23	Rabbath	1	Arab C	Amman	21 May
2.29	Bernard	Q	WCh	Osaka	27 Aug	2.23	Samoylenko	4	NCp	Kyiv	3 Aug
2.27	Campioli	1		Formia	26 May						

2.22	Stroobants	16 Sep	2.21	Diaz	15 Jul	2.20	Benko	26 May	2.20	Goleshev	30 Jun
2.21	Belt	5 May	2.20	Fritz	28 Apr	2.20	Chubsa	2 Jun	2.20	Lloyd	4 Aug
2.21	Nuyens	13 Jun	2.20	Boros	19 May	2.20	Ukhov	17 Jun	2.20	Al-Mannai	18 Aug
2.21	Boswell	14 Jul	2.20	G Ciotti	26 May	2.20	Aleksejev	20 Jun			

Drugs disqualification: 2.26 Jesse Lipscombe # CAN 4.4.80 1 Sánchez Santo Domingo 12 May

JUNIORS

See main list for top 8 juniors. 11 performances by 7 men to 2.24. Additional marks and further juniors:

Huang	2.24	1		Shijiazhuang	5 Aug					
Nartov	2.26	1	NCp	Yalta	12 Jun	2.24i	2		Dresden	24 Jan
	2.26	3	WUG	Bangkok	11 Aug	Best out: 2.20 Al-Mannai QAT 1 Verviers 18 Aug				
2.22	Jason	House	USA	15.5.88	1				Tallahassee	10 Mar

Mark		Name	Nat	Born	Pos	Meet	Venue	Date
2.22		Wang Chen (10)	CHN-Y	27.2.90	1	WY	Ostrava	14 Jul
2.22	Sergey	Mudrov	RUS-Y	8.9.90	2	WY	Ostrava	14 Jul
2.22	Sylwester	Bednarek	POL	28.4.89	1		Opole	21 Sep
2.21	Liam	Zamel-Paez	AUS	4.8.88	1	NC	Brisbane	9 Mar
2.21	Grant	Lindsey	USA	11.11.88	1		Waco	20 Apr
2.21	Jamal	Wilson	BAH	1.9.88	3	NC	Nassau	24 Jun
2.21	Andriy	Protsenko	UKR	20.5.88	2=	EJ	Hengelo	21 Jul
2.21	Silvano	Chesani	ITA	17.7.88	5	EJ	Hengelo	21 Jul
2.20		Qu Zhaobing	CHN-Y	11.6.91	1		Beijing	28 Apr
2.20	Josh	Hall	AUS-Y	3.4.90	3	WY	Ostrava	14 Jul
2.20	Alan	McKie (20)	GBR	14.10.88	1		London (Ha)	2 Sep

POLE VAULT

Mark		Name	Nat	Born	Pos	Meet	Venue	Date	Series
5.95	Brad	Walker	USA	21.6.81	1	AUS Ch	Brisbane	10 Mar	5.70/2 5.95/2 6.04/xxx
5.92					1	WACh	Perth	23 Feb	5.71/2 5.92/1 6.04/xxx
5.91					1	Athl	Lausanne	10 Jul	5.60/1 5.75/1 5.91/1 6.04/xxx
5.91					1	WAF	Stuttgart	23 Sep	5.60/2 5.76/3 5.86/x 5.91/2 6.16/xxx
5.86					1	WCh	Osaka	1 Sep	5.51/1 5.66/1 5.76/x 5.81/1 5.86/1 5.91/xxx
5.85					1		Rio Vista	12 May	5.60/2 5.85/3 6.04/x
5.91	Paul	Burgess	AUS	14.8.79	1		Perth	7 Jan	5.71/1 5.91/1 6.06/xxx
5.91	Steve	Hooker	AUS	16.7.82	2		Perth	7 Jan	5.71/3 5.91/3 6.01/xxx
5.87					2	Herc	Monaco	25 Jul	5.60/2 5.77/1 5.87/2 5.97/xxx
5.85					1	GP	Athína	16 Jun	5.65/1 5.75/2 5.85/2 6.01/xxx
5.90i	Björn	Otto	GER	16.10.77	1	NC	Leipzig	17 Feb	5.50/1 5.70/1 5.80/1 5.90/3 6.01/x
5.90					1		Leverkusen	10 Aug	5.50/1 5.70/2 5.80/2 5.90/2
5.88i					1	Spark	Stuttgart	3 Feb	5.60/1 5.78/2 5.88/2
5.86					2	WAF	Stuttgart	23 Sep	5.45/1 5.60/1 5.70/2 5.81/2 5.85/1 5.91/xx 5.96/x
5.82i					2		Cottbus	31 Jan	5.50/1 5.70/1 5.82/3 5.87/xxx
5.87	Danny	Ecker	GER	21.7.77	1	Herc	Monaco	25 Jul	5.50/2 5.70/1 5.82/3 5.87/1
5.86					1	ISTAF	Berlin	16 Sep	5.51/1 5.71/1 5.81/x 5.86/1 5.91/xxx
5.82i					1		Cottbus	31 Jan	5.50/2 5.70/2 5.82/2 5.92/xx-);
5.86	Tim	Mack	USA	15.9.72	1		Chula Vista	14 Jun	5.41/3 5.51/1 5.61/x 5.71/2 5.76/2 5.86/2 5.96/xxx
5.86	Romain	Mesnil	FRA	13.6.77	2	WCh	Osaka	1 Sep	5.66/2 5.81/1 5.86/2 5.91/xxx
5.82					3	Herc	Monaco	25 Jul	5.50/2 5.70/1 5.82/3 5.92/xxx
5.85i	Jeff	Hartwig	USA	25.9.67	1		Jonesboro	19 May	
5.83A					1		Xalapa	5 May	
5.83i	Fabian	Schulze	GER	7.3.84	2	Spark	Stuttgart	3 Feb	5.45/1 5.70/3 5.83/3 5.93/xxx
5.83	Tim	Lobinger	GER	3.9.72	1		Ingolstadt	16 Jun	5.50/2 5.60/1 5.70/2 5.83/2 5.91/xxx
5.82	Giovanni	Lanaro	MEX	27.9.81	1	MSR	Walnut	15 Apr	5.42/1 5.62/1 5.73/1 5.82/2 5.90/xxx
5.82	Spas	Bukhalov	BUL	14.11.80	1		Sofia	2 Jun	5.50/1 5.70/1 5.82/1 5.90/x
5.82	Jake	Pauli	USA	15.6.79	1		Cedar Falls	15 Jun	
	(28/13) and 16 performances at 5.81								
5.81	Igor	Pavlov	RUS	18.7.79	4	WCh	Osaka	1 Sep	
5.81	Yevgeniy	Lukyanenko	RUS	23.1.85	6	WCh	Osaka	1 Sep	
5.81	Aleksandr	Averbukh	ISR	1.10.74	7	WCh	Osaka	1 Sep	
5.80i	Viktor	Chistyakov (ex AUS)	RUS	9.2.75	2		Donetsk	10 Feb	
5.80i	Oleksandr	Korchmid	UKR	22.1.82	3		Donetsk	10 Feb	
5.80	Tommy	Skipper	USA	19.9.84	1	NCAA-r	Eugene	25 May	
5.77	Fábio Gomes	da Silva	BRA	4.8.83	1	SAmC	São Paulo	7 Jun	
	(20)								
5.76	Maksym	Mazuryk	UKR	2.4.83	11	WCh	Osaka	1 Sep	
5.75i	Lars	Börgeling	GER	16.4.79	3		Leipzig	9 Feb	
5.75	Daichi	Sawano	JPN	16.9.80	1		Shizuoka	30 Apr	
5.75	Pavel	Prokopenko	RUS	24.8.87	1	EU23	Debrecen	15 Jul	
5.75	Derek	Miles	USA	28.9.72	1		Chula Vista	21 Aug	
5.73	Russ	Buller	USA	10.9.78	2	MSR	Walnut	15 Apr	
5.72i	Daniel	Ryland	USA	6.8.79	1		Jonesboro	23 May	
5.72	Denys	Yurchenko	UKR	27.1.78	1	GP	Rieti	9 Sep	
5.71	Jon	Takahashi	USA	21.10.82	2		Chula Vista	14 Jun	

Mark		Name	Nat	Born	Pos	Meet	Venue	Date
5.71		Liu Feiliang	CHN	27.3.85	1		Guangzhou	20 Jul
	(30)							
5.71	Richard	Spiegelburg	GER	12.8.77	3	DLV	Bochum-Wattenscheid	12 Aug
5.71	Przemyslaw	Czerwinski	POL	28.7.83	4	DLV	Bochum-Wattenscheid	12 Aug
5.71	Alexander	Straub	GER	14.10.83	2		Königs Wusterhausen	9 Sep
5.70i	Sergey	Kucheryanu	RUS	30.6.85	1		Moskva	31 Jan
5.70i	Jérôme	Clavier	FRA	3.5.83	1		Eaubonne	2 Feb
5.70i	Ilian	Efremov	BUL	2.8.70	1		Sofia	3 Feb
5.70i	Adam	Kolasa	POL	2.8.75	4		Leipzig	9 Feb
5.70	Adam	Ptácek	CZE	8.10.80	1		Praha	5 Jun
5.70	Giuseppe	Gibilisco ¶	ITA	5.1.79	6	GP	Athína	2 Jul
5.70	Jesper	Fritz	SWE	13.9.85	2	EU23	Debrecen	15 Jul
	(40)							
5.70	Kevin	Rans	BEL	19.8.82	2	NA	Heusden-Zolder	28 Jul
5.70	Dmitriy	Starodubtsev	RUS	3.1.86	4	NC	Tula	1 Aug
5.70	Alhaji	Jeng	SWE	13.12.81	3		Göteborg	1 Aug
5.70i	Jeremy	Scott	USA	21.5.81	1		Jonesboro	6 Aug
5.70	Toby	Stevenson	USA	19.11.76	2		Chula Vista	18 Aug
5.67i	Leonid	Kivalov	RUS-J	1.4.88	1	NC-j	Penza	1 Feb
5.66		Kim Yoo-suk	KOR	19.1.82	1		Livermore, CA	16 Sep
5.65i	Aleksandr	Gripich	RUS	21.9.86	3=		Moskva	28 Jan
5.65i	Pavel	Gerasimov	RUS	29.5.79	5		Moskva	28 Jan
5.65i	Nicolas	Guigon	FRA	10.10.80	1		Carriéres-sous-Poissy	3 Feb
	(50)							
5.65	Denys	Fedas	UKR	24.8.85	3	EU23	Debrecen	15 Jul
5.65	Germán	Chiaraviglio	ARG	16.4.87	3	GP	Rieti	9 Sep
5.61	Jeff	Ryan	USA	8.12.80	4		Chula Vista	14 Jun
5.61	Steven	Lewis	GBR	20.5.86	1	NC	Manchester	28 Jul
5.61	Jan	Kudlicka	CZE-J	29.4.88	1		Breclav	25 Aug
5.61i		Yang Quan	CHN	8.12.86	1		Shanghai	15 Mar
5.60i	Ruslan	Yeremenko	UKR	31.7.78	2		Eaubonne	2 Feb
5.60i	Rens	Blom	NED	1.3.77	10	Spark	Stuttgart	3 Feb
5.60i	Brad	Gebauer	USA	19.1.84	1		Houston	3 Feb
5.60i	Darren	Niedermeyer	USA	2.4.82	3	NC	Boston (R)	24 Feb
	(60)							
5.60	Vladyslav	Revenko	UKR	15.11.84	2		Kyiv	18 May
5.60	Nick	Hysong	USA	9.12.71	3		Chula Vista	19 May
5.60A	Robison	Pratt	MEX	25.2.80	1		Provo	2 Jun
5.60	Stepán	Janácek	CZE	12.6.77	2		Praha	5 Jun
5.60	Damiel	Dossévi	FRA	3.2.83	2		Noisy-le-Grand	12 Jun
5.60	Andrej	Poljanec	SLO	10.11.84	1		Novo Mesto	19 Jun
5.60	Michal	Balner	CZE	12.9.82	1	NC	Trinec	1 Jul
5.60	Tobias	Scherbarth	GER	17.8.85	5	EU23	Debrecen	15 Jul
5.60	Artem	Kuptsov	RUS	22.4.84	5=	NC	Tula	1 Aug
5.60	Andrey	Chemov	RUS	13.7.83	7	NC	Tula	1 Aug
5.60		Yang Yansheng	CHN-J	5.1.88	1	NC	Shijiazhuang	3 Aug
	(70)							
5.60	Jurij	Rovan	SLO	23.1.75	1		New Orleans	26 Aug
5.58i	Renaud	Lavillenie	FRA	18.9.86	2		Aulnay-sous-Bois	7 Dec
5.57Ai	Paul	Gensic	USA	27.6.82	1		Albuquerque	10 Feb
5.55i	Robbert-Jan	Jansen	NED	22.7.83	1		Kirchberg	27 Jan
5.55	Dmitriy	Markov	AUS	14.3.75	1		Adelaide	27 Jan
5.55	Jordan	Scott	USA-J	22.2.88	1	Big 12	Lincoln	13 May
5.55	Tye	Harvey	USA	25.9.74	1		Livermore, CA	2 Jun
5.53i	Scott	Roth	USA-J	25.6.88	1		Seattle	3 Mar
5.52i	Brian	Mondschein	USA	9.1.83	1		Tsaotun	14 Mar
5.52	Ray	Scotten	USA	20.5.83	5	KansR	Lawrence	21 Apr
	(80)							
5.51	Rory	Quiller	USA	17.4.84	2	NCAA-r	Gainesville	25 May
5.50i	Joël	Soler	FRA	15.2.82	3		Bordeaux	13 Jan
5.50Ai	Derek	Mackel	USA	18.11.82	2		Albuquerque	13 Jan
5.50i	Yevgeniy	Mikhaylichenko	RUS	13.2.79	4		Moskva	24 Jan
5.50i	Nikolay	Lavrinenko	RUS	24.3.84	6		Moskva	24 Jan
5.50Ai	Pat	Manson	USA	29.11.67	1		Air Force Academy	2 Feb
5.50i	Giorgio	Piantella	ITA	6.7.81	1		Sempeter	4 Feb
5.50i	Nicolas	Durand	FRA	23.1.79	3		Aubière	9 Feb
5.50i	Charles	Andureu	FRA	13.2.85	6		Aubière	9 Feb
5.50i	Chip	Heuser	USA	9.2.85	1		Fayetteville	10 Feb
	(90)							
5.50i	Igor	Alekseyev	RUS	7.4.83	3		Chelyabinsk	15 Feb
5.50i	Hendrik	Gruber	GER	28.9.86	6	NC	Leipzig	17 Feb

Mark	Name		Nat	Born	Pos	Meet	Venue	Date
5.50i	Dennis	Leyckes	GER	20.4.82	7	NC	Leipzig	17 Feb
5.50i	Tyson	Byers	USA	18.5.83	3	NCAA	Fayetteville	9 Mar
5.50	Adam	Keul	USA	27.1.80	1		Nacogdoches	24 Mar
5.50	Dennis	Kholev	ISR	21.10.75	1		La Jolla	21 Apr
5.50	Dominic	Johnson	LCA	31.10.75	6		Chula Vista	19 May
5.50	Justin	Norberg	USA	18.7.77	1		Eagle Rock	2 Jun
5.50	Lázaro (100)	Borges	CUB	19.6.86	1		La Habana	7 Jun
5.50	Raphael	Holzdeppe	GER-J	28.9.89	1		Potsdam	9 Jun
5.50	Lukasz	Michalski	POL-J	17.8.88	1	NC-j	Biala Podlaska	28 Jun
5.50	Richard	Möcks	GER	15.10.81	2		Regensburg	30 Jun
5.50	Mikko	Latvala	FIN	8.7.80	1		Lapua	11 Jul
5.50	Xavier	Tromp	FRA	3.3.84	3		Longeville-lès-Metz	15 Jul
5.50	Yevgeniy	Ageyev	RUS-J	22.4.88	2	EJ	Hengelo	22 Jul
5.50	Oscar	Janson	SWE	22.7.75	5		Göteborg	1 Aug
5.50	Michel	Frauen	GER	19.1.86	3=		Leverkusen	10 Aug
5.50	Takafumi	Suzuki	JPN	25.5.87	2		Akita	7 Oct

5.45i	Dmitriy	Kuptsov	RUS	9.11.82	3 Feb
5.45	Scott	Martin	USA	8.3.84	13 May
5.45	Mike	Landers	USA	19.8.83	8 Jun
5.45	Matti	Mononen	FIN	25.11.83	3 Jul
5.45	Pavel	Burlachenko	RUS	7.4.76	3 Jul
5.45	Stéphane	Diaz	FRA	24.12.78	22 Jul
5.43i	McKane	Lee	USA	4.12.83	3 Mar
5.42i	Thorsten	Müller	GER	22.3.83	24 Feb
5.42i	Scott	Simpson	GBR	21.7.79	10 Mar
5.42	Javier	Gazol	ESP	27.10.80	18 Jul
5.41i	Graeme	Hoste	USA	1.5.86	10 Feb
5.41	Mitch	Greeley	USA	5.5.86	25 May
5.41i	Spencer	McCorkel	USA-J	15.2.89	6 Jun
5.41	Mark	Johnson	USA	24.11.83	9 Jun
5.41	Hiroki	Sasase	JPN-J	17.8.89	5 Aug
5.41i	Sébastien	Homo	FRA	27.4.82	7 Dec
5.40i	Nikolay	Ostapenko	RUS	12.10.86	20 Jan
5.40i	Laurens	Looije	NED	12.1.73	27 Jan
5.40i	Christian	Tamminga	NED	30.4.74	27 Jan
5.40i	Matteo	Rubbiani	ITA	31.8.78	28 Jan
5.40i	Roman	Gripich	RUS	.82	9 Feb
5.40i	Damien	Inocencio	FRA	29.7.77	9 Feb
5.40i	Olexandr	Bubka	UKR	9.9.86	10 Feb
5.40i	Sergiy	Horovyy	UKR	11.7.87	13 Feb
5.40i	Viktor	Derkach	UKR	8.11.83	13 Feb
5.40i	Luke	Cutts	GBR-J	13.2.88	24 Feb
5.40i	Michael	Hogue	USA		9 Mar
5.40i	Jason	Scott	USA	10.4.85	10 Mar
5.40	Takehito	Ariki	JPN	15.1.82	15 Apr
5.40	Randy	Flach	USA	25.12.82	12 May
5.40	Vincent	Favretto	FRA	5.4.84	20 May
5.40	Mikhail	Golovtsov	RUS	8.6.86	19 Jun
5.40	Mateusz	Didenkow	POL	22.4.87	20 Jun
5.40	Joe	Ive	GBR	12.5.87	23 Jun
5.40	Paul	Walker	GBR	15.8.85	23 Jun
5.40	Jarno	Kivioja	FIN	7.10.82	28 Jun
5.40	Sergey	Pogorelov	RUS-J	15.3.88	30 Jun
5.40	Fabrice	Fortin	FRA	2.2.80	5 Jul
5.40	Wout	van Wengerden	NED	16.2.87	15 Jul
5.40	Sergio	D'Orio	ITA	25.10.78	15 Jul
5.40	Okkert	Brits	RSA	22.8.73	29 Jul
5.40	Artem	Burya	RUS	11.4.86	31 Jul
5.40	Jason	Wurster	CAN	23.9.84	12 Aug
5.38Ai	Whitney	Neves	USA	4.84	24 Feb
5.38	Pierrick	Mille	FRA	20.5.84	16 Jul
5.36	Chris	Steddum	USA	21.5.80	13 Jun
5.35Ai	Adam	Sarafian	USA	28.3.86	20 Jan
5.35i	Paul	Terek	USA	20.10.79	27 Jan
5.35i	Gustaf	Hultgren	SWE	18.8.83	31 Jan
5.35i	Alexander	Streller	GER	27.2.82	4 Feb
5.35i	Konstadínos	Filippídis ¶	GRE	26.11.86	21 Feb
5.35	Yoshihiro	Asano	JPN	21.12.85	4 May
5.35	Paul	Litchfield	USA	27.11.80	5 May
5.35	Matt	Adkisson	USA		6 May
5.35	Chris	Ashcraft	USA	14.1.83	13 May
5.35	Seth	Harris	USA	5.5.84	13 May
5.35	Naoya	Kawaguchi	JPN	18.6.87	8 Jun
5.35	Nikólaos	Sidihákis	GRE	3.10.84	2 Jul
5.35	Yevgeniy	Olkhovskiy	ISR	22.12.83	3 Jul
5.35	Patrick	Schütz	SUI	16.3.83	14 Jul
5.35	Karsten	Dilla	GER-J	17.7.89	22 Jul
5.35	Marvin	Reitze	GER-J	24.9.88	22 Jul
5.35	Mohd Mohsen	Rabbani	IRI	20.4.83	27 Jul
5.35	Mikael	Westö	FIN	3.4.82	11 Aug
5.35	Vesa	Rantanen	FIN	2.12.75	20 Aug
5.35	Jere	Bergius	FIN	4.4.87	20 Aug
5.35	Akira	Onodera	JPN	27.4.80	7 Oct
5.35	Masafumi	Moribe (177)	JPN	29.1.84	7 Oct

Best outdoors

5.90	Otto	1		Leverkusen	10 Aug
5.83A	Hartwig	1		Xalapa	5 May
5.71	Börgeling	3		Köln	3 Jun
5.70	Kucheryanu	1	NC-23	Tula	19 Jun
5.70	Clavier	1	NC	Niort	4 Aug
5.66	Jer. Scott	1		Meadville	10 May
5.65	Chistyakov	1	NCp	Tula	7 Jul
5.63	Ryland	1		Aosta	7 Jul
5.61	Kolasa	1		Sopot	7 Jul
5.60	Niedermeyer	1		Madison	5 May
5.60	Kivalov	4		Sochi	26 May
5.60	Blom	2		Dessau	1 Jun
5.60	Gerasimov	4		Moskva	29 Jun
5.55	Guigon	3	NC	Niort	4 Aug
5.51A	Gebauer	1		El Paso	14 Apr
5.50	Gripich	6		Sochi	26 May
5.50	Jansen	1		Leiden	9 Jun
5.50	Alekseyev	5		Bydgoszcz	10 Jun
5.50	Soler	3		Noisy-le-Grand	12 Jun
5.50	Korchmid	1=		Lugano	15 Jun
5.50	Andureu	1	NC-23	Elancourt	30 Jun
5.50	Lavrinenko	4		Moskva	3 Jul

5.45	Roth	12 May
5.45	Heuser	8 Jun
5.45	Gruber	23 Jun
5.45	Lavillenie	4 Aug
5.45	Durand	4 Aug
5.42	Leyckes	6 Jun
5.41	Schulze	3 Jun
5.40	Yeremenko	2 Jun
5.40	Homo	8 Jun
5.40	Looije	9 Jun
5.40	Rubbiani	10 Jun
5.37	Gensic	21 Apr
5.37	Lee	4 Aug
5.36	Manson	28 Apr
5.35	Hoste	12 May
5.35	Hogue	8 Jun

Exhibition

5.82	Adam	Ptácek	CZE	8.10.80	1	Praha	7 Jun
5.72sq	Richard	Spiegelburg	GER	12.8.77	1	Silandro	3 Aug
5.62	Jan	Kudlicka	CZE-J	29.4.88	1	Kutná Hora	12 Aug
5.60	Nicolas	Durand	FRA	23.1.79	2	Bucuresti	2 Jun
5.40	Mathieu	Boisrond	FRA	8.1.77			2 Jun
5.40	Jonas	Campagnoni	FRA-J	18.11.88			2Jun

Drugs disqualification: 5.40 Konstadínos Filippídis ¶ GRE 26.11.86 16 Jun

Mark	Wind	Name		Nat	Born	Pos	Meet	Venue	Date

JUNIORS

See main list for top 8 juniors. 11 performances by 7 men to 2.24. Additional marks and further juniors:

Kivalov	5.60	4	Sochi	26 May	5.60	2	WUG	Bangkok	12 Aug
	5.60	1 EJ	Hengelo	22 Jul	5.50	11	NC	Tula	1 Aug
Kudlicka	5.50	2 NC	Trinec	1 Jul					
Scott	5.52	1 NC-j	Indianapolis	21 Jun					
5.41i	Spencer	McCorkel	USA	15.2.89	1			Jonesboro	6 Jun
	5.36				1			Black Springs	31 Mar
5.41	Hiroki	Sasase (10)	JPN	17.8.89	1			Saga	5 Aug
5.40i	Luke	Cutts	GBR	13.2.88	1		NC-j	Birmingham	24 Feb
	5.30				1			Loughborough	20 May
5.40	Sergey	Pogorelov	RUS	15.3.88	2			Zhukovskiy	30 Jun
5.35	Karsten	Dilla	GER	17.7.89	4		EJ	Hengelo	22 Jul
5.35	Marvin	Reitze	GER	24.9.88	5		EJ	Hengelo	22 Jul
5.34	Nico	Weiler	GER-Y	5.4.90	1			Gilroy	25 May
5.32	Nick	Frawley	USA	21.6.88	1			San Diego	12 May
5.25	Casey	Roche	USA	4.8.88	1		Jnr Oly	Walnut	29 Jul
5.21	Maston	Wallace	USA	2.7.89	1			Friendswood	13 Apr
5.20i	Viktor	Kozlitin	RUS	12.6.88	4			Penza	1 Feb
5.20i	Stéfanos	Koufídis (20)	GRE	14.5.88	2			Pireás	17 Feb
	5.20				1			Árgos	19 May
5.20	Jason	Colwick	USA	25.1.88	1			Austin	21 Apr
5.20	Yuya	Ariake	JPN	27.6.89	7=		NC	Osaka	30 Jun
5.20	Aleksey	Kovalchuk	RUS	22.7.88	4			Zhukovskiy	30 Jun
5.20	Nico	Dieckmann	GER	3.9.88	1		NC-j	Ulm	4 Aug
5.40ex	Jonas	Campagnoni	FRA-J	18.11.88	3=			Bucuresti	2 Jun

LONG JUMP

8.66	1.6	Loúis	Tsátoumas	GRE	12.2.82	1		Kalamáta			2 Jun
					8.34/1.0	x	x	8.66	p	p	
8.54	1.8	1	Veniz	Haniá	9 Jun	x	8.54	p	p	p	p
8.37	0.5	1	NC	Athína	17 Jun	x	8.37	p	x	p	p
8.57	0.0	Irving	Saladino	PAN	23.1.83	1	WCh	Osaka			30 Aug
					x	8.30/0.5	8.46/0.0	x	x	8.57	
8.53	-0.2	1	GP	Rio de Janeiro	13 May	8.17/0.3	7.52	p	8.20/-1.6	p	8.53
8.53	-1.2	1	FBK	Hengelo	26 May	x	8.33	x	8.25	8.32	8.53
8.49	1.3	1	Pre	Eugene	10 Jun	x	x	x	8.49	x	x
8.45	1.0	1	Hanz	Zagreb	4 Jul	8.45	x	p	8.13/1.0	8.37/0.6	p
8.38	0.3	Q	PAm	Rio de Janeiro	23 Jul	8.38	only jump				
8.36	0.6	1	Athl	Lausanne	10 Jul						
8.31i		1		Birmingham	17 Feb	8.10	8.22	x	x	8.31	p
8.31	0.1	1	GP	Rieti	9 Sep	8.24/1.6	p	p	8.31	p	x
8.28	-0.5	1	PAm	Rio de Janeiro	24 Jul	6.66	7.69	8.13	x	6.74	8.28
8.47	-0.2	Andrew	Howe	ITA	12.5.85	2	WCh	Osaka			30 Aug
					x	8.13/-0.1	x	8.12/0.7	8.20/0.2	8.47	
8.35	0.7	1	WAF	Stuttgart	23 Sep	7.84	x	8.35	x		
8.30i		1	EI	Birmingham	4 Mar	7.89	7.90	7.87	7.79	8.30	7.93
8.40w	2.4	1	NC	Padova	27 Jul	8.40w	x	8.10w/2.8	8.21/1.4	x	8.18/1.6
8.37	0.5	James	Beckford	JAM	9.1.75	1	Kuso	Warszawa			17 Jun
					7.79	x	8.01	8.31/-0.6	8.37	p	
8.35	1.3	1		Tallinn	22 Jul	7.76	7.92	x	x	8.02	8.35
8.34A	-0.1	Khotso	Mokoena	RSA	6.3.85	1		Pretoria			9 Mar
					x	8.18	x	8.34	8.18	x	
8.28	0.6	Q	WCh	Osaka	29 Aug	8.10	7.96	8.28			
8.32w	2.6	1	GP	Dakar	28 Apr	x	8.09w/4.4	7.90	8.32w		
8.31	0.0	Dwight	Phillips	USA	1.10.77	1	Vard	Réthimno			18 Jul
					7.80	8.22	8.12	8.04	8.31	8.20	
8.30	1.8	-	NC	Indianapolis	22 Jun	x	8.36w	x	7.97w	x	8.30/1.8
8.30	0.4	3	WCh	Osaka	30 Aug	8.30	x	x	8.02/0.3	x	8.22/0.0
8.27	1.0	*	Aragon	Zaragoza	28 Jul	8.18w/3.1	8.37w	x	x	x	8.27/1.0
8.26	0.8	*	Pre	Eugene	10 Jun	x	8.35w	8.19/0.0	x	x	8.26/0.8
8.31	0.7	Brian	Johnson	USA	25.3.80	2	Vard	Réthimno			18 Jul
					8.10	8.31	8.00	p	x	8.05	
8.29	1.9	Ruslan	Gataullin	RUS	1.12.79	1		Sochi			27 May
					7.58	7.86	7.77	8.03	7.78	8.29	
8.29	1.7	Chris	Tomlinson	GBR	15.9.81	2		Bad Langensalza			7 Jul
					8.21/1.2	8.00/1.8	8.19w/2.7	8.29	8.02/1.5	x	
8.26	0.7	Issam	Nima	ALG	8.4.79	3	Aragón	Zaragoza			28 Jul
		(30/10)			x	7.95w	7.89w	x	8.00	8.26	
8.25	1.2	Mohamed Salim	Al-Khuwalidi	KSA	19.6.81	1		Qatif			21 Mar

Mark	Wind	Name		Nat	Born	Pos	Meet	Venue	Date
8.25	0.2	Oleksiy	Lukashevych	UKR	11.1.77	4	WCh	Osaka	30 Aug
8.24	0.9	Miguel	Pate	USA	13.6.79	2	NC	Indianapolis	22 Jun
8.24	0.5	Walter	Davis	USA	2.7.79	4	NC	Indianapolis	22 Jun
8.22	0.8		Zhou Can	CHN	20.5.79	1	WCT	Suzhou	9 Jun
8.22	1.9	Trevell	Quinley	USA	16.1.83	*	NC	Indianapolis	22 Jun
8.22	-0.3		Li Runrun	CHN	24.2.83	1		Wuhan	7 Jul
8.21	1.4	Marcin	Starzak	POL	20.10.85	1		Salamanca	4 Jul
8.20	1.4	Luis Felipe	Méliz	CUB	11.8.79	2		Kalamáta	2 Jun
8.19	1.1	John	Moffitt	USA	12.12.80	1		Nuoro	11 Jul
		(20)							
8.19	0.8	Christian	Reif	GER	24.10.84	Q	WCh	Osaka	29 Aug
8.18	1.4	Gable	Garenamotse	BOT	28.2.77	*		Bad Langensalza	7 Jul
8.17	0.9	Wilfredo	Martínez	CUB	9.1.85	1	ALBA	Caracas	11 May
8.17	0.4	Tony	Allmond	USA	8.10.82	1		Sotteville	5 Jun
8.17	1.4	Rogerio	Bispo	BRA	16.11.85	1		Padova	8 Jul
8.17	2.0	Pétros	Katsís	GRE	13.6.83	1		Sparti	11 Jul
8.16	1.5	Nikolay	Atanasov	BUL	11.12.74	1	BalkC	Sofia	5 Jul
8.15		Iván	Pedroso	CUB	17.12.72	1		La Habana	15 Jun
8.13i		Salim	Sdiri	FRA	26.10.78	2		Paris	23 Feb
8.12	2.0	Nils	Winter	GER	27.3.77	1		Bad Camberg	3 Jun
		(30)							
8.12	1.1	Chris	Noffke	AUS-J	6.1.88	2		Nuoro	11 Jul
8.12	0.5	Ahmad Fayez	Marzouk	KSA	6.9.79	Q	WCh	Osaka	29 Aug
8.11	1.3	Ndiss Kaba	Badji	SEN	21.9.83	1		Alger	21 Jun
8.10	0.0	Arnaud	Casquette	MRI	16.4.78	2		Alger	21 Jun
8.10	-0.9	Nelson	Évora	POR	20.4.84	1	ECp-1B	Milano	23 Jun
8.10	0.2	Peter	Rapp	GER	29.5.83	1		Ebensee	7 Jul
8.10	0.5	Hussein	Al-Sabee	KSA	14.11.79	2	PArabG	Cairo	21 Nov
8.09i		Kafétien	Gomis	FRA	23.3.80	1	NC	Aubière	18 Feb
8.09	1.1	Louis	Tristán	PER	1.5.84	1		São Paulo	28 Feb
8.09	1.3		Zhang Xiaoyi	CHN-J	25.5.89	2	WCT	Suzhou	9 Jun
		(40)							
8.08	0.0	Ignisious	Gaisah	GHA	20.6.83	1		Abuja	5 May
8.07	0.8	Aarik	Wilson	USA	25.10.82	*	NC	Indianapolis	22 Jun
8.07	0.7		Su Xiongfeng	CHN	21.3.87	1		Wuhan	30 Oct
8.06i		Valeriy	Vasylyev	UKR	21.4.76	1		Zaporozhye	24 Jan
8.05	0.1	Dmitriy	Sapinskiy	RUS	13.10.83	1		Moskva	3 Jul
8.04		Yahya	Berrabah	MAR	13.10.81	1		Casablanca	12 May
8.04	0.5		Gao Hongwei	CHN	10.8.87	1		Zhaoqing	19 May
8.04A	0.3	Erivaldo da Cruz	Vieira	BRA	18.11.80	1		La Paz	1 Jun
8.04A	1.5	Joe	Allen	USA	7.7.78	Q		Provo	2 Jun
8.04	0.6	Kirill	Sosunov	RUS	1.11.75	2		Moskva	3 Jul
		(50)							
8.04	1.8	Christoph	Stolz	GER	17.1.80	7		Bad Langensalza	7 Jul
8.02i		Fabrizio	Donato	ITA	14.8.76	2	NC	Ancona	17 Feb
8.02	1.2	Tunde	Suleman	NGR	9.11.77	1		Ijebu Ode	3 Mar
8.02	-0.1	Rodrigo	de Araújo	BRA	12.11.79	1		Sertãozhino	19 May
8.02A	0.9	Bashir	Ramzy	USA	4.5.79	1eB		Provo	2 Jun
8.02	0.6	Robert	Crowther	AUS	2.8.87	1	WUG	Bangkok	12 Aug
8.01	1.2	Tim	Parravicini	AUS	25.4.81	1	NC	Brisbane	11 Mar
8.01	1.7	Hideaki	Suzuki	JPN	31.5.87	1		Tokyo	9 Jun
8.01	0.0	Konstantin	Safronov	KAZ	2.9.87	1		Almaty	10 Jun
8.00i		Danut-Marian	Simion	ROM	25.1.83	1		Bucuresti	27 Jan
		(60)							
8.00	0.6	Vladimir	Malyavin	RUS	4.3.73	3		Moskva	3 Jul
8.00	2.0	Nathan	Morgan	GBR	30.6.78	*		Salamanca	4 Jul
7.99	0.0	Jadel	Gregório	BRA	16.9.80	3	Nebiolo	Torino	8 Jun
7.99	1.1	John	Thornell	AUS	22.4.85	1		Gold Coast	29 Jun
7.99	0.5	Sergey	Slepukhin	RUS	6.3.87	4		Moskva	3 Jul
7.98	1.2	Tommi	Evilä	FIN	6.4.80	1		Äänekoski	14 Jun
7.98	1.8	Roman	Novotny	CZE	5.1.86	1	NC	Trinec	1 Jul
7.98	1.9	Fabrice	Lapierre	AUS	17.10.83	4		Nuoro	11 Jul
7.97i		Morten	Jensen	DEN	2.12.82	1	SWE Ch	Göteborg	25 Feb
7.97i		Tone	Belt	USA	10.2.87	1	NCAA	Fayetteville	9 Mar
		(70)							
7.96	1.8	Oslay	Vilches	CUB-J	13.7.88	5	NC/Barr	La Habana	25 May
7.96	1.0	Bogdan	Tudor	ROM	1.2.70	1		Bucuresti	27 May
7.96		Jairo	Guibert	CUB	22.2.84	2		La Habana	15 Jun
7.96	-0.2	Greg	Rutherford	GBR	17.11.86	3		Tallinn	22 Jul
7.96	0.6	Volodomyr	Zyuskov	UKR	29.8.81	3		Thessaloniki	30 Jul
7.96	-0.2	Andrejs	Maskancevs	LAT	11.10.86	2		Palermo	30 Sep

Mark	Wind	Name		Nat	Born	Pos	Meet	Venue	Date
7.96	0.5	Scott	Crowe	AUS	7.10.83	1		Canberra	1 Dec
7.95i		Scott	Mayle	USA	14.10.83	1		Akron	23 Feb
7.95i		Julien	Fivaz	SUI	9.1.79	1	NC	Magglingen	25 Feb
7.95	1.4	Jonathan	Chimier	MRI	6.8.82	1		Tourlaville	22 Jul
		(80)							
7.95	0.8		Chao Chih-Chien	TPE	30.9.83	2	WUG	Bangkok	12 Aug
7.95i		Jared	Randle	USA	14.11.87	1		Princess Anne	7 Dec
7.94	0.8	Michal	Rosiak	POL	9.5.86	1	EU23	Debrecen	13 Jul
7.94	1.6	Okoineme	Giwa-Agbomeirele	USA	30.11.78	1		New York	14 Jul
7.94	0.7	Stephan	Louw	NAM	26.2.75	3		Malles	4 Aug
7.93	0.0	Herbert	McGregor	JAM	13.9.81	7	NC/Barr	La Habana	25 May
7.93	-0.3		Kuang Li	CHN	13.8.84	5	WCT	Suzhou	9 Jun
7.93		Héctor	Fuentes	CUB-J	19.5.88	3		La Habana	15 Jun
7.93	0.5	Aleksandr	Petrov	RUS	9.8.86	1	NC-23	Tula	19 Jun
7.93	0.6	Petteri	Lax	FIN	12.10.85	•	NC	Lappeenranta	4 Aug
		(90)							
7.93	0.3	Esteban	Copland	VEN	12.10.79	1		Barinas	18 Dec
7.92A	1.5	Chris	Gillis	USA	16.11.83	2eB		Provo	2 Jun
7.92	1.9	Yeóryios	Tsákonas	GRE-J	22.1.88	1	NC-j	Thessaloniki	1 Jul
7.92	1.7		Kim Duk-hyung	KOR	8.12.85	1		Kwangju	13 Oct
7.91i		Astérios	Noúsios	GRE	25.2.79	2		Athína (P)	3 Feb
7.91	1.5	Reinier	Reyes	CUB	15.7.82	2		La Habana	1 Mar
7.91	0.1	Osbourne	Moxey	BAH	27.8.78	1	NC	Nassau	22 Jun
7.91	1.3	Jonathan	Martínez	ESP	29.1.86	1		Arganda del Rey	4 Jul
7.90	0.0	Mateusz	Parlicki	POL	14.4.84	1		Sosnowiec	13 May
7.90	0.9	Andrey	Kravchenko	BLR	4.1.86	1D		Götzis	26 May
		(100)							
7.90	0.7	Daisuke	Arakawa	JPN	19.9.81	1	NC	Osaka	29 Jun
7.90	1.0	Dimítrios	Diamadáras	GRE	18.7.84	1		Pátra	9 Jul

Mark	Wind	Name		Nat	Born	Date
7.89i		Olexandr	Patselya	UKR	3.7.83	3 Feb
7.89i		Vitaliy	Shkurlatov	RUS	25.5.79	11 Feb
7.89	1.0	Frédéric	Erin	FRA	23.4.80	11 Mar
7.89	0.0		Xie Feng	CHN	23.10.84	14 Apr
7.89	0.0		Weng Yongfeng	CHN-J	18.1.89	7 Jul
7.89	1.4	Carlos	Jorge	DOM	24.9.86	15 Jul
7.88i		Sebastian	Bayer	GER	11.6.86	17 Feb
7.88	-1.4	O'Darien	Bassett	USA		28 Apr
7.88	2.0	Anastásios	Makrinikólas	GRE	21.7.77	9 Jun
7.88	0.0	Tomasz	Mateusiak	POL	5.12.80	17 Jun
7.88	2.0	Jonathan	Moore	GBR	31.5.84	4 Jul
7.88	0.4		Ding Jie	CHN	21.4.87	7 Jul
7.88	-0.2	Josbert	Tinus	MAS	10.3.80	5 Oct
7.87i		Norris	Frederick	USA	17.2.86	27 Jan
7.87i		Dmytro	Bilotserkivskyy	UKR	25.3.85	3 Feb
7.87i			Yu Zhenwei	CHN	18.3.86	21 Mar
7.87	1.6	Stepán	Wagner	CZE	5.10.81	13 May
7.87	0.1	Dmitriy	Tarasyuk	RUS	12.12.80	27 May
7.87	1.2	Hildeberto	Almeida	POR	8.8.78	28 Jul
7.87	0.0	Jan	Zumer	SLO	9.6.82	4 Aug
7.87	1.2		Han Jinru	CHN	28.5.86	12 Aug
7.87	0.1	Jacob	Minah	GER	3.4.82	12 Aug
7.87	1.7	Henry	Dagmil	PHI	7.12.81	10 Dec
7.86i		Nikita	Lebedev	RUS	17.4.85	15 Feb
7.86	1.8	Yaw	Fosu-Amoah	RSA	8.10.81	16 Mar
7.86	0.6	Andriy	Makarchev	UKR	15.4.85	19 May
7.86	0.0		Wang Minsheng	CHN	7.4.85	9 Jun
7.86	1.0	Naohiro	Shinada	JPN	10.2.86	9 Jun
7.86	0.0	Ivan	Pucelj	CRO	11.7.81	20 Jun
7.86	0.0	Denis	Sinyavskiy	RUS	13.8.79	2 Aug
7.86	-0.3		Zhang Xin	CHN	24.4.83	4 Aug
7.85i		Oliver	Koenig	GER	31.1.81	17 Feb
7.85i		Trey	Hardee	USA	7.2.84	2 Mar
7.85	1.2	Keenan	Watson	RSA-J	3.3.88	31 Mar
7.85	-0.1	Hatem Mohamed	Mersal	EGY	20.1.75	5 May
7.85	0.2	Lucas	Jakubczyk	GER	28.4.85	6 May
7.85	0.8		Li Jinzhe	CHN-J	1.9.89	25 May
7.85	1.1	Barrett	Saunders	USA	27.3.85	25 May
7.85	-0.2	J.J.	Jegede	GBR	3.10.85	16 Jun
7.85	2.0	Michel	Tornéus	SWE	26.5.86	11 Aug
7.84i		Anton	Filatenkov	RUS	15.2.87	3 Feb
7.84		Tareq	Bougtaïb	MAR	30.4.81	29 Aor
7.84	1.0	Matt	Turner	USA	21.7.86	12 May
7.84	0.3	Sergio	dos Santos	BRA	13.5.76	19 May
7.84	1.7	Roman	Sebrle	CZE	26.11.74	26 May
7.84	0.5	Michal	Lukasiak	POL	7.3.84	23 Jun
7.84A	-2.0	Daimnler	Griego	COL	12.3.84	30 Jun
7.84	1.1	Gerri	PUarson	EST	1.6.84	1 Aug
7.83	1.7	Desmond	Hamilton	USA		12 May
7.83	0.6	Salah Abdelaziz	Al Haddad	KUW	7.4.86	21 Jun
7.83		Ahmed	Houmida	MAR	29.10.83	30 Jun
7.83	0.9	Tyrone	Harris	USA		15 Jul
7.83	0.5	Olivier	Huet	FRA-J	11.2.89	21 Jul
7.83		Hugo	Chila	ECU	22.7.87	8 Dec
7.82i		Buford	Williams	USA	9.1.85	7 Jan
7.82i		Adrian	Vasile	ROM	9.4.86	27 Jan
7.82		Chris	Kirk	GBR	6.9.85	5 May
7.82	0.7	Atanas	Rusenov	BUL	30.8.81	10 Jun
7.82	1.2	Thiago	Dias	BRA	2.3.84	21 Jun
7.82	0.7	Viktor	Gushchinskiy	RUS	12.8.78	3 Jul
7.82	1.1		Li Xin	CHN	2.7.81	7 Jul
7.82	0.4		Tian Dan	CHN	7.11.85	7 Jul
7.82	1.3	Yohei	Sugai	JPN	30.8.85	16 Jul
7.81i		Damion	McLean	USA		27 Jan
7.81	0.1		Yan Ying	CHN	11.4.83	14 Apr
7.81	1.4	Andre	Black	USA	21.5.87	5 May
7.81	-3.2	Charles	Bailey	USA		12 May
7.81	1.8	Daniel	Roper	USA	26.9.84	13 May
7.81	1.6	Jaanus	Uudmäe	EST	24.12.80	29 May
7.81	0.0	Joan Lino	Martínez	ESP	17.3.78	4 Aug
7.81		Mohammad	Arzandeh	IRI	30.10.87	11 Sep
7.80			Hong Seung-nam	KOR	5.9.86	29 Apr
7.80	-1.9	Alain	Bailey	JAM	14.8.87	12 May
7.80	2.0	Bryan	Clay	USA	3.1.80	26 May
7.80	0.0	Marijo	Bakovic	CRO	11.4.82	20 Jun
7.80	0.0		Cai Peng	CHN	28.3.83	7 Jul
7.80	-0.2		Tsai Yi-Da (179)	TPE	20.5.84	15 Sep

Wind assisted

Mark	Wind	Name		Nat	Born	Pos	Meet	Venue	Date
8.41	3.8	Tommi	Evilä	FIN	6.4.80	1	v SWE	Göteborg	8 Sep
					6.01w	x	x	x	8.41w p
8.37	2.4	Dwight	Phillips	USA	1.10.77	1	Aragón	Zaragoza	28 Jul

8.36 2.3 1 NC Indianapolis 22 Jun above
8.35 2.2 2 Pre Eugene 10 Jun see above
8.28 3.0 1 ModR Modesto 5 May 8.28w x 8.20/1.8 p x 8.10/1.0

Mark	Wind	Name		Nat	Born	Pos	Meet	Venue	Date
8.35	5.4	Tareq	Bougtaïb	MAR	30.4.81	1		Khémisset	14 Jul
8.34	2.5	Gable	Garenamotse	BOT	28.2.77	1		Bad Langensalza	7 Jul
					x		8.34w	8.09/0.6 8.12/1.5 7.93	8.18/1.4
8.26	3.1	Jadel	Gregório	BRA	16.9.80	2	GP	Dakar	28 Apr
8.26	w?	Thiago	Dias	BRA	2.3.84	1		São Paulo (Guarujá)	22 Jul
8.26	2.8	Trevell	Quinley	USA	16.1.83	2	Aragón	Zaragoza	28 Jul
8.15	2.2	Robert	Crowther	AUS	2.8.87	1		Cairns	17 Jun
8.11	3.3	Aarik	Wilson	USA	25.10.82	5	NC	Indianapolis	22 Jun
8.08A	3.3	Bashir	Ramzy	USA	4.5.79	Q		Provo	2 Jun
8.05	2.8	Nathan	Morgan	GBR	30.6.78	2		Salamanca	4 Jul
8.05	5.2	Salah Abdelaziz	Al-Haddad	KUW	7.4.86	2	AsiC	Amman	26 Jul
8.04	2.6	Jonathan	Moore	GBR	31.5.84	3		Salamanca	4 Jul
8.04	2.4	Hatem	Mersal	EGY	20.1.75	3		Nuoro	11 Jul
8.02	w?	Mauro	da Silva	BRA	26.12.86	2		São Paulo (Guarajá)	22 Jul
8.01	4.2	Chris	Gillis	USA	16.11.83	1		Fayetteville	4 May
8.00	5.3	Juho-Matti	Pimiä	FIN	28.12.84	2	v SWE	Göteborg	8 Sep
7.99	3.2	Héctor	Fuentes	CUB-J	19.5.88	1	NC/Barr	La Habana	25 May
7.97	2.8	Jairo	Guibert	CUB	22.2.84	2	NC/Barr	La Habana	25 May
7.97	3.6	Astérios	Noúsios	GRE	25.2.79	2		Thessaloniki	30 Jul
7.97	2.6	Petteri	Lax	FIN	12.10.85	1	NC	Lappeenranta	4 Aug
7.96	4.3	Ibrahin	Camejo	CUB	28.6.82	4	NC/Barr	La Habana	25 May
7.94	3.0	Norris	Frederick	USA	17.2.86	1	NCAA-r	Eugene	25 May
7.93	3.9	Matt	Turner	USA	21.7.86	2	NCAA-r	Eugene	25 May
7.92	3.1	Naohiro	Shinada	JPN	10.2.86	1		Tokyo	16 Sep

7.88	3.2	Randall	Flimmons	USA		24 May
7.87	3.1	Barrett	Saunders	USA	27.3.85	6 Apr
7.87	3.1	Yohei	Sugai	JPN	30.8.85	30 Apr
7.85	4.3	Eric	Babb	USA	10.5.85	21 Apr
7.85	2.6	Stanley	Gbabeke	NGR-J	24.7.89	19 May
7.85	2.4	Kazushi	Saeki	JPN	29.1.80	18 Aug
7.83	2.5	Andre	Black	USA	21.5.87	21 Apr
7.83	2.8		Hong Seung-nam	KOR	5.9.86	29 Apr
7.83	2.5	Nicola	Trentin	ITA	20.6.74	11 Jul
7.83	4.1	Corey	Vinson	USA		14 Jul
7.82	2.2	Janis	Karlivans	LAT	2.6.82	26 May
7.82	5.8	Daisuke	Komori	JPN	5.6.84	8 Sep
7.81	4.1	Francoesco	Agresti	ITA	20.10.77	11 Jul
7.80	4.2	Jefferson	Sabino	BRA	4.11.82	6 May
7.80	3.8	Dermillo	Wise	USA	7.11.83	13 May
7.80	3.2	Stefano	Tremigliozzi	ITA	7.5.85	26 May

Best at low altitude

8.28	0.6	Mokoena	Q	WCh	Osaka	29 Aug
	8.32w	2.6	1	GP	Dakar	28 Apr
8.03	0.0	Allen	4	Aragón	Zaragoza	28 Jul
7.98	1.0	Ramzy	7	NC	Indianapolis	22 Jun
7.86	0.5	Vieira				27 May
7.81	0.8	Chila				7 Jun

Best outdoors

8.01	1.8	Sdiri	2		Sotteville	5 Jun
7.95	0.9	Fivaz	1		Génève	9 Jun
7.94	0.0	Vasylyev	1		Kyiv	25 May
7.89	0.6	Donato				30 Sep
7.88	1.9	Gillis				23 Mar
7.91	0.5	Gomis	1	NC	Niort	5 Aug
7.90	0.6	Noúsios	4	Veniz	Haniá	9 Jun
7.96w	3.2	Jensen	1	MAI	Malmö	2 Jul
7.87	2.0	Jensen				2 Jul
7.85w	2.9	Belt				6 Apr

JUNIORS

See main list for top 5 juniors. 11 performances by 6 men to 7.89. Additional marks and further juniors:

Noffke	7.97	1.3	2	NC	Brisbane	11 Mar
	7.93	1.7	5		Salamanca	4 Jul
	7.89	1.9	*		Canberra	27 Jan
Zhang	8.03i		1		Shanghai	16 Mar
	7.90	0.0	1		Urumqi	19 Sep

7.89	0.0		Weng Yongfeng	CHN-J	18.1.89	4		Wuhan	7 Jul
7.85	1.2	Keenan	Watson	RSA-J	3.3.88	1		Durban	31 Mar
7.85	0.8		Li Jinzhe	CHN-J	1.9.89	1		Zhengzhou	25 May
7.83	0.5	Olivier	Huet	FRA-J	11.2.89	Q	EJ	Hengelo	21 Jul
7.78		Luis F.	Gutiérrez (10)	CUB	1.9.88	4		La Habana	15 Jun
7.75	1.7	Sumito	Minakawa	JPN-Y	26.9.90	1		Saga	4 Aug
7.73i		Michael	Morrison	USA	18.3.88	1		Lexington	23 Feb
7.73	0.4	Stanislav	Ionov	RUS	27.11.88	2	NC-j	Sochi	22 May
7.72i		Dmitriy	Abramov	RUS	.88	1		Sankt Peterburg	20 Jan
7.69	0.8	Daisuke	Yoshiyama	JPN-Y	17.10.90	2		Kofu	15 Jun
7.68	1.3	Tiberiu	Talnar	ROM	16.2.88	1		Bucuresti	12 Aug
7.67i			Zhao Xiaoxi	CHN	19.3.89	1		Shanghai	16 Mar
7.67A	1.2	Ethan	Alexander	RSA	27.1.88	7		Pretoria	13 Apr
7.65	0.8	Emeka	Okoli	NGR	13.7.90	2	NC	Lagos	19 May

Wind assisted 7 performances by two men to 7.90

Noffke	8.05	2.9	1		Sydney	13 Jan
	8.04	4.3	1		Canberra	27 Jan
	7.98	2.4	2		Brisbane	25 Feb
	7.96	5.5	5	Aragón	Zaragoza	28 Jul
	7.91	4.5	1		Sydney	17 Feb
	7.90	3.6	1		Brisbane	21 Jan

7.99	3.2	Héctor	Fuentes	CUB	19.5.88	1	NC/Barr	La Habana	25 May
7.85	2.6	Stanley	Gbabeke	NGR-J	24.7.89	1	NC	Lagos	19 May
7.74		Derrick	Locke	USA		1		Moore	5 May
7.72	2.9	Yasumichi	Konishi	JPN-Y	13.4.90	2		Saga	4 Aug
7.66	2.2	Zedric	Thomas	USA	21.3.88	1		Baton Rouge	5 May

MEN 2007

TRIPLE JUMP

Mark	Wind	Name	Nat	Born	Pos	Meet	Venue	Date	Series
17.90	0.4	Jadel Gregório	BRA	16.9.80	1	GP	Belém	20 May	17.66/-0.4 x 17.47/0.0 p 17.90 x
17.70	1.1				1	NC	São Paulo	24 Jun	x 16.80 p 17.19 16.15 17.70
17.59	0.3				2	WCh	Osaka	27 Aug	16.68 17.00/-0.6 x 15.09 17.59 17.28/0.6
17.74	1.4	Nelson Évora	POR	20.4.84	1	WCh	Osaka	27 Aug	17.41/0.3 x 17.74 p x 17.39/-1.7
17.51	1.8				1	GP	Madrid	21 Jul	x 17.18/1.2 x 17.26/1.8 x 17.51
17.35w	2.4				1	ECp-1B	Milano	24 Jun	17.05/1.3 x x17.35w
17.58	1.6	Aarik Wilson	USA	25.10.82	1	LGP	London (CP)	3 Aug	16.51 17.58 17.04/1.7 17.19/0.7 x x
17.50	1.0				1		Daegu	3 Oct	17.10 17.34/1.2 17.50/1.4 17.50/1.0 17.39/0.3 17.38/0.5
17.41	0.3				1	Spitzen	Luzern	28 Jun	17.41 x 16.91 16.87 16.79 16.76
17.34	0.6				2	WAF	Stuttgart	22 Sep	x x 16.94 17.34
17.31	0.6				5	WCh	Osaka	27 Aug	16.89 17.21 x 15.35 17.07 17.31
17.56i		Phillips Idowu	GBR	30.12.78	1	EI	Birmingham	3 Mar	17.56 17.25 p 14.12 16.47 x
17.35	0.9				1	Bisl	Oslo	15 Jun	17.21 17.35 16.52 p 16.81 x
17.56	-0.2	Christian Olsson	SWE	25.1.80	1	Gaz	Saint-Denis	6 Jul	17.25 17.42/-0.6 17.56 p p p
17.44i					1		Karlsruhe	11 Feb	17.16 16.92 17.17 17.44 p x
17.34i					1		Birmingham	17 Feb	x x 17.34 p p x
17.33	1.2				2	Bisl	Oslo	15 Jun	17.33 x x 17.30 x 16.95
17.33	1.1				1	ECp-1A	Vaasa	24 Jun	17.11/-0.2 17.33 p x
17.52	1.0	Osniel Tosca	CUB	30.6.84	1	ALBA	Caracas	10 May	17.09 x 17.15 p 15.73 17.52
17.39	1.4				2	Kuso	Warszawa	17 Jun	16.98 17.13 x 17.39 x x
17.35	0.3				2	GP	Belém	20 May	16.98 x 17.17 16.96 17.23 17.35
17.32	1.1				4	WCh	Osaka	27 Aug	16.71 x 17.32 x 17.20 17.27
17.31	0.5				2	Spitzen	Luzern	28 Jun	17.31 17.16 17.09 17.03 16.95 16.94
17.48	1.5	Danil Burkenya	RUS	20.7.78	1	Kuso	Warszawa	17 Jun	x 17.48 17.05 p x x
17.47i		Nathan Douglas	GBR	4.12.82	2	EI	Birmingham	3 Mar	17.08 17.22 17.47 x 17.41 x
17.43	0.0	Randy Lewis	GRN	14.10.80	3	LGP	London (CP)	3 Aug	17.02 17.22 x 17.06 x 17.43
17.40w	2.4				2	GP	Madrid	21 Jul	x 15.33w 17.09w 17.40w 17.24w 17.07
17.39i		David Giralt	CUB	26.8.84	1		Samara	3 Feb	17.37 17.23 17.39 x p p
17.37	2.0	Tareq Bougtaïb	MAR	30.4.81	1		Khémisset	14 Jul	
17.35	1.3	Dmitrij Valukevic	SVK	31.5.81	1		Kaunas	25 Jul	17.14 17.17 16.94w x x 17.35
17.35	0.7	Walter Davis	USA	2.7.79	1	WAF	Stuttgart	22 Sep	16.52 17.16 x 17.35
17.33	1.0				3	WCh	Osaka	27 Aug	17.33 x x x 17.22 x
17.32	-1.8	Marian Oprea	ROM	6.6.82	1	DNG	Stockholm	7 Aug	17.17 17.32 17.09 p p 17.24
		(31/14)							
17.30	0.0	Mykola Savolaynen	UKR	25.3.80	1		Kyiv	24 May	
17.29	1.6	Aleksandr Petrenko	RUS	8.2.83	1	ECp-S	München	24 Jun	
17.27	0.6	Zhong Minwei	CHN	9.4.87	1		Jinan	15 Jun	
17.26	1.9	Kenta Bell	USA	16.3.77	1		Clermont	8 Jun	
17.23	0.9	Leevan Sands	BAH	16.8.81	•	LGP	London (CP)	3 Aug	
17.15i		Aleksandr Sergeyev	RUS	29.7.83	3	EI	Birmingham	3 Mar	
		(20)							
17.13	1.7	Viktor Yastrebov	UKR	13.1.82	1		Kyiv	5 Aug	
17.13	1.9	Alexander Martínez	SUI	23.8.77	1		La Chaux de Fonds	12 Aug	
17.12i		Yoandri Betanzos	CUB	15.2.82	2		Samara	3 Feb	
17.11	-2.6	Gu Junjie	CHN	5.5.85	1	WCT	Suzhou	10 Jun	
17.10	1.4	Allen Simms	PUR	26.7.82	1		Carolina	17 Mar	
17.10	-0.4	Julien Kapek	FRA	12.1.79	1	NC	Niort	4 Aug	
17.10	1.7	Anton Andersson	SWE	12.3.81	1	NC	Eskilstuna	12 Aug	
17.09i		Yevgeniy Plotnir	RUS	26.6.77	2	NC	Volgograd	10 Feb	
17.07	0.9	Yoelbi Quesada	CUB	4.8.73	5	NC/Barr	La Habana	26 May	
17.04	-0.3	Renjith Maheswary	IND	30.1.86	1		Guwahati	23 Jun	
		(30)							
17.03	0.6	Wu Bo	CHN	17.6.84	2		Jinan	15 Jun	
17.02	0.7	Kim Duk-hyung	KOR	8.12.85	1	WUG	Bangkok	14 Aug	
17.01	1.7	Zhu Shujing	CHN	24.5.85	1		Guangzhou	25 Jul	
16.99	0.1	Dimítrios Tsiámis	GRE	12.1.82	4	ECp-S	München	24 Jun	
16.97	1.2	Lawrence Willis	USA	12.7.81	2	NC	Indianapolis	24 Jun	

Mark	Wind	Name		Nat	Born	Pos	Meet	Venue	Date
16.97	1.8	Fabrizio	Donato	ITA	14.8.76	1	NC	Padova	28 Jul
16.96	0.4	Pawel	Kruhlik	POL	25.8.83	1		Biala Podlaska	2 Jun
16.95	-0.1	Viktor	Gushchinskiy	RUS	12.8.78	1	Kuts	Moskva	12 Aug
16.94	2.0	Rafeeq	Curry	USA	19.8.83	1		Ried/Innkreis	28 Jul
16.94	0.0	Viktor	Kuznetsov	UKR	14.7.86	2	WUG	Bangkok	14 Aug
		(40)							
16.91	1.6	Konstadínos	Zalaggítis	GRE	13.12.80	8	GP	Madrid	21 Jul
16.90	1.8	Jefferson	Dias Sabino	BRA	4.11.82	1		São Paulo	13 Jun
16.90	0.9	Yevgen	Semenenko	UKR	17.7.84	2		Yalta	14 Jun
16.90	0.2	Takanori	Sugibayashi	JPN	14.3.76	1	NC	Osaka	30 Jun
16.89	1.9	Yordanis	Durañona	CUB-J	16.6.88	1		Santiago de Cuba	27 Jun
16.87	0.0	Alexis	Copello	CUB	12.8.85	2		La Habana	17 Mar
16.86	-1.3	Tosin	Oke	GBR	1.10.80	4	LGP	London (CP)	3 Aug
16.85	-0.9	Jacek	Kazimierowski	POL	7.2.74	5	ECp-S	München	24 Jun
16.84	0.4		Li Yanxi	CHN	26.6.84	3	NC	Shijiazhuang	5 Aug
16.81i		Michaël	Velter	BEL	21.3.80	1		Gent	27 Jan
		(50)							
16.81	-0.1	Colomba	Fofana	FRA	11.4.77	6	ECp-S	München	24 Jun
16.80	0.0	Ndiss Kaba	Badji	SEN	21.9.83	1	AfG	Alger	19 Jul
16.76	-0.1	Roman	Valiyev	KAZ	27.3.84	2		Guwahati	23 Jun
16.75A	0.8	Khotso	Mokoena	RSA	6.3.85	1		Secunda	26 Jan
16.75	-0.9	Leonardo	dos Santos	BRA	7.5.84	1	GP	Rio de Janeiro	13 May
16.75	0.1	Lyukman	Adams	RUS-J	12.6.88	1	NC-j	Sochi	24 May
16.74	0.4	Alwyn	Jones	AUS	28.2.85	*	NC	Brisbane	9 Mar
16.74	-0.3	Marc	Kellman	USA	6.6.83	4	NC	Indianapolis	24 Jun
16.73		Vladimir	Chicherov	RUS	2.4.85	2		Moskva	16 May
16.73	0.2		Cui Lifu	CHN-J	18.12.88	1		Wuhan	1 Nov
		(60)							
16.72i		Andreas	Pohle	GER	6.4.81	1	NC	Leipzig	18 Feb
16.72		Hugo	Mamba-Schlick	CMR	1.2.82	1	NC	Bafoussam	12 Aug
16.72		Amarjeet	Singh	IND	1.5.81	2		Bhubaneswar	7 Oct
16.70		Younés	Moudrik	MAR	1010.77	2		Khémissed	14 Jul
16.69i		Klim	Vorobyev	RUS	25.3.84	4	NC	Volgograd	10 Feb
16.68i		Paolo	Camossi	ITA	6.1.74	1		Celje	19 Jan
16.68		Dmitriy	Kolosov	RUS	8.6.86	3		Moskva	16 May
16.67	0.1	Ilya	Yefremov	RUS-J	20.3.88	2		Sochi	24 May
16.66	-0.4	Vasyl	Nishchyk	UKR	13.3.83	2		Kyiv	20 May
16.66	0.7	Mateusz	Parlicki	POL	14.4.84	*	Kuso	Warszawa	17 Jun
		(70)							
16.64i		Karl	Taillepierre	FRA	13.8.76	1	NC	Aubière	17 Feb
16.63i		Petar	Ivanov	BUL	5.9.85	1		Sofia	27 Jan
16.63	1.5	Anton	Boltenkov	RUS	29.6.85	3		Sochi	27 May
16.62	0.6	Benjamin	Compaoré	FRA	5.8.87	1		Forbach	27 May
16.62		Dmitriy	Platnitskiy	BLR-J	26.8.88	Q	WUG	Bangkok	13 Aug
16.61	1.3	Michele	Boni	ITA	2.4.81	1		Jesolo	25 May
16.61	0.0	Héctor	Fuentes	CUB-J	19.5.88	1	PAm-J	São Paulo	8 Jul
16.61	1.3		Chen Jinsen	CHN	16.10.85	2		Guangzhou	24 Jul
16.60	0.7	Fabrizio	Schembri	ITA	27.1.81	2		Jesolo	25 May
16.59	0.6	Bibu	Mathew	IND	30.3.81	*	AsiC	Amman	29 Jul
		(80)							
16.59	-0.1	Yuriy	Zhuravlyev	RUS	25.5.85	4	WUG	Bangkok	14 Aug
16.58	-0.3	Charles Michael	Friedek	GER	26.8.71	1		Garbsen	20 May
16.58	1.4	Arius	Filet	FRA	17.12.77	2		Bron	11 Jul
16.56i		Sébastien	Pincemail	FRA	21.2.79	4	NC	Aubière	17 Feb
16.56	1.9	Jaanus	Uudmäe	EST	24.12.80	1		Fayetteville	4 May
16.54	1.2	Dmitriy	Detsuk	BLR	9.4.85	1		Minsk	14 Jun
16.54i		Mantas	Dilys	LTU	30.3.84	1	NC	Kaunas	10 Feb
16.54i		Aleksey	Musikhin	RUS	8.11.75	5	NC	Volgograd	10 Feb
16.53i		Teddy	Tamgho	FRA-J	15.6.89	1		Eaubonne	23 Dec
16.51	1.6	Marcelo	da Costa	BRA	1.5.81	1		São José do Rio Preto	17 Mar
		(90)							
16.51	1.1	Julian	Golley	GBR	12.9.71	1		Budapest	7 Jul
16.51	0.5		Jia Yingli	CHN	16.2.84	5	NC	Shijiazhuang	5 Aug
16.50	0.5	Stanislav	Syachinov	RUS	24.9.82	1		Vladivostok	3 Jun
16.49	1.3	Nikólaos	Dontás	GRE	8.4.86	1	NC-23	Thessaloniki	30 Jun
16.49		Mohamed Youssef	Al-Shahabi	BRN-J	26.7.89	1		Manama	7 Oct
16.45		Alex	Thomas	IND	16.4.79	1		Guwahati	15 Feb
16.45		Zafar	Iqbal	PAK	10.4.82	1	NC	Karachi	12 Apr
16.45	-0.4	Mohamed	Hazouri	SYR	.83	5		Guwahati	23 Jun
16.45	1.8	Marius-Alin	Anghel	ROM	13.5.86	1	BalkC	Sofia	4 Jul

Mark	Wind	Name		Nat	Born	Pos	Meet	Venue	Date
16.44	1.8	Theerayut (100)	Philakong	THA	27.2.84	1	SEAG	Nakhon Ratchasima	7 Dec

16.43	0.3	Hugo	Chila	ECU	22.7.87	20 May
16.43	0.7	Larry	Achike	GBR	31.1.75	10 Jun
16.42	0.3	Igor	Spasovkhodskiy	RUS	1.8.79	3 Aug
16.41	1.8		Zhao Peng	CHN	8.12.85	22 Jul
16.41	0.4		Jiang Wei	CHN-J	16.5.89	14 Aug
16.41	-0.3		Kim Dong-hyun	KOR-J	5.6.89	17 Aug
16.40	1.5	Michael	Perry	AUS	30.9.77	9 Mar
16.40	0.8	Brandon	Rhoulac	USA	13.12.83	18 Mar
16.40	0.0	Andrejs	Batagelj	SLO	9.9.80	3 Jun
16.40	1.0	Thomas	Moede	GER	26.7.77	3 Jun
16.40	1.4	Osviel	Hernández	CUB-J	.89	28 Jun
16.39i		Andrés	Capellán	ESP	10.6.85	18 Feb
16.39i			Kong Guanyong	CHN-J	18.3.88	20 Mar
16.39	1.2	Stanislav	Ionov	RUS-J	27.11.88	24 May
16.39	0.2	Anders	Møller	DEN	5.9.77	25 Aug
16.38		Afshin	Daghri Hemadi	IRI	15.7.78	8 May
16.37i		Jaroslav	Dobrovodsky	SVK	13.12.84	28 Jan
16.37i		Pávlos	Galaktiádis	GRE	15.5.84	11 Feb
16.36	0.2	Thiago	Dias	BRA	2.3.84	16 May
16.36	1.7	Davy	Manga	FRA	6.5.83	26 May
16.35		Roger	Haitengi	NAM	12.9.83	31 Mar
16.35		Tuan	Wreh	LBR	23.11.79	5 May
16.34		Alonzo	Moore	USA	17.1.83	5 May
16.34	1.4	Hirotaka	Horiuchi	JPN	8.2.86	21 Jul
16.34i		Yevgeniy	Ektov	KAZ	1.9.86	1 Nov
16.33i		Wilbert	Walker	JAM	7.1.85	10 Feb
16.33	0.6	Muhammad	Halim	USA		6 May
16.33	0.8	Alexandr	Petrov	RUS	8.9.86	20 Jun
16.33	-0.2	Gary	White	GBR	16.6.85	15 Jul
16.32	1.0	Andrew	Owusu	GHA	8.7.72	19 Jul
16.31i		Aleksandr	Vorobey	BLR	28.12.81	27 Jan
16.31	1.6	Samyr	Laine	USA	17.7.84	21 Apr
16.31	1.0	Aleksey	Tsapik	BLR-J	4.8.88	18 Aug
16.30i		Daniel	Donovici	ROM	5.3.80	11 Feb
16.30A	-0.9	Tumelo	Thagane	RSA	3.7.84	9 Mar
16.30	0.7	Sergey	Yarmak	RUS	21.3.86	27 May
16.30	0.7	Abdoulaye	Diarra	FRA-J	27.5.88	19 Jul
16.29i		Andre	Black	USA	21.5.87	10 Mar
16.29	1.0	Dmytro	Tyden	UKR	17.1.86	14 Jun
16.29	-0.6	Adrian	Swiderski	POL	27.9.86	15 Jul
16.28	0.5	Johan	Meriluoto	FIN	22.3.74	9 Sep
16.26		Mike	Whitehead	USA	13.6.85	4 May
16.25	1.8		Dong Bin	CHN-J	22.11.88	27 May
16.25	1.8	(144)	Ko Dae-young	KOR	15.2.85	11 Oct

Wind assisted

17.55	2.5	Leevan	Sands	BAH	16.8.81	2	LGP	London (CP)	3 Aug
					16.78 17.16 17.55w 17.23 16.03 16.76				
17.41	3.5	Aleksandr	Petrenko	RUS	8.2.83	1	Veniz	Haniá	9 Jun
					x 17.02w x 17.41w x p				
17.21	5.4	Yoandri	Betanzos	CUB	15.2.82	2	NC/Barr	La Habana	26 May
17.19	2.5	Renjith	Maheswary	IND	30.1.86	1	AsiC	Amman	29 Jul
17.18	2.2	Viktor	Yastrebov	UKR	13.1.82	4	Kuso	Warszawa	17 Jun
17.15	2.6	Alexis	Copello	CUB	12.8.85	4	NC/Barr	La Habana	26 May
17.09	2.5		Wu Bo	CHN	17.6.84	1		Guangzhou	24 Jul
17.06	3.5	Fabrizio	Donato	ITA	14.8.76	1		Barletta	6 Sep
17.03	2.4		Kim Duk-hyung	KOR	8.12.85	1		Kwangju	11 Oct
16.85	4.6	Mateusz	Parlicki	POL	14.4.84	1		Warszawa	27 May
16.80	3.8	Alwyn	Jones	AUS	28.2.85	1	NC	Brisbane	9 Mar
16.78	5.0	Jaanus	Uudmäe	EST	24.12.80	1		Fayetteville	21 Apr
16.71	2.8	Kazuyoshi	Ishikawa	JPN	6.11.82	1		Gifu	23 Sep
16.64	5.2	Bibu	Mathew	IND	30.3.81	3	AsiC	Amman	29 Jul
16.60	6.3	Mohamed	Hazouri	SYR	.83	4	AsiC	Amman	29 Jul
16.58	3.6	Carl	White	USA	10.2.82	1		Abilene	24 Mar
16.55	4.0	Andrew	Owusu	GHA	8.7.72	1		Nashville	21 Apr

16.44	2.3	Davy	Manga	FRA	6.5.83	28 Apr
16.42	2.4	Teddy	Tamgho	FRA-J	15.6.89	12 May
16.41	2.6	Dennis	Fernández	CUB	23.1.86	26 May
16.39	4.6	Tuan	Wreh	LBR	23.11.79	14 Jul
16.38	6.2	Jason	Kidza-Sewenyana	RSA	3.1.82	31 Mar
16.37	2.1	Thiago	Dias	BRA	2.3.84	7 Mar
16.37	4.1	Shardae	Boutte	USA	2.10.85	21 Apr
16.37	2.4	Rayon	Taylor	JAM	11.4.86	9 Jun
16.32	2.8	Abdenor	Benaldjia	FRA	18.3.83	22 Jul
16.30	3.5	Johan	Meriluoto	FIN	22.3.74	20 Jun
16.29	4.6		Yang Yang	CHN-J	23.6.89	24 Jul
16.27A	2.8	Martin	Eriksson	SWE	15.6.71	14 Jul
16.27	3.7		Liu Zhiqiang	CHN		24 Jul
16.27	2.8		Yoo Jae-hyuk	KOR-J	13.5.89	11 Oct

Best outdoors

17.35	0.9	Idowu	1	Bisl	Oslo	15 Jun
17.18	1.2	Douglas	4	Bisl	Oslo	15 Jun
17.10	0.8	Giralt	1		Kortrijk	13 Jul
		17.18w 2.2	3	NC/Barr	La Habana	26 May
16.96	0.0	Betanzos	3		Baie Mahault	1 May
16.88	0.0	Plotnir	3	NC	Tula	3 Aug
		16.96w 3.4	1	ECCp	Albufeira	27 May
16.83	-1.0	Sergeyev	3	Znam	Zhukovskiy	9 Jun
16.72	1.4	Pohle	1		Zeulenroda	3 Jun
16.68	0.3	Vorobyev	5	NC	Tula	3 Aug
16.56	1.9	Camossi	2		Barletta	6 Sep
16.50		Velter	3		Liège (NX)	25 Jul
16.48	-0.1	Dilys	2		Kaunas	25 Jul
16.45	0.8	Pincemail	3		Bron	11 Jul

16.37	1.0	Capellán	14 Jul
16.35	-0.3	Tamgho	20 Jul
16.30	0.3	Vorobey	24 Jun
16.27	0.0	Donovici	27 Jul
16.26	2.0	Ektov	6 Jul
16.25	0.8	Black	26 May

JUNIORS

See main list for top 8 juniors. 10 performances by 7 men to 16.59. Additional marks and further juniors:

Durañona	16.78	-0.4	6	NC/Barr	La Habana	26 May	16.70	1	La Habana	7 Jun
Adams	16.63	0.5	4	Znam	Zhukovskiy	9 Jun				
Plotnitskiy	16.59	1.4	1		Biala Podlaska	24 Jun				

16.41	0.4		Jiang Wei	CHN	16.5.89	6	WUG	Bangkok	14 Aug
16.41	-0.3	(10)	Kim Dong-hyun	KOR	5.6.89	1		Andong	17 Aug
16.40	1.4	Osviel	Hernández	CUB	.89	2		Santiago de Cuba	28 Jun
16.39i			Kong Guanyong	CHN	18.3.88	2		Beijing	20 Mar
16.39	1.2	Stanislav	Ionov	RUS	27.11.88	3		Sochi	24 May
16.31	1.0	Aleksey	Tsapik	BLR	4.8.88	1	v3N-j	Valmiera	18 Aug
16.30	0.7	Abdoulaye	Diarra	FRA	27.5.88	Q	EJ	Hengelo	19 Jul

Mark		Name		Nat	Born	Pos	Meet	Venue		Date
16.25	1.8		Dong Bin	CHN	22.11.88	2	NC-j	Zhengzhou		27 May
16.23	0.6		Ma Le	CHN	26.4.88	Q	NC-j	Zhengzhou		26 May
16.23	0.9	Zuheir	Sharif	USA	7.10.88	2	PAm-J	São Paulo		8 Jul
16.23	-0.3	Luis F.	Gutiérrez	CUB	1.9.88	1		São Paulo		6 Aug
16.22	0.3	Yeóryios	Tsákonas (20)	GRE	22.1.88	3	NC	Athína		15 Jun
		16.23w 2.2				8	Veniz	Haniá		9 Jun
Best out: 16.35	-0.3	Teddy	Tamgho	FRA	15.6.89	4	EJ	Hengelo		20 Jul
Wind assisted										
16.42	2.4	Teddy	Tamgho	FRA	15.6.89	4		Montgeron		12 May
16.29	4.6		Yang Yang	CHN	23.6.89	3		Guangzhou		24 Jul
16.27	2.8		Yoo Jae-hyuk	KOR	13.5.89	1	NG-j	Kwangju		11 Oct

SHOT

Mark		Name		Nat	Born	Pos	Meet	Venue		Date
22.43		Reese	Hoffa	USA	8.10.77	1	LGP	London (CP)		3 Aug
					21.35	21.33	x	21.32	21.58	22.43
22.04	1	WCh	Osaka	25 Aug	21.81	21.61	22.04	x	21.91	21.58
21.84	1	AlabR	Tuscaloosa	25 Mar	20.74	x	21.19	x	21.23	21.84
21.77	1	GS	Ostrava	27 Jun	21.55	21.77	21.41	x	x	21.35
21.75i	2	Mill	New York	2 Feb	20.78	21.50	21.75	x		
21.65	2	Pre	Eugene	10 Jun	20.68	21.65	x	x	x	x
21.47	1	NC	Indianapolis	23 Jun	21.38	21.43	21.26	21.15	21.47	x
21.47	1	City S	Cork	30 Jun	20.95	x	x	20.90	21.47	x
21.37	1	SGP	Doha	11 May	20.25	20.70	20.97	21.37		
21.36	3	adidas	Carson	20 May	20.83	21.23	21.31	20.69	x	21.36
21.32i	1		Valencia	10 Feb	20.75	20.97	20.98	21.26	x	21.32
21.31i	1		Nordhausen	19 Jan	20.07	21.25	21.31	x	20.74	x
21.30	1	GP	Gorée Island	27 Apr	20.94	x	21.30	20.43	x	21.12
21.96		Christian	Cantwell	USA	30.9.80	1	adidas	Carson		20 May
					20.69	21.96	20.87	20.84	x	20.80
21.88i	1	Mill	New York	2 Feb	21.31	21.88	x	x		
21.83	1	Pre	Eugene	10 Jun	21.39	x	x	x	21.04	21.83
21.72i	1	NC	Boston	25 Feb	21.72	21.06	21.09	21.29	21.23	x
21.72	1	DrakeR	Des Moines	28 Apr	20.54	20.84	20.95	21.13	21.72	x
21.68	2	GS	Ostrava	27 Jun	21.35	20.92	x	21.68	x	x
21.66	2	LGP	London (CP)	3 Aug	20.67	x	x	x	x	21.66
21.43	1		Melbourne	6 Mar	19.81	20.05	19.85	20.55	20.45	21.43
21.36i	2	BIG	Boston	27 Jan	20.51	21.31	21.36	21.31		
21.31i	2		Valencia	10 Feb	19.90	19.96	21.12	20.97	x	21.31
21.30	1	ModR	Modesto	5 May	20.72	20.69	21.30	19.52	x	x
21.61		Joachim	Olsen	DEN	31.5.77	1		København		13 Jun
					20.84	x	21.61	20.62	20.82	20.89
21.61		Adam	Nelson	USA	7.7.75	2	WCh	Osaka		25 Aug
					21.47	21.61	x	x	x	x
21.47	2	adidas	Carson	20 May	x	21.47	x	x	20.76	x
21.57i		Dan	Taylor	USA	12.5.82	1	BIG	Boston (R)		27 Jan
					21.16	21.21	21.40	21.57		
21.57i		Mikulás	Konopka	SVK	23.1.79	1	EI	Birmingham		2 Mar
					21.32	21.57	x	21.36	21.14	21.40
21.27		Andrey	Mikhnevich	BLR	12.7.76	3	WCh	Osaka		25 Aug
		(30/7)			19.97	21.27	20.88	20.75	20.81	
21.19		Rutger	Smith	NED	9.7.81	3	LGP	London (CP)		3 Aug
21.00		Peter	Sack	GER	27.7.79	1		Schönebeck		10 Jun
20.87		Tomasz	Majewski	POL	30.8.81	5	WCh	Osaka		25 Aug
		(10)								
20.82i		Pavel	Lyzhin	BLR	24.3.81	2	EI	Birmingham		2 Mar
20.81		Russ	Winger	USA	2.8.84	4	Pre	Eugene		10 Jun
20.77		Anton	Lyuboslavskiy	RUS	26.6.84	1	NC	Tula		1 Aug
20.75		Ralf	Bartels	GER	21.2.78	1		Neuwied-Engers		27 Jun
20.72		Dylan	Armstrong	CAN	15.1.81	1	Jerome	Burnaby		8 Jun
20.69		Milan	Haborák	SVK	11.1.73	1		Szolnok		26 May
20.67		Miroslav	Vodovnik	SLO	11.9.77	6	WCh	Osaka		25 Aug
20.61		Sultan Abdulmajid	Al-Hebshi	KSA	23.2.83	1	UKR Ch	Donetsk		5 Jul
20.60		John	Godina	USA	31.5.72	1		Phoenix		7 Apr
20.60		Dorian	Scott	JAM	1.2.82	1	FlaR	Gainesville		7 Apr
		(20)								
20.56		Noah	Bryant	USA	11.5.84	1		Los Angeles		28 Apr
20.53		Robert	Häggblom	FIN	9.8.82	1		Lapua		11 Jul
20.52		Scott	Martin	AUS	12.10.82	4	GP	Madrid		21 Jul
20.47		Yuriy	Belov	BLR	20.3.81	1	ECp-1B	Milano		23 Jun
20.38		Pavel	Sofyin	RUS	4.9.81	1	Znam	Zhukovskiy		9 Jun

Mark	Name		Nat	Born	Pos	Meet	Venue	Date
20.35	Ryan	Whiting	USA	24.11.86	1		Tempe	28 Apr
20.35	Petr	Stehlik	CZE	15.4.77	1	Danek	Turnov	22 May
20.29	Jeff	Chakouian ¶	USA	20.4.82	3	ModR	Modesto	5 May
20.27i	Garrett	Johnson	USA	24.5.84	4	GP	Birmingham	17 Feb
20.24i	Sheldon	Battle	USA	23.6.83	4	NC	Boston (R)	25 Feb
	(30)							
20.22i	Dmitriy	Goncharuk	BLR	17.7.70	2	NC	Mogilev	8 Feb
20.21	Yves	Niaré	FRA	20.7.77	1		Chelles	23 May
20.21	Mika	Vasara	FIN	22.10.83	1		Eurajoki	13 Jun
20.20	Chang Ming-Huang		TPE	7.8.82	2		Neuwied-Engers	27 Jun
20.20	Yuriy	Bilonog	UKR	9.3.74	2	NC	Donetsk	5 Jul
20.18i	Maris	Urtans	LAT	9.2.81	1		Riga	3 Feb
20.11	Luka	Rujevic	SRB	14.10.85	1		Novi Sad	9 Jun
20.09i	Conny	Karlsson	FIN	30.12.75	6	EI	Birmingham	2 Mar
20.09	Hamza	Alic	BIH	20.1.79	1		Bar	1 May
20.07	Rhuben	Williams	USA	14.2.82	2		Tuscaloosa	25 Mar
	(40)							
20.06	Ivan	Yushkov	RUS	15.1.81	1		Adler	22 Apr
20.05	Sean	Shields	USA	10.2.83	2		La Jolla	21 Apr
20.01i	Gaëtan	Bucki	FRA	9.5.80	1		Mondeville	27 Jan
20.01	Nedzad	Mulabegovic	CRO	4.2.81	2		Zagreb	20 Jun
20.01	Maksim	Sidorov	RUS	11.5.86	1	WUG	Bangkok	14 Aug
19.98i	Steve	Manz	USA	19.9.81	1		Houston	10 Feb
19.96	Carl	Myerscough	GBR	21.10.79	2	ECp-S	München	23 Jun
19.95	Taavi	Peetre	EST	4.7.83	1		Valga	5 Jun
19.94	Mitchell	Pope	USA	21.1.84	1		Durham	6 May
19.93	Andriy	Semenov	UKR	4.7.84	1		Kyiv	25 Jul
	(50)							
19.91i	Gheorghe	Guset	ROM	28.5.68	1	NC	Bucuresti	10 Feb
19.90	Marco Antonio	Verni	CHI	27.2.76	1		Santiago	17 Mar
19.90	Andrey	Sinyakov	BLR	6.1.82	1		Minsk (Staiki)	28 Jul
19.88	Mark	Edwards	GBR	2.12.74	1		Loughborough	20 Jun
19.88	Antonin	Zalsky	CZE	7.8.80	1		Brno	25 Jul
19.87	Jakub	Giza	POL	26.9.85	1	EU23	Debrecen	12 Jul
19.85	Chris	Figures	USA	8.10.81	1		Los Angeles	21 Apr
19.84	Aleksandr	Grekov	RUS	6.5.85	1	NC-23	Tula	19 Jun
19.83	Lajos	Kürthy	HUN	22.10.86	1		Budapest	8 Jun
19.81	Vince	Mosca	USA	23.1.80	3		La Jolla	21 Apr
	(60)							
19.79	Dominik	Zielinski	POL	25.4.80	2eA		Halle	19 May
19.78	Andriy	Borodkin	UKR	18.4.78	2		Kyiv	3 Aug
19.76i	Detlef	Bock	GER	15.8.74	3		Nordhausen	19 Jan
19.76	Justin	Anlezark	AUS	14.8.77	1		Brisbane	17 Jun
19.75	Alexis	Paumier	CUB	21.1.75	1		La Habana	16 Feb
19.75	Carlos	Véliz	CUB	12.8.87	3	PAm	Rio de Janeiro	24 Jul
19.72	Milan	Jotanovic	SRB	11.1.84	1	NCAA-r	Gainesville	26 May
19.70	Navpreet	Singh	IND	15.6.78	1	AsiC	Amman	28 Jul
19.67	Germán	Lauro	ARG	2.4.84	1		Buenos Aires	26 May
19.66	Raigo	Toompuu	EST	17.7.81	1		Eagle Rock	12 May
	(70)							
19.63	Cory	Martin	USA	22.5.85	1	SEC	Tuscaloosa	13 May
19.57	Kevin	Bookout	USA	12.2.83	1		Fayetteville	21 Apr
19.57	Mehdi	Shahrokhi	IRI	23.5.85	1		Tehran	1 Jul
19.56	Zsolt	Bíber	HUN	31.5.76	3		Szolnok	26 May
19.56	Khaled Habash	Al-Suwaidi	QAT	10.10.84	1	PArabG	Cairo	21 Nov
19.52	Grigoriy	Panfilov	RUS	17.5.80	2	ECCp	Albufeira	26 May
19.52	Marco	Schmidt	GER	5.9.83	1		Kehl	30 Jun
19.52i	Bryan	Vickers	USA	14.1.85	1		Findlay	1 Dec
19.48	Manuel	Martínez	ESP	7.12.74	1		Rivas Vaciamadrid	29 Jun
19.47	Zack	Lloyd	USA	10.10.84	2		Tucson	16 Mar
	(80)							
19.44i	Westley	Stockbarger	USA	5.6.85	1	SEC	Lexington	24 Feb
19.44	Kresimir	Rada	CRO	3.11.81	1		Split	25 Feb
19.43	Jon	Kalnas	USA	18.4.80	1		Newark, DE	5 May
19.42	Georgi	Ivanov	BUL	13.3.85	2	BalkC	Sofia	5 Jul
19.42	Yasser	Ibrahim	EGY	2.5.84	3	PArabG	Cairo	21 Nov
19.40i	Ivan	Emilianov	MDA	19.2.77	1	NC	Chisinau	11 Feb
19.40i	Adam	Kuehl	USA	19.1.84	5	NCAA	Fayetteville	10 Mar
19.39	Will	Denbo	USA	24.2.84	2	Pac-10	Stanford	12 May
19.39	Daniel	Vanek	SVK	18.1.83	1	NC	Dubnica nad Váhom	1 Jul

Mark	Name		Nat	Born	Pos	Meet	Venue	Date
19.38i	Soslan	Tsirikhov	RUS	25.3.84	2	NC	Volgograd	9 Feb
	(90)							
19.36i	Shawn	Best	USA	4.9.84	6	NCAA	Fayetteville	10 Mar
19.34	Germán	Millán	ESP	21.5.79	1		La Laguna	14 Jul
19.33	Jamie	Beyer	USA	29.12.76	4		Cuxhaven	14 Jul
19.31	Janus	Robberts	RSA	10.3.79	1		Pretoria	9 Mar
19.30	Asmir	Kolasinac	SRB	15.10.84	2		Banja Luka	5 May
	19.40 dq for irregular entry				1		Sremska Mitrovica	2 Jun
19.29i	Seppo	Kujala	FIN	24.9.80	3	NC	Rovaniemi	18 Feb
19.29	Jesse	Roberge	USA	2.10.78	5	MSR	Walnut	15 Apr
19.24	Anthony	Greer	USA	22.10.83	Q	NCAA	Sacramento	7 Jun
19.24	Odinn Björn	Thorsteinsson	ISL	3.12.81	1		Hafnafjördur	16 Aug
19.23	John	Caulfield	USA	22.8.84	2		Los Angeles	28 Apr
	(100)							

Mark	Name		Nat	Born	Date
19.22i	Niklas	Arrhenius	SWE	10.9.82	17 Feb
19.22	Oleg	Korotkov	RUS	16.3.80	9 Jun
19.22	Andréas	Anastasópoulos	GRE	2.4.76	15 Jun
19.22		Guo Yanxiang	CHN	29.1.87	29 Oct
19.21i	Remigius	Machura	CZE	7.1.86	26 Jan
19.21i	Marco	Dodoni	ITA	5.9.72	10 Feb
19.20i	Marco	Di Maggio	ITA	22.5.83	18 Feb
19.20	Dragan	Peric	SRB	8.5.64	1 May
19.19	Tepa	Reinikainen	FIN	16.3.76	23 Jun
19.18	Ahmed Hassan	Gholoum	KUW	31.5.80	18 May
19.18	Marco	Fortes	POR	26.9.82	1 Jun
19.18	Sven-Eric	Hahn	GER	17.10.80	17 Jun
19.14	Miháil	Stamatóyiannis	GRE	20.5.82	9 Jun
19.13	Krzysztof	Krzywosz	POL	1.10.83	4 Aug
19.11i	Leszek	Sliwa	POL	20.9.79	11 Feb
19.11	Justin	Clickett	USA	12.4.85	9 Jun
19.10i	José María	Peña	ESP	18.8.82	17 Feb
19.10	Reinaldo	Proenza	CUB	20.11.84	8 Jun
19.08		Zhang Enqi	CHN	2.4.83	21 Apr
19.08	Jeremy	Silverman	USA	28.1.83	19 May
19.04	Brian	Hallett	USA	20.5.79	28 Apr
19.04		Yao Yongguang	CHN	6.1.83	2 Aug
19.02	Roelie	Potgieter	RSA	20.3.80	19 Jul
19.01	Kim	Christensen	DEN	1.4.84	12 May
19.01	Paolo	Capponi	ITA	25.3.76	23 Jun
19.00i	Aleksandr	Lobynya	RUS	31.5.84	21 Jan
19.00	Daniel	Anglés	ESP	11.4.85	29 Jun
19.00	Dubravko	Brdovcak	CRO	25.3.78	28 Jul
18.98i	Kyle	Helf	CAN	17.3.86	24 Feb
18.98i		Zhang Qi	CHN	2.4.84	21 Mar
18.96	Steve	Marcelle	USA	9.9.86	12 May
18.96	Dave	Adamek	CAN	6.2.84	26 May
18.95i	David	Nichols	USA	13.1.85	24 Feb
18.95	Mosfata	Abdel Maati Ali	EGY	14.1.87	21 Nov
18.93	Chris	Gaviglio	AUS	3.10.77	26 Aug
18.93	Paolo	Dal Soglio	ITA	29.7.70	30 Sep
18.91	Grzegorz	Pankau	POL	23.1.84	30 Jun
18.90	Jarred	Sola	USA	8.4.85	7 Jun
18.90	Borja	Vivas	ESP	26.5.84	16 Jun
18.88	Kimani	Kirton	JAM	16.5.84	9 Jun
18.86i	Erik	van Vreumingen	NED	15.6.78	17 Feb
18.85	Wim	Blondeel	BEL	25.12.73	5 Aug
18.82	Erik	Whittsitt	USA	8.11.83	27 Apr
18.79	John	Danielson	USA	4.4.85	7 Apr
18.74		Tian Yingchun	CHN	29.5.79	2 Aug
18.73	Eddy	Cardol	NED	6.5.78	1 Jul
18.73		Jia Peng	CHN	12.1.84	2 Aug
18.73		Zhang Jun	CHN	11.4.83	19 Sep
18.68	Andrzej	Mrozik	POL	29.2.84	30 Jun
18.68	Saurabh	Vij	IND	14.6.87	2 Sep
18.67	Yibulayin	Abudula	CHN	8.1.81	15 Apr
18.66i	Lance	Pfeiffer	USA	24.11.83	9 Feb
18.63	Robert	Harting	GER	18.10.84	6 Jul
18.62i	Nick	Robinson	USA-J	26.1.88	17 Feb
18.62	Váios	Tíggas	GRE	16.10.78	6 Jun
18.62		Zhao Zhongjun	CHN	28.12.83	2 Aug
18.61i	Andy	Fryman	USA	3.2.85	2 Feb
18.61	Robert	Dippl	GER	21.10.83	22 Jul
18.60	Antonio	Lora	ESP	13.4.76	9 Jun
18.58i	Gavin	Ball	USA	14.10.84	24 Feb
18.57i	Shane	Maier	USA	18.5.84	25 Feb
18.55	Tomas	Fajardo	USA	28.11.83	21 Apr
18.55	Christopher	Götz	GER	10.4.83	6 Jun
18.55	Meshari	Suroor Saad	KUW	2.7.87	21 Nov
18.54	Vladislav	Tulácek	CZE-J	9.7.88	28 Aug
18.52	Amin	Nikfar	IRI	2.1.81	31 Mar
18.51	Auston	Papay	USA	10.2.85	11 May
18.49i	Margus	Hunt	EST	14.4.87	23 Jan
18.49i	Amir	Alvand	IRI	22.3.83	22 Feb
18.49	Yoger	Medina	VEN	5.9.73	14 Jul
18.48	Tony	Thompson	USA	12.3.80	20 Apr
18.48	Nick	Gretz	USA	3.9.84	27 Apr
18.47	Satoshi	Hatase	JPN	18.12.82	1 Jul
18.43i	Nate	Englin	USA	24.4.86	24 Feb
18.43	John	Langhauser	USA	6.2.85	26 May
18.42	Jan	Marcell	CZE	4.6.85	12 Jul
18.41i	Karl	Erickson	USA	1.6.82	17 Feb
18.41i		Wang Like	CHN-J	2.4.89	16 Mar
18.40i	Jarred	Rome	USA	21.12.76	3 Feb
18.39	Rashaud	Scott	USA	15.7.86	23 Mar
18.37	Philipp	Barth	GER	26.12.83	22 Jul
18.37		Wang Guangtu	CHN	15.11.87	2 Aug
18.35	Stuart	Gyngell	AUS	25.11.63	3 Feb
18.35i	John	Hickey	USA	29.9.87	25 Feb
18.34i	Patrick	Whalen	USA	25.2.86	17 Feb
18.33	Kemal	Mesic	BIH	4.8.85	26 May
18.32i	Dmitriy	Kunats	BLR	6.7.84	19 Jan
18.32	Tilman	Northoff	GER	18.6.69	7 Jul
18.32	Candy	Bauer (188)	GER	31.7.86	22 Jul

Best outdoors

Mark	Name	Pos	Meet	Venue	Date
21.18	Taylor	2	DrakeR	Des Moines	28 Apr
20.23	Battle	4	ModR	Modesto	5 May
20.14	Urtans	1	Takac	Beograd	29 May
20.07	Johnson	1		London (He)	4 Aug
20.02	Lyzhin	3		Cottbus	20 Jun
19.94	Konopka	2		Szolnok	26 May
19.62	Guset	1	NC	Bucuresti	27 Jul
19.43	Bucki	4		Villeneuve d'Ascq	8 Jun
19.42	Goncharuk	1eB	EThCp	Yalta	18 Mar
19.38	Manz	6	GP	Zagreb	4 Jul

Mark	Name	Date
19.19	Kuehl	24 Mar
19.09	Vickers	25 May
19.07	Kujala	13 Jun
19.03	Dodoni	11 Jul
19.02	Emilianov	27 Jul
18.93	Bock	19 May
18.93	Sliwa	17 Jun
18.82	Machura	5 Jun
18.80	Stockbarger	28 Apr
18.80	Peña	29 Jun
18.77	Nichols	26 May
18.77	Lobynya	31 Jul
18.75	van Vreumingen	1 Jul
18.67	Helf	16 Mar
18.58	Zhang Qi	19 May
18.57	Tsirikhov	9 Jun
18.56	Di Maggio	7 Jun
18.47	Alvand	21 Aug
18.41	Best	19 May
18.32	Hickey	21 Apr
18.30	Pfeiffer	25 May

Irregular: 20.40 Dragan Peric SRB 8.5.64 1 Sokoloc 10 Aug

Mark	Name		Nat	Born	Pos	Meet	Venue	Date
			JUNIORS					
18.62i	Nick	Robinson	USA-J	26.1.88	6		Flagstaff	17 Feb
	17.89				1		Los Angeles (Ww)	3 Mar
18.54	Vladislav	Tulácek	CZE-J	9.7.88	1		Praha	28 Aug
18.41i		Wang Like	CHN-J	2.4.89	2		Shanghai	16 Mar
18.06i	Aaron	Studt	USA	25.5.88	1		Minneapolis	16 Fe
	17.96				3		Athens, GA	16 Mar
18.06	Darius	Savage	USA	18.1.88	4		Los Angeles	28 Apr
17.99i	Stanislav	Seheda	UKR	22.1.89	4		Sumy	13 Feb
17.83A	J.P.	Hofmann	RSA	1.5.88	3		Pretoria	9 Mar
17.78	Nikola	Kišanic	CRO	17.5.88	3		Varaždin	12 May
17.74i		Xu Zhongnan	CHN	13.11.89	7		Beijing	21 Mar
17.69	Eric	Plummer	USA	24.5.89	1		Princeton	1 May
17.67	Niko	Hauhia	FIN	9.2.89	1		Kotka	11 Jul
17.62	Bo	Taylor	USA	5.1.88	3		Northridge	17 Mar
17.57i	António Vital	Silva	POR	23.1.88	2	NC	Espinho	18 Feb
6kg Shot		8 performances by 8 men to 19.75						
19.95	Stanislav	Seheda	UKR	22.1.89	1		Kyiv	16 Jun
19.95	Niko	Hauhia	FIN	9.2.89	1		Hämeenkyrö	5 Jul
19.95	Aleksandr	Bulanov	RUS	26.12.89	1	EJ	Hengelo	22 Jul
19.85	Vladislav	Tulácek	CZE	9.7.88	1		Bílina	14 Aug
19.81	António Vital	Silva	POR	23.1.88	1	NC-j	Viseu	7 Jul
19.79	Nick	Robinson	USA	26.1.88	1		Eagle Rock	3 Jun
19.77	Yeóryios	Yeromarkákis	GRE	17.3.88	Q	EJ	Hengelo	21 Jul
19.69	Rosen	Karamfilov	BUL	4.1.89	1	NC-w	Sofia	25 Mar
19.63	Nikola	Kišanic	CRO	17.5.88	1		Zagreb	20 Jun
19.59	J.P.	Hofmann	RSA	1.5.88	1		Pretoria	13 Apr
19.37	Aleksandr	Bolshakov	RUS	1.1.88	2		Zhukovskiy	29 Jun
19.28	Pavel	Shustitski	BLR	26.6.88	1	NC-j	Grodno	30 Jun
19.25	Michał	Bosko	POL	25.7.88	1		Slupsk	5 Aug
19.22	Ivan	Shariy	UKR	12.3.88	2		Kyiv	16 Jun
19.19i	Lukasz	Kutek	POL	9.1.88	1		Brzeszcze	3 Feb
19.03	David	Storl	GER-Y	27.7.90			Biberach	16 Jun
19.02i	Lukasz	Haratyk	POL	18.8.88	2		Spala	13 Jan
18.98	Emanuele	Fuamatu	AUS	27.10.89	1		Sydney	10 Nov
18.96	Konstantin	Lyadusov	RUS	2.3.88	2	NC-j	Sochi	22 May
18.93	Milos	Markovi	SRB	22.11.89	1		Kragujevac	8 Sep

DISCUS

72.02	Gerd	Kanter		EST	6.5.79	1eA		Salinas		3 May
					70.52	68.02	x	x	72.02	68.60
70.93	1		Helsingborg	28 Jun	70.93	68.79	x	x	70.73	70.14
70.92	2		Kaunas	25 Jul	66.79	x	66.62	69.92	x	70.92
70.36	1		Kópavogur	8 Jul	63.68	63.96	65.61	69.96	70.36	67.91
70.16	1		Helsingborg	11 Aug	67.42	67.88	70.16	x	67.46	65.92
70.12	1		Valga	5 Jun	62.57	70.12	63.19	65.70	x	66.64
69.08	1		Tartu	5 Jul	x. x	69.08	x	68.57	67.25	
68.94	1	WCh	Osaka	28 Aug	64.89	65.37	68.94	x	65.22	68.84
68.84	1		Rakvere	24 Jul	68.84	only throw				
68.43	2	Vard	Réthimno	18 Jul	67.82	65.78	x	68.06	x	68.43
68.09	2		Helsingborg	15 Sep	x	x	x	x	x	68.09
67.84	1	Danek	Turnov	22 May	x	64.41	x	66.14	67.84	66.49
71.56	Virgilijus	Alekna		LTU	13.2.72	1		Kaunas		25 Jul
					65.29	67.65	67.62	67.37	x	71.56
70.51	1	Bisl	Oslo	15 Jun	67.95	70.51	65.94	67.16	x	x
70.43	1	GP	Athína	2 Jul	x	66.44	67.69	67.97	x	70.43
70.01	1		Vilnius	18 Apr	69.60	69.49	66.09	70.01	x	x
69.97	1		Halle	19 May	68.88	66.43	68.02	x	69.97	68.86
69.90	1		Klaipeda	13 Jul	67.18	66.36	67.45	69.90	x	x
69.67	1	Vard	Réthimno	18 Jul	65.78	69.67	x	66.10	66.12	68.08
69.43	1		Bydgoszcz	10 Jun	68.97	64.70	69.43	68.54	68.28	x
68.74	1	GP	Madrid	21 Jul	65.65	60.67	65.18	66.19	68.74	63.93
68.68	1	Ubartas	Vilnius	26 May	68.68	68.00	67.35	68.22	68.46	67.30
68.51	1	SGP	Doha	11 May	x	64.96	65.03	68.51		
68.19	1		Salôn-de-Provence	2 Jun	63.96	63.00	68.19	66.26	68.05	x
69.97	Frantz	Kruger (RSA)		FIN	22.5.75	1		Helsingborg		15 Sep
					69.97	x	x	x	x	x
68.37	Jarred	Rome		USA	21.12.76	1		Wailuku		16 Apr
					68.37	x	x	65.80	x	64.37
68.26	Mario	Pestano		ESP	8.4.78	2	GP	Athína		2 Jul
					61.25	64.91	x	64.88	65.56	68.26

Mark	Name		Nat	Born	Pos	Meet	Venue	Date
67.98	Ian	Waltz	USA	15.4.77	2		Wailuku	16 Apr
				65.19	67.98	66.24	x x	64.78
67.95	Ehsan	Hadadi	IRI	21.1.85	1	Klim	Minsk (Staiki)	9 Jun
67.88	1	Tehran	24 May	x	64.70	x	64.11 66.83	67.86
	(30/7)							
67.63	Rutger	Smith	NED	9.7.81	3		Helsingborg	15 Sep
66.93	Robert	Harting	GER	18.10.84	1		Schönebeck	10 Jun
66.61	Piotr	Malachowski	POL	7.6.83	3		Kaunas	25 Jul
	(10)							
66.58	Omar	El-Ghazaly	EGY	9.2.84	2		Helsingborg	28 Jun
66.56	Märt	Israel	EST	23.9.83	4		Helsingborg	15 Sep
66.45	Gábor	Máté	HUN	9.2.79	4		Kaunas	25 Jul
66.42	Zoltán	Kövágó	HUN	10.4.79	5		Kaunas	25 Jul
65.77	Niklas	Arrhenius	SWE	9.9.82	2eA		Salinas	17 May
65.39	Stanislav	Alekseyev	RUS	10.2.82	1		Samara	9 Aug
65.29	Michael	Möllenbeck	GER	12.12.69	2		Schönebeck	10 Jun
65.01	Hannes	Kirchler	ITA	22.12.78	1		Bolzano	4 Jun
64.98	Adam	Kuehl	USA	19.1.84	3eA		Salinas	17 May
64.96	Vikas	Gowda	IND	5.7.83	4eA		Salinas	17 May
	(20)							
64.95	Bogdan	Pishchalnikov	RUS	26.8.82	1	NC	Tula	3 Aug
64.94	Stanislav	Nesterovskyy	UKR	31.7.80	1		Kyiv	17 Jun
64.74	Casey	Malone	USA	6.4.77	5eA		Salinas	17 May
64.68	Frank	Casañas	CUB/ESP	18.10.78	1		Uden	4 Aug
64.52	Abbas	Samimi	IRI	9.6.77	2		Tehran	16 Jul
64.41	Aleksander	Tammert	EST	2.2.73	Q	WCh	Osaka	26 Aug
64.34	Ercüment	Olgundeniz	TUR	7.7.76	3	EThCp	Yalta	17 Mar
64.21	Andrzej	Krawczyk	POL	11.4.76	2		Sopot	7 Jul
64.20	Rashid	Al-Dosari	QAT	8.5.81	3	NA	Heusden-Zolder	28 Jul
64.14	Mikko	Kyyrö	FIN	12.7.80	2		Jalasjärvi	29 Jun
	(30)							
64.04	Michael	Robertson	USA	19.12.83	1	NC	Indianapolis	24 Jun
63.69	Gregg	Garza	USA	6.1.85	1	Pac-10	Stanford	12 May
63.61	Will	Conwell	USA	12.9.82	1eB		Salinas	16 May
63.44	Yves	Niaré	FRA	20.7.77	1		Chelles	9 May
63.37	Emeka	Udechuku	GBR	10.7.79	1		London (He)	4 Aug
63.26	Dariusz	Slowik	CAN	15.8.77	4	ModR	Modesto	5 May
63.18	Aleksandr	Borichevskiy	RUS	25.6.70	2		Samara	9 Aug
63.17	Mika	Loikkanen	FIN	20.2.74	5		Helsingborg	15 Sep
63.07	Sultan M.	Al-Dawoodi	KSA	16.6.77	2		Kyiv	17 Jun
62.99	Benn	Harradine	AUS	14.10.82	3		Helsingborg	28 Jun
	(40)							
62.95	Jason	Morgan	JAM	6.10.82	1		Monroe, LA	28 Apr
62.91	Lois Maikel	Martínez	CUB	3.6.81	2		Bilbao	23 Jun
62.87	Jason	Tunks	CAN	7.5.75	1		London, ON	16 Jul
62.79	Mykyta	Nesterenko	UKR-Y	15.4.91	1		Kyiv	22 May
62.76	Doug	Reynolds	USA	11.8.75	1		Lexington	14 Jun
62.76	Olgierd	Stanski	POL	4.4.73	1		Lublin	14 Jun
62.76	Oleksiy	Semenov	UKR	27.6.82	1		Kyiv	3 Aug
62.68	Erik	Cadée	NED	15.2.84	1		Eindhoven	14 Jul
62.62	Sergiu	Ursu	ROM	26.4.80	1	NC-w	Bucuresti	10 Mar
62.43	Jorge	Balliengo	ARG	5.1.78	1		Rosario	24 Mar
	(50)							
62.36	Rustan	Khlybov	BLR	15.2.83	1		Minsk (Staiki)	18 May
62.14	Sergiy	Pruglo	UKR	18.11.83	2		Kyiv	25 Jul
62.13	Bertrand	Vili	FRA	6.9.83	1		Auckland	19 Dec
62.12	Gerhard	Mayer	AUT	20.5.80	1		Schwechat	17 May
62.04	Martin	Maric	CRO	19.4.84	2eB		Salinas	17 May
61.93	Spirídon	Arabatzís	GRE	2.6.78	1		Iráklio	20 May
61.78	Germán	Lauro	ARG	2.4.84	1		Buenos Aires	9 Sep
61.72	Pavel	Lyzhin	BLR	24.3.81	2		Minsk (Staiki)	18 May
61.66	Aaron	Neighbour	AUS	2.12.77	1		Melbourne	13 Jan
61.65	Scott	Martin	AUS	12.10.82	1		Christchurch	21 Feb
	(60)							
61.58	Hannes	Hopley	RSA	26.1.81	1		Savona	26 Jun
61.58	Yasser	Ibrahim	EGY	2.5.84	2	AfrG	Alger	18 Jul
61.49		Wu Tao	CHN	3.10.83	1	NC	Shijiazhiang	3 Aug
61.45	Daniel	Schaerer	SUI/USA	20.10.85	2eB		Salinas	16 May
61.43	Diego	Fortuna	ITA	14.2.68	3		Donnas	15 Jul
61.39	Westley	Stockbarger	USA	5.6.85	1	NCAA-r	Gainesville	25 May
61.38	James	Dennis	USA	25.2.76	2eB		Salinas	3 May

Mark	Name		Nat	Born	Pos	Meet	Venue	Date
61.22	Jean-Baptiste	Tiercelin	FRA	1.2.77	1		Maisons-Laffitte	30 May
61.21	Dmitriy	Sivakov	BLR	15.2.83	3	ECp-1B	Milano	24 Jun
61.13	Pavlo	Karsak	UKR	11.11.87	1		Kyiv	19 May
	(70)							
61.12	Yemi	Ayemi	NGR	10.10.86	2	NCAA-r	Gainesville	25 May
61.10	Martin	Wierig	GER	10.6.87	1	EU23	Debrecen	14 Jul
61.08	Darius	Savage	USA-J	18.1.88	2	TexR	Austin	6 Apr
61.08	Libor	Malina	CZE	14.6.73	1		Humpolec	22 Sep
61.05	Karl	Erickson	USA	1.6.82	1		Chula Vista	14 Jun
61.00	Aleksandr	Malasevich	BLR	7.4.77	2		Minsk (Staiki)	28 Jul
60.93	Michal	Hodun	POL	17.2.83	2		Lublin	14 Jun
60.70	Heinrich	Seitz	GER	6.4.80	1		Bad Schwalbach	14 Jul
60.70	Dmytro	Isnyuk	UKR	4.7.85	4		Kyiv	3 Aug
60.68	Dmitriy	Shevchenko	RUS	13.5.68	2	NC	Tula	3 Aug
	(80)							
60.64	Luke	Sullivan	USA	4.6.76	4eB		Salinas	3 May
60.57	Kibwe	Johnson	USA	17.7.81	1	MSR	Walnut	15 Apr
60.56	Mohammed	Samimi	IRI-J	18.9.88	3		Tehran	24 May
60.48	Dan	Austin	USA	12.4.83	4	TexR	Austin	6 Apr
60.47	Matt	Lamb	USA	27.9.86	4	NCAA-r	Eugene	25 May
60.46	Ivan	Hryshyn	UKR-J	26.7.88	5		Kyiv	3 Aug
60.42	Derek	Randall	USA	15.6.83	1		Austin	21 Apr
60.40	Clendon	Henderson	USA	1.8.84	Q	NCAA	Sacramento	6 Jun
60.39	Nick	Petrucci	USA	10.11.75	7eA		Salinas	17 May
60.25	Gaute	Myklebust	NOR	29.4.79	1		Oslo	13 May
	(90)							
60.22	Graham	Hicks	AUS	14.12.78	3		Sydney	17 Feb
60.11	Pedro José	Cuesta	ESP	22.8.83	1		Leiria	21 Jul
60.10	Shigeo	Hatakeyama	JPN	9.3.77	1		Toin	3 Jun
60.10	Yuriy	Bilonog	UKR	9.3.74	3	NC	Donetsk	6 Jul
60.09	Sergey	Gribkov	RUS	30.4.85	1		Moskva	16 May
60.07	Mihai-Liviu	Grasu	ROM	21.4.87	2		Zalau	5 May
60.00	Konrad	Szuster	POL	21.1.84	3		Lublin	14 Jun
59.90	Vyacheslav	Ivashkin	RUS	6.3.74	2		Adler	11 Feb
59.78	Yuriy	Seskin	RUS	7.7.66	Q	NC	Tula	2 Aug
59.75	Ronald	Julião	BRA	16.6.85	1		São Caetano do Sul	27 May
	(100)							

59.73	Roman	Ryzhyy	UKR	17.1.85	9May	58.51	Nate	Rolfe	USA	28.10.85	17 Mar
59.55	Bartosz	Ratajczak	POL	18.3.85	27May	58.41	Sergey	Ryzhenko	RUS	1.7.83	2 Jun
59.53	Sascha	Hördt	GER	27.4.84	10 Jun	58.39	Sultan	Abdulmajid Al Hebshi	KSA	23.2.83	16 Oct
59.47	Cristiano	Andrei	ITA	14.5.73	26 Jun	58.38	Antonin	Zalsky	CZE	7.8.80	2 Jun
59.39	Sean	Shields	USA	10.2.83	21 Apr	58.37	Sheldon	Battle	USA	23.6.83	21 Apr
59.39	Jouni	Waldén	FIN	9.1.82	15 Sep	58.37	Drew	Ulrick	USA	13.1.85	12May
59.37	Nabil	Kiram	MAR	1.5.82	24 Jun	58.32	Róbert	Fazekas	HUN	18.8.75	22May
59.24	Jan	Marcell	CZE	4.6.85	13 Jul	58.30	Yeóryios	Tsolakídis	GRE	25.6.82	3 Jun
59.22	Pertti	Hynni	FIN	14.2.60	5 Aug	58.25	Jason	Rider	USA	25.2.83	25May
59.21	Russ	Winger	USA	2.8.84	28 Apr	58.21	Kyrylo	Chuprynin	UKR	22.7.75	6 Jul
59.16	Jorge	Grave	POR	5.9.82	20 Jun	58.16	Apostolos	Parellis	CYP	24.7.85	14 Jul
59.15	Juha	Lahdenranta	FIN	12.6.76	15 Sep	58.15	John	Harper	USA	8.2.83	12May
59.12	Johannes	van Wyk	RSA	16.3.80	17 Mar	58.08	Marco	Zitelli	ITA	5.2.82	8 Sep
59.10	Aleksandr	Shtepa	RUS	15.5.79	11 Feb	58.07		Li Shaojie	CHN	26.11.75	3 Aug
59.10	Justin	Anlezark	AUS	14.8.77	16 Feb	58.05	Stefano	Lomater	ITA	23.4.74	8 Mar
58.95	Vadim	Hranovschi	MDA	14.2.83	4 Jul	58.05	Loïc	Fournet	FRA	12.5.77	14 Jun
58.90	Margus	Hunt	EST	14.7.87	15 Jun	58.00	Markus	Münch	GER	13.6.86	10 Jun
58.88	Jason	Schutz	USA	24.9.84	6 Jun	58.00	Taavi	Peetre	EST	4.7.83	15 Jun
58.79		Wu Jian	CHN	25.5.86	20May	57.97		Xin Jia	CHN-J	1.3.88	3 Aug
58.72	Tulake	Nuermaimaiti	CHN	8.3.82	3 Aug	57.94	Nikolay	Sedyuk	RUS-J	29.4.88	27May
58.71	Stéfanos	Kónstas	GRE	16.5.77	3 Jun	57.94	Nikólaos	Loukópoulos	GRE	2.6.83	22 Jul
58.68	Musaeb	Al-Momani	JOR	28.8.86	19May	57.90	Yunior	Lastre	CUB	26.10.81	10 Mar
58.68		Choi Jong-bum	KOR	22.8.81	14 Oct	57.85	Oskars	Silcenoks	LAT	21.8.83	10 Aug
58.67	Ahmed Mohamed	Dheeb	QAT	29.9.85	28 Jul	57.84	Kevin	Brown	GBR	10.9.64	1 Sep
58.52	Giovanni	Faloci	ITA	13.10.85	11 Feb	57.82	Aleksandr	Demidovich (150)	BLR	.85	19May

Downhill

63.79	Emeka	Udechuku	GBR	10.7.79	1		Birmingham	1 Jul

2, Abdul Buhari GBR 26.6.82 59.80, 3. Marcus Gouldbourne GBR 12.6.81 58.43, 3. Mark Wiseman GBR 9.2.69 58.41

JUNIORS

See main list for top 4 juniors. 10 performances by 4 men to 58.90. Additional marks and further juniors:

Nesterenko	60.60	1	Kyiv	19 Apr	59.29	5	Lugano	19 Jun
	60.37	5	Kyiv	17 Jun				
Samimi	60.02	1	Tehran	21 Aug	59.10	3	Tehran	11 Sep

Mark	Name		Nat	Born	Pos	Meet	Venue	Date
Savage	59.93 1c2	Austin		6 Apr				
57.97		Xin Jia	CHN	1.3.88	5	NC	Shijiazhuang	3 Aug
57.94	Nikolay	Sedyuk	RUS	29.4.88	3		Sochi	27 May
56.46	Cameron	Carter	USA	3.6.88	2		San Diego	12 May
56.17	Dmitriy	Chebotaryov	RUS	9.10.88	3		Samara	9 Aug
55.65	Brett	Morse	GBR	11.2.89	1		London (He)	4 Aug
55.60	Seyed Ali	Shahrokhi (10)	IRI	12.3.88	3		Tehran	16 Jul
54.93	Rosen	Karamfilov	BUL	4.1.89	1		Sofia	4 Aug
54.03	Mikhail	Dvornikov	RUS	10.8.89	4		Samara	9 Aug
53.50	Anton	Tikhomirov	RUS	29.4.88	5		Adler	22 Apr

1.75kg Discus

Mark	Name		Nat	Born	Pos	Meet	Venue	Date
63.40	Ivan	Hryshyn	UKR	26.7.88	1		Kyiv	17 Jun
	62.79 1 v3N	Valmiera		18 Aug	62.27	Q	EJ Hengelo	19 Jul
	62.28 1 EJ	Hengelo		21 Jul	10 performances by 3 men to 61.50.			
62.72	Nikolay	Sedyuk	RUS	29.4.88	1		Hengelo	21 Jul
	62.43 1 NC-wj	Adler		19 Feb	61.86	1	Adler	11 Feb
	62.28 1	Zhukovskiy		30 Jun	61.69	1	NC-j Sochi	24 May
61.93	Marin	Premeru	CRO-Y	29.8.90	1		Cakovec	9 Sep
61.15	Darius	Savage	USA	18.1.88	1	NC-j	Indianapolis	21 Jun
60.75	Mikhail	Dvornikov	RUS	10.8.89	2		Adler	11 Feb
60.65	Mohammad	Samimi	IRI	18.9.88	1		Tehran	22 Aug
60.04	Rosen	Karamfilov	BUL	4.1.89	1		Halle	19 May
59.47	Gordon	Wolf	GER-Y	17.1.90	2		Halle	19 May
59.45	Luke	Bryant	USA	5.12.88	1	PAm-J	São Paulo	6 Jul
59.40	Anton	Tikhomirov	RUS	29.4.88	2		Adler	22 Apr
59.19	Antonio Vital	Silva	POR	23.1.88	1		Lisboa	23 Jun
59.14	Joni	Mattila	FIN	30.11.88	1		Alavieska	20 May
59.01	Michal	Pietraszko	POL	12.4.88	1	NC-j	Biala Podlaska	28 Jun
58.85	Artur	Hoppe	GER	3.5.88	3		Halle	19 May
58.69	Clinton	Williams	RSA	3.8.88	2		Port Elizabeth	9 Feb
58.31	Pavel	Shustitski	BLR	26.6.88	1	NC-j	Grodno	1 Jul
57.97	Dmitriy	Chebotaryov	RUS	9.10.88	3	NC-wj	Adler	19 Feb
57.82	Fredrik	Amundgård	NOR	12.1.89	1		Helsingborg	8 Jul
57.33	Andrew	Peska	AUS	23.3.89	1		Melbourne	23 Oct
57.29	Yeóryios	Trémos	GRE	21.3.89	1		Iráklio	3 Jun

Downhill

Birmingham 1 Jul: 1. Brett Morse GBR 11.2.89 63.30, 2. Chris Scott GBR 21.3.88 57.53.

HAMMER

Mark	Name		Nat	Born	Pos	Meet	Venue	Date	Series
83.63	Ivan	Tikhon	BLR	24.7.76	1	WCh	Osaka	27 Aug	x x 79.35 x 80.77 83.63
	82.61				2	GP	Rieti	9 Sep	78.98 80.05 77.75 80.27 82.61 81.30
	82.58				1	Kuso	Warszawa	17 Jun	77.85 80.78 82.58 x 80.17 78.80
	82.05				1	WAF	Stuttgart	23 Sep	81.07 78.53 79.95 82.05
	81.29				1		Dubnica	16 Sep	75.92 77.72 80.40 x 81.29 x
	81.18				1		Brest	27 Apr	77.04 77.90 x 79.04 79.43 81.18
	81.03				1	NCp	Minsk (Staiki)	1 Jun	79.87 ? 81.03 ?
	81.01				1	Klim	Minsk (Staiki)	9 Jun	
82.94	Vadim	Devyatovskiy	BLR	20.3.77	1		Minsk (Staiki)	28 Jul	80.72 x 82.80 81.86 80.76 82.94
	81.57				4	WCh	Osaka	27 Aug	76.28 80.95 x 81.22 81.57 81.20
	80.45				5		Bydgoszcz	10 Jun	77.52 75.68 78.44 80.45 78.97 x
82.62	Koji	Murofushi	JPN	8.10.74	1	GP	Rieti	9 Sep	78.79 79.76 79.67 x 80.46 82.62
	80.46				6	WCh	Osaka	27 Aug	76.94 79.46 80.38 79.56 80.13 80.46
82.30	Primoz	Kozmus	SLO	30.9.79	1		Bydgoszcz	10 Jun	79.13 x 79.47 71.72 82.30 81.28
	82.29				2	WCh	Osaka	27 Aug	80.68 79.62 82.12 x x 82.29
	80.54				1	Odlozil	Praha	13 Jun	76.36 77.06 79.62 76.86 x 80.54
81.60	Libor	Charfreitag	SVK	11.9.77	3	WCh	Osaka	27 Aug	x 80.93 79.10 76.88 81.60 80.48
	80.87				3		Bydgoszcz	10 Jun	79.72 x 80.87 78.25 79.60 78.86
	80.61				Q	WCh	Osaka	25 Aug	80.61 only throw
	80.36				1	MSR	Walnut	15 Apr	77.02 x 80.36 77.67 p 76.36
	80.35				2	Kuso	Warszawa	17 Jun	x 75.46 80.35 x 77.28 77.45
81.40	Krisztián	Pars	HUN	18.2.82	2		Bydgoszcz	10 Jun	x 78.08 81.38 80.90 80.64 81.40
	81.36				1	Vard	Réthimno	18 Jul	x 80.23 x 81.36 79.18 79.89
	80.93				5	WCh	Osaka	27 Aug	78.29 79.49 79.55 79.63 77.29 80.93
	80.28				1		Lahti	25 Jul	72.40 76.85 80.28 79.34 77.29 77.81

Mark	Name		Nat	Born	Pos	Meet	Venue	Date
80.70	Szymon	Ziólkowski	POL	1.7.76	4		Bydgoszcz	10 Jun
				x 79.25 x 80.70 x 79.64				
80.68	Markus	Esser	GER	3.2.80	1		Leverkusen	10 Aug
				80.43 x x 80.68 x 80.20				
80.57	1	Rhede	29 Jul	x 78.22 x x 78.20 80.57				
80.45	1	Schönebeck	10 Jun	79.12 77.66 79.79 80.45 78.21 78.78				
80.31	Esref	Apak	TUR	3.1.82	2		Minsk (Staiki)	28 Jul
	(30/9)							
80.00	Igor	Vinichenko (10)	RUS	11.4.84	1		Adler	11 Feb
79.83	Miloslav	Konopka	SVK	23.1.79	Q	WCh	Osaka	25 Aug
79.12	Aleksey	Zagornyi	RUS	31.5.78	1		Moskva	3 Jul
78.89	Dilshod	Nazarov	TJK	6.5.82	1		Dushanbe	16 Jun
78.61	Pavel	Krivitskiy	BLR	17.4.84	3		Minsk (Staiki)	28 Jul
78.60	Aleksandr	Vashchilo	BLR	30.8.81	4		Minsk (Staiki)	28 Jul
78.35	Olli-Pekka	Karjalainen	FIN	7.3.80	9	WCh	Osaka	27 Aug
78.21	Nicola	Vizzoni	ITA	4.11.73	1	ECCp	Albufeira	26 May
78.10	A.G.	Kruger	USA	18.2.79	1	NC	Indianapolis	22 Jun
78.03	Kirill	Ikonnikov	RUS	5.3.84	2		Sochi	26 May
77.92	Karsten	Kobs	GER	16.9.71	2		Schönebeck	10 Jun
	(20)							
77.65	Marco	Lingua	ITA	4.6.78	1		Nice	29 Apr
77.60	Artem	Rubanko	UKR	21.3.74	1		Kyiv	25 May
77.60	Nicolas	Figère	FRA	19.5.79	1		Reims	17 Jul
77.57	Andras	Haklits	CRO	23.9.77	1		Varazdin	7 Jul
77.38	Jim	Steacy	CAN	29.5.84	1		Calgary	16 Jun
77.24	Aleksandr	Kozulko	BLR	8.12.83	3	Klim	Minsk (Staiki)	9 Jun
77.18	Adrián	Annus	HUN	28.6.73	1		Szombathely	25 May
77.18	David	Söderberg	FIN	11.8.79	1		Vilppula	3 Jul
77.14	Ali Mohamed	Al-Zankawi	KUW	27.2.84	solo		Al-Kuwait	11 Sep
	77.07				1		Al-Kuwait	4 Mar
76.95	Frédéric	Pouzy	FRA	18.2.83	1		Sedan	13 May
	(30)							
76.73	Chris	Harmse	RSA	31.5.73	1	AfG	Alger	21 Jul
76.73	Jens	Rautenkrantz	GER	11.4.82	2		Rhede	29 Jul
76.51	Yevgen	Vynogradov	UKR	30.4.84	1	NC	Donetsk	4 Jul
76.32	Dmitriy	Shako	BLR	27.5.79	1		Vitebsk	14 Jan
76.32	Andrey	Vorontsov	BLR	24.7.75	2		Minsk (Staiki)	17 May
76.22	Igors	Sokolovs	LAT	17.8.74	1	NC	Valmiera	3 Aug
76.13	Valeriy	Svyatokho	BLR	20.7.81	7		Bydgoszcz	10 Jun
76.00	Mohsen	Anani	EGY	25.5.85	1		Cairo	8 Oct
75.95	Kibwe	Johnson	USA	17.7.81	1		Cleveland	7 Jul
75.93	Alexándros	Papadimitríou	GRE	18.6.73	3		Nikiti	4 Aug
	(40)							
75.68	Dmitriy	Velikopolskiy	RUS	27.11.84	2		Adler	4 Feb
75.49	Fatih	Eryildirim	TUR	1.3.79	1		Ankara	13 May
75.49	Christophe	Épalle	FRA	23.1.69	2		Reims	17 Jul
75.39	Aleksey	Korolyov	RUS	5.4.82	3		Sochi	26 May
75.24	Maciej	Palyszko	POL	2.1.78	1		Skórcz	29 Sep
75.20	Dorian	Collaku	ALB	2.6.77	1		Espoo	22 Sep
75.12	Andrey	Azarenkov	RUS	26.9.85	3	NCw	Adler	21 Feb
75.03	Lorenzo	Povegliano	ITA	11.11.84	1		Majano	27 May
75.00	Vadim	Khersontsev	RUS	8.7.74	2		Adler	22 Apr
74.98	Dário	Manso	POR	1.7.82	1		Lisboa	28 Apr
	(50)							
74.95	Markus	Kahlmeyer	GER	20.1.82	1		Braunschweig	1 Jul
74.92	Yuriy	Shayunov	BLR	22.10.87	1	EU23	Debrecen	15 Jul
74.88	Ioánnis	Barlís	GRE	26.11.79	2	NC	Athína	17 Jun
74.80	Sergey	Litvinov	BLR	27.1.86	7	Klim	Minsk (Staiki)	9 Jun
74.74	Lukás	Melich	CZE	16.9.80	3		Rhede	29 Jul
74.71	Patric	Suter	SUI	17.5.77	1		St. Gallen	2 Jun
74.63	Michael	Mai	USA	27.9.77	3		Provo	2 Jun
74.56	Igor	Tugay	UKR	22.3.75	1		Kyiv	3 Aug
74.47	Benjamin	Boruschewski	GER	23.4.80	1		Köln	16 Jun
74.39	Jacob	Freeman	USA	5.11.80	3	NC	Indianapolis	22 Jun
	(60)							
74.39	Pavel	Sedlácek	CZE	5.4.68	1		Breclav	25 Aug
74.24	Travis	Nutter	USA	9.2.75	2		Tucson	19 May
74.18	Yevgeniy	Aydamirov	RUS	18.6.87	1	NC-23	Tula	19 Jun
74.13	Sergey	Kirmasov	RUS	25.3.70	3	NC	Tula	2 Aug
74.09	Cosmin	Sorescu	ROM	11.7.75	1		Bucuresti	11 Aug

Mark	Name		Nat	Born	Pos	Meet	Venue	Date
74.08	Hiroaki	Doi	JPN	2.12.78	1		Inba	16 Jun
73.71	Yuriy	Voronkin	RUS	18.5.79	4	NCp	Tula	7 Jul
73.65	Juan Ignacio	Cerra	ARG	16.10.76	1		Santa Fé	1 Sep
73.50	Kristóf	Németh	HUN	17.9.87	3		Veszprém	21 Jul
73.46	Stamátios	Papadoníou	GRE	3.5.84	1		Kalamáta	21 Jul
	(70)							
73.44	Oleksiy	Sokyrskyy	UKR	16.3.85	1		Kyiv	16 Jun
73.26	Paddy	McGrath	USA	1.7.71	1		West Point	2 Jun
72.72	Noleisis	Bicet	CUB	6.2.81	1		La Habana	15 Feb
72.69	Anatoloy	Pozdnyakov	RUS	1.2.87	3	NC-23	Tula	19 Jun
72.40	Giovanni	Sanguin	ITA	14.5.69	2		Palermo	30 Sep
72.39	Vladimir	Maska	CZE	6.2.73	1		Plzen	25 Aug
72.34	Vítor	Costa	POR	28.5.74	4		Sotteville	5 Jun
72.30	Lasse	Luotonen	FIN	16.6.83	1		Pori	29 Aug
72.27	Andy	Frost	GBR	17.4.81	1		London (He)	4 Aug
72.17	Marcel	Lomnicky	SVK	6.7.87	3	EU23	Debrecen	15 Jul
	(80)							
72.06	Pellegrino	Delli Carri	ITA	4.8.76	1		Foggia	23 Jun
71.87	Jake	Dunkleberger	USA	6.10.84	1	NCAA	Sacramento	8 Jun
71.81	Bengt	Johansson	SWE	7.7.73	2		Västerås	2 Jun
71.67		Ma Liang	CHN	22.7.84	1	WCT	Suzhou	8 Jun
71.61	Mattias	Jons	SWE	19.11.82	1		Pocatello	7 Apr
71.46	Zsolt	Németh	HUN	9.11.71	3	NC	Székesfehérvár	28 Jul
71.42	Cory	Martin	USA	22.5.85	1	SEC	Tuscaloosa	11 May
71.40	Yosvany	Suárez	CUB	20.12.72	2		Santiago de Cuba	10 Mar
71.32	Petri	Mättölä	FIN	1.7.86	1		Kotka	7 Jun
71.20	Nick	Owens	USA	6.1.85	2	NCAA	Sacramento	8 Jun
	(90)							
71.19	James	Parker	USA	3.12.75	2		Eugene	5 May
71.01	Moisés	Campeny	ESP	27.5.79	1		Barcelona	21 Jul
70.96	Juha	Kauppinen	FIN	16.8.86	1		Helsinki	23 Jul
70.95	Ahmed	Abderraouf Mohamed	EGY	12.2.80	1		El Maadi	31 Aug
70.89	Roberto	Janet	CUB	29.8.86	3		Santiago de Cuba	10 Mar
70.84		Lee Yun-chul	KOR	28.3.82	1		Andong	22 May
70.67	Roman	Rozna	MDA	25.3.76	2	Rom IC	Bucuresti	10 Jun
70.63		Zhao Yihai	CHN	29.3.85	1	NC	Shijiazhiang	2 Aug
70.60	Vadym	Hrabovyy	UKR	5.4.73	3		Kyiv	16 Jun
70.58	Sergiy	Karpovych	UKR	23.4.81	2		Kyiv	18 May

Mark	Name		Nat	Born	Date	Mark	Name		Nat	Born	Date
	(100)					69.07	Sven	Möhsner	GER	30.1.86	10 Mar
70.32	Oleg	Sinkevich	BLR	16.1.83	17 May	69.05	Wil	Fleming	USA	11.4.82	4 Jun
70.30	Bergur Ingi	Pétursson	ISL	5.10.85	3 Sep	69.04	Konstadínos	Stathelákos	GRE	30.12.87	17 Jun
70.20		Wan Yong	CHN	22.7.87	8 Jun	68.94	David	Paul	USA	6.3.84	11 May
70.15	Jérôme	Bortoluzzi	FRA	20.5.82	17 Jul	68.88	Maksym	Tyhomyrov	UKR	23.3.77	23 May
70.14	Yegor	Agafonov	RUS	7.2.83	12 May	68.73	Lucais	MacKay	USA	13.4.80	28 Apr
70.05	Hassan	Mohamed Mahmoud	EGY	10.2.84	31 Aug	68.68	Erik	Jiménez	CUB	17.9.81	8 Jun
70.01	Saber	Souid	TUN	9.3.81	21 Jul	68.65	Dameion	Smith	USA	3.8.79	9 May
69.89	Aleksey	Fedotov	RUS	28.12.86	19 Jun	68.46	Giovanni	Mondanaro	ITA	16.4.77	3 Jun
69.72	Rich	Ulm	USA	3.5.77	2 Jun	68.42	Simon	Bown	GBR	21.11.74	19 Aug
69.64	Andrey	Volkov	RUS	11.12.85	19 Jun	68.30	Oleksandr	Myahkyh	UKR	7.5.86	25 May
69.60	Spiridon	Zoullién	GRE	21.6.81	17 Jun	68.20	Mikhail	Levin	RUS	10.4.86	21 Apr
69.57	Adam	Midles	USA	24.9.83	28 May	68.20	Andreas	Sahner	GER	27.1.85	25 Aug
69.53	Marco	Felice	ITA	20.10.79	20 May	68.18	Massimo	Marussi	ITA	5.4.84	28 Jul
69.44	Turgay	Cabukel	TUR	17.6.85	30 Jun	68.15	Dusan	Král	CZE	12.6.83	30 Jun
69.43	Kamilius	Bethke	GER	21.5.85	8 Sep	68.15		Qi Dakai	CHN	23.5.87	30 Oct
69.20	Benjamin	Siart	AUT	11.1.84	19 Aug	68.09	Andy	Nicholas	USA	8.2.83	11 May
69.17	Hiroshi	Noguchi	JPN	3.5.83	7 Oct	68.09	Tuomas	Seppänen (135)	FIN	16.5.86	14 Jul

Drugs disqualification: 76.41 Ilya Konavalov RUS 4.3.71 (2) Adler 4 Feb

JUNIORS

Mark	Name		Nat	Born	Pos	Meet	Venue	Date
67.23		Dan Zhangcheng	CHN	14.12.88	5		Suzhou	8 Jun
66.62		Zhou Heng	CHN	23.7.88	2		Zhaoqing	18 May
65.86	Dimítrios	Filladitákis	GRE	16.9.88	4		Trípoli	27 May
65.35	Adrian-Cristian	Pop	ROM	13.6.88	3		Bucuresti	10 Jun
65.10	Artem	Vynnyk	UKR	1.1.88	4		Kyiv	18 May
64.90	Aleksandr	Lobazov	RUS	11.5.88	1		Sankt-Peterburg	14 Jan
64.36	Aleksey	Romanov	RUS	12.3.89	3		Sankt Peterburg	23 Dec
64.15	Alex	Smith	GBR	6.3.88	4		London	4 Aug
64.04	Khaled	Shawky Mahmoud	EGY	3.1.89	4		El Maadi	26 Oct
63.89	Walter	Henning (10)	USA	24.1.89	10c3	PennR	Philadelphia	28 Apr
63.79	Sergey	Tsitsorin	BLR	27.2.88	11		Staiki	1 Jun
63.78	Ibrahim	Bada	NGR	2.2.88	1	NC	Lagos	19 May

6kg Hammer

Mark	Name		Nat	Born	Pos	Meet	Venue	Date
75.43	Igor	Sergeyev	RUS	7.8.89	1		Zhukovskiy	29 Jun
74.48	Artem	Vynnyk	UKR	1.1.88	1	NC-j	Mykolaiv	21 Jun
74.33	Sergey	Tsitsorin	BLR	27.2.88	Q	NC-j	Grodno	30 Jun
	73.38 Q EJ Hengelo 21 Jul						8 performances by 7 men to 73.00	
73.88	Denis	Lukyanov	RUS	11.7.89	2		Zhukovskiy	29 Jun
73.59	Walter	Henning	USA	24.1.89	1	NC-j	Indianapolis	22 Jun
73.29	Dimítrios	Filladitákis	GRE	16.9.88	1		Iráklio	3 Jun
73.06	Alex	Smith	GBR	6.3.88	1		Varaždin	7 Jul
72.82	Arno	Laitinen	FIN	9.3.88	1		Äänekoski	11 Jul
72.62	Adrian-Cristian	Pop	ROM	13.6.88	1	Balk-j	Kragujevac	8 Sep
71.16	Yevgeniy	Shaytor (10)	BLR	28.1.88	2	NC-j	Grodno	30 Jun
70.82	James	Bedford	GBR	29.12.88	1		Liverpool	17 Jun
70.79	Sergey	Kalamoyets	BLR	.88	2	Klim	Minsk (Staiki)	9 Jun
70.77	Sándor	Pálhegyi	HUN	4.11.88	1	NC-wj	Budapest	4 Mar
70.73	Samuli	Heinänen	FIN	12.3.88	2		Kaustine	28 Jun
70.43	Antonio Vital	Silva	POR	23.1.88	1		Viseu	7 Jul
70.32	Bartlomiej	Molenda	POL	16.7.88	1		Pozna	16 Jun
70.20	Sergey	Bakachov	BLR	25.4.88	3		Grodno	30 Jun

JAVELIN

Mark	Name		Nat	Born	Pos	Meet	Venue	Date						
91.29	Breaux	Greer	USA	19.10.76	1	NC	Indianapolis	21 Jun	82.51	91.29	p	p	p	p
90.71					1	adidas	Carson	20 May	90.71	87.25	89.44	86.49	x	87.58
88.73					2	Bisl	Oslo	15 Jun	x	88.73	x	x	85.60	83.31
86.78					Q	WCh	Osaka	31 Aug	64.49	79.67	86.78			
91.23	Tero	Pitkämaki	FIN	19.12.82	1		Lapinlahti	22 Jul	80.22	82.91	91.23	x	x	x
90.33					1	WCh	Osaka	2 Sep	81.62	89.16	83.64	87.72	x	90.33
89.70					1	Gaz	Saint-Denis	6 Jul	87.71	87.88	85.08	89.70	x	82.73
89.43					1	NC	Lappeenranta	5 Aug	85.04	89.43	x	x	p	p
88.78					1	Bisl	Oslo	15 Jun	85.27	88.78	x	82.31	80.62	82.84
88.67					Q	NC	Lappeenranta	4 Aug	72.04	75.00	88.67			
88.58					1	ISTAF	Berlin	16 Sep	83.23	88.58	p	p	p	p
88.19					1	WAF	Stuttgart	23 Sep	88.19	x	82.02	x		
87.78					1		Kuortane	3 Jun	87.78	86.60	x	85.00	x	84.48
87.44					2	WK	Zürich	7 Sep	x	69.68	83.70	87.44	x	x
87.30					1	VD	Bruxelles	14 Sep	84.92	79.22	84.26	85.18	83.14	87.30
90.73	Vadims	Vasilevskis	LAT	5.1.82	1		Tallinn	22 Jul	x	86.75	81.37	76.54	90.73	p
87.56					1		Dessau	1 Jun	x	83.63	87.56	85.13	x	x
87.37					Q	WCh	Osaka	31 Aug	x	72.80	87.37			
89.51	Andreas	Thorkildsen	NOR	1.4.82	1	WK	Zürich	7 Sep	89.51	p	p	p	p	p
89.49					1	DNG	Stockholm	7 Aug	82.80	89.49	86.02	p	p	p
88.61					2	WCh	Osaka	2 Sep	82.78	88.61	x	82.80	x	87.33
88.36					1	GGala	Roma	13 Jul	88.36	x	85.60	p	p	p
87.79					3	Bisl	Oslo	15 Jun	86.36	84.27	x	86.05	85.99	87.79
87.64					1	ECp-2	Odense	24 Jun	80.51	87.64	82.89	81.85		
87.24					2		Kuortane	3 Jun	87.24	84.13	83.37	x	x	x
87.46	Sergey	Makarov	RUS	19.3.73	1		Moskva	29 Jun	79.53	81.05	84.94	85.28	83.16	87.46
87.32					1	Znam	Zhukovskiy	9 Jun	84.64	81.29	85.13	84.24	87.32	84.32
87.05					2		Dessau	1 Jun	81.96	83.01	82.17	86.32	83.68	87.05
86.56					1	NC	Tula	31 Jul	84.10	83.00	84.26	82.40	x	86.56
86.71	Aleksandr (30/6)	Ivanov	RUS	25.5.82	2	Znam	Zhukovskiy	9 Jun						
85.93	Guillermo	Martínez	CUB	28.6.81	1		Fortaleza	16 May						
85.75	Magnus	Arvidsson	SWE	20.2.83	1	GP	Osaka	5 May						
84.52	Robert	Oosthuizen	RSA	23.1.87	6	WCh	Osaka	2 Sep						
84.35	Tero (10)	Järvenpää	FIN	2.10.84	Q	WCh	Osaka	31 Aug						
84.06	Teemu	Wirkkala	FIN	14.1.84	3		Kuortane	3 Jun						
84.02	Jarko	Koski-Vähälä	FIN	21.11.78	2		Lapinlahti	22 Jul						
83.98	Scott	Russell	CAN	16.1.79	2		Fortaleza	16 May						
83.94	Ilya	Korotkov	RUS	6.12.83	2		Moskva	29 Jun						
83.70	Jarrod	Bannister	AUS	3.10.84	1	NC	Brisbane	10 Mar						
83.38	Igor	Janik	POL	18.1.83	7	WCh	Osaka	2 Sep						
83.35A	Eriks	Rags	LAT	1.6.75	1		Potchefstroom	7 Apr						
83.34	Igor	Sukhomlinov	RUS	13.2.77	1B	EThCp	Yalta	18 Mar						

Mark	Name		Nat	Born	Pos	Meet	Venue	Date
82.96	Hardus	Pienaar	RSA	10.8.81	1		Oudtshoorn	17 Feb
82.78	Peter	Esenwein	GER	7.12.67	1		Luzern	28 Jun
	(20)							
82.71	Antti	Ruuskanen	FIN	21.2.84	1		Joensuu	22 Aug
82.55	Kolyo	Neshev	BUL	30.5.82	1	NC-w	Sofia	25 Mar
82.46	Stephan	Steding	GER	29.1.82	1		Garbsen	1 May
82.34	Esko	Mikkola	FIN	14.2.75	2		Tampere	20 Jun
82.23	Mark	Frank	GER	21.6.77	1		Schönebeck	10 Jun
82.23	Ainars	Kovals	LAT	21.11.81	3	WUG	Bangkok	11 Aug
82.02	Viljo	Toivanen	FIN	18.8.84	1		Joensuu	7 Jun
81.99	Mike	Hazle	USA	22.3.79	1		Huelva	13 Sep
81.01	Yervásios	Filippídis	GRE	24.7.87	1		Kalamáta	2 Jun
80.88	Harri	Haatainen	FIN	5.1.78	1		Nokia	22 Aug
	(30)							
80.73	Josh	Robinson	AUS	4.10.85	2		Brisbane	20 Jan
80.58	Voldemars	Lusis	LAT	7.12.74	2		Riga	13 Jun
80.53	Annier	Boué	CUB	3.4.84	1		La Habana	21 Jun
80.45	Elefthérios	Karasmanákis	GRE	16.8.78	1		Pátra	9 Jul
80.38		Park Jae-myong	KOR	15.12.81	1		Goyang	29 Apr
80.34	Stefan	Wenk	GER	13.3.81	3		Schönebeck	10 Jun
80.31	Ari	Mannio	FIN	23.7.87	4		Kuortane	3 Jun
80.27	Gerbrand	Grobler	RSA	26.1.83	5		Dessau	1 Jun
80.24	Tino	Häber	GER	6.10.82	1		Bad Köstritz	8 Jul
80.21		Qin Qiang	CHN	18.4.83	1	WCT	Suzhou	10 Jun
	(40)							
79.85	Yukifumi	Murakami	JPN	23.12.79	1	NC	Osaka	29 Jun
79.81	Vitolio	Tipotio	FRA	17.7.75	8	Gaz	Saint-Denis	6 Jul
79.58	Christian	Nicolay	GER	4.3.76	3eA		Halle	19 May
79.56	Aleksandr	Vieweg	GER	28.6.86	1	EU23	Debrecen	14 Jul
79.48	Jonas	Lohse	SWE	15.5.87	1	NC-23	Uddevalla	25 Aug
79.45A	Pablo	Pietrobelli	ARG	24.6.80	1		Bogotá	30 Jun
79.45	Vitezslav	Vesely	CZE	27.2.83	1		Turnov	29 Sep
79.43	Stefan	Müller	SUI	20.9.79	4		Luzern	28 Jun
79.06	Oleksandr	Tertychnyy	UKR	5.10.85	1		Kyiv	19 May
79.04	Nick	Nieland	GBR	31.1.72	1	BIG	Bedford	10 Jun
	(50)							
78.97	Gabriel	Wallin	SWE	14.10.81	3		Göteborg	1 Aug
78.94	Yeóryios	Iltsios	GRE	28.11.81	1	NC	Athína	17 Jun
78.67	Matthias	De Zordo	GER-J	21.2.88	1		Mannheim	23 Jun
78.65	Tom	Goyvaerts	BEL	20.3.84	1		Beveren	1 Sep
78.57	Alexon	Maximiano	BRA	12.10.82	4		Fortaleza	16 May
78.38	Felix	Loretz	SUI	13.11.75	3	ECp-1A	Vaasa	24 Jun
78.32	Miroslav	Guzdek	CZE	3.8.75	1		Opava	7 Aug
78.17	Jan	Syrovátko	CZE	11.2.85	9	SGP	Doha	11 May
78.15	Csongor	Olteán	HUN	8.4.84	1		Veszprém	21 Jul
78.08	Matija	Kranjc	SLO	12.6.84	1		Tarvisio	19 Aug
	(60)							
78.08	Stuart	Farquhar	NZL	15.3.82	19Q	WCh	Osaka	31 Aug
78.07	Vadim	Yevtyukhovich	BLR	24.5.81	1	NC-w	Brest	3 Feb
78.07		Chen Qi	CHN	10.3.82	1	AsiC	Amman	29 Jul
78.03A	Tommie	du Toit	RSA	17.8.82	2		Potchefstroom	2 Feb
78.03A	Noraldo	Palacios	COL	8.7.80	2		Bogotá	30 Jun
78.01	Victor	Fatecha	PAR-J	10.3.88	6		Fortaleza	16 May
77.99	Daniel	Ragnvaldsson	SWE	3.1.76	4		Göteborg	1 Aug
77.94	Francesco	Pignata	ITA	14.2.78	1		Palermo	29 Sep
77.88	Roman	Avramenko	UKR-J	23.3.88	Q	EJ	Hengelo	19 Jul
77.76		Wang Qingbo	CHN-J	24.5.88	1	NGP	Urumqi	20 Sep
	(70)							
77.70	Mihkel	Kukk	EST	8.10.83	1		Tallinn	1 Aug
77.68A	Brian	Erasmus	RSA	28.2.80	3		Potchefstroom	2 Feb
77.68	Tomas	Intas	LTU	15.9.81	3		Kaunas	25 Jul
77.65	Júlio César	de Oliveira	BRA	4.2.86	1		São Caetano do Sul	14 Jul
77.54	Manuel	Nau	GER	2.7.77	2		Immenshausen	26 Jul
77.29	Risto	Mätas	EST	30.4.84	6	WUG	Bangkok	11 Aug
77.24	Leigh	Smith	USA	28.8.81	1	MSR	Walnut	15 Apr
77.17	Kalle	Sillanpää	FIN	4.12.83	6		Kuortane	3 Jun
77.16	Levente-Andrei	Bartha	ROM	8.3.77	1	CISM	Hyderabad	17 Oct
77.15	Peter	Blank	GER	10.4.62	4		Rehlingen	28 May
	(80)							
77.04	Karlis	Alainis	LAT	18.6.85	4		Riga	13 Jun
76.97	Arley	Ibargüen	COL	17.10.82	3	ALBA	Caracas	10 May

Mark	Name		Nat	Born	Pos	Meet	Venue	Date
76.80	Ioánnis-Yeóryios	Smaliós	GRE	17.2.87	3	NC	Athína	17 Jun
76.77	Melik	Janoyan	ARM	24.3.85	1		Artashat	27 May
76.74	Marko	Jänes	EST	29.8.76	3	ECp-2A	Odense	24 Jun
76.58	Andis	Anskins	LAT	25.1.79	2	NC	Valmiera	4 Aug
76.35	Tanel	Laanmäe	EST-J	29.9.89	1		Tartu	5 Jul
76.28	Oleksandr	Pyatnytsya	UKR	14.7.85	3	EU23	Debrecen	14 Jul
76.19	Mikko	Löppönen	FIN	29.9.83	3		Savonlinna	16 Sep
76.13	Mika	Aalto	FIN	11.3.82	5		Kuortane	12 Aug
	(90)							
76.09	Seppo	Hirvonen	FIN	1.11.82	5		Savonlinna	16 Sep
76.08	Lars Møller	Laursen	DEN	3.3.82	4	ECp-2A	Odense	24 Jun
76.07	Kazuki	Yamamoto	JPN	8.10.83	1		Miyoshi	13 May
76.06	Oleg	Statsenko	UKR	22.10.80	1	NC	Donetsk	5 Jul
75.96	Andrus	Värnik	EST	27.9.77	24Q	WCh	Osaka	31 Aug
75.75	Franz	Burghagen	GER-J	16.3.89	1		Sindelfingen	11 Feb
75.68	Mervyn	Luckwell	GBR	27.11.84	1		Loughborough	11 Aug
75.67	Ken	Arai	JPN	22.12.81	2	NC	Osaka	29 Jun
75.67	Tim	Werner	GER	25.9.80	2		Immenhausen	26 Jul
75.66	Heiko	Väät	EST	25.8.74	2		Tallinn	23 May
	(100)							
75.66	Marko	Kantanen	FIN	17.4.78	1		Alarjärvi	30 May

Mark	First name	Last name	Nat	Born	Date
75.65	Christian	Fusenig	GER	9.5.78	24 Jun
75.55	Petr	Frydrych	CZE-J	13.1.88	8 Sep
75.50	Adrian	Markowski	POL	14.10.78	30 Jun
75.50	Thomas	Smet	BEL-J	12.7.88	18 Sep
75.49	Marián	Bokor	SVK	17.4.77	1 Jul
75.45	Spiridon	Lebésis	GRE	30.5.87	17 Jun
75.34		Jung Sang-jin	KOR	16.4.84	2 Jun
75.30	Teemu	Pasanen	FIN	24.5.77	12 Jun
75.28	Keita	Yamada	JPN	1.6.87	3 Nov
75.26	Björn	Lange	GER	15.6.79	3 Jun
75.22	Konstadinos	Vertoúdos	GRE	5.1.86	30 Jun
75.21	Tony	Bonura	USA	1.10.82	14 Apr
75.21	Oliver	Dziubak	AUS	30.3.82	9 Dec
75.18	Manuel	Fuenmayor	VEN	3.12.80	13 Apr
75.15	Vladislav	Shkurlatov	RUS	30.3.83	21 Feb
75.08	Aleksey	Tovarnov	RUS	20.1.85	26 May
75.02A	Willie	Human	RSA	8.3.82	20 Feb
74.99		Liu Yanhong	CHN	20.4.83	20 Sep
74.94	Denis	Davydov	RUS	25.9.82	1 Aug
74.92	Neil	McLellan	GBR	10.9.78	22 Jun
74.92	Ignacio	Guerra	CHI	15.9.87	27 Oct
74.80	Shae	Murray	USA	28.9.84	6 Jun
74.75		Li Yu	CHN	9.3.87	20 Sep
74.74	Gustavo	Dacal	ESP	30.3.77	30 Jun
74.72	Trevor	Snyder	CAN	2.6.82	11 May
74.71	Justin	St.Clair	USA	17.5.79	21 Jun
74.69	Yudel	Moreno	CUB	24.2.83	16 May
74.57	Berenger	Demerval	FRA	29.4.82	4 Feb
74.55	Yutaro	Tanemoto	JPN	30.11.84	3 Nov
74.54	Vladimir	Chizhov	RUS	5.8.75	9 Aug
74.52		Jiang Xingyu	CHN	16.3.87	1 Nov
74.50	Robert	Szpak	POL-J	31.12.89	5 May
74.42	Daniel	Kratzmann	AUS	19.2.81	25 Feb
74.41	Nicklas	Wiberg	SWE	16.4.85	27 May
74.41	Jérôme	Haeffler	FRA	12.5.82	12 Jul
74.40	Diego	Moraga	CHI	6.10.76	19 May
74.38	Aleksandr	Ashomko	BLR	18.2.84	3 Feb
74.29	Karol	Jakimowicz	POL	15.6.87	14 Jul
74.29	Philippe	Traulle	FRA	26.8.87	5 Aug
74.26	John	Hetzendorf	USA	27.1.77	21 Jun
74.16	Barry	Krammes	USA	1.9.81	21 Jun
74.16	Tomasz	Damszel	POL	25.3.72	30 Jun
74.10	Sean	Furey	USA	31.8.82	21 Jun
74.03	(145)	Song Dong-hyun	KOR	17.11.81	13 Oct

Downhill: 87.88 Antti Ruuskanen FIN 21.2.84 1 Savonlinna 16 Sep

JUNIORS

See main list for top 6 juniors. 10 performances by 4 men to 76.75. Additional marks and further juniors:

	Mark	Pos	Meet	Venue	Date	Mark	Pos	Meet	Venue	Date
de Zordo	78.59	1	EJ	Hengelo	22 Jul	77.74	1	NC-j	Ulm	5 Aug
	78.28	1		Rehlingen	24 Jun	77.51	1		Tomblaine	18 Sep
	77.94	1	NC-23	Hannover	25 Aug	77.48	3		Strasbourg	28 Jun

Mark	Name		Nat	Born	Pos	Meet	Venue	Date
75.55	Petr	Frydrych	CZE	13.1.88	2		Susice	8 Sep
75.50	Thomas	Smet	BEL	12.7.88	2		Tomblaine	18 Sep
74.50	Robert	Szpak	POL	31.12.89	1		Bialogard	5 May
73.71	Bartlomiej	Kempny (10)	POL	16.5.89	Q	EJ	Hengelo	19 Jul
73.35	Danila	Blinyayev	BLR	14.10.88	1	NC-w	Brest	3 Feb
73.28A	Fernie	Kitshoff	RSA	30.1.88	1		Potchefstroom	19 Sep
73.00	James	Campbell	GBR	1.4.88	1		Grangemouth	31 Jul
72.80	Chris	Hill	USA	26.2.88	Q	NCAA	Sacramento	6 Jun
72.51	Tuomas	Saari	FIN	17.3.89	1	v3N	Esbjerg	2 Sep
72.40	Ansis	Bruns	LAT	30.3.89	5	NC	Valmiera	4 Aug
72.05	Nobuhiro	Sato	JPN	28.4.88	1		Oita	21 Oct
71.95	Pavel	Penáz	CZE	3.12.88	1		Pardubice	14 Aug
71.77	Mohamed Ali	Kbabou	TUN	27.6.88	3	AfG	Alger	22 Jul
71.56		Wei Zheng (20)	CHN		1c2		Beijing	21 Apr

PENTATHLON

3881	7.07	65.33	23.04	46.86	4:53.39	Tomás	Dvorák	CZE	11.5.72	1	Prerov	1 May
3755	6.88w	54.28	22.98	46.96	4:33.99	Päärn	Brauer	EST	21.11.82	1	Tallinn	24 May
3653	7.09	62.25	22.39	34.98	4:46.66	Patrick	Spinner	GER	28.11.85	1	Immenhausen	25 Jul
3613	6.95	59.89	23.53	37.32	4:32.41	Matthias	Laube	GER	24.5.83	1	Kirchzarten	7 Jul

DECATHLON

Mark	Name			Nat	Born	Pos Meet	Venue			Date
8697	Roman	Sebrle		CZE	26.11.74	1	Kladno			20 Jun
	10.94/0.6	7.84/1.4	16.47	2.12	48.99	14.39/-0.7	47.66	4.80	68.87	4:40.44
8676		Sebrle				1 WCh	Osaka			1 Sep
	11.04/-0.2	7.56/-0.1	15.92	2.12	48.80	14.33/-0.3	48.75	4.80	71.18	4:35.32
8644	Maurice	Smith		JAM	28.9.80	2 WCh	Osaka			1 Sep
	10.62/0.7	7.50/0.0	17.32	1.97	47.48	13.91/-0.2	52.36	4.80	53.61	4:33.52
8617	Andrey	Kravchenko		BLR	4.1.86	1	Götzis			27 May
	10.86/0.2	7.90/0.9	13.89	2.15	47.46	14.05/-0.1	39.63	5.00	64.35	4:29.10
8586	Dmitriy	Karpov		KAZ	23.7.81	3 WCh	Osaka			1 Sep
	10.70/-0.2	7.19/0.0	16.08	2.06	47.44	14.03/-0.2	48.95	5.00	59.84	4:39.68
8553		Karpov				2	Kladno			20 Jun
	10.90/0.6	7.54/1.4	16.36	2.03	47.75	14.42/-0.7	52.24	5.00	55.66	4:40.28
8553		Kravchenko				1	Talence			28 Sep
	10.98/0.2	7.73/0.8	14.00	2.13	47.17	14.08/-1.1	44.08	5.15	64.08	4:48.99
8518		Sebrle				2	Götzis			27 May
	11.10/-0.5	7.84/1.7	15.58	2.09	49.27	14.52/-0.1	45.15	4.80	70.09	4:39.92
8493	Bryan	Clay		USA	3.1.80	3	Götzis			27 May
	10.40/-0.5	7.80w/3.7	15.30	2.09	48.41	13.97/-0.1	36.14	4.80	69.09	4:51.32
8492		Kravchenko				1 EU23	Debrecen			13 Jul
	11.02/-0.2	7.71w/3.5	13.44	2.14	47.61	14.22/-0.3	43.31	5.10	59.80	4:30.83
8475	Aleksey	Drozdov		RUS	3.12.83	4 WCh	Osaka			1 Sep
	10.97/0.2	7.25/-0.3	16.49	2.12	50.00	14.76/1.4	48.62	5.00	63.51	4:36.93
8373		Drozdov				4	Götzis			27 May
	11.10/0.0	7.20/1.2	15.97	2.12	50.63	15.02/0.0	47.04	5.00	68.97	4:39.62
8371	André	Niklaus		GER	30.8.81	5 WCh	Osaka			1 Sep
	11.12/0.2	7.42/0.4	14.12	2.06	49.40	14.51/-0.2	44.48	5.30	63.28	4:32.50
8357	Aleksey	Sysoyev		RUS	8.3.85	6 WCh	Osaka			1 Sep
	10.80/-0.2	7.01/-0.3	16.16	2.03	48.42	14.59/-0.3	49.76	4.90	57.75	4:36.16
8352	Tom	Pappas		USA	6.9.76	1 NC	Indianapolis			23 Jun
	11.00/-0.5	7.50/0.3	16.43	2.05	48.81	14.12/1.9	46.34	5.00	59.70	4:59.69
8340		Niklaus				5	Götzis			27 May
	11.07/0.2	7.49/0.4	13.83	2.06	49.38	14.34/-0.1	45.73	5.00	62.87	4:30.92
8298	Romain	Barras (10)		FRA	1.8.80	3	Kladno			20 Jun
	11.17/0.6	7.10/0.6	15.12	2.00	48.50	14.30/-0.7	45.39	5.00	62.06	4:27.31
8298		Smith				2	Talence			28 Sep
	10.89/0.2	7.08/0.0	16.72	1.98	48.07	14.01/-1.1	53.83	4.55	51.36	4:39.17
8278		Smith				1 PAm	Rio de Janeiro			24 Jul
	10.84/-0.8	7.27/0.8	16.93	1.97	47.99	14.06/-0.2	53.24	4.40	50.23	4:40.12
8271	Janis	Karlivans		LAT	2.6.82	6	Götzis			27 May
	11.13/0.2	7.82w/2.2	15.01	2.06	49.10	14.86/-0.6	47.95	4.70	60.55	4:43.62
8269	Arthur	Abele		GER	30.7.86	1	Ratingen			17 Jun
	10.84/0.5	7.42/1.1	13.43	2.04	48.51	13.93/1.3	37.95	4.60	65.23	4:18.00
8267		Sysoyev				1 NC	Zhukovskiy			15 Jul
	10.99/0.5	7.15/1.9	15.51	2.15	49.52	14.97/0.3	48.18	4.90	57.65	4:39.64
8262		Barras				7 WCh	Osaka			1 Sep
	11.36/-0.5	7.13/0.4	15.03	2.00	49.32	14.36/-0.2	44.51	5.00	65.74	4:25.75
8257	Yordani	García		CUB-J	21.11.88	8 WCh	Osaka			1 Sep
	10.73/0.7	7.15/0.2	14.94	2.09	49.25	14.08/-0.2	42.91	4.70	68.74	4:55.42
8255	Norman	Müller		GER	7.8.85	7	Götzis			27 May
	10.91/0.2	7.49/0.9	14.58	1.91	48.26	14.53/0.0	44.43	5.00	62.06	4:34.23
8244		Müller				2	Ratingen			17 Jun
	10.89/0.5	7.40/0.7	14.44	1.86	47.30	14.56/1.3	45.10	5.00	61.54	4:32.35
8243		Abele				9 WCh	Osaka			1 Sep
	10.87/0.7	7.17/0.0	13.58	2.00	48.58	13.92/-0.2	41.28	4.70	65.24	4:21.69
8241		Smith				8	Götzis			27 May
	10.71/-0.5	6.84/-0.8	17.25	2.03	47.79	13.83/-0.1	51.68	4.50	46.71	4:43.64
8239	Pascal	Behrenbruch		GER	19.1.85	2 EU23	Debrecen			13 Jul
	10.84/-0.2	7.01/0.8	16.10	2.02	50.40	14.13/-0.3	49.55	4.40	69.55	4:50.09
8215	Jake	Arnold		USA	3.1.84	1 NCAA	Sacramento			7 Jun
	11.12/2.0	6.88w/2.2	14.15	2.02	48.38	14.20/1.8	44.42	5.30	58.80	4:34.22
	(30/16)									
8179	Arkadiy	Vasilyev		RUS	19.1.87	3 EU23	Debrecen			13 Jul
	10.93w/2.7	7.41/0.8	14.62	1.99	50.02	14.55/-0.3	46.94	4.60	63.08	4:32.21
8156	Leonel	Suárez		CUB	1.9.87	1	Santiago de Cuba			11 Mar
	10.8h/-1.2	7.25/0.0	12.80	2.14	49.0h	14.2h/-1.2	42.10	4.30	70.35	4:27.1h
8134	Paul	Terek		USA	20.10.79	1	Desenzano del Garda			6 May
	11.08/0.8	7.28/0.8	15.36	2.00	49.52	15.45/-1.4	45.62	5.00	58.23	4:27.55

Mark	Name		Nat	Born	Pos	Meet	Venue	Date
8101	Aleksandr	Parkhomenko	BLR	22.3.81	1	ECp-S	Tallinn	8 Jul
	11.37w/2.2	7.12/-1.0 16.34	1.98	50.42	14.75/-0.2		43.45 4.70 68.63	4:32.97
(20)								
8099	Jacob	Minah	GER	3.4.82	1	WUG	Bangkok	13 Aug
	10.75/-0.6	7.87/0.1 13.80	1.92	47.79	14.38/-0.2		42.38 4.80 52.66	4:41.11
8047	Hans	Van Alphen	BEL	12.1.82	2	WUG	Bangkok	13 Aug
	11.16/-0.9	7.49/0.9 15.39	1.83	48.25	14.85/-0.1		45.32 4.40 60.79	4:21.05
8042	Alberto	Juantorena	CUB	27.6.77	1		La Habana	22 Jun
	10.7h	7.40/1.0 13.35	2.11	49.3h	14.8h		45.18 4.60 59.30	4:38.6h
8028	Nikolay	Shubenok	BLR	4.5.85	1		Minsk (Staiki)	19 May
	11.10	6.94 15.19	2.06	49.45	14.40		41.60 4.50 59.60	4:24.90
8020	Tomás	Dvorák	CZE	11.5.72	4		Kladno	20 Jun
	11.09/-0.2	7.63w/2.8 16.70	1.91	50.60	14.98/0.8		42.22 4.60 66.56	4:49.87
8017	Attila	Zsivoczky	HUN	29.4.77	12	WCh	Osaka	1 Sep
	11.44/-0.5	7.00/-0.1 15.13	2.09	50.58	14.82/1.4		46.80 4.80 59.63	4:35.55
7977	Carlos Eduardo	Chinin	BRA	3.5.85	3	PAm	Rio de Janeiro	24 Jul
	10.88/-0.8	7.76/0.5 13.44	2.09	48.36	14.52/-0.3		37.01 4.30 51.95	4:23.99
7974	François	Gourmet	BEL	28.12.82	15	WCh	Osaka	1 Sep
	10.67/0.7	7.15/0.3 13.74	1.85	47.98	15.02/-0.3		39.87 5.00 57.73	4:25.51
7964	Oleksiy	Kasyanov	UKR	26.8.85	4	EU23	Debrecen	13 Jul
	10.75/-0.2	7.59/1.4 14.45	1.96	48.35	14.84/-0.3		42.89 4.10 55.84	4:27.35
7963w	Joe	Detmer	USA	3.9.83	2	NCAA	Sacramento	7 Jun
	10.97/1.2	7.24W/4.7 11.76	1.93	47.77	14.62w/2.2		40.43 4.80 52.92	4:04.11
(30)								
7963	Hans Olav	Uldal	NOR	16.12.82	1	ECp-2	Maribor	8 Jul
	10.95/0.9	7.23w/2.4 13.88	1.95	50.47	14.59/-0.3		44.78 4.50 63.81	4:31.77
7961	Edgars	Erins	LAT	18.6.86	1	NC	Valmiera	16 Jun
	10.81/-0.1	7.04/-0.9 13.95	1.91	48.08	14.80/0.3		48.17 4.30 52.97	4:15.74
7955	Pelle	Rietveld	NED	4.2.85	5	EU23	Debrecen	13 Jul
	10.90w/2.7	7.27/1.8 13.80	1.87	48.67	14.62/-0.3		35.84 4.90 63.35	4:26.35
7947	Michael	Schrader	GER	1.7.87	1		Bernhausen	20 May
	10.87/0.9	7.56/-0.8 12.96	1.95	48.47	15.00/0.7		40.80 4.80 55.50	4:29.46
7922	Josef	Karas	CZE	20.8.78	5		Kladno	20 Jun
	11.04/0.6	7.42/0.7 14.79	1.97	49.89	15.21/0.8		50.05 4.50 51.47	4:34.24
7916	Julien	Choffart	FRA	5.11.78	3	ECp-S	Tallinn	8 Jul
	11.18/1.5	7.29w/2.3 13.72	2.01	49.49	14.78/0.6		43.96 4.80 55.57	4:35.43
7912	Lars	Albert	GER	9.2.82	11		Götzis	27 May
	11.19/0.2	7.19/0.3 15.23	1.94	51.69	15.09/-0.6		48.58 4.70 62.48	4:41.84
7912	Mattias	Cerlati	FRA	25.10.83	4	ECp-S	Tallinn	8 Jul
	11.09w/2.2	7.52/-1.0 14.86	1.98	50.91	15.30/-0.2		46.06 4.80 57.33	4:46.12
7902	Yunior	Díaz	CUB	28.4.87	2		Santiago de Cuba	11 Mar
	10.4h/-1.2	7.55/1.1 13.80	1.93	45.9h	14.2h/-1.2		36.97 4.30 52.40	4:36.2h
7901	Ryan	Harlan	USA	25.4.81	1		Ponce	27 May
	11.18/-2.5	7.17w/2.3 16.38	2.06	49.97	14.36/-0.2		43.45 4.80 57.31	5:17.00
(40)								
7884	Nikolay	Tishchenko	RUS	4.2.77	1		Sochi	27 May
	11.12	7.53 13.60	1.97	49.76	14.45		44.76 4.60 50.99	4:32.22
7877	Eugène	Martineau	NED	14.5.80	5	ECp-S	Tallinn	8 Jul
	11.39w/2.2	7.22/0.9 14.01	1.98	50.86	14.93/-0.2		44.23 4.70 64.09	4:34.14
7874	Frédéric	Xhonneux	BEL	11.5.83	3	ECp-1	Szczecin	8 Jul
	11.33w/2.2	7.18/1.5 13.11	1.95	49.74	15.15/1.7		43.09 4.90 59.83	4:22.47
7871	Chris	Richardson	USA	25.11.80	1	MSR	Azusa	11 Apr
	11.00/1.4	7.52 13.68	2.01	50.04	14.86w/3.7		48.41 4.16 59.57	4:46.75
7870	Aleksandr	Kislov	RUS	4.11.84	2		Sochi	27 May
	11.02	7.10 14.67	2.03	49.57	14.39		37.13 4.90 51.50	4:33.89
7870	Nicklas	Wiberg	SWE	16.4.85	12		Götzis	27 May
	11.21/-0.8	7.11/1.5 13.31	2.06	49.15	15.00/-0.6		37.67 4.00 74.41	4:25.21
7838	Raven	Cepeda	USA	26.6.86	1		Des Moines	12 May
	11.06w/2.6	6.63/0.2 15.55	1.94	51.28	14.43/1.8		42.66 5.15 51.13	4:31.85
7838w	Vitaliy	Smirnov	UZB	25.10.78	3		Arles	3 Jun
	10.90w/7.1	6.56w/2.7 14.89	1.95	50.59	14.90/0.9		46.33 4.70 56.56	4:28.63
7838	Hamdhi	Dhouibi	TUN	24.1.82	1	AfG	Alger	19 Jul
	10.88/1.7	6.83/0.6 13.89	1.85	48.65	14.36/0.1		41.52 5.00 52.99	4:31.08
7834	Andres	Raja	EST	2.6.82	6	ECp-S	Tallinn	8 Jul
	11.06/-0.7	7.50/-0.1 14.35	1.86	49.34	14.34/-0.6		41.51 4.70 58.89	4:51.04
(50)								
7825	Iván Scolfaro	da Silva	BRA	30.7.82	1		São Paulo	27 May
	10.94w/2.3	7.28w/2.3 13.30	1.96	49.94	14.78/-0.3		41.19 4.60 61.26	4:38.80
7824		Yu Bin	CHN	26.11.85	1		Chengdu	15 Apr
	10.93/0.0	7.36/0.0 14.02	2.00	50.41	14.78/0.1		39.85 4.70 60.98	4:51.63

Mark	Name		Nat	Born	Pos	Meet	Venue	Date
7813	Agustin	Félix	ESP	14.3.79	5	Déca	Talence	23 Sep
	11.23/0.4 7.35/0.4 13.91		2.01 51.82		14.88/-0.2 43.68 5.05 58.02			4:53.50
7808	Jangy	Addy	USA	2.3.85	3	NCAA	Sacramento	7 Jun
	10.91/1.2 7.40/1.2 15.56		1.93 49.12		13.96/1.9 45.74 3.90 58.69			5:05.72
7804	Chris	Boyles	USA	2.5.80	5	NC	Indianapolis	23 Jun
	11.35/0.3 7.18w/2.3 15.33		2.08 51.09		14.90/1.4 41.33 5.00 53.70			4:52.79
7798	Chris	Randolph	USA	25.4.84	2	MSR	Azusa	12 Apr
	11.45/1.4 7.00 13.16		2.07 49.62		14.79w/3.7 41.47 4.86 54.74			4:29.47
7777	Aleksandr	Korzun	BLR	17.3.85	1	NC-23	Minsk (Staiki)	8 Jun
	10.67/0.3 7.51/-0.1 13.66		2.03 49.54		14.73/0.2 36.00 4.40 57.32			4:47.28
7775	Rudy	Bourguignon	FRA	16.7.79	6	Déca	Talence	23 Sep
	11.34/0.2 7.15/0.0 14.09		1.92 50.51		15.57/-0.2 44.51 5.15 59.17			4:43.00
7760	Joost	van Bennekom	NED	18.1.81	1		Hexham	22 Jul
	10.83/1.4 7.46w/2.3 13.78		2.05 49.33		14.74/-0.3 36.72 4.65 51.97			4:49.09
7760	Mustafa	Abdur-Rahim	USA	29.9.82	1	v GER	Bernhausen	19 Aug
	10.85/-0.6 7.00/0.5 14.19		1.88 48.51		14.41/0.5 44.31 4.10 54.30			4:27.88
	(60)							
7737	Atis	Vaisjuns	LAT	27.9.82	4	ECp-1	Szczecin	8 Jul
	11.23w/3.0 7.02w/3.8 13.85		2.01 50.27		15.06/-0.3 42.99 4.80 55.80			4:39.58
7734	Edward	Dunford	GBR	15.9.84	1		Stoke-on-Trent	9 Sep
	10.95w/3.8 6.96/1.7 14.21		1.99 50.67		13.99w/2.1 41.99 4.25 59.93			4:47.69
7732	Chris	Helwick	USA	18.3.85	1		Knoxville	12 Apr
	11.24/0.0 6.81/0.0 13.05		2.01 50.75		15.04w/3.0 42.77 4.75 65.12			4:40.51
7730w	Brent	Newdick	NZL	31.1.85	5		Arles	3 Jun
	10.99w/7.3 7.30w/3.9 14.30		1.92 53.29		14.41/0.9 44.67 4.80 56.92			4:51.29
7729	Jason	Dudley	AUS	10.11.84	1		Townsville	30 Sep
	11.23/1.6 7.02 15.32		1.94 50.26		15.29/-1.2 49.84 4.80 58.63			5:12.02
7724	Indrek	Turi	EST	30.7.81	1		Brezice	7 Oct
	11.44/0.0 6.79/0.0 13.79		2.08 51.76		14.59/-1.3 39.85 4.80 62.08			4:38.97
7706	Erik	Surjan	AUS	22.6.83	1	NC	Brisbane	10 Mar
	11.09/-2.0 7.55/1.3 14.49		1.90 52.22		14.68/0.2 44.30 4.50 58.69			4:51.10
7704	Masimo	Bertocchi	CAN	27.9.85	1	NC	Windsor	13 Jul
	10.93w/3.6 6.93/0.7 13.27		1.99 49.33		14.82/-2.9 42.74 4.90 52.75			4:51.93
7703	Dawid	Pyra	POL	27.3.87	5	ECp-1	Szczecin	8 Jul
	10.94w/2.2 7.14/1.4 12.83		1.95 48.77		14.41/1.7 37.85 4.70 57.71			4:48.10
7697	Mikhail	Logvinenko	RUS	19.4.84	3		Sochi	27 May
	11.21 7.27 12.70		2.00 49.22		14.37 40.17 4.60 47.54			4:26.84
	(70)							
7695 h	Yosley	Azcuy	CUB	5.12.81	2		La Habana	22 Jun
	10.8h 7.31/1.6 14.22		1.99 49.3h		14.4h 42.07 4.40 57.50			5:02.4h
7685	Alexis	Chivás	CUB	7.11.83	7	WUG	Bangkok	13 Aug
	11.04/-0.9 7.50/0.4 15.16		1.86 51.69		14.69/-0.1 47.13 4.20 59.29			4:55.95
7681	Vasiliy	Kharlamov	RUS	19.1.86	7	EU23	Debrecen	13 Jul
	11.27w/2.7 7.31w/3.0 13.13		1.90 50.75		15.05/-0.3 43.83 4.70 56.77			4:32.41
7680	Aleksandr	Zyabrev	RUS	16.5.87	2	NC	Zhukovskiy	15 Jul
	10.86/0.2 7.09/0.0 14.12		1.88 48.53		14.84/0.3 39.19 4.50 50.93			4:27.99
7678	Ahmad Hassan	Moussa	QAT	17.6.81	1	AsiC	Amman	28 Jul
	10.85/0.9 7.16w/2.3 14.40		1.83 50.14		14.78/1.0 41.01 4.20 66.40			4:44.95
7667w	Hadi	Sepehrzad	IRI	19.1.83	2	AsiC	Amman	28 Jul
	10.84/1.0 7.05w/6.7 15.85		1.86 50.87		14.69/1.0 49.17 4.30 54.84			5:02.58
7664	Neil	Hines	USA	3.6.83	4	NCAA	Sacramento	7 Jun
	11.36/2.0 6.71w/2.8 14.24		2.05 50.63		15.36/1.9 41.87 4.70 58.10			4:33.91
7659	David	Gervasi	SUI	1.8.83	1	NC	Frauenfeld	17 Jun
	11.41/-1.2 6.92/0.0 14.32		2.01 50.36		14.53/-0.9 41.11 4.90 52.44			4:47.33
7656	Hiromasa	Tanaka	JPN	28.9.81	1		Wakayama	22 Apr
	10.74w/2.6 6.81w/4.0 12.18		1.84 49.23		15.46/0.8 42.30 5.00 63.74			4:48.08
7654	Andrey	Nedra	RUS	18.11.80	4		Sochi	27 May
	11.23 7.16 14.03		2.00 10.41		14.86 44.30 4.70 49.32			4:45.58
	(80)							
7640	Cliff	Caines	CAN	18.1.79	2	NC	Windsor	13 Jul
	11.23/-2.3 6.33/0.9 14.05		2.05 50.46		15.78/-1.5 42.87 4.70 58.31			4:24.06
7628w	Luis Alberto	de Araújo	BRA	27.9.87	7		Arles	3 Jun
	10.80w/6.8 7.56w/5.1 13.93		1.89 50.61		14.30/0.6 41.84 4.20 52.19			4:49.04
7627	Andriy	Klimarchuk	UKR	20.1.85	2		Yalta	14 Jun
	11.40/0.0 7.29w/2.3 13.42		2.07 50.15		15.07/1.7 41.04 4.30 53.32			4:31.62
7626	Tarmo	Riitmuru	EST	31.1.86	11	ECp-S	Tallinn	8 Jul
	11.32/1.5 7.38w/3.2 13.37		1.98 50.40		15.20/0.6 40.51 4.60 52.90			4:31.14
7613	Jaakko	Ojaniemi	FIN	28.8.80	1	NC	Lappeenranta	5 Aug
	11.02/-0.4 7.39/1.0 14.88		1.93 50.17		15.56/0.9 39.69 4.25 61.37			4:47.67
7609		Kim Kun-woo	KOR	29.2.80	1		Kwangju	12 Oct
	11.19/0.7 7.08/-0.8 12.90		1.94 48.95		15.18/0.8 35.30 4.90 49.18			4:17.47

Mark	Name		Nat	Born	Pos	Meet	Venue	Date
7609	Daisuke	Ikeda	JPN	15.4.86	1		Maebashi	14 Oct
	11.30/0.0	6.90/-0.6 12.77	1.92	49.81	14.85/1.5	38.25 4.60	62.83	4:29.29
7603	Matt	Chisam	USA	3.7.82	1		Dallas	15 Jul
	11.31w/2.7	6.61/0.3 13.81	1.93	51.78	14.77/1.6	43.34 4.85	60.87	4:41.83
7602	Ben	Hazell	GBR	1.10.84	3		Woerden	26 Aug
	11.26/1.1	7.11w/2.4 13.59	1.93	49.46	15.35/0.7	42.37 4.40	56.62	4:31.29
7592	Daniel	Almgren	SWE	30.11.79	1	v 2N	Visby	10 Jun
	11.01w/2.2	7.29/1.2 12.50	2.00	49.23	15.28/1.1	35.42 4.23	55.69	4:19.10
	(90)							
7584	Ryan	Olkowski	USA	19.4.80	1		Dallas	3 Jun
	10.59/1.1	7.12/0.5 13.05	1.98	48.10	15.11/-1.2	37.07 4.80	46.63	4:53.13
7583	Mykola	Shulha	UKR	26.11.82	1		Kyiv	4 Aug
	11.23/1.6	6.89/-0.3 14.85	1.94	49.84	14.93/0.6	44.57 4.40	53.53	4:45.52
7578	Mike	Marsh	USA	20.3.80	2		Dallas	3 Jun
	10.92/0.0	6.81/1.6 13.47	1.92	49.99	14.61/-1.4	41.75 4.70	51.78	4:43.54
7577	Stefan	Hommel	GER	3.9.84	7		Ratingen	17 Jun
	10.98/1.2	7.32/1.1 15.23	1.86	49.19	14.77/0.9	45.56 4.30	48.45	4:59.53
7561	Brandon	Hoskins	USA	29.5.85	7	NCAA	Sacramento	7 Jun
	11.05/1.2	6.89/2.0 13.82	1.87	49.44	15.04/1.5	41.97 4.30	59.83	4:38.37
7556	Jarrod	Sims	AUS	11.6.84	2	NC	Brisbane	10 Mar
	11.18/-2.0	7.34/1.6 12.10	2.02	49.14	15.19/0.2	36.88 4.50	52.49	4:31.32
7556w	Wilfred	Gouacide	FRA	5.9.82	8		Arles	3 Jun
	10.70w/6.8	7.55w/4.8 14.53	1.83	49.50	15.83/1.8	41.30 4.30	53.30	4:45.74
7555	Steffen	Fricke	GER	25.3.83	4	v USA	Bernhausen	19 Aug
	11.28/-0.1	7.02/-0.3 14.10	2.03	48.94	15.35/0.8	41.90 4.30	48.29	4:31.72
7552	Yevgen	Nikitin	UKR	9.1.85	2		Kyiv	4 Aug
	11.12/1.6	6.57/-0.1 13.28	1.91	49.37	15.39/0.6	43.27 4.80	52.11	4:28.97
7545	Attila	Szabó	HUN	16.7.84	1	NC	Budapest	16 Sep
	11.03/1.4	7.29/0.9 14.09	2.02	51.00	15.09/-0.6	39.36 4.30	53.91	4:46.04
	(100)							

Mark	Name		Nat	Born	Date
7542	Scott	McLaren	NZL	22.2.82	11 Nov
7541		Zhu Hengjun	CHN	5.2.87	9 Jun
7533w	Damien	Beauvir	FRA	20.3.84	3 Jun
7532	Jari	Olli	FIN	3.4.77	8 Jul
7529	Johannes	Schwuchow	GER	28.2.85	20 May
7526	Yuji	Oshima	JPN	12.10.83	22 Apr
7520	Andrey	Bashtanov	RUS	23.4.84	15 Jul
7517	Paolo	Mottadelli	ITA	7.6.79	27 Jul
7517	Jamie	Adjetey-Nelson	CAN	20.5.84	13 Aug
7514w	Guillaume	Barras	FRA	1.6.83	3 Jun
7509	Erik	Larsson	SWE	3.2.80	8 Jul
7505	Péter	Skoumal	HUN	6.7.80	8 Jul
7504	Gonzalo	Barroilhet	CHI	19.3.86	8 Jun
7497	Marcin	Drózdz	POL	21.3.83	10 Jun
7494	Päärn	Brauer	EST	21.11.82	10 Jun
7488	Patrick	Spinner	GER	28.11.85	19 Aug
7484	Marian	Geisler	GER	10.8.84	17 Jun
7484	Pavel	Andreyev	UZB	24.11.78	28 Jul
7479	Álvaro	Contreras	ESP	27.1.82	3 Jun
7473	Aki	Heikkinen	FIN	24.2.80	10 Jun
7473	Boualem	Lamri	ALG	26.3.81	19 Jul
7470	David	Gómez	ESP	13.2.81	5 Aug
7466	Eelco	Sintnicolaas	NED	7.4.87	26 Aug
7464		Lin Qingquan	CHN	6.4.87	2 Nov
7460	Luca	Ceglie	ITA	24.10.79	7 Jul
7457		Vu Van Huyen	VIE	8.8.83	8 Dec
7449	Mikko	Halvari	FIN	4.3.83	8 Jul
7441	Pulimootil	Joseph Vinod	IND	4.3.79	28 Jul
7432	Chiel	Warners	NED	2.4.78	7 Jul
7416w	Kyle	McCarthy	AUS	23.1.82	3 Jun
7412	Dmitriy	Starodubtsev	RUS	3.1.86	22 Sep
7408	Maxime	Gonguet	FRA	19.4.87	16 Jun
7405	Yuriy	Blonskyy	UKR	9.7.79	14 Jun
7404w	Damien	Camberlein	FRA	5.2.80	3 Jun
7404	Steffen	Kahlert	GER	30.5.87	9 Sep
7403	Franck	Logel	FRA	8.1.85	16 Jun
7402	Benjamin	Jensen (137)	NOR	13.4.75	8 Jul

Best without wind assistance

Mark	Name		Nat	Born	Pos	Meet	Venue	Date
7825	Vitaliy	Smirnov	UZB	25.10.78	2		Desenzano del Garda	6 May
	11.36/0.8	6.85/1.9 15.08	1.94	49.91	14.92/-0.7	43.85 4.70	58.67	4:27.16
7652	Hadi	Sepehrzad	IRI	19.1.83	*	AsiC	Amman	28 Jul
	wih 6.99w/3.6 LJ							
7616	Joe	Detmer	USA	3.9.83	3		Bernhausen	19 Aug
	11.17/-0.6	7.03/0.8 12.49	1.91	47.48	15.21/0.7	38.02 4.50	54.10	4:18.43

7502 de Araújo 6 May | 7482 Newdick 11 Nov | 7472 Gouacide 6 May

JUNIORS

Mark	Name		Nat	Born	Pos	Meet	Venue	Date
8257	Yordanis	Garcia	CUB-J	21.11.88	8	WCh	Osaka	1 Sep
	10.73/0.7	7.15/0.2 14.94	2.09	49.25	14.08/-0.2	42.91 4.70	68.74	4:55.42
8113		García			2	PAm	Rio de Janeiro	24 Jul
	10.67/-0.8	7.14/0.6 14.57	2.03	49.96	14.01/-0.2	45.93 4.50	63.75	4:51.74
8013		García			1	Barr/NC	La Habana	25 May
	10.88/1.5	7.06w/3.0 15.39	1.99	49.98	14.40/1.0	38.96 4.80	65.63	4:47.72
7378	Mateo	Sossah	FRA	28.4.88	9	NCAA	Sacramento	7 Jun
	11.80/0.5	6.84/1.9 11.11	2.02	50.84	14.94/0.9	40.91 4.40	55.36	4:18.60
7366	Mohammed	Jassem Al-Qaree	KSA	11.5.88	1	ArabC	Amman	21 May
	10.93/-2.5	7.60w/2.3 12.14	2.01	50.35	14.3h/1.0	36.97 4.40	52.52	5:22.52
7349	Larbi	Bouraada	ALG	10.5.88	3	AfG	Alger	19 Jul
	11.15/1.7	6.61/0.7 10.66	2.00	49.54	15.28/0.1	32.28 4.50	59.16	4:18.09

Mark	Name		Nat	Born	Pos	Meet	Venue	Date
7346		Guo Weizhao	CHN	2.1.88	3	WCT	Suzhou	9 Jun
	10.91/-0.7 6.86/-0.6 12.08 2.00 49.31 14.93/1.5 33.43 4.40 55.13 4:46.98							
7316	Michael	Morrison	USA	18.3.88	2	SEC	Tuscaloosa	11 May
	11.17/-0.1 7.18/-0.3 12.13 1.94 50.01 15.01/0.2 35.40 4.75 54.87 5:02.80							
7123	Ashton	Eaton	USA	21.1.88	2	Pac10	Stanford	6 May
	10.81/-0.2 7.23/0.1 11.88 1.92 49.19 14.66/1.0 36.57 3.95 36.92 4:39.72							
7078	Nick	Adcock	USA	2.4.88	8	Big12	Lincoln	12 May
	11.22/0.7 6.39/0.4 13.05 2.01 48.88 14.99/-0.7 27.24 4.05 56.38 4:42.05							
7068	Cory	Roberts	USA	25.3.88	3		Nacogdoches	5 May
	11.38w/2.1 6.29/-0.5 12.03 1.92 49.32 15.03/1.7 35.68 4.45 51.12 4:39.95							
Junior Implements 99cm 110mh, 6kg SP, 1.75kg DT								
7908	Matthias	Prey	GER	9.8.88	1	EJ	Hengelo	20 Jul
	11.11/0.3 7.36/-0.9 16.26 1.86 50.43 14.06/0.0 47.45 4.40 57.33 4:50.04							
	7751 1-j Ratingen 17 Jun				7585 1		Bernhausen	20 May
7766	Eduard	Mikhan	BLR	7.6.89	1		Minsk (Staiki)	8 Jun
	10.89/0.2 7.53/-0.2 14.56 2.00 49.51 15.03/0.2 41.54 4.30 50.54 4:38.20							
7560	Rok	Deržani	SLO	11.1.88	2	EJ	Hengelo	20 Jul
	10.76/0.3 7.09/0.4 13.13 1.98 49.00 14.03/0.0 34.40 4.40 43.76 4:30.99							
7524	Rico	Freimuth	GER	14.3.88	3	EJ	Hengelo	20 Jul
	10.99/0.1 6.61/-0.2 14.98 1.89 50.85 14.47/-0,1 45.65 4.40 40.76 4:45.92							
7516	Mateo	Sossah	FRA	20.4.88	4	EJ	Hengelo	20 Jul
	11.74/-0.7 6.80/-1.1 13.01 2.07 49.80 14.82/-0.1 40.08 4.50 50.94 4:23.78							
7504	Simon	Hechler	GER	15.6.88	5	EJ	Hengelo	20 Jul
	10.88/0.3 7.20/0.1 13.66 1.86 50.59 14.57/0.0 36.57 4.40 56.55 4:42.42							
7458	Karol	Bodula	POL	23.6.88	6	EJ	Hengelo	20 Jul
	11.30/0.1 6.58/0.6 14.73 1.89 51.56 14.57/0.0 44.88 4.40 53.26 4:38.38							
7435	Quentin	Jammier	FRA	24.7.88	1		Nice	16 Jun
	11.28/2.9 6.57/2.6 14.76 1.92 50.25 15.43/-1.5 42.28 4.40 53.55 4:31.71							
7394	Jonas	Fringeli	SUI	12.1.88	1		Hochdorf	23 Sep
	11.60/0.1 7.06/0.6 14.15 1.97 50.34 14.48/0.1 40.24 4.00 46.19 4:23.11							
7389	Kevin	Chaffre	FRA	27.7.88	1	NC-j	Compiègne	7 Jul
	11.33/1.3 7.46/0.2 12.38 2.01 50.25 14.48/0.0 37.93 4.50 42.10 4:43.04							
7379	Benjamin	Davies	USA	1.9.89		USA	Knoxville	29 Jul
	11.11/1.3 6.35 16.15 1.75 49.51 14.72/-1.4 40.68 4.55 57.88 5:01.15							
7348	Lars Vikan	Rise	NOR	23.11.88	1		Vejle	24 Jun
	11.72/-1.6 6.61/1.0 16.34 1.89 50.70 15.64/-0.2 46.48 4.13 56.79 4:45.93							
7337	Florian	Geffrouais	FRA	5.12.88	2		Nice	16 Jun
	11.13/2.9 6.60/1.5 14.16 1.83 50.47 15.41/-1.5 40.17 4.30 57.39 4:32.04							
7337	Andreas	Züblin	SUI	18.2.88	1	NC-j	Frauenfeld	16 Jun
	11.26/-1.0 6.53/0.1 15.06 1.98 53.44 14.38/1.5 36.12 4.80 51.69 4:51.00							
7317	Adam	Nejedlý	CZE	3.2.88	8	EJ	Hengelo	20 Jul
	11.30/0.1 6.96/-0.4 13.06 1.98 50.83 14.44/0.0 39.82 4.20 49.73 4:45.15							
7296	Bruno	Carton-Delcourt	BEL	15.2.88	1	NC-j	Beveren	26 Aug
	11.53/0.7 6.92/1.7 12.98 1.90 50.92 14.95/0.9 39.90 4.50 50.89 4:33.59							

4 X 100 METRES RELAY

37.78	USA	Patton 10.28, Spearmon 9.22, Gay 9.05, Dixon 9.23	1	WCh	Osaka	1 Sep
37.89	JAM	Anderson 10.60, Bolt 9.05, N Carter 9.40, Powell 8.84	2	WCh	Osaka	1 Sep
37.90	GBR	Malcolm 10.43, Pickering 9.06, Devonish 9.23, Lewis-Francis 9.18	3	WCh	Osaka	1 Sep
37.99	BRA	de Lima 10.25, Ribeiro 9.22, de Morães 9.33, Viana 9.19	4	WCh	Osaka	1 Sep
38.02	JAM	Thomas, Mullings, N Carter, Powell	1h2	WCh	Osaka	31 Aug
38.03	JPN	Tsukahara 10.44, Suetsugu 9.08, Takahira 9.35, Asahara 9.16	5	WCh	Osaka	1 Sep
38.10	USA	Martin, Spearmon, Patton, Dixon	2h2	WCh	Osaka	31 Aug
38.21	JPN	Tsukahara , Suetsugu, Takahira, Asahara	3h2	WCh	Osaka	31 Aug
38.27	BRA	de Lima , Ribeiro, de Morães, Viana	1h1	WCh	Osaka	31 Aug
38.30	GBR	Edgar, Pickering, Devonish, Lewis-Francis	1	ECp-S	München	23 Jun
38.33	GBR	Malcolm, Pickering, Devonish, Lewis-Francis	2h1	WCh	Osaka	31 Aug
38.35	USA	"Red" Gay, Spearmon, Patton, Crawford	1	PennR	Philadelphia	28 Apr
38.38	USA	"B" Grimes, Dixon, Wiggins, X Carter	1	LGP	London (CP)	3 Aug
38.40	FRA	Nthépé, Alerte, De Lepine, Mbandjock	2	ECp-S	München	23 Jun
38.40	USA	Patton Spearmon, Gay, Dixon	1	WK	Zürich	7 Sep
38.43	NGR	Metu, I Chukwu, Oriala, Fasuba	4h2	WCh	Osaka	31 Aug
38.56	GER	Blum, Helmke, Kosenkow, Reus	3	ECp-S	München	23 Jun
38.56	GER	Ostwald, Unger, Kosenkow, Reus	5h2	WCh	Osaka	31 Aug
38.60	Florida State University (USA)	Bolden, Dix, Garvin, Clark	1	NCAA	Sacramento	8 Jun
38.62	POL	Rogowski, Chyla, Jedrusinski, Kuc	4	ECp-S	München	23 Jun
38.62	GER	Ostwald, Unger, Kosenkow, Reus	6	WCh	Osaka	1 Sep
38.63	ITA	Verdecchio, Collio, Cerutti, Riparelli	1		Génève	8 Jun

22 performances by teams from 10 nations

Mark	Nat	Name	Pos	Meet	Venue	Date
38.73	AUS	Shirvington, Miller, Williams, Rouge-Serret	6h2	WCh	Osaka	31 Aug
38.81	CAN	Adu-Bobie, Henry, Connaughton, Barnett	1h2	PAm	Rio de Janeiro	27 Jul
38.95	THA	U-tas, Sondee, Suwannarangrsi, Suwonprateep	1	SEAG	Nakhon Ratcha.	10 Dec
39.02	TRI	M Thomas, Burns, Callender, Bledman	2h1	PAm	Rio de Janeiro	27 Jul
39.05	RSA	Krone, Julius, Snyman, Vries	5h1	WCh	Osaka	31 Aug
39.08	RUS	Volkov, Yegorychev, R.Smirnov, Teplykh	6h1	WCh	Osaka	31 Aug
39.13	GRE	Steryioúlis, Vássou, Goúsis, Gavélas	5	ECp-S	München	23 Jun
39.16	ZIM	Makusha, Mvumvure, Dzingai, Banda	3	AfG	Alger	20 Jul
39.23	CUB	Lescay, Y Hernández, Herrera, Vizcaíno	1	ALBA	Caracas	9 May
39.24	SUI	Baumann, Schneeberger, Cribari, Kundert	4	WK	Zürich	7 Sep
	(20)					
39.30	CHN	Wang Xiaoxu, Zhang Peimeng, Du Bing, Yin Hualong	3	WUG	Bangkok	9 Aug
39.34	NED	Beck, Hoogmoed, Heisen, Spier	2	DNG	Stockholm	7 Aug
39.37	POR	Gonçalves, Abrantes, Martins, Nascimento	2	EU23	Debrecen	15 Jul
39.41	AHO	Kwidama, Raphaela, Mariano, Martina	3h1	PAm	Rio de Janeiro	27 Jul
39.47	NZL	Bearda, Dolphin, Brown, Donaldson	2		Sydney	17 Feb
39.49	GHA	Adade, Amoo, Duah, Mfum	1h2	AfG	Alger	19 Jul
39.51	QAT	Al-Shahwani, Francis, Aosman, Al-Waleed	3	DNG	Stockholm	7 Aug
39.51A	MRI	Casquette, Edwards, Louis, Coiffic	1	IOG	Antanarivo	16 Aug
39.53	KSA	Habeeb, Al-Kahes, Mubarak, Al-Bishi	1		Amman	20 May
39.53	FIN	Hämäläinen, Hongisto, Jokinen, Åstrand	3	EU23	Debrecen	15 Jul
	(30)					

39.54	CIV	19 Jul	39.80	COL	8 Jun	40.01	CAY	15 Jul	40.17	BUR	20 Jul	40.36	ROM	4 Jul
39.55	SLO	23 Jun	39.82	TPE	2 Jun	40.01	VEN	20 Dec	40.17	EGY	23 Nov	40.38	MAR	23 Nov
39.57	ESP	10 Jul	39.84	IND	29 Jul	40.05	ECU	8 Jun	40.26	IRI	16 Jul	40.44	LAT	23 Jun
39.68	UKR	23 Jun	39.90	MAS	10 Dec	40.07	PAN	9 May	40.27	HUN	15 Jul	**Hand timed**		
39.69	CZE	22 May	39.91	ARG	8 Jun	40.10	SIN	10 Dec	40.32	HKG	2 Nov	40.2	PAK	13 Apr
39.69	BEL	23 Jun	39.91	BAH	28 Jul	40.11	EST	23 Jun	40.33	IRL	23 Jun	**Best at low altitude**		
39.74	SKN	27 Jul	39.93	BOT	19 Jul	40.12	OMA	23 Nov	40.34	BAR	9 May	39.64	MRI	20 Jul
39.79	INA	10 Dec	40.00	BUL	4 Jul	40.16	SEN	30 Jun	40.36	SWE	23 Jun			

Mixed nation team: 38.30 Arkansas Alumni USA/TRI 1 MSR Walnut 15 Apr
Kimmons, Spearmon, Gay, Armstrong/TRI

JUNIORS

Mark	Nat	Name	Pos	Meet	Venue	Date
39.43	USA	Wims, Crawford, Stevenson, Williams	1	PAm-J	São Paulo	7 Jul
39.47	JAM	Marsden, McKenzie, Jerwis, Blake	1	Carifta	Providenciales	8 Jul
39.73	CHN	(Guangzhou) Zhao Haohuan, Su Bingtian, Li Haolun, Liang Jiahong	2		Wuhan	2 Nov
39.81	JPN	Abiko, Eriguchi, Kobayashi, Kumamoto	6		Osaka	5 May
39.81	GER	Christ, Reus, Hering, Brandt	1	EJ	Hengelo	22 Jul
39.83	GBR	Sobodu, Nelson, Fagan, Yearwood	2	EJ	Hengelo	22 Jul
40.11	TRI	Glasgow, Bacchus, Morgan, Bledman	2	PAm-J	São Paulo	7 Jul
40.21	FRA	Figaro, Lesourd, Mignot, Nubret	3	EJ	Hengelo	22 Jul
40.23	POL	Paruzel, Oganiaczyk, Wojciechowski, Zaczek	1h2	EJ	Hengelo	21 Jul
40.40	COL	Riascos, Gómez, Valencia, Maturana	3	PAm-J	São Paulo	7 Jul
40.53	ITA	Demichei, Demonte, Berdini, Galvan	1		Firenze	3 Aug
40.58	CUB	Betanzos, Lesacay, Skyers, Moya	3	Barr/NC	La Habana	26 May
40.59	NED	Van Betuw, Tromp, Codrington, Susanna	2h1	EJ	Hengelo	21 Jul

4 X 200 METRES RELAY

1:21.37	World Express (USA)	1	FlaR	Gainesville	6 Apr
1:21.65	Baylor University C Thomas, Betters, Harts, R Witherspoon	1	DrakeR	Des Moines	27 Apr
1:21.73	Florida State University	1	PennR	Philadelphia	28 Apr

4 X 400 METRES RELAY

2:55.56	USA	Merritt 44.4, Taylor 43.7, Williamson 44.32, Wariner 43.10	1	WCh	Osaka	2 Sep
2:59.18	USA Red Rock	45.9, Brew 44.9, Merritt 44.0, Williamson 44.4	1	PennR	Philadelphia	28 Apr
2:59.18	BAH	Moncur 45.2, Mathieu 45.0, A Williams 44.54, C Brown 44.41	2	WCh	Osaka	2 Sep
3:00.04	USA Blue	Neville 46.2, Spearmon 44.9, Clement 44.4, B.Jackson 44.5	2	PennR	Philadelphia	28 Apr
3:00.04	Baylor University USA	Witherspoon 45.6, Betters 44.4, Mutai 45.18, Summers 44.88	1	NCAA	Sacramento	9 Jun
3:00.05	POL	Plawgo 45.5, Dabrowski 44.6, Marciniszyn 44.81, Kozlowski 45.15	3	WCh	Osaka	2 Sep
3:00.37	BAH	McKinney 45.9, Mathieu 44.9, C Brown 44.52, A Williams 45.03	1h1	WCh	Osaka	1 Sep
3:00.44	JAM	Gonzalez 45.9, Green 46.0, Ayre 44.2, Blackwood 44.3	3	PennR	Philadelphia	28 Apr
3:00.64	BAH	McKinney 45.2, C Brown 45.3, A Williams 45.6, Mathieu 44.5	4	PennR	Philadelphia	28 Apr
3:00.76	JAM	Blackwood 45.4, Chambers 44.3, Green 44.50, Ayre 46.54	4	WCh	Osaka	2 Sep
3:00.99	JAM	Blackwood 46.4, Chambers 45.5, Green 44.44, Ayre 44.63	2h1	WCh	Osaka	1 Sep
3:01.07	Texas A&M Un USA	McCombs 45.9, Robinson 45.0, Pitre 45.49, Oliver 44.67	2	NCAA	Sacramento	9 Jun
3:01.07	RUS	Dyldin 46.3, Frolov 45.4, Svechkar 45.00, Alekseyev 44.38	3h1	WCh	Osaka	1 Sep
3:01.22	GBR	Steele 46.4, Tobin 45.4, Buck 45.23, Rooney 44.17	4h1	WCh	Osaka	1 Sep
3:01.46	USA	B.Jackson 45.7, Clement 45.3, Williamson 44.58, Taylor 45.85	1h2	WCh	Osaka	1 Sep
3:01.62	RUS	Dyldin 46.2, Frolov 44.9, Svechkar 45.31, Alekseyev 45.20	5	WCh	Osaka	2 Sep

Mark	Nat	Name	Pos	Meet	Venue	Date
3:01.66	Baylor Un USA	Witherspoon 45.7, Betters 45.0, Mutai 45.9, Summers 45.1	1	NCAA-r	Des Moines	26 May
3:01.70	POL	Kozlowski 46.18, Marciniszyn 45.10, Rysukiewicz 46.08, Dabrowski 44.34	1	ECp-S	München	24 Jun
3:01.77	GER	Schultz 45.9, Gaba 45.3, Bos 45.93, Swillims 44.66	2	ECp-S	München	24 Jun
3:01.92	GBR	Steele 45.7, Strachan 45.9, Rooney 44.94, Caines 45.38	3	ECp-S	München	24 Jun
	20 performances by teams from 6 nations					
3:02.21	GRE	Régas 46.8, Doúpis 45.4, Grávalos 45.41, P Iakovákis 44.57	4	ECp-S	München	24 Jun
3:02.44	JPN	Yamaguchi, Horigome, Y Ota, Kanemaru	1	GP	Osaka	5 May
3:02.48	DOM	Santa, Peguero, Tapia, Sánchez	3	PAm	Rio de Janeiro	28 Jul
3:02.59	AUS	Wroe 45.7, Grant 45.4, Mulcahy 45.27, Ormrod 46.15	6h1	WCh	Osaka	1 Sep
	(10)					
3:02.92	TRI	Modibo 45.5, Toppin 46.1, Solomon 45.56, Quow 45.79	5h2	WCh	Osaka	1 Sep
3:03.16	BOT	Masheto, Ngwigwa, Makwala, Molefe	1	AfG	Alger	22 Jul
3:03.65	FRA	Kadri 47.2, Panel 45.0, Lahaye 45.99, Venel 45.43	6	ECp-S	München	24 Jun
3:03.99	NGR	Lawal, Weigopwa, Isaiah, James	2	AfG	Alger	22 Jul
3:04.01	CAN	Barnett, Vadeboncoeur, Kunkel, Christopher	1	Jerome	Burnaby	8 Jun
3:04.36	BRA	de Almeida, Bargas, Vasconcelos, Fernandes	1	SACh	São Paulo	9 Jun
3:04.74	KSA	H H Al-Bishi, Hamdan Al-Bishi, Al-Salhi, Al-Sabyani	1	PArab	Cairo	24 Nov
3:04.84	ZIM	Ndebele, Nyongani, Chikomo, Banda	3	AfG	Alger	22 Jul
3:05.11	ITA	Turchi, Salvucci, Galletti, Barberi	1	ECp-1B	Milano	24 Jun
3:05.14	BEL	K Borlée 46.5, Beyens 45.9, Schoeps 46.66, Duerinck 46.10	7	ECp-S	München	24 Jun
	(20)					
3:05.32	ALG	Chérifi, Madi, Louahla, Rahmani	4	AfG	Alger	22 Jul
3:05.61	ROM	Pavel, Câmpeanu, Suciu, Vieru	2	ECp-1B	Milano	24 Jun
3:05.71	CZE	Hruby, Jirán, Jares, Klofác	4	EU23	Debrecen	15 Jul
3:05.72	PUR	Amador, Culson, Carrasquillo, Martinez	2	Sánchez	Santo Domingo	12 May
3:05.88	VEN	Céspedes, Silvera, Rivas, Rodríguez	2	SACh	São Paulo	9 Jun
3:06.00A	KEN	(Armed Forces)	1	NC	Nairobi	14 Jun
3:06.30	ESP	Ujakpor, Ezquerro, Testa, Reina	1	ECp-1A	Vaasa	24 Jun
3:06.37	UKR	Rachkovskyy, Knysh, Tverdostup, Zyukov	2		Wattenscheid	12 Aug
3:06.44	RSA	H Kotze, Dreyer, Cilliers, de Beer	4	WUG	Bangkok	14 Aug
3:06.52	SUD	Maki, Kaki, Adam Dar, Abubakar	2	PArab	Cairo	24 Nov
	(30)					

3:06.65 SEN 21 Jul	3:06.95 CHN 5 Aug	3:07.32 NED 12 Aug	3:08.22 IRL 24 Jun	3:08.64 IRI 29 Jul
3:06.78 SWE 24 Jun	3:07.08 HUN 15 Jul	3:07.74 SLO 24 Jun	3:08.25 THA 8 Dec	3:09.06 DEN 24 Jun
3:06.83 TUN 24 Nov	3:07.10 MAR 24 Nov	3:07.94 IND 29 Jul	3:08.43 POR 24 Jun	3:09.26 SVK 24 Jun
3:06.84 CUB 10 May	3:07.15 SRI 19 Jun	3:07.95 MAS 8 Dec	3:08.53 PHI 8 Dec	3:09.52 SUI 12 Aug
				3:09.67 PAN 9 Jun

JUNIORS

Mark	Nat	Name	Pos	Meet	Venue	Date
3:05.70	TRI	Hewitt, Toppin, Morgan, Forte	1	PAm-J	São Paulo	8 Jul
3:06.15	USA	Simmons, Ward, Dutch, Nellum	2	PAm-J	São Paulo	8 Jul
3:06.17	JAM	Coote, Hylton, Peart, Blake	3	PAm-J	São Paulo	8 Jul
3:07.94	BEL	Gillet, Froidmont, Ghislain, Haeck	1h2	EJ	Hengelo	21 Jul
3:08.17	POL	Ciepiela, Porzadny, Krzewina, Wojciechowski	2h2	EJ	Hengelo	21 Jul
3:08.21	GBR	Levine, Davis, Persent, McGrath	1	EJ	Hengelo	22 Jul
3:08.64	GER	Nabow, Krüger, Schneider, Schembera	2	EJ	Hengelo	22 Jul
3:08.68	BRA	Cardoso, Gomes, de Souza, Alves	1	SAm-J	São Paulo	1 Jul
3:08.86	CAN	Barnett, Dargie, ?, ?	5	PennR	Philadelphia	28 Apr
3:09.10	FRA	Naprix, Francois, Rollamd, Fonsat	4	EJ	Hengelo	22 Jul
3:09.28	BAH		3	Carifta	Providenciales	9 Apr
3:09.90	KEN		1	Af-J	Ouagadougou	12 Aug
3:10.20	JPN	Takebe, Sakamoto, Irie, Sato	1		Fukushima	26 Aug
3:10.78	PUR	de Jesús, Benítez, Lopez, Santiago	5	PAm-J	São Paulo	8 Jul
3:11.12	ITA	Berdini, Capotosti, Severi, Galvan	1	vFRA-J	Firenze	4 Aug
3:11.65	ESP	Orozco, Guerrero, García, Cabello	3h1	EJ	Hengelo	21 Jul

4 X 800 METRES RELAY

Mark	Name	Pos	Meet	Venue	Date
7:18.43	University of Southern California	1	TexR	Austin	7 Apr

4 X 1500 METRES RELAY

Mark	Name	Pos	Meet	Venue	Date
15:17.91	Randwick (AUS) Farrelly, Hunt, Woods, Woods, Roff	1		Sydney	17 Nov

4 X 110 METRES HURDLES

Mark	Nat	Name	Pos	Meet	Venue	Date
53.36	USA	Bramlett, Moore, Payne, Merritt	1	DNG	Stockholm	7 Aug

3000 METRES TRACK WALK

Mark	First name	Surname	Nat	Born	Pos	Meet	Venue	Date
11:00.5+	Francisco Javier	Fernández	ESP	6.3.77	1	in 5k	Villeneuve d'Ascq	8 Jun
11:06.8+	Erik	Tysse	NOR	4.12.80	1	in 5k	Askim	10 Aug
11:22.4	Jarrod	Tallent	AUS	17.10.84	1		Sydney	17 Feb
11:27.0	Michael	McCagh	AUS	16.4.86	2		Sydney	17 Feb
11:27.7	Adam	Rutter	AUS	24.12.86	3		Sydney	17 Feb

Mark	Name		Nat	Born	Pos	Meet	Venue	Date
11:32.0+	Ilya	Markov	RUS	19.6.72	1	in 5k	Kielce	15 Sep

11:36.83+ Ivano Brugnetti ITA 1.9.76 27 Jul

Indoors: 11:41.27+ Grzegorz Sudol POL 28.8.78 18 Feb

5000 METRES TRACK WALK

Mark	Name		Nat	Born	Pos	Meet	Venue	Date
18:27.34	Francisco Javier	Fernández	ESP	6.3.77	1		Villeneuve d'Ascq	8 Jun
18:32.46	Erik	Tysse	NOR	4.12.80	1	NC	Askim	10 Aug
18:35.54	Yohann	Diniz	FRA	1.1.78	1		Paris	17 Jun
18:40.97A	Eder	Sánchez	MEX	21.5.86	1		Xalapa	5 May
18:45.05	Hatem	Ghoula	TUN	7.6.73	2		Paris	17 Jun
18:46.08A	Jefferson	Pérez	ECU	1.7.74	2		Xalapa	5 May
18:50.27		Diniz			2		Villeneuve d'Ascq	8 Jun
18:50.51		Diniz			1		Lomme	6 May
18:54.03	Juan Manuel	Molina	ESP	15.3.79	1		Gavá	30 Jun
18:59.37	Robert	Heffernan	IRL	28.2.78	2		Gavá	30 Jun
18:59.43	Luke	Adams	AUS	22.10.76	1		Melbourne	24 Feb
19:00+	Ivano	Brugnetti	ITA	1.9.76	1	in 20k	Milano	17 Mar
19:08.55+		Fernández			1	in 10k	San Sebastián	5 Aug
19:20.38	Ilya	Markov	RUS	19.6.72	1		Kielce	15 Sep

Mark	Name		Nat	Born	Date
19:32.47A	Álvaro	García	MEX	18.10.83	5May
19:32.5	Benjamín	Sánchez	ESP	10.3.85	11 Feb
19:35.86A	Adrián	Herrera	MEX	6.4.84	5May
19:37.29	Hervé	Davaux	FRA	22.8.78	6May
19:40.27	Chris	Erickson	AUS	1.12.81	24 Feb
19:44.65A	David	Mejia	MEX	7.12.86	5May

Indoors

Mark	Name		Nat	Born	Pos	Meet	Venue	Date
18:08.86	Ivano	Brugnetti	ITA	1.9.76	1	NC	Ancona	17 Feb
18:24.13	Francisco Javier	Fernández	ESP	6.3.77	1		Belfast	17 Feb
18:30.91	Aleksandr	Yargunkin	RUS	6.1.81	1		Yekaterinburg	7 Jan
18:33.95	Ivan	Kuznetsov	RUS	11.9.83	2		Yekaterinburg	7 Jan
18:39.58		Fernández			3		Yekaterinburg	7 Jan
18:56.31	Ilya	Markov	RUS	19.6.72	4		Yekaterinburg	7 Jan
19:04.74	João	Vieira	POR	20.2.76	1	NC	Espinho	17 Feb
19:11.58		Heffernan			2	NC	Belfast	17 Feb
19:22.62	Alessandro	Gandellini	ITA	30.4.73	2	NC	Ancona	17 Feb
19:24.38	Tim	Seaman	USA	14.5.72	1	NC	Boston (R)	24 Feb
19:28.63	Kevin	Eastler	USA	14.10.77	2	NC	Boston (R)	24 Feb
19:28.83	André	Höhne	GER	10.3.78	1	NC	Leipzig	17 Feb
19:29.23	Jean-Jacques	Nkouloukidi	ITA	15.4.82	3	NC	Ancona	17 Feb

Mark	Name		Nat	Born	Date
19:32.79	Grzegorz	Sudol	POL	28.8.78	18 Feb
19:36.42	Colin	Griffin	IRL	3.8.82	17 Feb
19:41.5	Aleksandr	Prokhorov	RUS	22.1.86	6 Jan
19:41.53	Andrey	Talashko	BLR	31.5.82	17 Feb
19:42.12	Rafal	Augustyn	POL	14.5.84	18 Feb

10,000 METRES TRACK WALK

Mark	Name		Nat	Born	Pos	Meet	Venue	Date
38:07.65	Francisco Javier	Fernández	ESP	6.3.77	1	NC	San Sebastián	5 Aug
39:00.0	Ivano	Brugnetti	ITA	1.9.76	1	in 20k	Milano	17 Mar
39:11.78	Robert	Heffernan	IRL	28.2.78	1	NC	Dublin	22 Jul
39:21.51		Shin Il-yong	KOR	17.2.79	1		Andong	22 May
39:25.58		Pak Chil-sung	KOR	8.7.82	2		Andong	22 May
39:31.51		Kim Hyun-sub	KOR	31.5.85	3		Andong	22 May
39:51.85	Colin	Griffin	IRL	3.8.82	2	NC	Dublin	22 Jul
39:54.47	Yuki	Yamazaki	JPN	16.1.84	1		Akita	8 Oct
39:56.3	Ingus	Jenevics	LAT	29.4.86	1		Murjani	28 Apr
40:02.88	Sergey	Morozov	RUS-J	21.3.88	1	EJ	Hengelo	21 Jul
40:07.3	Carsten	Schmidt	GER	29.5.86	1		Jüterbog	11 May
40:08.71	André	Höhne	GER	10.3.78	1	NC	Erfurt	21 Jul
40:13.2	Erik	Tysse	NOR	4.12.80	1		Strandebarm	10 Jun
40:15.79	Koicho	Morioka	JPN	2.4.85	2		Akita	8 Oct

Mark	Name		Nat	Born	Date
40:20.82	Giorgio	Rubino	ITA	15.4.86	29 Sep
40:21.84		Cui Zhili	CHN	11.1.83	22 Apr
40:28.02	Jamie	Costin	IRL	1.6.77	22 Jul
40:31.39	Lorenzo	Civallero	ITA	8.8.75	29 Sep
40:31.5	Vladimir	Parvatkin	RUS	10.10.84	22 Jun
40:36.84	Benjamin	Sánchez	ESP	10.3.85	5 Aug
40:39.21	Alex	Schwazer	ITA	26.12.84	27 Jul
40:41.39	Alessandro	Gandellini	ITA	30.4.73	29 Sep

Indoors

Mark	Name		Nat	Born	Pos	Meet	Venue	Date
40:04.38	Andriy	Kovenko	UKR	25.11.73	1	NC	Sumy	14 Feb
40:06.15	Sergey	Chernov	BLR	5.2.79	1	NC	Mogilyov	9 Feb
40:06.19	Andrey	Stepanchuk	BLR	12.6.79	2	NC	Mogilyov	9 Feb

JUNIORS

Mark	Name		Nat	Born	Pos	Meet	Venue	Date
40:02.88	Sergey	Morozov	RUS	21.3.88	1	EJ	Hengelo	21 Jul
40:51.75		Li Gaobo	CHN	4.5.89	1		Guangzhou	19 Jul
40:54.15	Yusuke	Suzuki	JPN	2.1.88	3	NG	Yuwa	8 Oct
40:54.88	Matteo	Giupponi	ITA	8.10.88	2	EJ	Hengelo	21 Jul

Mark	Name		Nat	Born	Pos	Meet	Venue	Date
41:06.32	Lluis	Torlá	ESP	2.10.89	3	EJ	Hengelo	21 Jul
41:07.04	Eiki	Unami	JPN	10.5.88	1		Toyama	21 Oct
41:07.51	Manel	Torlá	ESP	2.10.89	4	EJ	Hengelo	21 Jul
41:39.43		Chu Yafei	CHN	5.9.88	4		Guangzhou	19 Jul
41:42.08		Wang Hao	CHN	16.8.89	4		Beijing	22 Apr
41:49.91	Stanislav	Yemelyanov	RUS-Y	8.5.90	1	WY	Ostrava	14 Jul

10 KILOMETRES ROAD WALK

Mark	Name		Nat	Born	Pos	Meet	Venue	Date
38:19	Ivano	Brugnetti	ITA	1.9.76	1		Fiumicino	9 Sep
38:25	Francisco Javier	Fernández	ESP	6.3.77	1		San Fernando	3 Feb
38:25	Ilya	Markov	RUS	19.6.72	2		San Fernando	3 Feb
38:28+	Vladimir	Kanaykin	RUS	21.3.85	1=	in 20k	Saransk	29 Sep
38:28+	Valeriy	Borchin	RUS	3.7.86	1=	in 20k	Saransk	29 Sep
38:28+	Igor	Yerokhin	RUS	4.9.85	1=	in 20k	Saransk	29 Sep
38:28+	Sergey	Morozov	RUS-J	21.3.88	1=	in 20k	Saransk	29 Sep
38:36+		Fernández			1	in 20k	La Coruña	2 Jun
39:19+	Hatem	Ghoula	TUN	7.6.73	2	in 20k	La Coruña	2 Jun
39:22+	Nathan	Deakes	AUS	17.8.77	3	in 20k	La Coruña	2 Jun
39:23	Erik	Tysse	NOR	4.12.80	1		S fteland	25 Ma
39:25		Fernández			1		Granollers	2 Dec
39:28+		Han Yucheng	CHN	16.12.78	4	in 20k	La Coruña	2 Jun
39:29	Giorgio	Rubino	ITA	15.4.86	2		Fiumicino	9 Sep
39:32		Brugnetti			2		Granollers	2 Dec
39:35+		Brugnetti			1=	in 20k	Leamington	20 Ma
39:35+	Yohann	Diniz	FRA	1.1.78	1=	in 20k	Leamington	20 Ma
39:42+	Eder	Sánchez	MEX	21.5.86	5	in 20k	La Coruña	2 Jun
39:49+	Robert	Heffernan	IRL	28.2.78	4	in 20k	Leamington	20 Ma
39:50	Jean-Jacques	Nkouloukidi	ITA	15.4.82	3		Fiumicino	9 Sep
39:58	Marco	Giungi	ITA	30.10.74	1		Chieti	24 Jun
40:04+	Takayuki	Tanii	JPN	14.2.83	1=	in 20k	Nomi	25 Mar
40:04+	Koichiro	Morioka	JPN	2.4.85	1=	in 20k	Nomi	25 Mar
40:05+	Ivan	Trotskiy	BLR	27.5.76	6=	in 20k	Leamington	20 May
40:06+	Sergey	Chernov	BLR	5.2.79	8	in 20k	Leamington	20 May

JUNIORS

Mark	Name		Nat	Born	Pos	Meet	Venue	Date
38:28+	Sergey	Morozov	RUS	21.3.88	1=	in 20k	Saransk	29 Sep
	40:25 1 ECp-J Leamington 20 May	40:27 1 NC-wj Adler 17 Feb						
40:32	Aleksey	Barchaykin	RUS	22.3.89	1	NC-j	Cheboksary	16 Jun
40:49	Miguel Ángel	López	ESP	3.7.88	2	ECp-J	Leamington	20 May
40:57	Edikt	Khaybullin	RUS	29.5.89	2	NC-wj	Adler	17 Feb
41:09	Dmitriy	Shorin	RUS	26.3.88	3	NC-wj	Adler	17 Feb
41:20	Anton	Sivakov	RUS	19.1.89	4	NC-wj	Adler	17 Feb
41:30	Pavel	Samoylenko	RUS	13.3.88	3	NC-J	Cheboksary	16 Jun
41:31		Zhang Rui	CHN	12.1.89	1	NC-j	Beijing	20 Aug
41:43	Stanislav	Yemelyanov	RUS-Y	8.5.90	1	NC-Y	Cheboksary	16 Jun
41:46	Manel	Torlá	ESP	2.10.89	4	ECp-J	Leamington	20 May
41:49	Lluis	Torlá	ESP	2.10.89	5	ECp-J	Leamington	20 May
41:55	Víctor	Mendoza	ESA	16.11.88	1		San Salvador	3 Feb

20 KILOMETRES WALK

Mark	Name		Nat	Born	Pos	Meet	Venue	Date
1:17:16	Vladimir	Kanaykin	RUS	21.3.85	1	RWC	Saransk	29 Sep
1:17:36		Kanaykin			1	NC	Cheboksary	17 Jun
1:18:50	Francisco Javier	Fernández	ESP	6.3.77	1		La Coruña	2 Jun
1:18:51		Fernández			1		Shenzhen	24 Mar
1:18:56	Valeriy	Borchin	RUS	3.7.86	1	NC-w	Adler	17 Feb
1:18:56	Ilya	Markov	RUS	19.6.72	2	NC	Cheboksary	17 Jun
1:18:58	Yohann	Diniz	FRA	1.1.78	1	ECp	Leamington	20 May
1:19:03		Li Gaobo	CHN-J	4.5.89	2		Shenzhen	24 Mar
1:19:14	Sergey	Bakulin	RUS	13.11.86	3	NC	Cheboksary	17 Jun
1:19:15		Han Yucheng	CHN	16.12.78	2		La Coruña	2 Jun
1:19:21	Igor	Yerokhin	RUS	4.9.85	2	NC-w	Adler	17 Feb
1:19:34	Nathan	Deakes (10)	AUS	17.8.77	3		La Coruña	2 Jun
1:19:36	Ivano	Brugnetti	ITA	1.9.76	2	ECp	Leamington	20 May
1:19:52		Fernández			1	NC	Santa Eularia des Riu	4 Mar
1:19:57	Viktor	Burayev	RUS	23.8.82	3	NC-w	Adler	17 Feb
1:20:07	Andrey	Ruzavin	RUS	28.3.86	4	NC-w	Adler	17 Feb
1:20:08	Eder	Sánchez	MEX	21.5.86	3		Shenzhen	24 Mar
1:20:09		Yerokhin			3	ECp	Leamington	20 May
1:20:11.72t		Li Gaobo			1		Wuhan	2 Nov
1:20:12	Andrey	Krivov	RUS	14.11.85	4	NC	Cheboksary	17 Jun

Mark	Name		Nat	Born	Pos	Meet	Venue	Date
1:20:13	Ivan	Trotskiy	BLR	27.5.76	4	ECp	Leamington	20 May
1:20:15	Robert	Heffernan	IRL	28.2.78	5	ECp	Leamington	20 May
1:20:16		Lu Ronghua	CHN	21.2.83	4		Shenzhen	24 Mar
1:20:16	Dmitriy	Yesipchuk	RUS	17.11.74	5	NC	Cheboksary	17 Jun
1:20:20	(20)	Park Chil-sung	KOR	8.7.82	1		Goyang	1 May
1:20:21		Brugnetti			1		Rio Maior	14 Apr
1:20:26		Sánchez			1		Kraków	23 Jun
1:20:30	Luke	Adams	AUS	22.10.76	5		Shenzhen	24 Mar
1:20:31	Erik	Tysse	NOR	4.12.80	2		Kraków	23 Jun
1:20:32	André	Höhne	GER	10.3.78	6	ECp	Leamington	20 May
	(30/23)							
1:20:40	Hatem	Ghoula	TUN	7.6.73	3		Kraków	23 Jun
1:20:42	João	Vieira	POR	20.2.76	7	ECp	Leamington	20 May
1:20:44	Juan Manuel	Molina	ESP	15.3.79	4		Kraków	23 Jun
1:20:54		Kim Hyun-sub	KOR	31.5.85	2		Goyang	1 May
1:21:02	Sergey	Chernov	BLR	5.2.79	8	ECp	Leamington	20 May
1:21:09	Takayuki	Tanii	JPN	14.2.83	1	AsiC	Nomi	25 Mar
1:21:11	Ivan	Kuznetsov	RUS	11.9.83	6	NC-w	Adler	17 Feb
	(30)							
1:21:14	Jefferson	Pérez	ECU	1.7.74	6		Shenzhen	24 Mar
1:21:14	Vladimir	Stankin	RUS	2.1.74	6	NC	Cheboksary	17 Jun
1:21:17	Giorgio	Rubino	ITA	15.4.86	10	ECp	Leamington	20 May
1:21:20.69t		Wang Hao	CHN-J	16.8.89	2		Wuhan	2 Nov
1:21:21	Benjamín	Sánchez	ESP	10.3.85	5		Rio Maior	14 Apr
1:21:25	Jarrod	Tallent	AUS	17.10.84	7		Shenzhen	24 Mar
1:21:26		Wei Yang	CHN-J	26.3.89	8		Shenzhen	24 Mar
1:21:30	Koichiro	Morioka	JPN	2.4.85	2	AsiC	Nomi	25 Mar
1:21:36		Zeng Guoqiang	CHN	25.10.84	9		Shenzhen	24 Mar
1:21:41.59t	Marco	Giungi	ITA	30.10.74	2		Formia	18 Mar
	(40)							
1:21:47		Shin Il-yong	KOR	17.2.79	1	NG	Kwangju	11 Oct
1:21:50	Andrey	Talashko	BLR	31.5.82	2	NC	Nesvizh	14 Apr
1:21:56	Sergey	Sergachev	RUS	10.7.87	4	RWC	Saransk	29 Sep
1:21:57	José Ignacio	Díaz	ESP	22.11.79	14	ECp	Leamington	20 May
1:21:58	Beniamin	Kucinski	POL	1.6.82	15	ECp	Leamington	20 May
1:22:06		Dong Jimin	CHN	10.10.85	13		Shenzhen	24 Mar
1:22:08	Rafal	Augustyn	POL	14.5.84	16	ECp	Leamington	20 May
1:22:11.67t		Chu Yafei	CHN-J	5.9.88	3		Wuhan	2 Nov
1:22:12	Sérgio	Vieira	POR	20.2.76	10		La Coruña	2 Jun
1:22:12	Nikolay	Seredovich	BLR	25.1.84	1	NC	Grodno	5 Jul
	(50)							
1:22:13	Aleksandr	Prokhorov	RUS	22.1.86	5	RWC	Saransk	29 Sep
1:22:22	Andriy	Kovenko	UKR	25.11.73	1	NC-w	Yevpatoriya	17 Mar
1:22:24	Aleksandr	Yargunkin	RUS	6.1.81	8	NC	Cheboksary	17 Jun
1:22:26	Denis	Simanovich	BLR	20.4.87	3	NC	Nesvizh	14 Apr
1:22:29.46t		Zhang Xuezhi	CHN	6.7.87	4		Wuhan	2 Nov
1:22:31	Andrés	Chocho	ECU	4.11.83	7		Kraków	23 Jun
1:22:52	Aleksandr	Kuzmin	BLR	24.3.81	2	NC	Grodni	5 Jul
1:22:52	Vitaliy	Talankov	BLR	29.4.82	1		Alytus	15 Sep
1:22:53	Recep	Celik	TUR	10.8.83	8	Rus-w	Adler	17 Feb
1:22:56	Kevin	Eastler	USA	14.10.77	12		La Coruña	2 Jun
	(60)							
1:22:59		Lee Dae-ro	KOR	12.3.80	3	NG	Kwangju	11 Oct
1:23:01	Andrey	Stepanchuk	BLR	12.6.79	1		Grodno	6 Oct
1:23:05		Wang Zhiping	CHN	11.12.83	15		Shenzhen	24 Mar
1:23:06	Ken	Akashi	JPN	6.11.76	1		Tokyo	1 Jan
1:23:06A	David	Kimutai	KEN	19.8.69	1		Nairobi	15 Jun
1:23:07	Isamu	Fujisawa	JPN	12.10.87	2		Tokyo	1 Jan
1:23:07		Cui Zhili	CHN	11.1.83	16		Shenzhen	24 Mar
1:23:08	Takafumi	Higuma	JPN	3.9.82	3		Tokyo	1 Jan
1:23:08	Horacio	Nava	MEX	20.1.82	17		Shenzhen	24 Mar
1:23:11	Sergey	Safarov	RUS	28.10.83	9	NC-w	Adler	17 Feb
	(70)							
1:23:12	Artem	Valchenko	UKR	3.4.84	2	NC-w	Yevpatoriya	17 Mar
1:23:14	Luis Manuel	Corchete	ESP	14.5.84	19	ECp	Leamington	20 May
1:23:17	Akihiro	Sugimoto	JPN	20.10.81	3	AsiC	Nomi	25 Mar
1:23:18	Aleksey	Kanayev	RUS	30.5.86	10	NC-w	Adler	17 Feb
1:23:19	Ingus	Janevics	LAT	29.4.86	2		Alytus	15 Sep
1:23:20A	Omar	Segura	MEX	24.3.81	1		Naucalpan	10 Mar
1:23:21.19t	Alex	Schwazer	ITA	26.12.84	1		Milano	17 Mar

Mark	Name		Nat	Born	Pos	Meet	Venue	Date
1:23:23	José Antonio	González	ESP	15.6.79	7		Rio Maior	14 Apr
1:23:23		Li Jianbo	CHN	14.11.86	2	NC	Beijing	20 Aug
1:23:27	Masato	Yoshihara	JPN	14.3.77	4	AsiC	Nomi	25 Mar
	(80)							
1:23:28		Chen Zhong	CHN-J	1.6.88	19		Shenzhen	24 Mar
1:23:28	Rolando	Saquipay	ECU	21.7.79	2	PAm	Rio de Janeiro	22 Jul
1:23:31	Ruslan	Dmytrenko	UKR	22.3.86	3	NC-w	Yevpatoriya	17 Mar
1:23:32		Zhang Hong	CHN	25.4.78	20		Shenzhen	24 Mar
1:23:36		Wu Guosong	CHN	21.4.87	21		Shenzhen	24 Mar
1:23:37	Fortunato	D'Onofrio	ITA	12.2.81	20	ECp	Leamington	20 May
1:23:37	Hassane	Sbai	TUN	21.4.84	9		Kraków	23 Jun
1:23:38	Tim	Seaman	USA	14.5.72	13		La Coruña	2 Jun
1:23:38	Anatoliy	Kukushkin	RUS	12.2.86	7	RWC	Saransk	29 Sep
1:23:40	Babubhai	Panocha	IND	5.9.80	1	NC	Jamshedpur	24 Oct
	(90)							
1:23:42.98t		Cui Zhide	CHN	11.1.83	1	CISM	Hyderabad	15 Oct
1:23:43A	Cristian D.	Berdeja	MEX	21.6.81	2		Naucalpan	10 Mar
1:23:45A	Gustavo	Restrepo	COL	27.7.82	1		La Virginia Risralda	18 Mar
1:23:45		Gao Lianzuo	CHN	30.8.85	22		Shenzhen	24 Mar
1:23:45.76t		Bo Xiangdong	CHN	1.10.87	5		Wuhan	2 Nov
1:23:46		Gao Chao	CHN-J	4.1.89	23		Shenzhen	24 Mar
1:23:49.14t		Yang Tao	CHN-J	12.12.89	6		Wuhan	2 Nov
1:23:53		Zhu Hongjun	CHN	18.8.83	14		La Coruña	2 Jun
1:23:53	Grzegorz	Sudol	POL	28.8.78	2	NC	Poznan	30 Jun
1:23:54.58t		Zhang Rui	CHN-J	21.1.89	7		Wuhan	2 Nov
	(100)							

Mark	Name		Nat	Born	Date
1:23:55	Noe	Hernández	MEX	15.3.78	24 Mar
1:23:58		Kang Wenduo	CHN	9.10.83	24 Mar
1:24:01	Maik	Berger	GER	17.2.79	24 Mar
1:24:03	Daniel	García	MEX	28.10.71	2 Jun
1:24:06	Rodrigo	Flores Plata	MEX	14.8.72	10 Jun
1:24:07.61t	Marco	De Luca	ITA	12.5.81	18 Mar
1:24:09	Eric	Guevara	MEX	25.8.80	10 Jun
1:24:09.5At	Claudio Erasmo	Vargas	MEX	9.12.74	10 Jun
1:24:11		Zou Cuizhi	CHN	11.1.83	20 Aug
1:24:13	José David	Domínguez	ESP	29.7.80	2 Jun
1:24:13.0t	Juan Manuel	Cano	ARG	12.12.87	7 Oct
1:24:14	Pyotr	Trofimov	RUS	18.12.83	17 Feb
1:24:14	Silviu	Casandra	ROM	27.10.75	14 Apr
1:24:17	Artur	Brzozowski	POL	29.3.85	30 Jun
1:24:18	Predrag	Filipovic	SRB	5.10.78	24 Mar
1:24:19	Mikel	Odriozola	ESP	25.5.73	1 May
1:24:22	Jean-Jacques	Nkoukoukidi	ITA	15.4.82	1 May
1:24:22		Si Tianfeng	CHN	17.6.84	20 Aug
1:24:22.7At	Luis Fernando	López	COL	3.6.79	5 May
1:24:23	Michael	Krause	GER	23.9.85	21 Apr
1:24:25.37t	James	Rendón	COL	7.4.85	8 Jun
1:24:27		Zhang Ronglong	CHN	2.11.84	20 Aug
1:24:27.49t	Lorenzo	Civallero	ITA	8.8.75	17 Mar
1:24:28	Alessandro	Gandellini	ITA	30.4.73	1 May
1:24:31	José Alejandro	Cambil	ESP	26.1.75	4 Mar
1:24:31	Ivan	Losyev	UKR	26.1.86	1 Jun
1:24:35	Daniele	Paris	ITA	18.10.84	14 Apr
1:24:40	Yusuke	Suzuki	JPN-J	2.1.88	28 Oct
1:24:41	Oleksiy	Kazanin	UKR	22.5.82	1 Jun
1:24:42.79t		Zhao Jianguo	CHN-J	19.1.88	2 Nov
1:24:43.64t		Li Rui	CHN	15.10.87	2 Nov
1:24:44	Mohamed	Ameur	ALG	1.11.84	3 May
1:24:45	Diogo	Martins	POR	14.8.84	20 May
1:24:46	Rustam	Kuvatov	KAZ	9.11.77	17 Feb
1:24:47	Donatas	Skarnulis	LTU	21.10.77	20 May
1:24:48	Yusuke	Yachi	JPN	2.1.80	1 Jan
1:24:48		Liu Guangjun	CHN-J	7.9.89	24 Mar
1:24:52	Konstantin	Maksimov	RUS	17.6.82	17 Feb
1:24:53	Jamie	Costin	IRL	1.6.77	24 Mar
1:24:54	Tadas	Suskevicius	LTU	22.5.85	15 Sep
1:24:55.09t		Xu Faguang	CHN	17.5.87	2 Nov
1:24:58	Chris	Erickson	AUS	1.11.81	28 Jan
1:25:00		Ai Bin	CHN	20.6.87	24 Mar
1:25:00	Francisco	Arcilla	ESP	14.1.84	15 Apr
	(144)				

Other best track times

1:21:30.01	Rubino	1	Formia	18 Mar
1:24:05.03	Wei Yang			2 Nov
1:24:50.61	Wu Guosong			2 Nov
1:24:59.50	D'Onofrio			17 Mar

??: Mar 18, Guatemala: Allan Segura CRC 1:22:53, Bernardo Calvo CRC 1:22:59

JUNIORS

See main list for top 8 juniors. 10 performances by 8 men to 1:24:00. Further juniors:

Li Gaobo 2+ 1:21:16 6 La Coruña 2 Jun

Wang Hao 1:23:19 1 NC Beijing 20 Aug

Mark	Name		Nat	Born	Pos	Meet	Venue	Date
1:24:40	Yusuke	Suzuki	JPN	2.1.88	1		Takahata	28 Oct
1:24:42.79t		Zhao Jianguo	CHN	19.1.88	9		Wuhan	2 Nov
1:24:48		Liu Guangjun	CHN	7.9.89	27		Shenzhen	24 Mar
1:25:26		Wang Leilei	CHN	14.2.89	10	NC	Beijing	20 Aug
1:25:26	Eiki	Unami	JPN	10.5.88	2		Takahata	28 Oct
1:25:35		Yang Tao	CHN	12.12.89	30		Shenzen	24 Mar
Best track time: 1:24:05.03	(10)	Wei Yang	CHN	26.3.89	8		Wuhan	2 Nov

30 KILOMETRES WALK

2:04:16+	Vladimir	Kanaykin	RUS	21.3.85	1	in 35k	Adler	17 Feb
2:04:54+	Sergey	Kirdyapkin	RUS	16.1.80	2	in 35k	Adler	17 Feb
2:05:35+	Oleg	Kistkin	RUS	13.5.83	3	in 35k	Adler	17 Feb
2:05:50+	Igor	Yerokhin	RUS	4.9.85	4	in 35k	Adler	17 Feb
2:06:27+	Jarrod	Tallent	AUS	17.10.84	1	in 20M	Canberra	10 Jun

MEN 2007

Mark	Name		Nat	Born	Pos	Meet	Venue	Date
2:06:40+	Sergey	Melentyev	RUS	14.12.76	5	in 35k	Adler	17 Feb
2:11:17+	Alexander	Schwazer	ITA	26.12.84	1	in 50k	Rosignano Solvay	11 Feb
2:11:52	Sergiy	Budza	UKR	6.12.84	1	NC-w	Yekpatoriya	17 Mar

2:13:16	Colin	Griffin	IRL	3.8.82	10 Mar	2:13:54+ ?		Zhao Chengliang	CHN	1.6.84	15 Apr
2:13:16	Oleksiy	Kazanin	UKR	22.5.82	17 Mar	2:13:54+	Yuki	Yamazaki	JPN	16.1.84	15 Apr
2:13:52+	Chris	Erickson	AUS	1.12.81	10 Jun	2:13:54+	Takayuki	Tanii	JPN	14.2.83	15 Apr

35 KILOMETRES WALK

2:26:09	Vladimir	Kanaykin	RUS	21.3.85	1	NC-w	Adler	17 Feb
2:28:47	Sergey	Kirdyapkin	RUS	16.1.80	2	NC-w	Adler	17 Feb
2:30:28	Oleg	Kistkin	RUS	13.5.83	3	NC-w	Adler	17 Feb
2:32:55+	Alexander	Schwazer	ITA	26.12.84	1	in 50k	Rosignano Solvay	11 Feb
2:33:39	Igor	Yerokhin	RUS	4.9.85	4	NC-w	Adler	17 Feb
2:34:26	Sergey	Melentyev	RUS	14.12.76	5	NC-w	Adler	17 Feb
2:36:03+ ?		Zhao Chengliang	CHN	1.6.84	1=	in 50k	Kobe	15 Apr
2:36:03+	Yuki	Yamazaki	JPN	16.1.84	1=	in 50k	Kobe	15 Apr
2:36:03+	Takayuki	Tanii	JPN	14.2.83	1=	in 50k	Kobe	15 Apr
2:36:14	Sergey	Sergachev	RUS	10.7.87	1	NCp	Chelyabinsk	8 Sep
2:36:21+	Trond	Nymark	NOR	28.12.76	1	in 50k	Leamington	20 May

2:36:54+	Aleksey	Voyevodin	RUS	9.8.70	20May	2:37:33+	Nathan	Deakes	AUS	17.8.77	1 Sep
2:36:55+	Yuriy	Andronov	RUS	6.11.71	20May	2:37:39+	Yohann	Diniz	FRA	1.1.78	1 Sep
2:37:07	Denis	Langlois	FRA	10.10.68	8 Apr	2:37:41+	Marco	De Luca	ITA	12.5.81	20May

50 KILOMETRES WALK

3:36:04	Alex	Schwazer	ITA	26.12.84	1	NC	Rosignano Solvay	11 Feb
3:40:53	Denis	Nizhegorodov	RUS	26.7.80	1	NC	Cheboksary	17 Jun
3:40:57	Vladimir	Kanaykin	RUS	21.3.85	1	ECp	Leamington	20 May
3:41:31	Trond	Nymark	NOR	28.12.76	2	ECp	Leamington	20 May
3:41.51	Oleg	Kistkin	RUS	13.5.83	3	ECp	Leamington	20 May
3:41:52	Aleksey	Voyevodin	RUS	9.8.70	4	ECp	Leamington	20 May
3:42:55	Yuriy	Andronov	RUS	6.11.71	5	ECp	Leamington	20 May
3:43:53	Nathan	Deakes	AUS	17.8.77	1	WCh	Osaka	1 Sep
3:44:22	Yohann	Diniz	FRA	1.1.78	2	WCh	Osaka	1 Sep
3:44:26	(10)	Zhao Chengliang	CHN	1.6.84	1	AsiC	Kobe	15 Apr
3:44:38		Schwazer			3	WCh	Osaka	1 Sep
3:44:45	Jarrod	Tallent	AUS	17.10.84	1	NC	Melbourne	16 Dec
3:46:08	Jesús Ángel	García	ESP	17.10.69	6	ECp	Leamington	20 May
3:46:56	Santiago	Pérez	ESP	15.1.72	7	ECp	Leamington	20 May
3:46:57		Nizhegorodov			4	WCh	Osaka	1 Sep
3:47:04	Marco	De Luca	ITA	12.5.81	8	ECp	Leamington	20 May
3:47:40	Yuki	Yamazaki	JPN	16.1.84	2	AsiC	Kobe	15 Apr
3:48:07	Rafal	Fedaczynski	POL	3.12.80	9	ECp	Leamington	20 May
3:49:27		Yu Chaohong	CHN	12.12.76	1		Shenzhen	25 Feb
3:50:08	Takayuki	Tanii	JPN	14.2.83	1		Takahata	28 Oct
3:50:46		Sun Chao	CHN	8.1.87	2		Shenzhen	25 Feb
3:50:53	Francisco José	Pinardo (20)	ESP	15.3.75	10	ECp	Leamington	20 May
3:51:11	Sergey	Melentyev	RUS	5.12.76	2	NC	Cheboksary	17 Jun
3:51:32	Colin	Griffin	IRL	3.8.82	1		Dudince	24 Mar
3:51:34	Eddy	Riva	FRA	17.4.73	11	ECp	Leamington	20 May
3:51:48	David	Boulanger	FRA	11.12.74	12	ECp	Leamington	20 May
3:51:52	Erik	Tysse	NOR	4.12.80	5	WCh	Osaka	1 Sep
3:51:59	Vitaliy	Talankov	BLR	29.4.82	13	ECp	Leamington	20 May
3:52:07	Xavier	Moreno	ECU	15.11.79	1	PAm	Rio de Janeiro	28 Jul
3:52:17	António	Pereira	POR	10.7.75	14	ECp	Leamington	20 May
	(30/28)							
3:52:35	Horacio	Nava	MEX	20.1.82	2	PAm	Rio de Janeiro	28 Jul
3:52:49	Adam	Rutter (30)	AUS	24.12.86	2	NC	Melbourne	16 Dec
3:53:19	Luke	Adams	AUS	22.10.76	3	NC	Melbourne	16 Dec
3:53:24		Li Jianbo	CHN	14.11.86	3	AsiC	Kobe	15 Apr
3:53:30	Jamie	Costin	IRL	1.6.77	15	ECp	Leamington	20 May
3:53:57	Ingus	Janevics	LAT	29.4.86	1	NC	Jürmala	9 Jun
3:54:10	Milos	Bátovsky	SVK	26.5.79	2	1 NC	Dudince	24 Mar
3:54:19		Xing Shucai	CHN	4.8.84	4		Shenzhen	25 Mar
3:54:23	Donatas	Skarnulis	LTU	21.10.77	3		Dudince	24 Mar
3:54:24	Maik	Berger	GER	17.2.79	1		Zittau	21 Apr
3:54:42		Zou Cuizhi	CHN	11.1.83	5		Shenzhen	25 Mar
3:55:05		Zhao Jianguo	CHN-J	19.1.88	2	NC	Beijing	22 Aug
	(40)							

Mark	Name		Nat	Born	Pos	Meet	Venue	Date
3:55:08	Tim	Berrett	CAN	23.1.65	1		Ferreira do Alentejo	3 Mar
3:55:14	Augusto	Cardoso	POR	13.12.70	16	ECp	Leamington	20 May
3:55:19	Mikel	Odriozola	ESP	25.5.73	6	WCh	Osaka	1 Sep
3:55:21	Diego	Cafagna	ITA	9.7.75	2	NC	Rosignano Solvay	11 Feb
3:55:22	Grzegorz	Sudol	POL	28.8.78	1		Bad Deutsch Altenburg	7 Oct
3:55:35		Gadasu Alatan	CHN	27.1.84	3	NC	Beijing	22 Aug
3:55:45		Xu Faguang	CHN	17.5.87	4	NC	Beijing	22 Aug
3:55:55	Ken	Akashi	JPN	6.11.76	4	AsiC	Kobe	15 Apr
3:55:57	Duane	Cousins	AUS	13.7.73	4	NC	Melbourne	16 Dec
3:56:04	Omar	Zepeda	MEX	8.6.77	3	PAm	Rio de Janeiro	28 Jul
	(50)							
3:56:11		Guan Weilong	CHN	22.3.85	5	NC	Beijing	22 Aug
3:56:16	José Alejandro	Cambil	ESP	26.1.75	19	ECp	Leamington	20 May
3:56:43		Hou Yang	CHN	8.7.85	6	NC	Beijing	22 Aug
3:57:01	Denis	Langlois	FRA	10.10.68	20	ECp	Leamington	20 May
3:57:08	Jesús	Sánchez	MEX	23.3.76	2		Zittau	21 Apr
3:57:18	Nikolay	Matyukhin	RUS	13.12.68	3	NC	Cheboksary	17 Jun
3:57:41	Antón	Kucmin	SVK	7.6.84	21	ECp	Leamington	20 May
3:57:44	Jorge	Costa	POR	20.3.61	22	ECp	Leamington	20 May
3:57:48	Tadas	Suskevicius	LTU	22.5.85	1	SWE Ch	Stockholm	10 Oct
3:57:59	Antti	Kempas	FIN	3.10.80	23	ECp	Leamington	20 May
	(60)							
3:58:10	Oleksiy	Shelest	UKR	27.3.73	24	ECp	Leamington	20 May
3:58:16	Sébastien	Biche	FRA	1.2.73	1	NC	Reims	28 Oct
3:58:22	Jarkko	Kinnunen	FIN	19.1.84	10	WCh	Osaka	1 Sep
3:58:27		Si Tianfeng	CHN	17.6.84	7	NC	Beijing	22 Aug
3:58:44	Hatem	Ghoula	TUN	7.6.73	4		Santa Eularia des Riu	4 Mar
3:58:46	Yuriy	Chesnokov	RUS	12.12.79	4	NC	Cheboksary	17 Jun
3:59:02	Chris	Erickson	AUS	1.12.81	5	NC	Melbourne	16 Dec
3:59:22	Roman	Bilek	CZE	29.9.67	1	NC	Prerov	1 Sep
3:59:27	Artur	Brzozowski	POL	29.3.85	2		Bad Deutsch Altenburg	7 Oct
3:59:51	Salvador	Mira	ESA	23.8.84	4	PAm	Rio de Janeiro	28 Jul
	(70)							
3:59:56	Igors	Kazakevics	LAT	17.4.80	25	ECp	Leamington	20 May
3:59:58		Zhang Ronglong	CHN	2.11.84	8	NC	Beijing	22 Aug
4:00:48	Andreas	Gustafsson	SWE	10.8.81	26	ECp	Leamington	20 May
4:01:24	Sergey	Korepanov	RUS	15.7.84	5	NC	Cheboksary	17 Jun
4:01:36	Luis	García	GUA	13.9.74	5	PAm	Rio de Janeiro	28 Jul
4:01:48	Hervé	Davaux	FRA	22.8.78	2		Dublin	17 Jun
4:02:02	Sergey	Sergachev	RUS	10.7.87	6	NC	Cheboksary	17 Jun
4:02:02	Sergiy	Budza	UKR	6.12.84	1		Ivano-Frankivsk	2 Oct
4:02:07	Takafumi	Higuma	JPN	3.9.82	3		Takahata	28 Oct
4:02:27	Oleksiy	Kazanin	UKR	22.5.82	27	ECp	Leamington	20 May
	(80)							
4:02:50	Alessandro	Mistretta	ITA	6.3.71	3	NC	Rosignano Solvay	11 Feb
4:03:01	Maciej	Rosiewicz	POL	31.7.77	3		Bad Deutsch Altenburg	7 Oct
4:03:05		Yu Guoping	CHN	13.6.86	9	NC	Beijing	22 Aug
4:03:10	Freddy	Hernández	COL	25.4.78	6	PAm	Rio de Janeiro	28 Jul
4:03:20	Dario	Privitera	ITA	17.3.79	4	NC	Rosignano Solvay	11 Feb
4:03:37	Zoltán	Czukor	HUN	18.12.62	28	ECp	Leamington	20 May
4:03:42	Nenad	Filipovic	SRB	5.10.78	29	ECp	Leamington	20 May
4:03:42	Konstandinos	Stefanópoulos	GRE	11.7.84	30	ECp	Leamington	20 May
4:03:51		Bai Xuejin	CHN	6.6.87	10	NC	Beijing	22 Aug
4:03:53		Han Yucheng	CHN	16.12.78	7		Shenzhen	25 Mar
	(90)							
4:04:06	Darren	Bown	AUS	30.6.74	6	NC	Melbourne	16 Dec
4:04:08	Yusuke	Yachi	JPN	2.1.80	5	AsiC	Kobe	15 Apr
4:04:10A	Claudio	Vargas	MEX	9.12.74	3		Naucalpan	11 Mar
4:04:23	Andriy	Kovenko	UKR	25.11.73	1		Ivano-Frankisk	1 Oct
4:04:25	David	Sánchez	ESP	23.8.73	5	NC	Santa Eularia des Riu	4 Mar
4:04:26	Mesias	Zapata	ECU	8.1.81	1		Hauppage	28 Oct
4:04:44A	Rodrigo	Flores	MEX	14.8.72	4		Naucalpan	11 Mar
4:04:52	José Francisco	Gutiérrez	ESP	13.6.83	6	NC	Santa Eularia des Riu	4 Mar
4:04:52	Álvaro	García	MEX	18.10.83	1	PAmCp	Camboriu	22 Apr
	(100)							

Mark	Name		Nat	Born	Date
4:05:05		Wu Guosong	CHN	21.4.87	25 Mar
4:05:09	Alessandro	Garozzo	ITA	3.9.84	11 Feb
4:05:38	Aleksandar	Rakovic	SRB	13.4.68	20May
4:05:44	Kevin	Eastler	USA	14.10.77	28 Jan
4:06:03	Fredrik	Svensson	SWE	10.9.73	10 Oct
4:06:29	Mário José	dos Santos	BRA	10.9.79	28 Jan
4:06:55	Aleksey	Kronin	RUS	23.7.70	17 Jun
4:06:59		Kang Wenduo	CHN	9.10.83	25Mar
4:07:09	Cristian	Bascuñán	CHI	8.3.83	31Mar
4:07:43	Dusan	Majdan	SVK	8.8.87	24Mar

Mark	Name		Nat	Born	Date	Mark	Name		Nat	Born	Date
4:07:49	Cédric	Houssaye	FRA	13.12.79	28 Oct	4:08:46	Ricardas	Rekst	LTU	10.10.87	10 Oct
4:07:53	Andrey	Trofimov	RUS	3.6.87	17 Jun	4:08:59	Semyon	Lovkin	RUS	14.7.77	17 Jun
4:08:30	Andrey	Stepanchuk	BLR	12.6.79	11 Mar	4:09:54	Phillip	Dunn (116)	USA	12.6.71	28 Jan

JUNIORS

Mark	Name		Nat	Born	Pos	Meet	Venue	Date
3:55:05	Zhao Jianguo		CHN	19.1.88	2	NC	Beijing	22 Aug
	3:59:00	6	Shenzhen	24 Mar				
4:12:23	Matteo	Giupponi	ITA-J	8.10.88	2		Scanzorosciate	21 Oct

100 KILOMETRES WALK

Mark	Name		Nat	Born	Pos	Meet	Venue	Date
9:05:36	Zoltán	Czukor	HUN	18.12.62	1		Scanzoroscaite	21 Oct
9:11:51	Andrey	Stepanchuk	BLR	12.6.79	2		Scanzoroscaite	21 Oct
9:24:15	Oleksandr	Romanenko	UKR	26.6.81	3		Scanzoroscaite	21 Oct
9:42:18	Igors	Kazakevics	LAT	17.4.80	4		Scanzoroscaite	21 Oct
9:51:34	Andriy	Kovenko	UKR	25.11.73	5		Scanzoroscaite	21 Oct
9:59:45	Roberto	Defendeti	ITA	30.5.68	6		Scanzoroscaite	21 Oct

WOMEN'S WORLD LISTS 2007

60 METRES INDOORS

Mark	Name		Nat	Born	Pos	Meet	Venue	Date
7.10	Kim	Gevaert	BEL	5.8.78	1s2	EI	Birmingham	3 Mar
	7.12				1	EI	Birmingham	4 Mar
7.13	Tezdzhan	Naimova	BUL	1.5.87	1	BalkC	Pireás	21 Feb
7.14	Kerron	Stewart	JAM	16.4.84	1	SEC	Lexington	25 Feb
	(4/3)							
7.15	Courtney	Champion	USA	10.6.86	2	SEC	Lexington	25 Feb
7.16	Laverne	Jones	ISV	16.9.81	1	Spark	Stuttgart	3 Feb
7.16	Yevgeniya	Polyakova	RUS	29.5.83	1	NC	Volgograd	9 Feb
7.16	Sani	Roseby	USA	5.2.82	1	NC	Boston (R)	25 Feb
7.17	Virgen	Benavídes	CUB	31.12.74	1		Chemnitz	23 Feb
7.17	Carmelita	Jeter	USA	24.11.79	2	NC	Boston (R)	25 Feb
7.17	Jeanette	Kwakye	GBR	20.3.83	1s1	EI	Birmingham	3 Mar
	(10)							
7.18	Marina	Kislova	RUS	7.2.78	2	NC	Volgograd	9 Feb
7.19	Larisa	Kruglova	RUS	27.10.72	1h1		Moskva	28 Jan
7.19	Juanita	Broaddus	USA	12.5.85	1h2		Baton Rouge	2 Mar
7.20	Kelly-Ann	Baptiste	TRI	14.10.86	3	SEC	Lexington	25 Feb
7.20	Daria	Onysko	POL	30.7.81	3	EI	Birmingham	4 Mar
7.22	Ekateríni	Thánou	GRE	1.2.75	1r2	NC	Athína (P)	10 Feb
7.22	Sina	Schielke	GER	19.5.81	2		Chemnitz	23 Feb
7.22	Gloria	Asumnu	USA	22.5.85	1		Houston	24 Feb
7.22	Marshevet	Hooker	USA	25.9.84	3	NC	Boston (R)	25 Feb
7.23	Angela	Daigle-Bowen	USA	28.5.76	4	NC	Boston (R)	25 Feb
	(20)							
7.23	Johanna	Manninen	FIN	4.4.80	2h2	EI	Birmingham	3 Mar
7.24	Irina	Khabarova	RUS	18.3.66	1		Yekaterinburg	7 Jan
7.24	Yuliya	Gushchina	RUS	4.3.83	2		Volgograd	21 Jan
7.24	Victoria	Jordan	USA-Y	26.2.90	1r2		Houston	10 Feb
7.24	Amber	Plowden	USA	4.8.80	5	NC	Boston (R)	25 Feb
7.24	Susanna	Kallur	SWE	16.2.81	3s2	EI	Birmingham	3 Mar
7.24	Svetlana	Nabokina	RUS	5.6.83	1		Moskva	21 Dec
7.25A	Damola	Osayomi	NGR	26.6.86	1		Albuquerque	20 Jan
7.25	Alena	Nevmerzhitskaya	BLR	27.7.80	1h	NC	Mogilyov	8 Feb
7.25	Mariya	Bolikova	RUS	23.5.77	3s1	NC	Volgograd	9 Feb
	(30)							
7.25	Laura	Turner	GBR	12.8.82	1	NC	Sheffield	11 Feb
7.25	Alexandria	Anderson	USA	28.1.87	1h1	Big 12	Ames	23 Feb
7.26	Svetlana	Nabokina	RUS	26.1.82	2		Moskva	13 Jan
7.26	Magdalena	Khristova	BUL	25.2.77	2		Sofia	3 Feb
7.26	Shayla	Mahan	USA-J	18.1.89	1		Lexington	17 Feb
7.26A	Jeneba	Tarmoh	USA-J	27.9.89	1r3		Pocatello	17 Feb
7.27	Ebonie	Floyd	USA	21.10.83	1h5	Tyson	Fayetteville	9 Feb
7.27	Verena	Sailer	GER	16.10.85	2	NC	Leipzig	17 Feb
7.27	Bettina	Müller-Weissina	AUT	12.7.73	2h5	EI	Birmingham	3 Mar
7.28	LaKya	Brookins	USA-J	28.7.89	1r1		Clemson	2 Dec
	(40)							
7.28	Cleo	Tyson	USA	1.5.86	1h2		State College	26 Jan
7.28	Mikele	Barber	USA	4.10.80	2	BIG	Boston (R)	27 Jan
7.28	Montell	Douglas	GBR	24.1.86	5s2	EI	Birmingham	3 Mar
7.28	Nongnuch	Sanrat	THA	26.8.83	1	AsiC	Macau	30 Oct

Mark	Wind	Name		Nat	Born	Pos	Meet	Venue	Date
7.29A		Sherry	Fletcher	GRN	17.1.86	1h1		Albuquerque	19 Jan
7.29		Muriel	Hurtis-Houairi	FRA	25.3.79	1		Mondeville	27 Jan
7.29		Sheri-Ann	Brooks	JAM	11.2.83	3	BIG	Boston (R)	27 Jan
7.29A		Bianca	Knight	USA-J	2.1.89	2r3		Pocatello	17 Feb
7.29		Samantha	Henry	JAM-J	25.9.88	1h2		Baton Rouge	2 Mar
7.29		Simone	Facey	JAM	7.5.85	2h2	NCAA	Fayetteville	9 Mar

Outdoor times during 100m:
27 Aug Osaka: 7.02 Veronica Campbell, 7.03 Lauryn Wlliams, 7.04 Torri Edwards & Kim Gevaert, 7.06 Christine Arron

100 METRES

Mark	Wind	Name		Nat	Born	Pos	Meet	Venue	Date
10.89	1.0	Veronica	Campbell	JAM	15.5.82	1	NC	Kingston	23 Jun
10.90	2.0	Torri	Edwards	USA	31.1.77	1	adidas	Carson	20 May
10.90	-0.7		Campbell			1	Golden	Shanghai	28 Sep
10.91	2.0		Campbell			2	adidas	Carson	20 May
10.93	1.2		Campbell			1	GP	New York	2 Jun
10.95	2.0	Me'Lisa	Barber	USA	4.10.80	2	adidas	Carson	20 May
10.96	1.2		Edwards			2	GP	New York	2 Jun
10.97	-0.7	Sanya	Richards	USA	26.2.85	2	Golden	Shanghai	28 Sep
10.99	-0.1		Campbell			1s2	WCh	Osaka	27 Aug
11.00	0.0		Edwards			1	Athl	Lausanne	10 Jul
11.01	1.2	Allyson	Felix	USA	18.11.85	3	GP	New York	2 Jun
11.01	0.6		Edwards			1h4	NC	Indianapolis	21 Jun
11.01	-0.2		Campbell			1	WCh	Osaka	27 Aug
11.01	-0.2	Lauryn	Williams	USA	11.9.83	2	WCh	Osaka	27 Aug
11.02	-0.9		Edwards			1	NC	Indianapolis	22 Jun
11.02	0.8	Mikele	Barber	USA	4.10.80	1	PAm	Rio de Janeiro	24 Jul
11.02	-0.3		Edwards			1s1	WCh	Osaka	27 Aug
11.02	-0.2	Carmelita	Jeter	USA	24.11.79	3	WCh	Osaka	27 Aug
11.03	1.0	Kerron	Stewart	JAM	16.4.84	2	NC	Kingston	23 Jun
11.03	0.8		Edwards			1	GGala	Roma	13 Jul
11.03	-0.5		L Barber			1	DNG	Stockholm	7 Aug
11.04	-0.3	Tezdzhan	Naimova (10)	BUL	1.5.87	1		Plovdiv	1 Jul
11.04	-0.6		Campbell			1		Thessaloníki	30 Jul
11.04	-0.1	Christine	Arron	FRA	13.9.73	2s2	WCh	Osaka	27 Aug
11.05	2.0		Jeter			4	adidas	Carson	20 May
11.05	1.0	Sheri-Ann	Brooks	JAM	11.2.83	3	NC	Kingston	23 Jun
11.05	0.2		Edwards			1	Vard	Réthimno	18 Jul
11.05	-0.5		Richards			2	DNG	Stockholm	7 Aug
11.05	-0.2		Edwards			4	WCh	Osaka	27 Aug
11.05	-0.2	Kim	Gevaert	BEL	5.8.78	5	WCh	Osaka	27 Aug
		(30/13)							
11.06	2.0	Marshevet	Hooker	USA	25.9.84	5	adidas	Carson	20 May
11.06	1.4	Angela	Williams	USA	30.1.80	1		Clermont, FL	9 Jun
11.09	0.8	Stephanie	Durst	USA	6.1.82	1h3	NC	Indianapolis	21 Jun
11.09	1.1	Yevgeniya	Polyakova	RUS	29.5.83	1	NC	Tula	31 Jul
11.10	1.5	Brianna	Glenn	USA	18.4.80	1h2	NC	Indianapolis	21 Jun
11.10	0.6	Muna	Lee	USA	30.10.81	2h4	NC	Indianapolis	21 Jun
11.12	0.9	Debbie	Ferguson-McKenzie	BAH	16.1.76	1		Luzern	28 Jun
		(20)							
11.13	1.3	Ebonie	Floyd	USA	21.10.83	1s2	NCAA	Sacramento	6 Jun
11.13	0.8	Mechelle	Lewis	USA	20.9.80	4h3	NC	Indianapolis	21 Jun
11.13	0.8	Rachelle	Smith	USA	30.6.81	5h3	NC	Indianapolis	21 Jun
11.13	1.3	Susanthika	Jayasinghe	SRI	17.12.75	3h1	WCh	Osaka	26 Aug
11.14	1.7	Sally	McLellan	AUS	19.9.86	1h3	WCh	Osaka	26 Aug
11.15	0.8	Damola	Osayomi	NGR	26.7.86	2h8	WCh	Osaka	26 Aug
11.15	0.6	Chandra	Sturrup	BAH	12.9.71	1q4	WCh	Osaka	26 Aug
11.16	2.0	Sani	Roseby	USA	5.2.82	6	adidas	Carson	20 May
11.16	1.0	Simone	Facey	JAM	7.5.85	4	NC	Kingston	23 Jun
11.17	2.0	Aleen	Bailey	JAM	25.11.80	7	adidas	Carson	20 May
		(30)							
11.17	1.8	Tahesia	Harrigan	IVB	15.2.82	1		Donnas	15 Jul
11.18	0.9	Sherry	Fletcher	GRN	17.1.86	1h4	PAm	Rio de Janeiro	23 Jul
11.19	1.5	Gloria	Asumnu	USA	22.5.85	3h2	NC	Indianapolis	21 Jun
11.19	1.3	Laura	Turner	GBR	12.8.82	1		Loughborough	11 Aug
11.20	0.2	Lucimar	de Moura	BRA	22.3.74	1	SAmC	São Paulo	7 Jun
11.20	2.0	Guzel	Khubbieva	UZB	2.5.76	1	Kozanov	Almaty	9 Jun
11.21	0.6	Tiffany	Townsend	USA-J	14.6.89	1		Austin	11 May
11.21	-1.2	Alexandria	Anderson	USA	28.1.87	2	Big 12	Lincoln	13 May
11.21	1.7	Samantha	Henry	JAM-J	25.9.88	1	NC-j	Kingston	23 Jun

Mark		Name		Nat	Born	Pos	Meet	Venue	Date
11.21	0.3	Sina	Schielke	GER	19.5.81	1		München	23 Jun
		(40)							
11.22	1.3	Kelly-Ann	Baptiste	TRI	14.10.86	1		Baton Rouge	24 Mar
11.22	0.9	Franca	Idoko	NGR	15.6.85	3	GP	Athína	2 Jul
11.22	0.8	Vida	Anim	GHA	7.12.83	3h8	WCh	Osaka	26 Aug
11.24	1.7	Chauntae	Bayne	USA	4.4.84	2s1	NCAA	Sacramento	6 Jun
11.24	0.9	Cydonie	Mothersill-Modibo	CAY	19.3.78	4	GP	Athína	2 Jul
11.24		Marina	Kislova	RUS	7.2.78			Sankt Peterburg	3 Jul
11.24	0.8	Lynne	Layne	USA-J	1.4.88	1	PAm-J	São Paulo	6 Jul
11.25	2.0	Angela	Daigle-Bowen	USA	28.5.76	8	adidas	Carson	20 May
11.25	1.2	Yekaterina	Grigoryeva	RUS	21.4.74	2		Sochi	26 May
11.25	1.3	Tracy-Ann	Rowe	JAM	17.9.85	2s2	NCAA	Sacramento	6 Jun
		(50)							
11.26	1.2	Lashauntea	Moore	USA	31.7.83	3	MSR	Walnut	15 Apr
11.26	0.0	Ivet	Lalova	BUL	18.5.84	1	Takac	Beograd	29 May
11.26	-1.1	Tameka	Clarke	BAH	9.11.80	1		Atlanta	2 Jun
11.26	0.8	Wyllesheia	Myrick	USA	21.11.79	6h3	NC	Indianapolis	21 Jun
11.26	0.8	Jeanette	Kwakye	GBR	20.3.82	4h8	WCh	Osaka	26 Aug
11.27	1.7	Rakia	Al-Gasara	BRN	6.9.82	1h2	Arab C	Amman	19 May
11.27	1.9	Jeneba	Tarmoh	USA-J	27.9.89	1		Sacramento	2 Jun
11.27	1.2	Johanna	Manninen	FIN	4.4.80	1	ECp-1A	Vaasa	23 Jun
11.27	0.6	Nombulelo Constance	Mkenku	RSA-J	30.6.89	2	AfG	Alger	19 Jul
11.27	1.7	Amandine	Allou Affoué	CIV	29.8.80	4h3	WCh	Osaka	26 Aug
		(60)							
11.28	1.2	Inna	Eftimova	BUL-J	19.6.88	1	NC-j	Sofia	9 Jun
11.28	0.8	Montell	Douglas	GBR	24.1.86	1s1	EU23	Debrecen	12 Jul
11.29	0.9	Tonette	Dyer	USA	28.3.83	4	MSR	Walnut	15 Apr
11.29	1.3	Virgil	Hodge	SKN	17.11.83	4	NCAA-r	Des Moines	26 May
11.30	0.8	Shataya	Hendricks	USA-J	15.8.89	1		Jacksonville	17 Mar
11.30	0.9	Barbara	Pierre	USA	28.4.87	1	NCAA-2	Charlotte	26 May
11.30	1.2	Yelena	Bolsun	RUS	25.6.82	3		Sochi	26 May
11.31	0.9	Jessica	Onyepunuka	USA	3.5.86	5	MSR	Walnut	15 Apr
11.31	1.5	Sasha	Springer-Jones	TRI	17.3.78	1	NC	Port of Spain	23 Jun
11.31	1.0	Shelly-Ann	Fraser	JAM	27.12.86	5	NC	Kingston	23 Jun
		(70)							
11.31	0.3	Muriel	Hurtis-Houairi	FRA	25.3.79	5	Gaz	Saint-Denis	6 Jul
11.31	1.8	Verena	Sailer	GER	16.10.85	1h4	EU23	Debrecen	12 Jul
11.32	-0.3	Iryna	Shtangeyeva	UKR	6.2.82	1		Kalamáta	2 Jun
11.32	1.7	Carol	Rodríguez	PUR	16.12.85	5s1	NCAA	Sacramento	6 Jun
11.32	0.7	Laverne	Jones	ISV	16.9.81	1rB	Bisl	Oslo	15 Jun
11.32	1.2	Joice	Maduaka	GBR	30.9.73	2	ECp-1A	Vaasa	23 Jun
11.32	1.1	Natalya	Rusakova	RUS	12.12.79	3	NC	Tula	31 Jul
11.33	0.0	Shalonda	Solomon	USA	19.12.85	1		Greensboro	21 Apr
11.33	0.6	Nickeisha	Anderson	JAM	15.3.85	2	ModR	Modesto	5 May
11.33	2.0	Alexis	Weatherspoon	USA	27.7.83	9	adidas	Carson	20 May
		(80)							
11.34	-0.7	Michelle	Perry	USA	1.5.79	1	GP	Melbourne	2 Mar
11.34	1.3	Juanita	Broaddus	USA	12.5.85	2		Baton Rouge	24 Mar
11.34	1.3	Shakera	Reece	BAR-J	31.8.88	1	Carifta	Providenciales	7 Apr
11.34	0.0	Shericka	Williams	JAM	17.9.85	3	Takac	Beograd	29 May
11.34	1.0	Peta-Gaye	Dowdie	JAM	18.1.77	7	NC	Kingston	23 Jun
11.35	2.0	Emma	Ania	GBR	7.2.79	3		Coral Gables	14 Apr
11.35	1.5	Virgen	Benavídes	CUB	31.12.74	1	ALBA	Caracas	9 May
11.35	0.7	Geraldine	Pillay	RSA	25.8.77	3rB	Bisl	Oslo	15 Jun
11.35	1.0	Schillonie	Calvert	JAM-J	27.7.88	8	NC	Kingston	23 Jun
11.35	1.2	Roxana	Diaz	CUB	17.5.81	1		Alcalá de Henares	7 Jul
		(90)							
11.35	-0.6	Ekateríni	Thánou	GRE	1.2.75	4		Thessaloniki	30 Jul
11.36	1.6	Bianca	Knight	USA-J	2.1.89	1		Austin	6 Apr
11.36	1.1	Crystal	Cox	USA	28.3.79	1		Chapel Hill	13 Apr
11.36	-1.9	Yuliya	Gushchina	RUS	4.3.83	1h		Tula	18 Jun
11.36	1.2	Susanna	Kallur	SWE	16.2.81	3	ECp-1A	Vaasa	23 Jun
11.36	1.1	Natalya	Safronnikova	BLR	28.2.73	3	ECp-S	München	23 Jun
11.36	1.2	Victoria	Jordan	USA-Y	26.2.90	1	Jnr Oly	Walnut	29 Jul
11.36	1.8	Sylviane	Félix	FRA	31.10.77	1h1	NC	Niort	3 Aug
11.36	1.3	Emily	Freeman	GBR	24.11.80	3	LEAP	Loughborough	11 Aug
11.37	1.8	Mae	Koime	PNG	14.12.83	2	AUS Ch	Brisbane	10 Mar
		(100)							
11.37	-1.7	Josephine	Onyia	ESP	15.7.86	1	ECCp	Albufeira	26 May
11.37	2.0	Anastasiya	Vinogradova	KAZ	13.9.86	2	Kozanov	Almaty	9 Jun

Mark	Wind	Name		Nat	Born	Pos	Meet	Venue	Date
11.37	1.7	Shayla	Mahan	USA-J	18.1.89	1		Jackson, MI	9 Jun
11.37	2.0	Asha	Philip	GBR-Y	25.10.90	1	NC-j	Bedford	19 Jun
11.37	-0.1	Anita	Pistone	ITA	29.10.76	1		Pergine Valsugana	7 Jul

Mark	Wind	Name		Nat	Born	Date
11.38	1.5	Mileydis	Lazo	CUB	7.9.81	9 May
11.38	1.7	Audra	Dagelytė	LTU	26.3.81	6 Jul
11.38	0.5	Carima	Louami	FRA	12.5.79	12 Aug
11.38	-0.2	Irina	Khabarova	RUS	18.3.66	26 Aug
11.38	0.4	Juthamas	Thawoncharoen	THA	21.12.81	7 Dec
11.39	0.5	Daria	Korczynska (Onysko)	POL	30.7.81	26 May
11.39	1.3	María	Karastamáti	GRE	10.12.84	15 Jun
11.39	1.6	Nataliya	Pogrebnyak	UKR-J	19.2.88	21 Jun
11.39	0.5	Olivia	Borlée	BEL	10.4.86	12 Aug
11.40	1.4	Cynthia	Niako	CIV	25.9.83	31 Mar
11.40	1.7	Patrice	Potts	USA	9.9.87	21 Apr
11.40	1.9	Nolle	Graham	JAM	12.9.81	28 Apr
11.40	-0.7	Ashton	Purvis	USA-Y	12.7.92	28 Apr
11.40	1.3	Yolanda	Goff	USA	14.1.85	6 Jun
11.41	1.7	Melanie	Kleeberg	AUS	27.12.81	27 Jan
11.41	1.1	Anastacia	Leroy	JAM	11.9.87	29 Mar
11.41	0.0	Gloria	Kemasuode	NGR	30.12.79	5 May
11.41	0.3	Yuliya	Chermoshanskya	RUS	6.1.86	9 Jun
11.41		Rosemar	Coelho Neto	BRA	2.1.77	22 Jul
11.42	2.0	Porscha	Lucas	USA-J	18.6.88	14 Apr
11.42	0.5	Endurance	Ojokolo	NGR	29.9.75	27 May
11.43	1.7	Crystal	Attenborough	AUS	1.8.83	27 Jan
11.43	0.1	Lakecia	Ealey	USA	22.1.86	11 May
11.43	1.3	Gabrielle	Mayo	USA-J	26.1.89	19 May
11.43	1.2	Sandra	Möller	GER	16.3.80	26 May
11.43	0.7	Ezinne	Okparaebo	NOR-J	3.3.88	2 Jun
11.43	0.2	Felipa	Palacios	COL	1.12.75	7 Jun
11.43	-1.1	Jade	Bailey	BAR	10.6.83	16 Jun
11.43		Bettina	Müller-Weissina	AUT	12.7.73	5 Aug
11.43	-0.5	Hanna	Mariën	BEL	16.5.82	23 Aug
11.43	0.4	Sherone	Simpson	JAM	12.8.84	9 Sep
11.44	1.0	Shareese	Woods	USA	20.2.85	21 Apr
11.44	1.2	Brittany	Long	USA-J	7.9.89	19 May
11.44	1.9	Cherelle	Garrett	USA-J	7.5.89	2 Jun
11.44	1.2	Natalya	Murinovich	RUS	27.5.85	2 Jun
11.44	1.0	Yelizaveta	Bryzgina	UKR-J	28.11.89	19 Jun
11.44	1.0	Iryna	Shepetyuk	UKR	13.2.82	19 Jun
11.44	0.8	Rosângela	Santos	BRA-Y	20.12.90	6 Jul
11.44	0.3	Sari	Keskitalo	FIN	6.4.85	12 Jul
11.44	0.6	L´ónie	Mani	CMR	21.5.77	18 Jul
11.44	0.2	Cathleen	Tschirch	GER	23.7.79	21 Jul
11.45	0.8	Odeika	Bent	USA-J	14.12.88	17 Mar
11.45	0.6	Natalya	Ivoninskaya	KAZ	22.2.85	9 May
11.45A	0.0	Thatiana	Regina Ignácio	BRA	2.7.83	3 Jun
11.45	1.5	Consuella	Moore	USA	29.8.81	21 Jun
11.45	1.8	Yevgeniya	Gerasimova	RUS	25.5.84	30 Jun
11.46	0.3	Halyna	Tonkovyd	UKR	7.6.85	18 May
11.46A	1.1	Melinda	Smedley	USA	11.2.81	2 Jun
11.46	1.4	Chryste	Gaines	USA	14.9.70	9 Jun
11.46	0.7	Ewelina	Klocek	POL	20.3.87	17 Jun
11.46	0.7	Dorota	Jedrusinska	POL	4.2.82	17 Jun
11.46	1.0	Lizet	Assegbede	UKR	18.10.85	19 Jun
11.46	0.0	LaKya	Brookins	USA-J	28.7.89	21 Jun
11.46	0.9	Véronique	Mang	FRA	15.12.84	11 Jul
11.47	1.9	Latonia	Wilson	USA	30.11.84	12 May
11.47	-1.1	Marie	Woodward	USA	2.12.79	2 Jun
11.47A	0.0	Luciana	dos Santos	BRA	10.2.70	3 Jun
11.47	0.3	Yelena	Nevmerzhitskaya	BLR	27.7.80	14 Jun
11.47			Vu Thi Huong	VIE	7.10.86	23 Jun
11.48	1.7	Fiona	Cullen	AUS	31.8.79	24 Feb
11.48	-1.1	Felicia	Fant	USA		2 Jun
11.48	1.0	Anyika	Onuora	GBR	28.10.84	6 Jun
11.48	0.3	Lina	Grincikaitė	LTU	3.5.87	12 Jul
11.48	0.2	Katja	Wakan	GER	27.6.81	21 Jul
11.48	1.2	Tatjana	Mitic	SRB	19.8.83	29 Jul
11.49	0.0	Alexis	Joyce	USA	5.9.83	21 Apr
11.49	1.5	Jessica	Foreman	USA	27.5.87	12 May
11.49	1.9	Fabienne	Béret-Martinel	FRA	22.12.77	30 Jun
11.49	0.9	Delphine	Atangana	CMR	16.8.84	11 Jul
11.49	0.7		Jiang Lan	CHN-J	27.6.89	29 Oct
11.50	1.8	Jakki	Bailey	USA	4.10.84	3 Mar
11.50	1.9	Nikki	Martin	USA	24.2.85	6 Apr
11.50	1.5	Antonette	Carter	USA	16.2.84	15 Apr
11.50	0.9	Amandi	Rhett	USA	29.6.82	15 Apr
11.50	-0.2	Yuna	Mekhti-Zade	RUS	12.3.86	3 Jul
11.50	1.8	Myriam	Soumaré	FRA	29.10.86	12 Jul
11.50	1.1	Ruddy	Zang Milama	GAB	6.6.87	27 Jul
11.50	1.2		Chen Jue	CHN-J	23.3.88	29 Oct
11.51	1.7	Elizabeth	Adeoti	USA-J	12.6.88	14 Apr
11.51	2.0	Nicole	Brown	USA	28.10.85	22 Apr
11.51	1.8	Kiamesha	Otey	USA	28.5.81	4 May
11.51	0.8	Larica	Urbina	USA	26.8.84	12 May
11.51	-1.4	Thaissa	Presti	BRA	7.11.85	16 May
11.51	1.3	Yeorgia	Koklóni	GRE	7.5.81	15 Jun
11.51	1.0	Olga	Andreyeva	UKR	14.5.85	19 Jun
11.51	1.5	Ayanna	Hutchinson	TRI	18.2.78	23 Jun
11.51	1.7	Edita	Lingytė	LTU	17.1.80	6 Jul
11.51	-0.3	Olena	Chebanu	UKR	4.1.81	10 Aug
11.51	0.7		Wang Jing	CHN-J	26.3.88	29 Oct
11.52	1.8	Saori	Kitakaze	JPN	3.4.85	30 Apr
11.52	0.6	Dominique	Duncan	USA-Y	1.1.90	12 May
11.52	0.0		Qin Wangping	CHN	16.6.82	18 May
11.52	1.5	Kellie	Wells	USA	16.7.82	24 May
11.52	2.0	Elisabeth	Davin	BEL	3.6.81	3 Jun
11.52	0.8	Bárbara	Leôncio (200)	BRA-Y	7.10.91	6 Jul

Wind assisted

Mark	Wind	Name		Nat	Born	Pos	Meet	Venue	Date
10.95	2.6		L Barber			1h1	NC	Indianapolis	21 Jun
11.02	2.6		L Williams			2h1	NC	Indianapolis	21 Jun
11.04	2.3	Kim	Gevaert	BEL	5.8.78	1	NC	Heusden-Zolder	28 Jul
11.09	4.5	Laura	Turner	GBR	12.8.82	1		Budapest	7 Jul
11.10	2.6	Lashauntea	Moore	USA	31.7.83	3h1	NC	Indianapolis	21 Jun
11.11	2.6	Alexandria	Anderson	USA	28.1.87	4h1	NC	Indianapolis	21 Jun
11.13	4.2	Latonia	Wilson	USA	30.11.84	1		Fayetteville	21 Apr
11.15	3.5	Carol	Rodríguez	PUR	16.12.85	1h1	NCAA	Sacramento	6 Jun
11.15	2.6	Ivet	Lalova	BUL	18.5.84	2		Bydgoszcz	10 Jun
11.19	4.8	Virgil	Hodge	SKN	17.11.83	1		Fort Worth	21 Apr
11.19	2.6	Joice	Maduaka	GBR	30.9.73	3		Bydgoszcz	10 Jun
11.19	2.6	Alexis	Weatherspoon	USA	27.7.83	5h1	NC	Indianapolis	21 Jun
11.21	4.5	Shelly-Ann	Fraser	JAM	27.12.86	2		Budapest	7 Jul
11.23	2.4	Josephine	Onyia	ESP	15.7.86	1		La Laguna	5 May
11.23	2.4	Laverne	Jones	ISV	16.9.81	3		Cork	30 Jun
11.24	4.2	Yolanda	Goff	USA	14.1.85	2		Fayetteville	21 Apr
11.24	2.4	Jeanette	Kwakye	GBR	20.3.82	4		Cork	30 Jun
11.24	2.2	Virgen	Benavídes	CUB	31.12.74	2h3	PAm	Rio de Janeiro	23 Jul
11.26	3.5	Jessica	Onyepunuka	USA	3.5.86	2h1	NCAA	Sacramento	6 Jun
11.27	3.1	Alexis	Joyce	USA	15.9.83	1		Clermont, FL	19 May
11.28	6.0	Bianca	Knight	USA-J	2.1.89	1		Pearl, MS	5 May
11.28	2.3	Murielle	Ahoure	USA	23.8.87	1h3	NCAA-r	Gainesville	25 May
11.29	2.8	Nickeisha	Anderson	JAM	15.3.85	1	KansR	Lawrence	21 Apr
11.29	2.4	Candyce	McGrone	USA-J	24.3.89	1h1	NC-j	Indianapolis	21 Jun

Mark	Wind	Name		Nat	Born	Pos	Meet	Venue	Date
11.29	2.8	Shayla	Mahan	USA-J	18.1.89	2h2	NC-j	Indianapolis	21 Jun
11.30	6.5	Genna	Williams	BAR	3.11.84	1		Des Moines	13 May
11.30	3.0	Natalya	Rusakova	RUS	12.12.79	2h2	Znam	Zhukovskiy	9 Jun
11.30	2.4	LaKya	Brookins	USA-J	28.7.89	2h1	NC-j	Indianapolis	21 Jun
11.31	4.5	Brittany	Long	USA-J	7.9.89	1		Orlando	2 Jun
11.33	3.1		Vu Thi Huong	VIE	7.10.86	2	AsiC	Amman	26 Jul
11.34	3.1	Nicole	Whitman	USA	9.11.80	2		Clermont, FL	19 May
11.36	2.5	Melinda	Smedley	USA	11.2.81	4	ModR	Modesto	5 May
11.36	2.6	Antonette	Carter	USA	16.2.84	7h1	NC	Indianapolis	21 Jun

Mark	Wind	Name		Nat	Born	Date
11.37	3.6	Melanie	Kleeberg	AUS	27.12.81	27 Jan
11.37	2.8	Carima	Louami	FRA	12.5.79	3 Aug
11.39	2.6	Lakecia	Ealey	USA	22.1.86	28 Apr
11.39	2.2	Myriam	Soumaré	FRA	29.10.86	30 Jun
11.39	w?	Rosemar	Coelho Neto	BRA	2.1.77	22 Jul
11.40	3.1	Jamee	Jones	USA	20.7.84	24 Mar
11.40	2.7	Yuliya	Chermoshanskya	RUS	6.1.86	9 Jun
11.41	2.8	Yvonne	Mensah	CAN	15.5.85	21 Apr
11.42	5.1	Erica	Broomfield	CAN	17.10.77	12 May
11.43	4.5	Derval	O'Rourke	IRL	28.5.81	7 Jul
11.44	2.7	Luciana	dos Santos	BRA	10.2.70	14 Apr
11.44	2.5	Delphine	Atangana	CMR	16.8.84	5 Jun
11.45	2.7	Thaissa	Presti	BRA	7.11.85	14 Apr
11.45	2.1	Jakki	Bailey	USA	4.10.84	13 May
11.45	2.6	Dorota	Jedrusinska	POL	4.2.82	10 Jun
11.45	2.8	Maki	Wada	JPN	18.11.86	6 Oct
11.46	4.2	Larica	Urbina	USA	26.8.84	21 Apr
11.46	2.9	Kia	Davis	USA	23.5.76	20 May
11.47	2.5	Fiona	Cullen	AUS	31.8.79	21 Jan
11.47	3.3	Sakie	Nobuoka	JPN	24.8.77	30 Apr
11.47	6.0	Chisato	Fukushima	JPN-J	27.6.88	20 May
11.47	2.6	Fabienne	Béret-Martinel	FRA	22.12.77	10 Jun
11.48	6.6	Lisa	Nolting	USA	31.7.84	21 Apr
11.48	2.6	Nelly	Banco	FRA	17.2.86	30 Jun
11.48	5.3	Saori	Kitakaze	JPN	3.4.85	15 Jul
11.48		Svetlana	Nabokina	RUS	26.1.82	9 Aug
11.49	3.8	Nikki	Martin	USA	24.2.85	26 May
11.50	4.2	Leslie	Cole	USA	17.5.79	21 Apr
11.50	4.8	Kourtnee	Jones	USA	8.1.85	21 Apr
11.50	6.6	Kandice	Bell	USA	7.8.83	21 Apr
11.50	2.4	Glory	Alozie	ESP	30.12.77	5 May
11.50	2.4	Janice	Davis	USA	27.10.84	6 Jun
11.50	3.5	Shana	Solomon	USA	20.10.87	6 Jun
11.50	2.4	Belén	Recio	ESP	11.8.80	4 Jul
11.51	2.8	Courtney	Patterson	USA	10.2.85	15 Apr
11.51	2.8	Joanna	Hayes	USA	23.12.76	21 Apr
11.51	2.8	Saliha	Ozyurt	TUR	21.4.80	12 May
11.51	6.5	Andrea	Norris	USA	2.2.86	13 May
11.51	6.5	Jeanne	Roberts	USA	1.7.87	13 May
11.51	2.8	Kenyanna	Wilson	USA-J	27.10.88	21 Jun
11.51	2.8	Sandra	Gomis	FRA	21.11.83	3 Aug
11.52	2.3	Jacqua	Williams	USA	6.1.87	20 Apr
11.52	2.4	Kadi-Ann	Thomas	GBR	10.2.86	23 Jun

Best at low altitude

Mark	Wind	Name	Date
11.49	0.1	Smedley	28 Apr
11.49	0.3	L dos Santos	21 Jun
11.50	0.3	Ignácio	21 Jun

Doubtful timing

Mark	Wind	Name		Nat	Born	Pos	Meet	Venue	Date
11.12	1.3	Nicole	Whitman	USA	9.11.80	1		Orlando	3 Mar
11.33		Suslaidis	Giralt	CUB	19.8.87	1		Valencia, VEN	15 Aug

Hand timed

Mark	Wind	Name		Nat	Born	Pos	Meet	Venue	Date
11.0	1.9	Carol	Rodríguez	PUR	16.12.85	1		Eugene	7 Apr
11.1	1.5	Guzel	Khubbieva	UZB	2.5.76	1h1	Kozanov	Almaty	9 Jun

Mark	Wind	Name		Nat	Born	Date
11.2		Sasha	Springer-Jones	TRI	17.3.78	20 May
11.3	0.5	Misleydis	Lazo	CUB	7.9.81	21 Jun
11.3	-0.6	Rosemar	Coelho Neto	BRA	2.1.77	11 Jul
11.3		Crystal	Attenborough	AUS	1.8.83	23 Jul

Mark	Wind	Name		Nat	Born	Pos	Meet	Venue	Date
11.0w		Shayla	Mahan	USA-J	18.1.89	1		Warren	18 May

JUNIORS

See main list for top 11 juniors. 9 performances by 7 women to 11.32. Additional marks and further juniors:

Layne 11.31 0.0 1 NC-j Indianapolis 21 Jun 11.26w 2.8 1h2 NC-j Indianapolis 21 Jun
Eftimova 11.32 1.0 1h1 NC-j Sofia 2 Jun

Mark	Wind	Name		Nat	Born	Pos	Meet	Venue	Date
11.37	1.7	Shayla	Mahan	USA	18.1.89	1		Jackson, MI	9 Jun
11.37	2.0	Asha	Philip	GBR-Y	25.10.90	1	NC-j	Bedford	19 Jun
11.39	1.6	Nataliya	Pogrebnyak	UKR	19.2.88	1	NC-j	Mykolaiv	21 Jun
	11.37- 06								
11.40	-0.7	Ashton	Purvis	USA-Y	12.7.92	1	MSR	Walnut	28 Apr
11.42	2.0	Porscha	Lucas	USA	18.6.88	5		Coral Gables	14 Apr
11.43	1.3	Gabrielle	Mayo	USA	26.1.89	1		Greensboro	19 May
11.43""	0.7	Ezinne	Okparaebo	NOR	3.3.88	1		Florø	2 Jun
11.44	1.2	Brittany	Long	USA	7.9.89	1		Atlanta	19 May
11.44	1.9	Cherelle	Garrett (20)	USA	7.5.89	3		Sacramento	2 Jun
11.44	1.0	Yelizaveta	Bryzgina	UKR	28.11.89	1		Kyiv	19 Jun
11.44	0.8	Rosângela	Santos	BRA-Y	20.12.90	2	PAm-J	São Paulo	6 Jul

Wind assisted See main lists for top 5 juniors. '' Not permitted as a record as run in reverse direction
Townsend 11.26w 2.9 1h5 TexR Austin 6 Apr 5 performances by 5 women to 11.29

200 METRES

Mark	Wind	Name		Nat	Born	Pos	Meet	Venue	Date
21.81	1.7	Allyson	Felix	USA	18.11.85	1	WCh	Osaka	31 Aug
22.18	2.0		Felix			1	adidas	Carson	20 May
22.21	0.8		Felix			1s1	WCh	Osaka	30 Aug
22.31	1.6	Rachelle	Smith	USA	30.6.81	1	GP	New York	2 Jun
22.31	-0.2	Sanya	Richards	USA	26.2.85	1q1	WCh	Osaka	29 Aug
22.32	0.5	Ebonie	Floyd	USA	21.10.83	1	NCAA-r	Des Moines	26 May
22.34	0.4		Felix			1	NC	Indianapolis	24 Jun
22.34	1.7	Veronica	Campbell	JAM	15.5.82	2	WCh	Osaka	31 Aug
22.35	0.3		Felix			1	BrGP	Sheffield	15 Jul

Mark	Wind	Name		Nat	Born	Pos	Meet	Venue	Date
22.38	-1.6	Muriel	Hurtis-Houairi	FRA	25.3.79	1h1	NC	Niort	4 Aug
22.39	0.8		Campbell			1	NC	Kingston	24 Jun
22.41	1.3	Kerron	Stewart	JAM	16.4.84	1	NCAA-r	Columbia, MO	26 May
22.42	1.7		Stewart			1	NCAA	Sacramento	9 Jun
22.43	0.7	Tezdzhan	Naimova	BUL	1.5.87	1	NC	Sofia	17 Jun
22.43	0.4		Richards			2	NC	Indianapolis	24 Jun
22.44	0.3		Richards			2	BrGP	Sheffield	15 Jul
22.44	0.8		Campbell			2s1	WCh	Osaka	30 Aug
22.46	2.0	Lashauntea	Moore	USA	31.7.83	2	adidas	Carson	20 May
22.49	0.4	Simone	Facey (10)	JAM	7.5.85	1	Big 12	Lincoln	13 May
22.49	-0.1	Debbie	Ferguson-McKenzie	BAH	16.1.76	1	GP	Athína	2 Jul
22.50	-0.1		Hurtis-Houairi			2	GP	Athína	2 Jul
22.50	1.1		Felix			1h1	WCh	Osaka	30 Aug
22.50	-0.4		Richards			1s2	WCh	Osaka	30 Aug
22.51	1.1	Stephanie	Durst	USA	6.1.82	1		Bydgoszcz	10 Jun
22.51	0.8		Stewart			2	NC	Kingston	24 Jun
22.51	0.8	Torri	Edwards	USA	31.1.77	3s1	WCh	Osaka	30 Aug
22.52	-0.1		Stewart			1	SEC	Tuscaloosa	13 May
22.52	2.0	Cydonie	Mothersill-Modibo	CAY	19.3.78	3	adidas	Carson	20 May
22.52	0.0		Stewart			1s2	NCAA	Sacramento	7 Jun
22.52	0.7	Laverne	Jones	ISV	16.9.81	1		Salamanca	4 Jul
		(30/15)							
22.55	1.1	Susanthika	Jayasinghe	SRI	17.12.75	2h1	WCh	Osaka	29 Aug
22.60	-0.5	Aleen	Bailey	JAM	25.11.80	1q4	WCh	Osaka	29 Aug
22.61	1.0	Natasha	Hastings	USA	23.7.86	1h4	NCAA-r	Gainesville	25 May
22.62	0.4	Kim	Gevaert	BEL	5.8.78	1r1	GP	Athína	2 Jul
22.67	1.4	Alexandria	Anderson	USA	28.1.87	2	Big 12	Lincoln	13 May
		(20)							
22.67	1.7	Sherry	Fletcher	GRN	17.1.86	4	NCAA	Sacramento	9 Jun
22.68	-1.0	Virgil	Hodge	SKN	17.11.83	1h1	NCAA-r	Des Moines	25 May
22.68	0.7	Roxana	Díaz	CUB	17.5.81	2		Salamanca	4 Jul
22.70	1.3	Gloria	Asumnu	USA	22.5.85	2	NCAA-r	Columbia, MO	26 May
22.70	-1.2	Lauryn	Williams	USA	11.9.83	1	Vard	Réthimno	18 Jul
22.71	1.9	Natalya	Rusakova	RUS	12.12.79	1	NC	Tula	2 Aug
22.72	-2.0	Iryna	Shtangeyeva	UKR	6.2.82	1		Yalta	13 Jun
22.73	0.4	Mikele	Barber	USA	4.10.80	1h5	NC	Indianapolis	23 Jun
22.74	1.7	Shalonda	Solomon	USA	19.12.85	1h1	SEC	Tuscaloosa	11 May
22.74	1.7	Shareese	Woods	USA	20.2.85	6	NCAA	Sacramento	9 Jun
		(30)							
22.75	1.2	Yuliya	Gushchina	RUS	4.3.83	1h		Tula	19 Jun
22.76	-0.8	Sherone	Simpson	JAM	12.8.84	2		Kingston	5 May
22.76	2.0	Tonette	Dyer	USA	28.3.82	5	adidas	Carson	20 May
22.78	0.8	Sheri-Ann	Brooks	JAM	11.2.83	3	NC	Kingston	24 Jun
22.78	1.9	Yelena	Bolsun	RUS	25.6.82	2	NC	Tula	2 Aug
22.79	0.4	Porsche	Lucas	USA-J	18.6.88	3	Big 12	Lincoln	12 May
22.80	0.4	Rakia	Al-Gassra	BRN	6.9.82	3r1	GP	Athína	2 Jul
22.82	0.1	Carmelita	Jeter	USA	24.11.79	1		Eagle Rock	12 May
22.84	0.3	Samantha	Henry	JAM-J	25.9.88	1h5	SEC	Tuscaloosa	11 May
22.84	0.9	Tiffany	Townsend	USA-J	24.6.89	1		Austin	12 May
		(40)							
22.85	0.9	Natalie	Knight	USA	24.10.86	1h1	NCAA-r	Gainesville	25 May
22.88	-1.5	Christine	Arron	FRA	13.9.73	1h3	NC	Niort	4 Aug
22.90	2.0	Muna	Lee	USA	30.10.81	6	adidas	Carson	20 May
22.90	0.2	Yuliya	Chermoshanskaya	RUS	6.1.86	1	NC-23	Tula	19 Jun
22.93	0.0	Ionela	Târlea	ROM	9.2.76	1	NC	Bucuresti	28 Jul
22.95	1.5	Kelly-Ann	Baptiste	TRI	14.10.86	1rA		Baton Rouge	31 Mar
22.95	0.5	Chauntae	Bayne	USA	4.4.84	4	NCAA-r	Des Moines	26 May
22.96	0.3	Debbie	Dunn	USA	26.3.78	1		Lauderdale Lakes	7 Apr
22.97	0.3	Cathleen	Tschirch	GER	23.7.79	1	DLV	Bochum-Wattenscheid	12 Aug
22.98	0.9	Tahesia	Harrigan	IVB	15.2.82	1		Donnas	15 Jul
		(50)							
23.00	1.0	Christine	Amertil	BAH	18.8.79	2		Auburn	21 Apr
23.00	-0.5	Lucimar	de Moura	BRA	22.3.74	1	SAmC	São Paulo	9 Jun
23.00	1.8	Ivet	Lalova	BUL	18.5.84	1	ECp-1B	Milano	24 Jun
23.00		Olesya	Zykina	RUS	7.10.80	1		Irkutsk	18 Aug
23.03	0.6	Carol	Rodríguez	PUR	16.12.85	2h2	NCAA	Sacramento	7 Jun
23.03	0.1	Felipa	Palacios	COL	1.12.75	2s1	PAm	Rio de Janeiro	25 Jul
23.05	1.6	Mechelle	Lewis	USA	20.9.80	4	GP	New York	2 Jun
23.05	1.1	Joice	Maduaka	GBR	30.9.73	4		Bydgoszcz	10 Jun
23.06A	0.8	Adrienne	Power	CAN	11.11.81	1		San Luis Potosi	17 May

Mark	Wind	Name		Nat	Born	Pos	Meet	Venue	Date
23.06		Lyudmila	Zuyenko	RUS	6.9.83	1		Sankt-Peterburg	4 Jul
		(60)							
23.07	1.6	Nadine	Palmer	JAM	9.2.83	5	GP	New York	2 Jun
23.07	1.1	Monika	Bejnar	POL	10.3.81	5		Bydgoszcz	10 Jun
23.08	1.2	Krista	Simkins	USA	27.12.86	1		College Park	21 Apr
23.08	0.8	Peta-Gaye	Dowdie	JAM	18.1.77	5	NC	Kingston	24 Jun
23.11	1.9	Brooklynn	Morris	USA	27.3.86	1rB		Baton Rouge	31 Mar
23.11	-1.9	Latonia	Wilson	USA	30.11.84	2h4	NC	Indianapolis	23 Jun
23.11	-0.1	Jeanette	Kwakye	GBR	20.3.82	1		Cuxhaven	14 Jul
23.12	0.6	Anastacia	Leroy	JAM	11.9.87	1		Kingston	31 Mar
23.12	1.7	Crystal	Cox	USA	28.3.79	1		Chapel Hill	14 Apr
23.12	-0.6	Sani	Roseby	USA	5.2.82	1rB		Baie Mahault	1 May
		(70)							
23.12	1.9	Halyna	Tonkovyd	UKR	7.6.85	2		Kyiv	19 May
23.13	0.4	Wyllesheia	Myrick	USA	21.11.79	3h5	NC	Indianapolis	23 Jun
23.14	1.1	Olivia	Borlée	BEL	10.4.86	2	NC	Bruxelles	5 Aug
23.14	0.3	Vida	Anim	GHA	7.12.83	2	DLV	Bochum-Wattenscheid	12 Aug
23.15	0.3	Jessica	Ennis	GBR	28.1.86	1H4	WCh	Osaka	25 Aug
23.17	0.5	Britni	Spruill	USA	30.5.86	2h4	NCAA-r	Gainesville	25 May
23.17	0.5	Bianca	Knight	USA-J	2.1.89	1	PAm-J	São Paulo	8 Jul
23.17	1.3	Hanna	Mariën	BEL	16.5.82	1h2	NC	Bruxelles	4 Aug
23.18	1.9	Aymée	Martínez	CUB-J	17.11.88	2	ALBA	Caracas	10 May
23.18	2.0	Moushami	Robinson	USA	13.4.81	8	adidas	Carson	20 May
		(80)							
23.18	0.0	Angel	Perkins	USA	10.5.84	1		Eagle Rock	3 Jun
23.18	1.5	Eleni	Artymata	CYP	16.5.86	1	NC	Nicosia	5 Jull
23.19	-0.2	Carla	Grace	USA	6.6.86	2h3	Big 12	Lincoln	12 May
23.19	0.3	Damola	Osayomi	NGR	26.7.86	3	DLV	Bochum-Wattenscheid	12 Aug
23.20	1.2	Ashlee	Kidd	USA	26.7.85	2		College Park	21 Apr
23.21	0.9	Angela	Daigle-Bowen	USA	28.5.76	2	ModR	Modesto	5 May
23.21	-0.2	Olena	Chebanu	UKR	4.1.81	6q1	WCh	Osaka	29 Aug
23.22		Natalya	Safronnikova	BLR	28.2.73	5		Moskva	29 Jun
23.23A	0.7	Connie	Moore	USA	29.8.81	1		Provo	1 Jun
23.23	0.5	Schillonie	Calvert	JAM-J	27.7.88	2	PAm-J	São Paulo	8 Jul
		(90)							
23.24	0.4	Victoria	Jordan	USA-Y	26.2.90	1h3	Jnr Oly	Walnut	26 Jul
23.24	0.2	Amandine	Allou Affoué	CIV	29.8.80	4h6	WCh	Osaka	29 Aug
23.25	1.2	Patrice	Potts	USA	9.9.87	3		College Park	21 Apr
23.25	-2.0	Marshevet	Hooker	USA	25.9.84	1rB	GP	Madrid	21 Jul
23.25	-0.8	Guzel	Khubbieva	UZB	2.5.76	5h4	WCh	Osaka	29 Aug
23.26	0.0	Lynne	Layne	USA-J	1.4.88	2h3	SEC	Tuscaloosa	11 May
23.26	2.0	Jessica	Onyepunuka	USA	3.5.86	1h2	NCAA-r	Eugene	25 May
23.26	1.6	Monique	Henderson	USA	18.2.83	7	GP	New York	2 Jun
23.26	0.1	Ewelina	Klocek	POL	20.3.87	1h4	EU23	Debrecen	13 Jul
23.27	0.4	Tresha	Henry	JAM	23.9.83	5	Big 12	Lincoln	13 May
		(100)							
23.27	0.0	Geraldine	Pillay	RSA	25.8.77	3	GP	Belém	20 May
23.27	0.0	Emily	Freeman	GBR	24.11.80	1		Bratislava	5 Jun
23.27	2.0	Inna	Eftimova	BUL-J	19.6.88	1	NC-j	Sofia	10 Jun

23.28	0.0	Tracy-Ann	Rowe	JAM	17.9.85	24 Mar
23.28	-0.3	Franca	Idoko	NGR	15.6.85	27 May
23.28	0.8	Anneisha	McLaughlin	JAM	6.1.86	24 Jun
23.28	1.9	H.P.Sujani	Buddika	SRI	15.4.82	28 Jul
23.28	-1.3	Kadi-Ann	Thomas	GBR	10.2.86	13 Aug
23.29	-2.6	Laura	Turner	GBR	12.8.82	10 Jun
23.29	-0.6	Nelly	Banco	FRA	17.2.86	14 Jul
23.29	0.0	Aleksandra	Fedoriva	RUS-J	13.9.88	30 Jul
23.30	-2.0	Faní	Halkiá	GRE	2.2.79	24 Jun
23.30	1.9		Vu Thi Huong	VIE	7.10.86	28 Jul
23.31	1.0	Jacqua	Williams	USA	6.1.87	25 May
23.32	1.2	Kandace	Tucker	USA	12.4.84	21 Apr
23.32	-2.0	Yelena	Nevmerzhitskaya	BLR	27.7.80	24 Jun
23.32	-3.8	Shericka	Williams	JAM	17.9.85	30 Sep
23.33	0.4	Thaissa	Presti	BRA	7.11.85	24 Jun
23.34	-1.0	Murielle	Ahoure	USA	23.8.87	26 May
23.34	-0.3	Davita	Prendergast	JAM	16.12.84	26 May
23.34	-1.0	Yekaterina	Grigoryeva	RUS	21.4.74	27 May
23.34	1.6	Jeneba	Tarmoh	USA-J	27.9.89	1 Jun
23.34	0.4	Alexis	Weatherspoon	USA	27.7.83	23 Jun
23.34	1.8	Kadiatou	Camara	MLI	4.5.81	21 Jul
23.35	0.9	Michelle	Perry	USA	1.5.79	5 May
23.35	-0.3	Christy	Ekpukhon	NGR	6.2.85	27 May
23.35		Nadezhda	Belousova	RUS	18.1.86	29 May
23.36	-0.2	Marta	Jeschke	POL	2.6.86	14 Jul
23.36	0.9	Rosemar	Coelho Neto	BRA	2.1.77	14 Jul
23.36	0.1	Makelesi	Bulikiobo	FIJ	23.10.77	19 Aug
23.37	-0.7	Jade	Bailey	BAR	10.6.83	16 Jun
23.37	-0.2	Yelena	Novikova	RUS	27.10.85	14 Jul
23.37	-0.2	Hayley	Jones	GBR-J	14.9.88	21 Jul
23.38	-0.1	Anyika	Onuora	GBR	28.10.84	14 Jul
23.38	0.3	Carolina	Klüft	SWE	2.2.83	25 Aug
23.38	1.1	Montell	Douglas	GBR	24.1.86	9 Sep
23.39	-0.6	Novlene	Williams	JAM	26.4.82	21 Apr
23.39	0.1	Nicole	Ireland	USA	23.4.82	12 May
23.39	0.8	Phara	Anacharsis	FRA	17.12.83	12 Aug
23.40	0.0	Donna	Fraser	GBR	7.11.72	9 Jun
23.40	-0.4	Johanna	Manninen	FIN	4.4.80	22 Jul
23.40	0.3	Kelly	Sotherton	GBR	13.11.76	25 Aug
23.42	0.5	Sheena	Johnson	USA	1.10.82	21 Apr
23.42A	-1.0	Racheal	Nachula	ZAM-Y	14.1.90	5 May
23.42	0.3	Jessica	Cousins	USA	10.4.85	11 May
23.42	-2.0	Maryna	Mindareva	UKR	22.8.82	13 Jun
23.42	-1.0	Chalonda	Goodman	USA-Y	29.9.90	16 Jun
23.42	0.7	Emma	Ania	GBR	7.2.79	4 Jul
23.42	0.1	Olga	Andreyeva	UKR	14.5.85	13 Jul
23.43	0.0	Deedee	Trotter	USA	8.12.82	12 May
23.43A	1.2	Nomb. Constance	Mkenku	RSA-J	30.6.89	27 May

Mark	Wind	Name		Nat	Born	Date
23.43	1.2	Marina	Kislova	RUS	7.2.78	27 May
23.43	0.2	Sari	Keskitalo	FIN	6.4.85	9 Jun
23.43	0.8	Rosemarie	Whyte	JAM	8.9.86	24 Jun
23.44	-1.7	Teona	Rodgers	USA-J	26.6.89	4 May
23.44	0.2	Nora	Edletzberger	AUT	1.6.77	10 Jun
23.44	-1.0	Brittany	Long	USA-J	7.9.89	16 Jun
23.44	1.1	Myriam	Soumaré	FRA	29.10.86	17 Jun
23.44	0.0	Fabienne	Feraez	BEN	6.8.76	1 Jul
23.44	0.7	Belén	Recio	ESP	11.8.80	4 Jul
23.44	1.9	Anna	Geflikh	RUS	5.7.83	2 Aug
23.44	0.2	Daria	Korczynska	POL	30.7.81	17 Oct
23.45	1.3	Nivea	Smith	BAH-Y	18.2.90	9 Apr
23.45	1.6	Victoria	Howard	USA	14.5.87	4 May
23.45	0.6	Lina	Grincikaité	LTU	3.5.87	13 Jun
23.45	1.3	Ciara	Sheehy	IRL	12.8.80	11 Aug
23.46		Justine	Bayiga	UGA	15.1.79	24 May
23.46	-2.1	Iryna	Shepetyuk	UKR	13.2.82	13 Jun
23.46	0.0		Jiang Lan	CHN-J	27.6.89	1 Nov
23.47	0.7	Nandelle	Cameron	TRI	21.10.83	24 Jun
23.47	0.8	Tatyana	Levina	RUS	28.2.77	4 Jul
23.47	1.3	Yelizaveta	Bryzgina	UKR-J	28.11.89	21 Jul
23.47	1.5	Johanna	Kedzierski	GER	10.6.84	22 Jul
23.48A	-1.4	Darlenis	Obregón	COL	21.2.86	5 May
23.48	1.4	Solen	Désert	FRA	2.8.82	20 May
23.48	1.6	Cynthia	Niako	CIV	25.9.83	27 May
23.48	0.1	Angelique	Smith	USA	22.2.86	28 May
23.48	0.1	Elisabeth	Slettum	NOR	31.8.86	13 Jul
23.48	1.9		Zou Yiting	CHN	17.9.86	28 Jul
23.49	1.2	Lasadies	McClain	USA		12 May
23.49	0.3	Sina	Schielke	GER	19.5.81	1 Jun
23.49	-1.7	Nataliya	Pogrebnyak	UKR-J	19.2.88	13 Jun
23.49	-2.1	Oksana	Shcherbak	UKR	24.2.82	13 Jun
23.49	1.7	Ashley	Collier	USA-Y	4.2.92	28 Jul
23.50	1.7	Ashton	Purvis	USA-Y	12.7.92	28 Apr
23.50	0.2	Tatyana	Chernova	RUS-J	29.1.88	23 May
23.50	-1.9	Bárbara	Leoncio	BRA-Y	7.10.91	15 Jul
23.51	0.4	Monique	Williams	NZL	23.9.85	17 Feb
23.51	1.0	Leslie	Cole	USA	17.5.79	12 May
23.51	0.0	Sylviane	Félix	FRA	31.10.77	30 Jul
23.52	0.0	Daniela	Reina	ITA	15.5.81	20 May
23.52	2.0	Janice	Davis	USA	27.10.84	25 May
23.52	2.0	Deanna	Goodwin	USA	26.1.85	25 May
23.52A	2.0	LaBrittney	Horton	USA		28 May
23.52	-0.2	Xenia	Vdovina	RUS	15.4.87	19 Jun
23.52	0.1	Léonie	Mani	CMR	21.5.77	28 Jun
23.52	0.0	Angela	Morosanu	ROM	26.7.86	28 Jul
23.52	1.3	Joanne	Cuddihy (198)	IRL	11.5.84	11 Aug

Wind assisted

Mark	Wind	Name		Nat	Born	Pos	Meet	Venue	Date
22.39	2.7		Campbell			1		Fayetteville	21 Apr
22.80	2.7	Latonia	Wilson	USA	30.11.84	2		Fayetteville	21 Apr
22.84	2.6	Victoria	Jordan	USA-Y	26.2.90	1	Jnr Oly	Walnut	28 Jul
22.87	2.6	Carol	Rodríguez	PUR	16.12.85	1	NCAA-r	Eugene	26 May
22.93	2.3	Bianca	Knight	USA-J	1.1.89	1	NC-j	Indianapolis	22 Jun
22.94	2.3	Lynne	Layne	USA-J	1.4.88	2	NC-j	Indianapolis	22 Jun
22.95	2.6	Marshevet	Hooker	USA	25.9.84	1		Austin	21 Apr
23.02		Brittany	Long	USA-J	7.9.89	1		Atlanta	21 Apr
23.02A	2.4	Crystal	Cox	USA	28.3.79	1		Provo	2 Jun
23.03	3.6	Natalya	Safronnikova	BLR	28.2.73	1h	NC	Grodno	6 Jul
23.04	2.4	Kia	Davis	USA	23.5.76	1		New York	14 Jul
23.05	2.1	Wyllesheia	Myrick	USA	21.11.79	2		Cork	30 Jun
23.07	2.9	Jessica	Cousins	USA	10.4.85	1		Fayetteville	21 Apr
23.10	5.1	Cynthia	Niako	CIV	25.9.83	2		Lake Buena Vista	24 Mar
23.10	5.1	Charlette	Greggs	USA	20.10.83	3		Lake Buena Vista	24 Mar
23.12	2.8	Sakie	Nobuoka	JPN	24.8.77	1rB	MSR	Walnut	15 Apr
23.12	2.2	Nelly	Banco	FRA	17.2.86	1	NC-23	Elancourt	30 Jun
23.15	2.1	Emily	Freeman	GBR	24.11.80	3		Cork	30 Jun
23.15	2.4	Damola	Osayomi	NGR	26.7.86	1h1	AfG	Alger	21 Jul
23.20	2.4	Jeneba	Tarmoh	USA-J	27.9.89	1		Sacramento	2 Jun
23.21	4.8	Donniece	Parrish	USA	4.11.85	1		Lincoln	5 May
23.24	2.4	Ashton	Purvis	USA-Y	6.7.92	2		Sacramento	2 Jun
23.24	2.3	Candyce	McGrone	USA-J	24.3.89	4	NC-j	Indianapolis	22 Jun
23.26A	w?	Tsholofelo	Thipe	RSA	12.9.86	1		Pretoria	27 Oct

Mark	Wind	Name		Nat	Born	Date
23.27	2.2	Anneisha	McLaughlin	JAM	6.1.86	15 Jul
23.28	2.6	Monique	Williams	NZL	23.9.85	11 Mar
23.30	2.9	Tominique	Boatright	USA	19.1.86	21 Apr
23.30	2.6	Chalonda	Goodman	USA-Y	29.9.90	28 Jul
23.31	4.5	Reyare	Thomas	TRI	23.11.87	24 Jun
23.33	2.6	LaTasha	Kerr	USA	30.11.83	21 Apr
23.35	2.4	Aliann	Pompey	GUY	9.3.78	14 Jul
23.36	2.7	Yolanda	Goff	USA	14.1.85	21 Apr
23.36	3.2	Sabina	Veit	SLO	2.12.85	1 Jul
23.37	3.0	Lee	McConnell	GBR	9.10.78	31 Jul
23.38	2.6	Mae	Koime	PNG	14.12.83	11 Mar
23.38	5.1	Nicole	Whitman	USA	9.11.80	24 Mar
23.38	2.1	Amanda	Kotze	RSA	26.2.86	31 Mar
23.38	2.1	Cindy	Stewart	RSA	14.11.85	31 Mar
23.38	2.1	Donna	Fraser	GBR	7.11.72	30 Jun
23.38	2.6	Dominique	Duncan	USA-Y	7.5.90	28 Jul
23.41	2.8	Natalya	Murinovich	RUS	27.5.85	9 Jun
23.41	3.1	Grazyna	Prokopek	POL	20.4.77	4 Aug
23.42	4.5	Nandelle	Cameron	TRI	21.10.83	24 Jun
23.42mx	4.2	Sally	McLellan	AUS	19.9.86	29 Jun
23.45	2.5	Crystal	Attenborough	AUS	1.8.83	20 Jan
23.46	2.6	Melanie	Kleeberg	AUS	27.12.81	11 Mar
23.46A	2.4	Melinda	Smedley	USA	11.2.81	2 Jun
23.47	3.2	Lakeisha	Martin	USA		21 Apr
23.48	3.2	Semoy	Hackett	TRI-J	27.11.88	17 Jun
23.50	3.2	Shakera	Reece	BAR-J	31.8.88	8 Apr

Best at low altitude

Mark	Wind	Name		Nat	Born	Date
23.51	0.7	Adrienne	Power	CAN	11.11.81	25 Jul

Indoors

Mark	Name		Nat	Born	Pos	Meet	Venue	Date
22.46		Stewart			1r2	SEC	Lexington	25 Feb
22.90	Kelly-Ann	Baptiste	TRI	14.10.86	2r2	NCAA	Fayetteville	9 Mar
22.92	Courtney	Champion	USA	10.6.86	1r1	NCAA	Fayetteville	9 Mar
22.97A	Bianca	Knight	USA-J	2.1.89	1		Pocatello	17 Feb

Mark	Name		Nat	Born	Date
23.31+	Nicola	Sanders	GBR	23.6.82	3 Mar
23.33	Tatyana	Levina	RUS	28.2.77	25 Jan
23.41	Natalya	Murinovich	RUS	27.5.85	10 Feb
23.50	Mareike	Peters	GER	9.1.86	18 Feb

Hand timed: 23.2 –0.9 Susana Clement CUB-J 18.8.89 1r1 La Habana 8 Jun
22.8w 3.9 1 Santiago de Cuba 28 Jun

Short course: 22.77 1.2 Louise Ayétotché CIV 3.6.75 1 Carson 13 Apr

Mark	Wind	Name		Nat	Born	Pos	Meet	Venue	Date

JUNIORS

See main list for top 9 juniors. 10 performances (inc. 1 indoors) by 4 women to 23.17. Additional marks & further juniors:

Lucas 23.05 -0.6 1h2 Big 12 Lincoln 12 May 23.07w 2.3 3 NC-j Indianapolis 22 Jun
Henry 22.85 0.4 1h1 NCAA Sacramento 7 Jun 22.94 1.2 1 NC-j Kingston 24 Jun
22.92 -0.3 4s1 NCAA Sacramento 7 Jun 23.15 -1.0 1h1 NCAA-r Columbia 25 May

Mark	Wind	Name		Nat	Born	Pos	Meet	Venue	Date
23.29	0.0	Aleksandra	Fedoriva (10)	RUS	13.9.88	3		Thessaloniki	30 Jul
23.34	1.6	Jeneba	Tarmoh	USA	27.9.89	1h3		Sacramento	1 Jun
23.37	-0.2	Hayley	Jones	GBR	14.9.88	1	EJ	Hengelo	21 Jul
23.42A	-1.0	Racheal	Nachula	ZAM-Y	14.1.90	1B		Gaborone	5 May
23.42	-1.0	Chalonda	Goodman	USA-Y	29.9.90	1		Greensboro	16 Jun
23.43A	1.2	Nombulelo Constance	Mkenku	RS	30.6.89	1	S.Af Ch	Windhoek	27 May
23.44	-1.7	Teona	Rodgers	US	26.6.89	1		Winter Park	4 May
23.44	-1.0	Brittany	Long	US	7.9.89	2		Greensboro	16 Jun
23.45	1.3	Nivea	Smith	BAH-Y	18.2.90	1	Carifta	Providenciales	9 Apr
23.46	0.0		Jiang Lan	CHN	27.6.89	1		Wuhan	1 Nov
23.47	1.3	Yelizaveta	Bryzgina (20)	UKR	28.11.89	1s2	EJ	Hengelo	21 Jul

Wind assisted 10 performances by four women to 23.09. See main lists for 7 juniors.

Townsend 23.01 2.1 1 Denton 27 Apr 23.09 2.1 1 Denton 28 Apr
Long 23.05 1h1 Atlanta 21 Apr 23.05 3.6 1h4 Orlando 2 Jun

Mark	Wind	Name		Nat	Born	Pos	Meet	Venue	Date
23.30	2.6	Chalonda	Goodman	USA-Y	29.9.90	2	Jnr Oly	Walnut	28 Jul
23.38	2.6	Dominique	Duncan	USA-Y	7.5.90	3	Jnr Oly	Walnut	28 Jul

300 METRES

Mark	Name		Nat	Born	Pos	Meet	Venue	Date
36.64	Nicola	Sanders	GBR	23.6.82	1		Glasgow	3 Jun
Indoors								
36.0+	Nicola	Sanders	GBR	23.6.82	1	in 400m	Birmingham	3 Mar
36.33	Allyson	Felix	USA	18.11.85	1	Tyson	Fayetteville	9 Feb
36.42	Deedee	Trotter	USA	8.12.82	2	Tyson	Fayetteville	9 Feb
36.67	Francena	McCorory	USA-J	20.10.88	1r1		Blacksburg	12 Jan
36.93	Shalonda	Solomon	USA	19.12.85	2r1		Blacksburg	12 Jan
Drugs disqualification								
36.99	Vanya	Stambolova ¶	BUL	28.11.83	1		Sofia	3 Feb

During 400m races

24 Jun USA Ch Indianapolis: 35.8 Deedee Trotter, 35.9 Natasha Hasting & Sanya Richards, 36.3 Mary Wineberg
31 Aug WCh Osaka: 35.73 Novlene Williams, 35.9 Natalya Antyukh, 36.12 Christine Ohurogu, 36.17 Nicola Sanders, 36.3 Deedee Trotter, 36.4 Ana Guevara

400 METRES

Mark	Name		Nat	Born	Pos	Meet	Venue	Date
49.27	Sanya	Richards	USA	26.2.85	1	ISTAF	Berlin	16 Sep
49.27		Richards			1	WAF	Stuttgart	23 Sep
49.29		Richards			1	VD	Bruxelles	14 Sep
49.36		Richards			1	WK	Zürich	7 Sep
49.52		Richards			1	Gaz	Saint-Denis	6 Jul
49.61	Christine	Ohuruogu	GBR	17.5.84	1	WCh	Osaka	29 Aug
49.64	Deedee	Trotter	USA	8.12.82	1	NC	Indianapolis	23 Jun
49.65	Nicola	Sanders	GBR	23.6.82	2	WCh	Osaka	29 Aug
49.66	Novlene	Williams	JAM	26.4.82	1s1	WCh	Osaka	27 Aug
49.66		N Williams			3	WCh	Osaka	29 Aug
49.70	Allyson	Felix	USA	18.11.85	1	DNG	Stockholm	7 Aug
49.72		Richards			2	DNG	Stockholm	7 Aug
49.77		Richards			1	GGala	Roma	13 Jul
49.77		Sanders			1s2	WCh	Osaka	27 Aug
49.79		Richards			1	LGP	London (CP)	3 Aug
49.84	Natasha	Hastings	USA	23.7.86	2	NC	Indianapolis	23 Jun
49.93	Natalya	Antyukh	RUS	26.6.81	2s2	WCh	Osaka	27 Aug
50.02		Richards			1s1	NC	Indianapolis	22 Jun
50.06		N Williams			1	NC	Kingston	24 Jun
50.10		Antyukh			1	NC	Tula	2 Aug
50.12		N Williams			2	WAF	Stuttgart	23 Sep
50.15		Hastings			1	NCAA	Sacramento	9 Jun
50.15	Ami Mbacké	Thiam	SEN	10.11.76	2	GGala	Roma	13 Jul
50.16		Ohuruogu			1s3	WCh	Osaka	27 Aug
50.16	Ana Gabriela	Guevara	MEX	4.3.77	4	WCh	Osaka	29 Aug
50.17		Felix			2	LGP	London (CP)	3 Aug
50.17		Trotter			5	WCh	Osaka	29 Aug
50.19		Guevara			2s1	WCh	Osaka	27 Aug
50.20		Ohuruogu			3	WAF	Stuttgart	23 Sep
50.21		N Williams			1h4	WCh	Osaka	26 Aug
	(30/10)							

Mark	Name		Nat	Born	Pos	Meet	Venue	Date
50.22	Tatyana	Veshkurova	RUS	23.9.81	2	NC	Tula	2 Aug
50.24	Mary	Wineberg (Danner)	USA	3.1.80	3	NC	Indianapolis	23 Jun
50.31	Ilona	Usovich	BLR	14.11.82	3s1	WCh	Osaka	27 Aug
50.37	Shericka	Williams	JAM	17.9.85	4s2	WCh	Osaka	27 Aug
50.52	Natalya	Nazarova	RUS	26.5.79	3	NC	Tula	2 Aug
50.73	Joanne	Cuddihy	IRL	11.5.84	4s1	WCh	Osaka	27 Aug
50.78	Tatyana	Levina	RUS	28.2.77	4	NC	Tula	2 Aug
50.81	Olesya	Zykina	RUS	7.10.80	1s2	NC	Tula	31 Jul
50.82	Monique	Henderson	USA	18.2.83	5	NC	Indianapolis	23 Jun
50.84	Yelena	Migunova	RUS	4.1.84	5	NC	Tula	2 Aug
	(20)							
50.90	Amantle	Montsho	BOT	4.7.83	4s3	WCh	Osaka	27 Aug
50.98	Tatyana	Firova	RUS	10.10.82	6	NC	Tula	2 Aug
50.99	Christine	Amertil	BAH	18.8.79	2	PAm	Rio de Janeiro	25 Jul
51.00	Indira	Terrero	CUB	29.11.85	1	NC/Barr	La Habana	26 May
51.00	Shereefa	Lloyd	JAM	2.9.82	5s3	WCh	Osaka	27 Aug
51.01	Yulyana	Yushchenko	BLR	14.8.84	1		Minsk (Staiki)	11 Aug
51.04	Zhanna	Kashcheyeva	RUS	27.7.82	2s1	NC	Tula	31 Jul
51.06	Kseniya	Zadorina	RUS	2.3.87	1	NC-23	Tula	19 Jun
51.07	Lee	McConnell	GBR	9.10.78	5s1	WCh	Osaka	27 Aug
51.11	Christy	Ekpukpon	NGR	6.2.85	2		Brazzaville	27 May
	(30)							
51.13	Svetlana	Pospelova	RUS	24.12.79	1		Sochi	26 May
51.16	Olga	Shulikova	RUS	12.4.85	2	NC-23	Tula	19 Jun
51.19	Monique	Hennagan	USA	26.5.76	2	BrGP	Sheffield	15 Jul
51.20	Joy	Eze	NGR	23.4.87	2	AfG	Alger	20 Jul
51.24	Davita	Prendergast	JAM	16.12.84	4	NC	Kingston	24 Jun
51.25A	Gabriela	Medina	MEX	3.3.85	1		Xalapa	5 May
51.25	Lyudmila	Litvinova	RUS	8.6.85	1	EU23	Debrecen	13 Jul
51.27	Shana	Cox	USA	22.1.85	2	NCAA	Sacramento	9 Jun
51.36	Ebonie	Floyd	USA	21.10.83	1		Berkeley	28 Apr
51.40	Monica	Hargrove	USA	30.12.82	1	Nebiolo	Torino	8 Jun
	(30)							
51.42	Solen	Désert	FRA	2.8.82	2	NC	Niort	4 Aug
51.44	Shade	Abugan	NGR-Y	17.12.90	3	AfG	Alger	20 Jul
51.46	Ashlee	Kidd	USA	26.7.85	3	NCAA-r	Gainesville	26 May
51.47	Laverne	Jones	ISV	16.9.81	2	KansR	Lawrence	21 Apr
51.47	Moushami	Robinson	USA	13.4.81	7	NC	Indianapolis	23 Jun
51.52	Patricia	Hall	JAM	16.10.82	1	FlaR	Gainesville	6 Apr
51.59	Ionela	Târlea	ROM	9.2.76	3h4	WCh	Osaka	26 Aug
51.61A	Muna	Jabir Ahmed	SUD	6.1.87	1	E.AfCh	Kampala	31 May
51.61	Aliann	Pompey	GUY	9.3.78	1		New York	13 Jul
51.62	Olga	Tereshkova	KAZ	26.10.84	1	WUG	Bangkok	11 Aug
	(40)							
51.63	Jessica	Beard	USA-J	8.1.89	1		Columbus	2 Jun
51.66	Debbie	Dunn	USA	26.3.78	3		Kingston	5 May
51.70	Nadezhda	Belousova	RUS	18.1.86	4	NC-23	Tula	19 Jun
51.71	Tamsyn	Lewis	AUS	20.7.78	1	NC	Brisbane	10 Mar
51.72A	Esther	Akinsulie	CAN	22.4.84	1		San Luis Potosi	17 May
51.72	Bobby-Gaye	Wilkins	JAM-J	10.9.88	1	PAm-J	São Paulo	7 Jul
51.73	Angel	Perkins	USA	10.5.84	6s2	NC	Indianapolis	22 Jun
51.74	Sonita	Sutherland	JAM	9.8.87	4	adidas	Carson	20 May
51.74	Anna	Jesien	POL	10.12.78	1		Warszawa	26 May
51.74	Aymée	Martínez	CUB-J	17.11.88	4h4	WCh	Osaka	26 Aug
	(50)							
51.75	Kia	Davis	USA	23.5.76	2		Atlanta	12 May
51.76	Kaliese	Spencer	JAM	6.4.87	1		Kingston	19 May
51.76	Yelena	Novikova	RUS	27.10.85	5	NC-23	Tula	19 Jun
51.78	Nawal	El Jack	SUD-J	17.10.88	3		Abuja	5 May
51.80	Kineke	Alexander	VIN	21.2.86	1s2	NCAA	Sacramento	8 Jun
51.81	Asami	Tanno	JPN	25.9.85	8s1	WCh	Osaka	27 Aug
51.85A	Adrienne	Power	CAN	11.11.81	1		San Luis Potosi	19 May
51.85	Fabienne	Féraez	BEN	6.8.76	2	Nebiolo	Torino	8 Jun
51.85	Faní	Halkiá	GRE	2.2.79	1	ECp-S	München	23 Jun
51.86	Barbara	Petráhn	HUN	16.9.78	3h3	WCh	Osaka	26 Aug
	(60)							
51.88	Anastasiya	Ovchinnikova	RUS	16.10.84	3s1	NC	Tula	31 Jul
51.88	Danijela	Grgic	CRO-J	28.9.88	2	WUG	Bangkok	11 Aug
51.89	Josiane	Tito	BRA	8.8.79	1		São Paulo	7 Mar
51.89	Irina	Khlyustova	BLR	14.6.78	2		Minsk (Staiki)	11 Aug

Mark	Name		Nat	Born	Pos	Meet	Venue	Date
51.90	Carol	Rodríguez	PUR	16.12.85	1		Los Angeles	28 Apr
51.91	Tonette	Dyer	USA	28.3.82	1		Eugene	27 May
51.91	Jenna	Martin	CAN-J	31.3.88	2	PAm-J	São Paulo	7 Jul
51.92	Jessica	Cousins	USA	10.4.85	4	NCAA	Sacramento	9 Jun
51.93	Oksana	Shcherbak	UKR	24.2.82	1	NC	Donetsk	5 Jul
51.94	Jana	Rawlinson	AUS	9.11.82	1	ECCp	Albufeira	26 May
	(70)							
51.97	Nicole	Leach	USA	18.7.87	2		Los Angeles	28 Apr
51.97	Latosha	Wallace	USA	24.3.85	1	Pac-10	Stanford	13 May
51.98	Claudia	Hoffmann	GER	10.12.82	1		Gent	15 Jul
51.99	Daniela	Reina	ITA	15.5.81	6s2	WCh	Osaka	27 Aug
52.03A	Carline	Muir	CAN	1.10.87	2		San Luis Potosi	17 May
52.03	Clora	Williams	JAM	26.11.83	5	NCAA	Sacramento	9 Jun
52.04	Monika	Bejnar	POL	10.3.81	3	Kuso	Warszawa	17 Jun
52.04	Yelena	Ildeykina	RUS	16.6.83	1		Samara	9 Aug
52.06	Marilyn	Okoro	GBR	23.9.84	1		Génève	9 Jun
52.07	Darya	Safonova	RUS	21.3.80	1		Chelyabinsk	13 Jul
	(80)							
52.08	Anastasiya	Kochetova	RUS	18.9.83	2h1	NC	Tula	31 Jul
52.09A	Nadia	Cunningham	JAM	25.5.78	2		San Luis Potosi	19 May
52.09	Antonina	Yefremova	UKR	19.7.81	4	WUG	Bangkok	11 Aug
52.10	Teodora	Kolarova ¶	BUL	29.5.81	2	ECp-1B	Milano	23 Jun
52.10	Svetlana	Usovich	BLR	14.10.80	5		Moskva	29 Jun
52.11A	Markita	James	USA	28.6.83	4		Xalapa	5 May
52.13	Olga	Zavgorodnya	UKR	6.1.83	2	NC	Donetsk	5 Jul
52.14	Olga	Kotlyarova	RUS	12.4.76	3h		Tula	18 Jun
52.14	Zuzanna	Radecka-Pakaszewska	POL	2.4.75	1	NC	Poznan	1 Jul
52.14	Anastasiya	Kapachinskaya	RUS	21.11.79	5s1	NC	Tula	31 Jul
	(100)							

52.16	Maria Laura	Almirão	BRA	20.9.77	22 Jun
52.17	Trish	Bartholomew	GRN	23.10.86	9 Jun
52.19	Kenyata	Coleman	USA	21.4.86	6 Jun
52.19	Fatou Binetou	Fall	SEN	23.8.81	4 Aug
52.20	Natalya	Ivanova	RUS	25.6.81	26 May
52.20	Donna	Fraser	GBR	7.11.72	23 Aug
52.22	Nataliya	Pygyda	UKR	30.1.81	5 Jul
52.23	Oluoma	Nwoke	NGR	6.9.85	18 May
52.23	Makelesi	Bulikiobo	FIJ	23.10.77	26 Aug
52.24	Susana	Clement	CUB-J	18.8.89	26 May
52.27A	Zudikey	Rodríguez	MEX	14.3.87	31 Mar
52.28	Demetria	Washington	USA	31.12.79	22 Jun
52.28	Anastacia	Leroy	JAM	11.9.87	24 Jun
52.29	Najah	Floyd	USA	7.2.85	12 May
52.31A	Lucimar	Teodoro	BRA	1.5.81	3 Jun
52.31	Yelena	Voynova	RUS	10.3.85	19 Jun
52.31	Thélia	Sigère	FRA	3.6.85	12 Aug
52.32	Antonina	Krivoshapka	RUS	21.7.87	18 Jun
52.32	Brandi	Cross	USA-J	20.1.88	7 Jul
52.33	Deonna	Lawrence	USA	21.3.86	21 Apr
52.33	Cynthia	Rooks	USA	18.2.84	13 May
52.35	Becky	Horn	USA	12.5.86	12 May
52.38	Grazyna	Prokopek	POL	20.4.77	11 Aug
52.39	Tatyana	Azarova	KAZ	2.12.85	9 Jun
52.40	Jessica	Young	USA	6.4.87	26 May
52.40	Ruky	Abdulai	GHA	8.8.85	26 May
52.42	Tsvetelina	Kirilova	BUL	14.7.77	4 Aug
52.43	Agnieszka	Karpiesiuk	POL	17.4.82	1 Jul
52.44	Carey	Easton/Marshall	GBR	16.11.79	17 Jun
52.45	Yevgeniya	Isakova	RUS	27.11.78	18 Jun
52.45	Yuliya	Krevsun	UKR	8.12.80	5 Aug
52.46	Ginou	Etienne	HAI	12.1.85	20 Apr
52.46	Anna	Kozak	BLR	22.6.74	5 Jul
52.46	Tjipekapora	Herunga	NAM-J	.88	19 Jul
52.47	Ronetta	Smith	JAM	2.5.80	5 May
52.48	Tsholofelo	Thipe	RSA	12.9.86	18 Jul
52.50	Deborah	Jones	USA	30.3.85	12 May
52.51	Elizabeth	Muthoka	KEN	.79	24 May
52.51	Meshawn	Graham	USA-Y	26.5.90	2 Jun
52.53A	Estie	Wittstock	RSA	15.9.80	5 May
52.59	Marie-Angelique	Lacordelle	FRA	19.1.87	5 Aug
52.61	Virginie	Michanol	FRA	18.6.85	5 Aug
52.65	Sherone	Simpson	JAM	12.8.84	17 Feb
52.65	Phara	Anacharsis	FRA	17.12.83	22 Jul
52.66	Kou	Luogon	LBR	11.6.84	19 Jul
52.67	Ebony	Eutsey	USA-Y	3.5.92	8 Jul
52.68	Tominique	Boatright	USA	19.1.86	12 May
52.69	Johnsie	Liles	USA	25.5.85	26 May
52.70	Nathandra	John	SKN	6.11.84	8 Jun
52.70	Angela	Morosanu	ROM	26.7.86	27 Jul
52.71	Chauntae	Bayne	USA	4.4.84	13 May
52.73	Brooklyn	Morris	USA	27.3.86	21 Apr
52.73	Sheila	Ferreira	BRA	11.12.80	23 Jun
52.74	Monique	Williams	NZL	23.9.85	10 Mar
52.74	Alycia	Williams	USA	8.1.85	24 Mar
52.76		Huang Xiaoxiao	CHN	3.3.83	31 Mar
52.76	Natalya	Lavshuk	RUS	1.1.80	27 May
52.76	Amanda	Kotze	RSA	26.2.86	18 Jul
52.77	Eliana	Pacheco	VEN	14.1.79	19 Dec
52.78	Keva	Wilkins	JAM	20.10.83	26 May
52.79		Tang Xiaoyin	CHN	29.4.85	21 Apr
52.79	Dimítra	Dóva	GRE	2.7.74	15 Jun
52.80	Shareese	Woods	USA	20.2.85	15 Apr
52.80	Krystal	Cantey	USA	27.6.87	12 May
52.82	Nedyalka	Nedkova	BUL	15.3.77	16 Jun
52.85	Ariel	Burr	USA	10.4.86	26 May
52.85	Vicky	Barr	GBR	14.4.82	28 Jul
52.86	Emmily	Pinheiro	BRA	3.11.85	23 Jun
52.87	Olesya	Krasnomovets	RUS	8.7.79	17 Jun
52.88	Alexandria	Anderson	USA	28.1.87	21 Apr
52.88	Dominique	Darden	USA	9.12.83	1 May
52.88	Viktoriya	Shalygina	RUS	3.8.85	18 Jun
52.89	Shevon	Stoddart	JAM	21.11.82	19 May
52.89A	Justine	Bayiga	UGA	15.1.79	3 Jun
52.90A	Nallely	Vela	MEX	8.2.86	5 May
52.90	Kseniya	Ustalova	RUS-J	14.1.88	30 Jun
52.91	Kandace	Tucker	USA	12.4.84	21 Apr
52.91	Nina	Gilbert	USA	17.4.84	8 Jun
52.91	Alissa	Kallinicou	CYP	24.5.85	23 Jun
52.92	Deanna	Goodwin	USA	26.1.85	13 Apr
52.92	Sekinat	Adesanya	NGR-J	25.7.88	5 May
52.92	Alexandria	Spruiel	USA		26 May
52.93	Menike	Wickramasinghe	SRI	10.9.77	15 Oct
52.94	Martina	Naef	SUI	23.4.80	11 Aug
52.95	Ajoke	Odumosu	NGR	27.10.87	13 May
52.95	Anna	Verkhovskaya	RUS-J	11.1.88	30 Jun
52.96	Katie	Baker	USA	14.11.86	12 May
52.96	Bozena	Lukasik	POL	16.2.85	13 Jul
52.97	Angelina	Popova	RUS-J	4.10.90	7 Jun
52.98A	Shunte	Thomas	USA	5.7.84	14 Apr
52.98	Lucia	Klocová	SVK	20.11.83	17 Jun
52.99A	Racheal	Nachula	ZAM	14.1.90	5 May

Mark	Name		Nat	Born	Date	Mark	Name		Nat	Born	Date
52.99	Faye	Harding	GBR	7.9.85	7 May	53.01	Chitra K.	Soman	IND	10.7.83	23 Jun
53.00	Stephanie	Smith	USA	27.6.85	24 Mar	53.02	Brigita	Langerholc	SLO	23.7.76	23 Jun
53.00	Oksana	Ilyushkina	UKR	25.5.74	12 Jun	53.04	LaTonya	Loche (198)	USA	8.10.85	25 May

Indoors

Mark	Name		Nat	Born	Pos	Meet	Venue	Date
50.02		Sanders			1		Birmingham	3 Mar
51.48	Kineke	Alexander	VIN	21.2.86	2r2	NCAA	Fayetteville	10 Mar
51.93	Angela	Morosanu	ROM	26.7.86	4	EI	Birmingham	3 Mar
52.00	Grazyna	Prokopek	POL	20.4.77	3s1	EI	Birmingham	2 Mar

Mark	Name		Nat	Born	Date	Mark	Name		Nat	Born	Date
52.62	Emma	Duck	GBR	9.2.81	17 Feb	52.82#	Nikiesha	Wilson	JAM	28.7.86	25 Feb
52.74	Jenna	Harris	USA	28.1.85	9 Mar	52.93	Olga	Zaytseva	RUS	10.11.84	3 Feb
52.81	Brigita	Langerholc	SLO	23.7.76	11 Feb	53.04	Natalya	Peryakova	RUS	4.3.83	25 Jan

Best at low altitude: 52.04 Medina 2 Kuso Warszawa 17 Jun

52.56 Wittstock 20 Jul 52.69 Cunningham 4 Aug 52.77Akinsulie 24 Jul

Doubtful timing/irregular conditions: Mobile 14 Apr: 1. Ajoke Odumosu NGR 27.10.87 50.46, 2. Natalie Dixon TRI 29.4.83 52.22, 3. Clarisse Moh FRA 6.12.86 52.58

JUNIORS

See main list for top 7 juniors. 11 performances by 7 women to 51.91. Additional marks and further juniors:

Name	Mark	Pos	Meet	Venue	Date	Mark	Pos	Meet	Venue	Date
Abugan	51.49	3		Brazzaville	27 May	51.78	3s2	AfG	Alger	19 Jul
Beard	51.91	3	PAm-J	São Paulo	7 Jul					
El Jack	51.83	4	AfG	Alger	20 Jul					

Mark	Name		Nat	Born	Pos	Meet	Venue	Date
52.24	Susana	Clement	CUB	18.8.89	2	NC/Barr	La Habana	26 May
52.32	Brandi	Cross	USA	20.1.88	4	PAm-J	São Paulo	7 Jul
52.46	Tjipekapora	Herunga (10)	NAM	.88	2s1	AfG	Alger	19 Jul
52.51	Meshawn	Graham	USA-Y	26.5.90	2		Columbus	2 Jun
52.67	Ebony	Eutsey	USA-Y	3.5.92	1		Lisle	8 Jul
52.90	Kseniya	Ustalova	RUS	14.1.88	1		Zhukovskiy	30 Jun
52.92	Sekinat	Adesanya	NGR	25.7.88	6		Abuja	5 May
52.95	Anna	Verkhovskaya	RUS	11.1.88	2		Zhukovskiy	30 Jun
52.97	Angelina	Popova	RUS	4.10.90			Sankt=Peterburg	7 Jun
53.07	Aleksandra	Zaytseva	RUS	10.6.89	1	NC-j	Sochi	23 May
53.10	Robin	Reynolds	USA-Y	22.2.94	1	NC-y	Lisle	8 Jul
53.13	Jaimee-Lee	Hoebergen-Starr	AUS	17.2.88	1		Sydney	13 Jan
53.15	Jasmine	Joseph (20)	USA-Y	1.1.91	1		Sacramento	2 Jun

600 METRES

Mark	Name		Nat	Born	Pos	Meet	Venue	Date
1:25.08+	Janeth	Jepkosgei	KEN	13.12.83	1	in 800m	Rieti	9 Sep
1:25.84	Brigita	Langerholc	SLO	23.7.76	1		Ljubljana	3 Jun
1:26.57	Vanja	Perisic	CRO	5.7.85	2		Ljubljana	3 Jun
1:26.7+	Maria	Mutola	MOZ	27.10.72	2	in 800m	Osaka	28 Aug
1:26.79+	Hasna	Benhassi	MAR	1.6.78	3	in 800m	Osaka	28 Aug
1:27.32+	Mayte	Martínez	ESP	17.5.76	4	in 800m	Osaka	28 Aug
Indoors								
1:25.81	Jennifer	Meadows	GBR	17.4.81	1		Manchester	7 Jan

800 METRES

Mark	Name		Nat	Born	Pos	Meet	Venue	Date
1:56.04	Janeth	Jepkosgei	KEN	13.12.83	1	WCh	Osaka	28 Aug
1:56.17		Jepkosgei			1s3	WCh	Osaka	26 Aug
1:56.29		Jepkosgei			1	GP	Rieti	9 Sep
1:56.84	Hasna	Benhassi	MAR	1.6.78	2s3	WCh	Osaka	26 Aug
1:56.98	Maria	Mutola	MOZ	27.10.72	3s3	WCh	Osaka	26 Aug
1:56.99		Benhassi			2	WCh	Osaka	28 Aug
1:57.62	Mayte	Martínez	ESP	17.5.76	3	WCh	Osaka	28 Aug
1:57.63	Yuliya	Krevsun	UKR	8.12.80	1	WUG	Bangkok	14 Aug
1:57.87		Jepkosgei			1	WAF	Stuttgart	23 Sep
1:58.11	Svetlana	Usovich	BLR	14.10.80	1s1	WCh	Osaka	26 Aug
1:58.14	Olga	Kotlyarova	RUS	12.4.76	1	NC	Tula	3 Aug
1:58.14		Martínez			2	WAF	Stuttgart	23 Sep
1:58.21		Mutola			1	Aragón	Zaragoza	28 Jul
1:58.22		Kotlyarova			4	WCh	Osaka	28 Aug
1:58.33		Mutola			1	Pre	Eugene	10 Jun
1:58.37	Svetlana	Cherkasova	RUS	20.5.78	2	NC	Tula	3 Aug
1:58.41	Brigita	Langerholc	SLO	23.7.76	4s3	WCh	Osaka	26 Aug
1:58.52		Langerholc			5	WCh	Osaka	28 Aug
1:58.56		Kotlyarova			2s1	WCh	Osaka	26 Aug
1:58.61	Kenia	Sinclair (10)	JAM	14.7.80	2	Pre	Eugene	10 Jun
1:58.62	Lucia	Klocová	SVK	20.11.83	3s1	WCh	Osaka	26 Aug
1:58.62		Jepkosgei			1	ISTAF	Berlin	16 Sep
1:58.63	Svetlana	Klyuka	RUS	27.12.78	3	NC	Tula	3 Aug

Mark	Name		Nat	Born	Pos	Meet	Venue	Date
1:58.63	Elisa	Cusma Piccione	ITA	24.7.81	4s1	WCh	Osaka	26 Aug
1:58.67		Sinclair			1		Thessaloníki	30 Jul
1:58.68		Usovich			2	GP	Rieti	9 Sep
1:58.75	Alice	Schmidt	USA	3.10.81	3	Pre	Eugene	10 Jun
1:58.76	Marilyn	Okoro	GBR	23.9.84	3	WAF	Stuttgart	23 Sep
1:58.77		Kotlyarova			1h4	NC	Tula	2 Aug
1:58.79		Mutola			1		Eugene	27 May
	(30/15)							
1:58.80	Oksana	Zbrozhek	RUS	12.1.78	1	Kuso	Warszawa	17 Jun
1:59.07	Hazel	Clark	USA	3.10.77	1	GP	New York	2 Jun
1:59.15	Treniere	Clement	USA	27.10.81	2	GP	New York	2 Jun
1:59.29	Alysia	Johnson	USA	26.4.86	1	NCAA	Sacramento	9 Jun
1:59.35	Katie	Erdman	USA	24.8.83	2	NCAA	Sacramento	9 Jun
	(20)							
1:59.37	Tamsyn	Lewis	AUS	20.7.78	3	Aragón	Zaragoza	28 Jul
1:59.39	Jennifer	Meadows	GBR	17.4.81	5s3	WCh	Osaka	26 Aug
1:59.46	Élodie	Guégan	FRA	19.12.85	6s3	WCh	Osaka	26 Aug
1:59.49	Yelena	Soboleva	RUS	3.10.82	1	Znam	Zhukovskiy	9 Jun
1:59.51	Amina	Aït Hammou	MAR	18.7.78	3s2	WCh	Osaka	26 Aug
1:59.52	Yekaterina	Kostetskaya	RUS	31.12.86	2	WUG	Bangkok	14 Aug
1:59.59	Mariya	Shapayeva	RUS	7.11.86	1h	NC-23	Tula	18 Jun
1:59.64	Ewelina	Setowska-Dryk	POL	5.3.80	2	Kuso	Warszawa	17 Jun
1:59.75	Diane	Cummins	CAN	19.1.74	1	PAm	Rio de Janeiro	24 Jul
1:59.76	Agnes	Samaria	NAM	11.8.72	4h6	WCh	Osaka	25 Aug
	(30)							
1:59.81	Tatyana	Paliyenko	RUS	18.11.83	5	NC	Tula	3 Aug
1:59.84	Marian	Burnett	GUY	22.2.76	2	JAM Ch	Kingston	24 Jun
1:59.85	Tetyana	Petlyuk	UKR	22.2.82	1		Kyiv	4 Aug
1:59.90	Anna	Alminova	RUS	17.1.85	1	NC-23	Tula	19 Jun
1:59.91	Nicole	Teter	USA	8.11.73	2		Eugene	27 May
2:00.02	Rosibel	Garcia	COL	13.2.81	2	PAm	Rio de Janeiro	24 Jul
2:00.07	Liliana	Popescu	ROM	5.2.82	5s1	WCh	Osaka	26 Aug
2:00.18	Jemma	Simpson	GBR	10.2.84	3	LGP	London (CP)	3 Aug
2:00.21	Corina	Dumbravean	ROM	15.4.84	1	NC	Bucuresti	28 Jul
2:00.27	Natalya	Shipitsyna	RUS	6.5.81	1		Chelyabinsk	14 Jul
	(40)							
2:00.34	Zulia	Calatayud	CUB	9.11.79	3	PAm	Rio de Janeiro	24 Jul
2:00.37	Olesya	Chumakova	RUS	23.7.81	6	NC	Tula	3 Aug
2:00.52	Natalya	Khrushchelyova	RUS	30.5.73	2		Chelyabinsk	14 Jul
2:00.74	Seltana	Aït Hammou	MAR	10.5.80	6h5	WCh	Osaka	25 Aug
2:00.77	Neisha	Bernard-Thomas	GRN	21.1.81	4	GP	New York	2 Jun
2:00.78	Mariya	Savinova	RUS	22.6.85	3		Chelyabinsk	14 Jul
2:00.85	Aimee	Teteris	CAN	24.6.79	3		Thessaloniki	30 Jul
2:00.86	Rebecca	Lyne	GBR	4.7.82	5	LGP	London (CP)	3 Aug
2:00.92	Jolanda	Ceplak ¶	SLO	12.9.76	1	Takac	Beograd	29 May
2:00.93	Yevgeniya	Zinurova	RUS	16.11.82	4		Chelyabinsk	14 Jul
	(50)							
2:01.02	Anna	Rostkowska (Zagórska)	POL	26.7.80	1		Slupsk	25 Aug
2:01.04	Yuliya	Fomenko	RUS	30.8.79	9	GS	Ostrava	27 Jun
2:01.05	Heather	Dorniden	USA	19.1.87	3	NCAA	Sacramento	9 Jun
2:01.08	Mihaela	Neacsu	ROM	3.5.79	4h1	WCh	Osaka	25 Aug
2:01.09	Irina	Krakoviak	LTU	16.11.77	6	Kuso	Warszawa	17 Jun
2:01.11	Irina	Maracheva	RUS	29.9.84	7	NC	Tula	3 Aug
2:01.12	Erin	Donohue	USA	8.5.83	2		Liège (NX)	25 Jul
2:01.13	Vanja	Perisic	CRO	5.7.85	1		Velenje	28 Jun
2:01.15	Monika	Gradzki	GER	21.9.79	7	Kuso	Warszawa	17 Jun
2:01.15	Faith	Macharia	KEN	9.2.76	2B	GP	Madrid	21 Jul
	(60)							
2:01.17	Madeleine	Pape	AUS	24.2.84	1		Stanford	29 Apr
2:01.28	Josiane	Tito	BRA	8.8.79	1h2	PAm	Rio de Janeiro	23 Jul
2:01.33	Natalya	Peryakova	RUS	4.3.83	3		Sochi	26 May
2:01.33	Sylwia	Ejdys	POL	15.7.84	8	Kuso	Warszawa	17 Jun
2:01.35	Laura	Finucane	GBR	3.8.86	8	Odlozil	Praha	13 Jun
2:01.40	Gulnara	Galkina	RUS	9.7.78	1h1	NC	Tula	2 Aug
2:01.42	Natalya	Koreyvo	BLR	14.11.85	4	EU23	Debrecen	14 Jul
2:01.49	Vicky	Griffiths	GBR	9.10.84	1		London (CP)	25 Aug
2:01.50	Charlotte	Best	GBR	7.3.85	3	WUG	Bangkok	14 Aug
2:01.56	Celia	Brown	GBR	22.1.77	2		London (CP)	25 Aug
	(70)							
2:01.57	Sandra	Teixeira	POR	13.3.78	1	NC	Lisboa (U)	29 Jul

Mark	Name		Nat	Born	Pos	Meet	Venue	Date
2:01.58	Lidia	Chojecka	POL	25.1.77	9	Kuso	Warszawa	17 Jun
2:01.59	Lisa	Corrigan	AUS	2.12.84	1		Canberra	27 Jan
2:01.63	Teodora	Kolarova ¶	BUL	29.5.81	2		Kalamáta	2 Jun
2:01.66	Ibtissam	Lakhaoud-Boucif	MAR	7.12.83	1		Castres	11 Aug
2:01.71	Leonora	Piuza	MOZ	14.4.78	1		Villefranche-sur-Saône	30 Jun
2:01.75	Morgan	Uceny	USA	10.3.85	4	NC	Indianapolis	24 Jun
2:01.76	Margarita	Fuentes-Pila	ESP	6.10.82	2		Rivas Vaciamadrid	29 Jun
2:01.77	Susan	Scott	GBR	26.9.77	9	Odlozil	Praha	13 Jun
2:01.78	Natalya	Pantelyeva	RUS	18.8.83	2h6	NC	Tula	2 Aug
	(80)							
2:01.78	Liz	Brathwaite	GBR	10.4.85	2		Mancheter (Str)	11 Aug
2:01.80	Zoya	Hladun-Nesterenko	UKR	10.3.83	2		Kyiv	4 Aug
2:01.84	Olga	Cristea	MDA	13.12.87	4	WUG	Bagkok	14 Aug
2:01.85	Anna	Luchkina	RUS	13.1.86	h	NC-23	Tula	18 Jun
2:01.86	Kerstin	Werner	GER	18.9.82	4	DLV	Bochum-Wattenscheid	12 Aug
2:01.88	Aneta	Lemiesz	POL	17.1.81	5	DLV	Bochum-Wattenscheid	12 Aug
2:01.89	Fatimoh	Muhammed	LBR	23.1.84	4	NCAA	Sacramento	9 Jun
2:01.94	Yekaterina	Martynova	RUS	12.6.86	4	NC-23	Tula	19 Jun
2:01.95	Emma	Jackson	GBR-J	7.6.88	3		Manchester	9 Jun
2:02.02	Sinimol	Paulose	IND	24.6.83	1	NC	Jamshedpur	26 Oct
	(90)							
2:02.06	Natalya	Tsyganova	RUS	7.2.71	10	Odlozil	Praha	13 Jun
2:02.09	Lauren	Austin	USA	3.4.86	5	NC	Indianapolis	24 Jun
2:02.16	Eléni	Filándra	GRE	12.1.84	3		Kalamáta	2 Jun
2:02.19	Nikeya	Green	USA	10.8.82	1		Kortrijk	13 Jul
2:02.20	Hilary	Stellingwerff	CAN	7.8.81	1		Ninove	11 Aug
2:02.22	Carmo	Tavares	POR	27.4.74	6	Aragón	Zaragoza	28 Jul
2:02.24	Geena	Gall	USA	18.1.87	5	NCAA	Sacramento	9 Jun
2:02.24	Nadezhda	Vorobyeva	RUS	30.5.77	3		Moskva	4 Jul
2:02.25	Larisa	Chzhao	RUS	4.2.71	5		Chelyabinsk	14 Jul
2:02.25	Sasha	Spencer	USA	4.8.79	1		Rovereto	12 Sep
	(100)							

2:02.28	Ysanne	Williams	JAM	25.9.80	24 Jun
2:02.29		Liu Qing	CHN	28.4.86	5 Aug
2:02.30	Juliana Paula	de Azevedo	BRA	12.6.83	6 Jun
2:02.34	Tatyana	Popova	RUS	5.1.84	4 Jul
2:02.34	Yevgeniya	Zolotova	RUS	28.4.83	2 Aug
2:02.36	Lenka	Masná	CZE	22.4.85	13 Jun
2:02.36	Nadiha	Touhami	ALG	10.2.78	1 Aug
2:02.38	Chanelle	Price	USA-Y	22.8.90	24 Jun
2:02.39		Truong Thanh Hang	VIE	1.5.86	8 Dec
2:02.41	Polina	Nikonorova	RUS	18.6.86	19 Jun
2:02.53	Mary Jane	Harrelson	USA	17.6.78	10 Jun
2:02.55	Svetlana	Kovgan	BLR	10.8.80	14 Jun
2:02.57	Temeka	Kincy	USA	16.8.85	9 Jun
2:02.57	Tiffany	McWilliams	USA	20.10.82	13 Jul
2:02.60	Halima	Hachlaf	MAR-J	6.9.88	16 Jun
2:02.64	Anita	Banovic	CRO	4.6.84	20 Jun
2:02.66	Yelena	Kofanova	RUS-J	8.8.88	4 Jul
2:02.67	Natalya	Fedotova	RUS	11.7.84	2 Aug
2:02.68	Nicole	Cook	USA	16.12.82	13 Jul
2:02.72	Melissa	de Leon	TRI	9.4.81	23 Jul
2:02.74	Antonella	Riva	ITA	3.9.81	15 Jul
2:02.84	Elena-Mirela	Lavric	ROM-Y	17.2.91	22 Jul
2:02.85	Lysaira	Del Valle	PUR	10.5.82	19 May
2:02.85	Frances	Santin	USA	27.7.80	29 Apr
2:02.87	Chiara	Nichetti	ITA	15.4.80	19 Sep
2:02.89	Sonja	Roman	SLO	11.3.79	1 Jun
2:03.04	Elisabette	Artuso	ITA	25.4.74	15 Jul
2:03.07	Alena	Rucklová	CZE	7.10.81	5 Jul
2:03.07	Egle	Uljas	EST	18.12.84	30 Jul
2:03.10	Virginie	Fouquet	FRA	9.9.75	25 Jul
2:03.12	Ilona	Usovich	BLR	14.11.82	2 Jun
2:03.12	Rebecca	Johnstone	CAN	30.9.84	21 Jul
2:03.22	Rebekah	Noble	USA	15.6.87	21 Apr
2:03.24mx	Abby	Westley	GBR	15.7.87	7 Aug
	2:03.90				30 May
2:03.28		Cao Kun	CHN-J	12.4.89	5 Aug
2:03.29	Ana H.	Peña	CUB	1.1.82	23 Jul
2:03.34	Meskerem	Legesse	ETH	28.9.86	10 Jun
2:03.35	Laetetia	Valdonado	FRA	4.8.77	29 May
2:03.35	Olga	Dubovik	RUS	10.9.76	18 Aug
2:03.41	Natalya	Lavshuk	RUS	22.2.80	22 Jul
2:03.47	Viktoriya	Tereshchuk	UKR	18.2.82	19 May
2:03.50	Joanna	Ross	GBR	18.2.81	21 Jul
2:03.50	Zhanna	Smolina	RUS	28.2.78	2 Aug
2:03.52	Irina	Gornova	RUS	3.11.86	26 May
2:03.54	Carine	Falhun	FRA	20.6.84	30 Jun
2:03.62	Korine	Hinds	JAM	18.1.76	5 May
2:03.64	Claire	Gibson	GBR	25.12.82	9 Jun
2:03.66	Anna	Mishchenko	UKR	25.8.83	7 Jul
2:03.67	José	van der Veen	NED	26.3.80	13 Jun
2:03.69	Anna	Eyfert	RUS	19.10.84	14 Jul
2:03.70	Anna	Yemashova	RUS	15.4.83	2 Aug
2:03.71	Jana	Hartmann	GER	23.10.81	4 Aug
2:03.72	Machteld	Mulder	NED-J	21.2.89	22 Jul
2:03.74	Yuliya	Rusanova	RUS	3.7.86	18 Jun
2:03.74	Veronika	Mrácková	CZE	20.6.82	27 Jun
2:03.75	Rikke	Rønholt/Albertsen	DEN	1.1.76	25 Aug
2:03.81		Liu Xiaoping	CHN	14.1.78	5 Aug
2:03.83	Tatyana	Suprun	BLR	16.2.86	14 Jun
2:03.84	Katarina	Zarudnaya	RUS-J	21.2.89	30 Jun
2:03.88	Sushma	Devi	IND	7.5.84	26 Oct
2:03.89	LaTavia	Thomas	USA-J	17.12.88	26 May
2:03.89	Johanna	Hallberg	SWE	29.10.79	22 Jul
2:03.90	Fatima	Lanouar	TUN	14.3.78	2 Jun
2:03.92	Hannah	England	GBR	6.3.87	20 May
2:03.92	Saida	El Mehdi	MAR	21.9.81	11 Aug
2:03.93	Julian	Clay	USA	2.11.77	4 Aug
2:03.94	Zoe	Buckman	AUS-J	21.12.88	11 Mar
2:03.94	Anna	Willard	USA	31.3.84	21 Apr
2:03.94	Janina	Goldfuss	GER	22.7.83	12 Aug
2:03.97	Jekaterina	Sakovic	LTU	18.7.81	14 Jun
2:04.00	Rachael	Ogden	GBR	23.7.79	21 Jul
2:04.00	Patricia	Conde	ESP	24.1.83	28 Jul
2:04.00	Iuliana	Popescu	ROM	12.7.81	28 Jul
2:04.00mx	Katrina	Wootton	GBR	2.9.85	5 Sep
	(174)				

Indoors

1:58.67	Tetyana	Petlyuk	UKR	22.2.82	1	Spark	Stuttgart	3 Feb
1:58.99	Jolanda	Ceplak ¶	SLO	12.9.76	1		Karlsruhe	11 Feb
1:59.82	Mihaela	Neacsu	ROM	3.5.79	1	BalkC	Pireás	21 Feb

Mark	Name		Nat	Born	Pos	Meet	Venue	Date
2:00.07	Teodora	Kolarova ¶	BUL	29.5.81	2	BalkC	Pireás	21 Feb
2:01.32	Aneta	Lemiesz	POL	17.1.81	3		Karlsruhe	11 Feb
2:01.67	Yevgeniya	Zolotova	RUS	28.4.83	1h4	NC	Volgograd	9 Feb
2:01.76	Mariya	Dryakhlova	RUS	24.4.84	2	NC	Volgograd	10 Feb
2:02.02	Zhanna	Smolina	RUS	28.2.78	2		Moskva	25 Jan

Mark	Name		Nat	Born	Date	Mark	Name		Nat	Born	Date
2:02.70	Rikke	Rönholt/Albertsen	DEN	1.1.76	3 Mar	2:02.94	Ilona	Usovich	BLR	14.11.82	27 Jan
2:02.84	Olga	Komyagina	RUS	10.2.74	24 Feb	2:03.53	Karen	Harewood	GBR	19.8.75	17 Feb
						2:03.70	Christy	Wurth-Thomas	USA	11.7.80	25 Feb

Drugs disqualification

Mark	Name		Nat	Born	Pos	Meet	Venue	Date
1:59.36	Teodora	Kolarova ¶	BUL	29.5.81	4	GP	Athína	2 Jul
1:59.86	Jolanda	Ceplak ¶	SLO	12.9.76	1		Lignano	15 Jul

JUNIORS

Mark	Name		Nat	Born	Pos	Meet	Venue	Date
2:01.95	Emma	Jackson	GBR	7.6.88	3		Manchester	9 Jun
	2:03.23 2 EJ Hengelo 22 Jul							
2:02.38	Chanelle	Price	USA-Y	22.8.90	7	NC	Indianapolis	24 Jun
	2:02.76 1 Greensboro 16 Jun			2:03.09	4s2	NC-j	Indianapolis	23 Jun
2:02.60	Halima	Hachlaf	MAR	6.9.88	4		Biberach	16 Jun
2:02.66	Yelena	Kofanova	RUS	8.8.88	5		Moskva	4 Jul
2:02.84	Elena-Mirela	Lavric	ROM-Y	17.2.91	1	EJ	Hengelo	22 Jul
	2:03.09 3 NC Bucuresti 23 Jul			10 performances by 6 women to 2:03.5				
2:03.28		Cao Kun	CHN	12.4.89	2	NC	Shijiazhuang	5 Aug
2:03.72	Machteld	Mulder	NED	21.2.89	3	EJ	Hengelo	22 Jul
2:03.84	Katarina	Zarudnaya	RUS	21.2.89	1		Zhukovskiy	30 Jun
2:03.89	LaTavia	Thomas	USA	17.12.88	3	NCAA-r	Columbia MO	26 May
2:03.94	Zoe	Buckman (10)	AUS	21.12.88	3	NC	Brisbane	11 Mar
2:04.06	Aleksandra	Uvarova	RUS	4.5.88	2		Zhukovskiy	30 Jun
2:04.10	Winny	Chebet	KEN-Y	20.12.90	1s1	WY	Ostrava	14 Jul
2:04.11	Alena	Fesenko	RUS	4.10.88	7r3		Moskva	4 Jul
2:04.54	Cristina	Vasiloiu	ROM	4.3.88	1		Bucure ti	27 May
2:04.57	Lindsey	de Grande	BEL	26.4.89	11		Liège (NX)	25 Jul
2:04.63	Irene	Jelagat	KEN	10.12.88	8	LGP	London (CP)	3 Aug
2:04.69	Nichole	Jones	USA	30.3.89	5s1	NCAA	Sacramento	7 Jun
2:04.86	Alison	Leonard	GBR-Y	17.3.90	7		Manchester	9 Jun
2:04.96	Anna Maria	Kesselring	GER	4.12.89	5	EJ	Hengelo	22 Jul
2:05.11	Olga	Bibik (20)	UKR-Y	5.2.90	3s1	WY	Ostrava	14 Jul

1000 METRES

Mark	Name		Nat	Born	Pos	Meet	Venue	Date
2:33.06	Mayte	Martínez	ESP	17.5.76	1		Huelva	13 Sep
2:34.35	Hasna	Benhassi	MAR	1.6.78	2		Huelva	13 Sep
2:36.95	Anna	Rostkowska (Zagórska)	POL	26.7.80	1		Miedzyzdroje	18 Aug
2:37.66	Diane	Cummins	CAN	19.1.74	3		Huelva	13 Sep

Mark	Name		Nat	Born	Date	Mark	Name		Nat	Born	Date
2:38.47	Natalya	Koreyvo	BLR	14.11.85	9 Sep	2:39.76	Sonja	Roman	SLO	11.3.79	9 Sep
2:38.91	Maria	Martins	FRA	1.4.74	15 Jul	2:39.84	Jennifer	Meadows	GBR	17.4.81	3 Jun
2:39.26	Faith	Macharia	KEN	9.2.76	3 Jun	2:39.89	Svetlana	Cherkasova	RUS	20.5.78	11 Sep
2:39.32	Tatyana	Paliyenko	RUS	18.11.83	13 Sep	2:39.89	Joanna	Ross	GBR	18.2.81	3 Jun
2:39.50	Erin	Donohue	USA	8.5.83	11 Sep	2:40.60	Svetlana	Klyuka	RUS	27.12.78	11 Sep
2:39.69	Jolanda	Ceplak ¶	SLO	12.9.76	3 Jun	2:40.87	Katrina	Wootoon	GBR	2.9.85	3 Jun

Indoors

Mark	Name		Nat	Born	Pos	Meet	Venue	Date
2:32.21	Oksana	Zbrozhek	RUS	12.1.78	1		Moskva	28 Jan
2:34.76	Tetyana	Petlyuk	UKR	22.2.82	2		Moskva	28 Jan
2:36.40	Mariya	Dryakhlova	RUS	24.4.84	3		Moskva	28 Jan
2:36.56	Yelena	Kanales	RUS	7.2.76	4		Moskva	28 Jan
2:37.31	Olesya	Chumakova	RUS	23.7.81	1rB		Moskva	28 Jan

Mark	Name		Nat	Born	Date	Mark	Name		Nat	Born	Date
2:38.31	Olga	Komyagina	RUS	10.2.74	28 Jan	2:38.61	Yevgeniya	Zolotova	RUS	28.4.83	28 Jan
2:38.42	Tatyana	Paliyenko	RUS	18.11.83	28 Jan	2:40.76	Gulnara	Galkina	RUS	9.7.78	28 Jan
2:38.60	Mariya	Shapayeva	RUS	7.11.86	28 Jan						

Best junior: 2:44.40 Polina Jelizarova LAT 1.5.89 1 Aizpute 15 Jul

1500 METRES

Mark	Name		Nat	Born	Pos	Meet	Venue	Date
3:57.30+	Yelena	Soboleva	RUS	3.10.82	1		Moskva	29 Jun
3:58.3		Soboleva			1	GP	Athína	2 Jul
3:58.75	Maryam	Jamal	BRN	16.9.84	1	WCh	Osaka	2 Sep
3:58.99		Soboleva			2	WCh	Osaka	2 Sep
3:59.0		Jamal			2	GP	Athína	2 Jul
3:59.91		Soboleva			1	Gaz	Saint-Denis	6 Jul
4:00.43		Jamal			1	Herc	Monaco	25 Jul
4:00.48	Gelete	Burka	ETH	15.2.86	1	Pre	Eugene	10 Jun
4:00.68		Burka			2	Gaz	Saint-Denis	6 Jul
4:00.69	Iryna	Lishchynska	UKR	15.1.76	3	WCh	Osaka	2 Sep
4:00.7	Yuliya	Fomenko	RUS	30.8.79	3	GP	Athína	2 Jul

Mark	Name		Nat	Born	Pos	Meet	Venue	Date
4:00.7+		Jamal			1	in 1M	Bruxelles	14 Sep
4:00.82	Daniela	Yordanova	BUL	8.3.76	4	WCh	Osaka	2 Sep
4:01.2	Olga	Yegorova	RUS	28.3.72	4	GP	Athína	2 Jul
4:01.23		Jamal			1	WAF	Stuttgart	22 Sep
4:01.44		Jamal			1	Bisl	Oslo	15 Jun
4:01.52	Mariem Alaoui	Selsouli	MAR	8.4.84	5	WCh	Osaka	2 Sep
4:01.58		Fomenko			2	Bisl	Oslo	15 Jun
4:01.82		Lishchynska			3	Bisl	Oslo	15 Jun
4:02.10	Viola	Kibiwott	KEN	22.12.83	6	WCh	Osaka	2 Sep
4:02.17		Lishchynska			3	Gaz	Saint-Denis	6 Jul
4:02.3		Selsouli			5	GP	Athína	2 Jul
4:02.46		Fomenko			7	WCh	Osaka	2 Sep
4:02.70+		Yegorova			1	in 1M	Moskva	29 Jun
4:02.8	Tatyana	Tomashova (10)	RUS	1.7.75	6	GP	Athína	2 Jul
4:02.88		Yegorova			4	Gaz	Saint-Denis	6 Jul
4:02.9+		Soboleva			2	in 1M	Bruxelles	14 Sep
4:02.98		Fomenko			2	Pre	Eugene	10 Jun
4:03.10+	Anna	Alminova	RUS	17.1.85	3		Moskva	29 Jun
4:03.2	Natalya	Pantelyeva	RUS	18.8.83	7	GP	Athína	2 Jul
	(30/12)							
4:03.31+	Gulnara	Galkina	RUS	9.7.78	4		Moskva	29 Jun
4:03.36+	Olesya	Chumakova	RUS	23.7.81	5		Moskva	29 Jun
4:03.4	Ibtissam	Lakhouad-Boucif	MAR	7.12.83	8	GP	Athína	2 Jul
4:03.62	Bouchra	Chaabi	MAR	22.9.80	2	Herc	Monaco	25 Jul
4:03.71	Sarah	Jamieson	AUS	24.3.75	5	Gaz	Saint-Denis	6 Jul
4:04.03	Siham	Hilali	MAR	2.5.86	4	Herc	Monaco	25 Jul
4:04.5	Olga	Komyagina	RUS	10.2.74	10	GP	Athína	2 Jul
4:05.10	Lidia	Chojecka	POL	25.1.77	9	Gaz	Saint-Denis	6 Jul
	(20)							
4:05.25	Lisa	Corrigan	AUS	2.12.84	1		Sydney	17 Feb
4:05.41	Nataliya	Tobias	UKR	22.11.80	1		Kalamáta	2 Jun
4:05.44	Agnes	Samaria	NAM	11.8.72	4	WAF	Stuttgart	22 Sep
4:05.48	Tetyana	Holovchenko	UKR	13.2.80	2		Kalamáta	2 Jun
4:05.55	Erin	Donohue	USA	8.5.83	1	NA	Heusden-Zolder	28 Jul
4:05.56	Kenia	Sinclair	JAM	14.7.80	1	adidas	Carson	20 May
4:05.62	Lauren	Fleshman	USA	26.9.81	5	GP	Rieti	9 Sep
4:05.65	Malindi	Elmore	CAN	13.3.80	10	Gaz	Saint-Denis	6 Jul
4:05.68	Treniere	Clement	USA	27.10.81	6	GP	Rieti	9 Sep
4:05.69	Hilary	Stellingwerff	CAN	7.8.81	11	Gaz	Saint-Denis	6 Jul
	(30)							
4:05.86	Shalane	Flanagan	USA	7.8.81	3	Pre	Eugene	10 Jun
4:05.91	Carmen	Douma-Hussar	CAN	12.3.77	6	Bisl	Oslo	15 Jun
4:05.98	Shayne	Culpepper	USA	3.12.73	2	adidas	Carson	20 May
4:06.19	Maria	Martins	FRA	1.4.74	8	Herc	Monaco	25 Jul
4:06.22	Lisa	Dobriskey	GBR	23.12.83	7	Bisl	Oslo	15 Jun
4:06.49	Dolores	Checa	ESP	27.12.82	9	Herc	Monaco	25 Jul
4:06.51	Saïda	El Mehdi	MAR	21.9.81	3		Kalamáta	2 Jun
4:06.65	Vivian	Cheruiyot	KEN	11.9.83	2	SGP	Doha	11 May
4:06.70	Stephanie	Twell	GBR-J	17.8.89	7	GP	Rieti	9 Sep
4:06.99	Iris	Fuentes-Pila	ESP	10.8.80	7s2	WCh	Osaka	31 Aug
	(40)							
4:07.23	Amy	Mortimer	USA	16.8.81	3	NA	Heusden-Zolder	28 Jul
4:07.45	Mestawet	Tadesse	ETH	19.7.85	2	GP	New York	2 Jun
4:07.48	Sylwia	Ejdys	POL	15.7.84	1		Kassel	6 Jun
4:07.52	Meselech	Melkamu	ETH	19.4.85	3	GP	Doha	11 May
4:07.81	Cristina	Vasiloiu	ROM-J	4.3.88	1	Rom IC	Bucuresti	10 Jun
4:07.86	Christy	Wurth-Thomas	USA	11.7.80	2	NC	Indianapolis	23 Jun
4:08.02	Daniela	Donisa	ROM-J	23.4.88	2	Rom IC	Bucuresti	10 Jun
4:08.02	Marina	Muncan	SRB	6.11.82	8s2	WCh	Osaka	31 Aug
4:08.10	Katrina	Wootton	GBR	2.9.85	11	GP	Rieti	9 Sep
4:08.30	Ragnhild	Kvarberg	NOR	23.3.81	2		Villeneuve d'Ascq	8 Jun
	(50)							
4:08.50	Emebet Etea	Bedada	ETH-Y	11.1.90	3		Villeneuve d'Ascq	8 Jun
4:08.60	Sonja	Roman	SLO	11.3.79	11s2	WCh	Osaka	31 Aug
4:08.61	Tatyana	Beltyukova	RUS	11.10.85	1rB	Znam	Zhukovskiy	9 Jun
4:08.73	Nicole	Teter	USA	8.11.73	5	adidas	Carson	20 May
4:08.74	Abby	Westley	GBR	15.7.87	1		Loughborough	20 May
4:08.77	Irina	Krakoviak	LTU	16.11.77	5		Bydgoszcz	10 Jun
4:08.86	Tiffany	McWilliams	USA	20.10.82	4	NC	Indianapolis	23 Jun
4:08.89	Alice	Schmidt	USA	3.10.81	6	adidas	Carson	20 May

Mark	Name		Nat	Born	Pos	Meet	Venue	Date
4:08.9	Corina	Dumbravean	ROM	15.4.84	12	GP	Athína	2 Jul
4:08.99	Sara	Hall	USA	15.4.83	5	NC	Indianapolis	23 Jun
	(60)							
4:09.0A	Florence	Kiplagat	KEN	27.2.87	1	NC	Nairobi	16 Jun
4:09.04	Meskerem	Legesse Assefa	ETH	28.9.86	5		Villeneuve d'Ascq	8 Jun
4:09.06	Rebecca	Lyne	GBR	4.7.82	1		Warszawa	19 Sep
4:09.11	Veronica	Nyarual Wanjiru	KEN-J	29.10.89	2	AfG	Alger	22 Jul
4:09.12	Nadiha	Touhami	ALG	10.2.78	1		Leverkusen	10 Aug
4:09.17	Mayte	Martínez	ESP	17.5.76	10	Bisl	Oslo	15 Jun
4:09.26	Fatima	Lanouar	TUN	14.3.78	2		Cuxhaven	14 Jul
4:09.34	Elisa	Cusma Piccione	ITA	24.7.81	3	ECp-1B	Milano	24 Jun
4:09.40	Kristine Eikrem	Engeset	NOR-J	15.11.88	2		Florø	2 Jun
4:09.51	Helen	Clitheroe	GBR	2.1.74	11rA	Athl	Lausanne	10 Jul
	(70)							
4:09.51	Wioletta	Frankiewicz (Janowska)	POL	9.6.77	2		Leverkusen	10 Aug
4:09.52	Jennifer	Rhines	USA	1.7.74	8	adidas	Carson	20 May
4:09.60	Lindsey	Gallo	USA	29.11.81	1		Stanford	29 Apr
4:09.64	Charlene	Thomas	GBR	6.5.82	1		Watford	30 Jun
	4:09.6+				11	in 1M	Bruxelles	14 Sep
4:09.93	Brie	Felnagle	USA	9.12.86	1	NCAA	Sacramento	9 Jun
4:10.00	Mika	Yoshikawa	JPN	16.9.84	2	GP	Osaka	5 May
4:10.08	Jemma	Simpson	GBR	10.2.84	1		Manchester	9 Jun
4:10.09	Lyubov	Pulyayeva	RUS	26.4.82	5	NC	Tula	31 Jul
4:10.26	Susan	Scott	GBR	26.9.77	2		Watford	30 Jun
4:10.27	Irene	Jelagat	KEN-J	10.12.88	2rB	Athl	Lausanne	10 Jul
	(80)							
4:10.29	Kara	Goucher	USA	9.7.78	8	Pre	Eugene	10 Jun
4:10.33	Mari	Järvenpää	FIN	29.11.81	3		Manchester (Str)	11 Aug
4:10.37mx	Donna	MacFarlane	AUS	18.6.77	1		Hobart	24 Feb
	4:12.22				4	GP	Osaka	5 May
4:10.38	Yekaterina	Volkova	RUS	16.2.78	2	NCp	Tula	8 Jul
4:10.41	Liliana	Popescu	ROM	5.2.82	1	NC	Bucuresti	27 Jul
4:10.57	Jenelle	Deatherage	USA	25.9.77	5	NA	Heusden-Zolder	28 Jul
4:10.62	Élodie	Guégan	FRA	19.12.85	7		Villeneuve d'Ascq	8 Jun
4:10.70	Natalya	Fedotova	RUS	19.7.84	3h1	NC	Tula	31 Jul
4:10.92	Irina	Maracheva	RUS	29.9.84	1		Samara	9 Aug
4:10.95	Olga	Kravtsova	BLR	25.6.81	1		Minsk	14 Jun
	(90)							
4:11.22		He Pan	CHN-J	1.5.88	1		Wuhan	30 Oct
4:11.34	Susan	Kuijken	NED	8.7.86	2	NCAA	Sacramento	9 Jun
4:11.36	Olga	Dubovik	RUS	10.9.76	1		Irkutsk	18 Aug
4:11.39	Juliana Paula	de Azevedo	BRA	12.6.83	2		Neerpelt	2 Jun
4:11.41	Yuriko	Kobayashi	JPN-J	12.12.88	10	Pre	Eugene	10 Jun
4:11.45	Eleonora	Berlanda	ITA	6.4.76	6		Bydgoszcz	10 Jun
4:11.57	Mary Jane	Harrelson	USA	17.6.78	13	adidas	Carson	20 May
4:11.60		Truong Thanh Hang	VIE	1.5.86	1	SEAG	Nakhon Ratchasima	7 Dec
4:11.66	Sinimol	Paulose	IND	24.6.83	1		Kolkata	13 May
4:11.67	Anne	Shadle	USA	1.12.82	16	adidas	Carson	20 May
	(100)							

Mark	Name		Nat	Born	Date
4:11.95	Veerle	Dejaeghere	BEL	1.8.73	8 Jun
4:11.96	Liz	Brathwaite	GBR	10.4.85	9 Jun
4:12.03	Yevgeniya	Khaliullina	RUS	22.1.84	31 Jul
4:12.06		Liu Qing	CHN	28.4.86	8 Jul
4:12.23	Inna	Poluskina	LAT	7.7.84	12 Aug
4:12.27	Yelena	Sidorchenkova	RUS	30.5.80	18 Aug
4:12.29	Arianna	Lambie	USA	12.6.85	9 Jun
4:12.30	Silvia	Weissteiner	ITA	13.7.79	2 Jun
4:12.31	Antje	Möldner	GER	13.6.84	14 Jul
4:12.32	Julia	Howard	CAN	8.11.83	28 Jul
4:12.34	Faye	Fullerton	GBR	31.5.84	9 Jun
4:12.38	René	Kalmer	RSA	3.11.80	22 Jul
4:12.44	Hannah	England	GBR	6.3.87	9 Jun
4:12.68	Alemitu	Bekele	TUR	17.9.77	1 Jul
4:12.72	Nicola	Gauld	GBR	28.3.82	25 Aug
4:12.79	Deirdre	Byrne	IRL	21.9.82	29 Apr
4:12.93	Miesha	Marzell-Arnold	USA	29.1.75	11 May
4:12.93	Roisín	McGettigan	IRL	23.8.80	15 Jul
4:12.99	Kajsa	Haglund	SWE	10.11.81	25 Aug
4:13.12	Megan	Brown	CAN	30.4.85	12 Aug
4:13.15	Ana Maria	Bordea	ROM	7.8.83	27 Jul
4:13.19	Georgie	Clarke	AUS	17.6.84	26 May
4:13.19	Rachel	Felton	GBR	27.6.79	25 Aug
4:13.22	Sushma	Devi	IND	7.5.84	13 May
4:13.3A	Margaret	Muriuki	KEN	21.3.86	16 Jun
4:13.30	Natalya	Pavlovskaya	RUS	30.4.75	8 Jul
4:13.33	Anna	Rostkowska	POL	26.7.80	19 Sep
4:13.38	Emma	Pallant	GBR-J	4.6.89	20 May
4:13.42	Sule Gedo	Utura	ETH-Y	8.2.90	2 Jun
4:13.45		Liu Nian	CHN-J	26.4.88	24 Jul
4:13.50	Natalya	Gorelova	RUS	18.4.73	8 Jun
4:13.55	Mimi	Belete	ETH-J	9.6.88	21 Jul
4:13.55	Kate	Reed	GBR	28.9.82	25 Aug
4:13.58	Molly	Huddle	USA	31.8.84	15 Jul
4:13.61	Esther	Chemtai	KEN-J	4.6.88	28 Jul
4:13.72	Hannah	Whitmore	GBR	24.2.84	9 Jun
4:13.82	Mable	Kunihira	UGA	31.1.83	9 Jun
4:14.0	Zulema	Fuentes-Pila	ESP	25.5.77	25 Jul
4:14.01	Rachael	Ogden	GBR	23.7.79	25 Aug
4:14.02mx	Adrienne	Herzog	NED	30.9.85	9 May
4:14.03	Ashu	Kasim Rabo	ETH	20.10.84	1 Jun
4:14.06	Sonja	Stolic	SRB	21.4.80	29 May
4:14.08	Kelly	Reid	IRL	17.6.78	25 Aug
4:14.10	Christine	Bardelle	FRA	16.8.74	8 Jun
4:14.20	Melissa	Cook	USA	22.11.79	15 Jul
4:14.20	Regina	Rakhimkulova	RUS	5.11.79	31 Jul
4:14.2	Mariya	Savinova	RUS	13.8.85	30 May
4:14.24	Dacia	Barr	USA	9.7.86	9 Jun

Mark	Name		Nat	Born	Pos	Meet	Venue	Date

Mark	First name	Surname	Nat	Born	Date
4:14.26	Zakia	Mrisho	TAN	19.2.84	8 Jul
4:14.35	Etalemahu	Kidane	ETH	14.2.83	28 Jul
4:14.39	Nikeya	Green	USA	8.10.82	10 Aug
4:14.45	Laura	Kenney	GBR	27.6.85	11 Aug
4:14.46	Lebogang	Phalula	RSA	9.12.83	9 Feb
4:14.53	Polina	Nikonorova	RUS	18.6.86	31 Jul
4:14.57	Anna	Mishchenko	UKR	25.8.83	22 Jul
4:14.70	Janeth	Jepkosgei	KEN	13.12.83	11 May
4:14.80	Anastasia	Starovoytova	BLR	4.11.82	17 May
4:14.83	Sabrina	Mockenhaupt	GER	6.12.80	6 Jun
4:14.85	Andrea	Grove	CAN	10.7.73	4 Aug
4:14.85	Aselefech	Assefa	ETH	12.12.87	10 Aug
4:14.97	Sasha	Spencer	USA	4.8.79	8 Jul
4:15.0A	Mercy	Kosgei Chelimo	KEN-J	10.10.89	16 Jun
4:15.12	Merat	Bahta Ogbagaber	ERI-J	89	22 Jul
4:15.14	Cack	Ferrell	USA	21.6.84	7 Jul
4:15.17	Megan	Metcalfe	CAN	27.1.82	6 Jun
4:15.17	Valérie	Lehmann	SUI	19.9.80	10 Aug
4:15.18	Ingvill	Måkestad	NOR	7.8.81	28 Jul
4:15.19	Flo	Jonsson	SWE	4.2.78	25 Aug
4:15.20	Natalie	Hughes	USA	18.12.82	10 Jun
4:15.27		Li Yong	CHN-J	18.6.88	9 Jun
4:15.28	Yelizaveta	Grechishnikova	RUS	12.12.83	31 Jul
4:15.32	Svetlana	Kovgan	BLR	26.8.80	2 Jun
4:15.33	Barbara	Parker	GBR	8.11.82	30 Jun
4:15.42	Nicole	Edwards	CAN	30.6.86	14 Jul
4:15.47	Sammary	Cherotich	KEN-Y	25.3.92	13 Jul
4:15.48	Natalya	Koreyvo (176)	BLR	14.11.85	17 May

Indoors

Mark	First name	Surname	Nat	Born	Pos	Meet	Venue	Date
4:03.73	Lidia	Chojecka	POL	25.1.77	1		Stockholm	20 Feb
4:05.81	Helen	Clitheroe	GBR	2.1.74	2		Stockholm	20 Feb
4:06.75	Sonja	Roman	SLO	11.3.79	3		Stockholm	20 Feb
4:11.35	Oksana	Zbrozhek	RUS	12.1.78	1		Sankt Peterburg	7 Jan
4:12.63	Yelena	Kanales	RUS	7.2.76	3	NC	Volgograd	10 Feb
4:13.43	Yuliya	Krevsun	UKR	8.12.80	3		Gent	4 Feb
4:14.12	Olesya	Syryeva	RUS	25.11.83	4	NC	Volgograd	10 Feb
4:14.65	Olesya	Tyurina	RUS	3.9.80	3		Sankt Peterburg	7 Jan
4:15.20	Tetyana	Mezentseva	UKR	17.1.72	5		Düsseldorf	6 Feb

JUNIORS

See main list for top 9 juniors. 11 performances by 6 women to 4:10.2. Additional marks and further juniors:

Twell	4:09.8+	11	in1M	Bruxelles	14 Sep					
Vasiloiu	4:09.06	1	ECp-1B	Milano	24 Jun	4:09.71	1		Bucuresti	2 Jun
Nyaruai	4:09.96	5	SGP	Doha	11 May	4:10.2A	2	WCT	Nairobi	28 Jul

Mark	First name	Surname	Nat	Born	Pos	Meet	Venue	Date
4:13.38	Emma	Pallant (10)	GBR	4.6.89	2		Loughborough	20 May
4:13.42	Sule Gedo	Utura	ETH-Y	8.2.90	4		Trento	2 Jun
4:13.45		Liu Nian	CHN	26.4.88	2		Guangzhou	24 Jul
4:13.55	Mimi	Belete	ETH	9.6.88	7		Brasschaat	21 Jul
4:13.61	Esther	Chemtai	KEN	4.6.88	10	NA	Heusden-Zolder	28 Jul
4:15.0A	Mercy	Kosgei Chelimo	KEN	10.10.89	4	NC	Nairobi	16 Jun
4:15.12	Merat	Bahta Ogbagaber	ERI	89	9		Alger	22 Jul
4:15.27		Li Yong	CHN	18.6.88	1	WCT	Suzhou	9 Jun
4:15.47	Sammary	Cherotich	KEN-Y	25.3.92	1	WY	Ostrava	13 Jul
4:15.58	Emma	Jackson	GBR	7.8.88	7		Manchester	11 Aug
4:16.06	Bizunesh	Urgessa (20)	ETH	18.6.89	3		Brazzaville	27 May

1 MILE

Mark	First name	Surname	Nat	Born	Pos	Meet	Venue	Date
4:15.63	Yelena	Soboleva	RUS	3.10.82	1		Moskva	29 Jun
4:17.75	Maryam	Jamal	BRN	16.9.84	1	VD	Bruxelles	14 Sep
4:20.10	Olga	Yegorova	RUS	28.3.72	2		Moskva	29 Jun
4:20.23	Gulnara	Galkina	RUS	9.7.78	3		Moskva	29 Jun
4:20.86	Anna	Alminova	RUS	17.1.85	4		Moskva	29 Jun
4:21.16		Soboleva			2	VD	Bruxelles	14 Sep
4:21.29	Olesya	Chumakova	RUS	23.7.81	5		Moskva	29 Jun
4:22.34		Jamal			1		Genève	9 Jun
4:22.66	Lisa	Corrigan	AUS	2.12.84	1	GP	Melbourne	2 Mar
4:23.40	Sarah	Jamieson	AUS	24.3.75	2	GP	Melbourne	2 Mar
	(10/8)							
4:24.79	Yuliya	Fomenko	RUS	30.8.79	4	VD	Bruxelles	14 Sep
4:24.84	Tatyana	Tomashova (10)	RUS	1.7.75	6		Moskva	29 Jun
4:25.01	Agnes	Samaria	NAM	11.8.72	5	VD	Bruxelles	14 Sep
4:25.35	Ibtissam	Lakhouad-Boucif	MAR	7.12.83	6	VD	Bruxelles	14 Sep
4:26.76	Carmen	Douma-Hussar	CAN	12.3.77	8	VD	Bruxelles	14 Sep
4:27.18	Natalya	Pantelyeva	RUS	18.8.83	7		Moskva	29 Jun
4:27.35	Erin	Donohue	USA	8.5.83	9	VD	Bruxelles	14 Sep
4:27.95	Charlene	Thomas	GBR	6.5.82	10	VD	Bruxelles	14 Sep
4:28.16	Stephanie	Twell	GBR-J	17.8.89	11	VD	Bruxelles	14 Sep
4:28.62	Hilary	Stellingwerff	CAN	7.8.81	12	VD	Bruxelles	14 Sep

Mark	First name	Surname	Nat	Born	Date
4:33.07+	Meseret	Defar	ETH	19.11.83	14 Sep
4:33.52	Donna	MacFarlane	AUS	18.6.77	2 Mar

Indoors

Mark	First name	Surname	Nat	Born	Pos	Meet	Venue	Date
4:31.35	Shayne	Culpepper	USA	3.12.73	2	BIG	Boston (R)	27 Jan
4:31.84	Christy	Wurth-Thomas	USA	11.7.80	3	BIG	Boston (R)	27 Jan
4:32.24i	Sara	Hall	USA	15.4.83	4	BIG	Boston (R)	27 Jan

Mark	First name	Surname	Nat	Born	Date
4:32.29	Mary	Cullen	IRL	17.8.82	20 Jan
4:32.48	Mestawet	Tadesse	ETH	19.7.85	9 Feb
4:32.50	Malindi	Elmore	CAN	13.3.80	9 Feb
4:33.43	Sarah	Schwald	USA	2.1.73	9 Feb
4:33.86	Lindsey	Gallo	USA	29.11.81	27 Jan
4:34.07	Meskerem	Legesse	ETH	28.9.86	9 Feb

Mark	Name		Nat	Born	Date	Mark	Name		Nat	Born	Date
4:34.67	Marina	Muncan	SRB	6.11.82	9 Feb	4:35.52	Katrina	Wootton	GBR	2.9.85	20 Jan
4:34.94	Shannon	Rowbury	USA	14.9.84	9 Feb	4:35.84	Collette	Douglas	USA	29.4.73	16 Feb

2000 METRES

Mark	Name		Nat	Born	Pos	Meet	Venue	Date
5:31.03	Gulnara	Galkina	RUS	9.7.78	1		Sochi	27 May
5:35.80	Liliya	Shobukhova	RUS	13.11.77	2		Sochi	27 May
5:36.43	Yelena	Soboleva	RUS	3.10.82	3		Sochi	27 May
5:36.52	Natalya	Pantelyeva	RUS	18.8.83	4		Sochi	27 May
5:37.52+	Meseret	Defar	ETH	19.11.83	1	in 3k	Bruxelles	14 Sep
5:40.03	Yelena	Sidorchenkova	RUS	30.5.80	5		Sochi	27 May
5:40.25+	Mariem Alaoui	Selsouli	MAR	8.4.84	1	in 3k	Monaco	25 Jul
5:40.49	Svetlana	Cherkasova	RUS	20.5.78	6		Sochi	27 May
5:41.21	Lyubov	Pulyayeva	RUS	26.4.82	7		Sochi	27 May
5:41.61	Yekaterina	Volkova	RUS	16.2.78	8		Sochi	27 May
5:42.60+	Olga	Komyagina	RUS	10.2.74	1	in 5k	Oslo	15 Jun
5:42.79+	Kara	Goucher	USA	9.7.78	1	in 3k	Rieti	9 Sep
5:47.10mx	Kim	Smith	NZL	19.11.73	1		Hamilton	13 Jan
Indoors								
5:38.95+i		Defar			1	in 3k	Stuttgart	3 Feb
5:39.2+i	Meselech	Melkamu	ETH	19.4.85	2	in 3k	Stuttgart	3 Feb
5:41.2+	Jo	Pavey	GBR	20.9.73	3	in 3k	Stuttgart	3 Feb
5:43.0+i	Shalane	Flanagan	USA	8.7.81	2	in 3k	Boston	27 Jan

Mark	Name		Nat	Born	Date	Mark	Name		Nat	Born	Date
5:46.5e+i	Lidia	Chojecka	POL	25.1.77	3 Feb	5:48.87i	Nataliya	Tobias	UKR	22.11.80	9 Feb
5:46.78i	Yelena	Kanales	RUS	7.2.76	7 Jan	5:49.49i	Regina	Rakhimkulova	RUS	5.11.79	7 Jan

3000 METRES

Mark	Name		Nat	Born	Pos	Meet	Venue	Date
8:24.51+	Meseret	Defar	ETH	19.11.83	1	in 2M	Bruxelles	14 Sep
8:27.24		Defar			1	WAF	Stuttgart	23 Sep
8:28.66	Vivian	Cheruiyot	KEN	11.9.83	2	WAF	Stuttgart	23 Sep
8:29.06	Priscah	Cherono	KEN	27.6.80	3	WAF	Stuttgart	23 Sep
8:29.52	Mariem Alaoui	Selsouli	MAR	8.4.84	1	Herc	Monaco	25 Jul
8:30.25		Cheruiyot			1	GP	Rieti	9 Sep
8:30.70		Cherono			2	GP	Rieti	9 Sep
8:34.99	Kara	Goucher	USA	9.7.78	3	GP	Rieti	9 Sep
8:35.03	Jennifer	Rhines	USA	1.7.74	2	Herc	Monaco	25 Jul
8:35.31	Kim	Smith	NZL	19.11.81	3	Herc	Monaco	25 Jul
8:35.34	Shalane	Flanagan	USA	7.8.81	4	Herc	Monaco	25 Jul
8:35.76+		Defar			1	in 5k	Oslo	15 Jun
8:35.92		Smith			4	GP	Rieti	9 Sep
8:36.1+		Cheruiyot			2	in 5k	Oslo	15 Jun
8:37.69+		Defar			1	in 2M	Carson	20 May
8:37.92+		Cherono			2	in 2M	Bruxelles	14 Sep
8:38.30	Lidia	Chojecka	POL	25.1.77	5	Herc	Monaco	25 Jul
8:38.97	Linet	Masai (10)	KEN-J	5.12.89	5	GP	Rieti	9 Sep
8:41.53	Jessica	Augusto	POR	8.11.81	6	Herc	Monaco	25 Jul
8:42.1+	Ejegayehu (20/12)	Dibaba	ETH	25.6.82	3	in 5k	Oslo	15 Jun
8:42.99	Mariya	Konovalova	RUS	14.8.74	1		Irkutsk	18 Aug
8:43.05+	Viola	Kibiwott	KEN	22.12.83	3	in 2M	Bruxelles	14 Sep
8:43.09+	Sylvia	Kibet	KEN	18.3.84	4	VD	Bruxelles	14 Sep
8:43.92	Lauren	Fleshman	USA	26.9.81	1	LGP	London (CP)	3 Aug
8:43.95	Olga	Komyagina	RUS	10.2.74	1	Znam	Zhukovskiy	9 Jun
8:44.13	Jo	Pavey	GBR	20.9.73	2	LGP	London (CP)	3 Aug
8:44.30	Liliya	Shobukhova	RUS	13.11.77	2	Znam	Zhukovskiy	9 Jun
8:44.45	Deena (20)	Kastor	USA	14.2.73	7	Herc	Monaco	25 Jul
8:44.73	Michelle	Sikes	USA	27.2.85	8	Herc	Monaco	25 Jul
8:46.71	Julie	Coulaud	FRA	7.8.82	9	Herc	Monaco	25 Jul
8:47.6e+	Meselech	Melkamu	ETH	19.4.85	2	in 5000	Ostrava	27 Jun
8:47.88	Philes	Ongori	KEN	19.7.86	1		Yokohama	21 Oct
8:47.92	Gulnara	Galkina	RUS	9.7.78	1	ECp-S	München	23 Jun
8:48.0e+	Gelete	Burka	ETH	15.2.86	3	in 5000	Ostrava	27 Jun
8:48.17	Mary	Cullen	IRL	17.8.82	3	BrGP	Sheffield	15 Jul
8:48.41	Sarah	Jamieson	AUS	24.3.75	3	LGP	London (CP)	3 Aug
8:48.63	Silvia	Weissteiner	ITA	13.7.79	2		Rovereto	12 Sep
8:50.33	Tatyana (30)	Petrova	RUS	8.4.83	1		Moskva	29 Jun
8:51.87	Dolores	Checa	ESP	27.12.82	3		Rovereto	12 Sep
8:51.94	Helen	Clitheroe	GBR	2.1.74	5	LGP	London (CP)	3 Aug
8:52.04	Belaynesh	Fikadu	ETH	28.3.87	2		Zagreb	4 Jul

Mark	Name		Nat	Born	Pos	Meet	Venue	Date
8:52.17	Sabrina	Mockenhaupt	GER	6.12.80	6	LGP	London (CP)	3 Aug
8:53.30	Kseniya	Agafonova	RUS	25.6.83	2	LGP	Moskva	29 Jun
8:53.34	Stephanie	Twell	GBR-J	17.8.89	7	GP	London (CP)	3 Aug
8:53.56	Marina	Ivanova	RUS	30.6.83	3		Moskva	29 Jun
8:53.9+	Lucy	Wangui	KEN	24.3.84	3	in 3k	Glasgow	3 Jun
8:53.94	Mercy	Cherono	KEN-Y	7.5.91	1	WY	Ostrava	11 Jul
8:54.12	Lisa	Dobriskey	GBR	23.12.83	1		Loughborough	20 May
	(40)							
8:54.21	Lyubov	Pulyayeva	RUS	26.4.82	4	Znam	Zhukovskiy	9 Jun
8:54.42	Ruth	Bisibori	KEN-J	2.1.88	4		Rovereto	12 Sep
8:54.52	Yuriko	Kobayashi	JPN-J	12.12.88	2		Yokohama	21 Oct
8:55.46	Malindi	Elmore	CAN	13.3.80	9	LGP	London (CP)	3 Aug
8:55.51	Alemitu	Bekele	TUR	17.9.77	1	BalkC	Sofia	5 Jul
8:56.07	Cristina	Vasiloiu	ROM-J	4.3.88	1		Bucuresti	3 Jun
8:56.98	Mahlet	Melese	ETH-Y	20.5.90	2	WY	Ostrava	11 Jul

Mark	Name		Nat	Born	Date	Mark	Name		Nat	Born	Date
8:57.29	Emebet Etea	Bedada	ETH-Y	11.1.90	28 Jun	9:01.21	Laura	Kenney	GBR	27.6.85	3 Aug
8:57.36	Jenelle	Deatherage	USA	25.9.77	15 Jul	9:01.24	Samira	Mezeghrane	FRA	29.12.79	15 Jun
8:57.82	Daniela	Yordanova	BUL	8.3.76	5 Jul	9:01.26	Felista	Wanjugu	KEN-Y	18.2.90	6 Aug
8:58.51	Molly	Huddle	USA	31.8.84	3 Aug	9:01.49+	Megan	Metcalfe	CAN	27.1.82	20 May
8:58.58	Wioletta	Frankiewicz	POL	9.6.77	15 Jul	9:01.67	Christine	Bardelle	FRA	16.8.74	15 Jun
8:58.67A	René	Kalmer	RSA	3.11.80	9 Mar	9:02.06	Gladys	Wairimu	KEN-Y	15.7.91	30 Jun
8:58.77	Natalya	Pavlovskaya	RUS	30.4.75	29 Jun	9:02.08	Bizunesh	Urgesa	ETH-J	18.6.89	28 Jul
8:58.77	Hatti	Dean	GBR	2.2.82	3 Aug	9:02.9	Olga	Kravtsova	BLR	25.6.81	19 May
8:58.81	Ayalew	Yimer	ETH	4.7.87	15 Jun	9:03.71	Donna	MacFarlane	AUS	18.6.77	17 Feb
8:59.60	Amy	Mortimer	USA	16.8.81	15 Jul	9:04.01	Irene	Kwambai	KEN	25.10.78	12 Sep
8:59.68mx	Katrina	Wootton	GBR	2.9.85	2 May	9:04.27+	Georgie	Clarke	AUS	17.6.84	20 May
	9:03.87				3 Aug	9:04.5mx	Sonia	O'Sullivan	IRL	28.11.69	16 Feb
8:59.86	Daniela	Donisa	ROM-J	23.4.88	23 Jun	9:04.63	Ai	Kinukawa	JPN-J	7.8.89	6 Aug
8:59.87	Evelyne	Wambui	KEN	4.4.86	30 Jun	9:04.80	Sara	Hall	USA	15.4.83	3 Aug
9:01.17	Kate	Reed	GBR	28.9.82	15 Jul	9:05.99	Simret	Restle	GER	4.5.84	6 Jun

Indoors

Mark	Name		Nat	Born	Pos	Meet	Venue	Date
8:23.72	Meseret	Defar	ETH	19.11.83	1	Spark	Stuttgart	3 Feb
8:23.74	Meselech	Melkamu	ETH	19.4.85	2	Spark	Stuttgart	3 Feb
8:30.31		Defar			1	BIG	Boston (R)	27 Jan
8:31.50	Jo	Pavey	GBR	20.9.73	3	Spark	Stuttgart	3 Feb
8:33.25	Shalane	Flanagan	USA	7.8.81	2	BIG	Boston (R)	27 Jan
8:38.14		Smith			3	BIG	Boston (R)	27 Jan
8:38.21	Lidia	Chojecka	POL	25.1.77	4	Spark	Stuttgart	3 Feb
8:44.30+	Tirunesh	Dibaba	ETH	1.6.85	1	in3k	Boston (R)	27 Jan
8:44.40	Marta	Domínguez	ESP	3.11.75	2	EI	Birmingham	4 Mar
8:44.81	Silvia	Weissteiner	ITA	13.7.79	3	EI	Birmingham	4 Mar
8:45.77	Sabrina	Mockenhaupt	GER	6.12.80	4	EI	Birmingham	4 Mar
8:47.25	Lisa	Dobriskey	GBR	23.12.83	5	EI	Birmingham	4 Mar
8:48.94	Regina	Rakhimkulova	RUS	5.11.79	1	NC	Volgograd	9 Feb
8:52.27	Yuliya	Vinokurova	RUS	17.6.72	2	NC	Volgograd	9 Feb
8:56.72	Sally	Kipyego	KEN	19.12.85	1		Seattle	27 Jan

Mark	Name		Nat	Born	Date	Mark	Name		Nat	Born	Date
9:00.60#	Arianna	Lambie	USA	12.6.85	27 Jan	9:03.47	Julia	Lucas	USA	4.3.84	3 Feb
9:01.02	Frances	Koons	USA	2.4.86	3 Feb	9:04.96	Malika	Asahssah	MAR	24.9.82	27 Jan
9:01.22	Sara	Hall	USA	15.4.83	2 Feb	9:05.73	Iris	Fuentes-Pila	ESP	10.8.80	27 Jan
9:02.73	Shannon	Rowbury	USA	14.9.84	10 Mar	9:05.91	Rosa María	Morató	ESP	19.6.79	27 Jan
9:03.37	Sentayehu	Ejigu	ETH	21.6.85	2 Feb	9:05.91	Elena	Romagnolo	ITA	5.10.82	18 Feb

JUNIORS

See main list for top 7 juniors. 10 performances by 9 women under 9:00.0. Additional marks and further juniors:

Mark	Name		Nat	Born	Pos	Meet	Venue	Date
Masai	8:42.54	4 WAF	Stuttgart	23 Sep				
8:59.86	Daniela	Donisa	ROM	23.4.88	2	ECp-1B	Milano	23 Jun
9:01.26	Felista	Wanjugu	KEN-Y	18.2.90	1		Saga	6 Aug
9:02.06	Gladys	Wairimu (10)	KEN-Y	15.7.91	2		Shizuoka	30 Jun
9:02.08	Bizunesh	Urgesa	ETH	18.6.89	1	Aragón	Zaragoza	28 Jul
9:04.63	Ai	Kinukawa	JPN	7.8.89	2		Saga	6 Aug
9:06.48	Sule	Utura	ETH-Y	8.2.90	3	WY	Ostrava	11 Jul
9:07.06	Obare	Doricah	KEN-Y	10.1.90	1		Kofu	18 Jun
9:07.65	Mimi	Belete	ETH	9.6.88	1		Merksem	25 Aug
9:09.41+		Jin Yuan	CHN	11.2.88	6	in 2M	Carson	20 May
9:09.8A	Irene	Cheptai	KEN-Y	4.2.92	1		Nairobi	13 Jun
9:10.38	Rui	Aoyama	JPN	15.4.89	2		Kofu	18 Jun

2 MILES

Mark	Name		Nat	Born	Pos	Meet	Venue	Date
8:58.58	Meseret	Defar	ETH	19.11.83	1	VD	Bruxelles	14 Sep
9:10.47		Defar			1	adidas	Carson	20 May
9:14.09	Priscah	Cherono	KEN	27.6.80	2	VD	Bruxelles	14 Sep
9:16.62	Sylvia	Kibet	KEN	18.3.84	3	VD	Bruxelles	14 Sep

Mark	Name		Nat	Born	Pos	Meet	Venue	Date
9:18.26	Viola	Kibiwott	KEN	22.12.83	4	VD	Bruxelles	14 Sep
9:22.89	Jessica	Augusto	POR	8.11.81	5	VD	Bruxelles	14 Sep
9:37.04	Megan	Metcalfe	CAN	27.1.82	2	adidas	Carson	20 May
9:38.39	Helen	Clitheroe	GBR	2.1.74				14 Sep
9:41.32	Kara	Goucher	USA	9.7.78				20 May
9:43.53	Georgie	Clarke	AUS	17.6.84				20 May
9:47.88	Amy	Rudolph	USA	18.9.73				20 May
Best Junior: 9:49.33		Jin Yuan	CHN	11.2.88	6	adidas	Carson	20 May
Indoors								
9:32.00	Jo	Pavey	GBR	20.9.73	1	GP	Birmingham	17 Feb
9:33.78	Lisa	Dobriskey	GBR	23.12.83	2	GP	Birmingham	17 Feb

5000 METRES

Mark	Name		Nat	Born	Pos	Meet	Venue	Date
14:16.63	Meseret	Defar	ETH	19.11.83	1	Bisl	Oslo	15 Jun
14:22.51	Vivian	Cheruiyot	KEN	11.9.83	2	Bisl	Oslo	15 Jun
14:30.18		Defar			1	GS	Ostrava	27 Jun
14:31.20	Gelete	Burka	ETH	15.2.86	2	GS	Ostrava	27 Jun
14:33.83	Meselech	Melkamu	ETH	19.4.85	3	GS	Ostrava	27 Jun
14:35.67	Tirunesh	Dibaba	ETH	1.6.85	1	GP	New York	2 Jun
14:36.52	Mariem Alaoui	Selsouli	MAR	8.4.84	1	G Gala	Roma	13 Jul
14:38.18		Burka			1	FBK	Hengelo	26 May
14:40.74	Florence	Kiplagat	KEN	27.2.87	2	FBK	Hengelo	26 May
14:42.00	Priscah	Cherono	KEN	27.6.80	3	FBK	Hengelo	26 May
14:44.51		Cherono			3	Bisl	Oslo	15 Jun
14:44.80	Shalane	Flanagan	USA	7.8.81	1	MSR	Walnut	13 Apr
14:44.93		Cheruiyot			1		Glasgow	3 Jun
14:45.22	Ejegayehu	Dibaba (10)	ETH	25.6.82	4	Bisl	Oslo	15 Jun
14:49.06		Defar			1	Golden	Shanghai	28 Sep
14:49.41	Kim	Smith	NZL	19.11.81	2	G Gala	Roma	13 Jul
14:50.15	Workitu	Ayanu	ETH	19.4.87	5	Bisl	Oslo	15 Jun
14:50.15	Philes	Ongori	KEN	19.7.86	1		Kofu	14 Oct
14:50.76		Melkamu			2		Glasgow	3 Jun
14:50.78		Cheruiyot			1	ISTAF	Berlin	16 Sep
14:51.72	Mestawet	Tufa	ETH	14.9.83	4	FBK	Hengelo	26 May
14:51.75		Flanagan			1	NC	Indianapolis	22 Jun
14:52.21	Deena	Kastor	USA	14.2.73	1	DNG	Stockholm	7 Aug
14:53.89		Melkamu			2	ISTAF	Berlin	16 Sep
14:55.02	Kara	Goucher	USA	9.7.78	3	ISTAF	Berlin	16 Sep
14:55.50	Linet	Masai	KEN-J	5.12.89	2	DNG	Stockholm	7 Aug
14:56.39	Jessica	Augusto	POR	8.11.81	3	G Gala	Roma	13 Jul
14:56.94		Cheruiyot			1	WAF	Stuttgart	22 Sep
14:57.26		Selsouli			6	Bisl	Oslo	15 Jun
14:57.29		L Masai			7	Bisl	Oslo	15 Jun
14:57.37	Sylvia	Kibet	KEN	18.3.84	2	WAF	Stuttgart	22 Sep
14:57.55	Lucy	Wangui	KEN	24.3.84	3		Glasgow	3 Jun
	(31/20)							
14:58.51	Jennifer	Rhines	USA	1.7.74	4	G Gala	Roma	13 Jul
15:00.02	Yekaterina	Volkova	RUS	16.2.78	1	NC	Tula	3 Aug
15:00.88	Elvan	Abeylegesse	TUR	11.9.82	5	WCh	Osaka	1 Sep
15:02.14	Belaynesh	Fikadu	ETH	28.3.87	5	FBK	Hengelo	26 May
15:02.28	Lauren	Fleshman	USA	26.9.81	3	DNG	Stockholm	7 Aug
15:02.65	Silvia	Weissteiner	ITA	13.7.79	6	ISTAF	Berlin	16 Sep
15:02.73		Xue Fei	CHN-J	8.8.89	1		Wuhan	31 Oct
15:02.96	Mariya	Konovalova	RUS	14.8.74	2	NC	Tula	3 Aug
15:03.95		Xie Fang	CHN-J	26.12.89	2		Wuhan	31 Oct
15:04.77	Jo	Pavey	GBR	20.9.73	9	WCh	Osaka	1 Sep
	(30)							
15:05.73	Kayoko	Fukushi	JPN	25.3.82	6	GGala	Roma	13 Jul
15:06.08		Zhang Yingying	CHN-Y	4.1.90	3		Wuhan	31 Oct
15:06.51	Lornah	Kiplagat	NED	1.5.74	6	FBK	Hengelo	26 May
15:08.03		He Pan	CHN-J	1.5.88	4		Wuhan	31 Oct
15:08.08	Evelyne	Wambui	KEN	4.4.86	1		Fukuroi	14 Oct
15:09.28	Michelle	Sikes	USA	27.2.85	3	NC	Indianapolis	22 Jun
15:09.84		Bai Xue	CHN-J	13.12.88	5		Wuhan	31 Oct
15:10.32	Sabrina	Mockenhaupt	GER	6.12.80	8	Bisl	Oslo	15 Jun
15:11.82	Olga	Kravtsova	BLR	25.6.81	13	WCh	Osaka	1 Sep
15:12.12	Malindi	Elmore	CAN	13.3.80	3	MSR	Walnut	13 Apr
	(40)							
15:12.48	Yelena	Sidorchenkova	RUS	30.5.80	3	NC	Tula	3 Aug
15:14.05	Esther	Maina	KEN	27.3.77	4	AfG	Alger	18 Jul
15:14.90	Bizunesh	Urgessa	ETH-J	18.6.89	2		Liège (NX)	25 Jul

Mark	Name		Nat	Born	Pos	Meet	Venue	Date
15:15.34	Kayo	Sugihara	JPN	24.2.83	1		Nobeoka	26 May
15:15.65	Winfrida	Kebaso	KEN	16.4.85	1		Yokohama	23 Sep
15:15.73	Megan	Metcalfe	CAN	27.1.82	4	MSR	Walnut	13 Apr
15:15.77	Nora	Rocha	MEX	18.12.67	5	MSR	Walnut	13 Apr
15:16.33	Simret	Sultan	ERI	20.7.84	5	AfG	Alger	18 Jul
15:16.39	Evelyne	Kimwei	KEN	25.8.87	2		Nobeoka	26 May
15:17.13	Molly	Huddle	USA	31.8.84	3		Liège (NX)	25 Jul
	(50)							
15:18.18	Sara	Slattery	USA	2.10.81	5	DNG	Stockholm	7 Aug
15:18.25	Aheza	Kiros	ETH	26.3.82	3	GP	New York	2 Jun
15:18.46	Gladys	Wairimu	KEN-Y	15.7.91	2		Yokohama	23 Sep
15:18.70	Irene	Kwambai	KEN	25.10.78	9	ISTAF	Berlin	16 Sep
15:19.04	Mary	Cullen	IRL	17.8.82	6	MSR	Walnut	13 Apr
15:19.72	Sally	Kipyego	KEN	19.12.85	7	MSR	Walnut	13 Apr
15:19.97	Eunice	Jepkorir	KEN	17.2.82	4	GS	Ostrava	27 Jun
15:20.28	Maryam	Jamal	BRN	16.9.84	8	FBK	Hengelo	26 May
15:20.29	Julia	Mombi	KEN	25.1.85	3		Yokohama	23 Sep
15:21.37	Yuriko	Kobayashi	JPN-J	12.12.88	2		Kumamoto	7 Apr
	(60)							
15:21.70	Sule	Utura	ETH-Y	8.2.90	10	FBK	Hengelo	26 May
15:21.74	Zakia	Mrisho	TAN	19.2.84	6	DNG	Stockholm	7 Aug
15:21.92	Yurika	Nakamura	JPN	1.4.86	1		Himeji	8 Dec
15:21.98	Mary Wanjohi	Wangari	KEN	4.10.86	3		Kumamoto	7 Apr
15:22.32	Pauline	Waruguru	KEN	26.8.80	3		Nobeoka	26 May
15:22.56	Sara	Hall	USA	15.4.83	8	MSR	Walnut	13 Apr
15:22.73	Yukiko	Akaba	JPN	18.10.79	1		Akita	5 Oct
15:23.17	Kseniya	Agafonova	RUS	25.6.83	5	GS	Ostrava	27 Jun
15:23.24	Etalemahu	Kidane	ETH	14.2.83	11	FBK	Hengelo	26 May
15:23.37	Veronica	Nyaruai Wanjiru	KEN-J	29.10.89	10	ISTAF	Berlin	16 Sep
	(70)							
15:24.25	Susanne	Wigene	NOR	12.2.78	9	G Gala	Roma	13 Jul
15:24.33	Esther	Chemtai	KEN-J	4.6.88	5		Liège (NX)	25 Jul
15:26.65	Ruth	Bisibori	KEN-J	2.1.88	11	ISTAF	Berlin	16 Sep
15:26.72		Zhu Xiaolin	CHN	20.2.84	2	WCT	Suzhou	8 Jun
15:26.88	Tetyana	Holovchenko	UKR	13.2.80	1	NC	Donetsk	7 Jul
15:27.57	Renee	Metivier-Baillie	USA	25.12.81	1		Stanford	29 Apr
15:27.72	Kate	O'Neill	USA	29.7.80	6		Liège (NX)	25 Jul
15:27.84	Sentayehu	Ejigu	ETH	21.6.85	10	Bisl	Oslo	15 Jun
15:27.98	Megumi	Kinukawa	JPN-J	7.8.89	1		Kounosu	22 Sep
15:28.31	Souad	Aït Salem	ALG	6.1.79	1		Longeville-lès-Metz	15 Jul
	(80)							
15:29.10	Kate	Reed	GBR	28.9.82	7		Liège (NX)	25 Jul
15:29.36		Chen Huirong	CHN-J	1.6.88	6		Wuhan	31 Oct
15:30.04	Mizuki	Noguchi	JPN	3.7.78	1		Amagasaki	16 Jun
15:30.06	Bethlehem	Moges	ETH		4	Golden	Shanghai	28 Sep
15:30.32	Christelle	Daunay	FRA	5.12.74	2		Longeville-lès-Metz	15 Jul
15:30.37	Sally	Chepyego	KEN	3.10.85	3	Oda	Hiroshima	29 Apr
15:30.61	Shayne	Culpepper	USA	3.12.73	9	MSR	Walnut	13 Apr
15:30.71	Yoko	Shibui	JPN	14.3.79	4	Oda	Hiroshima	29 Apr
15:31.21	Harun	Makida	ETH		6		Shanghai	28 Sep
15:31.34	Arianna	Lambie	USA	12.6.85	3		Stanford	29 Apr
	(90)							
15:31.94	Bilha	Kamau	KEN-J	2.7.88	1		Shibetsu	17 Jun
15:32.33	Ashu	Kasim	ETH	20.10.84	1	Takac	Beograd	29 May
15:32.37	Hilda	Kibet	KEN	27.3.81	12	FBK	Hengelo	26 May
15:32.75		Jiang Chengcheng	CHN	5.11.86	4	WCT	Suzhou	8 Jun
15:33.11	Yuliya	Vinokurova	RUS	17.6.72	4	NC	Tula	3 Aug
15:33.31	Mahlet	Melese	ETH-Y	20.5.90	1		Barcelona	2 Jun
15:33.40	Yoshimi	Ozaki	JPN	1.7.81	5		Hiroshima	29 Apr
15:33.63	Biruk Konjit	Tilahun	ETH	22.9.87	2		Shibetsu	17 Jun
15:33.70	Erba	Tiki Gelana	ETH	22.10.87	3		Shibetsu	17 Jun
15:33.90	Helah	Kiprop	KEN	.85	2		Trento	2 Jun
	(100)							

15:33.93	Jelena	Prokopcuka	LAT	21.9.76	7 Aug
15:33.95		Dong Xiaoqin	CHN	2.1.83	8 Jun
15:34.03	Rahab	Watetu Ndungu	KEN	19.10.78	7 Apr
15:34.19	Nathalie	De Vos	BEL	9.12.82	25 Jul
15:34.20	Ferhiwot	Goshu	ETH-J	.88	2 Jun
15:34.35	Hitomi	Niiya	JPN-J	26.2.88	29 Apr
15:34.41	Melissa	Cook	USA	22.11.79	21 Jul
15:34.41	Andrea	Grove	CAN	10.7.73	21 Jul
15:34.56	Treniere	Clement	USA	27.10.81	13 Apr
15:35.0	René	Kalmer	RSA	3.11.80	16 Mar
15:35.20	Alice	Timbilil	KEN	16.6.83	29 May
15:35.25		Zhu Yingying	CHN-J	18.8.88	28 Apr
15:35.36	Kumi	Akashi	JPN	23.8.81	7 Apr
15:35.37	Misaki	Katsumata	JPN	26.12.85	23 Dec
15:35.62	Yuka	Kakimi	JPN	4.4.86	23 Dec
15:35.76	Peninah	Chepchumba	KEN	14.1.85	2 Jun

Mark	Name		Nat	Born	Pos	Meet	Venue	Date
15:35.92	Tomomi	Yuda	JPN	28.5.85				19 May
15:36.18	Noriko	Matsuoka	JPN	2.5.79				23 Dec
15:36.25	Adriana	Fernández	MEX	4.4.71				26 May
15:36.42	Felista	Wambui	KEN	15.8.83				26 May
15:36.45	Benita	Johnson	AUS	6.5.79				2 Mar
15:36.56	Souad Aït	Kanbouchia	MAR	12.8.82				23 Jun
15:36.93	Akane	Taira	JPN	3.11.82				22 Sep
15:36.94		Xing Huina	CHN	25.2.84				28 Apr
15:37.08	Judit	Plá	ESP	2.5.78				23 Jun
15:37.54	Yoko	Miyauchi	JPN	19.6.83				26 May
15:37.6 mx	Hayley	Yelling	GBR	3.1.74				28 Jul
15:37.72	Silvia	Sommaggio	ITA	20.11.69				2 Jun
15:37.90	Yuka	Izumi	JPN	18.1.85				8 Dec
15:38.07	Fridah	Domongole	KEN	15.1.84				29 May
15:38.29	Yelizaveta	Grechishnikova	RUS	12.12.83				7 Jul
15:38.32	Beatrice	Chepchumba	KEN	25.11.83				2 Jun
15:38.40	Regina	Rakhimkulova	RUS	5.11.79				3 Aug
15:38.43	Leonor	Carneiro	POR	18.5.78				23 Jun
15:38.54	Mandi	Zemba	USA	1.7.83				13 Apr
15:38.63	Mai	Endo	JPN	22.12.86				26 May
15:38.64	Katie	McGregor	USA	2.9.77				7 Aug
15:38.66		Chen Rong	CHN-J	18.5.88				8 Jun
15:38.80	Megumi	Seike	JPN	26.2.87				5 Oct
15:38.84	Mizuho	Nasukawa	JPN	22.11.79				5 Oct
15:38.85	Christine	Bardelle	FRA	16.8.74				26 May
15:39.0+	Asmae	Leghzaoui	MAR	30.8.76				28 Jul
15:39.22	Nataliya	Berkut	UKR	30.5.75				7 Jul
15:39.74	Felista	Wanjugu	KEN-Y	18.2.90				1 Dec
15:39.94	Ryoko	Kizaki	JPN	21.6.85				1 Dec
15:40.12	Kazue	Kojima	JPN	14.10.87				1 Dec
15:40.68	Kaori	Urata	JPN	18.9.85				8 Dec
15:40.77	Peninah	Skarumba	KEN					29 May
15:40.95	Maya	Ino	JPN-J	5.2.88				8 Dec
15:41.10	Mary	Wangari Mureithi	KEN	9.4.78				7 Apr
15:41.16	Vincenza	Sicari	ITA	19.3.79				2 Jun
15:41.29	Amy	Rudolph	USA	18.9.73				2 Jun
15:41.31		Liu Nian	CHN-J	26.4.88				22 Apr
15:41.39	Aya	Manome	JPN	30.8.82				5 Oct
15:41.54	Kasumi	Nishihara	JPN-J	1.3.89				1 Dec
15:42.01	Cack	Ferrell	USA	21.6.84				27 Jul
15:42.04	Olga	Rosseyeva	RUS	1.8.81				3 Aug
15:42.12	Katrina	Wootton	GBR	2.9.85				9 Jun
15:42.14		Jiang Yuanyuan	CHN	20.12.86				8 Jun
15:42.20	Peninah	Arusei	KEN	23.2.79				17 Oct
15:42.59		Song Xiaoxue	CHN	13.2.87				30 Oct
15:42.66	Alessandra	Aguilar	ESP	1.7.78				2 Jun
15:43.40	Madoka	Ogi	JPN	26.10.83				5 Oct
15:44.07		Hao Xiaofan	CHN-J	9.12.89				30 Oct
15:44.29	Akiko	Matsuyama	JPN-J	24.7.89				8 Dec
15:44.33	Kazue	Ogoshi	JPN	2.3.81				26 May
15:44.55	Whitney	McDonald	USA	1.8.85				13 Apr
15:44.55	Renate	Rungger	ITA	6.9.79				2 Jun
15:44.63	Seika	Nishikawa	JPN	17.7.87				5 Oct
15:44.68	Jane	Wanjiku	KEN	14.6.79				10 Jun
15:44.81	Yukari	So	JPN	20.4.84				10 Jun
15:45.1	Yumi	Hirata	JPN	22.6.81				6 Oct
15:45.35	Galina	Yegorova	RUS	5.8.83				3 Aug
15:45.35	Michi	Numata	JPN-J	6.5.89				1 Dec
15:45.51	Hiroko	Miyauchi	JPN	19.6.83				26 May
15:45.74	Mika	Yoshikawa	JPN	16.9.84				29 Apr
15:45.87		Jia Chaofeng	CHN-J	16.11.88				30 Oct
15:45.96	Preeja	Sreedharan	IND	13.3.82				26 Oct
15:46.0	Yoshiko	Fujinaga (179)	JPN	15.8.81				6 Oct

Indoors

Mark	Name		Nat	Born	Pos	Meet	Venue	Date
14:27.42	Tirunesh	Dibaba	ETH	1.6.85	1	BIG	Boston (R)	27 Jan
15:30.17	Amy	Hastings	USA	21.1.84	1		Seattle	10 Feb
15:38.66	Marie	Davenport	IRL	24.1.75	3		Boston	10 Feb

JUNIORS

See main list for top 17 juniors. 13 performances by 8 women under 15:20.0. Additional marks and further juniors:

Masai 2+	15:02.74	4	WAF	Stuttgart	22 Sep	15:06.09 2	Shanghai	28 Sep
	15:12.05	4		Glasgow	3 Jun			

15:34.20	Ferhiwot	Goshu	ETH	.88	2		Barcelona	2 Jun
15:34.35	Hitomi	Niiya	JPN	26.2.88	6	Oda	Hiroshima	29 Apr
15:35.25		Zhu Yingying (20)	CHN-J	18.8.88	1		Beijing	28 Apr

10,000 METRES

31:00.27	Mestawat	Tufa	ETH	14.9.83	1		Valkenswaard	26 Jun
31:06.20	Florence	Kiplagat	KEN	27.2.87	1	NED Ch	Utrecht	17 May
31:13.67	Teyiba	Erkesso	ETH	28.9.82	2	NED Ch	Utrecht	17 May
31:17.30		Zhang Yingying	CHN-Y	4.1.90	1		Wuhan	2 Nov
31:17.31	Jennifer	Rhines	USA	1.7.74	1		Stanford	29 Apr
31:18.97	Ejegayehu	Dibaba	ETH	25.6.82	1		Barakaldo	14 Jul
31:20.63	Kim	Smith	NZL	19.11.81	2		Stanford	29 Apr
31:20.66	Aheza	Kiros	ETH	26.3.82	2		Barakaldo	14 Jul
31:21.25		Xie Fang	CHN-J	26.12.89	2		Wuhan	2 Nov
31:22.80	Nathalie	De Vos (10)	BEL	9.12.82	3	NED Ch	Utrecht	17 May
31:23.07		Chen Huirong	CHN-J	1.6.88	3		Wuhan	2 Nov
31:23.27	Yukiko	Akaba	JPN	18.10.79	1r2		Yokohama	23 Dec
31:25.15	Elvan	Abeylegesse	TUR	11.9.82	1	ECp	Ferrara	7 Apr
31:26.05		Tufa			1	AfG	Alger	21 Jul
31:26.08	Inga	Abitova	RUS	6.3.82	1	NC	Zhukovskiy	14 Jul
31:26.94	Jo	Pavey	GBR	20.9.73	1	NC	Watford	30 Jun
31:31.18	Edith	Masai	KEN	4.4.67	2	AfG	Alger	21 Jul
31:32.49		Bai Xue	CHN-J	13.12.88	4		Wuhan	2 Nov
31:32.52	Lucy	Wangui	KEN	24.3.84	1		Shizuoka	30 Apr
31:33.20		Wangui			1		Kobe	22 Apr
31:33.49	Etalemahu	Kidane	ETH	14.2.83	2		Valkenswaard	26 Jun
31:35.27	Megumi	Kinukawa (20)	JPN-J	7.8.89	2		Kobe	22 Apr
31:36.20	Evelyne	Kimwei	KEN	25.8.87	1		Gifu	21 Sep
31:36.56	Asmae	Leghzaoui	MAR	30.8.76	1	ESP Ch	Avilés	28 Jul
31:36.78	Irene	Kwambai	KEN	25.10.78	3	AfG	Alger	21 Jul
31:37.82	Katie	McGregor	USA	2.9.77	3		Stanford	29 Apr
31:38.16		Kimwei			3		Kobe	22 Apr
31:39.11	Philes	Ongori	KEN	19.7.86	4		Kobe	22 Apr

Mark	Name		Nat	Born	Pos	Meet	Venue	Date
31:39.32	Akane	Wakita	JPN	15.12.87	5		Kobe	22 Apr
31:39.84	Sally	Chepyego	KEN	3.10.85	6		Kobe	22 Apr
31:39.84		Song Xiaoxue	CHN	13.2.87	5		Wuhan	2 Nov
31:42.53		Kimwei			1		Kumagaya	19 May
31:45.00	Evelyne	Wambui	KEN	4.4.86	4	NED Ch	Utrecht	17 May
31:45.98	Bezunesh	Bekele	ETH	18.9.83	3		Valkenswaard	26 Jun
	(34/30)							
31:46.05	Ashu	Kasim	ETH	20.10.84	5	NED Ch	Utrecht	17 May
31:47.14	Kseniya	Agafonova	RUS	25.6.83	2	NC	Zhukovskiy	14 Jul
31:48.87	Yoko	Shibui	JPN	14.3.79	1		Fukagawa	11 Jul
31:50.45	Yoko	Miyauchi	JPN	19.6.83	7		Kobe	22 Apr
31:52.37	Marina	Ivanova	RUS	30.6.83	3	NC	Zhukovskiy	14 Jul
31:54.59	Kayo	Sugihara	JPN	24.2.83	8		Kobe	22 Apr
31:55.41	Tirunesh	Dibaba	ETH	1.6.85	1	WCh	Osaka	25 Aug
31:55.73	Julia	Mombi	KEN	25.1.85	1		Kobe	13 Oct
31:56.09	Sabrina	Mockenhaupt	GER	6.12.80	1	NC	Zeulenroda	5 May
31:56.61	Nora	Rocha	MEX	18.12.67	5		Stanford	29 Apr
	(40)							
31:56.72	Sally	Kipyego	KEN	19.12.85	6		Stanford	29 Apr
31:57.00	Deena	Kastor	USA	14.2.73	1	NC	Indianapolis	21 Jun
31:57.04	Dulce María	Rodríguez	MEX	14.8.72	7		Stanford	29 Apr
31:57.26	Amy	Rudolph	USA	18.9.73	8		Stanford	29 Apr
31:57.50	Megumi	Seike	JPN	26.2.87	2		Kobe	13 Oct
31:58.44	Derebe	Alemu	ETH	5.6.83	4		Valkenswaard	26 Jun
31:58.45	Biruk Konjit	Tilahun	ETH	22.9.87	3		Kobe	13 Oct
31:58.52	Olga	Kravtsova	BLR	25.6.81	1	NC	Grodno	5 Jul
31:59.98	Tetyana	Holovchenko	UKR	13.2.80	2	ECp	Ferrara	7 Apr
32:00.05		Liu Lijuan	CHN-J	1.4.88	6		Wuhan	2 Nov
	(50)							
32:01.43	Hayley	Yelling	GBR	3.1.74	6		Utrecht	17 May
32:02.05	Kara	Goucher	USA	9.7.78	3	WCh	Osaka	25 Aug
32:02.32	Adriana	Fernández	MEX	4.4.71	1		Abbotsford	10 Jun
32:03.02	Lidiya	Grigoryeva	RUS	21.1.74	4	NC	Zhukovskiy	14 Jul
32:06.54	Kiyomi	Ogawa	JPN	15.9.81	10		Kobe	22 Apr
32:09.28	Nataliya	Berkut	UKR	30.5.75	1	NC	Donetsk	4 Jul
32:09.50	Genet	Getaneh	ETH	6.1.86	5		Valkenswaard	26 Jun
32:13.58	Kayoko	Fukushi	JPN	25.3.82	1	NC	Osaka	29 Jun
32:13.95	Yoshimi	Ozaki	JPN	1.7.81	4		Gifu	21 Sep
32:15.15	Kate	O'Neill	USA	29.7.80	9		Stanford	29 Apr
	(60)							
32:16.83		Chen Rong	CHN-J	18.5.88	7		Wuhan	2 Nov
32:17.14	Megumi	Oshima	JPN	4.9.75	12		Kobe	22 Apr
32:18.07	Mary	Keitany	KEN	18.1.82	7	NED Ch	Utrecht	17 May
32:18.28	Akane	Taira	JPN	3.11.82	13		Kobe	22 Apr
32:18.57	Hiroko	Miyauchi	JPN	19.6.83	14		Kobe	22 Apr
32:18.87	Pauline	Waruguru	KEN	26.8.80	1		Kitakyushu	12 May
32:19.25	Bilha	Kamau	KEN-J	2.7.88	4		Kobe	13 Oct
32:20.86	Galina	Aleksandrova	RUS	15.10.76	5	NC	Zhukovskiy	14 Jul
32:21.04	Ruth	Wanjiru	KEN	11.9.81	4		Shizuoka	30 Apr
32:21.26	Noriko	Matsuoka	JPN	2.5.79	5		Kobe	13 Oct
	(70)							
32:21.42	Mary	Cullen	IRL	17.8.82	10		Stanford	29 Apr
32:21.79	Aya	Manome	JPN	30.8.82	15		Kobe	22 Apr
32:23.61	Rosa María	Morató	ESP	19.6.79	5	ECp	Ferrara	7 Apr
32:24.65	Yurika	Nakamura	JPN	1.4.86	7		Gifu	21 Sep
32:24.84	Irina	Timofeyeva	RUS	5.4.70	6	NC	Zhukovskiy	14 Jul
32:27.38		Zhu Xiaolin	CHN	20.2.84	1	WCT	Suzhou	10 Jun
32:28.35	Yuliya	Vinokurova	RUS	17.6.72	7	NC	Zhukovskiy	14 Jul
32:29.12		Xue Fei	CHN-J	8.8.89	1	NGP	Urumqi	20 Sep
32:29.53	Nadia	Ejjafini	BRN	8.11.80	1	pArab	Cairo	23 Nov
32:30.37	Amy	Hastings	USA	21.1.84	11		Stanford	29 Apr
	(80)							
32:31.21	Emily	Chebet	KEN	18.2.86	9	WCh	Osaka	25 Aug
32:31.85	Melissa	Cook	USA	22.11.79	12		Stanford	29 Apr
32:31.90	Blake	Russell	USA	24.7.75	1		Stanford	31 Mar
32:32.44	Doris	Changeywo	KEN	12.12.84	1	CISM	Hyderabad	15 Oct
32:33.28	Tomomi	Yuda	JPN	28.5.85	1r1		Yokohama	23 Dec
32:37.51	Yoshiko	Fujinaga	JPN	15.8.81	5		Fukagawa	11 Jul
32:37.98	Elva	Dryer	USA	26.9.71	13		Stanford	29 Apr
32:38.61	Marina	Haga	JPN	12.7.83	17		Kobe	22 Apr

Mark	Name		Nat	Born	Pos	Meet	Venue	Date
32:39.18		Jiang Chengcheng	CHN	5.11.86	3	NGP	Urumqi	20 Sep
32:39.29	Mai	Endo	JPN	22.12.86	18		Kobe	22 Apr
	(90)							
32:39.38		Wei Yanan	CHN	6.12.81	4	CISM	Hyderabad	15 Oct
32:40.58	Maria Elena	Valencia	MEX	25.5.83	1	MSR	Walnut	13 Apr
32:41.11	Zakia	Mrisho	TAN	19.2.84	1		Soffiano	29 Apr
32:42.95	Irina	Mikitenko	GER	23.8.72	2	NC	Zeulenroda	5 May
32:43.2	Jelena	Prokopcuka	LAT	21.9.76	1		Riga	16 Sep
32:43.31	Erba	Tiki Gelana	ETH	22.10.87	6		Fukagawa	11 Jul
32:44.13		Zhou Chunxiu	CHN	15.11.78	4	WCT	Suzhou	10 Jun
32:45.39	Kei	Terada	JPN	27.3.85	2		Miyoshi	13 May
32:45.94	Aine	Hoban	GBR	12.7.84	2		Stanford	31 Mar
32:46.28	Ikumi	Wakamatsu	JPN	22.6.74	7		Fukagawa	11 Jul
	(100)							

Mark	Name		Nat	Born	Date
32:47.5A	Magdeline	Chemjor	KEN	12.11.78	28 Jul
32:47.96	Hayley	Haining	GBR	6.3.72	30 Jun
32:47.98	Filomena	Cheyech	KEN	5.7.82	13 Oct
32:48.71	Ikuyo	Yamashita	JPN	17.6.85	19 May
32:48.92	Kazue	Ogoshi	JPN	2.3.81	3 Jun
32:49.72	Remi	Nakazato	JPN-J	24.6.88	3 Jun
32:50.63	Alicia	Craig	USA	14.6.82	21 Jun
32:52.34	Yuki	Kazama	JPN	29.11.85	30 Apr
32:52.39	Yukari	Sahaku	JPN-J	5.11.88	19 May
32:53.02	Yukako	Goto	JPN	16.9.73	30 Apr
32:53.13	Haruko	Okamoto	JPN	19.8.74	11 Jul
32:54.00		Jia Chaofeng	CHN-J	16.11.88	2 Nov
32:54.29	Yesenia	Centeno	ESP	27.6.71	28 Jul
32:54.41	Sara	Slattery	USA	2.10.81	23 Jul
32:55.10	Lidia	Chojecka	POL	25.1.77	5 May
32:55.11	Ryoko	Kizaki	JPN	21.6.85	9 Aug
32:55.94	Benita	Johnson	AUS	6.5.79	25 Aug
32:56.62	Miki	Ohira	JPN	28.6.81	19 May
32:57.53	Ayumi	Hashimoto	JPN	17.6.83	22 Apr
32:58.20	Michelle	Sikes	USA	27.2.85	19 Apr
32:59.88		Jiang Yuanyuan	CHN	20.12.86	10 Jun
33:00.23		Xi Qiuhong	CHN	4.9.84	10 Jun
33:01.30	Madoka	Ogi	JPN	26.10.83	29 Jun
33:01.56	Melissa	Grelli	USA		7 Jun
33:02.72	Viktoriya	Trushenko	RUS	19.7.84	14 Jul
33:05.42	Norie	Takahashi	JPN	22.4.80	22 Apr
33:05.79	Fatna	Maraoui	ITA	10.7.77	7 Apr
33:06.07		Zhu Yanmei	CHN	16.10.86	25 Jul
33:06.26	Whitney	McDonald	USA	1.8.85	31 Mar
33:06.35	Natalya	Sergeyeva	RUS	4.9.84	14 Jul
33:06.37	Olga	Minina	BLR	3.11.85	13 Jul
33:07.42	Valentina	Levushkina	RUS	20.4.82	14 Jul
33:08.30	Maya	Nishio	JPN	19.12.78	21 Sep
33:08.69	Irina	Sergeyeva	RUS	25.12.87	13 Jul
33:08.89	Harumi	Hiroyama	JPN	2.9.68	29 Jun
33:09.0A	Millecent	Gathoni	KEN		28 Jul
33:09.19	Isabel	Checa	ESP	27.12.82	7 Apr
33:09.27	Molly	Huddle	USA	31.8.84	21 Jun
33:09.38		Dong Xiaoqin	CHN	2.1.83	10 Jun
33:09.63	Alina	Alekseyeva	RUS	16.8.85	13 Jul
33:11.23	Julia	Lucas	USA	4.3.84	19 Apr
33:11.44	Mariko	Nakao	JPN	24.8.84	11 Jul
33:11.73	Ednalva	da Silva	CHN	10.12.76	20 Jun
33:12.08	Paula	Todoran	ROM	9.6.85	13 Jul
33:12.61	Mika	Okunaga	JPN	27.10.82	21 Sep
33:12.66	Yuka	Izumi	JPN	18.1.85	13 May
33:13.05	Oksana	Belyakova	RUS	9.9.75	14 Jul
33:13.51	Yumi	Hirata	JPN	22.6.81	11 Jul
33:14.24	Yumiko	Hara	JPN	9.1.82	29 Jun
33:14.97	Silvia	Sommaggio	ITA	20.11.69	7 Apr
	(150)				

JUNIORS

See main list for top 10 juniors. 12 performances by 10 women under 32:40.0. Additional marks and further juniors:

Zhang Y 32:30.23 2r2 Suzhou 10 Jun 32:33.81 2 Urumqi 20 Sep

Mark	Name		Nat	Born	Pos	Meet	Venue	Date
32:49.72	Remi	Nakazato	JPN	24.6.88	2		Kushiro	3 Jun
32:52.39	Yukari	Sahaku	JPN	5.11.88	6		Kumagaya	19 May
32:54.00		Jia Chaofeng	CHN	16.11.88	8		Wuhan	2 Nov
33:20.43	Karima Saleh	Jassem	BRN	18.2.88	6	CISM	Hyderabad	15 Oct
33:24.87	Furtuna	Zerergish	ERI-Y	.90	6	AfG	Alger	21 Jul
33:25.44		Chang Jinxue	CHN	9.3.88	9		Wuhan	2 Nov
33:38.92		Su Qian	CHN	4.11.88	11		Wuhan	2 Nov
33:39.04	Miho	Nomiyama	JPN	8.7.89	1		Fukuoka	4 May
33:46.47	Veronicah	Kanyi	KEN	6.2.88	1		Tokyo	19 May
33:49.14	Yuko	Nanba (20)	JPN	.89	3		Tokyo	19 May

10 KILOMETRES ROAD

Mark	Name		Nat	Born	Pos	Meet	Venue	Date
31:05	Lornah	Kiplagat	NED	1.5.74	1		San Juan	25 Feb
31:10+	Mary	Keitany	KEN	18.1.82	1	in HMar	Udine	14 Oct
31:10+		Kiplagat			2	in HMar	Udine	14 Oct
31:18+	Evelyne	Kimwei	KEN	25.8.87	1	in HMar	Sapporo	8 Jul
31:19+	Pamela	Chepchumba	KEN	8.3.79	3	in HMar	Udine	14 Oct
31:20+	Bezunesh	Bekele	ETH	18.9.83	4	in HMar	Udine	14 Oct
31:26	Hilda	Kibet	KEN	27.3.81	1		Schoorl	11 Feb
31:28+		Kimwei			5	in HMar	Udine	14 Oct
31:34+	Kayoko	Fukushi	JPN	25.3.82	1	in HMar	Marugame	4 Feb
31:36+	Deena	Kastor	USA	14.2.73	1	in 15k	Jacksonville	10 Mar
31:37+	Mizuki	Noguchi	JPN	3.7.78	2	in HMar	Sapporo	8 Jul
31:40+	Mara	Yamauchi	GBR	13.8.73	3	in HMar	Sapporo	8 Jul
31:40+	Atsede	Habtamu	ETH	26.10.87	6	in HMar	Udine	14 Oct
31:41+	Alice	Timbilil	KEN	16.6.83	7	in HMar	Udine	14 Oct
31:44	Sylvia	Kibet	KEN	28.3.84	1		Marseilles	1 May
31:46	Penninah	Arusei	KEN	23.2.79	1		Paderborn	7 Apr

Others where superior to track bests

Mark	Name		Nat	Born	Pos	Meet	Venue	Date
31:47	Joanne	Pavey	GBR	20.9.73	1		Manchester	20 May

Mark	Name		Nat	Born	Pos	Meet	Venue	Date
31:48	Anikó	Kálovics	HUN	13.5.77	2		Manchester	20 May
31:49	Eunice	Chepkorir	KEN	17.2.82	1		Barcelona	1 Apr
31:50	Rita	Jeptoo	KEN	15.2.81	3		Manchester	20 May
31:54	Erba	Tiki Gelana	ETH	22.10.87	1		Okayama	23 Dec
31:55	Jelena	Prokopcuka	LAT	21.9.76	4		Manchester	20 May
31:56	Zhor	El Kamch	MAR	15.3.73	1		Casablanca	20 May
31:56	Belaynesh	Fikadu	ETH	28.3.87	1		Tilburg	2 Sep
31:57	Luminita	Talpos	ROM	9.10.72	8	in HMar	Udine	14 Oct
31:58	Fridah	Domongole	KEN	15.1.84	2		Marseille	1 May
32:01+	Paula	Radcliffe	GBR	17.12.73	1	in HMar	Newcastle	18 Sep
32:02	Rehima	Kedir	ETH	11.12.85	1		Mobile	24 Mar
32:03	Jesica	Obare	KEN	.84	3		Marseille	1 May
32:06	Gladys	Cherono	KEN	.84	1		La Coruña	7 Oct
32:07	Kate	Reed	GBR	28.9.82	1	NC	Chichester	7 Oct
32:08	Meseret	Defar	ETH	18.11.83	2		San Juan	25 Feb
32:08	Vivian	Cheruiyot	KEN	11.6.83	1		Glasgow	13 May
32:08	Olivera	Jevtic	SER	24.7.77	1		Brcko	28 Jun
32:09	Pauline	Wangui	KEN	17.7.84	2		Casablanca	20 May
32:09+	Alina	Gherasim	ROM	16.11.71	11	in HMar	Udine	14 Oct
32:10	Tatyana	Petrova	RUS	8.4.83	2		Mobile	24 Mar
32:10	Irina	Mikitenko	GER	23.8.72	1		Berlin	4 Aug
32:10	Nadia	Ejjafini	BRN	8.11.80	1		Houilles	30 Dec
32:11	Anitha	Kiptum	KEN	.82	1		Hamburg	9 Sep
32:12	Amane	Gobena	ETH	9.11.82	2		Charleston	31 Mar
32:14	Emily	Chebet	KEN	18.2.86	2		New Orleans	7 Apr
32:15	Filomena	Chepchirchir	KEN	1.12.81	2		Hamburg	9 Sep
32:16	Pauline	Waruguru	KEN	26.8.80	1		Karatsu	11 Feb
32:17	Magdalene	Makunzi	KEN	.83	3		Casablanca	20 May
32:18	Rui	Aoyama	JPN-J	15.4.89	1		Yokohama	4 Feb
32:19	Mergia	Aselefech	ETH		2		Glasgow	13 May
32:20	Jemimah	Chelagat	KEN	.85	3		Mobile	24 Mar
32:20+	Benita	Johnson	AUS	6.5.79		in HMar	Berlin	1 Apr
32:20+	Chisato	Osaki	JPN	19.4.87	12	in HMar	Udine	14 Oct
32:21	Luminita	Talpos	ROM	9.10.72	1		Cape Elizabeth	4 Aug
32:21+	Irina	Timofeyeva	RUS	5.4.70	14	in HMar	Udine	14 Oct
32:21+	Atsede	Bayisa	ETH	16.4.87	15	in HMar	Udine	14 Oct
32:22	Berhane	Adere	ETH	21.7.73	1		Cardiff	29 Jul
32:24	Viktoriya	Trushenko	RUS	19.7.84	1		Zhukovskiy	29 Apr
32:25+	Hiromi	Ominami	JPN	15.11.75		in HMar	Sapporo	8 Jul
32:26	Alessandra	Aguilar	ESP	1.7.78	6		Manchester	20 May
32:28	Edna	Kiplagat	KEN	15.9.79	1		Green Bay	9 Jun
32:28	Fatiha	Klilech-Fauvel	FRA	1.2.75	1		Suresnes	24 Jun
32:28	René	Kalmer	RSA	3.11.80	1	NC	Stellenbosch	11 Aug
32:30	Pamela	Anesomuk	KEN	.82	1		Madrid	18 Nov
32:34	Catherine	Mutwa	KEN	12.9.79	2		Lahore	14 Jan

32:37+	Kazue	Ogoshi	JPN	2.3.81	25 Nov
32:38	Christelle	Daunay	FRA	5.12.74	25 Mar
32:38	Azalech	Masresha	ETH-J	88	20 May
32:38	Fatima	Maraoui	ITA	10.7.77	30 Sep
32:38+	Lidia	Simon	ROM	4.9.73	14 Oct
32:39+	Mary	Ptikany	KEN	.78	30 Sep
32:40	Jessica	Ruthe	NZL	31.5.79	4 Aug
32:40+	Rose	Cheruiyot	KEN	21.7.76	18 Nov
32:41	Michelle	Ross-Cope	GBR	31.1.72	20 May
32:42	Dire	Tune	ETH	19.6.85	25 Feb
32:42	Karoline	Bjerkeli Grøvdal	NOR-Y	14.6.90	29 Apr
32:43	Helen	Kiprop	KEN	9.9.76	25 Feb
32:43	Margaret	Maury	FRA	15.5.74	1 May
32:44	Helen	Clitheroe	GBR	2.1.74	31 Dec
32:45	Melanie	Kraus	GER	24.10.74	4 Aug
32:45	Dolores	Checa	ESP	2.1.74	18 Nov
32:46	Rose	Kosgei	KEN	22.8.81	18 Aug
32:46	Angelina	Mutuku	KEN	9.11.82	18 Aug
32:47	Susan	Chepkemei ¶	KEN	25.6.75	25 Feb
32:47	Natalya	Sergeyeva	RUS	4.9.84	29 Apr
32:51	Martha	Komu	KEN	23.3.83	16 Jun
32:52+	Karima	Saleh Jassem	BRN-J	18.2.88	30 Sep
32:53	Alice	Mogire	KEN	.87	9 Jun
32:53+	Alina	Ivanova	RUS	16.3.69	14 Oct
32:55	Liz	Yelling	GBR	5.12.74	20 May
32:55	Analia	Rosa	POR	28.2.76	29 Jul
32:55	Christine	Chepkemei	KEN		7 Oct
32:55+	Krisztina	Papp	HUN	17.12.82	14 Oct
32:56	Natalie	Harvey	GBR	19.1.75	25 Mar
32:56	Jessica	Augusto	POR	8.11.81	20 May
32:56	Beatrice	Omwanza	KEN	24.2.74	9 Jun
32:56	Anna	Thompson	AUS	11.12.76	22 Jul
32:56+	Olga	Glok	RUS	6.12.82	14 Oct
32:56	Joan	Aiyabei	KEN	17.5.79	21 Oct
32:57	Souad	Aït Salem	ALG	6.1.79	20 May
32:58	Alem Tsigay	Misganaw	ETH	.83	28 Apr
32:58	Caroline	Cheptanui	KEN	21.3.81	18 Aug
32:59	Olga	Rosseyeva	RUS	1.8.81	29 Apr
33:00	Rashida	Khayrutdinova	RUS	18.8.75	29 Apr
33:00	Alina	Alekseyeva	RUS	16.8.85	29 Apr
33:00	Sharon	Tavengwa	ZIM	9.12.83	11 Aug

Downhill

31:44	Ayalew	Yimer	ETH	4.7.87	1	Atlanta (34m)	4 Jul
31:52	Kate	Reed	GBR	28.9.82	2	Madrid (55m)	31 Dec
32:40	Kathryn	McGregor	USA	2.9.77	3	Atlanta	4 Jul

82m downhill: May 6, Toronto: 1. Florence Jepkosgei KEN 31:42, 2. Pauline Githuka KEN 32:48

+ intermediate time in longer race, A made at altitude of 1000m or higher, H made in a heptathlon, h made in a heat, qf quarter-final, sf semi-final, i indoors, Q qualifying round, r race number, -J juniors, -Y youths (born 1990 or later)

15 KILOMETRES ROAD

And see splits in 10 Miles below

Mark	Name		Nat	Born	Pos	Meet	Venue	Date
46:59+	Lornah	Kiplagat	NED	1.5.74	1	in HMar	Udine	14 Oct
47:01+	Mary	Keitany	KEN	18.1.82	2	in HMar	Udine	14 Oct
47:20	Deena	Kastor	USA	14.2.73	1	NC	Jacksonville	10 Mar
47:36	Bizunesh	Bekele	ETH	29.1.83	1		Nijmegen	18 Nov
47:37		Kiplagat			2		Nijmegen	18 Nov
47:46+	Pamela	Chepchumba	KEN	8.3.79	3	in HMar	Udine	14 Oct
47:46+	Bezunesh	Bekele	ETH	18.9.83	4	in HMar	Udine	14 Oct
47:52+	Kayoko	Fukushi	JPN	25.3.82	1	in HMar	Marugame	4 Feb
47:56+	Mizuki	Noguchi	JPN	3.7.78	1	in HMar	Sapporo	8 Jul
48:03+	Evelyne	Kimwei	KEN	25.8.87	5	in HMar	Udine	14 Oct
48:08+	Mara (11/10)	Yamauchi	GBR	13.8.73	2	in HMar	Sapporo	8 Jul
48:10+	Atsede	Habtamu	ETH	26.10.87	6	in HMar	Udine	14 Oct
48:19+	Alice	Timbilil	KEN	16.6.83	7	in HMar	Udine	14 Oct
48:44	Luminita	Talpos	ROM	9.10.72	1		Istanbul	28 Oct
48:49	Rose	Cheruiyot	KEN	21.7.76	3		Nijmegen	18 Nov
48:50+	Chisato	Osaki	JPN	19.4.87	9	in HMar	Udine	14 Oct
48:50+	Alina	Gherasim	ROM	16.11.71	10	in HMar	Udine	14 Oct
48:50	Derebe	Alemu	ETH	5.6.83	1		s'Heerenberg	2 Dec
48:51+	Akane	Taira	JPN	3.11.82	11	in HMar	Udine	14 Oct
48:52+	Irina	Timofeyeva	RUS	5.4.70	12	in HMar	Udine	14 Oct
48:56+	Atsede	Bayisa	ETH	16.4.87	14	in HMar	Udine	14 Oct
48:58	Jennifer	Rhines	USA	1.7.74	2	NC	Jacksonville	10 Mar
49:07+	Genet	Getaneh	ETH	6.1.86	15	in HMar	Udine	14 Oct
49:09+	Julia	Mombi	KEN	25.1.85		in HMar	Sapporo	8 Jul
49:11+	Philes	Ongori	KEN	19.7.86	1	in HMar	Yamaguchi	11 Mar
49:17+	Constantina	Tomescu	ROM	23.1.70	2	in HMar	Sendai	13 May
49:18+	Hiromi	Ominami	JPN	15.11.75		in HMar	Sapporo	8 Jul
49:22+	Kazue	Ogoshi	JPN	2.3.81	1	in HMar	Kobe	25 Nov
49:23+	Hilda	Kibet	KEN	27.3.81	1	in HMar	Den Haag	17 Mar
49:23	Lidia	Simon	ROM	4.9.73	1		Utica	8 Jul
49:26+	Yoshimi	Ozaki	JPN	1.7.81	17	in HMar	Udine	14 Oct
49:30+	Alina	Ivanova	RUS	16.3.69	18	in HMar	Udine	14 Oct
49:35+	Olga	Glok	RUS	6.12.82	19	in HMar	Udine	14 Oct
49:40	Elva	Dryer	USA	26.9.71	3	NC	Jacksonville	10 Mar
49:45	Anikó	Kálovics	HUN	13.5.77	1		Kerzers	17 Mar
49:45	Ashu	Kasim	ETH	20.10.84	2		Istanbul	28 Oct
49:51+	Yurika	Nakamura	JPN	1.4.86	3	in HMar	Okayama	23 Dec
49:56	Kathryn	McGregor	USA	2.9.77	4	NC	Jacksonville	10 Mar
49:58+	Harumi	Hiroyama	JPN	2.9.68	2	in HMar	Marugame	4 Feb
49:58+	Getenesh	Wami	ETH	11.12.74		in Mar	Berlin	30 Sep
49:59+	Krisztina	Papp	HUN	17.12.82	19	in HMar	Udine	14 Oct

50:04+	Yumiko	Hara	JPN	9.1.82	28 Jan
50:04+	Yoko	Shibui	JPN	14.3.79	28 Jan
50:06	Kate	O'Neill	USA	29.7.80	10 Mar
50:10+	Berhane	Adere	ETH	21.7.73	9 Sep
50:11+	Pauline	Wangui	KEN	17.7.84	9 Sep
50:13+	Yui	Sakai	JPN-J	19.1.88	8 Jul
50:16	Amelework	Fikadu	ETH		2 Dec
50:18+	Pauline	Waruguru	KEN	26.8.80	8 Jul
50:22	Miriam	Wangari	KEN	22.2.79	28 Oct
50:23	Irene	Kwambai	KEN	25.10.78	1 May
50:24+	Yuri	Kano	JPN	27.10.78	8 Jul
50:26+	Marina	Haga	JPN	12.7.83	11 Mar
50:26+	Aya	Manome	JPN	30.8.82	11 Mar
50:26+	Kiyoko	Shimahara	JPN	22.12.76	11 Mar
50:26+	Akane	Wakita	JPN	15.12.87	11 Mar
50:26+	Yoko	Miyauchi	JPN	19.6.83	11 Mar
50:26+	Tomoko	Ishii	JPN	14.10.83	11 Mar
50:26+	Yoshiko	Hosokawa	JPN	17.8.81	11 Mar
50:26+	Miyuki	Ando	JPN	25.3.80	11 Mar
50:26	Nina	Rillstone	NZL	15.4.75	8 Jul
50:26	Penninah	Arusei	KEN	23.2.79	2 Dec
50:27+	Yasuko	Hashimoto	JPN	12.8.75	4 Feb

10 MILES ROAD

Times at 15km in 2nd column

50:59+	47:36	Kara	Goucher	USA	9.7.78	1	in HMar	Newcastle (dh)	18 Sep
51:22+	47:53	Paula	Radcliffe	GBR	17.12.73	2	in HMar	Newcastle (dh)	18 Sep
51:44		Teyiba	Erkesso	ETH	28.9.82	1		Washington	1 Apr
52:30+		Liz	Yelling	GBR	5.12.74	1		Bath	25 Mar
52:49+		Pamela	Chepchumba	KEN	8.3.79	1=	in HMar	Philadelphia	16 Sep
52:49+		Alice	Timbilil	KEN	16.6.83	1=	in HMar	Philadelphia	16 Sep
52:58		Tatyana	Petrova	RUS	8.4.83	2		Washington	1 Apr
52:58	49:35	Belaynesh	Fikadu	ETH	28.3.87	1		Zaandam	23 Sep
53:08		Mai	Endo	JPN	22.12.86	1		Tsuchiura	15 Apr
53:09+		Edna	Kiplagat (10)	KEN	11.11.79	3	in HMar	Philadelphia	16 Sep
53:13+	49:32	Anikó	Kálovics	HUN	13.5.77	3	in HMar	Newcastle (dh)	18 Sep
53:16+		Magdalene	Makunzi	KEN	.83	1	in HMar	San Jose	14 Oct
53:26		Kathy	Butler	GBR	22.10.73	3		Washington	1 Apr
53:26+		Sharon	Cherop	KEN	16.3.84	4	in HMar	Philadelphia	16 Sep
53:27	49:53	Hilda	Kibet	KEN	27.3.81	2		Zaandam	23 Sep

Mark	Name		Nat	Born	Pos	Meet	Venue	Date
53:44	Pauline	Wangui	KEN	17.7.84	3		Zaandam	23 Sep
53:44	Rose	Cheruiyot	KEN	21.7.76	1		Portsmouth	28 Oct
53:51+	Hiromi	Ominami	JPN	15.11.75	5	in HMar	Philadelphia	16 Sep
53:52	Lidia	Simon	ROM	4.9.73	5		Washington	1 Apr

54:04+	Jane Mwikali	Muia	KEN	20.12.86	18 Sep
54:07	Galina	Aleksandrova	RUS	15.10.75	1 Apr
54:12+	Ashu	Kasim	ETH	20.10.84	16 Sep
54:12	Hayley	Yelling	GBR	3.1.74	28 Oct
54:13+	Rose	Kosgei	KEN	22.8.81	14 Oct
54:13	Mara	Yamauchi	GBR	13.8.73	28 Oct
54:16+	Angelina	Mutuku	KEN	9.11.82	16 Sep
54:20+	Megumi	Oshima	JPN	4.9.75	14 Oct
54:22	Filomena	Chepchirchir	KEN	1.12.81	23 Sep
54:26+	Olga	Kravtsova	BLR	25.6.81	16 Sep
54:26+	Nuta	Olaru	ROM	28.8.70	16 Sep
54:27	Dorota	Gruca	POL	5.12.70	1 Apr
54:27	Hellen	Musyoka	KEN		13 May

Point-to-point and wind assisted: 6 May, Philadelphia: 1. Naomi Wangui KEN 23.7.78 53:43, 2. Olga Romanova RUS 23.5.80 54:14.

20 KILOMETRES ROAD

See Half Marathon lists below to 67:20 – plus:

66:56	Alicia	Shay	USA	14.6.82	1	NC	New Haven	3 Sep
67:18	Elva	Dryer	USA	26.9.71	2	NC	New Haven	3 Sep

HALF MARATHON (/20KM)

Slightly downhill courses: Lisboa 69m, South Shields 30.5m

66:25	62:57	Lornah	Kiplagat	NED	1.5.74	1	WCh	Udine	14 Oct
66:48	63:18	Mary	Keitany	KEN	18.1.82	2	WCh	Udine	14 Oct
66:57dh	63:33	Kara	Goucher	USA	9.7.78	1	GNR	South Shields	30 Sep
67:08dh		Rita	Jeptoo	KEN	15.2.81	1		Lisboa	18 Mar
67:53dh	64:24	Paula	Radcliffe	GBR	17.12.73	2	GNR	South Shields	30 Sep
68:00	64:19	Kayoko	Fukushi	JPN	25.3.82	1		Marugame	4 Feb
68:06	64:40	Pamela	Chepchumba	KEN	8.3.79	3	WCh	Udine	14 Oct
68:07	64:40	Bezunesh	Bekele	ETH	18.9.83	4	WCh	Udine	14 Oct
68:22	64:48	Mizuki	Noguchi	JPN	3.7.78	1		Sapporo	8 Jul
68:28		Benita	Johnson (10)	AUS	6.5.79	1		Berlin	1 Apr
68:29	65:01	Atsede	Habtamu	ETH	26.10.87	5	WCh	Udine	14 Oct
68:30	65:00		Noguchi			1		Miyazaki	6 Jan
68:36dh		Susan	Chepkemei ¶	KEN	25.6.75	2		Lisboa	18 Mar
68:36			Keitany			1		Vitry-sur-Seine	1 Apr
68:39	65:03	Evelyne	Kimwei	KEN	25.8.87	6	WCh	Udine	14 Oct
68:43			Keitany			1		Lille	1 Sep
68:45	65:12	Mara	Yamauchi	GBR	13.8.73	2		Sapporo	8 Jul
68:45			Chepchumba			1		Philadelphia	16 Sep
68:54	65:21		Noguchi			1		Sendai	13 May
68:56		Alice	Timbilil	KEN	16.6.83	2		Philadelphia	16 Sep
68:56	65:23	Chisato	Osaki	JPN	19.4.87	7	WCh	Udine	14 Oct
68:57			Chepchumba			1		Azpeitia	31 Mar
68:58		Anikó	Kálovics	HUN	13.5.77	1		Milano	1 Apr
69:01	65:32	Luminita	Talpos	ROM	9.10.72	8	WCh	Udine	14 Oct
69:09	65:31		Timbilil			9	WCh	Udine	14 Oct
69:14	65:39	Alina	Gherasim	ROM	16.11.71	10	WCh	Udine	14 Oct
69:15	65:47	Atsede	Bayisa (20)	ETH	16.4.87	11	WCh	Udine	14 Oct
69:17	65:48	Akane	Taira	JPN	3.11.82	12	WCh	Udine	14 Oct
69:20	65:39		Kimwei			1		Okayama	23 Dec
69:23		Penninah (30/22)	Arusei	KEN	23.2.79	1		Ulrum	28 Jul
69:26	66:02	Yoshimi	Ozaki	JPN	1.7.81	13	WCh	Udine	14 Oct
69:28		Liz	Yelling	GBR	5.12.74	1		Bath	25 Mar
69:29	65:52	Irina	Timofeyeva	RUS	5.4.70	14	WCh	Udine	14 Oct
69:32	66:03	Alina	Ivanova	RUS	16.3.69	15	WCh	Udine	14 Oct
69:38	65:59	Deena	Kastor	USA	14.2.73	16	WCh	Udine	14 Oct
69:43	65:57	Hilda	Kibet	KEN	27.3.81	1		Den Haag	17 Mar
69:45	66:09	Julia	Mombi	KEN	25.1.85	1		Kobe	25 Nov
69:46		Irina (30)	Mikitenko	GER	23.8.72	2		Berlin	1 Apr
69:50	66:08	Philes	Ongori	KEN	19.7.86	1		Yamaguchi	11 Mar
69:50dh		Salina	Kosgei	KEN	16.11.76	3		Lisboa	18 Mar
69:53		Irene	Kwambai	KEN	25.10.78	2		Vitry-sur-Seine	1 Apr
69:53	66:22	Kazue	Ogoshi	JPN	2.3.81	2		Kobe	25 Nov
69:58+		Berhane	Adere	ETH	21.7.73	1=		London	22 Apr
69:58+	66:18	Constantina	Tomescu	ROM	23.1.70	1=		London	22 Apr
69:58+	66:18	Getenesh	Wami	ETH	11.12.74	1=		London	22 Apr
69:58+	66:18		Zhou Chunxiu	CHN	15.11.78	1=		London	22 Apr
69:58		Magdalene	Makunzi	KEN	.83	1		San Jose	14 Oct
69:58	66:25	Olga (40)	Glok	RUS	6.12.82	17	WCh	Udine	14 Oct

Mark		Name		Nat	Born	Pos	Meet	Venue	Date
70:08	66:35	Lidia	Simon	ROM	4.9.73	18	WCh	Udine	14 Oct
70:11		Edna	Kiplagat	KEN	11.11.79	3		Philadelphia	16 Sep
70:12+	66:31	Magarsa	Askale Tafa	ETH	27.9.84	1=	in Mar	Paris	15 Apr
70:12+		Asha	Gigi	ETH	15.10.73	1=	in Mar	Paris	15 Apr
70:13		Mary	Ptikany	KEN	.78	1	RdVin	Remich	30 Sep
70:17		Anne	Kosgei Chepkemboi	KEN	.80	1		Vigo	15 Apr
70:21		Sharon	Cherop	KEN	16.3.84	4		Philadelphia	16 Sep
70:23	66:48	Harumi	Hiroyama	JPN	2.9.68	2		Marugame	4 Feb
70:23	66:46	Yurika	Nakamura	JPN	1.4.86	3		Okayama	23 Dec
70:24+	66:45	Yumiko	Hara	JPN	9.1.82	1=	in Mar	Osaka	28 Jan
		(50)							
70:24+	66:45	Yoko	Shibui	JPN	14.3.79	1=	in Mar	Osaka	28 Jan
70:26		Caroline	Kwambai	KEN	9.9.75	1		Paris	11 Mar
70:26		Jane Mwikali	Muia	KEN	20.12.86	1		Bristol	9 Sep
70:27		Miriam	Wangari	KEN	22.2.79	2		Lille	1 Sep
70:29		Souad	Aït Salem	ALG	6.1.79	1		Ostia	25 Feb
70:30	66:49	Genet	Getaneh	ETH	6.1.86	19	WCh	Udine	14 Oct
70:30		Derebe	Alemu	ETH	5.6.83	1		New Delhi	28 Oct
70:32		Helena	Javornik	SLO	26.3.66	1		Klagenfurt	19 Aug
70:33dh		Catherine	Ndereba	KEN	21.7.72	2		New York (dh 30m)	5 Aug
70:33		Tigist	Tufa	ETH		3		Lille	1 Sep
		(60)							
70:35dh		Nina	Rillstone	NZL	15.4.75	3		New York	5 Aug
70:38		Nadia	Ejjafini	BRN	8.11.80	2		Milano	1 Apr
70:38		Rashida	Khayrutdinova	RUS	18.8.75	1	NC	Novosibirsk	8 Sep
70:40		Fatiha	Klilech-Fauvel	FRA	1.2.75	4		Lille	1 Sep
70:41	67:05	Hiromi	Ominami	JPN	15.11.75	6		Sapporo	8 Jul
70:43dh		Ana	Dias	POR	15.1.74	4		Lisboa	18 Mar
70:44		Filomena	Chepchirchir	KEN	1.12.81	1		Utrecht	9 Apr
70:47		Louise	Damen	GBR	12.10.82	1		Reading	25 Mar
70:52	67:19	Megumi	Seike	JPN	26.2.87	4		Matsue	18 Mar
70:53	67:19	Ikuyo	Yamashita	JPN	17.6.85	5		Matsue	18 Mar
		(70)							
70:53	67:20	Krisztina	Papp	HUN	17.12.82	20	WCh	Udine	14 Oct
70:54		Pauline	Chepkorir	KEN	.80	1		Muscat	2 Feb
70:55	67:19	Mikiko	Hara	JPN	6.2.86	6		Matsue	18 Mar
70:57		Marina	Haga	JPN	12.7.83	4		Yamaguchi	11 Mar
70:59		Aya	Manome	JPN	30.8.82	5		Yamaguchi	11 Mar
71:00		Kiyoko	Shimahara	JPN	22.12.76	6		Yamaguchi	11 Mar
71:00	67:19	Kei	Terada	JPN	27.3.85	7		Matsue	18 Mar
71:01		Akane	Wakita	JPN	15.12.87	7		Yamaguchi	11 Mar
71:02		Ayelech	Worku	ETH	12.6.79	2		Paris	11 Mar
71:02		Hilaria	Johannes	NAM	13.8.80	1		Swakopmund	16 Sep
		(80)							
71:03		Teyiba	Erkesso	ETH	28.9.82	2		Ra's Al Khaymah	9 Feb
71:03		Milkah	Jerotich	KEN	24.2.78	1		Frankfurt	4 Mar
71:03	67:35	Furtuna	Zegergish	ERI-J	.89	21	WCh	Udine	14 Oct
71:05dh		Yuri	Kano	JPN	27.10.78	4		New York	11 Mar
71:05	67:34	Christelle	Daunay	FRA	5.12.74	22	WCh	Udine	14 Oct
71:06		Yoko	Miyauchi	JPN	19.6.83	8		Yamaguchi	11 Mar
71:07		Alice	Mogire	KEN	.87	1		Hannover	6 May
71:08	67:27	Yasuko	Hashimoto	JPN	12.8.75	3		Marugame	4 Feb
71:09		Ryoko	Kizaki	JPN	21.6.85	1		Kyoto	11 Mar
71:09	67:35	Anna	Incerti	ITA	19.1.80	23	WCh	Udine	14 Oct
		(90)							
71:11	67:28	Hiroko	Miyauchi	JPN	19.6.83	3		Miyazaki	6 Jan
71:11		Dire	Tune	ETH	19.6.85	4		Ra's Al Khaymah	9 Feb
71:12	67:35	Vincenza	Sicari	ITA	19.3.79	24	WCh	Udine	14 Oct
71:14		Yoko	Yagi	JPN	14.4.80	4		Miyazaki	6 Jan
71:14dh		Merima	Denboba	ETH	21.8.74	5		Lisboa	18 Mar
71:14		Liliya	Shobukhova	RUS	13.11.77	1		Praha	24 Mar
71:14		Megumi	Oshima	JPN	4.9.75	2		San Jose	14 Oct
71:14		Nataliya	Berkut	UKR	30.5.75	4		New Delhi	28 Oct
71:15		Asuka	Kato	JPN	7.3.80	4		Marugame	4 Feb
71:15		Beatrice	Omwanza	KEN	24.2.74	1		Paderborn	7 Apr
		(100)							

71:16	Joan	Ayabei	KEN	17.5.79	20 May
71:18	Hayley	Haining	GBR	6.3.72	2 Sep
71:19	Ashu	Kasim	ETH	20.10.84	16 Sep
71:20dh	Madaí	Pérez	MEX	2.2.80	5 Aug
71:20	Pauline	Wangui	KEN	17.7.84	9 Sep
71:20	Angelina	Mutuku	KEN	9.11.82	16 Sep
71:22	Miho	Notagashira	JPN	17.8.83	6 Jan
71:22	Yoshie	Kurisu	JPN	21.8.85	18 Mar
71:23	Marta	Domínguez	ESP	3.11.75	4 Feb
71:23	Lenah	Cheruiyot	KEN	1.3.73	23 Sep

Mark	Name		Nat	Born	Date
71:24	Leila	Aman	ETH	24.11.77	24 Mar
71:24	Emmah	Kariuki	KEN	4.1.81	6 May
71:29	Hiroko	Shoi	JPN	18.6.80	18 Mar
71:29	Hellen	Cherono	KEN	22.2.84	16 Dec
71:29	Azalech	Masresha	ETH-J	88	21 Oct
71:31	Gladys	Cherono	KEN	.84	21 Oct
71:31	Roman	Gebregesesse	ETH		2 Dec
71:31	Hellen Nzembi	Musyoka	KEN	3.1.87	2 Dec
71:32	Caroline	Cheptanui	KEN	21.3.81	9 Feb
71:32	Pauline	Waruguru	KEN	26.8.80	8 Jul
71:33	Olga	Kravtsova	BLR	25.6.81	16 Sep
71:34	Tomoko	Ishii	JPN	14.10.83	11 Mar
71:34	Alessandra	Aguilar	ESP	1.7.78	31 Mar
71:35	Kayo	Sugihara	JPN	24.2.83	6 Jan
71:35	Evelyne	Lagat	KEN	12.8.80	14 Oct
71:37	Ruth	Wanjiru	KEN	11.9.81	6 Jan
71:38	Anna	Thompson	AUS	11.12.76	20 May
71:40	Agnes	Katunge	KEN	26.6.86	2 Dec
71:41	Fernanda	Ribeiro	POR	23.6.69	5 Oct
71:42	Elva	Dryer	USA	26.9.71	14 Jan
71:45	Yoshiko	Hosokawa	JPN	17.8.81	11 Mar
71:45	Yui	Sakai	JPN-J	19.1.88	8 Jul
71:45 ?	Jacqueline	Nytepi	KEN	.84	9 Dec
71:46	Nuta	Olaru	ROM	28.8.70	16 Sep
71:47	Kate	O'Neill	USA	29.7.80	14 Jan
71:52	Karima	Saleh Jassem	BRN-J	18.2.88	30 Sep
71:55	Ikumi	Wakamatsu	JPN	22.6.74	4 Feb
71:55	Luminita	Zaituc	GER	9.10.68	7 Oct
71:55	Yuko	Machida	JPN	11.8.80	14 Oct
71:56	René	Kalmer	RSA	3.11.80	1 Jul
71:57	Sabrina	Mockenhaupt	GER	6.12.80	22 Apr
71:58	Miyuki	Ando	JPN	25.3.80	11 Mar
72:00+	Bruna	Genovese	ITA	24.9.76	18 Nov
72:01+	Mari	Ozaki	JPN	16.7.75	28 Jan
72:01+	Inga	Abitova	RUS	6.3.82	28 Jan
72:01+	Lucy	Wangui	KEN	24.3.84	28 Jan
72:01	Yukie	Nakadomari	JPN	1.12.86	18 Mar
72:01	Katie	McGregor	USA	2.9.77	14 Oct
72:02	Sakura	Sato	JPN	17.11.84	4 Feb
72:02	Lisa Jana	Weightman	AUS	16.1.79	1 Jul
72:03	Edith	Masai	KEN	4.4.67	1 Apr
72:05+	Tomo	Morimoto	JPN	27.12.83	28 Jan
72:06	Lineth	Chepkirui	KEN-J	.88	8 Dec
72:07	Asami	Nishizawa-Obi	JPN	22.3.76	6 Jan
72:07	Caroline	Mutua	KEN	12.9.79	9 Feb
72:08	Selina	Chelimo	KEN	.73	9 Apr
72:09	Zahia	Dahmani	FRA	2.6.72	11 Mar
72:09	Dulce Maria	Rodriguez	MEX	14.8.72	1 Apr
72:09	Christine	Chepkonga	KEN	12.12.80	9 Apr
72:12	Asmae	Leghzaoui	MAR	30.8.76	9 Feb
72:14	Justyna	Bak	POL	1.8.74	25 Mar
72:14	Deborah	Toniolo	ITA	24.4.77	1 Apr
72:14dh	Hayley	Yelling	GBR	3.1.74	30 Sep
72:14	Daniela	Cârlan	ROM	18.9.80	14 Oct
72:15	Ednalva	da Silva	CHN	10.12.76	2 Sep
72:16	Haruko	Okamoto	JPN	19.8.74	4 Feb
72:16	Maria Elena	Valencia	MEX	25.5.83	10 Jun
72:16	Martha	Jiménez	MEX	19.1.65	10 Jun
72:17	Mai	Endo	JPN	22.12.86	1 Jul
72:18	Mikie	Takanaka	JPN	6.10.80	4 Feb
72:18	Malgorzata	Sobanska	POL	25.4.69	25 Mar
72:19		Jiang Chengcheng	CHN	5.11.86	21 Oct
72:20	Keiko	Nakasu	JPN	.86	18 Mar
72:21	Mindaye	Gishu Tilahun	ETH	18.8.86	25 Mar
72:25	Kaori	Takai	JPN	31.10.79	4 Feb
72:27	Fatna	Maraoui	ITA	10.7.77	27 May
72:28	Mihaela	Botezan	ROM	21.11.76	11 Feb
72:28	Michi	Inoue	JPN	26.6.85	18 Nov
72:31		Kim Kum-ok	PRK	9.12.85	11 Aug
72:31+	Helena Kiprop	Loshanyang	KEN	9.9.76	30 Sep
72:31+	Naoko	Sakamoto	JPN	14.11.80	30 Sep
72:32	Susanne	Pumper	AUT	1.9.70	28 Oct
72:33dh	Susan	Partridge	GBR	4.1.80	30 Sep
72:34		Lee Eun-jung	KOR	21.4.81	14 Oct
72:35	Tomomi	Hamasaki	JPN-J	17.1.88	11 Mar
72:36	Malika	Asahssah	MAR	24.9.82	20 May
72:36	Tabitha	Tsatsa	ZIM	18.9.72	27 May
72:37	Takami	Ominami	JPN	15.11.75	28 Jan
72:37	Olivera	Jevtic	SRB	24.7.77	23 Sep
72:38	Yuko	Sato	JPN	17.1.82	4 Feb
72:38	Akane	Mutazaki	JPN	10.1.86	11 Mar
72:38	Kirsten	Melkevik Otterbu	NOR	29.5.70	12 May
72:38	Mihret	Tadesse	ETH		14 Oct
72:39	Fatiha	Baouf	BEL	15.7.70	25 Mar
72:40	Penninah	Wanjiru	KEN	11.10.84	4 Feb
72:41	Selma	Borst	NED	6.9.83	14 Oct
72:42	Rieko	Sakane	JPN	1.10.82	4 Feb
72:42	Marisa	Barros	POR	25.2.80	5 Oct
72:42	Rose	Kosgei (199)	KEN	22.8.81	14 Oct
72:43	four women, 209 to 72:45				

Excessively downhill: 71:12 Kathy Butler GBR 22.10.73 1 Austin (114m) 28 Jan

Doubtful distance: 71:56 Magdalena Syombua KEN 1 Ngereny 22 Sep

JUNIORS

Mark		Name		Nat	Born	Pos	Meet	Venue	Date
71:03	67:35	Furtuna	Zegergish	ERI	.89	21	WCh	Udine	14 Oct
71:29		Azalech	Masresha	ETH	88	1		Reims	21 Oct
		71:59				4		Praha	24 Mar
71:45		Yui	Sakai	JPN	19.1.88	9		Sapporo	8 Jul
71:52		Karima	Saleh Jassem	BRN	18.2.88	2	RdVin	Remich	30 Sep
72:06		Lineth	Chepkirui	KEN	.88	1		Lagos	8 Dec
72:35		Tomomi	Hamasaki	JPN	17.1.88	2		Kyoto	11 Mar
72:44		Angeline	Nyiransabimana	RWA	10.1.88	31	WCh	Udine	14 Oct
72:45		Olga	Kimaiyo	KEN	.88	1		Chihuahua	21 Oct
72:59			Sun Lamei	CHN-Y	4.1.90	2		Beijing	21 Oct
73:18		Yukari	Sahaku (10)	JPN	5.11.88	18		Sapporo	8 Jul
73:50		Tomomi	Hamasaki	JPN	17.1.88	24		Sapporo	8 Jul
73:54		Akiho	Shigeta	JPN	14.2.88	16		Marugame	4 Feb
74:00		Yuri	Sugiyama	JPN	17.9.88	26		Sapporo	8 Jul

25–30 KILOMETRES ROAD

25 km	30 km	Name		Nat	Born	Pos		Venue	Date
1:22:50+	1:39:35+		Zhou Chunxiu	CHN	15.11.78	1=	in Mar	London	22 Apr
1:22:50+	1:39:36+	Getenesh	Wami	ETH	11.12.74	1=	in Mar	London	22 Apr
1:22:50+	1:39:36+	Lornah	Kiplagat	NED	1.5.74		in Mar	London	22 Apr
	1:40:38+	Constantina	Tomescu	ROM	23.1.70		in Mar	London	22 Apr
1:23:35+	1:40:45+		Wami			1	in Mar	Berlin	30 Sep
1:23:42+	1:40:54+	Yumiko	Hara	JPN	9.1.82	1	in Mar	Osaka	28 Jan
1:23:35+	1:40:56+	Magarsa	Askale Tafa	ETH	27.9.84	1	in Mar	Paris	15 Apr
1:23:42+	1:41:04+	Yoko	Shibui	JPN	14.3.79		in Mar	Osaka	28 Jan
1:24:23+	1:41:02+	Mizuki	Noguchi	JPN	3.7.78	1	in Mar	Tokyo	18 Nov
1:24:24+	1:41:03+	Salina	Kosgei	KEN	16.11.76	2	in Mar	Tokyo	18 Nov
1:24:27+	1:41:16+	Paula	Radcliffe	GBR	17.12.73	1	in Mar	New York	4 Nov

Mark		Name		Nat	Born	Pos	Meet	Venue	Date

MARATHON

Mark		Name		Nat	Born	Pos	Meet	Venue	Date
2:20:38	LW		Zhou Chunxiu	CHN	15.11.78	1		London	22 Apr
2:21:37	LW	Mizuki	Noguchi	JPN	3.7.78	1		Tokyo	18 Nov
2:21:45	LW	Getenesh	Wami	ETH	11.12.74	2		London	22 Apr
2:23:09	LW	Paula	Radcliffe	GBR	17.12.73	1		New York	4 Nov
2:23:12	L		Wei Yanan	CHN	6.12.81	1		Seoul	18 Mar
2:23:17	L		Wami			1		Berlin	30 Sep
2:23:31	LW	Salina	Kosgei	KEN	16.11.76	2		Tokyo	18 Nov
2:23:32	LW		Wami			2		New York	4 Nov
2:23:48	LW	Yumiko	Hara	JPN	9.1.82	1		Osaka	28 Jan
2:23:55	LW	Constantina	Tomescu	ROM	23.1.70	3		London	22 Apr
2:24:13	LW		Kosgei			4		London	22 Apr
2:24:39	LW	Mari	Ozaki	JPN	16.7.75	2		Osaka	28 Jan
2:24:43	LW	Yuri	Kano (10)	JPN	27.10.78	3		Osaka	28 Jan
2:24:46	LW	Lornah	Kiplagat	NED	1.5.74	5		London	22 Apr
2:24:51	L	Irina	Mikitenko	GER	23.8.72	2		Berlin	30 Sep
2:25:07	LW	Magarsa	Askale Tafa	ETH	27.9.84	1		Paris	15 Apr
2:25:08	L	Souad	Aït Salem	ALG	6.1.79	1		Roma	18 Mar
2:25:36	L	Pamela	Chepchumba	KEN	8.3.79	1		Milano	2 Dec
2:25:41	LW	Mara	Yamauchi	GBR	13.8.73	6		London	22 Apr
2:26:02	L		Jong Yong-ok	PRK	24.1.81	1		Pyongyang	8 Apr
2:26:08	L		Zhu Xiaolin	CHN	20.2.84	1	NC	Xiamen	31 Mar
2:26:13	LW	Jelena	Prokopcuka	LAT	21.9.76	3		New York	4 Nov
2:26:27	L	Helena (20)	Kiprop Loshanyang	KEN	9.9.76	3		Berlin	30 Sep
2:26:37	L	Hiromi	Ominami	JPN	15.11.75	1		Rotterdam	15 Apr
2:26:46	L	Hellen	Kimutai	KEN	28.12.77	2		Roma	18 Mar
2:26:52	L	Dire	Tune	ETH	19.6.85	1		Houston	14 Jan
2:26:54	L	Irina	Timofeyeva	RUS	5.4.70	4		Berlin	30 Sep
2:26:56	L		Kim Kum-ok	PRK	9.12.85	2		Pyongyang	8 Apr
2:27:02	D	Lenah	Cheruiyot	KEN	1.3.73	1		Venezia	28 Oct
2:27:05	L		Chen Rong	CHN-J	18.5.88	1		Beijing	21 Oct
2:27:19	L		Askale Tafa			1		Dubai	12 Jan
2:27:20	L		Zhang Yingying	CHN-Y	4.1.90	2		Beijing	21 Oct
2:27:25	L	Rose	Cheruiyot	KEN	21.7.76	2		Seoul	18 Mar
2:27:35	LW	Bruna (33/30)	Genovese	ITA	24.9.76	3		Tokyo	18 Nov
2:27:46	L		Bai Xue	CHN-J	13.12.88	3		Beijing	21 Oct
2:27:49	LW	Alevtina	Ivanova	RUS	22.5.75	1		Nagano	15 Apr
2:28:03	D	Shitaye	Gemeche	ETH	17.6.80	1		Treviso (dh 96m)	25 Mar
2:28:16	L	Magdeline	Chemjor	KEN	12.11.78	1		Amsterdam	21 Oct
2:28:17	D	Anikó	Kálovics	HUN	13.5.77	1		Carpi (dh 100m)	21 Oct
2:28:22	LW	Gulnara	Vygovskaya	RUS	6.9.80	2		Paris	15 Apr
2:28:25	L		Jo Bun-hui	PRK	29.11.79	3		Pyongyang	8 Apr
2:28:27	D	Anne	Kosgei Chepkemboi	KEN	.80	2		Venezia	28 Oct
2:28:33	L	Naoko	Sakamoto	JPN	14.11.80	5		Berlin	30 Sep
2:28:37	LW	Lidiya (40)	Grigoryeva	RUS	21.1.74	4		New York	4 Nov
2:28:39	LW	Akemi	Ozaki	JPN	12.10.77	4		Tokyo	18 Nov
2:28:47	L		Zhu Yingying	CHN-J	18.8.88	4		Beijing	21 Oct
2:28:49	LW	Yasuko	Hashimoto	JPN	12.8.75	1		Nagoya	11 Mar
2:28:53	L	Helena	Javornik	SLO	26.3.66	3		Roma	18 Mar
2:28:54	L		Pyo Un-suk	PRK	13.6.81	4		Pyongyang	8 Apr
2:28:54	LW	Christelle	Daunay	FRA	5.12.74	3		Paris	15 Apr
2:28:55	LW	Harumi	Hiroyama	JPN	2.9.68	2		Nagoya	11 Mar
2:28:56	L	Melanie	Kraus	GER	24.10.74	1		Frankfurt	28 Oct
2:29:01	L	Silviya	Skvortsova	RUS	16.11.74	1		Las Vegas	2 Dec
2:29:08	D	Atsede (50)	Bayisa	ETH	16.4.87	1		Istanbul	28 Oct
2:29:08	LW	Catherine	Ndereba	KEN	21.7.72	5		New York	4 Nov
2:29:11	LW	Asha	Gigi	ETH	15.10.73	4		Paris	15 Apr
2:29:12	L	Svetlana	Zakharova	RUS	15.9.70	2		Frankfurt	28 Oct
2:29:12	L	Kirsten Melkevik	Otterbu	NOR	29.5.70	3		Frankfurt	28 Oct
2:29:14	L	Ayelech	Worku	ETH	12.6.79	1		Hamburg	29 Apr
2:29:20	L	Alina	Ivanova	RUS	16.3.69	1		Dublin	29 Oct
2:29:22	L	Rose	Kerubo	KEN	28.10.76	2		Hamburg	29 Apr
2:29:24	LW	Takami	Ominami	JPN	15.11.75	3		Nagoya	11 Mar
2:29:27	L		Sun Weiwei	CHN	13.1.85	2	NC	Xiamen	31 Mar
2:29:28	L	Lidia (60)	Simon	ROM	4.9.73	1		Shanghai	25 Nov

Mark			Name	Nat	Born	Pos	Meet	Venue	Date
2:29:32	L		Lee Eun-jung	KOR	21.4.81	1		Seoul	4 Nov
2:29:33	L	Hellen	Cherono	KEN	22.2.84	3		Seoul	18 Mar
2:29:33	L	Sabrina	Mockenhaupt	GER	6.12.80	1		Köln	7 Oct
2:29:34	LW	Miki	Ohira	JPN	28.6.81	4		Nagoya	11 Mar
2:29:34	L	Lyubov	Morgunova	RUS	14.1.71	3		Nagano	15 Apr
2:29:37	L	Luminita	Zaituc	GER	9.10.68	1		Düsseldorf	6 May
2:29:38	LW	Julia	Mombi	KEN	25.1.85	5		Nagoya	11 Mar
2:29:41	L	Jemimah	Chelagat	KEN	.85	4		Frankfurt	28 Oct
2:29:47	LW	Benita	Johnson	AUS	6.5.79	7		London	22 Apr
2:30:08	L		Kim Chol-sun	PRK		5		Pyongyang	8 Apr
		(70)							
2:30:08	L	Mary	Ptikany	KEN	.78	1		Essen	13 May
2:30:09	LW	Haruko	Okamoto	JPN	19.8.74	6		Nagoya	11 Mar
2:30:10	L	Dorota	Gruca	POL	5.12.70	2		Amsterdam	21 Oct
2:30:12	L	Thabita	Tsatsa	ZIM	18.9.72	4		Seoul	18 Mar
2:30:14	L	Beáta	Rakonczai	HUN	25.6.77	2		Houston	14 Jan
2:30:16	DW	Madai	Pérez	MEX	2.2.80	3		Boston	16 Apr
2:30:22	D	Ornella	Ferrara	ITA	17.4.68	2		Carpi	21 Oct
2:30:30	L	Shiru	Deriba	ETH		4		Amsterdam	21 Oct
2:30:31	L	Natalya	Volgina	RUS	15.3.77	5		Roma	18 Mar
2:30:34	LW	Yuko	Manabe	JPN	8.2.79	7		Nagoya	11 Mar
		(80)							
2:30:35	D	Vincenza	Sicari	ITA	19.3.79	1		Padova	22 Apr
2:30:40	L	Lisa	Hunter-Galvan	NZL	25.6.69	5		Amsterdam	21 Oct
2:30:43	L	Hayley	Haining	GBR	6.3.72	6		Berlin	30 Sep
2:30:44	LW	Liz	Yelling	GBR	5.12.74	8		London	22 Apr
2:30:45	D	Justyna	Bak	POL	1.8.74	3		Carpi	21 Oct
2:30:46	L	Beatrice	Omwanza	KEN	24.2.74	3		Hamburg	29 Apr
2:30:55	LW	Reiko	Tosa	JPN	11.6.76	3	WCh	Osaka	2 Sep
2:30:56	L	Worknesh	Tola	ETH	3.6.77	5		Seoul	18 Mar
2:31:01	L	Hitomi	Niiya	JPN-J	26.2.88	1		Tokyo	18 Feb
2:31:02	L	Alevtina	Biktimirova	RUS	10.9.82	3		Rotterdam	15 Apr
		(90)							
2:31:04	LW	Kazue	Ogoshi	JPN	2.3.81	4		Osaka	28 Jan
2:31:08	LW	Mika	Okunaga	JPN	27.10.82	8		Nagoya	11 Mar
2:31:10	D	Malgorzata	Sobanska	POL	25.4.69	2		Istanbul	28 Oct
2:31:12	LW	Irene	Jerotich	KEN	.82	5		Paris	15 Apr
2:31:12	D	Olga	Glok	RUS	6.12.82	3		Istanbul	28 Oct
2:31:13	L	Zivile	Balciunaité	LTU	3.4.79	4		Hamburg	29 Apr
2:31:14	L		Zhang Shujing	CHN	13.9.78	3	NC	Xiamen	31 Mar
2:31:14	L		An Un-suk	PRK		6		Pyongyang	8 Apr
2:31:16	L	Maria Elena	Valencia	MEX	25.5.83	1	NC	Torreón	4 Mar
2:31:25	L	Leila	Aman	ETH	24.11.77	5		Hamburg	29 Apr
		(100)							

2:31:29	L		Zhang Xin	CHN-J	8.6.89	21 Oct
2:31:31	L	Marisa	Barros	POR	25.2.80	21 Oct
2:31:35	LW	Yuka	Ezaki	JPN	20.10.81	28 Jan
2:31:37	LW	Tomoko	Shimokawa	JPN	21.11.86	11 Mar
2:31:40	LW	Kiyoko	Shimahara	JPN	22.12.76	2 Sep
2:31:41	L	Leonor	Carneiro	POR	18.5.78	30 Sep
2:31:42	L	Larisa	Zyusko	RUS	27.4.69	29 Oct
2:31:43	L	Adenech	Zekiros	ETH	28.6.76	14 Jan
2:31:43	D	Soumiya	Labani	MAR	3.2.75	25 Mar
2:31:57	L	Lioudmila	Kortchaguina	CAN	26.7.71	27 May
2:32:01	L		Chae Eun-hee	KOR	20.7.82	18 Mar
2:32:03	LW	Rita	Jeptoo	KEN	15.2.81	2 Sep
2:32:10	L	Edith	Masai	KEN	4.4.67	29 Apr
2:32:10	L	Hilda	Kibet	KEN	27.3.81	21 Oct
2:32:14	L		Chang Jin-sook	KOR	10.1.83	1 Apr
2:32:21	L	Luminita	Talpos	ROM	9.10.72	29 Apr
2:32:24	L		Jang Hyon-ok	PRK		8 Apr
2:32:28	L	Martha	Markos	ETH	.85	21 Oct
2:32:33	LW	Alina	Gherasim	ROM	16.11.71	11 Mar
2:32:33	D	Liliya	Yadzhak	RUS	14.11.70	28 Oct
2:32:35	L		Kim Jong-hyang	PRK-J	7.2.88	8 Apr
2:32:41	L	Ulrike	Maisch	GER	21.1.77	28 Oct
2:32:48	L	Martha	Komu	KEN	23.3.83	21 Oct
2:32:50	D	Svetlana	Prétot	FRA	3.7.71	3 Jun
2:32:54	L	Merima	Denboba	ETH	21.8.74	14 Jan
2:33:00	P	Masayo	Kobayashi	JPN	4.2.80	9 Sep
2:33:08			Xie Sainan	CHN	3.11.86	11 Nov
2:33:10	L	Nailia	Yulamanova	RUS	6.9.80	13 May
2:33:11	L		Yang Fengxia	CHN-J	.89	21 Oct
2:33:19	P	Svetlana	Ponomarenko	RUS	28.11.69	4 Nov
2:33:22	L	Ayumi	Hayashi	JPN	7.6.82	1 Jul
2:33:25	L		Kim Sun-yong	PRK	5.8.80	8 Apr
2:33:25	LW	Susanne	Hahn	GER	23.4.78	15 Apr
2:33:25	L	Tsege	Worku	ETH	19.1.82	28 Oct
2:33:27	D	Mula	Seboka	ETH	13.1.84	3 Jun
2:33:27	L	Susanne	Pumper	AUT	1.9.70	7 Oct
2:33:27	L	Pamela	Kiyara	KEN	5.11.84	29 Oct
2:33:30	D	Lucilla	Andreucci	ITA	19.12.69	22 Apr
2:33:40	L		Lim Yon-hui	PRK		8 Apr
2:33:47	LW	Nuta	Olaru	ROM	28.8.70	28 Jan
2:33:48	L	Karina	Pérez	MEX	4.10.82	16 Dec
2:33:49	L	Berhane	Adere	ETH	21.7.73	7 Oct
2:33:50	LW	Yuko	Machida	JPN	11.8.80	11 Mar
2:33:51	LW	Yukako	Goto	JPN	16.9.73	28 Jan
2:33:52	L	Adriana	Pârtea	ROM	31.1.80	7 Oct
2:33:57	LW	Ayumi	Nakayama	JPN	10.9.85	11 Mar
2:33:58	L	Claudia	Dreher	GER	2.5.71	29 Apr
2:33:58	LW	Nina	Rillstone	NZL	15.4.75	2 Sep
2:33:59	L		Song Il-ok	PRK		8 Apr
2:34:00	L	Lucy	Muhami	KEN		16 Dec
2:34:03	LW	Miyuki	Ando	JPN	25.3.80	28 Jan
2:34:10	L	Yulia	Arfipova	UZB	7.3.81	28 Oct
2:34:14	LW	Mika	Hikichi	JPN	7.2.82	18 Nov
2:34:15	LW	Yoko	Shibui	JPN	14.3.79	28 Jan
2:34:15	L	María José	Pueyo	ESP	16.3.70	29 Apr
2:34:25	LW	Inga	Abitova	RUS	6.3.82	22 Apr
2:34:43	L	Oksana	Kuzmicheva	RUS	20.10.72	21 Oct
2:34:43	D	Genet	Selomie Kassa	ETH	.86	21 Oct

Mark Name Nat Born Pos Meet Venue Date

2:34:48	L	Fatima	Cabral	POR	14.1.72	29	Apr
2:34:50	LW	Asami	Nishizawa-Obi	JPN	22.3.76	28	Jan
2:34:50	L	Natalya	Kravets-Kulesh	BLR	25.5.78	7	Oct
2:34:50		Anzhelika	Averkova	UKR	13.3.69	21	Oct
2:34:52	L	Caroline	Kwambai	KEN	9.9.75	15	Apr
2:34:52	D	Ivana	Iozzia	ITA	18.2.73	28	Oct
2:34:58		Tetyana	Filonyuk	UKR	5.4.84	28	Oct
2:34:59	LW	Naoko	Uchida	JPN	25.12.81	11	Mar
2:35:00	L	Annemette	Aagard	DEN	11.4.72	29	Apr
2:35:00	L		Fang Guangxia	CHN		21	Oct
2:35:00	L	Marcella	Mancini	ITA	5.9.71	2	Dec
2:35:01	L	Haile Lemma	Kebelush	ETH	.86	18	Mar
2:35:01	L	Caroline Cheptanui	Kilel	KEN	21.3.81	18	Mar
2:35:01	L	Renata	Paradowska	POL	14.6.70	21	Oct
2:35:08	L	Anna	Rahm	SWE	12.10.81	29	Apr
2:35:09	DW	Deena	Kastor	USA	14.2.73	16	Apr
2:35:12	LW	Zahia	Dahmani	FRA	2.6.72	15	Apr
2:35:13	L	Jessica	Rodríguez	MEX	9.9.76	4	Mar
2:35:14	L	Emily Chepar	Kimuria	KEN	10.6.75	29	Apr
2:35:15	LW	Elva	Dryer	USA	26.9.71	4	Nov
2:35:18	L		Zeng Guang	CHN	9.5.86	21	Oct
2:35:21	L	Petra	Teveli	HUN	1.11.79	2	Dec
2:35:24	L		Jang Ok-ran	PRK		8	Apr
2:35:25	L		Choi Kyung-hee	KOR	13.9.81	28	Oct
2:35:25		Emily Samoei	Chepkemei	KEN	.80	9	Dec
2:35:28		Stefania	Benedetti	ITA	6.9.69	9	Dec
2:35:30	L	Hilaria	Johannes	NAM	13.8.80	29	Oct
2:35:33			Dai Yanyan	CHN	8.1.80	6	May
2:35:39	L	Abebe	Tola Eda	ETH	3.6.77	12	Jan
2:35:40		Mary	Akor	USA	25.9.76	17	Jun
2:35:46	L	Olivera	Jevtic	SRB	24.7.77	21	Apr
2:35:46	L	Yelena	Samokhvalova	RUS	21.11.80	29	Oct
2:35:47	LW	María	Abel	ESP	23.10.74	15	Apr
2:35:48	L	Angélica	Sánchez	MEX	11.12.75	4	Mar
2:35:50	P	Claudia	Camargo	ARG	30.3.71	6	May
2:35:51	LW	Maya	Nishio	JPN	19.12.78	11	Mar
2:35:51	D	Sisay	Measo Ardese	ETH	.80	25	Mar
2:35:53	L		Yun Sun-sook	KOR	28.5.72	21	Oct
2:35:56	P	Tatyana	Petrova	RUS	8.4.83	9	Dec
2:35:57	L	Angéline	Flückiger-Joly	SUI	28.2.74	30	Sep
2:36:05		Elizabeth	Chemweno	KEN	13.7.78	1	Apr
2:36:14	L	Patricia	Retiz (200)	MEX	17.3.71	4	Mar
2:36:15	L	Kate	O'Neill	USA	29.7.80	7	Oct
2:36:15	L	Irene	Mogaka	KEN	.85	2	Dec

Best on non-downhill course

2:29:24 L Anikó Kálovics HUN 13.5.77 1 Torino 15 Apr

Excessively downhill: 2:36:06 Deeja Youngqvist USA 30.3.77 6 Oct

JUNIORS

See main list for top 5 juniors. 10 performances by 10 women to 2:38:10. Additional marks and further juniors:

Mark		Name	Nat	Born	Pos	Venue	Date
2:31:29	L	Zhang Xin	CHN	8.6.89	6	Beijing	21 Oct
2:32:35	L	Kim Jong-hyang	PRK	7.2.88	8	Pyongyang	8 Apr
2:33:11	L	Yang Fengxia	CHN	.89	8	Beijing	21 Oct
2:37:00	L	Pak Jong-nyo	KOR-Y	10.7.90	14	Pyongyang	8 Apr
2:38:10	(10)	Zheng Wenrong	CHN	26.11.88	3	Shanghai	25 Nov
2:39:29		He Pan	CHN	1.5.88	2	Hangzhou	11 Nov
2:39:37		Liu Nian	CHN	26.4.88	3	Hangzhou	11 Nov
2:41:22	L	Su Qian	CHN	4.11.88	15	Beijing	21 Oct

100 KILOMETRES

Mark	Name		Nat	Born	Pos	Meet	Venue	Date
7:00:27	Norimi	Sakurai	JPN	20.4.71	1	WCp	Winschoten	8 Sep
7:16:23		Sakurai			1		Yubetsu	24 Jun
7:23:50	Hiroko	Sho	JPN	10.10.70	2		Yubetsu	24 Jun
7:26:44	Laurence	Klein (Fricotteaux)	FRA	22.1.69	2	WCp	Winschoten	8 Sep
7:27:12		Sho			3	WCp	Winschoten	8 Sep
7:39:18	Marina	Myshlyanova	RUS	16.6.66	4	WCp	Winschoten	8 Sep
7:40:36	Monica	Carlin	ITA	20.6.71	5	WCp	Winschoten	8 Sep
7:42:51	Magali	Reymonenq-Maggiolini	FRA	21.5.69	6	WCp	Winschoten	8 Sep
7:47:02	Birgit	Schönherr-Hölscher	GER	16.8.68	7	WCp	Winschoten	8 Sep
7:50:56	Martina	Gross	GER	24.1.60	8	WCp	Winschoten	8 Sep
7:51:54	Kami	Semick	USA	6.7.66	9	WCp	Winschoten	8 Sep
7:52:11		Schönherr-Hölscher			1	NC	Kienbaum	24 Mar
7:52:45	Helena	Crossan (10)	IRL	11.5.67	10	WCp	Winschoten	8 Sep
7:53:48	Marija	Vrajic	CRO	23.9.76	1	ITA Ch	Tarquinia	10 Nov
7:54:02	Paola	Sanna	ITA	19.3.77	2	NC	Tarquinia	10 Nov
7:54:21	Adela	Salt	GBR	18.2.73	11	WCp	Winschoten	8 Sep
7:57:32	Kazuho	Izutsu	JPN	16.10.62	12	WCp	Winschoten	8 Sep
	(17/14)							
8:01:59	Yoko	Yamazawa	JPN	7.1.68	3		Yubetsu	24 Jun
8:02:48	Patricia	Signorio-Baldacchino	FRA	3.2.63	13	WCp	Winschoten	8 Sep
8:06:20	Devon	Crosby-Helms	USA	23.6.82	15	WCp	Winschoten	8 Sep
8:09:04	Julie	Udchachon	USA	14.7.70	1		Madison	7 Apr
8:10:00	Karine	Herry	FRA	2.1.68	1	NC	Chavagnes-en-Paillers	19 May

8:11:33	Kazuko	Kono	JPN	.52?	24	Jun
8:14:46	Marion	Braun	GER	2.7.57	8	Sep
8:15:14	Connie	Gardner	USA	6.11.63	8	Sep
8:16:17	Carolyn	Smith	USA	4.6.65	8	Sep
8:16:21	Giovanna	Cavalli	ITA	7.5.59	8	Sep
8:16:43	Nadezhda	Karaseva	RUS	18.12.60	21	Apr
8:18:23 ?	Miho	Miyamoto	JPN	.81	24	Jun
8:18:33	Daniela	Da Forno	ITA	17.12.68	8	Sep
8:18:55	Mariko	Ozawa	JPN	28.7.66	8	Sep
8:20:28	Tazu	Isikawa (29)	JPN	28.9.75	24	Jun

24 HOURS

Mark		Name		Nat	Born	Pos	Meet	Venue	Date
236.848		Lyudmila	Kalinina	RUS	12.12.68	1	WCh	Drummondville	29 Jul
233.773		Connie	Gardner	USA	6.11.63	1	NC	Grapevine	18 Nov
233.307	t		Kalinina			1	EC	Madrid	6 May
233.137		Brigitte	Bec	FRA	7.4.64	2	WCh	Drummondville	29 Jul
232.920		Sumie	Inagaki	JPN	6.4.66	1		Soochow	25 Nov

Mark		Name		Nat	Born	Pos	Meet	Venue	Date
232.417		Michaela	Dimitriadu	CZE	23.12.73	1		Kladno	5 Aug
230.288		Galina	Yeremina	RUS	14.2.53	3	WCh	Drummondville	29 Jul
222.657		Karine	Herry	FRA	2.1.68	1	NC	Montigny-en-Gohelle	8 Apr
222.541		Irina	Reutovich	RUS	21.1.50	1		Sankt-Peterburg	2 Sep
221.940		Monica	Casiraghi	ITA	4.4.69	1		Monaco	25 Nov
221.383		Yasuko	Kanehira (10)	JPN	.55	4	WCh	Drummondville	29 Jul
220.312		Anne-Marie (12/11)	Vernet	FRA	15.12.67	1		Aulnat	11 Nov
217.776		Monique	Muhlen	LUX	31.10.52	5	WCh	Drummondville	29 Jul
216.402		Mary	Larsson	SWE	10.2.60	1		Apeldoorn	19 May
215.259		Kimie	Noto	JPN	10.1.52	6	WCh	Drummondville	29 Jul
213.410		Monika	Belau	GER	25.7.54	7	WCh	Drummondville	29 Jul
212.226	t	Sharon	Gayter	GBR	30.10.63	1		London (TB)	7 Oct
211.375			Chiou Shu-Jung	TPE	27.7.57	2		Soochow	25 Nov
211.167		Laurie	McGrath	CAN	7.12.67	8		Drummondville	28 Jul
210.749		Hiroko	Okiyama	JPN	21.4.62	3		Soochow	25 Nov
210.721	t	Rosario	Muñoz	ESP	5.5.61	3	EC	Madrid	6 May

Mark	Name		Nat	Born	Date
209.605 t	Irina	Koval	RUS	19.11.58	12 May
205.594	Christine	Bodet	FRA	8.5.58	8 Apr
204.604	Mami	Kudo	JPN	.64	25 Nov
204.595	Debra	Horn	USA	.59	18 Nov
204.566	Takao	Furuyama	JPN	.53	29 Jul
204.370	Carilyn	Johnson	USA	.67	18 Nov
204.236	Ilse	Sandberger	AUT	25.5.60	22 Jul
204.92	Marika	Heinlein	GER	.62	19 May
203.554t	Torill Fonn	Hartikainen	SWE	.67	6 May
203.174	Martine	Bertin	FRA	10.5.51	8 Apr
202.425t	Monika	Moling	ITA	4.2.74	23 Sep
201.965t	Vicky	Skelton	GBR	4.11.67	7 Oct
201.462t	Masae	Kamura	JPN	4.4.58	12 May
201.452	Jacqueline	Olivier	FRA	14.9.65	16 Sep
201.240t	Lorena	De Vito	ITA	2.11.62	6 May
200.835	Riyoko	Motoki	JPN	.51	25 Nov
200.478	Valery	Muskett	NZL	.54	29 Jul

Best track times

Mark	Name	Pos	Meet	Venue	Date
217.989	Casiraghi	2	EC	Madrid	6 May
210.208	Yeremina	1		Surgères	12 May

Indoors

Mark	Name		Nat	Born	Pos	Venue	Date
213.643	Nina	Mytrofanova	UKR	26.4.57	1	Brno	17 Mar
211.347	Sharon	Broadwell	NOR	10.11.61	1	Oslo	9 Dec
208.347	Edit	Bérces	HUN	16.5.64			9 Dec
201.350	Outi	Siimes	FIN	19.6.71			2 Dec

2000 METRES STEEPLECHASE

Mark	Name		Nat	Born	Pos	Meet	Venue	Date
6:20.66	Carrie	Messner-Vickers	USA	7.6.77	1		Nashville	5 May
6:22.30	Caroline	Chepkurui	KEN-Y	12.3.90	1	WY	Ostrava	14 Jul
6:22.49	Christine	Mayanga	KEN-Y	21.3.91	2	WY	Ostrava	14 Jul
6:25.30	Karoline Bjerkeli	Grøvdal	NOR-Y	14.6.90	3	WY	Ostrava	14 Jul
6:25.98	Kelly	Strong	USA	27.9.78	1		Seattle	16 Mar
6:26.23	Agnes	Tschurtschentaler	ITA	12.1.82	1		Rovereto	12 Jul
6:26.64	Dobrinka	Shalamanova	BUL	1.5.83	1		Sofia	19 May
6:26.72	Lisa	Galaviz	USA	30.11.79	2		Nashville	5 May
6:26.80	Kristine Eikrem	Engeset	NOR-J	15.11.88	1	NC-j	Tønsberg	4 Aug
6:29.81	Marta	Tigabea	ETH-Y	4.10.90	4	WY	Ostrava	14 Jul

Mark	Name		Nat	Born	Date
6:30.48	Dawn	Cromer	USA	24.11.79	5 May
6:30.8	Hatti	Dean	GBR	2.2.82	13 May
6:31.4A	Mercy	Njoroge	KEN	10.8.86	12 Jun
6:31.59	Polina	Jelizarova	LAT-J	1.5.89	30 Jun
6:32.45	Louise	Webb	GBR-Y	9.2.91	14 Jul
6:32.55	Sarah	Hopkinson	GBR-Y	11.8.91	14 Jul
6:32.69	Netsanet	Achamo	ETH	14.12.87	14 Apr
6:33.49	Sofia	Assefa	ETH	.87	14 Apr
6:33.54	Jessica	Gilfillan	AUS-Y	10.2.92	8 Jun
6:33.91	Kristen	Anderson	USA	16.6.83	5 May

JUNIORS

See main list for top 7 juniors. Further juniors:

Mark	Name		Nat	Born	Pos	Meet	Venue	Date
6:31.59	Polina	Jelizarova	LAT	1.5.89	1	NC-j	Riga	30 Jun
6:32.45	Louise	Webb	GBR-Y	9.2.91	5	WY	Ostrava	14 Jul
6:32.55	Sarah	Hopkinson	GBR-Y	11.8.91	6	WY	Ostrava	14 Jul
6:33.54	Jessica	Gilfillan	AUS-Y	10.2.92	1		Gold Coast	8 Jun
6:36.05	Danelle	Woods	CAN	19.3.89	1		Abbotsford	29 Jul
6:36.25	Diana	Sujew	GER-Y	2.11.90	7	WY	Ostrava	14 Jul
6:37.90	Sarah	Cornelsen	GER-Y	7.7.90	8	WY	Ostrava	14 Jul
6:38.68	Samantha	Carberry	AUS-Y	25.4.91	9	WY	Ostrava	14 Jul
6:39.03	Renata	Krasnova	RUS-Y	21.12.90	10	WY	Ostrava	14 Jul
6:39.36	Jessica	Furlan	CAN-Y	15.3.90	2		Abbotsford	29 Jul

3000 METRES STEEPLECHASE

Mark	Name		Nat	Born	Pos	Meet	Venue	Date
9:06.57	Yekaterina	Volkova	RUS	16.2.78	1	WCh	Osaka	27 Aug
9:09.19	Tatyana	Petrova	RUS	8.4.83	2	WCh	Osaka	27 Aug
9:11.68	Gulnara	Galkina	RUS	9.7.78	1	GP	Athína	2 Jul
9:13.35		Volkova			1	NC	Tula	31 Jul
9:14.35		Petrova			1	NC	Tula	31 Jul
9:14.37		Galkina			1	Znam	Zhukovskiy	9 Jun
9:14.52	Eunice	Jepkorir	KEN	17.2.82	2	GP	Athína	2 Jul
9:19.44		Jepkorir			1	Bisl	Oslo	15 Jun

Mark	Name		Nat	Born	Pos	Meet	Venue	Date
9:20.09		Jepkorir			3	WCh	Osaka	27 Aug
9:24.51	Ruth	Bisibori	KEN-J	2.1.88	1		Daegu	3 Oct
9:25.25		Bisibori			4	WCh	Osaka	27 Aug
9:25.51	Hanane	Ouhaddou	MAR	.82	1	NA	Heusden-Zolder	28 Jul
9:25.84		Jepkorir			1		Neerpelt	2 Jun
9:26.23	Rosa María	Morató	ESP	19.6.79	2	NA	Heusden-Zolder	28 Jul
9:26.25		Liu Nian	CHN-J	26.4.88	1		Wuhan	2 Nov
9:26.55	Yelena	Sidorchenkova	RUS	30.5.80	3	NC	Tula	31 Jul
9:26.63	Donna	MacFarlane (10)	AUS	18.6.77	2	Bisl	Oslo	15 Jun
9:26.80		Volkova			1	GP	Rieti	9 Sep
9:27.51	Sophie	Duarté	FRA	31.7.81	5	WCh	Osaka	27 Aug
9:28.03	Netsanet	Achano	ETH	14.12.87	2		Neerpelt	2 Jun
9:28.29	Roisin	McGettigan	IRL	23.8.80	3	NA	Heusden-Zolder	28 Jul
9:28.47	Veerle	Dejaeghere	BEL	1.8.73	3		Neerpelt	2 Jun
9:28.53	Cristina	Casandra	ROM	1.2.77	1	Vard	Réthimno	18 Jul
9:28.75	Lisa	Galaviz	USA	30.11.79	4	NA	Heusden-Zolder	28 Jul
9:28.86	Korine	Hinds	JAM	18.1.76	3	Bisl	Oslo	15 Jun
9:28.97	Wioletta	Frankiewicz (Janowska)	POL	9.6.77	3	GP	Athína	2 Jul
9:29.01		Duarté			5	NA	Heusden-Zolder	28 Jul
9:29.39		Casandra			1h3	WCh	Osaka	25 Aug
9:29.63		Casandra			6	WCh	Osaka	27 Aug
9:30.00		Volkova			2h3	WCh	Osaka	25 Aug
	(30/18)							
9:31.43	Julie	Coulaud	FRA	7.8.82	4	GP	Athína	2 Jul
9:32.05	Mekdes	Bekele (20)	ETH	20.1.87	5	Bisl	Oslo	15 Jun
9:32.35		Li Zhenzhu	CHN	13.12.85	1	WCT	Suzhou	10 Jun
9:32.36		Zhu Yanmei	CHN	16.10.86	2	WCT	Suzhou	10 Jun
9:33.19	Karoline Bjerkeli	Grøvdal	NOR-Y	14.6.90	4		Neerpelt	2 Jun
9:33.95	Jenny	Barringer	USA	23.8.86	1		Paris	8 Sep
9:34.28	Kristine Eikrem	Engeset	NOR-J	15.11.88	6	Bisl	Oslo	15 Jun
9:34.72	Anna	Willard	USA	31.3.84	2	NC	Indianapolis	23 Jun
9:37.50	Mardrea	Hyman	JAM	22.12.72	7	Bisl	Oslo	15 Jun
9:37.88	Ancuta	Bobocel	ROM	3.10.87	2	Vard	Réthimno	18 Jul
9:38.55	Christin	Johansson	SWE	26.1.78	7	NA	Heusden-Zolder	28 Jul
9:38.56	Hatti	Dean	GBR	2.2.82	3	BrGP	Sheffield	15 Jul
	(30)							
9:38.68	Minori	Hayakari	JPN	29.11.72	8	NA	Heusden-Zolder	28 Jul
9:39.40	Katarzyna	Kowalska	POL	7.4.85	1	EU23	Debrecen	15 Jul
9:39.50	Sigrid	Vanden Bempt	BEL	10.2.81	9	NA	Heusden-Zolder	28 Jul
9:39.95	Lindsey	Anderson	USA	23.5.85	1		Stanford	29 Apr
9:40.41	Élodie	Olivarès	FRA	22.5.76	9	Bisl	Oslo	15 Jun
9:41.11	Elena	Romagnolo	ITA	5.10.82	2	ECp-1B	Milano	23 Jun
9:41.14	Nataliya	Tobias	UKR	22.11.80	1		Kyiv	4 Aug
9:41.36	Fionnuala	Britton	IRL	24.9.84	10	NA	Heusden-Zolder	28 Jul
9:41.59	Helen	Clitheroe	GBR	2.1.74	6	WAF	Stuttgart	22 Sep
9:41.79	Stephanie	De Croock	BEL	4.3.79	11	NA	Heusden-Zolder	28 Jul
	(40)							
9:42.08	Dobrinka	Shalamanova	BUL	1.5.83	3	ECp-1B	Milano	23 Jun
9:42.47	Sara	Moreira	POR	17.10.85	3	EU23	Debrecen	15 Jul
9:42.97	Irini	Kokkinariou	GRE	14.2.81	1	NC	Athína	16 Jun
9:43.02	Mercy	Njoroge	KEN	10.6.86	5	SGP	Doha	11 May
9:43.06	Carrie	Messner-Vickers	USA	7.6.77	3		Thessaloniki	30 Jul
9:43.48	Valentyna	Horpynych	UKR	12.3.83	1		Yalta	13 Jun
9:43.95	Zulema	Fuentes-Pila	ESP	25.5.77	1		Barakaldo	14 Jul
9:45.20	Victoria	Mitchell	AUS	25.4.82	7	SGP	Doha	11 May
9:45.72	Zemzem	Ahmed	ETH	27.12.84	12	NA	Heusden-Zolder	28 Jul
9:45.96	Natalya	Izmodenova	RUS	1.1.81	4	NC	Tula	31 Jul
	(50)							
9:46.12	Turkan	Erismis	TUR	5.1.84	3	WUG	Bangkok	12 Aug
9:46.46	Gladys	Kipkemboi	KEN	15.10.86	12	Bisl	Oslo	15 Jun
9:46.52	Zenaide	Vieira	BRA	25.6.85	6		Neerpelt	2 Jun
9:47.24	Desiraye	Osburn	USA	5.8.84	5	NC	Indianapolis	23 Jun
9:47.41	Diana	Martin	ESP	1.4.81	2		Barakaldo	14 Jul
9:47.68	Kelly	Strong	USA	27.9.78	1		Stanford	31 Mar
9:48.14	Svetlana	Ivanova	RUS	18.8.83	5	NC	Tula	31 Jul
9:48.33		Jin Yuan	CHN-J	11.2.88	2		Eagle Rock	3 Jun
9:48.46	Sofia	Assefa	ETH	.87	13	NA	Heusden-Zolder	28 Jul
9:48.82	Barbara	Parker	GBR	8.11.82	3	NCAA	Sacramento	8 Jun
	(60)							

Mark	Name		Nat	Born	Pos	Meet	Venue	Date
9:48.87	Andrea	Mayr	AUT	15.10.79	1		Regensburg	9 Jun
9:49.03	Maria Teresa	Urbina	ESP	20.3.85	14	NA	Heusden-Zolder	28 Jul
9:50.02	Miranda	Boonstra	NED	29.8.72	16	NA	Heusden-Zolder	28 Jul
9:50.04	Habiba	Ghribi	TUN	9.4.84	1		Bordeaux	5 Jul
9:51.13	Sabine	Heitling	BRA	2.7.87	1	PAm	Rio de Janeiro	28 Jul
9:51.76	Liz	Wort	USA	23.9.83	4	NCAA	Sacramento	8 Jun
9:52.00	Salome	Chepchumba	KEN	29.9.82	8	GPF	Doha	11 May
9:52.10	Kassi	Andersen	USA	25.6.83	5	NCAA	Sacramento	8 Jun
9:53.24	Lauren	Fleshman	USA	26.9.81	1		London (Ha)	11 Aug
9:53.24	Amanda	Lorenzen	USA	16.11.83	1		Hillsdale	10 Jun
	(70)							
9:53.25	Verena	Dreier	GER	15.1.85	10		Neerpelt	2 Jun
9:53.95	Kristin	Anderson	USA	16.6.83	7	NC	Indianapolis	23 Jun
9:55.11	Tebogo	Masehla	RSA	6.10.79	4	AfG	Alger	20 Jul
9:55.19	Élodie	Mouthon	FRA	28.3.87	1h1	EU23	Debrecen	13 Jul
9:55.26	Agnes	Tschurtschentaler	ITA	12.1.82	6	Vard	Réthimno	18 Jul
9:55.43	Talis	Apud	MEX	5.1.82	2	PAm	Rio de Janeiro	28 Jul
9:56.6A	Consolata	Chemutai	KEN		3	NC	Nairobi	16 Jun
9:56.68	Nicole	Bush	USA	4.4.86	6	NCAA	Sacramento	8 Jun
9:57.02	Yoshika	Tatsumi	JPN	26.2.82	2	NC	Osaka	29 Jun
9:57.09	Kara	June	USA	10.8.82	2		Stanford	29 Apr
	(80)							
9:57.50	Irene	Pelayo	ESP	16.2.80	1		Santander	12 Jul
9:57.79	Julia	Hiller	GER	24.7.87	12		Neerpelt	2 Jun
9:57.98	Silje	Fjørtoft	NOR	23.6.87	15	Bisl	Oslo	15 Jun
9:58.08	Kate	McIlroy	NZL	26.8.81	7	Vard	Réthimno	18 Jul
9:58.7A	Mueni	Mutua	KEN-J	.88	4	NC	Nairobi	16 Jun
9:59.04	Oxana	Juravel	MDA	23.2.86	2	ECp-2B	Zenica	23 Jun
9:59.21	Bridget	Franek	USA	8.11.87		PennR	Philadelphia	26 Apr
10:00.09	Tatyana	Vilisova	RUS	27.11.79	2		Bordeaux	5 Jul
10:00.30		Chen Xiaofang	CHN	28.10.81	2	NC	Shijiazhuang	4 Aug
10:01.19	Amy	Fowler	USA	20.7.87	5h1	NCAA	Sacramento	6 Jun
	(90)							
10:01.28	Tina	Brown	GBR	22.8.76	3		Manchester	9 Jun
10:01.53	Lindsey	Allen	USA	30.6.86	6h1	NCAA	Sacramento	6 Jun
10:01.91	Haruna	Mori	JPN	12.4.82	3	NC	Osaka	29 Jun
10:01.94	Meriem	Méred	FRA	4.4.76	9		Villeneuve d'Ascq	9 Jun
10:02.24	Biljana	Jovic	SRB	2.3.85	2h2	EU23	Debrecen	13 Jul
10:02.50	Gwendoline	Desprès	FRA	27.11.83	5	NC	Niort	3 Aug
10:02.63	Irina	Bakhanovskaya	BLR	21.6.85	6h1	EU23	Debrecen	13 Jul
10:02.76		Zhao Yanni	CHN-Y	9.1.91	3	WCT	Suzhou	10 Jun
10:03.18	Yuliya	Ignatova	UKR	30.7.83	3	NC	Donetsk	6 Jul
10:03.2A	Irene	Limika	KEN	28.8.79	5	NC	Nairobi	16 Jun
	(100)							

10:03.23	Dawn	Cromer	USA	24.11.79	23 Jun
10:03.54	Claire	Entwistle	GBR	9.12.76	9 Jun
10:03.77	Emily	Brown	USA	6.7.84	31 Mar
10:03.91	Polina	Jelizarova	LAT-J	1.5.89	21 Jul
10:04.05	Lenka	Ptácková	CZE	14.1.85	9 Jun
10:05.22	Sariah	Long	USA	7.12.85	8 Jun
10:05.37	Marcela	Lustigová	CZE	11.11.82	26 May
10:05.43	Carolin	Lang	GER	28.2.86	2 Jun
10:05.95	Susanne	Lutz	GER	26.3.87	2 Jun
10:06.43		Wang Huan	CHN-J	12.1.89	2 Nov
10:06.45	Catherine	Parker	USA		6 Jun
10:06.54	Bouchra	Chaabi	MAR	22.9.80	18 May
10:06.74	Gladys	Chemweno	KEN-J	4.7.88	28 Jun
10:07.09	A'Havahla	Haynes	USA	1.3.84	8 Jun
10:07.25	Lindsay	Sundell	USA		26 May
10:07.30	Trina	Cox	USA	15.7.80	20 Apr
10:07.41	Jo	Ankier	GBR	5.8.82	9 Jun
10:07.72	Delilah	DiCrescenzo	USA	28.2.83	20 Apr
10:07.72A	Caroline	Chepkirui	KEN-Y	12.3.90	28 Jul
10:07.90	Clarisse	Cruz	POR	9.7.78	28 Jun
10:08.47	Brooke	Bennett	USA	13.3.85	6 Jun
10:08.54	Marnie	Ponton	AUS	16.3.84	3 Feb
10:08.64	Sarah	Madebach	USA	7.10.85	26 May
10:08.8A	Esther	Chebor	KEN	21.4.81	14 Jun
10:09.4A	Jane	Murage	KEN		3 Jun
10:09.53	Patricia	Lobo	BRA	6.4.83	22 Jun
10:09.57	Oksana	Ilyutchik	UKR	20.10.87	6 Jul
10:09.96	Jane	Rudkin	USA	15.5.80	3 Jun
10:10.01	Iwona	Lewandowska	POL	19.5.85	1 Jul

10:10.05		Xu Yinuo	CHN-J	23.12.88	2 Nov
10:10.06	Beatrice	Kiprop	KEN-J	7.8.89	12 Aug
10:10.57	Selien	De Schryder	BEL	10.11.86	19 May
10:10.59	Olga	Gorshkova	RUS	3.9.83	31 Jul
10:10.69	Rosa	Godoy	ARG	19.3.82	28 Apr
10:10.77	Heidi	Bouwhuis	USA	27.4.83	6 Jun
10:11.00	Agata	Drozdz	POL	15.5.84	1 Jul
10:11.03	Bethany	Nickless	USA	4.10.85	26 May
10:11.18	María	Pardaloú	GRE	21.4.84	16 Jun
10:12.02	Eva	Arias	ESP	8.10.80	30 Jun
10:12.56	Ángela	Figueroa	COL	28.6.84	14 Jul
10:12.60	Ulrika	Johansson	SWE	9.2.75	9 Sep
10:12.71	Tsehaye	Dagnachew	USA	26.6.85	12 May
10:13.0A	Jackline	Cheruto	UGA-Y	30.6.91	15 Jun
10:13.33	Shauneen	Garrahan	USA		25 May
10:13.45	Jillian	Sullivan	USA	19.7.85	5 May
10:13.58		Lu Minhong	CHN	25.10.86	10 Jun
10:13.72	Brianna	Dahm	USA	13.3.82	21 Jun
10:13.98	Danelle	Woods	CAN-J	19.3.89	7 Jul
10:14.52	Ljiljana	Culibrk	CRO	27.10.82	23 Jun
10:14.53	Arianne	Field	USA	8.11.84	6 Jun
10:14.63A	Thandi	Malindi	RSA	10.7.87	24 Feb
10:14.63	Alicia	Valtin	USA	25.3.84	26 May
10:14.66		Fang Xiaoyu	CHN	6.3.87	2 Nov
10:15.76	Julia	Rudd	USA	14.2.83	21 Jun
10:15.83	Stephanie	García	USA-J	3.5.88	26 May
10:16.78	Justyna	Mudy	POL	20.10.84	1 Jul
10:16.84	Aurélie	Casado	FRA	6.6.80	19 Jun
10:16.99	Amanda	King	NZL	31.7.84	5 May

Mark	Name		Nat	Born	Date
10:17.16	Simret	Restle	GER	4.5.84	19 Aug
10:17.26	Rachel	Carrizales	USA	29.11.86	6 Jun
10:17.30	Tirhas	Gebre	ETH-J		12 Aug
10:17.96	Stephanie	Pezzullo	USA		2 Jun
10:18.0A	Regina	Cherotich	KEN		21 Apr
10:18.48	Zsofia	Erdelyi	HUN	10.12.87	23 Jun
10:18.72	Irina	Orlova	RUS	28.12.85	19 Jun
10:18.76	Sudha	Singh	IND	25.6.86	25 Oct
10:18.83	Elena	Linn	USA	14.2.86	20 Apr
10:18.89	Stacie	Lifferth	USA	17.6.86	20 Apr
10:18.95	Maiko	Yamaguchi	JPN	19.5.82	15 Jul
10:19.12	Yasuko	Kitano	JPN	28.7.84	29 Jun
10:19.41	Emma	Quaglia	ITA	15.8.80	7 Jul
10:19.55	Andrea	Deelstra	NED	6.3.85	9 Jun
10:19.7A	Josephine	Kimuyu	KEN-J	.88	16 Jun
10:19.89	Sara	Trané	SWE	16.8.85	12 May
10:19.94	Michele	da Costa	BRA	23.1.79	20 May
10:20.00	Brittany	Somers (176)	USA	1.6.85	28 Apr

JUNIORS

See main list for top 7 juniors. 11 performances by 5 women to 9:50.0. Additional marks and further juniors:

Bisibori 2+	9:31.20	5h3	WCh	Osaka	29 Aug	9:31.99	1	AfG	Alger	20 Jul
Grøvdal	9:40.47	10	Bisl	Oslo	15 Jun	9:44.34	1	EJ	Hengelo	21 Jul
Engeset	9:47.35	2	EJ	Hengelo	21 Jul					

10:03.91	Polina	Jelizarova	LAT	1.5.89	3	EJ	Hengelo	21 Jul
10:06.43		Wang Huan	CHN	12.1.89	3		Wuhan	2 Nov
10:06.74	Gladys	Chemweno (10)	KEN	4.7.88	8		Luzern	28 Jun
10:07.72A	Caroline	Chepkirui	KEN-Y	12.3.90	4	WCT	Nairobi	28 Jul
10:10.05		Xu Yinuo	CHN	23.12.88	4		Wuhan	2 Nov
10:10.06	Beatrice	Kiprop	KEN	7.8.89	2	Afr-J	Ouagadougou	12 Aug
10:13.0A	Jackline	Cheruto	UGA-Y	30.6.91	2h1	NC	Nairobi	15 Jun
10:13.98	Danelle	Woods	CAN	19.3.89	1	PAm-J	São Paulo	7 Jul
10:15.83	Stephanie	García	USA	3.5.88	8	NCAA-r	Gainesville	26 May
10:17.30	Tirhas	Gebre	ETH		3	Afr-J	Ouagadougou	12 Aug
10:19.7A	Josephine	Kimuyu	KEN	.88	7	NC	Nairobi	16 Jun
10:20.43		Zhu Liping	CHN	8.5.88	6		Suzhou	10 Jun
10:20.64	Sarah	Hopkinson (20)	GBR-Y	11.8.91	6	NC	Manchester	29 Ju

60 METRES HURDLES INDOORS

7.84	Susanna	Kallur	SWE	16.2.81	1h1	EI	Birmingham	2 Mar
7.85		Kallur			1h1	Spark	Stuttgart	3 Feb
7.86	Gail	Devers	USA	19.11.66	1r2	Mill	New York	2 Feb
7.87	Lolo	Jones	USA	5.8.82	1		Karlsruhe	11 Feb
7.87		Kallur			1	EI	Birmingham	2 Mar
7.88		Kallur			1	Spark	Stuttgart	3 Feb
7.88		Jones			1	NC	Boston (R)	25 Feb
	(7/3)							
7.90	Priscilla	Lopes	CAN	26.8.82	1		Paris (B)	23 Feb
7.90	Irina	Shevchenko	RUS	2.9.75	2h1	EI	Birmingham	2 Mar
7.91	Joanna	Hayes	USA	23.12.76	2r2	Mill	New York	2 Feb
7.91	Josephine	Onyia	NGR/ESP	15.7.86	1h2		Valencia	10 Feb
7.91	Lacena	Golding-Clarke	JAM	20.3.75	2		Karlsruhe	11 Feb
7.92	Danielle	Carruthers	USA	22.12.79	2	NC	Boston (R)	25 Feb
7.93	Aleksandra	Antonova	RUS	24.3.80	1		Pireás	24 Feb
	(10)							
7.93	Nichole	Denby	USA	10.10.82	3	NC	Boston (R)	25 Feb
7.96	Perdita	Felicien	CAN	29.8.80	4r2	Mill	New York	2 Feb
7.97	Reina-Flor	Okori	FRA	2.5.80	1s2	NC	Aubière	18 Feb
7.97	Kirsten	Bolm	GER	4.3.75	3	EI	Birmingham	2 Mar
7.98	Vonette	Dixon	JAM	26.11.75	3	Spark	Stuttgart	3 Feb
7.98	Shantia	Moss	USA	27.10.85	1	NCAA	Fayetteville	9 Mar
7.99	Anay	Tejeda	CUB	3.4.83	2		Pireás	24 Feb
8.00	Nevin	Yanit	TUR	16.2.86	1h1	NC	Gent	18 Feb
8.00	Jessica	Ohanaja	NGR	6.12.86	2	NCAA	Fayetteville	9 Mar
8.01	Nickiesha	Wilson	JAM	28.7.86	1h1	NCAA	Fayetteville	9 Mar
	(20)							
8.01	Ashley	Lodree	USA	22.10.85	3	NCAA	Fayetteville	9 Mar
8.03	Sara	McGreavy	GBR	13.12.82	1	NC	Sheffield	10 Feb
8.03	Aurelia	Trywianska	POL	9.5.76	3h1		Karlsruhe	11 Feb
8.05	Tiffany	Ofili	USA	13.11.87	1		Notre Dame	3 Feb
8.05	Sarah	Claxton	GBR	23.9.79	2	NC	Sheffield	10 Feb
8.05	Flóra	Redoúmi	GRE	11.9.76	1	NC	Athína (P)	11 Feb
8.05	Candice	Davis	USA	26.5.85	4	NCAA	Fayetteville	9 Mar
8.06	Jenny	Adams	USA	8.7.78	4	Tyson	Fayetteville	9 Feb
8.06	Irina	Pepelyayeva	RUS	25.5.82	1		Yekaterinburg	18 Feb
8.06	Sheena	Johnson	USA	1.10.82	4	NC	Boston (R)	25 Feb
	(30)							
8.07	Eline	Berings	BEL	28.5.86	1	NC	Gent	18 Feb
8.07	Tatyana	Pavliy	RUS	18.5.78	2		Yekaterinburg	18 Feb
8.08	Dawn	Harper	USA	13.5.84	6	Tyson	Fayetteville	9 Feb

Mark		Name		Nat	Born	Pos	Meet	Venue	Date
8.08		Adrianna	Lamalle	FRA	27.9.82	1s1	NC	Aubière	18 Feb
8.09		Yenima	Arencibia	CUB	25.12.84	2		Valencia	10 Feb
8.09		Yuliya	Kondakova	RUS	4.12.81	h		Yekaterinburg	18 Feb
8.09		Tatyana	Dektyareva	RUS	8.5.81	h		Yekaterinburg	18 Feb
8.11		Kellie	Wells	USA	16.7.82	3	BIG	Boston (R)	27 Jan
8.11		Yekaterina	Shtepa	RUS	25.8.87	1	NC-j	Volgograd	14 Feb
8.13		Nia	Ali	USA-J	23.10.88	4h2	NCAA	Fayetteville	9 Mar
		(40)							
8.14		Glory	Alozie	ESP	30.12.77	2h1		Valencia	10 Feb
8.14		Edit	Vári	HUN	31.5.75	1		Budapest	11 Feb
8.14		Gemma	Bennett	GBR	4.1.84	2r2		Sheffield	18 Feb
8.15		Lucie	Martincová	CZE	4.1.82	1	NC	Praha	24 Feb
8.15		Colriece	Law	USA	2.9.86	2	SEC	Lexington	25 Feb
8.15		LaNeisha	Waller	USA	30.12.85	2	Big 10	Champaign	25 Feb
8.16		Olga	Korsunova	RUS	20.5.81	3		Volgograd	21 Jan
8.17		Yvette	Lewis	USA	16.3.85	1		State College	27 Jan
8.17		Jackie	Coward	USA-J	5.11.89	1		Lexington	17 Feb
8.17		Monique	Morgan	JAM	10.10.85	1s2	ECAC	Boston	4 Mar
		(50)							
8.18		Jessica	Ennis	GBR	28.1.86	3	NC	Sheffield	10 Feb
8.19		Kelly	Sotherton	GBR	13.11.76	4	NC	Sheffield	10 Feb
8.19		Andrea	Ivancevic	CRO	21.8.84	2		Budapest	11 Feb
8.19A		Andrea	Bliss	JAM	5.10.80	4=		Albuquerque	16 Feb
8.19A		Ebony	Foster	USA	26.7.83	4=		Albuquerque	16 Feb
8.19		Annette	Funck	GER	24.11.77	1h1	NC	Leipzig	18 Feb
8.19		Esen	Kizildag	TUR	30.9.80	2h1	NC	Gent	18 Feb
8.19		Alice	Decaux	FRA	10.4.85	3	NC	Aubière	18 Feb
8.19		Rebecca	Williams	USA	29.10.83	1	Big 12	Ames	24 Feb
8.19		Amber	Williams	USA	15.12.85	1		Akron	24 Feb
		(60)							

100 METRES HURDLES

Mark	Wind	Name		Nat	Born	Pos	Meet	Venue	Date
12.44	0.5	Michelle	Perry	USA	1.5.79	1	GGala	Roma	13 Jul
12.45	1.4	Virginia	Powell	USA	7.9.83	1	GP	New York	2 Jun
12.46	-0.1		Perry			1	WCh	Osaka	29 Aug
12.49	-0.1	Perdita	Felicien	CAN	29.8.80	2	WCh	Osaka	29 Aug
12.49	0.9	Susanna	Kallur	SWE	16.2.81	1	ISTAF	Berlin	16 Sep
12.50	-0.1	Delloreen	Ennis-London	JAM	5.3.75	3	WCh	Osaka	29 Aug
12.51	1.3		Perry			1	Pre	Eugene	10 Jun
12.51	-0.1		Kallur			4	WCh	Osaka	29 Aug
12.52	0.5		Kallur			1	VD	Bruxelles	14 Sep
12.55	-0.1		Perry			1s2	WCh	Osaka	28 Aug
12.55	-0.1		Powell			5	WCh	Osaka	29 Aug
12.56	-0.2		Perry			1	Gaz	Saint-Denis	6 Jul
12.57	0.2	Lolo	Jones	USA	5.8.82	1	Vard	Réthimno	18 Jul
12.58	1.4		Perry			1	adidas	Carson	20 May
12.58	1.3		Powell			2	Pre	Eugene	10 Jun
12.60	0.0		Perry			1	Athl	Lausanne	10 Jul
12.61	1.4		Powell			2	adidas	Carson	20 May
12.61	1.4		Jones			3	adidas	Carson	20 May
12.61	-0.1		Felicien			2s2	WCh	Osaka	28 Aug
12.61	0.5		Ennis-London			2	VD	Bruxelles	14 Sep
12.61	0.5		Perry			3	VD	Bruxelles	14 Sep
12.62	1.0		Ennis-London			1	NC	Kingston	24 Jun
12.62	0.0		Kallur			2	Athl	Lausanne	10 Jul
12.62	-0.1		Jones			6	WCh	Osaka	29 Aug
12.63	1.4	Angela	Whyte	CAN	22.5.80	4	adidas	Carson	20 May
12.63	-1.3		Powell			1	NC	Indianapolis	23 Jun
12.64	0.5		Kallur			1s1	WCh	Osaka	28 Aug
12.64	-0.1	Vonette	Dixon	JAM	26.11.75	7	WCh	Osaka	29 Aug
12.65	0.0		Ennis-London			1	PAm	Rio de Janeiro	25 Jul
12.65	0.0		Felicien			2	PAm	Rio de Janeiro	25 Jul
12.65	0.5		Whyte			2s1	WCh	Osaka	28 Aug
12.65	-0.1		Dixon			3s2	WCh	Osaka	28 Aug
12.65	-0.8		Perry			1	Golden	Shanghai	28 Sep
		(33/8)							
12.67	0.5	Josephine	Onyia (NGR)	ESP	15.7.86	2	GGala	Roma	13 Jul
12.67	1.4	Dawn	Harper (10)	USA	13.5.84	1	DLV	Bochum-Wattenscheid	12 Aug

WOMEN 2007

Mark	Wind	Name		Nat	Born	Pos	Meet	Venue	Date
12.71	1.7	Brigitte	Foster-Hylton	JAM	7.11.74	1		Kingston	5 May
12.71	0.0	Sally	McLellan	AUS	19.9.86	1	GP	Osaka	5 May
12.74	0.1	Damu	Cherry	USA	29.11.77	1	Herc	Monaco	25 Jul
12.75	-0.2	Adrianna	Lamalle	FRA	27.9.82	4	Gaz	Saint-Denis	6 Jul
12.76	0.2	Nevin	Yanit	TUR	16.2.86	2	Vard	Réthimno	18 Jul
12.80	1.8	Tiffany	Ofili	USA	13.11.87	1	NCAA	Sacramento	8 Jun
12.80	0.2	Nichole	Denby	USA	10.10.82	3	Vard	Réthimno	18 Jul
12.80	0.2	Anay	Tejeda	CUB	3.4.83	2h3	PAm	Rio de Janeiro	24 Jul
12.82	0.9	Priscilla	Lopes	CAN	26.8.82	1	GP	Rio de Janeiro	13 May
12.82	1.4	Jenny	Adams	USA	8.7.78	8	adidas	Carson	20 May
		(20)							
12.83	1.4	Aurelia	Trywianska	POL	9.5.76	1	Oda	Hiroshima	29 Apr
12.85	0.8	Anjanette	Kirkland	USA	24.2.74	1	ModR	Modesto	5 May
12.85	0.2	Lacena	Golding-Clarke	JAM	20.3.75	6s1	WCh	Osaka	28 Aug
12.88	0.2	Flóra	Redoúmi	GRE	11.9.76	5	Vard	Réthimno	18 Jul
12.88	1.4	Derval	O'Rourke	IRL	28.5.81	2	DLV	Bochum-Wattenscheid	12 Aug
12.89	-0.5	Yevgeniya	Snigur	UKR	7.3.84	1		Yalta	13 Jun
12.89	0.2	Danielle	Carruthers	USA	22.12.79	6	Vard	Réthimno	18 Jul
12.90	1.8	Sheena	Johnson	USA	1.10.82	2		Eugene	27 May
12.90	1.8	Candice	Davis	USA	26.5.85	2	NCAA	Sacramento	8 Jun
12.90	1.0	Tatyana	Pavliy	RUS	18.5.78	1	NC	Tula	1 Aug
		(30)							
12.91	1.8	Kristina	Castlin	USA-J	7.7.88	1	NCAA-r	Gainesville	26 May
12.93	1.8	Nickiesha	Wilson	JAM	28.7.86	3	NCAA	Sacramento	8 Jun
12.93	1.7	Kellie	Wells	USA	16.7.82	1		Bydgoszcz	10 Jun
12.95	2.0	Yevgeniya	Volodko	BLR	24.3.81	1		Minsk (Staiki)	28 Jul
12.95	1.0	Aleksandra	Antonova	RUS	24.3.80	2	NC	Tula	1 Aug
12.96	1.8	Fatmata	Fofanah	GUI	26.6.85	4	NCAA	Sacramento	8 Jun
12.97	0.1	Jessica	Ennis	GBR	28.1.86	1H	WCh	Osaka	25 Aug
12.97	0.4	Eline	Berings	BEL	28.5.86	5h4	WCh	Osaka	27 Aug
12.98	1.8	Queen	Harrison	USA-J	10.9.88	5	NCAA	Sacramento	8 Jun
12.99	1.8	Ashley	Lodree	USA	22.10.85	6	NCAA	Sacramento	8 Jun
		(40)							
13.00	1.4	Lauren	Smith	USA	27.8.81	6	GP	New York	2 Jun
13.00	1.7	Sarah	Claxton	GBR	23.9.79	2		Bydgoszcz	10 Jun
13.01	1.4	Gi-Gi	Johnson	USA	12.1.79	7	GP	New York	2 Jun
13.01	1.8	Jessica	Ohanaja	NGR	6.12.85	7	NCAA	Sacramento	8 Jun
13.01	1.0	Yekaterina	Shtepa	RUS	25.8.87	3	NC	Tula	1 Aug
13.02	1.4	Kumiko	Ikeda	JPN	10.1.81	2	Oda	Hiroshima	29 Apr
13.02	1.3	Natalya	Ivoninskaya	KAZ	22.2.85	1		Almaty	10 May
13.02	0.6	Toyin	Augustus	NGR	24.12.79	2		Chambéry	15 Jul
13.02	1.1	Andrea	Bliss	JAM	5.10.80	6	NA	Heusden-Zolder	28 Jul
13.03	2.0	Vashti	Thomas	USA-Y	21.4.90	1		Sacramento	2 Jun
		(50)							
13.04		Viktoriya	Gappova	RUS	27.1.84	1h		Sankt-Peterburg	3 Jul
13.04	2.0	Yuliya	Kondakova	RUS	4.12.81	2h1		Chambéry	15 Jul
13.04	0.4	Miriam	Bobková	SVK	2.3.79	7h2	WCh	Osaka	27 Aug
13.05		Anastasiya	Vinogradova	KAZ	13.9.86	1		Guwahati	23 Jun
13.06	1.2	Yvette	Lewis	USA	16.3.85	1s1	NCAA	Sacramento	6 Jun
13.06	0.8	Edit	Vári	HUN	31.5.75	1	ECp-1B	Milano	24 Jun
13.07	1.4	Alice	Decaux	FRA	10.4.85	1	NC-23	Elancourt	30 Jun
13.07	0.2	Christina	Vukicevic	NOR	18.6.87	7h2	WCh	Osaka	27 Aug
13.08	1.4	Shantia	Moss	USA	27.10.85	1h3		College Park	20 Apr
13.08	1.4	Fiona	Cullen	AUS	31.8.79	3	Oda	Hiroshima	29 Apr
		(60)							
13.08	0.8	Micol	Cattaneo	ITA	14.5.82	2	ECp-1B	Milano	24 Jun
13.08	1.4	Olga	Korsunova	RUS	20.5.81	1s2	NC	Tula	31 Jul
13.08	0.2	Jenny	Kallur	SWE	16.2.81	8h2	WCh	Osaka	27 Aug
13.09	1.3	Monique	Morgan	JAM	10.10.85	3h2	NCAA	Sacramento	6 Jun
13.12	0.8	Aleksandra	Fedoriva	RUS-J	13.9.88	1	EJ	Hengelo	22 Jul
13.13	1.8	Lyudmyla	Blonska	UKR	18.3.75	1H		Kyiv	3 Aug
13.14	1.8	Chiquita	Martin	USA	17.2.85	3	NCAA-r	Gainesville	26 May
13.14	0.9	Annette	Funck (Thimm)	GER	24.11.77	4	ECp-S	München	24 Jun
13.14		Svetlana	Topylina	RUS	6.1.85	1		Irkutsk	18 Aug
13.15	0.0	Kamilah	Salaam	USA	2.5.85	1		Atlanta	2 Jun
		(70)							
13.15	-0.1	Kirsten	Bolm	GER	4.3.75	6	Bisl	Oslo	15 Jun
13.15	0.6	Johanna	Halkoaho	FIN	13.1.77	1	PNG	Turku	1 Jul
13.15	0.5	Fanny	Gérance	FRA	4.1.81	2	NC	Niort	5 Aug
13.15	1.4	Irina	Lenskiy	ISR	12.6.71	5	DLV	Bochum-Wattenscheid	12 Aug

Mark	Wind	Name		Nat	Born	Pos	Meet	Venue	Date
13.15	0.1	Carolina	Klüft	SWE	2.2.83	2H1	WCh	Osaka	25 Aug
13.16	-0.8	Nadine	Faustin	HAI	14.4.76	7h3	WCh	Osaka	27 Aug
13.16	1.5	Mami	Ishino	JPN	10.1.83	1		Hiratsuka	21 Oct
13.17	0.7	Carolin	Nytra	GER	26.2.85	1		Mannheim	23 Jun
13.17	0.4	Eunice	Barber	FRA	17.11.74	2		Reims	17 Jul
13.18	1.7	Toni Ann	D'Oyley	JAM	25.10.81	5		Kingston	5 May
		(80)							
13.18	-0.4	LaNeisha	Waller	USA	30.12.85	4	NCAA-r	Columbia	26 May
13.18	1.6	Amber	Williams	USA	15.12.85	5s2	NCAA	Sacramento	6 Jun
13.18	0.0	Elizabeth	Davin	BEL	3.6.81	1		Génève	9 Jun
13.18	1.3	Glory	Alozie	ESP	30.12.77	2	NC	San Sebastián	5 Aug
13.20	0.1		Zhang Rong	CHN	5.1.83	1		Chengdu	14 Apr
13.20A	0.0	Brigith	Merlano	COL	29.4.82	1	Iriarte	Cochabamba	3 Jun
13.20	0.9	Cécile	Michot	FRA	2.6.74	3		Noisy-le-Grand	12 Jun
13.20	-0.3	Andrea	Miller	NZL	13.3.82	7	WUG	Bangkok	10 Aug
13.21	-0.4	Angel	Boyd	USA	25.2.85	6	NCAA-r	Columbia	26 May
13.21	1.2	Jackie	Coward	USA-J	5.11.89	1h2	NC-j	Indianapolis	21 Jun
		(90)							
13.21	0.1	Kelly	Sotherton	GBR	13.11.76	3H	WCh	Osaka	25 Aug
13.22	0.5	Gilvaneide	Oliveira	BRA	31.8.76	1		São Paulo	18 Apr
13.22	1.3	Tiffany	Johnson	USA	30.5.85	1	NCAA-r	Des Moines	26 May
13.22	0.7	Stephanie	Lichtl	GER	12.7.85	2		Mannheim	23 Jun
13.22	2.0	Yekaterina	Poplavskaya	BLR	7.5.87	2		Minsk (Staiki)	28 Jul
13.22	1.0	Mariya	Koroteyeva	RUS	10.11.81	6	NC	Tula	1 Aug
13.23	1.0	Ryanne	Dupree	USA	13.3.84	3h3	NCAA	Sacramento	6 Jun
13.23	2.0	Maila de Paula	Machado	BRA	22.1.81	3h1		Chambéry	15 Jul
13.24	0.0	Jennifer	Williams	USA	30.10.85	3		Baton Rouge	21 Apr
13.25	1.3	Jessica	Zelinka	CAN	3.9.81	1rB	MSR	Walnut	15 Apr
		(100)							
13.25	0.0	Nia	Ali	USA-J	23.10.88	1H	SEC	Tuscaloosa	10 May
13.25	0.9	Diana	Pickler	USA	9.12.83	1H	NCAA	Sacramento	7 Jun
13.25	0.9	Cindy	Billaud	FRA	11.3.86	4		Noisy-le-Grand	12 Jun
13.25	0.5	Joanna	Kocielnik	POL	11.3.83	1	NC	Poznan	1 Jul

13.26	1.9	Tavannia	Thompson	BAH	13.3.83	4 May
13.26	0.6	Hanna	Korell	FIN	16.3.79	1 Jul
13.26	1.2	Olena	Krasovska	UKR	17.8.76	5 Jul
13.26A		Zolymar	Febles	PUR	30.3.83	7 Jul
13.27	-1.0	Ashley	Brown	USA	23.10.85	13 May
13.27	0.7	Nadine	Hildebrand	GER	20.9.87	23 Jun
13.27	0.7	Anne-Kathrin	Elbe	GER	24.2.87	23 Jun
13.28	0.0	Joanna	Hayes	USA	23.12.76	22 Jun
13.28	1.2	Judith	Ritz	GER	16.6.83	29 Jul
13.28	0.4	Karin	Ruckstuhl	NED	2.11.80	25 Aug
13.28	-0.8		Liu Jing	CHN	8.8.77	28 Sep
13.29	0.0	Carmen	Ghilase	ROM	25.11.75	10 Jun
13.29	1.7	Yenima	Arencibia	CUB	25.12.84	7 Jul
13.29	-0.3	Gemma	Bennett	GBR	4.1.84	12 Aug
13.30	-0.5	Tamera	Thomas	JAM	10.3.83	31 Mar
13.30	1.9	MaKeatha	Cooper	USA	19.7.85	4 May
13.30	0.8	Petra	Seidlová	CZE	26.8.81	13 Jun
13.30	1.4	Tatyana	Dektyareva	RUS	14.6.84	31 Jul
13.31	1.9		He Liyuan	CHN	14.1.83	27 Jul
13.32	0.7	Marie Elisabeth	Maurer	AUT	10.2.83	11 May
13.32	2.0	Julian	Purvis	USA-Y	8.9.90	2 Jun
13.32	2.0	Ke'Nyia	Richardson	USA-J	6.9.89	2 Jun
13.32	0.4	Laetitia	Denis	FRA-J	4.2.88	29 Jul
13.33	1.3	Teona	Rodgers	USA-J	26.6.89	4 May
13.33	0.0	Nadine	Hentschke	GER	27.1.82	23 Jun
13.34	-0.4	Colriece	Law	USA	2.9.86	26 May
13.35	1.3	Tresha	Henry	JAM	23.9.83	6 Jun
13.35	0.9	Jacquelyn	Johnson	USA	8.9.84	8 Jun
13.35	-0.4	Femke	van der Meij	NED	20.5.85	9 Jun
13.36	1.7	Jessica	Czaikowski	CAN	20.4.84	5 May
13.37	-1.0	Rebecca	Williams	USA	29.10.83	13 May
13.37A	0.9	April	Williams	USA-J	20.4.89	2 Jun
13.37	1.3	Nancy	Searcy	USA	1.6.84	6 Jun
13.39	0.6	Aleesha	Barber	USA	16.5.87	25 May
13.39	-0.5	Nataliya	Zabrodskaya	UKR	6.9.77	13 Jun
13.39	0.3	Asuka	Terada	JPN-Y	14.1.90	21 Jul
13.40	0.0	Rosina	Hodde	NED	10.2.83	24 Jun
13.41	1.2	Samaiyah	Islam	USA	26.3.81	28 Apr
13.41	0.6	Monique	Johnson	USA	9.6.84	13 May
13.42	1.5	Funmi	Jimoh	USA	29.5.84	4 Apr
13.42	-0.4	Lorian	Price	USA	14.10.84	26 May
13.42	1.0		Sun Yawei	CHN	17.10.87	4 Jun
13.42	-0.6	Victoria	Schreibeis	AUT	9.1.79	1 Jul
13.42	0.7	Anastasiya	Solovyova	RUS	18.2.85	31 Jul
13.43	1.3	Arantza	Loureiro	ESP	22.2.81	5 Aug
13.43	0.5		Lee Yeon-kyung	KOR	15.4.81	13 Oct
13.44	1.9	Nikita	Holder	CAN	7.5.87	21 Apr
13.44	0.9	Andrea	Ivancevic	CRO	21.8.84	4 Jul
13.44	0.9	April	Garner	USA	25.12.83	14 Jul
13.44	1.8	Oksana	Kuzminok	UKR	7.8.83	3 Aug
13.44	-0.7	Sara	Aerts	BEL	25.1.84	9 Aug
13.45	0.2	Viorica	Tigau	ROM	12.8.79	5 May
13.45	-0.1	Sara	McGreavy	GBR	13.12.82	27 May
13.45	0.0	Sherrie	Willis	USA	6.6.85	2 Jun
13.45	1.9	Lyudmila	Klimova	RUS	8.3.80	9 Jun
13.45	0.2	Lucimara	da Silva	BRA	10.7.85	21 Jun
13.45	0.1	Lucie	Martincová	CZE	4.1.82	25 Aug
13.46	1.2	Janice	Josephs	RSA	31.3.82	2 Mar
13.46	1.6	Aleacna	Correa	CUB-J	22.6.89	25 May
13.46	1.9	Claudia	Troppa	ESP	14.2.85	9 Jun
13.46	-0.6	Daniela	Wöckinger	AUT	9.5.81	1 Jul
13.47	1.5	Tatyana	Chernova	RUS-J	29.1.88	30 May
13.47	1.5	Katey	Read	GBR	20.3.86	7 Jul
13.48	1.8	Shalina	Clarke	USA-J	8.8.88	25 May
13.48	1.9	Whitney	Holmes	USA	23.12.85	25 May
13.48	-0.8	Esen	Kizildag	TUR	30.9.80	27 Aug
13.49	0.0	Rahamatou	Drame	FRA	1.4.85	27 May
13.49	1.3	Hanna	Platitsyna	UKR	1.1.87	5 Jul
13.49	-2.8	Yekaterina	Gubina	RUS	19.6.85	7 Jul
13.49	0.0	Mirjam	Liimask	EST	25.10.83	7 Jul
13.49	0.0	Cindy	Roleder	GER-J	21.8.89	4 Aug
13.50	0.9	Salla	Rinne	FIN	22.5.80	7 Jul
13.50	1.3	Marina	Andryukhina	RUS-J	17.4.88	21 Jul
13.50	0.0	Anne	Marchewski	GER-J	11.4.88	4 Aug
13.50	-1.0	Lilli	Schwarzkopf	GER	28.8.83	10 Aug
13.51	1.3	Shermaine	Williams	JAM-Y	4.2.90	9 Apr
13.51	1.8	Anastasiya	Soprunova	KAZ	14.1.86	24 May
13.51	-0.4	Jennifer	Oeser	GER	29.11.83	26 May
13.51A	0.0	Fabiana	Morães	BRA	5.6.86	3 Jun
13.51	1.6	Radmila	Vukmirovic	SLO	23.11.79	3 Jul
13.51	0.5	Karin	Ertl	GER	23.6.74	8 Jul
13.51	1.5	Yuki	Sato	JPN	16.10.86	21 Oct

Mark	Wind	Name		Nat	Born	Pos	Meet	Venue	Date
13.51	-0.8	Dedeh	Erawati	INA	25.5.79				10 Dec
13.52	-0.7	Ronnetta	Alexander	USA	8.5.85				31 Mar
13.52	1.2	Theresa	Lewis	USA-J	23.3.88				5 May
13.52	0.4		Wang Jindan	CHN	1.4.87				2 Jun
13.52	1.7	Aliuska	López	ESP	29.8.69				7 Jul
13.52	1.1	Joanna	Bujak	FRA	30.8.79				5 Aug
13.53	-0.6	Fumiko	Kumagai	JPN	18.11.84				30 Jun
13.53		Anna	Odinokova	RUS	7.4.78				3 Jul
13.53	0.4	Annimari	Korte	FIN-J	8.4.88				3 Aug
13.54	-0.5	Margaret	Simpson (96)	GHA	2.8.82				20 Jul

Wind assisted

Mark	Wind	Name		Nat	Born	Pos	Meet	Venue	Date
12.50	4.3		Felicien			1	NC	Windsor	14 Jul
12.55	4.3	Angela	Whyte	CAN	22.5.80	2	NC	Windsor	14 Jul
12.64	2.2	Priscilla	Lopes	CAN	26.8.82	1	GP	Belém	20 May
12.72	3.8	Nichole	Denby	USA	10.10.82	1	KansR	Lawrence	21 Apr
12.75	2.1	Jenny	Adams	USA	8.7.78	1rA	MSR	Walnut	15 Apr
12.78	3.8	Joanna	Hayes	USA	23.12.76	2	KansR	Lawrence	21 Apr
12.80	4.0	Tatyana	Pavliy	RUS	18.5.78	1	Znam	Zhukovskiy	9 Jun
12.82	2.1	Kristina	Castlin	USA-J	7.7.88	1		College Park	21 Apr
12.83	2.1	Shantia	Moss	USA	27.10.85	2		College Park	21 Apr
12.86	4.0	Aleksandra	Antonova	RUS	24.3.80	2	Znam	Zhukovskiy	9 Jun
12.88	2.1	Candice	Davis	USA	26.5.85	2rA	MSR	Walnut	15 Apr
12.94	3.4	Lauren	Smith	USA	27.8.81	1		Fayetteville	21 Apr
12.95	4.0	Yuliya	Kondakova	RUS	4.12.81	3	Znam	Zhukovskiy	9 Jun
13.04	6.1	Tatyana	Chernova	RUS-J	29.1.88	1H		Arles	2 Jun
13.05	2.8	Alice	Decaux	FRA	10.4.85	1h1		Elanourt	30 Jun
13.10	4.0	Tatyana	Dektyareva	RUS	4.6.84	4	Znam	Zhukovskiy	9 Jun
13.14	2.7	Andrea	Miller	NZL	13.3.82	1		Auckland	4 Feb
13.17	2.2	Jackie	Coward	USA-J	5.11.89	3	NC-j	Indianapolis	21 Jun
13.18A	2.4	Brigith	Merlano	COL	29.4.82	1	NC	Medellín	4 May
13.19	4.5	Jessica	Zelinka	CAN	3.9.81	2H		Arles	2 Jun
13.20	2.2	Tiffany	Johnson	USA	30.5.85	1	DrakeR	Des Moines	28 Apr
13.23	2.5	Margaret	Macchiut	ITA	25.7.74	2	ECCp	Albufeira	27 May
13.23	3.1	Sara	McGreavy	GBR	13.12.82	2		Manchester	2 Jun

Mark	Wind	Name		Nat	Born	Date
13.26	2.2	April	Garner	USA	25.12.83	14 Jul
13.27	4.3	Jessica	Czaikowski	CAN	20.4.84	14 Jul
13.31	3.6	Jacquelyn	Johnson	USA	8.9.84	26 May
13.32	2.6	Tenaya	Jones	USA-J	22.3.89	29 Jul
13.34	3.2	Viorica	Tigau	ROM	12.8.79	28 Apr
13.34	2.6	Lorian	Price	USA	14.10.84	6 Jun
13.35	3.6	Nancy	Searcy	USA	1.6.84	26 May
13.36		Anastasiya	Solovyova	RUS	18.2.85	9 Aug
13.37	3.1	Fumiko	Kumagai	JPN	18.11.84	15 Jul
13.38	2.6	Latoya	James	USA-J	18.1.89	29 Jul
13.39	2.9	Funmi	Jimoh	USA	29.5.84	21 Apr
13.39	2.5	Esen	Kizildag	TUR	30.9.80	27 May
13.42	2.6	Shalina	Clarke	USA-J	8.8.88	6 Jun
13.43	2.7	Yanique	Booth	JAM	3.5.84	24 Mar
13.43	2.7	Rosvitha	Okou	FRA	5.9.86	29 Jul
13.46	2.1	Joanna	Bujak	FRA	30.8.79	11 Jul
13.47	3.9	Hayley	Cameron	AUS	21.4.84	27 Jan
13.47	3.7	Jenny	Snyder	USA	24.6.85	13 May
13.47	2.3	Michaela	Hejnová	CZE	10.4.80	9 Jun
13.48	2.6	Ulrike	Hebestreit	GER	19.3.81	16 Jun
13.48	2.1	Rahamatou	Drame	FRA	1.4.85	29 Jul
13.51	2.4	Sandra	Gomis	FRA	21.11.83	5 Aug
13.52	2.2	Jenna	Caffrey	USA-J	1.6.88	28 Apr
13.53	2.3	Valerie	Flournoy	USA	26.11.87	24 Mar
13.53	3.6	Amber	Peterson	USA		26 May
13.54	2.2	Denisa	Scerbová	CZE	21.8.86	17 Jun
13.54	3.6	Lucile	Berliat	FRA	7.12.82	11 Jul

Best at low altitude

13.27 0.0 Merlano 7 Jun 13.54 -0.1 Febles 26 May

Hand Timed

Mark	Wind	Name		Nat	Born	Pos	Meet	Venue	Date
12.7	0.8	Yenima	Arencibia	CUB	25.12.84	1		La Habana	8 Jun
13.0	-1.1	Gretchen	Quintana	CUB	30.6.84	1H		Santiago de Cuba	10 Mar
13.2	0.7	Aleacna	Correa	CUB-J	22.6.89	2		La Habana	8 Jun

JUNIORS

See main list for top 6 juniors. 12 performances by 4 women to 13.15. Additional marks and further juniors:

Castlin	13.02	-0.8	1	PAm-J	São Paulo	6 Jul	13.11	1.8	9	NCAA	Sacramento	8 Jun
	13.08	2.0	1h3	NC-j	Indianapolis	21 Jun	13.11	0.4	1h1	PAm-J	São Paulo	6 Jul
	13.10	1.2	5s1	NCAA	Sacramento	6 Jun	13.15	1.7	1h1		College Park	20 Apr
Harrison	13.07	1.2	2s1	NCAA	Sacramento	6 Jun	13.12	1.8	2	NCAA-r	Gainesville	26 May

Mark	Wind	Name		Nat	Born	Pos	Meet	Venue	Date
13.32	2.0	Julian	Purvis	USA-Y	8.9.90	2		Sacramento	2 Jun
13.32	2.0	Ke'Nyia	Richardson	USA	6.9.89	3		Sacramento	2 Jun
13.32	0.4	Laetitia	Denis	FRA	4.2.88	1	NC-J	Narbonne	29 Jul
13.33	1.3	Teona	Rodgers (10)	USA	26.6.89	1h1		Winter Park	4 May
13.37A	0.9	April	Williams	USA	20.4.89	2		Albuquerque	2 Jun
13.39	0.3	Asuka	Terada	JPN-Y	14.1.90	1		Iwamizawa	21 Jul
13.46	1.6	Aleacna	Correa	CUB	22.6.89	1h2	Barr/NC	La Habana	25 May
13.47	1.5	Tatyana	Chernova	RUS	29.1.88	3		Athína (F)	30 May
13.48	1.8	Shalina	Clarke	USA	8.8.88	2h2		Eugene	25 May
13.49	0.0	Cindy	Roleder	GER	21.8.89	1	NC-j	Ulm	4 Aug
13.50	1.3	Marina	Andryukhina	RUS	17.4.88	1h3	EJ	Hengelo	21 Jul
13.50	0.0	Anne	Marchewski	GER	11.4.88	2	NC-j	Ulm	4 Aug
13.51	1.3	Shermaine	Williams	JAM-Y	4.2.90	1	Carifta	Providenciales	9 Apr
13.52	1.2	Theresa	Lewis (20)	USA	23.3.88	1h2		Storrs	5 May

Wind assisted 6 performances by 3 women to 13.12 – see main list for top 3 juniors

Castlin	12.85	2.6	1h1	NCAA	Sacramento	6 Jun	13.07	2.2	1	NC-j	Indianapolis	21 Jun
Harrison	13.07	1.2	2s1	NCAA	Sacramento	6 Jun	13.12	1.8	2	NCAA-r	Gainesville	26 May

Mark	Wind	Name		Nat	Born	Pos	Meet	Venue	Date
13.32	2.6	Tenaya	Jones	USA	22.3.89	1	Jnr Oly	Walnut	29 Jul
13.38	2.6	Latoya	James	USA	18.1.89	2	Jnr Oly	Walnut	29 Jul
13.42	2.6	Shalina	Clarke	USA	8.8.88	7h1	NCAA	Sacramento	6 Jun
13.52	2.2	Jenna	Caffrey	USA	1.6.88	3	DrakeR	Des Moines	28 Apr

400 METRES HURDLES

Mark	Name		Nat	Born	Pos	Meet	Venue	Date
53.28	Tiffany	Williams	USA	5.2.83	1	NC	Indianapolis	24 Jun
53.29	Sheena	Johnson	USA	1.10.82	2	NC	Indianapolis	24 Jun
53.31	Jana	Rawlinson	AUS	9.11.82	1	WCh	Osaka	30 Aug
53.46		Rawlinson			1	Herc	Monaco	25 Jul
53.50	Yuliya	Pechonkina	RUS	21.4.78	2	WCh	Osaka	30 Aug
53.57		Rawlinson			1s1	WCh	Osaka	28 Aug
53.61		Pechonkina			1	NC	Tula	1 Aug
53.82		Pechonkina			1s2	WCh	Osaka	28 Aug
53.86	Anna	Jesien	POL	10.12.78	1s3	WCh	Osaka	28 Aug
53.92		Pechonkina			1	R.Chall	Moskva	5 Aug
53.92		Jesien			3	WCh	Osaka	28 Aug
53.97	Nickiesha	Wilson	JAM	28.7.86	2s3	WCh	Osaka	28 Aug
54.00		Pechonkina			1h3	NC	Tula	31 Jul
54.00		Huang Xiaoxiao	CHN	3.3.83	2s2	WCh	Osaka	28 Aug
54.04		Pechonkina			1	ECp-S	München	23 Jun
54.08	Natasha	Danvers-Smith	GBR	19.9.77	2s1	WCh	Osaka	28 Aug
54.10		Wilson			4	WCh	Osaka	30 Aug
54.11	Yevgeniya	Isakova	RUS	27.11.78	3s1	WCh	Osaka	28 Aug
54.14	Melaine	Walker (10)	JAM	1.1.83	1	Pre	Eugene	10 Jun
54.15		Williams			3s3	WCh	Osaka	28 Aug
54.15		Huang			5	WCh	Osaka	28 Aug
54.17		Jesien			1	WAF	Stuttgart	23 Sep
54.19		Rawlinson			2	WAF	Stuttgart	23 Sep
54.24	Yekaterina	Bikert	RUS	13.5.80	2	NC	Tula	1 Aug
54.24		Williams			1h2	WCh	Osaka	27 Aug
54.25		Rawlinson			1r2	GP	Athína	2 Jul
54.31		Walker			3	WAF	Stuttgart	23 Sep
54.32	Nicole	Leach	USA	18.7.87	1	NCAA	Sacramento	9 Jun
54.32		Walker			2	Herc	Monaco	25 Jul
54.34		Williams			1	Sánchez	Santo Domingo	12 May
	(30/12)							
54.36	Natalya	Ivanova	RUS	25.6.81	3	NC	Tula	1 Aug
54.38	Tetyana	Tereshchuk-Antipova	UKR	11.10.69	4s1	WCh	Osaka	28 Aug
54.40	Angela	Morosanu	ROM	26.7.86	1	GP	Athína	2 Jul
54.59	Sandra	Glover	USA	30.12.68	1		Kassel	6 Jun
54.78	Tatyana	Azarova	KAZ	2.12.85	1		Almaty	11 May
54.93	Muna	Jabir Ahmed	SUD	6.1.87	1	AfG	Alger	22 Jul
55.04	Zuzana	Hejnová	CZE	19.12.86	6s1	WCh	Osaka	28 Aug
55.12	Irina	Obedina	RUS	1.7.85	1	NC-23	Tula	19 Jun
	(20)							
55.21	Ulrike	Urbansky	GER	6.4.77	1	NC	Erfurt	22 Jul
55.21	Marina	Zafirova (Shiyan)	RUS	22.1.80	2h3	NC	Tula	31 Jul
55.37	Ajoke	Odumosu	NGR	27.10.87	1	DrakeR	Des Moines	28 Apr
55.41	Ionela	Târlea	ROM	9.2.76	5s3	WCh	Osaka	28 Aug
55.42	Shevon	Stoddart	JAM	21.11.82	4	PAm	Rio de Janeiro	25 Jul
55.43	Andrea	Blackett	BAR	24.1.76	2	GP	Athína	2 Jul
55.48	Markita	James	USA	28.6.83	2		Fortaleza	16 May
55.48	Anastasiya	Rabchenyuk	UKR	14.9.83	1	NC	Donetsk	7 Jul
55.49	Aïssata	Soulama	BUR	11.2.79	2	AfG	Alger	22 Jul
55.56	Dominique	Darden	USA	9.12.83	1		Ponce	19 May
	(30)							
55.58	Tina	Kron	GER	3.4.81	2	NC	Erfurt	22 Jul
55.62	Kaliese	Spencer	JAM	6.5.87	2	NC	Kingston	23 Jun
55.66	Faní	Halkiá	GRE	2.2.79	3h3	WCh	Osaka	27 Aug
55.71	Satomi	Kubokura	JPN	27.4.82	1		Shizuoka	30 Apr
55.72	Élodie	Ouédraogo	BEL	27.2.81	3	GP	Athína	2 Jul
55.81	Queen	Harrison	USA-J	10.9.88	3	NCAA	Sacramento	9 Jun
55.94	Shauna	Smith	USA	10.9.83	3		Kingston	5 May
55.94	Hristína	Hantzí-Neag	GRE	26.12.76	1	BalkC	Sofia	4 Jul
55.96	Lucimar	Teodoro	BRA	1.5.81	1		São Paulo	27 May
55.96	Joanna	Tilgner	GER	18.11.84	1		Cuxhaven	14 Jul
	(40)							
56.03	Tsvetelina	Kirilova	BUL	14.7.77	7s3	WCh	Osaka	28 Aug

Mark	Name		Nat	Born	Pos	Meet	Venue	Date
56.04	Lee	McConnell	GBR	9.10.78	4	BrGP	Sheffield	15 Jul
56.04	Olga	Adamovich	RUS	30.8.84	2h1	NC	Tula	31 Jul
56.14	Tatyana	Chernova	RUS-J	29.1.88	1		Zhukovskiy	30 Jun
56.18	Lamia	El Habz	MAR	19.5.84	2	NC	Meknès	30 Jun
56.18	Yelena	Ildeykina	RUS	16.6.83	7	NC	Tula	1 Aug
56.19	Josanne	Lucas	TRI	14.5.84	2		Atlanta	12 May
56.19	Erica	Mårtensson	SWE	24.6.79	6h4	WCh	Osaka	27 Aug
56.21	Krystal	Cantey	USA	27.6.87	2	NCAA-r	Gainesville	26 May
56.23	Aurore	Kassambara	FRA	26.10.79	1	NC	Niort	5 Aug
	(50)							
56.26	Benedetta	Ceccarelli	ITA	23.1.80	3	Kuso	Warszawa	17 Jun
56.27	Dora	Jémaa	FRA	15.7.85	4	ECp-S	München	23 Jun
56.28	Hanane	Skhiyi	MAR	5.7.83	3	NC	Meknés	30 Jun
56.33	Özge	Gürler	TUR	17.6.85	3	BalkC	Sofia	4 Jul
56.35	Latosha	Wallace	USA	24.3.85	4	NCAA	Sacramento	9 Jun
56.41	Yuliya	Mulyukova	RUS	1.12.85	2	NC-23	Tula	19 Jun
56.42	Anastasiya	Ott	RUS-J	7.9.88	1h	NC-j	Tula	18 Jun
56.42	Nagihan	Karadere	TUR	.84	4	BalkC	Sofia	4 Jul
56.42	Fabienne	Kohlmann	GER-J	6.11.89	1	EJ	Hengelo	21 Jul
56.46	Perry	Shakes-Drayton	GBR-J	21.12.88	2	EJ	Hengelo	21 Jul
	(60)							
56.48	Teodora	Kolarova ¶	BUL	29.5.81	1	NC	Sofia	17 Jun
56.48	Ilona	Ranta	FIN	28.10.82	4	WUG	Bangkok	13 Aug
56.53	Janet	Wienand	RSA	15.5.85	3		Luzern	28 Jun
56.53	Michelle	Carey	IRL	20.2.81	2		Uden	4 Aug
56.56	Joanna	Hayes	USA	23.12.76	3	MSR	Walnut	15 Apr
56.56	Svetlana	Gogoleva	RUS	11.12.85	3	NC-23	Tula	19 Jun
56.60A	Melinda	Sallins	USA	30.6.73	1		Provo	1 Jun
56.63	Phara	Anacharsis	FRA	17.12.83	8	Herc	Monaco	25 Jul
56.66	Sherlenia	Green	USA	22.3.85	1		College Park	21 Apr
56.70	Agnieszka	Karpiesiuk	POL	17.4.82	5	Kuso	Warszawa	17 Jun
	(70)							
56.71	Camille	Robinson	JAM	30.3.84	3	NCAA-r	Columbia, MO	26 May
56.73	Carlene	Robinson	JAM	30.3.84	3s1	NCAA	Sacramento	8 Jun
56.75	Yelena	Churakova	RUS	16.12.86	4	NC-23	Tula	19 Jun
56.80	Laia	Forcadell	ESP	6.6.82	2		Alcalá de Henares	7 Jul
56.81	Houria	Moussa	ALG	14.5.82	3		Thessaloniki	30 Jul
56.83	Martina	Naef	SUI	23.4.80	1	NC	Lausanne	29 Jul
56.86	Sherene	Pinnock	JAM	30.3.87	2	DrakeR	Des Moines	28 Apr
56.94	Janeil	Bellille	TRI-J	18.6.89	2	PAm-J	São Paulo	8 Jul
56.94	Mariya	Menshchikova	RUS	26.2.83	2h4	NC	Tula	31 Jul
56.97	Miriam	Barnes	USA	14.11.83	5	NCAA-r	Columbia, MO	26 May
	(80)							
56.98	Daimí	Pernia	CUB	27.12.76	1	ALBA	Caracas	11 May
56.98	Naim	Yisrael	USA	25.11.85	6	NCAA	Sacramento	9 Jun
57.00	Aleesha	Barber	USA	16.5.87	3	NCAA-r	Gainesville	26 May
57.01	Sara	Petersen	DEN	9.4.87	2	ECp-2A	Odense	23 Jun
57.04	Sheryl	Morgan	JAM	6.11.83	1	Big 12	Lincoln	13 May
57.04	Amanda	Kotze	RSA	26.2.86	2		Neerpelt	2 Jun
57.04	Manuela	Gentili	ITA	7.2.78	2	NC	Padova	28 Jul
57.07	Hanna	Rybakova	UKR	19.3.84	2	NC	Donetsk	7 Jul
57.08		Zhang Rongrong	CHN	27.1.84	2		Guangzhou	22 Jul
57.08		Wang Hui	CHN	1.6.87	9		Shanghai	28 Sep
	(90)							
57.09	Dalilah	Muhammad	USA-Y	7.2.90	1		Greensboro	16 Jun
57.10	Ieva	Zunda	LAT	20.7.78	1	NC	Valmiera	4 Aug
57.11	Galina	Pedan	KGZ	29.5.83	2		Almaty	10 Jun
57.11	Alena	Rücklová	CZE	7.10.81	6	Odlozil	Praha	13 Jun
57.11	Eilidh	Child	GBR	20.2.87	5	EU23	Debrecen	14 Jul
57.15	Ashley	Brown	USA	23.10.85	3h2	NCAA	Sacramento	7 Jul
57.20	Ryann	Krais	USA-Y	21.3.90	2	NC-j	Indianapolis	23 Jun
57.20	Sayaka	Aoki	JPN	15.12.86	2	NC	Osaka	1 Jul
57.21	Jackie	Coward	USA-J	5.11.89	3	PAm-J	São Paulo	8 Jul
57.21	Vassanee	Vinatho	THA	30.6.80	1	SEAG	Nakhon Ratchasima	7 Dec
	(100)							

Mark	Name		Nat	Born	Date
57.26	Emma	Duck	GBR	9.2.81	13 May
57.26		He Yu	CHN	26.6.86	22 Jul
57.27	Mary	Onyemuwa	NGR	4.12.83	19 May
57.31	Carla	Thomas	JAM	2.9.84	21 Apr
57.31	Erin	Crawford	USA	14.8.85	13 May
57.32	Mariya	Oprya	UKR	19.8.82	12 Jun
57.33	Meghan	Beesley	GBR-J	15.11.89	24 Jun
57.33	Andreea	Ionescu	ROM-Y	10.3.90	13 Jul
57.37	Patricia	Lopes	POR	11.7.82	14 Jul
57.37	Florence	Wasike	KEN	20.3.79	22 Jul
57.37	Nusrat	Ceesay	GBR	18.3.81	29 Jul
57.43	Chiquita	Martin	USA	17.2.85	6 Jun

Mark		Name	Nat	Born	Date
57.47	Jennifer	Grossarth	USA	5.83	22 Jun
57.47		Ruan Zhuofen	CHN	21.1.85	20 Sep
57.50	Higlecia	de Oliveira	BRA	19.4.86	24 Jun
57.51		Chen Yumei	CHN-J	10.1.88	1 Nov
57.52	Carole	Kaboud Mébam	CMR	17.9.78	30 Jun
57.53	Michelle	Burgher	JAM	12.3.77	5 May
57.53	Yelena	Golovankova	RUS	12.5.84	31 Jul
57.54	Darya	Korablyeva	RUS-J	23.5.88	30 Jun
57.54	Geraldine	Lecefel	FRA	28.1.84	12 Aug
57.55	Luciana	França	BRA	19.5.77	13 Jun
57.66	Elisa	Scardanzan	ITA	15.7.85	17 Jun
57.70	Kishelle	Paul	USA	20.12.87	26 May
57.72	Meka	Thompson	USA	10.1.74	22 Jun
57.73	Maiteland	Marks	USA	19.9.76	15 Jul
57.74	Perla Regina	dos Santos	BRA	29.1.82	20 May
57.74	Shana-Gaye	Tracey	JAM-Y	3.10.90	16 Jul
57.76	Ana	Berlinscaia	MDA	11.12.86	27 Jul
57.78	Gladys	Stephens	NGR	8.1.84	19 May
57.78	Shalina	Clarke	USA-J	8.8.88	28 May
57.78		Yu Qiuyue	CHN-J	18.11.88	3 Aug
57.78 mx	Zuzana	Bergrová	CZE	24.11.84	14 Aug
	57.83				1 Jul
57.79	Sara	Oresnik	SLO	3.6.84	12 May
57.79	Elaine	Paixão	BRA-J	15.6.88	24 Jun
57.79	Amélie	Fosse	FRA-J	21.11.89	29 Jul
57.83	Amber	Peterson	USA		8 Jun
57.85	Makiko	Yoshida	JPN	16.7.76	30 Jun
57.88	Elizabeth	Fairs	GBR	1.12.77	9 Jun
57.91	Nikolina	Horvat	CRO	18.9.86	13 Jul
57.92	Amanda	Fontes Dias	BRA	11.11.84	24 Jun
57.92	Tamara	Ruben	NED	11.6.82	1 Jul
57.93	Tameka	Jameson	USA-J	11.8.89	16 Jun
57.97	Alison	Erzinger	USA	18.6.83	12 May
57.97	Lara	Rocco	ITA	20.12.75	2 Jun
57.98	Laura Natalia	Sotomayor	ESP	22.4.86	1 Jul
57.99	Yelena	Maksimova	RUS	12.5.85	19 Jun
58.05	Andrea	Reid	JAM-J	28.3.89	17 Mar
58.06	Tatyana	Samarina	RUS	20.11.80	9 Aug
58.08	Norasheela	Mohd Khalid	MAS	27.9.79	1 Jun
58.09	Tatyana	Halayeva	UKR	12.9.86	20 Jun
58.10	Danielle	Gilchrist	USA-J	15.7.88	11 May
58.14	Tina	Polak	POL-J	12.7.88	20 Jul
58.15	Anwen	Rees	GBR	14.7.85	3 Aug
58.16	Stilianí	Dímoglou	GRE	18.11.84	16 Jun
58.16		Ding Jieqin	CHN-J	29.11.88	3 Aug
58.17	Marta	Chrust-Rozej	POL	29.9.78	2 Jun
58.18	Danielle	Brown	USA	6.6.87	25 May
58.20	Darya	Ukharskaya	RUS	12.4.85	19 Jun
58.22	Louise	Gundert	SWE	31.7.80	9 Jun
58.22	Ana Paula	Carvalho	BRA	11.12.78	23 Jun
58.23	Nicole	Dumpson	USA		14 Jul
58.23	Latoya	James	USA-J	18.1.89	29 Jul
58.24A	Callen	Nyakawa	KEN	10.12.86	16 Jun
58.25	Irina	Grebneva	RUS	5.2.85	20 Jun
58.26	Sarah	Wells	CAN-J	10.11.89	8 Jul
58.30	Claudia	Wehrsen	GER	18.10.84	14 Jul
58.32	Marta	Oliva	ITA	5.8.82	7 Jun
58.32		Deng Xiaoqing	CHN-J	13.6.89	6 Jul
58.35	Hanna	Titimets	UKR-J	5.3.89	22 Jun
58.35	Barbara	Gähling	GER	20.1.65	21 Jul
58.37	Janel	Grooms	USA		25 May
58.38	Faye	Harding	GBR	7.9.85	2 Jun
58.40	Lauren	Boden	AUS-J	3.8.88	11 Mar
58.40	Frederike	Schönfeld	GER	8.5.87	21 Jul
58.42	MacKenzie	Hill	USA	5.1.86	28 May
58.44	Judith	Riley	JAM-J	4.11.88	17 Mar
58.44	Chiaki	Ueda	JPN	19.10.87	30 Jun
58.46	Andrea	Sutherland	JAM-J	26.5.88	30 Mar
58.47	Chelsea	Shapard	USA	24.11.86	12 May
58.48	Sylvanie	Morandais (181)	FRA	14.7.79	15 Jul

Best at low altitude: 56.88 Sallins 3h2 NC Indianapolis 22 Jun

Hand timed

Mark		Name	Nat	Born	Pos	Meet	Venue	Date
57.0	Tacita	Bass	USA	28.10.79	3		Abuja	5 May
57.2A	Florence	Wasike	KEN	20.3.79	2	EfCh	Kampala	31 May

57.7 Dayami Lara CUB 27.10.85 8 Jun | 58.0 Catherine Obilor Chinwendu NGR 17.7.85 5 May

JUNIORS

See main list for top 9 juniors. 11 performances by 5 women to 56.78. Additional marks and further juniors:

Harrison	56.09	1	NCAA-r	Gainesville	26 May	56.25	1	PAm-J	São Paulo	8 Jul
	56.57	3		Atlanta	12 May	56.78	4s1	NCAA	Sacramento	8 Jun
Ott	56.47	1	NC-j	Sochi	23 May	56.55	2		Zhukovskiy	30 Jun

Mark		Name	Nat	Born	Pos	Meet	Venue	Date
57.33	Meghan	Beesley (10)	GBR	15.11.89	1	NC-J	Bedford	24 Jun
57.33	Andreea	Ionescu	ROM-Y	10.3.90	2	WY	Ostrava	13 Jul
57.51		Chen Yumei	CHN	10.1.88	1		Wuhan	1 Nov
57.54	Darya	Korablyeva	RUS	23.5.88	3		Zhukovskiy	30 Jun
57.74	Shana-Gaye	Tracey	JAM-Y	3.10.90	4		Ostrava	16 Jul
57.78	Shalina	Clarke	USA	8.8.88	2		Los Angeles	28 May
57.78		Yu Qiuyue	CHN	18.11.88	1h1	NC	Shijiazhuang	3 Aug
57.79	Elaine	Paixão	BRA	15.6.88	3	NC	São Paulo	24 Jun
57.79	Amélie	Fosse	FRA	21.11.89	1	NC-J	Narbonne	29 Jul
57.93	Tameka	Jameson	USA	11.8.89	3		Greensboro	16 Jun
58.05	Andrea	Reid (20)	JAM	28.3.89	1		Kingston	17 Mar

HIGH JUMP

2.07 Blanka Vlasic CRO 8.11.83 1 DNG Stockholm 7 Aug
1.87/1 1.92/1 1.95/1 1.98/1 2.01/1 2.03/2 2.07/3 2.10/xxx

Mark	Pos	Meet	Venue	Date	Series
2.06	1		Thessaloníki	30 Jul	1.83/1 1.89/1 1.95/1 1.99/1 2.02/2 2.06/2 2.10/xxx
2.05	1	GP	Madrid	21 Jul	1.84/1 1.92/2 1.95/1 1.98/1 2.01/1 2.05/1 2.10/xxx
2.05	1	WCh	Osaka	2 Sep	1.85/1 1.90/1 1.94/1 1.97/1 2.00/2 2.03/1 2.05/3 2.10/xxx
2.04	1	SGP	Doha	11 May	1.85/2 1.90/1 1.93/1 1.96/1 1.98/1 2.00/1 2.02/1 2.04/3 2.10/xxx
2.04	1	WK	Zürich	7 Sep	1.85/1 1.90/1 1.95/1 1.98/1 2.01/2 2.04/3 2.10/xxx
2.03	1	Herc	Monaco	25 Jul	1.85/1 1.90/1 1.94/1 1.97/1 2.00/1 2.03/1 2.06/xxx
2.03	1	VD	Bruxelles	14 Sep	1.85/1 1.90/1 1.96/1 2.01/1 2.03/1 2.10/xxx
2.02	1	Gaz	Saint-Denis	6 Jul	1.85/1 1.91/1 1.94/1 1.97/1 2.00/2 2.02/1 2.04/x 2.06/xx
2.02	1	GGala	Roma	13 Jul	1.85/1 1.90/1 1.95/1 1.98/1 2.00/2 2.02/1 2.05/xxx
2.02	1		Shanghai	28 Sep	1.85/1 1.91/1 1.97/1 2.00/1 2.02/1 2.10/xxx
2.01i	1		Bucuresti	9 Feb	1.85/1 1.89/1 1.95/1 2.01/2 2.03/xxx
2.00i	1		Göteborg	31 Jan	1.80/2 1.85/1 1.89/1 1.95/3 2.00.3 2.02/xxx
2.00i	1		Split	24 Feb	1.84/1 1.91/1 1.94/1 1.97/3 2.00/3 2.03/xxx

WOMEN 2007

Mark	Name		Nat	Born	Pos	Meet	Venue	Date	
2.00					1		Split	19 May	
2.00					1		Bydgoszcz	10 Jun	1.85/1 1.90/1 1.93/1 1.96/1 2.00/2 2.05/xxx
2.00					1	ECp-2B	Zenica	24 Jun	1.70/1 1.75/1 1.83/1 1.87/1 1.90/1 1.95/1 2.00/1 2.05/xxx
2.00					1		Moskva	29 Jun	1.85/1 1.92/1 1.96/1 1.98/1 2.00/1 2.05/xxx
2.00					1	ISTAF	Berlin	16 Sep	1.85/1 1.90/1 1.94/1 1.97/1 2.00/3 2.06/xxx
2.00					1	WAF	Stuttgart	22 Sep	1.85/1 1.90/1 1.94/1 1.97/1 2.00/1 2.05/xxx
2.05i	Tia	Hellebaut	BEL	16.2.78	1	EI	Birmingham	3 Mar	
									1.87/1 1.92/1 1.96/1 1.99/2 2.01/1 2.03/1 2.05/1 2.09/x
2.00i					1		Bruxelles	27 Jan	1.85/1 1.89/1 1.92/1 1.95/1 1.98/2 2.00/3 2.02/xxx
2.03	Antonietta	Di Martino	ITA	1.6.78	1	ECp-1B	Milano	24 Jun	
2.03					2=	WCh	Osaka	2 Sep	1.85/2 1.90/1 1.94/1 1.97/1 2.00/2 2.03/2 2.05/xxx
2.02					2	Nebiolo	Torino	8 Jun	1.80/1 1.85/1 1.89/1 1.92/1 1.95/1 1.98/1 2.00/2 2.02/3 2.04/xxx
2.00i					1		Banská Bystrica	13 Feb	1.80/1 1.85/1 1.88/1 1.91/1 1.94/1 1.97/3 2.00/2 2.02/xxx
2.03	Anna	Chicherova	RUS	22.7.82	2=	WCh	Osaka	2 Sep	
									1.85/1 1.90/1 1.94/1 1.97/1 2.00/2 2.03/2 2.05/xxx
2.01					1	NC	Tula	3 Aug	1.85/1 1.89/1 1.92/2 1.95/1 1.98/2 2.01/1 2.05/xxx
2.02	Kajsa	Bergqvist	SWE	12.10.76	1	Nebiolo	Torino	8 Jun	
									1.89/1 1.92/1 1.95/1 1.98/1 2.00/2 2.02/1 2.04/xxx
2.00					2	GGala	Roma	13 Jul	1.85/1 1.90/1 1.95/1 1.98/3 2.00/3 2.02/xxx
2.00					2	Herc	Monaco	25 Jul	1.85/1 1.90/1 1.94/2 1.97/2 2.00/2 2.03/xxx
2.02	Yelena	Slesarenko	RUS	28.2.82	1	Bisl	Oslo	15 Jun	
									1.85/1 1/90/1 1.93/1 1.96/1 1.98/1 2.00/1 2.02/1 2.04/xxx
2.02					1	ECp-S	München	24 Jun	1.85/1 1.89/1 1.92/2 1.95/1 1.98/3 2.00/1 2.02/1 2.05/xxx
2.01					2	WK	Zürich	7 Sep	1.85/1 1.90/2 1.95/1 1.98/1 2.01/3 2.04/xxx
2.01					2	VD	Bruxelles	14 Sep	1.85/1 1.90/1 1.93/1 1.96/2 1.99/1 2.01/2 2.03/xxx
2.00					2	Gaz	Saint-Denis	6 Jul	1.85/1 1.88/1 1.91/1 1.94/1 1.97/1 2.00/1 2.02/xx 2.04/x
2.00					4	WCh	Osaka	2 Sep	1.85 1.90 1.94 1.97/1 2.00/2 2.03/xxx
2.02	Ruth	Beitia	ESP	1.4.79	1	NC	San Sebastián	4 Aug	
									1.84/1 1.90/1 1.95/1 2.02/1 2.04/xxx
2.01i					1		Pireás	24 Feb	1.80/1 1.88/1 1.92/1 1.96/1 2.01/1 2.03/xxx
2.00	Yekaterina	Savchenko	RUS	3.6.77	1		Dudelange	1 Jul	
									1.74/1 1.78/1 1.81/2 1.84/1 1.87/1 1.90/1 1.92/1 1.94/1 1.96/3 1.98/1 2.00/1 2.03/xxx
2.00					5	WCh	Osaka	2 Sep	1.85/1 1.90/1 1.94/2 1.97/1 2.00/3 2.03/xxx
2.00	Vita	Palamar	UKR	12.10.77	2	Golden	Shanghai	28 Sep	
	(41/9)								
1.97i	Viktoriya	Klyugina (Slivka) (10)	RUS	28.9.80	1		Moskva	25 Jan	
1.97i	Mélanie	Skotnik	FRA	8.11.82	1	NC	Aubière	18 Feb	
1.97	Nicole	Forrester	CAN	17.11.76	2		Thessaloníki	30 Jul	
1.96i	Venelina	Veneva ¶	BUL	13.6.74	2		Hustopece	20 Jan	
1.96i	Destinee	Hooker	USA	7.9.87	1		Fayetteville	10 Feb	
1.96	Marina	Aitova	KAZ	13.9.82	4	SGP	Doha	11 May	
1.96	Svetlana	Shkolina	RUS	9.3.86	1	NC-23	Tula	19 Jun	
1.95i	Oana	Pantelimon	ROM	27.9.72	3		Bucuresti	9 Feb	
1.95i	Iryna	Kovalenko	UKR	12.6.86	1	NC	Sumy	12 Feb	
1.95A	Romary	Rifka	MEX	23.12.70	1		Ciudad de México	31 Mar	
1.95	Jessica	Ennis	GBR	28.1.86	1H		Desenzano del Garda	5 May	
	(20)								
1.95	Iva	Straková	CZE	4.8.80	1		Kladno	2 Jun	
1.95	Barbora	Laláková	CZE	2.5.81	1		Cottbus	20 Jun	
1.95	Amy	Acuff	USA	14.7.75	5	GGala	Roma	13 Jul	
1.95	Emma	Green	SWE	8.12.84	6	GGala	Roma	13 Jul	
1.95	Carolina	Klüft	SWE	2.2.83	1H	WCh	Osaka	25 Aug	
1.95	Romana	Dubnova	CZE	4.11.78	1		Olomouc	8 Sep	
1.94i	Yekaterina	Kuntsevich	RUS	13.7.84	3		Hustopece	20 Jan	
1.94i	Tatyana	Mnatsakanova	RUS	23.5.83	2		Moskva	25 Jan	
1.94	Tatyana	Efimenko	KGZ	2.1.81	1	AsiC	Amman	28 Jul	
1.94	Miruna	Mataoanu	ROM	4.6.83	Q	WCh	Osaka	31 Aug	
	(30)								
1.94	Lavern	Spencer	LCA	23.6.84	Q	WCh	Osaka	31 Aug	
1.94	Ariane	Friedrich	GER	10.1.84	2		Eberstadt	9 Sep	
1.94	Viktoriya	Styopina	UKR	21.2.76	3	CISM	Hyderabad	18 Oct	
1.93A	Anika	Smit	RSA	26.5.86	1		Potchefstroom	20 Feb	
1.93i	Marta	Mendía	ESP	18.5.75	Q	EI	Birmingham	2 Mar	
1.93i	Julia	Hartmann	GER	10.4.86	8Q	EI	Birmingham	2 Mar	
1.93	Adonía	Steryíou	GRE	7.7.85	1	NC	Athína	17 Jun	
1.93	Annett	Engel	GER	6.11.87	2	NC	Erfurt	21 Jul	
1.92i	Anne Gerd	Eieland	NOR	28.12.82	1		Kristiansand	21 Jan	
1.92i	Olena	Holosha	UKR	16.1.82	1		Zaporozhye	24 Jan	
	(40)								
1.92i	Yekaterina	Yevseyeva	KAZ-J	22.6.88	1		Tashkent	3 Mar	

Mark	Name		Nat	Born	Pos	Meet	Venue	Date
1.92i		Zheng Xingyuan	CHN-J	20.3.89	1		Beijing	21 Mar
1.92	Erin	Aldrich	USA	27.12.77	1		San Mateo	27 May
1.92	Anna	Ustinova	KAZ	8.12.85	1		Almaty	9 Jun
1.92	Ebba	Jungmark	SWE	10.3.87	2		Kil	10 Jun
1.92	Karolina	Gronau	POL	12.7.84	7	ECp-S	München	24 Jun
1.92	Persefóni	Hatzinákou	GRE	6.6.84	1	BalkC	Sofia	4 Jul
1.92	Lyudmyla	Blonska	UKR	18.3.75	2H	WCh	Osaka	25 Aug
1.92i	Aleksandra	Shamsutdinova	RUS	27.3.87	1		Omsk	22 Dec
1.91i	Viktoria	Leks	EST	28.9.87	1	NC	Tallinn	11 Feb
	(50)							
1.91i	Noengrothai	Chaipetch	THA	1.12.82	1	AsiG	Macau	31 Oct
1.91	Svetlana	Radzivil	UZB	17.1.87	1		Bishkek	3 Jun
1.91	Nadezhda	Dusanova	UZB	17.11.87	2		Pune	27 Jun
1.91		Bui Thi Nhung	VIE	21.1.83	1	NC	Ho Chi Minh	18 Oct
1.91	Ellen	Pettitt	AUS	13.5.86	1		Perth	2 Dec
1.90i	Tatyana	Kivimyagi	RUS	23.6.84	3		Moskva	13 Jan
1.90i	Inna	Gliznutsa	MDA	18.4.73	1	NC	Chisinau	10 Feb
1.90	Stephanie	Pywell	GBR	12.6.87	1		Loughborough	20 May
1.90	Kamila	Stepaniuk	POL	22.3.86	1		Warszawa	20 May
1.90	Viktoriya	Dobrynska	UKR	18.1.80	1		Kyiv	19 Jun
	(60)							
1.90	Miyuki	Aoyama	JPN	4.1.77	1		Osaka	23 Jun
1.90	Catherine	Drummond	AUS	14.12.87	1		Gold Coast	22 Dec
1.89i	Irina	Gordeyeva	RUS	9.10.86	1		Sankt-Peterburg	14 Jan
1.89i	Austra	Skujyté	LTU	12.8.79	1		Tallinn	23 Jan
1.89i	Tatyana	Grigoryeva	RUS	13.5.81	2		Moskva	26 Jan
1.89i	Darya	Kuntsevich	RUS	2.11.85	1		Samara	3 Feb
1.89i	Dóra	Györffy	HUN	23.2.78	1	NC	Budapest	17 Feb
1.89i	Julie	Crane	GBR	26.9.76	1		London (LV)	24 Feb
1.89i	Patricia	Sylvester	GRN	3.2.83	1	NCAA	Fayetteville	9 Mar
1.89	Marcoleen	Pretorius	RSA-J	25.7.89	1		Port Elizabeth	30 Mar
	(70)							
1.89	Kaylene	Wagner	USA	15.11.84	1	DrakeR	Des Moines	28 Apr
1.89	Olena	Demydova	UKR	16.6.82	2		Kyiv	18 May
1.89	Sharon	Day	USA	9.6.85	2	NC	Indianapolis	23 Jun
1.89	Natalija	Cakova	LAT	20.10.80	1	ECp-2A	Odense	24 Jun
1.89	Andreea	Ispan	ROM	2.6.78	2	BalkC	Sofia	4 Jul
1.89	Natalya	Mamlina	RUS-Y	16.3.91	1	WY	Ostrava	13 Jul
1.89	Maresa	Cadienhead	CAN	7.4.76	2	NC	Windsor	15 Jul
1.89	Doreen	Amata	NGR-J	5.6.88	1	AfG	Alger	19 Jul
1.88i	Susan	Moncrieff (Jones)	GBR	8.6.78	1		Cardiff	13 Jan
1.88i	Alina	Budnikova	RUS	22.10.83	3		Moskva	28 Jan
	(80)							
1.88i	Deirdre	Ryan	IRL	1.6.82	6		Gent	4 Feb
1.88i	Gema	Martín-Pozuelo	ESP	21.6.87	3	NC	Sevilla	17 Feb
1.88i	Karin	Ruckstuhl	NED	2.11.80	2=P	EI	Birmingham	2 Mar
1.88i	Kelly	Sotherton	GBR	13.11.76	2=P	EI	Birmingham	2 Mar
1.88	Marina	Matyukhina	RUS-J	17.5.88	1		Krasnodar	3 Jun
1.88	Mirela	Demireva	BUL-J	28.9.89	1	NC-j	Sofia	10 Jun
1.88		Qiao Yanrui	CHN-J	29.9.88	1	WCT	Suzhou	10 Jun
1.88	Irina	Glavatskikh	RUS	29.12.84	1		Hérouville	23 Jun
1.88		Li Shan	CHN	4.3.83	1		Wuhan	8 Jul
1.87i	Raffaella	Lamera	ITA	13.4.83	1		Caravaggio	14 Jan
	(90)							
1.87i	Karina	Vnukova	LTU	27.3.85	1	NC	Kaunas	9 Feb
1.87i	Erika	Wiklund	SWE-J	10.3.88	1		Nyköping	17 Feb
1.87i	María	Papayeoryíou	GRE	8.8.79	2	BalkC	Pireás	21 Feb
1.87i		He Yanhong	CHN	17.4.84	2		Beijing	21 Mar
1.87i	Sarah	Wilfred	USA	.85	1		New York	25 Feb
1.87	Raevan	Harris	USA	1.3.87	2	NCAA-r	Columbia	25 May
1.87	Caroline	Wolf	USA	13.2.85	2	NCAA-r	Des Moines	25 May
1.87	Jillian	Drouin	CAN	30.9.86	1=H	NCAA	Sacramento	7 Jun
1.87	Gaëlle	Niaré	FRA	12.3.82	H	NCAA	Sacramento	7 Jun
1.87	Kimberly	Jess	GER-Y	30.1.92	1		Kiel	9 Jun
	(100)							
1.87	Tatyana	Chernova	RUS-J	29.1.88	3	NC-23	Tula	19 Jun
1.87	Stefania	Cadamuro	ITA	23.2.79	2		Celle Ligure	27 Jun
1.87	Juana Rosario	Arrendel	DOM	16.6.78	3	NACAC	San Salvador	15 Jul
1.87	Caterine	Ibargüen	COL	12.2.84	4	PAm	Rio de Janeiro	25 Jul
1.87	Elena	Vallortigara	ITA-Y	21.9.91	1		Cesenatico	7 Oct

Mark	Name		Nat	Born	Date
1.86i	Elena	Brambilla	ITA	23.4.83	14 Jan
1.86i	Sophia	Sagonas	GER	18.9.81	21 Jan
1.86i	Alesya	Gerasimova	BLR-J	22.12.89	27 Jan
1.86i	Mariya	Nesterchuk	BLR-J	14.8.89	27 Jan
1.86i	Gwen	Wentland	USA	29.4.72	14 Feb
1.86i	Nataliya	Hapchuk	UKR-J	15.11.88	24 Feb
1.86i	Yuliya	Babayeva	RUS-J	22.5.88	24 Feb
1.86i	Sheena	Gordon	USA	26.9.83	24 Feb
1.86	Ann	Larsen	USA	28.2.83	24 Mar
1.86	Candeger	Oguz	TUR	16.7.80	13 May
1.86	Hanna	Melnychenko	UKR	24.4.83	19 May
1.86	Anna	Bogdanova	RUS	21.10.84	26 May
1.86	Yekaterina	Bolshakova	RUS-Y	23.4.91	27 May
1.86	Stine	Kufaas	NOR	7.4.86	9 Jun
1.86	Justyna	Kasprzycka	POL	20.8.87	9 Jun
1.86	Rita	Babos	HUN	21.10.80	17 Jun
1.86	Whitney	Evans	CAN	10.4.80	15 Jul
1.86	Olena	Motok	UKR	16.1.82	25 Jul
1.86	Hanna	Mikkonen	FIN	15.1.81	3 Aug
1.86	Yana	Maksimova	BLR-J	9.1.89	17 Aug
1.86	Serena	Capponcelli	ITA-J	24.1.89	15 Sep
1.86i	Brittney	Reese	USA	9.9.86	1 Dec
1.85i	Olga	Kychanova	RUS	14.7.75	20 Jan
1.85i	Olga	Kaliturina	RUS	9.3.76	26 Jan
1.85i	Yelena	Fedoseyeva	RUS	18.3.83	3 Feb
1.85i	Mariya	Nikolova	BUL	6.10.82	11 Feb
1.85	Yariagnis	Argüelles	CUB	18.4.84	15 Feb
1.85i	Renee	Hein	USA	6.1.85	18 Feb
1.85i	Vikki	Hubbard	GBR-J	13.7.89	25 Feb
1.85	Peaches	Roach	JAM	21.12.84	28 Apr
1.85	Victoria	Lucas	USA-J	18.9.89	12 May
1.85	Urszula	Domel	POL-J	21.7.88	13 May
1.85	Daniela	Rath	GER	6.5.77	26 May
1.85	Liene	Karsuma	LAT-J	27.1.88	26 May
1.85	Ruky	Abdulai	GHA	8.8.85	26 May
1.85	Elene	Meuti	ITA	26.6.83	26 May
1.85	Iveta	Srnková	SVK	2.5.87	5 Jun
1.85	Beatrice	Lundmark	SUI	26.4.80	9 Jun
1.85	Julia	Farmaka	CYP	20.4.78	9 Jun
1.85	Raquel	Álvarez	ESP	13.6.83	7 Jul
1.85	Lesyani	Mayor	CUB-J	8.7.89	8 Jul
1.85	Viktorija	Zemaityté	LTU	11.3.85	14 Jul
1.85	Anna	Iljustsenko	EST	12.10.85	22 Jul
1.85	Wanida	Boonyawan	THA	30.8.86	13 Aug
1.84i	Hannelore	Desmet	BEL-J	25.2.89	26 Jan
1.84i	Mariesa	Greene	USA	10.7.86	10 Feb
1.84i	Keneisha	Creary	JAM	2.3.85	17 Feb
1.84i	Jennifer	Klein	GER-J	3.4.88	18 Feb
1.84i	Kathryn	Holinski	GER	19.7.82	18 Feb
1.84i	Anna	Ksok	POL	29.9.83	18 Feb
1.84	Diana	Pickler	USA	9.12.83	4 Apr
1.84	Eliana Renata	da Silva	BRA	14.2.78	14 Apr
1.84	Beth	Castagno	USA	11.6.78	21 Apr
1.84	Rhonda	Watkins	TRI	9.12.87	12 May
1.84	Inika	McPherson	USA	29.9.86	25 May
1.84	Lacy	Wilson	USA	3.11.84	25 May
1.84		Xu Jie	CHN-J	2.1.89	4 Jun
1.84	Anne-Gaëlle	Jardin	FRA	2.11.79	8 Jun
1.84		Jiang Haiyan	CHN	19.12.79	10 Jun
1.84	Jenny	Isgren	SWE	16.4.81	10 Jun
1.84	Karolina	Blazej	POL	21.11.86	23 Jun
1.84	Anna	Nikitenko	RUS	30.8.84	7 Jul
1.84	Misha-Gaye	DaCosta	JAM-Y	25.9.90	13 Jul
1.84		Zhao Wei	CHN	11.9.83	3 Aug
1.84		Gu Xuan	CHN	19.11.87	3 Aug
1.84	Sandrine	Champion	FRA	29.8.80	4 Aug
1.84	Julia	Bennett	GBR	26.3.70	4 Aug
1.84	Georgiana	Zârcan (173)	ROM-J	30.5.88	12 Aug

Best outdoors

Mark	Name	Pos	Meet	Venue	Date
1.98	Hellebaut	2	SGP	Doha	11 May
1.96	Skotnik	1		Castres	11 Aug
1.93	Hooker	1	Big 12	Lincoln	12 May
1.93	Kovalenko	1		Yalta	12 Jun
1.92	Holosha	1		Kyiv	18 May
1.91	Yevseyeva	2	AsiC	Amman	28 Jul
1.90	Gliznutsa	2	ECp-2B	Zenica	24 Jun
1.90	Klyugina	3		Bühl	6 Jul
1.90	Pantelimon	1		Bucuresti	7 Jul
1.90	Shamsutdinova	1	NCp	Tula	8 Jul
1.89	Mnatsakanova	2=		Herrera	19 May
1.89	Eieland	1		Neerpelt	2 Jun
1.89	Leks	1		Türi	20 Jun
1.89	Györffy	1	ECp-1B	Milano	24 Jun
1.89	Mendía	2		Castellón	11 Aug
1.89	Y Kuntsevich	3	NC	Tula	3 Aug
1.89	Grigoryeva	1		Moskva	12 Aug
1.88	Kivimyagi	5		Kalamáta	2 Jun
1.88	Moncrieff	2	BIG	Bedford	10 Jun
1.88	Zheng Xingyuan	2	WCT	Suzhou	10 Jun
1.87	D Kuntsevich	2	NC-23	Tula	19 Jun
1.87	Ryan	1		Budapest	6 Jul
1.87	Sotherton	1H		Szczecin	7 Jul
1.87	Martín-Pozuelo	3	NC	San Sebastián	4 Aug

Mark	Name	Date
1.86	Wentland	26 Apr
1.86	Nesterchuk	2 Jun
1.86	Hapchuk	22 Jun
1.86	Papayeoryíou	4 Jul
1.86	Vnukova	14 Jul
1.86	Chaipetch	6 Oct
1.85	Hein	21 Apr
1.85	Gordon	28 Apr
1.85	Sagonas	26 May
1.85	Wiklund	27 Jun
1.84	Babayeva	30 Jun
1.84	Ruckstuhl	7 Jul
1.84	Skujyt	7 Jul
1.84	Hubbard	14 Jul

Exhibition: 1.93 Dóra Györffy HUN 23.2.78 3 Györ 16 Sep

Drugs disqualification

2.02i Venelina Veneva ¶ BUL 13.6.74 (1) Banská Bystrica 13 Feb
1.80/1 1.85/1 1.88/1 1.91/1 1.94/2 1.97/1 2.00/1 2.02/1 2.09/xxx
1.92 Alena Ivanova ¶ BLR 20.8.87 1 Grodno 30 Jun

JUNIORS

See main list for 12 top juniors. 7 (inc. 2 indoors) performances by 5 women to 1.89. Additional marks and further juniors:

Yevseyeva 2+ 1.89 2 NC Almaty 5 Jul

Mark	Name		Nat	Born	Pos	Meet	Venue	Date
1.86i	Alesya	Gerasimova	BLR	22.12.89	1		Mogilev	27 Jan
1.86i	Mariya	Nesterchuk	BLR	14.8.89	2		Mogilev	27 Jan
	1.86				1		Pinsk	2 Jun
1.86i	Nataliya	Hapchuk	UKR	15.11.88	1		Mogilev	24 Feb
	1.86				1	NC-j	Mikolayev	22 Jun
1.86i	Yuliya	Babayeva	RUS	22.5.88	3		Mogilev	24 Feb
1.86	Yekaterina	Bolshakova	RUS-Y	23.4.91	2		Sochi	27 May
1.86	Yana	Maksimova	BLR	9.1.89	1	v3N-J	Valmiera	17 Aug
1.86	Serena	Capponcelli	ITA-J	24.1.89	1		San Marino	15 Sep
1.85i	Vikki	Hubbard (20)	GBR	13.7.89	1		Birmingham	25 Feb
1.85	Victoria	Lucas	USA	18.9.89	1		Austin	12 May
1.85	Urszula	Domel	POL	21.7.88	1		Wroclaw	13 May
1.85	Liene	Karsuma	LAT	27.1.88	1		Murjani	26 May
1.85	Lesyani	Mayor	CUB-J	8.7.89	1	PAm-J	São Paulo	8 Jul

POLE VAULT

Mark	Name		Nat	Born	Pos	Meet	Venue	Date	
4.93i	Yelena	Isinbayeva	RUS	3.6.82	1		Donetsk	10 Feb	4.62/1 4.72/1 4.82/1 4.92/xx 4.93/1
4.91					1	Gaz	Saint-Denis	6 Jul	4.61/1 4.71/1 4.81/2 4.91/2 5.02/xxx
4.90					1	GGala	Roma	13 Jul	4.65/x 4.70/1 4.85/x 4.90/1 5.02/xxx
4.87					1	WAF	Stuttgart	22 Sep	4.67/2 4.77/1 4.82/1 4.92/xxx 4.87/1
4.85					1	Bisl	Oslo	15 Jun	4.60/x 4.65/1 4.75/1 4.85/3 4.95/xxx
4.84i					1		Bydgoszcz	14 Feb	4.64/1 4.74/x 4.84/1 4.94/xxx
4.83					1		Shanghai	28 Sep	4.65/1 4.83/3 5.02/xx
4.82i					1	Mill	New York	2 Feb	4.63/1 4.73/1 4.82/2 4.92/xxx
4.82					1	LGP	London (CP)	3 Aug	4.60/x 4.70/1 4.82/1
4.82					1	ISTAF	Berlin	16 Sep	4.62/1 4.77/1 4.82/1 5.02/xxx
4.81i					1		Paris (B)	23 Feb	4.66/2 4.81/3 4.94/xxx
4.80					1		Moscow	5 Aug	4.60/1 4.80/1 4.95/xxx
4.80					1	WCh	Osaka	28 Aug	4.65/1 4.80/2 5.02/xxx
4.80					1	WK	Zürich	7 Sep	4.65/1 4.75/x 4.80/2 4.93/xxx
4.80					1	VD	Bruxelles	14 Sep	4.65/1 4.80/1 4.90/x 5.02/xx
4.80					1		Daegu	4 Oct	4.65/1 4.80/1 4.93/xxx
4.73i					1		Birmingham	17 Feb	4.65/2 4.73/1 4.94/xxx
4.88	Jennifer	Stuczynski	USA	6.2.82	1	GP	New York	2 Jun	4.54/1 4.64/1 4.88/3 5.03/xxx
4.84					1	adidas	Carson	20 May	4.44/2 4.54/1 4.64/1 4.84/2 4.88/xpp
4.73					1		Brockport	21 Apr	4.41/2 4.61/1 4.73/1 4.84/xxx
4.82	Monika	Pyrek	POL	11.8.80	2	WAF	Stuttgart	22 Sep	4.40/1 4.60/1 4.72/1 4.77/x 4.82/1 4.87/xxx-x
4.75					4	WCh	Osaka	28 Aug	4.35/1 4.50/1 4.60/1 4.65/2 4.70/3 4.75/2 4.80/xxx
4.82	Svetlana	Feofanova	RUS	16.7.80	3	WAF	Stuttgart	22 Sep	4.40/1 4.50/1 4.60/2 4.67/2 4.72/1 4.82/2 4.87/xxx
4.80					2	VD	Bruxelles	14 Sep	4.40/1 4.55/1 4.65/1 4.70/2 4.80/3 4.85/xxx
4.76i					1	EI	Birmingham	4 Mar	4.38/1 4.48/1 4.58/1 4.66/1 4.71/xx 4.76/1
4.76					2	LGP	London (CP)	3 Aug	4.40/3 4.50/2 4.60/2 4.70/3 4.76/3 4.87/xxx
4.75					1	NC	Tula	3 Jul	4.40/1 4.50/1 4.60/1 4.70/1 4.75/1
4.75					3	WCh	Osaka	28 Aug	4.50/1 4.60/1 4.70/1 4.75/2 4.80/xxx
4.75					2	WK	Zürich	7 Sep	4.40/1 4.55/1 4.65/1 4.75/1 4.80/xx 4.85/x
4.75					2		Shanghai	28 Sep	4.45/1 4.55/1 4.65/1 4.75/3 4.83/xxx
4.74i					2		Bydgoszcz	14 Feb	4.44/3 4.54/1 4.64/1 4.74/2 4.84/xxx
4.75	Katerina	Badurová	CZE	18.12.82	2	WCh	Osaka	28 Aug	4.35/1 4.50/1 4.60/1 4.70/3 4.75/1 4.80/xxx
	(32/5)								
4.72i	Kym	Howe	AUS	12.6.80	2		Donetsk	10 Feb	
4.72i	Anna	Rogowska	POL	21.5.81	3		Donetsk	10 Feb	
4.72	Tatyana	Polnova	RUS	20.4.79	1		Rivas-Vaciamadrid	29 Jun	
4.71i	Yuliya	Golubchikova	RUS	27.3.83	2	EI	Birmingham	4 Mar	
4.70i	Carolin	Hingst	GER	18.9.80	1		Ludwigshafen	14 Jan	
	(10)								
4.70	Vanessa	Boslak	FRA	11.6.82	5	WCh	Osaka	28 Aug	
4.66i	Fabiana	Murer	BRA	16.3.81	2		Paris	23 Feb	
4.65	Anastasiya	Shvedova (Ivanova)	RUS	3.5.79	1	Odlozil	Praha	13 Jun	
4.64i	Pavla	Rybová (Hamácková)	CZE	20.5.78	4		Bydgoszcz	14 Feb	
4.64		Gao Shuying	CHN	28.10.79	2	GP	New York	2 Jun	
4.60Ai	April	Steiner	USA	22.4.80	2		Reno	19 Jan	
4.60Ai	Lacy	Janson	USA	20.2.83	1		Albuquerque	16 Feb	
4.60	Silke	Spiegelburg	GER	17.3.86	7	WAF	Stuttgart	22 Sep	
4.57	Chelsea	Johnson	USA	20.12.83	3=	GP	Madrid	21 Jul	
4.57	Julia	Hütter	GER	26.7.83	1=		Leverkusen	10 Aug	
	(20)								
4.56i	Naroa	Agirre	ESP	15.5.79	1	NC	Sevilla	17 Feb	
4.56	Anna	Battke	GER	3.1.85	1		Weissach im Tal	8 Jul	
4.55	Alana	Boyd	AUS	10.5.84	1		Perth	7 Jan	
4.54	Nicole	McEwen	USA	1.4.80	3	GP	New York	2 Jun	
4.53i	Becky	Holliday	USA	12.3.80	1		Jonesboro	14 Feb	
4.52i	Mary	Vincent (Sauer)	USA	31.10.75	2	Tyson	Fayetteville	9 Feb	
4.52i	Andree	Pickens	USA	17.6.80	1		Jonesboro	23 May	
4.52	Nastja	Ryshich/Ryjikh	GER	19.9.77	2		Rivas-Vaciamadrid	29 Jun	
4.52	Dana	Ellis	CAN	7.12.79	1		Chula Vista	18 Aug	
4.50i	Róza	Kasprzak	POL	9.4.82	2	NC	Spala	18 Feb	
	(30)								
4.50i	Joanna	Piwowarska	POL	4.11.83	9Q	EI	Birmingham	3 Mar	
4.50	Stacy	Dragila	USA	25.3.71	1		Eugene	27 May	
4.50	Aleksandra	Kiryashova	RUS	21.8.85	1	NC-23	Tula	18 Jun	

Mark	Name		Nat	Born	Pos	Meet	Venue	Date
4.50	Paulina	Debska	POL	27.9.85	1		Sopot	23 Jun
4.50	Jillian	Schwartz	USA	19.9.79	1		Luzern	28 Jun
4.46i		Zhang Yingning	CHN-Y	6.1.90	1		Shanghai	15 Mar
4.45i	Martina	Strutz	GER	4.11.81	4	NC	Leipzig	18 Feb
4.45	Carly	Dockendorf	CAN	31.12.83	2eA		Livermore	2 Jun
4.45	Tracy	O'Hara	USA	20.7.80	2eB		Livermore	2 Jun
4.40i	Krisztina	Molnár	HUN	8.4.76	2		Dresden	24 Jan
	(40)							
4.40i	Erica	Bartolina	USA	15.5.80	5	NC	Boston (R)	25 Feb
4.40i	Hanna-Mia	Persson	SWE	11.2.78	10=Q	EI	Birmingham	3 Mar
4.40i	Kate	Dennison	GBR	7.5.84	14Q	EI	Birmingham	3 Mar
4.40i	Linda	Berglund (Persson)	SWE	22.9.81	15Q	EI	Birmingham	3 Mar
4.40	Thórey Edda	Elisdóttír	ISL	30.6.77	4		Saulheim	3 Jun
4.40	Nataliya	Kushch	UKR	5.3.83	3	Kuso	Warszawa	17 Jun
4.40	Floé	Kühnert	GER	6.3.84	2		Mannheim	22 Jun
4.40	Kristina	Gadschiew	GER	3.7.84	3		Mannheim	22 Jun
4.40	Joana Ribeiro	Costa	BRA	15.8.81	2	NC	São Paulo	24 Jun
4.40	Vicky	Parnov	AUS-Y	24.10.90	2		Saulheim	30 Jun
	(50)							
4.40	Anna	Giordano Bruno	ITA	13.12.80	1		Trieste	21 Jul
4.40	Anna	Schultze	GER	26.5.85	1	NC-23	Hannover	25 Aug
4.40		Zhou Yang	CHN-J	16.5.88	1		Wuhan	2 Nov
4.38	Afrodíti	Skafída	GRE	20.3.82	4	ECp-S	München	23 Jun
4.36	Erin	Asay	USA	17.3.83	1		Eagle Rock	12 May
4.35	Bryson	Stately	USA	22.11.86	1	KansR	Lawrence	21 Apr
4.35	Kelsie	Hendry	CAN	29.6.82	1		Saskatoon	6 Jul
4.35	Maria	Rendin	SWE	28.7.82	2		Halmstad	14 Jul
4.35	Minna	Nikkanen	FIN-J	9.4.88	1	EJ	Hengelo	21 Jul
4.35	Yvonne	Buschbaum	GER	14.7.80	7	NC	Erfurt	22 Jul
	(60)							
4.35	Nicole	Büchler	SUI	17.12.83	3	WUG	Bangkok	10 Aug
4.35	Roslinda	Samsu	MAS	9.6.82	23=Q	WCh	Osaka	26 Aug
4.35	Takayo	Kondo	JPN	17.11.75	25Q	WCh	Osaka	26 Aug
4.35	Elizaveta	Ryshich	GER-J	27.9.88	5=		Beckum	9 Sep
4.33i	Tori	Anthony	USA-J	19.4.89	2		Seattle	10 Feb
4.33A	Elouise	Rudy	USA	30.12.85	1		Bozeman	4 May
4.32	Elisabete	Tavares	POR	7.3.80	1		Arras	15 Jul
4.31i	Elena	Scarpellini	ITA	14.1.87	1	NC-23	Genova	25 Feb
4.30i	Amélie	Delzenne	FRA	4.8.83	4		Eaubonne	2 Feb
4.30Ai	April	Kubishta	USA	5.7.85	1		Flagstaff	3 Feb
	(70)							
4.30i	Marta	Plewa	POL	17.12.83	4	NC	Spala	18 Feb
4.30i	Natalie	Moser	USA	19.2.86	2	NCAA	Fayetteville	10 Mar
4.30i	Yekaterina	Sultanova	RUS	31.12.84	3	NCAA	Fayetteville	10 Mar
4.30		Li Ling	CHN-J	6.7.89	1	WCT	Suzhou	9 Jun
4.30	Christina	Michel	GER-J	16.12.89	1		Potsdam	10 Jun
4.30	Karla Rosa	da Silva	BRA	12.11.84	3	NC	São Paulo	24 Jun
4.30	Anna Katharina	Schmid	SUI-J	2.12.89	1		Fribourg	14 Jul
4.30	Yarisley	Silva	CUB	1.6.87	3	PAm	Rio de Janeiro	23 Jul
4.30		Wu Sha	CHN	21.10.87	1	NC	Shijiazhuang	5 Aug
4.30	Alejandra	García	ARG	13.6.73	1		Buenos Aires	13 Aug
	(80)							
4.30	Denise	von Eynatten	GER	30.12.87	2	NC-23	Hannover	25 Aug
4.30	Vanessa	Vandy	FIN-J	14.5.89	1	v SWE	Göteborg	8 Sep
4.30	Arianna	Farfaletti-Casali	ITA	22.6.76	1		Donnas	15 Sep
4.30	Ikuko	Nishikori	JPN	5.1.80	1		Hamamatsu	3 Nov
4.30	Mami	Nakano	JPN	12.3.79	2		Hamamatsu	3 Nov
4.28i	Katelin	Rains	USA	20.8.87	1		Mankato	8 Dec
4.27i	Tamara	Diles	USA	5.11.82	1		Moscow	16 Feb
4.26i	Ellie	Spain	GBR	23.8.82	2		Wien	30 Jan
4.26	Jennie	Sewell	USA	21.2.84	1	NCAA-r	Des Moines	26 May
4.25i	Sabine	Schulte	GER	29.1.76	4		Bad Oeynhausen	9 Mar
	(90)							
4.25	Jodi	Unger	USA	28.12.84	2	NCAA	Sacramento	8 Jun
4.25	Ekateríni	Stefanídi	GRE-Y	4.2.90	1	NC-y	Athína	23 Jun
4.25	Simone	Langhirt	GER	19.1.84	1		Schweinfurt	8 Jul
4.25	Marion	Buisson	FRA-J	19.2.88	1	NC-j	Narbonne	29 Jul
4.25	Rianna	Galiart	NED	22.11.85	1		Amsterdam	1 Aug
4.25	Sandra-Helena	Tavares	POR	29.5.82	2	FRA Ch	Niort	5 Aug
4.25	Alixe	Auvray	FRA	24.1.85	4	NC	Niort	5 Aug

Mark		Name	Nat	Born	Pos Meet	Venue	Date
4.23	Michaela Ruth	Heitkötter	BRA/GER	22.3.85	4	Wipperfürth	6 Jul
4.22i	Jirina	Ptácniková	CZE	20.5.86	2	Praha	27 Jan
4.22Ai	Ingrid	Kantola	USA	8.2.86	2	Flagstaff	17 Feb
	(100)						
4.22i		Yang Jing	CHN	1.1.84	1	Toyota	3 Mar

4.21i	Kate	Soma	USA	13.2.83	10 Feb
4.21	Leila	Ben-Youssef	TUN	13.11.81	12 May
4.21	Anna Maria	Pinero	ESP	15.1.86	1 Jul
4.21	Cathrine	Larsåsen	NOR	5.12.86	3 Aug
4.20	Charmaine	Lucock	AUS	8.4.87	20 Jan
4.20	Rosanna	Ditton	AUS	7.6.79	27 Jan
4.20	Jacinta	Lynn	AUS	12.2.85	3 Feb
4.20i	Doris	Auer	AUT	10.5.71	10 Feb
4.20i	Vera	Chavdarova	BUL	19.11.80	10 Feb
4.20i	Kira	Sims	USA	1.3.82	25 Feb
4.20i	Jessie	Gallaher	USA	1.7.85	9 Mar
4.20i	Melinda	Owen	USA	30.10.84	10 Mar
4.20	Alizée	Dufraisse	FRA	13.6.87	22 Apr
4.20	Gabriella	Duclos-Lasnier	CAN-J	1.3.88	28 Apr
4.20	Stephanie	McCann	CAN	22.4.77	16 May
4.20	Anna	Fitidou	CYP	22.4.77	7 Jun
4.20	Marie	Bode	GER	11.9.87	9 Jun
4.20	Mariánna	Zahariádi	GRE-Y	25.2.90	23 Jun
4.20	Yuliya	Taratynova	BLR	25.5.83	23 Jun
4.20	Romana	Malácová	CZE	15.5.87	30 Jun
4.20	Slavica	Semenjuk	SRB	25.10.84	4 Jul
4.20	Alicia	Rue	USA-J	4.8.88	8 Jul
4.20	Karmen	Bunikowska	POL-J	21.3.88	21 Jul
4.20	Marie	Frachebois	FRA	26.7.84	22 Jul
4.20	Dimitra	Emmanouil	GRE	13.5.84	10 Aug
4.20	Dana Elvira	Cervantes	ESP	18.8.78	11 Aug
4.18i	Stephanie	Irwin	USA	14.3.86	9 Feb
4.17i	Tina	Sutej	SLO-J	7.11.88	20 Jan
4.16i	Petra	Olsen	SWE-Y	2.10.90	28 Jan
4.16	Melina	Hamilton	NZL	15.6.76	4 Mar
4.16	Kelly	Furr	USA	8.85	26 May
4.15i	Valeriya	Volik	RUS-J	15.11.89	15 Feb
4.15i	Sarah	Landau	USA	9.10.85	16 Feb
4.15i	Eleonor	Tavares	POR	24.9.85	17 Feb
4.15i	Kirsty	Maguire	GBR	5.7.83	24 Feb
4.15		Liu Dan	CHN-J	1.1.88	14 Apr
4.15	Evridíki	Prezerákou	GRE	8.3.75	11 May
4.15	Keisa	Monterola	VEN-J	26.2.88	30 Jun
4.15	Chloé	Mourand	FRA	20.10.87	12 Jul
4.15	Louise	Butterworth	GBR	22.2.85	4 Aug
4.15	Jennifer	Bassement	FRA	9.5.85	4 Aug
4.15		Li Caixia	CHN	23.8.87	5 Aug
4.15		Li Gaoqun	CHN	29.6.86	5 Aug
4.15	Nicola	Tietze	GER	22.5.85	25 Aug
4.15i	Ashley	Early	USA	4.9.87	1 Dec
4.14i	Angie	Aguilar	USA	3.10.83	24 Feb
4.14	Allison	Stokke	USA-J	22.3.89	24 Apr
4.14	Shade	Weygandt	USA-Y	24.1.91	12 May
4.12i	Ashley	Laughlin	USA	7.6.85	2 Mar
4.12i	Emily	Enders	USA	19.11.84	3 Mar
4.12	Vera	Neuenswander	USA		4 May
4.11i	Mallory	Peck	USA	18.8.87	24 Feb
4.11i	Adrianne	Vangool	CAN	30.10.85	24 Feb
4.11i	Laurence	Bago	FRA	3.3.80	24 Mar
4.11	Stevie	Marshalek	USA	1.6.85	27 Apr
4.11	Tiina	Taavitsainen	FIN	19.12.85	1 Jul
4.11	Rachel	Laurent	USA-J	21.9.89	1 Jul
4.10i	Sirine	Balti	TUN	31.10.83	13 Jan
4.10i	Anastasiya	Kiryanova	RUS	26.7.82	13 Jan
4.10i	Alisa	Vodopyan	RUS-J	7.4.89	15 Jan
4.10i	Alina	Kakoshinskaya	RUS	16.11.86	21 Jan
4.10i	Daniela	Höllwarth	AUT	24.8.87	21 Jan
4.10i	Agnes	Livebardon	FRA	31.5.80	28 Jan
4.10i	Anita	Tørring	DEN	19.1.79	4 Feb
4.10i	Katarzyna	Sowa	POL	19.11.85	7 Feb
4.10i	Nadine	Sonnabend	GER	28.1.81	9 Feb
4.10i	Kylie	Hutson	USA		9 Feb
4.10i	Brigitta	Pöll	AUT	17.3.79	10 Feb
4.10i	Anastasiya	Krupskaya	RUS	20.7.86	15 Feb
4.10i	Caroline	Bocquet	FRA	22.9.76	17 Feb
4.10Ai	Stephanie	Bagan	USA-J	15.7.88	23 Feb
4.10i	Lindsey	Walesheck	USA	25.8.85	23 Feb
4.10i		Liu Dan	CHN	3.4.80	20 Mar
4.10	Amy	Chow	USA	15.5.78	5 May
4.10	Jennifer	Green	USA	26.6.85	12 May
4.10	Patricia	dos Santos	BRA	13.6.84	16 May
4.10	Emma	Lyons	GBR	14.6.87	20 May
4.10	Zhanna	Bayandina	BLR-J	29.2.88	1 Jun
4.10	Anastasiya	Savehenko	RUS-J	15.11.89	8 Jun
4.10	Alevtyna	Ruyeva	UKR-J	13.3.88	12 Jun
4.10	Camille	Simon	FRA	24.4.86	20 Jun
4.10	Slavomíra	Slúková	SVK	18.11.80	30 Jun
4.10	Aurore	Pignot	FRA	24.12.79	6 Jul
4.10	Pascale	Gacon	FRA	31.10.83	12 Jul
4.10	Leah	Vause	CAN	4.5.87	21 Jul
4.10	Fiona	Harrison	GBR	30.11.81	29 Jul
4.10	Yekaterina	Kolesova	RUS-Y	4.9.90	18 Aug
4.10	Tomoko	Maeda	JPN	31.3.83	7 Oct
4.08i	Sarah	Hegna	USA	4.12.84	16 Feb
4.08	Ashley	McCallister	USA	.3.86	11 May
4.07Ai	Britany	Parker	USA	29.10.87	26 Jan
4.07	Jackie	Nguyen	USA	20.4.84	28 May
4.07	Lyudmila	Yeremina	RUS-Y	8.8.91	18 Aug
4.06i	Melanie	Buczko	USA	30.4.85	27 Jan
4.06i	Kelly	DiVesta	USA	20.10.85	10 Feb
4.06i	Elise	Carmignani	FRA	27.6.83	24 Mar
4.06	Erin	Mahony	USA	31.12.84	26 May
4.06	Kelley	Schulz	USA	14.6.85	26 May
4.06	Amanda	Alley	USA	9.3.87	26 May
4.06	Katelyn	Rodrigue	USA-J	29.1.88	26 May
4.06	Gloria	Gazzotti	ITA	29.6.84	8 Sep
4.06	Natasha	Benner (202)	GER-Y	1.1.90	9 Sep

Best outdoors

4.91	Isinbayeva	1	Gaz	Saint-Denis	6 Jul
4.70	Golubchikova	1	NCp	Tula	8 Jul
4.65	Howe	1		Saulheim	30 Jun
4.65	Murer	6=	WCh	Osaka	28 Aug
4.65	Hingst	3	Golden	Shanghai	28 Sep
4.60	Rogowska	8	WCh	Osaka	28 Aug
4.50	Steiner	1		Fayetteville	21 Apr
4.50	Janson	1		Fortaleza	16 May
4.50	Rybová	2	NC	Trinec	30 Jun
	4.51 ex	1		Kutná Hora	12 Aug
4.50	Agirre	8	GGala	Roma	13 Jul
4.45	Holliday	1eA		Livermore	2 Jun
4.45	Strutz	1		Mannheim	22 Jun
4.44	Vincent	2	adidas	Carson	20 May
4.40	Pickens	1		Tuscaloosa	24 Mar
4.40	Zhang Yingning	1	GP	Osaka	5 May
4.40	H Persson	1		Göteborg	29 Jun
4.40	Piwowarska	1		Warszawa	20 Jul
4.35	Molnár	3	SGP	Doha	11 May
4.35	Bartolina	1		Champaign	16 Jun
4.31	Dennison	3	Odlozil	Praha	13 Jun
4.30	Anthony	1		Folsom	10 Jun
4.30	Kasprzak	3	NC	Poznan	1 Jul
4.30	Delzenne	2		Reims	17 Jul
4.26	Kubishta	1	NCAA-r	Eugene	26 May
4.25	Scarpellini	2		Donnas	15 Sep

4.21	Soma	12 May
4.20	Auer	27 May
4.20	Plewa	2 Jun
4.20	Berglund	1 Aug
4.15	Diles	15 Apr
4.15	Sultanova	21 Apr
4.15	Yang Jing	28 Apr
4.15	Kantola	5 May
4.11	Early	20 Apr
4.10	Owen	28 Apr
4.10	Sutej	20 May
4.10	Bago	2 Jun
4.10	Vangool	8 Jun
4.10	Eleonor Tavares	16 Jun
4.10	Volik	29 Jun
4.10	Sowa	1 Jul
4.07	Olsen	30 Jun
4.06	Peck	21 Apr

Mark	Wind	Name		Nat	Born	Pos	Meet	Venue	Date

JUNIORS

See main list for 13 top juniors. 10 (inc. 2 indoors) performances by 5 women to 4.35. Additional marks and further juniors:

Zhang Y 4.40i 1 Beijing 20 Mar 4.35 23=Q WCh Osaka 26 Aug
Parnov 4.35 1 WY Ostrava 14 Jul
Nikkanen 4.35 19=Q WCh Osaka 26 Aug

Mark	Name		Nat	Born	Pos	Meet	Venue	Date
4.20	Gabriella	Duclos-Lasnier	CAN	1.3.88	1		Tempe	28 Apr
4.20	Mariánna	Zahariádi	GRE-Y	25.2.90	2	NC-y	Athína	23 Jun
4.20	Alicia	Rue	USA	4.8.88	1	PAm-J	São Paulo	8 Jul
4.20	Karmen	Bunikowska	POL	21.3.88	6	EJ	Hengelo	21 Jul
4.17i	Tina	Sutej	SLO	7.11.88	1		Ljubljana	20 Jan
4.16i	Petra	Olsen	SWE-Y	2.10.90	1		Malmö	28 Jan
4.15i	Valeriya	Volik (20)	RUS	15.11.89	1		Volgograd	15 Feb
4.15		Liu Dan	CHN	1.1.88	1		Chengdu	14 Apr
4.15	Keisa	Monterola	VEN	26.2.88	1	SAm-J	São Paulo	30 Jun

LONG JUMP

Mark	Wind	Name		Nat	Born	Pos	Meet	Venue	Date	Series
7.21	1.9	Lyudmila	Kolchanova	RUS	1.10.79	1		Sochi	27 May	7.21 6.80/-0.2 6.99/1.1 6.95/1.6 6.97/1.9 7.07/1.6
7.17	-1.3					1	NC	Tula	2 Aug	7.01/0.1 6.85/0.0 6.87/0.5 7.17 7.02/-0.5 p
6.96	0.5					Q	WCh	Osaka	27 Aug	6.47 6.96
6.92	-0.3					2	WCh	Osaka	28 Aug	x 6.84/0.4 x 6.71 6.63 6.92
7.15	1.0	Tatyana	Lebedeva	RUS	21.7.76	1	GP	Madrid	21 Jul	6.84/2.0 x 7.15 7.10w/2.2 p x
7.03	0.3					1	WCh	Osaka	28 Aug	6.73 7.03/0.7 7.03/0.3 x 6.98/0.1 p
6.90	1.0					1		Daegu	3 Oct	6.60 6.90 6.70 6.53 6.51 6.62
6.87	-1.9					1		Tallinn	22 Jul	x x 6.59 6.87 x 6.70
6.86	-0.9					1	Vard	Réthimno	18 Jul	6.70 6.70 6.86 6.71 6.74 x
7.11	0.1	Irina	Simagina	RUS	25.5.82	2		Sochi	27 May	6.77/0.5 7.07/1.0 x 6.99/1.9 6.93/1.9 7.11
7.08	0.7					2	NC	Tula	2 Aug	7.08 6.99/0.3 x 6.84/0.7 6.99/1.2 x
6.93	0.5					1		Moskva	29 Jun	x x 6.93 6.88/0.4 6.82/0.9 x
6.88	1.4					1	Déca	Paris (C)	8 Sep	6.80/0.6 6.88 6.58 x
6.88i						1		Ryazan	23 Dec	6.66 ? ? ? ? 6.88
7.01	2.0	Naide	Gomes	POR	10.11.79	2	GP	Madrid	21 Jul	6.81/1.8 6.84w/2.4 6.52 7.01 6.92/1.3 6.74
6.96	1.0					Q	WCh	Osaka	27 Aug	6.96 only jump
6.89i						1	El	Birmingham	3 Mar	6.73 6.72 x 6.69 6.89 x
6.87	0.7					4	WCh	Osaka	28 Aug	6.87 6.75/0.3 6.61 6.86/0.9 6.85/0.4 6.80/-0.3
6.95	0.6	Maurren	Maggi	BRA	25.6.76	Q	WCh	Osaka	27 Aug	6.95 p p
6.94A	1.0					1	Iriarte	Cochabamba	3 Jun	6.86/0.5 6.94 x 6.87/0.1 x x
6.91	1.0					1	SACh	São Paulo	8 Jun	6.64 6.77/0.4 6.83/0.4 6.65 p 6.91
6.93	1.6	Karen	Mey	RSA	31.5.84	1		Bad Langensalza	7 Jul	6.38 6.73 6.57 6.85/1.9 6.60 6.93
6.92	0.5	Oksana	Udmurtova	RUS	1.2.82	2		Moskva	29 Jun	6.92 6.77 6.88/0.9 6.54 6.81/-0.1 x
6.90	1.0	Tatyana	Kotova	RUS	11.12.76	3		Moskva	29 Jun	6.84 6.77 6.90 x 6.80 6.75
6.90	0.5					3	WCh	Osaka	28 Aug	6.80/-0.6 x 6.75/1.0 6.70 x 6.90
6.90	1.9	Bianca	Kappler	GER	8.8.77	2		Bad Langensalza	7 Jul	6.66 6.77 x x 6.63 6.90
6.85	0.1					Q	WCh	Osaka	27 Aug	x 6.85
6.89	0.3	Natalya	Lebusova (10)	RUS	4.4.78	3		Sochi	27 May	x 6.75 6.89 x x x
6.88	-0.1	Keila	Costa	BRA	6.2.83	1	GP	Belém	20 May	x x 6.64 6.71 6.80/-0.2 6.88
6.88	1.0	Lyudmyla	Blonska	UKR	9.11.77	1H	WCh	Osaka	26 Aug	x 6.70 6.88
6.85	-0.7	Olga	Rypakova	KAZ	30.11.84	1	WUG	Bangkok	10 Aug	x 6.46 6.49 6.82/0.7 6.85 6.64
6.85	1.0	Carolina (32/14)	Klüft	SWE	2.2.83	2H	WCh	Osaka	26 Aug	6.65 6.35 6.85
6.84	1.7	Concepción	Montaner	ESP	14.1.81	4	GP	Madrid	21 Jul	
6.83	-0.1	Brittney	Reese	USA	9.9.86	Q	WCh	Osaka	27 Aug	
6.82	0.3	Akiba	McKinney	USA	9.3.79	1	MSR	Walnut	15 Apr	
6.82	1.9	Rhonda	Watkins	TRI	9.12.87	1	NCAA-r	Eugene	25 May	
6.81	0.0	Anna	Nazarova	RUS	14.3.86	1	EU23	Debrecen	15 Jul	
6.80	0.9	Malgorzata (20)	Trybanska	POL	21.6.81	1	NC	Poznan	30 Jun	

Mark	Wind	Name		Nat	Born	Pos	Meet	Venue	Date
6.79i		Yargelis	Savigne	CUB	13.11.84	1	Spark	Stuttgart	3 Feb
6.79	0.1	Janice	Josephs	RSA	31.3.82	1	AfG	Alger	21 Jul
6.78	0.0	Lela	Nelson	USA	19.5.83	1H		Bernhausen	19 Aug
6.77	0.7	Viktoriya	Rybalko	UKR	26.10.82	Q	WCh	Osaka	27 Aug
6.77	-1.4	Oksana	Zhukovskaya	RUS	24.9.84	2		Gyumri	9 Sep
6.75	0.0	Oleksandra	Stadnyuk	UKR	16.4.80	1	Veniz	Haniá	9 Jun
6.73	1.2	Kumiko	Ikeda	JPN	10.1.81	1	GP	Osaka	5 May
6.73	0.9	Eunice	Barber	FRA	17.11.74	1	ECp-S	München	24 Jun
6.72	0.5	Viktoriya	Gurova	RUS	22.5.82	4		Sochi	27 May
6.72	0.8	Anna	Pyatykh	RUS	4.4.81	5		Moskva	29 Jun
		(30)							
6.72	1.6	Bronwyn	Thompson	AUS	29.1.78	4		Bad Langensalza	7 Jul
6.72	0.9	Grace	Upshaw	USA	25.9.75	5		Bad Langensalza	7 Jul
6.71	1.6	Brianna	Glenn	USA	18.4.80	2	MSR	Walnut	15 Apr
6.71	0.8	Oksana	Zubkovska	UKR	15.7.81	1		Kyiv	19 May
6.71	1.1	Alina	Militaru	ROM	10.4.82	1		Bucuresti	16 Jun
6.71	0.0	Yelena	Sokolova	RUS	23.7.86	3	EU23	Debrecen	15 Jul
6.70	1.0	Ruky	Abdulai	GHA	8.8.85	1		Fresno	24 May
6.69		Hrisopiyí	Devetzí	GRE	2.1.76	1	CISM	Hyderabad	16 Oct
6.68	0.6	Anna	Kovalenko	RUS	3.2.80	5		Sochi	27 May
6.68	0.9	Rose	Richmond	USA	29.1.81	6	GP	Madrid	21 Jul
		(40)							
6.68	-0.1	Kelly	Sotherton	GBR	13.11.76	3H	WCh	Osaka	26 Aug
6.67i		Ineta	Radevica	LAT	13.7.81	Q	EI	Birmingham	2 Mar
6.67	0.3	Marie	Collonvillé	FRA	23.11.73	4H	WCh	Osaka	26 Aug
6.66	0.0		Jung Soon-ok	KOR	23.4.83	1	NC	Daegu	1 Jun
6.66A	0.2	Eliane	Martins	BRA	26.5.86	1		La Paz	1 Jun
6.66	-0.2	Elva	Goulbourne	JAM	21.1.80	*	NC	Kingston	22 Jun
6.66	0.0	Chelsea	Hammond	JAM	2.8.83	*	NC	Kingston	22 Jun
6.65	-1.0	Nolle	Graham	JAM	12.9.81	1	Takac	Beograd	29 May
6.65	0.7	Jana	Veldáková	SVK	3.6.81	1		Kladno	2 Jun
6.65	0.0	Denisa	Scerbová	CZE	21.8.86	2	Veniz	Haniá	9 Jun
		(50)							
6.65	1.3	Anju Bobby	George	IND	19.4.77	2	AsiC	Amman	27 Jul
6.64	1.9	Karin	Ruckstuhl	NED	2.11.80	1		Leiden	9 Jun
6.63	1.2	Jackie	Edwards	BAH	14.4.71	1	NC	Nassau	22 Jun
6.61	2.0	Yuliya	Pidluzhnaya	RUS-J	1.10.88	Q		Sochi	23 May
6.61	1.2	Tatyana	Chernova	RUS-J	29.1.88	1H		Arles	3 Jun
6.61	0.5	Urszula	Gutowicz-Westhof	GER	13.7.77	2		Wesel	28 Jun
6.60	2.0	Tianna	Madison	USA	30.8.85	1	ModR	Modesto	5 May
6.60	0.7	Adina	Anton	ROM	6.10.84	1		Bucuresti	26 May
6.59i		Irina	Melnikova	RUS	14.5.75	1		Volgograd	21 Jan
6.59i		Marija	Sestak	SLO	17.4.79	1		Budapest	26 Jan
		(60)							
6.59	0.4		Chen Yaling	CHN	24.2.84	1	WCT	Suzhou	8 Jun
6.59	0.0	Marina	Pankova	RUS	16.11.82	5	NC	Tula	2 Aug
6.58		Yudelkis	Fernández	CUB	28.2.85	1		La Habana	9 Mar
6.58		Zhanna	Chernaya	RUS	24.7.84	1		Moskva	15 May
6.57i		Olesya	Kazanovskaya	RUS	12.7.82	2		Sankt Peterburg	7 Jan
6.57		Tisifenee	Taylor	USA	19.6.84	1		Moravian	21 Apr
6.57	2.0	Nina	Kolaric	SLO	12.12.86	*	NC-23	Ptuj	30 Jun
6.56	1.6	Kylie	Wheeler	AUS	17.1.80	1H	NC	Brisbane	10 Mar
6.56	-0.7	Jade	Johnson	GBR	7.6.80	2	ECp-1A	Vaasa	24 Jun
6.56	1.1	Valeria	Canella	ITA	6.2.82	1		Pergine Valsugana	7 Jul
		(70)							
6.55i		Ksenja	Balta	EST	1.11.86	1		Tallinn	23 Jan
6.55	0.4	Teresa	Dobija	POL	9.10.82	1		Biala Podlaska	23 Jun
6.54	0.6	Irina	Chernushenko (Stasyuk)	BLR	9.3.79	7	ECp-S	München	24 Jun
6.53i		Ivana	Spanovic	SRB-Y	10.5.90	1		Moskva	14 Feb
6.53	1.8	Laurice Cristina	Félix	BRA	28.5.81	1		São Paulo	28 Feb
6.53	0.2	Brenda	Faluade	USA	27.10.84	1	FlaR	Gainesville	6 Apr
6.53	1.9	Jovanee	Jarrett	JAM	15.1.83	1		Eugene	27 May
6.53	-0.9	Elise	Vésanes	FRA	25.1.84	1		Tours	10 Jun
6.53	1.7	Karolina	Tyminska	POL	4.10.84	2H		Kladno	20 Jun
6.53	1.8	Shameka	Marshall	USA	9.9.83	6	NC	Indianapolis	23 Jun
		(80)							
6.52i		Olga	Rublyova	RUS	28.10.74	4		Samara	3 Feb
6.52i		Panayióta	Koutsioumári	GRE	23.3.81	1	NC	Athína	10 Feb
6.52A	1.3	Kiamesha	Otey	USA	28.5.81	1		Provo	2 Jun
6.52	1.7	Jeomi	Maduka	USA	21.8.87	Q	NCAA	Sacramento	6 Jun

Mark	Wind	Name		Nat	Born	Pos	Meet	Venue	Date
6.52	-0.9	Tabia	Charles	CAN	6.4.85	1	NC	Windsor	14 Jul
6.52	1.3	Joanna	Skibinska	POL	21.2.85	4	EU23	Debrecen	15 Jul
6.52	-0.9	Ioánna	Kafetzi	GRE	30.5.76	2		Kalamáta	22 Jul
6.52	-0.3	Stilianí	Pilátou	GRE	28.3.80	3	WUG	Bangkok	10 Aug
6.51		Blessing	Okagbare	NGR-J	10.9.88	1		Ijebu Ode	2 Mar
6.51A	1.0	Alice (90)	Falaiye	CAN	24.12.78	2		El Paso	14 Apr
6.51		Francine	Simpson	JAM-J	1.11.89	1		Kingston	19 May
6.51	0.6	Olena	Svyrydenko	UKR	11.4.81	2		Yalta	13 Jun
6.51	0.3	Veronika	Shutkova	BLR	26.5.86	1		Minsk	14 Jun
6.50i		Yelena	Ivanova	RUS	16.3.79	3		Sankt Peterburg	20 Jan
6.50	0.8	Mindy	Neeley	USA	15.1.87	1		Los Angeles (Ww)	14 Apr
6.50	1.9	Ola	Sesay	USA	30.5.79	1		Lake Charles	12 May
6.50	0.1	Tania	Vicenzino	ITA	1.4.86	5	EU23	Debrecen	15 Jul
6.49	1.3	Tanika	Liburd	SKN	20.5.82	1		Houston	10 May
6.49	1.2	Nataliya	Sorokina	UKR	24.3.75	1		Praha	5 Jun
6.49	1.2	Natasha (100)	Harvey	USA	29.11.87	Q	NCAA	Sacramento	6 Jun
6.49	1.2	Darya	Klishina	RUS-Y	5.1.91	1		Penza	22 Jun

Mark	Wind	Name		Nat	Born	Date
6.48	-1.6	Julia	Mächtig	GER	1.1.86	27 May
6.48	0.3	Athanasia	Pérra	GRE	2.2.83	17 Jun
6.48	1.8	Olga	Zinovyeva	RUS	29.10.86	19 Jun
6.48	1.2	Sirkka-Liisa	Kivine	EST	22.6.77	1 Aug
6.47i		Amy	Harris	GBR	14.9.87	11 Feb
6.47	0.0	Martina	Darmovzalová	CZE	12.10.78	19 May
6.47	0.9	Yekaterina	Sidorenko	RUS	7.5.87	27 May
6.47		Natalia	Kilpelainen-Bäck	FIN	19.7.70	6 Jun
6.47	0.8	Eloyse	Lesueur	FRA-J	15.7.88	23 Jun
6.47	1.3	Antonia	Yordanova	BUL	17.8.76	4 Jul
6.47	1.4	Lauranne	Osse	FRA	5.4.85	5 Aug
6.47	0.3	Ida	Marcussen	NOR	1.11.87	26 Aug
6.46i		Viorica	Tigau	ROM	12.8.79	2 Mar
6.46	2.0	Funmi	Jimoh	USA	29.5.84	13 Apr
6.46	0.9	Liliya	Kulyk	UKR	27.1.87	19 May
6.46	0.5	Kateryna	Chernyavska	UKR	31.1.83	19 May
6.46	1.4	Olga	Sergeyenko	BLR	22.2.84	14 Jun
6.46	-0.1	Olga	Denisova	RUS	25.10.83	1 Aug
6.46	0.2	Anna	Bogdanova	RUS	21.10.84	26 Aug
6.46	0.5	Anastasiya	Zhuravlyeva	UZB	9.10.81	9 Sep
6.45	0.0	India	George	USA	22.12.86	12 May
6.45	0.0	Sachiko	Masumi	JPN	20.12.84	1 Jul
6.45	-0.1	Natacha	Vouaux	FRA	23.1.85	15 Jul
6.45			Wang Huiqin	CHN-Y	7.2.90	4 Aug
6.44i		Oksana	Potapova	RUS	12.9.84	3 Feb
6.44	-1.8	Mariya	Shumilova	RUS-Y	10.1.90	23 May
6.44	0.7	Amy	Seward	PUR	6.3.85	25 May
6.44	0.6	Antonette	Carter	USA	16.2.84	27 May
6.44	0.0	Hitomi	Nakano	JPN-Y	23.11.90	2 Jun
6.44	1.3	Jesenija	Volzankina	LAT	28.11.83	5 Jun
6.44	1.5	Yoleinis	Corbacho	CUB	17.9.83	6 Jun
6.44	0.6	Tia	Hellebaut	BEL	16.2.78	24 Jun
6.44	-0.2	Manuéla	Galtier	FRA-J	22.5.88	20 Jul
6.43i		Svetlana	Bolshakova	RUS	14.10.84	28 Jan
6.43	-0.8	Vanessa	Seles	BRA	26.10.81	18 Apr
6.43	0.0	Amadi	Chinazor	NGR	12.9.87	17 May
6.43	1.3	Olga	Pankova	RUS	13.8.76	9 Jun
6.42	0.5	Natalya	Kutyakova	RUS	28.11.86	19 Jun
6.42	0.6	Victoria	Schreibeis	AUT	9.1.79	7 Aug
6.41i		Daniela	Lincoln Saavedra	SWE	4.8.84	28 Jan
6.41	0.0	Renee	Williams	USA	6.6.85	14 Apr
6.41	-0.3	Katrin	van Bühren	GER	29.5.82	20 May
6.41	1.1	Olga	Kucherenko	RUS	14.2.85	19 Jun
6.41	1.7	Janay	DeLoach	USA	12.10.85	23 Jun
6.41	1.5	Olena	Kotchenko	UKR	5.3.86	5 Jul
6.40	-0.3	Jessica	Ennis	GBR	28.1.86	6 May
6.40	0.4	Nina	Kokot	SLO-J	15.5.88	19 Jun
6.40	0.9	Jamesha	Youngblood	USA-J	24.4.89	7 Jul
6.40	-0.1	Lauren	Boden	AUS-J	3.8.88	10 Aug
6.40	-0.7		Liu Huahua	CHN	20.9.84	19 Sep
6.39i		Olga	Goncharova	RUS	30.5.77	9 Feb
6.39	0.3	Luzia Maria	Teodoro	BRA	25.7.78	18 Apr
6.39	1.9	Gillian	Cooke	GBR	3.10.82	13 May
6.39	0.5		Zhang Lan	CHN-J	27.2.88	9 Sep
6.38i		Cornelia	Deiac	ROM-J	20.3.88	27 Jan
6.38i		Angelica	Badea	ROM	1.10.75	10 Feb
6.38i		Kwanya	Ferguson	USA		16 Feb
6.38	0.6	Olena	Shchors	UKR	6.3.84	26 May
6.38	-0.2	Claudia	Tonn	GER	18.4.81	27 May
6.38	0.9	Thaimi	O'Reilly	ITA	20.7.76	28 Jul
6.38	1.1	Saeko	Okayama	JPN	12.4.82	22 Sep
6.37i		Hanna	Melnychenko	UKR	24.4.83	27 Jan
6.37i		Natalya	Mamysheva	RUS	9.12.84	10 Feb
6.37	0.8	Olga	Balayeva	RUS	30.6.84	8 Jul
6.36i		Ernesta	Karaskiené	LTU	6.3.79	9 Feb
6.36	1.8	Jacinta	Boyd	AUS	10.2.86	10 Mar
6.36	0.6	Gi-Gi	Johnson	USA	12.1.79	28 Apr
6.36	1.2	Gretchen	Quintana	CUB	30.6.84	11 May
6.36	-0.3	Julie	Hollman	GBR	16.2.77	20 May
6.36i		Vonteena	Knotts	USA		1 Dec
6.35i		Lilli	Schwarzkopf	GER	28.8.83	28 Jan
6.35i		Arantza	Loureiro	ESP	22.2.81	18 Feb
6.35	1.1	Tameisha	King	USA	24.8.81	13 Apr
6.35	0.4	Toni	Smith	USA	13.10.84	28 Apr
6.35	1.9	Naroa	Agirre	ESP	15.5.79	12 May
6.35	1.2	Erica	McLain	USA	24.1.86	25 May
6.35	2.0	Ke'Nyia	Richardson	USA-J	6.9.89	2 Jun
6.35	0.3		Li Yanmei	CHN-Y	6.2.90	8 Jun
6.34	0.2	April	Williams	USA	12.1.84	4 May
6.34	-0.4	Simone	Oberer	SUI	8.4.80	6 May
6.34	-1.9	Yamilé	Aldama	SUD	14.8.72	18 May
6.34	1.3	Viola	Schmitt	GER	12.8.83	2 Jun
6.34	-0.3	Marina	Parkhomenko	BLR	28.5.81	8 Jun
6.34	1.3	Melanie	Bauschke	GER-J	14.7.88	9 Jun
6.34	0.3	Kelly	Proper	IRL-J	1.5.88	16 Jun
6.34	0.7	Kerrie	Taurima (187)	AUS	2.4.79	15 Dec

Wind assisted

Mark	Wind	Name		Nat	Born	Pos	Meet	Venue	Date
7.10	2.8	Tatyana	Kotova	RUS	11.12.76	1	ECCp	Albufeira	27 May
					x 7.10w x x				
6.96	2.5	Rhonda	Watkins	TRI	9.12.87	1	NCAA	Sacramento	7 Jun
					x 6.62 6.96w x 6.40 6.60				
6.87	2.2	Chelsea	Hammond	JAM	2.8.83	1	NC	Kingston	22 Jun
					6.63 6.65 6.66/0.0 6.49 6.87w 4.88				
6.81	2.7	Yargelis	Savigne	CUB	13.11.84	1		Baie Mahault	1 May
6.81	3.3	Malgorzata	Trybanska	POL	21.6.81	1		Herrera	19 May
6.80	2.1	Denisa	Scerbová	CZE	21.8.86	2	EU23	Debrecen	15 Jul
6.74	2.5	Grace	Upshaw	USA	25.9.75	1	NC	Indianapolis	23 Jun
6.74	2.2	Veronika	Shutkova	BLR	26.5.86	1		Olbia	21 Jul

Mark	Wind	Name		Nat	Born	Pos	Meet	Venue	Date
6.70	2.1	Olga	Kucherenko	RUS	14.2.85	2		Olbia	21 Jul
6.67	2.4	Elva	Goulbourne	JAM	21.1.80	2	NC	Kingston	22 Jun
6.64	3.6	Maho	Hanaoka	JPN	3.8.76	2		Shizuoka	30 Apr
6.62	3.0	Funmi	Jimoh	USA	29.5.84	1		Houston	23 Mar
6.62	4.8	Tanika	Liburd	SKN	20.5.82	2		Baton Rouge	21 Apr
6.61	2.3	Tianna	Madison	USA	30.8.85	7	GP	Madrid	21 Jul
6.59	2.7	Yudelkis	Fernández	CUB	28.2.85	2		Baie Mahault	1 May
6.59	2.8	Anna	Bogdanova	RUS	21.10.84	1H	NC	Zhukovskiy	15 Jul
6.58	2.8	Natasha	Coleman	USA	9.2.79	1		Baton Rouge	31 Mar
6.58	3.1	Antonette	Carter	USA	16.2.84	2eB	FlaR	Gainesville	6 Apr
6.58	3.7	Jade	Johnson	GBR	7.6.80	2		Cork	30 Jun
6.58	2.3	Valeria	Canella	ITA	6.2.82	1		Donnas	15 Jul
6.57	4.4	Alice	Falaiye	CAN	24.12.78	1		Austin	21 Apr
6.56	3.2	Jovanee	Jarrett	JAM	15.1.83	1		Auburn	7 Apr
6.56	2.5	Yosleiny	Gorbacho	CUB	17.9.83	1		Bilbao	23 Jun
6.55	3.0	Lauranne	Osse	FRA	5.4.85	2	NC	Niort	5 Aug
6.54	2.4	Jessica	Ennis	GBR	28.1.86	1		Manchester	2 Jun
6.53	3.9	Erica	McLain	USA	24.1.86	3	NCAA	Sacramento	7 Jun
6.50	2.2	Nataliya	Sorokina	UKR	24.3.75	4	NC	Donetsk	5 Jul
6.50	2.9	Blandine	Maisonnier	FRA	3.1.86	1H	EU23	Debrecen	15 Jul

6.47	3.0	Saeko	Okayama	JPN	12.4.82	30 Apr
6.43	2.9	Hyleas	Fountain	USA	14.1.81	23 Jun
6.43	2.7	Hanna	Melnychenko	UKR	24.4.83	8 Jul
6.42	3.0	Xenia	Atschkinadze	GER-J	14.1.89	2 Jun
6.40	3.8	April	Holliness	USA	27.5.82	21 Apr
6.40	4.7	Vanya	Stoyanova	BUL	21.1.87	23 Jun
6.40	2.7	Haoua	Kessely	FRA-J	2.2.88	8 Jul
6.40	3.1	Margrethe	Renstrøm	NOR	21.3.85	4 Aug
6.39	2.4	Jolanda	Keizer	NED	5.4.85	15 Jul
6.38	2.3	Yukari	Nakahara	JPN	19.2.85	15 Jul
6.37	4.4	Yuka	Sato	JPN	6.7.81	15 Jul
6.36	2.9	Scottesha	Miller	USA-J	14.1.88	12 May
6.36	5.1	Carlota	Castrejana	ESP	25.4.73	19 May
6.36	2.6	Trecia	Smith	JAM	5.11.75	2 Jun
6.36	3.5	Zuzana	Bicicková	CZE	7.9.81	28 Aug
6.35	2.2	Yah	Koïta	MLI	25.9.80	21 Jul

Best outdoors

6.66	0.0	Savigne	3	PAm	Rio de Janeiro	25 Jul
6.58	0.6	Sestak	1		Velenje	28 Jun
6.57	1.9	Kazanovskaya	1		Valkeala	12 Aug
6.47	0.9	Otey	1		Starkville	31 Mar
6.45	0.2	Rublyova	6	Veniz	Haniá	9 Jun
6.41	0.5	Spanovic	2	WY	Ostrava	15 Jul
6.38		Badea	2		Constanta	20 May
6.37	1.0	Harris	Q	EU23	Debrecen	14 Jul
6.35	-0.4	Radevica	11	GP	Doha	11 May
6.34	0.8	Schwarzkopf	2H		Ratingen	17 Jun

Best at low altitude

6.42	1.4	Falaiye	12 May

JUNIORS

See main list for top 6 juniors. 11 performances (inc. 1 indoor) by 7 women to 6.47. Additional marks & further juniors:

Pidluzhnaya	6.61	-1.9	1	NC-j	Sochi	23 May
Okagbare	6.50	1.5	1	NC	Lagos	17 May
Klishina	6.47	1.3	1	WY	Ostrava	15 Jul

Mark	Wind	Name		Nat	Born	Pos	Meet	Venue	Date
6.47	0.8	Eloyse	Lesueur	FRA	15.7.88	1		Mannheim	23 Jun
		6.47	1.9 1 NC-j Narbonne 28 Jul						
6.45			Wang Huiqin	CHN-Y	7.2.90	1		Qiaozhong	4 Aug
6.44	-1.8	Mariya	Shumilova	RUS-Y	10.1.90	3	NC-j	Sochi	23 May
6.44	0.0	Hitomi	Nakano (10)	JPN-Y	23.11.90	1		Kobe	2 Jun
6.44	-0.2	Manuéla	Galtier	FRA	22.5.88	1	EJ	Hengelo	20 Jul
6.40	0.4	Nina	Kokot	SLO	15.5.88	1		Novo Mesto	19 Jun
6.40	0.9	Jamesha	Youngblood	USA	24.4.89	1	PAm-J	São Paulo	7 Jul
6.40	-0.1	Lauren	Boden	AUS	3.8.88	6	WUG	Bangkok	10 Aug
6.39	0.5		Zhang Lan	CHN	27.2.88	1		Chongqing	9 Sep
6.38i		Cornelia	Deiac	ROM	20.3.88	2		Bucuresti	27 Jan
6.35	2.0	Ke'Nyia	Richardson	USA	6.9.89	2		Sacramento	2 Jun
6.35	0.3		Li Yanmei	CHN-Y	6.2.90	2	WCT	Suzhou	8 Jun
6.34	1.3	Melanie	Bauschke	GER	14.7.88	1		Potsdam	9 Jun
6.34	0.3	Kelly	Proper (20)	IRL	1.5.88	1		Limerick	16 Jun

Wind assisted

6.42	3.0	Xenia	Atschkinadze	GER	14.1.89	3		Dillingen	2 Jun
6.40	2.7	Haoua	Kessely	FRA-	2.2.88	1		Bondoufle	8 Jul
6.36	2.9	Scottesha	Miller	USA	14.1.88	1	Big12	Lincoln	12 May

TRIPLE JUMP

Mark	Wind	Name		Nat	Born	Pos	Meet	Venue	Date
15.28	0.9	Yargelis	Savigne	CUB	13.11.84	1	WCh	Osaka	31 Aug

Mark	Wind	Pos	Meet	Venue	Date	1	2	3	4	5	6
15.28						15.28	x	14.74w/2.1	14.73/1.4	x	p
15.09	2.0	1		Alcalá de Henares	7 Jul	14.63/1.0	14.52/0.8	14.76/1.5	15.09	14.55/-1.0	14.15
14.99	0.7	1	ALBA	Caracas	11 May	14.20	14.99	14.89/0.0	14.89w/2.2	14.88/1.7	x
14.92	0.7	1	GP	Rieti	9 Sep	14.66w/2.5	14.92	14.68/1.5	14.92/1.9	x	13.34
14.80i		1		Düsseldorf	6 Feb	14.13	14.66	14.80	x	p	p
14.80	0.5	1	PAm	Rio de Janeiro	27 Jul	14.33	14.46	14.54/-0.7	14.78/-0.3	14.80	x
14.78	0.4	1	WAF	Stuttgart	23 Sep	14.68/0.6	14.79	14.53/0.7	14.60/0.5		
14.73	0.0	1	Gugl	Linz	11 Sep	14.53/0.0	14.73	14.37	14.66/0.0	p	14.37

Mark	Wind	Name		Nat	Born	Pos	Meet	Venue	Date	Series
14.72	1.3					2	GP	Athína	2 Jul	14.72 x 14.03 x x 14.32
15.14	0.9	Tatyana	Lebedeva	RUS	21.7.76	1	GP	Athína	2 Jul	
										14.35 14.69/-0.6 15.08/0.8 15.14 14.96/-0.3 14.87/-0.5
15.10	0.4					1	Herc	Monaco	25 Jul	14.82/-0.1 14.90/-0.1 x 15.10 14.55/0.0 14.96/0.3
15.07	0.8					2	WCh	Osaka	31 Aug	14.75/0.4 14.79/0.5 14.78/0.3 x 15.07 15.01/1.0
14.97	0.3					1		Rovereto	12 Sep	14.53/0.8 14.73/1.3 x 14.70/0.8 14.59/0.0 14.97
14.86	-0.3					1	R.Chall	Moskva	8 Aug	14.79/-0.2 14.56/-0.8 14.53/-0.4 x 14.86 14.75/-0.5
14.75	0.5					2	GP	Rieti	9 Sep	14.37 14.70/2.0 14.68/1.8 14.75 14.72/1.0 14.70/1.2
14.72	0.6					3	WAF	Stuttgart	23 Sep	14.72 x x 14.70/0.5
15.09	-0.5	Hrisopiyí	Devetzí	GRE	2.1.76	Q	WCh	Osaka	29 Aug	
										15.09 only jump
15.04	-0.2					3	WCh	Osaka	31 Aug	15.04 x x x x 14.75/0.3
14.75	0.4					2	WAF	Stuttgart	23 Sep	x 14.65/0.2 14.75 x
15.01w	2.2					1	NC	Athína	17 May	15.01w p 14.52/0.8 x p 14.34
14.92	1.3	Marija	Sestak	SLO	17.4.79	1		Ljubljana	3 Jun	
										14.44 14.47 14.92 14.53/1.1 p p
14.72	0.2					5	WCh	Osaka	31 Aug	14.72 14.63/0.1 14.45 14.71/0.2 14.34 14.27
14.90	1.0		Xie Limei	CHN	27.6.86	1	NGP	Urumqi	20 Sep	
14.73	1.2					1		Bangkok	19 Jun	x 14.26 13.75 13.97 14.14 14.73
14.88	0.3	Anna	Pyatykh	RUS	4.4.81	4	WCh	Osaka	31 Aug	
										x x 14.55/-0.2 14.78/1.1 x 14.88
14.71	1.9					3	GP	Rieti	9 Sep	14.45 x x 14.71 x 14.46
14.79	0.4	Olga	Saladuha	UKR	4.6.83	1	WUG	Bangkok	13 Aug	
										14.25 14.79 14.36 x 14.63/0.5 14.73/0.6
14.71	1.3	Magdelin	Martínez	ITA	10.2.76	6	WCh	Osaka	31 Aug	
										x 14.52/0.0 14.71 14.52/0.5 x 14.62/0.1
14.70	2.0					4	GP	Rieti	9 Sep	14.35w 14.70 14.58 14.41 14.48 p
14.69	2.0	Teresa	N'zola Meso	FRA	30.11.83	1	ECp-S	München	23 Jun	
										x 13.97 14.16 14.69
14.69	1.6	Olga	Rypakova	KAZ	30.11.84	1	AsiC	Amman	28 Jul	
		(30/10)								14.69 x 14.65w 14.08 14.69 p
14.66		Mabel	Gay	CUB	5.5.83	1		La Habana	8 Mar	
14.64i		Carlota	Castrejana	ESP	25.4.73	1	EI	Birmingham	4 Mar	
14.58	0.0	Yamilé	Aldama	SUD	14.8.72	1		Kalamáta	2 Jun	
14.57	0.2	Keila	Costa	BRA	6.2.83	1	SAmC	São Paulo	9 Jun	
14.50i		Olesya	Bufalova	RUS	6.10.82	2	EI	Birmingham	4 Mar	
14.46	-1.2	Viktoriya	Gurova	RUS	22.5.82	3	ECp-S	München	23 Jun	
14.44	0.7	Maurren	Maggi	BRA	25.6.76	1		São Paulo	7 Mar	
14.41i		Oksana	Udmurtova	RUS	1.2.82	4	EI	Birmingham	4 Mar	
14.41	0.3	Yekaterina	Kayukova	RUS	9.10.86	1	NC-23	Tula	20 Jun	
14.41	0.1	Dana	Veldáková	SVK	3.6.81	2	WUG	Bangkok	13 Aug	
		(20)								
14.39	0.8	Athanasia	Pérra	GRE	2.2.83	2		Kalamáta	2 Jun	
14.39	0.4	Liliya	Kulyk	UKR	27.1.87	1	EU23	Debrecen	13 Jul	
14.36	-0.8	Yarianna	Martínez	CUB	20.9.84	2		La Habana	17 Mar	
14.35	1.9	Trecia	Smith	JAM	5.11.75	1	NC	Kingston	23 Jun	
14.31	0.2	Yelena	Ivanova	RUS	16.3.79	Q	NC	Tula	2 Aug	
14.31	0.6	Nadezhda	Bazhenova	RUS	22.9.78	3	NC	Tula	3 Aug	
14.29i		Adelina	Gavrila	ROM	26.11.78	1		Bucuresti	27 Jan	
14.28i		Svetlana	Bolshakova	RUS	14.10.84	3		Düsseldorf	6 Feb	
14.24	0.7	Malgorzata	Trybanska	POL	21.6.81	1		Biala Podlaska	2 Jun	
14.24	-0.3	Anastasiya	Taranova	RUS	6.9.85	2	NC-23	Tula	18 Jun	
		(30)								
14.21	1.8	Dailenis	Alcántara	CUB-Y	10.8.91	1		La Habana	1 Mar	
14.21	-0.3	Chinoye	Ohadugha	NGR	24.3.86	2	AfG	Alger	18 Jul	
14.20	0.1	Anna	Kuropatkina	RUS	3.10.85	3	NC-23	Tula	18 Jun	
14.19	1.8	Yusmay	Bicet	CUB	8.12.83	1		La Habana	15 Feb	
14.17	0.9	Kseniya	Priyemko	BLR	23.4.86	1		Minsk	14 Jun	
14.16	1.6	Níki	Panéta	GRE	21.4.86	1	NC-23	Thessaloniki	1 Jul	
14.15	-0.9	Erica	McLain	USA	24.1.86	1	Pac-10	Stanford	13 May	
14.15	1.5	Svitlana	Mamyeyeva	UKR	19.4.82	*		Yalta	14 Jun	
14.13	2.0	Blessing	Okagbare	NGR-J	10.9.88	1	NC	Lagos	19 May	
14.12	-0.3	Tatyana	Yakovleva	RUS	9.9.86	4	NC-23	Tula	18 Jun	
		(40)								
14.11	1.8	Tânia Ferreira	da Silva	BRA	17.12.86	5		Uberlândia	6 May	
14.10	0.4	Yudelkis	Fernández	CUB	28.2.85	3		La Habana	17 Mar	
14.10	1.1		Li Qian	CHN	17.9.84	2	NGP	Urumqi	20 Sep	
14.09	1.0	Katja	Demut	GER	21.12.83	2		Dessau	1 Jun	
14.09	1.8	Oleksandra	Stadnyuk	UKR	16.4.80	2		Yalta	14 Jun	
14.08i		Maria	Dimitrova	BUL	7.8.76	Q	EI	Birmingham	2 Mar	

Mark	Wind	Name		Nat	Born	Pos	Meet	Venue	Date
14.08	0.3	Shani	Marks	USA	24.8.80	1	NC	Indianapolis	21 Jun
14.04	0.6	Kaire	Leibak	EST-J	21.5.88	1		Valga	13 Jun
14.04	-0.1	Joanna	Skibinska	POL	21.2.85	1	NC	Poznan	1 Jul
14.03	1.5	Snezana	Rodic	SLO	19.8.82	2	NC	Nova Gorica	28 Jul
		(50)							
14.02i		Tabia	Charles	CAN	6.4.85	1		Notre Dame	3 Mar
14.02	0.7	Carolina	Klüft	SWE	2.2.83	*	v FIN	Göteborg	8 Sep
14.01	-1.4	Natalya	Safronova	BLR	11.7.74	1		Minsk (Staiki)	2 Jun
14.00i		Patricia	Sarrapio	ESP	16.11.82	1		Zaragoza	3 Feb
13.99i		Cristina	Bujin	ROM-J	12.4.88	1	NC-j	Bucuresti	24 Feb
13.98	1.2	Gita	Dodova	BUL	2.5.82	1		Sofia	24 Jun
13.96	1.0	Martina	Darmovzalová	CZE	12.10.78	1	ECp-1A	Vaasa	23 Jun
13.95	-0.5		Sha Li	CHN-J	14.8.88	1	NC-j	Chengdu	5 Jun
13.94	0.5	Anastasiya	Zhuravlyeva	UZB	9.10.81	1		Roma	30 May
13.93	1.5	Elena-Alina	Popescu	ROM	27.10.85	3		Alger	21 Jun
		(60)							
13.93	-0.4		Li Yanmei	CHN-Y	6.2.90	1		Wuhan	31 Oct
13.90	1.9	Svetlana	Semyonova	RUS	24.8.80	2		Istanbul	30 Jun
13.90	0.9		Liu Yanan	CHN	18.1.87	1		Wuhan	7 Jul
13.90	1.1	Biljana	Mitrovic-Topic	SRB	17.10.77	1	NC	Novi Sad	3 Aug
13.89	0.3		Lin Nuai	CHN	6.1.84	2		Zhaoqing	19 May
13.89	0.1	Simona	La Mantia	ITA	14.4.83	8	Nebiolo	Torino	8 Jun
13.88i		Yelena	Oleynikova	RUS	9.12.76	2		Moskva	28 Jan
13.88	1.4		Qiu Huijing	CHN	4.2.85	3		Zhaoqing	19 May
13.87	-0.5	Fernanda	Delfino	BRA	7.11.82	2	NC	São Paulo	21 Jun
13.87	0.5	Natalia	Kilpeläinen-Bäck	FIN	19.7.70	1	NC	Lappeenranta	4 Aug
		(70)							
13.85	0.0	Hanna	Knyazheva	UKR-J	25.9.89	2	EJ	Hengelo	22 Jul
13.85	1.3	Thitima	Muangjan	THA	13.4.83	1	SEAG	Nakhon Ratchasima	11 Dec
13.83	0.9	Iworima	Otonye	NGR	13.4.76	3	AfG	Alger	18 Jul
13.81		Tatyana	Titova	RUS	2.1.83	3		Samara	9 Aug
13.80i		Anna	Nazarova	RUS	14.3.86	1		Sankt Peterburg	21 Jan
13.79		Andriana	Banova	BUL	1.5.87	1		Dimitrovgrad	19 Jul
13.78	-1.3		Wang Huiqin	CHN-Y	7.2.90	1		Qiaozhong	3 Aug
13.78	1.6	Amy	Zongo	FRA	4.10.80	2	NC	Niort	3 Aug
13.76	1.5	Dímitra	Márkou	GRE	28.7.80	4	NC	Athína	15 Jun
13.76	1.5	Rakhima	Sardi	KGZ	11.4.86	3		Bangkok	19 Jun
		(80)							
13.76	0.0	Jennifer	Arveláez	VEN	28.10.82	1	NG	Barinas	19 Dec
13.75i		Irina	Beskrovnaja	SVK	28.12.82	2		Bratislava	28 Jan
13.75i		Anastasiya	Matveyeva	RUS-J	12.12.88	1	NC-j	Penza	2 Feb
13.75i		Alina	Dinu	ROM	2.9.82	1		Valencia	4 Feb
13.73		Alexandra	Zelenina	MDA	21.11.86	1		Chisinau	11 May
13.73	0.2	Yvette	Lewis	USA	16.3.85	1	NCAA	Sacramento	9 Jun
13.73	0.2		Xu Tingting	CHN-J	12.7.89	3	WCT	Suzhou	9 Jun
13.72		Keisha	Spencer	JAM	16.2.78	1		Lake Charles, LA	12 May
13.72		Yosleidis	Rivalta	CUB-Y	2.5.90	3		La Habana	15 Jun
13.72	0.0	Aneta	Sadach	POL	22.4.75	2	NC	Poznan	1 Jul
		(90)							
13.72	-0.9	Yelena	Parfyonova	KAZ	26.1.74	2	NC	Almaty	6 Jul
13.71	-1.4	Laurice Cristina	Félix	BRA	28.5.81	1		São Paulo	14 Apr
13.71	1.1	Veera	Baranova	EST	12.2.84	2		Volgograd	6 Jun
13.71	0.4	Alsu	Murtazina	RUS	12.12.87	5	NC-23	Tula	20 Jun
13.70		Natalya	Davydova	RUS	24.11.78	2		Moskva	16 May
13.68i		Ashia	Hansen	GBR	5.12.71	1	NC	Sheffield	10 Feb
13.68	-0.5		Yao Jiajia	CHN-J	7.4.88	2	NC-j	Chengdu	5 Jun
13.66	0.4	Ruslana	Tsyhotska	UKR	23.3.86	1		Kyiv	5 Aug
13.65	0.0	Olga	Pankova	RUS	13.8.76	1		Almaty	10 Jun
13.64	1.5	Sirkka-Liisa	Kivine	EST	22.6.77	1		Modena	19 May
		(100)							
13.64	0.3	Thaimi	O'Reilly	ITA	20.7.76	3	NC	Padova	27 Jul

13.63	0.0	Tetyana	Dyachenko	UKR	25.1.86	14 Jun
13.62	0.6		Hu Qian	CHN-J	14.1.89	31 Oct
13.61i		Aleksandra	Kotlyarova	UZB-J	10.10.88	17 Feb
13.61	1.1	Sheena	Gordon	USA	26.9.83	28 Apr
13.60	-1.9	Béatrice	Kamboulé	BUR	25.2.80	24 Apr
13.60i		Patricia	Sylvester	GRN	3.2.83	27 Jan
13.60	1.3	Simidele	Adeagbo	USA	29.7.81	5 May
13.60		Yanisleidis	Hodelín	CUB-J	27.8.88	8 Jun
13.60	1.2	Michelle	Vaughn	GUY	23.1.83	9 Jun
13.59	0.2	Nadia	Williams	GBR	17.11.81	16 Jun
13.59	1.2	Haoua	Kessely	FRA-J	2.2.88	7 Jul
13.59	0.0	Cristina	Nicolau	ROM	9.8.77	27 Jul
13.59	1.8	Tanja	Prudic	SLO	6.9.82	28 Jul
13.59	0.0		Yu Shaohua	CHN	4.1.85	4 Aug
13.58i		Ke'Nyia	Richardson	USA-J	6.9.89	11 Mar
13.58	0.0		Zhang Guihua	CHN	15.10.85	19 May
13.57i		Zinayda	Lifintseva	RUS	19.6.84	11 Feb
13.57		Livia	Pruteanu	ROM	22.12.81	19 May
13.57	1.7	Fabrícia	da Silva	BRA	9.5.82	26 May
13.57A	1.7	Amanda	Thieschafer	USA	27.4.82	2 Jun

Mark	Wind	Name		Nat	Born	Date
13.57	1.1	Irina	Litvinenko	KAZ	8.1.87	28 Jul
13.56	1.9	Liliana	Zagacka	POL	28.1.77	9 Jun
13.56	2.0	Nathalie	Marie-Nelly	FRA	24.11.86	30 Jun
13.55	1.0	Ronda	White	USA	25.8.82	2 Jun
13.55		Irina	Gumenyuk	RUS-J	6.1.88	8 Jun
13.54	1.1	Brandy	Depland	USA	2.1.84	31 Mar
13.54	0.7	Brenda	Faluade	USA	27.10.84	14 Apr
13.54	0.4		Duan Hongjie	CHN	1.2.84	23 Jul
13.53i		Yelena	Kiseleva	RUS	4.4.85	20 Jan
13.53i		Tomika	Ferguson	USA	8.12.85	3 Mar
13.53	1.6	Tiombé	Hurd	USA	17.8.73	21 Jun
13.53	1.2	Elina	Sorsa	FIN	22.7.86	23 Jun
13.52	0.4	Kimberly	Williams	JAM-J	3.11.88	28 Mar
13.52	1.1	Decontee	Kaye	USA	14.2.87	9 Jun
13.50	1.0	Fumiyo	Yoshida	JPN	25.4.81	29 Apr
13.50	1.9	Verónica	Davis	VEN	22.5.87	11 May
13.50	2.0	Petya	Dacheva	BUL	10.3.85	17 Jun
13.50	1.2	Colleen	Scott	JAM	18.8.74	21 Jun
13.49i		Susana	Costa	POR	22.9.84	18 Feb
13.49	-0.2		Jung Hye-kyung	KOR	13.4.81	3 Jun
13.49	-0.2		Wang Yu	CHN	18.7.87	9 Jun
13.48	2.0		Cai Lipiao	CHN-J	5.12.88	7 Jul
13.48	1.2	Sara	Fabris	ITA	17.8.84	29 Sep
13.46	0.9	Marta	Godinho	POR	24.6.80	28 Jul
13.45			Wang Ying	CHN	24.7.83	19 May
13.45	-0.5		Zhu Lirong	CHN-J	6.11.89	5 Jun
13.44	0.9	Yanelis	Veranes	CUB	20.7.87	1 Mar
13.44	0.8	Andrea	Linton	JAM	10.9.84	13 May
13.43	1.4	Paraskeví	Sidiropoúlou	GRE	9.11.78	9 Jun
13.42	0.0		Ngew Sin Mei	MAS	4.6.83	11 Dec
13.41A	0.0	Nelly	Tchayem	FRA	4.8.83	14 Apr
13.41	0.5		Luo Wen	CHN-J	2.10.88	22 Jul
13.41A		Vaovao	Rapitsaravolazandry	MAD	10.3.76	15 Aug
13.41	1.2	Snezana	Vukmirovic	SLO	19.8.82	13 Sep
13.40i		Francesca	Carlotto	ITA	30.9.77	18 Feb
13.40		Natalya	Vyatkina	BLR	10.2.87	17 May
13.40	0.0	April	Williams	USA	12.1.84	26 May
13.40	0.4		Sun Yan	CHN-Y	.91	3 Aug
13.39i		Olga	Savenkova	LAT	13.3.86	17 Feb
13.39	1.2	Emma	Green	SWE	8.12.84	23 Jun
13.38i		Renee	Williams	USA	6.6.85	17 Feb
13.38		Iryna	Yanchenko	UKR-J	22.3.88	30 May
13.38	0.8		Wu Ying	CHN	8.2.84	24 Jul
13.37i		Aleksandra	Fila	POL	17.8.83	28 Jan
13.37	-0.3	Annelie	Schrader	GER	19.12.79	17 Jun
13.37		Elena	Denkova	BUL	8.1.85	18 Jul
13.36	-0.1	Katja	Pobanz	GER	22.11.74	21 Jul
13.35i		Mukadder	Ulusoy	TUR	.82	21 Feb
13.35	2.0	Jamaâ	Chnaik	MAR	28.7.84	16 Jun
13.34	1.4	Toni	Smith	USA	13.10.84	13 May
13.34	1.5	Crystal	Manning	USA	15.4.86	8 Jun
13.34	1.6	Zignia	Gomis	FRA	19.8.82	3 Aug
13.33	0.0		Eun Jung-cho	KOR	10.3.81	1 May
13.33	-0.1	Lyvie-Paola	Laurent	FRA-J	24.12.88	22 Jul
13.33		Alyce	Williams	USA	8.1.85	27 Apr
13.32	1.0	Kamélia	Sahnoune	ALG	5.4.86	18 Jul
13.31	0.2	Anne	Neubauer	GER-J	2.9.89	22 Jun
13.30i		Ineta	Radevica	LAT	13.7.81	13 Jan
13.30i		Yvonne	Mensah	CAN	15.5.85	25 Feb
13.30		Diana	Plumaki (181)	UZB	20.3.85	25 May

Wind assisted

Mark	Wind	Name		Nat	Born	Pos	Meet	Venue	Date
15.10	2.7	Keila	Costa	BRA	6.2.83	1		Uberlândia	6 May
					15.09w/4.5	15.00w/3.7	p	15.10w p	14.75w/3.1
14.32	4.4	Laurice Cristina	Félix	BRA	28.5.81	2		Uberlândia	6 May
14.25	2.2	Oleksandra	Stadnyuk	UKR	16.4.80	2	Veniz	Haniá	9 Jun
14.24	4.6	Tabia	Charles	CAN	6.4.85	3		Uberlândia	6 May
14.17	2.3	Svitlana	Mamyeyeva	UKR	19.4.82	1		Yalta	14 Jun
14.17	5.8	Carolina	Klüft	SWE	2.2.83	1	v FIN	Göteborg	8 Sep
14.11	4.5	Shani	Marks	USA	24.8.80	1		Chula Vista	11 Aug
14.03	2.3		Sha Li	CHN-J	14.8.88	2	AsiC	Amman	28 Jul
14.01	2.5	Iworima	Otonye	NGR	13.4.76	2	NC	Lagos	19 May
13.90	3.6		Jung Hye-kyung	KOR	13.4.81	1	NG	Kwangju	13 Oct
13.83	2.5	Dímitra	Márkou	GRE	28.7.80	4	Veniz	Haniá	9 Jun
13.82	3.0	Ke'Nyia	Richardson	USA-J	6.9.89	1		Sacramento	2 Jun
13.80	5.2	Irina	Litvinenko	KAZ	8.1.87	3	AsiC	Amman	28 Jul
13.78	2.8	Kamélia	Sahnoune	ALG	5.4.86	5	AfG	Alger	21 Jun
13.75	3.2		Ngew Sin Mei	MAS	4.6.83	2	SEAG	Nakhon Ratchasima	11 Dec
13.71	3.4	Crystal	Manning	USA	15.4.86	1	Big 12	Lincoln	13 May
13.69	2.1	Elena	Denkova	BUL	8.1.85	2		Plovdiv	1 Jul
13.69	4.4	Marta	Godinho	POR	24.6.80	1	NC	Lisboa (U)	28 Jul
13.66	2.3	Jessica	Maussion	FRA	25.11.83	3	NC	Niort	3 Aug

Mark	Wind	Name		Nat	Born	Date
13.61	2.1	Dominike	Nkiruka	NGR	28.8.85	19 May
13.61	4.9	Paraskeví	Sidiropoúlou	GRE	9.11.78	11 Jul
13.61	3.1	Simidele	Adeagbo	USA	29.7.81	11 Aug
13.50	2.1	Lyvie-Paola	Laurent	FRA-J	24.12.88	22 Jul
13.45	2.2	Sohvi	Seppälä	FIN	16.7.83	4 Aug
13.42	3.1	Gillian	Kerr	GBR	10.11.83	30 Jun
13.41	6.9	Mariama	Cisse	FRA	14.9.85	1 Jul
13.40	2.7	Matja	Bratkic	SLO-Y	14.5.91	3 Jul
13.39	4.5	Ashika	Charan	USA-J	4.4.88	13 May
13.35	4.9	Yasmine	Regis	GBR	12.12.86	30 Jun
13.33	4.5	Ioánna	Grammatikopoúlou	GRE	19.10.83	12 May
13.33	2.1	Marianne	Schlachter	GER	4.2.85	13 May
13.32	2.3	Federica	De Santis	ITA	19.10.89	3 Aug
13.31	4.4	Ayanna	Alexander	TRI	20.7.82	24 Jun
13.31	2.2	Maria Natalia	Londa	INA-Y	29.10.90	28 Jul

Best outdoors

Mark	Wind	Name	Pos	Meet	Venue	Date
14.49	0.2	Bufalova	2	NC	Tula	3 Aug
14.47	1.8	Castrejana	4	GP	Athína	2 Jul
14.35	0.8	Udmurtova	7	GP	Athína	2 Jul
14.20	0.0	Gavrila	1	NC	Bucuresti	27 Jul
14.21w	2.6		1		Istanbul	30 Jun
13.95	-0.2	Dimitrova	1		Plovdiv	1 Jul
13.89	1.6	Charles	*		Uberlândia	6 May
13.81	1.2	Sarrapio	2	ECCp	Albufeira	26 May
13.71	1.7	Matveyeva	1		Zhukovskiy	29 Jun
13.57	1.3	Bujin				22 Jul
13.55	1.3	Richardson				8 Jul
13.33	-0.8	Ulusoy				29 Apr
13.30	1.4	Carlotto				9 Jun

JUNIORS

See main list for top 12 juniors. 11 performances (inc. 2 indoors) by 5 women to 13.86. Additional marks & further juniors:

Name	Mark	Wind	Pos	Meet	Venue	Date	Mark	Wind	Pos	Meet	Venue	Date
Leibak	13.90	-0.1	1	ECp-2A	Odense	23 Jun	13.86	1.2	11	GP	Athína	2 Jul
Sha Li	13.94	1.9	*	AsiC	Amman	28 Jul	13.86i		1		Shanghai	15 Mar
Li Yanmei	13.86	1.7	1		Guangzhou	23 Jul						

Mark	Wind	Name		Nat	Born	Pos	Venue	Date
13.62	0.6		Hu Qian	CHN	14.1.89	3	Wuhan	31 Oct
13.61i		Aleksandra	Kotlyarova	UZB	10.10.88	1	Moskva	17 Feb
13.60		Yanisleidis	Hodelín	CUB	27.8.88	2	La Habana	8 Jun

Mark	Wind	Name		Nat	Born	Pos	Meet	Venue		Date
13.59	1.2	Haoua	Kessely	FRA-	2.2.88	1		Bondoufle		7 Jul
13.58i		Ke'Nyia	Richardson	USA	6.9.89	1		New York (Arm)		11 Mar
		13.55	1.3			1	PAm-J	São Paulo		8 Jul
13.55		Irina	Gumenyuk	RUS	6.1.88	3		Sankt-Peterburg		8 Jun
13.52	0.4	Kimberly	Williams	JAM	3.11.88	1		Kingston		28 Mar
13.48	2.0		Cai Lipiao (20)	CHN	5.12.88	3		Wuhan		7 Jul

Best out: 13.57 1.3 Cristina Bujin ROM-J 12.4.88 3 EJ Hengelo 22 Jul

Wind assisted 2 performances by 2 women to 13.86. Additional performance and performer

Leibak		14.02	2.7 1	EJ	Hengelo	22 Jul				
13.50	2.1	Lyvie-Paola	Laurent	FRA-J	24.12.88	4	EJ	Hengelo		22 Jul

SHOT

Mark	Wind	Name		Nat	Born	Pos	Meet	Venue		Date
20.54		Valerie	Vili	NZL	6.10.84	1	WCh	Osaka		26 Aug
					19.89	19.74	19.80	x	19.95	20.54
20.40	2	WAF	Stuttgart	23 Sep	20.06	19.87	20.40	19.48		
20.03	1		Cairns	24 Aug	19.60	20.03	19.59	19.81	19.86	19.98
19.65	1		Rovereto	12 Sep	18.69	19.46	19.57	x	x	19.65
19.47	1		Auckland	24 Mar	19.47	19.29	19.33	x	18.74	19.20
19.45	Q	WCh	Osaka	26 Aug	19.45	only throw				
20.48		Nadezhda	Ostapchuk	BLR	12.10.80	2	WCh	Osaka		26 Aug
					20.04	x	19.17	x	x	20.48
20.45	1	WAF	Stuttgart	23 Sep	18.66	19.45	20.45	x		
20.34	1		Minsk (Staiki)	28 Jul	20.34	x	x	20.34	x	x
20.27	1		Minsk (Staiki)	11 Aug						
19.89i	1		Minsk	15 Feb						
19.54	1	NC	Grodno	6 Jul						
19.43	1	Gugl	Linz	11 Sep	18.47	x	19.03	19.34	19.43	19.29
19.40	1	Nebiolo	Torino	8 Jun	18.33	19.23	19.15	x	18.88	19.40
19.40	2		Rovereto	12 Sep	x	19.40	x	19.06	x	x
20.04		Petra	Lammert	GER	3.3.84	1		Zeven		26 May
					19.39	20.04	x	x	19.22	x
19.87	1		Biberach	16 Jun	19.87	x	19.71	x	19.85	x
19.78	1		Schapbach	17 Jun	18.88	19.78	x	19.06	18.93	x
19.61	1		Engers	27 Jun						
19.47	2	ECp-S	München	24 Jun	19.47	x	18.95	x		
19.34	1		Villeneuve d'Ascq	8 Jun						
19.34	1		Schönebeck	10 Jun	19.34	x	19.34	x	x	18.50
19.77		Nadine	Kleinert	GER	20.10.75	3	WCh	Osaka		26 Aug
					18.75	19.45	19.04	x	19.77	19.72
19.38	1		Bochum-Wattenscheid	12 Aug	18.64	19.15	19.13	x	19.06	19.38
19.36	3	WAF	Stuttgart	23 Sep	18.66	x	19.36	18.69		
19.35	1	Déca	Paris (C)	8 Sep	18.75	18.83	19.10	19.35		
19.69		Anna	Omarova	RUS	3.10.81	1	ECp-S	München		24 Jun
					18.41	x	19.69	x		
19.68	1	Znam	Zhukovskiy	9 Jun	17.92	18.09	18.45	19.68	18.19	18.56
19.34	1	NC	Tula	31 Jul	17.38	19.34	x	x	p	p
19.38			Li Ling	CHN	7.2.85	4	WCh	Osaka		26 Aug
					18.21	18.88	x	18.92	x	19.38
		(31/6)								
19.24		Yanina	Pravalinskaya (Korolchik)	BLR	26.12.76	1	Klim	Minsk (Staiki)		9 Jun
19.15		Chiara	Rosa	ITA	28.1.83	1	ECp-1B	Milano		24 Jun
19.13			Gong Lijiao	CHN-J	24.1.89	1	NC	Shijiazhuang		4 Aug
		(10)								
19.11		Anna	Avdeyeva	RUS	6.4.85	2	Znam	Zhukovskiy		9 Jun
19.09			Li Meiju	CHN	3.10.79	1	NGP	Urumqi		20 Sep
19.01i		Assunta	Legnante	ITA	14.5.78	1		Schio		20 Jan
19.01i		Irina	Khudoroshkina	RUS	13.10.68	1	NC	Volgograd		11 Feb
18.97		Misleydis	González	CUB	19.6.78	1		Bilbao		23 Jun
18.92		Jill	Camarena	USA	2.8.82	1		Stanford		31 Mar
18.91		Cleopatra	Borel-Brown	TRI	3.10.79	1		Arnhem		13 Jun
18.86		Yuliya	Leontyuk	BLR	31.1.84	2	Klim	Minsk (Staiki)		9 Jun
18.81		Yumileidi	Cumbá	CUB	11.2.75	2		Alcalá de Henares		7 Jul
18.74		Kristin	Heaston	USA	23.11.75	1	NC	Indianapolis		24 Jun
		(20)								
18.58i		Olga	Ryabinkina	RUS	24.9.76	3	NC	Volgograd		11 Feb
18.58			Liu Xiangrong	CHN-J	6.6.88	1		Wuhan		30 Oct
18.55i		Liz	Wanless	USA	18.11.81	1		Gainesville		27 Jan
18.53		Oksana	Gaus	RUS	9.7.81	4	NC	Tula		31 Jul
18.40		Sarah	Stevens	USA	2.4.86	2		La Jolla		21 Apr
18.27		Irina	Tarasova	RUS	15.4.87	2	NC-23	Tula		18 Jun
18.20		Irache	Quintanal	ESP	18.9.78	1		Barcelona		4 Jul

Mark	Name		Nat	Born	Pos	Meet	Venue	Date
18.18	Vivian	Chukwuemeka	NGR	4.5.77	1		Abuja	5 May
18.16	Jessica	Pressley	USA	27.12.84	1		Tempe	28 Apr
18.12i	Michelle	Carter	USA	12.10.85	2	NCAA	Fayetteville	9 Mar
	(30)							
18.08	Mailín	Vargas	CUB	24.3.83	2	ALBA	Caracas	9 May
18.08	Denise	Hinrichs	GER	7.6.87	2		Halle	19 May
18.03	Laurence	Manfrédi	FRA	20.5.74	1		Bron	11 Jul
18.02	Lieja	Tunks	CAN	10.3.76	1		London, ON	26 Jul
17.99	Elisângela	Adriano	BRA	27.7.72	1		São Caetano do Sul	14 Jul
17.88	Krystyna	Zabawska	POL	14.1.68	1		Siedlce	6 Jun
17.87i	Oksana	Chibisova	RUS	31.3.77	5	NC	Volgograd	11 Feb
17.80	Magdalena	Sobieszek	POL	4.5.86	2		Siedlce	6 Jun
17.72	Helena	Engman	SWE	16.6.76	5	Nebiolo	Torino	8 Jun
17.59i	Nadine	Beckel	GER	27.5.77	2		Sondershausen	24 Feb
	(40)							
17.48		Li Fengfeng	CHN	9.1.79	2		Wuhan	6 Jul
17.47	Abby	Ruston	USA	3.4.83	6	NC	Indianapolis	24 Jun
17.45i	Tatyana	Ilyushchenko	BLR	18.4.83	3		Minsk	15 Feb
17.42i	Kacey	Onwuchekwa	NGR/USA	22.11.85	1		New York	2 Feb
17.42	Iolanta	Ulyeva	KAZ	27.7.76	1		Almaty	9 May
17.42		Zhang Qiang	CHN	14.2.87	5	NGP	Urumqi	20 Sep
17.37	Anca	Heltne	ROM	1.1.78	1c2		Onesti	20 May
17.36	Jessica	Cérival	FRA	20.1.82	2		Bron	11 Jul
17.34		Li Li	CHN	22.2.87	2	NC-23	Chengdu	2 Jun
17.29	Rachel	Jansen	USA	26.7.84	1		Des Moines	13 May
	(50)							
17.28i	Ashley	Muffet	USA	16.9.86	1	SEC	Lexington	25 Feb
17.24	Irina	Kirichenko	RUS	18.5.87	3	NC-23	Tula	18 Jun
17.23	Natalia	Ducó	CHI-J	31.1.89	1		Santiago de Chile	25 Aug
17.21		Lee Mi-young	KOR	19.8.79	1	NC	Daegu	2 Jun
17.21	Denise	Kemkers	NED	11.4.85	4	EU23	Debrecen	12 Jul
17.21		Zhang Guirong	SIN	5.2.78	1	SEAG	Nakhon Ratchasima	11 Dec
17.18	Vera	Yepimashko	BLR	10.7.76	2		Minsk (Staiki)	1 Jun
17.18		Sun Huiying	CHN-J	17.7.89	3		Wuhan	30 Oct
17.17		Ma Qiao	CHN-J	28.9.89	7	NC	Shijiazhuang	4 Aug
17.14	Shernelle	Nicholls	BAR	28.2.84	2	Big 12	Lincoln	13 May
	(60)							
17.13i	Susan	King	USA	4.3.85	1		Jonesboro	1 Dec
17.12	Melissa	Boekelman	NED-J	11.5.89	1		Lisse	5 May
17.11i	Irini-Hrisovaládou	Terzoglou	GRE	2.2.79	1	BalkC	Pireás	21 Feb
17.11i	Gail	Lee	USA	25.5.84	1		Houston	24 Feb
17.09	Adriane	Blewitt	USA	24.5.80	2		Tucson	19 May
17.09	Ana	Po'uhila	TGA	12.10.79	2		Amiens	27 Jun
17.06	Christina	Schwanitz	GER	24.12.85	1		Igersheim	20 Oct
17.05	Mariam	Kevkhishvili	GEO	17.9.85	1	SEC	Tuscaloosa	12 May
17.03	Austra	Skujyté	LTU	12.8.79	1H	WCh	Osaka	25 Aug
17.02	Yoko	Toyonaga	JPN	15.4.77	20Q	WCh	Osaka	26 Aug
	(70)							
16.98	Kristin	Marten	GER	23.5.83	1		Thum	13 May
16.93i	Cristiana	Checchi	ITA	8.7.77	3	NC	Ancona	17 Feb
16.91	Agnieszka	Bronisz	POL	16.3.86	1		Warszawa	26 May
16.91	Josephine	Terlecki	GER	17.2.86	1	NC-23	Hannover	26 Aug
16.91		Mao Xiaoyan	CHN		6	WCT	Suzhou	8 Jun
16.90i	Robyn	Jarocki	USA	11.7.84	3	NC	Boston (R)	24 Feb
16.90	Andréa Maria	Pereira	BRA	8.12.73	2		São Caetano do Sul	3 Feb
16.87	Simoné	du Toit	RSA-J	27.9.88	1	NC	Durban	16 Mar
16.85	Joanne	Duncan	GBR	27.12.66	1		Eton	21 Jul
16.83	Brittany	Pryor	USA	16.2.86	2		Chapel Hill	11 May
	(80)							
16.79i		Zhang Chunjing	CHN	19.5.83	3		Shanghai	16 Mar
16.78	Zara	Northover	JAM	6.3.84	1		Princeton	13 May
16.77	Filiz	Kadogan	TUR	12.2.82	1		Izmir	21 May
16.77	Yaniuvis	López	CUB	1.2.86	1		La Habana	8 Jun
16.75i	Aline	Schäffel	GER	15.5.80	2	NC	Leipzig	18 Feb
16.75i		Li Bo	CHN-J	4.9.88	4		Shanghai	16 Mar
16.75	Katja	Kròl	GER	5.2.80	3		Halle	19 May
16.74	Elena	Hila	ROM	20.5.74	1c1		Onesti	20 May
16.74	Svitlana	Sakun	UKR	1.5.81	1		Kyiv	3 Aug
16.74	Jana	Kárníková	CZE	14.2.81	1		Ustĭ nad Labem	9 Aug
	(90)							

Mark		Name	Nat	Born	Pos	Meet	Venue	Date
16.71	Chandra	Brewer	USA	26.7.81	1		Nashvile	21 Apr
16.71		Jiang Limin	CHN-J	20.2.88	5		Wuhan	30 Oct
16.68		Wang Lihong	CHN	9.1.83	4		Beijing	28 Apr
16.68	Mariam	Ibekwe	NGR	29.10.69	2	NC	Lagos	18 May
16.63i	Aymara	Albury	BAH	25.7.85	2	SEC	Lexington	25 Feb
16.63	Eva	Massey	GBR	22.12.80	1	NC	Manchester	29 Jul
16.58		Lin Chia-Ying	TPE	5.11.82	3		Guwahati	23 Jun
16.57	Olympia	Menelaou	CYP	29.4.66	1		Póros	25 Jul
16.56	Ciera	Ayangbile	USA	17.7.85	1		Winston-Salem	23 Mar
16.56		Liu Xiaojing	CHN		1		Guangzhou	21 Jul

(100)

16.54	Nadia	Alexander	JAM	27.12.85	27 Apr
16.54	Martina	de la Puente	ESP	4.4.75	28 Jul
16.53		Yang Cui	CHN	15.8.84	8 Jun
16.51	Izabela	Koralewska	POL	29.1.85	19 May
16.49	Magnolia	Iglesias	ESP	25.5.79	12 May
16.46	Khadija	Talley	USA	18.8.86	12 May
16.44	Tatyana	Vorobey	BLR	5.11.87	9 Jun
16.41	Erin	Streater	USA	7.7.84	21 Apr
16.41	Viktoriya	Degtyar	UKR	5.11.83	23 May
16.40	Natalya	Sazanovich	BLR	15.8.73	7 Jun
16.37	Jeni	Steiner	USA	25.6.84	5 May
16.36i	Kenitra	Woods	USA	18.5.80	24 Feb
16.35	Luz Dary	Castro	COL	30.5.78	8 Jun
16.33i	Jere	Summers	USA	21.5.87	23 Feb
16.32i	Alena	Kopets	BLR-J	14.2.88	9 Feb
16.32	Janae	Strickland	USA	19.8.82	28 May
16.31	Natalya	Dobrynska	UKR	29.5.82	25 Aug
16.29	Veronica	Abrahamse	RSA	18.8.80	16 Mar
16.26	Kamaiya	Warren	USA	10.3.84	21 Apr
16.25i	Oksana	Zaharchuk	UKR	3.4.80	12 Feb
16.25	Rocío	Comba	ARG	14.7.87	20 May
16.25	Tetyana	Nasonova	UKR	15.12.76	5 Jul
16.24	Kimberly	Barrett	JAM	18.11.81	17 Mar
16.21	Ursula	Ruiz	ESP	11.8.83	11 Aug
16.19	Dani	Samuels	AUS-J	26.5.88	11 Feb
16.17	Margarita	Bernardo	DOM	26.2.72	7 Jul
16.16	Sheena	James	USA	3.12.84	24 Mar
16.16		Xiao Meng	CHN-Y	1.3.90	2 Jun
16.16	Rebecca	Peake	GBR	22.6.83	1 Jul
16.15	Sarah	Reed	USA		21 Apr
16.12i	Liz	Alabi	USA	18.4.84	24 Feb
16.11i	Liz	Podominick	USA	5.12.84	24 Feb
16.11	Marie-Patrice	Mondoloni	FRA	19.1.83	5 Aug
16.10	Isabell	von Loga	GER-J	3.2.88	4 Aug
16.09		Meng Qianqian	CHN-Y	6.1.91	8 Jun
16.09	Dijana	Sefcic	SRB	16.3.78	10 Jun
16.08	Heike	Koderisch	GER	27.5.85	20 May
16.07i	Sarah	Vance	USA	27.6.84	27 Jan
16.07	Sivan	Jean	ISR	25.6.85	17 Jun
16.06i	Stevi	Large	USA	11.2.86	12 Jan
16.06		Li Yue	CHN-J	.89	28 Apr
16.06	Juthaporn	Krasaeyan	THA	13.2.72	11 Dec
16.04i	Billie Jo	Grant	USA	4.4.85	13 Jan
16.04		Rong Jun	CHN-J	7.4.89	2 Jun
16.02	Stephanie	Jeffers	USA	10.6.85	31 Mar
16.01	Catherine	Timmermans	BEL	17.10.86	5 Aug
16.01		Zong Donghui	CHN	6.5.87	30 Oct
15.99		Wang Qiao	CHN	14.5.87	21 Jul
15.93	Amy	Haapanen	USA	23.3.84	12 May
15.92	Sharterika	Allen	USA	9.12.85	11 May
15.91	Alyona	Grishko	BLR-Y	25.1.90	14 Jul
15.89	Annie	Alexander	TRI	28.8.87	13 Jul
15.87i	Kelli	Burton	USA	5.7.84	27 Jan
15.87	Lindsay	Neuberger	USA	30.10.84	21 Apr
15.86i	Dayana	Octavien	HAI	10.6.82	11 Feb
15.86	Krishna	Lee	USA	25.7.86	25 May
15.86	Eleanor	Gatrell	GBR	5.10.76	7 Jul
15.85i	Lyudmila	Morunova	RUS	27.1.85	20 Jan
15.85	Keely	Medeiros (159)	BRA	30.4.87	9 Sep

Best outdoors

18.87	Khudoroshkina	1	NCp	Tula	8 Jul
18.85	Legnante	1		Pergine Valsugana	7 Jul
18.35	Wanless	1		Clermont	17 Mar
17.57	Carter	5	NC	Indianapolis	24 Jun
17.55	Beckel	2		Schönebeck	10 Jun
17.36	Onwuchekwa	4	NCAA	Sacramento	9 Jun
17.15	Chibisova	6	NC	Tula	31 Jul
16.96	Terzoglou	3		Nikiti	4 Aug
16.79	Checchi	2		Rieti	19 May
16.73	Schäffel	6		Gotha	6 Jul
16.71	Li Bo	6		Wuhan	30 Oct
16.60	Albury	2	DrakeR	Des Moines	28 Apr

16.43 Ilyushchenko 17 Mar | 16.25 Jarocki 12May | 16.21 Kopets 17Aug | 16.11 Zaharchuk 20 Apr | 16.00 Muffet 26 Apr

JUNIORS

See main list for top 9 juniors. 11 performances (inc. 2 indoors) by 2 women to 18.10. Additional marks & further juniors:

Gong L	19.07i	1		Shanghai	16 Mar	18.43	1		Cangzhou	15 Jun
	18.77	2		Zhaoqiang	18 May	18.38	Q	WCh	Osaka	26 Aug
	18.73i	1		Beijing	21 Mar	18.36	2		Wuhan	20 Oct
	18.66	8	WCh	Osaka	26 Aug	18.32	2		Suzhou	8 Jun
Liu X	18.38	3	NGP	Urumqi	20 Sep					

16.32i	Alena	Kopets (10)	BLR	14.2.88	3		Mogilev	9 Feb
	16.21				1	v3N-j	Valmiera	17 Aug
16.19	Dani	Samuels	AUS	26.5.88	1		Hobart	11 Feb
16.16		Xiao Meng	CHN-Y	1.3.90	7	NC-20	Chengdu	2 Jun
16.10	Isabell	von Loga	GER	3.2.88	1	NC-j	Ulm	4 Aug
16.09		Meng Qianqian	CHN-Y	6.1.91	12	WCT	Suzhou	8 Jun
16.06		Li Yue	CHN	.89	6		Beijing	28 Apr
16.04		Rong Jun	CHN	7.4.89	8	NC-20	Chengdu	2 Jun
15.91	Alyona	Grishko	BLR-Y	25.1.90	1	WY	Ostrava	14 Jul
15.82		Luo Aixia	CHN	16.11.88	2		Beijing	21 Apr
15.82	Eden	Francis	GBR	19.10.88	3		Birmingham	1 Jul
15.78		Cui Shuang (20)	CHN-Y	9.8.91	1		Suihua	29 Jul

Abbreviations and Symbols

+ intermediate time in longer race, A made at an altitude of 1000m or higher, D made in a decathlon, h made in a heat, qf quarter-final, sf semi-final, i indoors, Q qualifying round, r race number, -J juniors, -Y youths (b. 1990 or later)

DISCUS

Mark	Name		Nat	Born	Pos	Meet	Venue	Date
68.06	Franka	Dietzsch	GER	22.1.68	1		Halle	19 May
				x 68.06 x 62.77 64.54 67.87				
	66.61 1 WCh	Osaka	29 Aug	66.61 66.48 63.92 63.81 65.29 x				
	66.14 1 EThCp	Yalta	18 Mar	62.19 66.14 x 61.55 x x				
	65.55 1	Dessau	1 Jun	61.19 61.78 65.55 x 62.94 x				
	65.39 1	Bottnaryd	30 Jun	62.08 x 65.39 x 64.10 64.95				
	65.26 1	Schönebeck	10 Jun	65.16 61.45 64.61 63.93 65.26 x				
	65.17 Q WCh	Osaka	27 Aug	57.13 65.17				
	65.02 1	Zeulenroda	3 Jun					
	64.84 2 Kuso	Warszawa	17 Jun	64.84 60.89 61.77 62.47 63.56				
	64.61 1	Biberach	16 Jun	61.91 x x x 60.98 64.61				
	64.61 1 GS	Ostrava	27 Jun	62.55 x x 62.79 64.61 62.61				
67.67	Suzy	Powell	USA	3.9.76	1		Wailuku	14 Apr
				57.07 59.82 x 60.72 67.67 65.06				
	66.23 1c2	Wailuku	16 Apr	63.38 66.23 62.90 63.00 65.01 65.61				
	65.52 1	Salinas	3 May	59.81 65.52 64.36 61.54 61.94 x				
	65.34 2c1	Wailuku	16 Apr	62.24 62.29 63.81 65.32 62.43 65.34				
	65.17 1 ModR	Modesto	5 May	x 61.70 64.02 65.17 63.30 64.59				
67.37	Becky	Breisch	USA	16.3.83	1c1		Wailuku	16 Apr
				x 65.53 67.37 66.40 64.88 x				
	66.64 1	Salinas	17 May					
	66.06 2	Wailuku	14 Apr	55.20 63.72 x 58.12 66.06 x				
	65.78 2c2	Wailuku	16 Apr	61.07 65.78 56.75 64.90 65.46 64.55				
	64.95 2 ModR	Modesto	5 May	58.40 62.67 63.58 64.95 x 63.03				
66.18	Vera	Cechlová	CZE	19.11.78	1	Kuso	Warszawa	17 Jun
				65.61 66.18 x x x x				
	64.49 1 FBK	Hengelo	26 May	62.14 64.49 x x x 60.75				
65.78	Darya	Pishchalnikova	RUS	19.7.85	2	WCh	Osaka	29 Aug
				59.91 63.10 65.14 60.83 65.78 65.55				
65.60	Nicoleta	Grasu	ROM	11.9.71	1		Zalau	5 May
64.98		Sun Taifeng	CHN	26.8.82	1	WCT	Suzhou	9 Jun
64.97	Yania	Ferrales	CUB	28.7.77	1		Uberlândia	6 May
				x 55.95 x 64.97 x p				
	64.43 1	Bad Köstritz	8 Jul	61.49 64.43 x 63.56 x x				
64.87	Elizna	Naude	RSA	14.9.78	1		Stellenbosch	2 Mar
				64.87 x 60.67 x 62.16 x				
64.87	Irina	Yatchenko	BLR	31.10.65	1		Minsk (Staiki)	28 Jul
	(30/10)							
64.40	Kateryna	Karsak	UKR	26.12.85	1	EU23	Debrecen	13 Jul
63.90	Yarelis	Barrios	CUB	12.7.83	3	WCh	Osaka	29 Aug
63.89	Beth	Mallory-Lesch	USA	31.5.84	3		Wailuku	16 Apr
63.48	Melina	Robert-Michon	FRA	18.7.79	2	EThCp	Yalta	18 Mar
63.13	Joanna	Wisniewska	POL	24.5.72	Q	WCh	Osaka	27 Aug
62.98	Anna	Söderberg	SWE	11.6.73	3	GS	Ostrava	27 Jun
62.93	Nadine	Müller	GER	21.11.85	2		Halle	19 May
62.64		Song Aimin	CHN	15.3.78	2		Padova	7 Jul
62.57		Ma Xuejun	CHN	26.3.85	2		Zhaoqing	19 May
62.44	Nataliya	Semenova	UKR	7.7.82	1		Tallinn	22 Jul
	(20)							
62.41	Olena	Antonova	UKR	16.6.72	6	WCh	Osaka	29 Aug
62.31	Jana	Tucholke	GER	20.5.81	1		Leipzig	12 May
62.24		Li Yanfeng	CHN	15.5.79	3	NC	Shijiazhuang	4 Aug
62.20	Beatrice	Faumuina	NZL	23.10.74	1		Christchurch	21 Feb
62.07	Oksana	Yesipchuk	RUS	13.12.76	1	NCp	Tula	8 Jul
61.62	Wioletta	Potepa	POL	13.12.80	5	FBK	Hengelo	26 May
61.52	Dragana	Tomasevic	SRB	4.6.82	1	NC	Novi Sad	3 Aug
61.40	Stephanie	Trafton (Brown)	USA	1.8.79	3		Wailuku	14 Apr
61.30		Xu Shaoyang	CHN	9.2.83	1	AsiC	Amman	28 Jul
61.09	Elisângela	Adriano	BRA	27.7.72	1		São Caetano do Sul	14 Jul
	(30)							
60.91	Lyudmila	Kupriyanova	BLR	8.4.74	2		Minsk (Staiki)	28 Jul
60.65	Viktoriya	Boyko	UKR	20.1.74	3	NC-w	Yalta	11 Feb
60.47	Daniele	Samuels	AUS-J	26.5.88	2	WUG	Bangkok	12 Aug
60.20	Ellina	Zvereva	BLR	16.11.60	1	NC	Grodno	6 Jul
60.17	Cecilia	Barnes	USA	24.7.80	3	ModR	Modesto	5 May
59.74	Cristiana	Checchi	ITA	8.7.77	2	ECp-1B	Milano	23 Jun
59.60	Zhanna	Mozgunova	BLR	4.6.85	2		Minsk (Staiki)	18 May
59.51		Pan Saili	CHN-J	4.12.88	1		Wuhan	1 Nov
59.36	Zaneta	Glanc	POL	11.3.83	1		Warszawa	27 May

Mark	Name		Nat	Born	Pos	Meet	Venue	Date
59.29	Vera	Begic	CRO	17.3.82	1		Rijeka	5 Jun
	(40)							
59.08	Philippa	Roles	GBR	1.3.78	1		Cwmbran	14 Jul
58.80	Krishna	Poonia	IND	5.5.77	1		Patiala	2 May
58.77	Veronika	Watzek	AUT	13.8.85	1	NC	Gisingen	1 Jul
58.75	Olga	Chernogorova	BLR	30.1.82	2eB	EThCp	Yalta	18 Mar
58.62	Yuka	Murofushi	JPN	11.2.77	1		Gifu	13 May
58.52	Ulrike	Giesa	GER	16.8.84	5		Bad Köstritz	8 Jul
58.50	Katja	Kròl	GER	5.2.80	3		Dessau	1 Jun
58.18	Marzena	Wysocka	POL	17.2.69	2		Warszawa	27 May
58.09	Seema	Antil	IND	27.7.83	1		Kolkata	12 May
57.95	Heike	Koderisch	GER	27.5.85	3		Zeulenroda	3 Jun
	(50)							
57.90	Tsvetanka	Khristova	BUL	14.3.62	1		Plovdiv	1 Jul
57.73	Sarah	Stevens	USA	2.4.86	1	Pac-10	Stanford	12 May
57.67	Agnieszka	Krawczuk	POL	14.2.83	3		Warszawa	27 May
57.58		Jin Yuanyuan	CHN-Y	24.1.90	1		Beijing	20 Apr
57.58	Kelechi	Anyanwu	USA	27.12.85	1	NCAA	Sacramento	8 Jun
57.47	Oksana	Tuchak	RUS	27.3.73	1		Adler	11 Feb
57.22	Yarisley	Collado	CUB	30.4.85	1		La Habana	1 Mar
57.14		Yang Fei	CHN	20.7.87	2		Wuhan	1 Nov
57.12	Anita	Hietalahti	FIN	17.2.77	1		Jalasjärvi	29 Jun
57.05		Jiang Fengjing	CHN	28.8.87	3		Wuhan	1 Nov
	(60)							
57.04	Summer	Pierson	USA	3.9.78	6	ModR	Modesto	5 May
57.04	Svetlana	Ivanova/Savkova	RUS	10.7.85	3	Znam	Zhukovskiy	9 Jun
56.85	Jessica	Kolotzei	GER	6.4.85	2		Mannheim	23 Jun
56.84	Rhonda	Gullatte	USA	10.2.84	1		Marietta	27 May
56.81	Monique	Jansen	NED	3.10.78	1		Krommenie	17 Jun
56.78	Alla	Denisenko	RUS	26.1.83	1		Moskva	16 May
56.74	Zinaida	Sendriuté	LTU	10.6.84	1		Kaunas	3 Jun
56.72	Rachelle	Varner	USA	20.7.83	4		Salinas	16 May
56.68	Laura	Bordignon	ITA	26.3.81	2	NC-w	Bari	4 Mar
56.67	Sivan	Jean	ISR	25.6.85	1		Tel Aviv	8 May
	(70)							
56.56	Lieja	Tunks	CAN	10.3.76	2		Salinas	16 May
56.56	Olga	Olshevskaya	RUS	5.7.82	1		Bryansk	May
56.56	Yaima	Vives	CUB	16.12.85	1		La Habana	14 Jun
56.53	Tereapii	Tapoki	COK	19.4.84	1		Auckland	19 Dec
56.51	Irache	Quintanal	ESP	18.9.78	1		Barcelona	14 Jul
56.48		Ma Shuli	CHN	20.1.78	7	WCT	Suzhou	9 Jun
56.46	Katerina	Hutchinson	USA	10.6.85	5		Salinas	16 May
56.44	Novelle	Murray	CAN	31.8.84	1		Fresno	12 May
56.43	Dorothéa	Kalpakídou	GRE	21.9.83	5	Veniz	Haniá	9 Jun
56.36	Valentina	Aniballi	ITA	19.4.84	2	NC	Padova	27 Jul
	(80)							
56.34	Izabela	Koralewska	POL	29.1.85	1		Praha	19 May
56.31	Giorgia	Baratella	ITA	8.1.75	1		Donnas	21 Jun
56.17	Kateryna	Shyshkina	UKR	27.2.87	5	NC	Donetsk	6 Jul
56.16	Vera	Karmishina	RUS-J	6.11.88	1	EJ	Hengelo	22 Jul
56.13		Wang Bin	CHN	7.1.87	8	WCT	Suzhou	9 Jun
56.07	Ileana	Brîndusoiu	ROM	9.5.79	2	NC-w	Bucuresti	10 Mar
56.06	Maria	Pettersson	SWE	17.3.77	1		Helsingborg	28 Jun
56.02		Liu Linpeng	CHN	22.2.87	6	NC	Shijiazhuang	4 Aug
55.98		Tan Jian	CHN-J	20.1.88	4		Wuhan	1 Nov
55.85	Emily	Pendleton	USA-J	16.4.89	1		Oak Harbour	5 May
	(90)							
55.76	Sabine	Rumpf	GER	18.3.83	5		Kienbaum	12 Feb
55.75	Tanja	Mäkinen	FIN	2.3.80	2		Jalasjärvi	29 Jun
55.74	Dace	Ruskule	LAT	20.9.81	1	Big 12	Lincoln	11 May
55.73	Yelena	Machkanova	RUS	14.7.81	2		Moskva	16 May
55.70	Olga	Goncharenko	BLR	13.7.81	2		Minsk (Staiki)	11 May
55.55	Harwant	Kaur	IND	5.7.80	3		Patiala	2 May
55.53	Emilee	Strot	USA	12.5.86	4		Salinas	3 May
55.49	Rocío	Comba	ARG	14.7.87	4		Uberlândia	6 May
55.48	Grete	Snyder (Etholm)	NOR	25.1.76	1		Tønsberg	20 Jun
55.43	Magdaliní	Komótoglou	GRE	13.11.85	1		Thessaloniki	12 May
	(100)							

55.42	Sandra	Perkovic	CRO-Y	21.6.90	22 Jul
55.41	Teresa	Machado	POR	22.7.69	24 Feb
55.28	Eden	Francis	GBR-J	19.10.88	2 Sep
55.23	Tatyana	Kopytova	RUS	25.9.87	22 Apr
55.22	Rachel	Jansen	USA	26.7.84	27 Apr
55.21	Kara	Nwidobie-Sharpe	GBR	13.4.81	13 May

WOMEN 2007

Mark	Name		Nat	Born	Date
55.15	Monia	Kari	TUN	14.4.71	21 Jul
55.03	Aihaiti	Aziguti	CHN	31.10.81	9 Sep
55.02		Xi Shangxue	CHN-J	27.1.89	1 Nov
54.96	Aretha	Thurmond	USA	14.8.76	22 Jun
54.85	Olesya	Korotkova	RUS	21.12.83	27 May
54.82		Lin Xiaojing	CHN	8.1.86	28 Apr
54.79	Tai	Battle	USA	4.5.86	8 Jun
54.78	Monique	Nacsa	AUS	26.10.76	12 Jan
54.76	Abby	Emsick	USA	18.11.83	11 May
54.70	Jessica	Pressley	USA	27.12.84	31 Mar
54.67	Jennifer	Onyeagbako	USA	28.1.86	12 May
54.66	Melissa	Bickett	USA	16.4.82	22 Jun
54.65	Marina	Yakimova	BLR	27.5.86	9 Jun
54.65	Ahu	Sulak	TUR	27.8.81	27 Jul
54.63	Rachel	Longfors	USA	6.6.83	30 Mar
54.60	Julia	Bremser	GER	27.5.82	14 Jul
54.58	Emma	Carpenter	GBR	16.5.82	25 Aug
54.50	Shanna	Dickenson	USA	19.9.86	8 Jun
54.48		Chen Tingting	CHN-J	17.2.89	2 Nov
54.47		Ma Yanjie	CHN-J	16.4.88	28 Apr

Mark	Name		Nat	Born	Date
54.42	Brittany	Devereaux	USA	26.5.86	31 Mar
54.40	Katie	Richardson	USA	21.1.85	12 May
54.39	Emily	Fox	USA		9 May
54.34	Marie	LeJour	CAN	13.1.79	8 Jul
54.32	Sara	Ackman	USA	15.7.87	14 Apr
54.22	D'Andra	Carter	USA	17.6.87	6 Jun
54.17	Liliana	Cá	POR	5.11.86	3 Mar
54.06	Michelle	Carter	USA	12.10.85	6 Jun
54.05	Lara	Saye	USA	27.11.81	19 May
54.03	Olivia	Korte	USA	20.6.84	12 May
54.03		Liu Linming	CHN		19 May
54.01	Melissa	Boekelman	NED-J	11.5.89	5 May
53.98	Eha	Rünne	EST	25.5.63	6 Jul
53.96	Katarzyna	Jaworowska	POL	30.9.86	27 May
53.90	Astin	Steward	USA	15.5.85	13 May
53.90	Viktoriya	Bolbat	UKR-J	2.4.89	17 Jun
53.85	Svetlana	Strukova	BLR	.86	28 Apr
53.76	Christen	Clemson	USA	29.2.84	26 May
53.69	Britney	Rogers	USA	20.10.84	15 Apr
53.66	Dayana	Octavien	HAI	10.6.82	23 Jul
53.63	Annie	Alexander (147)	TRI	28.8.87	15 Jul

Downhill

61.92	Philippa	Roles	GBR	1.3.78	1	Birmingham	1 Jul
59.41	Kara	Nwidobie	GBR	13.4.81	2	Birmingham	1 Jul

Birmingham 1 Jul: 3. Dayana Octavien HAI 10.6.82 55.55, 4. Kirsty Law GBR 11.10.86 55.52

Training meeting: 66.68 Yarelis Barrios CUB 1 Kingston 3 Mar

60.55 62.20 64.20 66.68 x 63.11

JUNIORS

See main list for top 6 juniors. 10 performances by 3 women to 57.00. Additional marks and further juniors:

Samuels	60.44	13Q	WCh	Osaka	27 Aug	58.23	1		Christchurch	21 Feb
	60.40	1	NC	Brisbane	11 Mar	57.93	1		Sydney	23 Jun
	59.05	2		Canberra	27 Jan	57.06	2	GP	Melbourne	2 Mar
	58.48	1		Hobart	9 Feb					

55.42	Sandra	Perkovic	CRO-Y	21.6.90	2	EJ	Hengelo	22 Jul
55.28	Eden	Francis	GBR	19.10.88	1		London (He)	2 Sep
55.02		Xi Shangxue	CHN	27.1.89	6		Wuhan	1 Nov
54.48		Chen Tingting (10)	CHN	17.2.89	7		Wuhan	2 Nov
54.47		Ma Yanjie	CHN	16.4.88	7		Beijing	28 Apr
54.01	Melissa	Boekelman	NED	11.5.89	2		Lisse	5 May
53.90	Viktoriya	Bolbat	UKR	2.4.89	1-j		Kyiv	17 Jun
53.35		Wang Xi	CHN	8.9.89	9		Wuhan	1 Nov
53.20	Isabel V.	Gómez	CUB	12.10.88	3		La Habana	14 Jun
52.99	Anna-Katharina	Weller	GER	5.2.89	2		Gladbeck	1 Jul
52.78	Kylie	Spurgeon	USA	20.12.88	1		Edmond	19 Apr
52.21	Tamara	Apostolico	ITA	28.4.89	3	EJ	Hengelo	22 Jul
51.87		Li Wen-Hua	TPE	3.12.89	1	NG	Tainan	23 Oct
51.74	Irina	Rodrigues (20)	POR-Y	5.2.91	1	Eur Oly	Beograd	25 Jul

HAMMER

Note Lysenko and Khoroshikh failed a drugs test on 9 May 07. The ongoing enquiry into the particular circumstances of this may well mean the deletion of all their results from that date.

78.61	Tatyana		Lysenko	RUS	9.10.83	1		Sochi			26 May
					78.61	p	p	77.05	p	x	
	77.71	1	GS	Ostrava	27 Jun	77.32	77.71	x	73.69	75.91	76.13
	77.30	1		Adler	22 Apr	74.14	77.30	76.80	75.85	x	p
	77.01	1	Znam	Zhukovskiy	9 Jun	74.59	75.83	75.53	74.73	75.85	77.01
	76.74	1		Zagreb	4 Jul	75.26	76.24	76.74	72.48	x	75.30
	75.86	1	ECp	München	24 Jun	73.04	74.53	75.86	x		
	75.73	2	SGP	Doha	11 May	73.77	x	75.73	x		
	74.53	1		Adler	11 Feb	74.49	74.53	72.65	x	x	72.36
77.36	Gulfiya		Khanafeyeva	RUS	4.6.82	2		Sochi			26 May
					x	75.46	77.36	75.00	x	76.28	
	75.39	1	NCp	Tula	7 Jul	68.01	72.27	x	70.59	x	75.39
	74.32	2	Znam	Zhukovskiy	9 Jun	x	66.94	70.58	70.61	74.32	73.16
76.83	Kamila		Skolimowska	POL	4.11.82	1	SGP	Doha			11 May
					x	74.30	76.83	74.66			
	75.22	1		Tallinn	22 Jul	71.27	75.22	73.25	x	73.17	x
	73.75	4	WCh	Osaka	30 Aug	73.75	70.54	65.69	70.78	70.06	70.77
76.36	Yipsi		Moreno	CUB	19.11.80	1	Kuso	Waszawa			17 Jun
					71.75	76.36	x	71.03	69.36	69.95	
	75.65	1		Padova	7 Jul	x	73.55	74.49	75.14	x	75.65
	75.20	1	PAm	Rio de Janeiro	23 Jul	x	73.44	71.37	x	x	75.20
	74.90	1	NC	La Habana	27 May	x	x	74.90	73.20	x	73.10
	74.74	2	WCh	Osaka	30 Aug	72.84	x	x	74.33	70.87	74.74

Mark	Name		Nat	Born	Pos	Meet	Venue	Date
73.89					2		Zagreb	4 Jul
	x 73.89 72.14 72.51 73.68 x							
73.76					1	WAF	Stuttgart	22 Sep
	x 73.76 73.41 x							
76.21	Yelena	Konevtsova	RUS	11.3.81	3		Sochi	26 May
	73.70 73.97 75.55 74.54 76.21 73.13							
75.13					2	NCp	Tula	7 Jul
	71.38 73.61 73.47 71.17 72.17 75.13							
74.45					1		Moskva	3 Jul
73.95					1	NC	Tula	2 Aug
	71.06 73.19 x 73.95 x x							
75.77	Betty	Heidler	GER	14.10.83	1eA		Halle	19 May
	72.38 74.31 75.77 75.34 75.17 75.03							
75.21					1		Fränkisch-Crumbach	27 May
	70.68 75.21 74.72 72.43 74.81 73.26							
75.05					3	Kuso	Waszawa	17 Jun
	73.40 75.05 73.04 71.15 73.49 x							
74.94					1	NC	Erfurt	22 Jul
	67.85 70.66 x 74.94 x 74.61							
74.76					1	WCh	Osaka	30 Aug
	x 74.76 x 73.73 71.31 73.10							
73.94					1		Leverkusen	10 Aug
	70.54 73.94 x p p p							
75.08	Ivana	Brkljacic	CRO	25.1.83	2	Kuso	Waszawa	17 Jun
	71.46 x x 71.20 x 75.08							
74.69					Q	WCh	Osaka	28 Aug
	74.69 only throw							
74.62					3	SGP	Doha	11 May
	69.64 74.62 x 72.16							
74.87	Yekaterina	Khoroshikh	RUS	21.1.83	4		Sochi	26 May
	72.57 73.87 68.99 74.06 73.80 x							
74.86		Zhang Wenxiu	CHN	22.3.86	1	NC	Shijiazhuang	3 Aug
74.39					3	WCh	Osaka	30 Aug
	73.11 x 74.21 74.39 x							
74.30					1		Suzhou	8 Jun
	(30/9)							
73.94	Oksana	Menkova (10)	BLR	28.3.82	1		Minsk (Staiki)	1 Jun
73.71	Manuèla	Montebrun	FRA	13.11.79	1		Castres	11 Aug
73.45	Kathrin	Klaas	GER	8.2.84	2eA		Halle	19 May
73.21	Eileen	O'Keeffe	IRL	31.5.81	1	NC	Dublin	21 Jul
72.94	Jennifer	Dahlgren	ARG	27.8.84	1		Athens, GA	13 Apr
72.51	Brittany	Riley	USA	26.8.86	1	DrakeR	Des Moines	28 Apr
72.36	Olga	Kuzenkova	RUS	4.10.70	2	NC	Tula	2 Aug
71.96	Ester	Balassini	ITA	20.10.77	1		Abuja	5 May
71.83	Iryna	Sekachova	UKR	21.7.76	1		Kyiv	20 Apr
71.78	Yelena	Priyma	RUS	2.12.83	5		Sochi	26 May
71.74	Marina	Smolyachkova	BLR	10.2.85	2		Minsk (Staiki)	1 Jun
	(20)							
71.43	Clarissa	Claretti	ITA	7.10.80	1		Palermo	29 Sep
71.29	Darya	Pchelnik	BLR	20.12.81	1		Minsk (Staiki)	28 Jul
71.14	Arasay	Thondike	CUB	28.5.86	5	Kuso	Warszawa	17 Jun
71.11	Stéphanie	Falzon	FRA	7.1.83	1		Sasolburg	23 Jan
71.08	Amélie	Perrin	FRA	30.3.80	2		Strasbourg	28 Jun
70.62	Yelena	Matoshko	BLR	23.6.82	2		Minsk (Staiki)	28 Jul
70.36	Susanne	Keil	GER	18.5.78	1		Mannheim	23 Jun
70.33	Amber	Campbell	USA	5.6.81	1		Provo	2 Jun
70.10	Erin	Gilreath	USA	11.10.80	1		Clermont	17 Mar
69.91	Andrea	Bunjes	GER	5.2.76	4		Fränkisch-Crumbach	27 May
	(30)							
69.91	Nadezhda	Pavlyukovskaya	BLR	6.6.85	3	Klim	Minsk (Staiki)	9 Jun
69.56		Liu Yinghui	CHN	29.6.79	2	WCT	Suzhou	8 Jun
69.52	Nataliya	Zolotukhina	UKR	4.1.85	1		Kyiv	3 Aug
69.27	Katarzyna	Kita	POL	4.7.84	2	NC	Poznan	1 Jul
69.26	Kristal	Yush	USA	8.1.82	2		Provo	2 Jun
69.22	Martina	Danisová	SVK	21.3.83	1		Coolidge, AZ	10 Mar
69.11	Bethany	Hart	USA	10.4.77	1		West Point	2 Jun
69.07	Anita	Wlodarczyk	POL	8.8.85	1		Poznan	16 Sep
68.93	Jenny	Leatherman	USA	26.9.83	3		Provo	2 Jun
68.88	Alexándra	Papayeoryíou	GRE	17.12.80	1	NC	Athína	16 Jun
	(40)							
68.82	Yunaika	Crawford	CUB	2.11.82	3	NC/Barr	La Habana	27 May
68.77		Hao Shuai	CHN	19.7.87	2		Zhaoqing	18 May
68.70	Svetlana	Sudak-Torun (BLR)	TUR	20.3.71	3		Minsk (Staiki)	28 Jul
68.66	Berta	Castells	ESP	24.1.84	1		Valencia	9 Jun
68.65	Merja	Korpela	FIN	15.5.81	1	NC	Lappeenranta	4 Aug
68.60	Crystal	Smith	CAN	6.3.81	1		Lexington	14 Jun
68.56	Loree	Smith	USA	6.11.82	2		Tucson	19 May
68.49	Anna	Bulgakova	RUS-J	17.1.88	6		Sochi	26 May
68.48	Sanja	Gavrilovic	CRO	20.9.82	1		Bar	4 Aug
68.34	Jessica	Cosby	USA	31.5.82	1		Los Angeles (Ww)	13 Apr
	(50)							
68.31	Cecilia	Nilsson	SWE	22.6.79	1	NC	Eskilstuna	12 Aug
68.17	Inna	Sayenko	UKR	8.3.82	1		Kyiv	8 May

Mark	Name		Nat	Born	Pos	Meet	Venue	Date
68.16	Iryna	Novozhylova	UKR	7.1.86	1		Kyiv	18 May
68.07	Mihaela	Melinte	ROM	27.3.75	1	NC	Bucuresti	28 Jul
67.98	Stiliani	Papadopoúlou	GRE	15.3.82	4		Thessaloniki	30 Jul
67.92	Sultana	Frizell	CAN	24.10.84	1		Lethbridge	20 May
67.80	Mona	Holm	NOR	5.8.83	5eA		Halle	19 May
67.80	Zoe	Derham	GBR	24.11.80	2		Varazdin	7 Jul
67.78		Liao Xiaoyan	CHN	8.1.87	3		Zhaoqing	18 May
67.71	Sini	Pöyry	FIN	3.2.80	1		Keuruu	22 Jun
	(60)							
67.63	Lenka	Ledvinová	CZE	11.8.85	2	EU23	Debrecen	14 Jul
67.54	Britney	Henry	USA	17.10.84	1		Eugene	5 May
67.45	Marina	Marghieva	MDA	28.6.86	1		Chisinau	10 May
67.24	Bianca	Perie	ROM-Y	1.6.90	1	NC-w/j	Bucuresti	9 Mar
67.14	Vânia	Silva	POR	8.6.80	1		Leiria	3 Feb
67.09	Katalin	Divós	HUN	11.5.74	1		Veszprém	21 Jul
66.98	Éva	Orbán	HUN	29.11.84	4	MSR	Walnut	15 Apr
66.96	Rosa	Rodríguez	VEN	2.7.86	1		Valencia, VEN	14 Jul
66.93	Malgorzata	Zadura	POL	3.10.82	1		Lublin	14 Jun
66.83	Laëtitia	Bambara	FRA	30.3.84	2		Aulnay-sur-Odon	21 Jul
	(70)							
66.71	Vanda	Nickl	HUN	4.9.85	1		Veszprém	12 May
66.63	Olivia	Waldet	FRA	23.5.84	3		Forbach	27 May
66.60	Yelena	Kiseleva	RUS	24.3.79	7		Sochi	26 May
66.35	Dorotea	Habazin	CRO-J	14.6.88	1		Osijek	13 Jun
66.34	Sarah	Stevens	USA	2.4.86	2	NCAA-r	Eugene	26 May
66.31	Svitlana	Kovalchuk	UKR	3.1.84	1		Kyiv	25 May
66.24	Laura	Gibilisco	ITA	17.1.86	1		Siracusa	23 Jun
66.19	Silvia	Salis	ITA	17.9.85	2	NC	Padova	27 Jul
66.00	Brittany	Hinchcliffe	USA	24.7.82	7		Eugene	27 May
65.70	Marwa Ahmed	Hussein	EGY	19.6.78	1	AfG	Alger	19 Jul
	(80)							
65.67		Wang Yang	CHN	3.4.87	5		Zhaoqing	18 May
65.60	Bianca	Achilles	GER	17.4.81	1		Dortmund	16 May
65.58	Candice	Scott	TRI	17.9.80	4	NC/Barr	La Habana	27 May
65.40	Zalina	Marghieva	MDA-J	5.2.88	1	NC-w	Chisinau	11 Feb
65.36	Mateja	Greguric	CRO-J	27.5.88	1		Zenica	2 Jun
65.33	Leslie	Coons	USA	16.7.73	1		Irvine	28 Apr
65.20	Sarah	Hopping	USA	5.8.83	11	NC	Indianapolis	23 Jun
65.18	Amy	Haapanen	FIN	23.3.84	1		Irvine	6 Apr
65.09	Maris	Röngelep	EST	17.3.84	2		Kyiv	20 Jun
64.93	Simone	Mathes	GER	13.3.75	1eB		Halle	19 May
	(90)							
64.92	Malwina	Sobierajska	POL	22.4.85	4		Biala Podlaska	2 Jun
64.68	Paraskevi	Theodorou	CYP	15.3.86	3	GRE Ch	Athína	16 Jun
64.64	Kelly	Godsey	USA	1.1.86	1		Cambridge, MA	13 Jul
64.60	Natalya	Shayunova	BLR-J	11.9.89	1		Brest	27 Apr
64.60	Yuka	Murofushi	JPN	11.2.77	1	Oda	Hiroshima	29 Apr
64.59	Noémi	Németh	HUN	7.4.86	5	EU23	Debrecen	14 Jul
64.45	Lena	Solvin	FIN	4.7.86	3	NC	Lappeenranta	4 Aug
64.43	Carrie	Johnson	USA	19.10.84	2		Stanford	31 Mar
64.40	Johana	Moreno	COL	15.4.85	1		Bogotá	30 Jun
64.34	Carys	Parry	GBR	24.7.81	2		Loughborough	20 May
	(100)							

64.29	Ana	Susec	SLO	23.11.85	27 Jun
64.25		Yang Qiaoyu	CHN	14.9.85	18 May
64.18	Cari	Soong	USA	11.7.81	21 Apr
64.17	Mariya	Bespalova	RUS	21.5.86	3 Jul
64.11	Masumi	Aya	JPN	1.1.80	5 May
64.09	Oksana	Kondratyeva	RUS	22.11.85	7 Jul
64.05	Ariannis	Vichy	CUB-J	18.5.89	7 Jun
64.04		Wang Zheng	CHN	14.12.87	29 Oct
64.01		Yang Meiping	CHN	23.10.81	3 Aug
63.97	Melissa	Myerscough	USA	5.9.79	14 Apr
63.90	Tracey	Andersson	SWE	5.12.84	26 Jul
63.85	Robyn	Jarocki	USA	11.7.84	28 Apr
63.75	Loren	Groves	USA	7.2.86	29 Apr
63.70	Dolores	Pedrares	ESP	17.1.73	7 Jul
63.58	Katerina	Safránková	CZE-J	8.6.89	13 Jun
63.48	Weronika	Milkowska	POL	12.6.86	2 Sep
63.47	Annika	Hjelm	SWE	3.1.86	26 May
63.46	Veronica	Jatsek	USA	.86	11 May
63.46	Shirley	Webb	GBR	28.9.81	28 Jul
63.03	Kirsten	Münchow	GER	21.1.77	19 May
62.95	Zlata	Tarasova	RUS	2.12.86	12 May
62.95	Annika	Nurminen	FIN	27.12.87	13 Jul
62.94	Alicja	Filipkowska	POL	15.4.87	2 Jun
62.91	Katiusca María de Jesús		BRA	8.5.77	27 May
62.68	Kristen	Callan	USA	5.4.85	14 Apr
62.67	Laura	Douglas	GBR	4.1.83	12 Aug
62.66	Josiane	Soares	BRA	21.6.76	27 May
62.63	Brooke	Billett	AUS	9.7.80	28 Jan
62.42	Sarah	Bensaad	FRA	27.1.87	25 Jul
62.35	Jessica	Ponce de Leon	MEX	16.8.79	8 Jun
62.33	Jessica	Pressley	USA	27.12.84	28 Apr
62.28	Carolina	Pedersen	SWE	16.4.87	20 May
62.21	Anna	Dolegiewicz	USA	10.3.78	2 Jun
62.16	Amarilis	Almestica	PUR	12.2.81	17 Mar
62.15	Rebecka	Kvist	SWE	17.2.83	12 Aug
62.11	Yuliet	Hernández	CUB-Y	2.4.90	29 Jun
62.07	Yekaterina	Kireyeva	RUS	21.5.86	11 Feb
62.05	Adriana	Benaventa	VEN	19.10.84	14 Jul
62.00	Amy	Séné	FRA	6.4.85	16 Jun
61.85	Melanie	Motzenbächer	GER	2.3.86	27 May

Mark	Name		Nat	Born	Date
61.83	Yuliya	Rozenfeld	RUS	5.4.84	26 May
61.83	Stevi	Large	USA	11.2.86	26 May
61.79	Astin	Steward	USA	15.5.85	26 May
61.75	Alena	Krechik	BLR	20.7.87	9 Jun
61.74	Elisa	Palmieri	ITA	18.9.83	19 May
61.73	April	Phillips	USA	22.9.81	29 Apr
61.71	Emma	Johannesson	SWE	16.1.84	14 Jul
61.53	Karyne	Di Marco	AUS	14.3.78	11 Mar
61.50	Radka	Hejretová	CZE	17.5.87	28 Sep
61.44	Lucie	Vrbenská	CZE	12.5.77	30 Jun
61.42	Joana	Hahn	GER	7.2.86	19 Aug
61.36	Zubeyde	Yildiz	TUR	7.9.80	13 May
61.35	Yekaterina	Akulova	BLR	9.11.87	6 Jul
61.35	Marie	Hilmersson	SWE	14.1.81	1 Sep
61.34	Kirsi	Koro	FIN	22.6.76	23 Jul
61.30	Laci	Heller	USA	21.3.85	5 May
61.20	Jana	Hyjánková	CZE	20.1.81	30 Jun
61.13	Johana	Ramirez	COL	7.6.82	6 Oct
61.07	Chandra	Andrews	USA	4.9.83	26 May
61.07	Sarah	Holt	GBR	17.4.87	7 Jul
60.96	Susan	McKelvie	GBR	15.6.85	7 Jul
60.96	Katharina	Nowak	GER	13.5.85	29 Jul
60.94	Polina	Vashukova	RUS	10.8.87	11 Feb
60.94	Amy	Parkosewich	USA	26.7.81	2 Jun
60.93	Ozioma	Okolie	USA		26 May
60.90	Florence	Ezeh	TOG	29.12.77	27 May
60.87		Zhou Xiaoling	CHN-J	2.3.88	14 Apr
60.86	Liz	Alabi	USA	18.4.84	11 May
60.85	Romana	Grómanová	CZE	11.10.84	30 Apr
60.84	Rachel	Jansen	USA	26.7.84	13 May
60.82	Vanessa	Wilhelm	USA	24.11.79	13 Apr
60.82	Krishna	Lee	USA	25.7.86	26 May
60.81	Josefine	Berg	SWE	27.12.85	26 May
60.80	Idalmis	Rivera	CUB-J	17.3.88	21 Jun
60.78	Miki	Yamashiro	JPN	19.6.86	9 Jun
60.77	Odette	Palma	CHI	7.8.82	18 Nov
60.74	Ritu	Rani	IND	31.8.82	8 Oct
60.72	Svetlana	Cernei	MDA	20.11.86	1 Jun
60.69	Natalya	Karpuk	BLR	5.5.87	3 Feb
60.67	Irina	Karasyeva	RUS	8.3.82	2 Aug
60.66	Annabelle	Rolnin	FRA	28.12.87	6 Jun
60.57	Minna	Paavola	FIN	21.6.84	14 Jun
60.55	Tatayna	Khatantseva	RUS	18.2.81	2 Aug
60.52	Anna	Ksenofontova	RUS-J	24.1.88	4 Feb
60.51	Ashley	Harbin	USA		26 May
60.50	Natalie	Grant	JAM	25.5.81	11 May
60.49		Li Juan	CHN-J	6.2.88	2 Jun
60.48	Tamara	Burns	USA	21.12.83	19 Apr
60.43	Shanna	Dickenson	USA	19.9.86	13 Apr
60.41	Aymara	Albury	BAH	25.7.85	6 Apr
60.37	Sarah	Vance	USA	27.6.84	12 May
60.36	Emily	Turland	USA	26.4.84	17 Mar
60.36	Terri	Schwamb	USA		25 May
60.34	Keturah	Lofton	USA	24.7.82	5 May
60.27	Malvina	Cazac	MDA	11.4.85	11 Feb
60.26	Marynna	Karolina de Jesus	BRA-J	29.6.88	8 Jul
60.21	Liliya	Razinkova	UKR	29.11.85	4 Jul
60.19	Hannele	Kuutti	FIN	16.3.84	4 Aug
60.18	Nikola	Lomnická	SVK-J	16.9.88	17 Jun
60.10	Mélanie	Viniger (200)	FRA	16.7.84	3 Mar

Drugs disqualification

64.04	Susan Olufunke	Adeoye #	NGR	14.4.85	(2)	AfG	Alger	19 Jul

JUNIORS

See main list for top 6 juniors. 13 performances by 4 women to 65.46. Additional marks and further juniors:

Bulgakova	67.75	4		Moskva	3 Jul	66.49	5	NC	Tula	2 Aug
	66.80	1		Zhukovskiy	30 Jun	65.89	1	NC-j	Sochi	24 May
Perie	66.54	2	NC-w	Bucuresti	10 Mar	66.00	2	EThCp23	Yalta	18 Mar
	66.10	1	NC-j	Bucuresti	18 Aug	65.46	1	NC-wj	Bucurest	11 Mar
Habazin	66.08	1	NC-j	Zagreb	30 Jun					

64.05	Ariannis	Vichy	CUB	18.5.89	1		La Habana	7 Jun
63.58	Katerina	Safránková	CZE	8.6.89	3	v3N-j	Osijek	13 Jun
62.11	Yuliet	Hernández	CUB-Y	2.4.90	1		Santiago de Cuba	29 Jun
60.87	(10)	Zhou Xiaoling	CHN	2.3.88	1		Chengdu	14 Apr
60.80	Idalmis	Rivera	CUB	17.3.88	3		La Habana	21 Jun
60.52	Anna	Ksenofontova	RUS	24.1.88	2-j		Adler	4 Feb
60.49		Li Juan	CHN	6.2.88	3	NC-20	Chengdu	2 Jun
60.26	Marynna Karolina	de Jesus	BRA	29.6.88	1	PAm-J	São Paulo	8 Jul
60.18	Nikola	Lomnická	SVK	16.9.88	1		Ostrava	17 Jun
60.02	Gabi	Wolfarth	GER	6.9.89	3		Hannover	26 Aug
59.77	Yirisleidy L.	Ford	CUB-Y	1.1.91	2		La Habana	7 Jun
59.39	Laura	Redondo	ESP	3.7.88	1	NC-j	Castellón	8 Jul
59.37	Andriána	Papadopoúlou-Fatála	GRE-Y	21.1.90	2		Trípoli	27 May
59.19	Dóra	Lévai (20)	HUN	20.6.88	1	NC-23	Budapest	30 Jun

JAVELIN

WOMEN 2007

70.20	Christina	Obergföll	GER	22.8.81	1	ECp-S	München	23 Jun				
					64.16	70.20	65.77	62.80				
68.08	1		Halle	19 May	66.57	64.37	x	67.72	60.33	68.08		
67.88	1	GP	Athína	2 Jul	67.78	x	65.09	65.58	62.35	66.11		
67.04	1		Leverkusen	10 Aug	64.07	x	67.04	x	p	x		
66.95	1		Cottbus	20 Jun	62.39	x	63.90	64.08	66.95	x		
66.91	1	Athl	Lausanne	10 Jul	x	66.91	63.10	x	62.40	x		
66.59	1	NC	Erfurt	21 Jul	x	66.59	p	p	p	x		
66.46	2	WCh	Osaka	31 Aug	64.01	65.26	60.90	61.87	61.12	66.46		
65.42	1		Bochum-Wattenscheid	12 Aug	65.42	x	x	63.16	p,			
65.08	1		Kassel	6 Jun	56.77	57.92	61.12	x	x	65.08		
65.08	1		Berlin (Elstal)	15 Sep	64.21	64.07	65.36	59.56	x	60.64		
64.88	1		Versmold	8 Sep								
64.58	1	ISTAF	Berlin	16 Sep	63.58	x	x	63.20	64.58	63.04		
67.12	Barbora	Spotáková	CZE	30.6.81	1	WAF	Stuttgart	22 Sep				
					67.12	p	p	61.42				
67.07	1	WCh	Osaka	31 Aug	66.40	60.30	67.07	64.28	63.56	64.61		
66.08	2	GP	Athína	2 Jul	60.39	x	59.09	60.97	62.65	66.08		

Mark	Name		Nat	Born	Pos	Meet	Venue	Date	R1	R2	R3	R4	R5	R6
65.20					1	Pre	Eugene	10 Jun	53.25	55.84	61.67	x	65.20	57.76
65.19					1	ECCp	Albufeira	26 May	x	x	60.12	65.19		
64.94					1	GS	Ostrava	27 Jun	64.94	63.74	p	x	p	64.61
64.51					2	ISTAF	Berlin	16 Sep	61.05	64.51	p	p	p	64.07
64.49					3		Bochum-Wattenscheid	12 Aug	63.75	x	60.20	x	64.49	x
65.78	Steffi	Nerius	GER	1.7.72	2		Cottbus	20 Jun	x	65.78	x	64.56	x	x
65.72					2		Leverkusen	10 Aug	65.72	x	p	62.92	x	x
64.90					2	WAF	Stuttgart	22 Sep	62.90	64.90	x	64.26		
64.74					2		Halle	19 May	x	64.74	x	x	64.69	64.55
64.68					2		Bochum-Wattenscheid	12 Aug	x	63.73	x	64.68	p	p
64.49					3	ISTAF	Berlin	16 Sep	63.89	64.49	x	x	x	x
64.42					3	WCh	Osaka	31 Aug	59.89	59.75	59.96	64.42	62.38	x
64.41					2		Berlin (Elstal)	15 Sep	64.41	x	62.37	61.30	x	x
65.05	Goldie	Sayers	GBR	16.7.82	1		Loughborough	20 May	58.32	62.14	58.16	58.50	62.70	65.05
64.65	Sonia	Bisset	CUB	1.4.71	3	GP	Athína	2 Jul	60.83	x	59.76	60.94	64.65	59.12
	(31/5)													
64.29	Nikola	Brejchová	CZE	25.6.74	Q	WCh	Osaka	29 Aug						
64.28	Mariya	Abakumova	RUS	15.1.86	2	ECCp	Albufeira	26 May						
64.19	Kim	Kreiner	USA	26.7.77	1		Fortaleza	16 May						
63.65	Indre	Jakubaitytė	LTU	24.1.76	1		Kaunas	14 Sep						
63.58	Paula	Tarvainen	FIN	17.2.73	Q	WCh	Osaka	29 Aug						
	(10)													
63.35	Lada	Chernova	RUS	1.1.70	1	NC	Tula	1 Aug						
63.13	Sávva	Líka	GRE	27.6.70	5	WCh	Osaka	31 Aug						
62.80	Linda	Stahl	GER	2.9.85	Q	WCh	Osaka	29 Aug						
62.51A	Justine	Robbeson	RSA	15.5.85	1		Potchefstroom	2 Feb						
62.34	Urszula	Jasinska	POL	6.12.83	1		Sopot	6 May						
62.34	Osleidys	Menéndez	CUB	14.11.79	1	PAm	Rio de Janeiro	27 Jul						
62.23	Mariya	Yakovenko	RUS	6.1.82	3	NC-w	Tula	1 Aug						
62.19	Mercedes	Chilla	ESP	19.1.80	1	Aragón	Zaragoza	28 Jul						
62.09	Zahra	Bani	ITA	31.12.79	2	GS	Ostrava	27 Jun						
61.90	Felicia	Moldovan	ROM	29.9.67	2	Aragón	Zaragoza	28 Jul						
	(20)													
61.68	Olga	Ivankova	UKR	7.1.73	Q	WCh	Osaka	29 Aug						
61.66	Barbara	Madejczyk	POL	30.9.76	1		Villeneuve d'Ascq	8 Jun						
61.61		Chang Chunfeng	CHN-J	4.5.88	1	NC-j	Chengdu	4 Jun						
61.40	María de la C.	Álvarez	CUB	30.8.75	1		La Habana	21 Jun						
61.40	Buoban	Phamang	THA	27.12.86	1	WUG	Bangkok	14 Aug						
61.19	Monica	Stoian	ROM	25.8.82	2	WUG	Bangkok	14 Aug						
60.70	Mikaela	Ingberg	FIN	29.7.74	1		Kuortane	12 Aug						
60.63	Mareike	Rittweg	GER	1.6.84	2		Schönbeck	10 Jun						
60.58	Tetyana	Lyahovych	UKR	20.5.79	1	NC-w	Yalta	10 Feb						
60.39	Annika	Suthe	GER	15.10.85	1		Mannheim	22 Jun						
	(30)													
60.38	Oksana	Gromova	RUS	23.9.80	2	Vard	Réthimno	18 Jul						
59.96		Zhang Li	CHN	19.10.78	1	CISM	Hyderabad	18 Oct						
59.94	Christina	Scherwin	DEN	11.7.76	1	ECp-2A	Odense	23 Jun						
59.89		Song Dan	CHN-Y	5.7.90	1		Wuhan	2 Nov						
59.88	Claudia	Coslovich	ITA	26.4.72	1	NC	Padova	27 Jul						
59.74	Silvia	Cruz	POR	29.12.80	1	NC	Lisboa (U)	29 Jul						
59.70	Laverne	Eve	BAH	16.6.65	1	NC	Nassau	22 Jun						
59.69	Linda	Brivule	LAT	9.9.83	1		Riga	12 May						
59.65	Dana	Pounds	USA	5.6.84	1	NC	Indianapolis	22 Jun						
59.58	Alessandra	Resende	BRA	5.3.75	1		São Caetano do Sul	17 Mar						
	(40)													
59.52	Taina	Kolkkala	FIN	24.10.76	13Q	WCh	Osaka	29 Aug						
59.40	Natalya	Shimchuk	BLR	1.10.81	1	NC-w	Brest	3 Feb						
59.38	Jarmila	Klimesová	CZE	9.2.81	3	Odlozil	Praha	13 Jun						
59.36	Kimberley	Mickle	AUS	28.12.84	1		Perth	15 Dec						
58.87	Katharina	Molitor	GER	8.11.83	3		Kassel	6 Jun						
58.81	Yanet	Cruz	CUB-J	8.2.88	3	NC/Barr	La Habana	27 May						
58.76	Yekaterina	Rybko	RUS	5.6.82	2	NC-w	Adler	21 Feb						
58.68	Vivian	Zimmer	GER	22.7.87	4		Kienbaum	12 Feb						
58.61	Kathryn	Mitchell	AUS	10.7.82	1		Ballarat	8 Dec						
58.49	Martina	Ratej	SLO	2.11.81	1		Sentjur	6 May						
	(50)													
58.48	Vira	Rebryk	UKR-J	25.2.89	1	EJ	Hengelo	21 Jul						
58.48	Nadeeka	Lakmali	SRI	18.9.81	1		Colombo	1 Aug						

Mark	Name		Nat	Born	Pos	Meet	Venue	Date
58.39	Sunette	Viljoen	RSA	6.10.83	5	WUG	Bangkok	14 Aug
58.34	Esther	Eisenlauer	GER	29.10.77	1		Saarbrücken	19 Aug
58.03i	Kirsi	Ahonen	FIN	8.4.76	1		Pori	24 Feb
	55.89				6eB	EThCp	Yalta	17 Mar
57.98	Madara	Palameika	LAT	18.6.87	2		Riga	12 May
57.98	Marina	Novik	BLR	19.1.84	1		Minsk (Staiki)	28 Jul
57.93	Inga	Stasiulionyté	LTU	29.6.81	2		Kaunas	25 Jul
57.90	Rachel	Yurkovich	USA	10.10.86	1		Tempe	24 Mar
57.88		Li Lingwei	CHN-J	26.1.89	2	WCT	Suzhou	10 Jun
	(60)							
57.62	Rumyana	Karapetrova	BUL	7.2.82	1	BalkC	Sofia	5 Jul
57.57	Bregje	Crolla	NED	31.1.86	1		Kerkrade	17 Jun
57.55	Zuleima	Araméndiz	COL	23.9.75	2	SAmC	São Paulo	9 Jun
57.37	Laura	Cornford	AUS-J	11.6.88	1		Sydney	2 Feb
57.31	Annika	Petersson	SWE	10.1.79	1	NC	Eskilstuna	12 Aug
57.19	Emika	Yoshida	JPN	10.12.85	1	NC	Osaka	30 Jun
57.18		Xue Juan	CHN	10.2.86	1	NGP	Urumqi	19 Sep
57.17	Alexandra	Nasta-Tsisiou	CYP	2.7.81	19Q	WCh	Osaka	29 Aug
57.13	Pauliina	Laamanen	FIN	10.10.84	3		Eurajoki	13 Jun
57.06	Marina	Maksimova	RUS	20.5.85	4		Adler	4 Feb
	(70)							
57.01	Sinta	Ozolina	LAT-J	26.2.88	2	EJ	Hengelo	21 Jul
56.96	Stephanie	Hessler	GER	16.3.83	2		Longeville-lès-Metz	15 Jul
56.84	Nadia	Vigliano	FRA	24.6.77	1	NC	Niort	4 Aug
56.55	Tazmin	Brits	RSA-Y	8.1.91	1		Maputo	10 Jun
56.54	Sarah	Walter	FRA	5.5.78	6		Villeneuve d'Ascq	8 Jun
56.50	Ivana	Vukovic	CRO	18.5.86	1		Split	3 Mar
56.49	Lindy	Leveaux-Agricole	SEY	14.11.79	2	AfG	Alger	20 Jul
56.48		Fu Lin	CHN-J	21.2.89	3	WCT	Suzhou	10 Jun
56.45	Erma-Gene	Evans	LCA	25.1.84	1		Houston	11 May
56.42	Olivia	McKoy	JAM	1.12.73	1		Spanish Town	10 Mar
	(80)							
56.29		Kim Kyong-ae	KOR-J	5.3.88	1	NC	Daegu	2 Jun
56.26	Sandra	Schaffarzik	GER	22.6.87	4		Leverkusen	10 Aug
56.10	Maria	Negoita	ROM	6.12.86	4	EU23	Debrecen	15 Jul
56.06	Krista	Woodward	CAN	22.11.84	1		Tuscaloosa	25 Mar
56.03	Nora Aida	Bicet	CUB	29.10.77	7	GP	Madrid	21 Jul
55.93	Jelena	Jaakkola	FIN-J	7.3.89	1		Mannheim	22 Jun
55.92	Kateema	Riettie	JAM	5.12.73	3		Provo	2 Jun
55.88	Margaryta	Dorozhon	UKR	4.9.87	2		Kyiv	19 May
55.76	Marion	Bonaudo	FRA	12.9.82	1		Reims	17 Jul
55.56	Lindsey	Blaine	USA	14.12.84	1	NCAA	Sacramento	9 Jun
	(90)							
55.53	Galina	Kakhova	BLR	26.3.82	2		Minsk (Staiki)	18 May
55.41		Chang Jung-yeon	KOR	6.4.77	2	NC	Daegu	2 Jun
55.38	Leryn	Franco	PAR	1.3.82	5		Fortaleza	16 May
55.33	Yuki	Ebihara	JPN	28.10.85	Q	WUG	Bangkok	12 Aug
55.28	Dalila	Rugama	NCA	9.4.84	4	ALBA	Caracas	11 May
55.28		Wu Jie	CHN-J	26.9.89	5	NC-j	Chengdu	4 Jun
55.18A	Sabina	Moya	COL	27.1.77	2		Bogotá	30 Jun
55.17		Zhu Ying	CHN	15.12.87	3		Wuhan	2 Nov
55.08	Xénia	Frajka	HUN	24.1.82	1	NC	Székesfehérvár	29 Jul
55.07	Yelena	Makarova	RUS	21.12.81	5	Znam	Zhukovskiy	9 Jun
	(100)							

55.00	Franziska	Krebs	GER	11.10.85	22 Jun
54.98	Tiziana	Rocco	ITA	2.12.78	6 May
54.93	Yainelis	Ribeaux	CUB	30.12.87	27 May
54.83	Urszula	Kuncewicz	POL-J	11.6.88	21 Jul
54.77	Nathalie	Teppe	FRA	22.5.72	20 Jun
54.75	Yuko	Kojima	JPN	20.11.73	21 Oct
54.66	Oona	Sormunen	FIN-J	2.8.89	27 May
54.62		Zhang Ying	CHN-J	5.1.88	20 May
54.62		Zheng Ruixia	CHN	14.3.83	20 Jul
54.53	Jucilene	de Lima	BRA-Y	14.9.90	26 May
54.50	Panayióta	Touloumtzí	GRE	26.9.86	17 Mar
54.50	Marina	Buksa	BLR	19.10.87	9 Jun
54.47	Jana	Trakmann	EST	17.2.82	23 May
54.44	Lilli	Schwarzkopf	GER	28.8.83	26 Aug
54.43		Kim Hyun-joo	KOR	29.5.76	2 Jun
54.39	Susanne	Rosenbauer	GER	2.8.84	22 Apr
54.37	Carita	Hinkka	FIN-Y	1.4.91	19 Aug
54.34		Xu Xin	CHN	3.8.87	28 Apr
54.27	Nikolett	Szabó	HUN	3.3.80	26 May
54.25		Wang Beibei	CHN-J	22.1.89	2 Nov
54.15	Séphora	Bissoly	FRA	6.11.81	15 Jun
54.14		Zhang Li	CHN-J	17.1.89	20 May
54.11		Qu Shuangshuang	CHN	7.5.87	4 Jun
54.08	Karine	Hervieu	FRA	24.2.82	4 Aug
54.00	Sini	Kiiski	FIN-J	28.12.89	5 Jul
53.94		Gong Lijiao	CHN-J	24.1.89	16 Jun
53.88	Dayami	Delgado	CUB	14.3.85	15 Jun
53.81		Chiu Pei-Lien	TPE-Y	5.7.90	25 Apr
53.77	Anna	Raynor	USA	1.3.85	22 Jun
53.77	Bina	Ramesh	FRA	20.8.79	4 Aug
53.73	Ana Erika	Gutierrez	MEX	27.7.83	10 Jun
53.69		Wu Jie	CHN	25.4.85	21 Apr
53.67	Sofía	Ifadídou	GRE	10.1.85	9 Jun
53.58	Cecilia	Kiplangat	KEN	3.7.74	3 Mar
53.58	Miho	Miyamoto	JPN-J	14.9.88	22 Apr
53.53	Carolee	Gutierrez	USA		25 May

Mark		Name	Nat	Born	Date
53.48	Lilia	Dusmetova	UZB	11.2.81	19 Jun
53.43	Tatyana	Chernova	RUS-J	29.1.88	3 Jun
53.41	Ilse	Struys	BEL-J	21.2.88	9 Jun
53.40	Aleksandra	Pakhmutova	RUS	26.12.87	20 Jun
53.38		Zhu Jinqya	CHN	15.12.87	20 May
53.33	Margaret	Simpson	GHA	2.8.82	21 Jul
53.31	Yekaterina	Levoncheva	RUS-J	3.6.89	21 Feb
53.29	Takae	Seito	JPN	24.11.76	24 Jun
53.27	Ramona	Anghelas	ROM-J	3.7.88	26 May
53.22	Ana-Mirela	Termure	ROM	13.1.75	5 May
53.12	Hanaa Hassan	Ramadhan Omar	EGY	3.1.83	27 Mar
53.12	Linda	Selui	FRA	15.11.77	31 Mar
53.01	Xénia	Nagy (149)	HUN	29.3.86	26 Aug

JUNIORS

See main list for top 12 juniors. 10 performances by 6 women to 57.30. Additional marks and further juniors:

Chang C	60.88	1		Suzhou	10 Jun	58.43	1	NC	Shijiazhuang 2 Aug
Rebryk	57.97	1	v3N-j	Valmiera	17 Aug				
Cruz	57.34	1		La Habana	15 Jun				

54.83	Urszula	Kuncewicz	POL	11.6.88	3	EJ	Hengelo	21 Jul
54.66	Oona	Sormunen	FIN	2.8.89	1		Leppävirta	27 May
54.62		Zhang Ying	CHN	5.1.88	3		Zhaoqing	20 May
54.53	Jucilene	de Lima	BRA-Y	14.9.90	1		São Caetano do Sul	26 May
54.37	Carita	Hinkka	FIN-Y	1.4.91	1	NC-y	Kuopio	19 Aug
54.25		Wang Beibei	CHN	22.1.89	4		Wuhan	2 Nov
54.14		Zhang Li	CHN	17.1.89	5		Zhaoqing	20 May
54.00	Sini	Kiiski (20)	FIN	28.12.89	1-y		Pihtipudas	5 Jul

HEPTATHLON

Mark		Name	Nat	Born	Pos	Meet	Venue	Date
7032	Carolina	Klüft	SWE	2.2.83	1	WCh	Osaka	26 Aug
	13.15/0.1 1.95 14.81 23.38/0.3			6.85/1.0		47.98	2:12.56	
6832	Lyudmyla	Blonska	UKR	9.11.77	2	WCh	Osaka	26 Aug
	13.25/0.1 1.92 14.44 24.09/0.3			6.88/1.0		47.77	2:16.68	
6768w	Tatyana	Chernova	RUS-J	29.1.88	1		Arles	3 Jun
	13.04w/6.1 1.82 13.57 23.59w/5.2			6.61/1.2		53.43	2:15.05	
6733		Blonska			1	NC	Kyiv	4 Aug
	13.13/1.8 1.85 14.77 23.80/0.0			6.61/0.0		47.20	2:14.98	
6681		Klüft			1		Götzis	27 May
	13.27/-1.4 1.85 14.34 23.86/-1.3			6.62/-1.3		44.16	2:10.86	
6626		Blonska			2		Götzis	27 May
	13.53/-1.4 1.85 13.65 24.69/-2.7			6.57/0.3		51.53	2:12.18	
6510	Kelly	Sotherton	GBR	13.11.76	3	WCh	Osaka	26 Aug
	13.21/0.1 1.86 14.14 23.40/0.3			6.68/-0.1		31.90	2:11.58	
6469	Jessica	Ennis	GBR	28.1.86	4	WCh	Osaka	26 Aug
	12.97/0.1 1.89 11.93 23.15/0.3			6.33/0.1		38.07	2:11.39	
6439	Lilli	Schwarzkopf	GER	28.8.83	5	WCh	Osaka	26 Aug
	13.54/0.4 1.83 13.00 25.08/-0.2			6.17/0.4		54.44	2:12.76	
6437		Blonska			1		Talence	23 Sep
	13.54/0.1 1.82 13.72 24.71/0.8			6.46/0.8		49.13	2:17.02	
6399		Ennis			1	ECp-S	Szczecin	8 Jul
	13.05/0.9 1.87 12.89 23.65w/3.1			6.20w/2.5		37.38	2:10.91	
6388		Ennis			1		Desenzano del Garda	6 May
	13.12/0.2 1.95 12.13 23.68/0.6			6.40/-0.3		33.91	2:14.31	
6380	Austra	Skujyté	LTU	12.8.79	6	WCh	Osaka	26 Aug
	14.34/0.1 1.80 17.03 25.39/-0.4			6.28/0.7		52.63	2:23.64	
6378	Jennifer	Oeser	GER	29.11.83	7	WCh	Osaka	26 Aug
	13.51/0.4 1.83 14.21 24.41/0.1			6.25/-0.1		43.10	2:13.85	
6366		Oeser			3		Götzis	27 May
	13.51/-0.4 1.82 14.05 24.75/-2.1			6.17/-1.1		47.60	2:15.13	
6354		Blonska			1		Kladno	20 Jun
	13.72/-0.1 1.74 14.00 24.63/0.9			6.57w/2.1		48.01	2:16.93	
6343	Jessica	Zelinka	CAN	3.9.81	4		Götzis	27 May
	13.34/-1.4 1.79 13.98 24.39/-1.3			6.15/-0.5		42.71	2:10.93	
6343		Schwarzkopf			1		Ratingen	17 Jun
	13.56/1.8 1.70 13.41 24.90w/2.4			6.34/0.8		52.87	2:12.83	
6337		Skujyte			1	ECp-2	Maribor	8 Jul
	14.22/1.3 1.84 16.25 25.37/1.4			6.17w/2.2		48.13	2:19.01	
6327	Nataliya	Dobrynska (10)	UKR	29.5.82	8	WCh	Osaka	26 Aug
	13.89/0.1 1.77 16.31 24.91/-0.4			6.12/0.5		46.22	2:16.35	
6289	Anna	Bogdanova	RUS	21.10.84	1	NC	Zhukovskiy	15 Jul
	13.65/0.9 1.83 13.42 25.24w/2.1			6.59w/2.8		38.51	2:10.98	
6278	Margaret	Simpson	GHA	31.12.81	1	AfG	Alger	21 Jul
	13.54/-0.5 1.81 12.81 24.38			6.02/0.7		53.33	2:21.57	
6277		Skujyte			5		Götzis	27 May
	14.23/0.0 1.85 16.37 25.51/-2.6			6.10/-0.5		47.39	2:21.27	
6260	Karin	Ruckstuhl	NED	2.11.80	6		Götzis	27 May
	13.59/-1.4 1.79 14.04 24.62/-1.3			6.54/-0.4		36.60	2:13.37	

Mark	Name		Nat	Born	Pos	Meet	Venue	Date
6250		Oeser			2		Ratingen	17 Jun
	13.58/1.8 1.82 13.85 24.32/1.9 6.11/1.7 40.98 2:14.16							
6247		Dobrynska			2	NC	Kyiv	4 Aug
	14.04/1.8 1.76 15.70 24.91/0.0 6.18w/2.1 44.73 2:15.91							
6244	Marie	Collonvillé	FRA	23.11.73	9	WCh	Osaka	26 Aug
	13.63/0.9 1.83 12.12 25.01/-0.2 6.67/0.3 39.32 2:12.68							
6243		Bogdanova			10	WCh	Osaka	26 Aug
	13.71/-0.8 1.83 13.33 25.00/0.0 6.46/0.2 39.91 2:13.72							
6238		Dobrynska			2		Talence	23 Sep
	13.90/0.1 1.76 15.59 25.10/0.4 6.29/0.0 44.73 2:18.74							
6229		Sotherton			2	ECp-S	Szczecin	8 Jul
	13.28w/2.5 1.87 12.97 23.97w/3.1 6.36w/2.3 28.59 2:10.43							
	(30/14)							
6226	Ida	Marcussen	NOR	1.11.87	11	WCh	Osaka	26 Aug
	14.16/-0.8 1.68 13.00 24.59/-0.2 6.47/0.3 51.02 2:13.69							
6219	Viktoria	Zemaityté	LTU	11.3.85	1	EU23	Debrecen	15 Jul
	14.06/-0.5 1.85 13.70 24.67/-0.1 5.86/-0.5 49.24 2:16.99							
6219	Jolanda	Keizer	NED	5.4.85	2	EU23	Debrecen	15 Jul
	14.03/-0.5 1.76 14.50 24.88/-0.1 6.39w/2.4 44.94 2:17.47							
6205	Diana	Pickler	USA	9.12.83	1	TexR	Austin	5 Apr
	13.28/1.5 1.84 11.75 23.69w/2.3 6.15/0.7 41.97 2:19.08							
6200	Karolina	Tyminska	POL	4.10.84	1	NC	Torun	10 Jun
	13.96/-0.5 1.72 14.21 23.99/1.3 6.33/-0.4 37.97 2:09.89							
6199	Laurien	Hoos	NED	18.8.83	1		Woerden	26 Aug
	13.81/0.8 1.73 15.10 24.18/1.9 5.97/0.2 49.73 2:23.49							
	(20)							
6185	Olga	Kurban	RUS	16.12.87	2	NC	Zhukovskiy	15 Jul
	13.77/1.7 1.83 13.35 25.14/0.1 6.31w/2.1 40.05 2:13.13							
6184	Sonja	Kesselschläger	GER	20.1.78	3		Ratingen	17 Jun
	13.80/1.8 1.79 14.21 25.45w/2.4 6.28w/2.3 42.43 2:14.04							
6184	Kylie	Wheeler	AUS	17.1.80	12	WCh	Osaka	26 Aug
	13.87/0.9 1.80 13.00 24.44/0.1 6.42/0.0 38.49 2:12.81							
6162	Julia	Mächtig	GER	1.1.86	4		Ratingen	17 Jun
	14.16w/2.6 1.73 13.73 24.33/1.9 6.38/0.0 42.58 2:14.20							
6143	Hanna	Melnychenko	UKR	24.4.83	3	ECp-S	Szczecin	8 Jul
	13.66/0.9 1.84 13.34 25.15w/3.1 6.43w/2.7 37.28 2:17.05							
6112	Sylvie	Dufour	SUI	24.1.79	1	NC	Frauenfeld	17 Jun
	13.94/1.1 1.78 13.52 25.40/0.3 6.05/-0.7 48.74 2:17.43							
6108	Claudia	Tonn	GER	18.4.81	11		Götzis	27 May
	13.85/0.0 1.73 12.66 24.96/-2.4 6.38/-0.2 39.48 2:07.87							
6097	Kamila	Chudzik	POL	12.9.86	4	EU23	Debrecen	15 Jul
	14.05/-1.7 1.76 13.76 25.20/-0.6 6.16/1.4 49.51 2:21.69							
6096	Maren	Schwerdtner	GER	3.10.85	6		Ratingen	17 Jun
	13.58/1.8 1.73 14.03 24.25/1.9 6.06w/2.3 46.33 2:25.04							
6090	Hyleas	Fountain	USA	14.1.81	1	NC	Indianapolis	23 Jun
	13.81/-1.0 1.81 12.69 24.69/-1.2 6.43w/2.9 41.59 2:22.54							
	(30)							
6086	Yvonne	Wisse	NED	6.6.82	2		Náfplio	22 Jul
	13.63/-0.4 1.78 12.92 24.31/0.3 6.16/0.6 38.26 2:14.79							
6076	Gretchen	Quintana	CUB	30.6.84	1	ALBA	Caracas	11 May
	13.65/0.0 1.74 13.53 24.32/1.2 6.36/1.2 34.05 2:13.34							
6069	Irina	Naumenko	KAZ	13.2.80	1	NC	Almaty	6 Jul
	14.09/0.7 1.81 13.53 24.80/1.0 6.09/0.6 41.35 2:16.37							
6062	Olga	Levenkova	RUS	11.1.84	13		Götzis	27 May
	14.16/-1.2 1.76 13.61 25.45/-2.4 6.11/0.8 43.90 2:11.79							
6053	Julie	Hollman	GBR	16.2.77	2		Woerden	26 Aug
	13.96/0.8 1.76 12.14 24.36/1.9 6.32/1.2 42.40 2:17.15							
6025	Lyudmyla	Yosypenko	UKR	24.9.84	1		Kyiv	20 May
	14.07/0.0 1.79 12.42 24.32/-1.4 6.12/0.0 45.22 2:21.96							
6022	Lela	Nelson	USA	19.5.83	1		Bernhausen	19 Aug
	13.74/0.5 1.82 11.56 24.36/0.0 6.78/0.0 35.27 2:25.49							
6019	Aiga	Grabuste	LAT-J	24.3.88	17	WCh	Osaka	26 Aug
	13.84/-0.8 1.77 13.04 24.98/0.0 6.02/0.8 45.76 2:19.97							
6017	Denisa	Scerbová	CZE	21.8.86	15		Götzis	27 May
	13.60/-1.2 1.73 11.88 24.31/-1.3 6.46/-0.5 35.12 2:13.23							
6011	Svetlana	Sokolova	RUS	9.1.81	2		Sochi	27 May
	14.24 1.71 14.00 24.66 6.00 40.71 2:10.62							
	(40)							
6004	Marina	Goncharova	RUS	26.4.86	5	EU23	Debrecen	15 Jul
	14.21/0.2 1.64 13.91 25.05/-0.8 6.45w/2.2 40.89 2:12.57							

Mark	Name		Nat	Born	Pos	Meet	Venue	Date
6003	Aryiró	Strátaki	GRE	3.8.75	3		Náfplio	22 Jul
	14.03/-0.4 1.75 13.45 24.99/0.3 6.07/-0.3 44.30 2:18.30							
6002	Gi-Gi	Johnson	USA	12.1.79	3	NC	Indianapolis	23 Jun
	13.35/-1.0 1.66 13.31 23.90/-1.2 6.09/0.9 39.83 2:18.40							
5996	Simone	Oberer	SUI	8.4.80	16		Götzis	27 May
	13.63/-0.4 1.82 11.19 25.43/-2.1 6.16/-1.1 41.51 2:13.69							
5995	Linda	Züblin	SUI	21.3.86	20	WCh	Osaka	26 Aug
	13.63/0.9 1.65 12.43 24.75/-0.4 5.98/-0.2 49.85 2:16.72							
5984	Jackie	Johnson	USA	8.9.84	1	NCAA	Sacramento	8 Jun
	13.35/0.9 1.78 11.09 24.52/1.3 5.91/-0.5 45.58 2:19.54							
5982	Antoinette	Nana Djimou Ida	FRA	2.8.85	1	NC	Niort	4 Aug
	13.78/-0.2 1.68 13.21 24.74/0.7 5.90/-1.5 46.83 2:16.49							
5973	Bregje	Crolla	NED	31.1.86	6	EU23	Debrecen	15 Jul
	14.38/0.2 1.76 12.92 25.43/-0.8 5.48/-0.4 54.25 2:13.54							
5950	Sara	Aerts	BEL	25.1.84	2	ECp-2	Maribor	8 Jul
	13.60/1.3 1.75 13.49 24.20/1.4 5.76/0.2 40.08 2:19.52							
5942	Yasmiany	Pedroso	CUB	5.8.84	2	ALBA	Caracas	11 May
	13.89/0.0 1.80 14.24 25.56/1.2 6.13/1.2 41.93 2:27.10							
	(50)							
5912	Aleksandra	Butvina	RUS	14.2.86	2-23		Sochi	27 May
	14.58 1.70 14.52 24.75 6.17 38.60 2:16.03							
5911	Tatyana	Alisevich	BLR	22.1.69	1	NC	Minsk (Staiki)	8 Jun
	14.21/1.0 1.62 14.90 25.13/1.0 5.71/0.3 50.26 2:18.28							
5908	Fiona	Asigbee	USA	18.5.81	4	NC	Indianapolis	23 Jun
	13.77/-0.5 1.81 12.01 24.84/-1.9 6.17/0.8 36.51 2:18.82							
5904	Natalya	Kotova	RUS	13.5.83	3	NC	Zhukovskiy	15 Jul
	13.71/0.9 1.83 12.68 25.08w/2.1 6.16/0.5 35.17 2:21.04							
5897	Lucimara	da Silva	BRA	10.7.85	4		Desenzano del Garda	6 May
	13.63/0.5 1.77 11.32 24.63/0.6 6.05/0.2 39.08 2:16.41							
5894	Blandine	Maisonnier	FRA	3.1.86	10	EU23	Debrecen	15 Jul
	14.23/-1.7 1.76 11.27 24.78/-0.1 6.50w/2.9 35.39 2:13.52							
5894	Salla	Rinne	FIN	22.5.80	1	NC	Lappeenranta	4 Aug
	13.59/1.3 1.77 13.84 25.46/0.3 6.04/1.7 42.12 2:27.99							
5891	Anna	Nikitenko	RUS	30.4.84	3		Sochi	27 May
	15.14 1.83 13.10 25.93 6.39 36.66 2:11.71							
5890w	Jillian	Drouin	CAN	30.9.86	1		Storrs	5 May
	13.88w/4.6 1.84 12.22 24.71 6.07/1.3 41.13 2:28.16							
5889	Vassanee	Vinatho	THA	30.6.80	1	SEAG	Nakhon Ratchasima	11 Dec
	13.97/-0.2 1.79 11.82 24.74/0.0 6.30/0.0 34.90 2:16.85							
	(60)							
5883	Natalya	Roshchupkina	RUS	13.1.78	4	NC	Zhukovskiy	15 Jul
	14.70/0.9 1.77 14.69 25.48w/2.1 5.81/1.7 40.81 2:14.37							
5878	Marisa	De Aniceto	FRA	11.11.86	12	EU23	Debrecen	15 Jul
	14.18/-1.7 1.79 11.80 25.27/-0.8 5.70/1.5 45.17 2:12.88							
5876	Kaie	Kand	EST	31.3.84	1	NC	Rakvere	21 Jul
	14.06/1.6 1.71 12.57 25.49/0.0 6.10/0.3 40.66 2:11.86							
5869	Yuki	Nakata	JPN	10.3.77	23	WCh	Osaka	26 Aug
	13.82/0.9 1.74 11.31 25.28/-0.4 6.16/-0.1 43.26 2:17.61							
5864	Gaëlle	Niaré	FRA	12.3.82	2	NC	Niort	4 Aug
	14.55/-0.2 1.83 14.66 25.03/0.7 5.99/-0.7 33.59 2:19.32							
5844	Eliska	Klucinová	CZE-J	14.4.88	1	NC-j	Olomouc	10 Jun
	14.47/-0.1 1.78 12.80 25.30/0.6 5.89/0.1 44.14 2:18.63							
5841	Lyudmyla	Kovalyova	UKR	18.3.75	1		Yalta	14 Jun
	14.84/-2.1 1.75 13.75 25.82/-0.8 5.99w/3.4 42.84 2:14.24							
5831	Julie	Pickler	USA	9.12.83	2	NCAA	Sacramento	8 Jun
	13.96/1.8 1.75 11.84 24.70/1.3 5.95w/3.2 39.74 2:16.66							
5823	Vasilikí	Delinikóla	GRE	9.2.81	4		Náfplio	22 Jul
	13.74/-0.4 1.78 13.39 25.17/0.3 6.04/0.5 41.83 2:32.08							
5822	Oksana	Kuzminok	UKR	7.8.83	3		Kyiv	4 Aug
	13.44/1.8 1.73 12.77 24.81/0.0 6.10/0.7 37.49 2:24.98							
	(70)							
5820	Christine	Schulz	GER	30.1.84	6	Déca	Talence	23 Sep
	13.91/0.6 1.73 13.25 25.16/0.4 5.71/0.0 42.41 2:18.33							
5818	Ryanne	Dupree	USA	13.3.84	2	TexR	Austin	5 Apr
	13.40/1.5 1.66 12.39 24.81w/2.3 6.12/1.2 38.61 2:19.70							
5818	Ulrike	Hartz	GER	7.5.87	9		Ratingen	17 Jun
	14.28w/2.6 1.73 12.14 24.62w/2.4 6.02w/3.0 45.80 2:24.70							
5815	Svetlana	Kazanina	KAZ	31.10.71	2	NC	Almaty	6 Jul
	14.69/0.7 1.75 13.65 25.57/1.0 5.87/0.4 43.19 2:16.52							
5799	Jesenija	Volzankina	LAT	28.11.83	1	NC	Valmiera	16 Jun
	13.62/-0.1 1.74 13.03 25.05/0.3 6.17/1.1 38.03 2:27.89							

Mark	Name		Nat	Born	Pos	Meet	Venue	Date
5798	Roslyn	Gonse	GBR	1.3.82	4		Woerden	26 Aug
	14.13/0.8	1.73	13.56	24.93/1.1	5.81/0.0	42.52	2:23.17	
5794	Ashley	Selig	USA	23.2.84	5	NCAA	Sacramento	8 Jun
	13.98/1.0	1.78	11.44	24.50w/3.9	5.95/0.1	35.58	2:15.48	
5788	Iryna	Ilkevych	UKR	6.3.87	2		Yalta	14 Jun
	14.40/-2.1	1.78	10.97	24.66/-0.8	6.20w/3.9	37.06	2:16.07	
5779w	Aléna-Maria	Pádi	GRE	21.6.84	1	NC	Athína	10 Jun
	14.02w/5.5	1.72	11.59	25.00w/2.9	6.05w/2.5	37.00	2:12.54	
5774	Viorica	Tigau	ROM	12.8.79	5		Desenzano del Garda	6 May
	13.45/0.2	1.71	12.15	24.79/0.6	6.30/0.3	36.54	2:27.21	
	(80)							
5773	Ulrike	Hebestreit	GER	19.3.81	10		Ratingen	17 Jun
	13.48w/2.6	1.70	11.84	25.49w/2.4	5.97/1.9	40.43	2:17.60	
5767	Nadezhda	Sergeyeva	RUS	13.6.87	3-23		Sochi	27 May
	14.22	1.70	13.33	25.17	6.04	35.37	2:14.22	
5766	Elizete	da Silva	BRA	2.5.71	2	NC	São Paulo	22 Jun
	14.23/0.2	1.67	12.81	24.67/0.6	6.07/0.6	42.41	2:22.85	
5761	Marina	Parkhomenko	BLR	28.5.81	2	NC	Minsk (Staiki)	8 Jun
	13.96/0.1	1.59	12.36	25.13/1.0	6.34/-0.3	38.78	2:14.95	
5761	Jessica	Samuelsson	SWE	14.3.85	13	EU23	Debrecen	15 Jul
	14.47/-0.5	1.70	14.30	24.67/-0.6	5.53/1.4	37.58	2:12.25	
5741	Juana	Castillo	DOM	17.6.84	5		Ponce	27 May
	13.94/1.6	1.70	13.08	25.32/-1.1	5.56/0.5	42.79	2:16.64	
5727	Cecilia	Ricali	ITA	20.1.85	6		Desenzano del Garda	6 May
	14.14/0.7	1.74	11.32	25.75/1.2	6.09/1.7	37.35	2:12.00	
5724w	Bettie	Wade	USA	11.9.86	7	NCAA	Sacramento	8 Jun
	14.00/0.9	1.78	12.81	24.62/1.4	5.98W/4.3	31.25	2:20.76	
5716	Elisa	Trevisan	ITA	5.3.80	5	ECp-1	Tallinn	8 Jul
	13.97/-1.7	1.66	13.46	25.20/-0.8	5.96/1.2	42.62	2:25.88	
5716	Phyllis	Agbo	GBR	16.12.85	5		Woerden	26 Aug
	14.07/0.8	1.64	12.18	24.60/1.1	6.14/2.0	41.79	2:23.79	
	(90)							
5713	Magdalena	Szczepanska	POL	25.1.80	3	NC	Torun	10 Jun
	14.48/-0.5	1.75	13.02	25.61/1.3	5.77/-0.3	41.96	2:18.84	
5711	Gayle	Hunter	USA	9.4.86	8	NCAA	Sacramento	8 Jun
	13.68/1.8	1.63	11.29	24.03/1.3	6.13/-0.2	36.05	2:18.68	
5707	Niina	Kelo	FIN	26.3.80	2	NC	Lappeenranta	4 Aug
	14.23/1.3	1.56	15.02	25.99/0.3	5.77/0.1	52.75	2:27.92	
5693	Natalya	Tanana	BLR	1.1.83	3	NC	Minsk (Staiki)	8 Jun
	14.10/0.9	1.71	13.06	25.49/0.9	5.69/0.4	38.56	2:14.98	
5688	Yana	Panteleyeva	RUS-J	16.6.88	7		Desenzano del Garda	6 May
	14.49/0.7	1.77	12.52	26.06/1.2	5.94/0.8	41.97	2:20.74	
5684w	Louise	Hazel	GBR	6.10.85	8		Arles	3 Jun
	13.61w/4.5	1.67	11.07	24.97w/5.2	5.98/0.2	40.31	2:19.85	
5680	Claudine	Müller	SUI	27.2.80	6	ECp-1	Tallinn	8 Jul
	13.85/-1.0	1.75	11.16	25.10/1.9	6.07/1.2	40.06	2:26.20	
5679w	Alexandra	Barlet	FRA	17.2.77	9		Arles	3 Jun
	14.19w/6.1	1.67	12.71	25.87w/4.1	5.86/2.0	45.17	2:20.37	
5677	Annelies	Schrader	GER	9.12.79	4		Bernhausen	19 Aug
	13.90/0.5	1.67	11.88	25.64/0.0	6.08/0.0	47.10	2:28.98	
5674	Svetlana	Ladokhina	RUS	21.2.79	11	ECp-S	Szczecin	8 Jul
	14.13w/2.5	1.66	14.35	25.45w/3.1	5.63/1.0	40.31	2:19.25	
	(100)							

5657	Shevell	Quinley	USA	26.6.87	6 May
5653	Yana	Maksimova	BLR-J	9.1.89	8 Jun
5652	Zita	Óvári	HUN	28.5.84	8 Jul
5651	Franziska	Straubhaar	SUI	22.6.81	20 May
5649	Tatyana	Zhevnova	BLR	17.10.77	8 Jun
5649	Annett	Wichmann	GER	4.5.84	8 Jun
5644	Buky	Bamigboye	USA	21.8.87	5 May
5643		Liu Haili	CHN	24.12.84	10 Jun
5639w	Gabriela	Kouassi	FRA	18.11.79	8 Jun
5638	Danielle	McNaney	USA	1.5.83	19 Aug
5637	Melissa	Talbot	USA	23.4.84	12 May
5635	Romy	Gürbig	GER-J	1.3.88	17 Jun
5634	Sarah	Cowley	NZL	3.2.84	16 Dec
5633	Saskia	Triesscheijn	NED	16.6.81	18 May
5627	Michaela	Hejnová	CZE	10.4.80	8 Jul
5621	Liz	Roehrig	USA	19.11.85	30 Mar
5620w	Susan	Coltman	CAN	10.4.81	3 Jun
5609w	Abbie	Stechschulte	USA	28.4.85	5 Apr
5607	Nikol	Ogrodniková	CZE-Y	18.8.90	22 Jul

5605	Olga	Zinovyeva	RUS	29.10.86	27 May
5601w	Jade	Surman	GBR-J	27.3.89	3 Jun
5600	Heather	Biglow (Sterlin)	USA	12.4.74	6 May
5600w	Julie	Martin	FRA	28.10.79	8 Jul
5593	Francesca	Doveri	ITA	21.12.82	8 Jul
5592	Ashley	Wilhelm	USA	17.2.84	8 Jun
5591	Joanna	Grzesiak	POL	15.8.80	6 May
5590	Karin	Ertl	GER	23.6.74	12 Aug
5587	Etienne	Chaplin	USA	28.7.86	8 Jun
5577	Viktoriya	Dobrynska	UKR	18.1.80	4 Aug
5571	Elisa	Kirvesniemi	FIN	18.12.85	15 Jul
5563	Maija	Lasaroff	FIN	23.8.81	4 Aug
5545	Carolin	Schäfer	GER-Y	5.12.91	17 Jun
5543	Melry Neri	Caldeira	BRA	26.7.82	22 Jun
5542	Yuliya	Tarasova	UZB	13.3.86	6 May
5532	Ana	Capdevila	ESP	5.9.81	5 Aug
5529A	Yalitza	Rivera	PUR	10.5.85	5 May
5528	Ebe	Reier	EST-J	2.12.88	8 Jul
5526	Lauryn	Jordan	USA		12 Apr

Mark	Name		Nat	Born	Date
5524	Yuleydis	Limonta	CUB	14.3.82	11 Mar
5521	Inna	Ahkozova	UKR	16.9.84	20 May
5521	Shana	Woods	USA-J	7.7.88	21 Jun
5513	Yekaterina	Babich	BLR-J	12.12.88	8 Jun
5513	Rymma	Hula	UKR	31.12.85	14 Jun
5508h	Javur J.	Shobha	IND	14.1.78	24 Oct
5497	Maike	Goldkuhle	GER	10.3.80	29 Jul
5492h	Yasmina	Omrani	FRA-J	1.1.88	26 May
5490	Nia	Ali	USA-J	23.10.88	11 May
5476	Olga	Polomoshnova	RUS	26.8.87	27 May
5468	Elisa	Bettini	ITA	6.2.82	6 May
5465	Emilie	Boulleret	FRA	23.5.73	22 Jul
5465	Maryna	Brezhina	UKR	16.1.77	4 Aug
5462	Jana	Korešová	CZE	8.4.81	10 Jun
5462w	Sofía	Ifadídou	GRE	5.1.85	10 Jun
5458		Song Lijuan	CHN	2.2.87	20 Sep
5457	Bonnie	Meekins	USA	11.5.84	12 May
5452		Cao Lan	CHN	25.1.82	3 Aug
5451	Anika	Schütze	GER-Y	22.5.90	17 Jun
5449	Anna	Pakhmutova	RUS	26.12.87	27 May
5444	Nadja	Casadei	SWE	3.4.83	5 Aug
5442	Lauren	Foote	AUS	27.4.84	8 Apr
5437	Alina	Fyodorova	UKR-J	31.7.89	22 Jun
5436	Grace	Clements	GBR	2.5.84	10 Jun
5432	Jailma	de Lima	BRA	31.12.86	22 Jun
5425w	Iríni	Daniíl	GRE	18.4.83	10 Jun
5424	Marie	Burešová	CZE	6.5.85	10 Jun
5421	Yunna	Rykova	RUS-J	7.7.88	8 Jun
5415	Alena	Ivleva	RUS	31.7.74	15 Jul
5413	Valérie	Reggel	SUI	3.1.87	20 May
5413	Brianne	Theisen	CAN-J	18.12.88	8 Jul
5408	Julie	Delevallée	FRA	6.11.85	7 Jul
5406	Ulyana	Varukha	RUS	6.2.87	27 May
5402		Lai Xinming	CHN		21 Jul
5402	(173)	Fu Pengcheng	CHN	15.1.80	20 Sep

Best without wind assistance

Mark	Name		Nat	Born	Pos	Meet	Venue	Date
5822	Jillian	Drouin	CAN	30.9.86	3	NCAA	Sacramento	8 Jun
	14.14/0.9 1.87 11.99 25.02w/3.9			6.01w/3.1	38.16 2:24.33			
5722	Betty	Wade	USA	11.9.86	2		State College	12 May
	13.88/0.6 1.81 12.83 25.14/-1.7			6.03/-1.0	33.63 2:26.19			
5594	Louise	Hazel	GBR	6.10.85				5 Aug
5572	Susan	Coltman	CAN	10.4.81				26 Aug

JUNIORS

See main list for top 4 juniors. 10 performances by 8 women over 5600. Additional marks and further juniors:

Grabuste 6176 1 EJ Hengelo 22 Jul

Klucinová 5709 2 EJ Hengelo 22 Jul 5625 9 ECp-1 Tallinn 8 Jul

Mark	Name		Nat	Born	Pos	Meet	Venue	Date
5653	Yana	Maksimova	BLR	9.1.89	1	NC-j	Minsk (Staiki)	8 Jun
	15.34/0.8 1.83 13.50 26.00/0.2			5.64/0.5	39.88 2:16.21			
5635	Romy	Gürbig	GER	1.3.88	11		Ratingen	17 Jun
	14.07w/3.0 1.67 11.84 25.45/1.4			6.08/1.7	42.44 2:24.44			
5607	Nikol	Ogrodniková	CZE-Y	18.8.90	3	EJ	Hengelo	22 Jul
	14.07/-0.6 1.66 12.59 26.03/-0.5			5.62/0.6	48.15 2:23.33			
5601w	Jade	Surman	GBR	27.3.89	12		Arles	3 Jun
	13.96w/6.3 1.70 10.87 25.62w/6.5			6.11w/2.8	38.85 2:20.59			
5545	Carolin	Schäfer	GER-Y	5.12.91	12		Ratingen	17 Jun
	14.30w/3.0 1.64 11.93 24.62/1.4			5.54/0.8	42.91 2:20.78			
5528	Ebe	Reier (10)	EST	2.12.88	11	ECp-1	Tallinn	8 Jul
	14.17/-0.4 1.72 11.77 24.42/0.9			5.97/0.7	33.02 2:26.78			
5521	Shana	Woods	USA	7.7.88	1	NC-j	Indianapolis	21 Jun
	13.73/1.2 1.66 10.17 24.35/1.4			5.83w/3.1	39.22 2:24.76			
5513	Yekaterina	Babich	BLR	12.12.88	2	NC-23	Minsk (Stayki)	8 Jun
	14.85/0.4 1.74 13.23 25.64/0.7			6.00/-0.2	30.13 2:18.25			
5492h	Yasmina	Omrani	FRA	1.1.88	1		Lunel	26 May
	14.6h 1.72 11.66 25.0h			5.78	37.98 2:19.21			
5490	Nia	Ali	USA	23.10.88	1	SEC	Tuscaloosa	11 May
	13.25/0.0 1.69 10.47 24.00/0.4			5.95w/2.4	27.18 2:24.55			
5451	Anika	Schütze	GER-Y	22.5.90	13		Ratingen	17 Jun
	14.52w/3.0 1.67 10.63 24.77/1.4			6.16/1.3	33.95 2:21.95			
5437	Alina	Fyodorova	UKR	31.7.89	1	NC-j	Mykolaiv	22 Jun
	14.85/0.8 1.72 13.33 25.53/1.2			5.69w/2.2	34.70 2:22.82			
5421	Yunna	Rykova	RUS	7.7.88	1		Sankt-Peterburg	8 Jun
	14.42 1.67 11.21 25.88			6.00	37.09 2:21.34			
5413	Brianne	Theisen	CAN	18.12.88	1	PAm-J	São Paulo	8 Jul
	14.29/0.0 1.76 10.80 25.05/0.5			5.54/0.8	39.56 2:28.52			
5377	Ryann	Krais	USA-Y	21.3.90	2	NC-j	Indianapolis	21 Jun
	13.82/0.2 1.66 9.91 24.47/2.0			5.55w/3.0	32.66 2:16.96			
5372	Diana-Elena	Dumitrescu (20)	ROM	6.5.89	1		Bucuresti	12 Aug
	14.52/-1.4 1.70 13.22 25.83/-0.4			5.96/0.0	32.25 2:29.33			
5358	Nicole	Apitz	GER	15.9.88	2		Bernhausen	20 May
	14.63/-1.2 1.77 11.40 26.56/0.0			5.44/0.1	38.08 2:18.57			

DECATHLON

Mark	Name		Nat	Born	Pos	Meet	Venue	Date
6915	Margaret	Simpson	GHA	31.12.81	1		Réduit	19 Apr
	12.3 5.73 12.42 1.72 62.2			14.0	32.17 2.50 47.67 5:41.7			

4 X 100 METRES RELAY

Mark	Nat	Team	Pos	Meet	Venue	Date
41.98	USA	L.Williams 11.05, Felix 10.28, Barber 10.43, Edwards 10.22	1	WCh	Osaka	1 Sep
42.01	JAM	Brooks 11.05, Stewart 10.38, Facey 10.52, Campbell 10.06	2	WCh	Osaka	1 Sep
42.24	USA	Jeter, Lewis, Barber, L Williams	1h2	WCh	Osaka	1 Sep
42.70	JAM	Brooks, Stewart, Facey, Frazer	2h2	WCh	Osaka	1 Sep

Mark	Nat	Name	Pos	Meet	Venue	Date
42.75	BEL	Borlée 11.37, Marien 10.72, Ouédraogo 10.50, Gevaert 10.17	3	WCh	Osaka	1 Sep
42.78	RUS	Gushchina, Rusakova, Khabarova, Polyakova	1	ECp-S	München	23 Jun
42.82	GBR	Turner, Douglas, Freeman, Maduaka	3h2	WCh	Osaka	1 Sep
42.85	BEL	Borlée 11.37, Marien 10.72, Ouédraogo 10.50, Gevaert 10.17	1h1	WCh	Osaka	1 Sep
42.87	USA	"Red" Barber, Felix, Lee, L Williams	1	PennR	Philadelphia	28 Apr
42.87	GBR	Turner 11.13, Douglas 10.70, Freeman 10.55, Maduaka 10.49	4	WCh	Osaka	1 Sep
42.90	RUS	Khabarova, , Rusakova-Kresova, Gushchina, Polyakova	2h1	WCh	Osaka	1 Sep
42.93	USA	Lewis, Jeter, Joyce, C.Moore	1	GP	Osaka	5 May
42.97	RUS	Grigoryeva, Rusakova, Gushchina, Polyakova	5	WCh	Osaka	1 Sep
43.07	USA	Woods, Weatherspoon, Lewis, Barber	1h1	PAm	Rio de Janeiro	27 Jul
43.08	GER	Wakan, Tschirch, Kedzierski, Sailer	1		Bochum-Wattenscheid	12 Aug
43.09	FRA	Louami, Hurtis-Houairi, Banco, Arron	2	ECp-S	München	23 Jun
43.16	BLR	Shulyak, Safronnikova, Nevmerzhitskaya, Dragun	3h1	WCh	Osaka	1 Sep
43.17	BLR	Shulyak, Safronnikova, Nevmerzhitskaya, Dragun	1		Minsk	14 Jun
		(18 performances by teams from 8 nations				
43.25	POL	Jeschke, Korczynska, Jedrusinska, Klocek	2h2	WCh	Osaka	1 Sep
43.39	CHN	Tao Yujia, Chen Jue, Jiang Lan, Qin Wangping	4h1	WCh	Osaka	1 Sep
	(10)					
43.41	FIN	Hannula, Keskitalo, Ranta, Manninen	5h1	WCh	Osaka	1 Sep
43.46	CUB	Benavides, Arencibia, Lazo Tejeda	2h1	PAm	Rio de Janeiro	27 Jul
43.54	BRA	Presti, L dos Santos, de Moura, Ignacio	1	SACh	São Paulo	8 Jun
43.58	NGR	Kemasuode, Ojokolo, Osayomi, Idoko	6h1	WCh	Osaka	1 Sep
43.60	UKR	Chebanu, Tonkovyd, Shtangyeyeva, Shepetyuk	5	ECp-S	München	23 Jun
43.62	AUS	McClennan, Cullen, Attenborough, Kay	2	GP	Osaka	5 May
43.76	GHA	Addy, Amolofo, Dankwah, Anim	6h2	WCh	Osaka	1 Sep
43.81	PUR	Cruz, Morales, Gutierrez, Rodríguez	4	PAm	Rio de Janeiro	28 Jul
43.91	BUL	Eftimova, Lalova, Khristova, Naimova	1	BalkC	Sofia	4 Jul
43.92	THA	Jaksunin, Klomdee, Thavoncharoen , Saenrat	2	WUG	Bangkok	9 Aug
	(20)					
43.93	JPN	Ishida, M Takahashi, Nobuoka, Kitakaze	4	GP	Osaka	5 May
43.98	ITA	Pistone, Salvagno, Grillo, Levorato	1	ECp-1B	Milano	23 Jun
43.98	TRI	Hutchinson, Springer-Jones, Cameron, Ashby	3	NACAC	San Salvador	15 Jul
44.11	SKN	Liburd, Walwyn, Williams, Hodge	2h2	PAm	Rio de Janeiro	27 Jul
44.12	GRE	Kobídou, Koklóni, Boudá, Karastamáti	7	ECp-S	München	23 Jun
44.47	Terra i	Mar ESP Torrijos, Onyia, Troppa, Alozie	1	ECCp	Albufeira	26 May
44.48	CIV	Djaman, Ayetoche, Niako, Allou	3	AfG	Alger	20 Jul
44.53	COL	Merlano, Palacios, Brock, Obregón	4h2	PAm	Rio de Janeiro	27 Jul
44.72	LTU	Andrijauskité, Dagelyté, Lingyté, Tamosaityté	4h1	WUG	Bangkok	9 Aug
44.93	CZE	Mazácová, Dostálová, Bartonicková, Scerbová	1		Ostrava	17 Jun
	(30)					

44.94	BAH-J	8 Apr	45.14	IRL	23 Jun	45.38	SWE	23 Jun	45.62	VIE	10 Dec	45.84	ZIM	20 Jul
44.98	POR	23 Jun	45.24	IND	26 Oct	45.43	SLO	23 Jun	45.66	SUI	17 May	45.92	CYP	23 Jun
45.02	CMR	19 Jul	45.26	SEN	20 Jul	45.48	CAN	8 Jun	45.69	CRO	23 Jun	45.98	NED	21 Jul
45.03	DOM	12 May	45.34	CHI	8 Jun	45.49	NOR	23 Jun	45.77	SRB	4 Jul	45.99	PNG	7 Sep
45.10	NZL	17 Feb	45.38	TUR	23 Jun	45.61	HUN	23 Jun	45.79	ROM	23 Jun			

Mixed nation teams

Mark	Team	Pos	Meet	Venue	Date
43.05	Texas A&M University USA/JAM	1	NCAA	Sacramnto	8 Jun
	Adeoti, Lucas, Facey/JAM, Henry/JAM				
43.14	Louisiana State Un USA/NGR/GRN	2	NCAA	Sacramento	8 Jun
	Ohanaja NGR, Henry, Morris, Fletcher GRN				

JUNIORS

Mark	Nat	Name	Pos	Meet	Venue	Date
43.71	USA	K Wilson, Hendricks, McNary, Layne	1	PAm-J	São Paulo	7 Jul
43.98	BRA	Silva, Leoncio, Krasucki, Santos	2	PAm-J	São Paulo	7 Jul
44.41	JAM	(Edwin Allen HS) Briscoe, J Jones, Evans, K Smith	1		Kingston	5 May
44.52	GBR	Shand-Whittingham, Nelson, H Jones, Philip	1	EJ	Hengelo	22 Jul
44.69	TRI	B St.Louis, Hackett, S St.Louis, Giles	3	PAm-J	São Paulo	7 Jul
44.77	UKR	Titimets, Pohrebnyak, Yaroshchuk, Bryzhina	2h1	EJ	Hengelo	22 Jul
44.86	POL	Kociolek, Popowicz, Ceglarek, Wedler	1h2	EJ	Hengelo	21 Jul
44.94	BAH	White, Bodie, Rolle, N Smith	1	Carifta	Providenciales	8 Apr
45.21	GER	Möllinger, Gangnus, Strecker, Börner	1		Mannheim	23 Jun
45.47	FRA	Diawara, Gaydu, Amofa Diatuo, Pascal	2	vITA-j	Firenze	3 Aug
45.55	JPN	Nakano, Terada, Fukushima, Takeuchi	6		Osaka	5 May
45.70	SUI	Bieli, Arrieta, Humair, Reuse	2		Génève	9 Jun
45.71	COL	Caicedo, Idrovo, Hinestroza, Escobar	2	SAm-J	São Paulo	30 Jun
45.72	ITA	Balboni, Paoletta, Draisci, Palezza	3	vFRA-j	Firenze	3 Aug
45.73	SWE	Skugge, Collin, Backman, Eurenius	1		Esbjerg	1 Sep
45.98	THA		1		Hong Kong	8 Jul
45.98	NED	Vassell, Strijker, Bajon, Van Leuveren	3h1	EJ	Hengelo	21 Jul

Hand time: 45.8 CUB (La Habana) Alomá, Rivero, Despaigne, Bonne 1 Santiago de Cuba 30 Jun

4 X 200 METRES RELAY

Mark	Name	Pos	Meet	Venue	Date
1:31.56	University of South Carolina (USA) C Martin, Hastings, Giles, Solomon	1	PennR	Philadelphia	28 Apr
1:31.58	Louisiana State University Fletcher GRN, S Henry JAM, Morris USA, Baptiste TRI	2	PennR	Philadelphia	28 Apr
1:32.06	Texas A&M University (USA) Baker, Adeoti, K Carter, Lucas	3	PennR	Philadelphia	28 Apr

4 X 400 METRES RELAY

Mark	Nat	Name	Pos	Meet	Venue	Date
3:18.55	USA	Trotter 51.2, Felix 48.0, Wineberg 50.24, Richards 49.07	1	WCh	Osaka	2 Sep
3:19.73	JAM	S Williams 50.5, Lloyd 50.1, Prendergast 50.18, N Williams 48.93	2	WCh	Osaka	2 Sep
3:20.04	GBR	Ohuruogu 50.6, Okoro 50.9, McConnell 49.79, Sanders 48.76	3	WCh	Osaka	2 Sep
3:20.25	RUS	Litvinova 51.1, Nazarova 50.0, Veshkurova 49.79, Antyukh 49.40	4	WCh	Osaka	2 Sep
3:21.88	BLR	Yushchenko 51.4, Khlyustova 50.7, I Usovich 49.97, S Usovich 49.78	5	WCh	Osaka	2 Sep
3:23.37	USA	Trotter 51.3, Hennagan 50.1, Wineberg 50.78, Hastings 51.16	1h2	WCh	Osaka	1 Sep
3:23.49	RUS	Migunova 51.5, Nazarova 50.5, Litvinova 50.65, Levina 50.79	1h1	WCh	Osaka	1 Sep
3:23.67	BLR	Yushchenko 51.6, Khlyustova 51.3, S Usovich 50.34, I Usovich 50.40	1	ECp-S	München	24 Jun
3:24.70	USA	'Red' Wineberg, Felix, Robinson, Dunn	1	PennR	Philadelphia	28 Apr
3:25.14	BLR	Yushchenko 51.5, Khlyustova 51.1, Kozak 51.52, S Usovich 51.08	2h1	WCh	Osaka	1 Sep
3:25.45	GBR	McConnell 51.6, Fraser 51.6, Okoro 50.88, Sanders 51.34	2h2	WCh	Osaka	1 Sep
3:26.14	JAM	SWilliams 51.9, Le-Roy 52.8, Prendergast 50.66, Lloyd 50.83	3h1	WCh	Osaka	1 Sep
3:26.36	POL	Radecka 52.12, Bejnar 51.20, Wojcik 52.14, Prokopek 50.90	2	ECp-S	München	24 Jun
3:26.45	POL	Karpesiuk 53.1, Prokopek 50.7, Radecka 50.47, Jesien 52.10	3h2	WCh	Osaka	1 Sep
3:26.49	POL	Radecka 51.8, Prokopek 50.6, Setowska-Dyrk 52.58, Jesien 51.44	6	WCh	Osaka	2 Sep
3:26.58	RUS	U23 Shulikova, Zadorina, Novikova, Litvinova	1	EU23	Debrecen	15 Jul
3:27.04	CUB	Martínez 52.7, Pernía 51.6, Calatayud 51.56, Terrero 51.21	4h1	WCh	Osaka	1 Sep
3:27.05	CUB	Martínez 52.2, Pernía 51.8, Calatayud 52.20, Terrero 50.85	7	WCh	Osaka	2 Sep
3:27.14	MEX	Rodríguez 53.3, Medina 51.2, Vela 52.94, Guevara 49.70	4h2	WCh	Osaka	1 Sep
		(19 performances by teams from 8 nations)				
3:27.97	NGR	Abugan 51.9, Ekpukhon 51.7, Nwoke 52.03, Adesanya 52.34	5h1	WCh	Osaka	1 Sep
3:28.62	FRA	Anacharsis 53.4, Lacordelle 51.5, Michanol 52.75, Désert 50.94	3	ECp-S	München	24 Jun
3:28.67	UKR	Pygyda 52.5, Ilyushkina 52.3, Karandyuk 52.46, Shcherbak 51.46	4	ECp-S	München	24 Jun
3:28.89	BRA	Almirão 53.1, Pinheiro 52.5, Teodoro 51.1, Tito 52.2	5	PAm	Rio de Janeiro	28 Jul
3:29.52	GER	Hoffmann 52.6, Fink 51.6, Tilgner 52.59, Urbansky 52.77	5	ECp-S	München	24 Jun
3:30.17	JPN	Aoki 53.5, Tanno 51.6, Kubokara 52.88, Kida 52.18	6h2	WCh	Osaka	1 Sep
3:30.20	GRE	Sírou 54.8, Dóva 51.6, Hantzí-Neag 53.12, Halkiá 50.68	6	ECp-S	München	24 Jun
3:30.22	ROM	Crestincov, Popescu, Morosanu, Tirlea-	1	ECp-1B	Milano	24 Jun
3:31.07	ITA	Grasso, Ceccarelli, Riva, Reina	2	ECp-1B	Milano	24 Jun
3:32.14	CHN	Chen Jingwen, Tang Xiaoyin, Li Xueyi, Huang Xiaoxiao	1		Guwahati	23 Jun
3:32.37	CAN	Power 54.2, Akinsulie 51.6, Muir 53.6, Cummins 53.0	6	PAm	Rio de Janeiro	28 Jul
3:32.50	SLO (20)	Puc, Ceplak, Weit, Langerholc	3	ECp-1B	Milano	24 Jun
3:33.03	SWE	Dahlgren, Aruhn, Björkman, Klüft	2	ECp-1A	Vaasa	24 Jun
3:33.39	IND	Mand.Kaur, Manj.Kaur, Jose, Soman	1	AsiC	Amman	29 Jul
3:33.62	RSA	Wittstock, A Kotze, Vorster, Selemela	2	AfG	Alger	22 Jul
3:34.44A	KEN	Wasike, Muthoka, Zipporah, Nyarunda	1	EfCh	Kampala	31 May
3:34.44	CRO	Parlov, Banovic, Perisic, Grgic	1	ECp-2B	Zenica	24 Jun
3:34.62	POR	Carmo Tavares, Ratão, Lopes, M Carla Tavares	4	ECp-1B	Milano	24 Jun
3:34.84	SUD	El Jack, Omar, Hind, Jabir	3	AfG	Alger	22 Jul
3:34.88	SEN	Faye, Soumah, Paye, Fall	4	AfG	Alger	22 Jul
3:35.28	TRI-J	Bellille, S St Louis, A Walker, B St Louis	2	PAm-J	São Paulo	8 Jul
3:35.45	NED (30)	Krommendijk, van der Veen, Jaber, Schulte	3	ECp-1A	Vaasa	24 Jun

3:35.73	BUL	5 Jul	3:38.06	FIN	9 Sep	3:40.50	BEL	24 Jun	3:42.07	KAZ	27 Jun	3:43.88	ECU	28 Jul
3:35.79	LTU	24 Jun	3:38.26	THA	8 Dec	3:40.55	PNG	8 Sep	3:42.21A	COL	6 May	3:43.90	VIE	8 Dec
3:36.61	CZE	24 Jun	3:38.38	SUI	24 Jun	3:40.60	MYA	8 Dec	3:43.52		9 Jun	**Indoors**		
3:36.82	EST	24 Jun	3:38.39	IRL	24 Jun	3:40.84	LAT	24 Jun	3:42.59	AUS	9 Dec	3:37.59	KAZ	1 Nov
3:37.54	ESP	24 Jun	3:39.29	HUN	24 Jun	3:41.03	FIJ	8 Sep	3:42.88	MDA	24 Jun	3:38.25	THA	1 Nov
3:37.88	TUR	24 Jun	3:39.36	NOR	22 Jul	3:41.22	VEN	13 May	3:43.46	MAR	21 May			

JUNIORS

Mark	Nat	Name	Pos	Meet	Venue	Date
3:29.67	USA	Cross, Thomas, Jacobs, Beard	1	PAm-J	São Paulo	8 Jul
3:33.95	RUS	Fomina, Ott, Verkhovskaya, Ustalova	1	EJ	Hengelo	22 Jul
3:35.28	TRI	Bellille, S St.Louis, Walker, B St.Louis	2	PAm-J	São Paulo	8 Jul
3:35.36	JAM	Reid, Calvert, Henry, Cutenar	3	PAm-J	São Paulo	8 Jul
3:37.29	GBR	Beesley, H Jones, J Duck, Shakes-Drayton	2	EJ	Hengelo	22 Jul
3:37.32	GER	Ullmann Cremer, Schmidt, Kohlmann	3	EJ	Hengelo	22 Jul
3:37.82	FRA	Fosse, Denis, Manimba, Gayot	4	EJ	Hengelo	22 Jul
3:38.85	CAN	Wells, Smith, Martin, Hyacinthe	4	PAm-J	São Paulo	8 Jul
3:39.26	POL	Kielbasinska, Polak, Baumgart, Popowicz	5	EJ	Hengelo	22 Jul
3:39.67	ROM	Ionita, Ionescu, Rusu, Lavric	6	EJ	Hengelo	22 Jul
3:40.11	BLR	Boyko, Shavchuk, Boshko, Manko	7	EJ	Hengelo	22 Jul

Mark		Name	Pos	Meet	Venue	Date
3:42.12	ITA	Varisco, Romeo, Chessa, Bonfanti	2	vFRA-j	Firenze	4 Aug
3:42.12	UKR	Komuta, Yaroshchuk, Krasnoshchik, Mykhaylychenko	1	v3N-j	Valmiera	17 Aug
3:42.59	AUS	(NSW U18) Marks, Kingdom, Tauro, Keir	1		Sydney	9 Dec
3:43.36	CUB	Bonne, Méndez, Velazco, Clement	2	Barr/NC	La Habana	27 May
3:43.44	BRA	Miranda, Oliveira, dos Santos, Peixão	1	SAm-J	São Paulo	1 Jul
3:43.86	JPN	Shingu, Kitakata, Sakiyama, Fukai	1		Kyoto	17 Jun

4 X 800 METRES RELAY

		Pos	Meet	Venue	Date
8:18.54i	Moskovskaya Region RUS A Balakshina, N Pantelyeva, A Yemashova, O Chumakova	1	NC	Volgograd	11 Feb
8:18.78	University of Michigan (USA/CAN) G Gall 2:06.5, N Edwards CAN 2:05.7, A Willard 2:04.0, K Erdman 2:02.6	1	PennR	Philadelphia	28 Apr

4 X 1500 METRES RELAY

		Pos	Meet	Venue	Date
17:15.62	University of Michigan (USA/CAN) Erdman 4:22.0, Gall 4:21.4, Willard 4:13.9, Edwards CAN 4:18.3	1	PennR	Philadelphia	27 Apr

4 X 100 METRES HURDLES

		Pos	Meet	Venue	Date
53.54	University of South Carolina (USA) Martin, Young, Alexander, James	1	PennR	Philadelphia	28 Apr
53.73	Louisiana State University (USA) Wilson, Boyd, Davidson, Ohanaja	2	PennR	Philadelphia	28 Apr

3000 METRES WALK

12:25.01	Mayumi	Kawasaki	JPN	10.5.80	1		Naka	2 Jun
12:30.64	Sylwia	Korzeniowska	POL	25.4.80	1		Lomme	6 May
12:34.69	Kjersti	Plätzer	NOR	18.1.72	1	NC	Askim	10 Aug
12:38.75	Inês	Henriques	POR	1.5.80	1		Alcanena	25 Feb
Indoors								
12:03.94	Melanie	Seeger	GER	8.1.77	1	NC	Leipzig	17 Feb
12:12.23	Sabine	Zimmer	GER	6.2.81	2	NC	Leipzig	17 Feb
12:14.72	Elisa	Rigaudo	ITA	17.6.80	1	NC	Ancona	17 Feb
12:27.36	Sylwia	Korzeniowska	POL	25.4.80	1	NC	Aubière	17 Feb
12:32.04	Gillian	O'Sullivan	IRL	21.8.76	1		Nenagh	14 Jan
12:32.57	Inês	Henriques	POR	1.5.80	1	NC	Espinho	17 Feb
12:35.30	Olive	Loughnane	IRL	14.1.76	2		Nenagh	14 Jan

12:37.84	Zuzana	Malíková	SVK	2.8.83	14 Jan	12:44.00	Rossella	Giordano	ITA	1.12.72	17 Feb

5000 METRES WALK

20:28.05	Tatyana	Kalmykova	RUS-Y	10.1.90	1	WY	Ostrava	12 Jul
20:57.11	María	Vasco	ESP	26.12.75	1		Barcelona	2 Jun
21:07.7	Jolanta	Dukure	LAT	20.9.79	1		Murjani	28 Apr
21:11.21	Maria José	Poves	ESP	16.3.78	2		Barcelona	2 Jun
21:15.60+	Anisya	Kornikova	RUS-J	23.10.89	1	in 10k	Hengelo	19 Jul
21:19.95	Zuzana	Malíková	SVK	2.8.83	1		Banská Bystrica	6 May
21:21.14	Irina	Yumanova	RUS-Y	17.6.90	2	WY	Ostrava	12 Jul
21:23.10	Ryoko	Sakakura	JPN	9.5.76	1		Tama	15 Apr
21:27.52	Sachiko	Konishi	JPN	4.2.82	1		Osaka	23 Jun
21:38.27	Sylwia	Korzeniowska	POL	25.4.80	1		Bugeat	7 Jul

21:45.06	Beatriz	Pascual	ESP	9.5.82	2 Jun	21:52.70		Yi Qun	CHN-Y		21 Apr
21:45.46	Elisa	Rigaudo	ITA	17.6.80	28 Jul	21:56.63	Mayumi	Kawasaki	JPN	10.5.80	22 Sep
21:47.70		Yang Mingxia	CHN-Y	13.1.90	21 Apr	22:00.99		Cao Xi	CHN-Y		21 Apr

Indoors								
21:25.94	Yelena	Ginko	BLR	30.7.76	1		Minsk	17 Feb
21:33.3	Tatyana	Gudkova	RUS	23.12.78	1		Chelyabinsk	6 Jan
21:52.19	Yekaterina	Popova	RUS	10.12.87	1		Sankt-Peterburg	21 Jan

JUNIORS

See main list for top 3 juniors. Further juniors:

21:47.70		Yang Mingxia	CHN-Y	13.1.90	1		Beijing	21 Apr
21:52.70		Yi Qun	CHN-Y		2		Beijing	21 Apr
22:00.99		Cao Xi	CHN-Y		3		Beijing	21 Apr
22:15.4	Alena	Kostromitina	RUS	30.10.89	1		Chelyabinsk	16 May
22:16.04		Yang Shuo	CHN-Y	23.7.90	2		Guangzhou	19 Jul

10 KILOMETRES WALK

42:51	Kjersti	Plätzer	NOR	18.1.72	1		Søfteland	25 Mar
42:59	Anisya	Kornikova	RUS-J	23.10.89	1	NC-j/w	Adler	17 Feb
43:17		Kornikova			1	ECp-J	Leamington	20 May
43:18	Yelena	Shumkina	RUS-J	24.1.88	2	NC-j/w	Adler	17 Feb
43:18+	Olga	Kaniskina	RUS	19.1.85	1=	in 20k	Saransk	29 Sep
43:18+		Kornikova			1=	in 20k	Saransk	29 Sep

Mark	Name		Nat	Born	Pos	Meet	Venue	Date
43:27	Claudia	Stef	ROM	25.2.78	1	NC	Craiova	3 Mar
43:27.20 t		Kornikova			1	EJ	Hengelo	19 Jul
43:33	Irina	Yumanova	RUS-Y	17.6.90	3	NC-j/w	Adler	17 Feb
43:42+	Lyudmila	Arkhipova	RUS	12.9.78	3	in 20k	Saransk	29 Sep
43:46+	Tatyana	Korotkova	RUS	24.4.80	4	in 20k	Saransk	29 Sep
43:48	Vira	Zozulya	UKR	31.8.70	1		Ivano-Frankivsk	1 Oct
43:56+		Jiang Jing (10)	CHN	23.10.85	1	in 20k	Sesto San Giovanni	1 May
43:57+		Jiang Qiuyan	CHN	5.7.83	2	in 20k	Sesto San Giovanni	1 May
43:58+	Rita	Turova	BLR	28.12.80	3=	in 20k	Sesto San Giovanni	1 May
43:58+		Song Hongjuan	CHN	4.7.84	3=	in 20k	Sesto San Giovanni	1 May
43:58+		Bai Yanmin	CHN	29.6.87	3=	in 20k	Sesto San Giovanni	1 May
	(17/14)							
44:01	Jolanta	Dukure	LAT	20.9.79	1		Birstonas	5 May
44:05+	Tatyana	Sibilyeva	RUS	17.5.80	5	in 20k	Saransk	29 Sep
44:06	Yelena	Ginko	BLR	30.7.76	1		Alytus	15 Sep
44:09+	Mayumi	Kawasaki	JPN	10.5.80	1=	in 20k	Nomi	25 Mar
44:09+	Sachiko	Konishi	JPN	4.2.82	1=	in 20k	Nomi	25 Mar
44:13.87t	Susana	Feitor	POR	28.1.75	1	NC	Lisboa (U)	28 Jul
	(20)							
44:16.21t	Cristina E.	Lõpez	ESA	19.9.82	1	NACAC	San Salvador	13 Jul
44:18	Alina	Olaru	ROM	13.10.82	2	NC	Craiova	3 Mar
44:19	Sonata	Milusauskaité	LTU	31.8.73	2		Alytus	15 Sep
44:23+	Masumi	Fuchise	JPN	2.9.86	1	in 20k	Kobe	28 Jan
44:24+	Ryoko	Sakakura	JPN	9.5.76	2=	in 20k	Kobe	28 Jan
44:25	Tatyana	Kalmykova	RUS-Y	10.1.90	4	NC-j/w	Adler	17 Feb
44:39	Snezhana	Yurchenko	BLR	1.8.84	4		Alytus	15 Sep
44:44.77t	Elisa	Rigaudo	ITA	17.6.80	1		Milano	17 Mar
44:46.59t		Yang Mingxia	CHN-Y	13.1.90	1		Beijing	22 Apr
44:50+	Sabine	Zimmer	GER	6.2.81	7	in 20k	Sesto San Giovanni	1 May
	(30)							
44:51.52t	Inês	Henriques	POR	1.5.80	2	NC	Lisboa (U)	28 Jul
44:56	Nadezhda	Prokopuk	UKR	25.4.81	2		Ivano-Frankivsk	1 Oct
44:58+	Melanie	Seeger	GER	8.1.77	2=	in 20k	Rio Maior	14 Apr
45:08+	Olga	Mikhaylova	RUS	7.12.86	6	in 20k	Saransk	29 Sep
45:11	Veronica	Budileanu	ROM	27.2.76	3	NC	Craiova	3 Mar
45:17+	Tatyana	Shemyakina	RUS	3.9.87	2	in 20k	Osaka	31 Aug
45:18	Sylwia	Korzeniowska	POL	25.4.80	1		Zaniemysl	28 Apr
45:19.79t		Yi Qun	CHN-Y		2		Beijing	22 Apr
45:21+	Vera	Sokolova	RUS	8.6.87	7	in 20k	Saransk	29 Sep
45:21.74t	Rossella	Giordano	ITA	1.12.72	1		Alessandria	2 May
	(40)							
45:23.10t	Ana	Cabecinha	POR	29.4.84	3	NC	Lisboa (U)	28 Jul
45:28	Kumi	Otoshi	JPN	29.7.85	1		Tokyo	1 Jan
45:28+	Alena	Nartova	RUS	1.1.82	5=	in 20k	Leamington	20 May
45:28+	María	Vasco	ESP	26.12.75	5=	in 20k	Leamington	20 May
45:29	Gisella	Orsini	ITA	9.12.71	1		Chieti	24 Jun
45:30	Naomi	Hakamada	JPN	2.11.85	2		Tokyo	1 Jan
45:32+	Maria José	Poves	ESP	16.3.78	11=	in 20k	Leamington	20 May
45:32	Marie	Polli	SUI	28.11.80	1		Chiasso	9 Sep
45:33+	Jane	Saville	AUS	5.11.74	9=	in 20k	Sesto San Giovanni	1 May
45:33+	Beatriz	Pascual	ESP	9.5.82	13	in 20k	Leamington	20 May
	(50)							
45:34.52		Ye Chun	CHN	14.4.86	3		Beijing	22 Apr
45:42+	Svetlana	Solovyeva	RUS	6.11.86		in 20k	Debrecen	13 Jul
45:43+	Olive	Loughnane	IRL	14.1.76	26	in 20k	Fereira do Alente	3 Mar
45:48+		Shi Na	CHN	17.2.81	13	in 20k	Sesto San Giovanni	1 May
45:50	Brigita	Virbalité	LTU	1.2.85	2	1 NC	Druskininkai	9 Sep
45:52+	Zuzana	Malíková	SVK	2.8.83	1	in 20k	Dudince	24 Mar
45:53	Olga	Mazurenok	BLR-J	14.4.89	1	NC-j/w	Nesvizh	14 Apr
45:54+	Monica	Svensson	SWE	26.12.78	1	in 20k	Vallensbäek	5 May
45:55+		Yang Sha	CHN	16.1.86	5	in 20k	La Coruña	2 Jun
45:55	Lyudmila	Shelest	UKR	4.10.74	2	NCp	Mukachevo	20 Oct
	(60)							
45:55.77t	Vera	Santos	POR	3.12.81	4	NC	Lisboa (U)	28 Jul
45:58	Athiná	Papayiánni	GRE	18.8.80	2		Chiasso	9 Sep

46:00	Alena	Kostromitina	RUS-J	30.10.88	17 Feb
46:00	Olena	Shevchuk	UKR	23.3.86	1 Oct
46:01+		Liu Hong	CHN	12.5.87	1 May
46:01+	Natalya	Shiviryova	RUS	31.8.78	29 Sep
46:03	Cheryl	Webb	AUS	3.10.76	27 May
46:04	Katarzyna	Kwoka	POL	29.6.85	1 Sep
46:06+	Ana-Maria	Groza	ROM	1.6.76	20 May
46:07+	Larisa	Yemelyanova	RUS	6.1.80	29 Sep
46:15+	Mária	Gáliková	SVK	21.8.80	20 May
46:15	Lidia	Mongelli	ITA	3.8.80	10 Sep
46:16	Neringa	Aidietité	LTU	5.6.83	9 Sep
46:17+	Maria Teresa	Gargallo	ESP	15.10.69	20 May

Mark	Name		Nat	Born	Date
46:20	Barbora	Dibelková	CZE	26.5.83	15 Sep
46:21.51t		Wang Shanshan	CHN	16.6.87	23 Jul
46:25.82t		Kim Mi-jung	KOR	10.6.79	23 May
46:30	Megan	Szirom	AUS	18.8.77	2 Jun
46:32.67t		Han Jie	CHN	31.12.87	23 Jul
46:36	Yekaterina	Nigematzhanova	RUS-J	18.1.88	17 Feb
46:39+	Athanasía	Tsoumeléka	GRE	2.1.82	31 Aug
46:43	Paulina	Buziak	POL	16.12.86	1 Sep
46:44.30t		Yan Maoqing	CHN		22 Apr
46:44.55t	Júlia	Takács	HUN-J	29.6.89	4 Aug

Other best track times

44:29.56	Konishi	1	Akita	8 Oct
44:35.34	Kawasaki	2	Akita	8 Oct
44:52.90	Fuchise	1	Tokyo	10 Jun
45:46.90	Otoshi	3	Akita	8 Oct

46:01.31	Shi Na	23 Jul
46:04.56	Milusauskaité	4 Aug
46:17.59	Orsini	18 Mar
46:24.74	Shumkina	19 Jul
46:40.14i	Yurchenko	9 Feb
46:41.56	Kostromitina	19 Jul

JUNIORS

See main list for top 7 juniors. 10 performances by 6 women to 45:20. Additional marks and further juniors:

Shumkina 44:49 2 ECp-J Leamington 20 May best track: 46:24.74t 2 EJ Hengelo 19 Jul

Mark	Name		Nat	Born	Pos	Meet	Venue	Date
46:00	Alena	Kostromitina	RUS-J	30.10.88	5		Adler	17 Feb
	46:41.56				3	EJ	Hengelo	19 Jul
46:36	Yekaterina	Nigematzhanova	RUS-J	18.1.88	6		Adler	17 Feb
46:44.55t	Julia	Takács (10)	HUN	29.6.89	2		San Sebastián	4 Aug
46:47	Yelena	Alembekova	RUS-Y	30.6.90	1	NCp	Chelyabinsk	8 Sep
46:56	Natalya	Graber	RUS-Y	19.6.90	2	NCp	Chelyabinsk	8 Sep
46:59	Yelena	Pritushalova	RUS	16.9.89	2	NC-j	Cheboksary	16 Jun
47.01	Ana-Maria	Greceanu	ROM	12.5.89	4	ECp-j	Leamington	20 May
47:03	Jess	Rothwell	AUS	18.6.89	1		Melbourne	16 Dec
47:08	Oksan	Kirillova	RUS	18.7.88	3	NC-j	Cheboksary	16 Jun
47:11	Agnese	Pastare	LAT	27.10.88	3		Gdansk	1 Sep

20 KILOMETRES WALK

Mark	Name		Nat	Born	Pos	Meet	Venue	Date
1:26:47	Olga	Kaniskina	RUS	19.1.85	1	RWC	Saransk	29 Sep
1:27:10	Rita	Turova	BLR	28.12.80	1		Sesto San Giovanni	1 May
1:27:41	Kjersti	Plätzer	NOR	18.1.72	2		Sesto San Giovanni	1 May
1:27:52		Turova			1	ECp	Leamington	20 May
1:28:00	Anisya	Kornikova	RUS-J	23.10.89	2	RWC	Saransk	29 Sep
1:28:01		Turova			1		Rio Maior	14 Apr
1:28:13		Kaniskina			2	ECp	Leamington	20 May
1:28:25		Song Hongjuan	CHN	4.7.84	3		Sesto San Giovanni	1 May
1:28:29	Yelena	Ginko	BLR	30.7.76	3	ECp	Leamington	20 May
1:28:31	Alena	Nartova	RUS	1.1.82	1	NC-w	Adler	17 Feb
1:28:44		Turova			1		La Coruña	2 Jun
1:28:46	Tatyana	Korotkova	RUS	24.4.80	3	RWC	Saransk	29 Sep
1:28:48	Tatyana	Shemyakina	RUS	3.9.87	1	EU23	Debrecen	13 Jul
1:28:51	Tatyana	Sibilyeva (10)	RUS	17.5.80	2	NC-w	Adler	17 Feb
1:28:54		Plätzer			2		Rio Maior	14 Apr
1:28:56	Mayumi	Kawasaki	JPN	10.5.80	1	AsiC	Nomi	25 Mar
1:29:01	Lyudmila	Arkhipova	RUS	12.9.78	1	NCp	Chelyabinsk	8 Sep
1:29:02		Kaniskina			3	NC-w	Adler	17 Feb
1:29:10		Arkhipova			4	NC-w	Adler	17 Feb
1:29:15	Elisa	Rigaudo	ITA	17.6.80	4	ECp	Leamington	20 May
1:29:17	María	Vasco	ESP	26.12.75	5	ECp	Leamington	20 May
1:29:20		Arkhipova			4	RWC	Saransk	29 Sep
1:29:32	Melanie	Seeger	GER	8.1.77	3		Rio Maior	14 Apr
1:29:36	Masumi	Fuchise	JPN	2.9.86	1	NC	Kobe	28 Jan
1:29:41		Liu Hong	CHN	12.5.87	1		Shenzen	24 Mar
1:29:45		Jiang Jing	CHN	23.10.85	4		Sesto San Giovanni	1 May
1:29:53		Sibilyeva			5	RWC	Saransk	29 Sep
1:29:56	Irina	Stankina	RUS	25.3.77	1	NC	Cheboksary	17 Jun
1:30:02	Vira	Zozulya (20)	UKR	31.8.70	1	NC	Sumy	1 Jun
1:30:07	Tatyana	Kozlova	RUS	2.9.83	5	NC-w	Adler	17 Feb
	(30/21)							
1:30:12		Bai Yanmin	CHN	29.6.87	2		Shenzen	24 Mar
1:30:12	Sabine	Zimmer	GER	6.2.81	4		Rio Maior	14 Apr
1:30:16	Ryoko	Sakakura	JPN	9.5.76	2	NC	Kobe	28 Jan
1:30:19	Olga	Mikhaylova	RUS	7.12.86	2	NC	Cheboksary	17 Jun
1:30:22	Larisa	Yemelyanova	RUS	6.1.80	6	NC-w	Adler	17 Feb
1:30:24	Inês	Henriques	POR	1.5.80	7	ECp	Leamington	20 May
1:30:27		Jiang Qiuyan	CHN	5.7.83	4		Shenzen	24 Mar
1:30:34	Claudia	Stef	ROM	25.2.78	8	ECp	Leamington	20 May
1:30:37	Beatriz	Pascual	ESP	9.5.82	9	ECp	Leamington	20 May
	(30)							
1:30:48	María José	Poves	ESP	16.3.78	11	ECp	Leamington	20 May
1:30:49	Sachiko	Konishi	JPN	4.2.82	1		Takahata	28 Oct
1:30:53	Jane	Saville	AUS	5.11.74	6		Rio Maior	14 Apr

Mark		Name	Nat	Born	Pos	Meet	Venue	Date
1:30:58		Shi Na	CHN	17.2.81	5		Shenzen	24 Mar
1:31:10	Tatyana	Gudkova	RUS	23.1.78	2	NCp	Chelyabinsk	8 Sep
1:31:12	Snezhana	Yurchenko	BLR	1.8.84	12	ECp	Leamington	20 May
1:31:15	Susana	Feitor	POR	28.1.75	7		Rio Maior	14 Apr
1:31:18.79t		Song Xiaoling	CHN	21.12.87	2		Wuhan	1 Nov
1:31:20	Monica	Svensson	SWE	26.12.78	1		Vallensbäek	5 May
1:31:31	Svetlana	Solovyova	RUS	6.11.86	4	NC	Cheboksary	17 Jun
	(40)							
1:31:52.30t		Wang Shanshan	CHN	16.6.87	4		Wuhan	1 Nov
1:31:59	Svetlana	Vasilyeva	RUS	13.8.85	5	NC	Cheboksary	17 Jun
1:32:05	Natalya	Shiviryova	RUS	31.8.78	10	NC-w	Adler	17 Feb
1:32:05	Yekaterina	Yezhova	RUS	3.7.82	3	NCp	Chelyabinsk	8 Sep
1:32:12		Yang Sha	CHN	16.1.86	4		La Coruña	2 Jun
1:32:19	Zuzana	Malíková	SVK	2.8.83	1		Dudince	24 Mar
1:32:19.71t		Hie Jingjing	CHN-J	1.3.88	5		Wuhan	1 Nov
1:32:22	Antonina	Petrova	RUS	25.1.77	4	NCp	Chelyabinsk	8 Sep
1:32:25	Olive	Loughnane	IRL	14.1.76	2	POR Ch	Ferreira do Alentejo	2 Mar
1:32:29	Jolanta	Dukure	LAT	20.9.79	1	NC	Jurmala	9 Jun
	(50)							
1:32:30.36t		Sun Limin	CHN	6.2.87	6		Wuhan	1 Nov
1:32:34	Athiná	Papayiánni	GRE	18.8.80	8	RWC	Saransk	29 Sep
1:32:36	Aleksandra	Kudryashova	RUS-Y	18.7.90	11	NC-w	Adler	17 Feb
1:32:38	Rossella	Giordano	ITA	1.12.72	15	ECp	Leamington	20 May
1:32:39	Lyudmyla	Shelest	UKR	4.10.74	1	BLR Ch	Grodno	5 Jul
1:32:44	Nadezhda	Prokopuk	UKR	25.4.81	1	NC-w	Yevpatoriya	16 Mar
1:32:44 46?	Ana	Cabecinha	POR	29.4.84	9		Rio Maior	14 Apr
1:32:45	Sonata	Milusauskaité	LTU	31.8.73	11		Sesto San Giovanni	1 May
1:32:47	Sylwia	Korzeniowska	POL	25.4.80	16	ECp	Leamington	20 May
1:32:51	María Teresa	Gargallo	ESP	15.10.69	17	ECp	Leamington	20 May
	(60)							
1:32:53	Vera	Santos	POR	3.12.81	18	ECp	Leamington	20 May
1:32:56	Vera	Sokolova	RUS	8.6.87	9	RWC	Saransk	29 Sep
1:33:14	Alina	Olaru	ROM	13.10.82	1	BalkC	Galati	14 Apr
1:33:25	Zhanna	Golovnya	BLR	18.5.86	3	NC	Grodno	5 Jul
1:33:37	Svetlana	Tolstaya	KAZ	9.8.71	14	NC-w	Adler	17 Feb
1:33:40	Veronica	Budileanu	ROM	27.2.76	2	BalkC	Galati	14 Apr
1:33:54	Neringa	Aidietyté	LTU	5.6.83	22	ECp	Leamington	20 May
1:33:58	Athanasía	Tsoumeléka	GRE	2.1.82	7		Kraków	23 Jun
1:34:09	Ana-Maria	Groza	ROM	1.6.76	23	ECp	Leamington	20 May
1:34:11		Yang Mingxia	CHN-Y	13.1.90	1	NC-j	Beijing	21 Aug
	(70)							
1:34:12.31t		Chai Xue	CHN-J	21.10.88	7		Wuhan	1 Nov
1:34:16	Déspina	Zapounídou	GRE	5.10.85	3	BalkC	Galati	14 Apr
1:34:18	Mária	Gáliková	SVK	21.8.80	24	ECp	Leamington	20 May
1:34:21	Joanne	Dow	USA	19.3.64	1		Chula Vista	28 Jan
1:34:21.56t		Wang Xue	CHN-Y	14.2.90	8		Wuhan	1 Nov
1:34:27	Gisella	Orsini	ITA	9.12.71	1		Dublin	17 Jun
1:34:29		Song Jinzhao	CHN-J	16.1.88	8		Shenzen	24 Mar
1:34:39.71t		Han Jie	CHN	31.12.87	9		Wuhan	1 Nov
1:34:40	Cheryl	Webb	AUS	3.10.76	2		Canberra	28 Jan
1:34:42	Teresa	Vaill	USA	20.11.62	2		Chula Vista	28 Jan
	(80)							
1:34:44	Barbora	Dibelková	CZE	26.5.83	27	ECp	Leamington	20 May
1:34:44		Kim Mi-jung	KOR	10.6.79	1	NG	Kwangju	12 Oct
1:34:49	Katarzyna	Kwoka	POL	29.6.85	4	EU23	Debrecen	13 Jul
1:34:56	Zhanna	Drabenya	BLR	15.8.87	1		Minsk (Staiki)	2 Jun
1:34:57	Zuzana	Schindlerová	CZE	25.4.87	29	ECp	Leamington	20 May
1:35:04	Kumi	Otoshi	JPN	29.7.85	4	AsiC	Nomi	25 Mar
1:35:09	Anna	Sorokina	RUS-J	20.8.88	12	NC	Cheboksary	17 Jun
1:35:25	Lidia	Mongelli	ITA	3.8.80	30	ECp	Leamington	20 May
1:35:29	Natalya	Kozlova	RUS	17.4.87	13	NC	Cheboksary	17 Jun
1:35:32		Shi Tianshu	CHN-J	7.6.88	2	NC-j	Beijing	21 Aug
	(90)							
1:35:36	Claire	Woods	AUS	6.7.81	3		Canberra	28 Jan
1:35:39	Veronica	Colindres	ESA	9.7.86	1		San Salvador	3 Feb
1:35:39	Jurgita	Meskauskiené	LTU	27.8.76	31	ECp	Leamington	20 May
1:35:39		Sun Lihua	CHN	30.9.83	9		Shenzen	24 Mar
1:35:41	Marie	Polli	SUI	28.11.80	33	ECp	Leamington	20 May
1:35:41.84t		Li Leilei	CHN-J	18.8.89	10		Wuhan	1 Nov
1:35:42	Naomi	Hakamata	JPN	2.11.85	5	AsiC	Nomi	25 Mar

Mark	Name		Nat	Born	Pos	Meet	Venue	Date
1:35:49	Irina	Yezhova	RUS	25.6.86	14	NC	Cheboksary	17 Jun
1:35:50	Yekaterina	Popova	RUS	10.12.87	16	NC-w	Adler	17 Feb
1:35:57		Zheng Rongna	CHN	28.3.87	10		Shenzen	24 Mar

(100)

Mark	Name		Nat	Born	Date
1:36:06	Anastasia	Yatsevich	BLR	18.1.85	15 Apr
1:36:06	Olena	Miroshnychenko	UKR	1.3.77	17 Mar
1:36:11		Zhou Kang	CHN-J	24.12.89	21 Aug
1:36:22	Yeliz	Ay	TUR	9.11.77	17 Mar
1:36:28	Johanna	Jackson	GBR	17.1.85	13 Jul
1:36:29	Miriam	Ramón	ECU	10.2.73	17 Mar
1:36:32	Sandra	Zapata	COL	3.2.77	23 Jun
1:36:34	Evaggelía	Xinoú	GRE	22.11.81	14 Apr
1:36:34		Yu Miao	CHN-J	2.4.89	24 Mar
1:36:38	Brigita	Virbalité	LTU	1.2.85	13 Jul
1:36:54	Nina	Kovalchuk	UKR	26.1.87	17 Mar
1:36:54	Agnieszka	Dygacz	POL	18.7.85	24 Mar
1:36:55	Megan	Szirom	AUS	18.8.77	1 Jul
1:37:00		Yang Yawei	CHN	16.10.83	21 Aug
1:37:10	Olga	Yakovenko	UKR	1.6.87	17 Mar
1:37:10		Shi Yang	CHN	24.1.83	24 Mar
1:37:11	Evelyn	Nuñez	GUA	9.4.71	2 Jun
1:37:12	Lucie	Pelantová	CZE	7.5.86	13 Jul
1:37:13	Yelena	Ulyanova	RUS	4.7.85	17 Jun
1:37:17	Paulina	Buziak	POL	16.12.86	24 Mar
1:37:26	Yevdokiya	Korotkova	RUS	28.2.79	18 Feb
1:37:27		Ke Lijun	CHN-J	12.9.88	21 Aug
1:37:31		Xu Qing	CHN	17.4.85	21 Aug
1:37:37.48t	Valentina	Trapletti	ITA	12.7.85	7 Oct
1:37:38	Natalya	Rymar	RUS	16.3.83	17 Jun
1:37:41.20t		Pang Yingting	CHN	28.1.87	1 Nov
1:37:44.25t		Li Li	CHN	18.6.87	1 Nov
1:37:54	Tánia	Spindler	BRA	10.4.77	1 May
1:38:02	Anna	Pudovkina	RUS	29.3.85	17 Jun
1:38:04.97t		Qiao Li	CHN-J	5.5.88	1 Nov
1:38:05	Oksana	Chubenko	RUS	22.9.87	17 Feb
1:38:09	Irina	Lazareva	RUS	2.3.86	8 Sep
1:38:12		Yang Xiao	CHN-J	15.2.88	21 Aug
1:38:12	Tatyana	Zuyeva	BLR	22.3.83	5 Jul
1:38:14.26t	Leisis	Rodriguez	CUB	6.5.86	11 May
1:38:17.21t		Sun Huanhuan	CHN-Y	15.3.90	5 Jun
1:38:20	María Isabel	Pérez	ESP	4.7.79	2 Jun
1:38:22		Kim Sun-young	KOR-J	24.5.88	1 May
1:38:27	Aleksandra	Kubashova	RUS	19.8.86	17 Feb
1:38:28.36t		Yang Shuo	CHN-Y	23.7.90	5 Jun
1:38:33	Tatyana	Metlevskaya	BLR	14.9.84	15 Apr
1:38:47.20t		Song Jinzhao	CHN-J	16.1.88	3 Jun
1:38:50	Samantha	Cohen	USA	3.6.77	14 Oct
1:38:50	Amber	Antonia	USA	4.11.79	14 Oct
1:38:57	Júlia	Takács	HUN-J	29.6.89	2 Jun
1:38:58	Teresa	Marinelli	ITA	30.4.85	15 Jul
1:38:58	Olena	Shevchuk	UKR	23.3.86	17 Mar
1:38:59	Cristina	López	ESA	19.9.82	22 Jul
1:39:04	Edina	Füsti	HUN	24.6.82	9 Sep
1:39:11		Ye Chun	CHN	14.4.86	24 Mar
1:39:13	Olga	Povalyeva	RUS	19.10.84	17 Feb
1:39:19.77t	Geovana	Irusta	BOL	26.9.75	11 May
1:39:23		Zhang Guangcai	CHN-J	4.4.88	24 Mar
1:39:24	Maria	Shorokhova	RUS	24.12.85	17 Feb
1:39:24.14t	Jolene	Moore	USA	14.3.66	24 Jun
1:39:27	Emanuela	Perilli	ITA	19.5.73	3 Jun
1:39:30	Yarelis	Sánchez	CUB	2.1.82	28 Feb
1:39:31	Ayumi	Miyashita	JPN	13.9.82	28 Oct
1:39:32.5t	Cisiane	Lopes	BRA	17.2.83	21 Jun
1:39:33	Olga	Bezzubkova	RUS	4.2.86	17 Feb
1:39:33	Laura	Polli	SUI	7.9.83	9 Sep
1:39:34		Yuan Yufang	MAS	1.2.76	29 Apr
1:39:35	Nataliya	Klimashevskaya	UKR	12.1.83	17 Mar
1:39:48	Natalya	Ivanova	RUS	10.11.85	17 Feb
1:39:48	Ana-Maria	Greceanu	ROM-J	12.5.89	27 Jul
1:39:50	Agnieszka	Olesz	POL	27.8.79	30 Jun
1:39:54	Karina	Trofimova	RUS	30.4.87	17 Feb
1:39:56	Natalya	Kolotukhina	RUS	12.6.83	17 Feb

(168)

Other best track times

1:31:16.18 Liu Hong 1 Wuhan 1 Nov | 1:31:47.95 Bai Yanmin 3 Wuhan 1 Nov

Mark	Name		Date
1:36:42.8	Lidia	Mongelli	7 Oct
1:37:28.70	Teresa	Vaill	24 Jun
1:37:45.94	Sandra	Zapata	7 Jun
1:38:18.53		Zhou Kang	5 Jun
1:38:26.26	Miriam	Ramón	7 Jun
1:38:27.87		Ke Lijun	1 Nov
1:38:49.26	Tánia	Spindler	7 Jun
1:38:50.12		Yu Miao	1 Nov
1:39:36.48		Zheng Rongna	5 Jun
1:39:52.2	Lucie	Pelantová	17 Mar
1:39:52.2	Zuzana	Schindlerová	17 Mar

JUNIORS

See main list for top 10 juniors. 10 performances by 10 women to 1:35:45. Further juniors:

Mark		Name		Nat	Born	Pos	Meet	Venue	Date
1:36:11			Zhou Kang	CHN	24.12.89	4-j		Beijing	21 Aug
	1:38:18.53 t					5	NC-20	Chengdu	5 Jun
1:36:34			Yu Miao	CHN	2.4.89	12		Shenzhen	24 Mar
	1:38:50.12 t					15		Wuhan	1 Nov
1:37:27			Ke Lijun	CHN	12.9.88	6-j		Beijing	21 Aug
	1:38:27.87 t					14		Wuhan	1 Nov
1:38:04.97t			Qiao Li	CHN	5.5.88	13		Wuhan	1 Nov
1:38:12			Yang Xiao	CHN	15.2.88	7-j		Beijing	21 Aug
1:38:17.21t			Sun Huanhuan	CHN-Y	15.3.90	4	NC-20	Chengdu	5 Jun
1:38:22			Kim Sun-young	KOR	24.5.88	1		Goyang	1 May
1:38:28.36t			Yang Shuo	CHN-Y	23.7.90	6	NC-20	Chengdu	5 Jun
1:38:47.20t			Song Jinzhao	CHN	16.1.88	8	NC-20	Chengdu	3 Jun
1:38:57		Júlia	Takács	HUN	29.6.89	13		La Coruña	2 Jun

50 KILOMETRES WALK

Mark	Name		Nat	Born	Pos	Meet	Venue	Date
4:10:59	Monica	Svensson	SWE	26.12.78	1		Scanzorosciate	21 Oct
4:28:59	Kara	Boufflert	FRA	23.4.66	1		Charly-sur-Marne	18 Feb
4:33:42	Evaggelía	Xinoú	GRE	22.11.81	2		Scanzorosciate	21 Oct
4:49:17+	Jolanta	Dukure	LAT	20.9.79	3	in 100km	Scanzorosciate	21 Oct
4:51:43	Laura	Polli	SUI	7.9.83	4		Scanzorosciate	21 Oct
4:58:08	Lucie	Pelantová	CZE	7.5.86	5		Scanzorosciate	21 Oct

100 KILOMETRES WALK

Mark	Name		Nat	Born	Pos	Venue	Date
10:04:50	Jolanta	Dukure	LAT	20.9.79	1	Scanzorosciate	21 Oct
11:09:48	Valentina	Setrova	BLR	19.12.71	2	Scanzoroscaite	21 Oct

WORLD LIST TRENDS – MEN

This table shows the 10th and 100th bests in the year lists for 1988, 1992, 1996, 2000 and the last six years.

Men 10th Bests	*1988*	*1992*	*1996*	*2000*	*2002*	*2003*	*2004*	*2005*	*2006*	*2007*
100m	10.06	10.07	10.01	10.03	9.99	10.00	10.01	10.00	10.02	10.02
200m	20.18	20.15	20.17	**20.03**	20.21	20.15	20.17	20.21	20.19	20.06
400m	44.61	44.52	**44.51**	44.70	44.84	44.78	44.72	44.70	44.73	44.62
800m	1:44.10	1:44.33	**1:43.66**	1:44.06	1:43.93	1:44.22	1:44.09	1:44.34	1:43.93	1:44.27
1500m	3:34.61	3:33.80	3:33.00	3:32.01	3:32.37	3:31.61	**3:31.10**	3:31.95	3:31.85	3:32.13
5000m	13:17.48	13:10.47	12:59.19	12:58.70	13:01.98	**12:54.99**	12:59.04	12:56.13	12:56.41	13:02.89
10,000m	27:40.36	27:45.46	27:30.37	27:23.65	27:26.12	27:14.61	27:05.14	27:04.45	27:14.84	**27:00.30**
Marathon	2:08:49	2:09:30	2:09:15	2:07:47	2:07:06	**2:06:48**	2:07:43	2:07:46	2:07:14	2:07:19
3000mSt	8:16.04	8:13.65	8:12.54	8:10.23	**8:08.14**	8:09.37	8:11.44	8:09.43	8:11.36	8:09.72
110mh	13.36	13.33	13.24	13.24	13.30	13.28	13.22	13.23	13.22	**13.19**
400mh	48.65	48.60	48.28	48.40	48.25	48.50	**48.16**	48.24	48.57	48.26
HJ	**2.36**	2.34	2.34	2.34	2.32	2.32	2.32	2.33	2.33	2.34
PV	5.80	5.85	**5.90**	5.85	5.81	5.81	5.81	5.85	5.81	5.83
LJ	8.31	8.28	8.34	8.33	8.26	8.30	8.28	8.28	8.32	8.26
TJ	17.43	17.30	17.20	17.26	17.35	17.28	17.41	17.30	17.38	17.39
SP	21.16	20.93	20.78	21.27	21.11	21.14	21.14	20.94	20.85	20.87
DT	67.38	66.64	66.70	66.93	66.90	66.35	66.73	66.56	66.50	66.61
HT	**81.88**	80.46	79.52	81.36	81.59	80.89	80.90	80.00	80.54	80.00
JT	82.70	85.74	**87.12**	86.65	85.74	84.54	85.83	84.06	85.30	84.35
Decathlon	8387	8237	8462	8467	8175	8203	8285	8185	8310	8298
20kmW	1:20:10	1:20:32	1:19:31	1:19:18	1:20:36	1:19:35	1:19:30	1:18:30	1:19:12	1:19:34
50kmW	3:46:30	3:50:01	3:44:19	3:44:33	3:45:45	3:44:53	3:44:42	3:41:30	3:43:58	3:44:26

Peak years shown in bold. Other peaks: 100m 9.98 (1997), PV 5.90 (1998), LJ 8.35 (1997), TJ 17.48 (1985), SP 21.63 (1984), DT 68.20 (1982), Dec 8526 (1998)

Men 100th Bests	1988	1992	1996	2000	2002	2003	2004	2005	2006	2007
100m	10.34	10.32	10.27	**10.24**	10.27	10.26	10.26	10.29	10.27	10.25
200m	20.79	20.78	**20.66**	**20.66**	20.74	20.69	20.67	20.70	20.70	**20.66**
400m	45.99	45.98	45.91	**45.78**	45.99	45.83	45.86	45.98	45.90	45.91
800m	1:46.91	1:46.95	1:46.82	1:46.71	1:47.12	1:46.91	1:46.67	1:46.93	1:46.80	1:46.99
1500m	3:39.46	3:39.11	3:38.66	3:38.68	3:39.70	3:39.49	3:38.50	3:39.05	3:39.26	3:38.66
5000m	13:37.20	13:31.44	13:34.29	13:28.62	13:31.61	13:30.06	**13:25.52**	13:25.68	13:27.46	13:27.48
10,000m	28:27.28	28:30.42	28:20.9	28:15.98	28:27.17	28:22.29	28:21.4	28:22.85	28:21.98	**28:10.73**
Marathon	2:13:08	2:13:22	2:12:25	2:11:24	2:11:08	**2:10:38**	2:11:13	2:11:20	2:10:54	2:10:43
3000mSt	8:35.24	8:34.43	8:34.91	8:33.37	8:34.18	8:33.58	**8:31.06**	8:33.37	8:34.10	8:32.94
110mh	13.83	13.78	13.72	13.76	13.79	13.75	**13.70**	13.73	13.77	13.72
400mh	50.52	50.50	50.17	**50.06**	50.19	50.20	50.14	50.10	50.37	50.28
HJ	**2.24**	**2.24**	**2.24**	2.23	2.23	2.22	2.23	2.22	2.23	2.23
PV	5.50	5.50	5.50	**5.55**	5.50	5.50	5.50	5.50	5.50	5.50
LJ	7.93	7.93	7.94	7.93	7.90	7.92	**7.96**	7.90	7.90	7.90
TJ	**16.60**	16.59	16.56	16.48	16.41	16.43	16.55	16.42	16.43	16.44
SP	19.17	18.79	18.81	19.05	19.11	19.02	19.28	19.08	19.12	19.22
DT	60.84	59.80	59.82	60.16	59.72	59.62	60.05	59.50	59.63	59.75
HT	72.34	70.70	70.88	71.28	69.88	70.63	71.12	70.72	70.19	70.58
JT	76.48	76.40	76.20	76.06	76.60	76.17	76.31	76.10	75.98	75.66
Decathlon	7702	7567	7701	7633	7537	7512	7572	7490	7496	7545
20kmW	1:24:54	1:24:09	1:23:55	1:24:22	1:24:41	1:24:04	1:23:25	**1:22.48**	1:23:47	1:23:55
50kmW	4:06:34	4:07:33	4:06:31	4:04:34	4:07:43	4:06:54	4:05:13	4:05:04	4:13:16	4:04:52

Other peaks: 800m 1:46.54 (1999), 1500m 3:38.42 (1997), HJ 2.24 (also 1984, 1989), SP 19.48 (1984), DT 60.96 (1984), HT 73.06 (1984), JT 77.14 (1991), 50kmW 4:03:49 (1999)

Number of athletes achieving base level standards for world lists:

Men		2002	2003	2004	2005	2006	2007
100m	10.34	178	196	204	160	182	199
200m	20.85	153	177	179	166	174	187
400m	46.29	169	188	203	165	177	186
800m	1:47.99	177	200	218	200	201	202
1500m	3:41.4	155	156	204	207	204	203
5000m	13:42.0	182	185	205	199	196	218
10000m	28:42.0	168	174	195	185	191	230
HMar	62:45	165	194	197	196	168	232
Mar	2:13:15	204	199	213	196	220	224
3000St	8:40.0	151	154	166	167	156	156
110mh	13.95	166	185	202	199	195	196
400mh	50.85	185	187	189	192	158	159

		2002	2003	2004	2005	2006	2007
HJ	2.20	173	165	177	162	169	197
PV	5.35	157	173	180	167	168	177
LJ	7.80	160	157	167	157	164	179
TJ	16.30	122	125	148	138	125	137
SP	18.25	180	186	209	190	194	193
DT	57.80	142	140	150	140	151	150
HT	68.00	147	147	157	136	135	135
JT	74.00	153	147	155	146	137	145
Dec	7400	131	130	147	125	127	137
20kmW	1:25:00	112	133	149	162	143	144
50kmW	4:10:00	109	112	125	121	87	116

Notes: The 2007 marks were better than those of 2006: for 10th best 11-10 (1 tie), 100th best 14-5 (3 ties, base level standards 18-3 (2 ties)

WORLD LIST TRENDS – WOMEN

This table shows the 10th and 100th bests in the year lists for 1988, 1992, 1996 and the last seven years.

10th Bests	*1988*	*1992*	*1996*	*2000*	2002	*2003*	*2004*	*2005*	*2006*	2007
100m	**10.92**	11.07	11.03	10.99	11.05	11.05	11.04	11.05	11.08	11.04
200m	**22.24**	22.44	22.27	22.49	22.54	22.60	22.46	22.46	22.51	22.49
400m	49.90	50.30	50.32	50.04	50.80	50.59	50.19	50.38	50.14	50.16
800m	**1:56.91**	1:57.93	1:58.22	1:58.34	1:58.90	1:58.86	1:57.96	1:58.41	1:57.88	1:58.61
1500m	4:01.02	4:01.23	4:02.38	4:01.23	4:01.28	4:01.69	4:01.29	4:01.14	4:01.31	4:02.8
5000m	15:17.89	15:19.20	14:48.36	14:45.35	14:48.29	14:46.73	14:44.81	**14:43.87**	14:46.99	14:45.22
10000m	31:42.02	31:28.06	31:24.08	31:03.60	31:27.83	31:01.07	31:04.34	**30:55.67**	31:14.80	31:22.80
Marathon	2:28:40	2:27:42	2:27:41	2:24:33	**2:22:33**	2:23:07	2:24:27	2:23:59	2:23:22	2:24:23
3000mSt				10:02.60	9:47.87	9:44.95	9:39.84	9:35.51	9:27.35	**9:26.63**
100mh	12.73	12.76	12.69	12.70	12.75	12.72	**12.60**	12.66	12.66	12.67
400mh	54.49	54.70	54.40	54.41	54.72	54.60	**53.99**	54.47	54.47	54.14
HJ	1.98	1.96	1.98	1.98	1.97	**2.01**	2.00	1.97	1.98	1.97
PV	-	3.70	4.15	4.50	4.60	4.60	4.60	4.60	4.62	**4.70**
LJ	**7.07**	6.92	6.92	6.93	6.79	6.79	6.83	6.79	6.83	6.89
TJ	13.07	14.07	14.55	14.52	14.56	14.76	**14.78**	14.69	14.54	14.69
SP	20.81	19.78	19.46	19.32	19.20	19.10	19.29	19.05	19.10	19.13
DT	**70.34**	67.08	64.90	65.41	64.55	65.38	65.25	64.56	64.20	64.87
HT	-	56.40	61.84	69.36	68.70	71.12	72.57	73.08	**74.31**	73.94
JT *	68.42	65.02	66.14	**64.89**	63.89	62.89	63.07	62.64	63.20	63.58
Heptathlon	**6540**	6460	6406	6396	6151	6209	6287	6291	6356	6327
20kmW	Previously 10km standard event			1:28:06	1:28:46	1:28:17	1:27:52	1:28:01	1:28:26	1:28:51

Other peaks: 400m 49.74 (1984), 1500m 3:58.07 (1997), SP 20.85 (1987).
5000m succeeded 3000m as standard event from 1995. * Note new javelin from 1999.

100th Bests	1988	1992	1996	2000	2002	2003	2004	2005	2006	2007
100m	11.43	11.45	11.44	**11.36**	11.43	11.43	11.38	11.42	11.41	11.37
200m	23.32	23.36	23.32	23.21	23.35	23.31	**23.20**	23.29	23.28	23.27
400m	52.50	52.60	52.29	52.25	52.55	52.34	**52.14**	52.30	52.24	**52.14**
800m	2:01.66	2:02.80	2:02.96	2:02.51	2:02.65	2:02.38	2:01.98	2:02.58	2:02.31	2:02.25
1500m	4:11.70	4:11.80	4:11.87	4:11.18	4:12.37	4:11.37	4:10.34	4:12.12	4:11.61	4:11.67
5000m			15:35.62	15:29.36	15:36.99	15:43.15	**15:26.01**	15:29.96	15:31.57	15:33.90
10000m	33:11.31	33:05.80	32:56.63	**32:32.47**	32:46.11	32:43.76	32:37.88	32:34.11	32:42.44	32:46.28
Marathon	2:35:29	2:36:14	2:33:24	2:32:25	2:31:29	2:31:21	2:31:53	2:31:43	2:31:08	2:31:25
3000mSt						10:23.76	10:18.55	10:13.00	10:06.83	**10:03.2**
100mh	13.39	13.35	13.31	**13.22**	13.33	13.26	13.26	13.32	13.30	13.25
400mh	57.50	57.60	57.63	57.48	57.88	57.61	57.33	57.47	57.35	**57.21**
HJ	**1.88**	**1.88**	1.87	1.87	1.86	1.87	1.87	1.86	1.86	1.87
PV			3.60	4.10	4.10	4.15	4.20	4.20	4.20	**4.22**
LJ	**6.53**	6.45	6.50	6.49	6.43	6.46	6.50	6.48	6.51	6.49
TJ		13.16	13.45	13.68	13.64	13.67	**13.70**	13.62	13.66	13.64
SP	17.02	16.40	16.34	16.46	16.49	16.58	16.76	16.55	16.60	16.56
DT	57.40	56.20	56.86	56.22	55.20	55.15	56.32	55.93	55.92	55.43
HT			53.84	60.66	61.50	63.23	63.73	63.14	63.72	**64.34**
JT *	58.14	56.36	56.16	**55.55**	54.97	54.27	55.09	54.91	55.00	55.07
Heptathlon	**5741**	5661	5649	5647	5580	5622	5631	5650	5633	5674
20kmW				1:34:44	1:37:08	1:35:46	1:34:32	**1:34:11**	1:36:01	1:35:57

All-time record levels indicated in bold.
Other peaks: 800m 2:01.50 (1984), 1500m 4:10.22 (1984)), Mar 2:31:05 (2001), HJ 1.88 (also 1986, 1987, 1993), SP 17.19 (1987), DT 58.50 (1984)

Number of athletes achieving base level standards for world lists:

Women		2002	2003	2004	2005	2006	2007
100m	11.54	168	181	212	171	197	221
200m	23.54	148	180	198	177	190	214
400m	53.19	183	198	208	191	220	198
800m	2:04.0	159	183	210	174	161	174
1500m	4:15.5	155	193	191	169	171	176
5000m	15:45.0	151	156	187	165	173	171
10000m	33:15.0	152	166	153	161	159	150
HMar	72:59	179	194	183	205	194	236
Mar	2:36:00	185	198	182	189	192	198
3000mSt	10:20.0	70	84	107	142	160	176
100mh	13.54	177	183	221	180	180	196

Women		2002	2003	2004	2005	2006	2007
400mh	58.44	141	164	179	169	168	178
HJ	1.85	123	130	146	146	140	149
PV	4.05	139	151	179	213	207	211
LJ	6.33	169	191	201	186	210	193
TJ	13.30	173	185	201	174	172	181
SP	15.85	153	172	181	150	154	159
DT	53.65	143	136	147	160	145	146
HT	59.60	144	172	193	178	194	202
JT	53.00	148	130	156	151	141	149
Hep	5450	128	145	141	144	142	157
20kmW	1:40:00	144	164	175	173	162	168

Notes: The 2007 marks were better than those of 2006: for 10th best 11-10, 100th best 13-8, base level standards 18-3 (1 tie).

MEN'S INDEX 2007

Athletes included are those ranked in the top 100s at standard (World Championships) events (plus shorter lists for 1000m, 1M, 2000m and 3000m). Those with detailed biographical profiles are indicated in first column by:
* in this year's Annual, ^ featured in a previous year's Annual.

Name		Nat	Born	Ht/Wt	Event	2007 Mark	Pre-2007 Best
Aalto	Mika	FIN	11.3.82	178/88	JT	76.13	74.21- 05
Abate	Emanuele	ITA	8.7.85	190/75	110H	13.62	13.59- 06
Abdallah Afringi	Ali	ERI	2.11.82	170/52	5000	13:23.65	13:10.71- 06
Abderraouf Mohamed	Ahmed	EGY	12.2.80	187/106	HT	70.95	74.20- 06
Abdi	Youcef	AUS	7.12.77	178/66	1500	3:38.48	3:36.35- 02
					3kSt	8:18.34	8:21.98- 06
Abdirahman	Abdi	USA	1.1.77	178/60	3000	7:47.69	7:47.63- 01
					10,000	27:31.46	27:22.81- 06
					HMar	60:29dh	61:07- 06
Abdosh	Mohamed Ali	ETH	28.8.87	167/48	3000	7:45.96i, 7:54.7+	
					5000	13:13.08	13:01.44- 06
					10,000	27:04.92	
Abdur-Rahim	Mustafa	USA	29.9.82	175/85	Dec	7760	7937- 04
* Abele	Arthur	GER	30.7.86	184/80	Dec	8269	8012- 06
Abraham	Joseph	IND	11.9.81	166/66	400H	49.51	50.22- 06
Abrantes	Arnaldo	POR	27.11.86	176/70	200	20.48	21.20- 06
^ Aburaya	Shigeru	JPN	8.2.77	163/51	Mar	2:10:30	2:07:52- 01
Abyu	Tomas	GBR	5.5.78	/57	Mar	2:10:37	2:15:12- 05
* Adams	Luke	AUS	22.10.76	189/70	20kW	1:20:30	1:19:19- 05
					50kW	3:53:19	4:04:03- 02
Adams	Lyukman	RUS-J	12.6.88		TJ	16.75	15.97- 05
Adar	Jimmy	UGA	1.11.87	186/62	800	1:46.5A	1:47.4A- 06
Addy	Jangy	USA	2.3.85	190/93	Dec	7808	6938- 04
Adilo	Kasine	ETH			Mar	2:10:20	2:12:02- 05
Adimasu	Mesfin	ETH	5.3.85		Mar	2:09:49	2:10:45- 06
Adu-Bobie	Richard	CAN	12.1.85	183/77	100	10.29, 10.20w	10.28- 04
Ageyev	Yevgeniy	RUS-J	22.4.88		PV	5.50	5.20- 06
Aggoune	Khoudir	ALG	5.1.81	175/66	1500	3:38.15	3:38.58- 06
					5000	13:15.79	13:10.16- 06
Aguayo	Aaron	USA	27.7.84	180/64	3kSt	8:20.34	8:35.04- 06
Aish	Michael	NZL	24.7.76	175/60	10,000	27:46.37	27:53.28- 04
Akashi	Ken	JPN	6.11.76	169/59	20kW	1:23:06	1:24:25- 03
					50kW	3:55:55	3:54:11- 03
Akins	Tyrone	USA	6.1.86	180/79	110H	13.42	13.77- 06
* Akkas	Halil	TUR	1.7.83	175/60	2000	5:01.29	5:05.85i- 06
					3000	7:45.74i	7:51.62i- 06, 7:54.60- 05
					3kSt	8:18.43	8:22.00- 00
Alainis	Karlis	LAT	18.6.85	177/76	JT	77.04	77.03- 06
Al-Amri	Ali Ahmed	KSA	28.12.87	186/70	3kSt	8:23.61	8:21.87- 06
* Al-Azimi	Mohamed	KUW	16.6.82	176/70	800	1:44.55	1:44.13- 06
Albert	Lars	GER	9.2.82	197/93	Dec	7912	7920- 05
Al-Dawoodi	Ali Saadoun	QAT	29.6.84	169/54	10,000	28:04.74	29:05.93- 05
					HMar	60:39	63:47- 00
Al-Dawoodi	Sultan M.	KSA	16.6.77	180/110	DT	63.07	64.55- 06
Al-Dosari	Rashid	QAT	8.5.81	197/123	DT	64.20	64.43- 02
* Alekna	Virgilijus	LTU	13.2.72	200/130	DT	71.56	73.88- 00
Aleksejev	Marko	EST	14.2.79	196/80	HJ	2.23i	2.28- 05
Alekseyev	Denis	RUS	26.12.87	185/73	400	45.69	48.31- 04
Alekseyev	Igor	RUS	7.4.83		PV	5.50	5.65- 03
Alekseyev	Stanislav	RUS	10.2.82		DT	65.39	63.81- 06
Alemu	Gezahegn	ETH	.85		800	1:46.5A	1:46.5- 02
Alerte	David	FRA	18.9.84	192/83	200	20.33	20.37- 06
Alex	Sammy	KEN-J	1.6.89	177/58	5000	13:13.18	
					10,000	27:12.42	
Al-Haddad	Salah Abdelaziz	KUW	7.4.86		LJ	8.05w	7.88- 06
Al-Hebshi	Sultan Abdulmajid	KSA	23.2.83	180/103	SP	20.61	20.42- 06
Al-Housaoui	Idriss Abdulaziz	KSA	5.1.84		400H	50.25	51.28- 06
* Ali	Belal Mansoor	BRN	17.10.83	170/61	800	1:44.02	1:44.34- 05
					1000	2:15.23	2:21.45i- 06
					1500	3:31.49	3:33.86- 05
					1M	3:52.35	3:56.18- 06
Alic	Hamza	BIH	20.1.79	192/108	SP	20.09	20.09- 06
^ Aliu	Deji	NGR	22.11.75	187/75	100	10.22	9.95- 03, 9.9- 96
* Al-Khuwalidi	Mohamed Salim	KSA	19.6.81	188/82	LJ	8.25	8.48- 06
^ Allen	Charles	CAN	29.3.77	175/72	110H	13.66, 13.58w	13.23- 04
Allen	Joe	USA	7.7.78	195/89	LJ	8.04A, 8.03	8.06- 04
Alleyne	Richard	GBR	7.5.83	183/80	110H	13.71	14.00- 83
Allmond	Tony	USA	8.10.82	193/75	LJ	8.17	8.10, 8.35w- 04
Al-Mannai	Rashid	QAT-J	18.7.88	187/75	HJ	2.24i	2.10- 05

	Name		Nat	Born	Ht/Wt	Event	2007 Mark	Pre-2007 Best
	Almgren	Daniel	SWE	30.11.79		Dec	7592	7404- 06
	Alozídis	Minás	GRE	7.7.84	185/72	400H	49.16	49.31- 06
	Alozie	Anthony	NGR	18.8.86	168/66	100	10.24, 10.15w	10.39- 06
^	Al-Sabee	Hussein	KSA	14.11.79	187/85	LJ	8.10	8.35, 8.41w- 04
*	Al-Salhi	Mohammed	KSA	11.5.86	183/72	800	1:44.88	1:43.99- 06
	Al-Shahabi	Mohamed Youssef	BRN-J	26.7.89		TJ	16.49	16.42- 06
	Al-Suwaidi	Khaled Habash	QAT	10.10.84	188/105	SP	19.56	20.54- 05
	Al-Thawadi	Mohammed	QAT	18.11.81	178/70	110H	13.60, 13.55w, 13.59dt	13.89- 06
	Alves	Francisco Javier	ESP	3.9.80	170/53	3000	7:46.26	7:46.59i, 7:49.57- 06
	Al-Zankawi	Ali Mohamed	KUW	27.2.84	183/95	HT	77.14 solo, 77.07	76.97- 06
	Anani	Mohsen	EGY	25.5.85	187/117	HT	76.00	75.31- 05
	Anceschi	Stefano	ITA	18.6.84	193/84	200	20.3	20.86- 06
*	Anderson	Marvin	JAM	12.5.82	175/69	100	10.15, 10.03w	10.24- 03, 10.1w- 00
						200	20.06	20.65- 06, 20.36w- 05
	Andersson	Anton	SWE	12.3.81	195/90	TJ	17.10	16.49- 02
*	Andronov	Yuriy	RUS	6.11.71	180/68	50kW	3:42:55	3:42:06- 02
	Andureu	Charles	FRA	13.2.85	183/78	PV	5.50	5.70- 05
	Anghel	Marius-Alin	ROM	13.5.86		TJ	16.45	16.11i- 05, 15.70- 06
^	Angwenyi	Elkanah	KEN	5.2.83	176/62	1500	3:37.23	3:31.97- 06
^	Anlezark	Justin	AUS	14.8.77	188/130	SP	19.76	20.96- 03
^	Annus	Adrián	HUN	28.6.73	194/115	HT	77.18	84.19- 03
	Anskins	Andis	LAT	25.1.79	183/82	JT	76.58	81.80- 05
	Antmanis	Vladimir	RUS	12.3.84		400H	49.74	50.54- 06
*	Apak	Esref	TUR	3.1.82	186/100	HT	80.31	81.45- 05
	Arabatzís	Spirídon	GRE	2.6.78	188/105	DT	61.93	60.55- 04
	Arai	Ken	JPN	22.12.81	172/72	JT	75.67	75.06- 05
	Arai	Tomoyuki	JPN	14.6.81	173/64	100	10.12w	10.32- 06
	Arakawa	Daisuke	JPN	19.9.81	179/73	LJ	7.90	8.06- 02
	de Araújo	Luis Alberto	BRA	27.9.87		Dec	7628w, 7502	7386- 06
	de Araújo	Rodrigo	BRA	12.11.79		LJ	8.02	8.08- 04, 8.16w- 05
	Aritkulov	Ramil	RUS	1.3.78	178/67	800	1:46.86	1:45.28- 04
*	Armstrong	Dylan	CAN	15.1.81	190/125	SP	20.72	20.62- 06
*	Arnold	Dominique	USA	14.9.73	185/88	110H	13.17	12.90- 06
	Arnold	Jake	USA	3.1.84	191/91	Dec	8215	7870- 06
	Arrhenius	Niklas	SWE	9.9.82	194/120	DT	65.77	63.62- 04
*	Arvidsson	Magnus	SWE	20.2.83	191/100	JT	85.75	81.75- 06
	Asahara	Nobuharu	JPN	21.6.72	179/73	100	10.14	10.02- 01
	Asmerom	Bolota	USA	12.10.78	178/62	3000	7:45.84	7:48.59i- 04, 7:51.93- 02
						5000	13:15.16	13:26.80- 02
	Asmeron	Yared	ERI	3.2.79		HMar	60:28	62:44- 05
	Assefa	Girma	ETH	20.2.86	165/45	5000	13:16.87	13:24.62- 06
	10,000	27:43.67		27:44.12- 05		HMar	61:31	61:21- 06
	Assefa	Raji	ETH	18.2.86	166/50	10,000	27:15.68	27:42.97- 06
						HMar	60:31	61:47A- 05
	Assefa	Tesfaye	ETH	20.12.83		10,000	27:59.32	
	Atanasov	Nikolay	BUL	11.12.74	188/72	LJ	8.16	8.31- 03
*	Atkins	Derrick	BAH	5.1.84	185/84	100	9.91, 9.83w	10.08, 10.03w- 06
						200	20.50, 20.48w	20.69- 06
	Augustyn	Rafal	POL	14.5.84	178/71	20kW	1:22:08	1:21:36- 05
	Austin	Dan	USA	12.4.83	198/109	DT	60.48	63.40- 06
*	Averbukh	Aleksandr	ISR	1.10.74	178/76	PV	5.81	5.93- 03
	Avramenko	Roman	UKR-J	23.3.88	184/84	JT	77.88	76.01- 06
	Aydamirov	Yevgeniy	RUS	18.6.87	183/90	HT	74.18	71.01- 06
	Ayemi	Yemi	NGR	10.10.86	186/100	DT	61.12	56.50- 06
	Ayre	Sanjay	JAM	19.6.80	188/75	400	44.98	44.92- 02
	Azarenkov	Andrey	RUS	26.9.85	191/98	HT	75.12	72.89- 05
	Azcuy	Yosley	CUB	5.12.81	182/81	Dec	7695 h	7570- 06
*	Baala	Mehdi	FRA	17.8.78	183/65	1000	2:17.73	2:13.96- 03
	1500	3:31.01		3:28.98- 03		2000	4:56.56	4:53.12- 05
	Baaru Gitia	Philemon	KEN	20.5.81		HMar	61:52	61:25sc- 06
	Baba	Youssef	MAR	7.8.79	173/55	1500	3:32.13	3:33.01- 04
*	Bába	Jaroslav	CZE	2.9.84	196/82	HJ	2.29	2.37i, 2.36- 05
	Baday	Ahmed Ibrahim	MAR	12.1.79	174/60	3000	7:34.94	7:42.55- 06
						5000	13:03.82	13:09.46- 06
*	Baddeley	Andrew	GBR	20.6.82	186/70	800	1:46.32	1:46.62- 06
	1000	2:16.99		2:21:20- 04		1500	3:34.74	3:36.43- 05
						1M	3:51.95	3:56.13- 04
	Badji	Ndiss Kaba	SEN	21.9.83	192/79	LJ	8.11	8.20A, 8.03, 8.30Aw- 04
						TJ	16.80	16.30- 02, 17.15dq- 05
	Bai Xuejin		CHN	6.6.87	176/63	50kW	4:03:51	3:54:41- 05

Name		Nat	Born	Ht/Wt	Event	2007 Mark	Pre-2007 Best
Bailey	Daniel	ANT	9.9.86	178/77	100	10.25	10.19- 04
Bairu	Simon	CAN	8.8.83	173/57	5000	13:25.91	13:36.28- 06
					10,000	27:50.71	28:04.75- 05
Bakhet	Mohamed Abdu	QAT	25.12.87	165/62	HMar	61:38	
Bakhtache	Abdelkader	FRA	30.1.82	170/58	1500	3:38.24	3:38.90- 06
* Bakulin	Sergey	RUS	13.11.86	175/62	20kW	1:19:14	1:19:54- 06
Balch	Gareth	GBR	18.5.83	193/77	800	1:46.75	1:48.54- 05
Balliengo	Jorge	ARG	5.1.78	194/110	DT	62.43	66.32- 06
Balner	Michal	CZE	12.9.82		PV	5.60	5.45- 06
Banda	Lewis	ZIM	16.8.82	176/67	400	45.47	44.58- 04
Banı́ótis	Konstadinos	GRE	6.11.86	202/80	HJ	2.23	2.17- 06
Bannister	Jarrod	AUS	3.10.84	190/98	JT	83.70	78.06- 06
Barberi	Andrea	ITA	15.1.79	178/64	400	45.74	45.19- 06
Bargas	Rodrigo	BRA	4.2.86	182/75	400	45.77A	46.46- 06
Barlís	Ioánnis	GRE	26.11.79	182/100	HT	74.88	73.82- 03
Barnett	Brian	CAN	10.2.87	185/84	100	10.24A	10.60- 05
					200	20.31	20.70- 06
* Barras	Romain	FRA	1.8.80	194/86	Dec	8298	8416w, 8406- 06
Barré	Julien	FRA	21.2.84	182/62	800	1:46.67	1:47.53- 06
Barrett	Carl	JAM	21.4.75	185/90	100	10.25	10.30, 10.22w, 10.0w- 06; 10.1- 04
Barrios	Eugenio	ESP	3.11.76	192/76	800	1:46.48	1:44.84- 06
Barrios	Juan Luis	MEX	24.6.83	174/60	1500	3:37.71	3:39.28- 04
3000	7:42.86		7:37.64- 06		5000	13:11.37	13:27.89- 06
Barry	Trevor	BAH	14.6.83	190/77	HJ	2.26	2.23i- 06, 2.20- 05
* Bartels	Ralf	GER	21.2.78	186/128	SP	20.75	21.43i- 06, 21.36- 05
Bartha	Levente-Andrei	ROM	8.3.77	186/78	JT	77.16	78.66- 04
Barus	Benson	KEN	4.7.80		HMar	60:18	60:17- 06
					Mar	2:09:04	2:08:34- 06
Bashir	Daham Najim	QAT	8.11.79	171/60	1500	3:37.79	3:31.04- 05
					3kSt	8:32.29	8:32.48- 04
Batangdon	Joseph	CMR	29.7.78	180/75	200	20.4	20.31A, 20.3- 99, 20.31- 00
Bátovsky	Milos	SVK	26.5.79	178/65	50kW	3:54:10	3:54:08- 04
Battle	Sheldon	USA	23.6.83	188/120	SP	20.24i, 20.23	20.94- 05
Bauschinger	René	GER	12.6.85	180/67	800	1:46.89	1:47.04- 06
* Beckford	James	JAM	9.1.75	183/73	LJ	8.37	8.62- 97, 8.68w- 95
* Behrenbruch	Pascal	GER	19.1.85	196/96	Dec	8239	8209- 06
* Bekele	Kenenisa	ETH	13.6.82	160/54	1500	3:32.35	3:33.08- 06
1M	3:56.2+i		4:01.57i- 06		2000	4:58.98+,4:49.99i	5:00.32i- 04, 5:00.76+- 05
3000	7:25.79		7:30.67- 01		2M	8:13.51	8:05.12i- 06
5000	12:49.53		12:37.35- 04		10,000	26:46.19	26:17.53- 05
* Bekele	Tariku	ETH	21.1.87	165/52	3000	7:42.35	7:29.11- 06
2M	8:04.83		8:13.32i- 06		5000	13:01.60	12:53.81- 06
Belabbas	Mohamed-Khaled	FRA	4.7.81	178/65	3kSt	8:30.05	8:22.42- 06
* Bell	Kenta	USA	16.3.77	183/77	TJ	17.26	17.63- 02
Bellaabous	Fadil	FRA	15.6.86	184/69	400H	49.17	50.74- 05
* Bellani	Hicham	MAR	15.9.79	180/64	1500	3:33.71	
2000	4:59.9+				3000	7:37.93	7:33.71- 06
^ Belov	Yuriy	BLR	20.3.81	183/120	SP	20.47	21.14- 03
Belt	Tone	USA	10.2.87	190/80	LJ	7.97i, 7.85w	7.95- 06
^ Benjamin	Tim	GBR	2.5.82	183/75	400	45.28	44.56- 05
Bennett	LaRon	USA	25.11.82	183/75	400H	48.76	48.74- 05
Bensghir	Yassine	MAR	3.1.83	170/68	800	1:45.90	1:45.89- 05
1000	2:16.27				1500	3:33.04	3:35.04- 05
Berdeja	Cristian D.	MEX	21.6.81	169/58	20kW	1:23:43A	1:19:22- 05
Berger	Dominic	USA	19.5.86	181/79	110H	13.68, 13.54w	13.49- 06
Berger	Maik	GER	17.2.79	190/74	50kW	3:54:24	3:57:39- 04
Bergstedt	Sean	USA	4.5.85	183/73	400H	50.18	50.92- 06
Berhanu	Yirefu	ETH	1.1.86		Mar	2:09:01	2:16:17- 06
Bermejo	Javier	ESP	23.12.78	190/77	HJ	2.27	2.28- 04
Bernard	Martyn	GBR	15.12.84	196/83	HJ	2.30i, 2.29	2.27- 04
Berrabah	Yahya	MAR	13.10.81	186.75	LJ	8.04	8.33- 03
^ Berrett	Tim	CAN	23.1.65	179/66	50kW	3:55:08	3:50:21- 04
Berrian	Chris	USA	17.4.83	173/70	200	20.49	20.31- 06
Bertocchi	Masimo	CAN	27.9.85	195/85	Dec	7704	7147- 06
Best	Jahvid	USA-J	30.1.89	181/83	200	20.65	21.03- 06
Best	Shawn	USA	4.9.84	193/143	SP	19.36i	18.54- 05
* Betanzos	Yoandri	CUB	15.2.82	179/71	TJ	17.12i, 16.96, 17.21w	17.63, 17.67w- 06
^ Bett	Mark	KEN	22.12.76	180/64	3000	7:42.88+	7:36.66- 01
					5000	13:17.45	12:55.63- 00
Betters	LeJerald	USA-J	6.2.88	190/79	400	45.33	46.42- 05
Bettinelli	Andrea	ITA	6.10.78	194/82	HJ	2.30	2.31- 03

Name		Nat	Born	Ht/Wt	Event	2007 Mark	Pre-2007 Best
Beyens	Kristof	BEL	13.7.83	189/70	200	20.44	20.45- 05
Beyer	Jamie	USA	29.12.76	193/113	SP	19.33	21.13- 05
Biama	William	KEN	.85		Mar	2:09:53	-0-
Bíber	Zsolt	HUN	31.5.76	194/104	SP	19.56	20.81i, 20.55- 04
Bicet	Noleisis	CUB	6.2.81	193/103	HT	72.72	73.90- 06
Biche	Sébastien	FRA	1.2.73	173/57	50kW	3:58:16	
Bieniek	Michal	POL	17.5.84	197/73	HJ	2.30	2.36- 05
Bilek	Roman	CZE	29.9.67	174/61	50kW	3:59:22	3:56:03- 94
* Bilonog	Yuriy	UKR	9.3.74	200/135	SP	20.20	21.81- 03
					DT	60.10	65.53- 03
Bingham	Michael	USA	13.4.86	186/79	400	45.57	46.13- 06
Birech	Joseph Kiptoo	KEN	4.1.84		10,000	28:09.4A	
Birgen	John	KEN	8.5.74		Mar	2:09:20	2:09:08- 03
Birmingham	Collis	AUS	27.12.84	183/66	3000	7:46.01	8:16.81- 04
Bispo	Rogerio	BRA	16.11.85	180/75	LJ	8.17	8.21, 8.32Aw- 06
Biwott	Paul	KEN	18.4.78		Mar	2:09:56	2:08:17- 05
Biwott	Phillip Kiplagat	KEN	.77		Mar	2:10:27	2:14:29- 06
* Biwott	Yusuf	KEN	12.11.86	175/64	1500	3:35.09	3:34.04- 06
2000	4:59.48i		5:01.1+- 06		3000	7:33.39	7:34.40- 06
					5000	12:58.49	13:08.13- 06
^ Blackwood	Michael	JAM	29.8.76	190/79	400	45.05	44.60- 02
Blake	Yohan	JAM-J	26.12.89	178/70	100	10.11	10.33- 06
					200	20.62	20.92- 06
Blakely	Fernada	USA	28.9.81	185/79	400	45.24	45.25- 05
Blanco	José Luis	ESP	3.6.75	175/61	3kSt	8:22.47	8:12.86- 06
Blank	Peter	GER	10.4.62	194/93	JT	77.15	88.70- 01
Blanton	DaBryan	USA	3.7.84	179/74	100	10.12, 10.02w	10.07- 03
* Blaschek	Thomas	GER	5.4.81	189/83	110H	13.33	13.31- 05, 13.27w- 06
Bledman	Keston	TRI-J	8.3.88	183/75	100	10.14, 10.05w	10.32- 06
Blincoe	Adrian	NZL	4.11.79	181/61	1500	3:38.66	3:35.50- 05
					5000	13:17.28	13:21.73- 06
* Blom	Rens	NED	1.3.77	178/75	PV	5.60	5.81- 04
Blount	Elliot	USA	25.6.79	180/67	800	1:46.22	1:46.76- 04
Bo Xiangdong		CHN	1.10.87	180/66	20kW	1:23:45.76	1:23:54- 06
Bock	Detlef	GER	15.8.74	194/130	SP	19.76i, 18.93	20.72- 05
Bogdan	Mircea-Florin	ROM	6.5.82	184360	3kSt	8:23.12	8:27.29- 05
Bogdanov	Dmitriy	RUS	11.4.79	190/75	800	1:44.94	1:44.33- 06
Boit	Josphat	KEN	26.11.83	170/57	3000	7:43.30	7:45.72- 00
					10,000	27:47.57	28:07.27- 05
Bolden	Gregory	USA	30.6.84	175/75	100	10.21, 10.20w	10.24- 06, 10.15w- 05
* Bolt	Usain	JAM	21.8.86	196/88	100	10.03	
200	19.75		19.88- 06		400	45.28	45.35- 03
Boltenkov	Anton	RUS	29.6.85		TJ	16.63	15.98- 04
Bondarenko	Bohdan	UKR-J	30.8.89	195/72	HJ	2.25i	2.26- 06
Boni	Michele	ITA	2.4.81	194/86	TJ	16.61	16.06- 02
Bookout	Kevin	USA	12.2.83	203/118	SP	19.57	19.18- 06
* Borchin	Valeriy	RUS	3.7.86	178/63	20kW	1:18:56	1:20:00- 06
* Börgeling	Lars	GER	16.4.79	189/86	PV	5.75i, 5.71	5.85- 02
Borges	Lázaro	CUB	19.6.86	185/85	PV	5.50	5.30- 06
^ Borichevskiy	Aleksandr	RUS	25.6.70	194/120	DT	63.18	65.08- 99
Borisov	Yevgeniy	RUS	7.3.84	184/71	110H	13.56, 13.4	13.69, 13.67w- 06
Borodkin	Andriy	UKR	18.4.78	202/135	SP	19.78	20.38- 04
Boruschewski	Benjamin	GER	23.4.80	190/130	HT	74.47	72.73- 02
* Borzakovskiy	Yuriy	RUS	12.4.81	182/72	800	1:44.38	1:42.47- 01
^ Boswell	Mark	CAN	28.7.77	189/77	HJ	2.27i	2.35- 99
Boué	Annier	CUB	3.4.84	192/90	JT	80.53	76.26- 05
Bougtaïb	Tareq	MAR	30.4.81	180/75	LJ	7.84, 8.35w	8.21- 04
					TJ	17.37	17.06, 17.25w- 06
* Boukensa	Tarek	ALG	19.11.81	178/62	800	1:46.25	1:46.10- 06
1500	3:30.92		3:31.58- 06		2000	4:57.20	5:03.00i- 06
					1M	3:56.37	3:49.95- 05
Boulahfane	Kamel	ALG	1.7.76	178/63	1500	3:34.62	3:32.44- 04
Boulanger	David	FRA	11.12.74	176/64	50kW	3:51:48	3:51:36- 01
Bouramdane	Abderrahim	MAR	1.1.78		Mar	2:08:20	2:10:41- 06
Bourguignon	Rudy	FRA	16.7.79	185/82	Dec	7775	8025- 05
Bourifa	Migidio	ITA	31.1.69	171/55	Mar	2:10:30	2:09:07- 02
Bowen	Francis	KEN	12.10.73		HMar	61:13	62:58- 05
					Mar	2:10:41	2:10:49- 06
Bown	Darren	AUS	30.6.74	178/63	50kW	4:04:06	3:55:05- 01
^ Bownes	Shaun	RSA	24.10.70	194/90	110H	13.39A, 13.62	13.26- 01, 13.2A- 98

Name		Nat	Born	Ht/Wt	Event	2007 Mark	Pre-2007 Best
Boyles	Chris	USA	2.5.80	188/93	Dec	7804	7855- 06
* Bramlett	Ron	USA	22.10.79	181/68	110H	13.28	13.26- 04
Brathwaite	Ryan	BAH-J	6.6.88	186/75	110H	13.61	13.78- 06
Brenes	Nery	CRC	25.9.85	174/62	400	45.01	46.42- 05
Brew	Derrick	USA	28.12.77	185/82	400	45.02	44.29- 99
Brigg	Kane	AUS-J	14.1.88	185/78	HJ	2.24	2.21- 06
Brooks	Tom	USA	10.1.78	188/70	3kSt	8:27.34	8:28.24- 06
* Brown	Chris	BAH	15.10.78	178/68	400	44.45	44.48- 05
* Brown	Darrel	TRI	11.10.84	179/85	100	10.02, 9.88w	9.99- 05
					200	20.51	20.41- 01
Brown	Joel	USA	31.1.80	180/75	110H	13.31	13.22- 05
Brown	Russell	USA	3.3.85	182/70	1500	3:37.56	3:41.72- 05
Brown	Ryan	USA	17.9.84	175/64	800	1:46.71	1:46.29- 06
Brown	Xavier	JAM	21.2.83	187/86	200	20.2	20.50- 06
Browne	Dan	USA	24.6.75	178/67	10,000	28:10.73	27:42.19- 04
Bruce	Benjamin	USA	10.9.82	185/68	3kSt	8:32.74	8:32.68- 06
* Brugnetti	Ivano	ITA	1.9.76	175/62	20kW	1:19:36	1:19:40- 04
Brunson	Andrew	USA	4.4.86	185/77	110H	13.81, 13.63w	13.79, 13.70w- 06
Bryant	Noah	USA	11.5.84	185/120	SP	20.56	19.67- 06
Brzozowski	Artur	POL	29.3.85	172/65	50kW	3:59:27	4:18:25- 05
Buc	Bostjan	SLO	13.4.80	178/60	3kSt	8:26.42	8:16.96- 03
Bucki	Gaëtan	FRA	9.5.80	195/135	SP	20.01i, 19.43	19.86- 06
Buckley	Markino	JAM	16.4.86	191/79	400H	49.24	52.03- 04
Budza	Sergiy	UKR	6.12.84	180/72	50kW	4:02:02	3:59:31- 05
Bukhalov	Spas	BUL	14.11.80	186/85	PV	5.82	5.76i, 5.71- 06
Buller	Russ	USA	10.9.78	178/72	PV	5.73	5.81- 01
Bungei	Julius	KEN	16.6.84	173/58	400H	49.34	49.56- 04
* Bungei	Wilfred	KEN	24.7.80	172/60	800	1:44.14	1:42.34- 02
* Burayev	Viktor	RUS	23.8.82	176/58	20kW	1:19:57	1:18:06- 01
* Burgess	Paul	AUS	14.8.79	184/83	PV	5.91	6.00- 05
Burghagen	Franz	GER-J	16.3.89	186/88	JT	75.75	73.41- 06
* Burkenya	Danil	RUS	20.7.78	198/86	TJ	17.48	17.68- 04
* Burns	Marc	TRI	7.1.83	183/91	100	10.15, 10.06w	9.96- 05
* Busendich	Solomon	KEN	10.1.84	165/58	HMar	60:13	60:14- 06
Buzard	Aaron	USA	11.10.84	194/80	400	45.80	45.51- 06
Byers	Tyson	USA	18.5.83	186/82	PV	5.50i	5.40- 05
Cadée	Erik	NED	15.2.84	200/110	DT	62.68	61.51- 06
Cafagna	Diego	ITA	9.7.75	173/57	50kW	3:55:21	3:55:18- 05
Caines	Cliff	CAN	18.1.79		Dec	7640	7453- 06
Callander	Emmanuel	TRI	10.5.84	182/73	100	10.29, 10.18w	10.45- 06
Cambil	José Alejandro	ESP	26.1.75	176/66	50kW	3:56:16	3:51:32- 06
Camejo	Ibrahin	CUB	28.6.82	180/79	LJ	7.96w	8.34, 8.35w- 06
^ Camossi	Paolo	ITA	6.1.74	176/72	TJ	16.68i, 16.56	17.45- 00
Campbell	Clement	JAM	19.2.75	184/82	100	10.02, 9.92w	10.12- 06
					200	20.29	20.54- 06
Campbell	Dave	IRL	28.1.82	182/67	800	1:46.05	1:46.99- 06
^ Campbell	Milton	USA	15.5.76	178/75	400	45.48	44.67- 97
Campeny	Moisés	ESP	27.5.79	190/100	HT	71.01	75.42- 03
Campioli	Filippo	ITA	21.2.82	191/79	HJ	2.27	2.25- 06
* Cantwell	Christian	USA	30.9.80	198/145	SP	21.96	22.54- 04
Carabelli	Gianni	ITA	30.5.79	187/69	400H	49.11	48.84- 05
Cardoso	Augusto	POR	13.12.70	176/65	50kW	3:55:14	4:03:16- 06
Carelse	Ramsey	RSA	30.10.85	181/73	HJ	2.23	2.30- 05
Carne	Ben	GBR	11.6.86	181/79	400H	50.28	52.15- 06
Carney	James	USA	24.5.78	178/58	10,000	27:43.64	28:31.16- 04
Carriqueo	Javier	ARG	29.5.79	175/60	1500	3:38.62	3:42.01- 04
* Carter	James	USA	7.5.78	186/77	400H	47.72	47.43- 05
Carter	Matthew	USA	21.11.85	188/73	HJ	2.23	2.15- 04
Carter	Nesta	JAM	10.10.85	178/70	100	10.11	10.20- 06, 10.0- 04,
Carter	Randal	USA-J	7.4.89	183/84	HJ	2.23	2.19- 06
* Carter	Xavier	USA	8.12.85	191/89	200	19.92	19.63- 06
					400	45.26	44.53- 06
* Casado	Arturo	ESP	26.1.83	187/71	800	1:46.98	1:47.41- 06
1500	3:34.09		3:35.45- 06		1M	3:52.38	0
Casañas	Frank	CUB/ESP	18.10.78	184/101	DT	64.68	67.14- 06
Casquette	Arnaud	MRI	16.4.78	175/70	LJ	8.10	8.13A, 8.23w- 03; 8.12, 8.28Aw- 05
Castelo Branco	Thiago	BRA	6.11.79		110H	13.64	13.69- 05
Caulfield	John	USA	22.8.84	183/132	SP	19.23	19.91i, 18.88- 04
Cavallaro	Alessandro	ITA	22.2.80	170/60	200	20.56	20.42- 03
Celik	Recep	TUR	10.8.83	175/65	20kW	1:22:53	1:22:36- 06
Cepeda	Raven	USA	26.6.86	190/90	Dec	7838	7371- 06

	Name		Nat	Born	Ht/Wt	Event	2007 Mark	Pre-2007 Best
	Cerlati	Mattias	FRA	25.10.83	191/84	Dec	7912	7550- 05
	Cerra	Juan Ignacio	ARG	16.10.76	180/95	HT	73.65	76.42- 01
	Chabowski	Marcin	POL	28.5.86	170/50	3kSt	8:32.55	8:30.40- 05
	Chakouian ¶	Jeff	USA	20.4.82	183/118	SP	20.29	20.68- 06
*	Chambers	Ricardo	JAM	7.10.84	177/73	400	44.62	44.71- 06
	Chamney	Thomas	IRL	16.4.84	190/78	800	1:46.46	1:46.82- 06
	Chang Ming-Huang		TPE	7.8.82	194/130	SP	20.20	19.45- 06
	Chao Chih-Chien		TPE	30.9.83	170/65	LJ	7.95	7.71- 05
*	Charfreitag	Libor	SVK	11.9.77	191/117	HT	81.60	81.81- 03
	Chatbi	Jamel	MAR	30.4.84		3kSt	8:29.13	8:32.73- 06
	Chebet	Wilson	KEN	12.7.85		HMar	60:13	62:19- 05
*	Chebii	Abraham	KEN	23.12.79	172/63	3000	7:36.74	7:33.42- 06
						5000	12:59.63	12:52.99- 03
	Cheboiywo	Boaz	KEN	2.8.78	160/54	3000	7:45.76	7:35.65i- 06, 7:39.04- 05
						5000	13:20.72	13:19.56- 05
	Chebor	William Chebon	KEN	22.12.82		HMar	60:51	61:07- 06
*	Chéhibi	Mouhcine	MAR	28.1.78	182/70	800	1:45.32	1:44.16- 06
	Chelanga	Abraham	KEN	.84		Mar	2:10:15	
*	Chelanga	Joshua	KEN	7.4.73	168/56	Mar	2:08:14	2:07:05- 04
	Chelimo	Elijah	KEN	.87		3kSt	8:16.28	8:28.62- 05
	Chelimo	Nicholas	KEN			Mar	2:09:42	2:17:38- 06
	Chelimo	Stephen	KEN	9.8.85		HMar	61:03	
	Chemlal	Abdellatif	MAR	11.1.82	170/60	3kSt	8:17.71	8:21.00- 02
	Chemov	Andrey	RUS	13.7.83		PV	5.60	5.55- 06
	Chemweno	David	KEN	18.12.81	175/58	3kSt	8:20.57	8:09.09- 05
	Chen Jinsen		CHN	16.10.85	185/70	TJ	16.61	16.34- 06
	Chen Qi		CHN	10.3.82	186/75	JT	78.07	81.38- 04
	Chen Zhong		CHN-J	1.6.88	168/53	20kW	1:23:28	1:26:13- 06
	Chenonge	Hillary	KEN	30.5.85	172/57	5000	13:24.88	13:04.70- 05
						10,000	27:51.92	28:25.22- 06
*	Chepkirwok	Abraham	UGA-J	18.11.88	176/62	800	1:44.78	1:45.0 - 06
	Chérif	Abdoulaye Issa	SEN	22.10.84		400H	50.0 (49.97?)	50.73- 06
*	Cherkos Feleke	Abreham	ETH-J	23.9.89	158/52	5000	13:05.83	12:54.19- 06
	Chernov	Sergey	BLR	5.2.79	178/70	20kW	1:21:02	1:20:11- 06
	Cheruiyot	David	KEN	5.5.81		Mar	2:10:36	2:12:02- 06
*	Cheruiyot	Evans	KEN	5.10.82		HMar	59:05	59:29- 06
						Mar	2:09:16	
	Cheruiyot	Jonas	KEN	11.1.84	172/62	3000	7:34.37	
	2M	8:16.77				5000	13:07.30	12:59.08- 06
*	Cheruiyot	Robert K.	KEN	26.9.78	186/	HMar	60:38	59:21- 05
	Chesnokov	Yuriy	RUS	12.12.79	177/61	50kW	3:58:46	3:58:42- 06
	Chiaraviglio	Germán	ARG	16.4.87	192/77	PV	5.65	5.71- 06
	Chiba	Yoshihiro	JPN	29.4.79	178/65	400H	49.92	48.65- 01
	Chicherov	Vladimir	RUS	2.4.85		TJ	16.73	16.05i, 16.04, 16.25w- 06
	Chimier	Jonathan	MRI	6.8.82	175/75	LJ	7.95	8.28- 04, 8.29Aw- 03
	Chinin	Carlos Eduardo	BRA	3.5.85	195/83	Dec	7977	7426- 05
^	Chirchir	William	KEN	6.2.79	172/55	1500	3:36.82	3:29.29- 01
	Chisam	Matt	USA	3.7.82		Dec	7603	7403- 06
^	Chistyakov	Viktor (ex AUS)	RUS	9.2.75	203/83	PV	5.80i, 5.65	5.90, 5.95ex- 99
	Chivás	Alexis	CUB	7.11.83	180/84	Dec	7685	7629w- 06, 7624- 05
	Chocho	Andrés	ECU	4.11.83		20kW	1:22:31	1:23:14- 05
	Choffart	Julien	FRA	5.11.78	186/79	Dec	7916	7607- 05
*	Choge	Augustine	KEN	21.1.87	162/53	1500	3:31.73	3:32.48- 06
	1M	3:51.62		4:02.25- 06		2000	4:56.30i	
						3000	7:33.09i	7:28.75- 05
	Chopa	Andrew	TAN			HMar	61:40	
	Christian	Brendan	ANT	11.12.83	178/70	100	10.16, 10.10w	10.11, 10.06w- 04, 9.9- 02
						200	20.23	20.29- 03, 20.1- 02, 20.19w- 04
*	Christopher	Tyler	CAN	3.10.83	188/84	400	44.47	44.44- 05
	Chu Yafei		CHN-J	5.9.88	170/59	20kW	1:22:11.67	
	Chyla	Lukasz	POL	31.3.81	187/87	100	10.24w	10.20- 04
^	Cilliers	Ockert	RSA	21.4.81	186/76	400H	49.22A, 49.36	48.02A, 48.23- 04
	Ciotti	Giulio	ITA	5.10.76	188/78	HJ	2.23i	2.31- 06
	Ciotti	Nicola	ITA	5.10.76	188/78	HJ	2.27	2.30i- 02, 2.30- 03
	Cisneros	Osmar	CUB-J	19.11.89	186/80	400	46,05, 44.8dt	48.95- 06
						400H	49.57	
	Claesson	Mattias	SWE	26.7.86	183/69	800	1:46.43	1:46.46- 06
	Clark	Ben	USA	25.11.80	178/77	400H	49.79	49.89- 06
	Clark	Charles	USA	10.8.87	178/74	200	20.38	20.92, 20.91w- 06
	Clarke	Lerone	JAM	2.10.81	174/66	100	10.15	10.24- 05, 10.12w- 04
*	Clavier	Jérôme	FRA	3.5.83	185/73	PV	5.70	5.65i- 04, 5.63- 05

Name		Nat	Born	Ht/Wt	Event	2007 Mark	Pre-2007 Best
* Clay	Bryan	USA	3.1.80	180/83	Dec	8493	8820- 04
* Clement	Kerron	USA	31.10.85	188/84	100	10.23	
					200	20.49	20.65- 06, 20.40i- 05
					400	44.48	44.71- 06, 44.57i- 05
					400H	47.61	47.24- 05
Coachman	Golden	USA	24.7.84	188/78	800	1:46.79	1:49.28- 06
Cole	Brendan	AUS	29.5.81	187/81	400H	49.72	49.36- 06
Collaku	Dorian	ALB	2.6.77	184/108	HT	75.20	75.78- 05
Collazo	William	CUB	31.8.86	174/72	400	45.29	45.50- 05
* Collins	Kim	SKN	5.4.76	175/64	100	10.14	9.98- 02, 9.92w- 03
Collio	Simone	ITA	27.12.79	180/74	100	10.14	10.20, 10.14w- 04
Compaoré	Benjamin	FRA	5.8.87	188/80	TJ	16.62	16.61- 06
Conrad	Martin	GER	8.1.86	192/70	800	1:46.88	1:47.31- 06
Conwell	Will	USA	12.9.82	196/111	DT	63.61	60.98- 06
Conwright	Kaaron	USA	8.8.76	175/73	100	10.24	10.05A, 10.10- 00
Coolsaet	Reid	CAN	29.7.79	175/60	5000	13:21.53	13:23.30- 05
					10,000	27:56.92	28:39.54- 05
Cooper	Jermaine	USA	31.8.80	178/77	110H	13.67	13.54- 02, 13.52w- 01
Copello	Alexis	CUB	12.8.85	185/80	TJ	16.87, 17.15w	17.38- 06
Copello	Yasmani	CUB	15.4.87	196/86	400H	49.99	52.30- 06
Copland	Esteban	VEN	12.10.79	179/62	LJ	7.93	7.97- 00, 8.18Aw- 01
Corchete	Luis Manuel	ESP	14.5.84	185/73	20kW	1:23:14	1:24:48- 06
Costa	Jorge	POR	20.3.61	170/65	50kW	3:57:44	3:55:31- 04
da Costa	Marcelo	BRA	1.5.81	180/72	TJ	16.51	16.68- 04
Costa	Vítor	POR	28.5.74	183/105	HT	72.34	76.86- 04
Costin	Jamie	IRL	1.6.77	179/72	50kW	3:53:30	3:53:58- 03
Cotto	Héctor	PUR	8.8.84	190/81	110H	13.72	13.78- 05, 13.67w- 06
Cousins	Duane	AUS	13.7.73	178/66	50kW	3:55:57	3:53:19- 06
Couto	Kurt	MOZ	14.5.85	180/67	400H	49.12	50.29- 06
Craddock	Kevin	USA	25.6.87	193/84	110H	13.48	13.73- 06
* Cragg	Alistair	IRL	13.6.80	183/59	1500	3:36.18	3:39.24- 03
					3000	7:32.49	7:38.59i, 7:38.96- 04
					5000	13:07.10	13:08.97- 06
					10,000	27:39.55	28:20.29- 03
* Crawford	Shawn	USA	14.1.78	181/86	100	10.13, 9.96w	9.88, 9.86w- 04
					200	20.21	19.79- 04
Cribari	Marco	SUI	7.7.85	183/74	200	20.54	20.98- 06
Cronje	Johan	RSA	13.4.82	180/65	1500	3:37.67	3:35.58- 05
Crowe	Scott	AUS	7.10.83		LJ	7.96	7.89- 06
Crowther	Robert	AUS	2.8.87	188/77	LJ	8.02, 8.15w	8.00- 06
Cuesta	Pedro José	ESP	22.8.83	187/108	DT	60.11	58.75- 06
Cui Lifu		CHN-J	18.12.88	180/63	TJ	16.73	16.58- 06
^ Cui Zhide		CHN	11.1.83	182/73	20kW	1:23:42.98t	1:17:53- 05
Cui Zhili		CHN	11.1.83	176/63	20kW	1:23:07	1:25:00- 06
Culpepper	Alan	USA	15.9.72	185/59	10,000	27:50.05	27:33.93- 01
Culson	Javier	PUR	25.7.84	175/67	400H	49.07	49.48- 06
Curry	Rafeeq	USA	19.8.83	183/68	TJ	16.94	16.75- 06
^ Czapiewski	Pawel	POL	30.3.78	178/57	800	1:45.91	1:43.22- 01
Czerwinski	Przemyslaw	POL	28.7.83	184/80	PV	5.71	5.80- 06
Czukor	Zoltán	HUN	18.12.62	186/74	50kW	4:03:37	3:50:02- 95
Daba	Bekana	ETH-J	29.7.88	170/55	5000	13:06.52	
Dabrowski	Daniel	POL	23.9.83	182/72	400	45.33	45.38- 06
Dæhlin	Ådne Svahn	NOR	26.6.82	188/73	800	1:46.86	1:46.05- 05
Daigo	Naoyuki	JPN	18.1.81	182/66	HJ	2.30	2.33- 06
Damião	Manuel	POR	4.7.78	174/62	1500	3:38.49	3:34.37- 04
Davaux	Hervé	FRA	22.8.78	166/50	50kW	4:01:48	4:09:16- 06
Davide	Kléberson	BRA	20.7.85	175/67	800	1:45.47	1:46.56- 06
Davies	Stephen	GBR	16.2.84	180/67	1500	3:38.50	3:39.62- 06
Davis	Marquis	USA	14.8.80	188/91	100	10.27, 10.20w	10.11- 00, 10.00w- 06
					200	20.75, 20.56w	20.27- 00, 20.15w- 03
* Davis	Walter	USA	2.7.79	188/83	LJ	8.24	8.36- 06
					TJ	17.35	17.73i, 17.71- 06
De Lepine	Eddy	FRA	30.3.84	175/65	200	20.51	20.62- 04
De Luca	Marco	ITA	12.5.81	189/72	50kW	3:47:04	3:48:08- 06
de Villiers	Pieter	RSA	13.7.82	179/75	400H	48.89	48.46- 05
De Zordo	Matthias	GER-J	21.2.88	188/90	JT	78.67	71.67- 06
* Deakes	Nathan	AUS	17.8.77	183/66	20kW	1:19:34	1:17:33- 05
					50kW	3:43:53	3:35:47- 06
Deghelt	Adrien	BEL	10.5.85	180/68	110H	13.57	14.11- 05
Delli Carri	Pellegrino	ITA	4.8.76	182/97	HT	72.06	71.99- 06
Demczyszak	Mateusz	POL	18.1.86	176/62	3kSt	8:30.81	8:46.73- 06
* Demidyuk	Sergiy	UKR	5.6.82	195/80	110H	13.22	13.37- 04

Name		Nat	Born	Ht/Wt	Event	2007 Mark	Pre-2007 Best
Demma Daba	Bikila	ETH-J	18.7.89		3000	7:42.63	b.87?
Demps	Jeff	USA-Y	8.1.90	178/82	100	10.25	10.43w- 06
Demyanyuk	Dmytro	UKR	30.6.83	195/68	HJ	2.32	2.26- 04
Denbo	Will	USA	24.2.84	178/118	SP	19.39	19.07- 06
Dennis	James	USA	25.2.76	196/122	DT	61.38	63.54- 00
Dent	Martin	AUS	8.2.79	180/69	3kSt	8:24.54	8:28.98- 06
Derby	Brian	USA	18.2.81	178/79	400H	49.75	49.72- 03
Derevyagin	Aleksandr	RUS	24.3.79	178/80	400H	49.11	49.50- 04
Derrickson	Charles	USA	17.7.87	188/77	110H	13.63	14.17- 06
Desmet	Pieter	BEL	7.6.83	177/57	3kSt	8:15.02	8:20.31- 05
Detmer	Joe	USA	3.9.83	180/73	Dec	7963w, 7616	7536- 06
Detsuk	Dmitriy	BLR	9.4.85	196/78	TJ	16.54	16.25- 04
* Devonish	Marlon	GBR	1.6.76	183/76	100	10.06	10.13- 98
					200	20.33	20.19, 20.18w- 02
* Devyatovskiy	Vadim	BLR	20.3.77	194/120	HT	82.94	84.90- 05
Dhouibi	Hamdhi	TUN	24.1.82	190/85	Dec	7838	8023- 05
Di Cecco	Alberico	ITA	19.4.74	174/62	Mar	2:10:40	2:08:02- 05
Diamadáras	Dimítrios	GRE	18.7.84	180/65	LJ	7.90	8.12- 05
Dias	Thiago	BRA	2.3.84	188/71	LJ	8.26	8.00- 06, 8.03w- 03
Dias Sabino	Jefferson	BRA	4.11.82	192/94	TJ	16.90	17.22- 06
Diaz	Mickaël	FRA	28.10.86	195/80	HJ	2.24i, 2.21	2.23i -05, 2.18- 06
Díaz	José Ignacio	ESP	22.11.79	173/63	20kW	1:21:57	1:21:48- 06
Díaz	Yunior	CUB	28.4.87	187/6-	Dec	7902	7343- 06
Dickens	David	USA	19.3.85	188/82	400	45.91	46.29- 05
Dilling	Jim	USA	23.4.85	198/86	HJ	2.30	2.29i, 2.21- 06
Dilys	Mantas	LTU	30.3.84	182/78	TJ	16.54i, 16.48	16.34- 05
* Diniz	Yohann	FRA	1.1.78	185/66	20kW	1:18:58	1:20:20- 05
					50kW	3:44:22	3:41:39- 06
Disi	Dieudonné	RWA	24.4.78	178/67	10,000	27:22.28	27:53.51- 05
					HMar	59:32	61:26- 06
* Dix	Walter	USA	31.1.86	175/80	100	9.93	10.06, 9.96w- 05
					200	19.69	20.18- 05
Dixon	Leroy	USA	20.6.83	176/72	100	10.07	10.19- 05
* Djhone	Leslie	FRA	18.3.81	187/76	400	44.46	44.64- 04
Dlomo	Norman	RSA	18.4.75	168/45	Mar	2:10:39	2:14:17- 06
^ Dmitrik	Aleksey	RUS	12.4.84	191/69	HJ	2.30	2.34i- 05, 2.30- 04
Dmytrenko	Ruslan	UKR	22.3.86	180/62	20kW	1:23:31	1:27:16- 06
Dobson	Ian	USA	6.2.82	188/68	5000	13:18.87	13:15.33- 05
Dodson	Jeremy	USA	30.8.87	180/73	200	20.64	20.70A- 05
Doi	Hiroaki	JPN	2.12.78	179/103	HT	74.08	73.33- 03
Dolphin	James	NZL	17.6.83	187/82	200	20.65	20.60- 05
* Donato	Fabrizio	ITA	14.8.76	189/82	LJ	8.02i, 7.89	8.00- 06
					TJ	16.97, 17.06w	17.60- 00
Dong Jimin		CHN	10.10.85	178/64	20kW	1:22:06	1:18:45- 06
D'Onofrio	Fortunato	ITA	12.2.81		20kW	1:23:37	1:25:34- 06
Dontás	Nikólaos	GRE	8.4.86	189/76	TJ	16.49	15.68- 06
^ Dorival	Dudley	HAI	1.9.75	185/77	110H	13.63, 13.61w	13.25- 01
Dossévi	Damiel	FRA	3.2.83	182/82	PV	5.60	5.75- 05
* Doucouré	Ladji	FRA	28.3.83	183/75	110H	13.27	12.97- 05
* Douglas	Nathan	GBR	4.12.82	183/71	TJ	17.47i, 17.18	17.64- 05
Doulal	Saïd	MAR	17.12.79		800	1:46.7	1:46.53- 07
Douvalídis	Konstadínos	GRE	10.3.87	183/73	110H	13.49	13.78- 05
* Drozdov	Aleksey	RUS	3.12.83	184/80	Dec	8475	8350- 06
du Toit	Tommie	RSA	17.8.82		JT	78.03A	76.82A- 06
DuBose	Jacoby	USA	11.12.82		110H	13.65	13.81, 13.74w- 06
Dudley	Eric	USA	18.4.80	190/80	400H	49.58	49.59- 03
Dudley	Jason	AUS	10.11.84	187/89	Dec	7729	8001- 06
Duncan	Corenelius	USA	9.5.86	173/68	400	45.83	47.08- 06
Dunford	Edward	GBR	15.9.84	185/84	Dec	7734	7175- 05
Dunkleberger	Jake	USA	6.10.84	186/118	HT	71.87	71.34- 06
Dunkley	Julien	JAM	20.12.75	186/83	100	10.18w, 10.10dt	10.09- 03
Durand	Nicolas	FRA	23.1.79	176/71	PV	5.50i, 5.60ex	5.50- 02
Durañona	Yordanis	CUB-J	16.6.88	188/75	TJ	16.89	16.30- 05, 16.53w?- 06
Durotoye	Adeyote	NGR	9.5.86		100	10.0	10.42- 06
Dutch	Johnny	USA-J	20.1.89	180/82	400H	50.07	52.06- 05
* Dvorák	Tomás	CZE	11.5.72	186/90	Dec	8020	8994- 99
Dyldin	Maksim	RUS	15.5.87	185/78	400	45.64	46.98- 06
Dzingai	Brian	ZIM	29.4.81	168/64	100	10.26, 10.03w	10.36- 05, 10.19w- 01
					200	20.28	20.12- 04
Eastler	Kevin	USA	14.10.77	190/72	20kW	1:22:56	1:22:25- 03

	Name		Nat	Born	Ht/Wt	Event	2007 Mark	Pre-2007 Best
*	Ebuya	Joseph	KEN	20.6.87	176/60	3000	7:34.66	7:36.78- 06
						2M	8:18.33	8:23.21- 05
						5000	12:51.00	12:58.03- 06
*	Ecker	Danny	GER	21.7.77	192/80	PV	5.87	6.00i- 01, 5.93- 98,
	Edgar	Tyrone	GBR	29.3.82	183/79	100	10.13	10.19- 06, 10.04w- 03
	Edwards	Alonso	PAN-J	8.12.89	175/66	200	20.62	21.18- 06
	Edwards	Mark	GBR	2.12.74	180/115	SP	19.88	19.72- 00
	Edwards	Monzavous Rae	USA	7.5.81	183/77	100	10.09	10.08, 9.99w- 05
	Efremov	Ilian	BUL	2.8.70	191/84	PV	5.70i	5.73i- 04, 5.70- 98, 5.75sq- 03
	El Abubakr	Nagmeldin	SUD	22.2.86	171/61	400	45.25, 45.2	44.93- 05
	El Amri	Khalid	MAR	20.3.77	163/54	3000	7:37.77	7:34.77- 06
						5000	13:16.13	13:06.13- 06
						10,000	27:30.94	27:26.24- 05
	El Idrissi	Abdelaziz Naji	ITA/MAR	8.12.86		5000	13:21.39	
*	El-Ghazaly	Omar	EGY	9.2.84	196/120	DT	66.58	65.33- 06
	Ellerton	Andrew	CAN	18.11.83	181/68	800	1:46.66	1:46.25- 05
	Elliott	Kevin	USA	7.11.78	178/70	800	1:46.73	1:46.42- 06
*	Emedolu	Uchenna	NGR	17.9.76	183/79	100	10.23	9.97- 03
						200	20.66, 20.0	20.31- 02, 20.22w- 05
	Emilianov	Ivan	MDA	19.2.77	202/130	SP	19.40i	20.08- 03, 20.26i- 00
	Emmen	Tetlo	USA	24.1.84	180/70	800	1:46.67	1:46.89- 06
	Emrani	Dustin	USA	6.1.85	175/66	800	1:46.92	1:49.67- 06
^	Épalle	Christophe	FRA	23.1.69	194/116	HT	75.49	81.79- 00
	Erasmus	Brian	RSA	28.2.80	193/100	JT	77.68A	81.38A- 03
	Eraud	Guillaume	FRA	1.7.81	180/62	1500	3:38.16	3:39.03- 03
	Erickson	Chris	AUS	1.12.81	173/63	50kW	3:59:02	3:58:22- 06
	Erickson	Karl	USA	1.6.82	191/116	DT	61.05	61.12- 06
	Erins	Edgars	LAT	18.6.86		Dec	7961	7452- 06
	Ernst	Sebastian	GER	11.10.84	183/72	200	20.59	20.36- 04
	Ertiban	Abera	ETH-J	13.3.88		10,000	27:28.82	
	Eryildirim	Fatih	TUR	1.3.79	183/89	HT	75.49	75.03- 06
*	Esenwein	Peter	GER	7.12.67	188/100	JT	82.78	87.20- 04
*	España	Jesús	ESP	21.8.78	173/56	3000	7:43.29	7:38.26- 06
*	Esser	Markus	GER	3.2.80	180/99	HT	80.68	81.10- 06
^	Estévez	Reyes	ESP	2.8.76	187/70	1500	3:34.33	3:30.57- 99
*	Evilä	Tommi	FIN	6.4.80	194/83	LJ	7.98, 8.41w	8.19, 8.27w- 05
*	Évora	Nelson	POR	20.4.84	181/64	LJ	8.10	8.08i, 8.05- 06
						TJ	17.74	17.23- 06
	Eyears	Greg	AUS	21.8.81		110H	13.72	13.98- 05
	Ezzine	Hamid	MAR	5.10.83	174/60	3kSt	8:09.72	8:19.37- 06
	Falil	Abdellah	MAR	.76		HMar	60:43	61:07- 03
	Famiglietti	Anthony	USA	8.11.78	173/57	3000	7:41.27	7:48.08i- 02, 7:50.70- 04
						5000	13:11.93	13:24.47- 06
						3kSt	8:27.64	8:17.91- 04
*	Farah	Mohamed	GBR	23.3.83	175/65	3000	7:41.86	7:38.15- 06
						5000	13:07.00	13:09.40- 06
	Farmer	Kyle	USA	15.4.83	186/87	100	10.23	10.30- 05, 10.24w- 05
	Farnosov	Andrey	RUS	9.7.80	182/66	3kSt	8:31.18	8:25.68- 06
	Farquhar	Stuart	NZL	15.3.82	190/97	JT	78.08	81.70- 06
*	Fasuba	Olusoji	NGR	9.7.84	175/78	100	10.07	9.85- 06, 9.8A- 05
	Fatecha	Victor	PAR-J	10.3.88	190/98	JT	78.01	76.79A - 06
	Faulk	Dexter	USA	14.4.84	187/75	110H	13.34	13.60, 13.53w- 04
	Fedaczynski	Rafal	POL	3.12.80	160/50	50kW	3:48:07	3:56:13- 05
	Fedas	Denys	UKR	24.8.85	177/73	PV	5.65	5.50- 06
	Fekadu	Asnake	KEN	.82		Mar	2:10:27	2:15:13- 06
	Félix	Agustin	ESP	14.3.79	179/77	Dec	7813	7845- 06
*	Ferguson	Kenneth	USA	22.3.84	186/73	400	45.91	46.59- 02
						400H	48.15	48.51- 05
	Fernandes	Raphael	BRA	8.11.84	178/67	400H	49.29	49.89- 05
	Fernández	Álvaro	ESP	7.4.81	180/67	1500	3:36.40	3:32.88- 04
*	Fernández	Francisco Javier	ESP	6.3.77	175/65	20kW	1:18:50	1:17:22- 02
	Feyisa	Tadesse	ETH	.81		HMar	61:42	
	Fifton	Rikki	GBR	17.6.85	180/78	100	10.16	10.39, 10.37w- 06
^	Figère	Nicolas	FRA	19.5.79	177/91	HT	77.60	80.88- 01
	Figures	Chris	USA	8.10.81	180/111	SP	19.85	20.09- 05
	Fikadu	Habtamu	ETH-J	13.3.88	165/48	10,000	27:06.47	
	Filet	Arius	FRA	17.12.77	182/67	TJ	16.58	17.15- 01
	Filipovic	Nenad	SRB	5.10.78	182/72	50kW	4:03:42	4:13:14- 02
	Filippídis	Yervásios	GRE	24.7.87	186/86	JT	81.01	79.42- 05
	Findlay	Adrian	JAM	1.10.82	179/70	400H	49.34	49.64- 04
	Findlay	Mark	GBR	20.3.78	188/80	100	10.26, 10.24w	10.25- 05
	Fitschen	Jan	GER	2.5.77	178/61	3000	7:46.74	7:46.22- 03
						5000	13:14.85	13:26.68- 03
	Fivaz	Julien	SUI	9.1.79	178/74	LJ	7.95	8.27- 03

	Name		Nat	Born	Ht/Wt	Event	2007 Mark	Pre-2007 Best
	Flores	Rodrigo	MEX	14.8.72	170/60	50kW	4:04:44A	
	Fofana	Colomba	FRA	11.4.77	186/76	TJ	16.81	17.21- 05
	Fomenko	Pavel	RUS	29.6.76	198/76	HJ	2.30	2.32i, 2.31- 02
	Ford	Jacoby	USA	27.7.87	175/79	100	10.23	10.50, 10.21w- 05
	Fortuna	Diego	ITA	14.2.68	188/116	DT	61.43	64.69- 00
	Fountain	Mark	AUS	10.3.82	188/73	1500	3:37.42	3:35.38- 06
						1M	3:55.58i, 3:58.86	3:53.24- 05
	Francique	Alleyne	GRN	7.6.76	188/75	400	44.95	44.47- 04
*	Francis (NGR)	Samuel	QAT	27.3.87	190/80	100	9.99	10.44- 06
	Frank	Mark	GER	21.6.77	187/91	JT	82.23	84.88- 05
*	Frater	Michael	JAM	6.10.82	170/67	100	10.03, 9.95w	10.03- 05
	Frauen	Michel	GER	19.1.86	179/70	PV	5.50	5.20- 06
	Frederick	Norris	USA	17.2.86	183/79	LJ	7.94w	7.75- 05, 7.87w- 06
	Freeman	David	PUR	28.4.82	170/61	800	1:46.94	1:47.66- 02
	Freeman	Jacob	USA	5.11.80	193/129	HT	74.39	72.60- 05
	Fricke	Steffen	GER	25.3.83		Dec	7555	7221- 05
^	Friedek	Charles Michael	GER	26.8.71	184/80	TJ	16.58	17.59- 97
	Fritz	Jesper	SWE	13.9.85	186/78	PV	5.70	5.60- 06
	Frolov	Vladislav	RUS	24.7.80	187/79	400	45.63	45.09- 06
	Frösén	Oskari	FIN	24.1.76	194/85	HJ	2.28	2.31i- 04, 2.30- 01
	Frost	Andy	GBR	17.4.81	189/115	HT	72.27	72.62- 06
	Fueki	Yasuhiro	JPN	20.12.85	181/71	400H	50.07	50.73- 06
	Fuentes	Héctor	CUB-J	19.5.88	183/70	LJ	7.93, 7.99w	7.28- 05
						TJ	16.61	16.63- 05, 16.71w- 06
	Fujisawa	Isamu	JPN	12.10.87		20kW	1:23:07	
	Fujita	Atsushi	JPN	6.11.76	166/52	Mar	2:10:23	2:06:51- 00
	Gaba	Kamghe	GER	13.1.84	202/94	400	45.84	45.47- 06
	Gabius	Arne	GER	22.3.81	188/68	5000	13:27.48	13:30.74- 06
	Gadasu	Alatan	CHN	27.1.84	173/60	50kW	3:55:35	3:40:23- 05
	Gailes	Tyree	USA	24.2.83	170/77	100	10.32, 10.19w	10.11- 04, 10.03w- 03
*	Gaisah	Ignisious	GHA	20.6.83	186/70	LJ	8.08	8.43, 8.51w- 06
	Gallardo	Sergio	ESP	22.3.79	180/68	800	1:46.66	1:46.65- 01
	1500	3:33.43		3:34.95- 06		1M	3:52.85	3:56.78- 03
	Galván	David	MEX	6.4.76	172/60	5000	13:12.18	13:27.99- 99
						10,000	27:33.96	27:37.69- 00
	Gao Chao		CHN-J	4.1.89	/65	20kW	1:23:46	
	Gao Hongwei		CHN	10.8.87	184/72	LJ	8.04	7.40- 02
	Gao Lianzuo		CHN	30.8.85	166/46	20kW	1:23:45	1:22:55- 05
	García	Alberto	ESP	22.2.71	163/45	3000	7:46.61i	7:32.98i- 03, 7:36.53- 01
	García	Álvaro	MEX	18.10.83		50kW	4:04:52	4:08:51- 06
*	García	Jesús Ángel	ESP	17.10.69	172/64	50kW	3:46:08	3:39:54- 97
	García	Luis	GUA	13.9.74	174/62	50kW	4:01:36	3:53:31- 03
	García	Víctor	ESP	13.3.85	173/56	3kSt	8:30.00	8:43.97- 06
*	García	Yordani	CUB-J	21.11.88	193/88	Dec	8257	7879h- 06
*	Garenamotse	Gable	BOT	28.2.77	183/75	LJ	8.18, 8.34w	8.27- 06
	Gari	Roba	ETH	12.4.82		3kSt	8:15.05	8:30.20- 05
	Garland	Dale	GBR	13.10.80	185/74	400H	49.79	49.85- 05
	Garrett	LaBronze	USA	9.11.76	181/75	400H	49.61	48.61- 04
	Garso	Yakob	ETH-J	.88		3kSt	8:29.99	
	Garvin	Michael Ray	USA	29.9.86	174/83	100	10.21, 10.10w	10.46- 05
						200	20.58	20.75- 06
	Garza	Gregg	USA	6.1.85	193/109	DT	63.69	59.17- 06
	Gataullin	Ruslan	RUS	1.12.79	184/77	LJ	8.29	8.13- 06
*	Gay	Tyson	USA	9.9.82	183/73	100	9.84, 9.76w	9.84- 06
						200	19.62	19.68- 06
	Gaymon	Justin	USA	13.12.86	175/70	400H	49.25	50.20- 06
	Gebauer	Brad	USA	19.1.84	178/73	PV	5.60i, 5.51A	5.51- 06
*	Gebremariam	Gebre-egziabher	ETH	10.9.84	178/56	5000	13:10.29	12:52.80- 05
						10,000	26:52.33	26:53.73- 04
	Gebremedhin	Mekonnen	ETH-J	11.10.88	180/64	1500	3:36.04	3:41.00- 06
	Gebremeskel	Dejene	ETH-J	24.11.89	178/53	5000	13:21.05	
	Gebretsadik	Bekele	ETH	27.9.86	166/50	10,000	27:52.78	28:05.97- 06
*	Gebrselassie	Haile	ETH	18.4.73	164/53	10,000	26:52.81	26:22.75- 98
				58:55- 06		Mar	2:04:26	2:05:56- 06
	HMar	59:24dh						
	Gemechu	Kidane	ETH	23.6.85		HMar	61:38	
*	Geneti	Markos	ETH	30.5.84	175/55	3000	7:32.69i	7:37.0i- 04, 7:38.11- 05
						5000	13:07.65	13:00.25- 05
	Gensic	Paul	USA	27.6.82	183/82	PV	5.57Ai	5.50- 04
*	Gerasimov	Pavel	RUS	29.5.79	190/80	PV	5.65i, 5.60	5.90- 00
	Gervasi	David	SUI	1.8.83		Dec	7659	7519- 05

Name		Nat	Born	Ht/Wt	Event	2007 Mark	Pre-2007 Best
* Gharib	Jaouad	MAR	22.5.72	176/66	HMar	60:43dh	59:56dh- 04, 60:51- 05
					Mar	2:07:54	2:07:02/2:17:12?- 04
Ghirmai	Filmon	GER	25.1.79	168/52	3kSt	8:22.23	8:20.50- 03
* Ghoula	Hatem	TUN	7.6.73	180/67	20kW	1:20:40	1:19:02- 97
					50kW	3:58:44	3:59:56- 02
^ Gibilisco ¶	Giuseppe	ITA	5.1.79	183/79	PV	5.70	5.90- 03
Gilbert	Brant	USA	8.10.81	183/82	100	10.21w	10.46- 05
Gillick	David	IRL	9.7.83	188/80	400	45.23	45.67- 06
Gillis	Chris	USA	16.11.83	183/75	LJ	7.92A, 8.01w	7.97, 8.04w- 06
* Giralt	David	CUB	26.8.84	182/72	TJ	17.39i, 17.10, 17.18w	17.31- 03
Gitau	Daniel	KEN	1.10.87	175/57	5000	13:24.94	13:41.55- 06
					10,000	27:44.73	28:05.96- 06
Giungi	Marco	ITA	30.10.74	174/60	20kW	1:21:41.59t	1:19:49- 02
Giwa-Agbomeirele	Okoineme	USA	30.11.78	183/79	LJ	7.94	7.97i- 03, 7.93- 01, 8.17w- 05
Giza	Jakub	POL	26.9.85	186/113	SP	19.87	18.81- 06
Gnaligo	Mathieu	BEN	13.12.86	177/73	400	45.89	46.43- 05
* Godina	John	USA	31.5.72	193/129	SP	20.60	22.20- 05
^ Golley	Julian	GBR	12.9.71	186/80	TJ	16.51	17.06- 94
Gomis	Kafétien	FRA	23.3.80	183/67	LJ	8.09i, 7.91	8.21- 04
Gonçalves	Rafael	POR	12.5.77	176/70	HJ	2.23	2.18- 04
Goncharuk	Dmitriy	BLR	17.7.70	190/112	SP	20.22i, 19.42	20.33- 95
* Gonzales	Jermaine	JAM	26.11.84	190/72	400	45.78	44.85- 06
González	José Antonio	ESP	15.6.79	178/65	20kW	1:23:23	1:24:25- 06
Gouacide	Wilfred	FRA	5.9.82	181/81	Dec	7556w, 7472	7468- 05
* Goucher	Adam	USA	18.2.75	178/64	1500	3:37.13	3:36.64- 01
					1M	3:56.6	3:54.17- 99
* Goumri	Abderrahim	MAR	21.5.76	167/60	Mar	2:07:44	-0-
Gourmet	François	BEL	28.12.82	179/80	Dec	7974	7950- 05
Goúsis	Anastásios	GRE	7.7.79	177/75	200	20.11	20.44- 04
Gowda	Vikas	IND	5.7.83	206/110	DT	64.96	64.69- 05
Goyvaerts	Tom	BEL	20.3.84	200/91	JT	78.65	73.09- 06
Graham	Sean	USA	6.3.80	180/67	3000	7:47.69	7:46.9 - 06
					5000	13:23.50	13:29.30- 06
Grasu	Mihai-Liviu	ROM	21.4.87	190/110	DT	60.07	58.70- 06
Gray	Brent	USA	16.9.86	183/75	100	10.29, 10.24w	10.76- 06, 10.65w- 05
					200	20.51	21,41- 06
Grayman	James	ANT	11.10.85	193/63	HJ	2.27	2.15- 05
Green	Leford	JAM	14.11.86	186/89	400	45.71	45.82- 06
Green	Steven	GBR	15.1.83	188/76	400H	50.17	50.90- 03
Greene	David	GBR	11.4.86	183/75	400H	49.58	49.91- 06
Greene	Joe	USA	20.11.87	188/77	400H	49.92	50.52- 06
Greer	Anthony	USA	22.10.83	188/130	SP	19.24	17.72- 06
* Greer	Breaux	USA	19.10.76	188/102	JT	91.29	87.68- 04
* Gregório	Jadel	BRA	16.9.80	202/102	LJ	7.99, 8.26w	8.22- 04
					TJ	17.90	17.73- 05
Grekov	Aleksandr	RUS	6.5.85	190/100	SP	19.84	18.91- 06
Gribkov	Sergey	RUS	30.4.85		DT	60.09	57.88- 05
Griffin	Colin	IRL	3.8.82	182/68	50kW	3:51:32	0
Griffin	Robert	USA-Y	12.2.90	190/88	400H	49.56	
Griffiths	Dean	JAM	27.1.80	180/72	400H	49.30	48.55- 03
^ Grimes	Mickey	USA	10.10.76	185/84	100	10.01, 9.99w	9.99- 03
Gripich	Aleksandr	RUS	21.9.86	190/80	PV	5.65i, 5.50	5.40- 05
Grobler	Gerbrand	RSA	26.1.83	194/84	JT	80.27	80.32A- 03
Groce	James	USA-J	12.5.88	188/78	400	45.89	47.12- 06
Gruber	Hendrik	GER	28.9.86	192/80	PV	5.50i	5.20- 06
Grueso	Daniel	COL	30.7.85	180/68	200	20.66A	20.71A- 06
Gu Junjie		CHN	5.5.85	186/63	TJ	17.11	17.23- 04
Guan Weilong		CHN	22.3.85	171/58	50kW	3:56:11	4:05:33- 06
Guibert	Jairo	CUB	22.2.84	175/71	LJ	7.96, 7.97w	7.70- 02, 7.94w- 06
Guigon	Nicolas	FRA	10.10.80	181/60	PV	5.65i, 5.55	5.75- 04
* Guset	Gheorghe	ROM	28.5.68	185/138	SP	19.91i, 19.62	21.04i- 06, 20.84- 99
^ Gushchinskiy	Viktor	RUS	12.8.78	202/84	TJ	16.95	17.33i- 06, 17.22- 04
Gustafsson	Andreas	SWE	10.8.81	180/67	50kW	4:00:48	
Guta	Abiyote	ETH	1.1.85		10,000	27:30.67	
Gutiérrez	José Francisco	ESP	13.6.83	179/66	50kW	4:04:52	4:07:26- 06
Guzdek	Miroslav	CZE	3.8.75	191/93	JT	78.32	85.74A- 02
^ Haatainen	Harri	FIN	5.1.78	186/85	JT	80.88	86.63- 01
Häber	Tino	GER	6.10.82	185/76	JT	80.24	79.88- 04
^ Haborák	Milan	SVK	11.1.73	191/106	SP	20.69	20.87- 04
* Hachlaf	Abdelkader	MAR	3.7.79	182/68	3kSt	8:17.03	8:08.78- 06
Hadadi	Ehsan	IRI	21.1.85	198/115	DT	67.95	65.25- 05

Name		Nat	Born	Ht/Wt	Event	2007 Mark	Pre-2007 Best
Häggblom	Robert	FIN	9.8.82	183/115	SP	20.53	20.28- 06
Haklits	Andras	CRO	23.9.77	189/103	HT	77.57	80.41- 05
* Hall	Ryan	USA	14.10.82	180/64	10,000	28:07.93	-0-
HMar 59:43			-0-		Mar	2:08:24	-0-
Hamamraoui	Abdelghani	ALG	.83		1500	3:37.59	3:39.09- 05
^ Hammad	Abderahmane	ALG	27.5.77	189/70	HJ	2.28	2.34- 00
Han Gang		CHN	10.11.78	177/65	Mar	2:08:56	2:13:22- 05
* Han Yucheng		CHN	16.12.78	182/60	20kW	1:19:15	1:18:31- 05
					50kW	4:03:53	3:36:20- 05
Hanany	Mickaël	FRA	25.3.83	198/78	HJ	2.25	2.30A- 06, 2.24- 03
Harcourt	Alex	USA	.85	182/77	400	45.87	46.57- 04
Harlan	Ryan	USA	25.4.81	190/93	Dec	7901	8171- 04
Harmse	Chris	RSA	31.5.73	184/118	HT	76.73	80.63- 05
Harper	Jacey	TRI	20.5.80	183/77	100	10.28, 10.15w	10.10- 05
Harradine	Benn	AUS	14.10.82	198/115	DT	62.99	63.65- 05
Harris	Jebreh	USA	22.9.78	178/66	800	1:45.92	1:45.91- 06
Harris	Marcus	USA	5.5.83		HJ	2.23	2.24i- 06, 2.20- 04
^ Harris	Otis	USA	30.6.82	188/77	400	45.78	44.16- 04
^ Harris	Rickey	USA	29.9.81	176/73	400	45.64	44.84- 02
					400H	48.98	48.16- 02
Harris	Tora	USA	21.9.78	190/83	HJ	2.31i, 2.30	2.33- 06
* Harting	Robert	GER	18.10.84	201/115	DT	66.93	66.02- 05
* Hartwig	Jeff	USA	25.9.67	190/82	PV	5.85i, 5.83A	6.03- 00
^ Harvey	Tye	USA	25.9.74	186/73	PV	5.55	5.93i- 01, 5.80- 00
* Hassan	Abdullah Ahmad	QAT	4.4.81	170/54	3000	7:47.68	7:43.01- 99
10,000 27:33.87			26:38.76- 03		HMar	61:46	62:36- 04
Hassan	Yahya Ibrahim	KSA	6.2.86	165/70	100	10.28, 10.24w	10.28, 10.21w- 06
Hatakeyama	Shigeo	JPN	9.3.77	184/99	DT	60.10	58.00- 05
Haverney	Matthias	GER	21.7.85	198/78	HJ	2.23	2.25- 05
Hazell	Ben	GBR	1.10.84	186/87	Dec	7602	7554- 06
Hazle	Mike	USA	22.3.79	183/93	JT	81.99	79.15- 05
Hazouri	Mohamed	SYR	.83	178/65	TJ	16.45, 16.60w	16.67- 05
Heard	Jason	USA	11.7.83	178/73	100	10.26, 10.18w	10.39- 04
Heffernan	Robert	IRL	28.2.78	173/55	20kW	1:20:15	1:20:25- 02
Heikkilä	Jussi	FIN	21.3.83	180/76	400H	50.28	50.37- 02
Helmke	Till	GER	6.5.84	183/80	200	20.37	20.47- 04
Helwick	Chris	USA	18.3.85	193/89	Dec	7732	7780- 05
^ Hemingway	Matt	USA	24.10.72	201/81	HJ	2.25Ai, 2.23	2.38i- 00, 2.34- 03
Henderson	Clendon	USA	1.8.84	186/102	DT	60.40	55.46- 06
Henry	Anson	CAN	9.3.79	188/79	100	10.20, 10.12Aw	10.12- 06, 10.04w- 02
Herms	René	GER	17.7.82	195/80	800	1:45.89	1:44.14- 04
Hernández	Freddy	COL	25.4.78	173/60	50kW	4:03:10	
* Hernández	Yoel	CUB	12.12.77	184/77	110H	13.23	13.24- 99, 13.20w- 00
Herrera	Michael	CUB	5.6.85	176/75	200	20.31	20.89- 05, 20.5w- 06
Herring	Aubrey	USA	19.9.78	183/77	110H	13.51, 13.45w	13.31- 06
* Heshko	Ivan	UKR	19.8.79	180/70	1500	3:35.03	3:30.33- 04
Hession	Paul	IRL	27.1.83	186/75	100	10.18	10.42- 06
					200	20.30	20.56- 06, 20.40w- 05
Heuser	Chip	USA	9.2.85	186/79	PV	5.50i, 5.45	5.45i, 5.40- 06
Hicks	Antwon	USA	12.3.83	187/73	110H	13.36	13.35- 05
Hicks	Graham	AUS	14.12.78	193/120	DT	60.22	61.77- 05
Hierrezuelo	Sergio	CUB	15.3.82	175/70	400	45.6dt	47.06- 01
					400H	49.90	49.11- 05
* Higuero	Juan Carlos	ESP	3.8.78	180/60	800	1:45.87	1:46.00- 03
					1500	3:32.18	3:31.57- 06
Higuma	Takafumi	JPN	3.9.82		20kW	1:23:08	1:24:31- 04
					50kW	4:02:07	4:02:42- 04
Hill	Richard	GBR	12.2.86	180/68	800	1:46.90	1:45.10- 06
Hilliard	Thomas	USA	16.7.84	186/75	110H	13.61	13.90- 06
					400H	49.63	50.55- 06
Hines	Neil	USA	3.6.83	188/84	Dec	7664	7259- 06
Hirvonen	Seppo	FIN	1.11.82	174/95	JT	76.09	74.08- 03
Hodun	Michal	POL	17.2.83	195/115	DT	60.93	61.02- 06
* Hoffa	Reese	USA	8.10.77	182/133	SP	22.43	22.11i, 21.96- 06
Hogans	Obra	USA	29.6.82	188/80	200	20.83, 20.65w	20.91- 04
					400	45.66	45.28- 03
Hogarth	Kim	NZL	18.12.75	178/70	3kSt	8:29.12	8:40.94- 06
Höhne	André	GER	10.3.78	185/72	20kW	1:20:32	1:20:00- 05
* Holliday	Trindon	USA	27.4.86	165/72	100	10.02	10.47, 10.43w- 05
* Holm	Stefan	SWE	25.5.76	181/69	HJ	2.38i, 2.35	2.40i- 05, 2.36- 04
Holzdeppe	Raphael	GER-J	28.9.89	178/69	PV	5.50	5.42- 06

Name		Nat	Born	Ht/Wt	Event	2007 Mark	Pre-2007 Best
Hommel	Stefan	GER	3.9.84	188/81	Dec	7577	7746- 06
Hondrokoúkis	Dimítrios	GRE-J	26.1.88	193/72	HJ	2.24	2.21- 06
Hongisto	Visa	FIN	9.4.87	186/82	200	20.56	20.99- 06
Hoogmoed	Guus	NED	27.9.81	187/80	100	10.15	10.25, 10.21w- 05
					200	20.48	20.58, 20.41w- 05
* Hooker	Steve	AUS	16.7.82	187/82	PV	5.91	5.96- 06
Hopkins	Keith	USA	14.4.86	190/77	110H	13.76, 13.59w	13.96, 13.74w- 06
^ Hopley	Hannes	RSA	26.1.81	181/105	DT	61.58	67.66- 04
Horák	Peter	SVK	7.12.83	197/83	HJ	2.30i, 2.27	2.27- 06
Horiguchi	Takashi	JPN	26.9.79	165/52	10,000	28:07.57	28:30,45- 05
Hoskins	Brandon	USA	29.5.85	188/91	Dec	7561	7529- 06
Hou Yang		CHN	8.7.85	175/55	50kW	3:56:43	4:00:19- 05
* Howe	Andrew	ITA	12.5.85	184/73	200	20.53	20.28- 04
					LJ	8.47	8.41- 06
Hrabovyy	Vadym	UKR	5.4.73	190/108	HT	70.60	79.82- 02
Hryshyn	Ivan	UKR-J	26.7.88	202/100	DT	60.46	49.12- 05
Huang Haiqiang		CHN-J	8.2.88	192/75	HJ	2.30	2.32- 06
Huang Hao		CHN	7.10.87	178/55	110H	13.67	13.93- 06
Hughes	Robby	USA	10.10.78	182/80	110H	13.36	13.26A, 13.30, 13.24w- 06
Hurtault	Erison	USA	29.12.84	182/75	400	45.40	46.12- 06
Hutcherson	Orentheus	USA	18.11.76		400H	49.93	49.61- 05
Hutchinson	Eugene	USA	29.9.83	188/77	HJ	2.25	2.26- 06
Hyett	Gareth	NZL	13.2.80	178/58	1500	3:38.63	3:44.64- 04
^ Hysong	Nick	USA	9.12.71	183/77	PV	5.60	5.90- 00
* Iakovákis	Periklís	GRE	24.3.79	185/76	400H	48.35	47.82- 06
Iakovákis	Sotirios	GRE	20.9.82	184/72	400H	50.10	49.9- 05, 50.65- 06
Iannelli	Angelo	ITA	27.7.76	175/61	3kSt	8:26.96	8:22.06- 99
Ibargüen	Arley	COL	17.10.82		JT	76.97	71.73- 06
Ibrahim	Yasser	EGY	2.5.84	185/127	SP	19.42	18.99- 06
					DT	61.58	56.14- 05
* Idowu	Phillips	GBR	30.12.78	192/89	TJ	17.56i, 17.35	17.68- 02
Iglehart-Summers	Quentin	USA	15.6.87	193/80	400	45.62	46.02- 06
* Iguider	Abdelaati	MAR	25.3.87	170/52	1500	3:32.75	3:32.68- 06
					3000	7:41.95	8:00.15i- 06
Ihara	Naoki	JPN	22.4.82	178/70	400H	49.89	50.15- 04
Ikeda	Daisuke	JPN	15.4.86	185/80	Dec	7609	7269- 06
Ikonnikov	Kirill	RUS	5.3.84	185/100	HT	78.03	71.32- 04
Iltsios	Yeóryios	GRE	28.11.81	187/95	JT	78.94	79.72- 06
Ilyichev	Ivan	RUS	14.10.86		HJ	2.28i, 2.24	2.25i, 2.24- 06
^ Inocêncio	Matheus	BRA	17.5.81	192/94	110H	13.63	13.33- 04
Inose	Tomohisa	JPN	17.9.87		400H	50.21	51.92- 06
Intas	Tomas	LTU	15.9.81	200/108	JT	77.68	82.94- 04
* Ioannou	Kyricaos	CYP	26.7.84	193/66	HJ	2.35	2.30i- 06, 2.28- 04
Iqbal	Zafar	PAK	10.4.82		TJ	16.45	15.79- 04
Isaac	Uche	NGR	10.4.81	168/82	100	10.23	10.49- 03
Ishikawa	Kazuyoshi	JPN	6.11.82	178/70	TJ	16.71w	16.98- 04
Isnyuk	Dmytro	UKR	4.7.85	193/106	DT	60.70	57.20- 06
Israel	Märt	EST	23.9.83	190/115	DT	66.56	63.20- 06
* Ivanov	Aleksandr	RUS	25.5.82	194/100	JT	86.71	88.90- 03
Ivanov	Georgi	BUL	13.3.85	188/108	SP	19.42	19.51- 05
Ivanov	Petar	BUL	5.9.85		TJ	16.63i	16.40- 04
Ivashkin	Vyacheslav	RUS	6.3.74		DT	59.90	62.08- 06
* Ivuti	Patrick	KEN	30.6.78	165/52	HMar	59:27	59:31- 00
Iwafune	Yoichi	JPN	12.6.85	184/74	110H	13.69	13.83- 06
Iwamizu	Yoshitaka	JPN	20.6.79	174/53	3kSt	8:23.31	8:18.93- 03
* Jackson	Bershawn	USA	8.5.83	173/69	400	45.06	45.45- 05
					400H	48.13	47.30- 05
James	Godday	NGR	9.1.84	186/76	400	45.70	44.99- 06
Janácek	Stepán	CZE	12.6.77	189/79	PV	5.60	5.76- 02
Jänes	Marko	EST	29.8.76	186/83	JT	76.74	78.50- 06
Janet	Roberto	CUB	29.8.86	187/95	HT	70.89	68.43- 06
Janevics	Ingus	LAT	29.4.86	191/74	20kW	1:23:19	1:26:21- 06
					50kW	3:53:57	3:56:32- 06
* Janik	Igor	POL	18.1.83	200/112	JT	83.38	82.86- 06
* Jankú	Tomás	CZE	27.12.74	191/75	HJ	2.34i, 2.30	2.34- 06
Janoyan	Melik	ARM	24.3.85		JT	76.77	68.39- 06
Jansen	Robbert-Jan	NED	22.7.83	175/67	PV	5.55i, 5.50	5.35- 06
Janson	Oscar	SWE	22.7.75	192/90	PV	5.50	5.87- 03
* Järvenpää	Tero	FIN	2.10.84	188/95	JT	84.35	84.95- 06
* Jawher	Mushir Salem	BRN	13.6.78	182/66	3000	7:35.99	7:35.35- 01
(Mucheru	Leonard	KEN)			5000	13:02.89	12:59.79- 05

Name		Nat	Born	Ht/Wt	Event	2007 Mark	Pre-2007 Best
Jedrusinski	Marcin	POL	28.9.81	188/74	200	20.31	20.31- 02, 20.14w- 05
Jelks	Mark	USA	10.4.84	170/66	100	10.04, 10.02w	10.02, 10.01w, 9.8w- 05
* Jeng	Alhaji	SWE	13.12.81	185/77	PV	5.70	5.80- 06
Jennings	Karl	CAN	14.5.79	188/82	110H	13.63	13.47- 04
Jensen	Morten	DEN	2.12.82	189/81	LJ	7.97i, 7.96w	8.25- 05
* Jeylan	Ibrahim	ETH-J	12.6.89	158/52	5000	13:17.99	13:09.38- 06
					10,000	27:50.53	27:02.81- 06
Ji Wei		CHN	5.2.84	194/83	110H	13.40	13.85- 06
Jia Yingli		CHN	16.2.84	184/72	TJ	16.51	16.44- 06
Jifar	Tariku	ETH	18.7.84		HMar	61:28	62:02- 03
Jiles-Tindall	Julius	USA	14.2.86	183/86	110H	13.66	13.94- 05
* Jiménez	Antonio David	ESP	18.2.77	178/63	3kSt	8:21.33	8:11.52- 01
Johansson	Bengt	SWE	7.7.73	190/102	HT	71.81	76.32- 01
John	Alexander	GER	3.5.86	185/77	110H	13.59	13.74- 06
* Johnson	Allen	USA	1.3.71	178/70	110H	13.23	12.92- 96
Johnson	Brandon	USA	6.3.85	175/68	400H	49.02	48.59- 05
* Johnson	Brian	USA	25.3.80	196/91	LJ	8.31	8.33- 05
Johnson	Chris	USA	28.4.82	183/77	100	10.21	10.22- 05, 10.18w- 04
Johnson	Dominic	LCA	31.10.75	185/77	PV	5.50	5.70A- 00, 5.65- 98
Johnson	Garrett	USA	24.5.84	193/122	SP	20.27i, 20.07	20.84- 06
Johnson	Jody	USA	13.11.85	175/78	200	20.64	-0-
Johnson	Jonathan	USA	5.3.82	177/73	800	1:44.69	1:44.77- 04
^ Johnson	Joshua 'J.J.'	USA	10.5.76	191/91	100	10.01, 9.92	9.95- 02
					200	20.32, 20.30w	19.88- 01
Johnson	Kibwe	USA	17.7.81	189/108	DT	60.57	65.11- 05
					HT	75.95	78.25- 05
^ Johnson	Patrick	AUS	26.9.72	177/73	100	10.17, 10.12w	9.93, 9.88w- 03
					200	20.48	20.35- 06, 20.25w- 03
Jonas	Dusty	USA	19.4.86	193/82	HJ	2.27	2.28- 06
Joncheray	Pierre	FRA	9.9.82	187/69	HMar	61:36	
Jones	Alwyn	AUS	28.2.85	189/72	TJ	16.74, 16.80w	16.79- 06
Jones	Garry	USA	24.7.84	175/70	100	10.19,10.12w	10.23A,10.38- 06, 10.26w- 04
Jons	Mattias	SWE	19.11.82	187/110	HT	71.61	71.31- 06
* Joseph	Fabiano	TAN	24.12.85	158/48	HMar	60:14	60:52- 03
Jotanovic	Milan	SRB	11.1.84	184/123	SP	19.72	19.57- 06
Juantorena	Alberto	CUB	27.6.77	186/72	Dec	8042	7769- 04
Julião	Ronald	BRA	16.6.85	194/110	DT	59.75	58.71- 06
Julius	Leigh	RSA	25.3.85	170/66	100	10.25	10.27- 05, 10.21w- 06
					200	20.65, 20.39w	20.44- 04, 20.37w- 05
Kabiru	Mbuthi Davis	KEN	1.5.83	170/57	10,000	27:45.63	27:46.38- 04
Kaczmarek	Michal	POL	19.9.77	183/60	3kSt	8:31.28	8:33.23- 02
Kahlmeyer	Markus	GER	20.1.82	189/110	HT	74.95	71.87- 05
* Kaki	Abubaker	SUD-J	21.6.89	171/60	800	1:43.90	1:45.78- 06
Kakonzi	Francis	KEN	.77		800	1:46.8A	1:47.2A- 04
Kales	John	KEN	.84		HMar	60:47	
Kalnas	Jon	USA	18.4.80	180/109	SP	19.43	19.67i- 02, 19.52- 04
Kamal	Ali Abubaker	QAT	8.11.83	169/58	1500	3:38.42	3:36.98- 04
					3kSt	8:21.20	8:23.06- 06
* Kamani	Bayano	PAN	17.4.80	188/79	400H	48.70	47.84- 05
* Kamathi	Charles	KEN	18.5.78	165/51	10,000	27:36.12	26:51.49- 99
* Kamel	Youssef Saad	BRN	29.3.83	184/70	800	1:43.87	1:43.11- 04
					1500	3:34.59	3:34.45- 06
Kamzee	Josphat	KEN	.84		HMar	61:50	63:03A- 06
Kanayev	Aleksey	RUS	30.5.86		20kW	1:23:18	1:27:28- 06
* Kanaykin	Vladimir	RUS	21.3.85	170/60	20kW	1:17:16	1:21:11+- 05
					50kW	3:40:57	3:40:40- 05
Kanda	Musa	KEN	.73		Mar	2:10:40	2:19:18- 06
Kandie	Daniel	KEN	.77	183/70	800	1:46.27	
Kandie	Solomon	KEN	28.8.78	173/64	3kSt	8:32.03	8:31.23- 04
Kanemaru	Yuzo	JPN	18.9.87	177/73	400	45.64	45.41- 06
Kangogo Kimutai	Willy	KEN	12.2.84	175/57	10,000	27:52.35	28:21.62- 05
Kantanen	Marko	FIN	17.4.78	183/98	JT	75.66	78.08- 04
* Kanter	Gerd	EST	6.5.79	196/126	DT	72.02	73.38- 06
^ Kaouch ¶	Adil	MAR	1.1.79	170/60	1500	3:35.8+, 3:30.77dq	3:31.10- 06
1M	3:51.14		3:51.62- 99		3000	7:45.51	7:39.52- 99
Kapek	Julien	FRA	12.1.79	178/70	TJ	17.10	17.38- 06
Karas	Josef	CZE	20.8.78	190/88	Dec	7922	7849w, 7837- 06
Karasmanákis	Elefthérios	GRE	16.8.78	185/98	JT	80.45	79.70- 05
* Kariuki	John	KEN	10.11.86	172/54	5000	13:18.39	13:12.12- 05
					10,000	27:30.50	27:14.84- 06

Name		Nat	Born	Ht/Wt	Event	2007 Mark	Pre-2007 Best
* Karjalainen	Olli-Pekka	FIN	7.3.80	194/118	HT	78.35	83.30- 04
Karlivans	Janis	LAT	2.6.82	195/87	Dec	8271	7851- 04
Karlsson	Conny	FIN	30.12.75	195/120	SP	20.09i	20.78- 01
* Karpov	Dmitriy	KAZ	23.7.81	198/98	Dec	8586	8725- 04
Karpovych	Sergiy	UKR	23.4.81	191/110	HT	70.58	74.01- 04
Karsak	Pavlo	UKR	11.11.87	204/96	DT	61.13	49.04- 06
Kasyanov	Oleksiy	UKR	26.8.85	191/82	Dec	7964	7599- 06
Katsís	Pétros	GRE	13.6.83	181/71	LJ	8.17	7.86i, 7.79- 04
Kauppinen	Juha	FIN	16.8.86	181/99	HT	70.96	68.09- 06
Kawakita	Naohiro	JPN	10.7.80	181/75	400H	49.83	49.17- 06
Kazakevics	Igors	LAT	17.4.80		50kW	3:59:56	4:09:23- 06
Kazanin	Oleksiy	UKR	22.5.82	170/58	50kW	4:02:27	3:56:44- 05
Kazimierowski	Jacek	POL	7.2.74	187/76	TJ	16.85	16.77- 02, 16.89w- 04
Kebede	Tsegaye	ETH	.87		Mar	2:08:16	
Kebenei	Ernest	KEN	.83		HMar	61:50	63:51A- 06
Kéchi	Heni	FRA	31.8.80	186/75	400H	49.76	49.89- 02
Keddo	Eric	JAM	1.7.84	186/77	110H	13.71, 13.68w	13.72- 05
* Keflezighi	Mebrahtom	USA	5.5.75	170/58	10,000	27:41.26	27:13.98- 01
^ Keïta ¶	Naman	FRA	9.4.78	196/86	400H	48.90	48.17- 04
Keitany	Haron	KEN	.84	183/70	1500	3:37.75	3:41.5A- 06
Kelai	John	KEN	29.12.76		Mar	2:09:30	2:09:09- 05
Kelley	Kai	USA	8.11.86	188/82	110H	13.59	13.82- 06
Kellman	Marc	USA	6.6.83	188/79	TJ	16.74	16.43i, 15.97- 06
Kemboi	David	KEN	.75		Mar	2:09:46	
Kemboi	Elias	KEN	10.3.84		Mar	2:09:36	2:15:01- 06
* Kemboi	Ezekiel	KEN	25.5.82	175/62	3kSt	8:05.50	8:02.49- 03
Kemboi	Nicholas	KEN-J	18.12.89	178/59	1500	3:36.13	3:33.72- 06
Kemboi	Peter	KEN	.78		Mar	2:09:21	2:13:16- 06
Kemboi Kiyeng	David	KEN	.83		Mar	2:09:08	2:10:08- 06
Kempas	Antti	FIN	3.10.80	191/66	50kW	3:57:59	3:59:01- 05
Kenei	Josphat Kiprotich	KEN	.78		Mar	2:07:42	2:08:51- 06
Kennouche	Abdesslam	ALG	7.10.80	186/73	800	1:46.24	1:46.47- 04
					1500	3:38.11	3:33.46- 04
Keul	Adam	USA	27.1.80	193/88	PV	5.50	5.70- 05
Kgosimang	Kabelo Mmono	BOT	7.1.86	184/70	HJ	2.29	2.30- 06
Khadar	Samir	ALG	10.6.86	182/60	1500	3:37.25	3:36.60- 06
Khamis	Adam Ismail	BRN-J	12.2.89	171/65	5000	13:19.27	13:35.48- 06
Kharlamov	Vasiliy	RUS	19.1.86		Dec	7681	7806- 02
^ Khersontsev	Vadim	RUS	8.7.74	192/106	HT	75.00	81.26- 01
Khlybov	Rustan	BLR	15.2.83	201/133	DT	62.36	60.77- 06
Kholev	Dennis	ISR	21.10.75	187/80	PV	5.50	5.71- 02
Kiama	Charles Munyeki	KEN	2.11.86		HMar	61:04	61:34A- 05
Kibet	Leonard	KEN-J	16.12.88		800	1:45.7A	1:48.48- 06
* Kibet	Luke	KEN	12.4.83		Mar	2:10:27	2:08:52- 05
Kibet	Sammy	KEN	.82		HMar	61:16	
Kibiwott	Charles	KEN	8.8.74		Mar	2:09:45	2:06:52- 06
Kibiwott	Francis	KEN	15.9.78		HMar	59:26	60:29- 06
Kibiwott	Stephen	KEN	.80		HMar	61:54	61:15- 06
Kibore	Felix (ex KEN)	QAT-J	18.2.88	173/55	3000	7:44.30	
					5000	13:20.89	13:22.92- 06
Kibwalei	Elijah	KEN	.84		3kSt	8:23.38	8:22.82- 06
* Kifle	Yonas	ERI	24.3.77	168/55	HMar	59:30	61:05- 02
					Mar	2:07:34	
Kiflemariam	Samson	ERI	23.1.84	168/54	HMar	60:52	62:11- 05
* Kigen	Moses Kipkosgei	KEN	10.1.83		5000	13:21.13	13:07.47- 06
					HMar	60:39	61:17- 06
Kigen	Wilfred	KEN	23.2.75	173/52	Mar	2:07:33	2:08:29- 05
* Kikaya	Gary	COD	4.2.78	184/75	200	20.64	20.40- 06
					400	44.60A, 44.77	44.10- 06
Kim Duk-hyung		KOR	8.12.85	180/68	LJ	7.92	7.77- 06
					TJ	17.02, 17.03w	17.07- 06
Kim Hyun-sub		KOR	31.5.85	176/56	20kW	1:20:54	1:21:45- 06
Kim Kun-woo		KOR	29.2.80	181/79	Dec	7609	7824- 06
Kim Yoo-suk		KOR	19.1.82	191/84	PV	5.66	5.63- 06
Kimaiyo	Paul	KEN	4.3.80		HMar	61:49	60:15- 05
Kimeli	Patrick	KEN-J	22.4.89		10,000	27:35.85	
Kimurine	Isaac	KEN	.86		5000	13:26.60	
Kimutai	David	KEN	19.8.69	165/57	20kW	1:23:06A	1:20:40A- 96
Kimutai	Philemon	KEN	12.8.83	174/58	1500	3:38.40	3:39.24- 04
King	Max	USA	24.2.80	168/60	3kSt	8:31.26	8:33.06- 05

Name		Nat	Born	Ht/Wt	Event	2007 Mark	Pre-2007 Best
Kinnunen	Jarkko	FIN	19.1.84	187/69	50kW	3:58:22	3:56:54- 06
Kinyanjui	Nephat	KEN	30.6.77		Mar	2:08:09	2:11:18- 06
* Kipchirchir	Alex	KEN	26.11.84	188/63	800	1:45.55	1:45.0A- 06, 1:45.54- 05
1500	3:31.58		3:30.46- 04		1M	3:52.10	3:50.25- 03
* Kipchoge	Eliud	KEN	5.11.84	167/52	3000	7:33.06	7:27.72- 04
5000	12:50.38		12:46.53- 04		10,000	26:49.02	
Kipchoge	Gilbert	KEN	4.5.83	183/73	800	1:45.34	1:45.43- 06
Kipchumba	Hillary	KEN			HMar	61:32	
* Kipchumba	Robert	KEN	24.2.84	170/62	HMar	60:34dh	59:28- 06
Kipchumba Rutto	Ronald	KEN	8.10.87	173/63	3kSt	8:32.10	8:16.69- 05
Kipkemboi	Laban	KEN	30.12.77	172/66	Mar	2:08:38	2:08:39- 02
Kipkemboi Kigen	Wilson	KEN	15.9.80		Mar	2:09:56	2:08:34- 05
* Kipketer	Sammy	KEN	29.9.81	166/52	10,000	27:14.04	26:49.38- 02
Kipkorir	David Mandago	KEN	15.12.74		Mar	2:09:59	2:08:38- 06
Kipkorir	Edwin	KEN-J	3.9.89	158/52	3000	7:40.88	
Kipkorir	Henry	KEN			3kSt	8:32.2A	
Kipkorir	Jonathan Kosgei	KEN	.82		HMar	60:59	60:47- 06
					Mar	2:10:25	2:10:18- 06
^ Kipkosgei	Luke	KEN	27.11.75	176/57	HMar	61:18	62:01- 06
Kiplagat	Benjamin	UGA-J	4.3.89		5000	13:22.67	13:43.0A- 06
					3kSt	8:21.73	8:34.14- 06
Kiplagat	Bernard	KEN-J	10.8.88	174/57	2000	5:00.82	
3000	7:37.69				5000	13:26.30	
Kiplagat	Bisluke	KEN-J	8.8.88	175/59	3000	7:44.62	7:53.10- 05
					3kSt	8:20.43	8:18.11- 06
Kiplagat	Richard	KEN	3.7.87	178/64	800	1:45.1A	1:50.03- 06
Kiplagat	Richard	KEN	5.1.81		10,000	28:06.43	
Kiplagat	Shadrack	KEN	9.12.77		HMar	60:35	62:31- 06
					Mar	2:07:53	2:13:36- 06
Kipleting Biwott	Stanley	KEN	.86		HMar	61:20	
Kipngeno Siele	Geoffrey	KEN	10.4.84	170/55	5000	13:21.74	13:36.12- 05
					10,000	27:29.43	27:41.78- 05
Kiprono	Hillary	KEN	.85		3kSt	8:32.94	
Kiprono	Nicholas	UGA	7.11.87		HMar	60:57	64:32- 06
* Kiprop	Asbel	KEN-J	30.6.89	186/70	1500	3:35.24	
					3000	7:42.32	
* Kiprop	Boniface	UGA	12.10.85	167/53	5000	13:07.46	12:57.11- 06
					10,000	28:05.66	26:39.77- 05
Kiprop	Francis	KEN	4.6.82	172/54	HMar	60:17	60:50- 06
					Mar	2:09:49	2:10:40- 06
Kiprop Rotich	Hosea	KEN	2.8.79		Mar	2:08:11	2:10:17A- 06
Kiprotich	Peter	KEN	.79		Mar	2:08:49	2:10:57- 06
Kiprotich	Stephen	UGA-J	18.4.89	168/54	5000	13:27.40	
* Kiprotich	Wesley	KEN	1.8.79	179/64	3kSt	8:14.88	8:05.68- 04
* Kipruto	Brimin	KEN	31.7.85	176/54	1500	3:36.27	3:35.23- 06
					3000	7:43.20i	7:47.33- 06
2000	4:58.76i				3kSt	8:02.89	8:04.22- 05
Kipruto	Sammy	KEN	22.11.78		HMar	61:33	62:06- 03
Kipruto	Silas	KEN	.84	184/66	5000	13:13.95	
Kipsang	Salim	KEN	22.12.79	172/52	Mar	2:07:29	2:08:04- 05
Kipsang	William	KEN	26.6.77		HMar	60:25	62:53- 02
Kipsang Kwambai	James	KEN	.76		HMar	61:03dh	60:22- 04
* Kipsiro	Moses	UGA	2.9.86	174/59	3000	7:32.03	7:36.47+- 06
					5000	12:50.72	13:01.88- 06
^ Kiptanui	Timothy	KEN	5.1.80	171/58	1500	3:37.61	3:30.04- 04
Kiptoo	Mark	KEN	21.6.76		3000	7:38.83	
					5000	13:12.60	
Kiptum	Bernard	KEN	8.10.86	173/64	1500	3:34.04	3:33.23- 06
* Kipyego	Bernard	KEN	16.7.86	160/50	5000	13:13.40	13:09.96- 05
					10,000	26:59.51	27:04.45- 05
* Kipyego	Michael	KEN	2.10.83	162/58	3kSt	8:11.62	8:10.66- 05
Kirchler	Hannes	ITA	22.12.78	191/98	DT	65.01	62.72- 05
Kirk	Sherridan	TRI	11.2.81	178/72	800	1:46.50	1:45.43- 05
Kirkpatrick	Ryan	USA	10.9.78	173/59	5000	13:19.68	13:31.68- 06
^ Kirmasov	Sergey	RUS	25.3.70	180/118	HT	74.13	82.62- 98
* Kirui	Abel	KEN	4.6.82		HMar	60:11	61:15- 06
					Mar	2:06:51	2:15:22- 06
Kirui	Barnabas	KEN	12.12.85	163/55	3kSt	8:20.36	8:45.61- 06
* Kirui	Paul	KEN	5.2.80		HMar	61:07	60:18- 06
					Mar	2:07:12	2:06:44- 06

Name		Nat	Born	Ht/Wt	Event	2007 Mark	Pre-2007 Best
Kirwa Kiprono	Jackson	KEN	.86		HMar	60:52	63:13- 06
Kirwa Tarbei	Philemon	KEN	20.10.78		HMar	61:27	62:42- 06
					Mar	2:10:24	
* Kirwa Yego	Alfred	KEN	28.11.86	175/56	800	1:44.50	1:43.89- 06
Kisang Kipchumba	Philemon	KEN	.77		HMar	60:55	61:27- 06
Kislov	Aleksandr	RUS	4.11.84		Dec	7870	7598- 05
Kiss	Dániel	HUN	12.2.82	195/73	110H	13.60	13.53- 06, 13.49dw- 05
Kistkin	Oleg	RUS	13.5.83		50kW	3:41.51	
Kitamura	Satoru	JPN	4.2.86	161/51	10,000	28:00.22	28:12.81- 04
Kivalov	Leonid	RUS-J	1.4.88		PV	5.67i, 5.60	5.50- 06
Klimarchuk	Andriy	UKR	20.1.85	183/76	Dec	7627	7400- 05
^ Klyugin	Sergey	RUS	24.3.74	192/82	HJ	2.24i	2.36- 98
Koborsi	Rob	USA	4.10.83	178/62	3000	7:46.16	7:48.4 - 06
* Kobs	Karsten	GER	16.9.71	196/125	HT	77.92	82.78- 99
Koech	Charles	QAT	29.12.83		5000	13:24.26	
					HMar	61:27	61:48- 06
Koech	George	KEN-J	.88		800	1:46.8A	1:48.5A- 06
Koech	Jackson	KEN	26.12.78	166/52	Mar	2:10:28	2:08:02- 05
^ Koech	Justus	KEN	19.3.80	175/60	800	1:44.86	1:44.16A- 03
Koech	Matthew	KEN	1.1.83		HMar	60:57	62:56- 06
* Koech	Paul Kipsiele	KEN	25.11.81	168/57	1500	3:37.92	3:38.87- 01
3000	7:33.46i		7:33.93- 05		3kSt	7:58.80	7:56.37- 05
Koekemoer	Pieter	RSA	12.1.82		400H	49.04	49.44A, 49.68- 06
* Kogo	Micah	KEN	3.6.86	170/60	3000	7:38.67	7:44.57- 06
5000	13:10.68		13:00.77- 06		10,000	26:58.42	26:35.63- 06
Kogo	Paul Kipkemei	KEN	.83		Mar	2:10:39	2:13:48- 06
Koike	Takayuki	JPN	12.10.84	181/69	400H	49.78	49.23- 05
Kojima	Shigeyuki	JPN	25.9.79	173/68	100	10.24, 10.14w	10.20- 00, 10.12w- 99
Kolasa	Adam	POL	2.8.75	196/91	PV	5.70i, 5.61	5.75- 01
Kolasinac	Asmir	SRB	15.10.84	185/103	SP	19.30, 19.40irreg	17.88- 05
Kolesnikov	Vadim	RUS	24.5.85		HJ	2.24i	2.25- 06
Kolosov	Dmitriy	RUS	8.6.86		TJ	16.68	16.00- 05
* Kombich	Isaac	KEN	16.10.85	183/73	800	1:45.15	1:44.24- 06
* Komen	Daniel Kipchirchir	KEN	27.11.84	175/60	1500	3:31.75	3:29.02- 06
1M	3:48.28		3:48.49- 05		3000	7:37.47i	7:31.98- 05
Komen	Edwin	KEN	.80		Mar	2:08:45	2:13:26- 06
* Komen	Willy	KEN	22.12.87	168/55	3kSt	8:11.18	8:14.00- 06
* Komon	Leonard Patrick	KEN-J	10.1.88	172/57	3000	7:39.07	7:37.69- 06
					5000	13:04.79	13:04.12- 06
* Konopka	Mikulás	SVK	23.1.79	193/110	SP	21.57i, 19.94	20.66- 01, 20.87i-dq- 02
* Konopka	Miloslav	SVK	23.1.79	189/102	HT	79.83	81.33- 04
Korchmid	Oleksandr	UKR	22.1.82	188/89	PV	5.80i, 5.50	5.81- 05
Korepanov	Sergey	RUS	15.7.84		50kW	4:01:24	
* Korir	John Cheruiyot	KEN	13.12.81	172/57	10,000	27:26.31	26:52.87- 02
Korir	Paul	KEN	15.7.77	180/64	1500	3:37.29	3:30.72- 03
* Korir	Shadrack	KEN	14.12.78	170/54	1500	3:31.18	3:31.96- 06
1M	3:52.78		3:55.72- 01		2000	4:55.72i	4:56.62- 01
3000	7:37.35i		7:37.50- 06		2M	8:23.94i	8:14.84i- 06, 8:19.53- 05
Korolyov	Aleksey	RUS	5.4.82		HT	75.39	72.56- 05
Korotkov	Ilya	RUS	6.12.83		JT	83.94	78.23- 06
Korzun	Aleksandr	BLR	17.3.85	194/76	Dec	7777	7567- 06
Kosenkow	Alexander	GER	14.3.77	178/68	200	20.63	20.55- 04
Kosgei	Collins	KEN	4.8.86	178/64	3kSt	8:14.32	8:18.70- 06
Kosgei	James	KEN	.84		3000	7:42.64	
					3kSt	8:13.66	8:34.1- 05
* Kosgei	Paul	KEN	22.4.78	175/57	HMar	61:26dh	59:07- 06
					Mar	2:09:31	
* Kosgei	Reuben	KEN	2.8.79	170/55	3kSt	8:07.12	7:57.29- 01
Kosgei	Shadrack	KEN	24.11.84	176/60	3000	7:41.51	7:42.22- 05
					5000	13:11.85	13:01.06- 05
Koski-Vähälä	Jarko	FIN	21.11.78	194/97	JT	84.02	84.12- 05
Kotur	Milan	CRO	15.4.86		400H	50.14	50.15- 05
Kotze	Hennie	RSA	4.2.84		110H	13.67A, 13.91	13.64A- 05, 13.4A- 06
* Kövágó	Zoltán	HUN	10.4.79	204/127	DT	66.42	69.95- 06
* Kovals	Ainars	LAT	21.11.81	192/100	JT	82.23	85.95- 06
Kovenko	Andriy	UKR	25.11.73	174/64	20kW	1:22:22	1:21:53- 05
					50kW	4:04:23	3:59:38- 06
Kozlowski	Kacper	POL	7.12.86	177/66	400	45.80	46.60- 05
* Kozmus	Primoz	SLO	30.9.79	188/106	HT	82.30	81.21- 03
Kozulko	Aleksandr	BLR	8.12.83	200/98	HT	77.24	75.02- 06

Name		Nat	Born	Ht/Wt	Event	2007 Mark	Pre-2007 Best
Kranjc	Matija	SLO	12.6.84	181/81	JT	78.08	76.04- 05
* Kravchenko	Andrey	BLR	4.1.86	187/84	LJ	7.90	7.68i, 7.66, 7.72w- 05
					Dec	8617	8013- 06
^ Krawczyk	Andrzej	POL	11.4.76	195/112	DT	64.21	65.56- 05
Kristensen	Bjørnar Ustad	NOR	26.1.82	172/57	3kSt	8:16.75	8:23.65- 06
Krivitskiy	Pavel	BLR	17.4.84	188/100	HT	78.61	78.62- 06
Krivov	Andrey	RUS	14.11.85	178/67	20kW	1:20:12	1:22:21- 05
^ Kronberg	Robert	SWE	15.8.76	181/86	110H	13.51	13.35- 01
Krone	Christiaan	RSA	30.8.84	188/82	100	10.25	10.43A- 01, 10.2, 10.42w- 04
					200	20.51	21.29A- 05
Kruger	A.G.	USA	18.2.79	193/118	HT	78.10	79.26- 04
* Kruger	Frantz (ex RSA)	FIN	22.5.75	203/125	DT	69.97	70.32- 02
Kruhlik	Pawel	POL	25.8.83	180/58	TJ	16.96	16.72i, 16.42- 06
^ Krummenacker	David	USA	24.5.75	190/79	800	1:46.75	1:43.92- 02
* Krymarenko	Yuriy	UKR	11.8.83	187/65	HJ	2.34i, 2.27	2.33- 05
Kuang Li		CHN	13.8.84	182/60	LJ	7.93	7.94- 04
Kucheryanu	Sergey	RUS	30.6.85	185/73	PV	5.70	5.65- 06
Kucinski	Beniamin	POL	1.6.82	182/62	20kW	1:21:58	1:20:34- 05
Kucmin	Antón	SVK	7.6.84	180/64	50kW	3:57:41	4:03:34- 06
Kudlicka	Jan	CZE-J	29.4.88	183/72	PV	5.61, 5.62ex	5.30- 06
Kuehl	Adam	USA	19.1.84	188/116	SP	19.40i	18.40- 05
					DT	64.98	63.89- 06
Kujala	Seppo	FIN	24.9.80	186/111	SP	19.29i, 19.07	19.22- 05
Kukk	Mihkel	EST	8.10.83		JT	77.70	71.18- 06
Kukushkin	Anatoliy	RUS	12.2.86		20kW	1:23:38	1:26:25- 06
Kumagai	Masanori	JPN	20.10.86		100	10.23w	10.58- 06
Kundert	Andreas	SUI	1.10.84	185/76	110H	13.59	13.72- 06
* Kunkel	Adam	CAN	24.2.81	180/77	400H	48.24	48.77- 06
Kuptsov	Artem	RUS	22.4.84	183/64	PV	5.60	5.70- 03
Kurgat	Sammy	KEN	.75		Mar	2:08:38	2:15:20- 06
Kürthy	Lajos	HUN	22.10.86	190/125	SP	19.83	19.10- 06
Kuzin	Oleksandr	UKR	21.10.74	179/63	Mar	2:07:33	2:10:09- 06
Kuzmin	Aleksandr	BLR	24.3.81	178/69	20kW	1:22:52	1:22:06- 05
Kuznetsov	Ivan	RUS	11.9.83	173/56	20kW	1:21:11	1:21:00- 05
Kuznetsov	Viktor	UKR	14.7.86	190/67	TJ	16.94	16.84i, 16.58- 04
Kwoba	George	KEN	9.11.74	183/73	400	45.77A	46.09A- 04, 46.0A- 06
Kyyrö	Mikko	FIN	12.7.80	191/106	DT	64.14	63.27- 05
* Laâlou	Amine	MAR	13.5.82	178/57	800	1:43.94	1:43.25- 06
Laanmäe	Tanel	EST-J	29.9.89		JT	76.35	69.37- 06
* Lagat	Bernard	USA	12.12.74	175/61	1000	2:16.25	2:18.70- 00
1500	3:33.85+		3:26.34- 01		1M	3:50.56	3:47.28- 01
					3000	7:38.77, 7:32.43i	7:33.51- 00
Lahaye	Mathieu	FRA	25.12.83	181/75	400	45.90	47.08- 06
^ Lahlafi	Brahim	FRA	15.4.68	172/62	HMar	61:00	61:39dh- 94
^ Lahssini	El Hassan	FRA	1.1.75	175/62	10,000	27:59.93	27:50.73- 02
Lakhal	Irba	FRA	12.2.75	168/61	3kSt	8:28.82	8:20.45- 04
Lamb	Matt	USA	27.9.86	187/105	DT	60.47	57.84- 06
Lamdassem	Ayad	ESP	11.10.81	175/63	10,000	27:56.60	27:46.67- 06
Lanaro	Giovanni	MEX	27.9.81	183/77	PV	5.82	5.71Ai- 06, 5.65- 05
Lancaster	Kyle	USA	15.8.83	196/80	HJ	2.23	2.31A- 05, 2.29- 04
Langat	David	KEN	.80		3kSt	8:31.0A	8:24.5A- 06
Langat	Festus	KEN	.85		HMar	61:04dh	61:58- 05
Langlois	Denis	FRA	10.10.68	172/60	50kW	3:57:01	3:47:31- 05
Lapierre	Fabrice	AUS	17.10.83	179/66	LJ	7.98	8.19- 06
* Larry	Lionel	USA	14.9.86	175/68	400	44.67	45.38- 06
Latvala	Mikko	FIN	8.7.80	182/82	PV	5.50	5.66- 01
Lauckner	Benjamin	GER	3.4.87	190/82	HJ	2.26	2.20- 06
Lauro	Germán	ARG	2.4.84	186/110	DT	61.78	60.30- 06
					SP	19.67	19.78- 06
Laursen	Lars Møller	DEN	3.3.82		JT	76.08	72.29- 06
Lavillenie	Renaud	FRA	18.9.86	176/69	PV	5.58i	5.25i, 5.22- 06
Lavrinenko	Nikolay	RUS	24.3.84		PV	5.50	5.50- 04
Lax	Petteri	FIN	12.10.85	186/83	LJ	7.93, 7.97w	7.80- 06
Laynes	Jeff	USA	3.10.70	180/88	100	10.16	10.01- 96, 9.9- 95
LeBlanc	Mike	CAN	25.2.87	182/82	100	10.17, 10.16w	10.59- 05
^ Lee Bong-ju		KOR	11.10.70	168/56	Mar	2:08:04	2:07:20- 00
Lee Dae-ro		KOR	12.3.80	169/58	20kW	1:22:59	1:21:52- 03
Lee Hup-Wei		MAS	5.5.87	178/62	HJ	2.24	2.20- 05
Lee Yun-chul		KOR	28.3.82	188/110	HT	70.84	69.07- 06
* Lel	Martin	KEN	29.10.78	171/54	HMar	60:10dh	59:30dh- 06, 59:42- 05
					Mar	2:07:41	2:06:41- 06

Name		Nat	Born	Ht/Wt	Event	2007 Mark	Pre-2007 Best
Lemoncello	Andrew	GBR	12.10.82	187/68	3kSt	8:23.74	8:30.12- 05
Lescay	David	CUB-J	19.2.89	178/69	200	20.4	21.62- 06, 21.4- 05
Lett	Alleyne	GRN	7.1.83	193/97	110H	13.52	13.68, 13.49w- 05
Letting	Edwin	KEN	15.5.84	172/62	800	1:45.54	1:45.99- 06
Lewandowski	Marcin	POL	13.6.87	178/58	800	1:45.52	1:46.69- 06
Lewis	Elvis	USA	30.4.87	187/75	400	45.82	46.76- 06
Lewis	Randy	GRN	14.10.80	188/74	TJ	17.43	17.34- 04
Lewis	Steven	GBR	20.5.86	191/79	PV	5.61	5.50- 06
* Lewis-Francis	Mark	GBR	4.9.82	180/85	100	10.17	10.04, 9.97?w-01
Leyckes	Dennis	GER	20.4.82	184/77	PV	5.50i, 5.42	5.50- 06
* Li Gaobo		CHN-J	4.5.89	176/55	20kW	1:19:03, 1:20:11.72t	1:18:07- 05
Li Jianbo		CHN	14.11.86	172/50	20kW	1:23:23	1:19:34- 05
					50kW	3:53:24	3:43:02- 06
Li Runrun		CHN	24.2.83	185/70	LJ	8.22	7.89- 05
Li Xiangyu		CHN	21.10.85	176/61	800	1:46.67	1:46.45- 06
Li Yanxi		CHN	26.6.84	176/55	TJ	16.84	17.15- 05
^ Lichtenegger	Elmar	AUT	25.5.74	187/83	110H	13.68	13.33- 99
Lima	Jessé Farias de	BRA	17.2.81	191/79	HJ	2.29	2.30- 06
de Lima	Vicente Lenilson	BRA	4.6.77	166/65	100	10.14A, 10.18	
							10.13, 10.11w- 04, 10.08Aw- 02, 10.0- 03
					200	20.56	20.39- 04
* Limo	Benjamin	KEN	23.8.74	178/65	2M	8:15.90	8:10.59- 06
					5000	13:16.66	12:54.99- 03
* Limo	Felix	KEN	22.8.80	174/58	Mar	2:07:47	2:06:14- 04
* Limo	Richard	KEN	18.11.80	167/53	Mar	2:06:45	-0-
Limo Ndiwa	Remi	KEN-J	3.2.88	173/55	1500	3:35.10	3:38.31- 0
2000	5:00.74. 4:59.02i			2M 8:18.70	3000	7:38.62	
* Lincoln	Dan	USA	20.10.80	190/70	3kSt	8:28.32	8:08.82- 06
Lindsey	Justin	USA	25.8.79		110H	13.70	13.82- 02
Lingua	Marco	ITA	4.6.78	179/94	HT	77.65	77.66- 06
Lipscombe #	Jesse	CAN	4.4.80	186/79	HJ	2.26dq	2.20- 00
Little	Gregory	JAM	20.2.83	168/56	400H	49.71	48.95- 05
Littleton	Will	USA	14.10.83	188/79	HJ	2.28	2.23- 06
Litvinov	Sergey	BLR	27.1.86	183/93	HT	74.80	73.98- 05
Liu Feiliang		CHN	27.3.85	188/68	PV	5.71	5.70- 05
* Liu Xiang		CHN	13.7.83	188/74	110H	12.92	12.88- 06
Liu Xiaosheng		CHN-J	5.1.88	190/74	400	45.79	46.91- 05
Llanos	Enrique	PUR	7.5.80		110H	13.72	13.72, 13.69w- 05
Lloyd	Chris	DMA	10.10.80	178/62	200	20.56	20.62- 06
					400	45.40	45.46- 06
Lloyd	Zack	USA	10.10.84	191/141	SP	19.47	19.17- 06
* Lobinger	Tim	GER	3.9.72	193/86	PV	5.83	6.00- 97
Logvinenko	Mikhail	RUS	19.4.84		Dec	7697	7570- 05
Lohse	Jonas	SWE	15.5.87	202/11	JT	79.48	66.42- 06
Loikkanen	Mika	FIN	20.2.74	195/120	DT	63.17	62.93- 01
Lomnicky	Marcel	SVK	6.7.87	180/90	HT	72.17	69.53- 06
Lomong	Joseph Lopez	SUD/USA	1.1.85	178/67	800	1:45.79	1:47.00- 06
					1500	3:37.07	3:45.96- 06
* Longosiwa	Thomas	KEN	14.1.82	175/57	3000	7:32.79	
					5000	12:51.95	13:35.3A- 06
López	Yeimar	CUB	20.8.82	184/73	800	1:44.58	1:46.61- 05
Löppönen	Mikko	FIN	29.9.83	191/96	JT	76.19	75.99- 06
Loretz	Felix	SUI	13.11.75	181/90	JT	78.38	78.56- 02
Louw	Stephan	NAM	26.2.75	187/76	LJ	7.94	8.17A- 99, 8.16- 03
Lu Ronghua		CHN	21.2.83	174/60	20kW	1:20:16	1:18:39- 05
Luchianov	Ion	MDA	31.1.81	178/67	3kSt	8:23.83	8:26.17- 04
Luckwell	Mervyn	GBR	27.11.84	192/108	JT	75.68	72.37- 06
Luis	Yacnier	CUB	24.1.82	179/75	400H	49.82	48.83- 04
* Lukashevych	Oleksiy	UKR	11.1.77	175/70	LJ	8.25	8.27- 00
Lukezic	Chris	USA	24.4.84	173/58	1500	3:36.95	3:33.28- 06
* Lukyanenko	Yevgeniy	RUS	23.1.85	190/80	PV	5.81	5.60- 06
Luotonen	Lasse	FIN	16.6.83	188/100	HT	72.30	71.85- 06
Lusis	Voldemars	LAT	7.12.74	187/102	JT	80.58	84.19- 03
Lynsha	Maksim	BLR	6.4.85	190/72	110H	13.66	13.81, 13.70w- 05
Lyuboslavskiy	Anton	RUS	26.6.84	190/137	SP	20.77	20.75i- 06, 20.71- 05
* Lyzhin	Pavel	BLR	24.3.81	189/110	SP	20.82i, 20.02	20.92- 04
					DT	61.72	61.30- 06
Ma Liang		CHN	22.7.84	186/100	HT	71.67	71.01- 03
Maaroufit	Mourad	MAR	.82	178/62	5000	13:15.87	13:56.76- 06
* Maase	Kamiel	NED	20.10.71	191/71	Mar	2:08:21	2:08:31- 03

Name		Nat	Born	Ht/Wt	Event	2007 Mark	Pre-2007 Best
Maataoui	Ali	MAR	15.12.80	180/60	1500	3:37.71	3:35.52- 05
3000 7:36.70			7:56.96i- 02		2M	8:19.33	
Macharia	Isaac	KEN	25.11.80		HMar	60:48	60:53- 06
Macharinyang	Hosea	KEN	12.6.86	160/45	3000	7:46.93	7:54.29- 06
5000 13:09.85			13:19.43- 06		10,000	27:58.41	28:11.0A- 05
* Mack	Tim	USA	15.9.72	188/78	PV	5.86	6.01- 04
Mackel	Derek	USA	18.11.82	178/75	PV	5.50Ai	5.51- 06
MacLeod	Jared	CAN	3.4.80	183/74	110H	13.55	13.54- 05
Macrozonaris	Nicolas	CAN	22.8.80	181/78	100	10.29, 10.11Aw	10.03A,10.13- 03, 9.91w- 02
Madi	Nabil	ALG	9.6.81	180/69	800	1:44.54	1:44.63- 06
Maeda	Katsuhiro	JPN	19.4.81	167/54	10,000	27:55.17	28:10.66- 03
Maggidi	Itai	ISR	9.1.81	173/59	3kSt	8:30.51	8:25.04- 06
Maheswary	Renjith	IND	30.1.86	177/72	TJ	17.04, 17.19w	16.54- 06
Mai	Michael	USA	27.9.77	188/123	HT	74.63	74.40- 04
Maïga	Ibrahima	MLI	14.3.79	176/68	400H	49.13	50.14- 06
Maillard	Sébastien	FRA	2.5.81	184/81	400H	49.65	49.10- 03
Maindi	Elias	KEN	.80		HMar	61:53	63:06- 06
Maiyo	David	KEN	5.11.76		Mar	2:10:19	2:13:00- 05
Maiyo	Jonathan	KEN-J	.88		HMar	60:10	
* Majewski	Tomasz	POL	30.8.81	204/135	SP	20.87	20.83i- 04, 20.66- 06
Makabe	Takeshi	JPN	3.2.82	165/53	10,000	27:53.78	28:14.03- 05
* Makarov	Sergey	RUS	19.3.73	192/100	JT	87.46	92.61- 02
* Makau	Patrick	KEN	2.3.85		HMar	58:56	
Makhloufi	Rabia	ALG	.86		3kSt	8:23.56	8:37.55- 06
* Malachowski	Piotr	POL	7.6.83	194/125	DT	66.61	66.21- 06
Malasevich	Aleksandr	BLR	7.4.77	200/115	DT	61.00	65.80- 04
^ Malcolm	Christian	GBR	3.6.79	174/67	100	10.32, 10.22w	10.11, 10.09w?- 01
Malina	Libor	CZE	14.6.73	193/115	DT	61.08	67.13- 01
^ Malone	Casey	USA	6.4.77	203/109	DT	64.74	66.58A- 02
Malyavin	Vladimir	RUS	4.3.73	188/75	LJ	8.00	8.25- 00
Mamba-Schlick	Hugo	CMR	1.2.82		TJ	16.72	16.44- 06
Mannio	Ari	FIN	23.7.87	185/104	JT	80.31	79.68- 06
Manso	Dário	POR	1.7.82	183/117	HT	74.98	74.27- 06
* Manson	Andra	USA	30.4.84	196/75	HJ	2.33i, 2.30	2.32- 04
^ Manson	Pat	USA	29.11.67	178/75	PV	5.50Ai, 5.36	5.85- 94
Mansour	Najim	ALG-J	8.6.88		800	1:46.82	1:48.06- 06
Manyim	Philip	KEN	24.3.78	175/64	Mar	2:08:01	2:07:41- 05
Manz	Steve	USA	19.9.81	183/120	SP	19.98i, 19.38	20.29i, 20.20- 06
Manzano	Leonel	USA	12.9.84	165/57	1500	3:35.29	3:37.13- 05
Marciniszyn	Marcin	POL	7.9.82	185/72	400	45.77	45.54- 06
Marda	Musabeker	MAR	4.2.82		10,000	27:59.69	
					HMar	61:48	
Maregu	Joseph	KEN	.77		HMar	59:45	61:20- 06
Maric	Martin	CRO	19.4.84	196/115	DT	62.04	57.94- 06
^ Markov	Dmitriy	AUS	14.3.75	181/80	PV	5.55	6.05- 01
* Markov	Ilya	RUS	19.6.72	174/65	20kW	1:18:56	1:18:17- 05
Marsh	Mike	USA	20.3.80		Dec	7578	7587- 05
Martin	Cory	USA	22.5.85	196/125	SP	19.63	18.85- 05
					HT	71.42	69.97- 06
* Martin	Rodney	USA	22.12.82	180/73	200	20.06	20.14- 06
* Martin	Scott	AUS	12.10.82	190/130	SP	20.52	20.38- 06
					DT	61.65	64.00- 06
Martín	Eliseo	ESP	5.11.73	172/61	3kSt	8:22.91	8:09.09- 03
^ Martín	Luis Miguel	ESP	11.1.72	180/67	3kSt	8:28.89	8:07.44- 02
* Martina	Churandy	AHO	3.7.84	180/68	100	10.06	10.06, 10.04A, 9.76Aw- 06
					200	20.20	20.27A- 06, 20.32, 20.31w- 05
Martineau	Eugène	NED	14.5.80	180/79	Dec	7877	8114- 05
* Martínez	Alexander	SUI	23.8.77	184/82	TJ	17.13	17.51- 05
Martínez	Gerardo	MEX	9.3.79	194/81	HJ	2.30	2.25- 05
* Martínez	Guillermo	CUB	28.6.81	188/95	JT	85.93	87.17- 06
Martínez	Jonathan	ESP	29.1.86	178/73	LJ	7.91	7.65i- 06. 7.57- 04
* Martínez	José Manuel	ESP	22.10.71	176/62	Mar	2:10:12	2:08:09- 03
Martínez	Lois Maikel	CUB	3.6.81	185/90	DT	62.91	67.45- 05
* Martínez	Manuel	ESP	7.12.74	185/132	SP	19.48	21.47- 02
Martínez	Wilfredo	CUB	9.1.85	184/68	LJ	8.17	8.04- 05
Marwa Mkami	Dickson	TAN	6.3.82	166/55	3000	7:42.94	8:04.01- 04
5000 13:25.18			13:26.43- 06		10,000	27:38.58	28:47.49- 06
					HMar	60:24	61:57- 06
Marzouk	Ahmad Fayez	KSA	6.9.79	186/73	LJ	8.12	8.39- 06
* Masai	Moses	KEN	1.6.86	168/54	3000	7:47.29	7:49.1A- 05
5000 13:08.81			13:13.28- 06		10,000	26:49.20	27:03.20- 06

	Name		Nat	Born	Ht/Wt	Event	2007 Mark	Pre-2007 Best
	Masai Ndiwa	Allan	KEN			HMar	61:39	64:28- 05
	Masheto	Lesiba	BOT	1.11.84	173/62	400	45.41	46.20- 05
	Maska	Vladimir	CZE	6.2.73	190/115	HT	72.39	81.28- 99
	Maskancevs	Andrejs	LAT	11.10.86	186/78	LJ	7.96	7.83- 05
^	Mason	Germaine	GBR	20.1.83	195/80	HJ	2.30	2.34- 03
	Mason	Michael	CAN	30.9.86	187/70	HJ	2.27	2.23- 06
	Masztak	Kamil	POL	16.7.84	184/66	100	10.21w	10.43- 05
	Mätas	Risto	EST	30.4.84	190/87	JT	77.29	80.53- 06
*	Máté	Gábor	HUN	9.2.79	199/104	DT	66.45	66.54- 00, 66.99dh- 03
	Matebor	Albert	KEN	20.12.80		HMar	61:39	63:03- 06
						Mar	2:09:33	2:11:52- 06
*	Matelong	Richard	KEN	14.10.83	179/65	3kSt	8:06.66	8:05.96- 04
*	Mathathi	Martin Irungu	KEN	25.12.85	167/49	5000	13:22.13	13:03.84- 04
						10,000	27:09.90	27:08.42- 05
	Mathew	Bibu	IND	30.3.81	173/68	TJ	16.59, 16.64w	16.31- 06
	Mathieu	Michael	BAH	24.6.83	180/78	400	45.22	45.90- 06
	Mathiszik	Willi	GER	17.6.84	185/70	110H	13.61	13.64, 13.58w- 05
	Matsumiya	Takayuki	JPN	21.2.80	163/49	5000	13:13.20	13:29.50- 05
						Mar	2:10:04	2:10:20- 06
	Matsumiya	Yuko	JPN	21.2.80	165/49	Mar	2:09:40	2:09:18- 05
	Matthys	Thomas	BEL	4.9.85	183/62	800	1:46.77	1:45.75- 06
	Mättölä	Petri	FIN	1.7.86	183/90	HT	71.32	66.15- 06
	Matyukhin	Nikolay	RUS	13.12.68	179/68	50kW	3:57:18	3:40:13- 99
	Maximiano	Alexon	BRA	12.10.82	187/92	JT	78.57	75.84- 05
	Mayer	Gerhard	AUT	20.5.80	191/93	DT	62.12	62.85- 05
	Mayle	Scott	USA	14.10.83	185/79	LJ	7.95i	7.92- 05
	Mays	Jermaine	GBR	23.12.82	186/66	3kSt	8:30.41	8:31.04- 06
*	Mazuryk	Maksym	UKR	2.4.83	190/85	PV	5.76	5.75- 04
	Mbandjock	Martial	FRA	14.10.85	187/84	100	10.16	10.45- 06
	Mbogo	Elijah	KEN-J	.88		HMar	61:40	
	Mbote	Jason	KEN	5.1.77	170/58	Mar	2:07:51	2:08:13- 06
	Mburu Mugo	Kennedy	KEN			Mar	2:10:13	
	McAdams	Josh	USA	26.3.80	190/68	3kSt	8:21.36	8:34.10- 06
	McCormick	Nick	GBR	11.9.81	188/72	1500	3:38.46	3:35.74- 05
	McCoy	Reuben	USA	16.3.86	186/75	400H	49.27	49.22- 06
	McDougal	Josh	USA	1.6.85	175/64	5000	13:20.43	13:52.94- 05
	McDowell	Jonathan	USA	28.10.84	178/79	110H	13.60	14.42, 14.02w- 06
	McFarlane	Danny	JAM	14.2.72	185/81	400H	48.32	48.00- 04
*	McGrath	Paddy	USA	1.7.71	183/120	HT	73.26	77.49- 99
	McGregor	Herbert	JAM	13.9.81		LJ	7.93	7.78- 06, 7.98w- 05
	McIlroy	James	GBR	30.12.76	180/68	800	1:46.69	1:44.65- 05
	McKenzie	Ramone	JAM-Y	15.11.90	184/73	200	20.58	21.17- 06
	McKinney	Nathaniel	BAH	19.1.82	175/79	400	45.68	45.85- 04
	Mehkhissi Benabbad	Mahiedine	FRA	15.3.85	190/79	3kSt	8:14.22	8:28.25- 06
*	Mekonnen	Deresse	ETH	20.10.87	175/60	1500	3:36.41	
	Melentyev	Sergey	RUS	5.12.76	178/68	50kW	3:51:11	3:57:10- 05
	Meleshenko	Yevgeniy	KAZ	19.1.81	185/75	400H	49.56	48.46- 01
	Melesse	Gashaw	ETH	26.9.78	170/52	Mar	2:09:53	2:08:03- 06
	Melich	Lukás	CZE	16.9.80	186/105	HT	74.74	79.36- 05
^	Méliz	Luis Felipe	CUB	11.8.79	177/76	LJ	8.20	8.43- 00
	Melly	Paul	KEN	4.1.81		1500	3:37.04	3:40.4A- 05
	Meng Yan		CHN	30.9.80	188/68	400H	49.47	49.03- 06
*	Menjo	Josphat Kiprono	KEN	20.8.79	168/50	2M	8:18.96	
						5000	13:06.69	13:09.24- 06
						10,000	27:04.61	27:29.45- 06
*	Merga	Deriba	ETH	26.10.80	160/54	10,000	27:02.62	
						HMar	59:16	60:45- 06
						Mar	2:06:50	-0-
	Merlino	Justin	AUS	10.12.86	183/83	110H	13.55	14.15- 06
*	Merritt	Aries	USA	24.7.85	188/75	110H	13.09	13.12- 06
*	Merritt	LaShawn	USA	27.6.86	188/82	200	19.98	20.10- 06
						400	43.96	44.14- 06
	Mersal	Hatem	EGY	20.1.75	186/79	LJ	8.04w	8.31- 99
	Mesfin Tariku	Nahom	ETH-J	3.6.89		3kSt	8:17.21	8:26.20- 06
*	Mesnil	Romain	FRA	13.6.77	188/82	PV	5.86	5.95- 03
	Metu	Obinna	NGR-J	12.7.88	183/75	200	20.63	20.91- 06
	Michalski	Lukasz	POL-J	17.8.88	189/76	PV	5.50	5.30- 06
	Mikhaylichenko	Yevgeniy	RUS	13.2.79	185/77	PV	5.50i	5.70- 02
*	Mikhnevich	Andrey	BLR	12.7.76	201/135	SP	21.27	21.69- 03
	Mikkola	Esko	FIN	14.2.75	185/95	JT	82.34	84.27- 04
*	Miles	Derek	USA	28.9.72	191/82	PV	5.75	5.85i- 05, 5.82- 01
*	Milkevics	Dmitrijs	LAT	6.12.81	182/72	800	1:44.37	1:43.67- 06

	Name		Nat	Born	Ht/Wt	Event	2007 Mark	Pre-2007 Best
	Millán	Germán	ESP	21.5.79	190/97	SP	19.34	18.70- 06
	Miller	Adam	AUS	22.6.84	186/83	100	10.17	10.26- 06
	Minah	Jacob	GER	3.4.82	189/80	Dec	8099	7776- 06
	Mira	Salvador	ESA	23.8.84		50kW	3:59:51	4:12:53- 06
	Mistretta	Alessandro	ITA	6.3.71	172/58	50kW	4:02:50	3:51:33- 99
	Mitchell	Jacobi	BAH	4.1.86	180/73	200	20.66	21.20- 03
	Mitchell	Michael	USA	16.5.81	180/70	100	10.18w	10.22- 05, 10.07w- 04
	200	20.33		20.59- 00		400	45.88	46.08- 05
	Mitchell	Robert	GBR	14.9.80	190/78	HJ	2.23i	2.25- 01
	Mitchum	Eric	USA	2.8.84	188/82	110H	13.23	13.38- 04
	Mitei	Enock	KEN	26.11.80	172/52	HMar	61:01	60:32- 04
	Mîtîcov	Andrei	MDA	15.11.86	177/70	HJ	2.24	2.18- 06
	Mitsuya	Yu	JPN	18.12.84	166/49	5000	13:18.32	13:31.30- 05
	Möcks	Richard	GER	15.10.81	182/76	PV	5.50	5.60- 04
	Modibo	Ato	TRI	19.6.79	188/75	400	45.12	44.87- 01
	Moffatt	Keith	USA	20.6.84	203/84	HJ	2.28i, 2.25	2.30- 06
*	Moffitt	John	USA	12.12.80	185/75	LJ	8.19	8.47- 04
	Mogusu	Mekubo	KEN	25.12.86	165/51	10,000	27:52.79	27:44.94- 06
						HMar	59:48	61:28- 05
	Mohajershojaei	Ehsan	IRI	21.3.83	178/60	800	1:45.90	1:46.46- 04
*	Mohamed	Mustafa	SWE	1.3.79	172/54	3kSt	8:05.75	8:14.67- 06
	Mohammed	Hakeem	USA	.85	182/73	400	45.37	46.44- 06
*	Mokoena	Khotso	RSA	6.3.85	190/73	LJ	8.34A, 8.28, 8.32w	8.39, 8.45w- 06
						TJ	16.75A	17.25- 05
	Molefe	California	BOT	2.5.80	172/62	400	45.36	45.23- 05
*	Molina	Juan Manuel	ESP	15.3.79	173/67	20kW	1:20:44	1:19:44- 05
*	Möllenbeck	Michael	GER	12.12.69	200/120	DT	65.29	67.64- 02
	Moncur	Avard	BAH	2.11.78	196/82	400	44.86	44.45- 01
	Mondschein	Brian	USA	9.1.83	188/80	PV	5.52i	5.53- 06
	Monteiro	Edivaldo	POR	28.4.76	175/68	400H	49.31	49.10- 04
	Montenegro	Luis	CHI	6.10.81	183/64	400H	50.18	50.17- 06
*	Moore	Anwar	USA	5.3.79	182/75	110H	13.12, 13.00w	13.23, 13.20w- 05
	Moore	Carlos	USA	8.5.84	180/73	100	10.20	10.07- 06
	Moore	Jonathan	GBR	31.5.84	180/74	LJ	8.04w	8.03- 02
	Moradi	Sadjad	IRI	30.3.83	182/67	800	1:46.40	1:44.74- 05
	Morales	Ignacio	CUB	28.1.87	183/69	110H	13.4, 13.3w	14.33, 14.2- 05
	Moran	Ed	USA	27.5.81	180/58	5000	13:20.35	13:25.87- 05
						10,000	27:43.13	
	Moreira	José Carlos	BRA	28.9.83	168/63	100	10.16A, 10.31	10.23A, 10.24- 06
	Moreno	Xavier	ECU	15.11.79	168/60	50kW	3:52:07	4:05:38- 05
	Morgan	Jason	JAM	6.10.82	186/114	DT	62.95	57.49- 06
	Morgan	Nathan	GBR	30.6.78	187/86	LJ	8.00, 8.05w	8.26- 03
	Morioka	Koichiro	JPN	2.4.85	183/65	20kW	1:21:30	1:22:46- 06
	Morrison	Paul	CAN	25.9.80	180/60	5000	13:22.39	13:26.57- 04
	Mortimer	James	NZL	1.3.83	188/85	110H	13.71	13.88- 06
	Mosca	Vince	USA	23.1.80	189/127	SP	19.81	20.66- 06
*	Mosop	Moses	KEN	17.7.85	172/57	3000	7:45.83	7:36.88- 06
	5000	13:07.89		12:54.46- 06		10,000	26:49.55	27:08.96- 05
*	Mottram	Craig	AUS	18.6.80	188/72	1500	3:38.2+	3:33.97- 06, 3:32.7+?- 05
	1M	3:54.54		3:48.98- 05		3000	7:35.00	7:32.19- 06
	2M	8:03.50		8:11.27- 05		5000	13:04.97	12:55.76- 04
^	Moudrik	Younés	MAR	1010.77	176/72	TJ	16.70	16.80- 05
	Mourhit	Hassan	BEL	2.1.82	177/60	1500	3:37.47	3:40.98- 06
	Moussa	Ahmad Hassan	QAT	17.6.81	188/80	Dec	7678	7730- 04
*	Moustaoui	Mohammed	MAR	2.4.85	174/60	1500	3:32.67	3:32.51- 06
	2000	5:00.98i				3000	7:46.82i	7:49.57- 05
	Moxey	Osbourne	BAH	27.8.78	175/79	LJ	7.91	8.19- 02
*	Moya	Víctor	CUB	24.10.82	196/80	HJ	2.33	2.35- 05
	Muge	Edward	KEN	26.6.83		10,000	28:04.86	
	Mulabegovic	Nedzad	CRO	4.2.81	189/100	SP	20.01	20.15- 03, 20.31ex- 04
*	Mulaudzi	Mbulaeni	RSA	8.9.80	171/62	800	1:43.74	1:42.89- 03
						1000	2:15.86	2:18.45A- 03
	M ller	Norman	GER	7.8.85	195/84	Dec	8255	8129- 06
	Müller	Stefan	SUI	20.9.79	190/96	JT	79.43	82.07- 06
	Müller	Wolfram	GER	8.7.81	190/65	1500	3:37.85	3:35.50- 03
	Mullings	Steve	JAM	29.11.82	173/68	100	10.05, 9.91w	10.05, 10.04dq, 9.96w- 04
						200	20.54	20.27, 20.22dq, 19.90w- 04
	Murakami	Yukifumi	JPN	23.12.79	185/92	JT	79.85	81.71- 04
*	Murofushi	Koji	JPN	8.10.74	187/100	HT	82.62	84.86- 03
	Murozuka	Kenta	JPN	12.2.86	171/57	10,000	28:04.40	28:27.36- 06
	Musikhin	Aleksey	RUS	8.11.75	187/80	TJ	16.54i	17.02- 04

Name		Nat	Born	Ht/Wt	Event	2007 Mark	Pre-2007 Best
Musinde	Tom	KEN	22.4.79	179/78	100	10.26, 10.0A	10.1A- 05
Mutai	Abel	KEN-J	2.10.88		3kSt	8:29.76	8:35.38- 06
Mutai	Edward	KEN	28.8.84		3000	7:45.43	8:10.72- 04
* Mutai	Emmanuel	KEN	1.4.78		HMar	60:51dh	60:49- 06
					Mar	2:06:29	-0-
Mwangi	Daniel Muchunu	KEN	1.1.84	176/62	10,000	28:05.30	28:13.34- 03
Mwangi Macharia	James	KEN	23.6.84	178/58	Mar	2:10:27	2:19:39- 05
Mwaniki	Joseph	KEN-J	29.11.88	165/54	HMar	61:52	
Mwanzia	Musau	KEN	.83		HMar	61:37	62:04- 06
Mwera	Samwel	TAN	3.6.85	175/54	800	1:46.24	1:45.28- 05
* Myburgh	Alwyn	RSA	13.10.80	188/71	400H	48.64	48.09- 01
Myers	Rob	USA	5.8.80	172/59	1500	3:36.49	3:34.89- 05
^ Myerscough	Carl	GBR	21.10.79	209/149	SP	19.96	21.92- 03
Myklebust	Gaute	NOR	29.4.79	195/120	DT	60.25	63.32- 05
^ Nagel	Morné	RSA	23.2.78	183/77	100	10.0A	10.13A- 02, 10.13- 03
					200	20.32A, 20.59	20.11A, 20.34- 02
Naimadu	Nicodemus	KEN	24.4.84	175/57	10,000	28:06.26	
					3kSt	8:25.71	8:29.82- 06
Naito	Masato	JPN	31.7.80	185/75	110H	13.43	13.46, 13.45w- 06
* Narisako	Kenji	JPN	25.7.84	185/74	400H	48.44	47.93- 06
Nartov	Oleksandr	UKR-J	21.5.88	182/67	HJ	2.30i, 2.26	2.28- 05
Nau	Manuel	GER	2.7.77	190/90	JT	77.54	83.04- 00
Nava	Horacio	MEX	20.1.82	175/62	20kW	1:23:08	1:22:53- 04
					50kW	3:52:35	3:48:22- 06
Nazareno	Franklin	ECU	24.4.87	182/72	100	10.22A	10.45,10.1A, 10.33Aww- 06
					200	20.47A	21.21, 20.6A, 20.76w- 06
Nazarov	Dilshod	TJK	6.5.82	187/115	HT	78.89	77.63- 05
* Ndambiri	Josphat Muchiri	KEN	12.2.85	172/52	5000	13:18.49	13:05.33- 05
					10,000	27:28.38	27:04.79- 06
Ndebele	Nelton	ZIM	6 .6.85		400	45.7A	47.27- 05
Ndirangu	Augustine Gatimu	KEN	.84		10,000	28:10.57	28:29.41- 06
Ndirangu	Simon	KEN	1.11.85		10,000	27:38.56	27:31.29- 05
Ndiso	Denis Musembi	KEN	31.12.83		HMar	61:47	61:24- 03
Ndiwa	Cornelius	KEN-J	.88		1500	3:37.41	
Nedra	Andrey	RUS	18.11.80		Dec	7654	7496- 06
Neighbour	Aaron	AUS	2.12.77	198/130	DT	61.66	59.55- 06
Nellum	Bryshon	USA-J	1.5.89	185/78	200	20.43	20.94- 06
					400	45.38	46.20- 06
* Nelson	Adam	USA	7.7.75	183/115	SP	21.61	22.51- 02
Nelson	Tim	USA	27.2.84		10,000	28:04.46	28:45.32- 05
Németh	Kristóf	HUN	17.9.87	190/97	HT	73.50	70.99- 05
^ Németh	Zsolt	HUN	9.11.71	190/110	HT	71.46	81.56- 99
Neshev	Kolyo	BUL	30.5.82		JT	82.55	72.21- 06
Nesterenko	Mykyta	UKR-Y	15.4.91	202/97	DT	62.79	55.80- 06
Nesterovskyy	Stanislav	UKR	31.7.80	198/110	DT	64.94	62.59- 05
Neville	David	USA	1.6.84	193/77	400	45.24	44.75- 06
Newdick	Brent	NZL	31.1.85	189/89	Dec	7730w, 7482	7681- 06
* Ngatuny	Gideon	KEN	10.10.86	173/54	5000	13:12.62	13:15.9 - 06
					10,000	27:11.36	27:28.42- 06
Ngeno	Collins	KEN	14.4.83		3kSt	8:27.73	8:24.3A- 06
Ngeny	Joseph	KEN	20.7.77		Mar	2:10:25	2:09:27- 06
Ngetich	Caleb	KEN	20.1.81	175/60	3kSt	8:17.90	8:15.21- 06
Ngimba	Ezekiel	TAN	17.8.85		HMar	61:28	
Ngoepe	Samson	RSA	28.1.85		800	1:46.99	1:48.53A- 05
Niaré	Yves	FRA	20.7.77	195/120	SP	20.21	20.06- 06
					DT	63.44	58.56- 05
Nicolay	Christian	GER	4.3.76	189/88	JT	79.58	84.54- 03
Niedermeyer	Darren	USA	2.4.82	190/84	PV	5.60	5.20- 06
Nieland	Nick	GBR	31.1.72	190/100	JT	79.04	85.09- 00
^ Nieto	James	USA	2.11.76	193/79	HJ	2.27	2.34- 04
Nikitin	Yevgen	UKR	9.1.85	186/75	Dec	7552	7531- 06
* Niklaus	André	GER	30.8.81	190/84	Dec	8371	8316- 05
* Nima	Issam	ALG	8.4.79	186/74	LJ	8.26	8.17, 8.37w- 06
Nishchyk	Vasyl	UKR	13.3.83	190/80	TJ	16.66	16.15- 06
Nixon	Greg	USA	12.9.81	179/79	200	20.43	20.89, 20.60w- 06
					400	45.31	
* Nizhegorodov	Denis	RUS	26.7.80	180/61	50kW	3:40:53	3:35:29- 04
Njenga	Daniel	KEN	7.5.76	176/61	Mar	2:09:45	2:06:16- 02
Njeru	Micah	KEN-J	5.8.88	166/53	10,000	27:48.40	28:21.29- 06
Njoroge	Simon	KEN			Mar	2:09:46	2:18:13- 06

	Name		Nat	Born	Ht/Wt	Event	2007 Mark	Pre-2007 Best
	Njui	Cyrus	KEN	11.2.86	169/51	10,000	27:56.63	28:00.88- 06
	Noffke	Chris	AUS-J	6.1.88	188/76	LJ	8.12	7.95, 8.00w- 05
	Noguchi	Kenji	JPN	23.2.75	160/50	10,000	28:03.83	28:13.63- 03
	Norberg	Justin	USA	18.7.77	191/82	PV	5.50	5.75- 05
	Noúsios	Astérios	GRE	25.2.79	185/74	LJ	7.91i, 7.90, 7.97w	8.00- 00
	Novotny	Roman	CZE	5.1.86	180/73	LJ	7.98	7.84- 06
	Nowak	Marcin	POL	2.8.77	174/71	200	20.50dt	20.51- 00
	Nowicki	Bartosz	POL	26.2.84	187/70	800	1:46.81	1:48.62- 06
	Nowill	Peter	AUS	15.6.79	178/69	3kSt	8:26.94	8:22.85- 04
	Nthiwa	Patrick	KEN	30.6.83		3kSt	8:30.0A	8:27.63- 04
	Nurudeen	Selim	NGR	1.2.83	183/75	110H	13.59	13.61, 13.57w- 04
	Nutter	Travis	USA	9.2.75	178/95	HT	74.24	74.86- 05
	Nuyens	Martijn	NED	18.11.83		HJ	2.24i	2.16- 06
	Nyamu	Julius	KEN	1.12.77	178/66	3kSt	8:15.66	8:07.59- 01
	Nyasango	Cuthbert	ZIM	17.9.82	168/59	10,000	27:57.34	28:43.7- 04
						HMar	60:26	60:59- 06, 60:29Asc- 04
*	Nymark	Trond	NOR	28.12.76	180/64	50kW	3:41:31	3:41:30- 06
	Nyongani	Young Talkmore	ZIM	2.9.83	172/70	400	45.40	44.96A- 05, 45.09, 44.9- 04
*	Obikwelu	Francis	POR	22.11.78	195/79	100	10.06, 9.99w	9.86- 04, 9.84w- 06
						200	20.38	19.84- 99
	Obrist	Christian	ITA	20.11.80	186/66	800	1:46.65	1:46.19- 05
						1500	3:35.32	3:35.74- 02
	Obuon	Paulvince	KEN	18.11.83	188/84	200	20.54	20.97- 04
	Odom	Marlon	USA	4.12.82	193/79	110H	13.52, 13.50w	13.66, 13.45w- 06
*	Odriozola	Mikel	ESP	25.5.73	180/62	50kW	3:55:19	3:41:47- 05
	Ohashi	Yuji	JPN	5.9.83	185/70	110H	13.55	13.57- 05, 13.54w- 06
^	Ojaniemi	Jaakko	FIN	28.8.80	193/87	Dec	7613	8192- 02
	Oke	Tosin	GBR	1.10.80	178/77	TJ	16.86	16.65- 02, 16.75w- 04
	Okken	Arnoud	NED	20.4.82	182/65	800	1:45.88	1:45.64- 01
	Olgundeniz	Ercüment	TUR	7.7.76	203/120	DT	64.34	63.49- 04
*	Olijar	Stanislav	LAT	22.3.79	190/80	110H	13.38	13.08- 03
	Olinger	Brian	USA	2.6.83	178/62	3kSt	8:19.29	8:19.56- 05
	de Oliveira	Júlio César	BRA	4.2.86	185/97	JT	77.65	78.91- 06
*	Oliver	David	USA	24.4.82	188/93	110H	13.14	13.20- 06
	Olkowski	Ryan	USA	19.4.80	188/81	Dec	7584	7895- 04
	Olmedo	Manuel	ESP	17.5.83	179/60	800	1:45.13	1:45.30- 04
*	Olsen	Joachim	DEN	31.5.77	184/142	SP	21.61	21.63i- 04, 21.57- 02
*	Olsson	Christian	SWE	25.1.80	192/78	TJ	17.56	17.83i, 17.79- 04, 17.92w- 03
	Olteán	Csongor	HUN	8.4.84	184/91	JT	78.15	74.98- 03, 77.38irr- 06
	Omole	Demi	USA	29.7.85	178/73	100	10.10	10.11, 9.96w- 06
	Omori	Terukazu	JPN	3.9.79	174/55	10,000	27:51.90	27:43.94- 04
	Ondara	Macdonald	KEN	8.12.84		HMar	61:11	61:21- 06
	Oni	Samson	GBR	25.6.81	183/74	HJ	2.28	2.24- 06
*	Onnen	Eike	GER	3.8.82	194/83	HJ	2.34	2.28- 06
*	Oosthuizen	Robert	RSA	23.1.87	188/101	JT	84.52	83.07- 06
*	Oprea	Marian	ROM	6.6.82	190/77	TJ	17.32	17.81- 05
	Osovnikar	Matic	SLO	19.1.80	177/75	100	10.13	10.14, 10.12w- 06
						200	20.51	20.47- 04
*	Otto	Björn	GER	16.10.77	188/84	PV	5.90	5.85- 06
^	Ottoz	Laurent	ITA	10.4.70	180/69	400H	50.13	48.52- 96
	Ou Yongjian		CHN	1.7.84	185/80	400H	49.87	50.22- 06
	Owens	Nick	USA	6.1.85	190/118	HT	71.20	70.02- 06
^	Owusu	Andrew	GHA	8.7.72	180/75	TJ	16.32, 16.55w	17.23- 98
	Padgett	Travis	USA	13.12.86	174/77	100	10.09, 10.05w	10.00- 06
	Palacios	Noraldo	COL	8.7.80	173/75	JT	78.03A	79.09- 06
	Palli	Niki	ISR	28.5.87	186/76	HJ	2.27i, 2.25	2.30- 06
	Palomeque	Rubén	ESP	14.8.80	174/58	3kSt	8:23.21	8:26.53- 06
	Palyszko	Maciej	POL	2.1.78	186/112	HT	75.24	80.89- 03
	Panel	Brice	FRA	13.6.83	180/69	400	45.54	46.26- 06
	Panfilov	Grigoriy	RUS	17.5.80		SP	19.52	19.95- 04
	Panocha	Babubhai	IND	5.9.80		20kW	1:23:40	
	Papadimitríou	Alexándros	GRE	18.6.73	185/115	HT	75.93	80.45- 00
	Papadoníou	Stamátios	GRE	3.5.84	191/117	HT	73.46	68.92- 05
*	Pappas	Tom	USA	6.9.76	196/95	Dec	8352	8784- 03
	Park Chil-sung		KOR	8.7.82	173/61	20kW	1:20:20	1:22:14- 06
	Park Jae-myong		KOR	15.12.81	180/95	JT	80.38	83.99- 04
	Parker	James	USA	3.12.75	180/107	HT	71.19	79.20- 04
	Parkhomenko	Aleksandr	BLR	22.3.81	182/82	Dec	8101	8136- 06
	Parlicki	Mateusz	POL	14.4.84	187/78	LJ	7.90	7.62- 06, 7.64w- 05
						TJ	16.66, 16.85w	16.41, 16.48w- 06
	Parravicini	Tim	AUS	25.4.81	190/84	LJ	8.01	8.18, 8.20w- 05

Name		Nat	Born	Ht/Wt	Event	2007 Mark	Pre-2007 Best
* Pars	Krisztián	HUN	18.2.82	188/104	HT	81.40	82.45- 06
Parson	Rynell	USA-Y	11.7.90	173/70	100	10.23	10.43- 06
Parsons	Tom	GBR	5.5.84	190/78	HJ	2.29	2.24- 06
* Pate	Miguel	USA	13.6.79	188/84	LJ	8.24	8.59i, 8.45- 02, 8.46A- 03
* Patton	Darvis	USA	4.12.77	183/75	100	10.11	10.00- 03, 9.89w- 04
					200	20.49	20.03- 03
Pauli	Jake	USA	15.6.79	191/86	PV	5.82	5.80- 04
Paumier	Alexis	CUB	21.1.75	191/100	SP	19.75	20.78- 00
* Pavlov	Igor	RUS	18.7.79	187/83	PV	5.81	5.90i- 05, 5.80- 04
* Payne	David	USA	24.7.82	185/81	110H	13.02	13.31- 06
Peçanha	Fabiano	BRA	5.6.82	186/73	800	1:44.60	1:45.40- 05
^ Pedroso	Iván	CUB	17.12.72	176/70	LJ	8.15	8.71, 8.96Aw- 95, 8.79w-92
Peetre	Taavi	EST	4.7.83	192/119	SP	19.95	20.30- 04
Peguero	Arizmendi	DOM	7.8.80	173/76	400	44.92	45.48- 06, 45.2- 03
Pereira	António	POR	10.7.75	173/68	50kW	3:52:17	3:58:39- 06
Peremota	Igor	RUS	14.1.81	191/80	110H	13.47	13.37- 06
Peresta	Andrew	USA	12.10.85	180/77	400H	49.90	50.97- 05
Pérez	César	ESP	7.4.75	172/63	3kSt	8:23.40	8:13.06- 06
* Pérez	Jefferson	ECU	1.7.74	174/59	20kW	1:21:14	1:17:21- 03
Pérez	Lisvany	CUB	24.1.82	198/76	HJ	2.27	2.29- 05
Pérez	Santiago	ESP	15.1.72	179/70	50kW	3:46:56	3:45:55- 98
^ Peric	Dragan	SRB	8.5.64	186/115	SP	20.40	21.77- 98
Perry	Preston	USA	13.9.83	171/68	100	10.14	10.46- 05, 10.01Aw- 06
Perry	Willie	USA	16.5.87	178/73	200	20.57	20.42- 06
* Pestano	Mario	ESP	8.4.78	195/120	DT	68.26	68.00- 04
* Petrenko	Aleksandr	RUS	8.2.83	183/75	TJ	17.29, 17.41w	17.09- 06
Petrov	Aleksandr	RUS	9.8.86		LJ	7.93	7.32- 06
Petrucci	Nick	USA	10.11.75	197/129	DT	60.39	66.35- 03
Philakong	Theerayut	THA	27.2.84	174/60	TJ	16.44	16.58- 06
* Phillips	Dwight	USA	1.10.77	181/82	100	10.20, 10.06w	10.14- 05, 10.11w- 00
					LJ	8.31, 8.37w	8.60- 04
Phillips	Isa	JAM	22.4.84	193/84	400H	48.51	49.36- 06
Phillips	Richard	JAM	26.1.83	188/75	110H	13.42	13.39- 04
Piantella	Giorgio	ITA	6.7.81	181/75	PV	5.50i	5.55- 04
* Pickering	Craig	GBR	16.10.86	181/82	100	10.14	10.22- 05
Piedra	Byron	ECU	9.8.82	174/65	1500	3:37.88	3:39.31- 04
Pienaar	Hardus	RSA	10.8.81	190/88	JT	82.96	84.50- 03
Pietrobelli	Pablo	ARG	24.6.80	180/82	JT	79.45A	75.58- 06
Pignata	Francesco	ITA	14.2.78	191/81	JT	77.94	81.67- 05
Pimiä	Juho-Matti	FIN	28.12.84	171/70	LJ	8.00w	7.57, 7.58w- 06
Pinardo	Francisco José	ESP	15.3.75	179/64	50kW	3:50:53	3:51:40- 05
Pincemail	Sébastien	FRA	21.2.79	186/84	TJ	16.56i, 16.45	16.95- 03
Pishchalnikov	Bogdan	RUS	26.8.82	197/107	DT	64.95	64.19- 06
* Pitkämaki	Tero	FIN	19.12.82	195/92	JT	91.23	91.53- 05
Platas	Gustavo	ESP	19.2.81	180/65	1500	3:38.17	3:42.60- 05
Platnitskiy	Dmitriy	BLR-J	26.8.88	189/80	TJ	16.62	16.29- 06
* Plawgo	Marek	POL	25.2.81	183/72	400H	48.12	48.16- 01
Plotnir	Yevgeniy	RUS	26.6.77	196/85	TJ	17.09i, 16.88, 16.96w	17.21- 06
Pohle	Andreas	GER	6.4.81	178/65	TJ	16.72	16.99- 04
Pokrop	Hubert	POL	2.11.85	173/60	3kSt	8:31.31	8:37.97- 05
Poljanec	Andrej	SLO	10.11.84	182/77	PV	5.60	5.50- 06
Pollmächer	André	GER	22.3.83	179/58	10,000	27:55.56	28:22.56- 06
Polonet	Vickson	KEN	2.7.85		1500	3:38.1A	3:39.91- 05
Poole	Teddy	USA	.86	175/73	200	20.48w	21.48- 05
Pope	Mitchell	USA	21.1.84	196/150	SP	19.94	19.03- 06
Poplawski	Radoslaw	POL	16.1.83	176/61	3kSt	8:30.09	8:17.32- 04
Porter	Jeff	USA	27.11.85	188/84	110H	13.57	13.93- 06
Pouzy	Frédéric	FRA	18.2.83	184/88	HT	76.95	74.03- 05
Povegliano	Lorenzo	ITA	11.11.84	187/102	HT	75.03	72.52- 06
* Powell	Asafa	JAM	23.11.82	190/88	100	9.74	9.77- 05
					200	20.00	19.90- 06
Pozdnyakov	Anatoloy	RUS	1.2.87		HT	72.69	68.60- 06
Pratt	Robison	MEX	25.2.80	197/80	PV	5.60A	5.70Ai- 06, 5.61- 05
Prezelj	Rozle	SLO	26.9.79	193/73	HJ	2.27	2.31i- 04, 2.30- 06
Prince	Damian	USA	23.10.86	193/81	400H	49.21	50.91- 06
Privitera	Dario	ITA	17.3.79	173/62	50kW	4:03:20	4:20:10- 05
Probasco	Nate	USA	10.7.83	188/90	200	20.64	20.59, 20.49w- 05
Prokhorov	Aleksandr	RUS	22.1.86	176/62	20kW	1:22:13	1:20:51- 06
Prokopenko	Pavel	RUS	24.8.87	184/84	PV	5.75	5.40- 06
Pröll	Martin	AUT	21.3.81	175/58	3kSt	8:32.49	8:13.74- 05
Prowell	Lee	GUY	11.1.75		100	10.23w	10.49- 03

	Name		Nat	Born	Ht/Wt	Event	2007 Mark	Pre-2007 Best
	Pruglo	Sergiy	UKR	18.11.83	187/109	DT	62.14	62.74- 04
	Pseret	Benjamin	KEN	.80		Mar	2:10:18	2:13:46- 06
	Ptácek	Adam	CZE	8.10.80	178/65	PV	5.70, 5.82ex	5.81i- 03, 5.80- 02
	Pugh	Marcus	USA	30.4.86	182/73	200	20.66	21.03- 05, 20.84w- 04
	Pyatnytsya	Oleksandr	UKR	14.7.85	186/84	JT	76.28	72.20- 06
	Pyra	Dawid	POL	27.3.87	189/81	Dec	7703	0
	Qin Qiang		CHN	18.4.83	179/94	JT	80.21	78.15- 06
*	Quesada	Yoelbi	CUB	4.8.73	181/71	TJ	17.07	17.85- 97, 17.97w- 95
	Quiller	Rory	USA	17.4.84	190/82	PV	5.51	5.25- 06
	Quinley	Trevell	USA	16.1.83	198/91	LJ	8.22, 8.26w	8.17- 05
*	Quiñónez	Jackson	ESP	12.6.80	190/91	110H	13.33	13.34- 06
	Quow	Renny	TRI	25.8.87	170/66	400	45.35	45.74- 06
	Rabbath	Jean-Claude	LIB	12.7.77	188/82	HJ	2.24i, 2.23	2.27- 04
	Rada	Kresimir	CRO	3.11.81	199/134	SP	19.44	19.09- 05
	Ragnvaldsson	Daniel	SWE	3.1.76	184/89	JT	77.99	78.54- 05
*	Rags	Eriks	LAT	1.6.75	183/93	JT	83.35A	86.47- 01
	Raja	Andres	EST	2.6.82	187/80	Dec	7834	7809- 06
*	Ramaala	Hendrick	RSA	2.2.72	168/60	Mar	2:07:56	2:06:55- 06
^	Ramadhani	Samson	TAN	25.12.82	168/56	Mar	2:10:43	2:08:01- 03
	Ramohube	Onnanye	BOT	2.3.79	183/68	HJ	2.25A	2.20- 05
	Ramolefi	Ruben	RSA	17.7.78	174/56	3kSt	8:20.18	8:20.40- 05
*	Ramzi	Rashid	BRN	17.7.80	172/65	800	1:45.64	1:44.05- 06
						1500	3:35.00	3:29.14- 06
	Ramzy	Bashir	USA	4.5.79	185/86	110H	13.61	13.64- 02
						LJ	8.02A, 7.98, 8.08Aw	8.15- 04
	Randall	Derek	USA	15.6.83	191/109	DT	60.42	61.14- 06
	Randle	Jared	USA	14.11.87	185/73	LJ	7.95i	
	Randolph	Chris	USA	25.4.84	188/82	Dec	7798	7872- 06
	Randriamihaja	Joseph-Berlioz	MAD	30.11.75	188/75	110H	13.55	13.46- 04. 13.3- 03
	Rankin	Jonathan	USA	9.2.82	178/64	1500	3:35.72	3:35.26- 05
						1M	3:54.24	3:55.63- 05
	Rans	Kevin	BEL	19.8.82	187/80	PV	5.70	5.70i, 5.65- 06
	Rapp	Peter	GER	29.5.83	197/86	LJ	8.10	8.00- 05
	Rashad	Ahmad	USA	12.12.87	175/70	100	10.33, 10.20w	10.52, 10.37w- 05
						200	20.56	21.02, 20.73w- 05
	Rassioui	Badr	MAR	.86	179/66	1500	3:36.04	3:38.28- 06
	Rautenkrantz	Jens	GER	11.4.82	189/95	HT	76.73	76.21- 06
*	Reed	Gary	CAN	25.10.81	175/66	800	1:44.03	1:43.93- 06
	Reid	Orlando	JAM	3.7.82	188/72	100	10.19, 10.17w	10.28, 10.07w- 06
						200	20.51	20.54- 06
	Reif	Christian	GER	24.10.84	195/85	LJ	8.19	7.90- 06
*	Reina	Antonio Manuel	ESP	13.6.81	186/71	800	1:45.32	1:43.83- 02
	Ren Longyun		CHN	12.10.87	171/58	10,000	28:08.67	29:10.77- 06
						Mar	2:08:15	2:15:13- 06
	Repcík	Jozef	SVK	3.8.86	186/72	800	1:46.45	1:46.43- 06
	Restrepo	Gustavo	COL	27.7.82	165/60	20kW	1:23:45A	1:22:01- 05
	Revenko	Vladyslav	UKR	15.11.84	180/65	PV	5.60	5.80- 05
	Reyes	Luis Alexander	CUB	22.10.77	174/78	100	9.9	10.43- 98, 10.3- 03
	Reyes	Reinier	CUB	15.7.82	180/69	LJ	7.91	7,81- 05
	Reynolds	Doug	USA	11.8.75	196/124	DT	62.76	66.76- 99
	Richardson	Chris	USA	25.11.80	193/91	Dec	7871	7605- 06
	Rietveld	Pelle	NED	4.2.85	184/75	Dec	7955	7309- 05
	Riitmuru	Tarmo	EST	31.1.86		Dec	7626	7144- 06
	Riley	Jonathon	USA	29.12.78	175/58	5000	13:19.92	13:21.11- 04
	Rimmer	Michael	GBR	3.2.86	180/71	800	1:45.17	1:45.23- 06
	Riparelli	Jacques	ITA	27.3.83	183/75	100	10.25	10.36- 04
	Riseley	Jeff	AUS	11.11.86	191/75	800	1:46.35	1:49.0- 06
						1500	3:38.56	3:48.91- 06
	Riter	Trent	USA	15.6.82	183/68	800	1:46.62	1:47.78- 04
	Ritzenhein	Dathan	USA	30.12.82	170/52	3000	7:39.03	7:43.95- 05
	5000	13:16.06		13:16.61- 06		2M	8:11.74	8:23.45- 05
	Riva	Eddy	FRA	17.4.73	185/65	50kW	3:51:34	3:53:18- 03
	Rizki	Monder	BEL	16.8.79	176/66	3000	7:46.94	7:42.84- 04
^	Robberts	Janus	RSA	10.3.79	196/130	SP	19.31	21.97- 01
	Roberge	Jesse	USA	2.10.78	193/136	SP	19.29	19.68- 06
	Robertson	Michael	USA	19.12.83	198/111	DT	64.04	64.89- 04
	Robinson	Bennie	USA	6.7.82	176/79	100	10.24	10.40- 04
	Robinson	Josh	AUS	4.10.85	187/95	JT	80.73	79.92- 06
*	Robinson	Khadevis	USA	19.7.76	183/74	800	1:44.27	1:43.68- 06
*	Robles	Dayron	CUB	19.11.86	192/80	110H	12.92	13.00- 06
*	Rock	Andrew	USA	23.1.82	188/75	400	45.12	44.35- 05

	Name		Nat	Born	Ht/Wt	Event	2007 Mark	Pre-2007 Best
*	Rodgers	Michael	USA	24.4.85	178/73	100	10.10, 10.07w	10.29, 10.18w- 06
	Rodríguez	Álvaro	ESP	25.5.87	185/66	1500	3:37.04	3:39.28- 06
	Rodríguez	Ángel David	ESP	25.4.80	178/66	100	10.18	10.24, 10.20w- 06
	Roff	Jeremy	AUS	22.11.83	183/70	1500	3:38.20	3:39.58- 06
	Rogowski	Przemyslaw	POL	9.2.80	185/78	100	10.23w	10.40- 06
	Rohatinsky	Josh	USA	7.3.82	180/62	5000	13:25.53	13:47.57- 05
						10,000	27:55.86	28;39.93- 05
*	Rome	Jarred	USA	21.12.76	194/140	DT	68.37	67.51- 04
	Romero	Juan Carlos	MEX	15.12.77		10,000	28:10.14	28:32.61- 06
	Rono	Daniel	KEN	13.7.78		Mar	2:09:36	2:10:15- 06
	Rono	Geoffrey	KEN	21.4.87	175/60	800	1:46.92	1:47.10- 05
						1500	3:35.72	3:34.60- 06
	Rono	Vincent	KEN		165/55	1500	3:37.96	3:40.20- 06
	Rooney	Martyn	GBR	3.4.87	198/79	400	45.47	45.35- 06
*	Rop	Rodgers	KEN	16.2.76	172/52	Mar	2:07:32	2:07:34- 06
	Rosiak	Michal	POL	9.5.86	186/70	LJ	7.94	7.73- 05, 7.84w- 06
	Rosiewicz	Maciej	POL	31.7.77	173/68	50kW	4:03:01	4:03:07- 06
	Ross	Joshua	AUS	9.2.81	185/81	100	10.08	10.12- 05
						200	20.53, 20.51w	20.78- 04
	Roth	Scott	USA-J	25.6.88	180/73	PV	5.53i	5.31- 06
*	Röthlin	Viktor	SUI	14.10.74	172/60	Mar	2:08:20	2:09:56- 04
	Rotich	James	KEN	22.12.78		Mar	2:07:12	2:09:25- 06
	Rovan	Jurij	SLO	23.1.75	187/81	PV	5.60	5.61- 04
	Rozna	Roman	MDA	25.3.76	190/105	HT	70.67	76.62- 03
	Rubanko	Artem	UKR	21.3.74	191/110	HT	77.60	80.44- 04
	Rubino	Giorgio	ITA	15.4.86	176/55	20kW	1:21:17, 1:21:30.01t	1:22:05- 06
*	Rudisha	David	KEN-J	17.12.88	182/70	800	1:44.15	1:46.3A- 06
	Ruiz	Diego	ESP	5.2.82	182/68	1500	3:36.22	3:39.01- 06
	Rujevic	Luka	SRB	14.10.85	200/132	SP	20.11	19.73- 06
	Rupp	Galen	USA	8.5.86	180/62	10,000	27:33.48	28:15.52- 05
	Russell	Scott	CAN	16.1.79	206/122	JT	83.98	84.41- 05
*	Rutherford	Greg	GBR	17.11.86	188/84	LJ	7.96	8.26- 06
	Ruto	Nahashon	KEN	23.9.77	176/66	800	1:46.26	1:46.5A- 04
	Rutter	Adam	AUS	24.12.86	168/54	50kW	3:52:49	0
	Ruuskanen	Antti	FIN	21.2.84	190/85	JT	82.71, 87.88dh	84.10- 06
	Ruzavin	Andrey	RUS	28.3.86	175/70	20kW	1:20:07	1:21:51- 05
	Ryan	Jeff	USA	8.12.80	188/79	PV	5.61	5.50- 06
*	Rybakov	Yaroslav	RUS	22.11.80	198/82	HJ	2.38i, 2.35	2.38i- 05, 2.34- 03
	Ryland	Daniel	USA	6.8.79	185/82	PV	5.72i, 5.63	5.85i, 5.70- 05
*	Sack	Peter	GER	27.7.79	192/135	SP	21.00	20.83- 06
	Safarov	Sergey	RUS	28.10.83	178/67	20kW	1:23:11	1:22:02- 05
	Safronov	Konstantin	KAZ	2.9.87	184/68	LJ	8.01	7.93- 06
*	Saidy Ndure	Jaysuma (ex GAM)	NOR	1.1.84	192/72	100	10.06	10.26- 04, 10.18w- 05
						200	19.89	20.47- 06, 20.14w- 05
	Saito	Hitoshi	JPN	9.10.86	179/67	200	20.64	21.02- 06
	Sajdok	Stanislav	CZE	22.7.83	190/75	110H	13.74, 13.71w	13.68, 13.65w- 06
*	Saladino	Irving	PAN	23.1.83	183/70	LJ	8.57	8.56, 8.65w- 06
	Salem	Jamal Bilal	QAT	12.9.78	178/62	5000	13:19.31	13:06.81- 06
	Sales	Thiago	BRA	12.8.86		400H	50.25	51.19- 06
	Sambu	Ezra	KEN	4.9.78	175/70	400	45.73A	44.43A, 44.98- 03
	Samimi	Abbas	IRI	9.6.77	203/110	DT	64.52	64.98- 04
	Samimi	Mohammed	IRI-J	18.9.88	190/95	DT	60.56	55.23- 06
	Samoei	Stephen	KEN	20.6.82		10,000	28:07.65	28:36.71- 06
	Samoylenko	Vitaliy	UKR	22.5.84	196/74	HJ	2.23	2.20i- 06
	Samuels	J-Mee	USA	20.5.87	165/64	100	10.22, 10.13w	10.08, 10.05w- 05
						200	20.63w	20.32A- 05, 20.58- 04
	Sánchez	Benjamín	ESP	10.3.85	185/72	20kW	1:21:21	1:22:24- 06
	Sánchez	David	ESP	23.8.73	176/63	50kW	4:04:25	3:56:00- 99
*	Sánchez	Eder	MEX	21.5.86	176/67	20kW	1:20:08	1:19:02- 05
*	Sánchez	Fólix	DOM	30.8.77	178/73	400H	48.01	47.25- 03
	Sánchez	Jesús	MEX	23.3.76	175/61	50kW	3:57:08	4:04:29- 04
	Sandiku	Tesfaye	ETH	.83		HMar	61:36	
*	Sands	Leevan	BAH	16.8.81	190/73	TJ	17.23, 17.55w	17.50- 02
	Sands	Shamar	BAH	30.4.85	178/73	110H	13.47	13.67- 02
	Sang	Elijah	KEN	.83		Mar	2:10:13	2:15:33- 06
	Sang	Silas	KEN	21.8.78	171/56	HMar	60:34	60:56- 06
	Sanguin	Giovanni	ITA	14.5.69	185/100	HT	72.40	74.52- 97
	dos Santos	Leonardo	BRA	7.5.84	183/65	TJ	16.75	16.46- 05, 16.58w- 03
*	dos Santos	Marílson	BRA	6.8.77	174/58	5000	13:22.11	13:19.43- 06
	10,000	27:28.12		27:48.49- 06		HMar	59:33	62:12- 00
						Mar	2:08:37	2:08:48- 04

	Name		Nat	Born	Ht/Wt	Event	2007 Mark	Pre-2007 Best
	Sapinskiy	Dmitriy	RUS	13.10.83	192/84	LJ	8.05	8.17- 06
	Sappleton	Aldwyn	JAM	21.12.81	180/74	800	1:46.84	1:47.57- 03
	Saquipay	Rolando	ECU	21.7.79	166/57	20kW	1:23:28	1:19:21- 05
*	Sato	Atsushi	JPN	8.5.78	170/55	HMar	60:25	61:37- 02
						Mar	2:07:13	2:08:36- 04
	Sato	Yuki	JPN	26.11.86	178/59	10,000	27:51.65	28:07.02- 06
	Savage	Darius	USA-J	18.1.88	193/145	DT	61.08	
	Savolaynen	Mykola	UKR	25.3.80	189/76	TJ	17.30	17.16i- 04, 17.08- 02
*	Sawano	Daichi	JPN	16.9.80	182/70	PV	5.75	5.83- 05
	Sbai	Hassane	TUN	21.4.84		20kW	1:23:37	1:22:32- 06
	Scales	Mardy	USA	10.9.81	173/73	100	10.24	10.07, 10.02w- 04
	Scarr	Adam	GBR	7.5.85	191/82	HJ	2.24	2.25- 06
	Schaerer	Daniel	SUI/USA	20.10.85	195/115	DT	61.45	56.46- 06
	Schembera	Robin	GER-J	1.10.88	186/67	800	1:46.07	1:47.29- 06
	Schembri	Fabrizio	ITA	27.1.81	183/74	TJ	16.60	16.86- 06
	Scherbarth	Tobias	GER	17.8.85	195/81	PV	5.60	5.55- 06
	Schlangen	Carsten	GER	31.12.80	189/68	1500	3:36.54	3:38.04- 06
	Schmidt	Marco	GER	5.9.83	202/106	SP	19.52	18.20- 06
	Schneeberger	Marc	SUI	5.7.81	185/76	200	20.47	20.78- 04
	Schnelting	Daniel	GER	9.3.86	195/93	200	20.62	20.68- 05
	Schrader	Michael	GER	1.7.87	183/83	Dec	7947	-0-
^	Schultz	Ingo	GER	26.7.75	201/96	400	45.67	44.66- 01
*	Schulze	Fabian	GER	7.3.84	192/79	PV	5.83i, 5.41	5.81- 06
*	Schwazer	Alex	ITA	26.12.84	182/72	20kW	1:23:21.19t	1:21:38- 06
						50kW	3:36:04	3:41:54- 05
	Sciandra	Livio	ITA	23.9.80	187/73	800	1:45.93	1:46.26- 04
^	Scigaczewski	Tomasz	POL	18.11.78	188/80	110H	13.73, 13.71w	13.29- 99, 13.25w, 13.0- 98
	Scott	Bryan	USA	1.3.85	184/75	400H	49.78	49.86- 05
*	Scott	Dorian	JAM	1.2.82	185/136	SP	20.60	20.52i, 20.33- 06
	Scott	Jeremy	USA	21.5.81	206/91	PV	5.70i, 5.66	5.70i- 03, 5.56- 04
	Scott	Jordan	USA-J	22.2.88	188/84	PV	5.55	5.22- 05
*	Scott	Leonard	USA	19.1.80	181/84	100	10.09	9.91-06, 9.83w-99
	Scotten	Ray	USA	20.5.83		PV	5.52	5.55- 05
*	Sdiri	Salim	FRA	26.10.78	185/80	LJ	8.13i, 8.01	8.27i- 06, 8.25- 05, 8.29w- 03
	Seaman	Tim	USA	14.5.72	175/64	20kW	1:23:38	1:22:02- 04
*	Sebrle	Roman	CZE	26.11.74	186/88	Dec	8697	9026- 01
	Sedlácek	Pavel	CZE	5.4.68	198/111	HT	74.39	79.56- 96
	Sedoc	Gregory	NED	16.10.81	179/74	110H	13.37	13.51, 13.46w- 04
	Segura	Omar	MEX	24.3.81	170/57	20kW	1:23:20A	1:20:25- 05
	Seitz	Heinrich	GER	6.4.80	188/97	DT	60.70	62.63- 04
	Sellers	Scott	USA	16.8.86	190/72	HJ	2.33	2.27i, 2.26- 04
	Semenenko	Yevgen	UKR	17.7.84	178/67	TJ	16.90	17.03- 06
	Semenov	Andriy	UKR	4.7.84	204/115	SP	19.93	19.26- 06
	Semenov	Oleksiy	UKR	27.6.82	204/115	DT	62.76	62.46- 05
	Seoud	Amr Ibrahim	EGY	10.6.86	180/70	100	10.11w	10.48- 06
						200	20.64	20.93- 04
	Sepehrzad	Hadi	IRI	19.1.83		Dec	7667w, 7652	7490- 06
	Seredovich	Nikolay	BLR	25.1.84	176/58	20kW	1:22:12	1:20:34- 06
	Serem	Samson	KEN	.85	178/64	1500	3:36.86	3:42.4A- 05
	Sergachev	Sergey	RUS	10.7.87		20kW	1:21:56	
						50kW	4:02:02	
	Sergeyenkov	Artem	RUS	10.6.86	188/76	400	45.86	46.80- 06
*	Sergeyev	Aleksandr	RUS	29.7.83	191/81	TJ	17.15i, 16.83	17.23i, 17.11- 04
	Seskin	Yuriy	RUS	7.7.66	196/110	DT	59.78	64.58- 88
	Shahrokhi	Mehdi	IRI	23.5.85	188/100	SP	19.57	18.85- 05
	Shahween	Mohamed Othman	KSA	15.2.86	182/68	1500	3:38.18	3:42.13- 06
	Shako	Dmitriy	BLR	27.5.79	192/92	HT	76.32	77.92- 06
*	Shami	Mubarak Hassan	QAT	2.12.80	174/63	HMar	60:47	60:31dh- 04, 61:09- 05
						Mar	2:07:19	2:09:22- 05
	Shapoval	Viktor	UKR	17.10.79	198/75	HJ	2.28i, 2.26	2.26- 03
	Sharman	William	GBR	12.9.84	188/82	110H	13.68	13.49, 13.45w- 06
	Sharpe	Fred	USA	21.8.78	173/70	400H	50.13	48.86- 03
	Shaw	Brandon	USA	11.9.81	176/64	800	1:46.20	1:47.32- 06
	Shay	Ryan	USA	4.5.79	178/68	10,000	28:03.44	28:18.81- 04
	Shayunov	Yuriy	BLR	22.10.87	187/95	HT	74.92	
	Shebto	Moustafa	QAT	4.7.86	176/59	3000	7:46.38	7:57.23- 06
						3kSt	8:25.11	8:18.52- 04
	Shelest	Oleksiy	UKR	27.3.73	173/64	50kW	3:58:10	3:56.23- 05
^	Shevchenko	Dmitriy	RUS	13.5.68	200/140	DT	60.68	70.54- 02
*	Shi Dongpeng		CHN	6.1.84	191/75	110H	13.19	13.28- 06

	Name		Nat	Born	Ht/Wt	Event	2007 Mark	Pre-2007 Best
	Shields	Sean	USA	10.2.83	196/117	SP	20.05	20.11- 06
	Shimizu	Daisuke	JPN	2.8.82	182/62	10,000	28:10.68	29:00.39- 04
	Shin Il-yong		KOR	17.2.79	174/67	20kW	1:21:47	1:21:29- 04
	Shinada	Naohiro	JPN	10.2.86		LJ	7.86, 7.92w	7.87- 03
	Shubenok	Nikolay	BLR	4.5.85	190/75	Dec	8028	7517- 06
	Shulha	Mykola	UKR	26.11.82	188/81	Dec	7583	7574- 06
	Shunk	Adam	USA	29.8.79	183/75	HJ	2.26	2.30- 05
	Shustov	Aleksandr	RUS	13.8.84		HJ	2.31	2.28- 06
	Si Tianfeng		CHN	17.6.84	183/70	50kW	3:58:27	3:42:55- 05
	Sidorov	Maksim	RUS	11.5.86		SP	20.01	18.52- 06
	Siele	David	KEN-J	.88		3000	7:47.37	
	Sigei	Matthew	KEN	30.4.83		Mar	2:09:39	2:09:17- 03
	Sigei	Robert Kipngetich	KEN	3.1.82	165/53	3000	7:39.02	7:40.47- 05
	5000	13:06.71	13:19.95- 03			10,000	27:04.18	27:46.06- 04
*	Sihine	Sileshi	ETH	29.9.83	165/48	3000	7:44.?+	7:29.92- 05
	5000	12:50.16	12:47.04- 04			10,000	26:48.73	26:39.69- 04
	Sillanpää	Kalle	FIN	4.12.83	186/85	JT	77.17	76.12- 06
*	Silnov	Andrey	RUS	9.9.84	198/83	HJ	2.36i, 2.30	2.37- 06
	Silva	Andrés	URU	27.3.86	180/76	400	45.89	45.02- 06
						400H	50.14	50.46- 06
	da Silva	Anselmo Gomes	BRA	22.3.81	188/85	110H	13.52	13.31A- 05, 13.40- 06
*	da Silva	Fábio Gomes	BRA	4.8.83	178/74	PV	5.77	5.65- 06
	da Silva	Iván Scolfaro	BRA	30.7.82	188/80	Dec	7825	7711- 05
	da Silva	Mauro	BRA	26.12.86		LJ	8.02	7.39- 05
*	Silva	Rui	POR	3.8.77	175/65	1500	3:35.92	3:30.07- 02
	Simanovich	Denis	BLR	20.4.87		20kW	1:22:26	1:28:04- 05
	Simion	Danut-Marian	ROM	25.1.83	190/78	LJ	8.00i	8.12- 03
	Simms	Allen	PUR	26.7.82	178/75	TJ	17.10	17.26i, 17.17- 03, 17.19w- 05
*	Simotwo	Suleiman	KEN	21.4.80	182/70	1500	3:31.89	3:31.67- 06
						1M	3:53.08	3:50.82- 05
	Sims	Jarrod	AUS	11.6.84	183/77	Dec	7556	7217- 06
	Singh	Amarjeet	IND	1.5.81	179/76	TJ	16.72	16.58- 06
	Singh	Navpreet	IND	15.6.78	186/135	SP	19.70	19.93- 04
	Singoei	Philip	KEN	31.12.75		Mar	2:07:57	2:08:18- 06
	Sinyakov	Andrey	BLR	6.1.82	189/117	SP	19.90	19.62- 06
	Sivakov	Dmitriy	BLR	15.2.83	190/120	DT	61.21	60.62- 05
	Sjöqvist	Erik	SWE	4.12.72	183/71	5000	13:25.37	13:23.24- 03
	Skarnulis	Donatas	LTU	21.10.77	185/68	50kW	3:54:23	3:55:43- 06
	Skipper	Tommy	USA	19.9.84	186/86	PV	5.80	5.79- 06
	Skoog	Henrik	SWE	17.4.79	185/71	3kSt	8:31.72	8:25.55- 03
	Slattery	Steve	USA	14.8.80	180/73	3kSt	8:15.69	8:17.87- 05
	Slepukhin	Sergey	RUS	6.3.87		LJ	7.99	7.21- 05
	Slobodenyuk	Vadym	UKR	17.3.81	189/74	3kSt	8:25.15	8:24.15- 06
	Slowik	Dariusz	CAN	15.8.77	196/123	DT	63.26	64.56- 04
	Smaliós	Ioánnis-Yeóryios	GRE	17.2.87	192/80	JT	76.80	77.25- 05
	Smirnov	Vitaliy	UZB	25.10.78	191/86	Dec	7838w, 7825	8021- 03
	Smith	Calvin	USA	10.12.87	180/75	400	45.52	46.17- 06
	Smith	Leigh	USA	28.8.81	198/95	JT	77.24	82.33- 06
*	Smith	Maurice	JAM	28.9.80	190/90	Dec	8644	8349- 06
	Smith	Max	NZL	20.10.84	181/61	1M	3:56.46	3:59.33i- 06, 4:01.14- 04
	Smith	Paul	USA	29.5.84	175/70	200	20.63A	20.65A- 06
*	Smith	Rutger	NED	9.7.81	197/129	SP	21.19	21.62- 06
						DT	67.63	65.51- 05
	Snochowski	Rafal	POL	31.10.83	186/70	3kSt	8:31.54	0
	Söderberg	David	FIN	11.8.79	185/100	HT	77.18	78.83- 03
*	Sofyin	Pavel	RUS	4.9.81	200/120	SP	20.38	20.68i, 20.59- 06
*	Soi	Edwin	KEN	3.3.86	168/53	3000	7:34.07	7:31.84- 06
	5000	13:10.21	12:52.40- 06			2M	8:16.98	
	Sokolov	Aleksey	RUS	14.11.79	175/62	Mar	2:09:07	2:11:39- 06
	Sokolovs	Igors	LAT	17.8.74	185/100	HT	76.22	74.32- 06
*	Sokolovskyy	Andriy	UKR	16.7.78	196/80	HJ	2.35i, 2.30	2.38- 05
	Sokyrskyy	Oleksiy	UKR	16.3.85	185/95	HT	73.44	71.95- 06
	Soler	Joël	FRA	15.2.82	176/66	PV	5.50	5.51i- 05, 5.50- 04
	Solinsky	Chris	USA	5.12.84	185/73	1500	3:37.27	3:42.13- 04
	3000	7:36.90	7:53.14i- 05, 8:12.1- 03			5000	13:12.24	13:27.94- 06
	Solomon	Duane	USA	28.12.84	191/73	800	1:45.69	1:47.45- 06
*	Som	Bram	NED	20.2.80	179/66	800	1:45.61	1:43.45- 06
	Sondee	Wachara	THA	9.4.83	175/72	100	10.33, 10.21dt	10.38- 06
	Songok	Boniface	KEN	25.12.80	172/57	3000	7:35.88	7:30.62- 04
						5000	13:16.74	12:55.85- 05

Name		Nat	Born	Ht/Wt	Event	2007 Mark	Pre-2007 Best
* Songok	Isaac	KEN	25.4.84	170/54	1M	3:56.17	3:54.56- 01
3000 7:38.10			7:28.72- 06		5000	13:15.70	12:48.66- 06
Sorescu	Cosmin	ROM	11.7.75	188/95	HT	74.09	76.46- 03
^ Sosunov	Kirill	RUS	1.11.75	195/86	LJ	8.04	8.41i- 97, 8.38- 98, 8.48w- 95
de Souza	Éder Antônio	BRA	15.10.86	189/85	110H	13.58	13.79- 05
de Souza	Hudson	BRA	25.2.77	180/65	1500	3:36.32	3:33.25- 05
de Souza	Márcio	BRA	24.1.75	181/74	110H	13.79, 13.5w?	13.38- 99
Spank	Raul	GER-J	13.7.88	190/75	HJ	2.24	2.23- 06
Speaight	Neil	GBR	9.9.78	191/79	1500	3:38.33	3:38.65i- 06, 3:40.62- 05
* Spearmon	Wallace	USA	24.12.84	188/78	100	9.96	10.11- 06
					200	19.82	19.65- 06
Spence	Lancford	JAM	15.12.82	188/75	400	45.80	44.77- 05
Spence	Mike	USA	20.5.78	173/60	3kSt	8:31.65	8:35.26- 04
Spiegelburg	Richard	GER	12.8.77	182/77	PV	5.71, 5.72sq	5.85- 01
^ Sposób	Grzegorz	POL	12.2.76	200/87	HJ	2.28i, 2.24	2.34- 04
Stallworth	Joel	USA	18.1.83	193/82	400	45.40	46.99- 06
Stankin	Vladimir	RUS	2.1.74	184/71	20kW	1:21:14	1:17:23- 04
Stanski	Olgierd	POL	4.4.73	196/98	DT	62.76	64.20- 00
Starodubtsev	Dmitriy	RUS	3.1.86		PV	5.70	5.65i, 5.61- 06
Starzak	Marcin	POL	20.10.85	178/63	LJ	8.21	8.09- 06
Statsenko	Oleg	UKR	22.10.80	189/97	JT	76.06	79.44- 03
Steacy	Jim	CAN	29.5.84	191/111	HT	77.38	75.96- 06
Steding	Stephan	GER	29.1.82	202/104	JT	82.46	82.13- 04
Steele	Andrew	GBR	19.9.84	190/82	400	45.31	46.21- 06
Steele	Bryan	JAM	23.3.84	179/73	400	45.85	46.49- 04
					400H	49.48	49.02- 06
Steele	Edino	JAM	6.1.87	175/68	200	20.58, 20.37w	20.75- 06
					400	45.77	45.81- 06
Stefanópoulos	Konstandinos	GRE	11.7.84	179/66	50kW	4:03:42	4:08:48- 05
* Steffensen	John	AUS	30.8.82	180/71	400	44.82	44.73- 06
Stehlik	Petr	CZE	15.4.77	185/102	SP	20.35	20.96- 04
Stepanchuk	Andrey	BLR	12.6.79	176/65	20kW	1:23:01	1:22:17- 01
Stevens	Kendall	USA	26.1.83	184/75	100	10.18	10.28, 10.17w- 06
* Stevenson	Toby	USA	19.11.76	186/82	PV	5.70	6.00- 04
Stockbarger	Westley	USA	5.6.85	190/120	SP	19.44i	18.19- 06
					DT	61.39	57.50- 06
Stolz	Christoph	GER	17.1.80	188/78	LJ	8.04	7.87- 06
Straub	Alexander	GER	14.10.83	180/73	PV	5.71	5.60- 06
Stroobants	Stijn	BEL	15.4.84	193/73	HJ	2.25i, 2.22	2.20- 05
Su Xiongfeng		CHN	21.3.87	183/70	LJ	8.07	7.75- 06
Suárez	Alejandro	MEX	30.11.80	175/60	10,000	27:43.92	28:17.65- 01
Suárez	Leonel	CUB	1.9.87	180/72	Dec	8156	7357- 06
Suárez	Yosvany	CUB	20.12.72	181/95	HT	71.40	73.93- 06
Suciu	Florin	ROM	18.5.83	178/62	100	10.24	10.54- 06
* Sudol	Grzegorz	POL	28.8.78	174/60	20kW	1:23:53	1:21:03- 05
					50kW	3:55:22	3:49:09- 04
* Suetsugu	Shingo	JPN	2.6.80	178/68	100	10.23	10.03- 03
					200	20.20	20.03- 03
Sugibayashi	Takanori	JPN	14.3.76	185/65	TJ	16.90	17.02- 00
Sugimachi	Mahau	BRA	13.11.84	184/78	400H	49.30	49.62- 06
Sugimoto	Akihiro	JPN	20.10.81	162/54	20kW	1:23:17	1:21:09- 04
Sugut	Harry	KEN	4.5.85	160/54	10,000	27:51.34	28:57.82- 06
Sukhomlinov	Igor	RUS	13.2.77	182/100	JT	83.34	80.20- 06
Suleman	Tunde	NGR	9.11.77	175/68	LJ	8.02	7.85- 98
^ Sullivan	Kevin	CAN	20.3.74	183/70	1500	3:34.16	3:31.71- 00
1M 3:56.21			3:50.26- 00		3000	7:40.17i	7:42.17i, 7:43.89- 06
					5000	13:19.27	13:27.29- 05
Sullivan	Luke	USA	4.6.76	188/114	DT	60.64	60.06- 98, 61.06dh- 99
Summerside	Seth	USA	14.2.84	183/70	3000	7:43.82	8:07.79i- 06
					10,000	28:02.51	
Sun Chao		CHN	8.1.87	173/63	50kW	3:50:46	4:04:07- 03
Surjan	Erik	AUS	22.6.83	191/93	Dec	7706	7621- 05
Suskevicius	Tadas	LTU	22.5.85		50kW	3:57:48	4:05:17- 06
Suter	Patric	SUI	17.5.77	192/115	HT	74.71	80.51- 03
Suzuki	Hideaki	JPN	31.5.87	185/68	LJ	8.01	7.82- 06
Suzuki	Takafumi	JPN	25.5.87	182/72	PV	5.50	5.21- 06
Svoboda	Petr	CZE	10.10.84	195/83	110H	13.64	13.87- 04, 13.84w- 06
Svyatokho	Valeriy	BLR	20.7.81		HT	76.13	81.49- 06
Swillims	Bastian	GER	9.12.82	191/91	400	45.44	45.83- 04
Syachinov	Stanislav	RUS	24.9.82		TJ	16.50	15.92- 06

Name		Nat	Born	Ht/Wt	Event	2007 Mark	Pre-2007 Best
Symmonds	Nick	USA	30.12.83	180/75	800	1:44.54	1:45.83- 06
Syrovátko	Jan	CZE	11.2.85	178/72	JT	78.17	76.48- 06
* Sysoyev	Aleksey	RUS	8.3.85	194/96	Dec	8357	8108- 06
Szabó	Attila	HUN	16.7.84		Dec	7545	7536- 06
Szebeny	Miklós	HUN	13.3.87	183/75	100	10.17w	10.46- 06
Szuster	Konrad	POL	21.1.84	196/96	DT	60.00	57.42- 05
Szymkowiak	Tomasz	POL	5.7.83	176/58	3kSt	8:26.52	8:25.45- 06
* Tadese	Zersenay	ERI	8.2.82	160/56	2M	8:19.34	
10,000	27:00.30		26:37.25- 06		HMar	58:59	59:05- 05
Tadesse	Dereje Raya	ETH	24.1.87		5000	13:25.34	13:42.66- 06
					10,000	27:51.51	27:52.54- 06
Tadili	Achraf	CAN	8.7.80	180/68	800	1:45.84	1:45.05- 03
* Taher	Tareq Mubarak	BRN	24.3.84	178/68	3kSt	8:07.12	8:11.36- 06
* Tahri	Bouabdellah	FRA	20.12.78	191/68	1500	3:36.13	3:34.85- 02
3000	7:38.41i		7:41.41i- 02, 7:42.49- 05		5000	13:12.29	13:24.05- 99
					3kSt	8:09.06	8:06.91- 03
^ Taillepierre	Karl	FRA	13.8.76	176/64	TJ	16.64i	17.45- 05
Takada	Shingo	JPN	26.9.85	184/72	200	20.64w	21.39- 06
Takahashi	Jon	USA	21.10.82	180/79	PV	5.71	5.61- 04
Takahira	Shinji	JPN	18.7.84	179/62	200	20.52	20.35- 06
Takezawa	Kensuke	JPN	11.10.86	170/52	5000	13:19.00	13:22.36- 06
					10,000	27:45.59	28:19.22- 06
Talam	Henry	KEN	12.2.81		3kSt	8:22.57	
Talankov	Vitaliy	BLR	29.4.82	176/68	20kW	1:22:52	1:23:08- 05
					50kW	3:51:59	4:06:26- 04
Talashko	Andrey	BLR	31.5.82	173/65	20kW	1:21:50	1:19:12- 06
Taleb	Brahim	MAR	16.2.85	182/70	3kSt	8:07.02	8:14.75- 06
Tallent	Jarrod	AUS	17.10.84	178/60	20kW	1:21:25	1:21:36- 06
					50kW	3:44:45	3:55:08- 06
* Tamesue	Dai	JPN	3.5.78	170/67	400H	48.73	47.89- 01
Tamgho	Teddy	FRA-J	15.6.89	184/67	TJ	16.53i, 16.35, 16.42w	15.68- 06
* Tammert	Aleksander	EST	2.2.73	196/126	DT	64.41	70.82- 06
Tanaka	Hiromasa	JPN	28.9.81	177/73	Dec	7656	7803- 06
Taneli	Heikki	FIN	12.6.80	191/80	HJ	2.24	2.27- 05
Tanii	Takayuki	JPN	14.2.83	166/57	20kW	1:21:09	1:20:39- 04
					50kW	3:50:08	3:47:23- 06
Tanonaka	Tasuku	JPN	23.9.78	185/79	110H	13.59, 13.51w	13.55, 13.51w- 06
Tanui	Mark	KEN	.77		HMar	61:53	61:52- 05
Taragon	Wilfred	KEN	9.6.85		5000	13:15.91	13:21.74- 06
10,000	27:33.02		28:22.2A- 06		HMar	60:42	60:46- 06
* Taylor	Angelo	USA	29.12.78	188/84	200	20.60	20.67- 97
400	44.05		44.68- 01		400H	48.45	47.50- 00
* Taylor	Dan	USA	12.5.82	198/145	SP	21.57i, 21.18	21.59- 06
Taylor	Logan	USA	3.4.86	183/70	110H	13.71	14.32, 14.19w- 06
Taylor	Mark	AUS	29.5.80		HJ	2.23	2.19- 06
* Tegenkamp	Matt	USA	19.1.82	186/66	1500	3:34.25	3:35.96- 06
3000	7:35.68		7:34.98- 06		2M	8:07.07	8:16.50- 06
					5000	13:07.41	13:04.90- 06
Teixeira	Maurício	BRA	22.3.82		400H	50.08	50.10- 05
^ Terek	Paul	USA	20.10.79	186/83	Dec	8134	8312- 04
Terer	Philemon	KEN	.85		HMar	61:51	
* Tereshin	Andrey	RUS	15.12.82	195/77	HJ	2.35i, 2.34	2.36i- 06, 2.32- 05
* Tergat	Paul	KEN	17.6.69	183/61	Mar	2:08:06	2:04:55- 03
Tertychnyy	Oleksandr	UKR	5.10.85	188/87	JT	79.06	73.26- 06
Tesfay	Michael	ERI	23.9.76	178/62	HMar	60:39	
Thamer	Kamal Ali	QAT-J	12.11.88	179/66	3kSt	8:25.71	8:20.29- 06
Theuri	James Kibocha	FRA	30.10.78	171/52	HMar	61:36	60:54- 05
Thomas	Alex	IND	16.4.79		TJ	16.45	16.16- 06
Thomas	Chris	USA	9.2.81	178/76	110H	13.60	13.66, 13.65w- 05
Thomas	Courtney	USA	4.3.87	173/70	200	20.52	21.28- 05
* Thomas	Donald	BAH	1.7.84	190/75	HJ	2.35	2.24- 06
* Thomas	Dwight	JAM	23.9.80	185/82	100	10.15, 10.07w	10.00- 05
					200	20.32	20.41- 04
Thompson	Floyd	USA	22.11.79	185/73	800	1:46.11	1:46.78- 03
* Thompson	Kemel	JAM	25.9.74	180/75	400H	49.28	48.05- 03
* Thompson	Richard	TRI	7.6.85	188/80	100	10.09, 9.95w	10.27, 10.26w- 06
* Thorkildsen	Andreas	NOR	1.4.82	188/90	JT	89.51	91.59- 06
* Thörnblad	Linus	SWE	6.3.85	180/78	HJ	2.38i, 2.31	2.34- 06
Thornell	John	AUS	22.4.85	178/64	LJ	7.99	8.08- 06
Thorsteinsson	Odinn Björn	ISL	3.12.81	200/128	SP	19.24	18.20- 06

	Name		Nat	Born	Ht/Wt	Event	2007 Mark	Pre-2007 Best
	Thuo	John	KEN	27.11.85		3000	7:46.65	
	Tickner	Frank	GBR	12.10.83	175/62	3kSt	8:31.40	8:45.78- 06
	Tiercelin	Jean-Baptiste	FRA	1.2.77	186/95	DT	61.22	59.26- 06
*	Tikhon	Ivan	BLR	24.7.76	186/110	HT	83.63	86.73- 05
	Tinsley	Michael	USA	21.4.84	183/80	400H	48.02	48.25- 06
	Tipotio	Vitolio	FRA	17.7.75	182/87	JT	79.81	80.34- 02
	Tishchenko	Nikolay	RUS	4.2.77	195/93	Dec	7884	8043- 04
	Tobin	Robert	GBR	20.12.83	190/75	400	45.90	45.01- 05
	Todoo Rotich	William	KEN	.80		HMar	61:48	60:12- 06
						Mar	2:09:53	2:11:31- 06
	Toivanen	Viljo	FIN	18.8.84	186/96	JT	82.02	80.57- 06
	Tola	Tadesse	ETH	31.10.87	172/55	3000	7:43.70	8:02.23- 06
	5000	13:18.82		13:19.47- 06		10,000	27:04.89	28:15.16- 06
						HMar	61:37	
*	Tomlinson	Chris	GBR	15.9.81	197/81	LJ	8.29	8.27- 02, 8.28w- 04
*	Ton	Svatoslav	CZE	20.10.78	192/75	HJ	2.30	2.33- 04
	Toompuu	Raigo	EST	17.7.81	188/118	SP	19.66	19.28- 05
^	Topic	Dragutin	SRB	12.3.71	197/77	HJ	2.27	2.38- 93
	Torrance	Jamaal	USA	20.7.83	173/69	400	45.19	46.40- 06
	Torres	Jorge	USA	22.8.80	170/62	10,000	27:42.91	28:14.43- 06
	Torro	Osku	FIN	21.8.79	183/68	HJ	2.27	2.26i, 2.25- 06
*	Tosca	Osniel	CUB	30.6.84	178/60	TJ	17.52	17.17- 04
	Townsend	Fred	USA	19.2.82	188/82	110H	13.71	13.76, 13.71w- 04
*	Trammell	Terrence	USA	23.11.78	188/84	100	10.21	10.04- 00
						110H	12.95	13.02- 05
	Traoré	Bano	FRA	25.4.85	180/65	110H	13.54	13.86- 06
	Tristán	Louis	PER	1.5.84	185/75	LJ	8.09	8.09A- 06
	Tromp	Xavier	FRA	3.3.84	191/86	PV	5.50	5.55i, 5.50- 06
	Troode	Chris	AUS	10.2.83	184/84	400	45.42	45.42- 06
	Troop	Lee	AUS	22.3.73	176/55	Mar	2:10:31	2:09:49- 03
	Trotskiy	Ivan	BLR	27.5.76	167/50	20kW	1:20:13	1:19:40- 03
	Tsákonas	Yeóryios	GRE-J	22.1.88		LJ	7.92	7.49- 05
	Tsao Chih-Hao		TPE	21.9.81		HJ	2.23	2.15- 05
*	Tsátoumas	Loúis	GRE	12.2.82	187/76	LJ	8.66	8.34- 03, 8.37w- 04
	Tsiámis	Dimítrios	GRE	12.1.82	178/67	TJ	16.99	17.55- 06
	Tsirikhov	Soslan	RUS	25.3.84		SP	19.38i, 18.57	19.47- 06
	Tsukahara	Naoki	JPN	10.5.85	180/75	100	10.15	10.25- 06
						200	20.60	20.35- 06
	Tsushima	Yosuke	JPN	24.12.81	184/72	400H	49.79	50.22- 03
	Tsvetkov	Mikhail	RUS	4.5.80	194/73	HJ	2.26i, 2.25	2.30i- 02, 2.30- 03
	Tucker	Steven	AUS	3.12.82	188/81	100	10.22w	10.46- 05
^	Tudor	Bogdan	ROM	1.2.70	187/70	LJ	7.96	8.37- 95
	Tugay	Igor	UKR	22.3.75	185/108	HT	74.56	78.85- 05
*	Tunks	Jason	CAN	7.5.75	200/125	DT	62.87	67.88- 98
	Turi	Indrek	EST	30.7.81	187/85	Dec	7724	8122- 03
	Turner	Andrew	GBR	19.9.80	184/77	110H	13.27	13.38, 13.24w- 06
	Turner	Matt	USA	21.7.86	193/82	LJ	7.84, 7.93w	7.54A, 7.59Aw- 06
*	Tysse	Erik	NOR	4.12.80	184/59	20kW	1:20:31	1:19:38- 06
						50kW	3:51:52	3:54:37- 06
	Udechuku	Emeka	GBR	10.7.79	176/125	DT	63.37, 63.79dh	64.93- 04
	Ueno	Masahide	JPN	10.9.83	178/70	100	10.26, 10.16w	10.28- 06
	Ueno	Yuichiro	JPN	29.7.85	183/57	5000	13:21.49	13:35.68- 06
	Uhlík	Michal	CZE	9.3.80	187/69	400H	50.14	49.43- 05
*	Ukhov	Ivan	RUS	29.3.86	192/83	HJ	2.39i, 2.20	2.37i, 2.33- 06
	Uldal	Hans Olav	NOR	16.12.82	184/86	Dec	7963	8018w- 06, 7752- 05
	Uliczka	Steffen	GER	17.7.84	179/65	3kSt	8:32.79	8:37.65- 06
^	Unger	Tobias	GER	10.7.79	180/72	200	20.48	20.20- 05
	Ursu	Sergiu	ROM	26.4.80	202/127	DT	62.62	63.78- 03
	Urtans	Maris	LAT	9.2.81	188/120	SP	20.18i, 20.14	19.40- 06
	Uudmäe	Jaanus	EST	24.12.80	188/75	TJ	16.56, 16.78w	16.57i, 16.48- 06, 16.69w- 05
	Väät	Heiko	EST	25.8.74	184/82	JT	75.66	77.94- 04
	Vaden	Jordan	USA	15.9.78	181/75	100	10.21	10.20- 06
						200	20.17	19.98- 06
	Vaisjuns	Atis	LAT	27.9.82	183/80	Dec	7737	7721- 06
	Valcárcel	Jorge	CUB-J	16.4.88	192/79	200	20.4	20.95, 20.5w- 06
	Valchenko	Artem	UKR	3.4.84	185/66	20kW	1:23:12	1:23:05- 05
	Valiyev	Roman	KAZ	27.3.84	190/73	TJ	16.76	16.98- 06
*	Valukevic	Dmitrij	SVK	31.5.81	186/78	TJ	17.35	17.57- 03
	Van Alphen	Hans	BEL	12.1.82	191/88	Dec	8047	7411- 06
	van Bennekom	Joost	NED	18.1.81	185/81	Dec	7760	7638- 06
	van der Burgt	Ate	NED	17.3.78	184/73	1500	3:38.19	3:40.75- 06

Name		Nat	Born	Ht/Wt	Event	2007 Mark	Pre-2007 Best
van der Westen	Marcel	NED	1.8.76	192/86	110H	13.63	13.43- 05
van Deventer	Juan	RSA	26.3.83		1500	3:37.58	3:37.54- 06
Van Koolwijk	Krijn	BEL	30.8.81	181/62	3kSt	8:20.86	8:17.11- 05
* van Zyl	L.J. (Louis)	RSA	20.7.85	186/75	400H	48.24	48.05- 06
Vanek	Daniel	SVK	18.1.83	188/110	SP	19.39	18.77- 06
Vanryckeghem	Vincent	BEL	18.1.87		400H	50.25	52.70- 06
Vargas	Claudio	MEX	9.12.74		50kW	4:04:10A	3:51:35- 04
* Värnik	Andrus	EST	27.9.77	182/100	JT	75.96	87.83- 03
Vasara	Mika	FIN	22.10.83	194/120	SP	20.21	20.18- 06
Vashchilo	Aleksandr	BLR	30.8.81	197/120	HT	78.60	78.80- 06
Vasilache	Stefan	ROM	9.5.79	190/79	HJ	2.27i, 2.24	2.30- 03
* Vasilevskis	Vadims	LAT	5.1.82	187/82	JT	90.73	90.43- 06
Vasilyev	Arkadiy	RUS	19.1.87	191/90	Dec	8179	7728- 06
Vasylyev	Valeriy	UKR	21.4.76	189/82	LJ	8.06i, 7.94	8.21- 04
Veldhuyzen	Eelco	NED	19.7.84		400H	50.19	50.72- 06
Velikopolskiy	Dmitriy	RUS	27.11.84		HT	75.68	74.18- 06
Véliz	Carlos	CUB	12.8.87	185/120	SP	19.75	18.05- 06
Velter	Michaël	BEL	21.3.80	187/73	TJ	16.81i, 16.50	17.00- 06
Verni	Marco Antonio	CHI	27.2.76	188/114	SP	19.90	21.14- 04
Vesely	Vitezslav	CZE	27.2.83	186/84	JT	79.45	75.98- 06
Viana	Sandro	BRA	26.3.77	188/77	200	20.43A, 20.47	20.98- 05
Vickers	Bryan	USA	14.1.85	191/132	SP	19.52i, 19.09	19.60i, 18.45- 06
Vieira	Erivaldo da Cruz	BRA	18.11.80	184/80	LJ	8.04A	8.18A- 06, 7.99- 02
* Vieira	João	POR	20.2.76	174/58	20kW	1:20:42	1:20:09- 06
Vieira	Sérgio	POR	20.2.76	174/58	20kW	1:22:12	1:20:58- 97
Viera	Heber	URU	29.4.79	180/74	200	20.59	20.46A, 20.52- 02
Vieweg	Aleksandr	GER	28.6.86	192/92	JT	79.56	78.18- 06
Vilches	Oslay	CUB-J	13.7.88	170/65	LJ	7.96	7.42- 05
Vili	Bertrand	FRA	6.9.83	185/108	DT	62.13	60.45- 06
Villani	Matteo	ITA	28.8.82	179/63	3kSt	8:32.45	8:28.63- 06
Villanueva	Eduardo	VEN	29.12.84	171/62	800	1:46.33	1:48.21- 06
Vincek	Zeljko	CRO	16.6.86		400	45.69	45.90- 05
Vinichenko	Igor	RUS	11.4.84	191/108	HT	80.00	74.26- 06
Vivancos	Felipe	ESP	16.6.80	183/75	110H	13.56, 13.52w	13.41- 06
Vizcaíno	Henry (Jenris)	CUB	16.5.80	176/78	100	10.18, 9.8	10.20- 05
Vizzoni	Nicola	ITA	4.11.73	193/126	HT	78.21	80.50- 01
* Vodovnik	Miroslav	SLO	11.9.77	197/115	SP	20.67	20.76- 06
Vorobyev	Klim	RUS	25.3.84		TJ	16.69i, 16.68	16.52i, 16.42- 06
* Voronin	Vyacheslav	RUS	5.4.74	191/78	HJ	2.32i, 2.30	2.40- 00
Voronkin	Yuriy	RUS	18.5.79	184/83	HT	73.71	78.69- 03
Vorontsov	Andrey	BLR	24.7.75	191/105	HT	76.32	80.54- 06
* Voyevodin	Aleksey	RUS	9.8.70	178/65	50kW	3:41:52	3:38:01- 03
Vries	Sherwin	RSA	22.3.80	179/74	200	20.60A	20.20A, 20.35- 03
Vynogradov	Yevgen	UKR	30.4.84	195/98	HT	76.51	76.06- 06
^ Wade	Larry	USA	22.11.74	187/83	110H	13.38	13.01- 99
Wagne	Abdoulaye	SEN	30.1.81	180/75	800	1:46.12	1:45.08- 03
^ Walerianczyk	Aleksander	POL	1.9.82	195/78	HJ	2.30	2.36- 03
* Walker	Brad	USA	21.6.81	188/86	PV	5.95	6.00- 06
Walker	Josh	USA	6.5.82	185/73	110H	13.68, 13.56w	13.32- 04
Walker	Juan	USA	19.8.85	178/79	110H	13.80, 13.70w	13.88- 06
Wallin	Gabriel	SWE	14.10.81	193/94	JT	78.97	80.71- 04
* Waltz	Ian	USA	15.4.77	186/122	DT	67.98	68.91- 06
Wambua Mutiso	Joseph	KEN			Mar	2:10:34	2:17:13- 04
Wang Hao		CHN-J	16.8.89	182/64	20kW	1:21:20.69	
Wang Qingbo		CHN-J	24.5.88	182/78	JT	77.76	76.25- 06
Wang Zhiping		CHN	11.12.83	172/56	20kW	1:23:05	1:20:05- 06
Wanjiku	Samuel Ndungu	KEN-J	4.4.88	166/53	10,000	27:48.03	
* Wanjiru	Samuel	KEN	10.11.86	164/52	5000	13:18.25	13:09.5e+- 05
10,000	27:20.99		26:41.75- 05		HMar	58:33	59:16- 05
					Mar	2:06:39	-0-
Wanjuki	Jacob	KEN	16.1.86	178/52	10,000	27:51.39	28:11.47- 06
Warga	Sahle	ETH	.81	182/64	3000	7:43.67	7:43.27- 05
					5000	13:06.51	13:17.41- 05
* Wariner	Jeremy	USA	31.1.84	188/67	200	20.35	20.19- 06
					400	43.45	43.62- 06
Waugh	Ainsley	JAM	17.9.81	186/84	200	20.70, 20.62w	20.36- 05
Weakley	Ian	JAM	24.2.74	180/68	400H	49.74	48.55- 03
* Webb	Alan	USA	13.1.83	175/64	800	1:43.84	1:46.09- 04
1500	3:30.54		3:32.52- 05		1M	3:46.91	3:48.92- 05
Wei Yang		CHN-J	26.3.89	175/55	20kW	1:21:26	

Name		Nat	Born	Ht/Wt	Event	2007 Mark	Pre-2007 Best
* Weidlinger	Günther	AUT	5.4.78	169/53	HMar	61:42	
					3kSt	8:15.35	8:10.83- 99
Weigopwa	Saul	NGR	14.6.84	176/67	400	45.62	45.00- 04
Wells	Evander	USA	7.12.87	173/73	200	20.43	21.05, 20.98w- 06
Wenk	Stefan	GER	13.3.81	192/83	JT	80.34	83.94- 06
Werner	Tim	GER	25.9.80	190/85	JT	75.67	82.66- 02
Werrmann	Jens	GER	29.6.85	188/69	110H	13.63	13.60- 06
White	Carl	USA	10.2.82		TJ	16.58w	16.10i- 01, 16.03- 02
* Whiting	Ryan	USA	24.11.86	190/116	SP	20.35	19.75- 06
Wiberg	Nicklas	SWE	16.4.85	193/84	Dec	7870	7883- 06
Wibowo	Suryo Agung	INA	8.10.83	170/62	100	10.25	10.32- 03
Wierig	Martin	GER	10.6.87	202/108	DT	61.10	57.37- 06
Wiggins	Ernest	USA	18.6.82	183/77	100	10.14w, 10.16dt	10.20- 04, 10.11w- 05
* Wignall	Maurice	JAM	17.4.76	186/75	110H	13.29	13.17- 04
Williams	Andrae	BAH	11.7.83	185/82	400	45.26	44.90- 05
^ Williams	Bernard	USA	19.1.78	183/81	100	10.22	9.94- 01
					200	20.47	20.01- 01
* Williams	Chris	JAM	15.3.72	178/68	100	10.18, 10.03w	10.05, 10.04w- 00
					200	20.17	20.02- 00
* Williams	Derrick	USA	25.3.82	180/73	400H	48.26	48.68- 06
Williams	Ivory	USA	2.5.85	173/77	100	10.13, 10.11w	10.27- 02, 10.05w- 05
* Williams	Jesse	USA	27.12.83	184/75	HJ	2.33	2.32- 06
Williams	Jonathan	BIZ	29.8.83	178/67	400H	48.88	49.10- 06
Williams	Rhuben	USA	14.2.82	176/102	SP	20.07	19.75- 04
Williams	Ricardo	JAM	29.9.76	183/73	100	10.19, 10.13w	10.20- 03, 10.07w- 02
					200	20.35	20.33- 00, 20.20w- 03
Williams	Rubin	USA	9.7.83	175/70	200	20.40	20.47- 06
Williams	Siraj	LBR	5.3.84	178/70	400	45.77	46.64- 06
* Williamson	Darold	USA	19.2.83	188/77	400	44.68	44.27- 05
Williamson	Simeon	GBR	16.1.86	184/77	100	10.10	10.24, 10.22w- 05
Willie	Kelly	USA	7.9.82	177/72	100	10.22	10.13, 10.04w- 06
Willis	Lawrence	USA	12.7.81	188/73	TJ	16.97	16.94- 04
* Willis	Nick	NZL	25.4.83	183/68	1500	3:35.85	3:32.17- 06
					1M	3:55.09	3:52.75- 06
* Wilson	Aarik	USA	25.10.82	191/88	LJ	8.07, 8.11w	8.04A- 06, 7.97- 04, 8.00w,8.17i- 05
					TJ	17.58	17.32- 06
Wilson	Ryan	USA	19.12.80	188/79	110H	13.02	13.22- 06
Wims	Scott	USA-J	30.5.88	175/75	100	10.24	10.43- 06
					200	20.61	21.15- 06
Winger	Russ	USA	2.8.84	191/120	SP	20.81	20.05- 05
Winter	Nils	GER	27.3.77	187/84	LJ	8.12	8.21- 05
Wirkkala	Teemu	FIN	14.1.84	187/85	JT	84.06	82.82- 06
* Wissman	Johan	SWE	2.11.82	180/75	200	20.30	20.38- 06, 20.26w- 05
					400	44.56	45.57- 04
Witherspoon	Brian	USA	5.6.85	188/86	200	20.65	21.09- 06
Witherspoon	Reggie	USA	31.5.85	173/77	200	20.32	20.71i- 06, 21.04- 05
					400	45.56	45.42- 05
Wolski	Robert	POL	8.12.82	181/63	HJ	2.27i	2.31- 06
Wondimu	Eshetu	ETH	26.1.82		10,000	27:11.93	
					HMar	60:08	
Woods	John	USA	19.6.82	174/76	100	10.16A, 10.29	10.25, 10.16Aw- 05
^ Woody	Joey	USA	22.5.73	188/78	400H	49.92	47.97- 98
Worku	Bado	ETH-J	22.7.88	173/60	5000	13:22.50	13:18.08- 05
Wright	Decosma	JAM	1.9.82	188/91	110H	13.67	13.58- 06
Wright	O'Neil	LBR	3.5.80		400H	50.26	49.55- 05
Wroe	Sean	AUS	18.3.85	182/75	400	45.25	45.35- 06
Wu Bo		CHN	17.6.84	174/60	TJ	17.03, 17.09w	16.90- 06
Wu Guosong		CHN	21.4.87	173/55	20kW	1:23:36	1:23:06- 06
					50kW	4:05:05	3:59:51- 05
Wu Tao		CHN	3.10.83	191/100	DT	61.49	64.28- 05
Wu Youjia		CHN	6.5.83	185/72	110H	13.65	13.55- 05
Wyatt	Reggie	USA-Y	17.9.90	188/73	400H	50.10	
Wynne	William	USA-Y	30.1.90	183/75	400H	49.70	51.67- 06
Xhonneux	Frédéric	BEL	11.5.83		Dec	7874	7902- 05
* Xing Shucai		CHN	4.8.84	172/60	50kW	3:54:19	3:37:58- 05
Xing Yanan		CHN	17.6.83	183/70	110H	13.54	13.69, 13.64w- 06
Xu Faguang		CHN	17.5.87	178/69	50kW	3:55:45	
Yachi	Yusuke	JPN	2.1.80	172/55	50kW	4:04:08	3:55:19- 06
Yahata	Kenji	JPN	4.11.80	185/77	110H	13.58	13.90- 03
Yamaguchi	Yuki	JPN	22.2.84	174/63	400	45.91	45.18- 03

Name		Nat	Born	Ht/Wt	Event	2007 Mark	Pre-2007 Best
Yamamoto	Kazuki	JPN	8.10.83	190/90	JT	76.07	77.47- 04
Yamazaki	Yuki	JPN	16.1.84	178/64	50kW	3:47:40	3:43:38- 06
Yang Quan		CHN	8.12.86	172/53	PV	5.61i	5.50i- 06, 5.40- 05
Yang Tao		CHN-J	12.12.89	173/53	20kW	1:23:49.14t	1:24:08- 06
Yang Yansheng		CHN-J	5.1.88	189/75	PV	5.60	5.54- 06
Yarbrough	John	USA	16.8.85	193/89	110H	13.45, 13.43w	13.56, 13.55w- 06
Yarbrough	Linnie	USA	9.9.82	191/82	110H	13.34, 13.33dt	13.67, 13.49w- 06
Yargunkin	Aleksandr	RUS	6.1.81	182/68	20kW	1:22:24	1:20:22- 04
Yastrebov	Viktor	UKR	13.1.82	185/73	TJ	17.13, 17.18w	17.32- 04
Yatich	James	KEN	22.10.84		HMar	60:48	62:04- 06
Yator	Bellor	KEN	.84	160/	Mar	2:09:48	2:12:32- 06
Yator	Jacob	KEN	5.8.82		HMar	61:10	61:48- 05
Yefremov	Ilya	RUS-J	20.3.88	179/68	TJ	16.67	16.45- 05
Yegezu	Lishan	ETH	6.10.85	173/59	3000	7:44.39	
					5000	13:17.99	
Yego	Daniel	KEN	28.8.79	167/52	Mar	2:09:04	2:08:16- 05
Yemmouni	Mounir	FRA	12.10.83	184/63	1500	3:34.52	3:32.97- 04
^ Yeremenko	Ruslan	UKR	31.7.78	193/78	PV	5.60i, 5.40	5.84i, 5.80sq- 05, 5.70- 01
Yerokhin	Igor	RUS	4.9.85	168/56	20kW	1:19:21	
Yesipchuk	Dmitriy	RUS	17.11.74	178/66	20kW	1:20:16	1:19:32- 06
Yevtyukhovich	Vadim	BLR	24.5.81		JT	78.07	1:18:05- 01
Yin Jing		CHN-J	23.5.88	184/65	110H	13.68	78.12- 06
Yoshihara	Masato	JPN	14.3.77	169/55	20kW	1:23:27	14.05, 14.02w- 06
Yoshikata	Masahira	JPN	23.8.82	175/65	400H	49.53	1:22:00- 00
Yousif	Rabah	SUD	11.12.86	183/73	400	45.72	48.66- 05
Yu Bin		CHN	26.11.85	186/80	Dec	7824	46.33- 05
* Yu Chaohong		CHN	12.12.76	175/63	50kW	3:49:27	7705- 05
Yu Guoping		CHN	13.6.86	170/60	50kW	4:03:05	3:36:06- 05
Yuda	John	TAN	9.6.79	162/53	HMar	60:39	3:45:46- 01
* Yurchenko	Denys	UKR	27.1.78	174/74	PV	5.72	60:02- 02
Yushkov	Ivan	RUS	15.1.81	193/115	SP	20.06	5.85i- 05, 5.81- 03
^ Zagornyi	Aleksey	RUS	31.5.78	197/130	HT	79.12	20.57- 05
Zaizan	Ioan	ROM	21.7.83	183/73	800	1:46.99	83.43- 02
Zalaggítis	Konstadínos	GRE	13.12.80	187/75	TJ	16.91	1:47.54- 06
Zalsky	Antonin	CZE	7.8.80	200/108	SP	19.88	17.43- 02
Zaman	Sultan Khamis	QAT	23.7.85	180/65	3000	7:46.70	20.71- 04
Zapata	Mesias	ECU	8.1.81		50kW	4:04:26	7:48.50- 03
Zasimovich	Sergey	KAZ	11.3.86	192/72	HJ	2.30	4:21:30- 06
Zaytsev	Artyom	BLR	7.12.84	202/75	HJ	2.28i	2.23- 06
Zeller	Clemens	AUT	2.7.84	185/72	400	45.83	2.27- 05
Zeng Guoqiang		CHN	25.10.84	176/65	20kW	1:21:36	46.63- 06
Zepeda	Omar	MEX	8.6.77		50kW	3:56:04	1:22:39- 05
Zerguelaine	Anter	ALG	4.1.85	177/60	1500	3:34.32	3:49:01- 05
Zewdie	Tefere Maregu	ETH	23.10.82	178/60	3000	7:36.34	3:31.95- 05
					5000	13:11.32	7:41.92- 06
Zhang Hong		CHN	25.4.78	180/70	20kW	1:23:32	13:06.39- 04
Zhang Ronglong		CHN	2.11.84	172/60	50kW	3:59:58	1:22:09- 04
Zhang Rui		CHN-J	21.1.89	176/65	20kW	1:23:54.58t	4:13:24- 04
Zhang Xiaoyi		CHN-J	25.5.89	186/65	LJ	8.09	1:27:53- 06
Zhang Xuezhi		CHN	6.7.87	187/65	20kW	1:22:29.46	8.17- 06
* Zhao Chengliang		CHN	1.6.84	170/62	50kW	3:44:26	1:26:22- 05
Zhao Jianguo		CHN-J	19.1.88	170/58	50kW	3:55:05	3:36:13- 05
Zhao Yihai		CHN	29.3.85	183/90	HT	70.63	3:41:10- 06
Zhong Minwei		CHN	9.4.87	186/71	TJ	17.27	69.94- 05
Zhou Can		CHN	20.5.79	184/68	LJ	8.22	16.34- 06
Zhu Hongjun		CHN	18.8.83	175/68	20kW	1:23:53	8.13i- 04, 8.11- 99
Zhu Shujing		CHN	24.5.85	181/63	TJ	17.01	1:17:41- 05
Zhu Zhi		CHN	25.8.82	184/70	400H	49.97	17.03- 06
Zhuravlyev	Yuriy	RUS	25.5.85		TJ	16.59	49.88- 05
Zielinski	Dominik	POL	25.4.80	192/140	SP	19.79	16.40- 06
Zilali	Abdelhakim	FRA	20.6.83	188/73	3kSt	8:25.42	19.69- 06
* Ziólkowski	Szymon	POL	1.7.76	192/120	HT	80.70	8:40.42- 05
Zlatnar	Damjan	SLO	16.12.77	187/72	110H	13.56	83.38- 01
Zou Cuizhi		CHN	11.1.83	179/65	50kW	3:54:42	13.62- 04
Zouaoui Dandrieux	Vincent	FRA	12.10.80	188/72	3kSt	8:16.55	4:09:04- 02
* Zsivoczky	Attila	HUN	29.4.77	193/82	Dec	8017	8:22.82- 05
Zumer	Jan	SLO	9.6.82	189/75	100	10.34, 10.22w	8554- 00
Zyabrev	Aleksandr	RUS	16.5.87		Dec	7680	10.21- 06
^ Zyuskov	Volodomyr	UKR	29.8.81	190/75	LJ	7.96	8.31- 05

WOMEN'S INDEX 2007

Athletes included are those ranked in the top 100s at standard (World Champs) events (plus shorter lists for 1000m, 1M, 2000m, 3000m and 3000m St). Those with detailed biographical profiles are indicated in first column by:
* in this year's Annual, ^ Featured in a previous year's Annual, # old javelin.

Name		Nat	Born	Ht/Wt	Event	2007 Mark	Pre-2007 Best
* Abakumova	Mariya	RUS	15.1.86	179/80	JT	64.28	60.12- 06
Abdulai	Ruky	GHA	8.8.85	170/60	LJ	6.70	6.36, 6.79w- 06
* Abeylegesse	Elvan	TUR	11.9.82	159/40	5000	15:00.88	14:24.68- 04
					10000	31:25.15	30:21.67- 06
* Abitova	Inga	RUS	6.3.82	153/47	10000	31:26.08	30:31.42- 06
Abugan	Shade	NGR-Y	17.12.90	163/52	400	51.44	51.95- 06
Achano	Netsanet	ETH	14.12.87	171/57	3kSt	9:28.03	10:10.11- 06
^ Achilles	Bianca	GER	17.4.81	181/125	HT	65.60	68.40- 99
* Acuff	Amy	USA	14.7.75	188/66	HJ	1.95	2.01- 03
Adamovich	Olga	RUS	30.8.84		400H	56.04	57.01- 05
* Adams	Jenny	USA	8.7.78	165/55	100H	12.82, 12.75w	12.63, 12.61w- 01
* Adere	Berhane	ETH	21.7.73	170/48	HMar	69:58+	67:32- 03
^ Adriano	Elisângela	BRA	27.7.72	180/95	SP	17.99	19.30- 01
					DT	61.09	61.96- 98, 62.23dq- 99
Aerts	Sara	BEL	25.1.84	181/65	Hep	5950	5736- 04
Agafonova	Kseniya	RUS	25.6.83		3000	8:53.30	8:58.62- 06
5000	15:23.17		15:25.60- 06		10000	31:47.14	32:47.52- 06
Agbo	Phyllis	GBR	16.12.85	176/70	Hep	5716	5541- 06
* Agirre	Naroa	ESP	15.5.79	177/64	PV	4.56i, 4.50	4.50- 06
Ahmed	Zemzem	ETH	27.12.84	164/48	3kSt	9:45.72	
Ahonen	Kirsi	FIN	8.4.76	170/70	JT	58.03i/55.89	60.98- 06
Ahoure	Murielle	USA	23.8.87	167/57	100	11.28w	11.42- 06
Aidietyté	Neringa	LTU	5.6.83	177/64	20kW	1:33:54	1:39:50- 06
^ Aït Hammou	Amina	MAR	18.7.78	165/49	800	1:59.51	1:57.82- 03
Aït Hammou	Seltana	MAR	10.5.80	166/47	800	2:00.74	1:59.59- 06
Aït Salem	Souad	ALG	6.1.79	158/50	5000	15:28.31	15:07.49- 06
HMar	70:29		70:26- 06		Mar	2:25:08	2:28:22- 06
* Aitova	Marina	KAZ	13.9.82	180/60	HJ	1.96	1.95- 06
Akaba	Yukiko	JPN	18.10.79	158/44	5000	15:22.73	15:11.17- 05
					10000	31:23.27	32:54.14- 99
Akinsulie	Esther	CAN	22.4.84	170/60	400	51.72A	52.91- 06
Albury	Aymara	BAH	25.7.85		SP	16.63i, 16.60	17.23- 06
Alcántara	Dailenis	CUB-Y	10.8.91	163/56	TJ	14.21	12.63- 06
* Aldama	Yamilé	SUD	14.8.72	173/62	TJ	14.58	15.29- 03
Aldrich	Erin	USA	27.12.77	186/62	HJ	1.92	1.97i- 98, 1.95- 00
Aleksandrova	Galina	RUS	15.10.76	175/63	10000	32:20.86	32:11.52- 02
Alemu	Derebe	ETH	5.6.83		10000	31:58.44	31:04.49- 04
					HMar	70:30	70:45- 03
Alexander	Kineke	VIN	21.2.86	173/60	400	51.80, 51.48i	51.35- 06
Al-Gasara	Rakia	BRN	6.9.82	170/65	100	11.27	11.34- 06
					200	22.80	23.02- 06
Ali	Nia	USA-J	23.10.88	168/60	100H	13.25	13.63, 13.55w- 06
Alisevich	Tatyana	BLR	22.1.69	173/63	Hep	5911	6173- 05
Allen	Lindsey	USA	30.6.86	162/50	3kSt	10:01.53	10:26.71- 05
Allou Affoué	Amandine	CIV	29.8.80	160/52	100	11.27	11.30- 04
					200	23.24	23.08A- 05, 23.14- 04
Alminova	Anna	RUS	17.1.85	165/50	800	1:59.90	2:02.02- 06
1500	4:03.10+		4:04.72- 06		1M	4:20.86	
^ Alozie	Glory	ESP	30.12.77	156/52	100H	13.18	12.44, 12.4w- 98
Álvarez	María de la C.	CUB	30.8.75	165/62	JT	61.40	61.57- 00, 63.02#- 95
Aman	Leila	ETH	24.11.77		Mar	2:31:25	2:27:54- 04
Amata	Doreen	NGR-J	5.6.88	189/68	HJ	1.89	1.70- 05
* Amertil	Christine	BAH	18.8.79	168/53	200	23.00	22.58- 05
					400	50.99	50.09- 05
An Un-suk		PRK			Mar	2:31:14	
Anacharsis	Phara	FRA	17.12.83	177/58	400H	56.63	-0-
Andersen	Kassi	USA	25.6.83	178/60	3kSt	9:52.10	9:44.68- 04
Anderson	Alexandria	USA	28.1.87	175/60	100	11.21, 11.11w	11.12, 11.10w- 06
					200	22.67	22.96- 05
Anderson	Kristin	USA	16.6.83	170/52	3kSt	9:53.95	9:57.98- 06
Anderson	Lindsey	USA	23.5.85	163/48	3kSt	9:39.95	10:20.91- 05
Anderson	Nickeisha	JAM	15.3.85	157/52	100	11.33, 11.29w	11.37- 06
Ania	Emma	GBR	7.2.79	166/54	100	11.35	11.32- 06
Aniballi	Valentina	ITA	19.4.84	176/77	DT	56.36	53.22- 06
Anim	Vida	GHA	7.12.83	168/58	100	11.22	11.14- 04, 11.0- 02
					200	23.14	22.81- 06

Name		Nat	Born	Ht/Wt	Event	2007 Mark	Pre-2007 Best
Anthony	Tori	USA-J	19.4.89	170/60	PV	4.33i, 4.30	4.11- 06
Antil	Seema	IND	27.7.83	183/85	DT	58.09	64.84- 04
Anton	Adina	ROM	6.10.84	173/57	LJ	6.60	6.80- 04
Antonova	Aleksandra	RUS	24.3.80	162/60	100H	12.95, 12.86w	12.78- 06
* Antonova	Olena	UKR	16.6.72	182/95	DT	62.41	67.30- 04
* Antyukh	Natalya	RUS	26.6.81	182/73	400	49.93	49.85- 04
Anyanwu	Kelechi	USA	27.12.85	173/82	DT	57.58	49.72- 06
Aoki	Sayaka	JPN	15.12.86	162/51	400H	57.20	57.08- 06
Aoyama	Miyuki	JPN	4.1.77	172/56	HJ	1.90	1.92- 04
Apud	Talis	MEX	5.1.82	163/50	3kSt	9:55.43	11:00.45-=02
Araméndiz	Zuleima	COL	23.9.75	172/75	JT	57.55	59.09A- 01, 61.72#- 96
Arencibia	Yenima	CUB	25.12.84	173/53	100H	13.29, 12.7	13.29- 05, 13.1- 04, 13.13w- 01
Arkhipova	Lyudmila	RUS	12.9.78	167/55	20kW	1:29:01	1:28:52- 05
^ Arrendel	Juana Rosario	DOM	16.6.78	191/60	HJ	1.87	1.97- 02
* Arron	Christine	FRA	13.9.73	177/64	100	11.04	10.73- 98
					200	22.88	22.26- 99
Artymata	Eleni	CYP	16.5.86		200	23.18	23.51- 06
Arusei	Penninah	KEN	23.2.79	160/39	HMar	69:23	70:54- 06
Arveláez	Jennifer	VEN	28.10.82	170/53	TJ	13.76	13.65A- 02
Asay	Erin	USA	17.3.83	168/55	PV	4.36	4.28Ai- 06, 4.20- 05
Asigbee	Fiona	USA	18.5.81	173/61	Hep	5908	6030- 06
Askale Tafa	Magarsa	ETH	27.9.84		HMar	70:12+	75:55- 06
					Mar	2:25:07	2:27:57- 06
Assefa	Sofia	ETH	.87	166/48	3kSt	9:48.46	10:17.48- 06
Asumnu	Gloria	USA	22.5.85	168/59	100	11.19	11.49- 03, 11.38w- 06
					200	22.70	23.56- 05
Augusto	Jessica	POR	8.11.81	165/44	3000	8:41.53	8:57.65i- 05. 9:02.36- 04
2M	9:22.89				5000	14:56.39	15:15.76- 04
Augustus	Toyin	NGR	24.12.79	160/52	100H	13.02	12.89- 04
Austin	Lauren	USA	3.4.86	178/62	800	2:02.09	
Auvray	Alixe	FRA	24.1.85	162/51	PV	4.25	4.10- 06
Avdeyeva	Anna	RUS	6.4.85	170/90	SP	19.11	18.45- 06
Ayangbile	Ciera	USA	17.7.85		SP	16.56	15.61i, 15.13- 06
Ayanu	Workitu	ETH	19.4.87	170/55	5000	14:50.15	14:50.51- 06
Azarova	Tatyana	KAZ	2.12.85	166/51	400H	54.78	57.02- 05
de Azevedo	Juliana Paula	BRA	12.6.83	159/54	1500	4:11.39	4:16.25- 06
* Badurová	Katerina	CZE	18.12.82	167/55	PV	4.75	4.52- 04
Bai Xue		CHN-J	13.12.88	155/45	5000	15:09.84	15:29.06- 05
10000	31:32.49		31:28.88- 05		Mar	2:27:46	2:37:07- 03
Bai Yanmin		CHN	29.6.87	170/51	20kW	1:30:12, 1:31:47.95t	1:27:37- 05
* Bailey	Aleen	JAM	25.11.80	170/64	100	11.17	11.04- 04
					200	22.60	22.33- 04
^ Bak	Justyna	POL	1.8.74	174/52	Mar	2:30:45	2:41:50- 06
Bakhanovskaya	Irina	BLR	21.6.85		3kSt	10:02.63	10:13.8- 06
* Balassini	Ester	ITA	20.10.77	173/73	HT	71.96	73.59- 05
Balciunaité	Zivile	LTU	3.4.79	160/43	Mar	2:31:13	2:25:15- 05
Balta	Ksenja	EST	1.11.86	167/53	LJ	6.55i	6.80- 06
Bambara	Laëtitia	FRA	30.3.84	180/75	HT	66.83	61.67- 05
Banco	Nelly	FRA	17.2.86	161/53	200	23.29, 23.12w	23.69- 06
* Bani	Zahra	ITA	31.12.79	173/73	JT	62.09	62.75- 05
Banova	Andriana	BUL	1.5.87		TJ	13.79	13.48i, 13.02, 13.43w- 06
Baptiste	Kelly-Ann	TRI	14.10.86	160/54	100	11.22	11.08- 06, 11.04w- 05
					200	22.95, 22.90i	22.73- 06
Baranova	Veera	EST	12.2.84	174/61	TJ	13.71	14.06- 06
Baratella	Giorgia	ITA	8.1.75	176/82	DT	56.31	56.18- 01
Barber	Aleesha	USA	16.5.87	168/53	400H	57.00	60.04- 05
* Barber	Eunice	FRA	17.11.74	175/68	100H	13.17	12.78- 01, 12.62w- 05
					LJ	6.73	7.05- 03
* Barber	Me'Lisa	USA	4.10.80	160/52	100	10.95	11.03- 06, 10.87w- 05
* Barber	Mikele	USA	4.10.80	157/50	100	11.02	11.27- 06
					200	22.73	22.98- 00, 22.71w- 01
Barlet	Alexandra	FRA	17.2.77	185/63	Hep	5679w	5678- 02
Barnes	Cecilia	USA	24.7.80	175/86	DT	60.17	58.47- 05
Barnes	Miriam	USA	14.11.83	173/60	400H	56.97	57.06- 06
Barringer	Jenny	USA	23.8.86	165/50	3kSt	9:33.95	9:53.04- 06
* Barrios	Yarelis	CUB	12.7.83	172/89	DT	63.90, 66.68ex	61.01- 06
Bartolina	Erica	USA	15.5.80	168/57	PV	4.40i, 4.35	4.40- 04
Bass	Tacita	USA	28.10.79		400H	57.0	57.31- 01
Battke	Anna	GER	3.1.85	173/58	PV	4.56	4.20- 05
Bayisa	Atsede	ETH	16.4.87		HMar	69:15	70:26- 05
					Mar	2:29:08	2:37:48- 06

	Name		Nat	Born	Ht/Wt	Event	2007 Mark	Pre-2007 Best
	Bayne	Chauntae	USA	4.4.84	166/59	100	11.24	11.15A, 11.26- 06
						200	22.95	22.87A, 22.77i- 06
^	Bazhenova	Nadezhda	RUS	22.9.78	176/63	TJ	14.31	14.65i- 02, 14.60- 01
	Beard	Jessica	USA-J	8.1.89		400	51.63	51.89- 06
	Beckel	Nadine	GER	27.5.77	190/89	SP	17.59i, 17.55	18.59- 03
	Bedada	Emebet Etea	ETH-Y	11.1.90	160/45	1500	4:08.50	4:10.48- 06
	Begic	Vera	CRO	17.3.82	169/69	DT	59.29	60.73- 06
*	Beitia	Ruth	ESP	1.4.79	192/71	HJ	2.02	2.00- 03
	Bejnar	Monika	POL	10.3.81	173/57	200	23.07	22.91- 06
						400	52.04	51.68- 05
	Bekele	Alemitu	TUR	17.9.77		3000	8:55.51	
	Bekele	Bezunesh	ETH	18.9.83	145/38	10000	31:45.98	31:10.68- 05
						HMar	68:07	71:23- 04
	Bekele	Mekdes	ETH	20.1.87	174/57	3kSt	9:32.05	9:46.67- 06
	Bellille	Janeil	TRI-J	18.6.89	172/60	400H	56.94	59.76- 06
	Belousova	Nadezhda	RUS	18.1.86		400	51.70	55.91- 05
	Beltyukova	Tatyana	RUS	11.10.85		1500	4:08.61	4:13.83- 06
	Benavídes	Virgen	CUB	31.12.74	165/56	100	11.35, 11.24w	11.14, 11.10w- 99
*	Benhassi	Hasna	MAR	1.6.78	166/55	800	1:56.84	1:56.43- 04
						1000	2:34.35	2:33.15- 99
	Berglund (Persson)	Linda	SWE	22.9.81	178/58	PV	4.40i, 4.20	4.40- 06
^	Bergqvist	Kajsa	SWE	12.10.76	175/59	HJ	2.02	2.08i- 06, 2.06- 03
	Berings	Eline	BEL	28.5.86	162/53	100H	12.97	13.27- 06
	Berkut	Nataliya	UKR	30.5.75	172/53	10000	32:09.28	31:08.89- 04
						HMar	71:14	70:26- 03
	Berlanda	Eleonora	ITA	6.4.76	172/49	1500	4:11.45	4:07.54- 05
	Bernard-Thomas	Neisha	GRN	21.1.81	163/64	800	2:00.77	2:00.13- 06
	Beskrovnaja	Irina	SVK	28.12.82	174/66	TJ	13.75i	14.07- 06
	Best	Charlotte	GBR	7.3.85		800	2:01.50	2:03.9mx- 04, 2:04.01- 05
	Bicet	Nora Aida	CUB	29.10.77	178/78	JT	56.03	63.32- 04
	Bicet	Yusmay	CUB	8.12.83	183/73	TJ	14.19	14.61, 14.67w- 04
^	Bikert	Yekaterina	RUS	13.5.80	182/68	400H	54.24	53.72- 04
	Biktimirova	Alevtina	RUS	10.9.82		Mar	2:31:02	2:25:12- 05
	Billaud	Cindy	FRA	11.3.86	168/57	100H	13.25	13.48- 04, 13.46w- 06
*	Bisibori	Ruth	KEN-J	2.1.88	170/55	3000	8:54.42	
	5000	15:26.65				3kSt	9:24.51	10:12.0A- 05
^	Bisset	Sonia	CUB	1.4.71	171/69	JT	64.65	67.67- 05, 68.24#- 97
^	Blackett	Andrea	BAR	24.1.76	160/54	400H	55.43	53.36- 99
	Blaine	Lindsey	USA	14.12.84	180/75	JT	55.56	50.47- 06
	Blewitt	Adriane	USA	24.5.80	178/79	SP	17.09	18.29- 05
	Bliss	Andrea	JAM	5.10.80	172/63	100H	13.02	12.83- 05
*	Blonska	Lyudmyla	UKR	18.3.75	175/62	100H	13.13	13.38- 05
	HJ	1.92		1.87- 03		LJ	6.88	6.76- 05
						Hep	6832	6448- 06
	Bobková	Miriam	SVK	2.3.79	170/58	100H	13.04	13.44- 02
	Bobocel	Ancuta	ROM	3.10.87	163/52	3kSt	9:37.88	9:46.19- 06
	Boekelman	Melissa	NED-J	11.5.89	177/76	SP	17.12	17.66- 06
*	Bogdanova	Anna	RUS	21.10.84	178/66	LJ	6.46, 6.59w	6.09- 06
						Hep	6289	5785- 06
*	Bolm	Kirsten	GER	4.3.75	181/70	100H	13.15	12.59- 05
	Bolshakova	Svetlana	RUS	14.10.84	174/59	TJ	14.28i	14.17- 06
	Bolsun	Yelena	RUS	25.6.82	168/62	100	11.30	11.36- 04, 11.35w- 05
						200	22.78	22.64- 04
	Bonaudo	Marion	FRA	12.9.82	174/65	JT	55.76	56.28- 03
	Boonstra	Miranda	NED	29.8.72	175/58	3kSt	9:50.02	9:45.87- 06
	Bordignon	Laura	ITA	26.3.81	180/78	DT	56.68	57.98- 05
	Borel-Brown	Cleopatra	TRI	3.10.79	168/93	SP	18.91	19.48i, 18.90- 04
	Borlée	Olivia	BEL	10.4.86	176/62	200	23.14	22.98- 06
*	Boslak	Vanessa	FRA	11.6.82	170/57	PV	4.70	4.70- 06
	Boyd	Alana	AUS	10.5.84	171/61	PV	4.55	4.40- 06
	Boyd	Angel	USA	25.2.85	163/54	100H	13.21	13.25, 13.04w- 06
	Boyko	Viktoriya	UKR	20.1.74	180/84	DT	60.65	63.43- 01
	Brathwaite	Liz	GBR	10.4.85	172/54	800	2:01.78	2:03.10- 06
*	Breisch	Becky	USA	16.3.83	180/100	DT	67.37	63.53- 05
	Brejchová	Nikola	CZE	25.6.74	178/75	JT	64.29	65.91- 04
	Brewer	Chandra	USA	26.7.81	175/77	SP	16.71	16.91- 05
	Brîndusoiu	Ileana	ROM	9.5.79	176/83	DT	56.07	59.96- 03
	Brits	Tazmin	RSA-Y	8.1.91	169/72	JT	56.55	49.00- 06
	Britton	Fionnuala	IRL	24.9.84		3kSt	9:41.36	9:49.20- 06
	Brivule	Linda	LAT	9.9.83	184/74	JT	59.69	56.36- 04
*	Brkljacic	Ivana	CRO	25.1.83	170/65	HT	75.08	71.34- 06

Name		Nat	Born	Ht/Wt	Event	2007 Mark	Pre-2007 Best
Broaddus	Juanita	USA	12.5.85	168/55	100	11.34	11.32- 05
Bronisz	Agnieszka	POL	16.3.86	174/73	SP	16.91	16.78- 06
Brookins	LaKya	USA-J	28.7.89	165/52	100	11.46, 11.30w	11.45- 06
* Brooks	Sheri-Ann	JAM	11.2.83	168/55	100	11.05	11.19- 06
					200	22.78	22.80, 22.74w- 05
Brown	Ashley	USA	23.10.85	168/55	400H	57.15	59.64- 06
Brown	Celia	GBR	22.1.77	160/50	800	2:01.56	2:04.76- 05
Brown	Tina	GBR	22.8.76	174/55	3kSt	10:01.28	9:48.57- 05
Büchler	Nicole	SUI	17.12.83	161/55	PV	4.35	4.15- 05
Budileanu	Veronica	ROM	27.2.76	179/58	20kW	1:33:40	1:32:47- 06
Budnikova	Alina	RUS	22.10.83	182/60	HJ	1.88i	1.88i, 1.86- 05
* Bufalova	Olesya	RUS	6.10.82	165/56	TJ	14.50i, 14.49	14.50- 06
Bui Thi Nhung		VIE	21.1.83	167/53	HJ	1.91	1.94- 05
Buisson	Marion	FRA-J	19.2.88	176/60	PV	4.25	4.02i, 4.00- 06
Bujin	Cristina	ROM-J	12.4.88	171/52	TJ	13.99i, 13.57	14.06i- 06, 13.72- 05
Bulgakova	Anna	RUS-J	17.1.88		HT	68.49	67.79- 06
^ Bunjes	Andrea	GER	5.2.76	175/80	HT	69.91	70.73- 04
* Burka	Gelete	ETH	15.2.86	165/45	1500	4:00.48	3:59.60- 05
3000	8:48.0e+		8:25.92- 06		5000	14:31.20	14:40.92- 06
Burnett	Marian	GUY	22.2.76	156/50	800	1:59.84	1:59.47- 04
^ Buschbaum	Yvonne	GER	14.7.80	170/57	PV	4.35	4.70- 03
Bush	Nicole	USA	4.4.86	172/54	3kSt	9:56.68	10:01.04- 06
Butler	Kathy	GBR	22.10.73	175/55	HMar	71:12dh	71:05- 06
Butvina	Aleksandra	RUS	14.2.86		Hep	5912	5275- 05
Cabecinha	Ana	POR	29.4.84	168/52	20kW	1:32:44	1:31:02- 06
Cadamuro	Stefania	ITA	23.2.79	178/58	HJ	1.87	1.91- 00
Cadienhead	Maresa	CAN	7.4.76	168/55	HJ	1.89	1.95- 02
Cakova	Natalija	LAT	20.10.80	179/61	HJ	1.89	1.86- 06
* Calatayud	Zulia	CUB	9.11.79	169/59	800	2:00.34	1:56.09- 02
Calvert	Schillonie	JAM-J	27.7.88	166/57	100	11.35	11.21- 06
					200	23.23	23.14- 06
Camarena	Jill	USA	2.8.82	180/91	SP	18.92	19.26i, 19.02- 06
Campbell	Amber	USA	5.6.81	170/91	HT	70.33	69.52- 05
* Campbell-Brown	Veronica	JAM	15.5.82	163/61	100	10.89	10.85- 05
					200	22.34	22.05- 04
Canella	Valeria	ITA	6.2.82	171/58	LJ	6.56, 6.58w	6.48i, 6.31- 06
Cantey	Krystal	USA	27.6.87	168/60	400H	56.21	56.83- 05
Carey	Michelle	IRL	20.2.81	167/57	400H	56.53	56.52- 06
* Carruthers	Danielle	USA	22.12.79	173/62	100H	12.89	12.56- 04
Carter	Antonette	USA	16.2.84	170/57	100	11.50, 11.36w	11.33, 11.08Aw- 06
					LJ	6.44, 6.58w	6.50, 6.56w- 05
Carter	Michelle	USA	12.10.85	175/104	SP	18.12i, 17.57	18.56i- 06, 18.26- 05
* Casandra	Cristina	ROM	1.2.77	168/50	3kSt	9:28.53	9:31.96- 04
Castells	Berta	ESP	24.1.84	174/79	HT	68.66	68.87- 04
Castillo	Juana	DOM	17.6.84	183/73	Hep	5741	5860- 06
Castlin	Kristina	USA-J	7.7.88	170/57	100H	12.91, 12.82w	13.73- 06
* Castrejana	Carlota	ESP	25.4.73	188/70	TJ	14.64i, 14.47	14.60- 05
Cattaneo	Micol	ITA	14.5.82	174/63	100H	13.08	13.15- 06
Ceccarelli	Benedetta	ITA	23.1.80	170/51	400H	56.26	54.79- 05
* Cechlová	Vera	CZE	19.11.78	178/78	DT	66.18	67.71- 03
^ Ceplak ¶	Jolanda	SLO	12.9.76	168/55	800	2:00.92, 1:59.99i, 1:59.86dq	1:55.19- 02
Cérival	Jessica	FRA	20.1.82	185/100	SP	17.36	17.44- 04
Chaabi	Bouchra	MAR	22.9.80	158/45	1500	4:03.62	4:06.95- 04
Chai Xue		CHN-J	21.10.88	168/50	20kW	1:34:12.31	1:31:37- 05
Chaipetch	Noengrothai	THA	1.12.82	165/49	HJ	1.91i, 1,86	1.91- 04
Champion	Courtney	USA	10.6.86	175/63	200	22.92i	23.53- 03, 22.98i- 05
Chang Chunfeng		CHN-J	4.5.88	179/68	JT	61.61	58.72- 06
Chang Jung-yeon		KOR	6.4.77	174/74	JT	55.41	60.92- 04
Changeywo	Doris	KEN	12.12.84		10000	32:32.44	32:10.28- 05
Charles	Tabia	CAN	6.4.85	178/64	LJ	6.52	6.52i, 6.46- 06
					TJ	14.02i, 13.89, 14.24w	13.94, 14.17w- 06
Chebanu	Olena	UKR	4.1.81	170/60	200	23.21	22.97- 06
Chebet	Emily	KEN	18.2.86	157/45	10000	32:31.21	31:33.39- 06
Checa	Dolores	ESP	27.12.82	168/52	1500	4:06.49	4:16.37- 04
					3000	8:51.87	9:34.33i- 05, 9:57.3- 03
Checchi	Cristiana	ITA	8.7.77	175/69	SP	16.93i, 16.79	18.64i- 03, 18.59- 05
					DT	59.74	56.48- 06
Chelagat	Jemimah	KEN	.85		Mar	2:29:41	2:35:12- 06
Chemjor	Magdeline	KEN	12.11.78		Mar	2:28:16	
Chemtai	Esther	KEN-J	4.6.88	163/50	5000	15:24.33	16:06.13- 05
Chemutai	Consolata	KEN		162/48	3kSt	9:56.6A	

	Name		Nat	Born	Ht/Wt	Event	2007 Mark	Pre-2007 Best
	Chen Huirong		CHN-J	1.6.88	164/44	5000	15:29.36	16:24.05- 06
						10000	31:23.07	34:49.08- 06
	Chen Rong		CHN-J	18.5.88	160/45	10000	32:16.83	32:51.38- 06
						Mar	2:27:05	2:34:57- 06
	Chen Xiaofang		CHN	28.10.81	166/52	3kSt	10:00.30	9:50.88- 03
	Chen Yaling		CHN	24.2.84	174/66	LJ	6.59	6.62- 06
	Chepchirchir	Filomena	KEN	1.12.81	165/43	HMar	70:44	71:30- 06
*	Chepchumba	Pamela	KEN	8.3.79	155/44	HMar	68:06	69:09- 05
						Mar	2:25:36	2:29:48- 06
	Chepchumba	Salome	KEN	29.9.82	166/52	3kSt	9:52.00	9:26.07- 06
^	Chepkemei ¶	Susan	KEN	25.6.75	164/48	HMar	68:36dh	65:44- 01
	Chepkorir	Pauline	KEN	.80		HMar	70:54	
	Chepyego	Sally	KEN	3.10.85	160/42	5000	15:30.37	15:06.26- 06
						10000	31:39.84	
*	Cherkasova	Svetlana	RUS	20.5.78	172/57	800	1:58.37	1:56.93- 05
						2000	5:40.49	
	Chermoshanskaya	Yuliya	RUS	6.1.86	176/65	200	22.90	23.06- 05
	Chernaya	Zhanna	RUS	24.7.84		LJ	6.58	6.24- 04
	Chernogorova	Olga	BLR	30.1.82	182/90	DT	58.75	61.33- 06
	Chernova	Lada	RUS	1.1.70	172/75	JT	63.35	61.25- 06, 61.34#- 96
*	Chernova	Tatyana	RUS-J	29.1.88	189/63	100H	13.47, 13.04w	13.70- 06
	400H 56.14					HJ	1.87	1.80- 06
	LJ 6.61			6.35- 06		Hep	6768w	6227- 06
	Chernushenko (Stasyuk)	Irina	BLR	9.3.79		LJ	6.54	6.65- 06
	Cherono	Hellen	KEN	22.2.84	165/45	Mar	2:29:33	2:30:56- 06
	Cherono	Mercy	KEN-Y	7.5.91		3000	8:53.94	9:24.2- 06
*	Cherono	Priscah	KEN	27.6.80	160/47	3000	8:29.06	8:40.55- 06
	2M 9:14.09					5000	14:42.00	14:35.30- 06
	Cherop	Sharon	KEN	16.3.84		HMar	70:21	73:57- 05
*	Cherry	Damu	USA	29.11.77	163/59	100H	12.74	12.44- 06
	Cheruiyot	Lenah	KEN	1.3.73		Mar	2:27:02	2:33:44- 06
^	Cheruiyot	Rose	KEN	21.7.76	163/48	Mar	2:27:25	2:27:09- 06
*	Cheruiyot	Vivian	KEN	11.9.83	155/39	1500	4:06.65	4:23.0A- 00
	3000 8:28.66			8:38.86- 06		5000	14:22.51	14:47.43- 06
	Chibisova	Oksana	RUS	31.3.77	177/87	SP	17.87i, 17.15	18.62- 05
*	Chicherova	Anna	RUS	22.7.82	180/57	HJ	2.03	2.04i, 2.00- 03
	Child	Eilidh	GBR	20.2.87		400H	57.11	59.53- 04
*	Chilla	Mercedes	ESP	19.1.80	170/60	JT	62.19	63.20- 06
*	Chojecka	Lidia	POL	25.1.77	166/46	800	2:01.58	1:59.97- 99
	1500 4:05.10, 4:03.73i			3:59.22- 00		3000	8:38.30, 8:38.21i	8:31.69- 02
	Chudzik	Kamila	POL	12.9.86	176/64	Hep	6097	5438- 06
	Chukwuemeka	Vivian	NGR	4.5.77	178/90	SP	18.18	18.43- 03
	Chumakova	Olesya	RUS	23.7.81	165/50	800	2:00.37	2:00.38- 05
	1000 2:37.31i			2:36.70i- 04		1500	4:03.36+	4:02.55- 05
						1M	4:21.29	4:31.17- 05
	Churakova	Yelena	RUS	16.12.86		400H	56.75	
^	Chzhao	Larisa	RUS	4.2.71	172/57	800	2:02.25	1:57.33- 05
*	Claretti	Clarissa	ITA	7.10.80	170/70	HT	71.43	71.98- 06
*	Clark	Hazel	USA	3.10.77	178/55	800	1:59.07	1:57.99- 05
	Clarke	Tameka	BAH	9.11.80	163/54	100	11.26	11.33- 03
	Claxton	Sarah	GBR	23.9.79	165/57	100H	13.00	12.93- 06, 12.91w- 04
	Clement	Treniere	USA	27.10.81	159/50	800	1:59.15	1:59.59- 05
						1500	4:05.68	4:03.32- 06
	Clitheroe	Helen	GBR	2.1.74	168/57	1500	4:09.51, 4:05.81i	4:01.10- 02
	3000 8:51.94			8:58.33- 02		3kSt	9:41.59	-0-
	Coleman	Natasha	USA	9.2.79		LJ	6.58w	6.21- 01
	Colindres	Veronica	ESA	9.7.86		20kW	1:35:39	1:42:37- 06
	Collado	Yarisley	CUB	30.4.85	178/65	DT	57.22	54.46- 05
*	Collonvillé	Marie	FRA	23.11.73	163/54	LJ	6.67	6.44- 06
						Hep	6244	6350- 97
	Comba	Rocío	ARG	14.7.87	179/100	DT	55.49	58.78- 06
	Cook	Melissa	USA	22.11.79	165/50	10000	32:31.85	33:03.03- 04
	Coons	Leslie	USA	16.7.73	175/74	HT	65.33	66.76- 04
	Cornford	Laura	AUS-J	11.6.88	176/74	JT	57.37	54.99- 05
	Corrigan	Lisa	AUS	2.12.84	165/45	800	2:01.59	2:03.38- 04
	1500 4:05.25			4:09.93- 06		1M	4:22.66	4:31.08- 06
	Cosby	Jessica	USA	31.5.82	173/77	HT	68.34	70.78- 06
	Coslovich	Claudia	ITA	26.4.72	170/70	JT	59.88	65.30- 00, 65.55#- 98
	Costa	Joana Ribeiro	BRA	15.8.81	174/60	PV	4.40	4.31- 05
*	Costa	Keila	BRA	6.2.83	170/62	LJ	6.88	6.63- 05
						TJ	14.57, 15.10w	14.17- 06

Name		Nat	Born	Ht/Wt	Event	2007 Mark	Pre-2007 Best
Coulaud	Julie	FRA	7.8.82	169/53	3000	8:46.71	8:58.83i- 06, 9:19.96- 05
					3kSt	9:31.43	
Cousins	Jessica	USA	10.4.85	165/55	200	23.42, 23.07w	23.96- 04
					400	51.92	53.28- 06
Coward	Jackie	USA-J	5.11.89	167/55	100H	13.21, 13.17w	13.59, 13.27w- 06
					400H	57.21	59.31- 06
Cox	Crystal	USA	28.3.79	190/79	100	11.36	11.31- 04
					200	23.12, 23.02Aw	22.58- 04
Cox	Shana	USA	22.1.85	171/57	400	51.27	51.15- 06
Crane	Julie	GBR	26.9.76	178/60	HJ	1.89i	1.90i- 05, 1.89- 04
* Crawford	Yunaika	CUB	2.11.82	165/75	HT	68.82	73.16- 04
Cristea	Olga	MDA	13.12.87	166/52	800	2:01.84	2:01.29- 04
Crolla	Bregje	NED	31.1.86	170/60	JT	57.57	54.68- 06
					Hep	5973	5711- 06
Cruz	Silvia	POR	29.12.80	175/85	JT	59.74	57.16- 06
Cruz	Yanet	CUB-J	8.2.88	165/75	JT	58.81	54.20- 06
Cuddihy	Joanne	IRL	11.5.84	184/65	400	50.73	51.09- 06
Cullen	Fiona	AUS	31.8.79	172/64	100H	13.08	13.19- 02, 13.14w, 13.0- 03
Cullen	Mary	IRL	17.8.82	165/54	3000	8:48.17	9:00.61- 06
5000	15:19.04		15:25.80- 06		10000	32:21.42	32:39.59- 06
Culpepper	Shayne	USA	3.12.73	165/55	1500	4:05.98	4:06.33- 04
1M	4:31.35i		4:33.62- 98		5000	15:30.61	15:01.36- 04
* Cumbá	Yumileidi	CUB	11.2.75	183/100	SP	18.81	19.97- 04
* Cummins	Diane	CAN	19.1.74	165/50	800	1:59.75	1:58.39- 01
					1000	2:37.66	2:34.14- 02
Cunningham	Nadia	JAM	25.5.78		400	52.09A, 52.69	52.98- 02
Cusma Piccione	Elisa	ITA	24.7.81	167/49	800	1:58.63	1:58.90- 06
					1500	4:09.34	4:09.55- 06
Dahlgren	Jennifer	ARG	27.8.84	180/115	HT	72.94	72.01- 06
Daigle-Bowen	Angela	USA	28.5.76	157/57	100	11.25	11.23- 04, 11.09w- 05
					200	23.21	22.59- 05
Damen	Louise	GBR	12.10.82		HMar	70:47	0
Danisová	Martina	SVK	21.3.83	180/100	HT	69.22	73.84- 06
* Danvers-Smith	Natasha	GBR	19.9.77	175/61	400H	54.08	54.02- 03
Darden	Dominique	USA	9.12.83	165/57	400H	55.56	54.88- 06
Darmovzalová	Martina	CZE	12.10.78	172/54	TJ	13.96	13.98- 02
Daunay	Christelle	FRA	5.12.74	163/43	5000	15:30.32	15:30.94- 04
HMar	71:05		72:37- 03		Mar	2:28:54	
Davin	Elizabeth	BEL	3.6.81	164/54	100H	13.18	13.40- 06
* Davis	Candice	USA	26.5.85	170/62	100H	12.90, 12.88w	13.07A. 13.10, 13.05w- 06
Davis	Kia	USA	23.5.76	168/55	200	23.04w	23.34, 23.18w- 05
		(now LBR)			400	51.75	51.63- 04
Davydova	Natalya	RUS	24.11.78		TJ	13.70	13.11- 06
Day	Sharon	USA	9.6.85	173/60	HJ	1.89	1.93- 05
De Aniceto	Marisa	FRA	11.11.86	162/55	Hep	5878	5880- 06
De Croock	Stephanie	BEL	4.3.79	170/55	3kSt	9:41.79	9:48.65- 05
De Vos	Nathalie	BEL	9.12.82	157/42	10000	31:22.80	31:45.94- 06
Dean	Hatti	GBR	2.2.82	164/52	3kSt	9:38.56	9:51.12- 06
Deatherage	Jenelle	USA	25.9.77	175/59	1500	4:10.57	4:07.87- 04
Debska	Paulina	POL	27.9.85	165/51	PV	4.50	4.35- 06
Decaux	Alice	FRA	10.4.85	165/65	100H	13.07, 13.05w	13.42- 06
* Defar	Meseret	ETH	19.11.83	155/42	2000	5:37.52+	
3000	8:24.51+, 8:23.72i		8:24.66- 06		2M	8:58.58	
					5000	14:16.63	14:24.53- 06
Dejaeghere	Veerle	BEL	1.8.73	164/52	3kSt	9:28.47	9:32.69- 06
Dektyareva	Tatyana	RUS	4.6.84		100H	13.30, 13.10w	13.04- 06
Delfino	Fernanda	BRA	7.11.82	173/51	TJ	13.87	13.69- 05
Delinikóla	Vasilikí	GRE	9.2.81	175/61	Hep	5823	5909- 03
Delzenne	Amélie	FRA	4.8.83	168/52	PV	4.30	4.25- 05
Demireva	Mirela	BUL-J	28.9.89		HJ	1.88	1.86- 06
Demut	Katja	GER	21.12.83	176/55	TJ	14.09	13.96i- 04, 13.96- 06
Demydova	Olena	UKR	16.6.82	178/62	HJ	1.89	1.86- 06
^ Denboba	Merima	ETH	21.8.74	168/48	HMar	71:14dh	69:36- 04
* Denby	Nichole	USA	10.10.82	163/52	100H	12.80, 12.72w	12.62- 04
Denisenko	Alla	RUS	26.1.83		DT	56.78	58.26- 06
Denkova	Elena	BUL	8.1.85	182/55	TJ	13.37, 13.69w	13.67- 06
Dennison	Kate	GBR	7.5.84	171/59	PV	4.40i, 4.31	4.35- 06
Derham	Zoe	GBR	24.11.80	180/118	HT	67.80	65.85- 06
Deriba	Shiru	ETH			Mar	2:30:30	
Désert	Solen	FRA	2.8.82	178/60	400	51.42	51.52- 05
Desprès	Gwendoline	FRA	27.11.83	162/48	3kSt	10:02.50	10:05.12- 06

Name		Nat	Born	Ht/Wt	Event	2007 Mark	Pre-2007 Best
* Devetzí	Hrisopiyí	GRE	2.1.76	170/60	LJ	6.69	6.83- 06
					TJ	15.09	15.32- 04
* Di Martino	Antonietta	ITA	1.6.78	169/58	HJ	2.03	1.98- 01
Dias	Ana	POR	15.1.74	169/50	HMar	70:43dh	70:28- 03
Diaz	Roxana	CUB	17.5.81	178/60	100	11.35	11.31A- 02, 11.42- 01
					200	22.68	22.69- 03
* Dibaba	Ejegayehu	ETH	25.6.82	160/46	3000	8:42.1+	8:35.94- 06
5000	14:45.22	14:32.74- 04			10000	31:18.97	30:18.39- 05
* Dibaba	Tirunesh	ETH	1.6.85	160/47	3000	8:44.30+i	8:29.55- 06
5000	14:35.67, 14:27.42i	14:30.40- 06			10000	31:55.41	30:15.67- 05
Dibelková	Barbora	CZE	26.5.83	172/55	20kW	1:34:44	1:29:05- 05
* Dietzsch	Franka	GER	22.1.68	183/95	DT	68.06	69.51- 99
Diles	Tamara	USA	5.11.82	176/69	PV	4.27i	4.35Ai- 02, 4.25- 06
Dimitrova	Maria	BUL	7.8.76	170/55	TJ	14.08i, 13.95	14.52- 04
Dinu	Alina	ROM	2.9.82	178/62	TJ	13.75i	14.32i, 14.17- 03
^ Divós	Katalin	HUN	11.5.74	180/84	HT	67.09	70.79- 01
* Dixon	Vonette	JAM	26.11.75	170/62	100H	12.64	12.67- 05
Dobija	Teresa	POL	9.10.82	175/62	LJ	6.55	6.14- 06
Dobriskey	Lisa	GBR	23.12.83	170/58	1500	4:06.22	4:05.42mx - 05, 4:06.21- 06
2M	9:33.78i				3000	8:54.12, 8:47.25i	9:02.85- 05
* Dobrynska	Nataliya	UKR	29.5.82	182/77	Hep	6327	6387- 04
Dobrynska	Viktoriya	UKR	18.1.80	176/63	HJ	1.90	1.86- 06
Dockendorf	Carly	CAN	31.12.83	165/59	PV	4.45	4.20- 05
Dodova	Gita	BUL	2.5.82		TJ	13.98	13.74, 13.94w- 06
* Domínguez	Marta	ESP	3.11.75	163/52	3000	8:44.40i	8:28.80- 00
Donisa	Daniela	ROM-J	23.4.88	165/50	1500	4:08.02	4:21.69- 05
Donohue	Erin	USA	8.5.83	166/57	800	2:01.12	2:02.57- 06
1500	4:05.55	4:14.57- 06			1M	4:27.35	4:28.99- 06
Dorniden	Heather	USA	19.1.87	166/55	800	2:01.05	2:02.77- 06
Dorozhon	Margaryta	UKR	4.9.87	180/75	JT	55.88	57.68- 06
Douglas	Montell	GBR	24.1.86	173/64	100	11.28	11.52- 06
* Douma-Hussar	Carmen	CAN	12.3.77	170/57	1500	4:05.91	4:02.29- 05
					1M	4:26.76	4:28.43i- 05, 4:33.62- 03
Dow	Joanne	USA	19.3.64	172/61	20kW	1:34:21	1:32:54- 04
Dowdie	Peta-Gaye	JAM	18.1.77	170/61	100	11.34	11.03A, 11.06- 99, 10.98w- 00
					200	23.08	22.51- 00, 22.25w- 99
D'Oyley	Toni Ann	JAM	25.10.81	180/64	100H	13.18	12.92- 02
Drabenya	Zhanna	BLR	15.8.87		20kW	1:34:56	
* Dragila	Stacy	USA	25.3.71	172/62	PV	4.50	4.83- 04
Dreier	Verena	GER	15.1.85	166/52	3kSt	9:53.25	9:48.90- 06
Drouin	Jillian	CAN	30.9.86	167.58	HJ	1.87	1.81- 06
					Hep	5890w, 5822	5287- 06
Drummond	Catherine	AUS	14.12.87		HJ	1.90	1.80- 05
Dryakhlova	Mariya	RUS	24.4.84	174/58	800	2:01.76i	1:58.26- 06
					1000	2:36.40i	
Dryer	Elva	USA	26.9.71	165/51	10000	32:37.98	31:21.92- 05
du Toit	Simoné	RSA-J	27.9.88	184/113	SP	16.87	17.13- 05
* Duarté	Sophie	FRA	31.7.81	170/54	3kSt	9:27.51	10:07.73- 05
Dubnova	Romana	CZE	4.11.78	180/58	HJ	1.95	1.96- 05
Dubovik	Olga	RUS	10.9.76		1500	4:11.36	4:15.48- 06
Ducó	Natalia	CHI-J	31.1.89		SP	17.23	16.36- 06
Dufour	Sylvie	SUI	24.1.79	176/65	Hep	6112	6033- 03
Dukure	Jolanta	LAT	20.9.79	165/55	20kW	1:32:29	1:31:02- 06
Dumbravean	Corina	ROM	15.4.84	167/50	800	2:00.21	2:00.46- 06
					1500	4:08.9	4:02.24- 06
Duncan	Joanne	GBR	27.12.66	173/86	SP	16.85	17.13- 06
Dunn	Debbie	USA	26.3.78	168/57	200	22.96	23.01- 03
					400	51.66	51.12- 04
Dupree	Ryanne	USA	13.3.84	170/63	100H	13.23	13.38- 06
					Hep	5818	5606- 06
* Durst	Stephanie	USA	6.1.82	168/58	100	11.09	11.13- 06
					200	22.51	22.48, 22.46w- 02
Dusanova	Nadezhda	UZB	17.11.87		HJ	1.91	1.85- 06
Dyer	Tonette	USA	28.3.83	183/66	100	11.29	11.20- 04
200	22.76	22.34- 04			400	51.91	51.15- 04
Ebihara	Yuki	JPN	28.10.85	164/66	JT	55.33	57.47- 06
Edwards	Jackie	BAH	14.4.71	172/64	LJ	6.63	6.80- 96, 6.89Aw- 95
* Edwards	Torri	USA	31.1.77	163/52	100	10.90	10.93- 03, 10.86w- 06
					200	22.51	22.28- 03
Efimenko	Tatyana	KGZ	2.1.81	187/70	HJ	1.94	1.97- 03
Eftimova	Inna	BUL-J	19.6.88	165/54	100	11.28	11.67- 06

Name		Nat	Born	Ht/Wt	Event	2007 Mark	Pre-2007 Best
(Eftimova)					200	23.27	24.01- 06
Eieland	Anne Gerd	NOR	28.12.82	175/58	HJ	1.92i, 1.89	1.93- 03
Eisenlauer	Esther	GER	29.10.77	180/75	JT	58.34	57.20- 06
Ejdys	Sylwia	POL	15.7.84	162/50	800	2:01.33	2:03.22- 06
					1500	4:07.48	4:09.94- 06
^ Ejigu	Sentayehu	ETH	21.6.85	160/45	5000	15:27.84	14:35.18- 04
Ejjafini	Nadia	BRN	8.11.80	165/50	10000	32:29.53	33:19.3- 06
					HMar	70:38	70:43- 06
Ekpukpon	Christy	NGR	6.2.85	168/61	400	51.11	51.75- 06
El Habz	Lamia	MAR	19.5.84	175/60	400H	56.18	58.89- 06
El Jack	Nawal	SUD-J	17.10.88	163/50	400	51.78	51.19- 05
El Mehdi	Saïda	MAR	21.9.81		1500	4:06.51	4:08.60- 04
^ Elisdóttír	Thórey Edda	ISL	30.6.77	181/64	PV	4.40	4.60- 04
* Ellis	Dana	CAN	7.12.79	162/57	PV	4.52	4.51- 05
Elmore	Malindi	CAN	13.3.80	168/53	1500	4:05.65	4:02.64- 04
3000	8:55.46		8:51.90- 06		5000	15:12.12	
Endo	Mai	JPN	22.12.86	159/39	10000	32:39.29	32:47.80- 06
Engel	Annett	GER	6.11.87	192/72	HJ	1.93	1.90i- 05, 1.90- 06
Engeset	Kristine Eikrem	NOR-J	15.11.88	162.47	1500	4:09.40	4:19.58- 06
					3kSt	9:34.28	10:27.3- 06
Engman	Helena	SWE	16.6.76	171/	SP	17.72	17.51- 06
* Ennis	Jessica	GBR	28.1.86	164/57	200	23.15	23.56- 06
100H	12.97		13.19- 06		HJ	1.95	1.91- 06
LJ	6.54w		6.24- 06, 6.25w- 05		Hep	6469	6287- 06
* Ennis-London	Delloreen	JAM	5.3.75	178/67	100H	12.50	12.51- 04
Erdman	Katie	USA	24.8.83	177/60	800	1:59.35	2:03.86- 05
Erismis	Turkan	TUR	5.1.84	174/50	3kSt	9:46.12	9:50.32- 05
Erkesso	Teyiba	ETH	28.9.82	160/40	10000	31:13.67	31:41.26- 04
					HMar	71:03	70:00- 05
Evans	Erma-Gene	LCA	25.1.84	170/70	JT	56.45	55.00- 06
Eve	Laverne	BAH	16.6.65	179/77	JT	59.70	63.73- 00, 64.78#- 89
Eze	Joy	NGR	23.4.87	175/56	400	51.20	52.02- 06
Facey	Simone	JAM	7.5.85	162/53	100	11.16	11.22, 11.0- 04
					200	22.49	22.71- 04
Falaiye	Alice	CAN	24.12.78	168/55	LJ	6.51A, 6.57w	6.63A- 00, 6.59- 04, 6.69w- 06
Faluade	Brenda	USA	27.10.84	160/50	LJ	6.53	6.43- 06
Falzon	Stéphanie	FRA	7.1.83	170/66	HT	71.11	68.84- 06
Farfaletti-Casali	Arianna	ITA	22.6.76	158/51	PV	4.30	4.31- 02
* Faumuina	Beatrice	NZL	23.10.74	185/125	DT	62.20	68.52- 97
Faustin	Nadine	HAI	14.4.76	160/56	100H	13.16	12.74- 04
Fedoriva	Aleksandra	RUS-J	13.9.88	165/52	100H	13.12	13.48- 06
Fedotova	Natalya	RUS	19.7.84		1500	4:10.70	4:19.70- 06
* Feitor	Susana	POR	28.1.75	160/52	20kW	1:31:15	1:27:55- 01
* Felicien	Perdita	CAN	29.8.80	163/63	100H	12.49	12.46, 12.45w- 04
* Felix	Allyson	USA	18.11.85	168/57	100	11.01	11.04- 06
200	21.81		22.11A- 03, 22.11- 06		400	49.70	51.12- 05
Félix	Laurice Cristina	BRA	28.5.81	178/68	LJ	6.53	6.28- 00
					TJ	13.71, 14.32w	13.44- 06
Félix	Sylviane	FRA	31.10.77	174/58	100	11.36	11.15- 98
Felnagle	Brie	USA	9.12.86	170/52	1500	4:09.93	4:20.81- 05
* Feofanova	Svetlana	RUS	16.7.80	164/53	PV	4.82	4.88- 04
Féraez	Fabienne	BEN	6.8.76	175/57	400	51.85	51.47- 06
* Ferguson-McKenzie	Debbie	BAH	16.1.76	167/59	100	11.12	10.91- 02
					200	22.49	22.19- 99
Fernández	Adriana	MEX	4.4.71	163/59	10000	32:02.32	31:10.12- 00
Fernández	Yudelkis	CUB	28.2.85	174/63	LJ	6.58, 6.59w	6.74A- 04, 6.70- 05
					TJ	14.10	14.03- 03
* Ferrales	Yania	CUB	28.7.77	180/86	DT	64.97	66.00- 06
Ferrara	Ornella	ITA	17.4.68	153/40	Mar	2:30:22	2:27:49- 04
Fikadu	Belaynesh	ETH	28.3.87	157/45	3000	8:52.04	9:02.85- 06
					5000	15:02.14	15:59.95- 06
Filándra	Eléni	GRE	12.1.84	176/60	800	2:02.16	2:01.68- 05
Finucane	Laura	GBR	3.8.86	170/61	800	2:01.35	2:03.73- 04
Firova	Tatyana	RUS	10.10.82	178/64	400	50.98	50.08- 06
Fjørtoft	Silje	NOR	23.6.87	170/50	3kSt	9:57.98	10:34.94- 06
* Flanagan	Shalane	USA	7.8.81	165/50	1500	4:05.86	4:09.27- 04
2000	5:43.0+i				3000	8:35.34, 8:33.25i	8:54.43- 05
					5000	14:44.80	15:05.08- 04
Fleshman	Lauren	USA	26.9.81	173/54	1500	4:05.62	4:11.27- 06
3000	8:43.92		8:43.95- 05		5000	15:02.28	15:02.52- 05
					3kSt	9:53.24	

Name		Nat	Born	Ht/Wt	Event	2007 Mark	Pre-2007 Best
Fletcher	Sherry	GRN	17.1.86	168/55	100	11.18	11.47, 11.35w- 05
					200	22.67	23.44- 06
Floyd	Ebonie	USA	21.10.83	168/57	100	11.13	11.29, 11.13Aw- 06
200	22.32		22.63- 06		400	51.36	51.66- 06
Fofanah	Fatmata	GUI	26.6.85	178/64	100H	12.96	13.27, 13.20w- 06
* Fomenko	Yuliya	RUS	30.8.79	166/54	800	2:01.04	1:57.07- 06
1500	4:00.7		3:55.68- 06		1M	4:24.79	
Forcadell	Laia	ESP	6.6.82	173/55	400H	56.80	57.11- 05
Forrester	Nicole	CAN	17.11.76	192/72	HJ	1.97	1.94- 01
* Foster-Hylton	Brigitte	JAM	7.11.74	170/62	100H	12.71	12.45- 03
* Fountain	Hyleas	USA	14.1.81	170/60	Hep	6090	6502- 05
Fowler	Amy	USA	20.7.87	165/52	3kSt	10:01.19	10:08.12- 06
Frajka	Xénia	HUN	24.1.82	178/66	JT	55.08	58.12- 03
Franco	Leryn	PAR	1.3.82		JT	55.38	54.68- 04
Franek	Bridget	USA	8.11.87	160'50	3kSt	9:59.21	-0-
* Frankiewicz (Janowska)	Wioletta	POL	9.6.77	177/54	1500	4:09.51	4:03.09- 04
					3kSt	9:28.97	9:17.15- 06
Fraser	Shelly-Ann	JAM	27.12.86	160/52	100	11.31, 11.21w	11.57- 03
Freeman	Emily	GBR	24.11.80	163/55	100	11.36	11.40- 06
					200	23.27, 23.15w	23.25- 06
* Friedrich	Ariane	GER	10.1.84	178/59	HJ	1.94	1.92- 04
Frizell	Sultana	CAN	24.10.84	178/100	HT	67.92	66.42- 05
Fu Lin		CHN-J	21.2.89	177/75	JT	56.48	51.32- 06
Fuchise	Masumi	JPN	2.9.86	161/45	20kW	1:29:36	1:33:59- 06
Fuentes-Pila	Iris	ESP	10.8.80	169/53	1500	4:06.99	4:04.25- 02
Fuentes-Pila	Margarita	ESP	6.10.82	170/58	800	2:01.76	2:03.83- 06
Fuentes-Pila	Zulema	ESP	25.5.77	166/52	3kSt	9:43.95	9:40.36- 06
Fujinaga	Yoshiko	JPN	15.8.81	170/51	10000	32:37.51	31:47.82- 01
* Fukushi	Kayoko	JPN	25.3.82	161/45	5000	15:05.73	14:53.22- 05
10000	32:13.58		30:51.81- 02		HMar	68:00	67:26- 06
Funck (Thimm)	Annette	GER	24.11.77	173/57	100H	13.14	13.14- 03
Gadschiew	Kristina	GER	3.7.84	179/57	PV	4.40	4.35- 06
Galaviz	Lisa	USA	30.11.79	160/46	3kSt	9:28.75	9:40.58- 05
Galiart	Rianna	NED	22.11.85		PV	4.25	4.20- 06
Gáliková	Mária	SVK	21.8.80	161/55	20kW	1:34:18	1:34:38- 05
* Galkina	Gulnara	RUS	9.7.78	174/56	800	2:01.40	
1500	4:03.31+		4:01.29- 04		1M	4:20.23	4:22.68- 04
2000	5:31.03		5:56.57i- 04		3000	8:47.92	8:41.72i, 8:49.48- 04
(née Samitova)					3kSt	9:11.68	9:01.59- 04
Gall	Geena	USA	18.1.87	172/57	800	2:02.24	2:02.73- 06
Gallo	Lindsey	USA	29.11.81	166/50	1500	4:09.60	4:05.75- 05
* Gao Shuying		CHN	28.10.79	180/66	PV	4.64	4.53- 05
Gappova	Viktoriya	RUS	27.1.84		100H	13.04	13.08- 07
Garcia	Rosibel	COL	13.2.81	167/52	800	2:00.02	1:59.58- 06
García	Alejandra	ARG	13.6.73	172/58	PV	4.30	4.43- 04
Gargallo	María Teresa	ESP	15.10.69	162/46	20kW	1:32:51	1:30:41- 03
Gaus	Oksana	RUS	9.7.81	183/95	SP	18.53	18.78- 06
* Gavrila	Adelina	ROM	26.11.78	174/55	TJ	14.29i, 14.20. 14.21w	14.76i, 14.75- 03
Gavrilovic	Sanja	CRO	20.9.82	179/69	HT	68.48	67.72- 03
* Gay	Mabel	CUB	5.5.83	186/71	TJ	14.66	14.57i- 04, 14.52- 03
Gemeche	Shitaye	ETH	17.6.80	150/39	Mar	2:28:03	2:26:15- 02
Genovese	Bruna	ITA	24.9.76	161/50	Mar	2:27:35	2:25:35- 01, 2:25:28dh- 06
Gentili	Manuela	ITA	7.2.78	163/49	400H	57.04	57.35- 04
* George	Anju Bobby	IND	19.4.77	177/62	LJ	6.65	6.83- 04
Gérance	Fanny	FRA	4.1.81	171/61	100H	13.15	13.21- 00, 13.10w- 02
Getaneh	Genet	ETH	6.1.86		10000	32:09.50	
					HMar	70:30	
* Gevaert	Kim	BEL	5.8.78	170/60	100	11.05, 11.04w	11.04- 06
					200	22.62	22.20- 06
Gherasim	Alina	ROM	16.11.71	166/46	HMar	69:14	69:10- 99
Ghribi	Habiba	TUN	9.4.84	170/57	3kSt	9:50.04	9:51.49- 05
Gibilisco	Laura	ITA	17.1.86	162/85	HT	66.24	64.01- 05
Giesa	Ulrike	GER	16.8.84	183/93	DT	58.52	60.63- 05
Gigi	Asha	ETH	15.10.73	165/48	HMar	70:12+	69:53dh- 05
					Mar	2:29:11	2:26:05- 04
^ Gilreath	Erin	USA	11.10.80	177/92	HT	70.10	73.87- 05
Ginko	Yelena	BLR	30.7.76	165/53	20kW	1:28:29	1:28:11- 05
Giordano	Rossella	ITA	1.12.72	170/51	20kW	1:32:38	1:29:12- 97
Giordano Bruno	Anna	ITA	13.12.80	171/65	PV	4.40	4.32- 06
Glanc	Zaneta	POL	11.3.83	188/82	DT	59.36	56.15- 05
Glavatskikh	Irina	RUS	29.12.84	180/56	HJ	1.88	1.90i- 04, 1.87- 03

Name		Nat	Born	Ht/Wt	Event	2007 Mark	Pre-2007 Best
Glenn	Brianna	USA	18.4.80	168/55	100	11.10	11.27- 06, 11.15w- 01
					LJ	6.71	6.68, 6.70w- 05
Gliznutsa	Inna	MDA	18.4.73	184/65	HJ	1.90	1.95- 99
Glok	Olga	RUS	6.12.82		HMar	69:58	74:10- 06
					Mar	2:31:12	2:37:01- 04
* Glover	Sandra	USA	30.12.68	173/59	400H	54.59	53.32- 05
Godinho	Marta	POR	24.6.80	160/50	TJ	13.46, 13.69w	13.22- 04
Godsey	Kelly	USA	1.1.86		HT	64.64	62.92- 06
Goff	Yolanda	USA	14.1.85	161/52	100	11.24w	11.50- 06
Gogoleva	Svetlana	RUS	11.12.85		400H	56.56	58.93- 06
* Golding-Clarke	Lacena	JAM	20.3.75	168/57	100H	12.85	12.68, 12.67w- 05
Golovnya	Zhanna	BLR	18.5.86		20kW	1:33:25	
* Golubchikova	Yuliya	RUS	27.3.83	175/57	PV	4.71i, 4.70	4.60- 06
* Gomes	Naide	POR	10.11.79	181/70	LJ	7.01	6.82, 6.84w- 06
Goncharenko	Olga	BLR	13.7.81	185/95	DT	55.70	59.06- 01
Goncharova	Marina	RUS	26.4.86		Hep	6004	5760- 05
* Gong Lijiao		CHN-J	24.1.89	175/80	SP	19.13	17.92- 06
Gonse	Roslyn	GBR	1.3.82	171/60	Hep	5798	5578w- 05, 5567- 06
* González	Misleydis	CUB	19.6.78	178/80	SP	18.97	19.10- 06
Gorbacho	Yosleiny	CUB	17.9.83		LJ	6.56w	6.37- 06
Gordeyeva	Irina	RUS	9.10.86		HJ	1.89i	1.88- 04
* Goucher	Kara	USA	9.7.78	170/58	1500	4:10.29	4:05.14- 06
2000	5:42.79+				3000	8:34.99	8:41.42- 06
5000	14:55.02		15:08.13- 06		10000	32:02.05	31:17.12- 06
					HMar	66:57dh	-0-
^ Goulbourne	Elva	JAM	21.1.80	170/50	LJ	6.66, 6.67w	
							7.16A- 04, 6.86-01, 6.96w- 03, 6.91i- 02
Grabuste	Aiga	LAT-J	24.3.88	176/68	Hep	6019	5443- 06
Grace	Carla	USA	6.6.86	175/62	200	23.19	23.49- 06
Gradzki	Monika	GER	21.9.79	172/59	800	2:01.15	2:00.16- 06
Graham	Nolle	JAM	12.9.81	167/59	LJ	6.65	6.63, 6.67w- 01
* Grasu	Nicoleta	ROM	11.9.71	176/88	DT	65.60	68.80- 99
* Green	Emma	SWE	8.12.84	180/62	HJ	1.95	1.97- 05
Green	Nikeya	USA	10.8.82	176/60	800	2:02.19	2:02.24- 06
Green	Sherlenia	USA	22.3.85	170/59	400H	56.66	-0-
Greggs	Charlette	USA	20.10.83	170/57	200	23.10w	22.85, 22.74w- 05
Greguric	Mateja	CRO-J	27.5.88		HT	65.36	55.15- 06
Grgic	Danijela	CRO-J	28.9.88	175/61	400	51.88	50.78- 06
Griffiths	Vicky	GBR	9.10.84	160/50	800	2:01.49	2:03.19- 06
* Grigoryeva	Lidiya	RUS	21.1.74	163/48	10000	32:03.02	30:32.72- 06
					Mar	2:28:37	2:25:10- 06
Grigoryeva	Tatyana	RUS	13.5.81		HJ	1.89	1.96- 03
Grigoryeva	Yekaterina	RUS	21.4.74	177/71	100	11.25	11.13- 98
Gromova	Oksana	RUS	23.9.80	178/75	JT	60.38	61.12- 03
Gronau	Karolina	POL	12.7.84	180/60	HJ	1.92	1.84- 04
Grøvdal	Karoline Bjerkeli	NOR-Y	14.6.90	167/52	3kSt	9:33.19	9:55.95- 06
Groza	Ana-Maria	ROM	1.6.76	167/53	20kW	1:34:09	1:29:31- 04
Gruca	Dorota	POL	5.12.70	159/46	Mar	2:30:10	2:27:46- 05
^ Gudkova	Tatyana	RUS	23.1.78	170/60	20kW	1:31:10	1:25:18- 00
Guégan	Élodie	FRA	19.12.85	169/55	800	1:59.46	2:00.90- 05
					1500	4:10.62	4:24.51- 02
* Guevara	Ana Gabriela	MEX	4.3.77	173/61	400	50.16	48.89- 03
Gullatte	Rhonda	USA	10.2.84		DT	56.84	57.43- 05
Gürler	Özge	TUR	17.6.85	163/52	400H	56.33	57.59- 06
* Gurova	Viktoriya	RUS	22.5.82	178/63	LJ	6.72	6.49i- 03
					TJ	14.46	14.74i- 05, 14.65- 04
* Gushchina	Yuliya	RUS	4.3.83	175/62	100	11.36	11.13- 06
					200	22.75	22.53- 05, 22.52w- 06
Gutowicz-Westhof	Urszula	GER	13.7.77	179/57	LJ	6.61	6.62- 05
^ Györffy	Dóra	HUN	23.2.78	175/55	HJ	1.89, 1.93ex	2.00- 01
Haapanen	Amy	FIN	23.3.84		HT	65.18	59.79- 04
Habazin	Dorotea	CRO-J	14.6.88		HT	66.35	59.70- 05
Habtamu	Atsede	ETH	26.10.87		HMar	68:29	
Haga	Marina	JPN	12.7.83	171/48	10000	32:38.61	32:34.15- 06
					HMar	70:57	72:04- 06
Haining	Hayley	GBR	6.3.72	166/54	Mar	2:30:43	2:31:51- 06
Hakamata	Naomi	JPN	2.11.85		20kW	1:35:42	1:40:49- 05
* Halkiá	Faní	GRE	2.2.79	175/64	400	51.85	50.56- 04
					400H	55.66	52.77- 04
Halkoaho	Johanna	FIN	13.1.77	165/55	100H	13.15	13.23- 05
Hall	Patricia	JAM	16.10.82	170/57	400	51.52	51.45- 06

Name		Nat	Born	Ht/Wt	Event	2007 Mark	Pre-2007 Best
Hall	Sara	USA	15.4.83	163/48	1500	4:08.99	4:14.83- 06
					1M	4:32.24i	4:35.02- 06
					5000	15:22.56	15:20.88- 06
Hammond	Chelsea	JAM	2.8.83	175/60	LJ	6.66, 6.87w	6.57- 04
Han Jie		CHN	31.12.87	170/53	20kW	1:34:39.71	1:33:08- 06
Hanaoka	Maho	JPN	3.8.76	171/60	LJ	6.64w	6.82- 01
^ Hansen	Ashia	GBR	5.12.71	173/64	TJ	13.68i	15.16i- 98, 15.15- 97
Hantzí-Neag	Hristína	GRE	26.12.76	170/56	400H	55.94	56.15- 05
Hao Shuai		CHN	19.7.87	178/65	HT	68.77	65.72- 06
Hara	Mikiko	JPN	6.2.86	160/46	HMar	70:55	
* Hara	Yumiko	JPN	9.1.82	163/43	HMar	70:24+	69:28- 02
					Mar	2:23:48	2:24:19- 05
Hargrove	Monica	USA	30.12.82		400	51.40	51.95- 06
* Harper	Dawn	USA	13.5.84	168/57	100H	12.67	12.80A, 12.86- 06
Harrelson	Mary Jane	USA	17.6.78	170/54	1500	4:11.57	4:07.37- 01
* Harrigan	Tahesia	IVB	15.2.82	157/50	100	11.17	11.13A, 11.02w- 06; 11.29- 05,
					200	22.98	23.07- 06
Harris	Raevan	USA	1.3.87		HJ	1.87	1.78- 05
Harrison	Queen	USA-J	10.9.88	165/57	100H	12.98	
					400H	55.81	
Hart	Bethany	USA	10.4.77	172/73	HT	69.11	69.65- 05
Hartmann	Julia	GER	10.4.86	181/62	HJ	1.93i	1.87- 05
Hartz	Ulrike	GER	7.5.87	181/72	Hep	5818	5522- 06
Harvey	Natasha	USA	29.11.87	175/64	LJ	6.49	6.53- 06
Hashimoto	Yasuko	JPN	12.8.75	163/46	HMar	71:08	68:55- 01
					Mar	2:28:49	2:25:21- 05
* Hastings	Amy	USA	21.1.84	163/46	5000	15:30.17i	15:52.06- 06
					10000	32:30.37	33:17.89- 06
Hastings	Natasha	USA	23.7.86	173/63	200	22.61	23.66- 04, 23.08i- 05
					400	49.84	51.34- 05
Hatzinákou	Persefóni	GRE	6.6.84	184/61	HJ	1.92	1.87- 05
Hayakari	Minori	JPN	29.11.72	164/48	3kSt	9:38.68	9:41.21- 05
* Hayes	Joanna	USA	23.12.76	165/58	100H	13.28, 12.78w	12.37- 04
					400H	56.56	54.57- 99
Hazel	Louise	GBR	6.10.85	167/56	Hep	5684w, 5594	5894- 06
He Pan		CHN-J	1.5.88	170/51	1500	4:11.22	4:14.69- 06
					5000	15:08.03	15:44.88- 06
He Yanhong		CHN	17.4.84	173/54	HJ	1.87i	1.84- 04
Heaston	Kristin	USA	23.11.75	180/127	SP	18.74	18.68- 05
Hebestreit	Ulrike	GER	19.3.81		Hep	5773	5697- 06
* Heidler	Betty	GER	14.10.83	174/80	HT	75.77	76.55- 06
Heitkötter	Michaela Ruth	BRA/GER	22.3.85		PV	4.23	4.00i, 3.97- 04
Heitling	Sabine	BRA	2.7.87	167/52	3kSt	9:51.13	10:04.71- 05
Hejnová	Zuzana	CZE	19.12.86	170/54	400H	55.04	55.83- 06
* Hellebaut	Tia	BEL	16.2.78	182/66	HJ	2.05i, 1.98	2.03- 06
Heltne	Anca	ROM	1.1.78	175/76	SP	17.37	17.51- 99
* Henderson	Monique	USA	18.2.83	170/54	200	23.26	22.71- 04
					400	50.82	49.96- 05
Hendricks	Shataya	USA-J	15.8.89	164/52	100	11.30	11.51- 06
Hendry	Kelsie	CAN	29.6.82	170/59	PV	4.35	4.46- 05
* Hennagan	Monique	USA	26.5.76	173/55	400	51.19	49.56- 04
Henriques	Inês	POR	1.5.80	156/48	20kW	1:30:24	1:30:28- 06
Henry	Britney	USA	17.10.84	170/82	HT	67.54	68.17- 05
Henry	Samantha	JAM-J	25.9.88	160/52	100	11.21	11.68- 06
					200	22.84	24.07- 03
Henry	Tresha	JAM	23.9.83	168/57	200	23.27	23.61, 23.15w- 06
Hessler	Stephanie	GER	16.3.83	166/65	JT	56.96	57.00- 03
Hie Jingjing		CHN-J	1.3.88	168/45	20kW	1:32:19.71t	1:29:50- 06
Hietalahti	Anita	FIN	17.2.77	177/80	DT	57.12	57.90- 04
Hila	Elena	ROM	20.5.74	180/98	SP	16.74	18.73i- 99, 18.73- 02
Hilali	Siham	MAR	2.5.86	161/58	1500	4:04.03	4:08.15- 04
Hiller	Julia	GER	24.7.87	170/55	3kSt	9:57.79	10:11.67- 06
Hinchcliffe	Brittany	USA	24.7.82	170/75	HT	66.00	64.69- 06
* Hinds	Korine	JAM	18.1.76	163/54	3kSt	9:28.86	9:30.12- 05
* Hingst	Carolin	GER	18.9.80	170/60	PV	4.70i, 4.65	4.66- 04
Hinrichs	Denise	GER	7.6.87	181/81	SP	18.08	18.21i, 17.56- 06
^ Hiroyama	Harumi	JPN	2.9.68	160/47	HMar	70:23	69:41- 01
					Mar	2:28:55	2:22:56- 00
Hladun-Nesterenko	Zoya	UKR	10.3.83	169/58	800	2:01.80	2:02.01- 06
Hoban	Aine	GBR	12.7.84	173/53	10000	32:45.94	33:44.22- 06
Hodge	Virgil	SKN	17.11.83	168/54	100	11.29, 11.19w	11.33, 11.07w- 06
					200	22.68	22.89A, 22.57w- 06

Name		Nat	Born	Ht/Wt	Event	2007 Mark	Pre-2007 Best
Hoffmann	Claudia	GER	10.12.82	171/62	400	51.98	51.79- 06
Holliday	Becky	USA	12.3.80	160/52	PV	4.53i, 4.45	4.47- 03
Hollman	Julie	GBR	16.2.77	180/69	Hep	6053	6135- 02
Holm	Mona	NOR	5.8.83	169/78	HT	67.80	64.89- 06
Holosha	Olena	UKR	16.1.82	183/60	HJ	1.92	1.90- 02
Holovchenko	Tetyana	UKR	13.2.80	164/54	1500	4:05.48	4:05.01- 06
5000 15:26.88			15:35.83- 05		10000	31:59.98	
Hooker	Destinee	USA	7.9.87	193/72	HJ	1.96i, 1.93	1.92i, 1.90- 06
Hooker	Marshevet	USA	25.9.84	175/67	100	11.06	11.09- 06, 11.03w- 05
					200	23.25, 22.95w	22.75, 22.70w- 06
Hoos	Laurien	NED	18.8.83	178/63	Hep	6199	6291- 05
Hopping	Sarah	USA	5.8.83		HT	65.20	66.96- 06
Horpynych	Valentyna	UKR	12.3.83	161/48	3kSt	9:43.48	9:49.73- 05
* Howe	Kym	AUS	12.6.80	176/63	PV	4.72i, 4.65	4.62- 06
* Huang Xiaoxiao		CHN	3.3.83	181/62	400H	54.00	54.18- 05
Huddle	Molly	USA	31.8.84	163/48	5000	15:17.13	15:32.55- 04
Hunter	Gayle	USA	9.4.86		Hep	5711	5411- 04
Hunter-Galvan	Lisa	NZL	25.6.69		Mar	2:30:40	2:33:51- 05
* Hurtis-Houairi	Muriel	FRA	25.3.79	180/68	100	11.31	10.96- 02
					200	22.38	22.31- 99
Hussein	Marwa Ahmed	EGY	19.6.78	168/110	HT	65.70	68.48- 05
Hutchinson	Katerina	USA	10.6.85	180/82	DT	56.46	57.73- 06
Hütter	Julia	GER	26.7.83	169/57	PV	4.57	4.52- 06
^ Hyman	Mardrea	JAM	22.12.72	168/52	3kSt	9:37.50	9:27.21- 05
Ibargüen	Caterine	COL	12.2.84	165/59	HJ	1.87	1.93A- 05, 1.91- 04
Ibekwe	Mariam	NGR	29.10.69		SP	16.68	16.42- 98
Idoko	Franca	NGR	15.6.85	168/59	100	11.22	11.53- 03
Ignatova	Yuliya	UKR	30.7.83	166/59	3kSt	10:03.18	9:59.83- 06
* Ikeda	Kumiko	JPN	10.1.81	166/53	100H	13.02	13.04, 12.90w- 06
					LJ	6.73	6.86- 06
Ildeykina	Yelena	RUS	16.6.83	165/52	400	52.04	51.48- 05
					400H	56.18	55.49- 04
Ilkevych	Iryna	UKR	6.3.87	172/56	Hep	5788	5952- 06
Ilyushchenko	Tatyana	BLR	18.4.83	178/85	SP	17.45i, 16.43	18.06- 06
Incerti	Anna	ITA	19.1.80		HMar	71:09	70:56- 04
* Ingberg	Mikaela	FIN	29.7.74	174/66	JT	60.70	64.03- 00, 67.32#- 97
* Isakova	Yevgeniya	RUS	27.11.78	168/54	400H	54.11	53.93- 06
Ishino	Mami	JPN	10.1.83	169/52	100H	13.16	13.26- 06
* Isinbayeva	Yelena	RUS	3.6.82	174/66	PV	4.93i, 4.91	5.01- 05
Ispan	Andreea	ROM	2.6.78	189/68	HJ	1.89	1.88i- 05, 1.88- 06
Ivankova	Olga	UKR	7.1.73	173/72	JT	61.68	60.74- 05
Ivanova ¶	Alena	BLR	20.8.87	188/55	HJ	1.92dq	1.85- 06
Ivanova	Alevtina	RUS	22.5.75	160/43	Mar	2:27:49	2:30:26- 02
^ Ivanova	Alina	RUS	16.3.69	163/52	HMar	69:32	70:11- 04
					Mar	2:29:20	2:25:34- 01
Ivanova	Marina	RUS	30.6.83		3000	8:53.56	9:07.03- 06
			3		10000	31:52.37	34:21.66- 04
Ivanova	Natalya	RUS	25.6.81	183/69	400H	54.36	55.04- 06
Ivanova	Svetlana	RUS	18.8.83	173/60	3kSt	9:48.14	9:38.48- 06
Ivanova	Yelena	RUS	16.3.79	175/64	LJ	6.50i	6.77- 06
					TJ	14.31	14.39- 04
Ivanova/Savkova	Svetlana	RUS	10.7.85		DT	57.04	57.62- 05
Ivoninskaya	Natalya	KAZ	22.2.85	176/54	100H	13.02	13.20- 05
Izmodenova	Natalya	RUS	1.1.81	167/52	3kSt	9:45.96	9:35.51- 05
Jaakkola	Jelena	FIN-J	7.3.89	172/74	JT	55.93	50.22- 06
Jabir Ahmed	Muna	SUD	6.1.87	175/60	400	51.61A	53.34- 04
					400H	54.93	56.55- 06
Jackson	Emma	GBR-J	7.6.88	178/60	800	2:01.95	2:04.43- 06
Jakubaityté	Indre	LTU	24.1.76	177/70	JT	63.65	60.59- 05
* Jamal	Maryam	BRN	16.9.84	155/44	1500	3:58.75	3:56.18- 06
1M 4:17.75					5000	15:20.28	14:51.68- 05
James	Markita	USA	28.6.83	178/62	400	52.11A	52.00- 06
					400H	55.48	54.47- 06
* Jamieson	Sarah	AUS	24.3.75	172/57	1500	4:03.71	4:00.93- 06
1M 4:23.40			4:29.15- 06		3000	8:48.41	8:49.46- 04
Jansen	Monique	NED	3.10.78		DT	56.81	51.91- 05
Jansen	Rachel	USA	26.7.84		SP	17.29	16.50i, 16.46- 06
Janson	Lacy	USA	20.2.83	178/68	PV	4.60Ai, 4.50	4.58- 06
Jarocki	Robyn	USA	11.7.84		SP	16.90i, 16.25	17.05i, 16.77- 06
Jarrett	Jovanee	JAM	15.1.83	170/62	LJ	6.53, 6.56w	6.52- 06
Järvenpää	Mari	FIN	29.11.81	168/53	1500	4:10.33	4:16.94- 06

Name		Nat	Born	Ht/Wt	Event	2007 Mark	Pre-2007 Best
Jasinska	Urszula	POL	6.12.83	169/70	JT	62.34	57.11- 06
^ Javornik	Helena	SLO	26.3.66	163/52	HMar	70:32	69:22- 04
					Mar	2:28:53	2:27:33- 04
* Jayasinghe	Susanthika	SRI	17.12.75	170/62	100	11.13	11.04- 00
					200	22.55	22.28- 00
Jean	Sivan	ISR	25.6.85	171/92	DT	56.67	56.16- 06
Jelagat	Irene	KEN-J	10.12.88	162/45	1500	4:10.27	4:08.88- 06
Jémaa	Dora	FRA	15.7.85	154/45	400H	56.27	56.69- 06
* Jepkorir	Eunice	KEN	17.2.82	164/48	5000	15:19.97	15:09.05- 04
					3kSt	9:14.52	10:19.0A- 05
* Jepkosgei	Janeth	KEN	13.12.83	167/47	800	1:56.04	1:56.66- 06
* Jeptoo	Rita	KEN	15.2.81		HMar	67:08dh	69:56- 06
Jerotich	Irene	KEN	.82		Mar	2:31:12	2:32:42- 06
Jerotich	Milkah	KEN	24.2.78		HMar	71:03	71:22- 06
* Jesien	Anna	POL	10.12.78	168/56	400	51.74	51.92- 06
					400H	53.86	53.96- 05
Jess	Kimberly	GER-Y	30.1.92	181/61	HJ	1.87	1.83- 06
* Jeter	Carmelita	USA	24.11.79	163/53	100	11.02	11.48- 06, 11.43w- 03
					200	22.82	23.54- 06
Jiang Chengcheng		CHN	5.11.86	170/52	5000	15:32.75	15:49.79- 03
					10000	32:39.18	32:38.66- 05
Jiang Fengjing		CHN	28.8.87	180/75	DT	57.05	56.05- 06
* Jiang Jing		CHN	23.10.85	164/51	20kW	1:29:45	1:27:19- 05
Jiang Limin		CHN-J	20.2.88	179/125	SP	16.71	17.51- 04
Jiang Qiuyan		CHN	5.7.83	160/48	20kW	1:30:27	1:28:01- 05
Jimoh	Funmi	USA	29.5.84	173/64	LJ	6.46, 6.62w	6.44- 06
Jin Yuan		CHN-J	11.2.88	173/51	3kSt	9:48.33	
Jin Yuanyuan		CHN-Y	24.1.90	170/65	DT	57.58	53.18- 06
Jo Bun-hui		PRK	29.11.79	157/48	Mar	2:28:25	2:27:22- 06
Johannes	Hilaria	NAM	13.8.80		HMar	71:02	73:35- 06
Johansson	Christin	SWE	26.1.78	166/53	3kSt	9:38.55	9:40.90- 06
Johnson	Alysia	USA	26.4.86	170/61	800	1:59.29	2:01.80- 06
* Johnson	Benita	AUS	6.5.79	166/50	HMar	68:28	67:55- 04
					Mar	2:29:47	2:22:36- 06
Johnson	Carrie	USA	19.10.84	178/86	HT	64.43	63.47- 06
Johnson	Chelsea	USA	20.12.83	175/62	PV	4.57	4.60- 06
Johnson	Gi-Gi	USA	12.1.79	165/61	100H	13.01	12.92- 06
					Hep	6002	6192- 05
Johnson	Jackie	USA	8.9.84	173/64	Hep	5984	5987- 06
^ Johnson	Jade	GBR	7.6.80	185/72	LJ	6.56, 6.58w	6.80- 04
* Johnson	Sheena	USA	1.10.82	165/58	100H	12.90	12.75- 04
					400H	53.29	52.95- 04
Johnson	Tiffany	USA	30.5.85	168/62	100H	13.22, 13.20w	13.58, 13.24w- 06
Jones	Laverne	ISV	16.9.81	171/59	100	11.32, 11.23w	11.25- 04, 11.22w- 05
200	22.52		22.81- 04		400	51.47	53.39A- 04, 53.78- 05
* Jones	Lolo	USA	5.8.82	168/60	100H	12.57	12.56- 06
Jong Yong-ok		PRK	24.1.81	153/40	Mar	2:26:02	2:26:12- 02
Jordan	Victoria	USA-Y	26.2.90	162/50	100	11.36	11.57- 05, 11.38w- 06
					200	23.24, 22.84w	23.66- 05, 23.45w- 06
Josephs	Janice	RSA	31.3.82	160/60	LJ	6.79	6.54- 06
Jovic	Biljana	SRB	2.3.85	176/59	3kSt	10:02.24	10:04.60- 06
Joyce	Alexis	USA	15.9.83	157/52	100	11.49, 11.27w	11.45- 01
June	Kara	USA	10.8.82	165/52	3kSt	9:57.09	10:12.79- 06
Jung Hye-kyung		KOR	13.4.81	166/53	TJ	13.49, 13.90w	13.77- 06
Jung Soon-ok		KOR	23.4.83	169/54	LJ	6.66	6.68- 06
Jungmark	Ebba	SWE	10.3.87	178/59	HJ	1.92	1.85i, 1.84- 06
Juravel	Oxana	MDA	23.2.86	160/48	3kSt	9:59.04	10:22.82- 05
Kadogan	Filiz	TUR	12.2.82	187/95	SP	16.77	17.16- 03
Kafetzi	Ioánna	GRE	30.5.76	165/55	LJ	6.52	6.71- 04
Kakhova	Galina	BLR	26.3.82	167/62	JT	55.53	59.48- 01
^ Kallur	Jenny	SWE	16.2.81	170/62	100H	13.08	12.85- 05
* Kallur	Susanna	SWE	16.2.81	170/61	100	11.36	11.30- 06
					100H	12.49	12.52- 06
* Kálovics	Anikó	HUN	13.5.77	175/57	HMar	68:58	69:16- 02
					Mar	2:28:17	2:26:44dh- 06
Kalpakídou	Dorothéa	GRE	21.9.83	184/90	DT	56.43	56.76- 06
Kamau	Bilha	KEN-J	2.7.88	153/40	5000	15:31.94	
					10000	32:19.25	
Kanales	Yelena	RUS	7.2.76	158/48	1000	2:36.56i	2:32.91i- 06
Kand	Kaie	EST	31.3.84	175/63	Hep	5876	5860- 06
* Kaniskina	Olga	RUS	19.1.85	160/43	20kW	1:26:47	1:26:02- 06

Name		Nat	Born	Ht/Wt	Event	2007 Mark	Pre-2007 Best
Kano	Yuri	JPN	27.10.78	152/39	HMar	71:05dh	70:28- 03
					Mar	2:24:43	
Kantola	Ingrid	USA	8.2.86	173/59	PV	4.22Ai, 4.15	3.84i- 06, 3.81- 05
* Kapachinskaya	Anastasiya	RUS	21.11.79	176/64	400	52.14	50.59- 03
* Kappler	Bianca	GER	8.8.77	180/62	LJ	6.90	6.71- 04
Karadere	Nagihan	TUR	.84		400H	56.42	58.70- 06
Karapetrova	Rumyana	BUL	7.2.82	171/74	JT	57.62	61.78- 06
Karmishina	Vera	RUS-J	6.11.88		DT	56.16	50.28- 06
Kárniková	Jana	CZE	14.2.81	187/85	SP	16.74	16.97- 06
Karpiesiuk	Agnieszka	POL	17.4.82	183/64	400H	56.70	55.88- 06
Karsak	Kateryna	UKR	26.12.85	183/88	DT	64.40	62.75- 06
Kashcheyeva	Zhanna	RUS	27.7.82		400	51.04	52.95- 03
Kasim	Ashu	ETH	20.10.84		5000	15:32.33	
					10000	31:46.05	34:05.2 - 05
Kasprzak	Róza	POL	9.4.82	180/58	PV	4.50i, 4.30	4.50- 06
Kassambara	Aurore	FRA	26.10.79	169/58	400H	56.23	56.43- 05
* Kastor	Deena	USA	14.2.73	163/48	3000	8:44.45	8:42.59- 00
5000	14:52.21		14:51.62- 00		10000	31:57.00	30:50.32- 02
					HMar	69:38	67:34- 06
Kato	Asuka	JPN	7.3.80	157/40	HMar	71:15	72:22- 05
Kaur	Harwant	IND	5.7.80	165/70	DT	55.55	63.05- 04
Kawasaki	Mayumi	JPN	10.5.80	167/52	20kW	1:28:56	1:31:19- 04
Kayukova	Yekaterina	RUS	9.10.86		TJ	14.41	14.15- 06
Kazanina	Svetlana	KAZ	31.10.71	175/64	Hep	5815	6228- 99
Kazanovskaya	Olesya	RUS	12.7.82		LJ	6.57	6.47i, 6.51uc- 05; 6.42- 06
Kebaso	Winfrida	KEN	16.4.85	163/46	5000	15:15.65	15:14.46- 06
^ Keil	Susanne	GER	18.5.78	172/66	HT	70.36	72.74- 05
* Keitany	Mary	KEN	18.1.82		10000	32:18.07	
					HMar	66:48	
Keizer	Jolanda	NED	5.4.85	183/67	Hep	6219	5760- 05
Kelo	Niina	FIN	26.3.80	178/69	Hep	5707	5956- 06
Kemkers	Denise	NED	11.4.85	182/81	SP	17.21	16.79- 06
Kerubo	Rose	KEN	28.10.76	/49	Mar	2:29:22	2:34:19- 04
* Kesselschläger	Sonja	GER	20.1.78	177/66	Hep	6184	6287- 04
Kevkhishvili	Mariam	GEO	17.9.85	186/91	SP	17.05	17.21?- 04, 16.18= 05
* Khanafeyeva	Gulfiya	RUS	4.6.82	170/84	HT	77.36	77.26- 06
Khayrutdinova	Rashida	RUS	18.8.75	162/51	HMar	70:38	76:10- 06
Khlyustova	Irina	BLR	14.6.78	175/62	400	51.89	51.87- 06
* Khoroshikh	Yekaterina	RUS	21.1.83	172/73	HT	74.87	76.63- 06
^ Khristova	Tsvetanka	BUL	14.3.62	175/85	DT	57.90	73.22- 87
^ Khrushchelyova	Natalya	RUS	30.5.73	172/55	800	2:00.52	1:56.59- 04
Khubbieva	Guzel	UZB	2.5.76	173/62	100	11.20, 11.1	11.26- 04
					200	23.25	23.16- 04
* Khudoroshkina	Irina	RUS	13.10.68	182/100	SP	19.01i, 18.87	20.32- 96
Kibet	Hilda	KEN	27.3.81	159/45	5000	15:32.37	15:32.07- 04
					HMar	69:43	71:40- 04
* Kibet	Sylvia	KEN	18.3.84	157/44	3000	8:43.09+	8:40.09- 06
2M	9:16.62				5000	14:57.37	15:02.54- 06
* Kibiwott	Viola	KEN	22.12.83	157/45	1500	4:02.10	4:06.64- 04
2M	9:18.26				3000	8:43.05+	8:40.14- 03
Kidane	Etalemahu	ETH	14.2.83	158/44	5000	15:23.24	15:04.34- 04
					10000	31:33.49	
Kidd	Ashlee	USA	26.7.85	179/67	200	23.20	23.52- 06
					400	51.46	51.57- 06
Kilpeläinen-Bäck	Natalia	FIN	19.7.70	168/58	TJ	13.87	14.18- 03
Kim Chol-sun		PRK			Mar	2:30:08	2:33:19- 06
Kim Kum-ok		PRK	9.12.85		Mar	2:26:56	2:29:25- 06
Kim Kyong-ae		KOR-J	5.3.88		JT	56.29	54.11- 06
Kim Mi-jung		KOR	10.6.79	165/56	20kW	1:34:44	1:31:39- 05
Kimutai	Hellen	KEN	28.12.77		Mar	2:26:46	2:25:53- 03
* Kimwei	Evelyne	KEN	25.8.87	146/40	5000	15:16.39	15:14.15- 05
10000	31:36.20		31:16.50- 06		HMar	68:39	68:41- 06
King	Susan	USA	4.3.85		SP	17.13i	15.15- 06
Kinukawa	Megumi	JPN-J	7.8.89	152/38	5000	15:27.98	15:28.13- 06
					10000	31:35.27	
* Kipkemboi	Gladys	KEN	15.10.86	156/45	3kSt	9:46.46	9:32.68- 06
Kiplagat	Edna	KEN	11.11.79		HMar	70:11	69:32- 06
* Kiplagat	Florence	KEN	27.2.87	155/42	1500	4:09.0A	
5000	14:40.74		15:32.34- 06		10000	31:06.20	
* Kiplagat	Lornah	NED	1.5.74	166/49	5000	15:06.51	14:51.95mx- 02, 14:56.43- 03
HMar	66:25		66:34- 01		Mar	2:24:46	2:22:22- 03

Name		Nat	Born	Ht/Wt	Event	2007 Mark	Pre-2007 Best
Kiprop	Helah	KEN	.85		5000	15:33.90	16:15.27- 06
Kiprop Loshanyang	Helena	KEN	9.9.76		Mar	2:26:27	2:28:51- 06
Kipyego	Sally	KEN	19.12.85	168/52	3000	8:56.72i	
5000	15:19.72		16:13.39- 06		10000	31:56.72	
Kirichenko	Irina	RUS	18.5.87		SP	17.24	16.19- 06
Kirilova	Tsvetelina	BUL	14.7.77	173/53	400H	56.03	56.51- 99
^ Kirkland	Anjanette	USA	24.2.74	172/66	100H	12.85	12.42- 01
Kiros	Aheza	ETH	26.3.82	152/42	5000	15:18.25	15:09.34- 06
					10000	31:20.66	31:35.81- 06
Kiryashova	Aleksandra	RUS	21.8.85	162/54	PV	4.50	4.30- 05
Kiseleva	Yelena	RUS	24.3.79		HT	66.60	63.90- 06
Kislova	Marina	RUS	7.2.78	167/63	100	11.24	11.09- 01
Kita	Katarzyna	POL	4.7.84	169/97	HT	69.27	67.61- 06
Kivimyagi	Tatyana	RUS	23.6.84	185/64	HJ	1.90i, 1.88	1.98- 04
Kivine	Sirkka-Liisa	EST	22.6.77	172/56	TJ	13.64	13.76- 03
Kizaki	Ryoko	JPN	21.6.85	156/45	HMar	71:09	71:43- 05
Klaas	Kathrin	GER	8.2.84	168/72	HT	73.45	71.67- 06
* Kleinert	Nadine	GER	20.10.75	190/90	SP	19.77	20.06- 05
Klilech-Fauvel	Fatiha	FRA	1.2.75	157/42	HMar	70:40	72:34- 05
Klimesová	Jarmila	CZE	9.2.81	172/78	JT	59.38	62.60- 06
Klishina	Darya	RUS-Y	5.1.91		LJ	6.49	6.33- 06
Klocek	Ewelina	POL	20.3.87	171/62	200	23.26	23.63- 06
* Klocová	Lucia	SVK	20.11.83	176/53	800	1:58.62	2:00.28- 06
Klucinová	Eliska	CZE-J	14.4.88	177/68	Hep	5844	5468- 06
* Klüft	Carolina	SWE	2.2.83	178/65	100H	13.15	13.15- 05
HJ	1.95		1.94- 03		LJ	6.85	6.97- 04
TJ	14.02, 14.17w		13.87- 04		Hep	7032	7001- 03
Klyugina (Slivka)	Viktoriya	RUS	28.9.80	178/54	HJ	1.97i, 1.90	1.94- 99
* Klyuka	Svetlana	RUS	27.12.78	170/62	800	1:58.63	1:57.21- 06
Knight	Bianca	USA-J	2.1.89	163/60	100	11.36, 11.28w	11.26- 06
					200	23.17, 22.97Ai, 22.93w	22.94- 06
Knight	Natalie	USA	24.10.86	170/59	200	22.85	23.18, 23.12w- 05
Knyazheva	Hanna	UKR-J	25.9.89	178/61	TJ	13.85	13.28- 06
Kobayashi	Yuriko	JPN-J	12.12.88	163/46	1500	4:11.41	4:07.86- 06
3000	8:54.52		8:52.33- 05		5000	15:21.37	15:31.90- 06
Kochetova	Anastasiya	RUS	18.9.83		400	52.08	51.21- 06
Kocielnik	Joanna	POL	11.3.83	178/64	100H	13.25	13.50, 13.24w- 06
Koderisch	Heike	GER	27.5.85	188/87	DT	57.95	55.09- 05
Kohlmann	Fabienne	GER-J	6.11.89	170/57	400H	56.42	58.88- 05
Koime	Mae	PNG	14.12.83	158/52	100	11.37	11.71- 06
Kokkinariou	Irini	GRE	14.2.81	170/55	3kSt	9:42.97	9:53.07- 06
Kolaric	Nina	SLO	12.12.86		LJ	6.57	6.35, 6.37w- 06
Kolarova ¶	Teodora	BUL	29.5.81	171/57	400	52.10	53.53- 06
800	2:01.63, 2:00.07i, 1:59.36dq		2:00.00- 06		400H	56.48	57.50- 06
* Kolchanova	Lyudmila	RUS	1.10.79	175/60	LJ	7.21	7.11- 06
^ Kolkkala	Taina	FIN	24.10.76	173/73	JT	59.52	64.06- 00, 66.00#- 95
Kolotzei	Jessica	GER	6.4.85	186/86	DT	56.85	56.16- 05
Komótoglou	Magdaliní	GRE	13.11.85	180/75	DT	55.43	54.85- 06
* Komyagina	Olga	RUS	10.2.74	162/48	1500	4:04.5	4:02.32- 00
2000	5:42.60+		5:39.06+- 01		3000	8:43.95	8:35.67i- 06, 8:42.58- 99
Kondakova	Yuliya	RUS	4.12.81	170/57	100H	13.04, 12.95w	13.27- 04
Kondo	Takayo	JPN	17.11.75	160/56	PV	4.35	4.35- 04
* Konevtsova	Yelena	RUS	11.3.81	183/77	HT	76.21	75.07- 06
Konishi	Sachiko	JPN	4.2.82	154/43	20kW	1:30:49	1:32:21- 05
Konovalova	Mariya	RUS	14.8.74	178/62	3000	8:42.99	8:30.18- 99
					5000	15:02.96	14:58.60- 99
Koralewska	Izabela	POL	29.1.85	172/85	DT	56.34	56.66- 05
Koreyvo	Natalya	BLR	14.11.85	172/49	800	2:01.42	2:01.47- 04
Kornikova	Anisya	RUS-J	23.10.89	165/51	20kW	1:28:00	0
^ Koroteyeva	Mariya	RUS	10.11.81	175/63	100H	13.22	12.60- 04
Korotkova	Tatyana	RUS	24.4.80	165/57	20kW	1:28:46	1:27:35- 04
Korpela	Merja	FIN	15.5.81	170/75	HT	68.65	67.33- 05
Korsunova	Olga	RUS	20.5.81		100H	13.08	12.91- 06
Korzeniowska	Sylwia	POL	25.4.80	165/52	20kW	1:32:47	1:30:31- 06
* Kosgei	Salina	KEN	16.11.76	162/58	HMar	69:50dh	67:52dh- 06
					Mar	2:23:31	2:23:22- 06
Kosgei Chepkemboi	Anne	KEN	.80		HMar	70:17	71:47- 06
					Mar	2:28:27	2:30:09- 02
Kostetskaya	Yekaterina	RUS	31.12.86	168/59	800	1:59.52	2:05.95- 03
* Kotlyarova	Olga	RUS	12.4.76	180/66	400	52.14	49.77- 04
					800	1:58.14	1:57.24- 06

Name		Nat	Born	Ht/Wt	Event	2007 Mark	Pre-2007 Best
Kotova	Natalya	RUS	13.5.83		Hep	5904	6060- 06
* Kotova	Tatyana	RUS	11.12.76	182/60	LJ	6.90, 7.10w	7.42- 02
Kotze	Amanda	RSA	26.2.86	180/64	400H	57.04	60.76A- 06
Koutsioumári	Panayióta	GRE	23.3.81	165/58	LJ	6.52i	6.66- 06
Kovalchuk	Svitlana	UKR	3.1.84	180/80	HT	66.31	62.31- 03
Kovalenko	Anna	RUS	3.2.80		LJ	6.68	6.75- 02
Kovalenko	Iryna	UKR	12.6.86	183/60	HJ	1.95i, 1.93	1.95i- 03, 1.93- 04
Kovalyova	Lyudmyla	UKR	18.3.75	174/62	Hep	5841	6230- 99
Kowalska	Katarzyna	POL	7.4.85	177/57	3kSt	9:39.40	9:42.50- 06
Kozlova	Natalya	RUS	17.4.87	168/54	20kW	1:35:29	1:36:11- 05
Kozlova	Tatyana	RUS	2.9.83	163/57	20kW	1:30:07	1:27:30- 05
Krais	Ryann	USA-Y	21.3.90	173/55	400H	57.20	
Krakoviak	Irina	LTU	16.11.77	167/53	800	2:01.09	2:01.03- 05
					1500	4:08.77	4:03.19- 05
Kraus	Melanie	GER	24.10.74	164/48	Mar	2:28:56	2:27:58- 00
Kravtsova	Olga	BLR	25.6.81	165/48	1500	4:10.95	4:05.76- 05
5000	15:11.82		14:47.75- 05		10000	31:58.52	33:03.09- 06
Krawczuk	Agnieszka	POL	14.2.83	180/78	DT	57.67	58.01- 06
Kreiner	Kim	USA	26.7.77	175/76	JT	64.19	62.44- 06
Krevsun	Yuliya	UKR	8.12.80	170/54	800	1:57.63	2:00.49- 02
Kròl	Katja	GER	5.2.80	193/93	SP	16.75	17.12i- 03, 17.00- 01
					DT	58.50	58.20- 03
Kron	Tina	GER	3.4.81	173/55	400H	55.58	56.10- 05
Kubishta	April	USA	5.7.85	165/57	PV	4.30Ai, 4.26	4.10- 06
Kubokura	Satomi	JPN	27.4.82	161/52	400H	55.71	56.19- 06
Kucherenko	Olga	RUS	14.2.85		LJ	6.41, 6.70w	6.72, 6.80w- 06
Kudryashova	Aleksandra	RUS-Y	18.7.90	168/56	20kW	1:32:36	
Kühnert	Floé	GER	6.3.84	174/58	PV	4.40	4.41- 02
Kuijken	Susan	NED	8.7.86	168/52	1500	4:11.34	4:19.72- 05
Kulyk	Liliya	UKR	27.1.87	170/56	TJ	14.39	14.01- 06
Kuntsevich	Darya	RUS	2.11.85		HJ	1.89i, 1.87	1.88- 06
Kuntsevich	Yekaterina	RUS	13.7.84	174/58	HJ	1.94i, 1.89	1.94- 06
Kupriyanova	Lyudmila	BLR	8.4.74		DT	60.91	64.20- 06
Kurban	Olga	RUS	16.12.87	171/61	Hep	6185	5675- 06
Kuropatkina	Anna	RUS	3.10.85		TJ	14.20	14.13- 06
Kushch	Nataliya	UKR	5.3.83	170/56	PV	4.40	4.51i- 06, 4.50- 04
* Kuzenkova	Olga	RUS	4.10.70	176/76	HT	72.36	75.68- 00
Kuzminok	Oksana	UKR	7.8.83		Hep	5822	5269- 06
Kvarberg	Ragnhild	NOR	23.3.81	168/53	1500	4:08.30	4:07.14- 06
* Kwakye	Jeanette	GBR	20.3.82	162/52	100	11.26, 11.24w	11.44- 06
					200	23.11	23.34- 06
Kwambai	Caroline	KEN	9.9.75	148/37	HMar	70:26	69:45- 01
Kwambai	Irene	KEN	25.10.78	170/52	5000	15:18.70	14:49.32- 06
10000	31:36.78		30:55.67- 05		HMar	69:53	69:52- 01
Kwoka	Katarzyna	POL	29.6.85	168/52	20kW	1:34:49	1:41:13- 05
La Mantia	Simona	ITA	14.4.83	177/65	TJ	13.89	14.69- 05, 14.71w- 04
Laamanen	Pauliina	FIN	10.10.84	172/69	JT	57.13	56.40- 06
Ladokhina	Svetlana	RUS	21.2.79	171/67	Hep	5674	6056- 06
Lakhaoud-Boucif	Ibtissam	MAR	7.12.83	170/52	800	2:01.66	2:02.70- 06
1500	4:03.4		4:08.22- 06		1M	4:25.35	
Lakmali	Nadeeka	SRI	18.9.81	163/59	JT	58.48	54.00- 05
Laláková	Barbora	CZE	2.5.81	178/58	HJ	1.95	1.99i, 1.94- 06
* Lalova	Ivet	BUL	18.5.84	168/55	100	11.26, 11.15w	10.77- 04
					200	23.00	22.51, 22.36w- 04
Lamalle	Adrianna	FRA	27.9.82	170/58	100H	12.75	12.67- 06
Lambie	Arianna	USA	12.6.85	170/50	5000	15:31.34	15:44.23- 06
Lamera	Raffaella	ITA	13.4.83	175/56	HJ	1.87i	1.89- 05
* Lammert	Petra	GER	3.3.84	182/85	SP	20.04	19.81- 05
* Langerholc	Brigita	SLO	23.7.76	170/56	800	1:58.41	1:58.51- 00
Langhirt	Simone	GER	19.1.84	174/56	PV	4.25	4.20- 05
Lanouar	Fatima	TUN	14.3.78	165/52	1500	4:09.26	4:06.91- 00
Layne	Lynne	USA-J	1.4.88	165/55	100	11.24	11.70- 06
					200	23.26, 22.94w	24.07i- 06, 24.51, 24.05w- 05
Leach	Nicole	USA	18.7.87	170/60	400	51.97	52.27- 06, 52.19i- 04
					400H	54.32	55.35- 06
Leatherman	Jenny	USA	26.9.83		HT	68.93	66.78- 06
* Lebedeva	Tatyana	RUS	21.7.76	171/61	LJ	7.15	7.33- 04
					TJ	15.14	15.36i, 15.34- 04
Lebusova	Natalya	RUS	4.4.78	180/66	LJ	6.89	6.93- 06
Ledvinová	Lenka	CZE	11.8.85	180/80	HT	67.63	65.13- 06
Lee	Gail	USA	25.5.84	173/	SP	17.11i	16.18- 06

	Name		Nat	Born	Ht/Wt	Event	2007 Mark	Pre-2007 Best
*	Lee	Muna	USA	30.10.81	173/50	100	11.10	11.04, 10.97w- 03
						200	22.90	22.36, 22.22w- 04
	Lee Eun-jung		KOR	21.4.81	167/50	Mar	2:29:32	2:26:17- 04
	Lee Mi-young		KOR	19.8.79	174/81	SP	17.21	17.62- 05
	Legesse Assefa	Meskerem	ETH	28.9.86	161/50	1500	4:09.04	4:22.51A- 06
^	Leghzaoui	Asmae	MAR	30.8.76	155/40	10000	31:36.56	31:16.94- 01
*	Legnante	Assunta	ITA	14.5.78	183/110	SP	19.01i, 18.85	19.20i- 02, 19.04- 06
	Leibak	Kaire	EST-J	21.5.88	177/58	TJ	14.04	14.43- 06
	Leks	Viktoria	EST	28.9.87	183/57	HJ	1.91i, 1.89	1.90i- 06, 1.87- 05
	Lemiesz	Aneta	POL	17.1.81	167/53	800	2:01.88, 2:01.32i	1:59.93- 06
	Lenskiy	Irina	ISR	12.6.71	176/54	100H	13.15	12.80- 02
	Leontyuk	Yuliya	BLR	31.1.84	180/82	SP	18.86	18.86- 06
	Leroy	Anastacia	JAM	11.9.87	170/57	200	23.12	23.25- 06
	Leveaux-Agricole	Lindy	SEY	14.11.79	172/65	JT	56.49	57.86- 05
	Levenkova	Olga	RUS	11.1.84	172/60	Hep	6062	6231- 06
	Levina	Tatyana	RUS	28.2.77	173/60	400	50.78	50.98- 04
	Lewis	Mechelle	USA	20.9.80	168/55	100	11.13	11,50, 11.38w- 00
						200	23.05	23.62- 00
*	Lewis	Tamsyn	AUS	20.7.78	168/57	400	51.71	51.51- 00
						800	1:59.37	1:59.21- 00
	Lewis	Yvette	USA	16.3.85	173/62	100H	13.06	13.14- 06
						TJ	13.73	13.75i, 13.73- 06
	Li Bo		CHN-J	4.9.88	181/89	SP	16.75i, 16.71	16.66- 06
	Li Fengfeng		CHN	9.1.79	176/110	SP	17.48	19.13- 06
	Li Leilei		CHN-J	18.8.89	160/46	20kW	1:35:41.84t	
	Li Li		CHN	22.2.87	174/115	SP	17.34	17.49- 05
	Li Ling		CHN-J	6.7.89	185/70	PV	4.30	4.15- 06
*	Li Ling		CHN	7.2.85	179/85	SP	19.38	19.05- 06
	Li Lingwei		CHN-J	26.1.89	172/75	JT	57.88	58.87- 06
*	Li Meiju		CHN	3.10.79	173/85	SP	19.09	19.05- 05
	Li Qian		CHN	17.9.84	168/50	TJ	14.10	14.09, 14.16w- 06
	Li Shan		CHN	4.3.83	180/60	HJ	1.88	1.87- 04
	Li Yanfeng		CHN	15.5.79	179/80	DT	62.24	64.34- 04
	Li Yanmei		CHN-Y	6.2.90	171/56	TJ	13.93	
	Li Zhenzhu		CHN	13.12.85	168/45	3kSt	9:32.35	9:48.63- 06
	Liao Xiaoyan		CHN	8.1.87	175/65	HT	67.78	65.53- 05
	Liburd	Tanika	SKN	20.5.82	163/52	LJ	6.49, 6.62w	6.56, 6.62w- 05
	Lichtl	Stephanie	GER	12.7.85	176/58	100H	13.22	13.30- 06
*	Líka	Sávva	GRE	27.6.70	168/70	JT	63.13	62.89- 04
	Limika	Irene	KEN	28.8.79	160/45	3kSt	10:03.2A	9:39.51- 01
	Lin Chia-Ying		TPE	5.11.82	168/82	SP	16.58	16.76- 06
	Lin Nuai		CHN	6.1.84	172/54	TJ	13.89	13.87- 06
*	Lishchynska	Iryna	UKR	15.1.76	163/53	1500	4:00.69	4:00.04- 06
	Litvinenko	Irina	KAZ	8.1.87	173/61	TJ	13.57, 13.80w	13.42- 06
	Litvinova	Lyudmila	RUS	8.6.85	177/60	400	51.25	51.99- 06
*	Liu Hong		CHN	12.5.87	164/55	20kW	1:29:41, 1:31:16.18t	1:28:26- 06
	Liu Lijuan		CHN-J	1.4.88	163/45	10000	32:00.05	
	Liu Linpeng		CHN	22.2.87	179/70	DT	56.02	58.88- 05
	Liu Nian		CHN-J	26.4.88	169/50	3kSt	9:26.25	
	Liu Xiangrong		CHN-J	6.6.88	182/84	SP	18.58	16.94- 06
	Liu Xiaojing		CHN			SP	16.56	
	Liu Yanan		CHN	18.1.87	168/55	TJ	13.90	13.62- 05
	Liu Yinghui		CHN	29.6.79	180/86	HT	69.56	72.51- 05
	Lloyd	Shereefa	JAM	2.9.82	164/53	400	51.00	51.39- 05
	Lodree	Ashley	USA	22.10.85	167/54	100H	12.99	13.00A, 13.13, 12.95Aw- 06
	Long	Brittany	USA-J	7.9.89	172/62	100	11.31w	11.54, 11.52w- 06
						200	23.44, 23.02w	24.22- 05
	Lopes	Priscilla	CAN	26.8.82	168/67	100H	12.82, 12.64w	12.60- 06
	López	Yaniuvis	CUB	1.2.86	180/71	SP	16.77	16.92- 06
	Lorenzen	Amanda	USA	16.11.83	168/52	3kSt	9:53.24	
	Loughnane	Olive	IRL	14.1.76	160/49	20kW	1:32:25	1:30:29- 03
	Lucas	Josanne	TRI	14.5.84	170/55	400H	56.19	55.29- 06
	Lucas	Porsche	USA-J	18.6.88	170/56	200	22.79	23.22- 06
	Luchkina	Anna	RUS	13.1.86		800	2:01.85	2:06.15- 06
	Lyahovych	Tetyana	UKR	20.5.79	173/78	JT	60.58	63.07- 04
*	Lyne	Rebecca	GBR	4.7.82	173/52	800	2:00.86	1:58.20- 06
						1500	4:09.06	4:06.85- 06
*	Lysenko	Tatyana	RUS	9.10.83	180/85	HT	78.61	77.80- 06
	Ma Qiao		CHN-J	28.9.89	185/150	SP	17.17	16.61- 06
	Ma Shuli		CHN	20.1.78	175/70	DT	56.48	62.50- 05
*	Ma Xuejun		CHN	26.3.85	185/90	DT	62.57	65.00- 06

Name		Nat	Born	Ht/Wt	Event	2007 Mark	Pre-2007 Best
Macchiut	Margaret	ITA	25.7.74	171/48	100H	13.23w	13.03- 06
* MacFarlane	Donna	AUS	18.6.77	176/57	1500	4:10.37mx	4:15.83- 06
					3kSt	9:26.63	9:25.05- 06
Machado	Maila de Paula	BRA	22.1.81	167/62	100H	13.23	12.86- 04
^ Macharia	Faith	KEN	9.2.76	165/55	800	2:01.15	1:58.34- 01
Machkanova	Yelena	RUS	14.7.81		DT	55.73	59.40- 04
Mächtig	Julia	GER	1.1.86	187/76	Hep	6162	6066- 06
* Madejczyk	Barbara	POL	30.9.76	180/81	JT	61.66	64.08- 06
* Madison	Tianna	USA	30.8.85	168/60	LJ	6.60, 6.61w	6.89, 6.92w- 05
Maduaka	Joice	GBR	30.9.73	172/65	100	11.32, 11.19w	11.23- 06
					200	23.05	22.83- 99
Maduka	Jeomi	USA	21.8.87	188/73	LJ	6.52	6.18i, 6.14, 6.23w- 06
* Maggi	Maurren	BRA	25.6.76	178/66	LJ	6.95	7.26A- 99, 7.06- 03, 7.17w- 02
					TJ	14.44	14.53- 03
Mahan	Shayla	USA-J	18.1.89	160/50	100	11.37, 11.29w	11.53, 11.47w- 06
Maina	Esther	KEN	27.3.77	162/42	5000	15:14.05	15:45.07- 02
Maisonnier	Blandine	FRA	3.1.86	179/65	LJ	6.50w	6.06- 06
					Hep	5894	5529- 06
Makarova	Yelena	RUS	21.12.81	168/72	JT	55.07	55.41- 05
Makida	Harun	ETH			5000	15:31.21	
Mäkinen	Tanja	FIN	2.3.80	170/74	DT	55.75	53.64- 06
Maksimova	Marina	RUS	20.5.85		JT	57.06	55.50- 06
Makunzi	Magdalene	KEN	.83		HMar	69:58	70:05- 06
Malíková	Zuzana	SVK	2.8.83	175/50	20kW	1:32:19	1:32:14- 06
Mallory-Lesch	Beth	USA	31.5.84		DT	63.89	59.35- 05
Mamlina	Natalya	RUS-Y	16.3.91		HJ	1.89	1.81- 06
Mamyeyeva	Svitlana	UKR	19.4.82	175/65	TJ	14.15, 14.17w	13.73- 03
Manabe	Yuko	JPN	8.2.79	158/41	Mar	2:30:34	2:39:15- 04
Manfrédi	Laurence	FRA	20.5.74	175/92	SP	18.03	18.69i, 18.68- 00
Manninen	Johanna	FIN	4.4.80	170/58	100	11.27	11.33- 01, 11.26w- 03
Manning	Crystal	USA	15.4.86	173/64	TJ	13.34, 13.71w	12.72- 05, 12.84w- 04
Manome	Aya	JPN	30.8.82	160/46	10000	32:21.79	32:28.02- 05
					HMar	70:59	71:46- 06
Mao Xiaoyan		CHN			SP	16.91	
Maracheva	Irina	RUS	29.9.84		800	2:01.11	2:04.91- 05
					1500	4:10.92	4:18.84- 06
Marcussen	Ida	NOR	1.11.87	173/64	Hep	6226	6020- 06
Marghieva	Marina	MDA	28.6.86	183/72	HT	67.45	61.88- 06
Marghieva	Zalina	MDA-J	5.2.88		HT	65.40	65.50- 06
Mariën	Hanna	BEL	16.5.82	169/67	200	23.17	22.68- 06
Márkou	Dímitra	GRE	28.7.80	176/53	TJ	13.76, 13.83w	14.05- 00
Marks	Shani	USA	24.8.80	173/67	TJ	14.08, 14.11w	13.89- 06
Marshall	Shameka	USA	9.9.83	163/54	LJ	6.53	6.66i, 6.58, 6.59w- 06
Marten	Kristin	GER	23.5.83	184/90	SP	16.98	17.87- 04
Mårtensson	Erica	SWE	24.6.79	165/57	400H	56.19	56.75- 06
Martin	Chiquita	USA	17.2.85	166/55	100H	13.14	13.59, 13.39w- 06
Martin	Diana	ESP	1.4.81	162/50	3kSt	9:47.41	9:47.52- 06
Martin	Jenna	CAN-J	31.3.88	173/65	400	51.91	54.27- 06
Martínez	Aymée	CUB-J	17.11.88	168/52	200	23.18	22.99- 05
					400	51.74	52.04- 05
* Martínez	Magdelin	ITA	10.2.76	174/63	TJ	14.71	15.03, 15.24Aw- 04
* Martínez	Mayte	ESP	17.5.76	168/56	800	1:57.62	1:58.29- 02
1000 2:33.06 2:38.68i, 2:43.68- 05					1500	4:09.17	4:05.05- 05
Martínez	Yarianna	CUB	20.9.84	168/56	TJ	14.36	14.28- 06
Martín-Pozuelo	Gema	ESP	21.6.87	187/71	HJ	1.88i, 1.87	1.84i- 05, 1.83- 06
Martins	Eliane	BRA	26.5.86		LJ	6.66A	6.41- 05
Martins	Maria	FRA	1.4.74	162/53	1500	4:06.19	4:04.55- 03
Martynova	Yekaterina	RUS	12.6.86		800	2:01.94	2:00.85- 06
* Masai	Edith	KEN	4.4.67	168/55	10000	31:31.18	30:30.26- 05
* Masai	Linet	KEN-J	5.12.89	170/55	3000	8:38.97	
					5000	14:55.50	
Masehla	Tebogo	RSA	6.10.79	160/45	3kSt	9:55.11	10:01.14- 06
Massey	Eva	GBR	22.12.80	170/88	SP	16.63	16.32i, 16.15- 03
Mataoanu	Miruna	ROM	4.6.83	175/58	HJ	1.94	1.87- 04
^ Mathes	Simone	GER	13.3.75	175/77	HT	64.93	67.97- 04
Matoshko	Yelena	BLR	23.6.82		HT	70.62	66.84- 05
Matsuoka	Noriko	JPN	2.5.79	156/44	10000	32:21.26	31:49.89- 06
Matveyeva	Anastasiya	RUS-J	12.12.88		TJ	13.75i, 13.71	12.79- 06
Matyukhina	Marina	RUS-J	17.5.88		HJ	1.88	1.75- 05
Maussion	Jessica	FRA	25.11.83	167/58	TJ	13.66w	13.12- 05
Mayr	Andrea	AUT	15.10.79	174/53	3kSt	9:48.87	9:56.78- 05

Name		Nat	Born	Ht/Wt	Event	2007 Mark	Pre-2007 Best
^ McConnell	Lee	GBR	9.10.78	178/64	400	51.07	50.82- 02
					400H	56.04	55.25- 06
McEwen	Nicole	USA	1.4.80	175/60	PV	4.54	4.45- 06
* McGettigan	Roisin	IRL	23.8.80	170/55	3kSt	9:28.29	9:32.04- 06
McGreavy	Sara	GBR	13.12.82	164/60	100H	13.45, 13.23w	13.20- 06
McGregor	Katie	USA	2.9.77	173/52	10000	31:37.82	31:21.20- 05
McGrone	Candyce	USA-J	24.3.89		100	11.54, 11.29w	
					200	23.24w	
McIlroy	Kate	NZL	26.8.81	170/60	3kSt	9:58.08	9:32.54- 06
McKinney	Akiba	USA	9.3.79	160/55	LJ	6.82	6.83- 06
McKoy	Olivia	JAM	1.12.73	165/73	JT	56.42	61.10- 05
McLain	Erica	USA	24.1.86	170/62	LJ	6.35, 6.53w	6.53- 06
					TJ	14.15	14.01- 05
* McLellan	Sally	AUS	19.9.86	166/60	100	11.14	11.36- 06
					100H	12.71	12.95- 06
McWilliams	Tiffany	USA	20.10.82	178/58	1500	4:08.86	4:06.30- 06
Meadows	Jennifer	GBR	17.4.81	152/47	800	1:59.39	2:00.16- 06
Medina	Gabriela	MEX	3.3.85		400	51.25A, 52.04	52.37- 06
Melese	Mahlet	ETH-Y	20.5.90	156/44	3000	8:56.98	9:37.9A- 06
					5000	15:33.31	
^ Melinte	Mihaela	ROM	27.3.75	174/92	HT	68.07	76.07- 99
* Melkamu	Meselech	ETH	19.4.85	158/47	1500	4:07.52	4:09.77- 03
2000	5:39.2+I				3000	8:47.6e+, 8:23.74i	8:34.73- 05
					5000	14:33.83	14:37.44- 06
Melnikova	Irina	RUS	14.5.75	169/57	LJ	6.59i	6.76- 03
Melnychenko	Hanna	UKR	24.4.83	178/58	Hep	6143	6055w/6010 - 06
Mendía	Marta	ESP	18.5.75	176/59	HJ	1.93i, 1.89	1.96i- 04, 1.95- 03
Menelaou	Olympia	CYP	29.4.66	180/68	SP	16.57	16.71- 01
* Menéndez	Osleidys	CUB	14.11.79	178/80	JT	62.34	71.70- 05
Menkova	Oksana	BLR	28.3.82	183/79	HT	73.94	76.86- 06
Menshchikova	Mariya	RUS	26.2.83		400H	56.94	56.21- 06
Méred	Meriem	FRA	4.4.76	166/48	3kSt	10:01.94	10:04.76- 01
Merlano	Brigith	COL	29.4.82	174/64	100H	13.20A, 13.18Aw	13.41- 04
Meskauskiené	Jurgita	LTU	27.8.76		20kW	1:35:39	1:38:11- 99
Messner-Vickers	Carrie	USA	7.6.77	160/52	3kSt	9:43.06	9:39.68- 05
Metcalfe	Megan	CAN	27.1.82	157/54	5000	15:15.73	15:30.65- 06
Metivier-Baillie	Renee	USA	25.12.81	160/50	5000	15:27.57	15:15.78- 05
Mey	Karen	RSA	31.5.84	168/57	LJ	6.93	6.60- 06
Michel	Christina	GER-J	16.12.89	170/58	PV	4.30	4.05- 05
Michot	Cécile	FRA	2.6.74	170/57	100H	13.20	13.06- 02
Mickle	Kimberley	AUS	28.12.84	166/65	JT	59.36	58.56- 06
Migunova	Yelena	RUS	4.1.84	174/67	400	50.84	50.93- 05
Mikhaylova	Olga	RUS	7.12.86	171/51	20kW	1:30:19	1:33:10- 06
* Mikitenko	Irina	GER	23.8.72	158/49	10000	32:42.95	31:29.55- 01
HMar	69:46		70:09- 06		Mar	2:24:51	0
Militaru	Alina	ROM	10.4.82	174/58	LJ	6.71	6.73- 04
Miller	Andrea	NZL	13.3.82	170/67	100H	13.20, 13.14w	13.47- 05
Milusauskaité	Sonata	LTU	31.8.73	163/53	20kW	1:32:45	1:30:53- 03
Mitchell	Kathryn	AUS	10.7.82	170/78	JT	58.61	58.81- 06
* Mitchell	Victoria	AUS	25.4.82	165/53	3kSt	9:45.20	9:30.84- 06
Mitrovic-Topic	Biljana	SRB	17.10.77	180/60	TJ	13.90	13.78- 02
Miyauchi	Hiroko	JPN	19.6.83	154/41	10000	32:18.57	32:22.12- 05
					HMar	71:11	71:21- 05
Miyauchi	Yoko	JPN	19.6.83	153/41	10000	31:50.45	32:18.05- 05
					HMar	71:06	70:04- 06
Mkenku	Nombulelo Constance	RSA-J	30.6.89	158/52	100	11.27	11.58- 06
Mnatsakanova	Tatyana	RUS	23.5.83		HJ	1.94i, 1,89	1.82- 06
* Mockenhaupt	Sabrina	GER	6.12.80	156/45	3000	8:52.17, 8:45.77i	8:44.65- 03
5000	15:10.32		15:03.47- 04		10000	31:56.09	31:21.28- 05
					Mar	2:29:33	
Moges	Bethlehem	ETH			5000	15:30.06	
Mogire	Alice	KEN	.87		HMar	71:07	
* Moldovan	Felicia	ROM	29.9.67	169/70	JT	61.90	63.89- 02, 69.26#- 96
Molitor	Katharina	GER	8.11.83	182/76	JT	58.87	57.58- 06
^ Molnár	Krisztina	HUN	8.4.76	168/51	PV	4.40i, 4.35	4.55- 06
Mombi	Julia	KEN	25.1.85	164/46	5000	15:20.29	15:17.19- 04
10000	31:55.73		31:39.89- 04		HMar	69:45	70:20- 06
					Mar	2:29:38	2:37:50- 06
Moncrieff (Jones)	Susan	GBR	8.6.78	177/62	HJ	1.88	1.95- 01
Mongelli	Lidia	ITA	3.8.80	155/49	20kW	1:35:25	1:38:09- 06
* Montaner	Concepción	ESP	14.1.81	170/56	LJ	6.84	6.92- 05

	Name		Nat	Born	Ht/Wt	Event	2007 Mark	Pre-2007 Best
*	Montebrun	Manuèla	FRA	13.11.79	175/92	HT	73.71	74.66- 05, 75.20dh- 03
	Montsho	Amantle	BOT	4.7.83	173/64	400	50.90	52.14- 06
	Moore	Connie	USA	29.8.81	165/63	200	23.23A	22.62- 06, 22.60i, 22.45w- 04
*	Moore	Lashauntea	USA	31.7.83	170/56	100	11.26, 11.10w	11.26- 04, 11.25w- 05
						200	22.46	22.63, 22.37w- 04
*	Morató	Rosa María	ESP	19.6.79	158/46	10000	32:23.61	0
						3kSt	9:26.23	9:42.51- 06
	Moreira	Sara	POR	17.10.85	163/50	3kSt	9:42.47	10:27.72- 05
	Moreno	Johana	COL	15.4.85	177/	HT	64.40	65.51- 06
*	Moreno	Yipsi	CUB	19.11.80	168/70	HT	76.36	75.18- 04
	Morgan	Monique	JAM	10.10.85	168/60	100H	13.09	13.16- 05, 13.06w- 06
	Morgan	Sheryl	JAM	6.11.83	170/57	400H	57.04	56.81- 02
	Morgunova	Lyubov	RUS	14.1.71	159/45	Mar	2:29:34	2:26:33- 00
	Mori	Haruna	JPN	12.4.82	166/50	3kSt	10:01.91	10:07.65- 06
	Morosanu	Angela	ROM	26.7.86	178/57	400	51.93i	52.48- 05
						400H	54.40	55.37- 06
	Morris	Brooklynn	USA	27.3.86	170/55	200	23.11	23.03, 22.84i, 22.99w- 06
	Mortimer	Amy	USA	16.8.81	175/59	1500	4:07.23	4:06.55- 06
	Moser	Natalie	USA	19.2.86		PV	4.30i	4.10- 06
	Moss	Shantia	USA	27.10.85	173/59	100H	13.08, 12.83w	13.18, 13.12w- 06
*	Mothersill-Modibo	Cydonie	CAY	19.3.78	170/54	100	11.24	11.08, 11.02w- 06
						200	22.52	22.39, 22.26w- 05
	de Moura	Lucimar	BRA	22.3.74	167/64	100	11.20	11.17A- 99, 11.24- 05
						200	23.00	22.60A, 22.75- 99
	Moussa	Houria	ALG	14.5.82		400H	56.81	56.66- 06
	Mouthon	Iodie	FRA	28.3.87	167/55	3kSt	9:55.19	10:33.26- 06
	Moya	Sabina	COL	27.1.77	162/70	JT	55.18A	62.62A- 02
	Mozgunova	Zhanna	BLR	4.6.85		DT	59.60	57.82- 06
^	Mrisho	Zakia	TAN	19.2.84	165/45	5000	15:21.74	14:43.87- 05
						10000	32:41.11	33:19.25- 02
	Muangjan	Thitima	THA	13.4.83	168/53	TJ	13.85	13.49- 05
	Muffet	Ashley	USA	16.9.86		SP	17.28i	16.52- 06
	Muhammad	Dalilah	USA-Y	7.2.90	170/52	400H	57.09	58.75- 06
	Muhammed	Fatimoh	LBR	23.1.84	170/60	800	2:01.89	2:05.28- 05
	Muia	Jane Mwikali	KEN	20.12.86		HMar	70:26	71:59- 04
	Muir	Carline	CAN	1.10.87	180/67	400	52.03A	52.38- 05
	Müller	Claudine	SUI	27.2.80	178/62	Hep	5680	5526- 06
	Müller	Nadine	GER	21.11.85	192/95	DT	62.93	59.35- 05
	Mulyukova	Yuliya	RUS	1.12.85		400H	56.41	55.84- 06
	Muncan	Marina	SRB	6.11.82	165/49	1500	4:08.02	4:11.23- 03
*	Murer	Fabiana	BRA	16.3.81	172/64	PV	4.66i, 4.65	4.66- 06
	Murofushi	Yuka	JPN	11.2.77	170/64	DT	58.62	56.84- 99
						HT	64.60	67.77- 04
	Murray	Novelle	CAN	31.8.84	173/85	DT	56.44	54.45- 05
	Murtazina	Alsu	RUS	12.12.87		TJ	13.71	12.94- 06
*	Mutola	Maria	MOZ	27.10.72	162/61	800	1:56.98	1:55.19- 94
	Mutua	Mueni	KEN-J	.88		3kSt	9:58.7A	10:46.5A- 06
	Myrick	Wyllesheia	USA	21.11.79	163/54	100	11.26	11.24- 06
						200	23.13, 23.05w	22.94- 04
	Naef	Martina	SUI	23.4.80	175/64	400H	56.83	56.97- 06
*	Naimova	Tezdzhan	BUL	1.5.87	163/54	100	11.04	11.23, 11.11w- 06
						200	22.43	22.99- 06
	Nakamura	Yurika	JPN	1.4.86	165/50	5000	15:21.92	15:23.75- 06
	10000	32:24.65		32:52.94- 05		HMar	70:23	70:03- 06
	Nakano	Mami	JPN	12.3.79	166/57	PV	4.30	4.31- 04
	Nakata	Yuki	JPN	10.3.77	167/55	Hep	5869	5962- 04
	Nana Djimou Ida	Antoinette	FRA	2.8.85	177/68	Hep	5982	6089w- 05, 5981- 06
	Nartova	Alena	RUS	1.1.82	167/52	20kW	1:28:31	1:28:51- 06
	Nasta-Tsisiou	Alexandra	CYP	2.7.81	176/68	JT	57.17	57.20- 06
*	Naude	Elizna	RSA	14.9.78	180/87	DT	64.87	63.17A- 05
	Naumenko	Irina	KAZ	13.2.80	180/63	Hep	6069	6140- 03
	Nazarova	Anna	RUS	14.3.86		LJ	6.81	6.66- 06
						TJ	13.80i	13.58- 03
*	Nazarova	Natalya	RUS	26.5.79	168/57	400	50.52	49.65- 04
*	Ndereba	Catherine	KEN	21.7.72	160/45	HMar	70:33dh	67:54- 01
						Mar	2:29:08	2:18:47- 01
	Neacsu	Mihaela	ROM	3.5.79	170/58	800	2:01.08, 1:59.82i	1:59.78- 05
	Neeley	Mindy	USA	15.1.87	168/55	LJ	6.50	6.07- 06
	Negoita	Maria	ROM	6.12.86	171/74	JT	56.10	54.24- 05
	Nelson	Lela	USA	19.5.83	180/64	LJ	6.78	6.59, 6.61w- 06
						Hep	6022	5903- 06

Name		Nat	Born	Ht/Wt	Event	2007 Mark	Pre-2007 Best
Németh	Noémi	HUN	7.4.86		HT	64.59	64.09- 05
* Nerius	Steffi	GER	1.7.72	178/69	JT	65.78	66.52- 05, 69.42#- 96,
Ngew Sin Mei		MAS	4.6.83	168/51	TJ	13.42, 13.75w	13.74- 04
Niako	Cynthia	CIV	25.9.83		200	23.48, 23.10w	23.14, 22.99w- 06
Niaré	Gaëlle	FRA	12.3.82	182/72	HJ	1.87	1.93- 03
					Hep	5864	
Nicholls	Shernelle	BAR	28.2.84	183/93	SP	17.14	15.11i, 14.92- 05
Nickl	Vanda	HUN	4.9.85		HT	66.71	66.61- 06
Niiya	Hitomi	JPN-J	26.2.88	164/44	Mar	2:31:01	
Nikitenko	Anna	RUS	30.4.84		Hep	5891	5481- 06
Nikkanen	Minna	FIN-J	9.4.88	169/52	PV	4.35	4.21i, 4.17- 06
Nilsson	Cecilia	SWE	22.6.79	178/88	HT	68.31	69.03- 06
Nishikori	Ikuko	JPN	5.1.80	165/54	PV	4.30	4.36- 06
Njoroge	Mercy	KEN	10.6.86		3kSt	9:43.02	9:50.63- 05
Nobuoka	Sakie	JPN	24.8.77	164/54	200	23.12w	23.33- 04, 23.22w- 05
* Noguchi	Mizuki	JPN	3.7.78	150/40	5000	15:30.04	15:34.36- 99
HMar 68:22			67:43- 06		Mar	2:21:37	2:19:12 05
Northover	Zara	JAM	6.3.84		SP	16.78	16.56- 05
Novik	Marina	BLR	19.1.84		JT	57.98	57.23- 06
Novikova	Yelena	RUS	27.10.85	176/62	400	51.76	
Novozhylova	Iryna	UKR	7.1.86	175/71	HT	68.16	66.30- 06
Nwidobie	Kara	GBR	13.4.81	178/83	DT	59.41dh	57.27- 05
Nyaruai Wanjiru	Veronica	KEN-J	29.10.89	165/43	1500	4:09.11	4:08.22- 06
					5000	15:23.37	15:13.1A- 05
Nytra	Carolin	GER	26.2.85	175/63	100H	13.17	13.28- 05
* N'zola Meso	Teresa	FRA	30.11.83	168/53	TJ	14.69	14.07, 14.17w- 06
Obedina	Irina	RUS	1.7.85	170/58	400H	55.12	55.32- 06
Oberer	Simone	SUI	8.4.80	176/61	Hep	5996	6052- 05
* Obergföll	Christina	GER	22.8.81	175/78	JT	70.20	70.03- 05
Odumosu	Ajoke	NGR	27.10.87	172/53	400	52.95, 50.46dt	52.99- 06
					400H	55.37	56.09- 06
* Oeser	Jennifer	GER	29.11.83	176/64	Hep	6378	6376- 06
Ofili	Tiffany	USA	13.11.87	172/62	100H	12.80	13.37, 13.15w- 06
Ogawa	Kiyomi	JPN	15.9.81	158/38	10000	32:06.54	31:59.56- 05
Ogoshi	Kazue	JPN	2.3.81	161/41	HMar	69:53	70:11- 01
					Mar	2:31:04	2:32:11- 05
Ohadugha	Chinoye	NGR	24.3.86	175/64	TJ	14.21	13.81- 05
Ohanaja	Jessica	NGR	6.12.85	173/60	100H	13.01	13.14, 13.10w- 06
O'Hara	Tracy	USA	20.7.80	165/55	PV	4.45	4.60- 05
Ohira	Miki	JPN	28.6.81	169/49	Mar	2:29:34	
* Ohuruogu	Christine	GBR	17.5.84	175/70	400	49.61	50.28- 06
Okagbare	Blessing	NGR-J	10.9.88		LJ	6.51	6.16- 06
					TJ	14.13	13.38- 06
Okamoto	Haruko	JPN	19.8.74	154/40	Mar	2:30:09	2:27:01- 02
* O'Keeffe	Eileen	IRL	31.5.81	170/80	HT	73.21	69.36- 05
Okoro	Marilyn	GBR	23.9.84	165/64	400	52.06	52.02- 06
					800	1:58.76	1:59.75- 06
Okunaga	Mika	JPN	27.10.82	161/43	Mar	2:31:08	2:29:56- 06
Olaru	Alina	ROM	13.10.82	168/54	20kW	1:33:14	1:34:01- 06
* Oleynikova	Yelena	RUS	9.12.76	178/57	TJ	13.88i	14.83- 02
Olivarès	Élodie	FRA	22.5.76	170/55	3kSt	9:40.41	9:33.12- 02
Oliveira	Gilvaneide	BRA	31.8.76	171/59	100H	13.22	13.19A- 03, 13.23- 00
Olshevskaya	Olga	RUS	5.7.82		DT	56.56	61.31- 06
* Omarova	Anna	RUS	3.10.81	180/108	SP	19.69	18.40- 06
Ominami	Hiromi	JPN	15.11.75	165/48	HMar	70:41	68:45- 04
					Mar	2:26:37	2:23:26- 04
Ominami	Takami	JPN	15.11.75	167/47	Mar	2:29:24	2:23:43- 02
Omwanza	Beatrice	KEN	24.2.74		HMar	71:15	71:15- 06
					Mar	2:30:46	2:27:19- 04
O'Neill	Kate	USA	29.7.80	160/45	5000	15:27.72	15:21.66- 04
					10000	32:15.15	31:34.37- 04
Ongori	Philes	KEN	19.7.86	159/45	3000	8:47.88	8:54.90- 07
5000 14:50.15	15:08.3mx- 04, 15:09.49- 05				10000	31:39.11	31:18.85- 06
					HMar	69:50	70:00- 06
Onwuchekwa	Kacey	NGR/USA	22.11.85		SP	17.42i, 17.36	16.92- 06
Onyepunuka	Jessica	USA	3.5.86	176/60	100	11.31, 11.26w	11.31- 03
					200	23.26	23.60- 04
* Onyia	Josephine	ESP	15.7.86	166/60	100	11.37, 11.23w	11.46- 06
		(ex NGR)			100H	12.67	12.78, 12.70w- 06
Orbán	Éva	HUN	29.11.84	173/75	HT	66.98	69.10- 06
O'Reilly	Thaimi	ITA	20.7.76	174/60	TJ	13.64	13.97- 05

Name		Nat	Born	Ht/Wt	Event	2007 Mark	Pre-2007 Best
* O'Rourke	Derval	IRL	28.5.81	168/57	100H	12.88	12.72- 06
Orsini	Gisella	ITA	9.12.71	161/49	20kW	1:34:27	1:31:57- 05
Osaki	Chisato	JPN	19.4.87	157/41	HMar	68:56	
Osayomi	Damola	NGR	26.7.86	163/63	100	11.15	11,31A, 11.13Aw- 06, 11.34- 04
					200	23.19, 23.15w	23.36A, 23.16Aw- 06
Osburn	Desiraye	USA	5.8.84	165/50	3kSt	9:47.24	
Oshima	Megumi	JPN	4.9.75	160/43	10000	32:17.14	31:34.01- 04
					HMar	71:14	69:59- 05
Osse	Lauranne	FRA	5.4.85	177/70	LJ	6.47, 6.55w	6.45- 06
* Ostapchuk	Nadezhda	BLR	12.10.80	180/90	SP	20.48	21.09- 05
Otey	Kiamesha	USA	28.5.81		LJ	6.52A, 6.47	6.54- 02
Otonye	Iworima	NGR	13.4.76	174/62	TJ	13.83, 14.10w	13.87- 06
Otoshi	Kumi	JPN	29.7.85		20kW	1:35:04	1:35:08- 06
Ott	Anastasiya	RUS-J	7.9.88		400H	56.42	56.28- 06
Otterbu	Kirsten Melkevik	NOR	29.5.70	170/50	Mar	2:29:12	2:31:20- 06
Ouédraogo	Élodie	BEL	27.2.81	173/59	400H	55.72	57.43- 06
Ouhaddou	Hanane	MAR	.82	158/46	3kSt	9:25.51	9:58.54- 06
Ovchinnikova	Anastasiya	RUS	16.10.84		400	51.88	51.10- 05
Ozaki	Akemi	JPN	12.10.77	157/44	Mar	2:28:39	2:28:51- 06
* Ozaki	Mari	JPN	16.7.75	162/46	Mar	2:24:39	2:23:30- 03
Ozaki	Yoshimi	JPN	1.7.81	155/41	5000	15:33.40	15:28.55- 04
10000	32:13.95		31:47.23- 05		HMar	69:26	73:03- 06
Ozolina	Sinta	LAT-J	26.2.88	182/67	JT	57.01	56.38- 06
Pádi	Aléna-Maria	GRE	21.6.84	174/63	Hep	5779w	5769- 06
Palacios	Felipa	COL	1.12.75	168/60	200	23.03	
							22.85A- 05, 22.74Aw, 22.7w- 97, 22.8A- 98, 23.05- 99
* Palamar	Vita	UKR	12.10.77	187/66	HJ	2.00	2.01- 03
Palameika	Madara	LAT	18.6.87	184/74	JT	57.98	54.19- 06
Paliyenko	Tatyana	RUS	18.11.83		800	1:59.81	2:00.96- 06
Palmer	Nadine	JAM	9.2.83	173/68	200	23.07	23.44- 00
Pan Saili		CHN-J	4.12.88	176/80	DT	59.51	58.52- 05
Panéta	Níki	GRE	21.4.86	168/55	TJ	14.16	13.20, 13.66w- 06
Pankova	Marina	RUS	16.11.82		LJ	6.59	6.43, 6.50w- 06
Pankova	Olga	RUS	13.8.76		TJ	13.65	14.47- 04
Panteleyeva	Yana	RUS-J	16.6.88	170/63	Hep	5688	5985- 06
^ Pantelimon	Oana	ROM	27.9.72	179/61	HJ	1.95i, 1.90	1.99- 00
* Pantelyeva	Natalya	RUS	18.8.83	170/56	800	2:01.78	1:59.21- 06
1500	4:03.2		4:00.81- 06		1M	4:27.18	4:46.66- 04
					2000	5:36.52	
Papadopoúlou	Stiliani	GRE	15.3.82	175/86	HT	67.98	68.14- 05
Papayeoryíou	Alexándra	GRE	17.12.80	176/76	HT	68.88	70.03- 06
Papayeoryíou	María	GRE	8.8.79	183/61	HJ	1.87i	1.89- 05
Papayiánni	Athiná	GRE	18.8.80	168/55	20kW	1:32:34	1:28:58- 04
Pape	Madeleine	AUS	24.2.84		800	2:01.17	2:05.38- 06
Papp	Krisztina	HUN	17.12.82	170/54	HMar	70:53	75:03- 03
Parfyonova	Yelena	KAZ	26.1.74	171/54	TJ	13.72	14.23- 05
Parker	Barbara	GBR	8.11.82	173/52	3kSt	9:48.82	10:13.69- 03
Parkhomenko	Marina	BLR	28.5.81		Hep	5761	5589- 04
Parnov	Vicky	AUS-Y	24.10.90	173/53	PV	4.40	4.32- 06
Parrish	Donniece	USA	4.11.85		200	23.21w	24.31- 05, 24.06i- 06
Parry	Carys	GBR	24.7.81	173/72	HT	64.34	62.60- 06
Pascual	Beatriz	ESP	9.5.82	163/64	20kW	1:30:37	1:30:22- 04
Paulose	Sinimol	IND	24.6.83	160/60	800	2:02.02	2:02.02- 06
					1500	4:11.66	4:10.51- 06
* Pavey	Jo	GBR	20.9.73	162.51	2000	5:41.2+	5:41.4i, 5:41.6- 05
3000	8:44.13, 8:31.50i		8:31.27- 02		5000	15:04.77	14:39.96- 06
2M	9:32.00i				10000	31:26.94	-0-
Pavliy	Tatyana	RUS	18.5.78	168/61	100H	12.90, 12.80w	12.92- 06, 12.85w- 05
Pavlyukovskaya	Nadezhda	BLR	6.6.85	180/76	HT	69.91	67.40- 05
Pchelnik	Darya	BLR	20.12.81	185/97	HT	71.29	71.08- 05
* Pechonkina	Yuliya	RUS	21.4.78	180/67	400H	53.50	52.34- 03
Pedan	Galina	KGZ	29.5.83	166/62	400H	57.11	56.16- 04
Pedroso	Yasmiany	CUB	5.8.84	179/75	Hep	5942	5695- 06
Pelayo	Irene	ESP	16.2.80	163/50	3kSt	9:57.50	9:54.14- 06
Pendleton	Emily	USA-J	16.4.89		DT	55.85	52.64- 06
Pereira	Andréa Maria	BRA	8.12.73	173/94	SP	16.90	16.78- 06
* Pérez	Madai	MEX	2.2.80	157/45	Mar	2:30:16	2:22:59- 06
Perie	Bianca	ROM-Y	1.6.90	170/62	HT	67.24	67.38- 06
Perisic	Vanja	CRO	5.7.85		800	2:01.13	2:00.42, 2:00.20ip- 06
Perkins	Angel	USA	10.5.84	170/59	200	23.18	23.07, 22.85w- 01
					400	51.73	52.06- 03

Name		Nat	Born	Ht/Wt	Event	2007 Mark	Pre-2007 Best
^ Pernia	Daimí	CUB	27.12.76	173/59	400H	56.98	52.89- 99
Pérra	Athanasia	GRE	2.2.83	167/55	TJ	14.39	14.39- 04
Perrin	Amélie	FRA	30.3.80	171/85	HT	71.08	71.38- 06
* Perry	Michelle	USA	1.5.79	173/64	100	11.34	11.57- 01, 11.55w- 97
					100H	12.44	12.43- 05
Persson	Hanna-Mia	SWE	11.2.78	178/61	PV	4.40	4.40i- 06, 4.36- 05
Peryakova	Natalya	RUS	4.3.83		800	2:01.33	
Petersen	Sara	DEN	9.4.87		400H	57.01	57.65- 06
Petersson	Annika	SWE	10.1.79	176/74	JT	57.31	56.70- 00
* Petlyuk	Tetyana	UKR	22.2.82	174/60	800	1:59.85, 1:58.67i	1:57.34- 06
					1000	2:34.76i	2:35.67i- 06
Petráhn	Barbara	HUN	16.9.78	168/55	400	51.86	51.50A- 06, 51.85- 01
Petrova	Antonina	RUS	25.1.77	162/52	20kW	1:32:22	1:27:14- 03
* Petrova	Tatyana	RUS	8.4.83	156/48	3000	8:50.33	8:44.13- 06
					3kSt	9:09.19	9:22.82- 06
Pettersson	Maria	SWE	17.3.77		DT	56.06	54.19- 06
Pettitt	Ellen	AUS	13.5.86	182/62	HJ	1.91	1.91- 06
Phamang	Buoban	THA	27.12.86	166/56	JT	61.40	61.31- 06
Philip	Asha	GBR-Y	25.10.90	166/52	100	11.37	11.45- 06
Pickens	Andree	USA	17.6.80	158/61	PV	4.52i, 4.40	4.27i, 4.11- 06
Pickler	Diana	USA	9.12.83	178/64	100H	13.25	13.64- 06
					Hep	6205	5855- 06
Pickler	Julie	USA	9.12.83	178/64	Hep	5831	5734- 06
Pidluzhnaya	Yuliya	RUS-J	1.10.88		LJ	6.61	6.48- 05
Pierre	Barbara	USA	28.4.87		100	11.30	11.66- 06
Pierson	Summer	USA	3.9.78	180/84	DT	57.04	59.46- 04
Pilátou	Stilianí	GRE	28.3.80	172/56	LJ	6.52	6.80i- 03, 6.75- 02, 6.77w- 05
Pillay	Geraldine	RSA	25.8.77	178/64	100	11.35	11.07- 05
					200	23.27	22.78- 05
Pinnock	Sherene	JAM	30.3.87	167/55	400H	56.86	56.67- 06
* Pishchalnikova	Darya	RUS	19.7.85	190/103	DT	65.78	65.55- 06
Pistone	Anita	ITA	29.10.76	165/53	100	11.37	11.55- 00
Piuza	Leonora	MOZ	14.4.78	164/55	800	2:01.71	2:01.76- 06
Piwowarska	Joanna	POL	4.11.83	173/60	PV	4.50i, 4.40	4.53- 06
* Plätzer	Kjersti	NOR	18.1.72	174/54	20kW	1:27:41	1:27:53- 00
Plewa	Marta	POL	17.12.83	163/53	PV	4.30i, 4.20	4.25- 06
Polli	Marie	SUI	28.11.80	162/48	20kW	1:35:41	1:35:47- 04
* Polnova	Tatyana	RUS	20.4.79	173/66	PV	4.72	4.78- 04
Polyakova	Yevgeniya	RUS	29.5.83	164/58	100	11.09	11.45- 06
^ Pompey	Aliann	GUY	9.3.78	165/55	400	51.61	50.93- 04
Poonia	Krishna	IND	5.5.77	181/84	DT	58.80	61.53- 06
Popescu	Elena-Alina	ROM	27.10.85	172/52	TJ	13.93	13.87- 06
Popescu	Liliana	ROM	5.2.82	179/65	800	2:00.07	2:00.06- 03
					1500	4:10.41	4:15.17- 01
Poplavskaya	Yekaterina	BLR	7.5.87	173/59	100H	13.22	13.63- 06
Popova	Yekaterina	RUS	10.12.87	168/48	20kW	1:35:50	
* Pospelova	Svetlana	RUS	24.12.79	169/58	400	51.13	49.80- 05
* Potepa	Wioletta	POL	13.12.80	189/86	DT	61.62	66.01- 06
Potts	Patrice	USA	9.9.87		200	23.25	24.19- 05
Po'uhila	Ana	TGA	12.10.79	176/99	SP	17.09	16.92- 05
Pounds	Dana	USA	5.6.84	158/64	JT	59.65	59.64- 06
Poves	María José	ESP	16.3.78	168/52	20kW	1:30:48	1:31:55- 05
* Powell	Suzy	USA	3.9.76	178/73	DT	67.67	65.48, 69.44dh- 02
* Powell	Virginia	USA	7.9.83	178/63	100H	12.45	12.48- 06
Power	Adrienne	CAN	11.11.81	167/57	200	23.06A	23.41- 05
					400	51.85A	52.90- 06
Pöyry	Sini	FIN	3.2.80	182/88	HT	67.71	69.16- 04
* Pravalinskaya (Korolchik)	Yanina	BLR	26.12.76	187/87	SP	19.24	20.61- 01
Prendergast	Davita	JAM	16.12.84	173/60	400	51.24	51.29- 06
Pressley	Jessica	USA	27.12.84	178/100	SP	18.16	17.19- 06
Pretorius	Marcoleen	RSA-J	25.7.89	185/65	HJ	1.89	1.78- 06
Priyemko	Kseniya	BLR	23.4.86		TJ	14.17	13.59- 06
Priyma	Yelena	RUS	2.12.83	167/63	HT	71.78	70.09- 06
* Prokopcuka	Jelena	LAT	21.9.76	168/51	10000	32:43.2	30:38.78- 06
					Mar	2:26:13	2:22:56- 05
Prokopek	Grazyna	POL	20.4.77	170/51	400	52.00i, 52.38	51.29- 04
Prokopuk	Nadezhda	UKR	25.4.81	163/50	20kW	1:32:44	1:33:27- 06
Pryor	Brittany	USA	16.2.86		SP	16.83	15.55- 06
Ptácniková	Jirina	CZE	20.5.86	174/65	PV	4.22i	4.27- 06
Ptikany	Mary	KEN	.78		HMar	70:13	69:43- 06
					Mar	2:30:08	2:29:45- 05

Name		Nat	Born	Ht/Wt	Event	2007 Mark	Pre-2007 Best
Pulyayeva	Lyubov	RUS	26.4.82	170/57	1500	4:10.09	4:12.89- 06
2000 5:41.21					3000	8:54.21	9:18.21- 06
Purvis	Ashton	USA-Y	6.7.92		200	23.50, 23.24w	24.32, 24.12i- 06
* Pyatykh	Anna	RUS	4.4.81	175/64	LJ	6.72	6.57i, 6.53- 05
					TJ	14.88	15.02, 15.17w- 06
Pyo Un-suk		PRK	13.6.81		Mar	2:28:54	2:33:57- 00
* Pyrek	Monika	POL	11.8.80	170/54	PV	4.82	4.76i, 4.75- 06
Pywell	Stephanie	GBR	12.6.87	175/56	HJ	1.90	1.86- 06
Qiao Yanrui		CHN-J	29.9.88	178/54	HJ	1.88	1.88- 06
Qiu Huijing		CHN	4.2.85	169/49	TJ	13.88	14.11- 05
Quintana	Gretchen	CUB	30.6.84	179/68	100H	13.0	13.58, 31.1- 06
					Hep	6076	5931- 06
Quintanal	Irache	ESP	18.9.78	174/82	SP	18.20	17.20- 04
					DT	56.51	59.16- 04
Rabchenyuk	Anastasiya	UKR	14.9.83	177/64	400H	55.48	54.73- 06
* Radcliffe	Paula	GBR	17.12.73	173/54	HMar	67:53dh	65:40- 03
					Mar	2:23:09	2:15:25- 03
Radecka-Pakaszewska	Zuzanna	POL	2.4.75	172/58	400	52.14	51.58- 05
Radevica	Ineta	LAT	13.7.81	173/56	LJ	6.67i	6.80- 05
Radzivil	Svetlana	UZB	17.1.87	180/58	HJ	1.91	1.91- 06
Rains	Katelin	USA	20.8.87	168/59	PV	4.28i	3.81i, 3.66- 06
Rakhimkulova	Regina	RUS	5.11.79		3000	8:48.94i	8:57.51i- 06
Rakonczai	Beáta	HUN	25.6.77	171/56	Mar	2:30:14	2:29:54- 03
Ranta	Ilona	FIN	28.10.82	164/52	400H	56.48	56.82- 06
Ratej	Martina	SLO	2.11.81	178/69	JT	58.49	57.49- 06
* Rawlinson	Jana	AUS	9.11.82	181/68	400	51.94	50.43- 03
					400H	53.31	53.22- 03
Rebryk	Vira	UKR-J	25.2.89	174/65	JT	58.48	59.64- 06
Redoúmi	Flóra	GRE	11.9.76	168/59	100H	12.88	12.86- 04
Reece	Shakera	BAR-J	31.8.88	165/55	100	11.34	11.97- 06
Reed	Kate	GBR	28.9.82	168/50	5000	15:29.10	15:46.53- 06
* Reese	Brittney	USA	9.9.86	173/64	LJ	6.83	6.31- 04
Reina	Daniela	ITA	15.5.81	163/47	400	51.99	51.18- 06
Rendin	Maria	SWE	28.7.82	172/61	PV	4.35	4.30- 06
Resende	Alessandra	BRA	5.3.75	166/67	JT	59.58	58.21- 06
Rhines	Jennifer	USA	1.7.74	160/50	1500	4:09.52	4:15.57- 02
3000 8:35.03 8:50.72- 00					5000	14:58.51	14:55.18- 06
					10000	31:17.31	31:24.16- 06
Ricali	Cecilia	ITA	20.1.85	174/58	Hep	5727	5610- 05
* Richards	Sanya	USA	26.2.85	173/61	100	10.97	11.28- 03
200 22.31 22.17- 06					400	49.27	48.70- 06
Richardson	Ke'Nyia	USA-J	6.9.89	173/59	TJ	13.58i, 13.55, 13.82w	12.97- 06
Richmond	Rose	USA	29.1.81	168/61	LJ	6.68	6.84, 6.93w- 06
Riettie	Kateema	JAM	5.12.73		JT	55.92	54.91- 05
Rifka	Romary	MEX	23.12.70	180/64	HJ	1.95A	1.97- 04
* Rigaudo	Elisa	ITA	17.6.80	168/56	20kW	1:29:15	1:27:49- 04
* Riley	Brittany	USA	26.8.86	173/89	HT	72.51	66.30- 06
Rillstone	Nina	NZL	15.4.75	175/55	HMar	70:35dh	70:49- 05
Rinne	Salla	FIN	22.5.80	176/65	Hep	5894	5849- 06
Rittweg	Mareike	GER	1.6.84	173/73	JT	60.63	60.06- 06
Rivalta	Yosleidis	CUB-Y	2.5.90	183/74	TJ	13.72	13.51- 06
* Robbeson	Justine	RSA	15.5.85	167/58	JT	62.51A	62.80- 06
Robert-Michon	Melina	FRA	18.7.79	178/87	DT	63.48	65.78- 02
Robinson	Camille	JAM	30.3.84	165/53	400H	56.71	56.14- 02
Robinson	Carlene	JAM	30.3.84	165/53	400H	56.73	56.76- 06
Robinson	Moushami	USA	13.4.81	167/55	200	23.18	22.93- 06
					400	51.47	50.38- 05
Rocha	Nora	MEX	18.12.67	168/56	5000	15:15.77	15:06.54- 98
					10000	31:56.61	32:08.82- 00
Rodic	Snezana	SLO	19.8.82	180/66	TJ	14.03	14.18- 05
Rodríguez	Carol	PUR	16.12.85	175/60	100	11.32, 11.15w, 11.0	11.32, 11.05Aw- 06
200 23.03, 22.87w 22.23A, 22.80- 06					400	51.90	51.51- 06
Rodríguez	Dulce María	MEX	14.8.72	157/54	10000	31:57.04	31:25.33- 05
Rodríguez	Rosa	VEN	2.7.86		HT	66.96	64.22- 06
* Rogowska	Anna	POL	21.5.81	171/55	PV	4.72i, 4.60	4.83- 05
Roles	Philippa	GBR	1.3.78	180/100	DT	59.08, 61.92dh	62.89- 03
Romagnolo	Elena	ITA	5.10.82	165/50	3kSt	9:41.11	9:52.38- 06
Roman	Sonja	SLO	11.3.79	165/54	1500	4:08.60, 4:06.75i	4:08.30- 04
Röngelep	Maris	EST	17.3.84	176/80	HT	65.09	65.05- 06
* Rosa	Chiara	ITA	28.1.83	178/112	SP	19.15	18.71- 05

	Name		Nat	Born	Ht/Wt	Event	2007 Mark	Pre-2007 Best
	Roseby	Sani	USA	5.2.82	158/50	100	11.16	11.42- 99
						200	23.12	23.52- 99
^	Roshchupkina	Natalya	RUS	13.1.78	182/70	Hep	5883	6633- 00
	Rostkowska (Zagórska)	Anna	POL	26.7.80	174/54	800	2:01.02	2:00.04- 04
						1000	2:36.95	
	Rowe	Tracy-Ann	JAM	17.9.85	170/63	100	11.25	11.44- 05
^	Rublyova	Olga	RUS	28.10.74	175/65	LJ	6.52i	6.90, 7.01w- 95
	Rücklová	Alena	CZE	7.10.81	164/61	400H	57.11	55.87- 05
*	Ruckstuhl	Karin	NED	2.11.80	181/65	HJ	1.88i, 1.84	1.85- 04
	LJ	6.64		6.58- 05		Hep	6260	6423- 06
^	Rudolph	Amy	USA	18.9.73	176/55	10000	31:57.26	31:18.96- 05
	Rudy	Elouise	USA	30.12.85		PV	4.33A	4.16- 06
	Rugama	Dalila	NCA	9.4.84	164/59	JT	55.28	53.09- 04
	Rumpf	Sabine	GER	18.3.83	176/95	DT	55.76	60.75- 05
	Rusakova	Natalya	RUS	12.12.79	180/68	100	11.32, 11.30w	11.18, 11.15w- 06
						200	22.71	22.53- 06
	Ruskule	Dace	LAT	20.9.81	178/78	DT	55.74	59.68- 04
	Russell	Blake	USA	24.7.75	168/51	10000	32:31.90	31:35.25- 05
	Ruston	Abby	USA	3.4.83	170/91	SP	17.47	16.32- 06
*	Ryabinkina	Olga	RUS	24.9.76	190/87	SP	18.58i	19.65- 05
	Ryan	Deirdre	IRL	1.6.82	183/62	HJ	1.88i, 1.87	1.92- 06
	Rybakova	Hanna	UKR	19.3.84	178/57	400H	57.07	59.28- 05
	Rybalko	Viktoriya	UKR	26.10.82	177/60	LJ	6.77	6.82, 6.87w- 06
	Rybko	Yekaterina	RUS	5.6.82		JT	58.76	59.48- 06
*	Rybová (Hamácková)	Pavla	CZE	20.5.78	170/66	PV	4.64i, 4.50	4.60- 03
*	Rypakova	Olga	KAZ	30.11.84	183/64	LJ	6.85	6.63- 06
						TJ	14.69	
	Ryshich	Elizaveta	GER-J	27.9.88	174/49	PV	4.35	4.35- 06
*	Ryshich/Ryjikh	Nastja	GER	19.9.77	170/58	PV	4.52	4.63- 06
	Sadach	Aneta	POL	22.4.75	176/59	TJ	13.72	13.99- 03
	Safonova	Darya	RUS	21.3.80		400	52.07	52.62- 04
^	Safronnikova	Natalya	BLR	28.2.73	174/60	100	11.36	11.05- 03, 10.9- 98
						200	23.22, 23.03w	22.68- 01, 22.3- 98
^	Safronova	Natalya	BLR	11.7.74	176/60	TJ	14.01	14.65- 00
	Sahnoune	Kamélia	ALG	5.4.86		TJ	13.32, 13.78w	12.91, 13.11Aw- 06
	Sailer	Verena	GER	16.10.85	166/50	100	11.31	11.43- 06
	Sakakura	Ryoko	JPN	9.5.76	164/47	20kW	1:30:16	1:31:43- 06
	Sakamoto	Naoko	JPN	14.11.80	161/43	Mar	2:28:33	2:21:51- 03
	Sakun	Svitlana	UKR	1.5.81	176/93	SP	16.74	17.48i, 17.22- 06
	Salaam	Kamilah	USA	2.5.85	168/64	100H	13.15	13.91- 04, 13.81w- 06
*	Saladuha	Olga	UKR	4.6.83	175/55	TJ	14.79	14.41, 14.50w- 06
	Salis	Silvia	ITA	17.9.85	179/72	HT	66.19	65.61- 06
	Sallins	Melinda	USA	30.6.73	178/64	400H	56.60A, 56.88	56.06- 97
*	Samaria	Agnes	NAM	11.8.72	166/56	800	1:59.76	1:59.15- 02
	1500	4:05.44		4:13.22- 02		1M	4:25.01	
	Samsu	Roslinda	MAS	9.6.82	160/50	PV	4.35	4.40- 06
	Samuels	Daniele	AUS-J	26.5.88	182/82	DT	60.47	60.63- 06
	Samuelsson	Jessica	SWE	14.3.85	176/65	Hep	5761	5967- 06
*	Sanders	Nicola	GBR	23.6.82	172/60	400	49.65	50.68- 06
	Santos	Vera	POR	3.12.81	164/59	20kW	1:32:53	1:30:41- 06
	Sardi	Rakhima	KGZ	11.4.86	172/56	TJ	13.76	13.54- 06
	Sarrapio	Patricia	ESP	16.11.82	168/58	TJ	14.00i, 13.81	13.89- 06
*	Savchenko	Yekaterina	RUS	3.6.77	180/60	HJ	2.00	1.98i- 04, 1.97- 03
*	Savigne	Yargelis	CUB	13.11.84	165/53	LJ	6.79i, 6.66, 6.81w	6.77, 6.88w- 05
						TJ	15.28	14.91- 06
^	Saville	Jane	AUS	5.11.74	164/53	20kW	1:30:53	1:27:44- 04
	Savinova	Mariya	RUS	22.6.85		800	2:00.78	2:05.91- 06
	Sayenko	Inna	UKR	8.3.82	177/80	HT	68.17	68.11- 06
*	Sayers	Goldie	GBR	16.7.82	171/69	JT	65.05	61.45- 05
	Scarpellini	Elena	ITA	14.1.87	178/60	PV	4.31i, 4.25	4.15- 05
	Scerbová	Denisa	CZE	21.8.86	175/61	LJ	6.65, 6.80w	6.68- 04
						Hep	6017	5828- 06
	Schaffarzik	Sandra	GER	22.6.87	175/65	JT	56.26	60.45- 06
	Schäffel	Aline	GER	15.5.80	178/84	SP	16.75i, 16.73	16.91- 03
*	Scherwin	Christina	DEN	11.7.76	176/67	JT	59.94	64.83- 06
	Schielke	Sina	GER	19.5.81	170/58	100	11.21	11.16, 11.10w- 02
	Schindlerová	Zuzana	CZE	25.4.87	173/62	20kW	1:34:57	1:52:53- 06
	Schmid	Anna Katharina	SUI-J	2.12.89		PV	4.30	3.70- 06
	Schmidt	Alice	USA	3.10.81	180/64	800	1:58.75	1:59.29- 05
						1500	4:08.89	4:12.12- 05
	Schrader	Annelies	GER	9.12.79	176/63	Hep	5677	5615- 01

Name		Nat	Born	Ht/Wt	Event	2007 Mark	Pre-2007 Best
Schulte	Sabine	GER	29.1.76	169/58	PV	4.25i	4.40, 4.43sq- 02
Schultze	Anna	GER	26.5.85	173/61	PV	4.40	4.40i- 06, 4.36- 05
Schulz	Christine	GER	30.1.84	179/62	Hep	5820	6199- 05
Schwanitz	Christina	GER	24.12.85	185/112	SP	17.06	18.84- 05
* Schwartz	Jillian	USA	19.9.79	173/63	PV	4.50	4.61i- 06, 4.60- 04
* Schwarzkopf	Lilli	GER	28.8.83	174/63	Hep	6439	6420- 06
Schwerdtner	Maren	GER	3.10.85	182/72	Hep	6096	5865- 06
Scott	Candice	TRI	17.9.80	180/100	HT	65.58	71.45- 05
Scott	Susan	GBR	26.9.77	168/56	800	2:01.77	1:59.02- 06
					1500	4:10.26	4:09.00- 05
* Seeger	Melanie	GER	8.1.77	166/49	20kW	1:29:32	1:28:17- 04
Seike	Megumi	JPN	26.2.87	163/49	10000	31:57.50	0
					HMar	70:52	
* Sekachova	Iryna	UKR	21.7.76	165/72	HT	71.83	74.31- 06
Selig	Ashley	USA	23.2.84	175/63	Hep	5794	5775- 05
* Selsouli	Mariem Alaoui	MAR	8.4.84	165/49	1500	4:01.52	4:07.13- 06
2000 5:40.25+					3000	8:29.52	8:41.67i, 8:45.96- 06
					5000	14:36.52	15:04.46- 06
Semenova	Nataliya	UKR	7.7.82	178/85	DT	62.44	63.11- 03
Semyonova	Svetlana	RUS	24.8.80		TJ	13.90	14.02- 05
Sendriuté	Zinaida	LTU	10.6.84	188/89	DT	56.74	57.26- 06
Sergeyeva	Nadezhda	RUS	13.6.87	175/63	Hep	5767	5786- 05
Sesay	Ola	USA	30.5.79	173/64	LJ	6.50	6.63- 04
* Sestak	Marija	SLO	17.4.79	178/56	LJ	6.59i, 6.58	6.50- 06
					TJ	14.92	14.53- 06
Setowska-Dryk	Ewelina	POL	5.3.80	171/56	800	1:59.64	1:58.96- 06
Sewell	Jennie	USA	21.2.84		PV	4.26	4.15- 05
Sha Li		CHN-J	14.8.88	178/65	TJ	13.95, 14.03w	14.01- 06
Shadle	Anne	USA	1.12.82	162/47	1500	4:11.67	4:08.60- 05
Shakes-Drayton	Perry	GBR-J	21.12.88	174/60	400H	56.46	57.52- 06
Shalamanova	Dobrinka	BUL	1.5.83	165/50	3kSt	9:42.08	9:56.75- 05
Shamsutdinova	Aleksandra	RUS	27.3.87		HJ	1.92i, 1.90	1.89i, 1.85- 06
Shapayeva	Mariya	RUS	7.11.86		800	1:59.59	2:01.69- 06
Shayunova	Natalya	BLR-J	11.9.89		HT	64.60	62.95- 06
Shcherbak	Oksana	UKR	24.2.82	175/60	400	51.93	51.23- 06
Shelest	Lyudmyla	UKR	4.10.74	166/54	20kW	1:32:39	1:30:45- 05
* Shemyakina	Tatyana	RUS	3.9.87	161/51	20kW	1:28:48	
Shi Na		CHN	17.2.81	160/50	20kW	1:30:58	1:28:22- 05
Shi Tianshu		CHN-J	7.6.88	174/55	20kW	1:35:32	
* Shibui	Yoko	JPN	14.3.79	165/46	5000	15:30.71	15:18.92- 02
10000 31:48.87			30:48.89- 02		HMar	70:24+	69:20- 02
Shimahara	Kiyoko	JPN	22.12.76	154/43	HMar	71:00	70:16- 06
Shimchuk	Natalya	BLR	1.10.81	179/77	JT	59.40	62.01- 06
Shipitsyna	Natalya	RUS	6.5.81		800	2:00.27	2:02.4 - 06
Shiviryova	Natalya	RUS	31.8.78	164/54	20kW	1:32:05	1:29:50- 05
Shkolina	Svetlana	RUS	9.3.86		HJ	1.96	1.92- 05
^ Shobukhova	Liliya	RUS	13.11.77	169/50	2000	5:35.80	
3000 8:44.30		8:27.86i- 06, 8:34.85- 04			HMar	71:14	
Shtangeyeva	Iryna	UKR	6.2.82	170/56	100	11.32	11.31- 05
					200	22.72	23.21- 05
Shtepa	Yekaterina	RUS	25.8.87	168/55	100H	13.01	13.33- 06
Shulikova	Olga	RUS	12.4.85	167/53	400	51.16	
Shutkova	Veronika	BLR	26.5.86		LJ	6.51, 6.74w	6.64- 05
Shvedova (Ivanova)	Anastasiya	RUS	3.5.79	174/63	PV	4.65	4.55- 04
Shyshkina	Kateryna	UKR	27.2.87	176/72	DT	56.17	50.70- 05
* Sibilyeva	Tatyana	RUS	17.5.80	159/42	20kW	1:28:51	1:27:33- 01
Sicari	Vincenza	ITA	19.3.79	165/45	HMar	71:12	72:39- 05
					Mar	2:30:35	2:34:52- 06
Sidorchenkova	Yelena	RUS	30.5.80	165/53	2000	5:40.03	5:47.21i- 06
5000 15:12.48			-0-		3kSt	9:26.55	9:27.35- 06
Sikes	Michelle	USA	27.2.85	177/57	3000	8:44.73	9:33.29- 05
					5000	15:09.28	16:07.44- 06
da Silva	Elizete	BRA	2.5.71	167/61	Hep	5766	5669A- 99, 5618- 06
da Silva	Karla Rosa	BRA	12.11.84	168/58	PV	4.30	4.20- 05
da Silva	Lucimara	BRA	10.7.85	174/64	Hep	5897	5611- 06
da Silva	Tânia Ferreira	BRA	17.12.86		TJ	14.11	13.87, 13.92Aw- 06
Silva	Vânia	POR	8.6.80	172/79	HT	67.14	68.82- 04
Silva	Yarisley	CUB	1.6.87	169/68	PV	4.30	4.20- 06
* Simagina	Irina	RUS	25.5.82	171/60	LJ	7.11	7.27- 04
Simkins	Krista	USA	27.12.86	163/52	200	23.08	23.71- 03, 23.62w?- 05

	Name		Nat	Born	Ht/Wt	Event	2007 Mark	Pre-2007 Best
^	Simon	Lidia	ROM	4.9.73	157/44	HMar	70:08	68:34- 00
						Mar	2:29:28	2:22:54- 00
	Simpson	Francine	JAM-J	1.11.89		LJ	6.51	5.91- 06
	Simpson	Jemma	GBR	10.2.84	168/55	800	2:00.18	1:59.99- 06
						1500	4:10.08	4:19.77- 03
*	Simpson	Margaret	GHA	31.12.81	162/53	Hep	6278	6423- 05
*	Simpson	Sherone	JAM	12.8.84	163/50	200	22.76	22.00- 06
*	Sinclair	Kenia	JAM	14.7.80	167/54	800	1:58.61	1:57.88- 06
						1500	4:05.56	4:07.11- 05
	Skafída	Afrodíti	GRE	20.3.82	167/60	PV	4.38	4.48- 05
	Skhiyi	Hanane	MAR	5.7.83		400H	56.28	58.05- 05
	Skibinska	Joanna	POL	21.2.85	177/53	LJ	6.52	5.68- 06
						TJ	14.04	12.59- 06
*	Skolimowska	Kamila	POL	4.11.82	180/105	HT	76.83	75.29- 06
*	Skotnik	Mélanie	FRA	8.11.82	182/59	HJ	1.97i, 1.96	1.97i- 03, 1.95- 05
*	Skujyté	Austra	LTU	12.8.79	188/75	HJ	1.89i, 1.84	1.89i, 1.86- 06
						SP	17.03	17.05- 06
						Hep	6380	6435- 04
	Skvortsova	Silviya	RUS	16.11.74		Mar	2:29:01	2:27:02- 02
	Slattery	Sara	USA	2.10.81	173/52	5000	15:18.18	15:08.32- 06
*	Slesarenko	Yelena	RUS	28.2.82	178/57	HJ	2.02	2.06- 04
	Smedley	Melinda	USA	11.2.81	163/58	100	11.46A, 11.36w	11.27, 11.24w- 04
	Smit	Anika	RSA	26.5.86		HJ	1.93A	1.91- 06
	Smith	Crystal	CAN	6.3.81		HT	68.60	66.34- 06
*	Smith	Kim	NZL	19.11.81	166/49	3000	8:35.31	8:47.06- 06
						5000	14:49.41	14:50.46i- 05, 14:56.58- 06
						10000	31:20.63	31:21.00- 05
	Smith	Lauren	USA	27.8.81	168/55	100H	13.00, 12.94w	13.04A, 13.25- 04
	Smith	Loree	USA	6.11.82	168/89	HT	68.56	70.03- 05
*	Smith	Rachelle	USA	30.6.81	163/59	100	11.13	11.17, 11.02w- 05
						200	22.31	22.22- 05
*	Smith	Shauna	USA	10.9.83	178/64	400H	55.94	54.21- 05
*	Smith	Trecia	JAM	5.11.75	185/77	TJ	14.35	15.16- 04
	Smolina	Zhanna	RUS	28.2.78		800	2:02.02i, 2:03.50	1:59.33- 05
*	Smolyachkova	Marina	BLR	10.2.85	179/76	HT	71.74	72.75- 06
	Snigur	Yevgeniya	UKR	7.3.84	171/63	100H	12.89	12.95- 06
	Snyder (Etholm)	Grete	NOR	25.1.76	183/72	DT	55.48	59.48- 03
^	Sobanska	Malgorzata	POL	25.4.69	165/50	Mar	2:31:10	2:26:08- 01
	Sobierajska	Malwina	POL	22.4.85	179/86	HT	64.92	64.24- 05
	Sobieszek	Magdalena	POL	4.5.86	178/75	SP	17.80	17.58- 06
*	Soboleva	Yelena	RUS	3.10.82	176/66	800	1:59.49	1:57.28- 06
						1500	3:57.30+	3:56.43- 06
						1M	4:15.63	
						2000	5:36.43	5:40.75i- 06
*	Söderberg	Anna	SWE	11.6.73	177/85	DT	62.98	64.54- 99
	Sokolova	Svetlana	RUS	9.1.81	176/70	Hep	6011	6591- 04
	Sokolova	Vera	RUS	8.6.87	151/42	20kW	1:32:56	1:40:03- 06
	Sokolova	Yelena	RUS	23.7.86	173/76	LJ	6.71	6.53- 06
*	Solomon	Shalonda	USA	19.12.85	169/56	100	11.33	11.09, 11.07w- 06
						200	22.74	22.36, 22.30w- 06
	Solovyova	Svetlana	RUS	6.11.86	169/50	20kW	1:31:31	1:38:22- 06
	Solvin	Lena	FIN	4.7.86	163/73	HT	64.45	63.13- 06
*	Song Aimin		CHN	15.3.78	177/83	DT	62.64	65.33- 03
	Song Dan		CHN-Y	5.7.90	173/71	JT	59.89	59.09- 06
*	Song Hongjuan		CHN	4.7.84	166/50	20kW	1:28:25	1:26:46- 04
	Song Jinzhao		CHN-J	16.1.88	162/49	20kW	1:34:29	1:34:56- 06
	Song Xiaoling		CHN	21.12.87	167/49	20kW	1:31:18.79t	1:28:23- 06
	Song Xiaoxue		CHN	13.2.87	170/52	10000	31:39.84	33:29.60- 06
	Sorokina	Anna	RUS-J	20.8.88		20kW	1:35:09	1:52:42.0t- 06
	Sorokina	Nataliya	UKR	24.3.75	174/58	LJ	6.49, 6.50w	6.61- 06
*	Sotherton	Kelly	GBR	13.11.76	180/66	100H	13.21	13.22- 06
						HJ	1.88i, 1.87	1.85- 04
						LJ	6.68	6.68- 04
						Hep	6510	6547- 05
	Soulama	Aïssata	BUR	11.2.79	172/57	400H	55.49	56.45- 05
	Spain	Ellie	GBR	23.8.82	172/68	PV	4.26i	4.21- 06
	Spanovic	Ivana	SRB-Y	10.5.90	175/62	LJ	6.53i, 6.41	6.48i- 06, 6.43- 05
	Spencer	Kaliese	JAM	6.4.87	173/59	400	51.76	51.56- 06
						400H	55.62	55.11- 06
	Spencer	Keisha	JAM	16.2.78	176/61	TJ	13.72	14.06i, 13.97- 00, 14.26w- 04
	Spencer	Lavern	LCA	23.6.84	180/54	HJ	1.94	1.94- 05
	Spencer	Sasha	USA	4.8.79	163/52	800	2:02.25	2:01.56- 03
*	Spiegelburg	Silke	GER	17.3.86	173/62	PV	4.60	4.56- 06
*	Spotáková	Barbora	CZE	30.6.81	182/80	JT	67.12	66.21- 06
	Springer-Jones	Sasha	TRI	17.3.78	165/54	100	11.31	11.53- 00

Name		Nat	Born	Ht/Wt	Event	2007 Mark	Pre-2007 Best
Spruill	Britni	USA	30.5.86	164/54	200	23.17	23.47- 06
Stadnyuk	Oleksandra	UKR	16.4.80	170/55	LJ	6.75	6.64- 04
					TJ	14.09, 14.25w	14.34i- 06, 14.09- 05
Stahl	Linda	GER	2.9.85	172/63	JT	62.80	57.17- 06
^ Stankina	Irina	RUS	25.3.77	165/50	20kW	1:29:56	1:25:29- 00
Stasiulionyté	Inga	LTU	29.6.81	176/66	JT	57.93	62.27- 05
Stately	Bryson	USA	22.11.86	165/57	PV	4.35	4.15- 06
* Stef	Claudia	ROM	25.2.78	160/48	20kW	1:30:34	1:27:41- 04
Stefanídi	Ekateríni	GRE-Y	4.2.90	171/57	PV	4.25	4.37i, 4.30- 05
Steiner	April	USA	22.4.80	175/58	PV	4.60Ai, 4.50	4.45- 04
Stellingwerff	Hilary	CAN	7.8.81	158/48	800	2:02.20	2:02.55- 05
1500	4:05.69		4:05.86- 06		1M	4:28.62	
Stepaniuk	Kamila	POL	22.3.86	184/66	HJ	1.90	1.86- 05
Steryíou	Adonía	GRE	7.7.85	179/59	HJ	1.93	1.86- 06
Stevens	Sarah	USA	2.4.86	178/83	SP	18.40	17.91i, 17.46- 06
DT	57.73		53.95- 06		HT	66.34	65.69- 06
* Stewart	Kerron	JAM	16.4.84	175/61	100	11.03	11.03- 06
					200	22.41	22.65- 06
Stoddart	Shevon	JAM	21.11.82	165/52	400H	55.42	54.47- 05
Stoian	Monica	ROM	25.8.82	169/67	JT	61.19	58.89- 06
Straková	Iva	CZE	4.8.80	187/65	HJ	1.95	1.96i- 03, 1.93- 04
Stratáki	Aryiró	GRE	3.8.75	173/60	Hep	6003	6235- 06
Strong	Kelly	USA	27.9.78	168/54	3kSt	9:47.68	9:48.90- 06
Strot	Emilee	USA	12.5.86	183/90	DT	55.53	54.24- 06
Strutz	Martina	GER	4.11.81	160/53	PV	4.45	4.50- 06
* Stuczynski	Jennifer	USA	6.2.82	180/64	PV	4.88	4.68i, 4.66- 06
^ Sturrup	Chandra	BAH	12.9.71	163/55	100	11.15	10.84- 05
^ Styopina	Viktoriya	UKR	21.2.76	178/58	HJ	1.94	2.02- 04
^ Sudak-Torun (BLR)	Svetlana	TUR	20.3.71	174/90	HT	68.70	69.80- 05
Sugihara	Kayo	JPN	24.2.83	161/44	5000	15:15.34	15:17.20- 06
					10000	31:54.59	31:47.60- 06
Sultan	Simret	ERI	20.7.84	169/50	5000	15:16.33	15:18.69- 05
Sultanova	Yekaterina	RUS	31.12.84	165/55	PV	4.30i, 4.15	4.30i, 4.20- 04
Sun Huiying		CHN-J	17.7.89	181/91	SP	17.18	15.24- 06
Sun Lihua		CHN	30.9.83	162/44	20kW	1:35:39	1:30:16- 05
Sun Limin		CHN	6.2.87	174/55	20kW	1:32:30.36t	1:30:39- 05
Sun Taifeng		CHN	26.8.82	187/90	DT	64.98	62.98- 06
Sun Weiwei		CHN	13.1.85	160/45	Mar	2:29:27	2:25:15- 02
Suthe	Annika	GER	15.10.85	175/78	JT	60.39	61.38- 04
Sutherland	Sonita	JAM	9.8.87	174/64	400	51.74	51.13- 06
Svensson	Monica	SWE	26.12.78	166/60	20kW	1:31:20	1:32:51- 06
Svyrydenko	Olena	UKR	11.4.81	182/71	LJ	6.51	6.54- 06
Sylvester	Patricia	GRN	3.2.83	175/55	HJ	1.89i	185- 06
Szczepanska	Magdalena	POL	25.1.80	178/63	Hep	5713	6115- 04
Tadesse	Mestawet	ETH	19.7.85	168/51	1500	4:07.45	4:04.61- 06
Taira	Akane	JPN	3.11.82	161/45	10000	32:18.28	32:12.67- 05
					HMar	69:17	70:26- 05
Talpos	Luminita	ROM	9.10.72	164/47	HMar	69:01	70:08- 02
Tan Jian		CHN-J	20.1.88	179/80	DT	55.98	57.01- 05
Tanana	Natalya	BLR	1.1.83		Hep	5693	5312- 06
Tanno	Asami	JPN	25.9.85	162/48	400	51.81	51.80- 05
Tapoki	Tereapii	COK	19.4.84		DT	56.53	57.61- 06
Taranova	Anastasiya	RUS	6.9.85	178/61	TJ	14.24	14.20- 05
Tarasova	Irina	RUS	15.4.87		SP	18.27	17.11- 06
* Târlea	Ionela	ROM	9.2.76	169/54	200	22.93	22.35- 99
400	51.59		49.88- 99		400H	55.41	53.25- 99
Tarmoh	Jeneba	USA-J	27.9.89	167/59	100	11.27	11.24- 06
					200	23.34, 23.20w	23.14- 06
* Tarvainen	Paula	FIN	17.2.73	167/68	JT	63.58	64.90- 03
Tatsumi	Yoshika	JPN	26.2.82	161/44	3kSt	9:57.02	
Tavares	Carmo	POR	27.4.74	168/52	800	2:02.22	2:01.94- 05
Tavares	Elisabete	POR	7.3.80	170/54	PV	4.32	4.32i- 06, 4.25- 03
Tavares	Sandra-Helena	POR	29.5.82	166/55	PV	4.25	4.21i- 05, 4.20- 03
Taylor	Tisifenee	USA	19.6.84	158/52	LJ	6.57	6.41- 06
Teixeira	Sandra	POR	13.3.78	170/52	800	2:01.57	2:01.55- 06
* Tejeda	Anay	CUB	3.4.83	165/59	100H	12.80	12.72- 06, 12.6- 02
Teodoro	Lucimar	BRA	1.5.81	178/67	400H	55.96	55.94- 04
Terada	Kei	JPN	27.3.85		10000	32:45.39	33:01.69- 04
					HMar	71:00	70:53- 04
* Tereshchuk-Antipova	Tetyana	UKR	11.10.69	185/63	400H	54.38	53.37- 04
Tereshkova	Olga	KAZ	26.10.84	172/53	400	51.62	51.77- 06

Name		Nat	Born	Ht/Wt	Event	2007 Mark	Pre-2007 Best
Terlecki	Josephine	GER	17.2.86	182/78	SP	16.91	16.75- 06
Terrero	Indira	CUB	29.11.85	168/54	400	51.00	53.07- 03
Terzoglou	Irini-Hrisovaládou	GRE	2.2.79	175/86	SP	17.11i, 16.96	19.10- 03
^ Teter	Nicole	USA	8.11.73	172/57	800	1:59.91	1:57.97- 02
					1500	4:08.73	4:04.19- 02
Teteris	Aimee	CAN	24.6.79	163/48	800	2:00.85	2:00.21- 06
^ Thánou	Ekateríni	GRE	1.2.75	165/56	100	11.35	10.83, 10.77w- 99
Theodorou	Paraskevi	CYP	15.3.86		HT	64.68	59.85- 06
* Thiam	Ami Mbacké	SEN	10.11.76	183/70	400	50.15	49.86- 01
Thipe	Tsholofelo	RSA	12.9.86		200	23.26A	24.40A, 23.7A- 06
Thomas	Charlene	GBR	6.5.82	166/52	1500	4:09.64	4:20.60mx- 05, 4:20.74- 06
					1M	4:27.95	
Thomas	Vashti	USA-Y	21.4.90	170/54	100H	13.03	14.16- 05, 13.92w- 06
* Thompson	Bronwyn	AUS	29.1.78	177/68	LJ	6.72	7.00- 02
* Thondike	Arasay	CUB	28.5.86	168/71	HT	71.14	69.26- 06
Tigau	Viorica	ROM	12.8.79	171/60	Hep	5774	6289- 00
Tiki Gelana	Erba	ETH	22.10.87	165/45	5000	15:33.70	
					10000	32:43.31	
Tilahun	Biruk Konjit	ETH	22.9.87	155/42	5000	15:33.63	
					10000	31:58.45	
Tilgner	Joanna	GER	18.11.84	170/55	400H	55.96	57.57- 06
^ Timbilil	Alice	KEN	16.6.83	155/45	HMar	68:56	
Timofeyeva	Irina	RUS	5.4.70	156/48	10000	32:24.84	31:40.14- 00
HMar	69:29		70:35- 05		Mar	2:26:54	2:25:29- 01
Tito	Josiane	BRA	8.8.79	168/52	400	51.89	52.30- 03
					800	2:01.28	2:01.47- 02
Titova	Tatyana	RUS	2.1.83		TJ	13.81	13.83- 05
Tobias	Nataliya	UKR	22.11.80	160/49	1500	4:05.41	4:02.52- 06
					3kSt	9:41.14	
Tola	Worknesh	ETH	3.6.77		Mar	2:30:56	2:25:42- 03
Tolstaya	Svetlana	KAZ	9.8.71	172/52	20kW	1:33:37	1:28:38- 02
^ Tomasevic	Dragana	SRB	4.6.82	175/80	DT	61.52	63.63- 06
* Tomashova	Tatyana	RUS	1.7.75	164/50	1500	4:02.8	3:56.91- 06
					1M	4:24.84	4:38.13- 01
* Tomescu	Constantina	ROM	23.1.70	165/48	HMar	69:58+	68:07+- 06
					Mar	2:23:55	2:21:30- 05
Tonkovyd	Halyna	UKR	7.6.85	174/63	200	23.12	23.35, 23.16w- 06
* Tonn	Claudia	GER	18.4.81	182/70	Hep	6108	6373- 06
Topylina	Svetlana	RUS	6.1.85		100H	13.14	13.31- 06
* Tosa	Reiko	JPN	11.6.76	167/45	Mar	2:30:55	2:22:46- 02
Touhami	Nadiha	ALG	10.2.78	175/60	1500	4:09.12	4:05.25- 04
Townsend	Tiffany	USA-J	14.6.89	163/50	100	11.21	11.65, 11.75w- 06
					200	22.84	24.55- 06
Toyonaga	Yoko	JPN	15.4.77	164/90	SP	17.02	17.57- 04
Trafton (Brown)	Stephanie	USA	1.8.79	193/102	DT	61.40	61.90- 04
Trevisan	Elisa	ITA	5.3.80	166/55	Hep	5716	5844- 04
* Trotter	Deedee	USA	8.12.82	178/60	400	49.64	49.80- 06
Truong Thanh Hang		VIE	1.5.86	165/50	1500	4:11.60	4:17.66- 06
Trybanska	Malgorzata	POL	21.6.81	177/61	LJ	6.80, 6.81w	6.71- 06
					TJ	14.24	13.94- 06
^ Trywianska	Aurelia	POL	9.5.76	174/59	100H	12.83	12.74- 03
Tsatsa	Thabita	ZIM	18.9.72		Mar	2:30:12	2:32:09- 06
Tschirch	Cathleen	GER	23.7.79	167/54	200	22.97	23.38- 06
Tschurtschentaler	Agnes	ITA	12.1.82	160/45	3kSt	9:55.26	9:58.44- 06
^ Tsoumeléka	Athanasía	GRE	2.1.82	158/47	20kW	1:33:58	1:29:12- 04
Tsyganova	Natalya	RUS	7.2.71	162/50	800	2:02.06	1:56.60- 00
Tsyhotska	Ruslana	UKR	23.3.86	166/49	TJ	13.66	13.13- 04
Tuchak	Oksana	RUS	27.3.73	187/82	DT	57.47	64.25- 99
Tucholke	Jana	GER	20.5.81	185/90	DT	62.31	60.48- 04
* Tufa	Mestawat	ETH	14.9.83	157/45	5000	14:51.72	14:59.05- 06
					10000	31:00.27	
Tufa	Tigist	ETH			HMar	70:33	
Tune	Dire	ETH	19.6.85		HMar	71:11	71:16+- 05
					Mar	2:26:52	2:30:48- 05
Tunks	Lieja	CAN	10.3.76	183/95	SP	18.02	18.82- 03
					DT	56.56	58.93- 02
Turner	Laura	GBR	12.8.82	168/55	100	11.19, 11.09w	11.38- 06
* Turova	Rita	BLR	28.12.80	174/55	20kW	1:27:10	1:26:11- 06
Twell	Stephanie	GBR-J	17.8.89	165/48	1500	4:06.70	4:12.76- 06
1M	4:28.16				3000	8:53.34	9:07.41- 06

Name		Nat	Born	Ht/Wt	Event	2007 Mark	Pre-2007 Best
* Tyminska	Karolina	POL	4.10.84	178/61	LJ	6.53	6.59- 06
					Hep	6200	6402- 06
Uceny	Morgan	USA	10.3.85	168/57	800	2:01.75	2:04.32- 06
* Udmurtova	Oksana	RUS	1.2.82	174/64	LJ	6.92	7.02- 06
					TJ	14.41i, 14.35	
Ulyeva	Iolanta	KAZ	27.7.76	172/90	SP	17.42	18.04i- 02, 17.82- 00
Unger	Jodi	USA	28.12.84	168/62	PV	4.25	4.24- 06
* Upshaw	Grace	USA	25.9.75	178/65	LJ	6.72, 6.74w	6.84- 04, 6.99w- 03
^ Urbansky	Ulrike	GER	6.4.77	174/62	400H	55.21	54.57- 00
Urbina	Maria Teresa	ESP	20.3.85	177/53	3kSt	9:49.03	10:05.74- 06
Urgessa	Bizunesh	ETH-J	18.6.89	155/44	5000	15:14.90	
* Usovich	Ilona	BLR	14.11.82	167/55	400	50.31	50.69- 06
* Usovich	Svetlana	BLR	14.10.80	164/52	400	52.10	50.79- 04, 50.55i- 05
					800	1:58.11	1:58.17- 05
Ustinova	Anna	KAZ	8.12.85	178/59	HJ	1.92	1.92i- 05, 1.92- 06
Utura	Sule	ETH-Y	8.2.90		5000	15:21.70	
Vaill	Teresa	USA	20.11.62	162/48	20kW	1:34:42	1:33:23- 01
Valencia	Maria Elena	MEX	25.5.83		10000	32:40.58	
					Mar	2:31:16	2:30:53- 06
Vallortigara	Elena	ITA-Y	21.9.91	179/56	HJ	1.87	1.85- 06
Vanden Bempt	Sigrid	BEL	10.2.81	173/58	3kSt	9:39.50	9:35.28- 04
Vandy	Vanessa	FIN-J	14.5.89	162/50	PV	4.30	3.85- 06
Vargas	Mailín	CUB	24.3.83	176/80	SP	18.08	17.50- 06
Vári	Edit	HUN	31.5.75	172/61	100H	13.06	13.17- 02
Varner	Rachelle	USA	20.7.83	175/86	DT	56.72	57.93- 04
* Vasco	María	ESP	26.12.75	156/45	20kW	1:29:17	1:27:36- 04
Vasiloiu	Cristina	ROM-J	4.3.88	162/50	1500	4:07.81	4:12.01- 06
					3000	8:56.07	9:41.98i- 06, 9:44.87- 05
Vasilyeva	Svetlana	RUS	13.8.85	168/50	20kW	1:31:59	1:32:25- 05
Veldáková	Dana	SVK	3.6.81	178/59	TJ	14.41	14.21i, 14.19- 06
Veldáková	Jana	SVK	3.6.81	177/59	LJ	6.65	6.66- 06
^ Veneva ¶	Venelina	BUL	13.6.74	179/61	HJ	1.96i, 2.02idq	2.04- 01
Vésanes	Elise	FRA	25.1.84	171/60	LJ	6.53	6.46- 04
* Veshkurova	Tatyana	RUS	23.9.81	180/70	400	50.22	49.99- 06
Vicenzino	Tania	ITA	1.4.86	167/60	LJ	6.50	6.18- 06
Vieira	Zenaide	BRA	25.6.85	175/57	3kSt	9:46.52	9:53.40- 06
Vigliano	Nadia	FRA	24.6.77	181/72	JT	56.84	56.25- 06
* Vili	Valerie	NZL	6.10.84	193/123	SP	20.54	20.20- 06
Vilisova	Tatyana	RUS	27.11.79		3kSt	10:00.09	9:50.14- 04
Viljoen	Sunette	RSA	6.10.83	168/63	JT	58.39	61.59- 03
Vinatho	Vassanee	THA	30.6.80	170/57	400H	57.21	56.40- 03
					Hep	5889	5630- 98
^ Vincent (Sauer)	Mary	USA	31.10.75	164/59	PV	4.52i, 4.44	4.65- 02
Vinogradova	Anastasiya	KAZ	13.9.86	174/55	100	11.37	11.91, 11.78w- 06
					100H	13.05	13.30- 06
Vinokurova	Yuliya	RUS	17.6.72		3000	8:52.27i	8:56.45i- 06, 9:23.16- 00
5000	15:33.11		15:42.15- 00		10000	32:28.35	33:18.02- 05
Vives	Yaima	CUB	16.12.85	180/80	DT	56.56	54.60- 06
* Vlasic	Blanka	CRO	8.11.83	192/75	HJ	2.07	2.05i -06, 2.03- 04
Vnukova	Karina	LTU	27.3.85		HJ	1.87i, 1.86	1.83- 02
Volgina	Natalya	RUS	15.3.77		Mar	2:30:31	2:27:32- 06
* Volkova	Yekaterina	RUS	16.2.78	169/55	1500	4:10.38	4:09.03- 05
2000	5:41.61		5:55.91i- 06		5000	15:00.02	
					3kSt	9:06.57	9:20.49- 05
Volodko	Yevgeniya	BLR	24.3.81		100H	12.95	13.17- 04
Volzankina	Jesenija	LAT	28.11.83	174/59	Hep	5799	5996- 06
von Eynatten	Denise	GER	30.12.87		PV	4.30	3.80- 06
Vorobyeva	Nadezhda	RUS	30.5.77	168/56	800	2:02.24	2:00.47- 02
Vu Thi Huong		VIE	7.10.86	166/51	100	11.47, 11.33w	11.49- 05
Vukicevic	Christina	NOR	18.6.87	178/60	100H	13.07	13.34- 06
Vukovic	Ivana	CRO	18.5.86		JT	56.50	55.05- 06
Vygovskaya	Gulnara	RUS	6.9.80	154/41	Mar	2:28:22	2:32:51- 06
Wade	Bettie	USA	11.9.86		Hep	5724w, 5722	5354- 06
Wagner	Kaylene	USA	15.11.84	186/64	HJ	1.89	1.92- 04
Wairimu	Gladys	KEN-Y	15.7.91	162/45	5000	15:18.46	
Wakamatsu	Ikumi	JPN	22.6.74	155/41	10000	32:46.28	
Wakita	Akane	JPN	15.12.87	160/48	10000	31:39.32	
					HMar	71:01	
Waldet	Olivia	FRA	23.5.84	177/79	HT	66.63	65.52- 05
* Walker	Melaine	JAM	1.1.83	165/53	400H	54.14	54.87- 06

Name		Nat	Born	Ht/Wt	Event	2007 Mark	Pre-2007 Best
Wallace	Latosha	USA	24.3.85	173/57	400	51.97	53.58- 06
					400H	56.35	57.57- 06
Waller	LaNeisha	USA	30.12.85		100H	13.18	13.77, 13.5- 06
Walter	Sarah	FRA	5.5.78	173/64	JT	56.54	62.53- 03
Wambui	Evelyne	KEN	4.4.86	162/49	5000	15:08.08	15:06.74- 05
					10000	31:45.00	31:30.86- 06
* Wami	Getenesh	ETH	11.12.74	153/44	HMar	69:58+	70:22+- 06
					Mar	2:21:45	2:21:34- 06
Wang Bin		CHN	7.1.87	176/70	DT	56.13	55.92- 06
Wang Hui		CHN	1.6.87	169/47	400H	57.08	57.00- 04
Wang Huiqin		CHN-Y	7.2.90	168/52	TJ	13.78	13.18- 06
Wang Lihong		CHN	9.1.83	168/75	SP	16.68	17.87i- 05, 17.64- 04
Wang Shanshan		CHN	16.6.87	168/50	20kW	1:31:52.30t	1:30:02- 06
Wang Xue		CHN-Y	14.2.90	159/44	20kW	1:34:21.56t	1:31:37- 05
Wang Yang		CHN	3.4.87	175/65	HT	65.67	60.94- 06
Wangari	Mary Wanjohi	KEN	4.10.86	163/50	5000	15:21.98	15:08.28- 05
Wangari	Miriam	KEN	22.2.79		HMar	70:27	71:54- 05
* Wangui	Lucy	KEN	24.3.84	154/42	3000	8:53.9+	8:56.41- 06
5000	14:57.55		14:56.09- 06		10000	31:32.52	31:05.90- 04
Wanjiru	Ruth	KEN	11.9.81	156/44	10000	32:21.04	31:56.21- 03
Wanless	Liz	USA	18.11.81	181/107	SP	18.55i, 18.35	18.59- 06
Waruguru	Pauline	KEN	26.8.80	153/46	5000	15:22.32	15:25.36- 06
					10000	32:18.87	32:00.25- 06
Watkins	Rhonda	TRI	9.12.87	178/64	LJ	6.82, 6.96w	6.56- 06
Watzek	Veronika	AUT	13.8.85	184/75	DT	58.77	57.35- 06
Weatherspoon	Alexis	USA	27.7.83	165/55	100	11.33, 11.19w	11.34, 11.31w- 05
Webb	Cheryl	AUS	3.10.76	165/53	20kW	1:34:40	1:31:43- 04
^ Wei Yanan		CHN	6.12.81	160/48	10000	32:39.38	31:54.86- 01
					Mar	2:23:12	2:24:02- 01, 2:20:23dq- 02
Weissteiner	Silvia	ITA	13.7.79	163/46	3000	8:48.63, 8:44.81i	8:50.35- 06
					5000	15:02.65	15:26.92- 06
Wells	Kellie	USA	16.7.82	163/	100H	12.93	13.25- 04, 13.17w- 06
Werner	Kerstin	GER	18.9.82	172/57	800	2:01.86	2:03.37- 06
Westley	Abby	GBR	15.7.87	168/57	1500	4:08.74	4:16.23- 06
* Wheeler	Kylie	AUS	17.1.80	180/64	LJ	6.56	6.57- 03, 6.66w- 04
					Hep	6184	6298- 06
Whitman	Nicole	USA	9.11.80	170/57	100	11.34w, 11.12dt	11,55, 11,33w- 05
* Whyte	Angela	CAN	22.5.80	170/57	100H	12.63, 12.55w	12.69- 04
Wienand	Janet	RSA	15.5.85		400H	56.53	55.82A, 56.31- 06
* Wigene	Susanne	NOR	12.2.78	168/50	5000	15:24.25	14:48.53- 05
Wiklund	Erika	SWE-J	10.3.88		HJ	1.87i, 1.85	1.86- 04
Wilfred	Sarah	USA	.85		HJ	1.87i	1.84- 06
Wilkins	Bobby-Gaye	JAM-J	10.9.88		400	51.72	52.85- 06
Willard	Anna	USA	31.3.84	168/52	3kSt	9:34.72	10:06.83- 06
Williams	Amber	USA	15.12.85		100H	13.18	13.55- 05
* Williams	Angela	USA	30.1.80	156/52	100	11.06	11.04, 10.96w- 99
Williams	Clora	JAM	26.11.83	167/54	400	52.03	51.06- 06
Williams	Genna	BAR	3.11.84		100	11.30w	11.47- 04
Williams	Jennifer	USA	30.10.85	167/56	100H	13.24	13.40, 13.23w- 06
* Williams	Lauryn	USA	11.9.83	157/57	100	11.01	10.88- 05
					200	22.70	22.27- 05
* Williams	Novlene	JAM	26.4.82	170/57	400	49.66	49.53- 06
* Williams	Shericka	JAM	17.9.85	164/52	100	11.34	
					400	50.37	50.24- 06
* Williams	Tiffany	USA	5.2.83	157/57	400H	53.28	53.79- 06
Wilson	Latonia	USA	30.11.84	160/52	100	11.47, 11.13w	11.67- 06, 11.66w- 03
					200	23.11, 22.80w	23.37- 05
* Wilson	Nickiesha	JAM	28.7.86	173/64	100H	12.93	13.64- 06
					400H	53.97	56.77- 06
* Wineberg (Danner)	Mary	USA	3.1.80	178/61	400	50.24	51.27- 06
Wisniewska	Joanna	POL	24.5.72	178/88	DT	63.13	63.97- 99
Wisse	Yvonne	NED	6.6.82	180/60	Hep	6086	6026- 05
Wlodarczyk	Anita	POL	8.8.85	178/88	HT	69.07	65.53- 06
Wolf	Caroline	USA	13.2.85		HJ	1.87	1.86- 06
Woods	Claire	AUS	6.7.81		20kW	1:35:36	1:35:18- 06
* Woods	Shareese	USA	20.2.85	164/57	200	22.74	22.95, 22.70w- 06
Woodward	Krista	CAN	22.11.84		JT	56.06	54.24- 06
Wootton	Katrina	GBR	2.9.85	170/54	1500	4:08.10	4:09.65i, 4:10.58- 06
^ Worku	Ayelech	ETH	12.6.79	165/47	HMar	71:02	
					Mar	2:29:14	2:31:11- 06
Wort	Liz	USA	23.9.83	178/60	3kSt	9:51.76	10:05.39- 05

Name		Nat	Born	Ht/Wt	Event	2007 Mark	Pre-2007 Best
Wu Jie		CHN-J	26.9.89	161/53	JT	55.28	55.91- 06
Wu Sha		CHN	21.10.87	172/64	PV	4.30	4.30- 03
Wurth-Thomas	Christy	USA	11.7.80	165/52	1500	4:07.86	4:05.00- 06
					1M	4:31.84i	4:36.08i- 06
Wysocka	Marzena	POL	17.2.69	178/85	DT	58.18	64.57- 05
Xie Fang		CHN-J	26.12.89	164/52	5000	15:03.95	15:37.08- 06
					10000	31:21.25	
* Xie Limei		CHN	27.6.86	168/50	TJ	14.90	14.54- 06
Xu Shaoyang		CHN	9.2.83	173/70	DT	61.30	62.54- 02
Xu Tingting		CHN-J	12.7.89	182/65	TJ	13.73	13.72- 06
Xue Fei		CHN-J	8.8.89	163/47	5000	15:02.73	15:20.44- 06
					10000	32:29.12	
Xue Juan		CHN	10.2.86	174/65	JT	57.18	62.93- 03
Yagi	Yoko	JPN	14.4.80	159/43	HMar	71:14	70:06- 06
Yakovenko	Mariya	RUS	6.1.82	176/84	JT	62.23	60.83- 05
Yakovleva	Tatyana	RUS	9.9.86	176/53	TJ	14.12	14.08- 06
Yamashita	Ikuyo	JPN	17.6.85	157/43	HMar	70:53	
* Yamauchi	Mara	GBR	13.8.73	160/52	HMar	68:45	69:24- 06
					Mar	2:25:41	2:25:13- 06
Yang Fei		CHN	20.7.87	186/90	DT	57.14	
Yang Jing		CHN	1.1.84	170/57	PV	4.22i	4.40- 05
Yang Mingxia		CHN-Y	13.1.90	160/43	20kW	1:34:11	
Yang Sha		CHN	16.1.86	161/43	20kW	1:32:12	1:29:33- 05
Yanit	Nevin	TUR	16.2.86	163/52	100H	12.76	12.88- 06
Yao Jiajia		CHN-J	7.4.88	173/50	TJ	13.68	13.08- 06
* Yatchenko	Irina	BLR	31.10.65	186/105	DT	64.87	69.14- 04
* Yefremova	Antonina	UKR	19.7.81	176/61	400	52.09	50.70- 02
* Yegorova	Olga	RUS	28.3.72	160/48	1500	4:01.2	3:59.47- 05
					1M	4:20.10	4:25.54i- 00
Yelling	Hayley	GBR	3.1.74	152/45	10000	32:01.43	31:45.14- 04
Yelling	Liz	GBR	5.12.74	174/56	HMar	69:28	70:00+- 04, 70:51- 06
					Mar	2:30:44	2:30:58- 03
Yemelyanova	Larisa	RUS	6.1.80	164/52	20kW	1:30:22	1:27:23- 03
Yepimashko	Vera	BLR	10.7.76		SP	17.18	17.78- 05
Yesipchuk	Oksana	RUS	13.12.76	183/95	DT	62.07	63.68- 00
Yevseyeva	Yekaterina	KAZ-J	22.6.88	174/58	HJ	1.92i, 1.91	1.88- 06
Yezhova	Irina	RUS	25.6.86	164/48	20kW	1:35:49	1:35:57- 06
Yezhova	Yekaterina	RUS	3.7.82	166/51	20kW	1:32:05	1:32:04- 05
Yisrael	Naim	USA	25.11.85	168/60	400H	56.98	60.30- 06
* Yordanova	Daniela	BUL	8.3.76	165/52	1500	4:00.82	3:59.10- 04
Yoshida	Emika	JPN	10.12.85	165/60	JT	57.19	55.60- 05
Yoshikawa	Mika	JPN	16.9.84	155/38	1500	4:10.00	4:11.00- 06
Yosypenko	Lyudmyla	UKR	24.9.84	175/63	Hep	6025	5782- 05
Yuda	Tomomi	JPN	28.5.85	159/42	10000	32:33.28	
Yurchenko	Snezhana	BLR	1.8.84	164/53	20kW	1:31:12	1:30:33- 06
Yurkovich	Rachel	USA	10.10.86	180/77	JT	57.90	54.82- 06
Yush	Kristal	USA	8.1.82	175/75	HT	69.26	64.94- 06
Yushchenko	Yulyana	BLR	14.8.84	173/56	400	51.01	51.46- 06
^ Zabawska	Krystyna	POL	14.1.68	183/92	SP	17.88	19.42- 92
Zadorina	Kseniya	RUS	2.3.87	173/59	400	51.06	51.81- 06
Zadura	Malgorzata	POL	3.10.82	171/85	HT	66.93	64.13- 05
Zafirova (Shiyan)	Marina	RUS	22.1.80	168/52	400H	55.21	55.14- 05
^ Zaituc	Luminita	GER	9.10.68	165/50	Mar	2:29:37	2:26:01- 01
^ Zakharova	Svetlana	RUS	15.9.70	158/48	Mar	2:29:12	2:21:31- 02
Zapounídou	Déspina	GRE	5.10.85	166/55	20kW	1:34:16	1:36:50- 05
Zavgorodnya	Olga	UKR	6.1.83	171/57	400	52.13	52.54- 06
* Zbrozhek	Oksana	RUS	12.1.78	167/49	800	1:58.80	1:58.06- 04
1000	2:32.21i		2:39.39i- 05		1500	4:11.35i	4:08.16- 05
Zegergish	Furtuna	ERI-J	.89		HMar	71:03	
Zelenina	Alexandra	MDA	21.11.86		TJ	13.73	13.91- 06
* Zelinka	Jessica	CAN	3.9.81	175/61	100H	13.25,13.19w	13.08- 06
					Hep	6343	6314- 06
Zemaityté	Viktoria	LTU	11.3.85	184/65	Hep	6219	6021w- 06, 5913- 05
Zhang Chunjing		CHN	19.5.83	176/85	SP	16.79i	18.28- 05
Zhang Guirong		SIN	5.2.78	182/98	SP	17.21	18.57- 05
Zhang Li		CHN	19.10.78	172/75	JT	59.96	60.02- 00
Zhang Qiang		CHN	14.2.87	180/90	SP	17.42	17.61- 06
Zhang Rong		CHN	5.1.83	174/65	100H	13.20	13.11- 05, 13.03w- 01
Zhang Rongrong		CHN	27.1.84		400H	57.08	55.91- 05
Zhang Shujing		CHN	13.9.78	158/55	Mar	2:31:14	2:23:17- 02
* Zhang Wenxiu		CHN	22.3.86	181/102	HT	74.86	74.15- 06

Name		Nat	Born	Ht/Wt	Event	2007 Mark	Pre-2007 Best
Zhang Yingning		CHN-Y	6.1.90	170/42	PV	4.46i, 4.40	4.45- 06
Zhang Yingying		CHN-Y	4.1.90	165/47	5000	15:06.08	
10000 31:17.30					Mar	2:27:20	
Zhao Yanni		CHN-Y	9.1.91	170/60	3kSt	10:02.76	10:16.99- 06
Zheng Rongna		CHN	28.3.87	161/50	20kW	1:35:57	1:39:23- 06
Zheng Xingyuan		CHN-J	20.3.89	180/52	HJ	1.92i, 1.88	1.92- 05
* Zhou Chunxiu		CHN	15.11.78	163/44	10000	32:44.13	31:09.03- 05
HMar 69:58+			70:19+- 05		Mar	2:20:38	2:19:51- 06
Zhou Yang		CHN-J	16.5.88	174/63	PV	4.40	4.30- 06
* Zhu Xiaolin		CHN	20.2.84	166/50	5000	15:26.72	15:22.35- 05
10000 32:27.38			32:39.60- 03		Mar	2:26:08	2:23:57- 02
Zhu Yanmei		CHN	16.10.86	174/53	3kSt	9:32.36	10:01.93- 06
Zhu Ying		CHN	15.12.87	176/70	JT	55.17	
Zhu Yingying		CHN-J	18.8.88		Mar	2:28:47	2:32:44- 06
Zhukovskaya	Oksana	RUS	24.9.84		LJ	6.77	6.44- 06
Zhuravlyeva	Anastasiya	UZB	9.10.81	170/60	TJ	13.94	14.55- 05
Zimmer	Sabine	GER	6.2.81	165/48	20kW	1:30:12 (13?)	1:27:56- 04
Zimmer	Vivian	GER	22.7.87	179/69	JT	58.68	60.14- 04
Zinurova	Yevgeniya	RUS	16.11.82		800	2:00.93	2:02.2 - 06
Zolotova	Yevgeniya	RUS	28.4.83	166/59	800	2:01.67i, 2:02.34	2:00.10- 06
Zolotukhina	Nataliya	UKR	4.1.85	180/77	HT	69.52	69.73- 04
Zongo	Amy	FRA	4.10.80	163/49	TJ	13.78	14.01- 06
Zozulya	Vira	UKR	31.8.70	166/56	20kW	1:30:02	1:28:19- 03
Zubkovska	Oksana	UKR	15.7.81	175/63	LJ	6.71	6.60- 06
Züblin	Linda	SUI	21.3.86	171/63	Hep	5995	5764- 06
Zunda	Ieva	LAT	20.7.78	164/54	400H	57.10	55.59- 04
Zuyenko	Lyudmila	RUS	6.9.83		200	23.06	23.28i- 06, 23.63- 01
^ Zvereva	Ellina	BLR	16.11.60	186/96	DT	60.20	71.58- 88
* Zykina	Olesya	RUS	7.10.80	170/60	200	23.00	22.55- 05, 22.3- 99
					400	50.81	50.15- 01

2008 World Indoor Lists - continued from p. 606 – **Women's Pentathlon**

4655	Austra	Skujyte	LTU	12.8.79	5	WI	Valencia	7 Mar
	8.84	1.81	17.00	6.22	2:21.23			
4641	Lilli	Schwarzkopf	GER	28.8.83	1	NC	Frankfurt-am-Main	27 Jan
	8.55	1.81	14.83	6.24	2:16 59			
4632	Denisa	Scerbová	CZE	21.8.86	1	v3N	Sheffield	3 Feb
	8.20	1.78	12.12	6.59	2:15.19			
4617	Olga	Kurban	RUS	16.12.87	2	NC	Sankt-Peterburg	3 Feb
	8.41	1.83	13.42	6.43	2:19.97			
4566	Claudia	Tonn	GER	18.4.81	2	NC	Frankfurt-am-Main	27 Jan
	8.78	1.78	12.86	6.43	2:10.71			
4537	Kamila	Chudzik	POL	12.9.86	2	NC	Spala	16 Feb
	8.45	1.69	15.28	6.40	2:20.85			
4523	Sonja	Kesselschläger	GER	20.1.78	3	NC	Frankfurt-am-Main	27 Jan
	8.53	1.78	14.94	6.09	2:19.85			
4522	Marina	Goncharova	RUS	26.4.86	3	NC	Sankt-Peterburg	3 Feb
	8.56	1.74	13.35	6.38	2:14.85			
4496	Jacquelyn	Johnson	USA	8.9.84	1	NCAA	Fayetteville	15 Mar
	8.23	1.78	11.86	6.16	2:13.45			
4471	Yana	Panteleyeva	RUS	16.6.88	4	NC	Sankt-Peterburg	3 Feb
	8.61	1.83	13.56	6.27	2:24.50			
4458	Yelena	Prokhorova	RUS	16.4.78	5	NC	Sankt-Peterburg	3 Feb
	8.77	1.74	14.00	6.28	2:16.96			
4428	Jessica	Samuelsson	SWE	14.3.85	1	NC	Göteborg	16 Mar
	8.62	1.70	14.51	6.15	2:17.49			
4423	Yvonne	Wisse	NED	6.6.82	3	NC	Gent	3 Feb
	8.45	1.74	11.64	6.19	2:11.21			

4380	Christine	Schulz	GER	30.1.84	17 Feb
4379	Oksana	Kuzminok	UKR	7.8.83	26 Jan
4378	Julia	Machtig	GER	1.1.86	27 Jan
4377	Viktoria	Dobrinska	UKR	18.1.80	23 Feb
4370	Olga	Levenkova	RUS	11.1.84	3 Feb
4366	Bettie	Wade	USA	11.9.86	15 Mar
4363	Anna	Nikitenko	RUS	30.8.84	10 Jan
4355	Kaie	Kand	EST	31.3.84	16 Feb
4355	Blandine	Maissonier	FRA	3.1.86	1 Mar
4348	Diana	Pickler	USA	9.12.83	9 Mar
4334	Simone	Oberer	SUI	8.4.80	17 Feb
4332	Lyudmila	Kovalyova	UKR	18.3.75	26 Jan
4325	Tatyana	Vtorushina	RUS	17.11.85	6 Jan
4321	Jana	Koresová	CZE	8.4.81	9 Feb
4296	Julie	Pickler	USA	9.12.83	9 Mar
4281	Yulia	Ignatkina	RUS	23.9.82	3 Feb
4263	Bregje	Crolla	NED	31.1.86	3 Feb
4256	Aleksandra	Butvina	RUS	14.2.86	23 Feb
4256	Shevell	Quinley	USA	26.6.87	15 Mar

3000 METRES WALK

12:10.23	Elisa	Rigaudo	ITA	17.6.80	1	NC	Genova	23 Feb
12:12.57	Melanie	Seeger	GER	8.1.77	1	NC	Sindelfingen	23 Feb
12:24.06	Sylwia	Korzeniowska	POL	25.4.80	1	NC	Bordeaux	16 Feb

WORLD INDOOR LISTS 2008 – MEN

60 METRES

! In late 2007, # Oversized track (over 200m)

6.51	Olusoji	Fasuba	NGR	9.7.84	1		Valencia	9 Feb
6.51	Richard	Thompson	TRI	7.6.85	1h2	NCAA	Fayetteville	14 Mar
6.54!	Samuel	Francis	QAT	27.3.87	1	AsiG	Macau	30 Oct
6.54	Mike	Rodgers	USA	24.4.85	1	NC	Boston (R)	24 Feb
6.54	Dwain	Chambers	GBR	5.4.78	2=	WI	Valencia	7 Mar
6.54	Kim	Collins	SKN	5.4.76	2=	WI	Valencia	7 Mar
6.54	Trindon	Holliday	USA	27.4.86	2	NCAA	Fayetteville	15 Mar
6.55	Simone	Collio	ITA	27.12.79	2		Valencia	9 Feb
6.55	Jaysuma	Saidy Ndure	NOR	1.7.84	1		Gent	24 Feb
6.56!	Yahya Saed	Al-Kahes	KSA	19.2.86	2	AsiG	Macau	30 Oct
6.56	Leroy	Dixon	USA	20.6.83	2	NC	Boston (R)	24 Feb
6.57	Craig	Pickering	GBR	16.10.86	1	v4N	Glasgow	26 Jan
6.57	Simeon	Williamson	GBR	16.1.86	2	GP	Birmingham	16 Feb
6.57	Rae	Edwards	USA	7.5.81	3	NC	Boston (R)	24 Feb
6.57	Lukasz	Chyla	POL	31.3.81	1		Chemnitz	29 Feb
6.58		Wen Yongyi	CHN	3.1.87	1		Shanghai	26 Jan
6.58	C.J.	Spiller	USA	15.8.87	1		Chapel Hill	2 Feb
6.58	Daniel	Bailey	ANT	9.9.86	1		Houston	2 Feb
6.58	Vicente Lenilson	de Lima	BRA	4.6.77	1h1		Paris (B)	22 Feb

6.59	Leonard	Scott	USA	19.1.80	1 Feb
6.59	Ryan	Scott	GBR	20.2.87	13 Feb
6.59	Harry	Aikines-Aryeetey	GBR	29.8.88	26 Feb
6.59	Rubin	Williams	USA	9.7.83	14 Mar
6.60	Maksim	Lynsha	BLR	6.4.85	15 Feb
6.60A	Emanuel	Parris	CAN	7.10.82	16 Feb
6.60	Marius	Broening	GER	24.10.83	23 Feb
6.60	Ivory	Williams	USA	2.5.85	24 Feb
6.60	DaBryan	Blanton	USA	3.7.84	24 Feb
6.60	Andrey	Yepishin	RUS	10.6.81	7 Mar
6.60	Travis	Padgett	USA	13.12.86	15 Mar
6.61	Rikki	Fifton	GBR	17.6.85	16 Feb
6.61	Jason	Heard	USA	11.7.83	24 Feb
6.61	Greg	Bolden	USA	30.6.84	24 Feb
6.61	Adam	Harris	USA	21.7.87	2 Mar
6.62	four men				

200 METRES

20.19	Wallace	Spearmon	USA	24.12.84	1	Tyson	Fayetteville	15 Feb
20.36	Rubin	Williams	USA	9.7.83	1r2	NCAA	Fayetteville	15 Mar
20.50	Charles	Clark	USA	10.8.87	2r2	NCAA	Fayetteville	15 Mar
20.66	Arman	Dixon	USA	25.6.86	1		Boston (Allston)	1 Mar
20.67	J-Mee	Samuels	USA	20.5.87	1r1	NCAA	Fayetteville	15 Mar

20.70	Walter	Dix	USA	31.1.86	16 Feb
20.72	Evander	Wells	USA	7.12.87	14 Mar
20.73	Willie	Perry	USA	16.5.87	15 Mar
20.76	Chris	Dykes	USA	15.8.87	14 Mar
20.79	Michael	Garvin	USA	29.9.86	14 Mar
20.80	Jordan	Vaden	USA	15.9.78	15 Feb
20.82	LaShawn	Merritt	USA	27.6.86	8 Mar
20.83	Antonio	Sales	USA-J	26.1.89	2 Mar

300 Metres: 32.53 Tyler Christopher CAN 3.10.83 1 Winnipeg 2 Feb

400 METRES

45.67	Tyler	Christopher	CAN	3.10.83	1	WI	Valencia	9 Mar
45.94	Justin	Gaymon	USA	13.12.86	1	SEC	Fayetteville	2 Mar
46.02	Chris	Lloyd	DMA	10.10.80	2	GP	Birmingham	16 Feb
46.02	Andretti	Bain	BAH	1.12.85	1h2	NCAA	Fayetteville	14 Mar

46.04	Calvin	Smith	USA	10.12.87	2 Mar
46.04	Johan	Wissman	SWE	2.12.82	9 Mar
46.08!		Wang Liangyu	CHN	9.8.84	31 Oct
46.22	Maksim	Dyldin	RUS	15.5.87	8 Feb
46.26	Chris	Brown	BAH	15.10.78	9 Mar
46.27	Joel	Phillip	GRN	12.9.87	15 Mar
45.81#	Greg	Nixon	USA	12.9.81	9 Feb
46.13#	Miles	Smith	USA	24.9.84	16 Feb

800 METRES

1:44.81	Abubaker	Kaki Khamis	SUD-J	21.6.89	1	WI	Valencia	9 Mar
1:44.91	Mbulaeni	Mulaudzi	RSA	8.9.80	2	WI	Valencia	9 Mar
1:45.26	Youssef Saad	Kamel	BRN	29.3.83	3	WI	Valencia	9 Mar
1:45.58	Yuriy	Borzakovskiy	RUS	12.4.81	1	Spark	Stuttgart	2 Feb
1:45.72	Dmitrijs	Milkevics	LAT	6.12.81	4		Valencia	9 Jun
1:45.76	Dmitrij	Bogdanov	RUS	11.4.79	5	WI	Valencia	9 Mar
1:46.33	Richard	Kiplagat	KEN	3.7.87	1	GP	Birmingham	16 Feb
1:46.36	Yuriy	Koldin	RUS	1.11.83	1r2	NC	Moskva	8 Feb
1:46.38	Wilfred	Bungei	KEN	24.7.80	2	Spark	Stuttgart	2 Feb
1:46.48	Nick	Symmonds	USA	30.12.83	6	WI	Valencia	9 Mar
1:46.77#	Elias	Koech	KEN	4.6.85	1		Ames	16 Feb
1:46.95	Khadevis	Robinson	USA	19.7.76	1	NC	Boston (R)	24 Feb

1:47.06	Jozef	Repcík	SVK	3.8.86	16 Feb
1:47.20	Abraham	Chepkirwok	UGA	18.11.88	2 Feb
1:47.28#	Shaun	Smith	JAM	19.4.83	16 Feb
1:47.32	Damien	Moss	GBR	2.9.82	16 Feb
1:47.32	Eugenio	Barrios	ESP	3.11.76	16 Feb
1:47.33#	Adam	Mach	USA	1.1.87	8 Mar
1:47.37	Jakub	Holusa	CZE	20.2.88	29 Jan
1:47.42	Bartosz	Nowicki	POL	26.2.84	10 Feb
1:47.49	Sebastian	Keiner	GER-J	22.8.89	6 Jan
1:47.64	Richard	Hill	GBR	12.2.86	29 Jan

1000 METRES

2:15.77	Abubaker	Kaki Khamis	SUD-J	21.6.89	1	GE Galen	Stockholm	21 Feb
2:16.96	Richard	Kiplagat	KEN	3.7.87	2	GE Galen	Stockholm	21 Feb
2:17.06	Belal	Mansoor Ali	BRN	17.10.83	2		Gent	24 Feb
2:17.78	Abdesslam	Kennouche	ALG	7.10.80	3	GE Galen	Stockholm	21 Feb
2:18.13	Suleiman	Simotwo	KEN	21.4.80	3		Gent	24 Feb
2:18.48	Johan	Cronje	RSA	13.4.82	4	GE Galen	Stockholm	21 Feb

2:18.54	Geoffrey	Rono Kipkoech	KEN	21.4.87	24 Feb
2:18.58	Christian	Obrist	ITA	20.11.80	21 Feb
2:18.84	James	McIlroy	GBR	30.12.76	24 Feb

1500 METRES

3:34.80	Daniel Kipchirchir	Komen	KEN	27.11.84	1		Athína (P)	13 Feb
3:35.23	Bernard	Lagat	USA	12.12.74	1	GP	Birmingham	16 Feb
3:35.46	Suleiman	Simotwo	KEN	21.4.80	2		Athína (P)	13 Feb
3:35.51	Deresse	Mekonnen	ETH	20.10.87	3		Athína (P)	13 Feb
3:36.38	Belal	Mansoor Ali	BRN	17.10.83	4		Athína (P)	13 Feb
3:36.63	Mekonnen	Gebremedhin	ETH	11.10.88	1		Valencia	9 Feb
3:36.74	Juan Carlos	Higuero	ESP	3.8.78	5		Athína (P)	13 Feb
3:37.31	Rashid	Ramzi	BRN	17.7.80	3h3	WI	Valencia	7 Mar
3:38.10	Youssef	Baba	MAR	7.8.79	6		Athína (P)	13 Feb
3:38.13	Arturo	Casado	ESP	26.1.83	4		Valencia	9 Feb
3:38.47	Carsten	Schlangen	GER	31.12.80	1	NC	Sindelfingen	24 Feb
3:38.68	Shadrack	Korir	KEN	14.12.78	3	GP	Birmingham	16 Feb
3:38.82	Mulugeta	Wondimu	ETH	28.2.85	1		Leipzig	17 Feb
3:38.84	Rui	Silva	POR	3.8.77	4	GP	Birmingham	16 Feb

3:39.28	Johan	Cronje	RSA	13.4.82	16 Feb
3:39.42	Isaac	Sang	KEN	24.8.78	10 Feb
3:39.42	Michael	East	GBR	20.1.78	16 Feb
3:39.48	Diego	Ruiz	ESP	5.2.82	9 Feb
3:39.51	Reyes	Estévez	ESP	2.8.76	16 Feb
3:39.56	Brimin	Kipruto	KEN	31.7.85	16 Feb
3:39.60	Christoph	Lohse	GER	26.11.83	24 Feb
3:39.73	James	McIlroy	GBR	30.12.76	16 Feb
3:39.81	Cornelius	Ndiwa	KEN	.88	16 Feb
3:39.83	Mounir	Yemmouni	FRA	12.10.83	3 Feb
3:39.86	Guillaume	Éraud	FRA	1.7.81	10 Feb
3:40.01	Geoffrey	Rono	KEN	21.4.87	22 Feb
3:40.28	Youssef	Saad Kamel	BRN	29.3.83	9 Feb
3:40.47	Stefan	Eberhardt	GER	10.10.88	10 Feb
3:40.63	Sergio	Sánchez	ESP	1.10.82	9 Feb
3:40.66	Nick	Willis	NZL	25.4.83	7 Mar

1 MILE

3:55.93	Nick	Willis	NZL	25.4.83	1	Tyson	Fayetteville	15 Feb
3:56.00#	Steve	Sherer	USA	5.5.81	1		Seattle	2 Feb

3:57.50	Kevin	Sullivan	CAN	20.3.74	15 Feb
3:57.51	Bernard	Lagat	USA	12.12.74	1 Feb
3:57.81	Steve	Sherer	USA	5.5.81	15 Feb
3:57.82	Robert	Myers	USA	5.8.80	15 Feb
3:57.90	Craig	Mottram	AUS	18.6.80	1 Feb
3:58.34	Boaz	Lalang	KEN		15 Feb

2000 Metres: 5:00.61+ Kenenisa Bekele ETH 13.6.82 1 in 2M Birmingham 16 Feb

3000 METRES

7:31.09	Tariku	Bekele	ETH	21.1.87	1	Spark	Stuttgart	2 Feb
7:34.50	Craig	Mottram	AUS	18.6.80	1	BIG	Boston (R)	26 Jan
7:34.6+	Kenenisa	Bekele	ETH	13.6.82	1	in 2M	Birmingham	16 Feb
7:34.65	Bernard	Lagat	USA	12.12.74	1	GE Galen	Stockholm	21 Feb
7:34.8+	Paul Kipsiele	Koech	KEN	10.11.81	2	in 2M	Birmingham	16 Feb
7:36.70	Edwin	Soi	KEN	3.3.86	2		Valencia	9 Feb
7:38.03	Abreham	Cherkos Feleke	ETH-J	23.9.89	2	Spark	Stuttgart	2 Feb
7:38.11	Shadrack	Korir	KEN	14.12.78	3	Spark	Stuttgart	2 Feb
7:38.58	Daniel Kipchirchir	Komen	KEN	27.11.84	4		Valencia	9 Feb
7:38.63	Abraham	Chebii	KEN	23.12.79	3	GE Galen	Stockholm	21 Feb
7:40.92	Bekane	Daba	ETH	29.7.88	4	Spark	Stuttgart	2 Feb
7:41.81	Markos	Geneti	ETH	30.5.84	2	BIG	Boston (R)	26 Jan
7:42.12	Gari	Roba	ETH	12.4.82	6		Valencia	9 Feb
7:43.86	Mohamed-Khaled	Belabbas	FRA	4.7.81	1		Gent	24 Feb
7:45.10	Andrew	Baddeley	GBR	20.6.82	3	BIG	Boston (R)	26 Jan
7:45.39	Brimin	Kipruto	KEN	31.7.85	8		Valencia	9 Feb
7:45.61	Rui	Silva	POR	3.8.77	9		Valencia	9 Feb
7:46.0+	Mohamed	Farah	GBR	23.3.83	5	in 2M	Birmingham	16 Feb
7:46.09	Bikila	Demma Daba	ETH-J	18.7.89	5	GE Galen	Stockholm	21 Feb
7:46.13	Ali	Maataoui	MAR	11.12.80	10		Valencia	9 Feb
7:46.39	Nahom	Mesfin Tariku	ETH-J	3.6.89	3		Gent	24 Feb
7:47.09	Isaac	Sang	KEN	24.8.78	4		Gent	24 Feb

7:47.81	Jonas	Cheruiyot	KEN	11.1.84	8 Feb
7:48.94	Adrian	Blincoe	NZL	4.11.79	26 Jan
7:49.31	Sultan	Khamis Zaman	QAT	23.7.85	16 Feb
7:49.47	Surendra	Kumar Singh	IND	1.10.78	16 Feb
7:50.37#	David	McNeill	AUS	6.10.86	16 Feb

2 MILES

8:04.35	Kenenisa	Bekele	ETH	13.6.82	1	GP	Birmingham	16 Feb
8:06.48	Paul	Koech Kipsiele	KEN	10.11.81	2	GP	Birmingham	16 Feb
8:13.28	Abraham	Chebii	KEN	23.12.79	3	GP	Birmingham	16 Feb
8:16.49	Markos	Geneti	ETH	30.5.84	4	GP	Birmingham	16 Feb

8:18.92	Bekane	Daba	ETH	29.7.88	5	GP	Birmingham	16 Feb
8:20.95	Mohamed	Farah	GBR	23.3.83	6	GP	Birmingham	16 Feb

5000 Metres: 13:32.01 Alistair Cragg IRL 13.6.80 1 Tyson Fayetteville 15 Feb

60 METRES HURDLES

7.33	Dayron	Robles	CUB	19.11.86	1		Düsseldorf	8 Feb
7.44	Yevgeniy	Borisov	RUS	7.3.84	1	EICp	Moskva	16 Feb
7.46		Liu Xiang	CHN	13.7.83	1	WI	Valencia	8 Mar
7.47	David	Oliver	USA	24.4.82	1	NC	Boston (R)	24 Feb
7.50	Anwar	Moore	USA	5.3.79	1h2	NC	Boston (R)	24 Feb
7.52	Allan	Scott	GBR	27.12.82	1		Glasgow	12 Jan
7.52	Jackson	Quiñónez	ESP	12.6.80	1	NC	Valencia	24 Feb
7.53	Antwon	Hicks	USA	12.3.83	1	Mill	New York	1 Feb
7.53	Allen	Johnson	USA	29.3.77	2	NC	Boston (R)	24 Feb
7.53	Andrew	Brunson	USA	4.4.86	1	NCAA	Fayetteville	14 Mar
7.53	Jason	Richardson	USA	4.4.86	2	NCAA	Fayetteville	14 Mar
7.54	Thomas	Blaschek	GER	5.4.81	2	Spark	Stuttgart	2 Feb
7.54	Joel	Brown	USA	31.1.80	3	NC	Boston (R)	24 Feb
7.58	Dexter	Faulk	USA	14.4.80	5	NC	Boston (R)	24 Feb
7.58	Ronald	Forbes	CAY	5.4.85	3	NCAA	Fayetteville	14 Mar
7.59	Igor	Peremota	RUS	14.1.81	1		Moskva	27 Jan
7.60	Yoel	Hernández	CUB	12.12.77	4		Karlsruhe	10 Feb
7.60	Stanislav	Olijar	LAT	22.3.79	5		Karlsruhe	10 Feb
7.61	Maurice	Wignall	JAM	17.4.76	2h5	WI	Valencia	8 Mar
7.62	Maksim	Lynsha	BLR	6.4.85	1		Mogilyov	16 Feb
7.63	Petr	Svoboda	CZE	10.10.84	1h1		Luxembourg	19 Jan
7.63	Felipe	Vivancos	ESP	16.6.80	2		Zaragoza	2 Feb

7.64	Damjan	Zlatnar	SLO	16.12.77	29 Jan
7.64	Artur	Noga	POL	2.5.88	10 Feb
7.65	Aries	Merritt	USA	24.7.85	26 Jan
7.65	Ryan	Brathwaite	BAR	6.6.88	16 Feb
7.65	Willi	Mathiszik	GER	17.6.84	17 Feb
7.65	Stanislav	Sajdok	CZE	22.7.83	23 Feb
7.65	Paulo	Villar	COL	28.7.78	26 Feb
7.65		Shi Dongpeng	CHN	6.1.84	8 Mar
7.66	Dominik	Bochenek	POL	14.5.87	10 Feb
7.66	Ty	Akins	USA	6.1.86	14 Mar
7.67	Jangy	Addy	USA	2.3.85	8 Feb
7.67	Robert	Kronberg	SWE	15.8.76	9 Feb
7.68	Ladji	Doucouré	FRA	28.3.83	19 Jan
7.68	Erik	Balnuweit	GER	21.9.88	24 Feb
7.68	Shawon	Harris	USA	1.7.85	14 Mar
7.69	Descosma	Wright	JAM	1.9.82	8 Feb
7.69	Samuel	Coco-Viloin	FRA	19.10.87	22 Feb
7.69	Adrien	Deghelt	BEL	10.5.85	8 Mar
7.69	Ryan	Fontenot	USA	4.5.86	14 Mar

HIGH JUMP

2.38	Yaroslav	Rybakov	RUS	22.11.80	1	NC	Moskva	10 Feb
2.37	Andrey	Silnov	RUS	9.9.84	1		Arnstadt	2 Feb
2.37	Stefan	Holm	SWE	25.5.76	1	NC	Malmö	24 Feb
2.36	Ivan	Ukhov	RUS	29.3.86	1		Hustopece	19 Jan
2.36	Andrey	Tereshin	RUS	15.12.82	2	NC	Moskva	10 Feb
2.35	Linus	Thornblad	SWE	6.3.85	2	NC	Malmö	24 Feb
2.33	Aleksey	Dmitrik	RUS	12.4.84	5	NC	Moskva	10 Feb
2.32	Jesse	Williams	USA	27.12.83	2		Banská Bystrica	5 Feb
2.32	Kyriakos	Ioannou	CYP	26.7.84	1		Novi Sad	7 Feb
2.31	Dusty	Jonas	USA	19.4.86	1	NCAA	Fayetteville	15 Mar
2.30	Eike	Onnen	GER	3.8.82	1		Wuppertal	18 Jan
2.30	Michael	Mason	CAN	30.9.86	1		Seattle	19 Jan
2.30	Dmytro	Demyanyuk	UKR	30.6.83	1		Zaporozhye	27 Jan
2.30	Victor	Moya	CUB	24.10.82	4		Banská Bystrica	5 Feb
2.30	Filippo	Campioli	ITA	21.2.82	2		Novi Sad	7 Feb
2.30	Dragutin	Topic	SRB	12.3.71	3		Novi Sad	7 Feb
2.30	Samson	Oni	GBR	25.6.81	1	NC	Sheffield	9 Feb
2.30	Aleksandr	Shustov	RUS	13.8.84	6	NC	Moskva	10 Feb
2.30	Andra	Manson	USA	30.4.84	1	NC	Boston (R)	23 Feb
2.30	Jaroslav	Bábá	CZE	2.9.84	1	NC	Praha	24 Feb
2.29	Scott	Sellers	USA	16.8.86	1	Big 12	Lincoln	1 Mar
2.28	Eduard	Malchenko	RUS	24.11.86	1		Moskva	19 Jan
2.28	Donald	Thomas	BAH	1.7.84	8		Arnstadt	2 Feb
2.28	Vyacheslav	Voronin	RUS	5.4.74	6		Banská Bystrica	5 Feb

2.27	Svatoslav	Ton	CZE	20.10.78	19 Jan
2.27	Peter	Horák	SVK	7.12.83	19 Jan
2.27	Rozle	Prezelj	SLO	26.9.79	19 Jan
2.27	Konstadínos	Baniótis	GRE	6.11.86	26 Jan
2.27	Yuriy	Krymarenko	UKR	11.8.83	27 Jan
2.27	Jamie	Nieto	USA	2.11.76	12 Feb
2.27	Javier	Bermejo	ESP	23.12.78	13 Feb
2.27	Andriy	Sokolovskyy	UKR	16.7.78	17 Feb
2.27	Grzegorz	Sposob	POL	12.2.76	17 Feb
2.27	Yevgeniy	Shishakov	RUS	27.2.88	2 Mar
2.27	Ilya	Krivetskiy	RUS	24.8.86	2 Mar
2.26	Pavel	Fomenko	RUS	29.6.76	19 Jan
2.26	Joe	Kindred	USA	15.9.87	26 Jan
2.26	Raul	Spank	GER	13.7.88	3 Feb
2.26	Michal	Bieniek	POL	17.5.84	9 Feb
2.25	eleven men				

POLE VAULT

5.90	Yevgeniy	Lukyanenko	RUS	23.1.85	1	WI	Valencia	9 Mar
5.85	Brad	Walker	USA	21.6.81	2	WI	Valencia	9 Mar
5.81	Igor	Pavlov	RUS	18.7.79	2	Spark	Stuttgart	2 Feb
5.81	Maksym	Mazuryk	UKR	2.4.83	1	Mast	Donetsk	16 Feb
5.81	Tim	Lobinger	GER	3.9.72	2	GE Galen	Stockholm	21 Feb
5.80A	Derek	Miles	USA	28.9.72	1		Reno	4 Jan
5.80	Jérôme	Clavier	FRA	3.5.83	1		Limoges	2 Feb
5.80	Danny	Ecker	GER	21.7.77	2	NC	Sindelfingen	23 Feb
5.80	Steve	Hooker	AUS	16.7.82	3	WI	Valencia	9 Mar
5.76	Fabian	Schulze	GER	7.3.84	3	Spark	Stuttgart	2 Feb
5.76	Sergey	Kucheryanu	RUS	30.6.85	1		Paris (B)	22 Feb
5.75	Pavel	Gerasimov	RUS	29.5.79	3		Moskva	27 Jan
5.75	Alexander	Straub	GER	14.10.83	1	GP	Birmingham	16 Feb
5.75	Tobias	Scherbarth	GER	17.8.85	2		Chemnitz	29 Feb
5.71	Giovanni	Lanaro	MEX	27.9.81	1		Azusa	16 Feb
5.71	Alhaji	Jeng	SWE	13.12.81	1		Donetsk	16 Feb
5.71	Leonid	Kivalov	RUS	1.4.88	3	GE Galen	Stockholm	21 Feb
5.71	Steven	Lewis	GBR	20.5.86	1		Tsaotun	14 Mar
5.71	Jeremy	Scott	USA	1.5.81	1		Jonesboro	13 Mar
5.70A	Toby	Stevenson	USA	19.11.76	2		Reno	4 Jan
5.70	Björn	Otto	GER	16.10.77	2		Dormagen	25 Jan
5.70	Dmitriy	Starodubstev	RUS	3.1.86	5		Moskva	27 Jan
5.70	Tommy	Skipper	USA	19.9.84	1	Mill	New York	1 Feb
5.70	Jeff	Hartwig	USA	25.9.67	5	Spark	Stuttgart	2 Feb
5.70	Denys	Yurchenko	UKR	27.1.78	1		Potsdam	9 Feb
5.70	Romain	Mesnil	FRA	13.7.77	1	NC	Bordeaux	17 Feb
5.70	Renaud	Lavillenie	FRA	18.9.86	3		Paris (B)	22 Feb

5.68	Raphael	Holzdeppe	GER-J	28.9.89	1 Mar
5.65	Lars	Börgeling	GER	16.4.79	29 Jan
5.65	Daichi	Sawano	JPN	16.9.80	8 Mar
5.65	Rory	Quiller	USA	17.4.84	8 Mar
5.62		Liu Feiliang	CHN	27.3.85	27 Jan
5.61	Russ	Buller	USA	10.9.78	12 Jan
5.61	Malte	Mohr	GER	24.7.86	8 Feb
5.61	Spas	Bukhalov	BUL	14.11.80	16 Feb
5.61	Fabio	Gomes da Silva	BRA	4.8.83	16 Feb
5.61	Graeme	Hoste	USA	1.5.86	1 Mar
5.60	Pavel	Prokopenko	RUS	24.8.87	19 Jan
5.60	Damiel	Dossévi	FRA	3.2.83	8 Feb
5.60	Dmitriy	Kuptsov	RUS	9.11.82	9 Feb
5.60	Adam	Ptácek	CZE	8.10.80	13 Feb
5.60	Ray	Scotten	USA	20.5.83	16 Feb
5.60	Jacob	Pauli	USA	15.6.79	23 Feb

LONG JUMP

8.42	Irving	Saladino	PAN	23.1.83	1		Athína (P)	13 Feb
8.24	Mohamed	Al Khuwailidi	KSA	19.6.81	1	AsiC	Doha	16 Feb
8.18	Chris	Tomlinson	GBR	15.9.81	1	Spark	Stuttgart	2 Feb
8.13	Brian	Johnson	USA	25.3.80	1		Baton Rouge	1 Feb
8.12	Norris	Frederick	USA	17.2.86	1		Seattle	29 Feb
8.12	Reindell	Cole	USA	16.2.88	1	NCAA	Fayetteville	14 Mar
8.10	Wilfredo	Martínez	CUB	9.1.85	1	NC	Valencia	23 Feb
8.08	Khotso	Mokoena	RSA	6.3.85	1	WI	Valencia	8 Mar
8.03	Peter	Rapp	GER	29.5.83	1		Luxembourg	19 Jan
8.03	Nikolay	Atanasov	BUL	11.12.74	1		Plovdiv	20 Jan
8.03	Ruslan	Gataullin	RUS	1.12.79	1		Samara	2 Feb
8.03	Rogerio	Bispo	BRA	16.11.85	2		Samara	2 Feb
8.02	Oleksandr	Soldatkin	UKR	26.4.86	1		Donetsk	18 Jan
8.02	Volodomyr	Zyuskov	UKR	29.8.81	1		Moskva	27 Jan
8.02	Nelson	Évora	POR	20.4.84	1		Espinho	2 Feb
8.00	Kafétien	Gomis	FRA	23.3.80	1	NC	Bordeaux	17 Feb

7.98	Loúis	Tsátoumas	GRE	12.2.82	13 Feb
7.98	Marcin	Starzak	POL	20.10.85	16 Feb
7.98	Salim	Sdiri	FRA	26.10.78	17 Feb
7.97	Ngonidzashe	Makusha	ZIM	11.3.87	14 Mar
7.96	Andriy	Makarchev	UKR	15.4.85	21 Jan
7.95!	Jared	Randle	USA	14.11.87	7 Dec
7.95	Dmytro	Bilotserkivskyy	UKR	25.3.85	26 Jan
7.95	Danut	Simion	ROU	25.1.83	26 Jan
7.95	Fabrizio	Donato	ITA	14.8.76	2 Feb
7.95	Héctor	Fuentes	CUB	19.5.88	29 Feb
7.94	Astérios	Noúsios	GRE	25.2.79	2 Feb

TRIPLE JUMP

17.75	Phillips	Idowu	GBR	30.12.78	1	WI	Valencia	9 Mar
17.47	David	Giralt	CUB	26.8.84	2	WI	Valencia	9 Mar
17.33	Nelson	Évora	POR	20.4.84	1		Karlsruhe	10 Feb
17.27	Randy	Lewis	GRN	14.10.80	2		Karlsruhe	10 Feb
17.27	Fabrizio	Donato	ITA	14.8.76	4	WI	Valencia	9 Mar
17.14	Dmitrij	Valukevic	SVK	31.5.81	5	WI	Valencia	9 Mar
17.13	Aarik	Wilson	USA	25.10.82	Q	WI	Valencia	7 Mar
17.13	Osniel	Tosca	CUB	30.6.84	6	WI	Valencia	9 Mar
17.11	Yoandris	Betanzos	CUB	15.2.82	3		Karlsruhe	10 Feb
17.02	Yevgeniy	Plotnir	RUS	26.6.77	1		Moskva	12 Jan
16.99	Alexis	Copello	CUB	12.8.85	5		Karlsruhe	10 Feb

16.99	Mykola	Savolaynen	UKR	25.3.80	2		Gent	24 Feb
16.94	Teddy	Tamgho	FRA-J	15.6.89	1	NC	Bordeaux	16 Feb
16.93	Danil	Burkenya	RUS	20.7.78	1	NC	Moskva	9 Feb
16.92	Fabrizio	Schembri	ITA	27.1.81	1		Saronno	1 Feb
16.89	Kenta	Bell	USA	16.3.77	1		Gainesville	25 Jan
16.86	Lyukman	Adams	RUS	12.6.88	2		Moskva	12 Jan
16.85	Vladimir	Letnicov	MDA	7.10.81	1	NC	Chisinau	3 Feb
16.84		Li Yanxi	CHN	26.6.84	1		Shanghai	26 Jan
16.83	Viktor	Kuznetsov	UKR	14.7.86	1	NC	Sumy	24 Feb
16.82	Momchil	Karailiev	BUL	21.5.82	1	NC	Sofia	2 Feb
16.82	Tarik	Bougtaïb	MAR	30.4.81	6		Gent	24 Feb
16.81	Aleksandr	Petrenko	RUS	8.2.83	2		Moskva	20 Jan
16.81	Viktor	Yastrebov	UKR	13.1.82	2	NC	Sumy	24 Feb

16.73	Leevan	Sands	BAH	16.1.81	16 Feb	16.61	Dimítrios	Tsiámis	GRE	12.1.82	2 Feb
16.73	Paolo	Camossi	ITA	6.1.74	24 Feb	16.61	Pawel	Kruhlik	POL	25.8.83	23 Feb
16.72	Nathan	Douglas	GBR	4.12.82	10 Feb	16.61	Dmitriy	Kolosov	RUS	8.6.86	2 Mar
16.69	Karl	Taillepierre	FRA	13.8.76	16 Feb	16.60	Viktor	Gushchinskiy	RUS	12.8.78	20 Jan
16.67	Brandon	Roulhac	USA	13.12.83	25 Jan	16.60	Sherif	El-Sherif	UKR-J	2.1.89	24 Feb
16.67	Andrés	Capellán	ESP	10.6.85	7 Mar	16.59	Jacek	Kazimierski	POL	2.7.74	2 Feb
16.64	Roman	Valiyev	KAZ	27.3.84	27 Jan	16.59	Rafeeq	Curry	USA	10.8.83	23 Feb

SHOT

22.40	Adam	Nelson	USA	7.7.75	1	Tyson	Fayetteville	15 Feb
22.18	Christian	Cantwell	USA	30.9.80	1		Warrensburg	22 Feb
21.73	Ryan	Whiting	USA	24.11.86	1	NCAA	Fayetteville	14 Mar
21.49	Reese	Hoffa	USA	8.10.77	Q	WI	Valencia	7 Mar
21.29	Russ	Winger	USA	2.8.84	2	NCAA	Fayetteville	14 Mar
20.93	Tomasz	Majewski	POL	30.8.81	3	WI	Valencia	7 Mar
20.89	Rutger	Smith	NED	9.7.81	1	NC	Gent	16 Feb
20.88	Peter	Sack	USA	27.7.79	1		Leipzig	17 Feb
20.83	Scott	Martin	AUS	12.10.82	Q	WI	Valencia	7 Mar
20.82	Andrey	Mikhnevich	BLR	12.7.76	4	WI	Valencia	7 Mar
20.68	Miroslav	Vodovnik	SLO	11.9.77	1		Slovenska Bistrica	23 Feb
20.66	Garrett	Johnson	USA	24.5.84	1	NC	Sheffield	9 Feb
20.62	Dorian	Scott	JAM	1.2.82	Q	WI	Valencia	7 Mar
20.38	Daniel	Taylor	USA	112.5.82	4	Mill	New York	1 Feb
20.25	Mark	Edwards	GBR	2.12.74	1		Loughborough	3 Feb
20.24	Robert	Häggblom	FIN	9.8.82	1		Kuressaare	28 Feb
20.23	Hamza	Alic	BIH	20.1.79	1	Balk	Athína (P)	8 Feb
20.13	Milan	Haborák	SVK	11.1.73	1		Budapest	16 Feb
20.11	Pavel	Sofyin	RUS	4.9.81	1	NC	Moskva	8 Feb
20.08	Marco	Fortes	POR	26.9.82	2		Valencia	9 Feb
20.07	Yuriy	Bilonog	UKR	9.3.74	1	NC	Sumy	23 Feb
20.05	Chris	Figures	USA	8.10.81	1		Flagstaff	2 Feb

19.94	Steve	Manz	USA	19.9.81	24 Feb	19.75	Manuel	Martínez	ESP	7.12.74	7 Mar
19.91	Dylan	Armstrong	CAN	15.1.81	2 Feb	19.72	Yuriy	Belov	BLR	20.3.81	23 Feb
19.86	Carl	Myerscough	GBR	21.10.79	7 Mar	19.71	Maris	Urtans	EST	9.2.81	6 Feb
19.82	Mikulás	Konopka	SVK	23.1.79	12 Feb	19.64	Milan	Jotanovic	SRB	11.1.84	14 Mar
19.81	Ivan	Yushkov	RUS	15.1.81	8 Feb	19.60	Zack	Lloyd	USA	10.10.84	1 Mar
19.75	Andrey	Sinyakov	BLR	6.1.82	2 Feb	19.52!	Brian	Vickers	USA	14.1.85	1 Dec
						19.50	Borja	Vivas	ESP	26.5.84	2 Feb

35 LB WEIGHT

25.26	Libor	Charfreitag	SVK	11.9.77	1		Nampa	2 Feb
25.12	Kibwe	Johnson	USA	17.7.81	1	NC	Boston (R)	24 Feb
24.28	A.G.	Kruger	USA	18.2.79	1		Kent	12 Jan
23.30	James	Parker	USA	3.12.75	1		Seattle	16 Feb
23.29!	Jacob	Freeman	USA	5.11.80	1		New York	1 Dec
22.99	Arnaldo	Cueto	USA	5.5.81	1		Flagstaff	2 Feb
22.71	Yegor	Agafonov	RUS	7.2.83	1	NCAA	Fayetteville	15 Mar
22.42	Chris	Rohr	USA	28.12.85	2	Big 12	Lincoln	29 Feb
22.24	Jake	Dunkleberger	USA	6.10.84	2	NCAA	Fayetteville	15 Mar

22.08	Jérôme	Bortoluzzi	FRA	20.5.82	23 Feb	22.02	Jon	Pullum	USA	3.5.87	15 Mar
22.02	Walter	Henning	USA-J	24.1.89	15 Mar	21.93	Simon	Wardhaugh	AUS	14.1.86	15 Mar

HEPTATHLON

6371	Bryan	Clay	USA	3.1.80	1		WI	Valencia	9 Mar
	6.71	7.75	16.21	2.09	7.86	5.00		2:55.64	
6234	Andrey	Kravchenko	BLR	4.1.86	2		WI	Valencia	9 Mar
	7.19	7.63	14.29	2.15	8.11	5.30		2:46.49	
6229	Dmitriy	Karpov	KAZ	23.7.81	2			Tallinn	16 Feb
	7.07	7.21	16.23	2.07	7.99	5.15		2:43.69	
6136	Aleksandr	Pogorelov	RUS	10.1.80	1		NC	Sankt-Peterburg	3 Feb
	7.09	7.80	15.34	2.09	8.08	4.90		2:52.95	

6129	Mikhail	Logvinenko	RUS	19.4.84	2	NC	Sankt-Peterburg	3 Feb
	7.13	7.59	14.47	2.00	7.94	5.00	2:40.50	
6119	Aleksey	Sysoyev	RUS	8.3.85	3	NC	Sankt-Peterburg	3 Feb
	7.01	7.14	16.59	2.12	8.34	4.90	2:45.64	
6008	Donovan	Kilmartin	USA	11.6.84	1		Nampa	2 Feb
	7.08	7.52	14.39	2.06	8.28	5.25	2:56.15	
5978	Arkadiy	Vasilyev	RUS	19.1.87	3		Tallinn	16 Feb
	7.12	7.37	15.01	2.01	8.06	4.95	2:49.56	
5963	Andre	Niklaus	GER	30.8.81	4		Tallinn	16 Feb
	7.19	7.19	13.39	2.04	8.04	5.05	2:41.27	
5951	Gonzalo	Barroilhet	CHI	19.3.86	1	NCAA	Fayetteville	15 Mar
	7.19	7.42	13.74	2.02	7.98	5.05	2:49.30	
5949	Andres	Raja	EST	2.6.82	1	NC	Tallinn	3 Feb
	7.06	7.31	14.65	1.98	8.00	4.80	2:45.22	
5906	Raven	Cepeda	USA	26.6.86	1		Cedar Falls	2 Feb
	7.09	6.89	15.08	1.99	8.06	5.00	2:46.64	
5892	Roman	Sebrle	CZE	26.11.74	5		Tallinn	16 Feb
	7.12	7.58	15.13	2.07	8.14	4.55	2:55.49	

5883	Mustafa	Abdur-Rahim	USA	29.9.82	12 Jan
5878	Darius	Draudvila	LTU	29.3.83	2 Feb
5859	Ashton	Eaton	USA	21.8.88	2 Feb
5851	Jake	Arnold	USA	3.1.84	9 Mar
5842	Chris	Boyles	USA	2.5.80	26 Jan
5836	Jangy	Addy	USA	2.3.85	1 Mar
5836	Josh	Hustedt	USA	1.6.84	15 Mar
5829	Eduard	Mikhan	BLR-J	7.6.89	16 Feb
5829	Alexey	Drozdov	RUS	3.12.83	16 Feb
5827	Eelco	Sintnicolaas	NED	7.4.87	3 Feb
5822	Massimo	Bertocchi	CAN	27.9.85	19 Jan
5795	Nick	Adcock	USA	3.4.88	1 Mar

5000 METRES WALK

18:33.06	Ivano	Brugnetti	ITA	1.9.76	1	NC	Genova	23 Feb
18:51.46	Robert	Heffernan	IRL	28.2.78	1	NC	Belfast	26 Jan

19:14.33	Giorgio	Rubino	ITA	15.4.86	9 Feb
19:21.51	Lorenzo	Civallero	ITA	8.8.75	23 Feb
19:23.48	Alessandro	Gandellini	ITA	30.4.73	16 Feb
19:23.82	Andrey	Stepanchuk	BLR	12.6.79	19 Jan

10,000 METRES WALK

39:26.79	Ivan	Trotskiy	BLR	27.5.76	1	NC	Mogilyov	22 Feb
39:42.19	Sergey	Chernov	BLR	5.2.79	2	NC	Mogilyov	22 Feb
39:55.58	Andrey	Stepanchuk	BLR	12.6.79	3	NC	Mogilyov	22 Feb

WORLD INDOOR LISTS 2008 – WOMEN

60 METRES

7.06	Angela	Williams	USA	30.1.80	1	WI	Valencia	7 Mar
7.08	Jeanette	Kwakye	GBR	20.3.83	2	WI	Valencia	7 Mar
7.09	Yevgeniya	Polyakova	RUS	29.5.83	1	NC	Moskva	8 Feb
7.09	Franca	Idoko	NGR	15.6.85	1		Chemnitz	29 Feb
7.09	Tahesia	Harrigan	IVB	15.2.82	3	WI	Valencia	7 Mar
7.13	Kelly-Ann	Baptiste	TRI	14.10.86	1	SEC	Fayetteville	2 Mar
7.15	Kim	Gevaert	BEL	5.8.78	2	GP	Birmingham	16 Feb
7.16	Svetlana	Nabokina	RUS	26.1.82	1h1		Moskva	27 Jan
7.16	Bianca	Knight	USA-J	2.1.89	1h3	NCAA	Fayetteville	15 Mar
7.17	Christine	Arron	FRA	13.9.73	1		Paris (B)	22 Feb
7.17	Alexandria	Anderson	USA	28.1.87	2	NCAA	Fayetteville	15 Mar
7.18	Samantha	Henry	JAM	25.9.88	2A		New York (Arm)	8 Feb
7.19	Jessica	Young	USA	6.4.87	1		Fayetteville	15 Feb
7.19	Damola	Osayomi	NGR	26.7.86	1		Chapel Hill	16 Feb
7.20	Oksana	Dragun	BLR	19.4.81	1h	NC	Mogilyov	22 Feb
7.20	Yuliya	Nesterenko	BLR	15.6.79	1	NC	Mogilyov	22 Feb

7.21	Alexis	Joyce	USA	5.9.83	24 Feb
7.21	Carmelita	Jeter	USA	24.11.79	24 Feb
7.21	Virgen	Benavides	CUB	31.12.74	29 Feb
7.22	Mikele	Barber	USA	4.10.80	24 Feb
7.22	Gloria	Asumnu	USA	22.5.85	1 Mar
7.22	Nickeisha	Anderson	JAM	15.3.85	1 Mar
7.23	Natalya	Murinovich	RUS	27.5.85	27 Jan
7.23	Anna	Geflikh	RUS	5.7.83	8 Feb
7.23	Marina	Kislova	RUS	7.2.78	8 Feb
7.23	Verena	Sailer	GER	16.10.85	23 Feb
7.23	Simone	Facey	JAM	7.5.85	1 Mar
7.23	Laverne	Jones-Ferrette	ISV	16.9.81	7 Mar
7.23	Lakecia	Ealey	USA	22.1.86	15 Mar
7.24	Josephine	Onyia	ESP	15.7.86	13 Feb
7.24	Emma	Ania	GBR	7.2.79	27 Feb
7.24	Guzel	Khubbieva	UZB	2.5.76	7 Mar
7.25	three women				

200 METRES

22.40	Bianca	Knight	USA-J	2.1.89	1r2	NCAA	Fayetteville	15 Mar
22.62	Nickeisha	Anderson	JAM	15.3.85	2r2	NCAA	Fayetteville	15 Mar
22.81	Alexandria	Anderson	USA	28.1.87	3r2	NCAA	Fayetteville	15 Mar
22.83	Porscha	Lucas	USA	18.6.88	4r2	NCAA	Fayetteville	15 Mar
22.94	Simone	Facey	JAM	7.5.85	1r1	NCAA	Fayetteville	15 Mar
23.01	Samantha	Henry	JAM	25.9.88	1h1	SEC	Fayetteville	1 Mar
23.02	Anastasiya	Kapachinskaya	RUS	21.11.79	1h2	NC	Moskva	9 Feb

23.07	Kelly-Ann	Baptiste	TRI	14.10.86	1h3	SEC	Fayetteville	1 Mar

23.14	Natalie	Knight	JAM	24.10.86	15 Mar
23.16	Anna	Geflikh	RUS	5.7.83	10 Feb
23.20	Virgil	Hodge	SKN	17.11.83	15 Mar
23.22	Courtney	Champion	USA	10.6.86	14 Mar
23.26	Jeneba	Tarmoh	USA-J	27.9.89	1 Mar
23.28	Olesya	Zykina	RUS	7.10.80	22 Feb

300 Metres: 37.26 Svetlana Pospelova RUS 24.12.79 1r6 Moskva 12 Jan

400 METRES

51.09	Olesya	Zykina	RUS	7.10.80	1A	NC	Moskva	10 Feb
51.10	Natalya	Nazarova	RUS	26.5.79	2	WI	Valencia	9 Mar
51.41	Shareese	Woods	USA	20.2.85	3	WI	Valencia	9 Mar
51.42	Olga	Zaytseva	RUS	10.11.84	1h6	NC	Moskva	8 Feb
51.53	Antonina	Yefremova	UKR	19.7.81	4	WI	Valencia	9 Mar
51.55	Svetlana	Pospelova	RUS	24.12.79	1		Moskva	29 Jan
51.58	Yulia	Gushchina	RUS	4.3.83	2h4	NC	Moskva	8 Feb
51.63	Olesya	Forsheva	RUS	8.7.79	2		Moskva	29 Jan
51.75	Christy	Ekpukhon	NGR	6.2.85	1		Chemnitz	29 Feb
51.80	Ilona	Usovich	BLR	14.11.82	1	NC	Mogilyov	22 Feb
51.85	Moushami	Robinson	USA	13.4.81	3s1	WI	Valencia	8 Mar
51.88	Tatyana	Levina	RUS	28.2.77	2h6	NC	Moskva	8 Feb
51.95	Krista	Simkins	USA	27.12.86	1h1	NCAA	Fayetteville	14 Mar
51.96	Tatyana	Firova	RUS	10.10.82	1h1	NC	Moskva	8 Feb

52.10	Anast.	Kapachinskaya	RUS	21.11.79	21 Feb
52.10	Trish	Batholomew	GRN	23.10.86	2 Mar
52.12	Brandi	Cross	USA	20.1.88	2 Mar
52.15	Moya	Thompson	JAM	19.2.81	16 Feb
52.17	Antonina	Krivoshapka	RUS	21.7.87	2 Mar
52.23	Mary	Wineberg	USA	3.1.80	25 Jan
52.32	Jenna	Martin	CAN	31.3.88	2 Mar
52.34	Monica	Hargrove	USA	30.12.82	15 Feb
52.35	Nataliya	Pygyda	UKR	30.1.81	23 Feb
52.47	Kelly	Sotherton	GBR	13.11.76	16 Feb
52.48	Jessica	Beard	USA-J	8.1.89	15 Mar
52.51	Oksana	Sukhachova	RUS	4.9.84	8 Feb
52.52	Svetlana	Usovich	BLR	14.10.80	22 Feb
52.52	Kseniya	Karendyuk	UKR	21.6.86	23 Feb
52.57	Shana	Cox	USA	22.1.85	15 Feb
52.61	Tsvetelina	Kirilova	BUL	14.7.77	8 Feb
52.63	Anastasia	Ovchinnikova	RUS	16.10.84	8 Feb
52.52#	Ashlee	Kidd	USA	26.7.85	2 Feb

500 Metres: 1:08.52 Natalya Nazarova RUS 26.5.79 1r4 Moskva 12 Jan

1:09.18! Shana Cox USA 14 Dec, 1:09.41 Tatyana Firova RUS 12 Jan, 1:09.52 Olesya Forsheva 8.7.79 7 Jan

600 METRES

1:25.23	Tatyana	Firova	RUS	10.10.82	1r2		Moskva	27 Jan
1:25.91	Ilona	Usovich	BLR	14.11.82	1		Mogilyov	2 Feb

1:26.42	Irina	Khlyustova	BLR	14.6.78	2 Feb
1:26.53	Natalya	Ignatova	RUS	6.5.81	27 Jan
1:26.92	Tatyana	Paliyenko	RUS	18.11.83	27 Jan
1:27.00	Marina	Shiyan	RUS	22.1.80	27 Jan

800 METRES

1:56.49	Yelena	Sobolyeva	RUS	3.10.82	1	NC	Moskva	9 Feb
1:58.84	Natalya	Ignatova	RUS	6.5.81	2	NC	Moskva	9 Feb
1:59.46	Mariya	Savinova	RUS	22.6.85	3	NC	Moskva	9 Feb
1:59.48	Maria	Mutola	MOZ	27.10.72	1		Karlsruhe	10 Feb
1:59.58	Tetyana	Petlyuk	UKR	22.2.82	1s1	WI	Valencia	8 Mar
1:59.71	Mariya	Shapayeva	RUS	7.11.86	4	NC	Moskva	9 Feb
1:59.73	Jenny	Meadows	GBR	17.4.81	2s2	WI	Valencia	8 Mar
2:00.36	Elisa	Cusma	ITA	24.7.81	3s2	WI	Valencia	8 Mar
2:00.41	Liliana	Popescu	ROU	5.2.82	1	Balk	Athína (P)	8 Feb
2:00.68	Mayte	Martínez	ESP	17.5.76	3	GE Galen	Stockholm	21 Feb
2:00.75	Ewelina	Setowska-Dryk	POL	5.3.80	4	GE Galen	Stockholm	21 Feb
2:00.79	Mihaela	Neacsu	ROU	3.5.79	3h4	WI	Valencia	7 Mar
2:01.25	Jemma	Simpson	GBR	10.2.84	2	GP	Birmingham	16 Feb
2:01.33	Élodie	Guegan	FRA	19.12.85	3		Karlsruhe	10 Feb
2:01.33	Marilyn	Okoro	GBR	23.9.84	1		Sheffield	17 Feb
2:01.41	Kenia	Sinclair	JAM	14.7.80	1	Tyson	Fayetteville	15 Feb
2:01.73	Nicole	Teter	USA	8.11.73	4h4	WI	Valencia	7 Mar

2:01.84	Zoya	Hladun	UKR	10.3.83	10 Feb
2:01.85	Tamsyn	Lewis	AUS	20.7.78	7 Mar
2:01.95	Yekaterina	Martynova	RUS	12.6.86	8 Feb
2:01.96	Yuliya	Rusanova	RUS	3.7.86	2 Mar
2:02.03	Olga	Kotlyarova	RUS	12.4.76	8 Feb
2:02.08	Tatyana	Paliyenko	RUS	18.11.83	13 Feb
2:02.15	Tatyana	Andrianova	RUS	10.12.79	8 Feb
2:02.27	Yevgeniya	Zinurova	RUS	16.11.82	8 Feb
2:02.27	Marian	Burnett	GUY	22.2.76	8 Mar
2:02.28	Irina	Maracheva	RUS	29.9.84	8 Feb
2:02.31	Tatyana	Popova	RUS	5.1.84	22 Feb
2:02.34	Olesya	Chumakova	RUS	23.7.81	13 Feb
2:02.45	Larisa	Chzhao	RUS	4.2.71	8 Feb
2:02.51	Yelena	Kofanova	RUS	8.8.88	8 Feb
2:02.59	Yuliya	Fomenko	RUS	30.8.79	26 Jan
2:02.59	Susan	Scott	GBR	26.9.77	16 Feb

1000 METRES

2:34.67	Yuliya	Fomenko	RUS	30.8.79	1		Yekaterinburg	17 Feb
2:37.63	Yekaterina	Martynova	RUS	12.6.86	1r3		Moskva	12 Jan
2:38.24	Mariya	Shapayeva	RUS	7.11.86	2r3		Moskva	12 Jan

2:39.31	Anastasiya	Fesenko	RUS	17.6.82	12 Jan
2:39.55	Yevgeniya	Zinurova	RUS	16.11.82	12 Jan

1500 METRES

3:57.71	Yelena	Sobolyeva	RUS	3.10.82	1	WI	Valencia	9 Mar
3:59.41	Yuliya	Fomenko	RUS	30.8.79	2	WI	Valencia	9 Mar
3:59.75	Gelete	Burka	ETH	15.2.86	3	WI	Valencia	9 Mar
3:59.79	Maryam	Jamal Yusuf	BRN	16.9.84	4	WI	Valencia	9 Mar
4:03.33	Liliana	Popescu	ROU	5.2.82	1	NC	Bucuresti	15 Feb
4:03.68	Yekaterina	Martynova	RUS	12.8.86	3	NC	Moskva	10 Feb
4:04.19	Daniela	Yordanova	BUL	8.3.76	5	WI	Valencia	9 Mar
4:05.90+	Olga	Komyagina	RUS	10.2.74	2	in 1M	Moskva	27 Jan
4:06.04+	Yelena	Sidorchenkova	RUS	30.5.80	3	in 1M	Moskva	27 Jan
4:07.41	Olesya	Chumakova	RUS	23.7.81	4	NC	Moskva	10 Feb
4:07.46	Sylvia	Kibet	KEN	18.3.84	1		Karlsruhe	10 Feb
4:08.12	Sonja	Roman	SLO	11.3.81	3h2	WI	Valencia	8 Mar
4:08.43	Bouchra	Ghézielle	FRA	19.5.79	3		Karlsruhe	10 Feb
4:08.88	Lisa	Dobriskey	GBR	23.12.83	4	GE Galen	Stockholm	21 Feb
4:09.07	Susan	Scott	GBR	26.9.77	5	GE Galen	Stockholm	21 Feb

4:10.09	Siham	Hilali	MAR	2.5.86	8 Mar
4:10.3	Nataliya	Tobias	UKR	22.11.80	19 Feb
4:10.32	Hilary	Stellingwerff	CAN	7.8.81	10 Feb
4:10.56	Christy	Wurth-Thomas	USA	11.7.80	8 Mar
4:10.91	Tetyana	Petlyuk	UKR	22.2.82	22 Feb
4:11.17	Jemma	Simpson	GBR	10.2.84	8 Mar
4:11.29	Celia	Brown	GBR	22.1.77	29 Jan
4:11.79	Elena	Antoci	ROU	16.1.75	15 Feb
4:12.22	Helen	Clitheroe	GBR	2.1.74	21 Feb
4:12.34	Olesya	Tyurina	RUS	3.9.80	10 Feb

1 MILE

4:20.21	Yelena	Sobolyeva	RUS	3.10.82	1		Moskva	27 Jan
4:23.49	Olga	Komyagina	RUS	10.2.74	2		Moskva	27 Jan
4:24.14	Kimberly	Smith	NZL	19.11.73	1		Boston (Allston)	8 Feb
4:24.53	Yelena	Sidorchenkova	RUS	30.5.80	3		Moskva	27 Jan
4:27.18	Christy	Wurth-Thomas	USA	11.7.80	1	Tyson	Fayetteville	15 Feb
4:27.36	Olesya	Chumakova	RUS	23.7.81	4		Moskva	27 Jan

4:31.84	Jenelle	Deatherage	USA	25.9.77	15 Feb
4:31.90	Liliya	Shobukhova	RUS	13.11.77	19 Jan
4:32.28	Megan	Metcalfe	CAN	27.1.82	19 Jan

2000 METRES

5:36.95+	Gelete	Burka	ETH	15.2.86	1	in 3k	Birmingham	16 Feb
5:38.79+	Meseret	Defar	ETH	19.11.83	1	in 3k	Stuttgart	2 Feb
5:39.85+	Meselech	Melkamu	ETH	19.4.85	1	in 3k	Valencia	9 Feb

5:40.26	Mariya	Konovalova	RUS	14.8.74	7 Jan
5:40.95	Yelena	Zadorozhnaya	RUS	3.12.77	7 Jan

3000 METRES

8:27.93	Meseret	Defar	ETH	19.11.83	1	Spark	Stuttgart	2 Feb
8:29.48	Meselech	Melkamu	ETH	19.4.85	1		Valencia	9 Feb
8:31.94	Gelete	Burka	ETH	15.2.86	1	GP	Birmingham	16 Feb
8:33.37	Tirunesh	Dibaba	ETH	1.6.85	1	BIG	Boston (R)	26 Jan
8:35.86	Mariem	Alaoui Selsouli	MAR	8.4.84	2		Valencia	9 Feb
8:36.59	Ejegayehu	Dibaba	ETH	25.6.82	2	BIG	Boston (R)	26 Jan
8:41.82	Sylvia	Kibet	KEN	18.3.84	4	WI	Valencia	8 Mar
8:44.57	Olga	Komyagina	RUS	10.2.74	5	WI	Valencia	8 Mar
8:44.61	Yelena	Sidorchenkova	RUS	30.5.80	1	NC	Moskva	10 Feb
8:46.29	Jessica	Augusto	POR	8.11.81	2	GP	Birmingham	16 Feb
8:48.48	Kimberly	Smith	NZL	19.11.73	6	WI	Valencia	8 Mar
8:48.56	Megan	Metcalfe	USA	27.1.82	4h2	WI	Valencia	7 Mar
8:49.11	Silvia	Weissteiner	ITA	13.7.79	7	WI	Valencia	8 Mar
8:49.52	Mariya	Konovalova	RUS	14.8.74	3	NC	Moskva	10 Feb

8:50.42	Lisa	Dobriskey	GBR	23.12.83	16 Feb
8:50.69	Katrina	Wootton	GBR	2.9.85	16 Feb
8:51.02	Helen	Clitheroe	GBR	2.1.74	16 Feb
8:54.16	Elena	Antoci	ROU	16.1.75	16 Feb
8:54.24	Sonja	Roman	SLO	11.3.81	8 Feb
8:54.51	Hanane	Ouhaddou	MAR	.82	22 Feb
8:54.68	Sabrina	Mockenhaupt	GER	6.12.80	8 Feb
8:54.97	Christy	Wurth-Thomas	USA	11.7.80	26 Jan
8:55.19	Shannon	Rowbury	USA	14.9.84	23 Feb
8:55.39	Daniela	Donisa	ROU	23.4.88	8 Feb
8:56.73	Alemitu	Bekele	TUR	17.9.77	8 Feb

2 MILES

9:10.50	Meseret	Defar	ETH	19.11.83	1	BIG	Boston (R)	26 Jan
9:13.94	Kimberly	Smith	NZL	19.11.73	2	BIG	Boston (R)	26 Jan

50 Metres Hurdles: in 60mh at Stockholm 21 Feb: 1. Susanna Kallur SWE 6.76, 2. Josephine Onyia ESP 6.75+

60 METRES HURDLES

7.68	Susanna	Kallur	SWE	16.2.81	1		Karlsruhe	10 Feb
7.77	Lolo	Jones	USA	5.8.82	2		Karlsruhe	10 Feb
7.84	Josephine	Onyia	ESP	15.7.86	1h4	WI	Valencia	8 Mar
7.85	Damu	Cherry	USA	29.11.77	2h2		Karlsruhe	10 Feb
7.89	Yevgeniya	Volodko	BLR	24.3.81	1		Mogilyov	26 Jan
7.90	Anay	Tejeda	CUB	3.4.83	2h1		Karlsruhe	10 Feb
7.90	Candice	Davis	USA	26.10.85	2	NC	Boston (R)	24 Feb
7.91	Priscilla	Lopes-Schliep	CAN	26.8.82	1		Gent	24 Feb

7.92	Angela	Whyte	CAN	22.5.80	1		Moscow	8 Feb
7.93	Lacena	Golding-Clarke	JAM	20.3.75	3	GE Galen	Stockholm	21 Feb
7.94	Vonette	Dixon	JAM	26.11.75	3	Spark	Stuttgart	2 Feb
7.94	Tiffany	Ofili	USA	13.11.87	1	NCAA	Fayetteville	14 Mar
7.98	Aleksandra	Antonova	RUS	24.3.80	1	NC	Moskva	8 Feb
7.99	Aurelia	Trywianska	POL	9.5.76	3h1		Karlsruhe	10 Feb
7.99	Tatyana	Dektyarova	RUS	14.6.84	2		Paris (B)	22 Feb
7.99	Mariya	Koroteyeva	RUS	10.11.81	3		Paris (B)	22 Feb
8.00	Danielle	Carruthers	USA	22.12.79	5	Spark	Stuttgart	2 Feb
8.00	Yuliya	Kondakova	RUS	4.12.81	2	NC	Moskva	8 Feb
8.00	Kellie	Wells	USA	16.7.82	4		Düsseldorf	8 Feb
8.01	Olga	Korsunova	RUS	20.5.81	3	NC	Moskva	8 Feb
8.01	Kristi	Castlin	USA	7.7.88	1h1		Blacksburg	9 Mar

8.02	Micol	Cattaneo	ITA	14.5.82	8 Mar
8.03	Christina	Vukicevic	NOR	18.6.87	10 Feb
8.03	Queen	Harrison	USA	10.9.88	14 Mar
8.04	Fatmata	Fofanah	GUI	26.6.85	12 Jan
8.04	Dawn	Harper	USA	13.5.84	8 Feb
8.04	Miriam	Bobková	SVK	2.3.79	10 Feb
8.05	Perdita	Felicien	CAN	29.8.80	1 Feb
8.05	Eline	Berings	BEL	28.5.86	8 Mar
8.06	Nevit	Yanit	TUR	16.2.86	24 Feb
8.06	Yevgeniya	Snigur	UKR	7.3.84	8 Mar
8.07	Sarah	Claxton	GBR	23.9.79	16 Feb
8.08	Joanna	Hayes	USA	23.12.76	1 Feb
8.08	Reina-Flor	Okori	FRA	2.5.80	17 Feb
8.08	Adrianna	Lamalle	FRA	27.9.82	22 Feb
8.08	Shantia	Moss	USA	27.10.85	14 Mar
8.08	Jessica	Ohanaja	NGR	6.12.85	14 Mar
8.09	Yekaterina	Poplavskaya	BLR	7.5.87	26 Jan
8.09	Derval	O'Rourke	IRL	28.5.81	13 Feb
8.09	Nickiesha	Wilson	JAM	28.7.86	14 Mar

HIGH JUMP

2.05	Blanka	Vlasic	CRO	8.11.83	1		Weinheim	27 Feb
2.02	Yelena	Slesarenko	RUS	28.2.82	1		Brno	12 Feb
2.02	Ariane	Friedrich	GER	10.1.84	2		Weinheim	29 Feb
2.01	Vita	Palamar	UKR	12.10.77	3	WI	Valencia	9 Mar
2.00	Yekaterina	Savchenko	RUS	3.6.77	1	Iagar	Bucuresti	17 Feb
1.99	Tia	Hellebaut	BEL	16.2.78	1P	WI	Valencia	7 Mar
1.99	Ruth	Beitia	ESP	1.4.79	4	WI	Valencia	9 Mar
1.98	Tatyana	Kivimagi	RUS	23.6.84	1		Moskva	20 Jan
1.98	Anna	Chicherova	RUS	22.7.82	2	Iagar	Bucuresti	17 Feb
1.98	Emma	Green	SWE	8.12.84	1	NC	Malmö	23 Feb
1.98	Iva	Straková	CZE	4.8.80	1		Cejkovice	14 Mar
1.97	Barbora	Laláková	CZE	2.5.81	1		Trinec	21 Jan
1.97	Antonietta	Di Martino	ESP	1.6.78	1	GE Galen	Stockholm	21 Feb
1.96	Svetlana	Shkolina	RUS	9.3.86	2		Göteborg	29 Jan
1.96	Marina	Aitova	KAZ	13.9.82	1		Cottbus	30 Jan
1.95	Amy	Acuff	USA	14.7.75	1		Fresno	21 Jan
1.95	Yekaterina	Yevseyeva	KAZ	22.6.88	1		Karaganda	26 Jan
1.95	Romana	Dubnova	CZE	4.11.78	1=		Eaubonne	8 Feb

1.92!	Alexandra	Shamsutdinova	RUS	27.3.87	22 Dec
1.92	Viktoria	Klyugina	RUS	28.9.80	19 Jan
1.92	Viktoria	Styopina	UKR	21.2.76	30 Jan
1.92	Iryna	Kovalenko	UKR	12.6.86	8 Feb
1.92	Jessica	Ennis	GBR	28.1.86	10 Feb
1.91!	Noengrothai	Chaipetch	THA	1.12.82	31 Oct
1.91	Inna	Gliznutsa	MDA	18.4.73	9 Jan
1.91	Karina	Vnukova	LTU	27.3.85	26 Jan
1.91	Dora	Györffy	HUN	23.2.78	26 Jan
1.91	Tatyana	Efimenko	KGZ	2.1.81	16 Feb
1.91	Anna	Ustinova	KAZ	8.12.85	16 Feb
1.91		Zheng Xingjuan	CHN-J	20.3.89	27 Feb
1.90	Kimberly	Jess	GER-Y	30.1.92	6 Jan
1.90	Olena	Holosha	UKR	26.1.82	16 Jan
1.90	Natalya	Mamlina	RUS-Y	16.3.91	17 Jan
1.90	Lavern	Spencer	LCA	23.6.84	19 Jan
1.90	Sharon	Day	USA	9.6.85	21 Jan
1.90	Persefóni	Hatzinákou	GRE	6.6.84	2 Feb
1.90	Nicole	Forrester	CAN	17.11.76	5 Feb
1.90	Svetlana	Radzivil	UZB	17.1.87	22 Feb
1.90	Adonía	Steryiou	GRE	7.7.85	24 Feb
1.90	Romary	Rifka	MEX	23.12.70	8 Mar
1.89	Yekaterina	Kuntsevich	RUS	13.7.84	7 Jan
1.89	Gwen	Wentland	USA	29.4.72	19 Jan
1.89	Tatyana	Grigoryeva	RUS	13.5.81	25 Jan
1.89	Annett	Engel	GER	6.11.87	10 Feb
1.89	Doreen	Amata	NGR	5.6.88	15 Feb
1.89	Kamila	Stepaniuk	POL	22.3.86	16 Feb
1.89	Julia	Hartmann	GER	10.4.86	17 Feb
1.89	María	Papayeoryíou	GRE	8.8.79	17 Feb
1.89	Chaunte	Howard	USA	12.1.84	23 Feb
1.89	Olena	Demydova	UKR	16.6.82	1 Mar
1.89	Viktoriya	Dobrynska	UKR	18.1.80	1 Mar
1.89	Ebba	Jungmark	SWE	10.3.87	14 Mar

POLE VAULT

4.95	Yelena	Isinbayeva	RUS	3.6.82	1	Mast	Donetsk	16 Feb
4.75	Yuliya	Golubchikova	RUS	27.3.83	1		Athína (P)	13 Feb
4.75	Jenn	Stuczynski	USA	6.2.82	2	WI	Valencia	8 Mar
4.71	Svetlana	Feofanova	RUS	16.7.80	1		Bydgoszcz	20 Feb
4.70	Monika	Pyrek	POL	11.8.80	1	NC	Spala	24 Feb
4.70	Fabiana	Murer	BRA	16.3.81	3=	WI	Valencia	8 Mar
4.65	Carolin	Hingst	GER	18.9.80	2		Athína (P)	13 Feb
4.64	Jillian	Schwartz	USA	19.9.79	2=	Tyson	Fayetteville	15 Feb
4.64	Lacy	Janson	USA	20.2.83	2=	Tyson	Fayetteville	15 Feb
4.62	Anna	Rogowska	POL	21.5.81	4	Mast	Donetsk	16 Feb
4.60	Vanessa	Boslak	FRA	11.6.82	1		Limoges	2 Feb

4.60	Anastasia	Shvedova	RUS	3.5.79	2	NC	Moskva	10 Feb
4.60	Julia	Hutter	GER	26.7.83	1	NC	Sindelfingen	24 Feb
4.53	Pavla	Rybová	CZE	20.5.78	1		Bad Oeynhausen	29 Feb
4.52	Silke	Spiegelburg	GER	17.3.86	6	Mast	Donetsk	16 Feb
4.52	Nataliya	Kushch	UKR	5.3.83	7	Mast	Donetsk	16 Feb
4.52	Tatyana	Polnova	RUS	20.4.79	8	Mast	Donetsk	16 Feb
4.52	Lisa	Ryshich	GER	19.9.77	9=	Mast	Donetsk	16 Feb
4.50	Aleksandra	Kiryashova	RUS	21.8.85	1		Sankt-Peterburg	21 Dec
4.50	Anna	Battke	GER	3.1.85	2	NC	Sindelfingen	24 Feb
4.50	Chelsea	Johnson	USA	20.12.83	3	NC	Boston (R)	24 Feb
4.45	April	Steiner	USA	22.4.80	5	NC	Boston (R)	24 Feb
4.45		Li Ling	CHN-J	6.7.89	1		Beijing	26 Feb
4.45	Naroa	Agirre	ESP	15.5.79	Q	WI	Valencia	7 Mar
4.42	Martina	Strutz	GER	4.11.81	1		Hamburg	3 Feb
4.42	Erin	Asay	USA	17.3.83	1		Seattle	16 Feb

4.41	Nicole	McEwen	USA	1.4.80	8 Feb
4.40	Kristina	Gadschiew	GER	3.7.84	18 Jan
4.40	Kate	Dennison	GBR	7.5.84	2 Feb
4.40	Becky	Holliday	USA	12.3.80	16 Feb
4.40	Mary	Vincent	USA	31.10.75	16 Feb
4.40	Elisabete	Tavares	POR	7.3.80	23 Feb
4.40	Joanna	Piwowarska	POL	4.11.83	24 Feb
4.40	Nikoléta	Kiriakopoúlou	GRE	21.3.86	24 Feb
4.40	Valeria	Volik	RUS-J	15.11.89	1 Mar
4.39	Tracy	O'Hara	USA	20.7.80	15 Feb
4.32	Kate	Conwell	USA	13.2.83	16 Feb
4.31	Sandra	Tavares	FRA	29.5.82	9 Feb
4.31	Rianna	Galiart	NED	22.11.85	9 Feb
4.31	Katelin	Rains	USA	20.8.87	14 Mar
4.30	Lelsie	Hendry	CAN	29.6.82	26 Jan
4.30A	April	Kubishta	USA	5.7.85	2 Feb
4.30	Anna	Schmid	SUI-J	2.12.89	3 Feb
4.30	Afrodíti	Skafída	GRE	20.3.82	8 Feb
4.30	Yekaterina	Sultanova	RUS	31.12.84	9 Feb
4.30	Dana	Cervantes	ESP	18.8.78	16 Feb
4.30	Vanessa	Vandy	FIN-J	14.5.89	23 Feb
4.30A	Elouise	Rudy	USA	30.12.85	1 Mar
4.30	Anastasiya	Savchenko	RUS-J	15.11.89	1 Mar
4.30	Andree	Pickens	USA	17.6.80	2 Mar

LONG JUMP

7.00	Naide	Gomes	POR	10.11.79	1	WI	Valencia	9 Mar
6.96	Irina	Simagina	RUS	25.5.82	1	GE Galen	Stockholm	21 Feb
6.89	Maurren	Maggi	BRA	25.6.76	2	WI	Valencia	9 Mar
6.87	Olga	Kucherenko	RUS	14.2.85	1		Krasnodar	15 Jan
6.87	Brittney	Reese	USA	9.9.86	1	SEC	Fayetteville	1 Mar
6.85	Hrysopíyi	Devetzí	GRE	2.1.76	1	Balk	Athína (P)	8 Feb
6.85	Karin	Mey	RSA	31.5.83	3	GE Galen	Stockholm	21 Feb
6.84	Eloyse	Lesueur	FRA	15.7.88	1		Gainesville	25 Jan
6.82	Lyudmila	Kolchanova	RUS	1.10.79	1		Samara	2 Feb
6.78	Tatyana	Kotova	RUS	11.12.76	4	GE Galen	Stockholm	21 Feb
6.77	Yargelis	Savigne	CUB	13.11.84	1		Linz	31 Jan
6.76	Marina	Pankova	RUS	16.11.82	2		Samara	2 Feb
6.68	Blessing	Okagbare	NGR	10.9.88	2	NCAA	Fayetteville	14 Mar
6.66	Ineta	Radevica	LAT	13.7.81	4	Spark	Stuttgart	2 Feb
6.66	Concepción	Montaner	ESP	14.1.81	3		Valencia	9 Feb
6.65	Yelena	Sokolova	RUS	23.7.86	1		Krasnodar	20 Jan
6.63	Oksana	Udmurtova	RUS	1.2.82	1		Tartu	20 Feb
6.61	Tatyana	Chernova	RUS	29.1.88	1P		Tallinn	16 Feb
6.60	Oksana	Zhukovskaya	RUS	24.9.84	3		Samara	2 Feb
6.60	Ksenija	Balta	EST	1.11.86	1	NC	Tartu	10 Feb
6.60	Oleksandra	Stadnyuk	UKR	16.4.80	1	NC	Sumy	23 Feb
6.60	Natasha	Harvey	USA	29.11.87	3	NCAA	Fayetteville	14 Mar

6.59	Denisa	Scerbová	CZE	21.8.86	3 Feb
6.58	Jovanee	Jarrett	JAM	15.1.83	8 Feb
6.57	Lyudmila	Blonska	UKR	9.11.77	16 Feb
6.56	Melanie	Bauschke	GER	14.7.88	3 Feb
6.56	Bianca	Kappler	GER	8.8.77	29 Feb
6.54	Natalya	Lebusova	RUS	4.4.78	9 Feb
6.54	Karolina	Tyminska	POL	4.10.84	16 Feb
6.53	Valeria	Canella	ITA	6.2.82	20 Jan
6.52	Ivana	Spanovic	SRB-J	10.5.90	8 Feb
6.52	Shaquainia	Lundy	USA	18.7.86	29 Feb
6.51	Anna	Bogdanova	RUS	21.10.84	3 Feb
6.51	Viktoriya	Rybalko	UKR	26.10.82	16 Feb
6.51	Irina	Chernushenko	BLR	9.3.79	23 Feb
6.51	Janice	Josephs	RSA	31.3.82	8 Mar
6.50	Oksana	Zubkovska	UKR	15.7.81	9 Jan
6.50	Lela	Nelson	USA	19.5.83	26 Jan
6.50	Jacquelyn	Johnson	USA	8.9.84	29 Feb
6.50	Shara	Proctor	AIA	16.9.88	1 Mar
6.50	Anna	Nazarova	RUS	14.3.86	2 Mar
6.50	Erica	McLain	USA	24.1.86	14 Mar

TRIPLE JUMP

15.08	Marija	Sestak	SLO	17.4.79	1		Athína (P)	13 Feb
15.05	Yargelis	Savigne	CUB	13.11.84	1	WI	Valencia	8 Mar
15.00	Hrysopíyi	Devetzí	GRE	2.1.76	2	WI	Valencia	8 Mar
14.94	Oksana	Udmurtova	RUS	1.2.82	1		Tartu	20 Feb
14.78	Adelina	Gavrila	ROU	26.11.78	1		Bucuresti	3 Feb
14.58	Olga	Rypakova	KAZ	30.11.84	4	WI	Valencia	8 Mar
14.54	Olesya	Bufalova	RUS	6.10.82	1		Krasnodar	15 Jan
14.53	Teresa	Nzola Meso	FRA	30.11.83	3		Athína (P)	13 Feb
14.52	Olga	Saladuha	UKR	4.6.83	1	NC	Sumy	24 Feb
14.51	Anna	Pyatykh	RUS	4.4.81	1	NC	Moskva	10 Feb

14.47	Yamilé	Aldama	SUD	14.8.72	5	WI	Valencia	8 Mar
14.32	Viktoriya	Gurova	RUS	22.5.82	4	NC	Moskva	10 Feb
14.30		Xie Limei	CHN	27.6.86	1		Beijing	26 Feb
14.28	Alsu	Murtazina	RUS	12.12.87	1	NC-23	Penza	2 Mar
14.26	Kaire	Leibak	EST	21.5.88	1	NC	Tartu	9 Feb
14.24	Athanasía	Pérra	GRE	2.2.83	1		Athína (P)	26 Jan
14.20	Erica	McLain	USA	24.1.86	1	NCAA	Fayetteville	15 Mar
14.17	Biljana	Topic	SRB	17.10.77	2	Balk	Athína (P)	8 Feb
14.17	Svitlana	Mamyeyeva	UKR	19.4.82	2	NC	Sumy	24 Feb
14.08	Yelena	Ivanova	RUS	16.3.79	1		Volgograd	19 Jan
14.07	Cristina	Bujin	ROU	12.4.88	2	NC	Bucuresti	15 Feb

14.03	Magdelin	Martinez	ITA	10.2.76	24 Feb
14.00	Snezana	Rodic	SLO	19.8.82	8 Feb
13.97	Dana	Veldáková	SVK	3.6.81	23 Feb
13.95		Xu Tingting	CHN-J	12.7.89	26 Jan
13.94	Patricia	Sarrapio	ESP	16.11.82	23 Feb
13.94	Shakeema	Welsch	USA	10.11.76	24 Feb
13.94	Natalya	Kutyakova	RUS	28.11.86	2 Mar
13.92	Petra	Dacheva	BUL	10.3.85	26 Jan
13.90	Alina	Popescu	ROU	27.10.85	2 Feb
13.88	Tatyana	Yakovleva	RUS	9.9.86	22 Feb
13.87	Shani	Marks	USA	24.8.80	24 Feb
13.86	Paraskeví	Papahrístou	GRE-J	17.4.89	2 Feb
13.86	Paraskeví	Sidiropoúlou	GRE	9.11.78	2 Feb
13.84	Anna	Kuropatkina	RUS	3.10.85	26 Jan
13.82	Kimberly	Williams	JAM	3.11.88	15 Mar

SHOT

20.35	Nadezhda	Ostapchuk	BLR	12.10.80	1	NC	Mogilyov	22 Feb
20.19	Valerie	Vili	NZL	6.10.84	1	WI	Valencia	9 Mar
19.68	Christina	Schwanitz	GER	24.12.85	1		Chemnitz	29 Feb
19.09	Anna	Omarova	RUS	3.10.81	1	NC	Moskva	10 Feb
19.09		Li Meiju	CHN	3.10.79	3	WI	Valencia	9 Mar
18.93	Nadine	Kleinert	GER	20.10.75	2		Chemnitz	29 Feb
18.88	Anna	Avdeyeva	RUS	6.4.85	2	NC	Moskva	10 Feb
18.81	Anca	Heltne	ROU	1.1.78	1		Bucuresti	3 Feb
18.81	Denise	Hinrichs	GER	7.6.87	1	NC	Sindelfingen	23 Feb
18.77		Li Ling	CHN	7.2.85	1		Beijing	27 Feb
18.75	Misleidis	González	CUB	19.6.78	4	WI	Valencia	9 Mar
18.68	Chiara	Rosa	ITA	28.1.83	5	WI	Valencia	9 Mar
18.63	Petra	Lammert	GER	3.3.84	2	NC	Sindelfingen	23 Feb
18.56	Assunta	Legnante	ITA	14.5.78	1		Schio	24 Jan
18.52		Liu Xiangrong	CHN	6.6.88	2		Beijing	27 Feb
18.47	Cleopatra	Borel-Brown	TRI	3.10.79	7	WI	Valencia	9 Mar
18.45	Elizabeth	Wanless	USA	18.11.81	1		Anderson	9 Feb
18.18	Irina	Khudoroshkina	RUS	13.10.68	3	NC	Moskva	10 Feb
18.16	Yumileidis	Cumba	CUB	11.2.75	3		Chemnitz	29 Feb
18.13	Helena	Engman	SWE	16.6.76	1		Nordhausen	18 Jan
18.12		Gong Lijiao	CHN-J	24.1.89	1	AsiC	Doha	14 Feb
18.11	Jill	Camarena	USA	2.8.82	1	NC	Boston (R)	23 Feb
18.03	Abby	Ruston	USA	3.4.83	2	NC	Boston (R)	23 Feb

18.00	Oksana	Gaus	RUS	9.7.81	19 Jan
17.92	Vera	Yepimashko	BLR	10.7.76	19 Jan
17.83	Mariam	Kevkhishvili	GEO	17.9.85	15 Mar
17.78	Sarah	Stevens	USA	2.4.86	16 Feb
17.78	Kristin	Heaston	USA	23.11.75	23 Feb
17.58	Gail	Lee	USA	25.5.84	22 Feb
17.54	Yuliya	Leontyuk	BLR	31.1.84	26 Jan
17.46	Krystyna	Zabawska	POL	14.1.68	24 Feb
17.44	Magdalena	Sobieszek	POL	4.5.86	2 Feb
17.42	Annie	Alexander	TRI	28.8.87	1 Mar
17.33	Oksana	Chibisova	RUS	31.3.77	10 Feb

20 LB WEIGHT

25.34	Brittany	Riley	USA	26.8.86	1	NCAA	Fayetteville	14 Mar
23.68	Amber	Campbell	USA	5.6.81	1		Chapel Hill	16 Feb
22.62	Kristal	Yush	USA	8.1.82	2	NC	Boston (R)	24 Feb
22.04	Jessica	Pressley	USA	27.12.84	2	NCAA	Fayetteville	14 Mar

21.71	Erin	Gilreath	USA	11.8.80	24 Feb
21.62	Astin	Steward	USA	15.5.85	14 Mar
21.53	Veronica	Jatsek	USA	.86	2 Mar

PENTATHLON

4867	Tia	Hellebaut	BEL	16.2.78	1	WI	Valencia	7 Mar
	8.54	1.99	13.85	6.41	2:16.42			
4852	Kelly	Sotherton	GBR	13.11.76	2	WI	Valencia	7 Mar
	8.25	1.81	14.57	6.45	2:09.95			
4771	Lyudmila	Blonska	UKR	9.11.77	1		Tallinn	16 Feb
	8.32	1.81	14.30	6.57	2:16.00			
4769	Karolina	Tyminska	POL	4.10.84	1	NC	Spala	16 Feb
	8.50	1.72	14.69	6.54	2:06.52			
4762	Anna	Bogdanova	RUS	21.10.84	1	NC	Sankt-Peterburg	3 Feb
	8.43	1.75	17.06	6.36	2:18.11			
4758	Nataliya	Dobrinska	UKR	29.5.82	2		Tallinn	16 Feb
	8.43	1.75	17.06	6.36	2:18.11			
4717	Tatyana	Chernova	RUS	29.1.88	3		Tallinn	16 Feb
	8.38	1.78	12.80	6.61	2:10.10			

Continued on page 595

WORLD INDOOR CHAMPIONSHIPS 2008

At Valencia, Spain 7-9 March

The 12th IAAF World Indoor Championships were the third in the series to be staged in Spain and Valencia rose to the challenge admirably. World records are precious commodities, but on the final day Yelena Soboleva broke her own mark of a month earlier by front-running the 1500m, and her 3:57.71 was the only new championship record. We then had another terrific run from the gun from Abubaker Kaki who became the youngest ever world indoor champion at 18 years 262 days. Another 'world record' came as Tia Hellebaut cleared 1.99 in the high jump for the best ever in a combined events competition. Maria Mutola competed in a record ninth World Indoors and won a record ninth medal and Natalya Nazarova matched Mutola by winning a seventh gold as she took a fifth relay gold to go with two individual titles. Stefan Holm excelled with a fourth world indoor high jump title and it was number three for Yelena Isinbayeva and Meseret Defar. Manuel Martínez tied the men's record of Javier Sotomayor with an eighth world indoor appearance (at shot). The superpowers Russia and USA headed the medal table, but 16 nations won gold , 36 medals of any colour and 50 placed athletes in the top eights.

MEN – 60 Metres (7)

1. Olusoji Fasuba NGR	6.51
2= Dwain Chambers GBR	6.54
2= Kim Collins SKN	6.54
4. Michael Rodgers USA	6.57
5. Vicente de Lima BRA	6.60
6. Uche Isaac NGR	6.63
7. Simeon Williamson GBR	6.63
8. Andrey Yepishin RUS	6.70

400 Metres (9)

1. Tyler Christopher CAN	45.67
2. Johan Wissman SWE	46.04
3. Chris Brown BAH	46.26
4. Nery Brenes CRC	46.65
5. Maksim Dyldin RUS	46.79
6. Sean Wroe AUS	46.93

800 Metres (9)

1. Abubaker Kaki SUD-J	1:44.81
2. Mbulaeni Mulaudzi RSA	1:44.91
3. Yusuf Saad Kamel BRN	1:45.26
4. Dmitrijs Milkevics LAT	1:45.72
5. Dmitriy Bogdanov RUS	1:45.76
6. Nick Symmonds USA	1:46.48

1500 Metres (8)

1. Deresse Mekonnen ETH	3:38.23
2. Daniel K Komen KEN	3:38.54
3. Juan Carlos Higuero ESP	3:38.82
4. Arturo Casado ESP	3:38.88
5. Rashid Ramzi BRN	3:40.26
6. Mekon. Gebremedhin ETH	3:40.42
7. Suleiman Simotwo KEN	3:41.04
8. Youssef Baba MAR	3:44.50
dq. Nick Willis NZL	(5th)

3000 Metres (9)

1. Tariku Bekele ETH	7:48.23
2. Paul Kipsiele Koech KEN	7:49.05
3. Abreham Cherkos ETH-J	7:49.96
4. Edwin Soi KEN	7:51.60
5. Craig Mottram AUS	7:52.42
6. Mohammed Farah GBR	7:55.08
7. Ali Maataoui MAR	7:58.93
8. Sergio Sánchez ESP	7:59.74

60 Metres Hurdles (8)

1. Liu Xiang CHN	7.46
2. Allen Johnson USA	7.55
3= Yevgeniy Borisov RUS	7.60
3= Stanislav Olijar LAT	7.60
5. Thomas Blaschek GER	7.64
6. Allan Scott GBR	7.65
7. Jackson Quiñónez ESP	7.66
8. Yoel Hernández CUB	7.91

High Jump (8)

1. Stefan Holm SWE	2.36
2. Yaroslav Rybakov RUS	2.34
3= Kyriakos Ioannou CYP	2.30
3= Andra Manson USA	2.30
5. Victor Moya CUB	2.27
6= Dragutin Topic SRB	2.27
6= Jesse Williams USA	2.27
8. Michael Mason CAN	2.27
9. Jaroslav Bába CZE	2.23

Pole Vault (9)

1. Yevgeniy Lukyanenko RUS	5.90
2. Brad Walker USA	5.85
3. Steve Hooker AUS	5.80
4. Jérôme Clavier FRA	5.75
5. Tim Lobinger GER	5.70
6. Maksym Mazuryk UKR	5.70
7. Alhaji Jeng SWE	5.70
8. Derek Miles USA	5.60

Long Jump (8)

1. Khotso Mokoena RSA	8.08
2. Chris Tomlinson GBR	8.06
3. Mohamed Al-Khuwalidi KSA	8.01
4. Gable Garenamotse BOT	7.93
5. Nikolay Atanasov BUL	7.90
6. James Beckford JAM	7.85
7. Marcin Starzak POL	7.74
8. Wilfredo Martínez CUB	7.72

Triple Jump (9)

1. Phillips Idowu GBR	17.75
2. David Giralt CUB	17.47
3. Nelson Évora POR	17.27
4. Fabrizio Donato ITA	17.27
5. Dmitrij Valukevic SVK	17.14
6. Osniel Tosca CUB	17.13
7. Aarik Wilson USA	16.88
8. Danil Burkenya RUS	16.84

Shot (7)

1. Christian Cantwell USA	21.77
2. Reese Hoffa USA	21.20
3. Tomasz Majewski POL	20.93
4. Andrey Mikhnevich BLR	20.82
5. Rutger Smith NED	20.78
6. Dorian Scott JAM	20.29
7. Scott Martin AUS	20.13
8. Peter Sack GER	20.05

Heptathlon (8-9)

1. Bryan Clay USA	6371
2. Andrey Kravchenko BLR	6234
3. Dmitriy Karpov KAZ	6131
4. Mikhail Logvinenko RUS	5984
5. Donovan Kilmartin USA	5951
6. Andres Raja EST	5894
dnf. Roman Sebrle CZE	
dnf. Aleksandr Pogorelov RUS	

4 x 400 Metres Relay (9)

1. USA	3:06.79
J Davis, J Torrance, G Nixon, K Willie	
2. JAM	3:07.69
M Blackwood, E Steele, A Findlay, D Barrett	
3. DOM	3:07.77
A Peguero, C Santa, P Mejia, Y Tapia	
4. POL	3:08.76
5. GBR	3:09.21
6. RUS	3:15.38

WOMEN – 60 Metres (7)

1. Angela Williams USA	7.06
2. Jeanette Kwakye GBR	7.08
3. Tahesia Harrigan IVB	7.09
4. Kim Gevaert BEL	7.22
5. Yevgeniya Polyakova RUS	7.24
6. Oludamola Osayomi NGR	7.26
7. Franca Idoko NGR	7.30
8. Alexis Joyce USA	7.37

400 Metres (9)

1. Olesya Zykina RUS	51.09
2. Natalya Nazarova RUS	51.10
3. Shareese Woods USA	51.41
4. Antonina Yefremova UKR	51.53
5. Angela Morosanu ROU	53.07
6. Moushami Robinson USA	53.10

800 Metres (9)

1. Tamsyn Lewis AUS	2:02.57
2. Tetyana Petlyuk UKR	2:02.66
3. Maria Mutola MOZ	2:02.97
4. Mayte Martínez ESP	2:03.15
5. Jennifer Meadows GBR	2:03.51
6. Elisa Cusma Piccione ITA	2:03.76

1500 Metres (9)

1. Yelena Soboleva RUS	**3:57.71**
2. Yuliya Fomenko RUS	3:59.41
3. Gelete Burka ETH	3:59.75
4. Maryam Yusuf Jamal BRN	3:59.79
5. Daniela Yordanova BUL	4:04.19
6. Liliana Popescu ROU	4:07.61
7. Bouchra Ghézielle FRA	4:08.66
8. Siham Halali MAR	4:15.54
dnf. Sonja Roman SLO	–

3000 Metres (8)

1. Meseret Defar ETH	8:38.79
2. Meselech Melkamu ETH	8:41.50
3. Mar. Alaoui Selsouli MAR	8:41.66
4. Sylvia Kibet KEN	8:41.82
5. Olga Komyagina RUS	8:44.57
6. Kimberley Smith NZL	8:48.48
7. Silvia Weissteiner ITA	8:49.11
8. Jessica Augusto POR	8:49.78

60 Metres Hurdles (8)

1. Lolo Jones USA	7.80
2. Candice Davis USA	7.93
3. Anay Tejeda CUB	7.98
4. Lacena Golding-Clarke JAM	8.01
5. Aleksandra Antonova RUS	8.02
6. Yevgeniya Snihur UKR	8.12
7. Yuliya Kondakova RUS	10.19
8. Josephine Onyia ESP	43.72

High Jump (9)

1. Blanka Vlasic CRO	2.03
2. Yelena Slesarenko RUS	2.01

3. Vita Palamar UKR 2.01
4. Ruth Beitia ESP 1.99
5. Marina Aitova KAZ 1.95
6. Amy Acuff USA 1.95
7. Yekaterina Savchenko RUS 1.93
8= Ariane Friedrich GER 1.93
8= Iva Straková CZE 1.93

Pole Vault (8)
1. Yelena Isinbayeva RUS 4.75
2. Jennifer Stuczynski USA 4.75
3= Monika Pyrek POL 4.70
3= Fabiana Murer BRA 4.70
5. Svetlana Feofanova RUS 4.60
6. Anna Rogowska POL 4.55
7. Pavla Rybová CZE 4.50
8. Anna Battke GER 4.45
9. Naroa Agirre ESP 4.40

Long Jump (9)
1. Naide Gomes POR 7.00
2. Maurren Maggi BRA 6.89
3. Irina Simagina RUS 6.88
4. Eloyse Lesueur FRA 6.60
5. Concepción Montaner ESP 6.57
6. Ineta Radevica LAT 6.54
7. Keila Costa BRA 6.48
8. Janice Josephs RSA 6.39

Triple Jump (8)
1. Yargelis Savigne CUB 15.05
2. Hrisopiyí Devetzí GRE 15.00
3. Marija Sestak SLO 14.68
4. Olga Rypakova KAZ 14.58
5. Yamilé Aldama SUD 14.47
6. Olha Saladuha UKR 14.32
7. Olesya Bufalova RUS 14.31
8. Xie Limei CHN 14.13

Shot (9)
1. Valerie Vili NZL 20.19
2. Nadezhda Ostapchuk BLR 19.74
3. Li Meiju CHN 19.09
4. Misleydis González CUB 18.75
5. Chiara Rosa ITA 18.68
6. Christina Schwanitz GER 18.55
7. Cleopatra Borel-Brown TRI 18.47
8. Anna Omarova RUS 17.75

Pentathlon (7)
1. Tia Hellebaut BEL 4867
2. Kelly Sotherton GBR 4852
3. Anna Bogdanova RUS 4753
4. Nataliya Dobrynska UKR 4742
5. Austra Skujyte LTU 4655
6. Karolina Tyminska POL 4580
7. Tatyana Chernova RUS 4543
8. Lyudmila Blonska UKR 4474

4 x 400 Metres Relay (9)
1. RUS 3:28.17
Y Gushchina, T Levina, N Nazarova, O Zykina
2. BLR 3:28.90
A Kozak, I Khlyustova, S Usovich, I Usovich
3. USA 3:29.30
A Perkins, M Barnes, S Woods, M Robinson
4. CZE 3:34.53
5. ROU 3:36.79
6. POL 3:36.97

WORLD CROSS-COUNTRY CHAMPIONSHIPS 2008

Edinburgh, GBR, 30 March

History was made at the 36th IAAF World Cross Country Championships in Edinburgh's Holyrood Park as for the first time Ethiopians won all four races. Despite a series of mishaps, the great Kenenisa Bekele won a record sixth 12k victory and, with a team silver as well, won an astonishing 27th World Cross medal. He had missed a connecting flight at Heathrow, had a stomach upset overnight and had to stop to put on his shoe after about 2k losing about 15 sec, and yet still came through to win. Tirunesh Dibaba came back from injury to sprint clear and take a third women's title (and a 14th World Cross medal as senior and junior) as Gelete Burka "blew up" on the final hill. Dibaba's younger sister Genzebe took the junior race in grand style. Very few European nations fielded full teams in any race and top European-born finishers were 24th, 23rd, 15th and 16th in the four races below – Hilda Kibet in the women's race being an ex-Kenyan. The Kenyan men won their 21st senior title in 23 years and their 20th junior men's in 21 years while Ethiopia won both women's titles – the seniors for the 10th time in 12 years and the juniors for the sixth time.

Senior Men 12km
1. Kenenisa Bekele ETH 34:38
2. Leonard Komon KEN 34:41
3. Zersenay Tadese ERI 34:43
4. Joseph Ebuya KEN 34:47
5. Moses Masai KEN 35:02
6. Felix Kibore QAT 35:15
7. Gideon Ngatuny KEN 35:16
8. Ahmad A Hassan QAT 35:18
9. Habtamu Fikadu ETH 35:19
10. Bernard Kipyego KEN 35:24
11. Hosea Macharinyang KEN 35:24
12. Augustine Choge KEN 35:26
13. Moses Kipsiro UGA 35:29
14. Mark Kiptoo KEN 35:39
15. Sileshi Sihine ETH 35:40
16. Berrnard Kiprop UGA 35:41
17. Gebre Gebremariam ETH 35:59
18. John Thuo KEN 36:00
19. Jorge Torres USA 36:03
20. Yonas Kifle ERI 36:09
21. Dereje Debele ETH 36:10
22. Sultan Khamis Zaman QAT 36:12
23. Teklemariam Medhin ERI 36:13
24. Juan Carlos de la Ossa ESP 36:15
25. Mubarak H Shami QAT 36:17

166 of 179 finished

Team 6 to score; 15 teams completed

1. KEN	39	6. UGA	211
2. ETH	105	7. USA	301
3. QAT	144	8. ESP	353
4. ERI	164	9. AUS	400
5. MAR	197	10. ALG	425

Junior Men's 8km
1. Ibrahim Jeylan ETH 22:38
2. Ayele Abshero ETH 22:40
3. Lucas Rotich KEN 22:42
4. Benjamin Kiplagat UGA 22:43
5. Titus Mbishei KEN 22:45
6. Mathew Kisorio KEN 22:51
7. Peter Some KEN 22:55
8. Geofrey Kusuro UGA 22:56
9. Amanuel Mesel ERI 23:00
10. Levy Omari KEN 23:03
11. Hunegnaw Mesfin ETH 23:03
12. Stephen Kiprotich UGA 23:09

108 of 109 finished

Team 4 to score; 15 teams completed

1. KEN	21	6. USA	138
2. ETH	28	7. CAN	188
3. UGA	37	8. ALG	200
4. JPN	119	9. GBR	202
5. MAR	136	10. AUS	222

Women's 8km
1. Tirunesh Dibaba ETH 25:10
2. Mestawet Tufa ETH 25:15
3. Linet Masai KEN 25:18
4. Doris Changeywo KEN 25:34
5. Hilda Kibet NED 25:35
6. Gelete Burka ETH 25:35
7. Priscah Cherono KEN 25:36
8. Margaret Wangari KEN 25:46
9. Meselech Melkamu ETH 25:51
10. Grace Momanyi KEN 25:54
11. Benita Johnson AUS 25:56
12. Lineth Chepkurui KEN 26:05
13. Asmae Leghzaoui MAR 26:06
14. Koren Jelela ETH 26:12
15. Liz Yelling GBR 26:13
16. Aselefech Mergia ETH 26:28
17. Kareema Jasim BRN 26:29
18. Emily Brown USA 26:36
19. Saadia B Haddioui FRA 26:36
20. Lisa Weightman AUS 26:37
21. Hayley Yelling GBR 26:39
22. Katie McGregor USA 26:40
23. Molly Huddle USA 26:40
24. Kathy Newberry USA 26:42
25. Simret Sultan ERI 26:43

90 of 95 finished

Team 4 to score; 12 teams completed

1. ETH	18	6. GBR	116
2. KEN	22	7. ERI	150
3. AUS	84	8. POR	165
4. USA	87	9. ESP	175
5. MAR	100	10. JPN	207

Junior Women's 6km
1. Genzebe Dibaba ETH 19:59
2. Irene Cheptai KEN 20:04
3. Emebet Etea ETH 20:06
4. Delvine Meringor KEN 20:06
5. Emebet Bacha ETH 20:11
6. Jackline Chebii KEN 20:11
7. Betelhem Moges ETH 20:13
8. Dorcas Kiptarus KEN 20:17
9. Tigist Memuye ETH 20:27
10. Yukino Ninomiya JPN 20:30
11. Bitaw Yehune ETH 20:33
12. Christine Muyanga KEN 20:34

65 of 66 finished

Team 4 to score; 8 teams completed

1. ETH	16	5. CAN	99
2. KEN	20	6. USA	100
3. JPN	57	7. AUS	133
4. GBR	95	8. RUS	203